DICTIONARY OF
MEDIEVAL LATIN
FROM BRITISH SOURCES

FASCICULE III
D–E

DICTIONARY OF
MEDIEVAL LATIN
FROM BRITISH SOURCES

Fascicule III D-E

PREPARED BY

R. E. LATHAM, M.A., O.B.E., F.S.A.

AND

D. R. HOWLETT, M.A., D.PHIL., F.S.A.

WITH THE ASSISTANCE OF

A. H. POWELL, M.A., AND R. SHARPE, M.A.

UNDER THE DIRECTION OF A COMMITTEE
APPOINTED BY THE BRITISH ACADEMY

LONDON · *Published for* THE BRITISH ACADEMY
by OXFORD UNIVERSITY PRESS
1986

Oxford University Press, Walton Street, Oxford OX2 6DP
Oxford New York Toronto
Delhi Bombay Calcutta Madras Karachi
Kuala Lumpur Singapore Hong Kong Tokyo
Nairobi Dar es Salaam Cape Town
Melbourne Auckland
and associated companies in
Beirut Berlin Ibadan Nicosia

Oxford is a trade mark of Oxford University Press

Published in the United States
by Oxford University Press, New York

British Library Cataloguing in Publication Data
Dictionary of medieval Latin from British sources.
Fasc. III, D–E
1. Latin language, Medieval and modern—
Dictionaries—English
I. Latham, R. E.   II. Howlett, D. R.   III. British Academy
477   PA2891

ISBN 0 19 726023 3

Printed in Great Britain
at the University Printing House, Oxford
by David Stanford
Printer to the University

MEMBERS OF THE COMMITTEE

PREFACE TO FASCICULE III

THE third fascicule of the Dictionary is the first to carry the name of the second editor, Dr David Howlett. For much of the time since the publication of Fascicule II in 1981 the project has been conducted in two bases, the Clarendon Building in Oxford, where Dr Howlett and Mr Richard Sharpe, assisted by Mrs Lorna Lyons, have assembled a working library that, together with the Dictionary's files, attracts a stream of Medieval scholars, and the Public Record Office, where Mrs Avril Powell is assisted by Miss Joyce Batty. The Committee is very conscious of the crucial part played by the Bodleian Library and the Public Record Office, whose hospitality has been no less vital than the continued and generous support of the British Academy. It is grateful also for the contributions of Dom Frederick Hockey, the Revd Canon Bernard Wigan, and the late Mr J. H. Ward, who have excerpted texts; the staff of the Literary and Linguistic Computing Centre of the University of Cambridge and Mr Kieran Devine of the Queen's University, Belfast, who have supplied computer-produced concordances; and Prof. J. D. Latham, who has provided etymologies for words borrowed from Arabic.

We regret that this fascicule appears as long as five years after the second. The delay has been for technical reasons that inevitably affect the changeover to a new (and markedly cheaper) technology. But we are confident that users of the Dictionary will admire this product of the combined skills of the Literary and Linguistic Computing Centre in Cambridge and the Oxford University Press. It is hoped that the inclusion of a sense 1 in lemmas and a change in type size for cross references will prove helpful.

This fascicule contains a Bibliography revised and enlarged by Dr Howlett and Mr Sharpe, who are grateful for suggestions from Prof. C. N. L. Brooke, Dr A. Burnett, Dr M. Lapidge, the Revd Dr P. O. Lewry, O.P., Dr C. Page, Mr A. J. Piper, and Prof. A. G. Rigg.

Work on Fascicule IV (F–G–H) is far advanced. It is the earnest wish of the staff and of the Committee that its publication will not be long delayed. The Editor would be glad to receive addenda and corrigenda for any of the published fascicules and notice of current work on British Medieval Latin.

DICTIONARY OF
MEDIEVAL LATIN
FROM BRITISH SOURCES

Fascicule III   D-E

BIBLIOGRAPHY
FROM FASCICULE III

THE BRITISH ACADEMY
20–21, CORNWALL TERRACE
REGENT'S PARK, LONDON NW1 4QP

BIBLIOGRAPHY

This bibliography is intended to include all sources used in the Dictionary, except a few that have been cited so rarely that it has seemed simpler to make the citations bibliographically adequate in themselves. Its arrangement is in alphabetical order of short-titles by which a work is cited in the Dictionary and to which it is meant as a key. It is hoped that use will make readers familiar with the means by which short-titles have been allocated, and that it may therefore become a useful bibliographical handbook. To this end an attempt has been made to include all British Latin authors whose work is in print besides some whose work is not. But a truly comprehensive listing is not practical in this arrangement, nor could one contemplate listing the huge archival resources, printed and unprinted, in public and private collections all over the country. But a very large sample of records, especially public and monastic, has been quarried in print and in manuscripts, so that the language of such documents is amply represented. With respect to literary, technical or other works, 'it is hoped' (as R.E. Latham wrote in Fascicule I, p. ix) 'that no significant class or period of writing has been wholly disregarded.' Since the bibliography first appeared in Fascicule I (1975), it has increased in size by more than a third, the majority of the additions being named authors or additional work by authors.

The revision has also included the addition of new editions of works already cited. This has entailed some duplication in the bibliography, where two or more editions may now be listed. The word 'also' indicates a further edition not used by the Dictionary; the words 'superseded by' indicate that a new edition is cited. Where possible, citation is by the same means as previously: thus Ordericus Vitalis is now cited from the edition by Mrs Chibnall using book and chapter as the main reference, supplemented by the page number of the old edition which is given in the margin of the new edition. The letters of John of Salisbury are cited by a double system: J. SAL. *Ep.* 143 (209 p. 324) indicates the letter numbered 143 in Giles's edition reprinted in *Patrologia Latina*, now numbered 209 in the edition of Millor and Brooke to which the page-number refers. It would be foolish to persist in using defective editions when better ones have become available, but conversion may impose an unwelcome complication in references. It will help the editors and users of the Dictionary if scholars preparing new editions of texts bear in mind the need of a stable means of citation or a convenient means of conversion.

Means of citation in use in the Dictionary vary considerably, though the most convenient and practical is in general adopted. In most cases, passages from published prose works are cited by reference to the pages of the edition specified in the bibliography. In some cases, however, if this edition indicates the foliation of a principal manuscript or the pagination of a widely-available work (e.g. *Patrologia Latina*), it has been judged preferable to take this as the basis of reference. Alternatively, where works are divided into books and chapters or editorially numbered sections, these will generally serve for more than one edition and are preferred. Likewise in collections of numbered documents the number will often give a more precise reference. In both these cases, it may be desirable to add the page-number. Passages of verse are cited where possible by line or stanza, but in case of lengthy verse texts without line-numbers, reference will be by page or folio. In citations direct from manuscript, again the most practical system is adopted, be this folio and column, membrane, rotulet or whatever. Where any doubt may arise the method of reference is indicated in square brackets at the end of the entry in the bibliography.

Citations from glossaries such as *WW*, in which words are listed or indexed alphabetically, usually omit any page-reference.

Citations from sources of diverse content (e.g. Rymer's *Foedera*, *Archaeologia*, English Historical Review) usually include some indication of the nature of the document cited; letters or other documents included in chronicles are distinguished where practicable from the actual writing of the chronicles.

Dates of sources are generally noted in the bibliography. In the case of chronicles, a citation is usually accompanied by a *sub anno* date (s1215) to facilitate reference between different chroniclers' accounts of the same event. In the case of documents, a date is given with each quotation. In some cases this date forms an essential part of the reference: thus '**1263** assumatis omnibus particulis solucionis *Cl* 295' refers to p. 295 of the published volume of Close Rolls covering the years 1261–4; '**1423** eisdem viciis .. assuetus, .. que quidem assuetatio ex ipsa iteracione decernatur *Reg. Cant.* III 518' refers to the

published Register of Henry Chicheley, archbishop of Canterbury 1414–43, Vol. III p. 518. In some cases two dates are given: **1139** (1381) indicates a document of the former date quoted from an inspeximus of the latter; **939** (13c) marks a charter preserved in a later cartulary or transcript.

The quotation-slips were made by many hands over many years and the editing of the Dictionary is similarly a long-term project, its staff liable to change over the years: it is almost inevitable, therefore, that a few works may have been cited indifferently, e.g. by page or number. It is hoped that these are scarce enough not to tax the patience of the reader zealous enough to trace the sources quoted.

Abbat. Abingd. *De abbatibus Abbendoniae* [Abingdon, Berks] (12c.), in *Chr. Abingd.* II app. II 268–95.

ABBO Abbo of Fleury, of Ramsey [*ob.* 1004]: **Edm.** *Vita S. Eadmundi* [*ob.* 870], ed. M. Winterbottom, Three Lives of English Saints, Toronto Med. Latin Texts (1972) 67–87 [by cap.]; also in *Mem. S. Edm.* I 1–25. **QG** *Quaestiones grammaticales*, ed. A. Mai, *Classici Auctores e Vaticanis Codicibus Editi* V (1833) 329–49 [by sect.]; superseded by ed. A. Guerreau-Jalabert, (Paris, 1982) [by sect. of Mai & sect. of Jalabert (in brackets)]; **prol.** verse prologue, in *Chr. Rams.* xxvii–xxviii [by line].

Abbotsford Club publications (Edinburgh, 1883–66).

Abbr. Orig. *Rotulorum originalium in curia scaccarii abbreviatio* (Hen. III–Ed. III), 2 vols. RC (1805, 1810).

Abbr. Plac. *Placitorum abbreviatio* (Ric. I–Ed. III), RC (1811).

Ac. A. Bicknor The enrolled account of Alexander Bicknor, Treasurer of Ireland, 1308–14 (PRO E. 372/171), *Anal. Hib.* XXX (1982) 15–46.

Ac. Almon. Peterb. The book of William Morton [*ob.* a1471], Almoner of Peterborough monastery 1448–67, Northants Rec. Soc. XVI (1954).

A. CARPENTER Destruct. Vit. Alexander Carpenter (*alias* Fabricius) [*fl.* 1430]: *Destructio* (or *destructorium*) *vitiorum* (Cologne, 1480, etc.) [by part & cap.].

Ac. Bailiff Percy Percy Bailiff's rolls of the fifteenth century, Surtees Soc. CXXXIV (1921).

Ac. Beaulieu Account-book of Beaulieu Abbey [Hants] and manor of Faringdon [Berks] (c1270), ed. S. F. Hockey, Camd. 4th S. XVI (1975).

Ac. Bridge House Accounts and rental of the Bridge House properties (1404–), MS Guildhall RO, London.

Ac. Bridge Masters Bridge Masters' Account rolls (1381–1405), MS London Guildhall RO.

Ac. Build. Hen. III Building Accounts of King Henry III, ed. H. M. Colvin (Oxford, 1971).

Ac. Chamb. Cant. Chamberlains' Accounts of the city of Canterbury (1393–1536), HMC Rep. IX App. 1 (1883) 131–77.

Ac. Chamb. Chesh Accounts of the Chamberlains of the county of Chester 1301–60, Lancs & Chesh Rec. Soc. LIX (1910); *v. et.* Pipe Chesh.

Ac. Chamb. Winchester Chamberlains' Accounts of the city of Winchester (1378–), MS Winchester City Archives, Hants RO.

Ac. Chamb. York York City Chamberlains' Account rolls 1396–1500, Surtees Soc. CXCII (1980).

Ac. Churchw. Bath Churchwardens' Accounts of the church of St. Michael without the North Gate, Bath, 1349–1575, ed. C. B. Pearson, Arch. Soc. Som, supplements to vols. XXIII–XXVI (1877–80) [contin. pag.].

Ac. Churchw. Glast. Churchwardens' Accounts of St. John's Glastonbury (1366–1574), Som & Dors N. & Q. IV (1894–5) 89–96, 137–44, 185–92, 235–40, 281–88, 329–36, 379–84; (1584–1610), *ib.* V (1896–7) 45–8, 93–6.

Ac. Churchw. Sal. Churchwardens' Accounts of St. Edmund and St. Thomas, Salisbury (1443–1702), Wilts Rec. Soc. I (1896).

Ac. Churchw. Som Churchwardens' Accounts of Somerset parishes 1349–1560, Som Rec. Soc. IV (1890).

Ac. Coll. Wint. Account rolls, MS Winchester College.

Ac. Cornw Ministers' Accounts of the Earldom of Cornwall, 1296–7, Camd. 3rd S. LXVI, LXVIII (1942, 1945) [contin. pag.].

Ac. Dom. Ep. Wint. Household roll (1393) of William of Wykeham, Bishop of Winchester [1366–1404], MS Winchester College.

Ac. Durh. Extracts from the Account rolls of the Abbey of Durham (1278–1580), Surtees Soc. XCIX, C, CIII (–284, –576, –989) (1898–1901).

Ac. Ep. Bath. Household roll (1337–8) of Ralph of Shrewsbury, Bishop of Bath and Wells [*ob.* 1363], Som Rec. Soc. XXXIX (1924) 72–174.

Ac. Esch. v. LTR.

Ac. Exec. Ep. Exon. Accounts of the Executors of Thomas, Bishop of Exeter (1310), Camd. Soc. NS X (1874) 1–45.

Ac. Exec. Ep. Lond. Account of the Executors of Richard, Bishop of London (1303), Camd. Soc. NS X (1874) 47–116.

Ac. Exec. W. Merton Accounts of the Executors of Walter de Merton (1277–8), in *Rolls Merton* 90–169.

Ac. Foreign Exchequer Rolls of Foreign Accounts (Pipe Office) (1368–), MS PRO (E. 364) [letters represent consec. rotulet nos.]: E. 364/1, in *Ac. Foreign Hen. III* 1–73; E. 364/21, Med. Stud. XLII (1980) 261–87; E. 364/27, *ib.* 288–307.

Ac. Foreign Hen. III Foreign Accounts, Henry III (1219–34), Pipe R. Soc. NS XLIV (1974–5) [1982].

Ac. Galley Newcastle The 'Newcastle' Galley A.D. 1296, *Arch. Aeliana* 4th S. II (1926) 161–193.

ACHARD Achard of St. Victor (*alias* of Bridlington), Bishop of Avranches [*ob.* c1171]: **Discret.** *De discretione animae et spiritus et mentis*, in Grabmann Studies 252–62; **Serm.** *Sermones*, ed. J. Chatillon, Textes philosophiques du moyen âge XVII (1970) [by no. & sect.]; **Trin.** *De Trinitate* (extr.), RTAM XXI (1954) 299–306; also cited from J. CORNW. *Eul.*.

Ac. Havener Cornw Haveners' Accounts (1517–), Duchy of Cornwall, MS PRO (E. 306).

Ac. H. Derby Expeditions made by Henry, Earl of Derby 1390–1 and 1392–3, accounts kept by his treasurer, Camd. Soc. NS LII (1894).

Ac. Jarrow Inventories and account rolls of the Benedictine house of Jarrow and Monkwearmouth (1303–1537), Surtees Soc. XXIX (Durham, 1854) 1–136.

Ac. LChamb. Lord Chamberlain's department, Accounts (1483–), MS PRO (L.C. 9); English version from L.C. 5.

Ac. Lenton Lenton Priory (Notts), estate accounts (1296–8), Thoroton Soc. XIX (1959).

Ac. Linlithgow Account of work done at the Peel of Linlithgow (c1302), in *Ac. Palaces Scot.* lxiii–lxviii.

Ac. Man. Cant. Manorial Accounts, Christchurch, Canterbury, MS Canterbury Cathedral Library; *v. et. DCCant.*

Ac. Man. Coll. Wint. Manorial Accounts, MS Winchester College.

Ac. Man. Westm. Manorial Accounts, MS Westminster Abbey.

Ac. Man. Wint. Manorial Accounts, MS Winchester Cathedral Library.

Ac. Mayor Winchester Accounts of the Mayor of Winchester (1354–), MS Winchester City RO.

Ac. Obed. Abingd. Accounts of the Obedientiars of Abingdon Abbey (1322–1532), Camd. Soc. NS LI (1892).

Ac. Palaces Scot. Accounts of the Masters of Works for building royal palaces Scotland, I (1529–1615), Scot. RO (1957); *v. et.* Ac. Linlithgow.

Ac. Sheriffs Sheriffs' Accounts (Hen. III–), MS PRO (E. 199).

Ac. Shorwell v. FormMan Shorwell.

Ac. Stratton Accounts and surveys (1271–89) of the Wiltshire lands of Adam de Stratton [*fl.* 1265–90], Wilts Rec. Soc. XIV (1959); *v. et. CourtR A. Stratton.*

Ac. Swinfield Household expenses (1289–90) of Richard de Swinfield, Bishop of Hereford [1283–1317], Camd. Soc. LIX, LXII (1854–5).

Acta SS. Ben. *Acta sanctorum ordinis S. Benedicti*, ed. J. Mabillon and Th. Ruinart, 9 vols. (Paris, 1668–1701).

Acta SS. Boll. *Acta sanctorum quotquot toto orbe coluntur*, ed. J. Bollandus *et al.* (Antwerp, etc., 1643–).

Acta Univ. Andr. *Acta facultatis artium universitatis S. Andree* (1413–1588), ed. A. I. Dunlop, SHS 3rd S. LIV, LV (1954) [contin. pag.].

Acta Wulf. et Ruff. v. V. Wulf. et Ruff.

Act. Cant. *Acta Stephani Langton* (1207–28), Cant. & York Soc. L (1950).

Act. Ep. English Episcopal *Acta*, I (1980–) [by date, diocese, & no.].

Act. Hen. II Recueil des actes de Henri II concernant les provinces françaises (1138–89), ed. L. Delisle and E. Berger, Acad. des Inscriptions, etc., Chartes et Diplômes III, intro. & 3 vols. (1909–27) [by p.].

ActPC Proceedings and ordinances of the Privy Council of England (1386–1542), 7 vols. RC (1834–7).

ActPCIr Acts of the Privy Council in Ireland (1556–71), HMC Rep. XV app. III (1897) 1–256.

Ac. Trin. Dublin Account roll of the Priory of the Holy Trinity, Dublin (1337–46), ed. J. Mills, Royal Soc. of Antiquaries of Ireland, extra vol. (1891).

AcWardr Wardrobe accounts: 1300 *Liber quotidianus contrarotulatoris garderobae* (1299–1300), Soc. of Antiquaries of London (1787) [by p.]; 1310–11, MS BL Cotton Nero C VIII; also used with *Chanc. Misc., KRAc, TRBk.*

Ac. Wearmouth (1321–1534), in *Ac. Jarrow* 139–232.

Ac. Wellingb. Wellingborough manorial Accounts, 1258–1323, from account rolls of Crowland Abbey, Northants Rec. Soc. VIII (1936).

Ac. W. Wales v. MinAc. W. Wales.

AD. BUCKF. Adam of Buckfield [*fl.* 1243]: **An.** *In I de Anima* (extr.), Revue néoscolastique de philosophie XLII (1939) 433–8; **Metaph.** *Sententia super secundum Metaphysicae*, in *Med. Thinkers* 101–44.

AD. BURLEY Quaest. Adam Burley [*fl.* 1318–28]: Four questions by Adam Burley on the *liber sex principiorum*, Med. Stud. XXXIII (1970) 63–90 [by sect.].

AD. DORE Pictor Adam of Dore [*fl.* 1200] [attrib.]: *Pictor in Carmine*, Arch. XCIV (1951) 151–66.

AD. EASTON Def. Adam of Easton, Cardinal [*ob.* 1397]: *Defensorium* (extr.), EHR LI (1936) 675–80.

ADEL. Adelard of Bath [*fl.* 1120]: **Abac.** *Regulae abaci*, Bullettino di bibliografia e di storia delle scienze matematiche e fisiche XIV (1881) 91–134; **Alch.** *Libri ysagogarum Alchorismi in artem astronomicam* Abhandlungen zur Geschichte der Mathematik VIII (1898) 3–27 [I–III only]; superseded by ed. A. Allard, *Corpus Scriptorum Latinorum Paravianum*; **Astr.** *De opere astrolapsus* (*c*1142–6) (extr.), in *Med. Sci.* (1927) 21, 25, 28–9; **CA** *De cura accipitrum*, Allard Pierson Stichting, Afdeling voor mod. lit. wetenschap (1937); **ED** *De eodem et diverso* (*c*1109), BGPM IV i (1903) 3–34; **Elk.** *Ezich Elkauresmi per Athelardum Bathoniensem ex arabico sumptus*, Danske Videnskabernes Selskabs Skrifter, Historisk og Filoso-

fisk Afdeling VII iii (Copenhagen, 1914) 1–231 [by cap.]; **Euclid** *Translatio Euclidis* (extr.), Abhandlungen zur Geschichte der Mathematik II (1880) 143–66; **MC** *Mappae clavicula*, Arch. XXXII (1847) 187–244 [by cap.]; checked against American Philosophical Soc. Trans. LXIV iv (1974) 1–128; **QN** *Quaestiones naturales*, BGPM XXXI i (1934) 1–91 [by cap.].

ADEL. BLANDIN. Dunst. Adelard of Blandinium [*fl. a*1011]: *Epistola de vita S. Dunstani*, in *Mem. Dunst.* 53–68 [by cap.].

AD. EYNS. Adam of Eynsham [*ob. p*1233]: **Hug.** *Magna vita S. Hugonis* [Bishop of Lincoln, *ob.* 1200], ed. D. H. Farmer and D. L. Douie, 2 vols., Med. Texts (1961–2) [by bk. & cap.]; **Visio** *Visio monachi de Egnesham* [Eynsham] (*c*1197), OHS LI (1908) 285–371 [by cap]; also in *Anal. Boll.* XXII (1903).

AD. MARSH Ep. Adam Marsh (de Marisco) [*ob.* 1257]: *Epistolae* (mainly *c*1250), in *Mon. Francisc.* I 77–489 [by no.].

Admin. Ir. H. G. Richardson and G. O. Sayles: The Administration of Ireland, 1172–1377, IMC (Dublin, 1963).

AD. MUR. Adam Murimouth [*ob.* 1347]: **Chr.** Chronicle (*Continuatio Chronicarum*) (1303–47), RS XCIII (1889) 1–219; **app.** appendix, text of MS BL Cotton Nero D x (1340–4), *ib.* 220–53; **Cont. A** *Continuatio* (1337–77), ed. T. Hog, Eng. Hist. Soc. (1846) 171–227; **Cont. B** *Continuatio continuationis* (1377–80), *ib.* 228–43.

AD. SCOT Adam Scot (*alias* of Dryburgh) [*fl.* 1180]: **OP** *De ordine canonicorum Ordinis Praemonstratensis*, PL CXCVIII (1855) 439–610; **QEC** *De quadripartito exercitio cellae*, PL CLIII 799–884; **Serm.** *Sermones*, PL CXCVIII 97–440; **Sol.** *Soliloquiorum de instructione animae libri duo*, *ib.* 843–72; **TGC** *De triplici genere contemplationis*, *ib.* 795–842; **TT** *De tripartito tabernaculo*, *ib.* 609–792; **Vir. Relig.** *Sermones ad viros religiosos*, ed. F. Petit (Tongerloo, 1934) [by no. & sect.]; **Vita** *De vita et conversatione magistri Adae Cartusiensis*, *v. Chr. Witham.*

AD. USK Adam of Usk [*ob.* 1430]: *Chronicon* (1377–1421), ed. E. M. Thompson, 2nd ed. (1904).

AD. WODEHAM Adam Wodeham, O.F.M. [*ob.* 1358]: **Cont.** *De divisione et compositione continui contra Chatton*, Franciscan Studies XXVI (1966) 267–88 [*cf.* W. CHATTON *Cont.*]; **Lect. B** *Lectura secunda super I Sententiarum* (extr.): prol. q.3 *Traditio* XXXVIII (1983) 235–52; d. 1 q. 1, Franciscan studies XXXVII (1977) 72–102; d. 23 q. 1, CIMA XXXV (1980) 38–55 [complete edn. by Franciscan Institute in prep.]; **Sent. Abbr.** *Super quattuor libros Sententiarum* [abbreviated by Henry Totting of Oyta] (Paris, 1512).

ÆLF. Ælfric, Abbot of Eynsham [*ob. c*1025]: **Æthelwold** *Vita S. Æthelwoldi*, ed. M. Winterbottom, Three Lives of English Saints, Toronto Med. Latin Texts (1972) 17–29; also in *Chr. Abingd.* II app. 1, 253–66; **CH I pref.** Catholic Homilies, First S., preface, ed. B. Thorpe, The Homilies of the Anglo-Saxon Church (London, 1846) I 1–3; **CH II pref.** Catholic Homilies, Second S., preface, EETS Sup. S. V (1979) 1–2; **Coll.** Colloquy, ed. G. N. Garmonsway (1939) [by col. of *WW*]; **EC** *De ecclesiastica consuetudine*, ed. B. Fehr, Die Hirtenbriefe Ælfrics (Hamburg, 1914) 234–49 [by cap.]; **Ep.** *Epistolae*: *Ep.* 2, *ib.* 35–57; *Ep.* 2a, 222–7; *Ep.* 3, 58–67 [by sect.]; **Gl.** Glossary or vocabulary [attrib.], in *WW* 104–67; **Gram.** Grammar and Glossary, ed. J. Zupitza, Ælfrics Grammatik und Glossar (Berlin, 1880); **Lives pref.** Lives of Saints, preface, EETS LXXVI (1881) 2–4; **Regul. Mon.** *Regulae Monasticae*, ed. M. Bateson in *Comp. Swith.* 174–98; **Sup.** Supplement to Glossary, in *WW* 168–91; **Swith.** *Historia translationis et miraculorum S. Swithuni*, Acta SS. Boll. July I (1712) 328–30; superseded by Winchester Studies IV ii [by cap.].

ÆLF. BATA Ælfric Bata [*fl.* 1005]: Colloquies, in *Early*

Schol. Coll., no. 4, 27–66; no. 5 *Colloquia difficilia*, 67–74; no. 6 *Ælfrici colloquium ab A. B. auctum*, 75–101 [by no. & sect.].

ÆLNOTH Cnut Ælnoth [*fl.* 1085–1109]: *Historia ortus, vitae, et passionis S. Canuti*, *Acta SS. Boll.* July III (1723) 127–42 [by sect.]; also ed. M. C. Gertz, *Vitae SS. Danorum* (Copenhagen, 1908) 77–136.

Aen. Laur. *Aenigmata Laureshamensia* (or *Anglica*), *CCSL* CXXXIII (1968) 345–58 [by no. & line].

ÆTHELW. Æthelweard [*ob. c*998]: Chronicle (Creation – 975), ed. A. Campbell, Med. Texts (1962) [by date, bk., & cap.].

ÆTHELWALD, Bishop of Lindisfarne [*ob.* 740], *v. Cerne.*

ÆTHELWALD [*fl. a*700], *v. Carm. Aldh.*

ÆTHELWOLD Æthelwold, Bishop of Winchester [*ob.* 984]: **Ep.** *Epistola*, in *Mem. Dunst.* 361–2; *v. et. Bened. Æthelwoldi*, charters in *CS* 1046–7, 1138, 1147, 1149–59, 1190, *Conc. Syn.* I 121–33, and *RegulC; cf.* ÆLF. *Æthelwold*, WULF. *Æthelwold.*

ÆTHELWULF Abb. Æthelwulf [*fl.* 810]: *Carmen de abbatibus cellae suae*, ed. A. Campbell (Oxford, 1967) [by line].

AFH *Archivum Franciscanum Historicum* I– (Quaracchi, 1908–).

AFP *Archivum Fratrum Praedicatorum* I– (Rome, 1931–).

AGNELLUS Hen. Thomas Agnellus, Archdeacon of Wells [*fl.* 1180]: *Sermo de morte et sepultura Henrici regis junioris* (*c* 1183), in COGGESH. 263–73.

Agnus Castus *Agnus Castus*, a Middle English Herbal [15c.], ed. G. Brodin (Uppsala, 1950) [by f.].

AHDLMA Archives d'histoire doctrinale et littéraire du moyen age, I– (Paris, 1926–).

Aids Inquisitions and Assessments relating to feudal Aids, etc. (1284–1431), 6 vols. HMSO (1899–1920).

AILR. Ailred (*alias* Æthelred) of Rievaulx [*ob.* 1166]: **An.** *Dialogus de anima*, Med. & R. Stud. sup. I (1952) 65–157 [by f.]; superseded by *CC cont. med.* I (1971) 683–754 [by bk. & cap.]; **Comp. Spec. Car.** *Compendium speculi caritatis*, *CC cont. med.* I 171–240 [by bk., cap., & col. of *PL* CXCV]; **Dilect. Dei** *Sermo de dilectione Dei*, *ib.* 241–4 [by cap.]; **Ed. Conf.** *Vita S. Edwardi regis*, *PL* CXCV (1855) 739–90 [*cf. V. Ed. Conf. metr.*]; **Gen. Regum** *De genealogia regum Anglorum*, in *Hist. Angl. Script.* X 347–70; **Inst. Inclus.** *De institutione inclusarum*, *CC cont. med.* I 635–82 [by cap.]; **Jes.** *De Jesu puero duodenni* [sermon on *Luke* ii 42], *PL* CLXXXIV (1854) 849–70; superseded by *CC cont. med.* I 245–78 [by bk. & cap.]; **Nin.** *Vita S. Niniani*, ed. A. P. Forbes, Lives of St. Ninian and St. Kentigern, Historians of Scotland V (Edinburgh, 1874) 137–57 [by cap.]; **OP** *Oratio pastoralis*, *CC cont. med.* I 755–63 [by cap.]; **Sanct.** *De sanctimoniali de Wattun*, *PL* CXCV 789–96; **Serm.** *Sermones*, *PL* CXCV 209–500; **Spec. Car.** *Speculum caritatis*, *ib.* 501–620; superseded by *CC cont med.* I 2–161 [by bk., cap., & col. of *PL* CXCV]; **Spir. Amicit.** *De spirituali amicitia*, *CC cont. med.* I 279–350 [by bk., cap., & col. of *PL* CXCV]; **Spir. Amicit. Abbr.** *Abbreviationes de spirituali amicitia*, *ib.* 351–63 [by bk. & cap.]; **SS Hex** *De sanctis ecclesiae Haugustaldensis* (634–1154), Surtees Soc. XLIV (1864) 173–203 [by cap.]; **Stand.** *Relatio de standardo*, in *Chr. Steph.* III 181–99 [by f.].

ALB. LOND. DG Alberic of London [*fl.* 1200]: *De diis gentium et illorum allegoriis*, Scriptores rerum mythicarum latini tres Romae nuper reperti (Zelle, 1834) 152–256 [by cap. & sect.].

ALCH. Alchfrith [*fl. c*770]: **Ep.** *Epistola Alchfridi anachoritae ad Higlacum lectorem et presbiterum*, ed. W. Levison, England and the Continent in the eighth century (Oxford, 1946) app. IX 297–300; **Or.** *Orationes*, in *Cerne* 143–5, 155–6.

ALCUIN Alcuin (Albinus) [735–804]: **ad Beatum** Alcuin to Beatus of Liébana, ed. W. Levison, England and the Continent in the Eighth Century (Oxford, 1946), app. XI 318–23; **Carm.** *Carmina*, in *PLAC* I (1881) 220–351 [by no. & line]; **CR** *Carmina rhythmica*, *ib.* IV (1923) 903–10; **Didasc.** *Opera didascalica: Disputatio Pippini regis et nobilissimi juvenis cum Albino*, *PL* CI 975–80; *De cursu et saltu lunae ac bissexto* [attrib.; an editorial conflation], *ib.* 981–1002 [*v. et. Gram., Orth., Rhet.*]; **Dogm.** *Opera dogmatica: De fide sanctae et individuae Trinitatis*, *PL* CI 9–58 (*pref.* = *Ep.* 257); *De Trinitate ad Fredegesium quaestiones XXVIII*, *ib.* 57–64 (*pref.* = *Ep.* 289); *Libellus de processione spiritus sancti*, *ib.* 63–84 (*pref.* = *Ep.* app. 3); *Contra haeresim Felicis*, *ib.* 85–120 [*v. et. Haer.*]; *Adversus Felicem*, *ib.* 119–230 (*pref.* = *Ep.* 23, 202, 203); *Adversus Elipandum*, *ib.* 231–300 (*pref.* = *Ep.* 200, 201, 166); *Alcuinus filiae in Christo*, *ib.* 299–304 (= *Ep.* 204); **Dub.** *Opera dubia: Confessio fidei*, *PL* CI 1027–98; *Disputatio puerorum*, *ib.* 1097–1144; *Propositiones ad acuendos juvenes*, *ib.* 1145–60; *Varia*, *ib.* 1161–70; **Ep.** *Epistolae*, ed. E. Duemmler, *MGH Ep. Carol. Aevi* II (1895) 1–481 [by no.; letters to Alcuin cited as *Ep. Alcuin.*]; **Exeg.** *Opera exegetica: In Genesim*, *PL* C 516–66 (*pref.* = *Ep.* 80); *Super Geneseos i 26*, *ib.* 565–8; *Brevis expositio decalogi*, *ib.* 567–70; *Enchiridion or Expositio in Psalmos poenitentiales*, *ib.* 569–640 (*pref.* = *Ep.* 243); *In Canticum*, *ib.* 641–64; *In Ecclesiasten*, *ib.* 667–720 (*pref.* = *Ep.* 251); *Interpretationes nominum Hebraicorum*, *ib.* 725–34; *In Joannis evangelium*, *ib.* 737–1008 (*pref.* = *Ep.* 214, 196, 213); *Explanatio in tres S. Pauli epistolas*, *ib.* 1009–84; *Expositio Apocalypsis*, *ib.* 1087–1156; **Gram.** *Grammatica*, *PL* CI 849–902; **Haer.** *Contra haeresim Felicis*, Studi e teste CCLXXXV (1980) 55–99 [by sect.]; **Hag.** *Opera hagiographica: De vita S. Martini*, *PL* CI 657–64; *Vita S. Richarii*, *ib.* 681–94 (*pref.* = *Ep.* 306) [*v. et Vedast., WillP, WillV*]; **Liturg.** *Opera liturgica: Liber sacramentorum*, *PL*, CI 445–66; *De Psalmorum usu*, *ib.* 465–508; *Officia per ferias*, *ib.* 509–612 (*pref.* = *Ep.* 304); *De baptismi caerimoniis*, *ib.* 611–14 (= *Ep.* 134; *cf. Ep.* 137 p.214); **Moral.** *Opera moralia: De virtutibus et vitiis*, *PL* CI 613–38 (*pref.* = *Ep.* 305); *De animae ratione*, *ib.* 639–50 (= *Ep.* 309); *De confessione peccatorum*, *ib.* 649–56 (= *Ep.* 131); **Orth.** *Orthographia*, ed. H. Keil, *Grammatici Latini* VII (1878) 295–312 [by p. of ed. Putschius 2327–50]; also ed. A. Marsili (Pisa, 1952); **Rhet.** *De rhetorica*, ed. C. Halm, *Rhetores Latini minores* (1863) 525–50 [by sect.]; **SS Ebor** *Versus de pontificibus et sanctis Eboracensis ecclesiae*, in *PLAC* I 169–206 [by line]; also ed. P. Godman, Med. Texts (1984); **Suppos.** *Opera supposita: De divinis officiis*, *PL* CI 1173–1286; *Homiliae*, *ib.* 1300–1308 (etc.); *Libellus sacrarum precum*, *ib.* 1383–1406; **Vedast.** *Vita S. Vedasti episcopi Atrebatensis* [*ob.* 539], *MGH Script. rer. Merov.* III (Hanover, 1896) 414–27; **WillP** *Vita S. Willibrordi* (prose), ed. B. Krusch and W. Levison, *MGH Script. rer. Merov.* VII (Hanover & Leipzig, 1920) [by cap.]; **WillV** *Vita S. Willibrordi* (verse), in *PLAC* I (1881) 207–20 [by sect. & line].

ALDH. Aldhelm, Bishop of Sherborne [*ob.* 709]: **Aen.** *Aenigmata*, *MGH Auct. Antiq.* XV (1919) 97–149 [by no. & line]; **CE** *Carmina ecclesiastica*, *ib.* 3–32 [by no. & line; *v. et. Carm. Aldh.*]; **Ep.** *Epistulae*, *ib.* 475–503 [by no.; letters to Aldhelm cited as *Ep. Aldh.*]; **Met.** *De metris etc.*, *ib.* 59–96 [by cap.]; **PR** *De pedum regulis*, *ib.* 150–204 [by cap.]; **VirgP** *De virginitate* (prose), *ib.* 226–323 [by cap.]; glosses in *GlN* sect. 1–18, and ed. L. Goossens, The Old English Glosses of MS Brussels, Royal Library 1650 (Brussels, 1974); **VirgV** *De virginitate* (verse), *ib.* 350–471 [by line].

ALDR. Margin. Aldred, Provost of St Cuthbert's, Chester-le-Street [*fl.* 970]: *Marginalia*, ed. W. J. P. Boyd (Exeter, 1975) [by no.]; *v. et. John, Luke, Mark, Matthew, Rit. Durh.*

Alea Evang. *Alea Evangelii* (10c.), ed. J. A. Robinson, The Times of Saint Dunstan (Oxford, 1923) 173–7.

ALEXANDER OF HALES *v.* HALES.

ALEX. BATH Mor. Alexander of Bath, Dean of Wells [*c*1190–1210]: *Moralia super Evangelia* (extr.), ed. E. J. Dobson, Moralities on the Gospels, a new source of Ancrene Wisse (Oxford, 1975) [by bk., cap., & p.].

ALEX. CANT. Alexander of Canterbury [12c.]: **Dicta** *Liber ex dictis beati Anselmi*, in *Mem. Anselm* 108–95; **Mir.** *Miracula*, *ib.* 196–270 [by no., version, & p.]; **V. Anselmi** *Brevis vita Anselmi* (extr.), in EADMER *HN* cxx–cxxvii; superseded by ALEX. CANT. *Dicta*, *Mir.*

ALF. ANGL. Alfredus Anglicus (of Shareshull) [*fl.* 1200]: **Cor** *De motu cordis*, BGPM XXIII i–ii (1923) 1–96 [by cap.]; **Met.** *In meteora* (extr.), in Grabmann Studies 463–71; **Min.** *Mineralia* or *De congelatione et conglutinatione lapidum* [transl. of Avicenna], in *Theatrum Chem.* IV 883–7; also ed. E. J. Holmyard and D. C. Mandeville (1927), 45–55; **Plant.** *De plantis* [transl. of Nicholas of Damascus *via* Arabic], ed. E. H. F. Meyer (Leipzig, 1841).

ALMA *Archivum Latinitatis medii aevi* (Bulletin du Cange), I– (Brussels, 1924–).

Alph. *Alphita*, a medico-botanical glossary (14c.), ed. J. L. G. Mowat, *Anecd. Oxon.* I ii (1887); Eng. recension of *Alphita*, ed. S. de Renzi, *Collect. Salern.* III (1854) 272–322.

Altercatio *Altercatio magistri et discipuli* (*a*994), ASE I (1972) 108–120 [by line].

Ambrosden Parochial antiquities attempted in the history of Ambrosden [Oxon], ed. White Kennett, 2 vols. (Oxford, 1818).

A. MEAUX Susanna Alan de Melsa [*fl.* 1210]: Poem on Susanna, Studi Medievali, NS III (1950) 41–50.

AMUND. John Amundesham [*fl.* 1440]: *Annales monasterii S. Albani* (1421–40), 2 vols. *Chr. Mon. S. Alb.* V.

Anal. Boll. *Analecta Bollandiana*, I– (Brussels, 1882–).

Anal. Cist. *Analecta Sacri Ordinis Cisterciensis*, I– (Rome, 1945–).

Anal. Etheldr. v. RIC. ELY.

Anal. Hib. *Analecta Hibernica*, incl. reports of IMC, I– (Dublin, 1930–).

Anal. Hymn. *Analecta hymnica medii aevi*, ed. G. M. Dreves and C. Blume, 55 vols. (Leipzig, 1886–1922) [by vol. & no.].

Analog. Cant. Pilg. Analogues of Chaucer's Canterbury Pilgrimage (15c. docs.), ed. F. J. Furnivall and R. E. G. Kirk, Chaucer Soc. NS XXXVI (1903).

AncC Ancient Correspondence (Hen. II–), MS PRO (S.C. 1).

AncCh Ancient Charters royal and private prior to A.D. 1200, Pipe R. Soc. X (1888) [by no.].

AncD Ancient Deeds (12c.–), MS PRO (var.).

AncExt Ancient Extents (John–Hen. VI), MS PRO (E. 142).

AncIndict Ancient Indictments (Ed. I–), MS PRO (K.B. 9).

AncPet Ancient Petitions (Hen. III–), MS PRO (S.C. 8).

AncrR The Latin text of the Ancrene Riwle (early 14c. transl. from Eng., attrib. S. GAUNT), EETS CCXVI (1944); Eng. text cited from EETS CCXLIX and CCLXVII.

AND Anglo-Norman Dictionary, ed. L. W. Stone and W. Rothwell, I– (London, 1977–).

ANDRÉ Hen. VII Bernard André of Toulouse [*ob. p*1520]: *De vita atque gestis Henrici Septimi historia*, in *Mem. Hen. VII* 1–130: *Vita* (1497) 1–75; *Annales* (1504–8) 77–130.

ANDR. S. VICT. Andrew of St. Victor, Abbot of Wigmore [*fl.* 1150]: **Comm.** *Commentarii* (extr.), ed. B. Smalley, The Study of the Bible in the Middle Ages (Oxford, 1941) 86–144, 271–89; **Eccles.** *Commentarius in Ecclesiasten*, ed. G. Calandra (Palermo, 1948).

Anecd. Oxon. *Anecdota Oxoniensia*. Texts, documents, & extracts chiefly from MSS in Bodl., Mediaeval & Modern S., I–XV (Oxford, 1882–1929).

Anecd. Poet. *Anecdota quaedam poetica*, Surtees Soc. LXX (1878) 72–89 [by no. & line].

Anglia *Anglia*, Zeitschrift für englische Philologie, I– (Halle, 1878–).

Anglia Sacra *Anglia sacra, sive collectio historiarum de archiepiscopis et episcopis Angliae* (–1540), ed. H. Wharton, 2 vols. (1691).

Anglo-Scot. Rel. Anglo-Scottish Relations, 1174–1328, ed. E. L. G. Stones, Med. Texts (1965).

Ann. Ang. & Scot. *Annales Angliae et Scotiae* (1292–1300), in *Chr. Mon. S. Alb.* II 371–408.

Ann. Berm. *Annales monasterii de Bermundeseia* [Bermondsey, Surrey] (1042–1432), in *Ann. Mon.* III 423–87.

Ann. Burton *Annales de Burton* [Staffs] (1004–1263), in *Ann. Mon.* I 183–500.

Ann. Cambr. *Annales Cambriae* (444–1288), RS XX (1860).

Ann. Cestr. *Annales Cestrenses* or Chronicle of the Abbey of St. Werburgh at Chester (Creation–1297), Lancs & Chesh Rec. Soc. XIV (1887).

Ann. Dunstable *Annales prioratus de Dunstaplia* [Beds] (Incarnation–1297), in *Ann. Mon.* III 1–420; also ed. T. Hearne, *Chronicon seu annales prioratus de Dunstaple*, 2 vols. (Oxford, 1733) [–1241 attrib. R. DE MORINS].

Ann. Durh. Durham annals (1207–86), Surtees Soc. CLV (1940); docs. (13c.), *ib.* 85–202.

Ann. Ed. I *Annales Regis Edwardi Primi* (3 frags., 1285–1307), in *Chr. Mon. S. Alb.* II 435–99.

Ann. Hen. IV *Annales Henrici Quarti, Regis Angliae* (1399–1406), in *Chr. Mon. S. Alb.* III 280–420.

Ann. Lond. *Annales Londonienses* (1195–1311), in *Chr. Ed. I & II* I 3–251.

Ann. Margan *Annales de Margan* [Margam, Glam] (1066–1232), in *Ann. Mon.* I 1–40.

Ann. Midi *Annales du Midi*, I– (Toulouse, 1899–).

Ann. Mon. *Annales Monastici*, RS XXXVI, 5 vols. (1864–9); *v. Ann. Berm.*, *Ann. Burton*, *Ann. Dunstable*, *Ann. Margan*, *Ann. Osney*, *Ann. Tewk.*, *Ann. Wav.*, *Ann. Wint.*, *Ann. Worc.*, WYKES.

Ann. Osney *Annales monasterii de Oseneia* [Oxon] (1016–1347), in *Ann. Mon.* IV 3–352 [first text]; *v. et.* WYKES.

Ann. Paul. *Annales Paulini* [St. Paul's, London] (1307–41), in *Chr. Ed. I & II* I 253–370.

Ann. Ric. II *Annales Ricardi Secundi, Regis Angliae* (1392–9), in *Chr. Mon. S. Alb.* III 153–280.

Ann. Scot. *Annales regni Scotiae* (1291–2), in *Chr. Mon. S. Alb.* II 233–368.

Ann. S. Edm. *Annales S. Edmundi* [Bury St. Edmunds] (1032–1212), in *Mem. S. Edm.* II 1–25 complemented by *ANQuellen* 107–55.

Ann. Tewk. *Annales monasterii de Theokesberia* [Tewkesbury, Glos] (1066–1263), in *Ann. Mon.* I 41–180.

Ann. Wav. *Annales monasterii de Waverleia* [Waverley, Surr] (Incarnation–1291), in *Ann. Mon.* II 127–411.

Ann. Wint. *Annales monasterii de Wintonia* [Winchester] (519–1277), in *Ann. Mon.* II 3–125.

Ann. Worc. *Annales prioratus de Wigornia* [Worcester] (Incarnation–1377), in *Ann. Mon.* IV 365–564.

ANQuellen F. Liebermann: Ungedruckte Anglo-Normanische Geschichtsquellen (Strasbourg, 1879).

ANSELM Anselm, Archb. of Canterbury [*ob.* 1109], *Opera omnia*, ed. F. S. Schmitt, 6 vols. (Seckau, Rome, Edinburgh, 1938–61) [by vol. & p.]: **Azym.** *Epistola de sacrificio azimi et fermentati*, II 221–32; **Casus Diab.** *De casu diaboli*, I 227–76; **CurD** *Cur Deus homo*, II 37–133; **Ep.** *Epistolae*, III 93–294, IV, V [letters to Anselm cited as *Ep. Anselm.*]; **Gram.** *De grammatico*, I 141–68; **Incarn.** *Epistola de incarnatione Verbi*: **A** I 277–90, **B** II 1–35; **Lib. Arb.** *De libertate arbitrii*, I 201–26; **Medit.** *Meditationes*, III 76–91; **Misc.** *Miscellanea Anselmiana*, in *Mem. Anselm* 295–360; **Mon.** *Monologion*, I 1–87; **Or.**

Orationes, III 1–75; **Orig. Pecc.** *De conceptu virginali et de originali peccato*, II 135–73; **Praesc.** *De concordia praescientiae* [2 recensions] II 243–88; **Proc. Sp.** *De processione spiritus sancti*, II 175–219; **Prosl.** *Proslogion*, I 89–122; **Resp. Ed.** *Ad proslogion responsio editoris*, I 130–9; **Resp. Insip.** *Ad proslogion responsio Gaunilonis pro insipiente*, I 125–9; **Sacr.** *Epistola de sacramentis ecclesiae*, II 239–42; **Ver.** *De veritate*, I 169–99; [*v. et. Simil. Anselmi*; *cf.* ALEX. CANT., EADMER *Beat.*, *V. & Mir. Anselmi*].

ANSELM BURY Mir. Virg. Anselm, Abbot of Bury St. Edmunds [1121–48]: *Miracula S. Virginis Mariae*, Univ. of Wisconsin Stud. in Social Science & History XII (1927) 15–61 [by cap.; letter to Anselm cited as *Ep. Anselm. Bur.*].

Antiq. Antiquity, a quarterly journal of archaeology, I– (Cambridge, 1927–).

Antiq. Cant. W. Somner: Antiquities of Canterbury, 2nd ed. (1703).

Antiq. J. Society of Antiquaries of London, Journal, I– (1921–).

Antiq. Salop R. W. Eyton: Antiquities of Shropshire, 12 vols. (1854).

Antiq. Warw. W. Dugdale: Antiquities of Warwickshire (Coventry, 1765).

APScot Acts of the Parliaments of Scotland (1124–1567), 2 vols. RC (1844, 1814) [pag. not contin.]; *v. et. Iter Cam., Iter Cam. Artic., Leg. IV Burg., Quon. Attach., RegiamM, Stat. Gild. Berw.*

Arch. Aeliana, Society of Antiquaries of Newcastle-upon-Tyne, I– (1822–).

Arch. *Archaeologia*, Society of Antiquaries of London, I– (1775–).

Arch. Bridgw. Bridgwater borough Archives, 1200–1485, 5 vols. Som Rec. Soc. XLVIII, LIII, LVIII, LX, LXX (1933–71) [by no.].

Arch. Cambr. *Archaeologia Cambrensis*, Cambrian Archaeological Association, seven series, I– (London & Cardiff, 1846–); **Orig. Docs.** Original documents, I (1877) [issued with 4th ser. I–VIII (1870–77), contin. pag. i–ccclviii]; II [issued with 4th ser. IX, X, XIV, (1878–83), contin. pag. i–lxxii, incomplete]; III [issued 1912–15].

Arch. Cant. *Archaeologia Cantiana*, Kent Archaeological Society, transactions, I– (1858–).

Archd. Buck. The courts of the Archdeaconry of Buckingham, 1483–1523, Bucks Rec. Soc. XIX (1975) [by no.].

Arch. Gironde, Archives historiques du départment de la Gironde, I–XLIX (Paris & Bordeaux, 1859–1914).

Arch. Hist. Camb. R. Willis & J. W. Clark: Architectural History of the University of Cambridge, 4 vols. (Cambridge, 1886).

Archiv für Gesch. der Medizin Archiv für Geschichte der Medizin, ed. K. Sudhoff, I– (Leipzig, 1908–).

Arch. J. Archaeological Journal, Royal Archaeological Institute of Great Britain and Ireland, I– (1844–).

Arch. Mun. Bordeaux Archives municipales de Bordeaux, I– (1867–).

Arch. Ox. Mediaeval Archives of the University of Oxford (*c*1179–*c*1571), OHS LXX, LXXIII (1917, 1919).

Arch. Soc. Derb Derbyshire Archaeological Society, Journal, I– (1879–); Rec. S., I– (1965–).

Arch. Soc. Essex Essex Archaeological Society, transactions, I– (Colchester, 1858–); occasional publications, I– (Colchester, 1946–).

Arch. Soc. Norf Norfolk Archaeology, I– (Norwich, 1846–).

Arch. Soc. Salop Shropshire Archaeological Society, transactions, I– (Shrewsbury, 1878–).

Arch. Soc. Som Somersetshire Archaeological Society, proceedings, I– (Taunton, 1851–).

Arch. Soc. Suss v. Collect. Suss.

Arch. Soc. Yorks Yorkshire Archaeological Association: **J.** Journal, I– (Leeds, 1870–); **Rec. S.** Record Series I– (Leeds, 1885–).

Ars notaria Treatise on conveyancing (extr.) [attrib. Simon O., Filius Columbae, *fl.* 1400], JRL Bull. XXIII (1939), 438–44; *v. et. Dictamen*.

Arthur & Gorlagon (13c.), ed. G. L. Kittredge, Harvard Studies in Philology and Literature VIII (1903) 150–62 [by cap.].

Artic. Cam. v. Iter Cam. Artic.

ASC Anglo-Saxon Charters, I– (British Academy, 1973–).

ASCHAM Ep. Roger Ascham [1515–68]: *Epistolarum libri IV* (1703).

AS Chr. Anglo-Saxon Chronicle; cited by date alone as source for Latin chroniclers; *Annales Domitiani Latini*, MS BL Cotton Domitian A VIII (wr. *p*1058), cited from Med. Stud. IX (1947) 243–72.

AS Church M. Deanesly: Sidelights on the Anglo-Saxon Church (1962).

ASD An Anglo-Saxon Dictionary, ed. J. Bosworth and T. N. Toller (Oxford, 1898); **Add.** Enlarged addenda and corrigenda, ed. A. Campbell (Oxford, 1972); **Sup.** Supplement, ed. Toller (Oxford, 1921).

ASE Anglo-Saxon England, I– (Cambridge, 1972–).

ASHENDEN AM John Ashenden (*alias* Eastwood), Fellow of Merton [*fl.* 1338–57]: *Summa astrologiae judicialis de accidentibus mundi* (Venice, 1489) [by f.].

AS Hymns The Latin Hymns of the Anglo-Saxon Church, with an Interlinear Anglo-Saxon Gloss (11c.), Surtees Soc. XXIII (1851).

AS Inscr. E. Okasha: Hand-list of Anglo-Saxon non-runic Inscriptions (Cambridge, 1971) [by no.].

ASPR The Anglo-Saxon Poetic Records, ed. G. P. Krapp and E. V. K. Dobbie, 6 vols. (New York, 1931–42).

ASSER Alf. Asser, Bishop of Sherborne [*ob. c*909]: *De rebus gestis Ælfredi* (Oxford, 1904) [by cap.]; *v. et. Chr. S. Neoti.*

AssessR Cornw Duchy of Cornwall Assession Rolls (1300–), MS PRO (E. 306).

Assize Clar. The Assize of Clarendon (1166), in R. HOWD. II 248–52 [by sect.]; also in *SelCh.* 170–3.

AssizeR Durh The Assize Rolls for Co. Durham (1235–6, 1242), Surtees Soc. CXXVII (1916) 1–105.

AssizeR Lincs The earliest Lincolnshire Assize rolls (1202–9), Lincs Rec. Soc. XXII (1926).

AssizeR Northants The earliest Northamptonshire Assize Rolls (1202–1203), Northants Rec. Soc. V (1930).

AssizeR Northumb Three early Assize Rolls for the county of Northumberland (1256, 1269, 1279), Surtees Soc. LXXXVIII (1891).

ASTON John Aston (*alias* Ashton) [*fl.* 1382], *v. Ziz.*.

A. TEWK. Alan, Prior of Tewkesbury [*ob.* 1202]: **Ep.** *Epistolae*: 1–9, 10(11)–14(15), ed. J. A. Giles, Caxton Soc. (1846), 33–58; also *PL* CXC 1475–88; 10, 16–50, ed. M. A. Harris, *Studia Monastica* XVIII (1976) 77–108, 299–351 [by no.]; **Prol. Thom.** Prologue to J. SAL. *Thom.*, in *Becket Mat.* II 299–301; **Add. Thom.** Additions to J. SAL. *Thom.*, *ib.* 323–52 [by cap.].

Auct. Brit. *Auctores Britannici Medii Aevi*, I– (British Academy, 1969–).

Augm. Bk. Exchequer, Augmentation Office, Miscellaneous Books (12c.–), MS PRO (E. 315).

AVESB. Robert of Avesbury [*ob. a*1360]: *De gestis mirabilibus Regis Edwardi Tertii*, RS XCIII (1889) 279–471 [by f.].

AYLWARD Thomas Aylward [*ob.* 1413]: Life of William of Wykeham, ed. G. H. Moberley (1887) 287–91 [ed. 1893 315–20]; *cf.* HEETE *Wykeham*.

B. *Auctor B.* [*fl.* 1000]: **Ep.** *Epistola B. ad Æthelgarum archiepiscopum* (*a*990), in *Mem. Dunst.* 385–8; **V. Dunst.** *Vita S. Dunstani* [*ob.* 988] *auctore B.*, in *Mem. Dunst.* 3–52 [by cap.].

Babio *De Babione* (? c1180), ed. E. Faral (Paris, 1948) [by line].

BACON Roger Bacon [*ob.* 1294], *Opera hactenus inedita*, ed. R. Steele *et al.*, 16 vols. (1905–40) [by vol. & p.]: I *Metaphysica de vitiis contractis in studio theologiae*; II–IV *Communia naturalia*; V *Secretum secretorum*; VI 2–198 *Compotus*; 199–211 *Kalendarium*; 212–67 *Compotus v.* GROS. *Comp.*; VII *Quaestiones supra undecimum primae philosophiae Aristotelis*; VIII *Quaestiones supra libros IV Physicorum Aristotelis*; IX 1–83 *De retardatione accidentium senectutis* [attrib.], 84–9 *Summaria expositio epistolae predictae*; 90–5 *De universali regimine senum*; 96–7 *De balneis senum*; 98–102 *De compositione medicinarum*; 103–19 *Antidotarius*; 120–43 *De conservatione juventutis*; 144–9 *De graduatione medicinarum*; 150–79 *De erroribus medicorum*; 181–6 *Liber sex scientiarum* (extr.); 186–208 *De diebus creticis*; X *Quaestiones supra libros primae philosophiae Aristotelis*; XI 1–170 *Quaestiones alterae supra libros primae philosophiae Aristotelis*; 171–252 *Quaestiones supra De plantis*; 253–312 *Metaphysica vetus Aristotelis*; XII 1–158 *Quaestiones supra librum de causis*; 159–87 *Liber de causis*; XIII *Quaestiones supra libros octo Physicorum Aristotelis*; XIV 1–134 *Liber de sensu et sensato*; 135–208 *Summa de sophismatibus et distinctionibus*; XV 1–190 *Summa grammatica*; 191–359 *Summulae dialectices*; XVI *Communia mathematica*; other works cited individually: **CSPhil.** *Compendium studii philosophiae, Fr. Rogeri Bacon Opera inedita*, RS XV (1859) 393–519; **CSTheol.** *Compendium studii theologiae*, ed. H. Rashdall, Brit. Soc. Franciscan Studies III (Aberdeen, 1911); **Gram. Gk.** The Greek Grammar of Roger Bacon and a fragment of his Hebrew Grammar (Cambridge, 1902) 3–196; **Gram. Heb.** Hebrew Grammar, *ib.* 202–8; **Maj.** *Opus majus* (1267), ed. J. H. Bridges, 3 vols. (Oxford, 1897–1900), *corrigenda* in vol. III; **Min.** *Opus minus* (1267), RS XV 313–89; **Mor. Phil.** *Moralis philosophia*, ed. E. Massa (Zürich, 1953) [part VII of *Maj.*; supersedes ed. of 1897–1900 II 223–404 and III 144–151]; **MS** *De multiplicatione specierum*, w. *Maj.* II 407–552; superseded by ed. D. C. Lindberg, Roger Bacon's Philosophy of Nature (Oxford, 1983, 1–269; **NM** *De nullitate magiae*, RS XV 523–51; **Persp.** *Perspectiva* (Frankfurt, 1614); **SC** *De speculis comburentibus*, ib. 168–204; superseded by ed. D. C. Lindberg, Roger Bacon's Philosophy of Nature (Oxford, 1983), 272–341; **Sign.** *De signis*, *Traditio* XXXIV (1978) 75–136; **Tert.** *Opus tertium* (1267), RS XV 3–310; **sup.** [additional portions of *Tert.*], Brit. Soc. Franciscan Studies IV (1912).

BACONTHORPE John Baconthorpe [*ob.* 1346]: **Post. Matth.** *Postilla super Matthaeum* (extr.), *Carmelus* II (1955) 260–74; **Quaest. Sent.** *Quaestiones in IV libros Sententiarum* (Cremona, 1618), I, II 1–582; **Quodl.** *Quodlibetorum libri IV*, ib. II 583–779; **Sent.** *Opus super IV sententiarum libris* (Paris, 1484).

BAD. AUR. Johannes de Bado Aureo (of Guildford) [*fl.* 1400]: *Tractatus de armis* [2 versions], ed. E. J. Jones, Mediaeval Heraldry (Cardiff, 1943) 95–212.

Baga Secr. *Baga de secretis* (1477–), MS PRO (K.B. 8).

BAKER Geoffrey le Baker (*alias* Walter of Swinbroke) [*fl.* 1350]: *Chronicon* (1303–56), ed. E. M. Thompson (Oxford, 1889) [by f.]; *cf.* MORE *Chr. Ed. II.*

BALD. CANT. Baldwin, Archb. of Canterbury [*ob.* 1190]: **Commend. Fid.** *De commendatione fidei*, PL CCIV (1855) 571–640; **Sacr. Alt.** *De sacramento altaris*, ib. 641–774; **Tract.** *Tractatus*, ib. 403–572 [by no. & col.].

BALE Index John Bale [*ob.* 1563]: *Index Britanniae Scriptorum*, ed. R. L. Poole and M. Bateson, *Anecd. Oxon.* IX (1902).

BALSH. Adam of Balsham (*alias* de Parvo Ponte) [*ob.* 1181]: **AD** *Ars disserendi* (*Dialectica Alexandri*) (1132), ed. L. Minio-Paluello, Twelfth century logic, texts and studies I (Rome, 1956) 1–68 [by cap.]; **AD rec. 2** [second

recension, possibly by NECKAM], *ib.* footnotes and 69–111 [by cap.]; **Ut.** *De utensilibus*, in *N. & E.* XXXIV (1891) 33–59 [*vv. ll.* checked with variants in A. Scheler, Jahrb. für rom. Lit. VIII (1867) 75–93].

Bannatyne Club publications, 133 vols. (Edinburgh, 1823–67).

Bannatyne Misc. Miscellany of original papers relating to the history of Scotland, 3 vols. Bannatyne Club (1827–55).

Banstead History of Banstead in Surrey (selected docs. 1086–), ed. H. C. M. Lambert, 2 vols. (Oxford, 1912, 1931).

Baronial Reform E. F. Jacob: Studies in the period of Baronial Reform (Oxford, 1925).

BART. ANGL. Bartholomaeus Anglicus (*alias* de Glanville) [*fl.* 1230–50]: *De proprietatibus rerum* (Cologne, 1472) [by bk. & cap.]; bks. III–IV also ed. R. J. Long, Toronto Med. Latin Texts (1979).

BART. EXON. Pen. Bartholomew of Exeter [*ob.* 1184]: *Liber poenitentialis*, ed. A. Morey, Bartholomew of Exeter (Cambridge, 1937) 175–300 [by cap.].

BATES An. John Bates, Carmelite [*ob.* 1429]: *Quaestiones de Anima* (extr.), *Carmelus* XXIV (1977) 112–26.

BBAdm *Monumenta juridica* or the Black Book of the Admiralty (14c.–15c.), 4 vols. RS LV (1871–6).

BBC British Borough Charters (1042–1660), ed. A. Ballard, J. Tait, and M. Weinbaum, 3 vols. (Cambridge, 1913–43): I 1042–1216; II 1216–1307; III 1307–1660 [by date & p.].

BB Christ Church The Black Book of Christ Church Cathedral, Dublin (compiled 1340), extr. facsimile in RC Rep. (Ireland) I (1810–15) 308–9; MS Christ Church Cathedral Library, Dublin.

BBExch *Liber niger Scaccarii* or the Little Black Book of the Exchequer (*temp.* Hen. III), MS PRO E. 164/12, ed. T. Hearne, 2nd ed. 2 vols. (1771); *v. et. Domus Reg.*, KYMER, W. WORC. *Anecd.*

BBHouseh *Liber niger domus Regis Angliae, etc.*, ed. A. R. Myers, The Household of Edward IV (1959) 76–197.

BB Lismore The Black Book of Lismore, frags. ed. J. Ware, Antiquities of Ireland (1704–5).

BB S. Aug. v. Reg. S. Aug.

BB St. Davids The Black Book of St. Davids: an extent of lands etc. in 1326, Cymmrodorion Rec. S. V (1902); (extr.) also in *Tribal System* app. C, 97–100.

BB Wint. The Black Book of Winchester [Corporation] (15c.–16c.), ed. W. H. B. Bird (Winchester, 1925).

B. COTTON Bartholomew Cotton [*ob.* c1298]: **Arch.** *Liber de archiepiscopis et episcopis Angliae* (582–1228), RS XVI (1859) 345–418; **HA** *Historia Anglicana* (449–1298), *ib.* 1–344;

BEAUFEU Cervisia Robert Beaufeu (*alias* de Bello Foco or de Bello Fago), canon of Salisbury [*fl.* 1190]: *Versus de commendatione cervisiae*, Rev. Ben. L (1938) 139–40 [by no. & line; *cf.* P. BLOIS *Cervisia, Vinum*].

Becket Mat. Materials for the history of Thomas Becket, Archb. of Canterbury, 7 vols. RS LXVII (1875–85); *v.* A. TEWK. *Thom.*, BECKET *Ep.*, BEN. PET., *Ep. Becket*, GRIM, H. BOS. *Thom.*, J. SAL. *Thom.*, *V. Thom. A & B*, W. CANT., W. FITZST.

BECKET Thomas Becket, Archb. of Canterbury [1162–70]: **Ep.** *Epistolae*, in *Becket Mat.* V–VII [by no.; letters to Becket cited as *Ep. Becket*]; **Sim.** Satire against the Simoniacs [attrib.], in *Poésies Pop.* 175–7.

Becket to Langton C. R. Cheney: From Becket to Langton (Manchester, 1956).

Bec M. Morgan: The English lands of the Abbey of Bec (Oxford, 1946).

BEDE Bede the Venerable [673–735]: **Acts** *In Acta* (p709), PL XCII 937–996; **AM** *De arte metrica*, ed. H. Keil, *Grammatici Latini* VII (1878) 227–60 [by p. of ed. Putschius 2349–2383]; superseded by *CCSL* CXXIIIA

(1975) 81–141 [by p.]; **Apoc.** *In Apocalypsin* (*a*716), *PL* XCII 129–206; **Cant.** *In Cantica canticorum libri VI* (*a*731), *CCSL* CXIXB (1983) 167–375 [by col. of *PL* XCI]; **Chr.** *Chronica Maiora*, *CCSL* CXXIIIB (1977) 463–544; **CuthbP** Prose Life of St. Cuthbert (*c*721), ed. B. Colgrave, *Two Lives of St. Cuthbert* (1940) 141–306 [by cap.]; **CuthbV** Metrical Life of St. Cuthbert, ed. W. Jaager (Leipzig, 1935) [by line]; also *PL* XCIV 575–90; **Egb.** *Epistola ad Ecgbertum episcopum* (734), ed. C. Plummer, *Baedae Opera Historica*, I 405–23 [by cap.]; **Ezra** *In Ezram et Neemiam*, *CCSL* CXIXA (1969) 235–392 [by col. of *PL* XCI; Bks. I and II are commentaries on Ezra, Bk. III on Nehemiah (sometimes known as 2 Ezra)]; **Gen.** *Libri quatuor in principium Genesis* (*p*721), *ib.* CXVIIIA (1967) [by col. of *PL* XCI 9–190]; **HA** *Historia abbatum* [Benedict, Ceolfrid, Eosterwin, Sigfrid, Hwætberht] (*p*716), ed. C. Plummer, *Baedae Opera Historica*, I 364–87 [by cap.]; **Hab.** *In canticum Abacuc*, *CCSL* CXIXB (1983) 381–409 [by col. of *PL* XCI]; **HE** *Historia ecclesiastica gentis Anglorum* (731), ed. C. Plummer, *Baedae Opera Historica* 2 vols. (Oxford, 1896) I 5–360 [by bk. & cap.]; also ed. B. Colgrave and R. A. B. Mynors, Med. Texts (Oxford, 1969); **HE Cont.** ed. Plummer, I 361–3; **Hom.** Homilies, *CCSL* CXXII (1955) 1–143; [this contains all the genuine homilies of Bede; cited by bk. & no. of *CCSL*, & col. of *PL* XCIV]; **Hymn.** *Liber hymnorum, etc.*, *CCSL* CXXII (1955) 405–73 [by no. & line or stanza; *cf.* Ps.-Bede *Hymn.*]; **Kings** *In Regum librum XXX quaestiones*, *CCSL* CXIX (1962) 289–322 [by col. of *PL* XCI]; **Luke** *In Lucae evangelium expositio*, *CCSL* CXX (1960) 1–425 [by col. of *PL* XCI]; **Mark** *In Marci evangelium expositio*, *CCSL* CXX (1960) 427–648 [by col. of *PL* XCI]; **Mart.** Martyrology (prose) [attrib.], *PL* XCIV 797–1148; **Nom. Loc.** *Nomina locorum ex beati Hieronimi presbiteri et Flavi Josephi collecta opusculis*, *CCSL* CXIX (1962) 273–87; **Orth.** *De orthographia*, ed. H. Keil, *Grammatici Latini* VII 261–94 [by p. of ed. Putschius 2775–2804]; superseded by *CCSL* CXXIIIA (1975) 7–57 [by p.]; **Pleg.** *Epistola ad Pleguinam* (708), ed. C. W. Jones, *Bedae Opera de Temporibus*, Med. Acad. of America XLI (1943), 307–15 [by cap.]; **Prov.** *In Proverbia*, *CCSL* CXIXB (1983) 23–163 [by col. of *PL* XCI]; **Retract.** *Liber retractationis in Actus Apostolorum PL* XCII 995–1032; **Sam.** *In primam partem Samuhelis libri IIII*, *CCSL* CXIX (1962) 1–272 [by col. of *PL* XCI]; **ST** *De schematibus et tropis*, ed. C. Halm, *Rhetores Latini minores* (1863) 607–18 [by p.]; superseded by *CCSL* CXXIIIA (1975) 142–171 [by p.]; **Tab.** *De tabernaculo* (*a*729), *CCSL* CXIXA (1969) 1–139 [by col. of *PL* XCI]; **Temp.** *De temporibus* (703), ed. C. W. Jones, *Bedae Opera de Temporibus* 293–303 [by cap.]; **Templ.** *De templo*, *CCSL* CXIXA (1969) 141–234 [by col. of *PL* XCI]; **Tob.** *In Tobiam*, *CCSL* CXIXB (1983) 3–19 [by col. of *PL* XCI]; **TR** *De temporum ratione*, ed. C. W. Jones, *Bedae Opera de Temporibus*, Med. Acad. of America XLI (1943) 175–291 [by cap.]; also *CCSL* CXXIIIB 263–460; **Wict.** *Epistola ad Wicthedum* (708), *Opera de Temporibus* 317–25 [by cap.].

Beds Hist. Rec. Soc. Bedfordshire Historical Record Society, publications, I– (Apsley Guise, Bedford, 1913–).

BEKINSAU John Bekinsau [*ob.* 1559]: *De supremo et absoluto regis imperio*, in *Monarchia* I 735–56.

BEKYNTON Thomas Bekynton, king's secretary [*ob.* 1465]: Official [diplomatic] correspondence, 2 vols. RS LVI (1872); **App. 285** Dialogue in praise of William of Wykeham (incl. Life of Bekynton) [attrib. Chaundler], *ib.* II 321–6.

BELETH RDO John Beleth [*fl.* 1182]: *Rationale divinorum officiorum* (*a*1190), *PL* CCII (1855) 13–166 [by cap. & col.]; superseded by *CC cont. med.* XLI, XLIA (1976) [by cap. & col. of *PL*].

Bened. Æthelwoldi The Benedictional of Saint Æthelwold, ed. G. F. Warner and H. A. Wilson (Oxford, 1910).

Bened. Rob. Benedictional of Archbishop Robert (10c.), HBS XXIV (1903).

BENET Chr. John Benet, vicar of Harlington [*ob. c*1471]: Chronicle (1400–1462), Camd. Misc. XXIV, Camd. 4th S. (1972) 175–232.

BEN. GLOUC. Dubr. Benedict of Gloucester [*fl.* 1150]: *Vita S. Dubricii*, in *Anglia Sacra* II 654–61.

BEN. PET. Benedict of Peterborough [*ob.* 1193]: **Gesta** *v. G. Hen. II*, *G. Ric. I*; **Mir. Thom.** *Miracula S. Thomae Cantuariensis*, in *Becket Mat.* II 21–281 [by bk. & cap.]; **Pass. Thom.** *Passio S. Thomae Cantuariensis*, *ib.* II 1–19 [by frag.].

Best. Bestiary from MS Ii. iv. 26 in the University Library, Cambridge (12c.), ed. M. R. James, Roxb. Club (1928) [by serial no. (*cf.* pp. 28–34) & f.].

Beunans Meriasek Beunans Meriasek (1504), ed. W. Stokes (1872) [Latin stage directions cited by p. of MS in marg.].

BEVER *v.* J. Lond.

BGPM Beiträge zur Geschichte der Philosophie des Mittelalters, I–XLII (Münster, 1891–1970); NS I– (Münster, 1970–).

Bibl. Chem. *Bibliotheca chemica curiosa*, ed. J.-J. Manget, 2 vols. (Geneva, 1702).

Bibl. Vet. Pat. *Maxima bibliotheca veterum patrum et antiquorum scriptorum ecclesiasticorum* (–1600), ed. M. de la Bigne, 27 vols. (Lyon, 1677).

BILLINGHAM Richard Billingham, Fellow of Merton [*fl.* 1344–61]: **Sens.** *De sensu composito et diviso* (extr.), ed. A. Maierù, A Giuseppe Ermini (Spoleto, 1970) 387–93; **Spec.** *Speculum puerorum* (or *De probationibus terminorum* or *Terminus est in quem*), ed. L. M. de Rijk, Some 14c. tracts on the *Probationes Terminorum*, *Artistarium* III (1982) 45–186 [five recensions].

BIRCHINGTON Arch. Cant. Stephen Birchington [*fl.* 1382] [attrib.]: *Vitae archiepiscoporum Cantuariensium* (597–1369), in *Anglia Sacra* I 1–48.

BISSET Proc. Baldred Bisset (*alias* Bissait), Rector of Kinghorn [*fl.* 1300]: *Processus contra figmenta regis Angliae*, ed. T. Hearn, *Scotichronicon*, 5 vols. (Oxford, 1722), III 883–905.

BL British Library; supersedes BM, British Museum.

BLAKMAN Hen. VI John Blakman [*ob. p*1457]: *De virtutibus et miraculis Henrici VI*, ed. M. R. James (Cambridge, 1919).

BLANEFORD Henry de Blaneford [*fl.* 1330]: Chronicle (1323–4), in *Chr. Mon. S. Alb.* III 129–52.

BLUND *v.* J. Blund.

BM Ch. Facsimiles of royal and other Charters in the British Museum, I (1070–98) (1903) [no more pub.].

BNB Bracton's Note Book, extracts from *CurR*, *temp.* Hen. III, made for Henry de Bracton [*ob.* 1268], ed. F. W. Maitland, 3 vols. (1887) [by p.]; *v. et.* Bracton.

Bodl. Bodleian Library, Oxford.

BOECE Hector Boece (Boethius) [*ob.* 1536]: *Scotorum historiae a prima gentis origine libri XIX* (–*c*1436) (Paris, 1526) [by f.].

Boldon Bk. Boldon Buke, survey of possessions of see of Durham (1183), Surtees Soc. XXV (1852) [by p.].

BONIF. Boniface (*alias* Winfreth) [*ob.* 755]: **AG** *Ars* [*grammaticalis*], ed. A. Mai, *Classici auctores e codicibus Vaticanis editi* VII (1835) 475–548; superseded by *CCSL* CXXXIIIB (1980) 1–99 [by p. of Mai]; **Aen.** *Aenigmata* (*Virt. et Vit.*), *CCSL* CXXXIII (1968) 273–343 [by line]; also ed. E. Duemmler, in *PLAC* I; **Carm.** *Carmina*, in *PLAC* I (1881) 16–20 [by no. & line]; **Ep.** *Epistolae*, ed. M. Tangl, Briefe des heiligen Bonifatius und Lullus, *MGH Ep. selectae* I (1916) [by no.; letters to Boniface and others cited as *Ep. Bonif.*]; **Met.** *De caesuris et metris*, ed. T. Gaisford, *Scriptores Latini rei metricae* (1837) 577–85; superseded by *CCSL* CXXXIIIB (1980) 109–113.

Borough Cust. Borough Customs, 2 vols. Selden Soc. XVIII, XXI (1904, 1906).

BOSO Boso, monk of St. Albans [*ob.* 1181]: **V. Pont.** *Vitae Romanorum Pontificum*, ed. L. Duchesne, Le *Liber Pontificalis* (Paris, 1892) II 351–446.

Bower, Walter, Abbot of Inchcolm [*ob.* 1449], *v.* Fordun *Cont.*

BRACTON Henry de Bracton (*alias* Bratton) [*ob.* 1268] [attrib.]: *De legibus et consuetudinibus Angliae* (*c*1258), ed. G. E. Woodbine, 4 vols. (New Haven, Conn., 1915–42) [by f.]; *v. et. BNB.*

BRADW. Thomas Bradwardine, Archb. of Canterbury [1290–1349]: **AM** *Ars memorativa* [attrib.], ed. B. Politus, *Quaestio de modalibus* (Venice, 1505); **AS** *Arithmetica speculativa* (Paris, 1495, etc.); **CD** *De causa Dei contra Pelagium libri III* (1344), ed. H. Savile (1618); **Conseq.** *Textus consequentiarum* [attrib.], CIMA XLII (1982) 92–150; **Cont.** *De continuo* (extr.), in *Sci. Mech.* 232–4; **Fut.** *De futuris contingentibus*, Recherches augustiniennes XIV (1979) 281–336 [by sect.]; also in Grabmann Studies (extr.), 1169–80; **GS** *Geometria speculativa* (Paris, 1511, etc.); **Inc.** *De incipit et desinit*, CIMA XLII (1982) 47–83; **Insol.** *Insolubilia*, AHDLMA XXXVII (1970) 285–306 [by sect.]; **Log.** *Opus artis logicae* [attrib.], CIMA XLII (1982) 152–64; **Prop.** *De proportione velocitatum in motibus* (1328), ed. H. Lamar Crosby (Madison, Wisc., 1955); **Sermo** *Sermo epinicius* [attrib.], AHDLMA XXV (1958) 295–329.

BRAKELOND Jocelin of Brakelond [*ob. p*1214]: *Cronica de rebus gestis Samsonis abbatis monasterii S. Edmundi* [Suff] (1173–1202), ed. H. E. Butler, Med. Texts (1949) [by f.].

BRAMIS Wald. John Bramis (*alias* Bromis), monk of Thetford [14c.]: *Historia regis Waldei* [transl. from French], ed. R. Imelmann, Bonner Studien zur englischen Philologie IV (1912) [by bk & cap.].

Brev. Aberd. *Breviarium Aberdonense* (1509–10), 2 vols. Bannatyne Club (1854).

Brev. Ebor. *Breviarium ad usum insignis Ecclesiae Eboracensis* (printed from ed. 1493), Surtees Soc. LXXI, LXXV (1880, 1883).

Brev. Hyda The monastic Breviary of Hyde Abbey, Winchester, HBS LIX, LXXI, LXXVI, LXXVIII, LXXX (1932–42) [by f.].

Brev. Sal. The Salisbury Breviary, or great breviary, text of the 1531 ed., ed. F. Procter and C. Wordsworth, 3 vols. (Cambridge, 1882, 1879, 1886).

BRINKLEY Richard Brinkley, O.F.M. [late 14c.]: **Summa** *Summa Logicae* (extr.), Franciscan Studies XL (1980) 79–101 [by part & cap.].

BRINTON Serm. Thomas Brinton (*alias* Brunton), Bishop of Rochester [1373–89]: Sermons, Camd. 3rd S. LXXXV, LXXXVI (1954) [by no. & p.].

Brokage Bk. Southampt. The Brokage Books of Southampton: 1439–40 Southampton Rec. Soc. XL (1941); 1443–4, Southampton Rec. S. IV, VI (1960, 1961).

BROMPTON John Brompton [*fl.* 1436] [attrib.]: *Chronicon* (588–1198), in *Hist. Angl. Script. X* 728–1284 [by col.].

BROMYARD Summa John of Bromyard [*fl.* 1390]: *Summa praedicantium*, 2 vols. (Venice, 1586).

Bronnen Bronnen tot de Geschiedenis van den Handel met Engeland Schotland en Ierland (1150–1585), ed. H. J. Smit, 4 vols. Commissie van advies voor's Rijks Geschiedkundige LXV, LXVI, LXXXVI, XCI (The Hague, 1928–50).

Brunton *v.* Brinton.

Brutus *Brutus* Eine metrische Paraphrase der *Historia Regum Britannie* für den Durhames Bischof Hugo de Puiset (1190), Mittellateinisches Jahrbuch XI (1976) 204–23 [by line].

BR Will. I *Brevis relatio de origine Willelmi Conquestoris* (*a*1135), ed. J. A. Giles, *Scriptores rerum gestarum Willelmi Conquestoris*, Caxton Soc. (1845) 1–26.

BRYGG Itin. Thomas Brygg [14c.]: *Itinerarium in Terram Sanctam domini Thomae de Swynburne* (1392–3), Archives de l'orient latin II (Paris, 1884) 378–88.

Bucks Rec. Soc. Buckinghamshire Archaeological Society, Records Branch, publications, I–VI (1937–45); Buckinghamshire Record Society, publications, VII– (1947–).

Building in Eng. L. F. Salzman: Building in England down to 1540, a documentary history (Oxford, 1952).

Bull. DuC v. ALMA.

Burley *v.* Ad. Burley, W. Burley.

Bury St. Edm. M. D. Lobel: The borough of Bury St. Edmund's (Oxford, 1935), app. I, docs. (*c*1190–1479) 171–95.

BUTLER William Butler [*fl.* 1410]: *Determinatio*, ed. M. Deanesly, *The Lollard Bible* (Cambridge, 1920) 399–418.

BYRHT. Byrhtferth of Ramsey [*fl.* 1000]: **HR** *Historia regum* (616–888), capp. 1–35, 40–50, 53–80, in S. Durh. II 3–91 [by cap.] (*cf.* M. Lapidge, Byrhtferth of Ramsey and the early sections of the *Historia Regum* attributed to Symeon of Durham, ASE X (1981) 97–122; **Man.** Manual, EETS CLXXVII (1929) 2–246; epilogue also *Speculum* III (1928) 516–19; cf. H. Henel, Byrhtferth's Preface: the Epilogue of his Manual?, *Speculum* XVIII (1943) 288–302; **V. Ecgwini** *Vita S. Ecgwini*, ed. J. A. Giles, *Vita quorundum Anglo-Saxonum* (*sic*), Caxton Soc. (1854) 349–96; **V. Osw.** *Vita S. Oswaldi Archiepiscopi Eboracensis* [*ob.* 992] (wr. *c*1000), in *Hist. Church York* I 399–475.

CAIUS John Caius (*alias* Keyes) [1510–73]: **Anim.** *De rariorum animalium historia libellus* (1570), ed. E. S. Roberts, The Works of John Caius (Cambridge, 1912) [by f.]; **Can.** *De canibus Britannicis libellus* (1570), *ib.*

Cal. Bart. v. Cart. Bart.

Cal. ChancR Var. Calendar of various Chancery Rolls (1277–1326), HMSO (1912).

CalCh Calendar of Charter Rolls (1226–1516), 6 vols. HMSO (1903–27); *v. et. ChartR, RChart.*

CalCl Calendar of the Close Rolls (1272–), HMSO (1900–); *v. et. Cl.*

Cal. CourtR Chester Calendar of County Court, City Court, and Eyre Rolls of Chester, 1259–97, w. inquest of military service, 1288, Chetham Soc. NS LXXXIV (1925).

Cal. Deeds Ormond Calendar of Ormond deeds (1170–1603), 6 vols. IMC (Dublin, 1932–43).

Cal. Doc. France Documents preserved in France, illustrative of the history of Great Britain and Ireland (918–1206), ed. J. H. Round, HMSO (1899) [by no.].

CalExch The antient kalendars and inventories of the Treasury of H. M. Exchequer, 3 vols. RC (1836).

CalFineR Calendar of Fine Rolls (1272–1509), 22 vols. HMSO (1911–63); *v. et. FineR.*

CalIMisc Calendar of Inquisitions Miscellaneous (1219–), HMSO (1916–) [by no.].

Cal. IPM Calendar of inquisitions *post mortem etc.*: 1st S., vol. I– (Hen. III–) (1904–); 2nd S., vol. I– (Hen. VII–) (1898–) [by no.].

Cal. Ir. Calendar of documents relating to Ireland (1171–1307), 5 vols. HMSO (1875–86).

Cal. Just. Ir. Calendar of the Justiciary Rolls of Ireland, 3 vols. (Dublin, 1905–56): I (1295–1303), II (1305–7), III (1308–13).

Cal. LBLond. Calendar of Letter Books preserved at the Guildhall [London], ed. R. R. Sharpe, A–L (Ed. I–Hen. VII), 11 vols. (1899–1912).

Cal. Liberate Calendar of Liberate Rolls (1226–72), 6 vols. HMSO (1916–64) [vol. VI by no.; others by p.].

Cal. Mayor's CourtR Lond. Calendar of early Mayor's Court Rolls at the Guildhall, London (1298–1307), ed. A. H. Thomas (1924).

CalMem Calendar of Memoranda rolls (Exch) (Michaelmas 1326–Michaelmas 1327), HMSO (1968).

CalPat Calendar of Patent Rolls (1232–), III– HMSO (1906–); *v. et. Pat.*

Cal. Pl. Mem. Lond. Calendar of Plea and Memoranda Rolls of the City of London (1323–1482), ed. A. H. Thomas, 7 vols. (1926–1961).

Cal. RCoron Lond. Calendar of Coroners' Rolls of the City of London (1300–78), ed. R. R. Sharpe (1913).

Cal. RecogR Chester Calendar of Recognizance Rolls of Chester (13c.-1830), PRO Deputy Keeper's Reps. 36, 37, 39, app. II, sep. pub. (1875–8).

Cal. Scot. Calendar of documents relating to Scotland (1108–1509), 4 vols. Scot. RO (1881–8).

Cal. Scot. Mary Calendar of State Papers relating to Scotland and Mary, Queen of Scots (1547–1603), 13 vols. in 14, Scot. RO (1898–1969).

Cal. SPScot Calendar of State Papers relating to Scotland (1509–1603), Scot. S., 2 vols (1858).

Camb. Antiq. Soc. Cambridge Antiquarian Society, publications, 4° S., 2 vols. (1840–9); New 4° S. I– (1908–); 8° S. I– (1859–).

CAMD. Br. William Camden [1551–1623]: *Britannia* (1586) [by p. of ed. 1600].

Camd. Misc. The Camden Miscellany, I– , Camd. Soc. XXXIX (1847) *et alia*.

Camd. Soc. Camden Society, publications: I–CV (1808–70); NS New Series, I–LXII (1871–99); Camd. 3rd S. I–XCIV (1900–63); Camd. 4th S. I– (1964–); 3rd and 4th S. pub. by RHS.

CAMPSALL Richard of Campsall, fellow of Balliol and Merton Colleges [*ob. a*1360]: **Anal. Pri.** *Quaestiones super librum Priorum Analyticorum*, ed. E. A. Synan, The Works of Richard of Campsall, 2 vols. (Toronto, 1968–82), I 37–306 [by sect.]; **Log.** *Logica Campsale Anglici* [formerly attrib.], *ib.* II 76–420 [by sect.]; **Mat.** *Utrum materia possit esse sine forma, ib.* II 24–31; **Not.** *Notabilia de contingentia et praescientia Dei, ib.* II 38–43 [by no.]; **Univ.** *Contra ponentes naturam, ib.* II 14–17.

Canon. Edm. Rich *Quadrilogus*, docs. in support of the canonization of Edmund Rich (wr. 1241–2), ed. C. H. Lawrence, Lives of Edmund Rich (1960) 187–202.

Canon. G. Sempr. Un procès de canonisation (1201–2); le livre de Saint Gilbert de Sempringham [*ob.* 1189], ed. R. Foreville, (Lille, 1943) [by f.].

CANON Phys. John Canon (*alias* Canonicus) [*fl.* 1320]: *Quaestiones super octo libris Physicorum Aristotelis* (Padua, 1475); (extr.), *Opusc. & Text.* XVIII (1937) 57–63.

Canon. S. Osm. *Registrum in causa canonizationis beatae memoriae Osmundi* [*ob.* 1099] (wr. 1424–56), ed. A.R. Malden, The Canonization of St Osmund, Wilts Rec. Soc. (Salisbury, 1901), 1–90; other docs., *ib.* 93–246.

Cant. Cath. Pri. R. A. L. Smith: Canterbury Cathedral Priory (597–1540) (Cambridge, 1943).

Cant. Coll. Ox. Canterbury College, Oxford, ed. W. A. Pantin OHS VI, VII, VIII (1947–50) [I–II contin. pag.; III sep.].

Cantica Die monastischen Cantica im Mittelalter und ihre altenglischen Interlinear-versionen (10c.), ed. M. Korhammer (Munich, 1976) 254–351 [by no. & stanza].

CANTLOW Orig. Cantab. Nicholas Cantlow [*ob.* 1441]: *Historiola de antiquitate et origine Universitatis Cantabrigiensis*, ed. T. Hearne, in T. SPROTT *Chr.* 253–80.

Cant. & York Soc. Canterbury and York Society, publications, I– (London, 1909–).

Cap. Aug. Chapters of the Augustinian Canons, Cant. & York Soc. XXIX and OHS LXXIV (1922).

CAPGR. John Capgrave [1393–1464]: **Acts** *In Actus Apostolorum* (extr.), *v. Hen.* app. III; **Dunst.** *Vita et miracula Dunstani*, in *Mem. Dunst.* 325–53 [by cap.; *v. et. NLA*]; **Gen.** *In Genesim* (extr.), *v. Hen.* app. IV; **Hen.** *Liber de illustribus Henricis*, RS VII (1858) w. app. of extr. from

other works; **Symb.** *Commentarius super Symbola* (extr.), *v. Hen.* app. II.

Capt. Seis. Cornw *Captio seisinae Ducatus Cornubiae* (1337), MS PRO (E. 120); ed. P. L. Hull, Devon & Cornw Rec. Soc. NS XVII (1971).

CAREW Sent. Richard Carew [14c.]: *Commentarius in Sententias* (extr.), *AFH* LXXIII (1980) 497–513.

Carm. Aldh. *Carmina rhythmica* 1–5, *Aldhelmi Opera, MGH Auct. Antiq.* XV (1919) 523–37 (1 attrib. ALDH., 2–5 by Æthelwald) [by no. & line].

Carmelus *Carmelus: Commentarii ab Instituto Carmelitano editi* I– (Rome, 1954–).

Carm. Lew. *Carmen de bello Lewensi* [*c*1265], ed. C. L. Kingsford, The Song of Lewes (Oxford, 1890) 1–31.

Cart. Aberd. *Cartularium ecclesiae S. Nicholai Aberdonensis* (1328–), 2 vols. New Spalding Club (Aberdeen, 1888–92).

Cart. Antiq. *Cartae antiquae* (Ric. I–Ed. II), I (rolls 1–10), Pipe R. Soc. NS XVII (1939); II (rolls 11–20), *ib.* XXXIII (1960) [by p.]; rolls 21–46, MS PRO (C. 52).

Cart. Bart. Cartulary of St. Bartholomew's Hospital [London] (12c.-), calendar, ed. N. J. M. Kerling (1973).

Cart. Bath Two Chartularies of the Priory of St. Peter at Bath (9c.-) [specified as A or B], Som Rec. Soc. VII (1893) [by no.].

Cart. Beauchamp The Beauchamp Cartulary Charters 1100–1268, Pipe R. Soc. LXXXI (1980), [by no.].

Cart. Beaulieu Cartulary of the Abbey of Beaulieu [Hants] (13c.-), MS BL Loans 29/330, ed. S. F. Hockey, Southampton Rec. S. XVII (1974) [by f.].

Cart. Beauly Historical notices and charters of the Priory of Beauly, Ross-shire (13c.-), RHS Trans. IV (1876) 1–74; *v. et. Ch. Beauly.*

Cart. Bilsington Cartulary and Terrier of the Priory of Bilsington [Kent], ed. N. Neilson, Rec. Soc. & Econ. VII (1928): cartulary (mainly 13c.) 65–147; terrier (1567) 148–218.

Cart. Blyth Cartulary of Blyth Priory [Notts] (11c.-), Thoroton Soc. Rec. S. XXVII, XXVIII and HMC JP XVII (1973) [by no.].

Cart. Boarstall Boarstall [Bucks] Cartulary (1170–1498), OHS LXXXVIII (1930) [by no.].

Cart. Bonport Cartulaire de l'abbaye royale de Notre-Dame de Bonport [Norm.] (1190–1467), ed. J. Andrieux (Evreux, 1862).

Cart. Boxgrove Chartulary of Boxgrove Priory (13c.-), Sussex Rec. Soc. LIX (1960) [transl. only].

Cart. Brecon *Cartularium prioratus de Brecon* (12c.-), *Arch. Cambr.* 4th S. XIII (1882) 275–308; XIV (1883) 18–49, 137–68, 221–36, 274–311.

Cart. Brinkburn Cartulary of Brinkburn Priory [Northumb] (14c.), Surtees Soc. XC (1893).

Cart. Burton Abstract of Chartulary of Burton Abbey (1004–1437), Collect. Staffs V i (1884).

Cart. Bushmead Cartulary of Bushmead Priory (13c.), Beds Rec. Soc. XXII (1945) [by no.].

Cart. Canons Ashby Cartulary of the Priory of Canons Ashby [Northants] (late 13c.), MS BL Egerton 3033.

Cart. Carisb. Cartulary of Carisbrooke [I. of W.] (1114–), MS BL Egerton 3667.

Cart. Chertsey Chertsey Abbey Cartularies, 2 vols. in 3, Surrey Rec. Soc. XII (1915–63) [by vol. & no.; calendar only].

Cart. Chester Chartulary of the Abbey of St. Werburgh, Chester (10c.-early 14c.) w. addit. docs., Chetham Soc. NS LXXIX, LXXXII (1920–3) [contin. pag.].

Cart. Chich. Cartulary of the High Church of Chichester (12c.-17c.) [calendar], Sussex Rec. Soc. XLVI (1946) [by no.].

Cart. Ciren. Cartulary of Cirencester Abbey [Glos] (12c.-15c.), ed. C. D. Ross and M. Devine, 3 vols. (1964–77) [by no.].

Cart. Clerkenwell Cartulary of St. Mary's Priory, Clerkenwell [London], Camd. 3rd S. LXXVII (1949).

Cart. Cockersand Chartulary of Cockersand Abbey [Lancs] (12c.–16c.), 3 vols. in 7, Chetham Soc. NS XXXVIII–XL, XLIII, LVI, LVII, LXIV (1898–1909).

Cart. Colch. *Cartularium monasterii de Colecestria* [Essex] (11c.–13c.), 2 vols. Roxb. Club (1897).

Cart. Coldstream Chartulary of the Cistercian Priory of Coldstream [Berw] (12c.–16c.), Grampian Club (London, 1879).

Cart. Colne *Cartularium Prioratus de Colne* (12c.), Arch. Soc. Essex, occ. pub. I (1946) [by f.].

Cart. Dale Cartulary of Dale Abbey (13c.–   ), Arch. Soc. Derb, Rec. S. II and HMC JP XI (1967).

Cart. Darley Cartulary of Darley Abbey (late 12c.–13c.), ed. R. R. Darlington, 2 vols. (1945).

Cart. Dieul. Chartulary of Dieulacres Abbey (12c.–13c.), Collect. Staffs NS IX (1906) 291–362; **add.** *ib.* 363–6.

Cart. Dublin Chartularies of St. Mary's Abbey, Dublin, etc. (12c.–15c.), 2 vols. RS LXXX (1884).

Cart. Dunstable Digest of the Cartulary of Dunstable (late 12c.–17c.), Beds Hist. Rec. Soc. X (1926).

Carte Nativ. *Carte Nativorum*, a Peterborough Abbey cartulary (14c.), Northants Rec. Soc. XX (1960) [by no.].

Cart. Eye Cartulary of Eye Priory [Suff] (13c.), MS Essex RO D/DBy Q 19.

Cart. Eynsham Eynsham Cartulary (1005–1539), OHS XLIX, LI (1907–8); *v. et.* AD. EYNS. *Visio.*

Cart. Fount. Abstracts from charters contained in Chartulary of Fountains Abbey [Yorks] (12c.–15c.), ed. W. T. Lancaster, 2 vols. (1915) [English summary].

Cart. Glam. *Cartae et alia munimenta quae ad Dominium de Glamorgancia pertinent* (†5c. [11c.]–18c.), ed. G. T. Clark, 6 vols. (Cardiff, 1910) (–224, –712, –1176, –1632, –2096, Index) [some docs. cited from fuller text in first ed. 1885–93].

Cart. Glast. Great Chartulary of Glastonbury (12c.–16c.), Som Rec. Soc. LIX, LXII, LXIV (1947–56).

Cart. Glouc. *Historia et Cartularium Monasterii S. Petri Gloucestriae* (12c.–14c.), 3 vols. RS XXXIII (1863–7); *v. et. Hist. Glouc.*

Cart. God's House Southampt. Cartulary of God's House, Southampton (12c.–15c.), Southampton Rec. S. XIX, XX (1976) [by no.].

Cart. Godstow Cartulary of Godstow Abbey [Oxon] (15c.), MS PRO KR Misc. Bks. E. 164/20 [by f.].

Cart. Guisburn *Cartularium prioratus de Gyseburne* [Yorks], Surtees Soc. LXXXVI, LXXXIX (1889–94) [by no.].

Cart. Harrold Records of Harrold Priory, incl. Cartulary (12c.–16c.), Beds Hist. Rec. Soc. XVII (1935).

Cart. Healaugh Chartulary of the Augustinian priory of St John of the Park of Healaugh (12c.–16c.), Arch. Soc. Yorks, Rec. S. XCII (1936) [by f.].

Cart. Heming Heming, monk of Worcester [*fl.* 1096]: *Chartularium ecclesiae Wigorniensis* (8c.–11c.), ed. T. Hearne, 2 vols. (1723); *v. et. Cart. Worc.*

Cart. Holyrood *Liber Cartarum S. Crucis, munimenta ecclesie S. Crucis de Edwinesburg* (12c.–16c.) (extr.), Bannatyne Club LXX (1840).

Cart. Hosp. S. John Cartulary of the Hospital of St. John, Oxford (13c.–   ), OHS LXVI, LXVIII, LXIX (1914–16).

Cart. Norm. Cartulaire de Jersey et des autres Îles normandes (11c.–14c.), 6 pts. Soc. jers. (1918–24) [contin. pag.].

Cart. Lennox *Cartularium comitatus de Levenax* [Stirlingshire] (13c.), Maitland Club (1833).

Cart. Lewes Chartulary of the Priory of St. Pancras of Lewes (c1089–   ), compiled 1444, Sussex Rec. Soc. XXXVIII, XL (Lewes, 1932–4) [by f.; mainly transl.].

Cart. Lindores Chartulary of the Abbey of Lindores [Fife] (12c.–15c.), SHS XLII (1903) [by no.].

Cart. Missenden, Cartulary of Missenden Abbey (12c.–14c.), Bucks Rec. Soc. II, X, XII (1938–62) [by no.].

Cart. Mont. S. Mich. Cartulary of St. Michael's Mount (Hatfield House MS no. 315), ed. P. L. Hull, Devon & Cornwall Rec. Soc., N.S. 5 (1962) [by no.].

Cart. Newent Cartulary of Newent [Glos] (13c.), MS BL Add. 15668 ff. 50–68 [by f.].

Cart. Newm. *Chartularium Abbathiae de Novo Monasterio* [Northumb] (12c.–15c.), Surtees Soc. LXVI (1878).

Cart. Newnham Cartulary of Newnham Priory (12c.–15c.), Beds Hist. Rec. Soc. XLIII pts. 1 and 2 (1963–4).

Cart. Osney Cartulary of Oseney Abbey (12c.–16c.), OHS LXXXIX–XCI, XCVII, XCVIII, CI (1929–36).

Cart. Percy The Percy Chartulary, Surtees Soc. CXVII (1911) [by no.].

Cart. Pontefr. Chartulary of Pontefract (12c.–13c.), Arch. Soc. Yorks, Rec. S. XXV, XXX (1899, 1902).

Cart. Rams. *Cartularium monasterii de Rameseia* [Hunts] (11c.–14c.), 3 vols. RS LXXIX (1884–93).

Cart. Rievaulx *Cartularium Abbathiae de Rievalle* [Yorks] (12c.–16c.), Surtees Soc. LXXXIII (1889).

Cart. Rufford Rufford [Notts] Cartulary (12c.), MS BL Loans 41 ff. 1–16.

Cart. Sallay Chartulary of Sallay in Craven (12c.–14c.), Arch. Soc. Yorks, Rec. S. LXXXVII, XC (1933–4) [by no.].

Cart. Sandford Sandford Cartulary (12c.–13c.), Oxfordshire Rec. Soc. XIX, XXII (1938–41) [by no.].

Cart. S. Denys Southampt. Cartulary of the Priory of St. Denys, Portswood, Southampton (1157–   ), compiled *p*1342, MS BL Add. 15314; Southampton Rec. S. XXIV, XXV (1981).

Cart. S. Fridesw. Cartulary of the Monastery of St. Frideswide at Oxford (11c.–16c.), OHS XXVIII, XXXI (1895–9).

Cart. S. Greg. Cant. Cartulary of the Priory of St. Gregory, Canterbury (late 11c.–13c.), Camd. 3rd S. LXXXVIII (1956) [by no.].

Cart. Shrews. Cartulary of Shrewbury Abbey (11c.–   ), ed. U. Rees, 2 vols. (Aberystwyth, 1975).

Cart. S. Neots Cartulary of the Priory of St. Neots [Hunts] (12c.–15c.), MS BL Cotton Faustina A IV.

Cart. Staff. The Staffordshire Chartulary (1072–1237), Collect. Staffs II pt. 1 (1881) 178–276.

Cart. S. Thom. Hosp. Chartulary of the Hospital of St. Thomas Martyr, Southwark (1213–1525), calendar, ed. F. G. Parsons, private pub. (1932).

Cart. Stoke by Clare Cartulary of Stoke by Clare [Suff] (*p*1250), MS BL Cotton App. xxi.

Cart. Tutbury Cartulary of Tutbury Priory (12c.–15c.), Collect. Staffs 4th S. IV and HMC JP II (1962) [by no.].

Cart. Tynemouth Tynemouth Cartulary (7c.–16c.), ed. W. S. Gibson, History of the monastery at Tynemouth, 2 vols. (1846–7), app. i–clxvii.

Cart. Wardon Cartulary of Old Wardon (12c.–15c.), Beds Hist. Rec. Soc. XIII (1930) [by f.].

Cart. Whitby *Cartularium Abbathiae de Whiteby* [Yorks] (11c.–16c.), Surtees Soc. LXIX, LXXII (1879, 1881).

Cart. Winchcombe v. Reg. Winchcombe.

Cart. Worc. Cartulary of Worcester Cathedral Priory, Register I (*c*1240), Pipe R. Soc. NS XXXVIII (1968) [by no.]; *v. et. Cart. Heming.*

Cart. York Cartulary of the treasurer of York Minster and related documents (12c.–   ), compiled 15c., Borthwick Texts and Calendars: Records of the Northern Province V (1978).

Catal. Durh. Catalogues of the Library of Durham Cathedral from the Conquest to the Dissolution, Surtees Soc. VII (1838).

Catal. MSS AS N. R. Ker: Catalogue of Manuscripts Containing Anglo-Saxon (Oxford, 1957) [by p.].

Ann. Paul., G. Ed. II Bridl., G. Ed. III Bridl., J. LOND. *Commend. Ed. I,* MORE *Chr. Ed. II, V. Ed. II.*

Chr. Evesham *Chronicon abbatiae de Evesham* [Worcs], RS XXIX (1863): (*c*700–1214) [attrib. T. MARLB.], based on DOMINIC *V. Ecgwini* I pp. 1–27, *Translatio S. Ecgwini* pp. 27–38, DOMINIC *V. Ecgwini* II pp. 39–67; continued as *V. Ecgwini* III (*-c*1200), pp. 69–108, and *Chr.* (1200–1214), pp. 109–257; **Cont. A** Continuation (1214–1418), 257–310; **Cont. B.** (1418–1539), 338–40.

Chr. Hen. II & Ric. I Chronicles of the reigns of Henry II and Richard I, 2 vols. RS XLIX (1867); *v. G. Hen. II, G. Ric. I.*

Chr. Hen. VI & Ed. IV Brief notes of occurrences under Hen. VI and Ed. IV, Three fifteenth-century chronicles, Camd. Soc. NS XXVIII (1880) 148–63.

Chr. Holyrood *Chronicon Coenobii Sanctae Crucis Edinburgensis* (40 B.C.–1163), Bannatyne Club (1828).

Chr. Kirkstall The Kirkstall Chronicle (1355–1400), JRL Bull. XV (1931) 121–37.

Chr. Louth *Chronicon abbatiae de Parco Lude* [Louth Park, Lincs], w. app. of docs. (1066–1404), ed. E. Venables, Lincs Rec. Soc. I (1891).

Chr. Man *Chronica regum Manniae et Insularum* (1000–1374), ed. P. A. Munch and J. Goss, Manx Society XXII (text and transl.), XXIII (docs.) (Douglas, 1874).

Chr. Melrose *Chronica de Mailros* (731–1270), Bannatyne Club (1835).

Chr. Mon. S. Alb. *Chronica monasterii S. Albani*, 7 vols. in 12, RS XXVIII (1863–70): I WALS. *HA*, 2 vols.; II *Ann. Angl. & Scot., Ann. Ed. I, Ann. Scot.,* RISH.; III *Ann. Hen IV, Ann. Ric. II,* BLANEFORD, *Op. Chr.,* TROKELOWE; IV *G. S. Alb.* w. appendices, 3 vols.; V AMUND., *Chr. S. Alb. (1422–31),* w. appendices, 2 vols.; VI *Reg. Whet.,* 2 vols.; VII *Ps.-*RISH., WALS. *YN.*

Chr. Northern A Northern Chronicle (extr. 1399–1430), in *Eng. Hist. Lit. 15c.* 279–91.

Ch. Roff. Charters of Rochester, ed. A. Campbell, ASC I (1973) [by no.].

Chr. Peterb. *Chronicon Petroburgense* (1122–1289), Camd. Soc. XLVII (1849) 1–155; **app.** *Liber niger monasterii S. Petri de Burgo* (1125–8), *ib.* 157–83; *cf. Chr. Angl. Peterb.*

Chr. Pont. Ebor. *Chronica Pontificum Ecclesiae Eboracensis* (601–1519), in *Hist. Church York* II: **A** Anon. (601–1140, wr. *a*1150) 312–87; **B** *v.* T. STUBBS *Chr.*; **C** Anon. (1374–1519), 422–45.

Chr. Rams. *Chronicon Abbatiae Rameseiensis* [Hunts] (10c.-*c*1200), RS LXXXIII (1886); *v. et.* GOSC. *Mir. Iv.*

Chr. S. Alb. The St. Albans Chronicle (1406–20) [attrib. WALS.], ed. V. H. Galbraith (1937); supersedes WALS. *HA pt. 2,* 272–336; 1422–31 *Chronicon rerum gestarum in monasterio S. Albani a quodam auctore ignoto compilatum,* in *Chr. Mon. S. Alb.* V pt. 1 1–69.

Chr. S. Edm. The St. Edmundsbury Chronicle 1296–1301, EHR LVIII (1943) 51–78.

Chr. S. Neoti *Chronicon fani S. Neoti sive annales* (44–914), ed. W. H. Stevenson, Asser's Life of King Alfred (Oxford, 1904) 117–45; superseded by ed. D. N. Dumville, The Anglo-Saxon Chronicle: a collaborative edition, XVII (Woodbridge, 1985).

Chr. Southern A Southern Chronicle (earliest times–1422) (prob. wr. *c*1426) [possibly used up to 1400 by compiler of *Eul. Hist. Cont.*] (extr. 1399–1422), in *Eng. Hist. Lit. 15c.* 275–8.

Chr. Sprotti v. T. SPROTT *Chr.*

Chr. Steph. Chronicles of the reign of Stephen, Henry II and Richard I, 4 vols. RS LXXXII (1884–9); *v.* AILR. *Stand.,* DEVIZES, *G. Steph.,* H. HUNT. *Ep. ad Warinum,* RIC. HEX. *Stand.,* STEPH. ROUEN, TORIGNY, W. NEWB.

Chr. St. Mary's Chronicle of St. Mary's Abbey [York] (1112–1323), Surtees Soc. CXLVIII (1934) 1–80; *v. et. Cust. St. Mary's,* STEPH. WHITBY.

Ch. Rufford Rufford Charters (12c.–13c.), Thoroton Soc.

Rec. S. XXIX, XXX, XXXII, XXXIV (1972–81) [by no.].

Chr. Wallingf. The Chronicle attributed to John of Wallingford (449–1035) (wr. *a*1258), Camd. Misc. XXI, Camd. 3rd S. XC (1958).

Chr. Westm. Chronicle (1381–94) [formerly attrib. J. MALVERN] (wr. late 14c. by a monk of Westminster), in HIGD. IX 1–283 [by p.]; superseded by ed. B. F. Harvey, Med. Texts (1981) [by p. of MS].

Chr. Witham Witham Charterhouse Chronicle, a fragment (13c.) *De vita et conversatione Magistri Adae Cartusiensis* [prob. AD. SCOT] *secundum quod habetur in Cronica Domus de Witham,* JRL Bull. XVI (1932) 482–506.

Ch. Sal. Charters and documents illustrating the history of the cathedral, city, and diocese of Salisbury (1109–1300), RS XCVII (1891).

Ch. Stirling Charters and documents relating to the Royal Burgh of Stirling (1124–1705), ed. R. Renwick (Glasgow, 1884).

Ch. Str. Marc. Five Strata Marcella Charters, National Library of Wales Journal V (1947) 50–4.

CIMA Cahiers de l'Institut du moyen âge grec et latin, I– (Copenhagen, 1969–).

CIREN. Richard of Cirencester [*ob.* 1401]: *Speculum historiale* (447–1066), 2 vols. RS XXX (1863–9).

Cîteaux Cîteaux: *Commentarii Cistercienses,* I– (Westmalle, 1950–).

CLAPWELL, Richard, *v.* KNAPWELL.

Clovesho Various councils and synods held at Clovesho [unidentified] (716–825), in *Conc. HS* III (1871) and *CS.*

Cl *Rotuli litterarum clausarum* or Close Rolls: 1204–27, 2 vols. RC (1833, 1844) [by p. & col.]; 1227–72, 14 vols. HMSO (1902–38) [by p.]; 1272– , MS PRO (C. 54) [by roll & m.; *v. et. CalCl*]; **Frag.** Close Roll fragments 1215–16, Pipe Roll Soc. NS XXXI 127–44; **sup.** Close Rolls supplementary: 1244–66, HMSO (1975); later rolls, MS PRO (C. 55).

COGGESH. Ralph de Coggeshall, abbot of Barnwell [*fl.* 1207–24]: **Chr.** *Chronicon Anglicanum* (1066–1224), RS LXVI (1875) 1–208 [by f.], references to COGGESH. only are to *Chr.*; **Visio** *Visio Thurkilli,* ed. P. G. Schmidt (Leipzig, 1978).

COLET John Colet, Dean of St. Paul's [*ob.* 1519]: **Corp. Myst.** *De compositione sancti corporis Christi mystici,* in *Ep.* 183–95; **Cel. Hier.** The Celestial Hierarchy (wr. ? 1498), ed. J. H. Lupton, Two treatises on the hierarchies of Dionysius (1869) 163–96; **Eccl. Hier.** The Ecclesiastical Hierarchy, *ib.* 197–272; **Ep.** *Epistolae,* ed. J. H. Lupton, Letters to Radulphus (1876) 165–82 [*v. et. Ep. Erasmi*]; **In 1 Cor.** *Enarratio in primam epistolam S. Pauli ad Corinthios* (wr. ? *a*1499), ed. J. H. Lupton (1874); **In 1 Pet.** *Enarratio in primam B. Petri epistolam* [attrib.], in *Ep.* 283–303; **Rom. Enarr.** *Enarratio in epistolam B. Pauli ad Romanos* (wr. ? 1498–9), ed. J. H. Lupton (1873); **Rom. Exp.** *Epistolae B. Pauli ad Romanos expositio,* in *Ep.* 197–281; **Sacr. Eccl.** *De sacramentis ecclesiae* (wr. ? 1499), ed. J. H. Lupton (1867); **Stat.** Statutes, in *Reg. S. Paul.* 217–36, 237–49; **Stat. Cantar.** *Excerpta ex libro statutorum ea quae concernunt capellanos ad cantarias suas admittendos,* ed. W. S. Simpson, *Arch.* LII (1890) 161–7.

Collect. Aen. *Collectiones aenigmatum Merovingicae aetatis,* CCSL CXXXIII, 2 vols. (1968); *v. Aen. Laur.,* BONIF. *Aen.,* HWÆTBERHT *Aen.,* TATWINE *Aen. & Ars.*

Collect. Ox. *Collectanea,* 4 vols. OHS V, XVI, XXXII, XLVII (1885–1905).

Collect. Salern. *Collectio Salernitana,* 5 vols. (Naples, 1852–9); *v. et. Alph.*

Collect. Staffs Collections for a history of Staffordshire, William Salt Archaeological Society, since 1936 known as Staffs Rec. Soc., I– (1880–).

Collect. Stories A Collection of Stories and Sketches: *Petronius Redivivus* (12c.), ed. M. L. Colker, *Analecta*

Dublinensia, Med. Acad. of America LXXXII (Cambridge, Mass., 1975) 195–235.

Collect. Suss Sussex archaeological collections, Arch. Soc. Suss, I– (1853–).

Collect. W. Worc. William of Worcester's collections respecting the wars of the English in France and Normandy (1427–50), ed. *Letters and papers illustrative of the wars of the English in France*, RS XXII (1864) II 519–72.

Commend. Ed. I v. J. LOND.

Comm. Lond. J. H. Round: *The Commune of London and other studies* (1899).

Comm. Sph. Commentary on the Sphere of Sacrobosco [attrib. M. SCOT], in SACROB. *Sph.* 247–342.

Comp. Dom. Buck. *Compota domestica familiarum de Bukingham et d'Angoulême*, 1443, 1452, 1463; *annexae expensae cujusdam comitis* 1273, Abbotsford Club (1836).

Compilatio *Compilatio de gestis Britonum et Anglorum* [concluding portion (1422–7)], Camd. Soc. NS XXVIII (1880) 164–85.

Comp. Swith. Compotus rolls of the obedientiaries of St. Swithun's Priory, Winchester (14c.–16c.), Hants Rec. Soc. (1892); *v. et.* ÆLF. *Regul. Mon.*

Comp. Worc. I Early compotus rolls of the Priory of Worcester (1278–1352), Worcs Hist. Soc. (1908); II Compotus rolls of the Priory of Worcester (14c. and 15c.), *ib.* (1910).

Conc. *Concilia Magnae Britanniae et Hiberniae* (446–1717), ed. D. Wilkins, 4 vols. (1737) [superseded in part by *Conc. HS* & *Conc. Syn.*].

Conc. HS Councils and ecclesiastical documents relating to Great Britain and Ireland (200–1295), ed. A. W. Haddan and W. Stubbs, 3 vols. (Oxford, 1869–78); *v. et. Clovesho*, EGB. *Dial.*, *Pen.*, THEOD. *Pen.*

Concl. Loll. XII Twelve Conclusions of the Lollards (1396), EHR XXII (1907) 292–304 [by no.]; other versions in R. DYMMOK pp. 30, 53, 71 *etc.*, *Ziz.* 360–69.

Concl. Loll. XXXVII Thirty-seven Conclusions of the Lollards (*c*1383), EHR XXVI (1911) 741–9 [by no.].

Conc. Scot. *Concilia Scotiae, Ecclesiae Scoticae statuta* (1225–1559), ed. J. Robertson, 2 vols. Bannatyne Club (1866).

Conc. Syn. Councils and Synods: I (871–1204) ed. D. Whitelock, M. Brett, and C. N. L. Brooke (Oxford, 1981), 2 pts (–562, –1151); II (1205–1313) ed. F. M. Powicke and C. R. Cheney (Oxford, 1964), 2 pts. (–723, –1393) [by date & p.].

Const. Clar. The Constitutions of Clarendon (1164), in GERV. CANT. I 178–80 [by cap.]; also in *SelCh* 163–7.

Consuet. Monach. v. RegulC.

Contra Relig. Simul. *Tractatus B. Gregorii Pape contra religionis simulatores* (12c. or 13c.), ed. M. L. Colker, *Analecta Dublinensia*, Med. Acad. of America LXXXII (Cambridge, Mass., 1975) 17–51.

CONWAY Def. Mend. Roger Conway (*alias* Chonnoe) [*ob.* 1360]: *Defensio religionis mendicantium* (*c*1357), in *Monarchia* II 1410–1344 (*recte* 1310–1328, 1333–1344) [by p. as printed & *recte*].

CONYNGTON Richard Conyngton, O.F.M. [*ob.* 1330]: **Paup.** *Tractatus de paupertate fratrum minorum AFH* XXIII (1930) 70–105, 340–60; **QO** *Quaestiones ordinariae* (extr.), *ib.* XXIX (1937) 430–38; **Quodl.** *Quodlibeta* I q. 1, Franciscan Studies XXVI (1966) 53–9; **Resp.** *Responsiones ad rationes papales*, *ib.* XXIV (1931) 355–69.

Cop. Pri. S. Andr. *Copiale Prioratus Sanctiandree*, the letter-book of James Haldenstone, Prior 1418–43, w. app. of docs. 1378–1450, ed. J. H. Baxter (St. Andrews, 1930).

CoramR *Coram Rege* Rolls (1272–1702), MS PRO (K.B. 27); roll 151 (Trinity 1297), British Record Society Index Library XIX (1898).

Corp. Gloss. Lat. *Corpus Glossariorum Latinorum*, I–V,

ed. G. Goetz (Leipzig, 1923, 1888–94); VI and VII *Thesaurus glossarum emendatarum*, ed. Goetz (Leipzig, 1899–1901).

Corp. Script. Mus. *Corpus Scriptorum de Musica*, I– (Rome, 1950–).

Correct. Alch. *Correctorium alchemiae* (? *a*1200) [attrib. RIC. MED.], in *Theatrum Chem.* II 385–406 [by cap.].

COTTON *v.* B. COTTON, J. COTTON.

Couch. Furness Coucher Book of Furness Abbey [Lancs], 2 vols. in 6, Chetham Soc. NS IX, XI, XIV (= I, –260, –536, –706), LXXIV, LXXVI, LXXVIII (= II, –288, –583, –880) (1886–1919); *v. et.* R. ESK.

Couch. Kirkstall Coucher Book of the Cistercian Abbey of Kirkstall, [Yorks] (late 12c.–14c.), Thoresby Soc. VIII (1904) [by no.].

Couch. Selby Coucher Book of Selby (late 12c.–13c.), Arch. Soc. Yorks, Rec. S. X, XIII (1891–3).

Council in North R. R. Reid: *The King's Council in the North* (1921).

Courtauld Institute *v.* Warburg Institute.

CourtR A. Stratton Court Rolls of the Wiltshire Manors of Adam de Stratton [*fl.* 1265–90], Wilts Rec. Soc. XXIV (1970); *v. et. Ac. Stratton*.

CourtR Banstead Court Rolls of the manor of Banstead, MS Surrey RO; *v. et. Banstead*.

CourtR Carshalton Court Rolls of the manor of Carshalton (Ed. III–Hen. VII), Surrey Rec. Soc. II (1916).

CourtR Castle Combe Court Rolls of the manor of Castle Combe [Wilts] (extr., 1460–1700), in *Hist. Castle Combe* 233–337.

CourtR Chalgrave Court Roll of Chalgrave Manor (1278–1313), Beds Rec. Soc. XXVIII (1950).

CourtR Chester v. Cal. CourtR Chester.

CourtR Court Rolls, various (13c.–), MS PRO (S.C. 2).

CourtR Hales Court Rolls of the manor of Hales (1270–1307), 3 pts. in 2 vols. Worcs Hist. Soc. (1910–33).

CourtR Ingoldmells Court Rolls of the manor of Ingoldmells [Lincs] (1291–1569), ed. W. O. Massingberd (1902).

CourtR Lancs Some Court Rolls of the manors of Thomas, Earl of Lancaster (1323–4), Lancs & Chesh Rec. Soc. XLI (1901).

CourtR Lygh Court Rolls of the manor of Lygh [Abbotsleigh, Som] (1461–1507), MS Bristol University.

CourtR Nursling Court Roll of the manor of Nursling [Hants] (1413), MS mun. Herriard Park [Hants].

CourtR Ottery St. M. Court Rolls of Ottery St. Mary [Devon] (15c.), MS Exeter City Library.

CourtR Ramsey Court Rolls of the Abbey of Ramsey [Hunts] and of the Honor of Clare [Suff] (1255–1384), ed. W. O. Ault (New Haven, Conn., 1928).

CourtR Ruthin Court Rolls of the Lordship of Ruthin [Denb] (1294–6), Cymmrodorion Rec. S. II (1893).

CourtR Tempsford Court Roll of the manor of Tempsford [Beds] (1604), MS Bedford RO D.D. BS 1276.

CourtR Tooting Beck Court Rolls of Tooting Beck manor (1246–1422), ed. G. L. Gomme, London County Council (1909).

CourtR Wakefield Court Rolls of the manor of Wakefield (1274–1331), Arch. Soc. Yorks, Rec. S. XXIX, XXXVI, LVII, LXXVIII, CIX (1901–45).

CourtR Wimbledon Extracts from the Court Rolls of the Manor of Wimbledon (1461–1864), for use of Wimbledon Common Committee, ed. P. H. Lawrence, 3 vols. (1866–9) [by date, vol. & p.].

CourtR Winchester Winchester Court Rolls (1269–19c.), MS Winchester City Archives.

COWTON Sent. Robert Cowton, O.F.M. [*fl.* 1300]: *Commentarius in Sententias* (extr.): prologi, qq. 2, 5, 6, 7, BGPM XLII iii (1970) 257–321; q. 4, Franciscan Studies XXXI (1971) 8–40; I dd. 38, 39, ed. H. Schwamm, *Robert Cowton O.F.M.* (Innsbruck, 1931) 5–23; III q. 1, ed. V. Nadalin, *Roberti de Cowton Quaestio Disputata*

(Rome, 1961) 31–58; III d. 3, ed. B. Hechich, *Bibliotheca Immaculatae Conceptionis* VII (Rome, 1958) 72–116; III d. 23, BGPM XLII iii (1970) 322–30; III d. 33, *Studia Anselmiana* III–IV (1935) 70–112; III d. 36, RTAM XXII (1955) 273–86 [by bk., dist., q. & p.].

CRATHORN Univ. Magister Crathorn, O.P. (*alias* William Crowthorn) [14c.]: *Quaestio de universalibus* (extr.), *Opusc. & Text.* XVIII (1937) 9–44.

Crawley N. S. B. and E. C. Gras: The economic and social history of an English village [Crawley, Hants] (909–1928), (Cambridge, Mass., 1930); *v. et. Pipe Wint.*

CRICKLADE Robert of Cricklade, Prior of St. Frideswide's [*fl.* 1157–88]: **Conn.** *De connubio patriarchae Jacob*, MS Bodl. Laud misc. 725; (extr.) RHS Trans. 4th S. XIX (1936) 31–2, and in *Collect. Ox.* II 161–2; **Ep.** Letter to Benedict of Peterborough, *v.* BEN. PET. *Mir. Thom.* II 52; **Plin.** *Defloratio Naturalis Historiae Plinii*, ed. K. Rück, Sitzungsberichte der Bayerischen Akademie der Wissenschaften, Phil.-hist. Kl. 1902, 265–85 [prefaces only cited]; **Spec. Fid.** *Speculum Fidei*, MS Corpus Christi Camb. 380; (extr.) RHS Trans. 4th S. XIX (1936) 37–8 [by bk. & cap.].

CROMPE Henry Crompe (*alias* Crump) [*fl.* 1380], *v. Ziz.*

Croyl. Pseudo-Ingulf [14c.]: *Historia monasterii Croyland* [Crowland, Lincs] (616–1089), ed. J. Fell and W. Fulman, *Rerum Anglicarum Scriptorum Veterum* (Oxford, 1684) I 1–107; **Cont. A** *Continuatio* (*temp.* Will. II–1117) [wrongly attrib. P. BLOIS], *ib.* 108–32; **Cont. B** (1149–1470), *ib.* 451–546; **Cont. C** (1459–86), *ib.* 549–78; **Cont. D** (Oct. 1485–Apr. 1486), *ib.* 581–93.

CS *Cartularium Saxonicum* (604–975), ed. W. de G. Birch, 3 vols. (1885–99) [by no.; checked in light of P. H. Sawyer, Anglo-Saxon Charters (1968)].

Cumb & Westmor Antiq. Soc. Cumberland and Westmorland Antiquarian and Archaeological Society, transactions, I– (Kendal, 1886–).

CurR *Curia Regis* Rolls (1194–1272), HMSO I– (1922–), in prog. [I–X by p.; XI– by no.]; later rolls, MS PRO (K.B. 26) [by r.]; **CurR PR** 1194–5 Pipe R. Soc. XIV (1891), 1196–8 *ib.* XXXI 69–118 (1955); **CurR RC** (1194–1200), 2 vols. RC (1835).

Cust. Abingd. *De consuetudinibus Abbendoniae* (*c*1190), in *Chr. Abingd.* II app. III 296–334.

Cust. Battle Custumals of Battle Abbey [Suss] 1283–1312, Camd. Soc. NS XLI (1887).

Cust. Bened. Customary of the Benedictine Monasteries of St. Augustine, Canterbury, and St. Peter, Westminster, HBS XXIII, XXVIII, (1902–4); *v. et. Cust. Cant.*, *Cust. Cant. Abbr.*, *Cust. Westm.*

Cust. Bleadon Custumal of Bleadon [Som] (13c.), ed. E. Smirke, Archaeological Institute of Great Britain & Ireland, Memoirs of Wiltshire and Salisbury (1851) 182–210.

Cust. Bury St. E. v. Kal. Samson.

Cust. Cant. Customary of St. Augustine's, Canterbury (*c*1330–40), in *Cust. Bened.* I 1–433; **Abbr.** Earlier customary (? *c*1245), *ib.* II 249–318; *v. et. Cust. Westm.*

Cust. Eton Old customs of Eton College (prob. *temp.* Mary), in *Stat. King's Cantab.* 626–33.

Cust. Eynsham Customary of the abbey of Eynsham [Oxon], ed. A. Gransden, *Corpus consuetudinum monasticorum* II (Siegburg, 1963) [by marginal no.].

Cust. Fordwich *Custumale villae de Fordewico* [Fordwich, Kent] (15c.), ed. C. E. Woodruff, History of the town and port of Fordwich (Canterbury, 1895) 233–81 [by cap.].

Cust. Glast. *Rentalia et Custumalia abbatum monasterii B. Mariae Glastoniae* (1235–61), Som Rec. Soc. V (1891).

Cust. Heacham Custumal of Heacham [Norf] (13c.), MS Norfolk RO L'Estrange papers, Q. 33.

Cust. Kent Manors Custumal of the Archbishop's manors in Kent (1285), MS DCCant. E. 24. 1–91.

Cust. Loventon, Cust. Malling v. Cust. Suss.

Cust. Norm. *Statuta et consuetudines Normannie* (*a*1200), ed. E.-J. Tardif (Rouen, 1881) [by cap. & sect.].

Cust. Norw. Customary of the cathedral priory church of Norwich (*c*1280–), HBS LXXXII (London, 1948).

Cust. Rents N. Neilson: Customary Rents (12c.–15c.) (Oxford, 1910).

Cust. Roff. *Custumale Roffense* (compiled ? *a*1320 by John de Westerham), ed. J. Thorpe (1788).

Cust. S. Malling, Cust. Slyndon v. Cust. Suss.

Cust. St. Mary's Custumal of St. Mary's Abbey [York], with extracts from the Ordinal (*c*1300), Surtees Soc. CXLVIII (1934) 80–109, 109–23; *v. et. Chr. St. Mary's.*

Cust. Suss Sussex Custumals (13c.–14c), Sussex Rec. Soc. XXXL, LVII, LX (1925, 1959, 1962) [transl. only; quotations from MS]; II incl. custumals (1285) of Loventon, 16–21; Malling, 111–20; S. Malling, 30–47; Slyndon, 1–10; Tangmere, 11–16; Terring, 21–30 [by date, place, vol. & p.].

Cust. Swith. Consuetudinary of the house of St. Swithin in Winchester (14c.), ed. G. W. Kitchen, Winchester Cathedral Records I (1886).

Cust. Tangmere v. Cust. Suss.

Cust. Taunton Medieval Customs of the manors of Taunton and Bradford on Tone (13c.), Som Rec. Soc. LXVI (1962).

Cust. Terring v. Cust. Suss.

Cust. Waltham Custumal of Waltham Abbey [Essex] (*c*1230), MS BL Cotton Tiberius C IX [by f.].

Cust. Westm. Customary of St. Peter's, Westminster (*c*1266), in *Cust. Bened.* II 1–247; *v. et. Cust. Cant.*, *Cust. Cant. Abbr.*

Cust. York v. Ord. Ebor.

CUTCL. John de Rupescissa (*alias* Cutliffe or Rochetaillade) [*fl.* 1350]: **CL** *De confectione veri lapidis philosophorum*, in *Theatrum Chem.* III 189–97; also in *Bibl. Chem.* II 80–3; **LL** *Liber lucis*, in *Theatrum Chem.* III 284–98 [by cap.] also in *Bibl. Chem.* II 84–7; **Proph.** *Prophetia*, in *Fasc. Rerum Expet.* II 494–6; **QE** *De consideratione quintae essentiae omnium rerum* (Basel, 1561); **VM** *Vade mecum in tribulatione*, in *Fasc. Rerum Expet.* II 496–508.

CUTHB. Cuthbert, Abbot of Wearmouth and Jarrow [*ob. p*764]: **Ep.** *Epistolae*, *v. Ep. Bonif.*; **Ob. Baedae** *De obitu Baedae*, ed. C. Plummer, *Baedae Opera Historica*, I clx–clxiv; *vv. ll.* The manuscripts of Cædmon's Hymn and Bede's Death Song, ed. E. V. K. Dobbie (New York, 1937), *Medium Ævum* VIII (1939) 41–4, and BEDE *HE*, Med. Texts (1969) 580–86.

Cuthb. Hib. *Libellus de ortu S. Cuthberti de historiis Hiberniensium exceptus* (*c*1186) [attrib. R. COLD.], Surtees Soc. VIII (1838) 63–87 [by cap.].

Cuxham Manorial records of Cuxham [Oxon] (*c*1200–1448), Oxfordshire Rec. Soc. L and HMC JP XXIII (1976); bailiff's account 1316–17, in *Hist. Agric.* II 617–30.

Cymmrodorion Rec. S. Honourable Society of Cymmrodorion, Record S., I–XIII (1892–1936).

Cymmrodor Y Cymmrodor, Cymmrodorion Soc. of London, publications, I– (1877–).

Danelaw Documents illustrative of the social and economic history of the Danelaw, ed. F. M. Stenton, Rec. Soc. & Econ. V (1920).

DAN. WINT. Daniel, Bishop of Winchester [*ob.* 745], *v. Ep. Bonif.*

DASTIN John Dastin [*fl.* 1320]: **Ros.** *Rosarium, secretissimum philosophorum arcanum comprehendens*, in *Bibl. Chem.* II 309–24 [by cap.]; **Visio** *Visio super artem alchemicam*, *ib.* 324–6.

Davenports T. P. Highet: The early history of the Davenports of Davenport, Chetham Soc. 3rd S. IX (1960).

DB Domesday Book (1086), ed. A. Farley, 2 vols. (1783) [by f.]; **Add.** *Additamenta*, 2 vols. (1816); *v. et. Dom. Exon., Inq. Ely, Lib. Wint.*

D. BEC. Daniel of Beccles [*fl.* ? 1180]: *Urbanus magnus*, ed. J. G. Smyly (Dublin, 1939).

DB Exon. v. Dom. Exon.

DCCant. Muniments of Dean and Chapter of Canterbury, incl. some listed in HMC Rep. IX app. 1 (1883) 72–129, and Var. Coll. I (1901) 205–81; *v. et. Ac. Man. Cant., Doc. G. Chart.*

DCChich. Muniments of Dean and Chapter of Chichester, incl. some listed in HMC Var. Coll. I (1901) 187–204.

DCDurh. Muniments of the Dean and Chapter of Durham, incl. miscellaneous charters, MS Durham.

DCEbor. Muniments of the Dean and Chapter of York, incl. *Registrum antiquum de actis capitularibus* (1335–42), MS York Reg. K.

DCLichf. Muniments of the Dean and Chapter of Lichfield, incl. testimony (1252), Arch. Soc. Derb V (1883) 150–6.

DCLinc. v. Chap. Linc.

DCornw MS records in Duchy of Cornwall R.O. (London).

DCSal. Muniments of Dean and Chapter of Salisbury, incl. some listed in HMC Var. Coll. I (1901) 338–88.

DC S. Paul. Muniments of Dean and Chapter of St. Paul's, incl. some listed in HMC Rep. IX app. 1 (1883) 1–72.

DCWestm. Muniments of Dean and Chapter of Westminster Abbey, MS.

DCWint. Muniments of the Dean and Chapter of Winchester, MS.

D. EDW. Anat. David Edwardes [*ob. c*1542]: *In anatomicen introductio* (1532) [by sign.].

Deeds Balliol The Oxford Deeds of Balliol College (13c.–), OHS LXIV (1913).

Deeds Mon. & Ep. Ir. Irish Monastic and Episcopal Deeds, ed. N. B. White, IMC Ormond Deeds Series (Dublin, 1936).

Deeds Newcastle Early Deeds relating to Newcastle-upon-Tyne, Surtees Soc. CXXXVII (1924).

Deeds Wards Deeds and Evidences, Court of Wards (12c.–), MS PRO (Wards 2).

DEE Monas John Dee [*ob.* 1608]: *Monas Hieroglyphica* (1564), in *Theatrum Chem.* II 178–215.

De lib. arb. *Carmen de libero arbitrio* (*c*975), ed. M. Lapidge, ASE I (1972) 126–36 [by line].

DENE, W. *v. Hist. Roff.*

Deorum Imag. *De deorum imaginibus* (14c.), in *Mythographi Latini*, ed. T. Muncker, 2 vols. (Amsterdam, 1681), II 301–30 [by cap.].

Descr. Constant. Une description de Constantinople (*c*1100), Revue des études byzantines XXXIV (1976) 245–63.

DEVIZES Richard of Devizes [*fl.* 1190]: *Chronicon de tempore regis Richardi I*, ed. J. T. Appleby, Med. Texts (1963) [by f.; N.B. some rearrangement of ff. in this ed.]; also in *Chr. Steph.* III 381–454.

Dial. Scac. *De necessariis observantiis scaccarii dialogus* (*c*1178) [attrib. Richard Fitzneal (*ob.* 1198), ed. C. Johnson, Med. Texts (1950) [by bk. & cap., incl. serial letters given in ed. A. Hughes *et al.* (Oxford, 1902)].

DICETO Ralph de Diceto, Dean of St. Paul's [*ob.* 1202], *Radulphi de Diceto opera historica*, 2 vols. RS LXVIII (1876): **Abbr. Norm.** *Abbreviatio de gestis Normannorum*, II 241–67 [mainly abbr. from W. JUM.]; **Chr.** *Abbreviationes chronicorum* (Creation–1147), *ib.* I 3–263; **Opusc.** II 175–241, 267–85; **YH** *Ymagines historiarum* (1148–79), *ib.* I 267–440, II 3–174.

Dictamen Treatise on Dictamen, a medieval treatise on letter-writing, with examples, from the Rylands Latin MS. 394 [attrib. Simon O., Filius Columbae, *fl.* 1400], JRL Bull. XIII (1929), 333–82; *v. et. Ars notaria.*

Dieta *Dieta*, verses on Diet (15c.), EETS XXXII ii (1868) 56–7.

Dietarium *Dietarium*, verses on Diet (*c*1460), EETS XXXII i (1868) 55–9.

Dieul. Chronicle of Dieulacres Abbey [Staffs] (1381–1403) (wr. *a*1413), JRL Bull. XIV (1930) 164–81 [by f.].

Digby Plays The Digby Plays (1480–90), EETS Extra S. LXX (1869); superseded by EETS CCLXXXIII (1982).

Dign. Dec. *Dignitas decani ecclesiae cathedralis S. Patricii* (*c*1190–16c.), ed. N. B. White, IMC (1957) [by no.].

Dign. Peer Reports from the Lords Committees touching the dignity of a Peer of the Realm, 5 vols. 3rd ed. (1829) [vols. III–V contain app. of docs.].

Dip. Corr. Ric. II Diplomatic correspondence of Richard II, Camd. 3rd S. XLVIII (1933).

DipDocC Diplomatic Documents, Chancery *Miscellanea* bundles 27–32 (Hen. III–Hen. VII), MS PRO (C. 47); *v. et.* Chanc. Misc.

DipDoc Diplomatic documents preserved in the Public Record Office (1101–), HMSO vol. I– (1964–).

DipDocE Diplomatic Documents of the Exchequer (Hen. I–), MS PRO (E. 30).

Dist. Mon. *Distinctiones monasticae et morales* (*c* 1220), MS Paris, Bibliothèque Mazarine 3475; (extr.), ed. A. Wilmart, *Mémorial Lagrange* (Paris, 1940), 307–46 [by no.], and J. B. Pitra, *Spicilegium Solesmense* II–III (Paris, 1855), *passim* [by vol. & p.; see List of sections, III 452–3].

Ditchley Pps. Ditchley Papers, MS County Hall, Oxford.

D. LOND. Ep. Master David of London, ? prebend of Brownswood [*fl.* 1175]: *Epistolae*, ed. F. Liverani, *Spicilegium Liberianum* I (Florence, 1863), 603–28 [by no.].

DL Records of the Duchy of Lancaster, MS PRO: **Ac. Var.** Accounts various (Ed. I–) (D.L. 28); **Cart. Misc.** *Cartae Miscellaneae* (Hen. I–) (D.L. 36); **ChancR** Chancery Rolls (Ed. III–Hen. VII) (D.L. 37); **Couch.** Coucher Book (D.L. 42/1 and 2), incl. extr. in N. Riding Records NS II–VI (1895–7); **CourtR** Court Rolls (Ed. I–) (D.L. 30); **DeedsL** Deeds Series L (12c.-) (D.L. 25); **Forest Proc.** Forest Proceedings (Hen. III–) (D.L. 39); **MinAc** Ministers' Accounts (Ed. I–) (D.L. 29); **Misc. Bk.** Miscellaneous Books (John-) (D.L. 42); **Rent. & Surv.** Rentals and Surveys (Hen. III–) (D.L. 43).

D. MORLEY Daniel of Morley (*alias* Merlai) [*fl.* 1170–1200]: *De naturis inferiorum et superiorum libri II*, ed. K. Sudhoff, Archiv. für die Gesch. der Naturwissenschaften und Technik VIII (1917) 6–40; *vv. ll.*, *ib.* IX 50–1; superseded by MLJ XIV (1979) 204–55.

Doc. Bec Select Documents of the English lands of the Abbey of Bec [Norm.], Camd. 3rd S. LXXIII (1951).

Doc. Bev. Beverley Town Documents, Selden Soc. XIV (1900).

Doc. Bury Feudal Documents of the Abbey of Bury St. Edmunds (11c.–12c.), ed. D. C. Douglas, Rec. Soc. & Econ. VIII (1932) [by no.].

Doc. Bury Sup. Twelfth-century documents from Bury St Edmunds Abbey, EHR XCII (1977) 806–19.

DocCantab Documents relating to the University and Colleges of Cambridge, 3 vols. (1852).

Doc. Coll. Wint. Winchester College muniments; *v. et. Ac. Dom. Ep. Wint., Ac. Man. Coll. Wint.*

DocCOx Oxford City Documents (1268–1665), OHS XVIII (1891).

Doc. Eng. Black Monks Documents illustrating the activities of the English Black Monks, 1215–1540, Camd. 3rd S. XLV, XLVII, LIV (1931–7).

Doc. Eng. Mint The *De Moneta* of Nicholas Oresme and English Mint Documents, ed. C. Johnson, Med. Texts (1956) 50–106.

DocExch Documents illustrative of English history in the 13th and 14th centuries, selected from the records of the Queen's Remembrancer of the Exchequer, ed. H. Cole, RC (1844).

Doc. Francisc. Franciscan papers, lists and Documents, ed. A. G. Little, (Manchester, 1943); *v.* DOCKING, MELTON.

Doc. Francisc. Ir. Materials for the history of the Franciscan province of Ireland, ed. E. B. Fitzmaurice and A. G. Little (Manchester, 1920).

Doc. G. Chart Documents concerning land transfers (1570–1630), MS (copies) DCCant. Parish Reg. I [Great Chart, Kent].

Doc. Gros. Robert Grosseteste at the papal curia, Lyons 1250. Edition of the documents, *Collectanea Franciscana* XLI (1971) 350–93.

Doc. Interdict. Interdict Documents (1207–13), ed. P. M. Barnes and W. R. Powell, Pipe R. Soc. NS XXXIV (1960).

Doc. Ir. Historic and municipal Documents of Ireland 1172–1320, RS LIII (1870); *v. et. Chain Bk. Dublin.*

Doc. Kingswood Documents relating to the abbey of Kingswood [Wilts] (1240–1442), HMC Rep. V (1876) app. 335–8.

DOCKING Thomas Docking [*ob. p*1269]: extr. from biblical commentaries, in *Doc. Francisc.* 98–121.

Doc. Leeds Documents relating to the manors and borough of Leeds, 1066–1400, Thoresby Soc. XLV (1957).

Doc. Robertsbr. Documents relating to Robertsbridge Abbey, Sussex (1160–1537), HMC Rep. LXXVII, DeLisle and Dudley MSS I (1925) 33–171.

Doc. Scot. Documents illustrative of the history of Scotland (1286–1306), ed. J. Stevenson. 2 vols. Scot. RO (Edinburgh, 1870).

Doc. S. Paul. Documents illustrating the history of St. Paul's Cathedral (1262–1798), Camd. Soc. NS XXVI (1880).

Doc. Theob. Documents relating to Theobald Archbishop of Canterbury 1139–61, ed. A. Saltman, Theobald Archbishop of Canterbury (London, 1956), 233–549 [by no. & letter].

Doctus dicetur *Doctus dicetur*, verses on table manners (15c.), EETS XXXII pt. ii (1868) 26–9.

Doc. T. Waleys T. Kaeppeli: Le Procès contre Thomas Waleys O.P. Étude et documents (Rome, 1936), 93–247; *v. et.* T. WALEYS.

Doc. W. Abb. Westm. Documents illustrating the rule of Walter de Wenlok, abbot of Westminster, 1283–1307, Camd. 4th S. II (1965).

Dom. Cant. Domesday *Monachorum* of Christ Church, Canterbury (12c.), ed. D. C. Douglas, RHS (1944) 75–110.

Dom. Chesh Cheshire Domesday roll (*temp.* Ric. I–1289), calendar and fragments, ed. G. Ormerod, A memoir on the Cheshire Domesday roll (1851).

DOMERH. Glast. Adam de Domerham [*ob.* 1291]: *Historia de rebus gestis Glastoniensibus* (1126–1291), ed. T. Hearne (Oxford, 1727) pt. ii; *cf.* W. MALM. *Glast.*

Dom. Exon. Exeter Domesday (1086), in *DB Add.* I 1–493 [by f.].

DOMINIC Dominic, Prior of Evesham [*fl.* 1125]: **Mir. Virg.** *Miracula S. et perpetuae Virginis Mariae*, MS Balliol Coll. Ox. 240 ff. 137–48 [by f.]; **V. Ecgwini** *Vita S. Ecgwini* [*ob.* ? 717], ed. M. Lapidge, Book I, *Anal. Boll.* XCVI (1978) 77–98; Book II, in *Chr. Evesham* 39–67 corrected by *Anal. Boll.* XCVI (1978) 104 [by bk. & cap.; *cf.* T. MARLB.].

Dom. S. Aug. An eleventh-century inquisition of St. Augustine's Canterbury (compiled 13c.), ed. A. Ballard, Rec. Soc. & Econ. IV pt. 2 (1920) [by p.].

Dom. S. Paul. The Domesday of St. Paul's (1181, 1222 etc.), Camd. Soc. LXIX (1858).

Domus Reg. *Constitutio domus Regis* [*c*1136], in *Dial. Scac.* (1950) 129–35; also in *BBExch* 341–59.

Drama K. Young: The Drama of the medieval Church, 2 vols. (Oxford, 1933, repr. 1967).

Dryburgh *Liber S. Mariae de Dryburgh* [Berwickshire] (1153–17c.), Bannatyne Club (1847).

DuC Du Cange: *Glossarium mediae et infimae Latinitatis,* condito a Carolo Dufresne, domino du Cange, rev. ed. 8 vols. (Paris, 1840–50).

Dugdale Soc. Dugdale Society, publications [on the history of Warwickshire], I– (1921–).

DUMBELER John Dumbeler [14c.]: *Practica vera alkimica e libris magistri Ortholani* (1386), in *Theatrum Chem.* IV 912–34.

DUMBLETON Summa John Dumbleton, fellow of Merton [*ob. c*1349]: *Summa logicae et naturalis philosophiae* (extr.), in *Sci. Mech.* 317–25.

DUNS John Duns Scotus [*ob. c*1308]: **Gram.** *De modis significandi sive grammatica speculativa* [attrib.], *Opera Omnia* (Paris, 1891–5) I 1–50; **Metaph.** *Quaestiones super libros Metaphysicorum Aristotelis I–XII, ib.* VII [by bk., q. & p.]; **Ord.** *Ordinatio,* ed. Scotist Commission, *Opera Omnia* (Rome, 1950–), I– ; **Praedic.** *In librum praedicamentorum quaestiones* (or *Super praedicamenta*), *Opera Omnia* (Paris, 1891–5) I 437–538; **Prim. Princ.** *De primo rerum omnium principio, ib.* IV 722–99; also ed. M. F. Garcia, (Quaracchi, 1910) 625–702; **PW** Philosophical writings (extr.), ed. A. Wolter (Edinburgh, 1962); **Sent.** *Quaestiones in primum et secundum librum Sententiarum, Opera Omnia* (Paris, 1891–5) VIII–XIII [by bk., dist., q., & sect.]; partly superseded by *Ord.*; **Sent. cont.** *Quaestiones in tertium et quartum librum Sententiarum, ib.* XIV–XXI; **Univ.** *In universam logicam quaestiones* (or *Super universalia Porphyrii quaestiones acutissimae*), *ib.* I 51–435.

DUNST. Dunstan, Archb. of Canterbury [*ob.* 988]: **Classbk.** St. Dunstan's classbook from Glastonbury, ed. R. W. Hunt, *Umbrae Codicum Occidentalium* IV (Amsterdam, 1961); **Vers.** Poem, ed. M. Lapidge, ASE IV (1975) 108–9 [by line]; *v. et.* charter in *CS* 880.

EADMER Eadmer, monk of Canterbury [*ob. c*1124]: **Beat.** *De beatitudine coelestis patriae, PL* CLIX 587–606; superseded by *Mem. Anselm* 273–91 [by cap.]; **Breg.** *Vita S. Bregwini* [*ob.* 765], *Acta SS. Boll.* Aug. V (1754) 831–5; **Conc. B. M.** *De conceptione S. Mariae, PL* CLIX, 301–318; also ed. H. Thurston and T. Slater (Freiburg, 1904); **Ep. ad Glast.** *Epistola ad Glastonienses, PL* CLIX 799–808; **Ep. ad mon. Wig.** *Epistola ad monachos Wigornienses, ib.* 807–808; **Excell. B. M.** *De excellentia virginis Mariae, ib.* 557–80; **Gabr.** *Consideratio de beatissimo Gabriele archangelo,* Revue des sciences religieuses XV (1935) 371–9; **Greg.** *De ordinatione beati Gregorii Anglorum apostoli, ib.* 207–19; **HN** *Historia novorum in Anglia* (960–1122), RS LXXXI (1884) [by p. of MS (in margin)]; **Mir. Anselmi** *Descriptio miraculorum Anselmi,* in *V. Anselmi* 152–71; **Mir. Dunst.** *Quaedam de miraculis quae idem pater [Dunstanus] fecit,* in *Mem. Dunst.* 223–49 [by cap.]: **Mir. Osw.** *Miracula S. Oswaldi,* in *Hist. Church York* II 41–59 [by cap.]; **Miser.** *Scriptum Eadmeri peccatoris ad commovendam super se misericordiam beati Petri janitoris regni caelestis,* Revue des sciences religieuses XV (1935) 192–206; **Odo** *Vita S. Odonis* [attrib.], *Acta SS. Boll.* July II (1721) 67–73 [by cap.]; also in *Anglia Sacra* II 78–87; **Pet.** *Vita beati Petri primi abbatis* [*ob.* ? 607], Revue des sciences religieuses XV (1935) 354–61; **Rel. Audoeni** *De reliquiis S. Audoeni, ib.* 362–70; also (extr.) in GERV. CANT. I 7–9; **Sanct.** *Sententia de memoria sanctorum quos veneraris,* Revue des sciences religieuses XV (1935) 190–91; **V. Anselmi** *Vita Anselmi,* ed. R. W. Southern, Med. Texts (1962) 1–151 [by bk. & cap.]; *v. et. Simil. Anselmi;* **V. Dunst.** *Vita S. Dunstani Archiepiscopi Cantuariensis,* in *Mem. Dunst.* 162–222 [by cap.]; **Virt.** *De quattuor virtutibus quae fuerunt in Beata Maria, PL* CLIX 579–86; **V. Osw.** *Vita S. Oswaldi Eboracensis archiepiscopi,* in *Hist. Church York* II 1–40 [by cap.]; **Wilf.** *Vita Wilfridi Episcopi Eboracensis, ib.* I 161–226 [by cap.]; **Wilf. Brev.** *Breviloquium vitae S. Wilfridi* [attrib.], *ib.* I 227–37.

Early Arith. The Earliest Arithmetics in English, ed. R. Steele, EETS Extra S. CXVIII (1922 for 1916).

Early Schol. Coll. Early Scholastic Colloquies, ed. W. H. Stevenson, *Anecd. Oxon.* XV (1929) [by no. & sect.; *v. et.* ÆLF. BATA].

Early Sci. Ox. R. T. Gunter: Early Science in Oxford, OHS LXXVII, LXXVIII (1923); *v. Nav. Ven., Turquet, WALLINGF.*

EASTON *v.* AD. EASTON, S. EASTON

EASTWOOD *v.* ASHENDEN.

Eccl. Doc. v. Episc. Som.

ECCLESTON Adv. Min. Thomas Eccleston [*fl.* 1250]: *De adventu fratrum minorum in Angliam*, ed. A. G. Little, Collection d'études sur l'histoire religieuse du moyen-âge VII (Paris, 1909); supersedes *Mon. Francisc.* II 3–28; also ed. A. G. Little (Manchester, 1951).

Eccl. & Synag. *Altercatio ecclesiae contra synagogam et synagogae contra ecclesiam* (10c.), Revue du moyen âge latin X (1954) 53–123.

E. Chanc. Proc. Early Chancery Proceedings (1377–1558), MS PRO (C. 1).

E. Ch. Chesh Facsimiles of Early Cheshire Charters (*c*1146–*c*1237), Lancs & Chesh Rec. Soc. (1957) [by no.].

E. Ch. Northants Facsimiles of Early Charters from Northamptonshire collections, Northants Rec. Soc. IV (1930) [by no.].

E. Ch. Ox. Facsimiles of Early Charters in Oxford muniment rooms (*c*1097–1251), ed. H. E. Salter (1929) [by no.].

E. Ch. Scot. Early Scottish Charters prior to 1153, ed. A. C. Lawrie (Glasgow, 1905) [by no.].

E. Ch. S. Paul. Early Charters of the Cathedral Church of St. Paul, London (9c.–13c.), Camd. 3rd S. LVIII (1939) [by p.].

E. Ch. Wessex Early Charters of Wessex (7c.–11c.), ed. H. P. R. Finberg (Leicester, 1964).

E. Ch. Yorks Early Yorkshire Charters, 13 vols.: I–III, ed. W. Farrer (Edinburgh, 1914–16); IV–XII & Index, ed. C. T. Clay, Arch. Soc. Yorks, Rec. Soc., Extra S. (1935–65) [by vol. & no.].

Econ. Condit. N. Neilson: Economic Condition of the manors of Ramsey Abbey [Hunts] (1898); *v. et. MinAc Wistow.*

Econ. HR Economic History Review, I– (1927–).

EDDI Eddi (*alias* Stephanus) [*ob.* 731]: Life of Bishop Wilfrid (*a*720), ed. B. Colgrave (Cambridge, 1927) [by cap.]; also ed. W. Levison, *MGH Script. rer. Merov.* VI (Hanover, 1913) 169–263.

EDMUND Edmund Rich, Archb. of Canterbury [*ob.* 1240]: **BVM** *Psalterium beatae Mariae virginis, Anal. Hymn.* XXXV (1900) 137–52 [by quinq. & stanza]; **Or.** *Oratio*, ed. W. Wallace, Life of St. Edmund of Canterbury (1893) 586–8; **Serm.** *Sermo*, in M. PAR. *Edm.* 55; also ed. Wallace, 584–6; **Spec. Relig.** *Speculum religiosorum*, ed. H. P. Forshaw, *Auct. Brit.* III (1973) 30–110 [by sect.].

Educ. Ch. A. F. Leach: Educational Charters and documents, 598–1909 (Cambridge, 1911).

ED. UPTON Edward Upton, Principal of St Edmund Hall [*fl.* 1340–1400]: **Term.** *Terminus est in quem* (1390), ed. L. M. de Rijk, Some 14c. tracts on *Probationes Terminorum, Artistarium* III (1982) 189–208.

EEC N. S. B. Gras: The Early English Customs system (13c.–16c.) (Cambridge, Mass., 1918).

EE County Court W. A. Morris: The Early English County Court (13c.–14c.) (Berkeley, Calif., 1926).

EE Text given by agreement of Epinal glossary (8c.) and first Erfurt glossary (? 8c.). *Cf. Corpus Glossariorum Latinorum* V (Leipzig, 1894) 337–401, and W. M. Lindsay, The Corpus, Epinal, Erfurt and Leyden glossaries, Philol. Soc. VIII (1921).

EETS Early English Text Society, publications, I– (1864–).

E. FAVERSHAM Eustace of Faversham [*ob. p*1244]: Life of Edmund Rich, Archb. of Canterbury [*ob.* 1240], ed.

C. H. Lawrence, St. Edmund of Abingdon (Oxford, 1960) 203–21.

EGB. Ecgberht, Archb. of York [*ob.* 766]: **Dial.** Dialogue, in *Conc. HS* III 403–13; **Pen.** Penitential, *ib.* 416–31 [by cap. & sect.]; **Pont.** *Pontificale Ecgberhti* (8c.–10c.), Surtees Soc. XXVII (1853).

EHR English Historical Review, I– (1886–).

ELMER CANT. Elmer (*alias* Æthelmer), Prior of Canterbury [*ob.* 1137]: **Ep.** *Epistolae*, ed. R. Anstruther, in H. Los. *Ep.* 213–33; superseded by ed. J. Leclercq, *Studia Anselmiana* XXXI (1953) 62–109 [by no. & sect.]; **Exc.** *Excitatio mentis in inquisicionem Dei*, ed. Leclercq, ibid. 110–114 [by sect.]; **Quer.** *Querimonia de absentia vultus Dei, PL* CLVIII 809–14 [by col.]; **Record.** *Recordationes beneficiorum Dei, ib.* 709–22 [by col.]; **Serm.** *Sermo*, ed. Leclercq, *Studia Anselmiana* XXXI (1953) 114–17 [by sect.].

ELMH. Thomas Elmham, Treasurer of St. Augustine's, Canterbury [*ob. c*1427]: **Cant.** *Historia monasterii S. Augustini Cantuariensis*, RS VIII (1858); **Hen. V** *Henrici V, Angliae Regis, gesta* (1413–16) [attrib.], ed. B. Williams, Eng. Hist. Soc. (1850) 1–108; superseded by *G. Hen. V*; **Hen. V Cont.** Continuation, *ib.* 109–63 (1417–22) [anon.], [abbr. of *Ps.*-ELMH. *Hen. V* 90–338]; **Metr. Hen. V** *Liber metricus de Henrico V*, in *M. Hen. V* 77–166 [by line].

ELVEDEN Cal. Walter de Elveden, fellow of Gonville Hall [*fl.* 1360]: Calendar (1387) (extr.), in *SB* 5–7.

Enc. Emmae *Encomium Emmae Reginae* [*ob.* 1052] (wr. 1040–2), Camd. 3rd S. LXXII (1949) [by bk. & cap.].

Enf. Stat. Lab. B. H. Putnam: The Enforcement of the Statute of Labourers 1349–59 (New York, 1908).

Eng. Abbots to Cîteaux Letters from the English Abbots to the Chapter at Cîteaux, 1442–1521, Camd. 4th S. IV (1967).

Eng. Aust. Fri. F. Roth: English Austin Friars, 1249–1538, 2 vols. (New York, 1966).

Eng. Carols The Early English Carols, ed. R. L. Greene, 2nd ed. (Oxford, 1977) [by no.].

Eng. Clergy A. H. Thompson: The English Clergy in the later middle ages (Oxford, 1947).

Eng. Dip. Admin. G. P. Cuttino: English Diplomatic Administration, 2nd ed. (Oxford, 1971).

Eng. Feudalism F. M. Stenton: The first century of English Feudalism 1066–1166 (Oxford, 1932).

Eng. Field Syst. H. L. Gray: English Field Systems, Harvard Hist. Studies XII (Cambridge, Mass., 1915).

Eng. Friars B. Smalley: English Friars and antiquity in the early 14th century (Oxford, 1960).

Eng. Fur Trade E. M. Veale: The English Fur Trade in the later middle ages (1966).

Eng. Gilds The original ordinances of more than one hundred early English Gilds, EETS XL (1870).

Eng. Hist. Lit. 15c. C. L. Kingsford: English Historical Literature in the 15th century (Oxford, 1913).

Eng. in Manorial Docs. English in Manorial Documents of the thirteenth and fourteenth centuries, Mod. Philol. XXXIV (1936–7) 37–61.

Eng. Justice D. M. Stenton: English Justice 1066–1215 (Philadelphia, 1964).

Eng. Pol. Tracts Four English Political Tracts of the later middle ages, Camd. 4th S. XVIII (1977).

Eng. Roy. Chap. J. H. Denton: English Royal Free Chapels (1100–1300) (Manchester, 1970).

Eng. Roy. Writs Facsimiles of English Royal Writs (1044–1100), presented to V. H. Galbraith, ed. T. A. M. Bishop and P. Chaplais (1957) [by no.].

Eng. Sec. Cath. K. Edwards: The English Secular Cathedrals in the middle ages, rev. ed. (Manchester, 1967).

Eng. Weights Select tracts relating to English Weights and Measures (1100–1742), Camd. Misc. XV, Camd. 3rd S. XLI (1929).

Enr. Chester Palatinate of Chester, Enrolments (1307–), MS PRO (Chester 2).

Entries William Rastell [*ob.* 1565]: Collection of Entries etc. [by p. of ed. 1670, which contains additions to ed. 1564].

EpAcOx *Epistolae academicae Oxonienses* (*Registrum* F) (1421–1509), OHS XXXV, XXXVI (1898) [by p.].

Ep. ad amicum *Epistolae ad amicum* (12c.), ed. M. L. Colker, *Analecta Dublinensia*, Med. Acad. of America LXXXII (Cambridge, Mass., 1975) 91–163 [by no.].

Ep. Alcuin. v. ALCUIN *Ep.*

Ep. Aldh. v. ALDH. *Ep.*

Ep. Alex. III *Variorum epistolae ad Alexandrum III*, PL CC 1359–1466.

Ep. Anselm. v. ANSELM *Ep.*

Ep. Anselm. Bur. A twelfth-century letter from Bury St. Edmunds Abbey, Rev. Ben. LXXXII (1972) 96–7; *v. et.* ANSELM BURY.

Ep. B. ad Archiep. v. B. Ep.

Ep. Becket v. BECKET *Ep.*

Ep. Bonif. v. BONIF. *Ep.*

Ep. Cant. *Epistolae Cantuarienses* (1185–1211), in *Mem. Ric. I*, II 1–561 [by no.].

Ep. Erasm. *Opus epistolarum Des. Erasmi Roterdami*, letters to Erasmus (1484–1536), ed. P. S. & H. M. Allen 12 vols. (1906–58) [by vol. & no.].

Ep. G. Foliot v. G. FOLIOT *Ep.*

Ep. Glasg. Letter in praise of Jocelin, bishop of Glasgow [*ob.* 1199], by R. of Melrose, ed. A. P. Forbes, St. Ninian and St. Kentigern (Edinburgh, 1874) 308–12.

Epigr. Milredi Epigrams from a codex of Milred Bishop of Worcester (745–775), ed. M. Lapidge, EHR XC (1975) 798–820.

Epigr. Misc. *Epigrammata miscellanea* (12c.), in *Sat. Poets* II 156–62.

Epinal Gl. v. EE.

Ep. Innoc. III Selected Letters of Pope Innocent III (1198–1216) concerning England, ed. C. R. Cheney and W. H. Semple, Med. Texts (1953) [by no.].

Episc. Som. *Historiola de primordiis Episcopatus Somersetensis*, (–1175) (wr. *temp.* Hen. II), Camd. Soc. VIII (1840) 9–28; **doc.** ecclesiastical documents (11c.–16c.), *ib.* 43–91.

Ep. J. Exon. v. J. EXON *Ep.*

Ep. J. Sal. v. J. SAL. *Ep.*

Ep. Lanfr. v. LANFR. *Ep.*

Ep. Peckham v. PECKHAM *Ep.* [by no.]; *cf. Reg. Cant.*

Erf. 2 & 3 The second and third Erfurt glossaries as quoted in W. M. Lindsay, The Corpus, Epinal, Erfurt and Leiden glossaries, Philol. Soc. VIII (1921); *v. et. EE.*

ERIUG. Per. John Scotus (*alias* Eriugena) [*fl.* 850]: *Periphyseon, de divisione naturae libri V*, ed. I. P. Sheldon-Williams *et al.*, *Scriptores Latini Hiberniae* VII, IX, XI (Dublin, 1968–) [by col. of *PL* CXXII].

EschF Escheators' Files (Hen. III–Ric. III), MS PRO (E. 153).

E. Schools Yorks Early Yorkshire Schools, Arch. Soc. Yorks, Rec. S. XXVII, XXXIII (1899, 1903).

Estate Bk. H. de Bray Estate Book of Henry de Bray (*c*1289–1340), Camd. 3rd S. XXVII (1916).

Estates Crowland F. M. Page: The Estates of Crowland Abbey [Lincs] (*c*1258–1528) (Cambridge, 1934).

Eul. Hist. *Eulogium (historiarum sive temporis), chronicon ab orbe condito usque ad 1366, a monacho quodam Malmesburiensi exaratum*, 3 vols. RS IX (1858–63); **Annot.** *Id.* Annotations incorporated in parts of text, II and III; **Chr. Brev.** *Chronicon brevius* (–1364), III 243–313; **Cont.** *Continuatio eulogii* (1361–1413), III 333–421.

EUSEBIUS *v.* HWÆTBERHT.

Exc. Hist. S. Bentley: *Excerpta historica* (13c.–16c.) (1831).

ExchScot *Rotuli Scaccarii Regum Scotorum*, The Exchequer Rolls of Scotland (1264–1579), 23 vols. Scot. RO (Edinburgh, 1878–1908) [by date & p.].

ExcRFin *Excerpta e rotulis finium* (1216–72), 2 vols. RC (1835–6); *v. et. FineR.*

Exp. Hymn. *Expositio Hymnorum* (11c.), ed. H. Gneuss, Hymnar und Hymnen im englischen Mittelalter (Tübingen, 1968) 265–413 [by no. & stanza].

Expug. Terrae Sanctae *De expugnatione Terrae Sanctae per Saladinum libellus* (1186–8), in COGGESH. *Chr.* 209–62 [by f.].

Ext. Alien Pri. Extents of Alien Priories (1293–1483), MS PRO (E. 106).

Ext. Guern. The Extentes of Guernsey 1248 and 1331, ed. H. de Sausmarez, Soc. guernesiaise (1934).

Ext. Hadleigh *Extenta manerii de Hadleghe* (1305), Suffolk Institute of Archaeology Proc. III (1863), app. A 229–52.

Extr. Chr. Scot. *Extracta e variis cronicis Scocie*, ed. W. B. D. D. Turnbull, Abbotsford Club (1842).

ExtrR Extract Rolls or *extracta donationum* (1229–1352), MS PRO (C. 59).

Eyre Berks The roll and writ file of the Berkshire Eyre of 1248, Selden Soc. XC (1973) [by no.].

Eyre Chester Pleas before Justices in Eyre in counties of Chester and Flint (1306–1500), MS PRO (Chester 17).

Eyre Kent The Eyre of Kent, 1313–14, Selden Soc. XXIV, XXVII, XXIX (= Year Bk. Ed. II, nos. V, VII, VIII) (1909–13).

Eyre Lincs Rolls of Justices in Eyre for Lincolnshire (1218–19), Selden Soc. LIII (1934) 1–440;

Eyre Lond. The Eyre of London (1321), 2 vols. Selden Soc. LXXXV, LXXXVI (= Year Bk. Ed. II, no. XXVI, pts. 1 and 2) (1968–9).

Eyre Salop Roll of the Shropshire Eyre (1256), Selden Soc. XCVI (1981).

Eyre Worcs Rolls of Justices in Eyre for Worcestershire (1221), Selden Soc. LIII (1934) 441–665.

Eyre Yorks Rolls of Justices in Eyre for Yorkshire (1218–19), Selden Soc. LVI (1937).

Fabr. Exon. Accounts of the Fabric of Exeter Cathedral 1279–1353, Devon & Cornw Rec. Soc. NS XXIV (1981).

FABRICIUS *v.* A. CARPENTER.

Fabr. Westm. v. Ac. Build. Hen. III.

Fabr. York Fabric Rolls of York Minster (14c.–17c.), Surtees Soc. XXXV (1859) 1–120; app. of docs. (12c.–18c.), *ib.* 121–334.

Fasc. Rerum Expet. *Fasciculus Rerum Expetendarum*, ed. E. Brown, 2 vols. (1690).

Fasti Sal. *Fasti ecclesiae Sarisburiensis* (634–19c.), ed. W. H. Rich Jones (1879).

FAVENT Thomas Favent [*fl.* 1390]: *Historia de modo et forma mirabilis Parliamenti apud Westmonasterium* (1386–8), Camd. Misc. XIV, Camd. 3rd. S. XXXVII (1926).

Fees *Liber feodorum*, Book of Fees (1198–1293), 3 vols. (–636,–1483, index) HMSO (1920–31).

FELIX Guthl. Felix of Crowland [*fl.* 730]: Life of St. Guthlac [*ob.* 716] (prob. wr. 730–40), ed. B. Colgrave (Cambridge, 1956) [by cap.].

Feod. Durh. *Feodarium Prioratus Dunelmensis* (15c.), w. other docs. (11c.–16c.), Surtees Soc. LVIII (1871).

FERR. Kinloss Johannes Ferrerius of Riva (Piedmont) [*ob. p*1574]: *Historia Abbatum de Kynlos* [Moray] (1150–1537), ed. W. D. Wilson, Bannatyne Club (1839).

Feudal Eng. J. H. Round: Feudal England, historical studies on the 11th and 12th centuries (1895).

Feudal Man. Feudal Manuals of English History, ed. T. Wright (London, 1872) 88–124 (14c.), 125–153 (15c.).

Fig. *Tractatus de figuris sive de notis* (*c*1350), ed. G. Reaney, *Corp. Script. Mus.* XII (1966) 40–51.

Finc. The Priory of Finchale [Durh], charters, inventories, account rolls etc., Surtees Soc. VI (1837).

FineR Chancery Fine Rolls (1204–1641), MS PRO (C. 60); *v. et. CalFineR, ExcRFin, RFin*].

Fines Feet of Fines (Hen. II–), MS PRO (C.P. 25).

Fines Northumb & Durh Feet of fines for Northumberland & Durham 1196–1272, Newcastle upon Tyne Rec. S. X (1931) [by no.].

Fines P. Hen. II, Ric. I Feet of Fines (1182–99): 1182–96 Pipe R. Soc. XVII (1894); 1196–7 ibid. XX (1896); 1197–8 ibid. XXIII (1898); 1198–9 ibid. XXIV (1900) [by no.].

Fines P. Lincs Feet of Fines for Co. Lincoln (1196–1216), Pipe R. Soc. NS XXIX (1954) [by no.].

Fines P. Norf Feet of Fines for Norfolk (1198–1202), Pipe R. Soc. NS XXVII (1950).

Fines P. Norf & Suff Feet of Fines for Norfolk (1201–15) and for Suffolk (1199–1214), Pipe R. Soc. NS XXXII (1958) [by no.].

Fines P. Ric I v. Fines P. Hen. II.

Fines RC *Fines siue pedes finium siue finales concordiae in curia Domini Regis* (1195–1214), RC (1835, 1844): I Beds, Berks, Bucks, Cambs, Cornw; II Cumb, Derbs, Devon, Dorset.

Fines Suss Abstract of feet of Fines relating to Sussex, 1190–1249, Sussex Rec. Soc. II (1903); 1249–1307, *ib.* VII (1908) [by no. (contin.)].

Fines Warw Warwickshire Feet of Fines (abstr.), Dugdale Soc. XI, XV, XVIII (1932–43): I (1195–1284), II (1284–1345), III (1345–1509) [by date & no.].

Fines Yorks *Pedes finium Ebor.* (1199–1214), Surtees Soc. XCIV (1897).

Firma Burgi T. Madox: *Firma Burgi* (1726).

FISHACRE Richard Fishacre [*ob.* 1248]: **Quaest.** *Quaestio de ascensione Christi*, Med. Stud. XL (1978) 43–55; **Sent. Prol.** *Commentarium in libros Sententiarum, Prologus, ib.* XXXIV (1972) 79–98; **Serm.** *Sermones* (as listed by Schneyer): 1, *AFP* LII (1982) 83–7.

FITZRALPH *v.* RIC. ARMAGH.

FITZTHEDMAR Arnold Fitzthedmar, alderman of London [1201–*c*1274], *v. Leg. Ant. Lond.*

Fleta *Fleta seu commentarius juris Anglicani* (*c*1290), ed. J. Selden (1647); superseded by Selden Soc. LXXII (1955), LXXXIX (1972), in prog. [all bks. cited by p. of ed. 1647].

FLETE Westm. John Flete [*ob.* 1469]: History of Westminster Abbey (to 1386), ed. J. A. Robinson (Cambridge, 1909).

Flor. Hist. *Flores historiarum* (Creation–1327) [attrib. 'Matthew of Westminster'; to 1249 probably by M. PAR.], 3 vols. RS XCV (1890).

FL. WORC. Florence of Worcester [*ob.* 1118]: Chronicle (450–1117), ed. B. Thorpe, 2 vols. Eng. Hist. Soc. (1848–9) I, II 1–70; **Cont. A** (1118–41), *ib.* II 71–136 *v.* J. WORC.; **Cont. B** (1152–1265), *ib.* II 136–96 *v.* TAXTER *Chr. Bury; cf.* B. COTTON 136–40; **Cont. C** (1266–95), *ib.* II 196–279 *v. Chr. Bury Cont. A.*

F. MALM. V. Aldh. Faricius of Malmesbury [*ob.* 1117]: *Vita Aldhelmi*, PL LXXXIX (1863) 63–84.

Foed. T. Rymer: *Foedera, conventiones, literae et acta publica ab anno 1101 usque ad nostra tempora*, 20 vols. (1704–35) [addit. entries (1066–1383) from RC ed., 4 vols. in 7 (1816–69)].

FOLC. Folcard [*fl.* 1066]: **Carm.** *Carmen de S. Vigore*, ed. L. d'Achery *et al., Spicilegium* (Paris, 1723) II 342; **V. Bertini** *Vita S. Bertini* [*ob.* 698], *Acta SS. Boll.* Sept. II (1748) 604–13 [by cap.]; **V. Bot.** *Vita S. Botulfi* [*ob.* 680], *Acta SS. Boll.* June III (1701) 402–3 [by cap.], *vv. ll.* from *Acta SS. Ben.* III 4–7; **V. Bot. Pref.** Preface, ed. T. D. Hardy, Descriptive Catalogue, RS XXVI (1862–71) I 373–4; **V. J. Bev.** *Vita S. Johannis episcopi Eboracensis* (St. John of Beverley) [*ob.* 721] (wr. *a*1070), in *Hist. Church York* I 239–60 [by cap.].

FORDUN John Fordun [*ob. c*1385]: **Chr.** *Chronica gentis Scotorum (alias Scotichronicon)*, I–V (Creation–1153), ed. W. F. Skene, Historians of Scotland I (Edinburgh, 1871), 1–253 [by bk. & cap.]; **GA** *Gesta annalia* (1153–1385), *ib.* 254–353 [by cap.]; **Cont.** *Scotichronicon, cum supplemento et continuatione Walteri Boweri* (Creation–1447), ed. W. Goodall, 2 vols. (1759) [VI–XVI (1153–1447) by bk. & cap.].

Forest Bk. Sherwood The Sherwood Forest Book (*TRBk* 76), Thoroton Soc. Rec. S. XXIII (1965).

FormA T. Madox: *Formulare Anglicanum*, or a collection of ancient charters and instruments (1066–1547) (1702).

Form. Hist. Doc. H. Hall: Formula book of official Historical Documents, 2 vols. (Cambridge, 1908–9): I Diplomatic docs.; II Ministerial and judicial records.

FormMan Legal and Manorial Formularies, edited in memory of J. P. Gilson (Oxford, 1933): I text of MS BL Add. 41201 (*c*1300), 1–24; II text of PRO Wards 2, box 56, 197/5 (*c*1300), 25–49.

FormMan Shorwell Specimen accounts of the Manor of Shorwell, I. of W. (*c*1258), MS Caius Coll. Camb. 205 pp. 367–91.

FormOx Formularies which bear on the history of Oxford *c*1204–1420, OHS NS IV, V (–255, –491) (1942).

Form. S. Andr. The St. Andrews *Formulare* (1514–46), Stair Soc. VII, IX (1942–4).

FORTESCUE John Fortescue [*c*1394–1476]: **Def. Lanc.** *Defensio juris domus Lancastriae*, Works I (1869) 503–10 [by cap.]; **LLA** *De laudibus legum Angliae*, ed. S. B. Chrimes (Cambridge, 1942) [by cap.]; **NLN** *De natura legis naturae*, Works I (1869) 63–184 [by bk. & cap.]; **Tit. Edw.** *De titulo Edwardi comitis Marchiae, ib.* 63*–74* [by cap.].

Found. Holyrood *Historia miraculosae fundationis monasterii Sanctae Crucis prope Edinburgh* (1128), Bannatyne Misc. II, Bannatyne Club (1836) 9–31 (incl. app.).

Found. Waltham The Foundation of Waltham Abbey [Essex], *De inventione Sanctae Crucis* (wr. *a*1200), ed. W. Stubbs (1861) [by cap.].

Frag. Rit. Dunst. *Fragmenta ritualia de Dunstano* (11c.), in *Mem. Dunst.* 440–57.

Franciscan Studies Franciscan Studies I– (St Bonaventure, N.Y., 1941–).

Franziskanische Studien Franziskanische Studien I– (Münster, 1914–).

FREE John Free (*alias* Phreas) [*ob.* 1465]: **Ep.** *Epistolae*, Journal of Comparative Literature I (1903) 47–65; **LC** *De laude calvitii* [transl. of Synesius], *Erasmi Moriae Encomium* (Basel, 1519) 40–63.

Free Peasantry F. M. Stenton: The Free Peasantry of the Northern Danelaw, w. app. of charters (12–13c.), Bull. Soc. Royale des Lettres (Lund, 1926) 74–185.

FRIDUG. Fridugisus [*fl.* 800]: *De substantia nihili et tenebrarum*, ed. C. Gennaro (Padua, 1963).

FRITH. Frithegod of Canterbury [*fl.* 950]: *Breviloquium vitae beati Wilfridi*, ed. A. Campbell (Zurich, 1950), 1–62 [by line; for emendations *v. ALMA* XXV (1955) 71–98].

GAD. John of Gaddesden [*ob. a*1350]: *Rosa medicinae* or *Rosa Anglica* (Venice, 1502) [by f. & col.].

G. AMIENS Hast. Guy, Bishop of Amiens [*ob.* 1075]: *Carmen de Hastingae proelio* (*c*1068), ed. C. Morton and H. Muntz, Med. Texts (1972) [by line].

Gaol Del. Cambs A Cambridgeshire Gaol Delivery Roll 1332–1334, ed. E. G. Kimball, Cambr. Antiq. Rec. Soc., IV (1978).

Gaol Del. Gaol Delivery Rolls (1271–1476), MS PRO (J.I. 3).

Gaol File Wales Gaol Files, writs (1513–), MS formerly PRO Wales 4, now Aberystwyth, National Library of Wales.

GARDINER Stephen Gardiner, Bishop of Winchester [*ob.* 1555]: **Bucher** Answer to Bucher (1541), ed. P. Janelle, Obedience to Church and State, three political tracts (Cambridge, 1930) 174–211; **CC** *Confutatio Cavillationum* (1552) (Louvain, 1554); **Legat.** Address to the Legates (1529), ed. Janelle, 1–9; **Reg.** *Registrum, v. Reg. Wint.*; **Si sedes** Tract on Fisher's execution (1535), ed.

Janelle 22–65; **VO** *De vera obedientia oratio* (1535), *ib.* 67–171; supersedes *Monarchia* I 716–32.

GARL. John of Garland [*ob. p*1258]: **Aeq.** *Fragmentum ex libro de aequivocis* [attrib.], *PL* CL (1854) 1589–90; **Dict.** *Dictionarius* (*a*1230), ed. T. Wright, Vocabularies.. 10c.–15c. (1857) I 120–38 [readings checked against A. Scheler, Jahrb. rom. Lit. VI (1865) 142–62, 287–321, 370–9; glosses printed in *Cultura Neolatina* XXXIX (1979) 11–20]; **Epith.** *Epithalamium* (begun *c*1230), MS BL Cotton Claudius A x [by bk., line & f.; some refs. checked w. MS Bodl. Digby 65]; superseded by ed. A. Saiani, Biblioteca di *Quadrivium* III, V, VIII, X (Bologna, 1965–) [by bk. & line]; **GS** *Georgica spiritualia* (*c*1220) (extr.), Mélanger Paul Fabre (Paris, 1902) 274–8 and *Speculum* VIII (1933) 358–77; **Hon. Vit.** *Exempla honestae vitae* (1258), ed. E. Habel, Romanische Forschungen XXIX i (1911) 131–54 [by line]; **IO** *Integumenta Ovidii*, ed. F. Ghisalberti (Milan, 1933) [by line]; **Mor. Scol.** *Morale scolarium* (1241), ed. L. J. Paetow, Two medieval satires on the university of Paris (Berkeley, Calif., 1927), 185–260 [by line]; **Mus.** *De musica mensurabili positio, Introductio musicae, De musica mensurabili,* in *Script. Mus.* I (1864) 97–117, 157–75, 175–82; superseded by GARL. *Mus. Mens.*; **Mus. Mens.** *De musica mensurabili,* ed. E. Reimer, Beihefte zum Archiv für Musikwissenschaft X–XI (Wiesbaden, 1972) [by cap.]; **Myst. Eccl.** *De mysteriis ecclesiae* (1245), ed. F. W. Ott, *Codices Bibliothecae Academicae Gissensis* (Giessen, 1842) 131–48 [by line]; **add.** additional (alternative) lines to above, *ib.* 148–51 [by p.]; **Poems** Poems, *Anal. Hymn.* L (1907) 546–57 [by no. (1–9) & stanza]; **PP** *Parisiana Poetria,* ed. T. Lawlor (New Haven, Conn., 1974); **SM** *Stella Maris* or *Miracula B. Mariae Virginis* (1248–9), ed. E. F. Wilson, (Cambridge, Mass., 1946) [by line]; **Syn.** *Opus synonymorum* [attrib.], *PL* CL (1854) 1578–90; **Tri. Eccl.** *De triumphis ecclesiae,* ed. T. Wright, Roxb. Club (1856) [by p.]; **Unum** *Unum Omnium,* MS Bodl. Rawl. G. 96 pp. 1–90; *cf.* Revue de linguistique romaine XLIII (1979) 164–77.

GASCOIGNE Loci Thomas Gascoigne [*ob.* 1458]: *Loci e libro veritatum,* passages selected from Gascoigne's Theological Dictionary, illustrating the condition of Church and State, 1403–58, ed. J. E. T. Rogers (Oxford, 1881).

GAS Gesetze der Angelsachsen, ed. F. Liebermann, 3 vols. (Halle, 1903); I multicolumned text [by p., title in brackets]: **Cons. Cnuti** *Consiliatio Cnuti* (1130–5); **Duellum** *Benedictio scuti et baculi ad Duellum* (1067–1130); **Inst. Cnuti** *Instituta Cnuti* (*c*1110); **Jud. Dei** *Judicium Dei rituale* (*c*850–*c*1210); **Leg. Ed.** *Leges Edwardi Confessoris* (1130–5); **Leg. Hen.** *Leges Henrici primi* (1114–18), also ed. L. J. Downer (Oxford, 1972); **Leg. Will.** *Legum Willelmi articuli Londoniis retractati* (*c*1210); **Leis Will.** *Leis Willelme* [OF and Lat.] (*c*1200); **Lib. Lond.** *Libertas Londoniensis* (*c*1133–*c*1154); **Ps.-Cnut** Pseudo-Cnut *Constitutiones de foresta* (? *c*1184); **Quad.** *Quadripartitus* (*c*1114), incl. *Argumentum* and *Rectitudines singularum personarum.*

Gavelkind W. Somner: A Treatise of Gavelkind (1660).

G. BURTON Modw. Geoffrey, Abbot of Burton [*ob.* 1151]: *Vita S. Modvennae virginis,* MS BL Royal 15 B IV ff. 76–88.

G. COLD. Geoffrey of Coldingham [*fl.* 1214]: **Durh.** *Liber Gaufridi sacristae de Coldingham de statu ecclesiae Dunelmensis* (1152–1214), in *Hist. Durh. Script.,* Surtees Soc. IX (1839) 3–31 [by cap.]; **Godr.** *Vita S. Godrici* [*ob.* 1170], *Acta SS. Boll.* May V (1685) 70–85 [by cap.; *cf.* R. COLD. *Godr.*]; *v. et. V. Bart. Farn.*

G. CORNW. Guy Warw. 'Girardus Cornubiensis': *Historia Guidonis de Warwyke* [attrib.] (? 14c.), in *Ann. Dunstable,* ed. T. Hearne, II 825–30.

G. CRISPIN Gilbert Crispin, Abbot of Westminster [*ob.* 1117]: **Disp.** *Disputatio Christiani cum gentili de fide*

Christi, Med. & R. Stud. III (1954) 58–77; **Ep.** Correspondence, ed. J. A. Robinson, Gilbert Crispin (1911), 77–84 [by no.]; **Ep. sup.** La lettre de Gilbert Crispin sur la vie monastique (*c*1110), *Studia Anselmiana* XXXI (1953) 120–23; also Med. & R. Stud. III (1954) 99–104; **Herl.** *Vita domini Herluini abbatis Beccensis* [*ob.* 1078], ed. Robinson, 85–110; **Jud. & Chr.** *Disputatio Judaei et Christiani,* ed. B. Blumenkrantz (Utrecht, 1956); **Pecc.** *Probatio de illa peccatrice que unxit pedes Domini,* Med. & R. Stud. III (1954) 105–112; **Serm.** *Sermo in ramis palmarum, ib.* 112–15; **Simon.** *De simoniacis,* ed. Robinson, 111–24.

G. Durh. *Gesta Dunelmensia* (1300), Camd. Misc. XIII, Camd. 3rd S. XXXIV (1924).

G. Ed. II Bridl. *Gesta Edwardi de Carnarvon auctore canonico Bridlingtoniensi,* in *Chr. Ed. I & II* II 25–92.

G. Ed. III Bridl. *Gesta regis Edwardi tertii auctore canonico Bridlingtoniensi* (to 1339, w. brief additions to 1377), in *Chr. Ed. I & II* II 93–151; *v. et. G. Ed. II Bridl.*

GERV. CANT. Gervase of Canterbury [*ob. c*1210]: **AP** *Actus pontificum Cantuariensis ecclesiae* (582–1205), Historical Works of Gervase of Canterbury, 2 vols. RS LXXIII (1879–80), II 325–414; **Chr.** *Chronica Gervasii* or Greater Chronicle (1135–99), *ib.* I 84–594; **Combust.** *De combustione et reparatione Cantuariensis ecclesiae, ib.* I 3–29; **GR** *Gesta Regum* or Lesser Chronicle [deriv. from G. MON., W. MALM. etc.], II 3–106; **cont.** continuations (1208–1328), *ib.* II 106–324; **Imag.** *Imaginationes,* speeches concerning dispute between Archb. of Canterbury and Abbot of St. Augustine's, *ib.* I 29–83; **MM** *Mappa Mundi, ib.* II 414–49.

GERV. CIC. Gervase of Chichester [*fl.* 1170]: **Hom.** Homilies on martyrdom of Thomas Becket (incomplete), MS BL Royal 3 B x ff. 113– , frag. in GERV. CANT. II app. I xlviii–ix; **Mal.** Commentary on Malachi, MS BL Royal 3 B x ff. 2–112v; **Vers.** Verses prefacing *Mal.* in GERV. CANT. II app. I xlvii–viii.

GERV. LOUTH Gervase, Abbot of Louth Park [*fl.* 1139–47], *v. Mem. Gerv. Louth.*

GERV. MELKLEY Gervase of Melkley (*alias* de Saltu Lacteo) [*fl.* 1210]: **AV** *Ars versificatoria,* MS Balliol Coll. Ox. 273 ff. 153–76; extr. ed. E. Faral, Les Arts poétiques du xiie siècle (Paris, 1924) 328–30; superseded by ed. H. J. Gräbener, (Münster, 1965); **Vers.** verses (extr.), ed. Faral, 36, and in GERV. CANT. I xxxvii.

GERV. TILB. Gervase of Tilbury [*fl.* 1210]: *Otia imperialia* (1211), *Scriptores rerum Brunsvicensium* I (1707) 881–1004, some readings supplied from *ib.* II (1710) 751–84 [by bk. & cap.]; (extr.) II 10, 16–17, 20 also in COGGESH. 419–49 [Med. Texts edition in prep.].

Gesch. Stahlhofes v. Steelyard.

G. EVERSLEY Geoffrey of Eversley (*alias* Gaufridus Anglicus) [*ob.* 1283]: *Ars scribendi epistolas,* MS Perugia, Biblioteca communale 338 ff. 1–67 [by f.].

G. FOLIOT Ep. Gilbert Foliot, Bishop of Hereford and London [*ob.* 1178]: Letters and charters, ed. A. Morey and C. N. L. Brooke (Cambridge, 1967) [by no.; letters to G. Foliot cited as *Ep. G. Foliot*].

G. FONT. Inf. S. Edm. Geoffrey de Fontibus [12c.]: *Liber de infantia S. Eadmundi,* in *Mem.* S. Edm. I 93–103; superseded by *Anal. Boll.* XCV (1977) 34–42 [by sect.].

G. Hen. II *Gesta regis Henrici secundi* [wrongly attrib. BEN. PET.], in *Chr. Hen. II & Ric. I* I 1–361, II 1–71.

G. Hen. V *Gesta Henrici V* (1413–16) (wr. 1416–17), ed. F. Taylor and J. S. Roskell, Med. Texts (1975) [by cap.; some refs. in Fasc. I are to ELMH. *Hen. V*].

G. Herw. *Gesta Herwardi incliti exulis et militis* [*fl.* 1070] (wr. *c*1150), Lestorie des Engles RS XCI (1888) I 339–404 [by f.].

Ghost Stories Ghost stories (*c*1400), by a monk of Byland [Yorks], ed. M. R. James, *EHR* XXXVII (1922) 413–22; two more ghost stories, ed. H. E. D. Blakiston, ibid. XXXVIII (1923) 85–7.

G. HOYLAND Gilbert of Hoyland (*alias* of Swineshead) [*ob.* 1172]: **Ascet.** *Tractatus ascetici, PL* CLXXXIV (1854) 251–90; **Ep.** *Epistolae, ib.* 289–98; **Serm.** *Sermones in Cantica, ib.* 11–252.

GILB. Gilbertus Anglicus [*ob. c*1250]: *Compendium medicinae* (Lyon, 1510) [by bk., f., & col.].

GILDAS Gildas [*fl.* 540]: **EB** *De excidio et conquestu Britanniae* (? *a*549), *MGH Auct. Antiq.* XIII (Berlin, 1894) 25–85 [by cap.]; **Ep.** *Epistulae ad Vinnianum fragmenta, ib.* 86–8 [by sect.]; **Pen.** *Praefatio Gildae de poenitentia, ib.* 89–90 [by sect.]; *vv. ll.* from L. Bieler, The Irish Penitentials (Dublin, 1963) 60–64.

Gild Camb. Cambridge Gild records (14c.), ed. M. Bateson, Camb. Antiq. Soc., 8° S., XXXIX (1903).

Gild Merch. C. Gross: The Gild Merchant (1066–17c.), 2 vols. (Oxford, 1890).

GIR. Giraldus Cambrensis [*ob. c*1223], *Giraldi Cambrensis Opera*, 8 vols. RS XXI (1861–91): **Ad. S. Langton** *Epistola ad Stephanum Langton* (*c*1215), I 401–7; **Æthelb.** *Vita regis et martyris Æthelberti* [King of East Anglia, *ob.* 794], EHR XXXII (1917) 222–36 [by cap.]; **Catal. Brevior** *Catalogus brevior librorum suorum*, I 421–3; **DK** *Descriptio Kambriae* (1194), VI 153–227 [by bk. & cap.]; **David** *Vita S. Davidis* [*ob.* ? *a*600], III 377–404; **EH** *Expugnatio Hibernica* (*c*1188), V 205–411 [by bk. & cap.]; also ed. A. B. Scott & F. X. Martin (Dublin, 1978); **Ep.** *Epistulae*, ed. R. B. C. Huygens, *Speculum Duorum* (Cardiff, 1974) 156–282 [by no. & p.]; **Galf.** *De vita Galfridi* (*c*1195), RS IV 355–431 [by bk. & cap.]; **GE** *Gemma Ecclesiastica* (*c*1197), II 3–364 [by dist., cap. & p.]; **Gir. Men.** *De Giraldo archidiacono Menevensi*, I 397–9; **Hug.** *Vita S. Hugonis*, VII 81–147 [by dist. & cap.]; **IK** *Itinerarium Kambriae* (*c*1191), VI 2–152 [by bk. & cap.]; **Invect.** *De invectionibus* (*c*1203), Y Cymmrodor XXX (1920) 77–237 [by bk. & cap.]; **JS** *De Jure et Statu Menevensis Ecclesiae* (*c*1218), RS III 99–373 [by dist. & p.]; **sup.** passages omitted from Rolls edition, *Medium Ævum* IV (1935) 144–52; **LS** *Epistola ad capitulum Herefordense de libris a se scriptis*, RS I 409–19; **PI** *De Principis Instructione* (*c*1217), VIII 5–329 [by dist. & cap.]; **RG** *De rebus a se gestis* (*c*1205), I 3–122 [by bk. & cap.]; **Rem.** *Vita S. Remigii* [2nd version *c*1214; incl. lives of various bishops of Lincoln, 1094–1200, and other later–12c. bishops], VII 3–80 [by cap.]; **Retr.** *Retractationes*, I 425–7; **SD** *Speculum Duorum*, ed. Y. Lefèvre, *Speculum Duorum* (Cardiff, 1974) 2–152; **Spec.** *Speculum Ecclesiae* (*c*1220), RS IV 3–354 [by dist. & cap.]; pref. ed. R. W. Hunt, *Viator* VIII (1977) 189–213; **Symb.** *Symbolum Electorum*, RS I 197–395 [by bk.]: I *Epistulae* 201–335 [by no. & p.]; II *Metra* 337–87 (including so-called *Juvenilia*) [by no. & p.; nos. 28–31, 33 not cited]; III *Orationes*, IV *Praefationes* [not cited]; **TH** *Topographia Hibernica* (*a*1188), V 1–204 [by bk. & cap.]; also 1st recension, ed. J. J. O'Meara, RIA Proc. LII (1949) C, 113–78.

GLA Carl Prantl: Geschichte der Logik in Abendlande, 4 vols. in 3 (Leipzig, 1867–70).

Gl. AN Glasg. The Glasgow Latin – French Glossary (13c.), *Medium Aevum* XXV (1957) 156–63 [by f.]; supplemented by P. Meyer, Documents manuscrits de l'ancienne littérature de la France conservés dans les bibliothèques de la Grande Bretagne (Paris, 1871) 123–6 [also in Archives des missions scientifiques et littéraires NS IV (1867) 156–9], and Jahrb. rom. Lit. VII (1866) 37–8.

Gl. AN Ox. The Anglo-Norman Vocabularies in MS Oxford, Bodleian Library, Douce 88 (13c.) [*vv. ll.* from St. John's College, Oxford, MS 178], *Medium Ævum* XLIX (1978) 7–24 [by no.].

GLANV. Ranulf Glanvill [*ob.* 1190]: *De legibus et consuetudinibus Regni Angliae* (*c*1185) [attrib.], ed. G. D. G. Hall, Med. Texts (1965) [by bk. & cap.]; also ed. G. E. Woodbine (New Haven, Conn., 1932).

Gl. Arch. H. Spelman: *Glossarium archaiologicum* (1664).

GlC An eighth-century Latin – Anglo-Saxon Glossary (Cambridge, Corpus Christi College MS 144), ed. W. M. Lindsay (Cambridge, 1921); *cf.* Philol. Soc. VIII (1921); *Interpretatio nominum Hebraicorum et Graecorum* cited from ed. J. H. Hessels (Cambridge, 1890); *v. et. EE, Erf.* 2 & 3, and *Gl. Leid.*

Gl. Castelnou The fourteenth-century medico-botanical glossary of Raimon de Castelnou, Leeds Philos. & Lit. Soc. XV vi (1974) 135–225.

GlD Old English Glosses, mostly dry point, Journal of English and Germanic Philology LX (1961) 441–50.

Gl. Durh. The Durham Glossary of the names of worts (11c.), in *Leechdoms* III 297–305.

GlH The Harley Latin – Old English Glossary (BL MS Harley 3376; 10c.), ed. R. T. Oliphant (The Hague, 1966), checked with MS [by letter & no.].

Gl. Leid. A late 8th-century Latin – Anglo-Saxon glossary preserved in Leiden University, ed. J. H. Hessels (Cambridge, 1906).

GlM Old English Glosses (A Collection), ed. H. D. Meritt (New York & London, 1945) [by sect. & no.].

Gl. Nautique Nouveau glossaire nautique d'Augustin Jal; révision de l'édition publiée en 1848, I– (Paris, 1970–).

GlN Old English Glosses chiefly unpublished, ed. A. S. Napier (Oxford, 1900) [by sect. & no.].

Gl. Nomin. A Nominalistic Glossary, a harvest of medieval theology, ed. H. A. Oberman (Cambridge, Mass., 1963) 459–76.

Gloss. Poems Glossarial Poems of medical terminology from Canterbury (10c.), ASE IV (1975) 103–4.

GlP The Old English Prudentius Glosses at Boulogne-sur-Mer (11c.), ed. H. D. Meritt (Stanford, Calif., 1959) [by no.].

GlS Anglo-Saxon Scratched Glosses in Corpus Christi College, Cambridge, Manuscript, ed. *Otium et Negotium*, Studies in Onomatology and Library Science presented to Olof von Feilitzen (Stockholm, 1973) 210–214.

GlSid The vernacular entries in the *Glossae in Sidonium* (*c*1200), Zeitschrift für französische Sprache und Literatur LXXXIX (1979) 135–50.

G. MON. Geoffrey of Monmouth [*ob.* 1154]: *Historia regum Britanniae* (1136), ed. A. Griscom (1929) [by bk. & cap.]; *v. et. V. Merl.*

G. NOTT. Geoffrey, Archdeacon of Nottingham [*fl.* 1140]: **Thurst.** Verses on Thurstan, Archb. of York [quoted in *V. Thurst.*], in *Hist. Church York* II 268–9 [by line]; **Visio** Vision of Thurstan, *ib.* 267–8 [by line].

GODEMAN Verses on the Benedictional of St. Æthelwold (10c.), ed. M. Lapidge, ASE IV (1975) 105–6 [by line].

GOSC. Goscelin, monk of Canterbury [*ob.* ? *c*1108]: **Æthelb.** *Vita S. Æthelburgae virginis, Studia Monastica* VII (1965) 398–417 [by cap.]; **Aug. Maj.** *Vita S. Augustini, historia major* (? *c*1094), *PL* LXXX (1850) 41–94; **Aug. Min.** *Historia minor, PL* CL (1854) 743–63; **Edith** *Vita S. Edithae* [ob. 984] (*c*1080), *Anal. Boll.* LVI (1938) 34–101, *Translatio ejusdam, ib.* 265–307; **Ed. Mart.** *Passio S. Eadwardi regis et martyris* [*ob.* 978] (*c*1080) [attrib.], ed. C. E. Fell, Edward King and Martyr (Leeds, 1971); **Hild.** *Lectiones de S. Hildelitha, Studia Monastica* VII (1965) 455–8 [by cap.]; **Just.** *Vita S. Justi archiepiscopi Cantuariensis* [*ob.* 627], *Acta SS. Boll.* Nov. IV (1925) 535–7 [by sect.]; **Lib. Confort.** *Liber confortatorius* (*c*1081), *Studia Anselmiana* XXXVII (1955) 26–117; **Lib. Mild.** *Libellus contra inanes S. Mildrethae usurpatores*, Med. Stud. XXXIX (1977) 68–96 [by cap.]; **Mellitus** *De adventu B. Melliti in Britanniam* (extr.), in FLETE *Westm.* 38–40; **Milb.** *Vita S. Milburgae* [attrib.] (extr.), ed. H. P. R. Finberg, Early charters of the West Midlands (Leicester, 1961) 201–204; **Mir. Aug.** *Libellus de miraculis S. Augustini* (*c*1094), *Acta SS. Ben.* I (1668) 535–59; **Mir. Iv.** *Miracula S. Ivonis*, in *Chr. Rams.* app. II lix–lxxxiv; **Transl. Æthelb.** *Translatio SS. Æthelbur-*

gae, Hildelithae, ac Wulfildae, Studia Monastica VII (1965) 435–54 [by f.]; **Transl. Aug.** *Historia translationis S. Augustini* (*p*1099), *PL* CLV (1880) 13–46; **V. Iv.** *Vita S. Ivonis episcopi* (*c*1090), *ib.* 81–90; **V. Mild.** *Vita S. Mildrethae* [*ob. c*740] (*c*1090), ed. D. W. Rollason, The Mildrith Legend (Leicester, 1982) 108–43 [by cap.]; **Werb.** *Vita S. Werburgae* [*ob. c*700] (11c.) [attrib.], *ib.* 93–110; also EETS LXXXVIII (1887) xix–xxvi; **Wulfh.** *Vita S. Wulfhildae* [*ob. c*1000] (*p*1086), *Anal. Boll.* XXXII (1913) 10–26 [by cap.]; superseded by *Studia Monastica* VII (1965) 418–34 [by cap.]; **Wulsin** Life of St. Wulsin of Sherborne (*c*1070), *Rev. Ben.* LXIX (1959) 68–85 [by cap.].

GOWER John Gower [*ob.* 1408], Complete works, ed. G. C. Macaulay: **Carm.** *Carmina varia*, IV (1902) 343–5 and 355–68 [by p. & line]; **CT** *Chronica tripartita* (*p*1399), 314–43 [by part & line]; **VC** *Vox clamantis* (begun 1381, finished *a*1399), 3–313 [by part & line]; **VP** *Carmen super vitiorum pestilentia* (1396–7), 346–54 [by line].

Grabmann Studies Aus der Geisteswelt des Mittelalters. Studien und Texte Martin Grabmann gewidmet, edd. A. Lang, J. Lechner, & M. Schmaus, BGPM Suppl. III (1935).

Grampian Club publications (London, 1869–80; Edinburgh, 1882–91).

GRAYSTANES Robert de Graystanes [*fl.* 1330]: *Historia de statu Ecclesiae Dunelmensis* (1214–1336), in *Hist. Durh. Script.* 33–123 [by cap.].

Great RB Bristol Great Red Book of Bristol (13c.–16c.), Bristol Rec. Soc. II, IV, VIII, XVI, XVIII (1931–1953).

GREG. Mir. Rom. Gregory (Magister Gregorius) [*ob. p*1200]: *De mirabilibus Urbis Romae*, ed. M. R. James, EHR XXXII (1917) 531–54, also ed. G. M. Rushforth, Journal of Roman Studies IX (1919) 14–48; superseded by ed. R. B. C. Huygens (Leiden, 1970) [by cap.].

Grey Friars Lond. C. L. Kingsford: The Grey Friars of London, British Soc. Franciscan Studies VI (1915).

Grey Friars Ox. A. G. Little: The Grey Friars in Oxford, OHS XX (1892).

G. Ric. I *Gesta Ricardi* (*c*1157–99) [wrongly attrib. BEN. PET.], in *Chr. Hen. II & Ric. I* II 71–252.

GRIM Edward (or Everardus) Grim [*fl.* 1170–85]: **Pass.** *Passio S. Thomae*, in *Thes. Nov. Anecd.* III 1737–46; **Thom.** *Vita S. Thomae* (*c*1175), in *Becket Mat.* II 353–450 [by cap.]; **app.** appendix, *ib.* 451–8.

G. Roman. *Gesta Romanorum* (*c*1340), ed. H. Oesterley (Berlin, 1872).

GROS. Robert Grosseteste, Bishop of Lincoln [1235–53], Die philosophische Werke [incl. some works of doubtful attribution], ed. L. Baur, BGPM IX (1912) 1–274 [by p.]: 1–7 *De artibus liberalibus* (*a*1209); 7–10 *De generatione sonorum* (*a*1209); 10–32 *De sphaera* (*a*1220); 32–6 *De generatione stellarum* (*a*1225); 36–41 *De cometis* (*c*1222) [= shorter text of *Com.*]; 41–51 *De impressionibus aëris seu de prognosticatione* (*a*1220); 51–9 *De luce seu de inchoatione formarum* (*c*1225); 59–65 *De lineis, angulis et figuris seu de fractionibus et reflexionibus radiorum* (*c*1230); 65–72 *De natura locorum*; 72–8 *De iride* (*c*1230); 78–9 *De colore* (*c*1230); 79–84 *De calore solis* (*c*1230); 84–7 *De differentiis localibus*; 87–9 *De impressionibus elementorum*; 90–92 *De motu corporali et luce*; 92–100 *De motu supercaelestium*; 101–106 *De finitate motus et temporis*; 106–111 *De unica forma omnium* [= *Ep.* 1 pp. 1–7]; 112–119 *De intelligentiis* [= *Ep.* 1 pp. 8–17]; 120–26 *De statu causarum*; 126–9 *De potentia et actu*; 130–43 *De veritate*; 143–5 *De veritate propositionis*; 145–7 *De scientia Dei* [= *Quaest. Theol.* I]; 147–50 *De ordine emendandi causatorum a Deo* (or *De aeternitate filii in divinis*); 150–241 *De libero arbitrio*; 241–74 *De anima* [attrib.]; other works as follows: **Anal. Post.** *Commentarius in Posteriorum analyticorum libros*, ed. P. Rossi (Florence, 1981); **Cess. Leg.** *De cessatione legalium* [part 1 only] (London, 1658); (extr. from part 2), Franciscan Studies XVI (1956) 3–18 [complete edn. for

Auct. Brit. in prep.]; **Cista** *Ordinatio de pecunia deposita in cista*, in *StatOx* 74–6; **Com.** *De cometis, Isis* XIX (1933) 19–25; **Comp.** *Compotus factus ad correctionem communis Kalendarii nostri*, in BACON VI 212–67; **Const.** *Constitutiones* (= *Ep.* 52*), in *Conc. Syn.* II 265–78; **Deus est** 'Deus est' (*De confessione* II), Franciscan Studies XXX (1970) 239–93; **Dicta** MS Lincoln Cathedral 188 and 303 [by cap.]; (extr.) in *Fasc. Rerum Expet.* II 258–305 [by no. & p.]; no. 60, Franciscan Studies XXIV (1964) 153–8; **DM** *De decem mandatis*, ed. R. C. Dales, *Auct. Brit.* [in prep.]; **Dot.** *De dotibus*, Med. Stud. XLIV (1982) 83–109 [by cap.]; **Ep.** *Epistolae* (*a*1210–53), RS XXV (1861) [by no.] [*Ep.* 1 = pp. 106–19 in Baur's ed.]; **Eth. Nic.** *Aritotelis Ethica Nicomachea* [transl.], ed. R. A. Gauthier, *Aristoteles Latinus* XXVI/1–3 iii–iv (Leiden, 1972–3); **Flux.** *De fluxu et refluxu maris* (*c*1227), *Isis* LVII (1966) 459–68; **Gram.** Grammar, v. Ps.-GROS. *Gram.*; **Hexaem.** *Hexaemeron*, ed. R. C. Dales and S. Gieben, *Auct. Brit.* VI (1982) [by bk. & cap.]; **Kal.** *Kalendarium* (*c*1220), Arkiv för Matematik, Astronomi och Fysik II ii (1916) 15–41; **Oper. Sol.** *De operationibus solis*, RTAM XLI (1974) 62–91; **Phys.** *Commentarius in VIII libros Physicorum Aristotelis*, ed. R. C. Dales, (Boulder, Col., 1963); **Phys. Sum.** *Summa Physicorum*, ed. J. E. Bolzan and C. Lértora Mendoza (Buenos Aires, 1972); **Post. Mark** *Postillae super evangelium Marci* (extr.), ed. H. Glunz, History of the Vulgate in England (Cambridge, 1933), 356–9; **Ps.-Andr.** *Pseudo*-Andronicus περὶ παθῶν [transl.], ed. Glibert-Thirry (Leiden, 1977); **Ps.-Dion.** *Pseudo*-Dionysius, *De divinis nominibus, De mystica theologia, De caelesti hierarchia, De ecclesiastica hierarchia* [all transl.], ed. P. Chevallier, *Dionysiaca*, 2 vols. (Paris & Bruges, 1937–50) [text R]; **Ps.-Dion. MT** *Pseudo-Dionysii de mystica theologia* [transl. & comm.], ed. U. Gamba (Milan, 1942); **Quaest. Theol.** *Quaestiones theologicae* [attrib.], ed. D. A. Callus, in Powicke Studies 194–209; **Reg.** *Registrum*, v. *Reg. Linc.*; **Sang.** *De sanguine Christi*, in M. PAR. *Maj.* VI 138–44; **Summa** v. Ps.-GROS. *Summa*; **Templ.** *Templum Dei*, ed. J. Goering and F.A.C. Mantello, Toronto Med. Latin Texts (1984) [by cap. & sect.]; **Test. Patr.** *Testamenta XII patriarcharum* [transl.], *Patrologia Graeca* II 1025–1150.

Growth Eng. Ind. W. Cunningham: The Growth of English Industry and commerce during the early and middle ages (Cambridge, 1896).

G. S. Alb. *Gesta abbatum monasterii S. Albani* [Herts] (793–1396), in *Chr. Mon. S. Alb.* IV, 3 vols. (1867–9): I 1–324 (793–1255) [mainly by M. PAR]; I 325–II 109 (1248–1308) [anon.]; II 111–III 372 (1308–96) [by WALS.]; III 373–535 (1349–1401) [anon.].

G. SOUTHWICK Conf. Guy, Prior of Southwick [*ob. c*1217]: *De virtute confessionis* (*a*1198), RTAM VII (1935) 340–52.

G. STANFORD Cant. Gilbert of Stanford, Cistercian [12c.]: *Super Canticum canticorum* (extr.), Studia Anselmiana XX (1948) 205–30.

G. Steph. *Gesta Stephani* (1135–54) [attrib. Robert of Lewes, Bishop of Bath 1136–66], ed. K. R. Potter and R. H. C. Davis, Med. Texts (1955; rev. ed. 1976) [by cap.]; also in *Chr. Steph.* III 3–136.

Gt. Cause Ed. I Edward I and the throne of Scotland 1290–1296, an edition of the record sources for the Great Cause (Oxford, 1978), vol. II.

Guild Cert. Chancery Guild Certificates (1388–9), MS PRO (C. 47/38–46); *cf.* (extr.) in *Eng. Gilds.*

GUISBOROUGH *v.* W. GUISB.

G. Walth. *Gesta Waldevi comitis* [*ob.* 1076] (wr. ? 12c.), ed. F. Michel, Chroniques Anglo-Normandes, 3 vols. (Rouen, 1836–40), II 99–142.

G. WINT. Godfrey of Winchester [*ob.* 1107]: **Epigr.** *Epigrammata*, in *Sat. Poets* II 103–47 [by no.]; superseded by ed. H. Gerhard, Der *Liber Proverbiorum* des

Godefrid von Winchester (Würzburg, 1974) [by no.]; **Epigr. Hist.** *Epigrammata historica*, in *Sat. Poets* II 148–55 [by no.].

HADRIAN IV Pope Hadrian IV (*alias* Nicholas Breakspear of St. Albans) [*ob.* 1159]: *Epistolae et privilegia*, *PL* CLXXXVIII 1361–1640 [by no.].

H. ALBUS Hugh Albus (*alias* Candidus), monk of Peterborough [*ob.* a1175]: Chronicle (656–1155), ed. W. T. Mellows (Oxford, 1949); supersedes *Hist. Angl. Script.* II 1–94.

Hal. Durh. *Halmota Prioratus Dunelmensis*, from Halmote Court or Manor Rolls (1296–1384) (extr.), Surtees Soc. LXXXII (1889) [vol. II not pub.].

HALES Alexander of Hales [*ob.* 1245]: **An.** *Expositio super tertium de Anima* [attrib.] (Oxford, 1481); **Fat.** *Quaestio de fato*, Franziskanische Studien XIX (1932) 23–39; **Qu.** *Quaestiones disputatae 'antequam esset frater'* [sometimes wrongly referred to as *Summa Abendonensis*], *Bibliotheca Franciscana scholastica medii aevi* XIX–XXI (Quaracchi, 1960); **Sent.** *Glossa in quatuor libros Sententiarum Petri Lombardi*, *ib.* XII–XV (1951–7); **Summa** *Summa theologica* [a compilation based on writings of HALES and others], 5 vols. (1924–48).

HAM. S. ALB. Hamelin of St. Albans [*fl.* 1100]: *Liber de monachatu* (extr.), in *Thes. Nov. Anecd.* V 1453–6.

Hants Rec. Soc. Hampshire Record Society, publications, I– (Winchester, 1889–).

HANV. John de Hanville (*alias* Hauville, or de Alta Villa) [*fl.* 1184]: *Architrenius*, in *Sat. Poets* I 240–392 [by bk. & p.]; superseded from Fasc. III by ed. P. G. Schmidt (Munich, 1974) [by bk. & line].

HARCLAY Henry of Harclay, Chancellor of Oxford [*ob.* 1317]: **Adv.** *Quaestio de secundo adventu Christi*, ed. F. Pelster, Archivio italiano per la storia della pietà I (1951) 53–82; **Aetern.** *Quaestio utrum mundus potuit fuisse ab aeterno*, AHDLMA L (1983) 231–55; **Forma** Disputed question on the plurality of Forms, Essays in honour of Anton Charles Pegis (Toronto, 1974) 129–59; **Idea** Questions on the Divine Ideas, Med. Stud. XXIII (1961) 166–93; **Immort.** Questions on Immortality, *ib.* XIX (1957) 89–107; **Praedest.** Questions on Predestination, Franciscan Studies XL (1980) 195–223; **Thom.** *Sermo de laudibus S. Thomae Cantuariensis* (extr.), in *Anglia Sacra* II 524n., repr. in GIR. *JS* I pp. 125–6n.; **Trin.** *Utrum Pater, Filius, et Spiritus Sanctus sint unum principium respectu creaturae vel tria* (MS Vat. Burgh. 171 ff. 17v–20v), Franciscan Studies XLI (1981) 281–335 [by sect.]; **Univers.** *Utrum universale significet aliquam rem extra animam, aliam a singulari vel supposito* (MS Vat. Burgh. 171 ff. 7vb–12rb), Franciscan Studies XXXI (1971) 186–234 [by sect.]; **Univoc.** Question on the Univocity of Being (extr.), Med. Stud. XVI (1954) 1–18.

HAUBOYS John Hauboys (*alias* Hanboys) [*fl.* p1350]: *Summa super musicam continuam et discretam*, in *Script. Mus.* I 403–48.

HAUDLO Robert de Haudlo (*alias* Handlo) [*fl.* 1326]: *Regulae*, in *Script. Mus.* I 383–403.

H. AVR. Henry of Avranches [*ob.* 1260]: **CG** *Commoda grammaticae* (? 1219) (extr.), ed. J. P. Heironimus and J. C. Russell, (Colorado Springs, 1929) 10–26 [by f. & line]; **prol. & epil.** prologue and epilogue, in Poems (Cambridge, Mass., 1935) 58–9; **Guthl.** *Vita S. Guthlaci* [*ob.* 714], MS Cambridge University Library Dd. 11. 78 [by f. & line]; **Hugh** Metrical Life of St. Hugh, Bishop of Lincoln [*ob.* 1200] (*c*1220) [attrib.], ed. J. F. Dimock (Lincoln, 1860); **Poems** The shorter Latin poems relating to England, ed. J. C. Russell and J. P. Heironimus (Cambridge, Mass., 1935) [complete poems by no. & line; extr. by no. & p.; *v. et.* M. CORNW.].

H. BOS. Herbert of Bosham [*ob. c*1185]: **CE** *Causa exsilii B. Thomae*, *PL* CXC (1893) 1413–16; **Ep.** *Epistolae*, *ib.* 1415–74 [by no. & col.; *v. et. Ep. Becket*]; **Gl. Pref.** *Praefationes in Glossam Magnam*, ed. H. Glunz, History

of the Vulgate in England (Cambridge, 1933), 342–50; **Hom.** *Homilia in festo S. Thomae*, *PL* CXC 1403–14; **LM** *Liber melorum*, *ib.* 1293–1404; **Psalt.** Commentary on *Psalterium juxta Hebraeos* (extr.), RTAM XVIII (1951) 29–65; **Thom.** *Vitae S. Thomae*, in *Becket Mat.* III 155–534 [by bk. & cap.; this version differs somewhat from *PL* CXC 1073–1292].

HBS Henry Bradshaw Society, publications, I– (1891–).

HCA High Court of Admiralty, records, MS PRO: **Act Bk.** Instance and Prize courts, Acts (1524–) (H.C.A. 3); **Crim.** Oyer and terminer records, criminal (1535–) (H.C.A. 1); **Libel** Libels, etc. (1519–) (H.C.A. 24); **Warrant Bk.** Warrant books (1541–) (H.C.A. 38).

H. CANDIDUS *v.* H. ALBUS.

H. CANTOR Hugh the Chanter (*alias* Sottovagina), Precentor of York [*ob. c*1139]: History of the Church of York (1066–1127), ed. C. Johnson, Med. Texts (1961) [by f.]; **Cont.** Additions (–1153), in *Hist. Church York* II 220–27; **Vers.** *Versus*, in *Sat. Poets* II 219–29 [by p.].

H. DE BURGO Henry de Burgo, Prior of Lancercost [*ob.* 1315], Verses, *v. Lanercost*.

HEETE Robert Heete [*ob. c*1432]: **Catal. Coll. Wint.** *Libri B. Mariae prope Winton'* (*temp.* Hen. V, Hen. VI), Arch. J. XV (1858) 62–74; **Wykeham** Life of William of Wykeham [1324–1404], ed. G. G. Moberly, Life of William of Wykeham (1887) 293–308, 2nd ed. (1893) app. E, 321–36; *cf.* AYLWARD.

HENGHAM Ralph de Hengham, Chief Justice [*ob.* 1311]: **Judic. Esson.** *Judicium Essoniorum*, ed. G. E. Woodbine, Four 13th-century law tracts (New Haven, Conn., 1910) 116–42; **Magna** *Summa Magna* (a1275), *Radulphi de Hengham Summae*, ed. W. H. Dunham, (Cambridge, 1932) 1–50 [by cap.]; **Parva** *Summa Parva* (p1285), *ib.* 51–71 [by cap.].

Heresy Tri. Norw. Heresy Trials in the diocese of Norwich, 1428–31, Camd. 4th S. XX (1977).

HERFORD Nicholas Herford, Fellow of Queen's College [*fl.* 1390], *v. Ziz.*

HERM. ARCH. Herman of Bury St Edmunds, archdeacon [*ob. c*1095]: *Liber de miraculis S. Eadmundi* [*ob.* 870], in *Mem. S. Edm.* I 26–92 [by cap.]; also ed. F. Liebermann, in *ANQuellen* 202–81; *v. et.* SAMSON.

HERRISON Abbr. Chr. John Herrison [*fl.* 1460]: *Abbreviata chronica* (1377–1469), Camb. Antiq. Soc., 4° S., II (1840).

Hexham The Priory of Hexham, Surtees Soc. XLIV, XLVI (1863–4); *v. et.* AILR. *SS Hex*, J. HEX., RIC. HEX.

HEYTESBURY William Heytesbury, fellow of Merton [*ob. c*1372]: **Prob.** *Probationes conclusionum* (Venice, 1494) f. 188v.–203v.; also (extr.) in *Sci. Mech.* 287–9; **Reg.** *Regulae solvendi sophismatum* (Venice, 1494) f. 9v.–52; also (extr.) in *Sci. Mech.* 238–42, 277–83.

H. FAVERSHAM Haymo of Faversham [*ob.* 1243]: *Ordines*, ed. S. J. P. van Dijk, Sources of the Modern Roman Liturgy, 2 vols. (Leiden, 1963), II.

H. HARTLEPOOL Hugh of Hartlepool [*ob. c*1302]: Sermon (1291), in *Theol. Ox.* 192–204.

H. HUNT. Henry, Archdeacon of Huntingdon [*ob.* ? 1155]: **CM** *Epistola ad Walterum de contemptu mundi*, RS LXXIV (1879) 297–320 [by cap.]; **Ep. ad Warinum** *Epistola ad Warinum de regibus Britonum*, in TORIGNI 65–75; **HA** *Historia Anglorum* I–VIII (55 B.C.-A.D. 1154), RS LXXIV (1879) 1–292 [by bk. & cap.]; **HA IX** *De miraculis* (extr.), *ib.* xxv–xxx; **HA X** *De summitatibus*, *v. supra* CM, *Ep. ad Warinum* [remainder not printed]; **HA XI** *Epigrammata*, in *Sat. Poets* II 163–74 [by p.].

HIGD. Ralph Higden [*ob.* 1364]: *Polychronicon* (Creation–1352), 9 vols. RS XLI (1865–86) [by bk. & cap.]; **Cont. A** Continuation (–1381) [attrib. J. MALVERN], *ib.* VIII 355–428; **Cont. B** (1381–94), *v.* Chr. Westm.

HIL. RONCE. Hilarius of Ronceray [*fl. c*1125]: *Versus et ludi*, ed. J. B. Fuller (New York, 1929).

Hist. Abb. Jarrow *Historia abbatum, auctore anonymo* (*c*716), ed. C. Plummer, *Baedae Opera Historica* (Oxford, 1896) I 388–404 [by cap.]; *v. et.* HWÆTBERHT *Ep.*

Hist. Agric. J. E. Thorold Rogers: A History of Agriculture and Prices in England (1259–1793), 7 vols. (Oxford, 1866–92) [by vol. & p.].

Hist. Angl. Script. *Historiae Anglicanae scriptores varii*, ed. J. Sparke, 2 parts (1723); *v.* Chr. Angl. Peterb., H. ALBUS, SWAFHAM, WHITTLESEY.

Hist. Angl. Script. X *Historiae Anglicanae Scriptores X*, ed. R. Twysden (1652); *v.* AILR. *Gen. Reg.*, BROMPTON, THORNE.

Hist. Arthuri *Vera historia de morte Arthuri* (13c.), ed. M. Lapidge, Arthurian Studies I (1981) 84–92.

Hist. Bart. N. Moore: The History of St. Bartholomew's Hospital, 2 vols. (1918).

Hist. Brit. Iron & Steel Ind. H. R. Schubert: History of the British Iron and Steel Industry (*c*450 B.C.-A.D. 1775) (1957).

Hist. Castle Combe G. P. Scrope: History of Castle Combe (1852).

Hist. Cath. Cant. J. Dart: The History and antiquities of the Cathedral Church of Canterbury (1726).

Hist. Chess H. J. R. Murray: A History of Chess (Oxford, 1913).

Hist. Chester G. Ormerod: The History of the County Palatine and City of Chester, 2nd ed. (1882).

Hist. Ch. Peterb. S. Gunton: The History of the Church of Peterborough (1686).

Hist. Church York Historians of the Church of York and its Archbishops, 3 vols. RS LXXI (1879–94); *v.* BYRHT. *V. Osw.*, Chr. Ebor. Metr., Chr. Pont. Ebor., EADMER *V. & Mir. Osw.*, Wilf., Wilf. Brev., FOLC. *V. J. Bev.*, G. NOTT., H. CANTOR *Cont.*, H. PONTEFR., KETEL *J. Bev.*, Mir. *J. Bev.*, Mir. Will., Misc. Scrope, S. DURH. *Ep. Hug.*, SENATUS *Osw.*, T. STUBBS *Chr.*, V. Thurst., V. Will.

Hist. Cuthb. *Historia de S. Cuthberto* [*ob.* 687] (10c.), in S. DURH. I 196–214.

Hist. Durh. Script. *Historiae Dunelmensis scriptores tres*, Surtees Soc. IX (1839), appendix of documents [sep. pag.; by p.]; *v. et.* G. COLD., GRAYSTANES, *Hist. Durh.*

Hist. Durh. William de Chambre [*fl.* ? 1356] *et al.*: *Continuatio historiae Dunelmensis* (1336–1571), in *Hist. Durh. Script.* 127–56 [by cap.].

Hist. Eng. Bar H. Cohen: History of the English Bar (–1450) (1929).

Hist. Eng. Coron. P. E. Schramm: History of the English Coronation, transl. L. G. W. Legg (Oxford, 1937).

Hist. Exch. T. Madox: History of the Exchequer (1066–1327) (1711).

Hist. Fordwich v. Cust. Fordwich.

Hist. Francisc. Eng. A. G. Little: Studies in English Franciscan History (Manchester, 1917).

Hist. Glouc. *Historia monasterii S. Petri Gloucestriae* (681–1390), in *Cart. Glouc.* I 3–125.

Hist. Imbank. W. Dugdale: The History of Imbanking and drainage (1772).

Hist. Llanthony History of Llanthony (12c), *Studia Celtica* XII/XIII (1977–8) 126–31 (*cf. MonA* VI 128–34).

Hist. Meriadoci *Historia Meriadoci* (*c*1250), ed. J. D. Bruce, Modern Language Association of America XV (1900) 339–97; checked against revised ed., *Hesperia* Ergänzungsreihe II (Göttingen, 1913).

Hist. Merton Texts concerning Gilbert, founder of Merton Priory, *Studia Monastica* XII (1970) 248–70 [by f.].

Hist. Newc. J. Brand: History and antiquities of Newcastle upon Tyne, 2 vols. (1789).

Hist. Northumberland J. Hodgson: History of Northumberland, 3 vols. in 7 (Newcastle, 1820–58).

Hist. Roff. *Historia Roffensis* (1314–50) [attrib. William Dene], with supporting docs. [by f. of MS BL Cotton Faustina B v; some refs. may be to pp. of *Anglia Sacra* I 356–77].

Hist. Shrewsb. H. Owen and J. B. Blakeway: A History of Shrewsbury, 2 vols. (1825).

Hist. S. Paul. W. Dugdale: The History of St. Paul's Cathedral in London, ed. H. Ellis (1818).

Hist. Staffs S. Shaw: The History and Antiquities of Staffordshire, 2 vols. (1798, 1801).

Hist. Tynemouth v. Cart. Tynemouth.

Hist. Wells *Historia major* (704–1408) *et minor* (704–1367) *Wellenses*, ed. J. A. Robinson, *Collectanea* I, Som Rec. Soc. XXXIX (1924) 48–71.

H. KIRKSTALL Hugh, monk of Kirkstall [*fl.* 1200] *v.* SERLO GRAM.

H. LEXINGTON *v. Reg. Linc.*

H. LOS. Herbert de Losinga, Bishop of Norwich [*ob.* 1119]: **Ep.** *Epistolae*, ed. R. Anstruther (Brussels, 1846) 1–107 [by no.]; *cf.* collation in Goulburn and Symons I 418–23; **Serm.** Sermons, ed. E. H. Goulburn and H. Symonds, Life, Letters, and Sermons (1878) II 2–430.

HMC Historical Manuscripts Commission: **JP** Joint Publications Series (with county record societies), I– (1962–). **Rep.** Reports, I– (1874–).

HMSO His [Her] Majesty's Stationery Office.

H. NEWCASTLE Hugh of Newcastle [*fl.* 1320]: **Sent.** *Commentarius in primum Sententiarum* (extr.), Franziskanische Studien XX (1933) 193–222; **Vict.** *De victoria Christi contra Antichristum* (wr. 1319), (Nuremberg, 1471); (extr.) *N. & E.* XXXV (1896) 232–8.

HOLCOT Robert Holcot [*ob.* 1349]: **Comm.** Commentaries (extr.), in *Eng. Friars* 321–37, 358–9, 366–8; **Ecclus.** *In librum Ecclesiastici* [i–vii] *Jesu filii Sirach expositio* (Venice, 1509); **Mor.** *Moralitates*, w. *Wisd.* (Basel, 1586), 709–48; **Quodl.** *Quodlibeta* (1332), MS BL Royal 10 C VI: *Utrum theologia sit scientia* (*Quodl.* I q. 1), Med. Stud. XX (1958) 128–53; *Utrum Deus posset scire plura quam scit* (*Quodl.* I q. 6), Speculum XXXIX (1964) 59–64; **Sermo** *Sermo Finalis*, Med. Stud. XI (1949) 220–4; **Wisd.** *Super Sapientiam Salomonis* (Basel, 1586).

Holy Rood-Tree Latin Versions [12c.], ed. A. S. Napier, History of the Holy Rood-Tree, EETS CIII (1894) 41–62.

HON. Honorius 'Augustodunensis' [12c.]: **Eluc.** *Elucidarium sive dialogus de summa totius Christianae theologiae*, PL CLXXII 1109–76; **GA** *Gemma animae, ib.* 541–738; **Inev.** *Inevitabile sive dialogus de libero arbitrio, ib.* 1192–1222; **Sig.** *Sigillum beatae Mariae, ib.* 495–518; **Spec. Eccl.** *Speculum ecclesiae, ib.* 807–1108.

HOPEMAN Heb. Thomas Hopeman, O.P. [14c.]: Commentary on Hebrews (extr.), *AFP* XXV (1955) 334–44 [by f.].

HORN Mir. Just. Andrew Horn [*ob.* 1328]: Latin verses prefatory to Le Mireur à justices (*c*1290), Selden Soc. VII (1895) 1.

Hosp. in Eng. The Knights Hospitallers in England, report to Grand Master (1338), Camden Soc. LXV (1857).

HOTHBY John Hothby [*ob.* 1487]: **Cant. Fig.** *De cantu figurato*, in *Script. Mus.* III 330–2; **Contrap.** *Regulae super contrapunctum* (version Fa), *ib.* 333–4; superseded by *Johannes Hothby de arte contrapuncti*, ed. G. Reaney, *Corp. Script. Mus.* XXVI (1977) 101–3; another text (version Fl), *ib.* 63–9 [by version & p.]; **Prop.** *Regulae super proportionem*, in *Script. Mus.* III 328–30.

Househ. Bk. Durh. Household Book (bursar's accounts) of the monastery of Durham 1530–4, Surtees Soc. XVIII (1844).

Househ. Eleanor Court and Household of Eleanor of Castille in 1290, ed. J. C. Parsons (Toronto, 1977).

Househ. Isabella The Household Book of Queen Isabella of England (1311–12), MS BL Cotton Nero C VIII ff. 121–52, ed. F. D. Blackley and G. Hermansen (Edmonton, Alberta, 1971).

HOWDEN v. J. HOWD., R. HOWD.

H. PONTEFR. Hugh, monk of Pontefract [*fl.* 1140]: Verses on Thurstan, Archb. of York [quoted in *V. Thurst.*], in *Hist. Church York* II 261–5 [by line].

H. READING (I) Hugh, Abbot of Reading [*ob.* 1164]: **Adjut.** *Vita S. Adjutoris, PL* CXCII (1855) 1345–52; **Dial.** *Dialogorum libri VII, ib.* 1141–1248 [by bk. & col.]; **Ep.** *Epistolae, ib.* 1131–8 [by no. & col.]; **Fid. Cath.** *Super fide catholica, ib.* 1323–46; **Haeret.** *Contra haereticos, ib.* 1255–98 [by bk. & col.]; **Hexaem.** *Tractatus in hexaemeron, ib.* 1247–56; **Mem.** *Tractatus de memoria, ib.* 1299–1324.

H. READING (II) Cel. Hugh, Abbot of Reading [*ob.* 1207]: Epistle to Celestine III (*c*1197), in Wilkinson Essays 29–31.

H. SALTREY H. of Saltrey [Hunts] [*fl.* 1150]: *Purgatorium S. Patricii,* ed. J. Colgan, *Triadis Thaumaturgae Acta* (Louvain, 1647) 273–80 [by sect.]; *cf.* M. PAR. *Maj.* II 192–203.

H. SOTTOVAGINA v. H. CANTOR.

H. SULLY Lib. Henry de Sully (de Soliaco), Abbot of Glastonbury [*ob.* 1195]: *Liber,* an inquisition of the manors of Glastonbury Abbey of the year 1189, ed. J. E. Jackson, Roxb. Club (1882).

HUBERT Gros. Frater Hubertus [13c.]: *De vita beati Roberti quondam Lincolniensis episcopi* [*ob.* 1253], *Med. & Hum.* NS I (1970) 246–51 [by line].

HUGEB. Hugeburg (Hygeburh) [*fl. c*778]: **Will.** *Vita Willibaldi episcopi Eichstetensis* [? 700–86], *MGH Scriptores* XV (Hanover, 1887) 86–106 [by cap]; **Wynn.** *Vita Wynnebaldi abbatis Heidenheimensis* [*ob.* 761], *ib.* 106–17 [by cap.].

Hug. Soc. Huguenot Society of London, publications, I– (Lymington, 1887–).

Hund. Highworth The Rolls of Highworth Hundred (1257–87), Wilts Arch. Soc., Rec. Branch, XXI, XXII (Devizes, 1966–8).

Hund. & HundR H. M. Cam: The Hundred and the Hundred Rolls (1930).

HundR Hundred Rolls (Hen. III – Edw. I), MS PRO (S.C. 5); *v. et.* Hund.

Hund. *Rotuli hundredorum* (Hen. III–Ed. I), 2 vols. RC (1812–18); *v. et. HundR.*

Hunt Essays Medieval Learning & Literature: essays presented to Richard William Hunt (Oxford, 1976).

Husb. Walter of Henley: Husbandry, ed. D. Oschinsky (Oxford, 1971) [AN and ME; cited as source of passages in *Fleta; cf.* Senesch.].

HWÆTBERHT Hwætberht (*alias* Eusebius), Abbot of Wearmouth and Jarrow [*ob. c*744]: **Aen.** *Aenigmata, CCSL* CXXXIII (1968) 209–71 [by no. & line]; **Ep.** *Epistola,* in *Hist. Abb. Jarrow* 30.

H. WILE An. Henry of Wile [Wylye, Wilts] [*ob.* 1329]: *Commentarius de Anima,* MS Magdalen Coll. Ox. 63; (extr.), Franciscan Studies XXVIII (1968) 231–48.

H. WODSTONE Henry of Wodstone, O.F.M. [*ob. c*1290]: *Contra Judaeos,* ed. A.G. Little, British Society for Franciscan Studies X (1922) 153–4.

Hymn. Cant. The Canterbury Hymnal, ed. G. R. Wieland, Toronto Med. Latin Texts (1982).

IAQD Inquisitions *ad quod damnum* (Hen. III–Ric. III), MS PRO (C. 143).

ICrim Criminal Inquisitions (Hen. III–Hen. VI), MS PRO (C. 144).

IHR Bull. Institute of Historical Research, Bulletin, I– (London, 1925–).

Illust. Scot. Illustrations of Scottish history, 12th to 16th century, ed. J. Stevenson, Maitland Club (1834).

IMC Irish Manuscripts Commission, publications, I– (Dublin, 1931–).

IMisc Miscellaneous Inquisitions (1218–1485), MS PRO (C. 145).

Incept. Ox. Four graduation speeches from Oxford manuscripts (*c*1270– 1310), Med. Stud. XLIV (1982) 138–80.

Inchaffray Charters relating to the Abbey of Inchaffray, Perth, SHS 1st S. LVI (1908) [by p.].

Indict. (Assizes) Indictments, S. E. Circuit (1559–), MS PRO (Assizes 35).

Inq. Cantab. *Inquisitio comitatus Cantabrigiensis* (1086), ed. N. E. S. A. Hamilton (1876); *v. et. Inq. Ely.*

Inq. Ely *Inquisitio Eliensis* (1086), in *DB Add.* I 495–528 [by f.]; also ed. N. E. S. A. Hamilton, in *Inq. Cantab.* 97–195 [differs from DB text].

Inq. Glast. Inquisition of the manors of Glastonbury abbey (1189), ed. J. E. Jackson, Roxb. Club (1882).

Inq. Non. *Nonarum inquisitiones in Curia Scaccarii* (*temp.* Ed. III), ed. G. Vanderzee, RC (1807).

Instr. Nov. *Instructio noviciorum secundum consuetudinem ecclesiae Cantuariensis* (? 13c.), in LANFR. *Const.* 133–49 [by f.].

Inst. Sempr. *Institutiones B. Gilberti ordinis de Sempringham* (*c*1148), pp. *xxix–*lix, in *MonA* VI, between pp. 946 and 947; [roman pag. in ed. 1846 differs from that in ed. 1817–30].

Invent. Ch. Ch. Inventories of Christchurch Canterbury (1294–18c.), ed. J. W. Legg and W. H. St. J. Hope (1902).

Invent. Exch. Inventories of goods and chattels: 1207–8, Pipe R. Soc. NS XXXI 119–25; later rolls (John–), MS PRO (E. 154).

Invent. Med. The inventory of John Hexham, a fifteenth-century apothecary (1415), Medical History IX (1965) 79 [by no.].

Invent. Norw. Archdeaconry of Norwich, Inventory of church goods (1368), Norf Rec. Soc. XIX, 2 vols. (1947–8).

Invent. S. Paul. Inventories of St. Paul's Cathedral, London: 1245 *Arch.* L (1887) 464–500; 1402 *ib.* 500–518; 1445 *ib.* 518–24.

Invent. York *Inventarium omnium librorum pertinentium ad domum fratrum Heremitarum Sancti Augustini* (1372), N. & Q., 1st S., I (1850) 83–4; also ed. M. R. James, *Fasciculus Joanni Willis Clark dicatus* (Cambridge, 1909), 19–83.

IPM Inquisitions *post mortem,* MS PRO: Hen. III (C. 132); Ed. I (C. 133); Ed. II (C. 134); Ed. III (C. 135); Ric. II (C. 136); Hen. IV (C. 137); Hen. V (C. 138); Hen. VI (C. 139); Ed. IV (C. 140); Ric. III (C. 141); Hen. VII, Hen. VIII etc., (C. 142).

IRELAND Imm. Conc. John Ireland, Rector of Hawick [*fl.* 1480]: *De immaculata conceptione virginis Mariae* (extr.), ed. M. Esposito, EHR XXXIV (1919) 68–71 [by f.].

Isis Isis, I– (Brussels & Cambridge, Mass., 1913–).

IS. STELLA Isaac of Stella [*c*1110–*c*1167]: **An.** *De anima, PL* CXC 1875–90; **Can.** *De canone missae, ib.* 1889–96; **Serm.** *Sermones,* ed. A. Hoste, Sources chrétiennes CXXX, CCVII (1967–74) [by no., sect., & col.]; **sup.** *Collect.* OCR XLIII (1981) 34–55.

IssueR Issue Rolls of the Exchequer of Receipt (1240–1480), MS PRO (E. 403).

Iter Cam. *Modus procedendi in itinere camerarii infra regnum Scocie,* in *APScot* I app. IV, 329–38 [by cap.].

Iter Cam. Artic. *De articulis inquirendis in itinere camerarii,* in *APScot* I app. III, 316–18 [by cap.].

Itin. Mand. *Itinerarium Johannis Maundeville de mirabilibus mundi* [transl. *c*1400] (extr.), EETS CCLIII (1963).

Itin. Ric. *Itinerarium peregrinorum et gesta regis Ricardi* (*c*1200) [attrib. Ricardus de Templo, prior of Holy Trinity, London], in *Mem. Ric. I,* I 3–450 [by bk. and cap.; anon. source of Bk. I, ed. H. E. Mayer, *MGH* Schriften XVIII (Stuttgart, 1962)].

J. ACTON Comment. John of Acton (*alias* Ayton) [*ob.* 1350]: *Commentaria in constitutiones legatinas D. Othonis*

et D. Othoboni, pub. w. LYNDW. (Oxford, 1679) [sep. pag.].

Jahrb. rom. Lit. Jahrbuch für romanische und englische Literatur, I– (Berlin, 1859–).

Jan. Joannes Balbus Januensis: *Catholicon* (1286) (Mainz: J. Gutenberg, 1460; facs. 1971).

J. BATH John of Bath, ? monk of Dore [*fl.* 1200]: Notes on OSB. GLOUC. *Deriv.*, MS Hereford Cathedral Library P. V. 5 (extr.), Med. & R. Stud. IV (1958) 277–81.

J. BLUND An. John Blund [*ob.* 1248]: *Tractatus de anima* (*c*1200), ed. D. A. Callus and R. W. Hunt, *Auct. Brit.* II (1970) [by sect.].

J. BRIDL. St. John of Bridlington [*ob.* 1379], prophecies falsely attrib., *v. Pol. Poems* I 132–215; *V. J. Bridl. v. NLA* II 64–78.

J. BURGH PO John de Burgh [*ob.* 1386]: *Pupilla oculi* (Strasbourg, 1514) [by bk. & cap.].

J. BURY Glad. Sal. John of Bury [*fl.* 1420–70]: *Gladius Salomonis* (*c*1460) (extr.), in PECOCK *Repressor* II 566–613.

J. CARPENTER John Carpenter, Common Clerk of London [*ob. c*1441], *v. MGL.*

J. CORNW. John of Cornwall (*alias* de Sancto Germano) [*fl.* 1170]: **Canon.** *Libellus de canone mystici libaminis* [attrib.], *PL* CLXXVII (1854) 455–70; **Eul.** *Eulogium ad Alexandrum III Papam* (*c*1178), *PL* CXCIX (1855) 1043–86; superseded by Med. Stud. XIII (1951) 256–300 [by cap.]; **Merl.** *Prophetia Merlini* (*c*1156), ed. C. J. Greith, *Spicilegium Vaticanum* (Frauenfeld, 1838) 92–106, checked against ed. M. J. Curley, *Speculum* LVII (1982) 217–49; also in Études celtiques XIV (1974) 35–41; **Verb.** *Apologia de Verbo incarnato* [attrib.], *PL* CLXXVII (1854) 295–316; superseded by Franciscan Studies XVI (1956) 110–43.

J. COTTON John Cotton [12c.]: *Tractatus de musica, PL* CL (1854) 1391–1430; superseded by *Johannis Affligemensis De musica cum tonario*, in *Corp. Script. Mus.* I (1950).

JEWEL Apol. John Jewel [1522–71]: *Apologia ecclesiae Anglicanae* (1562) [by sign.]; also ed. J. Ayre, Parker Society (1848).

Jews Norw. V. D. Lipman: Jews of Medieval Norwich, Jewish Hist. Soc. (1967).

J. EXON. Joseph of Exeter [*fl.* 1190]: **Antioch.** *Antiocheis*, ed. L. Gompf, Joseph Iscanus Werke und Briefe (Leiden & Cologne, 1970) 212 [by line]; **BT** *De Bello Trojano, ib.* 77–211 [by bk. & line]; also ed. A. J. Valpy, Delphin Classics (1825); **Ep.** *Epistolae*, ed. Gompf, 220–8 [by no. & line; letter addressed to John cited as *Ep. J. Exon.*]; **Martin** *De Beato Martino, ib.* 218–9 [by line]; **Virg.** *De laudibus Virginitatis, ib.* 213–7 [by line].

J. FORD John of Ford [*ob. c*1200]: **Serm.** *Super extremam partem Cantici canticorum sermones CXX, CC cont. med.* XVII, XVIII (1970) [by no. & sect.]; **app.** *Sermo in dominica in Ramis palmorum, ib.* [by sect.]; **Wulf.** *Vita B. Wulfrici* [*ob.* 1154], Som Rec. Soc. XLVII (1932) [by cap.].

J. FURNESS Jocelin (*alias* Jordan) of Furness [*fl.* 1200]: **Helen** *Vita S. Helenae*, MS Corpus Christi Coll. Camb. 252 ff. 166v.–183v.; **Kentig.** *Vita S. Kentigerni*, ed. A. P. Forbes, Lives of St. Ninian and St. Kentigern, Historians of Scotland V (Edinburgh, 1874) 159–242 [by cap.; *cf. V. Kentig.*]; **Pat.** *Vita S. Patricii* (*c*1185), Acta SS. Boll. Mar. II (1668) 540–80 [by cap.]; **Walth.** *Vita S. Walthevi* [*ob.* 1159] (wr. *a*1215) [attrib.], Acta SS. Boll. Aug. I (1733) 248–76 [by cap.]; *cf.* WALTH. *Ep.*

J. GLAST. John of Glastonbury [*fl.* 1400]: *Historia de rebus Glastoniensibus* (foundation –1342), ed. T. Hearne, 2 vols. (Oxford, 1726) [contin. pag. w. app.]; superseded by ed. J. P. Carley, 2 vols. (Oxford, 1978) [by cap.]; *cf.* DOMERH. *Glast.*, W. MALM. *Glast.*, WYCH.

J. GODARD John Godard, Abbot of Newenham [*ob. p*1248]: **Ap.** *Apostropha in Virginem gloriosam, Anal.*

Cisterc. X (1954) 246–67; **Ep.** *Epistola ad sororem, ib.* 220–45.

J. HERD Hist. IV Regum John Herd [*ob.* 1588]: *Historia Quatuor Regum Angliae* (Ed. IV, Ed. V, Ric. III, Hen. VII), Roxb. Club (1868).

J. HEX. HR Cont. John of Hexham [*fl.* 1180]: Continuation (1130–53) of S. DURH. *HR*, in S. DURH. II 284–332.

J. HOLLAND John of Holland [*fl.* 1370]: **Mot.** *De Motu* (extr.), in *Sci. Mech.* 248–50, 268–9n.

J. HOWD. John of Howden [*ob.* 1275]: **CA** *Canticum amoris*, Surtees Soc. CLIV (1939) 206–40 [by stanza]; **Cant.** *Quinquaginta cantica, ib.* 8–117 [by stanza]; **Cyth.** *Cythara, ib.* 118–75 [by stanza & line]; **Gaudia** *Quindecim gaudia, ib.* 1–7 [by stanza & line]; **Lira** *Lira, ib.* 203–5 [by stanza & line]; **O Mira** *O mira creatura, ib.* 241–2 [by stanza]; **Ph.** *Philomena*, Hymnologische Beiträge IV (Leipzig, 1930) [by stanza]; **Sal.** *Quinquaginta salutationes*, Surtees Soc. CLIV 176–93 [by stanza & line]; **Viola** *Viola, ib.* 194–202 [by line].

J. KELSO Ep. John, Abbot of Kelso [*fl.* 1170]: Letter to Adam of Dryburgh, *PL* CXCVIII (1855) 623–8; *v. et.* AD. SCOT *TT.*

J. LOND. John of London (*alias* John Bever) [*ob. c*1311]: **Brutus** *Tractatus de Bruto abbreviato* [prose & verse compilation based on G. MON.] (extr.), Mod. Philol. XXXIV (1937) 121–31; **Commend. Ed. I** *Commendatio lamentabilis in transitu magni Regis Edwardi* (1307), in *Chr. Ed. I & II* II 1–21.

J. MALVERN John of Malvern [*ob.* 1414], *v. Chr. Westm.*, HIGD. *Cont. A.*

J. MASON Ep. John Mason [*c*1270–1350]: A formulary of letters from St. Augustine's, Canterbury (1307–50), ed. W. A. Pantin, in Wilkinson Essays 192–219.

J. MIRFIELD John Mirfield [*fl.* 1390]: **Brev.** *Breviarium Bartholomei* (extr.), ed. P. H. S. Hartley and H. R. Aldridge, Johannes de Mirfeld of St Bartholomew's Smithfield, his life and works (Cambridge, 1936) 46–94; **Flor.** *Florarium Bartholomei* (extr.), *ib.* 114–62; **SB** *Sinonoma Bartholomei* [attrib.], *v. SB.*

J. NORFOLK John Norfolk, fellow of All Souls [*ob.* 1467]: *In artem progressionis summula*, in *Rara Math.* 94–106.

John The Gospel according to Saint John, ed. W. W. Skeat (Cambridge, 1878), cited from the Lindisfarne Gospels, wr. *c*697, glossed 970 [by cap. & verse].

JOHN DE ALTA VILLA *v.* HANV.

JOHN DE S. GERMANO *v.* J. CORNW.

JOHN DUNS SCOTUS *v.* DUNS.

JOHN LUTTERELL *v.* LUTTERELL.

JOHN PECKHAM (*alias* PECHAM or PATCHAM) *v.* PECKHAM.

JOHN SCOTUS ERIUGENA *v.* ERIUG.

JOHN WYCLIF *v.* WYCL.

JO. READING Sent. John of Reading, O.F.M. [*fl. c*1320]: *In Sententias* I d. 3 q. 3, Franciscan Studies XXIX (1969) 77–156; **prol.** q. 2, *ib.* XXVI (1966) 40–51.

JOSEPH CANT. Joseph, monk of Christ Church, Canterbury [*ob. p*1114]: Pilgrimage to Constantinople and Jerusalem (*c*1090), EHR XXV (1910) 293–5.

J. OXFORD John of Oxford, monk of Luffield [*fl.* 1268–84]: *De placitis et curiis tenendis* (*c*1270) (extr.), in *CBaron* 68–78.

J. READING John of Reading [*ob. c*1369]: *Chronica*, ed. J. Tait (Manchester, 1914) [by f.].

JRL Bull. Bulletin of the John Rylands University Library of Manchester, I– (Manchester, 1903–).

J. RODINGTON John of Rodington, O.F.M. [*ob.* 1348]: **Consc.** *Quodlibet de conscientia* (extr.), in Grabmann Studies 1125–68; **Sent.** *In primum Sententiarum* (Milan, 1506).

J. ROUS Hist. Reg. Angl. John Rous (*alias* Ross) [*ob.* 1491]: *Historia Regum Angliae* (–1485), ed. T. Hearne, 2nd ed. (Oxford, 1745).

J. SAL. John of Salisbury [*ob.* 1180]: **Anselm** Life of St. Anselm [abridged from EADMER *V. & Mir. Anselmi*], *PL*

CXCIX (1855) 1009–40; **Enth. Phil.** *Entheticus de dogmate philosophorum*, ed. C. Petersen (Hamburg, 1843); superseded from Fasc. IV by *Traditio* XXXI (1975) 137–93 [by line]; **Enth. Pol.** *Entheticus in Policraticum*, in *Pol.* (ed. 1909) 1–11; **Ep.** *Epistolae*, *PL* CXCIX (1855) 1–378; superseded by ed. W. J. Millor, H. E. Butler, and C. N. L. Brooke, Med. Texts, 2 vols. (1955–79) [by no. of *PL* & no. of Med. Texts (in brackets); letters to John cited as *Ep. J. Sal.*]; **Hist. Pont.** *Historiae pontificalis quae supersunt* (1148–52), ed. R. L. Poole (Oxford, 1927); superseded by ed. M. Chibnall, Med. Texts (1956) [by cap.]; **Memb.** *Carmen de membris conspirantibus* [attrib.], *PL* CXCIX (1855) 1005–8; **Met.** *Metalogicon* (1159), ed. C. C. J. Webb (Oxford, 1929) [by col. of *PL* CXCIX]; **Pol.** *Policraticus* (1159), ed. C. C. J. Webb, 2 vols. (Oxford, 1909) [by col. of *PL*]; **SS** *De septem septenis* [attrib.], *PL* CXCIX 945–964; **Thom.** *Vita S. Thomae*, in *Becket Mat.* II 302–22 [by cap.; v. et. A. TEWK. *Prol. Thom.*].

J. SCAWBY John of Scawby (Schalby) [*c*1324]: *Vita episcoporum Lincolniensium*, in GIR. VII 193–216.

J. SEWARD John Seward [1364–1345]: Miscellaneous writings, Med. & Ren. Stud. I (1941–3) 85–104.

J. SHEPPEY Fab. John of Sheppey [*ob.* 1360]: *Fabulae*, ed. L. Hervieux, Les Fabulistes latins IV (Paris, 1896) 417–50 [by no.].

J. SHIRWOOD Arithm. John Shirwood, Bishop of Durham [*ob.* 1494]: *Liber de arithmomachia* (Rome, 1482).

J. ST. GILES John of St. Giles [*fl.* 1230]: **Exp.** *Experimenta*, MS Bodl. 786 ff. 170–71v; **Serm.** *Sermones*, ed. M. M. Davy, Les Sermons universitaires parisiens de 1230–31, Études de philosophie médiévale XV (Paris, 1931), 271–98.

J. TILB. AN John of Tilbury [*fl.* 1170]: *Epistola de arte notaria* (extr.), ed. V. Rose, Hermes VIII (1874) 310–26.

J. TYNEMOUTH John of Tynemouth, monk of St. Albans [*ob.* *c*1348]: **Hist. Aur.** *Historia Aurea* (extr.), EHR XLIII (1928) 208–15; **Sanct.** *Sanctilogium Angliae, Walliae, Scotiae, et Hiberniae v.* NLA.

Judas Story The Latin Judas Story (? 12c.), EETS CIII (1894) 68–70.

Jus Feudale Sir Thomas Craig [*ob.* 1608]: *Jus Feudale* (1603) [by p. of ed. 1655].

JustIt Assize Rolls etc. (1201–1482), MS PRO (J.I. 1).

J. WALDEBY Ave John Waldeby, O.S.A. [*c*1315–*c*1372]: *Tractatus in salutationem angelicam*, ed. M. J. Morrin, *Studia Augustiniana Historica* II (Rome, 1975) 81–153.

J. WALEYS John Waleys (*Wallensis*) [*ob.* *c*1285], *Opera* (Lyon, 1511): **Brev. Sap.** *Breviloquium de sapientia sanctorum*, ff. 195–200v. [by cap.]; **Brev. Virt.** *Breviloquium de quatuor virtutibus cardinalibus*, ff. 200v.–16 [by cap.]; **Commun.** *Communiloquium* or *Summa collationum ad omne genus hominum*, ff. 1–139v. [by bk., dist., & cap.]; **Compend.** *Floriloquium sive compendiloquium de vita et dictis illustrium philosophorum*, ff. 140–94 [by bk., dist., & cap.]; **Schak.** *Comparatio mundi ad ludum schakarum*, *Speculum* VI (1931) 463–5 (addition to *Commun.* I 10. 7); **V. Relig.** *Ordinarium* or *Alphabetum vitae religiosae*, *Opera* ff. 217–55 [by cap.].

J. WALLINGF. *v.* Chr. *Wallingf.*

J. WHYTEFELD *Pref. Catal.* John Whytefeld [14c.]: Catalogue of the library of St. Martin's Dover (1389), *v. Libr. Cant. Dov.* 407–9, 434.

J. WORC. John, monk of Worcester [*fl.* 1140]: Chronicle (1118–40), ed. J. R. H. Weaver, Anecd. Oxon. XIII (1908); supersedes FL. WORC. II 71–136.

J. YONGE Vis. Purg. Pat. James Yonge [*fl.* 1425]: *Memoriale super visitatione Laurentii Ratholdi ad Purgatorium S. Patricii* (*c*1411), *Anal. Boll.* XXVII (1908) 43–60 [by cap.].

Kal. M. A. *Medii Aevi Kalendarium*, ed. R. T. Hampson (1841) vol. I: I (10c.) 397–420; II (11c.) 422–33; III (11c.) 435–46; IV (14c.) 449–60.

Kal. Met. Un témoin Anglo-Saxon du calendrier d'York (*c*800), Rev. Ben. XLVI (1934) 65–8.

Kal. Samson The Kalendar of Abbot Samson [*ob.* 1212] of Bury St. Edmunds [Suff], Camd. 3rd S. LXXXIV (1954): *Liber de consuetudinibus monasterii S. Edmundi* (*c*1186–91), 1–72 [by f.]; charters (1182–1211), 73–170 [by no.].

KB ContrR King's Bench Controlment Rolls (1329–), MS PRO (K.B. 29).

Kelso *Liber S. Mariae de Calchou*, 2 vols. Bannatyne Club (1846) [by no.].

KETEL J. Bev. William Ketel [*fl.* 1150]: Miracles of St. John of Beverley, in *Hist. Church York* I 261–91.

KILLINGWORTH Alg. John Killingworth [*ob.* 1445]: *Algorismus* (extr.), EHR XXIX (1914) 707–17.

KILMINGTON Richard Kilmington [*ob.* *a*1362]: **Soph.** *Sophismata* (extr.), ed. C. Wilson, William Heytesbury (Madison, Wisc., 1956) 163–8 [by no.].

KILWARDBY Robert Kilwardby, Archbishop of Canterbury [*ob.* 1279]: **ad Petrum** *Epistola ad Petrum de Confleto* (1277), ed. F. Ehrle, Archiv für Literatur- und Kirchengeschichte des Mittelalters V (1889), 603–35, repr. in F. Ehrle, Gesammelte Aufsätze zu englischen Scholastik (Rome, 1970), 18–44 [by p.]; cf. BGPM XX v (1922) 36–69; **Don.** *In Donati Artem majorem III*, ed. L. Schmücker (Brixen, 1984); **Ep.** *Epistolae*, w. *Jejun.* 177–85; **Injunc.** Injunctions for Merton College (1276), ed. H. W. Garrod (Oxford, 1929); **Jejun.** *Sermo in capite jejunii* (MS Trin. Coll. Camb. B. 15. 38 ff. 208v–212v), ed. E. M. F. Sommer-Seckendorff, Studies in the life of Robert Kilwardby, O.P. (Rome, 1937) 163–76; **Nec. Inc.** *De necessitate incarnationis* (extr.), RTAM VIII (1936) 98–100; **NR** *De natura relationis*, ed. L. Schmücker (Lenggries, 1980) [by cap.]; **NT** *De natura theologiae* (= *Prologus in Sententias*), ed. F. Stegmüller, *Opusc. & Text.* XVII (1935); **OS** *De ortu scientiarum*, ed. A. G. Judy, *Auct. Brit.* IV (1976) [by sect.]; **Pass.** *Sermo in dominica in Passione* (MS Trin. Coll. Camb. B. 15. 38 ff. 212v–215v), AFP LII (1982) 101–113; **Prisc.** *Super Priscianum Majorem* [attrib.], CIMA XV (1975); **Quomodo Deus** *Quomodo Deus sit homini philosopho cognitus* (extr.), in *N. & E. (Hauréau)* V 116–30; **Resp.** *Responsio de XLIII quaestionibus*, *Archivum Fratrum Praedicatorum* XLVII (1977) 10–50; **Sent.** *Quaestiones in III Sententiarum*, ed. E. Gössmann, Texte aus der mittelalterliche Geisteswelt X (Munich, 1982); **SF** *De Spiritu fantastico*, MS Balliol Coll. Ox. 3 [by f.]; **SP** *De spiritu phantastico*, MS Balliol Coll. Ox. 3; ed. P. O. Lewry, *Auct. Brit.* [by f.]; **Summa** [attrib.], *v. Ps.*-GROS; **Temp.** *De tempore* (extr.), in Grabmann Studies 855–61; superseded by ed. P. O. Lewry, *Auct. Brit.* [by sect.].

King's Serjeants J. H. Round: The King's Serjeants and Officers of State, with their Coronation Services (1911).

Kingsthorpiana A calendar of documents in the church chest of Kingsthorpe [Northants] (*c*1350–1705), ed. J. H. Glover (1883).

King's Works History of the King's Works, ed. H. M. Colvin, I– HMSO (1963–).

KNAPWELL Richard Knapwell (*alias* Clapwell) [*fl.* 1286]: **Form.** *Quaestio disputata de unitate formae*, ed. F. E. Kelley, Bibliothèque thomiste XLIV (1982); **Not.** *Notabilia super primum Sententiarum usque ad distinctionem XIX*, AHDLMA III (1928) 185–200; **Quare** *Correctorium corruptorii 'Quare'*, Bibliothèque thomiste IX (Kain, 1927); **Quodl.** *Quodlibet* (extr.), Zeitschr. kath. Theol. LII (Innsbruck, 1928) 473–91.

KNIGHTON Henry Knighton [*c*1366]: *Chronicon* (939–1366), 2 vols. RS XCII (1889–95) I, II 1–123; **Cont.** [anon.] (1377–95), II 124–322.

KR Records of the Exchequer, King's Remembrancer, MS PRO: **Ac** Accounts, Various (Hen. II–) (E. 101); **AcCust** Customs Accounts (Ed. I–) (E. 122); **Eccl.** Ecclesiastical documents (John–) (E. 135); **Ext. & Inq.**

Extents and Inquisitions (Hen. III–) (E. 143); **Forest Proc.** Forest Proceedings (Hen. III–) (E. 146); **Invent.** v. Invent. Exch.; **Mem** Memoranda Rolls (1216–) (E. 159); **Mem. PR** Memoranda Roll 1230–1, Pipe R. Soc. NS XI (1933); **Misc.** *Miscellanea* (Hen. II–) (E. 163); **Misc. Bks.** Miscellaneous Books, 1st S. (Hen. III–) (E. 164); **Spec. Comm.** Special Commissions (Eliz. I–) (E. 178); **Writs** (Hen. III–) (E. 202).

KYKELEY Kykeley, O.F.M. [*fl. c*1300]: *Quaestio de cooperatione divina*, *Bohoslovia* X (Lviv, 1932) 194–228.

KYMER Gilbert Kymer, Dean of Salisbury [*ob.* 1463]: *Diaetarium de sanitatis custodia* (1424) (extr.), in *BBExch* 550–9 [by cap.].

KYN. John Kynyngham (*alias* Cunningham) [*ob.* 1399], v. *Ziz*.

Lancs & Chesh Rec. Soc. Lancashire and Cheshire Record Society, publications, I– (1879–).

Land-ch. J. Earle: A handbook to the Land-charters and other Saxonic documents (Oxford, 1888).

Lanercost *Chronicon de Lanercost* [Cumb] (1201–1346), 2 vols. Bannatyne Club (1839).

LANFR. Lanfranc, Archb. of Canterbury [*ob.* 1089]: **Annot. Cassian.** *Annotatiunculae in Cassiani collationes*, *PL* CL (1854) 443–4; **Cel. Conf.** *De celanda confessione libellus*, *ib.* 625–32; **Comment. Paul.** *Commentaria in epistolas S. Pauli*, *ib.* 101–406 [partly checked w. ed. L. d'Achery (1648) which more clearly distinguishes Lanfranc's from earlier notes]; **Const.** Monastic constitutions, ed. M. D. Knowles, Med. Texts (1951) 1–132 [by p. of Giles's ed. (in marg.)]; reprinted w. extra notes as *Corpus consuetudinum monasticarum* III (Siegburg, 1967); v. et. *Instr. Nov.*; **Corp. & Sang.** *De corpore et sanguine Domini*, *PL* CL 407–42; **Ep.** *Epistolae*, *ib.* 516–51 [by no.]; superseded by ed. H. Clover and M. Gibson, Med. Texts (1979) [by no. of *PL* & no. of Med. Texts (in brackets); letters to Lanfranc cited as *Ep. Lanfr.*]; **Sermo** *Sermo sive sententiae*, *PL* CL 637–40.

Langley R. L. Storey: Thomas Langley and the bishopric of Durham 1406–1437 (1961); **app.** Report of inquisition by royal commissioners (1433), MS PRO (C. 49 roll 23), in *Langley* app. B 245–62.

LANGTON, v. J. LANGTON, S. LANGTON.

LANTFR. Lantfred [*fl.* 980]: **Ep.** *Epistola Lantfrithi ad Wintonienses*, in *Mem. Dunst.* 369–70; **Mir. et Transl. Swith A** *Historia translationis et miraculorum S. Swithuni* (extr.), *Acta SS. Boll.* July I (1719) 331–7, complemented by **B** *S. Swithuni Wintoniensis episcopi translatio et miracula*, *Anal. Boll.* IV (1885) 377–410, and **pref. Swith.** *ib.* 372–7; all superseded by LANTFR. *Swith.*; **Swith.** *Translatio et miracula S. Swithuni*, ed. M. Lapidge, Winchester Studies IV pt. ii [by cap.].

LATHBURY Lam. John Lathbury, O.F.M. [*fl.* 1350]: *Liber moralium super Threnis Jeremiae* (Oxford, 1482).

Latin Stories A selection of Latin Stories of the 13th and 14th centuries, ed. T. Wright (1842).

LAVENHAM Richard Lavenham, Carmelite [*ob.* ? *p*1399]: **Log.** *Summulae logicales*, Franciscan Studies XL (1980) 377–409 [= cc. 1–9, 12], supplemented by Med. Stud. XXXV (1973) 44–59 [= cc. 10, 11] [by cap. & p.]; **Oblig.** *Obligationes*, Revista critica di storia della filosofia XXXIII (1978) 226–41 [by sect.]; **Scire** *Scire*, Med. Stud. XLVI (1984) 13–30 [by sect.]; v. et. *Ziz*.

Law & Cust. Sea Documents relating to the Law and Custom of the Sea (1205–1767), 2 vols. Navy Rec. Soc. XLIX, L (1915–15).

Law Merch. Select cases concerning the Law Merchant A.D. 1270–1638, 3 vols. Selden Soc. XXIII, XLVI, XLIX (1908–32).

Laws Romney Marsh The Charter or Laws and Customs of Romney Marsh, ed. H. de Bathe (London, 1686): documents (13c.–14c.), 1–55; charter (1360), 55–75.

LBLond. Letter Books of the City of London, MS Corpo-

ration of London RO; extr. in *MGL* I 534–739 [by f.]; v. et. *Cal. LB Lond.*

LC *Lexicon Chymicum* (1652), ed. W. Johnson, in *Bibl. Chem.* I 217–90 [cited only to elucidate other passages].

L. DURH. Laurence, Prior of Durham [*ob.* 1154]: **Brig.** *Vita S. Brigidae*, *Acta SS. Boll.* Feb. I (1658) 172–85 [by cap.]; also *Vitae SS. Hiberniae e codice Salmanticensi* (Brussels, 1965) 1–37; **Cons.** *Consolatio de morte amici*, ed. U. Kindermann (Breslau, 1969); **Dial.** *Dialogi*, Surtees Soc. LXX (1880) 1–61 [by bk. & line]; **Ep.** Letter to Ailred (pref. to *Brig.*), *Sacris Erudiri* XI (1960) 263–5; **Hypog.** *Hypognosticon* (extr.), Surtees Soc. LXX (1880) 62–71.

LEDREDE Richard de Ledrede, Bishop of Ossory [*ob. c*1361]: **Carm.** *Carmina* (extr.), HMC Rep. X app. V 242–53 [*cf. RBOssory HMC*]; also ed. E. Colledge (Toronto, 1974) and R. L. Greene (Oxford, 1974); superseded by Latin Hymns of Richard Ledrede, ed. T. Stemmler (Mannheim, 1975) [by no. & line]; **Kyteler** v. *Proc. A. Kyteler*.

Leechdoms Leechdoms, wortcunning and starcraft of early England, ed. O. Cockayne, 3 vols. RS XXXV (1864–6).

Leeds Philos. & Lit. Soc. Leeds Philosophical and Literary Society, Lit. & Hist. Sect., proceedings, I– (Leeds, 1925–).

LEEKE Laurence Leeke, Prior of Norwich [*ob.* 1357]: *Historiola de vita et morte Willelmi Bateman Norwicensis episcopi* [*ob.* 1355], ed. F. Peck. *Desiderata Curiosa* (1735) II, Bk. VII item 1 [by sect.].

Leet Coventry The Coventry Leet Book (1420–1555), 4 vols., EETS CXXXIV, CXXXV, CXXXVIII, CXLVI (1907–13).

Leet Norw. Leet jurisdiction in the city of Norwich, Selden Soc. V (1891).

Leg. Ant. Lond. *De antiquis legibus liber*, London Chronicle (1178–1274) of Arnold Fitzthedmar [*ob.* ? 1274], w. app., Camd. Soc. XXXIV (1846).

Leg. Baronum v. Quon. Attach.

Leg. Hen. v. GAS.

Leg. IV Burg. *Leges et consuetudines quatuor burgorum, Berewic, Rokisburg, Edinburg, et Strivelin* (*c*1270), in *APScot* I 15–44 [by cap.].

Leg. Wall. *Liber legum Howell Da*, ed. H. D. Emanuel, The Latin texts of the Welsh Laws (Cardiff, 1967): 109–58 Redaction A (*a*1200); 193–259 Redaction B (*c*1250); 276–90 Redaction C (*p*1258); 316–97 Redaction D (*c*1280); 434–509 Redaction E (14c.) [by letter & p.].

LESLEY RGScot John Lesley (*alias* Leslie), Bishop of Ross [*ob.* 1596]: *De origine, moribus, et rebus gestis Scotorum* (Rome, 1578).

Let. Ch. Ch. Letters relating to the Priory of Christ Church Canterbury (14c.–16c.), Camd. Soc. NS XIX (1877).

Let. R. Joseph The Letter Book of Robert Joseph (1530–33), OHS NS XIX (1957) [by no.].

LEVINS Manip. Peter Levins [16c.]: *Manipulus Vocabulorum* (1579), EETS XXVII (1867).

Lib. Ant. Linc. *Liber antiquus de ordinationibus vicariarum tempore Hugonis Wells Linc. Ep.*, *1209–35* (Lincoln, 1888).

Lib. Cust. Northampt. *Liber Custumarum*, the book of the ancient usages of Northampton to 1448, ed. C. A. Markham (Northampton, 1895).

Lib. Eli. *Liber Eliensis* (499–1171), Camd. 3rd S. XCII (1962) [by bk. & cap.]; v. et. RIC. ELY, T. ELY.

Liberate Liberate Rolls, Chancery (1200–1436), MS PRO (C. 62) [v. et. *Cal. Liberate*]; **(Exch)** Liberate Rolls, Exchequer, MS PRO (1219–1306) (E. 403); **RC** *Rotuli de Liberate* (1200–4) etc., RC (1844).

Lib. Evesham *Officium ecclesiasticum abbatum secundum usum Eveshamensis monasterii* (1282–1316), HBS VI (1893).

Lib. Exempl. *Liber exemplorum ad usum praedicantium*

(13c.), ed. A. G. Little Brit. Soc. Franciscan Studies I (Aberdeen, 1908).

Lib. Hyda *Liber monasterii de Hyda* [Hants] (455–1023), RS XLV (1866).

Lib. Kilken. *Liber primus Kilkenniensis* (1231–1586), IMC (Dublin, 1931).

Lib. Landav. *Liber Landavensis*, ed. J. Rhys and J. G. Evans, The Text of the Book of Llan Dâv (Oxford, 1893).

Lib. Mem. Bernewelle *Liber memorandorum ecclesie de Bernewelle* [Cambs] (1092–1296) (wr. 1295–6, w. later addit. to 1304), ed. J. W. Clark (Cambridge, 1907); *v. et. Obs. Barnwell.*

Lib. Monstr. *Liber Monstrorum* (*c*700), ed. F. Porsia (Bari, 1976).

Lib. Prot. *Liber protocollorum S.* [*i. e.* Cuthbert Simon] *notarii publici et scribae capituli Glasguensis* (1499–1513), 2 vols. Grampian Club (Glasgow, 1875); *v. et. Rent. Glasg.*

Libr. Cant. Dov. The ancient Libraries of Canterbury and Dover, three catalogues, ed. M. R. James (Cambridge, 1903).

Lib. Regal. *Liber regalis seu ordo consecrandi regem, etc.* (14c.), Roxb. Club (1870); also in *Rec. Coronation* 81–112 [by f.].

Lib. Wint. *Liber Wintoniae*, ff. 1–12b (*c*1110) and ff. 13b–33 (1148), in *DB Add.* I 529–62 [by f.].

LINACRE Emend. Lat. Thomas Linacre [*ob.* 1524]: *De emendata structura Latini sermonis* (1524) [by f.; some refs. to ed. Leipzig, 1591].

Linc. Chapter Acts v. Chap. Linc.

Linc. Rec. Soc. Lincoln Record Society, publications, I– (1911–).

Lit. Cant. *Literae Cantuarienses* (14c.–16c.), 3 vols. RS LXXXV (1887–9).

Little RB Bristol The Little Red Book of Bristol (1331–1574), ed. F. B. Bickley, 2 vols. (Bristol, 1900).

Lit. Wall. *Litterae Walliae* (1217–92), preserved in *Liber A* [*TR Bk.* 274] in the PRO, ed. J. G. Edwards (Cardiff, 1940) [by no.]

Lives Ed. Conf. Lives of Edward the Confessor, RS III (1858); *v. V. Ed. Conf., V. Ed. Conf. Metr.*

LIV. Hen. V Titus Livius de Frulovisiis [15c.]: *Vita Henrici V regis Angliae* (*p*1437), ed. T. Hearne (Oxford, 1716) [by f.].

Lond. Ed. I & II M. Weinbaum: London unter Edward I und Edward II, 2 vols. (Stuttgart, 1933).

Loseley MSS Manuscripts of W. M. Molyneux of Loseley Park [Surrey], HMC Rep. VII (1877) 596–681.

L. & P. Hen. VIII Letters and Papers illustrative of the reign of Henry VIII, 21 vols. & 2 vols. *addenda*, HMSO (1884–1932).

L. & P. Ric. III–Hen. VII Letters and Papers illustrative of the reigns of Richard III and Henry VII, 2 vols. RS XXIV (1861–3).

L. SOMERCOTE Lawrence of Somercote, canon of Chichester [13c.]: *Tractatus sive summa de formis electionum episcoporum faciendarum* (1254), ed. A. von Wretschko (Weimar, 1907); also in *Stat. Linc.* II cxxv–cxlii.

LTR Records of the Exchequer, Lord Treasurers's Remembrancer and Pipe Office, MS PRO: **Ac** Accounts Miscellaneous (Ed. II–)(E. 358); **AcCust** Customs Accounts (Ed. I–Eliz. I) (E. 356); **AcDecl** Declared Accounts, Pipe Office (1500–) (E. 351); **AcEsch** Escheators' Accounts (1323–) (E. 357); **AcWardr** Wardrobe and Household Accounts (1257–1548) (E. 361); **Enr Estr** Enrolled Estreats (Ed. VI–) (E. 362); **Mem** Memoranda Rolls (1216–) (E. 368); **Mem PR** Memoranda Rolls 1199–1200 and 1207–8, Pipe R. Soc. NS XXXI (1943) and XXXI (1957); **MiscR** Miscellaneous Rolls (Hen. II–) (E. 370).

LUCIAN Chester Lucian, monk of St. Werburgh's, Chester [*fl.* 1200]: *Liber Luciani de laude Cestriae* (*c*1195), Lancs & Chesh Rec. Soc. LXIV (1912) 1–78.

Ludus Angl. *Ludus Anglicorum* (14c.), ed. D. W. Fiske, Chess in Iceland (Florence, 1905), 162–5.

Ludus Coventriae *Ludus Coventriae* or the plaie called *Corpus Christi*, ed. K. Block, EETS Extra S. CXX (1922 for 1917, repr. 1960) [by f.].

Luke The Gospel according to Saint Luke, ed. W. W. Skeat (Cambridge, 1874), cited from the Lindisfarne Gospels, wr. *c*697, glossed 970 [by cap. & verse].

LUPSET Ep. Thomas Lupset [*ob.* 1530]: Letters, ed. J. Archer Gee, Life and Works of Thomas Lupset (New Haven, Conn., 1928) 295–321.

LUTTERELL John Lutterell [*ob.* 1335]: **Occam** *Libellus contra doctrinam Guilelmi Occam*, ed. F. Hoffmann, Erfurter theologische Studien VI (Leipzig, 1959) 3–102 [by sect.]; **Visio Beat.** *Epistula de visione beatifica, ib.* 103–19 [by f.].

LYNDW. William Lyndwood [*ob.* 1446]: *Provinciale* (Oxford, 1679) [by p. & serial letter]; *v. et. J. ACTON.*

Magna Carta *Magna Carta* (1215), in *SelCh* 292–302 [by cap.]; (1216), *ib.* 336–9 [by cap.].

MAIDSTONE Clement Maidstone (*alias* Maydeston) [*ob.* *c*1456]: Tracts, HBS VII (1894) 1–237.

Maitland Club publications, I–LXXV (Glasgow, 1829–59).

MAJOR John Major (*alias* Mair) [*ob.* 1550]: *Historia Majoris Britanniae* (Paris, 1521; new ed. Edinburgh 1740) [by bk. & cap.].

MALACHY Ven. Malachias Hibernicus, Franciscan, Archb.-elect of Tuam [*fl.* 1280]: *Tractatus de veneno* (Paris, 1518); also (extr.) ed. M. Esposito, EHR XXXIII (1918) 359–61 [by f.].

MALDON Ps. Thomas Maldon, O. Carm. [*ob.* 1404]: *Lectura in Psalmum cxviii*, MS Balliol Coll. Ox. 80 ff. 190–232; (extr.), *Carmelus* XXIX (1982) 193–235 [by f.].

M. ALNWICK Martin of Alnwick (*alias* Martinus Anglicus), O.F.M. [*ob.* 1336]: **Prop.** *De veritate et falsitate propositionis*, ed. L. M. de Rijk, Some 14c. tracts on the *Probationes Terminorum, Artistarium* III (1982) 7–33.

Mandeville J. H. Round: Geoffrey de Mandeville, a study of the anarchy (1892).

Man. Ebor. *Manuale et processionale ad usum insignis Ecclesie Eboracensis* (14c.), Surtees Soc. LXIII (1875) 1–207.

Manners Manners and household expenses of England in the 13th and 15th centuries, Roxb. Club LVII (1841): Household roll of Eleanor, Countess of Leicester (1265), 3–115; Accounts of the executors of Eleanor, Queen Consort, (1291), 116–45.

Man. Sal. *Manuale ad usum percelebris ecclesiae Sarum* (prob. mainly 15c.; printed Rouen, 1543), ed. A. J. Collins, HBS XCI (1960); also ed. W. G. Henderson in abbreviated form, *Man. Ebor.* app. 1*–112*.

MAP NC Walter Map [*ob.* *c*1210]: *De nugis curialium*, ed. M. R. James, *Anecd. Oxon.* XIV (1914); superseded by Med. Texts (1983) [by bk., cap., & f.]; *cf. Ps.-MAP.*

March. S. Wales The Marcher lordships of S. Wales (1415–1536), select docs., ed. T. B. Pugh (Cardiff, 1963).

Mark The Gospel according to Saint Mark, ed. W. W. Skeat (Cambridge, 1871), cited from the Lindisfarne Gospels, wr. *c*697, glossed 970 [by cap. & verse].

Mart. Hist. H. Quentin: Les Martyrologes historiques du moyen âge (Paris, 1908).

Matth. The Gospel according to Saint Matthew ed. W. W. Skeat (Cambridge, 1887), cited from the Lindisfarne Gospels, wr. *c*697, glossed 970 [by cap. & verse].

Mayor's CourtR Lond. Mayor's Court Rolls (1298–1307), MS Corp. of London RO: *v. et. Cal. Mayor's CourtR Lond.*

M. CORNW. Michael of Cornwall [*fl.* 1250]: **Hen.** *Versus magistri Michaelis Cornubiensis contra magistrum Henricum Abrincensem* (*c*1254), ed. A. Hilke, Festgabe zum 60. Geburtstage von Hermann Degering (Leipzig, 1926) 125–154 [by line]; **Mansel** *De crure J. Mansel curando*

(1243), ed. J.P. Heironimus and J.C. Russel, The Shorter Latin poems of Henry of Avranches relating to England (Cambridge, Mass., 1935), app. A p. 157 [by line; *cf.* H. AVR. *Poems*]; **Montfort** Lament on death of Simon de Montfort (*c*1265) [attrib.], ed. J. O. Halliwell, Camd. Soc. XV (1840) 139–46 [by p.].

M. CRISPIN Lanfr. Milo Crispin [*ob. c*1150]: *Vita B. Lanfranci*, PL CL (1854) 19–58.

Meaux *Chronica monasterii de Melsa* [Yorks] (1150–1406), 3 vols. RS XLIII (1866–8).

MED Middle English Dictionary, ed. H. Kurath, S. M. Kuhn, and R. E. Lewis, vol. I– (Ann Arbor, Mich., & Oxford, 1956–).

Med. Admin. Hist. T. F. Tout: Chapters in the Administrative History of Medieval England, etc., 6 vols. (Manchester, 1920–33).

Med. Bor. Snowd. E. A. Lewis: The Mediaeval Boroughs of Snowdonia, Univ. Wales Hist. Stud. I (1912).

Med. Cult. C. H. Haskins: Studies in Mediaeval Culture (Oxford, 1929).

Med. E. Anglia D. C. Douglas: The social structure of Medieval East Anglia (Oxford, 1927).

Med. Eng. Sheriff W. A. Morris: The Medieval English Sheriff to 1300 (Manchester, 1927).

Med. Fenland H. C. Darby: The Medieval Fenland (Cambridge, 1940).

Med. & Hum. *Medievalia et Humanistica*, I–XVII (Boulder, Colorado, 1943–1966); NS I– (Cambridge, 1970–).

Medit. Farne *Meditationes* (*c*1350), by a solitary of Farne, ed. D. H. Farmer, *Studia Anselmiana* XLI (1957) 158–245 [by f.]; (extr.) also ed. W. A. Pantin, EHR LIX (1944) 162–86.

Medium Ævum Soc. of Med. Languages & Lit., journal, I– (Oxford, 1932–).

Med. Mason D. Knoop and G. P. Jones: The Medieval Mason (Manchester, 1933).

Med. & R. Stud. Mediaeval and Renaissance Studies, I– Warburg Inst. (1941–).

Med. Sci. C. H. Haskins: Studies in the history of Mediaeval Science (Cambridge, Mass., 1924).

Med. Stage E. K. Chambers: The Medieval Stage, 2 vols. (Oxford, 1903).

Med. Stud. Mediaeval Studies, Pontifical Inst. of Med. Stud., Toronto, I– (New York & Toronto, 1939–).

Med. Texts [Nelson's] Medieval Texts (Edinburgh, 1949–65) [incl. earlier volumes called Medieval Classics]; continued as Oxford Medieval Texts (Oxford, 1967–).

Med. Thinkers Nine Mediaeval thinkers, ed. J. R. O'Donnell (Toronto, 1955).

Medulla *Medulla Grammatice* (Latin – Latin-English Dictionary), MS Stonyhurst A. 1. 10 (*s.* xv^{in}) [by f.; mostly cited from *MED*].

Melrose *Liber Sancte Marie de Melros* [Roxb] (1124–1625), 2 vols. Bannatyne Club (1837) [by no.].

MELTON William Melton [*fl.* 1420–30]: *Sermo in die Parasceues* (1431), in *Doc. Francisc.* 247–56.

Mem. Anselm Memorials of St Anselm, ed. R. W. Southern and F. S. Schmitt, Auct. Brit. I (1969).

Mem. Beverley Memorials of Beverley Minster [Yorks] (1286–1347), 2 vols. Surtees Soc. XCVIII, CVIII (1897, 1903).

Mem. Dunst. Memorials of Saint Dunstan, Archb. of Canterbury [*ob.* 988], RS LXIII (1874); *v.* ADEL. BLANDIN. *Dunst.*, B. *V. Dunst.*, CAPGR. *Dunst.*, EADMER *V. & Mir. Dunst.*, *Frag. Rit. Dunst.*, OSB. *V. & Mir. Dunst.*, W. MALM. *Dunst.*

Mem. Fount. Memorials of the abbey of St. Mary of Fountains [Yorks], docs. (12c.–16c.), 3 vols. Surtees Soc. XLII, LXVII, CXXX (1863–1918); *v. et.* SERLO. GRAM. *Mon. Font.*, SWYNTON *Mem.*

Mem. Gerv. Louth Memorials of Gervase, Abbot of Louth Park [*fl.* 1139–47], *Anal. Cist.* VII (1951) 38–45: *Lamentatio Gervasii*, a memoir of Gervase, *Epistola Gervasii de absolutione*.

Mem. Hen. VII Memorials of King Henry VII, RS X (1858); *v.* ANDRÉ *Hen. VII*.

Mem. Hen. V Memorials of Henry V, RS XI (1858); *v.* ELMH. *Metr. Hen. V*, REDMAN, *Vers. Hen. V*.

Mem. Ir. Memoranda Rolls of Ireland (extr., 1312–16), in *Doc. Ir.* 312–58; MS PRO Dublin.

Mem. Parl. *Memoranda de Parliamento* (1305), RS XCVIII (1893) [by no.].

Mem. Pri. East. Henry of Eastry, Prior of Christ Church, Canterbury [*ob.* 1331]: *Memoriale*, MS BL Cotton Galba E IV ff. 1–186.

Mem. Ric. I Chronicles and Memorials of the reign of Richard I, 2 vols. RS XXXVIII (1864–5); *v. Ep. Cant.*, *Itin. Ric.*

Mem. Ripon Memorials of the church of Ripon [Yorks], 4 vols. Surtees Soc. LXXIV, LXXVIII, LXXXI, CXV (1882–1908) [by vol. & p.].

MemR Memoranda Rolls: 1199, Pipe R. Soc. XXI (1943); 1231–3, HMSO (in prep.); *v. et.* CalMem, KRMem, *LTRMem.*

Mem. S. Edm. Memorials of St. Edmund's Abbey [Suff], 3 vols. RS XCVI (1890–6); *v. et.* ABBO *Edm.*, *Ann. S. Edm.*, G. FONT., HERM. ARCH., SAMSON.

Mem. York York Memorandum Book, 3 vols. Surtees Soc. CXX, CXXV, CLXXXVI (1912–73).

Mens. & Disc. (Anon. IV) *Anonymi IV de Mensuris et Discantu* (13c.), in *Script. Mus.* I (1864) 327–65; superseded by ed. F. Reckow, Der Musiktraktat des Anonymus 4, 2 vols. (Wiesbaden, 1967) I 22–89.

METHLEY Tract. Richard Methley (*alias* Richard Furth), Carthusian [*fl. c*1480]: Spiritual treatises (MS Trinity Coll. Camb. O. 2. 56), *Scola amoris languidi*, *Dormitorium dilecti dilecti*, *Refectorium salutis*, facs. ed. J. Hogg, *Analecta Carthusiana* LXIV ii (1978) [by f.].

MFG Medieval Farming Glosssary of Latin and English words taken mainly from Essex records (1200–1600), ed. J. L. Fisher (London, 1968).

MGH *Monumenta Germaniae Historica* (Hanover, etc., 1826–).

MGL *Munimenta Gildhallae Londoniensis*, 3 vols. in 4, RS XII (1859–62).

MIDDLETON Richard Middleton (*alias* de Mediavilla) [*c*1249–*a*1308]: **Form.** *De gradu formarum*, ed. R. Zavalloni, Philosophes médiévaux II (1951), 35–169; **QD** *Quaestio disputata de privilegio Martini IV*, ed. F. M. Delorme (Quaracchi, 1925) 1–78; **Quodl.** *Quodlibeta* (Brescia, 1591) [w. *Sent.*; sep. pag.]; **Sent.** *Quaestiones in Sententias*, 4 vols. (Brescia, 1591) [by bk. & p.]; **Serm.** Three sermons, ed. E. Hocedez, *Spicilegium Sacrum Lovaniense* VII (1925) 490–509; **Unit.** *Quaestio de unitate formae*, ed. Zavalloni, 173–80.

Midlothian *Registrum Domus de Soltre* [Haddington], *necnon Ecclesiae Collegiatae S. Trinitatis prope Edinburgh, etc.* (1153–1612), Bannatyne Club (1861).

MILEMETE Nob. Walter de Milemete: *De nobilitatibus regum* (*c*1327), ed. M. R. James, Roxb. Club (1913).

MILTON Sacr. William of Milton (*alias* Meliton) [ob. 1261]: *De Sacramentis, Bibliotheca Franciscana scholastica medii aevi* XXII, XXIII (–502, –1158) (Quaracchi, 1961).

MinAc Essex Ministers' Accounts, MS Essex RO; *v. et.* MFG.

MinAc Ministers' and receivers' Accounts (S. I Hen. III–Ric. III; S. II Hen. VII–Chas. II) MS PRO (S.C. 6).

MinAc Westm., Wint. (etc.) *v. Ac. Man. Westm. etc.*

MinAc Wistow Ministers' Accounts for Wistow [Hunts], in *Econ. Condit.* app. [sep. pag.].

MinAc W. Wales Ministers' Accounts for West Wales 1277–1306, pt. I, ed. M. Rhys, Cymmrodorion Rec. S. XIII (1936).

Mir. Audoeni *Miracula S. Audoeni, Acta SS. Boll.* Aug. IV (1739) 825–40; *v. et. V. & Transl. Audoeni.*

Mir. Crisp. *Miraculum quo B. Maria subvenit Willelmo Crispino seniori* (*a*1100), *PL* CL (1854) 735–44.

Mir. Cuthb. *Capitula de miraculis et translationibus S. Cuthberti* (*a*1130), capp. 1–7 in S. DURH. I 229–61, capp. 8–21, *ib.* II 333–62 [by cap.].

Mir. Cuthb. Farne Miracles of St. Cuthbert at Farne (wr. *c*1200), in *Anal. Boll.* 70 (1952) 9–19 [by sect.].

Mir. Fridesw. *Miracula S. Frideswidae* [*ob.* ? 735], [attrib. Philip, prior 1175–91], *Acta SS. Boll.* Oct. VIII (Brussels, 1853) 568–89 [by cap.].

Mir. Furs. *Miracula S. Fursei abbatis Latiniacensis* [*ob.* 650], *Acta SS. Ben.* II 309–14; *v. et. V. Furs.*

Mir. Hen. VI *Henrici VI Angliae regis miracula postuma* (*c*1500), ed. P. Grosjean, *Subsidia Hagiographica* XXII (Brussels, 1935) [by bk. & cap.].

Mir. J. Bev. Miracles of St. John of Beverley, in *Hist. Church York* I: **A** (*c*1175) 293–320; **B** (12c. or 13c.) 321–5; **C** (*c*1275) 327–47.

MIRK Man. John Mirk, Prior of Lilleshall, Salop [*fl.* 1400]: *Manuale sacerdotis*, MS BL Harl. 5306 ff. 1–61v.

Mir. Montf. The Miracles of Simon de Montfort (*c*1280), ed. J. O. Halliwell, Camd. Soc. XV (1840) 67–110; *v. et.* M. CORNW. *Montfort.*

Mir. Nin. *Miracula Nyniae Episcopi*, in *PLAC* IV ii–iii (1923) 943–62 [by line].

Mir. Odulphi v. T. MARLB. *Odulph.*

Mir. Will. *Miracula quaedam S. Willelmi* [*ob.* 1154] (? *c*1285), in *Hist. Church York* II 531–43; *v. et. V. Will.*

Mir. Wist. v. T. MARLB. *Wistan.*

Mir. Wulfst. Miracles of St. Wulfstan [*ob.* 1095] (*c*1240), Camd. 3rd S. XL (1928) 115–88.

Misae *Rotuli Misae*: 1209–10, in *Liberate RC* 109–71; 1212–13, in *DocExch* 231–69.

Misc. Bannatyne v. Bannatyne Misc.

Misc. Chester Miscellanea (1311–), MS PRO (Chester 38).

Misc. LChamb. Lord Chamberlain's department, Miscellanea (1516–), MS PRO (L.C. 5).

Misc. Scrope Miscellanea relating to Archb. Scrope (1399–1405), in *Hist. Church York* II 292–311.

Misc. Wells Dean Cosyn and Wells Cathedral Miscellanea, Som. Rec. Soc. LVI (1941).

Miss. Ebor. *Missale ad usum insignis Ecclesie Eboracensis* (12c.–15c.), Surtees Soc. LIX–LX (1874).

Miss. Heref. *Missale ad usum percelebris ecclesiae Herfordensis* (14c.), ed. W. G. Henderson (Leeds, 1874).

Miss. Leofric The Leofric Missal (11c.), ed. F. E. Warren (Oxford, 1883).

Miss. R. Jum. The Missal (1013–17) of Robert of Jumièges [Archb. of Canterbury, 1051–2], HBS XI (1896).

Miss. Rosslyn The Rosslyn Missal (late 13c.), HBS XV (1899).

Miss. Sarum The Sarum Missal (? early 14c.), ed. J. Wickham Legg (Oxford, 1916).

Miss. Westm. *Missale ad usum ecclesie Westmonasteriensis* (1362–86), HBS I, V, XII (1891–7).

M. KIRKHAM Salom. Maurice, Prior of Kirkham [*fl.* 1170]: Against the Salomites (extr.), Journal of Theological Studies XXXV (1934) 287–97.

MLJ Mittellateinisches Jahrbuch I– (Cologne, 1966–).

MLLM *Mediae Latinitatis lexicon minus*, ed. J. F. Niermeyer and C. van de Kieft (Leyden, 1954–76).

MLW Mittellateinisches Wörterbuch, I– (Munich, 1967–).

Mod. Comp. Brevia *Modus componendi brevia* (*p*1285), ed. G. F. Woodbine, Four 13th-century Law Tracts, (New Haven, Conn., 1910) 143–62.

Mod. Philol. Modern Philology, I– (Chicago, 1903–).

Mod. Ten. CBaron *Modus tenendi curiam baronum cum visu franci plegii* (1510), ed. C. Greenwood (1915).

Mod. Ten. Parl. *Modus tenendi parliamentum* (14c.), ed. T. D. Hardy, RC (1846); also ed. M. V. Clarke, Medieval representation and consent (1936) 373–92.

Monarchia *Monarchia S. Romani Imperii*, ed. M. Goldast, 3 vols. (Hanover & Frankfurt, 1611–14); *v.* CONWAY *Def. Mend.*, OCKHAM *Dial.*, *Disp. & Err. Pap.*, PAUL. ANGL. *ASP*, RIC. ARMAGH *Def. Cur.* [many irregularities in pagination; note especially that from p. 1335 (*recte* 1235 *bis*) to p. 1428 (*recte* 1328) most page numbers are wrong by 100].

MonA W. Dugdale: *Monasticon Anglicanum*, ed. J. Caley *et al.*, 6 vols. in 8 (1817–30); also 3 vols. (1661–82) and 6 vols. in 8 (1846); *v. et. Inst. Sempr.*.

MonExon *Monasticon Dioecesis Exoniensis*, ed. G. Oliver (Exeter, 1846).

Mon. Francisc. *Monumenta Franciscana*, 2 vols. RS IV (1858–82) [partly superseded by ECCLESTON *Adv. Min.* (1909)]; *v. et.* AD. MARSH.

Mon. Hib. & Scot. *Vetera monumenta Hibernorum et Scotorum historiam illustrantia* (1216–1547) [mainly papal letters], ed. A. Theiner (Rome, 1864).

Mon. Rit. *Monumenta ritualia Ecclesiae Anglicanae, etc.*, ed. W. Maskell, 3 vols. (Oxford, 1882).

Mon. Tithes G. Constable: Monastic Tithes from their origins to the 12th century (Cambridge, 1964).

MORE Chr. Ed. II Thomas de la More [*fl.* 1327–47] [attrib.]: *Vita et Mors Edwardii II*, in *Chr. Ed. I & II*, II 297–319 [copied w. minor variations from BAKER].

MORE Ut. Thomas More [*ob.* 1535]: *Utopia* (1518), ed. J. H. Lupton (Oxford, 1895).

MOROW Thomas Morow, Abbot of Paisley [15c.]: Appeal to Council of Basel (1424), *Monumenta Conciliorum Generalium seculi decimi quinti*, 4 vols. (Vienna, Basel, 1857–1935), I 53–60.

MORTON, William *v. Ac. Almon. Peterb.*

M. PAR. Matthew Paris [*ob. c*1259]: **Abbr.** *Abbreviatio Chronicorum Angliae* (1000–1255), in M. PAR. *Min.* III 159–348; **Edm.** Life of Edmund Rich, Archb. of Canterbury [*ob.* 1240], ed. W. Wallace, Life of St. Edmund of Canterbury (1893) 543–88 [here attrib. E. FAVERSHAM]; superseded by C. H. Lawrence, Life of St. Edmund of Abingdon (Oxford, 1960) 222–89; **Flor.** *v. Flor. Hist.*; **Gesta** *v. G.S. Alb.*; **Maj.** *Chronica majora* (Creation–1259), 7 vols. RS LVII (1872–83); **Min.** *Historia Anglorum sive historia minor* (1066–1253), 3 vols. RS XLIV (1866–9).

M. RIEVAULX Matthew, precentor of Rievaulx (*alias* Nicolaus Rievallensis) [*fl.* 1210]: Miscellany of verse, sermons and letters, Rev. Ben. LII (1940) 15–84 [by no. of calendar, pp. 30–48]: 20–22, ed. E. Faral, Les Arts poétiques (Paris, 1924) 24–6 [*cf.* VINSAUF *Interdict.*]; 63 and 65, *Studia Anselmiana* XXXVII (1955) 175–9; **app.** additional verses, Rev. Ben. LII (1940) 48–51 [by no.].

M. SCOT Michael Scot [*ob. c*1235]: **Alch.** *De arte alchimiae* [attrib.] (extr.), in *Med. Cult.* 149–56; **An.** *De anima* **Intr.** *Liber Introductorius*, MS Escorial f. III 8 ff. 32v–53v; also (extr.), in *Med. Sci.* cap. xiii; **Lumen** *Lumen luminum*, ed. J. Wood Brown, Enquiry into the Life and Legend of Michael Scot (Edinburgh, 1897) 240–68; **Mot.** *De motibus celorum* [transl. from al-Biṭrūjī], ed. F. Carmody (Berkeley, Calif., 1952); **Part.** *Liber Particularis* (extr.), in *Med. Sci.* cap. xiii; **Phys.** *Liber Physiognomiae* (Pavia, 1515) [by cap.]; **Sol** *Quaestio curiosa de natura solis et lunae* (*p*1235) [attrib.], in *Theatrum Chem.* V 713–22; **Sphera** *v. Comm. Sph.*

MSS Ir. Facsimiles of national manuscripts of Ireland, 5 vols. (1874–84).

MunAcOx *Munimenta academica* or Documents illustrative of life and studies at Oxford (1214–1549), 2 vols. RS L (1868).

MunCOx *Munimenta civitatis Oxoniae* (1285–1545), OHS LXXI (1920).

Mun. K's Lynn King's Lynn Muniments, MS Norfolk RO.

Mun. Merton Merton [College] Muniments (with facsimiles) (*c*1154–1519), ed. P. S. Allen and H. W. Garrod (Oxford, 1928).

Mun. Univ. Glasg. *Munimenta almae universitatis Glasguensis* (1453–1727), ed. C. Innes, Maitland Club (1854).

MUSCA *v. Chr. Dale.*

Mus. Mens. (Anon. VI), *De musica mensurabili* (1391), in *Script. Mus.* III (1869) 398–403.

MYLN Dunkeld Alexander Myln [*ob. c*1548]: *Vitae Dunkeldensis ecclesiae Episcoporum* (1127–1515), Bannatyne Club (1823); **app.** compotus rolls (1513–16) in reissue, Bannatyne Club (1831).

Natura Deorum *Liber de Natura Deorum* (12c), Med. Stud. XXXIV (1972) 2–72 [by cap.].

Nav. Ven. *Navicula de Venetiis* (*a*1400), in *Early Sci. Ox.* II 375–9 (*cf. ib.* 38–41).

N. DUNSTABLE Nicholas of Dunstable [*fl.* 1225]: **Chr.** The Chronicle of the election of Hugh, Abbot of Bury St. Edmunds and later Bishop of Ely [attrib.], in *Mem. S. Edm.* II 29–130; also ed. R. M. Thomson, Med. Texts (Oxford, 1974); **Rel.** *De pace Veneta Relatio* [attrib.], *Speculum* L (1975) 29–32 [by f.].

NEB New English Bible (Oxford & Cambridge, 1961–70).

NECKAM Alexander Neckam (*melius* Nequam) [*ob.* 1217]: **AD** *Ars disserendi* [attrib.], *v.* BALSH. *AD rec. 2;* **Avianus** *Novus Avianus,* ed. L. Hervieux, Les Fabulistes latins III (Paris, 1894) 462–7; **Corrog.** *Corrogationes Promethei,* MS Bodley 550 [by f.]; also (extr.) in *N. & E.* XXXV (1897) 641–82, and *Med. Sci.* 363–4; **DS** *De laudibus divinae sapientiae,* RS XXXIV (1863) 355–503 [by bk. & line]; **Eccles.** *Commentarium in Ecclesiastem III 1–11,* MS Magdalen Coll. Ox. 139; **Fab.** *Fabulae* or *Novus Aesopus,* ed. L. Hervieux, Les Fabulistes latins II (1894) 392–416 [by no. & line]; **NR** *De naturis rerum,* RS XXXIV (1863) 1–354 [by bk. & cap.]; **Poems** Poems [attrib.], ed. M. Esposito, EHR XXX (1915) 450–71; complemented by MLJ II (1965) 111–29; **Sac.** *Sacerdos ad altare* [attrib.], MS Caius Coll. Camb. 385; (extr.) in *Med. Sci.* 361–76; **Sal.** *De prevaricatione Salamonis et ejus penitentia,* Med. & R. Stud. IV (1958) 29–31; **SS** *Speculum speculationum,* ed. R. M. Thomson, *Auct. Brit.* [in prep.]; **Ut.** *De nominibus utensilium,* ed. T. Wright, Vocabularies I (1857) 96–119 [by p.]; *vv. ll.* from ed. A. Scheler, Jahrb. rom. Lit. VII (1866) 58–74, 155–73; glosses printed in Revue de linguistique romane XLIII (1979) 239–62; **VM** *De vita monachorum* [attrib.], in *Sat. Poets* II 175–200.

NEN. HB 'Nennius' [attrib.]: *Historia Brittonum* (early 9c.) *cum additamentis Nennii,* MGH *Auct. Antiq.* XIII (1898) 143–219.

N. & E. Notices et extraits des MSS de la Bibliothèque Nationale, I– (1787–); **(Hauréau)** Notices et extraits de quelques manuscrits latins de la Bibliothèque Nationale, ed. B. Hauréau, 6 vols. (Paris, 1890–3).

NETTER DAF Thomas Netter of Walden [*ob.* 1430]: *Doctrinale antiquitatum fidei Ecclesiae Catholicae* (1426–7), 3 vols. (Venice, 1571) [Vol. I by p., II and III by f.]; *v. et. Ziz.*.

New Spalding Club (formerly Spalding Club), publications, (Aberdeen, 1877–).

N. FAKENHAM Nicholas of Fakenham, O.F.M. [*ob. c*1407]: **Concl.** *Conclusiones,* Two *questiones* on the Great Schism, *AFH* LXX (1977) 121–7; **Determ.** *Determinatio de schismate facta Oxoniae* (1395), *AFH* I (1908) 582–600, *ib.* II (1909) 79–91.

NGML *Novum Glossarium Mediae Latinitatis* (800–1200), ed. F. Blatt *et al.,* L–O (Copenhagen, 1957–) [in prog.].

NIC. S. ALB. Nicholas, monk of St. Albans [*fl.* 1180]: **Concept.** *De celebranda conceptione beatae Mariae contra beatum Bernardum,* Rev. Ben. LXIV (1954) 92–117; **Ep.** *Epistola ad Petrum Cellensem,* PL CCII 622–8.

NIG. Nigel Wireker [*fl.* 1190]: **Cur.** *Tractatus contra curiales et officiales clericos,* in *Sat. Poets* I 146–53 (verse), 153–230 (prose); also ed. A. Boutemy, Nigellus de Longchamp dit Wireker I (Paris, 1959), 144–210; **Ely** *Versus ad Episcopum Eliensem* [William Longchamp, *ob.* 1197], *ib.* 231–9; **Ep.** *Epistola ad Willelmum, Medium Ævum* XXXIX (1970) 17–20; **Eust.** *Vita metrica S. Eustacii,* Zeitschrift für deutsches Alterthum 24 (1880) 242–54 [by line]; **Laur.** *Passio S. Laurencii,* MS BL Cotton Vespasian D XIX ff. 28–45 [by f. & col.]; **Mir. BVM** *Miracula S. Virginis Mariae, ib.* ff. 5–24 [by f. & col.]; **Paul.** *Vita Pauli primi heremitae, ib.* ff. 45v.–52; ed. L. M. Kaiser, Classical Folia XIV (1969) 63–81 [by f. & line]; **Poems** Unprinted poems, Cotton Vespasian D XIX ff. 1–53 (incl. *Laur., Mir. BVM,* and *Paul.*); (extr.), *Speculum* VII (1932), 398–423; **SS** *Speculum stultorum,* ed. J. H. Mozley and R. R. Raymo (Berkeley, Calif., 1960) [by line]; also in *Sat. Poets* I 3–145.

NLA *Nova Legenda Angliae,* collected by J. TYNEMOUTH [*ob. c*1348], w. additions by CAPGR. [*ob.* 1464] *et al.,* ed. C. Horstman, 2 vols. (Oxford, 1901); **prol.** prologue, prob. wr. for ed. 1516; *v. et. V. Erkenwaldi.*

N. OCKHAM QD Nicholas of Ockham, O.F.M. [1242–1320]: *Quaestiones disputatae de dilectione Dei,* ed. C. S. Alarcón, *Spicilegium Bonaventurianum* XXI (Grottaferrata, 1981).

Non-Cycle Plays Non-Cycle Plays and Fragments, ed. N. Davis, EETS Sup. S. I (1970) [by no. & line].

Norf. Arch. v. Arch. Soc. Norf.

Norm. Inst. C. H. Haskins: Norman Institutions (Cambridge, Mass., 1918), w. app. of docs. 241–343.

Northants Rec. Soc. Northamptonshire Record Society, publications, I– (1924–).

North Durh. J. Raine: History and Antiquities of North Durham (1830–52); **app.** appendix of documents [by no.].

Norw. Cath. Pri. Norwich Cathedral Priory in the fourteenth century, JRL Bull. XX (1936) 105–30.

Nott. Med. Stud. Nottingham Mediaeval Studies, I– (Cambridge, 1957–).

N. & Q. Notes and Queries, I– (1849–).

N. Riding Rec. Soc. North Riding Record Society, publications, I– (London, 1884–).

Nunnam. The Book of Nunnaminster. An Ancient manuscript of the Eighth or Ninth Century, ed. W. de G. Birch, Hants Rec. Soc. (1889).

Oak Bk. Southampt. The Oak Book of Southampton (*c*1300), 3 vols. Southampton Rec. Soc. (1910–11).

O. BATTLE Odo of Canterbury, abbot of Battle [*ob.* 1200]: **Ep.** *Epistolae:* 1–4 (*a*1175) in *Ep. Alex.* III 1396–8, 1464–6; 5 (1187) in *Ep. Cant.* 28; 6, ed. J. Mabillon, *Vetera Analecta* (Paris, 1675), I 349–59 (cf. *Studia Anselmiana* XXXI 128 n. 3); 7 (*a*1200) in *Becket Mat.* II xlix [by no.]; **Kings** *Tractatus in libros Regum,* ed. C. de Clercq (Ventimiglia, 1980); **Serm.** *Sermones,* ed. C. de Clercq (Brussels, 1983).

Obed. Abingd. *De obedientiariis abbatiae Abbendonensis* [Abingdon, Berks] (late 13c.), in *Chr. Abingd.* II app. IV 336–417.

ObitR Durh. The Obituary Roll of William Ebchester and John Burnby, priors of Durham, etc. (1233–15c.), Surtees Soc. XXXI (1856).

Obs. Barnwell The Observances in use at the Augustinian Priory at Barnwell [Cambs] (1295–6), ed. J. W. Clark (Cambridge, 1897); *v. et. Lib. Mem. Bernewelle.*

Obsess. Durh. *De obsessione Dunelmi* (*c*1090), in S. DURH. I 215–20 [by cap.].

O. CANT. Odo, Archb. of Canterbury [*ob.* 959]: **Const.** *Constitutiones,* PL CXXXIII 945–50 [by no.]; superseded by *Conc. Syn.* I 69–74; **Ep.** *Epistola, ib.* 949–52; superseded by *Conc. Syn.* I 65–7; **Pref. Frith.** *Praefatio Frithegodi,* in FRITH. 1–3 [by line].

O. CHERITON Odo of Cheriton [*ob.* 1247]: **Cant.** *Expositiones super Cantica canticorum* [attrib.] (extr.), AHDLMA XXXII (1956) 61–9; **Fab.** *Fabulae*, ed. L. Hervieux, Les Fabulistes latins IV (Paris, 1896) 171–255 [by no.]; **add.** additional fables: **A** first series, MS BL Harl. 219, *ib.* 361–86; **B** second series, MSS BL Harl. 219 and Bodl. Douce 169, *ib.* 387–404 [by no.]; **Par.** *Parabolae, ib.* 265–343 [by no.].

OCKHAM William of Ockham [*ob.* 1349]: **Brev.** *Breviloquium de potestate Papae* (1341–2), ed. L. Baudry, Études de philosophie médiévale XXIV (Paris, 1937); **Dial.** *Dialogus* (1332–?), in *Monarchia* II 392–957 (recte 394–957); **Disp.** *Disputatio super potestate praelatis ecclesiae atque principibus terrarum commissa, ib.* I 13–18; **Dub.** *Opera dubia et spuria: Tractatus minor logicae, Elementarium logicae, Tractatus de praedicamentis, Tractatus de relatione, Centiloquium theologicum, Tractatus de principiis theologiae*, ed. E. Buytaert *et al.*, *Guillelmi de Ockham Opera Philosophica* VII (St. Bonaventure, N.Y., in prep.); **Elench.** *Expositio super libros Elenchorum Aristotelis*, ed. F. del Punta, *Guillelmi de Ockham Opera Philosophica* III (St. Bonaventure, N.Y., 1979); **Err. Papae** *Compendium errorum Johannis papae XXII* (1338), in *Monarchia* II 957–76; **Expos. Aurea** *Expositio aurea*, ed. E. A. Moody *et. al.*, *Guillelmi de Ockham Opera Philosophica* II (St. Bonaventure, N.Y., 1978); also ed. M. de Benevento (Bologna, 1496; facsimile, Farnborough 1964) [by signature]; **I. & P.** *De imperatorum et pontificum potestate* (1346–7), ed. C. K. Brampton (Oxford, 1927); **I. & P. Sup.** supplementary text, ed. W. Mulder, *Archivum Franciscanum Historicum* XVI 469–92, XVII 72–97 (Quaracchi, 1923–4); **Misc. Phil.** *Brevis summa libri Physicorum, Summula philosophiae naturalis* and *Quaestiones super librum Physicorum Aristotelis*, ed. S. F. Brown, *Guillelmi de Ockham Opera Philosophica* VI (St Bonaventure, N.Y., 1984); **Phys.** *Expositio in libros Physicorum*, ed. V. Richter et al., *Guillelmi de Ockham Opera Philosophica* IV, V (St Bonaventure, N.Y., 1984); **Pol.** *Opera politica*, ed. J. G. Sikes *et al.*, 3 vols. (Manchester, 1940–56); vol. I ed. 2 (1974) [some refs. in Fasc. II are to both eds., refs. from Fasc. III onwards are to ed. 2]: I 1–221 *Octo quaestiones de potestate Papae* (*c*1340); 223–71 *An Princeps, pro suo succursu scilicet guerrae, possit recipere bona ecclesiarum, etiam invito Papa* (*c*1338); 273–86 *Consultatio de causa matrimoniali* (*c*1342); I 287–II 858 *Opus nonaginta dierum* (*c*1332); III 1–17 *Epistola ad Fratres Minores* (1334) [also ed. C. K. Brampton (Oxford, 1929)]; 19–156 *Tractatus contra Joannem* [*XXII*] (1335); 157–322 *Tractatus contra Benedictum* [*XII*] (1337–8); **Qu.** *Quaestiones variae*, ed. G. J. Etzkorn *et al.*, *Guillelmi de Ockham Opera Theologica* VIII (St. Bonaventure, N.Y., 1983); **Quodl.** *Quodlibeta VII*, ed. J. C. Wey, *Guillelmi de Ockham Opera Theologica* IX (St. Bonaventure, N.Y., 1981); **Sacr. Alt.** *De sacramento altaris* (? 1323), ed. T. Bruce Birch (Burlington, Iowa, 1930); **Sent.** *Quaestiones in quatuor libros Sententiarum* (*c*1320), ed. G. Gál, S. F. Brown *et al.*, *Guillelmi de Ockham Opera Theologica* I–VII (St. Bonaventure, N.Y., 1967–) [by vol. & p.]; **Summa** *Summa logicae* (Oxford, 1675); superseded by ed. P. Boehner *et al. Guillelmi de Ockham Opera Philosophica* I (St. Bonaventure, N.Y., 1974) [by bk. & cap.].

OCREATUS Helceph N. Ocreatus [*fl.* 1150]: *Prologus in Helceph ad Adelardum Batensem*, fragm. in Abhandlungen zur Gesch. der Mathematik III (Leipzig, 1880) 129–39.

ODINGTON Walter Odington of Evesham [*fl.* 1320]: *De speculatione musicae*, in *Script. Mus.* I 182–250; superseded by *Walteri Odington Summa de speculatione musicae*, in *Corp. Script. Mus.* XIV (1970) 42–146.

OED A New English Dictionary on historical principles, ed. J. A. H. Murray, H. Bradley, W. A. Craigie (Oxford, 1888–1928) [later known as Oxford English Dictionary].

Offic. Evesham *Officium ecclesiasticum abbatum secundum usum Eveshamensis monasterii* (1282–1316), HBS VI (1893).

Offic. Kentig. Office of St. Kentigern (13c.), ed. A. P. Forbes, St. Ninian and St. Kentigern (Edinburgh, 1874) xciv–c.

Offic. R. Rolle *Officium de S. Ricardo heremita et legenda de vita ejus*, EETS XX (1866, rev. ed. 1920), xix–xlv.

Offic. Sal. *De officiis ecclesiasticis tractatus* (p1215), in *Reg. S. Osm.* I 1–185 [by cap.].

Offic. S. Andr. *Liber officialis* [*curie consistorialis*] *S. Andree* (1513–88), Abbotsford Club (1845).

OHS Oxford Historical Society, publications, I–CI(1885–1936); NS I– (1939–).

Op. Chr. *Opus Chronicorum* (1259–95), in *Chr. Mon. S. Alb.* III 3–59.

Opusc. & Text. *Opuscula et textus historiam ecclesiae eiusque vitam atque doctrinam illustrantia, series scholastica*, ed. M. Grabmann and F. Pelster, I–XXI (Münster, 1926–56).

Ord. Cartus. *Ordinarium Cartusiense* (*c*1500), tracts on the Mass, HBS XXVII (1904) 97–110.

Ord. Ebor. Ordinal and customary of St. Mary's Abbey, York (*c*1400), HBS LXXIII, LXXV, LXXVI (1934, 1936, 1937).

Ord. Ely Ely chapter Ordinances and visitation records (1241–1515), Camd. Misc. XVII, Camd. 3rd S. LXIV (1940) 1–3, 24–8, 36–43; v. et. Vis. Ely.

Ord. Exon. *Ordinale Exoniense* (*c*1337), HBS XXXVI, XXXVIII (1909).

ORD. VIT. Ordericus Vitalis [*ob. c*1143]: *Historia ecclesiastica* (–1141), ed. A. Le Prévost, 5 vols. (Paris, 1838–55); superseded by Med. Texts, ed. M. Chibnall, 6 vols. (1969–80) [by bk., cap., & p. of ed. Le Prévost].

Or. Eli. *Orationes Elienses*, prayers from Ely (14c.), *Studia Monastica* I (1959) 390–92.

Orthog. Gall. *Orthographica Gallica* (13c.), ed. J. Stürzinger, Altfranzösische Bibliothek VIII (Heilbronn, 1884) 1–27 [*cf. Medium Ævum* VI (1937) 193–209]; also ed. Selden Soc. XXVII (1912) xliv–xlvii.

Ort. Walw. *De ortu Walwanii* (*alias* Gwalchmai), ed. J. D. Bruce, Modern Language Association of America XIII (1898) 390–432, checked against revised ed., Hesperia Ergänzungsreihe II (Göttingen, 1913).

OSB. Osbern of Canterbury [*fl.* 1090]: **Ep.** *Epistolae, v. Ep. Anselm.* IV 6–10, 13–14; **Mir. Dunst.** *Liber Miraculorum*, in *Mem. Dunst.* 129–61 [by cap.]; **Mus.** *De vocum consonantiis ac de re musica* [attrib.], ed. J. Smits van Waesberghe, *Divitiae Musicae Artis* series A Xa (Amsterdam, 1979); **Transl. Elph.** *Historia de translatione corporis S. Elphegi*, in *Anglia Sacra* II 143–7; **V. Dunst.** *Vita S. Dunstani*, in *Mem. Dunst.* 69–128 [by cap.]; **V. Elph.** *Vita S. Elphegi* (*alias* Ælfheah), *archiepiscopi Cantuariensis* [*ob.* 1012], in *Anglia Sacra* II 122–42; also *PL* CXLIX 375–94.

OSB. BAWDSEY Osbert of Bawdsey [*fl.* 1149]: *De expugnatione Lyxbonensi* (1147) [attrib.], in *Mem. Ric.* I, I cxlii–clxxxii; checked w. MS facs. in Conquista de Lisboa em 1147, ed. R. de Azevedo (Coimbra, 1962); also ed. C. H. David (New York, 1936).

OSB. CLAR. Osbert of Clare [*ob. c*1136]: **Anna** *Sermo et versus in honorem S. Annae*, Annales de Bretagne XXXVII (1925–6) 13–33 [by f.]; **Ep.** *Epistolae*, ed. E. W. Williamson (Oxford, 1929) [by no.]; **Mir. Edm.** *Liber de miraculis S. Eadmundi, v.* SAMSON; **V. Ed. Conf.** *Vita S. Edwardi Confessoris*, *Anal. Boll.* XLI (1922) 64–131 [by cap.].

OSB. GLOUC. Osbern of Gloucester [*fl.* 1150–75]: **Deriv.** *Liber Derivationum, Classici auctores e Vaticanis codicibus editi*, VIII, ed. A. Mai (1836); **pref.** Med. & R. Stud. IV (1958) 275–7.

OSW. Vers. Oswald of Ramsey [*fl.* 1000]: On composing verse, ed. M. Lapidge, ASE IV (1975) 106–7 [by line].

OTTERB. Thomas Otterbourne [*fl.* 1400]: *Chronica Regum Angliae* (–1420), ed. T. Hearne, *Duo rerum Anglicarum scriptores veteres* I (1732) 1–283.

OXNEAD John of Oxnead [*ob. c*1293]: **Chr.** *Chronica* (–1292), RS XIII (1859) [corrected ed.]; **Chr. Min.** *Chronica minora* (–1294, cont. to 1503), *ib.* 412–39; **S. Ben. Holme** Early history of the Abbey of St. Benet Holme [*alias* Hulme (Norf)], *ib. app.* I 289–300.

PALMER Thomas Palmer [*fl.* 1415]: *De translatione sacrae scripturae*, ed. M. Deanesly, The Lollard Bible (Cambridge, 1920) 418–37.

Parl. Ir. Parliaments and councils of mediaeval Ireland, ed. H. G. Richardson and G. O. Sayles, I (1290–1420) IMC (Dublin, 1947).

Parl. Writs Parliamentary Writs and writs of military summons etc. (1272–1327), 2 vols. in 4, RC (1827–34).

Pass. Æthelb. *Passio S. Æthelberti martyris* [King of East Anglia, *ob.* 794] (wr. ? *c*1100), EHR XXXII (1917) 236–44 [by cap.].

Pass. Indracti *Passio S. Indracti* (wr. ? 11c.), ed. M. Lapidge, Ireland in Early Mediaeval Europe, edd. D. Whitelock *et al.* (Cambridge, 1982), 199–204 [by f. of MS Digby 112].

Paston Let. The Paston letters, 1422–1509, ed. J. Gairdner, 3 vols. (1895) [by no.], also ed. *Id.*, 6 vols. (1904); superseded by Paston Letters and papers of the fifteenth century, ed. N. Davis, 3 vols. (Oxford, 1971–) [by no.].

Pat. Hib. Hen. V *Transcripta omnium litterarum patentium .. sub testimonio loca-tenentium Hiberniae temp. R. Hen. V*, in *RSelecti* 39–80.

PAT. HIB. Soph. Patricius de Hibernia [*fl.* 1280]: *Sophisma 'Homo est animal'*, CIMA XXIV (1978) 16–34.

Pat *Rotuli litterarum patentium* or Patent Rolls: 1201–16 RC (1835); 1216–32, Patent Rolls, 2 vols. HMSO (1901, 1903); 1232– MS PRO (C. 66) [by roll & m.]; *v. et. CalPat, Pat Sup.*

Pat Sup. Patent Rolls Supplementary (1275–), MS PRO (C. 67).

PAUL. ANGL. ASP Paulus (*alias* Thomas) Anglicus, canonist [*fl.* 1400]: *Aureum speculum Papae*, in *Monarchia* II 1527–58.

P. BLOIS Peter of Blois [*ob.* 1212]: **Caro & spir.** *Cantilena de lucta carnis et spiritus*, PL CCVII (1855) 1127–30; **Cervisia** *Responsio contra cervisiam*, *ib.* 1155–8 [*v. et.* BEAUFEU *Cervisia*]; **Contra Clericos** *Contra clericos voluptati deditos*, *ib.* 1129–36; **Dict.** *De arte dictandi* [abridgement of work by Bernard of Meung], *ib.* 1127–8; **Ep.** *Epistolae*, *ib.* 1–560 [by no.]; **Euch.** *Tractatus de eucharistiae mysteriis*, *ib.* 1135–54; **Guthl.** *Vita S. Guthlaci* [*ob.* 716], in *NLA* II 698–719; **Opusc.** *Opuscula* [incl. some of doubtful authenticity], *ib.* 777–1126; **Perf. Jud.** *Contra perfidiam Judaeorum*, *ib.* 825–70; **Poems** Poems, *ib.* 1127–58; **Serm.** *Sermones*, *ib.* 559–776; **Sil.** *De silentio servando*, *ib.* 1125–8; **Vinum** *Versus de commendatione vini*, *ib.* 1155–6.

P. BRADLAY Peter Bradlay, fellow of Balliol [*fl.* 1305]: **Anal. Pri.** A Question by Peter Bradlay on the Prior Analytics, Med. Stud. XXX (1968) 3–21 [by sect.]; **Cat.** Master Peter Bradlay on the Categories, *ib.* XXIX (1967) 275–327 [by sect.].

P. BRIDL. Philip of Bridlington, O.F.M. [*fl.* 1300], *v. Quaest. Ox.* 344–7.

P. CORNW. Peter of Cornwall [*ob.* 1221]: **Disp.** *Liber disputationum contra Symonem Judaeum* (extr.), in Powicke Studies 143–56; **Panth. prol.** *Prologus in primam partem Pantheologi*, RHS Trans. 4th S. XIX (1936) 38–42; **Rev.** *Liber Revelationum* (*c*1200), MS Lambeth Palace Library 51 [by bk. & cap.]; (extr.) I 183–4, 200–203, 205, II 891–4, ed. C.J. Holdsworth, Cîteaux XIII (1962) 193–204; (extr.) I 5, *Anal. Boll.* XCVII (1979) 410–16.

Peasants' Rising The Peasants' Rising and the Lollards, docs. 1381–99, ed. E. Powell and G. M. Trevelyan (1899).

PECKHAM John Peckham (*alias* Pecham or Patcham), Archb. of Canterbury [*ob.* 1292]: **Aetern.** *Quaestio disputata utrum mundus potuit ab aeterno creari*, *Patristica & Mediaevalia* I (Buenos Aires, 1975) 85–101; **An.** *Tractatus de anima*, ed. G. Melani, Biblioteca di Studi Francescani I (Florence, 1948); **Bibl.** *Divinarum sententiarum Librorum Biblie* Paris, 1513); **Cant. Paup.** *Canticum pauperis pro dilecto*, *Bibliotheca Franciscana ascetica medii aevi* IV (2nd ed., Quaracchi, 1949) 133–205; **Def. Mend.** *Defensio fratrum mendicantium*, Brit. Soc. Franciscan Studies II (Aberdeen, 1910) 148–97 [by line]; **Ep.** *Registrum epistolarum fratris Johannis Peckham*, 3 vols. RS LXXVII (1882–5) [by no.]; **Exp. Thren.** *Expositio Threnorum* (or *In Lamentationes Jeremiae*), S. Bonaventurae Opera Omnia VII (Quaracchi, 1895) 607–51 [by bk. & cap.]; **Kilw.** *Tractatus contra fratrem Robertum Kilwardby*, ed. F. Tocco, La Quistione della povertà nel secolo xiv (Naples, 1910), 219–75, cited from reprint, Brit. Soc. Franciscan Studies II (1910) 121–147 [*cf.* KILWARDBY]; **Paup.** *Tractatus pauperis*, prol. & cc. 1–6, ed. A. van den Wyngaert (Paris, 1925); cc. 7–9. ed. F. Delorme, Studi Francescani 3rd S. IV (1932) 47–62, 164–93; c. 10, ed. A.G. Little, Brit. Soc. Franciscan Studies II (Aberdeen, 1910), 27–55; cc. 11–14, ed. F. M. Delorme, *Collectanea Franciscana* XIV (1944) 90–117; c. 15, ed. F. M. Delorme, *Richardi de Mediavilla quaestio disputata de privilegio Martini papae IV* (Quaracchi, 1925) 79–88; c. 16, ed. Little, (as above) 63–87 [by cap. & p.]; **Persp.** *Perspectiva communis*, ed. L. Gavricus (Venice, 1504) [by bk. & cap.]; also ed. D. C. Lindberg, John Pecham and the science of optics (Madison, Wisc., 1970); **Phil.** *Philomena* (=*Poems* 9), *Anal. Hymn.* L (1907) 602–16; **Poems** Miscellaneous poems, in *Anal. Hymn.* L (1907) 597–600 [by no. (1–8) & stanza]; **Puer. Obl.** *Quaestio de pueris oblatis*, *Archivum Franciscanum Historicum* VIII (Quaracchi, 1915) 414–49; **QA** *Quaestiones tractantes de anima* (*c*1270), BGPM XIX v–vi (Münster, 1918); **QD** *Quaestio disputata, De humanae cognitionis ratione anecdota quaedam S. Bonaventurae et discipulorum* (Quaracchi, 1883) 179–82; **QR** *Quodlibet Romanum*, ed. F. M. Delorme, *Spicilegium Pontificii Athenaei Antoniani* I (Rome, 1938); **Reg.** *Registrum*, *v.* Reg. Cant.; **Serm.** *Sermones* (extr.), in *Powicke Studies* 269–82; **Trin.** *De trinitate* (London, 1510).

PECOCK Reginald Pecock, Bishop of Chichester [*ob. c*1460]: **Abbr.** *Abbreviatio* (1447), *Repressor*, RS XIX (1860) II 615–19; **Collect.** *Collectanea*, ed. J. Foxe, *Commentarii rerum in ecclesiis gestarum* (Strasburg, 1554) ff. 199v.–223v.

Peramb. Dartmoor S. Rowe: A Perambulation of the forest of Dartmoor and the Venville precincts, 3rd ed. (1896).

PETRUS Petrus Alfonsi, physician to Henry I [1067–*c*1120]: **DC** *Disciplina clericalis*, ed. A. Hilka and W. Söderhjelm (Heidelberg, 1911); also PL CLVIII (1854) 671–706; **Dial.** *Dialogus Christiani cum Judaeo*, PL CLVII (1854) 535–672, checked against ed. K. P. Mieth (Berlin, 1982); **Drac.** *De dracone*, *v.* WALCHER *Drac.*; **Peripat.** Letter to the Peripatetics of France, Sefarad III (1943) 97–105.

P. HIB. Petrus de Hibernia [*fl.* 1240–60]: **Determ.** *Determinatio utrum membra essent facta propter operationes vel operationes facta propter membra*, ed. C. Baeumker, Sitzungsberichte der Bayerischen Academie der Wissenschaften, phil.-hist. Kl. 1920, Heft 8; **Periherm.** *Glosulae in librum Aristotelis peri Hermeneias*, CIMA XLIII (1982) 13–44.

Pickering The honor and forest of Pickering [Yorks], ed. R. B. Turton, N. Riding Rec. Soc. I–IV (1894–7).

Pipe Chesh Cheshire in the Pipe Rolls (1158–1301), Lancs & Chesh Rec. Soc. XCII (1938); **app.** Account of

Chamberlain of Chester (1301), *ib.* 187–220; *v. et. Ac. Chamb. Chesh.*

Pipe Cloyne *Rotulus Pipae Clonensis* (1364–1403) w. other docs., ed. R. Caulfield (Cork, 1859).

Pipe Ir. The Irish Pipe Roll of 14 John, 1211–12, Ulster J. of Arch. 3rd S. IV Sup. (Belfast, 1941).

Pipe Pipe Rolls or Great Rolls of the Exchequer: 1130, 1155–8, 2 vols. RC (1833, 1844, repr. in facsimile HMSO, 1929–30); 1158– Pipe R. Soc., I– (1884–) [by p.]; 1242, ed. H. C. Cameron, Yale Historical Publications (New Haven, Conn., 1918) [by p.]; later Rolls, MS PRO (E. 372); **(Chanc.)** Chancellor's Roll (E. 352) [duplicate of Pipe; cited as *v. l.* or to supply deficiency].

Pipe R. Soc. Pipe Roll Society for the publication of the Great Rolls of the Exchequer, publications, I– (1884–).

Pipe Wint. Pipe Rolls of the Bishopric of Winchester (1208–1454): 1208–9 ed. H. Hall (1903); 1210–11 ed. N. R. Holt (Manchester, 1964); later rolls, MS PRO Eccl. 2; *v. et. Crawley.*

PLAC *Poetae Latini aevi Carolini*, ed. E. Duemmler *et al.*, 4 vols. *MGH* (Berlin, 1881–1923).

Planct. Univ. Ox. *Planctus Universitatis Oxoniensis contra laicos* (1354), in *Collect. Ox.* III (1896) 170–9 [by line].

Pl. Anglo-Norm. *Placita Anglo-Normannica* (Will. I–Ric. I), ed. M. M. Bigelow (1879).

Plant. & Tudor Chester R. H. Morris: Chester in the Plantagenet and Tudor reigns (Chester, 1895).

PlCrGlouc Pleas of the Crown for the county of Gloucester (1221), ed. F. W. Maitland (1884).

Pl. K. or J. Pleas before the King or his Justices (1198–1202), Selden Soc. LXVII, LXVIII, LXXXIII, LXXXIV (1932–67) [by no.].

Pl. Mem. Lond. Plea and Memoranda Rolls of the City of London (1323–1484), MS Guildhall RO; *v. et. Cal. Pl. Mem. Lond.*

PL *Patrologiae cursus completus. Series Latina*, ed. J.-P. Migne, 221 vols. (Paris, 1844–64); **Sup.** *Supplementum*, ed. A. Hamman, 4 vols. (Paris, 1958–71).

PlRChester Plea Rolls, Palatinate of Chester (1259–), MS PRO (Chester 29).

PlRCP Plea Rolls (*Placita de Banco*), Court of Common Pleas (1272–), MS PRO (C.P. 40).

PlRExch Plea Rolls, Exchequer of Pleas (1235–), MS PRO (E. 13).

PlRJews Jewish Plea Rolls (1219–87), MS PRO (E. 9); *v. et. SelPlJews.*

PlRMarshalsea Plea Rolls, *Aula Regis* or Marshalsea Court (Ed. II–), MS PRO (E. 37).

Plusc. *Liber Pluscardensis* VI 15–XI (1141–1445), ed. F. J. H. Skene, Historians of Scotland VII (Edinburgh, 1877) [by bk. & cap; earlier portion omitted by ed. as adding nothing material to FORDUN].

PN English Place-names, arr. by county, series published by the English Place-name Soc. I– (Cambridge, 1924–); **Elements** English place-name elements, ed. A. H. Smith, XXV, XXVI (1956); **Intro.** Introduction to the survey of English place-names, ed. A. Mawer and F. M. Stenton, I (1924).

Poem Edm. Rich Un poème en l'honneur de Saint Edmond de Cantorbéry, *Anal. Boll.* XXXII (1913) 5–9.

Poem S. Greg. Poem on St. Gregory [*ob.* 604] (10c. MS), in *Poésies pop.* 237–8;

Poem S. Thom. Poem on St. Thomas Becket [*ob.* 1170] (*a*1200), in *Poésies pop.* 70–93.

Poésies pop. Poésies populaires latines du moyen âge, ed. E. du Méril (Paris, 1847).

Pol. Poems Political poems and songs (1327–1483), 2 vols. RS XIV (1859–61); *v. et.* J. BRIDL., R. MAIDSTONE, W. PETERB.

Pol. Songs Political songs of England (John–Ed. II), Camd. Soc. VI (1839).

Pont. Bernham The Pontifical Offices used by David de

Bernham, Bishop of S. Andrews, ed. C. Wordsworth (Edinburgh, 1885).

Pont. Ebor. *Liber pontificalis Archiepiscopi Eboracensis* (12c.), Surtees Soc. LXI (1875).

Pont. Exon. *Liber pontificalis Episcopi Exoniensis* [Edmund Lacy, *ob.* 1455] ed. R. Barnes (Exeter, 1847).

Pont. Sal. Pontifical of Salisbury (13c.–15c.) (extr.), in *Mon. Rit.* I 3–272, II 154–365.

Poole Essays Essays in history presented to R. L. Poole, ed. H. W. C. Davis (Oxford, 1927).

Port Bk. Port Books (1565–1798), MS PRO (E. 190).

Port Bk. Southampt. Port Books of Southampton: 1427–30 Southampton Rec. Soc. (1913); 1435–6 Southampton Rec. S. VII (1963); 1439–40, *Ib.* V (1961); 1469–81, Southampton Rec. Soc. XXXVII, XXXVIII (1937–8).

Powicke Studies Studies in medieval history presented to F. M. Powicke, ed. R. W. Hunt, W. A. Pantin, and R. W. Southern (Oxford, 1948).

PP *Promptorium parvulorum sive clericorum dictionarius Anglo-Latinus princeps, auctore fratre Galfrido Grammatico dicto* (1440), ed. A. L. Mayhew, EETS Extra S. CII (1908).

PQW *Placita de Quo Warranto* (Ed. I–Ed. III), RC (1818).

Praest. *Rotuli de Praestito*: 1205–6, in *DocExch* 270–6; 1210–11, in *Liberate RC* 173–253; 1212–16, in Pipe R. Soc. NS XXXVII (1964).

Praxis F. Clarke: *Praxis in curiis ecclesiasticis* (1596), 2nd ed. (1684) [by cap.].

Prejudice & Promise C. L. Kingsford: Prejudice and promise in 15th-century England (Oxford, 1925).

Prests Books of Prests of the King's wardrobe for 1294–5, presented to J. G. Edwards, ed. E. B. Fryde (Oxford, 1962).

Pri. Cold. Correspondence etc. of the Priory of Coldingham [Berwick] (1261–15c.), Surtees Soc. XII (1841).

Proc. A. Kyteler Narrative of the Proceedings against Dame Alice Kyteler 1324, by R. de Ledrede, Bishop of Ossory [*ob.* 1360], Camd. Soc. XXIV (1843); *v. et.* LEDREDE.

Process. Sal. Ceremonies and Processions of the Cathedral Church of Salisbury (*c*1445), ed. C. Wordsworth (Cambridge, 1901).

Proc. J. P. Proceedings before Justices of the Peace in the 14th and 15th centuries, ed. B. H. Putnam (London, 1938).

Proc. PC v. Act. PC.

Proc. v. Crown L. Ehrlich: Proceedings against the Crown (1216–1377) (Oxford, 1921).

PRO Public Record Office, Chancery Lane, London.

Prov. Durh. Durham Proverbs (11c.), *Speculum* LVI (1981) 291–5 [by no.].

Psalt. B Glosses in the Blickling Psalter (Roman, 8c.), EETS LXXIII (1880) 253–63.

Psalt. Sal. The Salisbury Psalter (Gallican, *c*975, glosses *c*1100), EETS CCXLII (1959 for 1955–6) [by psalm & verse].

Psalt. Vesp. The Vespasian Psalter (Roman, 8c., glosses 9c.), ed. S. M. Kuhn (Ann Arbor, Mich., 1965) [by psalm & verse].

Ps.-ANSELM Medit. *Pseudo*-Anselm: *Meditationes*, PL CLVIII 709–820 [assigned where possible to authors; *v.* Revue d'ascétique et mystique VIII (1927) 272–82].

Ps.-BEDE Hymn. *Hymni* [included among BEDE's in *PL* but not authentic], *PL* XCIV 605–21, 627–8, 633–4 [by col.].

Ps.-ELMH. Hen. V *Pseudo*-Elmham: *Vita et gesta Henrici V* (*c*1446), ed. T. Hearne (Oxford, 1727) [by cap.]; *cf.* ELMH., *G. Hen. V.*

Ps.-GOSC. Pseudo-Goscelin: *Milb. v.* GOSC. *Milb.*; *Swith. v.* ÆLF. *Swith.*; *Werb. v.* GOSC. *Werb.*

Ps.-GROS. *Pseudo*-Grosseteste: **Gram.** *Tractatus de Grammatica* (13c.), ed. K. Reichel, Veröffentl. des Grab-

mann-Instituts XXVIII (Munich, 1976); **Summa** *Summma theologica* (*c*1270), in BGPM IX (1912) 275–643 [possibly by KILWARDBY].

Ps.-INGULF *v. Croyl.*

Ps.-MAP Latin poems commonly attributed to Walter Mapes (12c.-), Camd. Soc. XVI (1841); *cf.* MAP; *v. et.* WALT. WIMB.

Ps.-OCKHAM *Pseudo*-Ockham: **Princ. Theol.** *Tractatus de principiis theologiae* (*a*1550) [made up chiefly of extracts from OCKHAM], ed. L. Baudry, Études de philosophie médiévale XXIII (Paris, 1936).

PS Privy Seal Warrants, MS PRO (C. 81) [cited as providing OF equivalent of letters patent etc.].

PS Rec. Council and Privy Seal Records (Ed. III–Eliz. I), MS PRO (E. 28).

Ps.-RIC. Anat. *Pseudo*-Galen: *Anatomia vivorum* [wrongly attrib. RIC. MED.], ed. R. Töply (Vienna, 1902) [by cap.].

Ps.-RISH. *Chronicon de duobus bellis* (1264–5) [attrib. RISH.], in *Chr. Mon. S. Alb.* VII 491–565.

P. SUTTON Peter of Sutton, O.F.M. [*fl.* 1310]: **QD** *Quaestiones disputatae* [attrib.], Franciscan Studies XXIV (1964) 103–43; **Quodl.** *Quodlibeta* [attrib.], *ib.* XXIII (1963) 72–139; **Univoc.** *Quaestio de univocatione entis Dei et creaturarum*, Collectanea Franciscana III (1933) 8–25.

Pub. Works Public Works in medieval law, Selden Soc. XXXII, XL (1915, 1923).

PULL. Robert Pullen (*alias* Pullus) [*ob. c*1147]: **CM** *Sermo de omnibus humanae vitae necessariis* or *de contemptu mundi*, Gregorianum XXXI (1950) 199–223; **Sent.** *Sententiarum theologicarum libri VIII* (*c*1133), *PL* CLXXXVI (1854) 639–1010.

PURVEY John Purvey [*ob. ? p*1427], *v. Ziz.*

P. VERG. Polydore Vergil [*ob.* 1555]: *Anglicae historiae libri XXVII* (–1538) (Basle, 1556) [by bk. & p.]; **Camd.** Bks. XXIV (XXVI) and XXV (XXVII), ed. D. Hay, Camd. 3rd S. LXXIV (1950) [supersedes ed. 1556 for these 2 bks.]; **Praef.** Preface to GILDAS *EB* (prob. Antwerp, 1525); **Vat. Extr.** from *Anglica Historia*, Vatican MSS I and II, ed D. Hay, Polydore Vergil (Oxford, 1952) 199–207.

Quadr. Reg. Spec. *De quadripartita regis specie* (*a*1400), possibly by John Thorpe, Treasurer of Ireland 1393–4, Camd. 4th S. XVIII (1977) 22–39.

Quaest. Ox. *Quaestiones disputatae*, in *Theol. Ox.* 104–32 (*a*1290), 287–362 (*c*1301).

Quaest. Salern. The Prose Salernitan Questions, an anonymous collection dealing with science and medicine written by an Englishman *c*1200 with an appendix of ten related collections, *Auct. Brit.* V (1979) [by collection & no.].

Qui majora cernitis Poem (*c*1225) addressed to John of Garland, ed. D. Guerri, Studi Literari e Linguistici dedicati al Pio Rajna (Milan, 1911).

Quon. Attach. *Quoniam attachiamenta, sive leges Baronum* (? 14c.), ed. J. Skene, in *RegiamM* I 105–31; also Stair Soc. XI (1947) 305–81 [by cap.; preferred to text in *APScot* I app. II 283–95].

Rara Math. *Rara Mathematica*, ed. J. O. Halliwell (1839).

R. BASEVORN Robert de Basevorn [fl. 1320]: **Praedic.** *Forma praedicandi*, ed. T. M. Charland, *Artes Praedicandi*, Publications de l'Institut d'études médiévales d'Ottawa VIII (1936) 233–323 [by cap.].

R. BATTLE Ralph, Prior of Rochester and Abbot of Battle [*c*1040–1124]: **Octo** *De octo a monachis observandis*, *Studia monastica* XI (1969) 26–9.

RBExch The Red Book of the Exchequer (12c.–16c.), 3 vols. (–445, –806, –1081) RS XCIX (1896).

RB Heref. The Red Book of the Hereford bishopric estates (13c.), Camd. Misc. XV, Camd. 3rd S. XLI (1929).

RB Kildare The Red Book of the Earls of Kildare (1185–1519), ed. G. Mac Niocaill, IMC (Dublin, 1964).

R. BOCKING Ric. Cic. Ralph Bocking [*ob.* 1270]: Life of St. Richard of Wych, Bishop of Chichester [*ob.* 1253], *Acta SS. Boll.* Apr. I (1675) 282–318 [by bk. & cap.].

RB Ormond The Red Book of Ormond (*c*1197–*c*1547), ed. N. B. White, IMC (Dublin, 1932).

RB Ossory The Red Book of Ossory (14c.–16c.) (extr.), ed. W. Carrigan, History of the Diocese of Ossory (Dublin, 1905) IV 363–93; **HMC** The Red Book of the diocese of Ossory, summarized w. extr., HMC Rep. X app. V (1885) 219–56, *cf. ib.* app. VII, VIII; *v. et.* LEDREDE.

R. BROMWICH Sent. Richard of Bromwich, O.S.B. [*fl.* 1300]: Commentary on the Sentences (extr.), RTAM V (1933) 206–17.

R. BURY Richard of Bury (*alias* d'Aungerville), Bishop of Durham [1281–1345]: **Ep.** *Liber Epistolaris*, ed. N. Denholm-Young, Roxb. Club (1950); (extr.) also in *FormOx* I 1–79; **Phil.** *Philobiblon*, ed. E. C. Thomas (1888) [by cap. & sect.]; also ed. A. Altamura (Naples, 1954); **Reg.** *Registrum*, v. *Reg. Durh.*

RB Worc. The Red Book of Worcester, surveys of Bishops' Manors (chiefly 12c.–13c.), ed. M. Hollings, 4 parts, Worcs. Hist. Soc. (1934–50).

R. CANT. Reginald of Canterbury [*fl.* 1112]: **Malch.** *Vita S. Malchi*, ed. L. R. Lind (Urbana, Ill., 1942) [by bk. & line]; **Poems** Poems, ed. F. Liebermann, Neues Archiv XX (1888) 521–56 [by no. & line]; further poems in *Sat. Poets* II 259–67 [by p.], and *Anal. Hymn.* L (1907) 370–87 [by no. (287–98) & stanza].

RChart *Rotuli chartarum* 1199–1216, RC (1837); *v. et. ChartR, CalCh.*

R. COLD. Reginald of Coldingham [*ob. c*1173]: **Cuthb.** *Libellus de admirandis B. Cuthberti* [*ob.* 687] *virtutibus*, Surtees Soc. I (1835) [by cap.]; **Godr.** *De vita et miraculis S. Godrici, heremitae de Finchale* [*ob.* 1170], Surtees Soc. XX (1847) [by sect.]; **Osw.** *Vita S. Oswaldi regis et martyris* [*ob.* 642] (wr. 1165), in *S. Durh.* I app. III 326–85 [by cap.; incomplete].

RCoron Coroners' Rolls (Hen. III–Hen. VI), MS PRO (J.I. 2).

RCoron Lond. Coroners' Rolls, MS Corporation of London RO, calendared (1913).

R. COURÇON Robert de Courçon [*ob.* 1219]: **Summa** *Summa* (extr.), in *N. & E.* XXXI (1884) 261–74; **cap.** capitula, Med. Stud. IX (1947) 83–107; **Us.** *De usura* (extr.), ed. G. Lefèvre (Lille, 1902).

RC Record Commission publications (1802–52); **Rep.** Reports and proceedings, various, I–IX (1719–1839).

R. DE MONTE *v.* TORIGNI.

R. DE MORINS *v. Ann. Dunstable*, RIC. ANGL.

R. D'ESCURES Ralph d'Escures, Archb. of Canterbury [*ob.* 1122]: **Ep.** *Epistola de causis ecclesiae Eboracensis*, in *Hist. Church York* II 228–51; **Serm.** *Sermo*, *PL* CLVIII 644–9.

R. DE TEMPLO *v. Itin. Ric.*

RDomin *Rotuli de dominabus* (1185), Pipe R. Soc. XXXV (1913).

R. DYMMOK Roger Dymmok [*ob. ? c*1418]: *Liber contra XII errores et hereses Lollardorum* (? 1395), Wycl. Soc. (1923).

Rec. Aberdeen Early records of the burgh of Aberdeen (1317–1407), ed. W. C. Dickinson, SHS 3rd S. LXIX (1957).

Rec. Barts. Records of St. Bartholomew's, Smithfield [London] (12c.-), ed. E. A. Webb (Oxford, 1921); *v. et.* J. MIRFIELD.

Rec. Burford Manuscripts of the extinct corporation of Burford, Oxfordshire (1350-), HMC Var. Coll. I (1901) 29–64.

Rec. Caern. The Record of Caernarvon (1258–16c.), ed. H. Ellis, RC (1838).

Rec. Coronation English Coronation Records (9c.-), ed. L. G. W. Legg (1901); *v. et. Lib. Regal.*

Rec. Crondal Records relating to the hundred and manors

of Crondal [Hants] (*c*880–17c.), pt. 1 Historical and manorial, Hants Rec. Soc. (1891).

Rec. Edinb. Extracts from the Records of the Burgh of Edinburgh, 1403–1571, 3 vols. Scottish Burgh Rec. Soc. (1869–75).

Receipt Exch A. Steel: The Receipt of the Exchequer, 1377–1485 (Cambridge, 1954).

ReceiptR Enrolments and registers of receipts, Receipt Rolls, MS PRO (E. 401).

Rec. Elton Elton [Hunts & Northants] manorial Records 1279–1351, Roxb. Club (1946).

Rec. Eton Calendar of Eton College Records (12c.-), ed. N. Blakiston, I– (1939–) [TS copy at PRO; by vol. & no.].

Rec. Gild Camb. Cambridge Gild Records (14c.), Cambridge Antiq. Soc. 8° S. XXXIX (1903).

Rec. Leic. Records of the Borough of Leicester (1103–1835), ed. M. Bateson *et al.*, I–VI (London, 1899–1901; Cambridge, 1905–23, Leicester, 1965–7); NS I–II (1196–1930) (Leicester, 1927–33).

Rec. Lewes Records of the Rape of Lewes (1265–15c.), Sussex Rec. Soc. XLIV (Lewes, 1939).

Rec. Lincoln's Inn Records of Lincoln's Inn (1420–), ed. W. P. Baildon *et al.*, 7 vols. (1896–1968).

Rec. Lostwithiel Records of the Corporation of Lostwithiel [Cornw] (1190–), HMC Var. Coll. I (1901) 327–37.

Rec. Merton Records of Merton Priory [Surrey] (1114–1539), ed. A. Heales (1898).

Rec. Norw. Records of the City of Norwich (1086–), ed. W. Hudson and J. C. Tingey, 2 vols. (Norwich, 1906–10).

Rec. Nott. Records of the borough of Nottingham (1155–), ed. J. Raine *et al.*, 9 vols. (London & Nottingham, 1882–1956).

RecogR Chester v. Enr. Chester.

Rec. Prescot Selection from Prescot court leet and other Records (1447–1600), Lancs & Chesh Rec. Soc. LXXXIX (1937).

Rec. Reading Records of the Borough of Reading (1431–1654), ed. J. M. Guilding, 4 vols. (London, 1892–6).

Rec. Scot. Documents and Records illustrating the history of Scotland (1236–1306), ed. F. Palgrave, RC (1837).

Rec. Soc. & Econ. Records of the social and economic history of England and Wales, 9 vols. British Academy (1914–35); new series, I– British Academy (1972–).

Rec. Stan. Records relating to the Stannaries of Cornwall (*c*1197–), ed. E. Smirke, The Case of Vice against Thomas, (1843), appendix [sep. pag.].

Rect. Adderbury Adderbury *rectoria* (14c.–15c.), Oxfordshire Rec. Soc. VIII (1926).

Rec. Templars Records of the Templars in England: inquest (1185) 1–135, charters etc. 137–236, Rec. Soc. & Econ. IX (1935).

RecusantR Exchequer, Recusant Rolls (1592–), MS PRO (E. 376, E. 377); (extr.) Cath. Rec. Soc. XVIII, LVII, LXI.

Rec. Wardr. Records of the Wardrobe and Household, 1285–6, ed. B. F. & C. R. Byerley, HMSO (1977) [by no.].

REDMAN Hen. V Robert Redman [*ob.* 1540]: *Henrici quinti illustrissimi Anglorum regis historia* (1413–22) (wr. *a*1540), in *Mem. Hen. V* 1–59.

Reg. Aberbr. *Registrum Abbatiae de Aberbrothoc* [Arbroath, Angus] (1178–1536), 2 vols. Bannatyne Club (1846–56).

Reg. Aberd. *Registrum episcopatus Aberdonensis* (12c.–), 2 vols. Spalding Club XIII, XIV (1845).

Reg. All Saints Dublin *Registrum ecclesiae Omnium Sanctorum juxta Dublin* (12c.–15c.), ed. R. Butler (Dublin, 1845).

Reg. Ant. Linc. *Registrum antiquissimum* of the Cathedral Church of Lincoln (1061–), Linc. Rec. Soc. XXVII, XXVIII, XXIX, XXXII, XXXIV, XLI, XLVI, LI, LXII, LXVII, LXVIII (1931–73).

Reg. Armagh Registers of the Archbishops of Armagh: 1418–39 John Swayne, w. some earlier and later entries, HMSO (Belfast, 1935); 1443–56 John Mey, HMSO (Belfast, 1972).

Reg. Bath Registers of the Bishops of Bath and Wells: 1407–24 Nicholas Bubwith, Som Rec. Soc. XXIX, XXX (1914); 1425–43 John Stafford, *ib.* XXXI, XXXII (1915, 1916) [by date, vol., & p.].

Reg. Black Pr. Register of Edward the Black Prince (1346–8, 1351–65), 4 vols. HMSO (1930–3).

Reg. Brechin *Registrum Episcopatus Brechinensis* [Brechin, Angus] (1165–), 2 vols. Bannatyne Club (1856).

Reg. Brev. *Registrum brevium tam originalium quam judicialium* (mainly 15c.), 4th ed. (1687): **Orig.** pt. 1 (*Originalia*) 1–321 [by f.]; **Jud.** pt. 2 (*Judicialia*) 1–85 [by f.].

Reg. Burgh Aberd. Extracts from the council register of the Burgh of Aberdeen (1398–1625), 2 vols. Spalding Club XII, XIX (Aberdeen, 1844–8).

Reg. Butley The Register or chronicle of Butley Priory, Suffolk (1510–35), ed. A. G. Dickens (Winchester, 1951).

Reg. Cant. Registers of the Archbishops of Canterbury, Cant. & York Soc. (1928–): 1207–28 Stephen Langton, L (1950), *v. Act. Cant.* [*v. et.* S. LANGTON]; 1279–92 John Peckham, LXIV, LXV (1968–9) [*v. et.* PECKHAM]; 1294–1313 Robert Winchelsea, LI, LII (1956) [*v. et.* WINCHELSEA]; 1366–8 Simon de Langham, LIII (1956); 1414–43 Henry Chichele, XLII, XLV–XLVII (1937–47); 1454–86 Thomas Bourchier, LIV (1957); 1559–75 Matthew Parker, XXXV, XXXVI, XXXIX (1928–33) [by date, vol., & p.].

Reg. Carl. Registers of the Bishops of Carlisle, Cant. & York Soc. (1913–): 1292–1324 John de Halton, XII, XIII (1913) [by date, vol., & p.].

Reg. Clogher Fragments of a lost register of the diocese of Clogher (wr. 1525), Arch. Soc. Louth IV (Dundalk, 1920) 226–7.

Reg. Coll. Exon. *Registrum Collegii Exoniensis* [Oxford] (1314–), OHS XXVII (1894).

Reg. Congreg. Registers of Congregation, University of Oxford: 1448–63 Register Aa, OHS NS XXII (1970); others MS University Archives.

Reg. Dunferm. *Liber cartarum abbatiae de Dunfermelyn* [Fife] (12c.-), Bannatyne Club (1842) [by no.].

Reg. Durh. *Registrum Palatinum Dunelmense*: 1311–16 Richard de Kellawe, 4 vols. RS LXII (1873–8); 1333–45 Richard d'Aungerville of Bury (extr.), Surtees Soc. CXIX (1910) 10–64 [*v. et.* R. BURY]; 1406–37 Thomas Langley, *ib.* CLXIV, CLXVI, CLXIX, CLXX, CLXXVII, CLXXXII (1956–70) [*v. et. Langley*]; 1494–1501 Richard Fox, *ib.* CXLVII (1932); 1530–59 Cuthbert Tunstall, *ib.* CLXI (1952) 1–131; 1561–76 James Pilkington, *ib.* 140–82 [by date, vol., & p.].

Reg. Ebor. Registers of the Archbishops of York: 1215–55 Walter Gray, Surtees Soc. LVI (1872) [1215–24 are missing]; 1266–79 Walter Giffard, *ib.* CIX (1904); 1279–85 William Wickwane, *ib.* CXIV (1907); 1286–96 John le Romeyn, *ib.* CXXIII, *ib.* CXXVIII 1–203 (1913, 1916); 1296–9 Henry of Newark, *ib.* CXXVIII 205–35; 1300–4 Thomas of Corbridge, *ib.* CXXXVIII, *ib.* CXLI (1925, 1928); 1305–6 John of Cracumbe, vicar-general, *ib.* CXLV (1931) 1–2; 1306–15 William Greenfield, *ib.* CXLV 3–288, CXLIX, CLI, CLII, CLV (1931–8) [by date, vol., & p.]; 1317–40 William Melton, Cant. & York Soc. LXX, LXXI (1977–8).

Regesta PR *Regesta Pontificum Romanorum* (1198–1304), ed. A. Potthast, 2 vols. (Berlin, 1874–5) [by no.].

Regesta *Regesta Regum Anglo-Normannorum*, ed. H. W. C. Davis *et al.*, 4 vols. (Oxford, 1913–69): I (1066–1100);

II (1100–35); III (1135–54); IV (facsimiles, 1135–54) [by date & no. (or p. of appendix)].

Regesta Scot. *Regesta Regum Scottorum*, ed. G. W. S. Barrow, 2 vols. (Edinburgh, 1960–71): I (1153–65, w. earlier docs. not incl. in *E. Ch. Scot.*); II (1165–1214) [by no.].

Reg. Ewell Register or memorial of Ewell [Surrey] (wr. 1408) w. notes on priors of Merton, ed. C. Deeds (1913) 1–135, w. undated custumal 135–8 and other 15c. docs.

Reg. Exon. Registers of the Bishops of Exeter, ed. F. C. Hingeston-Randolph, 10 vols. (1889–1915): 1138–55 Robert Chichester, I (1889) 2; 1194–1206 Henry Marshall, I 2; 1214–23 Simon de Apulia, I 2–4; 1224–44 William Briwere, I 5–7; 1245–57 Richard Blondy, I 7 [these five are frags.]; 1258–80 Walter Bronescombe, I 8–305; 1280–91 Peter Quivil, I 309–95; 1292–1307 Thomas de Bytton, *ib.* 399–437; 1307–26 Walter de Stapeldon, II (1892); 1327 James de Berkeley, III (1894) 1–33; 1327–69 John de Grandisson, III 37–603, IV, V (1894–9); 1370–94 Thomas de Brantynham, VI, VII, (1901–6); 1395–1419 Edmund Stafford, VIII (1886); 1420–55 Edmund Lacy [*v. et. Reg. Heref.*], IX, X (1909–15) [this last vol. superseded and cont. by Devon & Cornw Rec. Soc. pubs. NS VII, X, XIII, XVI, XVIII (1963–72), = Cant. & York Soc. LX–LXIII, LXVI (1963–72)].

Reg. Gasc. A *Gascon Register A* (1318–19), ed. G. P. Cuttino, 3 vols. (London, 1975–6).

Reg. Glasg. *Registrum Episcopatus Glasguensis* (12c.-), 2 vols. Bannatyne Club (1843).

Reg. Godstow The English Register of Godstow nunnery, near Oxford [mainly Eng. transl. (c1450) of Latin docs.], EETS CXXIX, CXXX, CXLII (1911); *v. et. Vis. Godstow.*

Reg. Heref. Registers of the Bishops of Hereford, Cant. & York Soc.: 1275–82 Thomas de Cantilupo, II (1907); 1283–1317 Richard de Swinfield, VI (1909); 1317–27 Adam de Orleton, V (1908); 1327–44 Thomas de Charlton, IX (1913); 1344–61 John de Trillek, VIII (1912); 1361–70 Lewis de Charltone, XIV (1914); 1370–5 William de Courtenay, XV (1914); 1375–89 John Gilbert, XVIII (1915); 1389–1404 John Trefnant, XX (1916); 1404–16 Robert Mascall, XXI (1917); 1417–20 Edmund Lacy, XXII (1918) 1–128 [*v. et. Reg. Exon.*]; 1420–2 Thomas Poltone, *ib.* [sep. pag.] 1–25; 1422–48 Thomas Spofford, XXIII (1919); 1449–50 Richard Beauchamp, XXV (1919) 1–17; 1451–3 Reginald Boulers, *ib.* [sep. pag.] 1–26; 1453–74 John Stanbury, *ib.* [sep. pag.] 1–203; 1474–92 Thomas Myllyng, XXVI (1920); 1504–16 Richard Mayew, XXVII (1921); 1516–35 Charles Bothe, XXVIII (1921) 1–360; 1535–8 Edward Foxe (extr.), *ib.* 361–80; 1538–9 Hugh Coren (extr.), *ib.* 381–2; 1539 Edmund Boner (extr.), *ib.* 383–5 [all by date, vol., & p.]; index vol. 1275–1535 (Hereford, 1925).

Reg. Holm Cultram Register and records of Holm Cultram [Cumb] (12c.-), Cumb & Westmor Antiq. Soc., Rec. S. VII (1929).

Reg. Hosp. S. John Register of the Hospital of St. John the Baptist, Dublin (c1190–16c.), ed. E. St. J. Brooks, IMC (1936) [by no.].

RegiamM *Regiam Majestatem* (14c.), ed. J. Skene, 2 vols. (Edinburgh, 1609), I ff. 8–104v. [by bk. & cap.; other texts cited by vol. & f.]; also in Stair Soc. XI (1947) 280–304 [by bk. & cap.; preferred to text in *APScot* I app. 1 231–77].

Regim. Princ. *Tractatus de regimine principum ad regem Henricum VI* (1436–7), Camd. 4th S. XVIII (1977) 40–173.

Reg. Kilmainham *Registrum de Kilmainham*: Register of the chapter acts of the Hospital of St. John of Jerusalem in Ireland (1326–39), ed. C. McNeill, IMC (1932).

Reg. Linc. Rolls and Registers of the Bishops of Lincoln, Lincoln Rec. Soc.: 1209–35 Hugh de Welles, III, VI, IX

(1912–14); 1235–53 Robert Grosseteste, XI (1914) 1–507 [*v. et.* GROS.]; 1254–8 Henry de Lexington, *ib.* 509–14; 1258–79 Richard Gravesend, XX (1925) [all the above vols. also Cant. & York Soc. I (1909), III (1907), IV (1908), X (1913), XXXI (1925)]; 1280–99 Oliver Sutton, XXXIX, XLIII, XLVIII, LII, LX, LXIV– (1948–); 1405–19 Philip Repingdon, LVII, LVIII (1963) [by date, vol., & p.; some MS refs. by f.].

Reg. Lond. Registers of the Bishops of London, Cant. & York Soc.: 1304–13 Ralph Baldock, VII (1911) 1–168 and 174–6; 1313–16 Gilbert Segrace, *ib.* 169–73; 1317–18 Richard Newport, *ib.* 177–94; 1318–38 Stephen de Gravesend, *ib.* 195–320; 1362–75 Simon de Sudbury, XXXIV, XXXVIII (1927, 1938) [by date, vol., & p.].

Reg. Magdalen A Register of members of St. Mary Magdalen College, Oxford, 1st S. 8 vols. (1853–85); 2nd S. 8 vols. (15c.-) (1894–1915).

Reg. Malm. *Registrum Malmesburiense* (c685–14c.), 2 vols. RS LXXII (1879–80).

Reg. Merton *Registrum annalium Collegi Mertonensis* [Oxford] 1483–1603, OHS LXXVI, NS XXIII, XXIV (1921–76).

Reg. Moray *Registrum episcopatus Moraviensis* (1160–), Bannatyne Club (1837).

Reg. Newbattle *Registrum S. Marie de Neubotle* [Midloth] (1140–), Bannatyne Club (1849) [by no.].

Reg. North. Historical papers and letters from the Northern Registers (1265–1413), RS LXI (1873).

Reg. Paisley *Registrum monasterii de Passelet* [Renf] (1163–1529), Maitland Club (1832).

Reg. Pinchbeck Walter Pinchbeck [*fl.* c1333]: Pinchbeck Register of the Abbey of Bury St. Edmunds (1286–7), ed. Lord F. Harvey, 2 vols. (Brighton, 1925) [by f.].

Reg. Plympton Register of Plympton Priory [Devon] (10c.–13c.), MS Bodl. James 23 (18c) 151–70 [by p. of MS].

Reg. Pri. Worc. *Registrum Prioratus B. Mariae Wigorniensis* (1235–c1285), Camd. Soc. XCI (1865).

Reg. Richm. *Registrum Honoris de Richmond* [Yorks] etc. (1087–), app. w. sep. pag., ed. R. Gale (1722).

Reg. Roff. Cap. Capitular Register of Rochester Cathedral (1142–8), MS BL Cotton Domitian A x.

Reg. Roff. Ep. Registers of the Bishops of Rochester, Cant. & York Soc.: 1319–52 Hamo de Hethe [*alias* Hythe] (incl. 12c. and 13c. charters), XLVIII, XLIX (1948) [by f.].

Reg. Roff. *Registrum Roffense*, records of the Diocese and Cathedral Church of Rochester (600–17c.), ed. J. Thorpe (1769).

Reg. Rough Register of Daniel Rough, common clerk of Romney, 1353–80, Arch. Soc. Kent, Kent Recs. XVI (1945).

Reg. Sal. Registers of the Bishops of Salisbury, Cant. & York Soc.: 1297–1315 Symon de Gandavo, XL, XLI (1934) [*v. et.* S. GAUNT]; 1315–30 Roger Martival, LV, LVI, LVII, LVIII, LIX (1959–72) [by date, vol., & p.].

Reg. S. Andr. *Liber cartarum Prioratus S. Andree* [Fife] (12c.–15c.), Bannatyne Club (1841) [by f.].

Reg. S. Aug. Register of St. Augustine's Abbey, Canterbury, ed. G. J. Turner and H. E. Salter, 2 vols. Rec. Soc. & Econ. II, III (1915–24).

Reg. S. Bees Register of the Priory of St. Bees [Cumb] (early 12c.), Surtees Soc. CXXVI (1915).

Reg. S. Ben. Holme Register of the Abbey of St. Benet of Holme [*alias* Hulme] 1020–1210, Rec. Soc. Norf II, III (1932).

Reg. S. Osm. *Vetus registrum Sarisberiense alias dictum registrum S. Osmundi Episcopi* (10c.–13c.), 2 vols. RS LXXVIII (1883–4); *v. et. Offic. Sal.*

Reg. S. Paul. *Registrum statutorum et consuetudinum Ecclesiae Cathedralis S. Pauli Londinensis* (674–19c.), ed. W. Sparrow Simpson (1873).

Reg. S. Thom. Dublin Register of the Abbey of St. Thomas, Dublin (12c.-), RS XCIV (1889) [by no.].

Reg. Stoneleigh Leger Book or Register of Stoneleigh Abbey [Warw] (12c.–14c.), Dugdale Soc. XXIV (1960).

Reg. Temp. *Registrum temporalium* (14c.), MS Kent RO (DRcR3 Rochester).

Reg. Tristernagh Register of the Priory at Tristernagh [Westmeath] (13c.), ed. M. V. Clarke, IMC (Dublin, 1941).

RegulC *Regularis concordia Anglicae nationis monachorum sanctimonialiumque* (c970) [attrib. Æthelwold] (*ob.* 984)], ed. T. Symons, Med. Texts (1953) [by sect.]; AS cited from *De consuetudine monachorum* (Lat. & AS), *Anglia* XIII (1891) 365–454.

Regul. Recl. *Regulae reclusorum*, ed. L. Oliger, *Antonianum* III (1928) 151–90, 299–320: I *Ordo anachoritalis vitae* (13c.), 170–83; II *Regula eremitarum* (14c.), 299–312; III *Regula eremitarum Oxoniensis* (14c.), 312–30 [by no. & sect.]; v. et. ROB. PRESB.

Reg. Wetherhal Register of the priory of Wetherhal [Cumb], Cumb & Westmor Antiq. Soc. (1897).

Reg. Whet. *Registrum Johannis Whethamstede* [Abbot of St. Albans] (1420–40, 1451–65), in *Chr. Mon. S. Alb.* VI 2 vols. (1872–3).

Reg. Winchcombe *Landboc sive registrum monasterii de Winchelcumba* [Glos] (798–1422), ed. D. Royce, 2 vols. (Exeter, 1892–1903).

Reg. Wint. Registers of the Bishops of Winchester, Cant. & York Soc. and Hants Rec. Soc.: 1282–1304 John de Pontissara, XIX, XXX (1915–24) [also pub. Surrey Rec. Soc. I, VI (1916–24)]; 1305–16 Henry Woodlock, XLIII, XLIV (1940–1); 1316–19 John de Sandale, Hants Rec. Soc. (1897) 3–264; 1320–3 Rigaud de Asserio, *ib.* 387–606; 1346–66 William Edington, MS Hants RO [by vol. & f.]; 1367–1404 William de Wykeham, 2 vols. Hants Rec. Soc. (1896–9); 1520–30 Thomas Wolsey, Cant. & York Soc. XXXII (1926); 1531–2, 1553–5 Stephen Gardiner, *ib.* XXXVII (1930) 1–91 [*v. et.* GARDINER]; 1551–3 John Poynet, *ib.* 93–103; 1556–9 John Whyte, *ib.* XVI (1914) [by date, vol., & p.].

Reign of Hen. VII A. F. Pollard: The Reign of Henry VII, 3 vols. (1913–14).

Reliq. Antiq. *Reliquiae Antiquae*, scraps from ancient MSS, ed. T. Wright and J. O. Halliwell, 2 vols. (1841–3).

Remonstr. Ir. Remonstrance of Domnall O Neill, king of Ulster, and others to Pope John XXII (1318), ed. T. Hearne, *Scotichronicon*, 5 vols. (Oxford, 1722) III 908–26; also in FORDUN *Cont.* II 259–67.

Rent. Glasg. Rental book of the diocese of Glasgow (1509–70) [bound w. *Lib. prot.*], 2 vols. Grampian Club (1875).

Rent. Glouc. Rental of all the houses in Gloucester (1455), ed. R. Cole (Gloucester, 1890).

Rent. Ottery St. M. Rental of Ottery St. Mary [Devon] (? 14c.), MS BL Add. 28838.

Rent. Pri. Nuneaton Nuneaton Priory Rental, MS BL Add. 49466.

Rent. S. Andr. *Rentale S. Andreae*, Chamberlain and Granitar accounts of the Archbishopric (1538–46), SHS, 2nd S. IV (1913).

RentSurv. Rentals and Surveys (Hen. III–), MS PRO: **P** Portfolios (S.C. 12); **R** Rolls (S.C. 11).

Rep. PR Ir. Reports respecting the Public Records of Ireland (1810–25), 3 vols. RC (1815–29).

R. ESK Richard of Esk, monk of Furness [15c.]: Metrical preface, in *Couch. Furness* I 21–3; superseded by Cumb & Westmor Antiq. Soc. NS LIII (1954) 98–109 [by line].

Responsio *Responsio discipuli* (a994), *ASE* I (1972) 122–6 [by line].

Rev. Ben. Revue bénédictine, I– (1884–).

Rev. Downside Downside Review, I– (1880–).

RFin Fine Rolls, ed. T. D. Hardy, *Rotuli de Oblatis et Finibus* (1199–1216), RC (1835) 197–605; *v. et. CalFinR, ExcRFin, FineR, ROblat.*

RGasc Roles Gascons: 1242–1307, 3 vols. in 4 (Paris,

1885–1906) [by p.]; IV (1307–17), HMSO (1962) [by no.]; later rolls, MS PRO (C. 61).

R. HOWD. Roger Howden (*alias* Hovedene) [*ob.* ? 1201]: *Chronica* (732–1201), 4 vols. RS LI (1868–71).

RHS Royal Historical Society; **Trans.** Transactions, I– (1873–).

RHYG. Rhygyfarch [*ob.* 1099]: **David** *Vita S. Davidis* [6c.], ed. J. W. James (Cardiff, 1967), 1–28 [first text; by cap.]; **Vesp.** additional text in MS BL Cotton Vespasian A XIV (c1200), ibid. [second text; by cap.].

RIA Proc. Proceedings of the Royal Irish Academy, I– (Dublin, 1841–), section C.

RIC. ANGL. Ricardus Anglicus [? Richard de Morins, Prior of Dunstable (*ob.* 1242)]: **Summa** *Summa de ordine judiciario* (c1196), ed. L. Wahrmund, Quellen zur Gesch. des römisch-kanonischen Processes im Mittelalter, II iii (Innsbruck, 1915) [by cap.]; **Summa Brevis** *Summa brevis super decreta* (extr.), *Traditio* VII (1949–51) 353–5; **Summa Quaest.** *Summa quaestionum* (extr.), *ib.* 355–8.

RIC. ARMAGH Richard Fitzralph, Archb. of Armagh [*ob.* 1360]: **AP** Autobiographical prayer (= *Summa contra Armenos* XIX 35), ed. L. L. Hammerich, The beginning of the strife between Richard Fitzralph and the Mendicants (Copenhagen, 1938) 18–22; **Def. Cur.** *Defensio curatorum*, in *Monarchia* II 1391–1410 (*recte* 1291–1310) [by p. as printed & *recte*]; **Paup. Salv.** *De pauperie salvatoris* I–IV, in WYCL. *Dom. Div.* 129–476 [by bk. & p.; rest unprinted]; **Sent.** Commentary on the Sentences (extr.), JRL Bull. XLV (1963) 390–422; also in G. Leff, Richard Fitzralph, Commentator of the Sentences (Manchester, 1963); **Serm.** *Sermones* (extr.), ed. Hammerich 30–42; **Summa** *Summa contra Armenos* (Paris, 1512); **Unusq.** The proposition *Unusquisque*, ed. Hammerich 53–84.

RIC. CORNW. Richard Rufus of Cornwall, O.F.M. [*fl.* 1235–59]: **Quaest.** *Quaestio utrum Christus in triduo mortis fuerit homo* (*Sent.* III d. 22), RTAM XVI (1949) 275–80; **Opin.** *Opiniones notatae in libros Sententiarum*, Franciscan Studies XXXV (1975) 149–93 [by bk. & no.]; **Sent.** *Commentarius in Sententias* (extr.): I d. 2, Franziskanische Studien XXXVIII (1956) 187–202; II d. 17, Revue néoscolastique de philosophie XLII (1939) 439–45.

RIC. ELY Etheldr. Richard, Prior of Ely [*ob.* c1194]: *Analecta S. Etheldredae*, Acta SS. Boll. June IV 577–82; *v. et. Lib. Eli.*, T. ELY.

RICHARD KNAPWELL (*alias* CLAPWELL), *v.* KNAPWELL.

RIC. HEX. Richard, Prior of Hexham [*ob.* p1154]: **Hist. Hex.** History of the church of Hexham (c674–c1114), Surtees Soc. XLIV (1864) 1–62 [by bk. & cap.]; **Stand.** *De gestis Regis Stephani et de bello standardii* [sic] (1135–8), in *Chr. Steph.* III 139–78 [by f.]; also in Surtees Soc. XLIV 63–106.

RIC. MED. Ricardus Medicus (*alias* Anglicus) [*ob.* 1252]: **Anat.** *Anatomia* (= *Micrologus* III) (a1200), ed. K. Sudhoff, Archiv für Gesch. der Medizin XIX (Leipzig, 1927) 209–39 [*cf.* Ps.-RIC. *Anat.*]; **Correct.** v. *Correct. Alch.*; **Pract.** *Practica* (= *Micrologus* IV), ed. H. Hellriegel (Leipzig, 1934); **Signa** *Signa pronostica infirmitatum* (= *Micrologus* V), earlier part ed. H. E. Beusing, Leben und Werks des Ricardus Anglicus (Leipzig, 1922).

RIC. SWYN. Richard Swyneshed, fellow of Merton (*alias* the Calculator) [*ob.* p1354]: **Calc.** *Calculationes* (c1350) (Padua, 1477, etc.); also (extr.) in *Sci. Mech.* 298–304; **Mot.** *De motu* [attrib.], in *Sci. Mech.* 245–6.

RIDEWALL John Ridewall, O.F.M. [*fl.* 1340]: **Apoc.** *Lectura in Apocalypsim* (c1330) (extr.), in *Eng. Friars* app. I 312–14; **CivD** Commentary on *De Civitate Dei* (c1334) (extr.), *Medium Ævum* XXV (1957) 140–53; **Fulg.** *Fulgentius metaforalis*, ed. H. Liebeschütz (Leipzig, 1926).

RINGSTEAD Prov. Thomas Ringstead [*ob.* 1366]: *In*

Proverbia Salomonis (Paris, 1515, under name of HOLCOT or T. WALEYS).

RIPLEY George Ripley [*ob.* 1490]: *Opera omnia chemica* (Cassell, 1649): 1–100 *Liber XII portarum*; 101–122 *Liber de mercurio et lapide philosophorum*; 123–78 *Medulla philosophiae chemicae*; 179–224 *Philorcium alchymistarum*; 226–94 *Clavis aureae portae* [transl. from Eng.; not cited]; 295–313 *Pupilla alchemiae*; 314–22 *Terra terrae philosophicae*; 323–36 *Concordantia Raymondi Lullii et Guidonis philosophi Graeci*; 337–65 *Viaticum seu Varia practica*; 366–420 *Accurtationes et practicae Raymundinae*; 421–6 *Cantilena*; 427–39 *Epistola ad regem Edwardum quartum* [transl. from Eng.; not cited]; **Axiom.** *Axiomata philosophica*, in *Theatrum Chem.* II 109–118 [summary of *Liber XII portarum*].

RISH. William of Rishanger [*ob.* p1312]: *Chronica* (1259–1307), in *Chr. Mon. S. Alb.* II 1–230.

Rit. Durh. *Rituale ecclesiae Dunelmensis* (10c., gl. 970 or 981), Surtees Soc. X (1839); superseded by Surtees Soc. CXL (1927).

Rit. Gilb. *Gilbertine Rite* (a1265), HBS LIX, LX (1921–2).

R. LEWES *v.* G. Steph.

RL *Royal Letters* 1216–72, 2 vols. RS XXVII (1862–6); 1399–1413, 2 vols. RS XVIII (1860–64, rev. ed. 1965).

R. MAIDSTONE Richard of Maydistone [*ob.* 1396]: **Conc.** *De concordia inter regem Ricardum II et civitatem Londoniensem* (1393), in *Pol. Poems* I 282–300; **PP** *Protectorium pauperis* (c1380), *Carmelus* V (1958) 132–80 [by f.].

R. MARSTON Roger Marston, O.F.M. [*ob.* c1300]: **QD** *Quaestiones disputatae*, *Bibliotheca Franciscana scholastica medii aevi* VII (Quaracchi, 1932): 1–148 *De emanatione aeterna quaestiones VII*; 149–200 *De statu naturae lapsae quaestiones II*; 201–454 *De anima quaestiones X*.

R. MELROSE *v.* Ep. Glasg.

R. MELUN Robert of Melun, Bishop of Hereford [*ob.* 1167]: **DP** *Quaestiones de divina pagina*, ed. R. M. Martin, *Spicilegium Sacrum Lovaniense* XIII (1932) [by sect.]; **Paul.** *Quaestiones theologicae de epistolis Pauli*, *ib.* XVIII (1938); **Sent.** *Sententiae*, *ib.* XXI (1947), XXV (1952) [by vol. & p.]; **Summa** *Summa theologiae* or *Sententiarum* (extr.), *PL* CLXXXVI 1011–62; superseded by *Sent.*.

R. MERTON Rainald of Merton [12c.]: *Epistola de vita venerabilis Guidonis Meritonensis ecclesiae canonici* (wr. a1151), Med. Stud. XXXI (1969) 255–61 [by f.].

RMS Scot *Registrum magni sigilli regum Scotorum* (1306–1668), 11 vols. Scot. RO (1882–1914, vol. I, 2nd ed. 1912) [by date & no.].

R. NIGER Ralph Niger [*ob.* a1200]: **Chr. I** *Chronicle* [incl. cont.] (Creation–1199), ed. R. Anstruther, Caxton Soc. (1851) 1–104; **Chr. II** (Incarnation–1162, w. cont. to 1178), *ib.* 105–91; **Mil.** *De re militari et triplici via peregrinationis Jerosolimitane*, ed. L. Schmugge (Berlin, 1977) [by bk. & cap.]; **MR** *Moralia regum* (a1189), cap. 19, Med. & R. Stud. I (1943) 249–52; **Vers.** *Verses*, in GERV. TILB. II 3.

RNorm *Rotuli Normanniae* 1200–5, 1417–18, RC (1835); 1203 fragm. of Norman Roll of 5 John, Pipe R. Soc. NS XXI (1943) 87–8.

ROB. ANGL. (I) Robertus Anglicus (*alias* of Chester, Ketene, etc.), translator from Arabic [*fl.* 1140]: **Alch.** *Liber de compositione alchemiae* [attrib.], in *Bibl. Chem.* I 509–19 [recension 3]; also ed. L. Stavenhagen, *A Testament of Alchemy* (Hannover, N.H., 1974) [recension 1]; **Alg.** *Liber restaurationis et oppositionis numeri* [transl. of the Algebra of Al-Khowirasmi (c825)], ed. L. C. Karpinski (Ann Arbor, Mich., 1915); **add.** *addita quaedam pro declaratione Algebrae*, *ib.* 128–56. **Chr. Mend.** *Chronica mendosa et ridiculosa Saracenorum* (Basle, 1550); **Jud.** *Judicia Alkindi* (extr.), EHR XXX (1915) 63; **Koran** Latin version of the Koran, bound w. *Chr. Mend.*

ROB. ANGL. (II) Robertus Anglicus [*fl.* 1270]: Commentary on the Sphere of Sacrobosco, in SACROB. *Sph.* 143–198.

ROB. BACON Psalt. Robert Bacon [*ob.* 1248]: *Tractatus super psalterium* (extr.), in RHS Trans. 4th S. XXX (1948) 1–19.

ROB. BRIDL. Dial. Robert of Bridlington [*fl.* 1150]: The Bridlington Dialogue, Exposition of the Rule of St. Augustine for the life of the clergy, [ed. R. P. Lawson] (London, 1960).

ROBERT GROSSETESTE *v.* GROS.

ROBERT KILWARDBY *v.* KILWARDBY.

ROBERT PULLEN *v.* PULL.

ROBERTSON Rolloc George Robertson: *Vita et mors Ricardi Rolloc* (1599), Bannatyne Club (1826).

ROB. FLAMB. Pen. Robert of Flamborough, canon of S. Victor [*fl.* 1220]: *Liber Poenitentialis* (c1208–15), ed. J. J. F. Frith (Toronto, 1971) [by sect.].

ROblat *Oblata* Rolls, ed. T. D. Hardy, *Rotuli de Oblatis et Finibus* (1199–1216), RC (1835) 1–196; *v. et.* RFin.

ROB. PRESB. Robertus presbyter [? 12c.]: *Admonitiones praesertim de eucharistia*, in *Regul. Recl.* 183–90.

ROBYNS Com. John Robyns [*ob.* 1558]: *De Cometis* (extr.), in *Rara Math.* 48–54.

ROG. FORD Roger of Ford [*fl.* 1170]: **LP** *Lac Parvulorum* [attrib. Roger of Byland], *Anal. Cist.* VII (1951) 224–31 [on authorship, *v. Studia Monastica* XXII (1980) 83–8]; **Maria** *Orbis opes pereant*, verses on the Virgin, *Collectanea Ordinis Cisterciensium Reformatorum* VI (1939) 48–54.

ROG. NOTT. Roger Nottingham, O.F.M. [*fl.* 1343]: **Insol.** *Insolubilia*, Med. Stud. XXVI (1964) 260–70 [by sect.]; **Intr. Sent.** *Introitus ad Sententias*, *ib.* XXV 270–9 [by sect.].

ROG. SWYN. Roger Swynesheld [*fl.* 1330]: **Insol.** *Insolubilia*, AHDLMA XLVI (1979) 180–220 [by sect.]; **Oblig.** *Obligationes*, *ib.* XLIV (1977) 249–85.

ROLLE Richard Rolle of Hampole [*ob.* 1349]: **AM** *Contra amatores mundi*, ed. P. F. Theiner (Berkeley, Calif., & Los Angeles, 1968); **Apoc.** *Tractatus super Apocalypsim*, ed. N. Marzac (Paris, 1968); **IA** *Incendium amoris*, ed. M. Deanesly (Manchester, 1915); **Judic.** *Judica me Deus*, ed. J. P. Daly, Elizabethan and Renaissance Studies XCII:14 (Salzburg, 1984); **MA** *Melos Amoris*, ed. E. J. F. Arnould (Oxford, 1957).

Rolls Merton The early Rolls of Merton College, Oxford (1274–1300), w. app. of charters, OHS, NS XVIII (1964); *v. et.* Ac. Exec. W. Merton.

Romania *Romania* I– (Paris, 1872–).

RomR *Roman Rolls* (1306–58), MS PRO (C. 70).

R. ORFORD Robert of Orford (*alias* de Tortocollo) [*fl.* 1290]: **Reprob.** *Reprobationes dictorum a fratre Aegidio in primum Sententiarum*, Bibliothèque thomiste XXXVIII (1968); **Sciendum** *Correctorium corruptorii 'Sciendum'* [attrib.], *ib.* XXXI (1956).

Rot. Gros. et Lex. v. Reg. Linc.

Roxb. Club Roxburghe Club, publications (1814–).

Royal Writs Royal Writs in England from the Conquest to Glanvill, Selden Soc. LXXVII (1959).

RParl Ir. Parliaments and councils of mediaeval Ireland (1296–1421), ed. H. G. Richardson and G. O. Sayles, I– IMC (Dublin, 1947–).

RParl *Rotuli Parliamentorum* (1278–1552), 7 vols. (1767–83; index I–VI 1832); other rolls MS PRO (C. 65); **Exch** Exchequer S. MS PRO (S.C. 9), nos. 3, 4, 14, 21, and 22 printed in *DocExch* 55–82, 129–38, 1–54, no. 8 in *RParl Ined.* 30–45, no. 12 in *Mem. Parl.* 1–188, 232–314; **Ined.** *Rotuli parliamentorum Anglie hactenus inediti* (1279–1373), Camd. 3rd. S. LI (1935).

R. PARTES Robert Partes [*ob.* 1172]: Poems, *Speculum* XII (1937) 215–50 [by p.].

RR K's Lynn Red Registers of King's Lynn [Norf]

(c1307–c1395), ed. H. Ingleby, 2 vols. (King's Lynn, 1919–22).

RScacNorm *Magni rotuli scaccarii Normanniae* (1180–1201), ed. T. Stapleton, 2 vols. Soc. of Antiquaries of London (1840–44).

RScot *Rotuli Scotiae*, 2 vols. RC (1814–19): I (1291–1377), II (1377–1509) [by date, p., & col.].

RSelecti *Rotuli selecti ad res Anglicas et Hibernicas spectantes* (1205–1431), ed. T. Hunter, RC (1834); *v. et. Pat. Hib. Hen. V.*

R. SHREWSB. Robert, Prior of Shrewsbury [*ob.* 1168]: *Vita et translatio S. Wenefredae* (wr. c1140), *Acta SS. Boll.* Nov. I (1887) 708–31 [by cap.].

RS Rolls Series. *Rerum Britannicarum Medii Aevi Scriptores* or Chronicles and Memorials of Great Britain and Ireland during the Middle Ages, I–XCIX, (1858–97).

RTAM *Recherches de théologie ancienne et médiévale,* I– (Louvain, 1929–).

RUDBORNE Thomas Rudborne [*fl.* 1460]: *Historia major de fundatione et successione ecclesiae Wintoniensis* (164–1138), in *Anglia Sacra* I 177–286.

Runica Manuscripta R. Derolez: *Runica Manuscripta,* the English tradition (Bruges, 1954).

Rutland MSS Accounts of the estates of the Duke of Rutland (16c.), MS Belvoir Castle.

RWL Revised Medieval Latin Word-List from British and Irish Sources, ed. R. E. Latham (1965, reissued w. sup. 1981).

SACKVILLE *v.* SICCAV.

Sacr. Ely Sacrist Rolls of Ely (1291–1360), ed. F. R. Chapman, 2 vols. (Cambridge, 1907).

Sacr. Lichf. Sacrist's Roll of Lichfield [Staffs] Cathedral (1345), Arch. Soc. Derb IV (1882) 107–17.

SACROB. John de Sacro Bosco (*alias* of Holywood) [*fl.* 1230]: **AN** *Tractatus de arte numerandi,* in *Rara Math.* 1–26 [by cap.]; **Sph.** *De Sphaera,* ed. L. Thorndike, The Sphere of Sacrobosco (Chicago, 1949) 76–117; *cf. Comm. Sph.,* ROB ANGL II.

SÆWULF Sæwulf, monk of Malmesbury [*fl.* 1100]: *Relatio de peregrinatione ad Hierosolymam* (1103), ed. M. P. d'Avezac, Recueil de voyages et de mémoires IV, Société de géographie (Paris, 1839), 833–54.

Salter Essays Oxford Essays in medieval history presented to H. E. Salter (Oxford, 1934).

SAMSON Mir. Edm. Samson, Abbot of Bury St. Edmund's [Suff] [*ob.* 1212]: *Liber de miraculis S. Eadmundi* [attrib.; parts by OSB. CLAR.], in *Mem. S. Edm.* I 107–208 [by bk. & cap.]; *v. et. Kal. Samson.*

Sanct. Bev. *Sanctuarium Beverlacense* (c1478–1539), Surtees Soc. V (1837) 112–211 [by no.].

Sanct. Durh. *Sanctuarium Dunelmense* (1464–1524), Surtees Soc. V (1837) 1–90 [by no.].

Sat. Poets Anglo-Latin Satirical Poets and epigrammatists of the 12th century, 2 vols. RS LIX (1872); *v. Epigr. Misc.,* G. WINT., HANV., H. CANTOR *Vers.,* H. HUNT. *HA* XI, NECKAM *VM,* NIG., R. CANT. *Poems,* SERLO BAY.

SAUTRY William Sautry (*alias* Sawtrey), Priest of St. Margaret's, Lynn [*ob.* 1401], *v. Ziz.*

SB *Sinonoma Bartholomei,* a medico-botanical glossary (14c.) [attrib. J. MIRFIELD], ed. J. L. G. Mowat, *Anecd. Oxon.* I (1882); *cf.* ELVEDEN.

Sci. Mech. M. Clagett: The Science of Mechanics in the Middle Ages (Madison, Wisc., 1959), *v.* BRADW. *Cont., Prop.,* DUMBLETON, HEYTESBURY, J. HOLLAND, RIC. SWYN. *Calc.*

Scone *Liber Ecclesiae de Scon,* ed. W. Smythe, Maitland Club (1843) [by no.].

Scot. Grey Friars The Scottish Grey Friars, ed. W. M. Bryce, 2 vols. (Edinburgh, 1909).

Scot. RO Scottish Office, General Register House, Edinburgh 2.

Scot. Saints Lives of the Scottish Saints, ed. J. Pinkerton, revised W. M. Metcalfe, 2 vols. (Paisley, 1889).

Script. Mus. *Scriptorum de musica medii aevi novam seriem a Gervertina alteram collegit nuncque primum edidit* E. Coussemaker, 4 vols. (1864–76); *v.* GARL. *Mus.,* HAUBOYS, HAUDLO, HOTHBY, *Mens. & Disc. (Anon. IV), Mus. Mens. (Anon. VI),* ODINGTON, TUNST.

Scrope v. Grosvenor The Scrope and Grosvenor controversy (1385–90), ed. N. H. Nicolas, 2 vols. (1832).

Sculp. Lap. *De Sculpturis Lapidum* (13c.), *Arch.* XXX (1844) 449–53.

S. DURH. Simeon of Durham [*ob.* c1130], *Symeonis Dunelmensis Opera,* 2 vols. RS (1882–5): **Durh.** *Historia ecclesiae Dunelmensis* (635–1096), I 3–135 [by bk. & cap.]; **Durh. Cont. A** (1096–1144), I 135–60; **Durh. Cont. B** (1141–54), I 161–9; **Ep. Hug.** *Epistola ad Hugonem decanum Ebor. de archiepiscopis Ebor.* (? a1110), I 222–8 [by cap.]; **HR** *Historia Regum* (888–1129) [attrib.], *ib.* II 91–283 [by cap.; *v. et.* BYRHT. *HR*]; **HR Cont.** *v.* J. HEX.

Seals Sir Christopher Hatton's book of Seals (12c.–13c.), ed. L. C. Lloyd and D. M. Stenton, Northants Rec. Soc. XV (1950) [by no.].

S. EASTON Stephen of Easton, Abbot of Fountains [*ob.* 1252]: **ET** *Exercitium triplex,* ed. A. Wilmart, Revue d'ascétique et de mystique XI (1930) 361–74; **Medit.** *Meditationes de gaudiis B. V. M.,* *ib.* X (1929) 391–414; **Psalm.** *De informatione mentis circa psalmodiam diei et noctis,* Cîteaux XXIII (1972) 259–88 [by sect.]; **SN** *Speculum novitii, Collectanea Ordinis Cisterciensis Reformatorum* VIII (1946) 45–68.

Sea Terms Middle English Sea Terms, ed. B. Sandahl, I– (Upsala, 1951–).

SECHEVILLE *v.* SICCAV.

Seignorial Admin. N. Denholm-Young: Seignorial Adminstration in England (Oxford, 1937).

SelBEyre Select Bills in Eyre (1292–1333), Selden Soc. XXX (1914).

SelCCant Select Cases from the ecclesiastical courts of the province of Canterbury c1200–1301, Selden Soc. XCV (1981).

SelCChanc Select Cases in Chancery (1346–1471), Selden Soc. X (1896).

SelCCoron Select Cases from the Coroners' rolls (1265–1413), Selden Soc. IX (1895).

SelCCouncil Select Cases before the King's Council (1243–1482), Selden Soc. XXXV (1919).

SelCExchCh Select Cases in the Exchequer Chamber before all the Justices of England (1377–1461), Selden Soc. LI (1933).

SelCExchPl Select Cases in the Exchequer of Pleas (Hen. III–Ed. I), Selden Soc. XLVIII (1932).

SelCh Select Charters and other illustrations of English constitutional history to the reign of Ed. I, ed. W. Stubbs, 9th ed. (1913).

SelCivPl Select Civil Pleas I (1200–3), Selden Soc. III (1890) [no more pub.].

SelCKB Select Cases in the Court of King's Bench (Ed. I–Ed. III), 7 vols. Selden Soc. LV, LVII, LVIII, LXXIV, LXXVI, LXXXII, LXXXVIII (1936–71).

SelCReq Select Cases in the Court of Requests (1497–1569), Selden Soc. XII (1898).

SelCWW Select Cases of procedure Without Writ under Hen. III, Selden Soc. LX (1941).

Selden Soc. Selden Society, publications [of legal records], I– (1888–).

SelPlAdm Select Pleas in the Court of Admiralty, 2 vols. Selden Soc. VI, XI (1892–7).

SelPlCrown Select Pleas of the Crown I (1200–1225), Selden Soc. I (1887) [no more pub.].

SelPlForest Select Pleas of the Forest (1209–1334), Selden Soc. XIII (1901).

SelPlJews Select Pleas, Starrs, and other records from the Rolls of the Exchequer of the Jews (1220–84), Selden Soc. XV (1902).

SelPlMan Select Pleas in Manorial and other seignorial

courts, I (Hen. III–Ed. I), Selden Soc. II (1889) [no more pub.].

SelPlStarCh Select Pleas of the Court of Star Chamber (1477–1544), 2 vols. Selden Soc. XVI, XXV (1903–11).

SENATUS Senatus, Prior of Worcester [*ob.* 1207]: **Ep.** *Epistolae*, MS Bodl. 633 [by no. & f.]; (extr.), RTAM XIX (1952), 206–7, 218–20; **Ep. Conc.** *Epistola de Concordia* (=*Ep.* 2), ed. C. H. Turner, Early Worcester Manuscripts (Oxford, 1916), xlv–li; **Ep. Ox.** Letters relating to Oxford (*Epp.* 4, 6 extr.), in *Collect. Ox.* II 180–82; **Osw.** *Vita S. Oswaldi archeipiscopi* [*ob.* 992], in *Hist. Church York* II 60–97; **Wulfst.** *Vita S. Wulfstani* [*ob.* 1095] (abbr. from W. MALM. *Wulfst.*) [attrib.], Camd. 3rd S. XL (1928) 68–108 [cf. W. MALM. *Wulfst. Abbr.*].

Senesch. The Seneschaucy, printed w. *Husb.* (1971) [cited as source of passages in *Fleta*].

SERLO BAY. Serlo of Bayeux (*alias* Parisiacensis) [*ob.* c1122]: Verses, in *Sat. Poets* II 208–12, 233–58.

SERLO GRAM. Serlo Grammaticus [*ob.* c1207]: **Bell. Stand.** *De bello inter regem Scotie et barones Anglie* (1138) [attrib.], in SERLO WILT. 7–9; **Mon. Font.** *Narratio de fundatione Fontanis Monasterii* (c1207) [dictated by Serlo to Hugh of Kirkstall], in *Mem. Fount.* I 1–129.

SERLO WILT. Serlo of Wilton [*ob.* c1180]: Poems ed. J. Öberg, *Studia Latina Stockholmiensia* XIV (1965) [by no. & line].

Serm. Beauchamp Sermon on the anniversary of the death of Thomas Beauchamp, Earl of Warwick (*p* 1401), *Traditio* XXXIV (1978) 385–401 collated w. MS Bodl. Laud misc. 709 ff. 72–80v. [by f.].

SessPBeds Sessions of the Peace for Bedfordshire 1355–59, 1363–64, HMC JP XVI (1969).

SessPCambs Some Sessions of the Peace in Cambridgeshire (1340, 1380–3), ed. M. M. Taylor, Camb. Antiq. Soc. 8° S. LV (1942).

SessPEssex Essex Sessions of the Peace (1351, 1377–9), ed. E. C. Furber, Arch. Soc. Essex, occ. pub. III (1953).

SessPLincs Some Sessions of the Peace in Lincolnshire (1360–96), 3 vols. Linc. Rec. Soc. XXX, XLIX, LVI (1936–62).

SessPNorthants Rolls of Northamptonshire Sessions of the Peace (1314–16, 1320), ed. M. Gollancz, Northants Rec. Soc. XI (1940).

Sess. Pps. H. of C. Sessional Papers printed by order of the House of Commons, I– (1693–).

SessPSalop The Shropshire Peace Roll, 1400–14 (Shrewsbury, 1959).

SessPWarw Rolls of the Warwickshire and Coventry Sessions of the Peace (1377–97), ed. E. G. Kimball, Dugdale Soc. XVI (1939).

S. FAVERSHAM Simon of Faversham [chancellor of Oxford 1304–6]: **An.** *Quaestiones super tertium de Anima*, AHDLMA IX (1934) 309–68; **Elench.** *Quaestiones super librum Elenchorum*, ed. S. Ebbesen *et al.* (Toronto, 1984); **Porph.** *Questiones libri Porphyrii*, Archivio di filosofia I (1931) 16–29; **Praed.** *Quaestiones super libros praedicamentorum*, Memorie della Reale Accademia dei Lincei 6th S. III iv (Rome, 1930); **Soph.** *Sophisma Universale est Intentio*, Med. Stud. XXXI (1969) 3–14; *vv. ll. ib.* XXXIII (1971) 360–4.

S. FOUGÈRES Vitalis Stephen of Fougères [*ob.* 1178]: Life of St. Vitalis of Savigny, *Anal. Boll.* I (1882) 355–90.

S. GAUNT Simon of Ghent, Chancellor of Oxford, Bishop of Salisbury [*ob.* 1315]: **AncrR** Latin translation of *Ancrene Riwle* [attrib.], *v. AncrR*; **Reg.** *Registrum, v. Reg. Sal.*; **Serm.** University Sermon on Ash Wednesday (1293), in *Theol. Ox.* 205–15.

SHIRWOOD William Shirwood (*alias* Shyreswood), Treasurer of Lincoln [*fl.* 1260]: **Insol.** *Insolubilia* [attrib.], AHDLMA XXXVII (1970) 248–61 [by sect.]; **Log.** *Introductiones in logicam*, *Traditio* XXXIX (1983) 222–91; also ed. M. Grabmann, Sitzungsberichte der

Bayerischen Akad. der Wissenschaften, Phil.-hist. Abt. (1937), Heft 10; **Syncat.** *Syncategoremata*, Med. Stud. III (1940) 48–93; *v. et. GLA.*

SHR Scottish Historical Review I– (Glasgow, Edinburgh, Aberdeen, 1903–28, 1943–).

SHS Scottish History Society, publications, I– (Edinburgh, 1887–).

SICCAV. John de Siccavilla (*alias* Sackville or de Sècheville) [*ob.* c1295]: **PN** *De principiis naturae*, ed. R. M. Giguère, Univ. Montreal, Institut d'etudes médiévales XIV (Montreal & Paris, 1956).

SIGAR Visio Orm Sigar, Priest of Newbald [*ob.* c1130]: *Vita et visio et finis simplicis Orm* (c1126), *Anal. Boll.* LXXV (1957) 76–82 [by sect.].

SILGRAVE Henry of Silgrave (*alias* Sulgrave) [*ob.* a1292]: *Chronicon* (449–1274), ed. C. Hook, Caxton Soc. (1849).

SIM. HENTON Simon of Henton (*alias* Hinton) [*fl.* 1250]: **Exc.** *Exceptiones a Summa*, ed. P. A. Walz, *Angelicum* XIII (1936) 290–368; **Post. Mor.** *Postillae morales in prophetas minores*, MS New Coll. Ox. 45; **Summa** *Summa, J. Gersonii Opera Omnia* (Antwerp, 1706), I 233–422.

Simil. Anselmi *Liber de S. Anselmi similitudinibus*, PL CLIX (1865) 605–708 [by col.]; superseded by *Mem. Anselm* 39–104 [by sect.].

Simon. Haer. *De Simoniaca haeresi carmen* (? c1091), *MGH Libelli de lite* III (Hanover, 1897), 615–17.

S. Jers. Société jersiaise: I (1876) Extente de l'Île de Jersey (1331), PRO (E. 101/89/15); II (1877) 1–13, Extente des Îles de Jersey etc. (1274), PRO (C. 47/10/5/1); 14–48, Inquisitions dans les Îles de Jersey et Guernesey (1274), PRO (C. 47/10/1–3); XVIII (1903) Rolls of the Assizes held in the Channel Islands, etc. (1309), PRO (J.I. 1/1160–61).

SKELTON John Skelton [*ob.* 1529]: Poetical works, 2 vols. (1843).

S. Langton F. M. Powicke: Stephen Langton (Oxford, 1928).

S. LANGTON Stephen Langton, Archb. of Canterbury [*ob.* 1228]: **Acta** *v. Act. Cant.*; **BVM** *Psalterium beatae Mariae virginis*, *Anal. Hymn.* XXXV (1900) 153–71 [by quadr. & stanza]; **Chron.** Commentary on the book of Chronicles, ed. A. Saltman (Ramat Gan, 1978); **Gl. Hist. Schol.** *Glossa in Historiam scholasticam* (extr.), AHDLMA VI (1931) 39–51; **Quaest.** *Quaestiones* (extr.), Franciscan Studies XIV (1954) 362–73 and New Scholasticism IV (1930) 131–58; cited also from MS St John's Coll. Camb. 57 ff. 171–346; **Ruth** *Glossa in Ruth*, AHDLMA VI (1931) 86–126; **Sent.** *Commentarius in Sententias*, BGPM XXXVII i (1952) 1–153; **Serm.** *Sermones*: 1–4 (=Schneyer nos. 192, 169, 375 & *s.n.*) Selected Sermons of Stephen Langton, Toronto Med. Latin Texts (1980) [by no. & sect.]; 5 (=Schneyer no. 177), *Manuscripta* XX (1976) 101–4; 6–8 (=Schneyer nos. 304, 27, 22), *Traditio* XXXVI (1980) 243–8, 250–8, 260–8 [by no. & sect.]; **Summa** *Summa magistri Stephani Langton de hiis quae dicuntur de Deo*, MS St John's Coll. Camb. 57 ff. 147–70.

S. MEPHAM Spec. Simon Mepham, Archb. of Canterbury [d. 1333]: *Speculum regis Edwardi III* (c1332) [attrib. Simon Islip], ed. J. Moisant (Paris, 1891), 127–69 [by sect.].

SOMERSET Quer. John Somerset, physician [*ob.* c1455]: *Querimonia* (c1451), in *Ps.-*ELMH. *Hen.* V 347–50.

Som Rec. Soc. Somerset Record Society, publications, I– (1887–).

Southampton Rec. Soc. Southampton Record Society, publications, I– (Southampton, 1905–); Southampton Records S., I– (Southampton, 1951–).

Spalding Club publications (Aberdeen, 1839–71) [cont. as New Splading Club].

SP Dom. Eliz. State Papers Domestic, Eliz. I, MS PRO (S.P. 12–13), calendared in 7 vols. (1856–71).

Spec. Alch. *Speculum Alchemiae* (? 13c.) [attrib. BACON], in *Theatrum Chem.* II 377–85.

Spec. Eccl. *Speculum ecclesiae* [transl. from AN version of EDMUND *Spec. Relig.*], ed. H.P. Forshaw, Edmund of Abingdon, *Speculum religiosorum* and *Speculum ecclesiae*, *Auct. Brit.* III (1973) 31–111 [by sect.]; also in *Bibl. Vet. Pat.* XXV (1677) 316–27.

Spec. Incl. *Speculum inclusorum* (14c.), ed. L. Oliger, *Lateranum* IV i (1938) [by cap. & sect.].

Spec. Laic. *Speculum laicorum* (c1290), ed. J. T. Welter (Paris, 1914) [by cap.].

Speculum *Speculum*, a journal of Mediaeval Studies, I– (Boston, Mass., 1926–).

SPELMAN Asp. Sir Henry Spelman [*ob.* 1641]: *Aspilogia* (wr. c1595) (London, 1654).

SP Hen. VIII State Papers, foreign and domestic, Henry VIII, MS PRO (S.P. 1).

SP Ir. State Papers Ireland (1509–1603), MS PRO (S.P. 60–3), calendared in 11 vols. (1860–1912).

Spons. Mariae The Spousells of the Princess Mary (1508), Camd. Misc. IX, Camd. NS LIII (1893).

Sports & Pastimes J. Strutt: Sports and Pastimes of the people of England, 7th ed. (1903).

S. SIM. Itin. Simon Simeon [*fl.* 1325]: *Itinerarium ab Hybernia ad Terram Sanctam* (c1322–23), ed. M. Esposito, *Scriptores Latini Hiberniae* IV (Dublin, 1960) [by cap.].

Staffs Rec. Soc. v. Collect. Staffs.

Stair Soc. Stair Society, publications, I– (Edinburgh, 1936–).

STANBR. Vulg. John Stanbridge [*ob.* 1510]: *Vulgaria*, EETS CLXXXVII (1932) 1–30.

STANIHURST Hib. Richard Stanihurst of Dublin [*ob.* 1618]: *De rebus in Hibernia gestis* (Antwerp, 1584).

Stans Puer *Stans puer ad mensam*, verses on behaviour of page at table [attrib. GROS.], EETS XXXII pt. 2 (1868) 30–3; checked against recensions, *Vivarium* V (1967) 56–82.

Staple Bk. Bristol Staple Court Books of Bristol (1509–1601), Bristol Rec. Soc. V (1934).

Starrs Starrs and Jewish charters (1182–1280) preserved in the British Museum, w. illustrative docs. etc., ed. I. Abrahams *et al.*, 3 vols. Jewish Hist. Soc. (1930–2).

StatCantab The original Statutes of Cambridge University, ed. M. B. Hackett (Cambridge, 1970).

StatCCOx Statutes of Corpus Christi College, Oxford, in *Stat. Coll. Ox.* II.

Stat. Coll. Ox. Statutes of the Colleges of Oxford, 3 vols. (1853) [by coll., vol., & p.]; *v. et. StatCCOx*.

Stat. Durh. The Statutes of the cathedral church of Durham, Surtees Soc. CXLIII (1929).

Stat. Ebor. *De consuetudinibus et ordinationibus antiquitus usitatis et observatis* (13c.–14c.), in *Stat. Linc.* II 91–135.

Stat. Eton Eton College Statutes (1444–5), in *Stat. King's Cantab.* 477–625.

State Tri. Ed. I State Trials of the reign of Ed. I, 1289–93, Camd. 3rd S. IX (1906).

Stat. Gild. Berw. *Statuta gildae apud Berwicum facta* (c1250–94), in *APScot* I app. II, 89*–96*.

Stat. Heref. *Consuetudines et statuta ecclesiae Herfordensis* (c1280), in *Stat. Linc.* II 36–85; later additions, *ib.* 86–9.

StatIr Early Statutes of Ireland (1204–1482), ed. H. F. Berry *et al.*, 4 vols. PRO Ireland (Dublin, 1907–39).

Stat. King's Cantab. The ancient laws of the fifteenth century for King's College, Cambridge (1443–1674), ed. J. Heywood and T. Wright (1850) 1–298; app. docs. (1444–85); *v. et. Ch. Eton, Cust. Eton, Stat. Eton, Vis. Eton.*

Stat. Lich. Statutes of Lichfield cathedral (c1190), in *Stat. Linc.* II 11–25; select Lichfield statutes (12c.–16c.), *ib.* 26–35.

Stat. Linc. Statutes of Lincoln Cathedral, ed. H. Bradshaw

and C. Wordsworth, 2 vols. in 3 (Cambridge, 1892–7); *cf. Stat. Ebor., Stat. Heref., Stat. Lich.*

Stat. Man J. F. Gill: Statutes of the Isle of Man (1883).

Stat. Mich. Cantab. The Statutes of Michael House under the seal of Harvey de Stanton (1324), ed. J. B. Mullinger The University of Cambridge to 1535 (Cambridge, 1873) app. D 640–45.

Stat. Ottery St. M. *Ordinatio et statuta beatae Mariae de Otery*, ed. J. N. Dalton, The Collegiate Church of Ottery St. Mary (Cambridge, 1917): *Tabula*, 81–5; *Ordinacio primaria* (1338), 85–115; fragments of register, 127–31; *Statuta collegii* (1339), 133–259; other documents (14c.–16c.), 260–302.

StatOx *Statuta antiqua Universitatis Oxoniensis*, ed. S. Gibson (Oxford, 1931).

Stat. Sal. Statutes and customs of the cathedral church of Salisbury, ed. C. Wordswoth and D. Macleane (1915).

Stat. Wells *Ordinale et statuta ecclesiae cathedralis S. Andreae Wellensis* (c1150), ed. H. E. Reynolds, Wells Cathedral (Leeds, 1881) 1–113.

Staura Civ. *Staura civitatum* (a1401), *Anglia* LXXXV (1967) 128–9 [by line].

Steelyard J. M. Lappenberg: Urkundliche Geschichte des Hansischen Stahlhofes zu London, 2 pts. in 1 vol.; app. of docs. w. sep. pag. 1–218 (Hamburg, 1851).

Stenton Misc. A medieval Miscellany for D. M. Stenton, ed. P. M. Barnes and C. F. Slade, Pipe R. Soc. NS XXXVI (1962).

STEPH. HARD. Stephen Harding, Abbot of Cîteaux [*ob.* 1134]: **Bibl.** *Censura de aliquot locis Bibliorum, PL* CLXVI 1373–6; **Carit.** *Carta Caritatis, ib.* 1377–84; **Ep.** *Epistolae, PL* CLXXXII 149–52, 157–8; **sup.** additional letter, *Collectanea Ordinis Cisterciensis Reformatorum* III (1936–7) 66–9; **Exord.** *Exordium ordinis Cisterciensium, PL* CLXVI 1501–10; **Serm.** *Sermo in obitu praedecessoris sui, ib.* 1375–6.

STEPH. ROUEN Stephen of Rouen [*ob.* c1170]: *Draco Normannicus* (1118–69), in *Chr. Steph.* II 585–757 [by bk. & line]; **addit.** *additamenta* 758–62; **app.** appendix of miscellaneous verse 765–79.

STEPH. WHITBY Stephen of Whitby, Abbot of St. Mary's, York [*ob.* 1112]: *De fundatione abbatiae S. Mariae Virginis Eboraci*, in *MonA* III 544–6.

Stewards' Bk. Southampt. The Stewards' Books of Southampton (1428–39), Southampt. Rec. Soc. XXXV, XXXIX (1935–9).

STOKES Peter Stokes, Carmelite [*ob.* 1339], *v. Ziz.*

STONE Chr. John Stone, monk of Christ Church, Canterbury [*ob.* c1480]: Chronicle (1415–71), Camb. Antiq. Soc. 8° S. XXXIV (1902) 1–152.

Stonor Pps. The Stonor Letters and Papers (1290–1483), 2 vols. Camd. 3rd S. XXIX, XXX (1919); **Sup.** Camd. Misc. XIII, *ib.* XXXIV (1924).

STRATFORD John Stratford, Archbishop of Canterbury [*ob.* 1348]: **Const.** Constitutions, *v. Conc.* II; **Serm.** Sermons (extr.): nos. 15, 22, 28, 29, EHR VIII (1893) 85–91; no. 22, Journal of Ecclesiastical History XXXIV (1983) 432–7; also contains list of sermons [by no. & p.].

StRealm Statutes of the Realm (1236–1713), 11 vols. in 12, RC (1810–28).

STRECCHE Hen. V John Strecche [*fl.* 15c.]: Chronicle of the reign of Hen. V, ed. F. Taylor, JRL Bull. XVI (1932) 146–87.

Stud. 14 Cent. M. V. Clarke: Fourteenth-century Studies (Oxford, 1937).

Studia Monastica *Studia Monastica* I– (Barcelona, 1959–).

STUDLEY Richard Studley: *Vita S. Roberti heremitae* [of Knaresborough, *ob.* c1235], *Anal. Boll.* LVII (1939) 365–74 [by cap.]; *cf. V. Rob. Knaresb.*

Suff Hund. E. Powell: A Suffolk Hundred [Blackbourne] in 1283 (Cambridge, 1910).

SULCARD Sulcard of Westminster [*fl.* c1080]: *De con-*

structione Westmonasterii, *Traditio* XX (1964) 80–91 [by f.].

SULGRAVE *v.* SILGRAVE.

Summa Abend. v. HALES.

Superst. Pharis. *De superstitione pharisaeorum* [*p*1360], Med. Stud. XXX (1968) 109–114 [by line].

Surrey Rec. Soc. Surrey Record Society, publications, I– (London & Guildford, 1916–).

Surtees Soc. Surtees Society, publications [concerning Northumbria *sensu latiore*], I– (Durham, 1835–).

Surv. Denb. Survey of the Honour of Denbigh, 1334, ed. P. Vinogradoff and F. Morgan, Rec. Soc. & Econ. I (1914); (extr.) also in *Tribal System* app. B, 49–96.

Surv. Devon T. Risdon [*ob.* 1640]: The chorographical description, or Survey of the County of Devon [printed from 17c. MS], rev. ed. (1811).

Surv. Durh. Hatf. Bishop Hatfield's Survey, a record of the possessions of the See of Durham (1345–81), Surtees Soc. XXXII (1857).

Surv. Linc. The Lincolnshire Domesday and the Lindsey survey (1115–18), Linc. Rec. Soc. (1924) 237–60.

Surv. Pembr. Survey of the lands of William, earl of Pembroke and Montgomery (1566–73) [w. earlier docs.], ed. C. R. Stratton, 2 vols. Roxb. Club (1909).

Surv. Wye A Survey of the manor of Wye [Kent] (*c*1450), ed. H. E. Muhlfeld (New York, 1933).

Sussex Rec. Soc. Sussex Record Society, publications, I– (Lewes, 1901–).

SWAFHAM Robert Swafham: *Historia coenobii Burgensis* [Peterborough] (1117–1245), in *Hist. Angl. Script.* 97–122; **app.** chronological summary of H. ALBUS, in H. ALBUS *app.* 133–9; *cf.* WHITTLESEY.

SWINESHEAD, R. *v.* RIC. SWYN., ROG. SWYN.

SWYNTON Mem. Thomas Swynton, Abbot of Fountains [resigned 1478]: Memorandum book (1446–58), in *Mem. Fount.* III 93–255.

Tap. Bayeux The Bayeux Tapestry (*a*1080), ed. D. C. Douglas, English Historical Documents II (1953) [by panel].

TATWINE Tatwine, Archb. of Canterbury [*ob.* 734]: **Aen.** *Aenigmata*, *CCSL* CXXXIII (1968) 143–208; **Ars** *Ars* [*de partibus orationis*], *ib.* 1–141 [by sect.].

TAXTER Chr. Bury John Taxter (*alias* Tayster): *Chronica Buriensis* (–1265), in *Chr. Bury* 1–33 [supersedes FL. WORC. *Cont. B*].

T. BUCKINGHAM Thomas of Buckingham, Fellow of Merton, Chancellor of Exeter [*ob. c*1356]: **QT** *Quaestiones theologicae* (extr.), ed. M. D. Chenu, *Studia Mediaevalia in honorem R. J. Martin* (Bruges, 1948) 234–41; **Sent.** *Quaestiones super libros Sententiarum* [published as Johannes Bokinham] (Paris, 1505) [by sign.].

T. CHOBHAM Thomas Chobham [*fl.* 1230]: **Conf.** *Summa confessorum*, *Analecta Mediaevalia Namurcensia* XXV (Louvain & Paris, 1968).

T. CLAXTON Thomas of Claxton, O.P. [*fl.* 1400]: **Analog.** *Quaestio de analogia entis*, ed. M. Grabmann, *Acta pontificiae academiae Romanae S. Thomae Aquinatis* NS VIII (1943) 125–53; **Esse** *Quaestio de distinctione essentiae et esse realis*, *ib.* 99–125.

T. ELY Etheldr. Thomas of Ely [*ob.* 1175]: **Acta** *Acta S. Etheldredae*, *Acta SS. Boll.* June IV (1707) 497–538; **Prol.** Prologue, *ib.* 493–4; **Transl.** Second translation of St. Etheldreda [*ob.* 679], *Lib. Eli.* II capp. 143–4; **Mir.** Miracles of St. Etheldreda, *ib.* III capp. 27–138 (*passim*); also *Acta SS. Boll.* June IV (1707) 538–76; *v. et.* RIC. ELY.

Terr. Fleet A Terrier of Fleet, Lincs (1316) w. other docs., ed. N. Neilson, Rec. Soc. & Econ. IV pt. 1 (1920).

Test. Ebor. *Testamenta Eboracensia* (*c*1300–1550), Surtees Soc. IV, XXX, XLV, LIII, LXXIX, CVI (1836–1902).

Test. Ep. Heref. The will of Peter de Aqua Blanca, Bishop of Hereford (1268), Camd. Misc. XIV, Camd. 3rd S. XXXVII (1926).

Test. Karl. *Testamenta Karleolensia* (1353–86), Cumb & Westmor Antiq. Soc., Extra S. IX (1893).

Texte aus der mittelalterlichen Geisteswelt Veröffentlichungen der Kommission für die Herausgabe ungedruckter Texte aus der mittelalterlichen Geisteswelt, Bayerische Akademie der Wissenschaften, I– (Munich, 1968–).

Text. Roff. *Textus Roffensis* [attrib. Ernulf, Bishop of Rochester (*ob.* 1124)], ed. P. H. Sawyer, Early Eng. MSS in facsimile VII, XI (Copenhagen, 1957–62) [*cf. Arch. Cant.* XXIII (1898) 94–112] [by folio; refs. to pp. are to T. Hearne's ed. 1720].

T. FRACKENHAM Thomas of Frackenham (*alias* Frakaham), Canon of Lessness [12c.]: **Spec. Hum.** *Speculum humilitatis*, *Studia monastica* I (1959) 129–36; **Spir. Amicit.** *Speculum spiritalis amicitiae* [based on AILR. *Spir. Amicit.* and *Spec. Car.*], *ib.* III (1961) 297–323.

Theatrum Chem. *Theatrum Chemicum*, ed. L. Zetzner, 6 vols. (Strasbourg, 1659–61).

THEOB. Theobald, archbishop of Canterbury [*ob.* 1161], *v. Ep. J. Sal.*; *cf. Doc. Theob.*

THEOD. Theodore of Tarsus, Archb. of Canterbury [*ob.* 690]: **Ep.** Letter to Æthelred, K. of Mercia (686), in EDDI 42; also in W. MALM. *GP* III and *Conc. HS* 171–2; **Pen.** *Paenitentiale*, in *Conc. HS* III 173–213 [by bk., cap., & sect.]; also ed. P. W. Finsterwalder, Die *Canones Theodori Cantuariensis* und ihre Ueberlieferungsformen (Weimar, 1929).

Theol. Ox. A. G. Little and F. Pelster: Oxford Theology and Theologians *c*1282–1302, OHS XCVI (1934).

Thes. Nov. Anecd. *Thesaurus novus anecdotorum*, ed. E. Martène and U. Durand, 5 vols. (Paris, 1717).

Thingoe J. Gage: The history and antiquities of Suffolk, Thingoe hundred (1838).

THOMAS ANGLICUS *v.* PAUL. ANGL.

THOMAS BRADWARDINE *v.* BRADW.

THOMAS DOCKING *v.* DOCKING.

Thoresby Soc. Thoresby Society, publications, I– (Leeds, 1891–).

THORNE William Thorne [*fl.* 1397]: *Chronica de rebus gestis abbatum S. Augustini Cantuariae* (578–1397), in *Hist. Angl. Script.* X 1753–2296.

Thoroton Soc. Thoroton Society, Record S. [mainly concerning Notts], I– (Nottingham, 1903–).

THURKILL Thurkill *compotista* [*fl.* 1115]: **Abac.** *Regunculae super abacum*, ed. E. Narducci, Bullettino di bibliografia e di storia delle scienze matematiche et fisiche XV (1882) 135–54 [by f.]; **Li.** *Epistola de libris*, *ib.* 127–8.

T. MARLB. Thomas of Marlborough, Abbot of Evesham [*ob.* 1236]: **Acta Prob.** *Acta proborum virorum* [based on lost work of DOMINIC], in *Chr. Evesham* 320–25; **Chr.** Chronicle (or *V. Ecgwini* III) (*c*700–1214), *v. Chr. Evesham* 69–257; **Ecgwine** *Vita S. Ecgwini* [*ob.* ? 717] [based on DOMINIC *V. Ecgwini*], *v. Chr. Evesham* 1–67; **Odulph** *Vita et miracula S. Odulphi* [canon of Utrecht, *ob. c*830] [based on lost work of DOMINIC], in *Chr. Evesham* 313–20; also *Acta SS. Boll.* June II (1742) 592–5; **Wistan** *Vita et miracula S. Wistani* [*ob.* 850] [attrib.], in *Chr. Evesham* 325–37.

T. MON. Will. Thomas of Monmouth [*ob. p*1172]: Life and miracles of St. William of Norwich [*ob.* 1144], ed. A. Jessopp and M. R. James (Cambridge, 1896) [by bk. & cap.].

Tonale Sal. *Tonale*, ed. W. H. Frere, The Use of Sarum, 2 vols. (Cambridge 1898–1901) II app. i–lxxix.

TORIGNI Robert de Torigni (*alias* de Monte) [*ob.* 1186]: **Access. Sig.** *Accessiones ad Sigebertum*, in *Chr. Steph.* IV 3–60; **Chr.** *Chronica* (1100–86), *ib.* 61–315; **Cont. Bec.** *Continuatio Beccensis* (1157–60), *ib.* 317–27; *v. et.* W. JUM. *Cont.*

TORKESEY John Torkesey: *Trianguli et scuti declaratio de proportionibus musicae mensurabilis*, ed. A. Gilles and G. Reaney, *Corp. Script. Mus.* XII (1966) 58–63.

Tout Essays Essays in medieval history presented to T. F. Tout, ed. A. G. Little and F. Pelster (Manchester, 1925).

Tout Papers T. F. Tout: Collected Papers, 3 vols. (Manchester, 1932–4).

Tract. Ebor. *Tractatus Eboracenses* [attrib. Gerard, Archb. of York (*ob.* 1108)], ed. H. Böhmer, *MGH Libelli de lite* III (Hanover, 1897) 645–87.

Tract. Ed. II *Tractatus pacis*, Edward II, the Lords Ordainers etc. (1312–13), Camd. Misc. XV, Camd. 3rd S. XLI (1929).

Tract. Peterb. & Ramsey Tract relating to Peterborough and Ramsey Abbeys (14c.), ed. T. Hearne, in T. Sprott *Chr.* (Oxford, 1719) 171–220; also in *MonA* II 571–9.

Traditio I– (New York, 1943–).

Transl. Audoeni *Variae translationes sacri corporis S. Audoeni, Acta SS. Boll.* Aug. IV (1739) 820–4; *v. et. V. & Mir. Audoeni.*

Transl. Ecgwini v. Chr. Evesham.

Transl. Edm. Rich *Historia translationis B. Edmundi* (*a*1254), in *Thes. Nov. Anecd.* III 1859–74.

Treat. J.P. Early Treatises on the practice of the Justices of the Peace in the 15c. and 16c., ed. B. H. Putnam (Oxford, 1924).

TreatyR Treaty Rolls (1234–), I– HMSO (1955–), [by vol. & no.]; later rolls, MS PRO (C. 76).

TREVET Nicholas Trevet (*alias* Trivet) [*ob.* 1328]: **Agam.** *Nicolai Treveti expositio L. Annaei Senecae Agamemnonis*, ed. P. Meloni (Cagliari, 1961); **Ann.** *Annales sex regum Angliae* 1136–1306, ed. T. Hog, Eng. Hist. Soc. (1845); **Herc. Fur.** *Nicolai Treveti expositio Herculis Furentis*, ed. V. Ussani (Rome, 1959); **Herc. Oet.** *Nicolai Treveti expositio L. Annaei Senecae Herculis Oetaei*, ed. P. Meloni (Rome, 1962); **Quaest.** *Quaestiones* (extr.), BGPM Suppl. II (1923) 52–62; **Thyestes** Il commento di Nicola Trevet al Tieste di Seneca, ed. E. Franceschini (Milan, 1938); **Troades** Commento alle *Troades* di Seneca, ed. M. Palma, Temi e Testi XXII (Rome, 1977).

Tribal System F. Seebohm: The Tribal System in Wales (1895), app. of docs. [sep. pag.]: 3–48 *v. Doc. Aberffraw;* 49–96 *cf. Surv. Denb.;* 97–100 *cf. BB St. Davids;* 101–105 *IPM* 5 Ed. I, MS PRO C. 133/78; 106 Indenture (1355).

Tri. W. Langton Records of the trial of Walter Langeton, bishop of Coventry and Lichfield 1307–12, Camd. 4th S. VI (1969).

TROKELOWE John of Trokelowe [*ob. p*1330]: *Annales* (1307–24), in *Chr. Mon. S. Alb.* III 61–127.

Trop. Wint. The Winchester Troper (from MSS 10c. and 11c.), HBS VIII (1894).

TR Records of the Exchequer, Treasury of the Receipt, MS PRO: **Bk** Receipt Books (Ed. I–) (E. 36); **Forest Proc.** Forest Proceedings (John–) (E. 32). **Scot. Doc.** Scottish documents (Hen. III–) (E. 39).

TRYVYTLAM Laus Ox. Richard Tryvytlam [*fl.* 1370]: *De laude universitatis Oxoniae*, in *Collect. Ox.* III 195–209 [by line].

T. SPROTT Chr. Thomas Sprott (*alias* Spott) [*fl. ?* 1270]: *Chronica* (wr. *c*1300) [attrib.], ed. T. Hearne (Oxford, 1719) 3–164 .

T. STUBBS Chr. Thomas Stubbs [*ob. ? p*1380]: *Continuatio chronicae de vitis Archiepiscoporum Eboracensium* (1147–1373), in *Hist. Church York* II 388–421; *cf. Chr. Pont. Ebor.*

T. SUTTON Thomas of Sutton (*alias* Anglicus), O. P. [*fl.* 1300]: **Duns** *Contra quodlibet Johannis Duns Scoti*, ed. J. Schneider, Texte aus der mittelalterlichen Geisteswelt VII (Munich, 1978); **Esse** *Tractatus de esse et essentia*, Studia Mediewistyczne XI (1970) 233–59; **Gen. & Corrupt.** *Expositionis in libros Aristotelis de Generatione et corruptione continuatio*, ed. F. E. Kelley, Texte aus der mittelalterlichen Geisteswelt VI (Munich, 1976); **Plur. Form.** *Contra pluralitatem formarum*, ed. P. Mandonnet, *S. Thomae Aquinatis Opuscula omnia* (Paris, 1927) V

308–46; **Prod.** *De productione formae substantialis*, AHDLMA XLVI (1979) 142–75; **Quaest.** *Quaestiones de reali distinctione inter essentiam et esse*, ed. F. Pelster, *Opusc. & Text.* V (1929); **QO** *Quaestiones ordinariae*, ed. J. Schneider, Texte aus der mittelalterlichen Geisteswelt III (Munich, 1977); **Quodl.** *Quodlibeta*, ed. M. Schmaus, Texte aus der mittelalterlichen Geisteswelt II (Munich, 1969); in fasc. I–II, some refs. to Revue néoscolastique de philosophie XXXVI, XXXVII (Louvain, 1934).

TUNST. Simon Tunsted [*ob.* 1369] [attrib.]: *Quattuor principalia musicae*, in *Script. Mus.* IV 201–98.

TURGOT Turgot, Bishop of St. Andrews [*ob.* 1115]: **Bede** *Venerabilis Bedae vita* [attrib., actually from S. Durh. *Durh.*], *PL* XC 53–68; **Marg.** *Vita S. Margaretae Scotorum reginae*, Surtees Soc. LI (1867) 234–54.

TURNER William Turner [*ob.* 1568]: **Av.** *Avium brevis historia* (Cologne, 1544) [by sign.]; also ed. A. H. Evans (Cambridge, 1903); **Herb.** *Libellus de re herbaria* (1538) [by sign.]; facsimile, ed. W. T. Stearn, Ray Soc. (1965), 41–60; **Herb Names** The names of Herbes in Greek, Latin, Englishe (1548) [by sign.]; Ray Soc. (1965), 79–142; some refs. in Fasc. I–II from *OED*.

Turquet *De Turketo* (*a*1350), in *Early Sci. Ox.* II 370–5.

T. WALEYS Thomas Waleys (*alias* Wallensis) [*ob.* 1350]: **CivD** Commentary on Augustine *de Civitate Dei* (printed 1468, etc.); **I&M** *De instantibus et momentis* (1333), in *Doc. T. Waleys* 157–83; **Praedic.** *De modo componendi sermones cum documentis*, ed. T. M. Charland, *Artes Praedicandi*, Publications de l'Institut d'études médiévales d'Ottawa VII (1936) 327–403; **Serm. Avin.** *Sermo Thomae Waleys Avinionii* (1333), in *Doc. T. Waleys* 93–108.

T. YORK Thomas of York [*ob. ? c*1260]: **Sap.** *Sapientiale* (extr. and cap. heading), ed. P. E. Longpré, Fr. Thomas d'York, O.F.M., La première somme métaphysique du XIIIᵉ siècle, *Archivum Franciscanum Historicum* XIX (Quaracchi, 1926) 875–930 [by bk. & cap.]; **Serm.** *Sermo de passione Jesus Christi*, Franciscan Studies XXIV (1964) 210–22.

Tyss. John Tyssington, O.F.M. [*ob. c*1395], *v. Ziz.*

UHTRED Uhtred of Boldon [*ob.* 1396]: **Contra querelas** *Contra querelas fratrum* (extr.), British Academy Proceedings XXXVII 332–42; **Inst.** *De prima institutione monachorum*, in *MonA* I xix–xxii; **Medit.** *Meditacio devota, Studia Anselmiana* XLIII (1959) 195–206; **Mon. V.** (extr.), Two treatises on the monastic life, in Powicke Studies 363–85.

UPTON Nicholas Upton [*ob.* 1457]: *De studio militari*, ed. E. Bysshe (1654); **app.** appendix of notes and documents [sep. pag.]; *v. et.* Ed. Upton.

VAC. Vacarius [*ob. c*1200]: **Assumpt.** *Tractatus de assumpto homine*, Med. Stud. XXI (1959) 162–75 [by sect.]; **Err.** *Liber contra multiplices errores*, Studi e testi CXV (1945) 475–583; **Lib. paup.** *Liber pauperum*, ed. F. de Zulueta, Selden Soc. XLIV (1927); **Mat.** *De matrimonio*, ed. F. W. Maitland, Law Quarterly Review L and LI (1897) 133–43 and 270–87 [by sect.].

Val. Eccl. *Valor ecclesiasticus* (1535), 6 vols. RC (1810–24).

Val. Norw. The Valuation of Norwich 1254, w. other docs. (1217–919), ed. W. E. Lunt (Oxford, 1926).

V. Anselmi Epit. An anonymous verse epitome of the life of St. Anselm [*p*1163], *Anal. Boll.* XCII (1974) 117–24 [by line].

V. Audoeni *Vita S. Audoeni* [*ob.* 684], *Acta SS. Boll.* Aug. IV (1739) 805–10; another Life *ib.* 810–19; another Life, *Anal. Boll.* V (1886) 67–146; *v. et. Mir. & Transl. Audoeni.*

V. Bart. Farn. *Vita Bartholomaei Farnensis* [*ob.* 1193] [attrib. G. Cold.], in *S. Durh.* I (1882) 295–325.

V. Begae *Vita S. Begae* (wr. 12c.), in *Reg. S. Bees* 497–520.

V. Bertell. *Vita S. Bertellini, Acta SS. Boll.* Sept. III (1750) 449–53 [by sect.].

V. Brig. *Vita IV S. Brigidae* (wr. *c*1200), ed. J. Colgan,

Trias Thaumaturga (Louvain, 1647) 546–63 [by bk. & cap.]; also in *Acta SS. Boll.* Feb. I (1658) 155–71.

VCH Victoria History of the Counties of England, ed. H. A. Doubleday, W. Page *et al.* (1900–).

V. Cuthb. *Vita S. Cuthberti* [*ob.* 688] (wr. *a*705), by a monk of Lindisfarne, ed. B. Colgrave, Two Lives of St. Cuthbert (Cambridge, 1940) 59–139 [by bk. & cap.].

V. Dunst. B. v. B. V. Dunst.

V. Ecgwini v. BYRHT. *V. Ecgwini, Chr. Evesham,* DOMINIC *V. Ecgwini,* T. MARLB. *Ecgwine.*

V. Ed. Conf. Metr. Metrical Lives of Edward the Confessor: I abridgement of AILR. *Ed. Conf.* (wr. *c*1450), in *Lives Ed. Conf.* 359–77; II (extr.) MS Caius Coll. Camb. 153, *ib.* 379–83 [both by line].

V. Ed. Conf. *Vita Aedwardi regis* [*ob.* 1066] *S. Bertini monacho ascripta* (wr. *c*1067) [attrib. GOSC.], ed. F. Barlow, Med. Texts (1962) [by f.]; also in *Lives Ed. Conf.* 389–435.

V. Ed. II *Vita Edwardi Secundi* [*ob.* 1327] (wr. ? *c*1326), Med. Texts (1957) [by marginal pp. from *Chr. Ed. I & II* II 155–289]; *v. et.* BAKER.

V. Edm. Rich Life of St. Edmund Rich, Archb. of Canterbury [*ob.* 1240]: **B** Anon. B, ed. W. Wallace, Life of St. Edmund of Canterbury (1893) 614–24; **C** Anon. C, *ib.* 589–612; **P** Anon. (Pontigny), in *Thes. Nov. Anecd.* III 1775–1826; *v. et. Canon Edm. Rich.*, EDMUND, E. FAVERSHAM, M. PAR. *Edm., Poem Edm. Rich.*

V. Erkenwaldi *De sancto Erkenwaldo episcopo et confessore* [*ob.* 693], in *NLA* I 391–408; also *Acta SS. Boll.* Apr. III (1675) 781–7.

Vers. Cant. Verses in windows formerly in the Choir of Canterbury Cathedral, Camb. Antiq. Soc. 8° S. XXXVIII 13–26.

Vers. Hen. V *Versus rhythmici de Henrico V* (? by a contemporary), in *Mem. Hen. V* 63–74 [by line]; *cf. pref.* xxviii–xl.

Vers. Peterb. Verses in paintings formerly in the Choir of Peterborough Cathedral, Camb. Antiq. Soc. 4° S. IX 180–1.

Vers. Peterb. Psalter Verses of the Peterborough Psalter in Brussels, Journal of the British Archaeological Association XXXIII (1970) 45–49.

Vers. S. Alb. Cloister Verses in windows formerly in the Cloister of St. Albans Abbey, Camb. Antiq. Soc. 8° S. VII 64–9.

Vers. S. Alb. Libr. Verses in windows formerly in the Library of St. Albans Abbey. Camb. Antiq. Soc. 8° S. VIII 219–20.

Vers. Worc. Verses in paintings formerly at Worcester priory, Camb. Antiq. Soc. 4° S. X 99–104, 112–15.

Vex. Will. *De injusta vexatione Willelmi* [*de S. Carilevo*] *episcopi* [*Dunelm.*] (? *p*1125), in S. DURH. I 170–95 [*cf.* EHR LXVI (1951) 32–41].

V. Furs. *Vita S. Fursei abbatis Latiniacensis* [*ob.* 650], *Acta SS. Ben.* II 300–309; *v. et. Mir. Furs.*

V. Greg. *Vita S. Gregorii* [*ob.* 604], by a monk of Whitby (*c*710) (extr.), ed. C. Plummer, *Baedae Opera Historica* II 389–91, and EHR III (1888) 305–10; superseded by ed. B. Colgrave (Lawrence, Kansas, 1968), 72–138 [by p. of MS].

V. G. Sempr. *Vita S. Gilberti de Sempringham* [*ob.* 1189] (wr. *c*1202), MS BL Cotton Cleopatra B I ff. 33–89v. [by f.; complements *Canon. G. Sempr.*]; extr. pp. *v–*xxix, in *MonA* VI, between pp. 946 and 947; *cf. Inst. Sempr.*

V. Gund. *Vita Gundulfi* [*ob.* 1108] (wr. *c*1120), The Life of Gundulf, Bishop of Rochester, ed. R. M. Thomson, Toronto Med. Latin Texts (1977) 1–71 [by cap.].

V. Har. *Vita Haroldi* [*ob.* 1066] (wr. *a*1216), ed. W. de G. Birch (1885) [by cap. & f.].

V. Hug. Metr. v. H. AVR. *Hugh.*

V. II Off. *Vitae duorum Offarum sive Offanorum Merciorum regum* [attrib. M. PAR.], ed. W. Wats (1639); *vv. ll.* from

R. W. Chambers, Beowulf, an introduction to the study of the poem (ed. 3, Cambridge, 1963) 217–43.

Villainage in Eng. P. Vinogradoff: Villainage in England, essays in English medieval history (Oxford, 1892).

VINSAUF Geoffrey de Vinsauf [*ob. p*1200]: **AV** *Documentum de modo et arte dictandi et versificandi*, ed. E. Faral, Les Arts poétiques du XIIe et du XIIIe siècle (Paris, 1924) 265–320 [by bk. & sect.]; **CR** *Summa de coloribus rhetoricis, ib.* 321–7; **Interdict.** [attrib.] Poèmes sur l'interdit de l'Angleterre, *ib.* 24–6, *v.* M. RIEVAULX (*Vers.*) 20–22; **PN** *Poetria nova, ib.* 197–262 [by line]; also ed. E. Gallo (The Hague, 1971) [corrects error in Faral's line-numbering at 520–4).

Vis. Derry *Acta* of Archb. Colton [*ob.* 1404] in his metropolitan Visitation of the Diocese of Derry, 1397, w. a rental of the See estates at the time, ed. W. Reeves (Dublin, 1850).

Vis. Ebor. Documents relating to diocesan and provincial visitations (1407–52), Surtees Soc. CXXVII (1916) 131–302.

Vis. Ely Ely Visitation recs., in *Ord. Ely* 4–23, 29–33, 44–67.

Vis. Eton Visitation of Eton College (1561), in *Stat. King's Cantab.* 634–8.

Vis. Godstow Visitation of Godstow nunnery by William, Bishop of Lincoln (1432), in *Reg. Godstow* EETS CXXIX lxxxi–lxxxvii.

Visio S. Thom. *Visio cujusdam de morte sancti Thome martiris* (wr. *c*1175), Mittellateinisches Jahrbuch IX (1974) 165–8 [by stanza].

Vis. Linc. 1420–49 Visitation of religious houses in the diocese of Lincoln, 3 vols. Linc. Rec. Soc. VII, XIV, XXI (1914–23) (=Cant. & York Soc. XVII, XXIV, XXXIII); 1517–31, Linc. Rec. Soc. XXXIII, XXXV, XXXVII (1940–7).

Vis. Norw. Visitations of the diocese of Norwich 1492–1532, Camd. Soc. NS XLIII (1888).

Vis. Southwell Visitations and memorials of Southwell [Notts] Minster (1469–1553), Camd. Soc. NS XLVIII (1891).

Vis. S. Paul. *c*1250 Visitations of churches belonging to St. Paul's Cathedral, Camd. Misc. IX, Camd. Soc. NS LIII (1895); 1295 *Visitatio facta in thesaura* (sic) *S. Pauli*, in *Hist. S. Paul.* 310–35 [also in *MonA*, ed. 1673, III 308–31].

Vis. Wells Visitation of religious houses and hospitals by Bishop's Vicar-general (Bath and Wells) (1526), Som Rec. Soc. XXXIX (1924) 207–25.

Vivarium *Vivarium*, journal for mediaeval philosophy and the intellectual life of the middle ages I– (Assen, 1963–).

V. Kenelmi Lives of St. Kenelm of Winchcombe [*ob.* 821]: **A** (early 10c.), MS Corpus Christi Coll. Camb. 367 ff. 45–8, ed. R. von Antropoff, Die Entwicklung der Kenelm-Legenda (Bonn, 1965), app. xxxiii–iv [by cap.]; **B** (*c*1074), MS Bodl. Douce 368 ff. 80–83v, *etc., ib.* ii–xxiv [by f.].

V. Kentig. *Vita S. Kentegerni* (wr. *a*1164), ed. A. P. Forbes, Lives of St. Ninian and St. Kentigern, Historians of Scotland V (Edinburgh, 1874) 243–52 [by cap.]; also in *Reg. Glasg.* I app. II lxxviii–lxxxvi.

V. Merl. *Vita Merlini* [attrib. G. MON.] (wr. *c*1150), ed. J. J. Parry (Urbana, Ill., 1925) [by line]; also ed. B. Clarke (Cardiff, 1973).

V. Montf. C. Bémont: Simon de Montfort .. sa vie (1208–65) (Paris, 1884); **app.** appendix of docs. 263–380; *v. et. Chr. Battle 1258–65.*

V. Neot. *Vitae S. Neoti* [*ob.* ? *c*875]: **A** (wr. *c*1100), ed. J. Whitaker (1809); superseded by ed. M. Lapidge (Cambridge, 1985) 111–42; **B** (wr. 12c.) *Acta SS. Boll.* July VII (1731) 319–29.

V. Odonis v. EADMER Odo.

V. Odulphi v. T. MARLB. *Odulph.*

V. Osw. v. BYRHT. *V. Osw.*

V. Ric. II *Historia vitae et regni Ricardi II monacho quodam de Evesham consignata* (*c*1404), ed. T. Hearne (Oxford, 1729).

V. Rob. Knaresb. *Vita S. Roberti juxta Knaresburgum* [*ob. c*1235] (wr.? 13c.), *Anal. Boll.* LVII (1939) 375–400 [by cap.]; *cf.* STUDLEY.

V. Rob. Newm. *Vita S. Roberti* [Abbot of Newminster, Northumb, *ob.* 1159] (wr.? 12c.), *Anal. Boll.* LVI (1938) 343–60 [by cap.].

VSB *Vitae Sanctorum Britanniae et Genealogiae* (11c.–12.), ed. A.W. Wade-Evans (Cardiff, 1944).

VSH *Vitae Sanctorum Hiberniae* (12c.–14c.), ed. C. Plummer, 2 vols. (Oxford, 1910).

V. Swith. *Vita S. Swithuni,* ed. M. Lapidge, *Winchester Studies* IV pt. ii (forthcoming) [by cap.]; also *Anal. Boll.* VII (1888) 374–80.

V. Thom. Lives of St. Thomas of Canterbury [*ob.* 1170]: **A** [attrib. Roger of Pontigny], in *Becket Mat.* IV 1–79 [by cap.]; **B** (wr. ? *a*1175), *ib.* 80–144 [by cap.].

V. Thurst. *Vita Thurstani archiepiscopi* [*ob.* 1140], in *Hist. Church York* II 259–69; *v. et* G. NOTT., H. PONTEFR.

V. Walth. v. J. FURNESS *Walth.*

V. Wenefr. *Vita S. Wenefredae* [7c.] (wr. ? 12c.), *Acta SS. Boll.* Nov. I (1887) 702–8 [by sect.]; also in *VSB* 288–308; *cf.* R. SHREWSB.

V. Will. *Vita S. Willelmi* [*ob.* 1154], in *Hist. Church York* II 270–91; *v. et. Mir. Will.*

V. Wist. v. T. MARLB. *Wistan.*

V. Wulf. et Ruff. *Acta SS. Wulfhadi et Ruffini martyrum, Acta SS. Boll.* July V (1727) 575–82 [by sect.]; also in *MonA* VI 226–30 and WHITTLESEY app. pp. 140–59.

Wager The Wager story (15c.), *Romania* LXXXVIII (1967) 408–16 [by f.].

WALCHER Walcher, Prior of Malvern [*ob.* 1135]: **Drac.** *De dracone* (1120), [based on PETRUS], *Sefarad* III (1943) 87–97; also (extr.), in *Med. Sci.* 116–17; **Exp.** *De experientia scriptoris* (*p*1092) (extr.), in *Med. Sci.* 114–15.

WALEYS *v.* J. WALEYS, T. WALEYS.

WALLINGF. Richard of Wallingford, Abbot of St. Albans [*ob.* 1336], Richard of Wallingford, ed. J. D. North, 3 vols. (Oxford, 1976): **Alb.** *Tractatus Albionis,* (1327) 1976), I 245–401; supersedes *Early Sci. Ox.* 349–70; **EPT** *Exafrenon pronosticacionum temporis,* I 179–243; **Eccl.** Ecclesiastical writings, I 527–54; **Horol.** *Tractatus horologii astronomici,* I 441–526; **Maud.** Canons to the tables of John Maudith and a related treatise, (extr.), I 3–19; **Or.** *Orationes,* in *G. S. Alb.* II 294–9; **Quad.** *Quadripartitum,* ed. North, I 21–169; supersedes *Isis* V (1923) 99–115, 359–63; **Rect.** *Tractatus rectanguli,* I 403–31; supersedes *Early Sci. Ox.* 337–48; **Sect.** *Tractatus de sectore,* I 170–8.

W. ALNWICK William of Alnwick, O.F.M. [*ob.* 1333]: **Aetern.** *Quaestio utrum asserere mundum fuisse ab aeterno fuerit de intentione Aristotelis* (*Determ.* q. 10), ed. F. A. Prezioso, L'Eternità aristotelica (Padua, 1962) 27–70; **An.** *Quaestiones de Anima,* Studia mediewistyczne VII (1966) 6–76; **Determ.** *Determinationes* (extr.), *Bibliotheca Franciscana scholastica medii aevi* X (Quaracchi, 1937), xxii–xlvi [*v. et. Aetern.*]; **QD** *Quaestiones disputatae, ib.*: 1–175 *De esse intelligibili quaestiones* VI; 179–605 *Quaestiones X de quodlibet;* **Sent.** *Commentarius in I Sententiarum,* prol. q. 2, Franciscan Studies XXVII (1967) 63–107.

WALS. Thomas Walsingham, monk of St. Albans [*ob. c*1422]: **AD** *De archana* (*sic*) *deorum,* ed. R. A. Van Kluyve (Durham, N. Carolina, 1968); **HA** *Historia Anglicana* (1272–1422), in *Chr. Mon. S.Alb.* I, 2 vols. (1863) [*v. et. Chr. S. Alb. 1406–20*]; **YN** *Ypodigma Neustriae* (–1419), *ib.* VII (1876); *v. et. Chr. Angl., G. S. Alb.*

WALT. ANGL. *Walterus Anglicus* [*fl. c*1200]: **Fab.** *Fabulae,* ed. K. McKenzie and W. A. Oldfather, Univ. of

Illinois Studies in language and literature V (1919) 49–214 [by no. & line]; also ed. L. Hervieux, Les Fabulistes latins II (1894) 317–91; **FabP.** prose version, ed. Hervieux, 383–91 [by no. & line].

WALT. EVESHAM *v.* ODINGTON.

WALTH. Ep. Waltheof, Abbot of Melrose [*ob.* 1159]: *Epistola de visione* (1159), *Studia Anselmiana* XLIII (1958) 96–100; *cf.* J. FURNESS *Walth..*

WALT. WIMB. Walter of Wimborne [*fl.* 1265]: **App.** Appendices, The Poems of Walter of Wimborne, ed. A. G. Rigg (Toronto, 1978) 281–314 [by no. & stanza]; **Carm.** *Marie Carmina, ib.* 188–277 [by stanza]; **Elem.** *Tractatus moralis super quatuor elementa* (extr.), *ib.* 316–25 [by p.]; MS Univ. Libr. Camb. Ii 2. 27 [by f.]; **Palpo** *De palpone, ib.* 38–70 [by stanza]; **Scel.** *De mundi scelere, ib.* 105–10 [by line]; **Sim.** *De symonia et avaritia, ib.* 113–43 [by stanza]; **Van.** *De mundi vanitate, ib.* 73–102 [by stanza]; **Virgo** *Ave Virgo Mater Christi, ib.* 146–83 [by stanza].

Warburg Institute Journal I–IV (1937–41); subsequently known as Journal of the Warburg and Courtauld Institutes V– (1942–).

War. Issue Exchequer of Receipt, Writs and Warrants for Issues, MS PRO (E. 404).

War. PS v. PS.

W. BERNHAM Ep. W. de Bernham, vicar of Inchture [*fl.* 1255]: Letters from Paris and Oxford, in *FormOx* 472–91 [by no.].

W. BURLEY Walter Burley [*ob. c*1345]: **Anal. Post.** *Expositio super libros Analyticorum Posteriorum* (Venice, 1497); **Conseq.** *De consequentiis,* Franciscan Studies XL (1980) 113–63; **Def.** *De definitione,* Med. Stud. XXVII (1965) 337–40; **Ente** *De Ente, Manuscripta* VII (1963) 105–8; **Form.** *De formis,* ed. F. J. Down Scott, Texte aus der mittelalterlichen Geisteswelt IV (Munich, 1970) 262–84 [by sect.]; **Insol.** *Insolubilia,* AHDLMA XXXVII (1970) 262–84 [by sect.]; **Periherm.** Treatises on Aristotle's *Liber Perihermeneias:* **B** *Commentarius medius,* Franciscan Studies XXXIII (1973) 45–134; **D** *Questiones,* Franciscan Studies XXXIV (1974) 202–95; **Pol.** Commentary on the Politics [of Aristotle] (extr.), in Wilkinson Essays 278–81; **Potent.** *De potentiis animae,* Med. Stud. XXXIII (1971) 88–113 [by sect.]; **Prop. Hypoth.** *De propositionibus hypotheticis,* part one, Franciscan Studies XXIII (1963) 14–67; **Pur. Log. Brev.** *De puritate artis logicae tractatus brevior,* ed. P. Boehner, Franciscan Institute Publications, Text S. XI (1955), 199–260; **Pur. Log. Long.** *De puritate artis logicae tractatus longior, ib.* 1–197; **Rel.** *De relativis,* Franciscan Studies XXII (1962) 159–71; **Suppos.** *De suppositionibus,* Franciscan Studies XXXII (1972) 31–64; **TP** *De toto et parte,* AHDLMA XXXIII (1966) 299–303; **Vit. Phil.** *Liber de vitis et moribus philosophorum et poetarum,* ed. H. Knust (Tübingen, 1886).

W. CANT. William of Canterbury [*fl.* 1170]: **Mir. Thom.** *Miracula S. Thomae,* in *Becket Mat.* I 137–546 [by bk. & cap.]; **V. Thom.** *Vita et passio S. Thomae, ib.* 1–136 [by bk. & cap.].

W. CHATTON Walter of Chatton, O.F.M. [*ob.* ? 1343]: **Cont.** *Quaestio de continuo,* Franciscan Studies XXVI (1966) 234–66; **Paup.** *De paupertate evangelica,* AFH XXV (1932) 36–58, 210–40; **Sent.** *Commentarium in Sententias:* **prol.** prologus, q. 2, in *Med. Thinkers* 235–69; I d. 3 q. 2, Franciscan Studies XXXI (1971) 90–126 [*cf. ib.* XXVII (1967) 199–212]; I d. 17 q. 1, *ib.* XXXVII (1977) 38–54, 55–65 [by bk., dist., q., & p.].

W. CHESTER Vers. Anselm. William, monk of Chester [*fl.* 1100]: Verses on Anselm, Archb. of Canterbury [*ob.* 1109], Rev. Ben. XCV (1985) 271–9 [by no. & line].

W. COMBE William, Cantor of Combe [*fl.* ? *c*1200]: Hymns to St Thomas of Canterbury, ed. J. A. Giles, *Anecdota Baedae,* Caxton Society VII (1851), 191–6, checked against MS. Bodl. 509 f. 12–14v.

W. COVENTR. *Memoriale fratris Walteri de Coventria* [attrib.] (*p*1293), 2 vols. RS LVIII (1872–3): I and II 1–195 (–1201) are derived from known chroniclers; II 196–279 (1202–25) [anon.], based on anon. chron. of Barnwell (*c*1227).

W. DAN. Walter Daniel [*fl.* 1170]: **Ailred** *Vita Ailredi Abbatis Rievall'* [*ob.* 1167] (wr. *c*1170), ed. F. M. Powicke, Med. Texts (1950) [by cap.]; **Ep.** *Epistola ad Mauricium* (*c*1170), *ib.* 66–81 [by f.]; **Sent.** *Centum sententiae*, *Sacris Erudiri* XI (1960) 287–374 [by no.]; (extr.), JRL Bull. VI (1922) 323–7; **Serm.** *Sermones*, *Sacris Erudiri* XI (1960) 374–83; (extr.), ed. Powicke, JRL Bull. 330–31 and Med. Texts (1950) xxiv–v [by f.].

W. DE CHAMBRE *v. Hist. Durh.*

W. DE MARA William de Mara, O.F.M. [*fl.* 1270]: **Decl.** *Declarationes seu examinationes de variis sententiis S. Thomae Aquinatis*, ed. F. Pelster, *Opusc. & Text.* XXI (1956) [by sect.].

W. DE MONTIBUS *v.* W. LEIC.

W. DONC. Aph. Phil. William of Doncaster [*fl.* ? early 12c]: *Explicatio aphorismatum philosophicorum*, Studien und Texte zur Geistesgeschichte des Mittelalters XI (Leiden & Cologne, 1976) [by no. & sect.].

W. DROGHEDA SA William of Drogheda, canonist [*ob.* 1245]: *Summa Aurea continens modum advocandi* [*etc.*] (*c*1239), ed. L. Wahrmund, Quellen zur Gesch. des römisch-kanonischen Processes im Mittelalter, II ii (Innsbruck, 1914) [by cap.].

WEALDHERE Ep. The letter from Bishop Wealdhere of London to Archbishop Brihtwold of Canterbury: the earliest original 'letter close' extant in the West (704–5), ed. P. Chaplais, Medieval Scribes, manuscripts & Libraries, Essays presented to N. R. Ker (London, 1978), 22–3 [supersedes *CS* 115].

WelshR Welsh Rolls (1276–95), MS PRO (C. 77).

WEND. Roger of Wendover [*ob.* 1236]: *Flores Historiarum* (1154–1235), 3 vols. RS LXXXIV (1886–9) [earlier portion (447–1153), incl. in ed. H. O. Coxe, 4 vols. Eng. Hist. Soc. 1841–4, is cited only in so far as it is incorporated in M. PAR. *Maj.* I and II].

WESSINGTON Resp. John Wessington (*alias* Washington), Prior of Durham [*ob.* 1446]: *Responsiones contra priorem studentium* (1422), in *Collect. Ox.* III 27–33.

West Coker M. Nathan: Annals of West Coker (Cambridge, 1957).

WEY Itin. William Wey (*alias* Way) [*ob.* 1476]: Itineraries .. to Jerusalem, 1458 and 1462; to St. James of Compostella, 1456, Roxb. Club (1857).

W. FITZST. Thom. William Fitzstephen [*ob.* 1190]: *Vita S. Thomae*, in *Becket Mat.* III 13–154 [by cap.]; **prol.** *prologus (Descriptio Londoniae)*, *ib.* 1–13 [by cap.].

W. FLEETE William of Fleet, O.S.A. [*fl. c*1368–80]: **Cath.** Writings on St Catherine of Siena, ed. R. Fawtier, Mélanges d'archéologie et d'histoire XXXIV (1914) 40–93; **Ep.** *Epistolae*, *Analecta Augustiniana* XVIII (1941) 308–24 [by no.].

W. GLASG. William of Glasgow [12c.]: *Carmen de morte Sumerledi* (*c*1164), in S. DURH. II 386–8 [by line].

W. GUISB. Walter of Guisborough [alias of Hemingford or Hemingburgh] [*ob.* ? *c*1315]: Chronicle (1048–1315), Camd. 3rd S. LXXXIX (1957); **Cont.** *De gestis Regis Edwardi Tertii et caeteris eventibus* (1327–46), ed. H. C. Hamilton, *Chronicon Domini Walteri de Hemingburgh*, Soc. of Antiquaries of London (1849), II 297–426.

WHITTINGTON Vulg. Robert Whittington: *Vulgaria* (1520), EETS CLXXXVII (1932) 31–128.

WHITTLESEY Walter of Whittlesey [*ob.* ? *c*1321]: *Historia coenobii Burgensis* [Peterborough] (1246–1321), in *Hist. Angl. Script.* 125–216; **app.** additions to H. ALBUS, in H. ALBUS *app.* 140–73; **Cont.** *Continuatio* (1321–38), in *Hist. Angl. Script.* 217–37; *cf.* SWAFHAM.

Wilkinson Essays Essays in medieval history presented to B. Wilkinson, ed. T. A. Sandquist and M. R. Powicke (Toronto, 1969).

WILL. ANGL. Willelmus Anglicus [*fl.* 1230]: **Astr.** *Opus astrolabii* [transl. of Al Zarkali] (extr.), ed. L. Sédillot, Mémoires sur les instruments astronomiques des arabes (Paris, 1841) 185–90; corrected and supplemented by *N. & E.* XXXV (1896) 633–40.

WILL. GLASG. Sum. William of Glasgow [*fl.* 1160]: *Carmen de Morte Sumerledi*, in S. DURH. II 386–8.

WILLIAM OF OCCAM *v.* OCKHAM.

WILLIB. Bonif. Willibald, Bishop of Eichstatt [*ob.* 786]: *Vita S. Bonifatii*, ed. W. Levison, *MGH* (Hanover, 1905) [by cap.].

Wills Dublin Register of wills and inventories in the diocese of Dublin (1457–83), R. Soc. Antiq. of Ireland, extra vol. (1898).

Wills Durh. Wills and inventories illustrative of the northern counties of England (11c.–), taken mainly from Durham Registry, Surtees Soc. II, XXXVIII, CXII, CXLII, (1835, 1860, 1906, 1929).

Wills N. Country North country Wills of York, Nottingham, Northumberland, Cumberland, Westmorland, *etc.* (1383–1604), Surtees Soc. CXVI, CXXI (1908–12).

Wills Richm. Wills and inventories from the registry of the Archdeaconry of Richmond, *etc.* (1442–1579), Surtees Soc. XXVI (1853).

Wills Wells Wells Wills (1528–36), ed. F. W. Weaver (1890).

WILL. William, perhaps Prior of Dover [14c.]: *Breviarium regulare musicae*, ed. G. Reaney *Corp. Script. Mus.* XII (1966), 15–31.

WILTON Thomas Wilton, Chancellor of St. Paul's [*fl.* 1288–1322]: **Act.** *Actus inaugurales*, AFH XXIV (1931) 7–11; **QD** *Quaestiones disputatae* (extr.), Studia mediewistyczne V (1964) 75–116.

Wilts Rec. Soc. Wilts Record Society, 3 vols. (1896–1902); also Wiltshire Record Society, publications, XXIII– (1967–); formerly Wiltshire Archaeological and Natural History Society, Records Branch, I–XXII (1939–66).

WINCHELSEA Robert Winchelsea, Archb. of Canterbury [*ob.* 1313]: **Quaest.** Two *Quaestiones*, in *Theol. Ox.* 137–45; **Reg.** *Registrum*, *v. Reg. Cant.*.

Windsor Castle W. H. St. John Hope: Windsor Castle, an architectural history (1086–), 2 vols. (1913).

WINFRETH *v.* BONIF.

W. JUM. William of Jumièges [*ob.* ? 1087]: *Gesta Normannorum ducum* I–VII (–1087), ed. A. Duchesne, *Historiae Normannorum scriptores antiqui* (Paris, 1619) 215–92 [by bk. & cap.]; **Cont.** Continuation (–1137), by TORIGNI, VIII, 292–317 [by bk. & cap.] [this ed. cont. many interpolations by ORD. VIT. and TORIGNI, subsequently excised by J. Marx in his ed. (Rouen & Paris, 1914)]; also *PL* CXLIX 779–914.

W. LEIC. Sim. William of Leicester (*alias* de Montibus) [*ob.* 1213]: *Similitudinarius*, MS Lincs RO Ancaster 16/1; MS Peterhouse Camb. 255.

W. MACCLESFIELD Quaest. William of Macclesfield [*ob.* 1303]: *Correctorium corruptorii 'Quaestione'* [attrib.], *Studia Anselmiana* XXXV (Rome, 1954) [by f.].

W. MALM. William of Malmesbury [*ob. c*1143]: **Amal.** *Abbreviatio Amalarii*, RTAM XLVIII (1981) 128–71 [by bk. & cap.]; **Dunst.** *Vita S. Dunstani*, in *Mem. Dunst.* 251–324 [by bk. & cap.]; **Glast.** *De antiquitate Glastoniensis Ecclesiae* (–1126), ed. T. Hearne, in DOMERH. *Glast.* (1727) pt. i; superseded by ed. J. Scott (Woodbridge, 1981) [by cap.]; **GP** *De gestis pontificum Anglorum* (*p*1125), RS LII (1870) [by bk. & cap.]; **GR** *De gestis regum Anglorum* (*c*1125), 2 vols. RS XC (1887–9) [by bk. & cap.]; **Greg.** *Deflorationes ex libris beati Gregorii papae* (extr.), *Studia Monastica* IV (1962) 309–11; **HN** *Historia novella* (1125–42), ed. K. R. Potter, Med. Texts (1955) [by cap.]; **Lam.** Commentary on Lamentations (extr.),

Studia Monastica IV (1962) 283–307; **Mir. Mariae** *De laudibus et miraculis S. Mariae*, ed. J. M. Canal, *Claretianum* VIII (1968) 111–236; **Polyh.** *Polyhistor*, ed. H. T. Ouelette (Binghamton, N. Y., 1982); **Wulfst.** *Vita Wulfstani* [*ob.* 1095], Camd. 3rd S. XL (1928) 1–67; **Wulfst. Abbr.** Abbreviated version, *v.* SENATUS *Wulfst.* [*v. et. Mir. Wulfst.*].

W. MERLE Temp. William Merle (*alias* Morley) [*ob.* 1347]: *Considerationes temperiei pro septem annis* (1337–44), MS Bodl. Digby 176 ff. 4–8v.; facs. ed. G. J. Symons (1891) [by f.].

W. NEWB. William of Newburgh [*ob. c*1200]: **Cant.** *Explanatio sacri epithalamii in matrem sponsi*, ed. J. C. Gorman, (Fribourg, 1960); **HA** *Historia rerum Anglicarum* (1066–1198), in *Chr. Steph.* I 1–408, II 409–500 [by bk. & cap.]; **Cont.** *Continuatio* (1199–1298), *ib.* II 501–83 [by p.]; **Serm.** *Sermones*, ed. T. Hearne (Oxford, 1719), III 819–902.

W. PAGULA William de Pagula [? Paull, Yorks], Vicar of Winkfield [*fl.* 1314–32]: **Ep.** *Epistola ad regem Edwardum III* (*c*1331), ed. J. Moisant (Paris, 1891) 83–123 [by sect.; on authorship, *v.* RHS Trans. V (1955) 107–8].

W. PETERB. Bell. Hisp. Walter of Peterborough [*fl.* 1370]: *De victoria belli in Hispania per principem Edwardum* (1367), in *Pol. Poems* I 97–122.

W. POIT. William of Poitiers, Dean of Lisieux [*ob. p*1087]: *Gesta Willelmi ducis Normannorum et Regis Anglorum* (*c*1075), ed. R. Foreville (Paris, 1952) [by bk. & cap.].

W. RAMSEY Cant. William of Ramsey [*fl.* 1200]: *Distinctio super cantica*, MS Prague 431; *Sacris Erudiri* X (1958) 335–52 [by f.].

W. RYMYNGTON William of Rymyngton, Prior of Sawley and Chancellor of Oxford [*fl.* 1372]: **Concl.** *XLV Conclusiones*, MS Bodl. 158 ff. 199–217; **Dial.** *Dialogus inter catholicam veritatem et haereticam pravitatem*, *ib.* ff. 188–97; **Medit.** *Meditationes* or *Stimulus peccatoris*, Cîteaux XVI (1965) 278–304; **Serm.** Two sermons to the northern clergy (1372–3), *ib.* XIX (1968) 46–67.

W. S. ALB. V. Alb. & Amphib. William of St. Albans [*fl.* 1178]: *Vitae SS. Albani et Amphibali, Acta SS. Boll.* June IV (1707) 149–59 [by cap.]; shorter version in M. PAR. *Maj.* I 149–54;

W. SAY Lib. Reg. Cap. William Say, Dean of the Chapel Royal: *Liber regiae capellae* (1449), HBS XCII (1961).

W. THETFORD Ep. William of Thetford, O.P. [*fl. c*1240]: Letters, Journal of Ecclesiastical History V (1954) 201–4.

WULF. Wulfstan of Winchester [*fl.* 1000]: **Æthelwold** Life of St. Æthelwold [*ob.* 984], ed. M. Winterbottom, Three Lives of English Saints, Toronto Med. Latin Texts (1972) 33–63 [by cap.]; also *Acta SS. Ben.* V 608–24; **Poems** Poems, *Anal. Hymn.* XLVIII 9–18, LI 164–6 [attrib.], *PL* CXXXVII 105; **Swith.** *Narratio metrica de S. Swithuno* [*ob.* 862] (wr. *c*993), ed. A. Campbell (Zürich, 1951) [by bk. & line].

WW Anglo-Saxon and Old English Vocabularies, ed. T. Wright and R. P. Wülcker, 2 vols. (1884) [mainly 10c. (? 11c.) or 15c.; undated entries are 15c.; for refs. *v.* vol. II (Index); cols. 1–54 superseded by *GlC*, cols. 192–257 by *GlH*; *v. et.* ÆLF. *Coll.* and ÆLF. *Gl.*]; earlier ed. T. Wright, 2 vols. (1857, 1873) [*v. et.* GARL. *Dict.*, NECKAM *Ut.*].

W. WARE Sent. William of Ware, O.F.M. [*fl.* 1300]: *Quaestiones super libros Sententiarum* (extr.): q. 19, BGPM Suppl. I (1913), 311–18.

W. WATERFORD Wycl. William of Waterford, O.F.M. [*ob.* 1397]: *Contra XVIII articulos Johannis Wiclef*, in *Fasc. Rerum Expet.* I 280–95.

W. WOODFORD William of Woodford, O.F.M. [*ob. p*1411]: **Def. Mend.** *Defensorium fratrum mendicantium contra Richardum Armachanum* (*c*1396) (extr.), Franciscan Studies XXXV (1975) 98–106; **Wycl.** *De causis condemnationis articulorum XVIII damnatorum Johannis Wyclif* (1396), in *Fasc. Rerum Expect.* I 191–265.

W. WORC. William of Worcester (*alias* Botonier) [*ob. c*1482]: **Anecd.** *Anecdota*, in *BBExch* II 522–41; **Ann.** *Annales rerum Anglicarum* (1324–1468; anon. cont. –1491), Letters and papers illustrative of the wars of the English, RS XXII (1864) II 743–93; **Collect.** *v. Collect. W. Worc.*; **Itin.** Itineraries, ed. J. H. Harvey, Med. Texts (1969).

WW Sup. The Old English Vocabularies in MS Oxford Bodley 730 (12c.), English Studies LXII (1981) 202–7 [by no.].

W. WYCUMBE V. Rob. Betun. William of Wycumbe, Prior of Lanthony [*fl.* 1150]: Life of Robert de Bethune [*ob.* 1148], Bishop of Hereford, in *Anglia Sacra* II 295–321 [by cap.].

WYCHE Richard Wyche [*fl.* 1400]: **Ep.** *Epistola*, EHR V (1890) 531–44; *v. et. Ziz.*

WYCH William Wych [*fl. a*1500]: *Liber monasterii B. Mariae Glastoniae quem Willelmus Wych monachus scribi fecit* (1342–1493), in J. GLAST. I 272–83.

WYCL. John Wycliffe [*ob.* 1384], Works of John Wyclif, Wyclif Soc. (1883–1924): **Act.** *De actibus animae*, w. *Misc. Phil.* I 1–127; **Apost.** *Tractatus de apostasia* (1889); **Blasph.** *Tractatus de blasphemia* (1893); **Chr. & Antichr.** *De Christo et Antichristo* (1383–4), w. *Pol.* II 653–92; **Civ. Dom.** *De civili dominio* (1375–6), 4 vols. (1885–1904); **Compl.** The Latin text of Wycliffe's Complaint (1382), *Speculum* VII (1932), 87–94; **Compos. Hom.** *De compositione hominis* (*c*1360) (1884); **Concl.** *De Eucharistia Conclusiones* XV (1381), in *Ziz.* 105–6; **Conf.** *De Eucharistia confessio* or *Tractatus minor de Eucharistia* (1381), in *Ziz.* 115–32; further text in Speculum VIII (1933) 503–10; **Decl.** *Declarationes Johannis Wickliff*, in WALS. *HA* I 357–63; **Dial.** *Dialogus sive Speculum ecclesie militantis* (1886); **Dom. Div.** *De dominio divino* (*a*1377) (1890); **Eccl.** *De ecclesia* (1378) (1886); **Ente** *Summa de ente*, MS Trin. Coll. Camb. B. 16. 2: I 3, I 4, II 1, II 3, II 6 (part), ed. M. H. Dziewicki, Wyclif Soc. (1909); **(Spec.)** A lost chapter of Wyclif's *Summa de Ente* (*a*1367), *Speculum* IV (1929) 339–46; **(Sum.)** I 1, I 2, ed. S. H. Thomson (Cambridge, 1930); also cited from *Wycl. & Ox.*; *v. et.* WYCL *Trin., Univ.*; **Ente Praed.** *De ente praedicamentali* (*p*1360) (1891); **Euch.** *De Eucharistia tractatus major* w. *Tractatus de Eucharistia et poenitentia sive de confessione* (1379) (1892); **Form.** *De materia et forma* (? 1365), w. *Misc. Phil.* I 163–242; **Incarn.** *Tractatus de benedicta Incarnacione* (1371) (1886); **Innoc.** *Tractatus de statu innocencie* (*c*1375–6), w. *Mand. Div.* (1922) 475–524; **Log.** *Tractatus de logica* (? 1361), 3 vols. (1893–9); **Mand. Div.** *Tractatus de mandatis divinis* (1375–6) (1922); **prol.** Prologue, *Speculum* VIII (1933) 201–2; **Min.** *Opera minora* (1913); **Misc. Phil.** *Miscellanea philosophica*, 2 vols. (1902–5) [*v. et.* WYCL. *Act., Form., Univ.*; other works of dubious authorship]; **Offic. Reg.** *Tractatus de officio regis* (1887); **Op. Evang.** *Opus evangelicum*, 4 vols. in 2 (1895–6); **Peccatum** *Differentia inter peccatum mortale et veniale*, w. *Mand. Div.* (1922), 527–33; **Pol.** Polemical works in Latin, 2 vols. (1883); **Potest. Pape** *De potestate Papae* (1379) (1907); **Quaest. Log.** *Quaestiones XIII logicae et philosophicae* (1360–2), w. *Ente Praed.* 221–306; **Serm.** *Sermones*, 4 vols. (1887–90); **Sim.** *De Simonia* (1379–80) (1898); **Trial.** *Trialogus cum supplemento Trialogi* (1382), ed. G. Lechler (Oxford, 1869); **Trin.** *Tractatus de trinitate* (= *Summa de ente* II 4), ed. A. du P. Breck (Boulder, Col., 1962); **Univ.** *Tractatus de universalibus* (= *Summa de ente* I 5 [6]), MS Prague University Library VIII G 23 ff. 1–84 [vv. ll. from MS IV H 9]; now ed. I. J. Mueller (Oxford, 1985); cf. *De universalibus*, in *Misc. Phil.* II 1–188 which is by Stanislav of Znojmo; **Ver.** *De veritate sacrae scripturae* (1378–9), 3 vols. (1905–7); **Versut.** *De versutiis anti-Christi*, EHR XLVII (1932) 95–103.

Wycl. & Ox. J. A. Robson: Wyclif and the Oxford schools,

the relation of the *Summa de Ente* to scholastic debates at medieval Oxford (Cambridge, 1961).

Wycl. Soc. The Wyclif Society [founded 1882, dissolved 1925], publications (1883–1924); *cf.* Note on Wyclif Soc. in Poole Essays 98–114.

WYKES Thomas Wykes (*alias* de Wyca) [c1222–91]: *Chronicon* (1066–1289) [attrib.], in *Ann. Mon.* IV 6–319 [second text; *v. et. Ann. Osney*]; **Vers.** Verses in praise of the young Edward (c1272), in *Pol. Songs* 132.

WYNTERTON Thomas Winterton [fl. 1390], *v. Ziz*.

Year Bk. Year Books (20–22 Ed. I, 30–35 Ed. I, 11–20 Ed. III), 20 vols. RS XXXI (1863–1900); Year Books of Ed. II etc., Selden Soc., Year Book S. I– (1903–).

York Plays The York Plays, ed. R. Beadle (1982) [by f.].

Ziz. *Fasciculi Zizaniorum Magistri Johannis Wyclif cum tritico* [attrib. NETTER], RS V (1858), incl. statements by or proc. against: ASTON, John (1382); CROMPE (Henry Crumpe) (1384, 1392); HERFORD (Nicholas Hereford) w. Philip Repyngdon (1382); KYN. (John Cunningham) (c1363); LANGTON, John (c1390); LAVENHAM, Richard (c1380); PURVEY, John (1401); SAUTRY, William (1399); STOKES, Peter (*ob.* 1399); SWYND. (William Swynderby) (1382); TYSS. (John Tyssyngton) (1382); WYCHE, Richard (c1401; *cf.* EHR V 531–44); WYNTERTON, Thomas (c1390); besides WYCL. *et al.*

D

D [CL]

1 D (letter of alphabet).

D littera propinqua est consonantibus his, CGLPRMT, quae succedunt in locum ejus, ut 'accipe', 'aggere' . . BEDE *Orth.* 7; interdum D littera geminatur, quoties ab ea sequens incipit syllaba et una pars orationis expletur, ut 'reddere' dicimus geminata D, 'reducere' autem simplici ALCUIN *Orth.* 2344; A ante D breviatur, ut 'Hyades' . . BACON *Tert.* 258; grossiores mute, sc. B, D, G, . . cum M et N non consillabicantur *Ps.*-GROS. *Gram.* 28.

2 musical note.

rotunda B cum D sonat ditonum TUNST. 215a.

3 numeral (= 500).

D . . est . . nota . . numeri cum quingentos [significat] BEDE *Orth.* 7; Latino more computando D notat quingentos BACON *Gram. Gk.* 82.

dab- v. et. daub-.

dabilis, (log.) admissible.

omnes proposiciones ypothetice comprehenduntur solum sub tribus speciebus, sc. sub condicionali, concessiva, et disjunctiva, cum non sit ~is proposicio ypothetica quin sit aliqua illarum explicite vel implicite WYCL. *Quaest. Log.* 233; ad argumentum nullam ~em esse transubstanciacionem hujusmodi . . NETTER *DAF* II 122a.

dabitis, a logical mood.

BACON XV 301 (v. celantes).

dabitura, dabura v. daubatura.

dabreiamim [Heb.], (bibl.) Chronicles.

iste liber Grece Paralipomenon, quod sonat 'residuorum' . . Hebraice . . dicitur Dabreiamin, quod sonat 'verba dierum' S. LANGTON *Chron.* 63.

daca v. Dacus 2b. **dacas** v. dorcas.

Dacensis, (w. *hachia*) Danish axe, pole-axe. *Cf. Dacus* 2b, *Danechius.*

1200 ei robavit j haccham Dacen[sem] *CurR* I 246.

daceria v. daieria a.

dacheum [cf. OF *dache*], (?) straw; but *cf. drasca.*

1296 in ~eo pro porcis, fabis plantandis . . et aliis minutis *DL MinAc* (*Kneesal, Notts*) 1/1 r. 1 (cf. ib. r. 6: in v saccis dacheo (*sic*) ad porcos).

Dachus v. Dacus. **dacium, ~ia** v. datium.

dacra, ~um, ~is [OF *dacre* < Frk. < decuria; *cf.* AN, ME *diker* < AS **dicor*], set of ten: **a** (of hides); **b** (of iron rods); **c** (of pairs of horse-shoes or gloves); **d** (of knives).

a c**1177** pro tacra coriorum (v. corium 1c); †a**1204** (1295) concessisse . . de coriis . . de ij ~is j quad. et, si j ~a per se venerit, quadrantem (*Ch. Regis*) *Reg. Wint.* II 742; **1216** tria lesta corei et xv daker' *Pat* 197a; **1218** concessimus . . xij ~as coriorum *Cl* 349a; **1224** de quolibet ~o coriorum, obolum *Pat* 433; **1242** v tacres coreorum *Cl* 470; **1275** attachiati sunt . . per iij diker' de coriis bovinis *SelPlMan* 145; **1284** nullus confrater gilde . . debet habere *lotte* neque *cavyl* cum alio in minori quam dim. quarterio pellium et dim. ~a coriorum *Stat. Gild. Berw.* 95*; **1300** de qualibet ~a coreorum, si vendantur per ~as, j d.; de dim. ~a vel iiij coreis vel iij et ij coreis, ob. (*Assisa Tollon.*) *APScot* I app. p. 305; **1323** [lastagium] de quolibet lasto coreorum siccorum, unde xx ~res faciunt lastum et x corea faciunt j ~em, *EEC* 209 (cf. ib. 183: de x †darkeris coreorum); **1379** pro xxiij dageris pellium vitulinarum (*CourtR Yarmouth*) *Bronnen* 576 (22); **1409** v albos pro quacumque †tarqua [MS: traqua] coriorum (*DipDocE* 374) *Foed.* VIII 576b; **1460** de custuma . . j laste et iij ~arum [et] v corriorum custumatorum *ExchScot* 33. **b** reddebat civitas de Glowecestre . . xxxvj dicras ferri et c virgas ferreas ductiles ad clavos navium regis *DB* I 162. **c 1195** reddendo inde mihi per annum x s. et iij ~as ferrorum equorum (*Ch.*) *Hist. Brit. Iron & Steel Ind.* 341; lastus coreorum consistit ex x dakris et quodlibet dakrum ex x coreis; dacrum vero cirotecarum ex x paribus; dacrum vero ferrorum equorum ex xx ferris *Fleta* 73. **d 1472** xx ~e cultellorum (*Ac. Cust. Scarborough*) *Bronnen* 1662 I (22).

dactalus v. dactylus.

dactylicus [CL < δακτυλικός]

1 dactylic.

cum praeter ultimum pedem ceteri omnes dactilica fungantur scansione ALDH. *Met.* 10 p. 91; metrum ~um exametrum, quod et heroicum vocatur BEDE *AM* 108; carmine versifico cum pede dactilico WULF. *Swith. pref.* 72; Creta . . / . . dactilicis primitus usa metris NECKAM *DS* V 968; posset queri quare [rithmus decasillabus] dicatur iambicus et non dactilicus GARL. *PP* 180.

2 of a date-palm (also fig.).

802 spinis . . quae . . apostolicam inrepserunt sedem, ex qua palma pietatis dactilico florens fructu crescere debuit ALCUIN *Ep.* 258; pergrandem ejecit . . . lapidem, instar lapilli dactilici *Mir. Hen. VI* I 14.

dactylus [CL < δάκτυλος], **~is**

1 finger.

~ulus, digitus *GlC* D 7; Marcus . . fertur pollicem sibi abscidisse et . . fuit colobo ~ilis . . dactilon digitus [interpretatur] GROS. *Post. Mark* 358.

2 dactyl (metrical foot); **b** (fig.). **c** dactylic poem.

dactilus excepto decurrat fine metrorum ALDH. *VirgV* 48; 'quaerite regna poli, quaerite regna poli,' 'quaerite' ~ylus, 'regnapo' ~ylus, 'liquae' spondeus BEDE *AM* 110; [versus] quartus Adonicus, in quo / dactilus exultat, trocheus inde comes GARL. *PP* 202; est sub ea [quantitate] pes, qui dividitur in ~alum, spondeum, trocheum etc. BACON XV 219. **b** quidam de sompnis vigilans repperit unum pedem longiorem alio. . ~alus . . fuit, cum uno pede longo et alio brevi constabat *Mir. Cuthb. Farne* 7. **c** eo volvente, canit quem dactilus, anno WULF. *Swith.* II 707.

3 date (fruit); *cf.* 2 *data.* **b** (w. *acetosus* or *Indicus*) tamarind. **c** almond.

dactilus ut dulcis frondenti vertice palmae / truditur ALDH. *VirgV* 168; **9..** ~ulus, *ficæppel odde palmæppel* *WW*; ad villam [*Zoar*] . . mellitis pomis, que ~ylos dicunt, fecundam W. MALM. *GR* IV 377; dactylus hanc [palmam] ditat NECKAM *DS* VIII 41; palmarum pomis, que ~ylos nominamus GERV. TILB. III 32; **1234** retineri faciat ad opus regis . . ij miliaria vel amplius de ~ilibus *Cl* 382; ubi est pilorum generatio necessaria, ut in superciliis et barba, fiat frequens inunctio. cortices avellanarum . ., teste amigdalarum, ossa ~ilorum et mirobolan[orum] GILB. I 78v. 2; **1285** xxviij lib. datilium empte pro coquina, precium libre iiij d. (*KRAc* 91/7) *Arch.* LXX 44; **1303** pro iiij^{xx}xiij libratis ficorum, racemorum, dattylorum et coriorum de Cyvyle [*Seville*] *EEC* 268; cameli quandoque vivunt de lapidibus sive ossibus que in ~ilis reperiuntur S. SIM. *Itin.* 46; quemadmodum ferrum est cibus struthioni et ossa dactilorum camelis NETTER *DAF* II 101; **1390** pro iiij lib. dattilorum *Ac. H. Derby* 8 (cf. ib. 171: pro xj lib. de datilibus); s**1404** in festo Palmarum papa . . duas palmas et duos ~alorum . . ramos portat plenos AD. USK 97; †frincan [? l. finicon = φοινίκων] ~ilus palme idem, et †finicen balanion ~ilus idem *Alph.* 65. **b** ~ili Indici recentes mundati a granis suis, quorum interiora sunt tenera ad modum cerebri BACON V 103; oxifenicia, i. tamarindi, i. ~alus acetosus *SB* 32; oxifenicia, †fincon [v. l. finicon], dicitur eciam ~ilus Indicus vel tamarindus *Alph.* 133. **c** hic ~ilis, A. *an almonde WW.*

Dacus [CL]

1 Dacian.

hic [Domicianus] . . de ~is et Germanicis triumphans HIGD. IV 12 p. 468.

2 Dane; *cf. Geta* = Goth. **b** (as sb. f.) Danish axe, pole-axe; *cf. Dacensis, Daneschus.*

Oinus ~us . ., Anunt ~us *DB* II 25b; de ~is seu Norensibus sive Scotis, qui Eboracam navigio venientes regnum infestare solebant H. CANTOR 1v.; s**1004** Suain rex ~orum . . venit ad Nordwic H. HUNT. *HA* VI 3; Rollo . . / gentis Dacorum gloria, gemma, decus NECKAM *DS* V 662; rex Dachus pugnax et rex Norvegius audax GARL. *Tri. Eccl.* 16; s**1240** percrebuerunt . . rumores in Anglia quod ~i disponebant ipsam hostiliter invadere M. PAR. *Maj.* IV 9; de quorum [Gothorum] stirpe processerunt ~i in Europa, Getuli in Africa, Amazones in Asia HIGD. I 17 p. 144 (cf. ib. 31 p. 320: ~i quasi Dagi de Gothorum genere procreati). **b** planat et hastas / Anglia, quas comitans Dacha bipennis erit GARL. *Tri. Eccl.* 28; **1276** domum suam spoliaverunt . . de iij securibus et de iij ~is et . . de ~a Scotenci *Hund.* II 111; hec ~a, *a pollex WW.*

daemericius v. dammaricius.

daemon [CL < δαίμων]

1 daemon, spirit (good or evil).

GERV. TILB. I 17 (v. calodaemon); BACON *Mor. Phil.* 21 (v. cacodaemon).

2 demon, evil spirit; **b** (possession by); **c** (worship of); **d** (invocation of). **e** (*fuga ~onum*) St. John's wort.

taceo . . quam mire ~ones effugavit *V. Cuthb.* I 7; sunt non nulli qui, spiritus gratia pleni, infirmos curant, mortuos suscitant, ~onibus imperant BEDE *Hom.* II 11. 161; **940** (12c) ubi cum ~onibus ferreis sartaginibus crudeli torqueantur in poena *CS* 763; phantasticis ~onum prodigiis seducti GOSC. *Mir. Iv.* lxxii; quando sepultus eris a demonibus rapieris D. BEC. 149; audivit . . animam comitis †~onicibus portari [v. l. ~onibus portatam] *Lib. Eli.* II 119; GERV. TILB. III 61 (v. effigies 3); ~ones aerea dicuntur animalia, quia corporum aereorum natura vigent nec per mortem dissolvuntur BART. ANGL. II 19; venerunt duo ~ones et sederunt ad sinistram, et unus bonus angelus stetit ad dextram ECCLESTON *Adv. Min.* 71; ~ones [ME: *deovel*] horribiles eos terrebunt *AncrR* 76; in his [libris] hierarchie celestis distinguuntur officia et ~onum tyrannides describuntur R. BURY *Phil.* 1. 18; c**1410** tunc auditori fiet signacio prona, / demone pejori, nisi des sibi grandia dona (*Vers. Exch.*) *EHR* XXXVI 59. **b** contigit . . puerum . . atrocissimo ~one vexari . . . missus est ad energuminum presbiter . . solitus . . per exorcismi gratiam immundos fugare spiritus BEDE *CuthbP* 41; discessere procul, qui me torquere solebant, / daemones ALCUIN *SS Ebor* 424; quos etenim doemon rabida possederat ira, / effusis precibus fidei virtute resolvit FRITH. 1315; notandum est . . energumenam fuisse a diabolo possessam, qui et per os ejus loquebatur. . . cum autem . . attulissent corpus Christi . ., respondit ~on . . GIR. *IK* I 12 p. 94 (= *Id. GE* I 18 p. 54: respondit demonium . .). **c 600** si fana . . bene constructa sunt, necesse est ut a cultu ~onum in obsequio veri Dei debeant commutari (*Lit. Papae*) BEDE *HE* I 30; qui immolant ~onis (*sic*) in minimis, j annum peniteat (*sic*); qui vero in magnis, x annos peniteat THEOD. *Pen.* I 15. 1; barbara . . agmina . . / quae . . lurida fana / daemonis horrendi decepta fraude colebant ALDH. *CE* 4. 4. 8; LANTFR. *Swith. pref.* (v. diaboleus); Guodenen et Thurum Freamque aliosque falsos deos, immo ~ones, colebant ORD. VIT. IV 5 p. 191; [Julianus] cuncta faciebat quibus placari ~ones solent AD. SCOT *TT* 714C; c**1218** sortilegi et maxime qui ~onibus immolaverunt *Conc. Syn.* 60 (cf. ib. 204, 1062). **d** reverti voluerit ad artem vestram pessimam eamque per ~ones . . excolere *V. Greg.* p. 98; asserentes illum malis artibus imbutum nec quicquam divino auxilio sed pleraque ~onum prestigio operari OSB. *V. Dunst.* 11; quod soleat populus litteratorum famam ledere, dicens illum loqui cum ~one quem in aliquo viderint excellentem opere W. MALM. *GR* II 167 (cf. ib. 205: nigromanticis artibus instructus . . ~ones territare et ad quodlibet officium impellere); falsi matematici . . desiderant adjutoria ~onum et faciunt carmina et karacteres et sacrificia secundum quod libri eorum pessimi docent, quorum aliquos demones fecerunt et tradiderunt pessimis hominibus et quorum aliquos ipsi matematici fecerunt instinctu et instructione demonum BACON V 6; ~onum invocator et cultor OCKHAM *Dial.* 469; rumpens vincla fugit demonis artis ope ELMH. *Metr. Hen. V* 104. **e** fuga ~onum, herba S. Johannis *SB* 22.

3 Satan, the Devil (usu. not dist. from 'a devil').

perditorum infaustus pater, veluti magnarum alarum unguiumque ~on GILDAS *EB* 34; Daemonis ut regnum . . /

Daedaleus [CL], worthy of Daedalus. **b** (conf. w. *dalus*).

huc illucque vagos stans circumducit ocellos, / Attica Daedalei tecta stupetque soli WULF. *Swith. pref.* 52. **b** ~ei tecti, *of daliscre þecene* [i.e. '*made of thatch from a marsh*'] *GlH* D 375.

Daedalinus, worthy of Daedalus.

s**1066** pennas manibus et pedibus nescio qua nexuerat arte ut ~o more volaret HIGD. VI 28 p. 222 (= W. MALM. *GR* II 225: Dedali more); huic puelle [Rosamunde] fecerat rex [Hen. II] . . cameram opere ~o sinuatam *Ib.* VII 22 p. 52.

daedalus [CL < δαίδαλος], skilful, crafty.

~a, ingeniosa *GlC* D 121; quenam mulierum / consequitur verum, mendax et dedala [*gl.:* deceptrix, ingeniosa] rerum? GARL. *Mor. Scol.* 642; capax gremium, mens dedala, lingua / tullia *Id. Epith.* I 103.

diruat ALDH. *VirgV* 314; GARL. *Tri. Eccl.* 1, *Meaux* I 75 (v. caro 7); Demone namque duce vincentur vespere Luce [*gl.*: quia per Diabolum ducti erant [Scoti] .. ad Angliam] (J. BRIDL.) *Pol. Poems* I 156, 158.

4 demon in human shape, devilish person.

hominum in specie demones revera *Poem S. Thom.* 86; ut homo homini ~on, ita homo homini lupus .. merito dicitur BEKINSAU 736.

daemoniacus [LL]

1 demoniac, (one) possessed by devil (sts. = epileptic). **b** (as sb. f.) (?) woman possessed by devil, witch.

infirmantes ~i professi sunt pro eo tantum futuro deseruisse demones et numquam iterum possessuros *V. Cuthb.* IV 18; ut per eas [reliquias] sint ~i curati BEDE *HE* III 11 *rub.*; daemoniăca quidem vel qualiter uxor ab illo / sit sanata ALCUIN *SS Ebor* 703; ~us, *deofelseoc* ÆLF. *Gl.*; caducus, ~us, .. *bræcseoca GlH* C 28; OSB. *Mir. Dunst.* 19 (v. daemonicus 2); in Italia quoniam ibi ~i abundare solent GIR. *GE* I 18; divinabat per os ~i *Latin Stories* 17; **s1202** mulier ~a .. evomuit duos nigros bufones HIGD. VII 32 p. 182 (= WEND. I 298: a demonibus obsessa; *Meaux* I 339: demonica); intellectus hujus proposicionis 'demonium habes' [*John* x 20] .. est iste: 'Judei dixerunt Christo "tu es ~us"' (KYN.) *Ziz.* 6; **s1381** rustici, ribaldi perditissimi, ganeones ~i .. portas Turris .. cum clamore .. sunt ingressi WALS. *HA* I 459; *wode*, arepticius .., demens, ~us *CathA*. **b 12..** quamdiu illum [lapidem] habueris, ab aliqua ~a ledi non poteris *Sculp. Lap.* 449.

2 demonic, devilish.

dira ~ae inlusionis temptatio ALCUIN *WillP* 22; relicta ~ae pravitatis caligine LANTFR. *Swith. pref.*; regina Francorum .. ~i furoris igne succensa EADMER *Wilf.* 7; instinctu ~o grangiam monachorum .. combussit juvenis quidam GIR. *IK* I 7 p. 68; *Flor. Hist.* I 421 (v. daemonicus 1); inexorabilis malignitas ~e rabiei AD. MARSH *Ep.* 1; **1268** quidam Judei .. ~o spiritu arrepti *MunAcOx* 37; *a devylle*, .. demon, diabolus ..; [*adj.*] ~us, diabolicus *CathA*.

daemonialis, demonic, devilish.

quantumcumque vales nisus preme demoniales R. CANT. *Malch.* VI 27; contra .. ~ium hostilitatum pervicacias procedamus ad bellandum AD. MARSH *Ep.* 16.

daemoniaticus [cf. LL daemoniacus], demoniac, possessed by devil.

freneticus i. ~us, insanus, amens, *gewitleasa GlH* F 696.

daemonicibus v. daemon 2a.

daemonicola, demon-worshipping.

in illa ~a plebe, in qua callidissima demonum factione falsorum deorum flagitia pro sacris colebantur AILR. *Spec. Car.* I 73. 529.

daemonicus [LL < δαιμονικός]

1 demonic, devilish.

non ~a sed divina virtute praediti BEDE *HE* I 25 (cf. ib. IV 13: a servitute ~a); **940** (13c) †sic [? l. si quis] ~e fermentationis stimulo incedens nostrum .. donum .. infringere probaverit *CS* 761 (cf. ib. 782, 784); ~o globo, *deofellicum geferscipe GlH* D 162; ausu ~o permoti HERM. ARCH. 2; nichil ~is insidiis intemptatum abit GOSC. *Mir. Iv.* lxii; reges qui .. ~is cultibus .. serviere FL. WORC. I 13; "ego .. ~is semper artibus inservii" W. MALM. *GR* II 204 (= *Flor. Hist.* I 421: demoniacis); indomiti tauri quidam distillat in aurem / demonicum nomen GARL. *Tri. Eccl.* 74 (cf. ib. 39: demonicas acies); David Saulem a ~a possessione liberavit BACON *Tert.* 299.

2 demoniac, (one) possessed by devil.

~um duci ad se praecepit OSB. *Mir. Dunst.* 19 p. 145 (cf. ib. p. 148: coeperamus ad domum in qua demoniacus sub magna custodia jacebat vinctus appropinquare); *Meaux* I 339 (v. daemoniacus 1a).

daemoniosus [LL], demoniac, (one) possessed by demons.

clamante et vociferante ~o, plurimorum aures horror invasit *V. Cuthb.* IV 15; filia ~a BEDE *Hom.* I 22. 104; eum .. in virtutibus quasi ~um et contraria Deo potestate miracula facientem abominationi habebant *Id. Sam.* (*1 Sam.* xxi 14–15) 657; et commune fuit viduis solamen et orbis, / claudis, contractis, leprosis, daemoniosis (*Vers. Anselmi de Lanfranco*) TORIGNI 50.

daemonium [CL < δαιμόνιον]

1 demon, evil spirit; **b** (possession by); **c** (worship of, also fig.); **d** (invocation of); **e** (w. ref. to *Psalm* xc 6).

716 quem .. videbat angelico .. umbraculo contra impetum ~iorum .. defensum BONIF. *Ep.* 10 p. 14; risum ~iorum BEDE *HE* V 12; **a804** est .. ipse [Judas] principi ~iorum traditus ALCUIN *Ep.* 281; **941** (15c) collocetur .. cum Tartarorum ~iis *CS* 769; signa crucis removent virtutes demoniorum NIG. *Laur.* 32v. 2; si forte rictibus ~iorum adimantur anime vestre AD. MARSH *Ep.* 45; habemus .. cum ~iis societatem OCKHAM *Dial.* 469. **b** judicatus est [diabolus] ab eo [Deo] cum .. ipse ~ia eiceret BEDE *Hom.* II 11. 160; ~ium cum sanguine evomuit OSB. *Mir. Dunst.* 8; crebro afflatus ~io, contumacis perfidie tormenta pendebat W. MALM. *GR* I 10; **s1381** nisi ~iis pleni fuissent, nequaquam in destruccionem .. ecclesie .. conspirassent WALS. *HA* II 9. **c** BEDE *HE* II 15 (v. arula a); puerum .. quem volebant [magi] sacrificare ~iis *G. Hen. II* I 257; **s1453** quia non Deo sed ~iis immolasti .. coluistique .. idolum avaricie *Reg. Whet.* I 112. **d** [magi] arte sua ~ia excitantes *V. Greg.* p. 97; responsum .. quod per †strigiles et veneficas suas a ~iis acceperat *Chr. Rams.* 329. **e 1187** negotium hucusque perambulans in tenebris in incursum versum est et ~ium meridianum *Ep. Cant.* 64; si [papa] .. vendicat habere dominium omnium bonorum ecclesie .., tunc est meridianum ~ium et capitalis discipulus Antichristi WYCL. *Sim.* (cf. id. *Ver.* III 163).

2 demon in human shape, devilish person.

uxor illius [Reinaldi filii regis], furiis agitata, non simplicem in ejus amplexus sexum sed dirum et horrendum offerebat ~ium *G. Steph.* I 48; clericos meos deos nomino, monachos ~ia DEVIZES 40v.

3 'devilry', possession by devil.

a devylry, ~ium *CathA*.

daemonologus, demonologer.

hec .. non est vox theologi sed ~i WYCL. *Ver.* II 133.

daenberum v. denberum. **daeria** v. daieria. **dafnoydes** v. daphnoides.

daga [AN *dage*, OF *dague* (?) < daca, cf. Dacus 2b], dagger.

1322 lego D. famulo meo .. unam ~am argenteam hernesiatam *FormA* 431; **1554** cum †diga [? l. daga] seu pugione †eruginata *Midlothian* 221 (v. aeruginare c).

dagardus, ~um [ME *daggard*], dagger.

s1387 extracto cultello, id est ~o, ejus cerebrum perforavit *V. Ric. II* 95 (= WALS. *HA* II 168: extracto cultello daggardo); **p1393** felonice interfecit Johannem Prechur .. cum uno daggardo *SelCCoron* 96; **1406** reportavit ~um quod asportavit *Reg. Heref.* 103; hic ~us, A. *a dagar WW*; **1492** cognoverunt se commisisse homicidium .. cum ~o *Sanct. Bev.* 169.

dagarius, ~ium [ME *daggar, daggere*], dagger.

s1348 [domine] habentes cultellos quos daggerios vulgariter dicunt in powchiis desuper impositis KNIGHTON II 58; **1349** Willelmum felonice interfecit cum quodam cultello qui vocatur *daggere* precii j d. *SelCCoron* 113; **1390** percussit .. Henricum cum quodam daggerio ex latere sinistro usque cor *Ib.* 100; **s1388** stringens ipsum per capicium, abstracto dagerio, dixit .. FAVENT 17; **1389** furati fuerunt unam permam et unum daggerum precii ij s. *Pat* 327 m. 19; **1399** j daggarium argento hernesiatum precii x s. .. felonice ceperunt *Ib.* 352 m. 12; †**13..** quilibet homo .. habens xv li. terre .. habeat .. capilium de ferro, ensem et cultellum qui dicitur *dagare*; habens xl s. et ultra usque ad c solidatas terre habeat archum et sagittas et daggarium et cultellum (*Fragm. Coll.*) *APScot* I 388b; **c1410** pro percussione cum gladio, cultello, sica vel daggario *StatOx* 205; **1423** de j ~io deargentato *Test. Ebor.* III 87; **1432** gladios, ~ia, *bouges*, et alia hernesia licita .. deferentes (*TreatyR*) *Foed.* X 508b; **1440** cum .. in magna aula placitorum nostrorum Westm' .. longum daggarium suum extraxerit *Pat* 445 m. 5; **1457** lego .. j ~ium harnesiatum cum *lokittes, chape*, et *rose* argenti *Fabr. York* 208; **s1488** J. F. .. cognovit se commisisse homicidium .. cum uno †gadar' [l. dagar' et] cum uno baculo *Sanct. Bev.* 195; **1496** gladios, ~ios, lanceas, et cultellos .. ferre (*DipDocE*) *Foed.* XII 583a.

dagera v. dacra a. **dagerius** v. dagarius. **dagg-** v. et. dag-. **daggerius** v. dagarius.

dagma [δάγμα], bite.

a990 si .. quidam importunus ~ate adsurgeret et diriperet enerviter miseris vivendi victum B. *Ep.* 386 (cf. ib. 390: praeripere ~ata).

dagnare v. damnare. **Dagus** v. Dacus.

1 daia [ME *dai*], 'day' (division of mullioned window). *Cf. dies* 1e, *diversorium* 1e.

1384 unam novam capellam .. cum ij fenestris in latere ejusdem nove capelle, qualibet fenestra de duabus daiis, et una fenestra in dicte nove capelle superiori parte vel capite cum iij daiis, dictis fenestris veruratis *Cl* 227 m. 29*d*.

2 daia [ME *daie* < AS *dǣge*], 'dey', dairy-maid.

ibi viij inter servos et ancillas et vaccarius et ~a *DB* I 180b (cf. ib.: j porcarius et ij bovarii et ~a); **1209** in corrediis iiij bovariorum, j haiwardi, j ~e per annum *Pipe Wint.* 51 (= *Crawley* 190); **c1224** (v. bubulcus a); **1234** debet habere .. totum lac de ovibus per diem Dominicam in comuni cum deia et serviente *Cust. Glast.* 138; **1243** invenire facias .. cuidam daye .. rationabiles solidos suos *Liberate* 19 m. 6; **s1255** daya nostra .. percussa a quodam ribaldo .. obiit *Ann. Tewk.* 157; **1264** in stipendiis xx feminarum adjuvancium dayas ad oves lactandas *MinAc* 1078/8 r. 2; in stipendio j deye per annum iij s.; in stipendiis j vaccarii et porcarii per annum vj s. *FormMan* 35; **1376** debet .. mulier honestior tocius ville esse daya, prout villa elegerit, pro caseo domini faciendo *IMisc* 208/4; **1398** de vij li. .. de lactagio xxvij vaccarum cum vitulis sic dimiss[arum] ~e manerii hoc anno ex convencione *Ac. Man. Coll. Wint.* (*Harmondsworth*).

daiaria v. daieria. **daiela** v. dala.

daieria [AN *dayerie* < ME *daie*], dairy, w. ref. to: **a** building; **b** department (or produce); **c** farm.

a 1160 ibi est .. j daeria et j boveria et iij parve domus gallinacee *Dom. S. Paul.* 132; **1209** in parietibus daerie et granarii faciendis *Pipe Wint.* 50 (= *Crawley* 190); **s1253** dayaria .. igne accensa .. est *Ann. Tewk.* 157; **1317** una domus vocata ~ia *Cl* 135 m. 19 *d.* (= *Cal.* p. 573: †daceria); **1330** ~ia, bovaria et bovaria (*sic*) ac cetere omnes domus .. sunt bene cooperte *Reg. Exon.* 574; **c1350** tenementa .. que debent tegere aulam abbatis et cameram et daeriam *Reg. S. Aug.* 193; **1351** quoddam plumbum .. in quadam dayeria in muro situatum cepit *SessPEssex* 125; **c1430** j plumbum in deiria (*Dimiss. S. Paul.*) *Camd. Misc.* IX p. xviii; **1446** reparacio .. j grangie et deire *Feod. Durh.* 184*n*. **b 1209** in custo daerie *Pipe Wint.* 53; **1242** in custu dayerie apud Cumbe *Pipe* 124; **1287** exitus herbagii et dayerie *Comp. Worc.* I 5; nec permittat [prepositus] quod aliquis .. quicquam .. deportet quod cedere posset .. daerie in decrementum [*Senesch.*: *en apeyrement de la dayerie*] *Fleta* 171; *Ib.* 172 (v. androchia); sequitur de daeria, ut de caseo etc. *FormMan* 14 (cf. ib. 47: butirum .. de x [lagenis] provenientibus de exitu dayrie); **1316** de cxxx petris iiij lib. casei venditi ut extra de exitibus ~ie *Cart. Glam.* (*ed.* 1885 *only*) I 216; **1337** in ij tubbys ad deyriam *Ac. Man. Cant.* (*Milton*); **1442** liberabit .. lix vaccas cum ij tauris pro daiera .. manerii AMUND. II app. 283. **c 1461** daiariam alias dictam *a wyke* vocatam Dangebrygge [*Essex*] *Pat* 498 m. 8 (= *Pat* 545 m. 19: dayriam); **1587** totam illam grangiam sive diariam suam de Turbutsey aceciam omnia et singula terras, tenementa .., pasturas, lesuras suas dicte diarie sive grangie spectancia *Pat* 1303 m. 1.

daila v. dala. **daimerettus** v. dammaricius.

daina [? cf. ME *dai wine*], (amount of grain *etc.* allowed for) day's work. **b** 'day-work' (measure of land). *Cf. daiwerca, handaina.*

1189 qualibet die faciet unam ~am (*Inq. Glast.*) *Villainage in Eng.* 288 (cf. ib. 295*n*.); **1234** dicit villata quod, quando falcant prato (*sic*) domini, debent habere j ~am de frumento, que continet j bussellum et dim. *Cust. Glast.* 13 (cf. ib. 37: inter festum S. Mich. et festum S. Martini debet triturare tres daynas, que si fuerint de frumento continent vj bus., si .. de fabis vel de ordeo, ij crannocos, si de avena xviij); **c1280** quilibet predictorum debet iiij *deywynes* per unum hominem *Cust. Battle* 74; debet facere qualibet die Veneris .. j †dayuam manualem *Cust. Bleadon* 202; Adam .. debet operari qualibet septimana per annum †dayuam manualem et faciet pro †dayua quicquid precipietur a serviente preter falcare *Ib.* 208. **b** Adam .. tenet mesuagium et ortum et j pecetam terre continentem j †dayuam terre *Ib.*; **c1260** dedi .. x dainias et dim. terre de libero tenemento meo *Cart. Glam.* 670; **1307** purpresturavit et assartavit j daynam de eodem feodo *Cart. Glast.* I 180; **1317** in j ~a terre *Fabr. Exon.* 88; **13..** J. Faber [tenet] j ~am [*of land of the highway in Newport, Som*] (*Wells MSS*) *HMC Rep.* XII i 328.

Daisios [*Δαίσιος*], a Macedonian month.

vocatur apud eos [Graecos] ipse .. Junius Deseos BEDE *TR* 14; [Junius] Grece Deseos *Miss. Jum.* 14.

daitida [ME *dai tide*], tide flowing by day.

13.. in portubus attachiamenta sive adjornaciones sunt similiter ordinatim (*sic*), sicut et res venales veniunt ad portum et exeunt portum, sc. de daytyda in daytydam, nec computari debent tide noctuales *Little RB Bristol* I 57.

daiwerca [ME *dai werk*], 'day-work', measure of land (var.): **a** (Kent); **b** (elsewhere in Eng.).

a 1204 confirmasse .. xiij acras terre et dim. et v *daiwercs* apud Hecham .. et et iij acras et ij *daiwercs* de bosco .. *RChart* 131b; **1208** confirmasse .. sex ~as prati in campo qui vocatur B. *Ib.* 179b; **1214** petit .. ij acras terre et vj deiwercas .. ut jus suum *CurR* VII 211; **1225** petit .. medietatem j acre et v deiwercarum terre *Ib.* XII 229; **1247** dedisse .. vij deiworcas terre cum domibus *Reg. S. Aug.* 508 (cf. ib. 248: tenere solet .. dim. acram et ij †wywercass' de terra); **12..** ij virgatas et ij diwercas et dim. bosci *ChartR* 116 m. 20; **12..** vij deyuercas et dim. prati mei *AncD* A 7201; **1310** ij acras et xj daywarcas terre .. unde j acra et dim. et xvj daywarce jacent in quodam campo vocato ate Hethe .. *Ib.* C 5076 (cf. ib. D 544, 572, A 11500); **a1330** non habentur de ten[ementis] in visu posit[is] nisi xv ~e terre, que faciunt j rodam et dim. terre *JustIt* 385 r. 47; **1432** J. B. tenet .. in mesuagio nuper Johannis M. j acram vj daywerc' et j perch' *Cart. Bilsington* 214. **b 1274** dominus rex habet .. in villa de Opministre [*Essex*] j daywrcam terre *Hund.* I 149; **1325** donacionem .. de vij deiwercis terre cum pertinenciis (*Ch. Bayham, Suss*) *MonA* VI 915a.

daiwercata [cf. ME *dai werk*], 'day-work', measure of land worked in one day.

c1270 sex daywercatas terre mee [*in Tilbury, Essex*] *Rec. Coll. Merton MS* no. 1257; **1339** Alis R. .. reddidit in manum domini j acram et j rodam iij daywercatas et terciam partem j daywercate terre .. ad opus Willelmi S. (*Ac. Man. Blackmore*) *Essex RO* D/DK, M 108 (cf. ib.: j cotagium et ij daywercatas terre); **1356** unam porcionem prati mei .. continent' unam daywercatam terre in toto

Doc. Coll. Wint. (*Cranfield, Beds*; *Elias ate Hethe to John Barnet*); **1383** de placito duarum ~arum terre et dim. (*Coggeshall, Essex*) *PlRCP* 491 r. 436; **1412** j virgatam et j daywerkatam [terre] *CatAncD* VI C 5314.

daiwerclanda, measure of land (Essex).

12.. in eadem crofta .. que .. continet in longitudine et latitudine quatuor deywerchland' *BL MS Cotton Nero* E VI f. 195.

dakaica [Ar. *daqīqa*, pl. *daqā'iq*], minute.

annus in menses xij, mensis in dies numero diversos, dies in horas xxiiij, hora in ~as [v. l. minuta] lx, ~a in lx zenias, id est secundas, dividitur ADEL. *Elk.* 2; *Ib.* 6 (v. decrescere 1a).

dakera v. dacra.

dakerhenna [Eng. *daker-hen*], corncrake.

aliqui ortygometram esse volunt Germanorum *scricam* et Anglorum ~am TURNER *Av.* G 4v.

dakrum v. dacra.

dala, ~us [AS *dāl*], 'dale', 'dole', portion of land (esp. meadow or marsh).

1084 donamus in eadem villa [*Northampton*] .. tres ~os prati et unum hulmum *MonA* V 190 (cf. *CalCh* IV 119); a**1190** j ~am terre *al crupht* et alteram ~am terre in minori Redeles et terciam ~am *al perier* de Fuerstrete, et quartam ~am *al perier* Ailred *Med. E. Anglia* 229; a**1190** totum pratum meum .. in deila que vocatur Ingenestang [*Lincs*] .., sc. ij acras prati *Ch. Gilb.* 57; a**1200** pro j daila .. in territorio .. ville de G. [*Grainthorpe, Lincs*] *Danelaw* 114; c**1200** j perticatam prati in latitudine in deila mea in longum ex aquilonari parte deile in quantum pratum durat *Reg. Ant. Linc.* IV 1144; c**1200** j ~am salse ad predictam terram pertinentem (*Ch. Westwood, Worcs*) *MonA* VI 1009a; dedit .. j dailam et xx carectatas turbarum in Waghna [*Wawne*] *Meaux* II 5; c**1250** concessi .. totam deleam meam .. in Wrengelfen [*Lincs*] *DL Cart. Misc.* II 232; c**1260** remiserunt .. consuetudines .. de dim. dola †terra [? l. terre] in parochia de Rokinges tam in marisco quam in susanna terra *Cart. Bilsington* 128 (cf. ib. 61); **1271** dedit .. totam daylam marisci tam de rossa quam de prato (*Ch. Nocton, Lincs*) *MonA* VI 342b; a**1272** j daylam continentem in se j acram prati [*Lincs*] *Ch. Gilb.* 46; **1285** relicta Godefridi G. [debet] ij vomeres de j della *Cust. Suss.* II 29; **1290** j dolam [prati] (*Leics*) *CalCh* II 381; c**1330** falcabit j sellionem de dolo domini (*Ext. Barrington, Cambs*) *Growth Eng. Ind.* 585; **1364** cum pomario suo et dola *Pipe Cloyne* 12; **1413** cepit de domino j daielam prati .. jacentem in le Hallemare vocatam Southdayle [*Lincs*] *CourtR* 186/2; **14..** dola Godewini jacet .. in marisco de Romene [*Kent*] (*Survey*) *Eng. Field Syst.* app. 543 (cf. ib. 286); **1567** tenet j dailam terre vocatam *a grepe* in Estfeld [*Som*] *Surv. Pembr.* 465.

dalbura v. daubatura.

daleth [LL < Heb.], Hebrew letter daleth.

similitudo .. litterarum '~h' et 'res' hunc apud Hebraeos saepe facit errorem BEDE *Gen.* (x 4) 116; Esdras .. scriba legisque doctor .. invenit litteras quibus nunc utuntur Hebraei ..: aleph, beth, gimel, deleth, he, vau, zai, eth, teth, ioth, caph, lamech, mem, nun, samech, ain, phe, sade, cof, res, sin, thau *Runica Manuscripta* 350; he, deleth, gimel, beth, aleph BACON *Gram. Heb.* 202.

dalf- v. delph-. **dalitaria** v. deleteria. **dalmata** v. dalmaticus 2.

dalmaticare [LL], to clothe w. a dalmatic.

sequitur benedictio cerei paschalis a diacono ~ato facienda *Miss. Ebor.* I 111.

Dalmaticus [CL]

1 Dalmatian, Croatian.

1457 an forte despicis Ungarios et ~os, homines feroces arcubus et sagittis invictissimos? (*Lit. Papae*) *Reg. Whet.* I 275.

2 (as sb. f. *sc. vestis*) dalmatic, wide-sleeved robe: **a** (worn by deacon or priest or unspec.); **b** (ornate, esp. as worn by bishop); **c** (as episcopal vestment granted to abbot or prior); **d** (worn by sovereign at coronation).

a ~a, tunica latas manicas habens *GlC* D 10; diaconi ~is vestiti EGB. *Pont.* 120; diacono ~a induto [AS p. 416: *diacone mid diacon rocce gescryddum*] *RegulC* 42; hora congrua ingrediatur diaconus capitulum .., alba .. et ~a indutus LANFR. *Const.* 111; Jocelinus [ep., ob. **1242**] .. tunicam et ~am ex albo panno in transverso virgatas nobis contulit *Cart. Bath* B 808 p. 155; **1246** fieri faciat .. ij paria tunicarum et †dalmatarum *Cl* 427; **1313** tuniculam et dealmaticam ejusdem secte *Pri. Cold.* 9; **1320** unum vestimentum integrum pro sacerdote, diacono et subdiacono, viz. unam casulam, tunicam et ~am de viridi panno de Tarys .. *Reg. Glasg.* 227; **1343** j tunicam cum almatica de cerico veterem (*KRAc* 67/10) *Arch. J.* XI 382; **1344** diaconus et subdiaconus induti ~a et tunica celebranti serviant (*Stat. Cotterstock*) *Eng. Clergy* 285; **1415** duo vestimenta integra pro sacerdote, exceptis ~a et capa *Reg. Cant.* II 188. **b** †c**693** (v. demandare 2); **796** aliquam benedictionem de ~is nostris vel palleis ad singulas sedes episcopales regni vestri .. direximus (*Lit. Caroli Magni*) *Ep. Alcuini* 100; s**1088** Lamfrancus .. ecclesie Roffensi misit ~am principalem de albo dyapre circumdatam aurifrisio *Flor. Hist.* II 20; **1238** in ij aurifrigiis ad tunicam et dealmaticam *Liberate* 12 m. 9; **1240** in j casula et almatica cum aurifratis *Ib.* 14 m. 22; **1268** episcopus qui .. ecclesiam detractaverit .. consecrare .. a ~e, tunice et sandalium usu .. noverit se suspensum *Conc. Syn.* 751; **1295** tunica et ~a de albo diaspro lineat' interius de rubeo sendato *Vis. S. Paul.* 322a (cf. ib. 321a: tunica et ~a de rubeo sameto cum stricto aurifrigio cum borduris in posteriori parte et floribus cum capitibus draconum de auro); **1310** (v. 2 clavis 1b). **c** a**1181** H. abbati S. Edmundi: .. te volentes prerogativa decorare honoris, tibi usum tunice atque ~e .. concedimus (*Lit. Papae*) *Reg. Pinchbeck* f. 3b; **1254** priori .. ecclesie S. Edmundi de Hatissel [*Athassel, Co. Tipperary*]: .. tibi .. et successoribus tuis .. utendi anulo, mitra, tunica, ~a, et cirothecis .. plenam concedimus .. facultatem *Mon. Hib. & Scot.* 59a; abbas, in festis principalibus et quasi, solet uti omnibus pontificalibus indumentis, id est tunica, ~a, et sandaliis *Cust. Cant.* 49; **1379** quod abbates monasteriorum Westmon', S. Albani, S. Edmundi de Bury, de Evesham, et S. Augustini Cantuar' .. gaudent .. usu mitre, annuli, chirothecarum, tunice, ~e, sandaliorum, et aliorum insignium pontificalium (*Lit. Papae*) *Conc.* III 143b. **d** s**1189** deinde induerunt eum vestimentis regalibus: primo viz. tunica, deinde ~a R. HOWD. III 10; c**1220** due broche auree ad pallium et ~am, quarum in una est saphirus et in alia perla (*Exch ReceiptR* 3) *Rec. Coronation* 55.

dalmaticula, little dalmatic.

1289 furtive .. furatus fuit unam almaticulam de serico *Gaol Del.* 36/1 r. 5; **1327** xxx cassibulas, xxx tuniculas, xl ~as .. ceperunt *MonA* III 109a.

dalph- v. delph-.

daltinus [Ir. *dailtín*], camp-follower, skirmisher.

ultimus omnium ordo cursorum numero concluditur, quos Hiberni ~os, nos Latine scurras, velites, seu servos a pedibus nominare possumus. isti inermes incedunt, ministros se praebent equitibus, sparos etiam amentatos vibrant, phaleras sordibus maculatas mundant STANIHURST *Hib.* 43.

dalum v. dolo 2. **dalus** v. dala. **dalvata** v. davacha. **dama** v. 1 & 2 damma. **damac-** v. damasc-. **damaisella** v. domicella 1a. **damala** v. dammula a.

damagium [OF *damage*], damage, injury.

1555 exonerari .. debet .. in recompensacione .. ~ii per ipsum sustenti (*MinAc*) *MonA* IV 283b.

damaricius, ~arium v. damm-.

Damascenus [CL < Δαμασκηνός]

1 Damascene, (citizen) of Damascus. **b** (w. *pannus* or as sb. m.) damask.

s**1129** in obsidione ~a H. HUNT. *HA* VII 40; s**1187** sub soldano ~orum Norahadino *Itin. Ric.* I 3. **b** **1445** j frontale de panno ~o aureo .. cum v paginibus de rubeo ~o *Invent. S. Paul.* 522; **1493** mutatorium damaseni glauci coloris (*Invent. Mon. S. Crucis*) *Bannatyne Misc.* II 23.

2 (w. *prunum*) damson. **b** (as sb.) damson tree.

1287 pro prunis damacenis emptis *TRBk* 201 p. 23; **1290** in prunis damacenis, x d. *Doc. W. Abb. Westm.* 173. **b** hec damasenus, A. *damyssyntre WW*; *a damysyn tre*, damisenus .. *CathA.*

1 Damascus [CL < Δαμασκός], (w. *pannus* or as sb. m.) damask.

1388 [frontellum] album auro intextum de panno ~i indentatum (*Invent. Westm.*) *Arch.* LII 229; [abbas T., ob. **1396**] duos pannos de ~o preciosos, floribus aquaticis aureis repletos, cum frontali consimili .. perquisivit *G. S. Alb. Cont.* III 380; **1411** ij amicte de ~o *Lit. Cant.* III 114; **1429** ij vestimenta, unum .. de viridi ~o *Test. Ebor.* II 5; **1442** j vestimentum panni ~i coloris nigri et albi *Reg. Cant.* II 609 (cf. ib.: j thoga ~i); **1445** j fanon' de albo ~o aureo *Invent. S. Paul.* 522; **1447** pro pannis sericis de ~o pro ij robis pro domino rege ad personam propriam *ExchScot* 267; **1470** pro *le haluynge* de nova secta blodii damaski *Ac. Churchw. Sal.* 13; **1501** iij rubee albe de ~o *Cant. Coll. Ox.* I 35.

2 damascus [AN *damasche*, OF *domesche*], domestic.

1251 clausus est parcus ille, ita quod bestie ~e non possint intrare *IMisc* 5/14.

damasenus v. Damascenus. **damaskus** v. 1 Damascus. **damerettus, damericeus** v. dammaricius. **damgnare** v. damnare. **damicula, ~illus, ~inus** v. damm-. **damicella** v. domicella. **damigeria** v. dangerum. **damila** v. dammula. **damisella** v. domicella. **damisenus** v. Damascenus.

1 damma, dama [CL], doe (esp. of fallow deer). **b** (usu. w. *masculus*) buck; *v. et.* dammus.

~ma, bestia, id est *eola GlC* D 12 (cf. *Gl. Leid.* 45. 20: ~ma, *elha*); BEDE *Sam.* 582 (v. dorcas); capio cervos, apros et ~mas [AS: *rann*] ÆLF. *Coll.* 92; c**1180** coria ~arum de parco suo *Act. Hen. II* II 151; **1189** ad capiendum omnes bestias preter cervum et cervam et damum et ~am *CalCh* I 7; **1217** †damnas (v. dammus); **1228** habere faciat .. xv ~mas vivas in .. foresta [de Clarendon'] *Cl* 25; **1237** (v. brokettus); **1293** (v. 1 bissus); **1387** de qualibet centena pellium .. cervorum, bissarum, damorum et ~arum *RScot* 87b; **1488** intraverant Novam Forestam .. et unam ~am fetantem .. occiderunt *DL Forest Proc.* 2/12. **b** scammate si regem pavidus quoque damma leonem / provocet *Altercatio* 5; **1446** sex ~as masculos et sex damas femellas *CalPat* *1494–1501* p. 99; **1488** unum ~am masculum vocatum *a buk DL Forest Proc.* 2/11; **1490** interficit unum ~am vocatum *a buk* (*Ib.* 3/16) *Pickering* I 141.

2 damma, ~um [ME *dam*], dam.

1281 de cignis, quia fere aves sunt et per dama fluminis vagantur *PlRCP* 42 r. 63; **1282** in ~o molendini faciendo de novo *Ac. Man. Cant.* (*Cliffe*); **1359** non liceat alicui .. facere ~as vel fordas aut alia impedimenta in aliquibus landeis, .. fossatis sive aquagiis communibus in marisco .., per quod rectus cursus aquarum .. impediatur *Laws Romney Marsh* 71; **1479** pro emendacione unius dampe apud Rilley *Ac. Durh.* 96.

dammaericius v. dammaricius.

dammare [ME *dammen*], to dam.

c**1370** solut' diversis operatoribus ad ramandum et ~andum contra meremium aquaticum .. molendini et *le baye MinAc* 900/18.

dammaricius, (w. *canis* or sim.) buckhound. **b** (w. *bernarius* or sim.) keeper of buckhounds.

1223 quod permittatis Willelmum B. habere canes suos damericeos currentes hac seisona in foresta nostra de N. sine arcubus et leporariis *Cl* 556b; mittimus ad vos Ricardum P. venatorem nostrum cum canibus nostris damerettis ad currendum ad damos in .. foresta sine arcu et leporariis *Ib.* 559b; cum canibus nostris dammaericiis *Ib.* 563a; **1225** cum canibus deimericiis ad currendum ad damas in foresta de Savernac *Cl* 84a; **1229** cum canibus daimerettis ad currendum ad damum in Nova Foresta *Cl* 207; **1237** [cum canibus] damariciis *Cal. Liberate* I 299; **1284** per serjanciam custodiendi unam meutam deynector' (*sic*) canum *JustIt* 48 r. 28; **1286** brachettum deymeretum (v. brachettus); **1290** venatori custodienti canes regis damerettos, existenti cum canibus suis in com. Suhamptes' ad venandum ad lepores (*AcWardr*) *Chanc. Misc.* 4/4 f. 51; **1312** daemericiis (v. canis 2a); **1366** balliva custodiendi canes domini regis damaricios *IAQD* 359/14. **b** **1312** (v. bernarius).

dammarium, deer-park.

J. N. prior claustralis [ob. **1491**] providebat ut in die anniversarii sui .. fratres haberent unam damam ex †damnario de Offeham; et ideo ampliavit parcum de Offenham *Chr. Evesham* 339 (= *MonA* II 39); **1543** in solutis Bochere custodi damarii apud Marewell iij s. *Ac. Coll. Wint.* (*Bursar, cust. necess.*).

dammicula, young fallow doe.

1274 de v damiculis, xxviij damis tempore ferm[isone] de exitu *MinAc* (*I. of W.*) 984/5 r. 1; **1354** canis suus ibat in parco domine affraiando damas et mactando j damynculam *CourtR* (*Suff*) 203/88 E 5.

dammillus, of fallow deer.

c**1520** in regardo dato Ricardo T. pro carnibus damillis pro domino priore *DCCant* DE 31 p. 15.

damminus, of fallow deer.

carnesque gruine / et pavonine, dammine sint et olores D. BEC. 2639; *Ib.* 2567 (v. capreolinus).

dammula [CL], young doe (usu. of fallow deer). **b** figure of doe.

8.. ~a, *hind* .., **10..** ~a, *da WW*; damula vel caprea .., *hræge* ÆLF. *Gl.*; damula diffugiens STEPH. ROUEN app. 769. 84; **1178** tamquam damula de manu diffugiunt (*Lit. Abbatis Clarev.*) *G. Hen. II* I 214; Christus resurgens a mortuis querit duntaxat pulmentarium .., non damulam, non cervum H. BOS. *Thom.* III 15; dignam dicit inediam mercede leonis, qui damulam lupis aufert ut eam devoret MAP *NC* IV 11 f. 52; damula .. vulnerata dracundeam .. comedit BART. ANGL. XVIII 34; **1361** cuidam homini portanti unam damalam *Ac. Durh.* 126; nemora .. cervis, damulis aliisque feris silvestribus .. referta FORDUN *Chr.* II 7; **1480** pro ij vaccis emptis pro sustentacione certarum damularum *ExchScot* 54. **b** **1500** vestimentum rubeum .. cum damilis aureis et volucribus intextis cum aurifrigerio *Invent. Ch. Ch.* 127.

dammulus, young buck.

9.. damulus, *don WW.*

dammus, damus, (fallow) buck. *V. et.* 1 *damma* b.

1189 ~um (v. 1 damma a); **1217** dedimus .. Sarr' episcopo xxx tam †damnos quam †damnas ad parcum suum restaurandum *Cl* 342b; **1223** ~morum, **1237** ~os (v. brokettus); **1255** mandatum est .. custodi foreste regis Essex' quod .. faciat capi xxx vel xl ~os ad opus regis et eos bene saliri *Cl* 116; **1272** reddere .. sex feras mediocres, sc. tres damos [? l. damas] masculos die S. Crucis in autumno .. et tres damas, sc. alterius sexus, in vigilia Purificacionis B. M. Virginis (*Concordia*) *G. S. Alb.* I 424; **1277** omnes ~os qui in ista pinguedine in parco de Bergenvenny

commode capi poterunt *Cl* 94 m. 3; **1279** non permittit canes .. habere percursum cujusdam ~y quem fugaverunt ad parcum suum *PQW* 752a; **1288** canes .. non currerunt ad aliquam bestiam de warenna, immo ad quemdam ~um, qui non est bestia de warenna *SelPlForest* cxxviii; **1292** ceperunt unam damam et unum fetonem ~i masculum *TR Forest Proc.* 13 m. 16; **1387** ~orum (v. 1 damma a); ~us, A. *a bukke* .., *dobuk WW*.

damna v. 1 damma.

damnabilis [LL] **(dampn-)**

1 (of persons): **a** subject to condemnation. **b** subject to damnation.

a **1238** si W. le FizNel, qui captus est pro malo retto .., per inquisitionem vel per judicium vel per patriam sit ~is, tunc significetis nobis occasionem quare est ~is antequam reddatis inde judicium *Cl* 80. **b** Cornelius [*Acts* x] mox minime ~is fuit, etsi non crederet Christum incarnatum H. Bos. *Thom.* III 13; defendens hereticam pravitatem ~ior est heretico Ockham *Dial.* 956 (*recte* 944); sequuntur multa que sonant contra fidem, sc. quod .. ista proposicio verificatur de Christo: 'aliquis homo est pessimus et ~is' (Kyn.) *Ziz.* 53.

2 (of actions, beliefs, *etc.*) damnable (or leading to damnation), abominable.

†**747** quia in luxuria .. etiam cum sanctimonialibus volutaris est vituperabile et ~e (*Lit. Bonif.*) W. Malm. *GR* I 80 (cf. Bonif. *Ep.* 73); **1178** per ~em predicationem (*Lit. P. Cardinalis*) *G. Hen. II* I 203; nec absentia nec exsilii causa justa poterit esse vel excusabilis, sed revera ~is et ~i ~ior H. Bos. *Thom.* IV 29; non ~e minus esse peccatum sacerdotis cum soluta quam .. soluti cum alterius sponsa Gir. *GE* II 12; sensus ~is multitudinis stulte Bacon *CSTheol.* 52; ~i ignorancia laborantes Ockham *Dial.* 458; **1378** omnis excommunicacio .. est timenda, eciam licet excommunicacio ecclesie sit humili excommunicato non ~is sed salubris (Wycl.) Wals. *HA* I 360; **1398** per ~em scismatis errorem (*Cl*) *Peasants' Rising* 53; **s1272** dico .. quod mortale et ~e est, dummodo unum competens sit, plura beneficia in simul retinere Fordun *Cont.* X 32; **s1455** ~is .. magis quam laudabilis .. triumphus *Reg. Whet.* I 177.

3 condemnatory.

'judicabit', i.e. comparationem sui judicabilem faciet et ~em Lanfr. *Comment. Paul.* (*Rom.* ii 27) 114.

damnabilitas [LL] **(dampn-),** damnation. **b** loss.

affeccio proprietatis in homine interiori preponderans sapit symoniam, apostasiam, blasfemiam, et ~atem perpetuam Wycl. *Blasph.* 47. **b** **1373** si .. appareat .. custodem [hospitalis] .. negligenciam seu ~atem .. versasse .., amoveatur *MonA* VI 737b.

damnabiliter [LL] **(dampn-),** damnably, culpably, or w. risk of damnation.

quia curiose exiit, ad hec mala ~iter pervenit Ad. Scot *QEC* 11. 819C; **s1190** W. Eliensis episcopus .. ecclesias, terras et possessiones .. ~iter sibi retinebat *G. Hen. II* II 143; seipsos multo gravius quam illos et ~ius seducunt Gir. *TH* III 29; plus appetunt ~iter occultari quam manu medicinali propalari salubriter et curari *Id. Spec.* III *pref.* p. 125; **1236** eosdem a lupo crudeliter occidi ~iter permittimus Gros. *Ep.* 28 p. 112; ~ius Ad. Marsh *Ep.* 8 (v. detorquere b); necesse est quod [peccatum mortale] depravet hominem morbo infinito, maxime animam .. in qua ~iter requiescit Bacon *CSPhil.* 406; **1294** in sententiam excommunicacionis .. per nos latam ~iter incidere non expavit *Reg. Carl.* I 19; **1382** Roberto antipape ~iter adherere *RScot* 45b; **c1530** (v. canonicus 6a).

damnaliter, damnably, culpably, or (?) *f. l.*

s1399 [rex] plures proceres regni Anglie .. interimere dampnaliter [? l. dampnabiliter] proposuit Ad. Usk 36.

damnare [CL] **(dampn-)**

1 to condemn (person), judge guilty; **b** (w. abl. of charge or offence); **c** (w. abl. of penalty or sentence); **d** (w. *ad*); **e** (fig., w. abstr. subj.).

latro nequaquam .. furem alium ~at Gildas *EB* 100; dicebant .. virum tantae auctoritatis .. nequaquam ~ari debere, sed .. culpis accusationum absolutum .. reverti Bede *HE* V 19; ~atus, *fordemed* Ælf. *Sup.*; nec ~etur vel judicetur [episcopus] priusquam legittimos accusatores .. habeat (*Leg. Hen.* 5. 24) *GAS* 551; Guillelmus [I] rex .. neminem nisi quem non ~are iniquum foret ~avit Ord. Vit. IV 1 p. 164; **s1191** (v. damnator); Christo .. imperanti obediunt venti et mare. .. solus homo .. ~at mundi factorem, vitam adimens illi per quem vivit Gerv. Tilb. I 1; **1339** nec est putanda .. juris intencio sic iniqua ut matrem et filium racione contraria simul ~et (*Lit. Regis Angliae*) Ad. Mur. *Chr.* 93. **b** criminibus stupri nitens damnare puellam Aldh. *VirgV* 1914; **s1071** abbati .. latronem .. aut alio crimine ~atum a supplicio liberare liceat *Chr. Battle* f. 23v.; **s1239** papa .. imperatorem .. heretica ~avit enormitate M. Par. *Maj.* III 590 (cf. 3c infra). **c** quamvis jamdudum damnaret carcere tetro / membra catervarum .. Aldh. *VirgV* 487; Eanfridum .. simili sorte ~avit Bede *HE* III 1; decomatione .. ~etur (*Leg. Hen.* 75. 1) *GAS* 591; **s1175** multitudinem callide convocatam .. sententia capitali ~avit Diceto *YH* I 401; *Ib.* II 118 (v. condemnare 1b). **d** ~ati erant et inprisonati ad dampnum c librarum *State Tri. Ed. I* 39. **e** ubi .. conscientia ~at, cogitationes increpant Bracton 2.

2 to condemn (action or doctrine), denounce. **b** to reject, spurn. **c** to disregard, treat contemptuously. **d** (w. inf.) to refuse.

atrocis damnans conubia regis Aldh. *VirgV* 441; diversitates .. ~andas Anselm II 240 (v. concorditer a); D. Bec. 75 (v. dedocere b). **b** ~are delicias, consuetas fastidire coctiones Serlo Gram. *Mon. Font.* 5. **c** de his qui ~ant Dominicam et indicta jejunia aecclesiae Dei Theod. *Pen.* I 11 *rub.* **d** conditor et legum nunc Justinianus abivit / set Dionisius has dampnat habere suas Gower *VC* VI 1276.

3 to damn (theol.). **b** to invoke damnation on. **c** (p. ppl. or gdv. as sb. pl.) the damned. **d** to condemn (doctrines, books, or statutes) as heretical or uncanonical. **e** (p. ppl.) accursed.

679 si aliquis aliter fecerit, a Deo se ~atum sciat *CS* 45; in nomine Jesu Christi, qui te [Satanam] de caelo ~avit Felix *Guthl.* 36; qui non vult ecclesiae januam sponte humiliatus ingredi, necesse habet in januam inferni non sponte ~atus introduci Bede *HE* V 14; **793** si quid peccati .. commiserit, abluat confessione .., ne ~etur in poena Alcuin *Ep.* 19; si vocem [daemonis] irati ferre non potuistis, societatem ~ati quo pacto sustinebitis? Osb. *V. Dunst.* 14; sunt quorum animus infantes ~ari debere, qui sine baptismo moriuntur, ob solam injustitiam .. non vult accipere Anselm (*Orig. Pecc.* 28) II 170; queritur utrum Deus possit salvare Judam et ~are Petrum Hales *Sent.* I 443; hec [racio] est impossibilis: 'aliquis ~atur contra predestinacionem Dei' Ockham *Pol.* II 729; ne .. gravitas criminum .. nos ~andos dejiciat in abyssum R. Bury *Phil.* 20. 251. **b** **12..** ex auctoritate Dei .. excommunicamus, ~amus, anatematizamus .. omnes conspiratores contra .. episcopos .. *Reg. Aberd.* II 36. **c** fetida ~atorum cadavera Aldh. *VirgP* 86; queritur cum †dagnandi [MS: damgnandi, l. dampnandi] qui in criminalibus exeunt, .. qua pena .. puniendi sint R. Melun *DP* 41; dampnant dampnati dampnatos D. Bec. 295; quia mala voluntas movet in ~atis, quod propterea demerentur Hales *Qu.* 689; **s1256** pro diabolo .. aut manifeste ~atis non est sperandum nec orandum M. Par. *Maj.* V 546; de animabus ~atorum et sanctorum Ockham *Dial.* 445. **d** **1382** cum .. declaratum fuerit quasdam conclusionum ipsarum hereticas esse, quasdam vero erroneas et determinacionibus ecclesie notorie repugnantes et ab ecclesia ~atas fuisse et esse, quas eciam ex abundanti sic ~atas esse declaramus (*Mandatum Cancellario Oxon.*) *Ziz.* 309; **1520** nonnulli domini temporales .. contra sacrorum canonum .. statuta edunt .. nonnulla statuta .. quibus prohibent .. eorum subditis .. ne .. eorum aliquis alterum suum tenandum citet .. ad judicium ecclesiasticum .. sub certa pena .. in dictis eorum ~atis statutis contenta *Conc. Scot.* I cclxxix; **1549** ut .. ordinarii .. deputent .. inquisitores .. qui inquirere teneantur de libris ~atis haereticorum *Ib.* II 117. **e** concedat Dominus .. episcopo suo .. in tranquillitate judicare .., presertim in his diebus ~atissimis Ad. Marsh *Ep.* 16.

4 to cancel, annul: **a** (deed, bond or sim.); **b** (tally).

a †**1026** (12c) proscribimus .. omnes antiquiores testamentorum litteras .. et ad nichilum ~amus *CD* 743; **1239** ~atum est cyrographum, quia Judeus honerator inde (*Chirog.*) *DCWestm.* 6692; **1243** carta ipsius R. .. ~etur *JustIt* 756 r. 3d.; **1259** reddidit .. litteras .., que ibidem laniate fuerant et ~ate Paris' per J. et R. clericos *Cl* 261; **1268** cum .. mercatores litteras .. Baldewini de quietancia detulerint, recognicio predicta ~etur et pro nullo habeatur *Cl* 525; **1286** retentis et ~atis .. litteris patentibus *RGasc* II 288; **1335** pro uno hanaperio empto pro ~atis litteris et billis de hoc termino imponendis *IssueR* 282. **b** **1225** tradidit .. vicecomiti Linc' unam talliam allocandam ad Scaccarium, que debuit esse ~ata, cujus pars inventa fuit in thesauro inter tallias ~atas *LTRMem* 8 r. 1 (1); **1286** iste tallie ~antur coram baronibus, eo quod alie loco earum innovantur *Cl* 103 m. 7; **1299** predicta tallia ~atur per thesaurarium et barones et liberatur in thesaurum cum eodem brevi *Pipe* 144 r. 28; **1462** omnes tallie cum foliis earundem pro eodem mutuo assignate sunt restitute et ~ate (*ReceiptR*) *Receipt Exch* 287.

5 to damage, hurt.

s1138 rex .. iterata eos obsidione ~avit, segetes eorum in agris vastans et cuncta solatia denegans J. Hex. *HR Cont.* 291; nec ille .. dominari querit, sed ~are, sed delere, sed a patria propellere Gir. *EH* I 8; a celo pupis damnatur [v. l. vexatur], ab aere prora H. Avr. *Hugh* 633; **c1250** sacrarium contritum et ~atum *Vis. S. Paul.* 9.

6 to block, seal (? *cf. dammare* or Fr. *condamner une porte*).

cum juxta portam [Exonie] equis desiluissent, offenderunt introitum forinsecus repagulis, intus seris ~atum W. Malm. *GP* II 95; id foramen [in mausoleo S. Etheldride] postea Athelwoldus .. et cemento et lapide ~avit *Ib.* IV 183; janue seris et repagulis ~entur! *Id. GR* II 202.

damnarium v. dammarium.

damnaticius [LL] **(dampn-),** condemned, damned. **b** (as sb.) criminal, convict.

Simonis vice te coerce, / quorum manet emulos in eorum merce / merces damnatitia W. Combe 193. **b** exosum .. et grave .. tolerare cogebantur ~ii Ad. Eyns. *Visio* 24; occurrit ei cum apparitorum turba quidam ~ius, qui ob commissum furtum .. ad meritum protrahebatur supplicium *Id. Hug.* V 9 p. 127.

damnatio [CL] **(dampn-)**

1 condemnation: **a** (of person); **b** (of doctrine or sim.).

a ecclesie .. prerogativam esse ut cujusque periculum ~onis declinantibus et ad eam confugium facientibus securitatem prestet Ad. Eyns. *Hug.* V 9 p. 127. **b** approbacio seu ~o summi pontificis catholici nonnunquam determinacio ecclesie appellatur Ockham *Pol.* III 71.

2 (theol.) damnation.

eam [gentem] ab aerumna perpetuae ~onis .. eripuit Bede *HE* IV 13; **930** (14c) (v. chirographum 1e); **1033** (12c) obligetur .. nodorum habenis perpetuae ~onis nisi resipiscat *CD* 752; promulgata est in te [Berengarium] ~onis sententia, privans te communione sanctae ecclesiae Lanfr. *Corp. & Sang.* 413C; Anselm II 256 (v. conqueri 1a); reprobatio sumitur pro effectu reprobationis, qui est ~o Hales *Sent.* I 414; item [valent bona opera] ad dimissionem cujusdam pene in Gehenna, ut sc. tolerabilior sit ~o *Id. Qu.* 434; hec misericordia, quam fecit pius rex Ricardus, ipsum .., ut credimus, a periculis ~onis et cruciatuum citius liberavit M. Par. *Maj.* III 215; **1323** utinam non sit ad ~onem anime mee! *Lit. Cant.* I 424; graciam reformando ac remittendo debitum ~onis eterne Ockham *Pol.* I 34; nec aliquid magis inducit extremam ~onem quam amor mundi Rolle *IA* 259; laborant quotidie in statu proprie ~onis Paul. Angl. *ASP* 1537.

3 damage, hurt.

723 ut ei nullus ullam contrarietatem vel ~onem adversus eum facere non debeat (C. Martel) *Ep. Bonif.* 22; nihil aliud in causa tante punitionis et ~onis erat nisi quod porcos pingues habebat Gir. *GE* II 34 p. 330; **1266** cum .. rebelles nostri .. dampna enormia perpetrando in .. regni nostri dampnum gravissimum .. ad majoris ~onis sue cumulum quendam de nunciis nostris .. ceperint et ei manum truncaverint *Cl* 240; **1438** decanus .. edificavit stabulum .. per cujus stillicidia dampnificatur tectum claustri, et eciam plures lapides .. de ipso muro ad hoc opus .. prostravit, per quod timetur de majori ~one in futurum (*Vis.*) *Stat. Linc.* II 374.

4 (?) contempt.

si pro ~one diei [Dominicae] jejunaverit, sicut Judeus abhominetur ab omnibus aecclesiis catholicis Theod. *Pen.* I 11. 3.

damnativus, leading to damnation.

secularis pompe vicio superato, in sui contemptu perseverans vires percepit adulterantis superbie ~as *NLA* (*J. Bridl.*) II 70.

damnator [LL] **(dampn-),** condemner.

coitus damnator iniqui R. Cant. *Malch.* II 504; **s1191** mittuntur et a dampnato [W. de Longo Campo] et a ~oribus nuntii ad ipsum regem .., quique pro parte sua ad accusandum vel excusandum sufficienter instructi Devizes 37v.; **s1196** ut .. ~ores ejus [Willelmi cum Barba] impios comprobarent, .. illi martyris nomen .. quesierunt W. Newb. *HA* V 21; esto .. caritativus corrector et non presumptuosus ~or [v. l. depravator] *Chr. Dale* 1; [Willelmus I] latronum fuit explorator sagacissimus et eorum ~or immiserabilis *Flor. Hist.* II 14; quid scit ~or talis, cum sacramentum sit porosum, si in poris lateat panis non triticeus Wycl. *Blasph.* 250.

damnatorius [CL], damnatory.

a ree conscientie ~io testimonio accusatus J. Furness *Walth.* 101.

damnificabilis (dampn-), hurtful.

mors bestiarum non est eis penalis pocius quam passio inanimati est ei ~is Wycl. *Ente* 296.

damnificare [LL] **(dampn-)**

1 to damage, hurt, cause loss (to): **a** (persons); **b** (things); **c** (absol.); **d** (w. dat.).

a hoc modis omnibus agitur ut paterfamilias, cui impensa perit et opera, ~etur J. Sal. *Pol.* 736D; **1196** litteras .. regis Anglie habuimus, quibus promittebat se ~atis omnibus .. recompensationem debitam prestiturum (*Lit. Archiep. Rotomag.*) Diceto *YH* II 145; **s1213** tutor habet potestatem in capite libero non ut pupillum .. in aliquo ledat vel ~et *Chr. Evesham* 232; **1227** ~atus est et deterioratus est et dampnum habet ad valenciam xx m. *CurR* XIII 88; **1260** cum .. melius sit cum securitate persone in bonis aliquantulum ~ari quam cum .. bonorum perditione totali .. crudelis mortis pene liberari (*Pat*) *Leg. Ant. Lond.* 68; [speculi] artifex ~atus est in c li. Parisiensibus Bacon *Tert.* 116; **1334** terras nostras .. ad populum .. gravandum seu ~andum ingredi *RScot* 276b; **1587** authoritatem .. Hispanos vi armata .. molestandi, ~andi, deprimendi, convincendi, et impugnandi *Pat* 1302 m. 7. **b** tene quod habes, quia conditionem / de facili posses damnificare tuam Nig. *SS* 204; **1322** manerium .. de T. plurimum ~atum extitit et existit, in grave ejusdem ecclesie detrimentum *Mon. Hib. & Scot.* 224a; **1350**

propter cistas que ~ate erant .. custodes cistarum .. super deficiente condempnentur ad reintegrandum dictas cistas *StatOx* 77; **1383** ad custodiendum .. terras ecclesiasticas .. et precipue tres villas de F. a malefactoribus .. illas ~are volentibus *Reg. Moray* 190; **1438** (v. damnatio 3). **c 1235** in quibus [boscis] de cetero ingressum injuste non habebunt nec ~abunt *CurR* XV 1430; **c1400** G. vada bacchando [MS: bacando] sunt D. vada dampnificando (*Vers.*) *Collect. Ox.* III 182. **d s1403** sicut ~avi regno, ita paratus sum damnum reformare *Eul. Hist. Cont.* III 397.

2 to fine, mulct.

1228 ~atus est de xv li. quas de .. manerio recepisse debuit *Cl* 130.

3 to condemn.

habet furcas, ubi ~at et suspendit captos cum manuopere *Hund.* II 31.

4 to injure spiritually, damn (theol.).

1378 non est possibile hominem excommunicari ad sui damnum nisi excommunicetur primo et principaliter a seipso .., cum oportet talem excommunicacionem originari a peccato ~ati. .. nemo debet nisi in causa Dei excommunicare .., cum .. amor ~ati debet superare .. appetitum temporalium quorumcunque (Wycl. *Decl.* 8, 9) Wals. *HA* I 359–60 (cf. *Ziz.* 250).

damnificatio [LL] **(dampn-),** damage, injury; **b** (theol.).

1309 quod .. processus contra eundem magis in .. archidiaconi ~onem quam juris execucionem fecimus ordinari *Reg. Cant.* 1057; **s1369** pestilencia .. per inundaciones .. sequebatur et magna bladi ~o Wals. *HA* I 309; in terra de S., que in presenciarum preter ~onem per aquas Humbrie pacifice retinetur *Meaux* I 95 & *n.*; Wycl. *Innoc.* 477 (v. dicere 10). **b** ~o vel deterioracio est homini quamlibet sic ditari [*w. ref. to Matth.* xvi 26], quia resistencia contra Deum incutit damnum Wycl. *Civ. Dom.* I 82; *Id. Ver.* III 205 (v. bonificatio).

damnificus [CL] **(dampn-),** hurtful, injurious.

causidicorum est lingua ~a, nisi eam .. funibus argenteis vincias J. Sal. *Pol.* 564B; **a1400** pro .. injuriis monasterio nostro .. irrogatis super precipiti precepcione et ~a detencione domus nostre de C. *Pri. Cold.* 78.

damnose [CL] **(dampn-),** hurtfully, injuriously.

cum verbum cohortationis ad te missum utiliter fuerit, in aliis forsitan ~e cadet G. Hoyland *Ascet.* 277B; **s1257** W. [de Valentia] .. in .. vicinos suos irreverenter, maxime in religiosos, ~e deseviens M. Par. *Maj.* V 634; **1343** sic jura corone nostre tam probrose quam ~e depereunt (*Lit. Regis*) Ad. Mur. *Chr.* 144.

damnosus [CL] **(dampn-),** hurtful, injurious, detrimental. **b** (theol.) leading to damnation.

a1180 si lis aliqua ~a intra ambitum messagii alicui eorum evenerit *BBC* (*Wells*) 112; lapides .. hostibus in conflictu ~issimos Gir. *TH* III 10; **1305** in loco nobis minus ~o et magis utili R. predicto *RGasc* III 462; **1308** intendit enervare composicionem factam, quod esset nobis et vobis ~um *Lit. Cant.* III 364; ~a est hodie studio Latinorum Greci sermonis inscicia R. Bury *Phil.* 10. 165; **1450** didicimus .. grave et ~um imminere periculum *Pri. Cold.* 169. **b 1457** ut ~e gentilitatis ritu deposito sacrosancto fidei merearis signaculo insigniri (*Lit. Papae ad Soldanum*) *Reg. Whet.* I 275.

damnum [CL] **(dampn-)**

1 loss, damage, injury; **b** (w. gen. of cause); **c** (w. gen. of thing lost); **d** (w. gen. of loser); **e** (w. *in* & abl.); **f** (w. *in* or *ad* & acc.); **g** (w. ref. to writ of *ad quod ~um*).

ne forte nos [Deus] .. vel temporalibus ~is .. affligat vel ad perpetuum perditionem .. tollat Bede *HE* IV 23 p. 266; **8.** .. ~um, *hendo WW*; magnum ~um [AS: *hynd*, l. *hynð*] et verecundia est homini nolle esse quod est Ælf. *Coll.* 100; unum molendinum quod .. maximum ~um facit regi et hominibus *DB* I 1; quilibet hoc [aliquid armorum] arripiat et ~um [AS: *hearm*] inde faciat, rectum est ut qui ~um fecit ~um etiam emendet (*Quad.*) *GAS* 363 (= *Inst. Cnuti* ib.: malum); inter dampna duo dampnum minus elige D. Bec. 1912; **1200** recognitores .. adesse .. ad dicendum que ~a ipsa habuit per illam disseisinam *CurR* I 274 (cf. ib. 275: de placito xv m. quas .. R. debuit reddidisse pro ~o quod eis fecit); **1339** cum .. injuriosa ~orum discrimina nobis mota fuerint (*Lit. Regis*) Ad. Mur. *Chr.* 91; Fortescue *LLA* 29 (v. consecutivus a). **b** atra venenorum non sensit damna nigrorum Aldh. *VirgV* 477 (cf. ib. 1671: damna latronis); **1002** (12c) sanctissimus vir [Job] in artiori suae ~o anxietatis *CD* 1295. **c** quamvis caecatus sentiret damna pupillae Aldh. *VirgV* 498; ceteras .. copias non sine magno exercitus sui ~o delevit Bede *HE* II 2; quam institutionem si .. aliquis .. infringere audebit, .. magne pecunie ~o obnoxius erit Ric. Hex. *Hist. Hex.* I 5; **1253** pro ~is equorum suorum .. in servicio regis *Cl* 188. **d s1221** [comes de Albemarlia] castrum suum de ~is aliorum munivit Wend. II 256. **e 1253** tali precio eos [pannos] eis habere faciat quod non sint in ~o, quia rex vult ipsum pocius esse in ~o quam ipsos *Cl* 191. **f 1247** destruxit bladum suum ad ~um suum j thrave frumenti et dedecus ij sol. *SelPlMan* 7; **1269** exierunt plures fere de foresta in libertatem, que ibi capte erant ad ~um domini regis et detrimentum foreste sue *SelPlForest* 44; **1269** pisces in ~um et dedecus ipsius asportaverunt *CBaron* 75; **1292** (v. 2 contemptus c); **1298** [bosci] afforestati .. ad tale ~um, viz. quod .. nichil de predictis boscis capere potuerunt .. *Cart. Boarstall* 574; **1341** multa .. attemptare presumpsit in .. populi nobis subditi ~um non modicum et gravamen (*Pat*) Avesb. 97; ad ~um ecclesie faciunt oppositum verbis Pauli Wycl. *Pol.* 19; **1433** sibi commissa abutitur potestate in ~um, prejudicium, et intolerabile gravamen prioris et prioratus *Pri. Cold.* 107. **g 1385** (v. ad 14a).

2 (leg.) compensation for injury, damages. **b** 'damages cleer' (payable to clerks).

1199 ~um disseisine est xviij m.; illud reddat *CurR* I 76; **1202** ipse quesivit versus eum dedecus et ~um ut de uxore sua *SelPlCrown* 44; **s1266** habeant terras suas quietas et ~a sua per consideracionem curie *Leg. Ant. Lond.* 89; petunt ~a sua versus predictos R. [et al.] *State Tri. Ed. I* 34 (cf. ib. 35: quod illi solummodo ~a intrarent et ad ~a teneantur qui se ~um fecisse cognoverunt); **1305** abbas recuperet ~a sua vj d. versus .. R. *SelPlForest* cxxvi; **1356** (v. 1 assidere 7d); **1375** unde ~a taxantur per juratores ad xiij s. iiij d. *Hal. Durh.* 128; **1564** reddat prefato A. pixidem .. cum .. carta .. vel dicta separabilia ~a sibi .. separatim adjudicata *Entries* 219b. **b 1280** quas .. concessit .. clericis dictorum justiciariorum de iiij^{xx} li. que ei adjudicate fuerunt pro ~is suis *SelCKB* I 69 (cf. ib. lxxxvi-viii); **1302** ~a x m., unde c s. cler[icis], xx s. mar[escallo] *JustIt* (*Durh.*) 226 r. 8d.; **1336** ~a xx m., unde clericis xx et marescallo dim. m. *SelCKB* V 85 (cf. ib. xiv).

3 game preserve (within which lord is entitled to compensation for damage done by animals).

1203 [in] illo bosco cepit porcos .. ut in ~o et in panagio et in defenso domini sui *CurR* II 231; **1236** cignos illos juste cepit et in ~o suo *Ib.* XV 1893; **1250** quia invenit illos [boves] in dompno [v. l. dampno] suo, illos inparcavit *Ib.* XIX 1686; **c1255** (v. cuniculus 2a); **1282** cum .. averia Fabiani .. in dompno suo apud Treruf [*Cornw*] inventa imparcare vellet *IMisc* 41/15 (*Cal.* 2249); possunt capciones advocari eo quod dici poterit quod averia capta fuerunt in loco certo in ~o suo, ut in parco vel alibi in suo separali *Fleta* 104 (cf. *1 Westm.* 35); **1330** ad capiendum .. animalia in ~is .. fratrum inventa *MonA* VI 1564b; si quis latronem in ~o suo invenerit cum furto, clamorem super illum statim levare debet cum cornu *RegiamM* IV 23. 2; si quis invenerit aucas vel capras in ~o suo (*Fragm. Collecta*) *APScot* I 364.

4 (theol.) spiritual injury, damnation.

s1178 qualiter Arriana heresis .. cum auctore suo in eternum ~um deperiit *G. Hen. II* I 214; **1378** (v. damnificare 4); **s1389** (v. capitositas).

damnus v. dammus.

1 dampa v. 2 damma.

2 dampa [ME *damp*], fire-damp (Notts).

1390 operentur in predicta minura, nichil eos impedientes salvis .. damp' et aqua (*Middleton MSS*) *HMC Rep.* IX 100.

damphius v. daphnis. **dampleon** v. daphnelaeon. **dampn-** v. et. damn-, daphn-, dominus 8d. **dampneleon, ~elicon, ~ilion** v. daphnelaeon. **damula, ~ulus** v. damm-. **damus** v. dammus, 1 danus. **damyncula** v. dammicula. **Danachius, Danachus** v. Daneschus. **Danageldum** v. Danegeldum. **danatio** v. donatio 1e.

1 Danaus [CL < *Δαναός*], Greek.

~i, Greci *GlC* D 8; in auxilium Michaelis, quem ~i de throno imperiali expulerant Ord. Vit. IV 3 p. 172.

2 Danaus v. 2 Danus.

†dandonare, *f. l.*

1274 antequam .. prisones finem fecerint de xx marcis .. Roberto †dandonandis [MS: dā (*at end of line*) donandis, ? l. dandis *or* donandis] pro deliberacione eorum sub plegiamento *Hund.* II 89a.

Danechius v. Daneschus.

Danegeldum, ~a, ~us [AS **Denegēld*], Danegeld (tax thought to have been instituted by Ethelred II).

1071 denegeldo (v. donum 3a); Stanford burgum regis dedit geldum T. R. E. pro xij *hundrez* et dim. in exercitu et navigio et in *Danegeld* *DB* I 336b; hec sunt jura que rex Anglie solus .. habet in terra sua ..: infractio pacis regie .., Denagildum, placitum brevium .. Denagildum, quod aliquando þingemannis dabatur, id est xij d. de unaquaque hyda per annum, si ad terminos non reddatur, wita emendetur (*Leg. Hen.* 10. 1 & 15) *GAS* 556, 559; Denegeldi redditio propter piratas primitus statuta est (*Leg. Ed. Conf.*) *Ib.* 634; **a1116** ut sit quieta de sciris et hundredis et murdro et Denegildo *Regesta* 1163; **1130** vic. r. c. de ~o *Pipe* 5; **1131** [cives London'] sint quieti de *scot* et de Danegildo et de *murdre* (*Ch. Hen. I*) *GAS* 525; **s1135** vovit [rex S.] quod Denegeldum, id est, ij s. ad hidam, quos antecessores sui accipere solebant singulis annis, in eternum condonaret H. Hunt. *HA* VIII 3 (cf. ib. V 29: **s991** statuerunt Angli .. quod .. censum Dacis persolverent; *AS Chr.*: *gafol*, tributum); **1166** r. c. de vij li. de veteri Daneg' de W. *Pipe* 37 [*last mention in Pipe*]; **c1170** dedisse .. Strettunam .. solutam ab omni terreno servicio .. et geldis et Danageldis et hornegeldis *Cart. Newm.* 197; **1175** (1337) quiete de .. schiris et tenemanetale et de †dangerio [MS: dang^{d}, i.e. Danegeldo] et de murdro *CalCh* IV 404; ad hos [predones] arcendos, a regibus Anglicis statutum est ut de singulis hidis regni jure quodam perpetuo ij s. argentei solverentur in usus virorum fortium qui perlustrantes et jugiter excubantes maritima impetum hostium reprimerent. quia igitur principaliter pro Dacis institutus est hic redditus, ~um vel ~us dicitur. hic .. annua lege .. sub indigenis regibus solvebatur usque ad tempora regis W. I .. raro .. temporibus ejus vel successorum ipsius solutus est, hoc est cum ab exteris gentibus bella vel opiniones bellorum insurgebant *Dial. Scac.* I 11 A; **1209** quiete sint .. de scutag' et Denegaldis *RChart* 185b; **1214** liberum .. de scutag' et geldis, Dengeldis, hidagiis *Ib.* 201b.

Danelaga [AS *Dena lagu*], Danelaw, (part of England subject to) Danish law.

si quis burhbotam vel brigbotam vel *fyrdfare* supersederit, emendet hoc erga regem cxx solidis in Anglorum laga, in Denalaga [AS: *on Dena lage*] sicut stetit antea (*Quad.*) *GAS* 353 (= *Cons. Cnuti*: in lege Danorum); legis Anglice trina est partitio .., alia enim Westsexie, alia Mircena, alia Denelaga est (*Leg. Hen.* 6. 2) *Ib.* 552; [rex W. I] propositis legibus Anglicanis secundum tripartitam earum distinctionem, hoc est Merchenelage, ~e, Westsexenelage, quasdam reprobavit, quasdam autem approbans illis transmarinas Neustrie leges .. adjecit *Dial. Scac.* I 16 A; in Denelahe (*Leis Will.*) *GAS* 505 (v. dominicus 3c); iste xv provincie .. orientales et boreales judicabantur olim lege illa que vocabatur Denelaga Higd. I 49 p. 86.

danerellus v. denerellus.

Daneschus, ~ius [cf. AS *Denisc*, AN *Danesche*, OF *Daneis*], Danish, (w. *hachia* or as sb. f.) Danish axe, pole-axe. *Cf. Dacus* 2b.

1200 de roberia .. j hache ~achie *CurR RC* II 244; **1231** ei dedit j plagam cum quadam hachia ~esch' in sinistra parte capitis *CurR* XIV 1737; **1250** vi et armis, sc. cum hachiis Denachiis, arcubus et sagittis *Ib.* XIX 2272; **1266** erigens quandam hachiam Deneschiam ad .. flammam extinguendam *ICrim* 616; **1270** ipsum percusciendo in capite cum hachia Denachia ter *CourtR Hales* 6; **1272** latrones dimiserunt unam achiam Denech' *SelCCoron* 24; **1274** abstulerunt ab eo quandam hackam †Denoscham precii xij d. *Hund.* II 99 (cf. ib.: quandam hackam Denescam de precio viij d.); **1276** ceperunt collobium suum et unam denescham *Ib.* 105; **1280** percussit ipsum quadam hachia Danech' unde mancha fuit de fraxino *JustIt* 759 r. 26 (ix); **1290** [cum] hacka Denesa *CallMisc* I 2321.

dangerosus, dangerous.

dawyngerows, domigerosus [v. l. domigeriosus] *PP*.

1 dangerium v. Danegeldum.

2 dangerium, ~um [OF *dangier, dongier* < *dominiarium; *form* domigerium *perh. orig. misr. of* doungerium]

1 due: **a** paid by tenant of vineyard (Norm.); **b** paid by tenant of 'den' for right to take wood or sim., or land subject to due (Kent & Suss; *cf. Cart. Bilsington* 16–21).

a c1160 G. .. dedit S. Stephano .. omne ~ium et consuetudines quas habebat in vineis S. Stephani que erant in terra sua *Act. Hen. II* I 282 (cf. ib.: ~ium et pressoragium de iij virgatis vinee). **b 1213** Neuingburn: .. de pannagio et ~o, xx s. *DCCant. Rental* 38/1 m. 3; **1268** consuetudines .. sicut hactenus tenentes facere consueverunt, *husbote, werbote, heibote, faldbote* et ~ium, pannag' et pasturam, *mortboys* et *suboys* de boscis [*in Kennington, Kent*] *ChartR* 60 m. 12; **1271** idem r. c. .. de iij s. vj d. de danger' pannag' *MinAc* (*Maidstone*) 1128/1; **1271** quod dongerium pannag' dictorum boscum valet per annum lxxij s. [*Folkestone*] *IPM* 40/7 r. 6; **1285** de xx s. receptis de donger' in Wald[is] hoc anno *MinAc* (*Ospringe*) 894/1; **1285** (15c) tenentes de Waldis habent communam cum omnibus bestiis suis excepto uno bosco domini incluso ..; et dominus suo tempore habet danger' *Cust. Suss* II (*Slyndon*) 5 (cf. ib. 10: tenentes de Slyndon' debent ad festum S. Mich. pro ~io de †Tuisteek', ne namientur tempore aperto, licet serentur aut non, ij s.); tenentes .. debent communare ubique excepto uno bosco incluso per annum excepto tempore pannagii vel ~ii, quod est domini, cum omnibus animalibus suis exceptis capris *Ib.* (*Terring*) 29; **1292** (14c) R. de C. tenere solet antiquitus in capite de domino abbate in .. manerio suo de Kenyngtone de nova terra et ~io quod dicitur *drofden* apud C. quod nunc tenent heredes Willelmi de C. ... E. et R. de C. tenere solent .. quoddam tenementum ibidem, de quo tenemento sunt nova terra et ~ium viij acre *Reg. S. Aug.* 236–7; **13..** Hervorthing' v s.: inde debetur *drofdenne*, *lesyeld* in certo, dongerium, et redditus hujusmodi cum consuetudine etc. .. Doclyndenne [etc.], inde redditum tantum, et non debetur ibi dongerium neque *drofdenne* debetur. .. summa ~ii in certo preter redditum in dennis supradictis per annum xix s., unde serviens de Kenyngtone annuatim habet respondere etc.; et debet preterea respondere de pannagio et dongerio de eisdem cum pannagium acciderit *Ib.* 235–6 (cf. ib. 246: Herverthingg' est de veteri terra et dongerio in Hathewoldenne. .. Parrok est de veteri terra set non dongerio in Benyndenne).

2 a authority of foresters (? incl. right to special dues). **b** (area of) authority or jurisdiction.

a 1235 [vic. Oxon'] venire faciat .. xij tam milites quam alios .. qui non sint de bailliva Thome de Langeleghe [forestarii regis] nec in dongerio nec potestate sua *CurR* XV 1054; **1241** [vic. Norhamt'] venire faciat .. iiij de .. militibus de comitatu suo qui minus sint in doungerio foreste regis ad videndum statum foreste regis *Cl* 364; **1267** quod .. libere et sine visu et liberacione et daungerio forestariorum .. capere possint et cariare estoveria sua *Cart. Osney* IV 41 (cf. ib. 343 [c**1280**]: absque daungerio forestarii seu viridarii); **1285** terras .. deafforestatas extra omnimodum doungerium et potestatem forestariorum, viridariorum, agistatorum, regardatorum, et ministrorum nostrorum foreste (*Ch. Vale Royal, Chesh*) *ChartR* 73 m. 32; **1289** est ibidem [*Chalton, Hants*] unus boscus in foresta .. et valet per annum v s. et non plus propter ~ium forestariorum *IPM* 53/15. **b** [repellitur a sacramento juratorum] si sit ita sub ejus [pro quo jurare debet] potestate quod ei possit imperari vel noceri vel hujusmodi, ut si in ~io [vv. ll. domigeria, damigerio] vel ita sub ejus manu quod possit per eum in aliquo gravari BRACTON 185; pudorem hujusmodi voco .. pati quandoque illorum ~ia [ME: *danger*] qui possent esse vestri servi *AncrR* 138 (cf. ib. 149: letari corde debetis si paciamini ~ium [ME: *danger*] a mancipio lavante discos); cum .. R. abbas [ob. **1310**] et conventus .. manerium de Wyfelesby .. in manibus propriis retinerent, abbas et canonici de Welleho- we .. ipsum manerium .., cum vix ad milliarium a monasterio suo distet et in domigerio ipsius manerii indies detinerentur, in usus suos .. redigere sunt conati *Meaux* II 225; **1359** loca .. in domigerio Anglicorum super marchias situata *Melrose* II 439; **1444** ipsum per pavimentum ville [de Beverlaco] ac per rura et devia per pedes, quousque domigerium habitatorum ville .. evasissent, ut proditorem traxerunt *Pat* 602 m. 13*d.*; *a dawnger*, domigerum, †rig- num [? l. regnum] *CathA.*

3 a liability, expense. **b** debt, hardship.

a p**1323** H. de Stokes, quondam officialis Northampto- nie, habuit meremium [boscorum de Pipewell'] .. pro edificio domorum .., nec audebant [abbates] resistere, quia aut pro denariis aut pro bladis semper fuerunt .. in daungerio dicti officialis *MonA* V 435a; s**1352** per justicia- rios .. emolumentum regi semper accrevit et †dominige- rium ad populum KNIGHTON II 74; pro ecclesiis .. stramentandis .. vicarius .. non habet stramentalia nisi ex empcione et hoc multociens cum magno domigerio *Reg. Rough* 297; abbas M. [ob. **1394**] magnam porcionem .. de lapidicina adquisivit, ubi sine domigerio .. sufficientes lapides extrahi possent ad opera .. monasterii *G. S. Alb.* II 361; s**1392** sic recuperaverunt cives .. libertates antiquas .. credebant autem Londonienses quod per hec dona domi- gerium evasissent ..; sed fefellit eos eorum opinio, quia coacti sunt expost solvere regi x millia librarum WALS. *HA* II 211. **b** c**1380** in magno ~io duco .. vitam meam, quia .. pecunia quam michi providet reverencia paternalis .. michi sufficere non poterit *FormOx* 390; fratres ibidem .. morabantur in magno domigerio, cum quidam pro eorum sustentacione .. mendicare compellebantur *G. S. Alb.* II 398; **1408** pro immenso domigerio in quo .. penes .. diversos .. creditores suos, quibus ipse in quammagnis summis est obligatus, stare dinoscitur *Pat* 378 m. 14.

dangio v. dunjo.

Danicus, Danish.

s**1035** Angli .. extinctos fuisse truculentia ~a suae gentis nobilissimos minime obliti sunt W. POIT. I 2; s**1051** ex quo .. Ægelredus .. id [vectigal] ~is solidariis solvi mandarat FL. WORC. I 204; viri bellicosi ~o more undique ferro vestiti GIR. *EH* I 21; dixisse memoratur lingua ~a *leit loupe*, quod Latine sonat 'sine salire' *Id. IK* II 7.

Danielitas, essential nature of Daniel.

quidditas et suppositum ibi non differunt nisi sicut ~as et Daniel T. SUTTON *Esse* 26 p. 43.

Danieliticus, (text) associated w. Daniel.

juxta quod Daniheliticum legitur: 'jam cognoscet omnis natio Deum esse solum in omni loco' [? cf. *Dan.* iv 14] HERM. ARCH. 37.

dano, 'soulscot', mortuary payment, or (?) *f. l.*

dano [? l. dona], *sawlsceat* vel *syndrig Godes lac* ÆLF. *Gl.*

dansa [OF *dance*], dance.

c**1200** debet novus residenciarius post cenam die SS. Innocencium ducere puerum suum cum daunsa et chorea et torchiis ad elemosinariam *Reg. S. Paul.* 129.

dantia, act of giving.

dominus temporalis .. committit ministro suo dacionem ministerialem ..; et, sicut oportet servum suum parere suis monitis, vel alias dacio non valebit, sic oportet ipsum ad mandata Dei .. conformare suum mandatum, vel aliter ~ia est injusta. et, si Paulus [qui recipit] .. sit injustus pro tempore dacionis et Petrus justus qui tribuit, tunc ~ia est justa et recepcio est injusta WYCL. *Civ. Dom.* I 258.

†dantulus [cf. DuC], *f. l.*

divites .. donis acceptis .. vaniglorium datorem deri- dent, et qui tertium gradum cognationis vel quartum computant aut concedunt †~o [MS: clanculo] centesi- mum genu numerare nesciunt J. FURNESS *Walth.* 43.

Danubianus, (?) Nubian.

S. SIM. *Itin.* 71 (v. corvus 1a).

1 danus [cf. δάνος, δανειστής], usurer.

†damus, fenerator *GlC* D 11.

2 Danus [ON *Danir*, AS *Dæne, Dene pl.*], Dane. **b** Danish. *Cf. Dacus.*

sunt Fresones, Rugini, Danai [AS: *Dæne, Dene*], Hunni, Antiqui Saxones, Boructuari BEDE *HE* V 9; **789** si spes ulla sit de ~orum conversione ALCUIN *Ep.* 6; a**941** (10c) cum consensu .. Æðelstani Angelsaxonum Denorumque glo- riosissimi regi[s] *CS* 648; oppidum .. quod sermone Saxonico Slesuuic nuncupatur, secundum vero ~os Haith- aby ÆTHELW. I 4; per pressuram ~orum *V. Ed. Conf.* 38v.; quod hereditatem eorum ~i invasione occupaverint W. POIT. I 1; Fin ~us *DB* I 153; hoc est consilium quod Ælfred rex et Godrún rex elegerunt .. quando Angli et ~i [AS: *Dene*] ad pacem .. convenerunt (*Quad.*) *GAS* 129; quomodo .. rex Willelmus leges Anglorum voluit dimitte- re et leges ~orum [v. l. †Danaorum] tenere (*Leg. Ed. Conf. rub.*) *Ib.* 671; W. MALM. *GR* II 125 (v. 1 coalescere 1a); a Dano, filio ejus [Antenoris], gens illa e Trojanis orta ~orum nomen accepit ORD. VIT. IX 3 p. 474; non inmerito metuens †Donaos [MS *in marg.*: ~os] 'et dona ferentes' [cf. Virgil *Aen.* ii 49] MAP *NC* V 4 f. 62v. **b** s**871** in loco qui Northuuorthige nuncupatur, juxta autem Danaam linguam Deoraby ÆTHELW. IV 2 (cf. ib. IV 3 [s**893**]: Danaa suda in Beamfleote loco .. ruit).

dapefer v. dapifer a.

daphne [LL < δάφνη], (w. *Alexandrina*) butcher's broom (*Ruscus*).

dapne, quam alii Alexandrinam vocant vel ypoglosson, folia habet †eximursine [v. l. oximyrsino] similia .. *Alph.* 48 (cf. ib. 6: Alexandrina, i. camedafne, respice in dapne).

daphnelaeon [δαφνέλαιον], laurel oil.

confice cum dampnileon et succo rute GILB. VII 353v. 2; laurus, i. dampnis; inde dampnococce et †dampnelicon [v. l. dampneleon], i. oleum confectum ex oleo et baccis lauri *Alph.* 95 (cf. ib. 47: †dampleon [v. l. dampnilion], i. oleum laurinum).

daphnis [LL < δαφνίς], laurel.

~is vel laurus, *laurbeam* ÆLF. *Gl.*; ~is Grece laurus dicitur Latine. .. et sunt duo genera ejus, sc. Delphica et Cypriaca BART. ANGL. XVII 48; rami cedri et dampnidis GILB. V 225v. 1; †damphius, laurus idem *SB* 17; dampnis *Alph.* 95 (v. daphnelaeon); dampnis, A. *a loreytre WW.*

daphnococcus [δαφνόκοκκος], laurel berry. *Cf. anacoccus.*

grana ij staphizagrie .., dapnococti, sinomi, petrolei, storacis rubei .. GILB. II 119. 2 (cf. ib. V 225v. 1: damnococti); bacce lauri, dampnococci idem; G. *bayes de lorer Alph.* 19.

daphnoides [CL < δαφνοειδής], (bot.) spurge laurel (*Daphne laureola*).

dafnoydes vel pentalon aut camedafne *Alph.* 48; ~es aliquibus eupatalon nonnullis camedaphne dicitur; herba- rii laureolam appellant, vulgus autem *laury* aut *lauriell* TURNER *Herb.* A4v.

dapicida, ~us, ~arius, carver (in royal house- hold).

1437 dilecto et fideli militi nostro, Edmundo Hunger- ford, uni de ~cidis nostris *Pat* 440 m. 8; **1457** unum ~scidarum nostrorum *RScot* II 379a (= *Foed.* XI 397b); **1462** uni ~scidorum nostrorum *Pat* 500 m. 20; **1468** considerantes .. cordiale servicium Jacquetti Haulte, ar- migeri, unius ~cidarium .. consortis nostre regine Anglie *Ib.* 521 m. 19.

dapicus, lavish.

large, †amplos .., dapsilis in dapibus, ~us, .., largus *CathA.*

dapifer, attendant at meals, sewer, steward: **a** (unspec. and var.; *cf. Eng. Feudalism* 73); **b** (royal, Eng.; *cf. King's Serjeants* 69, *Regesta* I *intr.* § 17); **c** (royal, Scot.; *cf. Regesta Scot.* I p. 32); **d** (mon.); **e** (fig.). *Cf. dispensator 2, senescallus.*

a praepositus hujus manerii [*Monkland, Heref*] consue- tudinem habebat T. R. E. ut, veniente domina sua in manerio, praesentaret ei xviij oras denariorum ut esset ipsa laeto animo; et ~fer et alii ministri habebant de eo x s. *DB* I 179b; si quis ~ferum vel quemlibet ministrum ita rebus suis prefecerit .. ut quodammodo locum ejus habeat .. (*Leg. Hen.* 42. 2) *GAS* 568 (cf. ib. 92. 18 p. 609: ad ~ferum vel ministrum manerii); **1127** testibus .. Godwino ~fero, Godwino camerario meo [sc. episcopi S. Andr.] *E. Ch. Scot.* 73; c**1160** Willelmo de Rothomago, dapefero *Dane- law* 280; **1203** R. .. dicit quod .. ad opus W. filii sui fecit dissaisinam sicut ~fer filii sui de baronia quam habet ex hereditate uxoris W. [Daci] *CurR* III 62; disce ministrare, dapibus sua jura parare. / .. / da juxta morem, dextra preeunte, saporem; / fercula sessorem dapifer locet ante priorem GARL. *Mor. Scol.* 400; episcopi, .. barones et hujusmodi magnates, milites, servientes, ~feros, pincer- nas .. et pistores sub suis fridbordis existentes .. ad standum recto et paci .. promptos habere debent *Fleta* 40 (cf. *GAS* 647, camerarius 4d); hic ~fer, A. *mettes gyffer* .., *a berere of mete WW.* **b 1067** Stigand ~fer *Regesta* 6a; Eudo ~fer *DB* I 343; rex Guillelmus .. Willelmo ~fero Normannie .. insulam Vectam.. dedit ORD. VIT. IV 7 p. 218; s**946** FL. WORC. 134 (v. cleptor); *manbote* in lege Anglorum .. comiti comitatus et ~fero regis xx s. (*Leg. Ed.*) *GAS* 638; [Arturus] assumpto Kaio ~fero et Bedeve- ro pincerna G. MON. X 3; **1200** R. de Curci ~fer regis *CurR* I 239; **1227** Radulfum filium Nicholai ~ferum nostrum *Pat* 162; **1583** unum ~ferarum (*sic*) camere nostre *Pat* 1234 m. 8. **c** c**1160** [teste] Waltero filio Alani ~fero *Regesta Scot.* I 162; a**1170** sciant .. Walterum filium Alani, ~ferum regis Scotie, religionis domum apud Passa- let .. fundasse *Reg. Paisley* 2; **1380** per comites de Carr .., ~feros domini regis ac seneschallos Scocie *Melrose* 483; **1453** J. comitem de Douglas .. et Robertum Liddale de Balmure primi ~feri (*sic*) .. Jacobi .. Scottorum regis .. ambassiatores *RScot* 363a. **d** a**1097** Radulfo ~fero .. abbatis [de S. Edmundo] *Regesta* p. 134; **11..** Edmundo ~fero monachorum *Feod. Durh.* 132*n.* **e** Simon [de Monteforti], legitime qui regum ducit habenas, / scrutatur rectas persequiturque vias, / largifluus dapifer dispensa- torque facetus, / promptus pincerna. munera larga pluunt GARL. *Hon. Vit.* 297; **1431** dummodo †dapsifero [? l. dāpifero] non desint sacra Lieo (*Vers.*) AMUND. I 299.

1 dapifera, dispenser (f., fig.). *Cf. dapiferia.*

Maria, fons dulcoris, / .. / dapifera saporis J. HOWD. *Viola* 115; virgo .. / panis vite dapifera LEDREDE *Carm.* 14. 5.

2 dapifera v. dapiferia.

dapiferatus, stewardship.

1142 do ei totam terram que fuit Eudonis dapiferi in Normannia et ~um ipsius (*Ch. M. Imp.*) *Mandeville* 167 (cf. *Act. Hen. II* I 7); **1158** rex Francorum .. recognovit quod custodia abbatie S. Juliani Turonensis ad me perti- net ex dignitate ~us mei *Act. Hen. II* I 194; s**1164** comes Carnotensis Tedbaudus despondit filiam L. regis Francie et ideo rex ei concessit ~um Francie, quem comes Ande- gavensis antiquitus habebat TORIGNI *Chr.* 222.

dapiferia, stewardship; **b** (as serjeanty).

1126 miles quidam, Odo nomine, .. ob gratiam cujus- dam consobrine sue, quam idem Odo conjugem duxerat, †~feram [? l. ~feriam] ecclesie et tria maneria de dominio sibi astrinxerat (*Scriptum H. abbatis*) DOMERH. *Glast.* 306. **b** p**1222** heres Isolde B. [tenet] Cumbam [*Wilts*] per ~iam *Fees* 341.

dapinare [CL], to provide food.

ȝeve mete, ~o *PP.*

dapiscida, ~us v. dapicida. **dapne** v. daphne. **dapno- coctus** v. daphnococcus.

daps [CL], feast, food; **b** (fig.).

sobolem numquam dapibus saturabo ciborum ALDH. *Aen.* 63 (*Corbus*) 8; ~is, cibus; ~es, cibi lautiores *GlC* D 16–17; ~es sibimet adpositas deferri pauperibus .. praece- pit BEDE *HE* III 6; **742** adfirmant se vidisse .. in Romana urbe .., quando Kalende Januarii intrant, .. mensas illa die vel nocte ~ibus onerare BONIF. *Ep.* 50; ~es vel fercula, *wista* vel *sand* ÆLF. *Gl.*; ~es, epule, *swetmete GlS* 213; nemo eo .. in ~ibus aliis sumptuosior vel sibi moderatior fuit W. MALM. *GR* V 407; non obstet dapibus pollex sumptis cocleari D. BEC. 1001; cum satis haberem ~is et minus rixe multoque minus cure quam nunc habeam GIR. *Invect.* I 13 p. 123 (cf. id. *GE* II 34 p. 331: satis .. ~is .. minusque laboris); s**1236** civibus .. Wintoniensibus co- quine et ~ium curam gerentibus M. PAR. *Maj.* III 338; GARL. *Mor. Scol.* 395 (v. dapifer a); hec ~s, *mete WW.* **b** diversa ~ium dogma et evangelici nectaris mellifua pan- debat mysteria HUGEB. *Wynn.* 6; ALCUIN *SS Ebor* 1232 (v. carnalis 4c).

dapsifer v. dapifer e.

dapsile [CL], copiously, lavishly.

†dapsele, †cupiose [l. copiose] *GlC* D 9.

dapsilis [CL], lavish, munificent, bountiful: **a** (of person or household); **b** (of action).

a [Loth] dapsilis et tribuens cunctis solamina victus ALDH. *VirgV* 2517; fuit en pia filia regis / dapsilis et clemens *Epigr. Milredi* 815; **9..** ~is, *rumheort WW*; largus vel ~is, *cystig* ÆLF. *Gl.*; erat egentibus ~is liberaliter ABBO *Edm.* 4; domino †vestram [? l. vestrā] nullam puto dapsiliorem R. CANT. *Poems* 261; hic non ~is sed prodigus erat ORD. VIT. IV 7 p. 219; ex paternis rebus et propriis ~is erat et liberalissimus *G. Herw.* 320b; hic .. presul J. [ob. **1303**] .., ~is, munificus et in retinendis militibus honora- bilis .. existens, honorem ecclesie .. querebat T. STUBBS 409; s**1469** (v. consiliosus a). **b** ALDH. *Ep.* 5 (v. deditio 1b); **745** (12c) ego C. rex .. terrae partem .. ~i .. liberalitate .. ad Maldunense monasterium largitus sum *CS* 170; **956** nostra ~i deditione perfruatur *Ib.* 961; dum quicquid victus habere videamur .., externis ~i jussu distribueras B. *V. Dunst.* 27.

dapsilitas [LL], munificence, bounty.

934 (14c) tota magnatorum generalitate sub ulnis regie ~atis ovanti *CS* 704; **942** (13c) inter innumeras quibus beavit utriusque certaminis catervas ~ates eternis provo- catur proverbiis *Ch. Burton* 5; **986** a vestrae .. ~atis

largitate sustentationem adipisci speramus (*Lit. Abbatis Blandin.*) *Mem. Dunst.* 381; W. MALM. *Glast.* 117 (cap. 79) (v. clamare 3a); contigit regem .. a quodam abbate .. inter reliquos sue ~atis appetitores adiri *Chr. Battle* f. 39; diceres tunc ~atem Burgundionum ipsum quoque vicisse luxum effusionis Anglicorum AD. EYNS. *Hug.* V 14 p. 164; parcas larga manus damnans, Albania Scotos / ponit in exemplum dapsilitate sua GARL. *Tri. Eccl.* 33; **s1305** papa episcopum Dunelmensem .., propter ~atem et cordis magnificenciam quas in eo reperit, fecit patriarcham Jerosolymitanum WALS. *YN* 236.

dapsiliter [CL], lavishly, bounteously.

refectionem quam dux praeparaverat ~er ad edendum BYRHT. *V. Osw.* 464; **c1043** (11c) cuidam meo optimati .. quandam ruris portiunculam .. impertior quatinus .. cuicumque placuerit cleronomo ~er concedat *CD* 769; Samson .., antiquorum homo morum, ipse liberaliter vesci et aliis ~er largiri W. MALM. *GP* IV 150.

†Dar, *f. l.*

Martius [vocatur] Hebraice †Dar [l. Adar] *Miss. R. Jum.* 11.

darapti, a logical mood.

BACON XV 301 (v. baroco).

darces v. darsus. **darchem** v. darsen.

Dardanus [CL], descended from Dardanus. **b** Trojan (w. ref. to *ludus Trojanus*).

Dardana proles [i.e. Ganymedes] ALDH. *Aen.* 57 (*Aquila*) 3. **b** hinc thessara, calculus, tabula, urio vel ~a pugna J. SAL. *Pol.* 399C.

dare [CL]

1 to give, grant, bestow: **a** (goods or sim.); **b** (land or sim.); **c** (bequest); **d** (absol.); **e** (inf. as sb.). **f** (phr. *pro suo dando* or sim.) on one's own initiative or authority. **g** (p. ppl. as sb. n.) gift.

a egenis eleemosynam esse dandam .. praedicantes, sed ipsi .. obolum non dantes GILDAS *EB* 66; illa desponsata .. reddatur ei pecunia quam pro ipsa dedit THEOD. *Pen.* II 15. 34; siquid pecuniae a divitibus accipiebant mox pauperibus dabant BEDE *HE* III 26; quisquis vestrum discere citius istum codicem possit, dabo illi illum ASSER *Alf.* 23; arator dat [AS: *sylð*] nobis panem et potum. tu [faber] quid das [AS: *sylst*] nobis .. nisi ferreas scintillas et sonitus tundentium malleorum? ÆLF. *Coll.* 99–100; multis multa dĕdi, que non cuperem michi dēdi SERLO WILT. II 30 p. 81; **1195** (v. canon 5); **1221** precium equi et carette x s., quos prior habet et ei dantur in elemosinam *PlCrGlouc* 100; **1342** R. Parker non custodit parcum domini, quia dat et vendit feras .. voluntate sua *CBaron* 103. **b** dedit ei locum mansionis in quadam insula BEDE *HE* V 11; **853** etc. (v. concedere 4a); **c1080** terra quam dedit Milo .. in maritagio cum filia sua Arphasto *Regesta* p. 124; de feodo in liberam elemosinam dato GLANV. IX 2; dabantur ville abbatis .. ad firmam BRAKELOND 121; **1219** legatus .. insulam dedit michi et heredibus meis in feodum perpetuo possidendam et tenendam nomine ecclesie Romane (*Lit. Regis Manniae*) *Mon. Hib. & Scot.* 11b. **c** **1100** si quis baronum .. meorum infirmabitur, sicut ipse dabit vel dare disponet pecuniam suam, ita datam esse concedo (*Ch. Hen. I*) *GAS* 522; **1386** do et lego pro omnimodis expensis sepulture mee faciendis .. cc li. (*Test.*) *FormA* 427. **d** duunt, dant, †tribuant; duit, det, †tribuit *GlC* D 376–7; qui cito dat bis dat; det ob hoc cito qui dare spondet / quisque dator D. BEC. 898; **1210** (v. attingere 9a); BRACTON 12 (v. deteriorare 1c); **c1350** rex esto justus, paciens, dans, ore venustus (*Neville's Cross*) *Pol. Poems* I 42; **c1380** cum loqui debuero mei patri semper una voce, prout .. cuculus .., "da! da! da!" *FormOx* 389. **e** D. BEC. 1607–09 (v. capere 2h); per dare [*gl.*: per donationem] regnare poteris celoque volare GARL. *Mor. Scol.* 84. **f** **1250** R., frater junior, tantum locutus est capitali domino quod ipse posuit eum in seisina pro suo dando, dum .. H. fuit in partibus transmarinis tanquam utlagatus *CurR* XIX 1984; **c1250** quidam nativus .. discessit per licenciam .. prioris et pro suo dante *CalIMisc* I 436; **1269** W. capellanus habet unum furnum ad ecclesiam S. Hylde in quo furniat bladum marinariorum et extraneorum pro suo dando, cum voluerint *AssizeR Northumb* 82; **1294** vic. numquam pro aliquo voluit facere execucionem vel aliud ad officium suum pertinens nisi pro suo dando *JustIt* 1095 r. 1; **c1320** levavit de quolibet homine transeunte .. j d. .. absque alio de suo dando (*Eyre*) *Lond. Ed. I & II* II 164; **1351** testamentum .. fabricatum coram .. commissario .. approbare fecerunt et inde acquietanciam pro suo dando indilate voluerunt *SessPEssex* 134; **1384** cum juratores .. de veredicto suo dicendo concordati fuissent, pro eo quod .. per magnum tempus jejuni fuerunt, .. in quadam domo in qua sub custodia fuerunt in publico requisiverunt quandam feminam .. quod eis portaret duos panes et unam lagenam cervisie pro suo dando *PlRCP* 492 r. 325b (*in sched.*). **g** donum, datum vel donatum, *gifu* ÆLF. *Gl.*; **†974** (12c) ego E. rex vexillifero signo throphei proprium datum corroboravi *CS* 1301; comes .., cujus actus sola locutio, cujus datum sola promissio H. HUNT. *HA* VIII 15; 'datum' significat per modum motus, eo quod est participium quod substantiam significat cum agere et pati et sic cum tempore; 'donum' autem nominaliter, et ideo abstrahit a tempore HALES *Sent.* I 183; **s1251** papa, largus in datis et in dandis prodigus M. PAR. *Maj.* V 237; **1427** ea [jocalia] que ex legacione vel dato pertinent .. officiis cancellarii vel procuratorum *StatOx* 232.

2 to pay: **a** (tax, toll, fine, or sim.); **b** (rent or sim.). **c** to give (pledge or earnest); *cf.* 3c *infra*. **d** to render (account).

a ut .. debita .. multa pecuniae regi ultori daretur BEDE *HE* IV 19 p. 249; **s876** rex pactum cum eis pacis confirmat, simulque pecuniam dando ÆTHELW. IV 3; burgenses dederunt xx naves regi una vice in anno *DB* I 1 (cf. ib.: dabant pro caballo transducendo iij d.); quando geldum dabatur T. R. E. .., dabat hida iij d. et ob. ante Natale Domini et tantumdem ad Pentecosten *Ib.* 56b; **1137** (v. canum); **1201** tenet ij carrucatas terre in Newinton' [*Cumb*] per sectam comitatus et de *hendemot*, unde scutagium dari non debet *Pipe* 255; **1203** tempore H. regis non dederunt toloneum in comitatu *SelPlCrown* 31; **s1473** (v. benevolentia d). **b** **c945** (10c) pro firma dabit hoc quod ego testificata sum *CS* 812; **1247** dat ij altilia de redditu annuo *SelPlMan* 10; **1253** burgenses dabunt firmam suam de burgo ad iiij anni terminos (*Ch. Bolton*) *EHR* XVII 293. **c** ex hoc dedit ille vadem *DB* II 103; **1100** si quis baronum .. foris fecerit, non dabit vadium in misericordia pecuniae suae (*Ch. Hen. I*) *GAS* 522; si .. accusatus ei vadium dare nolit [AS: *wedd sellan nelle*] (*Quad.*) *Ib.* 93; **1184** renuit dare wadium .. justiciis *Pipe* 101; **1221** si .. emerint .. mercandisam, ubi *ernes* dederint .. nullus .. a mercandisa sua eos elongabit *SelPlCrown* 98; **c1250** (v. arra a); **1275** (v. argentum 3b). **d** **s1406** laici nihil solvere volebant nisi eis daretur compotus de receptis *Eul. Hist. Cont.* III 409; **1468** de post non reperitur exinde dare computum *ExchScot* 577.

3 (w. abstr. obj.) to give, bestow, confer: **a** (help, favour, pardon, joy, or sim.); **b** (care, attention, or sim.); **c** ('faith', promise); *cf.* 2c *supra*; **d** (dignity, office, or sim.); **e** (opportunity, leave, power, authority, or sim.). **f** *dedimus potestatem* as name of writ; (*cf. Reg. Brev. Orig.* 151 *etc.*).

a ut mihi .. / .. veniam dantes commissa piacula solvant ALDH. *CE* 4. 13. 5; pax data manu regis vel suo brevi vel per suum legatum, si ab aliquo fuisset infracta, inde rex c s. habebat *DB* I 262b; **1211** [serviens regis] dedit ei pacem domini regis et recessit *CurR* VI 137; NECKAM *Ut.* (*gl.*) 103 (v. auxilium 1a); D. BEC. 2034 (v. basium); das gaudium J. HOWD. *Ph.* 47 (v. demulcere a). **b** primo .. sermo .. prorumpit .., daturus operam de singulis quae terra fovet *Lib. Monstr.* I *pref.*; lectioni operam dare gaudebant BEDE *HE* III 27; date operam ut libenter faciatis .. OSB. BAWDSEY clxi; [regina] operam et studium dederat ut .. *Arthur & Gorlagon* 7. **c** **1191** fidem dedit corporaliter cunctis videntibus quod insulam non exiret donec .. (*Lit. Ep. Eli.*) *G. Ric. I* 218; **1564** scholares .. fidem dent universitati etc. *StatOx* 393. **d** da, .. Pater, in hunc famulum tuum .. presbiterii dignitatem EGB. *Pont.* 22; **1102** archidiaconatus non dentur ad firmam (*Act. Conc. Lond.*) EADMER *HN* 163; cur in legibus Anglie non datur bacalariatus et doctoratus gradus FORTESCUE *LLA* 50; **1482** me dedisse .. Edwardo .. officium senescalli .. *FormA* 335. **e** si eis facultas abeundi daretur ALDH. *VirgP* 38; **a705** pontificem qui licentiam dedit baptizari illam sanctimonialem *Id. Ep.* 6 (8); [Eadbald] occasionem dedit ad priorem vomitum revertendi [cf. *2 Peter* ii 22] his .. BEDE *HE* II 5; *Ib.* II 8 (v. auctoritas c); data sibi optione *Ib.* III 25 p. 183; *Ib.* V 6 (v. 1 copia 3a); orat sibi pernoctandi ibidem licentiam dari OSB. *Mir. Dunst.* 2; nulla dabitur ei inde dilatio GLANV. II 1 (cf. 11f infra); **1313** sciatis quod dedimus potestatem tali monacho nostro petendi [et] exigendi W. de A. tanquam clericum nobis liberandum *Eyre Kent* I 124; OCKHAM *Pol.* I 77–8 (76) (v. capacitas 2a). **f** **1462** absque brevibus nostris .. de dedimus potestatem extra cancellariam nostram .. prosequendis *ChartR* 191 m. 5; **1508** coram .. commissionariis domini regis virtute cujusdam brevis de dedimus potestatem eisdem commissionariis per dictum dominum regem directi .. recognovit .. *Cl* 373 m. 20d.

4 (w. abstr. or inanim. subj.).

aethereum .. regnum / .., / cui dedit et dempsit nil mundi longa vetustas ALDH. *VirgV* 2875; Clementem .. / .. cui dat clementia nomen *Ib.* 525; GIR. *TH* II 28 (v. agnomen a); huic lacui mirabilis .. casus initium dedit *Ib.* II 9; nulla patitur ratio .. ut aliqua .. res sit per illud cui dat esse ANSELM (*Mon.* 3) I 16 (cf. 14c infra); quod ipsa [forma] non sit esse, cum tamen dicatur dare esse T. YORK *Sap.* II 29 *tit.*; hoc dat defectus humiditatis ei NECKAM *DS* VI 106; **1325** dicunt .. quod quar. mediocris frumenti valuit iiij s. viij d. et quar. simplicioris frumenti iiij s. vj d.; et, quia ij d. neque dant neque minuunt assisam panis, fiat examinacio panis secundum precium *CBaron* 145.

5 (w. pers. obj.): **a** to give in marriage. **b** to give as hostage. **c** to give as tenant or serf. **d** to entrust as ward. **e** to appoint, provide (to office or sim.); *cf. datio* 2.

a BEDE *HE* II 9 (v. conjunx); offerebat ut .. filiam fratris sui virginem illi conjugem daret *Ib.* V 19; **1100** si .. filia heres remanserit, illam dabo consilio baronum meorum cum terra sua (*Ch. Hen. I*) *GAS* 521; **c1110** ut det .. filiam suam Hugoni .. in uxorem *CalCh* IV 266; W. NEWB. *HA* II 18 (v. compar 2c); cui [Dermitio .. Rotherico] .. filiam suam se nuptui daturum spopondit GIR. *EH* I 10; Emelina data fuit .. Rogero *Meaux* I 165. **b** **s876** ipsi dant obsides ei ÆTHELW. IV 3; obsides dantur ab utraque parte *Enc. Emmae* II 14; super hoc ei [Rotherico] filium suum .. obsidem dedit [Dermitius] GIR. *EH* I 10. **c** **a1190** sciatis me dedisse .. conventui de B. Hugonem filium G. et humagium ejus cum omni sequela sua .. liberum et quietum de me .. *Danelaw* 26; **c1210** dedi et concessi .. Willelmum filium R. .. cum tota sequela sua .. sicut liberum hominem *E. Ch. S. Paul.* 201; **1258** dedisse .. G. G. servum nostrum *Inchaffray* 77; **c1280** dedi .. terram meam .. et R. nativum meum cum sua sequela *Couch. Furness* II 176. **d** infans pro infante potest dari ad monasterium Deo THEOD. *Pen.* II 14. 5; datus sum educandus .. abbati Benedicto BEDE *HE* V 24 p. 357. **e** cum episcopo, quem ei adjutorem fidei dederant BEDE *HE* I 25; postulans ab O. rege ut aliquos sibi doctores daret, qui gentem suam ad fidem Christianam converterent *Ib.* III 22; rex .. postulavit .. ut illis episcopus Ceadda daretur *Ib.* IV 3; **c1220** J. procurator abbatis .., datus ad componendum coram nobis *Reg. Malm.* I 404; [rex] hanc fossam, datis magistris operum, construi fecit per gentem suam armigeram *G. Hen. V* 6; **1518** (v. dativus 3a).

6 a (refl.) to devote oneself to (attacking). **b** to betake oneself, resort. **c** (absol. w. *obviam*, *cf.* CL refl.) to encounter. **d** (p. ppl.) inclined.

a sic pauco exercitu se certamini dedit BEDE *HE* III 24; **s1273** [in torneamento] dedit se Edwardus .. comiti ..; cum sepius se dare vellet, non adquievit in primis W. GUISB. 211; **s1184** (*conf. w.* 1139) [rex] David .. se dedit in Angliam cum magna fortitudine KNIGHTON I 139. **b** Angli .. a manibus hostium sunt elapsi .., sese .. dantes ad inhonesta refugia *Enc. Emmae* II 10. **c** **s1337** quibus [cardinalibus] .. episcopi .. dederunt obviam parum citra S. AD. MUR. *Chr.* 81; **s1351** Vasconici et Francigene ad invicem obviam sibi dantes AVESB. 121; cum statim nostri precursores equites eis dedissent obviam *G. Hen. V* 11; **1428** fiat .. processio .. per .. ecclesie ministros dantes .. nobis obviam *Conc.* III 509a. **d** juvenculum .. solum juvenili consilio datum GIR. *EH* II 36; [episcopi] seculo dediti et insatiabili secularitatis ambitioni dati *Id. GE* II 27 p. 300.

7 (w. Deity as recipient or sim.): **a** to render (praise), ascribe (glory), or sim. **b** to devote, consecrate (property). **c** to dedicate (a person or one's own life). **d** to give *pro Deo*; *cf. deodandum*.

a undarum gurgites, dantes gloriam Deo ab infidelibus denegatam, .. virgines marginibus restituunt ALDH. *VirgP* 51 (cf. ib. 52: da honorem Deo). **b** voto se obligans .. quia .. quartam partem ejus [insulae] simul et praedae Domino daret BEDE *HE* IV 14 p. 237; Eanmundus Christo indeptus quod dĕderat almo ÆTHELWULF *Abb.* 74. **c** dum dilubra dedit Christo atque sacella pudoris ALDH. *VirgV* 1685; gratias Deo referens, dedit filiam suam .. perpetua ei virginitate consecrandam BEDE *HE* III 24; si dicimus quia dabit se ipsum ad oboediendum Deo .., non erit hoc dare quod Deus .. exigat ANSELM (*CurD* II 11) II 110 (cf. datio 1d). **d** **1221** precium equi et carete, dim. m.; detur pro Deo pauperi sorori ejusdem W., que languida est *PlCrGlouc* 33.

8 (w. Deity as donor) to grant, bestow; **b** (absol.); **c** (p. ppl. as sb. n.; *cf. James* i 17) gift. *Cf.* 14b *infra*.

quanta Deus dederit devoto dona clienti ALDH. *VirgV* 686; dedit auxilium clemens defensor egentum *Ib.* 1764; Albanus dari sibi a Deo aquam rogavit BEDE *HE* I 7; hec vera est: 'tota Trinitas dat se.' .. dare enim est communicare effectum communem creature rationali, secundum quod dicimus: 'Filius datus est nobis in humana natura' HALES *Qu.* 176 (cf. datio 1e). **b** Deo dante GIR. *Invect.* I 13 p. 123; fiet, Domino dante, ut volueritis AD. MARSH *Ep.* 33; **1408** auctoritate .. Dunelm' episcopi proponentis, dante Domino, nos .. visitare .. vos citamus quatinus .. (*Citatio*) *Finc.* 29. **c** pater luminum, a quo descendit omne datum optimum AD. SCOT *Serm.* 146A; munditiam, celeste datum, servare monemur NECKAM *DS* VI 141; determinatum est .. de donatione Spiritus Sancti secundum quod dans et datum differunt HALES *Sent.* I 151; datum optimum gratie et glorie donum perfectum AD. MARSH *Ep.* 119.

9 to administer: **a** food or drink (sts. w. inf.); **b** Eucharist.

a rasuram [foliorum codicum] aquae inmissam ac potui datam BEDE *HE* I 1 p. 13; dedit illi per quendam familiarem suum venenum potare G. MON. VI 14; hec mihi, non illis, velut estimo, poma dabantur *V. Merl.* 1423; dabimus bibere aquam de sandal' GILB. VII 326v. 1 (cf. ib. 2: da medicinam provocantem flegma); antidotum quasi contra vicium aliquod datum, precipue quod datur per os *SB* 11. **b** si quis dederit aut acciperit (*sic*) communionem de manu heretici [etc.] THEOD. *Pen.* I 5. 7; cum viderent pontificem, celebratis in ecclesia missarum sollemniis, eucharistiam populo dare BEDE *HE* II 5; **1229** eukaristia .. ad infirmum deferatur et cum debita honestate infirmo detur *Conc. Syn.* 171.

10 to inflict; **b** (absol.).

primum inimicis .. strages dabant GILDAS *EB* 20; pestis .. nimiam dedit mortalibus plagam *Lib. Monstr.* III 5; legio quae .. magnas hostium strages dedit BEDE *HE* I 12; de sortilegis et liblacis mortem [v. l. †sortem] dantibus [AS: *morðdædum*] (*Quad.*) *GAS* 153; *BR Will.* I 3 (v. dorsata); **1321** (v. alapa a); **s1479** ipsum .. percussit et ei dedit plagam mortalem *Sanct. Durh.* 8. **b** ciconia statim dedit ei [serpenti] cum rostro super capud, et serpens statim occubuit O. CHERITON *Fab.* 65.

11 a to direct, turn. **b** to yield, submit, give up. **c** (w. *manum*, *in manum*, or sim.) to submit or pledge oneself. **d** to consign, commit. **e** to impose, lay down (restriction or sim.). **f** to assign, set (day for legal procedure).

a terga pro scuto fugantibus dantur et colla gladiis GILDAS *EB* 6; dum consternati mox omnes terga dederunt ALDH. *VirgV* 577 (cf. ib. 1371); **s891** barbari .. construunt classem, primnas dant ventis, volant rostra ad Anglicas partes ÆTHELW. IV 3; **s1270** quod illi videntes dederunt facies suas et, cesis aliquibus, ceteros in fugam converterunt W. GUISB. 208; **s1388** cum aliquantisper decertatum fuisset, Angli mox terga dederunt FORDUN *Cont.* XIV 54; **s1459** audiens .. rex .. dominos dedisse sibi dorsum aufugisseque *Reg. Whet.* I 345. **b** sopitus cum somno membra dedisset ALDH. *VirgV* 1275; viam dedisse BEDE *HE* I 7 (v. 2 cedere 4); mandavit canonicis ut unum de duobus eligerent, aut .. dare locum monachis aut suscipere habitum monachici ordinis WULF. *Æthelwold* 18 (cf. ib. 35: cum membra sopori dedisset); **1463** sponte .. cessit et dedit accionem suam quam habuit contra T. *MunAcOx* 700. **c** alii fame confecti .. manus hostibus dabant in aevum servituri GILDAS *EB* 25; putantes homines illos manum cito daturos fame et siti et obsessione coactos ASSER *Alf.* 54; *Enc. Emmae* II 13 (v. dexter 2b); debet prolocutor occisoris in manum dare [AS: *on hand syllan*] cognationi quod rectum ei per omnia faciet. deinde oportet ut prolocutori detur in manu [v. l. manum; AS: *þæt man sylle .. on hand*] cur interfector audeat .. ipse weram vadiare (*Quad.*) *GAS* 191; **1119** nulli sapienti dubium tam Theodorum quam ejus successorem in Eboraco primatum habuisse, .. quibus omnes .. manus dare consenserunt (*Lit. Archiep. Cant.*) *Hist. Church York* II 239 (cf. datio 3b). **d** dat venum, vendit *GlC* D 14 (cf. venumdare); donec [corpus] sepulturae daretur BEDE *HE* IV 9; ÆTHELW. IV 3 (v. dromo a); data in inferias villa in qua occubuerat, ut que .. conscia fuerat homicidii W. MALM. *GR* II 144; GIR. *TH* I 27 (v. 1 catellus d); **1381** precipitant edes, spoliant dant atque camino (*Mors Simonis*) *Pol. Poems* I 227. **e** datas sibi metas GERV. TILB. III 34 (v. approximare 1c); de istis non potest dari regula generalis OCKHAM *Pol.* III 49; **1449** ea submovere per que eisdem obstaculum de verisimili dandum putaretur *Lit. Cant.* III 199; COLET *Ep.* 267 (v. coercitrix). **f** tunc dabitur eo respectus [cf. 3e supra], et alius dies ei dabitur in curia GLANV. II 1; **1196** (v. audire 3c, chirographum 2b); **1219** milites dederunt ei diem ad quem ipse venit *CurR* VIII 66; ordinatum est .. quod nulli detur tardius vel maturius, sed omnes dies sint pariter omnibus communes in hac forma *Fleta* 86.

12 a to give, show (example or sign). **b** to give out, express (utterance), pronounce, impart (message or sim.); **c** (w. *conicere*, *intelligere*, or sim.); **d** (w. *in mandatis* or *praeceptis*).

a vobis exemplum dedit exemplaris iste vir ut, quemadmodum fecit ipse, et vos similiter faciatis. .. unde .. signa propter infideles data .. pretereo, ea sola viri exemplaris signa operum prosequens que fidelibus .. ad imitandum data sunt H. BOS. *Thom. pref.* p. 156; R. PARTES 241 (v. datrix); pseudoprophete Antichristi dabunt signa magna et prodigia OCKHAM *Dial.* 491; ut .. signum daret navigio sparso .. ad eum .. festinandi *G. Hen. V* 3. **b** prompta damus rogitanti verba silenter ALDH. *Aen.* 30 (*Elementum*) 7; quem consulta ferunt tali cum voce dedisse *Id. VirgV* 1486 (cf. ib. 2389: angelus ut dederat sancti praecepta pudoris); data oratione a presbytero BEDE *HE* III 11; hoc consilium do [AS: *þis geþeaht ic sylle*] omnibus operariis, ut unusquisque artem suam diligenter exerceat ÆLF. *Coll.* 100; sententiam dedit quam se dedisse postea .. penituit ABBO *Edm.* 15; data super illos suae auctoritatis benedictione OSB. *V. Dunst.* 42; non potuit dare responsum *DB* II 405b; **1253** det .. responsionem (v. deficere 6c); **s1260** judicium dare (v. colludere c); dederunt plenum consensum ad articulos appunctuatos *G. Hen. V* 20; quando aliquis habet prerogativam in choro vel in capitulo, in opcionibus, in processionibus, in vocibus dandis et hujusmodi LYNDW. 108 i. **c** cujus differentiae argumento conici et colligi datur quod virginitas sit quae .. spontaneo caelibatus affectu pudica perseverat ALDH. *VirgP* 19; qua de re conici datur quam pretiosa sit .. pudicitiae generositas *Ib.* 31; ut palam daretur intellegi quia .. illa .. intercapedo quietis .. caelitus donata est BEDE *HE* V 1; **s1191** Sabbati dies ad colloquendum prefixus infortunium aliquod exinde proventurum intelligere dedit quampluribus DICETO *YH* II 98; **1220** datum fuit ei intelligi quod terra sua capta fuit in manum domini sui *CurR* VIII 347; ista nos historia dat intelligentes, / quod .. *Latin Stories* 150; **1291** per literas suas dederunt intelligi quod .. *BBC* (*Ipswich*) 346; **1358** in locucione mea dans intelligere quasi ij essent sophiste *MunAcOx* 211; quid .. Augustinus .. senciat .. ex suo prologo .. datur intelligi J. BURY *Glad. Sal.* 596. **d** ait Cantuariensis se id in mandatis non dedisse A. TEWK. *Add. Thom.* 7; **s1217** rex vicecomiti de Notinham dedit in mandatis ut .. castellum .. complanaret WEND. II 219; **s1262** donec rex super aliud dedisset in preceptis *Leg. Ant. Lond.* 56; **1264** dedimus vicecomiti .. in preceptis quod ei inde .. seisinam rehabere faciat *Cl* 81; precipuis de familia domus regie dedit in mandatis ut .. necessaria providerent *Ps.*-ELMH. *Hen. V* 70.

13 to 'give', issue (formal letter or other document). **b** (p. ppl. as sb. f. or n.) date or dating clause. **c** (date of) regnal year. **d** (as sb. f.) document of specified date.

601 data die xv Kalendarum Juliarum (*Lit. Papae*) BEDE *HE* I 28; **1116** datum Laterani, Nonis Januarii (*Lit. Papae*) H. CANTOR 10v.; **1221** datum apud Dorcestre, anno .. mccxxj *Ch. Sal.* 116; **1237** dat' per manum .. cancellarii nostri, apud Wigorniam, xxj die Maii anno regni nostri xxj *Reg. S. Osm.* I 247; **1293** cartam domini H. regis .. datam anno regni sui liiij *PQW* 218a; **1296** data apud S., vij Idus Augusti *Lit. Cant.* I 24; **1297** datum apud C., xviij Kalendas Julii *Ib.* 25; **1321** acta et data apud G., xj die Decembris *Ib.* 56; **1398** [testamentum] scriptum et datum Oxonie die et anno Domini supradictis *Deeds Balliol* 35. **b** **s1095** adsunt .. praesul Wintoniensis ac cum eo R. capellanus regis vicesima quinta die mensis Aprilis, datarum autem die Maii septimo Kalendas HERM. ARCH. 45; **1169** est data rescripti post diem late sententie *Becket Mat.* VII 58; anno milleno sexageno data sexto / rex sacer Eduuardus celica regna capit GARL. *Tri. Eccl.* 17; **1255** post datum presentium litterarum *RGasc* I sup. 20; eo quod data brevis .. excesserat datam inquisicionis *State Tri. Ed. I* 29 (cf. ib. 37: non potuit dedicere .. quin datum illorum brevium precessit capcionem inquisicionis); **s1296** fuit ista litera [regis Scocie] sine data W. GUISB. 276; **s1326** datum bulle non fuit lectum *Ann. Paul.* 315; **13..** nulla acquietancia sive relaxacio portans datam extra Londonias solucionis .. allegetur *MGL* I 175; ut patet per datam obitus sui in capite istius capituli prenotatum (*sic*) ELMH. *Cant.* 137; **s1404** super .. anticipacione date facta per cameram pape AD. USK 91. **c** **s1272** die S. Cecilie magnates regni nominarunt Edwardum .. in regem .. ; et ex tunc cepit currere data sua et deinceps *Ann. Dunstable* 254; **s1307** (v. currere 6a); **1390** sic patet quod illa septima curia tenta fuit ante primam curiam, eo quod data domini regis [Ric. II] mutatur ante festum .. S. Joh. Baptiste *PlRCP* 490 r. 105; **s1216** facta est hec coronacio quinto Kalendas Novembris, a quo die .. descripta est data in brevibus regis Henrici CAPGR. *Hen.* 87. **d** **s1300** potestatem et effectum procuratorii .. per posteriorem datam totaliter revocando *G. Durh.* 40.

14 a (w. subj. or *ut* & subj.) to grant (that). **b** (w. dat. & inf.) to give (as attribute, right, or sim.). **c** (w. acc. & inf. or compl.) to make, cause. *Cf.* 3e, 8, 12c *supra*.

a laudibus eximiis da Augustinum resonemus WULF. *Poems* 142; da, quesumus, eorum .. solemnitas nostre sit tuitionis argumentum *Rit. Durh.* 62; da nobis .. ut .. apostoli tui .. solemnitas .. devotionem nobis augeat *Ib.* 81. **b** qualiter integritas .. / virginibus dederit nitidas gestare coronas ALDH. *VirgV* 1662; daque illi sophiae debriari fonte *Epigr. Milredi* 820; porosior est cui sic natura sonoro / esse dedit; quod sit siccior ecce liquet NECKAM *DS* VI 104; ecclesie sacre stilus exerit iste triumphos, / dans ex materia nomen habere libro GARL. *Tri. Eccl.* 7 (cf. ib. 27: scelerum causas sculptor in orbe dedit / .. / denarios primos argenti fecit Yonas, / rector Thessalie, quos numerare dedit); **1520** (v. commissio 3c). **c** o nos felices, .. quos, licet indignos et peccatores, hodierna lux tanti dabit martiris esse consortes AD. EYNS. *Hug.* IV 12 p. 59; sunt Alleluja quoque Gloria cantica festa; / dum suspenduntur, dant primum tempora mesta; / dat prius abjectas signare Sequentia gentes, / quod sit ei data lex GARL. *Myst. Eccl.* 150; J. HOWD. *Gaudia* 8. 10 (v. datrix); [rex] stultorum vile sibi consilium juvenile / legerat et sectam senium dedit esse rejectam GOWER *CT* I 16.

15 to grant (as condition or consequence). **b** (p. ppl. in abl. abs. w. *quod*) granted that.

nec hodie destitissent scriptores optimi, si non desiissent imperatores electi. da igitur Pirrum; dabis Homerum. da Pompeium; dabis et Tullium GIR. *TH intr.* p. 4. **b** **1293** dato quod [cc libras] ab eodem habuisset Baruncino nomine societatis, potuit esse quod .. pecuniam receptam .. dicto B. .. liberavit *RGasc* III p. xciv.; **s1311** dato quod nullus omnino tortor valeat inveniri in Anglia, utrum .. mittendum sit ad partes transmarinas ..? W. GUISB. *Cont.* 287; **s1339** dato quod excludi deberet Philippus .., rex Anglie .. nihil juris in .. regno Francie vendicare posset AD. MUR. *Chr.* 101; dato quod fecisset, non fuisset ad propositum CONWAY *Def. Mend.* 1336; cum non stetit per eos, dato quod aliquod infortunium in regno pretextu hujus fatigacionis .. inopinate novercaverit FAVENT 21; **1415** alios .. collectores .., dato quod primi .. ab hac luce subtracti fuerint, deputantes *Conc.* III 375.

16 to present (with). *Cf. donare*.

s1260 rex cingulo dedit militari Johannem *Flor. Hist.* II 456.

17 to make, perform.

dans David saltum manibus se tollit in altum AD. DORE *Pictor* 148 (*cf.* Ovid *Met.* IV 552).

darii, a logical mood.

BACON XV 301 (v. barbara).

darkera v. dacra a. **darmatio** v. dearmatio.

darsen [Ar. < Pers. *dār ṣīnī*, *Chinese wood*], cinnamon.

~sen, i. cinamomum illius terre, s[c]. Arabie *SB* 17; ~chem est cinamomum selectum purum *LC* 238.

darsus [OF *dars* < Gall.], dace.

cum salsa roche, darsi piscesque minores / cenentur D. BEC. 2650; pisces .. convenientes eligantur, ut sunt perchie, lucii, ~i GILB. I 36. 2; **1253** in ccc ~is et rochis emptis pro vivario in parco instaurando *Pipe Wint.* 159291 A r. 7; **1257** provideant regem .. de luciis, rochis, daris, et alio genere piscis aque dulcis *Cl* 153; pisces petrosi habentes squamas, sicut lucius, perchia, ruschi, †dorsi, rupelle, longisti GAD. 10v. 1; **1266** (1324) exceptis .. *darces* marinis (*Inq.*) *MGL* II 279 (cf. barsa); **1338** in rochis et daris emptis, xij d. *Ac. Ep. Bath* 126.

dartus [OF *dart* < Frk.; cf. AS *daroþ*], dart, javelin.

1293 pro .. empcionibus .. quarellorum, scutorum, .. ~orum et sagittarum *RGasc* III p. cxlin.; **1305** ~i; et pro xxvj *dartes* emptis pro municione [castrorum terre] *MinAc W. Wales* I 404; **c1335** vj botell' de darttis *IMisc* 128/19.

darus v. darsus. **dasaisitus** v. dissaisire 1a.

dasia [LL < δασεῖα], (mark of) rough breathing, aspirate. (*Cf.* Isid. *Etym.* I 19. 9).

~ia, hispidum *GlC Int.* 93; sciat .. librarius ubi scribere debeat sylen [v. l. silen], ubi †diasyan [v. l. dasian] NECKAM *Ut.* 169; antiquitus scripserunt pi litteram et ~iam in linea pro phi et F litteram in Latinis diccionibus BACON *Gram. Gk.* 51.

dasile v. rasilis.

1 data v. dare 13.

2 data, ~is [OF *date* < dactylus], date (fruit).

1238 de cera, amigdalis, et ~ibus capiendis: mandatum est ballivis Suthampton' quod Nicholaum .. quem rex mittit ad capiendum .. ceram, amigdalas, ~es, et ficus .. ad hoc admittant *Cl* 37; **1239** ut .. capiat .. racemos et ~as *Liberate* 13 m. 21; **1265** pro expensis Boleti cum j equo ducentis ~as et speceriam Kenilworthe *Manners* 23; **1389** ij lib. de ~is, viij d. *Ac. Durh.* 49.

datalicium v. dotalicius 1c.

datarius [cf. LL datarium = *date-clause*], papal official responsible for dating bulls *etc.*

~ius qui datam apponit PAUL. ANGL. *ASP* 1552; **1511** postquam nos eos [cardinales] .. per .. episcopum Concordiensem, ~ium nostrum, .. ad nos .. vocari feceramus (*Lit. Papae*) *Reg. Heref.* 123; queruntur hodie de nobis indulgentarii, ~ii, quaestores, lenones JEWEL *Apol.* H 3v.

datatim [CL], by giving in turn.

~im, adv., i. de dato in datum OSB. GLOUC. *Deriv.* 162.

datia v. datium.

daticius [LL *gl.*], prisoner of war. *V. et. dediticius.*

~ius Latinum non est, sed dediticius .. *GlC* D 15; *ȝoldman in were*, ~ius *PP* (cf. ib.: *prisoner takyn and ȝeldyn in werre*, †staticius).

datilis v. dactylus 3a.

datim, with gifts.

invictum Julium quem opipaverat / datimque dubia dea ditaverat / .. / mors preseps subito resupinaverat WALT. WIMB. *Sim.* 112.

datio [CL]

1 giving, bestowal, grant: **a** (of money, goods, *etc.*); **b** (of slave); **c** (of land *etc.*); **d** (w. Deity as recipient); **e** (w. Deity as donor); **f** (phil.).

a **933** (10c) pro .. episcopi E. placabilis pecuniae ~on[e] *CS* 694; 'ministerium', id est, administratio ~onis LANFR. *Comment. Paul.* (2 *Cor.* ix 12) 244; simoniacos qui ~one auri .. fiunt episcopi G. CRISPIN *Simon.* 111; in omni potatione, ~oni vel emptioni vel gilde vel ad quidlibet in hunc modum preparata (*Leg. Hen.* 81. 1) *GAS* 597; **s1140** si .. apostolicus .. eum [Turstinum] in archiepiscopum .. liberi pallii ~one confirmavit J. HEX. *HR Cont.* 303; *Alph.* 51 (v. dosis a); *Man. Sal.* 46 (v. desponsatio 1a); nulla vel pauca requiri .. nisi ~ones vel oblaciones pecunie vel munerum GASCOIGNE *Loci* 119. **b** servi alii natura, alii facti et alii emptione et alii .. sui vel alterius ~one servi (*Leg. Hen.* 76. 3) *GAS* 593. **c** **c1145** ista [j hide terre etc.] concessio et ~o facta et lecta fuit *Cart. Worc.* 439 (= *CurR* VI 181: donatio); **a1180** pro hac [terre in London'] ~one Robertus de P. dedit Roberto de R. ij bisandos auri. .. et huic ~oni affuit M. filius R. *AncD* A 2178; ecclesie ~o ad firmam .. est libere sponse Jesu Christi in servilem condicionem redactio GROS. *Ep.* 18. **d** quaerendum .. est cujusmodi esse debebit haec ~o. dare namque se non poterit Deo .., quasi non habenti, ut suus sit, quoniam omnis creatura Dei est. .. sic ergo intelligenda est ~o, quia .. ponet se ad honorem Dei .. ANSELM (*CurD* II 11) II 10. **e** ~onem carismatum in spiritu baptisma spiritus recte vocari testatur ipse [Christus (*Acts* i 5)] BEDE *Hom.* I 1. 25; licet gratia detur a Deo immediate, tamen notandum quia non sic ~o quod quodlibet donum, sed gratum †facientem [? l. faciens] GROS. *Quaest. Theol.* 198; queritur quare ~o active adscribitur divine essentie, passive autem dicta Filio vel Spiritui Sancto HALES *Sent.* I 153; tria sunt vocabula que temporaliter dicuntur, licet intelligitur eternum: apparitio, missio, ~o .. *Id. Qu.* 174 (cf. dare 8a); ~o Dei WYCL. *Dom. Div.* 214 (v. dominium 1d). **f** in manifestando quare [sapientes] potius dixerunt [formarum] datores quam extractores vel eductores, et quid sit formam dari et quid ~o forme T. YORK *Sap.* II 28 *tit.*; ad

illum sensum deducunt Augustinus, Anselmus, et alii theologi Deum esse ex necessaria ~one veritatis WYCL. *Act.* 90.

2 appointment, provision (of person). *Cf. dare* 5e.

1338 ad providendum .. prioratui de priore ydoneo, in casu quo ipsius collacio, provisio, ~o seu ordinacio ad nos debeat .. pertinere *Lit. Cant.* II 194; c**1520** ad ~onem et constitutionem executorum dativorum *Conc. Scot.* I cclxxxviii.

3 **a** giving, pledging (of faith); *cf. dare* 3c. **b** giving (of hand in token of submission); *cf. dare* 11c.

a c**1250** ubi sponsalia contrahuntur per verba de futuro, sive per fidei ~onem sive absque fidei ~one *Conc. Syn.* 643; a**1350** fidei ~one pro observandis .. universitatis statutis .. et consuetudinibus onerare magistros *StatOx* 67; **1364** convencionem .. et pactum fidele inierunt .. Hugonis fidei ~one vallata *Lit. Cant.* II 466. **b** **1119** manus ~onem, subjectionem et professionem Eboracensis .. ecclesie semper ecclesia Cantuariensis obtinuit (*Lit. Archiep. Cant.*) *Hist. Church York* II 239 (= *Conc.* I 403).

datis v. 2 data.

datisi, a logical mood.

BACON XV 301 (v. bocardo a).

datium, -ia [cf. It. *dazio*], form of toll.

1401 priorem [S. J. Jerusalem] .. transire .. sine solucione alicujus ~ii, pedagii, fundi navis, gabelle .. (*TreatyR*) *Foed.* VIII 234b; **1423** sine solucione ~ii, pedagii, gabelli (*Pat*) AMUND. I 125; **1485** (v. bulletta 2); **1490** exsisis, gabellis vel ~iis vini, frumenti etc... exceptis, quas exsisas, gabellas et ~ias .. subditi regis Anglie .. in civitate Pisarum solvent (*DipDoc* I 604) *Foed.* XII 391b.

dativus [CL]

1 **a** (gram.) dative, (as sb. m.) dative case. **b** ready to give, munificent. **c** (w. play on senses 1a and 1b).

a solet .. proceleumaticus a tertia declinatione per obliquos casus ~i et ablativi progigni ut 'nemoribus' ALDH. *PR* 125; post hunc [casum genitivum] ~us est, qui a dando dicitur, significans aliquid nos dare, ut 'do tibi illam rem' ALCUIN *Gram.* 868D; ~us *ys forgyfendlic*: .. huic homini do equum ÆLF. *Gram.* 22; glossa [*on Mark* ix 2] 'non potest Deus illam claritatem dare in terris quam potest in celis' .. potest determinare ex parte transitiva quoad ~um subintellectum, ut sit sensus: 'non potest dare illam claritatem discipulis in terris quam potest dare discipulis exsistentibus in celis' HALES *Sent.* I 442; ~us et accusativus prout perficitur res indigens aut res superfluens *Ps.*-GROS. *Gram.* 41. **b** contemplativi studiis et amore dativi / dogmatis attactus R. CANT. *Malch.* VI 425; si largitio plena / pectore festivo cunctis foret equa dativa,/ plurima que florent plene sine flore paterent D. BEC. 1631; tu .. / restauratrix et dativa / libertatis perdite WALT. WIMB. *Virgo* 61; **1346** rex exactivus, vecors, injustus oditur; / fortis diligitur, justus, racione dativus (*In Franciam*) *Pol. Poems* I 39; **1446** cum [sacramentale donum] .. sit insignium virtutum signum divine benediccionis ~um *Conc.* III 550b. **c** HANV. VI 263 p. 334 (v. ablativus 2a); **1370** quidam ballivus, armis jam nominātivus,/ voce vocativus tauri tauroque dativus [*gl.*: vel quia aliqua dona prebuit regi Anglie vel forte sibi concessit subjeccionem Scocie] .. (J. BRIDL.) *Pol. Poems* I 141–2; **15**.. si dativus fueris,/ quandocumque veneris, / genetivus eris (*Vers. adventicii*) *Reg. Whet.* II 297.

2 fit to be given.

1425 volo quod de uno cipho meo .. fiat unus calix bene .. ornatus .. ~us ecclesie de C. *Reg. Cant.* II 323.

3 dependent on or subject to appointment (and removal): **a** (of executor); **b** (of executorship or sim.); **c** (of prior); **d** (of priory).

a **1518** nobis .. ut bona .. decedentium .. in pios usus disponantur, executores ~os dare et deputare incumbit *Form. S. Andr.* I 74; c**1520** (v. datio 2); *Jus Feudale* 252 (v. executor 4c). **b** statuere .. qui episcopi debeant habere immunitatem tutele seu testamentarie, sive legitime sive ~e OCKHAM *Pol.* I 54. **c** dixit prior R. [ob. **1307**] .. quod prior de C. ~us est; ideo nec debet fidelitatem facere regi nec obedienciam episcopo S. Andree GRAYSTANES 27; **1331** prior de S. Neoto est prior ~us et amobilis ad voluntatem abbatis de Becco *PQW* 55b; **1395** (v. amotivus a); sic quod idem prior non est ~us, id est movendus ab eodem [loco] ad nutum abbatis .. nec alio modo nisi per viam privacionis, si hoc meruerit *G. S. Alb.* III 283; **1416** quod quidem domus sive prioratus cella monasterii .. et eidem monasterio subjecta dictusque prior ~us et ad nutum abbatis monasterii .. ammobilis existunt (*sic*) *Reg. Cant.* III 396. **d** **1331** prioratus [de Bello Loco] .. est ~us et .. cella abbathie de S. Albano *PQW* 26b; a**1494** idem prioratus fuit .. alienigena .. ac prioratus ~us et remobilis et non conventualis *Entries* 33b (cf. ib. 28: omnes prioratus ejusdem prioratus .. fuerunt ~i et remotivi).

dator [CL], giver, donor: **a** (var.); **b** (of land or sim.); **c** (of advice); **d** (w. ref. to Deity); **e** (phil.); *cf. datio* 1f.

a te nunc sancte speculator, / verbi Dei digne dator, / Hæddi, pie presul, precor THEOD. *Pen. vers. epil.*; ~or hilaris [cf. *2 Cor.* ix 7], qui numquam obliviscebatur accepti AILR. *Ed. Conf.* 745D; cum dator esse velis, videas cui munera dones D. BEC. 2197; abbas .. ait: "~or aliquando fui; nunquam tamen vobis accommodator fui vel ero" M. PAR. *Maj.* V 51; s**1431** (v. datorius). **b** do hiis domibus episcopum Bajocensem ad protectorem et liberatorem vel ~orem *DB* I 1. **c** consilii magni si nosti forte datorem J. SAL. *Enth. Pol.* 382C. **d** auctor et ~or evangelii Dominus BEDE *HE* III 25 p. 186; EGB. *Pont.* 19 (v. dispositor 1b); BACON VII 63 (v. collatio 6e). **e** inprimitur in anima intellectus formalis mediante primo ~ore formarum J. BLUND *An.* 344 (cf. ib. 361); T. YORK *Sap.* II 28 *tit.* (v. datio 1f).

datorius, recipient, donee.

peccator, licet videatur in facie ecclesie errantis habere dona Domini, non tamen vere est †dotarius, sed ex permissione divina injuste occupat hec ad tempus WYCL. *Civ. Dom.* I 12; s**1431** quia juxta leges civiles ~ius tenetur sequi in donacione voluntatem donatoris; sed voluntas est datoris quod [etc.] .. (*Sermo*) AMUND. I 297.

datrix [LL], (lavish) giver (f.).

mens tranquilla manusque datrix sermoque modestus / signa dabant quod ea filia pacis erat R. PARTES 241; des ergo, datrix gaudii, / vultum placatum filii J. HOWD. *Gaudia* 8. 10; methaphysica .. dicitur dea scienciarum quia .. dat necessitatem, .. unde dea et ~ix idem BACON XI 31; tota Trinitas, ut latrix vel ~ix muneris WYCL. *Dom. Div.* 210.

dattilus, ~ylus v. dactylus. **datum** v. dare 1g, 8c.

datus [CL], giving, gift.

955 (14c) ego A... ministro meo .. xvj mansas gratuito ~u tribuo *CS* 910.

daubare, ~iare [OF *dauber* < dealbare], to daub, plaster.

1280 in porcario faciendo, ~ando, et tegendo *Ac. Man. Cant.* (*Milton*); **1336** in j daubiatore conducto ad .. parietes [domus molendini] ~iandos *Ib.* (*Bocking*); **1336** in stipendiis .. hominum .. fodiencium argillum, illud similiter et aquam portancium infra castrum, mortarium inde faciencium ac ~ancium tam parietes quam astra .. domorum (*KRAc* 19/40) *Cal. Scot.* III app. 365; **1366** daubacio domorum: .. pro xj domibus de novo constructis ~andis et dealbandis ad tascam *KRAc* 483/23 m. 7; **1370** in stipendio Walteri G. dobiantis et dealbantis dictos muros *MinAc* 1253/17; **1373** in eisdem conductis ad dobandum in stabulo .. et doband' aluram inter aulam et coquinam *Ib.* 900/6; **1392** in salar' .. doubancium super parietes .. domus *Mem. Ripon* III 108; **1395** ad dobandum cameram et studia *Cant. Coll. Ox.* II 142; **1397** in m[ercede] j dowbantis parietes .. domus *Mem. Ripon* III 125; **1425** Johanni B. ~anti circa .. domum *Ib.* 152; **1477** (v. breidare); **1478** in solutis laboratori ad dawbandum et breydandum parietes *Ac. Chamb. Winchester*.

daubarius, dauber, plasterer.

1326 in servicio portancium .. lutum et sabulonem pro parietibus aule .. et servicio †tauberiorum [? l. dauberiorum] et cooperiencium *ExchScot* 56; **1397** Symoni dober' .. xx d. ..; item in feno et stramine ad dobandum *Cant. Coll. Ox.* II 144; **1498** in dabero, wallero et frethero *la sperys* emend[antibus] dicte domus *Ac. Churchw. Som* 196.

daubatio, daubing, plastering.

1305 in humo fodienda ad ~onem parietum nove domus *Ac. Man. Cant.* (*Milton*); **1339** in ix carcatis de *lom* emptis cum cariagio ad castrum pro ~one murorum *KRAc* 462/15 m. 4; **1366** (v. daubare); **1423** pro cc *stours* emptis pro dobacione super *kylnhouse* et alias (*sic*) locos *Fabr. York* 48.

daubator, ~iator, ~or [cf. AN *daubour*], dauber, plasterer.

1274 dabator': Roberto de G. per j diem, iiij d. *KRAc* 467/6/4 m. 2; **1286** in servicio Stephani ~oris, qui perjactavit longam cameram juxta turrim *Ib.* 460/27 A (3); **1305** in stipendio ~atoris pro daubatura nove aule *Ac. Man. Cant.* (*Milton*); **1336** in j ~iatore (v. daubare); **1415** j dawbatori cum suo famulo ad emendandum diversos defectus elemosinarie (*Ac. Obed. Westm.*) *Educ. Ch.* 310; **1449** pro dobatore cum famulo *Cant. Coll. Ox.* II 172; **1503** ~atori operanti in camera inferiori *Ib.* 237.

daubatura, daubura, daubing, plastering.

1237 perfici facias ~aturam et lambreschuram .. in nova capella *Liberate* 11 m. 13; **1305** (v. daubator); **1306** in aqua portanda ad dalburam pro parietibus nove salsarie temperandam et pro dictis parietibus auxiliar' daubandis *MinAc* 991/28; **1307** iij dauboribus cooperientibus cameram regis de ~ura *KRAc* 501/22 r. 3 (1); **1336** iiij hominibus cum iiij equis carientibus .. terram et turbas pro ~atura et pro coopertura diversarum domorum (*Ib.* 19/24) *Cal. Scot.* III app. 348; **1400** domos et muros in manerio .. existentes .. reparabunt et manutenebunt in coopertura et ~ura *AncD* D 300; **1425** eas [domos manerii] .. manutenebunt in coopertura straminis et in ~atura .. quolibet anno *FormA* 145; **1445** pro dabatura murorum *Cant. Coll. Ox.* II 170; **1454** pro doubura .. camere *Mem. Ripon* III 161; **1458** pro dabura j parietis *Ac. Chamb. Winchester*; **1483** reparabunt .. domum et cameram in daubitura, viz. cum *splynts* et *cley* mixt' cum stramine (*CourtR Great Waltham*) *OED* s. v. *splint sb.*; **1532** pro dalbura super iiij camina in vico S. Egidii ..; et in virgis et *dalbyngstours* pro eodem opere; et .. pro dalbura *le gavylls* tenementi Johannis Dixson *Househ. Bk. Durh.* 86; **1580** permittit tenementum suum fore ruinosum et in decassu ob defectum reparacionis, viz. tecture, dabiture et solidature (*CourtR Newborne, Suff*) *MS BL Add.* 21,046.

dauberius v. daubarius. **daubiare** v. daubare. **daubitura** v. daubatura. **daubor** v. daubator. **daubura** v. daubatura.

daucus [δαῦκος], parsnip, (?) carrot, or sim., (w. *Creticus*) *Athamanta cretensis*. *Cf. baucia*.

pastinaca, *feldmora*; ~us, *wealmora* ÆLF. *Gl.*; electuarium ducis: recipe .. cyperi, squinanti, ~i, yrcos, amomi folii GILB. V 228. 1 (cf. ib.: amomi, carui, ~i Cretici, apii); ~us: hujus due sunt species, agrestis et Creticus... ~us quandoque sumitur pro pastinaca *SB* 17; ~us Creticus, i. pastinaca domestica, G. *dauk*... ~us asininus assimilatur petrocillino sed folia ejus sunt pilosa .. *Alph.* 47; *Ib.* 30 (v. careum b); hic ~us, A. *clapwype WW*.

daungerium v. dangerium. **daunsa** v. dansa. **daunsella** v. domicella. **daurata** v. deaurare 3.

davacha, ~us, ~ata [Gael. *dabhach*], 'davach', measure of land (Scot.).

a**1195** illas vij *davahs* in forestam *Regesta Scot.* II 346; c**1200** tenebunt de .. episcopo terras quas habet in S., dimidias ~as *Reg. Moray* 12; a**1225** exceptis decimis bladi de ij ~is que sunt juxta castellum *Ib.* 17; c**1205** dedisse .. illum davach' qui vocatur Balegillegrand' *Reg. Aberbr.* I 49 (cf. *Regesta Scot.* II 466); c**1220** nos .. quietum clamasse .. conevetum et redditum que percipere solebamus .. in dimidia *davach* terre... quare volumus ut .. monachi de L. .. predictam dim. davacatam .. liberam teneant *Cart. Lindores* 33; **1233** me dedisse .. unam ~am terre que dicitur Sutheluthy *Reg. Aberd.* II 268; **1266** (17c) de sex †davatis terre, quas tenet hereditarie de domino rege *ExchScot* 26; **1325** ambulaverunt rectas metas .. inter dim. †davatam terre parci et terram de A. *Reg. Aberbr.* I 311; ita quod ille husbandus octavam partem unius †davate terre tenuerit vel plus *Quon. Attach.* 23; **1369** (v. baronia 1b); **1468** propter vastitatem quarte partis unius †dalvate *ExchScot* 545; **1484** de x li. †dawate de W. *Ib.* 279.

Davidicus (Daviticus) [LL], Davidic, of David. **b** (as sb. n.) Psalm.

odis Daviticis modulantes carmina sancta ALDH. *VirgV* 2415; lapidem .. more ~o de funda emittens EDDI 13; Davidicumque melos castra Dei reboant WULF. *Poems* 11; ad obtinendum decus Palestine et metropolim ~i regni ORD. VIT. IX 15 p. 599; ~a lyra GIR. *TH* III 12. **b** ceu praecinuit Davitica psaltes FRITH. 1134; illud proclamabat ~um: 'non nobis, Domine' [*Psalm* cxiii 1] AILR. *Ed. Conf.* 763B; cum Daviticum illud auribus nostris frequenter occurrat: 'ne occidas eos' [*Psalm* lix 11] DICETO *YH* II 76.

dawata v. davacha. **dawb-** v. daub-. **day-** v. et. dai-. **dayaria, ~eria** v. daieria. **dayeta** v. diaeta 3c. **dayla** v. dala. **dayria** v. daieria. **daytyda** v. daitida. **dayua** v. daina. **daywarca, daywrca** v. daiwerca. **daywerkata** v. daiwercata. **daywerchland'** v. daiwerclanda.

de [*as in* CL, *but used more extensively, like Fr.* de, *often in place of simple abl. or gen., esp. w. indeclinables, w. little care to avoid repetition*, e.g. **1227** debet .. vj li. .. de scutagio de Pictavia de feudis de Wahull' *LTRMem* 9 r. 6. *For use w. adv., prep., or conj.* v. et. deante, dearetro, decontra, deextra, deforas, deforis, deillinc, deinfra, deinter, deintro, deintus, deinvicem, dejuxta, depost, deprope, desicut, desub, desubter, desubtus, desuper, desupra, desursum, deultra, deversus, ibidem, longe, mane, noctu, plane, praesto, trans (mare). *The following exx. have been noted of* de *w. acc.*: **748** de illud [*corr. to* illo] (*Lit. Papae*) *Ep. Bonif.* 8 p. 173; s**893** exercitus qui de Gallias venerat partes ÆTHELW. IV 3; **1199** (v. 3b infra)].

1 (impl. separation) from (w. ref. to): **a** position at a distance; **b** departure or removal; **c** acceptance or exaction; **d** vantage-point; **e** distinction (w. compar. = than); **f** deliverance, deprivation, or abstention; **g** origin or descent; **h** tenure.

a **1220** manent ad xv leucas de Bertona *CurR* VIII 328; de licencia .. morandi de completorio fratribus concedenda *Cust. Westm.* 22; **1452** ecclesia .. de W., que distat per xiiij milliaria de H. *MunAcOx* 642. **b** leo de clatris rugibundus mittitur artis ALDH. *VirgV* 1235; mandavit se venisse de Roma BEDE *HE* I 25; †**676** (12c) ut nullus .. de ea cespitis conditione .. auferre quippiam .. praesumat *CS* 43; †**858** (12c) nullus .. licentiam .. habeat .. illam terram alicui dandi neque abstrahendi de illo loco *CS* 495; †**948** (12c) deleatur memoria ejus de libro viventium [cf. *Rev.* xxii 19] *CS* 860; *DB* I 5v. (v. emere 1c); W. MALM. *GR* II 201 (v. avironatus); de manu in gulam GIR. *Symb.* I 31 (v. continentia 3a); si unus de naufragio evaserit *Id. PI* I 20 p. 119; **1231** se subtraxerunt de terris et partibus suis *Pat* 434; BACON *Maj.* I 159 (v. abscindere b);

1275 subtrahat de predictis iij s. et j d. valorem j libre lane *SelPlMan* 141; **1289** adivit de portu in portum et de patria in patriam ad querendum .. Bryanum *Law Merch.* II 49 (cf. *Reg. Brev.* 71b: de patria ad patriam .. vagatur et discurrit). **c** accipe promeritam nostri de parte coronam G. AMIENS *Hast.* 479; *DB* I 2 (v. capere 3b); **c1095** (v. custuma 3b); **1266** per denarios mutuatos de abbate *ExchScot* 31; **1283** in pastura .. quam habemus de Willielmo P. *Cust. Battle* 32; **1294** quando .. rex exigit servicium de .. baronibus Anglie *SelPlMan* 76. **d** insulam .. quam .. de longe aspicere solemus BEDE *HE* I 1; jubens ut cito de muro specularetur si .. nuntii Renum transissent W. MALM. *GP* I 6. **e** volentes diffinicionem 'dominii' assignare, de 'dominio' secundum quod accipitur in jure distinguunt OCKHAM *Pol.* I 306; **a1300** qui minus tenuerit de una virgata *Pat* 247 m. 15. **f** sed nece de praesente simul salvavit eosdem ALCUIN *SS Ebor* 586; *DB* I 41b (v. acquietare 3a); **s1119** (v. divestire 2); **1130** quietum de superplus (v. clamare 7a); utrum dominia S. Ædmundi deberent esse quieta de communi misericordia BRAKELOND 139; **c1230** (v. custodire 3a); **1231** spoliaverunt ecclesiam .. de secundo meliori averio .. decedentium parochianorum *Reg. Malm.* I 388; **1277** (v. contravenire d); **1284** (v. defendere 1a); **1300** anime defunctorum de purgatorii ergastulo .. liberantur *Lit. Cant.* I 13; **s1303** *Flor. Hist.* III 115 (v. derobare a); **1309** (v. abstinere 1a); **1323** in .. xx acris prati .. de montibus talparum mondandis *MinAc* 1147/11 A 11; de .. heretica pravitate excusari OCKHAM *Dial.* 448; **1341** (v. abjudicare b); **1460** navis .. de quodam apparatu .. destituta *Pat* 488 m. 3*d*. **g** quae fuit Israhel claro de germine gentis / desponsata proco ALDH. *VirgV* 1676; de cujus stirpe multarum provinciarum regium genus originem duxit BEDE *HE* I 15; GLANV. VII 16 (v. corpus 5f); **1207** Reginaldus descendit de Eularia *CurR* V 46; **1219** ipse tenuit terram .. ut illam que ei descendit de .. fratre suo *Ib.* VIII p. x; HALES *Qu.* 930 (v. 2a infra); **1264** (v. caro 6b); **1307** obiit sine herede de se *Year Bk. 1 Ed. II* 2; de tribu Dan, de qua nonnulli Antichristum estimant nasciturum OCKHAM *Dial.* 524; de avo et proavo *Quon. Attach.* 56 (v. bondagium d); **1355** nativus de stipite *AssessR Cornw* 1 r. 21*d*.; **1399** nativi de sanguine *Pat* 304 m. 13*d*. **h** episcopus tenet S., et A. presbyter de eo *DB* I 5b; R. tenet de rege unum manerium quod C. tenuit T. R. E. *Ib.* 47; **1130** (v. caput 20c); **1322** recepi a priore et conventu .. unam domum .., tenendam et inhabitandam predictam domum .. de eisdem priore et conventu .. quamdiu .. eisdem .. placuerit, reddendo pro predicta domo .. annuatim .. xl s. *Lit. Cant.* I 17.

2 (w. ref. to construction or change) of, from: **a** material; **b** person; **c** person as having specified status or attribute; **d** condition or other abstr. **e** (w. adj.) from being; *cf. ex* 8.

a ALDH. *Aen.* 61. 6 (v. construere 1a); curavit .. majorem .. de lapide fabricare basilicam BEDE *HE* II 14; *Ib.* III 25 (v. componere 3a); secundum materiam de qua editum est ANSELM (*CurD pref.*) II 42; tertia interpretatio qua dicitur aliquid factum 'de nihilo' est cum intelligimus esse quidem factum sed non esse aliquid unde sit factum *Id.* (*Mon.* 8) I 23 (cf. DUNS *Ord.* IV 41); queritur, utrum hec [propositio] sit concedenda: 'de pane fit corpus Christi'. videtur quod non; 'de' enim uno modo tenetur materialiter, ut 'de carne B. Virginis fit corpus Christi' ..; item dicit potestatem, ut cum dicitur 'de Spiritu Sancto conceptus' [cf. 1g supra, 11 infra]... neutro predictorum modo dicitur hec HALES *Qu.* 930; 'e' et 'de' et 'ex' .. dicunt racionem materie ad formam *Ps.*-GROS. *Gram.* 56 (cf.ib. 190–1). **b** **1140** sciatis me fecisse comitem de Gaufrido de Magnavilla *Regesta* 273; **1230** Willelmus fecit atornatum suum de Rannulfo et Rannulfus de Willelmo, si ambo non poterunt venire *LTRMem* 11 r. 6. **c** **s1190** de veteri episcopo novum comitem factum G. COLD. *Durh.* 9; **s1191** Willelmus P. de priore Westmonasterii factus est abbas ejusdem loci *Flor. Hist.* II 106; dictus monachus .. de monacho simplici .. assumptus in abbatem fuerat .., deinde de abbate in abbatem .., ad cathedram sc. digniorem .. instans GIR. *Spec.* III 7 p. 163; **s1232** J. de Laci .. de barone comes effectus est M. PAR. *Maj.* III 230; fuit Hester elevata in reginam de paupere puella [ME: *ihehet to cwen of a poure meiden*] *AncrR* 58; de lauro nemus fructiferum .. et de rege conquestor nutu deifico procreantur *Ps.*-ELMH. *Hen. V* 29; **1472** (v. demonachus). **d** **c692** (8c) trado et de meo jure in tuo transscribo terram quae appellatur R. *CS* 81; arbor .. mutatur de venenositate ad comestibilitatem BACON IX 21; **s1382** [J. Wyclif] evangelium .. transtulit de Latino in Anglicam linguam KNIGHTON II 152; **c1430** quamvis fuerim .. transmutabilis .. de una qualitate in alteram *Reg. Whet.* II 398. **e** monasterium .. nunc grande de modico effectum BEDE *HE* IV 4; L. DURH. *Brig.* 4. 172D (v. efficere 6); GIR. *Spec.* III 15 (v. debriare 2b); **1316** ut de promptis .. efficiantur imposterum prompciores *RGasc* IV 1637.

3 **a** (w. ref. to time) from, since. **b** (w. *in* or *ad* & sb. repeated) from .. to (over a period or at regular intervals); **c** (w. sb. not merely denoting period).

a **c1228** requisitus quomodo predicta omnia sciret de tam longo tempore *Feod. Durh.* 255; **1276** assisam panis et cervisie .. habeurunt iste comes et predecessores sui de tam antiquo tempore quod non occurrit alicujus memorie qui nunc vivit *Hund.* II 178b; post crastinum Animarum ultimo preteritum, de quo crastino placitum continuatum fuit hic usque ad hunc diem *Entries* 122. **b** de die in diem ipsius causam examinandam dives negligens prolongabat R. COLD. *Cuthb.* 48; de die in diem renovantur in melius GIR. *TH* I 18; **1315** accusans teneatur suam accusacionem .. de octo in octo diebus prosequi *RGasc* IV 1626 (xx); **s1344** propositum de diebus in dies exstitit impeditum AD. MUR. *Chr.* 158; de quindena in quindenam .. debent panni linei lavari *Obs. Barnwell* 194; **1280** faciendo sectam ad curiam .. abbatis .. de tribus septimanis in tres septimanas *Reg. Malm.* I 252; **c1283** virgata T. .. debet semper j averagium de xij septimanis in xij septimanas *Cust. Battle* 122; **1294** faciendo servientibus pacis .. puturam de mense in mensem *IPM* 67/1; **1199** de †annum (*sic* MS) in annum *CurR* I 86 (cf. ib. 213 [**1200**]: de anno in annum); **1218** nichil clamant de terra illa nisi de anno in annum [*as yearly tenants*] de Henrico de M. *Eyre Yorks* 84; **1488** ut .. liberaret priores ceteros a gravi .. de anno quasi in annum vexacione *Reg. Whet.* I app. 461; **1534** quod .. teneantur reddere fidelem compotum de biennio in biennium *Stat-Ox* 337; **1290** quod .. taxacio illa fieri debeat de septennio in septennium *MunAcOx* 55; **1344** quod .. nos de nominibus illorum sic arestandorum .. de tempore in tempus redderemur cerciores (*Lit. Regis*) AD. MUR. *Chr.* 237. **c** **1219** defendit vim et injuriam .. de verbo in verbum [*categorically*] (*Pl. Judaeorum*) *DocExch* 309; **1285** cartas .. de verbo ad verbum [*word for word*] transcripsit *Cart. Chester* 83; **1220** habet terram .. per cartas omnium regum de rege in regem *CurR* VIII 249; **1224** reddet .. de scaccario ad scaccarium v m. *LTRMem* 7 r. 1a; **1242** habeant custodiam .. heredum successive de herede in heredem, si moriantur antequam ad .. etatem pervenerint *RGasc* I 156 (= *CalPat* 397); **1324** (v. curia 6a); **1336** gradientem de virtute in virtutem *Lit. Cant.* II 116; **1446** quas quidem .. treugas .. juramus facere .. observari de puncto in punctum (*TreatyR*) *Foed.* XI 111a.

4 (w. ref. to time): **a** by (day or night). **b** (w. *tempore* or *temporibus*) at, during. **c** (w. adj. n. abl., (?) *sc. tempore*).

a **1221** malefactores venerunt de nocte ad domum *PlCrGlouc* 19; gens [Albanie] occulos habet pictos et glaucos in pupilla, adeo ut melius de nocte videant quam de die BART. ANGL. XV 7; **s1254** M. PAR. *Maj.* V 478 (v. contrectare 2b); **1285** villa Oxon' non fecit sectam cum hoc evenit de die (*Eyre*) *DocCOx* 196; de luce ELMH. *Metr. Hen. V* 323 (v. dearmare b). **b** **1270** pro arreragiis expensarum .. quas fecit .. de tempore quo habuit custodiam [insule] *Cl* 306; **1290** si contingit querelam aliquam de temporibus retroactis factam .. innovari *MunAcOx* 47. **c** praedico .. quia .. post xx annos, de reliquo vobiscum permansura, regrediar GOSC. *Wulfh.* 9; W. MALM. *GP* I 6 etc. (v. ceterus 4); **1188** de proximo speramus .. oportunitatem vobis serviendi (*Lit. Regis Hungariae*) DICETO *YH* II 54; GIR. *TH* III 34 (v. denuo); **1271** in ducendo quendam palefridum de novo emptum ad opus nostrum *Liberate* 47 m. 12; **1374** de presenti nobis videtur melius consilium quod .. *Let. Ch. Ch.* 4; **s1451** satis de raro subsequitur victoria, ubi juvenes certamen ineunt contra senes *Reg. Whet.* I 8; **1452** dicat .. exequias de cero [i.e. sero] *MunCOx* 643.

5 **a** from among. **b** of (partitive or sim.). **c** (ellipt.) part of, some (of). **d** comprising. **e** per, in (expr. ratio).

a **c1130** sciatis me concessisse civibus meis Lundon' tenendum Middlesexe ad firmam .., ita quod ipsi cives ponent vicecomitem qualem voluerint de se ipsis (*Ch. Hen. I*) *GAS* 525; **c1215** (v. custodia 4d); **1315** (v. eligere 3d). **b** **680** si quilibet de nostris .. ad eos .. perrexerint ALDH. *Ep.* 4 p. 484; praecepit .. ut non confringeretur os de ossibus ejus NEN. *HB* 174; **790** (v. 2 carrata a); onus viri fortis de incenso ASSER *Alf.* 81; reddebat xviij libras, de quibus denariis habebat rex E. duas partes *DB* I 1; nichil de pecunia ejus habeat [AS: *nage heo his yrfes awuht*] (*Quad.*) *GAS* 55; **1199** (v. aretro 2c); minus stagni adicitur, plus de ere R. COLD. *Cuthb.* 81; **1225** v quarteria de †mestillum [? l. *mestillun*] *Cl* 41b; **1238** rex dedit medietatem de Alencestr' Willelmo *CurR* XVI 149C; de bove viginti fercula danda parant GARL. *Tri. Eccl.* 33; **1272** alii de societate eorum *SelPlForest* 38; liberabit .. de cereo .. xl lib. *Cust. Cant.* 104 (v. custos 8c); satis tibi inest de fortitudine, de decore, de rigore *Eul. Hist.* II 206; de anabulla quidem utimur lacte, de esula cortice radicis, de catapucia semine *SB* 42; **1415** vj panni de melioribus staminis integri *Ac. Durh.* 184. **c** adsumta ampulla, misit de oleo in pontum BEDE *HE* III 15; *Ib.* V 4 (v. consecrare 2d); **s883** papa misit regi Ælfredo de ligno Domini *AS Chr.*; **1238** kariare [fecit] apud A. de bosco domini regis ad rogum faciendum *CurR* XVI 149C; **1294** rogamus .. quod de hominibus vestris ad nos mittatis *RGasc* III 229; **1315** in cruce longa .. continentur: de ligno Dominico; de cunabulo Domini .. de virga Moysy *Invent. Ch. Ch.* 81. **d** venit Partholomus cum mille hominibus de viris et mulieribus NEN. *HB* 154. **e** **s1198** rex .. cepit de unaquaque carucata .. terre .. totius Anglie v s. R. HOWD. IV 36; **s1303** (v. custuma 6d); **1322** contribucionem subsidii v denariorum de marca nos .. contingentem .. optulimus .. persolvendam *Lit. Cant.* I 72; **1369** tronario percipienti j denarium de sacco pro feodo suo *ExchScot* 314; **1462** que minor est nova mensura .. per j bollam de celdra *Ib.* 133; **1405** archiepiscopo Ebor' pro expensis pro relaxacione decime de qualibet marca obolum *Ac. Durh.* 606.

6 about, concerning (w. ref. to): **a** person or property; **b** speech, thought, or sim.; **c** feeling, interest, or sim.; **d** charge, judgement, or sim.; **e** assurance, promise, or sim.;

a de barbosis mulieribus *Lib. Monstr.* I 22 *tit.*; ut quid de te fieri deberet agnoscerem BEDE *HE* V 12 p. 309; **c760** (12c) ne .. de eadem terra quippiam agere auderent *CS* 194; **c775** (12c) ita ut, quicquid de ea [terra] agere volueris, liberam .. potestatem teneas *Ib.* 260; quid dicimus de coco [AS: *be coce*]? ÆLF. *Coll.* 98; **c1080** de Anselmo plenam justiciam .. fieri precipio *Regesta* p. 126; **1205** quod nullus vicecomes de firma predicta .. intromittat *BBC* (*Huntingdon*) 122; **1208** fiat de ea sicut de convicta *SelPlCrown* 100; **1262** inde ut de re propria pro sua voluntate disposuit et ordinavit *Cl* 188. **b** **680** sacerdotes de privata propriae conversationis mundita gloriantes ALDH. *Ep.* 4 p. 484; **c705** de his .. implendis mea voce possis ammoneri *Ib.* 8 (11); de natura rerum et de temporibus libros singulos BEDE *HE* V 24 p. 359; *Ib.* III 27 (v. cogitare 1a); cum quaerenti de tacente unde loquatur respondetur 'de nihilo', id est 'non loquitur' ANSELM (*Mon.* 8) I 23; de quibus modo tetigimus AD. SCOT *OP* 523A; quoniam non nisi de aliquo aliquid enuntiari vel interrogari contingit, est autem 'de quo' quam 'quid de eo' prioris cognitionis, erit 'de quo' aliquid enuntiari vel interrogari conveniat et in arte docere et ex arte attendere primum, 'quid de eo' secundum BALSH. *AD* 12; respondit quod de rastura illa nichil scivit, de hoc quod dicunt quod breve exiit sub testimonio domini W. .., respondit quod de brevi illo non habet respondere *State Tri. Ed. I* 36; OCKHAM *Dial.* 407 (v. 10a infra); **s1459** ut velit .. nobis de et super illorum concessione certiorare *Reg. Whet.* I 325; **1524** de .. deponendo de et super ab eis inquirendis (v. consoror). **c** de casu meo.. dolebat BEDE *HE* V 6; ÆLF. *Coll.* 98 (v. curare 1a); cum homo contristatus sine causa dicitur contristatus de nihilo ANSELM (*Mon.* 8) I 23; *G. Herw.* 334b (v. admirari 1a); **1202** (v. condolere 1c); **1235** non pertinet ad eum de maritagio *CurR* XV 1461; quid ad te de mea canitie? *Latin Stories* 35; **1242** miramur de eo quod nondum est ei provisum *RGasc* I 140 (= *CalPat* 385); **1257** meror anxius animam meam .. affligit de eo quod .. presentie vestre jucunditatem .. adire non sufficio AD. MARSH *Ep.* 169; **s1322** rex de tanta gaudens victoria TROKELOWE 124; **s1385** (v. congaudere 1a); **1544** meum .. interesse et demandam que .. habeo .. de et in predicto archidiaconatu *FormA* 72. **d** non fuit summonitus de eo placito *DB* II 424; **c1105** praecipio quod homines episcopi .. juste tractentur de hoc quod summoniti sunt .. (*Ch. Wint.*) *EHR* XXXV 391; GLANV. XIV 3 (v. accusare 1a); **1218** de nullo tenementorum suorum ponatur in placitum *Pat* 151; **1219** (v. culpabilis 1c); **1221** (v. convincere 5a); **1226** ad audiendum judicium suum de eo quod nobis illam [firmam] non reddiderunt *LTRMem* 8 r. 2 (2); **1230** demanda que eis fit de hoc quod tenuerunt unum mercatum *Ib.* 11 r. 7; **1277** (v. contravenire d); **1382** eundem P. de pravitate heretica non convictum .. ad pristinum statum restituimus *Conc.* III 169b. **e** securi de victoria hostes invadite OSB. BAWDSEY clxxiv; si quis alium plegiaverit de stando ad rectum GLANV. X 5; **1216** etc. (v. confidere 1b); **1217** accepta securitate a Willelmo .. de xxx m. nobis reddendis *Pat* 49; **1218** juramentum nobis prestiterunt de moneta nostra fideliter conservanda *Ib.* 138; **1225** fecit nos securos .. de solvendo nobis .. scutagia .. *LTRMem* 7 r. 2 (1) *d*. (cf. ib. 8 r. 3 [**1226**]: recognovit se esse securum de Johanne Wac .. quod reddat .. x m.); **1259** (v. custodire 6b); manuceperunt Rogerum de habendo eum hic ad prefatum terminum *State Tri. Ed. I* 53; **1543** (v. cautio 1a).

7 in respect of, as regards: **a** life, limb, or property; **b** payment or service; **c** period of time; **d** var.; **e** (w. gd., gdv., or inf.). **f** (w. *se*) of or in itself, inherently. **g** (w. *ipso*) personally.

a **1201** minatus fuit ei de corpore et catallis suis *SelPlCrown* 3; **1220** cum debilis esset de corpore suo *CurR* VIII 335; mahamaverunt ipsum R. de dextro brachio suo *State Tri. Ed. I* 14; **1382** ipsum in tantum cominatus fuit de vita et membris suis .. quod vix de potencia sua de vita evasit *SessPCambs* 51. **b** de theloneo et de aliis consuetudinibus burgi xlix s. *DB* I 135v.; **1130** (v. auxilium 4a); **1167** debet l li. de misericordia *Pipe* 3; **1217** vij m. quas .. regi .. debuistis de vino capto *Pat* 25; **1230** concessimus Gerardo .. iij^{m} s. .. percipienda .. de annuo feodo *Pat* 398; **c1283** de omnibus aliis consuetudinibus et operibus debet eodem modo sicut W. *Cust. Battle* 9; **c1355** contra quam summam et de et pro ipsa summa .. solvimus .. liij s. *Meaux* III 99n. **c** **1169** in terris datis Adelize .. xv s. de tribus annis pro escambio terre sue *Pipe* 161; **1219** aretro sunt .. denarii de ij annis *CurR* VIII 117; **s1261** plenam habuerunt .. mercedem de xl diebus *Flor. Hist.* II 470; **1268** solvit de iij primis terminis et quietus est *Cl* 506. **d** **1218** ad videndum .. in quo statu foresta illa fuit de bosco et bestiis *Pat* 174; **1260** (v. custodire 6e); **c1375** in quadam camera .. continente de longitudine xxiiij pedes et xij in latitudine *Pri. Cold.* 54. **e** **1212** promisit se non compulsurum O. de solvendo sibi redditu *FormA* 82; **1216** de bersare in foresta (v. bersare); **1234** respondit quod noluit nec consilium suum fuit de mittendo ei litteras de conductu *CurR* XV 1031; **1310** pro expensis suis de veniendo in Angliam *RGasc* IV 357. **f** PECKHAM *QA* 4 (v. communicativus b); sicut se de se patet OCKHAM *Pol.* II 834; negare assercionem catholicam est de se malum *Id. Dial.* 426; in tali opere de se malo RIC. ARMAGH *Def. Cur.* 1404 (*recte* 1304); est bona religio de se GOWER *VC* IV 5; **1465** potestatem .. omnia .. faciendi .. que .. necessaria fuerint .., licet mandatum de se magis exigant speciale *Lit. Cant.* III 242; si in aliquo .. substantiali .. sit .. interlineatum .., hoc instrumentum de se non facit fidem *Praxis* 290. **g** quod de ipso viderat ac postmodum pro certo cognoverat .. protestatus est T. MON. *Will.* I 8.

8 by (a measure of quantity or degree).

1230 habuit .. unum mesuagium quod plus valuit de vj m. quam pecunia illa *CurR* XIV 207; **1231** (v. esseware 2);

1265 extenta prati quod vocatur P. extentam pratorum .. de S. et W. de xj s. annuis excedit *Cl* 151; c**1380** exoro quod de tanto vos meis precibus velit vestra bonitas inclinare ut .. *FormOx* 327; de quanto aliquis magis vel propinquius juvat ad consummacionem illius actus, de tanto .. magis meretur PAUL. ANGL. *ASP* 1552.

9 (instrumental or sim.) with (the aid of), by means of. **b** with, by (expenditure of). **c** by (a means of reckoning). **d** with (w. word expr. anointment or sim.); **e** (w. word expr. supply, equipment, adornment, or sim.); **f** (w. word expr. possession or sim.).

iiij evangelia de auro purissimo .. scribere jussit EDDI 17; apprehendens eum de mento BEDE *HE* V 2; percutiens ter super liminare de cambutta sua aut baculo EGB. *Pont.* 30; amputetur ei manus de qua furatus est [AS: *ðe he hit mid gedyde*] (*Quad.*) *GAS* 53; **1195** se lesit de sagittis viri sui *CurR RC* I 82; ligaverunt ei de restibus manus a tergo GIR. *GE* I 24 p. 65; **1220** traxit ad .. Willelmum de una sagitta *CurR* VIII 259; tu, Reginalde, potes de pontibus ire per undas / ponti GARL. *Tri. Eccl.* 44; **1289** dedimus .. licenciam .. faciendi domum fortem .. de muris et fossatis *RGasc* II 425; *State Tri. Ed. I* 51 (v. compeditare); c**1380** de celeriori remedio succurratur *FormOx* 225; mihi de facie notus FERR. *Kinloss* 52. **b** si plus opus esset, de pecunia ejus conducebatur *DB* I 1; **12..** *EHR* XVII 507 (v. 3 costus b); **1226** quousque pacatus fuit de .. firma *LTRMem* 8 r. 3 (3); s**1237** ut .. de juste utrique debitis satisfieret M. PAR. *Maj.* III 413; **1301** de .. vj m. argenti .. vobis interim satisfieri volumus *Reg. Cant.* 613; levavit unam novam boveriam .. de sumptibus xxij m. WHITTLESEY 143. **c** s**1397** (v. 2 cloca 1c); **1419** (v. 2 campana 2d); ab hora diei prima usque decem de campana STRECCHE *Hen. V* 175. **d** de adipe .. calciamenta sua liniantes *V. Cuthb.* III 5; lavas eam de aqua benedicta EGB. *Pont.* 118; de sanctificato / illinit hos oleo GARL. *Myst. Eccl.* 159; de aqua ro[sarum] .. irroretur GILB. II 94v. 2; stuellus .. de lardo perunctus *Ib.* IV 181v. 2. **e** **790** benefacite viduis .. de frumento, vino, et lardo ALCUIN *Ep.* 8; c**1160** (v. deforis 3a); **1212** (v. 2 cooperire 6b); duo fratres .. de aqua et manutergio eidem servient *Cust. Westm.* 2; c**1283** primam acram quam seminant de *bericorn Cust. Battle* 67; **1293** de tribus cursibus serviantur ad prandium et ad cenam de uno cursu *Reg. Malm.* II app. 383; **1295** concedit .. j selionem terre ad plantandum de fabis *CourtR Hales* 331; **1338** (v. broudare); s**1341** castrum .. de victualibus instaurare *Meaux* III 49; **1374** una pipa .. plena de vino *Pri. Cold.* app. p. lxxvi. **f** ij hidas de quibus fuit aecclesia saisita *DB* I 32; a**1128** precipio ut .. de hac custodia eum seisias *E. Ch. S. Paul* 216; **1219** donec ei provideret de x libratis terre *CurR* VIII 62; **1240** vestiti et seisiti de tenemento *BNB* III 290; **1249** Isabella dotabitur de tercia parte .. terre .. comitis *Cl* 225; **1425** de manerio .. possessionati fuerunt *Reg. S. Aug.* 574. **1485** ad intrandum ac seisinam .. capiendam .. de et in .. predictis terris *FormA* 209.

10 (w. abstr.): **a** by virtue of, in accordance with. **b** by way of, in the form of. **c** because of, on the ground of. **d** with (a symptom of emotion). **e** (w. adj. as sb. n. equivalent to adv.) in a (specified) manner; *cf. ex* 13c.

a rex .. de more familiariter .. ad Dei hominem accessit *V. Neot. A* 9; solito de more priorum G. AMIENS *Hast.* 795; qui alium de iniquitate [AS: *mid wo*] accusare voluerit (*Cons. Cnuti*) *GAS* 321 (= *Inst. Cnuti*: injuste); GLANV. VII 1 (v. consilium 1b); AD. EYNS. *Hug.* III 11 (v. conscientia 2b); si bos debetur de jure, duo rapiuntur / de facto H. AVR. *Hugh* 825–6; **1232** de voluntate sua carcavit eos de xl li. de panagio, .. unde non debent nisi xix li. *KRMem* 12 r. 12 *d.*; BACON *Tert.* 242 (v. bene 5); s**1270** lane extra regnum de licencia nostra ducte *Leg. Ant. Lond.* 136; **1275** de commissione (v. custodia 4a); **1276** clamat libertatem .. de j caruca terre de antiquitate *Hund.* II 178a; *State Tri. Ed. I* 15 (v. 1 consensus a); que quidem auxilia fiunt de gracia et non de jure *Fleta* 198; **1296** communitas villanorum .. de sua mera et spontanea voluntate sursum reddidit domino totum jus et clamium *SelPlMan* 172; **1314** quod Pater potuit producere omnem creaturam sine Filio producente de potencia absoluta etsi non de potencia ordinata (*Artic. Condemnati*) *MunAcOx* 100; electus [in regem Romanorum] nichil petere tenetur a papa de necessitate, sed tantum tenetur sequi informaciones ejus consonas fidei Christiane OCKHAM *Pol.* I 199. **b** liberata fuit Hugoni pro dim. carucata de escangio *DB* II 409; c**1160** pro hac donatione dedit michi R. .. iij m. argenti de recognicione *FormA* 42; c**1190** dedisse .. de adjectione .. mea j acram terre *Danelaw* 203; **1200** dedi eisdem monachis de incremento pratum unum *Couch. Kirkstall* 151; **1220** d m. .. Philippo .. de prestito habere faciatis *Pat* 250; **1220** habere faciatis de dono .. S. episcopo l robora *Ib.* 257; **1357** (v. custuma 3b); **1434** ut in precio j quar. et dim. ordii ad vj s. viij d. eidem annuatim per dominum priorem de elemosina concess[orum] *Ac. Durh.* 623. **c** his de causis ALDH. *VirgP* 59; **765** (12c) qua de re ego S. rex .. terram .. episcopo .. perdono *CS* 194; duo prima essonia possunt esse de infirmitate veniendi et tertium de reseantisa GLANV. II 20; totaque descendit de gravitate sua NECKAM *DS* IV 579; **1214** etc. (v. continere 7a); **1255** mortuus est et essoniatus de morte *SelPlForest* 35; **1287** (v. causa 4a). **d** quando ab eo aliquid postulatur, .. de hylari vultu prebeat *Cust. Westm.* 71. **e** de facili novit salsus abire sapor NECKAM *DS* IV 249; cum in presentia vestra ambo de pari stare potuerimus GIR. *Symb.* I 31 p. 327; **1209** in .. iiij carucis factis de novo et in carucis reparandis *Pipe Wint.* 50; s**1217** consuetudo est Romanis de levi causas adinvenire ubi materia prede subjacet malignantibus M. PAR. *Maj.* III 23; **1246** (v. belongum); **1264** (v. altus 1d); **1266** perdonacionem de pleno revocavimus *Cl* 277; de plano se ponit in veredicto eorum *State Tri. Ed. I* 20; de valde possibili WYCL. *Blasph.* 37 (v. dissolutio 3a); **1382** (v. difficilis 1b); de quibusdam dudum †fortuniis [? l. fortunis *or* infortuniis] in Anglia de miro motis FAVENT 1; **1449** (v. dare 11e); **1460** de quodam apparatu .. eidem navi de necesse spectante *Pat* 468 m. 3*d.*

11 by (agent or sim.).

1195 occisus fuit de burgatoribus *CurR RC* I 147; c**1230** si aliquis implacitatus fuerit de vicino suo *BBC* (*Salford*) 203; **1270** percepti erant .. de pluribus hominibus *SelPlForest* 55; **1306** summa precii .. debiti de .. Johanne per annum *Cust. Battle* 21; s**1307** de .. regni sapientibus .. correptus TROKELOWE 64; quamvis hoc prohibeatur de sacris canonibus OCKHAM *Dial.* 817.

12 (in compl.): **a** resulting from, established by. **b** appurtenant or belonging to, assigned to, associated w. **c** dependent on, subject to. **d** in receipt of. **e** in a state of. **f** made of. **g** of an age of. **h** approved by or as.

a haec terra est de emptione W. episcopi *DB* I 133v.; **1204** de .. perquisito meo (v. catallum 1c); **1228** pro reparacione ecclesie .. que est de fundatione antecessorum domini regis *Pat* 191; **1371** xvij paria linthiaminum, quorum v paria de empcione domini J. *Ac. Durh.* 130. **b** [Waleorde] fuit de vestitu monachorum *DB* I 31; unum manerium quod .. fuit de victu monachorum *Ib.* 41; c**1120** Bramcestre .. cum .. consuetudinibus quas ipse rex Anglie, si esset de mensa sua, posset ibi habere *Cart. Rams.* I 149; **1275** si probaverit .. quod de communitate dictorum R. et R. non extiterit *SelCMan* 154; **1275, 1279** (v. consilium 2b, 4a); **1313** de libertate (v. concivis a); **1448** de villatis et hundredis de et in quibus terre, tenementa et feoda predicta extiterint *Reg. Whet.* I 34. **c** **1230** (v. custodia 7a); **1294** exceptis bonis illorum qui sunt de potestate et dominio regis Francie (*Breve Regis*) B. COTTON 246; **1300** nullus scholaris .. de hujusmodi jurisdiccione .. cancellarii existens *MunAcOx* 79; si [papa est] vere hereticus, est de jurisdiccione catholicorum OCKHAM *Dial.* 519. **d** **1290** clerici et eorum familie et servientes et .. scriptores, barbitonsores, et alii homines de officio qui sunt de robis clericorum *MunAcOx* 52; dominus A., Willelmum O. .. de robis suis habens in comitiva *Proc. A. Kyteler* 17; **1419** illi de mistera cujus erat major et qui de sua liberata fuerant *MGL* I 26 (cf. *Reg. Cant.* II 351 [**1425**]: omnes homines de liberata mea); reus .. excipit contra testes .. quod sunt .. de roba ac stipendio partis producentis *Praxis* 49. **e** recognitores non fuerunt de uno et eodem assensu [*of one mind*] in suo veredicto *State Tri. Ed. I* 64; **1309** plures Anglicos homines nostros, qui non erant nec sunt de guerra, in mari et in terra depredaverunt *RGasc* IV 336 (cf. ib.: qui non erant de guerra adherebant illis de guerra); **1315** de consensu (v. abettator); **1323** tuiciones pro malefactoribus [Hibernicis] qui de guerra contra nos .. insurrexerunt ad certum tempus durature, infra quod dicti malefactores de pace fuerunt *Cl* 141 m. 40; **1344** ne qui .. armaturas quascumque eisdem Hibernicis, dum sic de guerra existant, ministrent *StatIr* I 364. **f** orientalis pars feretri est de argento *Lib. Eli.* III 50 (v. deauratura); **1388** primum par est de rubeo *velvett* (v. custos 10c). **g** **1235** dicit quod est de lx annis *CurR* XV 1304. **h** s**1274** Judei quedam animalia arbitrantur de lege sua, quedam non; de carnibus illorum que sunt de lege commedunt *Leg. Ant. Lond.* 172; **1337** per librum *del Domesday* et .. alia memoranda que sunt de recordo *SelCKB* V 98.

13 (in phr. qualifying thing, equivalent to gen.) of: **a** objective; **b** subjective; **c** indicative of material, value, function, *etc.*; **d** (w. *terminus*) indicative of date; **e** indicative of origin or location; **f** (of towns, rivers, *etc.*) equivalent to apposition.

a **716** admirandas visiones de illo redivivo qui nuper .. mortuus est BONIF. *Ep.* 10 p. 8; *DB* I 1 (v. custodia 4b); **1187** quasi de spiritualibus curam receperitis (*Lit. Archiepiscopi*) DICETO *YH* II 48; **1230** fecit ei visum tantum de j roda; .. et concedit quod, si de plus [*indecl.*] fecit ei visum, quod (*sic*) amittat terram *CurR* XIV 693; **1235** retinuit sibi .. maritagium de eo *Ib.* XV 1461; **1257** eleccionem .. de .. priorissa .. in abbatissam (v. custos 8a); s**392** de vulgo stragem non minimam facientes M. PAR. *Maj.* I 173 (cf. G. MON. V 16); s**887** de populo cedem nefariam commiserunt *Ib.* 424 (cf. W. JUM. I 6); **1298** (v. 1 carcagium); **1343** (v. cura 3a); c**1380** cum .. timeat .. sibi .. damnum de corpore suo et jacturam de rebus suis posse .. evenire *FormOx* 253. **b** s**1189** capella .. non habebit .. administrationem nisi de uno tantum presbitero seculari M. PAR. *Maj.* II 354 (= DICETO *YH* II 72: ministrabitur .. per unum solummodo sacerdotem). **c** benedictio vespertina de cotidianis diebus EGB. *Pont.* 81 *rub.*; ibi ij piscariae de viij s. et x d. *DB* II 2; **1200** litteras .. de protectione (v. clericus 2a); **1202** in brevi de cape etc. (v. brevis 10b); **1216** (v. canis 2a); **1230** debet iij dextrarios de precio *LTRMem* 11 r. 12 (1) *d.*; **1234** ad Scaccarium de Recepta *Cl* 467; **1242** (v. aurum 1a); **1245** capa fusca de panno serico *Invent. S. Paul.* 477; **1261** (v. arma 3a); s**1260** domorum quarumdam extitit religiosarum patronus, quarum quedam de monachis, quedam de canonicis, et quedam de sanctimonialibus infra suum erant dominium constructe *Flor. Hist.* II 446; **1267** (v. 2 cuppa 1a); c**1283** j picherum ad minus de ij galonibus *Cust. Battle* 36; **1300** (v. 3 color 1b); **1341** (v. 1 bargia a); **1404** j par de flakatis de iiij lagenis *Ac. Durh.* 398; a**1440** una cappa coloris purpurei de panno aureo operis sumptuosi AMUND. I app. 257. **d** **1198** placita de termino Pasche *CurR RC* I 138; **1199** breve est in ligamine de termino S. Yllarii *Ib.* II 88; **1218** ad Scaccarium nostrum de termino S. Hyllarii *Pat* 179. **e** **1153** (v. abbatia c); c**1155** cum dim. parte monasterii de Wikham *Ch. Gilb.* 4; **1173** (v. castellum 2a); **1238** (v. castrum 3a); c**1283** debet .. ij sectas ad curiam de Bello *Cust. Battle* 3; **1296** pannus de Worthstede *CalCl* 511; **1327** empcio vini de Rino *KRAc* 78/2 m. 3; s**1342** per partes de Caleys et omnium portuum de Caleys AD. MUR. *Chr.* 128; s**1345** (v. Atrebatensis); **1367** (v. caseus a); **1446** ultra pontem de Tyne *Ac. Durh.* 629. **f** insula de Wit *DB* I 38v.; civitas de Glowecestre *Ib.* 162; burgus de Warwic *Ib.* 238; c**1109** in villa de Cotis *Surv. Linc.* 4; c**1130** in insula de Oseneya *Cart. Osney* IV 14; a**1190, 1195** (v. 1 cultura 2a, 2b); **1276** (v. aqua 1c); usque ad flumen de Humbre BIRCHINGTON *Arch. Cant.* 1; in manerio nostro de Aukelande R. BURY *Phil.* 20. 253; **1368** infra castrum lacus de Levyn *ExchScot* 309; **1442** pro mundacione campi de Smythfeld (*Ac. Foreign*) *Analog. Cant. Pilg.* 25; **1483** inter villas de Aton et Barube *Sanct. Durh.* 23.

14 (in phr. qualifying pron.) of.

easdem consuetudines debent illi de Banneberga *DB* I 87v.; s**1204** de controversia inter nos et ipsos de Melros *Kelso* I 19; **1313** per avisamentum illorum de consilio nostro *RGasc* IV 1146 (cf. ib. 1153: a predicto nobili et illis de genere suo); c**1336** dominus T. S. et plures alii de patria et similiter illi de inquisicione *Ac. Durh.* 533; illi de ordine [Minorum] OCKHAM *Dial.* 427; s**1401** illi de Parliamento dixerunt .. *Eul. Hist.* III 388.

15 (in phr. qualifying person) of: **a** indicative of amount of land held; **b** indicative of office; **c** indicative of place of abode or origin.

a ad hoc manerium erant .. ij liberi homines de xlvii acris *DB* II 24; ibi ij soch[emanni] de ij bovatis terrae et dim. *Ib.* I 284; *Ib.* 128 (v. 1 bordarius a). **b** s**1121** (v. clericus 2a); a**1127** (v. baro 6a); **1205** (v. 2 bancus 3a) c**1283** per manum servientis de curia *Cust. Battle* 68; **1290** homines de officio (v. 12d supra); **1336** (v. clamator 2b); **1369** (v. camerarius 2c); **1384** quod nullus homo de lege sit .. justiciarius .. in propria patria sua *StRealm* II 36. **c** s**762** F. episcopus de Hwiterne obiit *AS Chr.*; s**1013** rex Æ. misit .. trans mare et Ælsigum abbatem de Burh *Ib.*; monachi de Suavesy *DB* I 195; **1159** monialibus de Carho *Pipe* 1; **1167** de sochemannis regis de eadem villa *Pipe* 118; s**1173** (v. burgensis 1); **1221** (v. baillivus 2b); s**1431** Johannes Scharpe de Wygmorelond motionem quamdam commovit in populo *Chr. S. Alb.* 63; c**1460** Johannes [Whethamstede] .. Roberto White de Ferneham in comitatu Surreie .. et Thome Sharp de dictis villa et comitatu salutem *Reg. Whet.* II 5.

16 (in phr. qualifying personal name, developing into hereditary surname) of: **a** indicative of office; **b** indicative of place of abode or origin; **c** (w. ref. to specific place-name). **d** (w. *eodem*, Scot.) of that ilk.

a **1130** Roberto de Sigillo *Pipe* 80; **1200** Herveotum de Camera *RChart* 58a; **1200** Willelmus de Capella *Ib.* 97a; **1200** Alanus de Scaccario *CurR* I 203; c**1200** hiis testibus .. Alano de Feria .., Philippo de Celario .., Gerardo de Coquina .., Buk de Bracino *Feod. Durh.* 16*n.* **b** **1130** Ernaldus de Bosco *Pipe* 88; c**1150** Rogero de Fraxino *E. Ch. S. Paul.* 29*n.*; **1195** Willelmum de Grava *Fines P. Ric. I* 49; **1202** terram Abrahe de Ponte *Fines P. Lincs* 95; **1199** Hervicus de Molendino *CurR* I 83; **1201** Nicholao de Quercu *Ib.* 397; **1204** Hugonem de Foresta *Ib.* III 108; **1222** nomina Juratorum: Lefchild de Marisco, Walterus de Mora .., Willelmus de Fonte, Edmundus de Marisco .., Jordanus de Bosco *Dom. S. Paul.* 52; **1236** Ricardus de Puteo *Fees* 594; **1243** Jacobus de Vado *Ib.* 767. **c** Alvredus de Merlebergh' .., Durandus de Glouuecestre .., Willelmus de Faleise .., Walscinus de Dowai .., Alvredus de Ispania *DB* I 64v.; **1196** Willelmus de Perci de Kenetebi *Pipe* 186; **1226** distringat Willelmum de Franketon', qui tenet villam de Franketon' *LTRMem* 8 r. 3; **1267, 1269** (v. cognomen a); **1283** pro Willelmo de Faencourt et G. de eadem *KRMem* 16 r. 6; **1309** pro Johanne de London' de Suthamton' cive Burdegale *RGasc* IV 186; Willelmus natus in Schelton et vocatus 'de Wodeforde', quia ibi erat nutritus cum quodam amico WHITTLESEY 151; **1326** Johannes de Ledecombe, filius Johannis Randolf de Ledecombe *KRMem* 103 r. 104; p**1440** in factura unius libri qui intitulatur Granarium Johannis de Loco Frumenti [*Wheathampstead*] AMUND. II app. 270. **d** **1450** [teste] Jacobo de Edmondstoune de eodem *Inchaffray* 144 (cf. ib. [c**1370**]: Rogerus de Makfen dominus de eadem); ib. 138 [**1444**]: Robertus de Mekven dominus ejusdem); **1461** compotum Archibaldi de Dundas de eodem *ExchScot* 47.

17 (in new comp., expr.): **a** (CL sense 'down') *v. decasatus*, 2 *decasus* 1, 1 *decisio*, *decolpare*, *decurribilis*, *defluentia* b, *defullare*, *deguttare*, *~atio*, *dependentia*, *desputare*, *devalare*, *devolatio*; **b** (intensification) *v. deaemulare*, *deaemulus*, *deagitare*, *deamelare*, *deargenteus*, *deastuppare*, *deblandiri*, *debroudatus*, *deburgare*, *decadere*, *decalcare*, *decastrare*, 2 *decasus* 2, *decharaxare*, *declausus* b, *decorrosivus*, *decorruere*, *decostare*, *decrassare*, *de-*

cruciare, decultor, defalcare, deflagitare, deflorare 2, *defossio, defucare, degradus, degrassator, deiterare, delanguidus, delugere, demacerare, ~atio, demanicatus, demartyrizare, dematurescere, demultare, demundare, demungere, denasci, denihilare, deornare* 2, *depasturare, depauperare, ~atio, ~ativus, ~ator, depejorare, depicatus, depictare, depinguere, deplacitare, deplanare, deplumare, deposse, depraedo, deprimare, deprivare, ~atio, depublicare, depulverare, depunctare, depuratio, depurpurare, dereinare, ~ium, derevocare, desequi, desteiniare, detingere, detrucidare, devetare, devigilare, deviolare, devitreare*; **c** (deprivation, removal, or separation) *v. deappellare, decaballare, decalceare, decanonizare, decapillare, ~atio, decaputiatus, decarcare, decarnellare, decarriare, decaudare, decomatio, decoronare, ~atio, decymare, ~ator, defluentia* a, *defluitio, defrondatio, ~ator, defruitio, defurfurare, defurnare, degranare, deincumbrare, deliliare, demediare, demembratio, deoculare, deparcare, depennare, deperatio, depetrare, depilatio, depotestare, derobare, ~atio,* 2 *despicari, despinare, desticulare, dethyrsare, detitulare, detogare, detrenchare, detunicare, deusitatus, deusus, devacuare, devanescere, devillare, ~atio, devirare, deviscerare*; **d** (reversal of action) *v. deaedificare, deafforestare, ~atio, dearmatio, dearrestare, ~atio, deartare, deauctorizare, deawarennare, decingere, declausus* a, *decopulare, decrudescere, dedamnificare, dedicere, dediligere, deeligere, deexaltare, ~atio, defatuare, defercire, defesantia, defieri, deforestare, ~atio, defrainnare, degelare, ~atio, deglomerare, dehabilitare, dehereditare, ~atio, dehospitari, deinstauratus, deinvadiare, dejejunare, delaqueare,* 2 *deligare, delucere, dememinisse, demiscere, demolimen,* 2 *demollire, demultiplicare, ~atio, denobilitari, denodare, deobligare, ~atio, deobstructio, deobstruere, deobstuppare, ~atio, deoneratio, deonustatio, deopinari, deoppilare, ~atio, ~ativus, deordinare, depalliare, deparietare, depatriare, depessulare, depignerare, dequadrare, deregulare, derudire, descandalizare* 2, *descire, desecrare, desepelire, destaurare, detegulare, ~atio, detumulare, dewarennare*; **e** (refusal) *v. deacceptare, ~atio, deacceptio, ~us, deallocare*; **f** (negation) *v. deadvocare, ~atio, deappetitus, deaptare, decontinuatio, decredere, decuratus, dedecenter, ~ia, dedignabundus, dedignanter, dedignosus, dedilectio, deferratus, deformaliter, deformiter, degenerositas,* 2 *delirus, demeritare, ~io, ~orie, ~orius, demonachari, ~us, denaturare, denuere, depatrissare, deposse* 2, *depraedicare. V. et.* 2 *dis-* 1.

18 (conf. w. *di-, dis-*): **a** (from CL or LL) *v. defamare, ~atio, ~ator, ~atorius,* 2 *decidere,* 2 *decisio, deferre, defugere, defundere, degredi, dejudicare, delabi, delacerare, delapidare, ~atio, deligere,* 1 *deluere, deminuere, demittere, derigescere, deripere, derivare, ~atio, ~ativus, deruere,* 1 *desecare,* 1 *desilire, despectare, despicere, destillare, destringere, deverberare*; **b** (from OF *de-* < *de-, di-, dis-*) *v. dearrestare, deastuppare, decarcare, decingere, decontinuatio, decopulare, decredere, dedicere, defesantia, deincumbrare,* 2 *deligare, depersonare, dereinare, derobare, ~atio, ~ator. V. et.* 2 *dis~* 2.

dea [CL], goddess: **a** (Classical); **b** (Northern); **c** (fig.).

a quamque deam stolidi dixerunt arte potentem, / aurea sternuntur fundo simulacra Minervae ALDH. *VirgV* 1332; Lamia dea silvae dicitur habens pedes similes caballi, caput, manus, et totum corpus pulchrum simili (*sic*) mulieris *GlC* L 29; imago dee [sc. Diane] responsa dabat G. MON. I 11; Ceres dea inter omnes deos deasque veterum ultimo in ordine posita est *Imag. Deorum* 329. **b** Eosturmonath .. quondam a dea illorum [Anglorum], quae Eostre vocabatur et cui in illo [mense] festa celebrabant, nomen habuit BEDE *TR* 15. **c** quibus imperialis / est dominus nummus, quibus est dea forma monete D. BEC. 1557; non serviunt veraciter Mammone et ficte dee SERLO GRAM. *Mon. Font.* 20.

deabilitare v. dehabilitare.

deacceptare [cf. CL acceptare], to refuse.

cum benignitas [Christi] .. exonerat filios suos .., ~are hanc libertatem foret spernere donum Dei WYCL. *Ver.* III 131; s**1423** intercedens quatenus ea non ~et paterna bonitas AMUND. I 152.

deacceptatio, [cf. acceptatio], refusal.

omnia mala ecclesie oriuntur ex ~acione autoritatis scripture WYCL. *Ver.* I 389.

deacceptio [cf. CL acceptio], refusal.

cum .. locorum differencia, complexionis fragilitas, ~o sive prescripcio non excusat quin pari evidencia qua carnalis copula alicui sacerdoti sit licita et cuilibet, vel e contra WYCL. *Ver.* II 261.

deacceptus [cf. CL acceptus], unacceptable, displeasing.

una talis missa est .. Deo odibilis et alia est .. Deo acceptabilis; .. patet ex hoc quod, ut sacerdos est Deo ~ior, est ministracio sua injustior WYCL. *Euch.* 112.

deacon- v. diacon-.

deacus, divine being or (?) *f. l. V. et. deicus.*

dico quod ibi sumitur 'deus' pro substantiis separatis, ut pro intelligentiis, quia philosophi posuerunt substantias separatas esse deos; vel dicendum quod omnes deaci [? l. deici] sunt dii, quia, sicut distinguit Boetius, participantes divinitatem et bonum divinum sunt dii BACON XIII 125.

deadema v. diadema. **deadvoatio** v. deadvocatio.

deadvocare [cf. CL advocare], to disavow, disclaim, disown, deny: **a** (obligation to) feudal lord; **b** (paternity of) child; **c** (responsibility for) alleged servant; **d** (title to) liberty; **e** (liability for) debt; **f** (connection w.) objects associated w. crime; **g** (responsibility for or intention to assert) action, claim, or sim.; **h** (w. inf., acc. & inf., or *quod*, sts. w. double neg.). *V. et. devocare* 3, *disadvocare.*

a **1180** W. de D. debet xx s., quia ~avit dominum suum *RScacNorm* I 16; **1249** H. ~avit ipsum in curia et dixit quod nichil de eo tenuit *CurR* XIX 1112; competunt domino .. duo remedia .., vel quod petat tenementum tenentis sui quod de eo tenere debuit in dominico, quia ~atus est per tenentem in cujus persona deficit obligatio, vel quod petat servitium .. BRACTON 81 (cf. ib. 81b: eo quod .. contra homagium suum .. ipsum malitiose et ad exheredationem suam ~averit); **1259** de servicio feodorum abbacie .., de quo regi faciendo .. episcopus asserit se medium esse inter regem et abbatem .. et unde .. abbas eum ~avit in curia regis *Cl* 411. **b** si [vir], cum generare non possit propter legitimum impedimentum, partum in utero vel editum ~averit et .. a domo sua amoverit BRACTON 70; ipso [puero] semel [ut filio] advocato, iterum ipsum ~are non poterit *Fleta* 14. **c** **1278** vicecomes .. non clamat nisi iiij servientes in baronia .. et, si plures sint .., ipsos ~at (*JustIt* 982) *EE County Court* 172. **d** **1281** qualitercunque [prior] ~et warennam ibidem ad presens .., idem prior et predecessores sui hactenus in .. terris suis warennam clamaverunt et hiis que ad warennam pertinent usi sunt *PQW* 391a; **1292** prior .. primo die itineris clamavit .. libertatem [sc. wreccum maris] .. et modo hac (*sic*) ~at *Ib.* 386b. **e** **1219** Furmentinus .. adjudicatus est in misericordia .., quia jam advocavit debitum illud quod prius ~averat (*Pl. Judaeorum*) *DocExch* 323. **f** **1255** invenerunt eum in domo Willelmi ..; et illuc inventus fuit unus arcus cum v parvis sagittis. .. et Willelmus .. ~avit arcum et sagittas nec scivit dicere cujus fuerunt *SelPlForest* 11; **1315** Agnes .., capta cum uno cipho .. furato .., ~at ciphum .. et defendit furtum *SessPNorthants* 67; **1400** quod .. dux .. haberet quecumque bona et catalla vocata manuopera capta vel capienda cum quacumque persona .. ac per eandem personam .. ~ata (*Ch. Regis de Duc. Lanc.*) *MGL* II 487 (cf. *RParl* III 654b [**1411**]: catalla vocata manuopera .. ~anda). **g** **1219** petit dampna sibi restitui que habuit per predictam districcionem, desicut justiciarii illam ~averunt (*Pl. Judaeorum*) *DocExch* 317; **1222** ~at quod narrator suus pro eo narravit *BNB* II 113; **1255** vicecomes .. factum eorum penitus ~avit *SelPlForest* 18; si donationes et cartas ~averit BRACTON 15; c**1264** ipsorum mala opera .. in presencia regie majestatis ~avimus et improbavimus *AncC* III 172 B; **1280** ex nunc eam [denunciacionem] revocat et ~at *RParl Ined.* 11; omnino ~at fracturam domorum suarum *G. S. Alb.* I 461; Willelmus ad predictum breve ~andum audiri non debet *State Tri. Ed. I* 34; **1345** presentant quod W. de H. tenet tres *stagges* in pastura domini, et quod terrarius hoc ~at *Hal. Durh.* 16. **h** **1200** comparuit et ~avit quod ipsa A. terram illam non habuit per eum *CurR* I 211; **1285** per hoc quod tenentes ~ant nichil tenere nec clamium tenere de eo qui districcionem fecit et advocavit, remansit qui distrinxit in misericordia et tenentes sui quieti, quibus pro illa deadvocacione .. pena infligi non potest (*Westm.* 2) *StRealm* I 72; non obstante deadvocacione qua abbas Glastonie ~averat se tenere feuda .. de episcopis Bathoniensibus DOMERH. *Glast.* 536; **1293** maneria illa de eodem comite tenere ~avit *RParl* I 97b; illas [acras terre] de ipso W. adtunc tenere omnino ~avit et disclamavit, per quas disclamacionem et deadvocacionem accio accrevit ipsi W. *Entries* 224.

deadvocatio [cf. CL advocatio], disavowal, disclaimer.

si tenens deadvocaverit illum qui distringit pro servitio, non tamen cessare debet districtio pro servitio, quia ista simul stare possunt, ~o et districtio BRACTON 82b; **1285** deadvoatio (v. advocatio 3c); **1285** etc. (v. deadvocare h).

deaedificare [cf. CL aedificare], to unbuild.

apud quandam castelli partem quidam Anglicus .., muri latus attingens et ab eodem paulatim lapides extrahens, sibimet sedem lustralem infra parietis viscera ~ando construxit *Ps.*-ELMH. *Hen. V* 54 p. 135; **1537** pro licencia ~andi et prosternendi domum inhabitabilem tenementi sui nativi in Alburgh' [*Norf*] *CourtR* 192/15 r. 11.

deaemulare [cf. CL aemulari], to follow, emulate.

to folowe, assequi .., demulare, emulari *CathA.*

deaemulus [cf. CL aemulus], following, emulous.

folowynge, demulus, emulus, imitatorius, sequax *CathA.*

deafforestare [cf. 1 afforestare, forestare], to disafforest, remove (land or residents) from forest status. *V. et. deforestare, difforestare, disafforestare, exforestare.*

1184 quod nullus .. faciat aliquam forstallationem feris suis .. inter forestam suam et boscos vel alia loca per ipsum [regem] vel progenitores suos ~atos (*Ass. Forest.* 16) R. HOWD. II 248*n.*; **1203** r.c. de lx m. .. pro manerio suo de S. ~ando *Pipe* 6; **1204** concessimus hominibus de Cornubia qui finem fecerunt nobiscum pro Cornubia deaforestanda, .. quod, si qui venati fuerint .. infra divisas deaforestatas .. et non fuerint participes finis quem .. fecerunt pro deaforestacione predicta .., quod (*sic*) .. misericordiam nostram incidant *Pat* 40a; **1204** sciatis nos omnino deaforestasse forestam de Browuda de omnibus que ad forestam et forestarios pertinent; quare .. precipimus quod predicta foresta et homines in ea manentes .. sint deaforestati inperpetuum *RChart* 122a; **1209** milites et homines manentes in Brewode in Salopsir' dant domino regi c m. ut ipsi et heredes eorum sint inperpetuum ~ati *SelPlForest* 9; **1215** omnes foreste que aforestate sunt tempore nostro statim ~entur *Magna Carta* 47; **1217, s1225, 1293** (v. 1 afforestare); s**1225** ut xij milites vel liberi homines eligerentur ad deambulandum metas forestarum, ut .. que foreste remanere ut fuerunt prius et que ~ari debeant discernatur WEND. II 286; **1227** (v. deawarennare); **1275** rex H. diaforestavit (*sic* MS) dictum mariscum *Hund.* I 252; **1284, 1296** (v. dewarennare). **1377** quod dicta placea .. sit omnino ~ata inperpetuum *Reg. Brev. Jud.* 83b; *a foreste*, foresta; .. ~are est forestam destruere *CathA.*

deafforestatio [cf. afforestatio], disafforestation. *V. et. deforestatio, difforestatio, disafforestatio.*

1204 deaforestacione *Pat* 40a (v. deafforestare); **1204** collectoribus pecunie de ~one Devon' etc. *Cl* 10b; **1205** preter concessionem .. quam fecimus Willelmo .. de ~one manerii sui de S. .., concessimus eidem .. ut habeat percursum canum .. suorum usque ad coopertum foreste nostre *RChart* 153b; **1275** post ~onem foreste de Horewell' *Hund.* II 284; s**1300** ut .. ~ones .. a rege sepius concessas sed hactenus opere non completas .. fieri juberet discretas *Flor. Hist.* III app. 303; **1397** (v. 2 dominium 1b).

deafragma v. diaphragma.

deagitare [cf. CL agitare], (?) to debate or decide.

1266 (17c) eo quod causa pro qua x li. debentur non fuit ~ata in Fyfe *ExchScot* 32.

dealbare [CL], **~iare**

1 to whitewash; **b** (fig.).

s**1183** (v. deforis 2d); **1195** pro aula .. ~anda, xlix s. *Pipe* 142; **1212** (v. coquina 1d); **1240** cameram ubi milites jacent ~ari et lineari .. faciatis *Cl* 178; **1255** pars calcis posita fuit ad murum †dealbiatidum [l. ~iandum]; et statim cecidit ~iata *Hund.* II 41; **1296** in mercedes Duncani pictoris pro hurdicea galee ~anda ad tachiam *Ac. Galley Newcastle* 178; **1366, 1370** (v. daubare); **1395** una biga calcis pro capella ~anda *Cant. Coll. Ox.* II 141; **1437** plaustranti et ~anti parietes *Ac. Obed. Abingd.* 113; **1452** ad progettand' et ~and' muros petrinos turris campanarum *Ac. Churchw. Som* 185. **b** ut quicquid mecum confuse depinxi, sapientis discretioni ~andum supponam ADEL. *ED* 3; adulator vitia cujusque ~at J. SAL. *Pol.* 483A; talibus verbis facinus .. ~at et colorat GIR. *Symb.* I 31 p. 326; ficta / forma, dealbatus paries et hypocrita verbum / se simulans VINSAUF *PN* 744 (cf. *Acts* xxiii 3; *Math.* xxiii 27).

2 a to refine (silver). **b** to 'blanch' (payment of farm), adjust to offset deficiency in assay (*cf. albus* 6, *blancus* 2). **c** to silver (alch.; *cf. albus* 5d). **d** to coat w. silver or tin.

a **1196** pro una huchia facienda et una fabrica et utensilibus faciendis ad ~andum argentum *Pipe* 20; **1280** magister .. monetam reddet domino regi coctam et ~atam et paratam in omnibus *RBExch* 985; **1452** in j *blanchyngbasyn* pro moneta ~anda et mundificanda *KRAc* 294/7. **b** quod solutum est in thesauro et ~atum detrahitur. .. post hec .. que alias soluta sunt .. per acervos disponuntur et hec per subtractionem xij denariorum e singulis libris ~antur, sicut que in thesauro solvuntur ~ata per combustionem *Dial. Scac.* II 28; **1229** [denarii] positi ad examen ignis lacaverunt in primo assaio xiiij d. et in secundo xij d. .. ~atur libra ad vij denarios, salvo regi

clamio ad combustionem ut, si plus cadat in tercia combustione, plus ∼etur (*LTRMem* 11 r. 7) *Hist. Exch.* 193*n.* **c** ex argento et ramo ∼ato cum medicina fit plus argentum in apparentia M. Scot *Part.* 295 (cf. ib. 297: sulphuris .., suffumigatio cujus ∼at setam zallam et folia rose et lilii); pulvis iste .. laborat perfecte in sole et optime constringit mercurium et ultra modum ∼at erem *Id. Alch.* 154; Dastin *Ros.* 6 (v. coquere 3b); ∼a cuprum et habes magisterium Ripley 225 (*recte* 224); tunc habebis mercurium .. albissimum instar lactis, atque hoc est nostrum lac virginis, menstruum ∼atum, et argentum vivum nostrum philosophice exuberatum *Ib.* 309. **d** s**1297** pollardi deintus erant de cupro et stanno, deforis autem tenuiter ∼ati, ut †appararent [l. apparerent] de argento *Ann. Angl. & Scot.* 380; **1329** in x lib. stanni pro clavis ∼andis *ExchScot* 125.

3 a to taw (hide, in making white leather or parchment). **b** to bleach (cloth). **c** to blanch (almonds).

a 1198 in custamento .. ∼andi coria ferarum *Pipe* 147; **1211** in loricis ∼andis *Pipe Wint.* 42; **1226** (v. corium 1b); **1306** in percameno ∼ato *MinAc* 856/15 m. 2; **1310** in corio j affri ∼ando ad emendacionem harnes' *Ib.* 992/8; **1318** (v. corium 1c); **1345** in vij correis equinis et stircinis .. ∼andis pro harnas' carrectariorum *Ac. Durh.* 544. **b 1292** pro manutergiis ∼andis et telis *Sacr. Ely* II 7; **1316** [*linen cloth placed on lord's common*] ∼andam *CourtR Wakefield* IV 108. **c** lac amigdalarum dulcium ∼atarum Gad. 5v. 2.

4 a to whiten, make white; **b** (w. ref. to complexion); **c** (fig., w. ref. to baptism or absolution); **d** (fig., w. ref. to Premonstratensian habit).

a parietes lavans secundum prophetam [*Psalm* l 9] super nivem ∼avit Eddi 16; sanguis superfluus in muliere pregnante .. ∼atus transit in lactis naturam Ric. Med. *Anat.* 228; s**1255** propter senium, quod caput suum ∼averat M. Par. *Maj.* V 523; melius est .. ut [oleum] decoquatur in aquis temperatis .. donec purgetur et ∼etur Bacon *NM* 547; frequens inunccio cum oleo olive dentes ∼at Gad. 119v. 2; calor [materiam] humidam denigrat et siccam ∼at Upton 102. **b** ponitur in unguento ∼ante faciem cum cerusa et marmore albo .. et pinguedine gallinacea, quod optimum est mulieribus volentibus habere faciei dealbacionem Gad. 134. 1; fuco adulterine fallacie facies suas colorant et ∼ant Rolle *IA* 266; ejus [gerse] usus est ad facies ∼andas *Alph.* 74. **c 618** (13c) ego Ædbaldus rex .., quem .. Augustinus .. ∼atum fonte baptismatis sanctorum collegio copulavit *CS* 13; E. rex Cantuariorum ad fidem Christi correctus, ejus baptismo ∼atus cum sua enituit natione *V. Greg.* p. 86; ut is qui Domino peccaverat .. ablutus sit .. et super nivem ∼atus Bede *Tab.* 459; ecclesia, .. Christi .. sponsa ∼ata O. Cant. *Const.* 1. **d** vallis .. ista virtutum floribus erit ∼ata *Chr. Dale* 6.

5 to clothe in white; **b** (w. ref. to novices at time of profession); **c** (w. ref. to Cistercian habit).

procedit ∼atus .. clericorum cuneus Samson *Mir. Edm.* I 5 p. 124. **b** s**1270** statutum est .. quod novicii .. in sexta feria semper suam facient (*sic*) professionem atque .. in Dominica ∼entur *Cust. Westm.* 226; nullus eorum [noviciorum] antequam ∼etur, licet sacerdos fuerit, vinum in calicem fundere consuevit *Cust. Cant.* 270. **c** s**1099** cenobium Cisterciense incipitur, principium ordinis ∼ati Diceto *Chr.* 232.

dealbatio [LL]

1 whitewashing.

1236 in ∼one claustri *Invent. Ch. Ch.* 114; **1329** pro j celdra calcis albe empta pro ∼one .. camere *ExchScot* 125; **1345** pro ∼one et perjactatione parietum capelle *MinAc* 1120/12 r. 2 (1) *d.*; **1358** pro ∼one, ocriacione, et vernacione camere (*KRAc* 472/4) *Building in Eng.* 159; cum dicitur .. '*A* est ∼o parietis', illud nomen verbale .. '∼o' non significat principaliter .. parietem albam, sed denotat medium †quo [v. l. quod] competit tali .. parieti (Wynterton) *Ziz.* 203; **1422** (v. brusca 2).

2 a 'blanching' (allowance for deficiency in assay); **b** silvering (alch.).

a s**1248** pro opere aurifabrili, id est monetationis, quam vulgariter ∼onem vocabant, pro qualibet libra xiij d. solvebantur M. Par. *Maj.* V 18; c**1285** (v. denarius 4b); **1297** (v. albus 6a). **b** ∼o eris perfecta secundum Barbanum Saracenum de Alap M. Scot *Alch.* 154; ignis in solucione semper erit lenis, .. in ∼one continuus, in rubificacione fortis Dastin *Ros.* 6; ex hoc [sc. mercurio sublimato] excluduntur omnes ∼ones, citrinaciones [etc.] Ripley 392.

3 a tawing (of hide). **b** bleaching (of cloth).

a in ∼one j corii equini et j corii affri *Ac. Beaulieu* 141; **1276** in ∼one corii j jumenti de morina *Ac. Stratton* 191; **1283** cuidam pelletario pro ∼one c pellium agnorum *Ac. Wellingb.* 32; **1287** pro ∼one iij loricarum et iij parium de coopertur' *KRAc* 351/28 m. 3; **1306** in ∼one corii j bovis, iiij d.; item in ∼one coriorum ij porcorum, iiij d. *MinAc* 856/15 m. 2; **1533** pro tannacione et ∼one ij pellium equorum *Househ. Bk. Durh.* 158. **b 1302** pro ∼one linee tele *Sacr. Ely* II 18; **1395** cum suicione et ∼one .. napirie *Ac. Durh.* 598.

4 whitening, turning white; **b** (w. ref. to complexion).

quelibet species flegmatis, cum plenaria fiat ejus resolutio, urinam reddet tenuem et albam ..; unde in qualibet specie potest fieri .. plenaria resolutio et ∼o et ejusdem attenuatio Gilb. I 307v. 2; sicut ∼o vadit in unam speciem coloris et est unus motus specie, et hec ∼o est unus motus numero Bacon II 144. **b** Gad. 134. 1 (v. dealbare 4b); alcanna .. valet ad mundificacionem et ∼onem cutis *Alph.* 7.

5 wearing of white; **b** (by novices at profession). *V. et. exalbatio.*

circulum .. princeps ob reverenciam sue ∼onis ipso die feret continue capite denudato W. Say *Lib. Reg. Cap.* 92. **b** si forte radatur conventus dum sic novicii in albis existunt, radi debent post ∼onem priusquam alicubi in conventu appareant *Cust. Cant.* 273; s**1422** quatenus .. singulos novicios ad ipsum [juramentum professionis] in eo loco [sc. in capitulo] prestandum inducerent in die ∼onis eorundem Amund. I 98.

dealbativus, whitening (fig.), purificatory.

sic nubes peccati dissolvitur in pluviam lachrymarum .. sordium purgativam et super nivem ∼am anime peccatricis Bradw. *CD* 395c.

dealbator [LL]

1 whitewasher; **b** (fig.).

1212 (v. 1 appositor); **1253** in stipendiis .. Ade ∼oris cum serviente *Ac. Build. Hen. III* 268. **b** procedant nunc ∼ores potentum, susurrent aut .. preconentur principem non esse legi subjectum J. Sal. *Pol.* 527b.

2 whittawyer.

1184 [rex] precipit quod nullus tannator vel ∼or coriorum maneat in forestis suis extra burgum (*Ass. Forest.* 15) R. Howd. II 247*n.*

dealbescere, to become white.

pone istas formas cere in sole calido .. verte eas sepe ex omni parte donec ∼ant Gad. 134. 1.

dealbiare, ∼iatidum v. dealbare.

dealis [cf. LL dealiter], godlike, deiform. *Cf.* 1 *dialis.*

∼ibus, i. deificis, *godlicum GlH* D 404; **1432** ipsa .. ∼is effigies .. illud propheticum [*Psalm* xci 16] emisit: 'longitudine dierum replebo eum' (J. Carpenter) *MGL* III 462.

dealitas [LL], divinity.

uterus Mariae .. erat talis ac tanta quae decenter in se ∼atem Filii Dei sicut lana susciperet Alcuin (*Adv. Felicem* 6. 9) *Dogm.* 210d.

deallocare [cf. allocare], **a** to disallow (item in account); *v. et. disallocare* a, *dislocare* 2. **b** to disappoint (petitioner).

a 1327 cujus quidem summe particule cancellantur et ∼antur eidem J. in rotulis de particulis predictis *LTRMem* 99 r. 50. **b 1456** quod .. comes [Devon'] ab eadem peticione sua ∼etur *Entries* 50.

dealmatica v. dalmaticus 2. **dealtea (diaalthaea)** v. 1 dia 1. **deamant-** v. diamandus.

deambulacrum [LL], (surrounding) walk, gallery (*cf. 1 Kings* vii 2).

∼um, circuitus, *embgong GlH* D 407.

deambulare [CL]

1 to walk (about). **b** (trans.) to walk in or on. **c** (w. *in*) to collide with (fig.). **d** (of fire) to run through. **e** (of skin disease) to move about.

V. Cuthb. IV 16 (v. ductus 1); spatiatur, ∼at *GlC* S 443; videas .. istam [puellam] ∼ando productis filis quasi telam ordiri Gir. *IK* I 2; *Id. Spec.* III 13 (v. curia 10c); sicut volo ∼are propter sanitatem; ad quam tamen deambulationem sequitur fatigatio, si excedat vires animales R. Marston *QD* 405; in ecclesia vel oratorio nunquam .. sibi complacuit .. huc illucve, ut moris est mundanorum, ∼are Blakman *Hen. VI* 6. **b** quisquis ut ignotis haec deambulat atria plantis Wulf. *Swith. pref.* 47; castra in hunc modum ∼ant G. Mon. I 9 (cf. ib. 17: perveniens ad T. fluvium ∼avit litora); sibi parant [indigestionis] remedium .. per deambulationes, dicentes: "eamus et ∼emus pratorum purpuream vernantiam!" J. Godard *Ep.* 223; Machomet .. dixit: ".. Jesus maximus, dum predicando partes Jerusalem ∼aret.." M. Par. *Maj.* III 357. **c** de Pica Petrillo, ∼ante in nos et debachante cum illo, quid dicam? Gir. *Invect.* I 13. **d** fenestre, que illinite erant pice, accendebantur, et ignis ∼abat totam domum Gilb. I 6. 1. **e** Gad. 25. 2 (v. deambulativus).

2 to perambulate, beat bounds: **a** (intr.); **b** (trans.).

a 1133 sicut vicini et scientes de illa terra in circuitu ∼averunt (*Cart. Heref.*) *Royal Writs* 73; c**1228** vidit liberos homines de H. perambulare divisas .., sed non fuit unus ∼antium *Feod. Durh.* 294. **b** s**1225** (v. deafforestare); c**1228** interfuit .. ubi episcopus ∼abat divisas bosci *Feod. Durh.* 258; a**1256** concessisse .. communam .. sicut G. cum aliis probis hominibus eam .. ∼avit *BBC* (*Rathcool*) 75.

deambulatio [CL]

1 walking about. **b** sheep-walk.

cum tamen ∼one et circuitione viarum potius quam diligenti investigatione rerum Peripatheticos imitentur J. Sal. *Pol.* 663a; J. Godard *Ep.* 223 (v. deambulare 1b); R. Marston *QD* 405 (v. deambulare 1a). **b 1588** damus .. communiam pasture, pasturacionem et ∼onem pro dc ovibus *Pat* 1321 m. 12.

2 perambulation, beating of bounds.

1204 debet x m. .. pro habenda ∼one *Pipe* 137; **1219** (v. deambulator b); c**1228** requisitus an prior .. interesset dicte ∼oni divise, dicit quod non *Feod. Durh.* 259; **12..** si .. dicta terra .. per aliquam particulam terre circumjacentem per recognicionem vel per ∼onem augeatur *Reg. Dunferm.* 317.

deambulativus, (med.) mobile, diffusive.

[dolor] ∼us est ex ventositate grossa leviter se diffundens per partes corporis Gilb. II 89v. 1; humor .. extensivus fleumaticum agravativus melancolicum significat, ∼us ventositatem Bacon V 85; formica ∼a .. vocatur ignis Persicus; .. et vadit de loco in locum deambulans Gad. 25. 2.

deambulator, traverser, rambler. **b** beater of bounds, surveyor.

c**1000** vates futurorum, invisibilium spectator, poli ∼or, ipse quoque corpore in alta sublatus (*Sermo*) *Mem. Dunst.* 455. **b 1219** pone per .. salvos plegios omnes illos ∼ores quod sint coram consilio nostro .. [responsuri] quare deambulacionem illam [de foresta nostra] fecerunt sine precepto nostro *Cl* 386a; **1606** omnium .. forestariorum, rangiatorum, laundariorum, ∼orum .. *Pat* 1714 m. 13.

deambulatorius [cf. LL deambulatorium]

1 made for walking in. **b** (of justice or seal) itinerant.

disponam .. hypodromum et per gyrum arcus ∼ios (*V. Thomae Apost.*) Ord. Vit. II 8 p. 311. **b** a justiciis errantibus, quos nos ∼ios vel perlustrantes judices nominamus *Dial. Scac.* I 8 d; expressam habet imaginem et inscriptionem cum ∼io curie sigillo *Ib.* I 15.

2 (as sb. n.): **a** walk, gallery or sim. **b** passage. **c** aisle. **d** (w. *facere*) to clear a way.

a s**1174** (v. ascensorium b); **1193** pro ∼iis circa castellum *Pipe* 83; **1250** quod .. cameram regis cum oriolo et ∼io in circuitu super aquam versus orientem juxta capellam regis in .. Turri .. reparari faciant *Cl* 300; respicit consuetudinem Palestine, ubi domus in superiori parte plane sunt, unde, si non fuerint muri in circuitu vel ∼ia, periculum est magnum et occasio labenti (Docking *in Deut.* xxii 8) *Doc. Francisc.* 106; xvj .. cerei ponantur in superiori ∼io circa magnum altare *Obs. Barnwell* 76; s**1091** flamme .. ∼ium penes infirmitorium ac totum ipsum infirmitorium .. uno impetu depaste sunt *Croyl.* 97; quelibet earum [ecclesiarum Saracenorum] habet unam turrim altam ad modum campanilis et turris ∼ium externum, in quo stant eorum sacerdotes .. ad populum .. excitandum S. Sim. *Itin.* 28; **1533** Henrico Plummer pro *ly casting of ledde* pro ∼io presidentis (*Journal Queens' Coll.*) *Arch. Hist. Camb.* II 31*n.* **b 1267** a domo sua .. facere possit quandam aleyam seu ∼ium ultra vicum S. Nicholai Lond' usque ad eandem ecclesiam *Pat* 85 m. 28; **1378** in factura unius ∼ii de aula ad *le ymppeyard Ac. Durh.* 131; s**1438** in renovacione ∼ii, que (*sic*) ab illa camera ducit ad aulam Amund. II 199 (= *Reg. Whet.* I 456). **c** a**1447** in ala sive ∼io australi ecclesie ex opposito feretri S. Albani Amund. I app. 437; **1458** infra ecclesiam cathedralem Glasg' .. in navi sive ∼io ejusdem ex parte boriali *Reg. Glasg.* 392; **1504** infra ecclesiam collegiatam de Dalketh in navi sive ∼io ejusdem *Midlothian* 323. **d** s**1403** H. Percy .. irrupit in exercitum regis et fecit ∼ium in medio exercitus usque ad fortissimos regis custodes *Eul. Hist. Cont.* III 397.

deamelare [cf. esmallare], to enamel.

1329 calicem argenteum deauratum habentem .. sex nodos ∼atos in medio *Pat* 172 m. 22.

deamentro v. 1 diameter 2a.

deangustatio, constriction or (?) removal of constriction.

illa aquositas cum .. superfluitate .. per concavitatem venarum ad epar vel renes mandatur, que per vasa .. distensa libere non †valent [? l. valet] expelli, humoribus qui influunt ei obviantibus, istaque ∼one fit valida compressio spiritus Gilb. VII 312v. 1.

deante [LL]

1 (prep.) from before.

Deus .. alienigenas a facie nostra conteret et ipsorum robur ∼e suam presentiam disperdet *V. Neot. A* 16.

2 (adv.) formerly.

s**1262** pro quodam Rogero Talebot ∼e ministrum (*sic*) ipsius comitis [Glovernie] Gerv. Cant. *GR Cont.* 217.

deappellare [cf. CL appellare], to call away.

s1119 ipse [G. archiep. Vienn., in papam raptus], ~atus officio, parum agere voluit donec ab illis qui Rome erant quod isti fecerant confirmatum accepit H. CANTOR 15.

deappetitus [cf. CL appetitus], distaste, disinclination.

tales [anime] actus consecuntur quascunque potencias anime . ., sed distinccius potenciam volutivam, que eciam non solum habet appetitum vel ~um, quod est volucio vel nolucio, sed habet actus sperandi vel desperandi . ., et sic de multis actis compositis WYCL. *Act.* 2.

deaptare [cf. CL aptare], to unfit, disable.

quemadmodum . . caliditas movet et humiditas disponit, frigiditas finit . . et siccitas ~at et possibilitati contradicit et inobedientiam prestat, cum sit fortior passivarum GILB. I 6v. 2.

deaquilon (diachylon) v. 1 dia 1. **dearctare** v. deartare. **dearest-** v. dearrest-.

dearetro [al. div.; cf. aretro], in arrear.

1346 quod reddat ei iiij li. vj s. viij d. qui de a retro sunt de annuo redditu *Reg. Roff. Ep.* f. 185.

deargentatus [LL], silver-plated; **b** (fig.).

rex [Willelmus I] Roffensem ecclesiam . . in tantum dilexit ut . . ei . . dorsale . . unum cum feretro ~o dimitteret *Text. Roff.* 210v. (= *Flor. Hist.* II 17); **c1180** reddendo mihi . . annuatim una calcaria ~a (*Middleton MSS*) *HMC* 69 p. 18; **1278** (v. calcar 1b); **s1300** Gallici . . hanc monetam fabricaverant, que non erat argentea sed superficialiter ~a RISH. 195; frenum ~um *Cust. Cant.* 363; **1376** noduli de latone ~i (*LBLond.* H f. 42) *MGL* I 604; **1377** pannum de serico quadratum purpureum quatuor hastis ~atis sustentatum . . gestabunt barones de V Portibus *Lib. Regal.* 5v. (cf. *MGL* II 477); **1423** vij ciphi, unde j cum cooperculo ~o *Ac. Obed. Abingd.* 92; **1427** j zonam argenteam . . cum cultello †deargententato *Mem. Ripon* I 329; **1450** j zonam ~am *MunAcOx* 605. **b** ecce habes epistolam . . non auream vel deauratam, set ferream et ~am W. DAN. *Ep.* 62c.

deargenteus [cf. CL argenteus], silver-plated.

1315 tabula lignea ex una parte ~ea et deaurata *Invent. Ch. Ch.* 84; **1388** cathedre sunt tres pontificales, quarum una est ~ea (*Invent. Westm.*) *Arch.* LII 240.

dearmare [CL], to disarm; *v. et. disarmare.* **b** (of fortifications) to dismantle, demolish.

si quis injuste quemquam ~averit (*Cons. Cnuti*) *GAS* 351; **1203** dies datus est Rogero . . et Meurico ad audiendum judicium suum de duello invadiato . .; et tunc veniant ~ati *CurR* II 192 (cf. ib. VIII 272 = *SelPlCrown* 126). **b** quanta dearmarunt regis de luce lapilli [*gl*: bombardorum], / tanta rearmata nocte fuere loca ELMH. *Metr. Hen. V* 323.

dearmatio, demolition.

[hostes] per . . muros et turres, quamdiu fuerunt armati, necnon per ruinas, cancellos et fracta foramina post †darmacionem ipsorum, . . insidiantes *G. Hen. V* 6.

dearrestare [cf. arrestare, OF *desarrester*], to release from arrest or seizure: **a** (persons); **b** (goods *etc.*); *v. et. disarrestare.*

a 1317 fiduciam . . dearestandi, quietandi et deliberandi . . omnes de gentibus . . comitis [Lanc'] (*Pat*) *Foed.* III 667b. **b 1278** si . . innotuisset vobis . . fecissetis ~ari . . mercimonia predicta *RGasc* II 70 (= *Foed.* II 127b); **1294** precipimus quod omnes lanas, pelles lanutas, que . . fuerint †arrestata . . sine dilacione dearestari facias (*Breve Regis*) B. COTTON 246; **1315** quod . . mercimonia illa ~ari . . facerent (*CoramR*) *Law Merch.* II 86; **1335** (v. dearrestatio b); **1372** breve pro mercatoribus Flandrie, de bonis suis dearestandis (*LBLond.* G f. 28b) *MGL* I 541.

dearrestatio, release from arrest: **a** (of persons); **b** (of goods *etc.*).

a 1312 circa dearestacionem et deliberacionem Benedicti et Edwardi *Foed.* III 309b (= *TreatyR* I 503). **b 1295** cum nos mercatoribus regni Scocie . . concessimus quod naves eorum, lanas, coria, et alia mercimonia ad regnum nostrum . . possint adducere . ., super quorum averiorum ~one, si que per gentes vestras tenentur, ad vos magistrum E. . . duximus destinandum . . (*Lit. Regis Francie*) *Doc. Scot.* II 3; **1335** mandamus quod . . naves . . per vos . . arestatas . . dearestari . . permittatis. . . ballivis . . de S. Bothulfo [consimile breve] ad hujusmodi dearestaciones faciendas *RScot* 379a.

deartare [cf. 1 artare 1a], to restore to former width.

14.. quod . . permittat B. . . dearctare quandam viam . . quam C. injuste . . arctavit *Reg. Brev. Orig.* 199b.

dearticulate, point by point.

hec ~e dico, ideo quod nullus Curiensium se credere debeat excusatum PAUL. ANGL. *ASP* 1553.

deasceare [CL], to cut into shape.

~ato, i. dolato, *geholedum GlP* 475.

deasp- v. diaspr-.

deastuppare [cf. astuppare, AN *desestoper, destuper*, OF *destoupper*], to stop up, block. *V. et. distuppare.*

1223 deastupavit [v. l. distupavit] unam gutteram, per quam aqua superhabundavit *CurR* XI 1072.

deauctorizare [cf. auctorizare], to deprive of authority, discredit.

s1253 propter judicium justiciariorum, ne viderentur, dum regium lucrum sitirent, ~ari *G. S. Alb.* I 341.

deaurare [LL]

1 to gild; **b** (prov.). **c** (fig.) to enrich, reward. **d** (fig.) to gloss over. **e** (p. ppl.) clad in gold.

~atas simulacrorum effigies ALDH. *VirgP* 47; **c750** (v. argenteus 1a); **840** (11c) dedit . . unam cuppam ~atam in duobus pundis *CS* 430; Alfwara [ob. **1007**] dedit . . sacerdotalia ornamenta et v marcas auri . . ad hec omnia ~anda *Chr. Rams.* 84; **s1040** cassidem ex parte ~atam FL. WORC. I 195; **1155** pro auro ad ~anda frena *Pipe* 4; duos libellos nostros . . cum duobus unciis auri, quibus ~ari possent, . . transmisimus GIR. *Symb.* I 30; **1199** (v. calcar 1b); **1242** pro pondere iiij d. ob. puri auri ad septrum B. Edwardi ~andum *Liberate* 16 m. 6; si lapis . . quo cambiatores examinant aurum pulverizetur . ., de hoc liquore liniantur [capilli] et ~abuntur GILB. II 77v. 2; per liberum servicium . . j paris calcarium †deauratariorum [? l. deauratarum] HENGHAM *Magna* 1; **1298** j cuppa de cupro †deauratus [l. deaurata] (*Invent. S. Paul.*) *Arch.* L 463; WHITTLESEY 169 (v. argentum 1a); **1377** (v. campanella d); **1406** currus et *wherle* garnit' infra cum panno †adaureo [MS: adaur'] cla[vis] de cupr[o] †deaureo [MS: deaur'] . . (*KRAc* 406/10) *Arch.* LXVII 181; **1431** j ciphum argenteum stantem super tres leones parcellatim ~at' *Reg. Cant.* II 439; argenteos calices quaquaversum ~atos FERR. *Kinloss* 73. **b** rite scelus ratus est lutum deaurare *Poem S. Thom.* 85; NECKAM *NR* II 180 (v. castigate). **c c717** quantos labore proprios adquaesieris, de tantis ante tribunal aeterni regis dux futurus ~atus gaudebis (ECGBURG) *Ep. Bonif.* 13; Phoroneus rex, qui . . primus Grecorum studia ~avit MAP *NC* IV 3 f. 45v.; sine tribulatione non ~atur animus auro sapientie NECKAM *NR* II 55. **d s1189** Ricardus . . matri sue . . honorem exhibere curavit, ut in obsequio materno quod in patrem commiserat ~atum omnibus appareret DICETO *YH* 68. **e** Romanus pontifex . ., collabentibus ecclesiis, . . non modo purpuratus sed ~atus incedit J. SAL. *Pol.* 624A.

2 to strip of gold or (?) to stain w. blood. *Cf. deauratio* 2.

~abit illud [frenum] aquila rupti federis (*Proph. Merlini*) G. MON. VII 3.

3 (p. ppl. as sb. f. or m.) dory (fish). *Cf. dorea.*

1248 quod fieri faciant . . cccc pastillos, unde una pars sit de salmonibus et alia pars de turbuttis et alia pars de ~atis *Cl* 54; pisces scamosi aque dulcis . . currentis, lucii . ., darsi, pertice, †alande [l. alause], daurate GILB. II 95. 2; **1299** item †doracum [l. doratum] meliorem pro v d. *MGL* II 118.

deauratio [LL]

1 gilding. **b** (fig.) glossing over (w. play on ἐπίχρυσος ; *cf.* 1 *apocrisis*).

tanta est virtus vivi argenti ut sine ejus beneficio non possit fieri ~o NECKAM *NR* II 55; *RBExch* 979 (v. 3 casus 1e); **1355** in parciali ~one ejusdem pelvis *DCCant.* DE 3 f. 2; **1404** ij par de *bedys* pro ~one in vitro colorato *Ac. Durh.* 397; **1452** Thome Goldsmyth pro . . ~one j *knopp* pro magna murra *Ib.* 147; *CathA* (v. 1 apocrisis); **1516** pro iij quar. *les* auri pro ~one j stelle super ymaginem B. M. et cuidam pictori pro pictione et ~one ejusdem stelle *Fabr. York* 97. **b c1200** exponitur ypocrisis Latine deauracio, / et nullum viciosius est vicium hoc vicio (*Hypocr. Prelatorum*) *EHR* V 322.

2 stripping off of gold or (?) bloodshed. *Cf. deaurare* 2.

erit ~o in templis, nec acumen gladiorum cessabit (*Proph. Merlini*) G. MON. VII 3.

deauratura, gilding.

orientalis pars feretri est de argento cum ~a [v. l. deaurata] per loca *Lib. Eli.* III 50 (cf. ib.: ymagines de argento sine ~a).

deaureus v. deaurare 1a.

deawarennare [cf. awarennare], to diswarren, remove (land) from warren status. *V. et. dewarennare, diswarennare.*

1227 quod tota warenna de Stanes . . sit deawarrenata [*Cal.*: †dewarrenata] et deafforestata inperpetuum *ChartR* 19 m. 5 (cf. *Cl* 197b, *MGL* I 136); **1279** consideratum est quod warenna . . †deawarrerantur *PQW* 741a (cf. ib.: rex concessit . . quod omnes terre in com. [Surr'] . . disaforestarentur et †deawaranentur).

debacari v. debacchari.

debacchantia, fury, savagery.

hoc quippe sacrilegi opus omnem . . Neronis . . aliorumve hostium Christi excedit ~iam H. BOS. *Thom.* IV 9.

debacchari [CL], **~are,** to rage, vent fury (on); **b** (w. *in* & acc.); **c** (of animal); **d** (of elements); **e** (w. abstr. subj.). **f** (p. ppl.) frantic, furious.

coepit quasi . . freniticus . . sartagines basiare, in quibus diu . . debachatus et . . ludificatus abscedit ALDH. *VirgP* 50; totas eorum provincias ~ando pervagatus BEDE *HE* II 20; **934** (10c) filios . . rictibus ~ando venenosis mordaciter dilacerat *CS* 702 (= *MonA* I 59b: †debactando); ne ipsi ~arentur propter captionem apostoli LANFR. *Comment. Paul.* (*Phil.* i 12) 308; **s1365** (v. comitiva 2e); debacor, A. *to wex wilde WW.* **b** [Maximus] tanta insania in dominos ~atus est . . GILDAS *EB* 13; Caduallo . . ita debachatus est in Saxones ut ne sexui quidem muliebri . . parceret G. MON. XII 9; pontifices suum sic archipresulem judicantes, quin potius linguis in archipresulem suum . . ~antes H. BOS. *Thom.* III 33; GIR. *Invect.* I 13 (v. deambulare 1c); potenciam . . qua posset secundum libitum in subjectos ~are OCKHAM *Dial.* 873. **c** lupus . . toto malignitatis impetu debaccando grassabatur R. COLD. *Godr.* 51. **d** videres . . ventorum flabra debachando insurgere *Id. Cuthb.* 75; cum turbulenta debacantur maria *Ps.*-ELMH. *Hen. V* 115. **e s1296** contra . . regem . . bella debacancia *Chr. S. Edm.* 63; **1399** virus pestiferum [nobilium rebellancium] in persone nostre prejudicium . . ~avit (*Lit. Reg. Romanorum*) BEKYNTON I 288; mutua inquietandi debacantur conamina *Ps.*-ELMH. *Hen. V* 102. **f 9..** debachatus, *wedende WW*; **s1305** W. Waleys . . Nerone vesania ~atior *Flor. Hist.* III 123.

debacchatio [LL], fury, frenzy; **b** (of animals); **c** (of abstr.).

c675 (14c) contra hanc . . cartulam . . sacrilega debacacione venire *CS* 107; rabiem proprie debacationis . . in familiam effudit PULL. *CM* 203; **s1263** [barones] non erubescebant . . consueto ~onis genere . . depopulare provincias WYKES 139; **s1381** nebulonum debaccaciones *V. Ric. II* 30. **b** boves . . in mare propinquum . . quasi furibunda debacatione precipitati sunt GIR. *GE* I 54. **c s1455** letus . . quod sic evaderet nec majus damnum susciperet in tanti strepitus debaccacione *Reg. Whet.* I 172.

debactari v. debacchari. **debata** v. debatum.

debatabilis [cf. OF *debatable*], debatable, disputable (Scot.): **a** (of lands); **b** (of matters).

a 1457 super perambulacione facta de marchiis terrarum ~ium *Reg. Dunferm.* 454; **1489** ad inspiciendum *le fischgarth* de Esk et terras ~es ibidem adjacentes *RScot* 490a. **b 1466** in quadam causa . . versus quamdam peciam terre . ., cujus diocesis . . est inter . . episcopos S. et B. debatabiles [? l. debatabilis] seu †litigiosos *Reg. Brechin* I 191; **1475** in quibusdam causis ~ibus . . desuper nonnullis decimis et aliis rebus inter eosdem ~ibus *Midlothian* 71; **1492** super . . querelis et questionibus . . inter eosdem ~ibus *Reg. Moray* 241.

debatare [cf. OF *debatre* < CL debattuere], to dispute.

1458 si . . accio, variacio, aut debata sit mota inter aliquos serviencium, . . aliquorum parcium . ., extunc . . nullus . . parcium . . manuteneat . . aliquem illorum qui sic volunt placitare, variare aut ~are *Reg. Whet.* I 306.

debatarius, ~or [cf. OF *debateor*], brawler.

1374 [*W. R. indicted for being*] communis ~arius *Cal. Pl. Mem. Lond.* II 181; **1417** transgressores, rebelles, ~ores, et omnes alios malefactores *RNorm* 164.

debatum, ~a [cf. OF *debat*], debate, dispute. **b** brawl.

1313 pretextu cujusdam ~i inter B. de B. militem et B. de G. domicellum super alta jurisdiccione *RGasc* IV 1020 (cf. ib. 1626 p. 472b [**1315**]: in dicta bastida . . non fiat ~um de non vendendo bladum et alia victualia); **1335** potestatem ad . . tractandum . . super guerrarum discordiis, dissensionibus, controversiis et ~is quibuscumque *RScot* 387a; **1343** ad tractandum . . super universis et singulis questionibus, querelis, controversiis, arestis, demandis et †delatis [cf. *Foed.* V 366: debatis] (*Lit. Regis*) AD. MUR. *Chr.* 137; **1431** cum plures querele, dissensiones, et ~e nuper exorte fuerint inter . . abbatem de S. Albano . . et W. F. (*Arbitratio*) AMUND. I 266; **1447** super controversia et ~a motis inter . . magistrum J. M. canonicum . . et dominum J. M. capellanum . . super jure de recto cujusdam tenementi (*Conventio*) *Reg. Glasg.* 367; **b 1366** in quadam ~a inter . . Henricum F. . ., unum pagettorum officii saucerie hospicii nostri et G. Portour de officio squillarie . ., predictus G. auriculam ipsius H. in ore suo iracunde et maliciose cepit et momordit *Pat* 274 m. 5.

debaudatus v. debroudatus.

debellare [CL]

1 to fight, go on fighting.

1316 adversus . . regem . . conspirantes . . jam diucius unanimiter ~arunt *Conc.* II 458b; **1327** (v. comproditor); ante maritagium puelle Orwen illi duo reges [Elfridus et Athelbertus] semper ~abant *Eul. Hist.* II 379; eo usque ~arunt donec demum vi armorum . . dissipata est fortitudo eorum *G. Hen. V* 7.

2 (trans.) to subdue, defeat: **a** (person, also fig.); **b** (w. inanim. obj., also fig.).

a exercitum ad ~andum Aedilfridum colligit copiosum BEDE *HE* II 12 p.110; hi non jam hostes sed homines, non rebelles sed ~ati GIR. *EH* I 14; blande debellaturus Achivos / prevelat fraudes J. EXON. *BT* III 161; **s1221** Johannes Presbyter .. mandaverat caliphe .. quod eum ~aturus esset COGGESH. *Chr.* 119; **s1265** (v. commarchio 2); **s1346** (v. decaballare); non solum alios sed et se ipsum sufficit ~are FORTESCUE *LLA* 37. **b** fragoribus / turgentis Tithis tellurem / debellantis per terrorem (ÆTHELWALD) *Carm. Aldh.* 2. 52; **s1270** cum per duos dies et totidem noctes eam [Tonicam] ~aret .., castrum .. sibi subjugavit B. COTTON 144; ibi est locus a majori constructive, sicut hic: 'rex potest ~are castrum, ergo miles' R. MARSTON *QD* 305; **1413** (v. assilire 2b).

3 (Scot.) to wage judicial duel against.

si .. aliquem appellent de .. aliquo .. malefacto per quod duellum possit oriri, bene liceat eis .. in curia regis vel in aliqua alia curia defendentem ~are per interpositam personam, si .. (*Stat. Alex. II* 8) *APScot* I 70.

debellatio [LL], fighting, attacking; **b** (w. subj. gen.); **c** (w. obj. gen.).

partem illam quam subjugare nequibat diris ~onibus infestare laboravit G. MON. V 2; **s1322** depredaciones .. et ~ones hostiles cum equis et armis *G. Ed. II Bridl.* 77. **b** **s1118** continua ~o jam dictorum principum .. regem vexavit H. HUNT. *HA* VII 30. **c** **1383** pro salvacione .. marchiarum .. ac ~one et destruccione Scotorum *RScot* 59b; **s1415** peciere suppliciter ut rex .. cessaret ab eorum ~one WALS. *HA* II 308; **1587** subditos nostros .. commissos in resistenciam et ~onem Hispanorum *Pat* 1320 m. 7*d*.

debellator [CL], subduer or (?) attacker (also fig.). **b** (?) rebel.

Hilarius .. Arianae perfidiae fortissimus ~or ALCUIN (*Adv. Elipand.*) *Dogm.* 279A; imbellium ~or, rebellium blanditor GIR. *EH* II 16. **b** **s1283** membra ejus [David, fratris Leulini] in quatuor partes desecta in penam †depellatoris *Lanercost* 112.

debellatrix [LL], subduer (f.).

carnis munditiam .., quam .. omnium vitiorum potentem quandam ~icem agnoscit AILR. *SS Hex* 6; **1234** (v. dissolutio 4b).

debellio, warfare or (?) *f. l.*

1339 Scotis .. per nequam debellionis [v. l. rebellionis] demenciam contra naturalem dominum calcitrare conantibus (*Lit. Regis*) AD. MUR. *Chr.* 95.

debentura, debenture.

1427 per billas de ~a, indenturas, et alias evidencias *RParl* IV 324b.

debēre [CL]

1 to owe: **a** money or goods (also absol.); **b** service (feud. or man.); **c** service (fig.); **d** oneself (fig.); **e** penalty; **f** (with *quod* or *hoc* .. *quod*) the fact that (fig.). **g** (pr. ppl. as sb.) debtor (Gasc.).

a ~ita pensio, *gedaebeni geabuli GlC* D 69; primo .. abacum, i. e. abaci scientiam ingrediens, debitores cum debitis propone, et .. numerum eorum qui ~ent et eorum que ~entur .., summamque ex eorum multiplicatione descendentem diligenter ordina THURKILL *Abac.* 56; **c1131** omnes debitores qui civibus debita ~ent eis reddant vel in London' se disrationent quod non ~ent (*Ch. Hen. I*) *GAS* 525; Haugustaldensis ecclesia .. nec propter synodum nec propter crisma .. episcopo Dunelmensi .. aliquod debitum seu aliquam consuetudinem ~et RIC. HEX. *Hist. Hex.* II 3; **1198** Rogerus .. venit et recognovit quod ~et Nicolao .. xx s. de debito R. vicecomitis *CurR* I 51; H. AVR. *Hugh* 825 (v. de 10a); **1243** (v. catallum 2a); **1253** (v. creatio 2a); **1282** mandamus quatinus .. [Reymundo] vadia cum arreragiis et ~enda quamdiu in servicio nostro fuerit .. liberetis *RGasc* II 263. **b** **1166** ~eo inde regi servitium de l militibus *RBExch* 348; **1199** ~entur ei de feudo illo viij s. annuatim de firma et preterea forinsecum servicium *CurR* I 114; **1228** (v. consuetudo 3a); **1239** ~ent sectam (v. comitatus 6b); **1279** (v. columbar 1); **c1283** W. B. ~et omnes consuetudines et opera sicut W. S. *Cust. Battle* 10; **1294** omnes isti ~ent corporale servicium quando dominus rex exigit servicium suum de comitibus et baronibus Anglie *SelPlMan* 76 (cf. ib. 64 [**1258**]: omnes qui ~ent servicium per corpora); **c1357** pro operibus suis annualibus ~itis manerio de F. *Ac. Durh.* 558. **c** quid ~erent [AS: *hwæt sceoldon*] mihi [accipitres] nisi scirem domitare eos? ÆLF. *Coll.* 95. **d** totum me illi ~eo semperque ~ebo SERLO GRAM. *Mon. Font.* 117. **e** quaecunque illi ~ebantur supplicia BEDE *HE* I 7. **f** omne compositum ut subsistat indiget iis ex quibus componitur et illis ~et quod est ANSELM (*Mon.* 17) I 31; hoc .. nostre diligentie digne ~eri non diffido, quod .. exemplo virtutis .. vigor accrescat GIR. *TH pref.* 2 p. 21. **g** **1289** mandamus .. ut .. debitores Petri .. compellatis .. ad solvendum Petro .. debita .. de quibus docuerint per eorundem ~encium confessionem *RGasc* II 433.

2 (p. ppl.) due, merited, fitting.

in altiore dignitate positis .. ~itum denegare honorem GILDAS *EB* 4; a Christo remuneratore nostro ~itum victoriae triumphum percepturi ALDH. *VirgP* 11; diem ~ita solemnitate recolimus BEDE *Hom.* I 13. 226; ~itus usus, i. congruus, *neadgewuna* vel *geneadod bryce GlH* D 388; ~itum, *rihtlice* vel *wurþlice GlP* 886; ~itum solvat officium AILR. *Inst. Inclus.* 645; ~ita funeris obsequia *Dial. Scac.* II 4 D; luna ~ita luminositate destituta GIR. *TH* II 3; sic mundi machina in esse ordine ~ito servaretur BART. ANGL. IV 4; **1300** (v. allocantia); **1455** perdonavimus .. abbati .. contemptus .. unde .. caderet in demandam ~itam seu in finem et redempcionem aut in alias penas *Reg. Whet.* I 196.

3 (p. ppl. as sb. n.) debt, due; **b** (payable to crown). **c** (w. *in*) (involved) in debt.

in burgo habet Normannus ij burgenses, unum in vadimonio contra eundem et alterum pro ~ito *DB* II 438; THURKILL *Abac.* 56, **c1131**, RIC. HEX. *Hist. Hex.* II 3 (v. 1a supra); **1224** de denariis quo[s] recepisti .. de ~etis (*sic*) nostris *Cl* 636a; **1290** nolentes quod aliquid a Christianis predictis racione ~itorum predictorum .. exigatur preterquam ~ita principalia tantum que a Judeis .. receperunt *SelPlJews* xli; **1306** acsi recognicio illa de mero ~ito ju[x]ta formam statuti .. facta fuisset *Cl* 115 m. 3; **1408** in j equo griseo recepto de Roberto .. pro malo ~ito vij li. *Ac. Durh.* 401; **1448** (v. componere 7c). **b** †**964** (12c) habeat .. ipsum *hundred* cum omnimodis ~itis quae rex antea in eo habuit .. et proprii juris ~itum transgressionis *CS* 1135; haec terra non geldavit nec ullum ~itum reddidit *DB* I 158v.; tota civitas ex omnibus ~itis reddebat T. R. E. xv li. et v s. et iij d. in uno anno *Ib.* II 107; **1217** etc. (v. clarus 5b); **1238** etc. (v. atterminare 2b); **1297** pro quodam ~ito ix li. et vj s. quos .. debuit regi de pluribus ~itis [? i.e. *debts to be collected by the accountant*] *SelCExchPl* 155; **1322** capiendo pro quolibet animali capto et detento in falda pro ~ito domini regis .. j ob. *IPM* 69/6; **1333** ~ita .. de viridi cera (v. 1 cera 2c). **c** **1203** R. B., qui in nostro ~ito est *CurR* II 252; **1227** fuit in ~ito domini regis pro Judeis *LTRMem* 9 r. 3 (2) *d.*; **1380** officium [feretrarii] est in ~ito diversis *Ac. Durh.* 423.

4 (p. ppl. as sb. n.) debt: **a** (fig); **b** (w. ref. to death); **c** (original sin); **d** (conjugal rights); **e** (excretion).

a nunc persolvo ~itum multo tempore antea exactum GILDAS *EB* 1. **b** cum generale mortis naturae ~itum suprema sorte persolverit ALDH. *VirgP* 24; si dominus ejus .. ~ita carnis solverit *Dial. Scac.* II 4 D; **1338** (v. caro 4e); **1419** non ita disposuit [omnium gubernator] ut finetenus alicui .. a solucione communis ~iti parceret *Reg. Cant.* I 60; antequam ad annos pubertatis .. pervenerat, nature ~itum persolvit *Plusc.* VII 30. **c** **957** (14c) idem crimen eademque poena quasi per ~itum primae praevaricationis ad operandam .. iniquitatem omnes jure constrinxit *CS* 995. **d** quod cum causa sobolis coitur, aut ut ~itum reddatur aut .. ut fornicatio evitetur PULL. *Sent.* 948C; queritur si conjugati, in quibus est subsecuta carnalis copula, possint negare ~itum, uno proponente .. converti ad monasterium HALES *Sent.* IV 508. **e** W. CANT. *Mir. Thom.* II 65 (v. contentivus a); R. COLD. *Godr.* 242 (v. constipatio 2).

5 (w. inf.) to be bound, obliged: **a** (by duty or right); **b** (by rule or custom); **c** (by necessity). **d** to have the right, be entitled.

a et pastores, qui exemplo esse omni plebi ~uerint, .. vino madidi torpebant resoluti GILDAS *EB* 22; duplam .. vitam, / quam rector debet justa discernere lance ALDH. *VirgV* 833; eos quos defendere ~uerat inermes reliquit BEDE *HE* II 2; ÆLF. *Ep.* 20 (v. columna 1d); concessa est [j hida] eidem in vita sua tantum tenere, et post mortem ejus ad aecclesiam ~ebat redire *DB* I 47; fremunt .. canonici quod terras que sue deberent famulari ecclesie T. archiepiscopus monachis dederit W. MALM. *GP* IV 155; **1265** vobis, qui ordinacionum .. conscii estis et testes esse ~etis *Cl* 67; **1275** quos quidem lv s. .. T. ~uit solvisse ad festum S. Mich. *SelPlMan* 146; **1287** purpresturas .. in postremum statum reduci †debilant [l. debebant] *Bury St. E.* 175; **1312** (v. consuetudinarius 1b); **1327** appropriacionis causas .. sufficientes esse et de jure sufficere ~ere .. declaramus *Lit. Cant.* I 263. **b** offensus quis ab aliquo ~et hoc indicare abbati GILDAS *Pen.* 18; nec in fine dactilus ~et poni nec spondeus in quinto loco ALDH. *Met.* 10 p. 90; habere solet .. insula [Hii] rectorem .. abbatem presbyterum, cujus juri .. ipsi episcopi ordine inusitato ~eant esse subjecti BEDE *HE* III 4 p. 134; omni die ~eo [AS: *ic sceal*] arare integrum agrum ÆLF. *Coll.* 90; **1234** (v. 2 daia); BRACTON 4 (v. consuetudo 2a); **c1283** ~et invenire j hominem ad falcandum *Cust. Battle* 5; **1321** communitas .. defendit jus suum .. et dicit quod non ~et eis .. respondere *MGL* II 365; **1326** (v. colonus a). **c** dic illi quia, velit nolit, ~et ad monasteria venire BEDE *HE* V 9 (cf. ib. 12: nunc ad corpus reverti et rursus inter homines vivere ~es); **s1270** dixit quod illa peticio fuit .. contra honorem Dei .., cum Christiani ~erent subjici Judeis et per eos maritari *Leg. Ant. Lond.* app. 234; **1337** ex quo facto ~eret .. manifestum obloquium exoriri *Lit. Cant.* II 155; **1465** proventus .. ecclesie .. decrescere ~ere verisimiliter formidatur in futurum *Ib.* III 241. **d** '~ere' et 'non ~ere' dicitur aliquando improprie, ut cum dico quia '~eo amari a te' ANSELM (*Ver.* 8) I 188 (cf. debitor b); homo qui de curia sit regis .. in domo alicujus civis Lundon' .. hospitari non ~et (*Lib. Lond.*) *GAS* 672; ~et .. percipere j panem *Cust. Battle* 13; **1334** racione ballive sue ~uit fugare leporem .. in foresta *SelPlForest* 67 (cf. ib.: ~uit habere corticem .. quercuum ..).

6 (p. ppl. as sb. n.) obligation, duty: **a** (w. *ex* or *pro*); **b** (w. *ultra* or *supra*); **c** (w. *sub*); **d** (w. *contra*).

a imberbi satrape ad nefas agendum non ex ~ito sed sponte sua gratanter adherebant ORD. VIT. XII 5 p. 329; **s1170** eo [T. archiepiscopo] .. pro ~ito pastoralis officii exulante, episcopus Dunhelmensis sicut universi pene per Angliam coepiscopi .., suspensionis sententiam accepit G. COLD. *Durh.* 5; **1301** ad quod servicium faciendum omnes regnicole ex ~ito tenentur *Melrose* I 351. **b** coloni .. non vexentur ultra ~itum [OF: *si de lour droite cense noun*] (*Leis Will.*) *GAS* 512; ipse certe supra suscepti officii ~itum, cujus .. onus grande, sed ipse etiam supra ~itum munificus H. BOS. *Thom.* II 11. **c** **1220** vobis .. precipientes sub ~ito sacramenti vestri nobis prestiti *Pat* 226; **1265** vobis mandamus sub ~ito fidelitatis quibus (*sic*) nobis estis astricti .. *Cl* 67; injunget eis sub ~ito juramenti quod secreta capituli nemini revelabunt *Cust. Cant.* 15. **d** **1356** contra fidei et ligeancie sue ~itum contra nos .. surrexerunt (*Lit. E. de Balliolo*) AVESB. 132.

7 (w. inf.): **a** shall, should (as auxiliary vb. used in dependent clause in indeterminate sense). **b** would (conditional). **c** to be about to, on the point of. **d** to be supposed or alleged to.

a Cuthbertus ad .. Lugubaliam civitatem rogatus advenit, quatinus ibidem sacerdotes consecrare, sed et ipsam reginam .. benedicere ~eret BEDE *CuthbP* 28; **1169** quam paterne .. regiam sepius excellentiam .. exortati fuerimus ut .. archiepiscopum tibi reconciliare ~eres (*Lit. Papae*) DICETO *YH* I 333; **1216** ipsi obsides dederunt quod, nisi quieti esse ~eant .., quod (*sic*) in prisonam nostram .. revertentur *Pat* 12; **1272** non videtur juri consonum quod .. Elena de seisina sua impediri ~eat *Cl* 534; **s1303** (v. 2 comitas b); **s1313** pro eo quod [justiciarii] non ~erent ibidem tenere placita sua tempore messis, dederunt homines Cancie .. regi ccc li. *Ann. Paul.* 274; **1375** sub ea spe .. quod benevolenciam vestram in justa peticione favorabilem .. ~eamus .. invenire *FormOx* 227; **1405** procurabunt quod .. privilegia .. concessa .. inviolabiliter .. ~eant observari *Lit. Cant.* III 96. **b** **1289** videtur sibi quod hoc bene facere potest, quia homo extraneus est ..; et, si ipse illum non duxisset, †quidem [l. quidam] alius extraneus predictum peregrinum duxisse ~uit *Rec. Leic.* I 206. **c** dum venire ~ebat ad capere [promotionem], ova simul et obolum perdidit DEVIZES 29v.; **1218** Brianus ~uit balneare .. et submersus fuit *Eyre Yorks* 288; **1221** sicut ~uit facere legem, venit idem A. et levavit eum *PlCrGlouc* 6; **1301** quidam H. ~uit ligare carectam suam oneratam de feno; per infortunium cecidit .. per quod fregit collum *SelCCoron* 59; positis .. quibusdam .. qui .. secum commeasse ~uerant, in quolibet comitatu ubi de prodicione .. timebatur *G. Hen. V* 3; *Ib.* 1 (v. cornix 1b). **d** calumniantur .. ad opus regis per singulos annos ij m. .., et hoc per concessionem .. Osuuoldi pro bello quod contra G. P. facere ~uit *DB* I 36v.; dicunt se audisse quod rex W. ~uerit eam [terram] dare Walleno *Ib.* 208; **1195** audierunt dici quod J. filius E. ~ebat vi concubuisse cum filia Johannis de C. *CurR PR* I 96; **1234** suggestum fuit quod idem G. dixisse ~uit quedam verba .. in despectu domini regis *BNB* II 665; **s1255** Judei .. imprisonati .. pro morte cujusdam pueri quem ~uerant necasse apud Lincolniam *Leg. Ant. Lond.* 23; **1291** nullam fecit mencionem .. de die, hora neque loco nec eciam de modo quo ipsam rapuisse ~uit *Eyre Kent* I 111; **1359** pardonavimus Willelmo .. de eo quod .. vij ollas eneas .. furatus fuisse ~uerat *Pat* 258 m. 14; **1393** de eo quod ipse .. vj li. argenti .. felonice, ut dicitur, asportare ~uisset *Ib.* 337 m. 5.

8 (inf. as sb.) due (Gasc.). *V. et.* 2 *debetum, deverium.*

1254 petivimus ab eis nostrum ~ere, sc. .. custodiam castri et honoris de Gensac *RGasc* I 545 (cf. *CalPat* 299).

deberium v. deverium.

1 debetum v. debere 3a.

2 debetum, (Gasc.) due, custom (seasonal monopoly of wine). *V. et. debere* 8.

1254 retinuit sibi dominus ~um vini, hoc est quod singulis annis per unum mensem .. non vendatur ab aliquo vinum in burgo Genciac' nisi a domino; et potest dominus ponere cartonem ad j d. plus quam primo vendetur *RGasc* I 546 (cf. *CalPat* 356); **1289** licet .. consuetum sit quod castellani .. annis singulis vendant per xv dies mensis Maii racione ~i vina excrescencia in loco .., inquiratis de valore dicti ~i et, si .. burgenses valorem ipsius nobis assignare voluerint, tunc .. ~um cessare faciatis *Ib.* II 530; **1316** cum in .. villa [S. Macarii] habeamus quoddam devarium vocatum '~um', viz. quod vina aliqua per primos xv dies Maii .. non vendantur nisi vina nostra *Ib.* IV 1661.

debilare v. debere 5a.

debilire, to weaken.

scimus quod Deus multis modis nobis absconditis potest facere miracula, ut ignem posset Deus sic unire et applicare passo, ipsum [ignem, sc. agens] juvando ac passum ~iendo, quod quantumlibet velociter ageret in unum, dimittendo aliud WYCL. *Ente Praed.* 155.

debilis [CL]

1 weak, infirm, lacking in force: **a** (of person); **b** (of pulse); **c** (of abstr.).

a lurida debilium fomentat membra virorum ALDH. *VirgV* 701; ~is vel enervatus, *lame* ÆLF. *Gl.*; ~e, *lef GlP*

104; elemosinarius .. in eas .. domos in quibus mulieres aegrae vel ~es jacent nunquam introeat LANFR. *Const.* 154; pro defensione pauperum ~iumque .. exsurge ORD. VIT. VIII 5 p. 295; **11..** pace fracta / vi redacta / fortes trudunt debiles *Anecd. Poet.* 7. 7; statuerunt ut viri forciores .. in mercatum fugerent, ~iores vero .. remanerent in urbe *Ps.*-ELMH. *Hen. V* 123. **b** GAD. 102v. 1 (v. caprizare 2b). **c** illud causatum quod est posterioris esse habet esse ~ius et instabilius J. BLUND *An.* 293; frigiditas est elementaris qualitatis quedam activa proprietas ~ior in actione quam caliditas BART. ANGL. IV 2; istud argumentum videtur satis ~e R. MARSTON *QD* 197.

2 a (of artefacts) worn (out). **b** (of goods or land) poor, inferior, defective. **c** (of coinage) debased. **d** (of wine or ale) weak, dilute.

a c**1300** gradale ~e et aliud vetus; ij troperia ~ia ..; iij paria vestimentorum ~issima (*Vis.*) *Ch. Sal.* 369; **1342** crux portabilis ~is est et inhonesta (*Vis. Totnes*) *EHR* XXVI 111 (cf. ib. 113: una fiola deficit et alia ~is); **1370** ij lecti cum *boterflies* ~es *Ac. Durh.* 130; **1393** de .. vestimentis unum erit de ~ioribus pro diebus ferialibus et aliud melius pro diebus Dominicis *Lit. Cant.* III 24; **1464** [lego] servo meo j tunicam ~em *Test. Ebor.* II 264. **b 1304** totum bonum braseum et totum ~e braseum *Cant. Cath. Pri.* 211; **1311** sunt in grava .. xxxiij acre de subbosco ~i, quia totum fere spine et tribuli *Cust. Battle* 139; **1324** quar. melioris frumenti valuit .. vij s. et quar. mediocris frumenti vj s. et quar. ~is frumenti v s. iiij d. *CBaron* 139 (cf. ib. 138: tradidit Johanni .. j mill' leschie ~ioris quam ipse emit de eo); **1329** pratum mariscosum et ~e *IPM* 16/22 r. 4. **c 1222** insinuatum fuerat quod cum H. de T. pro lxxx li. ~is monete patrie pacificari volebamus (*AncC* IV 160) *RL* I 185; c**1250** de moneta mea .., quam mecum portavi tam in Anglia quam Parisius, quia ~is fuit nec legalis, mu[l]tum amisi *FormOx* 488; **1425** si alique monetarum predictarum sunt per ij d. forciores vel ~iores ad libram, custodes debent deliberare illam tanquam bonam *Pat* 439 m. 18. **d** carnes .. cum vino ~issimo GILB. I 23. 2; **1259** [de] ~ioribus [? l. de vilioribus] vinis que sunt in custodia sua faciat habere .. j dolium vini .. *Cl* 431; c**1230** si braciatrices ~em et insufficientem servisiam et contra assisam braciaverint *Doc. Bec* 113; de ~i servisia, de assisa fracta et de falso pane *FormMan* 13; **1351, 1448** (v. cervisia 1c).

debilitamentum, weakening, impairment.

s**1308** P. Gavastone .. multa in corone ~um et ligii domini sui et regni sedicionem .. perpetravit *G. Ed. II Bridl.* 34.

debilitare [CL], to weaken, enfeeble, impair: **a** (bodily organ, person, or nation); **b** (building); **c** (abstr.). **d** (w. abl.) to dock, deprive (of).

a multos .. ~atis membris, mancos aut loripedes, .. reddidit ORD. VIT. VIII 5 p. 301; deleta magna ex parte et plurimum ~ata natione ista GIR. *TH* III 6; a**1230** egrotante uno capellano et alias ~ato *Conc. Syn.* 181; **1428** quia ipse tunc .. fuit oculorum visu ~atus .. non potuit .. abjuracionem legere *Heresy Tri. Norw.* 79. **b 1250** (v. decadere 1b). **c** †**1083** (12c) eos, si qui nisu contrario talia [proposita] ~are praesumerent, perpetuo .. anathemate .. feriens *Ch. Durh.* 3 (= S. DURH. *Durh.* IV 2); quidquid valet ad astruendam unam partem destruit alteram, et quidquid unam ~at alteram roborat ANSELM (*Gram.* 1) I 146; tota ratio tua ~ata est ADEL. *QN* 4; ut concupiscentiam possit ~are BALD. CANT. *Tract.* 6. 463D; in tantum potest [tepiditas] ~ari quod ex se non generat similem immutationem J. BLUND *An.* 293; quando .. forma aeris ~atur, tunc forma ignis in aere imprimitur BACON VIII 17; sicut lumen, secundum quod magis recedit a suo fonte, ~atur continue R. MARSTON *QD* 233; auxit nostris potenciam, quam prius ~averat et emarcuerat, victualium penuria *G. Hen. V* 13. **d** s**1424** corona .. ~ata redditibus *Plusc.* XI 2.

debilitas [CL]

1 weakness, infirmity: **a** (of body); **b** (of mind); **c** (of community); **d** (of matter); **e** (of artefact); **f** (astr.).

a cum pudicitia non in ~ate sit corporis sed in animi voluntate ÆLF. *Ep.* 2. 80; BEN. PET. *Mir. Thom.* II 41 (v. 2 contractus 1a). **b 1345** propter senectutem suam et pro ~ate anime *Hal. Durh.* 16. **c 1388** considerantes ~atem et penuriam .. burgi *ExchScot* 200. **d** magnum consistit in extencione partium continui, que est causa ~atis, et parvum in earum compressione, que est causa fortitudinis BACON VIII 17. **e 1425** propter ~atem et confracciones ejusdem [navis] posita fuit in quodam *dok* supra *stokes* (*Ac. Foreign* 59 r. 22 *d.*) *OED* s. v. *stock* 13. **f** sunt et alie fortitudines et ~ates, quas planete mutuo accipiunt a se invicem, ut per aspectum bonum accipit planeta unus ab alio fortitudinem, per malum autem ~atem GROS. 44.

2 (of coinage) underweight.

1282 allocatur eisdem [custodibus monete] pro fortitudine ferlingorum xliiij s. ij d. .. debent adhuc pro ~ate denariorum et obolorum xiiij li. xj s. v d. quad., qui debent poni in emendacione monete *KRAc* 230/21.

debilitatio [CL], weakening, impairment. **b** (penal) mutilation.

robur detrimentum et ~o sumebat incrementum *Mir. Fridesw.* 106; [pisces] non discernunt inter medios colores propter ~onem visus ex continua †apparitione [? l. apertione] *Ps.*-RIC. *Anat.* 28; que quidem restauracio non fit sine deperdicione vel ~one humidi radicalis DUNS *Sent.* II 19 i 1; WYCL. *Act.* 82 (v. deperdibilis). **b** aliis .. ~o membrorum inflicta est ex sententia curie ORD. VIT. VIII 5 p. 297.

debiliter, weakly, w. little force.

enervatius, i. ~ius, *sleaclice, þweorlice GlH* E 271; ut color adurens eliminat nigredines et ~iter agens albedines BACON VII 21; Aristoteles [*De Gen.* ii 9] dicit .. quod elementa ~ius agunt respectu celi quam organa respectu artificis *Id. Maj.* I 379; que sic videntur ~iter videntur, quia per radios tantum fractos PECKHAM *Persp.* III 15; *waykly*, basse, ~iter, effeminate *CathA.*

debitator v. dubitatio a.

debitatus, indebted.

1415 lego .. xx li. viz. pro commemoracione anime mee et animarum parentum meorum et .. omnium aliorum quibus ~us existo *Reg. Cant.* III 407.

debite, duly, properly.

illaborato judicio non contentus, superate difficultatis non solum effectum sed et effectivum ~e circumspiciat BALSH. *AD rec.* 2 124; **1226** executionem hujus negocii, si ~e facta fuerit et mature *Pat* 104; **1301** Johannem de Baliolo .. ~e prefecimus in regem Scottorum (*Lit. E. Regis*) W. GUISB. 342; s**1308** liberius peccabatur, eo quod non esset qui ~e peccantes argueret GRAYSTANES 30; **1331** abbas .. tempore suo ~e usus est libertatibus illis *PQW* 25b; s**1407** princeps .. delicta et rapinas hujusmodi ~e, prout decet, faciet castigari *Chr. S. Alb.* 26; **1540** plene, integre †debiterque *Pat* 689 m. 51.

debitor [CL], debtor. **b** one under obligation (sts. w. inf., *ut*, or *in* & acc.).

~or, i. obnoxius, reus vel *neadgylda GlH* D 389; THURKILL *Abac.* 56 (v. debere 1a); si quis moriens ~or .. testamenta .. fecerit .. (*Leg. Hen.* 75. 11) *GAS* 593; c**1131** (v. debere 1a); distinguendum est circa ~ores et debita ut in quibus fides oblata locum habeat, et in quibus non, tibi constet *Dial. Scac.* II 13 A; ~or ille respondit .. se ei pecuniam reddidisse GIR. *GE* I 52; **1218** etc. (v. capitalis 7c); **1264** plegios inveni subscriptos .., quorum quilibet ~or principalis pro me devenit et pro me manucepit solvere dictas xl m. .. si in solucione dicte pecunie defecero *Cl* 377; **1271** inquirat que debita regis .. vicecomites regis .. a diversis ~oribus regis .. receperint (*LTRMem* 45) *EE County Court* 171. **b** si vere debeo [a te amari], ~or sum reddere quod debeo et in culpa sum si non amor a te ANSELM (*Ver.* 8) I 188; qui eam [consuetudinem] tenere ~ores non sunt AD. SCOT *OP* 465A; **1271** singulis de regno nostro .. in exhibicionem justicie sumus ~ores *Cl* 332; qui ~or est ut catholicam veritatem defendat, ~or est ut .. resistat catholicam veritatem impugnanti OCKHAM *Dial.* 626; **1441** (v. creditor 1b).

debitorium, (Gasc.) due.

1220 debetis tenere terras suas in manu vestra usque heredes sui pervenerint ad annos discretionis .. et reddiderint ~ia vestra (*AncC* IV 107) *RL* I 95.

debitrix [CL], one (f.) indebted or under obligation. **b** (as adj.) due.

illa ~ix egregia .. repudit officium W. MALM. *Mir. Mariae* 146; multa sunt que debes [anima mea], quia multa sunt que promisisti. .. in omni quod potes .. ecclesie .. ~icem te agnosce AD. SCOT *Sol.* 859D; de ove que timore lupi fecit se ~icem cervo WALT. ANGL. *FabP.* 26 *tit.*; **1240** caro .. ut mortis ~ix vergit in occasum *Conc. Syn.* 305; Minerva .. jam ad Britanniam .. accessit, ut se Grecis et barbaris ~icem ostendat R. BURY *Phil.* 9. 157. **b 956** (10c) referre ~ices gratias oportet ei *CS* 965.

1 debitus, ~**um** v. debere.

2 debitus, debt or due.

a**716** (11c) ab omni ~u vel pulsione regum censuris liberas eos (*sic*) esse .. statuimus *CS* 91.

deblandiri [cf. CL blandiri], to flatter.

to fage, adulari .., blandiri, ~iri .. *CathA.*

deblaterare [CL], to babble, noise; **b** (intr.).

diblaterare, divulgare OSB. GLOUC. *Deriv.* 179; ita mendacium lingua deblaterat WALT. WIMB. *Palpo* 59. **b** tu qui deblateras verbis inanibus / de celi circulis .., / dic .. *Id. Carm.* 396.

debotus v. devovere 6a. **debraudatus,** ~**itus** v. debroudatus.

debriare [LL]

1 to inebriate, intoxicate (also *s. pass.*); **b** (w. divine inspiration); **c** (w. pride or other sin); **d** (w. blood-lust).

plures dĕbrians impendo pocula Bacchi ALDH. *Aen.* 78 (*Cupa vinaria*) 1; regiis .. dapibus farcitus et poculo ~iatus ÆLNOTH *Cnut* 48; presbyter ~iatus et extra modestie briam longe positus GIR. *GE* II 27 p. 303; cum [Mahumet] in palatio sederet vino ~iatus meracissimo M. PAR. *Maj.* I 270; *to be dronkyn*, deebriare, madere .., *to make dronkyn*, deebriare, ebriare, inebriare *CathA.* **b** qui .. sobrio jam calice ~iandi ferventem gratiae spiritalis .. complectantur amorem BEDE *Sam.* 508; dum sese alterutrum caelestis sapientiae poculis ~iarent *Id. CuthbP* 28; *Epigr. Milredi* 820 (v. dare 14b); **801** Sancti Spiritus gratia ~iatus ALCUIN *Ep.* 213; †**1066** (11c) archipraesul .. memet .. mandatis divinis saepissime ~iavit *CD* 715; daque illum [v. l. illi] sophiae dĕbriari fonte, cui jam / suspiravit ovans (*Epitaph. Bedae*) W. MALM. *GR* I 62; discipuli .. typicos sermones ejus [Anselmi] scripto retinuerunt, quibus affatim ~iati non solum sibi sed et aliis multis .. profecerunt ORD. VIT. IV 10 p. 245; c**1150** istis rivis debriatus, / hoc liquore satiatus, / fons hoc rore fecundatus, / dignus es memoria (*De Hugone Cancellario*) *Anecd. Poet.* 10. 65; loquebatur in capitulo monachorum verbum Dei et .. quasi musto quodam pretiosis rerum spiritualibus pigmentis condito jocundissime ~iabat, vino licet meracissimo Scripturarum jugiter potatos AD. EYNS. *Hug.* I 14; debrietur mens summe sobria / voluptatis ex abundantia J. HOWD. *Ph.* 626; o anima .., cur non omnem capacitatem extendis ut tanti amoris dulcore tantilla .. totaliter deebrieris? BRADW. *CD* 628A. **c 1091** ut nullus mortalium elationis tumore ~iatus dominationem .. exerceat *Cart. Eynsham* I 35 (= *MonA* III 15b); sua malitia ~iati EADMER *HN* 229; palpones .. / incautos debriant potu mendacii WALT. WIMB. *Palpo* 74; **1245** seculo dediti, deliciis ~iati, Deum postponunt (*Lit. Fred. Imp.*) M. PAR. *Maj.* IV 477; **1326** quidam filii Belial, paternis mendaciis ~iati, .. mendaciter divulgarunt quod .. (*Lit. Episc. Lond.*) *Reg. Heref.* 359; s**1382** [J. Purveye] majus de ejus [Johannis Wyclyf] documentis ~iatus KNIGHTON *Cont.* 179; s**1402** rex .. majori audacia ~iatus *Chr. Pont. Ebor. C* 431. **d** sanguinis innocentis effusione ~iati ad palatium archiepiscopi .. recurrerunt BEN. PET. *Pass. Thom.* 7.

2 a to steep (in blood). **b** to soak, flood; **c** (fig.).

a 1188 norunt hec reges, quorum cruore gladii Romani sunt crebrius ~iati (*Lit. Fred. Imp.*) WEND. I 146. **b** [monachi] terram .. aquis abunde superinductis .. salis amaritudine purgare et ~iare .. deque sterili effecta ad pristinam revocare fecunditatem .. non cessarunt GIR. *Spec.* III 15 p. 229; s**1254** omnes terras .. invenerunt maris salsugine ~iatas M. PAR. *Maj.* V 461; *Ann. Berm.* 468 (v. brecca a). **c** quibus [rivis gratie et severitatis] ~iata superficies terre sanctorum .. semen producit in fructum vite eterne *V. Har.* 8 f. 12b.

debriatio, intoxication (fig.).

post gratiam praedicationis, post ~onem potus spiritalis BEDE *Tab.* 415.

debrius, intoxicated.

in illa cena in qua me poculo ~ius culpare studuit BEDE *Pleg.* 17.

debroudatus, ~**itus** [cf. broudare], embroidered.

[A. abbas, ob. **1268**] ecclesiam .. ornamentis variis decoravit, sc. .. vj parium albarum cum parruris de India brudatis, ij capparum cum scutis †de baudatis [? l. debraudatis] et pluribus aliis OXNEAD *S. Ben. Holme* 299; ymaginibus ~a .. vestimenta *Ord. Exon.* I 13; p**1368** j casulam de scarleto debroydat' cum aparatu *Invent. Norw.* 42; **1382** lectum meum bluetum ~atum *DCLinc. Reg. Linc.* 1363–97 f. 257*d.*; **1396** capam .. rubiam cum *perles* debrauditam *Invent. Ch. Ch.* 104.

†**debuare,** *f. l.*

1309 dantes eidem [procuratori] potestatem †debuandi [? l. debatandi *or* deputandi], defendendi, excipiendi *Reg. Cant.* 1144.

deburgare [cf. burgare; OF *burgier*], to burgle, break into. **b** (?) to break out from (gaol; *cf.* E. G. Kimball *Gaol Del. Cambs* 8–9).

1275 bladum cujusdam hominis .. furatus fuit de nocte et domum illius ~avit *Hund.* I 275; **1298** ecclesia †defurgata fuit .. per ipsum latronem *Rec. Leic.* I 360; **1340** cum .. quemdam S. .. felonice ~antem grangiam .. cepisset .., permisit eum evadere *SessPCambs* 12; **1346** ipse simul cum aliis .. felonice ~avit prisonam .. archiepiscopi Ebor' de Rypon et J. .. et R. .. clericos convictos .. a dicta prisona cepit et abduxit *Pat* 216 m. 9; **1376** felonice receptavit quandam J. .., sciens ipsam J. ~asse domum cujusdam J. P. *Pat* 294 m. 13. **b 1332** Rogerus ~avit [felonice] prisonem domini regis castri Cant' .. unde indictatus est, venit per vicecomitem nunc ductus, et allocutus qualiter de .. felonia ejusdem deburgerie se velit acquietare, dicit quod non est culpabilis .. *Gaol Del. Cambs* 1.

deburgaria, gaol-breaking.

1332 (v. deburgare b).

deburgatio, burglary.

1334 J. O. .. et J. R. .. capti pro ~one grangie H. de T. felonice deburgate *Gaol Del. Cambs* 46.

debursare [OF *desborser*], to disburse. *V. et.* *eursare.*

set cum aurum debursatur / mox despectus honoratur P. BLOIS *Carm.* 26.33; c**1516** in summa v^m ducatorum .. per ipsos .. persolvendorum, deponendorum et ~andorum in eventum promotionis .. dicti A. .. in .. cardinalem *Form. S. Andr.* I 115.

debutare v. dubitare 1a.

decaballare [cf. OF *deschevaler*], to unhorse.

s1346 rex Francie . . sagittatus bisque per regem Anglie †debellatus [v. l. decaballatus, ut dicebatur, vix] aufugit HIGD. VII 44 p. 342 (cf. *Ann. Osney* 352; AD. MUR. *Cont.* 176).

decachordus [LL < δεκάχορδος], ten-stringed (instrument; also fig.).

1154 Apollo, si te videret, . . / decachordum temperaret, tuas laudes personaret OSB. CLAR. *Ep.* 38; **c1160** quem sequitur decimo crysopressus [cf. *Rev.* xxi 20] . .; ibi namque in sanctis martyribus est vite perfectio, ubi in spirituali ∼o reperta fuerit legis divine plenitudo *Ib.* 41 p. 152 (cf. ib.: cum . . decem pretiosi lapides ad ∼um divine legis respiciant); Cassiodorus [*De Artibus* V] ait: "decalogi ∼us." BACON *Tert.* 233 (cf. id. *CSPhil.* 442: [vocabula Greca] . . decacordon . .); *of tene stringis*, decacordus *CathA.*

decacontarche v. decarcha. **decada** v. decas.

decadere [cf. CL cadere]

1 a to decay, fall into ruin; *v. et.* 1 *decidere* 1b. **b** (p. ppl. *decasus*) fallen, ruined; *v. et. decasatus, discaëtus.*

a 1392 permisit ∼ere ibidem unum columbar' *IMisc* 252/12 r. 1 (cf. ib. r. 3: permisit ∼ere ibidem tria alia tenementa nativa). **b 1250** muri cujusdam camere . . multum debilitantur et ∼i sunt *CalIMisc* I p. 30; **1335** due shoppe in Fleshmongerestret nichil reddiderunt, quia decasse *Comp. Swith.* 271; **1336** pro stipendiis x hominum . . removencium . . petras de veteri muro castri ∼o (*KRAc* 19/40) *Doc. Scot.* III 366; **1374** ad cariandum petras de stagno predicto alias ∼as *Doc. Leeds* 112; **1423** in stipendio plumbiarii emendantis defectus j partis porticus capelle . . ∼e *Ac. Obed. Abingd.* 97; **1452** de . . proficuis . . de arboribus et lignis in parco et warrena . . crescentibus et postea ventis obrutis vel ∼is *Entries* 74b; **1558** x muros luti et lapidum . . fore ruinosos et totaliter ∼os ob defectu reparacionis *Ib.* 699.

2 to be deducted. *V. et.* 1 *decidere* 4b.

1248 debent reddere . . xx s. ix d. Turonensium; sed modo ∼unt inde singulis annis ij d. de quadam domo . . quam episcopus prosternere fecit *CalIMisc* I 55 (*Guernsey*) p. 16.

decagesima, suggested name for Sunday preceding Septuagesima. (*Cf. Ps.*-Ambrose *Serm.* 15. 2).

798 si qui . . fuissent qui decimam ebdomadam addere . . voluissent . ., non propter numerum ebdomadarum '∼a' seu quolibet alio nomine . . sed octogesimam . . nuncupare debuissent ALCUIN *Ep.* 144 (cf. dominicus 7a).

decagium v. dicagium.

decagonum [δεκάγονον], decagon.

id est latus ∼i circuli cujus *AF* est semidiametrum WALLINGF. (*Quad.*) I 42.

decaisatus v. decasatus.

decaladismus [dub.], disease causing loss of hair.

capilli . . ablati . . et a capite precisi ipsum turpe reddunt, ut patet in allopicia et in ∼o BART. ANGL. V 2.

decalagus v. decalogus 2.

decalcare [cf. CL calcare], to knock down, trample on or defile. *V. et. deculcare, disculcare.*

s1252 [ventus] ecclesias plumbo projecto ∼avit M. PAR. *Maj.* V 272; **1275** major Linc[olnie] cepit de W . . j equum . . in regia via, hernisium suum de dicto equo extrahendo et in luto enormiter ∼ando *Hund.* I 334a; **1324** fecit transgressionem Waltero A. et bona et catalla sua de assensu uxoris sue invito marito de domo sua asportavit diversis vicibus, uxorem suam sepissime ∼ando *CBaron* 138; *to defoulle*, attaminare . ., calcare . ., conculcare . ., ∼are *CathA.*

decalceare [cf. CL calceare, discalceare, OF *deschaucier*], to unshoe, take off footwear.

discalceatum [v. l. ∼eatum] BRACTON 356b, **s1274** ∼iatus (v. discalceare 2a).

decalogus [LL < δεκάλογος]

1 decalogue, ten commandments. **b** (fig.) enactment. **c** (?) set of ten (w. pun on *denarius*).

tabulae ∼i litteris sulcatae recondebantur ALDH. *VirgP* 45; 'triginta cubitos' [*Exod.* xxvi 8] . . ecce hic . . numerum . . denarium habes et hunc tertio multiplicatum, quo patenter insinuatur virtus eorum qui ∼um Legis in fide S. Trinitatis . . perficiunt BEDE *Tab.* 431; *Id. Gen.* 96 (v. denarius 11); Pharisei, Legis pre ceteris emulatores, in pitaciis scribebant ∼um, ut illum semper quasi ante oculos haberent appensum H. BOS. *LM* 1333A; dico quod ∼us ratione sui non dicitur 'occidere' [cf. 2 *Cor.* iii 6], sed hoc dicitur propter prohibitionem eorum que ibi erant, eo quod corruptio humana magis tribuit in contrarium propter prohibitionem HALES *Qu.* 366; AD. MARSH *Ep.* 180 (v. denarius 1c); **s1318** moliebatur iniqua persuasio reproborum dignitatem presulatus et instituta ∼i, quibus in Lege [cf. *Lev.* xxi 18] ab altari suo cecos et claudos Christus evellere precepit, . . profanare *Flor. Hist.* III 182; quandoque idem preceptum in diversis locis replicatur; unde et decem precepta ∼i Exodi xx c[apitulo] describuntur, que tamen Deuteronomii v replicantur OCKHAM *Pol.* II 746; *the ten commawndmentis*, decem precepta, ∼us *CathA.* **b c1430** cum ipsum [aurum] miserimus ad excambium, ejusdem primitias offerimus camsoribus cogimurque . . eis dare quantum regie legis ∼us decreverat dari eis *Reg. Whet.* II app. 419. **c 1323** mittimus vobis ∼um sterlingorum pro novis botulis emendis *Lit. Cant.* I 99.

2 (? by conf. w. *catalogus*) list.

s1262 S. Ricardus . . canonizatus est et sanctorum dechalogo ascriptus *Flor. Hist.* II 475 (cf. RISH. 12: papa Urbanus B. Ricardum catalogo sanctorum ascripsit); **1387** progenitorum nostrorum . ., quorum multi sanctorum decalago reperiuntur ascripti *Dip. Corr. Ric. II* 50.

decalvare [LL], to deprive of hair by shaving or scalping; **b** (fig.).

quamvis flava caesaries raderetur et [puella] per publicum ∼ata traheretur ALDH. *VirgV* 47; ∼atum, decollatum, *besceoren GlH* D 11; ad Pascha et ad festum S. Marie Magdalene et ad festum Omnium SS. ad minus ∼entur sorores *Inst. Sempr.* lvi; isti . . in ipsa Jerusalem Christum Domini [i.e. S. Thomam] ∼arunt . ., patrem suum in ipso matris sue utero ∼antes H. BOS. *Thom.* VI 9 (cf. corona 4c, decoronare b); 'quare ergo te ∼asti?' [cf. Macrobius II 5. 7] R. NIGER *Chr. II* 109; *to make belde*, †decalvere, decapillare *CathA.* **b** jam videmus philosophos ∼atos [sc. discipulis privatos], . . quorum sectam nemo [est] qui profiteatur, nemo qui sequatur AILR. *Serm.* 457B; hunc [montem] latices decalvavere profusi / fulmineique imbres, nudum spoliatur utroque / crine caput J. EXON. *BT* I 412; P. BLOIS *Opusc.* 1009 (v. depilate); J. FORD *Serm.* 49. 12 (v. exsoporare); MAP *NC* I 25 (v. 2 celare f); per Chore [*Num.* xvi], qui 'calvus' interpretatur, hypocrite designantur, qui, cum interius sint ∼ati omnibus graciis atque donis . ., virtutes exterius simulant ELMH. *Cant.* 243.

decalvatio [LL], shaving to the scalp (fig.). **b** scalping.

in subtillissima novacula judicii virtutes omnes . . abrasit. que sane extollentie vanitas, quia ∼onem hanc velut meritum et causam precesserit J. FORD *Serm.* 64. 4. **b** in hac [S. Thome] ∼one, in decoronatione hac, in hac tam dura . . capitis tonsione, ubi testa capitis cum corona unctionis separatur a capite H. BOS. *Thom.* VI 9 (cf. id. *LM* 1300C).

decambium [cf. cambium], exchange. *V. et. excambium* 1.

c1152 dedisse . . x acras de foresta mea . . ad dandum in ∼ium pro terra ubi fiat [virgultum] *Act. Hen. II* I 44.

decana [cf. decanus 3], senior nun (Angers).

1161 testes . . O. abbatissa, H. celleraria, T. ∼a *Act. Hen. II* I 336.

decanalis, decanal, belonging to a dean.

s1256 quidam . ., in ecclesiam Ebor' . . clanculo intrantes, inquisiverunt . . quod . . esset stallum decani; et responsum est 'hoc', demonstrato stallo ∼i M. PAR. *Maj.* V 586; **1261** cum a decano jure ∼i cognoscente fuerit appellatum *Conc.* I 757a; **1307** inter manerium ∼e . . et toftum Willelmi M. *Reg. Ant. Linc.* III 119; **13..** ad dignitatem ∼em ecclesie Linc' *Stat. Linc.* I 340; **1437** decanus, inconsulto capitulo, edificavit stabulum . . infra mansum . . ∼em *Ib.* II 374.

decanatim, by deanery.

in tantum quod potest . . per se vel ejus deputatos ∼im vel ecclesiatim visitare *Lib. Landav.* 281.

decanatus

1 deanery, office of dean: **a** (of secular cathedral); **b** (of collegiate church or chapel); **c** (of Arches).

a s1166 quia archipresul Jocelinum Sar' episcopum . . suspendisset, eo viz. quod ∼um Saresberiensis ecclesie contra interdictum . . pape et suum, inconsultis quibusdam . . canonicis . . quorum erat . . decanum suum eligere, cuidam de aulicis clericis . . contulisset H. BOS. *Thom.* IV 18; **s1193** archiepiscopus . . dedit ∼um illum [Eboraci] Simoni Apulo, clerico suo R. HOWD. III 221; **1221** cum . . in ecclesia tua ∼um . . et alias personatus provide ordinaris . ., nos . . ordinationem ipsam . . confirmamus (*Lit. Papae*) *Mon. Hib. & Scot.* 18b (cf. ib. 68a); **1280** decanus Linc' . . pro ecclesiis quas habet in nostra diocesi suo ∼ui appropriatis juravit nobis canonicam obedienciam *Reg. Ebor.* 70; **s1306** [papa] prefecerat eum [nepotem suum] in cardinalem et ∼us Lincolniensem et Londoniensem . . ei dedit GRAYSTANES 27; **1393** ∼u vacante *Reg. Heref.* 51; **1542** unacum . . auctoritate presentandi personas ydoneas ad curas seu vicarias, . . ecclesiarum seu capellarum . . eidem ∼ui [Moraviensi] unitarum *Form. S. Andr.* II 195. **b 1141** [terre] qu[e] pertinent ad ∼um S. Martini London' *Regesta* 529; **s1177** Gwido decanus . . resignavit in manu domini regis ∼um suum S. Crucis de Waltham *G. Hen. II* 134 (cf. ib. 174); **1203** contulimus . . Petro de R. ∼um B. Martini de And[egavia] *Pat* 22b; **1217** ∼um capelle nostre Walengeford' *Pat* 27; **1259** tua peticio continebat quod . . J. rex Anglorum advocatiam ∼us ecclesie B. Michaelis de Pencris [*Penkridge, Staffs*] . . concessit archiepiscopatui Dublin' (*Lit. Papae*) *Ch. Hib.* 29; **s1282** mandavit rex archiepiscopo quod citare faceret . . procuratores ∼uum et capitulorum ecclesiarum collegiatarum ipsius et suffraganeorum suorum diocesium *Chr. Peterb.* 58; ab liberam regiam capellam collegiatam in castro de Bruggenorth sitam, uno ∼u et v prebendis . . dotatam BROMPTON 989. **c 1320** R. nuper Cantuarie archiepiscopus, ∼us de Arcubus Londoniis, qui est jurisdiccionis sue exempte, personaliter usitatus *MGL* I 446 (cf. arcus 4f, g).

2 (rural) deanery, office (or area of jurisdiction) of rural dean: **a** (Eng.); **b** (W.); **c** (Ir.); **d** (Sc.). *Cf. diaconatus* 2.

a *GAS* 651 (v. decanus 2b); suggeritur ei a decano vicini loci mulierculam quamdam in ∼u suo, . . plurimas ad se divinando turbas pertrahere populorum AD. EYNS. *Hug.* V 8; **1206** ad ∼um pertinet corrodium unius servientis . . et visitatio ecclesiarum vallis *Chr. Evesham* 210 (cf. *Becket to Langton* 122); **c1218** sint in quolibet ∼u duo vel tres viri . . qui excessus . . prelatorum . . episcopis denuncient *Conc. Syn.* 75; **c1293** ∼us de Taverham, in quo sunt parochie xviij *Val. Norw.* 363; **s1320** [episcopus] apud Frakenham commorans per unum mensem ∼um de Iselham visitando *Hist. Roff.* f. 34v.; **1403** predicti capellani officium ∼us Christianitatis . . seu . . aliud officium per quod possint . . subtrahi aut . . impediri nullatenus . . assumant *Cl* 251 m. 17d. **b** cum . ., generale tallagium per episcopatum faciens, ∼ui de Elevein v li. sibi reddendas . . episcopus [Menevensis] imposuisset GIR. *JS* 1 p. 142; **12..** annuus census debitus episcopo Landavensi . . de quibusdam ecclesiis in ∼u de Bergaveny *Cart. Glam.* 939; **p1254** (v. decanus 8b). **c 1265** habebunt ipse [archiepiscopus Ardmachanus] et successores sui . . in singulis v ∼uum . . dyocesis [Midensis], sc. Diuelek [etc.] . ., duas stationes et in quolibet aliorum ∼uum, qui sex sunt numero, unicam tantum stationem *Reg. S. Thom. Dublin* 81. **d 12..** taxacio ecclesiarum . . per episcopatum Aberdonensem : ∼us de Mar . .; ∼us de Buchania . . *Reg. Aberd.* II 52; **1293** W. . . S. Andree episcopus . . decanis de Merskis et de Hadingtoun: . . ab ecclesiis . . in ∼ibus vestris existentibus . . *Dryburgh* 182; **13..** infrascriptos ad confessiones virorum ecclesiasticorum nobis subjectorum audiendum . . stabilimus per singulos ∼us *Conc. Scot.* II 66; **1540** de cotis receptis de decanis omnium ∼uum synodorum annorum viz. mdxxxix et mdxl *Rent. S. Andr.* 36.

decandicare, to whiten.

to make white, albare, de-, . . candidare, candicare, ∼are *CathA.*

decania [LL]

1 tithing. *Cf. decena.*

bis in anno conveniant in hundretum suum quicunque liberi . . ad dinoscendum . . si ∼ie plene sint, vel qui . . recesserint vel superacreverint (*Leg. Hen.* 8. 1) *GAS* 554; *Ib.* 552 (v. centuria 2b).

2 deanery: **a** (of cathedral); **b** (rural); **c** (unspec.).

a decanum Lincolnie . ., cui juxta morem ecclesie sue . . in B. V. natalitio, utpote nuper in ∼ie dignitatem sublimato, solempne convivium instruere . . incumbit AD. MARSH *Ep.* 142. **b s1108** (v. archidiaconatus a); **c1170** quod in nostra ∼ia vidimus . . fideliter testamur *Cart. Glam.* 151. **c s1074** [Gregorius VII] decrevit . . ut . . damnaretur . . emptor et venditor cujuscunque officii, ut puta episcopatus, abbatie, prepositure, ∼ie vel decimationis ecclesie W. COVENTR. I 90; *a deynrie*, ∼ia *CathA.*

decanonizare, to deprive of the status (or nature) of a canon.

s1256 in domo S. Trinitatis London', duo . . canonici dum . . sepe contenderent . . unus eorum . . alterum interfecit. . . proh dolor! ambo isti canonici ∼ati . . ante summi Judicis tribunal . . quid poterunt respondere? M. PAR. *Maj.* V 571.

decanonus, *metri gratia* for *decimus nonus.*

13.. ter triples ternam senam denam decanonam; / sic cito percipies urbs tua quare ruit (*Vers.*) MAP *NC* [*ed. James*] app. p. 260 (cf. ib. 261: littera decimanona); ELMH. *Metr. Hen. V* 53 (v. decaquartus).

decantare [CL]

1 to sing; **b** (w. theme as obj.). **c** to play (mus.). **d** to sing in opposition (fig.), to deny; *cf. de* 17d, f.

ut . . ymnista . . carmen triumphale . . ∼et ALDH. *VirgP* 18; cum . . solitas Domino laudes ∼aret BEDE *HE* IV 7; *Latin Stories* 123 (v. cantilena 1). **b** [libri] Lucani proelia Caesaris et Pompei ∼antis ALDH. *Met.* 10 p. 83; archanorum spiritalium mysteria ∼ata BEDE *Hom.* II 16. 185. **c** citharedus . . alterius modi melum modulans juncide . . ∼abat in cithara H. BOS. *LM* 1300B. **d 1168** supervenerunt . . nuntii legatorum . .; minime coarantes, nam quicquid cecinerat alius, alius in curia ∼abat J. SAL. *Ep.* 244 (272 p. 562).

2 (eccl.) to sing, chant: **a** (creed, psalm, or sim.); **b** (mass).

a Ambrosius . . admonet ut verba symboli matutinis semper horis fideles quique ∼ent BEDE *Egb.* 5 (cf. ib.: idiotas . . haec ipsa sua lingua discere ac . . ∼are facito);

vovit .. quia .. cotidie psalterium totum .. ~aret *Id. HE* III 27; sic .. ~ans 'Gloria Patri et Filio et Spiritui Sancto' .. ultimum e corpore exhalavit spiritum CUTHB. *Ob. Baedae* clxiv; in prima oratione ~et tres primos paenitentiae psalmos *RegulC* 16; **985** (12c) ~ante psalmigrapho: 'Domini est terra ..' [*Psalm* xxiii 1] *CD* 652; decantare Deo cepit psalmos cum leticia HIL. RONCE. 1. 127; *G. S. Alb.* II 106 (v. departire 1a); **s1349** (v. Christicola); ~ari fecit statim per capellam suam angelicum hymnum 'Te Deum' *G. Hen. V* 16. **b** missas a sacerdote in Quadragesima ~andas GIR. *GE* I 49 p. 133; due misse .. solempniter ~ate *Cust. Cant.* 397; missa de Spiritu ~ata *Hist. Roff.* f. 63.

3 (of birds) to sing, warble.

avis ~ans melodias quasdam Paradisi O. CHERITON *Fab.* 78.

4 to recite.

si numerum mensium singulorum .. memoriter ~are consuescas BEDE *TR* 22.

5 **a** (w. acc. & dat.) to ascribe (in song). **b** to proclaim, declare.

a judicem universorum .. rex propheticus .. longanimem esse declarat [cf. *Psalm* cii 8] et .. ei se misericordiam cum judicio ~are manifestat ÆLNOTH *Cnut prol.* 2 p. 127. **b** quod me audires a lascivientibus rusticis inter hereticos per pocula ~ari BEDE *Pleg.* 307; **797** sicut ab omnibus in terminis paschalibus verissime ~atur et firmissime tenetur ALCUIN *Ep.* 126; alma fides .. securam se defensore Sadio ~are non timeat MAP *NC* III 2 f. 37v.

decantatio [LL], (eccl.) singing, chanting: **a** (of creed, psalm, or sim.); **b** (of mass).

a plures ecclesiae magistri ~onem alleluiae tempore quadragesimali intermittendam esse sanxerunt BEDE *Hom.* II 16. 185; per crebram symboli vel orationis sacrae ~onem *Id. Egb.* 6; cum ~one [AS p. 390: *mid sange*] canonici cursus .. operentur *RegulC* 25; explicitis septenorum psalmorum ~onibus BYRHT. *V. Osw.* 468; **1271** post ~onem hymni angelici *Ch. Sal.* 352; **1389** psalmorum ac officiorum ~onibus non refrenatis *Reg. Heref.* 13; **1452** Spiritus Sancti gracia per ~onem ymni 'veni Creator Spiritus' .. invocata *Reg. Whet.* I 13. **b** ~one missarum .. officium beatificant perficiendi funeris *V. Ed. Conf.* 56v.; **1360** (v. cantaria 2b); **1451** processiones .. cum ~one letanie misse *Reg. Heref.* 10.

decānus [LL; cf. δεκᾱνός]

1 (astr.) decan, segment of ten degrees (of zodiac).

unumquodque signum dividitur in tres partes equales, et unaqueque constat ex x gradibus que vocantur facies et alio nomine ~i GROS. 44; facies signorum accipiuntur per divisionem cujuslibet signi in tres partes equales, et unaqueque constat ex x gradibus; que [partes] vocantur facies et alio modo ~i BACON *Maj.* I 261; meminit .. hujus virginis et matris partum in primo Virginis ~o notatum fuisse *Ps.*-GROS. *Summa* 282 (cf. BACON *Tert.* 49); facies signorum distinguuntur per ~os WALLINGF. (*EPT*) I 204.

2 **a** leader of ten men. **b** tithingman (later app. conf. w. rural dean; *cf.* 8a *infra*); *cf. decenarius.*

a ~us, i. princeps militibus vel *tyna aldor GlH* D 9; erant .. dux populi Moyses et sub eo .. chiliarche, ecatontarche, pentecontarche, †decacontarche [l. decarche], id est millenarii, centenarii, quinquagenarii, ~i BELETH *RDO* 12. 26C (cf. *Exod.* xviii 25); sequantur quemlibet preceptorem x vicarii, et sequantur quemlibet vicarium ductores x, et quemlibet ductorem x ~i, et sequantur quemlibet ~um x homines BACON V 150. **b** sapientiores .. impesuerunt justiciarios super quosque x friborghas, quos ~os possumus dicere; A. autem *tyenþe heved* vocati sunt, hoc est 'caput de decem' (*Leg. Ed.*) *GAS* 651 (cf. *Leg. Ed. Retr.* ib.: ~us episcopi, in cujus decanatu pax fracta fuerit, reliquos x [solidos habebat]).

3 monastic officer subordinate to (provost and) abbot, prior. (*Cf. Regula S. Benedicti* 21, 65, *Antiq. J.* XX (1940) 22–5).

docente consilio a ~ibus facto .. reliquias ossium sancti Cudberhti .. probatissimi viri de sepulchro proposuerunt elevare *V. Cuthb.* IV 14; in primo anno illic veniens cubicularius fuit aecclesiae, et in secundo erat ~us in monasterio HUGEB. *Will.* 5; constitui debet aliquis frater qui totius claustri sub ~o [AS p. 433: *decane*] curam gerat *RegulC* 57; [Deus] elegit .. reges, pontifices, duces, ~os, praepositos caeterosque ecclesiae suae rectores B. *V. Dunst.* 2; discipuli Dunstani .. electi ut essent .. praepositi, ~i, abbates, episcopi, etiam archiepiscopi *Ib.* 15; Egelnothus [ob. **1038**] .. ecclesie Christi ~us. erant enim tunc temporis Cantuariensis ecclesie monachi quasi canonici cathedrales .. prepositum suum ~um vocabant, quem nos post adventum Lamfranci priorem appellamus GERV. CANT. *AP* 361.

4 canon or sim. (Byzantine).

Justinianus .. fecit ecclesiam Constantinopoli .. et in ea psallentes dcccl ~os, i.e. canonicos R. NIGER *Chr. II* 134.

5 dean, president of cathedral chapter: **a** (Fr.); **b** (Eng.; *cf. Eng. Sec. Cath.* 138 *seqq.*); **c** (W.); **d** (Ir.); **e** (Sc.). **f** (w. *major*) dean as dist. from subdean.

a de adventu Normannorum .. Dudo Veromandensis ~us studiose scripsit ORD. VIT. VI 10; **c1152** ~us B. Marie Rothomagensis et canonicus ejusdem ecclesie de prebenda de A. .. habuerunt .. consuetudines suas liberas *Act. Hen. II* I 45; **c1161** ego .. Stephanus ~us Andegavensis *Ib.* 336; **s1286** magister E. Lamberti, ~us S. Martini Turonensis FORDUN *Cont.* XI 6. **b** **c1052** hac declaratur inscriptione Ægelwinum ~um Wigornensis aecclesiae .. terram .. emisse *CD* 807; **1091** dignitas ~i est et omnium canonicorum ut episcopo in nullo respondeant nisi in capitulo [etc.]. .. ~us omnibus canonicis et .. vicariis praeest quo ad regimen animarum et correctionem morum *Stat. Sal.* 28–29; [W. ep. Dunelm', ob. **1096**] monumentum apud monachos habet quod .. priorem loci hoc insigni extulerit ut in toto episcopatu ~us et vicedominus esset W. MALM. *GP* III 133; **a1100** [archiepiscopus] statuit ~um, thesaurarium, cantorem, dans cuique digne et ecclesie .. et personarum honore H. CANTOR 3v.; **1111** dominus W. ~us et ceteri canonici S. Pauli *E. Ch. S. Paul.* xxx; **1127** nullus in ~um nisi presbyter .. constituatur (*Conc. Lond.* 4) J. WORC. 24; rex [Will. I] quemdam externum monachum super eos [monachos de Ely] constituere voluerat ex eis pro quibus .. miserat de gente Francorum monachis, ut in omnibus ecclesiis Anglorum ~os constitueret et prepositos *G. Herw.* 330b; **1226** mandamus quatinus omnes suffraganeos nostros vocetis ut veniant London' .. et vocent ~os cathedralium et archidiaconos suos (*Lit. Archiep. Cant.*) *Conc. Syn.* 156; **c1237** ~i officium est, cum omnibus canonicis et vicariis in animarum regimine, morum correctione et juredictione premineat, causas omnes ad capitulum spectantes audire et judicio capituli terminare .. *Stat. Linc.* I 280; **1333** (v. capitulum 6a); Sarum presul adest, hic qui fuit ante decanus, / Jon Chaundler dictus ELMH. *Metr. Hen. V* 1330. **c** Jocelinus ~us [? Menevensis] GIR. *Symb.* I 7 p. 218; **1236** magister Gwydo ~us ecclesie Bangor' *Pat* 46 m. 6. **d** **c1265** P. .. archiepiscopus Ardmacanus .., Joseph ~us et capitulum *Cart. Dublin* 327; **1260** ~o et capitulo ecclesie Dublin' (*Lit. Papae*) *Ch. Hib.* 29; **1476** [teste] magistro J. Alleyn, ~o Dubliniensi *Reg. S. Thom. Dublin* 494. **e** **1128** [teste] A[iulfo] ~o [S. Andree] *E. Ch. Scot.* 81; **1256** ~us pro majore parte anni tenetur continue residere vel interpollatim *Reg. Glasg.* II 46; **1362** ecclesie cathedrali Abbirdonensi necnon ~o et canonicis ibidem residentibus *Reg. Aberd.* I 96. **f** **1214** ~us eum [canonicum] instituet ..; absente autem majore ~o, subdecanus .. id exequetur *Stat. Linc.* II 138; H. AVR. *Hugh* 703 (v. concorditer c); **1242** testibus S. ~o majore [et al.] ego S. ~us Moraviensis ecclesie subscribo *Cart. Beauly* 37; **1255** statuisti quod major ~us sicut in Saluberiensi ecclesia eligatur (*Lit. Papae*) *Mon. Hib. & Scot.* 70a; **1270** domino W. ~o majori Linc' *Cl* 301.

6 dean of collegiate church or chapel (incl. peculiars). **b** Dean of Arches.

H. [de Blois] episcopus illius ecclesie [Wint'], tunc quidem ~us noster *Found. Waltham.* 13; **c1108** Waltero ~o et canonicis S. Crucis de Waltham *Ib.* app. p. 55 (= *Regesta* 1984); **1141** Rogerus episcopus Sar', ~us .. ecclesie [S. Martini London'] *Regesta* 529; varie sunt consuetudines in ecclesiis Anglicanis: quedam habent ~um, quedam non P. BLOIS *Ep.* 212. 497B; **1276** ballivus [archiepiscopi] de Otteley [Yorks] et †decennus [MS: decanus] tenuit in capitulo placita ad coronam regis spectancia *Hund.* I 106b; **s1323** magister J. de Stratforde .., qui, cum, ~us Londoniensis existens, in artibus inter omnes clericos hujus facultatis reputaretur .. excellentissimus .. BLANEFORD 147; **1413** ad disposicionem unius eorum [capellanorum infra castrum de Belvere], qui ut ~us inter eos habebitur *Reg. Cant.* II 23; **1437** ad .. capellanum nostrum Ricardum Praty .., regie capelle nostre ~um BEKYNTON I 54; jurisdiccionem .. in foro .. consciencie .. exercet ~us capelle W. SAY *Lib. Reg. Cap.* 56. **b** **1227** ~us de Arcubus *CurR* XIII 210; **1267** (v. arcus 4g).

7 senior bishop (*doyen*) of Canterbury province (office held by bishop of London).

s1109 episcopus Lundoniensis inter alios episcopos est ~us ecclesie Cantuariensis EADMER *HN* 2; **s1100** Londoniensis episcopus, archiepiscopi Cantuar', immo tocius Anglie, ~us *Flor. Hist.* II 34; **s1278** J. episcopus London', tanquam ~us ceterorum episcoporum provincie Cantuar', bis convocavit episcopos apud Londonias ad tractandum de communibus negociis reipublice provincie Cantuar' *Ib.* III 52; **1261** archiepiscopus aut episcopus London', tanquam ~us episcoporum, cum aliquibus sibi associatis episcopis .. requirant (*sic*) eum [episcopum arrestatum] *Conc. Syn.* 674 (cf. ib. 827 *n.*2); habet .. archiepiscopus Cant' in collegio episcoporum episcopos Londinense[m] ~um, Winton' cancellarium, Lincoln' vicecancellarium .. LYNDW. 317 e.

8 rural dean: **a** (Eng.); **b** (W.); **c** (Ir.); **d** (Sc.); **e** (Eng. mon.; *cf. Becket to Langton* 122*n.*).

a ~us episcopi *GAS* 651 (v. 2b supra); **s1108** (v. archidiaconatus a); **s1156** [teste] Waltero ~o de Rudestein *E. Ch. Yorks* II 1209; **s1156** venerunt duo ~i episcopi Cicestrie .. locutique cum abbate obtulerunt ei litteras domini pape A., instantes ut responsum ejus super his .. archidiacono Cicestrie H. referrent *Chr. Battle* f. 63v.; J. SAL. *Pol.* 580A (v. archidiaconus); **1181** ecclesia de Cadendona est in dominio canonicorum. .. ~us loci colligit denarium B. Petri et solvit archidiacono *Dom. S. Paul.* 148; **1206** Willelmus ~us patrie .. testatus est quod interdictum ville factum fuit pro decimis feni .. et non molendini *CurR* IV 70; ~us dicitur qui decem presbiteris ad minus est prelatus GIR. *PI* I 19 p. 110; [clerici ecclesie] statim ~o suo plebano et postea, simul cum eo, loci illius archidiacono miraculum hoc significarunt *Id. Hug.* II 4; *Chr. Evesham* 83 etc. (v. Christianitas 3c); **1222** statuimus ut ~i rurales nullam causam matrimonialem .. audire presumant *Conc. Syn.* 113 (*gl.* LYNDW. 79 m: sc. racione officii sui ..; nam, cum tales ~i rurales non sint perpetui .., racione consuetudinis prescribere non possunt. .. alia racio hujus constitucionis potuit esse quia, ut communiter, tales ~i rurales sunt imperiti et juris ignari); **1224** (v. capitulum 7a); **1279** precipimus .. archidiaconis .. quatenus constitutionem [contra concubinarios] .. faciant per se vel eorum officiales vel saltem per ~os rurales .. recitari *Conc. Syn.* 837 (*gl.* LYNDW. 14 e: sunt hi ~i temporales ad aliquid ministerium sub episcopo .. exercendum constituti .. nec habent institucionem canonicam tanquam in beneficia ..; et dicuntur ~i eo quod decem clericis sive parochiis presunt); **1326** a tempore .. Stephani quondam archiepiscopi Cantuar', qui archidiaconatum Cantuar' contulit Simoni fratri suo et in augmentum jurisdiccionis dicti archidiaconi concessit eidem archidiacono et successoribus suis creacionem omnium ruralium ~orum vestre diocesis Cantuar' *Lit. Cant.* I 181; **1419** T. Lyes, ~us de Aukland *Pri. Cold.* 92. **b** nunciantes ex parte ~i et capituli finium illorum [de Elvein et Melenith] quod eorum ecclesias .. visitare non deberet GIR. *RG* I 5; **p1254** estimatio ecclesiarum decanatus Landavie facta per Eneam rectorem de Magh'an, ~um [et al.] *Val. Norw.* 314. **c** **1189** ut nullus .. episcopus, archidiaconus, ~us aut eorum officiales in ecclesiis vestris .. [excommunicationis] sententiam audeat promulgare (*Lit. Papae*) *Cart. Dublin* I xxin. **d** **a1180** testibus .. R. ~o de Thevidal', P. ~o de Cludesdal' .. *Reg. Glasg.* 41; **1310** (v. Christianitas 3c); a1400 episcopo de N. vel archidiacono, ~o vel eorum officiali *Conc. Scot.* I ccxxxvii; **1559** quod statutum circa officium ~orum ruralium .. debite execucioni demandetur *Ib.* II 160. **e** **c1155** predictus abbas et quisque successorum ejus sit ~us de omnibus ecclesiis que date sunt ecclesie sue in Derbisira *Cart. Darley* II 596; **s1206** necesse est ut monachi sint ~i, quia, si abbas discessisset, nisi monachus est ~us non esset aliquis qui ministros regis ausus est excommunicare *Chr. Evesham* 195; **1255** qui [abbas] cum auctoritate ipsius episcopi ~um instituet predicte leuge circa monasterium adjacentis *Chr. Battle* [*ed. Brewer*] app. 192.

9 (acad.): **a** dean of college. **b** head of college. **c** dean of faculty (Sc.).

a **1274** de officio ~orum: de scholaribus aliqui de discretioribus eligantur, qui sub .. custode tanquam ejus coadjutores .. agere teneantur; adeo ut numero cuilibet vicenario vel etiam decenario .. presit unus (*Merton*) *Stat. Coll. Ox.* I 25 (cf. ib. 26: scholares .. sub custode et aliis prepositis, vicenariis, et ~is .. mensam communem habeant); **1359** statuimus .. ut quotannis, cum primarius lector eligitur, ~us eciam, qui quasi morum et discipline magister sit, .. eligatur (*Clare Coll.*) *DocCantab* II 177; **1382** v socii .., qui sub .. custode .. scholarium et sociorum curam et regimen habeant .., quos .. sic prefectos ~os volumus nuncupari (*New Coll.*) *Stat. Coll. Ox.* I 37; **1507** duos praeponimus humeros, i.e. duos ~os .., eritque eorum officium sociorum scholasticorum doctrinae providere, virtutis et studii incrementa augere [etc.] (*Balliol*) *Ib.* I 11. **b** **1526** per nomen ~i et canonicorum collegii Thomae Wolsey cardinalis Ebor' (*Cardinal*) *Ib.* II 6. **c** **1413** ego juro quod ero obediens facultati arcium et ~o ejusdem (*Juramentum Bachalar. St. Andr.*) *OED* s. v. *dean* 8; **1453** facultatem, ~os, procuratores, nacionum regentes et scholares in .. universitate *Mun. Univ. Glasg.* I 119; **1549** magister J. Mayr, ~us facultatis theologiae universitatis S. Andree *Conc. Scot.* II 84.

10 dean of guild: **a** (Sc.) **b** (Eng.).

a **c1250** [transgressor] puniatur secundum arbitrium aldirmanni, feryngmannorum, ~i et aliorum confratrum gilde *Stat. Gild. Berw.* 6; **1494** [teste] J. Fowlare, ~o gilde [*Haddington*] *Scot. Grey Friars* II 21; **1559** ~us gilde dicte civitatis [*S. Andree*] *Ib.* 203; **1518** quos dies .. volumus assignari ~is dictarum artium [lathomorum, carpentariorum etc.] et magistris fabrice dicti altaris .. pro apprenticiis et introitibus magistrorum ad libertates dictarum artium et de *le dewites* predictis ~is .. propterea debitis *Form. S. Andr.* I 6; **1536** ~um artis .. pistorie *Offic. S. Andr.* 135. **b** **1389** aldermannus habebit ij laginas servisie die generali, quilibet scabinus unam laginam servisie, ~us unum *potel Guild Cert.* (*King's Lynn*) 42/239.

decapiciatus v. decaputiatus.

decapillare [cf. OF *descheveler*], to crop (the hair of). **b** to scalp.

1290 de prisona ductus fuit .. in ferris et ~atus, tanquam priso (*CoramR*) *Law Merch.* III 11; *CathA* (v. decalvare a). **b** truncetur ei nasus et aures et superlabrum aut ~etur [AS: *do man* .. *hine hættian*] (*Quad.*) *GAS* 335 (= *Inst. Cnut* ib.: auferatur .. corium capitis cum capillis, quod Angli dicunt *behætian*).

decapillatio, removal of hair, depilation.

subtilitas in .. tinctura capillorum vel lexive superciliorum ~one vel eorum erectione cum humida strictione *AncrR* 69.

decapitare [LL], to behead, decapitate: **a** (person); *v. et. excapitare*; **b** (animal). **c** to top (tree). **d** (fig.).

a eum arrepto pugione spiculator uno ictu ~ando hac luce privavit ABBO *Edm.* 10; **s1075** comes Waltheofus jussu regis W. . . securi ~atur FL. WORC. I 12; [Albanus] hospite servato decapitatus obit L. DURH. *Hypog.* I 4 p. 68; **1239** de catallis ij latronum †decapitus [MS: decapit(atorum)] *Pipe Chesh.* 44; Hengistus Saxon fidei corruptor ab hoste / Aurelio captus decapitatus obit GARL. *Tri. Eccl.* 72; **s1272** cum invenissent Hibernici corpus ejus, ~averunt eum W. NEWB. *HA Cont.* 562; **s1305** quia utlagatus fuit [W. Waleys] nec postea ad pacem domini regis restitutus, decolletur et ~etur (*Recordum Placiti*) *Ann. Lond.* 142; **s1326** Hugo [Despenser] . . ~atus et quarteratus fuit caputque suum positum super pontem London' AVESB. 78; quosdam prelatos statuerunt exoculare / altius et natos proceres tunc decapitare *Vers. Hen. V* 162. **b** cicade quedam . . dulcius . . ~ate quam integre . . canunt. unde et pastores . . eas ~are solent GIR. *TH* I 21. **c** **1432** J. B. ~avit j quercum super communam domini *CourtR Banstead*. **d** **c1119** qui Arfastus [episc. Norwic.], suam ~atam ecclesiam inveniens, querimoniam suam ante regem . . deposuit (*Eccl. Estangl.*) *EHR* XL 227.

decapitatio, beheading, decapitation. **b** topping (of trees).

rememoratur abbas sancti [Eadmundi] sanctae ~onis ac . . innuit monachis utrum . . caput . . martyris decollatum cum corpore jam sit solidatum HERM. ARCH. 20; **s1186** de Hugonis de Laci, a securibus male securi, dolo Hibernensium . . ~one GIR. *EH* II 35; **s1312** [P. de Gavastone] abscissione capitis est peremptus. ista . . comitis ~o . . odium . . inter regem et comites suscitavit *G. Ed. II Bridl.* 44; **1337** pro ~one iiij felonum decapitatorum ad sectam regis (*KRAc* 19/40) *Cal. Scot.* III 391; licet . . clerici mereantur puniri tali †decapicione WYCL. *Blasph.* 196 (cf. ib.: si utilius esset ecclesie et persone decapitate mori aliter); **s1381** episcopus . . Johannem [Littestere] . . addixit . . ~oni WALS. *HA* II 8; **s1415** ~onis sentenciam subiere *Id. YN* 457. **b** **13..** translata est carecta spinea ad ~onem quercuum, que nunquam revertebatur ad spinas et tribulos cariand' (*Ch. Pipewell*) *MonA* V 435a (cf. ib. 435b: de ~one quercuum in Personeswode).

decapitio v. decapitatio. **decapitus** v. decapitare.

decapolis [LL < δεκάπολις], district containing ten cities.

~is est ut ipso nomine probat regio decem urbium trans Jordanem BEDE *Mark* (vii 31) 203; **9..** ~eas, *tienceastro WW*.

decaputiatus [cf. caputiare], unhooded (in token of humility).

1365 steterunt super scabell' decapiciati in Gilhalda *Pl. Mem. Lond.* A 10 m. 6; nonne luxuriosus . . prosternitur meretrici? nonne ~us impendit talibus reverencias mundiales? WYCL. *Mand. Div.* 164.

decaquartus, *metri gratia* for *decimus quartus*.

qua sedet Henricus quintus diademate regni, / a Conquestoris rex deca quartus humo; / Edmundo regi Ferrilatus est deca †quartus [? l. nonus] ELMH. *Metr. Hen. V* 52–3.

decarcare [cf. AN *decharger*, OF *deschargier*] to unload: **a** (goods); **b** (ship). *V. et. discarcare* 1, 2, *dischargiare*.

a **1151** nullus extraneus potest ~are apud Rothomagum [vinum] in celario *Act. Hen. II* I 20 (= *Regesta* 729: †decartare); **1258** mercatores Leycestrie qui . . venient ad Stanford' cum panno seu lana . . easdem marcandisas facient cariari ad schopas . . et ibidem facient easdem . . †decariari [? l. decarcari] et aperiri *Rec. Leic.* I 79. **b** **1225** quod navem illam que est in portu . . ~ata vinis, . . arestari faciat *Cl* 28b.

decarcha [cf. δεκάρχης], leader of ten men.

†decacontarche BELETH *RDO* 12. 26c (v. decanus 2a).

†decare, *f. l.*

1534 Willelmus . . felonice nuper †decavit [? l. necavit] Radulphum *Sanct. Bev.* 437.

decariare v. decarcare a, decarriare.

decarius [cf. denarius, *infl. by* decem etc.], (w. *numerus*) number ten.

sicut . . dividitur . . comitatus in plura centenaria, ita centenarium unum in plures decimationes, sicut centum unum in plures ~ios numeros (*Cons. Cnuti*) *GAS* 618.

decarnellare [cf. carnellare, 1 carnellus], to strip of battlements.

1250 murus inter turrem et aulam domini regis dekarnelatus est per partes *CalIMisc* I p. 30 (cf. ib.: duo turelli dekarnellati); murus degarnelatus *Ib.* p. 31.

decarraxare v. decharaxare.

decarriare [cf. 1 carriare], to carry away.

c1395 fimum super eandem placeam terre jacentem decariare debet (*Anc. Indict.*) *Pub. Works* II 62.

decartare v. decarcare a.

decas [LL < δεκάς], decade, group of ten. **b** period of ten years. **c** period of ten days.

numerus centenarius . . decem ~adibus impletur BEDE *Gen.* 85; **798** (v. concurrere 4c); **s878** rex ruit, octoginta quippe cum eo ~ades ÆTHELW. IV 3; figure jubilee ~adis addita litera in hunc modum vixit ille annis lx GIR. *GE* II 8 p. 205; **1426** in Novo Testamento venerabilis est ~as, sicut et fructus spiritus denis exponitur germinare virtutibus *Reg. Cant.* III 136; *tene*, decem, deca, ~ades Grece . ., *twenty*, viginti . ., duodecades [? l. duo ~ades] *CathA*; quique bis inde dias bis septem bis decas letras / si cadit in lucem domini numeralis eandem (*Tab. Fest. Mobil.*) *Brev. Sal.* I. **b** post tertiam annorum ejus †~adam [?l. ~adem] BEDE *Sam.* 520; per Septuagesimam, in cujus septima ~ade filii Israel acceperunt redeundi licentiam [cf. *Jer.* xxv 11–12] BELETH *RDO* 62. 69B; **s1461** finiunt acta in anno decimo . .; de cujus laboris finitione . . scribitur . . in hiis verbis metrificacionis: 'hac nunc in decade, numerus qui dicitur esse, / in qua tocius residet perfeccio legis . .' *Reg. Whet.* II 420. **c** Pentecostes . . festum . . quod post v ~ades Pasche celebratur, unde et vocabulum sumpsit *Ord. Ebor.* II 330.

decasatus [cf. decadere], fallen down, ruined, decayed. *V. et decadere*.

1308 levare faciat domum suam decaisatam sub forisfactura tocius tenementi sui *CourtR Tooting Beck* 243; **c1465** circa reedificacionem ecclesie et sedilium infra ecclesiam per ruinam ecclesie decassatorum *Ac. Churchw. Glast.* 235 (cf. ib. 236: pro nova reedificacione navis [ecclesie] decassate); **1587** capellam modo ~am et prophanatam *Pat* 1265 m. 19; **1588** capellam . . decaisatam sive prophanatam *Ib.* 1295 m. 17.

decaschemus [δεκάσχημος; cf. LL decaschematistus], having ten possible forms.

ex hac triplici sillabarum definitione . . omnis metrorum ratio monstratur et qui versus monoscemi, qui pentascemi vel qui decascemi cum xxiiij temporibus, excepto si trocheo terminentur, rite dicantur ALDH. *Met.* 9 (cf. id. *Ep.* 1 = W. MALM. *GP* V 195); versus xv sillabarum . . x scematibus, ut ille prior, componitur. nam sicut in illo xiv sillabarum dactilus decies variatur, ita in hoc spondeus toties invertitur. . . ergo hujuscemodi versus decascemi dicuntur *Ib.* 10 p. 86.

decastrare [cf. CL castrare], to castrate.

si propter temptationes se ~ant, sciant et intelligant nullomodo esse peccatum si non sit voluntarium. . . canones vero dampnant illos qui semetipsos sponte ~ant corporaliter ÆLF. *Ep.* 2. 81–3.

decassatus v. decasatus. **decassus**, v. decadere 1b.

1 decasus v. decadere 1b.

2 decasus [cf. 3 casus]

1 a (of building) collapse, ruin, decay. **b** (fig.) downfall. **c** (of grain) decay, rotting.

a **1260** menia . . ~ui preparantur et in magna parte ceperunt ~um *CalIMisc* I p. 89; **12..** dictum molendinum [aquaticum], ~um paciens, a nullo prorsus meruit relevari *Meaux* II 49; **1388** solebant esse ibidem ij bercarie. . . et possunt esse ibidem vj^{c} bidentes, unde c oves matrices; et modo nichil, quia in ~u *IMisc* 240/13; **1482** quod . . prioratus . ., per incuriam . . prioris . . edificia . . prioratus collabi permittendo, ad . . ~um et ultimatam destruccionem †incidi . . non dubitatur *Reg. Heref.* 83; **1483** de redditu . . columbaris . . nichil hoc anno, quia . . columbare est totaliter . . in ~u et nulla districcio ibidem inveniri potest hoc anno *Comp. Swith.* 377; **1573** diversa cotagia . . in tam magna ruina et ~u existencia ut . . redditus eorundem . . cito penitus extinguentur *Pat* 1104 m. 7. **b** dubito prope quod generalis / decasus nostre prosperitatis adest GOWER *VC* VII 1242. **c** **1300** in ~u et exsiccacione iij quarteriorum [frumenti] *AcWardr* p. 111; **1313** (v. exsiccatio 1a).

2 loss, deficit, depreciation. **b** loss in coining or assay. *Cf. casura*.

1271 cum . . aretro sint . . vij li. . . in ~u elemosinarum de eadem firma *Cl* 316; quia accepimus . . quod . . concessimus . . hundredum de O. . ., quod . . consuevit reddere per annum vicecomiti xvj m., unde decidere debent . . Waltero . . iiij m., . . vobis mandamus quod predictum †decesum [MS: decasum] eidem W. †allocatis [MS: allocetis] et ipsum inde exoneretis *Ib.* 438; **1290** de ~u dicte avene mensurate per mensuram Scocie (*Pipe* 128) *Doc. Scot.* I 208; **1297** (v. caput 11e); **1346** in ~u firme tenementi Johannis P., quia combustum erat, vj s. viij d. *Sacr. Ely* II 128; **1426** [prior] habet sub se cellerarium . ., qui . . laboret . . ad . . reformandum quicquid ~us aut descrescentie contigerit in materia supradicta AMUND. I 218; **s1454** officia [camere etc.] stant pro nunc nequaquam in incremento sive in statu solito, immo verius in decremento in ~uque non modico pejoranturque in receptis suis annuis *Reg. Whet.* I 128; **1464** ~us [ville de Southwike] lxxvij s.; et precipua causa ~us predicti fuit . . propter nimiam oppressionem tenencium factam per J. H. defunctum *Feod. Durh.* 119; **1524** se exonerat . . de vj li. xij s. de ~ibus hujus compoti *Ac. Durh.* 666; **1581** pro eo quod maxima pars mercatorum in . . civitate [Ebor'] commorancium in magnam paupertatem et ~um ducantur (*Pat* 1201) *Gild Merch.* II 281. **b** **1259** ~um auri regis et sumptus quos W. . . apposuit in nova moneta . . auri . . fabricanda . . eidem W. in exitibus cambii regis allocari faciant *Cl* 415; **a1272** [cambitor] capiat de qualibet libra veteris monete . . x d. ad opus monetariorum pro †decensu ad ignem *RBExch* 983; **1280** allocabuntur . . magistro [monete] j d. et j quad. in ~u argenti ad ignem et j d. et ob. in emendacione cujuslibet libre monete *Ib.* 985.

decasyllabus [LL < δεκασύλλαβος], having ten syllables (in a line).

rithmus decasillabus iambicus . ., sicut habetur in rithmo 'de querela Edippi', sic: 'diri patris infausta pignora' GARL. *PP* 180.

decatertius, *metri gratia* for *decimus tertius*.

mcccc decatercius astra movebat / annus Verbigene, tuus xx sexque patebat *Vers. Hen. V* 59.

decaudare [cf. caudare], to dock, deprive of tail. **b** (fig.) to curtail, diminish.

[archiepiscopus] terribili sententia damnavit unum de regalibus qui . . equos . . ad ipsius contumeliam ~avit GRIM *Thom.* 74; **13..** minabatur . . monachis quod, si ipse aliquos illorum inveniret equites, equos ~aret (*Reg. Pipewell*) *MonA* V 437a; ~o, *to kytte of the tayle WW*. **b** GOWER *VC* V 819 (v. apocope 1b).

decausa [Ar. *daqīq*], gut.

tharme, intestinum, . . lien, ~a, zirbus, omasus . . *CathA*.

1 decedere [CL]

1 to depart, withdraw; *v. et.* 1 *discedere* 1. **b** to be taken away.

illo prae inopia rerum ab episcopatu ~ente atque ad alia loca secedente BEDE *HE* IV 12; **s1095** (v. 2 conductus 1c); **1200** (v. chevalchea). **b** fratre immatura morte intercepto ejusdemque nominis filio . . in pugna extincto . ., multum felicitati sue decessisse . . suspiravit W. MALM. *GR* I 17.

2 to decease; *v. et.* 1 *discedere* 3; *cf.* 1 *decidere* 2b. **b** (pr. ppl. as sb.) decedent, deceased.

illis ~entibus cum successisset aetas tempestatis illius nescia GILDAS *EB* 26; ambo . . / decedunt mundo Dominique feruntur ad aulam BEDE *CuthbV* 654; rex . . vita decessit *Id. HE* V 23; **759** (15c) ~entibus primis testibus *CS* 186; **813** (17c) illis viventibus seu ~entibus *CS* 342; **s1152** quem [statum] totiens creditur [ecclesia Dunelm'] immutasse quotiens †descendente suo pontifice, in alterius regimen visa est successisse G. COLD. *Durh.* 2; cum bona confessione ~entibus . . obsequium debitum persolvatur GIR. *EH* I 35; subito casu . . in fata decessit *Id. PI* III 2 p. 229; **1225** antequam R. descederat (*sic*) *BNB* III 116; **1363** cum magister . . in fata decesserit *Lit. Cant.* II 440; quidam nobilium ascendencium marcialia decesserunt in †facta [l. fata] *Ps.*-ELMH. *Hen. V* 45 p. 110; **1503** obiit et ab hac luce decessit *Sanct. Durh.* 92. **b** **1237** (v. communis 7a); **1309** in periculum anime ~entis *Deeds Balliol* 337; **1353** junior masculus . . puerorum post decessum . . patris sui vel . . matris sue possidebit tenementum dicti ~entis (*Cust. Bradf.*) *Som Rec. Soc.* LXVI 85.

2 decedere v. 1 decidere 1a.

decem [CL], ten.

nos decem et septem genitae sine voce sorores ALDH. *Aen.* 30 (*Elementum*) 1; cum dicis ~em, unguem indicis in medio figes artu pollicis BEDE *TR* 1; **c795** ~im (*sic*) praecepta sunt legis . .; ~im minas dedit Christus [*Luke* xix 13] ALCUIN *Ep.* 81; **798** (12c) terram centum et ~em manentium *CS* 291; **9..** ille ~em, *se tyn WW*; **s1240** duodecim milites . . fuerunt electi in asisa . ., et consenserunt partes in ~em, quia duo non comparuerunt M. PAR. *Maj.* IV 53.

December [CL], **~rius**, December (adj. or sb.).

September mensis, October, November, et ~er principalem sui retinent appellationem, significantes nomine quoti sint a verno mense, id est Martio BEDE *TR* 12 (cf. ib. 15: [apud Anglos] ~er *Giuli*, eodem quo Januarius nomine, vocatur); hoc bellum rex Osuiu . . xvij^{a} die Kalendarum ~rium . . confecit *Id. HE* III 24; **s1184** mense ~rio GERV. CANT. *Chr.* 325 (cf. ib.: xiiij [diebus] in ~rio); **1199** dat' . . apud Pictavis iiij die Decemb[ris] anno regni nostri primo *RChart* 62b; **s1258** prima nocte ~ris fuit tonitrus . . in triste auspicium, quod semper solet tonitrus significare hiemalis M. PAR. *Maj.* V 724; **1267** hoc anno fuit solsticium hyemale idibus ~ris per xij dies ante Nativitatem Domini BACON *Maj.* I 272; **s1422** natus est . . dominus meus rex mense ~rio. . . ex antiqua consuetudine tenet mensis iste nomen suum '~er', quasi 'decimus imber', ex decade virtutem suam eructans CAPGR. *Hen.* 126.

Decembrica, winter feast, Saturnalia.

hec libertas ideo dicta est ~a quod olim apud ethnicos moris fuerit ut hoc mense servi . . velut quadam libertate donarentur BELETH *RDO* 120. 123C.

decemnovennalis (decenno-) [LL], consisting of 19 years.

680 patrum regulam . ., qui in Niceno concilio decemnovenalem laterculi circulum per ogdoadam et endicadam usque ad finem mundi recto tramite decurs[ur]um . . sanxerunt ALDH. *Ep.* 4; decemnovenalis circuli ordinem

primus Eusebius .. ob .. diem Paschae inveniendum composuit, eo quod luna .. post tantum temporis ad eundem redeat anni solaris diem BEDE *TR* 44; *Ib.* 56, ALCUIN *Ep.* 126 etc. (v. cyclus 3c); **779** anno decemnovenali primo lunari xvij *CS* 230; circulus ~is, *se niganteoþa getælcircul* ÆLF. *Gl.*; **977** (11c) xvij° anno cicli †decenovelis *Land Ch.* 295; ciclum decennovalem GERV. CANT. *Chr. pref.* 90 (cf. ib. 112: ciclus ~is); **1214** anno quinto decimo regni J. regis Anglie ciclo decem †novali [? l. nonali] currente per decem et octo *AncD* B 5129; **1238** anno gratie mccxxxviij, cicli .. ~is quarto (*Chirog.*) *FormA* 133; cyclus lunaris incipit in quarto anno cycli decennovenalis et continet xix annos sicut noster cyclus BACON *Tert.* 214.

decempeda [CL], ten-foot measuring rod.

gaade, to mete with londe, ~a *PP.*

decemplex [CL], tenfold.

~ex .. sexies, *six siþum tynfeald GlP* 950.

decena (decenn-), ~ia, ~um, ~ium [cf. LL decenus, AN *deseine*, OF *dizeine, disaine*]

1 tithing, frankpledge group (of ten men mutually responsible for law-abiding conduct); **b** (dist. acc. identity of tithing-man); **c** (dist. acc. locality). (*Cf.* W. A. Morris *The Frankpledge System* (1910) pp. 86–103). *Cf. decimatio* 5, *decimus* 5.

1214 Walterus .., quem Stephanus .. apellavit de societate latronum et de quo testatum fuit quod ipse est legalis homo, committitur in custodia ~e sue *CurR* VII 100; **1227** ad duo lagehundreda per annum venire debent omnes homines .. ville [*Godalming, Sur*] de capitalibus ~nis ..; de subdecennis nullus homo venire debet *Ib.* XIII 88; **1246** curia presentat quod N. B. non est in ~a et tenet terram; ideo distringatur *SelPlMan* 8; **12..** debet summonire docinnas de Northilede ad omnes curias Glastonie *Cust. Glast.* 177; **s1274** ballivus Eudonis .. in visu franciplegii sui .. inprisonavit J. .. hominem nostrum, quia in ipso visu per ~as illius curie de latrocinio fuerat indictatus *Ann. Dunstable* 261; **1274** ballivus .. capit de quolibet homine qui est in eorum dicena ij d. pro capite eorum injuste *Hund.* I 138; **1276** Gillelma tenet discenam in curia de Coy *Ib.* 53; **1277** (1355) ad .. curiam [de Hedyndone, *Oxon*] singulis annis inter festum S. Mich. et S. Martini venient iidem homines cum toto ac pleno dyceno *Cart. Boarstall* 538 (= *Ambrosden* I 454: †dyteno; cf. *CalPat 1354–8* 302: dyseno); **1287** ~ne sue [sc. magistri milicie Templi] sunt de collecta de diversis villis *PQW* 5b; **1292** respondebunt franciplegii .. pro dezennis suis omnia que ad pacem et coronam domini regis spectant *Cart. Burton* 59; **1345** de iiij s. de certo fine ~nie per annum *Comp. Swith.* 147; **1360** non sunt jurati in dicena *CourtR Carshalton* 20 (cf. ib. 35 [**1392**]: in desena); **1375** non venit ad letam neque est in ~na domini regis *Leet Norw.* 65 (cf. ib. lvii); **c1430** fines pro licencia intrare in ~a et recedere *Cart. Ciren.* II 619. **b** **1191** A. faber et ~a ejus debet x s. quia non habuit quem plegiavit *Pipe* 90; **1197** ~a Herevei de H. r. c. de dim. m. pro fuga Willelmi Coci [etc.] *Ib.* 243; **1239** ~a Ricardi C. et Rogeri H. manuceperunt villatam de Hadfeld [*Essex*] adessendi coram justiciariis foreste *SelPlForest* 71; cum quis se posuerit in francum plegium alicujus vel ~nam vel ex antiquo secutus fuerit cum ~na, non poterit se retrahere cum voluerit BRACTON 124b; **1276** fuit quasi fugitivus pro multis latrociniis .. et fuit in desaino Mauricii filii Rogeri *Hund.* II 175; **c1280** (v. decenarius 3a); omnis .. xij annos habens et ultra in alicujus frithborgo esse debet et in ~na *Fleta* 40; **1315** (v. borgesalder); **1368** Johannes Bole in discena Johannis ate Stocke *CourtR* 178/51 r. 2; **1387** vic. regi computat de j m. de ~na Ricardi Fabri de Estone pro fuga (*Ch. Regis*) *G. S. Alb.* III 64. **c** **1219** committitur ~ne sue de Cestrehunt' [*Herts*] *CurR* VIII 144; **1278** de ~na de Moredenn' [*Dorset*] de auxilio vic. *PQW* 183a; **1285** nulla habuit catalla; sed fuit in ~na de Bunsey (*Eyre*) *DocCOx* 202; **1421** omnes terras et tenementa que nuper perquesivi .. infra ~ium de Stepham [*Kent*] *Reg. Cant.* II 216.

2 a (?) set of ten pairs (of gloves). **b** measure of iron. **c** measure of charcoal (? = *duodena*).

a **1312** iij ~na cyrotecarum *Reg. Leic.* I 375. **b** **1313** in dim. summa et j ~na ferri emptis, xj s. *Ib.* 284. **c** **1333** [in] carbonibus [em]ptis, qualibet ~a continente xxiiij [quarteria] carbonum, ad dictas blomas faciendas .., pro ~a iij s. iij d. (*MinAc* 890/25) *Arch.* LXIV 157 (cf. ib. 153).

3 a form of weekly payment. (*Cf. Cust. Rents* 193). **b** (*s. dub.*).

a **c1300** eadem .. xv maneria solvunt lij dizenas ad cameram S. Pauli (*Stat. Maj. S. Paul.*) *Dom. S. Paul.* 160; **c1300** de terminis statutis de solvendo firmas et disanas *DC S. Paul.* WD 5 f. 60b (*HMC* p. 69a). **b** **1292** Johanni de Maundeville pro detencione j ~ne et aliorum serviciorum in Netherlym [*Dorset*], xj li. x s. (*KRAc* 353/1 r. 3) *Manners* 126.

decenalis, a relating to a tithing. **b** (w. *numerus*) number ten.

a de omnibus villis totius regni sub decennali fidejussione debebant omnes esse, ita quod, si unus ex decem forisfaceret, novem haberent eum ad rectum (*Leg. Ed.*) *GAS* 645. **b** **1527** donec .. numerus .. procuratorum .. sub et infra numerum decennalem decreverit *Conc.* III 711a.

decenaria, tithing or (?) *f. l.*

s1286 [prior], requisitus quot habet decennarias [? l. ~ios], dicit quod habet in visu suo [franci plegii] quem tenet apud Dunestaple circiter xxx decennarias [? l. ~ios], et in visu suo quem tenet apud Flittewike circiter iiij decennarias [? l. ~ios], et similiter in visu suo quem tenet apud Howtone circiter iiij decennarias [? l. ~ios] capitales *Ann. Dunstable* 330 (= *PQW* 14a: decennar' *in all cases*); **1302** batellum appreciatur ad xij d. .. de quo precio ~ia [? l. ~ius] de Bensey cum tota ~ia [? l. decena] sua respondebit (*Inq. Coron.*) *DocCOx* 164.

decenarius (decenn-) [LL = CL denarius, *infl. by* septenarius etc.]

1 (w. *numerus* or as sb. m.) number ten.

ut .. citius ad memoriam revoces anno tali tale quid accidisse, per unius incrementum in x, per ~iorum multiplicationem in milia, rerum facilius poteris habere notitiam DICETO *Chr. prol.* 18; ~ius numerus est perfectio eorum que complectuntur quaternarium et circumdabunt in numeris BACON V 150; differencie signorum .. non pinguntur ultra numerum ~ium BAD. AUR. 134; **1440** si .. fuerit aliquis numerus [incepturorum] residuus ultra numerum ~ium *StatOx* 263.

2 captain of ten (Gasc.). *Cf.* AN *deceyner, dizeiner*, OF *disenier*.

1295 quilibet peditum .. capiet per diem ij d. et vicenarius et ~ius per diem iij d. (*Chanc. Misc.* 2/12) *RGasc* III cl (cf. ib.: †vimenarius [MS: vintenarius] iij d. et ~ius similiter).

3 tithingman, headborough, chief pledge (of frankpledge group); **b** (w. *capitalis*). **c** (?) ordinary member of tithing. *Cf. decimalis* 1. (*Cf.* W. A. Morris *The Frankpledge System* (1910) pp. 103–111).

1183 in terris datis Widoni qui fuit ~ius de Waltham *Pipe* 7; **1261** ballivi .. prioris presentare debent ~ium coram ballivis .. abbatis in plena curia ipsius prioris .. ad duos turnos .. abbatis *Cart. Ciren.* I 355; **1276** ~ii locorum illorum attachiati .. ad furcas illas expectasse debuerant donec [felones] ultimum spiritum exalassent *MonA* VI 809a (= *CalPat* 175); **1278** vic. Kancie .. distringat omnes dissenarios de baronia .. abbatis .. venire coram eo in com. ad respondendum quare nolunt presentare .. defaltas .. tenencium .. de baronia *RParl* I 4; **c1280** si R. at Mare sit ~ius, respondebit cum tota decenna sua per annum j m. (*Cust.*) *Crawley* 233; **1286** quod dezennarii presentant ad magnam curiam defectus spectantes ad coronam *BBC* (*Bakewell*) 369; **s1286** (v. decenaria); de custodibus hostiorum in itineribus .. ordinatum est quod de inventoribus, vicinis et aliis attachiatis villatis, iiij hominibus et preposito vel de ~iis nihil capiant *Fleta* 88 (cf. *StRealm* I 93 *n.*4); **1301** ~ii de P. secuti fuerunt ipsos .. cum hutesio volentes ipsos atachiare; et dictus dominus R. P. noluit permittere ~ios intrare curiam suam, set recettavit dictos R. et R. *SelCCoron* 58–9; **1315** (v. borgesalder); **1462** (v. 2 borgus); **1519** presentacio ~iorum, viz. vocatorum *le hedboroghes*, de Baroughby [*Lincs*] *CourtR* 183/116 m. 5. **b** **s1286** (v. decenaria); **1290** (v. capitalis 7a); tota villata debet †presentari [? l. presentare] per sex capitales ~ios *Chr. Peterb.* 110; **1368** capitales discenarii presentant quod dant domino de certo fine ij s. *CourtR* (*Herts*) 178/51 r. 2. **c** que .. presentacio non fuit advocata de ~iis suis de capitali plegio *Leet Norw.* 44 (cf. ib. xxix).

decenator, tithingman.

1266 Reginaldus C. factus fuit decennator *CourtR* (*Beds*) 154/34 m. 6; **1300** dicunt quod nulla vidua non solvantur (*sic*) [*tuthyngpeny*] nec facere solebant nec nullus ~at[or] infra officium suum nichil dant (*sic*) *RentSurv. P* 14/57 r. 3; **1415** hutesia .. presentata .. per sacramentum dussinatorum de novo electorum et juratorum *Rec. Nott.* II 104.

decendere v. descendere.

decendium, period of ten days.

1249 jam elapso ~io, id est diebus decem (*Lit. R. Cardinalis*) M. PAR. *Maj.* V 63; simile his videtur quod est infra ~ium appellandum; nam nulla racio magis cogebat ab inicio ad x dies quam ad xj vel ad ix BRADW. *CD* 234B.

decenia, ~ium v. decena 1c. **decenna** v. decena.

1 decennalis v. decenalis.

2 decennalis [LL < CL = *recurring every ten years*], lasting ten years.

~em .. fecerat continentiam GIR. *GE* II 18; **s1229** Soldanus .. coactus est cum Imperatore mediantibus treugis ~ibus componere WEND. II 364; **s1252** domum Girivallensem .. continuatis ~ibus persecutionibus non destitit fatigare M. PAR. *Maj.* V 356; prelium ~e Trojanum R. BURY *Phil.* 7. 113; **p1400** per absenciam ~em AMUND. I app. 415.

decennaria, ~ius v. decenar-. **decennia** v. decena 1a.

decennis [CL], ten years old. **b** (w. *novennis*) extending over nineteen years.

puerum, licet ~em, in paternum regnum promovere *Hist. Meriadoci* 345. **b** **680** secundum ~em novennemque Anatolii computatum ALDH. *Ep.* 4.

decennium [CL], period of ten years, decade.

peniteant .. iij annos in iiij feria et vj, et in iij xl[mis] hoc secundum canones ~ium judicatur THEOD. *Pen.* I 14. 24; per ~ium .. morbo laboraverat R. COLD. *Cuthb.* 53; **1316** transacto termino predicto ~ii *Kelso* 311.

decennovalis, ~enalis v. decemnovennalis. **decennus** v. decanus 6. **decenovelis** v. decemnovenalis. **decensia** v. decentia. **decensus** v. 2 decasus 2b, descensus.

decenter [CL], decently, fittingly, in a seemly manner; **b** (w. ref. to burial).

imperatoris insignibus, quae nec ~er usquam gessit, non legitime, sed ritu tyrannico GILDAS *EB* 13; virginitatis nobilitas .. multimoda mandatorum varietate ~er decoretur ALDH. *VirgP* 15; risus ille ~er significat gaudium novi testamenti BEDE *Gen.* (xvii 17) 164; ejusdem loci situm monasterialibus edificiis ~issime renovavit WULF. *Æthelwold* 23; **1194** ad .. molendina reparanda ~er *CurR RC* I 61; **c1214** hominibus meis concedo ne eant in exercitu extra Angliam nisi in Normanniam et in Britanniam, et hoc ~er (? *Ch. J. Regis*) *EHR* VIII 291; eos [subditos suos] ~issime ex suis relevans BLAKMAN *Hen. VI* 9. **b** corpus .. in porticu .. ~er sepultum est BEDE *HE* II 3; sanctorum pignora .. ~issime reposita GOSC. *Transl. Aug.* 39B; circa cujus [Gwydonis] sepulcrum et ipsa [uxor ejus] .. ~issime humata est G. CORNW. *Guy Warw.* 830.

decenti v. decere 4, ducenti.

decentia [CL], appropriate character or treatment.

decensia BACON VII 22 (v. congruitas a); **1315** capellam .. juxta ~iam qua convenit omnibus insigniis parochialibus volumus .. insigniri *Melrose* 407; ad ~iam judicis .. spectat quod habeat noticiam illarum legum et jurium secundum que est .. judicandum OCKHAM *Dial.* 633; **s1216** domum ubi ipsemet rex J. hospitabatur, contra regalem majestatem et ~iam, propriis manibus ignem imponendo combussit *Plusc.* VII 4; **1389** ad .. majorem †~ium [MS: ~iam] ministrancium in eadem proinde ordinabat .. (*Pat*) *MonA* VI 1309a; **1418** volo quod, ubi corpus meum sepelietur, ponatur lapis marmoreus juxta ~iam meam *Reg. Cant.* II 165.

decentus v. discantus. **decenum** v. decena.

decenus [LL = CL denus, *infl. by* septeni etc.; cf. decena], (pl.) ten each. **b** tenth, of ten. **c** (w. *numerus* or ellipt.) the number ten; **d** (in comp. numeral).

inibi milites ejus vicenos et duodenos ~osque [v. l. denos et duodenos] singula duxit per hospicia *Enc. Emmae* III 4. **b** primus .. [abaci] arcus singularis est vocatus, secundus ~us, tertius centenus, quartus millenus, quintus decenus millenus THURKILL *Abac.* 55v. (v. et. d infra). **c** si multiplicaveris per ~um singularem numerum, dabis unicuique digito x et omni articulo c; si multiplicaveris ~um per ~um, dabis unicuique digito c et omni articulo m BYRHT. *Man.* 232; THURKILL *Abac.* 58 (v. decimare 7). **d** *Ib.* 55v. (v. b supra).

deceptabilis v. deceptibilis. **deceptare, ~atio, ~ator** v. decept-.

deceptibilis, ~abilis, a deceptive, deceitful. **b** subject to deceit, fallible.

a **c625** spretis .. auguriorum ~abilibus [v. l. ~ibilibus] blandimentis (*Lit. Papae*) BEDE *HE* II 10 (cf. ib.: expulsa .. sollicitatione venenosi et ~ibilis Hostis); **c797** ~ibilis auri species ALCUIN *Ep.* 189; **1295** deceptus per capciosam astuciam ~ibilem aliquorum (*Lit. Papae*) B. COTTON 265; **1401** ad resistendum voluntati fraudabili et ~abili eorundem inimicorum nostrorum [sc. Saxonum] (*Lit. Oeni ad dominos Hiberniae*) AD. USK 73. **b** creatura racionalis .. est de se mutabilis intellectus; potest enim .. †decepi [l. decipi], dum id quod credit esse verum, re tali clam mutata, sit [? l. fit] falsum; quare et est similiter mutabilis, ~ibilis et peccabilis voluntatis BRADW. *CD* 527C.

deceptio [LL], deception, deceit, fraud; **b** (w. obj. gen.). **c** fraudulent manipulation. **d** being deceived, error, misconception.

ALDH. *VirgP* 53 (v. decipula b); solent gentiles .. ~onum tendere laqueos, dicendo .. BEDE *Hom.* II 9. 141; ab errore diabolicae ~onis *Ib.* II 6. 234; **855** (11c) qui in aliquo fraude vel disceptione .. istam libertatem .. minuere temptaverit *CS* 487; ~o, i. fraus, *lotwrænc, beswicung GlH* D 36; [philosophi Greci] possent cito multos .. dubiis ~onibus a statu certitudinis concutere M. PAR. *Min.* III 64; **s1262** rex se sensit falsis ~onibus circumventum RISH. 10; nullam aliam ~onem fecit in curia .. nec aliquam aliam falsitatem *State Tri. Ed. I* 25; sompnium dormiendo non reputetis nisi fantasma, quia ~o [ME: *gile*] ejus [sc. Traditoris infernalis] est *AncrR* 81; in tantis proditorum ~onibus et prodicionibus *Plusc. pref.* p. 4. **b** **c625** qua .. mentis ~one eos deos .. colentes sequimini .. repperire non possumus (*Lit. Papae*) BEDE *HE* II 10; ad ~onem stultorum *V. Greg.* p. 89; **a804** permissum est maligno spiritui ad ~onem ista [auguria] observantium facere ALCUIN *Ep.* 267; **1292** quod scriptum proposuit in ~onem domini regis *PQW* 114b; **1335** in nostri contemptum et ~onem manifestam *RScot* 310b; **1375** in ~onem populi *Leet Norw.* 64. **c** **1290** mercatores .. conqueruntur quod per ~onem tronagii et suptilitatem manuum ponderancium decipiuntur catallis suis *RParl* I 47b. **d** Gerebertus .. consulta statua ~onem suam et mortem suam cognovit

W. MALM. *GR* II 172; **1222** per ~onem amiserat hereditatem suam *BNB* II 136; didicimus .. quod decepta fuit, credens se esse impregnatam cum non esset. et ideo vobis mandamus quod propter illam ~onem non omittatis quin capiatis homagium predicti C. BRACTON 71; magister .. credidit quod Maius vocaretur .. nomine quod Novembri datur in Hebreo .. et sic deceptus est .. et ~o .. glossatoris fuit sicut magistri BACON *Tert.* 211.

deceptitas, state of being deceived or mistaken.

non .. posset esse racio quare Deus immediate deciperet; sed omnem decepcionem possibilem communicare potest causato, cum non sit magnum ipsum excedere in ~ate WYCL. *Act.* 126.

deceptiuncula, petty deception.

falsis ~is nostra bestia astringit animam COLET *Rom. Enarr.* 150.

deceptive, deceitfully.

1289 cum .. litteram a cancellaria nostra clam ~e subtraxerit *RGasc* II 354; **1332** idem T. summas illas sub colore lucri falso et ~e cepit et asportavit *Reg. Brev. Orig.* 290.

deceptivus [LL], deceptive, deceitful.

nec ubique transtulimus verbum ex verbo, sed sensum ex sensu, cavendo .., diligentissime ~os errores ÆLF. *CH pref.* I 1; 'profanas vocum novitates', [i.e.] ~as propositiones LANFR. *Comment. Paul.* (*1 Tim.* vi 20) 360; ratiocinatio .. ~a sophistica vocatur KILWARDBY *OS* 509; modicam certitudinem haberet homo in ejus doctrina .. si sit [Deus] plus ~us hominis quam aliqua res causata WYCL. *Act.* 125; quod Cristus .. fuit homo falsissimus, mendacissimus, et maxime ~us *Id. Ver.* II 1; **1573** ~as, injustas aut minus veras soluciones, allocaciones et deducciones *Pat* 1104 m. 6; **1588** talia ~a, covinosa sive fraudulenta devisamenta, A. *practices Entries* 207b.

deceptor [CL], deceiver; **b** (as title of Satan).

factiosus, fallax, ~or *GlC* F 47; ~or, *bepæcend* ÆLF. *Sup.*; pseudomenus, ~or OSB. GLOUC. *Deriv.* 480; plebem .. ~ores falsa vaticinantes suadebant ut .. non crederent J. SAL. *Pol.* 419A; si [oculi] in profundo sunt positi, dicimus quod callidus est et ~or GILB. III 129v. 2; auctores theologi moderni temporis canonistas tanquam .. fallaces, ~ores, cavillatores et ignaros .. despiciunt OCKHAM *Dial.* 401; *a begyler*, ~or *CathA*. **b** quando ~or infernalis [ME: *þe sweoke of helle*] allicere nititur ad aliquid quod videtur .. bonum *AncrR* 80.

deceptorie, deceitfully. **b** mistakenly.

incircumcisi questiones ~ie ceteris faciebant LANFR. *Comment. Paul.* (*Tit.* i 10) 369; **1254** transgressionem .. fecit ~ie ponendo in Judaismo nostro .. quoddam vadium cupreum tanquam argentum *RGasc* I 482 (cf. *CalPat* 313); **1311** quod Petrus de G... regem .. ad male faciendum ~ie et multiformiter induxit (*Ordinatio*) *V. Ed. II* 172; **1369** iidem .. reputant .. cedulam esse falsam et in ligula .. esse ~ie positam (*CoramR* 434) *EHR* XXXV 414; **1428** tales observancie [i.e. jejunia] a summis pontificibus erant ~ie institute (*Examinatio W. Whyte*) *Ziz.* 427. **b s1225** libertates generales .., pro quibus tantum cum rege J. decertatum fuit, licet nihil stabile vel solidum secundum pollicita redderetur vel observaretur, sunt ~ie [*ed:* ~iae] acclamate M. PAR. *Maj.* III 92.

deceptorius [CL], deceptive, deceitful. **b** erroneous, mistaken. **c** (as sb. f.) 'deceiver', die. **d** (as sb. n.) deceit.

~ias illas lacrimas judicabimus? AILR. *Spec. Car.* II 17. 565B; gradientes .. per eam [sc. vitam presentem] in .. fomento corporis, non jacentes in ea in ~io somno mentis AD. SCOT *Serm.* 253B; abjicite mel .. ~ie voluptatis P. BLOIS *Serm.* 724A; **s1254** breve .. in quo continetur hoc falsum et ~ium M. PAR. *Maj.* V 445; credis tu quod me decipies per verba tua blanda et ~ia? *Latin Stories* 114; **1438** ille dompnus R. maxime ~ius est, nec verum intimavit *Cant. Coll. Ox.* III 97; *false*, falsus, .. ~ius, dolosus *CathA*. **b** in hac opinione, quamquam ~ia, non solum ipse sed et patria fere tota .. tunc temporis erat GIR. *Invect.* V 15. **c** thessaras, i. *dez*, ~ias *GlSid* 143. **d** per inpostum, per deceptorium, / si negare vis adjutorium HIL. RONCE. 6. 46.

deceptrix [LL], deceiver, deceitful (f.).

~ix, fallax, seductrix, *biswica GlH* D 35; nebula que est nimietas ~icis indiscretionis AD. SCOT *Serm.* 123C; [vulpem] ~icem advertit mortuam se esse mentientem NECKAM *NR* II 125; fit ipsa cito credula blandiciis ~icis *Wager* f. 41a.

deceptuose, deceitfully.

1270 capellum false sive ~e factum, sc. mixtum vel de alio quam de lana factum *MGL* II 101.

deceptuosus, deceitful.

cui [gallo] illa [gallina]: "domine, nullo modo [exi]; multum ~a est [vulpes], et nescitur ad quem finem tendit" J. SHEPPEY *Fab.* 67.

1 deceptus v. decipere.

2 deceptus [LL], deceit, deceiving.

1398 in grave dampnum et ~um .. populi *Doc. Bev.* 42.

decēre [CL]

1 to befit, be fitting or becoming (for).

ea tantummodo [facere potuit] quae religiosam ejus linguam ~ebant BEDE *HE* IV 22 p. 259; **8..** non ~ent [? l. ~et], *ne riseð WW*; BIRCHINGTON *Arch. Cant.* 10 (v. Christianus 1e); sollicitudo decet animam discreta GOWER *VC* III 1971.

2 (w. inf.) to be intended, have a duty or right.

a690 nequaquam flagrans lichinus .. occulitur .., qui .. cunctus limpido lumine lucere ~uit [cf. *Matth.* v 15] ALDH. *Ep.* 5; nec decuit modio abscondi tam clara lucerna ALCUIN *WillV* 34. 53; **797** clementia regis omnium hominum .. excellere ~et consuetudines *Id. Ep.* 123; principaliter ~et Romanorum Imperator in armis suis aquilam portare BAD. AUR. 118.

3 (impers., usu. w. inf.) to befit, be right or fitting: **a** (w. acc.); **b** (w. dat.); **c** (absol.); **d** (w. *ut*).

a neglecto, ut ~et Christi discipulum, fucato ostro ALDH. *Ep.* 3; nos credere ~et nihil eum .. perdidisse BEDE *HE* II 1 p. 74; neminem perturbari ~et BALSH. *AD* 39; decuit te volvere pensa / et vacuare colum VINSAUF *PN* 519; H. AVR. *Guthl.* 77v. 2 (v. comparticipare a); quia .. non fecisti, ut ~uit vocationem tuam, dignos fructus penitentie ECCLESTON *Adv. Min.* 18. **b** c**800** audiens vestram laudabilem conversationem, sicut ~et vestre persone ALCUIN *Ep.* 302; nobis visum est nobis ~ere consilium cardinalis requirere H. CANTOR 7; **s1295** mercedem sue faccionis, ut ~et traditoribus, accepit *Eul. Hist.* III 164. **c** perfecte, ut decuit, postquam iam cuncta peregit / .. / extremum aetatis clauserat ipse diem *Epigr. Milredi* 810; construxit .. aecclesiam, ad quam eum, ut ~ebat, transtulit cum magna gloria ABBO *Edm.* 13; vix unum invenies qui .. diurnos labores enormius quam ~eret nocte non redimat GIR. *TH* III 27; **s1254** rex .., qui eum .. ultra quam debuit aut ~uit in episcopatum .. promoverat M. PAR. *Maj.* V 469. **d** nec ~et ut hoc faciant *Cust. Westm.* 173; **1298** ~et ut ministri .. tanto majori polleant sanctitate .. quanto .. *Lit. Cant.* I 25; alioquin .. ~eret ut summus sacerdos nove legis hujusmodi se implicaret OCKHAM *Pol.* I 41; **1481** ~et ut exultent .. Christicole quod .. *Reg. Cant.* 135.

4 (pr. ppl.) seemly, becoming, estimable.

ut .. non pertimescas libertatis aureae decenti nota inuri GILDAS *EB* 1; virguncula .. / pulchra comis cirrisque decens ALDH. *VirgV* 2177; montem .. qui .. gratia ~entissima .. situs est (*V. Albani*) BEDE *HE* I 7; c**980** †dicentissimo .. archipraesuli (*Lit. Ignoti*) *Mem. Dunst.* 376; praecellentissimus Augustinus et ~entissimi consortes sui GOSC. *Transl. Aug.* 34B; **1255** (v. comitiva 2a); **1270** ad sustentationem .. pauperum ~entium [? l. degentium] ibidem *Cl* 217.

5 ? *f. l.*

quo vitio cum †dēcenti [vv. ll. cum cedenti, concedenti, cum de centum; ? l. detenti] plerique laborent, / unum supra omnes Euripidem video G. WINT. *Epigr.* 110; profitentur se .. fidelem regulam observare, sed alienis consuetudinibus †decenti [? l. detenti], magis ex occasione quam ex veritate sanctam regulam sepius †jubenter [? l. jubentur] audire SERLO GRAM. *Mon. Font.* 12.

decernere [CL]

1 to decide, determine (the outcome of). **b** to appoint. **c** (w. dat.) to assign, allot (to). **d** to sentence (person to punishment). *V. et. discernere* 5.

abas ~at GILDAS *Pen.* 18; per me fata virum dicunt decernere Parcas ALDH. *Aen.* 45 (*Fusum*) 6 (cf. ib. 74. 6: cum tereti bellum decernere saxo); decernat igitur judex clemencia / si debent recipi tot testimonia WALT. WIMB. *Carm.* 294. **b 1580** virtute cujusdam commissionis in ea parte a .. convocatione decretae *StatOx* 417. **c** seva mihi genitrix atroxque est lena decreta, / crudelisque pater pardus HWÆTBERHT *Aen.* 46 (*Leopardus*) 1; episcopatus .. Guintonie Diuuanio ~itur. †dercernitur quoque pontificalis Alclud Eledenio G. MON. IX 15; Vulcano famuli, qui fulmina fabricent, ~untur Brontes et Steropes et Pyracmon ALB. LOND. *DG* 10. 5. **d 1325** Robertum .. carcerali pene subeunde non decrevimus *Lit. Cant.* I 151.

2 (w. inf.) to decide, resolve.

671 fateor .. me .. decrevisse .. Natalis Domini sollemnitatem ibidem .. celebrare ALDH. *Ep.* 1; cum .. illi soli servire decrevisset BEDE *HE* IV 21 p. 253; †**704** (c800) aliquantulum (*sic*) agri partem .. donare decrevimus *CS* 111; cum .. nutrix .. ad aecclesiam pergere .. decrevisset WULF. *Æthelwold* 5; arma sumere decreverunt GIR. *EH* I 3; **s1406** si sic ~erent eum contempnere *Chr. S. Alb.* 3; [imperator] decrevit in propria persona .. labores assumere *G. Hen. V* 18; **1565** ut .. cognoscatur quamnam ille partem .. defendere decreverit *StatOx* 383.

3 to decide (that something is so): **a** (w. pron. as obj.); **b** (w. acc. & inf. or compl.); **c** (w. *quia*); **d** (absol.).

a ad nihil aliud suspicor te hos [syllogismos] attulisse nisi ut, cum horum conclusionem aperte falsam cernerem, idem de similibus quos ego feceram ~erem ANSELM (*Gram.* 3) I 148. **b** verba quae naturae regulis produci majorum auctoritas decrevit ALDH. *PR* 116; hoc esse tutius communi consilio ~ebant BEDE *HE* I 23; **s1232** misit .. rex literas eis quos idoneos decreverat collectores quadragesime sibi concesse M. PAR. *Maj.* III 230; **1390** si decreveritis expediens *FormOx* 231. **c** decretum est communi consilio quia satius esset ut omnes .. ibi .. Domino deservirent quam inter rebelles fidei .. residerent BEDE *HE* II 5. **d** sit secundi generis [interrogationis elective] exemplum, in quo utrumque opinari liceat, 'an rethorica utilis sit', ut ejus scriptores probaverunt, 'an non', ut Lacedemones et Athici .. decreverunt BALSH. *AD rec.* 2 133.

4 to decide (that something should be done), decree, ordain: **a** (w. pron. as obj.); **b** (w. quasi-cognate acc.); **c** (w. acc. & inf. or compl.) **d** (w. *ut* or *quod*).

a 673 si consentirent ea quae a patribus canonice sunt antiquitus decreta custodire (*Conc. Hertf.*) BEDE *HE* IV 5. **b** nec statim ordinatio decreta, sed .. in .. sollemnitate paschali completa est *Ib.* IV 26 p. 273 (cf. id. *CuthbP* 24). **c** plura quae brevitatis causa omittenda decrevimus GILDAS *EB* 1; **680** nec Victorii paschalis laterculi curriculum .. posteris sectandum decreverunt ALDH. *Ep.* 4; hanc accipere debere tonsuram .. omnes qui in meo regno sunt clericos ~o BEDE *HE* V 21 p. 346; aliquanta [Germani] miracula .. scribenda decrevi NEN. *HB* 172; c**1230** (v. decimus 4b); **1236** (v. decretalis 2a). **d** cum esset .. decretum ut omnes per ordinem cantare deberent BEDE *HE* IV 22 p. 259; decreverunt ut cornibus .. ductilibus .. contenti essent ABBO *Edm.* 12; Dei judicio decretum erat .. ut homo qui sponte peccaverat nec peccatum nec poenam peccati vitare per se posset ANSELM (*CurD* 7) II 58; **1444** (v. 1 cistula a); **1515** decretum est quod unus quisque graduatus .. debeat .. orare pro bono statu archiepiscopi *StatOx* 331.

5 (p. ppl. *decretus* as sb. n.) decision, decree: **a** (unspec. & var.); **b** (papal or sim.). **c** (pl.) canon law (acad.).

a qui haec non tam nostra .. quam veteris novique testamenti ~a recusarit GILDAS *EB* 92; jus, ~um vel lex, *andweald* ÆLF. *Gl.*; ~um, i. institutum, statutum, diffinitum, judicium, .., placitum, *geþoht, laga, gesetnes GlH* D 2; ~um, *gerec GlP* 685; LANFR. *Comment. Paul.* 324 (v. chirographum 1e); a**1275** ~um electionis poterit fieri in hunc modum (*Const. Frat. Penit.*) *EHR* IX 123; c**1320** accelerata .. ~i sui [sc. episcopi defuncti] ultimi execucione (R. BURY *Ep.*) *FormOx* 57; c**1380** in vestrum ~um vestramve graciam se submittet *Ib.* 388; **1507** in complementum, execucionem et juxta formam et effectum cujusdam ~i et judicii redditi in curia Cancellarie domini regis *Cl* 371 m. 24*d.*; c**1517** ad observandum quoddam ~um arbitrale *Offic. S. Andr.* 119; illud dicitur ~um interlocutorium habens vim sententiae diffinitivae quando illud ~um est finale et non speratur alia sententia seu aliud ~um super illo articulo *Praxis* 244. **b** nunquam Romanorum ~a mutari a se saepe jam dicebat voluisse THEOD. *Pen.* I 5. 2; contra .. ~a synodalium totius orbis pontificum BEDE *HE* II 19; **735** quod peccati genus .. nec in antiquis canonibus nec in ~is pontificum patres .. usque enumerasse cognovi BONIF. *Ep.* 32 (cf. ib. 33: si hoc in catholicorum patrum ~is vel canonibus .. inveniretis); †**676** (12c) juxta sinodalia ~a *CS* 43; †**790** *for* 860 (11c) ea quae saecundum ~a canonum ac statuta synodalia salubriter defin[i]untur *CS* 502; c**1159** summi pontificis voluntas ~um est J. SAL. *Ep.* 23 (98); **s1243** [Innocentium IV] virum in ~is et jure canonico eleganter eruditum *Ann. Lond.* I 40; **1303** de uno pari ~orum vendito *Ac. Exec. Ep. Lond.* 52; **1337** Decretalia et ~a una cum glossa Hostiensis in ij voluminibus *Lit. Cant.* II 153; '~i auctoritate': .. dicitur ~um quod statuit papa de consilio cardinalium suorum ad nullius consultacionem LYNDW. 272 n; *Ib.* 297 h (v. decretalis 2a). **c** magistri regentes in ~is et legibus AD. MARSH *Ep.* 192; **1337** cum .. magister W. .. in universitate vestra .. incipere cupiat in ~is (R. BURY *Ep.*) *FormOx* 95; a**1350** doctores ~orum qui Oxonie seu Cantebrigie docuerunt *StatOx* 46; **s1372** T. de Brantone, doctor in ~is AD. MUR. *Cont. A* 213; **1543** magister A. B. .. bacchalaureus in ~is, qui per solita temporum curricula labori inherens in facultate ~orum studuit *Form. S. Andr.* II 309.

6 (by conf. w. *discernere*) to distinguish. *Cf. discernere* 3b.

in lumine Christi .. strictum callem .. ~amus a via lata et trita [cf. *Matth.* vii 14] COLET *Rom. Enarr.* 206.

1 decerpere [CL], to pluck, crop, gather; **b** (fig.). **c** to browse (on), root in. **d** (w. *viam*) to take. **e** to select, excerpt.

herbas arvorum buccis decerpo virentes ALDH. *Aen.* 86 (*Aries*) 2; dum vetita arboris poma ~eret BEDE *Mark* 155. **b** ALDH. *VirgV* 758 (v. contemplativus a); **1153** flores mundi gratissimos undequaque ~ens G. FOLIOT *Ep.* 108; quasdam primitias exultationis eterne ~unt P. BLOIS *Serm.* 691C; qui mee virginitatis primos ~ere flores dignus haberetur MAP *NC* IV 11 f. 52v. **c 1397** parochiani dicunt quod .. porci ejusdam [rectoris] ~ant cimiterium (*Vis. Heref.*) *EHR* XLV 93. **d** urbe relicta ~si viam altissimi nemoris MAP *NC* III 2 f. 36. **e** quae [nomina] de tertia declinatione ad regulam Ionici majoris ~simus ALDH. *PR* 132; de cujus scriptis aliqua ~ere .. commodum fore .. reor BEDE *HE* V 15; ea que magis .. necessaria mihi visa sunt ex libris Digestorum Justiniani et Codice ~endo VAC. *Lib. Paup.* 1; **s1409** hec premissa ~simus de epistola quam rex direxit pape *Chr. S. Alb.* 45.

2 decerpere v. discerpere.

decertare [CL], to contend, strive; **b** (w. inf.). **c** (w. acc. & inf.) to maintain (against opposition).

devincit humilis quisque doctor et Spiritus Sancti juvante gratia ~ans, aciem spirituum malignorum BEDE *Sam.* 575; **s1225** (v. deceptorie b); **c1239, s1253** (v. aries 2c); **s1388** (v. dare 11a). **b** monasterium .. fundaverunt .. secundam Romam .. in Anglia construere ~antes H. ALBUS 6; assunt pontifices mihi testes vera fatentes / decertant et in hac stare morique fide GARL. *Hon. Vit.* 128; **1236** ne ad processiones in annua visitatione et veneratione matris ecclesie aliqua parochia ~et cum vexillis suis alii parochie antecedere *Conc. Syn.* 205 (= GROS. *Ep.* 22). **c** dum .. quid in ignis incendio positum fuisset dubitarent, dum alii .. pannum dicerent, quidam vero .. lapidem fuisse ~arent R. COLD. *Cuthb.* 47.

decertatio [CL], contention, strife.

de ~onibus inter vicinos .., que frequenter insurgunt (*Leg. Ed.*) *GAS* 652; cum plures ~ones inter se commiscuissent G. MON. III 1; principum nostrorum gravis ob regni jura ~o GIR. *IK* II 13; DEVIZES 37v. (v. durus 3a); **s1206** vos †quot [MS: quos] hujus litis .. discertatio et cause decisio expectat *Chr. Evesham* 197.

decertator [LL], contender.

1236 hujusmodi ~ores inde matrem ecclesiam violant et inhonorant *Conc. Syn.* 205.

decessio [CL], decease. *V. et. discessio* c.

934 (14c) ut ille eam [telluris particulam] .. post suae ~onis transitum .. heredi .. derelinquat *CS* 704; **s1066** Haroldus .. quem rex ante suam ~onem regni successorem elegerat FL. WORC. I 224; **s1171** H. Guintoniensis episcopi .. felici fine ~o GIR. *EH* II 31; **c1230** post ejus vero ~onem meliorem bestiam percipere debet dominus *Doc. Bec* 30.

decessor [CL = *retiring magistrate*], predecessor.

634 vestra adquisitio ~orumque vestrorum (*Lit. Papae ad Archiep.*) BEDE *HE* II 18; [abbas] epistolam privilegii .. accepit instar illius quam .. ~or ejus Benedictus acceperat *Hist. Abb. Jarrow* 20; **c1155** ~orum vestrorum tempore J. SAL. *Ep.* 36 (7); Joseph [privilegium] obtinuit [*Gen.* xli 40] .. quod, si de humane sapientie artificio contingere potuisset, aliquem ~orum suorum ante eum meruisse crediderim *Id. Pol.* 434C; rex Henricus [I] .. omnes ~ores suos regimine tranquillo vicit MAP *NC* V 6 f. 67v.; **s1185** Baldewinus [archiepiscopus] .. iiij ecclesias, quas ~or ejus Ricardus .. ad alendos Christi pauperes .. assignaverat, .. subduxit *Ep. Cant. pref.* p. 2.

decessus [CL]

1 departure. *V. et.* 2 *discessus* a.

illis multum plorantibus, ac de subito ejus ~u turbatis, .. rogavit ut regulam .. servarent *Hist. Abb. Jarrow* 23.

2 decease; *v. et.* 2 *discessus* b; **b** (w. *civilis*) retirement into religion.

propinquante hora sui ~us BEDE *HE* IV 22 p. 261; **860** (15c) post suum ab luce ~um *CS* 499; **1088** uxor ejus .. tenebit ipsam terram in vita sua ..; sed post ~um vitae ejus recedet in manum abbatis (*Ch.*) *Chr. Rams.* 233; **1260** (v. barra 4a); **1301** ipse pre omnibus aliis propinquior est de sanguine ad terram illam habendam per ~um ejusdem capellani *SelPlMan* 125; **1537** ad quamlibet alienacionem seu ~um cujuslibet tenentis *MinAc Hen. VIII* 3352 m. 9d. **b** **1247** (v. civilis 4).

3 subtraction, deduction.

scientia .., cui ~us rerum potest fieri et accessus J. SAL. *Pol.* 445A.

decesus v. 2 decasus 2a. **decetare** v. disceptare. **decetero** v. ceterus 4.

†deceysenteia, *s. dub.*

1275 cepit de tota ~eia xl s. injuste postquam fuit acqu[i]et[ata] per patriam (*Kent*) *Hund.* I 213b.

dechalogus v. decalogus.

decharaxare [cf. charaxare], to write.

958 (12c) quorum nomina inferius decarraxata parent *CS* 1042.

deciatus [cf. decius], dice-shaped.

1355 pro iij duodenis clavorum pro eisdem [*henges*] cum capitibus deiciatis *KRAc* 471/6 m. 25 (cf. *Building in Eng.* 315: *dicehedenayles*).

decibilis [LL < decēre], seemly, meet.

sacrorum carminum modulamina seu ceteras Deo ~es laudes .. ex divinis inbutoribus didicerat B. *V. Dunst.* 31; *Ib.* 21 (v. 2 consessio a).

decicc- v. desicc-. **decicere** v. dedicere 1f.

decidentia, deficit.

1342 sic superexpendunt iiij^{xx}xix li. vij d. .., de quibus decidunt per superfluam allocacionem superius xxviij s. iiij d. .. summa ~ie patet. et sic est summa superexpense .. iii^{xx}xvij li. xij s. iij d. *ExchScot* 483; **1462** eidem [priori] per ~iam antiquarum firmarum terrarum de G., ut patet in rentali antiquo .., vij li. .. *Ib.* 91 (= *Reg. Brechin* II 420); **1482** *Ib.* 169 (v. croa).

1 decĭdere [CL]

1 to fall (down or off). **b** to fall into ruin; *v. et. decadere* 1a.

†decedit, ruit *GlC* D 67; flammarum globi ascendentes quasi de puteo magno rursumque ~entes in eundem BEDE *HE* V 12 p. 305; animadvertens circulum ferreum .. ~isse *Mir. J. Bev. A* 305; sic [bernace] .. in aquas ~unt GIR. *TH* I 15; horologium .. cum .. eriis pullulis, que ad completionem horarum .. ~ebant R. NIGER *Chr. II* 150. **b** **1221** (v. 1 decisio); **c1272** (v. 2 clausura 4a).

2 (of persons): **a** to sink. **b** to die; *cf.* 1 *decedere* 2. **c** (fig.) to fall morally. **d** to be degraded. **e** to desist, default (from).

a GILDAS *EB* 109 (v. ergastulum 2d); tactus infirmitate ~it in lectum BEDE *HE* V 13. **b** **1460** de hereyeldis certorum tenendorum ~encium per tempus compoti *ExchScot* 21. **c** animantia preter homines quelibet ea qua creata sunt vita gaudent .., quasi non ~erint a gracia creatoris MAP *NC* I 1 f. 7v.; decĭdo peccando, decīdo saxa secando H. AVR. *CG* f. 7. 21. **d** si clericus fuerit, proprio gradu ~at EGB. *Pont.* 10. **e** prius ego †ipsi [? l. ipse] .. penitus decrescam quam ab hac dubitatione ~am ADEL. *QN* 26; **c1128** si abbas in curia sua aliqua negligentia de justitia ~erit *E. Ch. Scot.* 74.

3 **a** to die down, abate. **b** (w. *ab*) to pass out of, be transferred from. **c** (pr. ppl.) passing, transitory.

a ventus ~ens in auram pacatissimam vertebatur R. COLD. *Cuthb.* 39. **b** rem ipsam .. dicet suam esse sed aliqua de causa ab ejus ~isse possessione GLANV. X 8. **c** ~ens, *gewitendi GlC* D 66.

4 (of payment or sim.): **a** to lapse, be omitted. **b** to be deducted, fall short; *v. et. decadere* 2; **c** (in assay).

a wita domini ~at, si .. ipsi coagentes non sint unius dominii (*Leg. Hen.* 94. 2a). *GAS* 611. **b** pro dim. hida, quae non est ibi, ~unt xx s. *DB* I 20v.; **1216** dedimus .. Philippo .. iiij^{xx} libratas terre .. in dominico nostro. .. si vero ei aliquod maritagium ei (*sic*) dederimus .., tantum ~et de illis iiij^{xx} libratis .. quantum maritagium illud valuerit *Pat* 21; **1257** rex commisit .. manerium de D. .. pro xl li. annuatim solvendis .., ita tamen quod .. ~ant .. singulis annis .. x li. pro manerio de H. *Cl* 63; **1271** *Cl* 438 (v. 2 decasus 2a); **1342** (v. decidentia); **1359** (v. clarus 5c); **1401** tantum ~at de solucione summe predicte quantum eis in redditibus .. contigerit provideri *Cl* 248 m. 8. **c** **1207** (v. casura 1b); **1248** sumpta .. una libra pluries nove monete et nove incisionis et in igne posita, †purgatura [? l. purgata] et examinata et extracta et in statera posita, inventum est quod non ~ebat (*sic*) de libra nisi vj d., unde secundum consuetudinem regni Anglie bona fuerat et legalis (*Exam. Monetae*) OXNEAD app. 316; **a1275** [argentum] de Monte Pessulano, quod est adeo bonum quod ~it libra examinata nisi in uno denario, vel in duobus ad plus. .. [denarii] Bruselenses ~unt in libra iij s. communiter *RBExch* 979 (cf. ib. 984: que assaia debet descidere unius oboli tantum et non magis neque minus).

2 decīdere [CL; *conf. w.* discindere]

1 to cut off, sever (also fig.). **b** to cut up, divide, separate. **c** to mutilate (fig.), diminish.

hi sunt qui instar Samson decisis virtutum crinibus .. deputantur ad molam AILR. *Spec. Car.* I 15. 519C; **1229** si textor .. tres telas a suis telariis descindat vel ~at *MonA* V 253b; si separetur vel decindetur (*sic*) quecunque pars [hominis], quod (*sic*) anima non sit ibi BACON VI 242 (cf. ib.: pars .. decissa); **s1382** mulieres .. productas ad conspectum publicum descissa cesarie .. circumduci fecerunt WALS. *HA* II 65. **b** singule partes [libri] in capitula sunt decise PULL. *Sent. prol.* 639; ferina / nunc est cum pipere croceo decisa minutim H. AVR. *Poems* 2. 222; *Id. CG* f. 7. 21 (v. 1 decidere 2c); mucro mortis habet descidere [vv. ll. discidere, decidere] / naturali compacta federe J. HOWD. *Ph.* 1033. **c** percatapsat, valde ~it *GlC* P 350; **s1296** rex .. Anglie .. monarchiam quondam tocius Britannie, per multa tempora decisam et truncatam, occupavit *Chr. S. Edm.* 63.

2 (p. ppl. *decisus*): **a** slashed (ornamentally). **b** cut short, concise.

a **1188** quod nullus habeat pannos ~os vel laceatos (*Conc. Geddington* 5) R. HOWD. II 337 (= W. NEWB. *HA* III 23); **a1350** nullus .. magister sotularibus liripipiatis vel ~is vel decollatis calciatus lectiones legat ordinarias *StatOx* 57. **b** sicut sermonis lubrici profluvia, sic ~e orationis angustias vitare propono BACON I 4.

3 to separate (seed) in the act of generation. *Cf. decisio* 3, *discindere* 2.

sperma maris naturaliter intendit imprimere formam ejus a quo ~itur *Ps.-*RIC. *Anat.* 40; sicut semen non est .. de veritate ejus a quo descinditur HALES *Qu.* 1302 (cf. ib. 1294: humiditas seminalis que fuit decisa a parentibus); ad nutrimentum hujusmodi humiditatis prime spermatice descinditur ab humiditatibus pars liquidior spermatica GILB. I 66. 2 (cf. ib. VI 243. 2: descendit sive descinditur sperma a nutrimento membrorum et producitur ad testiculos); virtus .. generativa .. accipit residuum alimenti et transmittit ad locum generationis et decindit, ut fiat individuum simile in specie BACON III 276; virtus que est in semine desiso *Id.* VII 11; semen †decisisum [l. decisum] a parentibus existens in matrice *Id.* VIII 67 (cf. ib. 68: homo in decisione seminis decindit prop[r]iam virtutem; planta decindit semen per virtutem maris et femine *Id.* XI 235; propter plantas et matres in animalibus, que in semine deciso perficiunt species in effectus completos *Id. Maj.* II 451; si pater creatus immediate ~eret a se filium, vere esset pater DUNS *Ord.* IV 65 (cf. ib. 64: actus ~endi semen).

4 to decide, determine (legal action or sim.).

1092 hanc litem ego canonice discindere cupiens .. *Cart. Worc.* 52 (= *Conc.* I 370a); GLANV. *prol.* (v. dirimere 2); hic longe velocius causas ~imus quam in ecclesiis episcopi vestri MAP *NC* V 7 f. 72; cum .. descidendis preesset causantium litibus AD. EYNS. *Hug.* V 16 p. 188; consequetur .. sic quod hujusmodi cause ecclesiastice nunquam descindentur: a seculari enim judice descindi non poterunt, nec ab ecclesiastico judice obstante regia prohibitione GROS. *Ep.* 72* p. 226; **1249** nos omnem materiam discordie taliter duximus ~endam *Reg. Aberbr.* I 168; [jus canonicum] forum conscientie discutit aut causas ecclesiasticas descindit BACON *Maj.* III 39; si per finem factum lis ~atur necnon HENGHAM *Magna intr.*; **s1293** si aliquid occurrat tam arduum quod per arbitros descindi nequeat, definiendum regibus reservetur RISH. 138; **1369** propter dubietatem inter .. abbatem et dominum J. .. ~endam in .. parliamento *ExchScot* 324; **c1386** duo aut unus ex ipsis ~ent et finient controversias *Reg. Aberd.* I 172; **1400** articuli decisi in congregacione magistrorum *StatOx* 189; **s1422** si glossam .. discusseris, decisum in eo conclusionaliter reperies: 'qui [etc.]' AMUND. I 96.

decidium v. discidium 2a.

deciduus [CL]

1 falling or liable to fall, declining (also fig.). **b** fleeting, transitory. **c** failing, ineffective; *cf.* 2 *desiduus.*

quemdam, nemoris dum scanderet alta, / .. / deciduum membris animam posuisse solutis BEDE *CuthbV* 677; ~um, quod cito cadit *GlC* D 113; ~o .. imbre, cadente, *of nyþerhreossendre þicnysse GlP* 165; deciduus tamen est cursus, quia tendit ad ima NECKAM *DS* I 335; ut frondes exigue facileque ~e ad vastissime arboris conferri putentur robur immensum AD. EYNS. *Hug.* V 18 p. 211; **s1245** in ~o regno Anglie .., multis nobilibus .. viduato *Flor. Hist.* II 305; **s1258** ejus dentes et ungues, scabri et liventes, quasi ~i, casum minabantur M. PAR. *Maj.* V 709; **14..** ~us, A. *lygtly fallen WW*. **b** ut .. habeas veram vitam, perennem profecto, non ~am GILDAS *EB* 32; **9..** ~am, *gewitendlic WW*; desidui .. imperii ÆLNOTH *Cnut* 6 (v. decurrere 5b); recedant igitur verba decidua WALT. WIMB. *Carm.* 207. **c** ergo age, deciduas precibus suppleto loquelas FRITH. 29.

2 (as sb. n.) amount lost (in process of preparation).

[in expensis sutorie:] in ~o fundacionis iij petr' [sepi] *Ac. Beaulieu* 212; summa [ferri grossi] cxlij quintalli. in extracto ad ferrum operatum lxix quintalli; in ~o scorie xxxiij quintalli; .. et remanent xl quintalli *Ib.* 266; caseus: .. in ~o exsiccacionis xj pondera *Ib.* 312.

1 decies [CL], ten times; **b** (in comp. numeral). **c** (w. *tantum*) name of a writ against juror taking a bribe (*cf. Reg. Brev. Orig.* 188v., *Stat. 38 Ed. III* c. 12); *cf. decimare* 3.

de caede ~es centenum milium exercitus Aethiopum GILDAS *EB* 41; sicut in illo [versu] xiv sillabarum dactilus ~es variatur, ita in hoc spondeus toties invertitur ALDH. *Met.* 10 p. 86; *Id. Ep.* 6 (v. centies); **s1223** non habito respectu ad multitudinem barbarorum, qui ~es excercitui suo superabundabant WEND. II 274 (= M. PAR. *Maj.* III 80: in decuplo). **b** sed decies nŏvem sunt et sex corporis ungues ALDH. *Aen.* 84 (*Scrofa praegnans*) 4; decies senas junxere puellas *Id. VirgV* 2413; **10..** ~es †senes, id est lx *WW*; in magnitudine sexta sunt 62 [stelle], quarum quelibet est ~es octies major tota terra BACON *Maj.* I 236; **s1355** ad ~es et quinquies c^{m} li. sterlingorum AVESB. 127. **c** **1393** cum .. prosecutus fuisset .. quoddam breve nostrum ~es tantum versus Willelmum T. coram .. justiciariis nostris de Banco *Pat* 338 m. 24; **1448** quod iidem abbas et conventus .. habeant .. omnimodas forisfacturas .. per brevia nostra .. de attinctis, ~es tantum, premunire facias, adjudicatis et adjudicandis *Reg. Whet.* I 33 (cf. *CalCh* VI 47).

2 decies v. 1 decius. **decim** v. decem. **decima** v. decimus 2–5.

decimabilis, tithable.

c1236 presumunt forenses judices causas pure ecclesiasticas judicialiter determinare, utpote utrum de lapidicinis et nemoribus .. debeant solvi decime, cum quid sit ~e solius sit ecclesie determinare GROS. *Ep.* 72* p. 221; sicut de aliis rebus ~ibus redditur decima postquam percepte fuerint, sic debent fieri de anno KILWARDBY *Jejun.* 168; **1330** de omnibus bonis nostris ~ibus solvimus decimam, ut tenemur *Lit. Cant.* I 335; **1341** de feno ~i *Inq. Non.* 425; **1397** pro .. garbis ~ibus *Ac. Obed. Abingd.* 61; **1405** infra fines et limites et loca ~ia parochie ejusdem ecclesie *Cl* 254 m. 9 (cf. AMUND. I 242).

decimalis

1 (w. *homo*) tithingman. *Cf. decenarius* 3.

sciat omnis presbiter et tungravius et ~es homines ut haec elemosina et jejunium proveniat (*Quad.*) *GAS* 261.

2 concerned w. (royal subsidy of) tenth.

s1254 pecunia ~is (v. decimus 3a); **s1432** processus . . in causa collecciocis ~is AMUND. I 300 *rub.* (cf. ib. 302: eum [priorem] deputare collectorem decimarum).

3 subject to or paid as tithe. **b** (w. *grangia* or *horreum*) tithe-barn.

vituli quoque et agniculi ~es erga Pentecosten . . aecclesiis persolvantur oportunis (*Paraph.*) *GAS* 253; **1236** omnes dicte decime, sive bladi, sive feni, seu ortorum, sive molendinorum, seu piscariorum, seu leguminum, seu nutrimentorum animalium et eorum exitus, sive quaruncunque rerum aliarum ~ium *Cart. Glast.* I 62; **1294** debitores farine ~is seu eorum homines dictam farinam cariantes *Reg. Paisley* 94; **1338** in lxiij gallinis ~ibus de vicario de B. *Ac. Durh.* 33; **c1360** campos ~es *Ib.* 564 (v. certificare 6); **1410** agni et lana ~es *Pri. Cold.* 86; **1437** (v. carbo 2a); salmones ~es . . oblatos FLETE *Westm.* 64; **1466** pro ~i feno prati de U. *ExchScot* 383; **1544** ubi nulli pisces ~es . . soluti fuerint *Form. S. Andr.* II 269. **b 1363** cum omnibus domibus super astantibus . . excepta grangia ~i *Pat* 268 m. 48; [abbas J., ob. **1379**] edificavit unam grangiam ~em *Chr. Evesham* 301; **1430** prior Dunelm' habet in eadem villa [*Brompton*] toftum et croftum situatum juxta grangiam ~em *Feod. Durh.* 76; **1464** orreum ~e cum uno tofto et crofto ibidem dimittitur cum decima ville [*Brompton*] *Ib.* 203; **1514** pro punctuacione super orrium ~e *Ac. Durh.* 161; **1583** totum illud horreum ~e nostrum cum pertinenciis *Pat* 1234 m. 15.

4 (?) *f. l.*

de . . j pari vestimentorum de *bustian* cum rubea cruce . . pro tempore †decimali [? l. quadragesimali, i.e. xl^ali^ *misread as* x^ali^] *Ac. Obed. Abingd.* 134.

5 (?) *f. l.*

cum . . A. sub cura T. . . extitisset et idem T. . . medicamenta . . pref[ato] A. necessaria, tres uncias †decimalium [? l. medicinalium] vocat[orum] *perles* . ., iiij pixides cordialibus plenas . . et xx quartas aque vite . . emisset *Entries* 187.

1 decimanus [CL], **a** (*sc. ager*) land subject to a tax of one tenth. **b** (*sc. limes*) boundary line.

a decumanus, *tiođe hafudæcer* ÆLF. *Gl.* **b** hi omnes [agri] accurate cardinibus et decumanis erant limitati BALSH. *Ut.* 46.

2 decimanus v. decimianus.

1 decimare [CL]

1 to decimate (misinterp. as killing 9 out of 10). **b** (in word-play) to end the life of.

s1011 grex monachilis et turba virilis, sed muliebris nec (*sic*) infantilis, ~atur; novem trucidantur; decimus vite reservatur; iiij monachis et dccc viris ~atorum summa perficitur FL. WORC. I 164 (cf. M. PAR. *Maj.* I 483: turba virorum et mulierum necnon parvulorum ~atur); **s1042** cum omnes interfecti essent nisi decima pars, . . fecerunt decimam ~ari H. HUNT. *HA* VI 20; germen albi draconis ex ortulis nostris abradetur et reliquie generationis ejus ~abuntur (*Proph. Merlini*) G. MON. VII 3. **b s1276** Gregorius decimus papa, qui decimas imposuit, decimo die mensis Januarii diem claudens extremum ~atus est apud civitatem Reatinam OXNEAD *Chr.* 248.

2 to complete the number ten.

s1087 ipse novem de mense dies Septembris habebas, / et tibi subtrahitur quod decimare queas G. WINT. *Epigr. Hist.* 5.

3 to pay back (a bribe) ten times over. *Cf.* 1 *decies* c.

s1365 statuitur quod [juratores] in talibus convicti accepta sic dona regis misericordie ~abunt J. READING 185.

4 to exact a tenth of; *cf. decimus* 3; **b** (eccl.) to exact tithe; *cf. decimus* 4.

s1188 cum ipsi duo reges Francie et Anglie possessiones tam clericorum quam laicorum, redditus ecclesiasticos et pecuniam singulorum violenta manu ~assent ad conficiendum iter Jerosolimitanum *Meaux* I 239; **s1254** venit episcopus Norwic' ad S. Albanum . . ut omnia bona ecclesie illius . . ad opus regis ~aret M. PAR. *Maj.* V 451; **c1370** [taurus, i.e. rex] festa rotundabit, segetes regni decimabit [*gl.*: i. expendet decimam partem segetis vel accipiet valorem decem segetum vel ab ecclesia] (J. BRIDL.) *Pol. Poems* I 149, 150. **b** vosque, capellani laicorum, dum decimatis / ecclesias et presbyteros decimis spoliatis, / cui non servitis altari participantes H. HUNT. *HA* XI 165.

5 to give or pay a tenth (of); **b** (absol.). **c** to endow w. a tenth (also fig. w. ref. to tithe; *cf. Heb.* vii 9–10).

arduum memoratu est quantum [Kedwalla] . . inservierit pietati, ut omnes manubias quas jure predatorio in suos usus transcripserat Deo ~aret W. MALM. *GR* I 34; **s855** dum [rex Adulfus] . . omne regnum Deo ~aret *Id. GP* II 75 p. 161; **s844** proavus meus . . totam terram suam ecclesiis et monasteriis ~avit (*Sermo Edgari*) AILR. *Gen. Regum* 361; appulsi [naute] . . S. Willelmo . . que in navi habebant universa ~arunt T. MON. *Will.* VII 17; **s1294** soluta prima porcione juxta taxacionem decime pretaxate, [rex] precepit secularium bona taxari et sibi per Angliam ~ari *Flor. Hist.* III 275. **b s1268** (v. decimus 3a); **s1428** concessum fuit regi . . novum tallagium inauditum: . . de quolibet feodo militari solverent vj s. viij d., si inde non ~averit (*sic*) *Chr. S. Alb.* 21. **c** benedicitur ac ~atur a Melchisedech Abram BEDE *Gen.* (xiv 20) 152; queritur adhuc circa hoc, cujus est decimatio, sc. utrum Christus ~atus [fuit] in lumbis Abrahe, cum fuit in lumbis Abrahe secundum carnem, sicut Levi fuit ~atus HALES *Qu.* 616.

6 (eccl.) to pay tithe (on); **b** (absol.); **c** (w. cognate acc.).

796 nos in fide catholica nati . . et edocti vix consentimus substantiam nostram pleniter ~are ALCUIN *Ep.* 110; **a1100** praecipio servientibus meis ut segetes meas de H. ~ent ad ostium granciae meae (*Ch.*) *Chr. Abingd.* II 33; **c1100** [rex Offa] ductus penitentia per regni fines mandat regalia maneria ~ari *Pass. Æthelb.* 11; ut . . omnis tainus ~et quicquid habet (*Quad.*) *GAS* 260; Ernulfus de Hesding . . decimarum ita curiosus ut, si horreum non ~atum jam intaxatum esset, omnia eici et incunctanter ~ari juberet W. MALM. *GP* V 274; **a1150** reddimus . . et super altare . . matris ecclesie nostre . . posuimus rectam decimam omnium rerum que ~ari debent de toto dominio de E. *Reg. S. Aug.* 508; **c1194** exhortor . . omnes tenentes de dominio meo . . ut †imitentur [? l. incitentur] exemplo meo ad ~andum bladum de dominio suo per garbas *Ch. Sal.* 53; initium et allectorium ad hec ~andum in Demetica . . datum fuerat per Giraldum GIR. *RG* I 4; **c1254** ex quibus, deductis . . expensis que . . deduci oportent, remanet vj li. xviij d. ad ~andum *Val. Norw.* 207; **12..** pulli aucarum ~antur. . . item omnes artes mechanice ~antur, mediante juramento, deductis expensis *Conc. Scot.* II 44; **1340** prepositus . . male ~avit omnia bona domini que ~anda fuerunt ad dampnum . . rectoris *CBaron* 105; blada . . fuerunt . . ~ata et separata *Entries* 635b. **b** scribimus et monachis: "fex religionis avare, / cur decimas rapitis, dum debetis decimare?" H. HUNT. *HA* XI 165; apparet . . te non recte ~asse, ideo fetorem hunc sensisti COGGESH. *Visio* 12; **1215** (v. bipartitor); **c1250** (v. decimus 4e); **1428** docuisti quod decime sunt a clericis et ecclesiis subtrahende . ., pro eo quod . . usque ad Gregorium X populus solis pauperibus libere ~abat (*Exam. W. Whyte*) *Ziz.* 428. **c a1100** haec iccirco recitavimus ut noscatur ubi eadem decima et quomodo debeat ~ari (*Ch.*) *Chr. Abingd.* II 33.

7 (math.) to move to tenth place (absol.).

singularis divisor sine differentiis . . sub se ponit denominationem . . si . . divisor fuerit decenus, secundat a se, . . si milies mille millenus, ~at, si decies milies mille millenus, undecimat, si centies . . milies mille millenus duodecimat THURKILL *Abac.* 58.

2 decimare v. decymare.

decimaria [LL = *tithe-law*], 'dimery', rectory entitled to tithe.

1554 totam rectoriam . . de Chartesey . . vocatam ~iam ibidem et omnes decimas bladorum cum omnibus aliis decimis tam majoribus quam minoribus ad dictam rectoriam sive ~iam spectantibus . . cum uno gardino ibidem vocato *le dymerye garden Pat* 874 m. 37.

decimarius [LL = *tithe-payer*], (?) tithe-collector, teinder (Scot.).

c1230 [teste] R. ~io *Inchaffray* 47.

decimatio [LL]

1 decimation. *Cf.* 1 *decimare* 1a.

Germanicus draco . . vigebit tandem paulisper; set ~o Neustrie nocebit (*Proph. Merlini*) G. MON. VII 3; **s1066** dux . . animavit eos [Normannos] contra Anglos . ., recitans . . seditiones quas fecerant, tum de Dacis . ., tum et de ~one et redecimatione Normannorum SILGRAVE 77; **s1042** facta ista ~one dolenda, videbatur Godwino . . quod numerus vivorum fuerat excessivus; jussit eos eodem modo . . decimari . . et facta secunda ~one pauci superstites remanserunt *Eul. Hist.* II 194–5.

2 exaction of tenth.

s1189 a tempore crucis suscepte ~o generalis rerum mobilium, facta per Angliam ad subventionem terre Jerosolimitane, tam clerum quam populum exactione violenta perterruit DICETO *YH* II 73; **s1229** procuratores . . promiserunt domino pape ex parte regis Anglorum ab universo regno Anglie et Hibernie ~onem omnium rerum mobilium ad guerram suam contra imperatorem sustinendam WEND. II 360; **s1268** (v. decimus 3a); **s1299** quomodo . . rex Anglie imposicione taxe et ~one cleri Anglie intendebat . . regnum Scocie subvertere FORDUN *Cont.* XI 35; **s1399** proclamando nullas de cetero ~ones ecclesiasticas in clero, quintam decimam in populo . . fieri *Misc. Scrope* 296.

3 (assessment or payment of) tithe (eccl.); **b** (w. gen. of source); **c** (w. gen. of recipient); **d** (w. ref. to *Heb.* vii 9–10; *cf. decimare* 5c); **e** area from which tithe is payable to a particular church.

9.. ~o, *teoþingsceat WW*; **c1100** dicit Dominus per prophetam: "apportate omnem ~onem in horreo meo, ut sit cibus servientibus in domo mea" [cf. *Malachi* iii 10] HAM. S. ALB. 1456 (cf. *Pat* [**1215**] 140a); expertus . . eo sibi per divinam gratiam rusticos proventus augeri quo studuisset nullam fraudem ~oni fieri W. MALM. *GP* V 274; **c1125** dedisse . . ecclesie S. Trin. de Dunfermelyn omnem ~onem de omnibus dominiis meis de D. nisi de illis que ad alias ecclesias pertinent *E. Ch. Scot.* 62; hi sunt qui . . ~ones et primitias ecclesiis subtrahunt J. SAL. *Pol.* 692D; in foresta que Dena dicitur, non ex ~one aliqua sed nomine proprio MAP *NC* II 9 f. 26; **c1214** consistit . . vicaria in †tota [l. toto] altalagio illius ecclesie, sc. in omnibus oblationibus et obventionibus et omnibus minutis ~onibus, salvis dicto R. [rectori] decimis bladi *Reg. Linc.* I 63; **c1230** concessisse . . monialibus . . omnes ~ones in B. *MonA* IV 492b; **1251** forma pacis inter nos et burgenses . . super ~onibus marinis *Studia Monastica* II 129; **1430** cum vesturis . . herbe et feni percipiendis sine ~one *Feod. Durh.* 25; **1521** racione arrendacionis et ~onis *Form. S. Andr.* I 103; in . . oblacionibus et minutis ~onibus cum profic' libri quadragesimalis *Val. Eccl.* V 140. **b 796** ~o substantiae nostrae valde bona est; sed melius est illam amittere quam fidem perdere ALCUIN *Ep.* 110; **c1040** quod homines . . Deo persolvere recusabant rerum suarum ~ones [AS: *on heora teođingsceattum*] (*MS Corpus Christi Coll. Camb.* 265) *GAS* 207; ut rectitudines Dei quoquo anno solvantur, que sunt . . juventutis ~o [AS: *geoguþe teođunge*] ad Pentecosten (*Cons. Cnuti*) *Ib.* 293; **c1100** fit rerum omnium ~o *Pass. Æthelb.* 11 (cf. 1 decimare 6a); **a1160** omnem ~onem molendinorum meorum *E. Ch. Yorks* VI 28; **1188** rectam ~onem . . foreste de P., de pannagiis [etc.] *Act. Hen. II* II 299; **c1200** me dedisse . . canonicis . . omnes decimas et ~ones et obvenciones . . illorum xv feudorum que teneo . ., tenendum et habendum eis ad eorum hospitum et pauperum sustentationem *Reg. S. Thom. Dublin* 404; **1235** ecclesia de C. habebit . . totam ~onem bladi pertinentem ad ecclesiam de H., excepta decima de terra ecclesie quam vicarius annuatim percipiet *Pri. Cold.* 241; **c1300** pro quolibet agno de v agnis reddatur obolus pro decima et pro vj agnis reddatur unus ad decimam; et, si vendantur ante ~onem, decimus denarius solvatur; et sic fiat de ~one lane *Conc. Syn.* 1392. **c c1160** concessisse ecclesiam de A. . . cum omni ~one canonicorum ejusdem ville, tam lane et casei quam bladi et omnium rerum unde decime Deo dantur *Reg. S. Osm.* I 221. **d** aut ~o sumitur pro oblatione decimarum, aut pro effectu . ., aut sumitur pro significato [sc. respectu purgationis facte] per Christum HALES *Qu.* 611 (cf. ib. 613: ~o vel est solutio decimarum vel purgatio signata per decimas: solutio facta fuit per Abraham, purgatio vero per Christum). **e s1074** (v. decania 2c); **1313** infra fines, limites seu ~ones ecclesie de S. *Augm. Bk.* I 5; **1345** percipiant nomine vicarie . . omnimodas oblaciones in . . ecclesia de F. et in quibuscumque locis infra fines et limites seu ~ones dicte ecclesie scituatis *Reg. S. Aug.* 347.

4 grant of a tenth (*cf. E. Ch. Wessex* 187–213).

855 (12c) ego Æđeluulfus rex . . pro ~one agrorum quam Deo donante ceteris ministris meis facere decrevi . . *CS* 486 (i).

5 tithing. *Cf. decena* 1, *decimus* 5.

a (*Cons. Cnuti*) *GAS* 193 (v. decimationarius); volumus ut omnis liber sit in centenario et in ~one [AS: *on teođunge*] positus (*Ib.*) *Ib.* 323; dividitur . . centenarium unum in plures ~ones (*Ib.*) *Ib.* 618 (cf. centenarius 4a).

decimationarius, tithingman. *Cf. decenarius* 3.

quodsi necessitas instet, primum nuncietur concionatori centenarii, qui deinde [nunciet] . . ~iis [AS: *đam teođingmannum*], id est singulis qui presunt decimationibus (*Cons. Cnuti*) *GAS* 193.

1 decimator, collector or receiver of tithe. **b** tithe payer or (?) tithe farmer.

c1160 convenit idem H. quod ipsam decimam faceret ac domos reddi ~ori S. Stephani [de Cadomo] *Act. Hen. II* I 274; **c1180** ~ores tam monachorum quam Gaufridi . . affidabunt quod jamdictas decimas fideliter congregabunt in loco quodam ex assensu utriusque partis assignato ibique in duas equas partes predicte decime dividentur *Ib.* II 131; si quis vendiderit acervum tritici ante ~orem, tam venditor quam emptor tenetur ad decimam J. BURGH *PO* IX 3. **b 1461** [episcopi] tam ipsos [abbatem et conventum] quam eorum . . ~ores, firmarios ac colonos laicos decimarum debitores ipsi monasterio pro solucione debitorum ac decimarum facta per eos excommunicant (*Lit. Papae*) *Reg. Aberbr.* II 122 (= *Mon. Hib. & Scot.* 435b); **1521** parochiani, arrendatores, ~ores, reddituarii, coloni, laboratores, censuarii, receptores, debitores, possessores et detentores fructuum *Form. S. Andr.* I 103.

2 decimator, ~**trix** v. decym-.

decimatus, (entitlement to) tithe.

1182 confirmasse . . ecclesie S. Martini de Albemarla . . alias ecclesias de Albemarla cum ~u et scol[is] et omnibus aliis pertinenciis suis *Act. Hen. II* II 211.

decimianus [CL], (designating a variety of pear).

est et decimanum pirum, tam minutum sc. ut x possint contineri manu OSB. GLOUC. *Deriv.* 197.

decimula, (little) tithe or tenth.

the tende, decima, ~a *CathA*.

decimus [CL]

1 tenth (also in comp. numeral). **b** (? in comp. ordinal used in place of cardinal); **c** (every) tenth, one out of ten.

aetatis decimus necnon et tertius annus ALDH. *VirgV* 1928; ~us [Hebraeorum mensis] Tebet Januario .. comparatur BEDE *TR* 11; appellentur [genera] secundum posite distinctionis ordinem primum, secundum, tertium, et sic usque ad ~um BALSH. *AD rec. 2* 131; **1214** anno quinto ~o (v. decemnovenalis); preter predictos x et octo modos rithmorum est nonus ~us GARL. *PP* 180; **1395** anno regni R. secundi ~o nono *Lit. Cant.* III 31. **b** s**1217** erant nutui suo dedite circiter ~e sexte naves .. sine naviculis comitantibus, que ad viginti sunt recensite M. PAR. *Maj.* III 29. **c 844** (12c) ego Æthelwlfus .. consilium salubre .. affirmavi, ut aliquam portionem terrarum hereditariam antea possidentibus omnibus gradibus, sive famulis et famulabus Dei .. sive laicis, semper ~am mansionem, ubi minimum sit tamen ~am partem in libertatem perpetuam perdonare dijudicavi *CS* 483; s**1040** omnibus comitibus preter ~os decapitatis; nam sors ~um quemque morti exemerat W. MALM. *GR* II 188; s**1042** novem semper excapitati sunt et ~us remansit H. HUNT. *HA* VI 20; presit singulis hominum novenis ~us (*Leg. Hen.* 8. 1a) *GAS* 554; c**1283** debet metere .. j acram de frumento .. et habere ~am garbam *Cust. Battle* 28; s**1295** W. GUISB. 258 (v. duodecimus 1b); **1370** (v. 1 carriare 1a);

2 (w. *pars* or as sb. f.) a tenth.

ut .. ~am frugum omnium .. partem pauperibus daret BEDE *HE* IV 27 p. 276; s**855** Æthelwulfus .. rex ~am totius regni sui partem ab omni regali servitio et tributo liberavit ASSER *Alf.* 11; Ethelwulfus .. ~am omnium hidarum infra regnum suum Christi famulis concessit liberam ab omnibus functionibus W. MALM. *GR* II 109; s**1042** (v. 1 decimare 1a); c**1235** de feudis ij militum .. et de dessima parte j militis *Fees* 449; s**1294** concessa est regi in subsidium werre sue medietas a clero, sexta a civibus et a reliquo populo ~a pars bonorum RISH. 143.

3 (as sb. f.): **a** aid or subsidy of one tenth of rents and chattels, incl. 'Saladin tithe' of 1188 (*cf. EHR* XXX 398–417, XXXII 49–89, XLI 332–57); **b** (w. *quintadecima*). **c** tenth payable to crown from benefice (*cf. Guide to P. R. O.* (1964) I 86).

a 1188 unusquisque ~am reddituum et mobilium suorum in elemosinam dabit ad subventionem terre Jerosolymitane hoc anno, exceptis .. (*Ord. Regis*) R. HOWD. II 335; s**1188** rex .. elegit clericos et laicos .. et .. misit eos per singulos comitatus ad ~as colligendas secundum .. preordinationem *G. Hen. II* II 33; s**1229** [pape cancellarius] recitavit literas domini pape in quibus exigebat ~as omnium rerum mobilium de tota Anglia, Hibernia et Wallia ab universis laicis et clericis ad guerram suam sustinendam .. contra Romanum imperatorem WEND. II 375; s**1254** ordine retrogrado et perverso coguntur prelati ~as persolvere laicis et inviti, unum tantum solatii refrigerium invenientes quod credebant, quando promittebatur, quod in succursum Terre Sancte .. pecunia decimalis expenderetur M. PAR. *Maj.* V 452; s**1268** licet non nisi per biennium clerus de ~is respondere deberent (*sic*), quia de primo anno decimationis jam satisfecerant, tamen ultro se obtulerunt episcopo [Norwicensi] ~as suas se daturos eciam de tercio anno .., tali pacto ut in decimando secundum taxationem W. quondam Norwicensis episcopi ~as suas possent contribuere FL. WORC. *Cont. C* 202; **1294** cum comites .. et .. alii de regno nostro in subsidium guerre nostre nobis ~am de .. bonis suis mobilibus .. concesserunt .., nos, ut ~a illa ad minus .. gravamen populi levetur .., assignavimus .. T. .. et R. .. ad dictam ~am .. colligendam (*Pat*) *Parl. Writs* I 27; **1323** (v. biennalis a); s**1336** papa revocavit sexannalem ~am concessam in subsidium Terre Sancte, pro eo quod rex Francie versus Terram Sanctam nimis distulit iter suum, et voluit quod solutum redderetur; sed in Anglia nihil fuit redditum, quia fuit per clerum regi concessum AD. MUR. *Chr.* 78; s**1337** fuit concessa regi per clerum ~a triennalis; item communitas regni concessit sibi triennalem ~am de burgis et civitatibus, item quintumdecimum denarium de forinsecis *Ib.* 80; **14..** nolumus quod idem W. [prebendarius] de hujusmodi bonis suis [sc. temporalibus prebende sue annexis], de quibus ~am nobis dat inter spiritualia, de .. ~a et quintadecima per laicos concessa oneretur *Reg. Brev.* 188; s**1432** (v. decimalis 2); **1451** dicit quod .. auctoritate .. Parliamenti ordinatum sit .. quod .. concessiones .. per .. regem .. facte de exoneracione .. ~arum spiritualium vel quintarum decimarum aut ~arum temporalium .. vacue forent *Reg. Whet.* I 63. **b 1333** pro quietacione ~e et quintedecime de bonis vestris in .. villa Bristoll' *RScot* I 231a; de ~is et quintisdecimis levandis *MGL* I 531; pecunia magna quintadecime et ~e in Anglia collecta GASCOIGNE *Loci* 205; **1488** taxatoribus et collectoribus ~e et quintedecime in comitatu Suthhampton salutem (*Breve*) *Reg. Merton* 112. **c 1561** penes rememoratorem primitiarum et ~arum hujus Scaccarii *PRO Cert. Second Admission* E. 333/7/293 f. 1 (cf. *DocCOx* 134 [**1585**]: nomina omnium et singulorum componentium cum regia majestate pro primitiis spiritualium suorum beneficiorum ac promocionum spiritualium .. una cum ~a parte clari annui valoris eorundem beneficiorum).

4 (as sb. f. *sc. pars*) tithe (eccl.), (Sc.) teind; **b** dist. acc. source; **c** dist. acc. season of payment; **d** dist. as great (garbal, rectorial *etc.*) or small (vicarial *etc.*); **e** dist. as personal (or privy) or predial; **f** appropriated, sts. dist. as particular or separate (partly exemplified also in b - e *supra*); (*cf.* G. Constable *Monastic Tithes* Cambridge 1964). **g** second teind (Sc.). **h** 'tithe' (fig. or allusive).

~as non est legitimum dare nisi pauperibus et peregrinis THEOD. *Pen.* II 14. 10; **747** [falsi pastores] lac et lanas ovium Christi oblationibus cotidianis ac ~is fidelium suscipiunt et curam gregis Domini deponunt (*Proc. Synod.*) BONIF. *Ep.* 78 p. 168; **786** de ~is dandis sicut in lege scriptum est [*Exod.* xxii 29 etc.] .. sicut sapiens ait: '.. plerumque contingit ut qui ~am non tribuit, ad ~am revertitur' (*Proc. Synod.*) AL-CUIN *Ep.* 3 p. 25 (= *Conc. HS* 456; cf. *GAS* 147); c**1055** (11c) sit haec terra libera ab omni servitio tam aecclesiastico quam seculari .., cum saca et *sokne, tolle* et *teame, ciricsceatte* et ~is *CD* 805; **1096** (v. consuetudo 4b); nonne laici murmurant si de ~is solvendis in sermone instituto mentio fiat? NECKAM *NR* II 7; c**1240** precipimus quod .. ~e ut ~e, non ut oblationes integre, persolvantur; quia, dum sub oblationis specie ~e prestantur a quibusdam, nonnunquam ecclesie non solum justis ~is sed et oblationibus consuetis et debitis defraudantur *Conc. Syn.* 383; **1297** vic. Kancie misit ministros suos ad domos rectorie ecclesie de T. ad triturandum ~as ibidem repositas pro xxxvij li., quas petit ab eodem priore *DCCant.* (*HMC*) 262; numquid credimus laicos debere subtrahere ~as et bona pauperum ab inferioribus sacerdotibus minus peccantibus et dare superioribus ..? WYCL. *Ver.* III 25; s**1382** docebant .. ceteri discipuli Wyclyf quod ~e sunt mere elemosine KNIGHTON *Cont.* 191; ~as et oblaciones Deo et ecclesie debitas amplissime persolvere studuit BLAKMAN *Hen. VI* 4; hec ~a, *tythe WW*. **b** a**1190** quatinus .. ~as vestras .. ecclesiis vestris .. plenarie .. persolvatis .., sc. de blado, de lino et lana, de caseo, de butiro, de agnis .. necnon et de ceteris omnibus non nominatis de quibus lex Christiana ~am dari postulat *Regesta Scot.* II 179; c**1194** me .. concessisse ~as bladi de dominio meo in Netheravene Deo et ecclesie ejusdem ville integre percipiendas, non per acras metendas sed per garbas collectas, viz. sine omni deductione expensarum que fiunt in metendo *Ch. Sal.* 53; **1228** mandatum est ballivo de Kaermerdin' quod de dominico regis de Kaermerdin' ~as feni ecclesie de Kaermerdin' dari faciat *Cl* 115; c**1230** ~as de omnibus que renovantur per annum .. dandas decernimus et potissime de molendinis et piscariis et fenis et apibus et de terris arabilibus et ad prata postea vel ad pasturam redactis *Conc. Syn.* 192; a**1251** promiserunt se daturos .. capellano .. ~am lactis vespertini et vitulorum mortuorum sive occisorum *Reg. Aberbr.* I 209; c**1260** statuimus .. quod ~e solvantur de artificibus, de mercatoribus et de lucro negotiationis, similiter de carpentariis et omnibus aliis stipendiariis operariis, viz. quod dent ~as de stipendiis suis .. *Ib.* 797 (*gl.* LYNDW. 191–7); c**1300** mandamus .. quod .. parochiani .. sine diminutione ~as inferius annotatas suis ecclesiis persolvant .. viz. ~am lactis a primo tempore sue innovationis .., de proventibus boscorum .., piscariorum .., warenarum, aucupitii .., turvarum in locis ubi fabricantur et fodiuntur [etc.] *Ib.* 1390–1 (*gl.* LYNDW. 199–201); **1417** de medietate ~e ecclesie de B. .., de ~a garbarum ville de H. .., de ~a minere carbonum Thome de B. *Ac. Durh.* 285; oblaciones minuti alteragii et albe ~e [? *tithe of dairy produce*] *Val. Eccl.* (*Cumb*) V 285; **1570** omnes illas ~as minutas et ~as privatas ac alteragia et ~as albas vocatas *the whyte tythes* necnon omnes ~as lini et canabi .. provenientes .. infra villam .. de Newbollde [*Warw*] *Pat* 1068 m. 23. **c 1403** de ~is autumpnalibus bladorum et feni et ~is quadragesimalibus et minutis oblatis capelle de W. *Ac. Durh.* 217; in ~is quadragesimalibus et aliis minutis ~is parochianorum *Val. Eccl.* V 115 (cf. ib. 158: in ~is paschalibus). **d** c**1200** retenta nobis quadam porcione minutarum ~arum, sc. agnorum, piscium, denariorum de piscibus ad ~am perveniencium, lane, casei, canabi *DCCant.* (*HMC*) 231; a**1228** ita quod .. episcopus Sar' et sui successores conferent .. cui voluerint idonee persone tertiam partem ~arum garbarum totius parochie de C. et omnes minutas ~as .. que debentur eidem ecclesie *Ch. Sal.* 106 (= *Ambrosden* I 288); **1245** portiones ejus [sc. vicarii] duxerunt exprimendas, viz. omnes minutas ~as et oblationes et altaragia cum tertia parte grossarum ~arum *Reg. S. Thom. Dublin* 385; **1304** quod ecclesia de Brechyn' habeat .. ecclesiam de M. .. cum omnibus terris et ~is tam majoribus quam minoribus ad predictam ecclesiam .. pertinentibus *Reg. Aberbr.* I 182; **1315** in grossis ~is et minutis ~is, ut de jure ecclesie *Year Bk.* XVII 196; **1362** ita quod ibidem ordinetur perpetuus vicarius qui totum alteragium .. habeat .. et inde solvat .. omnia onera .. ecclesie incumbencia, exceptis .. contribucionibus regiis et episcopalibus ~am garbalem tangentibus *Reg. Aberd.* I 99; **1546** singulas ~as garbales, nuncupatas parochiales, ecclesie de L. .. monasterio nostro .. unite *Dryburgh* 287. **e** c**1250** circa alias prestationes ~arum personalium credatur decimantium sacramento *Conc. Syn.* 490; **1315** cum omnibus ~is .. predialibus et personalibus *Melrose* 407; potest .. intelligi bene quod ~e prediales non debent subtrahi quin dentur dignis ecclesie quibus debentur, cum ~e debentur ecclesie, sive prepositus simpliciter bonus fuerit sive malus; ~e autem personales voluntarie supererogate possunt omnino subtrahi, sicut et alie elemosine, quando non adest qui digne reciperet. potest autem male intellegi quod ~e prediales debentur criminoso preposito WYCL. *Ver.* III 4–5; **1425** conclusiones .. nuper .. predicatas contra ~as personales et in nostra universitate .. necnon in .. consilio episcoporum .. damnatas *StatOx* 229; ~e personales alias *prive tithes Val. Eccl.* II 36 (cf. ib. 64: pro lactagio vitulorum et ~is privatis); **1588** ~as tam prediales quam personales *Pat* 1321 m. 9. **f** quibus [canonicis Lanfrancus] in terris, in ~is et in aliis redditibus tanta largitus est ut ad sustentationem eorum sufficientia esse viderentur EADMER *HN* 19 (cf. *Regesta* I p. 119; *DB* I 2v.); **1125** nullus abbas, nullus prior, nullus omnino monachus vel clericus ecclesiam sive ~am .. de dono laici sine proprii episcopi .. assensu suscipiat (*Conc. Lond.* 4) J. WORC. 20; **1167** (v. 1 constituere 4b); c**1250** pensiones et ~as separatas, quas viri religiosi qui non sunt de episcopatu nostro percipiunt in nostra diocesi, in manus nostras sequestramus *Conc. Syn.* 358 (cf. ib. 709 [c**1265**]: certas ~arum particularium portiones); **1255** abbas Colcestrie de ~is separatis vj m. *Val. Norw.* 224; *Ziz.* 394 (v. 2 appropriare 2c). **g** †**1175** cum frater meus concesserit .. episcopo Aberdonensi secundas ~as de omnibus redditibus, firmis, escaetis suis infra vicecomitatus de Aberden et de Banff *Regesta Scot.* II 193; **1261** nos .. confirmasse donacionem illam quam R. de Brus fecit .. abbati et conventui de L. de terra sua .. in G. .. in escambium secundarum ~arum quas .. consueverunt percipere de terris ejusdem R. .. *Cart. Lindores* no. 117 (cf. ib. p. lxiv); **1333** istud est rentale regis A. III vicecomitatuum de Aberden et de Banff de quo deduci debent secunde ~e ad opus episcopi Aberdonensis *Reg. Aberd.* I 55 (cf. ib. 199, 358); **1413** sumus .. informati quod ab antiquissimis temporibus ecclesia Brechinensis et episcopi ejusdem .. secundas ~as percipere consueverunt de .. proventubus domino regi pertinentibus infra balliam [de Kyncardin] .. *Reg. Brechin* I 35; **1469** pro secundis ~is debitis episcopo Aberdon' de .. thanagio de K. *ExchScot* 639. **h** Domino propriae decimas persolvere vitae ALCUIN *SS Ebor* 1094; '~as morientes': quasi diceret: "per hoc non possumus approbare Melchisedech fuisse immortalem .. quia ~as Abraham accepit .." LANFR. *Comment. Paul.* (*Heb.* vii 9) 391 (cf. decimatio 3d).

5 (as sb. f.) tithing. *Cf. decena* 1, *decimatio* 5.

si necesse sit in manibus, indicetur hominibus hundredi, et postea indicent hominibus ~arum [AS: *ðam teoðingmannum*] (*Quad.*) *GAS* 192 (= *Cons. Cnuti*: decimacionariis); ut omnis homo liber sit in hundreto et ~a (*Ib.*) *Ib.* 536; ut a duodecimo etatis sue anno in hundreto sit et ~a vel plegio liberali quisquis were vel wite vel jure (*sic*) liberi dignus curat estimari (*Leg. Hen.* 8. 2) *Ib.* 554; W. MALM. *GR* II 122 (v. centuria 2b); **1198** Godefridus de I. et ejus ~a, dim. m. *CurR RC* I 218.

6 (abl. sg. m. or n.) in the tenth place, tenthly (also in comp. numeral).

c**1160** (v. decachordus); **1279** ~o excommunicantur .. quicumque abstrahunt violenter reum ad ecclesiam .. confugientem *Conc.* II 35b (cf. *Conc. Syn.* 850); ~o cum dicit: "nempe," improperat Agamenon TREVET *Troades* 26; ~o est quis de pertinacia convincendus si .. OCKHAM *Dial.* 463 (cf. ib. 466: ~osexto potest papa .. convinci .. si ..; ~oseptimo de pertinacia .. potest quis convinci si ..).

decinctor, 'unbelter' (fig.), detractor.

a**1150** ~oribus ejus amici insultando resistant OSB. CLAR. *Ep.* 23 (cf. ib.: hunc .. cingulo letitie accingere).

decindere v. 2 decidere, discindere. **decinere** v. discinere.

decingere [cf. CL cingere], to ungird, unbelt. *V. et. discingere* 1a.

sine braccis et discinctum [v. l. decinctum] BRACTON 356b (v. et. decalceare); postea ~entes se exuant vetus staminum et, novo ordine retrogrado .. recingant se *Cust. Cant.* 10.

decipere [CL], **a** to ensnare, entrap, entice. **b** to beguile, deceive; **c** to cheat. **d** (w. abl. or *de*) to cheat of. **e** (pass.) to be mistaken.

a ignaros virorum more meretricis ~iebat *Lib. Monstr.* I 1; multis modis ~io [AS: *ic beswice*] aves, aliquando retibus, .. aliquando decipula [AS: *mid treppan*] ÆLF. *Coll.* 95; qui nos hamo, rethi, nassa / nititur decipere WALT. WIMB. *Virgo* 146; s**955** Edwius .. cuidam nobili abstulit uxorem, eo quod in ipsius pulchritudine ~eretur SILGRAVE 54; **1340** consueta est ~ere gallinas visinorum suorum *CBaron* 98. **b** egent sane populi, quibus praeestis vel potius quos decepistis, audire GILDAS *EB* 96; Judas Scarioth, strofa deceptus iniqua ALDH. *CE* 5. 5; ne .., siquid malificae artis habuissent, eum superando ~erent BEDE *HE* I 25; **930** (10c) massam humanae conditionis .. olim fraude falsitatis decoeptam *CS* 1343; ut nec antiqui hostis ~eretur simulatione fraudulenta ABBO *Edm.* 4; deludis, i. ~is, *bepæhst* vel *wægst GlH* D 129; Deus non ~it aliquem; tamen ~it per istum vel per illum, ut actio ad Deum referatur et imperfectio que est in verbo ad creaturam HALES *Sent.* III 503; sapientes .. viros sepius sic [traditor infernalis] decepit [ME: *he haveð* .. *swa bicherred*] *AncrR* 81. **c 1340** seminator ~it terram domini seminando, pro eo quod parum et parum furatur semen *CBaron* 103. **d** non erat qui posset eum ~ere de redditibus abbatie ad valentiam unius denarii BRAKELOND 128v.; **1235** postquam deceperat Willelmum .. de xxxvij d. quad. *CurR* XV 1306; **1290** ~iuntur catallis suis (v. deceptio c); **1295** (v. cautelose). **e** c**710** simoniacis .., qui in praesenti vita a deceptis hominibus putabantur digni perpetuae gloria coronae (*Ep. Ceolfridi*) BEDE *HE* V 21 p. 343; BRACTON 71, BACON *Tert.* 211 (v. deceptio d); *Id. Maj.* III 121 (v. Christus 2a); licet Joannes XXII fuerit juris peritus, tamen poterat ~i .. poterat ergo .. putare quod sufficeret Christianis ad excusandum ipsum, absque hoc

quod fateretur se errasse, confiteri catholicam veritatem OCKHAM *Pol.* III 83.

decipula [CL], trap, snare; **b** (fig.).

~a, *bisuicfalle GlC* D 33; ÆLF. *Coll.* 95 (v. decipere a); R. COLD. *Godr.* 89 (v. comprehendere 1a); habeat pedicam sive descipulam, qua lupi capiantur NECKAM *Ut.* 111; **s1303** mures et murelegos quos ~a [v. l. discipula] ceperant manducarunt *Flor. Hist.* III 113; *pyttfal*, ~a, avicipula *PP*; hec discipula, *a swyke WW*; *a felle for myse*, muscipula, ~a *CathA*. **b** muliebris audaciae muscipulam parvi pendens, callidae deceptionis ~am declinavit ALDH. *VirgP* 53; [immundi spiritus] pedestres incedunt cum per se ipsi clam ~as tendunt [*1 Sam.* xiii 4–5] BEDE *Sam.* 575; loetiferas vero scrobibus versute latentes / decipulas sensit Uuinfridus FRITH. 655; non tam philosophie species quam impietatis ~a est J. SAL. *Pol.* 440A; cui ejus [serpentis] delectat ~a [cf. *Job* xviii 10] displicet Domini disciplina MAP *NC* I 1 f. 7; rex Henricus [II] ad solitas discipulas se convertens GIR. *PI* III 2 p. 232; imperator .. non minus gloriabatur in actibus regis nostri quam detestabatur facciones et ~as Gallicorum *G. Hen. V* 25.

decipulator, deceptor, deceiver.

pellicator, fraudator, ~or OSB. GLOUC. *Deriv.* 468.

decipulosus, enticing, alluring.

~a, i. inlecebrosa, *leahterfulle* vel *forspenninga GlH* D 5.

decisibilis, decidable.

tolle omnem proprietatem .. et non est compossibile quin omnis casus ecclesie sit ~is secundum legem ewangelice caritatis WYCL. *Ver.* II 144.

1 decīsio [cf. 1 decidere,], ruin, decay. *Cf.* 2 *decasus* 1a.

1221 si edificium vetus sit .. paratum decidere .., domina illud sustinebit .., ita tamen quod, si heredes maliciose querantur de ~one edificiorum, .. mittantur .. legales homines .., qui videant deteriorationem domorum (*Responsio Itineris*) *MGL* I 68.

2 decīsio [CL]

1 a cutting down. **b** rending, wounding. **c** mutilation (fig.), curtailment. **d** division into parts. **e** division (of spoken sound), articulation. *Cf. discissio* 1.

a 1252 in .. combustione domorum et vinearum ac arborum ~one (*AncC* IV 148) *RL* II 73. **b** lacrime planctusque sequuntur / et gemitus fletuque madens decisio vultus HANV. VI 164 p. 330; **1282** eam .. sanguinolenta ~one vi subripuit et defloravit *Gaol Del.* 35 B r. 38. **c** ne Menevensis ecclesia .. in sua jurisdictione lesionem incurreret vel diocesis ~onem GIR. *RG* I 6 p. 39. **d** omne quod ~onem pati potest ex partibus compositum est R. MELUN *Sent.* II 3. **e** unum [lingue juvamentum] est ~o vocis et extractio litterarum, aliud .. conversio cibi masticati *Ps.*-RIC. *Anat.* 29;

2 cutting (of cloth *etc.*), retailing. *Cf. discissio* 1b.

a1155 mercator foranus .. videat ne ad incisionem [v. l. decisionem; OF: *a taille*] merces suas vendat (*Lib. Lond.*) *GAS* 674 (cf. *EHR* XVII 715); **1188** nullus extraneus .. vendat pannum ad ~onem nisi in nundinis *BBC* (*Bristol*) 212; **1200** quod nullus extraneus vendat pannos in civitate [*Dublin*] ad ~onem *RChart* 79a; **a1210** (1515) nulli mercatori extraneo liceat discisionem pannorum facere .. in villa *BBC* (*Kilkenny*) 285.

3 'decision', separation (of seed) in generation. *Cf.* 2 *decidere* 3.

tam parva est ~o seminis in mula quod non sufficit semen ad conceptum NECKAM *NR* II 159; si ~o est in generato, erit illa ex humiditate assumpta in generante HALES *Qu.* 1295; per descisionem KILWARDBY *SP* f. 28rb (v. discindere 2); virtus feminina dat semen unde fit corpus individui generandi; virtus vero masculina est motrix et primo movet ad hoc ut excitetur virtus feminina ad ~onem seminis BACON III 276; generatio per purgationem, sc. seminis desisionem *Id.* VII 10; *Id.* VIII 68 (v. 2 decidere 3); queritur an potentia generandi per ~onem seminis sufficit ad hoc quod sit sexus *Id.* XI 204; ad hunc intellectum Filius non est genitus de Patre vel de substancia Patris per ~onem sed per communicacionem substancie CONWAY *Def. Mend.* 1425 (*recte* 1325).

4 a termination. **b** settlement, decision.

a 1268 ut conficiendi testamenti .. adimat vite ~o facultatem *Conc. Syn.* 771. **b 1281** PECKHAM *Ep.* 173 (v. desolatio 2b); **c1300** usque ad diem prefixum ad finalem expedicionem et discisionem eleccionis negocii audiend[as] *DCCant. Reg.* Q f. 45a; **s1286** in regem Anglie E. .. ad ~onem questionis super jure regni .. consencierunt *Plusc.* VIII 3; **1434** (v. declaratio 1c).

3 decisio v. desitio b. **decisisus** v. 2 decidere 3.

decisivus, conclusive, decisive.

1291 tenent .. cardinales quod vester ad cismarinas .. partes adventus in tractatu prefato sit totius dubii ~us (*Rex Jerosolim. ad Ed. I*) *AncC* XVIII 155; **1303** ad apostolice sedis oracula ~a .. recurritur cum ex .. perplexitate .. hesitatur *Reg. Cant.* 655.

decisor, settler, decider (of dispute); **b** (w. ref. to proctor).

s1461 est sine lege necis vindex, sine judice juris / decisor, quia vi vult cuncta regi gladiali (*Vers.*) *Reg. Whet.* I 400. **b c1180** qui[a] ipse non potuit interesse, constituit quendam procuratorem, viz. V. de S., ~orem totius litis .., ratum habiturus quicquid V. inde finiret (*Cart. Trentham*) *Collect. Staffs* XI 323 (= *FormA* 22).

decisorius, decisive.

1311 constat tum per testes .. tum eciam per juramenta ~ia ex nostro officio principalibus personis delata *RGasc* IV 562; quaere utrum hoc juramentum sit litis decissorium vel necessarium *Praxis* 67.

decissus v. 2 decidere, discindere. **decit** v. dicere 1c. **decitera** v. sicera.

1 decius [cf. OF *de, des* < datum], dice, die.

a1183 dabit pro eis [terris] R. filio meo singulis annis iij ~ios eburneos *Cart. Glam.* 114; **1188** quod nullus ludat ad aleas vel ad ~ios (*Ord. Regis*) *G. Hen. II* II 32; plumbum .. per porum subtilem ~ii infundit, ut beneficio ponderositatis vergat tessera ad nutum suum NECKAM *NR* II 183; **1270** solebat ludere ad ~ios pluries cum .. Willelmo *ICrim* 2/17; **1277** de Abr' de Dorking' pro ludo ~ium (*sic*), iij s. *KRAc* 249/22; quibus .. concordat .. Ovidius [*Tristia* II 471–4] .., ubi agit de ludo ~iorum et illum damnat, eo quod non innititur racione sed casu fortuito ~iorum hominumque fortuna BRADW. *CD* 265B; omnes sedent et dicat primus Judeus jactans ~ios *Chester Plays* XVIA 120.

2 decius, tenth.

tene, decem ..; decimus, ~ius, decies *CathA*.

declamare [CL]

1 to declaim. **b** to proclaim, announce.

contionatur, *maðalade*, ~at *GlC* C 854; **1549** (v. declamatio 1a). **b** eum .. portarum vigiles caelestium .. quo erat ~abant *V. Greg.* p. 82; **1207** precipimus quod mercatum illud ei habere facias et facias illud per totam ballivam tuam .. ~ari *Cl* 82b; **c1236** [rex] precepit in dictis nundinis voce preconiali ~ari quod mercatores .. ad easdem nundinas nullas negotiationes exercere presumant GROS. *Ep.* 21.

2 to denounce, proscribe. **b** to cry down, devalue (currency).

in hac epistola, quicquid deflendo potius quam ~ando .. fuero prosecutus, ne quis me affectu cunctos spernentis .. sed condolentis patriae .. miseriis .. edicturum putet GILDAS *EB* 1; tante et tam ~ate per orbem [Cisterciensium] aviditatis bona, ut credimus, occasionem prestat intentio GIR. *IK* I 3; tanquam hostes publici per regni compita ~ati *Id. Invect.* I 10 p. 117; speculatores debent tales symoniacos hereticos alte et continue ~are WYCL. *Sim.* 104. **b 1484** ex eo quod dominus rex consideravit quod nigra moneta erat subito ~ata *ExchScot* 286; **1487** ex eo quod noluerunt dare nisi nigram monetam .. et illa moneta erat ~ata et sic deperdita *Ib.* 480 (cf. ib. lxvi-lxvii).

3 to disclaim (a right). *V. et. disclamare* 1.

1292 modo ~at quasdam libertates quas ipsemet in propria persona primo die itineris hic clamavit *PQW* 786a; **1293** quo ad *blodwyte* [etc.] dicit quod ipsas libertates ad presens ~at .. in isto comitatu; et quo ad liberam warennam .. dicit quod ipsam clamat per cartam .. regis *Ib.* 216b.

declamatio [CL]

1 declamation. **b** proclamation.

novum ~onis genus deliberando, demonstrando, judicando subortum est (*Quad.*) *GAS* 532; legantur .. libri .. quos decem Oratorum sententiis sub imagine ~onum scolarium [Seneca] illustravit J. SAL. *Pol.* 764B; **1549** inter baccalaureos .. junior primo declamabit, atque interim eligantur duo artium magistri ~onum praesides *StatOx* 359. **b** tunc ibi detur dies ex quo omnes loquele que in Banco fuerunt posite sunt et remanent sine die per publicam ~onem inde factam BRACTON 353b.

2 crying down, devaluation (of currency).

1486 de cv li. quas compotans obtulit .. compotorum rotulatori in *le plakkis* debito et legali tempore ante ~onem earundem *ExchScot* 363.

3 claim.

homines de hundredo .. moliebantur manerium hujus ecclesie .. suo juri mancipare; sed is abbas [F., ob. **1117**] .. ratiocinando ostendit ~onem eorum injustam esse *Chr. Abingd.* II 116.

declamatorium, shouting-house.

s1139 ecce totius episcopatus principale cenobium factum est civ[i]um diversorium et quoddam ~ium J. WORC. 56.

declarabilis, declarable, expressible.

quam intentionem principaliter logicus attendit, philosophus vero principalius rem naturalem quam intentionem communem ~em *Ps.*-GROS. *Summa* 334; Verbum formaliter declarat omne ~e DUNS *Ord.* VI 232.

declarare [CL]

1 to reveal, make clear, elucidate, demonstrate; **b** (w. acc. & inf., *quod*, or indir. qu.). **c** to declare, pronounce (w. compl.); **d** (w. cognate acc.). **e** (absol.) to clarify a decision; *cf. declaratio* 1c. **f** to 'declare' w. ref. to account (*cf. Guide to P. R. O.* (1964) I 70–1).

talia signa sacrum portendunt esse futurum, / prospera quod rerum liquido fortuna declarat ALDH. *VirgV* 987; D. .. Occidentalium Saxonum episcopus .. nonnulla mihi de historia .. provinciae ipsius .. litteris mandata ~avit BEDE *HE pref.* p. 7; quod ~ari vix verbo proprio potest, id translato inlustratur ALCUIN *Rhet.* 37; sanctus antistes Suuithunus, eodem tempore caelestibus signis ~atus et infra templi regiam gloriosissime translatus WULF. *Æthelwold* 26; propriam sic .. ~atam exponere visionem GOSC. *Transl. Aug.* 29A; ad ~andam sui potentiam GIR. *TH* II 19; **1302** (v. declarativus a); UPTON 256 (v. declaratio 1b); **1459** quemadmodum per exteriora vocis verborumque indicia ~atur passio animi (*Lit. Procerum*) *Reg. Whet.* I 341. **b** metrica nam Moysen declarant carmina vatem / jamdudum cecinisse prīsci vexilla tropei ALDH. *Aen. pref.* 17; quantum .. profecerit adhuc praesentia tempora ~ant BEDE *HE* II 4; **a1350** extitit ~atum procuratorum .. assercionem debere sufficere in hac parte *StatCantab* 319; ~ans quod .. controversia .. inter non habentes superiorem de sub celo celesti arbitrio ~atur, gladio exequente *G. Hen. V* 17; **1420** (v. declaratio 1b); **1421** (v. cauterium 2b). **c** papa [Bonifacius VIII] dictos cardinales deposuit, privavit, et inhabiles ~avit *Meaux* II 243; examinandus est .. an paratus sit corrigi vel .. possit .. pertinax ~ari OCKHAM *Pol.* III 51. **d** *Entries* 192 (v. declaratio 1d). **e 1439** ut vos .. possitis inter nos et .. dominum decanum .. arbitrari, laudare, diffinire, arbitraliter sentenciare .., interpretari, ~are, in scriptis vel sine scriptis *Stat. Linc.* II 195. **f 1504** abstractus separalium declaracionum diversorum receptorum, firmariorum et aliorum occupatorum in diversis portubus Anglie .., prout per separales declaraciones supra specificatas et inferius particulariter ~atas plenius apparet *LTR Ac. Decl.* 454 m. 1.

2 to clear (of a charge), exonerate.

1459 intendimus .. solummodo appetere hujusmodi habere graciam qua valeamus .. ~ari in hiis omnibus que objecta sunt .. contra nos (*Lit. Procerum*) *Reg. Whet.* I 342; **1460** non habebit libertatem antequam fuerit de dicta felonia ~atus *Doc. Bev.* 51.

declaratio [CL]

1 a revelation. **b** elucidation, explanation. **c** (clarification of) decision, settlement. **d** (leg.) declaration, statement of claim. **e** 'declaration' (of account); *cf. declarare* 1f.

a angelus est .. speculum .. immaculatum .. recipiens totam .. speciositatem .. deiformitatis et pure ~onis in seipso BART. ANGL. II 2. **b 1281** cum .. sint aliqua verba obscura in recordo illo, potest dominus rex .. accipere ~onem illius obscuritatis *SelCKB* I 88; sepe [in Scriptura] factum posterius premittitur et postmodum facta priora ad ~onem facti posterioris .. subnectuntur OCKHAM *Pol.* I 340; si Anglicana perspicacitas .. quicquam ad augmentum sciencie vel ~onem fidei promulgabat R. BURY *Phil.* 8. 134; **1420** peciit .. declarari que consuetudo .. consuevit observari; et ad ~onem hujusmodi faciendam .. *Conc. Scot.* II 77; **1423** super omnibus et singulis articulis ~one aliquali indigentibus *Cl* 273 m. 2*d.*; generaliter scias quod ad omnia illa arma que ego in diebus meis vidi habes regulas, ut credo, sufficientes ad dicendum super eorum discrecione et ~one naturaliter, dum tamen ad ea declaranda vel discernenda nimis avidus non fueris vel festinans UPTON 256. **c s1286** quod ejus decreto .. quoad ~onem juris regie successionis .. obedirent FORDUN *Cont.* XI 2; videtur congruere sigillum alicujus monasterii .. ad hujusmodi brige sive litigii ~onem .. prefato abbati fuisse transmissum ELMH. *Cant.* 123; **s1403** indulgencia pro fabrica ecclesie Ebor' cum †eclaracione privilegiorum aliorum *Fabr. York* 196 *rub.* (cf. ib. 197: quas quidem indulgencias per dominum T. S. .. declarari volumus); **1434** promiserunt se in solucione hujusmodi feodorum stare .. ordinacioni, voluntati, et ~oni venerabilis congregacionis magistrorum regencium *StatOx* 256 (cf. ib.: ad decisionem, terminacionem, et ~onem solucionis hujusmodi feodorum); **1439** super ambiguorum, dubiorum, et obscuritatum, tam in .. laudo .. quam eciam in .. registro aut statutis, interpretacione, exposicione, et ~one *Stat. Linc.* II 195. **d 1480** memorandum quod .. fiat ~o domino .. Cistercii de laboribus abbatis Woburnie habitis pro ecclesia de S. ultra ccc miliaria, et non potuit habere evidencias ullas ..; item fiat ~o quomodo .. abbas de T. fatigavit nos abbatem Woburnie pro colleccione subsidii comburendoque citacionem sibi factam *Eng. Abbots to Cîteaux* 83; **1560** videtur .. baronibus .. quod predictum breve et ~o .. modo et forma superius declarata ac materia in eisdem specificata minus sufficiens in lege existit *Entries* 192. **e 1504** (v. declarare 1f); **1526** uni officiar[io] in Recepta [Scaccarii] ad tallias scribendas et ~ones faciendas *SP Hen. VIII* XXXVII 1939 (9).

2 clearing (of a charge), exoneration.

1382 [ad] ~onem fame nostre tantis criminibus maculate (*Lit. contra N. Herford*) *Ziz.* 295; **1433** peciit omnia predicta pro ejus ~one irrotulari *Cl* 283 m. 4*d.* (cf. ib.: pro majori ~one ac vera et plana notificacione innocencie sue).

declarativus [LL], elucidatory, explanatory; **b** (as epithet of Giles of Rome).

s1281 idem clericus, quia videbatur sibi dictam peticionem suam nimis generalem, aliam a priore, ut dixit, ~am nobis .. porrexit *Chr. Peterb.* 89; **1302** capitula .. predicta sunt juris communis ~a, quia de contentis in illis fuerunt olim opposiciones inter doctores .., unde non inducunt jus novum set quod olim fuit dubium declarant illa capitula *Reg. Cant.* II 1118; dominus Nicholaus III in decretali illa ~a regule fratrum Minorum .. movet unum dubium Ric. Armagh *AP* 71. **b** sicut S. Thomas dictus est 'Doctor Communis' et venerabilis Egidius 'Doctor ~us' Capgr. *Hen.* 179.

declarator [CL], revealer. **b** settler (of dispute), arbiter.

~orem conjurationis utilitati reipublice perniciose Neckam *NR* II 155 p. 243. **b s1286** decreverunt .. pro .. E. †regi [l. rege] nuncios mittere .., ut in causa ipsa judex fieret superior ac juris utriusque ~or atque in ejus potencia partem contra quam sentenciam promulgaret .. debite coerceret Fordun *Cont.* XI 2 (cf. ib. 3: ut .. in causa juris utriusque partis ~or fieret); **1439** nos canonici .. vos .. arbitrum et arbitratorem, diffinitorem, arbitralem sentenciatorem .., dispositorem, pronunciatorem et ~orem super reformanda pace et concordia .. eligimus *Stat. Linc.* II 195.

declaratorius, declaratory, elucidatory.

s1299 bulla ~ia super exempcione et revocacione quorundam privilegiorum prius per eundem papam concessorum (*Chron. Aug.*) Elmh. *Cant.* 57; **1301** rescriptum [pape] ~ium de quibus fuerat decima persolvenda *Reg. Carl.* I 152; **1331** verba specialia eorundem verborum generalium ~ia .., veluti *flemansfleth*' et *utflach*' *PQW* 72a; possunt .. episcopi constituciones facere juris communis ~ias et revocatorias Lyndw. 70 r; **1503** literas patentes ~ias *RScot* 563a; si alius datus fuerat terminus probatorius ad id probandum, ad quod hae [positiones] sunt ~iae *Praxis* 148.

declaratrix, declaratory (f.).

s1301 rex E. misit pape B. litteras ~ices juris et dominii quod Anglia habet super regnum et reges Scocie Higd. VII 40 p. 290.

declausus [cf. CL decludere], unenclosed; *v. et. disclaudere* c. **b** closed.

1250 bene dicunt quod parcus debet esse clausus... set dicunt quod idem W. ob maliciam suam illum tenet ~um, ita quod averia .. intrant (*JustIt* 560) *SelCWW* 73. **b** spermate in matrice locato, oreque ejus ~o, si in dextra parte consistit .. fetus masculus efficitur *Quaest. Salern.* B 24.

declibius v. declivis 1a.

declinabilis [LL], (gram.) subject to inflection.

feower ðæra dæla synd ~ia, *þæt is declinigendlice* Ælf. *Gram.* 290; dividitur diccio in ~em et indeclinabilem *Ps.*-Gros. *Gram.* 34; iste differencie [construccionis] transitive et intransitive sunt de esse construccionis solum inter partes ~es et non inter partes indeclinabiles Bacon XV 107; opinio .. multorum modernorum dicentium quod sole monosyllabe indeclinabiles mutantur [in modo accentuandi], ~es vero non mutant accentum naturalem *Id. Tert.* 240.

declinacem v. declinare 6a.

declinantia, decline, deviation.

argumentum declaratum est superius .. de modo temptacionis et superacionis hominis ad peccandum, quomodo est propter adherenciam ad bonum conmutabile et ~iam ab inflexibili veritate Wycl. *Civ. Dom.* I 35.

declinare [CL]

1 (trans.) to bend down. **b** (intr.) to bow. **c** (trans., fig.) to bring low. **d** to bring to a close.

in exemplum feminarum .. quae .. vultum ~asse narrantur in terram [*Luke* xxiv 5] Bede *Hom.* II 10. 151; equus .. caput in terram ~are .. coepit *Id. HE* III 9; caput humiliter .. ~avit Wulf. *Æthelwold* 5; cujus oculi acute intuentur .. ciliis ~atis significant hominem malitiosum M. Scot *Phys.* 64; [amor] te declinat, ut hiems lilium J. Howd. *Ph.* 239. **b** vir Deo devotus, episcopo ~ans, ordinem subdiaconi sibi dare .. postulavit *V. Rob. Knaresb.* 1. **c** abominabile est .. anime liberalitatem in serviles delicias ~are Gir. *PI* I 4; longe stat justicia; falsum dominatur; / in plateis veritas lapsu declinatur [cf. *Is.* lix 14] Garl. *Epith.* I *Summa* 19; vix infirmatur post prandia qui spatiatur / aut declinatur in somnpnum quem moderatur *Id. Mor. Scol.* 414. **d** ~ata eadem die Bede *HE* III 25; ~ata jam die Herm. Arch. 6.

2 (intr.) **a** to grow weak. **b** to die down, abate. **c** to draw to a close.

a *Fleta* 165 (v. decrepitas). **b 1406** scismatice tempestatis procella ~at *Conc.* III 292b. **c s1087** Augusto mense ~ante W. Malm. *GR* III 282; jam die prope ~ante R. Cold. *Godr.* 231.

3 (trans.) to draw aside, divert.

8.. ~atur, *he bið aheld WW*; machinam contra fluvium ad dextram ~antes Osb. Bawdsey clxxv; **1169** Petri gladius .. Malco, nisi ~et ictum, amputabit auriculam J. Sal. *Ep.* 302 (295); si egritudo fuerit in manu, possumus †declivare materiam .. aut ad alteram manum aut ad pedem oppositum Gilb. VII 312. 2 (cf. ib.: ~are materiam ad locum oppositum).

4 (intr.) to deviate, diverge, tend; **b** (astr.); **c** (in morals or log.); **d** (w. ref. to quality). **e** to digress.

c710 fit ut numquam Pascha nostrum a septimana mensis primi tertia in utramvis partem ~et (*Ep. Ceolfridi*) Bede *HE* V 21 p. 337; deviat, i. errat, ~at, *on woh cerþ GlH* D 360; exorbitantes, i. circuientes, ~antes, *aswifende Ib.* E 690; **a1200** ~ando parum ad dexteram per exilem semitam *Feod. Durh.* 203n.; cor .. in medietate pectoris collocatum et in sinistrum ~ans Alf. Angl. *Cor* 4; Killingworth *Alg.* 714 (v. calculatorius b); Netter *DAF* I 298 (v. Christiformis b). **b** sol semper decurrit sub ecliptica; omnes alii planete ~ant vel versus septentrionem vel versus austrum Sacrob. *Sph.* 89; necesse est quod [sol] pluribus diebus moretur in medietate zodiaci que ~at ad septentrionem quam in altera parte zodiaci que ~at ad austrum Bacon VI 35. **c** militum Christi circiter x milia .. nequaquam a sanctae religionis tramite per obliquos anfractus dextra laevaque ~antia [cf. *Prov.* iv 27 etc.] Aldh. *VirgP* 36; ut ~emus [AS: *we bugon*] a malo et faciamus bona Ælf. *Coll.* 101; gradiens .. via regia [cf. *Num.* xxi 22], nec ~abat ad dextram extollendo se de meritis nec ad sinistram succumbendo vitiis humanae fragilitatis Abbo *Edm.* 4; **1296** ad aliud .. non intendimus .. nisi ad puram super hoc ~are justiciam *Reg. Cant.* 122; simpliciter dubitando, ad unam sc. partem magis quam ad aliam nequaquam explicite ~ando Ockham *Pol.* III 51. **d** color ejus ~at ad nigredinem Bart. Angl. IV 11; dieta epilepticorum temperata sit, ~ans ad caliditatem Gilb. II 111. 1; ad videndum ad que morbus ~et Gad. 18. 1; complexio .. multum ad sanguinis naturam ~ans Kymer 3; *Ib.* (v. densitas 2b). **e** a diverticulo ad materiam, a qua paulullum ~avimus, redeuntes *G. S. Alb.* I 82.

5 (intr.) to withdraw, resort, travel, pay a visit.

a1150 si clametur regi 'scachum', vel ab uno pedite, / declinare statim debet proximam ad tabulam (*Vers. Wint.*) *Hist. Chess* 515; debet senescallus .. mandare vicecomiti loci ubi dominus rex fuerit ~aturus quod .. *Fleta* 67; [archiepiscopus Ebor'] missis literis causa visitacionis faciende tempore Roberti [ob. **1283**] .. tunc Dunelmensis episcopi ~avit ibidem W. Guisb. 349; **1304** habeant senescalli .. receptaculum ad quod honeste valeant ~are *Ord. Ely* 25; **s1312** cum per villam de D... contingeret eos ~are Trokelowe 76; **1319** si Scoti ad nostros portus ~ant et nostri homines ad Scocie portus similiter ~averint (*Lit. Com. Flandriae*) *Foed.* III 771a; **1333** (v. declinatio 3); **s1355** latuit .. communitatem tocius exercitus quo [dux] proposuit ~are Avesb. 125; **1439** cum idem .. per vos .. ~averit *Cl* 289 m. 26.

6 (trans.) to avoid, shun, escape (from). **b** to reject, repudiate.

implenda non faciunt et prohibita non ~ant Gildas *EB* 98; declinat fercula pompae Aldh. *VirgV* 626; ut [columba] .. venturi raptum accipitris .. ~et Bede *Hom.* I 12. 62; regularem normam secutus .., devia queque ~ans Ælf. *Æthelwold* 10; si quis rectum ~et [AS: *riht forbuge*] vel aufugiat (*Quad.*) *GAS* 194; pagenses latrunculos fugiendo seu divertendo devitare possunt; versipelles vero bedellos nullatenus sine damno ~are queunt Ord. Vit. XII 34 p. 440; quia lucem cognovimus, pravorum operum tenebras ~emus Osb. Bawdsey clxxxi; **1308** fletum non possumus ~are (*Lit. Papae*) *Reg. Carl.* II 7; [rex] tunc excillabit et latronem generabit [*gl.*: nescio quis sit ille [MSS: iste] latro, si sit aliquis filius regis .. vel quod faciet populum suum latronem et predari ab eo †declinacem [MSS: declinantem], qui sibi victum et stipendia †prebeabat [MSS: praebebat] (J. Bridl.) *Pol. Poems* I 159–60. cum nullum medium tam gravis ulcionis funeree ~andi discrimina .. perpenderint *Ps.*-Elmh. *Hen. V* 69; omnem lasciviam .. ~averat Blakman *Hen. VI* 7. **b** Ric. Angl. *Summa* 16 (v. declinatorius b); **1301** an sit mittendum [ad papam] ad ~andum judicium vel ad excusandum *Anglo-Scot. Rel.* 89; **c1350** Lincolniensis episcopus protestabatur se .. suam [sc. archiepiscopi] jurisdiccionem velle in omnibus ~are *MunAcOx* 171; **1436** postquam fidem et ligeanciam .. proditorie ~averant *Cl* 287 m. 24 *d*.

7 to inflect (decline or conjugate).

sic .. 'jubeo', 'moveo', 'moneo' ~antur Aldh. *PR* 121; veteres 'huic famei', non 'huic fami', ~abant Bede *AM* 102; primus ordo, qui genitivo casu 'ae' regit, hoc modo ~atur: nominativo 'haec sancta' .. et pluraliter nominativo 'hae sanctae' Bonif. *AG* 21; **1222** requisitus quid esset 'clementissime', vel cujus casus, vel qualiter ~aretur, nescivit *Reg. S. Osm.* 304.

declinatio [CL]

1 decline, decay. **b** (w. *solis*) sunset. **c** (med.) abatement.

1231 in aeternis et increatis rationibus contuebimur omnium rerum creatarum existentias, formas et species, initia, profectus, status, ~ones et consummationes Gros. *Ep.* 6. **b** ab ortu usque ad ~onem solis fiat portagium sine requie *Stat. Gild. Berw.* 49. **c** quando secunda [febris] incipit prima nondum cessante, sed in prime ~one arripit Gilb. I 8. 1; quandoque in acutis in die vij urina apparet viridis .. et morbi ~onem significat *Ib.* VI 259. 2; nihil accipiat nisi in ~one paroxismi Gad. 18. 2.

2 deviation, divergence (also fig.). **b** (astr.) declination.

rectitudo est in nullo a se exitus aut ~o Gros. 135; Peckham *Persp.* III 2 (v. contiguatio a); negligencia ministrande ecclesie .. et ~o ad vitam seculi sunt illius heresis papalis manifestum indicium Wycl. *Sim.* 28. **b** arcus coluri qui intercipitur inter punctum solstitii estivalis et equinoctialem appellatur maxima solis ~o Sacrob. *Sph.* 90; Bacon IV 389, VI 9 (v. declivis 1a); de ~one stelle et latitudine ab ecliptica Wallingf. (*Rect.*) I 424; *Id.* (*Alb.*) I 290 (v. declivis 1a).

3 visit.

1333 ad nos .. velitis personaliter declinare, scientes quod hujusmodi ~o erit nobis afferens solacii relevacionem .. et vobis .. nullatenus onerosa *Lit. Cant.* II 41.

4 (gram.) inflexion (declension or conjugation) or inflected form. **b** (acad.) evening class in grammar.

nomina quae multiformi quinque ~onum radice .. pululasse noscuntur Aldh. *PR* 113; de secunda conjugatione in prima persona indicativi modi antibachius haud facile reperiri potest, quamvis in ceteris modorum et temporum ~onibus adsciscatur *Ib.* 124; si 'amem, ames, amet' ~o est verbi conjunctivi Bede *Orth.* 48; 'sensus' nomen est quartae ~onis *Ib.*; accusativus Graecus tertiae ~onis frequenter desinit in A: 'aera', 'aethera' Abbo *QG* 16 (35); omnia nomina quibus Latina utitur eloquentia v ~onibus inflectuntur Ælf. *Gram.* 21; **1103** in ~one et virtute grammaticae cognoscenda maxime intende Anselm (*Ep.* 290) IV 210; H. Los. *Ep.* 9 (v. conjugatio 1a); conjugacio est verborum sequens ~o *Ps.*-Gros. *Gram.* 50; ~o accidentalis est accentui et indeclinatio similiter Bacon *Tert.* 241. **b** vespertinum exercitium, quod ~o dicebatur, .. copiositate gramatice refertum erat J. Sal. *Met.* 855A.

declinativus [cf. declinare 6, *w. pun on* 7], repudiative.

passiva laborum / paupertas, vicii declinativa, malorum / ablativa, virum genitiva, dativa bonorum Hanv. VI 262 p. 334 (cf. ib. I 486 p. 257: species .. / .. nusquam declinativa).

declinatorie, by a declinatory plea.

1389 a premissis non recedendo set eisdem firmiter inherendo, excipiendo ~ie .. contra vos .. quod dicta commissio pretensa .. est .. revocata *Scrope v. Grosvenor* 9.

declinatorius, (leg.) declinatory. **b** (as sb. n.) declinatory plea.

1271 quod exceptionem proposuit [pro illa die] fori ~iam *SelCCant* 184; **1309** si persona ecclesiastica .. trahatur ad forum seculare in causis spectantibus ad cognicionem ecclesiasticam, non admittitur excepcio ~ia fori *Reg. Cant.* 1024; **1517** licet ego .. exceptionem legitimam .. fori vestri omnino ~iam in judicio coram vobis in medium produxerim *Form. S. Andr.* I 360. **b** cum vocati venerint, si judicium declinare voluerint, plenissime alias tractatum est de ~iis [v. l. declinationibus] judiciorum quibus vocati instrui possunt declinare Ric. Angl. *Summa* 16.

declinium v. declivis 2c. **declinosus** v. declivosus.
declivare v. declinare 3.

declivis [CL], **~ius, ~us**

1 downward sloping. **b** (geom. & astr.) slanting. **c** (w. *luna*) waning (w. ref. to disputed date of Easter). **d** bowed, downcast. **e** (morally) declining or erring. **f** inclined, tending.

declibius, inclinatus *GlC* D 127; collis non magnus declivo tramite flexus Æthelwulf *Abb.* 132; ~i, i. proni, inclinati, .. vel *aheldre GlH* D 23; mons ascendentis descendentisque per ipsum / limite declivi vexat utrumque gradum H. Avr. *Poems* 20. 122; rex .. quosdam milites .. ad ipsa ~a intersticia modis bellicis incolenda .. assignavit *Ps.*-Elmh. *Hen. V* 66. **b** dividit innumerus speram declivis orizon Hanv. VIII 416 p. 373; sol[i]us orbis solis et octava spera moventur secundum orbem signorum sine declinacione ..; alii enim orbes planetarum moventur super alios polos circulorum ~orum aliorum ab istis et abinvicem declinantes ad septentrionem et meridiem Bacon IV 389 (cf. ib.: per motus duos communes octo speris, sc. ~um et rectum); motus [solis] accipitur tripliciter... primus modus est per comparationem .. ad circulum declinationis in quo equinoctia et solstitia signantur. .. secundum primum modum dicitur annus circuli ~is, tempus sc. quo sol a puncto equinoctii vel solstitii movet secundum ordinem signorum .. donec redeat ad idem punctum *Id.* VI 9; an in tali diaphano lux habeat ~em incessum Peckham *Persp.* III 1; ponit semidiametrum umbre cum semidiametro lune adequari declinacioni circuli ~i ab ecliptica in termino eclipsis lunaris a nodo Wallingf. (*Alb.*) I 290; **c** publica declivae fiunt divortia lunae Frith. 252. **d** ~i, i... humiliati *GlH* D 23; ita erat curvatus somate ut ~i capite caelum vix posset cernere Lantfr. *Swith.* 37; cujus humilitas et patientia, quo ~ior atque mansuetior, eo sublimior est ante Deum Eadmer *HN* 129; [regina] ~a facie genibusque sepius flexis .. recessit Ælnoth *Cnut* 67; **c1423** non sine ~i vultus leticia *Reg. Whet.* II 406. **e** ad malum ~ioribus seculis inmane

quantum recrevere W. Malm. *Mir. Mariae* 138; rectificatque virum declivem regula virtus Hanv. VIII 283 p. 368. **f** dieta febricitantis debet esse ~is ad hanc complexionem Gilb. I 25v. 2; pulsus in quartana est ~is ad duriciem Gad. 16.1.

2 (as sb. n.) slope. **b** (*in ~o*) at an angle. **c** decline, close.

ecclesia sita est in ~io montis Syon Sæwulf 839; **1258** dim. acram que se extendit de B. . . in Q. . . per ~ium ex australi parte de H. *FormA* 161; **s1264** regalis exercitus . . occursurus eis ~um montis ascendit *Flor. Hist.* III app. 259; hinc jubet hos †punctis [v. l. punctus] rex reparare; sudes / terra fingendas dat declivo retinendas / versus eos, visu quo timor assit equis Elmh. *Metr. Hen. V* 421; **s1416** pernici gressu per ~ium montis descendere conabatur Wals. *YN* 469; *clyffe of a hylle*, ~um *PP*. **b** ut unusquisque affigeret ante se a fronte palum suum . . uno fine affixo in terram . . et alio in ~o versus hostes *G. Hen. V* 11. **c** quo [rege Edwardo] trahente decursum versus aevi †declinium, infirmatur . . et infirmatus finit hominem Herm. Arch. 22; cum ad ~ia lux diurna festinaret, Samson *Mir. Edm.* I 1 p. 109 (= Ciren. I 356: †~a); sunt cujuslibet egritudinis tempora iiij, principium, augmentum, status, et ~ium Ric. Med. *Signa* 32; **s1246** ejusdem anni in ~um tendente curriculo *Flor. Hist.* II 322.

declivitas [CL]

1 steepness (of descent).

s1297 via que . . deducit ad portum non in directum, ne nimia ~ate descendentes in precipicium vel ascendentes repere pocius manibus quam ambulare cogat, tenditur Rish. 174.

2 dullness.

a dullnes, ebitudo, ~as *CathA*.

declivosus, uneven, undulating.

ypocondriacos oportet post cibum per †declinosa loca ambulare, ut cibus fundum stomachi petat Gilb. II 15.2.

declivius, declivus v. declivis.

decludere [CL], **a** to unclose. **b** to disenclose. *V. et. discludere* 2. *Cf. declausus.*

a comes . . declusas [oppidi] fores ingrediens, ipsos fugientes . . prosequitur *Ps.*-Elmh. *Hen. V* 79. **b** **1275** dicunt quod dominus H. rex solebat annuatim habere ij s. redditus de una venella vocata Cattenelane dum exstiterat inclusa et in manu Galfridi B., quondam civis Lond'; item . . quod ipsa venella . . declusa fuit tempore turbacionis et ideo vacat *Hund.* I 415a.

declutire v. degluttire.

decoctio [LL]

1 cooking, baking. **b** decoction.

1279 supplicant quatinus . . panis fratrum . . l solidos ante ~onem ubique ponderet sterlingorum *Doc. Eng. Black Monks* I 116 (= *Cust. Cant.* 396). **b** detur ~o polip[odii], agar[ici] cum colatura cassief[istule] Gilb. I 45v. 2 (cf. ib. VII 321. 1: ~o que facit homines surgere a lecto, qua utantur in podagra); lava cum aqua ~onis furfuris Bacon IX 73; preter liquiriciam ad ~ones nullam rem medicinalem . . impendere consueverat *Cust. Cant.* 326; in dissinteria, quando paciens sedet in ~one aliquarum herbarum *SB* 20; *Ib.* 11 (v. apozema).

2 digestion. **b** maturation or sim.

quoniam . . ea que in stomachum descendunt . . in ipso stomacho digeri et decoqui patens est, ex tali item ~one fumum ascendere . . consequens est Adel. *QN* 20; recepto cibo in loco ~onis, primo sc. in stomacho Bart. Angl. IV 6; tunc corroborabitur stomacus super ~onem cibi Bacon V 74. **b** humor . . digeritur per plantarum membra et, cum sua ~one profecerit, turgescit in surculos J. Sal. *Pol.* 427d; albedo cum livido colore . . est signum diminute ~onis embrionis in matrice Bacon V 166.

3 smelting or sim.

quis adinvenit metallorum ~onem, alterius in alterum reductionem? Map *NC* I 1 f. 7v.; *Ps.*-Gros. *Summa* 634 (v. chalybs a); cathima auri dicitur id quod in ~one ab auro separatur *SB* 15; aurum de vena terre fit per ~onem *Alph.* 17.

decoctus, decocuere v. decoquere. **decoeptus** v. decipere b.

decollare [CL]

1 to behead; **b** (fig.); **c** (w. *caput* as obj.). **d** (?) to shave or scalp.

S. Babilas ~andi sortitus sententiam . . capite truncatur Aldh. *VirgP* 33; [S. Johannes Baptista] ~atus est in castello quodam Arabiae quod Macheronta nominant Bede *Hom.* II 23. 242; decretum est . . ut obsides [Turci] ~arentur *Itin. Ric.* IV 4; **1256** (v. depraedari 2); *Fleta* 16 (v. dismembrare b); **1276** [regno abjurato] arripuit iter suum et . . extra iter suum fugiendo . . fuit ~atus per villatam *SelCCoron* 37; **s1326** H. Despenser . . tractus, suspensus, et ~atus fuit Birchington *Arch. Cant.* 18; **1340** dictus [J.] †decollocetur et S. ad gaolam . . ducatur *CBaron* 99; unus collo suo grave vulnus inflixit, volens excerebrasse vel ~asse eum Blakman *Hen. VI* 17. **b** vae tibi, humana miseria; utinam ~areris Alch. *Ep.* 298. **c** abbas . . suis innuit monachis utrum . . caput hujus martyris ~atum cum corpore jam sit solidatum Herm. Arch. 20; **1322** idem T. cognovit se esse notorium et publicum latronem . .; per quod coronator in presencia predictarum iiij villatarum secundum consuetudinem comitatus Cestris' caput predicti T. ~are fecit *PlRChester* 34 r. 11d. **d 9..** (v. decalvare a).

2 (p. ppl., w. ref. to shoes) truncated (for ornament).

StatOx 57 (v. 2 decidere 2a).

decollatio [LL], beheading, decapitation. **b** (feast of) Decollation of St. John (29 Aug.).

sententiam ~onis accipiens Aldh. *VirgP* 43; ~o illa [S. Johannis Baptistae] in carcere et in obscuro patrata capitis ablatio Bede *Hom.* II 23. 241; **s1062** affirmante [Wlstano] se multo libentius ~oni quam tam alte ordinationi succumbere velle Fl. Worc. I 220; post illam Turcorum [obsidum] ~onem *Itin. Ric.* IV 7; **1280** clamat habere *hevedstok'*, hoc est ~onem latronum captorum cum manuopere *JustIt* (*Som*) 759 r. 8d.; nonne amens reputaretur qui . . recusaret . . punccionem acus pro ~one [ME: *bihavedinge*]? *AncrR* 62; **s1381** usi sunt . . judices . . ~onibus rusticorum, donec visum fuisset penam capitalem non correspondere tantis . . facinoribus . .; ob quam causam expost decreverunt omnes repertos sceleraciores . . protraccione [et] suspensione punire Wals. *HA* II 20. **b** ad terminum . . quem eis ponimus, id est ~o S. Johannis Baptiste [AS: *to ðæm dæg ðær beheafdunges seint Johannes þæs fulhteres*] (*Quad.*) *GAS* 147; Lanfr. *Const.* 134 (v. baptista 1b); **1203** a die Jovis, die sc. ~onis S. J. B., . . usque in xv dies sequentes *Pat* 33b; **1204** die Martis proxima post decolacionem S. J. B. *CurR* III 206; **1247** in festo ~onis S. J. B. *Melrose* I 230; cepit festum ~onis sue [sc. S. J. B.] in urbe illa [Jerosolima] celebrari, eo sc. die quo caput inventum fuerat et elevatum Higd. IV 5 p. 344; **13..** Augustus: . . iiij Kal., ~o S. J. B. (*Kal.*) *StatOx* 10; **s1430** in nocte ~onis S. J. B. *Chr. S. Alb.* 53.

decollator, beheader, executioner.

tunc ~or cum gladio eum quinquies in collo percussit Gascoigne *Loci* 227.

decollocare v. decollare 1.

decolor [CL], discoloured.

~or, i. deformis *GlH* D 20; ~or, pallidus, *æblæce vel æhiwe GlP* 270; planam . . lepre contagionem pretendebat; facies enim ~or, nodose manus, ulcerose tibie virum dehonestabant W. Cant. *Mir. Thom.* II 53.

decolorare [CL], to alter the colour of, to discolour. **b** to stain (fig.), tarnish, discredit; *v. et. discolorare* 1c.

~ant, desimulant, †depingant *GlH* D 21; Adel. *CA* 12 (v. 1 cera 3); R. Cold. *Godr.* 158 (v. decoriare f); **s1244** episcopus . ., quem . . ictericia ~averat . ., tussis desiccaverat M. Par. *Maj.* IV 330; peplis . . in quibus . . croceus color radiat, qui colorem ~ate faciei sofisticat suo fuco J. Godard *Ep.* 233; vultus . ., / quem Amoris omnipotencia / decolorat ut hiems lilia J. Howd. *Ph.* 209; egens sum et esuriens . ., ~atus ob absenciam amati mei Rolle *IA* 245. **b** cum [creatura] non vult quod debet . ., universitatis ordinem . . perturbat, licet potestatem aut dignitatem Dei nullatenus laedat aut ~et Anselm (*CurD* I 15) II 73; *Id. Or.* 7 (v. dominatus a); hortatur [Alcuinus] ne . . vestium luxui et gule intemperiei professionis sue reverentiam ~ent W. Malm. *GP* III 127; historiis quas suis poete ~avere figmentis J. Sal. *Pol.* 394a; quod primi parentes sue creationis nitorem peccato ~averint Pull. *Sent.* 646b (cf. ib. 752d); ad ~andam mutue fraternitatis famam A. Tewk. *Add. Thom.* 19.

decolorus [LL], discreditable.

[tres liberi Wihtredi] haud ~o [v. l. ~ato] exitu regnum [Cantie] continuavere W. Malm. *GR* I 15.

decolpare [AN *decolper*, OF *decoper*], to cut down, fell.

1228 mandatum est . . ut faciat ~ari in parco de Havering maeremium ad telarias faciendas *Cl* 49.

decomatio, scalping; *cf. extoppare*; or (?) *f. l.*

si quis dominum suum occidat . ., nullo modo se redimat, set decomatione [? l. decoriatione] vel e[viscer]atione . . dampnetur (*Leg. Hen.* 75. 1) *GAS* 591.

decomperere v. decooperire.

decompositus [LL], (gram.) derived from a compound; **b** (fig.).

[adverbia] ~a, id est, quae a compositis derivantur, ut ab 'indocto' 'indocte' a 'misericorde' 'misericorditer' Alcuin *Gram.* 886d; ~e figure sunt que ex compositis componuntur aut ex simplici et composito ut 'inexpugnabilis', 'inperteritus' *Ps.*-Gros. *Gram.* 41; συνθετον, quod est compositum, παρασυνθετον, quod est ~um Bacon *Gram. Gk.* 1 **b** c**1430** dominum Lincolniensem . ., qui, etsi compositus ~usque in diviciis fuerit ac derivativus in honore, semper tamen, ut loquamur cum grammaticis, in moribus est . . figure simplicis *Reg. Whet.* II app. 393.

deconclavi v. conclave 1a.

deconstare, to give a quittance.

1390 compotans non onerat [? sc. se] de custuma burgorum . ., quia custumarii non comparuerunt; nec potest ~ari sibi de custuma *ExchScot* 241.

decontinuatio [cf. CL continuatio], discontinuity. *V. et. discontinuatio* 1a.

ab una et eadem anima potest procedere regimentum per universitatem orbis, nec erit impedimentum quin ipsa sit propter ~onem in partibus mundi J. Blund *An.* 356.

decontra [CL], (adv.) on the opposite side. **b** (prep.) opposite.

frater . . qui in specula . . insulae longe de contra eventus ejusdem pervigil expectaverat horam Bede *CuthbP* 40; Moyses de contra e regione ignis depingitur Ad. Scot *TT* 734d. **b** stantis ~a illum proximi . . cerebrum excussit R. Cold. *Cuthb.* 110.

decooperire [LL], to uncover, reveal. *V. et. discooperire* 1b.

principium temporis coitus . . in masculo est post complementum annorum xiiij. . . [hinc] sibi vox mutatur, caput virge masculi ~itur M. Scot *Phys.* 2; *to schewe*, . . aperire, discooperire . ., retegere, †decomperere [? l. decooperire], ostendere . . *CathA*.

decopulare [cf. copulare 1a, AN *descopler*], to uncouple (hounds). *V. et. discopulare* a.

1255 fecit ~are duos brachettos, qui invenerunt unum cervum in bosco *SelPlForest* 34; **12..** ~averunt ibidem duos canes *Chanc. Misc.* 11/1/26.

decoquere [CL]

1 to boil (down). **b** to bake; **c** (fig.). **d** to execute by boiling. **e** (p. ppl.) parched, torrid.

jumento . . frustatim in aqua decocto Gir. *TH* III 25; ~atur fe[niculum], lactu[ca], portu[laca], scar[iola] in lacte mu' et papaver[is] et dentur coclearia duo in sero Gilb. I 65. 2; Bacon *NM* 547 (v. dealbare 4a); *SB* 11 (v. apozema); Upton 190 (v. colatura a). **b** **1286** quilibet burgensis possit construere sibi furnum . . in quo panem ~at *BBC* (*Bakewell*) 125; **1289** panem decocuet ad vendendum *RGasc* II 354. **c** **798** Alcuin *Ep.* 137 (v. compaginare 1c); ut . . immanis offense †dequoqueretur culpa W. Malm. *Mir. Mariae* 131; ut et illa, si quid priscarum culparum superesset, confessionis rubore ~eret *Ib.* 215; in ventris clibano per ignem misticum / Maria decoquit panem salvificum Walt. Wimb. *Carm.* 118. **d** **s1397** falsus monetarius . . ad mortem est decoctus Fordun *Cont.* XV 5. **e** jam estas decoctior in autumnum vergebat Gir. *PI* III 20.

2 (of disease, fever, *etc.*) to wear out, waste. **b** (of passion) to consume.

Heriberct diutina . . infirmitate ~itur Bede *CuthbP* 28 (= *Id. HE* IV 27 p. 275); septem . . diebus dira egritudine decoctus octavo die ad extrema pervenit Felix *Guthl.* 50; Folc. *V. J. Bev.* 11 (v. emaculare); cepit . . temporali languore decoctus ad eterna gaudia preparari R. Cold. *Godr.* 305; ex diuturnitate naufragii pedes decocti vel exulcerati solito mihi non famulantur incessu W. Cant. *Mir. Thom.* VI 161; languor continuus proprios si dequoquit artus D. Bec. 563; diutino febrium ardore decoctus Map *NC* III 2 f. 36; **s1356** alii terris congelati et . . tempestatis impetu decocti et contacti . . extincti sunt Fordun *Cont.* XIV 17. **b** suspiciosissima zelotipia decoctus Map *NC* II 22 f. 31.

3 to digest. **b** to mature, ripen. **c** (fig.) to ruminate, ponder.

[animalia] que calida sunt acceptos cibos melius digerunt . ., que vero frigida pejus. . . calidiora pinguedinem habent molliorem, utpote magis decoctam Adel. *QN* 7; [vinum tale] juvat digestionem . ., ducit cibum, ~it et perducit ipsum purificatum ad omnia membra que reguntur, et ~it cibum ipsum in eisdem membris donec convertatur in sanguinem subtilem et substantialem Bacon V 92. **b** **s1257** transiit . . annus . . sterilis. . . quicquid enim hiems seminaverat, quicquid ver promiserat, quicquid estas decoxerat, autumnalis inundatio suffocavit M. Par. *Maj.* V 660. **c** [Anselmus] has ratiocinationes secum diu decoctas in amantis sui Lanfranci sinum competenti evaporavit tempore W. Malm. *GP* I 45; quamvis sentencia pape . . tanta consilii moderacione concipi debeat tantaque maturitate paciencie ~i et tanta deliberacionis gravitate proferri Ockham *Dial.* 688.

4 to smelt, refine or sim. (esp. alch.); **b** (fig.).

macheram, / cujus erat vagina auri radiante metallo / predita decocti Wulf. *Swith.* I 280; aurea terra rubens, / que decocta diu tandem transibit in aurum Neckam *DS* VI 59; si . . cerusa decocta in olla rudi moveatur cum spatula ferrea Gilb. VII 351. 2; Dastin *Ros.* 18 (v. calcinatio). **b** decoquit hos mundus et, sicut in igne camini / aurum flamma probat, sic Deus urit eos Nig. *SS* 2362.

1 decor [CL; *sts. indistinguishable from* 1 decus]

1 beauty, charm: **a** of human form; **b** of place; **c** of artefact; **d** of literary style.

a in pulcherrimo pubertatis ~ore Aldh. *VirgP* 53; neque aliquos homines tanti ~oris ac venustatis esse posse

credebam BEDE *HE* IV 14; tuum [est], Christe, mortuos vivificare et imaginem tuam quam creasti in ~orem suum pristinum reformare WULF. *Æthelwold* 39; VINSAUF *PN* 562 (v. circinus 1b); †movent [? l. movet] luxuriam species ~oris alterius corporis ad corpus sibi amore conveniens M. SCOT *Phys.* 1; corruptor [virginum] .. oculos amittat propter aspectum ~oris quo virginem concupivit BRACTON 147. **b** delectatus suavitate et ~ore loci illius BEDE *HE* V 12 p. 309. **c** [Wilfridus] capitella columpnarum .. variis celaturarum figuris .. et picturarum et colorum grata varietate mirabilique ~ore decoravit RIC. HEX. *Hist. Hex.* I 3. **d** a**705** (CELLANUS) *Ep. Aldh.* III (9) (v. alburnus a); BEDE *HE* IV 22 (v. dignitas 1b).

2 embellishment, ornament (also fig.).

Hæddi, pie presul, precor, / pontificum ditum decor, / pro me tuo peregrino / preces funde Theodoro THEOD. *Pen. Verse epil.*; aedificium multifario ~ore ac mirificis ampliavit operibus BEDE *HE* V 20; ad ~orem et ornatum quem addere poterant [arbores] GIR. *TH* III 10; curia Romana .., / que decus atque decor urbis et orbis erat NIG. *SS* 2498; D. BEC. 137 (v. 1 decus a); nulla necessariis debetur gratia rebus. / concupiens igitur decus affectansque decorem, / Hugo domus domini rude vult componere claustrum H. AVR. *Hugh* 444; **1349** ad honorem Dei et ~orem ecclesie *Reg. Roff. Ep.* 245; in propugnaculis arma linee regalis ad ~orem in hastilibus prominebant *G. Hen. V* 15.

3 dignity, seemliness.

licet hoc non tantum ad artis praecepta pertineat quantum ad officii ~orem ALCUIN *Rhet.* 19.

2 decor [CL], beautiful.

residente .. papa B. Gregorio .., adsisterunt (*sic*) viri .. nimis vultu ~ores ÆTHELW. II 1; juvenes .. viderat ~ori rutilantes fulgore LANTFR. *Swith.* 2.

decoramen [CL], adornment, splendour.

conspexit .. / quendam pontificem miro decoramine comptum, / .. veluti celebrare paratum / missarum Domino sollempnia WULF. *Swith.* II 955; delatus Wintoniae ibidemque tumulatus cum regali ~ine HERM. ARCH. 17.

1 decōrare [cf. 1 decor], to beautify.

[ecclesiam] Hugo .. / .. egram / sanat, anum renovat, acrem dulcorat, egenam / fecundat, vilem decōrat turpemque decōrat H. AVR. *Hugh* 853.

2 decŏrare [CL; cf. 1 decus], to adorn, deck. **b** to fortify, arm. **c** to honour, glorify. **d** to decorate (w. emblem of knighthood).

aethereus per me decoratur Olimpus ALDH. *Aen.* 37 (*Cancer*) 4; **949** (14c) dedi cuidam meo homini .., ob studium quam (*sic*) mihi auri argentique fabrica sollicite deservit atque ~at, duas mansas *CS* 879; **970** (14c) quoddam ruris clima .. cuidam viduae sanctimonialique habitu ~atae .. largitus sum *CS* 1259; ut Galliarum honestos ecclesiarum usus [in] rudi Anglorum ecclesia ~ando (*sic*) [AS p. 368: *gewlitegende*] constitueret *RegulC* 5; erat .. vultu decorus, integer corpore, barba prolixa, cano ~atus capite W. JUM. IV 19; ecclesiam .. in cappis, casulis .. et aliis ornamentis .. ~avit EADMER *HN* 16; R. COLD. *Osw.* 51 (v. decusare); degenerantes animi, licet ad tempus morum venustate ~ari videantur .., in brevi revertuntur NECKAM *NR* II 132; absentia corporis ~ati etate et adornatione M. SCOT *Phys.* 1; puella .. ad modum ymaginis ornamentis pudicicie culcioribus ~ata *G. Hen. V* 15. **b** Brittannia .. munitionibus non improbabiliter instructis ~ata GILDAS *EB* 3; Arturus .. lancea dextram suam ~at, que nomine Ron vocabatur G. MON. IX 4. **c** ~ata totius orbis capita regni quodammodo dejecerat GILDAS *EB* 13; haec suprema suae decoravit tempora vitae, / purpureo sanctam perfundens sanguine carnem ALDH. *VirgV* 2006; atque adeo ingentis magno auxit munere doni / precipui decorans nobilitate gradus *Epigr. Milredi* 810; quod A. salubri verborum exhortatione predicavit, hoc Suuithunus miraculorum exhibitione mirifice ~avit WULF. *Æthelwold* 26; a**995** decurrato (v. eryceum); obsequ[i]is decorat Malchus dominos et adorat R. CANT. *Malch.* II 326; mille ducenti [monachorum] .. in ipsa die martirio ~ati G. MON. XI 13; vos estis in sublimitate papali ~atus BACON *Tert.* 62; donec eum decorat mansuete Petrus et orat W. PETERB. *Bell. Hisp.* 95. **d** P. BLOIS *Ep.* 94 (v. cingulum 2); **1259** quem rex cingulo milicie in proximo ~aturus est *Cl* 425.

decoratio [LL], decoration, adornment.

c**1238** quis suscepturus terrenum regem hospitio non mundat illud, honestat et decorat modis .. et impensis quibus potest .. donec habitaculum preparetur .. omni ~one acceptum GROS. *Ep.* 57 p. 178; BACON IX 82 (v. defensio 1e); **1401** j pannus viridis .. pro ~one circa feretrum *Ac. Durh.* 453.

decoriare [LL], to skin, flay: **a** (animals or unspec.); *v. et. discoriare* a; **b** (people); **c** (fig.); *v. et. discoriare* b. **d** to remove (skin). **e** to strip of adornment. **f** to scorch, burn off.

a deglu[b]it, ~avit *GlC* D 129; ~io, corium depono *GlH* D 19; oves ~iatas verubus affixas .. commedendo R. COLD. *Cuthb.* 29; cum .. oves seu armenta .. jugulassent ~iatisque ipsis carnes domi detulissent *Id. Godr.* 20; s**1423** cuniculi in Eywod .. fuerunt .. destructi et cervi et dame inhumane occisi et ~iati *Chr. S. Alb.* 5; *to flee* [v. l. *fla*], ~iare *CathA.* **b** s**1203** cum juramento quod .. omnes patibulo suspenderet aut illos vivos ~iaret WEND. I 319; s**1314** duo milites regni Francie, accusati super illicita commixtione carnali cum regina Navarrie et sorore sua, capiebantur, postea vivi ~iati et tandem in patibulo suspensi *G. Ed. II Bridl.* 46. **c** homines mei .. depredati sunt et spoliati, et ego .. jam eos nudos spoliarem, immo spoliatos ~iarem? EADMER *HN* 51. **d** cleptes .. excruciaretur .. ~ata pelle capitis cum crinibus LANTFR. *Swith.* 26. **e** s**1183** B. Martialis feretrum ~iavit et alia monasterii illius vasa aurea et argentea asportavit *G. Hen. II* I 299 (= R. HOWD. II 277: decorticavit). **f** exteriores asserum superficies ignis ~iaverat et nigra .. fuligine decoloraverat R. COLD. *Godr.* 158.

decoriatio, skinning (of animals).

1242 Goscelinus .. fugit pro ~one ovium furatarum *AssizeR Durh* 72.

decoronare [cf. coronare, OF *descoroner*], to decrown; *v. et. discoronare.* **b** to scalp; *cf. corona* 4c.

s**1170** dixit ei [Thome] vicecomes quod in igne et gladio terram intraverat; regem volebat ~are; .. omnes episcopos excommunicaverat pro servitio regis W. FITZST. *Thom.* 116. **b** s**1170** ita a lictoribus decalvatus ~atus est .. et .. moriens .. cecidit H. BOS. *Thom.* VI 8.

decoronatio, scalping.

H. BOS. *Thom.* VI 9 (v. decalvatio).

decorositas, beauty, elegance.

†**974** (14c) ecclesiam .. certemus polite ~atis munere exornare *CS* 1304.

decorosus [LL], beautiful.

'nemorosus', id est nemoribus plenus; sic '~us', 'speciosus' [etc.] ALDH. *PR* 135; puella pulchra facie atque ~a valde NEN. *HB* 177.

decorrosivus [cf. corrosivus], harshly critical, mordant.

veterum mordacior etas, / acrius in juvenes decorrosiva senectus HANV. I 66 p. 242.

decorruere [cf CL corruere], to decline.

1465 fructus .. in tantum ~erunt quod .. non sufficiunt *MonA* IV 178b (cf. *CalPat* 433).

decorticare [CL], to bark, peel; *cf. discoriare* c. **b** to husk (grain). **c** to skin. **d** (med.) to clear of (dead) skin. **e** to strip of adornment. **f** (fig.) to disfigure.

9.. ~avit, *berinde WW*; ~atum, .. *rindleas* ÆLF. *Sup.*; qui opera sua ad ostentationem magnificant ficum fructiferam ~ant et eam spoliant ALEX. BATH *Mor.* III 63 p. 138; virgas virides populeas .. quas .. ~ans posuit in canalibus HIGD. II 11 p. 32. **b** typsonas faciunt de ordeo; ~ant ipsa grana in pilo *GlC* T 357; formice .. grana que .. collegerunt solercius ~ant UPTON 162; far per genus molicionis fit de quolibet grano panifico, si solum retundetur exesis capitibus et ~etur *Alph.* 62. **c** **9**.. ~avit, .. *beflog WW*; ~atum, *æfelle* ÆLF. *Sup*; qua parte glacies caput [cadentis] excipit, totum radit, totum ~at W. FITZST. *Thom. prol.* 17. **d** coluber predicto modo preparatus [i.e. decoctus in vino etc.] et exbibitus vetulas ~at et rejuvenescere facit GILB. VII 344v. 1. **e** s**1183** (v. decoriare d). **f** audiveram .. garriencium philosophorum .. atque indoctorum Armenorum tumultum, qui fraudulenter .. ~abant tuam scripturam, ut ipsa quasi fetus sensus eis coloris varii parturiret RIC. ARMAGH *AP* 20.

decorticatio [CL], barking, stripping off bark.

1378 de cortic[e] dictarum quercuum nichil, quia prostrate fuerunt extra tempus decortic[acionis] (*Ac. Man. Hatfield Broad Oak*) *Essex R. O.* D/DC 18.

decorus [CL], beautiful, handsome. **b** neat, well kept. **c** orderly. **d** (w. abl.) adorned.

crispos juvenes et ~os *V. Greg.* p. 85; qui juvenes et ~i et vestium ornatu induti erant bene HUGEB. *Will.* 4; **10**.. ~us, speciosus, *wlitig WW*; hicque nitent fulvi nunc ornamenta metalli / cum serico gemmis croceo pretiosa decoris (*Vers.*) ÆLNOTH *Cnut* 44; pulcritudo [Helene] provinciales puellas superabat, nec uspiam adeo ~a reperiebatur G. MON. V 6. **b** D. BEC. 2205 (v. assellator). **c** cantus ~i ODINGTON 245 (140) (v. 2 conductus 4). **d** acies Redwaldi .. hirsute galeis .. et innumeris ~e vexillis H. HUNT. *HA* II 30.

decostare [cf. 2 costare], to cost.

1317 facit eam [domum] construi, que bene ~abit domino regi cccc vel d li. (*RGasc*) *Foed.* III 684b.

decrassare [cf. 1 crassare], to fatten.

to make fatte, crassare, con-, de-, id est valde crassare *CathA.*

decredere [cf. 1 credere], to disbelieve. *V. et. discredere* 1.

depositionem tabernaculi mei agilitate fatali agitari non ~o *Chr. Rams.* 103; et si hoc modo [v. l. hujusmodi] sim ego, non idcirco quod super me est de tanto viro ~ere licebit J. FORD *Wulf.* 19; fortassis quidam eorum qui hec audiunt angariantur; non ~o NETTER *DAF* I 489.

decrementum [CL]

1 decrease, diminution; **b** (w. ref. to moon or tide).

J. BLUND *An.* 144 (v. crementum 1a); s**1247** per mille annos ordo S. Benedicti tantum non suscepit ~um *Flor. Hist.* II 307; secundum .. materiam additam in augmentum erit crementum capillorum et secundum diminutam erit ~um et defectus GILB. II 75v. 2. **b** humida dum crescit Phebi soror, humida crescunt / et decrementi lege sequuntur eam NECKAM *DS* IV 467 (468); crementum et ~um lune GROS. *Com.* 23; ter ascendit mare cum incremento turgido sine ~o notabili vel reflexu M. PAR. *Maj.* V 30.

2 decrease in assessment or value. **b** wear and tear. **c** loss, disadvantage.

1252 pro ~o stauri per totam custodiam *DCCant. Reg.* H f. 173b; **1266** consuetudo .. immutata est ad †detrementum [MS app.: decrementum; *but cf.* detrimentum] ejusdem manerii *Cl* 252; **1272** medietas hundredi de S. in extenta xxxiij s. j d. cum incremento et ~o ejusdem *Cl* 505; **1415** in ~o redditus tenementi Chyld', unde reddi consuevit .. xvj s., et modo dimittitur .. pro xiij s. iiij d. *Ac. Obed. Abingd.* 79; **1437** ad damnum .. abbatis in ~o valoris manerii sui .. et infeccione negociorum suorum in hac parte c librarum (*Artic. Abbatis Westm.*) AMUND. II 130; s**1454** officia prius dicta stant pro nunc nequaquam in incremento sive in statu solito, immo verius in ~o *Reg. Whet.* I 128; **1533** petit allocacionem .. de v li. de decasu et ~o diversorum .. tenementorum *Ac. Durh.* 198; **1538** allocantur ei ij d. de decr[emento] firme j scalinge *MinAc S. II* 464 r. 6. **b** **1412** lego .. omnia utensilia mea .. ad usum suum occupanda et possidenda, racionabili usu et ~o eorundem medio tempore eidem B. allocato de premissis *Reg. Cant.* II 34. **c** ex hoc non modicum .. vobis possit contingere ~um MILEMETE *Nob.* 75; **1450** possessionum .. resumpcionem, que .. maximo nobis ~o fiet *MunAcOx* 293.

decrepedus, ~**idus** v. decrepitus.

decrepitas, decrepitude, old age.

quatuor aetates, pueritiam .. et juventutem, senectutem et ~atem ANSELM *Misc.* 318; **1227** si dictum onus [episcopatum Midensem] non obstante ~ate et gravitate suscipere voluerit in periculo anime sue *Cl* 179b; c**1254** abbas T. excusavit se per †decurpitatem *Doc. Eng. Black Monks* I 52; si priusquam senectutem nimiam attingerint (*sic*) vel per ~atem [v. l. decrepitationem], mahemium vel laborem nimium declinaverint, sic fuerint [pecora] electa *Fleta* 165.

decrepitatio, decrepitude (also fig.).

1007 (13c) in extrema ~one hujus senescentis mundi *Ch. Burton* 30; *Fleta* 165 (v. decrepitas).

decrepitus [CL], decrepit, enfeebled (esp. by age); **b** (as sb. m.); **c** (applied to abstr.).

decrēpita membra / suscitet ut vetulae ALDH. *VirgV* 602; homo senex ac ~us BEDE *Hom.* II 19. 207; ~a, *dobgendi GlC* D 46; **9**.. ~a, i. vetula, *forweren*, valde senex *WW*; viri ~i et senes cano capite AD. EYNS. *Hug.* V 14 p. 172; **1227** dicitur ipsum ita esse gravem et ~um quod non sufficere possit ad prelatie officium digne supplendum *Cl* 179b; homines languidos et ~os [v. l. †despitos] et .. languore detentos *Fleta* 222; **1381** decrepedus est et .. infirmitate detentus (*CoramR*) *Collect. Staffs* XIV 156; **1433** in .. relevacione .. tenencium meorum depauperatorum ~orum *Cl* 283 m. 15*d*.; s**1534** R. Norwic' episcopus cecus aut decrepidus *Reg. Butley* 61. **b** habetur instantia in senibus et ~is, qui nutriuntur non tamen augmentantur J. BLUND *An.* 53; infans, puer, adulescens, juvenis, vir, senex, ~us eandem rem secundum diversa esse signant BACON XIV 76; elemosina tantum decrepidis et debilibus .. est facienda (WYCHE) *Ziz.* 502; hic ~us, *a nald man* .., ille qui vadit cum baculo *WW*. **c** usque nonagenariam ~ae vetustatis senectam ALDH. *VirgP* 29; [aetas] mundi sexta .., ut aetas ~a ipsa, totius saeculi morte finienda BEDE *TR* 16; non propter ~am senectutem sed propter sapientiam presbiteri nominantur EGB. *Pont.* 11; propter ~am in eo senectutem ALCUIN (*Adv. Elipand.*) *Dogm.* 233A; [Alianor] Gallicos amplexus jam sibi ~os fastidiens GERV. CANT. *Chr.* 149; B. Ieronymus .. usque ad etatem ~am sacrarum litterarum indagator OCKHAM *Pol.* III 73.

decrescentia [CL], decrease, decline, waning; **b** (of moon or tide).

c**1423** si .. homo .. superseminaverit zizania [cf. *Matth.* xiii 25] .., faciet tellurem .. sterilitatis dispendio subjacere. paris permutacionis ~iam .. futuram fore conjicimus .. in arvo monastico scolarium studencium Oxonie *Reg. Whet.* II 390. **b** febres que accidunt in ~ia [lune], ut in tertia quadra et quarta BACON IX 190; *G. Hen. V* 24 p. 164 (v. flatus).

decrescere [CL]

1 to dwindle, grow less, wane; **b** (w. ref. to moon or tide); *v. et. discrescere.* **c** to decrease in duration; **d** (mus.). **e** to decline, decay, fail. **f** (w. *ab*) to decline from, fail in.

rota .. in xij dividitur signa, signum in gradus xxx, gradus in dakaikas lx, .. dakaika item in lx secundas,

secunda item in lx tertias, et ad hunc modum .. in infinitum rotae magnitudo descrescit ADEL. *Elk.* 6; commoda quaeque convalescant, incommoda ~ant ÆLNOTH *Cnut* 6; **c1150** (v. dominium 5d); per recessum *A* corporis a corpore luminoso magis ~it *A* umbra quam *B* umbra J. BLUND *An.* 141; juxta quod numerus fratrum cressit aut decressit *Cust. Westm.* 157; **1527** (v. decenalis b). **b** ut mihi lucifluae decrescit gloria formae, / sic augmenta latex rēdundans gurgite perdit ALDH. *Aen.* 6 (*Luna*) 3; eadem ratio est etiam lunae ~entis BEDE *TR* 25; dum mare ~it, [stagnum] eructat ad instar montis absortas aquas G. MON. IX 7; GARL. *SM* 969 (v. circumradiare); hebdomada lune prima decrescere fertur / humor, quem siccat lampade luna nova *Id. Tri. Eccl.* 31; de diversa apparitione figurationis luminis lunaris secundum quod crescit et ~it BACON *Maj.* II 109; luna oritur et occidit, crescit et ~it CHAUNDLER *Apol.* 29a. **c** sed plaga nostra dies decrescere, crescere cernit, / sol quia signifero tramite girat iter GARL. *Tri. Eccl.* 25. **d** TUNST. 256a (v. crescere 3b). **e** ADEL. *QN* 26 (v. 1 decidere 2e); ut .. semper vel crescant vel ~ant .. res humane GIR. *TH* III 12; **1257** Anglia diatim miserabile decrevit M. PAR. *Maj.* V 657; **1367** Dacia decrescit, Hibernia victa quiescit W. PETERB. *Bell. Hisp.* 94. **f** dicitur eis qui aderant 'venite', quia nimirum hoc ipsum numquam a divina contemplatione ~ere in divina contemplatione semper adcrescere est, et numquam corde recedere quasi quodam stabili motu est semper venire BEDE *Gen.* (xi 7) 125.

2 (of money): **a** to be deducted. **b** to be lost.

a c1356 brasiatrix .. non .. minuet quadrantem in gallonam [cerevisie] nisi pro xij denariis ~entibus in quarterio [brasei] (*Assisa Cervisiae*) *MunAcOx* 183; **1379** (*Assisa Panis*) *EHR* XIV 504 (v. crescere 2a). **b** per hoc quod vendunt mercandisas suas in domibus suis, nichil ~ere debet .. episcopo (*CurR*) *Law Merch.* II 2.

3 (trans.) to decrease, diminish. **b** (p. ppl. as adj.) small.

rapta ille superbit / casside, at impatiens captos decrescere visus J. EXON. *BT* I 322; si primo actionem criminalem criminaliter intentaverit, non poterit eam mutare nec agere civiliter, et sic ~ere appellum vel minuere BRACTON 140b; **12..** quibus diebus inceperunt facere caseum, et .. de numero augmentando et ~endo (*Artic. Visus*) *Reg. Malm.* I 202. **b** cum in ecclesiae suae longius protendendae aedificium, .. offendebat et angustum decretae machinae spatium GOSC. *Transl. Aug.* 34A.

decrescum [cf. AN, ME *decres*, OF *descrois*], decrease.

1302 unde computat in ~o mensure frumenti .. tam per desiccacionem .. quam per consumpcionem vermium *MinAc W. Wales* I 468.

decressere v. decrescere. **decrestista** v. decretista. **decretabile** v. decretalis 2a.

decretalis [CL]

1 a having the force of a decree, authoritative. **b** imposed by decree.

a apocriforum deleramenta .. procul eliminare .. patrum scita scriptis ~ibus sanxerunt ALDH. *VirgP* 24; **9..** ~ibus, *þæm rædendlicum WW*; [Lanfrancus] pauca ingenii monimenta reliquit, ~es epistolas et precipuam contra Beringerium W. MALM. *GP* I 44; **1455** hoc presens publicum ~e instrumentum [sc. decretum arbitrorum] manu michi satis recogniti notarii scriptum et signatum signo *Melrose* 570. **b** principes .. Judeorum .. sortes ponunt. quam vero sors designaverit regionem, ejus metropolis urbium ceterarum et oppidorum sortes applicabit, atque illud ~e explebit negotium cujus sors exierit T. MON. *Will.* II 11.

2 (w. *epistola* or as sb. f. or n.) decretal, papal decision on point of canon law. **b** (w. *liber* or as sb. m., f., or n.) book of decretals. **c** (acad.) decretals studied as part of canon law. **d** (adj. w. *causa*) case involving decretals.

c1180 Anacletus papa tertio suo ~i Lugdunensem ecclesiam primam inter occidentales ecclesias nominavit (*Lit. Archiep. Lugdun.*) DICETO *Chr.* 5; decretis et ~ibus epistolis operam prebens cum hora dabatur BRAKELOND 129v.; quam sit .. simoniacum prelatos ecclesiasticos .. pactionaliter eligere, canones aperte clamant et in ~ibus condemnant GIR. *Spec.* III 4; **s1231** frater Agnellus .. misit ad curiam et ~em que dicitur 'nimis iniqua' pro fratribus fieri impetravit ECCLESTON 75; **1232** in decretalibus istis / in quibus ecclēsias nulli prohibentur habere / quas habuere prius H. AVR. *Poem* 127. 126; **s1235** Gregorius papa IX, videns ~ium tediosam prolixitatem, sub quodam compendio eas eleganter abbreviatas et collectas sollenniter et autentice per totius mundi latitudinem legi precepit et divulgari. illas autem ab auctore ipsarum Gregorianas appellamus M. PAR. *Maj.* III 328; **1236** Alexander III in ~i quadam epistola natos ante matrimonium per bonum subsequentis matrimonii decernit esse legitimos GROS. *Ep.* 23 p. 89; ad hoc facit ~e cujus verba sunt hec: 'cum inter I. virum et B. mulierem divortii sententia canonice sit prolata ..' BRACTON 63; **s1317** papa septimum librum ~ium, a predecessore suo compositum et quasi ab ipso deletum, promulgavit, instituit, et confirmavit WALS. *HA* I 153; **1355** asserentes quod †decretibus et †decretabilibus [? l. decretis et decretalibus] .. obedire minime tenebantur *Mon. Hib. & Scot.* 269b; ~is epistola est quam statuit papa vel solus vel cum cardinalibus ad consultacionem alicujus LYNDW. 272 n (cf. ib. 297 h: nota quod ~es summorum pontificum sunt ejusdem auctoritatis sicut decreta que sunt in corpore canonum digesta). **b** **12..** in adventu nostro assignatus fuit michi quidam liber ~is, in quo nichil reperi preter textum nudum, corruptum, immo falsissimum *Ann. Durh.* 130 (cf. ib.: quedam ~es bene apparitate, decentes satis et utiles ac omnes addiciones plenissime continentes); **1291** quidam meus garcio Lumbardus .. ~es meas furtive surripuit *DCCant* (*HMC*) 260; **1295** lego .. filiolo meo ~es meos (*Test.*) *EHR* XV 525; **1337** legavit .. ~ia et Decreta una cum glossa Hostiensis in duobus voluminibus *Lit. Cant.* II 153; **1411** ~es glosate et bene audite; item Johannes in addicionibus super ~es; item Abbas super ~es; item Innocencius super ~es; item Johannes in Collectis super ~es; prima pars Johannis in Novella super ~es ..; item Hostiensis in summam super ~ium primum ..; item Repertorium Aureum super ~es *Ib.* III 121–2; **1434** lego .. par ~ium, sextum librum et Clementinas in j volumine *Reg. Cant.* II 534; *a Decretalles*, ~is *CathA*. **c c1260** quidam clericus dicebat se studuisse per xij annos et amplius in jure canonico et civili; dicebat se insuper legisse omnes libros legales et ~es *FormOx* 476; **1291** propositum mei fuerat .. Oxon' transtulisse ac legisse ~es *DCCant* (*HMC*) 260; **1333** statutum est quod legens ordinarie ~es .. obligetur quod .. complebit lecturam inferius annotatam, viz. quod uno anno per se et extra ordinarium suum legat primum, quartum, et quintum libros ~ium antiquarum una cum constitucionibus Clementinis, et quod ille qui secundo anno lecturus fuerit .. obligetur ad lecturam sexti libri, ac secundi et tercii antiquarum *StatOx* 133; **c1340** in jure civili et ~ibus insistendo et actualiter in eisdem ordinarie legendo et continuando *FormOx* 141; **1421** (v. audire 4). **d** tantam in causis ~ibus .. gratiam optinuit quod die quo ipsum causari velle notum .. fuerat tantus .. concursus extiterat quod vix domus .. capere poterat auditores GIR. *RG* II 1.

decretare, to decree, include in the form of a decree.

1422 cum .. sint nonnulle leges moribus utencium in contrarium hodie penitus abrogate, prout expresse ~atur *Conc.* III 416a; **s1425** jussit abbas .. curatis ut .. ipsi et [archiepiscopo] in pulsacionibus optatas impenderent reverencias, eas tamen ex liberalitate faterentur impensas et nullatenus ex ~ato jure AMUND. I 203; **1437** ut .. decima nec ~aretur nec exigeretur usque quo Greci ad unum de predictis applicuerint portum (*Bulla Conc. Basiliensis*) BEKYNTON II 20; **s1457** dicit doctor Gregorius, et ~atur dictum suum in Canone XV .., illa sacra iiij concilia .. non minoris honoris .. esse quam sunt iiij libri Sacri Evangelii *Reg. Whet.* I 282.

decretarius [CL], determined by decree.

1011 (13c) villas michi jure ~io assignatas *Ch. Burton* 33.

decretis v. decretalis 2a.

decretista, canon lawyer (specializing in *Decreta* and Decretals).

hic eorum quos legistas vel ~as vocant .. peritissimus habetur AD. EYNS. *Visio* 26; ideo legunt ~e primam clausulam S. LANGTON *Quaest.* f. 171; **s1249** Cistercienses monachi, ne amplius forent contemptui .. secularibus literatis, precipue legistis et ~is, novum impetrarunt privilegium M. PAR. *Maj.* V 79; **1252** hic .. ~e Justinianum extollunt et a latere medici predicant Galienum (*Lit. Magistrorum Tolosan.*) GARL. *Tri. Eccl.* 97; theologi et ~e, non instructi in talibus [studiis astrologicis], .. negligunt hec et abhorrent BACON *Maj.* I 394; iste probat se legistam, / ille vero †decrestistam, / inducens Gelasium (*Ruina Romae* 56) *Ps.*-MAP 219; lectores et bachalarios theologie et eciam ~as OCKHAM *Dial.* 696; **a1350** debent omnes theologi .., ~e, medici, et legiste in .. solempnitatibus in suis pilleis interesse *StatOx* 37; quis non haberet ~as suspectos, non parendo eis, .., dum eos viderint exequi ad ungwem partem legis sue sonantem ad fastum et questum seculi, aliam autem partem sonantem ad religionem .. postponere? WYCL. *Ver.* II 171; *a decree*, decretum; ~a qui legit decreta ..; *a lawyour*, .. canonista, causidicus, ~a *CathA*.

decretor, one who decrees, arbiter.

plures sancti patres hujus sancte institucionis ~ores ante hunc beatum Benedictum regule monastice normam sanxerunt UHTRED *Inst.* xix.

decretorius, involving *Decreta*.

1303 de j pari Decretorum vendito .. et .. de casibus ~iis cum repertorio Martiniani venditis *Ac. Exec. Ep. Lond.* 52.

decretum v. 1 decernere 5. **decretus** v. 1 decernere, decrescere, discernere.

decrevere [*backformed from* decrevi *perf. of* decernere], to decide.

705 ignarus fui quid de hac re tue relegionis praerogativa ~ere voluisset WEALDHERE *Ep.* 23.

decruciare [cf. CL cruciare], to torment.

hostis, / .. mea decrucians vinclis et verbere membra BEDE *Hymn* 16. 36.

decrudescere, to become less harsh.

1178 ~it in eo [Imperatore] severitas, et iracundia ejus mansuescit in gratiam P. BLOIS *Ep.* 48. 142A.

decrustare [LL], **a** to strip (bread) of crust. **b** to strip of adornment, despoil; **c** (fig.).

a 13.. panis monachi, ~atus secundum consuetudinem, debet ponderare lx s. et xx d. *Cart. Rams.* III 159. **b s1191** quicquid .. thesauri in auro et in argento et lapidibus pretiosis in abbatiis .. inventum est .. acceperunt, adeo ut cruces et feretra ~arentur *Ann. Wav.* 248; **s1193** ~ata sunt et feretra necnon cruces et philacteria *Ann. Cestr.* 42; **1297** [Scoti] domos, villas et castra, ecclesias atque monasteria .. incendiorum voragine ad areas et rudera ~atosque parietes redigunt *Reg. Cant.* 529 (= *Conc.* II 233a); si ecclesia exusta fuit, ita quod parietes sint combusti .. vel notabiliter eciam ~ati J. BURGH *PO* IX 1. **c** R. NIGER *Chr. II* 167 (v. annihilare 2b).

dectalis v. dactylus.

decubare [LL]

1 to lie down. **b** to lie (in sick-bed or child-bed). *V. et. decumbere.*

flectentes genua proni in terram ~ate (*Sermo*) OSB. BAWDSEY clxxiv. **b** languorem simulans leo decubat WALT. ANGL. (*ed.* 1894) app. II 6. 1; **s1216** rex .. in castro .. ~ans graviter infirmatus est B. COTTON 104; **1243** fratres domus nostre et infirmi ibidem ~antes *Ch. Sal.* 286; **s1301** [Scoti] mulieres in puerperio ~antes .. trucidarunt W. GUISB. 343; **1415** lego xx pauperibus ~antibus, A. *bedredyn Reg. Cant.* II 52; *lyyn yn or in chyldebedde*, ~o *PP*; *to ly in chilbed*, decumbere, †~ere .., *to lygg seke*, ~are, decumbere *CathA*.

2 (trans.) to establish firmly.

principes nostri .. castris delimitandis et ~andis insistunt et aggerem .. muniendis tentoriis circumducunt *Itin. Ric.* I 31.

decubatio [cf. LL decubare, decubitio], lying in sick-bed. *V. et. decubitus.*

s1377 per totum tempus sue [Ed. III] ~onis assiderat .. Alicia Pereres WALS. *HA* I 326.

decubiae [cf. CL excubiae], (lying in) child-bed.

s1341 regina .. peperit unam filiam in quodam manerio .., ubi jacuit in ~iis usque ad primam Dominicam mensis Octobris AD. MUR. *Chr.* 159; *lying yn of þe chyldbed*, hee ~ie *PP*; *a chilbed*, puerperium, ~ie *CathA*.

decubitus [cf. LL decubitio], (position of) lying. *V. et. decubatio.*

~us super ventrem est malum, quia .. dolorem signat J. MIRFIELD *Brev.* 58.

decucurrere v. decurrere.

deculcare [CL = *to tread down*], to impress. *V. et. decalcare, disculcare.*

si terras spolies celique circulum / cunctaque congreges in unum cumulum / que pulcritudine deculcant oculum, / Marie compara perduntque titulum WALT. WIMB. *Carm.* 186.

decultor [cf. CL cultor], cultivator. (*Cf. John* xv 2).

fructum qui non fecerit ~oris in vinea palmes abscidetur *Chr. Abingd.* I 123.

decumanus v. decimanus.

decumbere [CL], to lie down; **b** to lie (in sick-bed or child-bed). *V. et. decubare.*

~e, *hlyna GlP* 627; **1102** praecipio vobis ut .. omnem amodo honorem cuivis sancto debitum illi mortuo auferatis... filium autem ejus, qui ad tumbam ipsius ~it et ibi moratur, a villa depellite ANSELM (*Ep.* 237) IV 145; **s1170** corpus .. archiepiscopi .. quod a dextris altaris S. Benedicti decubuerat in pavimento, ante majus altare .. deportatum est DICETO *YH* I 344; ille hic intus est et cum domina mea in lecto suo ~it MAP *NC* IV 16 f. 58v.; *Ziz.* 393 (v. elemosynarius 3b). **b** [morbo] aucto post paucos dies decubuit W. MALM. *GP* I 48; *Itin. Ric.* I 61 (v. clinicus 1); cum morbo ~eret quo paulo post occubuit GIR. *IK* II 14; **1245** non possumus personaliter comparere cum in filii puerperio ~amus *Reg. Gasc. A* 436; Londoniis eger decumbens mense Novembri H. AVR. *Hugh* 1136; *CathA* (v. decubare 1b).

decunx, ten *unciae*, five sixths.

~x vel dextans, x unciae BEDE *TR* 4; ~x .., x uncie OSB. GLOUC. *Deriv.* 179.

decupedalis, ten feet long.

1404 x^c^ lignorum ~ium *Lit. Cant.* III 82.

decuplare [LL], to multiply by ten.

quod nomen Salvatoris octo [η] absoluta contineat, quia resurrectionis .. exemplum .. octava die resurgendo praestiterit; contineat et ~ata [$\eta \times \iota$] quia decalogus legis quomodo debeat impleri .. instituerit BEDE *Luke* 338; nostra sata decuplata nos fruge letificent (*Vers.*) W. FITZST. *Thom.* 71.

decuplatio, multiplication by ten.

~one .. totum opus texitur, quod ex nominis interpretatione signatur; abacus enim vel abax 'decuplex' interpretatur ADEL. *Abac.* 91.

decuplex, ten-fold.

ADEL. *Abac.* 91 (v. decuplatio); s**1338** (v. decuplus a).

decuplicatio, multiplication by ten.

ut in secundo loco scriptus secundus binarius j, xx accipiatur, et sic de ceteris deorsum dispositi †deduplicatione [? l. decuplicatione] OCREATUS *Helceph* 133.

decuplus [LL], ten-fold. **b** (as sb. m. or n.) ten-fold quantity; **c** (in comp. numeral).

hoc modo ~a scematum species alternatim inserta supputatur ALDH. *Met.* 10 p. 85; s**1338** sic non duplici sed †~i [? l. ~a *or* decuplici] contricione sunt attriti AD. MUR. *Chr.* 86*n.*; *tene*, decem .., denus, denarius, ~us *CathA.* **b** nec novissimus quadrans perdonabitur inde, quin ultra ~um exigetur hoc justitium HERM. ARCH. 27; secundus [limes] a x perprimorum per ~os primorum digitorum usque ad c; tertius vero a c usque ad mille per ~os secundorum OCREATUS *Helceph* 132; ~um invenit in eo †sapienciam [? l. sapiencie] ac prudencie super quam estimaverat W. DAN. *Ailred* 14; si .. regi resistere volueris, non solum archiepiscopatui [v. l. in archiepiscopatu] Cantuariensi sed in ~o, si tanti fuisset, cedere deberes A. TEWK. *Add. Thom.* 5; s**1223** (v. 1 decies a); plus in ~o laborant circa hujusmodi telam aranee construendam quam circa sententiam sermonis BACON *Tert.* 304; s**1296** hostes marini navigium suum in ~um numerositate superabant *Chr. S. Edm.* 63; s**1339** ubi .. rex Francie in ~o populi quam rex Anglie habuerat *Meaux* III 41. **c** diameter .. solis erit ~um octuplum ad diametrum lune, et quatuor quinte ejus BACON *Maj.* I 233.

decuratus [cf. curare 3a], uncared for.

c**1305** cum .. scripture in regula nostra nos moneant ut in curandis debilibus .. fratribus curam .. indefessam exerceamus .. inhumanum sit illos ~os negligere quibus .. constringimur .. subvenire (*Ordin. Abbatis*) *G. S. Alb.* II 103.

decuria [CL], group of ten men. **b** tithing, frankpledge group. *Cf. decena* 1.

†~io [? l. ~ia], numerus decem hominum *GlC* D 170. **b** s**872** [Alfredus] primus terram in .. comitatus, comitatus vero in centurias .. et [centurias] in ~ias, quas nunc tithingas vel thrithingas vocamus, distribuebat *Chr. Angl. Peterb.* 24 (cf. decimus 5); [Alvredus] centurias, quas dicunt *hundrez*, et ~ias, quas vocant *thethingas*, instituit OXNEAD *Chr.* 4.

decurialis [CL], municipal official.

curiales vel ~es, *burhgerefa* ÆLF. *Gl.*

decuriare, to banish from court, put out of court.

971 (12c) agatur .. de eo [procuratore] quod de regis agitur praeposito, ut videlicet, reo rite ~iato ac justo ordine depulso, illi qui dignus sit Christi designetur, uti regis solet praepositura, a nullo †decurium violata *CS* 1270 (cf. ib. 1297: ut .. reo rite †securato .. a nullo secularium .. possessione violata); *to putte out of curte*, ~iare *CathA.*

1 decurio v. decuria a.

2 decurio [CL], **a** commander of ten men. **b** royal official.

a ~o, i. ille qui preest x viris OSB. GLOUC. *Deriv.* 112; hic ~o, qui habet x milites *WW.* **b 10.** .. ~o, qui officium carum egerit .., ~o, consiliarius *WW*; nunc veltrariorum monstra, falconum circinnia, ~onum †torcias [? l. torciones] et nebulonum furias .. non timemus (*Quad. Arg.*) *GAS* 534; erat vir bonus ~o Harscoitus cognomento Musard apud dominum suum regem valde honoratus .., habens sub se milites *Lib. Eli.* III 38; domos .. sic prope .. manerium [de Shene] situari constituit ut futuri ~ones, viz. viri devoti, cum Cartusiensis ordinis viris sanctis .. optata devocionis intermiscerent solacia *Ps.*-ELMH. *Hen. V* 13; *cortyowre*, ~o curialis, curio *PP.*

decurium v. decuriare. **decurpitas** v. decrepitas. **decurrare** v. 2 decorare c.

decurrere [CL]

1 to run or roam (fig.). **b** (w. *ad*) to have recourse (to).

per ampla scripturarum stadia ~entes ALDH. *VirgP* 3 (cf. ib. 4: memoriale mentis ingenium per .. scripturarum arva late vagans .. ~it). **b** quid ad emendicata gentium exempla ~o? J. SAL. *Pol.* 518D; tunc ~endum erit ad communes eorum consanguineos, qui ad hoc vocandi sunt in curia ut per eos disquiratur eorum parentela GLANV. II 6; **1192** ad majoris et sanioris partis capituli ~etur arbitrium (*Stat. S. Paul.*) DICETO II lxxii.

2 to run (down, on, or out), flow (of fluids), pursue a course; **b** (fig., of speech, verse, or reckoning); **c** (p. ppl. *s. act.*).

de quo quadrifluis decurrunt flumina rivis ALDH. *CE* 4. 10. 8; videtur verisimile quod .. alter aliquis fluvius in eum ~at BEDE *Ezra* 868; fluxit, ~it, manavit, *fleow GlH* F 548; s**1135** ex corpore niger humor .. coria pertransiens ~ebat H. HUNT. *HA* VIII 2; EADMER *V. Anselmi* I 31 (v. 2 clausura 1e); quasi furente David .. saliva ei ~it in barbam AD. DORE *Pictor* 159; c**1250** (v. curba 3a). **b** dactilus excepto decurrat fine metrorum ALDH. *VirgV* 48; BEDE *TR* 1 (v. computus 1a); Job Moysi temporibus adaequatus dactylo spondioque ~it BONIF. *Met.* 111; R. COLD. *Osw.* 50 (v. dictamen 1c); totus sermo .. ad idem principium ~ebat et recurrebat P. CORNW. *Panth. prol.* 41; omnis sillogismus ~it super dici de omni vel dici de nullo BACON XV 290; ubi ~it sententia *Id. Tert.* 248 (v. 2 colon). **c** si fuerint bene haec aenigmata versu / .. / ritu dactilico recte decursa ALDH. *Aen. pref.* 27; purpureo carnis cruore rubris fibrarum rivulis decurso *Id. VirgP* 23.

3 to run, extend (in space).

nisi panuculae .. diversis colorum varietatibus fucatae inter densa filorum stamina ultro citroque ~ant ALDH. *VirgP* 15; **1427** (v. cursus 5f).

4 to run, extend (in time), remain in force. **b** (p. ppl. *decursus*) having elapsed.

680 decemnovenalem laterculi circulum .. usque ad finem mundi recto tramite decursurum ALDH. *Ep.* 4; **798** quinquagesimus [dies], qui ~it usque in diem sanctum resurrectionis dominicae ALCUIN *Ep.* 143 (cf. ib.: usque ad ultima tempora legis, quae per Moysen data est et †decucurrit [v. l. decurrit] in Christi .. tempora); nono ~enti spatio annorum [Petrus] Romae fungitur pontificatus officio ÆTHELW. I 1; DICETO *Chr. prol.* 1 (v. chronographia); **1278** si contingat .. hec .. ita non fieri ut .. lis inchoata coram priore B. Oswaldi .. suo Marte ~at *Reg. Heref.* 285. **b** septenis annorum ebdomadibus ~is ALDH. *Met.* 2; ~is bis quaternis dierum voluminibus FELIX *Guthl.* 10; ~is annis tribus ÆTHELW. II 7; paucis diebus ~is *G. Steph.* I 50; **1198** †decusso [? l. decurso] jam termino *Ep. Cant.* 467; **1330** multis ~is temporibus *Lit. Cant.* I 314; s**1347** Calesia, postquam obsessa est ~is xij mensibus, erat capta *Meaux* III 67.

5 (p. ppl. *s. pass.*): **a** traversed. **b** (of a race) having been run (fig.).

a tandem decurso concite / perlongi callis limite (ÆTHELWALD) *Carm. Aldh.* 2. 77; decursis civitatibus Gallicanis et Alpibus exsuperatis GIR. *GE* I 23. **b** desidui longaeva imperii meta decursa ÆLNOTH *Cnut* 6.

decurribilis, tending to run down, descending.

934 fortuna fallentis saeculi procax .. ad ima Cociti .. impudenter est ~is *CS* 702 (cf. ib. 718 [**937**]: decursibilis).

decursim [cf. CL cursim, LL discursim], at a run.

~im, adv., i. fugaciter OSB. GLOUC. *Deriv.* 92.

decursio [LL]

1 excursion, journey. **b** flow, flood (of tears); *v. et.* 2 *decursus* 1a.

tuus servulus ex peregrinatione .. veniens .. receptus est .. arbitrabatur eum ex mutatione melioratum, non ex terrarum longinqua ~one pejoratum fuisse *Ep. ad amicum* 146. **b** literulas tibi crebris lacrimarum ~onibus oblitas .. scripsi *Ib.* 129.

2 a course (of calculation). **b** lapse (of time); *v. et.* 2 *decursus* 2c.

a septinarius supputationum calculus simpla .. et septupla ~one ALDH. *Met.* 2. **b** s**1198** ~one sex mensium R. HOWD. IV 67.

1 decursus v. decurrere.

2 decursus [CL]

1 course, flow (of fluids); *v. et. decursio* 1b. **b** (w. *aquae*) watercourse.

perpes aquaeductum ~us .. arcuum fornicibus in edito sublimatus ALDH. *VirgP* 9; ista est causa quia menstruum non discurrit omni mense solito, quia efficitur cibus embrionis et habet ~um in stercus genitricis M. SCOT *Phys.* 10. **b 935** (12c) cum .. silvis, pratis, piscariis aquarumque ~ibus *CS* 707; c**1070** in bosco et plano, aquis et aquarum ~ibus *Regesta* p. 120; s**1316** R. de C. [et alii] .. in ~u aque tenencium coquinarii inter insulas de la Wike submersi sunt (*Chr. Abingd.*) *EHR* XXVI 730; **1407** edificabit unam domum .. juxta ~um aque prope viam regiam *Cart. Osney* II 409.

2 **a** course (of life). **b** way of the world, nature of things (*cf.* AN *decurs*). **c** course, lapse (of time); *v. et. decursio* 2b. **d** (?) sequence.

a 984 (11c) si viri vitae ~us supertranscenderit conjugis suae terminum *CD* 645; **1045** (12c) quatenus [terram illam] .. habeat quamdiu vivat; post generale vero istius ~us exitium .. cuicumque maluerit heredi .. derelinquat *CD* 778; HERM. ARCH. 22 (v. declivis 2b); **1504** post hujus vite ~um *StatOx* 313. **b** innuit antidotum fieri decursus amoris [OF: *nature requiert guerredon / d'amour*] WALT. ANGL. *Fab.* 40. 31; ut .. inter carnalium ~us .. cogitares nec hominem sed super hominem esse P. CORNW. *Panth. prol.* 41. **c** s**381** post ~um centum et nonaginta annorum ÆTHELW. I 1 (cf. ib. I 5 [s**534**]: in ipsius anni ~u); post tam diutinos mutue visionis intermissionum ~us AD. MARSH *Ep.* 97; elapsis temporum paucis decursibus WALT. WIMB. *Carm.* 262; **1271** per ~um temporis .. diffiniti *Ch. Sal.* 352; **1407** elapsis annorum ~ibus *StatOx* 199. **d** ubi prius apprehenditur substancia quam animal, et animal quam homo, [et homo] quam Sortes, commune †decursum [? l. deorsum] separat [Aristoteles] a materia; et de tali universali loquitur in littera BACON VIII 4; scietur descensus vel ~us primorum principiorum in ultimum principiatum in genere substantie SICCAV. *PN* 102.

decurtare [CL]

1 to dock, deprive of tail. **b** to cut off.

s**1170** equum .. archiepiscopi victualia deferentem ad dedecus et ignominiam ejus ~averat DICETO *YH* I 342. **b** s**1250** adhuc aliquorum [Sarracenorum] supervenientium capita, manus vel pedes mutilando ~abat M. PAR. *Maj.* V 153.

2 to cut short. **b** to abbreviate. **c** to diminish. **d** (w. abl.) to deprive (of).

c**710** ubi ad cervicem considerando perveneris, ~atam eam .. invenies coronam, ut merito talem Simoniacis et non Christianis habitum convenire cognoscas (*Ep. Ceolfridi*) BEDE *HE* V 21 p. 343; trabem ~avit F. MALM. *V. Aldh.* 72A; ~entur interiores [vestes, sc. femoralia] a zona tunice, manente suprema MAP *NC* I 25 f. 20. **b** satisne protractum tibi videor sermonem texuisse et quod in superioribus ~atum fuerat supplesse in fine? G. HOYLAND *Ascet.* 251; qui nomen meum [sc. Matheum] sincopat .. incurate ~asti M. RIEVAULX (*Ep.*) 74. **c** Judeus limites hereditarios ~abat, dicens quia tantummodo notus esset in Judea Deus P. BLOIS *Serm.* 24. 631B. **d** fratris mei .. honorem m militum .. vos feudo cc et xl militum ~astis W. FITZST. *Thom.* 102.

decurtatio [LL], shortening.

[multi] secundum hunc [stellarum] recessum ponunt vite ~onem BACON *Maj.* II 204.

decurtator, clipper (of coinage).

per falsarios et nummorum ~ores et detonsores *Dial. Scac.* I 3 E.

1 decus [CL], glory, honour; *cf.* 1 *decor.* **b** source of glory.

percipit inde decus reginae et sceptra sub astris BEDE (*Vers.*) *HE* IV 18 p. 248; hoc primum ~us Turchil armis Cnutonis auxit *Enc. Emmae* II 7; NIG. *SS* 929 (v. dedecus a); sint in amore tuo decus et decor ecclesialis D. BEC. 137; H. AVR. *Hugh* 444 (v. 1 decor 2); sic in quoddam innocentie non ignobile ~us sub novi baptismatis sacramento reflorescebat J. FORD *Wulf.* 5; GARL. *SM* 1003 (v. concatenare c). **b** NIG. *SS* 2498 (v. 1 decor 2); tantum temporis nostri ~us transitorie perire presens historia non permittit GIR. *EH* I 46; ille ~us et decor milicie, dux illustris *Ps.*-ELMH. *Hen. V* 114.

2 decus [cf. Prov. *dec*], boundary (Gasc.).

1283 habitatoribus ville nostre de Valencia .. infra ~os seu terminos .. bastide concedimus libertates .. *RGasc* II 208 (= *Foed.* II 260); **1308** quicquid est infra ~os predictos ex parte Alti Villaris remaneat de jurisdiccione .. Alti Villaris *Ib.* IV 216; **1310** extra ~os .. ville dominus rex habet totam jurisdiccionem *Reg. Gasc. A* I 26.

3 decus [LL < CL decussis], weight of ten *asses.*

ubi [luna] tertia est, multiplica iij per iiij; fiunt xij. partire per decem; decies asse ~us, et remanent duo puncti, id est sex partes BEDE *TR* 18.

decusare [cf. 1 decus], to decorate, adorn. *V. et.* 2 *decorare.*

editiore eas [reliquias] entheca ~are .. opere pretium duxi O. CANT. *Pref. Frith.* 36; a**975** praemia inaestimabili .. ornatu decussata (*Ep. ad Edgarum*) *Mem. Dunst.* 367; mentum rotunditate decenter composita ~atum, id est ornatum, decoratum R. COLD. *Osw.* 51; quidam quasi pueri nigri, capillo capitis ~ati qui rectius dici possunt pigmei, *Id. Godr.* 260; *arayn, or make honest*, orno .., ~o, decoro *PP*; *to make fare*, .. ornare .., ~are .., decorare *CathA.*

decusatio, decoration, adornment.

a fayrnes, pulcritudo, ~o, decor .., *wyrshipe*, honor .., decor, decus, ~o .. *CathA.*

decussatim [CL], crosswise.

illic planata decŭsatim [*corr. to* triviatim] vomere terra FRITH. 460; **972** his testibus consentientibus, quorum inferius nomina secundum uniuscujusque dignitatem utriusque ordinis decussatim Domino disponente caraxantur *CS* 1282 (cf. ib. 1046, *CD* 684, 1031 etc.).

decussus v. decurrere 4b, decutere.

decutere [CL], to strike down; **b** (fig.). **c** to shake off (fig.), get rid of.

decussit, percussit, projecit *GlC* D 28. **b** Teutonice animositatis colla vigore securis apostolice ~iens W. MALM. *GR* V 435. **c** Ecgberct decussa molestia egritudinis convaluit BEDE *HE* III 27; vestem poliens / et invisibiles plumas decutiens WALT. WIMB. *Palpo* 69.

decymare [cf. cymatio], to crop, lop.

to croppe, decimare ..; versus, decĭmo caulis frondes, sed decīmo garbas; / decĭmo flores, sed decīmo res meliores *CathA.*

decymator [cf. cymator], **~trix,** (?) cropper (m. or f.); but *cf.* 1 *decimator* a.

1268 item vj decimatoribus, ij equitatoribus, ij tassatoribus, iij quar. *Ac. Wellingb.* 6; **1311** in x decimatricibus, j tassatore xxij s. *Ib.* 108; *a cropper*, decimator, decimatrix *CathA*.

dedal- v. daedal-.

dedamnificare (dedampn-) [cf. damnificare 1], to indemnify.

1288 quatinus dictum regem [Majoricarum], qui per istam treugam .. est deceptus et dampnificatus in multis, restitui et ~ari faciatis (*Lit. Regis Franc.*) *Foed.* II 358a; **1426** ad debitam satisfaccionem .. faciendum et illos ~andum quibus bona illa pertinuerint (*TreatyR*) *Ib.* X 362a.

dedasculus v. didascalus.

dedbana [AS *dǣdbana*], accomplice in murder.

qui ad occidendum aliquem innoxium redbana vel ~a fuerit (*Leg. Hen.* 85. 3) *GAS* 600 (cf. ib. (*Quad.*) 286: si quis ordinatus homicidii particeps consilio vel auxilio fuisse [AS: *þæt he wære dædban oððe rædbana*] compelletur).

dedda v. dodda.

dedecenter [cf. CL decenter], disgracefully, unbecomingly.

1284 miramur .. qualiter vos et secrete et publice carnes audetis comedere ~er PECKHAM *Ep.* 582.

dedecentia [cf. CL decentia], disgrace.

tactus dolore .. super ~iis statum vestrum maculantibus AD. MARSH *Ep.* 162 (*Ad Comitissam Leic.*); **1283** quod nos .. plangimus longe plus quam nostro incommodo pro ~ia tante matris [sc. ecclesie] PECKHAM *Ep.* 393; **1284** Cham paterne irrisor ~ie [cf. *Gen.* ix 20–8] in posteritate sua meruit maledici *Ib.* 622 (= *Conc.* II 111).

dedecēre [CL], to disgrace, be unbecoming (to); **b** (absol.); **c** (impers.).

facile tibi est pervidere nullam amicitiam que bonos ~eat recipiendam AILR. *Spir. Amicit.* II 55. 676; **1451** neque aliis officiis ordinem nostrum ~entibus se .. intromittant (*Abbr. Stat.*) *Mon. Francisc.* II 96. **b** cum certum tibi fuerit quod nihil velit quod ~eat AILR. *Spir. Amicit.* III 131. 700; nobilis res est .. que omne quod ~et aspernatur J. SAL. *Pol.* 484B. **c** ~et, non †decit [l. decet] *GlC* D 106; ~et, non decet *GlH* D 38; satis ~et ministros vitae caelestis assensum prebere in mortem cujuslibet hominis ABBO *Edm.* 5; **1343** cum ~eat ut seculares de nostris capitulis aliqualiter intromittant *Conc.* II 726b.

dedecor [CL], disgraceful.

in fugam ~orem coactos *Ps.*-ELMH. *Hen. V* 97.

dedecorare [CL], to dishonour, disgrace; **b** (animal, by mutilation). **c** to disfigure.

~are, dehonestare, convitiare OSB. GLOUC. *Deriv.* 173. **b** equus ejus ad dedecus suum †~abitur desuper ballenro [*ed. Twiss*: decoriabatur de superiore labro]. .. canis, si secum habet, .. eodem modo ~abitur BRACTON 147b p. 418. **c** Midam regem .. Apollo .. asininis auribus ~avit ALB. LOND. *DG* 10. 7.

dedecorose [LL], disgracefully.

s**1214** imperator in fugam cum magna militum reversus est multitudine †dedicore [? l. dedecorose] *Plusc.* VII 2; Theobaldus ~e fugiens WALS. *YN* 34 (= W. JUM. IV 15: turpiter); s**1390** dominus Adam, cardinalis Anglicus, qui ~e depositus et privatus fuerat per .. papam, suo gradui .. restituitur *Id. HA* II 197; *G. S. Alb.* III 4 (v. collistrigium c).

dedecorosus [LL], disgraceful, dishonourable.

praesul injuriosus venire renuit, ne fieret ~us HERM. ARCH. 27; s**1386** [annus] Londoniensibus propter muliebrem meticulositatem .. ~us WALS. *HA* II 153; **1421** obliquus murus .. sicut nunc stat est indecens et ~us civitati *AncD* A 1995; s**1454** quod non minus ~um quam dolorosum restat unicuique religioso ad dicendum *Reg. Whet.* I 147; s**1473** neque .. vilis aut nostratibus ~a videri debet condicio apposita *Croyl. Cont. C* 558.

dedecus [CL], disgrace, shame. **b** sense of shame. **c** insult. **d** compensation for insult.

licet .. ad .. lupanar .. ad infame ~us natalium propriis exuta vestibus truderetur ALDH. *VirgP* 45; **9..** ~us, *unwlite oððe sconde WW*; ~us patula protestatione tuae serenitati profiteor B. *V. Dunst.* 1; ~us, *bysmor GlP* 656; rumpe fedus, quod tibi ~ori est G. MON. III 1; ut breve sit dēdecus longumque decus sit amicis NIG. *SS* 929 (cf. ib. 933: dēdecus in dominum papam damnumque redundat); si temporalis honor ~ore destruitur R. ROLLE *IA* 167. **b** primos homines vestiri non oportuit, quibus nihil ~oris inerat PULL. *Sent.* 752B. **c** s**943** rex ~us quod a Normannis perceperat .. aegre ferens W. JUM. IV 3; gravius ~oris quam damni dolore percussus GIR. *EH* I 1; **1247** (v. damnum 1f); s**1406** "non ita erit", ait Cantuariensis, ".. sed ipse luet predicatori ~us irrogatum" *Chr. S. Alb.* 2. **d** **1202** (v. damnum 2a).

dedere [CL]

1 to give, grant. **b** to give in marriage. **c** (w. *operam*) to give thought.

nec precor ut Phoebus linguam sermone loquacem / dedat ALDH. *VirgV* 27; de[di]dit obtutum caecorum lumina tangens *Ib.* 472; inque monasterio Domino se subdere temptant. / Eanmundus Christo indeptus quod dĕderat [? *for* dēderat *or* dēdĭderat] almo ÆTHELWULF *Abb.* 74; dapsilis ast, cunctis dedans (*sic*) ermenia vitae FRITH. 226; dedo, sponte trado, *ic forgyfe GlP* 177; multis multa dēdi que non cuperem michi dēdi SERLO WILT. 2. 30. **b** hanc pater et genetrix .. / .. satagebant dedere nuptis [= nuptiis] ALDH. *VirgV* 1985. **c** tres pueri .. nequaquam carnalis copulae voluptatibus operam ~idisse leguntur *Id. VirgP* 21.

2 (refl.): **a** to submit or devote oneself. **b** to betake oneself.

a normalis sese dedans (*sic*) sub regmine vitae FRITH. 74; monachus, qui cuncta relinquit, / se patribus dedit, dedens quasi servus obedit / judiciis R. CANT. *Malch.* III 528; edicimus ut .. a patria discedant, nisi se ~ant [AS: *gebugan*] et emendent (*Cons. Cnuti*) *GAS* 311 (= *Quad.*: nisi resipuerint); s**927** [barbari] se cum suis regnis Anglorum regi ~idere W. MALM. *GR* II 134; cives demum se Dermitio ~entes .. obsides .. tradiderunt GIR. *EH* I 3; s**1331** veniens Oxoniam .. levitatibus se ~ere, magnorum noticiam appetere GRAYSTANES 46. **b** *Enc. Emmae* II 5 (v. 1 batulus).

3 (p. ppl.) devoted.

India .., / idola quae coluit paganis dedita sacris ALDH. *CE* 4. 9. 3; baptizandi officio ~itus BEDE *HE* II 14; isque Deo dēditus cum tota mente fidelis ÆTHELWULF *Abb.* 584; [canonici] gule et ebrietati ~iti WULF. *Æthelwold* 16; catholicis regulari jugo ~itis [AS p. 370: *underþeoddum*] *RegulC* 7; vultis esse .. dulcibus verbis ~iti [AS: *underþeodde*], dolum intus alentes? ÆLF. *Coll.* 101; Vulfrico .. ~itior GOSC. *Transl. Aug.* 32C (v. concinnitas 1b); quamvis saeculari actui foret ~itus, totus tamen fuit fide Catholicus W. JUM. V 1; GIR. *GE* II 27 (v. dare 6d).

dedicare [CL]

1 to dedicate, consecrate, devote: **a** church or sim. (sts. w. God as subj.); **b** time; **c** person or sim.; **d** (p. ppl.) devoted.

a fecit ecclesiam episcopali sedi congruam .., quam .. archiepiscopus Theodorus in honore B. apostoli Petri ~avit BEDE *HE* III 25 p. 181; habentes .. vascula sacra et tabulam altaris vice ~atam *Ib.* V 10; hanc basilicam in honore sancti tui N. .. clementissime ~a EGB. *Pont.* 38; porticum .. ~ando .. sanctum Domino consecravit templum HUGEB. *Wynn.* 13; **933** basilicas in honore Dei sanctorumque ejus ~atas *CS* 694; c**1056** (v. 1 aula 2a); haec capella si fuit ~ata vel non *hundret* nescit *DB* II 281V.; sunt .. in eadem villa due adhuc alie ecclesie, una .. in honorem S. Marie semper Virginis ~ata RIC. HEX. *Hist. Hex.* I 4; **1229** in ecclesiis ~atis annus et dies dedicationis et nomen ~antis et nomen sancti in cujus honore ~ata est ecclesia .. scribantur circa majus altare *Conc. Syn.* 172; **1240** (v. consecrare 2a); **1342** majus altare stetit non ~atum a multis annis. .. et, quia [parochiani] non procurarunt dominum ad ~andum altare .., noviter sunt puniti (*Vis. Totnes*) *EHR* XXVI 111; **1429** locus .. ad cemeterium pro sepultura decedencium infra .. hospitale .. ~andus (*Pat*) AMUND. II 163. **b** lucida spiritui tempora, nocturna carni ~antes GIR. *TH* III 27. **c** [Samuel] Deo antequam nasceretur ~atus GILDAS *EB* 38; intravit .. regis filia Deo ~anda monasterium BEDE *HE* III 24 (cf. ib. IV 21 p. 257: ~ata Domino virginitate); super hunc famulum tuum .., Domine, placatus intende, quem tuis sacrariis serviturum in officium diaconi .. ~amus EGB. *Pont.* 20; AD. SCOT *TGC* 825B (v. arra c). **d** sanctissimi ac Deo immortali ~atissimi viri CHAUNDLER *Laud.* 111.

2 to assign, ascribe.

miraculum ~atur B. Yvoni rectissime, S. Benedicto .. ei favente GOSC. *Mir. Iv.* lxviii.

dedicatio [CL], dedication, consecration (or commemoration thereof): **a** (of church or sim.); **b** (of bishop).

a **685** (v. 1 basilica 1b); BEDE *HE* V 4 (v. consecrare 2d); ut altare .. celesti ~one sanctifices EGB. *Pont.* 50 (cf. ib. 53 *rub.*: oratio in ~one fontis); in conventu ducum, abbatum [etc.], qui eandem [aecclesiae veteris cenobii] cum omni gaudio caelebraverunt ~onem WULF. *Æthelwold* 40; pax sit .. ad ~ones euntibus (*Leg. Ed.*) *GAS* 629; c**1080** (v. consecrare 2a); sunt aliae festivitates quae magnifice celebrantur .., sunt autem hae: Epiphania .., festivitas S. Andree, ~o aecclesiae LANFR. *Const.* 130; a**1140** quod ego donavi ecclesie S. Wilfridi in ~one ejus *Mem. Ripon* 94; **1229** (v. dedicare 1a); **1262** [3 *Oct.*] hominibus .. transeuntibus ad festum ~onis ecclesie S. Pauli London' *Cl* 138; **1373** pro ~one altaris capelle infirmarie *Ac. Durh.* 210; *Reg. St. Bees* 389 (v. consecratio 1a); **1523** decernimus .. quod per totam civitatem London' atque suburbia ejusdem .. omnes et singuli dies festi, qui pro ~onibus ecclesiarum hactenus sparsim per diversos .. anni dies, juxta diem quo quevis ecclesia consecrata et Deo sive sanctis ejus dedicata fuerat, celebrari solebant, nunc de cetero in unum diem .. transferantur, viz. in tercium diem Octobris *Conc.* III 702b. **b** c**1170** donamus .. medietatem ecclesie de H. .. cum una cothlanda et viij acris, que fuerunt date in ~one Wlfwini episcopi de Dorcacestra [**1053**] *Cart. Eynsham* I 109.

dedicative [LL], affirmatively.

~e, confirmative *GlH* D 369.

dedicator [CL], sanctifier.

Deus, jejunii ceterarumque virtutum ~or atque amator EGB. *Pont.* 62.

dedicerant v. 2 dediscere.

dedicere [cf. OF *dedire, desdire*]

1 to deny, gainsay: **a** (action, accusation, or statement); **b** (previous statement by the speaker); **c** (absol.); **d** (w. inf.); **e** (w. *quod* & neg.); **f** (neg. w. *quin*). **g** (p. ppl. as sb. n.) denial.

a **1219** prior non potuit hoc ~ere *CurR* VIII 54; cum quis captus fuerit super mortuum cum cultello cruentato, mortem ~ere non poterit BRACTON 137; **1277** totum ~it de verbo ad verbum *SelPlJews* 95; dicunt quod quicquid factum fuit eo die .. fuit factum Willelmi .., quod Willelmus .. ~ere non potuit *State Tri. Ed. I* 36; s**1286** quia .. abbas non potuit ~ere subtractionem predictorum xx s. *Chr. Peterb.* 141; defendere debet omnem feloniam et verba per ordinem ~ere [v. l. †dediscere] *Fleta* 52; **1433** ex quo .. Johannes .. non ~it materiam per ipsum priorem .. allegatam (*Breve Regis*) AMUND. I 322; si reus .. de felonia .. rettatus crimen suum coram judicibus ~at FORTESCUE *LLA* 27. **b** **1253** G. dedixit .. coram iiij viridariis et iiij villatis quicquid prius dixerat coram senescallo et forestariis ..; et dixit quod W. de R. .. fecit eum per vim dicere hoc quod dixit *SelPlForest* 107; **1277** ut in .. presencia vestra .. quecumque contra personam nostram .. proposuerat ~eret .. et .. revocaret *RGasc* II 38. **c** **1221** hoc testatum est per villatam et per xij juratores; et ideo non potest ~ere *PlCrGlouc* 45; **1308** non potuit ~ere *Year Bk. 1 Ed. II* 38. **d** **1292** Willelmus .. dedixit tenere .. manerium de .. rege nunc .., per quod ~tum accio accrevit .. regi *PQW* 680a. **e** **1221** Georgius .. appellat Estmarum .. quod assultavit eum una cum Thoma filio suo. .. postea vero ~it quod non appellat Estmarum de facto, immo Thomam de facto et Estmarum de vi *PlCrGlouc* 21; **1258** presens fuit et ~it quod non ad presens debet servicium *SelCMan* 61; **1275** dedixerunt aperte et precise quod nunquam aliquem equum eidem J. vendiderunt .. nec aliquod contractum cum eodem fecerunt *Ib.* 151. **f** **1255** non potuit ~ere quin portaret arcum et sagittas *SelPlForest* 12; **1294** non .. potest ~i nec vult ~ere quin aperte .. bladum .. rectoris .. asportaverat *SelPlMan* 82; **1309** abbas non potest †decicere quin .. rex habebit catalla hominum .. abbatis felon[um] de latrocinio *PQW* 829a. **g** **1292** utrum ipse majus jus habeat tenendi predictum manerium .. an dominus rex nunc habendi racione predicti ~ti *PQW* 680a (cf. 1d supra).

2 to reject, repudiate (document, undertaking, or sim.).

1235 notum facimus .. quod nos de regno nostro Anglie et de terris nostris Wasconie et Pictavie .. assecuramus .. regem Navarie .. et homines suos ac res eorum usque ad unum an[n]um postquam predicta assecuracio ex parte nostra ~etur *TreatyR* I 21 (= *Foed.* I 340b; †ei dicetur); **1255** dedixit rotulum suum, dicendo quod .. *SelPlForest* 35; **1290** quedam scripta ~ta coram justiciariis (*LTRMem*) SelCKB I clxi (cf. ib. clx: carte ~te); **1330** Adam cognovit .. feloniam et devenit probator et appellat alios ..; et postea ~it appellum suum; ideo ipse suspendatur *Gaol Del.* 44 r. 3; **14..** quem .. finem .. placitando in eadem curia omnino dedixerunt *Reg. Brev. Orig.* 5b.

3 to contradict, give the lie to (person): **a** (w. dat.); **b** (w. acc.).

a **1220** Matillis dicit quod .. ipsa [carta] facta fuit tempore quo fuit desponsata Gaufrido .. et .. non fuit potens sui, quia non potuit ~ere viro suo *CurR* VIII 376; **1375** injunctum est omnibus tenentibus ville quod nullus eorum permittant (*sic*) uxores eorum .. ~ere aliquibus de vic[initate] *Hal. Durh.* 131; ergo magis paveant omnes dedicere nobis GOWER *VC* III 943. **b** **1307** J. de L. in misericordia, quia dedixit Henricum de H. in plena curia *CourtR Hales* 576.

4 to refuse.

cum aliquis dedixerit servicium petitum, sive debitum et solutum sive non *Fleta* 95 (cf. ib. 106: cum non jacuerit in ore tenentis .. ~ere demandam domini capitalis); s**1456** suggesserunt .. ipsi sibi [sc. Henrico VI] decere regem largum esse et liberalem neminique quicquam ~ere qui vellet ab ipso aliquid .. humiliter postulare *Reg. Whet.* I 248.

dedicius v. dediticius. **dedicore** v. dedecorose. **dediffi-cili** v. difficilis 1b.

dedignabundus, disdainful.

ut .. tumentem stomachum ex superbia non habeant; verba et vultum ~um non ostendant COLET *Stat. Cantar.* 166; ne Romani ~i secum cogitent accepisse se .. graciam spiritalem *Id. Rom. Exp.* (i 11) 207.

dedignanter [cf. LL dignanter], disdainfully, without compunction.

tibi nunc imputat .. quod ipsum ~er repulisti dum fuit placabilis MAP *NC* V 6 f. 67; Sapiens dicit: "si scirem deos

esse ignoscituros et homines ignoturos, ~er peccarem" BACON I 20; s**1324** quia voluntates occurrencium .. transfretacioni electorum .. rex discordes invenit, ipsam expedicionem usque ad tempus ~er prorogavit *Flor. Hist.* III 223; s**1366** quod factum principes Christiani .. moleste ac ~er ferebant J. READING 188.

dedignari [CL], **~are**

1 to disdain; **b** (w. inf.); **c** (w. dat.).

~or, *ic forhogige GlH* D 374; s**905** Æthelwoldus .. ejus [Edwardi] dominium ~abatur, asserens se non inferiorem W. MALM. *GR* II 125; s**617** Edelfridus rex ferus, ~ans et mirans quod aliquis ei auderet resistere H. HUNT. *HA* II 30. **b 799** te ipsum .. universae ecclesiae Christi conjunge, ut sis membrum .. illius capitis qui pro te suum sanguinem fundere non ~avit [v. l. dubitavit] ALCUIN *Ep.* 166 p. 271 (cf. ib.: ut [hoc] .. vestra .. humilitas recipere non ~etur); clerici elatione et insolentia .. preventi, adeo ut nonnulli eorum ~arentur missas suo ordine celebrare ÆLF. *Æthelwold* 12; [Rollo], ~atus genibus advolvi, apprehensum pedem regis ad os suum stans attraxit W. MALM. *GR* II 127; Teutones Francorum .. dedignati sunt habere consortium J. SAL. *Hist. Pont.* 24; Vasti regina ~atur intrare ad mandatum regis Assueri AD. DORE *Pictor* 165; indignum est Deo dare quod mundus ~atur habere GIR. *GE* II 8; **1469** pro .. libertate ecclesiastica .. mortem non ~avit appetere *Lit. Cant.* II 245. **c** caro quidem [Anselmi] infirmabatur magis et magis; sed generosus ille spiritus et Dei amore nobilis ecclesie ~abatur infirmitati J. SAL. *Anselm* 1035C.

2 to think fit or (?) *f. l.*

s**1394** rex, ejus [regine] mortem dolendo, illud .. manerium [de Shen'] solo prosterni fecit. set nec in locum aliquem, ubi sciebat illam perante fuisse, per totum annum introire dedignabatur [? l. dignabatur] preter in ecclesiam *V. Ric. II* 126.

dedignatio [CL], (occasion of) disdain, scorn.

de ira nascuntur rixe, contentiones, inflatio cordis, verba prava, ~o, blasfemia *Spec. Eccl.* 8; **1350** quatenus .. velitis pro conservacione honoris vestri ordinis ac vitandis scandalis et ~onibus plurimis, que sunt ex contrario proventura, rebellionem damnare predictam *(Cl) Mon. Francisc.* II app. 281; ~o, A. *dysdeygne WW.*

dedignosus, disdainful, scornful.

cujus oculi sunt quasi rubei vel vitiosi lachrymis vel sanguine significant hominem iracundum, superbum, ~um, crudelem, inverecundum M. SCOT *Phys.* 64; nares nasi stricte et subtiles significant hominem .. sagacem, ~um, mendacem, †fidelem [l. infidelem] *Ib.* 66; flamma pruinosa, nox clara, dies tenebrosa, / res dedignosa, socialis et ambiciosa GOWER *Carm.* p. 359.

dedilectio [cf. CL dilectio], lack of affection.

1423 vos nobis tale ~onis prebuistis indicium ut .. nec patris gratitudini dabatis caritatis debitum nec salutantem resalutastis (*Lit. Abbatis*) AMUND. I 146.

dediligere [cf. CL diligere], to banish from affection.

1177 quem semel dilexit, vix ~it; quem vero semel exosum habuit, vix in gratiam familiaritatis admittit P. BLOIS *Ep.* 66. 198B.

1 dediscere v. dedicere 1a.

2 dediscere [CL], to unlearn.

~ere, nescire *GlC* D 120; difficile a male consuetudinis loco receditur; difficile usus ~itur AILR. *Serm.* 411B; profecerant in uno dumtaxat: †dedicerant [? l. dedidicerant] modum, modestiam nesciebant J. SAL. *Met.* 869B; ne .. desidie vitia, quibus †si [? *omit*] tenerior etas imbuta fuerit, anni difficile ~ant maturiores GIR. *TH* I 12; [Henricus II] usu pravo, qui egre †didiscitur, ex juvenili primum insolentia proveniente sic jurare †consueverant [? l. consueverat] *Id. GE* I 54.

dediticius [LL], surrendered captive. *V. et. daticius.*

GlC D 15 (v. daticius); s**1070** Edgarus .., regis dedititius .., facto ad Scotos transfugio, jusjurandum maculavit W. MALM. *GR* III 251 (= M. PAR. *Min.* I 14: †dedicius).

deditio [CL]

1 surrender. **b** free gift.

universos.. aut occidit aut in ~onem recepit BEDE *HE* II 9; ~o, traditio spontanea, †*handgand GlC* D 70; ~o, i. traditio, *handgang GlH* D 371; ne defensores nostri opidi ad ~onem [*gl.*: *abandun*] cogantur NECKAM *Ut.* 104; s**1223** quosdam alios .. barones ad ~onem premere conabantur M. PAR. *Maj.* III 82. **b a690** quod gratuita caelitus munificentia Deique dapsili ~one receptantes .. adepti sunt ALDH. *Ep.* 5; *CS* 961 (v. dapsilis b).

2 authority, lordship, or (?) *f. l.*

s**886** omnis Anglia conversa est in deditione [? l. ditione] illius *ASChr.*

deditionaliter, w. reference to surrender.

dux, nolens incommoda eorum qui secum ~er agere coeperant, pretium dedit restituendarum aedium W. POIT. II 27.

dedocēre [CL], to 'unteach', cause to unlearn. **b** (p. ppl.) untaught.

dum divinatio sobrietatis mensuram excedit, .. non instruit sed suum ~et professorem J. SAL. *Pol.* 440B. **b** doctores dilige doctos; / dedoctus docti doctoris dogmata damnat D. BEC. 75.

dedolare [CL], to shape w. adze.

sanctos cineres .. in quibusdam vasculis ligneis ad hoc opus ~atis .. reposuerunt R. COLD. *Cuthb.* 40.

dedragma v. didrachma.

deducatrix, leader (f.).

in ipso monasterio est sancta imago sanctae Dei genitricis quae vocatur Odigitria ['Ὁδηγήτρια], quod est interpretatum ~ix, quia .. S. Maria .. deduxit eos [ij cecos] ad aecclesiam suam *Descr. Constant.* 249.

†deducatus, escort.

s**1245** assignatus est, rege miserante ei [Martino nuntio Pape] ~um [? *add* petenti *or sim.*] usque ad Doveram, dominus R. N. marescallus hospitii domini regis OXNEAD *Chr.* 175 (cf. M. PAR. *Maj.* IV 421).

deducere [CL]

1 a to lead, drive (animals). **b** (p. ppl. as sb. f.) beast of chase; *cf. deductus* 2a. **c** to lead, bring, escort (persons). **d** to lead out, plant (a colony).

a [me] pulchra puerpera prendit / et voti compos celsam deducit ad urbem ALDH. *Aen.* 60 (*Monocerus*) 9; quos [faunos] poeta Lucanus .. Orphei .. cantu ~tos cecinit *Lib. Monstr.* I 5; **1219** ita quod illos [boves et equos detentos] habere non potuit donec tulisset literas .. regis directas vicecomiti ut .. eos inde juste ~i faceret *CurR* VIII 29. **b 1549** quia fere et ~te in .. parco temporibus estivalibus minime habeant .. aliquam aquam pro earum sustentacione *Pat* 815 m. 19. **c** ALDH. *VirgP* 37 (v. donare 3d); quidam ex fratribus qui eum deduxerunt patriam rediere *Hist. Abb. Jarrow* 37; homo Dei commendavit nobis ut ~eremus illum ad te et sepeliremus eum tecum NEN. *HB* 216; haec a matre ~ta ad viri Dei tumulum obdormivit paululum WULF. *Æthelwold* 44; in celum ~ebaris OSB. *V. Dunst.* 40; FL. WORC. I 170 (v. derelinquere 2e); ad aliena regna .. a pristinis spiritibus malignis diduci, seduci ac illudi consuevit R. COLD. *Cuthb.* 122; s**1213** obtulerunt se .. cum civitate cruce signatis, ut tantummodo vita eis .. servaretur et ~erentur saltem uno die securi WEND. II 90; **1266** in cibo cc servientium quos .. comes de Mar deduxit secum in insulis *ExchScot* 11; J. HOWD. *Cant.* 38 (v. 1 cellarium 1d); **1293** ~tus est ad prisonam *SelCCoron* 128. **d** utrum Carthago diruatur .. an eo colonia ~atur ALCUIN *Rhet.* 8.

2 to bring (persons) to trial, deal with (judicially or otherwise). **b** (w. *de*) to put in possession of.

ne aliquis occidatur junior quam xv annorum, nisi se velit defendere aut fugere et in manus ire nolit, ut tunc ~atur [AS: *þæt hine man þonne lede*] sic in majori sic in minori, qualecumque sit (*Quad.*) *GAS* 183; unicuique domino magnum opus est ut hominem suum recte ~at [AS: *rihtlice healde*] (*Ib.*) *Ib.* 303; **1201** (v. 1 censura 1b); **1204** si alicubi arestati fuerint vel vexati contra libertates Wintonienses, ~antur et judicentur per cartam .. civium Wintoniensium *BBC* (*Ilchester*) 137; **1218** dictum est Rannulfo quod ~at eum [sc. tenentem suum] per judicium curie sue et quod distringat eum per feodum suum ad faciendum servicium suum *Eyre Yorks* 22; **1219** dubitatum fuit et non determinatum quo judicio ~endi sunt illi qui rettati sunt de latrocinio *Pat* 186; **1256** quod .. cives .. ~antur in compotis et retornis suis ad .. Scaccarium secundum leges et consuetudines .. Scaccarii, sicut vicecomites nostri Anglie in suis compotis ibidem ~untur *BBC* (*York*) 172; **1265** ipsos graviter molestavit et deduxit contra tenorem litterarum nostrarum *Cl* 142; **1294** custos prisone .. inculpatus fuit de hoc quod indebite ~it prisones custodie sue commissos .. et mulieres maxime, quas facit noctanter secum concumbere *PlRChester* 6 r. 11; **13**.. (1419) quod cives London' .. in itineribus suis ~antur per easdem leges per quas ~ebantur in itineribus tentis temporibus J. et H. .. regum *MGL* I 146. **b 1198** H. filius H. debet c li. ut juste ~atur de hereditate sua *Pipe* 3; **1206** Robertus .. et .. uxor ejus debent ccc m. .. pro habenda saisina medietatis ville de Caudebec [*Cumb*] unde Alexander .. habuit saisinam .., ita quod ipsi postea ~antur de tota villa *Pipe* 45.

3 a to bring out, produce (things). **b** to emit, shed. **c** to exact, levy. **d** to take away, deduct. **e** to except.

a c625 quos Deus .. ex primi hominis .. cognatione, ~tis per saecula innumerabilibus propaginibus, pullulare constituit (*Lit. Papae*) BEDE *HE* II 10; alii [homines] vadunt in fontem ad partem orientis et ~unt pisces ex ea parte NEN. *HB* 215; ut [sapientie lucerna] omnibus in commune ~ta pulchrius elucescat GIR. *TH* III *pref.* p. 139; tonus elevat aut deprimit aut mixtim sonum littere ~it BACON *Gram. Gk.* 129; **1288** capiunt [bladum] occulte in foro et illud .. ~unt extra forum in schoppis suis *Leet Norw.* 12. **b** s**1461** illis visis .. non poterant oculi nostri lacrymas non ~ere *Reg. Whet.* I 397. **c 1266** vicecomes .. exitus .. comitatuum plene ~ere non potuit *Cl* 265. **d** si sortem suam ~tis expensis .. recepit, .. possessionem restituat debitori BOSO *V. Pont.* 408; **1200** (v. casura 1b); **c1218** (v. defectus 1g); **1299** (v. defalcare 3a); **1302** ~tis racionabilibus misis et sumptibus *BBC* (*Berwick*) 99; **1333** *Reg. Aberd.* I 55 (v. decimus 4g); **1368** defalcata et ~ta illa summa pecunie *Melrose* 441; **c1470** (v. cristatio); **1598** decreverunt iiij solidos .. ex .. bedelli feodis ~endos *StatOx* 456. **e 1356** cancellarius .. clamat habere cogniciones omnium causarum .. et placitorum .. ubi clericus vel alius de juridiccione universitatis fuerit una parcium, ~tis placitis de morte vel mahemiis *MunAcOx* 174.

4 a to derive. **b** to conclude, infer, deduce (log.). **c** to lead (to a conclusion).

a verba ex triplici conjugatione ~ta ALDH. *PR* 117. **b** quamvis ex qualibet racione appellantis .. possit conclusio ista ~i OCKHAM *Pol.* I 332; *Id. Dial.* 488 (v. corollarie); hoc, propter errores in quarto capitulo ~tos ex ipso, non potest esse verum CONWAY *Def. Mend.* 1333; concedit magister quod album est nigrum quantum .. ad alia prius ~ta ex ista opinione (KYN.) *Ziz.* 12. **c** ratione argumentandi artificiosa hujusmodi, ut sophistica, ad contraria diduci posse videbit expertus BALSH. *AD* 95.

5 (usu. w. abstr. obj.) **a** to bring (to a condition or an end). **b** to bring forward, propose, offer. **c** to bring to notice or sim. **d** to adduce, refer for decision, bring before a court (leg.). **e** to take (into consideration). **f** to direct (attention).

a quod necessaria ratione veraciter esse colligitur, id in nullam ~i debet dubitationem ANSELM (*CurD* I 25) II 96; s**1153** ad hunc finem res ~ta est ut .. rex S. .. castellum .. everteret TORIGNI *Chr.* 174; WYCL. *Dom. Div.* 45 (v. definibilis); **1458** (v. devenire 4). **b 1220** ad hoc quod .. consilio nostro significastis ~tum fuisse vobis in pactum per justiciarium nostrum .. de faciendo vobis restitutione[m] illorum que posuistis in opere .. castri .. *Pat* 226. **c 1235** ad conscientiam magnitudinis vestre securi ~imus quecumque nostris utilitatibus .. noscimus expedire *TreatyR* 15; **1295** de causis .. ad nostram notíciam ~tis *Reg. Cant.* 55; **1330** prorogacionem .. termini .. publicare et in communem notíciam ~ere omnium quorum interest *Lit. Cant.* I 332; **1405** ad aures quarumdam nobilium personarum .. susurratorie deduxerunt quod .. (*TreatyR*) *Foed.* VIII 425; **1427** universitatis vestre noticie ~imus per presentes quod .. *FormOx* 461. **d c1236** feodus .. ~tus in controversiam (v. detentio 3a); **1248** dicta placita per ballivos nostros pertractentur et in judicium ~antur *BBC* (*Poole*) 197; **1343** appellacionibus .. frivolis ~tis viam ibi volentes precludere *Conc.* II 721a; **1348** dicit quod non potest eam terram ~ere in judicium *SelPlMan* 15; super omni revelato a Deo .. potest ~i questio seu dubitacio ad apostolice sedis examen OCKHAM *Pol.* III 244; **1428** invenimus .. nihil effectuale per partem adversam ~tum et probatum fuisse .. quod intencionem .. abbatis .. posset enervare (*Sententia W. Lyndewode*) AMUND. I 250. **e 1324** dispendiis variis que ex dissensione hujusmodi possent sequi necnon et impedimentis que ex ea .. possent .. ingeri .. in consideracione ~tis *TreatyR* I 638. **f c1410** ~ite igitur consideracionis intuitum [ad] coelectorum jura utriusque *FormOx* 198.

6 a (leg.) to settle, decide, conduct (plea, writ, dispute or sim.). **b** to transact, deal with (business). **c** (w. *mercatum*) to conduct, carry on.

a s**1198** responderunt .. Romanam curiam, per quam causa diducta est, consulendam fore GERV. CANT. *Chr.* 550; **1201** excessus qui inter eos emerserint .. inter eos ~antur secundum legem suam *SelPlJews* 2; **c1220** placita ad coronam pertinencia .. semper vidimus per servientes prioris Dunelm' attachiari et in curia eorundem .. presentari et ~i *Feod. Durh.* 219; **1221** loquela illa fuit ~ta .. coram justiciariis itinerantibus et terminata *PlCrGlouc* 31; **c1260** si aliquod breve .. regis .. liberatum fuerit, quod breve in comitatu sive in curia .. archiepiscopi Cant' ~i possit et terminari *Pat* 436 m. 6 (cf. *CalPat 1429–36* 421); s**1265** placita de Banco, que solebant ~i apud Westmonasterium, ~ta fuerunt in aula episcopi London' *Leg. Ant. Lond.* 84; **1448** quod predicta placita coram .. senescallo .. habeantur, ~antur, teneantur, audiantur, et terminentur *Reg. Whet.* I 54; **1549** ordinaciones penes officium procuratorum curiarum consistorialium et exercicium in eorum causis ~endis *Conc. Scot.* II 121 *rub.* **b 1297** istud negocium secrecius quo poterit ~atur *RGasc* III lxxxiv; **1378** onus relacionis super ~tis et communicatis inter nos reverencie vestre cercius faciende *FormOx* 232. **c c1160** omnes illi qui de mercato vivunt et mercatum ~unt infra quatuor divisas que pertinent civitati Lincolnie *BBC* (*Lincoln*) 108.

7 a to extend, draw out (in space). **b** (p. ppl.) extended, long. **c** (intr., of a road) to lead; **d** (fig.).

a montem .. quem lateribus longe lateque ~tum in modum aequoris natura complanat (*Passio Albani*) BEDE *HE* I 7; motuum localium super idem spacium .. ~torum velocitates (BRADW. *Cont.*) *Sci. Mech.* 233. **b** [Ethelstanus] statura .. que justam non excelleret, corpore ~to, capillo .. flavo W. MALM. *GR* II 134; calceus [Cupidinis] .., pedis instar factus, ut ipsos / exprimat articulos, cujus deductior [v. l. diductior] ante / pinnula procedit HANV. II 96 p. 261 (cf. ib. VIII 453 p. 374: neutrum deductius ortu /

surgit). **c** s**1297** RISH. 174 (v. declivitas 1). **d** confirmatur .. primo per [sc. argumentum] ~ens ad impossibile WYCL. *Ver.* I 111.

8 a to protract (in time). **b** to pass, spend (time or life).

a querela defendentis et calumniantis annis duobus diducta est neque finiri potuit R. COLD. *Godr.* 263. **b** in tali leticia quinquagesimales dies usque ad diem praefatum deduximus CUTHB. *Ob. Baedae* clxii; angeli .. noctem totam in hymnis et laudibus ~ebant W. S. ALB. *V. Alb. & Amphib.* 25; s**1235** cum intellexisset .. Caursinos .. vitam spurcissimam ~ere M. PAR. *Maj.* III 331; [abbas R., ob. **1235**] fuit .. vir pacificus .., cupiens in tranquillitate .. ~ere dies suos *Meaux* I 407.

9 (w. *in*) to multiply (by).

quadratum .. quod ex multiplicatione medietatis radicum in se ipsa ~te .. perficitur ROB. ANGL. *Alg.* 86.

deducibilis, (log.) deducible.

per hoc medium potissume est ~e actus generari vel circa idem objectum vel circa novum WYCL. *Act.* 26; cujus oppositum est manifeste ~e *Id. Compl.* 89.

deductio [CL]

1 transport, 'leading in' (of hay). **b** drawing off, flow. **c** carrying, escorting.

1453 pro falcacione et lucracione feni et ~one ejusdem feni .. prati de Row *ExchScot* 595. **b** euripus est ~o maris vel aquarum, quod fit secundum augmentum vel decrementum lune TREVET *Troades* 60. **c** ~o Christi in Egiptum nono die Januarii W. WORC. *Itin.* 278.

2 hunting, chase. *V. et.* 2 *deductus* 2a.

1252 mandatum est forestariis .. quod in .. foresta fieri faciant septem trencheyas ubi commodius fieri poterunt ad ~ones regis *Cl* 47.

3 deduction, subtraction.

c**1194** (v. decimus 4b).

4 (log.) deduction. **b** leading (of argument or sim.).

consimili ~one probabitur quod, si Sortes [i. e. Socrates] est homo et Sortes non est homo, Sortes est capra NECKAM *NR* II 173; hoc .. ~one infallibili .. ex scriptura vim sumente patere potest OCKHAM *Dial.* 819; oportet investigare quomodo locus ab auctoritate tenet in consequenciis et ~onibus et que sit racio sequele (KYN.) *Ziz.* 4; BEKINSAU 735 (v. devolvere 4a). **b** artificiosa adhibeatur rationum .. diductio BALSH. *AD* 59 (cf. ib. 42: ad diversa designanda verborum argumentis diductio).

5 (leg.) conduct of (case).

1549 [procuratores] explorent .. merita cause et .. suo patrocinio destituant [sc. causam] .. ubicumque in causae ~one de ejusdem injusticia apparuerit *Conc. Scot.* II 122.

6 (mus.) point in a monochord at which the note *ut* occurs.

~onum locum nominat ubi ista vox 'ut' in monocordo reperienda est. .. pro humana voce vij sufficiunt ~ones TUNST. 219a.

deductive, (log.) inferentially, by deduction.

cujus manifesta probacione ~e elici poterit quod cum Christo .. adunitur in amore *NLA* (*J. Bridl.*) II 75; argumenta .. istam veritatem probant lucide et ~e CONWAY *Def. Mend.* 1423 (*recte* 1323).

deductivus, eductive.

est caliditas .. formarum et specierum potencia in materia latenter existencium ad actum ~a ..; nam per caloris actionem aurum, es, argentum .. de lapidibus educuntur BART. ANGL. IV 1.

deductor [CL], guide, escort. **b** (w. *ferarum*) game-keeper.

cum .. a curia regis reverteretur, duces habens et ~ores Milonem .. et Paganum GIR. *IK* I 2 p. 34. **b** **1549** pro feodo ~oris ferarum forreste de Fekenham [*Worcs*] *Pat* 821 m. 3.

deductorium [LL], drain, conduit.

in una ecclesia Ytalie, ubi .. Sabbato S. Pasche hora baptizandi solebat aqua emanare .. et statim ex sese redire, nullo ~io apparente (SIG. GEMBLOUX) *Flor. Hist.* I 203.

1 deductus v. deducere.

2 deductus

1 (w. *aquae*) watercourse.

a**1290** extendit se super ~um aque apud Sadilbowe *Carte Nativ.* 317.

2 a chase (hunting or hawking). **b** sport, diversion.

a **1215** (v. cheverellus a); **1215** capere j cervum .. quam remocius poterit a loco ubi ~um nostrum habere consuevimus *Cl. Frag.* 135; **1253** viderunt homines .. fratris R. ferre unum leporem super unum baculum in ~u suo versus hospicium *SelPlForest* 111; **1278** cum ipse [rex] .. transiret per com. istum [*Herts*] pro ~u †amn' [MS: avium] suarum habendo ad aquam de Luye [*Lea*] (*JustIt* 323) *PQW* 284a; **1333** pro ~u regis cum falconibus suis *LTRMem* 105 r. 165 *d.*; **1368** (v. cornu 4b); **1416** concessimus .. H. duci Glouc' .. officium custodis .. forestarum nostrarum citra Trentam una cum officio magistri ~us nostri forestarum et parcorum *Pat* 398 m. 12; **1472** ~us noster cignorum infra mariscum de Wittelesmere [*Hunts*] .. tam per hamos, recia, fila viscata et ingenia quam per venatores, piscatores, aucipites et cignorum mutatores magnaliter devastatus existit *Pat* 529 m. 18*d.* **b** **1341** marinariis passantibus .. filias regis cum familia sua ultra aquam Thamisie pro recreacione et ~u earundem in gardinis ibidem habend' *KRAc* 389/11 m.1; **1429** aliquod gardinum pro ~u et solacio magistri sive custodis (*Pat*) AMUND. II 163; **1433** tempus autumnale, in quo magnatibus circa suas recreaciones et ~us .. intendere competebat *RParl* IV 420b.

deduplicatio v. decuplicatio. **deebriare** v. debriare 1a, b. **deedificare** v. deaedificare.

deeligere [cf. eligere 2], to reverse the election of.

quis ergo est ille elector qui vel accusat quem Deus approbat vel ~it quem Deus eligit? WYCL. *Sim.* 51.

deesse [CL], to be absent or lacking, to fail (w. dat. or abl. or absol.): **a** (of person); **b** (of thing or abstr.); **c** (w. inf.). **d** (w. *de*) to be missing (from), fall short (of).

a c**597** pro eo quod sacerdos alius in loco deest (*Lit. Papae*) BEDE *HE* I 27 p. 60; Ranulfo ad veniente de fuit Radulfus *DB* II 424 (cf. ib. 103: revocavit eum tutorem; set ipse sibi defuit); tempus cene, cui ~e non permittimur AILR. *Spir. Amicit. Abbr.* I 71. 670; nec deest qui rerum status attendat J. SAL. *Met.* 876B. c**1219** cum non desit qui .. viriliter se opponat (*AncC* IV 144) *RL* I 66; indignans equidem male prēesse, cupit bene dēesse H. AVR. *Hugh* 277; nulli dēest Dominus nisi desit primitus illi *Id. Poems* 2. 124; **1278** (v. defectus 4a); **1293** decenarius .. cum tota decena sua presentant G. le M. [et alios] .. ~e, quos manucap[iunt] ad proximam curiam *SelPlMan* 168. **b** ut .. lampadibus .. olei liquor oportunus defuisset ALDH. *VirgP* 32 (cf. ib. 47: licet .. passionis occasio defuisset); non defuit puniendis admonitio divinae pietatis BEDE *HE* IV 25; **8..** non deerit, *na wana bið WW*; deerat, *wana wæs GlP* 497; molinus et piscaria desunt pro superfacto W. de Braiose *DB* I 16v.; ANSELM I 26 (v. concipere 3c); Dominus tecum est et illius gratia tibi non deerit unquam W. S. ALB. *V. Alb. & Amphib.* 9; plus deest facultas, plus adest perniciosa voluntas GIR. *GE* II 23; 'avaro desunt omnia bona mundi' .. non videtur esse scolastice dicendum. nam de vi vocis hoc verbum '~e' importat negacionem respectu habitus; unde Ugucio .. et .. Januensis, ponendo differenciam inter 'abesse' et '~e', .. 'abest' inquiunt, 'quod longe est; deest quod deficit et non habetur' (KYN.) *Ziz.* 22. **c** **1326** per nostratum incuriam alicujus, eadem peticio defuit .. vobis mitti *Lit. Cant.* I 174. **d** adhuc capitulum unum de libro quem dictasti deest CUTHB. *Ob. Baedae* clxii; **1271** tantum decidat venditori de precio empcionis .. quantum defuerint [dolia] de antiqua mensura *Cl* 369 (cf. 2 decasus 2a).

deessentia, lack, want.

sic deest sibi [peccatori] premium quod pro legis observancia possideret; nec est talis carencia plus penalis quam carencia laureole, sc. ex ~ia doctoratus, martyrii aut virginitatis WYCL. *Civ. Dom.* II 160.

deexaltare [cf. exaltare 1d], to lower.

1334 ad gurgites illos, si eos .. inveniretis sic levatos et exaltatos fuisse, ~ari et in pristinum statum remitti faciendos *Cl* 155 m. 30*d.*; **1347** quod permittat ~are quoddam stagnum *Reg. Brev. Orig.* 199b.

deexaltatio [cf. exaltatio 1b], lowering.

1358 concordatum est .. quod occasione .. exaltacionis et ~onis molendinorum predictorum nullum generetur .. nocumentum molendino .. abbatis (*Compositio*) THORNE 2121.

deextra [*al. div.*], (w. acc.) from outside. **b** (adv.) to the outside.

1217 de extra ballivam (v. cheminagium); **1406** quod si quis ex dominis [cardinalibus] absentibus vel de extra collegium assumatur in papam *Conc.* III 287. **b** sanguis [qui] de extra deberet emitti intra retinetur ut cibus fetus *Quaest. Salern.* B 21.

defacere v. diffacere. **defacili** v. de 10e, facilis. **defaconare** v. desaconare.

defaecare [CL]

1 to purify, free from impurities (w. ref. to wine, ale, or sim., also fig.); *v. et. effaecare* a. **b** (by misinterp.) to stale (wine or ale). **c** to refine. **d** to free (land) from unwanted persons. **e** to free from error or sim.

merulenta ~ati nectaris defruta apothecis celestibus recondenda ALDH. *VirgP* 30; ~atum vinum, *gehluttrad win ÆLF. Gl.*; W. FITZST. *Thom.* 19, GAD. 123v. 2 (v. cervisia 1c); utrum de musto non ~ato .. [sanguis Domini] confici valeat, questio est GIR. *GE* I 8 p. 26; hoc .. de prelo purissimi torcularis in nostre memorie dolia ~andum transibat R. BURY *Phil.* 8. 134. **b** *stal, as drynke*, defecatus, meraxcis .., *stalyn, or make stale drynke*, ~o *PP*; servicia deficata, A. *stale ale WW*; *stale as ale*, ~atus *CathA.* **c** ADEL. *QN* 29 (v. detergere 2b); vis sensualis, .. ex subtilioribus elementis et ab hac carnali .. corpulentia .. ~atis .. compacta AILR. *An.* III 2. 42v.; ascendit .. ad cerebrum semen, ut spiritum vite animalis suscipiat. hoc longo defluxu ~ari oportuit, ut purum animal sanum produceret ALF. ANGL. *Cor* 15. 11; **1563** eadem [metalla] probare, ~are, liquefacere, purificare *Pat* 1173 m. 3. **d** [Henricus I] Flandrenses .. apud Ros velut in sentinam congessit, ut .. regnum ~aret W. MALM. *GR* V 401; s**1298** cum universas provincias Scocie rex E. ~asset necnon sue dicioni subjugasset RISH. 388. **e** expositis ad liquidum et ~atis peonum regulis ALDH. *PR* 137; ut, dissolutioris conversationis eorum [canonicorum] normam arctius innormans, senum canitiem vitiorum infectione puer [sc. Oswoldus] ~aret *Chr. Rams.* 22; ut sit Christiana undique versum ~ata religio PULL. *Sent.* 773A; c**1150** cultu ~ate religionis G. FOLIOT *Ep.* 84.

2 (p. ppl.) pure, clear; **b** (w. ref. to perception, thought, conduct, or sim.).

~atum, i. liquidum, purum, *ahluttrad GlH* D 55; maxime post pluvias aere ~atiori blavius seu saphirinus color apparet *Ps.*-GROS. *Summa* 620 (cf. ib. 641: aurum vero vivum argentum suum habet ~atissimum). **b** sensu †defectato [? l. meliorato, l. defecato], quia ebrietatis fumus penitus evanuerat W. MALM. *Mir. Mariae* 162; is cui mens sanior, oculus purior, vita est ~atior AILR. *Spec. Car.* III 26. 586B; licet aurium sensus purissimus et ~atissimus sit J. SAL. *Pol.* 758A; ~ate mentis agilitas R. COLD. *Cuthb.* 112; cor .. meditatione ~ata .. mundissimum AD. EYNS. *Hug.* II 2 p. 49; judicio ~atissimi intellectus WYCL. *Ver.* II 64.

defaecatio [LL], purification. **b** defecation.

†deficatio, i. purgatio *GlH* D 65; ~o vel purgatio, *hlyttrung ÆLF. Sup.* 179; *a clensynge*, colacio, ~o *CathA.* **b** utraque hec [restauratio et augmentum] embrioni sunt necessaria; fiunt autem cibi attractione, retentione, digestione, et ~one ALF. ANGL. *Cor* 13. 1.

defaenerare [CL = *to overwhelm w. debt, to ruin by extortion*], to bind, enslave (fig.). **b** (by misinterp.) to enrich.

Philippus [rex Francorum] .. illicitis ardoribus ~atus famulabatur W. MALM. *GR* V 404; Sampsonem .. Dalile lenociniis ~atum *Id. Mir. Mariae* 167; fenero componitur ~o, .. i. deservire OSB. GLOUC. *Deriv.* 233. **b** devenaravit, ditavit, donavit *GlC* D 118.

defalca v. defalta 1a.

defalcare [cf. falcare]

1 to mow. **b** to reap. **c** to cut down (fig.).

in lacus medio crusta pratum fecit, que .. tempore herbe tondende .. ad terram .. trahitur .. et sic ~ata sectiones recipit GERV. TILB. III 39; **1293** (v. diffortiare 3b); **1330** in j acra prati .. et pastura ij boum ubique excepto prato ipsius H. ~ato et gardino *ChartR* 117 m. 30; similiter de decima feni, si decima acra non ~ata est *Praxis* 140. **b** **1465** stipendia ~ancium grana *ExchScot* 322. **c** quia opportune ad spinas, cardones, et sizannia ~anda et extirpanda tunc temporis instetit messis .., a domicilio regis plures officiarios expulerunt FAVENT 13.

2 to cut down in amount or extent, diminish.

1246 quorum [minorum clericorum] portionem si contingat usque ad medietatem ~ari, peribit obsequium ecclesie *Conc. Syn.* 399; s**1285** condidit rex E. statuta, inter que jurisdiccionem ecclesiasticorum judicum ~avit *Flor. Hist.* III 63 (= *Ann. Worc.* 492); **1339** persecutor noster, Francorum regem se nominans, jura nostra vulnerat et ~at (*Lit. Regis E.*) AD. MUR. *Chr.* 92; eciam si Deus non sit in sua omnipotencia ~atus, potest saltem de plenitudine potestatis dare Christo actum hujusmodi cognitivum BRADW. *CD* 790C; papa sic signante vel ~ante fructus talis beneficii, laicus non tenetur ultra necessaria ad suum spirituale officium ministrare WYCL. *Sim.* 55; coitus talis si continuetur digestionem impedit, esurium ~at, siciem (*sic*) generat KYMER 19; s**1456** res regie .. per minus providam .. regis largicionem .. in se abbreviate ~ateque ac diminute erant *Reg. Whet.* I 249.

3 to deduct. **b** (w. dat.) to remit (by deduction from debt); **c** (impers. pass. w. *in*).

1299 ut de debito .. in quo ipsi W. tenemur .. ~etur quod racionabile fuerit seu eciam deducatur *RGasc* III 379; **1319** si contingat .. parcum iterato recludi, de dictis [decimis] .. ~abunt xx s. *Reg. Dunferm.* 591; **1368** ~ata et deducta illa summa pecunie *Melrose* 441; **1371** decime ac primicie / fidelium sunt hostie / divino date cultui; / .. /ascribi debet raptui, / si racione fatui / quicquid defalces latrie (*In Lollardos* 18) *Pol. Poems* I 237; **1402** de .. summa xl milium nobilium ~etur annuatim unum nobile (*TreatyR*) *Foed.* VIII 238b; s**1453** (v. computus 2a); **1458** se obligant allocare et ~are de precio predicto xiij solidos *Cl* 309 m. 40*d.* **b** **1452** pardonacio debitorum cum defalcacione eorumdem: et in diversis pecuniarum summis ~atis et pardonatis creditoribus defuncti *Test. Ebor.* III 152; **1472** licebit nobis .. porcionem istius quarte partis eisdem assignare ~ando dictis J. et I. .. valorem terre piscatoribus assignate in firma iij librarum *Reg. Aberbr.* II

169; **1479** asserencium se habere illas x m. sibi ~atas per literas regis *ExchScot* 567. **c 1538** ~atur .. compotanti in iij bollis ordei de decimis terre .. de K. de croppis annorum xxxvij et xxxviij, ex eo quod dicta terra fuerat vasta et non bene seminata *Rent. S. Andr.* 16.

defalcata v. defalta 1a.

defalcatio [cf. falcatio]

1 mowing.

1455 pro ~one et induccione feni pratorum de Faucland *ExchScot* 80.

2 clipping (of coins).

s1279 quia denarius qui (*sic*) findi in duas partes pro obolis et in iiij partes pro quadrantibus consuevit, ordinatum fuit ad tollendam occasionem ~onis monete quod rotundi essent denarii, oboli et quadrantes *Flor. Hist.* III 53 (cf. TREVET *Ann.* 300: moneta .. per tonsuram .. deteriorata).

3 remission (by deduction from debt, esp. in case of testator leaving insufficient legacy), discount.

si .. plura sint debita vel plus legatum fuerit .. ad que catalla defuncti non sufficiant .., fiat ubique ~o BRACTON 61; **1332** quo ad legata, paratus est .. solvere quatenus bona sufficiant, facta ~one de omnibus legatis *Reg. Roff. Ep.* f. 138; **1360** in solucione facta burgensibus solventibus dictam summam in Flandria pro ~one ejusdem pecunie solute in auro, xxxv li. *ExchScot* 48; **1391** ~o Symonis C. de v m.: .. S. .. remisit .. eisdem v m. annuas de dictis x li. annui redditus *Reg. Newbattle* 214; **1415** volo quod, si bona mea .. non sufficiant ad istud testamentum meum perimplendum, quod (*sic*) tunc ~o et diminucio fiat de legacionibus .. predictis *Reg. Cant.* II 68 (cf. ib. 220); **1430** fiat racionabilis ~o juxta ratam *ActPC* IV 34; *abatement or withdrawyng of mete or mesure or oper thyng*, subtraccio, ~o *PP*; **1452** (v. defalcare 3b); **s1453** volumus .. ut .. vadat residuum pecunie .. integraliter absque ~one sive abbreviacione ad manus suas *Reg. Whet.* I 117; **1540** quod .. plenam .. allocacionem, ~onem, deduccionem, et exoneracionem .. prefato R. .. de omnibus hujusmodi redditibus .. facient (*Pat*) *Cart. Glam.* 1922.

defalcatorius, tending to detract or diminish.

s1456 abbas .. sibi suspicari ceperat qualiter ipsa [billa porrecta in Parliamento] in revocacionem .. libertatis novelle noviter per .. regem .. ecclesie concesse derogatoria ~iaque multum erat *Reg. Whet.* I 259.

defallimentum, (fine for) default (Gasc.).

p1250 ballivi nobis mandant exercitum facere .. ubi necesse non est, ut possint .. a remanentibus .. aliquid extorquere, petentes ab eis ~um exercitus (*Querimonia*) *V. Montf.* app. 303.

defalta, ~um [cf. AN *defalt*, OF *defaute*]

1 (leg.) default, failure to appear in court as defendant, warrantor, juror, suitor or sim. **b** fine for default. **c** (w. *ponere in*) to put in (hold liable for) default. *Cf. defectus* 4b.

si quis .. de infidelitate rectatus tercio vocatus non comparet, quarto die ostendant summonitores tres ~as [OF: *defautes*] (*Leis Will.*) *GAS* 518; si alius terram ipsam .. per ~am waranti sui amiserit GLANV. III 4; **1198** preceptum fuit Gilleberto .. quod .. faceret rationabile escambium Acelino .. de dim. virgata terra .. quam idem A. perdidit per assisam per ~am ipsius G. *CurR* I 39; **1220** (v. deficere 6a); **1221** villata de S. non venit; et ideo in misericordia pro ~a; et veniat cras *SelPlCrown* 99; **1223** debet .. dim. m. pro diffalta *KRMem* 6 r. 17; **c1248** si .. contingat aliquos .. burgensium .. curie nostre .. interesse non posse, ballivi nostri absentiam suam nullo modo reputabunt †defalcatam *BBC* (*Poole*) 201; **1269** ~a tenentis in brevi de recto sic debet irrotulari .. *CBaron* 84; nullus amercietur pro ~a [v. l. †~u] alicujus summon[icionis] nisi coram rege vel justiciario tantum *Fleta* 64; **s1292** attornatorum ~a calumniata fuit per dominum J. de Balliolo *Ann. Scot.* 267; **1299** percipiet alia amerciamenta ejusdem visus, viz. de †defalcis tantum *PQW* 106b; **1312** pro defaulta cujusdam ancille, que interfuit quando equus percussit hominem at (*sic*) mortem *Reg. Cant.* 991; post tria essonia potest pars defendens facere tres ~as, que tolerantur propter lucrum curie. et pro qualibet ~a capietur una districcio. .. et pars conquerens potest taxare damna sua in absencia partis sue, quando fecerit ~am *Quon. Attach.* 4 (cf. *RegiamM* I 8); **1419** ut qui [in wardemoto] non .. respondet pro nomine suo et fecerit ~am notetur *MGL* I 37; **1489** tenentes .. faciunt ~um secte curie *Banstead* 361; **1597** non comparet sed ~um facit; cujus ~um recordatur ibidem *Law Merch.* III 88. **b 1199** (1285) sint quieti .. de summonitionibus et de defautis que ad hundreda et comitatus pertinent *CalCh* II 293; **1221** cum [non] solet primo die placiti ~a poni in manu petentis (*Quaest. Itineris*) *MGL* I 64. **c 1228** W. de B. .., qui non potest comparere coram baronibus de Scaccario .., habet litteras .. quod non ponatur in ~am propter absentiam suam *Cl* 118; **1233** preceptum est vicecomiti .. quod non ponat in ~am homines de L. quod non fuerunt coram illo ad comitatum *KRMem* 12 r. 9 *d.*; **1283** tenentes .. extra comitatum in negociis suis .. existentes in curia illa [abbatis] non ponantur in ~a nec aliquod dampnum incurrant propter absenciam (*Compositio*) THORNE 1933.

2 default, failure (in attendance at work). *Cf. defectus* 3b.

1269 T. L. est in misericordia pro ~a facta in opere domini *CBaron* 76; **1278** (v. decenarius 3a); **1301** [r. c.] de vij li. x s. ij d. receptis de ~a cementariorum et operariorum .. per dies per quos non operabantur *MinAc W. Wales* I 7.

3 a lack. **b** defect, flaw. **c** (w. *recti*) defect of justice.

a 1237 quia habuit ~am feni, venit ibi serviens suus et voluit emere unum mullonem propter necessitatem illam *BNB* III 213 (= *CurR* XV 1916: defectum). **b c1257** est .. crevacia magna infra turrellam .. que oportet refici, que ostensa fuit .. Henrico .. una cum aliis ~is prenominatis (*AncC* IV 3) *RL* II 125. **c** rite probata ~a per ~am recti in curia domini capitalis, vicecomes rectum teneat BRACTON 329b.

defamare [LL; CL *p. ppl. only*]

1 to defame, slander, denounce. **b** to disgrace. *V. et. diffamare* 2.

traducere, dehonestare, ~are *GlC* T 269; **s1239** ipsum .. nec capi mandavit, quamvis eum in sermonibus ~averat M. PAR. *Maj.* III 559; est in gravi forisfactura versus dominum regem et pudoriter ~atus *State Tri. Ed. I* 41; **1294** dicit se nunquam ~asse [predictum W.] immo veritatem dixisse, et veritas non est defamacio *SelPlMan* 82; **1296** deffamavit (v. 1 claviger 2a); **1427** (v. condemnare 1d). **b** si .. sorores religiose .. a .. regula .. deviant aut ~ate per malam .. vitam invenientur *Scot. Grey Friars* II 274.

2 to accuse (of): **a** (w. *de*); **b** (w. *super*); **c** (w. *pro*); **d** (w. *quod*). **e** (w. other). *V. et. diffamare* 3.

a s1208 exosum eum habuit uxor propria, quam de adulterio adulter ~avit *Flor. Hist.* II 137; **1281** clericis ~atis de morte Jordani *PQW* 425b; **1311** Templarius .. de magno crimine ~atus (*Dep. Templar.*) *Ann. Lond.* 189; **1461** enormia crimina .. de quibus .. ~atus .. existit *Mon. Hib. & Scot.* 431; **1499** persone ~ate vel suspecte de hujusmodi .. gravaminibus *Entries* 467. **b 12..** si [clerici] super hiis maleficiis fuerint ~ati *Reg. Aberd.* II 14; **1309** clericus super criminibus furti et roberie multipliciter ~atus *Reg. Carl.* II 9. **c 1257** M. PAR. *Maj.* VI 357 (v. carcer 1a). **d 1277** calumpniatur .. quod deberet ~asse homines domini de S. quod deberent falcasse in prato per diem dominicam *Hund. Highworth* 73; **1318** ~averunt curiam domini hic falso et maliciose quod nemo potest justiciam in curia optinere *CBaron* 127. **e** nullus ~atus tanquam receptator latrocinii debet puniri antequam malefactor fuerit convictus vel attayntus de latrocinio illo *Quon. Attach.* 83.

3 (by conf. w. *diffamare*) to publish abroad, make widely known. *V. et. diffamare* 1a.

quis sublimavit regnum Grecorum? quis eorum gesta per totum mundum perpetualiter ~avit? BACON V 58 (cf. *Reg. Cant. 1414–43* III 274).

defamatio, defamation, slander. **b** accusation. *V. et. diffamatio.*

1294 (v. defamare 1a); **1318** ~onibus pessimis .. nos impetunt *FormOx* 43; **1435** Agnes, que .. fuerat suscitatrix .. rumoris seu ~onis *MunAcOx* 509; **1553** vobis prohibemus ne .. placitum de ~one. .. in curia Christianitatis ulterius teneatis *Entries* 486b. **b 1239** potest .. accidere quod aliquis de clericis prenominatis per ~onem super homicidio vel furto vel hujusmodi crimine per regiam potestatem tradatur carcerali custodie GROS. *Ep.* 73 p. 239.

defamator, defamer, slanderer. *V. et. diffamator.*

articuli inquirendi in privata .. inquisitione. .. si sint ~ores vel rebelles sive noctivagi in burgo *Iter Cam.* 28; **1340** detractores et ~ores *FormOx* 170; **1341** omnes .. qui .. alicui .. crimen falso ex odii fomite maliciose imponunt, cum .. excommunicacionis sentencia .. in concilio Oxoniensi contra ~ores hujusmodi .. rite lata sint .. innodati (*Sententia Archiep.*) WALS. *HA* I 240 (= W. GUISB. *Cont.* II 379).

defamatorius, defamatory. *V. et. diffamatorius.*

1319 confisi de suis ~iis mendaciis et suggestionibus venenosis *FormOx* 50; **1465** verba .. opprobriosa, scandalosa, ~ia *MunAcOx* 713; quandam .. billam cum .. verbis vilipendiosis, scandalosis, et ~iis .. scribi fecit ac .. super ostium .. ecclesie S. Pauli .. infigi fecit *Entries* 13.

defatigare [CL], to fatigue, exhaust.

defitiget, ~et, fatiget, *suenceth GlC* D 51–2; †defigitet, i. ~et, lassat, *swencep GlH* D 46; quasi diffatigatus improbitate supplicum W. MALM. *GR* IV 337.

defatigatio [CL], fatigue, exhaustion.

secundum delicias ejus, sic defectio, sic ~o, sic languor et afflictio ejus J. FORD *Serm.* 1. 1.

defatuare [cf. CL fatuari], to cure of folly.

si tua proficiat illis correptio sana, / letifices super hiis fatuos quod defatuasti D. BEC. 404.

defaulta, defauta v. defalta. **defec-** v. et. defaec-, defet-, defic-.

1 defectare v. defaecare 2b.

2 defectare, to weaken, impair.

viole nimium humectant et stomachum infundunt et fastidium generant, quia os stomachi ~ant GILB. I 31. 2; si neutra causarum superabundet in excellentia, modum tamen excedat, virtutem ~at et dissolvit, et inde somniculositas .. fit *Ib.* II 106v. 2.

3 defectare v. devectare.

defectibilis [LL], subject to loss, impairment, or fault.

secundum Augustinum *De Fide ad Petrum* [III 25], anima est ~is, quia ex nihilo; ergo et mortalis. consequentia probatur, quia omne indefectibile est immortale; ergo omne ~e est mortale PECKHAM *QA* 16; sic debet fidelis in hac vita deffectibili congregare cumulos meritorum J. WALEYS *Commun.* f. 132; unde vult quod mensura media correspondeat illi quod habet moram indivisibilem et tamen ~em, ita quod potest ex se non esse, et illam mensuram ponit evum. nunc autem, sicut existencia angeli est indivisibilis et tamen ~is, ita et cogitacio ejus DUNS *Ord.* VII 223; putantes voluntatem divinam non esse universaliter efficacem, i.e. non frustrabilem, non ~em ullo modo BRADW. *CD* 5D; sequitur quod est dare potenciam ~em et potenciam indefectibilem equales WYCL. *Log.* II 137.

defectibilitas, liability to loss, impairment, or fault.

spiritaliter .. aqua est labilitas et ~as rationalis creature a bono .. in vitium GROS. *Hexaem.* IV 11; non est actualitas infinita infinita sine actu infinito; ergo nec ~as infinita sine defectu infinito PECKHAM *QA* 14; ob memoriam amisse immortalitatis et inflicte mortalitatis et ~atis J. WALEYS *V. Relig.* I 11. 224; quando velle aliquid pertinet ad defectum voluntatis, tunc posse velle illud est ex ~ate liberi arbitrii T. SUTTON *Quodl.* 371;

defectibiliter, fallibly or (?) *f. l.*

a1253 quoniam et in excelsis ~er [? l. indefectibiliter] presidemus ut domina et in terris .. vota virorum .. captivamus (*Lit. ad Regem Natalicium*) *Collect. Ox.* I 43.

defectio [CL], **a** weakness, defect. **b** (astr.) eclipse. **c** lack. **d** failure or omission. **e** shortening.

a sincopin, ~o stomachi *Gl. Leid.* 39. 47; ~o, *geteorung GlH* D 51; Ysaac de ea [medicina] loquitur, dicens: .. 'fluxui et †desectioni [v. l. defectioni] vesice repugnat' BACON IX 53; †sincopus est cordis ~o *SB* 39. **b** deliquium, ~o *GlC* D 95; eclipsis, ~o *Gl. Leid.* 27. 21; eclipsis, i. solis vel lune ~o, *onsprungennes GlH* E 18. **c** ex ipsa complexione sophistica .. principia .. sunt multipliciter: .. ex traductione, ex ~one, ex intellectione. .. ex ~one, cum an ut si 'aliquid' an ut si 'nichil' .. addi conveniat dubium ..; an ut si 'quid' addendum an ut si 'aliud' sic: 'hominem esse animal et non aliud est verum' - an 'aliud quam animal' an 'aliud quam hominem' ex adjungendorum ~one incertum BALSH. *AD* 89, 99 (cf. complexio 2b). **d** promisit rex .. dari illis victum et vestimentum absque ~one NEN. *HB* 176; **1457** quia nonnulla facta .. propter communis scribe ~onem irregistrata relicta .. ignorantur *StatOx* 285. **e** vitae nostrae terminus in ~one dierum exprimitur EGB. *Dial.* 412.

defectivitas, defectiveness, incompleteness.

a1290 questio est utrum generare conveniat Patri in divinis tanquam proprium. .. arguitur primo in communi quod non: generare non est in re nisi propter sui deffectivitatem *Quaest. Ox.* 123.

defectivus [LL]

1 defective, failing, inadequate. **b** (gram.) defective; **c** (phil. & theol.).

pater caelestis petitoribus suis suo timore et amore praeditis non ~a in caelis bona largitur BEDE *Hom.* II 14. 171; **1188** operum suorum fructum refectione non ~a percipiunt *Ep. Cant.* 289; dilectionem erga Deum, citra quam nihil est bonum .., nihil nisi prorsus ~um GIR. *PI* I 21 p. 143; **1282** cum .. in litera apostolica .. suppletum fuisset quod in .. litera precedenti .. fuerat ~um PECKHAM *Ep.* 256; **1296** fratrum .. numerus ~us *Reg. Cant.* 93; alia [donatio] incepta et ~a et post tempus confirmata; confirmatio enim omnem supplet defectum *Fleta* 178; **1311** modus eorum [magistrorum] statuendi est ~us, quia non habent tempus sufficiens ad deliberandum (*Acta Fratrum Predic.*) *Collect. Ox.* II 219; **1342** si alique consuetudines .. difficiles seu ~e existant .., major et aldermanni .. remedium congruum apponere possint (*Ch. Regis*) *MGL* II 443; **1342** missale insufficiens et ~um, eo quod omnes epistole et evangelia ferialia deficiunt in eodem (*Vis. Totnes*) *EHR* XXVI 113; **1353** corrigere corrupta et supplere ~a *Lit. Cant.* II 382. **b** verba ~a, .. ut 'libet', .. 'licet' ALDH. *PR* 113; 'odi, odisti' .. et praesenti tempore et praeterito perfecto sic declinatur: ideo ~um dicitur BEDE *Orth.* 39; sunt quaedam verba quae ex forma agendi in passivum perfectum vertuntur, quae etiam ~a appellantur secundi ordinis, ut 'soleo .., solitus sum' BONIF. *AG* 61; quia ~a esse verba introduxisti, subito ~a per singula accidentia opus habeo ut pandas mihi ALCUIN *Gram.* 882B; de †aerbis [l. verbis] ~is ÆLF. *Gram.* 203. **c** nec hac sola nativitate Christi ~a est potentia illius, qui omnipotens est, ut non posset illum hominem .. sibi .. naturalem

filium creare ALCUIN (*Adv. Felicem* 3. 3) *Dogm.* 164C; privatio .. nullius est factiva, immo a potius ~a SICCAV. *PN* 41.

2 a (of building or sim.) needing repair. **b** (of horse) unsound. **c** (med.) weak, ailing.

a 1334 domus .. ruinose et alias deffective *Reg. Heref.* 67; **1397** (v. defectus 3b); a**1400** tenebantur reparare .. pontem .., qui fuerat ~us *Meaux* III 80; **1417** quedam porta .. est ~a in defectu reparacionis *CourtR Banstead*; **1439** mansiones canonicorum multum sunt ruinose et ~e *Stat. Linc.* II 202; **1446** J. M. habet clausuram suam ~am .., per quam averia vicinorum consumunt novellas bosci domini *CourtR Carshalton* 61. **b 1378** qui quidem equus ~us fuit *Rec. Leic.* II 179; sciens equum illum .. in variis infirmitatibus ~um, viz. *spavens, splints* [etc.] *Entries* 9. **c** [pulvis gariofili etc.] consumit fleuma putridum .. et ~o stomacho subvenit BACON IX 127.

3 (of person) failing in duty, at fault.

1427 ita quod .. teneantur .. de ea [cista] compotum reddere, quantum in ipsis est, sub pena xl s. per eorum quemlibet ~um .. universitati .. solvendorum *StatOx* 232; **1434** quod [pandoxatores] .. sufficienter providerent de brasio ad pandoxandum pro rege et consuetudinariis suis .., sub pena xl solidorum, et hoc tocies quocies ~i inventi fuerint .. in premissis *MunAcOx* 507.

defectum v. deficere 1f, delinquere 1d, devehere.

defectuosus, a (of building) needing repair. **b** (of person) failing in duty, at fault.

a 1539 quorum mansiones ~e seu alias ruinate aut dirute .. fuerint *Form. S. Andr.* II 117; **1549** ecclesias tam in parietibus quam in tectis ruinosas aut ~as *Conc. Scot.* II 114. **b** si laici .. circa crimina secularia punienda in nullo invenirentur ~i OCKHAM *Dial.* 917; **13..** qui in hoc statuto ~us fuerit *Conc. Scot.* II 66; **1451** qui in his [psallendo etc.] ~i fuerint .., puniantur (*Abbr. Stat.*) *Mon. Francisc.* II 86.

defectus [CL]

1 deficiency, deficit, inadequacy, falling short. **b** (w. *aetatis*) nonage. **c** (w. *natalium*) illegitimacy. **d** (w. *sine*) without fail. **e** (astr.) eclipse. **f** (gram.) ellipsis. **g** defect in building or other artefact.

1209 in ~u gabuli terre Strong' tracte in dominium, ij s.; in ~u gabuli terre de A., v s., qui modo redduntur apud M.; summa quietanciarum et ~uum, xij s. *Pipe Wint.* 50 (= *Crawley* 188); sub ratione excellencie et ~us BACON VIII 18 (cf. conferentia 1); c**1283** deficit dim. virgata de acra et dim. illius jugi, et suppletur ~us ille .. de dim. virgata que est de M. *Cust. Battle* 123; **1356** pistor, cum inveniatur panis suus de quadra in ~u ponderis ij sol. vel infra, amercietur *MunAcOx* 182; **1410** ~us redditus: in ~u redditus terre Willelmi Stronge tracte in dominicum, per annum ij s. *Crawley* 295. **b** nati fuerant ei [Lud] duo filii .., qui ob ~um etatis regnum tractare nequivissent *Eul. Hist.* II 249. **c 1244** in .. diocesi tua multi consistunt ~um natalium patientes .. prelaturas et beneficia obtinentes *Mon. Hib. & Scot.* 43a. **d 690** (13c) ut ibi servienctium Deo preces protelentur atque pro vita mea sine ~u in conspectu Dei effundantur *CS* 41; **933** sciat se .. flammis sine ~u periturum *CS* 694. **e** dicunt .. lunam .. aliquando obscurari nullumque aliud sidus taliter eclipsim, hoc est ~um sui luminis, pati BEDE *TR* 7 (cf. ib. 27: de magnitudine vel ~u solis sive lunae); quomodo ~us solis et lune notari debeat ADEL. *Elk.* 33; J. SAL. *Pol.* 418C (v. coaptare 4b). **f** *Ps.*-GROS. *Gram.* 69 (v. dilucidus d). **g** c**1218** si .. rector .. domos ecclesie reliquerit dirrutas vel ruinosas, de bonis ejus ecclesiasticis tanta portio deducatur que sufficiat ad .. ~us ecclesie supplendos *Conc. Syn.* 82 (cf. *Reg. Aberd.* II 30); **1311** (v. conducere 2b); *Cust. Cant.* 161 (v. conductarius); **1321** si inveniatur ~us de filo vel textura .., solent ballivi .. hujusmodi ~um nunciare majori London' *PQW* 466b; librorum ~ibus quocies advertuntur est ocius occurrendum, quoniam nihil grandescit cicius quam scissura R. BURY *Phil.* 17. 226; **1359** quod ~us murorum et turellorum .. in locis quibus reparacione et emendacione .. indigent .. reparari et emendari faciatis *RScot* 842a; **1435** ~ubus [vestimentorum] remedium proponere *Reg. Brechin* 67; **1475** (v. conferre 9b).

2 lack, want, absence. **b** loss, hardship, calamity. **c** diminution.

quia [Judith] hoc .. non castitatis ~u fecisse memoratur ALDH. *VirgP* 57; **1188** (v. colorare 3e); s**1213** pro ~u cibariorum jejunavimus *Chr. Evesham* 238; **1238** ostenderunt nobis custodes cambii nostri Cant' quod ~um habebunt custodis unius cuneorum .. per mortem Ade *LTRMem* 12 r. 9d.; **1271** (v. durus 2b); s**1300** non sine magno ~u in esculentis et poculentis *G. Durh.* 48; ne propter ~um mutui colloquii cum amicis suis de non purgando se possit excusare *Proc. A. Kyteler* 37; **1333** [iiij^xx^ acre terre] devenerunt in manum .. comitis ob ~um sanguinis *IMisc (Ir.)* 36/20; **1337** de ~ibus librorum: .. deficit liber qui vocatur 'Logica vetus et nova ..', pro quo respondere habet frater W. de T. *Lit. Cant.* II 146; s**1349** tantus ~us extitit servorum quod non erat quis qui sciret quid facere deberet KNIGHTON II 62; **1417** (v. defectivus 2a); **1451** de ij s. vj d. de gardino marenie de D., quia in manu domini pro ~u tenentis *Ac. Durh.* 189. **b** virginitatis gratia, quae .. numquam ~u dirae mortalitatis marcescit ALDH. *VirgP* 18; non profectum jactando virtutum sed deflendo potius ~um quem sibi per curam pastoralem incurrisse videbatur BEDE *HE* II 1 p. 74 (cf. EADMER *V. Osw.* 23: in nullo sanctitatis opere ~um passus est propter onus sacerdotale); **798** ut, quantum me tristificat absentia illius, tantum vos laetificet praesentia, et ~us meus vester sit profectus ALCUIN *Ep.* 156; Roma .. incendium suum horruit sub Alarico; cotidianos imminentium ruinarum ~us deplorat GERV. TILB. II 17 p. 932; s**1300** priore .. per .. vij dies solo remanente et ~um non modicum paciente *G. Durh.* 48. **c** [rex] sanctus et christus Domini est; .. accepit unctionis regie sacramentum, cujus efficacia .. fidem ejus plenissimam faciet ~us inguinarie pestis et curatio scrophularum P. BLOIS *Ep.* 150.

3 (of persons): **a** (moral) shortcoming, fault, offence. **b** default (in performance of task *etc.*), negligence.

a HWÆTBERHT *Aen.* 4. 3 (v. chelydrus c); **1086** [homines] ad ea quae semper deficiunt, immo ad ipsum ~um, currendo toto affectu non timent ~um; et ad Deum numquam deficientem et suum auxilium promittentem non audent proficere timendo ~um... committe te totum auxilio Dei et non senties ~um in servitio Dei ANSELM (*Ep.* 117) III 253; est ..duplex ~us: primus est corruptionis in corporibus ..; alter est culpe in spiritibus secundum voluntatem HALES *Sent.* I 68; **1239** illum .. haberi Christi vicarium .. indigne fatemur, non ob dignitatis injuriam sed ob persone ~um (*Lit. F. Imp.*) M. PAR. *Maj.* III 586; s**1387** dederat rex duci G... commissionem .. ad inquirendum .. et judicandum de certis ~ibus, et precipue Michaelis atte Pool *Chr. Angl.* 380; **1447** dicunt .. quod Isabella .. fovet male viventes in corpore in domo sua; insuper quod .. est .. intolerabilis objurgatrix; item .. quod Christina .. filia .. Isabelle est in eisdem ~ibus *MunAcOx* 580; **1547** super quorumcumque excessibus, ~ibus, criminibus seu delictis .. ad forum ecclesiaticum spectantibus *Mem. Ripon* I 109. **b 1212** fecit ipse capi xx animalia .. pro ~u servicii domini sui, quod aretro fuit *CurR* VI 210; c**1215** aldermannus in garda sua videat arma singulorum .. et, si quis de armis suis fuerit in ~u, nomen ipsius inrotuletur (*Mun. Lond.*) *EHR* XVII 728; **1219** per ~um ipsorum W. et L., eo quod non reddiderunt firmam que pertinet ad terram illam, amiserunt seisinam *CurR* VIII 78; **1266** debet fieri diligens inquisicio utrum predicte terre jacuerunt vaste per ~um vicecomitis *ExchScot* 31; **1295** ne de negligencia seu deffectu valeatis reprehendi (*Lit. Regis Franc.*) *Doc. Scot.* II 2; **1303** si forte inveniatur ~us in aliquo ballivorum vel ministrorum (*Stat. de Nova Custuma*) *MGL* II 207; **1368** sub pena xl s. solvendorum per illum qui in deffectu reperitur *Hal. Durh.* 74; **1397** cancellus est defectivus in ~u rectoris et vicarii (*Vis. Heref.*) *EHR* XLIV 281; **1434** ad intencionem quod ipse supervideat .. quod celebraciones, soluciones .. et cetera premissa debite .. fiant .. et de ~ubus informet .. decanum .. pro reformacione eorundem *Reg. Cant.* II 594.

4 (leg.): **a** default of justice (by court or official). **b** default by party, suitor, or juror.

a hec sunt jura que rex .. solus .. habet in terra sua .. retenta: .. injustum judicium; ~us justitie; prevaricatio legis regie (*Leg. Hen.* 10. 1) *GAS* 556 (= *Royal Writs* 77: dejectus); c**1180** ne inde amplius clamorem audiam pro ~u recti (*Ch. Hen. II*) ELMH. *Cant.* 449 (cf. HENGHAM *Magna* 1); **1217** ne amplius .. pro ~u seisine ejusdem manerii ei faciende querelam audire debeamus *Pat* 29; **1278** cum ipsi barones in justicia facienda .. defuerint, custos noster .. portus et libertates suos in ~um eorundem ingrediatur ad plenam justiciam faciendam *BBC* (*Cinque Ports*) 178; **1285** super .. statutis in ~um legis et ad remedia editis (2 *Westm.* 47) *StRealm* I 95. **b** saisina .. terre adjudicata est eidem M. in curia mea pro ~u R. teste etc. GLANV. I 17; **1194** terra illa capta fuit in manu domini regis pro ~u ipsius G. *CurR RC* I 9; c**1200** (v. cadere 6a); **1219** saisina .. adjudicata est .. H[uberto] .. per ~um Reginaldi .. *Cl* 386b; **1282** senescallus, .. nolens Willelmum T. [tenentem] .. admittere .., ipsum posuit in ~u ac .. Willelmum C. [petentem] .. judicavit esse in possessionem .. manerii .. racione dicti ~us inducendum *RGasc* II 149; **1302** A... facit ~um versus J... in placito transgressionis (*Andover*) *Gild Merch.* II 298; **1309** ponitur in respectum .. pro ~u juratorum, quia nullus venit *Year Bk. 2 Ed. II* 53; **1439** redditus resolutus .. episcopo Dunelm' .. pro ~u secte curie .., xviij d. *Ac. Durh.* 73.

defed- v. diffoed-. **defencio** v. defensio.

defendere [CL]

1 to defend, protect; **b** (refl.). **c** (w. abstr. or inanim. subj.); **d** (p. ppl. *defensus* as sb. f. or n.) defence.

[sacerdotes] ecclesiasticos .. gradus .. tyrannico ritu acceptos ~entes GILDAS *EB* 66; Deus .. / cum forti famulas dextra defendit inermes ALDH. *VirgV* 2262; non habens scutum ad manum, quo regem a nece ~eret BEDE *HE* II 9; **956** (12c) maneat predictum rus defensum ab omni obstaculo *CS* 963; canes .. ut .. oves .. a lupis ~ant *Simil. Anselmi* 128; **1208** socii .. secundum posse suum wallam totius marisci contra mare ~ent *CurR* V 203; **1101** ad tenendum et ~endum regnum Anglie contra omnes homines *DipDoc* I 1; **1253** debemus .. ipsos [archiepiscopum etc.] in eandem monetam ab omni violentia deffendere *RGasc* I 273 (cf. *CalPat* 248); **1284** J. E. tenet villam de Laxton' per quoddam servicium ad ~endum quatuor comitatus de lupo *Aids* IV 18; **1360** dominus fideles suos subditos tenetur ~ere ac eciam garentire (*TreatyR*) *Foed.* VI 218a; ut demus .. honorem venerabilibus viris digne .. possedentibus et diffendentibus [v. l.: †diffidentibus] nobile regnum Scocie *Plusc. pref.* p. 4. **b** arcem munitam invenies, ut te ~es (*sic*) NEN. *HB* 181; si quis .. Dei judicium offerat quod se ~endo [*ed.* 1972: ~ente] fecerit [homicidium] (*Leg. Hen.* 80. 7b) *GAS* 597; **1203** Robertus, captus pro morte Rogeri .., qui v homines occiderat per insaniam, se ~endo, commissus est vicecomiti *SelPlCrown* 31; **1221** forestarii non potuerunt eum capere vivum et ipse †~idit se contra dominum regem *Ib.* 85; p**1393** J. B... felonice interfecit J. Prechur se deffendendo cum uno daggardo *SelCCoron* 96. **c** ALDH. *VirgV* 2672 (v. caetra b); **12..** (v. causon a). **d 1324** preter servicium et defens[am] wall[arum et] watergang[arum] *IPM* 82/6 r. 2; **1339** nec credimus .. quod arbiter .. rectus .. sic .. torqueat factum nostrum ut, quod nostram fecimus ad ~am [v. l.: †offensam], alterius .. putet injuriam vel offensam (*Lit. E. Regis*) AD. MUR. *Chr.* 97; **1354** guerram resumere nostram compellimur ad ~am *Reg. Exon.* 1159 (= *Conc.* III 34); AMUND. II 213 (v. deperdere 1b); *Ib.* I app. 428 (v. defossare); **1406, 1442** (v. dublettus 1b); c**1453** quesivit an ipse aliquid haberet in se quod sibi cedere posset in tuicionem et ~am *Reg. Whet.* I 111.

2 to warrant (title to) land or sim. *Cf. defensio* 2c.

738 (12c) si quis [hanc donationem] magis ~ere [et] augere voluerit *CS* 159; c**1215** ego et heredes mei hanc meam donationem prefatis monachis garantizare tenemur et ~ere *Cart. Boarstall* 25; c**1270** dictum jus patronatus dictis religiosis contra omnes homines warantizabimus inperpetuum et ~emus *Dryburgh* 9; **1300** Thomas et heredes sui warantizabunt et ~ent .. Radulfo et heredibus suis predictum manerium .. contra omnes homines ... et pro hac recognicione, warrentia, defensione, fine et concordia .. Radulfus concessit .. Thome predictum manerium ad totam vitam ipsius Thome *Reg. S. Thom. Dublin* 492.

3 a to 'defend' (land) as game preserve, or (by enclosure) as plough-land or meadow. **b** (p. ppl. *defensus* as sb. f. or n.) 'defence', (protection as) game preserve. **c** fowling preserve. **d** fishing preserve. **e** (period of) enclosure (of land) for cultivation or hay. *Cf. defensio* 3.

a 1225 post mortem .. regine [Alicie, ob. 1151], invenit .. R. avunculus noster dictum boscum ita defensum et ideo alios afforestavit *Cl* 80b; c**1260** quod possint habere communam cum catallis suis ex orientali parte .. ville .., exceptis bladis seminatis et pratis quando ~i debent *BBC* (*Warton*) 79. **b** rex W. tenet Windesores in dominio... ibi .. silva de l porcis de pasnagio et alia silva missa est in ~o *DB* I 56v.; silva missa est in ~o *Ib.* 176v.; a**1150** si ego meos [porcos] in parco meo vel in haia vel in aliquo alio ~o posuero *MonA* VI 221a; **1182** pasnagium porcis eorum in .. forestis, exceptis deffensis nostris *Act. Hen. II* II 216; c**1200** concedo .. pasturam .. dc ovibus per totam communam .. ville extra divisas .. ~i foreste *Cart. Sallay* 407; a**1210** liceat .. extra ~um meum communionem boscorum meorum habere *BBC* (*Kilkenny*) 56; **1216** ~am nostram (v. bersa a); **1220** ad inquirendum qui .. bosci positi fuerunt .. in ~um *Pat* 258 (cf. *Cl* 434b); **1279** engaranavit terras libere tenencium suorum et eas tenet indefenso (*sic*), ita quod nullus in eis fugare potest quin canes .. capti sint *PQW* 740a; s**1390** dux Lancastrie fecit magnam convocacionem magnatum regni ad venandum apud Leycestriam in foresta et ~a et in omnibus parcis suis ibidem KNIGHTON *Cont.* II 313. **c 1215** foreste .. deafforestentur et ita fiat de ripariis que per nos .. posite sunt in ~o *Magna Carta* 47; **1262** rex concessit .. Reginaldo .. quod riveare possit in ripariis regis que sunt in ~o in com. Suthampt' hac vice de gracia regis speciali *Cl* 164. **d 1200** de troytis captis in ~o nostro aque de Arches per homines .. archiepiscopi [Rotomagensis] *RChart* 59a; **1285** aque .. in quibus salmones capiuntur .. ponantur in ~o quoad salmones capiendos a die Nativitatis B. Marie [8 *Sept.*] usque diem S. Martini [10 *Nov.*] (*Westm.* 47) *StRealm* I 94. **e** a**1222** nullus poterit facere *inhoc* sive ~am in dictis terris sine communi .. assensu utriusque ville *Reg. Malm.* II 221; c**1228** ~um duravit quantum ad averia non pascenda per quindenam ante festum S. J. Baptiste [24 *June*] et per quindenam post *Feod. Durh.* 243; c**1230** si .. dominus poni faciat in ~um aliquam partem pasture sue ad falcandum *Doc. Bec* 41; inventa fuit ista arura ita quod dominus nullum ~um facere deberet in hieme, quod dicitur *wynterhaye Cust. Bleadon* 201; **1268** cum .. J... in ~um posuisset communam pasturam tocius warecte *Cart. Osney* IV 229; c**1280** totam .. terram .. et .. clausturam cum libera communa erbagii et mussi per omnia ~a mea omni tempore anni exceptis pratis meis quando .. in ~o ponuntur *Couch. Furness* II 276; dedi .. herbagium .. extra pratum et racionabiles ~as meas *FormMan* 4; **1308** terras suas vastatas .. in culturam redigere, parvo fossato et bassa haya includere et sic inclusas in ~o tenere *Reg. Winchcombe* I 301; *Meaux* II 220 (v. agistamentum 1); **1310** duo prata .. que sunt in ~o et que in ~o fore decernimus omni tempore anni mansura *Reg. Heref.* 456; **1329** vadiat communitati emendas, eo quod oves sue depascebant pasturam communitatis super S., que est in ~a usque ad tempus [etc.] (*Andover*) *Gild Merch.* II 326.

4 a to 'defend', maintain (land or tenement), be answerable for service or rent due from. **b** (refl.)

to maintain oneself (as tenant). **c** (w. land as subj., usu. refl.) be answerable for, assessed at. **d** (p. ppl. as sb. f.) assessment or assessed land; *cf. defensio* 4.

a 679 [terram] teneas possedeas tu, posterique tui in perpetuum ~ant *CS* 45; **690** (13c) ut teneat possideat ac ipsa semper successoresque ejus . . ~ant *CS* 40; †**799** (13c) [terram] teneatis posideatis, donetis . . vel quicquit exinde facere volueritis, liberam abeatis potestatem successoresque vestri ~ant in perpetuum *CS* 296; in Depbenham duas partes aecclesiae S. Mariae de xx acris habet Robertus ad ~endum *DB* II 305v.; quisquis terram suam juste ~erit [AS: *gewerod hæbbe*] teste comitatu, possideat sine calumnia (*Inst. Cnuti*) *GAS* 367 (= *Quad.*: adquietatam habet); **11..** (v. defensio 4); ~it illam dim. virgatam terre per servicium militis *RDomin* 35; alie xxij *cotsetlandes* sunt ad opera, sc. bubulci, porcarii, bedelli, pastores, claudentes sepes et curantes negotia camerarii; qui omnes ~unt domos et terram suam per tale servitium *Cust. Abingd.* 301; **1220** villanus fuit et terram suam defen[d]it per furcam et flagellum *CurR* IX 109 (= *BNB* III 374; †defendidit); *Leg. IV Burg.* 1 (v. 2 burgagium c); **1279** J. . . tenuit et ~it j hydam *Hund.* II 656a; **1387** impotens est predictam terram et tenementum manutenere et ~ere versus dominum (*CourtR Wilburton*) *EHR* IX 424. **b** **1211** R. serviens et E. prepositus r. c. de x li. xij d., preter iiij carucarios, j fabrum, j porcarium, ij bercarios, iij operatores, qui se ~unt per operationes suas *Pipe Wint.* 16 (= *Crawley* 196). **c** W. tenet dim. jugum, quod jacuit in gilda de Dovere et modo ~it se cum terra Osberti *DB* I 11v.; de hac terra tenet Ricardus R. viij hidas, quae pro iij hidis se defend[unt] modo *Ib.* 56v.; Bedeford T. R. E. pro dim. hundredo se ~ebat; terra de hac villa nunquam fuit hidata *Ib.* 209; **1138** manerium . ., quod se pro j hida ~ebat *Regesta* 132; terra sua . ., que se ~it pro feodo dim. militis, valet . . c s. *RDomin* 36; **c1200** preter hec sunt quedam terre que libero censu se ~unt et sunt sine opere *Chr. Battle* f. 21; **a1222** j hyda in W. que se ~it per militare servitium *Reg. Malm.* II 6; **1236** tria molendina . . reddunt pro mutura vj s. vj d. . . et ~unt se pro iij jugis in donis faciendis domino *Cust. Battle* 128; **1238** (v. bedellaria a); **c1250** villata de B. ~it (*sic*) versus regem pro x hydis et versus abbatem pro xj hydis et dim. *Cart. Rams.* I 475. **d** **1181** fuerunt ij hyde apud L. quarum una fuit in dominio, altera assisa; et fuit in defensa xl s. de Sandon' versus regem et reddebat canonicis j firmam plenam; modo defendebat (*sic*) se versus regem pro dim. m. et reddit modo canonicis xl s. *Dom. S. Paul.* 141.

5 a (refl.) to assert in defence of one's own opinion. **b** to defend by argument, maintain; **c** (acad.).

a 680 sacerdotes . . tonsuram S. Petri . . refutantes seque tali excusationis apologia pervicaciter ~entes . ., quod . . ALDH. *Ep.* 4. **b** qui de veritate sunt certi et qui . . approbant, et quam parati essent usque ad mortem ~ere OCKHAM *Pol.* III 263; S. Thomas . . ipsam [descripcionem simonie] approbat et declarat; hinc dicitur quod sensus descripcionis est catholice deffendendus WYCL. *Sim.* 14; **s1401** (v. degradare 1b); **s1457** si . . opiniones meas et posiciones ~ero, mors mihi est et ignis combustio. si vero non ~ero, incidam in linguis hominum *Reg. Whet.* I 284. **c** **1549** responsor tres ad minus theseis (*sic*) . . pronunciabit ea forma verborum qua velit eas ~ere *StatOx* 347; **1556** *Ib.* 372 (v. 3 casus 6).

6 (leg.): **a** (refl.) to defend oneself (against accusation or claim). **b** to defend (client or action) as advocate. **c** (w. *quod*) to assert in defence; *cf.* 7b *infra*.

a cum praesentibus accusatoribus acciperet locum se ~endi BEDE *HE* V 19 p. 166; qui . . inde accusatus fuerit per xl homines se ~it *DB* I 179; si Francigena compellet Anglicum per bellum . ., Anglicus . . ~at se [AS: *hine werige*] per bellum vel per judicium (*Quad., Inst. Will.*) *GAS* 484; [appellatus] ~et se per judicium aque vel ignis [OF: *s'en defende par juise*] (*Leis Will.*) *Ib.* 502; **1202** ~at se xij manu in adventu justiciariorum *SelPlCrown* 27; **1209** adjudicatum est ei ut ~at se secundum assisam foreste *SelPlForest* 5; **1209** si . . forisfactor . . factum negaverit et forestarius solus sit sine teste, ille debet se ~ere unica manu *Cart. Osney* V 95; [accusatus] habebit electionem utrum se velit ponere super patriam . . vel ~endi se per corpus suum BRACTON 137 (cf. ib. 142b: in his casibus . . tenetur quis se ~ere per patriam); **1269** consideratum est . . quod, quia bene se ~ebat, legitime deberet legem †inculpandi [? l. inculpati] vadiare *CBaron* 74. **b** [procurator] debet vicem ejus quem ~it obtinere. . . si autem non ~it, intelligitur dominus non defensus RIC. ANGL. *Summa* 20; militant . . etiam patroni causarum, qui . . laborantium spem vitamque ~unt W. DROGHEDA *SA* 33; **1275** idem W. pro iiij s. argenti manucepit secundum posse suum ~ere statum predicti Simonis, ne de suo corpore haberet vituperium et periculum, ita tamen quod idem S. se non subtraheret de querela *SelPlMan* 156; **s1330** (v. 2 causa 1a); **1345** cum . . sentencia lata fuerit . . Herefordensi ecclesia non deffensa preter sui culpam set ob culpam . . procuratoris *Reg. Heref.* 74; **1549** ne . . in foro ecclesie causas vel intendendas vel ~endas temere suscipiant *Conc. Scot.* II 121. **c** volunt ~ere per sacramentum . . quod ille . . liber homo fuit *DB* I 44v.

7 (leg.) to deny, rebut (accusation or claim). **b** (w. acc. & inf. or *quod*) to assert by way of rebuttal; *cf.* 6c *supra*. **c** (p. ppl. as sb. n.) rebuttal; *cf. defensio* 7. **d** (pr. ppl. as sb. or w. *pars*) defendant.

1199 A. venit et ~it omnem servitutem et dicit quod debet tenere . . terram per servicium x s. per annum *CurR RC* II 25; **1199** fratres Milicie Templi venerunt et ~unt jus abbacie *CurR* I 84; W. venit et ~it totum de verbo in verbum, si versus feminam et suniantam *Ib.* 100; **1200** J. dicit quod nullam summonicionem habuit respondendi, et ~it summonicionem; et prius ~it feloniam et roberiam *Ib.* 179; **1241** ego ~o feloniam vel latrocinium et quicquid super me dicitur *BBC* (*Newport*) 205; **1243** si quis alium appellaverit de tollagio coram vicecomitibus et culpatus non ~erit †nominatum [? l. nominatim] tollagium, quamvis ~eret de verbo in verbum, erit in misericordia vicecomitis quia non ~it tollagium et ad defensionem erga clamivum *MGL* I 115; **1248** veniunt et ~unt plenarie *SelPlMan* 8; **1275** sufficienter non responderunt ad incopamentum nec ~erunt verba que fuerint ~enda *Ib.* 147; si negaverit et crimen ~erit precise BRACTON 137; vadiat summonitus legem et ~at summonitionem per legem contra testificationem summonitorum *Ib.* 344b; J. . . ~it . . omnem mutacionem cujuslibet inrotulamenti, omnem facturam cujuslibet falsi brevis, omnem recepcionem denariorum ad hoc faciendum *State Tri. Ed. I* 43. **b** **1166** W. de W. [debet] iiij milites et dimidium; et preter hoc ex testimonio curie mee dimidium exigo, quem ipse se non debere ~it *RBExch* 186; **1201** ~it quod non est homo ejus nec unquam ei homagium fecit *SelPlCrown* 43; **1218** Emma venit et ~it quod numquam in viduitate sua fecit cartas illas *Eyre Yorks* 46; **1221** ~it quod nullum servicium ei a retro fuit *PlCrGlouc* 25; **1257** ~unt ipsi vim et injuriam et quod per ipsos non est mutatus modus talliandi *Leg. Ant. Lond.* 33. **c** de clamio petentis et de defenso tenentis . . curia ipsa suum recordum habebit GLANV. VIII 9; **s1263** rex Francie, propositis et defensis ac racionibus parcium plenius intellectis, protulit dictum suum *Flor. Hist.* II 486 (= *Ann. Lond.* 60). **d** **c1228** placita . . de arsona inter G. de B. appellantem et W. G. ~entem *Feod. Durh.* 218; **1269** ad legem vadiandam oportet ~entem offerre se facturum contra querentem et ejus sectam *CBaron* 84; **1285** legi . . que non permisit placitum aliquod poni coram justiciariis ad peticionem ~entis (2 *Westm.* 1) *StRealm* I 72; inter Thomam . . et Amiciam . . querentes et Nicholaum . . ~entem *State Tri. Ed. I* 84; si non venerit pars ~ens ad quartum diem, pars conquerens recuperabit . . damna taxata *Quon. Attach.* 4; **s1451** dicit quod ipse per aliqua per predictum ~entem placitata ab accione sua . . habenda precludi non debet *Reg. Whet.* I 63.

8 a (w. dat.) to deny, refuse. **b** to obstruct, prevent the enjoyment of.

a **1101** nec naves ~entur eis, si eas convenienter conducere voluerint *DipDoc* I 1; querat accusatus consilium et habeat ab amicis et parentibus suis, quod nulli jure debet ~i (*Leg. Hen.* 46. 4) *GAS* 570. **b** si quis aliquam aecclesiasticarum rectitudinum armis ~erit [AS: *forwyrne*], x s. . . emendet (*Inst. Cnuti*) *Ib.* 345 (= *Quad.* ib: prohibeat).

9 to prohibit, forbid, ban; **b** (w. neg. clause). **c** (p. ppl. *defensus* as sb. n.) prohibition; *cf. defensio* 8.

a1200 Walingefordenses . . insistebant ut regis assensum de foro ~endo adquirerent. . . rex . . precepit quidem interim mercatum ~i preter parva venalia. . . illi vero, accepta potestate a fori defensione abstinuerunt *Chr. Abingd.* II 227; **1212** quod omnes scotalle ~antur *MGL* II 86; **1279** anno regni regis Edwardi septimo defensa fuit †pratarum [MS: pratorum] falcacio *CalIMisc* I 1170; *RBExch* 997 (v. 1 billio a); **1300** predicti x s. fuerunt *pollard* et *crokard*, qui ~ebantur cito post recepcionem *Rec. Leic.* I 228; usuram Dominus defendit lege perhenni GOWER *VC* V 719. **b** **c1070** ~o ne aliquis de prefato jure ecclesie prescripte aliquid auferat vel minuat *Regesta* p. 120; **c1080** constanter ~o . . ut nullus amplius super hoc ei injusticiam faciat *Ib.* p. 125; **1101** neque ~am ei [baroni meo] quin eam [filiam suam] det, excepto si eam vellet jungere inimico meo (*Ch. Hen. I*) *GAS* 521; **s1119** quibus [episcopis] rex preceperat ut ~erent Eboracensi electo . . ne ab apostolico consecrationem acciperet H. CANTOR 18; **1184** ~it [rex] quod nullus ei forisfaciat de venatione sua nec de forestis in ulla re (*Ass. Foreste* 1) *G. Hen. II* I 323; **1231** debent principes qui eos [Judeos] tenent captivos ne occidantur ~ere et insimul ne Christianos usuris opprimant sevissime prohibere GROS. *Ep.* 5 p. 34; **c1285** monetam defensam ne reciperetur (v. denarius 4b); **1436** proclamari faciatis et ~i quod nullus extraneus . . bona seu mercandisas quecumque de partibus Flandrie in regnum nostrum . . adducat (*Cl*) *Foed.* X 654b. **c** **1212** servientes . . Walteri . . prohibuerunt ex parte . . regis quod nemo inde aliquid amoveret. . . et . . Walterus . . conquestus fuit de . . Ricardo et Alano T. quod . . asportaverunt catalla super ~um injuste *CurR* VI 293; **c1220** quatenus literas domini regis . . domino Lincolniensi et domino abbati de D. directas de ~o, quod non procedant de feodo laicali . ., nobis . . habere faciatis (*AncC* I 84) *RL* 161; **1263** vos, non obstante predicta carta, contra . . abbatem tanquam in ~um procedentes, . . communam . . priori adjudicastis . . contra tenorem carte nostre *Cl* 302; **1290** rex concessit et revocat ad voluntatem suam ~um suum quod prius inde fecit *RParl* I 50b.

10 (p. ppl. as sb.) (?) *f. l.*

1330 quo waranto clam[et] . . habere visum franciplegii . . et ponere eos in †defens' [? l. desenis, i.e. decenis] qui ponendi sunt *PQW* 583b.

defensa v. defendere 1d, 3b, 3e, 4d.

defensabilis, ~ibilis [LL = *that can be defended*]

1 fencible, fit for armed service: **a** (of men); **b** (of ships).

a in singulis trium [navium erant] homines ~abiles et victualia DEVIZES 33 p. 35; rex . ., cum . . per universas suarum partium partas munitiones viros ~abiles disposuisset *Ib.* 43 p. 84; **1213** debent . . escavingores eligi, qui . . videant illos qui debent de nocte vigilare, quod sint homines ~ibiles et decenter ad hoc armati *Comm. Lond.* 255; **1284** (v. attilliator); **1309** electis navibus illis easdem . . hominibus ~abilibus et ad arma potentibus muniri faciatis *RScot* 78a; **1312** cum . . ordinatum fuisset . . quod . . constabularius castri nostri [Dublin'] . . haberet in sua comitiva xij homines ~abiles *Doc. Ir.* 302; **1315** magnates et communitas regni concesserunt regi in auxilium guerre sue Scocie de qualibet villa in regno unum hominem peditem potentem et ~ibilem *RParl* I 351a; **1418** assignamus vos . . ad clerum vestre provincie, tam religiosos quam seculares, ydoneos et ~ibiles . . competenter arraiandum (*Pat*) *Reg. Heref.* 32 (= *Foed.* IX 601a: ~abiles); **c1422** mando . . quod venire facias . . omnes gentes ~ibiles villate tue inter etates xvj annorum et lx existentes . . competenter armatos et arraiatos . . et quod tunc sis ibidem . . habens . . nomina omnium hominum ~abilium villate tue *Treat. J. P.* 271; **1511** (v. arraiare 1a). **b** **1255** duas galyas bonas, grandes . . ac ~abiles *RGasc* I sup. 26; [V Portus] se . . regi Johanni obligaverunt invenire, quando . . rex habeat necessitatem de eis, . . lxxx naves ~abiles . . per xl dies KNIGHTON I 198 (= *Meaux* I 341: naves defensales).

2 (of weapons) defensive; *v. et. defensalis* 2. **b** (as sb. n.) defensive weapon.

1386 pro gonnis, springaldis, et aliis rebus ~abilibus . . ordinandis *RR K's Lynn* II 27. **b** **c1290** forisfacturam omnium gladiorum et aliorum ~ibilium *Entries* 425; **1472** quod nullus [presumat] . . cultellum, gestrum, vel aliud ~ibile trahere infra ecclesiam aut cimiterium (*Vis.*) *Fabr. York* 255.

3 a (of house) fortified. **b** (of buildings or sim.) proof, affording protection.

a haec terra . . in medio cujusdam silvae est posita, et ibi est domus una ~abilis *DB* I 184v. **b** †**1189** (14c) ita quod . . domus remaneat secura et ~ibilis contra sevitiam ignis advenientis (*Assisa Aedific.*) *MGL* I 329; **c1220** debent facere quandam gutteriam plumbeam super murum meum tam michi . . quam sibi . . acceptabilem et ~abilem *Cart. Osney* II 122; **c1300** shopum et solarium . . contra ventum et pluviam ~ibilia facient *FormA* 118; contra ventum et pluviam quoddam tenementum . . reparabunt . . et . . ~ibile facient *Entries* 136.

4 (of land) enclosed. *V. et. defensalis* 3. *Cf. defendere* 3e.

1267 sunt ibi xxiiij bovate de terris ~abilibus *IMisc* (*Cumb*) 14/10.

defensabiliter, ~ibiliter [LL], defensibly, so as to afford defence.

1587 locumtenentem et gubernatorem generalem subditorum nostrorum tam peditum quam equitum ~ibiliter armatorum *Pat* 1320 m. 7d.

defensaculum [LL], defence; **b** (w. gen. of thing warded off).

ardentis fidei ~o fretus ALDH. *VirgP* 28; latibulum, ~um *GlC* L 74; certabat fratrum devotio . . ~a speciali principi suo parare Augustino GOSC. *Transl. Aug.* 16c; exterius ad ~um medullaris substantie constituitur tereum, ut est cortex et testa GILB. VII 283. 1; *a defendynge*, . . defensio, ~um, munimen *CathA*. **b** ad ~um nocumenti extrinsecus advenientis *Ps.*-RIC. *Anat.* 42.

defensalis

1 (of men) fencible. *V. et. defensabilis* 1a.

1316 assignavimus vos ad communitatem populi nostri . . viz. omnes homines ~es inter etates xvj et lx annorum . . contra . . inimicos nostros . . levand' *RScot* 160a; **1319** homines pedites ~es et ad arma potentes *Ib.* 196b; **1335** quod . . nos . . de nominibus hominum . . armis ferreis armandorum ac de numero residuorum hominum ~ium de Northtrithingo . . reddatis cerciores *Cl* 156 m. 33d.; **s1385** ex omni parte Anglie de omni genere hominum ~ium ad eum multitudo . . confluebat *V. Ric. II* 61.

2 (of moat) defensive. *V. et. defensabilis* 2.

c1430 reformetur et fiat ~is more solito . . fossa premissa AMUND. I app. 430.

3 enclosed. *V. et. defensabilis* 4. *Cf. defendere* 3e.

1235 homines predicti Ade . . qui terram ~em de predicto Ada . . tenebunt habeant communam pasture in Schotton [*Northumb*] *Fines* 180/4/55.

defensamen, defence.

1438 ad vestre oratricis munimen perpetuum, hujus regni felix regimen et ecclesie catholice ~en *EpAcOx* 168.

defensare [CL]

1 to defend, protect; **b** (refl.); **c** (w. abstr. obj.); **d** (w. abstr. subj.).

defensante Deo sacrasque tuente puellas Aldh. *VirgV* 2240; **9.**. ~ante, *gescyldendum WW*; his defensor erat .., qui .. relictos inermes, quos ~aret, gladiis exposuit Gosc. *Aug. Maj.* 79A; multis diebus in ~ando [fossam subterraneam] frustra consumptis Osb. Bawdsey clxix; ut eam [insulam] contra regem W. .. ~aret *G. Herw.* 328b; **s1257** [archiepiscopus] Rofensis ecclesie .. invasit possessiones, quas potius ~are et tueri tenebatur M. Par. *Maj.* V 615. **b** qui cum sepius bello lacessiti se et suos ~arent fortiter Abbo *Edm.* 1; viriliter .. sese ~are *G. Steph.* II 94. **c** ad ~anda virtutum spiritalium perstabat castra Bede *Sam.* 524; tunc certe sunt acies virtutum in tuto, si istius clypei fuerint ~ate presidio H. Bos. *Thom.* II 6; Salvatoris clementia .. suum dignata est .. servum signo .. insignire quo .. illius contra probra infamancium .. ~aret honorem *V. Har.* 11 f. 14; virtus impugnacionis .. quam impugnatores .. ~are nituntur Ockham *Pol.* I 300; **a1434** pro juribus istius ecclesie ~andis *Stat. Linc.* I 15. **d** fuit difficillimum, quos ea natura loci maxime ~abat, expugnare W. Poit. I 25.

2 **a** (leg.) to defend, plead (a cause); **b** (absol.). **c** to defend by argument, maintain, justify.

a ut .. Romam pro sua ~anda causa pergerent W. Malm. *GP* III 109; **a1350** si .. pars rea contra formam venerit, .. habebitur [causa] pro non ~ata *StatOx* 91. **b** **802** postulantes, episcopo veniente, locum ~andi et disputandi cum eo Alcuin *Ep.* 245 p. 394. **c** non ausus ~are quod antea senseras Lanfr. *Corp. & Sang.* 411D; fraudes et mendacia ~amus Serlo Gram. *Mon. Font.* 19; propter asserciones catholicas, que erant a summis pontificibus catholice definite, approbate et ~ate Ockham *Pol.* III 298; hereses que sunt hodie per Antichristi discipulos publice deffensate Wycl. *Sim.* 68; quid est quod vos in tantam alienacionem incurritis ut hujuscemodi velitis ~are? Chaundler *Apol.* 24b.

defensatio [LL], defence; **b** (doctrinal).

illis [gentilium populis] pro idolorum ~one certantibus Bede *Sam.* 524; **802** ut rei et peccatores .. loca ~onis debuissent habere Alcuin *Ep.* 245 p. 397. **b** **1425** articulos .. pertinaciam et heresim in adhesione, sustentacione, et ~one ipsius dogmatizacionis erronee sufficienter concludentes *Reg. Cant.* III 127 (= *Conc.* III 443).

defensator [LL], defender (of doctrine).

omnis assercio, cujus pertinax ~or est vere hereticus, est vere heresis Ockham *Dial.* 420.

defensatrix [LL], defender (f.).

†**811** (12c) vexillum sanctae crucis .. ad hoc conquisivi ut animae meae .. contra tumultum pravorum tutatrix atque ~ix .. permansisset *CS* 338; **1399** ipsa [B. V. M.] .. nostrum omnium ~ix *Conc.* III 246b.

2 (leg.) defendant (fig.).

s1459 ab equa libracione cause litigialis inter actricem Justiciam et ~icem Misericordiam dependentis *Reg. Whet.* I 337.

defensibilis, ~**iter** v. defensabilis, ~iter.

defensio [CL]

1 defence, protection; **b** (of the realm or sim.); **c** (w. ref. to *burhbote*); **d** (w. ref. to self-defence); **e** (w. gen. of thing warded off). **f** means of defence.

de ~one itemque vastatione Gildas *EB* 2; explicare .. qualia S. Adelwoldus sustinuerit pro monachorum ~one pericula Wulf. *Æthelwold* 37; homicidium .. fit etiam pro ~one et justitia (*Leg. Hen.* 72. 1b) *GAS* 590; terra .. ventis exposita nullam .. solidi obstaculi ~onem habet Gir. *TH* I 6; **1257** quod omnes tenentes terras .., qui ~onem et salvationem habent per wallias et fossata maris, distringas ad wallias et fossata illa .. sustinenda *Cl* 281; **1293** †forsatum [MS: fossatum] .. levatum .. pro ~one et salvacione parcium istarum contra aquarum inundaciones (*Pat* 112 m. 11) *OED* s. v. *powdike*; **c1381** (v. catholicus 2a); inter has varias oppugnacionum et ~onum molestias *G. Hen. V* 6. **b** in patriae ~onibus *GAS* 532 (v. celebrare 1c); **c1128** omnia dona predicta .. quiete .. concedo .., ~one regni mei excepta et justitia regali *E. Ch. Scot.* 74; **c1230** quod non vadant .. ad exercitum nisi .. ad communem ~onem terre nostre (*Ch. Haverfordwest*) *EHR* XV 519; **1378** domino nostro regi in subsidium ~onis regni *Ac. Durh.* 181. **c** **770** terram liberam .. a cunctis operibus .. regis .. [praeter instructio]nibus pontium vel .. ~onibus arcium contra hostes *CS* 203 (cf. ib. 178). **d** **1366** Thomas W. in sua defencione vertebatur et Thomam H. percussit cum uno cultello *SelCCoron* 53; **1464** Willielmus .. contra suam voluntatem sed in ~onem sui corporis .. percussit .. Johannem *Sanct. Durh.* 1; **1476** sciatis me .. quemdam magistrum J. W. .. a commissis absolvisse .. et super irregularitate in homicidio commisso casuali, quam in ipsius defencione incurrebat, .. dispensasse *Reg. Whet.* II 247. **e** quidam sapientes dixerunt quod defendere hominem ab istis accidentibus potius spectabat ad decorationem quam ad ~onem infirmitatum Bacon IX 82. **f** **793** castigatio fortior est ~o quam sagittarum collectio et morum emendatio quam armorum congregatio Alcuin *Ep.* 21; Anselm III 10 (v. corpus 7b); **s1187** Salaadinus .. urbem obsidet. .. cives quas possunt ~ones objiciunt Wend. I 142.

2 **a** protection (feud.). **b** (?) territory under protection. **c** support, warranty (of title); *cf. defendere* 2.

a quaedam femina tenuit T. R. E. et potuit ire quo voluit; pro ~one sub abbatia se misit *DB* I 32v.; quidam liber homo hanc terram tenet ..; summisit se in manu Walterii pro ~one sui *Ib.* 36. **b** **c1113** dedi eis [monachis] omnes ecclesias non vacantes totius ~onis mee in quibus jus advocationis habeam (*Ch. R. de Candos*) *MonA* VI 1022a. **c** tu mihi promisisti sanum et mundum quod mihi vendidisti et plenam ~onem [AS: *fulle ware*] contra omnem postlocucionem (*Quad.*) *GAS* 399; **1196** Petrus .. et Rogerus .. dicunt quod tenent j virgatam terre de terra quam Eudo .. clamat versus Radulfum ..; et non ponent terram suam super ~onem Radulfi *CurR* I 17; **c1240** si forte pro defectu waran[tiza]tionis, acquietationis et ~onis mee vel heredum dicti canonici dampnum .. incurrerint *Cart. Osney* IV 503; in carta componenda .. primo ponendum est nomen donantis .. et statim postponi debet nomen recipientis. .. tercio ponitur res data. .. redditus eciam debet poni, pariter defencio, testimonium, cera, et data *FormMan* 1; **1300** (v. defendere 2); **c1311** pro hac concessione, tradicione, dimissione, warantia et defencione dedit michi .. ix m. *Deeds Balliol* 51; **c1350** cum warantizatione et ~one *Melrose* II app. 22.

3 **a** 'defence' (of land), reservation as game preserve. **b** 'defence' of fishery (during close season). **c** 'defence', seasonal enclosure or reservation (of ploughland or meadow). *V. et. defensus* 2, *cf. defendere* 3.

a omnes hae hidae wastae sunt. de his ix hidis una pars est in castellaria Alvredi Ewias et altera pars in ~one regis *DB* I 181v.; **1156** in eadem ~one de vasto et venacione facias esse .. forestas in qua fuerunt .. tempore H. regis avi mei *Act. Hen. II* I 109; **1267** in mense defenc' (v. donum 3b). **b** **c1394** dictus A. cum retibus suis tempore defencionis salmonum, viz. a festo Nativitatis B. M. V. [8 *Sept.*] usque diem S. Martini [11 *Nov.*], salmones, †salminiculos [? l. salmunculos] et fructus salmonum cepit .. et cum fructibus salmonum .. sic captorum porcos suos pavit cotidie durantibus defencionibus (*Anc. Indict.*) *Pub. Works* II 259. **c** **s1189** cum .. abbas de C. mariscum suum posuisset in ~one, sicut singulis annis fieri solet circa Rogationes, et acclamatum esset publice super pontem de Spalding' ut Hoilandenses et alii averia sua retinerent ab introitu marisci ut fenum posset liberius †esse [v. l. crescere], noluerunt ipsi *Croyl. Cont. B* 454 (cf. *Eng. Justice* 156); **1282** R. de H. in misericordia pro ovibus attachiatis in defencione; plegius messor *CourtR* (*Wilts*) 209/59 m. 7; **a1295** post messionem segetum .. usque ad tempus ~onis, viz. ad Purificacionem B. Marie [2 *Feb.*] *BBC* (*Tenby*) 84; **1301** quod mariscus ponatur in ~onem a die Annunciacionis B. Marie usque ad Ascencionem Domini, ita quod nulli porci nec alie bestie ibidem intrent (*Andover*) *Gild Merch.* II 296.

4 'defence', assessment of land (for service or rent) or land so assessed. *Cf. defendere* 4d.

a1130 in Scegla Henricus de A. [tenet] ij car[ucatas], que pertinent ad ~onem de Swepeston' (*Surv. Leic.*) *Feudal Eng.* 201 (cf. ib. 117); **11.**. teneant illam terram in liberam .. elemosinam absolutam ab omni .. terrena exactione, nisi quod monachi defendent eam infra iiij bancos hundredi per ~onem x et viij acrarum *Cart. Colch.* 171 (cf. *EHR* X 732); **1196** in perpetuam .. elemosinam quietam de .. omnibus .. consuetudinibus, exceptis danageldis per ~onem x acrarum *Fines P. Hen. II & Ric. I* 113.

5 defence by argument (doctrinal), assertion.

Terentio, qui .. prologos .. in ~onem sui velut apologiticos scenis dabat Aldh. *Met.* 10 p. 90; apologia, †defentio *GlC* A 679; propter .. manifestam ~onem damnabilium heresum et errorum Ockham *Pol.* III 320.

6 (leg. or sim.) defence (of accused party).

Bede *HE* III 19 (v. accusatio a); **1201** Petrus [appellatus] defendit totum .. ut liber civis Lincolnie; et, si non poterit habere ~onem per libertatem ville, offert defendere se per corpus suum *CurR* I 425; ad officium ejus [advocati] pertinet lapsa erigere, fatigata reparare, sue ~onis viribus W. Drogheda *SA* 33; si [accusatus] patriam elegerit, ad ~onem per corpus suum ex penitentia reverti non poterit Bracton 137; potest esse quod coheredes rem suam .. per judicium vel per malam ~onem amiserint Hengham *Parva* 8 p. 68; **1333** pars adversa emisit protestacionem quod contra nos .. suas justas diffenciones haberet *Lit. Cant.* II 17; **a1350** reus per se suam afferat ~onem *StatCantab* 323; **1549** explorent .. quo jure tam actio quam ~o nitatur *Conc. Scot.* II 121.

7 (leg.) rebuttal. *Cf. defendere* 7c.

1243 (v. defendere 7a); **1297** Isabella .. ~oni placiti quod est .. inter Elyam B. petentem et ipsam I. tenentem .. ad presens vacare non potest *RScot* 38b.

8 prohibition. *Cf. defendere* 9c.

c1080 precipio ut nullus super ~onem meam de illis terris aliquam calumpniam ei faciat *Regesta* I p. 125; **1102** ii qui insulam adipisci pridem cupierant .. ~onis obstaculum ibi instituere .. disponebant *Ib.* II no. 565 (= *Chr. Abingd.* II 51); **1167** H. G. r. c. de x m. pro molendino firmato super ~onem regis *Pipe* 178; **c1180** prohibeo firmiter ne quis in terra mea eorum [burgensium de Moravia] namum aliter capiat super meam plenariam ~onem *Regesta Scot.* 176; **c1206** *Ib.* 475 (v. contra 4c); †**1189** (14c) defendatur ne amplius edificant (*sic*); et, si ultra ~onem .. edificaverint, prisone mancipentur (*Assisa Aedific.*) *MGL* I 320; **a1200** (v. defendere 9a); **1224** posuit se idem B. in terram illam super ~onem domini regis pluries ei factam *CurR* XI 2761; **1300** breve de ~one domini regis ad emend' lanam .. nisi pro sterlingis *Rec. Leic.* I 234.

defensitare [CL], to defend.

monachi .. sese prout poterant ~abant, adversarios a choro propellentes W. Malm. *Glast.* 78; causam ~abat seseque .. immunem esse .. affirmabat Alex. Cant. *Mir.* 28 (I) p. 215.

defensive, defensively.

1457 sagittarii .. sint ~e arriati *Lit. Cant.* III 228 (v. arraiare 1a).

defensivus

1 defensive, protective: **a** (of arms); **b** (of a doublet or corslet); **c** (of fortifications or sim.); **d** (of ointment); **e** (of a leader).

a **1322** etc. (v. 2 arma 1c); **1369** rex .. necessitatur .. contra ipsorum [Francorum] violentiam et aggressus arma ~a resumere *Pri. Cold.* 39; **1403** quod arcus, sagittas, gladios, et omnia et singula arma et armaturas .. tam invasiva quam ~a vobis sursum reddant (*Pat*) *Foed.* VIII 331b; **1514** in expensis factis in armis ~is et equis cum victualibus et cariagiis versus regem Scottorum *Ac. Durh.* 662. **b** **1426** lego R. C. militi unum meum diploidem longum de velveto ~um *Reg. Cant.* II 362; **1451** loricis, deploidibus ~is [etc.] armati *Pat* 473 m. 16; **1460** (v. bomblastus); **1476** quod nulla persona .. gerat arma, viz. duploida, †defensum [MS: duploid' defensivum], gladium *March. S. Wales* 86; **1573** modo guerrino armati et arraiati, viz. .. gladiis .., loricis ~is, equis armatis, duploidis .. ac aliis armaturis *Pat* 1106 m. 24. **c** portus munitur claudentibus undique muris / cum defensivis turribus ante sitis Elmh. *Metr. Hen. V* 274; villulam .. ipsam menium summitas ~a tuetur *Ps.*-Elmh. *Hen. V* 85; **14.**. fossa ~a (v. defossare). **d** cura est primo, quousque ulcus carne repleatur, inungere labia ulceris .. cum unguento ~o Gad. 125. 1. **e** **s1187** baliste petrarieque, immo etiam clipeus, lorica, lancea et galea, effectu carent quia capite carent ~o M. Par. *Min.* I 443.

2 (as sb. f.) **a** (pl.) defences, musters. **b** fence.

a **s1153** [Stephanus] antiqua regni privilegia restaurare proponit. .. ~e locorum seu vicecomites locis statuentur statutis Diceto *YH* I 297; **s1198** in marchia principales ~e locorum prope munitionem illam que vocatur Castellum Matildis ad pugnam accincti (*sic*) concurrerunt hostiliter *Ib.* II 163. **b** **1585** preceptum .. est Johanni F. .. sufficienter facere ~am suam inter Johannem S. et seipsum *DL CourtR* 119/1838 m. 2d.

defensor [CL]

1 defender, protector. **b** guard-dog.

mox dedit auxilium clemens defensor egentum Aldh. *VirgV* 1764; horum [monachorum] plurimi .. orandi causa convenerant, habentes ~orem .. qui eos .. a barbarorum gladiis protegeret Bede *HE* II 2; Eadredus qui erat .. cenobii .. specialis amator atque ~or Wulf. *Æthelwold* 10; Neckam *Ut.* 104 (v. cataracta 1d); viri in parochia potentes, primo tanquam economi seu potius ecclesiarum patroni et ~ores a clero constituti Gir. *IK* II 4; Map *NC* III 2 (v. decantare 5b); **s1384** castrum esse omnino ~oribus .. destitutum Fordun *Cont.* XIV 47. **b** [villatici] per itinera dominis in praesidio sunt, quos a furibus defendunt; a qua re etiam canes ~ores jure dici possunt Caius *Can.* 8.

2 **a** warrantor (of title); *cf. defendere* 2. **b** tenant answerable for service or rent due from land; *cf. defendere* 4.

a Ranulfus P. calumpniatur hidam et xviij acras que jacent ad ecclesiam hujus manerii ..; et Ingelricus non fuit saisitus; set comes E. dedit cuidam suo militi, unde revocat †eam [? l. eum] ad ~orem *DB* (*Essex*) II 31v.; Newetona ten[ebat] j libera femina. .. hoc manerium fuit ad censum in ministerium Godrici pro xxx s.; sed G. non habuit eos, quia revocat ipsa regem addefensorem *Ib.* (*Norf*) II 125. **b** ipse R. tenet in B. j virgatam terre, cujus .. medietas est regis ..; sed R. eandem partem regis invasit et se ~orem facit *Ib.* (*Staffs*) I 249.

3 defender (of doctrine). **b** (w. *Fidei*) title bestowed on Henry VIII by Pope Leo X in 1521.

acerrimus veri Paschae ~or Bede *HE* III 25 p. 181; **9.**. ~or, adserto[r] *WW*; approbatores et ~ores illius constitutionis .. in qua .. erratur contra fidem .. sunt in hereticorum numero computandi Ockham *Pol.* III 271; *Ib.* I 327 (v. assertor a). **b** **1523** cum .. nobis significatum esset serenissimum .. regem .. a .. pontifice maximo .. Christianissimae fidei ~orem .. fuisse declaratum (*Lit. Ducis Venet.*) *Foed.* XIII 786a (cf. *Reg. Brev. Orig.* 307); **1553** anno regni serenissime .. domine nostre Marie Dei gracia Anglie, Francie, et Hibernie regine, Fidei ~oris, .. primo *StRealm* IV 197.

4 (leg.): **a** defendant. **b** (?) royal official presiding over court. **c** advocate, defending counsel. **d** champion fighting on behalf of appellee. **e** (?) professional champion, swordsman, bravo.

a quot persone solent in judiciis esse? quattuor: accusator cause, ~or cause, testes, judex. quo quisque utitur officio? .. ~or extenuatione ad minuendam causam ALCUIN *Rhet.* 16; in causis omnibus ecclesiasticis et secularibus legaliter et in ordine pertractandis alii sunt accusatores, alii ~ores, alii testes, alii judices (*Leg. Hen.* 5. 1) *GAS* 548; [in judicio aquae] jurent sacramenta et accusans et ~or quasi duellum ingressuri jurant (*Jud. Dei*) *Ib.* 418; insurgit alter in alterum, actor in ~orem FORDUN *Chr.* V 23. **b** de .. causis criminalibus vel capitalibus nemo querat consilium quin inplacitatus statim perneget sine omni petitione consilii ..; vel ejus affirmationem vel negationem ~or aut dominus prosequatur competenti termino comprobandam (*Leg. Hen.* 47. 1) *GAS* 571; ~or aut dominum de furto pulsatorum, si .. respectaverit erga vicinum diem vicinaliter et absque justitie majoris auctoritate condictum, curiam suam perdet (*Ib.* 26. 1) *Ib.* 562. **c** de rebus hereditatis sue interpellatus post xv annos ~orem habeat vel idem respondeat (*Ib.* 59. 9a) *Ib.* 578; **1313** tempore .. domini E., genitoris nostri, cause ipsum in diocesi Agenn' tangentes in civitate Agenn', vocato ~ore suo, consueverant ventilari [et] .. cause ille, pro eo quod copia ~orum hujusmodi necnon .. sani consiliarii in eadem civitate habundancius .. inveniri poterant .., utilius .. tractabantur *RGasc* IV 1110; multiplicantur legiste, juriste, et advocati, et ~ores malorum GASCOIGNE *Loci* 109. **d** si [compellatus] *untrum* sit, id est invalidus, .. querat sibi legalem ~orem [AS: *spalan*] (*Quad.*, *Inst. Will.*) *GAS* 484; **1269** de jure jurando pugilum pro terra: .. ~or a sinistris primo jurabit tenens appellatorem, qui erit a dextris, sic .. *CBaron* 77; **1276** L. filius J., ~or, qui vicit T. de D., probatorem, per duellum *Gaol Del.* 35/2 r. 56. **e** **1290** W. H., captus in societate Johannis de Wrytel', ~oris, pro suspicione burgerie cujusdam *Ib.* 36/1 r. 9.

defensorius [LL], defensive, protective. **b** (of leg. document) defensory.

'fendo' .. non est in usu; sed componitur defendo .. unde hic defensor, -ris, et ~ius, -a, -um OSB. GLOUC. *Deriv.* 218; **1450** in factura cujusdam magni muri densi et ~ii pro aqua ad .. molendinum includenda et conservanda *Ac. Durh.* 633; **1497** attachiamentum fossati ~ii sive capitis stagni vocati *a were CatAncD* VI C 3968. **b** **1310** procurator [archiepiscopi] .. peciit quod compelleretur .. episcopus per juramentum ipsis suis ~iis articulis respondere *Reg. Cant.* 1183.

2 (as sb. n.): **a** protective wrap or garment. **b** cover for eyes (of crab). **c** wrist-guard (for archery). **d** dripstone (arch.). **e** title of book.

a edituus ~ium lintheum sancto superpositum abstulit et pretiosius pallium sollenniter apparuit GOSC. *Mir. Iv.* lxxiii; **1451** unum ~ium, alias vocatum *le jacke*, cum parva tunica *MunAcOx* 622. **b** aliquibus animalibus ille extremitates protense duriores sunt nec retrahi possunt, set habent quedam ~ia supposita, quasi duos clipeos oculorum, ut patet in cancro *Ps.*-RIC. *Anat.* 26. **c** **1443** lego magistro W. L., quondam clerico meo, .. j *flatt bowe* et j ~ium argento ornatum *Test. Ebor.* II 91; *a brace*, ~ium, brachiale *CathA*; hoc ~ium, *a braser WW*. **d** **1507** cuidam lathamo versanti circa ~ium summitatis caminorum coquine ad propellandum (*sic*) impetum pluvie que illos antea descendere solebat *Cant. Coll. Ox.* II 249 (cf. *Building in Eng.* 101). **e** a**1452** in factura ~ii Exemptorum, cum aliis variis in eodem ..; item in factura ~ii Ecclesie (*Factura Librorum*) AMUND. II app. 269; **1529** alius [liber] qui vocatur ~ium Pacis *Conc.* III 720a.

defensum v. defendere, defensivus.

defensus

1 defence. *V. et. defensio* 1.

1397 in ~u sui ipsius cum uno baculo percuciebat unum de latronibus *SelCCoron* 101.

2 'defence' of land as game preserve. *V. et. defensio* 3. *Cf. defendere* 3.

haec silva est in ~u regis *DB* I 181.

defentio v. defensio.

deferator [cf. delator], bearer.

1554 unus ~orum caude nostre (v. cauda 3a).

deferatus v. deferratus. **deferb-** v. et. deferv-. **deferberare** v. deverberare.

defercire [cf. CL farcire], to empty.

to teme, evacuare, ~ire, haurire *CathA*.

†deferendo, *f. l.*

†deferendo [l. de ferrando] *MonA* VI 872b (v. clavarium a).

deferentia v. differentia.

deferratus [cf. CL ferratus], (of horse) unshod.

s**1250** in ferratura .. c equorum ~orum M. PAR. *Maj.* V 121; **1275** ferrabit palefridum .. regis cum venerit apud Man'efeld [*Notts*], si fuerit deferatus *Hund.* II 300b.

1 deferre [CL, *conf. w.* differre]

1 to drive, impel, move; **b** (astr.). **c** (pr. ppl. as sb. m. or n.) deferent, (planetary) orbit.

[Adamnan] vi tempestatis in .. Brittaniae littora delatus est BEDE *HE* V 16; [falcones] infatigabili velocitate ~untur GIR. *TH* I 12; infructuosa .. properatione ~imur insani MAP *NC* IV 13 f. 54v. **b** centrum epicicli semper ~tur in circumferentia deferentis SACROB. *Sph.* 114; quod orbis ~ens solem sit eccentricus BACON VI 35; *Id.* IX 194 (v. circulus 7c); dico quod circulus *EHG* est eccentricus ~ens stellam in epiciclo quesitus WALLINGF. (*Alb.*) I 278. **c** SACROB. *Sph.* 114 (v. 1b supra); in uno quoque istorum [sc. Saturno, Jove, et Marte] movetur centrum epicicli ab oriente ad occidentem et vocatur ~ens BACON IV 422 (cf. ib. 423: ~ens ejus [sc. Mercurii] totum, sicut ~ens Lune, movetur continue .. circa quoddam punctum); centrum equantis et ~entis Saturni WALLINGF. (*Alb.*) I 300.

2 to carry, transport; **b** (w. ship as subj.) **c** (w. ref. to corpse); **d** (w. ref. to processional cross); **e** (w. ref. to letter or sim.).

~t, i. .. portat *GlH* D 48; **9..** delatum, *geferedne oððe aledne WW*; ~ebant tabernaculum in hunc modum AD. SCOT *TT* 683A; duo pueri ad cereos ~endos *Offic. Sal.* 25; **1426** ipsum [confugam] a .. monumento violenter abstractum in navem ecclesie in suis brachiis detulerunt, eundem ab ecclesia ~re molientes *Lit. Cant.* III 148; **1456** presentabit quemdam nobilem puerum Rosenensen, qui in utero matris ad Turchiam delatus extitit BEKYNTON II 157. **b** **1258** ita quod quelibet navis .. sit ~ens xx et iiij equos *Cl* 297. **c** evulsum cadaveris lacertum et in sarcofago delatum ALDH. *VirgP* 32; cujus corpus honorifico agmine .. suam ~tur ad urbem BEDE *HE* I 21; **1214** ipsorum corpora differetis in cemeterio sepelienda *MunAcOx* 3; s**1424** delata sunt funera nobilium ducis T. et constabularii Francie .. ad monasterium FORDUN *Cont.* XV 35; **1431** volo quod corpus meum .. differatur usque ad portas civitatis Norwici et deinde in humeris hominum deportetur usque ad medium corpus ecclesie S. Trin. *Reg. Cant.* II 437. **d** episcopi .. hortantur quod [crux] uni eorum ~enda committatur W. CANT. *V. Thom.* I 25; **1268** (v. crux 5b); **1308** (v. delatio 3c). **e** dona [sc. pandecten et alia] que ~ret [papae] protulit *Hist. Abb. Jarrow* 29; qualiter decreta Romana regi detulerit FRITH. *tit.* 800 (cf. ib. *tit.* 810: quomodo rex delata scripta spreverit); hoc testatur omnis comitatus et ipse qui sigillum regis detulit *DB* I 169; si quis in nuncium regis eat et breve ejus ~at (*Leg. Hen.* 79. 2) *GAS* 595; HENGHAM *Magna* 4 (v. cavere 1c); **1293** in omnibus .. brevibus nostris .. que .. nomine nostro ~ri contigerit *PQW* 203a; **1332** inspexi litteras .. michi dilatas per commissarium vestrum *Lit. Cant.* I 467; c**1336** cuidam garcioni ~enti literas cujusdam mercatoris de London' *Ac. Durh.* 531; **1344** omnes illos quos .. literas, bullas, processus et hujusmodi in nostri .. prejudicium ~entes inveneris, ea (*sic*) ab ipsis capias et corpora hujusmodi ~encium capi et arestari .. facias (*Lit. Regis*) AD. MUR. *Chr.* 241; **1352** (v. defesantia b).

3 to carry about (on one's person), bear, wear: **a** (arms); **b** (clothing or ornaments); **c** (tonsure); **d** (yoke, fig.).

a s**1175** (v. cnipulus b); **1268, 1340** (v. 2 arma 1b); **1287** nullus .. ~at arcus vel sagittas in foresta .. extra viam regiam *SelPlForest* 64; **1289** arma .. per totum ducatum nostrum .. licite .. ~re *RGasc* II 450; **13..** (v. cultellus 1c); **1354** etc. (v. 1 clava b). **b** **1222** (v. anulus 1c); *V. Edm. Rich.* 1775 (v. cappa 1c); [S. Thomas] cilicium pro camisia ~ebat *Meaux* I 186; **1310** W. de M., ~ens habitum ordinis milicie Templi *Conc.* II 381; s**1312** [papa] inhibuit ne quis .. habitum illius [milicie Templi] ordinis ~ret vel reciperet T. STUBBS 414; *SB* 16 (v. cochlea 1a); c**1520** clericus non ~ens habitum suo ordini et statui congruentem *Conc. Scot.* I cclxxvii. **c** **1261** (v. corona 4b); **1301** se clericum ordinatum .. allegans tonsuramque ~ens *Reg. Cant.* 425; **1343** tonsuram congruam et aures patulas .. uniformiter ~entes (*Stat. Sibthorpe*) *Eng. Clergy* 272. **d** servitutis jugum ~re G. MON. IV 2; **1454** dissueti sepius tediose magis claustrale jugum ~unt (*Lit. ad Priorem*) *Reg. Whet.* I 145.

4 (w. inanim. subj.) to bear (a mark).

1278 tulit talliam suam ~entem in fine xv li. *Rec. Leic.* I 189.

5 to take away; **b** (w. abstr. obj.).

~t, i. .. deducit *GlH* D 48; congreget cantor de omnibus armariis libros et delatos; ponat in medio capitulo super extensa tapeta *Cust. Norw.* 67; **1375** quicquid colligerint infra campum differant per eosdem exitus *Hal. Durh.* 126. **b** a**1190** quicunque detulerit tholneum vel jura que .. predicte ville [*Rutherglen*] .. pertinuerunt *Regesta Scot.* 244 (= *BBC* 179); **12..** jura ordinariorum quandoque ~untur vel penitus enervantur *Reg. Aberd.* II 11.

6 to bring, fetch (to); **b** (w. dat.).

statuit .. sacrificium sibi novum .., panes viz. primitiarum duos, ad altare ~ri BEDE *Hom.* II 17. 194; detulerat, *brohte GlC* D 20; **9..** delaturos, *bringende WW*; mercator .. in civitatem .. trussellum ~ens *DB* I 263; s**1070** rex W. .. pecuniam .. auferri et in erarium suum jussit ~ri FL. WORC. II 5; ~to W. CANT. *Mir. Thom.* IV 44 (v. commensuratio 2c); **1217** lasta coriorum que .. marinelli .. eis abstulerunt in mari et ad castrum nostrum de S. .. distulerunt *Pat* 102; **1274** N. de M. tenet j virgatam terre .. per serganciam defferendi ij cultellos *Hund.* II 108; **1285** quod omnes qui tallias habent de debitis domini regis solutis vicecomitibus vel ballivis, quod (*sic*) tunc eas defferant ibidem coram thesaurario *Chr. Peterb.* 106; **1374** in stipendio iij hominum differencium petras et arrenam super stagnum *Doc. Leeds* 112; **1417** in expensis differentis liberacionem .. episcopi usque Farnham *Comp. Swith.* 364. **b** duo quidam dolium se viro Dei delaturos spoponderunt ALDH. *VirgP* 37; minister .. curie cum equo proprio monachorum singulis singulas ~re debet summas domibus *Chr. Battle* f. 18; **1266** pro harnesiis delatis .. regi *ExchScot* 10; **1351** cuidam garcioni .. ~enti venacionem priori de presento *Ac. Durh.* 552.

7 to refer (question for decision).

hoc quodam tempore quo contingit ad eum delatum sic judicavit THEOD. *Pen.* I 14. 29; **1082** res indeterminata permansit, donec ad praesentiam .. regis ~retur *Regesta* p. 122; in questione fidei que delata est ad apostolicam sedem OCKHAM *Pol.* III 263.

8 **a** to convey (message or sim.). **b** to state, announce. **c** to bear (testimony or sim.). **d** to delate, denounce, accuse. **e** (p. ppl. as sb. n.) accusation, charge.

a †**676** (12c) cum nobis evangelica .. dogmata .. fuissent delata *CS* 43; sensus particularis primo apprehendit res materiales per suas species, et ulterius depurando ad fantasiam ~untur BACON VIII 31. **b** ~t, nuntiat *GlC* D 92; Ricardus detulit quod Agnes .. partum edidit et de periculo .. evasit *Mir. Montf.* 80; ut quod per inculpatum ~tur per attornatum pronuncietur *Fleta* 50; si aliquid pro parte absencium possit interim allegari vel juritice diferri FAVENT 16. **c** de qua Alvricus detulit testimonium *DB* I 60v.; **1311** juramenta .. delata (v. decisorius). **d** ~t, accussat, unde delator dicitur *GlC* D 110; ~t, *wroegde Ib.* 122; delatur, i. ~tur, .. proditur *GlH* D 135; *V. Will.* 289 (v. defunctio); reum regi ~unt MAP *NC* V 5 (v. congerere d); s**1342** apud regem de infidelitate delatus FORDUN *Cont.* XIII 50. **e** s**1329** misit archiepiscopus .. clericos suos ad .. examinandum .. episcopum super compertis et delatis per capitulum Roffense in visitacione sua *Hist. Roff.* f. 53v; **1346** (v. 2 comperire 2c).

9 **a** (w. abstr. obj.) to render (service, deference, or sim.). **b** to defer, show consideration for, show deference to a person (*cf. Deut.* xxviii 50); **c** to defer to an institution or quality. **d** to defer, submit to a decision, regulation, or sim.

a ut omnes agnoscerent etiam torrentem martyri obsequium detulisse (*Passio Albani*) BEDE *HE* I 7; ut propensiori cura .. tibi servitutis officia ~amus, hoc .. altare dedicamus EGB. *Pont.* 41; cum [Lanfranco] Romam venienti .. [papa] assurgeret, professus hanc venerationem non se illius archiepiscopatui sed magisterio litterarum ~re W. MALM. *GP* I 42; nec Deo nec hominibus reverentiam ~ens RIC. HEX. *Stand.* 40b; venerationis obsequium, quod sibi archiepiscopus parabat ~re AD. EYNS. *Hug.* V 5 p. 102. **b** stultatus, qui ~re nescit *GlC* S 556; ~t, i. .. honorat *GlH* D 48; de talibus alias dixi, multum, ut decet, regie majestati ~ens W. MALM. *GP* I 45; s**1147** sancta illa edificia .. redigunt in favillam. non ~tur ordini SERLO GRAM. *Mon. Font.* 101; ~o Deo, parcens nature, que ab ipso est, et impugnans vitium, quod contra ipsum est J. SAL. *Met.* 827D; **1163** nos .. ei [regi Anglie] .. per omnia et in omnibus in quibus secundum Deum possumus ~re volentes (*Lit. Papae*) DICETO *YH* I 309; adeo ut natio .. Gualensium .., in inimicos suos .. sevissima, etiam inimicis vexillaris vasis hujus gestatoribus ~at H. BOS. *LM* 1335; tantam eorum esse perversitatem quod non magis ~rent pontifici quam persone cuilibet laicali AD. EYNS. *Hug.* V 10 p. 135; in multis pro pace bona deferre tenetur / Cesaribus magnis pontificalis apex GARL. *Tri. Eccl.* 22; quod neminem gravabunt per odium nec alicui ~ent per amorem BRACTON 116b; s**1312** cum mea rapuerint et homines meos occiderint, satis est verisimile quod michi nolunt ~re *V. Ed. II* 186. **c** s**1138** [rex David], ~ens dignitati et antiquitati ecclesie Hagustaldensis, pacem ei .. conservavit J. HEX. *HR Cont.* 290; quisquis non arridet divitibus etiam cum malefecerint .. videtur aut invidere fortune aut officio non ~re J. SAL. *Pol.* 630D. **d** **1178** appellationi vestre minime ~ens *Ch. Sal.* 42; s**1192** episcopus in nullo detulit sententie illi [archiepiscopi] *G. Ric. I* 237; c**1200** quorum [monachorum] appellationi [ad sedem apostolicam] .. debita devotione differre dignum duximus *Reg. S. Thom. Dublin* 478; nec ulli penitus juri vel scripto vel etiam consuetudinario delatum fuerat GIR. *Symb.* I 22 p. 265; **1242** quicumque sequeretur vel teneret hujusmodi placita [in curia Christianitatis], semper ad prohibitionem regiam supersedit et detulit prohibicioni sue *CurR* XVI 2021; s**1313** monachi .. magistrum T. .. elegerunt, non ~entes inhibicioni summi pontificis TROKELOWE 81; catholici non tenentur differre impugnacioni pape heretici nisi impugnantes interposuerint appellacionem legitimam OCKHAM *Dial.* 536; **1549** quatenus privilegiis sit ~endum *Conc. Scot.* II 92.

10 (w. dat.) to spare: **a** (person or thing); **b** (offence).

a cum terram B. Eadmundi, cui omnes predones detulerant, videret opulentam J. SAL. *Pol.* 807A; asserentes se Anglorum ecclesiis de cetero nullatenus ~re velle GIR. *IK* II 12; aliis quomodo male scribendo .. ~re valeret, qui sibi ipso .. minime ~re dignum duxit? *Id. Spec.* IV 15; s**1210** ignis .. succensus Londoniis ultra pontem maximam partem civitatis .. devoravit, nec ponti detulit,

quamvis elemento contrario .. superpositus *Ann. S. Edm.* 23; **s1219** cujus [urbis Jerosolymitane] muros .. evertit [Coradinus]; templo tantum et turri David detulit dominicoque sepulcro TREVET *Ann.* 204; **1221** nec timent Deum .. nec †differunt [MS: defferunt] ecclesie magis quam †torpedule [MS: torredule], qui xxxv ecclesias combusserunt (*Lit. Llewellini, AncC* IV 18) *RL* I 177; **1282** Anglici hactenus .. nulli sexui vel etati .. pepercerunt, nulli ecclesie vel loco sacro detulerunt (*Lit. Llewellini*) *Ep. Peckham* 341; **s1314** nec differebat ferocitas discurrencium ulli religioni vel clero *Flor. Hist.* III 158; hos colles transilit [cf. *Cant.* ii 8], quia illis ~t [ME: *forbereð ham and forbuweð*] donec crescant et de collibus fiant montes *AncrR* 149; **s1379** [Flandrenses] occidunt .. nostros, nulli parcentes, nulli ~entes WALS. *HA* I 401. **b** ibi .. remedium querimus ubi nec ejus excessibus nec vestris .. negligentiis .. ~etur GIR. *Symb.* I 3.

2 deferre v. 2 differre.

defervēre, ~escere [CL]

1 to burn (intr.). **b** (fig.) to burn w. zeal or anger. **c** to burn (trans., fig.) or ? *f. l.*

Martemque lacessit / qui gratis domitos tulerit defervēre tauros J. EXON. *BT* I 221. **b** pacis et justitie zelo ~ens, .. in male meritos juris rigore deseviens, .. cepit .. crudelitate notari GIR. *TH* III 50; ira vindice ~entes .. se in insidiis nocte contulerunt *Id. IK* I 4 p. 50. **c** procumbens dolio, defervens [? l. deferens] osculum, / cauponam deprecans ut [etc.] WALT. WIMB. *Carm.* 140.

2 to cool down; **b** (fig., of passion, w. pers. subj.); **c** (w. abstr. subj.).

tumores .. ~escentes resident, i. a fervore cessant GAD. 37v. 2. **b** **1145** ne .. ab ea quam hactenus erga vos habuimus caritate ~eamus G. FOLIOT *Ep.* 42; [porcus silvaticus] in iram excitatur, quod dum alium fervendo non possit ~escere, in se ipso †~escit [? l. fervescit] et voluntarie se spiculis invertit *Quaest. Salern.* N 57. **c** **c597** nisi prius ignis concupiscentiae a mente ~eat (*Lit. Papae*) BEDE *HE* I 27 p. 57; sensit .. per Angliam totam deferbuisse invasionem gulosam ad †revelationem [? l. relevationem] pauperum HERM. ARCH. 6; paulatim ~ente animi motu sedatus *V. Ed. Conf.* 44v.; quis est cujus ad hunc mirabilem intuitum non statim ira ~eat AILR. *Spec. Car.* III 5. 582B; quando sol occubuit? quando fervor tentationis deferbuit AD. SCOT *QEC* 13. 823C; cum jam deferbuisse deberet regis excandescentia W. FITZST. *Thom.* 72.

defesantia [AN *defesance*, OF *desfaisance*], 'defeasance', undoing. **b** (leg.) defeasance, (document specifying) condition on which a bond is made void.

1365 esset maximum detrimentum et deffesancia officii sui si predicti camerarii intromitterent cum eo in assignacionibus, solucionibus, seu aliis rebus quibuscumque thesaurarium tangentibus *Cl* 203 m. 25. **b** **s1327** †thesauriam abbatis ingressi, munimenta abbatis, cartas, obligaciones, ~ias .. et .. alias monasterii evidencias .. incendio consumpserunt (*Chr. Abingd.*) *EHR* XXVI 732; **1352** J. .. concedit .. quod, si .. H. vel alius nomine suo hanc ~iam secum deferens solvat predicto J. .. x li. .. ad diem supradictum .., ex tunc predicti .. [H. et] heredes .. sui de solucione predictarum xx li. absoluti sint .. et scriptum de statuto mercatorum inde eidem J. factum irritum sit et vacuum *Reg. Rough* 210 (cf. ib. 194 [**1376**]: *par un escript obligatorie et par une defesance sur ycelle*); **1384** obligaverunt se predictis R. et J. per quoddam statutum mercatorium in m m. sub tali ~ia, viz. quod .. *IMisc* 229/17 r. 5; **a1400** asserebat se obligatorium .. de c li. debiti nostri reperisse, cujus ~ia [v. l. diffesancia] minime haberetur *Meaux* III 209 (cf. ib. 19); **1431** sub certis condicionibus in quibusdam indenturis .. super ~ia ejusdem statuti [de stapula] confectis *Cl* 281 m. 7d.

defessio v. diffessio. **defeteri** v. diffiteri 1b.

defetisci [CL], to grow tired.

†defeciscor [? l. defetiscor], i. viribus privor *GlH* D 54; cibis deficientibus et ipsi ~entes *G. Steph.* I 23; ~or, fatigare, vexare, importunare OSB. GLOUC. *Deriv.* 177; *wery*, †aliolus, defessus itinere, lassus ..; *to wax wery*, †deficisci *CathA.*

deff- v. def-, diff-. **deffyamentum** v. diffidamentum. **defic-** v. et. defaec-.

deficere [CL]

1 (of thing or abstr., sts. w. dat. of person affected): **a** to fail, decline, run short. **b** (w. abstr. subj.) to fail, be ineffective. **c** (of truce) to expire. **d** (astr.) to be eclipsed (also fig. in pass.). **e** (of buildings) to be defective. **f** (p. ppl. as sb. n.) defect in building or artefact; *cf. defectus* 1f.

a flammas inferni .. nequaquam defecturas GILDAS *EB* 29; ante dies .. mihi .. / deficiet, totam quam possim pandere famam / virginibus castis fantem praeconia ALDH. *VirgV* 2783 (cf. ib. 907: oleum in vacua defecit lampade); ~iente .. omni membrorum officio BEDE *HE* V 5; timebant ne autumnale sibi deficeret tempus HUGEB. *Wynn.* 2; cum pecunia ~eret WULF. *Æthelwold* 29; *G. Steph.* I 23 (v. defetisci); in .. ede inextinguibiles posuit ignes, qui numquam ~iebant in favillas G. MON. II 10; pulsu debili et ~iente GILB. I 32. 2; **1221** per quod aqua eis ~it in villa *PlCrGlouc* 50; **s1255** post prandium et ~iente die *Leg. Ant. Lond.* 23. **b** si [mortuus] amicos habeat, qui audeant hoc facere [sc. eum mundificare contra advocantem], tunc ~it advocatio [AS: *berst se team*], sicut ille viveret et negaret (*Quad.*) *GAS* 226; instabat pia matrum sollicitudo, sed casso labore difficiebat W. CANT. *Mir. Thom.* II 67; ista allegacio videtur aperte ~ere OCKHAM *Dial.* 886. **c** **1230** ex quo voluerimus quod treuge .. ~iant, nos premuniemus inde .. vicecomitem per xiiij dies ante finem .. treugarum *Pat* 389. **d** querenti cur sol ~ere videatur, .. respondetur solem ~ere videri quoniam ei et videnti interponitur luna BALSH. *AD rec.* 2 151; si .. ad aspectum alicujus creature daretur divinitus lunam eclipsari, sola voluntate et aspectu existentis in terra luna ~eret *Ps.-* GROS. *Summa* 456; verus celi sol nube tegitur / et celorum celum †difficitur [vv. ll. diffinitur, dissuitur] J. HOWD. *Ph.* 977. **e** reficit .. domum et curiam, si defecerint *DB* I 205. **f** **1364** fossatum .. bene mundatur et non est aliquod defectum in eo (*CoramR*) *Pub. Works* I 71; **1493** ad scrutandum .. defecta vel injuria (*sic*) ad artem seu scienciam pannariorum pertinencia *Doc. Bev.* 102.

2 to fall short (of), be deficient; **b** (of money). **c** (pr. ppl. as sb.) deficit.

1321 *MGL* II 383 (v. denarius 10); preter istum principatum regalem sunt alii principatus regales diversimode ~ientes ab isto OCKHAM *Dial.* 795. **b** [manerium de T.] valet l li. .. R. dedit cuidam Anglico ad censum pro lx li.; set uno quoque anno ~iunt illi ad minus x li. *DB* II 38v.; **1275** ita quod idem A. ei allocaret de eadem pecunia valorem j libre lane, que de pondere viij librarum et dim. ~iebat *SelPlMan* 140; **1344, 1345** (v. 1 carata). **c** **a1350** statum est quod custodes cistarum, si contingat .. quod in eorum custodia ciste dampnificentur .., super ~iente condempnentur ad reintegrandum dictas cistas *StatOx* 77.

3 to be lacking or absent; **b** (in pass. form).

'conjux', quod nomen Priscianum in nominativo et vocativo cum additamento N litterae .. recolo disseruisse, licet in obliquis casibus penitus ~iat ALDH. *PR* 114; de feris et vermibus .. et venenosis omnibus hic ~ientibus GIR. *TH intr.* p. 7; **1220** (v. bonus 7d); **1337** (v. defectus 2a). **b** BEDE *ST* 612 (v. catachresis); **c1360** de aliis litteris que ~iuntur hic patet in notulis *Reg. Rough* 153; **c1400** quercus .. que in croppo ~iantur (v. croppa 2).

4 (of person): **a** to feel faint, swoon. **b** to decline, lose strength.

a HERM. ARCH. 40 (v. consessus 1a); supra modum admiror et fere in admiratione ~io quod .. R. MARSTON *QD* 412. **b** Guorthigirnus cum omnibus qui cum eo erant .. defecit; hic est finis Guorthigirni NEN. *HB* 191; **9..** occidimus, i. ~imus, *we giwitaþ WW*; **966** (10c) (v. cataclysma); **s1210** Matildis .. et W. filius ejus .. carcerali custodie deputati .. defecerunt *Ann. S. Edm.* 19 (= WEND. II 57: perierunt); **s1222** ambo, de tali crimine convicti, jussi sunt inter duos muros incarcerari quousque ~erent COGGESH. *Chr.* 119b; **s1293** aliqui milites .. sunt suspensi; quidam autem eligentes penitenciam secundum statutum miserabiliter defecerunt *Ann. Dunstable* 377.

5 (of person) to fail (in a task), be found wanting; **b** (w. dat. of person affected); **c** (w. inf.). **d** (w. *de*) to miss. **e** to fall short (of standard weight in selling goods). **f** to default (in payment). **g** to defect, desert.

delirantes, mente ~ientes *Gl. Leid.* 1. 37; quid prodest iter rectitudinis cepisse et ante consummatum ~ere? PULL. *Sent.* 928A; raro .. ~it qui sibi non diffidit GIR. *TH* I 12; GARL. *Myst. Eccl.* 240 (v. conflictus 2d); primus angelus ~iens, Lucifer *York Plays* f. 1v. **b** quamvis Deus non ~iat ecclesie sue .. in necessariis OCKHAM *Dial.* 828. **c** ydropisis non est nisi cum natura epati ~it mutare succum in humores GILB. VI 241. 2; ad Saladinum .. nuncios clam mittere non ~iens *Plusc.* VI 34. **d** **1268** cum pede suo dextro volebat eum percutere et de ictu ~iebat *Rec. Norw.* I 210; **1378** defecit de pedibus super scalam et cecidit in fornace et sic fuit scaterizata *SelCCoron* 91. **e** **a1250** quotienscumque pistor defecerit in pondere panis quadrantis citra ij s., quod tunc amercietur (*Assisa Panis*) *StRealm* I 200; **1324** E. J. ~iebat in pondere panis de ob. integr[i] frumenti v s. ij d.; habeat judicium *CBaron* 139 (cf. ib. 140: ~iebat de eodem pane viij s. vj d.). **f** **1215** si capitalis debitor defecerit in solutione debiti .., pleggii respondeant *Magna Carta* 9; **1264** (v. debitor a); **1286** si contingat .. Radulfum .. de predictis xl m. ad predictum terminum ~ere *FormA* 90; **1486** si .. in solucione .. deficerint (*sic*) *Reg. Aberbr.* II 246. **g** ut .. eos qui secum venerant, ne a fide ~erent, .. contineret BEDE *HE* II 9; **s1192** comes Johannes .. mandavit presto parari sibi navigium, ut putabatur, ad regem Francorum defecturus DEVIZES 38v.

6 (leg.) to default: **a** (w. ref. to default of justice or of backing by court or official); **b** (w. ref. to wager of law); **c** (of party to action or sim.); **d** (w. inf.); **e** (refl.); **f** (in pass. form).

a Aitardus .. revocat ad feudum episcopi B. de tenetura Alvredi antecessoris sui; et *hund*[*ret*] ei quod non pertin[ebat] ad antecessorem sum *DB* II 124v.; donec .. in curia ecclesiastica de recto defecerit (*Leg. Ed.*) *GAS* 630 (= *Leg. Ed. Retr.* ib.: nisi .. rectum defecerit; cf. curia 5g); **c1215** donec custos sokne in qua manserit ei defecerit in recto tenendo (*Mun. Lond.*) *EHR* XVII 714; **1220** R. .. dixit vicecomiti quod curia illa ei †deficerat [v. l. defecerit] de jure faciendo; et voluit probare defaltam *CurR* IX 80; **1221** de .. uno de juratoribus, qui dixit quod predicti duo homines deliberati fuerunt per comitatum, et alii xj et comitatus ei ~iunt *PlCrGlouc* 238; **1235** liberam habeat potestatem concordandi, justicia nostra nullam exigente inde consuetudinem .., donec burgenses in justicia defecerint (*Ch. Chard*) *EHR* XVI 109; **1269** si curia domini de recto defecerit, poterit loquela transferri vel ad comitatum vel ad justiciarios de Banco *CBaron* 69. **b** **1247** C. qui fuit in lege contra R. filium S. et defecit in lege *SelPlMan* 12; **1275** R. R. venit et incepit facere legem, sc. ipse et duo alii secum tantum; et ~iebant de iij hominibus. et R. T. optulit se similiter; et ~iebat omnino de sua lege, racione quod neminem habuit qui secum voluit facere legem *Ib.* 151; **1383** de Johanne .., quia defecit de lege versus Willelmum .., vj d. *Hal. Durh.* 180. **c** **a1122** (v. diratiocinamentum); si .. non poterat warantum suum habere, erat forisfactura et justicia; similiter de calumpniatore, si ~iebat (*Leg. Ed.*) *GAS* 647; **1167** quia defecit de appellatione de morte sororis sue in murdro *Pipe* 83 (cf. ib. 92: quia rettavit servientem regis de infidelitate et defecit); **1200** [tenentes] bis summoniti bis defecerunt *CurR* I 326; **1253** si aliquis implacitatus fuerit .. et per tres dies secutus fuerit, si testimonium habuerit .. quod adversarius suus defecerit ad hos tres dies, nullam postea det ei responsionem de illo placito (*Ch. Bolton*) *EHR* XVII 292; **1269** insufficienter negavit .. violenciam messori illatam tacendo; et remanet in misericordia xij d., quia defecit in negacione sua *CBaron* 76; **1271** si defecerit in secta per mortem vel infirmitatem, M. filia sua optulit se .. sequi vel probare *SelCCoron* 20; **1275** socii sui attachiati .. eisdem W. et A. de justicia defecerunt; unde W. et A. vocant ipsos .. detentores .. et debiti .. principales debitores *SelPlMan* 146; defecit in secta et improbacione sua per recognicionem suam propriam *State Tri. Ed. I* 44. **d** **1167** quia defecit venire coram justitiariis ad Scaccarium *Pipe* 137. **e** **a1135** desicut [abbas de Montisburgo] venit in curiam meam ut illam partem [ecclesie] disrationaret versus monachos de H. .. et illi defecerunt se illuc veniendi ad diem suum inde sumptum *Regesta* 1952; **c1228** prior non habet curiam nisi de *wrang* .. et de placitis terre per breve de recto donec curia se ~iat *Feod. Durh.* 252. **f** **c1230** si testimonium habuerit .. quod adversarius suus defectus sit *BBC* (*Salford*) 203.

7 (trans., leg.): **a** to 'defeat', annul; *cf. defieri* a. **b** (w. *condicionem*) to leave unfulfilled; *cf.* CL *condicio deficit*.

a **1227** Nicholaus .., qui finem fecit, eundem finem postea defecit *CurR* XIII 180; **1587** ad intencionem alterandi, ~iendi, molestandi .. statum hereditatis liberi tenementi .. alicujus persone *Entries* 359b. **b** **1540** quamvis vestra majestas .. precontractus .. declaracionem .. tanta instancia exegerit ut pro condicione contrahendi deinde matrimonii fuisse merito existimari possit, qua condicione defecta nihil ageretur *Conc.* III 854a.

8 (p. ppl. *defectus*), worn out, feeble.

decrepitos senes et ~as anus et ceteros .. debiles .. trucidaverunt RIC. HEX. *Stand.* 40b; motus .. post cibum .. etiam juvat seniores .. et omnem stomachum ad digestivam ~um GILB. II 105. 2.

deficilis v. difficilis 2. **deficio** (sb.) v. desitio a. **deficisci** v. defetisci. **deficitur** v. diffiteri.

†defictus, *f. l.*

1382 quid dicam de monachis Sancti Benedicti? / .. / nam non servant regulas quibus sunt astricti; / ab antiquo Mamona †minus sunt deficti† [? l. nimis sunt devicti] (*Contra Religiosos* 142) *Mon. Francisc.* I 596 (= *Pol. Poems* I 258).

defid- v. diffid-.

defieri, (leg.) to be 'defeated', annulled; *cf. deficere* 7a. **b** to be defaced; *cf. diffacere* b.

1220 quia finis factus fuit inter Simonem et predictos et finis non potest ~i sine Simone, consideratum est quod Simon summoneatur .. *CurR* VIII 311. **b** **15..** quod .. persone habentes auctoritatem accipiendi probacionem testamentorum .. super deliberacione sigilli et signi testatoris causarent idem sigillum ~i *Entries* 804.

defigere [CL]

1 to fasten, fix; **b** (fig.); **c** (w. ref. to vision). **d** (w. *animam*) to commit, pledge. **e** (p. ppl.) stable, well-ordered.

veluti portis martyrii sui trophaea ~erent GILDAS *EB* 11; **8..** difixisti, *ðu afesnadest* .., qui ~unt, *ðe afestniað WW*; gaude tibi sidera volvi / defigique polos HANV. VIII 330 p. 370; GIR. *Rem.* 27 (v. dormire 5a). **b** [Hostis] desperationis sagittam .. jaculavit, quousque in Christi militis mentis umbone defixa pependit FELIX *Guthl.* 29; ad hunc lapidem cordis dirigamus intellectum et ~ere studeamus in eo nostre mentis affectum S. LANGTON *Serm.* 4. 9; in B. Egidio tocius sue spei ancoram ~ens *Lib. Mem. Bernewelle* 39. **c** Pater omnipotens .. / .. defixit lumina terris ALDH. *VirgV* 1762; rex obstippo capite ~ens lumine terras .. conticuit [cf. Persius iii 80] ABBO *Edm.* 8; si in inferioribus .. intuitum nostrum ~amus, mulieris decorem tamquam supra secessus fecorem locatum repperiemus W. DONC. *Aph. Phil.* 7. 4; quid fiendum est si

quisquam viderit aliquem oculos in femina ~entem? ROB. BRIDL. *Dial.* 139; in ipsos solaris corporis radios aciem ~unt oculorum GIR. *TH* I 13. **d** ad oves proprias . ., pro quibus apud formidandum judicem suam animam defixit AD. MARSH *Ep.* 136. **e** defixa, i. stabilis, ordinata *GlH* D 64.

2 a to pitch (tent). **b** to plant (kisses or steps). **c** to bow, lay (knee or ear to ground).

a ut citius quis potuit tentorium terra ~ere OSB. BAWDSEY clvi; nisi fuisset clientum industria concurrencium ad cordas [tentorii] et †refigencium [*ed.*: defigencium] . . corruisset . . edificium *G. Hen. V* 24. **b** oscula dum supero defixit limpida sponso ALDH. *VirgV* 2138; illum pedum vestigia ad terram posse ~ere non crediderunt R. COLD. *Godr.* 232. **c** [Cuthbertum] curvatis genibus . . adorarunt. . . ille que eum videre non poterant . . "ubi est," inquiunt, "quem vocatis et (*sic*) genu ~itis?" *Id. Cuthb.* 31; aurem solo ~ens tanquam audivit gemitum W. CANT. *Mir. Thom.* III 1.

defigitare v. defatigare. **defigur-** v. diffigur-.

defindere [CL], to split.

to breke, . . findere, conf-, dif-, de- *CathA.*

definibilis (diff-), definable.

conceptus accidentis in se prior est et absolutus et ita ~is sine subjecto DUNS *Metaph.* VII 1. 350; ponit quod res simplices . . non sunt ~ia diffinicione proprie dicta *Ps.-*OCKHAM *Princ. Theol.* 54 (cf. ib.: ~e diffinicione proprie dicta, que est ex genere et differencia); ad tantam penuriam deducuntur aliqui quod dicunt nichil esse proprie ~e WYCL. *Dom. Div.* 45.

definire [CL] **(diff-)**

1 to limit, delimit, determine: **a** (spatially); **b** (qualitatively). **c** (p. ppl.) finite.

a determinat, ~it *GlC* D 206; tum illi congregati . . ~itam (*sic*) domui locum libraverunt HUGEB. *Wynn.* 11; **814** cum . . pascuis, pratis . ., aquis, mariscis . . quae umquam . . ad istam . . terram competebat (*sic*) aut nunc difinienda (*sic*) augendoque jure perpetuo donata constant *CS* 348; ~ire, i. . . disterminare *GlH* D 466; omne quod circumscribitur loco ~itur loco HALES *Sent.* I 378. **b** ~ientia priora sunt et etiam causa ~iti; set universalia sunt ~ientia; ergo universalia priora [sunt] et causa ipsius ~iti, quod est substantia BACON VII 3. **c** itaque nec impossibilis erit ~ita motio, nec infinitam incurret cause requisitio ADEL. *QN* 60.

2 to define, describe precisely; **b** (w. indir. qu., acc. & inf. or compl.). **c** (p. ppl. as sb. n.) thing defined.

a804 sapientia est, ut philosophi ~ierunt, divinarum humanarumque rerum scientia ALCUIN *Ep.* 307 p. 466; si, ut superius ~isti, ventus aer motus est ADEL. *QN* 60 (cf. ib. 14: dum talem essentiam tam male ~is); ~it ratio quod concipit intellectus J. SAL. *Pol.* 438B; Aristoteles . . ~it quantitatem per naturam divisibilitatis BACON *Tert.* 198. **b** ALCUIN *Rhet.* 7 (v. definitivus 1b); philosophorum scientias, quas earum rerum quae sunt et quae aliter esse non possunt cognitionem veritatis vetustas esse ~it OSB. *V. Dunst.* 8; noverat sapientiam, que de sursum est, primum quidem pudicam, deinde pacificam, ore apostolico ~iri [cf. *James* iii 17] AD. EYNS. *Hug.* III 11 p. 121; R. BURY *Phil.* 15. 193 (v. deiformis). **c** (GROS.) *GLA* III 89 (v. definitio 2a); si omne jus utendi esset usus, prima particula diffinicionis 'usus', que ponitur loco generis, esset convertibilis cum ~ito OCKHAM *Pol.* I 302.

3 to decide (on question of fact or right), assert or pronounce definitively; **b** (w. *de*); **c** (w. acc. & inf. or *quod*); **d** (w. indir. qu.).

in pedibus . . trina divisionis condicio ~itur ALDH. *PR* 112; malo de singulis dubitare quam . . quod ignotum . . est temere ~ire J. SAL. *Pol.* 449A; multa digna memoria hic facta . . oblivioni traduntur, de quibus aliquid magis pie arbitrari elegimus quam aliquid presumptuose ~ire *Chr. Evesham* 82. **b** ita ecclesia nec de questionibus fidei ~ire nec juridisccionem valet exercere OCKHAM *Pol.* III 9. **c** ~ivit apud se quod hec vita solitaria est magis similis vite Dei BACON *CSPhil.* 423; nolens leviter credere quod persona in tanto officio constituta hereses ~iret esse tenendas OCKHAM *Pol.* III 6. **d** que consuetudo sit magis approbanda . . non ~io GIR. *GE* I 7.

4 to decide (esp. judicially), determine, direct; **b** (w. abstr. subj.); **c** (w. *causam*); **d** (w. *sententiam*); **e** (w. *ut* or *quod*); **f** (w. acc. & inf.).

789 (12c) (v. chirographum 1b); †**814** (11c) hoc decretum ~iendo confirmavi *CS* 307; his ita ~itis . ., cogitabat quid adhuc addere potuisset ASSER *Alf.* 99; testes Willelmi nolunt accipere legem nisi regis E. usque dum ~iatur per regem *DB* I 44v.; que ad jus ~itum utrimque se habent ~itis prelocutionibus egent (*Leg. Hen.* 59. 2c) *GAS* 577; mulieres que fornicantur et partus suos extingunt . . antiqua diffinitio usque ad exitum vite removet ab ecclesia. nunc clementius ~itum: x annis penitea[n]t (*Ib.* 70. 16a) *Ib.* 589; respondit sese suam curiam habere et in illa ~iri debere quicquid aliquis in homines suos clamaret G. MON. IV 8; s**1234** ~itam pecuniam a vicecomitibus recipiendo M. PAR. *Maj.* III 296; quod . . habita . . deliberacione et tractatu recte fuerit ~itum *Fleta* 17; s**1293** (v. 2 decidere 4); ne plures simul de eisdem negociis ~iant OCKHAM *Dial.* 803. **b 673** omnibus placet . . quae ~ierunt sanctorum canones patrum nos quoque . . servare (*Conc. Hertf.*) BEDE *HE* IV 5; *Ib.* (v. definitio 4a); **c800** quicquid secus agamus quam regularis vita ~iat, remaneat apud nos tantum ALCUIN *Ep.* 223. **c** s**1070** de qua re . . decrevit . . papa oportere hanc causam . . audiri et episcoporum . . testimonio et juditio ~iri W. MALM. *GP* I 25; s**1119** causa audita . ., eam . . canonico et irrefragabili judicio ~iri H. CANTOR 19; noluit . . papa [Adrianus IV] diffinitivam promulgare sententiam, quinimmo causam ipsam . . episcopis committit ~iendam *Chr. Battle* f. 90v. **d 1178** controversia . . que . . per diffinitam sententiam decisa est (*Lit. Papae*) ELMH. *Cant.* 424 (= R. HOWD. II 149: diffinitivam). **e c1086** ~itum et concordatum fuit de silva de H. ut per medium partiretur *Regesta* p. 127; ~ivit rex quod qui terras possident eisdem . . utantur (*Ass. David* 26) *APScot* 10; **1373** ordinavimus, ~ivimus, et pronunciavimus quod lis . . predicta omnino quiescat *Reg. Paisley* 44; **1445** ~imus infringibiliter et ordinamus quod ante dissolucionem hujus capituli assignentur . . discreti . . monachi qui auctoritatem diffinitorum habeant ad colligendum . . omnes diffiniciones precedencium capitulorum *Doc. Eng. Black Monks* II 188. **f 1383** per concilium nostrum decretum et sencencialiter ~itum extitit . . processum versus fratrem H. [Crumpe] . . esse nullum (*Breve Regis*) *Ziz.* 315; **1427** laudo, †~o [? l. ~io], arbitror, et pronuncio in hiis scriptis . . rectorem S. Ebbe esse . . legitimum possessorem . . *FormOx* 463.

5 to decide (to act), resolve: **a** (w. *quod*). **b** (w. inf.).

a s**1304** [rex Anglie] de morte . . Roberti pertractavit et quod in die crastino eum vita privaret breviter deliberando ~ivit FORDUN *Cont.* XII 6. **b** sanctus vir . . idoneum praeponere ministrum supradicto gregi ~ivit WILLIB. *Bonif.* 8; **1425** divine bonitatis largitas . ., morbi excogitato remedio, ipsum [hominem] temporali unigeniti sui morte sanare ~iens . . *Conc.* III 447b; **c1430** priusquam pro Rachele . . fastidiatis torum Lye aut inter vos et sponsam habitam . . ~iatis divorcia celebrare *Reg. Whet.* II app. 445.

6 to end (intr.).

1320 litteras . . que sic incipiunt . . et sic difiniunt *Reg. Heref.* 125.

definis, limitless.

difinis, *suiðe micel GlC* D 327; difinis, valde magnus *GlH* D 461.

definite [CL], definitely, expressly.

excommunicatio . . non prius fieri debet quam diffinite, et non suspicione is qui sceleris arguitur anathemate dignus perpendatur PULL. *Sent.* 899B.

definitio [CL] **(diff-)**

1 a (spatial) delimitation. **b** determination, ascertainment. **c** extent, scope.

a ~o, i. terminatio *GlH* D 464. **b c710** in ~one et computo lunaris aetatis . . falluntur (*Ep. Ceolfridi*) BEDE *HE* V 21 p. 338. **c 1321** loquelam suspenderunt . . quousque istius calumnie ~o examinata fuerit *MGL* II 297.

2 definition, description; **b** (as rhet. device); **c** (as literary device).

ni . . prooemia omnemque hujus opusculi ~onem degeneri vitiorum stilo . . attaminando foedarem B. *V. Dunst.* 1; talem oportet dare ~onem libertatis arbitrii, quae nec plus nec minus illa contineat ANSELM (*Lib. Arb.* 1) I 208; est . . 'sensus' ~o, ut mihi quidem videtur, 'animati corporis exteriorum applicatione non levis mutatio'. que ~o ut fidem facere possit, prius ei fides astruatur ADEL. *QN* 13 (cf. ib.: est itaque plena ~onis nota terminique convertibilis paritas); quid verbis designetur dubitabile [est] et ~one indigens BALSH. *AD rec. 2* 109; utrum proprietas sit essentia divina vel Deus. . . ad id quod dicitur quod est omnino idem, dicendum quod intelligitur in iis que sunt eadem ~one; non autem eadem est ~o essentie secundum suum nomen et proprietatis. neutrum enim in se ~onem habet, cum non habeant priora quibus cognoscantur HALES *Sent.* I 338; ubi demonstratur diffinitum de sua ~one, non demonstratur nisi de sua ~one materiali; et medium proximum, quo ostenditur diffinitum de sua ~one materiali, est causa et ~o formalis diffiniti; et, si egeat ostendi illa ~o formalis de ~one materiali, demonstrabitur per medium, quod est ~o materialis respectu ~onis formalis, et idem medium est ~o formalis respectu ~onis materialis (GROS. *Anal. Post.* I 10. 2) *GLA* III 89; homicidium . . casuale, quod non est nequiter perpetratum, non est homicidium, ut [v. l. et] videri poterit per ejus ~onem *Fleta* 47; superflue ponitur 'pertinaciter' in ~one predicta [sc. quod dicitur hereticus omnis pertinaciter adherens errori] OCKHAM *Dial.* 439. **b** fiunt per . . ~onem legis quaestiones, dum alia ratione alter scriptum interpretari nititur, alia alter ALCUIN *Rhet.* 9. **c** ~o: [e. g.] 'consortis virtus est veri restis amoris, / sorte duos una menteque reque ligans' GARL. *PP* 122 (cf. id. *Hon. Vit.* 109).

3 authoritative pronouncement, rule.

'patuĕrunt' indicativi modi est temporis praeteriti perfecti, ubi semper E producitur . .; ast vero 'patuĕrint' . . in subjunctivo modo temporis praeteriti perfecti E semper fixa ~one corripitur ALDH. *PR* 136 (cf. id. *Met.* 6: si . . haec . . metricae ~onis regulis minime caruerint); dogma, doctrina vel difinitio *Gl. Leid.* 1. 35; **1258** in tractatu pacis quedam capitula continentur que nondum ~onem receperunt finalem (*Lit. Nuncii Papalis*) *Ann. Burton* 462; patet ex fine secunde partis ejusdem statuti, que est ~o ejusdem veritatis CONWAY *Def. Mend.* 1415 (*recte* 1315).

4 decision (esp. judicial), decree, settlement; **b** (w. *causae*); **c** (w. *negotii*). **d** (mon. or sim.) resolution (of chapter). **e** (w. *manus*) arbitrament of battle.

673 his capitulis in commune tractatis et definitis . ., placuit ut quaeque definita sunt unusquisque nostrum . . confirmaret; quam sententiam ~onis . . notario scribendam dictavi (*Conc. Hertf.*) BEDE *HE* IV 5; †**676** (12c) si quis . . contra hanc nostrae ~onis cartulam . . praesumere temptaverit *CS* 43 (cf. ib. 100, 307); **796** si quis . . contra hanc ~onis nostrae vel apostolici privilegii auctoritate[m] venire temptaverit (*Lit. Papae*) DICETO *Chr.* 128; s**957** publica res regum [Eadwigi et Eadgari] ex ~one sagacium sejuncta est, ut famosum flumen Tamesae regnum disterminaret amborum B. *V. Dunst.* 24; *GAS* 589 (v. definire 4a); s**1176** Gilebertus [dominus Galweie] . . precepit quod omnes alienigene qui in Galweia . . tenementum aliquod habebant exularent et qui huic ~oni consentire nollet capitalem subiret sententiam *G. Hen. II* I 126; non sinebatur contra eum judiciaria ~o sententialiter proferri AD. EYNS. *Hug.* IV 5 p. 26; **1237** (v. consecratio 1a); s**1298** (v. definitor a); **1365** ad sentencie nostre prolacionem et ~onem finalem procedimus *Lit. Cant.* II 476; **1445** (v. definire 4e); **1503** quod ordinaciones, declaraciones atque ~ones per . . Roffensem episcopum et cancellarium predictum . . mandato regio excogitatae inter autentica statuta incorporentur *StatOx* 308. **b** de causarum pertractatione et ~one vel descriptione (*Leg. Hen.* 3) *GAS* 547; ~onem cause . . presenti scripto intimare . . curavimus *Lib. Eli.* III 111; **1587** vobis . . examinacionem, revisionem, et ~ionem tocius cause . . committimus *Pat* 1300 m. 15. **c 1288** in nullam . . personarum . . nominatarum pro ~one dicti negocii auderemus . . consentire *Reg. Heref.* 188. **d** provisum fuit ut tantum xxxij administrationes essent in ordine . ., quia sc., cum electio ministri generalis ad solas pertineat ministros et custodes, si tot essent voces in electione vel ~one . ., vix expediri posset aliquid quod consensum tot personarum requireret ECCLESTON *Adv. Min.* 54; **1290** (v. definitor b); **1397** alii de capitulo Derensi rogantes ut ~ones et ordinaciones circa statum et regimen monasterii . . in scriptis dimitteret *Vis. Derry* 50; **1451** in omnibus . . capituli ~onibus sentencia plurium . . prevaleat (*Abbr. Stat.*) *Mon. Francisc.* II 14. **e** [J. de Veteri Castro] proposuit campum cepisse de nocte, quasi regem suum et dominum ligeum . . ad manus ~onem et campestre prelium incitaret *G. Hen. V* 1.

5 ending.

Oswaldus . . post orationum ~onem, post horarum determinationem, . . coepit . . membra solo prosternere sua BYRHT. *V. Osw.* 471.

definitiuncula [LL] **(diff-),** petty definition.

neque ei, qui extra conceptum humanae originis natus est, humanis diffinitiunculis praejudicare tentes ALCUIN (*Adv. Felicem* 3. 2) *Dogm.* 164A.

definitive [LL] **(diff-)**

1 a w. ref. to spatial determination (as dist. from confinement). **b** by definition.

a esse 'in loco' dicitur dupliciter: vel circumscriptive vel ~e HALES *Qu.* 761. **b** quid sit philosophia ~e sive descriptive J. WALEYS *Compend.* f. 143; BRADW. *CD* 606B (v. determinative); treuga ~e est securitas prestita personis et rebus ad tempus, discordia nondum finita UPTON 91.

2 definitively, decisively.

1205 ~e sentenciavimus et eisdem corpus . . Hugonis . . sententialiter adjudicavimus *Reg. S. Thom. Dublin* 393; **1233** judices . . istam amicabilem compositionem inter partes in perpetuum observaturam ~e ex consensu partium interlocuti sunt *Reg. Dunferm.* 222; **1234** adjudicavimus finaliter et ~e *Cart. Brecon* 285; **1259** mulierem ab impetitione . . sentencialiter et ~e absolvit *Cl* 19; plures alias asserciones in destruccionem regule nostre . . in eadem constitucione ~e determinat, asserit et affirmat OCKHAM *Pol.* III 8; **1466** laudamus, arbitramur ac pronunciamus ~e quod . . petant . . indulgenciam . . *MunAcOx* 722.

definitivus [CL] **(diff-)**

1 a pertaining to spatial determination. **b** pertaining to definition.

a magister recitavit . . tres opiniones de multiplicacione corporis [Christi], viz. dimensionalem, ~am, et virtualem; primas duas asseruit omnino esse falsas (*Concl. Wycl.*) *Ziz.* 107. **b** haec constitutio ~a dicitur, quia quid sit fur et quid sacrilegus definiendum ALCUIN *Rhet.* 7.

2 definitive, decisive (esp. of judicial sentence); **b** (as sb. f., *sc. sententia*).

si judici de causa liquet, tunc pronunciet ~am sententiam RIC. ANGL. *Summa* 106; AD. EYNS. *Hug.* IV 5 p. 26 (v. calculus 5b); **1221** adjudicata fuit demum dicto Lismer' episcopo episcopatus illius vera possessio et per sentenciam ~am assignata *Cl* 475b; ante ~am sentenciam

frustratorie causa dilacionis ad appellacionis auxilium convolavit OCKHAM *Pol.* I 54; appellacio vel est a gravaminibus .. vel a sentencia ~a seu decreto interlocutorio habente vim sentencie ~e *Praxis* 241. **b** numquid ille qui esset judex pape heretici potest .. in judicio papam hereticum detinere vel aliter circa ~am coartare? OCKHAM *Dial.* 653; **a1350** sive a gravamine sive a ~a ab ebdomadario ad .. cancellarium appelletur *StatOx* 93; [pape] statuerunt vel preceperunt ~am illam in sua forma CONWAY *Def. Mend.* 1423 (*recte* 1323).

definitor [CL] **(diff-),** deciding judge, arbiter. **b** (mon. or sim.) definitor, official regulating proceedings of chapter.

a1275 fratres .. non sint causarum secularium vel questionum ~ores, judices vel arbitrarii (*Const. Frat. Penit.*) *EHR* IX 126; **s1298** reges submiserunt se in viij arbitros, quorum sentenciis et diffinicionibus auctoritate domini pape roboratis pax inter eos soliditatis nancisseretur fundamentum. maturato igitur ~ores apostolorum petunt limina *Chr. S. Edm.* 69 (cf. W. GUISB. 317); **1314** (v. arbitrator); **s1386** rex .. compulsus est .. auditores et judicii ~ores eligere WALS. *HA* II 152; **1454** compromiserunt .. in .. viros .. electos .. et ordinatos coire, ab eis tamquam in arbitros compromissarios, .. compositores, laudatores, ~ores, et comites amicos sponte in se arbitrium suscipientes *Melrose* II 568. **b 1235** priori provinciali fratrum Predicatorum in Anglia et ~oribus in capitulo celebrando apud Eboracum GROS. *Ep.* 15 *rub.*; **s1240** sub ipso [fratre Haymone] celebratum est primum et ultimum capitulum generale ~itorum quod unquam fuit in ordine, propter insolentiam quidem eorum ECCLESTON *Adv. Min.* 87; **1255** habita .. collatione cum ~oribus capituli nostri generalis Mediolanis celebrati (*Lit. Prioris Praedicatorum*) *Ann. Burton* 434; **a1275** nos rector et priores provinciales ac ~ores capituli generalis (*Const. Frat. Penit.*) *EHR* IX 122; **1290** in .. generali capitulo abbatum et priorum .. ordinis .. super omnibus et singulis capitulum contingentibus .. ~ores seu provisores .. fuerunt electi, quorum diffiniciones ordinacionesve seu provisiones .. faciendas alii coabbates .. se .. servaturos .. promiserunt *Doc. Eng. Black Monks* I 129; **1396** presidens, ~ores, et abbates dicti capituli [generalis ordinis Cisterciensis] dictum J. H. .. verum abbatem monasterii de Dore .. pronunciaverunt *Pat* 344 m. 15; **1426** lego ordini fratrum Minorum in Anglia xl li. secundum discrecionem ejusdem ordinis et regni ac ~orum provincialis capituli .. disponendas *Reg. Cant.* II 357; **1445** (v. definire 4e).

definitorius, definitive, decisive.

quod finis secunde partis, sc. quod sine licencia proprii sacerdotis non poterit sibi confessum solvere vel ligare, sit diffinitoria CONWAY *Def. Mend.* 1413 (*recte* 1313).

defisus v. 2 diffidere. **defitigare** v. defatigare.

deflagitare [cf. CL flagitare], to importune.

to aske, .. ~are, .. flagitare cum clamore et pertinacia *CathA.*

deflare [CL], to blow on.

~at, incudit *GlC* D 128 (cf. *GlH* D 73).

deflectere [CL]

1 (trans.): **a** to incline downwards. **b** to turn, direct (also fig.). **c** to divert (fig.), wrest.

a quam beata conpunctione oculos ad terram deflexerint BEDE *Hom.* II 15. 177 (cf. id. *HE* III 19: oculos in inferiora ~ens). **b** cum ad finem scripturam suam deflexisset FELIX *Guthl.* 37 (cf. ib.: cursum suum .. ~ens); visum quoque .. circumquaque se per singula cursim †defleccente T. MON. *Will.* II 6 (cf. ib. II 14: via per diversorii deflexa dispendium); quedam animalia cornua habent flexibilia: hoc [est] ex humiditate, quia humiditas ~itur ad interiora et siccitas ad superiora *Quaest. Salern.* B 137. **c** BEDE *TR* 8 (v. dies 5a); conati sunt terram .. ad sue ditionis jura injuriosa injuste ~ere R. COLD. *Cuthb.* 46.

2 (intr.) to deviate (fig.).

si iter virtutum .. tenemus, si non a semita regulari .. ~imus BEDE *Hom.* I 13. 227.

deflenter, sorrowfully.

1417 qui ad ejus [Petri navicule] regimen se ingerunt .., quod ~er referimus, nec scientes nec potentes .. subvenire *Reg. Cant.* III 48 (= *Conc.* III 383a).

deflere [CL], to bewail, deplore. **b** (*form. pass.*, w. abstr. subj.). **c** to mourn (person).

quippe qui .. malorum cumulum lacrimosis querelis ~eam GILDAS *EB* 1; semper ex intimo corde ~eat culpam suam *Id. Pen.* 1; **680** peccatricem pollutae vitae piacula lugubriter ~entem ALDH. *Ep.* 4; cujus tam ~endae historiae [*2 Kings* xxiv] .. non opinor allegoriam esse reticendam BEDE *Kings* 735; si nostra errata, si miserias proximorum, debita lamentatione ~emus *Id. Hom.* II 13. 157; **†851** (11c) nisi digna satisfactione ~eat commissum *CS* 462; fides .. necessario tantum commissa ~et et ~enda cavet quantum [Deum et proximum] amat PULL. *Sent.* 839A (cf. ib. 655D); W. CANT. *Mir. Thom.* VI 52 (v. deformitas a); in me caritatis defectum et perpendo et ~eo J. FORD *Serm.* 35. 5. **b 956** (11c) omnia .. quae sollicitudo mortalis vitae in .. amicorum amisione conqueritur ac ~etur *CS* 978. **c** ~endi cives ab inimicis discerpuntur GILDAS *EB* 19; ipse [Orpheus] ad undam Strymonis raptam Eurydicen .. ~evit *Lib. Monstr.* II 7; [Jeremias] qui ~evit illum sanctum regem Josyam BELETH *RDO* 102. 107; pro hec cantu letitie ~emus extinctum Solem justitie HON. *GA* 666A.

deflexio [LL], deflexion.

difortium, ~o *GlC* D 172; astra septem, quae nunc septentrio / sursum levat et nunc deflexio / flectit austri certo judicio J. HOWD. *Ph.* 295.

deflexus v. deflectere, defluxus a.

deflorare [LL]

1 to deflower, deprive of bloom (fig.). **b** to deflower (sexually), ravish; **c** (w. virginity as obj.).

s946 quum multa felicitate regis [Edmundi] florerent successus, hus tandem miserabilis exitus ~avit *Chr. Rams.* 17; cum per quinquennium juventutem ejus [mulieris] languor et angor ~assent W. CANT. *Mir. Thom.* III 6; **s1388** rex .. jussit .. ut .. ecclesiam .. urticis, vepribus ~atam liliis et rosis ornarent KNIGHTON *Cont.* II 263. **b** Dina .. a Sichem .. concupiscitur, rapitur, opprimitur, ~atur [cf. *Gen.* xxxiv 2] P. BLOIS *Serm.* 634A; [clericus] totis nisibus virginem violare et ~are contendit GIR. *GE* I 34; **1199** duxit eam in domum suam et ~avit eam *CurR RC* II 82; **1206** Matillis .. queritur quod Willelmus .. in rapo eam ~avit *CurR* IV 232; **1243** (v. concubinare 1); [Anglia] gignit et lapidem gagatem, qui .. †deploratas prodit feminas per micturam OTTERB. 5; licet .. clerici .. occidant tenentes dominorum .. et difflorent uxores dominorum et reginam .., non potest punire eos per unum quadrantem WYCL. *Compl.* 91; *to defoulle*, .. maculare .., ~are .., stuprari *CathA.* **c** quod Aldredus .. virginitatem suam aliquociens ~averit W. DAN. *Ep.* f. 62c; nolite virginitatem meam ~are *Latin Stories* 117.

2 a to make excerpts from (a text). **b** to excerpt, select for quotation (sts. absol.). **c** (?) to select (as a gift).

a ut, eorum scripta ~ans, ea quae non dixerant illos dixisse finxerit BEDE *Wict.* 9; libellum Stephani cursim studui ~are HIGD. VII 25 p. 82. **b** de diversis rerum qualitatibus .. materiam nanctus, nunc grandem nunc gracilem creaturarum naturam considerans, strictim summatimque ~avi ALDH. *Met.* 5; aliqua ex his que .. Beda dixit ~abo W. MALM. *GR prol.*; Henricus .. fidissime .. decertavit, quemadmodum suis in locis in presenti historia plenius ~abimus *G. Steph.* I 38; sacrarum litterarum tractatores .. legi et, ut res dubia patefieret, testimoniorum hinc inde carptis, prout presens epistola edocet, ~avi H. BOS. *Ep.* 1417A; hec pauca .. ad edificacionem legencium ~are decrevi *NLA* (*Finan*) I 447. **c** optima quaeque dedit libens exenia miris / deflorata [v. l. efflorata] modis FRITH. 472.

defloratio [LL]

1 deflowering, ravishment.

perseverat inter eos sine actu conjugali conjugalis affectus et sine ~one virginitatis caste dilectionis amplexus AILR. *Ed. Conf.* 748A; omnis delibatio integritatis quedam ~o est virginitatis BALD. CANT. *Tract.* 7. 471D; si .. mulier .. visa fuerit per matronas nullam ~onis lesionem sustinuisse .., non audiatur *Cust. Norm.* 50. 1; **s1366** in .. adulteriis, virginum ac matronarum ~one et homicidiis convicti J. READING 190.

2 collection of excerpts, anthology.

quicquid ille largius dixerat in artum contrahens defloravit adeo splendide ut magis valere videatur ~o quam ingentis illius voluminis diffusio W. MALM. *GP* IV 164; prologus Rodberti Crikeladensis prioris Oxinfordie in ~onem naturalis historie Plinii secundi CRICKLADE *Plin. Prol.* (*tit.*).

deflorator [LL], deflowerer, ravisher.

audivimus .. puellarem pudicitiam expugnatam esse ipsamque defloratam ~orem sui minime nosse J. FURNESS *Kentig.* 1 p. 163.

deflorēre, ~escere [CL]

1, to shed bloom (fig.), wilt.

quomodo primus homo arbitrio floruit et ~uit PULL. *Sent.* 643B; ut pilis cadentibus caput ~eret W. CANT. *Mir. Thom.* IV 21; spes fuit in flore, sed flos defloruit NIG. *SS* 2037; id [sc. Grecorum militum] genus in illo ~uit exercitio Trojani exercitus MAP *NC* II 18 f. 30.

2 (?) to flourish.

abjecta seculi pompa, qua ante .. non parum ~uerat *Mir. Crisp.* 737D.

defluentia, (fig.) ebbing, melting away. **b** downfall.

expectavit turbe tumulantis ~iam *NLA* (*Decuman*) I 264. **b** causas .. humilitatis conspicere possumus .. respiciendo .. proximorum cotidianam ~iam *Spec. Laic.* 41.

1 defluere [CL]

1 to flow or float down. **b** (pr. ppl., w. ref. to hair or garment) flowing. **c** (w. *in lacrimas*) to burst into tears. **d** to spring (fig.), be derived. **e** (w. abstr. subj.) to pass (into).

ALDH. *VirgP* 32 (v. cuniculus 1a); ~entibus circa eum .. crustis glacierum BEDE *HE* V 12; quum .. sanies ex auribus ~xisset GOSC. *Mir. Iv.* lxvii; EADMER *Odo* 83 (v. confractio 1c); **1259** (v. 2 conductus 2a); BACON VIII 200 (v. depluere); ab ere campanarum liquefacto et ~ente *Croyl.* 97. **b** sunt mulieres, .. quae .. crines usque ad talos ~entes .. habent *Lib. Monstr.* I 28; ciclade cum fimbria .. ~enti *Lib. Regal.* 20v. (v. 1 cyclas 1a). **c** totus in lacrimas puer ~it MAP *NC* III 3 f. 40. **d** hoc donum in quorundam mentes de largitatis tuae fonte ~xit EGB. *Pont.* 109; cum communis nobilitatis vena Britonibus et Romanis ab Enea ~at G. MON. IV 2; sic capit exempla nullus de lege vetusta / quo testamentum defluit ecce novum GOWER *VC* VI 1240. **e** miseri / a quibus omne scelus vastum defluxit in orbem *De libero arbitrio* 37; post Ade peccatum concupiscentie pena ~xit in rationalia animalia et ita in mulieres *Quaest. Salern.* Ba 97.

2 a to fall, drop, droop (of crop or foliage). **b** to sink, lapse (fig.), abandon oneself.

a extabescit, languescens, ~it *GlC* E 438; frondes .. ~unt nisi multa sit humiditas *Quaest. Salern.* B 62; cum de arbore ista sublimi et fertili .. impossibile sit folium quodcumque ~ere J. FORD *Serm.* 52. 1; **13..** velut quercus ~entibus foliis *MonA* V 435a; marcescunt flores, defluit orta seges GOWER *VC* VI 1202. **b** ~it, *nyder asah GlN* 50. 42; per illicita desideria ~ximus HON. *Spec. Eccl.* 889B; **s1151** que [gens Pictaviensis], cum .. post belli sudores in bona quiete persistiterit, ilico tota ~it in voluptatem DICETO *Chr.* 294; sciam iter sanctorum currere / .. in Amoris flammam defluere / et in ejus mucronem ruere J. HOWD. *Ph.* 619.

2 defluere v. diffluere.

defluitio, emission (of breath).

de H .. dicendum quod dupliciter potest considerari, aut ipsius spiritus emissi in latum ~o .. aut simul cum hoc ipsorum laterum lingue ad dentes confraccio *Ps.*-GROS. *Gram.* 23.

defluus [CL], flowing down.

~us, inruens, fluens *GlH* D 10; fluo .. unde ~us, -a, -um, quod cito decurrit OSB. GLOUC. *Deriv.* 227; a capite ~um cum brachio detergens .. cruorem W. FITZST. *Thom.* 141.

defluxio [LL], ebb. **b** (fig.) decline, corruption.

de effluxione et ~one Occeani J. SAL. *Pol.* 640C. **b** prima ~o a luce veritatis mox ignorantie tenebras incurrit H. READING (I) *Haeret.* 1261A; in hujus ~onis tumultu multos sibi consentientes .. conmovit [Lucifer] GROS. *Hexaem.* IV 11 p. 132.

defluxus [CL]

1 flowing down or away. **b** outflow, estuary.

ALF. ANGL. *Cor* 15. 11 (v. defaecare 1c); similiter in mari dupplus †deflexus et resolutio; unde totum consumeretur, nisi esset dupplex restauratio huic dupplici †deflexui correspondens; et enim quidam †flexus [? l. fluxus] per meatus subterraneos .. et huic respondet regressio aquarum per flumina ad ipsum BACON VIII 22; continue creantur essencie .. qui mundum perficiunt; et non aliunde ex ~u accidencium tante imperficitur iste mundus WYCL. *Dom. Div.* 222. **b** dedit .. monasterio .. terras ab Inveralien proxime ad ~um Speae amnis FERR. *Kinloss* 25.

2 (fig.) decline, corruption.

est .. quibusdam a voluptuoso ~u cohercio claustrum GROS. *Hexaem.* IV 12 p. 135.

defodĕre [CL], **~ēre**

1 to dig, form by digging. **b** (p. ppl.) sunken, hollow. **c** (p. ppl. as sb. n.) pit, hole.

descendens in defossum sepulturae suae locum BEDE *Hom.* I 9. 47; defossum, †*bdolfn* [l. *bedolfen*] *GlM* 23. 349. **b** tandem oculus defossus ipsam fere palpebram occultando ademerat R. COLD. *Cuthb.* 70. **c** ille [Midas] celare nequiens nec palam proferre ausus, terram fodit et in defosso rem dixit et operuit ALB. LOND. *DG* 10. 7.

2 to bury.

genus quoddam humanum .. in hieme terris defossum legimus *Lib. Monstr.* I 9; hoc est talentum .. in terra ~eri [cf. *Matth.* xxv 25], id est scientiam spiritalem ad peccatorum opera converti BEDE *Kings* 736; defossae, absconsae, *hyddes GlM* 30. 79; W. MALM. *GR* II 199 (v. compilator 1).

3 to disinter, exhume.

c1086 corpora defunctorum, que ad ecclesiam Willelmi sepulta fuerant, ab hominibus ipsius Willelmi defossa sunt *Regesta* p. 127; si quis furem [cum dampnatis inhumatum] innoxiare velit .., adeat triplex ordalium. si mundus sit in ordalio, diffodiat cognatum suum [AS: *nime upp his mæg*]; si vero sit immundus, jaceat fur ubi jacebat (*Quad.*) *GAS* 230 (cf. ib. 221); si quis murdritus intra vij dies inhumetur .., non diffodiatur sine licentia justitie (*Leg. Hen.* 92. 12) *Ib.* 608.

defoedare [LL], to defile.

carnis illecebra, que honoris glorie insidiatur a latere .. ut .. quasi per vile lutum contaminet ipsam et ~et H. Bos. *LM* 1323A; Ysmaelita Syon gremium defedat, at illud / exornare studet Israelita pius Garl. *Tri. Eccl.* 109; exclusa per mortificationem carnis omni concupiscentia ~antis illecebre Ad. Marsh *Ep.* 11; sophismatibus artistarum, que ~averunt philosophiam Bacon *Tert.* 41; **1440** quod .. iste hostis ecclesie .. in loco originis sue .., quem .. pessimis doctrinis et faccionibus suis polluere et ~are temptavit, .. debitas lueret penas Bekynton I 189.

defoedatio, discoloration.

morphea est ~o coloris cutis propter corruptionem nutrimenti Gilb. III 170. 2; ictericia est cutis ~o universalis in croceitatem .. tendens Gad. 85. 2.

defoederare v. diffoederare. **deforare** v. devorare.

deforas [LL, al. div.], abroad (outside monastery). *V. et. deforis* 3a.

1346 nec monachum aliquem .. cum clochia .. permittimus ~as equitare *G. S. Alb.* II 453 (= *Conc.* II 730b: de foras).

deforc- v. diffort-.

deforestare [cf. forestare], to disafforest, remove (land) from forest status. *V. et. deafforestare, difforestare, disafforestare.*

1205 computate hominibus de Devonia c m. infra finem quem nobiscum fecerunt pro Devonia ~anda *Cl* 33a; **c1213** totam terram .. ~atam quam .. W. eis dedit *Reg. Paisley* 90; prefatam [silvam abbas] .. fraude versuta ~avit Gir. *Spec.* III 12 p. 206; **s1225** omnes .. nove foreste per Angliam sunt ~ate *Ann. Worc.* 417 (cf. Wend. II 286); **1236** concessisse abbati et conventui de M. .. omnes predictas terras, quas eis ~avimus *Melrose* 258; **1275** (v. diswarennare); **1279** clamat .. boscos suos inclusos .. tali waranto quod dominus H. rex .. ~avit omnes terras inter Use et Derwent *PQW* 201b.

deforestatio [cf. afforestatio], disafforestation. *V. et. deafforestatio, difforestatio, disafforestatio.*

1225 homines comitatus de Huntedon' debent xl m. pro ~one *LTRMem* 7 r. 17; **s1298** barones et prelati pecierunt ut [rex] .. cartam .. de foresta una cum ~one jam facta ratificaret *Flor. Hist.* III 297.

deforis [LL, al. div.]

1 (adv.) from outside. **b** from outside the immediate area. **c** from an external source.

T. Mon. *Will.* II 9 (v. deintus 1a); Noe .. arcam ingrediens, quam Dominus ~is includit [cf. *Gen.* vii 16] Ad. Scot *TGC* 821B; miles .. per portam [purgatorii S. Patricii] intravit, quam prior statim ~is observavit *Meaux* I 140; **1196** regum hostilitas .. possessiones ecclesie nostre ~is invadens (*Lit. Archiep. Rotomag.*) Diceto *YH* II 144; **1203** de nocte venit ad domum .. domini sui .. et firmavit ostia domus sue ~is .., ita quod nec ipse nec alii servientes domus exire potuerunt *CurR* II 195; **c1250** is .. poterat ita celari ut ~is aspicienti nullum interius haberi persuaderet *MonA* III 371a; nullus egredi debet oratorium .., si aliquis eum ~is vocaverit, absque .. licencia *Ord. Ebor.* I 6. **b** tunc [durante completorio] licet iis qui .. ante illam horam se expedire non possunt et fratribus qui de foris veniunt comedere in refectorio Lanfr. *Const.* 163; **a1190** quod nullus mercator qui sit extraneus et ~is sit residens in Lincolnia pro tingendis pannis suis (*Ch. Hen. II*) *Gild. Merch.* II 378; **1283** (v. deinfra). **c** **c1180** justitia, cujus acumine .. possis radere si quid eruginis conscientie intrinsecus adheserit seu ~is in ambiguis quid contigerit discutiendum A. Tewk. *Ep.* 10; inquirit an omnes anime ingrediantur in materia .. aut nunquid omnes adveniant ~is sive nulle Bradw. *CD* 86E.

2 on the outside, externally. **b** on an outside wall. **c** in relation to something external. **d** on the surface, superficially.

murus de foris altior longitudine stantis hominis Bede *CuthbP* 17; destinam non, ut antea, ~is in fulcimentum domus adposuerunt, sed intro .. ecclesiam .. posuerunt *Id. HE* III 17; debent esse coopertae crux, coronae, capsae, textus qui imagines ~is habent Lanfr. *Const.* 98; **s1066** ostendit ei dux .. relliquias que fuerant in magno vase cooperto pallio .., uno solo †filacerio [l. filaterio] ~is ostenso Silgrave 71; **c1250** calix argenteus intus et ~is deauratus *Vis. S. Paul.* 14; **s1255** cum .. scedula nuda .. sigillata per sigilla ~is dependentia *Ann. Osney* 110; res que adjuvant hoc totum de foris cum actione et abstersione subtili sunt liniamenta et ablutiones abstergentes Bacon VII 71; **1298** j bursa frettata ~is *Rec. Leic.* I 363; **1419** serviente ad arma tenente .. librum cum kalendario et ~is effigie crucifixi *MGL* I 24. **b** [mulieres] conducte .. ad metendum nullo modo introire clausuras nostras permittantur, set habeant domum hostium ~is habentem *Inst. Sempr.* *lxviii. **c** hujusmodi quedam est vis apprehensiva ~is, quedam est vis apprehensiva deintus; vis autem apprehensiva ~is est sensus, qui dividitur in v species, sc. visum, gustum, tactum, olfactum, auditum J. Blund *An.* 55. **d** si quis percusserit manum alterius de foris [AS: *utan*], si potest mederi, dentur ei xx s. (*Inst. Cnuti*) *GAS* 87 (= *Quad.*: extra); tu, quod habent alii deforis, intus habe; / sint tibi divitie, sed que comitentur ubique Nig. *Cur.* 147; **s1183** navem quandam que .. ~is aliquantum dealbata et refecta et in altum deducta fuerat *G. Hen. II* I 306; **s1297** (v. dealbare 2d); *Alph.* 102 (v. deintus 1c).

3 outside (of building or enclosed area). **b** publicly.

presbyter .. ingressum domus renuit, ~is autem commanendi locum annuit Herm. Arch. 11; **s1070** jacebant miseri homines per totam villam tam in domibus suis quam ~is .. fame consumpti *Chr. Evesham* 91; Northguicum obsident. .. vindex ~is exercitus cotidie crescit Ord. Vit. IV 13 p. 263; **c1160** apud T. est orreum .. plenum .. de frumento. .. tres tassi sunt ibi ~is *Dom. S. Paul.* 131; **s1174** hostes ~is agmine facto muris appropinquant Diceto *YH* II 386; deforis armigeri sint potu participantes D. Bec. 1473; antequam prima clausula legatur .., non debent .. qui ~is sunt fratres .. intrare *Obs. Barnwell* 156; **s1333** isti ~is .., satagentes villam .. optinere, machinas .. fieri faciebant; illi vero infra .. resistebant *G. Ed. III Bridl.* 111; **s1349** pons ligneus, subito elevatus, .. inclusit ingressos et exclusit ~is existentes Wals. *HA* I 274; deforis in campis stat primula cincta ligustris Gower *VC* 63. **b** **s1382** hec quidem erant verba monstrata ~is ad omnes dominos .. Italie per nuncios Wals. *HA* II 64.

4 (*quod deforis est*) besides, moreover, what is more.

quod ~is est, mendatis, quod [etc.] Gascoigne *Loci* 79.

5 (prep. w. acc.) outside.

si virga ~is sepem incaute missa sit (*Leg. Hen.* 90. 4a) *GAS* 605 (cf. deintus 2); ~is Bodeherste ad orientem est terminus leuge *Chr. Battle* f. 15; **1189** ascendendo per rivulum ~is .. fossatum (*Ch. Ric. I*) *MonA* V 594a (cf. *PQW* 130a).

deformaliter [cf. LL formaliter], in a nonformal sense.

dicitur quod katholicus loquitur equivoce de peccato, vel formaliter vel ~iter Wycl. *Sim.* 25.

deformare [CL]

1 to form, shape.

etiam laicis in hiis gratia affluebat, excepto quod per se litteras atramento ~atos legere nesciebant Ad. Eyns. *Hug.* I 10 p. 32.

2 to deform, mar (esp. morally); *cf. difformare.* **b** (pr. ppl.) disfiguring. **c** (p. ppl. as sb. n.) blemish.

non splendida .. argenti species turpiter ~atur Aldh. *VirgP* 9; matrona .. / .. Christi famulam sermone procaci / deformare studet *Id. VirgV* 1920; devenustat, ~at, *geatolhiwaþ GlH* D 353; **10..** ~atos, *geatelod WW*; hominem .. natura .. interiorem variis vitiorum maculis ~averat Gir. *EH* II 11; quod pater enormat baptismi forma reformat; / sed se deformat vendens quod gratia format Garl. *Mor. Scol.* 478; *V. Will.* 289 (v. defunctio). **b** lepra .. signat mistice symoniam. .. nullus morbus est isto .. ad solvendum continuitatem et formam ~ancior Wycl. *Sim.* 61. **c** **c1340** nos .. qui .. tenemur errata corrigere et ~ata in melius reformare *FormOx* 170.

3 to foul.

1424 plures sunt canes in domo ~antes claustra *Reg. Heref.* 72.

deformatio [CL], disfigurement; **b** (fig. or w. word play).

nec venusti capitis ~o .. statum cordis [virginis] inclinat Aldh. *VirgP* 47; **9..** ~o, *sio unwlitegung WW*; si quis serviens vulneratus fuerit in facie per magistrum suum, ita quod non possit sanari sine ~one .. (*Fragm. Coll.*) *APScot* I 374. **b** ~o .. per peccatum eicit eum extra paradisum Gros. *Hexaem.* XI 6; **s1238** suborta est discordia .. indecens inter gregem et pastorem [sc. archiep. Cant.] .., unde vocatus legatus ad reformationem illius ~onis .. priorem .. deposuit M. Par. *Maj.* III 492; inimici .. per quos falsidica .. informacio, imo ~o, ad aures plurimorum fidelium .. de gestis nostris .. dinoscitur pervenisse Ockham *Err. Papae* 958.

deformis [CL], deformed, misshapen (also fig. or w. word play). **b** (as sb. n.) deformity, (moral) blemish.

quid enim ~ius .. quam Deo timorem .. denegare Gildas *EB* 4; matronae rugosae forte figuram / vidit in extasi deformem fronte vetusta Aldh. *VirgV* 598; fedus, .. ~is, turpis vel *ful GlH* F 287; **9..** ~em, *atole* .., ~es, *unwlitig* .., **10..** ~is *hiwleas WW*; vir bonus post cenam fit melior, malus autem a cena redit ~ior Pull. *Sent.* 968D; dolens in sanctuario Dei fieri picturarum ineptias et ~ia quedam portenta Ad. Dore *Pictor* 142; pavo .. habet pedes ~issimos et rugosos Bart. Angl. XII 32; aperti sunt oculi .. ut sciam me nudum erubescamque rursus me ~em Chaundler *Apol.* 19a. **b** nisi te, Domine, donante, qui miris modis curas infirmitates nostras, formas ~ia Ailr. *Spec. Car.* II 28. 556A.

deformitas [CL], deformity, disfigurement; **b** (fig.). **c** harmful act.

ac si nil umquam in eo ~atis ac tumoris apparuisset Bede *HE* IV 30; [armiger] gladio precisam cratem manus defleverat. .. munere martyris evasit .. manci ~atem W. Cant. *Mir. Thom.* VI 52; degenerante quadam nature ~ate Gir. *TH* I 26; **1433** palacium .. gravis minabatur ~as et ruina *MonA* III 113a. **b** animae pulchritudo virtus est et ejus ~as vitium Alcuin *Moral.* 644; simul inerat splendor majestatis et ~as nostre mortalitatis Pull. *Sent.* 829C. **c** quia rex Alexander [II] tantas in Angliam ~ates et enormia mala cum suo exercitu perpetravit *Plusc.* VII 8 (= Fordun *Cont.* IX 31: molestias).

deformiter, unbeautifully. **b** disgracefully.

forma, .. unde ~iter Osb. Glouc. *Deriv.* 217; melius .. etsi non formose utcunque tamen vel ~iter formatus sit, forma .. citharedi imperitam peritiam indicante H. Bos. *LM* 1402D. **b** quam ~iter in subditos .. curia vindictam exercuerit noster explicare stilus abhorruit Gir. *IK* I 10; fedis voluptatibus ~ius inherere Ad. Marsh *Ep.* 244; impetus, ut memini, gravis est deformiter illis / quos sine jure Dei propria jura regunt Gower *VC* III 523.

defort- v. diffort-. **defortium** v. divortium.

defossare [cf. CL fossa, defossus *p. ppl. of* defodere], to dig.

14.. quedam fossa defensiva satis profunda et alta de campis elemosinarii .. ~ata ad defensam tam camporum ejus quam hortorum villanorum Amund. I app. 428.

defossio [cf. CL fossio], digging.

s1216 perrexerunt ad montem Thabor, ubi primo aquarum inopiam et postmodum per ~onem copiam repperrunt (Ol. Scholasticus) M. Par. *Maj.* III 10.

defossum v. defodere. **defotare** v. devotare 3. **defractio** v. diffractio.

defrainnare [OF *defraindre*], to dismantle.

1195 pro perreriis et mangonellis castri Cad[omi] †defranmand' et cameris emendandis *RScacNorm* I 185.

defraudare [CL], to defraud, cheat. **b** to acquire fraudulently. **c** (w. *spem*) to disappoint.

angelorum auxilio in .. angustiis .. non est ~atus *V. Cuthb.* I 4; ~at, fraudem facit *GlC* D 103; interrogans quid causae esset ut [? se] sine aliquo delicti peccato suis substantiis a regibus pro Deo donatis praedonum more ~arent Eddi 24; **c1327** suorumque desolatur militum stipamine, / dum dolose †desiandatur [MS: defraudatur] per †sudam [? l. fugam] Hoylandie (*Offic. T. Lanc.*) *Pol. Songs* 271; **s1364** Lombardi mercatores .. ~abant regem de mmm li. argenti quolibet anno *Eul. Hist.* III 234; **14..** prefatum I. .. de jure suo .. subdole machinantes †~ere *Reg. Brev. Orig.* 113b; **c1496** ad ~and' ipsos .. de bargania sua *Entries* 357b. **b** **964** (11c) nisi istud .. ad pristinum statum quod defra[u]davit redigat *CS* 1136; **1495** pro quolibet denario .. ~ato (v. cavere 2a). **c** sciebant .. quod spes eorum in sinu nostro reposita ~ari non poterat R. Bury *Phil.* 8. 140.

defraudatio [LL], defrauding, deprivation.

1253 non est .. alterum genus peccati .. tam odibile .. quam animas .. pastoralis officii .. ~one mortificare et perdere Gros. *Ep.* 128; **1265** quod .. prior de M. singulas travas de carucis suis .. eisdem .. fratribus subtraxerit in ~onem .. elemosine .. nostre *Cl* 111; absque gestus dolosa simulatione, absque operis perversa ~one J. Waleys *Commun.* 6; **1318** liberacionem panis et cervisie .. toto tempore vite sue sine ~one aliqua percipiet *FormA* 317; **1348** mercatores .. diversa .. coria .. ad diversas partes Scocie .. cariari faciunt in .. custume et subsidii nobis .. debitorum ~onem et amissionem manifestam *RScot* 712b.

defraudator [CL], defrauder, cheat.

qui .. habet collum breve valde est callidus ~or, astutus et dolosus Bacon V 170.

defraudere v. defraudare.

defremere [CL], to calm down (intr.), come to rest.

ut seditionum, sic externi belli, procella omnis ~uit W. Poit. I 59.

defricare [CL], to rub down (also fig.).

~atum, *abeowed GlH* D 77; **9..** ~abitur, *sie agniden WW*; nec .. ~ans labra colloquentium auricalco pigmentate adulationis R. Cold. *Osw. pref.* p. 327; *to rub*, fricare, con-, de-, per-, re-, *CathA*.

defringere [CL], to break down, crush, smash. **b** (p. ppl.) worn out, decrepit.

Egb. *Pont.* 96 (v. educare 3); demones, ostium ecclesie .. levi negotio ~entes, .. catenas diruperunt W. Malm. *GR* II 204; **c1300** *IMisc* 67/18 (v. devehere); **1346** ponte per gentes ville .. defracto [OF *in* Avesb. 105b: *ceaux de la ville .. debruserent le pount*] (*Lit. Confessoris Regis*) Ad. Mur. *Chr.* 213; **1372** (v. collum 3); **1383** molaris in prima molacione defractus fuit per infortunium *MinAc* 1209/15 r. 8 (2). **b** **1364** [*for calling S. de W., alderman*] falsum latronem et rusticum veterem et defractum *Cal. Pl. Mem. Lond.* II 15; **1437** in lavendria .. viij *towaylles* de panno lineo, unde iiij debiles et defracti *Ac. Obed. Abingd.* 110.

defrondare [LL], to lop, strip of branches.

1410 ~averunt salices .. ad valenciam ij carectatarum *splents* (*CourtR Gt. Waltham*) *OED* s. v. *splint*; *to twyste*, ~are *CathA*.

defrondatio [cf. CL frondatio], lopping.

1406 in ~one arborum et aliis diversis agendis, xij d. *Ac. Obed. Abingd.* 71.

defrondator [cf. CL frondator], lopper.

a twyster of trees, ~or *CathA*.

defrucatus, defructus v. defrutus.

defruitio [cf. LL fruitio], deprivation of enjoyment.

sitis cauti, ne contingat quod nullus de cetero ~one sit usus, quod non transeat in desolacionem cupido *Dictamen* 372.

defrustare [LL], to tear to bits.

defrustrare (*sic*) foro radium vel participare / cum sociis caveas D. Bec. 1749.

defrustis, torn.

c1250 duo rochetti, minor qui est integrum (*sic*) et major qui ~is *Vis. S. Paul.* 5.

defrustrare v. defrustare.

defrustrari [CL], to foil, disappoint.

spem defrustrante labore Nig. *SS* 229.

defrutus, ~atus [CL], boiled down, (w. *vinum* or as sb. n.) boiled down wine. **b** flat, stale.

nunc potius metuat defruti pocula virgo Aldh. *VirgV* 2512 (cf. id. *VirgP* 30: defecati nectaris ~a); ~um, *coerin GlC* D 19; **9..** ~i, *caerenes* .., *wines* .., †defrucatum [? l. defrutatum], *gesweted win WW*; ~um vinum, *gesoden win*, vel passum Ælf. *Gl.*; hec sumentem precipue exhilarat et reficit vinum passum et defructum [*gl.*: *saule*] Neckam *Ut.* 102. **b** *dollyd*, ~us; *dollyd as wyne or ale*, †defunctus, vapidus .., *palde as ale*, defructus *CathA*.

defucare [cf. CL fucare], to paint or caulk. **b** (fig.) to counterfeit.

1337 in rosco empto ad eandem galleam per vices ~andam *KRAc* 19/31 m. 5. **b** fortius timenda eorum .. amicitia ~ata quam inimicitia despicata Gir. *TH* III 21.

defugere [CL], to flee. *V. et. diffugere* 1.

dumque catervatim stridunt et spicula trudunt, / agmina defugiunt Aldh. *Aen.* 75 (*Crabro*) 10; **1285** si ~erint et testatum fuerit per vicecomitem quod non sunt inventi (2 *Westm.* 11) *StRealm* I 80 (= *Reg. Malm.* I 85: diffugerint); **1366** Thomas W. ~it; set ubi devenit nesciunt nec dicunt *SelCCoron* 53.

defullare [cf. fullare, AN *defuller*, OF *defoler*], to tread down, press.

1244 ~avit eum genibus suis super ventrem, ita quod †sthopivit sanguinem *JustIt* 175 r. 40.

defunctio [LL], decease.

†**a1046** (14c) volo quod in pretium sepulturae meae .. proveniant aecclesiae de R. xv librae de argento .. et catallis quae die ~onis meae apud me contigerit inveniri *CD* 971; quomodo posset .. mortem machinari ..; ad hanc ~onem malitie minister .. scelerum suorum congessit officinas ut eum ante tribunal publicum super incendii crimine criminaliter deferret, delatum vinceret, victum membrorum mutilatione .. deformaret *V. Will.* 289; quia dies ~onis sue non sibi foret dies judicii .. set dies potius misericordie Ad. Eyns. *Hug.* V 16 p. 198; **s1242** papa .. S. Edmundum Cantuar' septimo ~onis sue anno canonizavit *Ann. Worc.* 434; rex .. nunquam tristis nisi in ~one carorum suorum J. Lond. *Commend. Ed. I* 6; **1464** die aut nocte ~onis mee *MunAcOx* 706.

defunctorius [CL = *perfunctory*; cf. defungi 2b], death-dealing, killing.

[leena et leopardus] qualitates habent furentes, uritivas, ~as *Quaest. Salern.* N 2.

defunctus v. defrutus b, defungi.

defundere [CL]

1 to pour down. **b** to pour out; *v. et. diffundere* 1a. **c** to empty (a container).

qua croceos Titan radios defundit in orbem Aldh. *VirgV* 1073. **b** **1255** ij tynas ad aquam defund[end]am *CourtR Ramsey* 6. **c** **1213** pro quadam securi et j martello et j paletto et c clavis ad habendum in garderoba ad barillos ad denarios ~endos *Misae* 238.

2 to devolve or descend (to).

nulla mulier .. in jure corone [Anglie] .. succedere potest, sed ad heredes semper masculos ~endum est Fortescue *Def. Lanc.* 1.

defungi [CL]

1 (w. abl.) to complete the course (of life). **b** (p. ppl. *s. pass.*).

~itur, .. peragitur *GlH* D 74; nec vultum pristini coloris defunctus seculo immutaverat R. Cold. *Godr.* 308; **1408** Stephanus hoc seculo defunctus extitit, non tamen sepultus *Lit. Cant.* III 108. **b** ut .. centenarium munus defuncto agone virginitatis accipiant Egb. *Pont.* 108.

2 (absol.) to die; **b** (p. ppl. *defunctus* as sb. m. or f.).

pro defuncto monacho missa agatur Theod. *Pen.* II 5. 3; surgere ter fecit defuncta cadavera leto Aldh. *VirgV* 698; ambo in infantia defuncti et .. in ecclesia sepulti sunt Bede *HE* II 20; defunctus, *forðfaren*, ~itur, *forðfærð* Ælf. *Gl.*; uxores iiij villanorum nuper defunctorum *DB* I 166; **s688** Cedwalla rex perrexit ad Romam, ibi baptizatus, est septimo die defungitus Whittlesey app. f. 21 p. 159; **s1023** Wlstanus .. anno .. archiepiscopatus sui xx .. ~itur *Chr. Pont. Ebor. A* 342; **1334** patris sui defuncti tempore *SelPlForest* 26; Favent 18 (v. calvaria 2); **1491** avus meus simul cum Johanne .., Thoma [et al.] jam diffunctis *FormA* 411. **b** **634** ut .. is qui superstes fuerit alterum in loco ~i debeat episcopum ordinare (*Lit. Papae*) Bede *HE* II 18; ~i cadaver .. nondum .. humatum Aldh. *VirgP* 36; surgant canentes alte 'verba mea', si ~um aut breve pro ~o habeant Lanfr. *Const.* 106; omnibus vivis et ~is misericordiae tuae remedia distribuas Anselm (*Or.* 19) III 75; quod oraciones .. que fiunt pro vivis et ~is solummodo prosunt illis qui faciunt et non illis pro quibus fiunt Ockham *Pol.* II 235.

defurfurare [cf. CL furfur], to purify from bran.

panem peto farine tercio ~ate .., quia delicatius nutrit J. Godard *Ep.* 222.

defurgare v. deburgare.

defurnare, to take out of oven.

to drawe owen, ~are est de fornace extrahere *CathA*.

defusus v. diffundere. **deg** v. daeg. **degagiare** v. divadiare 2.

†**degalea,** *f. l.*

†sanguinem [l. sambucus] arbor est similis †degalee [? l. nuci †regali] in foliis *Alph.* 162 (cf. Dioscor. iv 171: καρύą βασιλικῃ).

degarnelare v. decarnellare.

degaudēre, to rejoice (? covertly).

~eo, A. *to joye by hynde WW*.

degelare [cf. CL gelare, OF *desgeler*; LL = *to be very cold*], to thaw; **b** (trans.).

~at, *thowes WW*; *to thowe*, ~are *CathA*. **b** aqua .. calida que attingit in superficie ~at sed cum sit penetrativa ad interiora non facit degelationem *Quaest. Salern.* L 3; **1496** xviij hominibus operantibus .. in ~ando aqueductum monasterii tempore magni gelu (*sic*) *Ac. Durh.* 654.

degelatio, thaw.

Quaest. Salern. L 3 (v. degelare b); *thowe*, gelicidium, ~o *CathA*.

degener [CL], ignoble, base, or degenerate (by birth or character).

~er, ignobilis *GlC* D 93; **c798** noli ~eris animi esse Alcuin *Ep.* 131; ~er, i. ignobilis, *aecnosle*, dissimilis parentibus; ~eri languore, *æcnoslum adle*, vel *unæþelre GlH* D 89–90; *B. V. Dunst.* 1 (v. definitio 2a); **s867** regem suum Osbrict abjecerant et alium ~erem .. acceperant H. Hunt. *HA* V 5; falcones .. tam generosi quam ~eres Gir. *TH* I 12; **s1256** uxorem .. genere nobilem sed moribus ~erem nimis et ignobilem M. Par. *Maj.* V 554; ~eris et suspiciosi est animi consiliarios probatos habere suspectos Fordun *Cont.* X 8; ~er, A. *unkynde WW*.

degenerare [CL], to degenerate (of person); **b** (of plant); **c** (of abstr.); **d** (pass.) to be debased, made less noble.

Romanae gentis, cujus nunc .. suboles .. avita bonitate ~avit Gildas *EB* 25 (cf. ib. 24: ~averat vinea illa olim bona in amaritudinem); ~averat, *misthagch GlC* D 179; Judaei .. a simplicitate patriarchae sui ~averunt Bede *Hom.* I 17. 93; ~ante, *geæcnosliendum GlH* D 100; consuetudinarium discidium coegerat populum superbum ~are G. Mon. XII 19; peccati effectum, ignorantiam tanquam ~aturam habentem, recusabat Pull. *Sent.* 794c; ~ans a patris .. sapientia filius *Found. Waltham* 14; dedecus est cuiquam generoso degenerare D. Bec. 110; Gir. *TH* I 26 (v. deformitas a); **1408** statum ecclesiae .. quem .. omnes ejusdem filii gratissimi, non ~antes, supportare tenentur *Finc.* 30. **b** **1456** (v. depatrissare). **c** quamvis.. nostrarum urbium partus et nativitas in homines devotiores consueverit ~are D. Lond. *Ep.* 3. **d** nisi fallor, valde ~ati sunt a nobis G. Mon. IV 1; **s1170** "non est dispersonatus, degradatus, minoratus vel ~atus [pater meus], si mihi ministret. ego enim sum filius regis et regine, ipse vero non" M. Par. *Min.* I 353.

degeneratio [LL], **a** degeneracy. **b** degradation.

a **1423** tantam in natura ~onem abhorrentes, qua moribus vel brutis animalibus dicamini deteriores (*Lit. Abbatis*) Amund. I 147. **b** **s1224** multis Anglie nobilibus causa .. ruine fuit .. Falcasius [de Breaute], mortis sc., paupertatis et ~onis *Flor. Hist.* II 182.

degenerositas [cf. CL generositas], ignobility.

duo proposuit tiranni legatus, apostasie enormitatem et subjeccionis ~atem *NLA* (*Edm. Rex*) II app. 585.

degerare v. dejerare.

degēre [CL *w.* LL *perf.* deguisse], **a** to spend, pass (time or life). **b** to live, dwell.

a absque cibo plures degebam marcida menses Aldh. *Aen.* 47 (*Hirundo*) 1; vitam compellor degere stando *Ib.* 96 (*Elefans*) 16; multos in .. monasterio ~ens annos Bede *HE* IV 25 p. 270; cum esset xxv annorum solitariam vitam ingressus, xv ~uit W. Malm. *GP* IV 182; **s1417** [R. abbas] cunctis postea diebus suis tranquillam et quietam ~uit vitam *Croyl. Cont. B* 513. **b** **686** vade in pace, vive cum Christo, ~e in Domino, Dominus sit tecum (Theod. *Ep.*) Eddi 43; stuppea cui fuerant pepli velamine texti, / donec degebat Aldh. *VirgV* 1516; **955** moniali in Wiltunensi monasterio ~enti *CS* 903; **9..** ~ebat, *lifde oðde drohte WW*; quamvis hic carneo septus velamine ~uisset in imis .., semper manebat in superis B. *V. Dunst.* 29; dum in corpore ~uit Gosc. *Mir. Iv.* lxvii; **1326** rebus ~ens in humanis *Lit. Cant.* III 401; conchilia dicuntur pisces ~entes in conchis *SB* 16; **s1337** A. de Moravia .. per totam yemem sequentem in foresta de P. ac in aliis locis occultis .. ~uit *Plusc.* IX 35.

degerere v. 1 digerere. **degest-** v. et. digest-.

degestare, to undo or (?) to cry down.

c1310 licet nonnulli sint qui precessorum bene gesta aliquando ~are conentur, dicere tamen non possunt .. successores .. quod patrimonium .. sit deminutum *MonA* II 306b.

degetit v. 1 digerere 3b. **degetus** v. 1 digitus 1a. **degladiare** v. digladiari. **deglobere, ~ire** v. deglubere.

deglomerare [cf. CL glomerare], to unfurl.

quosdam .. milites .., ~atis [MS: de glomeratis] vexillis in eorum fruicionem, dignis honoribus exaltavit *Ps.*-Elmh. *Hen. V* 19.

deglubere [CL], to skin, flay, strip bare.

Circius et Boreas quamvis et flamina Chauri / viribus horrendis studeant deglobere frontem Aldh. *Aen.* 69 (*Taxus*) 4; Id. *VirgV* 1204 (v. bursa 1); deglobere, i. *flean GlC* D 83; deglobere, spoliare vel *beflean GlH* D 88; **10..** deglobere, *behyldan WW*; Tiberius .. ait: "boni pastoris est pecus tondere, non †deglobire" R. Niger *Chr. II* 109 (= Suetonius *Tib.* 32. 2: deglubere; cf. M. Par. *Maj.* I 91: †deglutire).

degluttire, [CL] **(deglutire)**

1 to swallow, devour; **b** (absol.); **c** (fig.).

consumptum, i. devoratum, ~itum *GlH* C 1536; innoxius et inscius sobrie ad salubritatem sui cum omni facilitate hanc partem panis vel casei in nomine tuo signatam manducando ~iat (*Jud. Dei*) *GAS* 408; G. Mon. VII 4 (v. conglutire a); cetus ~it Jonam Ad. Dore *Pictor* 162; quod [terram illam] misceret in aqua et ea †uteretur †vos [? l. in os] declutiret *Mir. Montf.* 81; ~ivit eum quedam bellua monstruosa *Eul. Hist.* II 245 (= G. Mon. III 15: devoravit). **b** nullus panem intinctum accipiat .. excepto infirmo, qui propter ariditatem aliter nequeat ~ire Gir. *GE* I 9; fuit obtrusus in suo gutture quod non potuit .. ~ire Gascoigne *Loci* 35. **c** **c1157** micas et crustula [*w. ref. to treatise* de Panibus], Domino auctore, ~iam J. Sal. *Ep.* 85 (33); **1188** nisi quia Deus erat in vobis, forte vivos ~issent vos [cf. *Psalm* cxxiii 3] *Ep. Cant.* 253; etsi ipse [rex] ydropicus est, set ego aqua non ero quam ille ~iat Ad. Eyns. *Hug.* V 9 p. 124; **s1254** tantum denariis ~iendis intendebant M. Par. *Maj.* V 459; **1327** fructum paterne †libertatis [? l. liberalitatis] filiali manu importuna non .. decet colligere et ore avido ~ire (*Lit. Papae*) *Ann. Paul.* 336.

2 to engulf, overwhelm; **b** (fig.).

†**851** (11c) sicut illos duos [Dathan et Abiron] viventes dehiscens terra ~ivit [cf. *Num.* xvi 30] *CS* 462; ~itum, *ofertogen*, finitum *GlH* C 1536; terram eos ~ire velle putabant R. Cold. *Cuthb.* 65; **s1169** in Terra Promissionis .. terre motus .. villas subruit et innumera populorum millia hians terra ~ivit Fordun *Cont.* VIII 14. **b** Ad. Scot *Serm.* 267a (v. consumptrix); ut .. beatitudo miseriam absorbeat, vita mortem ~iat [cf. *1 Pet.* iii 2] P. Blois *Serm.* 557b; **s1247** (v. charybdis b); hoc idem agitante guerrarum Borea, in ~ientis †stille [? l. Scille] formidans deduci naufragium *Ps.*-Elmh. *Hen. V* 56.

3 *f. l.*

M. Par. *Maj.* I 91 (v. deglubere).

deglutitio, swallowing, absorption.

jam cessarent .. pulmonis .. operationes .. et non possit detineri coram re fetida et corrupta, nec etiam in hora deglu[ti]tionis *Ps.*-Ric. *Anat.* 25; panniculi ad duos orbes oculorum pervenientes ibi dilatantur per circumcinctum, ut intra se diglu[ti]tionem humorum possint accipere *Ib.* 26.

degniare v. divadiare 1a.

degradare [LL]

1 **a** (eccl. or mon.) to degrade in rank, demote; **b** (eccl.) to deprive of orders. **c** (var.). **d** to demean, humiliate.

a ~averit, deposuerit *Gl. Leid.* 2. 42; **s1070** in quo [Wintonie] concilio Stigandus Dorubernie archiepiscopus ~atur.. . abbates etiam aliqui ibi ~ati sunt, operam dante

rege ut quamplures ex Anglis suo honore privarentur Fl. Worc. II 5; s**1177** [episcopi] deposuerunt abbatissam [de Amesbiria] propter infamiam ipsius... et, ne .. abbatissa ⁓ata fame .. periret, rex spopondit ei se daturum .. singulis annis x m. *G. Hen. II* I 136; M. Par. *Min.* I 353 (v. dispersonare); si [canonici] de inobedientia et rebellione vel alio notorio deprehensi fuerint, debent a stallo ⁓ari et ad ostium [chori] post decanum vel in choro ultimi puerorum .. penitentiam agere *Offic. Sal.* 11; s**1211** Pandulfus dixit: "sancta †ecclesiae [l. ecclesia] non consuevit ⁓are archiepiscopum sine manifesta causa; sed assueta est principes sibi rebelles a summo ruere in deorsum" *Ann. Burton* 215; [v obedienciarii] pro inobediencia proclamati et a suis officiis sunt depositi et a stallis suis in choro, capitulo et refectorio ⁓ati sunt et ultimati .. atque inhabiles facti ad omne officium .. quoadusque dispensacionem .. mererentur *G. S. Alb.* II 198; **1423** (v. ceroferarius 1). **b** episcopus, presbiter, aut diaconus fornicationem facientes ⁓ari debent Theod. *Pen.* I 9. 1 (cf. ib. *rub.*: de his qui †⁓untur); c**1218** nullus [sacerdos] .. audeat revelare confessionem... si convictus fuerit, absque misericordia ⁓abitur *Conc. Syn.* 74; qui extra ecclesiam susceperunt ordines, qui non habent ordinem exsistentes in ecclesia, qui ⁓ati sunt, non habent potestatem [corporis Christi conficiendi] Hales *Sent.* IV 204 (cf. ib. 315: est clavis .. in †degredato ut in habente manum abscissam); **12..** statuimus clericos .. ab ecclesia esse defendendos donec exigente justicia .. a susceptis ordinibus rite ⁓entur *Reg. Aberd.* II 14 (= *Conc. Scot.* II 19); *Conc. Syn.* 105, Bracton 123b (v. degradatio 1b); quamvis .. principes seculi papam hereticum valeant judicare et punire .., ipsum tamen ⁓are non debent, tum quia talis degradacio sine periculo potest pretermitti, tum quia, sicut ordinare spectat ad habentem ordinem, ita ⁓are ad habentem ordinem spectat Ockham *Pol.* III 317; s**1401** statutum fuit editum de Lollardis ut .., si perseverarent pertinaciter opiniones suas defendere, ⁓arentur, et jurisdiccioni seculari committerentur Wals. *HA* II 247; s**1430** quidam presbyter Lollardus .. ⁓atus et .. in cinere conflagratus est *Chr. S. Alb.* 51. **c** s**1257** *Leg. Ant. Lond.* 36 (v. deponere 8c); †s**1239** (recte **1250**) obiit F. imperator, quondam excommunicatus et ⁓atus per papam *Ann. Lond.* 36; s**1312** convenientibus majore, aldermannis, et multis civium .., preceperunt .. Johanni L. vicecomiti quod faceret replegiare [Henricum B.] .. et dixerunt: ".. nisi feceris deliberacionem, ⁓emur (*sic*) te ab officio et a libertate tua" *Ib.* 220; [J. de Balliolo] genuit unum filium .., qui postea .. fuit rex per aliquod tempus et cum dedecore, suis demeritis exigentibus, ⁓atus est *Plusc.* VIII 14; s**1323** (v. calcar 1d); *to degrade*, ⁓are; *degradid*, ⁓atus ..; *to putte down*, .. deponere, deprimere, ⁓are *CathA.* **d** s**1170** (v. degenerare d).

2 (?) to rush down or (?) *f. l.*

aqua habens strictum exitum, cum †⁓are [v. l. †degurgidare; ? l. degurgitare] ceperit, parat in recessu largiorem meatum *Plusc.* IX 30.

degradatio [LL]

1 a (eccl. or mon.) degradation (in rank or status). **b** (eccl.) deprivation of orders. **c** (acad.) degradation. **d** (royal) deposition.

a papa .., rememorans gratuitam episcopi confessionem et eam quam sibi intulerant in ⁓one humiliter susceptam confusionem, .. letificavit omnes in episcopi reconciliatione *V. Ed. Conf.* 47; c**1150** ut, quotienscumque .. monachum .. fugitivum vel .. ejectum .. tandem .. per gratiam recipi contigerit, in ultimo gradu recipiatur; .. qui post lapsum redierint perpetuo ⁓onis sue intuitu .. humilientur *Lit. Cant.* III app. 355; **1423** (v. ceroferarius 1). **b** fit .. ordinatis suspensio; fit etiam, cum nimia est culpa, ⁓o. sed illa metam non figit, ista facit... utraque ab officii exercitio alienat; sed ab usu semovet altera minus, altera diutius Pull. *Sent.* 927C; si [clerici infames] post ⁓onem relaberentur in consimile flagitium, secundum publicas leges a seculari judice punirentur W. Cant. *V. Thom.* I 19; de episcopo qui sacerdotem animam parochiani sui diabolo commendantem pro xx s. de debita suspensionis et ⁓onis pena laxavit Gir. *GE* II 27 p. 303; s**1202** (v. depositio 7a); s**1222** sacerdos quidam et diaconus .. degradati fuerunt .. coram concilio a domino Cantuariensi... in ⁓one .., cum dominus C. casulam vel stolam vel aliud quid baculi pastoralis extremitate sublevando amoveret, hiis verbis usus est .. (W. Coventr. II 251) *Conc. Syn.* 105; **1239** sunt summi excessus quidam [canonicorum et al.] quibus congruam penam solus episcopus potest infligere, utpote excessus quibus debetur pena destitutionis et ⁓onis Gros. *Ep.* 73 p. 238; cum .. clericus .. de crimine convictus degradatur, non sequitur alia pena pro uno delicto vel pluribus ante ⁓onem perpetratis Bracton 123b; s**1385** de .. ⁓one sex cardinalium Wals. *HA* II 121 *rub.* **c** **1456** quod .. hujus statuti ordinacionem quilibet graduatus sub pena perjurii, incarceracionis, ⁓onis, et bannicionis teneatur .. observare *StatOx* 227 (cf. ib. 437). **d** s**1324** odium contra regem .. concipiens, Adam [episcopus Heref'] .. ad regis ⁓onem .. iracundie conceptе venenum propinavit Baker 103.

2 stairway. *Cf.* CL *gradatio.*

1272 in reparacione ⁓onis molendini *MinAc* 935/22 m. 1.

degradere v. degradare. **degradi** v. degredi 2b.

degradus [cf. CL gradus], stairway.

1288 concessi .. unum ⁓um pro tenentibus ipsorum religiosorum eundi ad solaria sua, que habent ultra dictam sopam meam *AncD* A 2019; **1332** extra ostium aule placitorum domini regis super ⁓us ejusdem aule *SelCKB* V 72.

degranare [DuC; cf. OF *desgrener*], to take out grain (from hopper), *i. e.* have it ground before another's.

1331 dictus capitalis tenens potest ⁓are in dicto molendino *S. Jers.* I 10.

degrassari [CL], to prowl in search of victims, to prey (on).

gradior .. componitur ⁓or, -aris, i. debacchari Osb. Glouc. *Deriv.* 178; lucius in vulgus [piscium] degrassatur propriosque / cives persequitur Neckam *DS* III 573.

degrassator [cf. CL grassator], robber, footpad.

gradior, .. inde ⁓or Osb. Glouc. *Deriv.* 249; sint in castro viri prudentes .., quorum censure rigore ⁓ores [v. l. degressatores; *gl.*: *envahures*, †*leverreyurs*] .., clepi, abactores .. fustigentur et puniantur Neckam *Ut.* 105.

degravare [CL], to overpower, subdue.

civitatem .. quot modis expeditius posset ⁓are *G. Steph.* I 30.

degredare v. degradare 1a.

degredi [CL]

1 to go down, descend.

digrediens, descendens *GlH* D 489.

2 to depart, go away. **b** to shamble. *V. et.* 2 *digredi* 1.

ecce repente meus ductor me linquerat atque / degrediens templo vacuis se condidit auris Æthelwulf *Abb.* 728; *Ib.* 324 (v. componere 6a); ⁓i, i. egredi *GlH* D 98. **b** *to schayle*, degradi *CathA.*

degressator v. degrassator. **deguadiare, deguajare** v. divadiare.

degulare [CL], to devour.

⁓are, devorare Osb. Glouc. *Deriv.* 179.

degulator [CL], glutton.

⁓or, gluto, heluo, ardelio Osb. Glouc. *Deriv.* 172; *a gluton*, ambro .., ⁓or, devorator *CathA.*

degurgitare [cf. CL egurgitare], to pour out or down.

Plusc. IX 30 (v. degradare 2).

degustare [CL], to taste; **b** (fig.).

quod prius Lucifer .. corruisset .. quam protoplaustus .. vetitam ⁓ans alimoniam in gastrimargiae voraginem cecidisset Aldh. *VirgP* 11; suavitatem carnis ⁓averunt *V. Cuthb.* II 4; libare, ⁓are *GlC* L 162; R. Cold. *Cuthb.* 118 (v. desuescere 1a). **b** ea quae mens rationabiliter de interna luce caritatis ⁓at Bede *Tab.* 473; ut is, quem antea ⁓ans quasi maximum rebar, jam permodicus mihi odor videretur *Id. HE* V 12 p. 307; o data vel raro vel nulli fercula, solis / degustanda viris! o felix mensa, Catoni / forsitan et nostro vix evo nota! Hanv. IX 458 p. 392; hos .. nostre diligentie fructus tue ⁓andos discretioni .. destinare proposui Gir. *IK* 1 *pref.* p. 8; scholares nonnulli .. indulgent studio liberalium; sed, dum singula ⁓ant, famelici relinquuntur Neckam *NR* II 186; tu [sc. corpus Christi], divino melle cum refluis, / degustatum famem exacuis J. Howd. *Ph.* 990; Ockham *Dial.* 776 (v. desiderium 1d); Fortescue *LLA* 54 (v. confundere 1e).

degustatio [CL], tasting; **b** (fig.).

periculum ad emptorem pertinet, nisi sit vinum, cujus periculum pertinet ad venditorem ante ⁓onem, nisi ⁓o remissa sit Vac. *Lib. Paup.* 148; cum ante se delicata cibaria ponerentur, ea debilibus et egrotantibus .. post modicam ⁓onem .. fecit communiter assignari Birchington *Arch. Cant.* 13. **b** ad premium et ⁓onem glorie quousque .. janua aperiatur per applicacionem passionis Christi Conway *Def. Mend.* 1417 (*recte* 1317).

degustator [LL], taster (fig.).

adhesio ista [Deo] non carnis, sed mentis est, in qua tria quedam naturarum auctor inseruit, quibus divine eternitatis compos efficeretur, particeps sapientie, dulcedinis ⁓or Ailr. *Spec. Car.* I 3. 507D; erat .. scripture sacre fervidus ⁓or *NLA* (*J. Bridl.*) II 69.

deguttare [cf. LL guttare]

1 to drip (intr.), fall in drops. **b** to drip (trans.), let fall. **c** to baste.

gutto componitur ⁓o, -as Osb. Glouc. *Deriv.* 256; s**1263** viderat .. corpus [Christiani mortui] conspersum et complutum circa crura et humeros quasi guttis cere mundissime, que quasi ⁓assent a cereis de celo missis Rish. 15; si [sanguis dominicus] super casulam vel albam ⁓et *Cust. Westm.* 219; plumbi fluxus liquefacti ubique ⁓abat *Croyl.* 97. **b** **1237** carpentarii debent erigere candelabrum .. et deponere et cereos in eodem illuminare et extinguere; et .. habebunt unum cereorum, quem voluerint, et ceram ⁓atam *Stat. Linc.* I 292; **1275** sceram ardentem ⁓averunt in †nazibus [l. naribus] illius, sic quod moriebatur *Hund.* I 274b (cf. ib. 384b). **c** †alii [l. alios] diversis metallis liquescentibus ⁓averunt H. Saltrey 9 (cf. M. Par. *Maj.* II 197: verubus transfixi ad ignem assati ⁓abantur a demonibus ex metallis liquefactis).

2 a to sprinkle, scatter. **b** to besprinkle, speckle.

a **1215** zonam de rubeo corio cum xj jaspidibus viridibus ⁓atis *Pat* 145b. **b** a**1170** vestimentum imperatricis ⁓atum auro Steph. Rouen *addit.* 759; **1245** fieri faciatis .. unum draconem rubeum aureo ⁓atum *Cl* 331; **1246** faciat .. lambruschuram .. camere depingi colore viridi et auro ⁓ari *Liberate* 22 m. 7; **1344** de panno velvetto ⁓ato *KRAc* 390/8 f. 9.

deguttatio, flow.

⁓o, -nis Osb. Glouc. *Deriv.* 256; sedet infantulus in matris gremio / et offert osculum humecto labio, / quod quidem osculum indulcat mixtio / salive tenuis et deguttacio Walt. Wimb. *Carm.* 223.

dehabilitare [cf. CL habilis], to injure, impair, or (?) *f. l.*

1378 in placito transgressionis, viz. quod ipsum deabilitavit [? l. debilitavit] in fama *Rec. Leic.* II 184.

dehereditare [cf. LL hereditare], to disinherit, deprive of inheritance. *V. et. dishereditare, exhereditare.*

illi quos S. rex ⁓averat H. Hunt. *HA* VIII 13 (cf. ib. 15: ab ipsis nequiter ⁓atis .. prius aggrediendus est); [Randulfus cancellarius] omnem vim sapientie sue convertit ad simplices †dehëritandos et pecunias eradendas *Id. CM* 9.

dehereditatio, disherison, disinheritance. *V. et. dishereditatio, exhereditatio.*

1200 de placito quare fecerunt humagium Roesie .. domine Willelmi Daci de tenementis suis que tenent .. de Willelmo, ad ⁓onem ipsius Willelmi *CurR* I 295.

dehinc [CL], thereafter. **b** therefrom, thence.

die ⁓c tertio Bede *HE* IV 11; qui primo .. caelum .., ⁓c [AS: *æfter*] terram .. creavit (Cædmon) *Ib.* 22 p. 260; ⁓c, i. deinde, abhinc .. vel *þonane* vel *forþan* *GlH* D 367; alleluia .. canitur, ⁓c [AS: p. 425: *þar æfter*] antiphona *RegulC* 49; acceperunt ⁓c duo episcopi manus regis Byrht. *V. Osw.* 437; s**1333** (v. descensus 4a). **b** dehinc humeris cymbam fert navita vimine textam Neckam *DS* III 913.

dehiscere [CL], to split open, gape, yawn. **b** to crack. **c** (fig.) to be undone. **d** (trans.) to undo, destroy, (perh.) to swallow (fig.).

cum tellus sponte dehiscit / et genus humanum tumbis emerserit atris Aldh. *VirgV* 1248; Bede *Tab.* 442 (v. compago b); ⁓at, *tocinit* *GlC* D75; †**851** (v. deglutire 2a); **931** (v. bustum b); ⁓ens, i. absorbens, subsidens .., patefaciens, scindens, vel *cinende* *GlH* D 402; capit unda fretumque dehiscit R. Cant. *Malch. preludium* 9; *Lib. Eli.* III 132 (v. consolidare 1a); si terra ⁓eret, si caelum patesceret W. Malm. *GR* III 268; limus .. profundi .. hyatu ⁓ens infinito Map *NC* IV 12 f. 54v. **b** solis ardore paludes ⁓ebant adustae *Lib. Monstr.* III 5. **c** Parisius discas ne Rome forte deiscas [*gl.*: deficias] Garl. *Mor. Scol.* 485. **d** temperantia omnis motus carnis illicitos absorbet et eorum ⁓it terrenitatem Gros. *Hexaem.* XI 24 p. 326.

dehonestamentum [CL], a disfigurement. **b** insult.

a scidit vestimentum, evellit pilos .., ut tali ⁓o corporis et indumenti .. omnium animos ad paenitentiam .. excitet Bede *Ezra* (ix 3) 874. **b** s**1382** (v. circumducere 1a).

dehonestare [CL]

1 a to dishonour, disgrace. **b** to treat disgracefully, insult. **c** to disfigure, mar, spoil.

a nec in comparatione hujuscemodi bonum ⁓ari video, sed .. propensius laudari Aldh. *VirgP* 9; **9..** ⁓are, *unweorðian* *WW*; non resistent adversum vos, quia nimirum, quos fidei ignorantie error ⁓at, hos proculdubio ex difficultate actionis cruciatus affligat (*Serm.*) Osb. Bawdsey clxxiii; cur ⁓ati honoris irreverenciam non percipitis? *NLA* (*J. Bridl.*) II 69. **b** c**740** sciat se .. Dei iram incurrere .. quoniam sanctissimam (*sic*) beatissimae V. M. locum deonestare conatus est *CS* 160; s**1138** [Scoti] priorem Hagustaldensem .. contumeliis et ludibrio ⁓averunt J. Hex. *HR Cont.* 298; in psalmis 'Gloria Patri' subticetur [in Adventu] .., quia multum ⁓ata est tunc Trinitas Beleth *RDO* 64. 71B (cf. ib. 85. 88D: passio Christi, in qua tota Trinitas a Judeis quasi ⁓ata videtur); sacerdotes ipsi .. sordium jactu ⁓antur Gir. *IK* I 12 p. 94; ⁓avit matrem misericordie et pudicitie sigillis *Latin Stories* 66; **1357** bachalarius .. magistrum .. per verba impropria ⁓avit .. fuerat ordinatum .. quod .. fateretur se publice deliquisse et quod honestaret personam quantum prius alias ⁓avit *MunAcOx* 203. **c** a**1400** nec habet vestem honestam .. preter unam tunicam, quam in equitando tantum ⁓abit quod expost cum honestate non sibi sufficiet sine nova *FormOx* 236; c**1410** urtica suo veneno malicie rosarum fragranciam inficit et ⁓at *Ib.* 425.

2 (? by misinterp.) to honour.

8.. cum ⁓averis, *ðonne ðu gearweorðas* *WW*.

dehonestas [LL], disgrace.

non possum ego illi respondendo ~atem inferre tantam quantam ipse sic loquendo intulit sibi ipsi W. BURLEY *Vit. Phil.* 202; **1376** epistola in missa capitulari [S. Greg. Cantuar'] legitur quotidie per unum canonicum indutum superpellicio nudo capite sine amita, ita quod colaria legencium, que aliquando sunt fracta, turpia et inhonesta, apparent laicis, in ~atem ordinis (*Vis.*) *Conc.* III 110b.

dehonestatio [LL], dishonour, disgrace, insult.

in cantico trium puerorum, sc. 'Benedicite' .. ['Gloria Patri'] nunquam cantatur, quia tunc Deo magna facta est ~o BELETH *RDO* 85. 88D; **s1381** [miles] confessus est se .. multum peccasse in ~one sacramenti WALS. *HA* I 451; **1416** in cimiterio ecclesie diebus Dominicis et festivis commune forum rerum venalium tenetur, .. in maximam ~onem ac divini cultus impedimentum (*Vis.*) *Fabr. York* 248.

dehonorare [LL], to dishonour, insult.

802 illud commune est omnibus ubique, quod moleste ferant suos ~are sanctos ALCUIN *Ep.* 249 p. 403; ~avistis justitiam et contumeliam veritati fecistis (*Serm.*) OSB. BAWDSEY clxxi; **s1256** abbas Clarevallensis [depositus] .., asserens se magis esse deoneratum quam ~atum .. M. PAR. *Maj.* V 596; Petrus regem honorare precepit [cf. *1 Pet.* ii 17]; iste [Benedictus XII] regem regum, Romanum viz. principem, ~at, blasphemat, vituperat, et confundit OCKHAM *Pol.* III 272; *to disworschippe*, ~are *CathA*.

dehonoratio [LL], dishonouring, disgrace.

cum alterius ~one non est aliquis honorandus OCKHAM *Pol.* I 172; contumelia, que est ~o alicujus per verba vel per facta .., peccatum est mortale J. BURGH *PO* X 5 f. 168v.; *a disworschepp*, ~o *CathA*.

dehortari [CL], to dissuade.

~or, †perhibeo [l. prohibeo] *GlH* D 401; ~or, -aris, i. dissuadere OSB. GLOUC. *Deriv.* 273; eos reos judico dehortantes eum *Poem S. Thom.* 89; quorum sententia est ad simile hortans vel †ad simile [v. l. a simili] ~ans NECKAM *Ut.* 105; cum inducitur alicujus rei narratio causa ortandi vel deortandi aliquem *Ps.*-GROS. *Gram.* 75.

dehortativus [LL], (gram.) dehortative, dissuasive.

sunt [adverbia] .. alia ~a, ut 'ne' ALCUIN *Gram.* 887D; *sume synd deortativa, þaet synd forbeodendlice oððe mistihtendlice*: ne .. neque .. nisi vel ni ÆLF. *Gram.* 225.

dehospitari, ~are, [cf. CL hospitari], to oust, dispossess, dislodge. **b** (?) to depopulate.

c1170 nec ego nec heredes mei poterimus ~ari predictum B. vel heredes suos ibidem hospitandos *E. Ch. S. Paul.* 134 (cf. ib. 87, 99); Aaron Judeus .. jactitabat se feretrum B. Albano nostro fecisse et ipsi ~ato hospitium de pecunia sua preparasse *G. S. Alb.* I 194; *Reg. S. Aug.* 382 (v. alligantia e); **12..** neque illum vel heredes suos poterimus ~are *AncD* A 1475; **1252** nullatenus poterimus .. Galfridum .. de predicta terra ~ari *FormA* 195; **1253** de domibus feiditorum .. habere faciat .. Gilberto .. unum hospicium de prestito nostro, ita quod nullus alius propter hoc ~etur *Cl* 177; **1290** fraus, collusio seu convencio non fiat per quod clerici †~antur [? l. ~entur] vel eorum hospicia fiant cariora *MunAcOx* 53 (cf. *MunCOx* 161). **b a1250** non poterunt predictam terram cum domibus ~ari, deteriorari nec diminuere *AncD* A 1932.

deia v. 2 daia.

deicere (dejic-) [CL]

1 to throw down. **b** (p. ppl.) low (in stature).

tecto vel longa incuria vel hostili manu dejecto BEDE *HE* II 16; diruit, dejecit *GlC* D 217; **c1072** si quis arborem incidit juxta regalem viam et eam super ipsam viam dejecerit *Pl. Anglo-Norm.* 8 (cf. *Powicke Studies* 24); BALSH. *Ut.* 47 (v. circumluvium); W. CANT. *Mir. Thom.* VI 114 (v. congerere a); W. FITZST. *Thom. prol.* 14 (v. consequi 1b) nonnullos movere solet .. quod fulmina frequenter ecclesias nostras et templa cadendo ~iunt GIR. *IK* I 12 p. 95; **s1387** (v. 1 contradictor a); THORNE 1785 (v. desideriose); **1534** equa .. in campis .. cecidit et dejecit predictum J. C. usque ad terram *Anc. Indict.* 531/136. **b** nec in pigmee brevitatis paupertatem dejectus *Ps.*-ELMH. *Hen. V* 6 (v. brevitas a).

2 (of fluids) to pour (down).

croceum [sulphur] .. dicitur cannellatum, quoniam in canellis .. ad hoc factis ~itur M. SCOT *Lumen* 264.

3 to cast down (fig.), lay low, depose. **b** (refl.) to humble oneself. **c** (p. ppl. *dejectus*) abased or depressed.

GILDAS *EB* 13 (v. 2 decorare c); inopinatum .. divinitus intercessit patrocinium, quo partis adverse ~eretur, de qua confidebat, potestas *Chr. Battle* f. 130v.; R. NIGER *Mil.* I 28 (v. 2 elevare 2c); **s1199** Christe, tui calicis predo fit preda Calucis; / ere brevi deicis, qui tulit era crucis (? MAP *Vers. de Ric. I*) HIGD. VII 31 p. 168; **s1229** papa [Honorius III], qui rebellem imperatorem .. estuabat ~ere WEND. II 360; **s1245** papa .. ad expugnandum ipsum Frethericum quem dejecerat, .. vicesimam postulavit *Flor. Hist.* II 304. **b** dum vident prelatum suum aliquantulum se ~ere et communem se exhibere, dedignantur eum venerari AD. SCOT *Serm.* 261C. **c** ~ior, i. humilior, *aworpenra GlH* D 419; elisa mens vel ~a, *forscrenct* ÆLF. *Gl.*

4 a to eject, banish. **b** to reject, abandon.

a 786 (v. detrudere 1a); postea gens nostra surget et gentem Anglorum trans mare viriliter ~iet NEN. *HB* 186; excussit, i. dejecit, *fram aswengde* vel *todraf GlH* E 751; actio .. datur contra eum qui vi dejecit, et datur ei qui vi dejectus est ad restitutionem possessionis rei immobilis qua quis vi dejectus est BRACTON 103b (cf. ib. 162: sufficit terror armorum, ut videatur armis dejecisse); de possessore dejecto a possessione sua *Leg. IV Burg.* 99 *rub.* **b** anathema, abhominabilis, dejectus *GlC* A 583; ego Nennius .. aliqua excerpta scribere curavi, quae hebitudo gentis Britanniae dejecerat, quia nullam peritiam habuerunt NEN. *HB* 143.

deiciatus v. deciatus.

deicida [LL], god-slayer.

ecce migrat qui per clementiam / deicidis precatur veniam J. HOWD. *Ph.* 851; *a slaer of goddis*, ~a *CathA*.

deicium v. deisium.

deicola [LL], worshipper of God (usu. Christian).

[basilicam] Hedde, pontifex petitus / ac cum amore accitus, / dedicavit deicola / atque clarus caelicola *Epigr. Milredi* 817; **935** (12c) ego Aþelstanus .. totius Britanniae orbis ~arumque .. curagulus *CS* 708; ~a Christi Oda sacris literis .. est traditus BYRHT. *V. Osw.* 410; †annuntiantur [? l. annuntiatur, *as* FLETE *Westm.* 40] circumquaque manentibus ~is ut accur[r]ant SULCARD 1635B (= *MonA* I 289); **1088** pax .. ~is omnibus *Regesta* 314; unde tristes ypocrite, leti semper ~e MAP *NC* I 1 f. 7; Petrus, stirps benivola, / huic patri successit, / qui quasi deicola / per mundum incessit PECKHAM *Def. Mend.* 254; Elie prophete, qui, licet putasset se solum ~am fuisse relictum, tamen fidem veram minime dereliquit OCKHAM *Pol.* III 16; nec †illorum [v. l. ullorum] mundi regnorum ~arum leges tanto evo inolite sunt FORTESCUE *LLA* 17.

deicus, divine. *V. et. deacus.*

lector advertat non hominum esse potentiam, sed ~e potius virtutis miram et potentissimam efficaciam *G. Steph.* I 64; statim de deico sinu mel liquitur / et ad virgineum favum transmittitur WALT. WIMB. *Carm.* 16; quam eligit proles ~a *Miss. Sarum* 911.

deidatorius, almoner.

1558 Franciscum Mallet, clericum .. ac nostrum ~ium *Pat* 930 m. 45.

deifer [LL], God-bearing. **b** missionary.

veneramur / viscera deifera WALT. WIMB. *Virgo* 55. **b** ~fer, pacifer, salutifer Augustinus GOSC. *Aug. Maj.* 59C; felix tellus sua fecunditate, sed felicissima tot ~ferorum advenarum, imo tot civium supernorum, hospitio *Ib.* 15. 60A (cf. id. *Aug. Min.* 747D: tellus .. felicissima tot ~ferorum ac civium supernorum primitiva hospitalitate).

deificare [LL], to deify, assimilate to God. **b** to worship as God. **c** to sanctify, canonize. **d** (p. ppl.) consecrated to God.

c1000 multo excellentius, salva fide, hic homo divinus praedicatur etiam Deus atque Dei filius et heres aeternus. Deus existebat, quia gratia et meritis ~atus (*Sermo*) *Mem. Dunst.* 457; nota .. Christi discipulos non .. fuisse passos quia de Christo predicabant, sed quia ipsum ~atum aiebant sine Romanorum auctoritate BELETH *RDO* 126. 133C; suos imperatores, quos de more populus Romanus fideliter jugulabat, ~avit fidelius J. SAL. *Pol.* 496A; [Deus est] perfectorum perfectio, ~atorum deificatio BART. ANGL. I 20; BACON *CSPhil.* 400 (v. christificare); ille Deus .. ~at deiformemque facit triplicem illam hierarchiam angelorum COLET *Cel. Hier.* 173. **b** laus Christo regi nato, / .. / a magis adorato, / .. / thure deificato LEDREDE *Carm.* 8. 5. **c** unde et ipsa [Radegunda, ob. **587**] fit sanctimonialis Pictavi ac post ~ata R. NIGER *Chr. II* 134. **d c717** deprecor te ut illius amicitiae in tuis ~atis orationibus recorderis (ECGBURG) *Ep. Bonif.* 13.

deificatio [LL], deification, apotheosis, assimilation to God.

BART. ANGL. I 20 (v. deificare a); **1253** unum peccaminum [pessimorum] est ipsius deitatis superessentialiter et supernaturaliter optime vilipensio; alterum vero deiformitatis et ~onis ex divini radii gratifica participatione essentialiter et naturaliter optime interemptio GROS. *Ep.* 128 p. 435.

deifice [LL], by divine assistance, divinely.

974 (12c) spatium omne prefatis cenobiis contiguum .. isdem sanctis locis in Wentana civitate ~e locatis aeterna largitus sum hereditate *CS* 1302; **982** (11c) aeterno genitore cum inclita prole sanctoque paraclyto in tribus tripudiante personis atque in una usia ~e omnia saeculorum jura .. gubernante *CD* 634.

deificus [LL], divine, godly. **b** (w. *contemplatio*) beatific vision.

de ~o tenore monachorumque decretis .. ruminans GILDAS *EB* 34; †nurus [l. nutus], potestas ~a *GlC* N 200; dealibus, i. ~is, *godlicum GlH* D 404; disciplinis innexus ~is B. *V. Dunst.* 5 (cf. ib. 25: moribus ~is .. instructus); **c1043** ego .. ~ae voluntatis permissione regali fretus dignitate *CD* 769; miraculum .. divinum, cujus cum se pius puer negaret conscium, totum constat celitus peractum et totum fuisse ~um ADEL. BLANDIN. *Dunst.* 2; quem latere noluit ~a virtus HERM. ARCH. 18; **1066** in eodem loco, ~ae videlicet Trinitatis *Regesta* I 4; succurre, deifica custos, / sancta fides *V. Ed. Conf.* 47v.; **s1125** anno incarnationis ~e mcxxv *Chr. Battle* f. 50v.; de laude gloriose ac ~e crucis *V. Har. prol.* f. 1; hoc opus ~um [Christi] conceptionis et nativitatis BACON *Maj.* I 267; **1432** septem ~e virtutes (J. CARPENTER) *MGL* III 459; **s1459** vis ad salvandum vis est ~a *Reg. Whet.* I 333. **b** quodsi angelica supernorum civium celsitudo .. ~ae contemplationis participio privabatur ALDH. *VirgP* 11; ~e contemplationis, *þære godlican* vel *godcundre besceawunga GlH* D 365; **c944** (13c) omnibus prudentibus, qui ~ae contemplationis beatitudinem in mentis suae hospitio cernere cupiunt *CS* 801 (cf. ib. 1043).

deiformis, god-like.

1166 quesitum est .. quo tendat, quod legitur et usurpatur a plurimis, quia ~iora sunt ea que non sunt quam ea que sunt J. SAL. *Ep.* 143; **c1238** taliter philosophantes viros cognominant .. Therapeutas .., quasi mundissimum .. et impertitum prestantes famulatum unientem ipsos in Dei specificam unitatem et ~em perfectionem GROS. *Ep.* 57 p. 176; hominibus factis ad imaginem Dei .. refectisque ad similitudinem ipsius per ~em limpidarum veritatum contemplationem AD. MARSH *Ep.* 92 p. 214; quantum ad .. speciei divine imitacionem, non habet racionem imaginis nisi quando ipsi Deo copulatur intelligendo et amando set sic ~is efficitur PECKHAM *QA* 198; hanc .. delectacionem felicissimam ac maxime ~em nos Christiani .. omnes concorditer expectamus BRADW. *CD* 58D; demonstravit hoc Xenocrates, ~is in constancia racionis, quem .. Phryne .. statuam definivit, non hominem R. BURY *Phil.* 15. 193; nec foret beatus ~is diligens modo Dei encia .., nisi Deum summe diligeret WYCL. *Mand. Div.* 139; mores viatorum reddere ~es J. BURY *Glad. Sal.* 568; COLET *Cel. Hier.* 173 (v. deificare a).

deiformitas, likeness to God.

c1238 eo quod congruat monacho .. 'solitarium sedere .., elevantem se super se' [*Lam.* iii 28], hominem in Dei formitatem (*sic*) GROS. *Ep.* 57 p. 176; **1253** (v. deificatio); BART. ANGL. II 2 (v. declaratio 1a); est intelligentia vel angelus .. imago Dei .., totam speciositatem pulcherrime ~atis et pure declarans in se ipso *Ps.*-GROS. *Summa* 422; anima gloriosa ex gloria habet ~atem in potencia intellectiva et voluntate. sed ex ~ate intellectus habet quod potest simul multa intelligere. .. ergo ex ~ate potencie motive habet quod potest corpus suum replicare simul super plures partes medii PECKHAM *QA* 135; puritas et lux et ~as inseparabiliter se habent COLET *Cel. Hier.* 173.

deiformiter, in the likeness of God.

per seipsum esse et per seipsam vitam 'deitatem' dicimus principaliter quidem et ~iter, et causaliter unum omnium superprincipale et superessenciale principium et causam BRADW. *CD* 150B; similiter potest intelligi quod sit Deus beatificativus creature racionalis, ut in ipso ~iter secundum intellectum et affectum perpetuo sit suspensa WYCL. *Mand. Div.* 132.

deila v. dala.

deillinc, thence.

~c multi odoris thi[mi]amata satis amene redolentia profluebant R. COLD. *Cuthb.* 38.

deimericius v. dammaricius a.

dein [CL], thereafter.

domo primum ac mutatis ~n mutuo vestibus occuluit GILDAS *EB* 11; nuper dein labentibus / binis brumae temporibus (ÆTHELWALD) *Carm. Aldh.* 2. 1; ~n, cum anno integro provincias Nordanhymbrorum .. dilaceraret, tandem Eanfridum .. damnavit BEDE *HE* III 1; ~n modicum requietus levavit se *Ib.* IV 20 p. 250; ~n .. apostolice apicem dignitatis .. cum reverentia adeuntes DOMINIC *V. Ecgwini* I 9.

deinceps [CL], **a** next, in turn, thereafter. **b** (w. *et sic* or sim.) and so on (successively). **c** from now (or then) on (continuously).

a hic medicus [Lucas] dudum sanabat vulnera carnis; / .. / uberius deinceps animarum crimina sontum / .. dempsit ALDH. *VirgV* 518; hactenus .. de ista dictum sit; ~s ad reliquas transeamus ADEL. *ED* 21; contigit interea .. Gerbertum .. incathedrari. ~s etiam, suscepti negotium honoris exequens, .. fit .. cardinalis .. et post pauca defuncto papa sedis illius .. gradum ascendit MAP *NC* IV 11 f. 53. **b** cum equivocari possint duo modis sex, tria decem, quatuor quindecim, quinque viginti et uno, et ~s similiter, uno semper crescente distantia BALSH. *AD rec. 2* 42; sciebat probare .. quod, ubi quatuor erant, ibi octo, et ubi sex, ibi duodecim, et sic ~s GIR. *GE* II 37 p. 350; *Fleta* 428 (v. duplicatio 3); WALLINGF. (*Quad.*) I 52 (v. completio 1b). **c** Picti .. tunc primum et ~s requieverunt GILDAS *EB* 21; ut .., qui existimabatur .. posterior, ~s divinae caritatis flamma succensus existat anterior ALDH. *VirgP* 10; multo ~s tempore vixit BEDE *HE* III 13; **745** (13c) sit .. praedicta possessio .. monasterii usibus mancipata ~s incessabili jugitate *CS* 170; **838** ex hac die et ~s *CS* 421; **s1102** et tunc et ~s habuit malignitatis sue complices W. MALM. *GR* V 397; **s1150** fuit prior depositus ibidem incarceratus quamdiu ~s vixit archiepiscopus GERV.

CANT. *Imag.* 48; **s1160** [abbas], intendens ~s soli Deo vacare . ., se conclusit *Meaux* I 107 (cf. concludere 2e).

deincumbrare [AN *desencumbrer*, OF *desencombrer*], to 'disincumber' (a church), rid of intruded incumbent.

1278 cum . . compertum sit . . quod vos ecclesiam infra tempus sex mensium . . contulistis ac ipsam incumbrastis, vobis mandamus quod predictam ecclesiam ~etis et ad presentacionem regine . . idoneam personam admittatis *Reg. Linc.* 81; **1278** episcopus [Ossoriensis] concedit . . quod ~abit . . ecclesiam et admittet idoneam personam ad presentacionem predictorum E. et M. *CoramR* 39 r. 16 (cf. *Cal. Ir.* I 1450).

deinde [CL]

1 a next, thereafter, in turn. **b** in the next place.

a qui cibum immolatum comederit, ~e confessus fuerit, sacerdos considerare debet personam THEOD. *Pen.* I 15. 5; Lucas . ., qui . . primo . . corporum valitudines . . ac ~e spiritales animarum incommoditates . . sanabat ALDH. *VirgP* 24; cum . . per mare ad Massiliam ac ~e per terram Arhelas pervenissent BEDE *HE* IV 1; **957** (14c) Adam . . culpa praevaricationis inventa . . ad inferos poenas luens de[s]cendit, ac ~e . . idem crimen eademque poena . . omnes jure constrinxit *CS* 995; cantavi nocturnam cum fratribus; ~e [AS: *æfter þa*] cantavimus . . matutinales laudes; post haec primam . .; ~e [AS: *syþþan*] tertiam ÆLF. *Coll.* 101; disserendi primo facultatem, inde artem, ~e scientiam posteriorum fugisse cognitionem necesse est BALSH. *AD* 6; NECKAM *DS* X 48 (v. dictio 3); GAD. 29v. 1 (v. denigrare 1a); **1431** (v. deferre 2c). **b 680** diversas ob causas Petrum . . hunc ritum sumpsisse asserimus: primitus, ut . . similitudinem Christi in capite gestaret . .; ~e, ut sacerdotes veteris et novi testamenti in tonsura . . discernerentur; postremo, ut idem apostolus suique successores . . ludibrium . . portarent ALDH. *Ep.* 4.

2 a on that side. **b** (w. *ex*) out of.

a hinc sedem cumula, †fultra [l. fulcra] deinde loca *Babio* 102. **b 1467** non cariabunt pisces ex ~e villam ad vendendum donec . . de . . inhabitantibus . . ville ipsos emere volentibus . . serviatur *Doc. Bev.* 58.

3 *f. l.*

1300 quomodo vis tu †deinde [? l. te inde] acquietare *Year Bk. 30–1 Ed. I* app. 540.

deinfra [LL], (prep. w. acc.) within.

1283 res comestibiles de foris apportate ad vendendum, que ~a mediam leucam erunt apportate . ., non vendantur donec primo ad placeam . . castri fuerint apportate *RGasc* II 210 (= *Reg. Gasc. A* 338).

deinotes [LL < δεινότης], cleverness.

est quedam potencia quam vocant ~oteta; hec autem est talis ut ad suppositam intencionem contendencia posset hec operari et sortiri ipsis BRADW. *CD* 61D.

deinstauratus, unstocked. *V. et. destaurare.*

12.. hec est extenta facta . . de terris et tenementis prioris de D. . ., quantum valeant instaurate et quantum ~e *MonA* IV 666b (= *CalIMisc* I 472).

deintegrare [CL = *to impair*], to dissect, analyse.

Grammatica . . sponsam seriatim ~avit locutionem OSB. GLOUC. *Deriv.* 239.

deinter [LL, al. div.]

1 (prep. w. acc.) between; **b** (w. ref. to disputants).

c1204 de Meresbech usque ad vadum ~er Rameshed et Driterum *Couch. Furness* II 100. **b 1121** placitum ~er episcopum Linc' et abbatem S. Augustini . . ita finitum est . . (*Cart. S. Aug. Cant.*) *KR Misc. Bk.* 27 f. 88b; terram . ., que ~er eos in calumnia fuit *Chr. Rams.* 225 (= *Cart. Rams.* I 244).

2 from between. **b** (?) from within.

venenatum . . animal, quod bufonem vocant, visum est reptans exire ~er femora mulieris *NLA* (*Malachy*) II 164. **b 1289** si homines de inter Dordoniam sint . . liberi ab omnibus pedagiis . . que percipiuntur inter Dordoniam *RGasc* II 504.

3 (adv.) inside.

1300 attachiata fuerunt [vellera] . . eo quod mala lana fuit volupata ~er *Rec. Leic.* I 229.

deintro [LL]

1 (adv.) within. **b** on the inside. **c** (w. *de*) from within.

fratribus ~o degentibus R. COLD. *Cuthb.* 102; ~o acclamantibus, "aquam, aquam," mulier ferventissimam attulit T. MON. *Will.* II 9. **b** clausis ~o capelle sue januis GIR. *GE* II 10 p. 215. **c** diabolum de ~o projicientes expellite R. COLD. *Cuthb.* 17.

2 (prep. w. acc.) within.

qui tunc temporis ~o insulam . . conversarunt R. COLD. *Cuthb.* 29 (cf. ib. 82: ~o ecclesiam . . subisse).

deintus [LL, al. div.]

1 (adv.) from within. **b** within. **c** on the inside.

rarum cum advenientibus ~us habens colloquium, et hoc per fenestram BEDE *CuthbP* 17; dum deforis illa [aquam] traderet et ~us illi susciperent T. MON. *Will.* II 9; commotio magna hinc a foris oppugnantium, inde ~us repugnantium *Itin. Ric.* II 16; **s1193** familiares Hoeli Seis oppidum Wiz . . insidiis cujusdam traditoris ~us ceperunt *Ann. Cambr.* 58; J. BLUND *An.* 55 (v. deforis 2c). **b s1160** capti sunt ~us milites lv *Flor. Hist.* II 75 (= M. PAR. *Maj.* II 216: intus); **s1314** illi ~us, non habentes unde obsidionis incommoda sustinerent, castrum reddere compelluntur *G. Ed. II Bridl.* 47. **c** sparget secundo desuper in circuitu ecclesiae ~us cum antiphona *Bened. Rob.* 80; **s1297** (v. dealbare 2d); radix illi [libanotidi] de foris nigra, de intus alba *Alph.* 102.

2 (prep. w. acc.) within.

si [animal] ~us sepem in virga se inpalaverit, non est solvendus (*Leg. Hen.* 90. 4b) *GAS* 605 (cf. deforis 5); **1199** de xl acris terre . . quas ipsi essartaverunt de foresta nostra de Scottor' [*Shotover, Oxon*] ~us ipsam forestam et †coneleiam [l. Coueleiam] *RChart* 2b.

deinvadiare [cf. invadiare], to redeem (from distraint).

1203 facias habere . . xx li. And[egavensium] ad equum suum ~iandum *RNorm* 79.

deinvicem [al. div.], w. respect to or about each other.

c1072 quoniam nobis nostrarum conscii sumus conscientiarum de invicem ANSELM (*Ep.* 4) III 104; proprium hoc habere solent amantes, ut vix quidquam sciant loqui nisi quod pertinet ad amorem, et tunc maxime cum vel ad invicem vel de invicem loquuntur AD. SCOT *Serm.* 303A.

Deipara [LL; cf. Θεοτόκος], Mother of God.

1521 ad reverentiam . . ~e assumptionis *Cant. Coll. Ox.* I 57; sacellum ex voto ~ae Virgini . . designat FERR. *Kinloss* 16; **1549** cum salutatione ad Virginem ~am *Conc. Scot.* II 121.

deira, ~ia v. daieria 1a. **deiscere** v. dehiscere.

deisium [OF *deis* < discus], high table or dais. *Cf. discus* 4a.

1236 faciat habere constabulario Turris London' denarios ad tabulas emendas ad mensas inde faciendas ad magnum ~ium regis in magna aula ibidem *Cl* 257; **1237** faciat . . desium aule tam coloribus . . quam aliunde emendari *Liberate* 12 m. 14; **1243** fieri faciant in gabulo ultra ~ium unam fenestram rotundam . .; depingi eciam faciant ultra idem ~ium regem et reginam sedentes cum barnagio suo *Cl* 23; **1244** verinas ad fenestras ex parte occidentali deicii regis fieri [faciat] *Liberate* 20 m. 3 (cf. ib. m. 13: aulam ultra ~ium per spatium v copularum lambruscari [faciat]).

deitas [LL]

1 divinity, godhead (Christian); **b** (as shared by man); **c** (non-Christian).

est namque in deitate manens substantia simplex; / in deitate manet quoque subsistentia triplex ALDH. *VirgV* 38–9; quia . . Christus et Deus et homo est, modo summa ~atis, modo humanitatis humilia loquendo designat BEDE *Hom.* II 12. 166; **800** Dominum nostrum Jesum Christum in utraque natura, ~atis viz. et humanitatis, . . verum filium profitentes, unigenitum viz. Patris unicum filium ALCUIN *Ep.* 199; cum . . Pater et Filius non differant in unitate ~atis, nec Spiritus Sanctus procedat de Patre nisi de ~ate, si eadem ~as est Filii, nequit intelligi quomodo procedat de ~ate Patris per ~atem Filii et non de ejusdem Filii ~ate, nisi forte quis dicat Spiritum Sanctum non procedere de ~ate Patris sed de paternitate, nec per ~atem Filii sed per filiationem ANSELM (*Proc. Sp.* 9) II 202; Patris et Filii equalitas . ., in quorum una ~ate unus generat ingenitus, alter generatur AD. SCOT *Serm.* 201C; rex summus, deitas ejus virgoque Maria / . . juratio non sit D. BEC. 1431; Filius Dei Deus noster se frequenter secundum infirmiorem sui partem se (*sic*) filium hominis dicebat, tacita Patris ~ate MAP *NC* V 6 f. 70v.; **1253** (v. deificatio a); 'deus' a ~ate et '~as' a datore dicitur BACON VII 63; [Saraceni], quamvis Christi ~atem et passionem negant, tamen eum super Moysen . . laudant S. SIM. *Itin.* 29; caro cujusque quasi mortua censetur comparatione carnis Christi . . quam ~as [ME: *þe quike goddede*] inhabitavit *AncrR* 33; **1381** in quacumque substancia creata est ~as realius et substancialius quam corpus Christi in hostia consecrata (*Conf. Wycl.*) *Ziz.* 125; *CathA* (v. divitas); COLET *Cel. Hier.* 174 (v. effictio). **b** recolens sis / quod Deus affligit quos vult deitate beari D. BEC. 185; sicut ~as presens erit cuilibet [electo], ita et humanitas BACON *Tert.* 188. **c** Macometus . ., cui cultum ~atis exhibent Saraceni DICETO *Chr.* 111; Titan . ., aliis detrusis, . . solus in sua ~ate permansit *Imag. Deorum* 316.

2 deity personified: **a** (Christian); **b** (other).

a ad ejus tumbam propitia ~as his signis revelat sanctum vivere secum in caelo *V. Ed. Conf.* 57; OSB. *V. Dunst.* 35 (v. 2 arrare b); **s1197** erant qui eorum emularentur . . fortunam, ymo ~atem indignarentur adeo fuisse propiciam G. COLD. *Durh.* 12; **c1205** seipso Deus est quia ~ate Deus est et ~as Deus est GROS. 108 (= *Ep.* 1); Pater est divinitas, Filius est ~as et Spiritus Sanctus est ~as, et simul sunt una divinitas et non ~ates BART. ANGL. I 7; ad irascendum . . ~atis pacienciam provocamus OCKHAM *Dial.* 534; Cristus est ~as, et ~as non potest esse pars creature, quia sic foret creatura perfeccior creatore WYCL. *Chr. & Antichr.* 661; [virginitas] splendet et in terris deitati nupta GOWER *VC* IV 649; **1420** speramus in dextera ~atis vobiscum faciente *Lit. Cant.* III 139; **1440** quod prestet Deitas, quod annuat ipsa potestas / que rotat astra poli (*Vers. J. Abbatis*) AMUND. II 247. **b** gaudeat, en quali deitas rugosa triumpho / molitur titulos! J. EXON. *BT* II 542.

deiterare [cf. CL iterare], to reiterate (complaints).

†tumque [? l. cumque] multum tumultuantes laici, quidam rationibus, quidam vero contumeliis, adversus episcopum ~arent et ipse ei[s] nullo modo respondere vellet . . *Vex. Will.* 182.

deividus, a imparting a vision of God. **b** (one) beholding God.

a Dunstanus in ecclesia cui praeerat ~is meditationibus inserviebat OSB. *V. Dunst.* 30. **b** vos, quibus scriptito, prece me tergite, / . . / solutum etiam a carnis cespite / inter deividos locari facite WALT. WIMB. *Palpo* 195; ave, virgo leta prole, / quam amictam vidit sole / Johannes deividus *Id. Virgo* 28.

deiwerca, ~worca v. daiwerca.

dejectio [CL]

1 throwing down, dismantling.

s1381 (v. confractio 1d); **1455** pro diversis instrumentis ad obsidionem et ~onem castri de Abircorne *ExchScot* 12 (cf. ib. 486).

2 downfall (fig.), abasement. **b** dejection, depression. **c** (astr.) 'dejection'.

angelicae superbiae ~onem, quam caveamus, ad memoriam nobis revocat BEDE *Hom.* II 23. 237D; Paulus nostri inimici vires effeminatas sufficienter noverat, quarum ~oni sui triumphi securus victoriose exprobrat [cf. *2 Tim.* iv 7] H. LOS. *Ep.* 13; **s1108** super ejus [monasterii] ~one magno compassionis dolore condoluit RIC. HEX. *Hist. Hex.* II 7; excellentiam domine hujus, per quam . . a tam estimabili [v. l. inestimabili] ~one erectus est mundus EADMER *Excell. B. M.* 578B; **c1155** quorum [abbatum electorum nec benedictorum] electionem, immo ~onem, dum apostolicis auribus intimarem *Lit. Cant.* III app. 366; epistolas . . quibus Davi mei ~onem . . vindicis animi vitio . . elaboravi GIR. *Symb. pref*; **s1229** quomodo nuntii regis Anglorum instabant Rome ad ~onem electi Cantuariensis WEND. II 360 *rub.*; **1265** ne domus nostra . . ad aliquam †dejicionem seu apporiacionem . . deveniat (*Lit. Abbatis*) *EHR* XXXIII 224. **b** in merore . . atque ~one sui vultus ALEX. CANT. *Mir.* 30 p. 219. **c** unusquisque planetarum dignitates suas in his signis optinet, sed et sublimationem et ~onem D. MORLEY 37.

dejector [CL], betrayer. **b** ejector, dispossessor.

~or, proditor *GlH* D 417. **b** [actio] duplex est in personam ~oris BRACTON 103b; queritur utrum ipse qui prius fuerit in possessione debet recuperare saisinam de ~ore antequam respondeat *Leg. IV Burg.* 99.

dejectus v. defectus 4a, deicere.

dejejunare [cf. LL jejunare], (refl.) to break fast.

[mulieres] in refectorium ut bibant sive se ~ent, . . de licencia duci possunt *Cust. Westm.* 170 (= *Cust. Cant.* 215).

dejerare [CL], to swear.

[sacerdotes] nomen daemonis, quo se censeri dixerit, et ~andi modos, quibus amoris sui foedus alterutrum pepigerint, prodendos esse praecipiunt BEDE *Luke* (viii 30) 438; dejurat, per †Dominum [? l. Deum] jurat *GlC* D 34; si mille dixeris impossibilia / palpo . . confirmat omnia, / per Deum degerans et evangelia WALT. WIMB. *Palpo* 71.

2 to forswear oneself, commit perjury.

c1159 nec prodest presbytero quod se tempore contractus subdiaconum fuisse juravit . ., cum idem disquirente eum episcopo Cicestrensi se ~asse confessus sit (THEOB.) *Ep. J. Sal.* 67 (99 p. 155); GLANV. II 19 (v. convincere 6a); **s1173** fidelitatem patris regis juraverat et . . in omnium oculis ~averat DICETO *YH* I 373; **s1188** rex . . cartis suis . . contradicere non erubuit vel ~are GERV. CANT. *Chr.* 418; **1245** [imperator] ~avit multociens (*Sententia Papae*) M. PAR. *Maj.* IV 448; **1303** per compurgatores . . quos non est verisimile odio seu optentu pecunie velle ~are *Reg. Cant.* 778; si, quando juravit, [debitor] credebat se non posse solvere vel non habebat causam probabilem quod posset solvere, utroque casu ~abat J. BURGH *PO* V 26 f. 83.

dejeratio [LL], perjury.

de quibusdam qui ipsa ~onis hora . . passione percussi sunt, quibusdam etiam . . infra annum perjurii damnum . . incurrerunt GIR. *GE* I 52.

dejicio v. deicere, dejectio 2a.

dejudicare [CL]

1 to judge, decide: **a** (w. matter as obj.); **b** (w. pers. obj.); **c** (absol.). *V. et. dijudicare* 2.

a spiritualis .. qui ex fide ~at omnia GARDINER *CC* 246. **b** Jeroboam, ~ans populum *GlC* Int. 180. **c** ut .. ipso .. audiente ac ~ante, quam immeritus eadem convicia sim perpessus appareat BEDE *Pleg.* 17.

2 to decide, determine, decree: **a** (w. inf.); **b** (w. acc. & inf.); **c** (w. *ut*). *V. et. dijudicare* 3.

a 811 rex has terrulas .. archipontifici donare .. firmiter pleniterque ~avit *CS* 335. **b** a**786** si rector rerum omnium istius vitae in itenere me longius super te sudare ~at (*Lit. Abb. Ripon*) *Ep. Bonif.* 131. **c 840** (11c) ibi Merciorum optimates ~averunt illi ut male ac injuste dispoliati essent in suo proprio *CS* 430.

3 to condemn (person). **b** to condemn (food) as unfit. *V. et. dijudicare* 4.

ipse [Juppiter] .. Thebanos ~avit, Grecos exaltavit ALB. LOND. *DG* 15. 7. **b 1330** panis pistorum captus et ~atus coram majore et aldermannis *MGL* III app. 420.

dejugare [CL], to detach.

cum a corona syderea, galeam stipante regalem, particula quedam hostili impulsu fuerit ~ata *Ps.*-ELMH. *Hen. V* 26.

†dejungere, *f. l.*

s**1215** proceres .. qui per scripta sua regi Francie se †dejunxerant [v. l. adjunxerant] HIGD. VII 33 p. 190.

dejurare v. dejerare 1.

dejuxta [cf. AN *dejuste*, OF *dejoste*], (adv.) alongside.

a**1200** tantum terre mee et more de juxta dedi eis et concessi ubi sufficienter possint exsiccare petas suas *Melrose* 87; a**1215** dedisse .. toftum continentem dim. acram juxta toftum Ricardi W. versus *north* et ibidem ~a duas acras terre et dim. versus *west Cart. Sallay* 82; **1260** domus magna Torald. domus parva ~a sub eodem culmo, que fuit Willelmi filii H. (*Rental*) *Cart. Osney* III 104.

dekarnel-, dekarnell- v. decarnell-. **del** v. le.

delabi [CL, *conf. w.* dilabi], to slip, fall down, descend; **b** (fig.). **c** to move imperceptibly, to slip into. **d** (of time) to slip by.

hoc tabulatum in extrema summitate murorum templi .. erat erectum, ne qui .. incaute progrediendo dilaberetur ad ima BEDE (*2*) *Kings* (vi 10) 723; est cisterna in ecclesia .. in quam stella dicitur esse dilapsa SÆWULF 848; W. CANT. *Mir. Thom.* VI 66 (v. crusculum); episcopus .., equo dilapsus, capiti suo mitram imponi fecit GIR. *RG* I 6 p. 35. **b** si in crimine dilabuntur H. READING (I) *Dial.* 6. 1216B; [vir] in summis rote gradibus quandoque constitutus, sed irremeabili descensu .. versus ima volubilitate dilapsus GIR. *EH* II 11; *Flor. Hist.* III 51 (v. comparativus). **c** tristior interea Frigius delabitur hospes / in portus, Salamina, tuos J. EXON. *BT* II 155 (cf. ib. VI 890: in Adriacas exul delabitur undas). **d** occulte velox delabitur etas D. BEC. 310.

delacerare [CL], to tear apart, mangle. **b** to wreck, ravage. *V. et. dilacerare.*

THEOD. *Pen.* I 7. 6 (v. dilacerare a); **1375** eam verberavit, pannos ~avit *Leet Norw.* 67. **b 1368** in parcella grangie frumenti ~ata turbine venti (*Ac. Man. Hutton*) *EHR* XXVI 336; **1378** pons .. defractus et ~atus *Pub. Works* I 139.

delaium [OF *delai*], delay.

1383 habita consideracione ad prorogacionem et delayum sic per curiam factum *Pl. Mem. Lond.* A 26 m.5.

delambere [CL], to lick (fig.).

ultionis justae .. ignis .. non quievit .. donec .. rubra occidentalem trucique oceanum lingua ~eret GILDAS *EB* 24; in hanc pelagus undis declivibus actum / proxima litoreis delambit tecta procellis J. EXON. *BT* III 256; mare .. quod .. tam Asiam quam Europam ~it GIR. *PI* III 20.

delamo v. dilanio.

delanguere [LL *gl.*] to languish, be feeble.

stipendiarius .. mira egritudine fere ad mortem usque ~ens *Mir. Hen. VI* I *prol.* p. 13.

delanguidus, enfeebled, dimmed.

hec anime tenebris intacta lucerna / splendeat exterius, nullo dilanguida [v. l. delanguida] fumo HANV. VII 470 p. 357.

delaniare v. dilaniare. **delanio** v. dilanio.

1 delapidare [CL], to pave w. stones, (p. ppl. as sb. f.) paved road.

agger, *eorðbyre* vel *geworht stræt*, strata vel ~ata ÆLF. *Gl.*

2 delapidare, ~atio v. dilapid-.

delapsus, descent, swoop.

volucris .. prepeti et precipiti dilapsu in unam [gruum] ruit W. CANT. *Mir. Thom.* VI 147.

delaqueare [cf. CL laqueare], to disentangle.

set juga, frena, fores, Pharaonis, criminis, Orci, / deles, delaqueas, conteris; una tria GARL. *Epith.* X 520.

delare v. delere 2b. **delargiri** v. dilargiri.

delarvare [cf. CL larvare], to mock.

larvas vestras derisorias .. notando, dicere vobis consuevimus quod .. vos ipsum deridere et ~are et in propriam .. faciem vestram .. expuere deberetis GIR. *SD* 32.

delassare [CL], to weary, exhaust.

membra pre labore vite ~ata BALD. CANT. *Sacr. Alt.* 738C.

delassatio, weariness, exhaustion.

post longam totius diei ~onem FERR. *Kinloss* 15.

1 delatare [*backformed from* delatus, *p. ppl. of* deferre]

1 to take away, carry off.

1361 dicit quod W. Hod ~averit quoddam †capionum *CourtR Carshalton* 16 (cf. 1 capero a).

2 to delate, accuse. *V. et. deferre* 8d; *cf. delator* 1.

1509 ad convocandum Alexandrum L. et suos complices dilatatos pro arte et parte interfectionis .. Georgii H. *Reg. Glasg.* 521.

2 delatare, ~ate, ~atio v. dilat-. **delatera** v. deleteria.

1 delatio [CL]

1 delation, denunciation, accusation.

non solum apud regem accusatio, sed etiam apud Romanum antistitem ab inimicis .. perlata fuerat ~o DOMINIC *V. Ecgwini* I 5; s**1096** plures illa ~o involvit, innocentes plane et probos viros W. MALM. *GR* IV 319; **1423** (v. circumducere 3).

2 movement.

sonus fit cum motu aeris propter successionem proprie ~onis BACON *Maj.* II 527; anathumatis, i. ~o fumi stomachi sursum ad caput *Alph.* 10.

3 ceremonial carrying or conveyance: **a** (of corpse to burial); **b** (of relics); **c** (of archiepiscopal cross).

a c**1228** C. de G. laicus .. de ~one mortuorum idem dicit quod W. decanus *Feod. Durh.* 226; a**1350** quod habeat [magister non regens] crucem universitatis et pannos honestiores in exequiis et in ~one corporis, si tempus sit serenum *StatOx* 62. **b** s**1429** speraverunt in Domino et martyre sancto ut post ~onem sui corporis cito post tristicia communis verteretur in gaudium *Chr. S. Alb.* 37. **c** c**1279** crucis .. nostre ~onem in ambitu monasterii vestri .. abhorretis .., quasi privilegiis vestris contrariam PECKHAM *Ep.* 64 (*ad Abbatem S. Augustini*); **1308** vobis [episcopo Lond'] .. mandamus quatenus .. faciatis .. inhiberi ne .. archiepiscopus [Ebor'] crucem suam coram se in nostra provincia .. erigi faciat seu deferri vel aliquis de sibi adherentibus crucem ipsam sic deferat seu ~oni ejusdem opem conferat seu assensum *Lit. Cant.* III 353.

4 bearing of arms.

1298 dimittimus sibi .. balliviam ville .. de Burgo cum juribus .. suis .. exceptis juramentis, facto duellorum, ~one armorum, deforciamento mulierum .. *RGasc* II 434 (cf. ib. 355); c**1340** sentencia excommunicacionis .. quam occasione ~onis armorum .. incurrebat *FormOx* 138 (cf. ib. *rub.*: super dilacione armorum).

5 bringing (of corn to mill).

a**1190** (v. bannalis).

2 delatio v. deletio.

3 delatio v. 3 dilatio.

1 delativus, (?) transmissive, informative.

dicendum quod omne quod in animo essencialiter est intelligitur actualiter et exprimit suam similitudinem in acie intelligencie. sed veritas dicit intencionem communem, que insplendet nobis in quantum ~a aliorum magis quam in racione objecti PECKHAM *QA* 221.

2 delativus v. dilativus.

delator [CL]

1 delator, informer, denouncer. **b** traitor.

GILDAS *EB* 8 (v. comminari a); **9..** ~oribus, *wregendum WW*; ~or, *wrohtbora* ÆLF. *Sup.*; canonum auctoritas prohibet ne .. quilibet de clero ~oris fungatur officio ABBO *Edm.* 15; c**1104** scitis quia ~ores, parvis magna addentes, mendaces solent esse ANSELM (*Ep.* 311) V 237; s**1096** proditionis apud regem accusatus ~oremque ad duellum provocans W. MALM. *GR* IV 319; GIR. *IK* I 4 (v. derisor). **b** s**1055** A. comes exul factus est propterea (sic) quod debuit esse ~or patriae *AS Chr.*

2 bearer (of letter). **b** conveyer, transmitter.

1299 cujus ~or quasdam alias literas apostolicas .. domino Edwardo .. directas .. exhibuit (*Lit. Papae*) *Ann. Lond.* 105; quid inde faciendum duxeritis nobis velitis rescribere per presencium ~orem *Reg. Brev. Orig.* 129. **b** spiritus sunt ~ores virtutum GAD. 37. 1.

delatorius [CL], incriminatory.

[Henricus I] pauperes opulentus, tributis et exactionibus inhians, ~iis hamis intercipiebat H. HUNT. *HA* VIII 1.

delatrare [LL; cf. CL oblatrare], to rail, carp.

1444 infamiam removere, ora unquam ~ancium per .. emendacionem defectuum obturare .. anelantes (*Vis. Westm.*) *EHR* XXXVII 87.

delatrix, a informer, denouncer (f.). **b** informant, bringer of tidings (f.).

a quia [cornix] alieni admissi ~ix fuit et conscia, coloris perdidit venustatem J. SAL. *Pol.* 502B; ut .. mulieris malitiose, proprii viri ~icis, redargueret nequitatem *G. Walth.* 118. **b** habeto lunam significatricem omnium rerum, quia .. post pauca ipsa luna est ~ix omnium planetarum BACON IX app. 207.

delatura [LL], (reward for) information, denunciation.

qui investigabit eam [furtivam carnem], habeat *þæt meldefeoh*, id est, pecuniam indicationis vel ~am [? l. ~ae] (*Quad.*) *GAS* 97; in quibusdam locis juramenti vel antejuramenti multa est distantia, sicut in ~a et pluribus aliis (*Leg. Hen.* 64. 1b) *Ib.* 583.

delatum v. debatum a.

1 delatus v. deferre.

2 delatus, (?) offer, proposal. *V. et. deferre* 8e.

s**1264** venerunt reges Anglie et Alemannie .., nitentes interficere sine ~u condicionis omnes sibi resistentes (*Bell. Lewes*) *EHR* XI 521.

3 delatus v. 2 differre. **delayum** v. delaium. **delea** v. dala.

delebilis [CL], delible, that can be obliterated.

creditum et character fidei non sunt ~ia, licet gratia fidei in hoc et in illo ~is sit HALES *Qu.* 1172.

delebiliter, delibly.

protrahantur occulte et ~iter deferens atque equans WALLINGF. (*Alb.*) I 300.

delebra v. dolabra d. **delebrum** v. delubrum c.

delectabilis [CL], delightful. **b** anxious to please.

quicquid jocundum ac ~e illatum sentitur ALDH. *VirgP* 7; **961** universa visibilia atque ~ia ornamenta hujus cosmi cotidie ab ipsis amatoribus transeunt *CS* 1075; ANSELM I 118 (v. delectatio); per montana amenissima loci ~is qui vocatur Balesham H. HUNT. *HA* VI 6; tanto labor hic ~ior .. quanto appetibilius ab aliis eligi quam bonus aliorum elector videri GIR. *EH intr.* p. 213; hanc .. felicitatem ~issimam et delectacionem felicissimam .. nos Christiani .. expectamus BRADW. *CD* 58D; *Ib.* 111A (v. durative). **b 836** pro redemptione animae meae placabile (*sic*) et dilectabile mente praedicta loca liberabo *CS* 416; intercilia significant hominem .. valde cupidum pulcrorum, vane fortune et plus crudelis (*sic*) quam ~is M. SCOT *Phys.* 63.

delectabilitas, delight.

trium enim est hec parilitas, / infinita delectabilitas J. HOWD. *Ph.* 208; ~as florum et fructuum *Spec. Incl.* 2. 2.

delectabiliter [CL], delightfully. **b** delightedly, w. delight.

haec .. poderis .. non uni cuilibet membro violenter imposita sed in toto est corpore ~iter consummata BEDE *Tab.* 480; amor, quam suaviter uris absentes! quam ~iter pascis presentes! AILR. *Serm.* 422B; id quod sumendum est quibusdam curiosis apparatibus sic procuro, quo magis gustum tangat ~iter prurientem J. GODARD *Ep.* 221; frater W. .., quoniam valide ad veritatem ambulat .., et docet acutius et ~ius tenet .. tam clerum quam populum ad visionem veritatis AD. MARSH *Ep.* 224. **b** c**675** domino venerabilier diligendo et ~iter venerando Wihtfrido ALDH. *Ep.* 3; dum hujus Patris Filiique proprietates communionemque ~iter intueor, nihil ~ius in illis contemplandum invenio quam mutui amoris affectum ANSELM (*Mon.* 49) I 64; post modulationes musicas, quibus ~iter diutius inservierat, Kyrieleyson .. jubilare .. incipiebat R. COLD. *Godr.* 273; s**1300** [T. filius regis] mulieris Francigene .. lac evomuit, donec adducta fuisset mulier Anglicana, de qua ~iter refocillabatur WALS. *HA* I 81; dominicus sermo debet audiri humiliter et ~iter ab omnibus Cristianis WYCL. *Ver.* II 138; omnipotens Creator, cui me oportet humiliter ac ~iter obedire CHAUNDLER *Apol.* 146.

delectamen, delight.

pulcritudinis et prudentiae ~ine omnium ejus temporum mulierum praestantissima *Enc. Emmae* II 16; fratres ad refectionis ~ina convocantur R. COLD. *Cuthb.* 81; omnis habet sua delectamina sensus H. AVR. *Poems* 27. 167; *joy*, .. beatitudo .., delectacio, ~en .. *CathA.*

delectamentum [CL], delight.

vis concupiscibilis . . est . . imperans motui cum appetitu ~i J. BLUND *An.* 55; amari et amare dulce est commercium tocius vite humane, eciam angelice atque divine ~um et beatitudinis precium ROLLE *IA* 214; in sirupis gustui afferentibus ~um BOECE 158v.

delectantia, active delight.

nec negandum est quin Deus . . delectatur et diligit quamlibet creaturam; sed, cum amor ille vel ~ia sit actus immanens, non potens incipere vel desinere esse, sicut est de dominio et ejus usu, negandum est illam delectacionem esse ejus dominium, possessionem vel usum WYCL. *Dom. Div.* 34.

delectare [CL], to delight, give pleasure (to); **b** (impers., w. inf.). **c** (pass., sts. w. *in* or inf.) to be delighted, take delight; **d** (intr. *s. pass.*).

sub obtuso grossioris chorde sonitu gracilium tinnitus . . latentius ~ant lasciviusque demulcent GIR. *TH* III 11 (cf. ib. 12: nihil amplius humanos vel jocundat vel ~at affectus). **b** maria terrasque spatiosas transmeare non tam piget quam ~at GILDAS *EB* 67; quos [versus] si vos habere ~at BEDE *CuthbP prol.*; ~at . . paucis sermonibus dicere quo ordine migraret [Baeda] a saeculo CUTHB. *Ob. Baedae* clx; *Ep. Bonif.* 116 (v. cithara a). **c** ob suavitatem divinae contemplationis ab humanis tacere ~abatur alloquiis BEDE *CuthbP* 1; dicens quia ipse . . ~aretur . . bibere cum eis *Id. HE* V 5; c**794** (v. desideranter); ALCUIN *Gram.* 850 (v. congratulari 2b); tali ac tanto studio . . rex magnopere ~atus [AS p. 367: *mærlice gegladud*] *RegulC* 4; WULF. *Æthelwold* 11 (v. delectatio); **1019** (14c) hujus amandae felicitatis gloria cordetenus ineffabili ~atus *CD* 730; HALES *Sent.* IV 217 (v. dolere 2a); BART. ANGL. XIII 27 (v. delphin a); **1335** ut . . in vestris honoribus †dilectemur *Lit. Cant.* III 101; accidentale vel contingens est Deo quod ~etur in existencia cujuscunque creature WYCL. *Dom. Div.* 34. **d** plura voluminis illius siqui scire ~at, . . in ipso . . volumine . . requirat BEDE *HE* V 17; sic corda vestra sanctificet Deus ut vobiscum, immo in vobis, habitare ~et EGB. *Pont.* 74; **1466** accidia est tedium boni spiritualis, ex quo homo nec in Deo nec in divinis laudibus ~at *Conc.* III 600b.

delectatio [CL], delight.

c**705** in quibuslibet corporeae ~onis voluptatibus execrandis ALDH. *Ep.* 8 (11); ~o, *lustbærnes* vel *lufsumnes GlH* D 141; quibus auditis delectatus rex magnam circa Dei famulum coepit habere ~onem WULF. *Æthelwold* 11; si multae et magnae ~ones sunt in rebus delectabilibus, qualis et quanta ~o est in illo qui fecit ipsa delectabilia? ANSELM (*Prosl.* 24) I 118; 'invidia est dolor de alieno bono'. . . qualiter ergo peccatum, cum ibi non sit ~o? dicendum quod est tristitia de alieno bono auferente nostrum vel minuente, sed est ~o in amando proprium bonum HALES *Sent.* II 357; ~o dilectionis est Dei fruitio; set ~o cognitionis est ipsius affectus BACON VII 120 (cf. ib. 121: propter †dilectationem); intensior dilectio, minor ~o DUNS *Ord.* II 57; BRADW. *CD* 58D (v. delectabilis a); WYCL. *Dom. Div.* 34 (v. delectantia).

delectatiuncula [CL], trivial pleasure.

vis pro ~a instantanea et turpissima Deum derelinquere? ROB. FLAMB. *Pen.* 6.

delectativus, delightful, productive of delight.

magis est ~um ex dilectione procedens quam ex cognitione, quam †illam [? l. illa] excellit; ergo sua [sc. prime cause] delectatio excellet (*sic*) cognitionem BACON VII 120.

delectator v. dilectator.

1 delectio

1 choice, selection.

menses integri hic requiruntur ~oni materie BACON *Min.* 318.

2 *f. l.*

946 (14c) si per culpam aliquam hujus †delectio [? l. delicti] successorumve suorum haec terra perdita fuerit *CS* 816.

2 delectio v. deletio.

1 delectus [cf. OF *delit*, It. *diletto*], delight.

†nundum [l. nondum] audivimus de illis secretis que pertinent ad ~um spiritus cum sapientia, ut de paradiso, purgatorio et inferno M. SCOT *Part.* 293; hec . . sufficiant ad presens de recitatione mirabilium mundi, que Deus fecit cum magno ~u ad instar joculatoris et adhuc facit continue *Ib.* 298*n*.

2 delectus, ~um v. deligere.

3 delectus v. delinquere 2c.

4 delectus v. dilectus.

5 delectus v. diligere.

delegare [CL]

1 a to assign as gift or bequest. **b** to transmit. **c** to commit, entrust; **d** (w. acc. & inf. pass.).

a dives ille caseum peroptimum viro Dei ~avit R. COLD. *Godr.* 231; c**1250** si quis non fuerit confrater hujus gilde et in extremis suis aliquid de bonis suis eidem gilde ~averit *Stat. Gild. Berw.* 4. **b** quando [lupus] prius videt hominem quia visibilis spiritus ad ipsum ~atur proprietatem quam habet corpori infundit *Quaest. Salern.* P 75. **c** jumentorum quorum ei custodia . . erat ~ata BEDE *HE* IV 22 p. 259 (cf. ib. III 16: cui suscipiendorum inopum erat cura ~ata); a**990** caeterum majestati vestrae curavimus †delegere [l. delegare] (*Lit. F. Abb. S. Vedasti*) *Mem. Dunst.* 384; inter hereditaria verba, que pater filio moriens ~avit, . . [Semei] decernitur occidendus [*cf. 1 Kings* ii 9] AILR. *Spir. Amicit.* III 26. 682D; **1204** utrum, si delegatus a principe causam sibi commissam alii ~are voluerit, nolentem delegationem suscipere, ad ipsam suscipiendam valeat coartare *Ep. Innoc. III* 22 (v. et. 2d infra); de jurisdictione ~ata, ubi quis ex se ipso nullam habet auctoritatem sed ab alio sibi commissam, cum ille qui ~at non sufficiat per se omnes causas sive jurisdictiones terminare BRACTON 108; sicut delegatus sepe ordinarie est inferior episcopo suo, quo tamen in casu ~ato sibi a papa potest esse superior OCKHAM *Pol.* I 84 (v. et. 2d infra). **d** [Henricus I] Radingie cenobium . . fundavit . . et corpus suum ibidem sepeliri ~avit *Eul. Hist.* III 57.

2 to delegate, appoint (person). **b** to dispatch. **c** (p. ppl. w. *judex*) judge delegate (eccl.). **d** (p. ppl. as sb.) delegate (var.); **e** (papal). **f** (gdv. as sb.) person to be delegated.

OSB. BAWDSEY clxxi (v. custos 1b); quod dicitur 'delegatus non potest ~are' intelligendum ad unam et certam causam delegatus VAC. *Lib. Paup.* 25 (v. et. 2d infra). **b** hunc . . / rex delegavit et eum sine labe fugavit GOWER *CT* III 84. **c** clericum, qui . . coram judicibus ~atis ecclesiam, a qua violenter ejectus fuerat, per sententiam demum evicerat GIR. *GE* II 27 p. 299; c**1210** citatio quandoque emanat a judice ordinario, quandoque a judice ~ato *FormOx* 276; **1233** cum quidam nobiles de regno nostro . . traherentur in causam coram judicibus a domino papa ~atis responsuri in partibus transmarinis *Cl* 303; si [judex] deligatus sit et warantum non habuerit ab ordinario, quod coram eo actum fuerit nullius erit momenti *Fleta* 430; **1303** judices principaliter ~ati inter partes . . a sede apostolica *Reg. Cant.* 470; licet nunc sint certi aut stati judices ~ati, tamen non habent commissionem ad universitatem causarum, sed tantum ad audiendum et terminandum causas appellationum ad regiam majestatem et curiam Cancellariae interpositarum *Praxis* 293. **d** in qua [Fresiorum] gente S. Wilbrordus positus est praedicator sedisque episcopalis in Trajecto castello ~atus est ALCUIN *WillP* 13; VAC. *Lib. Paup.* 25 (v. 2a supra); **1204**, OCKHAM *Pol.* I 84 (v. 1c supra); commissarius vel ~atus populi Romani OCKHAM *Dial.* 514. **e 1213** super ceteris capitulis si que fuerint dubitationes suborte . ., nisi per legatum vel ~atum domini pape de partium fuerint voluntate sopite, ad ipsius referantur arbitrium (*Pat*) WEND. II 73; **1245** indulgemus ut nullus ~atus aut subdelegatus, executor aut conservator, auctoritate sedis apostolice vel legatorum ipsius in vos seu monasterium vestrum excommunicationis . . sententias promulgare . . valeat absque mandato . . speciali (*Lit. Papae*) *Reg. Dunferm.* 277; s**1343** scripsit rex Anglie ~atis ac notariis graciarum domini pape . . sub hac forma W. GUISB. *Cont.* II 409 (cf. *Foed.* V 277). **f 1294** prout tibi et ~andis vel subdelegandis a te in hujusmodi negocio videbitur procedendum, plenam tibi et ~andis seu subdelegandis ipsius concedimus . . potestatem (*Lit. Papae*) B. COTTON 263.

delegatia, (eccl.) case referred to judges delegate.

1303 priori S. Greg. Cantuar' in quadam ~ia inter abbatem de B. et magistrum T. de C. rectorem de B. *Reg. Cant.* 469 *rub.*.

delegatio [CL], delegation, assignment, commitment.

†**974** (13c) liceat quod (*sic*) ipsi congregationi quod sibi per rectam ~onem collatum est perpetuo possidere *CS* 1310; isti, cum regia ~one curiam frequentare . . monerentur, . . scriptis regis adquiescere . . abnuerunt *G. Steph.* I 12; **1204** (v. delegare 1c); **1296** ordinacio . . super oblacionibus in trunco . . et de ~one clavium ejusdem *Reg. Cant.* 87 *rub.*; **1302** coram . . J. . . cardinali, qui ex ~one domini . . pape legacionis officio in Scoticanis partibus fungebatur *Melrose* 145; **1364** coram T. P. . ., cui . . episcopus Midensis causam hujusmodi non ex ~one apostolica audiendam commiserat *Mon. Hib. & Scot.* 327b.

delegativus, delegatory.

si nullo istorum modorum assellaverit, significat expulsive defectum et sensus ~e virtutis mortificationem, et ita mortem GILB. I 32. 1; Augustinus dicit verba antistitis esse solum ~a NETTER *DAF* I 325.

delegatorie, w. delegatory effect.

s**1378** [papa] scripsit episcopo Winton' ~ie in hec verba . . THORNE 2155.

delegatorius, acting as delegate.

s**1201** [papa] scripsit quibusdam conjudicibus ~iis in hec verba . . THORNE 1850.

delegere v. delegare c.

delegiatus, outlaw.

si quis ~us [v. l. diligiatus] legalem hominem accuset, funestam dicimus vocem ejus (*Leg. Hen.* 45. 5) *GAS* 570.

delenificus [CL], mollifying.

~us, i. blandiloquus; ~a, *bliþeword GlH* D 149–50; ~us, blandus OSB. GLOUC. *Deriv.* 180; sic inter curie coruscat lumina / per delinifica promotus famina WALT. WIMB. *Palpo* 16.

delenimentum [CL], mollification, blandishment.

delinimentum, *stracung* vel *olæcung* ÆLF. *Sup.*; pigebat hominem assuetum obsequiis, innutritum deliciis, carere delinimentis que ab ineunte fuerat expertus etate W. MALM. *GP* II 83; delinimentum, mulcedo OSB. GLOUC. *Deriv.* 178.

delenire [CL; *conf. w.* delinere], to soothe, mollify, cajole; **b** (refl.). **c** (w. abstr. obj.) to mitigate, allay.

delinuit, i. *geloccade*, *olehte GlH* D 118; iis qui . . vivum suis solebant ambitibus delinire se ab exsequiis defuncti subtrahentibus EADMER *V. Dunst.* 14; nove nupte blanditiis delinitus est W. MALM. *GR* II 205 (= *Eul. Hist.* I 394: †eam delinitus est); *V. Merl.* 712 (v. 1 apis 1); de illis . . qui mendaciis assentatoriis, tanquam si deliniri et demulceri possit sicut homo Deus, Dominum . . extollunt H. BOS. *Thom.* III 13 p. 213; s**1190** cum [episcopus Eliensis] ceteros vel confregisset terroribus vel arte et officiis delinisset W. NEWB. *HA* IV 14; in musicis instrumentis tanta sonoritatis dulcedine aures deliniunt et demulcent . . GIR. *DK* I 12; **1239** F. [imperator] . . matri ecclesie pro bonis mala retribuit et in eam, quam fucatis delinivit aliquando verborum fallaciis, virus effundere . . incepit (*Lit. Papae*) M. PAR. *Maj.* III 592; noverint . . neminem posse . . suavitate celica deliniri nisi ad Deum vere convertatur ROLLE *IA* 148; curantes regiam magestatem supplicis tractatus mediis delinire [v. l. delenire] *Ps.*-ELMH. *Hen. V* 103; *to fage*, adulari . ., blandiri . ., delinere . . *CathA*. **b** humanis laudibus et illecebris vane glorie sese delinire ROB. BRIDL. *Dial.* 173; precepit ei ut, quoties doloribus fatigatus esset . ., hujus cantici dulcedine se delinire atque solari meminisset R. COLD. *Godr.* 111. **c** c**1150** contentionis lites ratione devincere . . est . . motus inquietudinum ~ire *Ch. Durh.* 36a (= *Feod. Durh.* lxii: †delevire); diuturne famis duriciam in victualium plenitudine delinivit *G. Hen. V* 21.

delenitio, a blandishment, cajolery. **b** mitigation.

a lenio componitur . . hec delinicio OSB. GLOUC. *Deriv.* 304; *a fagynge*, blandicia . ., adulacio . ., delinicio . . *CathA*. **b 1439** ad minus . . aliquam dolorum delinicionem prestitisset tua grata societas BEKYNTON I 103.

deleramentum, ~are v. delir-.

delēre [CL]

1 to delete, expunge, obliterate (also fig.). **b** to exclude, expel, dismiss.

iiij superpossitionibus ~eat culpam GILDAS *Pen.* 7; **680** ALDH. *Ep.* 4 (v. chirographum 1e); **8.** . non ~ebitur, *ne bið adilegad WW*; **836** hanc libertatem scripsi . . ut . . meas iniquitates . . Deus ~ere faciat *CS* 416; †**948** (12c) si quis . . hoc memoriale meum corrumpere temptaverit . ., ~eatur memoria ejus de libro viventium [cf. *Rev.* iii 5] *CS* 860; *CS* 785 (v. destructor); dilitum, *gegniden GlH* D 515; **1016** (v. compingere b); **1157** (v. chirographum 2a); leo cum cauda ~ere propria vestigia consuevit BART. ANGL. II 5; WALS. *HA* I 153 (v. decretalis 2a); **1423** (v. circumducere 3). **b 1298** concesserunt . . burgenses quod Johannes de C. et Thomas de H. a balliva sua ~eantur *MunAcOx* 68; **1435** quod predictus T. ~eatur de societate et communitate . . burgensium *Lib. Kilken.* 59.

2 a to destroy, annihilate (also fig.). **b** to break, smash.

a ne penitus misera patria ~eretur GILDAS *EB* 17; totam ejus gentem . . ~ere atque exterminare decreverat BEDE *HE* III 24; tempore deleri gratia firma nequit WALT. ANGL. *Fab.* 40. 16; cunctis fere per diluvium jam ~etis, qualiter rerum istarum . . memoria . . retenta fuerit non indignum videtur dubitatione GIR. *TH* III 1; sunt positive verborum designationes . . superante transumptionis usu quasi ~ete BALSH. *AD rec. 2* 44; non efficacior est revocacio heresis ad ~endam heresim predictam quam sit vera penitencia ad ~endum peccatum precedens OCKHAM *Pol.* III 16. **b** timentes ne barbarorum irruptione ~erentur . . sacra ossa G. MON. XI 10; sub potencia faciendi domum comprehenditur potencia †delandi [l. delendi] sic et parandi et dirigendi parietes R. ORFORD *Reprob.* 76; **1297** clae . . ~eantur (v. cleta 2b).

deleteria [cf. LL deleterion], 'deletery', bane.

†delatera, *unlybbe*; *GlH* D 139; *a commonslaghter*, †dalitaria *CathA*.

deleth v. daleth.

deletio [CL], deletion, wiping out (fig.), annihilation.

abolitio, gestorum dilectio *GlC* A 84; liber vite recipit ~ones, juxta illud 'deleantur de libro' [*Rev.* iii 5] S. LANGTON *Quaest.* f. 279v.; s**1346** si . . Angli . . Scotorum †delectioni institissent (J. TYNEMOUTH *Hist. Aur.*) *EHR* XLIII 215; a**1428** frustra itur Jerusalem sive Romam, quia quicquid habebis ibi habebis hic, ut baptismum pro ~one

originalis peccati, et sic de aliis (R. Wyche) *Ziz.* 502; indulgencia est vera seu plena mali remissio seu deleccio Gascoigne *Loci* 86; *a doynge a-way*, †delacio, litura ..; *wastynge*, .. dilapidacio, ~o *CathA*.

deletrix [CL], destructive (f.).

ut rursus sit necesse ~ix peccati mors Christi adhibeatur Colet *Rom. Enarr.* 145.

deletus v. delere, dilectus c. **delevire** v. delenire c. **delf-** v. delph-.

delia, sort of mine or (?) *f. l.*

1517 de vj mesuagiis .. in Wynster [*Derb*] ac proficuo cujusdam minure ~ie [? l. delve] una cum officio discum portantis omnium minurarum ibidem *Fines* 6/29/21 (46).

delibare [CL]

1 to scrape, graze. **b** to skim off (fig.), pick out.

tenero delibat harenum / incessu J. Exon. *BT* III 231; ille arte Cidonum / fretus Itirea delibat cuspide frontem / principis *Ib.* V 323. **b** Hanv. I 137 (v. commendativus); hec .. cursim et breviter ~asse sufficiat Gir. *EH* I 46.

2 to offer as libation or sacrifice.

~atis, prolatis *GlC* D 204; ~or, i. immolor *GlH* D 123; si thura ydolo ~assem M. Rievaulx (*Ep.*) 56; *to do sacrifyce*, .. libare, de- .. *CathA*.

delibatio [LL]

1 skimming (fig.), picking out, pilfering.

est ~o prava ex aliqua re assumptio, ut ex pomis, vel ex cibo, vel ex potu Lanfr. *Comment. Paul.* (*Rom.* xi 16) 142D; cursim .. cuncta de cetero prosequemur, ut posteritati potius materie ~o quam historie narratio tradi videatur Gir. *EH* II *pref.* p. 307.

2 offering.

pauperes sufficienter recreati usque ad nove messis ~onem pascebantur J. Furness *Walth.* 55.

3 wasting away or (?) *f. l.*

fama ~onis [? l. debilitationis] ejus et egritudinis extreme .. multis viris sacris innotescens eosdem ad .. visitationem invitavit Gir. *David* 10.

deliberabilis, fit for delivery.

p1280 si modicum distet a moneta ~i, tunc quidem impeditur deliberacio; tamen facta levissima emendacione .. deliberabitur absque impedimento (*Tract. Nov. Mon.*) *RBExch* 1004.

1 deliberare [CL]

1 to deliberate, consider; **b** (refl.); **c** (w. indir. qu.); **d** (pass. *s. act.*).

delib[e]rat, cogitavit *GlC* D 45; **9..** †dileberaret, *gepohte WW*; **1169** (v. delusio); alternis ~ando sententiis ad contraria contendunt Gir. *EH* I 13; **1278** (v. deliberatorius b); **1290** inter se ~antes (v. curialitas 1c). **b s1384** capta fuit una treuga .., ut interim ambo regna consulcius et caucius ~arent se super articulis concordie tactis in .. tractatu *Chr. Westm.* 141. **c** ~avit aput se qualiter locum faceret memorabilem G. Mon. VIII 9; cum suis ~are inchoat quid agendum H. Bos. *Thom.* IV 15; Ric. Angl. *Summa* 27 (v. deliberatorius b); **1301** (v. denuntiatio 2b). **d 1411** voluerunt .. inter se ~ari, si in aliquo juvare possent *Conc.* III 334b; **1426** interrogatus .. utrum .. ad plenum ~atus fuisset de .. schedula in crastino .. legenda *Ib.* 461b; **s1454** vade ergo, et ~are solidius *Reg. Whet.* I 126.

2 to conclude, decide, resolve: **a** (w. inf.); **b** (w. acc. & inf.); **c** (w. *quod*); **d** (absol.).

a quamvis auctor integritatis virginale munus .. occultare .. ~aret Aldh. *VirgP* 44; miseros indigenas domo patriaque pellere ~ant; factumque est Abbo *Edm.* 1; **1100** Cantuariensis ecclesie dignitatem nec imminuimus nec imminuere ~amus (*Lit. Papae*) *Conc.* I 376b; Trophimus .. ~avit cemeterium .. constituere Gerv. Tilb. III 90. **b** totum genus Anglorum Brittaniae finibus erasurum se esse ~ans Bede *HE* II 20. **c 1420** ~atum fuit quod de bonis defunctorum mobilibus consueverunt fieri tres partes .. *Conc. Scot.* II 78. **d 949** (13c) ego Ælfric episcopus ~o *Ch. Burton* 10.

3 (p. ppl.) considered, thought out, planned.

alia .. superintulistis, quae .. memoria digna videbantur, si non ~ato et perfecto operi nova interserere .. minus congruum .. esse constaret Bede *CuthbP prol.*; **c1180** Johannes et ejus successores ipsos monachos suscipiant hospitio congruo et ~ato *AncD* A 2389; **1392** sciatis nos .. pro salute anime nostre .. ex ~ato consilio dedisse .. conventui .. de M. .. custumam l saccorum lane *ExchScot* 284.

2 deliberare [LL]

1 a to deliver, liberate (persons). **b** to try (accused persons held in gaol); *cf.* 2c *infra.* **c** to deliver, release (goods, esp. beasts seized in distraint) sts. w. dat.; *cf.* 3 *infra.*

a †delibor [l. deliberor], .. *ic beo onlesed GlH* D 123; **1194** mandamus ut ei terras suas .. restitui faciatis .., homines autem ejus captos vel retentos .. secundum consuetudinem Anglie faciatis .. replegiari et ~ari (*Lit. Regis*) R. Howd. III 274; **1202** misit ad vicecomitem ut vicecomes ~aret eum, ita quod vicecomes misit servientem et alios .., qui eum invenerunt in prisona et ~averunt *SelPlCrown* 20; **1206** ad clamorem quem fecit in domo in qua fuit inprisonatus venerunt quidam .. et fregerunt ostia et ~averunt eum *CurR* IV 216; **s1216** (v. condicionaliter c); **1227** mandatum est custodi gayole de Neugat' quod Rogerum .. et Matildem .., quos habet imprisonatos .., ~et et quo voluerint abire permittat *Cl* 2; **1248** dictus Howel dictum T[homam] .. et arma sua et catalla ~are et reddere debet *Cart. Glam.* 551; **s1262** qui potuerunt invenire plegios fuerunt ~ati per plegios *Leg. Ant. Lond.* 51; **1297** coram .. justiciariis .. ~ati fuerunt tanquam boni *SelCCoron* 89; **1333** ipsum a prisona .. interim ~ari facias per manucapcionem *RScot* 249a. **b s1279** dominus S. de P. [et al.] sedebant apud Gildhaldam London' ad ~andum dictos indictatos cives et carceratos *Ann. Lond.* 88. **c 1194** vobis .. precipimus quatinus .. ~etis in vestra potestate universas res .. archiepiscopi et canonicorum Rothomagensium .. et clericorum Normannorum et in pace de cetero habere permittatis (*Lit. Regis Franc.*) Diceto *YH* II 122; **1202** mandamus vobis quod catalla Gilberti .., que arestata sunt .., ~ari faciatis *Pat* 13a; **1221** Willelmus N. appellat Rogerum D. quod .. cepit averia sua et aliorum hominum .. et ea detinuit contra vadium et plegium, ita quod serviens hundredi quandam partem eis ~avit de catallis illis et quedam mortua fuerunt in parco ejusdem R. *SelPlCrown* 90; **1228** mandatum est ballivis Eboraci quod navem quam arestari fecerunt .. cum catallis in eadem navi contentis que sunt ejusdem Willelmi ei .. ~ari faciant *Cl* 20; **13..** per breve domini regis districciones sic capte fuerunt diliberate *Meaux* II 228; **a1400** quas oves .. per eos captas et ad communem clausuram .. ville legaliter inactas .. studuerunt .. curialiter vestris ~are *Pri. Cold.* 83; **14..** averia, bona et catalla predicta eisdem hominibus per sufficientem securitatem interim ~ari facias *Reg. Brev. Orig.* 14b.

2 a to free (from authority). **b** (w. *de*, sts. refl.) to relieve, clear, rid (of). **c** to deliver a gaol (by trying the prisoners held in it; *cf.* 1b *supra*). **d** (pass., of woman) to be delivered (of a child).

a c1157 (1286) clamo quietam abbatiam de H. et ab omni seculari potestate absolutam ~o *CalCh* II 327. **b s1266** quod custos castelli .. cum omnibus castellanis iiij dies ex gracia regis haberent ad castrum ~andum de bonis suis omnibus *Eul. Hist.* III 135; **1271** mercatores .. qui hujusmodi [sc. non recte latitudinis] pannos habent, se inde per vendicionem vel alio modo .. ~ent citra nundinas S. Botulphi *Cl* 365; **1311** capellarii qui emunt capellas de extraneis habent diem ad ~andum eos de eisdem capellis *MGL* II 103. **c 1207** mittimus .. Simonem de P. [et al.] .. ad ~andum gaolam nostram Linc' *Cl* 83b; **1220** constituimus vos justiciarios nostros ad ~andum gaolas Warrewici et Leircestre secundum consuetudinem regni nostri de prisonibus captis et in eis detentis *Pat* 229; **1221** suspensus fuit per judicium coram militibus missis a domino rege ad gaolam ~andam *SelPlCrown* 82; **1226** abbas de Rames' .. Walterum dimisit abire, ita quod libere ivit quo voluit, quousque audivit de adventu justiciariorum in partes illas ad .. gaolas ~andas *CurR* XII 2019; **1327** concessimus .. quod major civitatis [London'] .. sit unus justiciarius ad gaolam de Newgate ~andam assignandus (*Ch. Regis*) *Ann. Paul.* 327 (cf. *CalCh* IV 7); **1471** cum .. rex nunc .. concesserit .. quod senescallus noster, associatis sibi uno vel duobus legisperito vel legisperitis, .. sint justiciarii .. domini regis .. ad gaolam illam de prisonibus in ea existentibus .. ~andam (*Commissio Abbatis*) *Reg. Whet.* II 127. **d 1361** infra triduum ~ata fuit de quodam puero masculo mortuo *SelCCoron* 114.

3 to deliver, hand over, entrust: **a** (captive or sim.); **b** (land or sim.); **c** (custody of heir; once app. act. *s. pass.*); **d** (seisin); **e** (goods or money); **f** (document or sim.); **g** (keys, to gate-keeper). *Cf.* 1c *supra.*

a 1253 clericus fuit et .. ~atus archiepiscopo Cantuar' *SelPlForest* xcii; **s1324** [episcopus Heref'] ~atus est .. custodie Cantuar' archiepiscopi, donec rex discerneret quando ad objecta .. responderet Wals. *HA* I 172; **1364** comparuit .. episcopus .. petens nominatim R. .. N. .. et D. .. nativos homines suos sibi juste ~ari *Reg. Moray* 161; **s1497** (v. crux 6f). **b** de hoc manerio scira attestatur quod Edricus .. ~avit illum (*sic*) filio suo, qui erat in Abendone monachus, ut ad firmam illud teneret *DB* I 59 (cf. ib. 180: dicit comitatus quia, si vivum esset, hoc manerium appreciari possit sexies xx li.); heres tenebitur terram petitam .. ipsi mulieri ~are vel competens escambium suum eidem assignare Glanv. VI 11; **1200** comes confirmabit eidem [episcopo] donationem fratris sui de manerio de C. et illud ei ~abit secundum posse suum *CurR* I 241; **s1257** comitatus predictus cuidam Waltero de B. .. ~atus est *Plusc.* VII 22. **c 1214** tempore A. abbatis de Burgo ~averunt (*sic*) due custodie, que eum contingebant; et datum fuit intelligi domino regi quod custodie ille pertinebant ad dominum regem ..; et post, accessit idem abbas ad dominum regem et monstravit ei quod custodie ille fuerunt de feudo suo *CurR* VII 144; si [uxor] postmodum nupserit alteri viro vel pluribus successive, numquam ~abitur custodia vel maritagium in vita sua vel virorum Bracton 89b. **d 1392** assignavimus .. Ricardum [et al.] .. ad ~andam plenariam seisinam nomine nostro abbati et conventui B. Marie Eboraci de omnibus terris et tenementis .. que .. habemus in com. Cumbrie *Reg. S. Bees* 278; **1510** mandamus quatinus .. sasinam, .. statum et possessionem hereditariam .. predicti .. redditus .. priori et conventui .. ~etis et haberi faciatis *Melrose* 583; **1516** ballivus .. statum, possessionem corporalem et sasinam hereditariam .. gardiano dicti loci .. per terram et lapidem denariumque argenti dedit, tradidit, exhibuit pariterque ~avit *Scot. Grey Friars* II 12. **e 1261** si quid residuum fuerit ultra xx li., dicto J. ~ari faciatis *Pri. Cold.* 1; summa iij li. xv s. per talliam ~ata *FormMan* 13; **1325** in xiij ulnis de canab' ~atis pro velo ecclesie *Ac. Durh.* 167; **s1399** peciit .. quod rex faciat sibi ~are unum de melioribus dextrariis .. cum armis .., ac si ipsemet rex ad letale bellum ineundo perarmari deberet Ad. Usk 35; **1518** deliveravi (v. dominus 8d); **1535** colligent et recipient de tenentibus .. manerii xij s. .. et illos ballivo de C. .. ~abunt *Banstead* 366; **1542** lotrices venientes ad .. collegium pro linthiaminibus lavandis recipiendis aut ~andis stent infra .. porticum janue et non interius ingrediantur *Deeds Balliol* 323. **f** [justiciarius] fecit proclamari in itinere suo .. quod omnes qui coram eo implacitare voluissent brevia sua ~assent *State Tri. Ed. I* 11; **1321** duodene viij wardarum ~averunt justiciariis rotulos suos de articulis itineris *MGL* II 366; **c1390** ~ata est ei copia bille predicte *SelPlAdm* I 4; **1403** de xxix li. .. de arr[eragiis] hujus compoti, quorum nomina ~antur in quaterno *Ac. Durh.* 222; **1409** evidencias ~abit .. abbati et conventui *Reg. Paisley* 57; **1448** si .. cartas et munimenta .. eidem W. deliveraverit *Cl* 298 m. 14*d*.; **1534** sextus articulus ~atur, in aliud tempus commodius illi determinando *StatOx* 337; **1549** statuit .. synodus .. ut prothocolla sive libri et inbreviature notariorum defunctorum .. ad officialem .. diocesis .. ~entur *Conc. Scot.* II 112. **g 1395** claves portarum de Munkegate et posterne de Layrthorp †~ati [? l. ~ate] sunt Thome Belle, *sergeant Mem. York* I 155.

4 to leave (a place).

1291 consideratum est quod .. ~ent villam S. Yvonis, ne amplius de cetero redeant ibidem *Law Merch.* I 38.

deliberate, carefully, advisedly, w. consideration.

rediit et regi †deliberius [? l. deliberatius] locutus est W. Fitzst. *Thom.* 82; exponet vobis .. procurator .. viva voce factorum circumstantias, ut inde ~ius mentis vestre sententiam .. aperire valeatis Ad. Marsh *Ep.* 218; **s1298** [rex] ore proprio loquebatur ad eos qui vendebant mercimonia ut ~e [v. l. deliberare] componerent sarcinulas suas et sequerentur eum W. Guisb. 326; **1300** intendit .. rex super contentis in litteris [pape] quam cicius poterit commode eosdem [prelatos et barones] absentes et nunc presentes simul consulere et cum eisdem ~ius tractare *Reg. Cant.* 573; **1417** inspectis diligenter ordinacionis ipsius collegii litteris ac aliis in ea parte considerandis ~ius ponderatis *Reg. Cant.* I 159; satis ~e *Ib.* III 40 (v. diserte).

1 deliberatio [CL], deliberation (leading to action), consideration; **b** (rhet.). **c** decision.

c597 si ex ~one consentit, tunc peccatum cognoscitur perfici (*Lit. Papae*) Bede *HE* I 27 p. 61; ~o, *ymbðriodung GlC* D 62; qui per suae transgressionis ~onem .. perierat .. revocatus est ad vitam Egb. *Pont.* 65; presumeretur .. quod potius proveniret illud ex fervore animi quam ex mentis ~one Glanv. VII 1; post multas ~ones in hoc consilium denique resedit Gir. *EH* I 12; est propositum, prout de homine dicitur, ~o voluntate firmata; sed, quia in Deo non est ~o, dicetur propositum Dei scientia ordinans ut fiat voluntate firma Hales *Sent.* I 406; **1300** diliberacione .. habita *Reg. Cant.* 404; **1333** viso et examinato toto processu .. habitoque super contentis in eodem ~one pleniori *LTRMem* 105 r. 35*d*.; **1442** cum avisamento et ~one consilii nostri *Melrose* 563. **b** in judiciis saepius quid aequum sit quaeritur; in demonstratione quid honestum sit intellegitur; in ~one quid honestum et utile sit consideratur Alcuin *Rhet.* 5; non existimo aliquem prestantius consilium posse invenire quam istud. .. provide etenim providit nobis tua ~o Tulliano liquore lita G. Mon. IX 17. **c 1324** habito tractatu cum fratribus nostris .., ~onem ipsorum vobis significabo *Lit. Cant.* I 130; **1374** in liberacione facta domine regine, percipienti pro suis ornamentis per annum ex ~one concilii m li. *ExchScot* 458; nec erubescebant .. tenorem tocius dictaminis .. per ~onem nescio cujus nostre societatis improvisi de verbo in verbum extrahere Elmh. *Cant.* 224.

2 deliberatio

1 deliverance, liberation: **a** (of person); **b** (of country).

a s1141 presul Wintonie .. ad ~onem fratris sui mentem apposuit Fl. Worc. *Cont. A* 132; **1203** Guidoni .., qui venit ad nos pro ~one .. fratris sui *Pat* 31b; **1229** conventionem quam fecistis .. pro ~one corporis vestri a prisona nostra, in qua detenti estis capti .. in guerra nostra contra .. Leulinum, .. gratam habemus et acceptam *Pat* 239; **1258** ponantur in cippis et teneantur ibidem per octo dies integre sine aliqua ~one *BBC* (*Grimsby*) 295; **s1264** statuerunt parliamentum apud London', ubi .. tractarent de ~one domini Edwardi .. *Ann. Dunstable* 235; ipsum .. imprisonari fecit quousque H. uxor [sua] .. mutuata fuit xl s. .. et illos solvisset pro ~one sua *State Tri. Ed. I* 12; **1341** regi .. exoramus quatenus .. clericorum erepcionem a carcere sive ~onem dominacioni sue precipere placeat (*Lit. Archiep. Cantuar.*) W. Guisb. *Cont.* II 370; **1417** (v. 1 baillium 3); **s1436** qui David [Steuwart] in Anglia .. tunc erat in hostagio pro rege .. et ejus ~one *Plusc.* XI 9. **b**

s**1188** fiebat oratio .. pro ~one terre Jerusalem et Christianorum captivorum *G. Hen. II* II 53.

2 a relief, clearance (of land from flood water). **b** gaol delivery; *cf. deliberare* 2c; **c** (w. gen. of person tried).

a 1271 salvo mihi .. curs[u] aque super eandem peciam [terre] ad salvacionem et ~onem terre mee *AncD* A 3476. **b 1266** per ~onem carceris de illis ij annis, vj li. v s. *ExchScot* 23; **1273** ~o gayole de Newegate .. in crastino S. Margarete virginis *Gaol Del.* 35/1 r. 2; **1278** si aliquis captus per suspicionem .. veniendi ad comitatum plegios invenire non poterat, liceret servienti illi ipsum capere et ad prisonam ducere et inprisonatum detinere usque ad ~onem gayole (*Assize Westmor*) *EE County Court* 158; appellati .. debent .. plegios invenire quod de suspicione mali .. ad proximam ~onem gaole se acquietabunt *Fleta* 58; supplicaverunt ei [vicecomiti] quod dimitteret .. Gilbertum sub manucapcione usque ad proximam ~onem *State Tri. Ed. I* 55; **1320** commissus fuit penitencie prisone .. per .. justiciarios domini regis ad ~onem illam faciendam *SelCCoron* 81; s**1353** per fidem et plegios manucaptus ac domum rediens, diem ~onis gaole castri Ebor' expectabat *Meaux* III 84. **c 1340** juratores summoniti super ~onem Gilberti [capti per indictamentum] .. non veniunt *SessPCambs* 13.

3 a (power of) disposal. **b** delivery, conveyance (of land or sim.). **c** delivery, handing over (of goods, money or documents). **d** 'liverance' (Sc.), supply of provisions or money for (royal) household. **e** (w. *sui*) self-surrender.

a thesaurorum .. custos .. regis H. erarium .. ejus [regis S.] ~oni cum castello [Winton'] contradidit *G. Steph.* I 4 (cf. ib. 57: comes Alanus .. in carcerali squalore fuit addictus, donec .. castella sua illius [comitis Cestrie] ~oni permitteret); **1424** dederunt .. villam de Swintone .. cuidam Johanni Swyntone .., cujus ville ~onem virtute dicte donacionis pretense .. quidam W. .., custos sive tutor heredis dicti J. .., nunc clamat habere *Pri. Cold.* 98. **b** Berlei tenet Willelmus .. : [ibi] .. silva ad lx porcos, xiiij acr' prati .., xvij liberos (*sic*) homines, lxxx acr' terrae: hoc reclamat ex ~one ad perficiendum hoc manerium *DB* II 258; tunc recurrendum est ad antiquius .. feoffamentum, nullo habito respectu ad prioritatem ~onis [hereditatis] BRACTON 89b. **c 1349** quia non est consonum racioni quod quis pro impetracione brevium nostrorum pro jurium nostrorum defensione et eorundem brevium ~one excommunicetur *Reg. Brev. Orig.* 44; **1449** super ~one ornamentorum, rerum, bonorum et utensilium .. caucionem .. exhibere teneantur *Test. Ebor.* II 150; ipsum J. .. rogavit essendi de consilio suo in assisa .. et dedit et deliberavit eidem J. .. vj s. viij d. .., que quidem rogacio .. et denariorum ~o sunt eadem manutenencia .. unde .. queruntur *Entries* 429b. **d 1358** xxxij li. .. liberatas in diversis denariatis Patricio, clerico ~onis, ad usum regis *ExchScot* 562 (cf. ib. 587: Patricio clerico liberacionis domus regis); **1543** sub reversione summe xvj li. .. per tradicionem, ~onem et per ipsos (*sic*) pre manibus in pecunia numerata recepcionem dicte summe *Scot. Grey Friars* II 40. **e** quod ipse primus ab intelligentia vel anima separata cognoscatur 6 modis: uno modo per quandam collationem et ~onem sui ipsius ad suam causam; intelligit enim ut creatura, et per hoc intelligit suum creatorem BACON VII 119.

3 deliberatio v. delibratio.

deliberativus [CL], deliberative (rhet.).

ars rhetorica in tribus versatur generibus, id est demonstrativo, ~o, et judiciali. .. ~um est in suasione et dissuasione, ut in Regum legitur quomodo Achitophel suasit David citius perdere et quomodo Chusai dissuasit consilium ejus [*2 Sam.* xv 31–7] ALCUIN *Rhet.* 5; ~us sermo, in quo est suasio et dissuasio OSB. GLOUC. *Deriv.* 180; ~um genus cause tractant magnates et, deficiente accusatore, absolvendum esse tam senem quam juvenem pronuntiatum est NECKAM *NR* II 40.

deliberator [CL], deliverer, liberator; **b** (of beasts seized in distraint).

delyverar, ~or, liberator *PP*. **b** ballivi .. recipiant .. plegios de averiis retornandis .. ante quam liberacionem faciant averiorum. et, si quis alio modo plegios ceperit, respondeat ~or de precio averiorum *Fleta* 96.

deliberatorie, calmly, deliberatively.

iste .. estuosissimo ire incendio .. incanduit. .. sed, subtractis .. caloris jaculis, ad tempora reformacionis ~ie veniemus *NLA* (*J. Bridl.*) II 69; habeatis .. fideles consiliarios cum quibus possitis ~ie communicare *Regim. Princ.* 91.

deliberatorius, a (rhet.) deliberative. **b** (leg.) allowed for deliberation.

a nos .. quodam ~ii sermonis elogio alloquitur H. BOS. *Thom.* IV 15; nondum plene contuli cum magistro R. .. de personis aptis ad curam prebendalem, de quibus sermonem ~ium nobis imposuistis AD. MARSH *Ep.* 34. **b** inducie ~ie sunt que dantur reo tantum in judicio vocato, in quibus secum deliberet an cedat an contendat RIC. ANGL. *Summa* 27; **1225** pars monachorum citata, legitime ~iis optentis induciis, quasdam excepciones proposuit *Couch. Kirkstall* 267 (cf. *Meaux* I 431: ~ii[s] obtentis induciis); **1278** quod inducias ~ias juri consonas ad deliberandum super eodem articulo .. habere possit *Reg. Heref.* 162; tempus erat datum episcopo ad deliberandum, et ille .. recusat ~ium tempus sibi datum *Praxis* 88.

deliberius v. deliberate. **delibor** v. 2 deliberare. **delibra** v. delubrum e.

delibratio [LL], stripping of bark from trees.

1330 clamat .. habere .. corticem deliberacionis de dominicis boscis regis *PQW* 637a.

delibuere [CL *p. ppl. only*], to anoint, besmear (also fig.). **b** (p. ppl., fig.) steeped, filled. **c** stained, defiled.

liciis olei liquore ~utis ALDH. *VirgP* 36; ~utus, perunctus, infusus; ~uit, unxit *GlC* D 38–9; ~utus, *gesmirwid Ib.* D 264; **9..** †dilibatus, *gesmyred WW*; contigit ut ad laudem .. Trinitatis tertio mererer consecrari, ~utus .. sanctificati chrismatis perunctione ABBO *Edm.* 8; seram arripuit manu, quae .. eum est subsecuta quasi pessulus non esset in ea ac veluti foret oleo ~uta LANTFR. *Swith.* 27; **1228** (v. collyrium b); ~utus, A. *be bawdyd or untyd WW*. **b** c**770** multa sum laeticia ~utus (*Lit. Archiep. Ebor.*) *Ep. Bonif.* 124; **797** unde ego totus gaudio ~utus ALCUIN *Ep.* 125. **c** c**1106** ut sanguine et lacrimis pauperum ~utus thronum tantae dignitatis ascendat (*Lit. Archiep. Ebor.*) *Ep. Anselm.* (373) V 317.

delibutio, anointment.

ecclesie filius .. sacramentalis ~onis vel immemor vel dissimulator accepte GIR. *EH* I 46; non meritorum qualitatem sed potius sacramentalem ~onem attendit *Id. Galf.* II 10 p. 409.

delicabilis v. delitabilis.

delicaciter, delicately, gracefully.

ut [mulier] pedes tam flexibiles tamque ~iter articulatos haberet quod articulorum proceritate pariter et flexibilitate .. acu suere consueverit GIR. *IK* II 11.

delicate [CL], delicately, luxuriously.

ista .. tortis cincinnorum crinibus .. ~e componi .. satagit ALDH. *VirgP* 17; **8..** ~e, *estelice WW*; edidicit quod rex ille ~issime viveret in cibis pretiosis MAP *NC* V 2 f. 59v.

delicatia [cf. ME *delicacie*], delicacy, luxury.

1434 cum .. nonnulli .. hujusmodi sextis feriis .. ~iis et †aliis carnis illecibris et †ebricacionibus .. dediti ingurgitando se immississent *Reg. Heref.* 177.

1 delicatio, enjoyment.

[religiosi] ad tales [magnatos] accedere ob .. conviviorum ~onem vel pompaticam ostentacionem periculosum est J. WALEYS *V. Relig.* 251v.

2 delicatio v. deliquatio. **delicatudo** v. deliciositas.

delicatus [CL]

1 (of person): **a** delicate, tender, frail. **b** fastidious, self-indulgent.

a ~us, *wrast GlC* D 22; ~us, i. tenerus (*sic*) .., *unbrocheard*, vel *sefta* .., *mearuwe GlH* D 103; quem .. de opere absolvit ad quod etiam infirmos et ~os compellit? AILR. *Spec. Car.* III 36. 614A. **b** ~us, i. .. querulus *GlH* D 103; nec cibo nec veste ~us GIR. *EH* II 8; exterius ~i [ME: *estful*] *AncrR* 42 (v. deliciosus 2); s**1394** obiit ducissa Ebor' .., domina carnalis et ~a, mundialis .. et venerea OTTERB. 183; c**1410** plerumque contingit ut quod .. procuraverit parens studio diligenti dilicatus negligat filius animo contumaci *FormOx* 195.

2 a (of thing) fine, slender. **b** delicate, luxurious, splendid (of food, clothing *etc.*; also fig.).

a si ~iores, id est minores, nervi [AS: *ða smalan sinwe*] incisi fuerint, vj s. emendet (*Inst. Cnuti*) *GAS* 87 (= *Quad.* ib.: graciles). **b** a**705** cum memet .. ~ioribus solertiae cibis recreando ad vegetam usque pubertatem provexisti (ÆTHELWALD) *Ep. Aldh.* II (7); ornamentis vestium dilicatis decorari ALDH. *VirgP* 54 (cf. ib. 35: dilicatas defruti dilicias); non ullius inebriantis liquoris aut alicujus ~i libaminis haustum .. gustavit FELIX *Guthl.* 20; oblata .. ~iora .. et pretiosiora .., que .. a sobrietatis .. perfectione .. videri possent aliena H. BOS. *Thom.* III 16 p. 233; J. GODARD *Ep.* 22 (v. deliciosus 1b); **1260** j dolium boni vini et ~i *Cl* 322; **1293** ij s. .. ad emendum cibaria solito ~iora *Reg. Newbattle* 141; R. BURY *Phil.* 8. 120 (v. cilicium d); ~iori, ut reor, cibo non poterit dominus meus vesci CHAUNDLER *Apol.* 176.

deliciae [CL]

1 delights, pleasures. **b** choice food, dainties. **c** ornaments.

spernere dilicias et mundi linquere gazas ALDH. *VirgV* 761; recessit genus humanum ab Eden, id est a ~iis internorum bonorum BEDE *Gen.* 75; **8..** ~ias, *estas WW*; panem doloris et lacrimarum, quem esurio super copiam ~iarum ANSELM (*Or.* 16) III 67; viri molles et ~iis magis quam animi fortitudine affluentes *G. Steph.* I 58; voluntas .. ~ias appetit seculares et ad amores mundi et affectus et voluptates .. suspirat W. DAN. *Ailred* 22; [Hiberni] summas reputant ~ias labore carere GIR. *TH* III 10; NECKAM *DS* III 527 (v. deliciosus 1a); s**1256** [rex et regina Scotie] concupierunt .. regnum Anglie .., civitates et castra, fluvios et prata, silvas et agros .. contemplari, que inter omnium regnorum ~ias maxime comprobantur M. PAR. *Maj.* V 573. **b** [ostia fluminum] per quae .. transmarinae ~iae ratibus vehebantur GILDAS *EB* 3; dilicias, epulas regum luxusque ciborum / .. condo ALDH. *Aen.* 40 (*Piper*) 3; **9..** ~ias, *wista WW*; **966** (v. 1 aporiare 2); a**990** novimus inopes quosque .. cibis uti paupertinis, quibus rerum diversarum diliciae desunt B. *Ep.* 386 (cf. ib.: dulcoris ~ias); quicquid ~iarum regi infirmo deferebatur, ab eo illarum medietas Anselmo infirmanti mittebatur EADMER *HN* 13; NECKAM *DS* III 525 (v. delicium 1); [in Francia] gentes ad arma comedunt alitilia sua [sc. plebeiorum], ita ut vix ova eorum ipsis relinquantur pro summis vescendi ~iis FORTESCUE *LLA* 35; hee ~ie, *dantyths WW*. **c** a**705** tuos .. legimus fastos diversorum ~iis florum depictos (CELLANUS) *Ep. Aldh.* III (9); *MonA* II 437a (v. 2 crusta 2a).

2 (w. *flos* or sim., by misinterp. of OF *de lis*) fleur-de-lis, flower-de-luce, iris. **b** image of fleur-de-lis.

1418 reddendo unum florem ~iarum ad festum S. J. Baptiste *RNorm* 254. **b 1388** [frontellum] de armis Anglie et Francie in rubio et blodio velvecto cum leopardis et floribus ~iarum contextis (*Invent. Westm.*) *Arch.* LII 229; **1420** j septrum de cupro deaurato pro *le capstane* ad modum trium florum ~iarum operat' *Ac. Foreign* 59 r. 8(1)*d.*; **1443** j vestimentum .. cum floribus ~iarum de volucribus aureis intextis *Cant. Coll. Ox.* I 10; **1500** vestimentum album .. cum foliis ~iarum aurifrigiatum *Invent. Ch. Ch.* 127.

deliciari [LL], to be delighted, take pleasure. **b** (pr. ppl. *s. act.*) delightful.

s**1091** Robertum ducem .., qui tunc temporis ultra quam virum deceat in Normannia ~iabatur W. JUM. VIII 3; **1187** neque meliores sumus quam patres nostri, ut fluctus hujus seculi ~iando siccoque pede transvadare debeamus *Ep. Cant.* 97; in thalamo cordis deliciatur amor NECKAM *DS* V 150; dum jocundatur corpus, mens deliciatur *Id. Poems* 453; que mavult .. / .. includi modice sub paupere tecto / extra diviciis quam mundi deliciari H. AVR. *Poems* 2. 123; oblivisci non potest se .. de foedissima mercede .. ~iari JEWEL *Apol.* C 5v. **b** he [domine] subsistentibus a remotis videntur speciose, jucunde ac ~iantes; accedentibus autem visio penitus evanescit in fabulam GERV. TILB. III 43.

deliciora v. deliciosus 1b.

deliciose [LL], enjoyably, luxuriously, pleasurably, for pleasure. **b** splendidly.

diu ~e properando vivebant B. *V. Dunst.* 27; s**1151** anathem .. ad ignem lignorum viridium appositam studiose satis tractant ~e DICETO *YH* I 294; putant .. salamandrum .. in igne ~e commorari NECKAM *NR* I 17; **1242** austurcum regis .. recipiat et bene custodiat, non faciens eum volare nisi ~e, viz. semel vel bis ad plus in septimana *Cl* 73; sus gule habet hos porcelos, prepropere edere, nimis ~e [ME: *to esteliche*], nimis edaciter, nimium, nimis sepe *AncrR* 72; s**1383** viri de rebus bellicis expertes, ~e educati, in pace requieque nutriti WALS. *HA* II 92; indies ~ius agens, lurconibus, mimis, saltatoribus intentus BOECE 90v. **b** [abbas J., ob. **1260**] fecit eam [novam aulam] .. decentissime per manum Ricardi, monachi nostri, artificis optimi, pingi et ~e redimiri *G. S. Alb.* I 314.

deliciositas [LL], delicacy or delight.

delicatudo, elegantia vel ~as OSB. GLOUC. *Deriv.* 177; contraria sunt in modernis multis religiosis querentibus in alimentis ~atem ac curatam preparabilitatem, et sic de aliis J. WALEYS *V. Relig.* f. 236v.; ~as, A. *delyte WW*.

deliciosus [LL]

1 delicious, delightful. **b** (of food, clothing or sim.) delicate, sumptuous, luxurious.

~a. i. amabilior, laeta, *epgeorn* vel *estful GlH* D 104; delicie horribiles aut horror deliciosus / dicetur sapidum virus, amica lues NECKAM *DS* III 527 (cf. delicium 1); o regis quanta bonitas! pietas generosa / in vultu tanta! dulcedo deliciosa / in verbis, factis, aliis multis quoque rebus! ELMH. *Metr. Hen. V* 268; **1440** in illo ~o ortulo, ubi spirat nardus BEKYNTON I 114; *deliciouse*, ~us *CathA*. **b** vestibus atque cibis veterem mutaverat usum: / deliciosa nimis fugiens, nec vilia valde / sectatus fuerat ALCUIN *SS Ebor* 1485; **10..** sumptuosa, diliciosa *WW*; princeps triclinii, quia grossiora non poterat, utpote minime enutritus in his, ~a quidem sed parce admodum sumebat et sobrie H. BOS. *Thom.* III 16 p. 234; sepe loco vili latitant pretiosa, / continet urceolus vetus escas deliciosas D. BEC. 19; s**1135** regis .. corpus .., cujus os tam ~issimis et exquisitis cibis pasci solebat H. HUNT. *HA* VIII 2; lautiora ~ioraque venari contempno; sed, ut quevis grossa vel delicata fuerint oblata, ventrem .. sarcio J. GODARD *Ep.* 222; qui potest oblata commedere, comedat cum gratiarum actione; si non potest, doleat quia necesse habet querere ~iora [ME: *estfulre*] *AncrR* 32; prandia disposuit sibi †deliciora [? l. ~osa] sacerdos (*Vers.*) CAPGR. *Hen.* 21.

2 (of persons) fastidious, self-indulgent.

si cultiorem dicendi formam ~us exposcit auditor *Itin. Ric. prol.* p. 4; iracundi et tamen ~i [ME: *eastfule ancren*], asperi interius ubi deberet esse lenitas et exterius delicati ubi asperitas esse deberet *AncrR* 42.

delicium [CL], **~ius**

1 (source of) delight.

sed, si delicias murenam dicere cogor, / horrorem potero dicere delicium NECKAM *DS* III 526; **1336** talis erat dilectus tuus, o Rachel [cf. *Jer.* xxxi 15], nostra pulcherrima mulierum! confortate, filii, manus matris nostre dissolutas, que dilicium suum desiderabile osculorum suorum jam ablatum .. plorat! *Lit. Cant.* II 115; ~ium, A. *delyte WW*.

2 petted child, minion.

~ius, puer in deliciis amatus a domino *GlC* D 171; ~ius, A. *a cokenay WW*; *a coknay*, ambro, mammotropus, ~ius; versus 'delicius qui deliciis a matre nutritur' *CathA*.

delict- v. delinquere, derelinquere 2d, diligere 4a.

1 deligare v. delegare 2c.

2 deligare [cf. AN *delier*, OF *desliier* < LL disligare; CL = *to bind fast*], to unbind (person); *v. et. disligare* 1a. **b** to unmoor, detach (ship).

1271 Walterum .. et Ricardum .. garciones domus ligaverunt .., et Walterus .. ~avit se *SelCCoron* 16; **1356** ipsum [Johannem] ~avit et levavit (*CoramR*) *SelCKB* VI 109 (= *Controlment Roll*, ib. V cxxxix: diligavit). **b** quecumque naves partis adverse a navibus Anglicanis ~ari poterant, disruptis rudentibus, .. sese in fugam .. preparabant *Ps.*-ELMH. *Hen. V* 32.

1 deligere [CL; *conf. w.* diligere], to choose; **b** (w. inf.). **c** (p. ppl.) chosen, choice.

delegerunt, elegerunt *GlC* D 198; [Aþelwoldus] Wintoniensis ecclesie episcopus delectus [v. l. electus] est *V. Neot. A* 3; instar avis volans .. solitudinis secreta ~it, in qua .. similis fit pellicano solitudinis [cf. *Psalm* ci 7] AILR. *Serm.* 29. 482B; Calidonius heros / decreto procerum socio legatus Ulixe / deligitur J. EXON. *BT* IV 351; **1564** ut procuratores .. coarctentur talem ~ere pro respondente in praeviis disputationibus .. qui in comitiis sequentis anni respondeat *StatOx* 396. **b** cursum praesentis vitae finire delegerit in conversatione theorica FOLC. *V. Bot. pref.* 373; siquis extraneus in Oxeneford manere ~ens et domum habens sine parentibus ibi vitam finierit *DB* I 154v.; non agriculture delegit exercitia colere R. COLD. *Godr.* 11. **c** delecto quo primum milite caeso / invalidi fragiles perterreat agminis hastas FRITH. 600 (cf. ib. 705: miles †dilecte [MS: delecte]); paucis et delectis [v. l. electis] conceptis militibus munitionis arcem .. perfecit *V. Neot. A* 13.

2 deligere v. diligere.

deliliare, to deprive of lily-white purity, sully, darken.

est cui cana comam puerilis liliat etas / maturusque putrem vetulam deliliat annus HANV. I 284 p. 250; quos nulla criminis denigrat notula, / nulla deliliat cordis sordecula WALT. WIMB. *Palpo* 165; memor frontis quam mors deliliat J. HOWD. *Ph.* 1001.

delimare [CL = *to file down*]

1 to bring an end, (?) by wearing down.

~atum, conclusum [*corr. to* complexum] *GlC* D 47.

2 to mow down (fig.) or (?) to bespatter w. mud, denigrate (*cf. limus*).

celo redolentis lilia fame / livoris decerpit hiemps, .. / .. superos [v. l. superis] fragrancia morum / balsama delimat HANV. VI 110 p. 329.

delimitare [CL], to delimit, mark out.

castris ~andis *Itin. Ric.* I 31 (v. decubare 2).

delineare [CL], **~iare, ~ire,** to delineate, outline.

1298 non utantur .. frenis nisi cum una cruce dumtaxat in fronte et una in medio pectoralis stagno exterius ~itis *Reg. Cant.* 813; quod illa literis / deliniavit, hoc ego una praestiti MORE *Ut.* xciii.

delineatio [LL], delineation, portrayal.

1216 hic in margine inseritur ~o cujusdam avis grui similis cum his quoque verbis .. *Cl* 281b (*in margine cum imagine*); cf. crana 1b.

1 delinere v. delenire.

2 delinere [CL], **~ire,** to anoint, smear; **b** (prov.). **c** (fig.) to bribe, flatter; *cf. delenire* a. **d** (p. ppl.) honeyed (fig.).

quorum .. frontem [chrismate] ~ivimus EGB. *Pont.* 7; aliquando os matricis viscosis humoribus ~itur *Quaest. Salern.* B 13. **b** s**1236** [hoc] esset vulnus infixo ferro ~ire et cicatricem deformem, non medelam, procurare M. PAR. *Maj.* III 375. **c** s**1186** rex Anglorum .. sperabat .. regis Francie conatus pecunia mediante subvertere et commotum juvenis animum aureis et argenteis .. unguentis ~ire GERV. CANT. *Chr.* 336; nulli plus inimicantur papis .. quam illi domestici qui cessant eos corripere et statum suum et vitam suam non cessant blasphemo adulacionis oleo ~ire WYCL. *Sim.* 63. **d** s**868** Hinguarus .. vulpeculari astutia verbisque ~itis inducias ab Anglis impetravit H. HUNT. *HA* V 5.

deliniare v. delineare. **delinificus** v. delenificus. **delinimentum** v. delenimentum. **delinire,** v. delenire, delineare, 2 delinere.

1 delinitio v. delenitio.

2 delinitio, anointment.

fiat ~o circa palatum .. cum syrupo [etc.] GILB. I 74v. 1.

delinquere [CL]

1 to do wrong, offend (often w. internal acc.); **b** (w. dat. of person offended). **c** (pr. ppl. as sb.) offender, delinquent. **d** (p. ppl. *delictus* as sb. n.) misdeed, offence.

numquam divitibus .. siqua †~issent [v. l. deliquissent], reticebat BEDE *HE* III 5; **978** (? recte **974**) (18c) si non .. emendaverit .. quod contra nostrum deliquid decretum *CS* 1309; die quo contra regem deliquit *DB* I 196v.; quod homo illiteratus .. nesciret quantum ~eret W. MALM. *GP* I 23; quicquid ab eis ~itur, in istorum infamiam cuditur J. SAL. *Pol.* 502B; GIR. *GE* II 24 (v. appendicius 3b); **1221** quia illi multis modis deliquerunt versus dominum suum *SelPlCrown* 95; **1252** si homines de D. deliquerunt erga abbatem de H. *Cart. Dieul.* 357; *Cust. Westm.* 266 (v. certus 2c); **1297** Hybernici de densitate boscorum .. assumunt audaciam cicius ~endi *StatIr* I 208; **1321** si quis super premissis .. bis convictus et tercio †deliquierit *PQW* 456b. **b** c**1380** qui predicto A. sic .. deliquerunt *FormOx* 252; **1509** pro salute animarum eorum quibus deliqui *Scot. Grey Friars* II 138. **c** sciscitanti quoties ~entibus noxarum vincula enodanda forent [cf. *Matth.* xviii 22]. ALDH. *Met. intr.* 2 p. 68; secundum merita ~entium .. vindictae inferuntur LANFR. *Const.* 143; ut 'ignotum' dicitur tum quod ignoratum tum ~enti remissum BALSH. *AD* 53; **1318** (v. demerere 2e); **1588** potestatem .. ~entes .. juxta eorum demerita .. puniendi *Pat* 1320 m.16. **d** qui .. / sordida peccantis saecli delicta piarat ALDH. *VirgV* 2898; **749** (12c) pro expiatione ~orum suorum *CS* 140; **964** (12c) penam ~i, quae Anglice dicitur .. *gyltwyte CS* 1135; ~a mea, an eratis tam fore noxia futura cum animam meam vestra dulcedine potabatis? ANSELM (*Or.* 14) III 58; GIR. *GE* I 37 (v. derelinquere 1c); **1203** nec malecredunt eum de .. aliquo ~o facto eidem R. *SelPlCrown* 29; **1252** per aliquod ~um, transgressionem factam regule seu occasionem *Cl* 207 (= *RL* II 383: †defectum); **1257** cum contingit clericum pro ~o foreste defamari (*Artic. Cleri*) M. PAR. *Maj.* VI 356; **1313** ex quibuscumque †dil[i]ctis et causis contigerit adjudicari *PQW* 319a.

2 **a** (?) to abandon, desert; *cf. derelinquere*; **b** (absol.) or (?) *f. l.* **c** (?) to lose.

a ipsi per ignem transierunt et aquam et nos in mediis ignibus et fluctibus ~unt H. BOS. *Ep.* 19. 1450C; s**1228** benedictus Dominus .., qui non ~it [? l. derelinquit, *as Psalm* ix 11 etc.] confidentes in se GERV. CANT. *GR Cont.* 117; **b** **1249** J. et S. .. dicunt quod revera .. [alias] inplacitabant eum per consimile breve .. et dicunt quod ipse excepit contra eos quod non debuit illis ad aliud [v. l. illud] breve respondere, eo quod ipse non tenuit predictum manerium die quo breve inpetratum fuit, unde dicunt quod ipsi deliquerunt [v. l. reliquerunt] et recesserunt de brevi illo *CurR* XIX 946. **c** annominatio in litteris mutandis: 'o dilecte mihi, verum †delecte [? l. delicte] Johanni, / pre reliquis aliquis hec tibi forte feret' GARL. *PP* 120.

deliquamen, cleansing.

a clensynge, colacio, defecacio, deliquacio, ~en .. *CathA*.

deliquare [CL = *to strain* (*liquid*)], to freshen, brighten, or (?) *f. l.*

sic lilia primeva verni solis ~ata [? l. deliciata] teporibus .. leticia effusione lasciviunt MAP *NC* IV 3 f. 46.

deliquatio [cf. CL deliquare, delicare], draining off.

sudores fetidi mirro compescuntur: conservantur corpora in delicatione; in putredine dissolvuntur BART. ANGL. XVII 102; *CathA* (v. deliquamen).

deliquescere [CL = *to melt away*], to grow weak as water (*cf. Psalm* xxi 15).

s**1097** pagani .. animis delicuerunt et fuge indulserunt H. HUNT. *HA* VII 8; s**1138** acies .. Scotorum .. animo delicuit et fuge indulsit *Ib.* VIII 9 (= *Meaux* I 122: †delituit).

1 deliquium [CL],

1 eclipse.

~ium, defectio *GlC* D 95; ~ium, defectio solis *GlH* D 122; mortem annunciat mortis ymagine / luna deliquio celum vertigine WALT. WIMB. *Sim.* 164.

2 fault, offence.

vos .. pro meis precor orare ~iis LANTFR. *Swith. Ep.*; ~ium, .. defectum *GlH* D 122; **10..** [monachi] ex .. monasterio .. per proprium arbitrium egressi vel proprii reatu ~ii expulsi (*Paraph.*) *GAS* 249.

2 deliquium [LL], melting.

a meltynge, ~ium, liquamen, liquefaccio *CathA*.

1 deliramentum [CL], raving, absurdity.

sicut scismaticorum deleramenta garriunt ALDH. *VirgP* 8; garrula matronarum ~a FELIX *Guthl.* 12; **9..** deleramenta, *dofunge, dwolunge WW*; omnia ~a ejus familiares quasi clitellarii quibusdam nominis sui humeris portant J. SAL. *Pol.* 502C; nos eum reducimus syrenum cantibus et rhythmorum ~is P. BLOIS *Ep.* 76. 234A; cum tante gravitatis viros .. presumere audeam prophetare potius ~a mundi quam fabulari DEVIZES *prol.* 25; c**1370** licet verba mea appareant ~a et falsa propter occultum modum loquendi (J. BRIDL. *gl.*) *Pol. Poems* I 214; que .. increduli illi minime credere voluerunt, sed diliramenta et vana quedam deputaverunt BLAKMAN *Hen. VI* 21.

2 deliramentum [cf. 2 delirus], discord, strife.

a stryfe, agon .., decertacio, ~um .., discordia .. *CathA*.

1 delirare [CL], **a** to deviate, go astray (fig.). **b** to rave, go mad.

a **13..** tractatum fuit quod ipsi .. clamium .. nobis .. relaxarent. .. sed .., a dicto tractatu ~antes, asserebant se dictam relaxacionem .. non posse perficere absque .. consensu archiepiscopi *Meaux* III 118; c**1400** videns meas cartuarias .. per varios earum scriptores, qui suam nescient orthographiam .., in illarum sentenciis ~are (T. SAMPSON) *FormOx* 334. **b** †disipiscat, delerat *GlC* D 332; **9..** ~o, *ic dwolie*; ~as, *þu dwolast WW*; ~antes, mente deficientes *Gl. Leid.* 1.37; ut noveris me non ~are, sed scire que dico [etc.] ALEX. CANT. *Mir.* 38 p. 235; effeminate miles, belli delitias queris? plane ~as PULL. *CM* 212; si ita ~et quod manum porrigat [ME: *gef wurðeð swa wod þet he warpe hond*] *AncrR* 27.

2 delirare [cf. 2 delirus]

1 to be discordant, dispute.

descorder, .. dissonare, ~are *Gl. AN Ox.* f. 154v.; *to discorde* .., dissonare, ~are, discordare ..; *to stryfe* .., contendere .., ~are .., discordare *CathA*.

2 (trans.) to confute.

c**1400** Sampsonis ingeniosa subtilitas quamplurium Oxoniensium dictatorum argumenta penitus ~avit (T. SAMPSON) *FormOx* 334.

deliratio [CL], erratic behaviour, folly.

s**1159** inter L. Francorum regem et H. Anglorum principem, varia utriusque partis ~one, frequens bellici certaminis altercatio GIR. *EH* II 31 p. 374; senes qui jugi studio .. utuntur .. ~onis vitia non incurrunt *Id. SD* 64.

delire [LL], wildly, madly.

s**1378** ministri sceleris .. Roberti Haule cadaver .. horrende tractantes per sacratissimum locum chori .. foras ejiciunt, utpote ~e debacantes WALS. *HA* I 378.

delirium [CL], madness.

Pelagii ~io polluti BOECE 160.

1 delīrus [CL], **a** deviating. **b** raving, doting.

a H. AVR. *CG* 7v. 5 (v. 2 delirus). **b** ~us, insanus, brutus, insulsus, lymphatus OSB. GLOUC. *Deriv.* 174; quos diuturna nimis et ~a senectus extinguit GIR. *GE* II 8. p. 206; H. AVR. *CG* 7v. 5 (v. 2 delirus).

2 delĭrus [cf. 2 delirare, lyra], (playing the lyre) out of tune, discordant.

delīrus [*gl.*: deorsum lirare] hic cantat, delĭrus [*gl.*: demens vel qui male arat] montibus errat H. AVR. *CG* 7v. 5; *discordande*, ~us me[dio] co[rrepto], discors, dissonus ..; *oute of tune*, dissonus, ~us medio correpto, discors; versus: 'delĭro discordo, delīro devio dicas' *CathA*.

delitabilis [OF *delitable* < delectabilis], delightful.

predam certe desiderabilem / depredaris et †delicabilem J. HOWD. *CA* 143.

delitare v. dilacerare a. **delitere** v. delitescere.

delitescentia, concealment, secrecy.

argutatur signum non posse latere, quum hoc in loco totius sacramenti constituat ~iam GARDINER *CC* 692.

delitescere, ~iscere [CL], **delitēre** [LL], to lie hidden or go into hiding; **b** (refl.); **c** (w. abstr. subj.). **d** to play hide-and-seek.

antistes .. / delituit senis annorum cursibus intro / cisternae latebram descendens ALDH. *VirgV* 1026; etiam si fieri possit ut .. ~eam ubi .. me .. fluctus oceani .. a cunctorum mortalium, .. cognitione secludant BEDE *CuthbP* 8; ~ere, latere .., ~escere, moram facere *GlC* D 138, 196; dilitiscendo, *miþende*; dilituisse, i. celasse, *gedyrnan*; diliteo, -sco, lateo *GlH* D 516–18; huic spectaculo .. quidam nostrae religionis ~iscendo interfuit ABBO *Edm.* 11; EADMER *V. Anselmi* I 15 (v. commutare 1c); infra nemus .. ~ere G. MON. I 15 (v. divortium 1); [vulpes] infra cavernas montium ~ebit (*Proph. Merlini*) *Ib.* VII 4; noluit sub otio ~escere R. BOCKING *Ric. Cic.* I 60; s**1332** cum exercitu qui diliuit in latibulis *Hist. Roff.* f. 64; s**1458** (v. desubtus 2a). **b** s**1400** [Scoti] se ~entes ad frutices ac deviarum cavernarum .. abdita, a facie regis se subtraxerunt AD. USK 47. **c** Juliani martiris gloriam sub clandistino taciturnitatis latibulo ~escere non patiar ALDH. *VirgP*

36; in futuro punietur in opere quod hic male conscia ~escat in mente (*Serm.*) OSB. BAWDSEY clxxiii; carnalis concupiscentia .. in umbraculo desperationis ~escit R. COLD. *Cuthb.* 8; leticiam facietenus pretendens, †qui [? l. que] in animo minime ~ebat *Latin Stories* 88; officium testium est testificari veritatem justicie ~entis WYCL. *Civ. Dom.* I 25. **d** *pleyyn bukhyde*, angulo, ~eo *PP*.

deliti- v. delici-. **delituisse,** v. deliquescere, delitescere. **deliverare** v. 2 deliberare 3e. **della** v. dala. **delocissimus** v. velox. **deloricare** v. diloricare.

delphin, ~inus [CL < δελφίς], dolphin or porpoise; **b** (her.). **c** (astr.) Dolphin. **d** salmon.

Scylla .. luporum uterum et caudas ~inum [v. l. delfinorum] habuit *Lib. Monstr.* I 14; capiuntur saepissime et vituli marini et ~ines BEDE *HE* I 1; quid capis in mari? aleces et isicios, delfinos [AS: *mereswyn*] et sturias ÆLF. *Coll.* 94; ~in vel bocharius vel simones, *mereswin Id. Sup.* 180; delfini, i. simones vel *seolas GlN* 41. 2; tres ~ines siccis in arenis residentes repperit R. COLD. *Godr.* 12; delphinus cithare capitur dulcedine NECKAM *DS* III 419; illic porcus quem ~inum nominant, quem de genere militum esse vulgus autumat, porcina inter fluctus maris transumta latentem effigie GERV. TILB. III 63; ~ines qui et symones nominantur .. eo quod voces hominum sequuntur et ad vocem symphonie gregatim conveniunt [cf. Isid. *Etym.* XII 6. 11] et in armonia delectantur BART. ANGL. XIII 27 (cf. WALS. *HA* II 204); preterea delphin ludendo spargeret undas, / si ventura mari seva procella foret GARL. *Tri. Eccl.* 30 (cf. BACON V 10); **c1250** prior debet habere porpesium .. ad portus super terram S. Michaelis adductum... et debet habere medietatem delfini *Mon. Exon.* 255a; **1305** pro .. ij dolfinis, precii cujuslibet viij li. (*KRAc* 160/6) *RGasc* III app. cc; **1338** iij quarteria j delfini recentis *Ac. Durh.* 32; hic delfinus, *a porpas* .., hic dolfinus, A. *a dolfyn WW*. **b** Dolphinus Francie portat unum ~inum; nec oportet dicere ~inum planum sive ~inum de mari, quia speciale est videre ~inum .. pinnatum in dorso ..; sic ergo habes differenciam inter communem ~inum et ~inum de Nilo, qui semper est fortiter pinnatus in dorso UPTON 207. **c** Delphin, quem citharista puer revocavit ab undis, / invida dilecto fata fuisse gemit NECKAM *DS* I 377. **d** hec ~in, A. *sawmone WW*.

delphina [OF *daufine*], **~ella, ~issa,** wife of Dauphin, Dauphiness.

s1435 in qua [bargia] locata fuerat domina [Margareta] ~issa FORDUN *Cont.* XVI 12; **s1437** [Jacobus I] defunctus est .., relinquens post se filium suum J. II .. et sex filias, viz. Margaretam dalphinellam Francie [et al.] *Plusc.* XI 9; **s1445** Margareta ~a Francie cum rege et regina Francie ac cum proprio marito .. quasi regem et regnum ad nutum gubernavit *Ib.* 7.

delphinatus, a Dauphiné, lordship of the Viennois. **b** status of Dauphin.

a 1339 domicella de dalfinato de Viana *CalPat* 399; **1407** nos et ecclesia regni nostri ac dalphinatus Viennensis, pro nobis ac subditis nostris eorundem regni nostri et dalphinatus, decrevimus .. amplecti neutralitatem .. donec evulso schismate pax plantetur (*Lit. Regis Franciae*) BEKYNTON II 128. **b** UPTON 37 (v. banus); **s1420** hos [principes Franciae] rex [Henricus V] ita alloquitur: ".. civilium seditionum reliquias nobis persequendas statuo, quae in solo Carolo, qui vestro nuper judicio ~us honore est privatus, remanent" P. VERG. XXII 455.

delphinella v. delphina.

delphinensis, adherent of dauphin (afterwards Charles VII).

s1420 dum comes Sar' obsideret villam de Freney, commissum fuit bellum inter nostrates et ~es *Chr. S. Alb.* 124.

delphinianus, pertaining to dauphin (afterwards Charles VII).

s1423 rerum commutatio, quae adeo ~is rebus opportuna fuit ut de earum conservatione visum sit Deo cum primis curae fuisse P. VERG. XXIII 460.

delphininus, of dolphin or porpoise.

BEDE *CuthbP* 11 (v. coctura 1).

delphinion [LL < δελφίνιον], plant, (?) larkspur (*Delphinium*).

herba delfinion *Leechdoms* I 60; **10..** delfinion, *fugeleswyse WW*; †delfimon, *fugeles vise Gl. Durh.*.

delphinissa v. delphina.

1 delphinus v. delphin.

2 delphinus [OF *daufin*], dauphin, title (orig. pers. name) borne by: **a** lord of the Viennois; **b** (after 1349) eldest son of King of France.

a 1338 cum adherencia viri potentis et spectabilis, domini Imberti delfini de Vienna (*Lit. Ed. III*) *Foed.* V 10; **s1339** successit Philippus [V] .., qui de uxore suscitavit duas filias, una (*sic*) copulata in matrimonio comiti Flandrie, altera dolphino de Viennia AD. MUR. *Chr.* 100; **1345** Humbertus dalfinus Viennensis, de genere regio (*Lit. Papae*) *Ib.* 180; **s1354** nunciatum est .. Johannem [II] .. in regem Francie coronatum eundemque J. Karolo filio suo seniori, qui dictus est dolphinus de Vienna, ducatum Aquitannie contulisse WALS. *YN* 296; **s1356** rex Navarrie, factus est .. in .. ducatu [Normannie] ipsius regis [Johannis] et filii sui primogeniti ducis Normannie, tunc eciam dolphini de Vienna, locum tenens AVESB. 135; **s1349** successit patri Johannes Normanniae dux. hujus principatus initia ~i novo honore aucta se feliciter dederunt: siquidem id temporis mortuo sine liberis Humberto Delphinatium (*sic*) principe, qui Francum regem testamento haeredem fecerat, Carolus Joannis filius primus ~us creatur, unde mos natus ut regum filii, quibus regni ventura esset haereditas, ~i vocarentur P. VERG. XIX 377. **b s1413** dalphinus, regis Francorum filius, illi [Henrico V] / Carolus ascripsit verba jocosa nimis / Parisiusque pilas misit, quibus ille valeret / ludere cum pueris ELMH. *Metr. Hen. V* 155; **s1415** si non .. rex Gallicus vel dalphinus primogenitus ejus .. obsidionem illam [de Harfleu] vi prelii solveret *G. Hen. V* 8; **s1419** cum inter ipsum [ducem Burgundie] et dolphinum pretensum .. amicicie .. meridiem .. livoris eclipsarent tenebre *Ps.*-ELMH. *Hen. V* 75 p. 213; UPTON 207 (v. delphin b); **1518** conclusum est quod .. Francorum rex et dominus ~us .. assignabunt .. Marie .. donacionem propter nupcias .. (*DipDoc E* 817) *Foed.* XIII 635.

delta [LL < δέλτα], delta, fourth letter of Greek alphabet. **b** numberal (= 4).

~a, 'd', *Δ Runica Manuscripta* 351; est cithara cum xxiiij modis, in modum ~e litere componitur S. LANGTON *Chron.* 120; sciat .. librarius .. ubi scribere debeat .. ~a, ubi eta, ubi hee, ubi digama NECKAM *Ut.* 117; alphabetum Grecum .. alpha, vita, gemma, ~a, e pente, zita, ita, thita, iota, kappa, labda, mi, ni, xi, o micron, pi, ro, sima, taf, ypsilo, phi, chi, psi, o mega BACON *Maj.* I 75. **b** ~a, .. iiij *Runica Manuscripta* 351; hoc modo alfa .. significat unum, beta ij, gamma iij, ~a iiij, et sic deinceps usque ad decimam litteram, que est iota, que significat decem HARCLAY *Adv.* 80.

delubrum [CL], temple, shrine: **a** (pagan); **b** (Jewish); **c** (Christian or unspec.); **d** (fig.). **e** (? by misinterp.) statue or sacrifice.

a procum .. a superstitiosa ~orum cultura convertens ALDH. *VirgP* 40; pagana procul vulgi cultura manebat, / qua stetit antiquo dilubrum more dicatum *Id. VirgV* 1519; daemones .. qui hoc .. in ~is idolorum dicere et confiteri non desinunt BEDE *Luke* 437; **753** qui .. Fresorum .. fana et dilubra destruxit et aecclesias construxit BONIF. *Ep.* 109; ~a, templa idolorum *GlC* D 201; [Sudsaxonum] delūbra contritis pereunt velocius aris FRITH. 973. **b** curtinae veteris ~i .. ex auro, jacintho, purpura, bis tincto cocco .. fulsisse describuntur [cf. *Exod.* xxvi 1] ALDH. *VirgP* 15. **c** hic quoque Jacobus .. / dilubrum sancto defendit tegmine celsum *Id. CE* 4. 4. 5; intrant sidereo candentem (*sic*) luce dēlubrum / spiritus ÆTHELWULF *Abb.* 669; [Godwinus] fecit .. ecclesiam sacram execrabile pantheon et ~um lupanar MAP *NC* V 3 f. 60v.; hoc delebrum, i. ecclesia; .. hoc ~um, *a kyrk WW*. **d** dum dilubra dedit Christo atque sacella pudoris ALDH. *VirgV* 1685. **e** dilubra, statuae *GlC* D 237; delibra, sacrific[i]a *Ib.* 201; **9..** dilubra, *gield WW*.

delucēre, to lose brilliance, be dimmed.

meridies que nulla nubium nocturnitate picea ~ere didicit *Ps.*-ELMH. *Hen. V* 77 (cf. ib. 115: ~et lapis corone tue politissimus).

delucid- v. dilucid-. **delucior** v. 1 deluere.

deludere [CL], to delude, dupe. **b** to frustrate (an enterprise). **c** to mock.

sic .. / per totam noctem praeses diluditur amens, / defensante Deo sacrasque tuente puellas ALDH. *VirgV* 2239; Antichristus .. signis incautos videtur delusurus PULL. *Sent.* 888B; ÆLNOTH *Cnut* 127A (v. coaptare 1b); quod .. nequaquam ageret, nisi hinc eum falsa quedam felicitatis imago ~eret AILR. *Spec. Car.* I 22. 525C; est stolidi bis deludi, semel est sapientis D. BEC. 871; rex, videns se sic vicissim ~i et truphari verbis .., resumpsit arma *G. Hen. V* 19. **b** opus .. delusum *Ib.* 6 (v. contracuniculus). **c** audivi .. militem quendam sacerdotum avaritiam facete ~entem GIR. *GE* I 48.

deludium

1 mockery, deceitfulness. *Cf. eludium* a.

s1002 nisi fortune diludium ei [Sueino] invidisset et mors felicitatem interrupisset *Chr. Wallingf.* 62; speculari circa Dei altarium .. fabulosa vulpis et galli diludia AD. DORE *Pictor* 142.

2 playing-place.

playynge place, diludium *PP*; *a playnge place*, diludium *CathA*.

1 deluere [CL]

1 to wash away. **b** (p. ppl.) washed out, dilute. *V. et. diluere* 1.

~o, A. *to †wasty awey WW*; *to rince*, ~ere LEVINS *Manip.* 134. **b** ut tenella acies .. diluciores et quasi debiliores colores ad tempus intueatur COLET *Eccl. Hier.* 233.

2 (fig.): **a** to wash away, wipe out (guilt or crime). **b** to clear, discharge (debt). *V. et. diluere* 3.

a iij xl^{mas} ~at culpam GILDAS *Pen.* 11; numero sacratur eo quo deluit olim / inclitus ille David sua crimina WULF. *Swith. prol.* 452. **b 1491** in creacione novi abbatis nichil ~it .. monasterium in .. domus necessariis nisi ex provisione existebat provisum (*Vis.*) *Cart. Cockersand* III app. 1138.

2 deluere v. dolare.

delugēre [cf. CL lugēre], to deplore.

ut publice errata sua ad omnium exemplum ~eant COLET *Eccl. Hier.* 218.

delumbis [CL], lame (fig.), weak.

~em, i. enervem, eviratum, effeminatum, sine virtute *GlH* D 130; ~is, debilis OSB. GLOUC. *Deriv.* 178.

delumentum [cf. CL deluere], bath, washing. *V. et. dilumentum.*

~um, *ðhuehl GlC* D 56; ~um, i. lavatio, *þeal GlH* D 128.

delusio [LL], delusion, deception, mockery.

1169 Dunelmensis episcopus .. respondit .. deliberaturum se cum metropolitano suo super hoc et quicquid liceret .. se consulte facturum. meruit autem tali ~one favorem audientium et dilationem *Becket Mat.* VII 57; insula .. crastino .. similiter apparens eosdem juvenes simili ~one decepit GIR. *TH* II 12; **s1237** resonuit murmur .., eo quod totiens delusa est regia simplicitas, que ~o semper in dampnum reipublice dinoscitur redundare *Flor. Hist.* II 220; **s1265** (v. arrepticius b); **1295** statuimus ut .. [contemptor curie Cantuar'] parti .. lese ad .. dampna .. condempnetur et nihilominus pro ~one juris et judicis seu curie .. mulctetur *Conc.* II 209a; ~o que fit verbis generalibus, equivocis, multiplicibus et figurativis est dolus quidam et potest esse absque mendacio OCKHAM *Dial.* 638; **s1352** obprobrium esset duci Lanc' .. de loco recedere in ~onem tocius gentis Anglorum KNIGHTON II 72.

delusor [LL], deluder, deceiver.

qui divertit iter, qua se via publica monstrat, / mox perit infelix delusor ALCUIN *WillV* 15. 9; ita vir sanctus dolos ~oris in simplicitate sua elusit J. FORD *Wulf.* 88.

delusorie [LL], delusively, in mockery.

cum bene sciat [Deus] quod, nisi hoc intendat et velit, et hoc antecedenter et independenter respectu accionis seu passionis humane, inaniter et ~ie eam [graciam] offert BRADW. *CD* 613C.

delusorius, delusive, deceptive, illusory.

quam fallax et ~ia sit illa perniciosa felicitas P. BLOIS *Opusc.* 902; si [judex] judicium suum executioni demandare non posset, sic essent judicia ~ia BRACTON 107; **1345** expediens .. videbatur .., ne labor noster esset ~ius vel inanis, aliqua magis specifice presentare (*Lit. Papae*) AD. MUR. *Chr.* 184; **s1342** (v. derisorius a); talis revelacio de futuro potest esse erronea, ~ia atque falsa; potest enim oppositum evenire BRADW. *CD* 775D; quidam .. certas artes .. civitatis [London'], declaratis coram eis dilusoriis eorum intencionibus et propositis, per blandimenta et simulaciones .. in viscum ipsorum induxerunt FAVENT 5.

deluvius v. diluvium a.

delva [ME *delve*], **~us,** 'delve', dell, hollow.

a1195 [do] unum ~um, qui fuit Radulfi subtus Grimesflat *Feod. Durh.* 133n.; **1479** pro morte unius hominis .. in quadam ~a juxta Stony Stratford per ipsum interfecti *Sanct. Bev.* 230.

delyrus v. 2 delirus. **dema** v. demas.

demacerare [cf. CL macerare], to waste, wizen.

si membrum tale cum fractura demacratur, detur pacienti cibus et potus uberior GAD. 125. 1 (cf. ib. 24. 1: senes demacrati debent vitare acetum).

demaceratio, wasting away, wizened condition.

ferri durities .. spinam dorsi posterius jam exempta carne corroserat ..; dorsumque resupinari [vir] non poterat, quia nude spine dimaceratio id sufferre non sufficiebat R. COLD. *Cuthb.* 94.

demagogus [δημαγωγός], demagogue (*cf.* Aristotle *Pol.* V 8).

sunt ~i ducentes populum secundum voluntatem suam de beneplacito populi, non tanquam reges aut domini vel tyranni seu jus regendi populum .. habentes; sed quasi procuratores et concionatores seu monitores instigant populum ad illa que populo placent OCKHAM *Dial.* 795.

demainius v. dominius.

demanare [CL], to descend, be passed down (fig.).

quod in ea [ecclesia Romana] valet debet valere in minoribus, ut potestas primi cujuscunque ecclesie principis in succedentes ~et W. MALM. *GP* I 41.

demanda [OF *demande*], **~um, a** demand (for service or payment), exaction (esp. feud.). **b** (leg.) demand, claim, suit. **c** (w. *in*) subject to demand, in dispute.

a a1170 quod homines abbatis .. sint .. quieti .. ab omni theloneo et ~a aliqua per totam terram meam *Cart. Glam.* 105; **c1200** confirmavi .. burgensibus .. burgagia sua quieta ab omni servicio, consuetudine, et ~a seculari *BBC*

(*Walsall*) 43; **a1214** tenebunt .. in .. perpetuam elemosinam libere, quiete, et solute ab omnibus serviciis, exactionibus, et ~is *Melrose* I 60; **a1228** reddendo inde annuatim v m. .. pro omni servitio, ~a, et querela *Reg. S. Thom. Dublin* 9; **c1234** ita quod nos .. nunquam poterimus exigere nec clamare nullimodam ~am pro terra quam tenent .. *Starrs* I 4; **1280** petentibus quod ~am procuracionis ecclesie de M. C. .. in respectum poneremus *Reg. Heref.* 256 (cf. ib.: exaccionem procuracionis .. usque ad annum .. ponimus in respectum); **1320** faciendo inde sectam ad curiam justiciarie nostre .. pro omnimodis aliis serviciis, exaccionibus, consuetudinibus, et ~is *Reg. Newbattle* 58; **1429** (v. demandabilis); **1494** unde punicio caderet in ~um debitum seu in finem et redempcionem aut in alias penas pecuniarias *Foed.* XII 556 (= *CalPat* 474). **b** ut veniant ad curiam parati .. dicere quis eorum, id est petens an tenens, majus jus habeat in sua ~a GLANV. II 14; **1200** de ~is .. abbatis versus eundem J. de testamento patris sui *CurR* I 163; **1219** summoneatur quod sit in adventu justiciariorum pro parva ~a *Ib.* VIII 94; **1227** mandamus .. quod de ~a quam facitis Jeulano .. de redditu proveniente de terris comitis B. .. eidem J. pacem habere faciatis *Cl* 4; **1296** dicunt expresse quod .. Editha, que nunc petit .. porcionem .., nullum omnino jus habet in ~a sua *SelPlMan* 174; **1315** breve quod, si aliquis tulerit breve de errore, bona et catalla ipsius defendentis arestentur ad valenciam ~e et damnorum (*LBLond.* 38b) *MGL* I 620; **1341** quod .. prepositi .. possint .. amerciamentum taxare infra xij d. secundum quantitatem ~e seu secundum quantitatem transgressionis (*Ch. Tenby*) *EHR* XVI 103; **1343** (v. debatum a); **s1428** sopita .. lite .. factaque abbati super suis singulis ~is congrua desiderataque recompensa AMUND. I 260; **1456** quietum clamasse .. totum jus meum, clameum, titulum, ~um, et interesse (*Script. Indent.*) *Reg. Whet.* I 244; **1587** totum jus .., interesse et demaundam predicti E. *Pat* 1301 m. 1. **c 1258** cum abbas .. regem supplicaverit quod libertates suas, que diu extiterunt in ~a ad Scaccarium regis .., eidem abbati confirmaret, et rex mandaverit baronibus .. quod ~as illas .. ponerent in respectum *Cl* 204; provisum est quod denarii provenientes de sequestris ecclesiarum .. que diu extiterunt in ~a inter .. regem et episcopum Dunelm' .. deponantur in abbacia .. quousque .. *Cl* 460; **1262** cum quedam libertates quas abbas et monachi .. sibi vendicant .. adhuc sint in ~a ad Scaccarium nostrum *Cl* 163; **1377, 1387** (v. currere 8b); **1462** de .. una *cere* [*cherry tree*] viva existente in le North Orchard et in ~a existente inter Ricardum .. et Johannem .. *CourtR Lygh* 1 f. 2.

demandabilis, due to be exacted.

1429 quoad demandam .. herietti pro eodem manerio, pro eo quod heriettum predictum non est ~e nisi post mortem tenentis .., idem heriettum ponitur in respectum (*Indent.*) AMUND. I 271.

demandare [CL]

1 to assign. **b** to commit (to writing). **c** to put into (execution or effect).

abstrahens intellectus .. multitudinem .. bimembri divisione partitur, .. alteram ~ans arithmetice, alteram musice pleno jure reservans J. SAL. *Pol.* 439C. **b 796** nec aliquid novi litteris ~are possum quod tunc sermone tibi ingererem ALCUIN *Ep.* 102; multi .. sunt .. regressi, narrantes tormenta maxima se perpessos et gaudia se vidisse attestantes [cf. H. SALTREY 2]; quorum relationes jussit Patricius ad litteras ibidem ~ari *Meaux* I 139; **c1470** preteritorum gesta .., que, si scripture ~ata fuissent memorieque commendata, .. gerendi .. prestitissent exempla *StatOx* 285. **c** BRACTON 107 (v. delusorius); **c1273** quatinus .. tale remedium apponatur per quod mandatum domini regis execucioni debite ~etur *AncC* VII 67; **1279** quod [sentencie] per nos .. in nostra provincia †execucionem ~entur *MunAcOx* 40; **s1310** ordinaciones .., quarum virtus, debitis execucionibus ~ata, benignis foret .. defensio *Flor. Hist.* III 147; **s1307** hoc mandatum non potuit effectui ~ari AD. MUR. *Chr.* 10; **1313** volentes .. mandata nostra debito effectu[i] ~ari *Eyre Kent* I 79; **s1450** summa celeritate bullas execucioni ~avit *Reg. Whet.* I 151; ut fiat verbalis executio, est procedendum ut in ceteris causis quando sententiae sunt verbaliter executioni ~atae *Praxis* 275.

2 (w. pers. obj.) to entrust, invest (with).

†**c693** Berthwaldus .., qui in sedem .. Theodori .. subrogatus est .. primatumque omnium aecclesiarum Britanniae sortitus, cum sacro usu pallii ac venerabilis dalmaticae illic ~atus est (*Lit. Papae*) W. MALM. *GP* I 35.

3 (w. pers. obj.) to send, dispatch. **b** to consign (to a fate).

s1296 pecierunt obsessi .. ut possent quendam militem .. ad regem Scocie licite ~are, suam voluntatem experturum *Flor. Hist.* III 97. **b 1492** potestatem .. eorum quemlibet juxta eorum demerita castigandi et puniendi ultimoque supplicio ~andi (*Pat*) *Foed.* XII 486b.

4 to send word (of), report; **b** (w. indir. qu. or *quod*).

795 obsecro .. ut mihi ~are curaveris de prosperitate illius [sc. regis] ALCUIN *Ep.* 50; **796** per eos [regiae dignitatis missos] mihi ~are potestis quod vultis *Ib.* 101; prelatus .. extra monasterium moram facturus egressum suum dicet subpriori vel per alium ~abit *Obs. Barnwell* 54. **b 790** obsecro ut mihi ~es quid in illis agatur partibus ALCUIN *Ep.* 9; Theobaldi decet .. mores proponere, elemosinas ostendere, quam devotus emulator exstiterit .. patris nostri Job .. pro meo modulo posteris ~are *Croyl. Cont. A* 130; consilium nostrum est quod vos per litteras vestras capitulo ~etis quod visitacionem vestram .. continuare proponitis *G. Durh.* 41.

5 to send instructions, demand, require, claim; **b** (w. inf.); **c** (w. acc. & inf.); **d** (w. *ut* or *quod*). **e** (pr. ppl. as sb.) plaintiff, claimant.

790 sicut ~avi ei .. argentum quod de V. villa habeat ALCUIN *Ep.* 8; (*Quad.*) *GAS* 177 (v. ceapgildum); **1236** noluerunt [episcopi] .. rescribere domino regi in forma eis ~ata a domino rege per breve sum *BNB* III 135; **s1255** rex [Scotie] ad reginam accedere non potuit, sicut regina patri suo antea ~averat *Ann. Dunstable* 198; **1258** dicunt quod vicecomites ad duos turnos suos per annum ~ant personalem adventum .. baronum tenentium baronias suas in diversis .. comitatibus (*Pet. Baronum*) *Ann. Burton* 441; **s1312** responderunt barones: "utrum †~as [? l. ~atis] hoc per consuetudinem vel per facta regum?"; et dixerunt: "per consuetudinem" *Ann. Lond.* 218; **1318** salva lege et consuetudine burgorum, que est in certo defendendo *torte et noun rayson*, sc. *wrang and unlaw*, sine plus ~ando curiam suam (*Stat. Rob. I* c. 17) *APScot* 111; **1456** nec ego .. nec heredes mei .. aliquod jus .. in .. maneriis .. exigere .., vendicare aut ~are poterimus *FormA* 393; **1530** quod .. nihil ~aretur, reciperetur nec acciperetur per aliquem episcopum .. *Entries* 603. **b 796** quicquid tibi ~et domnus rex facere, mihi demandare studeas ALCUIN *Ep.* 112; **801** (14c) [rex] hoc coram synodo .. ascribere ~avit *CS* 302; **1012** (12c) hoc pro testaminis titulo hac inculcare †griphia ~avi *CD* 720; classem .. parari instituit suisque ad omnia paratos esse edicto proposito ~avit ÆLNOTH *Cnut* II 29. **c 1408** vos .. ordinamus nostrum in spiritualibus vicarium generalem ad .. electas personas canonice confirmandum et installandum seu installari ~andum (*Reg. Ebor.*) *Eng. Clergy* 190. **d 716** mihi moriens praecepit ut fratri illius .. ~arem ut ancillam quandam, quam .. communiter possederunt, .. manu mitteret BONIF. *Ep.* 10 p. 13 **a805** domino Jesu ~ante ut gratis spiritalia dona dentur ab omnibus ALCUIN *Ep.* 298; Oswoldus [ob. **922**] .. ~at .. toti fratrum congregationi ut .. nulla .. super hoc casu tristitia absorberentur *Chr. Rams.* 87; **s1235** optinuerunt litteras .. quibus ~atum fuit a domino papa ut infra quatuor menses .. causam terminarent *Flor. Hist.* II 215; **1236** vobis mandamus quod ~etis vicecomiti nostro Ebor' quod .. faciat inquisicionem *KRMem* 14 r. 9; **s1276** concessit dominus rex et ~avit per totum regnum Anglie quod carte de communibus libertatibus .. ab omnibus per omnia observarentur *Ann. Waverley* 386 (= *Ann. Wint.* 120: mandavit); **1365** papa .. archiepiscopo suis litteris ~avit ut .. dictas ecclesias restitueret *Lit. Cant.* II 473. **e** potest obici quod ~ans dotem suam habere non debet, eo quod .. vir suus .. non tenuit tenementum unde petit dotem in dominico HENGHAM *Parva* 3.

6 (w. pers. obj.) to demand the presence of, summon, cite; **b** (w. inf.).

1210 vicecomes Herefordie .. ~ari fecit eum in comitatu suo tanquam malefactorem; et, cum utlagari deberet .., mandavimus eidem vic. quod hoc differret donec in Angliam veniremus (*Scriptum Regis*) *BBExch* 383 (cf. ib. 384: sic de comitatu in comitatum ~atus et non comparens); **1221** ~ari facias proximo comitatu tuo Ricardum .. et Nicholaum .. ad instanciam et clamorem Willelmi .., qui eos apellat de roberia et pace nostra fracta, et sic de comitatu in comitatum eos ~ari facias .. usque ad quartum comitatum, ad quem, si non venerint .., eos utlagari facias *Cl* 474–5; **1321** [vic.] fuit primo amerciatus in isto itinere quia comparuit isto die reddens rotulos suos sine baga antequam fuit ~atus *MGL* II 297; J. T. comperuit ad respondendum prefato J. B. .. et fecit ~are ipsum J. B., ita quod idem J. B. non fuit prosecutus breve suum *Entries* 302. **b** [dominus Cantuariensis] ~atur sui presentiam coram domino papa exhibere A. TEWK. *Add. Thom.* 25; **s1450** quin .. abbas litteras .. dirigeret illi .. revocatorias ipsumque redire iterum ad monasterium districcius ~aret *Reg. Whet.* I 149.

demandatio [LL]

1 (w. *executioni*) putting into execution.

utrum haec ~o sententiae executioni obsit appellanti .. fuit maxime .. controversum *Praxis* 269.

2 demand, claim.

1467 rex .. remisit .. omnimodas acciones, execuciones, impeticiones ac ~ones quas versus ipsos .. habueirt *Entries* 86.

demandum v. demanda.

demanicatus [cf. CL manicatus], w. long sleeves.

crimina surgentis uteri, si quasque tumoris / desidior Natura notas incauta reliquit, / hos nova providit industria demanicatis / occultare togis HANV. II 152 p. 263.

demanium v. 2 dominium.

demarcescere [LL], to waste away, perish.

s823 Beornulf uno anno regnavit et ab Egbricto rege bello victus ~uit H. HUNT. *HA* IV 34 (cf. ib.: Estangli occiderunt Beornwlf).

demartyrizare [cf. LL martyrizare], to martyr.

s1311 ~ati sunt in dicto prelio [in planicie Damieti] pro Christo xv milia virorum *Flor. Hist.* III 335.

demas [cf. δέμας, *dat.* δέμαι; *oblique cases formed as* δῆμα, ~ατος], (human) body.

post cujus corporalem vivificae crucis passionem solibus quaterdenis commoratus in arvis, coelos petiit ~ate LANTFR. *Swith. pref.*; sanctus, mortalis saeptus ~atis velamine *Ib.*; signipotens in ea pausat quoque dēmate Suuiðhun WULF. *Swith. pref.* 263 (cf. ib. I 954: ubi sanctus erat vir dēmate pausans); **1007** (13c) in corpusculo ~atis nostri *Ch. Burton* 30.

dematurare [LL], to make haste.

c625 insiste ergo, gloriosa filia, et .. duritiam cordis ipsius .. mollire summopere ~a (*Lit. Papae*) BEDE *HE* II 11.

dematurescere [cf. LL maturescere], to reach maturity.

pesque reformidans molli juvenescere passu / lascivaque timens dematurescere culpa HANV. IX 444 p. 391.

demaunda v. demanda.

demeare [CL = *to descend*], to go across, to go around.

~are, transire; ~asse, circuisse *GlH* D 172–3; OSB. GLOUC. *Deriv.* 172 (v. demigrare a).

demediare [cf. CL medium], to remove from the midst of the living. *Cf. dimidiare* 2a.

cum finis eum ~iabit [AS: *ðonne him forðsið gebyrige*], habeat dominus quod relinquet (*Quad.*, *Rect.*) *GAS* 448.

demedius v. dimidius.

demegoria [δημηγορία], public address (w. ref. to *Farrago Annotationum in Genesim ex ore H. Zuinglii per L. Judae et G. Megandrum excerptarum*).

1530 libellos .. contraria fidei catholice .. dogmata continentes: .. ~iarum farrago annotacionum in Genesim ex ore Hildricii Zwingli *Conc.* III 720a.

demembrare [LL], to mutilate (person or image). **b** to dismember (dead body). **c** to break up (estate or sim.). *V. et. dismembrare.*

s1138 RIC. HEX. *Stand.* 40b (v. crucifigere 2b); **1202** Emma abscidit ei unum testiculorum suorum et Radulfus .. alterum et, postquam ita ~atus fuit .., Alanus .. reportavit eum in viam *SelPlCrown* 15; **1203** quod deliberetis Petrum clericum .. pro Ferrando balistario nostro, ita tamen quod .., si Ferrandus demenbratus sit, idem Petrus eodem modo demenbretur et reddatur pro eo *Pat* 25a; potest obici quod iste feloniam commisit ob quam suspensus fuit .. vel alio modo morti dampnatus vel ~atus HENGHAM *Parva* 3; **1389** aliquem .. cecum, mutum, surdum, ~atum, languidum perpetua vel temporali infirmitate *Guild Cert.* (*Hull*) 46/451. **b s1305** Willelmus Wallace .. Londoniis ~atur et ejus membra per diversa loca Anglie et Scocie .. turribus suspenduntur FORDUN *GA* 116; **s1322** Andreas de Harkeleye tanquam proditor .. distractus, suspensus, et decapitatus, visceribus combustis ~atus est *Ann. Osney* 346. **c** audieram abbatem respondentem se non posse ~are baroniam BRAKELOND 138v.; **1276** predicta serjancia ~ata fuit per eundem et arentata ad iij s. *Hund.* II 34; **s1147** cum vidisset episcopus J. [Glasguensis] episcopatum suum ~ari .., transfretavit FORDUN *Cont.* VIII 3; **1464** si illi redditus sint amoti, ~ati vel alienati a predicta domo *Reg. Aberbr.* II 142.

demembratio, a dismemberment, mutilation (of person). **b** breaking up (of empire).

a non absque damnosa obsidum ~one GIR. *EH* II 31; bonus princeps, pie seviens in perversos, effrenes quorundam impetus .. nunc cruciatibus corrigit, nonnunquam etiam ~one castigat *Id. PI* I 10 p. 36. **b 1186** [imperator] de facto Treverensis ecclesie subjunxit .. ut .. si secundum ordinationem vestram idem factum inconvulsum permanere deberet, videtur imperium ~onem et maximam sui juris imminutionem incurrisse (*Lit. Episcoporum Theutonicorum ad Papam*) DICETO *YH* II 45.

dememinisse [cf. CL meminisse], to forget.

vulgi cimba rapax [i.e. meretrix] .. / .. iteratis omnia carpit / naviglis, usuque vices impendere gratis / dememinit longo HANV. IX 258 p. 385; non ingratus ~it tante victorie gracias .. devotissime reddere largitori *Ps.*-ELMH. *Hen. V* 26.

demen- v. et. demem-. **demencionaliter** v. dimensionaliter. **demenia,** ~**ium** v. 2 dominium.

1 demens [CL], demented, mad: **a** (of person or unspec.); **b** (of action).

a qui regem caeli .. / vendidit argenti caecatus munere demens ALDH. *VirgV* 2594; ~tes, amentes *GlC* D 147; ~s, *gemendleas* ÆLF. *Gl.*; GAD. 132. 1 (v. amens a); **1392** Editha .. ~s et insanis (*sic*) submersa fuit in parvo puteo *SelCCoron* 49. **b** apostasia ~s regum Anglorum BEDE *HE* III 9.

2 demens v. demere. **demens-** v. dimens-, dimetiri.

dementare [LL], to dement, drive mad. **b** to infatuate. **c** to go mad. *V. et. amentare, ementare.*

quia .. cogitationem de corde progenitam diabolica tolerat arte ~atam BEDE *Hom.* I 22. 104; ~atus iste ex sua

predicamentali constitutione H. READING (I) *Fid. Cath.* 1327B; adjuro te .. ne mihi in aliquo molestiam facias, neque decipiendo ~are presumas R. COLD. *Godr.* 51; spiritus furoris duos ~averat W. CANT. *Thom.* III 52; **s1355** (v. dementia a). **b** Symon Magus .. diu populum magicis artibus ~averat HON. *Spec. Eccl.* 972 A; mulieres .. suis blanditiis etiam devotos ~ant ECCLESTON *Adv. Min.* 126. **c** *to ga owte of mynde*, ~are *CathA*.

dementer [CL], madly.

680 quis paschalis festi regulam .. refutans non potius se .. inextricabiliter obligandum quam ~er absolvendum .. arbitretur? ALDH. *Ep.* 4.

dementia [CL], madness; **b** (w. ref. to heresy).

ut Porphyrius rabidus .. ~iae suae ac vanitatis stilo hoc etiam adnecteret .. GILDAS *EB* 4; insanum vexat dementia cordis ALDH. *Aen.* 98 (*Elleborus*) 6; qua fiducia, vel qua ~ia potius .., ceci cecos .. ordinant! GIR. *GE* II 34 p. 335; **1212** de quodam stulto, qui est in prisona eo quod per ~iam congnoscit se esse latronem set non est culpabilis *CurR* VI 351; **1256** quidam .. capellanus demens in †demonicia [? l. demencia] sua de nocte ivit ad domum Hugonis .. et .. fregit tres bordas parietis *AssizeR Northumb* 94; **s1355** erat maxima ~ia predominans in Anglia et multis aliis provinciis, in tantum quod per centenos et millenos subito insanientes discurrerent et dementarentur per septimanam et quindenam, et quidam per mensem *Meaux* III 111. **b** quibus [Pelagianis] .. patres orthodoxi .. responderunt, nec eorum .. ~iam corrigere valebant BEDE *HE* I 10.

dementire [CL], to go mad, rave.

fere extra me factus, a mente transire et ~ire timebam GIR. *EH* II 30 (cf. id. *TH* II 48); **s1257** Willelmus [de Valentia], .. palam, ut vulgariter loquar, ~iens et notam ei [S. de Monte Forti] irreverenter proditionis imponens .. M. PAR. *Maj.* V 634 (cf. ib. 703).

dementiri, to give the lie to, accuse of lying.

1300 H. le S. acculpatus per majorem quod ~iebatur in presencia majoris .. Robertum G. *Rec. Leic.* I 230; **1339** T. .. cognovit quod predictum justiciarium .. dimentitus fuerit *CoramR* 315 r. 116 *sched.* (cf. ib.: T. non dedicit quin ipse dixit Johanni [sc. justiciario] quod ipse menciabatur (*sic*) quia idem J. prius sibi imposuit quod ipse mentitus fuisset).

demercio v. demeritio.

demere [CL], to take away (often w. dat.). **b** to subtract, deduct, except. **c** to rob.

magister, / sanguine purpureo demens peccamina mundi [cf. *John* i 29] ALDH. *VirgV* 1317; cui dedit et dempsit nil mundi longa vetustas *Ib.* 2875; FRITH. 916 (v. capsaces); **966** (v. cataclysma); **9..** ~ebat, *nom* .., ~psit, *gewonede* .., ~pto, *onweg adonum WW*; rebus mundi sua lumina Phebus / dempserat R. CANT. *Malch.* IV 186; Deus .. animo regis confidentiam solitam ~psit H. HUNT. *HA* IV 19; perempto / Hybero Lucio, qui .. / venerat ut fines Gallorum demeret illi [sc. Arturo] *V. Merl.* 1106; J. SAL. *Pol.* 503A (v. 1 communio 1b); cervus ait: "michi vestra necem clementia demat!" WALT. ANGL. *Fab.* 55. 7. **b** a quibus 21 ~ptis ROB. ANGL. *Alg.* 110 *n.*9; non addentes aut ~entes aut mutantes aliquid *Lib. Eli.* III 108; [filius] precipuus et uno ~pto primevus GIR. *TH* III 49; GARL. *Tri. Eccl.* 127 (v. chronographus); **1369** in solucione facta Johanni C. .. per .. acomodatum factum .., ut patet per literas regis ostensas super compotum, ~pto tercio denario .. *ExchScot* II 347; **1382** per custumam j laste cum dim. lasta, uno corio ~pto *Ib.* III 98. **c** [ancilla] tulit de farina domini sui et fecit sibi panem. .. tremere cepit qui[a] modium domini sui dempsum (*sic*) plenum non erat .. et furavit de farina monachorum et replevit modium quod prius ~psit HUGEB. *Wynn.* 12.

demerēre, ~ēri [CL]

1 a to earn. **b** to merit, deserve. **c** to merit (the society of). **d** (p. ppl. as sb. n.) merit.

a Lais .. grandem pecuniam ~ebat J. SAL. *Pol.* 622B. **b** Edgitha .. incorrupta .. virginitate et frequentibus excubiis Dei gratiam ~ebat W. MALM. *GR* II 218; **1220** consideratum est quod amittat pedem. et sciendum quod misericorditer agitur cum eo per consilium domini regis, cum majorem penam de jure ~uisset *CurR* VIII 278; *Ziz.* 182 (v. deobligatio). **c** [Athelwoldus] tonsoratus in clericum, non multo post .. est cucullatus in monachum; ordinatusque in monasterii decanum, hos doctrina, illos religione, omnes amore ~ebatur W. MALM. *GP* II 75 p. 165. **d** **1415** residuum .. bonorum meorum do .. ad remunerandum servientes meos familiares de parte inde secundum eorum ~ita juxta sanam discrecionem .. executorum *Reg. Cant.* II 68.

2 to be undeserving, unworthy (of), forfeit; **b** (absol.); **c** (w. inf.). **d** (p. ppl.) undeserving. **e** (as sb. n.) demerit, offence.

ut constet ipsum ab officio prophetie gratiam, quam ~uerat, accepisse J. SAL. *Pol.* 684B (cf. ib. 634A: inferiorum delicta bonum principem ~ent); quero si .. talis .. absolvi mereatur, cum etiam et Scaccarii sessionem et ipsam principis gratiam ~uerit *Dial. Scac.* I 8 E (cf. ib. II 10 H: clericus usuris inserviens dignitatis sue privilegium ~etur); tanquam tribus prioribus [hostiis], quarum perceptionem enormitate delicti ~uerat, divinitus ei, peracta penitentia, restitutis GIR. *GE* I 51 p. 147; citra quam [veritatem] omnis historia non solum authoritatem sed et nomen historie ~etur *Id. EH* I 46; **1223** tibi precipimus quod .. Ysabellam de dote sua .. resaisias .., cum dotem suam non ~uerit ex hoc facto *Cl* 562b; **1236** Ismael ~uit legitimationem et hereditatem quando lusit cum Isaac GROS. *Ep.* 23 p. 81; impia demeruit celi gens ista triumphos GARL. *Tri. Eccl.* 110; **s1324** erat et quedam baronia in partibus Essexie, quam Robertus de Brutz propter rebellionem dudum ~uit *V. Ed. II* 276; **1438** si quid displicencie .. in .. Johannem .., cum nil ~uerit, hisce de causis animo conceperitis BEKYNTON I 200. **b** theologus habet inquirere qua via contingat animam mereri et ~eri J. BLUND *An.* 22 (cf. ib.: ex quo theologus solum habet docere qualiter sit merendum et ~endum); potestas peccandi data est propter merendum, non ad ~endum S. LANGTON *Quaest.* f. 245; nonne Christus .., qui in nullo ~uit, a pessimis Judeis extitit crucifixus? *G. Durh.* 40; generale judicium .. ordinatur .. ad hoc, quod extunc cessat omnis status merendi et ~endi OCKHAM *Dial.* 750; **1461** hiis judex sit Radamantus, / .. / atque modum pene pensent †seu [l. ceu] demeruere (*Vers.*) *Reg. Whet.* I 396. **c** quia ipsorum elacio in .. principis obsidentis oculis graciam invenire ~uit, nichil hec primeva colloquia .. concludebant *Ps.*-ELMH. *Hen. V* 59. **d** **s1189** si rex Francie homines suos ~itos .. insurgit *G. Hen. II* 67. **e** plures sunt cause ~iti S. LANGTON *Quaest.* f. 221; BRACTON 107b (v. docere 1d); cum meritum et ~itum sint penes animam BACON III 286; **1296** cum .. nobis et regni nostri incolis .. dampna enormia .. intuleritis .., possessiones nostras et nostrorum .. injuste et sine nostris ~itis occupando (*Lit. J. Balliol*) *Anglo-Scot. Rel.* 71; citavit .. priorem et conventum .. ad conparendum .. responsuros super contemptu .. ac alias pro ~itis recepturos quod justicia suaderet *G. Durh.* 7; **1318** ad omnes eorum quos delinquentes .. contigerit inveniri juxta eorum ~ita justiciandos et puniendos *RScot* 188b; **s1332** racionabilius esset quod fama Johannis .. denigretur secundum suum ~itum quam prioris sine ~ito GRAYSTANES 46; sicut in voluntate vel affectu stat meritum quoad Deum, sic in errore affectus vel voluntatis stat ~itum quoad dyabolum WYCL. *Versut.* 101; *a mawgry*, †demercio, ~itum *CathA*.

demergere [CL], (trans.) to sink, submerge; **b** (as penalty; *cf.* keel-hauling); **c** (fig.). **d** to flood, inundate.

Hydra .. Eurydicen .. demersit in gurgitem *Lib. Monstr.* III 3; demersus est in sinu maris BEDE *HE* I 33; armenta vadunt in palude (*sic*) et ~ant (*sic*) se toto corpore nisi caput solum HUGEB. *Will.* 4 (cf. ib.: Petrus super undas ambulans .. ~atus est); **s1012** primum ad genua, mox ad femora, terre dimersi sumus (*Lit. Otberti Coloniensis*) W. MALM. *GR* II 174; illi qui ante festinantes precesserant cum ipsa via quam fecerant dimersi sunt *G. Herw.* 331b; R. COLD. *Cuthb.* 32 (v. 2 dissilire 1a); [rana] mergitur ut murem secum demergat WALT. ANGL. *Fab.* 3. 9; de .. philosopho in mari navigante, quem naute propter auri pondus quod vehebat ~ere cupieba[n]t ODINGTON 61; G. R. in mare dimersus cum filio regis .. obiit H. ALBUS 89; **s1400** cum .. ad mensam servi dominis eorum de potagio .. vel hujusmodi liquore servire deberent, statim [manice] in eis ~ebantur, de hujusmodi liquore prius gustantes quam domini *V. Ric. II* 172. **b** **s1191** marinarii si luserint, tribus diebus a summo navis in mare ~entur more marinariorum semel in die (*Stat. Peregrinorum*) *G. Ric. I* 131. **c** sensus conscientia remordente ad ima vel tartarum demersos GILDAS *EB* 66; ne lucernam verbi postulantis gurges neglegentiae ~at *Lib. Monstr.* II *pref.*; homo .. nullo modo potest resurgere nisi gratia relevetur, sed merito suo de peccato in peccatum usque in abyssum peccatorum .. ~atur nisi misericordia retineatur ANSELM (*Praesc.* III 8) II 275; [ranarum] demersit subitus guttura rauca timor WALT. ANGL. *Fab.* 19. 6; veritatem in .. profundum mare .. dimersam BEKINSAU 735; in illis prophetae aut manentes aut demersi Dei Spiritu prophetabunt JEWEL *Apol.* D 7. **d** **s1315** plagam hanc insequta est alia in Translacione S. Swithuni .., tanta viz. aquarum inundancia quod fluvii .. fruges et herbas .. demerserunt .. et viros et mulieres .. submerserunt GRAYSTANES 36; **1390** via .. ruinosa et dimersa toto tempore yemali *Pub. Works* I 182.

2 (intr.) to dive. **b** to sink, disappear.

tercio, more avicule mergule, jam usque ad fundum precipitanter ~endo descenderat R. COLD. *Cuthb.* 32. **b** quedam mulier cepit quondam spiritum et .. retulit quod vidit manus mulieris ~entes in carne spiritus *Ghost Stories* 419.

3 (trans.) to incline, bend down. **b** to hurl down.

dum .. caput gestaret demersum ferme usque ad genuculum LANTFR. *Swith.* 2. **b** cervus .. sese in ima .. praecipitii una cum canibus sequentibus demersit B. *V. Dunst.* 14.

demeritare [cf. CL meritare], to be unworthy of, forfeit.

to addylle mawgry .., *to addyl thanke*, demereri, ~are *CathA*.

demeritio, demerit.

a mawgry, demer[i]cio, demeritum .., *un thanke*, ~o, demeritum *CathA*.

demeritorie, through demerit, culpably.

nonne viro suo Anna viduatur cum anima fidelis, virtute qua nitebatur subtracta, ad tempus destituitur? quod quidem magis dispensatorie .. quam ~ie fit AD. SCOT *Serm.* 362C.

demeritorius, demeritorious, culpable.

salvatio et damnatio consequuntur ad motum liberi arbitrii meritorium vel ~ium HALES *Sent.* I 461; multi sunt actus, eciam meritorii et ~ii, qui nec sunt justi nec injusti, licet sint boni vel mali OCKHAM *Pol.* II 577; si propter hanc amiciciam aliquid contra divinam voluntatem ab amicis agatur, est amicicia perversa, fetida et immunda et multum ~ia ROLLE *IA* 263; ipsum occidere nequaquam ~ium aut punibile sed pocius meritorium et premiabile fuisse quis dubitat? BRADW. *CD* 47D; idem actus in prima medietate hore erit meritorius ex precepto et in secunda ~ius ex precepto opposito WYCL. *Act.* 21.

demeritum v. demerere 1d, 2e.

demersio [LL], immersion, submergence. **b** drowning. **c** (?) fluidity.

a798 sepulturam triduanam imitatur trina ~o [baptismatis] et ab aquis elevatio resurgentis instar est de sepulchro (*Lit. Papae*) *Ep. Alcuin.* 137; cum tertio a dimersione exsurgeret, .. subito a nautis accipitur R. COLD. *Cuthb.* 32; **s1402** in ypodromo paterno omnes equi patris sui [sc. Oweni] reperti sunt in alto cruore stetisse usque ad tibiarum ~onem WALS. *HA* II 254. **b** portum attingere maturantes .., subitam omnium ~onem timent R. COLD. *Cuthb.* 32; **s1393** aquarum inundancia .. domorum parietes diruit et viris .. ac mulieribus pene periculum ~onis intulit WALS. *HA* II 213. **c** si dominatur aque vis in quali, dominatur / in quanto; certam dat tibi flegma fidem. / sese debet aque dimersio quoque liquoris, / sed virtus variis est variata modis NECKAM *DS* IV 792.

Demeta, (pl.) inhabitants of Dyfed (S. Wales). **b** (p. ppl., by conf. w. *dimetiri*) measured.

~arum tyranne Vortipori GILDAS *EB* 31; **680** ultra Sabrinae fluminis fretum Demetarum sacerdotes ALDH. *Ep.* 4. **b** **9..** ~arum, *ametenra WW*.

demeter v. dimeter.

demetere [CL], to cut, mow (down); **b** (fig.).

caput .. absciditur .. velut lilium aut demessa rosa gratificatur, ut in conspectu Domini pretiosa mors sancti sui *V. Kenelmi B* f. 80v.; segetes falcem cultoris intactae expectabant, quas nec attrivit superba effusio nec demessuit pabulator W. POIT. II 2. **b** **s1016** in illo bello quod omnem florem provincie demessuit W. MALM. *GR* II 165; **s1069** omnis nobilitas popularis emarcuit, falce belli demessa *Id. GP* III 116.

Demeticus, belonging to Demetia (Dyfed, S. Wales).

per totam fere diocesim Menevensem, precipue ejus ~am regionem et Kereticam GIR. *RG* I 3; Keretice regionis princeps in ~am divertens provinciam *Id. David* 1.

demetire v. dimetiri. **demictare** v. demutare a.

demigrare [CL], to wander (away). **b** (fig.) to change one's occupation.

demeare, transire, transmeare, ~are OSB. GLOUC. *Deriv.* 172; **1148** utpote sedem certam aut locum proprium non habentes, sed negotiorum necessitate de loco ad locum ~antes G. FOLIOT *Ep.* 78. **b** *Itin. Ric.* I 17 (v. 1 colus b).

demigratio [CL], emigration (eccl.).

de his qui minis cessere tantum penarum, aut privatione facultatum territi aut ~one, sacrificaverunt ROB. FLAMB. *Pen.* 327.

deminu- v. et. diminu-.

deminuere [CL], to diminish, reduce; **b** (w. abstr. obj.) to lessen, weaken, impair. *V. et. diminuere 2.*

~te, *gewanude* vel *gelytlade GlH* D 163; **s1337** (v. consummatio d). **b** **805** hanc largitionem .. si quis ~erit, .. ~etur sibi gloria in Christo *CS* 322.

demirari [CL], to marvel at.

s1066 is, ~ans et urbane extollens modestiam inquirentem animos militum, num vellent dominum suum regem fieri, .. inquit .. W. POIT. II 29.

demiscēre [cf. CL miscēre], to 'unmix', separate.

Dominus noster ~uit et separavit ista, et peccatum dimisit et infirmitatem suscepit AILR. *Serm.* 12. 280B.

demiss- v. et dimiss-.

demisse [CL], at a low level. **b** in a low voice.

nasus .. nec nimis acute videtur exsurgere nec ~ius propatula latitudinis distensione protendendo extendere R. COLD. *Osw.* 51 p. 380; 'honeste tonsi' [cf. *Conc. Syn.* 116]: hec tonsura sic fiet ut aures sint patentes .. et hoc, si religiosus sit, altius, si secularis, dimissius LYNDW. 119 i. **b** proclamando, sed non nimis tarde vel dimisse sed tempore congruo et alte BRACTON 121.

1 demittere [CL]

1 to drop, let fall, let down. **b** to cast down, stoop, bow. **c** to set down, place.

~e frenum equi ALDH. *VirgP* 25; equus .. spumas ex ore ~ere .. coepit BEDE *HE* III 9; demissis straphis W. CANT. *Mir. Thom.* II 85 (v. 2 dependere 2); aves iste conchosos pisciculos contra litorea saxa sursum in aera deferunt et ~unt GIR. *TH* I 22; **1225** invenit .. Walterum super feminam illam braccis dimissis circa pedes *BNB* III 107; **s1263** lapis super caput ejus demissus est RISH. 15; residua pars hostie sicca existens .. in sanguinem dimittatur *Cust. Westm.* 218; GOWER *VC* I 1677 (v. cornu 7c). **b** quia hunc Deum esse didicerant, dimissis in terram vultibus adorant [cf. *Matth.* xxviii 17] BEDE *Hom.* II 8.145; nunc caput erigens parabas aliquid proferre in medium; sed .. iterum demisso capite tacebas AILR. *Spir. Amicit.* I 2. 661; unusquisque pudice dimissis luminibus ad ea tantum que sibi apposita sunt .. attendat *Cust. Westm.* 118. **c** ubi dimiserat sanguinem, consuetam vini reperit speciem EADMER *Odo* 70B; **c1218** laici .. flectant genua, maxime quando post elevationem hostia sacra dimittitur *Conc. Syn.* 79; altero fine [lancee] dimisso in terram *G. Hen. V* 16; **1427** volumus .. quod in die tricennalis nostri .. iiij .. luminaria circa corpus nostrum .. ardencia dimittantur *Reg. Cant.* II 391.

2 (p. ppl. *demissus*) low; **b** (of sound or voice). **c** lowly, unassuming.

terra valde ~a GIR. *TH* I 4 (cf. ib. 22: in .. arbore ~a .. nidificantes); crux quedam .., se subito .. in volatum erigens .., que ~ior prius extiterat .., parte inferiori .. coronam presbyteri tetigit *Id. GE* I 35. **b** voce ~a [v. l. dimissa voce] vocavit G. MON. XII 7; talia pone latens dimissa [v. l. demissa] voce canebat *V. Merl.* 169; dicitur sonus altus et ~us a veloci immutacione *Ps.*-GROS. *Gram.* 26; **s1235** quidam de fratribus Minorum necnon et aliqui de ordine Predicatorum .. missas clandestinas ~a voce celebrarunt M. PAR. *Maj.* III 333. **c** dimissa, i. humilia, *abogene, toslopene GlH* D 495; vestitus humilis et dimissus *Scot. Grey Friars* II 179.

2 demittere v. 2 dimittere.

demiurgus [LL < δημιουργός], speaker (of Parliament).

1555 ~us sive loquutor *CalPat* II 50.

demivirgata [OF *demivergee*], half virgate.

1381 redditus j demivirgatarii in opere: .. Thomas Outy pro sua ~a terre .. dat ad auxilium vicecomitis iij d. *(Rental) Econ. Condit.* app. 104.

demivirgatarius, tenant of half virgate.

1381 (v. demivirgata).

democratia [LL < δημοκρατία], democracy.

Periander .. dicebat .. ~iam pejorem tyrannide W. BURLEY *Vit. Phil.* 44; policia viciata et transgressa vocatur ~ia OCKHAM *Dial.* 796; democrachiam, que regimen est plurium malorum FORTESCUE *NLN* I 26 (cf. ib. II 46: aristocrachia, oligarchia, et democrachia).

demolimen, demolition, destruction.

wastynge .., dilapidacio, delecio, ~en .. *CathA*.

demolire [CL *dep.*], to demolish (building or sim.). **b** to devastate, destroy.

s881 plurima in regno Francorum monasteria a paganis ~ita sunt et concussa M. PAR. *Maj.* I 414 (= S. DURH. *HR* 97: desolata); ne faciat nocumentum .. in prosternendo, ~iendo vel destruendo injuriose .. quod juste factum est ab initio et levatum BRACTON 232b; **1327** quod .. penticia et fenestras .. et .. molendinos .. demollirent et ad terram prosternerent *Lit. Cant.* I 220; **s1355** edificia in suburbio .. ~iri fecerunt AVESB. 127; **1443** sic tenementa .. casibus fortuitis destruantur .. et demolliantur *Reg. Brechin* 94. **b** ubi neque erugo neque tinea ~itur [cf. *Matth.* vi 20] *V. Greg.* p. 101; ~itur, exterminatur *GlC* D 316; ob .. barb[ar]arum gentium seditionem, qua extraneorum alieni Franciam populorum praedones ~ire [v. l. ~iri] conabantur WILLIB. *Bonif.* 8 p. 43; ~itur, i. exterminatur, †*bid* [MS: *bið*] *forsworfen*, vel *forgniden GlH* D 157; **9**.. ~itus, *aiþende WW*; **s1011** provinciis a .. Danorum exercitu ferro flammaque ~itis FL. WORC. I 163 (= BIRCHINGTON *Arch. Cant.* 5: †~itur); **s1054** rex Henricus .. unum [agmen] .. ad ~iendum comitatum Ebroicensem ipse praefuit W. JUM. VII 24; **s1153** suos hostes immanissimos .. Dei providentia nil tale metuentes in eodem ~ivit tempore H. HUNT. *HA* VIII 35; mures infinitissimi .. vestes .. ~iendo corrodunt GIR. *TH* I 27; **s1248** (v. cucurbitinus); **1295** ne [vineam] vulpium demoliat .. voluptas [cf. *Cant.* ii 15] *Reg. Wint.* I 218; **1476** thesaurus .. nec effoditur per fures nec per tineas sive erugines .. ~itur *FormA* 336.

demolitio [CL], demolition. **b** destruction.

1431 incendia, demolliciones domorum et murorum .. *Cl* 281 m. 8*d*. **b** **1480** demolucionis seu dedicionis periculum expectant nisi .. fulciantur principum catholicorum favoribus *Pat* 545 m. 20.

demolitor [CL], destroyer.

1432 quilibet alicujus communitatis leges et jura violans .. tanquam ejus precipuus demollitor multipharie est puniendus *StatOx* 241.

1 demollire v. demolire.

2 demollire [LL = *to soften*], to deprive of softness, harden.

to make harde, durare .., ~ire, durificare *CathA*.

demollit- v. demolit-. **demolutio** v. demolitio b. **demon-** v. et. daemon-.

demonachari [cf. monachari], (w. *vitam*) to live unmonkishly.

vitam .. / demonachabatur moribus ipse malis NIG. *Mir. BVM* 12v. 1.

demonachus [cf. LL monachus], non-monk (w. play on *daemonicus*).

1472 ut vorago luxurie .. ab omnibus evitetur, que de monacho facit ~um et ipsius demonis habitaculum *Melrose* II 577.

demonicia v. dementia a.

demonstrabilis [LL], demonstrable, provable.

nec ex sola creatione sed ex creatorum gubernatione quod hec unitas nostra sit, et etiam aliquatenus quid sit ipsa, ~e H. BOS. *LM* 1354B; ego intelligo aliquam ~em veritatem et tu intelligis eandem; et ego intelligo te intelligere illam sicut me PECKHAM *QA* 59; quandoque dicitur [passio] proprium predicabile de proprio subjecto ~e *Ps.*-GROS. *Summa* 376; ita etiam acceptum est a lege quod Deus sit, et tamen non negatur Deum esse ~e DUNS *Ord.* II 237; WYCL. *Act.* 93 (v. concessibilis b); absoluta necessitas prior, utilior, conveniencior et ~ior quam conclusionis veritas doctrinalis in sciencia mathematica demonstrate (WYCL. *Ente* 139v.) *Wycl. & Ox.* 164.

demonstrabilitas, demonstrability.

aliqua que non possunt esse possunt demonstrari, cum possunt intellectui notari, et eadem racione omnia que non possunt esse; ergo nulla impossibilitas existendi impedit ~atem WYCL. *Log.* II 74.

demonstrare [CL]

1 to show, point out, draw attention to, display. **b** to put on parade, muster (troops).

angelum .. quem .. caecatus non viderat, digito quodammodo .. ~avit GILDAS *EB* 1; alius, .. sagittarum spicula .. depromens .., ut certos pupillarum conspectus ~et, .. strepente arcu et nervo stridente ad destinatum indeclinabiliter dirigit locum ALDH. *VirgP* 2; **679** juxta notissimos terminos a me †~atus [? l. ~atos] *CS* 45; **725** (10c) testium et consentientium huic donationi signa aeterna ~abo *CS* 144; accedens ad sacerdotem, a quo sibi sperabat iter salutis posse ~ari BEDE *HE* IV 23 p. 263; Dunstanus .. interrogabat haec sibi ~antem .. presbiterum WULF. *Æthelwold* 38; ~ant burgenses civitatis xlv mansiones terre unde habebant liij s. de gablo T. R. E. *Dom. S. Aug.* 10; BACON XV 187 (v. demonstrativus b); **1364** comparuit .. episcopus .. ~ans quoddam breve de capella .. super nativis recuperandis .. nobis directum *Reg. Moray* 161; **s1415** reductus est [papa] coramque concilio ~atus, non indumentis religiositatis redimitus sed brigantinorum more semivestitus WALS. *YN* 453. **b** **1404** de hominibus civitatis Cestrie arraiandis et ~andis *Enr. Chester* 77 r. 4*d*.

2 to demonstrate, make plain, give evidence (of); **b** (w. acc. & inf. or compl., indir. qu., or *quia*).

divinae legis regulas catholica praecessorum monimenta luce clariora ~ant ALDH. *Met.* 3; **c1150** (v. desicut a); J. SAL. *Met.* 919D (v. demonstrativus d); que sint que per eam que est a verbis notam non discerni .. evenit, ~andi modo ~andis accommodato distinguemus BALSH. *AD* 67 (cf. ib. 19: quoniam hujusmodi principia .. sunt distinctiora quam ut ~atorum distinctionibus conveniant); GROS. *Anal. Post.* I 10. 2 (v. definitio 2a); accidentia sciuntur et ~antur per substantiam BACON VII 125; quelibet passio non habet ~ari per 4 causas, quia passiones mathematice tantum ~antur per causam formalem, conjunctam tamen cum materia in qua est *Id.* XV 306; WALLINGF. *Quad.* 24 (v. commensurabilis a); †amphorismus est sermo brevis integre rei perfectum sensum ~ans *SB* 10; WYCL. *Log.* II 74 (v. demonstrabilitas). **b** regina Æ., cujus corpus vivens ante impollutum post mortem incorruptum manens adhuc ~at EDDI 19 (cf. ib. 56: tantum halitus et calida membra vivum eum ~abant); Deus ut qualis meriti vir fuerit ~aret, omni nocte super sepulchrum ejus lux apparuit BEDE *HE* I 33; quasi mortuus jacebat, halitu tantum pertenui quia viveret ~ans *Ib.* V 19; qualiter ad talium inventionem .. abundemus breviter ~andum BALSH. *AD* 82.

demonstrarius v. demonstratorius.

demonstratio [CL]

1 showing, bringing to notice. **b** display (of wares). **c** dramatic representation. **d** review, inspection; *cf. monstrum, ostensio.* **e** muster (of troops).

1583 super solam ~onem harum literarum *Pat* 1235. **b** **1444** Nicholao Bocher pro ~one sua apud Fratres pro die, j d. *Brokage Bk. Southampt.* I 45 (cf. ib. xxi). **c** **1516** in .. novellis datis super abbatem Salop' et famulos suos ad ludum et ~onem martiriorum Felicianae et Sabinae martirum in quarera post muros (*Ac. Bailiff*) *Hist. Shrewsb.* I 328 (cf. *Med. Stage* II 251). **d** habeant hii quatuor [primarii foreste] unam regalem potestatem .. quaterque in anno generales foreste ~ones et viridis et veneris forisfactiones, quas †*muchimut* dicunt, teneant (*Ps.-Cnut*) *GAS* 622. **e** **1373** in quodam loco vocato Barelond' juxta introitum .. castri [Glouc'], in quo ~o hominum ad arma et sagittariorum fieri solebat *Pat* 288 m. 6; **1385** ad supervidendum ~onem tam hominum ad arma quam sagittariorum qui in viagio predicto [episcopi Norwic'] transfretare debuissent *PlRCP* 496 r. 434; **1404** vobis precipimus .. quod ~onem ipsorum hominum ad arma et sagittariorum coram vobis capi et debite fieri faciatis *Enr. Chester* 77 r. 4 *d*.

2 **a** exposition (esp. rhet.), declaration. **b** (leg.) statement of case.

a ALCUIN *Rhet.* 5 (v. 1 deliberatio b); **1295** [*those things not expressly contained in the bill are declared* per racionabilem ejus] ~onem *Cal. Just. Ir.* I 43. **b** **1305** petit judicium de variacione brevis et sue ~onis *PlRCP* 155 m. 187*d*.; non potest dedicere .. quin ad .. dominum regem ad ecclesiam predictam .. pertinet presentare, prout .. dominus rex superius per ~onem suam supponit *Entries* 530b.

3 demonstration, proof (esp. log. or geom.).

J. SAL. *Met.* 919D (v. demonstrativus d); quod quoniam ignoranti incredibile, attendenti dubium, intelligenti certum, ejus plene ~oni non nisi arte cognita locus erit BALSH. *AD* 10; scientia est habitus per ~onem acquisitus; set substantie non est ~o BACON VII 125; cum prima ~o Euclidis sit potissima *Id.* IX 170; ~onum alia est universalis, alia particularis: .. ~o universalis ostendit hanc passionem 'habere 3' de triangulo; ~o particularis ostendit eandem de ysochele vel de gradato. de ~one est sciendum quod dupliciter fit: aut ostendit causam per effectum aut effectum per causam remotam *Id.* XV 312; DUNS *Metaph.* V 1. 189 (v. circularis 2d); veritatem geometricam et omnes alias quarumcunque scienciarum ~ones probatas OCKHAM *Dial.* 419; WYCL. *Act.* 119 (v. conicere 2a).

4 section, division (of library).

a1331 (v. distinctio 2d).

demonstrative [LL], demonstratively, by way of demonstration.

W. FITZST. *Thom. prol.* 9 (v. dialectice); quod scriptura illa [*Acts* iv 32] ~e supponat res usu consumptibiles quoad proprietatem seu dominium credentibus fuisse †communia patet OCKHAM *Pol.* I 355; cupio scire an .. existimes .. raciones quas allegas conclusionem tuam ~e probare *Id. Dial.* 414; aliquis per revelacionem vel ~e certificatus de una conclusione finitiva (KYN.) *Ziz.* 98.

demonstrativus [CL], demonstrative; **b** (gram.); **c** (rhet.); **d** (log.).

hic est amor relativus, / idem est demonstrativus / divine dulcedinis GARL. *SM* 1079; signa ~a et manifestativa morbi presentis GAD. 45v. 2. **b** [pronomina] sunt magis ~a quae non per casus declinantur, ut 'eccum', 'eccam' BONIF. *AG* 35; ~a *synd æteowigendlice*: 'en' .. 'ecce' ÆLF. *Gram.* 231; sunt pronomina ~a octo secundum 8 differencias quibus magis et minus fit cognitus qui demonstratur *Ps.*-GROS. *Gram.* 43; cum .. una [oratio] est hec, 'non ego solus ego', dicendum quod intelligitur ibi hoc verbum 'sum' per pronomen ~um. .. confert autem ad hoc actus demonstrandi, quia actualiter per pronomen demonstratur illud quod habet esse BACON XV 187 (cf. ib. 188: adverbia ~a). **c** ~um genus [artis rhetoricae], quod tribuitur in alicujus certae personae laudem vel vituperationem ut in Genesi [iv 4–5] de Abel et Cain legitur .. ALCUIN *Rhet.* 5. **d** [Posteriorum Analeticorum liber] continet artem demonstrandi. .. hec .. jam fere in desuetudinem abiit, eo quod demonstrationis usus vix apud solos mathematicos est. .. ad hec, liber quo ~a traditur disciplina ceteris longe turbatior est J. SAL. *Met.* 919D (cf. ib. 920C: non utique omnis scientia ~a est, sed illa dumtaxat que ex veris et primis est et immediatis); demonstrativa nunc contendit ratione NECKAM *DS* X 103; est [syllogismus] ~us, qui est ex necessariis et ex causis conclusionis certissimis faciens scientiam (SHIRWOOD) *GLA* III 16; *Ib.* 19 (v. disputatio 1); hoc ultimo modo est scientia habitus conclusionis ~e BACON VII 125; duo sunt [arguendi genera] ad intellectum, ut dyalecticum et ~um *Id. Tert. Sup.* 75; dialectica ac ~a scientia *Ps.*-GROS. *Summa* 300; racionis probabilis, non tamen ~e, imo nec necessarie DUNS *PW* 148; quod .. sit jure divino [papa hereticus] papatu privatus quidam racionibus plurimis ~is .. ostendunt OCKHAM *Pol.* I 59.

demonstrator [CL], a indicator. **b** demonstrator (log.).

a intellexit Elisabeth [cf. *Luke* i 41] .. quid illa exultatio sui significasset infantis, hoc est illius venisse matrem cujus ipse praecursor ac ~or esset futurus BEDE *Hom.* I 4. 17. **b** non omnis locus ~ori commodus est, utpote ab accidente, eo quod corruptibilium nec demonstratio nec scientia simpliciter est J. SAL. *Met.* 920D; profundus est in sententiis .., orator vehemens, efficax ~or *Id. Pol.* 672C; geometer vel ~or intelligit istam [majorem propositionem] in lineis rectis et ipse [syllogismus] coaptat eam recte et oblique BACON XV 313; oportuit logicam facere tractatum de modo raciocinandi in genere, prout abstrahit ab

omni materia propria vel communi, ad quam viz. respiceret tam ~or quam dialecticus raciocinari volens KILWARDBY *Quomodo Deus* (*extr.*) 122; quia simplices sequentes tales ~ores possent dubitare cui esset assenciendum, ideo tuta est via, .. auctoritas, circa [v. l. certa] que non potest fallere nec falli DUNS *Ord.* II 237.

demonstratorius [LL], index (finger).

secundus digitus nominatur index sive ~ius; pretium ejus, xv s. *Text. Roff.* f. 76 p. 40; ~ius, digitus qui dicitur index OSB. GLOUC. *Deriv.* 178; *lykpot fyngyr*, index, †demonstrarius [? l. ~atorius] *CathA.*

demorari [CL], **~are,** to remain (at a place), stay, reside: **a** (of person); **b** (of animal); **c** (of thing or abstr.).

a [tyrannos] inter altaria jurando ~antes et haec eadem .. paulo post .. despicientes GILDAS *EB* 27; **a705** aestivi temporis cursu .. tecum legendi studio conversatus ~abar (ÆTHELWALD) *Ep. Aldh.* II (7); venerat .. Agilberctus .. ad provinciam Nordanhymbrorum .. et apud eos aliquandiu ~abatur BEDE *HE* III 25 p. 183; **860** (14c) quam diu in ista transitoria vita ~atus fuerit *CS* 500; **s1042** illam mandavit ibidem quiete ~ari M. PAR. *Maj.* I 517 (= FL. WORC. I 197: manere jussit); **s1257** (v. carbo 2b); **1294** dum .. W. .. fuit in Gawaye .. et ~avit per xij dies (*KRAc* 331/2) *Doc. Scot.* I 428; **1439** in ecclesiis quarum rectores .. extra diocesim .. ~antur *Reg. Cant.* III 287 (cf. ib.: rectores qui .. moram trahunt extra dioceses); **1558** neque ille ullos exules in .. patria sua ~are permittet *ActPCIr* 54. **b** hippotami .. esse perhibentur majores elephantorum corporibus quos dicunt in .. fluvio .. ~ari *Lib. Monstr.* II 9; due vacce fuerunt .. in .. prato lutoso de nocte ~ate NIG. *Ep.* 18. **c** **1321** rotuli vicecomitum ~arunt versus justiciarios illo die *MGL* II 296; ut melodia perseveret ubi ~abatur tristicia [ME: *wher hevynes was*] ROLLE *IA* 244.

demoratio [LL = *dwelling*], delay.

c1090 mando .. ut partem de *craspeis* reddas G. abbati de Bello .. omni ~one et calumnia remota (*Breve Regis*) *Arch. Cant.* XLVII 109.

demordēre [CL], to bite. **b** (fig.) to backbite, slander.

†demorosos [l. demorsos], conrosos *GlH* D 156; *to bite*, mo[r]dere, de-, re- .. *CathA.* **b** si quid novum hic .. emerserit, non statim lividi vel contemnant vel ~eant GIR. *TH* II *pref.* p. 76.

demovēre [CL]

1 to remove, transfer. **b** (w. dat.) to bring (to).

remotio criminis est cum ejus intentio facti, quod ab adversario infertur, in alium, aut in aliud crimen, ~etur ALCUIN *Rhet.* 14; ~it saxum sepulchro surgens Christus integer *Cerne* 169. **b** cum sol 'mortalibus egris' igneum ~erat ortum FELIX *Guthl.* 19 (cf. ib. 41: cum sol aureum caelo ~erat ortum); *Ib.* 26 (v. crastinus 1a).

2 to oppress.

licet laboribus .. et infirmitate demotus [v. l. devictus] .., mane oratorium ingressus psallere cepit *NLA* (*Ric. Cic.*) II 335.

demps- v. et. dens-. **dempsum** v. demere c.

demptio [CL], taking away, removal.

c990 quid illos autumandum est inopes, si ita res se haberet, post melliti gustaminis ~onem egisse? B. *Ep.* 386; obesa corpora necessariam habent crebram sanguinis ~onem P. BLOIS *Ep.* 85. 260C.

demulare v. deaemulare.

demulcare [LL], to beat.

chastier, castigare, corripere, †demulgire *Gl. AN Ox.* f. 153v.

demulcēre [CL], to caress, fondle. **b** to soothe, flatter, appease. **c** to mitigate, soften.

[infantulus] blando manuum applausu caput et faciem ejus tangens, contrectans, complanans ~ebat *NLA* (*Walth.*) II 407; sic, sic, mater, demulces filium / et sic, per quem gaudes, das gaudium J. HOWD. *Ph.* 47. **b** mentem .. nec minarum ferocitas reflectit nec blandimentorum lenitas ~et ALDH. *VirgP* 33; subjectos .. corripiat justus in misericordia [cf. *Psalm* cxl 5] .. neque oleo noxiae consensionis eorum corda ~eat BEDE *Hom.* II 22. 217; terrigenasque tamen demulcet mente dolosa BONIF. *Aen.* 3 (*Cupiditas*) 7; **754** ille .. martyr .. nostra valde mesta majore letitia mitigat et ~it (*sic*) pectora (MILRED EPISC. WORC.) *Ep. Bonif.* 112; ~eat, blanditur, *olecce GlH* D 166; regina Dunstanum .. ~et alloquio OSB. *V. Dunst.* 23 p. 96; omne quod ~et abest et omne quod terret et cruciat presto est ELMER CANT. *Record.* 719C; H. BOS *Thom.* III 13 (v. delenire a); unde .. vox mea amati mei duriciam ~eret ROLLE *IA* 246; Salvatoris misericordiam devotis precibus ~endo *Ps.*-ELMH. *Hen. V* 61; LYNDW. 212 b (v. contristativus). **c** Mulciber dictus est quia ignis ferri duritiam emollit atque ~et ALB. LOND. *DG* 10. 5.

demulgare v. dimulgare. **demulgire** v. demulcare.

†demullare, *f. l.*

†demullo [l. tremulo], A. *to drede WW.*

demulsivus [cf. LL demulsus *p. ppl. of* demulcere], soothing, flattering, appeasing.

gavisa gaudio magno valde congratulando sibi sermonibus ~is *Wager* f. 43b.

demultare [cf. CL multare], to despoil.

si [papa et ecclesiastici prepositi] mercatores seculi in ministerio Christi preficiant et studeant precipue ad vitam secularem continuandum pauperes ecclesias ~are WYCL. *Civ. Dom.* I 391.

demultiplicare [cf. CL multiplicare], to diminish.

stat animam multiplicari per alimentum adveniens noviter assimilatum et ~ari per †partem [? l. partis] corporis abscisionem et sic acquirere et deperdere locum sine sui motu locali... habet tamen unum equivalens, quod dicitur multiplicacio vel demultiplicacio WYCL. *Log.* III 139.

demultiplicatio [cf. CL multiplicatio], diminution.

WYCL. *Log.* III 139 (v. demultiplicare).

demum [CL], at last, finally. **b** (w. *per*) for long.

c675 Hermionam .., quae .. despondebatur pridem .. Oresti ~umque sententia immutata Neoptolemo nupsit ALDH. *Ep.* 3; vixerat in terris .. / undecies denos et tres feliciter annos; / tunc demum .. / ivit ad aeterni castus consortia regni *Id. VirgV* 794; nihil alicujus cibi .. quatuor diebus et quatuor noctibus degustavit. .. quinta demum die, ecce angelus .. apparuit EDDI 56; **c710** expectamus adhuc .. tempus diei Dominicae, et sic ~um votiva Paschae nostri festa celebramus (*Ep. Ceolfridi*) BEDE *HE* V 21 p. 340; multo ~um interfluente tempore R. COLD. *Cuthb.* 27; **1221** (v. definitivus 2a); ~um finem loquendi faciamus AD. MARSH *Ep.* 1. **b** **1402** pacificare discordes et ad viam .. pacis reducere per ~um oberrantes *Reg. Cant.* I 410.

demundare [cf. CL mundare], to cleanse, scour.

1312 concessionem, quam .. Isabella fecit .. de licencia stagni et aqueductus molendinorum purgandi, ~andi et eciam ampliandi, .. confirmamus (*Pat*) *MonA* VI 205.

demungere [cf. mungere], to wipe clean. *V. et. emungere.*

to clense, .. mundare, e-, mungere, de-, e- .. *CathA.*

demutare [CL], to change. **b** to translate (bodies).

concupiscit ut per resurrectionem circumdetur stola ~atae carnis ABBO *Edm.* 16; jocos dicit, voces †demictat [l. demutat, *as* Cato *Orat.* 125] J. SAL. *Pol.* 758C; infirmitas .. labiorum .. nature beneficium tenuem ~avit in sibilum W. CANT. *Thom.* VI 117. **b** [Lanfrancus] jussit corpora sanctorum, que in orientali parte .. ecclesie humata erant, in occidentalem partem .. ~ari EADMER *Mir. Dunst.* 14.

demutatio [CL = *transformation*], change (of residence). **b** translation (of body).

"regulam," inquit, "B. Benedicti servare .. volo .. et idcirco in Gallia apud Floriacum, ubi ipsius patris reliquie dicuntur haberi, monachus fieri mente revolvo." .. hec patrie ~o .. utriusque voluntati complacuit EADMER *V. Osw.* 5. **b** corpus ipsius .. primo sepulture sue loco mansit immotum. sed .. Deus .. quorundam bene religiosorum mentes .. excitat atque ad ~onem illius affectum eis effectumque ministrat *Id. Wilf.* 57.

demuttire [LL], to be dumb.

to be dume, mutere .., mutire, de-, ob- *CathA.*

1 dena [AS *denu*], 'dean', 'dene', wooded valley. *Cf.* 1 *denna.*

c1200 concedo totam terram que pertinet ad demenium meum in cultura versus ~am de Haleton *Couch. Kirkstall* 116.

2 dena v. denarius.

3 dena v. 1 denna.

4 dena v. 2 denus 2b.

Denachius v. Daneschus. **Denagildum** v. Danegeldum. **denagium** v. dennagium. **Denalaga** v. Danelaga. **denarata, ~us** v. denariata. **denarentatus** v. denarius 6c. **denaria** v. deverium a.

denarialis, (w. *panis*) penny loaf.

s1386 dicebatur panem Anglie ~em vendi ibidem [apud le Sclus] pro xviij d. KNIGHTON *Cont.* II 212.

denariata, ~us, ~um

1 pennyworth: **a** (of goods, unspec.); **b** (of bread or ale); **c** (of rent); **d** (of land, w. ref. to yearly rental), 'pennyland'.

a omnis qui habuerit xxx ~as vive pecunie de suo proprio .. dabit denarium S. Petri (*Leg. Ed.*) *GAS* 634; **1233** nulla captio fiet in civitate .. preterquam ad opus domini comitis .. et hoc sit xiij ~i pro xij d., nisi tantummodo de cervisia *BBC* (*Chester*) 328; **1269** ex mutuo recepit denarios vel ~as tales sive catalla solvend' tali die *CBaron* 84; quod nullus extraneus mercator .. vendat in ~is, sed in grosso, et tunc in burgo et mercatoribus burgi (*Assis. Will.* 41) *APScot* I 61; [piscatores] frangunt et secant pisces in frusta et vendunt per ~as *Iter Cam.* 20; **1361** ut .. possit .. de bonis premissis duos ~us pro j d. vendere .. quousque perceperit x m. supradictas *Reg. Glasg.* 263; **1397** indentura de denariis et ~is liberatis per .. bursarium .. celerario *Ac. Durh.* 600; **c1430** isti sunt ~us ordinati .. per .. magistros de *cordewanercrafte* solvendi servientibus suis in eadem arte amplius quam eis solvere solebant ..: in primis pro aptacione xij parium de *les over leders*, j d. ob., ubi solvere solebant nisi j d. *Mem. York* I 193; ~us, A. *a penyworthe WW.* **b** **c1230** in die anniversarii mei .. c pauperes .. sustentabit in hac forma, viz. quod duo pauperes semper inter se habeant unam ~am panis *Ch. Sal.* 204; **1291** in uno dennarrato panis (*St. Ives*) *Law Merch.* I 39; **s1316** iiij ~us de grosso pane non sufficiebant uni simplici homini in die TROKELOWE 95; **c1330** valletti pistorum .. convicti fuerunt .. quod furati fuerunt .. duas denaratas de pane assaii *MGL* III app. 420; **1492** quod darent .. prefato J. B. unum ~um servitie *Entries* 607. **c** **1185** apud Cotesmore [*Oxon*] .. xix deneriat[us] in pratis quos tenet J.; item .. xx denariat[us] quos tenet magister W. *Rec. Templars* 55; **a1200** ponit se in magnam assisam de xvj ~is redditus in Wisebeche *CurR* I 3; **1222** de vij solidatis et iiij deneratis redditus in Merleberg' *Cl* 498a; **1253** ego Aaron .. dedi .. Galfrido G., civi London', sex marcatas et xix ~as quieti redditus annui in civitate London' *SelPlJews* 16; **1255** concessisse .. ij acras terre et dim. et ij ~as et ij gallinas annui redditus .. *MonA* IV 289 (cf. *CalCh* I 445); **1269** appropriavit sibi xij denarratas annui redditus de Johanne de U. pro j acra terre de dominico domini regis *SelPlForest* 48; **1278** concessi v m. et ij s. annui redditus in denariis et ~is, ut in redditibus, releviis, sectis, serviciis et omnimodis consuetudinibus (*Ch.*) THORNE 1927; [abbas R., ob. **1290**] perquisivit .. in villa S. Albani .. iiij mesuagia ...., viij solidatas et iiij ~us annui redditus *G. S. Alb.* I 472; **c1300** remisisse .. illos octo denaratos annui redditus quos mihi solvere consueverunt pro firmacione molendini sui *Cart. Burton* 76; **1322** fuit seisitus .. de xiij solidatis et iiij denaratis annui redditus *Cart. Glam.* 1094; **1341** recepisse in denariis et ~is contribucionem papalem nobis debitam de ecclesiis de K. et de K. *Reg. Glasg.* 251. **d** **c1095** xx deneratas terrae in Binham *Cart. Lewes* f. 13; **c1200** ponunt se in magnam assisam de xij deneriatis terre in Ferendon' [*Berks*] *CurR* I 3; **1224** replegiari faciat Philippo de B. unam marcatam terre et unam deneratam quas clamat tenere de domino rege in Mungumeri [*Wales*] *Cl* 592b; **1236** illam ~am terre *Melrose* I 203; **1247** quandam terram que ~a vulgariter dicitur (*Lit. Papae*) *Reg. Paisley* 123 (cf. ib. *rub.*: de terra ~a (*sic*) et ecclesia S. Colmaneli); **1259** cum rex nuper extendi fecerit maneria .. quorum extente pertingunt ad cix li. ix s. x d. et ob. et de quibus xxxvj librate ix solidate xi denarate et una obolata terre pertinent Matillidi de K. *Cl* 409; **c1260** terra de Drumfad' et de Glenop' [*in Carrick, Scot.*], sc. x ~e terre, valent per annum xl m. *IMisc* 10/21; **c1265** dedi .. iiij deneratas terre (*Cart. Hosp.*) *BL Cotton Nero* E vi f. 193 (cf. ib. 193v.: predictas iiij deyneratas terre); **1389** dedisse .. totam terram de Karynch [*N. Uist*] et iiij ~as in Ylara *Inchaffray* 136.

2 (pl.) goods sold retail (*cf.* AN *denarrees*, OF *denrees*).

1290 quod non liceat alicui carcare seu discarcare mercandisas aliquas seu denarratas nec forestallum facere de hujusmodi mercandisis seu deneratis emendo vel vendendo eadem nisi infra villam Novi Castri *RParl* I 26; **s1428** in his subterraneis .. minis erant edificia .. et vie et †vite [? l. vici] in modum vicorum civitatis divisi .., taberne eciam et omnia victualia et alia ~a *Plusc.* X 29; **1431** lego .. v m. in utensilibus et ~is *Test. Ebor.* II 16.

3 denerel (C. I.). *Cf. denerellus.*

1247 accepimus per inquisicionem .. quod homines nostri in .. insula [Gernes'] .. debent molagium, sc. de qualibet boveta terre j bussollum et duas denaratas frumenti ad parvam mensuram *Cl* 546; **1248** item debent melagium, sc. de qualibet bovata terre j bussellum et duas ~as frumenti .. ad parvum bussellum *Ext. Guern.* 25.

denariatim, at the rate of a penny each.

1432 lego ad distribuendum inter pauperes ~im .. c s. *Reg. Cant.* II 463; **1438** item [lego] pauperibus die sepulture mee ~im, si tot venerint, x s. *Ib.* 560.

denariatum v. denariata.

1 denariatus v. denariata.

2 denariatus, worth a penny.

Reg. Paisley 123 *rub.* (v. denariata 1d); **1408** in x gall[inis] ~is, x d. *Ac. Durh.* 53 (cf. ib. 187: de gallinis rentalibus).

denariolus, small penny. *V. et. denarius* 4.

c1203 si .. inciderint in forisfactum vel calumpniam de heynebuto, non dabunt nisi xij ~os forisfacto (*Ch.*) *Cumb & Westm Antiq. Soc.* NS XII 338.

denarium v. deverium.

denarius [CL]

1 consisting of ten units. **b** (w. *numerus* or as sb. m.) number ten. **c** (as sb. m.) set of ten (esp. w. ref. to Ten Commandments; *cf. decalogus*). **d** (? by analogy w. penny) unit.

prime illi [interrogationum disciplinalium] ~ie distinctioni non relinquuntur nisi ea ad que responderi oportet parte secunda BALSH. *AD rec.* 2 160; Architam Tarentinum

laudat auctorem ~ia predicamentorum distinctio NECKAM *NR* II 173 p. 285; AD. MARSH *Ep.* 180 (v. 1c infra). **b** c**798** eandem regulam perfectionis vel inperfectionis, quia prima unitas in suis numeris sub ~io servat, eandem et secundam in suis ~iis sub centenario servare necesse est ALCUIN *Ep.* 133; numeri fundamentum est unitas et ~ius THURKILL *Abac.* 55; si inter x fuerit [horoscopus], prima radiatio in area quinarii, id est prima, secunda vero in area ~ii, id est secunda, facienda est ADEL. *Elk.* 37; si multiplicare volueris radice numeri quinarii cum radice numeri ~ii ROB. ANGL. *Alg.* 100; instituta fuit decimatio in signum transgressionis facte ab homine, qui per novenarium significatur deficientem a ~io HALES *Sent.* IV 31 (cf. ib. III 470); ~ius, qui per excrescentiam unitatis excedit novenarium BART. ANGL. XIX 121; in ~io est unum et duo et tres et quatuor; si ergo †colligeris [? l. collegeris] hec, faciunt decem BACON V 150; tum numerus perfectus dicitur cujus partes aliquote ipsum precise constituunt, et non est nisi unus infra ~ium, viz. senarius *Id. Maj.* I 7; *tene*, decem, .. decies, denus, ~ius *CathA.* **c** virtutum profectibus .. productis ex vitalis decalogi ~io, secundum quod est apud ~iam effectum sanctitatem AD. MARSH *Ep.* 180 (v. et. 1a supra); sicut habetur in Henrico de Gandavo de ~io Predicamentorum DUNS *Metaph.* IV 2. 167b; [Henricus VI] ideo in hoc mense [Decembri] natus est ut ~ium mandatorum menti imprimat CAPGR. *Hen.* 126. **d** ROB. ANGL. *Alg.* 146, 128 (v. census 7a & b).

2 (silver) penny (orig. of 10 copper *asses*): **a** Continental (var.); **b** Eng. (sterling); **c** Scot. (*cf. ExchScot* II xcv *seqq.*).

a 743 ut annis singulis de unaquaque casata solidus, id est xij ~ii, ad aecclesiam .. reddatur (*Syn. Liftinas* [*in Hainault*]) *Ep. Bonif.* 56; haec ij maneria reddunt per annum lxx libras ~iorum Rodmensium *DB* I 104 (= *Dom. Exon.* 195: Rothomagensium); **1151** ita quod de vino alicujus civium Rothomagi quod ad servitium ducis accipietur quartus ~ius non cadat *Act. Hen. II* I 19; **1158** pro escambio ~iorum de †Monte Martin [l. moneta Martini, sc. Turonensis] *Pipe* 186; GIR. *GE* II 35 (v. Andegavensis); **1240** ~iis de Musc' *Liberate* 14 m. 2 (v. 3b infra); s**1247** l milia librarum ~iorum Vianensium, quorum quilibet ~ius valet tres obolos esterlingorum M. PAR. *Maj.* IV 624; s**1251** exceptis aliis ~iis communibus, sc. sterlingis, Turon[ens]ibus et Parisiensibus *Ib.* V 204 (cf. id. *Min.* III 103); **1253** (v. Burdegalensis); a**1275** (v. Coloniensis); **1282** iiij solidi et ij ~ii Turonensium grossorum; item ij Romanorum grossorum; qui, computat[o] uno Turonensium pro iij sterlinis et uno Romanorum pro duobus et dim., valent xij s. et d. xj sterlingorum (*Comp. Collectorum Apostol.*) *EHR* XXXII 52; **1285** iiij ~ios Turonensium parvorum *RGasc* II 263; **1300** quolibet sterlingo computato pro xj ~iis Turon' *AcWardr* p. 87. **b** a**831** pro conpetenti pecunia, id est iij milia ~iorum *CS* 318; c**930** ea conditione ut .. adferat octuaginta solidos ex meris ~iis *CS* 648; adhuc reddit x libras ~iorum de xx in ora *DB* I 172; componat de singulis, id est lxvj solidis et vj ~iis et tertiam partem unius ~ii [AS: *ðriddan dæl pæninges*] (*Quad.*) *GAS* 87; *overseunesse* judicetur, id est l solidorum in Westsexa—si erga comitem, [lx] solidorum erga hundretum, xxx solidorum ex v ~iis, qui faciunt v mancas—ut solidus ~iis xij computetur (*Leg. Hen.* 34. 3) *Ib.* 565; c**1236** de quibus debemus habere ij denerios et rex tertium *Cust. Battle* 126; si quis ~ium inveniat retonsum vel de alio cuneo quam de cuneis communibus Anglie, Hibernie et Scocie, statim illum faciat perforari et restitui ..; si quis autem falsum invenerit ~ium, illum statim frangi faciat, sed illum non restituat *Fleta* 33; s**1298** (v. coronare 5d); **1502** quod quilibet lector .. habeat pro stipendio .. suo .. pro quolibet anno xiij libras vj solidos et viij ~ios legalis monete Anglie *StatOx* 307. **c** c**1150** omnem decimationem ~iorum firme burgi [Dunfermelin] *E. Ch. Scot.* 209; c**1170** plenariam firmam, sc. l solidos et octo ~ios *Regesta Scot.* II 58; **1360** in defalcacione iiij[m] librarum solutarum in nobillis .., viz. de qualibet libra iiij ~ios *ExchScot* 56; **1374** cum .. in parliamento nostro .. ordinatum extitit .. quod moneta iiij ~iorum de Scocia ponatur et currat in valorem iij ~iorum *RScot* 964b (cf. *StRealm* I 395); **1434** et nil rec[eptum est] de Scoticis ~iis et *blankes*, quia expenduntur in oblacionibus fratrum *Ac. Durh.* 468; **1464** argenti fabricati in minutis ~iis et obolis *ExchScot* 292.

3 penny of specified metal: **a** silver; **b** gold; **c** base metal (tin or copper).

a †**888** (*for* 868) pro conpetenti pecuniam (*sic*) .., id est cxx ~ios (*sic*) argenteis *CS* 519; a**940** (v. argentum 2a); denārios primos argenti fecit Yonas / rector Thessalie GARL. *Tri. Eccl.* 27; *MGL* II 105 (v. argenteus 2a); **1372** reddant .. xij ~ios argenti (*Ch. Roby*) *EHR* XVII 295; **1403** de j ~io argenti de quolibet sacco lane ponderate *ExchScot* 572. **b** [W. de Breusa] singulis notariorum .. preter communia stipendia aureum annuatim ~ium dabat GIR. *IK* I 2 p. 23; **1270** in j ~io de Murcia iij solidos et in j ~io auri de nova moneta ij solidos *Liberate* 46 m. 3 (cf. ib. 14 m. 2 [**1240**]: pro v ~iis de Musc'); **1275** (v. aureus 2a); **1288** N... invenit ij ~ios de auro et J. emit eos pro iij quadrantibus *Leet Norw.* 19; **1339** iij milia ~iorum auri vocatorum scussellorum (*Pat*) *Foed.* V 133a; **1487** in ~iis aureis vocatis *unicornys ExchScot* 549. **c** c**1167** E. Lorimarius r. c. de v m. pro ~io stanneo *Pipe* 85; **1340** R... habet ~ios, obolos, quadrantes novos de moneta regis, set metallum unde fit est mixtum cum stagno *CBaron* 99; c**1370** venit de transmarinis per mercatores falsa moneta de cupro, que dicebatur *Lusscheburne*, habens formam ~ii Anglicani (J. BRIDL. *gl.*) *Pol. Poems* I 140.

4 (silver) penny: **a** dist. as reckoned by 'tale' (number) or weight (*cf.* 10 *infra*) and with or without 'blanching' (allowance for deficiency in assay); **b** dist. as 'small' or 'great' (sts. app. w. ref. to short weight, sts. to distinction of penny from groat; *cf. grossus*). *V. et. denariolus.*

a *DB* I 137 (v. albus 6a); haec civitas [*Hereford*] reddit regi lx libras ad numerum de candidis ~iis *Ib.* 179 (cf. candidus 2); [reddit] iiij ~ios blancas (*sic*) *Ib.* II 118 (cf. blancus 2a); *GAS* 426 (v. ad 9c); **1303** pro xij libris in ~iis numeratis *EEC* 278; **1313** furati fuerunt pecuniam .. in ~iis numeratis absconditis in quodam tasso bladi *Eyre Kent* I 78; **1367** quoad fabricacionem monete extat .. ordinatum .. quod libra argenti minuatur in pondere x ~iis ponderis, sic sc. quod de libra ponderis jam fiant xxix solidi et iiij ~ii numerales (*Stat. David II*) *APScot* I 144b. **b** c**1285** in Hibernia omnes fere locuntur .. de pluribus cambiis factis et de ~iis ultra modum adsis[e] r[egis]: primo de ~iis magnis electis de veteri moneta cambiatis pro †cujus li. xvj d.; item recepit parvam monetam .. de debitoribus regis per pondus et dealbacionem, quam quidem parvam monetam, defensam ne reciperetur, postmodum ut solveretur precepit propter excercitum regis versus Walliam *KRAc* 234/19 m. 2 (cf. *Cal. Ir.* III p. 8); **1316** pro precio magni ~ii oblatorii domini regis ponderantis vij d., oblati per ipsum dominum regem singulis diebus ad missam suam et postea redempti .. pro vij d. (*AcWardr*) *Arch.* XXVI 343; **1464** de lj li. ix s. provenientibus de cona ccclxxxv li. et xiiij unciarum argenti fabricati in grossis xij ~iorum et vj ~iorum ..; et vj li. vj s. ob. provenientibus de cona xciiij li. viij unciarum cum dimedia argenti fabricati in minutis ~iis et obolis *ExchScot* 292; **1517** invente fuerunt in cista communi .. in pecunia .. in dim. grossis, alias dictis ~iis de duobus, iij li. xv s. iiij d. *Fabr. York* 234.

5 penny payable to church, or religious house, given in alms, or sim.: **a** Peter-penny, Romescot; **b** reek-penny; *cf. fumagium*; **c** (var.).

a †**1031** ~ii quos Romae ad S. Petrum debemus (*Lit. Canuti*) FL. WORC. I 189 (cf. W. MALM. *GR* II 183; *GAS* 277; H. HUNT. *HA* VI 16); *DB* I 87v. (v. 6c infra); (*Leg. Ed.*) *GAS* 634 (v. denariata 1a); s**1031** Cnuto .. ~ium B. Petri denuo dedit, quum ante ab Edwardo filio Alvredi datus esset et ab Ethelwolfo rege R. NIGER *Chr. II* 157; [H. abbas, ob. **1133**] adquisivit legationem colligendorum ~iorum Rome in Anglia H. ALBUS 100; **1154** salva B. Petro et sacrosancte Romane ecclesie de singulis domibus annua unius ~ii pensione (*Lit. Papae*) DICETO *YH* I 301; c**1155** ecclesiam .. ab omni episcopali consuetudine absolutam excepto ~io B. Petri *Danelaw* 317; s**1164** domini pape auribus immurmurabant de archiepiscopi depositione, temptantes eum maximis promissis, tandem etiam adjecto quod ~ium annuum B. Petri, qui nunc a solis ascriptis glebe, nec tamen ab omnibus, datur in Anglia, rex faceret .. ab omni habitatore terre .. donari W. FITZST. *Thom.* 65; **1167** apostolico xlij li. pro ~iis B. Petri *Pipe* 58; **1181** decanus loci colligit ~ium B. Petri et solvit archidiacono *Dom. S. Paul.* 147 (cf. ib. 151: firmarius colligit ~ium B. Petri et sibi retinet); **1213** volumus .. ut de .. redditibus nostris .., salvis per omnia ~iis B. Petri, ecclesia Romana m. esterlingorum percipiat annuatim (*Ch. Regis*) WEND. II 75; s**727** statutum est .. per totum regnum Occidentalium Saxonum .. ut singulis annis de singulis familiis ~ius unus, qui Anglice *Rom-scot* appellatur, B. Petro et ecclesie Romane mitteretur M. PAR *Maj.* I 331; s**793** ex his omnibus provinciis dedit rex [Offa] .. ~ium B. Petri, .., quod (*sic*) Anglice *Romscot* appellatur *Ib.* 360 (cf. *V. II Off.* 30); c**1280** gravatur regnum Anglie eo quod dominus papa non est contentus illo subsidio quod vocatur ~ius S. Petri (*Lit. Baronum*) *DocExch* 353; **1310** recepimus de ~iis S. Petri m vj[c]ix li. xvij s. (*Lit. Collectorum Apostol.*) *EHR* XLI 354; c**1310** pro ~iis papalibus solvendis *Ac. Durh.* 510; **1453** de superplus ~iorum S. Petri vocatorum *Romscot MinAc* 1129/3 r. 5; numi illi argentei vocantur vulgo ~ii divi Petri, quos pontificius quaestor .. exigit P. VERG. IV 90. **b 1164** pia consuetudo .. ut de singulis sc. parrochiis vestris pro quaque domo ad operaciones ecclesie B. Cuthberti j ~ius annuatim consueverit exhiberi (*Lit. Papae*) *Hist. Durh. Script.* app. p. lii; **1276** si plures liberi proprium habentes in parentum pariter familia vivant, ad ~ios qui nuncupantur *rekpenys* minime arceantur (*Stat. Durh.*) *Conc. Syn.* 819; **1356** sacriste de ~iis fumalibus vj s. viij d. *Ac. Durh.* 122; postea [c**1300**] rediit [episcopus] revocatus et pro relaxacione sentencie [interdictus] dederunt de qualibet domo fumigante j ~ium .. cuilibet antistiti succedenti redeunti de Insulis *Chr. Man* 116. **c** c**1105** precipio quod presbiteri qui tenent ecclesias que sunt super terras dominicas monachorum Winton' bene eas acquietent de ~iis presbit[er]orum (*Ch. Wint.*) *EHR* XXXV 391; **1191** eo salvo quod ~ios S. Petri et ~ios de caritate persolvant, quos actenus solvere consueverunt *Cart. Glast.* I 2 (v. et. caritas 3c); c**1218** vicarius .. habebit de oblacionibus ad altare provenientibus j ~ium missalem [*mass-penny*] quocies celebraverit et ~ius provenerit *Lib. Ant. Linc.* 1; **1250** in decimis .. ville Spalding' .. cum ~iis missalibus et ~iis cum pane benedicto oblatis *Reg. Linc.* 114; W. clericus .. mensuratus ad comitem et ~io plicato convaluit *Mir. Montf.* 75; *Ib.* 74 (v. complicare 1b); c**1300** presbiteri stipendiarii .. juraburt .. quod ecclesiis parochialibus .. in quibus divina celebrantur eorumque rectoribus .. nullum .. inferent .. prejudicium circa oblaciones, porciones, obvenciones, ~ios pro requisitis, tricenalia vel jura *Conc. Syn.* 1383 (*gl.* LYNDW. 111 e: '~ios †perquisitos': aliqui libri habent sic, '~ios pro requestis'; et sunt hi ~ii qui in aliquibus partibus consueverunt dari curato pro habendis memoriis defunctorum; et ab aliquibus dicuntur ~ii memoriales, quia ut habeatur memoria defunctorum solent solvi; cf. ib. 237); **1360** racione decimi ~ii de .. terris de Menmur' .. priori et canonicis debiti *RMSScot* 214; **1378** presentando xx m. pro .. ~iorum synodalium oneribus supportandis *Reg. Aberbr.* II 35; **1389** decanus [gilde] habebit de quilibet (*sic*) fratre in collecta ~iorum animarum ['*soul-scot*'; cf. anima 5c] .. ij d. *Guild Cert.* (*Linc.*) 41/153; **1397** celerario et refectorario pro ~io S. Benedicti, iiij s. *Ac. Obed. Abingd.* 63 (cf. ib. 91).

6 penny payable to crown or lord (esp. feud. or man.): **a** third penny (of borough or county; *cf. EHR* XXXIV 62–4); **b** quota levied by crown; **c** (var.).

a de tercio ~io Sarisberie habet rex vj li., de tercio ~io Merleberge iiij li. .., de tercio ~io Malmesberie vj li. *DB* I 64v.; huic manerio Piretone adjacet tercius ~ius de tota scira Dorsete *Ib.* 75; tercius ~ius de placitis istius hundreti pertinebat T. R. E. huic manerio *Ib.* (*Chesh*) 263v.; *GAS* 614 (v. comitalis); *Ib.* 651 (v. comes 5); **1139** tertium ~ium redditus burgi Hereford quicquid unquam reddat et tertium ~ium placitorum totius comitatus Hereford (*Ch. Imperatricis*) *Mandeville* 288; **1141** *Ib.* 89 (v. comes 5); **1155** comiti Gloecestrie xx li. pro tercio ~io comitatus *Pipe* 49; c**1157** concessisse R. Lincolniensi episcopo tertium ~ium de wapentaco de Estowa ad firmam per x li. numero unoquoque anno *CalCh* IV 143; **1221** loquendum de xx li. de tertio ~io comitatus [Hereford'], que allocantur vicecomiti in corpore comitatus .., que proveniunt de placitis et perquisitis et non de firma assisa *LTRMem* 4 r. 12; **1331** concessimus .. wardam castri nostri de Lincoln' .. et xx libratas annui redditus .. pro tercio ~io comitatus Linc' (*Ch. Regis*) *Ambrosden* II 19. **b 1269** de vicesimo ~io assiso levando ad usus domini regis H. *Rec. Leic.* I 128; s**1269** ~ios provenientes de vicesimo ~io collecto per totam Angliam de omnibus liberis hominibus .., unde mencio superius facta est *Leg. Ant. Lond.* 125 (cf. ib. 122: liberi homines de regno Anglie .. dederunt domino regi vicesimam partem .. bonorum suorum mobilium ad expensas suas faciendas in itinere versus terram Jerosolimitanam); s**1294** rex .. in burgo morantibus indixit senarium ~ium a cunctis qui possederant sibi solvi *Flor. Hist.* III 91; s**1297** exigendo .. de populo octavum ~ium sibi dari *Ib.* 102 (cf. ib. 103: octonarium ~ium); s**1297** dederunt regi populus nonum ~ium, clerus Cantuariensis decimam [v. l. decimum], clerus Eboracensis quintam [v. l. quintum] *Eul. Hist.* III 168; c**1300** (v. denus 2b); s**1313** magnates, regis paupertatem considerantes, quintum decimum ~ium bonorum temporalium per totam Angliam sibi concedebant TROKELOWE 81. **c** istae consuetudines pertinent ad Tantone: *burgheristh*, latrones, pacis infractio, *hainfare*, ~ii de *hundret* et ~ii S. Petri, circieti *DB* I (*Som*) 87v.; ut .. renovarent pleggios suos et .. darent prefecto ~ium qui dicitur *borthselver* BRAKELOND 150; **1215** (v. 2 constabularius 2a); **1220** (v. carruca 3a); **1254** (v. crux 9b); **1279** predicti †denarentati [MS: den[arii] arentati] fuerunt domino regi et ipse vic. respondet de arentacione predictorum ~iorum *PQW* 337a; **1289, 1296** (v. capitalis 2a); **1382** summa ~iorum Calesie *EEC* 600 (cf. ib. 642 [**1444**]: †~ie [? l. ~ii] Calesie); **1505** denar' molend[ini] alias *treth melen*, viz. pro non virticione aque ad molendina nostra (*Bromefield & Yale*) *Pat* 597 m. 19.

7 (w. *Dei*), God's penny, earnest money.

c**1250** (v. arra a); **1301** (v. 2 contractus 2a); **1355** in ~iis Dei datis super nundinas S. Egidii pro diversis mercandisis emptis, v d. *Comp. Swith.* 242.

8 (pl. or collect.) money, cash. **b** (w. *ad*) at the expense (of); *cf. ad* 7a.

a**1123** emit terram .. de R. [et al.], qui ~ios inde receperunt (*Ch. B. Scriptoris*) *EHR* XIV 429; **1166** in singulis comitatibus ubi non fuerint gaiole fiant .. de ~iis regis et bosco ejus *Assize Clar.* 7; catalla cujuslibet nativi ita intelliguntur esse in potestate domini sui quod propriis suis ~iis versus dominum suum a villenagio se redimere non poterit GLANV. V 5; **1205** terra illa valet de reddit assiso viij li. v s. j d. exceptis operibus; et, si opera fuerint posita ad ~ium, valeret x li. ij s. vij d. *RNorm* 131; **1220** (v. deus 3d); **1221** non potuerunt deliberari antequam pacassent xlv m. in ~iis, exceptis aliis donis factis militibus suis [sc. captoris] *SelPlCrown* 95; **1253** †~ium quod ad hoc posueritis *RGasc* I 359 (= *Cl* 176: ~ios quos); **1269** (v. denariata 1a); in crastino die comitatus .., in quo fit collecta ~iorum regis [*money paid to crown*] *Fleta* 151; **1298** probatores qui ceperunt ~ios domini regis [*money paid by crown*] *Gaol Del.* 37/4 r. 2; **1345** invenitur quod servicia de Valle Dublin' subscripta soluta sunt ad Scaccarium in ~iis; viz: servicium archiepiscopi [et al.] .., qui omnes nunc clamant facere servicia .. ad castrum Dublin' per corpus suum (*Mem. Scac. Hib.*) *EHR* XVIII 508; **1404** deliberavit in ~iis levabilibus de tempore suo pro diversis debitorum debitis .. xl li. *Ac. Durh.* 399; ut ~ius acquiratur PAUL. ANGL. *ASP* 1533 (v. devotio 2c). **b 1225** precipimus quod navis illa cum rectoribus et marinellis .. sint ad ~ios nostros *Pat* 546; **1258** eis ad piscem illum ad regem cariandum habere faciat cariagium ad ~ios regis *Cl* 277; **1268** adducendo tecum milites .. quos perquirere poteris ad ~ios nostros *Cl* 382.

9 penny as minimal amount: **a** (w. neg. or *vix*); **b** (w. *ultimus*).

a patris tui satellites regale sic servant erarium ut vix unum tuis clientibus inde possis dare ~ium ORD. VIT. V 10 p. 377; BRAKELOND 128v. (v. decipere d); s**1213** nec quidem ~ium unum ad expensas itineris portare permisit WEND. II 97; c**1256** magni burgenses nunquam pacant ~ium *IMisc* 10/7; **1308** in nullo ~io ei tenetur *CourtR Wakefield* II 136;

ait puella: "amen dico tibi, nullum ~ium habebis" *Latin Stories* 121; **1365** dicit quod ipsi aliquem ~ium de ~iis regis predicto priori nunquam accomodavit *Cl* 203 m. 24; **1373** absque hoc quod .. misit xxx li. vel aliquem ~ium *SelCKB* VI 172; **1460** affirmavit quod nullum ~ium nec aliquam mundi pecuniam .. Johanni .. debet (*Assembly Bk. King's Lynn*) *Bronnen* 1506. **b 1350** quousque idem comes ultimum ~ium de redempcione sua domino regi persolvisset *SelCKB* VI 70; **s1373** eciam si contigerit me expendere omnia bona mea usque ad ultimum ~ium *Ghost Stories* 86.

10 penny as unit of weight, pennyweight.

c1100 justa [i.e. juxta] Gallos vicesima pars uncie ~ius est et xij ~ii solidum reddunt *Eng. Weights* 5 (cf. ib. 8); **1208** j cuppam deauratam .. ponderis lij solidorum vj ~iorum; .. [j c]uppam deauratam .. ponderis v marcarum, xj unciarum, x ~iorum *Invent. Exch.* p. 123; **1241** pro perlis ponderis iiij unciarum et viij ~iorum *Liberate* 15 m. 13; **a1250** quando quarterium frumenti venditur pro xviij d., tunc panis albus et bene coctus de quadrante de wastello ponderabit iiij libras x solidos et viij ~ios (*Assis. Panis*) *StRealm* I 199; **†1303** ~ius Anglicanus, qui vocatur sterlyngus, rotundus et sine tonsura ponderabit xxxij grana frumenti in medio spice; et uncia debet ponderare xx ~ios (*Assis. Pond.*) *Ib.* 204; **1321** assaiebantur balancie et pondera civitatis .. et invente sunt per omnes particulas concordantes ponderibus domini regis, excepto quod deficit de pondere viij marcarum civitatis pondus ij ~iorum oboli *MGL* II 383; **1425** inventum est dictam dim. unciam puri argenti post sumpcionem de igne excedere standardum predictum in allaio per unum ~ium ponder[is] ad libram *Pat* 419 m. 18.

11 reward (w. ref. to *Matth.* xx 9–10).

Dominus in carne apparens ~ium nobis regni celestis promisit. decalogum legis nos perficere posse .. concessit BEDE *Gen.* 96; post terminum hujus fluctivagi ponti valerem sumere partem aeterni ~ii BYRHT. *V. Ecgwini* 362; ~ius vitae monachilis .. esse debet perfectior quam clericalis ANSELM *Misc.* 305; decimum [caput] est .. de cavendo litigio ..; sed usque ad perfectionis ~ium .. dilectionem non perducimus si horribilem .. litigii tonitruum non devitamus AD. SCOT *OP* 515B; ~ium eterne remunerationis accepit a Domino J. FURNESS *Kentig.* 8 p. 177.

denarrata v. denariata.

denasci [cf. CL nasci], to be born (of).

s1245 reperit unum librum .. qui loquebatur de triplici mundo .. sic: 'in tercio mundo filius ~etur de Virgine Maria ..' *Meaux* II 72 (= HIGD. VII 36 p. 236: nascetur).

denaturare, to behave degenerately.

hec est gens illa que denaturat in aula, / potibus atque cibis dum manet ipsa tuis GOWER *VC* V 637 (cf. ib. I 979: o denaturans urbis natura prioris).

denberum, ~us [AS *denbǣr*], woodland pasture, esp. for swine (Kent). *Cf.* 1 *denna.*

759 (12c) adjectis iiij daenberis in communi saltu, hoc est Uuealdseuuestra Billincgden, [etc.] *CS* 194 (cf. ib. 260, 303); **764** (12c) cohaerent huic terrae in commune (*sic*) saltu ~i iij *CS* 195 (cf. ib. 779: *ða denbæro*); **804** (13c) cum .. xiij *denberende CS* 316 (= ELMH. *Cant.* 341: cum xiij *dennes* †glandis [l. glandes] portantibus); **838** (1000) adjectis iiij ~is, Hwætonstede, Heah dæn, Hese, Helman hyrst *CS* 418; **863** haec sunt pascua porcorum que nostra lingua Saxhonica ~a nominamus, hoc est Efreðingdenn, Bleccingdenn, [etc.] *CS* 507 (cf. ib. 496).

dencherus [? ME *daȝene chere*], a form of day-work (Chilhampton, Wilts), interp. by ed. as 'denshiring'.

1315 inveniet j hominem ad faciendum j dencher', viz. quolibet die Martis et Jovis operabili inter gulam Augusti [1 *Aug.*] et festum Decollacionis S. Johannis [29 *Aug.*] et eciam quolibet die operabili preter Sabbatum inter festum D. S. J. et festum S. Mich. et extenditur quodlibet opus valere quad., et non plus, quia non operabitur nisi usque horam diei primam. et, quia estimantur communibus annis advenire xxiiij dies operabiles ad hujusmodi dencherr' faciend[os], estimantur ~i cujuslibet virgate terre valere per annum in universo vj d. *Surv. Pembr.* app. 543 (cf. ib. lxii).

dendritis [CL < δενδρῖτις], sort of precious stone.

smaragdus, scythis et jaspis, heliotropius, ~es et hyacinthius ex utroque latere [corone] rutilare perhibentur ALB. LOND. *DG* 8. 7.

dendrolibanum [δενδρολίβανος], rosemary (*Rosmarinus*).

~um, i. ros marinus *SB* 17; ~um, libanotidos vel libantus, ros †marini [v. l. marinus], G. et A. *ros[e]maryn Alph.* 49; *rosemaryn*, ~um, herba est *CathA.*

denechus v. Daneschus. **Denegaldum** v. Danegeldum.

denegare [CL]

1 to refuse, deny (thing requested or sim.); **b** (w. abstr. subj.). **c** to decline to surrender. **d** (w. inf.) to refuse. **e** (w. acc. & inf.) to forbid, refuse to allow. *V. et.* 1 *deniare.*

GILDAS *EB* 67 (v. commessor); undarum gurgites, dantes gloriam Deo ab infidelibus ~atam ALDH. *VirgP* 51; **814** quod si quisque huic largitioni contradixerit, contradicat ei Deus et ~et ingressum caelestis vitae *CS* 346; **8..** ne ~es, *ne forwern ðu WW*; **s1095** utrum omnem subjectionem et obedientiam .. an illam solam .. quam pretenderet ex auctoritate Romani pontificis Anselmo ~assent EADMER *HN* 74; **1290** denicaverunt †Willelmum [? l. Willelmo] .. partem in lana paccanda *Rec. Leic.* I 215; **1310** denicavit districcionem communi serjanti *Ib.* 270; **c1332** cum nichil tanto domino in regno suo licite possit aut debeat ~ari J. MASON *Ep.* 17; **1381** (v. denegatio 1); inter prandendum tibi potus sit dĕnegandus *Dietarium* 60. **b** securae quietis spatium .. ecclesiastici regiminis sollicitudo ~abat ALDH. *VirgP* 59. **c 1268** iterato venit ad dictam heredem postulandam, et ipsam [mater et avia] ~averunt *JustIt* 618 r. 13*d*. **d 716** angeli precipiebant ei .. ut universa quae illi ostensa fuerunt credentibus .. manifestare non dubitaret, insultantibus autem narrare ~aret BONIF. *Ep.* 10; qui ab hominibus cognosci ~at, agnosci a feris .. quaerit FELIX *Guthl.* 39. **e 1268** Radulfum in forma communi replegiari ~asti *Cl* 476.

2 (w. acc. & inf. or absol.) to deny (a proposition).

non est grammaticus neque retor querit haberi; / Quintilianus eum deneget esse suum NIG. *Poems* 409; nemo simul potest .. exercere Christi ministerium et officium advocati. .. non inficior neque ~o P. BLOIS *Ep.* 26. 92A.

denegatio [LL]

1 refusal, denial (of request, right or sim.).

cognita condebitorum reversione et reditus ~one GILDAS *EB* 19; nec compelli debet ad hoc per ~onem actionis in assisa BRACTON 199; **s1297** clero in ~one persistente subsidii, rex ipsum a sua proteccione exclusit RISH. 168; **1305** cum .. a quodam gravamine et juris ~one per vos .. sibi .. illatis .. ad nostram audienciam duxerit appellandum *RGasc* III 465; **c1340** in hiis que .. non possunt absque ~one gracie ac juris injuria denegari *FormOx* 152; **1381** denegata est communio subditi regis Scocie trucidati, capti et depredati et dicta ~o communionis fuit proclamata in Anglia *RScot* II 38a; **1456** que sit pena .. ~onis fidelitatis .. domino BEKYNTON II 141.

2 denial (of occurrence).

785 saepe ex ignorantia sive etiam ex inprobitate contingit ut ~o rerum vere gestarum nascatur *CS* 247.

Denegeldum, ~gilda v. Danegeldum. **Denelaga, ~laha** v. Danelaga. **denerata, deneriat-** v. denariata.

denerellus, ~a [OF *denerel*], 'denerel', $\frac{1}{5}$ or $\frac{1}{6}$ of bushel (C. I.) *Cf. denariata* 3.

1309 reddit domino regi per annum ij buss' et j danerell' frumenti ad parvam mensuram *S. Jers.* XVIII 140; **1331** reddunt eidem tenentes de redditu vocato mellag' xxx quar. j bucellum iiij denerelas frumenti parve mensure et rase, .. viz. pro qualibet bovata viij denerelas frumenti *Ext. Guern.* 105 (cf. ib. 88: unde vj denerele faciunt bucellum; v. et. ib. p. v).

deneriata, ~ius, v. denar-. **deneschius, deneschus, denescus, denesus** v. Daneschus. **Denegeldum** v. Danegeldum. **denha** v. 1 denna. **deni** v. 2 denus.

1 deniare [OF *denier* < denegare], **a** to refuse, reject; *v. et. denegare* 1. **b** to condemn.

a justiciarius .. billam debet recipere et tradere eam .. juratoribus, ita quod .., si non sit verum, quod ~iant illam billam *State Tri. Ed. I* 69. **b 1287** ad quem diem predictus R. ~iatus est per verba recreancie *Gaol Del.* 36/1 r. 26*d*.

2 deniare v. dennere. **denicare** v. denegare 1a. **denichilare** v. denihilare.

denigrare [CL]

1 to blacken. **b** to dye black.

~atos lebetes et furviores fuligine caccabos ALDH. *VirgP* 50; fuscatus, i. ~atus .., *asweartad GlH* D 1001; cepit totum corpusculum ~ari W. CANT. *Mir. Thom.* III 33; [mulier] desecti, cruentati, jam ~ati .. corporis speciem minus discernere valens *V. Har.* 17 f. 21b; *G. S. Alb.* I 287 (v. caelatura 2a); sicut carbo primo ignitur, deinde ~atur GAD. 29v. 1; UPTON 102 (v. dealbare 4a). **b** habebit vestem clausam de blanketo ~ato *Cust. Cant.* I 278; **1392** pro j furra pro jupa domini ~ata *Ac. H. Derby* 280.

2 (fig.): **a** to blacken (character), denigrate, asperse. **b** to tarnish, defile, disgrace. **c** to darken, cast a gloom over. **d** (?) to overshadow, smother.

a s653 eorum innocentiam erga regem .. adulator sedulus ~abat M. PAR. *Maj.* I 288 (cf. ib. 474); **12..** malicia aliquorum, qui .. a me graciam ipsius [prioris] nituntur auferre et famam ~are *Ann. Durh.* app. 106; GRAYSTANES 46 (v. demereri 2e); **c1340** fama et status dictorum magistrorum leditur et ipsorum opinio multipliciter ~atur *FormOx* 170; **p1382** talia fingunt de viris catholicis, ut suam famam ~ent (WYCL.) *Ziz.* 283. **b** J. SAL. *Pol.* 699C (v. 1 committere 2c); cum per miserantis Opificis manum imago ipsius [sc. homo] ~ata reformatur H. BOS. *Thom.* IV 13; **s1173** comes [Flandrie] cum victoria simul et cum gaudio remeasset ad propria, nisi quia proditionis nota suos ~aret successus DICETO *YH* I 373; WALT. WIMB. *Palpo* 165 (v. deliliare); per incontinentie maculam famam suam .. ~avit GIR. *JS* 2 p. 161; ~antes statum regie dignitatis FAVENT 3; **1409** effrenata .. dissensionum .. continuacio, que .. morum venustatem, sciencie claritatem odoriferamque fame suavitatem fere .. ~averit *StatOx* 204; **1440** abusus quibus ecclesie status vel existimacio leditur et ~atur BEKYNTON II 94. **c 1436** quos constat rebellione intranea tranquillitatem nostri studii ~asse *EpAcOx* 142; **s1445** cujus [delphine] inopina .. mors .. multorum corda tam Francie quam Scocie dolore nimio ~avit *Plusc.* XI 7. **d** dicunt .. quidam quod apium †ravinum [l. raninum] ligatum super pulsus preservat a febre et curat; sed hoc erit aut dispergendo co[leram] aut ~ando calorem (*sic*) febris, quemadmodum dicit Ypo[crates] GILB. I 18v. 1; dolor membri major superveniens dolorem alterius membri ~at et ejus diminuit sensibilitatem, ut patet in freneticis BART. ANGL. V 1.

denigratio [LL]

1 blackening. **b** dyeing black.

niger .. componitur denigro, .. unde .. ~o OSB. GLOUC. *Deriv.* 373; cum colera in diversis locis putrefiat .., fit .. quasi quedam per adustionem [urine] ~o GILB. I 22v. 2; quanto fuerit magis dominium humidi, dummodo sit dominium calidi, tanto major erit fumus et caligo et ~o BACON XIV 67; contra lingue ~onem et adustionem fiat locio frequenter cum aqua rosata GAD. 7v. 1. **b 1325** pro viij ulnis panni pro capuciis cum ~one et tonsione ejusdem *Ac. Durh.* 166.

2 (fig.) blackening (of character), tarnishing.

illi ad .. delictorum recognitionem sua forte valuit confusio mihique fame et opinionis ~o ad spiritum humilitatis obtinendum .. plurimum profuit GIR. *Symb.* I 28 p. 299; **s1380** (v. calefurinus); **1384** in ~onem fame famosioris studii tocius orbis notabiliter cederet si hereticus condemnatus esset inter doctores catholicos tante universitatis receptus (*Inst. Notarii*) *Ziz.* 350; **s1391** papa .. videns hec in ~onem fame regie redundare WALS. *HA* II 200; **1482** in grave sui dispendium clericalique ordinis obprobrium ac gravamen [et] fame ~onem *Reg. Whet.* II 250.

denigrator, one who blackens (fig.), denigrator.

invidus percutitur mordax oblatrator, / thalami gemmiferi niger denigrator GARL. *Epith.* VI *Summa* 38.

denigrescere [LL], to turn black. **b** to grow dark.

niger .. componitur .. ~o OSB. GLOUC. *Deriv.* 373; **s1272** sirurgici .. medicamenta imponunt, sed .. videntes ~ere carnem mussitaverunt inter se W. GUISB. 209; *to make blak*, .. nigrescere, de- *CathA.* **b** in hoc tempore [hyeme] .. convalescunt frigora et exasperantur venti .., obscuratur aer, ~unt tempora BACON V 80.

denihilare [cf. nihilare], to annul. *V. et annihilare* 3a.

949 (13c) si qui .. hoc regale eulogium denichilent, ad nichilum redigantur *Ch. Burton* 8; **s1292** juramentum solemne in regis coronacione factum .. omnia alia juramenta incaute facta et privata .. extinguit et denichilat [v. l. annichilat] *Plusc.* VIII 17.

denique [CL], finally, in conclusion. **b** (in continuing argument, narrative, or sim.) next, moreover, and then.

vipera dira manum .. momordit; / sed Paulus gelidum non sensit vulnere virus / laedere ..; / denique .. celydrum / protinus in flammas torrendum tradidit atras ALDH. *CE* 4. 2. 29; **680** ~e solerter peto ut nullus post obitum nostrum hoc donativum in irritum facere praesumat *CS* 47; Osuald .. regna terrarum plus quam ulli majorum suorum .. consecutus est. ~e omnes nationes .. Brittaniae .. in dicione accepit BEDE *HE* III 7; ~e, postremo *GlC* D 285; expugnata ~e Bedefordia *G. Steph.* I 24; tertia [pars operis hujus] .. de gentis Hibernicae .. moribus ejusdemque per advenas expugnationibus, totam ~e gentis hujus .. producit historiam GIR. *TH intr.* p. 8; ~e, A. *at laste or forsothe WW*. **b** ~e plerumque, ut experti sumus, castitatis conscientia elationis pulsatur cenodoxia ALDH. *VirgP* 16; sub eodem ~e tempore .., cum quodam die .. psalmis .. incumberet, tunc antiquus hostis prolis humanae .. novas artes .. versat FELIX *Guthl.* 29; haec .. de se .. referre consuerat. ~e tempore quodam secreto, cum diacono suo .. conloquens, .. dolendo subjunxit .. BEDE *HE* II 1 p. 74; miles ~e, cum quo .. sacerdos mansitabat, ad limina .. apostolorum pervenire desiderabat BYRHT. *V. Osw.* 405.

1 denna [AS *denn*], den, woodland pasture, usu. for swine (esp. Kent), but not easily dist. from 1 *dena. Cf. denberum, drovedenna*; *v. Cart. Bilsington* 5 *seqq.*

ad ista iij solina sunt v denae *DB* I (*Kent*) 2; de silva regis habet Wadardus tantum quod reddit xvj d. per annum; et dimidiam denam tenet, quam T. R. E. quidam villanus tenuit *Ib.* 2v. (cf. ib.: de silva viij denae parvae et iij magnae); j denam silvae et j croftam *Ib.* (*Surrey*) 30v.; terciam partem unius denae *Ib.* (*Berks*) 56v.; **c1210** me dedisse et concessisse Radulfo de B. L. pro suo servicio denam de meo dominio apud meridiem castelli de C. *Cart. Carisb.* f. 69; **c1236** in villa de Wy [*Kent*] sunt xxvj juga servilia .. et j virgata .., que non habet nemus suum sine redditu sicud alia, et jugum unum .., sc. Henwode quod habet ~am suam per se *Cust. Battle* 133; **1239** abbas de Beggeham summonitus fuit ad respondendum .. quo waranto tenet j ~am cum pertinentiis in Elleford' [*Ayles-*

ford, Kent] *BNB* III 283 (cf. *CurR* XVI 24); **1286** sunt ibidem [*Boughton, Kent*] in ~is de Waldis due consuetudines que vocantur *heueshale* et *seuighale IPM* 45/1 r. 2; **1293** homines .. ~arum [de Wytheryngdenn etc.] bene cognoverunt quod ipsi simul cum hominibus hundredi de Eyhorn' [*Kent*] reparare debent medietatem .. pontis [de Eyhorn'] (*CoramR*) *Pub. Works* I 199 (cf. *CalPat 1348–50* 472); **1351** debent tenentes istarum ~arum sectam curie de Northbourne *Reg. S. Aug.* 78; **1458** iiij acras de terra ~e *Ib.* 111; **1406** indentura cujusdam ~e de Shlepyndenne in parochia de Smerdenne de ij s. annui redditus pro quadam consuetudine vocata *daungyr* (*DCCant.* B 3) *Cart. Bilsington* 20n.; **1441** super denham de Speldhurst [*Kent*] *Reg. Cant.* II 574; **1535** tenentes terrarum ~e de Hokrige .. in Wilda Kancie *Rutland MSS View of MinAc Salop etc.* p. 93.

2 denna, ~um, (use of) 'denne' or 'denes' (higher ground on sand-bank) at Yarmouth (Norf).

c**1157** nos [barones de Hastingges] concedimus .. S. Benedicto de H. terram illam apud Gernemut' quam tenet Adam .. in ~o *Reg. S. Ben. Holme* 133; **1238** mandatum est custodibus nundinarum de Jernem' quod baronibus de Rumenal [*Romney, Kent*] faciant habere ~as, strandas, et alia loca que in nundinis predictis habere consueverunt .. temporibus H. regis et R. regis et J. regis *Cl* 100; **1278** confirmasse .. baronibus nostris [V Portuum] .. quod habeant *den* et *strond* apud Gernemuth' secundum quod continetur in ordinacione per nos inde facta *ChartR* 66 m. 2 *sched.* (cf. S. Jeake *Charters of Cinque Ports*, (London 1728), p. 12).

3 denna v. 1 duna b.

dennagium [cf. Dutch *denne = flooring of a ship*], (naut.) dunnage, packing.

1298 in fretagio unius navis .. ducentis dolia et bladum .. et denagio ejusdem navis, construccione unius granarii in eadem navi ad bladum predictum .. *Pipe* 143 r. 21d. (*Northumb*); **1300** pro .. portagio et †quindagio [l. guindagio] ejusdem bladi, ~io ejusdem in ix navibus .. *AcWardr* p. 107 (cf. ib. p. 133: pro .. ~io navis dictum bladum cariantis inter loca predicta); **1306** pro ~io ejusdem avene in navi *KRAc* 369/11 f. 73; **1315** in bordis, lignis, stramine et feno, necnon et batellagio, ~io et circulagio .. victualium *Doc. Ir.* 330; **1336** (v. calfatatio); **1351** (v. dennere); **1377** in dcc *lattes* emptis pro ~io iiij navium pro .. victualibus cariandis usque London' *MinAc* 1096/6.

dennarratus v. denariata.

dennere, ~iare [cf. dennagium], (naut.) to 'dunnage'.

1300 in predictis bladis cariandis per diversa loca, predicta navi ~enda, cum lodmannis locatis *MinAc* 1132/10 m. 19; **1351** in denagio allocato de diversis hominibus in villis Cantebr', Ely, et Wysbech' ad predictas viij kelas deniandas pro dictis victualibus salvandis ne perirent in aqua, pro denagio cujuslibet kely xij d. viij s. *KRAc* 552/33 m. 7.

dennum v. 2 denna.

denobilitari [cf. CL nobilitare], to disennoble.

nobilis es generis nisi te denobiliteris; / ludicra sectatur qui se denobilitatur R. Cant. *Malch.* I 38–9.

denodare [cf. CL nodare]

1 to untie; **b** (fig.). *V. et. enodare* 1.

[novicii] sedendo coram lectis suis deponant calciamenta .. et, ~ato bracili anterius et extracto, inponant novis femoralibus *Cust. Cant.* 10. **b** mortis nodum denodavit / rosa, Deum que portavit Garl. *SM* 109; hic Veneris nodum strictum denodo *Id. Tri. Eccl.* 105; Wycl. *Incarn.* 77 (v. corrigia 2d).

2 to solve, resolve. **b** to explain. *V. et. enodare* 2.

satelles [regis], posteriori questionis parte, quam solvere nullatenus poterat, omissa, sic ~avit anteriorem .. Ben. Pet. *Pass. Thom.* 1 p. 3; s**1252** ut .. 'nodum querens in scirpo' [cf. Terence *Andr.* V 4. 38], .. perplexa ~aret M. Par. *Maj.* V 277. **b** **1187** scribimus in nube vobis .., nolentes omnibus exprimere vel ~are .. que .. papa vestre ecclesie .. indulsit *Ep. Cant.* 50.

denominabilis, (phil.) denominable.

accidencia .. informant sua subjecta et a se ~ia faciunt, ut 'magnum', 'parvum', 'album', 'nigrum', et ita in ceteris *Ps.*-Gros. *Summa* 343; non oportet quod [ille certus conceptus] insit utrique illorum [dubiorum] 'in quid', sed ut sic, vel est univocus eis ut determinabilis ad determinantes vel ut ~is ad denominantes Duns *PW* 7; eodem modo, quamvis sit ibi sapor, non tamen est ibi subjectum sustentans saporem ~em a sapore. ex quo sequitur plane quod quantitas non est subjectum informatum qualitatibus illis nec ~is ab eis. si enim substaret qualitatibus illis, vere esset ponderosa .., alba, dulcis vel amara Ockham *Sacr. Alt.* 272.

denominalis, (?) relating to source from which name is derived.

Augustinus loquens .. de veritate quiditatis et imitationis dicit: 'si veram [speciem] haberent, animus essent.' unde, sicut duplex est forma, exemplaris et essentialis, sic duplex est veritas, exemplaris et ~is Peckham *QA* 219.

denominanter, by way of assigning a name.

opus nature est opus prime intelligencie; nec dissentitur isti conclusioni nisi erronee intelligendo Deum univoce applicare vires cum creaturis et non summe ~er dicendo producere Wycl. *Ente Praed.* 132.

denominare [CL]

1 to denominate, distinguish by a name (derived from a spec. source). **b** to denominate (phil.), characterize. **c** to specify.

957 (14c) partem cujusdam telluris concedo .. in loco ubi a ruricolis ~atur At Lym *CS* 995; 'originale' ab 'origine' ~ari dubium non est Anselm (*Orig. Pecc.* 1) II 140; ab ipso [Merlino] ibidem invento ~ata est Kaermerdyn Gir. *IK* II 8; ubi non fuerit nisi unica villa in manerio, ~ari possunt uno nomine .., quia villa ~atur a manerio et manerium a villa e contrario Bracton 434. **b** Anselm I 159 (v. denominativus 1); dispositiones que ~ate sunt sunt ille que contracte sunt et habilitatem [dant] ad alicujus forme determinatam susceptionem Bacon VIII 29; motus naturalis ~atur a suo termino *Id.* XIII 91; Duns *PW* 7 (v. denominabilis); si actus tales odiendi per se mali essent forme absolute naturaliter bone, Deus ordinaret quod [he forme] ~arent subjecta odire Deum et taliter velle Wycl. *Act.* 23; *Ib.* 42 (v. efficienter); discrepat forma exemplaris a forma intrinseca in hoc quod nulla forma exemplaris ab intrinseco sed ab extrinseco ~at illud cujus est exemplar; e contra autem est de quacunque forma intrinseca *Id. Form.* 164 (cf. denominatio 1c). **c** iste consuetudines pertinent ad Tantone: *burgheristh* [etc.] .. has ~atas consuetudines reddunt in Tantone hae terrae .. *DB* I (*Som*) 87v.; si de hac re culpabilis es .. aut propter actam culpam ~atam sciens factores juvisti (*Jud. Dei*) *GAS* 420.

2 to nominate, assign, appoint. **b** to bequeath.

vicecomes .. ~avit illis constitutum tempus .., ut ambo adfuissent *DB* II 424; **1438** postquam aliquis pauperum hospitalis predicte (*sic*) decesserit vel amotus fuerit, alius pauper loco ejusdem per patronum .. ~etur *Cl* 289 m. 32d.; **1522** cum .. sedes S. Andree a primevo religionis Christiane exordio unicus Scotorum episcopus (*sic*) ~abatur alieque episcoporum regni Scocie sedes .. ab eadem .. derivate sunt *Form. S. Andr.* I 234. **b** de terra Tosti .. dicunt quod Eric frater ejus ~avit eam aecclesiae de Ramesy post mortem suam et fratris et sororis suae *DB* I (*Hunts*) 208v.

3 to denominate (math.).

dicimus differentias generis minutiarum denominationes esse, siquidem 5ae a quinario, 7ae a septenario, undecimae quoque ab undenario ~antur Adel. *Alch.* 2 p. 23.

denominatio [CL]

1 denomination, designation; **b** (rhet.); **c** (phil.). **d** description, specification. **e** (?) category. **f** (?) determinant.

s**1239** natus est domino regi .. filius primogenitus .. et est Eadwardus vocitatus, qui ~onem accepit a glorioso rege et confessore Eadwardo *Flor. Hist.* II 231; per ~ones membrorum visibilium intelliguntur invisibiles actiones celestium animorum Bart. Angl. II 3; ad unam mansionem pertinere poterunt plura tenementa et genera tenementorum .. diversis nominibus specificata, que cum ad mansionem pertineant .. non poterunt dici quod sint in tali villa specificata ~one mansionis Bracton 434; tale jus .. usitato vocabulo dicitur 'beneficium' et ita accipit ~onem ab accessorio et non principali Paul. Angl. *ASP* 1531. **b** quando sic minus commune ponitur pro magis communi, color est qui appellatur ~o Vinsauf *AV* II 4. 5 (cf. ib. 3. 25: exornatio rhetorica que appellatur ~o). **c** Bacon XV 206 (v. conservatio 1a; cf. denominative); non solum mentitur [Averroys] de nomine aggregati sed de nominatione propria ipsius forme et aggregati, quia dignius est aggregatum nominari †quam [? *omit*] forma propria ~one quam forma sua propria nominacione *Id. CSTheol.* 50; conveniunt omnes forme analoice in hoc quod quelibet denominat formatum, extendendo ~onem ad quodlibet nomen substanciale vel accidentale Wycl. *Form.* 163; est totus ubique sine dimensione, qui habet omnes ~ones hujusmodi satis equivoce et positive ac privative quodam modo infinite *Id. Trial.* 42. **d** **1298** debet ferre breve suum de manerio aut carucata sive per numerum acrarum terre .. ~o terre per virgatam .. in comitatu illo [*Norf*] non est cognita sive usitata *PIRCP* 125 m. 230d. **e** quod idem sit caro Christi et panis secundum speciem, et sic secundum substanciam indivisibilis, secundum speciem divisibilis, et sic de aliis ~onibus (Tyss.) *Ziz.* 152. **f** **1410** unde descendit hujusmodi confluencia finalis docebit eventus, qui est et esse debet cujuscumque rei ~o principalis *Fabr. York* 194 (cf. confluentia d).

2 **a** nomination (of person). **b** presentation (eccl.).

a **1416** feoffabunt .. episcopum †suas [? l. seu] alias personas ad suam ~onem in predicto tenemento *Deeds Balliol* 124; **1438** in quibus diverse persone ex confidencia et ad meam ~onem feoffati existunt *Reg. Cant.* II 576; **1517** panellum illud arraiatum fuit per R. nuper vicecomitem .. ad ~onem predicti J. et in favorem ejusdem J. *Entries* 116b. **b** s**1361** ecclesias parochiales .. quarum advocaciones et ~ones .. ex concessione .. regum Anglie .. habebamus *Meaux* III 116; s**1426** ~o ecclesie S. Mich. [*rub.*]: .. magistrum J.C. .. ad ecclesiam S. Mich. .. presentandum vobis nominamus *Lit. Cant.* III 148.

3 (math.): **a** denominator. **b** denomination, integral or rational number expressing ratio in the lowest terms.

a †adumbia [l. adverbia] a nominibus distorta ~ones vocamus: sic semel ab uno, bis a duobus Thurkill *Abac.* 57v.; Adel. *Alch.* 2 (v. denominare 3); vere ergo respondit divisio multiplicationi, quoniam in ~onibus sunt xxxiii, qui ducti fuerant in se ipsos ut inde produc[er]entur i o viii ix Ocreatus *Helceph* 137; accipe numerum ~onis parcium racionalium per se, et numerum dencium per se, si fuerint infra integrum ~onis, vel numerum qui superabundat ab integro ~onis per se, et cum illis duobus numeris intra 'Tabulam Proporcionis' distinctam per titulos Wallingf. (*Horol.*) I 450. **b** in superiori .. ponendi sunt divisores, in media dividenda, in inferiori .. ~ones Thurkill *Abac.* 57v.; diviso primo per secundum exit ~o; ergo ducta ~one in secundum producitur primum .. quia *B* est ~o proporcionis *C* ad *A*, ducta *B* in *A* producitur *C*, sicut diviso *C* per *B* exibit *A* Wallingf. (*Quad.*) 58.

denominative, derivatively, by derivation.

de 'grammatico' peto ut me certum facias utrum sit substantia an qualitas, ut, hoc cognito, quid de aliis quae similiter ~e dicuntur sentire debeam agnoscam Anselm (*Gram.* 1) I 145; quoniam genus univoce et non ~e, sic nec secundum quid predicatur J. Sal. *Met.* 905D; *Ib.* 895A (v. aequivoce a); aut nominative excommunicati .. aut saltem excommunicati †de nominative excommunicatorum participio H. Bos. *Thom.* IV 23; 'animal sanum', id est 'sanum' ~e dictum proprie, quia formaliter predicatur de animali et est in eo sicut accidens in subjecto Bacon XV 206 (cf. denominatio 1c); Gros. 130 (v. adjacenter).

denominativus [LL]

1 (gram. & phil.) denominative, derivative.

[nomina] alia principalia, ut 'mons' ..; alia derivativa, ut 'mons, montanus' ..; alia ~a, ut 'sanctus, sanctitas' Alcuin *Gram.* 860A; bonus *ys nama, þonne byð of ðam* bonitas *godnys* ~um *of ðam naman* Ælf. *Gram.* 17; si in 'grammatico' 'homo' intelligendus est cum 'grammatica', intelligendum est similiter in omnibus similibus ~is id quod denominatur cum eo a quo denominatur Anselm (*Gram.* 13) I 159; J. Sal. *Met.* 893B (v. consignificatio); Bacon XV 207 (v. cadentia b); augmentacio deest elemento secundum formalem et ~am inherenciam, licet insit secundum naturalem causanciam Wycl. *Log.* III 118; nomina connotancia subjectum et sibi accidentaliter inexistens vocantur ~a *Id. Ente Praed.* 21.

2 appointed.

~o termino profectionis, undecumque venerant repedarunt W. Jum. II 1.

denominator [LL = *one who names*], (math.) denominator.

si alicujus generis fraccionum fuerit numerus quadrandus, ~or radicis est subduplus ad ~orem numeri quadrandi Killingworth *Alg.* 716.

denoscere v. dinoscere. **Denoschus** v. Daneschus.

denotare [CL]

1 to mark, brand.

solent quorundam criminum rei in facie cauterio ~ari Ailr. *Serm.* 399C.

2 to note (in writing).

930 (14c) testibus .. quorum nomina subtus caracteribus depicta ~antur *CS* 669.

3 to indicate, denote.

s**1327** hoc verbum .. inventum est ad ~andum tercium Edwardum Ad. Mur. *Chr.* 55 (v. conquaestus 2b); Hothby *Cant. Fig.* 331 (v. circulus 1e).

4 to indicate w. disapproval, stigmatize, reproach; **b** (w. pers. obj.); **c** (w. compl.).

nullatenus ipsius in ulla epulationis aviditate vel modicus poterat ~ari excessus H. Bos. *Thom.* III 16 p. 231. **b** munus .. accipiat, ne sponsum vel sponsam .. in aliena patria exprobret aut in ceteris nuptiis ~et *G. Herw.* 323. **c** neque reum denoto Pharaonis Deum *Poem S. Thom.* 89.

denotatio [CL]

1 mark, brand (fig.).

hos infamiae ~one polluunt (*Quad. Dedic.*) *GAS* 531.

2 (?) note (of final concord).

1205 dies datus est .. ad recipiendum cirographum ... nos habemus den[otationem] *CurR* III 252 (cf. ib. 233: nos habemus notam. *But* (?) l. den[arios]).

3 token, expression.

1173 reverendo domino .. pontifici .. cum salute pronam debite subjectionis ~onem *Ch. Sal.* 37.

denote v. devote 1a. **denotus** v. dinoscere.

dens [CL]

1 tooth (human or unspec.); **b** (in spec. phr.). **c** (w. *invitis* or sim.) against one's will; *cf.* OF *maugre ses dents*.

numquam pignora tantum / improba sic lacerant maternas dente papillas Aldh. *Aen.* 1 (*Terra*) 3; clamare, ~tibus

frendere, spumare .. coepit BEDE *HE* III 11; **8..** ~s putridus, *forrotad toð WW*; adversi ~tes, *ða eahta forworden teþ betwux tuxum* ÆLF. *Gl.*; ~tes alii precisores, alii canini, alii molares (*Leg. Hen.* 93. 6) *GAS* 609; ~tes, qui sunt quasi mole nature ad conterenda dura cibaria .., in naturam ossium vergunt in exterioribus et eciam in interiori extremitate in natura[m] nervi, unde et dolere dicuntur propter radices RIC. MED. *Anat.* 223; VINSAUF *PN* 576 (v. compaginare 1a); dolor ~tium et alie varie infirmitates *Spec. Eccl.* 38; refert utrum fracti sint ~tes precisores, molares sive maxillares BRACTON 145; **s1258** (v. deciduus 1a); GAD. 92v. 1 (v. citrum); *Ib.* 118v. 1 (v. comminutivus a); "in hujus .. rei" inquit "evidenciam sigillum ~tibus meis impressi" .. ubi usque in presens in .. cera apparent ~tium vestigia pro sigillo ELMH. *Cant.* 119. **b** de deifico tenore monachorumque decretis sub ~te primum multa ruminans GILDAS *EB* 34 (cf. ib. 74: sub ~te ruminatis); non tamen arbitror quod .. / .. dentes stridant in potu forte bibentum ALDH. *VirgV* 2975; per ~tes [Dei] GIR. *PI* III 29 (v. Deus 3c); J. SAL. *Met. prol.* 823B (v. concurialis); armatus usque ad ~tes *Proc. A. Kyteler* 25 (v. armare 2a). **c** **1278** maledicebat dominum W. .., dicendo diabolus ipsum penderet et quod sederet in curia malagratis ~tibus suis (*Husting Roll*) *Lond. Ed. I & II* II 252; **1282** si aliquis Walensis emerit aliquam rem .., Anglicus qualiscunque superveniret et rem venditam dicto Walensi ab ipso auferret, invitis ~tibus suis (*Querela hominum de Ros*) *Ep. Peckham* 344 p. 449; **1320** respondit quod non nisi invitis ~tibus et hoc se defendendo *SelCKB* IV 92; **1413** quousque ipse essenciam predicti T. fratris sui invitis ejus ~tibus detegebat (*Indict.*) *Collect. Staffs* XVII 6; **1430** (v. concumbere a).

2 tooth (animal). **b** (serpent's) tooth typifying malice.

ut caper hirsutus rodit cum dente racemos ALDH. *VirgV* 2845; vibrat aper pro dente caput, nam verba superbit / reddere; sed dentem vix tenet ira trucem WALT. ANGL. *Fab.* 11. 3–4; piscis .. tres ~tes .. aureos habens GIR. *TH* II 10; scriptor habeat .. ~tem verris sive apri .. ad poliendum pergamum NECKAM *Ut.* 116; **1205** de redditu .. de quolibet bove qui non arat et habeat latas ~tes, obolus *RNorm* 135; securus ab ejus [apri silvestris] ~tibus [ME: *carles of his tuskes*] *AncrR* 105. **b** praesulis ut famam serpentis dente lacessant ALDH. *VirgV* 925; ne vituperationis suae ~te nostrae adrodet opus diligentiae *V. Greg.* p. 106; ex ~tibus detractionis bella plusquam civilia orta sunt NECKAM *NR* II 107; **1317** ~te detraccionis nos comedunt *FormOx* 16.

3 (in plant name): **a** henbane (*Hyoscyamus*). **b** (?) birdsfoot trefoil (*Lotus corniculatus*). **c** dandelion (*Taraxacum*).

a jusquiamus, caniculata, .. ~s caballinus idem, †G. [v. l. A.] *henesbane Alph.* 84 (cf. ib. 49: ~s cabellinus, respice in 'jusquiamus'). **b** ~s equinus, sulphuraca idem, herba est; ciperus idem secundum quosdam *SB* 17; ~s equinus vel ~s equi, sulphuraca herba, muscus de ca[m]po idem. stipitem habet rubeum, crescit ad modum ciceris et habet folia minuta sicut trifolium et florem croceum; A. *tynthare [tinetare] Alph.* 49 (cf. ib. 186: tercium [trifolii genus] habet florem croceum et vocatur ~s equinus et crescit in pratis; A. *honisoucles*). **c** caput monachi, ~s leonis idem, herba est *SB* 16; den[s] leonis, capud monachi idem, cui folium †lactessit [v. l. lactescit] in fractione; G. *dent de lion*, A. *doleroune* [cf. AS *dolhrune*] *Alph.* 49; potest fieri levissima medicina cum .. endivia vel rostro porcino, ~te leonis, scolopendria .. GAD. 4v. 2; *preste crowne*, quedam herba vel flos, glos, ~s leonis *CathA*; non desunt qui putent *dandelyon*, sive Latine mavis ~tem leonis .., hujus erratici intubi esse speciem TURNER *Herb.* B ii.

4 **a** tooth of comb. **b** tooth of file. **c** tine (of harrow or sim.); *cf.* 1 *cavilla* 4. **d** share-beam of plough. **e** cog. **f** bar of grating.

a **794** mirum animal duo habens capita et ~tes sexaginta, non elefantinae magnitudinis sed eburneae pulchritudinis ALCUIN *Ep.* 26; NECKAM *NR* II 40 (v. discriminare 1b); **1245** pecten argenteus, in medio deauratus cum gravatura, ~tibus albis *Invent. S. Paul.* 468. **b** incipit hec [vipera] limam rodere, lima loqui: / .. "dente meo pateris, non ego dente tuo" WALT. ANGL. *Fab.* 48. 4; nemo velit dente dentes corrodere lime [*gl.*: lima est supellex fabrilis ~tes habens innumerabiles] D. BEC. 452. **c** plaustrum, in similitudine arcae rotas habens intus; et ipsae ~tes habent qui rostra dicuntur in quibus frangent spicas *GlC* P 481; **1358** ~tes ha[r]ciarum .. et alia diversa ferralia .. asportavit *Proc. J. P.* 186; **1364** in ~tibus unius hercie elongandis cum ferro domini *MinAc* 1024/7. **d** GARL. *Dict.* 235 (v. 1 dentale 1a). **e** habita rota certi numeri ~cium, unam aliam rotam invenire que habeat quotlibet ~tes equales ~tibus rote date WALLINGF. (*Horol.*) I 444. **f** **1343** fecerunt in .. venella latrinas supra ~tes, quarum putredo cadit super capita hominum transeuncium *MGL* II 449.

5 (pl.) 'teeth' typifying power (of Satan).

†**693** (14c) sub diris ~tibus salamandri *CS* 121; nostram gentem .. de ~tibus antiqui hostis eripiens BEDE *HE* II 1 p. 78.

densanter, in dense masses.

cum .. viderimus .. ignitos .. globos .. divise variis in locis agiliter sese et ~er movere *G. Steph.* I 24.

1 densare [CL], to condense, thicken. **b** to serry. **c** to clothe thickly. **d** to cause to come thick and fast.

cornu serpentis aerem veneno infectum .. trahit ipsumque ~ando in sudorem commutat NECKAM *NR* II 98; per admixtionem [flegmatis] grossi ingrossati a frigiditate comprimente et dempsante GAD. 3. 2; *to make thyke*, ~are, con- .., spissare *CathA*. **b** [Anglorum] pars ibi magna perit, pars et densata resistit G. AMIENS *Hast.* 435; undique densantur acies GARL. *Tri. Eccl.* 63; **s1297** ~ata caterva *Ann. Angl. & Scot.* 381. **c** hic .. ~atus pellibus et epytogiis, clamidi penulam superducit J. SAL. *Pol.* 760B. **d** sperabatur laetitia, et ecce unde ~entur suspiria ANSELM (*Prosl.* 1) I 99.

2 densare v. drensare.

densatim, densely, thickly. **b** in serried ranks.

velut apis .. scripturae flosculos .. congregavit, quis praecordii sui cellulas ~im replevit ASSER *Alf.* 88; profundum .. fodere vallum, ramisque arborum ~im superinsertis .. recesserunt DICETO *Chr.* 163. **b** Anglis ut mos est, densatim progredientes G. AMIENS *Hast.* 367.

dense [CL], densely, in a mass.

deferentes illud [corpus] .. sub immenso murmure lugentium populorum feretrum ~issime ambientium OSB. *V. Dunst.* 45; denseo, .. unde ~e, ~ius, ~issime adverb. OSB. GLOUC. *Deriv.* 171; cadavera civium per vicos ~issime jacentia H. HUNT. *HA* VI 7.

densēre [CL], **~escere** [LL], to be or grow thick. **b** (w. abl.) to be thick with, to be crowded in. **c** to become condensed. **d** to come thick and fast.

in summo capitis densescit vertice vellus ALDH. *Aen.* 91 (*Palma*) 8; ~escit, †spissas [l. spissat], *þiccaþ GlH* D 180; ~eo, -es, -ui, verb. neut. et caret supino; inde ~esco, -is, verbum inchoat. OSB. GLOUC. *Deriv.* 171; *to be thyke*, ~ere, con-, constipare *CathA*. **b** inde prava seges glitibus densescet acerbis ALDH. *VirgV* 2725; [formicae] innumerae †numero [? l. innumero] densescunt milite vero R. CANT. *Malch.* IV 53. **c** aqua de inferioribus hausta, ex quibus aer ~escit et incrassatur ALB. LOND. *DG* 6. 4; aer facile spissatur in †aqua [? l. aquam], ut in uligine terre perpendimus, que ventis in altum agitata ~escit in pluviam GERV. TILB. I 7. **d** infidelis populi ad arces solo coequandas impetus undique densessit infestus W. MALM. *Mir. Mariae* 154; ~escunt murmurationes, fabricantur mendacia BRAKELOND 143v.

densilitas v. densitas 1.

densim, densely, thickly. **b** in multitudes.

cartulae rotellam .. ~im apicibus conscriptam B. *V. Dunst.* 33. **b** hoc ipsum quod retulit mihi ipse, alii jam ~im submurmurabant H. BOS. *Thom.* V 5 p. 473.

densio, density.

raritas lucis, densio tenebrarum, / translucidi dies et noctes umbrose J. HOWD. *Cant.* 567.

densitas [CL]

1 thick growth.

940 in .. silvis silvarumque ~atibus *CS* 748 (cf. *CD* 783); infra ~atem saltus ABBO *Edm.* 12; ne sit nimia crinium unguiumve ~as aut prolixitas PULL. *Sent.* 986D; milites .. in silvule ~ate absconditos MAP *NC* IV 15 f. 57v.; **s1260** (v. 2 cooperire 4b); **1285** in boscis .. in quibus propter eorum ~atem .. homicidia frequenter perpetrabantur *BBC* (*Carmarthen*) 66; **s1297** Scoti .. in nemorum densilitate [? l. densitate] delituerunt *Ann. Angl. & Scot.* 381.

2 density (of matter). **b** solidity (of human frame). **c** density (of formation). **b** darkness.

~as, i. spissitudo *GlH* D 183; iste [aer], humoris ~ate superante, propinquam aque servat sedem; illum raritas suffert, istum ~as subruit ADEL. *QN* 62; oratione motus, pater ~atem nebule dissipavit W. CANT. *Mir. Thom.* IV 13; si opacitas non erit in corporibus glorificatis, ergo nec gravitas nec ~as, que eam concomitantur, erunt in eisdem HALES *Qu.* 1307; FISHACRE *Quaest.* 49 (v. densus 2a); [ad visum] exigitur soliditas seu ~as rei vise, quia quod est omnino pervium non videmus BART. ANGL. III 17. **b** vir magnus et incompositus .., Brithmerus Budde, pro ~ate sic congnominatus *Lib. Eli.* II 85; puer erat .. ex nimia ~ate membrorum admodum rotundus *G. Herw.* 320v.; composicio vestri corporis in textura mediocriter est rara, porosa et pervia, aliquantulum compacta ~ate declinans KYMER 3. **c** testudo, ~as †ramorum [l. armorum] *GlC* T 56.

3 density (of darkness). **b** darkness.

in valle .. profunda ~as est tenebrarum magna *Simil. Anselmi* 99. **b** W. MALM. *GP* III 101 (v. dirigere 3f).

densitudo, thickness.

~o murorum ecclesie continet ij virgas W. WORC. *Itin.* 282.

densura, thickness, density.

a thyknes, ~a, densitas, spissitudo *CathA*.

densus [CL]

1 (of woodland or sim.) dense, thick. **b** (as sb. n.) thicket.

~issimis saltibus GILDAS *EB* 25; saltus nemorum densos pariterque frutecta / .. sub aethere spargo ALDH. *Aen.* 93 (*Scintilla*) 6; *of þiccam felde*, de ~o campo *GlH* D 145; in loco .. silvis ~issimis .. obsito GIR. *EH* I 5; **s1415** mirum est quod dempsissimam ausus sit aggredi Francorum silvam [i.e. exercitum] *Chr. S. Alb.* 93. **b** sic migrando mansit de ~o in condenso ÆTHELW. II 17; [lepores Hibernici] in ~o, tanquam vulpes, et in operto non in aperto diffugiunt GIR. *TH* I 24.

2 (of matter) dense. **b** thick, packed, coming thick and fast. **c** (as sb. n.) density, solidity.

universaliter conjuncta sunt gravitas et grossities vel densitas, ut patet in elementis. et quod est grossissimum vel ~issimum est gravissimum FISHACRE *Quaest.* 49. **b** agmine denso GILDAS *EB* 9; [nix] nimbo / densior et nebulis ALDH. *Aen.* 67 (*Cribellus*) 4; stipatur milite denso *Id. VirgV* 1408 (cf. ib. 1118: faretrarum densas sufferre sagittas); ~um, spissum *GlC* D 43; frequentes, ~os, multos, *gelomlican GlH* F 717; pridie transfertur arca densissima ab undis *Kal. M. A.* I 404; [nebularum] sicut quedam tenues sunt, ita alie ~e, alie ~issime; .. ~iores itaque .. in nubes primo concrescunt ADEL. *QN* 64; BART. ANGL. III 17 (v. diaphaneitas); quasi jam Satana .. ~os congressus constiparet AD. MARSH *Ep.* 244 p. 490; GARL. *Syn.* 353. 1584A (v. cirrus b); **1450** (v. defensorius 1a). **c** rarum et ~um ad generationem successivam ordinantur, et similiter calidum et frigidum HALES *Qu.* 1306; dispositiones contrarie que sunt circa materiam primam .. sunt materiales, et sic rarum et dempsum; et sic rarum et dempsum faciunt primam contrarietatem BACON XIII 37.

3 (of darkness) dense (also fig.).

ad ~am .. noctem *Lib. Eli.* III 43 (v. consumere 1b); in tenebris ignorancie dempsissimis BACON I 4 (cf. ib. 7: in signum dempsum ignorancie).

1 dentale [CL], **~ium**

1 'chep', share-beam (of plough); *cf. dentile* b, *dentorium* (*cf. Antiquity* XXVII 167). **b** (?) runner of sledge.

~ia, *sules reost GlC* D 80; ~e, prima in qua vomer inducitur quasi dens, †sive [MS: scilicet] est aratri pars, *sule reost* vel *þroc GlH* D 179; ~e, *cipp* ÆLF. *Gl.*; [aratro] supponatur dentile vel ~e, cui vomer .. infigatur NECKAM *Ut.* 112; diversa instrumenta aratri, stivam, trabem, et dentem sive ~ea GARL. *Dict.* 129; usus abest aratri vacat et dentale relictum GOWER *VC* I 283; ~e, *chyppe WW*. **b** corpus .. funebri deformitate transfiguratum—nam digiti ~ium trahe formam pretendebant W. CANT. *Mir. Thom.* II 71.

2 prong.

W. CANT. *Mir. Thom.* VI 114 (v. bidentalis).

2 dentale, (?) sort of stone.

unguentum citrinum. recipe boracis, .. amidi cristalli, entalis ~is [etc.] GILB. III 147. 1 (cf. ib. VII 342. 2: acuatur cum pulvere litargiri entalis †dentalio et apponatur; cf. ib. 345. 2: quibus addatur pulvis factus de belliricis marinis coralli al. entali ~i quidam lapides sunt); ~e lapis est *Alph.* 49; ~e lapis est *SB* 17.

dentalis [LL *gl.*], toothed.

instrumentum ~e [sc. pecten] *SB* 33.

dentare [CL *p. ppl. only*]

1 (p. ppl.) toothed: **a** (of man, as surname); **b** (of animal); **c** (of tool). **d** indented. **e** (her.) dancetté.

a Hamonem cognomine ~atum W. POIT. I 7. **b** **c1230** averium plene ~atum (v. bidentatus). **c** cum machinula .. ~ata *G. Steph.* I 29 (v. capistrare 2); [aurifaber] habeat et .. serram ~atam NECKAM *Ut.* 118; garcifer cum strigilibus asperis et ~atis strigilat equos GARL. *Dict.* 134. **d** duo scripta ad modum cyrograffi ~ata *State Tri. Ed. I* 13. **e** incisiones .. margines symboli afficiunt .. . vetustiores sunt imbricatae, ~atae, denticulatae SPELMAN *Asp.* 108.

2 to supply w. teeth. **b** to supply (plough) w. (?) share.

to tuthe, ~are *CathA*. **b** **1279** in ij carucis ~andis, j d. *Ac. Stratton* 230; **1297** in .. carucis ~andis, faciendis et emendandis *Ac. Cornw* I 60.

1 dentaria, (?) pellitory (*Parietaria*).

~ia, i. piretrum *SB* 17.

2 dentaria, ~iola, forceps.

hec ~ia, .. i. ferrum illud unde medici dentes tollunt OSB. GLOUC. *Deriv.* 161; *a tuthe yren*, ~ia, ~iola [v. l. tentaria, tentariola] *CathA*.

dentatio, (her.) dancette, fesse with indentations.

laterum incisiones: .. denticulatio .. . ~o, cum tribus tantum dentibus afficitur. denticulatio quum pluribus SPELMAN *Asp.* 105.

denticare, to squeak. *Cf. disticare*.

sorices ~ant ALDH. *PR* 131.

denticulatio, (her.) dancette, fesse with indentations.

SPELMAN *Asp.* 105 (v. dentatio).

denticulatus [CL], toothed, jagged. **b** (her.) dancetté.

~is trabium valliculis R. COLD. *Cuthb.* 43. **b** SPELMAN *Asp.* 108 (v. dentare 1e).

denticulus [CL], little tooth or fang. **b** tooth-like projection.

in ventris decubat lustro leunculus, / sed nullum territat ejus denticulus WALT. WIMB. *Carm.* 22; si cavant robora dura vermiculi, / dic, ubi fixi sunt isti denticuli? *Ib.* 407; pecten S. Neoti ex ossiculo duos digitos lato, insertis piscium ~is instar maxillae lupi fluviatilis (LELAND) *MonA* III 471a. **b** *Turquet* 371 (v. almuri).

dentile, a tooth-pick. **b** share-beam.

a ~e, *topsticca GlH* D 178. **b** NECKAM *Ut.* 112 (v. 1 dentale 1a).

dentorium, (?) share-beam. *Cf.* 1 *dentale* 1a.

1290 in novo cultro, v arcubus, iiij dentor', strugg', herciis et alio atillo ad carucas *Pipe* 136 r. 30*d*.

dentosus, toothed, tusked. **b** mordant.

ipsi excitabunt †aprium [l. aprum] ~um (*Proph. Merlini*) G. MON. VII 4 p. 392; *tothed,* dentatus, ~us *CathA.* **b** **1167** videntur [littere] supra modum ~is salibus habundare J. SAL. *Ep.* 232 (228).

dentriculus, pickerel.

pykerel, ~us, lucillus *PP*; **1466** Johanni C. portanti dim. *porpasse* . . iij s. iiij d.; et Roberto H. portanti tres ~os . . xij d. *Ac. Durh.* 91.

dentrix [cf. CL dentex], pike (? conf. w. dogfish). (*Cf.* Isid. *Etym.* XII 6. 23: *dentix* [*v. l. dentrix*]).

~ix, piscis qui plures habet dentes sicut lucius OSB. GLOUC. *Deriv.* 172; [pisces] diversi, utpote . . uranoscopus, ~ix [*gl.*: *lus,* canis marinus], megarus . . NECKAM *Ut.* 98; **1399** duas copulas piscium vocatorum *bremes* et iiij ~ices percipiendo annuatim *Pat* 351 m. 11 (= *PS*: iiij *pikes*); **1402** in xj ~icibus emptis, xxiij s. iiij d. *Ac. Durh.* 604; **1433** exenniis . . luciorum, ~icum [DuC: dentricium] et anguillarum et omnium aliorum piscium recencium *MonA* III 113b (cf. *Arch.* XV 69); **1446** pro stuffura pisci[s] salsi, *stokfysshe,* allecis, ~icium et . . aliorum victualium *Cl* 297 m. 27; **1462** in j ~ic' empto et dato domino de Montacu et domine uxori sue prandentibus infra hospitale (*Ac. Hosp. S. Leonardi*) *Fabr. York* 341; hic luceus, A. *pyke*; hic ~ix, idem *WW.*

dentura, indenture.

1470 remanebunt sine aliqua contradiccione, hiis ~is non obstantibus *Cart. Glam.* 1693.

denubere [CL], to marry.

Anglorum regina decens denupserat illi GARL. *Tri. Eccl.* 42.

denudare [CL]

1 to lay bare, denude. **b** to strip, deprive (of). **c** to reveal.

tumore deformi ~ato, cepit . . genua . . suis manibus confricare R. COLD. *Godr.* 232; W. CANT. *Mir. Thom.* II 35 (v. colligamentum a); [angeli] pedes habent, sed ~atos, quia liberos habent affectionum motus in Deum BART. ANGL. II 3; irati semper denudant nam tibi dentes GOWER *VC* I 411; **1428** coram solenni processione . . pedibus ~atis *Heresy Tri. Norw.* 34. **b** Dei benignitas, compatiens errori humani generis, quod ab antiquo serpente caelitus concessa ~atum gloria . . damnatur FOLC. *V. Bot.* 402; hujusmodi presidio ~atos RIC. ANGL. *Summa* 30 p. 47; non video quomodo differant tres dicte materie ~ate essentialiter KILWARDBY *OS* 285; universale . . a materia ~atum primo et per se intelligitur, singulare autem ex consequenti et per accidens BACON VIII 31; asserciones . . que erronee mihi videntur: . . quod omne dominium a perceptione temporalis commodi ~atum est inutile reputandum OCKHAM *Pol.* III 13; s**1398** familias . . comitum et omnium cum eis equitancium pecuniis ~avit *Eul. Hist. Cont.* III 379. **c** ut liberalitatis ingenue facies ~etur J. SAL. *Pol.* 764D; animi conceptum ~ans GIR. *EH* I 12; que verborum velata sunt dissimulatione pauca . . dignum duxi ~are NIG. *Ep.* 17.

2 to strip off, remove.

s**1305** plumbum monasterii S. Andree ~are ordinavit *Plusc.* IX 3 (= FORDUN *Cont.* XII 4: deponi); *to doffe,* exuere . ., ~are *CathA.*

denudatio [LL]

1 laying bare, clearing. **b** stripping, freeing (from). **c** exposure, revelation.

1371 in expensis pro ~one nove quarere . ., viz. iij rodas in grosso *Fabr. York* 6 (cf. *Building in Eng.* 124); **1447** ad ~onem corporis sui (v. despoliatio). **b** ad hoc quod aliquid intelligatur, exigitur unum a parte intelligentis, sc. immunitas a materia, et aliud a parte intelligibilis, sc. ~o intelligibilis a materia BACON VIII 31; *Id.* XI 12 (v. depuratio). **c** s**1164** prelati convocantur, ut, quanto generalior esset concilii celebratio, tanto manifestior fieret fraudis et malitie ~o DICETO *YH* I 315; scriptum est quod neminem laudabimus ante mortem suam, sed in fine erit ~o operum ejus BLAKMAN *Hen. VI* 3.

2 stripping off, removal.

~o tegularum in domo Jesu apertio est in vilitate litterae sensus spiritalis BEDE *Mark* (ii 4) 147; ficus [cf. *Joel* i 7] . . exsiccabitur ~one corticis [ME: *þurch þet hit is unhuled*] *AncrR* 49.

denuere [cf. CL abnuere], to reject, contradict.

hanc ejus posicionem Themistius . . posteriorque Avicenna ~erunt *Ps.*-GROS. *Summa* 362.

denumer- v. dinumer-.

denundinare [LL *gl.*], to advertise, sell, or buy in a market.

~at, notum facit *GlH* D 185; ~are, vendere vel publicare OSB. GLOUC. *Deriv.* 180; *to bere fro fayers,* ~are *CathA.*

denuntiare [CL]

1 to prophesy, announce, proclaim; **b** (w. acc. & inf. or *quod*). **c** to denote. **d** to specify.

illud propheticum, quod veterno illi populo ~iatum est GILDAS *EB* 21; **680** "ego", inquiens, ". . supremum . . examen . . diligenter . . ~iabo" ALDH. *Ep.* 4; episticula . . ~iatura [AS p. 445: *gecyþenne*] . . diem *RegulC* 67 (cf. depositio 3a); **1214** respondit . . quod non . . audivit Baldewinum ~iantem mortem domini regis *CurR* VII 170 (cf. ib.: Baldewinus, ut dicunt, respondit quod rex non erat vivens sed murdritus); *Mod. Ten. Parl.* 39 (v. clamatio 1b); S. SIM. *Itin.* 25 (v. columba 1c). **b** Romani, patriae ~iantes nequaquam se tam laboriosis expeditionibus posse frequentius vexari GILDAS *EB* 18; s**1347** rex Francie . . commovit Scotos . ., asserens et ~ians eis quod universale robur terre Anglicane stetit cum eorum rege in partibus transmarinis agente AD. MUR. app. 252. **c** BEDE *Sam.* 582 (v. dorcas). **d** J. SAL. *Pol.* 399B (v. calculus 3).

2 (w. acc. & inf. or compl.) to pronounce (formally); **b** (w. ref. to marriage banns). **c** (w. dat. & *ut*) to direct.

secundum mandatum domini pape cum fratribus et coepiscopis sollemnitatem ~iavimus sollemniter celebrandam *Canon. G. Sempr.* 137v.; c**1218** prohibitorias de conjugio de secundo et tertio affinitatis genere minime contrahendo . . vobis ~iamus auctoritate concilii abrogatas *Conc. Syn.* 89; **1228** ego donationem ab eo factam †~iam [l. ~iavi] irritam et inanem . . sed . . contradictores excommunicatos publice ~iavi *Reg. S. Osm.* II 83; s**1303** hic papa excommunicatos ~iavit omnes qui capcioni Bonifacii consenserunt AD. MUR. *Chr.* 6; s**1313** summus pontifex eleccionem illam . . nullam omnino esse ~iavit TROKELOWE 82; **1453** (v. derobator b). **b** **1224** ~ietur publice in ecclesiis quod nunquam sponsalia fiant nisi presente sacerdote et congregatis parochianis suis, et per tres dies solempnes trina fiat denuntiatio *Conc. Syn.* 134. **c** cavetur ne invito ~ietur ut testimonium dicat adversus socerum, generum [etc.] RIC. ANGL. *Summa* 30 p. 48.

3 to denounce, protest (against); **b** (w. pers. obj.).

nuncio componitur ~io, -as, quod et pro nunciare et pro prohibere dicitur OSB. GLOUC. *Deriv.* 379; c**1250** ut rectores . . excessus ~ient subditorum *Conc. Syn.* 487; s**1289** in tantum quod mitterent duos fratres Londoniam ad ~iandum episcopo impotenciam et debilitatem prioris et defectum regiminis GRAYSTANES 21; ne adversarii ecclesie . . aliud suggerant regie majestati quam ~iatum sit ecclesie et inventum de processu *Proc. A. Kyteler* 21; **1382** ad instanciam fratrum ~iancium *Ziz.* 335. **b** ~ia eum majori [sc. prelato] et convince eum ~iando per testes . . S. LANGTON *Quaest.* f. 171; nemo cogitur per aliquam legem alium accusare, licet per legem divinam et legem nature sepe cogamur alios ~iare OCKHAM *Pol.* III 274; **1407** (v. cito 4a).

4 (w. dat.) to renounce or (?) *f. l.*

c**1279** †~iantes [? l. renunciantes] . . pro nobis et heredibus nostris . . omni †jure [? l. juris] et facti remedio, excepcioni non facte promissionis [etc.] *Inchaffray* 102.

denuntiatio [CL]

1 announcement, proclamation. **b** marriage bann.

1214 Baldewinus . . defendit . . feloniam et ~onem mortis regis . . et dictum et factum et velle et cogitatum de ~one mortis domini regis *CurR* VII 171; c**1218** prohibemus ne ~ones scotallorum fiant in ecclesiis per laicos vel extra ecclesias per sacerdotes vel clericos *Conc. Syn.* 93. **b** ~ones legitime tribus Dominicis antequam matrimonium inter aliquos contrahatur fieri non omittantur GIR. *GE* I 13; **1224** (v. denuntiare 2b); **1236** dicit quod [desponsata fuit] . . in majore ecclesia . . cum solempnitate et facta ~one *BNB* III 162; c**1240** precipimus quod, cum matrimonia contrahenda fuerint, trina ~o per intervallum xv dierum inter quamlibet ~onem . . proponatur *Conc. Syn.* 375.

2 **a** warning. **b** denunciation.

a pauca de sapientia Salomonis quae exhortationem vel ~onem exprimunt GILDAS *EB* 62. **b** malorum hominum . . ~o GILDAS *EB* 105; **1227** mandamus quatinus contra . . regis Anglie . . personam ad ~onem vel prolationem . . sententie excommunicationis . . non procedas (*Lit. Papae*) *Pat* 152; †induciter [l. inducitur] presumptio . . ex ~one precedenti RIC. ANGL. *Summa* 33 p. 62; c**1245** de excessibus parochianorum suorum . . sacerdotes inquirant diligenter et que sine ~one ewangelica corrigere non potuerint decanis locorum . . referant corrigenda *Conc. Syn.* 428; **1246** (v. denuntiator); pars contraria comiti [Leicestr'] . . nihil horum facere . . voluit, quia onus probandi ~ones suas subire . . recusarunt AD. MARSH *Ep.* 30 p. 126; **1301** videtur esse deliberandum . . an [verba bulle] debeant vim habere ~onis, monicionis, citacionis seu artacionis *Anglo-Scot. Rel.* 89.

denuntiativus [LL], declaratory, prophetic.

titulus talis est ab interpretatione hujus nominis 'Maria', quod est 'stella maris', quia fit ~us stelle maris GARL. *SM pref.* p. 88; tunc adest vis intellectiva ~a figurarum seu similitudinum, et interpretationes sensibilium BACON V 131.

denuntiator [CL], denouncer.

1246 processit [papa] contra nos . . non per accusationis ordinem . . nec per denuntiationem, legitimo ~ore cessante (*Lit. F. Imp.*) M. PAR *Maj.* IV 539; **1289** cum hoc [bannum] procedat de voluntate Petri . . fratris dicti interfecti, ~oris mortis predicte *RGasc* II 499; **1382** comparuerunt . . fratres . . offerentes se ut ~ores ad probacionem premissorum per . . Willelmum negatorum *Ziz.* 335.

denuntiatorius, (w. *litterae*) letters denunciatory.

c**1545** sententiam excommunicationis . . promulgavimus literasque . . desuper ~ias in monasteriis ac ecclesiis . . emanari decrevimus *Conc. Scot.* I ccxcii; procurator actoris concipiet in scriptis literas ~ias excommunicationis praedictae *Praxis* 19.

denuo [CL], anew, afresh. **b** afterwards.

hostes, qui putabantur . . feliciter superati, ~o versa vice victores ad . . praelium provocant ALDH. *VirgP* 12; post v annos ~o accusatus BEDE *HE* V 19; c**956** (12c) mansas . . jam nuper tyrannide abstractas reddere procurat imperialis nostra potestas et . . eidem . . aecclesiae ~o immolat *CS* 936; aquam adportans et vasa ~o emundans ÆLF. *Æthelwold* 10; HAM. S. ALB. 1455 (v. cuculla a); tam enormiter in memoria Iesus fuerat ut psalmos, quos antea corde tenus . . noverat, . . quasi de novo recordantem videremus et literas etiam, quarum notitiam copiose habuerat, ~o mendicantem GIR. *TH* III 34; a puncto . . ad punctum ~o jam reversi *Id. IK* II 13; cum [prelatus] bene diccionem iturus vel ~o rediens acceperit *Obs. Barnwell* 46. **b** **1346** ut . . exeuntibus a completoriis nulla sit licencia ~o cuiquam quicquam loqui (*Const. Prov.*) G. S. *Alb.* II 455.

1 **Denus** v. 2 Danus.

2 denus [CL]

1 (pl., also in comp. numeral): **a** ten each. **b** ten.

a ut per annos ~os et novenos unum necesse esset solito dierum lunae numero auferri BEDE *TR* 42; partibus in illis [Britanniae Minoris] miles unus quinquaginta generat, sortitus more barbaro ~as aut amplius uxores W. POIT. I 44; s**1188** (v. 2 duodenus 1a). **b** [Brittannia] bis ~is bisque quaternis civitatibus . . decorata GILDAS *EB* 3; ad quorum tumbas . . / . . deni venere leprosi ALDH. *VirgV* 1447 (= *Id. VirgP* 36: x leprosi); quater denis et binis mensibus actus *Ib.* 258; **947** bis ~as mansas *CS* 820; **1426** (v. decas a).

2 (usu. in comp. numeral) tenth. **b** (as sb. f.) a tenth.

s**1187** actis milleno centeno septuageno, / septimus a deno dat Jerusalem Saladeno (*Vers.*) MAP *NC* V 3 f. 60; s**1274** Gregorius denus colliget omne genus (*Vers.*) *Flor. Hist.* III 29; **1339** (v. centenus 2); s**1460** (v. 2 duodenus 3); s**1484** mille †cccc [? l. c] quaterno l ter deno quoque quarto (*Vers.*) *Hist. Durh.* 10. **b** c**1300** compotus maneriorum solvencium ad ~as et ad denum denarium *Dom. S. Paul.* 154.

deobligare [cf. CL obligare], to release (from obligation). **b** (p. ppl.) disloyal.

si [eremita] proprium potest habere . ., numquid propter hoc ~atur a vinculo matrimonii? HALES *Sent.* IV 470; nisi alienus sacerdotis, functus vice proprii sacerdotis, audiendo parochianum eum equaliter ~aret ab omni confessione CONWAY *Def. Mend.* 1415 (*recte* 1314); diabolus . . semper debuit esse in rectitudine perpetua, sicut debet quelibet creatura racionalis nisi sit ~ata per graciam WYCL. *Ente* 22; omnis sacerdos conjugatus debet abstinere a carnali connubio nec presbiterari antequam ~etur quoad reddicionem debiti *Id. Ver.* II 263. **b** nec aliter videtur qualiter ad sensum scripture aliquis foret 'servus bonus' obligacior 'et fidelis' [cf. *Matth.* xxv 23], alius autem servus ~acior et nequam *Id. Dom. Div.* 24.

deobligatio [cf. CL obligatio], release (from).

primum modum sequitur absolucio pro ~one pene demerite (WYNTERTON) *Ziz.* 182.

deobstructio [cf. CL obstructio], clearance (of watercourse) from obstruction.

s**1327** inquisicio .. presentarunt quod .. in cursu aque de Nene .. obstruccio quedam erat facta .., ad quem deobstruendum .. abbas cum toto consilio suo .. nitebantur (*sic*) et tandem sumptibus propriis ~onem predictam .. obtinuit per decretum WHITTLESEY *Cont.* 229.

deobstruere [cf. CL obstruere], to clear, free (passage-way or watercourse) from obstruction. **b** to remove (an obstruction). *V. et. disobstruere.*

1278 preceptum est quod predicta via ~atur *JustIt* 132 r. 34*d*.; **1279** (v. bachelarius 2); **1322** posticum illum .. ~ere et ~ctum tenere tempore pacis *PlR Chester* 34 r. 15; **1342** hujusmodi ladas et trencheas ~ere tenentur et elargare *Cart. Rams.* I 175 (cf. *CalPat* 552); **14..** quod .. permittat C. ~ere quandam viam .. quam C. pater predicti A. .. injuste .. obstruxit *Reg. Brev. Orig.* 199b. **b 1362** quo ad omnes alias romas et estachias per ipsum episcopum .. de novo positas ad nocumentum .., consideratum est quod eradicantur (*sic*), ~entur (*sic*) et penitus deleantur (*CoramR*) *Pub. Works* II 305.

deobstuppare [cf. obstuppare], to clear, free (passage-way or watercourse) from obstruction. *V. et. disobstuppare.*

1313 de Christiana A., quia deobstupavit quandam gutteram .. per quam diversa sordia corruptibilia exeunt ad nocumentum vicinorum, xl d. *Leet Norw.* 56; **1368** fossatum predictum modo est in deobstupando per villatas predictas (*CoramR*) *Pub. Works* I 126; **1387** quare via .. sic de novo obstructa et obstupata deobstupari et aperiri non debeat (*Ib.*) *Ib.* 49.

deobstuppatio [cf. obstuppatio], clearance (of watercourse) from obstruction.

s**1331** [abbas] multum laborabat .. cum aliis abbatibus et dominis .. pro deobstupac[ione] de Welledam facienda *Chr. Rams.* app. 352; **1375** causa apparicionis [i.e. apercionis] et deobstupacionis sewerarum et fossatorum .. prioris (*Anc. Indict.*) *Pub. Works* I 285.

deoculare [cf. LL oculare], to blind. *V. et. disoculare, exoculare* 1a.

quia [Henricus I] consulem de M. .. in capcione positum ~avit CAPGR. *Hen.* 67 (= H. HUNT. *HA* VIII 1: exoculavit).

deodandus, (adj. or sb. f. or n.) deodand. (*Cf.* R. F. Hunnisett *The Medieval Coroner* (Cambridge, 1961) pp. 32–4). *Cf. dare* 7d.

1250 mandatum est vicecomiti Oxon' quod ~a que ad regem pertinet de molendino .. in quo Stephanus .. per infortunium fuit occisus .. apreciari faciat *Cl* 271; **1256** Gilbertus C. .. ducendo quoddam plaustrum doleo vini .. cecidit sub eodem plaustro et oppressus fuit. .. judicium: infortunium. precium vini, bovum et plaustri viij m. ij s. .. et Johannes .. et Gilbertus de W. falso appreciaverunt predictum ~um; ideo in misericordia *AssizeR Northumb* 97; batelli de quibus tales submersi fuerint apprietentur, et alia que sunt causa mortis alicujus; et sunt ~a pro rege, ut, si submersus fuerit quis in aqua dulci et non in mari, ubi nec navis nec meremium, si navis fracta fuerit, erit ~a, quia omnia erunt dominorum, si vivant, sicut eorum catalla. nec sunt ~a ex infortunio in mari, nec wreccum, nec etiam murdrum de occisis vel submersis in mari BRACTON 122; **1265** cum Ricardus .. in ducendo quandam bigam .. submersus extiterit .., per quod tu equos bigam illam trahentes una cum .. biga .. tanquam ~um cepisti in manum nostram *Cl* 228; hujusmodi que pro mortis causa reputantur .. appreciari debent. .. ex hiis autem provisum est quod pro animabus antecessorum regis omniumque fidelium defunctorum tanquam precium sanguinis distribuantur, et ideo ~a vocantur *Fleta* 38; **1293** abbas .. clamat habere *weyf*, deodand', catalla hominum suorum fugitivorum et felonum dampnatorum *PQW* 223b; c**1300** si W. obiit ex ictu equi, equus esset ~us *Year Bk.* 30–*1 Ed. I* app. II 528; **1314** elemosinam .. que ~a vocatur (v. convertere 7c); s**1341** ad relevamen debiti prioratus [prior] solvit de suis oblacionibus et ~is diversas pecunie summas *Hist. Durh.* 2; **1415** relaxavimus .. abbati et conventui .. catalla utlagatorum et felonum de se, †deudanda, vasta, impeticiones *Cart. Glam.* 1476; a**1470** inquiratur de hiis qui percipiunt vel concelant aliqua ~a admirallo .. spectancia, viz. naves vel batellas unde omnes viventes in eisdem naufragio perire videantur *BBAdm* I 242.

deodatus, (as sb. n.) deodand.

1263 mandatum est majori et vicecomitibus Lond' quod equum Johannis .., quem nuper tanquam ~um occasione submersionis cujusdam garcionis ipsius J. in aqua Thamis' .. arestavit (*sic*), eidem J. .. liberent de dono regis *Cl* 252; **1356** (v. administratrix); **1406** recepta: .. de lxij li. ix s. viij d. ex ~is per dominum H. Percy et alios amicos *Pri. Cold.* app. p. lxxx.

deodinare v. deordinare 2.

†Deona [cf. DuC s. v. Deonarii], Paulician heretic. (*Cf.* S. Runciman *The Medieval Manichee* (Cambridge, 1960) p. 122).

c**1167** quid de his hereticis qui apud vos †Deonas [? l. Telonarias, i.e. Publicanos] appellantur, deprehensis et palam convictis, agendum sit H. BOS *Ep.* 29. 1462B.

deonerare [CL = *to unload* (*fig.*)], to relieve of a burden (fig.). *Cf. disonerare* 1a.

s**1242** ~ata est regis Anglie prodiga sollicitudo, que .. Pictavensibus quolibet anno vij^m m. .. distribuere consuevit *Flor. Hist.* II 258; s**1251** ea in libro Additamentorum, ut hoc volumen ~etur, annotantur M. PAR. *Maj.* V 229; redditus, quos fratres solvebant diversis domibus .. religiosorum, redemit et fratres de illis redditibus ~avit ECCLESTON *Adv. Min.* 162; c**1270** dicit quod, nisi se dum sit minoris etatis ~et de custodia de qua .. abbas .. est in possessione de injuria .. Roberti .., nunquam de injuria illa ~abitur, cum per breve quod dicitur 'Ne vexes' non potest se ~are nisi de servicio de quo tenementum suum injuste oneratur *Couch. Furness* I 466; oportet respicere singula onera ballivi, videndo de quot quarteriis se ~averit ut equaliter sit oneratus *FormMan* 38; c**1380** hic oportet respicere supra in panello equorum et jumentorum de quot oneratus sit [ballivus] de adjuncturis, videndo ut hic sit de tot ~atus et de non pluribus *Reg. Rough* 221.

deoneratio, discharge of burden (fig.). *V. et. disoneratio.*

cum tali ~one bonorum fortune, que sunt pondus nature .., habilitati forent ecclesiastici ad influendum vitam spiritualem in populum WYCL. *Civ. Dom.* I 267; **1482** [ad] detentores predictarum summarum attachiandum et .. prosequendum .., literas quitancie et ~onis nomine nostro dandum .. necnon omnia .. facienda .. in premissis .. necessaria *Reg. Aberbr.* II 187.

deonestare v. dehonestare.

deonustatio [cf. onustare], disburdening.

[Mendicantes] in prima dotacione cum difficultate ad utilitatem pauperum, ad ~onem divitum et laboriosum eorum ministerium habentes in se ipsis parcum victum WYCL. *Civ. Dom.* III 12.

deopinari [cf. CL opinari], to unthink, reverse one's opinion of.

hos [duos episcopos] ego patres pauperum et refugium olim opinabar, ut ceteri; quod postea certius ~abar, ut ceteri P. BLOIS (*Quales*) *Opusc.* 1010.

deoppilare [LL *gl.*], to clear, deobstruct (med.). **b** (pr. ppl. as sb. n.) deobstruent, deoppilant (medicament).

si non tanta superfluat humiditas et omnino oppilet ventriculos cerebri .. prohibetque (*sic*) .. motum voluntarium in membris suppositis quousque iila pars ~etur GILB. II 114v. 1; BACON IX 129 (v. 1 deoppilatio); non tergatur sudor, quia tunc ~abit poros GAD. 7v. 2. **b** cum non fuerit distemperantia ca[lida] aut febris, insistas cum ~antibus subtiliantibus aliquantulum frigidis et calidis GILB. VI 261. 1; vel aliqua deopilancia ponantur vel portulaca GAD. 11. 1.

1 deoppilatio, clearance, deoppilation (med.).

sumatur hoc vinum cum aqua. .. omnem humiditatem superfluam totius corporis expellet et desiccabit et confortabit omnia membra interiora et deopilabit deopilatione perfecta. nam deopilatio facit currere spiritus per membra et naturalem calorem vigere in corpore .. intendit igitur medicus in deopilatione membrorum corporis .. cum re que confortet et deopilet .. et epar et renes et vesicam ab omni sordicie mundabit BACON IX 129; urina .. iterato fit alba per aliam opilacionem et facta deopilacione fit iterum rubea GAD. 12. 2.

2 deoppilatio v. depilatio 1.

deoppilativus, (as sb. n.) deobstruent, deoppilant (medicament).

si fit [sincopis] ex oppilatione [pororum], ~a exhibeantur GILB. IV 202. 2.

deordinare [cf. LL deordinatio]

1 to disorder. **b** (p. ppl.) inordinate, excessive; *v. et. disordinare.*

corpora gloriosa erunt incorruptibilia omnino et in sensibus nullatenus ~ari poterunt PECKHAM *QA* 164; si intendit lucrari rem necessariam, licet sit turpe lucrum racione intencionis ~ate, non credo quia teneatur restituere *Id. QR* 106; ubi predicti mores sunt, ibi merito respublica ordinatur et, ubi desunt, ~atur J. WALEYS *Commun.* f. 7; alii sunt qui se occupant in bonis .. et tamen, quia illa bona ~ant, perdunt tempus sic laborando *Id. V. Relig.* f. 225v.; misericordie succedit favor, favori deordinacio rectitudinis, ~ate rectitudini approximat injusticia CHAUNDLER *Apol.* 27a. **b** amor naturalis set ~atus quem [H. Despenser] .. gessit erga .. filium suum BAKER 100 (= MORE *Chr. Ed. II* 299: disordinatus).

2 to degrade. **b** to deprive of holy orders.

†deodinavit [MS: deordinavit], i. exauctoravit, *gehende GlH* D 400; s**1399** [Henricus IV] omnes duces ordinatos per regem Ricardum in ultimo parliamento ~avit *Chr. Southern* 275. **b** s**1223** ~avit eum [diaconum apostatam] archiepiscopus M. PAR. *Min.* II 254; Sergius IV papa .. omnes per Formosum papam ordinatos ~avit inique OCKHAM *Dial.* 475.

deordinate, in disorder.

1451 ne fratres ipsi propter defectum communis .. victus seorsum comedere et particulariter ac ~e vite necessaria sibi procurare cogantur (*Abbr. Stat.*) *Mon. Francisc.* II 92.

deordinatio [LL], disorder, breach of order, disturbance.

infinitas sapientie non posset pati ~onem creature respectu creatoris, sc. quod non serviret ei BACON *Tert. Sup.* 69; 'eo quod non sint qui veniant ad solemnitatem' [*Lam.* i. 4], id est propter interiorem universalem ~onem anime quantum ad vires cognitivas et motivas PECKHAM *Exp. Thren.* 613; a**1290** ~o facta per peccatum in voluntate *Quaest. Ox.* 126; ex defectu actus est intellectus culpabilis, cum non sit possibile ipsum inordinate velle nisi ipsemet sit causa ~onis hujusmodi tunc vel ante WYCL. *Mand. Div.* 440; quod quis potest peccare est pure a Deo; sed quod sit potencia ad peccandum est superfluitas humana, quam ~onem oportet auferre tamquam prepucium *Id. Ver.* III 150; **1451** quod omnes fratres .. in conventu sint una refeccione contenti, ad amovendas multas ~ones (*Abbr. Stat.*) *Mon. Francisc.* II 92; cum philosophia moralis humanis de moribus agat, de viciis, de virtutibus, de ordinacione sc. et de ~one hominis in Deum J. BURY *Glad. Sal.* 579.

deornare [LL *gl.*]

1 to strip of ornament.

in precipuis sollemnitatibus sacrista curabit ut ecclesia idonee ornetur et ~etur *Obed. Abingd.* 375.

2 to ornament.

zona de serico ~ata argento vel auro *Cust. Cant.* 362.

deorsum [CL]

1 down, downwards (also fig.); **b** (w. *in* or *versus*); **c** (w. *de*).

in giro volvens jugiter non vergo deorsum ALDH. *Aen.* 53 (*Arcturus*) 3; versis capitibus .. ~um ad terram .. pedes ad coelos sursum prominebant *V. Cuthb.* I 3; s**978** cuncti principes Angliae congregati in uno solario .. ceciderunt ~um *AS Chr.*; **10..** ~um, *nyðer WW*; cum de corpore vel sanguine Domini .. aliquo casu accidit ut cadat ~um LANFR. *Const.* 155 (= *Conc.* I 350b: †~im); incurvatus non possum nisi ~um aspicere ANSELM (*Prosl.* 1) I 100; W. DONC. *Aph. Phil.* 3. 41 (v. dextrorsum); quedam cogitationes .. trahunt cor nostrum ~um ut non possimus ascendere ad illud templum AILR. *Serm.* 237B; pedis usque deorsum / ad plantam NIG. *SS* 2557; BACON IV 330 (v. consimilitudo); *Id.* VIII 4 (v. 2 decursus 2d); GROS. 84 (v. condividere b); cortine, que .. ad ornandum monasterium dependi solent, ante octavum diem ~um poni non debent *Cust. Cant.* 115. **b** s**1211** a summo ruere in ~um (v. degradare 1a); **1389** inter ceteras lineas .. a summo versus ~um .. protractas (J. WHYTEFELD *Pref. Catal.*) *Libr. Cant. Dov.* 409. **c** inferius a capite solida colli compage, juncture gutturis ossium sibimet connexe de ~um aliquanto longius apparent R. COLD. *Osw.* 51 p. 380.

2 downstream (from): **a** (absol.); **b** (w. *aqua*); **c** (w. *pontem*).

a a**1260** (v. desursum 2b). **b** c**1400** (v. desursum 3b). **c 1512** inter muros ville Novi Castri super Tynam ~um pontem de Tyne *Sanct. Durh.* 161.

3 at the bottom.

cum baculo .. acutum ~um habente ferrum P. CORNW. *Rev.* I 6 f. 23vb.

deort- v. dehort-.

deosculari [CL], **~are,** to kiss. **b** to kiss goodbye (fig.).

[mulier] genuflectens et pedes ejus amplectens ~avit EDDI 18; **800** obsecro .. videam dulcissimos oculos Aquilae meae, ut eam amplecter (*sic*), ~er non solum ore sed etiam toto corde ALCUIN *Ep.* 194; **8..** adprehensumque ~atur, *gegripen and hio cyst WW*; in usu habebat .. singulis diebus .. xij pauperum pedes abluere, ~ando crine ac lintheo tergere, manibus aquam fundere EADMER *V. Osw.* 33; GIR. *IK* I 2 (v. ablambere a); [abbas] ~ato feretro redit in chorum .. ubi .. incepit cantor 'te Deum laudamus'; quod dum decantabatur, ~atur a priore et a toto conventu per ordinem BRAKELOND 127v.; ~ata est eum et procaci vultu blandiebatur *Latin Stories* 2; qui [abbas electus] cum .. fuerit admissus, texto ~ato, imponet cantor responsorium 'ecce vir prudens' *Cust. Cant.* 70. **b** ut patrem mundum et matrem concupiscentiam per abrenuntiationem mentis ~etur AD. SCOT *TT* 621D.

deosculatio [LL], kiss.

reginam matrem suam .. post dulces ~ones .. redire fecit cum archiepiscopo DEVIZES 32.

deosculatorius, (w. *pax* or as sb. n.) pax-board.

1340 j ~ium pacis argent' aymell' cum crucifixo (*AcWardr*) *TRBk* 203 p. 310 (cf. ib. p. 323: una pax ~ia); **1389** ~ia vitrea (*Invent.*) *Process. Sal.* 299; **1432** j calicem cum ij ur[c]eolis et ~io argenteis *Reg. Cant.* II 486; **14..** j novum dioscculatorium *Invent. Norw.* 30; **1498** dedi eis j ~ium, viz. *a paxbred*, deauratum cum ymagine Trinitatis (*Test. Archiep. Ebor.*) *BBExch* 673.

depacisci v. depecisci.

depalliare [cf. CL pallitus], to uncloak (fig.), disclose.

s**1249** nulla voluerunt racione latronum reatus ~iare nec nomina eorum .. revelare *Flor. Hist.* II 360; puerilis disputacio reperta est multiplici commoditate, viz. propter .. audaciam loquendi publice ~iandam (R. Hambury *Summa*) *OHS* NS XVI 173.

depannare [LL *gl.*], to strip, rip (clothes).

~o, -as i. dilacerare Osb. Glouc. *Deriv.* 460; nam in veste deaurata, / non in toga depannata, / sapit eloquentia Walt. Wimb. *Van.* 80; *to doffe*, exuere, deponere, ~are, denudare *CathA.*

deparcare [cf. parcare], to remove (cattle) from pound.

1276 parcus fractus fuit et .. averia ~ata fuerunt *KR Forest Proc.* 2/24.

deparcere v. depercere.

deparietare, to break down a wall.

to cast down walles, ~are, ex- *CathA.*

departire [LL], **~iri**

1 to distribute, apportion; **b** (dep.). **c** to dissipate. **d** (p. ppl.) particoloured. *Cf. dispertire.*

cum .. regi .. minister patinam obtulisset, que duos pisces pregrandes .. contineret, dedit ille magistro, ut accumbentibus duobus juxta se clericis ~iretur W. Malm. (*V. Aldh.*) *GP* V 240; abbas [J., ob. **1308**] fecit ut sconse ~ate (*sic*) essent in choro de nocte coram eis qui vellent in libris servicium suum decantare *G. S. Alb.* II 106. **b** omnes homines, ex utroque parente geniti, ~iuntur amorem in utrumque parentem Eadmer *Virt.* 585A. **c 1359** temporis discontinuacio animum suum [sc. erga labores scolasticos] nimis tabefecit, sed credimus .. quod ferven-cior diligencia, breviter ~ita, restaurabit *Lit. Cant.* II 387. **d 1421** lego eidem W. j vestimentum pro sacerdote, viz. j casulam, j amictam, j albam, j fanonem, j *stole* ~itum de *russet baudekyn* ex una parte et nigro *velvet* ex altera *Reg. Cant.* II 253; stragulata veste aut coloris ~iti, ut potest serviens, justiciarius non utetur Fortescue *LLA* 51.

2 a to dissolve (Parliament). **b** to depart, retire.

a parliamentum ~iri [v. l. dispartiri] non debet dummodo aliqua peticio pendeat indiscussa *Mod. Ten. Parl.* 45. **b** si idem R. ~iret a vicaria predicta aliquo tempore infra dictos vj annos *Entries* 162b.

departitio, dissolution (of Parliament).

~o parliamenti ita usitari debet .. *Mod. Ten. Parl.* 47.

depascentia, depasturage (fig.).

tercius error pastorum est quod non adaquant gregem suum cum aquis limpidis [cf. *Ezek.* xxxiv 18]... hoc autem est nequicia superaddita ~ie, qua herbis putridis depascunt se et subditos Wycl. *Ver.* II 231.

depascere, ~i [CL], **~are**

1 to graze (on), depasture; **b** (absol.).

rura per umbriferas depascor florida noctes Hwætberht *Aen.* 53 (*Ypotamus*) 6; **9..** ~or, *ic ete WW*; ne oves per suas [pastorum] iras torqueantur, sed ut pacifice in leticia suas ~ant pasturas *Fleta* 167; **1329** (v. defendere 3e); **1364** non fecerunt pro partibus *les lonyngys*, per quod frumentum Johannis .. depassabatur *Hal. Durh.* 27; **1372** bidentes domini de K. depasti fuerunt noctanter blada Ricardi *Ib.* 115; **1379** quod non permittant aucas .. conculcare nec ~ere blad[a] *Ib.* 157. **b 1296** decetero idem dominus nulla animalia habeat ~encia in communa .. nec in bosco *SelPlMan* 172; s**1306** dixerunt .. quidam quod [R. de Bruys] quasi insanus et ferus cum bestiis nemorum ~ebat *Meaux* II 278.

2 to pasture (animals); **b** (w. dat. of animal). **c** to feed (people); **d** (fig.).

c**1220** pastura .. in qua .. Thomas communam petiit ad octo boves cum bobus abbatis †~endis [*ed.:* ~endos] *Reg. Malm.* II 21; **1239** (v. depastio); **1287** si rectores .., ad quos cimiteriorum custodia dinoscitur .. pertinere, propria animalia vel aliena ibidem ~ant .. *Conc. Syn.* 1009; **1319** fratres depasti fuerunt oves suas in autumpno ante glaniatores *CBaron* 128; **1389** in uno bove depasto, xij s. *Ac. Durh.* 49; c**1422** habere debent communem pasturam in una pastura .. ad omnimoda averia sua ~enda .. tamquam pertinentem ad tenementa sua a tempore quo non existat memoria, per quod ipsi averia sua .. in communa sua predicta depascerunt (*sic*) (*Augm. Bk.* 169) *Treat. J. P.* 265; **1488** super hoc quod customarii videant quot pulli ibidem depast[i] sunt ultra etatem unius anni *DL CourtR* 127/1901 A m. 2. **b** c**1394** cum fructu salmonum .. porcis suis depastus fuit (*AncIndict*) *Pub. Works* II 265. **c 1299** quod ipse abbas xl ~at pauperes penitenciam .. injunximus *Reg. Cant.* 376; ab uxore propria ignotus .. est depastus G. Cornw. *Guy Warw.* 829; **1412** pro pauperibus scolaribus in die S. Nich. ~endis *StatOx* 215; c**1430** similes .. huic transgressionis populo qui, .. manna depastus angelico, iterum post has quas coxerat in Egipto carnes .. inhiabat [cf. *Exod.* xvi] *Reg. Whet.* II 388. **d** simili edulio quo altus est propheta depasta est anima mea M. Rievaulx (*Ep.*) 56; s**1454** jussit capellano ut ille ipsum [officiarium] verbis .. benevolis .. ~eret *Reg. Whet.* I 135.

3 to graze (land or crops w. animals).

prior cum bestiis suis propriis [herbam] illam ~ebat *Lib. Mem. Bernewell* 169; **1308** germina bosci sui cedui ibidem cum quibusdam averiis depasti fuerunt *Year Bk. 1 Ed. II* 21; **1357** de pas[tura] bidencium in bosco nihil, quia †dep[asta] cum hogastris domini *Crawley* 279; c**1560** quare .. clausum .. fregit et herbam .. cum .. averiis ~atus fuit, conculcavit et consumpsit *Entries* 608.

4 to devour (fig.), consume.

fama .. nunc illam depredatam provinciam, nunc istam combustione depastam mentiebatur *G. Steph.* II 107; *Ib.* 104 (v. conflagratio); ~or et non consumor; torqueor et non morior Ailr. *Ed. Conf.* 785D; sic fatur diroque animam depascitur estu J. Exon. *BT* I 244; iterum herbe nascuntur ad pastum; sic et illi [in inferno positi] morte depasti reviviscunt Gir. *GE* II 3; pastores a pascendo dicti, quia gregem pascere debent, non ~ere *Ib.* II 34 p. 334 (cf. depastor); flamme .. infirmitorium cum omnibus contiguis officinis uno impetu depaste sunt *Croyl.* 97.

depassare v. depascere 1a.

depastinare, (?) to dig up (vineyard).

~o, *to do away grapys WW.*

depastio [CL], (right of) grazing (also fig.).

merx popularis ei clerus, depastio civis, / est et plebs sevo preda cruenta viro L. Durh. *Dial.* II 53; **1239** ne .. pecora nostra in prefata pastura agistare vel depascere valeamus, sed ab omni ~one et agistatione imperpetuum simus exclusi *Rec. Leic.* I 39 (cf. *BBC* 72).

depastor, devourer (pun on *pastor*; *cf.* Gir. *GE* II 34 *s. v. depascere* 4).

s**1376** archiepiscopus .. et ejus suffraganei .. facti sunt ut canes muti, quippe qui non pastores sed ~ores erant et .. ovium desertores *Chr. Angl.* 104.

depasturare [cf. pasturare], to graze, depasture (absol.). **b** to pasture (animals).

1437 marisci ejusdem manerii [*Ebony, Kent*] submersi existunt, qua de causa bestie et animalia .. ~are nequeunt *Cant. Cath. Pri.* 203*n.*; **1567** de firma agistamenti xx animalium ~ancium infra separalem communem vocatam Southfeild *Rutland MSS MinAc 4–9 Eliz.* p. 91. **b 1542** pro bestiis et catallis domini ibidem ~andis et crassandis *Ib. MinAc 33–4 Hen. VIII* m. 43.

depastus, grazing.

14.. quoad fraccionem clausi et ~um bladorum [cum averiis] .., dixit quod .. *Reg. Brev. Jud.* 83.

depatriare, to leave home.

c**1452** ~ians redeundi metam tercium vicinis pollicebar crepusculum *Cant. Coll. Ox.* III 105; proposui ~iare me Ripley 179.

depatrissare [cf. CL patrissare], to be unlike one's father.

~antem filiam [sc. Dinam; cf. *Gen.* xxxiv] filiam nemo sapiens †appellarit [? l. appellavit] P. Blois (*Quales*) *Opusc.* 1029C; **1456** sicut granum interdum degenerat in lolium .., sic eciam aliquociens filius ~at a patre ac eciam a condicione omnium progenitorum suorum *Reg. Whet.* I 220.

depauperare [cf. CL pauperare]

1 to impoverish: **a** (person); **b** (purse); **c** (institution or sim.); **d** (endowment or estate).

a a**1180** si quis eorum ~etur, per quod oporteret ipsum burgagium suum vendere *BBC* (*Tewkesbury*) 70; [Will. I], spoliatis Anglis .. ac ~atis, suos Normannos .. locupletavit *G. S. Alb.* I 48; cum ipsum ditent et alios non ~ent *Correct. Alch.* 14; s**1242** dicunt [barones] quod per .. amerciamenta et .. auxilia .. omnes de regno ita gravantur et ~antur quod parum aut nihil habent in bonis M. Par. *Maj.* IV 187; ne .. religiosi per oneraciones indebitas .. ~entur *Fleta* 182; Ad. Mur. *Chr.* 174 (v. Clementinus b); s**1349** pecuniam magnam undique mutuans .. obiit .. et sic multos creditores ~ando destruxit *Hist. Roff.* f. 486; **1433** in sustentacione et relevacione pauperum .. et specialiter tenencium meorum ~atorum *Cl* 283 m. 15*d.*; Fortescue *LLA* 37 (v. depilatio 2). **b** loculis ~atis Ripley 187. **c** [cellerarius] domum suam .. antea pauperculam non solum amplius ~avit et .. apporiavit verum etiam .. fere funditus exterminavit Gir. *Spec.* III 16 p. 233; Mars duo regna ferus depauperat Garl. *Tri. Eccl.* 118; **1318** propter hoc quod regnum suum ~etur per alienaciones bonorum †deportatas [? l. deportatorum] extra regnum (*Stat. Rob. I* 24) *APScot* 113; **1437** una cum .. Rothomagensi ecclesia .. extenuata ~ataque Bekynton I 7; **1529** burgus jam penitus ~atur *Reg. Aberbr.* II 497. **d 1315** considerantes statum vestrum per diutinam guerre continuacionem adeo ~atum quod terras vestras more solito .. excolere non potestis *Melrose* II 407; **1421** beneficiis .. diminutis vel nimium ~atis *Reg. Heref.* 7.

2 (w. abl.) to starve, deprive (of).

videmus plantas et arbores .. beneficio nutrimenti ~atas arescere D. Morley 32; natura .. spirituum necessariis ~ata juvamentis .. dolet *Quaest. Salern.* B 17; sic [frigiditas] exteriorem cutis superficiem calore ~atam discoloratam facit Bart. Angl. IV 2.

depauperatio

1 impoverishment: **a** (of person); **b** (of institution or sim.); **c** (of estate).

a 1247 nos .. regni majores .. statuimus .. ut .. ipsi [clerici] hactenus ex nostra ~one ditati .. reducantur ad statum ecclesie primitive (*Scriptum conspiratorum Francorum*) M. Par. *Maj.* IV 593; c**1275** ad gravissimum damnum et ~onem ipsorum baronum [V Portuum] (*Querimonia*) *MGL* I 490; s**1283** ~o parochianorum per oppressiones varias occasione guerrarum *Chr. Peterb.* 63; **1306** statum nostrum, tum propter guerram Scocie, tum propter alia[s] depredaciones et ~ones .., minime sustinere valemus *Reg. Carl.* I 240; mulieres ex superbia .. grandia convivia preparant in suam ~onem (Wyche) *Ziz.* 376; s**1405** ~o mercatorum, in quibus esse deberent substancriales divicie regni, per excessivas elevaciones theoloneorum et custumarum *Eul. Hist. Cont.* III 405. **b 1252** remotarum incole regionum qui .. animarum curam negligunt et tamen pecuniam in magnam regni ~onem colligunt et asportant Gros. *Ep.* 131; a**1326** abbas .. bona prioratus .. in pios usus .. convertenda .. in usus proprios consumpsit .. in notoriam ipsius prioratus .. ~onem nimium condolendam (*Lit. Prioris de Binham*) *G. S. Alb.* II 135; **1437** considerata extenuacione et ~one notoria Rothomagensis .. ecclesie Bekynton I 11. **c 1405** omnia .. jocalia et vasa sua argentea ad status sui ~onem fuerunt invadiata *Cl* 254 m. 6.

2 starvation, deprivation.

ne humorum ~one .. subsequatur inanitio *Quaest. Salern.* B 18.

depauperativus, impoverishing.

cujus magnanimitatis et industrie regalis thesaurus exuberans nunquam pati didicit ~am diminucionis eclipsim *Ps.-*Elmh. *Hen. V* 76.

depauperator, impoverisher.

s**1252** rex .. factus est hinc avidus et alienigenarum amator et Anglorum ~or Oxnead *Chr.* 189 (= M. Par. *Maj.* V 283: regni dilapidator).

depecisci [CL]

1 to bargain for, bring on oneself.

~or, paciscor, pactum facere Osb. Glouc *Deriv.* 178 (cf. ib. 442).

2 to break a covenant.

~or, pacem rumpo Osb. Glouc. *Deriv.* 180; *to breke conande*, depacisci, diffidare *CathA.*

depectere [CL], to comb down.

de tertia correpta sed tempore praesenti: compescimus compescitis, .. ~imus ~itis Aldh. *PR* 132; in mulieribus, que comam nutrire solent, capilli compti et ad pulchram equalitatem depexi a vertice usque ad frontem discriminantur Bald. Cant. *Tract.* 8. 483A.

depectura v. depictura.

depeculari [CL], to steal or rob. **b** (p. ppl. *s. pass.*) stolen.

depilari, furari, clepere, ~ari, expilare Osb. Glouc. *Deriv.* 178. **b** ut pauperculae direpta et ~ata mulierculae redderentur Aldh. *VirgP* 37; **9..** ~ata, *þa ofdrifenan, oðde þa forstolenan WW*; *GlH* D 191 (v. depopulari a).

depeculatio [LL *gl.*], plundering.

~o, spoliatio, rapina Osb. Glouc. *Deriv.* 177; si furtum, latrocinium, templorum ~o .. atque id genus monstra alia mala sint Bekinsau 741.

depejorare [cf. LL pejorare], to harm.

ne ~entur [agni] frequentius in agro sumitur [decima] S. Langton *Quaest.* f. 340v.

depellator v. debellator b.

depellere [CL], to drive away, expel. **b** to dispel. **c** to remove. **d** to shove. **e** (naut.) to drive (seaward or shoreward).

quod eum pridem perfidia regno pulerit [v. l. depulerit] Bede *HE* III 7; nec .. ~i potuit [spiritus malignus] donec .. W. .. aquam illis benedictam direxerat Alcuin *WillP* 22; **9..** ~ar (*sic*), *ic adrife WW*; **1102** (v. decernere a); Hanv. IX 330 (v. detogare); neque .. est .. de apostolica sede .. depulsus Ockham *Pol.* III 308. **b** metum ~ens Gildas *EB* 71; ut furvas lumen noctis depelleret umbras Aldh. *Aen.* 58 (*Vesper sidus*) 7; Dominus noster .. reversus ut tetricas ignorantiae tenebras toto ~eret orbe Alcuin *Vedast* 416. **c 1428** omnes campane sunt ~ende et destruende ab ecclesiis *Heresy Tri. Norw.* 49. **d 1297** J. L. obvians ei et causa contencionis faciende cum scapula sua depulsit dictum D. semel et iterum *SelCCoron* 89. **e 1151** (v. clamor 4a); cum .. ad .. Connactici maris vastitates vi tempestatis depulsi fuissent Gir. *TH* III 26; **1217** ubicumque venerint .. tempestate sive alia necessitate depulsi, salvi sint .. cum nave sua *Pat* 125.

dependenter, dependently; **b** (gram. or log.).

1238 argui posses si temporalia assumeres quasi principalia et quasi eis ~er adnecterentur bona spiritualia GROS. *Ep.* 51 p. 150. **b** nec obest proposicionem esse ypotheticam, cum hoc quod secunda pars ~er significat ad aliam, quia sic est de copulativis quarum parcium posteriorum extrema referuntur ad extrema proposicionum priorum, ut hic .. 'S. currit et ille movetur' WYCL. *Log.* II 24.

dependentia

1 a suspension, hanging (of votive offering). **b** pendent position. **c** overhang (of cliff). **d** (med.) pendent protuberance, wart.

a 1410 expectabitur determinacio ecclesie antequam [sepulcrum archiepiscopi] hujusmodi adoracione ~ie cere vel aliarum rerum seu aliqua adoracione solenni honoretur *Fabr. York* 195. **b** [molares] superiores habent tres vel quatuor [radices] propter ~iam et gravitatem eorum GAD. 118v. 1. **c** castellum .. in ipsius alte rupis ~ia situatum *Ps.*-ELMH. *Hen. V* 118. **d** *SB* 9 (v. acrochordon).

2 a (leg.) pendency (of suit). **b** balance (of debt) pending.

a s**1283** propter litis ~iam inchoatam, sede Dunelmensi plena, inter ipsum archiepiscopum, episcopum et priorem Dunelmensem GRAYSTANES 19 p. 65. **b 1478** computans oneratur cum iij li. x s. ultra dictam summam [pendentem], eo quod dominus rex .. mandavit supersedere de levacione hujusmodi crescencie .. et nulla ~ia fuit post annum septuagesimum tercium *ExchScot* 490; **1539** summa totalis oneracionis frumenti cum arreragiis ultimi compoti preter ~ias restantes in pede *Rent. S. Andr.* 28.

3 a dependence (tenurial). **b** (mon.) dependency. **c** (eccl.) appendage.

a 1330 ad ~iam predictorum visuum [franciplegii] evidencius declarandam, dicit quod quidam H. .. fuit seisitus de predicto manerio .. et de visu franciplegii in eodem ut pertinente etc. *PQW* 514a. **b 1494** mandamus quatinus .. prioratum, ordinem, nomen et dignitatem ac ~iam hujusmodi [de Montefonte] supprimatis et extinguatis illumque in ecclesiam secularem collegiatam .. erigatis (*Lit. Papae*) *MonA* VI 483b; **1528** cum .. in monasterio S. Petri .. in villa .. de Ipswich sito nomen, dignitatem, ordinem et ~ias supprimendi et extinguendi .. licenciam .. concesserimus (*Lit. Papae*) *Ib.* III 614b (= *Foed.* XIV 240). **c 1542** reservatis .. eidem magistro A. decano .. omnibus et singulis †dictis [? l. dicti] decanatus ac parochialium ecclesiarum seu capellarum .. ac illis annexorum, connexorum et ~iarum eidem decanatui unitarum et pertinenciarum prefatarum fructibus *Form. S. Andr.* II 195.

4 dependence: **a** (gram.); **b** (log. or phil.). **c** adjunct, dependent (consequential) provision, or sim.; *cf. dependere* 4c.

a si quis .. obiceret .. quod nullum objectum debet alterius ~iam determinare et quilibet [casus] obliquus sit dependens, dicendum est quod, quamvis sit dependens quantum ad obliquitatem, non tamen quantum ad significationem substantie BACON XV 133; *Id. CSPhil.* 513 (v. 1 dependere 4a). **b** cum sit [anima separata] subjecta accidentibus carensque essentiali ~ia *Ps.*-GROS. *Summa* 463; nulla duo possunt esse terminancia totaliter ~iam alicujus ejusdem, quia tunc illud terminaret ~iam quo subtracto non minus terminaretur illa ~ia, et ita non esset ~ia ad illud. sed ad efficiens et eminens et ad finem dependent ali[qu]a essentialiter. ergo nulle due nature possunt esse primo terminancia ali[qu]a entia secundum illam triplicem ~iam DUNS *PW* 52; ordo essencialis .. videtur .. in dividi .. in ordinem eminencie et in ordinem ~ie. .. secundo modo 'prius' dicitur 'a quo aliquid dependet' et 'posterius' 'quod dependet ab illo' .., quia posterius eget priori, quam indigenciam possumus '~iam' appellare *Id. Prim. Princ.* 628–9 (cf. eminentia 4). **c1399** cum .. ad omnia et singula statuta, ordinaciones, et stabilimenta in ultimo parliamento .. edita .. cum omnibus ~iis et omnibus aliis que inde sequi possunt .. observandum .. sacramenta .. prestiterint (*Breve Ric. I*) *JRL Bull.* XV 119; **1406** cum universis suis circumstanciis, clausulis, ~iis *Melrose* II 528; **1429** cum .. causa .. fuerit et sit ad curiam Cantuariensem cum suis incidenciis, emergenciis, ~iis ac connexis (*Sententia*) AMUND. I 235; **1461** ad tractandum .. de et super certis .. negociis .. ac de et in .. negociis predictis procedendum .. et concludendum ceteraque omnia .. in premissis et eorum ~iis debita et requisita .. expediend[a] *RScot* 402a.

dependentium, pendent altar frontal. *V. et.* 1 *dependere* 1c.

1444 item duo ~ia ante altare, unum de *le arras* et aliud de serico †fustato [? l. fuscato]; item duo frontalia *Cart. Aberd.* I 63 (cf. ib. 64: T. C. .. decoravit .. altare cum duobus ~iis, viz. frontalibus .. circumeuntibus totum altare).

1 dependēre [CL], **~ēre**

1 to hang down (intr.). **b** (pr. ppl.) pendent, pendulous. **c** (as sb. n. pl.) objects pendent.

mafortibus .., quae vittarum nexibus assutae talotenus prolixius ~unt (*sic*) ALDH. *VirgP* 58; vinea .. deambulat ut quam pulchre in ea racemi ~eant videat *Simil. Anselmi* 16; GERV. CANT. *Combust.* 9 (v. corona 5d); **1245** omnia philateria et burse in quibus ~ebant reliquie reponuntur in thecis *Invent. S. Paul.* 472; J. BLUND *An.* 51, BART. ANGL. V 13 (v. caruncula b); *Cust. Westm.* 46 (v. cornu 8b); signum ad excitandum fratres in dormitorio ~ens invenire tenetur *Cust. Cant.* 106; s**1400** alie earum [manicarum] adeo late et longe fuerunt ut usque ad pedes .. ~erent *V. Ric. II* 172. **b** domum .. quam sera ~ente .. obfirmaverat W. CANT. *Mir. Thom.* II 3; GAD. 29. 1 (v. acrochordon). **c** cum rochetis militabunt et desubtus cincti erunt, ita quod zona vel ad eam ~encia non appareant *Obs. Barnwell* 46.

2 to be pending: **a** (of lawsuit); **b** (of writ); **c** (of debt).

a s**1239** cum causa excommunicationis sue coram .. papa sit proposita et ibi ~eat GERV. CANT. *GR Cont.* 168; s**1459** (v. defensatrix 2). **b 1236** dicit quod non debet ad hoc breve respondere, quia .. aliud breve ~it (*sic*) ad exigenda maneria unde nominatim dotatam se dicit esse *CurR* XV 1855; si aliud breve .. fuerit inter easdem partes ~ens a quo nondum recesserint *Fleta* 441; **1286** cum .. magnum breve de recto .. ~ens fuerit in .. curia mea *BBC* (*Bakewell*) 180. **c 1261** debita que .. ~eant terminanda *Cl* 431 (v. clarus 5b).

3 to be dependent, subject, subordinate; **b** (eccl. or mon.).

quamcicius .. dictatori seu scriptori per vos sit relatum, extunc ~et vestrum secretum in potestate alterius MILEMETE *Nob.* 70; Christus non impedivit dominacionem regum .., licet dominacionem ipsorum voluerit ~ere ab ipso OCKHAM *Pol.* I 94; salus Christianorum a Deo ~et *Id. Dial.* 568. **b 1296** capella de Burton', que ab eodem decanatu ~et *Reg. Cant.* 96; s**1323** ita quod prior habeat totam jurisdiccionem archidiaconalem in ecclesiis de Jarow et Weremuth Monachorum et capellis ab eis ~entibus GRAYSTANES 40; s**1458** licenciam .. ad ingrediendum singula loca a nostro cenobio ~encia *Reg. Whet.* I 318.

4 to depend, be dependent: **a** (gram.); **b** (log. or phil.); **c** (pr. ppl. as sb. n.) adjunct, dependent (consequential) provision; *cf. dependentia* 4c.

a omne adjectivum est ad alterum ~ens BACON XV 60; *Ib.* 133 (v. dependentia 4a); precedentis dictionis ultima mutatur in contrarium accentum, eo quod in eo non statur, sed ~et sermo et sententia ad aliud sequens, tanquam ad finem suum et terminum sue dependentie *Id. CSPhil.* 513; *Ps.*-GROS. *Gram.* 61 (v. divisivus b). **b** alia forma est que perficit sed non extenditur nec ~et quantum ad essenciam vel operacionem. cujusmodi est anima racionalis PECKHAM *QA* 190; activo naturali et passivo simul approximatis et non impeditis, sequitur actio necessaria quia non ~et essentialiter nisi ex eis tamquam ex causis prioribus DUNS *Ord.* I 5; WYCL. *Act.* 82 (v. deperdibilis). **c 1406** de et super omnibus .. contencionibus, questionibus .., demandis et discordiis .. cum omnibus suis circumstanciis, incidentibus, emergentibus, ~entibus et connexis inter nos .. et adversarium nostrum de Francia (*TreatyR*) *Foed.* VIII 433a; **1495** (v. conectere 1d).

2 dependĕre [CL], to pay, render.

~ere, persolvere, reddere, .. satis facere *GlC* D 150, 152; ~o, i. reddo .., *ic agylde GlH* D 193; **1156** omnipotenti Domino gratissimum ~imus famulatum (*Lit. Papae*) ELMH. *Cant.* 408; **1579** ut singuli .. non collegiati solvant annuatim denarium et quod quodlibet collegium pro rata porcione annui redditus pro quibuslibet xx annis ~at dragman (*sic*) annuatim *StatOx* 414.

2 to hang (trans.).

equo insidens demissis straphis gambas fluidas ~ebat W. CANT. *Mir. Thom.* II 85; alia tria crasseta .. inveniet in laternis, que ~i debent, unum viz. in medio partis claustri juxta ecclesiam .. *Cust. Westm.* 46; **1297** (v. chorda 6e); s**1307** per regales vicos tapetos aureos ~ebant *Ann. Lond.* 152; *Cust. Cant.* 115 (v. 1 cortina 3a).

3 to unhang, cut down.

1256 Eda .. suspendit se quodam peplo. .. et W. filius ejus primus inventor venit. et juratores testantur quod †non [*not in MS*], quando invenit eam pendentem, abcidit peplum et ~ebat ipsam *AssizeR Northumb* 122.

dependicium, a (eccl.) appurtenance; *cf. appendicius* 3a. **b** adjunct; *cf. appendicius* 3b, *dependentia* 4c.

a [temp. T. abbatis, ob. **1349**] archiepiscopus .. ecclesiam de E. .. cum suis juribus pertinenciis ac ~iis universis .. monasterio nostro .. incorporavit *Meaux* III 9. **b c1399** super quibus gravaminibus et eorum ~iis .. judicium capituli generalis sibi postulant .. exhiberi *Ib.* 260.

depennare, to pluck (bird); **b** (fig.).

1421 penne phavon': de xxx de exitu hoc anno et non plures, quia phavon' non fuerunt ~ati pro timore devor' [? l. devoracionis] (*MinAc Messing*) *Essex RO* D/DH X 29 (cf. ib.: de quibus [phavonibus] devor' cum vulpe in parco domini j). **b** jam depennatus olor est, equs excoriatus GOWER *CT* II 315.

deperatio, [cf. CL pera = *purse*], theft, robbery.

acerbae cervicositatis aporias injectaeque ~onis [*gl.*: furti] angilogias [*gl.*: i. molestas locutiones] .. indulcabo O. CANT. *Pref. Frith.* 44.

depercere [LL *gl.*], to spare.

nec sibi depercit [v. l. deparcit] in cetera livor, et ipsum / sevit in auctorem HANV. VI 112 p. 329.

deperdere [CL]

1 to lose. **b** (w. *operam*) to lose one's pains. **c** (w. *navem*) to wreck. **d** (pr. ppl.) (one) at loss, loser. **e** (p. ppl. as sb. n.) thing lost, loss.

1209 forestarii dubitaverunt quod ille cervum asportaverat quem rex interfecit in foresta et [qui] fuit ~itus *SelPlForest* 7; tam acquirere quam ~ere dominium WYCL. *Dom. Div.* 26. **b** s**1440** abbas .. contra ballivum de W. .. talem fecit defensam ac eciam resistenciam ut [ballivus] totam tam suam ~eret operam quam impensam AMUND. II 213. **c 1338** (v. ductor 3b). **d 1230** M. le Butiller manucepit .. quod dicta Luce inde non erit dampnificata nec ~ens *LTRMem* 11 r. 5. **e 1196** si decreverint quod [interdictum] injuste positum fuerit, ea que rex Francie de Andeliaco .. levaverit in ~ito erunt archiepiscopi [Rothomagensis] et archiepiscopus interdictum .. solvet (*Tractatus*) *EHR* XXVII 109; **1204** volumus quod idem T. terram illam habeat in restauramentum ~itorum suorum que pro servicio nostro sustinuit *Pat* 46b; **1206** quousque .. Willelmus et Arnaldus eis satisfecerint de ~itis et dampnis que ipsi eis fecerunt *Ib.* 66b; est illa vis [nutritiva] ad conservationem individui per restaurationem ~itorum J. BLUND *An.* 46; **1336** ad dampna, destrucciones, et ~ita que .. moniales sustinuerunt *RScot* 416b; **1403** quod absque non modico ~ito ibidem vendere nequibant *Cl* 252 m. 27; **1437** [excepta] tali mercandisa qualis .. in mari periclitata ac postea ad grandes custus et ~ita mercatoris adquisita fuerit et recuperata *FineR* 244 m. 19; **1492** in ipsorum .. inquietudinem et perturbacionem ~itumque et dispendium gravissima *Lit. Cant.* III 319.

2 (pass.): **a** to be lost (by wastage or destruction). **b** to be spoiled, made worthless.

a videns vineam suam tempesta fere ~itam *Spec. Laic.* 13; tunc [de nocte] nichil ~itur sicut sepe de die accidit [ME: *þer nis naut forloren*] *AncrR* 47; secunda [alteracio, sc. deperditiva] est quam precesserunt infinite qualitates successive ~ite, quarum nulla fuit bis ultimo ~ita, et infinitarum deperdiciones immediate sequentur, quarum nulla bis erit ultimo ~ita *Ps.*-OCKHAM *Princ. Theol.* 93. **b c1230** si quis caseus ~itus fuerit, tenetur restaurare *Doc. Bec* 59 (cf. deperire 3b); **1339** victualia .. ad .. castra .. nostra .. pro municione eorum missa quedam .. deteriorata et quedam †deperdita pro diutina detencione eorundem in aqua *RScot* 576b; **1487** (v. declamare 2b).

deperdibilis, losable.

si pars sit ~is et totum DUNS *Sent.* II 19.1; potencia est forma intrinseca potenti .., ita quod dependet ab ojecto in quod potest; sed solum est potencia talis ~is per alteracionem vel debilitacionem potentis WYCL. *Act.* 82.

deperditio [LL], loss.

contingit quandoque nutrimentum [corporis] fieri sine augmento, eo quod major est ~o per resolutionem quam sit per nutrimentum restauratio J. BLUND *An.* 55; **c1239** quem [Deum] nec ovis minime pili minimi ~o potest latere GROS. *Ep.* 127 p. 372; sine substantie sue immutatione seu ~one BART. ANGL. III 4; caro et os .. indigent .. nutrimento .. quia in ipsis est ~o propter actionem elementorum que debet restaurari in se BACON *Tert.* 157; utrum in omnibus partibus materie .. corporis organici fiat ~o et restauratio per alimentum dubitari potest *Ps.*-GROS. *Summa* 521; *Ps.*-OCKHAM *Princ. Theol.* 93 (v. deperdere 2a); nunquam fit acquisicio vel perdicio nominis alicujus sine acquisicione vel ~one alicujus significacionis seu significati illius BRADW. *CD* 753E; per talis dominii acquisicionem vel ~onem WYCL. *Dom. Div.* 26; s**1388** advocatus .. inhibuit factum, ne fieret major ~o pecuniarum THORNE 2187; sine ~one amoris divini NETTER *DAF* I 502; s**1430** videns .. opcionem abbatis rem fore, quoad ipsum, levissime ~onis, mox ille assensit AMUND. I 256.

deperditivus, involving loss.

alteracio est duplex, quedam acquisitiva et quedam ~a *Ps.*-OCKHAM *Princ. Theol.* 93 (cf. deperdere 2a).

deperditura, loss.

1573 remittimus .. prefato F.S. omnes et singulas forisfacturas et ~as .. bonorum et catallorum *Pat* 1105 m. 6; **1617** ad permagnum et generale dampnum subditorum nostrorum ac ~am nostri in customis et subsidiis nostris (*Pat*) *Gild Merch.* II 286.

deperire [CL]

1 a (of living being) to perish (utterly); **b** to languish, die (of love). **c** (of artefact) to be wasted. **d** (of abstr.) to fail, come to nothing.

a recte generatio reproba in undenario numero, et hoc in femina, terminatur ac ~it BEDE *Gen.* (iv 22) 75; vitam constare necesse est, aut †in [? *omit*] universum animal ~ire; id autem est mori ALF. ANGL. *Cor* 1. 4. **b** una erat cujus forma ~iens ad ejus dedecus acriores nervos incendit W. MALM. *Mir. Mariae* 183. **c** qui .. dum aratri stibam postergum respiciens neglegenter regeret, ruptis sulcorum glebulis jugerum occa nugaciter ~iret ALDH. *VirgP* 31;

~eunt .. res; oneratur debitis Map *NC* IV 11 f. 52. **d** s**1009** tanta tempestas facta est ut totum navigium Brihtrici ~iret et naves ad litus projecti sunt *AS Chr.*; [Lanfrancus] erat non inconsideratus dator, nec ~ibat ejus liberalitas, quam discretio et animi condiebat alacritas W. Malm. *GP* I 43; absit ut .. studia .. omissa ~eant Gir. *EH pref.* p. 224; peritiam ~isse Diceto *YH* I 291 (v. 1 condere 2d); **1218** tantum .. facientes .. ne negocium nostrum in hac parte ~eat pro defectu vestri *Pat* 149; **1419** (v. deterioratio 1c).

2 (w. dat.) to be lost (to), missing (from).

nullum de his crediderim ~ire celo quos egressos corpore tot patronorum excipit laus W. Malm. *GR* I 28; c**1140** sciens magnum mihi ex tua absentia consilium ~ire (*Lit. S. Bernardi*) Serlo Gram. *Mon. Font.* 83; **1225** assignando .. quantum conventui dinoscitur ~ire *Doc. W. Abb. Westm.* 220.

3 (in pass. form): **a** to be lost. **b** to be spoiled.

a quando .. defluit aliquid de vino et ~itur, tunc quandoque aer non potest dolium intrare Bacon VIII 203. **b** c**1230** si ullus [caseus] frangatur, ~eatur vel amittatur *Doc. Bec* 47 (cf. deperdere 2b).

deperitio, destruction, subversion.

ipsam hominum multitudinem in favorem abbatis nostri [R., ob. **1367**] et ~onem juris regii asseruit congregatam *Meaux* III 138.

depersonare [cf. OF *despersoner*] to 'disperson', disgrace, insult. *V. et. dispersonare.*

s**1170** hoc verbum consonum fuit dicto Henrici regis Anglie juniori[s], qui patri suo Henrico II regi in festo coronationis sue ministranti, ait "non es ~atus mihi ministrando, cum sis filius comitis, ego regis et regine" M. Par. *Maj.* IV 546; **1240** dictum J. de multimodis vituperiis et turpiloquiis, seductorem et infidelem appellando, ~avit in pleno hundredo *RentSurv R* 711.

depessulare [cf. CL pessulus], to unbolt.

ostia que reserat, aperit panditque, recludit, / ejusdem sensus 'depessulat' additur istis Garl. *Syn.* 187. 1581B (cf. *CathA* 260a).

depetrare [cf. CL petra], to stone, free from stones. **b** (? by conf.) to stand behind.

to stane, ~are, petras removere *CathA*. **b** ~o, *to by hynde stonde WW*.

depicatus [cf. CL picare], coated w. pitch.

e palude fluminis quasi ~us surrexit B. *V. Dunst.* 6.

depictare [cf. CL depictus, *p. ppl. of* depingere], to paint.

1317 depictand' clav' lapideo ad voutur' *Fabr. Exon.* 80; **1352** iij pictoribus ~antibus super dictum tabulamentum *KRAc* 471/6 m. 3.

depictio [LL], depiction, painting.

†**971** (12c) ego Ædelwine dux hoc donum triumphale agiae crucis propriae manus ~one impressi *CD* 567; hic non solum necessaria est ~o locorum et figuratio sed narratio eorum que depingi debent Bacon *Maj.* I 309; **1397** in ~one ymaginis S. Andree cum dorsorio *Ac. Durh.* 267; **1490** Johanni S. .. pro labore suo circa ~onem ad altare meum in ecclesia Ebor', xl s. *Fabr. York* 284.

depictura, painting.

1242 in ~is et aliis minutis operacionibus faciendis in castro Winton' *Liberate* 16 m. 4; **1243** lambruscari faciat .. cameram in qua garderoba regis est de plana lambruschura sine aliquo alio ornatu aut ~a *Cl* 19; **1308** circa ~as in camera depicta et ejusdem ~e historias reparandas et emendandas et eciam circa magnam aulam depingendam *KRAc* 468/16; tabernacula cum omnibus †depecturis altarium *Ord. Ebor.* II 178.

depignerare [cf. CL pignerare], to redeem (a pledge).

to take owt of wedde, ~are, ex- *CathA*.

depilare [CL *p. ppl. only*, LL depilari]

1 to strip bare of hair. **b** to pull (wool from a sheep). **c** (fig.) to strip (combs) in carding. **d** to form into strands or fibres.

depillat, i. runcat, radit, evellit *GlH* D 214; cum .. corpus ejus .. lepra profusum fuisset in tantum ut capillis capitis et superciliis ~aretur *Canon. G. Sempr.* 147v.; H. Avr. *CG* 8. 17 (v. 2a infra); locus ~andus .. fomentetur .. et suaviter fricetur et ~etur Gilb. II 78. 2; s**1253** Galfridus .. frater domini regis uterinus .., irascens contra quendam de .. regis cocis, .. caput suum ~avit, ita .. quod singulos singillatim pilos capillorum avelli jussit Oxnead *Chr.* 194; s**1258** [comes Gloverniе] enormiter extitit depilatus, quia ~atus, decoloratus .. M. Par. *Maj.* V 709; supercilia ~antur propter defectum nutrimenti Gad. 46. 2; folium .. ~etur *Ib.* 5v. 1 (v. domesticus 3b). **b** **1307** J. le D. et J. de R. capti pro suspicione latrocinii, eo [quod] deferebant lanam depillatam apud W. vendendam *Gaol Del.* 39/2 r. 2. **c** frustra ordietur aliquis telam, nisi pectines ferrei lanam pro capillis gerentes virtute igni molliendam longo et reciproco certamine sese prius ~averint [*gl.*: detrexerint] Neckam *Ut.* 107. **d** allumen rubeum .. depillatur ut allumen de pluma M. Scot *Lumen* 254 (v. et. alumen).

2 (scanned *depīlare*) to pillage, plunder. **b** to plagiarize.

depillat, i. .. distrahit *GlH* D 214; Osb. Glouc. *Deriv.* 178 (v. depeculari); quod vellem redditus peramplos relinquere propter pauperem cathedram ~atam undique et dilapidatam Gir. *Inv.* I 13; depīlat [*gl.*: †descunet] ora pīlis; non depīlat [*gl.*: spoliat] sine pīlis H. Avr. *CG* 8. 17; s**886** Aurelianis perveniunt, quam rebus omnibus ~atam tandem urbem combustione consumunt M. Par. *Maj.* I 424 (= W. Jum. I 7: distrahunt); s**1306** venit quidam cardinalis .. missus a latere pape .. ad Anglicanas ecclesias ~andum *Flor. Hist.* III 136; ut non sit villula una .. que non semel aut bis in anno hac nephanda pressura ~atur Fortescue *LLA* 35. **b** eum [Afranium] multa de libro Menandri ~ando sumpsisse P. Blois *Ep.* 92. 290B (cf. Macrobius *Sat.* I 6).

depilate, baldly (fig.).

nisi vigiles instanter excubando sibi providerint, que jam capita decalvavit †vicinia [? l. vicina] sua, me dolente, scabies eadem ~ius enudabit P. Blois (*Quales*) *Opusc.* 1009A.

depilatio

1 pulling out of hair. **b** pulling of wool. **c** loss of hair, baldness.

implicite prohibetur in hoc precepto omnis motus ire contra proximum, .. sive ore, ut contumelia, sive opere, ut percussio citra mortem et ~o et hujusmodi .. J. Burgh *PO* X 2 f. 163. **b** **1300** S. filius R. nocte captus pro ~one ovium .. et aliis latrociniis *Gaol Del.* 26 r. 5. **c** Gir. *TH* I 26 (v. abradere 1a); oppilatio narium, †deoppilatio superciliorum, gingivarum corrosio Gilb. VII 344. 2 (cf. ib. 345v. 1: contra ~onem superciliorum in leprosis); Gad. 45. 2 (v. alopecia a).

2 pillage, spoliation.

si [rex] .. manus suas cohibere nequit a ~one subditorum suorum, quo ipsemet eos depauperat Fortescue *LLA* 37.

depilator [LL *gl.*], raser (fig.), pillager, despoiler.

audiant prelati .. que tonsoribus ovium, in quibus subditorum ~ores dantur intelligi, accidere solent [cf. *Gen.* xxxi 19–24] Gir. *GE* II 34.

depilatorium, depilatory. **b** tweezer.

hec ~ia, si fuerint nimis spissa, cum urina propria rarefiant, non cum aqua, quoniam virtutem ~ii destrueret Gilb. II 78. 2 (cf. ib.: aliud ~ium suavius calcis vive et auripigmenti); psilotrum, ~ium idem *SB* 35. **b** hoc ~ium, *guigne Gl. AN Glasg.* f. 21.

depilis [CL], hairless.

~e, sine pilis *GlH* D 215.

depill- v. depil-.

depinctitare, to paint over.

1421 in una nova cruce .. ~anda ij s. j d. *Ac. Churchw. Glast.* 189.

depingere [CL]

1 to paint, depict, represent pictorially; **b** (w. image or sim. as obj.); **c** to form (written character or shape), set down (in writing). **d** to copy. **e** to portray (fig.), describe. **f** to conceive, fashion.

solem aut mare cum depicta videmus, non sicut est in se aut in re ita illa videmus Alex. Cant. *Dicta* 9; P. Blois *Ep.* 94 (v. clipeus 2a); O. Cheriton *Par.* 73 (v. diabolus 1d); **1243** (v. deisium); quomodo angeli in effigie corporali ~antur Bart. Angl. II 3; **1444** magistro W. E. pro armis Thome Langley depictis in diversis libris *Ac. Durh.* 713. **b** iconisma regale compto stemmate depictum Aldh. *VirgP* 60; imaginem Domini Salvatoris in tabula depictam Bede *HE* I 25; picturarum .. alie .., ut yconie, statue et figure et diversa picturarum genera que in vestibus vel in parietibus vel in vitrealibus ~untur Beleth *RDO* 85. 89C; **1268** crucem marmoream .. cum imagine Crucifixi .. et cum imagine B. Virginis cum Filio suo .. auro depictis *Cl* 15; c**1331** cuidam ~enti ymaginem S. Oswaldi *Ac. Durh.* 115. **c** †c**690** (12c) ego S. signum crucis manu propria depinxi *CS* 89; **945** (13c) ut ea quae communi tractatu salubri consilio ~untur rectis litterulis roborata confirmentur *CS* 807; **946** (14c) ego Edmund rex impressione signi sanctae crucis hoc donum .. ~ere jussi *CS* 816; **949** (12c) ego W. episcopus crucis modum depinxi *CS* 879; **960** scedula .. carraxata est et his testibus roborata, quorum nomina subtus litterulis depicta cernuntur *CS* 1056; grues in volatu litteram in aere ~ere videntur Neckam *NR* I 46. **d** **1159** Brito, de cujus manu [liber] avelli non potuit antequam totus ~eretur J. Sal. *Ep.* 81 (111). **e** venustum pudicitiae vultum componens diversis virtutum coloribus .. depinxi Aldh. *VirgV* 60; de his .. quae .. fuisse quondam poetae ac philosophi .. in suis litteraturis .. ~unt *Lib. Monstr.* II *pref.*; nigris coloribus phantasma tuum ~is Lanfr. *Corp. & Sang.* 409C; nisi variis verborum fucis veritas ~atur Dominic *V. Ecgwini* I 14; Adel. *ED* 3 (v. dealbare 1b); a**1160** ~o organum Sathane quod sub pallio hominis hujus .. vidimus latitare J. Sal. *Ep.* 77 (94); Homerus .. ~ens Hectoris arma *Croyl. Cont. A* 108. **f** ruminatis et gestibus praetenditis quae antea actor [v. l. auctor] vester depinxerat Gildas *EB* 74; incipit alea evangelii .. depicta a quodam Francone et a Romano sapiente *Alea Evang.* 173.

2 to paint (a surface). **b** to paint or stain (glass). **c** (w. *pannus* or sim.) to paint or (?) embroider. **d** to colour.

sicut sepulchrum depicto [AS: *metton*] mausoleo intus plenum fetore [cf. *Matth.* xxiii 27] Ælf. *Coll.* 101; s**1174** (v. 2 caelum 4a); **1242** quod .. capellam de Windlesores .. ~i optimis coloribus faciat *Cl* 514; **1264** quod .. camera nostra .., que jam depicta est, ad plenum perficiatur *Cl* 366; s**1325** (v. crux 4a); **1342** (v. 2 asser d); **1509** cum xij grossis papiri depicti *EEC* 562. **b** **1304** in clx pedes vitri depicti ad duas formas in nova vesteria *Fabr. Exon.* 35. **c** **1303** unus pannus depictus ad modum mappa (*sic*) mundi *DocExch* 278; **1415** (v. conopeum 3a); **1452** tria mappalia depicta *MunAcOx* 629; c**1500** pannus lineus depictus cum imagine crucifixi *Invent. Ch. Ch.* 128. **d** quantus .. quorundam vultus purpureus genarum rubor velut stibio depinxit ..! Aldh. *VirgP* 32; floris [sc. Christi] vultus sputis inficitur, / et flos vernans sputis depingitur J. Howd. *Ph.* 117.

3 to adorn, variegate.

septiformem .. calculum, qui misticis sacrorum canonum floribus ~itur Aldh. *Met.* 2; [mons] variis herbarum floribus depictus (*Passio Albani*) Bede *HE* I 7 p. 20 prius informem creaverat terram sub aquis, quam detectam postmodum multiplicibus depinxit formis Pull. *Sent.* 718C; seria sui negotia novis quibusdam natura ~it Gir. *TH* II *pref.* p. 75.

depinguere [cf. CL pinguefacere], to fatten (fig.), enrich, or (?) *f. l.*

da ei de rore caeli benedictionem et depingue [? l. de pingui], Domine, terrae ubertatem *Miss. Leofric* 9a.

depisicio v. depositio 5c.

deplacitare, to establish a claim to.

c**1080** facite ita esse socam et sacam inter episcopum W. et W. abbatem de Evesham; et ad istud ~andum sis .. in meo loco (*Breve Regis*) *MonA* I 610 (= *Regesta* 184); **1082** sicut abbas per cartas suas et per testes suos eas [consuetudines suas] ~are poterit *Royal Writs* 185 (= *Regesta* 154); episcopus dicit se hanc terram ~asse coram regina M. *DB* (*Warw*) I 238v.

deplanare [cf. planare], to trample flat.

s**1378** omnia loca in monasterio patencia ad parliamentum venientibus frequentata fuere. .. viridum claustri tanta luctancium et ad pilam ludencium exercitacione extitit ~atum quod nulla viriditatis vestigia in ibi sperabantur *Cart. Glouc.* I 53.

deplangere [CL], to deplore, grieve for; **b** (w. acc. & inf.).

deplangunt victum sub aquis ex parte relictum R. Cant. *Malch.* IV 650; ita flevit quoniam malis interurant futuri boni, quorum mala merito ~gebat Pull. *Sent.* 818C; filium .. quem mutum antea ~xerat multum anxie *Mir. J. Bev. A.* 311. **b** s**1327** fetorem .. fuisse penam maximam quam unquam sustinuit .. servus Dei ~xit Baker 107b.

deplēre [CL], to empty.

~ere, [de pleno] deducere *GlC* D 125; ~et, i. evacuat, exinanit *GlH* D 223.

deplicare [LL]

1 **a** to unfold. **b** to unfurl. **c** to fold back. *V. et. explicare* 1.

a **1295** prior .. pallium archiepiscopi in panno mundo plicatum recepit et dictum pallium ~avit *DCCant.* Q f. 26v. **b** s**1321** comes .. Lancastr' .., super eo quod vexillum ~atum contra regem erexerat, sentenciam suscepit capitalem *Hist. Roff.* 36v. **c** s**1327** cum rex Edwardus in lecto recumberet .., accesserunt ad eum et vestes a pedibus excucientes super caput ejus subito ~uerunt Knighton I 446.

2 to turn aside, deviate.

~at, i. declinat, deflectit *GlH* D 222; ~are, decedere, devitare Osb. Glouc. *Deriv.* 181.

deplois, deploys v. diplois.

deplorabiliter, deplorably.

1541 monachorum vita et professio .. temporum lapsu ~iter exorbitaverat (*Pat*) *MonA* I 106a.

1 deplorare v. deflorare 1b.

2 deplorare [CL], to deplore, lament, grieve (over); **b** (w. acc. & inf.).

propheta ~ans ait "incenderunt igni sanctuarium tuum [*Psalm* lxxiii 7]" etc. Gildas *EB* 25; quod germana petit deplorans anxia curis Aldh. *VirgV* 2048; W. Malm. *GP* I 44 (v. claudicare c); Pull. *Sent.* 852B (v. deploratio); in justitia illa meam ego ~o injustitiam J. Ford *Serm.* 35. 5; matris .. cineres semisepulte lacrimosis ~are singultibus

GIR. *IK pref.* p. 101. **S1255** (v. Cahursinus). **b** [frater] B. Cuthbertum eo die suam familiam deseruisse conquestuose ~avit R. COLD. *Cuthb.* 106.

deploratio [CL], lamentation.

gemitus ille sordet ante Deum qui feditatem anteactam deplorat, futuram exoptat, non quod ~o per se displiceat, sed quod ex adjuncto vigere non queat PULL. *Sent.* 852B.

deploratrix [cf. LL deplorator], loud in complaint (f.).

S1194 callet gens tua, que te [rege R.] sibi nunc reddito opum suarum claritatem secure ostentat, paulo ante paupertatis ~ix W. NEWB. *HA* IV 42.

deploratus, lament.

aruerant lacrime deploratusque; sepulchri / jam tacitus, jam siccus honos J. EXON. *BT* VI 402.

depluere [CL], to shower down.

si removeatur digitus, statim aqua descendet et ~et ab ea [clepsedra] BACON VIII 199 (*but* cf. ib. 200: quod amoto digito aqua non debeat defluere a clepsedra).

deplumare [cf. plumare], to pluck, strip of feathers; **b** (fig.). **c** (falc.) to 'plume'.

maritus .. [ciconiam] adulteram ~avit et dilaniavit NECKAM *NR* I 64; insultat cygnorum cetus; ~at damnatam, et sic frigori expositam mortis addicunt supplicio GERV. TILB. II 96; **S1129** venit in Normanniam avium .. multitudo, que gregatim volantes .. horribiliter sese ~antes pugnabant M. PAR. *Maj.* II 156 (cf. TORIGNI *Chr.* 116); probatio coctionis est ut pluma intus missa facile ~etur GILB. II 78. 2; **13..** abbacia in prima fundacione sua inter nemora .. frondosa .. sita fuit .., que nunc sicut avis ad coquinam que (*sic*) ~ata stat ex omni parte nuda *MonA* V 435 a; **1384** pavones .. prioris .. ~avit et plumas inde .. cepit et asportavit *PlRCP* 494 r. 76*d*.; *to pulle byrdes*, ~are *CathA*. **b** monachi .., sicut nisus alaudam territam, ita predam suam agnoscunt, milites sc. quos ~are possunt MAP *NC* I 25 f. 17v.; vidue .. et orphani non solum ~ari verum et excoriari solent GIR. *JS* 1 p. 136; sic quandoque de militibus videmus quod tantum dant religiosis quod totique (*sic*) remanent ~ati et heredes exheredati O. CHERITON *Fab.* 66; sicut dicitur impio militi rusticum quasi excorianti: "a, domine, benefacitis, quia oportet rusticos ~are [ME: *polkin and pilien*]" *AncrR* 23; **1441** domus [S. Antonii, London'] .. jam tristis .., desolata necnon ad extremam prope pauperiem ~ata BEKYNTON I 235; **1457** sic deplumatus Pavo fuit et spoliatus (*Vers. de R. Pecok*) *Reg. Whet.* I 288. **c** cum [accipiter] primam volucrem ceperit, ad libitum ~et et comedat ADEL. *CA* 2.

deponere [CL]

1 to lower; **b** (refl.) to dismount. **c** to lower (in rank or status); **d** (in pitch).

cum [Moyses] elevaret manus, vincebant filii Israel; si quando ipse ~ebat manus, vincebat Amalech [cf. *Exod.* xvii 11] AILR. *Serm.* 288B; W. FITZST. *Thom. prol.* 11 (v. contradictorius 1c). **b** quando [pueri] primo equitant nesciunt se ~ere set semper equitant donec cadunt H. HARTLEPOOL 202. **c** nobiles .. laborabat ~ere et ignobiles exaltare G. MON. III 17. **d 1091** cantor debet chorum regere quoad cantum et potest cantus elevare et ~ere *Reg. S. Osm.* I 214.

2 to take down; **b** (naut.). **c** to pull down, dismantle.

1237 (v. deguttare 1b); **S1325** (v. crux 4a); appositis vexillis .. regiis supra portas ville et depositis aliis adversariis *G. Hen. V* 8. **b** turgida ventosis deponens carbasa malis ALDH. *VirgV* 2807; viro Dei .. naviganti donec prospero cursu ostia [v. l. ad ostia] Hreni fluminis vela deposuit ALCUIN *WillP* 5. **c** multimodis machinationibus aggressi sunt choream [Gigantum] ~ere G. MON. VIII 12 (cf. ib.: [Merlinus] levius quam credi potest lapides deposuit); **1212** (v. claustrum 2a); **c1300** in .. muro vel fenestra .. nichil .. clamii .. habere me fateor, set .. tanquam .. non meum .. ad ~endum .. resingno (*Cart. S. Denys Southampt.*) *FormA* 233; **S1305** (v. denudare 2); **13..** pretor .. ibit semel propter firmam [regis] et alia vice, si placuerit ei, ~et hostium cujuslibet burgensis (*Cust. Preston*) *EHR* XV 497; *G. S. Alb.* III 447 (v. cristare 2); **1432** (v. dissolvere 1d).

3 to lay down, set in place. **b** to deposit, inter (human remains).

[munusculum] ante pedes ejus deposuit *V. Cuthb.* III 5; oblitus hoc [munus] alicubi ~ere, permisit suo in sinu permanere BEDE *HE* III 2; **1310** in loco .. ubi ~ebatur quoddam caput aureum *Conc.* II 362b; **1413** pro .. fenestra ~enda (v. cintra); *to sewe at the mete*, ~ere *CathA*; **1533** W. plumbario et suo servienti operantibus circa *le settyng* unius *tabbart* plumbi et removend' veteris gutture et ~entibus unam aliam de novo *Comp. Swith.* 221. **b** corpus incorruptibile .. in basilica deposuerunt *V. Cuthb.* IV 13; ne deposta voret funera labēs edax (*Vers.*) BEDE *CuthbP* 42; ecclesia .. in qua .. episcoporum .. sunt corpora deposita *Id. HE* V 8; quanta suspiria corpora vexant, / Thome depositum [sc. corpus] cum se conspectibus offert H. AVR. *Poems* 2. 94.

4 to deposit for safe-keeping; **b** (as pledge). **c** (p. ppl. *depositus* as sb. n.) deposit, object deposited. **d** (w. *in*) on deposit. **e** (?) repository. **f** preserve for fish.

depositum, *to healdenne*, vel *ædfæst tæht*, vel *becwyddod* ÆLF. *Gl.*; **S1070** (v. depopulatio b); *Collect. Stories* 201 (v. depositarius 1b); clericus .., propter pericula locorum deposita numerata pecunia sua apud fidelem matronam .., Romam profectus est W. CANT. *Mir. Thom.* IV 10; **1219** exemplata instrumentorum originalium penes nos deposita *Ch. Sal.* 93; libellus pro deposito: 'conqueror de N., apud quem deposui tales res .. quas negat se a me habuisse ..' W. DROGHEDA *SA* 211; **1258** (v. demanda c); OCKHAM *Dial.* 629 (v. depositor a); **1439** occasione tante summe per eundem H. eidem J. deposite ad custodiam *MunAcOx* 516; **1492** quod .. remittet commissionem alias depositam in bancho *Reg. Aberbr.* II 270. **b 1232** jocalia nostra que deposuimus in domo Novi Templi London' in tenantia pro mmm marcis *Pat* 490; **1291** volumus quod, si dictus apostata Fratribus Minoribus de Anglia est restitutus, quod (*sic*) a c marcis ~endis, quas pro dicto apostata requirendo ~ere tenebatur .., ad eas ~endas minime teneatur *Mon. Francisc.* II 45. **c** ~um, commendatum *GlC* D 100; ~um, i. commendatum, *læn GlH* D 211; lacrymis, quas angustia potentis ~i [sc. annuli perditi] extorserat, ejus [sancti] clementiam exposcit GOSC. *Transl. Aug.* 46B; aut debetur quid ex causa mutui .., aut ex commodato, aut ex locato, aut ex ~o .. GLANV. X 3; **1242** recognovit .. se recepisse xj m. xxv d. de priore de Monasterio Ederoso de ~o Henrici de Dun *KRMem* 20 r. 8; **1282** in diversis thesaurariis monasteriorum .. Anglie est summa ~orum de moneta veteri xxviiij^{m} ij^{c}xxxvij li. .. (*Comp. Collectorum Apostol.*) *EHR* XXXII 52. **d 1233** (v. 1 botellus b); **1240** una cum denariis quos .. commiserunt Martino suo monacho in ~o *Ib.* 18 r. 19; **1265** quia .. quedam summa pecunie S[imonis] de Monteforti .. residet in ~o in domo vestra (*Pat*) *Manners* 88; **1267** carta .. in equali manu ad Novum Templum Lond' de consensu partium in ~o liberetur *Cl* 392; **1291** quod exitus ejusdem terre in tempore medio recepti salvo reponantur in ~o et per manum camerarii Scocie .. conserventur (*Lit. Baronum Scotiae*) OXNEAD 283 (= TREVET *Ann.* 322: in salvo ~o); **1556** pecunie .. stent in ~o apud presidem collegii *StatOx* 367. **e 1317** in solutis custodi ~i conventus *Comp. Swith.* 401. **f 1254** in quodam ~o faciendo ad piscem .. vivarii in eo tenendum donec idem vivarium esset mundatum *Liberate* 30 m. 5.

5 to drop, shed, lose; **b** (w. ref. to excretion). **c** (w. *comam*) to accept tonsure. **d** (w. *coronam*) to abdicate. **e** (w. *carnem*) to die. **f** to take off (clothes or sim.); **g** (crusader's cross). **h** to put off (a role or character). **i** (w. abstr. obj.) to put aside, abandon. **j** (log.) to reject, refute (a proposition).

quo viso, abbas jussit ~i frustum WULF. *Æthelwold* 14; psalterium .. manibus suis firmiter adherens ~ere non prevaluit GIR. *IK* I 2; **1311** ~e crucem et dimitte in pace *Ann. Lond.* 184; hanc herbam [cervariam] cum cervi comedunt cornua ~ere dicuntur *Alph.* 54. **b 1280** confugientes ad ecclesiam .. custodiuntur .. ita arte quod non possunt exire locum sacrum causa superflui ponderis ~endi *Conc. Syn.* 884 (cf. ib.: exire .. pro obsceno pondere ~endo); **1406** cum nature pondus necessarie ~erent *Cal. LBLond.* I 49*n*. **c S728** *Chr. Abingd.* I 14 (v. 1 coma 1a); **S1020** de dono Ailrici, qui apud R. comam deposuit *Chr. Rams.* 197 (cf. ib. 147). **d S1403** ut .. convocato parliamento ad insinuacionem prelatorum et procerum coronam ~eret FORDUN *Cont.* XV 17. **e** carnem .. deposuit *NLA* I 309 (v. cohabitatrix). **f** deposito habitu saeculari monachus fieri maluit *Hist. Abb. Jarrow* 2; numquam .. vestimenta uda .. ~ere curabat BEDE *HE* V 12 p. 310; BYRHT. *V. Osw.* 437 (v. diadema 1a); **1248** deposuerunt tenam suam et habuit coronam de novo rasam *SelPlForest* 78; **1269** deposuit vestes suas et intravit in quadam aqua in .. gardino ad balniandum *SelCCoron* 12; cum venerint ad lectos suos, primo ~ent capucium furratum ..; postea sedendo coram lectis suis ~ant calciamenta, pedules et caligas ante formas *Cust. Cant.* 10; *Ib.* 49 (v. chirotheca 2b); *NLA* I 209 (v. chirotheca 2c). **g S1200** (v. crux 9a). **h** Thomas .. jam ecclesie consecratus, .. supra omnium spem mox deposito cancellario, antistitem vivens .., totum veterem hominem .. expulit [cf. *Eph.* iv 22] H. BOS. *Thom.* III 6 p. 192. **i 601** ut .. de corde errorem ~at (*Lit. Papae*) BEDE *HE* I 30; dum modo ille residens ad epulas tristitiam ~eret *Ib.* III 14; pueris pugnae interdixit certamen, dicens: "cessate .. a conflictu pugnaeque ~ite bellum" WILLIB. *Bonif.* 8 p. 49; quod quis teneatur heresim suam ~ere OCKHAM *Dial.* 460. **j** suppono ex eadem arte quod omnis posicio equivalet uni deposicioni .., quia, si ponitur quod tu es Rome, tunc ~itur ista 'tu non es Rome' ..; et ideo qui posuit unum contradictorium deposuit reliquum, et e contrario (HOLCOT) *GLA* IV 9 *n.27*; '~o' est nota tentandi si velit respondens depositam sibi proposicionem negare cum sibi proponatur (STRODE) *Ib.* 53 *n.* 192.

6 (gram.) to abandon (?) distinction between active and passive, (pr. ppl.) deponent.

'labor', quod si verbum fuerit ~ens, 'la-' producitur, ut 'lābitur ..' ALDH. *PR* 113; [verba] passiva, communia et ~entia utroque numero concordant *Ib.* 134; [verba] ~entia .. sunt R littera terminata, quae patientis formam (*sic*) et in verbo et in participio ~unt BONIF. *AG* 498; [verba] ~entia unam semper habent significationem, aut activam, ut 'sequor te' .., aut passivam, ut 'nascor a te' ALCUIN *Gram.* 875A; ~ens verbum, *þæt is, alecgende word*, ..; ~entia verba significant actum ÆLF. *Gram.* 122; BACON *Min.* 331 (v. confundere 3e).

7 to take away, remove; **b** (w. *ab*). **c** (w. abstr. obj.) to stop, avert. **d** (?) to set apart. **e** (p. ppl. as sb. f.) anchoress. **f** (w. *cum*) to put with, consign to same fate (as).

omnes kydelli .. ~antur penitus de Thamisia *Magna Carta* 33; **1294** si .. contingat ipsos .. transire .. per forestam prohibitam, .. corde arcuum ~antur *Reg. Paisley* 94; semen [camelee] acceptum coleram et flegma ~it *Alph.* 185; **c1435** paupertas, radices michi evertens, ~it virorem, florem et fructum *FormOx* 448. **b 1242** vidit .. unum parvum nigrum mastinum currentem ad unum broketum, et ipse secutus est et deposuit eum ab illo broketto *SelPlForest* 74; **c1247** concedo .. quod .. abbas et monachi mittant se in .. possessionem .. mansi mei .. et quod illi me ab illo manso ~ant *FormA* 356; eum .. in ferris .. invenit, unde eum a ferris ~i fecit *State Tri. Ed. I* 74. **c S1197** [Fulco] in Angliam quendam religiosum ad ~enda tempora commercii diebus Dominicis .. destinavit M. PAR. *Maj.* II 440 (cf. COGGESH. *Chr.* 95); **1339** [quod] wudewardus .. debeat portare in foresta hachettum et non arcum et sagittas, pro sinistra suspiccione venacionis ~enda (*CoramR*)*SelPlForest* xxvn. **d** J. filia G. W. est leprosa; ideo ~atur *CBaron* 134. **e c1218** de inclusis: moneat .. sacerdos viros inclusos .. ne mulierculam †recipiat [v. l. recipiant] de nocte in domo sua, similiter nec mulier masculum, nec deposita, sine testimonio sacerdotis et virorum fidedignorum *Conc. Syn.* 86. **f** qui cum fure stabit et conpugnabit cum fure ~atur [AS: *lecge hine man mid þam þeofe*] (*Quad.*) *GAS* 174.

8 to depose (from office): **a** (eccl. or mon.); **b** (royalty); **c** (var.). **d** to 'lay off', put out of employment.

a si quis episcopus .. vitium habuerit ebrietatis, aut desinat aut ~atur THEOD. *Pen.* I 1. 1; T. archiepiscopus deposuit eum de episcopatu BEDE *HE* IV 6; degradaverit, deposuerit *Gl. Leid.* 2.42; **1072** causa Alricii, qui olim Cicestrensis ecclesiae praesul dictus a suppositis legatorum nostrorum depositus est (*Lit. Papae*) *Conc.* I 326; si abbas longius a monasterio fuerit, ipse ~ere potest eos quos intellexerit non juxta proficuum aecclesiae res sibi commissas tractare LANFR. *Const.* 143; **S1154** hunc Willelmum [archiepiscopum Ebor'] Eugenius papa .. deposuerat TORIGNI *Chr.* 179; **S1177** (v. degradare 1a); **1213** sunt multe alie cause quare ~i debet abbas noster (*Accusatio*) *Chr. Evesham* 241; si ~atur sacerdos, licet ei relinquatur character, non relinquitur ei potestas consecrandi HALES *Sent.* IV 203; **S1296** P. et J. de Columna a cardinalatu per papam B. ~untur TREVET *Ann.* 340; **1342** archiepiscopus .. deposuit predictos fratres et sorores et statum eorundem adnullavit (*Inq.*) *Mem. Ripon.* I 228; **S1380** (v. electivus 2a). **b S1184** Baldewinus Mesellus .. in vita sua deposuit seipsum a regno *G. Hen. II* I 331; **S1245** si eum [F. imperatorem] .. auctoritas papalis .. ~eret M. PAR. *Maj.* IV 478; est dum depositus fortis Fredericus et alter / electus GARL. *Tri. Eccl.* 118; **S1214** Otho ab imperio judicio ecclesie depositus TREVET *Ann.* 191; **c1370** Saul rex, postquam audivit .. quod Deus ~eret eum de regno (J. BRIDL. *gl.*) *Pol. Poems* I 167; **S1403** (v. confundere 3c). **c S1245** Nicholaus depositus fuit .. a vicecomitatu et .. rex posuit in loco suo Johannem .. *Leg. Ant. Lond.* 12 (cf. ib. 36 [**S1257**]: Nicholaus [et alii] degradati sunt et depositi de ballivis suis); [Robertus de custodia] corporis et terrarum .. Simonis depositus fuit *State Tri. Ed. I* 77; **1375** (v. depositio 7c); **1549** ne ulli .. ad .. magisterii lauream recipiantur nisi .. ad hoc idonei fuerint reperti; alioqui ad proximam inferiorem classem ~antur *Conc. Scot.* II 105. **d 1326** (v. cremator).

9 a to put up (a prayer). **b** to lay, lodge (a complaint). **c** to 'depone', depose, testify (absol.); **d** (w. acc. & inf. or obj. clause). **e** (pr. ppl. as sb.) deponent.

a ferro vel aqua examinandi .., si orationem ibi [in ecclesia Glaston'] deposuerunt .., de salute sua tripudiarunt W. MALM. *Glast.* 18. **b c1119** (v. decapitare d); **c1228** vidit sepe homines episcopi eciam venientes ad curiam prioris et ~ere querelam et ibi accipere rectum de hominibus prioris *Feod. Durh.* 281; **1257** fratres .. contra monachos actionem injuriarum ~unt (*Narratio de Processu*) *Mon. Francisc.* II app. 270; **1301** antequam querelam judicialiter inde ~at *Reg. Cant.* 750; **1325** siquis apud .. regem .. querimonias deposuerit .. contra me occasione predicta .. *Lit. Cant.* I 152; **S1377** (v. coepiscopus 1). **c** deposuit .. cum aliis contra me. .. sed nonne recte testes hujusmodi precipites habendi sunt? GIR. *Invect.* I 13 p. 125; probavit .. abbas .. per monachos .. qui non ita bene deposuerunt sicut illi quos .. Johannes produxit *State Tri. Ed. I* 4; **1305** (v. dumtaxat 2); **a1350** quicunque in aliquo articulo contra dicta statuta [de malefactoribus] per duos vel tres testes de sciencia ~entes .. detectus fuerit *StatCantab* 326; super quibus dominus J. M. precontestis suus superius dixit et deposuit *Canon. S. Osm.* 68. **d 1311** tres [fratres in ordine militum Templi] deposuerunt se fore receptos cum abnegacione Christi. .. item lij fratres .. confitentur et ~unt quod ita est consuetudo .. (*Proc. v. Templar.*) *Ann. Lond.* 181 (cf. ib. 192: alius frater Templi ~it qualiter unus frater commiscuit se carnaliter cum alio); **S1376** intrantes parliamentum .. deposuerunt contra dominum de Latimer .. per os domini P. de la Mare quod inutilis regi et regno fuit *Chr. Angl.* 76; **1459** qui [clerici] interrogati uniformiter deposuerunt et per se determina-

verunt quod . . rex . . erat in possessione . . presentandi ad omnia vacancia beneficia . . *Conc. Scot.* II 79. **e** **1310** asserens . . quod esset in loco Templariorum London', exprimendo locum determinatum, de quo ~ens non recordatur *Conc.* II 362b; dicit quod . . vidit et novit quod . . puerum sic submersum et mortuum . . convicini sui de visu et sciencia istius ~entis de ipso flumine extraxerunt *Canon. S. Osm.* 74.

10 (acad.) to depose as to fitness of candidate. **b** (pr. ppl. as sb.) deponent. *Cf. depositio* 8b.

a**1350** quia magistrorum presentacionem sequitur eorumdem deposicio, statuit . . universitas . . ut nullus de cetero ad lecturam Sentenciarum . . admittatur nisi unus saltim magistrorum ~encium pro eodem utatur verbo sciencie, ceteris de credulitate saltim ~entibus *StatOx* 48 (cf. ib. 31: doctores juris civilis pro bachilariis in jure canonico ~ant sub hac forma: "Scio talem esse etc. in fide prestita, quatinus rectum sciendi judicium ad meam pertinere permittitur facultatem"). **b** **1597** si quis presentatus testimonio novem ~entium de scientia approbatus fuerit, tunc admitteretur *Ib.* 455.

deponibilis, deposable (from kingship).

si super regem esset totus populus, haec conclusio sequitur, quod pro populi arbitrio reges essent ~es MAJOR IV 18.

deponile, weft.

~e, *wefta GlC* D 57; ~e *weftan GlH* D 210.

depopulari, ~are [CL], to devastate, ravage, plunder; **b** (w. inanim. subj.); **c** (w. abl.) to rob, deprive (of); **d** (fig.).

testantur se cuncta insulae rupto foedere ~aturos GILDAS *EB* 23; graculus ater / qui segetum glumas . . / depopulare studet, carpens de messe maniplos ALDH. *VirgV* 226; exercitum suum contra Romam -are eam cogitando duxit *V. Greg.* p. 99; ecclesiam . . rebus ablatis omnibus ~atam BEDE *HE* IV 12; depeculatus, i. vastatus, depraedatus, -atus, *bescyred GlH* D 191; **10.** . ~ans, *idende WW*; ~atur civitas [Lunis], diruuntur . . moenia W. JUM. I 10; dicitur quod terram S. Edmundi ~anti martyr . . apparuerit W. MALM. *GR* II 179; **1148** omnes quicunque istius ecclesie possessiones abstulerint vel diripuerint vel ~ati fuerint *Cart. Colne* f. 10; cum [ecclesia] . . cum circumjacente regione sepius depredata et ~ata et diu deserta mansisset RIC. HEX. *Hist. Hex.* II 4; R. NIGER *Chr. I* 61 (v. derelinquere 2d). **b** in mortalitate illa quae plures ~avit regiones *V. Cuthb.* IV 6; ut [sol] non semper eisdem commoratus in locis fervoris aviditate mundanum ~etur ornatum BEDE *TR* 35. **c** cum mors in limine latrat, / marcida depopulans vitali pectora flatu ALDH. *VirgV* 2381. **d** evenit saepe ut, qui . . homicidam publice peccantem judicant, pejus odiorum malum, quo ipsi in secreta ~antur, non sentiant BEDE *Hom.* I 25. 108; ignis cupiditatis et libidinis . . late ~atur habitatores terre BALD. CANT. *Tract.* 2. 415C.

depopulatio [CL], devastation, plunder; **b** (w. subj. gen.).

suam gentem ab hostili paganorum ~one liberavit BEDE *HE* III 24; †**948** (v. condolere 1c); *G. Steph.* II 104 (v. conflagratio); Tancredus . . post ~onem regni sui singula reddere compelletur in quadruplum DEVIZES 30v.; s**1297** attendens strages et ~ones per Scotos sibi . . illatas FORDUN *Cont.* XI 30. **b** s**1070** rex W. monasteria totius Anglie perscrutari et pecuniam, quam ditiores Angli propter illius austeritatem et ~onem in eis deposuerant, auferri . . jussit FL. WORC. II 5.

depopulativus, devastating, destructive.

saxivoma in turrium et murorum apices ~is afflatibus minativa *Ps.*-ELMH. *Hen. V* 52 (cf. ib. 54: ~is incendiis).

depopulator [CL], ravager, waster.

expugnator regis Francorum et terre ipsius in igne et gladio ~or W. FITZST. *Thom.* 23; **1230** Willelmus Talebot terram illam . . reddidit cuidam W. quondam episcopo London' ut capitali domino suo, quia ipse W. T. fuit venditor et ~or totius hereditatis sue *CurR* XIV 610; BACON V 43 (v. destructor).

depopulatrix [LL], devastating, destructive (f.).

pessimam et ~icem et urendam incendiorum malitiam . . detestamur ROB. FLAMB. *Pen.* 315.

1 deportare [CL]

1 to exile, banish. **b** to eject, expel.

~atus, quem sua bona in exilium non secuntur *GlC* D 23 (cf. Isid. *Etym.* V 27. 30); ~atus, *to wite asent butan his gode* ÆLF *Sup.*; [accipitris pulli] instruuntur ad rapinam et a natali solo ~andi statim ab impiis parentibus compelluntur . . exulare GIR. *TH* I 12 p. 35. **b** mustelle . . per inferiora concipiunt et ore pariunt, quia virtus ~andi seu expellendi major est in illis circa superiora *Quaest. Salern.* P 65.

2 to carry (about); **b** (ceremonially); **c** (officially). **d** to wear (as ornament).

[scripta] civium exilii classe longius ~ata GILDAS *EB* 4; foris ~atus juxta parietem . . vidit hominem *V. Cuthb.* I 4; ut per plura loca ~atis beati martyris reliquiis plura virtutum signa fierent BEDE *Hom.* II 23. 242; qui alienis manibus fuerat ~atus, suis pedibus cucurrit OSB. *Mir. Dunst.* 4; vispillones, qui mortuos ad tumulandum ~ant *GlSid* 145. **b** aedituo hastam ~ante *RegulC* 41; dicitur . . Dominica in Ramis Palmarum quia illa die rami palmarum in processionibus ~antur . . BELETH *RDO* 94. 95B; **1268** (v. crux 5b); **1401** ij haste pro vexillo S. Cuthberti †deputande *Ac. Durh.* 454 (? l. deportando *as* ib. 461; cf. deputare 5a). **c** rex . . eundem . ., experta illius ingenti discrecione, suum privatum sigillum fecerat ~are HEETE *Wykeham* 297. **d** **1222** decrevimus ut moniales . . velum . . sericum non habeant nec in velo acus argenteas vel aureas audeant ~are *Conc. Syn.* 118.

3 **a** (w. sea as subj.) to carry (to). **b** (pass.) to be borne, move, fly. **c** to conduct, escort (bishop elect to altar). **d** to bring. **e** to import.

a mare fluctibus undans . . stipitem . . detulens . . ad hostium scopuli . . natantem ~avit *V. Cuthb.* III 4. **b** toto tempore . . [avis] circa arboris fastigia ~ata permansit R. COLD. *Godr.* 209; animalis spiritus ad veneria membra ~atur *Quaest. Salern.* Ba 96. **c** s**1228** facta electione . . cantetur sollemniter canticum 'Te Deum laudamus' et, si presens fuerit, electus ~ari debet cum cantico ad altare GERV. CANT. *GR Cont.* 126. **d** s**709** obiit Wilfridus in Undala et corpus eius ~atum est ad Hripe *AS Chr.*; s**1235** (v. classicus 4c); **1320** supplicavimus ipsi domino quatinus placeret eidem processum et recordum . . coram se . . preciperet (*sic*) ~ari . . sic . . rotulis hujusmodi contingentibus in medio ~atis, compertum extitit quod . . *DCCant.* (*HMC*) 281; **1337** de nominibus eorum qui hujusmodi apporta ibidem ~averint . . cancellarium nostrum . . certificantes (*Cl*) *Foed.* IV 730a; **1367** in casu quo . . litteras quiete clamacionis non procuraret ac eisdem abbati et conventui . . ~aret et exhiberet *Reg. Paisley* 29; s**1372** de comite Pembrogie cum taxa secum ad debellandum Franciam ~ata . . depredato et in Hispaniam captivato AD. USK 8; **1431** (v. deferre 2c); s**1485** ipso [corpore R. regis] non satis humaniter propter funem in collum adjectum usque ad Leicestriam ~ato *Croyl. Cont. C* 575. **e** a**1237** neque possunt [wesdarii] de aliquibus pannis quos ferunt . . tincturam facere neque aliquam mercem suam mutare, sed secundum quod eas ~ant communiter vendere *MGL* II 69; **1321** (v. deportatio 2c).

4 ? to bring out.

postquam classica que pulsantur pro mortuis . . fuissent ~ata et pulsata †notale pro dicto puero mortuo *Mir. Montf.* 91.

5 **a** to support. **b** to sustain, endure.

a **1440** solut' pro cordula l ulnarum ad ~andum pannos laterales aule, vj d. *Cant. Coll. Ox.* II 155. **b** si quis ordinatus calumniatur de homicidio . ., purget se cum parentibus suis qui possunt emendare aut ~are [AS: *mid beran oððe forebetan*] (*Inst. Cnuti*) *GAS* 287 (= *Quad.* ib.: quorum interest occisionis factionem tolerare vel emendare); **1422** desideriis affectantes hujusmodi onera claustralia cum mentis hilaritate continuo ~ari *Conc.* III 415b.

6 to relieve, treat favourably. *Cf. deportum.*

s**1257** rex . . voluit certificari qui divites fuerunt ~ati in tallagiis *Leg. Ant. Lond.* 31; s**1265** provisum fuit . . ut . . fuisset examinatum qui fuissent temporibus retroactis gravati et qui ~ati *Ib.* app. 240.

2 †deportare, *f. l.*

s**1388** lacrimabiliter . . †~antes [? l. deprecantes] ne . . tot sapientes legum Anglie necarentur *Chr. Kirkstall* 127.

deportatio [CL]

1 exile, banishment. **b** ejection, expulsion.

[Ovidius], qui an de conscientia alieni an proprii operis noxa ~onem meruerit incertum est J. SAL. *Pol.* 503A; in insulam ~o imperpetuum vel ad tempus, quod quidem exilium dici poterit abjuratio regni sive utlagatio BRACTON 136b; **1289** excercicium alte justicie in casibus mortis . . seu fustigacionis vel ~onis *RGasc* II 463. **b** [est] necessaria in partu ~o vel expulsio que . . est actio composita ex sensu anime et quodam motu naturali *Quaest. Salern.* P 65.

2 **a** carrying, escorting (also fig.). **b** bringing. **c** importing. **d** carrying away.

a debilis . . anima eget . . pia . . appellatione, misericordia, caritativa ~one ALEX. CANT. *Dicta* 17 p. 176; s**1228** nullus prorumpat in electionem [episcopi] . . antequam . . facta fuerit collatio, nec ad ~onem antequam fiat electio GERV. CANT. *GR Cont.* 125. **b** cum [vinum] defertur et visu percipitur, ex mentis attentione fit ipsius odoris attractio. . . et sic ex vini ~one mingendi voluntas excitatur *Quaest. Salern.* B 226. **c** **1321** quocienscumque aliquis de hansa predicta aliqua . . mercimonia . . in civitatem [London'] . . duxerit seu deportaverit, quietus esse debet de custuma danda pro eisdem . . in prima empcione, ~one et adduccione hujusmodi rerum . . in civitatem *PQW* 455b. **d** a**1553** [salmonum] captionem et ~onem illas *Entries* 665b.

deportator [LL], bringer.

1332 morosa tardacio ~oris pallii . . zelantibus honorem ecclesie Cantuariensis debet displicere *Lit. Cant.* I 477.

deportum [cf. OF *deport*], relief, favourable treatment. **b** (mon.) misericord, special indulgence or room in which it is allowed.

1275 mercatores dant domino pro favore et ~o xl s. *SelPlMan* 155. **b** **1298** monachi . . a carnium esu exceptis locis inferius annotatis abstineant, sc. quod solum in mensa magistri in infirmitorio et cameris infirmorum, in ~o et camera prioris aut aula hospitum . . vescantur carnibus *Reg. Cant.* 820 (cf. ib.: magister infirmarie . . premuniat octo fratres tantum . ., prout in ordine sunt priores, quod ~um suum recipiant, si voluerint, in septimana sequente; et, si aliquis ipsorum octo ~um suum recusaverit, ipse nichilominus sic recusans singulis diebus illius septimane misse . . teneatur interesse cum ceteris qui sunt in eodem ~o); **1331** ipsam aulam cum cameris et ~o pro dictis fratribus acceptamus *Lit. Cant.* I 393; **1411** novus locus pro ~o cum subtus celario *Ib.* III 115; **1506** item pro vino in ~o, iij d. *DCCant.* C 11 f. 113a.

deposcere [CL]

1 to request, seek, pray (for); **b** (w. abstr. subj.); **c** (w. inf. or acc. & inf.).

ab Egfrido rege . . omnique senatu ~enti [v. l. ~ente], ad episcopatum . . electus est *V. Cuthb.* IV 1; [Thebe] filium suum . . sibi in praemii loco ~it ALCUIN *Rhet.* 9; et genibus flexis veniam deposcere noxis (*Vers.*) ÆLNOTH *Cnut* 44; veniam a Deo, vobis intervenientibus, †~or [v. l. deprecor] J. FORD *Wulf.* 23. **b** nunc pedester ordo ~it ut trisillabos pedes . . patefacias ALDH. *PR* 117; competens ordo ~it ut . . tandem hominem ipsum . . introducamus GIR. *TH* III *intr.* p. 138; abbas, juxta quod sue ~it dignitas preferencie, in capite partis orientis claustri . . sedere solet *Cust. Westm.* 157 (cf. ib. 205: prout res ~erit). **c** tantum presbiterum aliquem secum mittere . . ~ebat *V. Cuthb.* II 8; sese . . prostravit, diu ~ens superni regis opulentissimum sibi adesse supplementum B. *V. Dunst.* 10; [pericula] a quibus [ecclesia] liberari ~it OCKHAM *Dial.* 829.

2 (w. pers. obj.) to entreat, beseech.

supplex deposce Tonantem / ut . . / aeternae pariter lucis migremus ad oras BEDE *CuthbV* 647; eos qui hec forte lecturi sunt . . submissa prece ~o ne mihi succenseant EADMER *Mir. Osw.* 11; s**714** quo in loco omnes qui eum [S. Guthlacum] pio affectu ~unt divine miserationis indulgentiam consequuntur M. PAR. *Maj.* I 328; s**1248** magnificentiam vestram ~entes quatinus . . in nostrum auxilium . . accedatis *Ib.* VI 147.

deposissio v. depositio 7c. **deposita** v. deponere 7e.

depositarius [CL]

1 depositary, recipient of deposit, bursar. **b** (as sb. n.) depository, place of storage; *v. et. depositorius* 1b.

nostram . . in ede sacra pecuniam vel penes fidum deponamus ~ium consignatam *Collect. Stories* 201; fidelis esto dispensator, quia tantum ~ius es NECKAM *NR* II 187; **1283** ne custodibus vel ~iis pecunie . . aliquid hujus occasione molestie vel gravaminis irrogaret PECKHAM *Ep.* 495 p. 637; **1283** compotus magistrorum J. de C., G. de C., et J. de P., ~iorum *Rolls Merton* 305; **1326** quod omnia debita que ex causa mutui seu depositi . . debebant necnon omnia nomina tam debitorum quam creditorum et ~iorum suorum . . nobis in scriptis traderent *Lit. Cant.* I 200; **1377** in liberacione facta Andree B. ~io custume deputato per regem *ExchScot* 553; **1457** concedimus . . potestatem . . deputandi . . receptores et ~ios pecuniarum occasione dictarum decimarum ac indulgenciarum acquisitarum *Mon. Hib. & Scot.* 404b. **b** **1301** quod nullus a secularibus deposicionem admittat pecunie, scriptorum vel alicujus rei notabilis preter . . licenciam prioris et tunc illud quod deponendum est in communi ~io . . reponatur *Reg. Cant.* II 876.

2 (mon., Winchester) obedientiary in charge of burials *etc. V. et. depositor* 2, *depositorius* 2. *Cf.* 1 *depositio* 3.

1395 compotus . . anniversarii: . . in solutis ~iis conventus pro pitancia *Comp. Swith.* 203.

depositicius, entrusted in deposit.

1516 pecuniam apud me ~iam Aegidio nostro persolutam esse non dubito (MORE) *Ep. Erasmi* II 481.

1 depositio [CL]

1 lowering; **b** (mus., in pitch). **c** turning downwards.

elevacio [accidencium sacramenti] significat [Christi] elevacionem in cruce; ~o, ~onem; fraccio, vulneracionem (TYSS.) *Ziz.* 164. **b** sive in elevacione sive in ~one cantus . . eum [precentorem] sequantur *Obs. Barnwell* 58. **c** GILB. V 214. 1 (v. catastropha b).

2 taking down, dismantling. **b** demolition.

s**1325** (v. crux 4a); **1470** item pro ~one *le crane* erecte in orto Collegii Regis (*Ac. Univ.*) *Arch. Hist. Camb.* III 14*n.* **b** **1447** [pro] ~one magni orrii hostillarii *Ac. Durh.* 145; **1461** pro prostracione et ~one . . cancelli *Ib.* 152.

3 laying in tomb, burial; **b** (w. ref. to observance of anniversary).

quaerant in suis codicibus, in quibus defunctorum est adnotata ~o BEDE *HE* IV 14 p. 234; mittitur et episcicula

ad vicina quaeque monasteria ejusdem [fratris] ~onis denuntiatura diem *RegulC* 67; **s992** sepeliuntur . . presulis artus in . . Virginis ede, loco viz. divinitus pridem designato. post hec annuntiatur ~o ejus his et illis . . EADMER *V. Osw.* 37; **s1130** de quo loco [Acca] post annos plusquam ccc ~onis sue a quodam presbytero divina revelatione translatus est S. DURH. *HR* 36; in die ~onis monachi omnia vestimenta [ejus] erunt camerarii *Obed. Abingd.* 388; **1458** tu per tua scripta plus laudis addideras . . nostro avunculo quam omnes voces ille superficiales que laudaverunt eum ore tenus a die sue ~onis usque in presens *Reg. Whet.* I 315. **b** in natale unius confessoris: . . qui illum fecit coruscare miraculis, vos exornet bonorum operum incrementis . ., quo, ejus exemplis eruditi et intercessione muniti cujus ~onis diem celebratis in terris, illi possitis in coelesti regione adjungi EGB. *Pont.* 93; cujus [B. Werburgae] ~o tertio Nonas Feb. celebratur GOSC. *Werb.* 106C; a die ~onis ejus [24 *Apr.*] jam anno transcurso, convenit undecunque maxima populi multitudo, utpote pro ~onis illius memoria excubias celebratura EADMER *Wilf.* 55; **1202** predicti confessoris domini ~onem [4 *Feb.*] annuam faciatis cum reverentia et sollemniter observari (*Lit. Archiep. Cant.*) *Canon. G. Sempr.* 138; instante festo ~onis B. Cuthberti [20 *March*], tante diei reverentie non deferens . ., misit [episcopus] clericos et laicos . . qui ne prior celebrare presumeret . . prohiberent G. COLD. *Durh.* 16; **c1220** concesserunt W. decanus Sar' et capitulum . . quod die anniversario ~onis nostre persone et canonici et vicarii ejusdem ecclesie habebunt pitancias quales solent habere solemnibus diebus *Ch. Sal.* 102; **s1261** papa . . constituit solemnizari diem ~onis ejus [R. Ep. Cicestr'] iij° nonas Aprilis OXNEAD *Chr.* 220; in ~one S. Swithini [2 *July*] . . prior inveniet j caseum . .; item in translatione ejusdem [15 *July*] inveniet ij caseos *Cust. Swith.* 15; **1416** festum ~onis . . S. Johannis *Conc.* III 379b (*gl.* LYNDW. 104 d: '~onis', i.e. obitus sive mortis; tunc namque justus homo deposita vetustate pene nascitur ad gloriam; et ideo dies mortis dicitur sanctorum natalis); **1504** da anime famule tue Elizabeth . . consortis H. septimi regis et fundatoris nostri, cujus anniversarium ~onis diem commemoramus, . . quietis beatitudinem *StatOx* 313.

4 deposit (for safe-keeping).

est . . thesaurus quedam vetus ~o pecunie vel alterius metalli cujus non extat memoria, ut jam dominum non habeat BRACTON 120; **c1261** super ~one pecunie de decima consilio magistri R. bene acquiescimus, quia satis tutus est modus, dummodo per mercatores inde cautio bona fiat (*AncC* VII 210) *RL* II 195; **1219** carta abbatis et conventus de W. de recognitione ~onis penes eos instrumentorum ecclesie Sar' *Ch. Sal.* 93 *rub.* (v. et. deponere 4a).

5 laying aside, shedding, casting off; **b** (w. ref. to excretion); **c** (of the fleshly tabernacle (*2 Pet.* i 14) or sim., euphem. for death). **d** (log.) rejection, refutation (of proposition).

s1327 astute . . circumvenerunt regem, promittentes sibi non parciorem honorem post honeris ~onem quam antea solebat ab omnibus habere regia celsitudo BAKER 106 (= MORE *Chr. Ed. II* 313: honoris ~onem). **b** [ad balneum] est utendum jejuno stomacho et post ~onem superfluitatum BACON IX 51 (cf. ib. 102). **c** certus sum quia tempus meae resolutionis instat et 'velox est ~o tabernaculi mei' BEDE (*CuthbP* 28) *HE* IV 27 p. 274; ea . . quae post ~onem corporalis sarcinae felix spiritus ejus in hoc saeculo dignatus est operari OSB. *Mir. Dunst.* 1; velox est ~o corporis mei W. MALM. *GP* (*Oswald*) III 115; *Chr. Rams.* 103 (v. decredere); **s1422** omnes hujus mundi . . strepitus una cum carnis ~one finaliter exuebat *Croyl. Cont. B* 515; *dede*, . . decessus, †depisicio [v. l. deposicio], exicium . ., mors . . *CathA*. **d** ~o est obligacio ad sustinendum aliquam proposicionem tanquam falsam (OCKHAM *Summa*) *GLA* IV 43 *n.* 169; (HOLCOT) *Ib.* 9 *n.*27 (v. deponere 5j).

6 taking away.

sunt etiam quedam [genera penarum] que dignitatis et ordinis inducunt ~onem BRACTON 104b.

7 deposition (from office): **a** (eccl. or mon.); **b** (from kingship); **c** (var.).

a 1102 non videtur, si alias [sacerdotes] digni fuerint, in eos ~onis sententiam dari (*Lit. Papae*) EADMER *HN* 159; ferunt quidam esse arcanam ~onis [archiepiscopi] causam W. MALM. *GR* III 267; **s1175** abbas de Burgo . . sententiam ~onis accepit DICETO *YH* I 402; **s1202** quod episcopus potestatem habebat . . errata usque ad ~onem et degradationem corrigere *Chr. Evesham* 110; **1267** (v. 1 cessio 2); **s1300** transactis tribus mensibus a suspensione prioris et ~one GRAYSTANES 23; **s1301** papa . . prelatis Anglie . . precepit sub pena excommunicacionis et ~onis ne . . regi . . decimam . . darent *Ann. Ed. I* 462; frater M. ante omnem ~onem et sentenciam latam contra ipsum a presidente . . OCKHAM *Pol.* I 294. **b** Pipinus . ., post ~onem Hilderici regis . . rex Francorum effectus, genuit Carolum Magnum HIGD. I 27 p. 282; **c1370** regina . . conspirabat ad ~onem mariti sui [Ed. II] de regno et ad filii sui elevacionem (J. BRIDL. *gl.*) *Pol. Poems* I 136; **s1399** quoniam de ~one regis Ricardi et sublimacione regis Henrici diversi diversa scripserunt CAPGR. *Hen.* 102. **c 1375** Henricus B. . . depositus et expulsus est ab omnibus concilio et congregacione in gildehalla . . faciendis . .; et, ut depositio et expulsio predicti H. . . firmius observentur . . *RR K's Lynn* II 118; **1456** rex noster . ., licet in mea ~one non interfuerit, tamen ipsius vehementer penitet (*Lit. Praepositi Regalis Collegii Cantab.*) BEKYNTON II 158.

8 a (leg.) deposition, testimony. **b** (acad.) deposition as to fitness of candidate (*cf. Theol. Ox.* 42).

a s1205 sicut per ~ones testium . . plenissime patebit *Chr. Evesham* 162; **1219** cum ~ones testium super his receptorum nobis . . transmisisset . ., ipsas . . fecimus inspici (*Lit. Papae*) *Reg. S. Osm.* II 6; **1301** ipsorum ~onibus . . non erat fides . . adhibenda *Reg. Cant.* 415; **1311** prout constabat . . per multas confessiones et ~ones magistri et preceptorum et fratrum coram multis prelatis et inquisitoribus heretice pravitatis in regno Francie factas (*Dep. Templar.*) *Ann. Lond.* 182; **1429** testibus . . receptis et . . juratis ac . . examinatis ipsorumque dictis et ~onibus ad . . curiam [Cantuariensem] transmissis (*Sententia in Curia de Arcubus*) AMUND. I 249; **1473** circa scripturam ~onum certorum personarum coram ymagine regis Henrici sexti . . offerencium *Fabr. York* 82. **b 1312** in tractatibus . . super inceptoribus in theologia et bacularriis pro legendis sentenciis licenciandis . ., in quibus solent omnium . . magistrorum theologie ibi presencium ante licenciacionem vota requiri et stricta ~o singulorum necessario obtineri (*Appellatio Fratrum Praedic.*) *Collect. Ox.* II 240; **a1350** (v. deponere 10a); **1391** consideratis . . meritis . . magistri A. de B. . ., quem . . ex magistrorum . . legitima ~one reperimus . . literarum studio actualiter insistendo . . se bene et laudabiliter habuisse *MunAcOx* 471; **a1477** non requiritur alia ~o quam exprimitur in hoc statuto *StatOx* 170.

2 depositio v. dispositio 2c.

depositor [CL]

1 a depositor of money; *cf. deponere* 4; **b** 'sewer', server at table; *cf. deponere* 3a.

a civitatis optimatibus . . ~orem [pecunie] sciscitantibus quam de muliere [furti rea] ferret sententiam W. CANT. *Mir. Thom.* IV 10; ~ori licet pro voluntate sua depositum revocare OCKHAM *Dial.* 629; **1413** vi rapuit a ~oribus expensarum ordinatarum pro . . ambassatoribus c nobilia *ExchScot* 189. **b** *seware ate mete*, ~or, sepulator, dapifer *PP*; ~or, A. *a sewer* . ., *a serofer in halle WW*; *a sewer at þe mete*, ~or, prepositor, discoforus *CathA*; **1489** Johannem Whytyng ~orem, alias dictum *sewer CalPat* 266.

2 (mon., Winchester) obedientiary in charge of burials *etc. V. et. depositarius* 2, *depositorius* 2. *Cf.* 1 *depositio* 3.

1387 expense consuete: . . ~oribus xiij s. iiij d. . . in solutis ~oribus die Animarum x s. *Comp. Swith.* 413.

depositorius

1 used for storage. **b** (as sb. n.) depository, place of storage; *v. et. depositarius* 1b.

12.. infra archam ~iam (*Const. Frat. Penit.*) *EHR* IX 124 (v. 1 capsula a). **b 12..** ut duo fratres . . statuantur, qui sub uno ~io ij clavium diversarum . . omnia deposita conservabunt *Ib.* 125.

2 (mon., Winchester) obedientiary in charge of burials *etc. V. et. depositarius* 2, *depositor* 2. *Cf.* 1 *depositio* 3.

1382 expense consuetudinarie [hordarii]: . . ~iis, xiij s. iiij d. *Comp. Swith.* 279; **1485** in solutis ~iis conventus *Ib.* 297.

depositum v. deponere 4.

deposse [cf. CL posse]

1 to be able.

1325 volentes . . subditorum nostrorum animarum saluti, ne . . sentencias incurrant predictas, quatinus tamen ~umus, precavere *Reg. Heref.* 314.

2 (?) to be unable, fail.

si cetera mundi / monstra triumphali potui consumere dextra, / in Phrygios (dicamne viros?) humanaque bella / depotuisse pudet J. EXON. *BT* I 289.

depost [LL, al. div.]

1 (adv.): **a** behind, at the rear. **b** afterwards, hereafter, thereafter.

a ceteris aciebus de post pro alis a lateribus constitutis *G. Hen. V* 4. **b s1394** dedit unum ciphum argenteum . . ac ~t dedit ad usum capituli . . alium ciphum majoris ponderis *Chr. Pont. Ebor. C* 426; **1447** juravit quod non de post portabit aliquod daggarium seu aliqua alia arma infra villam et universitatem *MunAcOx* 576; **1455** contrahentes matrimonium . . secum . . testes . . habeant, per quos . . matrimonium . . probari possit, si . . contingat id ~t denegari *Reg. Cant.* 23; **s1455** proposuerunt in omni parliamento ~t per septem annorum spacium . . tento . . *Reg. Whet.* I 181; **1468** (v. dare 2d); **c1470** quod . . hec ordinacio . . omnino cesset, tunc nullum ~t vigorem habitura *StatOx* 286.

2 (prep.): **a** from behind. **b** behind.

a 1198 qui novissimum fratrum . . in regem 'de post fetantes accepit' [*Psalm* lxxvii 70] (*Lit. Papae Electi*) *Ep. Cant.* 429. **b** videt iterum, quos prius, episcopos per pavimenta ecclesie de post altaris ulteriora procedere R. COLD. *Cuthb.* 38 (cf. ib. *rub.*: de fratre . . qui . . tres episcopos de post altare descendentes et regredientes perspexit); **s1397** in balneo ~t Albam Aulam AD. USK 14; baliste adversarie, que erant de post dorsum armatorum et ex lateribus *G. Hen. V* 13; ymago . . S. Georgii . ., habens ~t dorsum tapetam coccineam cum armis suis *Ib.* 15 p. 104 (cf. ib. in domo contigua ~t turrim).

depostulare [CL], to demand, require.

s1109 [rex Henricus] sacramenta ~ans de connubio filie sue ab imperatoris recepit legatis ad Pentecosten H. HUNT. *HA* VII 27.

depotare [LL = *to drink up*], to give to drink.

episcopus . . dixit: "da servo domini tui infirmanti aquam." . . ego jamjamque praecepto obediens per ter ~avi eum *V. Cuthb.* IV 7.

depotestare, to deprive of power.

R. de Glanvilla, regni rector et regis oculus, . . ~atus et custodie traditus DEVIZES 26.

depp- v. dep-.

depraedari [CL], **~are** [LL]

1 to plunder, rob, despoil (sts. w. abl. or *de*): **a** (district, building, or sim.); **b** (person); **c** (absol.); **d** (fig.).

a s676 Æðelredus rex Merciorum vastavit [*gl.*: vel ~avit] Cantiam *AS Chr.*; **793** ecclesia S. Cuðberhti . ., omnibus spoliata ornamentis, locus cunctis in Brittannia venerabilior, paganis gentibus datur ad ~andum. . . vineam electam vulpes ~arunt [cf. *Jer.* ii 21; *Cant.* ii 15] ALCUIN *Ep.* 16; **s1088** Willelmus de Owe . . regiam villam ~atur Beorchelaum [*Berkeley*] FL. WORC. II 24; **s1136** G. comes Andegavensis . . plurimas regiones ~avit ac destruxit RIC. HEX. *Stand.* 39; *Id. Hist. Hex.* II 4 (v. depopulari a); **1188** Salahadinus . . fines ejus vastavit et ~avit (*Lit. Regis Jerosolim.*) DICETO *YH* II 28; **s1265** S. de Monteforti junior . . Wyntonie civitatem ~avit *Ann. Lond.* 68; **s1315** J. Douglas ~atus est Hertilpol et totam orientalem plagam episcopatus GRAYSTANES 36; **1404** qui quandam navem . . de bonis et mercandisis hujusmodi ~ati fuerunt *Cl* 254 m. 27*d*. **b** ne et ~atae et insuper confusae a B. Petri pietate spectabiles personae in tanto recederent merore *V. Ed. Conf.* 47; **s1177** ubi mos erat ~are peregrinos S. Jacobi *G. Hen. II* I 132; **1254** cives . . ~atus est bonis suis contra pacem *Cl* 315; **s1264** hi qui cum rege erant burgenses et omnes alios ad extremum obolatum ~ati sunt *Ann. Dunstable* 230; **s1272** quidam maliciosi viri Belial . . proposuerunt quod . . insurgerent in aldermannos . . et illos ~arent de omnibus bonis et catallis suis *Leg. Ant. Lond.* 152; **1336** marinarii . . plures naves . . vi et armis ceperunt . . ac mercatores et alios homines in eisdem existentes de bonis et rebus suis ~ati fuerunt *RScot* 472b; **1347** (v. derobare a); **a1553** ipsum T. de xl li. . . felonice ~avit et spoliavit *Entries* 125. **c** qui ista confundunt, in delictis deferendo, in obsequiis deprimendo, in guerra blandiendo, in pace ~ando . . GIR. *DK* II 9; tunc simul unanimes lupus et canis, ursus in urbe / depredant GOWER *VC* I 960. **d** effeminatos a feminis viros debita virilitate femine ~antur GIR. *TH* I 12; qui horum alterutrum [sc. gloriam vel vindictam] sibi ipsi assumit, Deum ~atur [ME: *he robbeð God and reaveð*] *AncrR* 107; David . . cujus animam . . oculi ~ati fuerant [cf. *Lam.* iii 51] BLAKMAN *Hen. VI* 7.

2 to carry off as booty, steal.

Christiani superstitiosorum tam uxoribus quam etiam filiis necnon servis et ancillis ~atis ad propria redierunt WILLIB. *Bonif.* 8 p. 52; fur bona ~at ALCUIN (*Apoc.*) *Exeg.* 1110B; **s1214** ad tractandum quid . . a rege J. expeterent ad restitutionem bonorum que de prelatis ecclesie ~arat *Meaux* I 393; **1225** navem . . quam quedam mulier de Dublin' clamat esse suam et que ei ~ata fuit in costera Britannie *Cl* 86a; **1256** consuetudo comitatus talis est quod, quamcito aliquis capiatur cum manuopere, statim decolletur et ipse qui sequitur pro catallis ab ipso depridatis habebit catalla sua pro ipso decollando *AssizeR Northumb* 70; **1375** Johannes ~atus fuit . . duobus hominibus . . vij d. ob. *Leet Norw.* 64 (cf. ib. 65: Johanna Kempster . . ~avit de Petro de S. vj ulnas de *warp* de *brown* et est communis fur).

depraedatio [LL], depredation, plundering. **b** (w. obj. gen). theft, forcible seizure. **c** plunder, stolen property.

s796 Ceoluulfus rex Merciorum devastavit provinciam Cantuariorum miserabili ~one *AS Chr.*; **†884** (13c) vastancium crudelissima ~one hostium barbarorum *CS* 447; pervagabuntur diaboli . . hanc terram igne, ferro, et ~one hostili *V. Ed. Conf.* 55; suscepto in alteram vitam Lanfranco, ~ones ecclesiarum ubique in Anglia exerceri W. MALM. *GP* I 47; **1265** quod in mari nulle rapine seu . . ~ones aut homicidia committantur (*AncC* XII 12) *RL* II 289; **1285** in boscis . . in quibus ~ones et homicidia frequenter perpetrabantur *BBC* (*Carmarthen*) 66; **1296** in terrarum destruccionibus, . . subditorum suorum ~onibus (*Lit. Regis Scotiae*) FORDUN *Cont.* XI 26 (cf. *Anglo-Scot. Rel.* 70); **1450** perdonamus . . Johanni [Mortymer alias Cade], ceterisque secum . . associatis . . omnimoda murdra, insurrecciones . ., ~ones, spoliaciones, roberias . . et malefacta . . per ipsos . . facta, commissa sive perpetrata (*Pat*) *Lit. Cant.* III 206. **b** hostilis ~o bonorum ecclesie *Chr. Rams.* 325; **s1194** nunc villarum depopulacionibus, nunc ~onibus armentorum . . invigilare curabant DICETO

YH II 115; **1221** fugitivi sunt pro ~one carete robate *SelPlCrown* 105; **1227** nolumus quod homines .. qui dicuntur fuisse ad ~onem navis de Norweg' vexentur .. ea occasione quod ad predictam roberiam interfuisse debuerunt *Cl* 167b; **1265** cum .. comes [Derb'] minatus fuerit abbati et conventui de Bildewas de incendio domorum et ~one bonorum suorum *Cl* 64. **c** **1268** receptavit R. le W. cum sua ~one *JustIt* 618 r. 20*d*.

depraedativus, (as epithet of year) inflicting depredation.

s**1245** transiit annus ille .. regno Anglorum inimicus et ~us, Terre Sancte hostilis M. Par. *Min.* II 511; s**1255** transiit annus iste .. Anglie †depredatus [? l. ~ivus], Terre Sancte pestifer Oxnead *Chr.* 204.

depraedator [LL], plunderer, robber; **b** (as epithet of year).

maluit talis fuisse furti sacrilegus ~or quam tanto carere thesauro R. Cold. *Osw.* 48; Widonem .., patrie strateque publice ~orem, cepit W. Fitzst. *Thom.* 21; **1253** malefactores foreste et ~ores *SelPlForest* 111; supernorum illustrator, terrenorum gubernator, infernorum ~or (Peckham *Collatio in Passione*) *Powicke Studies* 279 *n.*5; **1265** attachientur ~ores illi .. et, si de robberia vel depredacione hujusmodi convicti fuerint, omnia dampna refundent conquerentibus *Cl* 132; **1270** monemus ut .. raptores et ~ores bonorum Deo dedicatorum .. ablata restituant *Conc.* II 23a; hec duo vicia ~oribus [ME: *grimme robberes*] comparantur *AncrR* 128; s**1381** "ubi est regni proditor? ubi communis vulgi ~or?" Wals. *HA* I 460; *pylowre or he þat pelyth oþer men*, pilator, ~or .., *ryfelowre*, ~or, spoliator *PP*. **b** s**1246** transiit annus ille .. adversarius Imperio, regnis quoque Francorum et Anglorum ~or M. Par. *Min.* III 15; s**1249** fluxit .. annus ille .. Francie, Anglie, Ytalie, et Germanie immisericors ~or et perturbator *Ib.* 68.

depraedatorius, predacious; **b** (as epithet of year).

volucres ~ie et rapaces P. Blois *Ep.* 61. 184B. **b** s**1248** transiit annus ille .. Germanie letifer, Francie et Anglie ~ius M. Par. *Min.* III 43.

depraedatus v. depraedativus.

depraedicare [LL = *to proclaim*], to deny in preaching.

quicquid predicabat unus [episcoporum] alter ~abat J. Sal. *Hist. Pont.* 24; **1166** timeo ne pontifices ipsi contra scripta sua venire cogantur et ~are quod predicant *Id. Ep.* 252 (174).

depraeditus v. deperdere 2b.

depraedo [cf. CL praedo], robber.

1268 villata .. dicit quod ~ones nec aliquos inimicos domini regis receptavit *JustIt* 618 r. 18 (cf. ib.: ~ones de Keni[l]wrth).

depraehendere v. deprehendere.

depravare [CL]

1 to twist, warp. **b** to pervert, corrupt. **c** to distort, misrepresent; **d** (w. ref. to text).

in humano corpore membrum .., quanquam languidum et vitio quolibet ~atum, non statim .. precidendum Gir. *PI* I 10 p. 34. **b** duabus feminis, quae nuper .. a Christi consortio apostataverant, eandem [Dorotheam] tradidit ~andam Aldh. *VirgP* 47; a sinceritate fidei ~atus Bede *HE* II 15; **9..** ~andam, *to mishworfenum* .., †deprevatum, *beþwyrad WW*; **811** pars illa quae rea et ~ata fuerit suae propriae partis rea privetur *CS* 332; exclusa per mortificationem carnis omni concupiscentia .., per contritionem spiritus omni vitio ~antis nequitie Ad. Marsh *Ep.* 11; Bacon *CSPhil.* 406 (v. depravatio 1). **c** ut nullus .. homo hoc quod constitutimus ~are aut minuere presumat (*Lit. Papae*) Dominic *V. Ecgwini* I 11; dicta nostra factaque omnia malitiose ~ant Jewel *Apol.* A 4v. **d** Bede *Retract.* 995 C (v. falsare 2b).

2 to denigrate, slander.

non ego criminibus quemquam depravo peractis Frith. 765; **13..** conversacionem monachorum nostrorum ~ando .. regis benevolentiam a nobis .. avertebat *Meaux* II 191; **1341** (v. conivere 2c); ~antes discipulos Cristi subsannio Wycl. *Ver.* III 166; **1381** jam mendicantes lacerant, / horum statum vituperant, / †depravunt vitam, opera (*In Lollardos* 41. 3) *Pol. Poems* I 244; quia [leccator] B. Virginis immaculata viscera deprav[av]erat .., effusa sunt viscera ejus *Latin Stories* 66; s**1404** Anglicorum sibi resistencium invidia suisque literis .. ipsum [presencium compilatorem] regi .. ~ancium Ad. Usk 85.

3 to restore (from deformed or debased condition).

adveniente igne .. dissolvet pura ab impuris .. et ita ~abuntur omnia et temperabuntur et ita erit perpetua vita *Quaest. Salern.* B 216.

depravatio [CL]

1 (moral) perversion, corruption.

quodlibet .. peccatum mortale est ~onis infinite; nam offendit divinam majestatem .., ergo necesse est quod depravet hominem morbo infinito Bacon *CSPhil.* 406.

2 slander.

pacietur contumelias, persecuciones et ~ones multiplices Wycl. *Ver.* III 172.

depravator [LL], perverter, misrepresenter.

aliter posset ~or scripture compaginare unum verbum de una oracione cum verbo de alia et dicere quod illa est scriptura sacra secundum quamlibet ejus partem et tamen notorie impossibilis Wycl. *Ver.* II 113; sic .. speculatores debent tales symoniacos .. declamare ..; et quicunque confessor, consultor vel ~or dicat contrarium caveat sibi de sentencia Domini [cf. *Ezek.* xxxiv 10] *Id. Sim.* 104.

2 blasphemer, slanderer.

uti hoc instruente exemplo sibi quisque precaveat ne divinis beneficiis ingratus ~or existat T. Mon. *Will.* VII 13; *Chr. Dale* 1 (v. damnator).

deprecabilis [LL], open to entreaty, exorable.

†**1068** (1335) precibus fratrum .. flexibilis ac ~is extiti *Regesta* 11; c**1220** ~is esto super servum tuum [cf. *Psalm* lxxxix 13] (*Oratio*) *Ch. Sal.* 213; erat rex Willelmus [I] ~is post victoriam M. Par. *Min.* I 12; **1337** cunctis in suis necessitatibus ex viscerosa caritate vos ~es exhibetis *FormOx* 99.

deprecari [CL *usu.* = *to deprecate or sim.*], **~are** [LL]

1 to pray, entreat: **a** (w. *ut*); **b** (w. inf.); **c** (w. *pro*); **d** (absol.); **e** (1st person sg. pres. indic. in parenthesis).

a Augustinus .. flectit genua sua ad Patrem Domini nostri .., ~ans ut visum caeco .. restitueret Bede *HE* II 2; c**792** has vobis literas dirigere praesumpsi, ~ans ut .. portitorem .. suscipere dignemini Alcuin *Ep.* 11; **1340** Salvatori nostro .. gracias .. exsolvimus, ~antes ut .. continuatis nos auxiliis prosequatur (*Lit. Regis*) Avesb. 90. **b** culpam confitens suam et quam patiebatur poenam apperiens et pro amore Christi se solvere depraecatus Alcuin *WillP* 20; **1464** volo, desidero et ~or et me et omnia mea .. cedere Deo *MunAcOx* 705. **c** pro aeterno regno semper laborare ac ~ari solebat Bede *HE* III 12; pauperes qui cotidie pro rege et omni populo Christiano ~antur *DB* II 372; s**1291** jussit rex crucem .. erigi ad regine memoriam, ut a transeuntibus pro ejus anima ~etur Rish. 121; **1353** cuilibet vidue pro anima mea ~anti et circa corpus meum vigilanti (*Testamentum*) *Feod. Durh.* 6*n*. **d** **705** tuque, obtime pater, utere prudenti consilio ut .. consentiam voci ~antium Wealdhere *Ep.* 23; cessit ~anti Bede *HE* II 12 p. 107; **901** (12c) ~anti (*sic*) .. familia Maldubiensis ecclesiae, aliquantulum terrae meae .. dedi praedictae familiae *CS* 589; nos mites ostendimus quando ~antibus aures .. inclinamus Bart. Angl. I 20; si non servire cuperem ~anti Ockham *Pol.* I 16. **e** **790** commendite (*sic*) .., ~or, nomen meum per .. amicos vestros Alcuin *Ep.* 10; sic ait: "o Philli, colludas, deprecor, illi" Garl. *PP* 26. 439. **2** (w. pers. obj.) to pray to, entreat, beseech; **b** (w. *ut* or sim.); **c** (w. inf.); **d** (w. acc. & inf.); **e** (w. *pro*). ~atus Dominum .. non est defraudatus *V. Cuthb.* I 4; monasterium in quo ipse rex .. ad ~andum Dominum verbumque audiendum advenire .. deberet Bede *HE* III 23; **1189** ubi Christus per constitutas diei et noctis horas ~abatur, nunc Mahumet .. laudatur (*Lit. Nuncii*) Diceto *YH* II 61. **b** ~antes eum [sc. Deum] toto corde .. ne ad internicionem usque delerentur Gildas *EB* 25; per ipsam .. te ~or quae te salvavit ne tu mihi sponsum nomines Aldh. *VirgP* 42; **796** (v. convalescere a); s**853** Merciorum rex per nuncios ~atus est Æthelwulfum .. ut ei auxilium conferret Asser *Alf.* 7; te ~or .. quatinus .. sospitatem mihi efficiat .. tua intercessio Gosc *Mir. Iv.* lxxiii; s**1116** (v. consentire 4b); **1323** rogamus vos et ~amus quod .. velitis .. mittere .. balsamum *Lit. Cant.* I 109. **c** **792** ut .. peregrinationis illius vias .. Pippinum regem subvenire †depraecamini [? l. ~emini] Alcuin *Ep.* 11; depraecata est per intercessionem sancti sui famuli divinam ei miserere clementiam *Id. WillP* 28; **1303** vos .. nostris necessitatibus compati .. ~amur *Chr. Rams. app.* 380; vestram nectaream linguam in laudes ejus alludere devote ~avi *Croyl. Cont. A* 108. **d** ~atus est Dominum ostendi sibi gloriam justorum Osb. *V. Dunst.* 17. **e** nonne melius esset .. Dominum pro eorum ~ari salute ..? Bede *CuthbP* 3; s**1066** fundata est ibidem [prope Hastinges] domus religiosorum .. pro eorundem [occisorum] animabus Deum imperpetuum ~atura *Flor. Hist.* I 598.

3 (sts. w. *ab*) to pray for, crave (a boon). **b** (absol.) to secure terms (of tenurial service); *cf. deprecatio* 3.

curationem parvulae a sacerdotibus ~antur Bede *HE* I 18; miles .. fatetur errorem, veniam ~atur W. S. Alb. *V. Alb. & Amphib.* 20 (= M. Par. *Maj.* I 151: a sancto veniam ~atur). **b** reddebat inde omnes consuetudines firmae sicuti reddebant antecessores sui, excepto rustico opere, sicut ~ari poterat a praeposito *DB* I (*Worcs*) 172v.; Godricus tenuit, serviens inde episcopo, ut poterat ~ari *Ib.* 173; K. et Godric tenuerunt et deserviebant sicut ab episcopo ~ari poterant *Ib.* 174.

4 to invite.

1285 ~abitur hospites domini ad cibum *Cust. Suss* II 1.

deprecatio [CL]

1 plea for forgiveness.

concessio est per quam non factum ipsum probatur ab reo, sed ut ignoscatur id petitur; cujus partes sunt duae, purgatio et ~o. .. ~o est cum et peccasse et consulto peccasse reus se confitetur et tamen ut ignoscatur postulat Alcuin *Rhet.* 15; *Ib.* (v. consulere 5e).

2 **a** prayer (to God). **b** entreaty. **c** object of prayer.

a cum .. apud divinam pietatem verbo ~onis ageret Bede *HE* II 12; depraecatio, frequens oratio *GlC* D 108; c**795** in secretis ~onum vestrarum intercessionibus Alcuin *Ep.* 42; Deus .., respice ad ~onem nostram (*Jud. Dei*) *GAS* 421; deprecor te ut exaudias verba ~onis meae (*Ib.*) *Ib.* 425; justa boni viri ~o .. apud Dominum audiri meruit [cf. *James* v 16] Gir. *PI* III 1; per affectum pie ~onis Ad. Marsh *Ep.* 121. **b** s**1187** Henrico .. rex Jerusalem .. et principes terre illius miserunt .. Templi magistros cum supplici ~one ut celerem succursum faceret Terre .. Sancte *G. Hen. II* I 331; sub ortacione comprehenduntur ~o et imperium, ~o quidem respectu majorum est, hortacio respectu parium, imperium respectu minorum *Ps.*-Gros. *Gram.* 59; rex Malcolmus .., quamvis .. tocius populi ~onibus exortatus [v. l. exoratus] .. nubere *Plusc.* VI 20 (= Fordun *Cont.* VIII 6: imprecacionibus); humillima deprecantes instancia ut ipsum .. favorabili vultu velitis ad infra recipere et nostre ~onis intuitu .. conclusionem .. demonstrare *Reg. Whet.* II app. 400. **c** Eve .. / †sumnus [l. somnus] erat atque quies jugis deprecatio Hil. Ronce. 1. 114.

3 boon-work (additional manorial service). *V. et. precaria.*

a**1128** quisquis eorum arat j acram et ij vicibus per ~onem inveniunt carrucas *Chr. Peterb.* app. 160; c**1310** debent arare ij acras de ~one *Reg. S. Aug.* 205.

deprecative, in the form of prayer.

presbyteri .. proponant quedam ypotetice .., quedam parenetice .., quedam prophonetice .., quedam proseutice, i.e. ~e Garl. *Dict.* 133.

deprecator [CL], (w. force of adj.) expressive of entreaty or request.

1176 Soltanus .. supplicavit imperio nostro et ~oribus usus est sermonibus et requisivit pacem (*Lit. Manuelis Imp.*) R. Howd. II 104 (= Diceto *YH* I 418: deprecatoriis).

deprecatorie, by way of entreaty or request.

1200 nos .. scribemus pro passagio nostrorum [hominum] .. ipsi archiepiscopo [Rothomag'] et ballivis suis ~ie, †et [? l. ut] ipsi preces nostras faciant *RChart* 59a; **1363** fuimus cum .. devota instancia ~ie requisiti quatinus .. contenta in litteris .. ratificare .. dignaremur *Lit. Cant.* II 441.

deprecatorius [LL]

1 expressive of entreaty or request; **b** (w. *litterae* or sim.). **c** (as sb. f. pl. or sg.) letter of request.

1176 (v. deprecator); succedit .. vox ista ~ia qua oramus sic: 'excita .. potentiam tuam ..' [*Psalm* lxxix 3] Ad. Scot *Serm.* 127B; c**1238** literas recepimus in forma ~ia ut T. clericum .. ad ecclesiam .. admitteremus Gros. *Ep.* 52; ~iam adjungo peticionem ut fratrem P. .. recommendare curetis .. fratribus vestris Ad. Marsh *Ep.* 178. **b** c**793** has .. ~ias cum magna humilitatis caritate litterulas tuae laudabili sapientiae dirigere curavi Alcuin *Ep.* 23; cunctorum pene totius ordinis priorum ~iis onustus litteris venit .. ad portam Cartusie Ad. Eyns. *Hug.* IV 13 p. 68; **1202** mercatores R. habent litteras domini regis patentes directas comitisse Flandrie ~ias quod eis reddi faciat pecuniam suam *Pat* 21b; per litteras suas ~ias et minatorias directas vicecomiti .. mandavit quod venire faceret illos *State Tri. Ed. I* 21; s**1470** responsio cuidam littere ~ie *Reg. Whet.* II 94 *rub.* **c** optimum .. videtur quod .. scribatis .. comiti ~ias efficaces, rationabiles, supplices Ad. Marsh *Ep.* 21; vidue .. me compulit obsecratio presentem ~iam vestre caritati destinare *Ib.* 232; ~ia pro domino J. M. super non residencia *Reg. Cant. 1294–1313* 411 *rub.*

2 (as sb. n.) (?) bead (of rosary). *Cf. deprecula.*

1350 iij paria deprecator' [? l. de precatoriis] *IMisc* 164/13.

deprecatus, entreaty.

c**1140** petitione et ~u Theobaldi hominis mei .. concessi .. ij croftulas .. *Reg. S. Osm.* I 342; piget nimiis grandium negotiorum importunitatibus causarum exilium humiles ~us ingerere Ad. Marsh *Ep.* 112.

deprecula, bead (of rosary).

1414 j par ~arum de argento, precii xiij s. iiij d. *Proc. J. P.* 304; *bedys*, .. ~e *PP*.

depredere v. deperdere 2b.

†deprehendare, *f. l.*

s**1317** villa Bristollis se reddidit castellanis ad eorum [civium] dampnum permaximum, quia eos pro eorum voluntate ~averunt [? l. depredaverunt] *Flor. Hist.* III 341.

deprehendere [CL]

1 (w. pers. obj.) to seize, catch; **b** (in the act of offending); **c** (w. *de* in ref. to the offence).

nonnulli miserarum reliquiarum in montibus deprehensi acervatim jugulabantur GILDAS *EB* 25; [frater meus] qui .. cum familia exulavit et pluries hostibus ~sus se redemit pecunia BACON *Tert.* 16. **b** saepe in furtis ~sus sum WULF. *Æthelwold* 46; **c1072** (v. detinere 2c); falsam mensuram in civitate faciens ~sus *DB* I 262v.; **1220** (v. 2 clericus 1a); BRACTON 152 (v. cognoscere 6a); **1559** quicumque procurator .. frivolam exceptionem .. exhibuerit seu aliter manifeste ~sus fuerit *Conc. Scot.* II 171. **c** de inobedientia .. ~si *Offic. Sal.* 11 (v. degradare 1a); primus modus quo potest quis de pertinacia ~di OCKHAM *Dial.* 448.

2 to detect: **a** (offender); **b** (offence or guilt); **c** (property thought to be stolen).

a Jonas sorte ~sus .. projicitur in mare AD. DORE *Pictor* 162. **b** tristitia .. quae de indignatione .. ~sae conscientiae extorquetur GILDAS *EB* 1; maritus crimen ~dit NECKAM *NR* I 64 (cf. ib.: ne a marito furtiva culpa ~deretur); at tandem dominus fraudem deprendit aselli *Id. Avianus* 466; **s1236** confusa est eorum [Bugarorum] superstitio et error ~sus M. PAR. *Maj.* III 361. **c** non sit quisquam alicujus advocationis dignus nisi credibile testimonium habeat unde venerit ei quod cum eo ~ditur [AS: *þæt him man æt befehþ*] (*Quad.*) *GAS* 327 (= *Inst. Cnuti* ib.: quod in manu sua vel in potestate captum est; v. et. deprehensor b).

3 to discover; **b** (w. acc. & inf., compl., or indir. qu.); **c** (w. *quia*).

sicut exterioris hominis natura, qui in propatulo formatus visibiliter conspicitur, haud difficillime ~di potest ALDH. *VirgP* 3; deprehaendo, *anfindo GlC* D 109; ~do, i. intelligo ..; deprendere, i. videre, intellegere *GlH* D 201–2; diabolum scurrae simillimum coram equitantibus deprendit saltantem OSB. *V. Dunst.* 21; vij sunt reliqui, vij discrimina vocum conficientes, quorum harmoniam Orpheus .. primus ~dit ALB. LOND. *DG* 8. 19; Eudoxus .. in excelsi montis acumine se posuit ut astrorum celique motus ~deret W. BURLEY *Vit. Phil.* 176. **b** conveniant .. singuli .. examine conscientiam suam, et ita ~ent an secundum rectam rationem sacerdotali cathedrae insideant GILDAS *EB* 92; si quis presbiter ordinatus ~dit se non esse baptizatum THEOD. *Pen.* II 2. 13; parentes .. sobolem cum adultam et jam pubescentem .. ~derent ALDH. *VirgP* 37; dispiciebat eos quos fide Christi inbutos opera fidei non habere ~dit BEDE *HE* III 21; **1075** (v. coemeterium); si .. tussientes audiverint, non esse indigenas ~dunt OSB. BAWDSEY cliv; cum .. ~disset [ornamentum] de Ely fuisse *Lib. Eli.* III 122; deprensum est hunc esse locum HANV. VIII 402 p. 373; filium .. vanis et frivolis studuisse ~sum GIR. *GE* II 37 p. 350; in quem cum respicerem .. in eadem illum ~di esse effigie et habitu et omnimoda qualitate qua fuerat vivus P. CORNW. *Rev.* I 205 p. 199. **c** archiepiscopus ~dit ad unius mussitationem quia se diffiduciasset rex W. CANT. *V. Thom.* II 37.

deprehensio [CL]

1 seizure, catching; **b** (of offender).

agmen .. apium .., quamdiu in conspectu meo fuerit, meum esse dici poterit, dum tamen possibilis sit ei ~o *Fleta* 175. **b** ea que .. per alios inplere possumus, veluti .. furis ~o VAC. *Lib. Paup.* 215.

2 detection (of guilt).

quia .. papa non debet reprehendi nec corripi, ideo in ~one incorrigibilitatis ejus .. modi speciales .. debent servari secundum eum OCKHAM *Pol.* III 321.

deprehensor, a seizer, catcher (of offenders). **b** discoverer (of property thought to be stolen).

a s1236 [Robertus Bugre] factus malleus hereticorum, accusator et ~or M. PAR. *Min.* II 388. **b** quodsi apud illum deprehensum fuerit et hujusmodi testimonium non habuit .., ~ori suum reddat (*Cons. Cnuti*) *GAS* 327.

deprendere v. deprehendere.

depresse [CL = *deeply*], at a low pitch.

distinguitur triplex accentus, acutus quando ab imo in altum sillaba elevatur, gravis quando tota sillaba ~e profertur, circumflexus quando circumflectitur ab imo in altum et postea deprimitur *Ps.*-GROS. *Gram.* 33.

depressio [CL]

1 depression, pressing down; **b** (astr.). **c** press, pressure.

videbis ~onem cordis et ~onem arterie et elevationem cordis et elevationem arterie simul fieri *Ps.*-RIC. *Anat.* 24; impressio non fit nisi in superficie, ut sigilli in cera, per elevationem quarundam partium superficiei et ~onem aliarum BACON *Maj.* II 432. **b** ~o Mercurii est in Piscibus, et ideo exaltatio Mercurii est in Virgine *Ib.* I 260; terciam differenciam, viz. elevacionis et ~onis, impossibile est salvare ponendo omnes celos esse concentricos DUNS *Sent.* II 14. 2. 6. **c s1308** ad .. coronacionem propter ~onem gencium dominus J. de B. per ruinam cujusdam muri .. fuit oppressus ad mortem *Ann. Lond.* 153.

2 (of sound) lowering in pitch or volume.

concrepantibus invicem trompis .. fit quedam tonorum discors concordia, dum .. singule singularum quodam modo repeterent exceptiones mutuas et vocum restaurarent ~ones *Itin. Ric.* II 13; cantoris officium est chorum in †canticum elevatione et ~one regere *Offic. Sal.* 3 (= *Conc.* I 498a: cantuum; *Stat. Linc.* I 283: cantus); tenor secundum elevacionem et ~onem vocis majori et minori inpetu expulse *Ps.*-GROS. *Gram.* 31; quia quibusdam viderentur tante elevaciones et ~ones simul nimis laboriose et tediose ODINGTON 101.

3 a (w. subj. gen.) oppression. **b** (usu. w. obj. gen., of person or institution) degradation, humiliation, impoverishment. **c** (of abstr.) abasement, enfeeblement.

a ob quarum [gentium] infestationem ac dirissimam ~onem [Britannia] legatos Romam .. mittit GILDAS *EB* 15. **b** super hac inverecunda ecclesie ~one .. eum [regem] implorarunt quatinus sue ecclesiam libertati redderet *G. Steph.* I 13; quod .. eum asseris verbis amaris culpam tuam exaggerare, magis sue caritati quam crudelitati, magis tue liberationi imputare debes quam ~oni AD. SCOT *Sol.* 849A; unde exclamandum non est: "o superbia monachorum!", sed, "o presumptio episcoporum! ~o monachorum!" GERV. CANT. *Imag.* 34; dixit rex: "si non procuraveritis privilegia ad ~onem hominum, .. poteritis principari principibus" ECCLESTON *Adv. Min.* 24; ad patrie defensionem et hostium ~onem BRACTON 35b; **s1263** propter ~onem et inopiam, que jam diu gleba deficiente in populo grassata est *Flor. Hist.* II 479; **1340** (v. concorditer a); **1377** forte in penam peccati populi .. evenit ut hec [apostolica] curia in ~onem secularium tantum hodie invalescit (WYCL. *Resp.*) *Ziz.* 267. **c 1192** papa in vestri ~one negotii plurima indignanter .. proponebat *G. Ric. I* 242; alii dicebant "non", talem emendationem honoris ~onem estimantes BRAKELOND 146v.; **1261** que in diminucionem et ~onem potestatis regie cedunt *Cl* 96; **1262** in .. enormem ~onem regie libertatis (*AncC* IV 39) *RL* II 208; **1298** in damnum et ~onem officii [fullonum] *MGL* II 127; **1388** graviter est districtus indebite et injuste in status ipsius J. K. ~onem manifestam *IMisc* 241/4 r. 1 (cf. *Reg. Brev. Orig.* 36b).

depressivus, oppressive, burdensome.

detestantes ~as temporalis sarcine cupidines AD. MARSH *Ep.* 86.

depressor, a oppressor. **b** repressor.

a Dei contemptor sortisque ejus ~or GILDAS *EB* 32; **c1356** forstallarius .. qui pauperum est ~or et tocius communitatis .. inimicus *MunAcOx* 184. **b** injurie ~or et atleta justicie MAP *NC* II 17 f. 28v.

depretiare [CL], **~iari** [LL], to devalue, depreciate. **b** to despise.

~o, prohibeo pretium *GlH* D 205; ~iatus, *wurðleas* ÆLF. *Gl.*; quid ita merces alienas ~iaretur et attenuaret rerum non suarum valentiam? (*V. Aldh.*) W. MALM. *GP* V 224; si personas que sibi assueverunt .. decretum fortune dissociet, fit plerumque ut utraque [persona] .. quasi exclusa ratione officii ~iatur J. SAL. *Pol.* 494B; arguit hunc [Mariam] pretio depretiasse suo NIG. *Mir. BVM* f. 20. **b** ~atus, [de]honoratus, vilis effectus *GlH* D 204; *to desspice*, .. dedignari, ~iari .., despicere *CathA*.

deprevatus v. depravare 1b. **deprid-** v. depraed-.

deprimare, to prime (w. paint).

1311 [*one painter*] deprimand' claves capellorum *Fabr. Exon.* 56.

deprimere [CL]

1 to press down, cast down, lower, sink (trans.). **b** to weigh down (fig.; also absol.). **c** to lay (sexually). **d** to lie down.

non obstetrices .. vel nares erigunt vel faciem ~unt vel tibias extendunt GIR. *TH* III 10; [navis] nunc in nubes effertur nunc in abyssum / deprimitur H. AVR. *Hugh* 627; si virga viri fit nimis brevis, tunc eleventur crura mulieris et caput ~atur in tantum quod sperma possit cadere in fundum matricis GAD. 77v. 2; **1382** fratres nunc et monachi vultum depresserunt (*Contra Religiosos* 276) *Mon. Francisc.* I 600. **b** quem gravi facinorum .. sarcina triste piaculi pondus ~it ALDH. *VirgP* 60 (cf. id. *VirgV* 2763: me materiae moles ceu sarcina grandis / deprimit); tuarum litterarum exhortatio .. fasculum ~entem patientie ponit in meritum *Ep. ad amicum* 20; sub fasciculis ~entibus anxie gemens non habuit requiem J. FORD *Wulf.* 51. **c** [pregnans juvencula] quamquam a viro depressa conceperit *V. Kentig.* 4. **d s1356** circa mediam noctem, cum omnes Anglici essent nudi in lectis ~entes AVESB. 134.

2 to lower (sound) in volume or pitch. **b** (p. ppl.) designating lowered volume or pitch.

GIR. *GE* II 25 (v. acuere 3); in hoc vocabulo 'facio' .. secunda et tercia sillaba ~untur BACON *Gram. Gk.* 5; si aliquis cantus per ignoranciam vel incuriam nimis elevetur aut ~atur *Cust. Westm.* 29 (= *Cust. Cant.* 91). **b** punctus .. depressus [sc.;] seu comma fit quandocunque est suspensiva constructio, quando .. versus incipit ab istis dictionibus, 'si' vel 'siquis', 'quoniam', 'quia', .. ita quod punctus depressus sit totius quod suspenditur, ut per illud quod sequitur versus compleatur BACON *Tert.* 249–50.

3 to put down, crush, suppress (person or institution). **b** to oppress, harass. **c** (pr. ppl.) oppressive.

s878 suos fideles .. flagellis adversitatum vult .. tangi, ut depressi de Dei misericordia non desperent *Chr. S. Neoti*; **s1245** etsi dignus multipliciter fuerit Fretherícus ~i et ab omni honore privari M. PAR. *Maj.* IV 478; **s1282** in Tunicio magna paganorum multitudo per .. P. regem Arragonie inter montium districtum fuit depressa *Meaux* II 177; **s1524** dictum prioratum [*Snape, Suff*] .. dissolvere et depressere ac ibidem priorem et monachos .. et omnia bona mobilia dissipavere et diripuere *Reg. Butley* 46. **b** quanto majori potentia et districtiori justitia .. [Henricus I] plures depresserat, aggravaverat, spoliaverat RIC. HEX. *Stand.* 37; Anglia sub Normannorum jugo misere depressa *Lib. Eli.* II 78; non solum ab hoste ~imur sed .. fame morimur M. PAR. *Maj.* I 182 (cf. G. MON. VI 4); **c1380** quidam .. ecclesie .. privignus .. N. domum nostram .. ~ere et .. spoliare non cessat *FormOx* 387 (= ib. 388: *empeirer nostre meisone*). **c c1340** ex ~enti extorsione regia, qua .. clerus affligitur *Ib.* 303; habet .. mundus .. gaudium lamentacionis .., ornatum abhominacionis, ducem seducentem, principem ~entem ROLLE *IA* 259.

4 a (w. abstr. subj. or agent) to depress, afflict, overwhelm. **b** (w. abstr. obj.) to lower, diminish, weaken.

a somno sopitus et sopore depressus ALDH. *VirgP* 36; ecclesiastica pastoralis curae sollicitudine depressum *Id. PR* 143 p. 202; corporis infirmitate depressus BEDE *HE* IV 21 p. 255; partu pena nulla deprimeris; / vim nature, Virgo, transgrederis J. HOWD. *Ph.* 6; **1198** constantiam mentis .., que nec ~i debet adversis nec prosperis elevari *Ep. Innoc. III* 1; **s1203** abbas noster .. ut semper consueverat ~i in adversis et elevari in prosperis *Chr. Evesham* 124; **s1321** alii, cujusque infirmitatis livore depressi *Flor. Hist.* III 206; nunc .. me ~unt languores †erumpuosi [l. erumpnosi] exilii ROLLE *IA* 244. **b s662** hec .. ejus [Wulferi] bona inficit et ~it gravis simonie nota W. MALM. *GR* I 76; omni calore depresso GIR. *GE* II 10; BRACTON 142 (v. comedere 1c); **1262** (v. commarchio 2); *Fleta* 51 (v. diabolus 1a); **1378** machinantes statum ipsius W. ~ere *IMisc* 216/7.

deprivare [cf. CL privare], to deprive; **b** (w. ref. to eccl. office).

non est mirum si aquosa superfluitas a capite descendens .. vitium capitis ~ata ca[lore] demonstret GILB. II 92. 2; ut alterentur homines ad sanitatem .. et ad bonos mores et ad eufortunia .. potest per hujusmodi procurari. et per contrarium qui digni sunt horum contrariis possunt in his omnibus ~ari BACON *Tert. Sup.* 15; **s1459** ecclesia, que dudum .. erat .. omnium princeps provinciarum .. usque pene in Indiam Ulteriorem .., stat modo quasi altera vidua, viduata hiis omnibus ac eciam ~ata *Reg. Whet.* I 333; **a1527** machinans ipsum T. de possessione cartarum .. callide et caute ~are *Entries* 5; **1565** omnibus libertatibus et privilegiis universitatis imperpetuum excludatur et ~etur *StatOx* 393. **b s1201** J. legatus .. multos .. ab administracione altaris amovendos .. judicavit et ~avit *Plusc.* VI 38; **c1520** (v. deprivatio); **s1553** [C. Tunstall] ~abatur episcopali omni auctoritate *Hist. Durh.* 16.

deprivatio [cf. CL privatio], deprivation (eccl.).

c1520 quamvis [archiepiscopus S. Andree] .. merito poterat ad eorum [rectorum etc.] ~ones a suis beneficiis et capellaniis .. procedere .. eosque actualiter deprivare et punire *Conc. Scot.* I cclxxi; **1550** cum episcopatus London' .. sit vacuus suoque idoneo pastore destitutus per ~onem Edmundi nuper loci .. episcopi (*Pat*) *Foed.* XV 223a; **1551** racione ~onis seu remocionis Stephani .. episcopi ab .. episcopatu (*Pat*) *Ib.* 253a.

deproeliare [LL < CL *intr. dep.*], to battle against.

ipse ad ~iandum mundi principem [cf. *2 Cor.* iv 4] promptus festinare non differt BEDE *Sam.* 615.

depromere [CL], to bring forth, produce, show. **b** to utter, declare, tell of; **c** (w. indir. qu.).

quis prior in mundo deprompsit tegmina vestis? ALDH. *Aen.* 77. 1; squalidus ut sablo .. / bratea flaventis depromit fila metalli *Id. VirgV* 173; ~at, proverat [i. e. proferat] *GlC* D 133; ~o, ostendo, praefero, protulero, exposuero, *geyppe GlH* D 219; ut .. quicquid in actionem ~pseris internum affectum sapiat *V. Gund.* 13; Verbum .. est .. imago de speculo semper ymaginem ~ente GROS. *Hexaem.* II 3. **b** tunc ait, audacter depromens fata futura ALDH. *VirgV* 1559; Eumenides quasdam mulieres vana historia ~it *Lib. Monstr.* I 45; talia mellifluo deprompserat ore sacerdos WULF. *Swith.* II 1003; cantum deprome suavem R. CANT. *Malch.* V 393; defuncto Henrico rege, libera, ut in mortuo solent, judicia populi ~ebantur H. HUNT. *HA* VIII 1; **s1177** venerunt .. ad ~endam calumniam suam *G. Hen. II* I 139; GIR. *EH* II 27 (v. comminatorius 1a); Urbanus III [ob. **1185**] .. concessit ut nulli .. liceret in nos .. excommunicationis .. sententiam promere; quam, si ~ta fuerit, decreverat omnino non tenere *Meaux* I 179; **s1388** postulaverunt ut [rex] .. veniret ad Westmonasterium, ubi voluerunt sibi ~ere vota sua *V. Ric. II* 99. **c** hortantur juvenem vero depromere fatu / qualiter exanimis .. / .. nigras posset penetrare latebras ALDH. *VirgV* 1415.

depromptio [LL], declaration.

dicere quod requiritur .. omnium peccatorum suorum singularis ~o .. foret .. blasfema WYCL. *Blasph.* 114.

deprope [LL, al. div.], near (or from near): **a** (adv.); **b** (prep. w. acc.); **c** (prep. w. abl.).

a indicat solatrix adeo [? l. a Deo] domunculam de prope ore et digito HERM. ARCH. 34; audiens ~e vocem humanam W. CANT. *Mir. Thom.* VI 148; funde manu gemina sine dampno de prope vina GARL. *Mor. Scol.* 405; quidam vident rem a longe distantem, de prope vero non BACON V 86; **1290** [rex] funus [regine] continue sequitur ad duas vel tres leucas ~e *DCCant.* (*HMC*) 258; **1316** ecclesiam .. et capellam .. monasterio .. ~e vicinas *Kelso* 310; **1332** archiepiscopi .. quando in diocesi vel ~e sunt presentes *Lit. Cant.* I 476; **c1340** cum .. armis ad suam [sc. regis] hic ~e forestam .. incedere non verentur *FormOx* 159; arcus est secreta temptacio quam emittit [diabolus] a longe; gladius, acutus, scindens de prope [ME: *keorvinde of nech*] *AncrR* 92; **s1434** archiepiscopum, pro tunc apud Harowe ~e hospitantem AMUND. I 371; ~e, A. *fro ny WW*. **b** **12..** ut facerent .. unum exterius fossatum per pasturam nostram .. incipiendo de prope .. pontem de F. *Meaux* I 410; **1305** eidem amoventi veterem terram, que fuit super predictam turrim ~e murum interioris ballii *KRAc* 486/17 *sched.* 2; Gallorum nobilitas .., ut de prope conjunccionem venerat .., diviserunt se in tres turmas *G. Hen. V* 13; processus inducciónis diversarum parcellarum terre .. jacencium ~e toftum de S. *Reg. Whet.* I 156 *rub.* **c** mausoleatus .. in villula †Suthtunc [l. Suthtune] dicta de prope loco martyrizationis HERM. ARCH. 1.

deproperare [CL], to hasten (w. inf.).

summi patris injuriam vindicare ~o GIR. *IK* I 1; **1245** (v. apostolus 2a).

depubes [CL], **~is,** (designating a sucking pig). **b** that has not yet reached puberty.

pubes .. componitur etiam ~es, -is, i. porcus suggens; et dicitur ~es quasi deorsum a setis OSB. GLOUC. *Deriv.* 409. **b** *berdeles*, ~is, impubis, investis, inverbis *CathA*.

depublicare [cf. CL publicare]

1 to take away, confiscate.

detrectus, depuplicatus *GlC* D 143.

2 to publish abroad (*cf.* AN *depublier*, OF *depopler*).

sicut qui occultam admittit offensam occulto curatur remedio, †in [v. l. ne] medicina publica ~et vulnus filii in dolorem matris ecclesie PULL. *Sent.* 863A.

depucellare [OF *despuceler*; cf. pucella], to deflower, ravish.

1286 Robertus .. vi cepit garciferam Ade Seel .. et ipsam depucelavit *Eyre Chester* 12 r. 3.

depudēre [CL], (impers.) to shame.

~uit .. te dum dissimulas, quod superius concessisti, ut ratione judice disputatio nostra constaret ADEL. *QN* 13.

depudicare [CL], to violate.

attendat locuples .. / qui centum virgines depudicaverat WALT. WIMB. *Sim.* 90.

depugnare [CL], to contend.

conluctantia, ~antia, *þa samwinnendan GlH* C 1619.

depuire v. depuvire.

depulsio [CL]

1 rebuttal, rejoinder.

intentio est propinquorum pupilli: "nostra est pecunia, de qua testatus non est propinquus noster"; ~o est: "immo nostra, qui heredes testamento patris sumus" ALCUIN *Rhet.* 11; ~o, rejectio, objectio *GlH* D 217; archiepiscopus lese majestatis corone regie arguitur, quia .. a rege citatus .. neque venisset neque idonee se excusasset. archiepiscopi ~o nullum locum habuit, allegata .. curie sue integritate W. FITZST. *Thom.* 40.

2 deposition (from office).

s948 Stephanus et Constantinus .. filii Romani imperatoris .. patrem de palatii solio deponunt et tonso capite ad .. insulam .. transmittunt .. post patris ~onem .. ad idem monasterium .. et ipsi .. transmittuntur (SIG. GEMBLOUX) DICETO *Chr.* 147.

depulsor [CL], deposer.

tu .., multorum tyrannorum ~or .., Maglocune GILDAS *EB* 33.

depulverare [cf. CL pulverare], **~izare,** to rub down, curry (horse).

cum .. custos palefredi episcopi Catanensis commissum sibi equum ~aret GERV. TILB. II 12 (cf. ib. 100: equum .. abstergere ac, ut moris est, ~are); **s1406** strigilem .., quod instrumentum pecten est ad ~isandum equos *Chr. S. Alb.* 2.

depunctare [cf. punctare], to punctuate.

fluvius inde egrediens est sacra scriptura, a Spiritu Sancto edita et eodem summi Dei digito ~ata S. LANGTON *Gl. Hist. Schol.* 43.

depurare [LL *p. ppl. only*]

1 to purify, cleanse, refine; **b** (w. ref. to 'humours'); **c** (w. ref. to 'ideas' or sim.).

corpus allevians .. et spiritum animalem ~ans *Quaest. Salern.* B16; ignis .. / depurat, purgat, dissolvit consolidatque / materiam NECKAM *DS* IV 7; aurum perfecte ~atum, quamvis per calorem dissolvatur, non in suo pondere minoratur BART. ANGL. IV 1; depuratur aqua ventis et sole per altum / aera dulcescit, que modo salsa fuit GARL. *Tri. Eccl.* 14; celi celorum, puritas depurata J. HOWD. *Cant.* 560; **1355** in xvj petris cepi ~ati *Sacr. Ely* II 163; **1360** in .. ij parvis manutergiis et ij cruettis pro ~end' (*sic*) in ecclesia *Ib.* 189; **s1382** sicut .. in terre visceribus includuntur aer et spiritus infecti et egrediuntur in terremotum et sic terra ~atur .., sic .. per condempnacionem [hereticorum] regnum fuit ~atum *Ziz.* 272; **1395** toga purpurea ingranata cum pelle ~ata *Test. Ebor.* III 4. **b** [aurum] corporis humores depurat purius NECKAM *DS* VI 25; GILB. VI 248. 2 (v. depuratorius). **c** BACON VIII 31 (v. deferre 8a); *Id.* XI 12 (v. depuratio 1c); si [intellectus] possibilis copulatur cum homine per phantasmata, aut [copulatur] per phantasma ut est in imaginacione aut per ipsum ut est jam ~atum et unitum intellectui PECKHAM *QA* 47; illa, que in creaturis repugnant propter imperfeccionem ac improprietatem quam sapiunt, ~ata secundum proprietates primarias in Deo se invicem consecuntur WYCL. *Dom. Div.* 231.

2 to clear away, remove by cleansing.

arterie causam motus trahunt a corde, cui pulmo flabellando ministrat et superflua ejus expellendo et ~ando RIC. MED. *Anat.* 220; superfluitates .. †deputare [v. l. depurare] *Ib.* 226 (v. collocare a); per activitatem illorum acetorum subtiliantur et ~atur omnes superfluitates partium [vitri] (M. SCOT *Alch.*) *Med. Cult.* 156.

3 to clear, discharge (debts).

1284 ut debita que adhuc veniunt in summonicionem Scaccarii, unde debitores proferunt tallias contra diversos vicecomites, ~entur et aquietentur (*Rhuddlan*) *StRealm* I 70.

4 to dirty, defile.

1399 pro lotura linthiaminum violatorum et †deputratorum per ducem Britannie et prepositum Colon' duobus vicibus *IssueR* 561 r. 13; *to file*, deturpare, ~are .. *CathA*.

depuratio

1 purification, cleansing, refinement; **b** (of 'humours'); **c** (of 'images' or 'ideas').

aque salse diligenti ~one dulces redduntur NECKAM *NR* II 1; qui de longe vident solum, spiritum habent multum set non subtilem set perturbatum et grossum et humidum, unde longo indigent intervallo ad sui ~onem BACON V 86. **b** discursus .. reumatis per spinam et venas transiens per humores diversos aut ab eis aliquid accipit aut digestionem eorum impedit et ~onem GILB. VII 312. 1. **c** hujusmodi species existentes in sensu in fantasia vel ymagine .. per majorem ~onem et denudationem a materia .. intellectui possibili repressentantur, et deinde intellectus agens irradians supra fantasmata ipsa penitus depurat a conditionibus materialibus BACON XI 12.

2 clearing away.

si diutius permittantur pira [in palea], fit major dissolutio quam possit fieri dissolutorum consumptio et ~o, quare marcescunt *Quaest. Salern.* Ba 111.

3 dregs, offscourings.

.. 'creavit Deus celum et terram' [*Gen.* i 1] .. per terram recte quatuor elementa designantur, quia, †sic [v. l. sicut] terra dicitur ~o elementorum, ita elementa corruptela et fex mundi appellantur; per terram itaque inferiora, per celum superiora intellexit D. MORLEY 23.

depurativus, purificatory.

allumen de Maroc est .. mundificative et ~e nature M. SCOT *Lumen* 256; [caliditas] virtute sua est ~a metallorum et rubiginis ipsorum consumptiva BART. ANGL. IV 1.

depuratorius, purificatory.

epar servit cordi virtute preparatoria et ~ia; unde, cum humores non depurantur nec preparantur, a vitio epatis sumitur principium erroris GILB. VI 248. 2.

depurgare [CL], to purge, cleanse; **b** (fig.).

rutilans in digitis aurum depurgatum NECKAM *Poems* 116; [herbe] cum bene superfluitates expellant, nutrimentum dicuntur habere incorruptum et ~atum *Quaest. Salern.* C 16. **b** ~atur anima quam [amor Christi] assumit sacris incendiis, nec remanet in ea quicquam rubiginosum aut obscurum ROLLE *IA* 272.

depurpurare [cf. CL purpurare], to dye purple.

quatuor Evangelia de auro purissimo in membranis ~atis coloratis .. scribere jussit EDDI 17.

1 deputare v. 1 deportare 2b.

2 deputare v. depurare 2.

3 deputare [CL]

1 **a** (w. compl. or acc. & inf.) to consider, reckon. **b** (w. *inter*) to reckon among. **c** (w. dat.) to assign to (a class).

a c597 nec haec dicentes culpam ~amus esse conjugium (*Lit. Papae*) BEDE *HE* I 27 p. 57; **797** similem eum ~antes Juliano ALCUIN *Ep.* 127; ~o hanc lectionem inscientibus puerulis .. aptandam fore ÆLF. *Gram.* 1; **a1090** alterius necessitatem propriam ~are LANFR. *Ep.* 10. 518B; qui parati sunt corrigi non sunt heretici ~andi OCKHAM *Pol.* II 847; **1460** de firmis terrarum .. ~atarum vastarum per dominum regem pro feris pascendis *ExchScot* 65; BLAKMAN *Hen. VI* 21 (v. 1 deliramentum). **b** **802** ut inter electorum numerum mereamur ~ari ALCUIN *Ep.* 254; Greci negantes Spiritum Sanctum procedere a Filio .. inter hereticos ~antur OCKHAM *Dial.* 419. **c** invitos spadones .. qui secundo eunuchorum gradui .. ~antur [cf. *Matth.* xix 12] ALDH. *VirgP* 21.

2 to ascribe, impute: **a** (to agent); **b** (to cause).

a **798** error scribentis quodammodo dictanti ~abitur ALCUIN *Ep.* 149; quare Scipioni hoc malum ~andum est *Id. Rhet.* 32; si ita ammonitus aliquid praetermiserit, sibimet ~et si dampnum ei evenerit (*Leg. Hen.* 49. 3b) *GAS* 572. **b** **799** nec .. segnities legentium benivolentiae magistri juste ~ari debebit ALCUIN *Ep.* 170; non conatum hunc meum praesumptioni ~es sed devotioni AILR. *Ed. Conf.* 782D; **s1066** quoniam [Haraldus] plus viribus propriis quam virtuti divine victoriam temere ~avit .., penas luit *Chr. Rams.* 179; que .., si dignabitur benignius excusare, distraccioni mentis vel festinancie aut inadvertencie ~et et ascribat OCKHAM *Pol.* I 217.

3 to allot, assign: **a** (to person or thing); **b** (to purpose). **c** to intend, plan.

a licet quidam centesimi fructus manipulos [cf. *Matth.* xiii 8] .. martiribus .. ~are soleant ALDH. *VirgP* 19; **c795** si alter corpori locus ~abitur, tamen animae .. requies vobiscum, credo, donabitur ALCUIN *Ep.* 42; **s888** [Alfredus] quartam [portionem census] clericis et doctoribus .. ~avit M. PAR. *Maj.* I 426; **1373** per demones raptus est in locum sibi divino judicio ~atum BRINTON *Serm.* 86; sacre scripture .. a Deo speciale ~atum est officium fundandi .. regimina, actus, leges .. et obsequia divina J. BURY *Glad. Sal.* 576; **s1404** (v. conclave 1d). **b** bene septima volatilia sive pecora in hostiam Domini ~ata sunt BEDE *Gen.* 105; **796** libros .. qui scribendi studio ~entur ALCUIN *Ep.* 114; horas certis .. solemniis ~atas AILR. *Ed. Conf.* 778D; **s1166** (v. concludere 1c); **s1191** in .. domibus ad convescendum .. ~atis DICETO *YH* II 99; **1191** preter liberam terram et .. decimas .., que in perpetuum ~abuntur in opus sacristarie *Ch. Sal.* 49; **1215** denarios .. ~andos subsidio Terre Sancte *Pat* 145b; **s1216** Westmonasterium, ubi locus est .. regie consecrationi ~atus *Ann. Lond.* 20; **1321** animalia ad waynagium terrarum ~ata *MGL* II 362; **1437** (v. deputatio 1). **c** **c1400** dum de manerio nostro de Croydon versus .. regem .. iter nostrum disposuimus, ~avimus nocturnam requiem in villa de Kyngeston *Lit. Cant.* III 73.

4 to commit, entrust. **b** (w. *scripto*) to put into writing.

mulierem .. cujus custodie [hircus] ~atus fuerat GIR. *TH* II 23; serviens .. respondeat sacriste de .. utensilibus sue custodie ~atis *Croyl.* 104; **1514** assistente ibidem vexillo S. Cuthberti ~ato in custodiam dompnorum Roberti S. [et al.] *Ac. Durh.* 663; *Ib.* 454 (v. deportare 2b). **b** clericus thesaurarii .. ~at scripto quantum vel a quo vel ob quam causam receperit *Dial. Scac.* I 3 A (cf. ib. I 51: cum in rotulo summa ejus scripto fuerit ~ata).

5 to consign, condemn: **a** (person); **b** (thing).

a **796** ~atus poenae (v. condonare 2e); **955** (12c) sit .. aeternis baratri .. ~atus incendiis *CS* 906; intelligens .. se esse pro tanti viri vindicta finitimae morti ferme ~atum B. *V. Dunst.* 14; W. POIT. I 3 (v. distractio 1); quendam hominem interfecit, ita quod fuit perpetue prisone ~atus BRACTON 276b; multi angeli ceciderunt in peccatum et ~ati sunt pene infernali BACON *Tert. Sup.* 56; **1276** de regno .. fuit ejectus et exilio ~atus *TreatyR* I 55; **s1304** monachi carceri apud Turrim ~ati *Ann. Lond.* 132. **b** alios vidi qui libros legis ~ant igni J. SAL. *Pol.* 808C.

6 to depute, appoint (person or agency); **b** (w. dat. or *ad*); **c** (w. compl. or *in* & acc.). **d** (p. ppl. as sb.) deputy; **e** (as title of governor as representative of sovereign). **f** (gdv.) person to be deputed.

~averat custodes, unumque praecipue qui ceteris in custodia praeesset JOSEPH CANT. 295; **s1307** Robertus le Bruys fere omnia castra .. Scocie adquisivit et custodes ~atos ibidem per patrem regis amovit AD. MUR. *Chr.* 11; **1335** assignavimus .. Johannem D. .. et Johannem de E. .. ad arestandum, per se vel per alios quos loco suo ~are voluerint, .. naves [etc.] *RScot* 337b; tres ~et inspectores .., qui librorum catalogum .. videant .. R. BURY *Phil.* 19. 243; **1511** famula ~ata, A. *a covent servante* (*Vis. Sheppey*) *EHR* VI 33. **b** milites ad excubias confessorum ~ati ALDH. *VirgP* 36; frater qui ad suscipiendos hospites ~atus est LANFR. *Const.* 153 (cf. ib.: per famulos sibi ~atos); itane .. tibi servientibus, tuis ~atis laudibus, .. claudes viscera pietatis? AILR. *Ed. Conf.* 785D; **c1220** viros religiosos nostri regiminis custodie ~atos *Reg. S. Thom. Dublin*

333; c**1239** non sufficiens fuit sue cure pastorali pastores sua reputatione idoneos singulis gregibus custodiendis ~asse GROS. *Ep.* 127 p. 381; **1242** nec aliqui incedant armati nisi specialiter fuerint ad custodiam pacis nostri ~ati *Cl* 483; BART. ANGL. II 18 (v. custodia 1a); *Cust. Westm.* 80 (v. descensus 1d); ROB. ANGL. II 154 (v. conjungere 2b); **1319** tallagia per homines gardarum ad hoc ~atos assessa (*Ch. Regis*) *MGL* I 142; **1333** ad ~and' sub vobis alios sufficientes ad premissa .. facienda *RScot* 250b. **c** **1293** R. J. custos porcorum ~atus per totam villatam *SelPlMan* 170; s**1296** rex Anglorum ~avit Robertum le Bruys et Johannem Comyn .. custodes regni Scocie AVESB. 81b; **1308** ad cujus [ecclesie Romanie] regimen voluit Christi clemencia Romanum pontificem vice sui ~are ministrum (*Lit. Papae*) *Reg. Carl.* II 2; **1328** vos suum [sc. prepositi] ~amus coadjutorem *Lit. Cant.* I 271; **1459** in coadjutorem .. ~are (v. coadjutorius c); **1543** vobis decano nomine nostro, quem ad hoc harum [x^m librarum] serie collectorem ~amus et ordinamus *Conc. Scot.* I cclv. **d** **1369** in solucione nuper facta cuidam ~ato regis Anglie apud Berewycum pro mutuo facto domino nostro regi in Anglia *ExchScot* 345; **1377** Willelmus [de Bardolf] perfecit servicium predictum per quendam ~atum suum *MGL* II 473 (cf. *Rec. Coronation* 143); **1382** injungentes vobis ac vestris commissariis sive ~atis .. quod .. (*Pat*) *Ziz.* 316; **1406** nisi in defectu majoris .. aut ministri seu ~ati sui (*Pat*) *MGL* II 435; **14..** ballivus .. colligere debet per se aut ~atum suum ad hoc assignatum custumam *Reg. S. Aug.* 151 (cf. *Hist. Fordwich* 255); **1537** officium .. per se vel sufficientem ~atum suum habuit .. *Entries* 75b. **e** **1533** eundem vicecomitem Lysle ~atum nostrum ville et marchiarum [Calesie] .. ordinavimus (*Pat*) *Foed.* XIV 452a; **1556** concordatum est per nos .. dominum ~atum et consilium ex una parte et comitem Tironie .. ex altera parte quod .. *ActPCIr* 7; **1588** de commissione pro Willelmo Fitzwilliams, domino ~ato Hibernie *Pat* 1321 m. 2 *rub.* **f** c**1333** cancellarius noster .. seu ~andus ab ipso *Reg. Brev. Orig.* 40b (cf. *CalPat* 491); **1335** damus eisdem .. ac ~andis ab eis potestatem .. illos .. quos sibi invenerint contrarios .. arestari faciendi *RScot* 338a.

deputatia, office of deputy (Calais). *V. et.* 2 *deputatus. Cf.* 3 *deputare* 6e.

1533 concedimus .. ~iam nostram sive officium ~ie nostre ville nostre Calesie (*Pat*) *Foed.* XIV 452a.

deputatio [LL]

1 assignment. *Cf.* 3 *deputare* 3b.

aliquando talia vocabula ['meum', 'tuum' etc.] important licitam potestatem utendi re aliqua vel usum rei vel ~onem alicujus rei ad usum alicujus OCKHAM *Pol.* I 309; **1437** civitatem Ferrariensem .. pro loco .. concilii transferendi nominamus, assignamus ac eciam deputamus. .. nulli ergo hominum liceat hanc paginam nostrorum [v. l. nostre] .. nominacionis, assignacionis, ~onis .., mandati .. et derogacionis infringere (*Lit. Papae*) BEKYNTON II 18 (cf. derogare a).

2 appointment. **b** deputation (collect.), body of deputies; *cf.* 3 *deputare* 6.

1339 illos quos idem T. sub se .. deputaverit ad hujusmodi homines eligend', arraiand', et triand', et qui juxta hujusmodi ~onem homines illos eligere, arraiare, et triare hactenus neglexerunt *RScot* 566a; **1341** inquisicio capta per abbatem de F. [et al.] .., virtute commissionis domini regis .. ad visitandum dictum hospitale commissarios sub certa forma ~onis *Mem. Ripon* I 223; **1344** qui .. circa .. negocia .. collegii .. promovenda .. ex nominacione, commissione vel ~one per .. eos .. ad quos pertinet fuerint occupati *Eng. Clergy* 289; **1368** deputent tunc procuratores [judices] de minus suspectis et eorum ~oni finaliter stetur *StatOx* 167; nec valet nuda eleccio, ~o prepositi vel acceptacio populi WYCL. *Ver.* II 172; **1478** prioris .. ejusdem loci [domus B. Marie de Tynemutha] prefixio, creacio, ~o et ordinacio .. ad nos .. solum .. pertinet *Reg. Whet.* II 185. **b** **1433** an debent ambassiatores nostri tenere et consentire quod per naciones, sicut olim, an per ~ones, ut jam, est inductum *Reg. Cant.* III 246 (= *Conc.* III 521).

deputatorius, (as sb. f. pl., *sc. litterae*) letters of appointment.

1312 supplicantes quatinus .. nobis et .. electo nostro assensum .. vestrum .. dignemini impertiri et domino .. episcopo vestris scribere ~iis ut ipse .. exequatur quod pertinet ad eundem *Cart. Glast.* I 122.

1 deputatus v. 3 deputare 6d, e.

2 deputatus, office of deputy (Calais). *V. et. deputatia. Cf.* 3 *deputare* 6a.

1533 deputaciam nostram sive officium ~us nostri [Calesie] (*Pat*) *Foed.* XIV 452a.

deputrare v. depurare 4.

depuvire [CL], to thrash, beat thoroughly.

depuire, verberare OSB. GLOUC. *Deriv.* 175 (cf. ib. 181: diloricare, deverberare, depuire).

dequadrare [cf. CL quadrare], to change from a square shape.

a**1270** [capa] alioquin dequadratur, / de quadrato rotundatur, / transit in almucium (*In Cissores*) *Pol. Songs* 53.

dequeri [CL], to deplore.

haut secus, exilium grate dequestus harene, / armenti princeps lunatum robur in ornos / asperat objectas J. EXON. *BT* I 299.

dequoquere v. decoquere 2a. **derainare, deraisnare, deraynare** v. dereinare. **derat-** v. dirat-. **deraubare** v. derobare a. **dercernere** v. decernere 1c.

dereddere [cf. CL reddere], to give back or (?) *f. l.*

c**1198** isti nostri sacrifices dereddere [? l. de reddere] non cogitant, / set ut revendant venditum occasiones suscitant (*Hypocr. Praelatorum* l. 21) *EHR* V 321.

deregare v. derogare a.

deregulare [cf. LL regulare], to disorder.

regulam deregulant vino crapulati / nec juri nec domino deferunt abbati (*Clarevall. et Clun.* 43) *Ps.*-MAP 238.

dereinare [AN *dereiner*, OF *deraisnier*; cf. ratiocinare, rationare]

1 to 'deraign', establish title (to); **b** (w. acc. & inf.). *V. et. diratiocinare, dirationare* 1.

c**1161** pressoragium Boerie .. totum est monachorum Majoris Monasterii. .. hoc enim disresnaverunt in curia domini H. regis Anglorum coram me [sc. senescallo Andegav'] *Act. Hen. II* I 335; c**1180** si contigerit quod via per medium pratum .. adversus eos deresnata fuerit, ipse R. viam dimittet .. et se tenebit ad illam que erga eos deresnata fuerit *Couch. Kirkstall* 85; c**1192** quam predictam terram ego Robertus †disreniavi [? l. disreinavi] per assisam coram justiciis regis apud Lincolniam *Danelaw* 113; a**1200** terram .. quam in curia mea contra filium Ricardi .. per bellum derainavit *DL Cart. Misc.* III 89; **1211** offert c s. pro habenda terra sua in A., quam ~avit tribus vicibus, prima vice versus Willelmum .. per breve de precipe in curia domini regis, secunda vice versus Johannem .. per breve de nova desaisina, tercia vice versus eundem J. per juramentum xxiiij militum per quos idem J. ipsum voluit attingere *CurR* VI 117; **1276** distringatur facere emendacionem Johanni .., sicut ~avit versus eundem *Hund. Highworth* 18 (cf. ib. 43: donec Ricardus .. ~avit); **1282** preceptum est distringere Philippum .. pro dim. m. quam Galfridus .. †disremit versus ipsum in ultima curia *CourtR Hales* 201. **b** O. episcopus .. de hac terra placitavit et disraisnavit testimonio Francigenarum esse suam *Dom. Exon.* 117 (= *DB* I 102v.: diratiocinavit).

2 (w. compl.) to adjudge.

12.. isti .. nichil aliud faciunt domino .. preter Willelmum .. et Johannem, qui deraynati fuerunt coram justiciariis .. villani; alii vero non sunt villani *IMisc* 19/13.

dereinium [AN *dereine*, OF *deraisne*], deraign, (procedure for) establishment of title.

1280 quod tale sit suum jus, sectam et †disremium [? l. disreinium] arram[avit] *CourtR Hales* 143.

derelicta, ~us v. derelinquere 2d, e.

derelictive, (?) residually. *Cf. derelinquere* 1d.

in Patre non solum est fecunditas ad generandum sed ad spirandum, et hoc a se; quia, si Pater non haberet ex se fecunditatem ad spirandum, sed haberet eam ~e ex produccione Filii .., sequitur, ut videtur, hoc impossibile quod Pater numquam haberet illam fecunditatem DUNS *Ord.* III 346.

derelinquere [CL]

1 to leave (behind); **b** (w. compl.). **c** to leave undone. **d** to leave (as result). **e** (p. ppl. *derelictus*) left, remaining.

joci vanitatem ~ens, consolari infantem cepit *V. Cuthb.* I 3; multociens promisi Deo me derelicturum hoc seculum et effecturum monachum *Descr. Constant.* 250; in recessu meo [curiam] totam agnosco; in reditu nichil aut modicum invenio quod dereliquerim MAP *NC* I 1 f. 7. **b** s**887** paganorum exercitus, Parisiam civitatem ~ens incolumem ASSER *Alf.* 84; **12..** universas arbores .. abscidebat, et ne unam †quidam [l. quidem] earum superstitem dereliquit *Meaux* II 49. **c** denomina[n]tur delicta quasi derelicta, quando viz. bona que facere potuimus non fecimus GIR. *GE* I 37. **d** recte signum dici potest quod se offert anime sed aliud a se ~it in anima *Ps.*-GROS. *Gram.* 32; BACON XIII 106 (v. concausa, concursus 1e). **e** binas caprarum pelles .. in quibus cornua capitum et ungule cum tibiis a genibus deorsum ~e pendebant ALEX. CANT. *Mir.* 31 p. 220.

2 to abandon, desert: **a** (land or building); **b** (person); **c** (office). **d** (p. ppl. *derelictus*) derelict. **e** (as sb. f.) relict, widow.

a erat eadem eremus, ut a Christicolis derelicta, sic a daemonibus possessa FOLC. *V. Bot.* 403; Francigeni .. perterriti .. terras sibi traditas ~entes fugerunt *G. Herw.* 328; **1324** licet idem Adam domum illam diu est dimiserit et dereliquerit et domus illa ad terram penitus sit prostrata *MunCOx* 44. **b** quia et hoc putabant aliquid ~endo populo commodi adcrescere GILDAS *EB* 18 (cf. BEDE *HE* I 12: quia et hoc sociis, quos ~ere cogebantur, aliquid commodi adlaturum putabant); s**831** in isto anno dereliquerunt Loduvicum et elegerunt Lotharium *Chr. S. Neoti*; alii proceres cordati socordem dominum dereliquerunt et sensatum regem utiliter expetierunt ORD. VIT. XI 10; judex secularis, .. postquam [aliquis] sibi fuerit tanquam hereticus ab ecclesia derelictus, non ignorat qua pena secundum jura civilia sit plectendus OCKHAM *Dial.* 407. **c** abbas potest pro humilitate cum permissione episcopi locum suum ~ere THEOD. *Pen.* II 6. 1. **d** coeperunt fana, quae ~a erant, restaurare BEDE *HE* III 30; s**686** hec [pestis] Ticinium depopulavit, adeo ut civitas habebatur pro ~o (*sic*) R. NIGER *Chr. I* 61; **1242** ea [castra] tanquam ~a et indefensa .. est ingressus *Cl* 531 (= *RGasc* I 28: †delicta); femina .. wayviari .. bene potest et pro ~a haberi cum pro aliqua felonia fugam ceperit BRACTON 125b. **e** ~a, *laf*, vel *forlæten wif* ÆLF. *Sup.*; s**1015** rex Ægelredus .. ~am Sigeferthi Aldgitham ad Maidulfi Urbem deduci precepit FL. WORC. I 170.

3 to bequeath; **b** (fig.).

Terram Repromissionis .. nepotibus et pronepotibus legitimae hereditatis jure perpetuo possidendam dereliquit ALDH. *VirgP* 12; **805** potestas ipsi datur ut .. terram .. cuicunque hominum voluerit in aeternam libertatem ~at *CS* 322; **853** unum aratrum .. sivi avendum .. et post dies ejus cuicumque hei eredi placuerit ~endum *CS* 467 (cf. ib. 519); **1012** (12c) villa cuidam matronae .. derelicta a viro suo *CD* 719; **12..** reliquam hereditatem .. filio suo .. dereliquit *Meaux* I 319; **b** posteris .. exemplum industriae ~ens ALDH. *PR* 143 p. 203; *CD* 769 (v. dinoscere 2a); jam senex .. uxorem duxit et .. extremum .. diem sortitus paranymphis pro fescenninis lugubres threnos dereliquit ORD. VIT. XI 8.

derepente [CL, al. div.], instantly, all at once.

reliqua [exercitus] ~e [v. l. repente] interierat aut tyrannum dextras petiverat *V. Neot. A* 11.

dereptio v. direptio. **deresnare** v. dereinare.

deretus [Gael. *deòraidh*], relic-keeper.

c**1190** donationem .. de ecclesia de Thelin cum tofto sacerdotis, tofto ~i cum omnibus rectitudinibus suis *Regesta Scot.* II 358; **1384** dedisse .. Thome de Lochane et heredibus suis .. officium derethy nostri de Terwas tenendum .. imperpetuum *Reg. Aberbr.* II 128.

derevestire v. direvestire.

derevocare [cf. CL revocare], to revoke, cancel.

s**1265** missis ad .. legatum et .. regem Francie literis de compromisso Lewensi penitus ~ato *Flor. Hist.* III 262.

deridēre [CL], to deride, mock; **b** (absol.).

cognati atque amici ~ebant eum *Descr. Constant.* 252; si .. considerarent quam convenienter hoc modo procurata sit humana restauratio, non ~erent nostram simplicitatem ANSELM (*CurD*) II 51; non .. me lector rugosa sanna ~eat si .. *G. Steph.* I 24; milite .. alios .. super ficta religione ~ente GIR. *TH* II 53; quod tamen ~et .. reproborum perfidia AD. MARSH *Ep.* 151; talia bona sperantes ~ent vel non ponderant GASCOIGNE *Loci* 41. **b** cum ululatu magno post eos ~entes vociferati sunt ORD. VIT. XI 3 p. 172; dicunt: "quid valet hec scientia vel illa?", ~endo, et non ut addiscant BACON *Tert.* 20.

derige v. dirigere 8b.

derigescere (dirig-) [CL], to become stiff; **b** (w. fear or amazement).

nec sic algore tepente in mortem anima fugiente ~uit W. MALM. *GP* I 17; statim manus ejus circa hastam ~uit et usque ad finem vite sue .. contracta permansit AILR. *SS Hex* 3; pre nimio frigoris squalore corpus ~uit R. COLD. *Godr.* 74. **b** †diriguere, pallescere *GlC* D 260 (cf. *Gl. Leid.* 35. 14 †diriguere, pro stupore pallescere); ~uit, i. obstipuit, horruit, induruit, *ablycde GlH* D 541; porrectis litteris dux fraudem miratus ~uit W. MALM. *GR* II 145; ad hec illi, fraude quasi jam intercepta, .. expalluere perterriti, dirriguere stupefacti T. MON. *Will.* VI 13; quibus ego visis pre timore totus ~ui AD. EYNS. *Hug.* V 4.

2 to stiffen (trans.).

R. COLD. *Cuthb.* 2 (v. bruchus).

deripere [CL], to snatch away, appropriate by force. *V. et. diripere* 2a.

~eret, i. vastarent *GlH* D 230.

derisibilis [LL]

1 deserving derision, ridiculous.

de corruptione kalendarii, que est intolerabilis omni sapienti et ~is ab omni computista BACON *Tert.* 272.

2 (as sb. n.) mockery, scorn.

[domina] de hoc toto [regis amore etc.] non curavit. nonne fuit hoc ~e mirandum [ME: *nes þis hoker wunder*]? *AncrR* 153.

derisio [LL], derision, mockery. **b** taunt. **c** laughing-stock, absurdity.

~o, *tælhleter* ÆLF. *Sup.*; ~o est ut talis misericordia Deo attribuatur ANSELM (*CurD* 1) II 93; hec ~o, quam de meo abscessu modo facitis, in magnum merorem vobis commutabitur W. MALM. *GP* III 100 p. 220; si ea in ~onem sive vanitatem proferrem, taceret spiritus qui me docet G. MON. VIII 10; VINSAUF *PN* 931 (v. antiphrasis);

querunt cum ~one: "quid valent hec?" BACON *Tert.* 20; **1356** de dampnis et ~one quibus ex vana missione hujusmodi subjaceremur (*TreatyR*) *Foed.* V 851. **b 1231** [littera] contumeliis et ~onibus gravida GROS. *Ep.* 4 p. 26; ducem servavit a ~onibus hostium WALS. *HA* I 405. **c 1218** nec miremur si . . facti simus . . ~o his qui in circuitu nostro sunt (*AncC* I 203) *RL* I 13; SICCAV. *PN* 203 (v. eclipsare a); quod . . contenditis summum pontificem superiorem esse per omnia, in ~ones mirabiles incidetis OCKHAM *Disp.* 15.

derisor [CL], mocker, scoffer.

8.. ~orem, *telend WW*; sicuti quidam regule nostre ~ores istum versiculum non habentes garriunt ROB. BRIDL. *Dial.* 159; derisor, latro, fallax, ferus esse caveto D. BEC. 39; jactator magnus derisorem cito querit WALT. ANGL. *Fab.* 23. 11; cleri ~ores et malignos delatores eodem solatio frequentissime fraudari videbis optato GIR. *IK* I 4.

derisorie [LL], mockingly, in derision.

s616 cum essent idolatre, ~ie dicebant episcopo in missarum solenniis: "quare non et nobis panem nitidum porrigis . .?" H. HUNT. *HA* III 20 (cf. BEDE *HE* II 5); GIR. *GE* I 48 (v. conflare 3c); **1236** quod reprehendis de brevis mei longitudine et ~ie vocas illud 'longum' meum GROS. *Ep.* 24; genua flectentes et ~ie dicentes: "ave, rex Judeorum!" EDMUND *Spec. Relig.* 99; quam indignanter, ~ie [ME: *on grim hoker*] et iracunde loquitur ei sponsus *AncrR* 29; **s1362** dirisorie (v. concordantia 3a); **s1397** (v. duketus).

derisorius [CL], **a** derisive. **b** ridiculous, absurd.

a erubescebat improperia que sibi fiebant ~ia, quod funambulus per murum exierat de Antiochia ORD. VIT. XI 2 p. 168; **s1242** non sine Francorum ~iis subsannationibus M. PAR. *Min.* II 463; **1299** (v. conviciatorius); **s1342** cardinales . . miserunt regi . . litteras ~ias [v. l. delusorias] AD. MUR. app. 224*n*. **b** caucionem invenient fidejussoriam, ne judicia sint ~ia *Fleta* 382; hoc per multas auctoritates . . posset ostendi; sed dicunt isti impugnatores quod est tam ~ium quod non oportet racionibus et auctoritatibus reprobare OCKHAM *Pol.* I 365; quod asseris mentalem simoniam non esse simoniam dictum videtur ~ium, cum simonia vocalis nunquam esset simonia nisi quia subordinatur mentali simonie PAUL. ANGL. *ASP* 1536.

derisus [CL], derision, mockery, joke.

ita ut in proverbium et ~um longe lateque efferretur GILDAS *EB* 6; cum . . illum [Christum] ~ui haberi . . viderent BEDE *Hom.* II 13. 155; non . . gravaret servos Dei . . ~u et obprobrio laicorum objurgantium *Tract. Ebor.* 681; ut pauperes, qui erant ~ui, vindicent in superbos PULL. *Sent.* 1007D; MAP *NC* IV 6 (v. devenustare b); GIR. *EH* II 36 (v. despectus 1a); [R. de Bruce] ab omnibus . . habitus est in sibilum, fabulam et ~um FORDUN *Cont.* XII 11.

derivare (diriv-) [CL]

1 to lead off, draw off: **a** (running water); **b** (w. ref. to poison). **c** (intr.) to flow (from).

a areola dicitur ubi aqua ~atur in ortum *Gl. Leid.* 10. 22; **†821** (14c) cum . . pratis, pascuis ~atisque cursibus aquarum *CalCh* IV 373 (= *Gl. Arch.* 173: †dirmatiisque; cf. *MonA* I 514b); **940** (12c) †diravatisque cursibus aquarum *CS* 759 (cf. ib. 767); velut fons . . qui in tria capita dividitur, e quibus rivi diversi . . ~antur *Simil. Anselmi* 9; **12..** tempore estivo decursus aque per . . seweram ad . . molendinum non solet ~ari *Meaux* II 49; **1283** rivus . . fontis vadit seu ~atur ad rivum del Coson *RGasc* II 192; **1290** dedi . . totam aquam . . ad stagnandum et †dirmandum *MonA* VI 1146 (= *CalCh* II 341: dirivandum). **b** horum [hominum quorum spiritus venenosi sunt] spiritus cum telo ad percussum ~atus subjectum . . corrumpit *Quaest. Salern.* B 269; quanto remotius ab origine [venenum] ~atur GIR. *TH* I 39. **c** ~avit, i. emanavit, fluit *GlH* D 232; **1289** in rivo ~ante a fonte *RGasc* II 489.

2 a to draw (streams of instruction or sim.). **b** (w. *ad notitiam*) to bring to notice. **c** to irrigate (fig.). **d** (geom.) to draw down.

a a705 paucos transmitte sermunculos illius pulcherrimae labiae tuae, de cujus fonte purissimo dulces ~ati rivi multorum possint reficere mentes (CELLANUS) *Ep. Aldh.* III 9; de vero lumine disputabo ut dirivetur ad eos quibus Christus donavit ut lumen sint *V. Greg.* p. 100; **793** sicut fons Paradisum irrigans quadrivido tramite latum diffunditur in orbem [cf. *Gen.* ii 10], sic fons caritatis . . in quattuor amoris rivos ~atur ALCUIN *Ep.* 19; temptavit . . vir Dei ultra Francorum regni fines caelestis doctrinae flumina ~are *Id. WillP* 9; Ariopago . ., unde . . officiorum jura quasi quidam salutis et vite rivuli ~arentur J. SAL. *Pol.* 390B; **1308** a qua [Romana ecclesia] veluti a primitivo fonte ad singulos alios ejusdem fidei rivuli ~antur (*Lit. Papae*) *Reg. Carl.* II 2; **c1338** (v. 1 copia 1b); cum dicat Christum abdicacionem proprietatis omnium rerum . . docuisse . . et apostolos in volentes perfecte vivere per doctrine ac vite ipsorum alveos hoc ipsum ~asse OCKHAM *Err. Papae* 963. **b** *Chr. Witham* 505 (v. conari b). **c** non valeo . . ab angusti pectoris exsiccato fonticulo tam spaciosam ~are abissum *Ps.*-ELMH. *Hen. V pref.* p. 3. **d** secundum . . latus . . a superiore loco dirivatum . . ad imum Luce esse describitur *Alea Evang.* 174.

3 (usu. in pass.) to derive, be derived; **b** (log., gram., or etym.). **c** to devolve (trans.), delegate. **d** to devolve (intr.).

~atur, descendit *GlH* D 231; pullulat in vulgi facinus vulgata voluptas / derivatque notam HANV. VII 439 p. 356; **c1239** reservatis sibi quibusdam majoribus, que potest ipse [papa] solus et que de potestate episcopali ~ata a potestate apostolica nullus potest episcopus GROS. *Ep.* 127 p. 364; a majoribus sumitur . . exemplum et a capite ~atur omnis malicia *V. Ed. II* 239; **1339** ad jus illud quod . . a matre . . non oritur sed in nepotem propagatum ad avo originaliter ~atur (*Lit. Ed. III*) *Chr. Ed. I & II* II 142; **c1407** cum vigor sensuum membris omnibus ~etur a capite *FormOx* 190. **b** futuri temporis participia a forma perfecta primae conjugationis ~ata ALDH. *PR* 137; idem Latine Petrus quod Syriace Cephas et in utraque lingua nomen a 'petra' ~atum est BEDE *Luke* 397; ex alio genere ~andi a 'vis' venit 'vilis' et 'viles' *Ps.*-GROS. *Gram.* 33; ['casus' et 'fortuna'] cause diverse sunt et repugnantes; non ergo secundum nomen dicetur vel ~abitur unum ab altero, quia ~atum et a quo ~atur debent communicare BACON VIII 108; *Id.* XV 207 (v. cadentia b). **c 1298** dum Deus in sua . . potencia ad nos . . multipharium ~ata . . collaudatur *Reg. Cant.* 279; **1425** si contingat . . magistrum J. T. ante completam execucionem testamenti . . mei in fata decedere . ., extunc volo quod modus et condicio suprascripta in personam magistri J. S. ~entur, et sic de primo in secundum, de secundo in tercium [etc.] *Reg. Cant.* II 353; UPTON 32 (v. derivative). **d** caput nobis Christus erit, ex quo omnis causa secunde regenerationis in nos ~asse videtur LANFR. *Comment. Paul.* (*Eph.* i 23) 290.

4 to divert or disperse.

†796 (13c) possessor illius terrae non habeat potestatem hanc terram a B. Albano diribare *CS* 280; **c805** (12c) terram . . dedi . . in vicissitudinem alterius agelluli in quaternis ~atum locis *CS* 324.

derivatio (diriv-) [CL]

1 effluence, overflow. **b** effluent (sb.). **c** passage from source.

s1268 pluviarum subsecute sunt inundationes et aquarum ~ones valde horribiles et durantes per xv dies *Ann. Osney* 215. **b** ubi Dominus fuit baptizatus . . stat crux lignea in medio, et parva ~o aquae stat illic et unus funiculus extensus supra Jordannem HUGEB. *Will.* 4. **c** longa ~one paulatim deficiens . . venenosus vigor GIR. *TH* I 39; ~o doloris ad superficiem corporis GILB. VII 311. 1.

2 a origination, derivation; **b** (etym., also fig.).

a si non es . . talis audaciae ut inter veridicas rationalis secundae a nuntiis ~onis creaturas [cf. *Psalm* viii 6] non pertimescas libertatis aureae decenti nota inuri GILDAS *EB* 1. **b** volebat [Brutus] ex ~one nominis [Brittanniae] memoriam habere perpetuam G. MON. I 16; qui horum singulorum prosequeretur ~ones . . magnam partem Latini extorqueret *Ps.*-GROS. *Gram.* 33; in te . . / primitivum derivatur; / talis derivatio / non est nota Prisciano WALT. WIMB. *Virgo* 60.

derivative [LL], derivatively, by delegation.

hodie omnia ista . . pertinent ad officium constabularii et marescalli . ., ~e tamen, quia eorum potestas derivata est et commissa per ducem belli UPTON 32.

derivativus (diriv-) [CL]

1 flowing away, effluent (adj.).

939 ut . . habeat xv mansas agelluli juxta ~is fluentium successibus *æt Cynetan CS* 734 (cf. ib. 752); **985** (13c) in campis, pascuis, pratis . . ~isque cursibus aquarum *CD* 1283.

2 derivative, secondary; **b** (etym., also as sb. n.).

~um, deductum, *scyriendlic GlH* D 539; putredo accidit dentibus aut ex causa primitiva aut ~a . . causa . . ~a fit intra aut extra GILB. III 160v. 2; ~um est cum vox a voce simili cum intencione descendat *Ps.*-GROS. *Gram.* 37; **c1430** (v. decompositus b). **b** *mys* Latine 'mus' . . interpretatur, et ex eadem prima positione ~um dicitur 'murius' vel 'murinus' ALDH. *Met.* 10 p. 95; ut 'passerinus', . . 'anserinus' et cetera ~a, quae superius de primitivis congessimus *Id. PR* 129; sunt omnia nomina propriae speciei, vel appellativae, principalis vel ~ae: propriae ut 'Julius'; appellativae, ut 'mons'; principalis, ut 'Julius'; ~ae, ut 'Julianus', 'montanus' ALCUIN *Gram.* 859C; 'extra', unde 'exterius' ~um est, locum significat FRIDUG. 136; A ante N breviatur . .; ~a vero producuntur, ut 'Spartānus' BACON *Tert.* 259.

derma [LL < δέρμα], skin.

~a, corium *GlH* D 242; ~a est pellis vel cutis *Gloss. Poems* 103; ~a, i. cutis; inde ostrocoderma *Alph.* 49.

derobare [AN *derober*, OF *desrober*], to rob, plunder. **b** to steal, carry off.

s1303 papa B. ~atus fuit in Campania Anagnie civitate et rex Anglie de thesauro suo per unicum latronem *Flor. Hist.* III 115 (cf. RISH. 222); **s1303** ingressi sunt ecclesiam [Anagnie] homines Schaire et spoliaverunt et ~arunt omnes clericos et laicos *Ann. Ed. I* 485; tanta est divisio in populo Romano, propter quod, qui sumus curtesani, . . singulis diebus expectamus quando erimus ~ati de . . aliis bonis nostris; nec possumus fugere . ., quia ex omni parte Rome sunt latrones et predones ad ~andum omnes transeuntes *Ib.* 491; venit domina Deveringham et conquesta est . . quod xl homines armorum et gentes pedites venerunt . . ad manerium domine . . et deraubaverunt eam bonis suis *Tract. Ed. II* 9; **1327** in succursum hominum piscatorum Anglie, qui indies . . ~ati et occisi extiterunt *KRMem* 103 r. 71*d.*; **1347** gemitus . . personarum miserabilium que, depredate et ~ate famisque subjecte angustie, clamant ad Dominum (*Lit. Papae*) AVESB. 111; **1392** ad instanciam N. C. ligei nostri, conquesti quod per quendam T. C. . . subditum vestrum in mari debuit ~ari *Dip. Corr. Ric. II* 100. **b s1303** thesaurus regis apud Westmonasterium ~atus *Flor. Hist.* III 115 *rub.*; **1318** breve missum ad inquirendum de navi disrobbata in mari per homines Alemannie (*LBLond.* E f. 74) *MGL* I 620; **1378** unum gladium de bonis ipsius V. . . felonice derobbaverunt, ceperunt, et asportaverunt *CoramR* 472 *rex* r. 18.

derobatio, robbery.

1444 predaciones, disrobaciones, incendia, et omnem facti actum et guerre viam *Cl* 294 m. 6*d.*; **1465** si . . aliquid contra presentes alligancias . . per aliquas incursiones . ., depredaciones, †deroboraciones . . attemptum fuerit (*TreatyR*) *Foed.* XI 556a.

derobator, robber. **b** (w. *viarum*) highwayman.

s1303 papa . . ~ores et spoliatores bonorum ecclesie Romane . . non absolvebat *Ann. Ed. I* 490. **b 1453** quod excommunicati . . denuncientur . . fures, latrones, . . viarum ~ores, pacis violatores . . (*Conc. Cashel*) *Conc.* III 565b.

derodere [CL], to gnaw away (partly fig.).

[quod] non aliquando . . bona ejus actio sit insidiatoris antiqui dente derosa BEDE *Sam.* 536; **793** ne vinea Domini vulpinis datur dentibus ad ~endum [*cf. Cant.* ii 15] ALCUIN *Ep.* 19; ne lupus insidians Christi deroderet agnos *Id. SS Ebor* 672.

derogamen, detriment.

1367 in divini cultus deminucionem et . . monasterii dampnum . . et egencium animarum ~en *Reg. Paisley* 32.

derogare [CL], (w. dat.) to derogate, detract (from), impugn. **b** (trans.) to revile, mock.

cum . . causam dissonantiae . . inquireret nec vellet Septuaginta translatorum fidei ~are BEDE *Gen.* 79; ~o, *ic ofteo* ÆLF. *Gl.*; non aliis apostolis ~at LANFR. *Comment. Paul.* (*Gal.* ii 6) 264; **c1150** (v. cavillatorie); libris eorum nunquam ~avi in aliquo J. SAL. *Pol.* 822B; cur tibi suave videtur absenti ~are, detrahere non audienti? AD. SCOT *Serm.* 223A; **1220** (v. collatio 6b); una [notio est] Spiritus Sancti tantum, sc. processio, nec aliquid ~at Spiritui Sancto quod tantum habet unam notionem BART. ANGL. I 4; **s1252** videns in hoc sibi [= OXNEAD 192: se] ~atum esse M. PAR. *Maj.* V 356; si melius quod omnis planta sit aromatica, et non ~et speciei BACON XI 233; *Chr. Dale* 1 (v. congaudere 2f); **1317** quibus . . nolumus in aliquo †deregari [? l. derogari] *Mon. Hib. & Scot.* 199a; **1437** ordinacionibus . . in contrarium facientibus . ., quibus omnibus . . ~amus ac ~atum esse . . declaramus, . . non obstantibus (*Lit. Papae*) BEKYNTON II 18; **1460** omnes qui furcas aut alia signa detestabilia signis aliquorum dominorum Anglie apposuerunt . . fame alicujus ~ancia *Mun-AcOx* 682. **b** ne . . livoris invidia criminemur aut . . suggillationis ludibrio ~emur ALDH. *VirgP* 58; **s1101** S. Blesensis . . comes pene ab omnibus ~abatur et . . verecundabatur eo quod de obsidione Antiochena turpiter aufugerit ORD. VIT. X 19 p. 118; **s1252** OXNEAD 192 (v. a supra); *to banne*, annathematizare, . . ~are, . . execrari *CathA.*

derogatio [LL < CL = *abrogation*], derogation, detraction. **b** (gram.) detraction, privation.

1073 linguas vestras ab omni ~one . . compescite LANFR. *Ep.* 47 (19); ille [dux Andegavensium] commendatum sibi [regis privignum] . ., legalitatis et future ~onis immemor, . . in carcere tenuit ORD. VIT. XI 16 p. 218; bonitatis . . serenitatem pestiferis . . persuasionibus ac ~onibus obnubilans, eorum corda unitatis . . quiete . . evacuat et . . . . rixarum fulminibus . . implet AD. SCOT *OP* 491C; **12..** quod non esset in ~onem regis vel regni *Ch. Sal.* 267; si . . eidem Radulpho [Yarewell; cf. *CalCl 1330–32* 570] prohibuerimus ne quicquam . . attentare presumeret per quod juri corone . . nostre derogari valeret in ~onem regie dignitatis nostre *Reg. Brev. Orig.* 37; **1333** in ~onem honoris domini regis et contemptum curie sue *LTRMem* 105 r. 41; videtur hec non esse laus scripture sed ~o quedam (KYN.) *Ziz.* 26; **s1398** processerunt . . ad alia . . Parliamentum tangencia . . in ~onem status Parliamenti WALS. *HA* II 227; ne . . proprie fragilitatis immemores in ~onis culpa capiantur *Ps.*-RISH. 491; **1437** (v. deputatio 1). **b** 'pro' multas significationes admittit: . . significat et ~onem, cum dicimus 'pro-fanus' locus, id est 'non sacer', quasi 'porro a fano' positus BONIF. *AG* 92.

derogativus [LL], derogatory. **b** detractive, privative (gram.).

c1378 quod . . foret . . honori ordinis nostri occasionaliter ~um et . . domino J. . . destructivum (*Excus. Wycl.*) *EHR* XLIII 77; prior J. [ob. **1401**] . . bullas eciam dignitati sui superioris ~as . . impetravit *G. S. Alb.* III 463. **b** 'in' praepositio nunc ~a, nunc adjectiva, ut 'firmus, infirmus' . ., 'infractus', id est 'valde fractus' BONIF. *AG* 90.

derogator [LL], derogator, detractor.

~ores dicuntur turpiloqui, unde dictum est derogat mihi, i. *mesdit GlSid* 149; *a banner*, .. ~or, execrator, imprecator *CathA*.

derogatorius [LL < CL = *modifying*], derogatory, detrimental; **b** (as sb. f., *sc. clausula*).

1306 premissa omnia in registro nostro inseri fecimus inviolabiliter permansura, statutis et consuetudinibus nostris presentibus litteris non ~iis in suo robore duraturis *StatOx* 101; **1432** dignetur vestra .. dominacio .. ante oculos sue sublimis discrecionis statuere quam sit prejudiciale ~iumque corone regie illas infringere libertates quas .. sui progenitores .. domibus concessere (*Supplicatio*) AMUND. I 309; cum .. clausulis ~iis juri alterius PAUL. ANGL. *ASP* 1556; **s1453** audiens .. billam dictam ~iam esse donacioni .. ducis Gloucestrie, [Johannes Skelton] mox contra eam .. se opposuit *Reg. Whet.* I 93; *Ib.* 259 (v. defalcatorius); **1502** dantes .. plenariam potestatem .. cuicumque privilegio .. alicui capitulo presentis tractatus quovis modo †~ie [l. ~io] .. renunciandi *RScot* 550b (cf. ib. 559b, *Foed.* XIV 782: dirogatorio). **b** **1462** non obstantibus .. ordinacionibus apostolicis et quibuscumque aliis .. indultis .. sub quibusvis verborum formis et cum quibuscumque eciam ~iarum ~iis aliisque melioribus et prohibitoriis clausulis .. *Mon. Hib. & Scot.* 437b (cf. *Conc.* III 683b, *Form. S. Andr.* II 255).

deronica, ~um, kind of herb or (?) *f. l.*

succi bedegar, zedoar', deronici [? l. doronici], serici, masticis .. ana ℥ iij .. valet in initio melancolie corque confortat GILB. IV 200v. 1; ~a vel veronica radix est parva utroque capite gracilis, in medio vero lacior *Alph.* 49.

derotionari v. dirationare. **dersa** v. dossa.

derta [Ar. *qūbā' misr. as drta*], (med.) impetigo.

si herpetes vel ~e circa crescant, curantur appositione saponis Sarracenici GILB. VII 336v. 2; aqua tartari .. ponatur super verucas et ~as et maculas et morpheas et impetigines et serpigines, et curat GAD. 134v. 2; zerna, ~a, serpigo est intensa inpetigo *Alph.* 49.

derudire [cf. CL rudis], to refine.

hic [Gregorius I] usum ecclesie ~ivit R. NIGER *Chr. II* 141.

deruere [CL], to tear down, demolish. *V. et. diruere.*

manebant exterminia civitatum ab hoste ~tarum ac desertarum BEDE *HE* I 22; ~ta, i. eversa, *ahwerfde GlH* D 236.

†desaconare, *f. l.*

1276 eo quod J. B. tenere voluerit inquisiciones suas ibi quasi ad libertatem suam †desaconare [MS: defaconare, ? l. diracionare] et quas tenere non deberet *Hund.* II 104.

desaevire [CL]

1 to rage, vent fury: **a** (of person or beast, or unspec.); **b** (of abstr.).

a bestia delituit, quae desaevire solebat ALDH. *VirgV* 554; **9..** ~iet, *grimsaþ WW*; **1171** satus .. erit eis regem .. sustinere, ut in vos valeant liberius ~ire D. LOND. *Ep.* 11; [comes] in male meritos juris rigore ~iens GIR. *TH* III 50; *Id. GE* I 34 (v. desperabiliter). **b** concupiscentia contra nos ~it BEDE *Sam.* 595; pestilentiae lues .. acerba clade diutius longe lateque ~iens *Id. HE* III 27; ~iente angustia T. MON. *Will.* VI 8 (v. devolvere 1b).

2 (?) to be appeased.

desevit, ab †iracuntia lenitur *GlC* D 168.

desafforestare v. disafforestare. **desainum** v. decena 1b. **desais-** v. dissais-. **desampar-** v. disempar-. **desca** v. discus 4.

descandalizare [LL]

1 to cause to stumble, offend.

'recessistis de via et ~astis plurimos in lege' [*Mal.* ii 8; *Vulg.*: scandalizastis] GILDAS *EB* 89.

2 to relieve from (sense of) offence.

si .. migras a conventu in separatam quietem .., si quam forte ex illa tua quiete scandalizari cognoveris, ~a eam et animum ejus in tranquillitate serena, quantum in te est, serva, suggesta sibi .. causa tue quietis. consulo etiam quod in omni meritoria actione ~es, si poteris, .. scandalizatas J. GODARD *Ep.* 242.

descantus v. discantus. **descarcare** v. discarcare 2. **descedere** v. decedere, 2 descendere.

1 descendere v. decedere 2a.

2 descendere [CL]

1 to descend, sink, come or go down. **b** (theol.) to descend. **c** (fig., w. *in se*) to shrink. **d** (math.) to descend (as through hundreds, tens, units). **e** (causative) to bring down.

[antistes] intro / cisternae latebram descendens usque profundam ALDH. *VirgV* 1027; vidit animam .. fratris .. cum agmine angelorum ~ere [v. l. ~entium] de caelo BEDE *HE* IV 3 p. 211; velut lupis vespertinis mos est clanculo ad plana ~ere ABBO *Edm.* 6; Domini .. exemplum, qui coram discipulis transfiguratus †descedentibus [l. descendentibus] illis de monte .. ait .. [cf. *Mark* ix 8] AILR. *Ed. Conf.* 761A; prora .. descensura sub undis W. CANT. *Mir. Thom.* III 46; DUNS *Ord.* II 68 (v. descensus 1a); **s1406** famulus .. illud optulit [predicatori] de gradibus ~enti *Chr. S. Alb.* 2. **b** dum Deus ad herebi vagas descenderit umbras ALDH. *VirgV* 455; **957** (12c) Adam .. ad inferos poenas luens decendit *CS* 995; si [Filius Dei] secundum corpus non ~it, ergo non ascendit; quod autem secundum corpus non ~it patet per hoc quod corpus illud non fuit in celo HALES *Qu.* 1470 (cf. ib.: forte diceretur quod '~ere' non dicitur ibi proprie, sed translative); an credimus quod is, in cujus conspectu non est aliqua creatura invisibilis .., non ~it liberare populum suum? AD. MARSH *Ep.* 244 p. 409. **c** felices quos non trahit ambitus! ardua nactus / non in se descendit honos J. EXON. *BT* I 41. **d** digiti et articuli in multiplicatione ascendunt, ita et denominationes in divisione ~unt THURKILL *Abac.* 58. **e** **1257** de j [juvenca capta] de Knaitho Goch, quia descend[it] averia sua de mont[ana] (*MinAc* 1094 / 11) *S. Wales Rec. Soc. Pub.* II 116 (cf. ib.: de Kidevor, quia non descend' predam suam).

2 a to go downstream. **b** (trans.) to sail (the sea). **c** (of ship) to put in, come ashore.

a profectus est Ceolfridus .. descensurus in mare per ostium Humbri fluminis *Hist. Abb. Jarrow* 31; major difficultas est per eum [fluvium] ascendere quam ~ere S. SIM. *Itin.* 41 (cf. ascendere 5a); princeps .. a .. castro suo Porcestrie in una navicula ad mare ~it *G. Hen. V* 3. **b** Patricius .. flatu prospero mare Hibernicum cum navi ~it NEN. *HB* 196. **c** **1243** de qualibet schuta ~ente in Soka Regine cum blado capiendus est j d. *MGL* III app. 447.

3 (of fluid, sound, light, *etc.*) to descend, flow or stream down (partly fig.); **b** (trans.).

~it pluvia serena sed copiosa BEDE *HE* IV 13; audivit .. vocem .. cantantium .. de caelo ad terras usque ~ere *Ib.* 3 p. 208; orientalis pars .. aquis .. alluitur .., quae .. cum maximis fluminibus ~unt in mare ABBO *Edm.* 2; Suirus .. apud Waterfordiam in mare ~it GIR. *TH* I 7; **1214** cursum aque que decendit a fontibus .. ad pontem torneicium per fossata Rochell' [*Gasc.*] usque ad mare *RChart* 196b; lux eterna primo super angelos influit et ipsis mediantibus ad nos ~it BART. ANGL. II 2; GILB. VII 309v. 2 (v. concatenatio 2); aqua non impeditur ~ere, sed ex natura sua propria quiescit superius BACON *Tert.* 165; ~it fluvius dulcis per mediam vallem, replens fossas *G. Hen. V.* 4. **b** **1507** (v. defensorius 2d).

4 to extend downhill (of slope, boundary, or road). **b** (of line) to slope down, descend.

c1185 locum in quo constructa est .. abbatia, sicut terra ~it de monte in Oudonem, et partem foreste, sicut via ~it versus domum Osberti *Act. Hen. II* II 380; **c1200** (v. clohus); **1221** sicut cheminum ~it versus Salopiam *Cl* 464a; **1294** per has divisas, viz. .. assendendo per quoddam †fossecum [l. fossetum] .. et sic de illo †fosseco .. usque ad caput de H., et sic per H. dessendendo usque ad metam de S. *Reg. Paisley* 94; **1320** et sic per mussam usque D. .., et inde .. usque P. et sic discendendo [? *add*: usque] mare *Cart. Cockersand* 298. **b** notularum ligatarum .. quedam tendunt ascendere, quedam ~ere *Mus. Mens.* (*Anon. VI*) 402.

5 (mus. or prosody) to descend (in scale): **a** (of singer); **b** (of phrase or sim.); **c** (pr. ppl. as sb. f., (?) *sc. mutatio*). **d** to 'descend' (in scale of colour).

a possumus ascendere et ~ere cum tenore per dissonancias HOTHBY *Contrap.* FL 63. **b** in E la mi fiunt due mutationes, sc. la mi et mi la, una ascendendo, una ~endo GARL. *Mus.* 160; periodus perfecte ~it BACON *Tert.* 248 (cf. 2 colon); quandocumque tenor ascendit contrapunctus debet ~ere HOTHBY *Contrap.* FL 63. **c** GARL. *Mus.* 167 (v. descensivus). **d** UPTON 101 (v. 3 color 1c).

6 (w. ref. to lineage or inheritance) to descend: **a** (of person); **b** (of property or title); **c** (dep.).

a flos virgulti de radice Jesse ~ens [*cf. Is.* xi 1] ALDH. *VirgP* 13; **1207** Reginaldus ~it de Eularia *CurR* V 46; **1226** heredibus suis de matre nostra descensuris *Pat* 98; pro defectu heredum recta linea ~entium BRACTON 21b; **1292** H. rex .. dedit .. Huberto .. et Margarete uxori sue et heredibus eorum de eisdem H. et M. decendentibus *PQW* 381a; ibi est j lectus .. de quo est stipes Houel ap T., de quo ~erunt David Vachan .., Walter ap D. .. *BB St. David's* 322; **1339** cum .. eidem Karolo .. ex ~entibus secum ab eodem Ph. masculus superstes proximior fuerit nullus nobis (*Lit. Ed. III*) WALS. *HA* I 202; ad genealogiam regum .. de .. prosapia .. Margarete .. ab Adam, viz. patre omnium racionabilium mortalium, linialiter discendencium procedendum est *Plusc.* VI 1. **b** si .. fuerint de illo stipite unde hereditas ~erit GLANV. XIII 11; *Ib.* VII 1 (v. ascendere 2c); **1198** (v. conquaestus 2b); **1201** sicut terram que habet ei ~ere a Cecilia .. cum einescia, cujus heres .. est *CurR* I 447; **1218** de Radulfo ~it jus .. terre .. Odoni filio suo *Eyre Yorks* 60; **1230** nec est heres .. Yonis nec aliquid ~it ad eam jure hereditario de hereditate ipsius Yonis *LTRMem* 11 r. 6d.; **1304** (v. descensus 6); **13..** que .. tenementa .. regi per prefatum (*sic*) escaetam ~ebant *Meaux* II 189; **14..** nihil ~ebat in feodo simplici post mortem .. patris sui *Reg. Brev. Orig.* 144; **1491** manerium .. michi .. jure hereditario .. discendebat *FormA* 411. **c** **s1308** antequam status corone ~atur, nulla ligiancia respicit personam (*Artic. Magnatum*) *G. Ed. II Bridl.* 33 (= *Ann. Lond.* 153: *avant ceo qe l'estat de la corone soit descendu*); **1399** in .. possessionibus et dominiis nobis .. jure hereditario in dominico, servicio vel reversione seu alias .. descensis (*Ch. Regis*) *MGL* III 487.

7 to derive, be derived: **a** (math.); **b** (etym.).

a THURKILL *Abac.* 56 (v. debere 1a). **b** quanta numerositas diccionum ab hac diccione 'vis' ~it *Ps.*-GROS. *Gram.* 33; 'consilium', prout sumitur pro deliberacione .., debet scribi per S; nam in casu hoc ~it a 'consulo' LYNDW. 18 d (cf. 1 concilium 1).

8 (of persons): **a** to work downwards (following a list). **b** (w. *ad* or *in* & acc., or w. dat.) to proceed, turn, 'get down' (to). **c** (w. *ex*) to argue, draw an inference (from).

a **1532** cantaria Roberti et Agnetis R., ~endo: Junii, .. solut' domino R. W., senescallo .. ; Julii, solut' domino H. B. [etc.] *Househ. Bk. Durh.* 99. **b** **s1249** (v. contributio b); **1282** volumus .. quod cum eodem .. super eodem negocio tractetis, ita quod in certos articulos ~atis *RGasc* II 157; **1338** ad eleccionem presidencium pro .. instanti capitulo continuo ~erunt *Conc.* II 627a; postquam .. quesivimus an expediret mundo uni imperatori subesse .., ad Romanum imperium ~amus, inquirentes primo a quo Romanum processit imperium OCKHAM *Dial.* 885 (recte 887); **s1385** compulsus est ergo papa, vellet nollet, paci ~ere et pacem petere *V. Ric. II* 59; **1411** sed hic .., pretermissis multis .. injuriis et .. obprobriis, ad aliquales causas hujusmodi malorum ~emus *FormOx* 188. **c** ex nulla particula narracionis ejusdem libelli potest ~ere nisi ex prima parte CONWAY *Def. Mend.* 1342.

9 (log.) to descend (towards particulars).

predicata .. que dicuntur de Deo .. sunt predicata transcendencia. .. quidquid convenit enti antequam ~at in genera est transcendens (DUNS) *OED* s. v. *transcendent* 4.

descendibilis, descendible, transmissible by inheritance.

reale est quod petimus regnum ~e preregnantis heredi FORTESCUE *NLN* II 50.

descensio [CL], **a** (astr.) 'descension'. **b** (theol.) descent. **c** descent, lineage.

a sicut in Ariete exaltatur sol per suam virtutem, sic in Libra est ejus ~o, cum sit signum oppositum Arieti GROS. 43. **b** cujus semel mirabilis / nos edocet descensio / pios sacra perenniter / ut lampet omnes gratia BEDE *Hymn* 7. 3; corpus plene glorificatum non movebitur; ergo non competit ei ascensio vel ~o HALES *Qu.* 1470. **c** dum magi Christum in vita Joseph fuisse regem Judeorum affirmant, alio quam hereditario ~onis titulo eum ibidem regnasse necessario confitentur FORTESCUE *NLN* II 11.

descensive, by descent (w. ref. to lineage).

1313 a quodam fratre ultimo genito quondam domini de B. suam traxerat originem ~e *RGasc* IV 826 (cf. compar 2a).

descensivus, (mus.) descending (in pitch).

ideo in cantu ~o ad ultimam descendentem debemus facere pausam, sicut patet in 'Kyrie eleyson' GARL. *Mus.* 167.

descensus [CL]

1 descent, fall. **b** descent (theol.). **c** downward direction (at table). **d** arrival (of guests), dismounting.

1231 de morte Ricardi .., quem Adam .. per decensum cujusdam sagitte, quam sursum traxerat, occidit *Cl* 552; [grave] prohibetur a ~u propter aliquid repugnans, vincens inclinacionem ejus .., quo amoto non impeditum descendit DUNS *Ord.* II 68. **b** ejus [Filii Dei] dicitur primo quod est in termino a quo est ~us, et iste terminus fuit celum HALES *Qu.* 1470. **c** D. BEC. 1063 (v. 1 ascensus 1b). **d** filii .. Israel .. numerentur .. in ~u in Egyptum S. LANGTON *Chron.* 78; frater qui ad suscipiendos hospites est deputatus, accepto rumore a famulo locutorii exterioris de hospitum decensu ibidem .. *Cust. Westm.* 80; ?**1461** (v. equester 2a).

2 (astr.): **a** setting. **b** 'descension'.

a GILB. I 74. 1 (v. ascensus 1d). **b** expectet donec eadem stella fuerit in majori suo ~u ROB. ANGL. (II) 181.

3 a movement or passage downstream. **b** downward flow (of fluid).

a in ~u ramusculorum natantium aves exterrentur NECKAM *NR* II 125; **1255** consuetudinem Mauritannie per ascensum et decensum fluvii de Gerunda *RGasc* I sup. 7. **b** aqua .. habet duos respectus. .. illa [comparatio] que est respectu ~us debetur ei in quantum est locabilis BACON *Tert.* 165 (cf. descendere 3a).

4 downward slope, declivity; **b** (of nose).

devexu[m], declibium, ~um *GlC* D 140; clivium, i. discensum, *helde, burghsteal GlH* C 1121; †**957** (14c)

terrarum limites: .. ab illo loco ad illam albam viam et tunc ad ~um obliquum [AS: *on þaeet* (sic) *sclæde*] *CS* 1000; **1205** terram assartatam que .. extendit se in decensum juxta campum de W. *RChart* 161b; **1337** quandam placeam .. vacuam una cum quodam decensu montis eidem placee contiguo *Pat* 426 m. 19; **s1333** magnus patuit Scotis prius ~us, et abruptus dehinc ascensus FORDUN *Cont.* XIII 28 (= *Plusc.* IX 28: discensus). **b** permaneant [novicii] .. cooperti capuciis .. usque ad ~um nasi *Cust. Cant.* 4.

5 (mus.) descent (in pitch).

quelibet dissonancia in ~u requirit consonanciam suam HOTHBY *Contrap. Fl* 63.

6 descent (w. ref. to lineage or inheritance).

MAP *NC* II 23 (v. conquisitor 2a); **1236** de narratione ~us in brevi de recto ab antecessore a tempore H. regis senioris (*Merton* 7) *StRealm* I 3; **1285** inter duos clamantes per unum ~um (2 *Westm.* 17) *Ib.* 82; **1304** una cum toto jure .. cujuscumque ~us .. quorumcumque tenementorum que ad me .. aliquo juris gradu descendere .. continget *Feod. Durh.* 58*n.*; **1321** in narrando nullum fecerunt ~um ab aliquo antecessorum suorum *MGL* II 365; **1330** (v. conquaestus a); **1333** eas tenet per ~um hereditarium *LTRMem* 105 r. 58; **1337** per †discessum hereditarium *Reg. Brev. Orig.* 88.

7 (log.) descent (towards particulars).

differentia .. aut sunt in recto discensu a generalissimo ad specialissima suscipientia predicationem generalissimi, et sic sunt species in predicamento; aut non, set a latere, ut differentiarum ~us et principiorum BACON XIII 259.

descept-, descern- v. disc-. **deschus** v. discus 4. **descidere, descindere** v. 1 & 2 decidere, discindere. **descipula** v. decipula.

descire [cf. CL scire], to 'unknow', unlearn.

ut nec magistrum diffiteretur in patre nec patrem in magistro ~iret P. BLOIS *Ep.* 217. 505; GIR. *TH* III 10 (v. desuescere 1b); *to forgete*, ~ire, dediscere, oblivisci .. *CathA.*

desciscere [CL], to defect, desert.

~ivit, *wiðstylde*, pedem retraxit *GlC* D 115; ~iscimus, recidimus *Ib.* 156; ~ivit, †voluit [l. noluit] *Ib.* 187; ~o, i. decipio, .. desero *GlH* D 254; hic est error .. quo carere si potuisses, nec a patrum nobilitate ~ivisses nec infame nomen .. incurrisses *Eccl. & Synag.* 86; ~ere, .. deserere OSB. GLOUC. *Deriv.* 180; **s1088** Odo .. livore ictus a rege ~ivit HIGD. VII 5 p. 322 (= KNIGHTON I 87: discivit).

descisio v. 2 decisio 3. **descissus** v. 2 decidere. **descistere** v. desistere b. **desconfectura** v. disconfitura. **descredere** v. discredere. **descrescere** v. decrescere 1a. **descrescio** v. 1 discretio 5b. **descretista** v. decretista.

describere [CL]

1 to describe (geom.), delineate.

ADEL. *Euclid* 155 (v. ducere 8e); tunc latus quadrati ~endi in glaciali [sphera oculi] subtenditur angulo recto pyramidis BACON *Maj.* II 60.

2 to write down, transcribe. **b** (p. ppl. as sb. n.) document.

bibliothecam .. ampliavit, ita ut .. iij pandectes faceret ~i *Hist. Abb. Jarrow* 20; magister dilecte, restat adhuc una sententia non descripta CUTHB. *Ob. Baedae* clxiii; **1115** descripta est hujus concessionis carta anno ab Incarnationis Domini mcxv *Chr. Abingd.* II 63; BACON *Tert.* 337 (v. columella b); **1454** ut patet per literas domini regis .. in superioribus rotulis descriptas *ExchScot* 614. **b** **s1106** quicquid de .. terra W. actitatum extitit, comes [Cestrensis] .. suo descripto roboravit; quod descriptum sigillo matris [sc. comitis] signari constitit *Chr. Abingd.* II 69.

3 to describe, recount (occurrence), depict (appearance) in words; **b** (w. acc. & inf.). **c** (her.) to blazon.

ut de monstruosis hominum partubus ~erem *Lib. Monstr. prol.*; vitam .. Cudbercti .. plano sermone descripsi BEDE *HE* V 24 p. 359; haec novem descripta maneria sunt de victu monachorum *DB* I 77; non omnes sanctos sed diversos sanctos descripsi *Descr. Constant.* 245; hec celi amplitudo ejusque forma, que a geometra ~itur, vulgari animo aut vix aut numquam patet ADEL. *QN* 25; fiunt .. tanti morientium gemitus, tanti invadentium furores, quantos et dolorosum est ~ere G. MON. XI 2; ut bellicam classem sermo succinctus ~at *Itin. Ric.* I 34; non ab re erit, descripto .. majori mundo, ipsum quoque minorem mundum .. parumper discribere HIGD. II *prol.* p. 174; **1431** prout inferius discribitur (*Cl*) *Foed.* X 487a. **b** adinstar illius mulieris .. quam Apocalipsis [xvii 3] super bestiam sedisse ~it ALDH. *VirgP* 17; Solinus .. in cxx milia passuum .. latitudinem Hibernie diffundi ~it GIR. *TH* I 3. **c** arma palata .. ~untur sic: 'portat arma palata de argento et azorio' BAD. AUR. 179.

4 to register, enrol. **b** to tax (also fig.).

cum ventum fuisset Glestoniam et descriptis omnibus ipse [Dunstanus] proscriptus fuisset OSB. *V. Dunst.* 27; **1549** ne quis officio procurandi sese ingerat, nisi cat[a]logo fuerit descriptus *Conc. Scot.* II 126. **b** jam exiit edictum a nostro imperatore Deo ut totus mundus ~atur, sicut terrenus ille imperator ~i voluit omnem mundum [cf. *Luke* ii 1] AILR. *Serm.* 220B; **s1168** fecit rex ditiores ex Anglia Judeos transfretare et reliquos in v^m m. ~ere GERV. CANT. *Chr.* 205.

descriptibilis, describable: **a** (geom.); **b** (phil.).

a latus quadrati ~is in sphera uvee BACON *Maj.* II 59. **b** motus uniformiter difformis .. terminatur ad gradum inclusive; quia aliter non esset dare gradum eis †intensissimus [? l. intensissimum] vel medium, et per consequens non esset ~is aliqua descripcione WYCL. *Log.* III 33; penitencia primo vel secundo modo .. non est ~is *Id. Blasph.* 143.

descriptio [CL]

1 the act of drawing or writing. **b** diagram. **c** map.

ort[h]ografia, discriptio litterarum *GlC* O 265; secundum ordinem ~onis nominum subsecuta est defunctio singulorum J. FURNESS *Walth.* 107. **b** tota substantia in 16 terminatur, ut subjecta docet ~o ROB. ANGL. *Alg.* 88*n.* **c** affero ~onem in albiori parte pellis, ubi civitates notantur per circulos rubeos BACON *Maj.* I 300.

2 survey; **b** (w. ref. to Domesday Book).

737 (11c) cartulam ~onis agri *CS* 156; **799** (c1000) contra hanc cartulam ~onis nostrae *CS* 296. **b** in anno quo facta est haec ~o *DB* I 3; de quo manerio nemo legatis regis reddidit rationem nec aliquis eorum venit ad hanc ~onem *Ib.* 164; †**1087** post ~onem totius Anglie *Regesta* p. 63.

3 description, account, definition.

~o anni Arabum ADEL. *Elk.* 1 *rub.*; Kambrie nostre ~onem vestre sanctitati destinare disposui GIR. *IK pref.* p. 155; ad hoc quod obicitur, sc. liberum arbitrium est 'facultas rationis et intellectus etc.' dicendum est quod illa ~o non est data per se secundum essentiam liberi arbitrii, sed est data secundum accidens J. BLUND *An.* 404 (cf. ib. 209: falsa est superior discriptio); **s1382** religiosi predicantes, qui nolunt .. scribere veram ~onem .. sacramenti .., sunt excommunicati KNIGHTON II 177; **1444** quod .. inventarium conficiatur .. cum discripcione et annotacione cujuscunque rei numero, pondere et mensura (*Vis. Westm.*) *EHR* XXXVII 88.

4 registration, enrolment for taxation. **b** contribution, tax.

ipsa totius orbis ~o quae a terreno rege facta memoratur [cf. *Luke* ii 1] caelestis opera regis manifeste designat BEDE *Hom.* I 6. 334; edictum Cesaris Augusti super orbis ~one AD. DORE *Pictor* 152. **b** omnium sibi auxilia asciscebat, vel in militibus mittendis vel in eris ~one reddenda *G. Steph.* II 75; **s1146** per totam Galliam fit ~o generalis; non sexus nec ordo, non dignitas quempiam excusavit quin auxilium regi conferret DICETO *Chr.* 256 (cf. id. *YH* I 372).

5 limit, ending.

cordis jocunditas aut exultacio / est vite terminus sive descripcio WALT. WIMB. *Sim.* 174.

descriptiuncula [CL], brief description.

nonnulli .. orationes per opuscula nostra varia dispersas .. in unum congestas et magnorum virorum ~as .. competenter adaptatas .. sibi largiri postulabant GIR. *LS* 413.

descriptive, by way of description. **b** by definition.

exemplariter hinc innotescant .. quatuor enuntiandi principiorum genera, et si nec ~e nec nominatim BALSH. *AD rec.* 2 18. **b** cum philosophus sit ~e amator sapientie WYCL. *Ver.* I 32.

descriptor [LL], describer, narrator.

licet ~or vite ipsius [Odulfi] .. id tacitum omiserit *Mir. Odulfi* 315; cosmographus, mundi ~or BACON *Gram. Gk.* 136; historie ~ores HIGD. I *prol.* (v. dimensor).

desculpere [LL], to carve, sculpture.

hec [archa] tota exterius premirabili celatura ~itur R. COLD. *Cuthb.* 43.

descurrere v. discurrere 3b.

†descurris, *f. l.*

9.. †~is [? l. de scurris; cf. *ASD* s. v. *þyle*], *hofðelum WW.*

descus, ~um v. discus 4.

1 desecare [CL, *conf. w.* dissecare], **a** to cut down. **b** to cut off.

a tigna .. ad planitiem terre sunt ~ta, quod aliter erui nequirent W. MALM. *GR* IV 324. **b** caput libens sanctissimum / jam dissecandum praebuit BEDE *Hymn* 10. 7; gentem Merciorum .. ~to capite perfido .. convertit *Id. HE* III 24.

2 desecare v. 2 dissecare.

desecrare [CL = *to consecrate*], to deprive of holy orders.

s1070 aliquot .. episcopi .. officio privati sunt. in iis fuit Stigantus Cantuariensis antistes, qui ~atus est P. VERG. IX 156.

desectio v. defectio a. **deseis-** v. dissais-. **deseminare** v. disseminare. **desena** v. decena 1a. **desenparare** v. disemparare. **desensio** v. dissensio. **Deseos** v. Daisios.

desepelire [cf. CL sepelire], to disinter.

1231 corpus illud fecerunt ~iri et .. omnes simul bene dicunt quod ipse est Rollandus et hoc vident per multa signa, sc. per quandam verucam in facie [etc.] *BNB* II 402; **1314** venit .. coronator et disspelliri (*sic*) fecit corpus *SelCCoron* 70.

deseptus v. dissaepire 1a.

desequi [cf. CL sequi], to accuse.

~untur, i. accusabant vel *meldadan GlH* D 263.

1 deserere [CL]

1 to abandon, forsake, let go: **a** (person); **b** (thing); **c** (abstr. or symbol.); **d** (in euphem. for death). **e** (p. ppl.) bereft; **f** (as sb. n.) lack, want.

a 706 si .. dominum, quem in prosperitate dilexerunt, .. ingruente .. adversitate ~uerint ALDH. *Ep.* 9 (12); *V. Cuthb.* IV 18 (daemoniacus 1a); obsecro .. ne me ~as, sed tui memor sis fidissimi sodalis BEDE *HE* IV 27 p. 274; si dominus .. eum [sc. hominem suum] in mortali necessitate ~at supervacue, forisfacere potest dominium suum erga eum (*Leg. Hen.* 43. 8) *GAS* 569; rex jacet extorris, solus, dīsertus, inermis GARL. *Tri. Eccl.* 81; **c1316** ut, nos fornace probacionis [cf. *Prov.* xxvii 21] nullatenus disserente, detur cum temptacione proventus *FormOx* 13. **b** classem absque valida manu non audebat ~ere ABBO *Edm.* 6; quando aliquam rem propter se non vis tenere sed ~ere, ut carbonem ignitum positum in nuda manu, tunc .. prius est non velle tenere quam velle ~ere ANSELM (*Casus Diab.* 3) I 239; temporalia cuncta .. plene ~uerunt SERLO GRAM. *Mon. Font.* 21. **c** an ad praedicationem Augustini suas ~ere traditiones deberent BEDE *HE* II 2; **798** Dominus tempore passionis suae opera .. non ~uit sanitatis ALCUIN *Ep.* 136; monachilem habitum ~ens ÆLF. *Æthelwold* 5; quatenus, cum possent ~ere justitiam et ex libertate servarent arbitrii, gratiam et laudem mererentur ANSELM (*CurD* II 10) II 107; **s1321** dum fidem regis ~endo baronibus adhesit TROKELOWE 110. **d** FELIX *Guthl.* 50 (v. corpusculum 1b); **947** (12c) postquam humani generis fragilitatem ~uerit et ad .. jucunditatis viam .. adierit *CS* 820. **e** membris deserta vigore / clinica FRITH. 1366 (cf. clinicus 1). **f** propter ~um victualium BRYGG *Itin.* 382.

2 (leg.): **a** to abandon, give up (an action). **b** to deny, fail to grant.

a intelligens placitum non duci per rectitudinem ad proficuum regis, placitum ~uit *DB* I 32; si appellans non prosecutus fuerit appellationem infra terminum juris .., ~ta est appellatio *Praxis* 280; **1593** cautio .. infra triduum .. interponatur; alias appellatio pro ~ta habeatur *StatOx* 449. **b 1314** implacitat visinos suos in curia domini regis .. antequam jus ei ~atur in curia propria (*Andover*) *Gild. Merch.* II 308; **1334** quod nullus faciat querelam alicui ministro domini regis antequam jus ei disser[a]tur in hundredo et curia (*Ib.*) *Ib.* 330.

3 to desert, leave, quit (place or occupation). **b** (p. ppl.) deserted, desolate. **c** (as sb. f. or n.) desert, wilderness. **d** (p. ppl. *s. act.*) having deserted.

draco .. / deserit obscurum .. tigillum ALDH. *VirgV* 2402; rex .. jussit abunde propinare hospitibus medonem, clausis foribus ne quis fugiendo potationem regalis convivii ~ere videretur ÆLF. *Æthelwold* 8; cervus fugit, avia silve / deserit WALT. ANGL. *Fab.* 55. 2; **s1225** parentum clam ~ens palatium WEND. II 290; **1283** hujusmodi artifices solent .. fugere tanquam fures artificium suum ~ando (*sic*) *AncC* XLVIII 177; ~uerunt locum et evanuerunt ab oculis nostris *G. Hen. V* 11 (cf. ib. 24: caraca .. ~uit visum nostrum). **b** GILDAS *EB* 26 (v. diruere a); squalida deserti procurans jugera ruris ALDH. *VirgV* 1457; Angulus .. usque hodie manere ~tus .. perhibetur BEDE *HE* I 15; **c1105** rex .. dedit mihi Ædnaham ~tam, quam ego .. mea propria pecunia inhabitavi et ecclesiam .. fabricavi *E. Ch. Scot.* 24; Hibernia .. vere terra ~ta, invia sed aquosa [cf. *Psalm* lxii 3] GIR. *TH* I 4; quod viso loco ~to in posterum diceretur a transeuntibus: 'hec fuit villa Beverlaci' *Mir. J. Bev. C* 341. **c** qui superfuerant silvis ac ~is abditisque speluncis se occultavere GILDAS *EB* 11; accola deserti vitam sine crimine ducens ALDH. *VirgV* 828; bestiae et dracones cognoverunt in ~o Salvatorem mundi *AS Inscr.* 105; ~tum vel heremus, *westen* ÆLF. *Sup.*; ~ta, sive [l. sic] vocata quae [l. quia] non seruntur, destituta, *alætan GlH* D 262; GARL. *Epith.* X 78, 80 (v. deservire 4c); dicunt quod apostoli tunc erant in casu necessitatis, quia erant in ~to OCKHAM *Pol.* II 766; pro mandato domini ~arum in Arabia BRYGG *Itin.* 387. **d s1349** tunc terra ob †~tum colonum, qui ipsam colere solebat, remansit inculta AD. MUR. *Cont. A* 178 (cf. WALS. *HA* I 273: ob defectum colonorum, qui nusquam erant).

4 (w. inf.) to cease or fail. *Cf. desinere.*

mihi .. fidem affectionis .. exhibere non ~it vestre suavitatis studiosa sollicitudo AD. MARSH *Ep.* 103; prelati, quando considerant .. quod mandatum pape est eis prejudiciale, ipsum ~unt adimplere OCKHAM *Dial.* 686.

2 deserere v. 3 disserere. **deseritatio** v. dishereditatio.

1 desertare [LL], to desert.

to forsake, .. derelinquere, deserere, invite relinquere, voluntate ~are, desinere .. *CathA*.

2 desertare v. dissertare. **desertatio** v. detentio 3a.

desertio [CL], desertion, abandonment: **a** (of duty, order, or sim.); **b** (leg., of appeal); **c** (of place).

a quoniam et naturam accusat spontanea, quam fecit in Adam, justitiae ~o ANSELM (*Orig. Pecc.* 27) II 170; pericula disercionis que est mercenarii, non pastoris (*Lit. O. Cardinalis*) *EHR* XV 97; **1392** primum [inconveniens] est contemptus proprii curati .., tercium ~o obediencie *Ziz.* 345; cum .. sit peccatum .. ~o ordinis universi FORTESCUE *NLN* II 21. **b** de forma allegandi ~onem appellationis *Praxis* 278 *rub.* **c 1285** quatenus, si quod de prefati loci [a fratribus ordinis Penitencie derelicti] ~one proponitur veritate fulcitur, ipsum .. vendas *Mon. Hib. & Scot.* 132a.

desertitudo v. disertitudo.

desertive, (?) by way of desertion.

si frenum mandatorum in eis dirumpitur .., statim fit emissarius, cui diabolus insidet, ducens a Deo ~e in voraginem viciorum WYCL. *Ver.* I 273.

desertivus, (as sb. f.) woman abandoned by husband.

ne quis Christianus .. uxorem ducat .. commatrem suam neque sanctimonialem neque ~am [AS: *on ælætan* .. *gewifige*] (*Cons. Cnuti*) *GAS* 291 (= *Quad.*: repudiatam; *Inst. Cnuti*: in alterius relicta, quam Angli vocant *oþres mannes ælæte*).

desertor [CL], deserter.

~orem propriae aecclesiae interdictum habemus in alia ministrare EGB. *Dial.* 6; quasi ~oris furtivo more discessit W. POIT. I 23; ~ores pugnae, quos in aliorum perniciem metus absolvit G. CRISPIN *Herl.* 88; P. BLOIS *Ep.* 69. 215B (v. emansor); milites xv castri ~ores ex desperatione scapham intrantes GIR. *IK* I 12; **s1377** (v. compastor); WYCL. *Ente* 182 (v. coangustare 1c); **1559** catholicae fidei et ecclesiasticae unitatis ~ores *Conc. Scot.* II 174.

desertus v. deserere, deservire, disertus.

deservire [CL]

1 to serve: **a** (absol.); **b** (w. dat.); **c** (w. abstr. subj.). **d** (pr. ppl. as sb.) servant.

a 984 (13c) dilecto fidelique ministro .. Elfwine .. pro ejus amabili humilique obsequio quo jugiter instanter ~it .. condono [etc.] *Ch. Burton* 24. **b** ut .. libera .. mente Domino ~irent BEDE *HE* II 5 (cf. ib. IV 29 p. 278: frater .. hospitum ministerio ~iens); uni / deservire Deo statuit simul omnibus horis ALCUIN *SS Ebor* 858; rex [Stephanus] misit ad episcopum, .. precipiens quatinus ecclesiam .. ab omni exactione .. liberam .. Christo Domino pacifice sineret ~ire *Chr. Battle* f. 58v.; **1301** *Reg. Wint.* I 129 (v. clericulus a); **1306** neque aliquis cogatur nobis ~ire, nisi fuerit conducticius qui pre aliis nobis pro racionabili stipendio ~ire tenetur *BBC* (*Swansea*) 131 (cf. 3a infra); diem .. quo prepotens urbs et castellum reddita novelle potenciori ~ire didicerant dicioni *Ps.*-ELMH. *Hen. V* 70. **c** canonica [scientia] .. theosophie ~it et subicitur *Ps.*-GROS. *Summa* 301. **d 1429** lego xvj ~ientibus meis, viz. cuilibet eorum vj s. viij d. *Reg. Cant.* II 408.

2 to serve (eccl.), officiate (at mass *etc.*): **a** (absol.); **b** (w. dat. of church or sim.); **c** (w. acc. of church or sim.). **d** to officiate (leg.).

a 1229 cum ecclesia .. ita tenuis esset in .. proventibus quod ad eam non spectarent .. proventus qui sufficere possent .. ministris .. in ea ~ituris *Pat* 249; **1249** parochiales ecclesie in quibus per vicarios ~itur (*Processus*) *G. S. Alb.* I 359; **1307** idem Ricardus [clericus] .. se elongavit de civitate London' usque Waltham et ibidem tunc per longum tempus ~ivit *Gaol Del.* 39/1 r. 9; **1356** capellano ~ienti in capella de C. *Ac. Durh.* 122. **b a1127** in dominicis preceptis frequenter legendo reperitur: 'qui altario ~iunt de altario vivant' [cf. *1 Cor.* ix 13] *E. Ch. S. Paul.* 44; **c1150** absentibus .. nobis sacerdos monachorum eidem capelle ~iet et omnes oblationes recipiet *Feod. Durh.* 131*n.*; **c1250** ut rectores ecclesiarum, vicarii et capellani qui ecclesiis ~iunt .. horas canonicas cantent in ecclesia cum nota et devotione *Conc. Syn.* 641 (cf. ib. 646: clerici infra sacros ordines constituti et alii qui ~iunt altari); **1448** monitus est quod decetero resideat et ecclesie ~iat in divinis *Eng. Clergy* 231; **1509** ut [abbas] aliquem canonicorum nullo modo sinat, sub occasione ~iendi curis monasterio nostro annexis, in patriam vagari, sed curis hujusmodi faciat per sacerdotes seculares deinceps ~iri (*Vis. Dorchester*) *EHR* IV 312. **c** †faniticus [l. fanaticus], qui templum diu deser[v]it *GlC* F 76; **a1192** sciatis me dedisse .. canonicis [B. Thome] .. capellam de castello meo, et ipsi faciant eam ~ire *Reg. S. Thom. Dublin* 20; **1245** abbas et conventus .. tenentur facere ~ire ecclesias memoratas per ydoneas .. personas continue juxta ritum fidei Christiane *Lit. Cant.* III app. 362 (cf. ib. 250). **d 1543** concedentes .. potestatem .. clericos .., notarios .., adjudicatores, serjandos, officiarios et alios juris ministros .. creandi .. et ipsos .. ad debite .. in eorundem officiis ~iendum jurare faciendi *Form. S. Andr.* II 219.

3 to serve (feud.), hold land by service; **b** (w. acc. of land held).

terra ecclesiae de Wirecestre: .. de eodem manerio tenet R. dispensator .. dim. hidam. .. Keneuuardus tenuit et ~iebat sicut episcopus volebat *DB* I 172v. (cf. ib. 174: tenuerunt et ~iebant sicut ab episcopo deprecari poterant); homines hundreti audierunt istum V. .. cognoscentem una vice .. quod .. ~iebat in R. et ad ultimum audivit hund[retus] istum eundem dicentem quod ~iebat erga Rogerum *Ib.* II 177; **a1122** episcopus concessit ei ij hidas .. in pheodo, quarum una est libera et fuit terra tani et altera de dominio, eotenus ut ~iat militari modo, viz. cum armis et equo *Cart. Bath A* 51; **1166** hoc faciunt homines mei mihi intelligere, quod pater meus ~iebat per xl milites *RBExch* 351; **1306** (v. 1b supra). **b** hanc terram ~ivit R. erga G. de M. per hoc quod ipse G. dixit ei quatinus rex sibi dederat servitium illius terrae *DB* II 97; **1100** militibus qui per loricas terras suas ~iunt (*Ch. Hen. I*) *GAS* 522; **a1128** x servientes, qui ~iunt terram per sergentariam *Chr. Peterb.* app. 161.

4 to earn, deserve. **b** (w. *pro*) to work for. **c** (p. ppl. *desertus* as sb. n. pl.) earned rewards, deserts.

volo .. ut inde gaudeant in ipsis locis qui haec dignius erga Deum et nos volunt ~ire [AS: *to Gode and to me geearnian willað*] (*Quad.*) *GAS* 147; volo esse domino meo fidelis .., ut me teneat sicut ~ire [AS: *earnian*] volo (*Ib.*) *Ib.* 397; folgario competit ut in xij mensibus ij acras habeat. .. si plus ~it [AS: *gyf he mare geearnian mæig*], ipsi commodum erit (*Ib. Rect.*) *Ib.* 450; mulier tunc temporis ita tenella fuit quod virum sustinere non posset, ita quod posset dotem ~ire BRACTON 302; **1314** quod nullus resettet mulierem neque hominem ad glenandum dummodo possint ~ire victum et stipendium (*Andover*) *Gild Merch.* II 308. **b 1430** pro eo quod maxima pars mercatorum in dicta civitate [Ebor'] commorancium, qui pro arte illa ~ierunt, in magnam †pauperitatem .. ducantur, racione quod illi qui pro arte illa nunquam ~iebant se intrudunt .. in mercandisis tradendis (*Pat*) *Ib.* 281. **c** omnis aromaticus pulvis fragescit in illa / quam per desertum sponsus in astra vocat: / "in celi deserta veni, que deseris orbem, / deserti nullis tu via nota viris" GARL. *Epith.* X 79 (cf. deserere 3c).

5 to pay: **a** (w. acc. of person); **b** (w. dat. of person).

a 1297 regie majestati supplicat Milo .. quod .., cum ex mandato suo Philippus .. sirurgicus .. Bernardo .. nepoti suo .. vulnerato .. curam fecerit et ipse ipsum in nullo ~ierit nec adhuc habeat unde ipsum possit ~ire, sibi placeat facere .. ut .. Philippus .. de ipso sit perpacatus (*Chanc. Misc.* 26/5) *RGasc* III app. p. cxcii; **1338** concessimus .. Johanni .. annuatim .. iiij s. .., sicuti unus armigerorum .. prioris pro stipendio suo ~itur ad scaccarium *Comp. Swith.* 161; **1389** camerario .. damus in mandatis quatenus eundem Johannem de predictis x li. singulis annis .. faciat ~iri *ExchScot* 208. **b 1329** Laurencio C., percipienti per annum xx m. .. quamdiu non ~iatur eidem de dicta summa in custuma burgi de Dunde *Ib.* 216.

6 to serve (food), provide, apportion.

1326 nec volumus quod occasione ferculi nostri .. prandium dicti conventus, de quo antiquitus communiter eis ~iri .. solebat, in aliquo pejoretur seu diminuatur *Melrose* 362; **1356** de quolibet ferculo .. j *parsay* coctum cum potagio, prout alicui confratrum .. in refectorio .. ~iri contigerit *Lit. Cant.* II 342; **1359** habebit .. Thomas .. corrodium, et ~ietur eidem mensa in cibariis *Ib.* 384; **1363** in reparacione j ciphi ad ~iendum *Ac. Durh.* 565.

7 (of thing or abstr.) to serve, be used (for): **a** (w. dat.); **b** (w. acc.); **c** (w. *ad* or *pro*).

a curia spectaculis communibus ~ire debet NECKAM *NR* II 165 (cf. cors 1c); rivulus qui aquatico molendino nostro .. ~it *G. S. Alb.* I 323 (cf. desiccativus); **1296** vj ulnis et dim. canabi .. ad ~iendum cabulis in foraminibus galee dum fuit trahenda *Ac. Galley Newcastle* 175; placida temporis oportunitas suis fructibus colligendis aptissime congruit et ~it *Ps.*-ELMH. *Hen. V* 71; **a1460** (v. attillio). **b** de specie .. visus que ~it operationem videndi coarctata in pyramide visuali BACON *Maj.* II 501; jussit rex [Hen. III] cuppam fieri .. argenteam .., quod quidem vas .. dominici corporis et sanguinis recondicionem plenius cernitur hactenus ~ire *Chr. Rams. pref.* livn. **c** Veneri et Mercurio solum argumenta eis in libro ascripta etiam ad hoc negotium ~iunt ADEL. *Elk.* 14; **c1334** ciphus .. de cristallo cum pede amallato qui dicitur 'desiderium'; et idem pes ~it ad quendam ciphum parvum de murra *Arch. J.* LIII 276; **1427** ij cumulos ponderum .., quorum unus .. ~it pro pane et pecuniis ponderandis et alius .. ~it pro speciebus et candelis ponderandis *MunAcOx* 284.

deservitio, service, officiation (eccl.).

1516 ad videndum .. ipsum [capellanum] a .. capellania amoveri .. propter non residenciam apud eandem et eciam non ~onem missarumve et suffragiorum celebracionem in eadem .. factam *Form. S. Andr.* I 388; **c1545** distringitur .. ut curato .. ecclesie de C. .. de v m. .. pro feodo et salario in ~one cure dicte ecclesie .. satisfaciat *Conc. Scot.* I ccxci (cf. ib. ccxc: pro ~one et ministracione in cura hujusmodi).

deses [CL], lazy, indolent.

†~is, *swaer GlC* D 26; dissides, i. tardi, *læte GlH* D 622; reses vel ~es vel piger, *slaw* ÆLF. *Sup.*; imprudens .. et ignavus et ~es erat ORD. VIT. VIII 11 p. 329; coactus est tandem divinum postulare suffragium, quia ~es a principio non quesierat humanum W. CANT. *Mir. Thom.* II 54; [prelati] in populi .. delinquentis correctione ~ides nimis sunt et negligentes GIR. *TH* III 28; HANV. II 151 (v. demanicatus); improperabant hostes nos sompnolentes et ~ides, quod super custodia nostra non potuimus melius vigilasse *G. Hen. V* 7.

deseverare [AN *deseverer*, OF *dessevrer* < disseparare], to 'dissever', remove.

1425 quia abbas ~aret ipsum de officio et alia importabilia sibi imponeret *Reg. Heref.* 72.

deshereditare v. dishereditare. **desiandare** v. defraudare a.

desiccabilis, that can be dried up.

si .. siccitas non potest desiccare nisi prius calor calefaciat, illa necessitas ordinis non est quia per calefaccionem fit objectum ~e presens sicco ut desiccetur, sed propter naturam istarum potenciarum activarum DUNS *Ord.* V 6.

desiccare [CL]

1 to dry (up), parch; **b** (w. ref. to hay or timber); **c** (fig.).

uva passa, ~ata *GlC* U 312; ~et, *adrugie GlH* D 301; vinum, crede, vetus corpus desiccat et urit D. BEC. 2706; in estate veneree actionis frequens exercitium nocet quia .. humiditatem consumendo corpus humanum .. extenuat et ~at *Quaest. Salern.* B 8; fontes .., quibus .. ~atis aquarum inopia tellus arescit GIR. *TH* II 7; affectus reliqui desiccant corpora; virtus / letitie corpus irrigat, ornat, alit NECKAM *DS* VI 29; **1223** molendinum omnino ~atum est et fractum, et vivarium similiter *BNB* III 483; corpora naturaliter calida cito crescunt .. ac impingua[n]tur vel desicantur M. SCOT *Phys.* 27; fratres .. manus suas .. lavabunt una cum suis cnipulis .. quos .. tali hora .. debent .. lavare et ~are tantum *Cust. Westm.* 174; DUNS *Ord.* V 6 (v. desiccabilis); DASTIN *Ros.* 14 (v. calcinare); thus .. vires habet calefacientes multum et ~antes *Alph.* 109 (cf. ib. 1: succus ~atus prunellarum). **b c1260** concessi .. aisiamenta super terram meam ad ~andum et cariandum fenum et bladum suum *Cart. Blyth* I 91; **1419** in *sleddyng* meremii ab orto palacii usque in aulam ejusdem ~andi *Fabr. York* 41. **c 1226** cum vix possibile sit fontem cupiditatis ~ari *Reg. S. Osm.* II 54.

2 to drain.

1279 si debeat waterfurgiare, debet ~are xx partitos (*Inq.*) *Dom. S. Paul* lxxix; **1329** racione ~andi manerium suum de C., quod situatum est in terra maresca .., obstruere fecit predictum cursum .. de terra et sabulone (*CoramR*) *Cart. Rams.* III 121; **1361** stagna .. ~are (v. caput 15a).

desiccatio [LL]

1 drying (up), desiccation.

cum aer exterior quidquid a terra traxerant estivali ~one eis [herbis] auferat, omne quod extra terre superficiem est marcendo moritur ADEL. *QN* 3; cum debilitatio insit corpori .. ex ~one et evacuatione oris stomaci *Quaest. Salern.* B 77; tradunt sancti xl annis ante Judicium vere appariturum arcum celi, quod etiam naturaliter ostendet aeris ~onem ceptam GERV. TILB. I 24; debilitas omnium membrorum propter digestionis impedimentum .. cum .. oris ~one GILB. VI 258. 1 (cf. ib. II 103. 1: ex nimia cerebri infrigidatione et ~one); nec omnia faciunt mirobolani et trifere per viam ~onis fleumatis BACON IX 51; apposicio medicaminis desiccativi et incarnativi mediocris ~onis GAD. 114. 1; **1399** in iiij *shep* de *charcole* emptis pro dessicacione thesaurarii, vestibuli et domus intus jacentis *Fabr. York* 17.

2 drainage.

1229 firmabunt .. stagnum .., ita quod nec per stagnum suum nec per aliud opus quod faciant †impidiatur [l. impediatur] ~o maresii *Reg. Dunferm.* 213; **1277** qualiter .. fieri poterit aqueductus ad ~onem terrarum et tenementorum predictorum *Pat* 96 m. 12*d*.

desiccativus [LL], parching, desiccative.

si [sperma] .. calidum habet [vim] ~am peremptoriam *Quaest. Salern.* B 13; si cadant [capilli] propter nimiam siccitatem .., abstinendi sunt a cibis ~is GILB. II 81. 2; **12..** rivulus qui .. molendino .. deservit .. propter ariditates estivales ~as .. officio .. curie non sufficit *G. S. Alb.* I 323; est [sal] .. per qualitatem siccitatis ~um *Ps.*-GROS. *Summa* 642; GAD. 114. 1 (v. desiccatio 1); **1307** pro alio unguento de rebus ~is cum balsamo (*KRAc* 368/30) *EHR* LXVII 173; ostre porphite .. dessicative sunt virtutis *Alph.* 132.

desiccatorius [LL], (as sb. n.) desiccatory plaster (med.).

appositis interim quibusdam ~iis, id attentare plurimorum curavit industria *Mir. Hen. VI* IV 141.

desiccatrix, maltster (f.).

hec ustrinatrix, *a kylme wyfe*; hec deciccatrix, idem est *WW*.

desicut, a (just) as, in the way that. **b** inasmuch as, since. **c** whereas, though.

a **1137** dedisse .. terram que est inter ecclesiam .. et fossatum, ∼ut fossatum se extendit in murum civitatis [Lincolnie] *CalCh* IV 103 (= *Regesta* 463); c**1150** ut .. terram suam habeant apud Sueiam [*Hants*], ∼ut signa foreste antiquitus posita demonstrabant *FormA* 302. **b** **1174** ∼ut ligiam fidelitatem fecerunt domino regi .., eos inde assecuraverunt *Anglo-Scot. Rel.* 2; **1199** ∼ut carta illa inde loquitur, non vult in curia domini regis respondere *CurR* I 85; **1248** ∼ut ipse nec antecessores sui nunquam alibi solebant placitare quam ibidem, non videbatur ei quod deberet ei respondere (*CurR*) *Cart. Glam.* 548; **1269** irrotulatur quod .. scriptum aliquod postmodum confectum sigillo predicto signatum nullius sit valoris, ∼ut sigillum illud maliciose extitit .. ablatum *Cl* 136; ∼ut excepcio illa debuit .. Johanni allocari .. et non .. Rogero, petit judicium si debeat .. Rogero .. respondere *State Tri. Ed. I* 21; **1306** quos malefactores .., ∼ut posse civitatis .. in .. hujusmodi necessitatibus ad vestram summonicionem .. est objectum, capere possetis et arestare (*Breve Regis*) *MGL* II 152. **c** **1221** mercatores salsarii .. non possunt habere stallagium in villa [Wigornie] nisi dent stallagium, ∼ut quieti sunt de stallagio per cartam *SelPlCrown* 89; **1221** petit sibi allocari quod mercator non sequitur, ∼ut vivus est et in plena sanitate *PlCrGlouc* 10; B., qui parvum tenementum habet .. de feodo ipsius A. .., non permittit ipsum A. parcum suum habere inclusum .., ∼ut [ipse B.] communam pasture habere poterit sufficientem extra parcum .. illum (*Forma brevis*) BRACTON 227b.

desidare v. desudare 3.

desiderabilis [CL]

1 desirable, acceptable, welcome: **a** (of thing or abstr.); **b** (of person); **c** (sexually).

a legebam .. admirandum legislatorem ob unius verbi dubitationem terram ∼em non introiisse [cf. *Num.* xx 12; *Psalm* cv 24] GILDAS *EB* 1; **667** ∼es litteras excellentiae vestrae suscepimus (*Lit. Papae*) BEDE *HE* III 29; **796** ut .. merear .. vobiscum ∼em audire vocem ALCUIN *Ep.* 117; **8..** thesaurus ∼is, *gewilniendlic goldhord WW*; illecebris ∼ibus ADEL. *ED* 15; ibi [in publica coquina] presto sunt omnia ∼ia W. FITZST. *Thom. prol.* 10; c**1218** apparet quod in hac vita maxime ∼e bonum et privilegiatum est matrimonium *Conc. Syn.* 87 (= *Ch. Sal.* 154: †desirabile); c**1239** dilectio est rerum optima, cui omne aliud ∼e non valet comparari GROS. *Ep.* 76; s**1269** annus .. Christicolis ∼is (v. devovere 2b); ROLLE *IA* 262 (v. collocutio a); **1347** ad pacem .. Deo placabilem, mundo †desirabilem (*Lit. Papae*) AVESB. 111b. **b** **797** vos .., viri fratres ∼es et venerabiles ALCUIN *Ep.* 129; *Ib.* 136, 265 (v. desiderabiliter 1); **958** [recte **956**] (14c) cuidam meo ∼i episcopo .. concedo *CS* 1029; totus ∼is Adrianus .. in porticum desiderantissimi patris Augustini gratissimus collega deponitur GOSC. *Transl. Aug.* 38A; quales ei nos modo existimus, talis et ipse [Christus] tunc apparebit nobis, amanti quidem amabilis et ∼is, non amanti vero odibilis et crudelis ROLLE *IA* 258. **c** unam [feminam] .. notavit miles .. super omnes regum delicias ∼em MAP *NC* II 12 f. 27.

2 eager, desirous; **b** (w. obj. gen.).

aquas illas percipere studio ∼iore satagebat R. COLD. *Cuthb.* 53. **b** **1458** reginam, que .. est ita ∼is dictarum unitatis, dileccionis, et concordie prout sibi est possibile (*Lit. Regis*) *Reg. Whet.* I 301.

desiderabiliter [LL]

1 desirably, so as to appear desirable.

798 domino ∼iter venerabili et venerabiliter desiderabili David regi salutem ALCUIN *Ep.* 136 (cf. ib. 265); ut .. sanctitatis prudentia .. exterminet secularis sapientie caligines, quam .. execratur sermo divinus [*James* iii 15], .. et .. conscendatis in eam .. sapientiam .. tam ∼iter divinitus descriptam [*Ib.* 17] AD. MARSH *Ep.* 102 p. 217.

2 eagerly, desirously.

nichil .. ∼ius expectabant quam medicum G. MON. VIII 14; **1312** fraudibus .. obviare ∼iter affectantes *Conc.* II 417b; **1321** exitum negocii reformacionis pacis .. ∼iter expectantes *FormOx* 65; **1407** attento .. vestram dominacionem †desirabiliter affectare bonum pacis *Lit. Cant.* III 103.

desideranter [CL], eagerly, desirously.

∼er .. multum auditur quod .. positus dicitur Dominus in resurrectionem multorum [cf. *Luke* ii 34] .. BEDE *Hom.* I 18. 81; c**794** haec .. communicare delector .. omnibus qui ∼er quaerunt ALCUIN *Ep.* 24; dum miles .. manum ∼er apposuisset .. ad sancti lecticam HERM. ARCH. 48; **1169** rogamus .. et consulimus ut .. ad colloquium .. ∼issime occurratis BECKET *Ep.* 602; cognosces illam .. pre ceteris venustam, ut possit decor opertus ex hiis que sunt aperta ∼er appeti MAP *NC* III 2 f. 37v.; vehementer ac ∼er et sperabatur et expectabatur GIR. *PI* III 31; **1267** mutuam pacem et concordiam nostram ∼er affectamus *Cl* 374; **1328** vestre eminencie .. filiali devocione †desideratissime [? l. ∼issime] supplicamus *Conc.* II 543b; **1438** hoc .. ∼er petimus BEKYNTON I 200.

desiderare [CL]

1 to desire, long (for): **a** (w. acc. or absol.); **b** (w. inf.); **c** (w. acc. & inf. or *ut*); **d** (w. personal obj. & *quod* or *ut*) to request (that); **e** (w. abstr. or inanim. subj.) to call for, require.

a a**705** pollicitans omni me ∼atae lectionis instrumento .. docendo imbuere (ÆTHELWALD) *Ep. Aldh.* II 7; ad caelestia quae semper amabam ac ∼abam praemia BEDE *HE* IV 3; ut ipse ∼abat, .. migravit ad regna caelestia *Ib.* III 27; quod maxime ∼abam, missas .. celebrari repperi CUTHB. *Ob. Baedae* clx; **8..** ∼at, .. *gegernð* .., ne ∼es, *ne †gewilnadi* [? l. *gewilna ðu*] *WW*; hoc est .. quod ∼o, quod omnibus votis antepono ABBO *Edm.* 8; **949** (13c) ego Æþelgar episcopus ∼o *Ch. Burton* 10; quaeram te [Domine] ∼ando, ∼em quaerendo ANSELM (*Prosl.* 1) I 100; s**1428** (v. demanda b). **b** nemo ibi pretiosis .. vestibus indui ∼at ubi a nullo valet videri ALDH. *VirgP* 55; monasterium .. in quo ∼abat .. patrui sui ossa recondere BEDE *HE* III 11; a**785** (12c) vitae caelestis praemia consequi ∼at *CS* 260; audiat .. qui nosse ∼at *G. Steph.* I 24; s**1172** (v. desiderium 1c); quod .. vocibus fieri nequit .. affectibus supplere ∼o AD. MARSH *Ep.* 11; c**1380** de statu vestro rumores bonos audire ∼o *FormOx* 319. **c** historiam .. latius propalari ∼as BEDE *HE pref.* p. 5; ecclesias .. immunes perdurare ∼ans *Ib.* IV 15 p. 238; ∼ante rege ut vir tantae eruditionis .. sibi .. sacerdos esset et doctor *Ib.* V 19 p. 325; **800** multum ∼o ut te habeamus praesentem ALCUIN *Ep.* 194; **836** in Deum meum ∼o et in ejus .. misericordiam confido ut .. Jhesus Christus meas iniquitates .. delere faciat *CS* 416; **1320** ∼antes ut hujusmodi reformacio .. roboretur effectibus *FormOx* 54. **d** **1471** te ∼amus quod ad (*sic*) gaolam illam de prisonibus in ea existentibus .. procedas deliberare *Reg. Whet.* II 127; *Ib.* I 9 (v. coenobialis). **e** grande vulnus grandioris curam medellae ∼at BEDE *HE* IV 23 p. 263; BRACTON 3 (v. coaequiparare).

2 **a** (pr. ppl.) desirous. **b** (pr. ppl. superl. *s. pass.*) dearly beloved (*cf.* 2c *infra* and *amare* 4b). **c** (gdv.) desired, beloved. **d** (p. ppl.) desired, beloved (*v. et.* 2a *supra*). **e** (p. ppl.) 'wanted' (of criminal).

a ∼antissimus scire .. quae in claustro sedendi sit religio G. CRISPIN *Herl.* 91; sunt medicine ∼a[n]tissimi et ad medicandum ardentissimi .., sed medicos ad medicandum venientes non ascultant GILB. II 103. 2. **b** **764** ∼antissimo et suavissimo .. amico Lullo episcopo (CUTHB.) *Ep. Bonif.* 116; **796** ∼antissime frater in Christo ALCUIN *Ep.* 113; ∼antissimus, i. qui ∼atur, *gelustfullesta GlH* D 293; locus .. cortinis ambitur, intusque a fidelibus domesticis ∼antissimus thesaurus perscrutatur GOSC. *Transl. Aug.* 18A; *Ib.* 38A (v. desiderabilis 1b); [virgo] mihi gratissima, mihi ∼antissima T. MON. *Will.* II 7 p. 81. **c** a**755** dominis sanctis et in Christo ∼andis patribus ac fratribus in monasterio Glestingaburg constitutis .. salutem (WIEHTBERT) *Ep. Bonif.* 101; **799** ∼ande pater ALCUIN *Ep.* 169; **1439** vestre paternitatis beneficia .., que in .. tocius cleri ∼andissimam excrescenciam redundant *EpAcOx* 185. **d** hic est ∼atus ille puer .., Philippus nomine, qui patri postea successit in regnum [Francie] H. BOS. *Thom.* IV 28 p. 445; de .. ∼atissima paradisi terrestris visione GIR. *TH* II 43; ipso ∼atissimo pacis negocio conclusum est .. *Ps.*-ELMH. *Hen. V* 91. **e** s**1217** diu quesitus et multum ∼atus Eustachius monachus .., pirata nequissimus M. PAR. *Maj.* III 27.

desiderat- v. et. desiderant-.

desiderativus [LL], desiderative, appetitive: **a** (gram.); **b** (phil.).

a 'facesso' et 'capesso' et 'viso' ∼a sunt .. : 'facesso', id est 'desidero facere' .. ALCUIN *Gram.* 883A; *sume word synd gecwedene* ∼a, *þæt synd gewilnigendlice*: .. lacero .., lacesso ÆLF. *Gram.* 214; tercius [sc. modus] optativus sive ∼us dicetur *Ps.*-GROS. *Gram.* 49 (cf. ib. 51: verba .. ∼a .. ut .. capesso, facesso). **b** hec corpora sunt animata et non habent de virtutibus anime misi virtutem intellectivam et ∼am GROS. 94; quod ex eadem virtute apprehensiva vel ∼a veniant diverse operaciones in corpore BACON IV 399; nonne Avicenna .. dicit quod proprietas faciendi miracula pendet ex virtute ∼a, que provenit ex anima prophete dignioris prophecie ..? BRADW. *CD* 56B; *a desyre*, .. appetitus .., desiderium, ∼a intencio *CathA*.

desiderator [LL], desirer, lover.

1093 desideratis ∼oribus suis, domno priori B. et aliis qui cum eo sunt fratribus, frater A. ANSELM (*Ep.* 147) III 293; **1188** quibus dominus prior .. tandem martyr accessit, ne videlicet ultra ∼or bonus differretur a regno *Ep. Cant.* 289; Gregorius, unus ex precipuis dilectoribus et ∼oribus, ejus dulcedinem erga nos .. exprimens G. STANFORD *Cant.* 213 *n.* 59; celestis regni ∼or *NLA* (*Brithun*) I 160.

1 desidēre [CL] **∼escere**, to loiter, be idle or negligent.

†desitescere, contemnere *GlC* D 105; ∼ere, neglegenter agere *Ib.* 116; ∼ens, negligens vel otium cupiens *Gl. Leid.* 2. 46; ∼ere torpescere, pigritari, relaxare OSB. GLOUC. *Deriv.* 174.

2 desidere v. 2 decidere 3, dissidere.

desideriose, eagerly, zealously.

1238 in quo mutue dilectionis .. roboratur integritas et ad prosperitatis augmentum ∼ius propagatur (*Lit. F. Imp.*) M. PAR. *Maj.* III 474; s**1055** hujus oratorii partem occidentalem pro dilatando suo monasterio [abbas] non tam prudenter quam ∼e .. dejecit THORNE 1785.

desideriosus, desirous, eager, zealous.

hoc [cf. *2 Sam.* vii] ∼us abbas non perpendens et ad sibi incessum opus frustra nitens .. templum suum a fronte diruit GOSC. *Transl. Aug.* 32C; affectuosa et ∼a .. patrie celestis exspectatio AD. SCOT *TT* 771C.

desiderium [CL]

1 desire, longing, striving; **b** (w. ref. to *Dan.* ix 23); **c** (w. *desiderare*; *cf. Luke* xxii 15); **d** (w. *habere*, w. acc., dat., or *in*). **e** object of desire, favourite (as name of cup).

carnalibus ∼iis GILDAS *EB* 70; **675** nostra parvitas .. ad consortium vestrum ardenti ∼io flagrabat ALDH. *Ep.* 2; indicavit ei ∼ium sibi inesse .. apostolorum limina visitandi BEDE *HE* V 19 p. 323; **8..** ∼ium veniens, †*cumede gewilung* [l. *cumende gewilnung*] *WW*; ad divini luminis intuitum simul et ∼ium GIR. *TH* I 13; ad curiam .. a rege vocatus, cui .. nil ∼io magis quam decipere *Id. PI intr.* app. p. lvii; duplex est ∼ium: est ∼ium rei cum non habetur .. et est ∼ium rei habite ut continuetur HALES *Sent.* I 22; in recuperacione ville de Harfleu, cui [rex] summis ∼iis insudaverat *G. Hen. V* 19; per sancta contemplacionis ∼ia sacre scripture vacabant et oracionibus CANTLOW *Orig. Cantab.* 268. **b** Daniel .. ab archangelo saepe 'vir ∼iorum' vocitatus ALDH. *VirgP* 21; s**1251** abbas Westm' .. erat utique tam voce quam corporali elegantia vir ∼iorum M. PAR. *Maj.* V 238; **1362** in Daniele, qui propter concupiscencias interne cognicionis voce angelica vir ∼iorum dicitur *Conc.* III 54a. **c** **1166** ∼io desideravi videre faciem vestram et loqui vobiscum BECKET *Ep.* 154; s**1172** rex .. Francie ∼io magno desiderabat videre filiam suam *G. Hen. II* I 34. **d** **1176** habebam in ∼iis ad vos .. reverti P. BLOIS *Ep.* 5. 13B; **1311** ∼io habeo quod possum .. interesse ubi .. fieret tractatus (*Lit. ad Abbatem*) *Chr. Rams.* app. 397; anime sancte .. gestant leticiam de visione essencie, sed adhuc ∼ium habent amplius †degustari [? l. degustare] OCKHAM *Dial.* 766. **e** c**1334** (v. deservire 7c).

2 expressed desire, request.

supplicantium .. ∼ia vel vota conplere BEDE *HE* I 7; **741** [? recte **750**] provabilibus ∼iis et petitionibus piis assensum semper praebere gloriosum constat esse *CS* 160; coeperunt fratres instantius meae pusillitati incumbere ut eorum ferventi ∼io satisfacerem ABBO *Edm. pref.*; quasi nova quedam Abisac [*1 Kings* i 15] regem .. mulcet obsequiis sed ∼iis non emollit AILR. *Ed. Conf.* 748B; qui .. nostris ∼iis militare studebant .. spe mercedis R. BURY *Phil.* 8. 134.

desidescere v. 1 desidere.

desidia [CL], laziness, indolence. **b** negligence, carelessness.

inertis ∼iae torpore tabescens ALDH. (*Alloc.*) *PR* 43 p. 203; illum ∼ias molles et marcida luxu otia sectantem et eo quod dederat privat BEDE *Luke* (xix 26) 566; desidia tutus es ipse tua WALT. ANGL. *Fab.* 11. 6; ∼ia plus se tenet ex parte anime, otium et pigritia respectu corporis; est enim horror laboris HALES *Qu.* 1560; BACON *CSPhil.* 409 (v. acedia). **b** ∼a, ignavia *Gl. Leid.* 2. 45; negligentie reatus judicatur quoties his, qui interim mori possunt, sacramentum istud [confirmationis] per ∼iam differtur PULL. *Sent.* 847A; ne currat tempus per ∼iam BRACTON 162; in .. caudam, in qua ex ∼ia clientum regalium erant evecciones regie *G. Hen. V* 12.

desidiose [LL], slothfully.

maledictus homo qui opus Dei facit negligenter et ∼e M. RIEVAULX (*Serm.*) 61.

desidiosus [CL], lazy, indolent: **a** (of person); **b** (of abstr.).

a quia non tam fortissimorum militum enuntiare trucis belli pericula mihi statutum est quam ∼orum, silui GILDAS *EB* 1; neque cum desidia Christi est quaerenda praesentia. et ideo forte non nulli quaerentes invenire non merentur, quia ∼i Christum requirunt BEDE *Luke* (ii 16) 334; ∼is ac vitae suae incuriosis *Id. HE* V 12; **9..** ∼orum, *slawera WW*; tu non vinosos reprobas et desidiosos H. AVR. *Poems* 93. 28. **b** in contemptum adducentur [adversarii], si eorum inertia, neglegentia, ignavia, ∼um studium et luxuriosum otium proferetur ALCUIN *Rhet.* 20; que tunc gesta sunt .. non videntur ∼o silentio supprimenda AD. EYNS. *Hug.* V 11 p. 138; s**1244** [Anglorum] patientia ∼a erat et humilitas infructuosa M. PAR. *Maj.* IV 311.

desidium v. discidium 2a.

1 desiduus v. deciduus.

2 desiduus [cf. DuC], sluggish (or long drawn out).

∼us, desidiosus *GlC* D 85 (cf. ib. 326: dissiduus, ignavus, desidiosus); ∼us, i. desidiosus, ignavus, diuturnus; disiduo, i. diuturne, *simle GlH* D 288.

desigillare v. dissigillare.

designabilis, 'designable', that can be specified.

enuntiatur [esse vel non esse] .. et de non nisi contradictive designato, ut cum sic dicitur: 'quod non est dictio non est contradictio'; de quo enim sic, non nisi secundum contradictionem ∼e BALSH. *AD rec.* 2 23; verissimum est tamen locum esse sub utroque axe ∼em, ubi per sex menses continue est dies et reliquos sex continua est nox *Ps.*-GROS. *Summa* 566.

1 designare [CL]

1 to mark, inscribe. **b** to demarcate (land).

957 (14c) attestantibus .. optimatibus quorum vocabula in hoc ~antur privilegio *CS* 995. **b 704** (8c) haec terra his locorum limitibus ~atur *Ib.* 111.

2 to designate, indicate, specify. **b** (w. pers. obj.) to designate, nominate (for office). **c** to assign (for a purpose). **d** (w. word *qua* word as subj.) to signify, mean, connote.

quandam puellam .. didicimus, .. cujus magnitudinem l pedibus ~abant *Lib. Monstr.* I 13; ~atum, i. demonstratum, manifestatum *GlH* D 291; illud [caput regis] respondebat designando locum patria lingua dicens "*her*, *her*, *her*", quod interpretatum Latinus sermo exprimit 'hic' ABBO *Edm.* 12; ut .. brevius edisseram, loquar tantum de 'Patre' et 'Filio', quoniam hae duae personae suis propriis vocibus aliae ab invicem aperte ~antur ANSELM (*Incarn. A* 5) I 285; residuum Tauri at Aquarii coacervatum vero Leonis et Scorpii ortum ~abit ADEL. *Elk.* 26; quid quibus verbis ~etur ex usus locutionum notitia comperire non incontingens; quibus autem et quot modis de quo dicatur disserendo ~andum, et ex his ~andi modis cujusmodi principiorum genera .., hec omnia .. sine artis preceptione comperiri non facile BALSH. *AD* 28; **1312** (v. circumferentia 2a). **b** interrex, ~atus rex *GlC* I 331; **743** si eum aptum cognoveris .., ea hora, qua te de presenti saeculo migraturum cognoveris, presentibus cunctis tibi successorem ~a, ut huc veniat ordinandus (*Lit. Papae*) *Ep. Bonif.* 51. **c** aliquid superfluum extra circulum ~are pro armilla suspensoria instrumenti WALLINGF. (*Alb.*) I 296. **d** 'plăgă,' si climata cardinalia ~at, pirrichius est ALDH. *PR* 113; 'numquam' tempus, 'nusquam' locum ~at *GlC* N 194.

3 to declare, make known; **b** (w. obj. clause).

800 H. duos libros S. Martini secum portavit, sicut in alia epistola tibi ~avi ALCUIN *Ep.* 194. **b** in monasterio ubi ejus animo labentia cuncta subterfuisse ipse ~at *V. Greg.* p. 75; ~asti que fuerunt in patribus .. merita pro quibus tanta Dei perceperint beneficia *Eccl. & Synag.* 59; †**1089** omnibus meis successoribus ~o quod .. dono .. ecclesiae .. de Seftesberia .. has terras *Regesta* p. 131.

4 to indicate allegorically, symbolize; **b** (w. acc. & inf. or obj. clause).

fontis designat Salvator jure figuram, / de quo quadrifluis decurrunt flumina rivis ALDH. *CE* 4. 10. 7; Jesus .. ascendens in caelos .. ecclesiam suam, quae saepe lunae vocabulo ~atur, .. luce replevit (*Ep. Ceolfridi*) BEDE *HE* V 21 p. 340; **798** (v. creatio 2); lupi .. in mense Decembri catulos habent .., rapine incommoda, que premature hic pullulant, ~antes GIR. *TH* II 26; cum longa coma .. ubique angeli depinguntur. .. capilli capitis ~ant cogitationes .. que oriuntur ex radice mentis BART. ANGL. II 3. **b** quem .. fructum propheticus sermo allegoricis enigmatibus explanans ~at virgultum in tipo .. Dei genetricis de radice Jesse .. pululasse ALDH. *Met.* 1; oportet eos .. formam .. coronae quam ipse [Dominus] in passione spineam portavit suo quemque in capite .. praeferre .., ut .. adversa se mundi et prospera contemnere ~ent (*Ep. Ceolfridi*) BEDE *HE* V 21 p. 343; NECKAM *NR* I 61 (v. designativus); identitas coloris purpurei ~at quod virtute sanguinis Christi .. similes ei erimus ELMH. *Cant.* 100; NETTER *DAF* II 39v. (v. circumincessio).

2 designare v. dissignare.

designatio [CL]

1 design, plan (arch.).

ita egit in calefactorio constituendo, relinquens veterem ~onem, quae a tergo domus adhuc conspicitur, et augustas [? l. angustas] aedes ponens FERR. *Kinloss* 32.

2 specification.

differt .. quod ex preter designata comperiendo multipliciter dicitur .. ab his .. que equivoce dicuntur, quoniam in eis duplex ~o, in hoc una BALSH. *AD* 80; *Ib. rec.* 2 44 (v. delere 2a).

3 indication, foreshadowing.

haec cordis exultatio futurae humiliationis exstitit ~o OSB. *Mir. Dunst.* 19 p. 147.

designativus [LL], (allegorically) indicative, symbolic.

'signum', 'mysterium', 'sacramentum' et si quid hujusmodi est dominicae passionis ~a nomina sunt LANFR. *Corp. & Sang.* 437C; viri religiosi quidam nigro utuntur habitu ut per hoc designetur se ad secularem vitam reverti non posse, licet et nigredo penitencie sit ~a NECKAM *NR* I 61.

designator [LL = *one who points out*], designer, architect.

novam Jerusalem .., cujus ~ores patriarchae, cujus mensores prophetae GOSC. *Aug. Min.* 750A.

desilare v. desselare. **desile** v. rasilis.

1 desilire [CL, *conf. w.* dissilire], to jump down, alight.

tremefactus ~uit [v. l. ~ivit] equo BEDE *HE* III 22; dissilivit, i. descendit, *gelihte*, vel dissilit *GlH* D 624; dissiluisse, *niþer GlN* 28. 19.

2 desilire v. 2 dissilire. **desimilis** v. dissimilis.

desinentia, cessation.

cum notum sit quod ~ia influencie tam nobilis esse, tamquam ad esse cujuslibet entis necessario requisite, tolleret omne esse universitatis encium WYCL. *Quaest. Log.* 262.

desinere [CL]

1 to cease: **a** (w. abl. or *ab*); **b** (w. inf.); **c** (absol. or unspec.).

a puer .. a garrula voce .. ~it *V. Cuthb.* IV 15; non desierat docendo plebem HUGEB. *Wynn.* 7; **1121** Stigandus .., convictus et depositus, a superba temeritate desivit (*Lit. Archiep. Cant.*) *Conc.* I 396b. **b** malos increpare non ~it GILDAS *EB* 89; illi .. oculorum fontibus .. faciem umectare jugiter non ~unt ALDH. *VirgP* 10; disipit, disinit [sapere] *GlC* D 244; mulierem dicit sanctam ecclesiam [cf. *John* xvi 21] .. quia spiritales filios Deo gignere numquam ~it BEDE *Hom.* II 13. 156; in loco .. usque hodie sanitates infirmorum .. celebrari non ~unt *Id. HE* III 9; desine grandevos jamjam vexare poetas *Altercatio* 56; solus es aeternus, quia solus omnium, sicut non ~is, sic non incipis esse ANSELM (*Prosl.* 13) I 110; **1258** fieri .. desierunt (v. caseus c); BACON III 262, WYCL. *Act.* 100 (v. desitio a); *A* aliquando fuit vel aliquando erit et nunc non est; ergo desiit vel †~iet [? l. ~et] esse (KYN.) *Ziz.* 37; s**1413** A. episcopus Northwicensis .. vivere desiit, licet sero *Chr. S. Alb.* 70. **c** si quis episcopus .. vitium habuerit ebrietatis, aut ~at aut deponatur THEOD. *Pen.* I 1. 1; concordia .. sopita .., triumphus .. ~it EDDI 19; des[i]isse, *tiorade GlC* D 185; **9**.. desivimus, *we geblunnon WW*; GIR. *TH intr.* (v. desistere c); **12**.. caduci plasmatis gens plusquam misera, / nunc es, nunc desinis velut effimera (*Humana Miseria*) *EHR* XXXII 403.

2 (of words) to end, terminate. *Cf. cadere* 7.

verborum genera .. quae perfectum tempus in -avi sillabas [v. l. syllaba] ~unt ALDH. *PR* 137; sunt nomina verbalia in -trix ~entia feminina, sicut masculina in -tor terminantia *Ib.* 126; ~entia, terminantia *GlH* D 294; similitudo ~ens est quod fit in simili coincidentia dictionum non casualium, hoc modo: 'nemo mei meminit. gladius, qui cetera finit, / mecum fedus init; me superesse sinit' VINSAUF *CR* 323; similiter ~ens est sub quo versus Leonini et rithmi inventi sunt. .. 'assit per maria mihi previa stella Maria, / dux pia, spes, venia, gloria, meta, via' GARL. *PP* 116.

3 (trans.) to leave.

quis a diabolo vexatus, suis mox fusis ad Dominum precibus .. non rediit sospes quem saevus desiit hospes? *V. Neot. A* 4.

desinibilis, liable to cease.

tempus, motus, et alia successiva sunt per se corruptibilia vel ~ia WYCL. *Ver.* III 123.

desinitio, cessation, bringing to an end; but *cf. desitio* or (?) *definitio*.

respectu termini accidentalis potest Deus facere quod aliquando non potuit. .. sed tamen propter deperdicionem sive ~onem talium veritatum Deus potest facere hoc et aliarum hujusmodi; non sequitur aliqua minoracio potencie a parte Dei (KYN.) *Ziz.* 101.

desintiria v. dysenteria.

desipa, dotard.

a dottrelle, ~a *CathA*.

desipere [CL], to act foolishly, lose one's wits; **b** (w. ref. to heretics or infidels).

disipit *GlC* D 244 (v. desinere 1b); ne quis .. pueriliter ~iens aestimet .. Domini nostri corpus excitatum a mortuis sustentaculo eguisse ciborum BEDE *Hom.* II 9. 143; nec / talia cures / verba profari: / te fore comptum / artibus et nos / posse poesim / fingere nullam. / desipis *Responsio* 54; nec aliquis ita ~uerit ut .. abnegare praesumat .. LANFR. *Corp. & Sang.* 424C; si tu ~ueris, perire estimas sapientiam? AILR. *Spec. Car.* I 6. 510C; statim postquam inceperimus sapere, mori cogimur aut ~ere MAP *NC* I 1 f. 7v. (cf. ib. V 3 f. 60v.: in id quod sibi sapit sapienter ~it); scienter ~io et prudenter pereo P. BLOIS *Serm.* 712D; s**1252** ut ejus nugis veluti joculatoris ~ientis .. omnes cachinnarent M. PAR. *Maj.* V 329; **1346** [Francigene naves] disperiunt, saliunt, dissipiunt, fugiunt (*In Franciam*) *Pol. Poems* I 36. **b** Affrica tota / desipit; Europe pars tenet una fidem GARL. *Tri. Eccl.* 79.

desipientia [CL], madness, folly; **b** (w. ref. to heresy).

lirima .. Grece ~ia est GROS. *Hexaem. proem.* 62; nuper accidit quemdam nobilem ad tantam ~iam melancolie vicio devenisse quod .. murilegum se putabat BART. ANGL. IV 11; quis .. anhelantibus ad Terre hujus [sc. Sancte] ereptionem non assistit nisi quem aut formidolosus horror ignavie aut perniciosus error dissipientie .. pervaserit? AD. MARSH *Ep.* 246 (bis) c. 8 p. 434; ad rabiem hominis et alienacionem et ~iam semen brusci da bibere GAD. 132v. 1. **b** s**1237** eorum [Grecorum] hec est ~ia: asserunt Spiritum Sanctum non a Filio sed a Patre solo procedere M. PAR. *Maj.* III 447.

desipiscere [LL], to go mad.

~it, sensum amisit .., †dispiscat, delerat *GlC* D 135, 332; fit .. ista passio [†ydroforbia] ex spuma rabidi canis projecta in aquam; si aliquis biberit, statim fit †ydroforbicus et ~it GILB. VII 355. 2.

desir- v. desider-. **desis** v. deses. **desisio** v. 2 decisio. **desistare** v. desistere a, drensitare.

desistentia, desistance.

1256 conventus et .. procuratores destiterunt ab omnibus litibus et questionibus propositis ex parte eorundem in curia Romana contra eundem electum et renunciaverunt eisdem ..; quam ~iam et renunciationem ipse electus .. acceptavit (*Pat*) *Mon. Francisc.* I app. 611; **1299** ab omni hostili invasione .. desistemus et ipsam ~iam seu sufferenciam per litteras patentes vobis tradendas approbavimus (*Lit. Custodum Scotiae*) *Foed.* II 859b.

desistere [CL], to desist, refrain, cease: **a** (w. abl. or *ab*); **b** (w. inf., usu. neg.); **c** (absol. or unspec.).

a 722 (v. educatio 1); his nisi desistas a pravo scismate, Iorvet, / incendere, miser, Plutoni consolidatus *Altercatio* 52; nec prius monstrum caedendo ~it quam flagellum tergo illius tribus in partibus comminutum apparuit OSB. *V. Dunst.* 26; ab incepto suadet ~ere NIG. *Ep.* 17; **1256, 1299** (v. desistentia); **1270** ab hujusmodi .. proposito .. ~antes (*sic*) *Cl* 235; WYCL. *Ver.* III 219 (v. contingenter). **b** ut .. porcinus paganorum strepitus .. contra .. ecclesiae castitatem .. grunnire ~eret ALDH. *VirgP* 45; pectoris intuitu desistit cernere numquam *Id. VirgV* 1033; febricitantes .. sanare non ~it BEDE *HE* IV 6; nec umquam eadem repetendo clamare destitit quoad omnes ad se perduxit ABBO *Edm.* 12; comes .. non destitit .. eam [ecclesiam] .. indesinenter ornare *Found. Waltham* 14; *AncrR* 42 (v. durus 2a); parum valet scienciam et virtutem habere et hiis uti penitus descistere MILEMETE *Nob.* 66. **c** ~e, cessa *GlC* D 192; **9**.. ~ens, *ablinnende WW*; nec hodie destitissent scriptores optimi, si non desiissent imperatores electi GIR. *TH intr.* p. 4.

desisus v. 2 decidere 3. **desitescere** v. 1 desidere.

desitio, cessation. **b** (w. *Parliamenti*) dissolution.

~o .. propriissime sumpta est instantanea et est corruptio finalis in *C* instanti; .. cum dicitur 'desinit esse', exponitur per privationem de presenti et positionem de preterito, ut 'nunc non est, set prius fuit' BACON III 262; inceptio et ~o sunt mutationes vel motus; set, quod contingit incipere moveri, et desinere [sc. contingit] *Ib.* XIII 293; eternum est quod est sine incepcione et ~one BRADW. *CD* 67A; ymaginantur quod omnia que jam sunt incipiant esse et alias desinant esse sine causa faciente incepcionem vel ~onem WYCL. *Act.* 100; dicens quod adnichilacio foret non accio sed conservacionis ~o (*Id. Ente*) *Wycl. & Ox.* 155 *n.* 2; obicitur per hoc quod videtur ex dictis .. eadem peccata in numero redire post sui disicionem *Id. Civ. Dom.* I 220; *a cessynge*, cessacio, †deficio [? l. desicio], intermissio *CathA*. **b** s**1459** in die †decisionis [MS: desicionis] Parliamenti, in quo die solent singula in eo inacta sive inactitata .. publice promulgari *Reg. Whet.* I 356.

desium v. deisium. **deska,** ~**us** v. discus. **desligare** v. disligare 1a.

desma [LL < δέσμα], (power of) binding.

Petrus ab altithrono donatus desmate Jesu [cf. *Matth.* xvi 19] FRITH. 296.

desolabilis, fit to be left desolate (*i. e.* unfit for occupation).

1291 fratres [Minores] .. in civitate vestra Exon' in loco ~i consistentes PECKHAM *Ep.* 717 (= *Conc.* II 175a).

desolamen, distress (esp. due to bereavement).

terni languoris ~ina uno medicamine reparavit R. COLD. *Cuthb.* 103; solus nosse potuit molem tanti ~inis quisque semel [v. l. quisquis simul] deflevisse potuit inrecuperabilem amissionem pignoris *Id. Godr.* 330; "heu, quam longa premunt nos desolamina!" dixit *V. Ed. Conf. Metr.* I 123.

desolare [CL], **a** to ravage, lay waste, leave desolate. **b** (of church) to leave vacant. **c** (w. abl. or *de*) to deprive. **d** to distress.

a Picti .. tunc .. requieverunt, praedas .. nonnumquam facientes. in talibus itaque indutiis ~ato populo saeva cicatrix obducitur GILDAS *EB* 21; BEDE *HE* IV 17 p. 245 (v. civitatula); s**881** plurima .. monasteria concussa sunt ac ~ata S. DURH. *HR* 97; letali clade deficiet populus et menia urbium ~abuntur (*Proph. Merlini*) G. MON. VII 4 p. 396; **1455** (v. confortatio 2); s**1455** ne ipsi domum alterius Jacob sic comederent destruerentve locum ejus aut nequiter in aliquo ~arent [cf. *Psalm* lxxviii 7] *Reg. Whet.* I 173. **b** ne diu ~etur ecclesia suo viduata pastore *V. Will.* 271. **c** ~atus meo satellite ABBO *Edm.* 8; c**1327** (v. defraudare a); **1344** sic .. eadem villa de bona pace habenda quasi ~ata maneret *SelCKB* VI 38. **d** suos .. ~atos et quasi animis consternatos conspiciens GIR. *EH* I 8; s**1189** venit .. nuntius referens reginam Francie fuisse defunctam. .. rex Francie .. vehementer ~atus est *Itin. Ric.* II 6; **1217** nullatenus ~emini in hiis que casu infortu[i]to ita acciderunt *Pat* 108; **1332** tediosum michi erit .. fratres

dimittere interius ~atos pro absolucionis beneficio non obtento *Lit. Cant.* I 451.

desolate, grievously.

multo ~ius dolendum nobis est quod, stantibus universis, soli demones et nos cecidimus MAP *NC* I 1 f. 7v.

desolatio [LL]

1 desolation, devastation; **b** (w. ref. to *Matth.* xxiv 15 *etc.*).

discedentibus inde ob ~onem plurimis incolarum BEDE *HE* IV 23 p. 266; erit miseranda regni ~o et aree messium in fructuosos saltus redibunt (*Proph. Merlini*) G. MON. VII 3; parum ante magnam illam ~onem per Hoelum filium Moreduci factam GIR. *IK* I 2; **s1185** cum .. civitatis sancte .. ~onem enarrassent, .. multitudinem .. ad suspiria provocarunt DICETO *YH* II 32; ex ista [Innocencii III et IV] usurpacione dicunt populorum strages, vastacionem civitatum, regionum et terrarum et alias ~ones innumeras .. accidisse OCKHAM *Pol.* I 86. **b** melius silentio lugemus .. his diebus damnatissimis 'abominationem ~onis stantem in loco sancto', que .. orbi universo imminere †prenuntiat [? l. prenuntiatur] AD. MARSH *Ep.* 48.

2 desolate condition, ruin (of institution or community); **b** (w. ref. to vacancy of religious house or see).

cum [Arturus] in urbem [Eboracum] venisset, visa sanctarum ecclesiarum ~one condoluit G. MON. IX 8; ut .. ad .. ducem Ailwinum .. dirigerentur, ei ingens hoc infortunium et fratrum ~onem indicaturi *Chr. Rams.* 86; **1188** dolori et ~oni materne [sc. ecclesie] et nostre volentes quidem sed non valentes lacrimas condignas impendere *Ep. Cant.* 179; **1319** ~onem studencium, immo quasi studii finale exterminium .., oculata fide cernimus *FormOx* 49; **1421** querelis .. super ~one universitatum .. occasione non promocionis graduatorum in eisdem factis et expositis pio compacientes affectu *Reg. Cant.* III 73; **1441** dolentes .. de ruina, miseria et ~one domus [S. Antonii, London'] BEKYNTON I 235; **1571** cum .. fecissent multas detestabiles .. proditiones .. in .. amissionem, dishereditationem, et dissolationem regni .. Anglie *Entries* 645. **b** **1219** cum .. cardinalis .. vidit Carleolensis ecclesie ~onem et ruinam .., eidem .. pastorem prefecit sue scientem domui caute disponere *Cl* 405a; **1242** ~oni domus vestre .. compatientes, licentiam [eligendi abbatissam] vobis .. duximus concedendam *RGasc* I 154 (cf. *CalPat* 396); **1281** de facto electi Wintoniensis suspiramus, attoniti quod tante ecclesie ~o et tam evidentis justicie decisio tanti tractu temporis suspenduntur PECKHAM *Ep.* 173.

3 distress (esp. on being forsaken or bereaved).

quatenus [discipuli] .. minus de sua ~one trepidarent, quos abeunte licet Domino Spiritus Sancti gratia consolandos esse sperarent BEDE *Hom.* II 11. 158; suam ~onem, quam tanto patre orbati se passuros non dubitabant, .. deflentes EADMER *V. Osw.* 34; presentiebant plures ejus in morte ~onem patrie AILR. *Ed. Conf.* 771C (cf. ib. 742D: ubique luctus, ubique clamor, ubique ~o); **s1306** [rex R.] nunc solus ab hostibus fugatus, nunc a servis suis despectus, in omni ~one permansit FORDUN *Cont.* XII 11; sibi non consolacionis sed ~onis prebetur materia et doloris OCKHAM *Pol.* I 232; **1401** tantam ~onem in cordibus prudencium pre .. perturbacione quam timent infra breve in .. regno evenire .. non memini me audisse BEKYNTON I 151.

desolator [LL], devastator, plunderer.

~or, vastator, *westend, tolysend* *GlH* D 309; **s1255** J. F., regis clericus .., B. Marie Ebor' et de Selebi cenobiorum ~or M. PAR. *Maj.* V 535; **1457** Johannes Soldanus .., Christianorum inimicus et ~or (*Lit. 'Soldani'*) *Reg. Whet.* I 269 (cf. continus).

desolatorie, w. devastating effect.

1432 pestilentissimos errores, sediciones, et excessuum enormitates singulis pene in provinciis ~ie †undiquam subortos *EpAcOx* 73.

desolatorius [LL], **a** devastating. **b** desolate, forsaken.

a infirmitatis .. multitudo non .. patiebatur cubiculum aliquo quietis deservire solatio, sed omni potius ~ie destitutionis incremento R. COLD. *Cuthb.* 96; *wastynge*, .. devastacio, desolacio, [*adj.*] ~ius *CathA.* **b** accidit ut in locis qui ~ii nunc temporis dicuntur fratres .. sine querela se poni permitterent ECCLESTON *Adv. Min.* 33; *forsakyn* [v. l. *forsaking*], desolatus, ~ius *CathA.*

desolatus, ruin.

s1321 o comes Lancastrie! .. si in primeva fide perdurasses, ad ~um nequaquam pervenisses *V. Ed. II* 271.

desolut-, desolv- v. dissol-. **desonantia, ~are, ~us** v. disson-. **desoneratio** v. disoneratio.

despectare [CL], to look down on, despise. *V. et. dispectare.*

~ans, i. despernens *GlH* D 279; *to desspice*, .. contempnere .., ~are, despicere, despicari .. *CathA.*

despectibilis [cf. LL despectabilis], lowly, contemptible.

Toronica .. civitas, muris quidem parvula et dispectibilis sed S. Martini patrociniis magna et laudabilis ALCUIN *WillP* 32; de monachis, qui mundo mortui sunt et non solum habitu ~i verum etiam ordine et professione totaliter segregati GIR. *Spec.* II 30.

despectio [CL]

1 looking down (fig.), contempt. **b** object of contempt (w. ref. to *Psalm* cxxii 4). **c** contemptuous usage, insult.

precepta [Dei] contumaci ~one contemnunt GILDAS *EB* 62; quadam .. superciliosa et notabili ~one P. BLOIS (*Penit.*) *Opusc.* 1092D (cf. contaminare 1b); cum predicamus ~onem temporalium ac aspiracionem .. ad eterna WYCL. *Civ. Dom.* II 9. **b** ab aliis .. diffamamur et derisioni habemur factique sumus opprobrium abundantibus et ~o superbis OCKHAM *Err. Papae* 958. **c** ~ones et derisiones a peccatore populo in Christi Domini passione .. factas *Eccl. & Synag.* 114; reditur .. contra comitem Leycestrie ad minarum sevitias, ad protervias exprobrationum .., ad indecentias ~onum AD. MARSH *Ep.* 30 p. 127; **s1294** inveniens castra sua prostrata per Walenses et dispeccionem et gravamina que Anglis fecerant *Ann. Dunstable* 386.

2 (recognition of) lowly condition.

ad montana conscendit, quia per humilitatem propriae ~onis ad sublimitatem debemus Deo devotae actionis ascendere BEDE *Gen.* (xii 8) 139.

despective, insultingly, disrespectfully.

ipsum [ducem Willelmum] 'pelliciarium' ~e vocitaverunt, eo quod parentes matris ejus pelliciarii extiterant W. JUM. VII 18; [Andegavenses] ab eisdem quibus impudenter nocuerunt hostili odio 'Hilibecci' ~e cognominati sunt ORD. VIT. XIII 26 p. 67; indignatus ille quod sibi [potum] ~e dedisset W. CANT. *Mir. Thom.* VI 74; **s1328** [R. de Brus] semper eam [uxorem suam] habuit exosam et ~e et iniquissime tractavit cum ea AD. MUR. *Chr.* 57*n.*

despectivus, disrespectful.

requiritur .. devota intencio ad memorandum sic sacramentaliter Salvatorem; quod si defuerit, est Christi irrisio et ~a super Christum humoris fetentis infusio WYCL. *Euch.* 178.

despector [LL], contemner.

sic Circes despector obit J. EXON. *BT* VI 951; idem A. per quosdam emulos suos et malefactores Dei et sanctorum locorum ejus dispectores .. extra .. ecclesiam vi et armis extractus fuit *Entries* 583.

despectuose, contemptuously, insultingly.

1337 (v. cippus 2); **s1326** Londonienses .. duxerunt episcopum in Chepe et ~e decollaverunt KNIGHTON I 434; **1389** litteras suas diffidencie omnibus subditis nostris apud Dantz existentibus ~e mandavit, guerrarum turbinem comminantes *Dip. Corr. Ric. II* 69; **s1419** corpora extra muros projecta crudeliter et ~e *Plusc.* X 25.

despectuosus, scornful.

[Cassibalaunus] indignatus de tributo suo non reddendo epistolam ~am Julio Cesari transmisit [cf. G. MON. IV 1] *Eul. Hist.* II 250.

1 despectus [CL]

1 contempt, scorn. **b** contemptuous usage, insult.

[quae] dispectui habita foras proicerentur BEDE *HE* III 22; ammonet gentes ne .. Judaeos ~ui habeant LANFR. *Comment. Paul* (*Rom.* xi 16) 142; vultus suos, utpote ab illo qui jam ipsis ~ui erat, avertebant EADMER *V. Dunst.* 6; Hibernici .. a .. Normannis in ~um et derisum habiti GIR. *EH* II 36; **12..** quamvis in tanto ~u haberemur *Chr. Evesham* 105; quidam puerulus .. nomen Domini cum ~u et irrisione mirabili blasphemavit *NLA* (*Modwenna*) II 211. **b** **1226** mandamus .. quatinus .. non torneatis, cum .. barones nostri ad mandatum nostrum .. torneare omiserint, quibus magnus videretur ~us si absque eis torneassetis *Pat* 71; **s1273** ego multa mala perpessus sum et ignominiam ac ~um supra omnes predecessores meos *Ann. Durh.* 31 (cf. GRAYSTANES 12); **1294** hiis exceptis .. qui ~um fecerunt mihi et heredibus meis *BBC* (*Chesterfield*) 220; **s1321** rex .. cupiens vindicari de ~u et rebellione .. sibi factis Londoniis WALS. *YN* 254.

2 contempt of court or other lawful authority, defiance; **b** (w. gen. of gd.). **c** fine for such contempt.

GAS 558 (v. 2 contemptus c); **1207** invenit plegios .. quod stabit recto de ~u curie *CurR* III 123; **1258** (v. deteriorare 2a); **s1260** ballivi in ~u regie majestatis .. nichil facere voluerunt *Leg. Ant. Lond.* 47; **1274** cepit de eadem villa j m. injuste pro dispectu Colecestr' ultra taxacionem primo factam *Hund.* I 144; **1281** in ~u curie abiit *SelPlMan* 66; **s1377** Florentini in ~um sacre Romane ecclesie quendam monachum missum a .. papa .. occiderunt *Chr. Angl.* 110. **b** **1283** J. de C. in misericordia quia habuit ~um eundi ad jurandum ad faciendam inquisicionem *RCoron* 209/59 r. 9. **c** qui exclamationem audierit et accurrere neglexerit, solvat ~um regis [AS: *þæs cinges oferhyrnesse*] (*Cons. Cnuti*) *GAS* 331; emendet .. domino aut regi plenum ~um [AS: *be fullan mundbryce*] (*Inst. Cnuti*) *Ib.* 343.

2 despectus v. 1 despicere. **despen-** v. dispen-.

desperabilis [LL], desperate, hopeless.

dispersiones solito ~iores GILDAS *EB* 19 (cf. ib. 23: ~em .. mentis hebetudinem); sed quod magis mirabile / mundo et desperabile (ÆTHELWALD) *Carm. Aldh.* 2. 136; uxoris velut mortuae disperabilem [v. l. de-] vitam revelavit *V. Cuthb.* IV 3; ratio rerum ~em intelligentiam ad deliberationem reducit perspicuam ADEL. *QN* 39; bellum tam ~is initii tam triumphali fine melior fortuna conclusit GIR. *EH* I 45; ~i languore detentus ECCLESTON *Adv. Min.* 7; repugnantiis confractis quantumcunque ~ium importunitatum AD. MARSH *Ep.* 25; **s1429** que in principio litis res adeo ~is fuerat quod jaceret inter causas mortuas AMUND. I 254.

desperabiliter [LL], desperately, despairingly.

filia archisinagogi ipsa est sinagoga, quae .. subito errorum languore consternata spiritales vitae vias ingredi ~iter omisit BEDE *Mark* (v 23) 180 (cf. id. *Luke* 441); que fere ~iter plorabatur AILR. *Ed. Conf.* 745A; in illos .. sic delinquentes et ~iter exorbitantes deseviandum .. decrevit GIR. *GE* I 34; continua .. cruciabantur .. afflictione, eo quidem vehementius quo prevaricante marchiso ~ius *Itin. Ric* I 66; non defuit perfidia que ~iter istud autumaverit AD. MARSH *Ep.* 245.

desperabundus, despairing.

impostores .. nunc tandem ~i DEE *Monas pref.* 191.

desperagatio v. disparagatio.

desperanter [CL], despairingly.

vel ~er meticulosus vel turpiter in fugam conversus GIR. *EH* I 4.

desperantia, despair.

diffidentia, disperantia, *ortreownes* *GlH* D 467.

desperare [CL], to despair (of): **a** (trans.); **b** (w. *de*); **c** (absol.); **d** (w. inf., or acc. & inf.); **e** (p. ppl. *s. act.*) despairing.

a ut .. grates pro sanitate agat .. mortalium ore ~ata GILDAS *EB* 72; quo miserabilius ipse ~ata salute periret BEDE *HE* V 14; **793** non est .. cuilibet conversio disperanda ALCUIN *Ep.* 23 p. 60; **c800** noli torrem de incendio raptum [cf. *Amos* iv 11] disperare *Ib.* 283; **9..** ~andum, *to ortruwienne* *WW*; diutino languore jam ~abat salutem et vitam GOSC. *Transl. Aug.* 27C; jejunat .. David pro salute parvuli ~ati AD. DORE *Pictor* 154; quod confessus sum cuidam seni, qui ~avit me O. CHERITON *Par.* 147. **b** BEDE *Hom.* I 8 (v. 1 despicere 2b); **s878** ut depressi de Dei misericordia non ~ent *Chr. S. Neoti*; **1202** eum .. vulneravit, ita quod de vita ejus ~abat *SelPlCrown* 28; **1226** fuit ipse portatus coram domino rege ut ille de cujus morte ~abatur *CurR* XII 1802 (= *BNB* III 541: disparabatur); **1384** (v. cruentare 2); **1408** ita quod ipse de vita sua disperabat *Mem. York.* I 176. **c** nullum perfectum credimus in baptismo, non ~amus tamen THEOD. *Pen.* II 4. 5; sic loquebatur miser ~ans BEDE *HE* V 13; **8..** ne †~is [l. ~es], *ne georwen ðu* *WW*; ut ~ans Deo in faciem bene diceret [cf. *Job* i 11] ABBO *Edm.* 5; nihil est difficile nisi cum ~es ADEL. *QN* 64; **1305** ecclesia .. surrexit et, ubi disparabat magis, ut Lucifer exorta est *Reg. Cant.* 673. **d** *V. Cuthb.* IV 15 (v. contulere); in hac intentione humana anima nullatenus se poterit exercere si ~et quo intendit se posse pervenire ANSELM (*Mon.* 75) I 83; vitium quo mens blasphema ~at .. Dei sapientiam .. posse .. sibi impensa refundere AD. MARSH *Ep.* 173; **s1241** capitis dolore ita acriter vexatus est ut in litteris proficere deinceps ~aret HIGD. VII 35 p. 216; **s1272** per fugam ~ans evadere RISH. 77; **1360** procurator citra incepcionem suam ad villam accedere disparavit *MunAcOx* 224. **e** ni desperatus medicantem spreverit aeger ALDH. *VirgV* 2660; miserata es mei ~ati penitus et nil tale .. sperantis GIR. *GE* II 12; **1228** tanquam de jure et justicia penitus ~ati *Cl* 108; ita ~ati sunt quod mortem appetunt HALES *Sent.* II 411; irreparabilia .. dierum damna .. ~ata deplorat anxietas AD. MARSH *Ep.* 51; **s1293** de pace et concordia penitus ~atus TREVET *Ann.* 328; **s1453** ~atus de subterfugio *Reg. Whet.* I 114.

desperate [LL], hopelessly.

in eo isti propensius et ~ius errant, quo .. a tyrannis .. emunt sacerdotia GILDAS *EB* 67.

desperatio [CL], desperation, despair.

puero in vitae ~one aestuanti GILDAS *EB* 72; trux desperatio mentis ALDH. *VirgV* 2646; cum nos in labore ac ~one [v. l. disperatione] positos cerneret BEDE *HE* V 1; FELIX *Guthl.* 29 (v. defigere 1b); **a796** magis haec potest esse .. disperatio fidei nostrae quam confirmatio causae tuae ALCUIN *Ep.* 58; disperatio, *ormodnes* *GlH* D 582; heu ~onis amaritudo! ANSELM (*Or.* 9) III 32; GIR. *TH intr.* (v. 1 diffidentia 1a); *Id. EH* I 13 (v. consolatio); ~o opponitur spei naturali, non spei virtuti HALES *Qu.* 1544; **1444** sunt in via gravis ~onis et perdicionis vite eorum *BBAdm* I 253.

desperativus, inclining to despair.

hec quidem [voluntas] dispensativa et eruditiva ad salutem; hec autem ~a ad finalem punicionem BRADW. *CD* 598B.

despicabilis [LL], contemptible, mean, wretched: **a** (of person); **b** (of horse); **c** (of abstr.).

a magis iconisma regale compto stemmate depictum laudatur quam dispicabilis persona pictoris veneratur Aldh. *VirgP* 60; R. dux .. ~ior quam antea fuerat suis effectus est Ord. Vit. XI 2 p. 163; leprosos .. libentius exhibebat quam alios pauperes .., illos autem ideo precipue quia, quanto sunt ~es abjectius .., tanto se sperat obsequium prestare Deo placentius Map *NC* V 5 f. 66v.; licet habitu ~is videretur, vultus tamen dignitate cognoscitur Gir. *GE* I 23; **s1221** peregrini .. ~es sunt effecti .., carnis curam perficiendo in desideriis W. Coventr. II 250; **s1227** papa .., in fratre .. habitum deformem, vultum ~em, barbam prolixam .. considerans, .. despexit eum Wend. II 329; **s1252** gestu, verbis, et habitu .. ~is, histrio potius quam sacerdos M. Par. *Maj.* V 329. **b s1232** Hubertum .. loris constrictum equo imposuerunt .., super equum, inquam, ~em *Ib.* III 228; **s1297** quidam miles cum parvo equo et ~i *Ann. Ed. I* 474; **s1322** comes Lancastrie .. ductus fuit extra villam .. sedans super ~e jumentum *Ann. Paul.* 303. **c** [Faritius] fuit .. non usquequaque ~is eloquentie W. Malm. *GP* V *prol.* p. 331; homuncionem .. ~is parentele *Id. GR* III 263; in tertia [gloria] ipsius fuerat humilitas ~is, in qua nec species nec decor H. Bos. *LM* 1345c; recedentes ab incommutabili veritate, illud incurrunt cum ~i ignominia quod ex inani gloria fugiunt Ad. Marsh *Ep.* 174.

despicabiliter [LL], **a** contemptuously, scornfully. **b** in a lowly fashion, so as to invite contempt.

a c1083 locum quem sacri corporis .. presentia illustrat neglegentiori quam ejus deceret sanctitatem servitio ~er destitutum conspexi *Ch. Durh.* 3; eum exinde cepit .. deligere cui primitus solebat ~er derogare T. Mon. *Will.* VII 13; cum puelle .. paganos Christianissime ~er contempsissent [cf. G. Mon. V 16] M. Par. *Maj.* I 173; neque iracunde aut indignando sive ~er aliquis erga alterum .. demonstrare debet *Cust. Westm.* 163. **b s1225** puella .. saccum et cilicium induit atque crines .. ~er precidit et .. naturalem .. corporis decorem in omnem studuit deformitatem transferre Wend. II 290.

1 despīcari [CL]

1 to despise, scorn. **b** (pr. ppl. w. gen. or (?) dat.) contemptuous (of).

~ari, despicere, deludere, subsannare Osb. Glouc. *Deriv.* 178; H. Avr. *CG* f. 8 (v. 2 despīcari); *to desspice*, .. dedignari .., despicere, ~ari *CathA.* **b** ambo hi .. impedimenta rerum temporalium evasere, ~antes mundanae philosophiae W. Poit. I 55.

2 (p. ppl. w. *inimicitia*) scornfully declared.

Gir. *TH* III 21 (v. defucare b); **s1189** premiserat imperator ad Saladinum .. litteras diffiduciatas ei et ~atas inimicitias .. denuntiantes *Id. PI* III 16.

2 despīcari [cf. CL spicari], to glean.

despīcor messem, liventem despīcor hostem H. Avr. *CG* f. 8. 12; *to glene*, aristare, conspicare et [conspica]ri, ~ari *CathA.*

despicatio [CL], scorn.

s1188 gravissimam Francorum regis .. indignationem .. et ~onem Gir. *PI* III 9.

1 despicere [CL, *conf. w.* dispicere]

1 to look down.

vix .. se subrigeret celo; ita semper inferiora despitiens dampnatus erat solo (*V. Aldh.*) W. Malm. *GP* V 262; respice retro te, ~e subter te et suspice supra te J. Godard *Ep.* 240.

2 to look at disdainfully, scorn; **b** (refl.); **c** (w. inf.). **d** (p. ppl. *despectus*) despised. **e** not worth looking at, inconspicuous.

non solum enim per vos virtutes Dei non annuntiantur, sed etiam pravissimis vestris apud incredulos quosque ~iuntur exemplis Gildas *EB* 107; quomodo .. virgo .. jugalitatis consortia .. refutans .. contempserit, despexerit [v. l. dispexerit], respuerit Aldh. *VirgP* 40 (cf. id. *VirgV* 1155: oscula virgineis dispexit [v. l. despexit] lubrica labris); odio habebat et dispiciebat eos Bede *HE* III 21; spretis atque dispectis puerilialis (*sic*) .. lasciviis Hugeb. *Wynn.* 1; **c793** noli dispicere animas .. filiorum quos genuisti Alcuin *Ep.* 23 p. 62; *Id. Ep.* 162 (v. 2 dis); **8..** qui ~it, *se ðe forsiohþ WW*; **933** ammonent ut ea .. non solum ~iendo sed etia[m] velut .. abominando fugiamus *CS* 694; me .. irate despexit Map *NC* V 6 (v. discidium 2b); tu qui summa potes, ne despice parva potentem Walt. Angl. *Fab.* 18. 23; **s1227** (v. despicabilis a); **s1306** (v. desolatio 3). **b** nullus se ipsum ~iat, nullus de sua salute disperet Bede *Hom.* I 8. 42. **c c597** mulieres .., dum se continere nolunt, ~iunt lactare quos gignunt (*Lit. Papae*) Bede *HE* II 27 p. 55; **c793** si tecum loquerer, non dispicerem tecum discere quae vera sunt Alcuin *Ep.* 23 p. 62; **a1085** litteras .. vix susceptas legere despexisti Lanfr. *Ep.* 29(27); magna .. abusio est .. quod illum prior honorare ~it qui eum priorem fecit Ad. Scot *OP* 568b; **s1176** missarum solenniis interesse ~iens Gerv. Cant. *Chr.* 259; **1281** scientes .., juxta Salvatoris sententiam [*Matth.* xii 30], contra nos esse qui nobiscum esse ~iunt Peckham *Ep.* 197 (= *Conc.* II 63); ~e videre eum Favent 19. **d** dispectus, *fraecuð GlC* D 331; multi me spernunt, cunctis dispectior en sum! Bonif. *Aen.* 9 (*Humilitas*) 3; dispectior, *forsewenlicra GlH* D 572; personis omnibus divo carens dogmate ~ior B. *V. Dunst.* 1; quanto quis propter Deum ~ior est in hoc saeculo, tanto magis exaltabitur in futuro Lanfr. *Comment. Paul.* (*1 Cor.* vii 22) 150. **e** calendris .. in colore fusca est et plumis ~a Upton 185.

2 despicere v. 2 dispicere.

despicienter, disdainfully, scornfully.

incolumitati restitutus, omnia ~er et superbe negat Map *NC* IV 6 f. 50.

despinare [cf. CL spina], to pull out thorns.

to drawe oute thornes, ~are, ex- *CathA.*

despitus v. decrepitus a. **desplic-** v. displic-.

despoliare [CL] **(disp-)**, to rob, strip, despoil (of). **b** to unsheathe (a sword).

801 (14c) cogitabat rex eum in aliqua parte suae hereditatis ~iare *CS* 302; **825** quaesitum fuerat .. quis cum injustitia et violentia fraudatus ~iatusque in sua persona fieret *CS* 384 (= *Conc. HS* 597); [Britones Romanos] cesos prosternunt, prostratos ~iant, ~iatos pretereunt, ut ceteros insequantur G. Mon. X 4; Christus fuit in tali hora ~iatus et totus nudus *Spec. Eccl.* 89; **s1263** destructum est Judaismum in Londoniis .. et quotquot Judei fuerunt inventi, nudi, ~iati et postea de nocte trucidati [sunt] *Leg. Ant. Lond.* 62; **1375** (v. coggo); **1408** Ricardus T. ~iavit Johannem P. .. de xx m. argenti *Reg. Heref.* 58; **s1454** ~iatur [cella] per viam impignoracionis de cunctis quasi ejus jocalibus *Reg. Whet.* I 141. **b** ~iatis gladiis in eum irrumpunt Asser *Alf.* 97.

despoliatio [LL] **(disp-)**, robbery, stripping, despoilment.

s1005 cum .. per Analaphum et Swanum ac eorum exercitus depredaciones, ~ones, et destrucciones assidue fierent *Croyl.* 56; **1447** pardonamus .. eidem R. omnimodas execuciones in ipsum post traccionem et suspendium sua ac ~onem corporis sui ad denudacionem corporis sui et tactum ejusdem cum cultello *Pat* 464 m. 18; **s1455** protegente .. martyre, salva stetit sua ecclesia .. ab omni gravi bonorum dispendio seu ~one *Reg. Whet.* I 172; de aliqua .. riota, captura et ~one facta per .. familiares seu servientes testatoris [sc. E. episcopi Sar', ob. **1524**] *Entries* 592b.

despoliator [LL], despoiler, (?) dispossessor.

1194 .. proditore et ~ore [*context corrupt*] *CurR RC* I 64.

despondēre [CL], to promise in marriage, betroth. **b** to plight troth to, espouse.

c675 Hermionam .., quae .. ~ebatur jure dotis Oresti Aldh. *Ep.* 3; ~et, valde promittit *GlC* D 41; **9..** ~i, *gesceatwyrpe WW*; si tunc in omni re concordent, adeat cognatio et ~eat eam [AS: *weddian heora magan*] *to wive and to rihtlive*, id est in uxorem et rectam vitam (*Quad.*) *GAS* 443; [rex] Berengariam .. sibi desspondi (*sic*) fecit Devizes 34v. (cf. contrahere 8a); **1301** ~erat filiam suam comiti Bolonie *Anglo-Scot. Rel.* 103; dispondeo, A. *to by hote or trowthe WW.* **b s1066** [Haroldus] nihil de pactis inter se et Willelmum cogitabat, liberatum se sacramento asserens, quod filia ejus quam ~erat citra nubiles annos obierat W. Malm. *GR* III 238; Abner reducit ad David Michol uxorem suam quam olim sibi ~erat Ad. Dore *Pictor* 166; **s1164** comes Carnotensis T. ~it filiam L. regis Francie Torigni *Chr.* 222.

desponsalia [LL], espousals.

pro ~ibus filie istius aliquod donativum extortirus R. Cold. *Cuthb.* 109; **1229** Willelmus .. dicit quod [filius suus] nunquam eam dotavit de tercia parte nec de aliqua terra; set bene concedit quod interfuit ~ibus [*corr. from* sponsalibus] et quod Cecilia adducta fuit ad domum suam et ibi celebratum fuit convivium *CurR* XIII 2070; **13..** contrahentes hujusmodi disponsalia *Conc. Scot.* II 69; **1450** predictus T. .. bigamus est, eo quod ipse ij uxores successive desponsavit .. quarum utramque infra ~ia carnaliter cognovit *Entries* 106; **1452** Johanne consorti mee xl li., una cum omnibus jocalibus .. que fuerunt ejusdem J. ante disponsalia inter nos celebrata *Test. Ebor.* II 163.

desponsalitia, espousals.

1200 dum placitum fuit inter .. Alexandrum et .. Agnetem de ~iis [v. l. sponsalitiis] ipsius Agnetis *CurR* I 309.

desponsare [CL]

1 to promise or give in marriage, betroth: **a** (woman); **b** (man). **c** (refl.) to pledge oneself to Christ (as nun). **d** (pass.) (?) to be dedicated, devoted.

a puellam disponsatam non licet parentibus dare alteri viro, nisi illa omnino resistat.. illa autem ~ata, si non vult habitare cum eo viro cui est ~ata, reddatur ei pecunia quam pro ipsa dedit Theod. *Pen.* II 12. 33–4; [virgo] proco fuerat .. / desponsata probo pactis sponsalibus arrae Aldh. *VirgV* 2068; **9..** terram .. dabit filio suo, si de ~ata muliere filium habet *CS* 812; potest homo pugnare sine forisfacto si alii obviet .. cum matre sua quae patri suo fuerit ~ata [AS: *ðe wære to æwum wife forgifen his fæder*] (*Quad.*) *GAS* 77; nec habeat nisi unam uxorem, quae sit ei legitime ~ata [AS: *þæt beo his beweddode wif*] (*Inst. Cnuti*) *Ib.* 291; huic et non alio me desponsate marito Nig. *Mir. BVM* f. 20v.; **a1230** nec fides de aliqua ~anda detur nisi presente sacerdote *Conc. Syn.* 190; **12..** unam filiam, que disponsata fuit Werrisio de P. *Reg. S. Thom. Dublin* 118; **1327** permissum est nativas nostras liberis hominibus ~ari *MonA* II 121a. **b c1370** 'Jo. dum sponsabitur annis', i. illo tempore quo Johannes disponsabitur (J. Bridl. *gl.*) *Pol. Poems* I 169; **c1400** ipse habet fratrem .. qui ~atur sorori domini W. C. Wyche *Ep.* 543. **c** M. Par. *Maj.* III 487 (v. anulus 1c). **d 1403** Ebor' ecclesia .., cui .. presidemus et medullatis affeccionibus inseparabiliter †dispensamur *Fabr. York* 197.

2 a to plight troth to, espouse. **b** (of priest) to celebrate the espousals of.

a mecum concumbe, quia hodie me ~asti; ego sum Venus, cujus digito apposuisti anulum W. Malm. *GR* II 205; uxor que fuit Petri de B. est de donatione domini regis, et Willelmus T. habet illam; sed nescitur a juratoribus si ~avit eam vel non *RDomin* 4; **1196** racionabilem dotem suam de terra que fuit Rannulfi .. viri sui, sc. [terciam partem] de illa de qua fuit seisitus die qua eam ~avit *CurR* I 18; in presbyteris .. nulla dispensatio locum habet, nisi forte per generale consilium .. de ~andis unicis et virginibus more Grecorum statueretur Gir. *GE* II 6; **s1198** [Otho] ~avit unicam filiam .. ducis Brebantie septennem Diceto *YH* II 163; **c1205** terram quam Walterus .. dedit mihi in maritagio cum filia sua quando eam ~avi *Reg. Aberbr.* I 64; **1225** (v. anulus 1c); **1226** si aliquis ~averit aliquam mulierem .. hereditatem habentem et .. ex ea prolem suscitaverit .., idem vir, si supervixerit ipsam uxorem suam, habebit .. custodiam hereditatis uxoris sue *Pat* 96; **s1238** ~avit solemniter Simon de Monteforti Alienoram filiam regis Johannis .., dictante verba et missam celebrante W. capellano capelle regie S. Stephani apud Westmonasterium in parvula capella regis .., tradente eam rege per manum eidem Simoni M. Par. *Maj.* III 471; Bracton 92 (v. dos 2a); **1502** dicto matrimonio .. per verba de presenti,. contracto .., rex Anglie .. dominam M. filiam suam .. ad limites regni Scocie transmittet .. et regi Scotorum ejusve commissario .. tradet .., ipseque dominus J. rex Scotorum eandem dominam M. .. in facie ecclesie secundum sacrorum canonum disposicionem solempniter disponsabit et in uxorem accipiet ipsamque deinceps tanquam uxorem suam legittimam .. tenebit *RScot* 553b. **b s1100** A. archiepiscopus .. ~avit Matildem filiam M. regis Scotie .. Henrico regi novo H. Hunt. *HA* VII 22; **s1121** [Adelhiza] in regni dominam electa .. regi ~abatur a W. Winton' episcopo J. Worc. 16.

desponsatio [LL]

1 espousal; **b** (dist. as first or second).

s1151 contigit quod L. rex Francorum a sponsa sua, filia consulis Pictaviensis, .. divideretur; Henricus igitur dux novus [Normannie] duxit eam... ea tamen ~o incentivum .. fuit.. discordie inter regem .. et .. ducem H. Hunt. *HA* VIII 31; **s1177** ducta est filia regis Anglie .. in quoddam palatium, ut ibidem ~onis .. sue diem gratius posset expectare... paucis itaque elapsis diebus .. desponsata fuit regi W. Sicilie *G. Hen. II* I 157; non puto urbem esse in qua sint probabiliores consuetudines .. in ~onibus firmandis, matrimoniis contrahendis, nuptiis celebrandis W. Fitzst. *Thom. prol.* 12; nullus .. presbyterorum propter baptisma quicquam exigere presumat .. nec propter ~onem Gir. *GE* I 13; **1199** de racionabili dote sua, que eam contingit ex dono Rogeri .. quondam viri sui, unde eam dotavit die ~onis sue *CurR* I 85; **1220** ipsa habuit breve ad officialem .. de probanda ~one *Ib.* IX 367; **c1240** laicos qui .. clamdestinis ~onibus interesse presumpserint excommunicamus *Conc. Syn* 376; non valet talis [uxori] donatio, maxime quia uxor cui donatum fuit numquam seisinam habuit ante ~onem Bracton 29; **s1299** cuncti fere principes nominati .. tante ~oni interesse gaudebant, quia nimirum regis Edwardi magnificentia .. cunctos attraxerat Rish. 192; verba [*Cant.* iii 11] .. non debent intelligi .. de ~one carnali neque de mundana leticia Ockham *Pol.* II 700; tenetur .. unusquisque .. sponsam suam dotare tempore ~onis *RegiamM* II 16. 2; dicuntur 'arre' annuli .. vel alie res dande sponse per sponsum; que dacio subarracio dicitur, precipue tamen quando fit per annuli dationem; et tunc vulgariter ~o vocatur *Man. Sal.* 46; **1442** liberentur .. filiabus meis postquam ad etatem xvj annorum pervenerint pro maritagiis suis .. tempore disponsacionum suarum *Reg. Cant.* II 614. **b c1430** in quarto cipho argenteo et deaurato dato filie Johannis H. .. in sua prima ~one v li. vj s.; item in quinto cipho argenteo et deaurato dato eidem filie in secunda sua ~one, vj li. xiij s. iiij d. Amund. II app. 257.

2 (fig.): **a** 'espousal' of church by monastery. **b** treaty of alliance.

a c1155 [*because the church was slenderly endowed*] die ~onis sue [sc. obedientie B. Marie de Monemuta] *Cal. Doc. France* 1146. **b** primo compaternitatis federa jungunt... postmodum ecclesiam intrantes .. misse celebratione et orationibus sacerdotum tanquam ~one quadam indissolubiliter federantur. ... o quoties in ipso ~onis hujus articulo a viris sanguinum .. inique funditur sanguis! Gir. *TH* III 22.

desponsio [LL]

1 espousal.

s1066 [Haroldus] filie [Willelmi] adhuc impubis ~one et totius patrimonii amplitudine donatus W. Malm. *GR* II

288 p. 280; s**1102** Agnes, uxor ejus [Gualterii comitis Buchingeham], .. Gualterium puerum post xv annos ~onis sue marito peperit ORD. VIT. XI 4 p. 184.

2 bishop's profession.

c**850** (12c) ego Deruulfus, ad episcopalem sedem .. electus Lundoniensis aecclesiae, .., cartulam meae confessionis et ~onis componens, .. profiteor illud observare quod servaverunt praedecessores mei *CS* 498.

desportare v. disportare. **despositio** v. dispositio 2b.

despotes [δεσπότης], **~us,** despot, master (of slaves). **b** (Byz.) prince.

OCKHAM *Pol.* I 28 (v. despoticus); plus potest in multis ~es seu dominus super servos suos .. quam possit imperator super sibi subjectos *Ib.* 197. **b 1438** ex parte Orientalium affuit personaliter serenissimus dominus imperator Romeorum cum dispoto, fratre suo germano (*Decr. Consil. Ferrar.*) *Cop. Pri. S. Andr.* 169.

despotia [δεσποτεία], despotism, absolute rule.

non tamen tyrannis proprie est ~ia OCKHAM *Dial.* 795.

despotice, despotically, absolutely.

quamvis [populus Romanus] .. omnem potestatem regulariter regendi propter bonum commune transtulerint in imperatorem, non tamen transtulerunt in ipsum potestatem dominandi seu regendi ~e OCKHAM *Pol.* I 150.

despoticus [δεσποτικός], despotic, absolute.

potencia motiva in homine est in obediencia servili respectu voluntatis que [Aristotelis] I Pol. cap. iij vocatur 'dispotica' DUNS *Sent.* II 42. 4. 16; si [homo] non compescit motus sensualitatis, habeo quod est contra racionem rectam, cum tamen racio sit respectu sensualitatis in principatu politico; si autem esset respectu ejus in principatu ~o, magis peccaret, si non compesceret LUTTERELL *Occam* 6; est aliqua multitudo que dicitur multitudo politica; et alia est multitudo que multum deficit a racione, et hec dicitur multitudo dispotica W. BURLEY *Comment. Pol. extr.* 281; licet .. quelibet prelacio ecclesiastica se excludat dominacionem que est respectu non liberorum, ita ut nullus prelatus ecclesie .. sit tali dominacione dominus Christianorum quorumcumque, que Grece vocatur 'despotes' .., quia principatus ecclesiasticus eciam supremus ex ordinacione Christi non est ~us OCKHAM *Pol.* I 28; principatus non dominativus seu ~us sed ministrativus *Id. I & P* 14 (cf. ib. 15: principatum dominancium, qui vocabulo sumpto ex Greco vocatur ~us).

despuere [CL], to spit (down). **b** (fig.) to reject.

to spitte, .. spuere, con-, ex-, de-.. *CathA*. **b** ~endo, reiciendo *GlH* D 276.

despumare [CL] **(disp-)**

1 to skim.

confice cum melle ~ato et uteris cum opus habueris *Leechdoms* I 376; bulli ipsum usque ad terciam sui partem et dispuma et distilla per filtrum M. SCOT *Lumen* 254; in melle rubeo bene bullito et fortiter dispumato pone pulverem nitri [etc.] GILB. VII 331. 2; modicum salis et mellis dispumati tepidi GAD. 22v. 2; mulsa est potus factus ex viij partibus aque et nona mellis ~ati *SB* 31 (cf. *Alph.* 12: dispumati); UPTON 190 (v. colatura a).

2 (intr.) to stop foaming, settle down.

ergo animos hebetes mendax audacia frontis / dissimulat clamorque minax despumat in ausus [? l. inausus] J. EXON. *BT* IV 288.

despumarium, ~atorium, skimmer.

a scomer, spumatorium, dispumatorium *CathA*; **1553** de .. v dispumariis, A. *fyve skommers Pat* 852 m. 29.

desputare [cf. CL sputare], to spit down or out.

to spitte, .. spuere .., sputare, de- ..; *to cast spyttynge*, ~are, exscreare *CathA*.

desquamare [CL], to descale.

~o, *unscale fysshe* STANBR. *Vulg.* 11.

dess- v. et. des-, dec-, desc-, diss-. **dessais-, desseis-** v. dissais-.

desselare [OF *desseler* < *dissellare], to unseat.

1221 eum assultavit et vulneravit et desilavit eum de equo suo *PlCrGlouc* 31.

dessendere v. 2 descendere. **desserere** v. 2 disserere 2. **dessicat-** v. desiccat-. **dessip-** v. dissip-. **desta** v. dextans. **destabilis** v. detestabilis. **destabiliter** v. detestabiliter a.

destare, a to cease, desist. **b** to stand behind.

a *to cese*, cessare, desinere, †descistere .., ~are *CathA*. **b** *to sstande be-hynde*, ~are *Ib.*

destaurare [cf. staurare], to unstock, deprive of stock. *V. et. deinstauratus.*

c**1095** pater meus ad mortem sua[m] dimiserat monachis totum mobile totius terre sue; et .. remiserunt michi monachi totum illud dimisum, ne ~etur tota terra mea *Cart. Lewes* f. 13.

desteiniare [OF *desteindre*], to 'distain', dye, or (?) embroider. *Cf.* 1 *distingere, steinare.*

1389 solutum pro j panno distainiato cum imaginibus *Ac. Bridge Masters* 8 m. 12; [T. abbas, ob. **1396**] contulit capelle S. Marie duos pannos optimos †destennatos [? l. desteiniatos], unde unus de gaudiis B. Virginis et alius de ymaginibus in tabernaculis situatis *G. S. Alb.* III 387.

desterarius v. dextrarius a.

desternere [LL], to unharness, unsaddle.

distrato [vv. ll. destrato, †distracto] equo trahens in domum et alligans ad parietem *V. Cuthb.* I 6; de querendo sibi serviente .., qui equos mane stratos ad vesperum destraret *Collect. Stories* 201; *onsadelyn hors or takyn a-wey fro hem byrdenesse*, disterno, -stravi .. et destravi *PP*.

destertere [CL], **a** to stop dreaming, wake up. **b** (by conf.) to dream, snore.

a ~ere, vigilare, expergiscere OSB. GLOUC. *Deriv.* 180. **b** ~uit, somniavit, *reat GlH* D 272.

destillabilis, distillable (matter).

de vitro vel quocunque omogenio, quantumlibet fortiter commixto, contingit partem subtilem aqueum vel aereum extrahi, semulento croceo derelicto, et longe facilius in vino, sanguine vel alio distillabili †omogenee [? l. omogeneo] WYCL. *Log.* III 77.

destillare (dist-) [CL]

1 (of fluids) to flow, trickle, ooze.

cortice inciso ~ans umor BEDE *Sam.* 674; humor ~at a capite ad pulmonem continue quasi pluvia *Ps.*-RIC. *Anat.* 41; aqua que condensatur in nubibus .. vi expressiva ventorum exprimitur et ~at in guttas *Quaest. Salern.* B 170; **1250** ~at pluvia per medium furnum, quia discoopertus est *CalIMisc* I p. 30; s**1220** [S. archiepiscopus] fecit per totam diem translacionis [S. Thome] vinum jugiter in canalibus per varia urbis loca ~are HIGD. VII 34 p. 200.

2 a (trans.) to exude, pour slowly. **b** to pour down (fig.). **c** (absol.) to exude or discharge moisture, drip.

a mel lentescens cerarum machina clausum / atque favi croceum destillans [v. l. distillans] flumine nectar ALDH. *VirgV* 1600; **930** (v. campulus b); favus melle redundans .. liquorem ~at dulcissimum L. DURH. *Brig.* 5. 175E; decoquatur cum aceto .. et ~etur in aurem GAD. 116v. 1. **b** tua labia / torrentes mellios sunt distillancia WALT. WIMB. *Carm.* 13; vindictam [Dei] .. ~ari WYCL. *Civ. Dom.* I 218 (v. dissipativus). **c** culmina antiquata tecti ~antia fenestraeque aperte .. et parietes incultae .. horribiles manebant EDDI 16; si .. oculus ~et, pro lacrimis detur aurea GILB. II 122. 1; **1323** quicumque nostrum tardius edificaverit super eundem murum gutteram faciet et sustentabit ~antem super terram suam propriam *Cart. Osney* I 130.

3 (alch.) to distill (trans. or intr.).

M. SCOT *Lumen* 266 (v. alembicum); auctores [alkimie] docent suas medicinas sublimare, ~are et resolvere BACON *Tert.* 40; ~a per alembicum lento igne vel claro in serpentaria; aqua que primo ~averit est optima GAD. 66v. 2 (cf. ib. 13. 1: purgetur cum aqua ~ata de floribus sambuci); *to stille waters*, stillare, ~are, *CathA*; cum .. xx quartas aque vite septies ~ate .. emisset *Entries* 187 (cf. decimalis 5).

destillatio [CL] **(dist-)**

1 dripping, trickling.

erat ibi saxi durities .. concava .., quia .. aquarum crebra ~o et refusio talem eam .. reddiderat GIR. *GE* II 10; c**1350** torticia .. teneantur hinc inde juxta altare a longe propter ~onem super vestimenta cavendam *Mon. Exon.* 273v.; adhuc in venis capillaribus secundum rorem causabilium et glutinum est †quantum sensibilis ~o et membrorum attraccio ad motus augmentacionis ultimum complementum WYCL. *Log.* III 112.

2 (alch.) distillation.

BACON IX 157 (v. attrenum); *Id. NM* 548 (v. 2 clavis 2b); post hec intendimus calcis propositionem et olei ~onem et aque exaltationem *Id. Min.* 314; aqua vite simplex fit de vino forti per viam ~onis in alembico GAD. 66v. 2.

destillatorius (dist-), (w. *vas* or as sb. n.) still, alembic.

GAD. 112. 1, *Alph.* 6 (v. alembicum); alembicum, ~ium idem *SB* 10; **13..** ejice quod in ~io, id est in olla, remansit *RBOssory (HMC)* 254; mensura latitudinis oris olle pro ~io fiendo W. WORC. *Itin.* 78; pone aquam .. in ~io et separa .. ab ea elementa RIPLEY 221.

destina [CL], prop, post. **b** lean-to.

sola illa ~a, cui incumbens [Aidan] obiit, ab ignibus .. absumi non potuit. .. unde, tertio aedificata ibi ecclesia, ~am illam non, ut antea, deforis in fulcimentum domus adposuerunt, sed intro ipsam ecclesiam in memoriam miraculi posuerunt BEDE *HE* III 17 p. 160; ~a vel postis vel fulcimen, *stipere* ÆLF. *Gl.*; evenit ut juvenis quidam .. tecta ecclesie .. invadendo conscenderet. .. cum manu altera .. ~e parietis clavum ligneum innitendo corriperet, mox pedibus cum subjectis virgultis avolantibus corruit R. COLD. *Cuthb.* 68. **b** in ecclesia .. Virginis mansitabat ..; cui etiam adhaerentem cellam sive ~am sive spelaeum sive alio quolibet nomine rectius nominari potest—non enim invenio qua id appellatione quam proxime vocem, cum non tam humani habitaculi quam formam gerat sepulcri—propriis laboribus fabricavit OSB. *V. Dunst.* 13.

destinare [CL]

1 to intend, appoint, assign; **b** (w. pers. obj.); **c** (w. inf.). **d** (absol. or w. inf.) to intend, purpose.

alius .. sagittarum spicula .. ad ~atum indeclinabiliter dirigit locum ALDH. *VirgP* 2; ubi ad locum ~atum morti venerat (*Passio Albani*) BEDE *HE* I 7; ~atus, i. missus, ordinatus, deputatus, vel *foreteohþad GlH* D 243 (cf. ib. D 688: distinat, i. disponit, contendit, mittit, *teohhaþ, asent*); †**948** (12c) hanc donationem ~avi ecclesiae Christi *CS* 860; **955** ut ex his [cassatis] binarum usus vernantibus ad ejus oracula monasterii, prout antiquitus ~abatur, indiscussus perseveret *CS* 903; s**1166** (v. concludere 1c); quibus .. monachis .. abbas .. quasdam .. observancias .. ~avit *Meaux* II 197 (cf. coenobialis). **b** praescivit famulos Omnipotens proprios, / destinat, amplificat hos *De libero arbitrio* 21; [Arturus] Piramum capellanum suum metropolitane sedi ~at G. MON. IX 8; Greci .. sortes in urnam ponebant et quos [sc. legatos] sors ~abat mittebant ALB. LOND. *DG* 9. 12. **c** c**1410** religio fulget monastica .. cum sic sue professionis alumpnos foveat et gubernet quod quosdam delicias ~at degustare claustrales, alios sudores disponit suscipere mundiales, nonnullos vero [etc.] *Form-Ox* 214. **d** dum erat in expeditione, jugulatus est, Morcanto ~ante NEN. *HB* 206; sin autem huc nunquam ~averit accedere LANTFR. *Swith.* 1; agmine toto / maximus innumeris fratres equare triumphis / destinat J. EXON. *BT* VI 489.

2 to send: **a** (gift or sim.); **b** (letter or sim.). **c** to dedicate.

a c**625** vobis direximus, .. speculum argenteum .., quod petimus ut eo benignitatis animo gloria vestra suscipiat quo a nobis noscitur ~atum (*Lit. Papae*) BEDE *HE* II 11; tria mala cum .. totidem rosis ad eundem Theophilum distinasse describitur ALDH. *VirgP* 47; Dei donum et subsidium eis divina providentia ~atum GIR. *TH* II 19; **1198** iiij anulos aureos .. tue magnitudini ~amus *Ep. Innoc. III* 1; s**1314** R. le Brus .. corpora comitis G. et baronis de C. .. regi Anglie .. pro sua voluntate sepelienda sine ullo precio ~avit TROKELOWE 87; nichil omnino preter panem et aquam comedet aut bibet, nisi illud tantummodo si quid ei a mensa fortasse fuerit ~atum *Cust. Cant.* 234 (cf. ib.: nisi ei aliquid commestibile a presidente ~etur). **b** c**710** utillimum duxi ad te .. has litteras ~are (BERHTWALD) *Ep. Bonif.* 7; **747** statuta .. quae hic sacerdotes nobiscum servanda decreverunt vobis emendanda et corrigenda distinamus BONIF. *Ep.* 78 p. 163; AD. MARSH *Ep.* 232 (v. deprecatorius 1c); **1295** receptis litteris vestris quas nobis ultimo ~astis (*Breve Regis*) *MGL* II 76; **1308** [rex Francie] multas et magnas nobis informaciones per nuncios et literas ~avit (*Lit. Papae*) W. GUISB. 388; **1327** litteram capituli nostri .. paternitati vestre .. †~amur [? l. ~amus] *Lit. Cant.* I 237. **c** fateor .. quod hoc opusculum .. ita perniciter ut sategistis dictare vobisque ~are nequiverim ALDH. *VirgP* 59; nulli libentius praesentem epistolam quam vestrae ~o sapientiae ANSELM (*Incarn.* 1) II 4; hujus Eulogii de pauperie mea gratie vestre ~ati J. CORNW. *Eul.* 21; in signum sue convalescencie quandam ymaginem cere apud Evesham ~avit *Mir. Montf.* 105.

3 to send, dispatch (person); **b** (in euphem. for death). **c** (absol.) to send for (a thing) or to (a place).

cui [sc. Britanniae] mox ~atur legio GILDAS *EB* 15; **a690** quia almae editum (*sic*) puerperae sobolem .. terris .. ~are dignatus est ALDH. *Ep.* 5; Colmanus .. primo venit ad insulam Hii, unde erat ad praedicandum verbum Anglorum genti ~atus BEDE *HE* IV 4; nuncios .. varias ad partes ~avit GIR. *RG* I 6; c**1210** decanum .. ad nos ~are curastis *Reg. Moray* 45; s**1213** rex Anglorum ~avit in succursum comitis .. fratrem suum [et alios] WEND. II 78; Oxonias ~atus *G. S. Alb.* II 299 (v. clericulus a); *Ps.*-ELMH. *Hen. V* 14 (v. ambasciatria). **b** s**1416** multis milibus perfidorum ad generum Cereris ~atis *Chr. S. Alb.* 98. **c 1241** dabunt eidem B. .. damos .. et damas .. quando ipsa B. racionabiliter pro eis ~averit *CurR* XVI 1408; rex .. ad civitatem Rotomagum .. ~avit, ut situm sciret civitatis STRECCHE *Hen. V* 167.

destinatio [LL], sending, dispatch.

misit [mulier] ad .. B. Wulfricum ut parceret ei ab egritudine hac et in aque sue benedicte ~one finem his malis imponeret J. FORD *Wulf.* 75; **1507** pro ~one duarum litterarum, ij d. (*Ac. W. Ingram*) *DCCant.* C 11 f. 115a.

destinator [LL], appointer, disposer (as title of Deity).

~orem .. excelsum .. precibus implorare debent quod .. ab eis futura mala avertat BACON V 61 (cf. BRADW. *CD* 42C).

destinctio, destinguere v. dist-.

†destinctus, *f. l.*

1204 †~a [? l. defuncta] Matillide, fuit Emma .. heres ejus *CurR* III 242.

destituere [CL]

1 to overthrow, undo.

~unt, *towuorpen*, ~tae, *toworpne GlC* D 30, 31; munera jus statuunt destituuntque simul NIG. *SS* 2596; sicut navis .. quatitur sine remige, sic regnum ~itur sine .. rege FORDUN *Cont.* X 1.

2 to abandon, leave uncared for. **b** (p. ppl.) deserted, destitute.

~it, *obgibeht GlC* D 24; sique ferae silvas piscesque marina fluenta / destituant *Altercatio* 10; W. MALM. *GR* II 165 (v. colligere 2b); horrea farciuntur; sola vero granaria ~untur GIR. *TH* I 5; si petis quo pacto suppetet antiquitatum copia posteris, quae nos ~erit, indicabo paucis FERR. *Kinloss pref.* 3. **b** distitutum, *ofgefen GlC* D 339; modo sunt ibi c domus, et xx sunt ita ~tae quod qui in eis manent geldum solvere non valent *DB* I 75; **1435** vestre gracie, ad cujus succursum .. habere solebant ~ti refrigerium juvaminis *FormOx* 445.

3 to cause to lack, to deprive (of): **a** (w. abl.); **b** (w. *ab*); **c** (w. *de*). **d** (p. ppl. w. gen.) destitute (of), devoid (of).

a quod .. ~ta pontifice provincia recte pariter divino fuerit ~ta praesidio BEDE *HE* III 7; *RegulC* 2 (v. coenobium); amicis ~tus [AS: *freondleas*] (*Quad.*) *GAS* 286 (v. consacramentalis); G. CRISPIN *Herl.* 104 (v. ducamen 1); **s1094** abbatie quamplures sunt in hac terra suis pastoribus ~te EADMER *HN* 57; **1259** salvo statu R. abbatis Glaston', ita quod sua possessione per hoc preter debitum exitum cause sue non distituatur *Cl* 411; **s1301** rex .. per Scotorum incursionem .. pecunia .. ~itur *Ann. Ed. I* 454; **1549** (v. deductio 6); **1550** (v. deprivatio). **b** orbatus, a fetibus ~tus *GlC* O 249; videbatur Haly quod sanguis, cum sit amicus nature, non possit putrefieri neque ~i a regimine nature, manens sanguis; sed, si accidat in eo destitutio, ut .. subtile ipsius convertitur in coleram [etc.] GILB. I 28v. 1 (cf. ib.: aduritur subtile ipsius [sanguinis] et ~itur a natura); BACON *Maj.* I 381 (v. deteriorare 1b); **1269** quod .. a communa quam habere debent .. ~antur contra legem *Cl* 112. **c** **c1380** cum de equo fueram ~tus, michi unum equum .. accommodasti *FormOx* 326; **1460** (v. de 1f). **d** **c1380** certis consociis taliter mutuavi quod pecunie permaneo ~tus *FormOx* 322.

4 to 'destitute', depose (esp. eccl.).

1239 invenit quedam que tenebantur per quosdam de familia imperiali, quibus non pepercit, sed eos statim ~it, restituens ~tos (*Responsio Imperialis*) M. PAR. *Maj.* III 553; *Obed. Abingd.* 395 (v. coquinarius 3b); **1261** compositio .. super .. modo instituendi et ~endi priores seu administratores in cella [B. Marie de Piltona] *Reg. Malm.* II 78; **1283** potestatem .. servitores .. retinendi, ponendi sive substituendi et eos ~endi et mutandi *RGasc* II 198; **s1327** allegabat .. archiepiscopus .. quod in multis casibus non potuit episcopus Dunelm' visitare [Allertonschir], quia nec ibi instituit nec ~it .. nec aliquid mere episcopale ibi exercet GRAYSTANES 42; nec instituere nec ~ere reges spectat ad papam OCKHAM *Pol.* I 85; **1372** [capellani] fuerunt instituti et ~ti .. per rectorem de W. *Reg. Lond.* I 209; **1427** quod nullam potestatem habuit .. archidiaconus Thewidalie clericos sui archidiaconatus deprivandi .. nec [debet] ipsos in beneficiis constituere nec ~ere sine mandato .. episcopi *Reg. Glasg.* 320.

5 *f. l.*

anima tres habet cellulas suis operationibus †destitutas [? l. constitutas *or* destinatas] *Quaest. Salern.* N 1.

destitutio [LL < CL = *desertion, betrayal*]

1 a deprivation, denial (of right or sim.). **b** deprived or destitute condition, sorry state. **c** (in word-play) undoing.

a si quisquam violenta recti ~one vel detentione in hundretis .. causam suam .. turbaverit .. (*Leg. Hen.* 7. 6) *GAS* 553; **1433** qui in ~onem sive destruccionem alieni privilegii talem procurat clausulam inseri .. (*Replicatio Abbatis*) AMUND. I 341. **b** R. COLD. *Cuthb.* 96 (v. desolatorius a); **1237** voluimus reformare statum [ecclesie Romane], ut sepe temptavimus; et ecce deformis ~o subintravit! (*Lit. Cardinalis*) M. PAR. *Maj.* III 445; **1328** imbecillitas corporis manifesta et membrorum ~o intolerabilis necnon alia senectutis incommoda *Lit. Cant.* I 271; **s743** Cuthbertus .. archiepiscopus .., animadvertens ~onem ecclesie cum presidebat, eo quod nullo honorabilis sepulture decore fulgebat THORNE 1772 (= ELMH. *Cant.* 317). **c** tres constituciones seu pocius ~ones hereticales .. legi et studui OCKHAM *Pol.* III 6 (cf. ib. 213: in iiij ~onibus Joannis XXII predictis).

2 'destitution' (from office), deposition (esp. eccl.).

c1158 institutionem et ~onem prioris Dovoriensis successorum .. reservamus arbitrio *Lit. Cant.* III app. 371; **1239** (v. degradatio 1b); **1325** institucio et ~o, visitacio quoque .. et .. omnimoda .. jurisdiccio .. pertinens ad episcopum Norwycensem *Lit. Cant.* I 153; **1340** ejus [magistri domus de B.] institucionem, eleccionem seu ~onem *Deeds Balliol* 287; ad quem pertinet institucio alicujus, ad eundem ~o spectat ejusdem OCKHAM *Dial.* 578; **1423** instituciones et ~ones beneficiorum *Reg. Cant.* III 516; **14..** [bulla] de institucionibus vel distitucionibus abbatum *Couch. Furness* I 109.

destitutorius, associated w. 'destitution' of official. *Cf. destituere* 4.

omne emolumentum institutorium vel ~ium quod de maneriis coquine assignatis progreditur .. coquinario deputatur *Obed. Abingd.* 392.

destornare v. distornare b. **destractus** v. destruere 3. **destrare** v. desternere. **destrarius** v. dextrarius. **destrauere** v. destruere 4a.

destrescia [AN *destresce*, OF *destrece* < *districtia], distress (leg.), distraint. *V. et* 3 *districtio* 5.

1194 curia recordata est summoniciones et ~ias ipsi R. rationabiliter factas *CurR RC* I 48.

destrib-, destric-, destring- v. distr-.

destringere [CL = *to strip off*]

1 (leg.) to distrain, compel by distraint (w. pers. obj.); **b** (w. *ad*); **c** (w. inf.). *V. et.* 2 *distringere* 5.

1253 comes .. vicecomites ~ere possit per terras *RGasc* I 277. **b** non possunt [domini] ad id [sc. werram suam manutenendam] tenentes ~ere de jure GLANV. IX 8; **1264** homines .. ad obsidionem .. faciendam nullatenus ~as vel eis super hoc molestiam inferas *Cl* 80. **c** **a1210** si ille qui [thelonum de burgensi K.] ceperit reddere .. contradixerit, per namia ejusdem loci unde ipse est, si inventa fuerint apud K., reddere ~atur *BBC* (*Kilkenny*) 196.

2 to distrain (property). *V. et.* 2 *distringere* 6a.

c1215 se nobis .. obligavit quod nunquam pro re aliqua predictans eleemosynam ~eret *Meaux* I 367; *BNB* II 229 (v. 2 distringere 6a); concedimus quod ballivi .. ~ant .. tenementa pro predicto redditu *Cust. Battle* 25; **1363** pro quibus [denariis] ~ere poterunt .. super terris de dote primaria ipsius cantarie *Lit. Cant.* III 63.

destructibilis, destructible.

nulla causa potest destruere aliquod ens propter repugnanciam sui effectus ad illud nisi suo effectui perfeccius et intensius esse det quam sit esse illius alterius ~is [v. l. destruibilis] DUNS *Ord.* II 171; quis non irracionabilior bestia posuerit bestiam Deum suum .. aut .. rem non omnipotentem sed debilem .., passibilem, interfectibilem, ~em eciam? BRADW. *CD* 10A.

destructilis [LL], destructible.

~em, *towyrpendlicne GlP* 462.

destructio [CL]

1 unbuilding, demolition; **b** (w. ref. to *burhbote*).

cum .. responsum accepisset nidos eorum ubique destruendos .., de castellis Norwagiensium hoc interpretantes .. in eorum ~onem Hibernienses .. insurrexerunt GIR. *TH* III 42; **1497** si aliquis .. reparaverit, edificaverit seu, ut vulgariter dicitur, imposuerit dictum *le Fisshgart* aut rumpat aut distruat, pro non attemptato reputabitur .., sic quod reparacio seu distruccio dicti *le Fysshgart* non impediat reformacionem aliorum attemptatorum *RScot* 533b. **b** **811** pontis instructionem contra paganos expeditionem atque arcis munitionem distructionemve *CS* 335; **822** nisi is iiij causis .., expeditione contra paganos ostes et pontes (*sic*) constructione seu arcis munitione vel ~one *Ib.* 370.

2 destruction, devastation; **b** (w. subj. gen.). **c** loss or (?) *f. l.*

nolebat de ipso manerio aliquid comedere pro ~one abbatiae *DB* I 164; **c1176** querela vestra super ~one et desolatione monasterii vestri (*Lit. Papae*) ELMH. *Cant.* 413; **1322** lamentabili .. indigencie .. quam scolaribus aule de Baliolo .. per terrarum suarum ~onem et bonorum derepcionem Scotorum intulit .. rabies *FormOx* 77; **1336** (v. deperdere 1e); **1347** ~ones ecclesiarum, monasteriorum, ac locorum sanctorum (*Lit. Papae*) AVESB. 111; abstinentia [in rege] .. cujus contrarium fuit causa ~onis regni Caldeorum *Quadr. Reg. Spec.* 32. **b** **1336** de x s. receptis de pomario .. et non plus propter ~onem guerre (*KRAc* 331/21) *Cal. Scot.* III 320. **c** **1327** dispendiosa destruccio [? l. distractio] vasorum argenteorum *Lit. Cant.* I 225 (cf. ib.: de vasis .. fraudulenter sublatis).

3 (leg.) waste.

1220 Maria .. fecit vastum et ~onem de gardino ipsius T. *CurR* VIII 358; **1221** vastum, exilium vel ~onem non facient de terris, hominibus vel boscis ejusdem manerii *Pat* 291; **1239** teneant prefatam pasturam .. libere et quiete absque ~one *BBC* (*Leicester*) 72; **1265** custodes vastum non possunt facere neque venditionem neque aliquam distructionem de hereditate illa (*Ch. Regis*) *Reg. Malm.* I 47; utrum dominus de residuo boscorum .. aliquid dare possit .. sine destruxcione facienda *FormMan* 26; **1427** absque impechiamento vasti seu distruccionis *Cart. Glam.* 1534.

4 (of persons) crushing, ruin.

1321 cum .. magnates .. occupassent castra .. et incarcerassent homines .. et alia plura fecissent in ~onem predictorum Hugonis et Hugonis [Dispensatorum] et amicorum suorum (*Act. Parl.*) G. *Ed. II Bridl.* 72 (= *StRealm* I 185: *en destruantz H. le D.* [etc.]); **s1340** comes Hannonie .. et alii .. in ~onem rebellium a dicta obsidione egredientes AVESB. 91b.

5 (of abstr.) impairment, subversion, abolition.

idem est principium remissionis forme et ~onis ejusdem; sed veniale non est principium ~onis caritatis; ergo nec remissionis HALES *Sent.* III 352; **1253** apostolice sedis sanctitas non potest nisi que in edificationem sunt et non ~onem GROS. *Ep.* 128 p. 437; **13..** asserentes eadem [recia] esse falsa in ~onem commoditatis aque Thamisie *MGL* I 385; quantum ad dictum de pictaciis, patet quod distruccio et exposicio scripture .. per talia additamenta est satis laudabilis WYCL. *Ver.* I 307.

destructivus [LL], destructive; **b** (log.).

ut quid igitur hec ciborum ~a refectio fiat semel sane constituto corpore? ADEL. *QN* 45; alia mala que .. sunt contraria sanitati, ~a corporis, corruptiva nature BACON V 68; **1363** ne scintilla tenuis ex desidia prelatorum in flammam transeat ~am *Doc. Eng. Black Monks* II 72; **c1370** 'estus Saturni', i. calor inordinatus sive ~us causatus ex natura Saturni (J. BRIDL. *gl.*) *Pol. Poems* I 209; filios dyaboli .. regnorum et dominorum temporalium ~os WYCL. *Sim.* 88. **b** BACON XV 322 (v. 2 constructivus).

destructor [LL], destroyer.

~ores ecclesiarum populique perversores abigebat WILLIB. *Bonif.* 7 p. 37; **†943** (14c) si quis .. donationis hujus ~or existere conatus fuerit, deleatur nomen ejus libro viventium *CS* 785; voti sui .. est violator et sancte, quam tenere promisit, hac in parte regule ~or AD. SCOT *OP* 545C; tales defensores, seu potius ecclesiarum ~ores, abbates se vocari fecere GIR. *IK* II 4 (cf. defensor 1a); qui fundit regni sui bona immoderate .., talis est depopulator reipublice, ~or regni, indignus et incompetens regimini BACON V 43; papa hereticus .., ~or ecclesie et subversor OCKHAM *Dial.* 600.

destructorius, destructive. **b** (as. sb. n.) destroyer (in title of book by Alexander Carpentarius).

solebat .. Peripateticus Palatinus [sc. Abailardus] omnibus his conditionibus obviare, ubi non sequentis intellectum antecedentis conceptio claudit aut non antecedentis contrarium consequentis ~ia ponit J. SAL. *Pol.* 453C; me .. sic emendes .. ne de me dicatur: 'destruxisti eum ab emundatione' [*Psalm* lxxxviii 45]; ~ius potius quam purgatorius mihi erit ille ignis terribilis, si expectavero eum P. BLOIS *Serm.* 49. 704D. **b** **1496** item ~ium Viciorum (*Invent.*) *Cant. Coll. Ox.* I 82 (cf. ib. 107).

destructus, demolition.

hic [S. de Islep, ob. **1366**] palacium Cantuariense, receptis ab executoribus J. archiepiscopi pro ~ibus domorum m marcis, fecit nobiliter reparari BIRCHINGTON *Arch. Cant.* 43.

destruere [CL]

1 to unbuild, demolish, uproot, smash.

[Martinus] paganorum destruxit fana profana, / jure tyrannorum sternens dilubra reorum ALDH. *VirgV* 690; pontifex ipse .. polluit ac ~xit eas quas ipse sacraverat aras BEDE *HE* II 13; elimino i. distruo limitem, .., expello, .. *ic ut anyde* vel *drife* vel *adyde GlH* E 192; G. AMIENS *Hast.* 678 (v. aggeries); aliae [masurae] sunt ~ctae in nova hospitatione archiepiscopi *DB* I 3v.; [Arturus] ecclesias usque ad solum ~ctas renovat G. MON. IX 8; BACON *Tert.* 46 (v. combustio 2b); **1320** tenementa vacua et distructa per longa tempora *Reg. S. Aug.* 372; **1356** cancellarius .. mensuras et pondera .. que falsa invenerit ~i faciat *MunAcOx* 178; **1497** (v. destructio 1a).

2 to destroy, devastate, ravage. **b** (w. *de*) to deprive, clear (of). **c** to kill (animals).

s1069 civitas Eboraca et tota regio circa .. a Francigenis ferro, fame, flamma ~cta est H. CANTOR 1; G. *Steph.* II 104 (v. conflagratio); **1219** facit ponere equas suas in bladis suis et ea penitus pascit et ~it *CurR* VIII 41; **1220** scidit et ~xit vij^xx^ arbores *Ib.* 358; **1278** bestie tocius villate ~xerunt omnes pisas crescentes super acram .. vicarii *SelPlMan* 90; **13..** oves .. segetes .. usque in terram ~entes *Pri. Cold.* 83. **b** **c1250** foresta de Carreck [*Westmor*] ~cta est de bestiis per forestarios, per canes et archeream et pro multitudine vaccariarum *CalIMisc* I 144; **1268** quia .. parci sui .. sunt ~cti de venacione *Cl* 4. **c** **12..** ibunt in forestam .., quando lupi habent catulos, ad illos capiendos et distruendos *DL Forest Proc.* 1/5 r. 14d.; **1285** quod salmunculi non capiantur nec ~antur per recia .. a medio April' usque ad Nativitatem S. J. Baptiste (2 *Westm.* 47) *StRealm* I 94.

3 (w. pers. obj.) to harass, crush, ruin.

exaltavit archiepiscopus dictam villam ad xvj li. [redditus]; et ideo .. est villa †destracta [? l. destructa] et homines †destracti *RDomin* 3; combustis urbibus et colonis ~ctis M. PAR. *Maj.* I 276 (= G. MON. XII 4: colonos .. tormentis affecit); **s1188** ~cti sunt Judei per Angliam *Leg. Ant. Lond.* 1; OCKHAM *Pol.* III 39 (v. confundere 3c); **s1349** (v. depauperare 1a); **1457** Christo, qui .. ~xit exercitum Magni Turchi *Reg. Whet.* I 278.

4 (w. abstr. obj.) to frustrate, impair, abolish. **b** (log.) to refute.

non ~amus illud quod consuetudo est in hac terra THEOD. *Pen.* II 6. 8; ut .. / .. regnum caeli, destructa

fraude maligni, / aedificet ALDH. *VirgV* 316; ~ctum regni statum recuperavit BEDE *HE* IV 24 p. 268; c**745** Dei opus ~i quaerunt (DAN. WINT.) *Ep. Bonif.* 64; **956** (12c) hoc donum .. ~iturus (*sic*) .. praecipitetur in Cociti palude *CS* 938; c**1102** in monasterio .., ubi minimi excessus negliguntur, ibi totus ordo paulatim dissipatur et ~itur ANSELM (*Ep.* 231) IV 137; si per veniale diminueretur caritas, ergo tot possent esse venialia quod totaliter ~eretur caritas HALES *Sent.* III 352; GILB. I 3. 2 (v. coaequalitas a); c**1375** nisi consiliarii odiant, immo †destrauant, avariciam primo in seipsis BRINTON *Serm.* 204. **b** ANSELM *Gram.* 21, J. SAL. *Met.* 906C (v. astruere 3a); BACON XV 322 (v. 2 constructivus); contra istas tres raciones simul instatur quod seipsas ~ant DUNS *Ord.* I 43; s**1406** predicavit .. magister T. Alkertone .. et ~xit racionibus evidentibus omnes prioris argucias *Chr. S. Alb.* 2.

destruibilis v. destructibilis. **destruxcio** v. destructio 3. **destulisse** v. differre 4b. **desturb-** v. disturb-. **desuadere** v. dissuadere.

desub [CL, al. div.], (prep. w. abl.): **a** from under, from beneath. **b** under, beneath. **c** below, downstream from.

a occurrunt filii protractumque de sub mensa thalamis inferunt AILR. *Ed. Conf.* 767B; ea pietas que hominem adjudicatum morti de sub manu ferientis eripuit *Id. SS Hex prol.* 175; tener pullus nuper progressus de sub alis maternis R. COLD. *Cuthb.* 133; de sub lapide eductus submersus emersit W. CANT. *Mir. Thom.* III 41; de sub pede montis .. tres .. fluvii nascuntur GIR. *TH* I 7; s**1252** sic .. de sub jugo Domini colla .. excusserunt [cf. *Gen.* xxvii 40] M. PAR. *Maj.* V 279; s**1257** nos de sub celo delere proponit *Ib.* 646; **1294** traxit de sub manto suo quandam cedulam *Reg. North.* 110; *G. Hen. V* 6 (v. 1 canella 2b). **b** c**1145** dedisse .. ecclesiam B. Marie de Hod cum terra et bosco ~b proximis montibus (*Ch. Newburgh*) *CalPat 1388–92* 161; c**1215** dim. acram ~b Atehil *Cart. Wardon* 38; philosopho .. inebriato .. librum de sub capite positum surripuit *Meaux* I 269 (= W. MALM. *GR* II 167: sub cervicali); de sub canopeo in trono quodam effigies magestatis in corpore solari .. rutilabat *G. Hen. V* 15 p. 110; **1436** una acra jacet ad crucem et ad spinam inter B. et N. ~b chimino et abuttat in chiminum *Cart. Osney* IV 303. **c** Nene .. extendit se .. ad Medeswell et ~b burgo *Tract. Peterb. & Ramsey* 209.

desubitare [cf. CL desubito], to take by surprise, attack suddenly.

si canis hominem ~et [AS: *toslite*] aut mordeat tacitus, in prima culpa reddantur vj s. (*Quad.*) *GAS* 63; si quis arcu vel balista ~anti vel pedico ad lupos .. capiendum posito dampnum .. recipiat, solvat qui posuit (*Leg. Hen.* 90. 2) *GAS* 605; non preoccupati, non ~ati, non adventus hujus ignari, quinimmo prescii potius et premuniti GIR. *IK* I 4; †desubitos [l. desubitatos] et improvisos nec .. tale timentes statim trucidaverunt universos *Id. PI* I 18 p. 97.

desubitatio, sudden attack.

de canum disubitatione [AS: *slite*] vel morsu (*Quad. rub.*) *GAS* 19; cujus inopinati eventus et ~onis causa .. in fugam sunt conversi GIR. *EH* I 21 (cf. ib. 4: nulla unquam violentia vel inopinata nulla preoccupatione, nulla ~one, .. animo consternatus).

desubitus v. desubitare.

desubter [LL, al. div.], (prep.): **a** (w. acc.) from beneath. **b** (w. abl.) beneath.

a exsiliens mater pueri .. de subter beluam .. contritum eripuit W. CANT. *Mir. Thom.* III 37. **b** viri .. gladiis ~er operimentis accincti R. COLD. *Cuthb.* 60.

desubtrahere, to remove.

to alyene, alienare, privare, ~ere, removere *CathA*.

desubtus [LL, al. div.]

1 (adv.) below. **b** here below, on earth.

a**1155** et inde sicut Glendi descendit in moram ~us per medium cacumen montis *MonA* III 265a; a**1190** sicut Pakedenbroc descendit in Ribbel ~us *Cart. Sallay* 124; c**1236** tantum terre †wannabilis [? l. wainiabilis] et prati quantum habui in Hethul ~us *FormA* 184; *Obs. Barnwell* 46 (v. 1 dependere 1c). **b** ecce duplex .. bonum ..: unum de subtus sumptum ad necessitatem in tempore; aliud desuper accipiendum ad felicitatem sine fine AD. SCOT *TGC* 838A.

2 (prep.): **a** (w. abl.) from beneath. **b** (w. abl.) beneath, below. **c** (w. acc.) below.

a s**1458** quia lucerna regiminis .. avunculi mei, ecclesie .. de Tynemutha prioris, que .. sub modio occultacionis delituit [cf. *Mark* iv 21 etc.], .. jam .. de subtus modio tollitur reponiturque .. super candelabrum *Reg. Whet.* I 312. **b** panno serico ~us reliquiis †positis [? l. posito] R. COLD. *Cuthb.* 35; **1255** cum .. supra muros veteres suburbii Burdegale, prout extenduntur a porta de subtus muro usque ad portam de A., domos .. construxisset *RGasc* I sup. 33. **c** a**1184** pratum illud de subtus pomarium de versus *west* ad caput culture *Cart. Sallay* 617.

desudanter, vigorously.

in agro progressus, operi suo ~er institit R. COLD. *Godr.* 124.

desudare [CL]

1 to sweat. **b** to exude moisture. **c** to succumb to sweating sickness.

usque ad nivatas .. rupium saxaces ~antes scandere conabant HUGEB. *Wynn.* 2; ~ans, *swætende GlH* D 313; redeunt .. per medium flamme .. inveniuntque B. Paulum .. quasi ~antem COGGESH. *Visio* 17; quare quidam comedendo ~ant et quidam non? *Quaest. Salern.* K 7. **b** si venereum opus .. prope fieri contigerit .., statim lapis guttis magnis ~abit GIR. *IK* II 7 p. 128; s**1313** decedente .. archiepiscopo .., ~ant oculi .. ecclesiasticorum et uberius resolvuntur in lacrimis *Flor. Hist.* III 154. **c** s**1508** saeviebat .. per omnia loca sudifica lues. principis quoque familiarium aliquot ~averunt; nec fuga tunc proderat .., quoniam mors omnia vincit ANDRÉ *Hen. VII* 128.

2 to labour (at); **b** (w. dat.); **c** (w. inf.).

in practicae conversationis studio ~ans ALDH. *VirgP* 29; spiritali agone ~antibus BEDE *Sam.* 613; ~ans, i. laborans, *winnende GlH* D 313; ne generi nostro obprobrium sit nos debiles fuisse rectores qui .. in id non ~avimus [v. l. ~averimus] G. MON. XII 6 (cf. RISH. 450); s**1195** rapinis, cedibus, incendiis populus atterebatur Christianus. .. eo namque tempore sub disciplina Domini ~abat W. NEWB. *HA* V 17; **1438** (v. congregare 2c). **b** ~ans cuicumque sciencie OCKHAM *Dial.* 802. **c** s**1293** premisit magnates .. in Vasconiam et ipse eos sequi continuo ~avit *Meaux* II 258.

3 (trans.) to elaborate, produce by labour.

commentariola .. quae praefatus divinae legis interpres .. ~a[vi]t ALDH. *VirgP* 49; **800** in quo [Felicis libello] multa inveniuntur .. contra veritatem apostolicae fidei inaniter ~ata ALCUIN *Ep.* 202; **811** has .. terrulas ideo collegere .. curavi ut facilius elaborare ac ~are sua propria in illis potuissent *CS* 332.

desudatio [CL], sweating, exudation.

quedam sunt accidentia morbi, ut calor et sudor ..; et quedam sunt supervenientia, ut dolor capitis .. et emunctiones plurime et sine causa facilis ~o GILB. I 33. 1; dicit Remigius quod a muliere procedit magis ~o quam semen *Ib.* VII 289. 2.

desuescere [CL], **desuēre**

1 to grow disaccustomed (to); **b** (trans.).

~evit, in [in] consuetudinem exit *GlC* D 173; cibi viliores .. gustantis palato dulcius sapiebant, eo forte quod diutius quippiam ora illius degustasse dissueverant R. COLD. *Cuthb.* 118; licet feminas videre non prohibemur, consilium tamen est ut videre dissuescamus AD. SCOT *OP* 534C; GARL. *Syn.* 584 (v. dormitare a); *to be unwonte*, dessuere, dessuescere, dissolere *CathA*. **b** ALCUIN *Carm.* 62. 29 (v. consuescere 1c); morbos cupiditatis si non potes opprimere, paululum dissue W. DONC. *Aph. Phil.* 12. 3; vitam quam hactenus assueverat nec ~escere novit nec descire GIR. *TH* III 10.

2 (p. ppl.): **a** unaccustomed. **b** unwonted, unfamiliar, contrary to custom.

a OSB. GLOUC. *Deriv.* 178 (v. desuetudo a); **1454** dissueti (v. assuescere 1b). **b** armorum gravitate dissuetorum pene suffocatur MAP *NC* IV 7 f. 51; est gravius quicquid desuetius H. AVR. *Poems* 20. 119; **1295** districcionem indebitam et hactenus dissuetam *Reg. Cant.* 23; **1325** nostris fratribus dissuetum et verecundum videtur ecclesiam nostram matricem .. sine culpa nostra supponere .. interdicto *Lit. Cant.* I 144.

desuetio, desuetude.

nolam .. quales bestiarum collo applicare solet antiquitas, ne in ~one insolescant *Found. Waltham* 5.

desuetudo [CL], desuetude, disuse. **b** unfamiliarity.

~o, quod aliquem desuetum facit OSB. GLOUC. *Deriv.* 178; hec [ars demonstrativa] utentium raritate jam fere in ~inem abiit J. SAL. *Met.* 919D (cf. ib.: ~ine exemplorum); imperatoris constitutionem invito populo .. fieri contingit et valet. ergo et durat, ut nec per ~inem abrogari possit nisi prius .. potestatem a principe amotam populus recipiat VAC. *Lib. Paup.* 15; VINSAUF *AV* II 3. 163 (v. comoedia a); **1222** nec vellemus quod herbergagia que nobis debetis per diuturnitatem temporis in dissuetudinem deducerentur *Pat* 355; **1281** ordinacionem .. a dissuetudine revocantes *Conc. Syn.* 900; **1328** hoc pocius sonat in dissuetudinem quam in consuetudinem seu libertatem *MGL* I 442; que sola consuetudine stabilitatem accipiunt, hec necesse est ~ine dirimantur R. BURY *Phil.* 11. 173. **b** aeris mutatio, ciborum dissuetudo et corporis exercitium .. †timorem [*ed.*: tumorem] vulneris innovabant W. CANT. *Mir. Thom.* II 27.

desultare [LL], to jump down. **b** (fig.) to gallop through, summarize.

to lepe down, desilire, ~are *CathA*. **b** **1457** arduis negociis implicatus ..; non possum omnia ~are *Reg. Whet.* I 278.

desultor [CL], rider who jumps from one horse to another.

~ores, †sive [l. sc.] nominati quod de equo in equum transiliebant *GlH* D 314.

desumere [CL], to select. **b** (w. *damnum*) (?) to effect a subtraction through loss.

1579 testimoniis e sacra scriptura aut interdum e patribus ~ptis *StatOx* 413. **b** pecus omnigenum pastoris munere demptum / in numero dampnum gregibus desumere nescit ÆTHELWULF *Abb.* 494.

desuper [CL, al. div.]

1 (adv.): **a** from above. **b** from on high (*i. e.* from God). **c** above, on top. **d** thereon.

a aspexit .. fusam ~er lucem omnia replevisse BEDE *HE* IV 21 p. 257; c**1192** si pro defectu fundamenti .. domus ~er cadat *Cart. Osney* II 9. **b** c**710** misso ~er Spiritu (*Ep. Ceolfridi*) BEDE *HE* V 21 p. 340; unde causaliter vel infra vel ~er ortum habeat GIR. *TH* II 13; **1416** eandem [sc. ecclesiam Norwic'] secundum discrecionem vobis ~er concessam tanquam sponsam divinitus datam dirigere studeatis *Reg. Cant.* I 33. **c** extento ~er papilione BEDE *HE* IV 17 p. 245; illa aecclesia est ~er patula et sine tectu HUGEB. *Will.* 4; altare sit ~er coopertum uno tantum lintheamine LANFR. *Const.* 114; D. BEC. 1287 (v. coopercu-lum 2c); **1285** (v. 1 constabularia 3). **d** mensam adposuit, praeparato cibo ~er quem habebat *V. Cuthb.* II 2; a**1130** concessit .. terram .. ad construendum ~er monasterium *Chr. Rams.* 259; **1252** unam fenestram ad warderobam nostram cum columpna et sede et uno banco ad reliquias nostras ~er ponendas *Liberate* 29 m. 13; **1270** totam terram cum edificiis ~er constructis *Reg. S. Bees* 309; **1342** cum hwarvagio unius hwarve et trium seudarum ~er existencium *IPM* 67/2 r. 9; **1386** j vestimentum rubeum de *velvet* cum *le Veronike* in granis rosarum ~er broudata *FormA* 428 (cf. ib. 429: unus alius equus .. cum uno homine ~er pro banerio meo); **1409** situm pro nova forgea ~er edificanda (*Aud. Durh.*) *EHR* XIV 517.

2 (adv.): **a** in addition; *cf. superplus*. **b** 'thereanent', on that matter.

a pratum x carucarum et xx s. ~er plus *DB* I 130v. **b** *Bened. Rob.* 80 (v. deintus 1c); **1453** quociescunque questio oritur ~er *Conc.* III 569; **1469** ut patet per indenturam ~er confectam *ExchScot* 621; **1504** in quibusdam indenturis .. ~er confectis *Cl* 364 m. 30d.

3 (prep.) above, upon, on to: **a** (w. abl.); **b** (w. acc.).

a ependiton, .. omnis vestis ~er aliis vestibus pendens *Gl. Leid.* 3. 56; in fornicibus ecclesie ~er tegulis se abscondit R. COLD. *Cuthb.* 82; **1327** in corbellis .. ~er turre (v. 2 corbellus 2a). **b** corpus .. adposuerunt ~er arcam BEDE (*CuthbP* 43) *HE* IV 28 p. 277; pollice ~er manubrium in longum extenso GIR. *TH* III 10; c**1180** croftam unam ~er villam de B. *FormA* 154; c**1220** concessi .. tres rodas ~er viam de H. *Cart. Sallay* 580; **1260** ascendendo .. usque ~er viam que vocatur le Haggestrete *Cl* 22; s**1346** rex Anglie cum exercitu suo venit ~er Cressy *Eul. Hist.* III 210; **1382** domum .. que sita est ~er viam regiam et quandam semitam .. *Comp. Swith.* 153; ~er pedem pontis in transversum itineris elevatur turris *G. Hen. V* 15; **1451** tonsuram ~er aures .. sibi fieri procurent (*Abbr. Stat.*) *Mon. Francisc.* II 89.

4 (prep. w. abl.) through, after, on account of.

qui pacem facit cum aliquo de vulnere .. quod inflixerit, distincte cum testibus .. finiat, ut ei sc. non requiratur .. quicquid postea contingat. sepe etenim fatigatio secuta est ~er natura, quae sanitatem intempestam doloribus obduxerit (*Leg. Hen.* 70. 11a) *GAS* 588.

desupra [LL, al. div.], (prep.) above. **b** (?) over and above.

a**1195** ~a crohas (v. croa). **b** **1441** computat solut' diversis fratribus .. pro pensionibus suis .., viz. cuilibet eorum c s. .. et solut' .. gardiano pro pensione sua .. cum xxx s. de supra solut' preceterum (*sic*) fratrum vj li. x s. *Cant. Coll. Ox.* II 160.

desurso v. sursa.

desursum [LL, al. div.]

1 (adv.): **a** from above; **b** from on high (*i. e.* from God). *V. et. esursum.*

a s**1261** tecto turris ex fulmine ~um in summitate incenso *Flor. Hist.* II 473; dicta est epiphania ab *epi* quod est 'supra' et *phanos* 'apparicio', quasi ~um facta apparicio, quasi per stellam HIGD. IV 5 p. 334 (cf. appritio 3d). **b** de his quae .. donis ~um perfecta .. descendunt [cf. *James* i 17] *V. Greg.* p. 80; a quo omne .. donum perfectum ~um descendit AD. SCOT *Serm.* 310B; **1198** per eam que ~um est sapientiam vestram [cf. *James* iii 15] *Ep. Cant.* 452; dicunt alii .. quod de sursum illabitur potius ad superna referri .. debere GIR. *DK pref.* p. 156; impetrant ~um [ME: *adun*] adjutorium .. Dei *AncrR* 90; **1474** ~um datum est ut inter nos et .. regem Scotorum .. tractatus haberetur *RScot* 444b.

2 (adv.): **a** up, upwards; **b** upstream.

a frater ille ~um se erexit R. COLD. *Cuthb.* 89 p. 191. **b** a**1260** stagnum [molendini] .. ulterius protendere et firmare ~um vel deorsum *Deed Bishop's Tawton* (*Devon R. O.*).

3 (prep.): **a** (w. abl.) above; **b** up (a stream) or upstream of.

a c**1260** magnum orreum Walentonie habet .. in altitudine sub trabe xxj pedes et dim., et ~um trabe xij pedes *Dom. S. Paul.* 130. **b** c**1200** a †dintello de Westerdene ~um Hameldun usque ad aquam Line et ~um Westerden' per transversum usque ad sursum †dintelli G. *Reg. Glasg.* I 75 (= ib. 74: *desus* Homeldon'; cf. duitellus); c**1400** in terra pertinente superiori molendino ~um aqua et deorsum *AncD* A 10323.

desutus v. 1 dissuere 1d. **deswarennare** v. diswarennare. **desyntiria** v. dysenteria.

detalea, ~ium [AN *detaille*, OF *detail*; cf. talea], retail. *V. et. retalea.*

1155 nullus in civitate C. vendat pannos per detaillum nisi sit de gilda mercatorum *BBC (Chichester)* 209; **1293** nec clamant mercandisas .. civitati [London'] ducere .. nisi per certam custumam .. et non ad vendendum .. extraneis mercatoribus ad revendendum, neque in grosso neque per detalliam (*Recog. Mercatorum Provinciae*) *MGL* II 70; **1421** ad detallium (v. beveragium a).

detectio [CL]

1 removal (of tiles), unroofing.

?**1471** tegulas .. juxta gutteram .. contigue jacentes ab eadem domo ipsorum R. et J. pro reparacione guttere .. ceperunt .., que quidem ~o tegularum est eadem fraccio domus .. unde .. R. et J. tulerunt accionem *Entries* 619b.

2 uncovering, unveiling.

quod crux velatur; quod fit detectio festo / Parasceves GARL. *Myst. Eccl.* 278; BACON IX 70 (v. detegere 2a).

3 disclosure, revelation. **b** (w. *caeli*) apocalypse. **c** (geographical) discovery.

s**651** rex Oswine .. Hunwaldi proditus ~one .. a prefecto suo .. peremptus est FL. WORC. I 20; lux est manifestatio et ~o coloris J. BLUND *An.* 149 (cf. ib. 122); est .. manumissio datio libertatis, id est ~o secundum quosdam, quia libertas que est de jure naturali per jus gentium auferri non potuit, licet per jus gentium fuerit obfuscata BRACTON 4; **1337** defectus librorum de primo (*sic*) ~one *Lit. Cant.* II 146; ~onem heretice pravitatis OCKHAM *Dial.* 463; secta nostra per ~onem equivocacionum et aliarum fallaciarum tollit argucias adversancium WYCL. *Conf.* 125; s**1453** cum siluisset [abbas] .. per annum .. et ultra .. nec venisset ad eum frater horum unus aut alius ad faciendum aliquam vel minimam in materia ~onem, cepit suspicari *Reg. Whet.* I 119; inquisitores .., quos episcopus et archidiaconus .. solent .. de inquisitis et compertis eorum judicium seu praesentationem aut, ut vocant, ~onem .. construendo juramento corporali onerare *Praxis* 323. **b** Pascha / subsequitur celi detectio facta Johanni GARL. *Myst. Eccl.* 338. **c** **1574** pars .. gubernatorum .. communitatis mercatorum Anglorum adventuratorum propter ~ones terrarum, territoriorum, insularum et principatuum mari et navigacionibus incognitis nec ante nuperrimam eorundem mercatorum periclitacionem mari frequentatorum *SelPlAdm* II 150.

detector [LL], revealer, informer.

13.. sub pena x marcarum, cujus medietas ~ori et alia dimidietas piis usibus applicetur *Conc. Scot.* II 66.

detegere [CL]

1 to unroof.

detecto domus culmine BEDE *HE* IV 21 p. 257; **1258** quod turellos castri .. qui detecti sunt .. cohoperiri faciant *Cl* 336.

2 **a** to remove (cover). **b** to uncover, display; **c** (fig.).

a illud quod abstergit .. et ~it ab eo [sc. sene] illud quod est mortuum supra faciem ejus detectione subtili et leni BACON IX 70. **b** ~at, denudat, aperit *GlH* D 320; PULL. *Sent.* 718c (v. depingere 3); detege quod galea horrendum, quod parma pudendum / occulit J. EXON. *BT* II 259; frontes suas habebunt detectas, ut sue corone circuli pateant intuentibus *Cust. Cant.* 214; manus, pedis, et lateris / vulnera detexit LEDREDE *Carm.* 26. 12. **c** tandem olla ~itur DEVIZES 33 p. 30.

3 to disclose, reveal. **b** (w. pers. object) to detect, inform against; **c** (w. acc. & inf.).

machina detegitur ALDH. *VirgV* 963; ob detectum sceleris reatum *Id. VirgP* 32 (cf. *WW* [**9..**]: ob detectum, *þære onwrigenan*); Arriana heresis .. in Nicena synodo detecta atque damnata BEDE *HE* I 8; non ~ere, non publicare, non manifestare *Gl. Leid.* 2. 118; rogo ut falsitatem ~ens aperias mihi veritatem ANSELM (*Gram.* 1) I 146; detexit visionem fratribus AILR. *Ed. Conf.* 779A; s**1293** (v. confiteri 2c); **1423** cuncta cupientes reformare .. que coram nobis in nostra visitacione detecta sunt (*Processus*) AMUND. I 102; a**1470** si aliquis .. detexit seu discooperuit consilium regis et sociorum suorum *BBAdm* I 221. **b** a**1350** (v. deponere 9c); c**1410** (v. comparticeps); **1434** cum .. Thomas et Agnes .. nobis .. fuerint detecti seu accusati *MunAcOx* 509; **1497** quidam .. C. .. detectus de furto et racione hujusmodi furti captus *Sanct. Durh.* 70; aliter .. detectus se purgare non potest propter incertitudinem et generalitatem detectionis *Praxis* 323. **c** **1261** cum privilegium dignitatis mereatur amittere qui concessa sibi abuti ~itur dignitate *Conc. Syn.* 684.

4 to cover, conceal.

culmina corrupta tecti renovans, artificiose plumbo puro ~ens EDDI 16; si quis culpabilis per aliquod maleficium .. peccatum suum vel furtum ~ere [*gl.*: tegere; AS: *giwoeria*] voluerit (*Jud. Dei*) *GAS* 411; loricam et galeam nigro panno detectam sub pallio .. ancille .. accepit *G. Herw.* 328.

detegulare [cf. tegulare], to untile.

1362 pretextu .. tempestatis .., unde tam plura edificia in terram prostrata et plurima ~ata et tegule inde .. confracte .. fuerunt (*Proclamatio*) *G. S. Alb.* III 47.

detegulatio [cf. tegulatio], untiling.

1472 laborantibus pro ~one et prostracione domus *MunCOx* 287.

detendere [CL = *to dismantle*], to defile, (?) ruin.

to defoulle, .. contaminare .., deprimere, ~ere, deturpare .. *CathA.*

detenebrare [cf. CL tenebrare], to make dark (fig.).

oculi eorum rete ~antur ne lumen veritatis valeant videre J. ST. GILES *Serm.* 366.

detenere v. detinere.

detentare [LL], to detain.

to halde behynde, detinere, ~are *CathA.*

detentatio [CL], (wrongful) detention.

1295 eundem .. a possessione seu verius ~one ecclesie memorate .. amoveri debere *Reg. Cant.* 34; 'titulus' in jure diversimode sumitur. est enim titulus quandoque idem quod ~o LYNDW. 46 n.

detentator [LL], (wrongful) detainer.

si forte princeps postulans non .. obtinet a subdito quod desiderat, .. aliquam super illa .. re questionem movet tanquam rei postulate molesto ~ori H. BOS. *Thom.* III 14 p. 221; **1310** quatinus .. cum ~oribus dictarum forisfacturarum .. financiam faciatis *RGasc* IV 401; c**1340** excommunicati sunt omnes .. qui .. tales res asportarunt et furtive contra voluntatem domini [detinuerunt] .., quos omnes et singulos malefactores seu ~ores .. in sententiam excommunicacionis majoris .. incidisse denunciamus *FormOx* 162.

detentio [CL]

1 (of things or unspec.) detention, keeping. **b** holding, keeping (open or closed). **c** occupation.

captio, ~o *GlC* C 167; **1189** eam [pennam de pellibus] quam ipse habuit statim vendidit, quia ex longa ~one perierat *Ep. Cant.* 322; possessio est corporalis rei ~o.. et possessio ideo dicitur rei ~o quia naturaliter tenetur ab eo qui ei insistit, id est corporaliter BRACTON 38b; **1266** bladum deterioratum et quasi nullius valoris per longam ~onem *ExchScot* 29; **1271** (v. deteriorare 3); **1339** (v. deperdere 2b); *SB* 17 (v. 2 colicus a). **b** **1199** pro detentione exclusarum (v. faeniso a). **c** s**1298** remissa majori parte exercitus et retentis qui ad ~onem ville [Berewici] possent sufficere TREVET *Ann.* 370.

2 (of persons) detention, keeping under restraint.

clericum promptum habuit .., qui statim audiens captionem suam et ~onem .. ad curiam Romanam propter ejusdem liberationem .. iter arriperet GIR. *JS* 6 p. 317; **1208** permittas .. Wilardum .. abire quiete, qui captus est et detentus occasione ~onis †Francigonarum *Pat* 85b; **1334** puniendum per arestaciones, imprisonamenta et ~ones corporum suorum *RScot* 276b; penam .. ~onis perpetue OCKHAM *Dial.* 888 (*recte* 884); s**1385** rex .. Sicilie .. cepit .. papam .. et per octo dies in privato loco secum tenuit .., quam quidem ~onem papa vocavit expost 'incarceracionem' WALS. *HA* II 121.

3 (wrongful) detention, detinue: **a** of land or sim.; **b** of rent, tithe or sim.; **c** of cash, goods, documents or sim.

a **1198** assisa venit recognitura si A. pater Walteri fuit seisitus .. de v acris terre .., quam terram Martinus .. tenet .. judicium: Walterus habeat seisinam, et Martinus in misericordia pro injusta ~one *CurR RC* I 154; **1217** occasione ulterioris ~onis castri sui, quod bona fide domino patri nostro commisit *Pat* 71; c**1236** una materia controversie est feodus .. detentus, deductus in controversiam juste vel injuste ~onis .. GROS. *Ep.* 72* p. 223; **1268** occasione ~onis ville nostre N. contra nos et captionis ejusdem *BBC (Northampton)* 40; s**1287** miles .. quemdam Judeum super ~one indebita cujusdam manerii sibi impignorati coram judicibus convenire decrevit RISH. 113; **1298** quoad possessionem vel proprietatem seu ~onem (*Lit. Papae*) *Foed.* II 821b (= W. GUISB. *ed. 1849* II 168: †desertationem); **1321** propter capciones, occupaciones, ~ones castrorum, villarum, maneriorum et aliarum rerum (*Act. Parl.*) *G. Ed. II Bridl.* 72 (= *StRealm* I 186: *prise, occupacion ou detenue*). **b** c**1200** causa que vertebatur .. super ~one consuetudinis cervisie et medonis *Reg. S. Thom. Dublin* 478; de dampnis suis que habuit occasione ~onis predicti redditus *State Tri. Ed. I* 92; curatus malus subditos excommunicans pro decimarum ~one (SWYND.) *Ziz.* 338. **c** **1194** pro misericordia sua in qua cecidit pro ~one j m. de redempcione domini regis *CurR RC* I 49; **1219** cepit ipse averia sua et imparcavit multociens et tenuit contra vadium et plegios, ita quod per ~onem averiorum et capcionem deterioratus est *CurR* VIII xiv (cf. ib. 154: defendit injustam captionem et ~onem contra vadium et plegios); **1246** super ~one cujusdam summe pecunie de xl m. annuis nobis .. debitis *Reg. Paisley* 25; **1269** (v. bos 1a); c**1340** illos .. qui de tali dicte rei [furtive asportate] ~one aliquid sciverint .. *FormOx* 162; ~onem oblacionum que solent a confitentibus sepe solvi eis qui eorum confessionem auscultant RIC. ARMAGH *Def. Cur.* 1397 (*recte* 1297); **1379** teneantur .. pecuniam .. ad cistas deferre et custodibus .. sine ulteriore ~one .. liberare *StatOx* 184; **14..** de ~one cujusdam scripti obligatorii .. traditi .. ut in equali manu .. custodiendi *Reg. Brev. Orig.* 28.

4 withholding, denial (of right).

defectus justitie ac violenta recti ~o .. secundum legem requisiti commune regis placitum est (*Leg. Hen.* 59. 19) *GAS* 579; *Ib.* 553 (v. destitutio 1a).

detentor [LL]

1 **a** detainer, captor (of captives). **b** maintainer, harbourer (of malefactors).

a quando .. vasalli alicujus domini .. pugnant contra invasores vel ~ores rerum, sive mobilium sive immobilium, aut hominum domini sui et capiunt res aut homines domini de manu detinencium sive occupancium OCKHAM *Pol.* I 132 (cf. 2c infra); **1377** quatenus vos .. omnes .. hujusmodi clericorum seu personarum ecclesiasticarum se .. bellicis actibus non immiscencium captores, ~ores, carceri mancipatores, compulsores .. excommunicatos publice nuncietis *Mon. Hib. & Scot.* 359a. **b** **1290** nos tam contra apostatam ipsum quam contra fautores seu ~ores ipsius .. procedemus prout deposcunt eorum demerita PECKHAM *Ep.* 708 (= *Mon. Francisc.* II 32).

2 (wrongful) detainer: **a** of land or sim.; **b** of tithe or sim.; **c** of goods, documents or sim.

a s**1155**, s**1181** (v. dominicus 4b); **1215** licebit .. regine repetere dotalicium suum ab omni ~ore extra regnum Anglie preterquam a nobis et successoribus nostris *Pat* 181b; c**1236** cum clericus ~or feodi laicalis, quem ingressus est per violentam spoliationem, convenitur a spoliato in foro laicali GROS. *Ep.* 72* p. 223; **1258** predictum militem et ceteros .. terre prenominate ~ores *Kelso* 295; **1339** occupatores et ~ores [terrarum regi forisfactarum] *RScot* 576a. **b** **1214** ~ores decimarum .. usque ad satisfactionem condignam anathematis vinculo feriantur *Conc. Syn.* 33; **1215** de laicis ~oribus decimarum .. statuta canonum renovamus *Pat* 140a; **1345** occultos ~ores decimarum, reddituum et aliorum bonorum (*Lit. Papae*) *Reg. Newbattle* app. p. 322. **c** si quem vel heredem vel alium rerum defuncti reppererint ~orem GLANV. VII 6; s**1259** rerum suarum raptores et ~ores excommunicationis .. sententia innodare *Flor. Hist.* II 433; **1287** debitores, ~ores seu occupatores bonorum *Deeds Balliol* 282; OCKHAM *Pol.* I 132 (v. 1a supra); s**1378** rex non potest concedere raptori vel fraudulento ~ori rei aliene ut gaudeat tali libertate quod non possit ad solvendum *Eul. Hist. Cont.* III 346; **1425** (v. concelator); **1434** si jura et munimenta .. per quoscunque detineantur abscondita, ~ores ipsos ad tradendum .. hujusmodi jura et munimenta .. compellatis (*Lit. Curiae Rom.*) AMUND. I 395; c**1520** quia nonnulli .. literas ordinarias suas .. a portatoribus .. manuforti rapiunt et detinent .., wlt [archiepiscopus] .. hujusmodi literarum raptores, captores, ~ores, laceratores et earundem execucionis impeditores .. sententiam excommunicacionis majoris incurrere *Conc. Scot.* I cclxxx.

3 withholder (of right).

1228 cum .. malefactoribus et juris alieni ~oribus videatur relinqui impunitas delinquendi *Cl* 108.

4 unlawful occupant, usurper: **a** of church or religious house; **b** of realm.

a s**1143** Gaufredum [de Magna Villa] adiit, monasterii sui ~orem *Chr. Rams.* 331; **1198** ~ores ipsarum [ecclesiarum] .. pena suspensionis .. percellentes *Ep. Cant.* 501; **1201** prebendas et cetera ecclesiastica beneficia si que vacant .., amoto quolibet illicito ~ore, tibi liceat idoneis personis assignare (*Lit. Papae*) GIR. *Invect.* III 10; c**1210** quatinus .., amoto quolibet illicito ~ore vel possessore, eam [ecclesiam] michi restituere faciatis *FormOx* 274. **b** in regni ~ores pacisque vestre turbatores GIR. *TH* III 48; ~orum Anglicani regni contra legitimum heredem Henricum Henrici regis .. nepotem inopinatus accidit occasus *Id. EH* II 31.

detentus v. decere 4, detinere.

detepescere [LL], to grow cold (fig).

rumor de ejus archiepiscopatu .. longinquitate temporis ~uerat W. MALM. *GP* I 47; c**1157** rigor discipline ecclesiastice in partibus illis adeo jam ~uit ut ibi .. scismatis seminarium pullulet J. SAL. *Ep.* 53 (87); studiorum ~uit omnis fervor ELMH. *Cant.* 309.

deterere [CL], to wear away, deprive by rubbing (also fig.). **b** to fritter away (fig). **c** (?) to wear down, exhaust. **d** to crush, break, destroy.

†detriturigine [l. detrita rubigine], *agnidine GlC* D 78; ⁓it, i. †prodit [l. perdit], diminuet *GlH* D 321; si [visibilis spiritus] in ipsa extensionis elongatione aliqua sui parte ⁓itur ADEL. *QN* 30; servum tuum duc ad vitam / post concissam et detritam / togam carnis putide WALT. WIMB. *Virgo* 162. **b** **1081** juvenilem aetatem in his [quaestionibus saecularium] detrivimus, sed accedentes ad pastoralem curam abrenuntiandum eis decrevimus LANFR. *Ep.* 33 (49); in talibus neniis nollem vitam ⁓ere *Id. Corp. & Sang.* 409C. **c** **s1378** insultum facit ad castrum, †deterius [*ed.*: deterrens; ? l. deterens] inclusos insuper cum . . machinis bellicis per longam moram WALS. *HA* I 388. **d** neque pro modico manuum Dei creatura †deterreatur [? l. deteratur; AS: *forspille* (*man*)] (*Cons. Cnuti*) *GAS* 311 (= *Quad.* ib.: dispereat); in lege Danorum quisquis justam legem †detererit [AS: *wyrde*] solvat legis fracturam (*Ib.*) *Ib.* 321; Bartolano . . pestilentie mucrone detrito GIR. *TH* III 3.

detergĕre [LL < CL detergēre]

1 to wipe away; **b** (fig.). **c** to cast away, reject.

Boreas . . sicco detergens nubila flatu *V. Merl.* 428; cum vetus effiueret in regnum mobile mundus / terrarumque notas ultrix detergeret unda J. EXON. *BT* II 353; W. FITZST. *Thom.* 141 (v. defluus); virtus est ei [lollio] ut putredinem vulnerum ⁓gere possit *Alph.* 105. **b** **601** ut . ., quanto in subjectis suis etiam aliena peccata ⁓serit, tanto etiam de peccatis propriis . . securior fiat (*Lit. Papae*) BEDE *HE* I 32; ob ⁓gendam rubiginem nostrorum facinorum ABBO *Edm.* 11; **a1078** cujus livoris dolorem nisi prius per satisfactionem ⁓sero ANSELM (*Ep.* 12) III 115; rogitate Dominum / . . / ut detergat si quas habet Eva sordes criminum HIL. RONCE. 1. 152; DOMINIC *V. Ecgwini* II 52 (v. dubietas a); W. MALM. *GR* V 400 (v. curialis 4a); ut . . canonicam . . obedientiam omni ambiguitate ⁓sa exibeatis *Chr. Battle* f. 65. **c** ⁓so tremoris pavore R. COLD. *Cuthb.* 30; **c1415** patris mei . . extat voluntas ut temporali pro commodo . . logicam ⁓gerem et legem civilem penitus excercerem *FormOx* 432.

2 to wipe clean (of). **b** (p. ppl.) clear, pure.

[crines] Hyale detergit, tersos in smegmate mergit R. CANT. *Malch.* IV 562; Oswaldus . . pedes pauperum lavit et osculans eos crine linitheoque ⁓sit EADMER *V. Osw.* 34; neque de superfluis saltem nostris more Magdalene [cf. *Luke* vii 38] pedes Domini ⁓gimus PULL. *Sent.* 917C; qui nares sordidas muscillaginibus / . . detergunt WALT. WIMB. *Palpo* 191. **b** scienti causas minime ⁓sas, . . quomodo tribuitur ei perfectio? EGB. *Dial.* 405; si . ., dum igneus . . spiritus in ⁓sam ac defecatam inciderit materiam, inde repercuti . . necesse est, ut quid, cum album vitrum et ⁓sissimum intuemur, simili causa vultus non referuntur? ADEL. *QN* 29; et jam rorificas noctis nudaverat umbras, / sed nondum detersa dies J. EXON. *BT* VI 854.

deteriatio v. deterioratio 2.

deterior [CL], worse.

quid te non ei regum omnium regi . . exhibes ceteris moribus meliorem, sed vice versa ⁓iorem? GILDAS *EB* 33; ⁓iora, *þa sæmran GlH* D 324; GLANV. X 6 (v. deterioratio 2); sanum consilium preponderat omnibus escis; / deterius nichil est, si dolus intus adest WALT. ANGL. *Fab.* 26. 20; ut mali ⁓rimi sunt, et nusquam pejores GIR. *TH* III 27; tempore semper in ⁓ius vergente *Id. GE* II 6; terre arrabiles vicinorum ⁓iores facte sunt BRAKELOND 160V.; **1234** non sit eis [hominibus abbatis] ⁓ius occasione istius placiti *CurR* XV 1277; **s1244** (v. calculus 5c); **s1304** quidam [Anglici] . . facientes cum . . Scotis alliganciam . . in centuplum effecti sunt Scotis ⁓iores W. GUISB. 363*n.*; **1342** (v. dies 3a); **1407** (v. cauterizare 1b).

deterioramentum, (liability for) damage.

1207 W. de Sully dat xx m. ut dominus rex eum quietum clamet [de] ⁓o et ruina molendini *Cart. Glam.* 306.

deteriorare [LL]

1 to make worse, harm, impair: **a** (person, community, or unspec.); **b** (thing); **c** (abstr.).

a inter regem . . et sanctum virum . . aliquando pax abundavit. aliquando vero aliquod spatium, olla fervente nequitiae, plures ⁓avit EDDI 45; **s1316** per hujusmodi dissensiones ⁓atur patria et . . leduntur indigene *V. Ed. II* 223; **s1324** Isabella regina . . diffamata vel ⁓ata fuit apud regem *Ann. Paul.* 308; si Deus posset dampnificare hominem sine causa peccati, tunc posset ⁓are innocentem auferendo ab illo graciam WYCL. *Innoc.* 479; promittunt . . quod defendunt jus et statum ecclesie, non ⁓ando sed meliorando matrem ecclesiam *Id. Sim.* 89. **b** **c1180** juraverunt quod fideles erunt . . de hoc tenemento non ⁓ando sed potius emendando *Cart. Osney* I 35; **1229** omnes balistas regis lesas et ⁓atas . ., que reparatione indigent, liberari faciat . . balistario regis ad ipsas reparandas *Cl* 181; quando [planete] sunt in oppositis locis suarum . . dignitatum, ⁓antur et destituuntur a naturali vigore BACON *Maj.* I 381; **s1279** moneta Anglie per tonsuram nimis ⁓ata RISH. 94 (v. et. circumcisio 1); res usu consumptibiles sunt ille que ipso usu . . vel penitus consumuntur quantum ad utentem vel ut communiter ⁓antur et tandem consumuntur OCKHAM *Pol.* I 304; **1335** libri, calices vel vestimenta . . vetustate corrupta vel alias enormiter ⁓ata *Eng. Clergy* 260; nonne est metallum maledictum quod ⁓atur, si nigrius et asperius eo fit quo magis limatur *AncrR* 107; **1438** diversos arcus pontis civitatis London' ⁓ari percipimus *Lit. Cant.* III 169. **c** **1214** jurabitis quod victualia . . rationabili pretio vendetis . . et . . graves . . non facietis constitutiones vel onerosas per quas conditio clericorum ⁓etur *MunAcOx* 2; **1220** (v. crucesignatio); **1221** plures fecerunt kayos super ripam per antiquam consuetudinem, et villa non est pejorata nec adventus navium per hoc ⁓atur *PlCrGlouc* 115; illi minores qui sunt sub tutela . . accipere . . poterunt tutore auctore et condicionem suam meliorem facere; dare autem non poterunt nec condicionem suam ⁓are BRACTON 12; **1289** forbarrat homines de civitate, . . per quod forum ⁓atur *Leet Norw.* 30.

2 (leg.) to injure, damage (so as to incur liability): **a** (person or community); **b** (property).

a **1200** R. . . queritur quod E. . . cepit averia sua et detinuit injuste . ., ita quod ⁓abatur ad valentiam xx s. *CurR* I 147; **1227** (v. damnificare 1a); **1258** conqueritur . . quod [Johannes] vetuit illi *lot* de pisce, unde communitas fuit ⁓ata quoad despectum per j cuvatam cervisie *Rec. Leic.* I 78; **s1260** de aliis transgressionibus versus ipsos narraverunt, unde ⁓ati sunt et dampnum habuerunt ad valentiam x li. *Leg. Ant. Lond.* 48; **1340** ipsam [Benedictam uxorem Willelmi] verberavit, vulneravit, et male tractavit et . . crines suos dilaceravit . ., unde iidem W. et B. ⁓ati sunt et dampnum habent ad valenciam xl s. *SessPCambs* 36. **b** **1204** queritur quod . . injuste ceperunt averia sua et ⁓averunt ad valentiam xxxvj m. . .; et . . defendunt prisam averiorum ejus et deteriorationem averiorum *CurR* III 200; **1311** si contingat nos . . dictos muros aut turellos . . operibus nostris in aliquo ⁓are . . *MunCOx* 19 (cf. ib. 20: quousque eisdem . . de dictis deterioracionibus . . plenarie fuerit satisfactum).

3 (of things) to grow worse, deteriorate (intr.).

⁓averunt, *wyrsadon GlH* D 323; deterire, vel ⁓are vel pejorare OSB. GLOUC. *Deriv.* 175; **1271** lana et pelles . . pro diuturna detencione eorundem de die in diem . . putrescent et ⁓abunt *Cl* 439; sunt quorum nec substancia ⁓at proveniente utilitate ex ipsis, sicut pecunie OCKHAM *Pol.* II 510.

4 (of patient or ailment) to grow worse, deteriorate: **a** (pass.); **b** (intr.).

a **s1199** ceperunt vulnera [regi] inflicta ⁓ari et nigrescere COGGESH. *Chr.* 96; egrotavit . . mulier usque ad mortem. . . filia vero, videns eam ⁓ari, adduxit . . vicinos . . *Latin Stories* 75. **b** contigit . . quandam . . matronam . . acrius ⁓antem fatigari R. COLD. *Cuthb.* 62; **1231** nunquam postquam percussus fuit [paralisi] non melioravit ei status suus . ., immo semper ⁓avit *BNB* II 488.

deterioratio [LL]

1 **a** deterioration, worsening. **b** decline in value, impoverishment. **c** wastage, decay.

a de regni ⁓one donec . . periret BEDE *Sam.* 693C; non licet angelo vel homini ad ⁓onem sed solum ad ecclesie edificacionem procedere WYCL. *Sim.* 108; *Id. Innoc.* 480 (v. charybdis b); **s1377** nemo ad sui ⁓onem excommunicatur . . nisi in causa Dei (WYCL. *Concl.*) WALS. *HA* I 354 (cf. *Ziz.* 250); si . . doleat quis esse secundus quia desiderat esse prior . ., prioritas in ⁓onem turpiter ducitur ELMH. *Cant.* 87. **b** **1214** si [obedientiarii] minus prudenter in officiis suis se habuerint . ., amoveantur . ., ne . . per moram fiat ⁓o obedientiarum *Chr. Evesham* 206; **1249** obedienciarii . . fideles reddant raciones, ut de melioracione vel ⁓one monasterii reddantur cerciores *Doc. Eng. Black Monks* I 36. **c** **1419** ne fides ipsarum [cartarum etc.] propter vetustatem et ⁓onem earundem deperire . . valeat (*Pat*) *MonA* VI 1107b.

2 injury, damage (involving financial liability).

1121 quicunque . . regis donativum quocunque ⁓onis genere pervertere presumpsisset (*Act. Curie Ep. Bath.*) *Hist. Exch.* 76 (cf. *MonA* II 268b); si [vadium] in custodia deterius factum fuerit . . per culpam creditoris, computabitur ei in debitum ad valentiam ⁓onis GLANV. X 6; **1204** (v. deteriorare 2b); **1221** mittantur ad edificia illa legales homines . ., qui videant †deteriationem domorum *MGL* I 68; **1261** muros et fossata curie sine ⁓one sustinebit *Reg. S. Thom. Dublin* 210; **1289** de H. W. pro forstallo et forbarramento puletarie ad ⁓onem fori *Leet Norw.* 32; **1311** (v. deteriorare 2b); **1335** in nostri dampnum et . . victualium ⁓onem *RScot* 336a; **1415** salvo . . passagio cum batellis suis . . absque ⁓one piscarie . . abbatis et conventus (*Arbitratio*) *Croyl. Cont. B* 510.

deterire v. deteriorare 3.

1 deterius v. deterere c.

2 deterius [CL], (adv.) worse.

⁓ius, *wyrs GlH* D 325; quanto . . potius debes manifestare, ne ⁓ius putrescat in corde? AD. SCOT *QEC* 34. 875A.

determinabilis [LL]

1 determinable, definable: **a** (spatially); **b** (log.). **c** (gram.) that can be modified.

a [angeli] in se ipsis situm non habent . . nec ad [assumpta] corpora propinquitatem aut remotionem habent lineari dimensione ⁓em GROS. 116 (= *Ep.* 1 p. 12). **b** est gradus discretum dominium qualitatis vel qualitatum . ., vel gradus est excessus qualitatis vel qualitatum ab optima compositione sensu ⁓i GILB. III 162V. 1; quod potencia practicans, cujus praxe noticia conformis est prior, sit aliquo modo ⁓is aliunde sive alii tamquam regule conformabilis in agendo DUNS *Ord.* I 181; *Id. PW* 7 (v. denominabilis); regula est, quando hoc verbum 'est' sine ⁓i precedente subjecto predicat secundum adjacens in particulari, tunc equipollet sue subalterne WYCL. *Log.* I 72. **c** ut non videatur determinatio cum proximo ⁓i debere solum continuari, debet aliquando separari ab utroque, sicut Genesis xl [21]: 'restituitque alterum in locum suum, ut porrigeret regi poculum; alterum suspendit in patibulo, ut conjectoris veritas probaretur'; debet enim elevari punctus post illud 'in patibulo', quia determinatio refertur ad utrumque; sed, si proximum debet determinare tantum, tunc post primum ⁓e debet fieri punctus elevatus BACON *Tert.* 250–1.

2 (of legal proceedings) determinable.

a1532 que inquisiciones coram nobis et non alibi sunt ⁓es *Entries* 601.

determinabilitas, determinability.

ex natura sua est determinatus [intellectus], vel determinabilis ea specie quam recipit, ut per speciem illius singularis, et tunc intellectus ille esset magis determinabilis quam intellectus noster; imo utroque modo sequitur determinacio vel ⁓as intellectus angelici magis quam sensus nostri DUNS *Sent.* II 19. 1.

determinare [CL]

1 to determine, define, fix: **a** (in space); **b** (in time); **c** (log.). **d** (p. ppl.) definite, perfect. **e** (gram.) to qualify or modify.

a ⁓at, definit *GlC* D 206; liber iste vij planetarum atque draconis statum continet a meridie quarte ferie usque ad meridiem quinte ⁓atum ADEL. *Elk. pref.*; propter hoc quod superficies ignis non est ⁓ata superficie aeris, ex quo videtur esse . . unum corpus BACON IV 325; cognicio organica, que inest secundum ⁓atam partem corporis DUNS *PW* 140; **1466** dubitacio quum incipit purgatorium, et quamdiu durabit, et de loco purgatorio, si est ⁓atus *MunAcOx* 716. **b** habetis licentiam loquendi in claustro vestro, sed ⁓atis et consuetis horis H. LOS. *Ep.* 48; [Æthericus, ob. **1034**] nullum certum ⁓avit diem quo vel accusatores vel accusati venientem operiri debuissent *Chr. Rams.* 122. **c** quando . . rectitudo ⁓ata contingenter convenit praxi, tunc non est objectum aliquod ⁓ans intellectum ad cognicionem rectitudinis ⁓ate antequam voluntas velit; nam illud contingens non ⁓atur ad alteram partem ante omnem actum voluntatis DUNS *Ord.* I 181; omne existens determinate subesse, quod non per se sufficienter ⁓atur ad esse, per aliquid aliud ⁓atur ad esse BRADW. *CD* 146B; qualitercunque [aliquid] determinate est, . . necessario est; sed tales veritates de preterito sunt ⁓ate et non possunt desinere esse; igitur sunt necessarie WYCL. *Act.* 65. **d** stellarum cursu et numero nihil est ⁓atius, nihil ordine stabilius ADEL. *QN* 74; si nascatur in decimo mense bene evadit . ., cum inveniat creaturam bene completam et ⁓atam M. SCOT *Phys.* 10. **e** nomen proprium tripliciter ⁓atur, aut per obliquum, aut per adjectivum, aut per verbum VINSAUF *AV* II 3. 49 (cf. ib. 79: verbum dupliciter ⁓atur, uno modo per adverbium, alio modo per dictionem casualem); BACON XV 258 (v. determinativus); *Id. Tert.* 251 (v. determinabilis 1c); omne adverbium ⁓at suum verbum in comparacione ad subjectum WYCL. *Conf.* 505.

2 to state precisely, specify; **b** (w. compl.).

nisi clamans ita discernat et ⁓et ut nulla dubitatio possit esse LANFR. *Const.* 173 (cf. clamare 4); quibus [astantibus] quum [mulier] miserabile[m] rei ⁓asset eventum GOSC. *Mir. Iv.* lxxix; Aristo[teles] . . causas resistentes putrefactionem ⁓at GILB. I 6v. 2 (cf. ib. 10. 2: tres species emitritei ⁓ate ab auctoribus); **1310** locum ⁓atum (v. deponere 9e); de terra et qualiter se dividit et in tribus partibus se extendit . . intendimus ⁓are *Eul. Hist.* II 10. **b** **c1233** salvis nobis . . omnibus . . que in dictis cartis . . nobis salvanda ⁓antur *Reg. Aberbr.* I 121.

3 to determine, decide, settle (a question or sim., sts. w. acc. & inf. or obj. clause): **a** (phil. or doctrinal; *cf.* 4a *infra*); **b** (leg. or administrative); **c** (w. *compotum*).

a sequitur ⁓are utrum duo spiritus possent esse in eodem loco intellectuali HALES *Sent.* I 381 (cf. ib. 378: secunda questio potest ⁓ari sic); OCKHAM *Pol.* I 297 (v. catholice); **s1377** [cancellarius universitatis Oxon'] vice omnium . . ⁓avit publice in scholis eas [conclusiones Johannis Wiccliff] veras esse sed male sonare in auribus auditorum *Eul. Hist. Cont.* III 348. **b** **705** ut . . ibi adunato concilio omnium dissimultatum causae ⁓entur WEALDHERE *Ep.* 22; quidam . . assident ad . . dubia ⁓anda que . . ex incidentibus questionibus oriuntur *Dial. Scac.* I 4 C (cf. 1 assidere 1b); **1190** ⁓atum est de clericis quod nulla occasione a secularibus potestatibus capientur nisi . . (*Artic. Cleri*) DICETO *YH* II 87; **1219** (v. deducere 2a); **s1250** ⁓atum est ut suam archiepiscopus . . exerceret jurisdictionem M. PAR. *Min.* III 314; **1251** ⁓averunt judices quod elemosina . . maneat in statu tali quo fuit *Cart. Sallay* 411; **1253** quod eis [burgensibus] concederet quod per xxiiij juratos . . omnia placita ipsos contingentia essent discussa et ⁓ata *Rec. Leic.* I 42; ante quam processus et tractatus . . plene ⁓e[n]tur *State Tri. Ed. I* 35; **1292** si aliquis aliquid fecerit contra coronam nostram quod non ⁓etur aliquo loco nisi infra libertatem ville predicte *BBC*

155; a1350 cancellarium adeat ut .. ~et an indigeat vel non indigeat advocato *StatOx* 89; **1459** (v. deponere 9d). **c 1533** pro compoto suo audiendo et ~ando *Ac. Durh.* 197; **1533** auditoribus hunc compotum ~antibus *Comp. Swith.* 222.

4 (acad.): **a** to 'determine' (a question; *cf.* 3a *supra*). **b** to qualify (by so doing) for master's degree (absol. or w. *acta*).

a 1282 (v. circulariter 2c); **a1350** *StatOx* 56 (v. determinatio 4a); **1549** cujus [questionis] ambigua et dubitaciones, dum in utramque partem enucleaverint, definient ~abuntque *Ib.* 345. **b a1255** quilibet [tempore] sue incepcionis antequam ~et fidem faciat .. de statutis universitatis .. custodiendis *StatCantab* 199; **1268** ut certa forma provideretur sub qua bachilarii arcium ~aturi ad ~andum .. forent admittendi *StatOx* 25 (= *MunAcOx* 34); **s1326** ~ans in artibus *G. S. Alb.* II 182; **1409** ut non liceat eis [determinatoribus] extra scholas xxxij .. ~are acta sua *MunAcOx* 240; **1414** quod ~antes admitterentur per decanum facultatis (*Acta Fac. Artium S. Andree OED* s. v. *regent* 3b).

5 to determine, make up one's mind (sts. refl.); **b** (p. ppl. w. *in*) determined, resolved (on).

s1460 tandem se ~ans concludebat finaliter et ~abat ipsum [manerium] vendicioni exponere *Reg. Whet.* I 357; *Ib.* 119 (v. concludere 6b). **b s1327** episcopus .. in necem Edwardi finaliter ~atus BAKER 107b.

6 to appoint, assign.

a1350 jurent sic electi quod .. ~ent .. partibus advocatos *StatOx* 89.

7 to bring to an end. **b** to come to an end.

~abit, *gesidode GlP* 828; de apoplexia: .. tales curationem suscipiunt, precipue si sensus .. in pedes .. seu etiam in manus .. descenderint; vel in paralisi ~abitur GILB. II 115. 1. **b** cum ~averit evangelium, ingredietur precentor incipiendo psalmum 'miserere' *Cust. Cant.* 385.

determinate, a (log.) determinately, definitely. **b** specifically, expressly.

a non potest esse summa natura alicubi et aliquando ~e ANSELM (*Mon.* 20) I 35; navale bellum fieri, item non fieri, possibile est; alterum tamen prescise et ~e verum est prescitum J. SAL. *Pol.* 444C; hujusmodi .. interrogabilia .. ad disciplinalem .. commoditatem ~e multiplicia appellentur BALSH. *AD rec. 2* 171; *Ib.* 172 (v. coherenter); corpora posita in aqua .. non poterunt elevari sub figuratione quacunque ab invicem ~e, set indeterminate, ut aliud corpus ingrediatur paulatim BACON IV 313 (cf. ib. VIII 96); BRADW. *CD* 146B, WYCL. *Act.* 65 (v. determinare 1c). **b** LANFR. *Const.* 174, *Cust. Westm.* 189 (v. clamator 4); si non ~e asserat illam [felicitatem] esse supremam perfeccionem nobis possibilem DUNS *Ord.* I 10; exemplum est de invitatis ad mensam alicujus, quibus illa que apponuntur coram omnibus simul et coram nullo ~e sunt eis communia antequam incipiunt actualiter uti ipsis OCKHAM *Pol.* I 360; statutum non obligat .. aliquem ad confitendum ~e et personaliter proprio sacerdoti CONWAY *Def. Mend.* 1338; FORTESCUE *LLA* 54 (v. confundere 1e).

determinatio [CL]

1 a limitation (of movement). **b** fixing (of time). **c** limitation, qualification (log.), restrictive clause. **d** qualification or modification (gram.).

a ~o sui motus est ex ordinatione ad hominem HALES *Qu.* 818. **b 1518** ~o scrutinii usque in proximum custodis adventum dilata est *Reg. Merton* 480. **c** quoties verba sanctorum vel ipsius Domini hujusmodi ~ones non habent J. CORNW. *Eul.* 21; fiunt interrogationes elective nec simplices nec simplicium coaptatione multiplices, sed ~one simplicibus adjecta BALSH. *AD rec. 2* 171; quibus .. consentire videmur, adjecta ~one ut de hiis essartis dicantur quieti 'que fuerant ante diem qua rex .. H. primus rebus humanis exemptus est' *Dial. Scac.* I 11 C; rex .. ait: "omnes he aberunt ~ones; nihil hic erit sophismatis" W. FITZST. *Thom.* 92; illud quod significatur ulterius per hunc terminum 'fugiendum' trahitur ad singulare per hanc ~onem 'ab hoc lupo' J. BLUND *An.* 260; quando in apprehensione previa nulla est ~o virtualis vel formalis de rectitudine praxis DUNS *Ord.* I 179; est fallacia .. quando in tali modo arguendi aliqua ~o ponitur in minori et in conclusione que non ponitur in majori OCKHAM *Pol.* I 343; syncategoreumata vel ~ones adverbiales (*Id. Quodl.*) *GLA* III 363*n.* 826. **d** ~onum alia adjectiva, alia partitiva GERV. MELKLEY *AV* 40; BACON *Tert.* 250 (v. determinabilis 1c); multe ~ones conveniunt corpori Christi, nominales, verbales et adverbiales (TYSS.) *Ziz.* 173.

2 specification, particularization.

ipsa ~o [fratris clamati] ab ordinibus vel officiis, si possit fieri, debet esse, hoc modo: 'domnus Eduuardus presbiter', .. 'magister infantum', .. vel aliquid hujusmodi, non 'archidiaconus', non 'Lundonensis', non aliquid cognomentum de saeculo LANFR. *Const.* 173 (cf. clamare 4).

3 determination, decision, settlement (of question or sim.): **a** (phil. or doctrinal); **b** (leg. or administrative).

a circa prime questionis ~onem sic procedatur HALES *Sent.* I 378; **1237** indigemus .. consilio in variorum .. casuum cotidie emergentium secundum Scripturarum intelligentiam sana et salubri ~one GROS. *Ep.* 40; docent diffinicionem pape ~oni ecclesie contrariam OCKHAM *Dial.* 635; [J. Wycclyf] in ultima ~one sua fortificavit partem suam validis argumentis (KYN.) *Ziz.* 73; **c1383** non tenentur fideles credere quod omnis ~o [ME: *determinacioun*] ecclesie Romane est undequaque .. ab ecclesia tanquam articulus fidei capienda *Concl. Loll. XXXVII* 746; **1397** R. S. recusat panem benedictum et aquam benedictam contra ~onem ecclesie (*Vis. Heref.*) *EHR* XLV 92; **1401** doctores catholici .., qui .. in obediencia et ~one sancte matris ecclesie radicantur *FormOx* 211. **b 1200** cum ~one querelarum que exorte sunt ex tenore carte *RChart* 69b; **1289** post ~onem .. inqueste *RGasc* II 291; **1300** totum negocium .. ad decisionem et ~onem sedis apostolice .. reducimus (*Lit. Papae*) *Ann. Lond.* 105; **1322** partes, .. lites declinare cupientes, quo ad decisionem et ~onem dissensionis predicte .. se nostre supposuerunt ordinacioni *Reg. Newbattle* 148; **1445** in ceteris que concernunt .. defensionem juris nostre ecclesie .. per ~onem consilii nostri procedimus BEKYNTON I 260; **s1405** conclusum est in concilio generali quod de qualibet domo ij d. darentur ..; cui ~oni gubernator [de Pertha] restitit MAJOR VI 10; **1542** si .. aliquis .. sociorum .. consilio, decreto, ordinacioni, et ~oni obedire recusaverit *Deeds Balliol* 322.

4 (acad.) 'determination' of question; *cf. determinare* 4a. **b** the act of 'determining' for master's degree; *cf. determinare* 4b.

c1301 dicitur ~one fratris Berengarii Predicatoris quod conceptus formati ab intellectu sunt plures *Quaest. Ox.* 327 (cf. ib. 39–42); **1311** cum .. fratres .. ordinis [Predicatorum] .. sint in possessione .. juris .. tenendi vesperias, disputaciones, ~ones ac alia que ad actus scolasticos pertinere noscuntur in scolis infra ambitum domorum ipsorum fratrum situatis *Collect. Ox.* II 252; **1314** quod fratres Predicatores Oxonie liberas habeant scolas in domo sua quantum ad lecciones, disputaciones, et ~ones *StatOx* 118; **a1350** lecciones .. legant .. duas ad plus in artibus, et hoc computando pro leccione summam vel ~onem sophismatum vel questionum, si illo die contigerit summam legi vel sophisma vel questionem determinari *Ib.* 56; **1466** [predicator] determinabit de simonia et de usura; et has perficiat ~ones per media accepta, ex scriptis sacris, ex originibus sanctorum et racione materiali, sicuti habebit locum *MunAcOx* 716. **b a1350** inhibet .. cancellarius .. ne aliqui tempore ~onis bachelariorum, ante hostia scolarum stantes .., transeuntes .. invite intrare compellant *StatOx* 25; **1409** quia per sollennes ~ones bachillariorum in facultate arcium nostra mater Oxonie universitas .. multipliciter honoratur *Ib.* 199; **1517** baccalaurie artium, completo prius post gradum baccalaureatus et ~ones triennio, .. ad gradum magistratus .. promoveantur *Stat. Coll. Ox.* II 59.

5 completion, end (of period or activity). **b** conclusion (of clausula).

post horarum ~onem BYRHT. *V. Osw.* 471 (v. definitio 5); usque ad creticam [febris] ~onem GILB. I 7. 2 (cf. criticus). **b** cadenciarum ~o prima finiri potest in uno dactilo cum spondeo precedente *Dictamen* 334.

6 (?) *f. l.*

si [responsalis] ~one [? l. de terminacione] respondeat, utpote si inde debeat judicium fieri et loquela terminari .., tunc debet judicium illud poni in respectum HENGHAM *Magna* 9 p. 33.

determinative, determinatively, decisively. *Cf. determinare* 3a, 4a.

[R. Grosseteste] de libero arbitrio .. scripsit .. unum libellum .. in quo magis disputative et inquisitive quam ~e aut definitive procedit BRADW. *CD* 606B; his omnibus astipulatur quod ~e dicit .. Augustinus cap. xxxj lib. primi de moribus ecclesie catholice, loquens de religione .. eremitarum NETTER *DAF* I 437.

determinativus [LL = *critical*], (gram. or log.) determinative.

alia sunt adverbia que determinare possunt compositionem [et] etiam rem verbi, ut 'vero', 'falso'.. faciunt tamen propositionem modalem solum, eo quod sunt compositionis ~a BACON XV 258; non semper illa intellectio prior est practica, sed tantum quando est ~a rectitudinis vel determinate rectitudinis ipsius praxis DUNS *Ord.* I 179 (cf. ib. 182: ex objecto .. quod est ex se primo ~um intellectus ad noticiam rectitudinis determinate ipsius praxis .. habetur hic noticia prior praxi et conformis).

determinator [LL]

1 determiner, decider: **a** (phil. or doctrinal); **b** (leg. or administrative).

a nullus .. est questionum intricatarum theologie facultatis ~or idoneus nisi fuerit in grammatica .. et logica et metaphysica et theologia perfectus OCKHAM *Pol.* I 596; sequitur .. quod ecclesia tales constituciones ordinando .. dedit eisdem fratribus auctoritatem .. ad peccandum .. et per consequens erravit in moribus vel sciencia; et sequitur quod .. non est ejus ~oribus adherendum CONWAY *Def. Mend.* 1343. **b 1434** ipsum dominum officialem in arbitrum, arbitratorem, laudatorem, et ~orem in premissis .. elegerunt et assumpserunt (*Compromissum*) AMUND. II 98; **1566** doctor W. [et al.] designantur .. ~ores utrum praelectores Graecae linguae et Hebraicae teneantur publice disputare *StatOx* 396.

2 (acad.) 'determiner' (bachelor qualifying for master's degree).

1268 si aliqui determinaturi .. non omnes illos [libros] quos secundum formam .. deberent audivisse rite audierint, dummodo alios libros .. audierint qui secundum magistrorum .. estimacionem .. sufficiunt .. ad officium ~orum admittantur *StatOx* 26; **1409** si numerus ~orum .. non excedat vicenarium, tunc omnes determinent simul *MunAcOx* 240; **1516** (v. 2 collector c).

deterraxas v. detrahere 3a.

1 deterrere v. deterere c.

2 deterrēre [CL]

1 to deter, discourage: **a** (person or unspec.); **b** (act).

a 596 nec labor vos itineris nec maledicorum hominum linguae ~eant (*Lit. Papae*) BEDE *HE* I 23; **s1179** dum [Caduallanus], pro scelerum immanitate semper ~itus, remeasset DICETO *YH* I 437; dissuadere nefas et deterrere fideles / a bellis cupio, dum fera bella cano GARL. *Tri. Eccl.* 63; *to flay* .., terrere, de-, ex- .., terrificare *CathA*. **b** prohibens punire flagello / deterrenda minis HANV. VIII 30 p. 360.

2 to terrify.

s1382 terre motus est magnus, .. multorum mortalium corda ~ens WALS. *HA* II 67; R. .. solebat egredi de sepulcro in noctibus et inquietare villanos et ~ere *Ghost Stories* 418.

deterrimus v. deterior.

detersio [LL], wiping.

[mundificatio] fit .. per ~onem cutis BACON IX 122.

detestabilis [CL], detestable, loathsome.

ad ~e prostibulum et invisum lupanar scortorum ALDH. *VirgP* 42; quem [annum] .. apostasia demens regum Anglorum ~em fecerat BEDE *HE* III 9; **9.** .. ~e, *ladlic WW*; **a1077** multos ~i invidia plenos LANFR. *Ep.* 17 (41); quamvis utrunque ~e nimis sit et abominabile GIR. *TH* II 23; **s1257** (v. Cultellifer); WYCL. *Compl.* 89 (v. cautela 3a); eam .. vir †destabilis sacrilego violare presumpsit intuitu *Brev. Hyde* f. 406; **1460** (v. derogare a).

detestabilitas [LL], loathsomeness.

1286 ~as facinoris est omnibus principibus .. in exemplum, et omnes debent assurgere ad vindictam (*Lit. Regis*) *Foed.* II 324a.

detestabiliter [LL], detestably. **b** w. loathing.

s1195 cujus [ducis Austrie] corpus .. jacuit inhumatum donec ~iter vermibus scateret M. PAR. *Min.* II 54; ~ius AD. MARSH *Ep.* 8 (v. detorquere b); **1368** alii, se penitenciarios nostros †destabiliter .., falso et mendaciter confingentes *Reg. Heref.* 51; **1432** (v. calamitose). **b** qui .. ventum favoris et laudis humane ~iter abhorrebat ut esset in Domino laudaretur anima sua (P. BLOIS *V. Guthl. prol.*) *NLA* II app. 699; amorem diviciarum ~iter reprobavit *Ib.* (*J. Bridl.*) II 76.

detestamen, curse.

a bannynge, detestatio, ~en, execramen, maledictum, malediccio *CathA*.

detestari [CL]

1 a to curse. **b** to detest, abhor; **c** (*s. pass.*); **d** (gdv.) detestable. **e** to repudiate, refuse to believe.

a †~are [? l. ~ari], *onseacan GlC* D 148. **b** non magnopere ~antur in filiis .. quod similiter ut patribus subinde venisse certissimum est GILDAS *EB* 67; **c710** simoniacam perfidiam tota mente ~or ac respuo (*Ep. Ceolfridi*) BEDE *HE* V 21 p. 344; **8.** .. ~or, *ic onscunige*, **9.** .. ~antur, *lapetteð WW*; GROS. 267 (v. contristabilis); **s1252** (v. cereus 1c); **1358** (v. catholicus 2b). **c s1098** factum est ut .. injustitia hominis eum [Anselmum] non equo judicio fatigantis .. ~aretur EADMER *HN* 111. **d** scortorum ~anda obscenitas ALDH. *VirgP* 45; ~anda omnibus morte BEDE *HE* III 14; **933** (10c) fortiter ~anda totillantis saeculi piacula *CS* 694; **s1166** (v. cauteriare 1c); ob ~andi criminis culpam GIR. *TH* II 9. **e** [generationem] sine mare obstinata malitia .. ~aris *Ib.* I 15; que detestari, que non valet inficiari, / omnia Judeus detegit immo Deus NIG. *Mir. BVM* f. 20v.

2 to denounce, condemn. **b** (w. acc. & inf.) to declare w. condemnation.

680 scisma .., quod psalmigraphi sententia [*Psalm* cxix 165] ~atur ALDH. *Ep.* 4. **b 1175** hoc [sc. pro perceptione crismatis nummos dari] simoniace heresis esse ~ata est sinodus et anathematizavit (*Conc. Westm.*) GERV. CANT. *Chr.* 253.

3 (w. inf.) to hate, be reluctant.

multum ~atus sum reverti ad corpus BEDE *HE* V 12 p. 309; **s1401** Scoti, cum Anglis pacem aut treugam tractare ~antes, diffidenciam et guerram Anglicis decreverant AD. USK 71.

detestatio [CL]

1 a curse, execration. **b** detestation, abhorrence. **c** detestable act, abomination. **d** repudiation.

a audivimus .. Jezabelem .. in prophetas Dei amara ~one saevisse B. *V. Dunst.* 22; **s1212** an talia in ~onem impietatis humane .. divina providerit dispositio quis ambigat, cum peccatum .., quod contra naturam Sodomitica produxit detestatio, ignis assumpsit? *Ann. S. Edm.* 24 (v. et. 1c infra); *CathA* (v. detestamen). **b** non detractationis personarum sed ~onis causa vitiorum GIR. *GE* II 27; rectitudinis emulatio et ~o pravitatis AD. MARSH *Ep.* 1 p. 78. **c** **s1212** (v. 1a supra); **1359** perversa ~o .. inolevit quod .. diebus Dominicis .. mercata .. fiunt *Conc.* III 43a. **d** hic inventor istius atque defensor verbalem, fictam et frivolam ponit ~onem seu revocacionem OCKHAM *Dial.* 750 (cf. id. *Err. Papae* 964: erroribus .. in tribus predictis suis ~onibus contentis).

2 testament.

si quis forte sine ~one [AS: *cwydeleas*] ex hac vita migraverit (*Cons. Cnuti*) *GAS* 357.

detestator [LL], **a** swearer, curser. **b** detester, abhorrer.

a non detestator sis impius; est Deus ultor / faminis enormis, lingue recolens maledicta. / adventus Christi, Natalis, passio, corpus, / .. / luna, dies, splendor solis juratio non sit D. BEC. 1421; *a banner*, devotator, derogator, ~ator, execrator *CathA*. **b** non iniquitatis auctor est, sed ~or BALD. CANT. *Tract.* 5. 422D.

detesticulare [cf. CL testiculari], to geld. *V. et. etesticulare.*

1330 est ad grave dampnum domini regis et haraciarum suarum .. si hujusmodi equi .. in eadem foresta teneantur nisi sint ~ati *Chanc. Misc.* 11/8/4.

dethyrsare [cf. CL thyrsus], to shred or strip (herbs).

shredyn wortys or herbys, detirso *PP*.

detinentia, detainment.

sanctitatis vestre presentiam propter nonnullas causarum cogentium ~ias personaliter .. adire non sufficio AD. MARSH *Ep.* 6.

detinēre [CL]

1 to hold in, confine. **b** to hold, possess. **c** (w. abstr. obj.) to hold fast, retain. **d** (intr.) to draw back, ebb.

virtus .. ~et aquas violenter superius—dico aquas que super celos sunt. sed aquas ~et sursum quia forte expedit .. FISHACRE *Quaest.* 47; ut liberentur naves detente TREVET *Troades* 54. **b** indignum judicantes eam [sc. insulam] ignavorum dominio ~eri ABBO *Edm.* 1; †**693** Berthwaldus .., quae a tempore .. G. Romani pontificis nunc usque sua aecclesia ~uit .. sortitus (*Lit. Papae*) W. MALM. *GP* I 35 (cf. demandare 2). **c** da ei, Domine, claves regni coelorum, ut .. quorum ~uerit peccata detenta sint EGB. *Pont.* 2. **d** cum jam ~uisset salsus fluvius et litora usque ad recentis aque alveolum exsiccasset *G. Hen. V* 25 p. 168.

2 (w. personal obj.) to detain, hold back; **b** (w. ref. to illness or disability); **c** (under constraint). **d** to restrain, prevent. **e** to keep.

cum quibus, fraterna caritate detentus, .. hactenus degui ABBO *Edm. pref.*; **1126** nisi amore curie ~eris *Ep. Anselm. Bury* 97; castigationibus, consiliis et suis interpositionibus eum longe ~et MAP *NC* III 3 f. 40; **1217** cum [legatus] episcopum pro negotiis suis secum ~uerit et adhuc ~eat *Pat* 71; Hercules .. descendens ad infernum non potuit ibi ~eri TREVET *Troades* 53. **b** in infirmitate .. ~ebatur *V. Cuthb.* I 4; acerbissimo langore ~a BEDE *HE* V 4; **s878** juvenis erat animoque juvenili detentus fuerat *Chr. S. Neoti*; nulla infirmitate detentus *State Tri. Ed. I* 82; **1301** capellanus, qui detentus fuit gravi infirmitate, quod (*sic*) nullo modo potuit accedere ad curiam *SelPlMan* 126; **1438** cecitate oculorum detentus *Cl* 288 m. 12. **c** **c1072** si quis in .. regali via sanguinem fuderit .., si dum hoc facit deprehensus atque detentus fuerit, regi emendabit *Pl. Anglo-Norm.* 8 (cf. *Powicke Studies* 24); **1197** Mattheum .. et Alanum .. captos ~uimus (*Lit. Regis R.*) *Foed.* I 96b; **1201** detentus fuit in gaolam *SelPlCrown* 7; **1208** (v. detentio 2); **1254** (v. clericalis 1d); detentus erat in prisona donec finem fecit cum .. comite *State Tri. Ed. I* 6; **1312** ipsos .. contra vadium et plegium et communem legem terre .. in carcere ~endo *RScot* 111a; **1382** (v. carceraliter); **1391** eum ~uit et non abhinc voluit eum abire *Leet Norw.* 71; **s1399** (v. carcer 1b). **d** **1228** omnes habitantes circa partes maritanas (*sic*) exleges .. efficiuntur et .. a juris sive justicie execucione ~entur suspensi *Cl* 108; plurimis cogentiis .. quominus cum ipso proficiscerer sum detentus AD. MARSH *Ep.* 32. **e** **1218** detenet (v. alopare a); **1520** contra [sacerdotes] focarias et concubinas publice ~entes *Conc. Scot.* I cclxxi.

3 to withold (wrongfully) (sts. w. dat. of claimant): **a** land or sim.; **b** rent, tithe or sim.; **c** goods or sim. **d** to detain (stray beasts).

a **798** (12c) rex Offa .. cenobium Coccham .. quanto tempore vixit ~uit et absque litterarum testimonio suis post se heredibus reliquid (*Clovesho*) *CS* 291; R. Pictavensis de terra quam S. Edmundus habet in hoc dim. hund[reto] tenuit socam; in Prelestuna de tinuit Warengerus ad feudum Rogeri *DB* II 139v.; **1181** preter R., quam occupatam ~et Robertus *Dom. S. Paul.* 144 (cf. ib. cx); **1202** (v. contradicere 6a); **1217** faciatis .. comitisse .. maritagium suum habere .., quod ei injuste ~etis *Pat* 103; **1236** (v. detentio 3a); **1265** x acras terre .. que fuerunt .. Ricardi .. occupavit et ~uit eidem *Cl* 45; **1299** (v. contra 6c); **1337** cum .. rege Francie, qui .. terras nostras .. nobis .. ~uit et adhuc ~et minus juste (*Cl*) *Conc.* II 623a; **1377** pia loca secularia .. invadere, .. occupare, occupata ~ere, diruere .. *Mon. Hib. & Scot.* 358b. **b** hoc manerium reddit per consuetudinem xij oves per annum... Radulfus hanc consuetudinem usque modo ~uit *DB* I 97; negat se ~uisse servitium *Ib.* II 381v. (cf. ib. 279: hunc [liberum hominem] ~uit N. aurifaber, et valet vj d.); **1214** cum hii qui decimas ~uerunt vel suripuerunt ad penitentiam accesserint, non admittantur nisi .. *Conc. Syn.* 33; **1246** medietatem pecunie detente ipsis plene relaxavimus *Reg. Paisley* 25; **1285** si quis ~eat domino suo servicium sibi debitum (2 *Westm.* 21) *StRealm* I 83; **1290** injuste et sine racione ~uit Johanni .. annuum redditum sibi debitum, viz. terciam partem j denarii *SelPlMan* 38; **1320** quare injuste ~et communi vie xij d. quos promisit *CBaron* 130. **c** **1200** (v. deteriorare 2a); **1218** reddi faciatis Rogero .. res suas quas Robertus .. et Vincencius .. ceperunt et ei ~ent *Pat* 150; **1219** Philippus .. petit versus Aliciam .. tres anulos aureos, quos ei injuste ~et *CurR* VIII 35; **1221** cepit averia sua et aliorum .. in communi pastura de N. .. et ea ~uit contra vadium et plegium *SelPlCrown* 90; **s1407** rex .. non solverat .. custodibus Calesie sua vadia, quare ipsi ~uerunt lanas mercatorum *Eul. Hist. Cont.* III 411. **d** **1313** equum .. quem .. probavit esse suum, qui detentus fuit nomine *estray Eyre Kent* I 81.

detingere [cf. CL tingere], to dye, tinge (fig.).

aspice spinosum caput meum, vide corpus meum sanguine ubique detinctum *Spec. Laic.* 20.

detirsare v. dethyrsare.

detitulare [cf. titulare], to debase (title).

proprie nam venditor artis / detitulat titulos quos ingerit J. EXON. *BT* II 349.

detogare [cf. CL togatus], to divest, unclothe (fig.).

inguina Democritus castrat / .. / .. fratresque togatos / detogat et Veneris geminum depellit avito / mancipium tecto HANV. IX 330 p. 387.

detonare [CL], to thunder out (fig.); **b** (an utterance). **c** to make thunderous, fill w. sound.

persecutionis .. ~ante procella, fuga conceditur Christianis W. NEWB. *Serm.* 893. **b** respondens talia fatur. / .. / haec ubi detonuit .. ÆTHELWULF *Abb.* 747. **c** cantibus angelicis spatium totius aeris ~ari audiebatur FELIX *Guthl.* 50 p. 159.

detonatio, bang.

actio baculi facientis ~onem in percutiendo BACON VII 19.

detondēre [CL], to shear, shave, tonsure.

detonsa, intonsa *GlH* D 330; forpices .. de quibus fama celebrior est illius quondam detonsos fuisse crines R. COLD. *Cuthb.* 42; *to schave*, radere .., tondere, re-, de- *CathA*; die eadem qua detonsus primum fuit FERR. *Kinloss* 63; *Ib.* 70 (v. convertere 8b).

detonsor, clipper (of coins).

Dial. Scac. I 3 E (v. decurtator).

detorchiare [cf. torchiare], to plaster, (p. ppl. as sb. m. or n.) plasterwork (*cf. Building in Eng.* 223).

1212 non cooperiat de arundine nec de junco nec de aliquo modo straminis neque stipula, nisi sit de tegula vel cingula vel bordo vel .. de plumbo aut †estra [? l. extra] ~iato [? l. de torchiato] *MGL* II 87.

detorquēre [CL], to wrench. **b** (fig.) to distort, pervert.

~eri, deflecti *GlH* D 332; detorsit, *æthræt GlP* 630; [carcannus] nates et anum ~endo corrodebat R. COLD. *Cuthb.* 20. **b** malorum corda per injustitiam detorta ad justitiae regulam diriguntur BEDE *Luke* (iii 5) 352; cum conspiciantur .. suavissimam sanctitatem .. in luxum sordide voluptatis tanto detestabilius quanto damnabilius .. ~ere AD. MARSH *Ep.* 8 p. 88.

detorsio, deflexion, conversion.

si non sit honeste / in casu dicto, fiat detorsio casus / in casum seriemque stude contexere vocum, / ut rude thema nove forme sibi sumat amictum VINSAUF *PN* 1682.

detractare, ~abilis, ~atio v. detrect-.

detractio [CL]

1 'drawing' (dragging of criminal to execution).

s†**1184** (recte **1196**) de ~one Wilhelmi cum Barba: hoc anno W. .. detractus fuit et suspensus *Leg. Ant. Lond.* 2; **s1283** David frater Liwelini corporis ~oni atque suspensioni, capitis detruncacioni, combustioni .. adjudicatus est OXNEAD *Chr.* 262.

2 a taking away. **b** (math.) subtraction. **c** retraction. **d** withholding, reservation.

a qualiter .. Dominus .. tria ab eis [Gallis] subtraxit: .. tercio potenciam eorum per ~onem nobilium et virorum forcium .. in hiis preliis *G. Hen. V* 17. **b** ut hujus ~onis [v. l. diminutionis] labor minuatur, subjecta est tabula secundum xxviij numerum coacervata ADEL. *Elk.* 5. **c** **s1059** [Berengarius] dixit corpus Domini non transmutari in formam panis et vini.. qui vero .., ab errore revocatus, sanctus postea factus est. cujus error et ~o ad sui laudem in Decretis conscribitur *Eul. Hist.* I 382. **d** **s1213** facio .. homagium Deo et .. pape .. ad tenendum regnum Anglie de eo sine ~one aliqua (*Juramentum J. Regis*) *Ib.* III 107.

3 a mauling. **b** distraction, diversion of interest; *cf. distractio* 5.

a boviculi: in ~one a canibus, ij *Ac. Beaulieu* 118. **b** **1423** ut studio oracionis liberius insisteret minusque occasionem ~onis interpolacionisque materiam inveniret AMUND. I 108.

4 detraction, disparagement, back-biting.

adloquitur omnes ut .. ab odiis, ~onibus, et scandalis caveant *Hist. Abb. Jarrow* 25; qui .. ~onibus aurem libenter aperit .., hanc animae suae portam mortis efficit BEDE *Luke* 417; **802** non sint murmurationes inter vos, .. non invidiae, non ~ones [cf. *1 Pet.* ii 1] ALCUIN *Ep.* 250; in peccati abrenuntiatione, non alterius ~one, baptizamur LANFR. *Cel. Conf.* 627C; **1191** quia id proculdubio in ~onem ordinis vestri ac nominis redundaret *Ep. Cant.* 357; cogitatur et dicitur in Galonem ~o, sed in Sadium fit ~onis ostensio MAP *NC* III 2 f. 38; BRAKELOND 143v. (v. 2 consuere 2); susurratio est diminutio boni alterius per sermonem immanifestum et ~o per sermonem manifestum [cf. *2 Cor.* xii 20] HALES *Sent.* II 183; causas pervertit mordax detractio; virtus / in vitium quadam proximitate cadit GARL. *Tri. Eccl.* 40; **1317** (v. dens 2b); S. Gregorius ter ei apparuit et ter blande de sua tenacia et detraxione †sine ~one [? *gl.*: sive ~one] corripuit BROMPTON 734.

detractivus, disparaging, slanderous.

c1340 viperina quadam mordacitate linguam suam docentes loqui mendacia ~a *FormOx* 169.

detractor [CL], detractor, back-biter.

8.. cum ~oribus, *mid telendum WW*; ~ores et murmuratores apostolus Deo odibiles appellat [cf. *Rom.* i 30] H. LOS. *Ep.* 48; multi ~ores †oblactaverunt [l. oblatraverunt], dicentes quia accepit de sacristia quod voluit [etc.] BRAKELOND 130; dic mihi, detractor, quid garris? GARL. *Hon. Vit.* 43; mendacium falsi testis vel ~oris *Fleta* 335; **s1321** in quibusdam .., non solum sue felicitati, immo pocius ~oribus divine dispensacioni, sic desevit rectum judicium judicis omnium ut .. *Flor. Hist.* III 207.

detractorie, slightingly, w. deprecation.

si odis peccatum tuum, quare ornate de eo loqueris? .. loquere confusibiliter et quasi multum ~ie, sicut velles confundere diabolum *AncrR* 121.

detractorius, disparaging, back-biting.

sermo ~ius murmuratio mordens procul sit ab ore .. monachi H. LOS. *Ep.* 48; unde fit ut ~iis linguis hinc potius exponar *Dial. Scac.* II 28 B; **1192** o labia ~ia, o lingua maledica et dolosa P. BLOIS *Ep.* 89. 279C; seruntur verba ~ia et fratres .. fratricide efficiuntur NECKAM *NR* II 107; **1299** (v. conviciatorius); verbum perniciosum .. est multiplex, sc. hereticum, mendax, ~ium [ME: *bacbitunge*], adulatorium *AncrR* 21; **1345** ne fama volatilis, fictis et ~iis conducta relatibus, vos .. aliud de nobis sentire faciat (*Lit. Regis*) AD. MUR. *Chr.* 168.

detractus [CL = *omission, taking away*], detraction, back-biting.

os duplex odias; ad mensam non paciaris / detractus *Dietarium* 22.

detradere v. detrudere 2.

detrahere [CL]

1 to drag away, pull off. **b** to strip off (crusader's cross).

peplorum amicula, sceleratis manibus membratim detracta, nequaquam a sanctis artubus spoliari valuerunt ALDH. *VirgP* 50; opima spolia, quae dux ~it *GlC* O 219; **8..** ut †~et [l. ~at] *þet he ut atio WW*; **9..** detracta, *fram atoge* (*sic*) *WW*; sibi calciamenta detraxit R. COLD. *Godr.* 41; tunica scissa, que propter distensionem corporis ~i non poterat W. CANT. *Mir. Thom.* II 40; sonus tanquam corium carni ~eretur *Ib.* VI 83; Cambises judici pellem detraxerat / sedemque judicis detracta texerat WALT. WIMB. *Carm.* 572. **b** Gaufrido .. et Willelmo, detracta sibi cruce, domi sedere permissis DEVIZES 26v.

2 a to 'draw' (criminal), to drag to execution; *v. et. distrahere* 2; *cf. detrectare* 4. **b** to bring into court (as defendant).

a si homo dominum suum occiderit, .. detractus suspendatur *Cust. Norm.* 35. 5; **1221** eum occiderunt ... et

ideo ~antur et tunc suspendantur *SelPlCrown* 116; **s1255** [Judeus] per pedes proprios caude vivus equi alligatur, super quem confestim ascendens quidam juvenis subductis calcaribus eundem in cursum velocius excitavit et nefandum .. per vicos et plateas .. civitatis spectante populo ~ebat *Ann. Burton* 345; *Fleta* 16 (v. dismembrare b); **1305** (v. devalare); **1318** (v. avalare c). **b c1236** cum talis ~eret talem in placitum in curia Christianitatis de laico feodo suo (*Breve*) Gros. *Ep.* 72* p. 234.

3 a to maul, tear to pieces; *v. et. distrahere* 1a. **b** (refl.) to be distraught; *cf. distrahere* 5b.

a †deterraxas [l. detraxisti], disrupisti *GlH* D 328 (cf. ib. D 337: detraxit, confregit); **1239** damus ille .. fuit absque plaga .. et fere detractus cum porcis *SelPlForest* 71. **b s1166** reges occulto odio sese ~ebant [v. l. distrahebant] *Flor. Hist.* II 80.

4 to subtract, omit. **b** to detract.

ut omnes illi versus qui supra dictum numerum videntur excedere, detractis sinaliphis, ad xvij .. redigantur Aldh. *Met.* 10 p. 84; directa summa ab ea ipsa xxviij anni ~endi, quotiens ab ea ~i possunt Adel. *Elk.* 5; clementie est aliquid ultrici ~ere sententie Gir. *PI* I 7 p. 22; **c1500** vobis .. statuta .. domus .. corrigendi .. ac eis addendi et ex ipsis ~endi .. plenam .. concedimus .. facultatem (*Lit. Papae*) *Deeds Balliol* 310. **b** uxoris ad fidem conversio nihil ~it imperio mariti Gardiner *VO* 96.

5 to disparage, speak slightingly (of): **a** (w. dat. or absol.); **b** (w. acc.).

a insusurrare, i. occulte ~ere, *diglice tælan* Ælf. *Sup.*; **s1014** frequenter ipsi martyri [S. Edmundo] ~ere et illum nil sanctitatis habere fuit ausus dicere Fl. Worc. I 168; manifeste videtur insanie illi ~ere discipline que omnes alias instruit J. Sal. *Met.* 873B; Ad. Scot *Serm.* 223A (v. derogare a); si virtuosum precessero, ut fiam invidiosus, clam ~ent Map *NC* IV 13 f. 55; sciens .. canes suos, emulos sc. et detractores, ~endo dicere illum familiaritatem principum affectare Gir. *GE* II 22; **1268** predicavit pro parte comitis, partem comitis justificando et parti regis ~endo *JustIt* 618 r. 17*d*.; **1339** ~encium informacio emula vel sinistra (*Lit. Regis*) Ad. Mur. *Chr.* 98; [Parisienses] Anglicanas subtilitates, quibus palam ~unt, vigiliis furtivis addiscunt R. Bury *Phil.* 9. 156. **b** qui alienum revelat consilium quod sibi injungitur celandum, proditor fit, cum alium ~it Milemete *Nob.* 83.

detrans v. dodrans 2. **detraxio** v. detractio 4.

detrectabilis, provoking detraction, unpraiseworthy.

et si vita sacerdotum valde detractabilis fuerit Netter *DAF* II 20a.

detrectare (detract-) [CL]

1 to reject, repudiate. **b** (w. inf.) to refuse. **c** (w. acc. & inf.) to forbid, grudge.

~avit, *forsooc GlC* D 71; dum tauri juga ~ant Gir. *DK* I 17; Albanus .. ~ando fugam .. celebravit exordium W. Newb. *Serm.* 887; [advocatus] pactiones violat, ~at transactiones P. Blois *Ep.* 26. 92B. **b** confidentes in virtute sua, conditoris adjutorium quaerere ~ant Bede *Hom.* I 4. 20; officium .. suscipere vel susceptum digne gerere ~ant *Id. Luke* (xix 20–21) 565; quousque .. servitii debitum mihi ~as exhibere? W. Jum. IV 14; **s1109** [archiepiscopus Ebor'] suscepit a ministro, R. sc. Lundoniensi episcopo, quod ~averat suscipere a magistro [sc. archiepiscopo Cant'] W. Malm. *GP* III 120; ad regratiandum redire ~arunt Ad. Marsh *Ep.* 11; **1268** (v. Dalmaticus 2b); **a1380** si ~averint comparere, pena .. bannicionis .. percellantur *StatOx* 88; **s1314** articulos .. ad effectum ~avit perducere Wals. *HA* I 140. **c** tantam naturalium bonorum gratiam in unum congeri livida natura ~ans .., niveo candori nevum adjecit Gir. *TH* III 49.

detrectatio (detract-) [CL], detraction, disparagement, back-biting.

lacerans homines trux detractatio linguae Aldh. *VirgV* 2729; ~o, vituperatio, *tæl GlH* D 336; illis delectationem, istis ~onem .. prestans Gir. *EH* II 32; **s1134** intumuit superbia, minis, maledictionibus et ~onibus M. Par. *Min.* I 247 (= *Id. Maj.* II 160: detractionibus); **1423** ut ~onis et susurri vicia a vestri congregacione penitus elongentur *Reg. Cant.* III 518.

detrementum v. decrementum 2a.

detrenchare [cf. trenchare], to provide w. an outflow trench.

1330 quandam seweram .. vocatam Skyterflekdyk' ~avit, per quam trencheam aqua a predicta sewera .. exivit (*CoramR*) *Pub. Works* I 221.

detricale v. dextralis 2a.

detrimen, loss. *V. et. detrimentum* 2.

s1230 rex .. cum exercitu suo, qui multa jam passus est thesauri sui cum ~ine diminutionem M. Par. *Min.* II 326.

detrimendum v. detrimentum 2a.

detrimentosus [CL], harmful.

Knighton II 144 (v. compassiosus).

detrimentum [CL]

1 decrease. **b** (astr.) waning.

[amphibrachus] cum praedictis pedibus parem divisionis non servat regulam, sed triplum condicionis incrementum contra simplum temporis ~um repugnat Aldh. *PR* 121. **b** Bede *TR* 43 (v. crementum 1b); **798** (v. augmentum 1b); [luna] juxta sui vel incrementa vel ~a Gir. *TH* II 3; apoplexia .. que in cremento lune accidit pessima est .., que vero apoplexia venit in ~o lune minus molesta Gilb. II 114v. 2.

2 loss, harm, damage, detriment; **b** (involving financial liability; *cf. deterioratio* 2).

absque fidei ~o debitum denegare honorem Gildas *EB* 4; sed detrīmenta rogi penitus ludibria faxo Aldh. *Aen.* 15 (*Salamandra*) 2; tum luscus tortor sensit detrīmenta pupillae *Id. VirgV* 1319; Bede *HE* II 5 (v. crementum 1c); ~um, *wonung GlC* D 177; **836** si anima ejus ~um patietur *CS* 416; omne pecus perdat ad †detrimendum et ignominiam sui (4 *Eadgar, Versio* C) *GAS* 213; coegit Britones .. recurrere, nec sine ~o suorum G. Mon. X 4; **s1117** multi procerum regis recesserunt ab eo, quod maximo ei fuit ~o H. Hunt. *HA* VII 29; **1269** *SelPlForest* 44 (v. damnum 1f); duplicatis cubitis reclinatur in codicem .. ad libri non modicum ~um R. Bury *Phil.* 17. 220. **b 1294** dominus R. subtraxit tres annos de termino suo de ecclesia de R., quam habet ad firmam de dicto domino R., ad ~um suum xxx s. *SelPlMan* 116.

detrituriginе v. deterere a.

detrivere [*backformed from* detrivi *perf. of* deterere], to dash, crush.

manus .. in remigiis retinendis jam defecerant, undisque .. supercadentibus de viribus lascescientium remigia ipsa ex parte detraxerant partemque residuam ipsi renitentes ~endo confregerunt R. Cold. *Cuthb.* 23.

detrucidare [cf. CL trucidare], to slaughter.

quis est qui vos .. ~ando elidat? R. Cold. *Cuthb.* 30.

detrudere [CL]

1 to thrust away, fend off, expel. **b** to get rid of.

sed tiro infracta tectus testudine Christi / horrida vulnifici detrudit spicula ferri Aldh. *VirgV* 2701; **786** si quis .. sceleri adhaeserit, si episcopus est aut ullus ex sacerdotali gradu, ex ipso ~datur et a sancta hereditate deiciatur Alcuin *Ep.* 3 p. 24; ~sis, i. expulsis, proturbatis, exclusis, precipitatis, *onbesceofenum GlH* D 334. **b** Salomon .. omnes montes in circuitu ejus [sc. templi] altitudine ~sit Sæwulf 843; si qua tibi vilis res sit qua sis oneratus, / illam collaudes cunctis, illam venereris; / sic citius vilem poteris detrudere mercem D. Bec. 607.

2 to thrust (into confinement).

ecclesiae sequipedas in latebras lautumiae diri tortores ~dunt Aldh. *VirgP* 50; R. Cold. *Cuthb.* 20 (v. carcer 1a); Gerv. Tilb. I 17 (v. caliginosus); **c1245** sacerdotes cum filiabus spiritualibus luxuriantes .. in artissimum monasterium ~dantur *Conc. Syn.* 427; **1282** constabularius de Ruthelan fecit eundem †detradi in carcerem injuriose *Ep. Peckham* 351; **s1306** qui .. diris carceribus ~duntur *Flor. Hist.* III 133; ad agendum perpetuam penitenciam in monasterio ~datur Wycl. *Blasph.* 122; **s1381** regina ac maritus suus .. capiuntur et in custodiam ~duntur *V. Ric. II* 34.

detruncare [CL]

1 to mutilate, cut up: **a** (person); **b** (animal); **c** (inanim. obj.). **d** to lop (tree). **e** to cut off (limb or head). **f** (?) to eradicate (hair).

a cum sic torperent et mortis amara timerent, / jam detruncandi, jugulandi, mortificandi R. Cant. *Malch.* V 148; **s1170** [T. archiepiscopus] sicut verus Christi martyr ~atur *Chr. Melrose* 84; **s1250** proposuerunt cives .. archiepiscopum .. in frusta ~are M. Par. *Maj.* V 124; rex Francorum .., cui oblata fuit pars corporis [S. Edmundi], respondit: "non placeat Deo ut pro me ~etur quod Deus integrum conservavit" *Ib.* 113; [Venus] hos reddit fures, illos suspendit ac istos / detruncat Garl. *PP* 216. 1875; **1309** eos .. mandant suspendi patibulis vel capitibus ~ari *Reg. Cant.* 1034. **b 786** equos .. ~atis (v. 2 cauda 1a). **c** fures .. libros enormiter ~antes, qui pro epistularum chartulis schedulas laterales abscindunt R. Bury *Phil.* 17. 223. **d 1242** in vj quercubus prosternendis .. et eisdem ~andis et cariandis usque N. *Pipe* 307. **e s1272** membris ~atis (v. corpus 1d); capite ~ato Fortescue *LLA* 13 (v. corpus 1a). **f** si accidit juvenibus propter calidum fumum .. caput ascendentem, unde ~entur capilli et †deutrucentur Gilb. II 81. 2.

2 to curtail.

ecclesie termini .. sunt restricti, sincopati, et ~ati .. et possessionum .. sunt spoliate *Remonstr. Ir.* 913.

detruncatio [LL], mutilation (of person), cutting off (of limb). **b** detruncation, curtailing.

[Henricus I] principio regni .. ad membrorum ~onem, post ad pecunie solutionem proclivior W. Malm. *GR* V 411; in condempnatos ultrices manus mittunt, ut alios suspendio, alios membrorum ~one vel aliis modis juxta quantitatem perpetrati sceleris puniant *Dial. Scac.* II 7 B; si ad ultionem ~onis ejus .. cives .. vellent insurgere W. Fitzst. *Thom.* 132; **s1267** quod, si .. quis quempiam de suis invaderet .., capitis ~one vel suspendio plecteretur Wykes 209. **b 1280** per ~onem .. officii cultus divinus videatur minui Peckham *Ep.* 126.

detrusio [LL], thrusting (into confinement).

1214 pro quo peccato .. xv annorum debetur penitentia et postmodum ~o in monasterium *Conc. Syn.* 26.

detuberare, to nap or burl (cloth); hence *detuberatio*, *~ator*, *~atrix*. *Cf. extuberare* 2.

to noppe, ~are, -tor, -trix, & -cio *CathA*.

detulere [*backformed from* detuli *perf. of* deferre], (pr. ppl.) carrying. *Cf. contulere.*

mare .. stipitem .. ~ens *V. Cuthb.* III 4 (v. 1 deportare 3a).

detumescere [CL], **detumēre,** to sink down, subside: **a** (of swelling); **b** (of sea); **c** (fig.).

a tumor .. paulatim a superficie ~escens corporis ad viscerum interiora perlapsus est Bede *CuthbP* 8; paullatim ~escente gutture via voci .. aperitur Ailr. *SS Hex* 9; cepit venter .. paulatim ~ere naturalemque .. statum recipere W. Cant. *Mir. Thom.* II 40; quidam .. tumefactam habebat faciem .. post meridiem ~escebat sed visum amittebat *Quaest. Salern.* P 96; vidit omnino pedem ~uisse *Canon. G. Sempr.* 150; **1244** ceci nati vident .., hydropici ~escunt (*Lit. Abb. Pontiniaci*) M. Par. *Maj.* IV 325. **b** luna .. cum ultra medietatem jam tumescit .., occidentis equora .. intumescunt ..; eadem .. decrescente .., paulatim tumor ille ~escit Gir. *TH* II 3; detumet unda, silet Auster, Boreas flat Garl. *Tri. Eccl.* 33. **c 1157** in adventum .. regine .. et .. cancellarii .., qui .. procellam michi ~uisse dixerunt J. Sal. *Ep.* 96 (31); spiritus hominis tribus modis deficit et ~escit Bald. Cant. *Tract.* 9. 486D; statim ~ui .. et residerunt turgide conceptiones mee J. Ford *Wulf.* 50; officiales prelatorum .. sunt sanguisuge eorum, qui intumescunt et ~escunt Gir. *GE* II 33 p. 329.

detumulare [cf. CL tumulare]

1 to disentomb.

s1002 fecit .. ~ari duos ejus socios .. et simul cum S. Yvone Rameseiam .. transferri *Chr. Wallingf.* 63.

2 to entomb or (?) *f. l.*

s1200 cum sancti viri [Hugonis ep. Linc.] corpus ad detumulandum [v. l. tumulandum] .. deportaretur Oxnead *Chr.* 111 (cf. R. Howd. IV 142).

detunicare [cf. CL tunicare], to uncloak (fig.), disclose.

s1192 donec omnia que Salahadinus duci .. mandaverat palam ~aret M. Par. *Min.* II 32; **s1252** ~ata est malitia Judaica *Id. Maj.* V 345; **s1240** suas proprias proditiones manifeste toti mundo ~averunt *Flor. Hist.* II 243.

deturbare [CL], **a** to expel, dislodge. **b** to uproot. **c** to disrupt. **d** to depose. **e** to harass.

a dis[s]ipat, ~at *GlC* D 240; fortissimis .. heroibus hostiles acies a foribus basilicae ~antibus Ælnoth *Cnut* 56; [Lanfrancus] ~atis veteribus fundamentis, suscitavit in ampliorem statum omnia W. Malm. *GP* I 43. **b c1290** si .. rectores .. arbores in hujusmodi crescentes cimiteriis, que quidem arbores .. loca .. ubi plantate fuerint non modicum condecorant .., evulserint, †deturpaverint seu radices extirpaverint *Conc. Syn.* 1124. **c s1012** dum quisque carissimos hospites .. cogeretur prodere et amplexus gladio ~are W. Malm. *GR* II 165 p. 191. **d 1559** reginam .. de regali statu .. ~are (v. compassare). **e** concilians et demulcens superos, ~ans et exterrens inferos Eadmer *Virt.* 583D; diabolus .. hiis sermonibus irrecuperabiliter ~atus [v. l. †deturpatus] nimia verecundia recedebat J. Yonge *Vis. Purg. Pat.* 9.

1 deturpare v. deturbare.

2 deturpare [CL]

1 to dirty, befoul, pollute. **b** (of fire) to ravage.

[Dunstanum] luto ~atum [canes] magis monstrum quam hominem putaverunt B. *V. Dunst.* 6; Ethelredus fontes ~avit quum a B. Dunstano baptizaretur R. Niger *Chr. II* 154; **1360** (v. caenulentus a); **1416** si terra dominica .. per hujusmodi mineram .. vel per cariagium carbonum .. fuerit ~ata vel conculcata *Cl* 266 m. 20*d*.; propter porcos et animalia alia que possent illud [cimiterium] ~are Lyndw. 253 c; **1493** M. T. ~at cotidie aquam currentem in villa cum puteo suo *CourtR Ottery St. Mary* 104; **1510** cimiterium ~atur cuniculis *Vis. Linc.* I 38. **b** ecclesiam .. que combustione ~ata fuerat H. Hunt. *HA* VIII 23; **s1346** totam circa regionem incendio .. ~avit *Meaux* III 57.

2 (w. ref. to persons or animals): **a** to disfigure. **b** (?) to bring to a shameful end. **c** to violate, dishonour (sexually). **d** to corrupt (morally), deprave, disgrace. **e** to defame, insult.

a leprosi . ., quos . . cutis callositas elefantino tabo ~ans . . maculaverat ALDH. *VirgP* 36; virgo . ., quia . . pubertatis decorem membrorum suorum ~aret inequalitas W. CANT. *Mir. Thom.* II 36; manibus tumoris emormitatis [? l. enormitate] ~atis *Mir. Fridesw.* 99; in hujusmodi avibus [sc. pavonibus] pedes et tibie scabie ~antur *Quaest. Salern.* C 13; **s1256** [fossores] fulgur terrestre . . ita combussit . . et ~avit ut semper sibi inutiles viderentur M. PAR. *Maj.* V 600. **b s1307** sic majores proditores Scocie mortui sunt et ~ati *Meaux* II 278 (cf. ib. app. 286). **c** ut illam . . fedo coitu suo ~are nequivit G. MON. X 3; qui regis Wallie reginam adulterio ~averit MAP *NC* II 22 f. 31; **s1216** sororem . . meam sponsam Christi, quam dilexi, proponit ~are rex W. GUISB. 155. **d †960** (12c) si . . aliquis frenetico ~atus spiritu hanc . . syngrapham . . demere conaverit *CS* 765; sordidarum scabenti ~atus meditationum prurigine BYRHT. *HR* 3; si de tiranni . . apparenti quis prosperitate tristatur, nequaquam ~atur invidie macula J. SAL. *Pol.* 702B; **1239** se ipsum mendacio suo in aliorum detractione ~at (*Lit. Papae*) M. PAR. *Maj.* III 606. **e** Egelwino ~ato verbis et minis a rege iniquo HERM. ARCH. 6; eum infamibus verbis ~avit ORD. VIT. XII 4 p. 324; **s1212** [rex] Robertum . . minis et conviciis . . cepit ~are *Flor. Hist.* II 143.

3 (w. abstr. obj.) to disfigure, corrupt.

virginitas . ., / quam non deturpat peccati scaeva cicatrix ALDH. *VirgV* 2469; bonum est malorum colloquia vitare; mores enim ~ant W. DONC. *Aph. Phil.* 10. 7; qui in vitiis ratione abutuntur, ipsum motum rationalem ~ant AILR. *Serm.* 25. 464D; **1158** ut gloriam regni tanto ~aret opprobrio J. SAL. *Ep.* 99 (37); per varias criminum maculas ecclesie faciem ~ant H. BOS. *Thom.* IV 11 p. 342; ne tantam summam bonorum unus ~et excessus BRAKELOND 160v.; **1258** puritatem in baptismo susceptam, peccatis postmodum ~atam *Conc. Syn.* 593; ne per ignoranciam seu desidiam divinum officium videatur apud nos in aliquo ~ari *Cust. Cant.* 38.

deturpatio, defacement, disfigurement. **b** debasement.

post destructionem omnium statuarum que Rome fuerunt et ~onem GREG. *Mir. Rom.* 6; BRADW. *CD* 168B (v. deturpativus). **b s1247** visum est multis discretis quod utilius foret materiam mutare quam formam alterare, cum ratione materie et non forme talem suscepisset moneta ~onem M. PAR. *Maj.* IV 633.

deturpativus, corruptive.

perfeccius est omni ~o posse resistere, ne quid deturpacionis paciatur ab illo, et per consequens non posse penitus pollui, quam sic posse BRADW. *CD* 168B.

deudandum v. deodandus.

deultra [LL, al. div.], (prep.) from beyond, across. **b** beyond.

scintille . . ~a muros altissimos †evolebant [? l. evolabant] R. COLD. *Cuthb.* 39; **1169** si quis laicus venerit de ultra mare . ., exquiratur utrum portet aliquid quod sit contra honorem domini regis (*Artic. Regis*) GERV. CANT. *Chr.* 215; **1212** in ccxij lodis mine cariandis ~a . . aquam de I. usque . . loturam de Bromyegg' *MinAc* (*Derb*) 1146/11 m. 12; *fra be yonde*, ~a *CathA*. **b 1419** do . . omnia bona et catalla mea . . tam citra mare quam ~a mare *Cl* 269 m. 8*d*.; **s1461** venerunt . . usque in campum de ultra villam jacentem *Reg. Whet.* I 408.

deunculus, godling.

799 magnum Deum eum nominavit [Paulus], . . non ~um quendam, qualem nova quorundam fingit praesumptio ALCUIN *Ep.* 166 p. 273.

deunx [CL], one *uncia* short of *libra* or *as*, eleven twelfths.

sive horam unam . . seu certe aliud aliquod . . temporis spatium in xij partiri vis, ipsa duodecima pars uncia est; reliquas undecim partes ~cem appellant BEDE *TR* 4 (cf. ib. ~x sive iabus: xj unciae); ponamus . . nomen, postremo quantum unaqueque in se contineat: . . as, . . ~x, . . semunciedeunx dextans, . . dodrans, . . duella, . . dragma, . . dimidia sextula THURKILL *Abac.* 61v.

deus [CL]

1 god: **a** (Classical); **b** (Northern); **c** (other); **d** (phr.).

a prisca nefandorum contemnens fana deorum ALDH. *VirgV* 561 (cf. ib. 1389: exhausta veterum virtute deorum); BEDE *TR* 8 (v. dies 5a); templum ipsa superbum / prima petit solitoque deos implorat honore J. EXON. *BT* III 261; Jupiter ut centum taurorum sanguine fuso, / sic capitur minimi thuris amore deus WALT. ANGL. *Fab.* 22. 18; per quos superi, id est dii, jurant TREVET *Troades* 32; Mercurius . . ab antiquis gentilibus sextus deus esse dicebatur *Deorum Imag.* 6; Jupiter et Juno et ceteri, qui sunt in ore hominum et mentibus, et de quorum fraternitate fama celebratur; atque ex his alii nati sunt, qui putantur dii BRADW. 80 (cf. ib.: feriantur qui deos sibi fabricant . . homines, animalia, arbores, ignem, aut quamcunque rem talem. tales fuerunt quidam gentiles antiqui, qui homines quosdam vivos, quosdam vero mortuos, deos sibi fecerunt); AMUND. I 138 (v. chronicus 4). **b** *Blodmonath*, 'mensis immolationum', [nominatur] quod in eo pecora quae occisuri erant [Angli] diis suis voverent BEDE *TR* 15; suspecti sunt . . quia, si pervenirent ad satrapam [Antiquorum Saxonum] . ., averterent illum a diis suis *Id. HE* V 10; WILLIB. *Bonif.* 6 (v. devotare 1a); ALCUIN *SS Ebor* 158 (v. cultura 4b); ÆTHELW. I 3 (v. devincere 1b); W. MALM. *GR* I 5 (v. dies 5e); ORD. VIT. IV 5 (v. daemon 2c). **c** paganorum prima est [secta] minus de Deo scientium; nec habent sacerdotium, sed quilibet pro voluntate sua fingit sibi deum et colit quod vult. . . deinde sunt idololatre, qui sacerdotes habent . . et orationes certas . . et ponunt plures deos, nullum autem omnipotentem. in tertio gradu sunt Tartari, qui unum deum adorant omnipotentem et colunt, sed nihilo minus ignem venerantur et limen domus BACON *Maj.* II 370 (cf. 3a infra); BRADW. *CD* 14D (v. 1 brodium). **d** dii boni! GIR. *TH* III 53.

2 (phil.) god as first cause or sim.

coepi mecum quaerere si forte posset inveniri unum argumentum . . solum ad astruendum quia deus vere est ANSELM (*Prosl. proem.*) I 93; ADEL. *QN* 76 (v. dissentire 2); an deus in omni tempore sit, qui semper est, an in nullo, qui temporalis non est BALSH. *AD rec. 2* 133; queritur utrum hoc nomen 'deus' debeat habere plurale HALES *Sent.* I 228; prima causa omnium, hoc est deus, nullam habet materiam nec formam J. BLUND *An.* 284; BACON XIII 125 (v. deacus); deus . . est finis hujus scientie [theologie] et efficiens, non igitur materia. . . deus . . non habet partes integrales, cum sit omnino simplex, nec subjectivas, cum sit singularis ex se; nec habet principia, cum sit primum principium, nec passiones . . DUNS *Ord.* I 91; in primis firmissime supponatur quod deus est summe perfectus et bonus, in tantum quod nichil perfeccius vel melius esse posset. hec autem supposicio posset evidenter ostendi ex magnitudine perfeccionis et bonitatis ipsius, que est simpliciter infinita, sicut racionibus philosophicis et theologicis posset multipliciter demonstrari BRADW. *CD* 1CD.

3 Christian (or Jewish) God; **b** (phr.); **c** (oaths). **d** (w. *pro*) gratis.

ungebantur reges non per Deum GILDAS *EB* 21; **601** Constantinus . . Romanam rempublicam a perversis idolorum cultibus revocans omnipotenti Deo Domino nostro Jesu Christo secum subdidit. . . et nunc itaque vestra gloria cognitionem unius Dei, Patris et Filii et Spiritus Sancti, regibus et populis sibimet subjectis festinet infundere (*Lit. Papae*) BEDE *HE* I 32; **s704** sancta synodus respondit: "Wilfrithus Deo amabilis episcopus canonice defensionis suae protectionem exposuit" EDDI 53; alma Deus Trinitas, quae saecula cuncta gubernas BEDE (*Hymn*) *HE* IV 18 p. 247; **738** (12c) sciat se in die judicii rationem Deo redditurum *CS* 159; *CS* 416 (v. desiderare 1c); O Dee cunctipotens cosmi qui regmina flectis *De libero arbitrio* 167; Dei justitiam [AS: *Godes riht*] dictis et factis . . amplectamur (*Quad.*) *GAS* 301; Dominum Christum Jesum dicimus verum Deum et verum hominem ANSELM (*CurD* I 8) II 59 (cf. ib. II 6 p. 101: necesse est ut eam [satisfactionem] faciat deus-homo); sit Deus in primis super omnia corde colendus D. BEC. 20; nihil placet plus Deo . . quam recognitio peccati HALES *Sent.* IV 270; in quarto gradu sunt Judei, qui plus secundum suam legem deberent sentire de Deo et veraciter aspirare ad Messiam, qui est Christus. . . quinto loco sunt Christiani, qui legem Judeorum spiritualiter peragunt et addunt ad ejus complementum fidem Christi BACON *Maj.* II 370 (cf. 1a supra); **1314** quod Deus Pater potuit produxisse creaturam ante Verbum origine, natura vel tempore . . (*Articuli reprobati*) *MunAcOx* 100; **1340** dileccionem vestram . . per Dei misericordiam obsecramus quatinus soli Deo vivo nos . . devotis oracionum instanciis recommendare curetis (*Lit. Regis*) AVESB. 90; **1400** nec possunt Dei viventis manus evadere [cf. *Heb.* x 31] *Lit. Cant.* III 74; Deus Optimus Maximus [cf. CL: Jupiter Optimus Maximus] DEE *Monas pref.* p. 184. **b** auxiliante Deo ALDH. *VirgV pref.* 34; suffragante Deo *Id. VirgV* 1015 (cf. *CS* 43); Deo favente BEDE *HE* I 16; Deo volente *Ib.* IV 26 p. 271; **738** (12c) in nomine Domini Dei nostri *CS* 159; **†749** (12c) hanc donationem Deo teste . . concedo, ut . . ab omnibus operibus oneribusque, auctore Deo, servientes absoluti maneant *Ib.* 178 (cf. *Chr. Evesham* 116: Deo teste . . veni huc propter vos); **c763** (12c) pro amore Dei *Ib.* 194; **c1070** Willelmus Dei gratia rex Anglie *Regesta* p. 120 (cf. gratia); statim post 'Deo gratias' (*Instr. Novic.*) LANFR. *Const.* 382; quod Deus avertat! *Ib.* 164; rex . . dedit Rogero Deus Salvæt Dominas *DB* II 21v.; [W. de Breusa] in omni sermone suo Deum anteponere consuevit, dicens . . "si Deo placuerit" vel "per Dei gratiam futurum est ita" GIR. *IK* I 2; **1227** (v. benedicere 2b); non placeat Deo! M. PAR. *Maj.* V 113 (v. detruncare 1a); **1339** cor habentes pacificum, novit Deus (*Lit. Regis*) AD. MUR. *Chr.* 91; **1340** quia, novit Deus, nichil foret . . accepcius (*Lit. Regis*) AVESB. 88b; **s1342** elegit . . locum in quo, Deo juvante, pugnaret AD. MUR. *Chr.* 127 (cf. ib. 227: Deo adjuvante); ignoscat ei Deus! THORNE 1864 (v. 1 cameraria 3a); det Deus! *G. Hen. V* 25 (v. devoratio d). **c** [Willelmus I], talia "per resurrectionem et splendorem Dei" pronuntians, quod soleret ex industria talia sacramenta facere, que ipso hiatu oris terrificum quiddam auditorum mentibus insonarent W. MALM. *GR* III 281 (cf. ORD. VIT. IV 13 p. 264); [Henricus II] "per oculos", inquit, "Dei, seu gorgiam, sive strumellos, avis illa evadere non poterit . .!", quoniam usu pravo . . sic jurare consueverant (*sic*), sicut et . . Henricus primus "per mortem Dei" GIR. *GE* I 54; terrarum principes alii in omni sermone sacramentis enormibus utentes, per mortem Dei, per oculos, per pedes et dentes, per gorgiam atque strumellos, fatue nimis et indiscrete jurare presumunt *Id. PI* III 29 p. 318; [abbas] ait: " . . per os Dei!" BRAKELOND 153v.; **s1258** [Henricus III] . . respondit: " . . per caput Dei!" M. PAR. *Maj.* V 706 (cf. caput 1b); **s1259** rex Alemannie . . respondit, jurans per guttur Dei *Ib.* 733. **d** hospicium sibi pro Deo petiit MAP *NC* II 14 f. 27v.; **1220** sicut hoc fecit pro Deo et non pro denariis *CurR* VIII 277; **1221** (v. dare 7d; cf. deodandus); **1382** per custodes sigilli pro Deo, quia pauper *Pat* 314 m. 37*d*.

4 *deus hujus saeculi* [*2 Cor.* iv 4], (sts. interp. as) the Devil.

'deus hujus saeculi', quasi diceret: "qui non solum invisibiles creaturas sed etiam hoc †invisibile [? l. visibile] saeculum regit". potest et ita †construit [? l. construi]: "in quibus Deus excaecavit mentes infidelium hujus saeculi"; quia, si de diabolo dictum est 'deus hujus saeculi', sic intelligitur in Evangelio [*John* xii 31] 'princeps mundi hujus' LANFR. *Comment. Paul.* (*2 Cor.* iv 4) 227A; celestis sanctuarii pervasoribus, quos . . deus hujus seculi excecavit AD. MARSH *Ep.* 111; deus hujus seculi sic cecavit eos WYCL. *Sim.* 14.

5 'god' (fig.): **a** (w. ref. to *Phil.* iii 9); **b** (w. ref. to *Exod.* xxii 9); **c** (applied to man). **d** (w. *pater*) godfather.

a 'noster', ait 'venter deus est' R. CANT. *Malch.* II 377; horum deus venter est et ciphi prelati (*Divers. Ord.* 170) *Ps.*-MAP 234. **b** si latet [fur], dominus domus applicabitur ad deos [*gl*: id est, judices] et jurabit . . (*Quad.*) *GAS* 37. **c** hic [Bledgabred] omnes cantores quos retro etas habuerat . . [superabat], ita ut deus joculatorum diceretur G. MON. III 19; DEVIZES 40v. (v. daemonium 2); **a1270** 'ego dixi, dii estis;' [*Psalm* lxxxi 6] . . dii revera, qui potestis / in figuram nove vestis / transmutare veterem (*In Cissores*) *Pol. Songs* 51–2. **d** qui [baptizandum] introduxerit . ., quem Dionysius vocat 'susceptorem' — eum arbitror quem nunc apud nos 'deum patrem' — hominem sacerdotibus et ministris exuendum . . tradit COLET *Eccl. Hier.* 210 (cf. ib. 212: deus pater ille quem D. vocat 'susceptorem').

deusitatus, deprived by non-use.

dicere poterunt quod, quamvis ita usi non essent [libertate] . ., tamen, cum carta eorum antenata sit et libertas anterior, non sunt ~i, quia numquam antea evenit casus quod (*sic*) uti possent BRACTON 57b.

deusus, deprived, or (?) deprivation, by non-use.

dum tamen non sit ~us, hoc est, quod non amittat [jura] per non-usum, sicut dici poterit de servitutibus, de pastu pecoris, et aliis consimilibus BRACTON 423.

deuterogamia [LL *gl.* < δευτερογαμία], second marriage.

~iae, secundae nuptiae *GlC* D 164; ~ie, secunde nuptie OSB. GLOUC. *Deriv.* 173; *the secund weddynge*, bigamia, ~ia *CathA*.

Deuteronomicus, Deuteronomic.

commenta . . nullam . . a ~o praecepto . . authoritatem habentia BEKINSAU 748.

Deuteronomium [LL < Δευτερονόμιον], (in etym. sense) second law. **b** Deuteronomy; **c** (fig.).

~ium, secunda lex *GlC Int.* 83 (cf. ib. D 155: ~ium, iteratio legis); ~ium 'lex secunda' interpretatur OCKHAM *Dial.* 915. **b 802** de servis fugitivis in ~io [xxiii 15–16] legitur . . ALCUIN *Ep.* 246; gestare etiam precipitur [rex] in manibus assidue deutronomium, quatinus inspectione justitie continua erudiatur ad expediendum populi negotia R. NIGER *Mil.* II 17; ut habetur ~ie (*sic*) xi BACON *Maj.* I 328; cum nostra translatio habeat 'onocrotalum' . . tam in ~io [xiv 18] quam in Levitici †secundo [(*recte* xi 18] *Id. Min.* 353; **1396** prima pars Biblie, in qua Genesis, Exodus, Leviticus, Numerus (*sic*), ~ius (*sic*) . . (*Invent.*) *Meaux* III app. lxxxiv (cf. ib. lxxxix: Deutronomium glosatum). **c** en rudis instrumenti, quod arbitror ~ii recapitulatione rite signari, plura in propatulo sita . . suffragantur ALDH. *Met.* 2.

deuterosis, [LL < δευτέρωσις], 'deuterosy', tradition supplementary to Jewish law.

sacerdotii veteris ac legis cui serviebat dignitas . . per ~es Pharisaeorum veri sensus erat luce privata BEDE *Sam.* (*1 Sam* iii 3) 519 (cf. id. *Mark* 254, *citing Jerome*); ~in, novitatem *GlC* D 49.

deuterus [LL < δεύτερος], second.

autentus ~us *Trop. Wint.* 62.

deutinum v. diutinus. **deutronomium** v. Deuteronomium b. **deutrucare** v. detruncare 1f.

devacuare [cf. CL vacuare], to empty (or wind off).

devacuatrices sunt que ~ant fila, vel mulieres aurisece; ~ant [v. l. devastant] et secant tota corpora frequenti coitu, [dum] ~ant et secant aliquando marsupia scolarium Parisiensium [*gl*.: devacuatrices dicuntur G. *desvuideresses*] GARL. *Dict.* 135.

devacuatrix, woman who winds off thread, spinster.

GARL. *Dict.* 135 (v. devacuare); *cylke woman*, ~ix *PP*.

devad- v. divad-. **devag-** v. divad-, divag-.

devalare [OF *devaler*], to strike down, cut down.

1247 percussit ipsum cum quodam palo supra sinistrum humerum, ita quod ~avit ei humerum illum *JustIt* 455 r. 1; **1305** detrahatur . . per medium civitatis usque Elmes et . . ibidem suspendatur et postea ~etur et . . decolletur (*Proc. W. Waleys*) *Ann. Lond.* 141.

devanescere [cf. CL vanescere], to fade away. *V. et. evanescere* 3a.

morbus . . ad inferiora membra descendit ibique demum lanceatus cito devanuit *Mir. Hen. VI* III 88.

devaricare v. divaricare 1a. **devarium** v. deverium.

devastare [CL], to devastate, lay waste (land or buildings, or absol.). **b** (leg.) to commit waste on. **c** to wear out, consume; **d** (fig.); *cf. devacuare.*

regiones impia clade longe lateque ~ans BEDE *HE* III 16; haec terra ~ata est; sed quando T. recepit valebat x s. *DB* (*Beds*) I 216v.; **1305** ecclesias . . sediciose mactavit, combussit et ~avit (*Proc. W. Waleys*) *Ann. Lond.* 141; **s1355** quamplures . . villas . . cepit et . . in eundo et redeundo per incendium ~avit AVESB. 127; **s1461** in omni loco per quem venerant . . depredantes, despoliantes ~antesque *Reg. Whet.* I 388; invadit agellos; / omnia divastans ferro consumit et igne J. HERD *Hist. IV Regum* 53. **b** **1363** dicunt quod priorissa de L. ~avit boscum suum de S. contra assisam foreste (*Inq.*) *Ambrosden* II 140; **1404** presentant quod predictus J. parcellam terre . . ~avit *CourtR Banstead.* **c** **1284** ad sagittas emend' ad opus peditum suorum, quia sagitte eorum erant quasi ~ate *KRAc* 351/9 m. 1; **1411** hoc gutterium fuit antiquum, ~atum et perditum *Lit. Cant.* III 115; **1503** duo tapeta de albo, quasi †devasta [? l. ~ata], cum floribus . . et aquilis in medio *Invent. Ch. Ch.* 132. **d** ira . . mentem intus ~at AD. MARSH *Ep.* 159.

devastatio [LL], devastation.

ante ~onem provincie Northanhymbrorum, que dccclxxv° anno . . ab Haldene Dano facta est RIC. HEX. *Hist. Hex.* I 19; **1260** progressuri . . versus partes Marchie nostre ad ~onem partium earundem *Cl* 268; **1318** occupacionibus et ~onibus castrorum et villarum *Lit. Cant.* III 397; **s1322** tanta karistia subsequta est istam ~onem in episcopatu . . GRAYSTANES 39; **s1461** per viam depredacionis, despoliacionis seu ~onis *Reg. Whet.* I 389.

devastator [LL], devastator, ravager.

1338 pluribus aliis supervenientibus de Wallia, qui multum confluunt de die in diem et sunt magni ~ores *Hosp. in Eng.* 35.

devastatrix, (fig.) devastator, ruiner (f.).

mors, humane condicionis ~ix *NLA* (*J. Bridl.*) II 66.

devastus v. devastare c.

devectare [LL], to carry, transport.

defectare, *wegan* vel *beran GlM* 28. 489; ~are, seorsum portare OSB. GLOUC. *Deriv.* 179.

†devectio, *f. l.*

Augustus . . facetus in jocis ut †~o [l. de Vettio], Julia, †Greuclo [l. Greculo] . . [cf. Macrob. *Sat.* II 4] R. NIGER *Chr. II* 108.

devectus v. devehere, devexus 1b.

devehere [CL], to carry, transport.

†defectum, aportatum *GlC* D 137; dum illuc devectus fueris R. COLD. *Godr.* 285; **c1300** devectus fuit sub rota molendini et per cursum rote currentis defractus fuit et obrutus *IMisc* 67/18; *to bere*, . . portare . ., vehere, de-, con-, ad- . . *CathA.*

develare [CL], to unveil; **b** (fig.).

~are, discooperire OSB. GLOUC. *Deriv.* 178; si develatam faciem monstraverit aut non, / perstringat visum cassibus ille tuum J. SAL. *Enth. Pol.* 381A; ~ato capite *Ps.-*ELMH. *Hen. V* 107. **b** menti et calamo rerum velamina mandat, / que develanti possint venisse magistro / mentis in aspectum HANV. III 184 p. 281.

1 devellere [CL], to pull out.

qui clavi . . nunquam ~i vel extrahi possent nisi . . malleo violenti (*sic*) . . dirui potuissent R. COLD. *Cuthb.* 46.

2 devellere v. divellere. **devenerare** v. defaenerare.

1 devenire [CL], **~iri**

1 (of persons) to come (to); **b** (w. inf.); **c** (w. *ad*) to turn to, get down to. **d** (w. *ad*) to come by, acquire.

quidam abbas . . adsolebat ad verbocinium praefati viri ~ire FELIX *Guthl.* 43; freneticus quidam . . ~it ibi vespere BEDE *HE* IV 3 (cf. ib. V 10: illas ~iens in partes); ut fortunatos felix devenit ad Anglos *Altercatio* 23; si ad id loci ~ire contingeret quo viri sancti caput jaceret ABBO *Edm.* 12; ÆLNOTH *Cnut* 44 (v. doxa a); **s1049** rex E. misit illuc H. episcopum et E. episcopum et ~erunt illuc *AS Chr.*; ad Hibernica litora forte ~it GIR. *TH* III 1; **1232** sint liberi in omnibus locis in regno nostro Anglie, ac corpora et sanguines eorundem, ubicumque ~iantur (*sic*) *Pat* 484. **b** cum praefatus clericus . . Guthlacum . . †tonderare [v. l. tondere] ~isset FELIX *Guthl.* 35. **c** ergo tandem ~iamus ad necessaria immediata DUNS *Ord.* I 26. **d** **1295** nec constat quod ipse bono modo ad eam [navem] ~it *RParl* I 137b.

2 (of things): **a** to come, be brought. **b** to come to, into the possession of; **c** (w. *ad* or *in manum*); **d** (w. *ad proficuum* or *opus*); **e** (w. ref. to writ directing inquiry what lands *etc.* have come to the king); **f** (w. *in*) to come to be included in.

a **s1428** versus Parisium, unde provisiones eorum [mercatorum] sibi ~erunt *Plusc.* X 29. **b** qui redditus ad heredes . . Johannis de Melsa [ob. **a1200**] . . postea ~iebat *Meaux* I 302*n.*; lex nature paucioribus fuit contenta, que memorialiter per patres ad filios ~erunt DUNS *Ord.* I 86; cum . . ad eum [Alveredum] totum regnum [Anglorum] ~isset *Plusc.* VI 16; **14..** nisi terra ~iatur domino feodi pro defectu heredis *Reg. Brev. Orig.* 3; **1437** mercandisas . . [ad] possessionem suam ~tas (*Chanc. Misc.*) *Law Merch.* III 119; **1583** non obstante aliquo titulo . . nobis . . antehac accreto, devoluto aut aliquo modo ~to *Pat* 1235 m. 25. **c** **1266** custodiam terrarum . . que ~it ad manum nostram *Cl* 281; **1268** (v. coffrarius 2a); **1273** castrum et manerium . . que ad manum suam ~erunt *SelCKB* I 2; nisi tenementum illud ~erit in manum capitalis domini pro defectu heredis HENGHAM *Magna* 1; **1322** obligo me . . et . . bona mea . . ad quorumcumque manus ~erint in futurum *Lit. Cant.* I 84; **1378** habent diem ad ostendendum . . que bona . . venerunt ad manus . . coronatoris et ad cujus manus residuum ~erit *Hal. Durh.* 149; **1382** ad cujus manum dictus equus ~iebat totaliter ignorant *Mem. York* I 45. **d** **1340** sic cepit j m. ultra taxacionem suam, que nunquam ~it ad proficuum regis *SelCKB* V 124; **1341** in diversis averiis . . abductis . . ne ~irent ad opus regis *MinAc* 1120/11 r. 14. **e** **1573** commissio in natura brevis de ~erunt post mortem Francisci Conyers *Pat* 1105 m. 27*d.* **f** **1227** preceptum est vicecomiti quod inquirat quantum de propresturis civitatis Ebor' ~erit in fossata civitatis Ebor' *LTRMem* 9 r. 5.

3 (of persons or things): **a** to come to a destination or fate (phr. *quo ~it?*, 'what has become of him or it?'). **b** (w. *in*) to turn into. **c** to become (w. sb. as compl.); **d** (w. adj. as compl.).

a quo tendebam, quo ~i? ad quid aspirabam, in quibus suspiro? ANSELM (*Prosl.* 1) I 99; **1198** (v. devocare 3b); **1221** mater ejus . . fuit inprisonata . . et nescitur quo ~it *PlCrGlouc* (cf. ib. 97: nesciunt ubi ipse ~it); **1275** dictam juvencam . . abduxerunt . ., set quo postea ~erunt nesciunt *CourtR Wakefield* I 49; **1275** nesciunt quo tota pecunia ~it *Hund.* I 202; **1286** nescivit quo vetus rotulus ~it (*LTRMem*) *SelCKB* I clix; de me vero nullus vestrum curet quo ~iam *Spec. Laic.* 52. **b** scio quid fieret de cancellario si in ipsa furoris hora inter manus gesticulantis ~isset in pomum DEVIZES 33v. **c** ~iens monacus reddidit terram *DB* II 363v.; **1174** W. rex Scottorum ~it homo ligius domini regis contra omnem hominem de Scocia et de omnibus aliis terris suis (*Conventio*) *Anglo-Scot. Rel.* 1; **s1177** rex . . terras Hibernie familiaribus suis distribuit . . et fecit eos ~ire inde homines suos et Johannis filii sui *G. Hen. II* I 162; **a1180** ipse homo noster legitimus ~iet *Kelso* 117; **1220** abbas queritur quod H., R., et M. injuste ~erunt homines ipsius S. *CurR* VIII 310 (cf. ib. 279: cognovit furtum et ~it probator); **1255** ~ti sunt tenentes Hospitalariorum *Hund.* II 69; dicere debet hec verba: "~io homo vester de tenemento quod de vobis teneo" BRACTON 80; **1298** J. . . ~it ballivus manerii de L. *MGL* II 95; **s1365** multi nobiles . ., data fidelitate, sui legii ~erunt J. READING 166; **1379** ~erunt plegii de J. . . de bono *geste* suo *Hal. Durh.* 154; *Ps.-*ELMH. *Hen. V* 82 (v. conquirere 2c). **d** ut . . totum mihi compleat quod in nostra praelocutione fuit quando suus ~i [AS: *þa ic to him gebeah*] et ejus elegi voluntatem (*Quad.*) *GAS* 397; **1378** causa quod allecia . . ~erunt ita cara et mali coreagii *IMisc* 220/3; [mulieres] carnes coctas comederunt; taliter et pingues ~erunt (*Brut*) *Eul. Hist.* III 217.

4 (sts. w. abstr. subj.) to come (to a stage, condition, or sim.).

si adulterium perpetraverit, . . et in †conscientia ~it populis [? l. conscientiam ~it populi], projiciatur extra ecclesiam THEOD. *Pen.* I 9. 5; **s1009** hoc ad nichilum omnino ~it *AS Chr.*; quando ~isti in hanc paupertatem venisti ad me . . petens aurum *Descr. Constant.* 251; **a1214** in dubium ~ire (v. 3 casus 1c); **c1228** ad quem finem postea ~it negocium nescit *Feod. Durh.* 243; BART. ANGL. IV 11 (v. desipientia a); **1268** (v. casura 1a); cum in transgressione fuisset placitum et ad inquisicionem capiendam ~erit *State Tri. Ed. I* 49; **1437** rem eo ~isse (v. conspicere c); **1458** proventus annui . . ecclesie . . in eam jam diu ~erunt et deducti sunt tenuitatem et notoriam exilitatem . . quod . . (*Reg. Ebor.*) *Eng. Clergy* 126.

5 (of time) to come, arrive.

cum septimus dies infirmitatis ipsius ~isset FELIX *Guthl.* 50 p. 154; **1379** cum turnus suus ~erit *Hal. Durh.* 157 (v. calefacere 1a).

2 devenire v. deviare 1b.

deventio, a coming (into possession); *cf. devenire* 2c. **b** becoming; *cf. devenire* 3c.

a **1586** ad dies eorum [monasteriorum] dissolucionis, suppressionis . ., sursum reddicionis aut ~onis ad manum . . regis *Entries* 488. **b** **s1401** comes de Donbar . . homo legeus regis Anglie devenit, sibi omnia possessiones et castra sua in regno Scocie habita reddendo; tamen dicebatur quod Scoti . . eadem ad usum regis Scocie occupabant, sic quod hujus ~o et redditus . . minime regi Anglie videbantur proficere AD. USK 65.

devenustare [CL], to disfigure, mar. **b** to portray as ugly. **c** to disgrace. **d** (by conf.) to beautify.

~at, deformat, *geatolhiwaþ GlH* D 353; ut paucorum scelus multitudinis innocentiam ~et OSB. BAWDSEY clxxvii; quod debitam mensuram minuit vel excedit . . gratiam pulchritudinis ~at BALD. CANT. *Tract.* 7. 469D; **s1450** super muros ejus irreverenter urinam emittendo, decorem domus Domini in quantum potuit ~avit *Croyl. Cont. B* 527. **b** quem [pictorem] . . exorabat Morpheus ne personam suam ~aret ad . . populi derisum MAP *NC* IV 6 f. 48v. **c** faciebant que . . personas omnium operis testimonio ~ent J. SAL. *Pol.* 479D; turpis rei geste narratio . . ~are videtur artificem GIR. *TH* III 25. **d** ~are, ornare, comere, vernare, limpidare, deflorare, clarificare OSB. GLOUC. *Deriv.* 181; polire, sculpere, celare, pingere, ~are *Ib.* 474.

deverberare [CL]

1 to strike, beat soundly. *V. et. diverberare* 2, *everberare.*

Arturus . . nefandum gladio ~at nec requievit donec . . totum mucronem capiti impressit G. MON. X 3.

2 to cleave. *V. et. diverberare* 1.

[beluae] auras marmoreis ~ant spumis *Lib. Monstr.* II *pref.*; deferberat, disjungit *GlC* D 175; OSB. GLOUC. *Deriv.* 181 (v. depuvire).

deverculum [cf. diverticulum], course, route, path.

homo . . monoculus (unius . . ocelli . . carebat lumine) . . tendit ad murum . . . ast ubi occurrit, ita eum contigit directo cursu sagitte ipsius obvium habere ~um, ut oculum illum caligantem . . sagitta percuteret *Mir. Hen. VI* II 50.

deverium, ~ia [OF *deveir* < debēre], 'devoir', duty, customary payment: **a** (Continental); **b** (Scot.). *Cf. debere* 8.

a **1259** super omnibus juribus, libertatibus et ~iis . . que ad nos pertinent . . in districtu nostro Vasconie *RGasc* I sup. lxxxviii; **1289** duo comitatus . . Gerardo de A. . . jure hereditario revertebant et ipse . . regi Anglie suum ~ium faciebat *Ib.* II 397; **1297** tantum solvet de deberio quantum aliquis vicinus . . solvit de terra sua *Ib.* III cxci; **1315** aliis juribus et diveriis ad nos spectantibus *Ib.* IV 1367; **1316** †denaria [? l. devaria] inde eidem P. . . debita . . restituti faciant *Ib.* 1748; **1416** solvendo custumas, gabella et ~ia pro tempore debita (*Tractatus*) *Ps.-*ELMH. *Hen. V* 33; **1440** bona sua capi ac ~ia nostra [Cales'] perdi formidantes *Pat* 448 m. 13 (= *Cal.* p. 492: †denaria). **b** **1348** marinariis . . dicta vina, pannos et alia necessaria . . traducendo . . salvum . . conductum . . habere faciatis, dum tamen custumas et ~ia inde solvant ut debebunt *RScot* 724a; **1354** xx m. quas ipsi [Fratres Minores de Berewico] de elemosina nostra annuatim percipiunt de ~iis de vendicione lanarum, coriorum et pellium lanutarum *Ib.* 774a; **1370** quod . . burgus de Dunbarre habeat pro bondis suis totum comitatum Marchie, sic tamen quod liceat burgensibus . . de Hadyngtona . . emere lanas, pelles, coria et alia mercimonia . ., solventes inde custumariis nostris in Dunbarre . . custumam et alia ~ia *RMSScot* 340; **1398** omnia alia devoria et jura *Reg. Moray* 358; **1462** terre, piscaciones, redditus aut devoria sibi [abbati] . . et conventui . . spectantes *Reg. Aberbr.* II 124; **1477** compotum . . de . . receptis suis et expensis per firmas et devorias dicte warde *Exch-Scot* 431; **1489** pro . . avenis, pultreis et aliis minutis devoriis *Ib.* 87; **1538** unam devoriam vocatam *lye kain* extendentem ad xl s. *Reg. Dunferm.* 531; **1562** cum . . multuris et divoriis . . molendini *Dryburgh* 300.

devers- v. et. divers-.

deversus [al. div.; cf. OF *devers*], towards. **b** situated towards, adjacent to.

1253 venit . . senescallus foreste de versus swanimotum de C. transiens per mediam forestam *SelPlForest* 112. **b** **a1184** (v. desubtus 2c); **c1190** concessi . . terram meam a vico ~us *le sud* usque ad vicum ~us *le nord*, que est inter terram quam R. filius A. tenet . . et vicum ~us *le west Cart. Osney* I 310; **1198** (v. ericius 4).

devert- v. divert-. **devest-** v. divest-.

devetare [cf. CL vetare], forbid.

1275 conqueritur . . de ballivis . . de Tremetoune, qui injuste ~arunt †pre emere [l. preemere] pisces in libera pola de Sutton' nisi redderent eis tributum *Hund.* I 76b.

devexitas [CL], steepness. **b** slope.

s1098 inter locorum intercepti angustias, ut neque ascendere neque propter montis ~atem descendere valuissent (WILL. TYR.) M. PAR. *Maj.* II 79. **b** ego . ., nec . . in montis cacumen cum Moyse nec etiam cum Josue in ullam ductus montis ~atem [cf. *Exod.* xxiv 3] H. BOS. *Thom.* III 5.

devexus [CL]

1 sloping (downwards), steep. **b** (as sb. m. or n.) declivity, slope (partly fig.). **c** brought low. **d** (fig. w. ref. to age) declining, old.

per devexa ac lubrica / clivosi ruris latera (ALDH.) *Carm. Aldh.* 1. 153; divexum, i. inclinatum, descensum, pronum, *stæþlepe GlH* D 736; praecipitium .. immensa profunditate ~um B. *V. Dunst.* 14; per ~a montium latera GIR. *EH* I 17; **s1075** in silva que erat in ~o montis supercilio *Chr. Man* 52. **b** ardua sectari necnon devexa caveri, / dum calles gemini dispari tramite tendunt ALDH. *VirgV* 762; *GlC* D 140 (v. descensus 4a); **9..** divexa, *þa healdan WW*; praerupta, i. ~a, *cludas GlP* 456; ferunt .. quod .. multitudo .. avium ab eodem loco .. descendat atque in ~u (*sic*) montis .. consideat ALEX. CANT. *Mir.* 36 (I) p. 233 (cf. ib. II: per ~um montis); propugnacula in †devectum [v. l. devexum] surrigi .. jussit *G. Steph.* I 30. **c** cum sole ~o in brumalem [circulum] plena est [luna], ipsam solstitiali scandere circulo nox longissima prodit BEDE *TR* 17. **d** †dinexa [? l. devexa], i. vetusta, *þe ealdan GlH* D 492.

2 concave, hollow. **b** (as sb. n.) vault.

aurea devexi dum format sidera caeli ALDH. *VirgV* 743; **9..** divexi, *þæs hwalfan WW*; NECKAM *DS* IX 411 (v. convexus a); ~as .. plicaturas RIC. MED. *Anat.* 214 (v. cellula 2a). **b** stellam .. que volavit per ~um poli inter nos et boream *G. Hen. V* 1.

deviare [LL]

1 to deviate, turn aside, go astray; **b** (fig.); **c** (impers. pass.). **d** (theol.) to fall from grace.

GlH D 360 (v. declinare 4a); **s1205** abbas, ut a me declinaret, per Mediolanum ~iando iter faciens, .. moram fecit *Chr. Evesham* 144; **1227** volens actu baculi bovem suum ~iantem castigare *Cl* 198b; **1230** magna flotta navium nocte precedenti ~iavit a domino rege et declinavit ad portum (*AncC* VI 124) *RL* I 364; GROS. 63 (v. deviatio a); recte ire uno modo contingit, set ~iare pluribus BACON VIII 89; **s1357** a recta via ~iando .. captus est *Plusc.* IX 44. **b** cum a recto tramite ~int GILDAS *EB* 1; ne a bono ~iemus itinere BEDE *Hom.* I 2. 28; **c798** ne claviger regni caelestis abiciat quos a suis ~iasse intellegit doctrinis ALCUIN *Ep.* 137 p. 215; a via veritatis .. non habentes pastorem ~iabunt B. *V. Dunst.* 32; si ab angeli vestri custodia ~iastis, reconciliari studete Domino (*Serm.*) OSB. BAWDSEY clxxi (cf. custos 1b); tenemur regulam observare, nec ab ea sine gravi offensa possumus ~iare AD. SCOT *OP* 579D; quod si †indistorta [l. in distorta] et amfractuosa via et vita ~iant et exorbitant et currant in invio et non in via H. BOS. *Thom.* III 30; **s1189** sunt .. barones et clerici qui .. nullatenus a vero ~iabunt [cf. *Exod.* xxiii 2] GERV. CANT. *Chr.* 448; dicentes .. se malle longe ~iare regem in eorum absentia quam ipsis presentibus .. exorbitare GIR. *PI* III 13; **c1381** dicunt quod isti †deveniant [? l. deviant] / et vanam vitam somniant (*In Lollardos* 37) *Pol. Poems* I 243. **c** immaniter ~iaretur a justitia si .. solus .. patronus noster obumbraretur silentio W. MALM. *GP* V *prol.* p. 330; KILWARDBY *OS* 586 (v. directe a); **s1459** citissime .. tam a fide quam a fidelitate ~iatur *Reg. Whet.* I 347. **d** auctorem deseruimus, ad proditorem ~iavimus PULL. *Sent.* 745A; a veritate, virtute, vita cecidit et ~iavit homo J. SAL. *Pol.* 819C.

2 (w. abstr. subj.) to diverge, be discrepant.

ut .. aliquantulum ab incepto digressionem faciam — neque enim a re quam tenemus multum ~iat OSB. *V. Dunst.* 15; deviet a desiderio professio numquam WALT. ANGL. *Fab.* 41. 17; **1221** cum unus solus justiciarius itinerans sit in Hybernia quod a consuetudine regni nostri Anglie plurimum ~iat in quo semper plures fuerint justiciarii itinerantes *Cl* 451a; omnis ignorantia a ratione ~iat BACON *CSPhil.* 394; quod .. notant plures chronicatores obitum ejusdem [Æthelberti] xxj anno fuisse ab adventu .. Augustini, videntur media ab extremitatibus ~iare ELMH. *Cant.* 137.

3 (trans.): **a** to turn aside, lead out of the way. **b** (fig.) to mislead, lead astray. **c** to wrest, misapply.

a [Godwinus] ~ians eum [Alfridum] a Londonia induxit eum in villa nuncupata [Geldefordia] *Enc. Emmae* III 4; virtus .. martyris mulierculam liberans et ab oculis ducentium ~ians HERM. ARCH. 2. **b** rex .. me quoque a veritate non ~iatum [MS: †deviaviatum] inveniet *G. Herw.* 332b; **1262** litium, quas .. mendacii pater, ut gregem dominicum a via ~iet veritatis, seminare satagit, fluctibus involuti *Conc.* I 758a; **1345** dolore cordis affligimur quod aliqui .. te ~iasse videntur ab hujusmodi proposito et ad illa que Deo displicent .. induxisse (*Lit. Papae*) AD. MUR. *Chr.* 186; ut monachos, sic canonicos, quos deviat error GOWER *VC* IV 351. **c** idem non valet dicere quod omnis substancia est composicio exacta et potencia, quia racio predicta primo competeret potencie et ab illa ~iaretur ad composicionem, quod non contingit generi substancie WYCL. *Ente. Praed.* 36.

deviatio [LL], deviation, turning aside, going astray; **b** (fig.). **c** (theol.) fall from grace.

ille [radius] qui cadit ad angulos inequales deviat ab incessu recto quem habuit in corpore priore .., et ista ~o vocatur fractio radii GROS. 63. **b** quamvis sua [Dei] potentia non sit potens in productione talium effectuum — posse agere malum .. et hujusmodi — non propter hoc dicitur impotens, quia hujusmodi effectus non sunt ex potentia set ex impotentia. .. est enim malum deformitas, deffectus, vel ~o operis, cujusmodi conditiones ex impotentia proveniunt BACON VII 99; pro .. ~one a fide est .. judicandus OCKHAM *Dial.* 946. **c** fuit .. tempus ~onis in genere humano, ab Adam usque ad Moysen, quo declinaverunt homines a cultu Dei BELETH *RDO* 55. 60C; duo sunt status, unus ab exordio mundi usque ad Christum, qui dicitur ~onis .. HIGD. I 4 p. 30; tunc ecclesia per cantus meroris representat primorum parentum ~onem J. BURGH *PO* IV 11 f. 28E.

deviativus, involving deviation (fig.).

1415 synodus Constanciensis .. declarat recessum per .. Johannem papam XXIII ab hac civitate .. clandestine et .. in habitu dissimulato .. fuisse .. illicitum .., schismatis .. nutritivum, a voto, promissione, et juramento per dominum J. .. prestitis ~um (*Sententia*) WALS. *HA* II 303 (= *Id. YN* 454).

deviator, deviator.

materia nostra .. neque est ex corrosivis aut .. rebus extraneis quibus hodie utuntur ~ores in tenebris palpitantes RIPLEY 118.

deviaviatum v. deviare 3b. **devid-** v. divid-.

devigentia, 'unthrift.'

a thryfte, vigencia; *wn thryfte*, ~ia *CathA.*

devigere [? CL], to thrive ill, fail in vigour.

to thryfe, vigere, re-; *to not thryfe*, ~ere *CathA.*

devigilare [cf. CL vigilare], to waken (trans.), rouse.

[abbas T., ob. **1396**] ante matutinas frequenter .. surgere consuevit, nullum ~ando, nullum inquietando, donec tempus esset pulsandi ad matutinas *G. S. Alb.* II 400; *to wakyn*, ~are, expergifacere, a sompno excitare *CathA.*

devillare [cf. CL villa], to leave town, go away from the district; **b** (eccl. or mon.); **c** (acad.). *V. et. evillare* a.

1320 episcopus ~averat ante prefixionem diei [ad tractandum de negocio] *RParl Ined.* 89; **1325** absentavit se in autumpno et noluit metere bladum domini nec vicinorum pro stipendio suo, set ~avit contra ordinacionem bilegis *CBaron* 146 (cf. birelagia); **1379** [amerciati] quia ~averunt in autumpno pro excessivo stipendio capiendo (*CourtR Ramsey*) *EHR* XLV 214; **1405** quod nullus debet ~are propter lucrum qui capere potest j d. per diem ad mensam, sub pena xx d. (*Ib.*) *Ib.*; **1414** ~avit, vicinis suis ibidem †incognitis, [MS: incognit(us)], ad propositum ad interficiendum dominum regem (*AncIndict* 204/1/11) *EHR* XXIX 104; **1416** licencia ab ipso domino cancellario [Anglie] petita et optenta, die illo ~avit versus civitatem London', penes .. custodem rotulorum se divertendo, ac .. sigillum .. eidem .. liberavit (*Cl*) *Foed.* IX 386a. **b c1300** [canonici] residentes ~are .. volentes licenciam petere debent a decano (*Stat.*) *Reg. S. Paul.* 17; **1326** ad tunc ~aturus erat dictus .. decanus *Stat. Linc.* I 352; **a1335** nulli fratrum ibidem in termino commoranti liceat .. extra alicubi pernoctare sine licencia abbatis .., nisi forte quis in comitiva prioris in negociis domus arduis ~antis exiverit (*Const. Abb. R.*) *G. S. Alb.* II 203; [A. abbas, ob. **1334**] constituit .. ut fratres ~antes ita cotidiana gaudeant porcione sicut domi personaliter residentes J. GLAST. 268; **1399** nullus .. deferat .. cultellum .., nisi contigerit eum ~are (*Pat*) *MonA* VI 1389b; **14..** primo die accessus abbatis ad domum cum ~averit AMUND. II app. 321. **c 1337** si aliquem famulorum .. ~are contingat, nichil omnino percipiat interim pro communa *StatOx* 137; **1484** si contingat te ~are, id est, te absentem esse per spacium vj dierum ab universitate ad minus, quod facias .. deliberari clavem [librarie] uni sociorum collegii usque ad tui reventum *Reg. Merton* 52.

devillatio, leaving town, 'going down' (acad.).

1424 pro ~one (*Mun. Barnstaple*) Poole *Essays* 423.

devincere [CL]

1 to defeat, vanquish; **b** (p. ppl. as sb. m.). **c** to win (battles).

devictis atque amotis subregulis BEDE *HE* IV 12; cum quis insidias regi per verba minatur / rex illi cedat ne devictus videatur (*Vers. Corpus*) *Hist. Chess* 519; hec est hominis exterriti vox et devicti MAP *NC* III 2 f. 37; **1197** (v. 3 casus 4d); quasi clamat se devictum [ME: *ȝeiȝed cravant*] *AncrR* 109; AD. MUR. *Chr.* 55 (v. conquaestor b). **b** Hengest et Horsa .. nepotes fuere Vuoddan regis barbarorum, quem post infanda dignitate ut deum honorantes sacrificium obtulerunt pagani, victoriae causa sive virtutis, divictusque, ut humanitas saepius credit hoc quod videt ÆTHELW. I 3. **c** per quod consilium [Alexander] suos hostes oppressit, bella devicit, .. obsessit castra MILEMETE *Nob.* 23.

2 (fig.) to overcome, subdue.

sacerdos / aethera glauca petit devicta morte triumphans ALDH. *VirgV* 1066 (cf. ib. 198: devicta carne rebelli); multorum unanima intentione devictus BEDE *HE* V 6; solis fulgorem sui .. gloria ~ens DOMINIC *V. Ecgwini* I 8; **c1150** lites ratione ~ere (v. delenire c); **1283** nos, ipsius ministri devicti precum instancia, concessimus ei .. ut .. PECKHAM *Ep.* 481; **c1340** hostilis est devicta malicia J. MASON *Ep.* 77. p. 207.

devincire [CL]

1 to bind; **b** (fig.).

devinxit, *geband GlC* D 81; devinxit, i. ligavit *GlH* D 362; copiosis ferri ponderibus eum concatenatum devincierat (*sic*) R. COLD. *Cuthb.* 20; *to bynde* .., cathenare .., vincire, de-, re- .. *CathA.* **b** horribile juramenti sacramentum, quo se devinxit GILDAS *EB* 28; quis debilitas artus devinxerat atra FRITH. 1317; antequam in Britannia Christiana religio dilataretur, nobilibus orti natalibus, germana nativitate et caritate devincti, studiis mox initiantur caelestibus FOLC. *V. Bot.* 2; ebrietate devinctos *G. Herw.* 328 (v. conviva a).

2 to constrain.

inolita consuetudo me devinxerat ne exteriorem cultum mutarem *V. Greg.* p. 76.

devincte, w. firm attachment (fig.).

dilexisse bonos et eis devinctius uti / innuit esse bonum HANV. VIII 213 p. 366.

deviolare [cf. CL violare], to violate; **b** (sexually).

sic vetus hic serpens, paradisum qui violavit, / claustra magis sancta deviolare cupit GOWER *VC* IV 456. **b** alterius sponsam presumens deviolare *Ib.* 673.

devirare [cf. CL vir]

1 to unman.

Venus .. / .. magica devirat arte viros GARL. *Tri. Eccl.* 105.

2 to enfeeble or (?) strip of verdure.

c1435 cum ceperit flores arbor parturire .., si obvius adversetur urens flatus, ~ata languescit *FormOx* 448.

devirginare [CL], to deprive of virginity, deflower; **b** (fig.).

non quod Dominus noster sacri ventris hospitium, quod ingressus sanctificarat, egressus ~asse credendus sit BEDE *Luke* (ii 23) 342; **9..** ~avit, *mægðhade benom WW*; ~o, .. i. virginitates auferre OSB. GLOUC. *Deriv.* 599. **b** per mare adhuc tunc nullis ~atum ratibus aut remis MAP *NC* IV 4f. 47; mores devirginat, illos / corrumpit GARL. *Epith.* I 107.

devirginatio [CL], loss of virginity.

si sponso fuerat inhonoracio / facta vel virgini devirginacio WALT. WIMB. *Carm.* 588.

devis- v. divis-.

deviscerare, to disembowel.

to drawe oute bowells, ~are, eviscerare, exenterare *CathA.*

devitare [CL], to shun, avoid, escape; **b** (w. inf.).

eis proficiebat immaturae mortis supplicium .., quo fratrum .. suorum .. poenas cito exitu ~abant GILDAS *EB* 19; quidam discrimen †duobus [? l. dubiis] / devitantes cum saltibus (ALDH.) *Carm. Aldh.* 1. 152; ~ando quod noxium est BEDE *HE pref.* p. 5; **957** (14c) omnium virtutum amator, qui nos cupit ~are malum sectarique bonum [cf. *1 Pet.* iii 17] *CS* 988; **c1025** si quis michi adherentium huic ordinationi resistens hoc ~at [AS: *onscunað*] (*Versio C*) *GAS* 213; si quis rectitudinem ~ans effugiat [AS: *riht forbuge and uthleape*] (*Cons. Cnuti*) *Ib.* 195 (= *Quad.*: declinet vel aufugiat); **1132** (v. considerare 3a); ORD. VIT. XII 34 (v. declinare 6a); quis puer non ~et dominum? MAP *NC* III 3 f. 40; **1342** erroris damnabilis devio excecati, suarum animarum excidia non ~ant *Conc.* II 704a. **b** quia de his .. aliquantulum prolixe diximus, diutius his immorari ~amur AD. SCOT *TT* 771A.

devitatio [LL], avoidance.

necessaria est discripcio, ut sit concupiscencie insidiantis cauta ~o J. WALEYS *V. Relig.* I 11 f. 235; ad objectum in contrarium dicendum quod homo numquam recipit solucionem que ad plenam pertinet amicicie restitucionem quamdiu durat inimicicia, tamen valet ad ~onem majoris offense PECKHAM *QR* 102.

devitiare

1 to defile.

to defoulle, attaminare .., ~iare .. *CathA.*

2 to correct, free from corruption.

to amende, emendare, corrigere, ~iare, corripere *CathA.*

devitreare [cf. vitreare], to glaze thoroughly.

hoc affunde supra .. plumbum in magno vase terreo bene ~eato RIPLEY 304.

devius [CL]

1 out of the way, inaccessible: **a** (of place); **b** (of person). **c** (as sb. n.) out of the way place.

a oberrantes per devia / dumosi ruris limina (ÆTHELWALD) *Carm. Aldh.* 2. 61; ~ia †callus [l. callis],

horweg stig GlC D 72; loca ∼ia, *ungefera stowa GlS* 213; s**1400** ∼iarum cavernarum (v. delitescere b). **b** hostillarius .. ita disponet quod omnes adventantes .. collacioni intersint et benediccionem .. recipiant, nisi forte tali hora cum ∼ius fuerit abbas *Cust. Westm.* 85. **c** ∼ium, *sloh*; ∼ia, †sive [l. sc.] sunt loca secreta et abdita, quasi extra †via [l. viam] vel invia, sine via, *orwegnes GlH* D 356–7; R. Cant. *Malch.* IV 620 (v. cursitare a); disgregati .. Romani partim ∼ia et nemora, cogente timore, carpebant G. Mon. X 12; s**1100** visibiliter diabolus apparuit hominibus in saltibus et ∼iis, transeuntes allocutus W. Malm. *GR* IV 331; **1444** (v. 2 dangerium 2b).

2 (fig.) straying, erring. **b** (as sb. n.) deviation, error. **c** false trail. **d** devious device.

ut ad corrigendos ∼ios nec desit in ore correptio nec dormitet in corde oratio W. Malm. *GP* V 215; a fide .. ∼ios Diceto *YH* I 318 (v. cauteriare 1c); **1514** (v. divinator). **b** ∼iis, erroribus *GlH* D 358; cum manifestum sit quod ipsa [ecclesia] deviat, .. ipsi [cardinales] principaliter causant hoc ∼ium Wycl. *Blasph.* 67. **c** ipse, regulare m normam secutus, una cum sibi subjectis ∼ia quaeque declinans Ælf. *Æthelwold* 10; etsi aliqui, relicto veritatis tramite, per ∼ia erroris incedere maluerunt Lanfr. *Corp. & Sang.* 426c; artis .. viam sine ∼iis permeare volenti Balsh. *AD rec.* 2 18; **1339** omni dimisso ∼io ad viam obedientie redeat omnemque faciat semitam suam rectam (*Lit. Regis*) *G. Ed. III Bridl.* 146; **1342** (v. devitare a); Jesu .., via sine ∼io, veritas sine nubilo et vita sine termino Ric. Armagh *AP* 18; terminus potencie et officii ministri ecclesie, ne evagetur in ∼ium, est signandus Wycl. *Blasph.* 66. **d** notato toto ∼io quo potest injuste occupare bona ecclesie *Id. Ver.* III 49.

devocare [CL = *to call down or away*]

1 (w. compl.) to call (? imprecisely). **b** to denounce as.

sic quelibet essencia, vel propria passio qua essencia per se tendit in finem, potest ∼ari accio Wycl. *Act.* 41. **b** **1404** nuper .. T[homam] M[erke] .., dudum Karliolensem episcopum, nostris .. episcopis ∼antes immeritum .., quod eiceretur ab ecclesia .. a vestre beatitudinis clementia .. meruimus optinere *FormOx* 202.

2 **a** (w. *in dubium* or sim.) to call in question, challenge the validity of. **b** (w. *in irritum*) to annul. **c** (w. pers. obj.) (?) to challenge or accuse.

a †**741** (? *recte* **750**) ne hodiernam donationem nostram futuri temporis abnegare valeat et in ambiguum ∼are praesumptio *CS* 160; quae fuit scientia mutabilitate rerum .. in opinionem poterit ∼ari J. Sal. *Pol.* 451B; c**1170** quidam malitiose conantur in dubium ∼are quo .. servitio H. de Laci pro manerio de H. .. debeat respondere G. Foliot *Ep.* 378; a**1208** ne quod in presentia nostra actum est a posteris ∼etur in dubium *Reg. Malm.* II 9; c**1220** ne .. processu temporis ∼aretur in dubium quod esset .. laudabiliter ordinatum *Reg. Cant.* 1414–43 IV 164. **b** **1138** quoniam electio canonicorum Lundoniensium citra conscientiam et assensum decani facta fuit .., nos eam auctoritate B. Petri ∼amus in irritum (*Sententia Ep. Hostiensis*) Diceto *Chr.* 251; a**1160** omnibus in irritum ∼atis que post appellationem presumpta sunt J. Sal. *Ep.* 93 (78); sicut dona ejus [sc. regis] revocari vel repeti non debent, sic nec regis dimissa .. nequeunt (*sic*) in irritum ∼ari *Dial. Scac.* I 8 F. **c** ut, si quis alium ibi quacunque dev[o]cet occasione, si placet, palam faciat (*Leg. Hen.* 81. 1) *GAS* 598.

3 to disavow: **a** feudal lord or vassal; **b** accomplice; **c** (claim to) tenement; **d** (responsibility for) document. *V. et. deadvocare.*

a **1180** de Roberto R. xxx s., quia ∼avit dominum suum *RScacNorm* I 16 (cf. ib. 19: quia dominus suus ∼avit eum). **b** **1198** B. .. ∼avit eum, et nescitur quo devenit *CurR RC* I 208. **c** **1201** dixerat quod Willelmus .. illas [terras] tenuit, et non tenuit, quia ipse ∼avit illa masagia *CurR* II 10. **d** **1203** ad judicium de juratoribus, qui ∼averunt scriptum suum *SelPlCrown* 31.

devocatio v. devotio 2c.

devolare [CL], to fly (down).

to flee, volare, con-, de-, e-, volitare *CathA.*

devolatio, flying down.

Gardiner *CC* 374 (v. avolatio a).

devolutio [LL = *corruption*]

1 occurrence, passage, course (of time).

s**871** post ∼onem pugnae praedictae illius anni post Pascha Æthelw. IV 2; c**1550** secundum cursum et ∼onem annorum a toto tempore .. concurrent[ium] *Entries* 623b.

2 **a** passage, transmission (of property or sim.). **b** devolvement (of task). **c** transference (of legal proceedings).

a contingit .. quod quibusdam subvenitur provocacione ad warantum in personalibus accionibus per ∼onem alicujus rei mobilis de manu in manum, cum seisitus nichil deliquerit *Fleta* 408; **1345** donum Dei, qui nobiscum in ∼one dicti regni [Francie] suam mirificavit graciam (*Lit. Ed. III*) Ad. Mur. *Chr.* 165. **b** **1451** ad .. electores eleccio revertatur, nisi scienter eligant indignum, quo casu ad .. vicarium [provincialem] illa vice .. provisio hujusmodi devolvatur. et eadem fiat ∼o si electores die ad eligendum custodem vel gardianum assignata eligere pretermittant (*Abbr. Stat.*) *Mon. Francisc.* II 106. **c** **1311** advocati vel procuratores in causis .. per viam appellacionis .. ad Ebor' curiam devolvendis contra ipsas ∼ones nullatenus cavillentur *Conc.* II 411a; **1342** in prosequendis directis appellacionibus in nostra curia [de Arcubus] .. si pars appellans .. plura gravamina .. introducat, pars appellata teneatur ad omnia contestari, neque audietur volens ad effectum ∼onis unum fateri exile gravamen .. et partem appellantem a revocacione excludere ceterorum *Ib.* 692a; **1542** [*that .. they had proceeded*] ad ∼onem .. cause appellacionis hujusmodi *Form. S. Andr.* II 198; **1549** absoluciones nulle dentur ante ∼onem *Conc. Scot.* II 126.

devolutorium, yarnwindle.

a garwyndelle, ∼ium, girgillus *CathA.*

devolvere [CL]

1 **a** to unroll, unfold. **b** to roll over, into or away. **c** to sink or fall (to a worse state).

a *to falde*, plicare .., volvere ..; *to unfalde*, explicare .., ∼vere *CathA.* **b** [mulier] deseviente angustia humi misera ∼vitur, .. quasi furiis agitetur per pavimentum volutans T. Mon. *Will.* VI 8; lignis .. per equora ∼utis Gir. *TH* I 15; sceptrum obliquavi, lesa racione, et sphera aurea nescio quo ∼vitur Chaundler *Apol.* 18b; ∼vo, A. *to turne upsodoun WW.* **c** qui evangelicae non consentit veritati, errat de via donec in ultimam perditionis foveam ∼vatur Alcuin (*Adv. Felicem*) *Dogm.* 88c; a sericis in cilicium ∼vitur *Ep. Glasg.* 309.

2 (pass., of time) to roll by, elapse.

s**819** paucis mensibus a patris obitu ∼utis *Croyl.* 7; **13**.. cum xxij anni dictorum xxxvj annorum fuissent ∼uti *Meaux* III 144.

3 (refl.) to discharge oneself.

1285 sicut tenens amitteret tenementum petitum si vocasset ad warantum, et warantus se posset ∼vere de warantia (2 *Westm.* 6) *StRealm* I 77; **1309** non potest se ∼vere quin eisdem J., D., et E. juxta formam in .. nota contentam [? recognoscat] *Year Bk.* 2 *Ed. II* 76.

4 (pass.): **a** (of persons) to be involved (in). **b** (of goods) to be consigned, put up (for).

a in magnos errores .. ob apparentem sed fallacem deduccionem imprudentes ∼uti sunt Bekinsau 735. **b** quod remanserit post festum S. Martini vendicioni ∼vatur *Fleta* 168 (cf. *Senesch.* 96: *seit vendu*).

5 (pass.) to be transmitted (to), devolve (upon): **a** (of kingdom or kingship); **b** (of inheritance, possession, chattel, or sim.); **c** (of knowledge); **d** (of right or authority); **e** (of task or obligation).

a ad nostrates in posterum totius regni dominium ∼vetur Gir. *EH* I 9; ad ipsum [Hen. II] .. regni jura .. sunt ∼uta *Id. PI* II 1; s**1272** post mortem regis regnum ∼utum est filio suo .. Edwardo *Leg. Ant. Lond.* 152; **1340** cum regnum Francie .. sit ad nos jure serenissimo ∼utum (*Lit. Ed. III*) Avesb. 88b; aut recurrendum est ad leges de usibus feodorum, per quas excluduntur omnes petentes et ∼utum est regnum ipsum ad dominum superiorem Fordun *Cont.* XI 7. **b** **1259** si hereditas aliqua .. ad plures heredes participes ejusdem ∼vatur (*Prov. Westm.* 2) *StRealm* I 8; **1265** cum manerium .. occasione turbacionis habite in regno nostro ad manum nostram .. ∼utum existat *Cl* 143; **1283** tenementa ∼uta ad manerium de M. pro quibus custos ejusdem manerii facit opera *Cust. Battle* 12; s**1237** comes Cestrie ultimus moritur et deficiente herede ∼utus est in possessionem regiam comitatus Trevet *Ann.* 221; [nos libri] .. ∼vimur .. in laicorum dominium R. Bury *Phil.* 4. 72. **c** [antiqui] multas nobis inventiones reliquerunt in scriptis; plurime ∼ute sunt ad nos parentatim a primis Map *NC* I 1 f. 7v. **d** **1237** [cum] justiciarii diem dedissent nimis diffusum, intra quem ∼vi potuit collacio ad episcopum per lapsum sex mensium *BNB* III 206; **1243** ad quos .. de jure .. ∼vebatur .. ecclesie providendi potestas *RGasc* I 160 (cf. *CalPat* 400); **12**.. si violencia .. vel furtum fiat in terris ad ecclesiam .. pertinentibus, [h]ujus emolumentum ad personas ecclesiasticas ∼vatur *Conc. Scot.* II 46; s**1283** jurisdiccio ad ipsum tunc ∼vi minime poterat, eo quod .. erat excommunicatus Graystanes 19; **1325** jus providendi eidem ecclesie ista vice .. est ad alios ∼utum *Lit. Cant.* I 136; **1330** cum hujusmodi opcio et admissio ad nos .. racione custodie .. possent ∼vi *Ib.* 318; ∼uta est potestas transferendi imperium ad summum pontificem Ockham *Pol.* I 87; **1408** beneficiorum .. que ad nos .. mere pertineant vel jure ∼uto .. infra nostram provinciam quovismodo poterunt pertinere (*Reg. Ebor.*) *Eng. Clergy* 191. **e** s**1226** et sic lapso tempore ∼veretur electio ad curiam Romanam Wend. II 302; c**1239** nisi forte ipsa correctio ∼vatur ad episcopum Gros. *Ep.* 127; s**1239** (v. celebrare 2d); **1451** (v. devolutio 2b).

6 (of legal proceedings or sim.) to be transferred.

1303 in causis .. ad curiam nostram ∼utis et ∼vendis *Reg. Cant.* 474; **1311** (v. devolutio 2c); s**1304** fuit negocium ad Romanam curiam ∼utum Ad. Mur. *Chr.* 5; **1350** archiepiscopus .. pronunciavit .. negocium confirmacionis hujusmodi ad audienciam suam propter negligenciam episcopi fore legitime ∼utum *MunAcOx* 171; **1354** litibus .. ad Romanam curiam legitime ∼utis *Lit. Cant.* II 328; **1414** causa .. forisfacture coram .. custodibus divolvatur *Doc. Bev.* 110.

devorare [CL], to devour (also fig.). **b** (fig.) to consume, destroy.

si .. quis sacrificium aliquod perdat, .. relinquens illud feris et alitibus ∼andum Gildas *Pen.* 9; **680** reliquias epularum .. immundis ∼andas porcis proiciunt Aldh. *Ep.* 4; discerpit, deforat *GlC* D 267; leo .. eos rapere et ∼are cupiens Hugeb. *Will.* 4; sto super eas [oves] .. cum canibus, ne lupi ∼ent [AS: *forswelgen*] Ælf. *Coll.* 91; *Itin. Ric. IV* 14 (v. crocodilus a); non hic ursa ∼at Gir. *TH* I 38; Ad. Marsh *Ep.* 193 (v. 1 cessio 2). **b** [Hercules] sese moriturum flammis ad ∼andum involvit *Lib. Monstr.* I 12; Ad. Marsh *Ep.* 48 (v. conflagratio); duriciam Gallicorum, quam nec lac caprinum demulcens nec vinum ulcionis ∼ans .. poterunt emollire *G. Hen. V* 25 p. 180.

devoratio [LL], devouring; **b** (w. ref. to *Rev.* xii 5). **c** engulfing. **d** destruction.

Epicureorum satis supersticiose vestigia complens, tandem in ∼one lassatus est *Ep. ad amicum* 15; agris jacetis .. bestiis in ∼onem W. S. Alb. *V. Alb. & Amphib.* 33; canibus ovium ∼oni assuetis *Latin Stories* 108. **b** ut draconis evadat ∼onem Ad. Scot *Serm.* 328A; draco .. perseverat in insidiis ad divine prolis ∼onem Ad. Marsh *Ep.* 92. **c** s**1360** inundaciones maritime .. qualibet quindena tumescentes .. ∼onem dicte ville [de Ravensere Odd] nunciantes *Meaux* III 120. **d** det Deus .. ut uterque et Francorum et Anglie gladius .. a propria ∼one cesset! *G. Hen. V* 25 p. 180.

devorator [LL], devourer; **b** (fig.) destroyer.

consumptor, i. ∼or, *gifre, grædig, glut GlH* C 1535; s**1419** vocati sunt [Scoti] a Gallis ∼ores vini et multonum epulones Fordun *Cont.* XV 31. **b** ecce, ille jam sevus ∼or [sc. diabolus] exiit! R. Cold. *Cuthb.* 17 p. 35; intrudere pro pastore ∼orem Ad. Marsh *Ep.* 247 *cap.* 16 p. 458; pluralitates habentes .. vocantur ∼ores et destructores salutis animarum Gascoigne *Loci* 68.

devoratrix [LL], devourer (f., fig.).

nequaquam .. superbiae balenam, ceterarum virtutum ∼icem, humilitatis cercilo declinant Aldh. *VirgP* 10; quid est terra? .. vivencium nutrix, ∼ix omnium W. Burley *Vit. Phil.* 378.

devorium, ∼ia v. deverium. **devort-** v. divort-.

devotare [CL]

1 to curse.

affectum .. asinae .., nolentis se vehiculum fore tiarati magi [Baalaam; cf. *Num.* xxii] devoturi [v. l. ∼aturi] populum Dei Gildas *EB* 1; testium personas .. ultrix divini potentatus censura eisdem cladibus, quibus perjurantes ∼abant, .. percussit Aldh. *VirgP* 32; devotaturus populum cum pergere vatis / vellet *Id. VirgV* 58; ∼aturus, *wergendi* .., ∼aturi, maledicturi *GlC* D 25, 180; magna .. aderat copia paganorum, qui et inimicum deorum suorum intra se diligentissime ∼abant Willib. *Bonif.* 6 p. 31; ∼o, *ic wyrge* Ælf. *Gl.*; quidam clericus, cum ad aleas omnia que habuit .. amisisset, cepit se ∼are, Deum blasphemare .. Gir. *GE* II 32.

2 to swear, vow.

s**1102** [Robertus] comitatum Cantie .. exigebat .., improbus adeo ut .. se ∼aret non induturum chlamydem nisi .. sibi refusam consequeretur hereditatem W. Malm. *GR* V 397; numquam ab obsequela martyris .. recessuram se ∼avit Ciren. I 363 (= Samson *Mir. Edm.* I 8: devovit).

3 to forswear (? by misinterp. of Aldh. *VirgP* 32; *cf.* 1 *supra*).

†defotabat, *forsuor GlC* D 84; *to breke vowe*, ∼are, devovere *CathA.*

devotatio [LL]

1 curse, malediction, indignation.

c**895** quia .. tandem evigilastis .., mucronem ∼onis retrahentes, .. benedictionem vobis mittimus (*Lit. Papae*) W. Malm. *GP* I 38; a**988** misit F. pontifex .. ad regem Eaduueardum, motus cum magna iracundia ac ∼one, et mandavit .. maledictionem contra benedictionem quam beatus papa Gregorius .. genti Anglorum antea misit, nisi .. *Conc. Syn.* 167; ∼o, *wergnes* vel *gehat* Ælf. *Gl.*

2 devotion or (?) *f. l.*

'magnificat' sequitur, per quod dĕvŏtatio [? l. dēvōtio] surgit Garl. *Myst. Eccl.* 263 (cf. J. Glast. 201: †devocatione [v.l. devotione]).

devote [LL]

1 devoutly, w. religious zeal. **b** w. superstitious credulity.

quae sententia [*John* xiii 14] et ad litteram et ad mysticum sensum recte accipi et ∼e debet impleri Bede *Hom.* II 5. 132; subdiaconi .. quinquagenarium ∼e [AS p. 445: *estfullice*] psallant *RegulC* 67; divino se ∼e commisit medicamento Gosc. *Mir. Iv.* lxiii; concine devote, lege

distincte, manifeste/ psalmos psallendo D. BEC. 161; a1296 cum satis comederint .., ~e gracias Deo .. agentes .. revertantur in claustrum (*Ord. Abbatis*) *Reg. Malm.* II 384; quando voluerunt de Deo sincere cogitare et ~e orare [ME: *makien clene bonen*] *AncrR* 50; B. Dionysius .. †denote [l. devote] invocat auxilium eucharistie (TYSS.) *Ziz.* 137 (cf. ib. 22: †denote dictum); devotissimus .. Christiane religionis sacramentorum .. cultor .. extiterat. in hujusmodi enim opere nudato capite ~ius insedere [v. l. incedere] solebat BLAKMAN *Hen. VI* 6. **b** medicus .. per carmina et characteres, licet fictos, utiliter .. potest adhibere .., ut ~ius et avidius medicina recipiatur BACON *NM* 527.

2 devotedly, eagerly, earnestly; **b** (w. ref. to entreaty).

793 ut pietas vestra placide perlegat quod caritas nostra ~e conscripsit ALCUIN *Ep.* 19 p. 56; affectuose vel ~e, *holdlice* ÆLF. *Sup.*; s**1066** paratus sum in hac expeditione cum omnibus meis ~e proficisci H. HUNT. *HA* VI 27; militibus .. sibi convocatis .., sed et predonum, qui undecumque ~e concurrerant, robustissima manu *G. Steph.* II 83; s**1151** Pictavienses .. anathem .. obvolutam reticulo ~e requirunt DICETO *YH* I 294 (cf. deliciose); **1217** rogantes quatinus .. auxilium vestrum .. efficaciter impendatis et ~e *Pat* 25; **1260** pro laudabili servicio quod barones nostri .. nobis ~e impenderint *BBC* (*Cinque Ports*) 166; c**1335** (v. coaptare 5c). **b** a**792** ~issime te flagito ut dona .. mihi .. transmittere curaveris ALCUIN *Ep.* 11; ~issime obsecro .. ut .. haec .. in .. corde plantent O. CANT. *Const. pref.*; **1202** universitatem vestram humiliter et ~e rogamus ut .. *Pat* 18a; stimulat amor .. ut, quod .. viva voce nequaquam feci hactenus, per .. litteram vobis ~e suadeam AD. MARSH *Ep.* 96; s**1265** paterne compassionis intuitu ~ius supplicando GRAYSTANES 10; **1438** humiliter ac ~issime supplicamus BEKYNTON I 3.

devotio [CL]

1 offering (to God). **b** devotional exercise, worship, prayer. **c** expression of respect.

c**980** (12c) ego Æðelred rex hanc meam ~onem signo crucis confirmavi *CD* 1284; pro aliis cereis ~one oblatis *Cust. Cant. Abbr.* 279; **1393** quia .. hiis diebus .. ~ones vivorum ab ecclesiis plus solito subtrahuntur *Lit. Cant.* III 21; **1458** recept' .. v s. viij d. ex ~onibus confratrum aliunde provenientibus *Ac. Durh.* 477; **1535** cantaria .. valet in pecuniis numeratis collectis ex ~one parochianorum .. iij li. *Val. Eccl.* II 9 (cf. ib.: vacat, quia non est perpetuitas set ~o parochianorum). **b** a**795** aperi tibi caelum primum per praedicationis ~onem ALCUIN *Ep.* 28; †**833** (15c) memor .. ecclesiae Croylandensis, quae .. vigiliis et orationibus .., elemosinis et innumeris aliis ~onibus .. pro seculo peccatore .. violentiam regno caelorum ingerit [cf. *Matth.* xi 12.] die ac nocte *CS* 409; post humillimam piae confessionis ~onem OSB. *V. Dunst.* 16; **1190** quatinus .. audientes ex sonis ad ~onem compunctionis provocentur J. EXON. *Ep.* 3; **1408** oratorium devotum .. construxit, ubi populus .. confluunt (*sic*) causa ~onis et pro missis in ibi audiendis *Lit. Cant.* III 110; **1409** insolencie clamorose .. frequenter impediunt et perturbant ~onem celebrantis *Fabr. York* 245; c**1430** ~ones abolitas suo pristino statui restituere seu in melius reformare AMUND. I app. 421; **1459** in vigiliis, jejuniis .. ceterisque omnibus et singulis ~onibus spiritualibus *Reg. Whet.* I 327; *Ib.* II 373 (v. commemor); quod .. timorem habuerat filialem ad Dominum patet in quammultis actis et ~onibus BLAKMAN *Hen. VI* 4. **c** **1219** ut ad obsequia et condignas ~ones vobis [cardinalibus] .. artius teneamur obligati *Pat* 211.

2 a devotion (to God), devoutness, pious zeal; **b** (w. *cordis* or *mentis*). **c** devotion, affection, loyal support.

a miro ~onis fervore ALDH. *VirgP* 29; **718** ~one sincerissima Dei mandata sunt observanda (DAN. WINT.) *Ep. Bonif.* 11; c**760** (12c) Deus non quantitatem muneris sed ~onem offerentium semper inquirit *CS* 194; responso ab omnibus cum omni ~onis affectu, ut mos est, 'amen' LANFR. *Const.* 152; [Lanfranci] ingens in Deum ~o W. MALM. *GP* I 44; mira illi circa Dei cultum ~o AILR. *Ed. Conf.* 745C; crevit amor populi, laus et devotio cleri NIG. *Mir. BVM* f. 13; quid Hebraica veritas, quid interpretes LXX, vel ante Legem senserint .. vel sub Lege, pari ~one, pari fide, dijudica DICETO *Chr. prol.* 18; GARL. *Myst. Eccl.* 263 (v. devotatio 2); ad ~onem confert illa que expressa sunt in Novo Testamento sub figura velata fuisse in Veteri DUNS *Ord.* I 86; s**1377** [rex E.] pretulit et alia penitencie et ~onis signa *Chr. Angl.* 145. **b** **718** haec cum cordis ~one facientes (DAN. WINT.) *Ep. Bonif.* 11; cui ardens inerat ~o mentis ad martyrium ocius pervenire (*Passio Albani*) BEDE *HE* I 7; magna mentis ~one HUGEB. *Wynn.* 2; **786** (v. devovere 2c). **c** a**705** humillima subjectae ~onis instantia .. insistens (ÆTHELWALD) *Ep. Aldh.* II (7); **797** quantum mea ~o considerare potuit, melius est ea facere quae suadeo quam omittere ALCUIN *Ep.* 128; ~o, i. obsequio, bonitas, honor, *estfulnes GlH* D 349; quamvis et mea voluntas tantum ~onis erga eundem patrem et dominum nostrum obtinere debeat ut .. OSB. *V. Dunst.* 2; AILR. *Ed. Conf.* 782D (v. deputare 2b); apud vestram paternitatem filialis me .. excusabit ~o (*Lit. ad Archiep.*) H. BOS. *Thom.* I 1; c**1200** (v. deferre 9d); **1220** [legatus], qui ob ~onem vestram [sc. papae] et .. ecclesie reverentiam .. circa agenda nostra .. insudat *Pat* 267; omni qua potuerunt †devocacione [v. l. devocione] et affectu summo pontifici literas dirigentes flagitabant .. J. GLAST. 201; in omnibus his [graciis curie Romane] tota ~o consistit ut denarius acquiratur PAUL. ANGL. *ASP* 1533.

3 'devotion', 'devoutness' (as title).

1188 ~onis tue litteras .. ad nos destinatas .. suscepimus (*Lit. F. Imp. ad Salahadinum*) *Itin. Ric.* I 18; **1239** quocirca ~onem tuam monemus et exhortamur .., mandantes .. (*Lit. Papae ad O. Legatum*) M. PAR. *Maj.* III 572; **1243** rex priori et conventui S. Trin. Cantuar' .. ~onem vestram monendam duximus .. *Cl* 65; **1258** B. Cantuar' archiepiscopus .. fratri R. .. Coventr' et Lychfeld' episcopo. .. ~onem vestram rogamus, monemus et exhortamur *Conc. Syn.* 571; **1327** vigeat vestra ~o sancta in Christo (*Lit. Prioris Cantuar' Suppriori Wygorn'*) *Lit. Cant.* I 242.

devotionalis, devotional, (w. *tabula*) (?) paxboard.

1423 in capella: .. iij pixides pro oblacionibus inponendis; vij tabule ~es in diversis locis pendentes *Ac. Obed. Abingd.* 98.

devovēre [CL]

1 (refl.) to 'devote' oneself (sacrificially, to death).

Decios duces Romanorum se pro suis exercitibus ~isse percelebre est J. SAL. *Pol.* 518B.

2 to devote, vow, pledge (esp. as thank-offering): **a** (w. acc. or absol.); **b** (refl.); **c** (w. *se* & inf.); **d** (w. inf.).

a [mulier caeca] illuminata .., sicut ~erat, in viduitate quoad vixit Deo devota permansit GOSC. *Mir. Iv.* lxix; totum quod vivo, totum quod scio, vestre ~eo utilitati AILR. *Serm.* 422C; sanitati redditus, iter ad limina S. Jacobi ~it R. COLD. *Godr.* 171; ~et ad tumbam martyris oblationem muneris W. CANT. *Mir. Thom.* III 22. **b** his populus visis se sacris devovet undis FOLC. *Carm.* 23; cum .. se Deo plenius ~ere deberent GIR. *GE* II 23; s**1269** transit annus .. cunctis Christicolis desiderabilis propter affectum regum et procerum qui se ~erunt ad liberationem Terre Sancte RISH. 64. **c** se ipsum famulum Christi venturum fore .. ~it FELIX *Guthl.* 18; **786** haec [synodi] decreta .. cum omni devotione mentis .. se in omnibus custodire ~erunt ALCUIN *Ep.* 3 p. 27; [ego] qui me sub Christo solo vivere .. ~erim ABBO *Edm.* 8; secundum tuam regulam ~i me vivere ANSELM (*Or.* 15) III 62. **d** adamato illius loci .. situ velut a Deo sibi donato, omnes dies vitae suae illic degere .. ~erat FELIX *Guthl.* 25.

3 to dedicate (literary work).

quoniam ad te maxime ~eo hoc [opusculum] ÆTHELW. III *prol.* p. 26 (cf. ib. IV 3 p. 39: tibi ergo hoc opus ~eo, gratissima); sanctitatem vestram, cui presentem librum .. ~i, exoro [etc.] P. CORNW. *Disp.* 153.

4 (p. ppl. *devotus* w. dat.): **a** devoted, attached. **b** held in devotion, cherished.

a dum .. peplum ferret gemini / Christo devotus ALDH. *VirgV* 683; Brittaniam .. confessionis Deo ~ae gloria sublimavit BEDE *HE* I 6 (cf. ib. III 25: Deo ~a femina); **838** praesidente huic eadem (*sic*) Deo ~e congregatione C. archiepiscopo *CS* 421; operam dabat .. regem Deo ~um efficere EADMER *HN* 15; miles .. habebat uxorem .. B. Marie valde ~am *Latin Stories* 31; **1219** ut, de ~is vobis ~iores effecti, ad uberes gratiarum actiones vobis assurgere debeamus *Pat* 209; licet isti imperatores ~i exstiterint .. sacerdotibus et clericis OCKHAM *Pol.* I 52. **b** **961** addo his meis petitionibus rem quamdam nimis mihi ~am, hoc est, ut .. monachos .. ad nos usque mittatis (*Lit. A. Comitis Flandr.*) *Mem. Dunst.* 361.

5 (p. ppl. *devotus*) devout, pious: **a** (of person); **b** (of abstr.). **c** (of place or sim.) hallowed.

a sequitur dominum devota juvencula Christum ALDH. *VirgV* 1743; agrorum Christi cultor devotus ALCUIN *SS Ebor* 81; cum ~a plebe .. ad B. Yvonis .. tumbam confluente GOSC. *Mir. Iv.* lxx; mulieres .. malitiose suis blanditiis etiam ~os dementant ECCLESTON *Adv. Min.* 126; **1315** dum populus Christianus reddatur ~ior *Melrose* 407; audivi a viris sanctis ac ~issimis OCKHAM *Disp.* 13; c**1430** in Christo ~e domine *Reg. Whet.* II app. 402. **b** **604** (12c) inquirere qualiter .. ~issimam voluntatem debeamus offerre *Ch. Roff.* 1; propter .. spontaneam ~ae subjectionis famulatum ALDH. *VirgP* 6; ut .. salutaria .. precibus sollicitis et ~is quaeramus actionibus BEDE *Hom.* II 12. 164; frater devoti pectoris ALCUIN *SS Ebor* 812; **957** (14c) portionem terrae .. mente ~a concedo *CS* 988; per ~iorem sanctimoniam AD. MARSH *Ep.* 247; **1265** per ~a pietatis opera *Reg. Malm.* I 418; ex corde rogamus ~issimo (*Lit. J. Abbatis*, ob. **1316**) *Chr. Rams.* app. 401; s**1377** dictis .. quibusdam ~is orationibus super regem *MGL* II 479. **c** †**1084** quia .. virorum illustrium ~a institutio diuturnitatis senio frequentius aboletur *Ch. Durh.* 4; **1304** in loco ~o seu sanctificato *FormOx* 8; **1338** in loco quem .. archiepiscopus .. pro consecracionis munere impendendo fore duxerit congruum et ~um *Lit. Cant.* II 189; BRYGG *Itin.* 381 (v. cinctura b); **1432** ad celebrandum ibidem [Rome] in locis ~ioribus .. pro anima mea *Reg. Cant.* II 488 (cf. ib.: ad faciendum ymaginem S. Michaelis honestam, magnam, ~am ac principalem in ecclesia parochiali de M.).

6 (p. ppl. *devotus*) devoted, loyal: **a** (of person or unspec.); **b** (of abstr.). **c** (as sb. m.) devoted servant or friend, liegeman.

a levius ferenda est livida ~i vibex amici quam adulatio fallax inimici ALDH. *VirgP* 58; **838** (10c) dabo debotissimo episcopo meo .. terrae partem *CS* 418; ~us, i. largus, honorabilis, *cystig*, voluntarius, dedicatus, promissus *GlH* D 343; **1219** domino suo Ph. .. regi Francie ~us consanguineus suus H. .. rex, salutem *Pat* 205; **1227** prelati terre nostre efficax auxilium nobis facere .. concesserunt, ad quod .. T. Norwic' episcopus .. se inter ceteros, sicut decuit, exhibuit ~um *Pat* 114. **b** ~ae fraternitatis vincula ALDH. *Met.* 2; **1218** grates vobis referimus multiplices et ~as *Pat* 152; ~issimam subjecti famulatus obedientiam AD. MARSH *Ep.* 1; s**1402** magister apud Tyburn' ~um sermonem predicavit .. juravitque .. quod contra regem H. non deliquit *Eul. Hist. Cont.* III 393. **c** supplicem ~i vestri petitionem AD. MARSH *Ep.* 11 (cf. ib. 104; ~issimi vestri .. caritas); **1340** ad nostrorum solacium ~orum (*Lit. Regis*) AVESB. 89.

7 (? infl. by OF *desvoer* < **disvocare*) to abjure, renounce, disapprove; *cf.* *devocare* 3. **b** (w. inf.) to refuse.

esum carnis devovet inde lupus WALT. ANGL. *Fab.* 47. 4; [Cistercienses] ecclesiarum possessiones ~erunt et omnimodas injustas adeptiones MAP *NC* I 24 f. 17; magnum [est] innate bonitatis indicium ipsa que necdum vitaveris vitia animi judicio ~ere GIR. *IK* I 3 p. 39; curiam ~ens in perpetuum .. ejusdemque fallacias .. longe post terga relinquens GIR. *PI pref.* 1 p. lix. **b** s**1134** [dux Robertus] flens et ejulans ~it manducare M. PAR. *Maj.* II 160.

8 to curse.

intellegibilis asinae .. nolentis se vehiculum fore tiarati magi [sc. Baalam] devoturi populum Deum GILDAS *EB* 1.

devulgare v. divulgare.

dewarennare [cf. warennare], to diswarren, remove (land) from warren status. *V. et. deawarennare, diswarennare.*

1284 quod omnes terre eidem burgo assignate dewarrenate et deafforestate sint *BBC* (*Conway*) 108; **1292** quod terre ipsius J. in .. villa rem[aneant] dewarrennate *PQW* 118a; **1296** quod omnes terre .. burgo [de Bello Marisco] adjacentes ~entur et deafforestentur *Rec. Caern.* 158.

dewlegg', dewillegg' v. douellegia. **dexeris** v. xyris.

dexia [δεξία], right hand (used in swearing; *cf.* *Philological Soc. Trans.* 1953 p. 17).

non igitur coeptum dissolvit dexia [*corr. to* inertia] votum FRITH. 456.

dextans [CL], five-sixth (of *as*), ten *unciae*.

si [aliquod temporis spatium] in sex partiris, sexta pars sextans, quinque reliquae ~ans vel, ut alii, distas [v. l. destas] vocitantur BEDE *TR* 4 (cf. ib.: decunx vel ~ans: x unciae); THURKILL *Abac.* 61v. (v. deunx).

dexter [CL]

1 right (as opposed to left). **b** (her.) dexter. **c** (as sb. m. or f., sg. or pl.) the right.

nec quadratum agmen nec dextrum cornu aliive belli apparatus GILDAS *EB* 6; genus utriusque sexus .. ~eram mammam virilem .., sinistram habet muliebrem *Lib. Monstr.* I 19; conversus ad ~rum iter BEDE *HE* V 12 p. 307; ~ro cornu, *fram swiþre healfe GlH* D 414; tene jubente poli rutilabit dextimus axis? FRITH. 685; sint duo .. pueri in ~era parte [AS p. 410: *on swyðran dæle*] chori qui .. psallant .. 'kyrie eleison', duoque similiter in sinistra parte qui respondeant 'Christe eleison' .. demum pueri ~erioris [AS p. 410: *swiþran*] chori repetant quae supra *RegulC* 37; si inter nonum et duodecimum [gradum Arietis] dicetur [sol] ~er et accedens ADEL. *Elk.* 15; G. MON. X 6 (v. cornu 9); M. SCOT *Phys.* 57 (v. confert). **b** BAD. AUR. 198 (v. cornu 8c); fissure in sinistro cornu incipiunt et protrahuntur ad ~eram partem scuti UPTON 243. **c** hunc Gabrihel .. praedixerat ante / dextris altaris promens oracula vati [cf. *Luke* i 11] ALDH. *VirgV* 403; [sinus] occidentalis supra se, hoc est ad ~eram sui, habet urbem Alcluith BEDE *HE* I 12; ad ~eram altaris *Ib.* III 17; vidit .. Jesum stantem a ~ris Dei [cf. *Mark* xiv 19 etc.] *Ib.* V 14; in circuitu aecclesiae per parietes de ~ra in ~ro faciens crucem cum pollice EGB. *Pont.* 40; †**1012** (12c) infra civitatis Wentanae moenia ad septemptrionis ~ram *CD* 720; s**1170** a ~ris altaris (v. decumbere a); s**1175** R. Ebor' archiepiscopus male tractatur .., quia voluit sedere ad ~ram legati in consilio FL. WORC. *Cont. B* 154; a ~ra J. BLUND *An.* 112 (v. dextrorsum); s**1236** justitiario foreste fercula a ~ris regis in mensa disponente M. PAR. *Maj.* III 338; prelatus .. dicet confessionem diacono a ~ris, subdiacono a sinistris *Obs. Barnwell* 112; **1315** iij morsi amalati, quilibet cum Crucifixo a ~ris et Annunciacione a sinistris amalat' *Invent. Ch. Ch.* 74; WYCL. *Log.* III 8 (v. dextralis 1a); ponens aciem suam anteriorem .. a ~ris *G. Hen. V* 12 p. 82 (cf. 1 ala 2a).

2 (w. *manus* or as sb. f.) right hand (partly fig.); **b** (given as pledge); **c** (joined in battle); **d** 'right hand man', principal agent.

armet sed dextram capulus ceu parma sinistram ALDH. *VirgV* 2853 (cf. ib. *pref.* 14: exiguos defendens dextera); inposuit ~eram suam capiti ejus BEDE *HE* II 12; protegat

atque regat Christi vos dextera, fratres (*Vers.*) ALCUIN *Ep.* 273; **933** (10c) per omnipotentis ~eram *CS* 694; abscondebat elemosinam in sinu pauperum advenientium, ut nesciret sinistra quid faceret ejus ~ra [cf. *Matth.* vi 3] GOSC. *Wulfh.* 5; facundia .. est preditus, sed ~era frigidus et plus lingua quam lancea lucratus ORD. VIT. XII 5 p. 328; **s1125** monetarios .. fecit ementulari et manus ~ras abscidi H. HUNT. *HA* VII 36; penitentia ductus .., ferro ~eram fratricidam circulavit T. MON. *Will.* VI 10; Pauli dextra tenet gladium, sed leva libellum NECKAM *DS* V 239; AD. EYNS. *Hug.* IV 6 (v. ambidexter 1b); **1390** (v. congerere d); *the ryghtehande*, ~era vel ~ra causa metri; versus: 'dextera pars hominis, sed bruti dicito dextram' *CathA.* **b** non .. parvi pendenda est haec ~ris firmata affinitas [cf. *Gal.* ii 9] ALDH. *Met.* 4; electis internuntiis, praemittit ad naves Cnutonis qui ~ras Danis dent et accipiant ab eis *Enc. Emmae.* II 13; datis ~ris in pristinam concordiam redierunt W. JUM. VI 2; oscula dans ad fidem ac ~ram W. POIT. I 3; **s1387** multi .. ad dandum ~ras dominis paraverunt WALS. *HA* II 168. **c** Britones .. ~ris hostium ~ras suas confestim conserunt G. MON. IX 4; *V. Merl.* 1058 (v. 1 conserere 2a); postquam ~eras cum hostibus viriliter miscuissent *G. Hen. V* 16 p. 120. **d** *Cust. Westm.* 96 (v. coadjutor); cujus [celerarii] ~er[a] manus et specialis coadjutor .. esse debet granatarius *Cust. Cant.* 134; **s1335** ejus [archiepiscopi Cant'] tyrannidem metuentes, utpote quia ~era regis et tocius regni procurator, promotor et patrocinator THORNE 2069.

3 favourable, propitious.

~rum, i. prosperum, felicem *GlH* D 413 (cf. ib. 415: ~eriora, prosperiora).

dextera- v. dextra-.

dextere [CL], on the right, (hence) auspiciously.

de oculo dextro dextre, de sinistro sinistre sibi successit BEN. PET. *Mir. Thom.* III 13; auguriorum quedam fiunt ante, quedam post, quedam dextre, quedam †sinister [l. sinistre] M. SCOT *Phys.* 57.

1 dexterior, dextimus v. dexter 1a.

2 dexterior [ME *dexter*], dyer.

1505 solut' Thome Court ~ori x d. *DCCant.* C 11 f. 113; **1517** ~ori pro coleracione .. panni (v. coloratio 1c).

dextraliolum [LL], bracelet.

a bee, armilla, brachiale, dextrale, dextrariolum *CathA.*

dextralis [LL], situated on the right; **b** (fig.). **c** southern (esp. w. ref. to Wales).

tripliciter dicitur 'ad dextrum': primo modo summe dextrum, sicut est quilibet punctus linee ~is et omne quod secundum se totum est ad talem punctum — voco autem lineam ~em que protenditur versus dextrum usque ad finem mundi orthogonaliter correctam super lineam longitudinalem WYCL. *Log.* III 8. **b** **c1430** (v. ambisinister). **c** aliis vallum inter duo flumina .. a ~i parte ejusdem villae facientibus ASSER *Alf.* 35 (cf. ib. 79: usque ad regionem Dexteralium Saxonum, quae Saxonice Suth-Seaxum appellatur); **s1166** cui [Henrico II] Owinus et Catwaladrus cum Nortwalensibus, Resus vero cum ~ibus, Owinus de Keweilauc et Jorwerth Choch cum Powissensibus viriliter †resisterunt *Ann. Cambr.* 50; in Sudwallia, quam Kambri 'Deheubarth', id est ~em Wallie partem, vocant GIR. *IK* I 2.

2 (as sb. n.) arm-band. **b** (as sb. m. or f.) hand-axe.

ista .. lacertos ~ibus ornari .. concupiscit ALDH. *VirgP* 17; ~ia, brachialia *GlC* D 178; **9..** ~ia, *earm oððe earmgegirelan WW*; assumpsit ~ia [= *Judith* x 3: dextraliola] J. SAL. *Pol.* 795D; fragor gemmarum, qui limbo tornatili dextraria manuum perornaverat, ex contactu baculi pastoralis .. personabat R. COLD. *Cuthb.* 68; de quodam .. a ~i ferreo liberato T. MON. *Will.* VI 10 *rub.*; †dextreolis addas armillas atque monile GARL. *Syn.* 543. 1587C [v. l. et †detricale, armillas, adde monile (cf. DuC s.v. dextrale)]; *CathA* (v. dextraliolum). **b** ~is, i. †sextre abilis [l. dextrae habilis], *handæx GlH* D 411; *an axe*, ascia, .. ~is, securila *CathA.*

dextraliter, on the right (fig.).

c1437 qualiacunque de mea simplici persona sinistre reportata fuerint, ~er tamen semper gradiar promptusque ero in omnibus ad consenciendum hiis mediis que Deo et paci .. complacere poterunt *Reg. Whet.* II app. 381.

dextrare [cf. LL dextratio], to accompany on the right.

1177 [imperator] recepto a nobis pacis osculo, nos devote ~avit et cum reverentia qua decuit et devotione nos ad altare in ecclesiam introduxit. .. sequenti vero die .. dextro latere nostro devote suscepto, nos in ecclesiam introduxit (*Lit. Papae*) *G. Hen. II* I 189 (cf. FL. WORC. *Cont. B* 154: F. imperator abrenuncians schisma apud Venetias ~avit papam A.); **s1193** ~avit archiepiscopum Lundoniensis episcopus, sinistravit Wintoniensis, et sic in sede sua .. collocatus est DICETO *YH* II 112.

dextraria v. dextralis 2a. **dextrariolum** v. dextraliolum.

dextrarius [cf. OF *destrier*], 'destrier', war-horse; **b** (w. *equus*).

1130 r. c. de lx m. argenti et iij ~iis pro terra patris sui *Pipe* 5; **c1150** pro hac concessione .. dedit mihi .. j falvum dexterarium bonum *Danelaw* 363; **c1160** propter hanc donationem Johannes donavit Gaufrido R. in recognitionem j destrarium et j anulum auri die qua ipse J. .. fecit humagium *Ib.* 338; **s1167** equo ejus militari, quem ~ium vocant, ablato W. NEWB. *HA* II 11; W. FITZST. *Thom. prol.* 11 (v. clunis a); **s1198** (v. 2 cooperire 2b); parcitur ~io itineranti, ut ad laborem majorem reservetur NECKAM *NR* II 158 p. 260; solebat .. abbas ~ios nutrire et in equis elegantioris forme plus forte justo gloriari P. CORNW. *Rev.* I 205 p. 199; **1217** ij desterarii et x austurci *KRMem* 2 r. 2d.; ~ium e claustris .. fecit produci Arabicum, .. sola regia sella dignum *Hist. Meriadoci* 387; si commutatur alicui dextrarius, illi / sepius expatians fata sinistra gerit GARL. *Tri. Eccl.* 63; est man[n]us magnus dextre dextrarius aptus *Id. Syn.* 399. 1585A; **1291** (v. cursorius 2a); **s1298** ~ius [v. l. distrarius (DuC)] regis incaucius a puero custoditus W. GUISB. 326; **1312** pro restauro unius destrarii sui clari badii cum stella (*Muster Roll*) *Cal. Scot.* III 395; jam .. ~iorum phalere preelecte pigritantibus asinis substernuntur R. BURY *Phil.* 5. 78; hec erat illa dies asino dextrarius in qua / succubuit GOWER *VC* I 639; **s1399** Thomas Dymmoc, miles, in ~io totaliter armatus .. aulam intravit AD. USK 34 (cf. *Cl* 303 m. 4); *a steed*, asturcio, ~ius *CathA.* **b** ne perirent homines salvis jumentis, equos destrarios pretiosos perimebant *Itin. Ric.* I 67; **1224** tres equos dexterarios *LTRMem* 6 r. 7d.; **c1250** [G. de Mandeville] extorsit a nobis .. equum ~ium optimum *MonA* IV 143b.

dextraura v. estrahura. **dextre** v. dextere. **dextreolum** v. dextralis 2a.

dextrocherium [LL], arm-band.

dextrocerium, i. brachiale, armillum, *earmbeag GlH* D 410; dextrochirium, *brad earmbeah ÆLF. Sup.*; ~ium, .. i. torques aurea OSB. GLOUC. *Deriv.* 169.

dextrorsum [CL], towards or on the right.

ad mensam ~um et sinistrorsum fratres cum archiepiscopo sedere .. coguntur G. CRISPIN *Herl.* 105; ADEL. *QN* 13 (v. ante 1b); motus .. directus est alius sursum, alius deorsum, alius ~um, alius sinistrorsum W. DONC. *Aph. Phil.* 3. 41; queritur quare contingat audire sonum venientem ab anteriori parte et a posteriori, et a dextra et a sinistra, et similiter non contingat videre ante et retro; similiter ~um et sinistrorsum J. BLUND *An.* 112; in hoc loco matricis ~um et sinistrorsum locavit natura testiculos parvos RIC. MED. *Anat.* 233.

dextus v. discus 4b. **deya** v. 2 daia. **deyeria** v. 2 diaria. **deymeretus, deynectorius** v. dammaricius. **deynerata** v. denariata. **deyria** v. daieria. **deyuerc-, deywerch-, deywerk-** v. daiwerc-. **dezamperare** v. disemparare. **dezen-** v. decen-.

1 dia (dya) [CL < διὰ]

1 made of, (orig. w. Gk. gen.) in names of electuaries or other confections composed of spec. ingredients (listed here alphabetically).

~aloes [*aloe*], epithimia faciens ad dolorem stomachi GILB. V 215v. 1. ~althaea [*marsh mallow*]: inunctiones de dyaltea *Ib.* II 119. 1 (cf. GAD. 17. 1: in causa calida fiat inunccio cum dialtea); **1322** dealtea *KRAc* 379/3; **1414** dialtia, vj lib. dim., xij d. (*EschF* 1066/1) *Invent. Med.* 50. ~ambra [? *amber or ambergris*]: recipe .. cimini .., ambre [etc.]; amoto cimino erit diambra GILB. IV 188v. 2; **1322** p[ulvis] dia ambr' libra j et quart' j, precium iiij s. *War. Issue* 482. ~anison [*anise*] GILB. I 34. 2 (cf. GAD. 34v. 2: dianisum). ~anthos [? *rosemary*]: cum mixtura dyanthos et dyasene *Ib.* I 54. 2; dyanthos, que consumit fleuma et melancoliam cerebri BACON IX 125 (cf. GAD. 66. 2). ~aroma [*spice* (ἄρωμα)]: utatur electuariis calidis, ut ~cimino, dyatrion pi[pereon], dyaroma GILB. III 145v. 2. ~asphaltum [*bitumen*]: **1349** xlv lib. rosyne; xij lib. diaspaltum; xxv lib. ambre (*KRAc* 391/15) *Arch.* XXXI 71.

~basilicon [*basil*] GILB. V 208. 2. ~boraginum [*borage*]: ~borraginum optimum in .. causis melancholie exhibeatur *Ib.* II 100. 2 (cf. GAD. 14. 2: purgetur cum .. sale ~boraginato). ~butirum [*butter*] *Ib.* III 161. 2.

~calamentum [*calamint or sim.*] *Ib.* IV 188. 2 (cf. GAD. 24. 1). ~cameron [cf. DuC] facit asmaticis .. et omni imbecillitati stomachi *Ib.* IV 200v. 2; ~cameron quod digestionem confortat et fleumaticas superfluitates consumit BACON IX 125; **1307** pro electuario precioso quod vocatur ~cameron (*KRAc* 368/30) *EHR* LXVII 174 (cf. GAD. 68. 2). ~cappare [*caper*] GILB. VI 263v. 2 (cf. GAD. 17. 2). ~careon (v. caryon a). ~caryophyllatum [*cloves*]: utantur .. ~gariofilato GILB. II 100. 1; **1313** pro iij lib. ~gariofilati, prec' lib. xviij d. *KRAc* 374/19 f. 14d.. ~castoreum [*scent-glands of beaver*] GILB. II 115v. 1 (cf. GAD. 65v. 2). ~ceraseos [*cherry*] *Ib.* V 210. 2. ~chylon [*various juices* (χυλῶν)]: contra enfraxim epatis detur ~kilon, quod fit de succo apii, seni, scariole GILB. I 51v. 1; in viatico vocatur ~quilon, quod recipe scariole, apii, feniculi, petrosilli ana BACON IX 177; **1307** de aquilon (*KRAc* 368/30) *EHR* LXVII 173; **1322** ~culon (*KRAc* 379/3) *Cal. Scot.* III 142; **1322** ~quiloti libre iiij *War. Issue* 482; si [apostema] non rumpatur, valet ~quilon ad dissolvendum et mollificandum GAD. 28. 2. ~cicoreatum [*chicory*] GILB. I 17v. 2 (cf. GAD. 7v. 1). ~cinnamomum [*cinnamon*]: confortantia epar .. ut ~nisum et ~cinamomum GAD. 73v. 2. ~citron [*citron or sim.*]: **1285** pro ix lib. de dyacitron .. ad opus ejusdem [*regine*] *KRAc* 351/12 m. 2. ~codion [*poppy*]: si [vigilie] sint ex nimio fluxu, detur suc[arum] ro[saceum] cum sir[upo] ro[sarum] et dyacodion dyapapa[veris] GILB. II 107. 1 (cf. GAD. 130. 1); †~conidon, dyapapaveris idem *SB* 18. ~costum [*costmary or sim.*] GILB. VI 263v. 2 (cf. GAD. 34. 2: idropisis de causa calida utatur ~costo). ~cubebe [*cubeb*] *Ib.* VI 256v. 2 (cf. GAD. 33. 1). †~cucurma [? *cucumber or colocynth* (cf. cucurbita)]: ~a valens ad duriciem splenis *Ib.* VI 256v. 2. †~cusi [? *ivy* (κισσός) *or cassia*]: in analempsia .. electuaria sint dyamargariton .., dyaciminum, ~cusi .. et ea que ventositatem excludunt *Ib.* II 112. 2. ~cydonites [*quince*]: dyacitonitem *Ib.* II 95v. 2 (cf. ib. 113. 1: omne .. antidotum excepto .. dyacitonite); **1253** pro vj li. et dim. de ~citoniton v s. v d. *KRAc* 349/10 (cf. ib.: diacetonit'); **1322** p[ulvis] ~citoiniton, libre ij, precium iiij s. *War. Issue* 482; ~citonitem GAD. 7v. 2 (cf. ib. 22v. 2). ~cyminum [*cumin*]: da diaciminium ventosis dulceque vinum GARL. *Mor. Scol.* 597; utantur .. ~cimino GILB. II 100. 1; ~ciminum .. et .. similia, que digestionem confortant BACON IX 92 (cf. GAD. 40v. 1).

†~disnia [? l. ~clisma (διάκλυσμα), *lotion*]: revertatur ad electuaria ca[lida]: commisceantur dyanthos .. vel dyadragag[antum] vel dyadisnia ana GILB. IV 188. 1.

~galanga [*galingale*] GILB. I 33v. 2 (cf. GAD. 24. 1: ~a .., si tussis sit); cf. infra †dialogon. ~glitis [*burdock* (cf. 3 *glis*)] lappa major .., ~is idem, G. *gletonere Alph.* 84. ~grydium [*scammony* (δακρύδιον)]: quod ~gridium medicine, hoc est scientia penitentie H. BOS. *Thom.* III 18; cum esula vel ~gredio GILB. II 96v. 2; quidam voluerunt quod .. radix laxativorum esset ~gridium BACON IX 108; addatur modicum scamonee vel ~gridii et esule GAD. 6v. 2 (cf. ib. 7. 1: nihil est ~cridium nisi scamonea cocta); **1357** (v. drachma 2a); ~gridium, scamonia idem; succus est cujusdam herbe in transmarinis partibus nascentis *Alph.* 50; **1534** ~gradyon *Rec. Nott.* III 192.

~hermis [? cf. Hermes]: medicina m[elanco]licorum adhibeatur, et utantur dyahermis, pillulis fetidis [etc.] GILB. II 112v. 1. ~hyssopus [*hyssop*]: ~ysopus *Ib.* IV 188. 1; utatur .. ~isopo GAD. 34. 2 (cf. ib. 54. 2: electuaria ~ysopi [etc.]).

~iris [*iris, orris*]: ~iris valens asmaticis GILB. IV 188v. 2 (cf. ib. 1: ~yris; *Ib.* VI 240v. 1: dyaris); ea que purgant et aperiunt pectus, ut diarris et ~prasium BACON IX 24; ~iris GAD. 55v. 2. ~iteon [*willow* (ἰτεών)]: salix, †icea idem; arbor est; inde dyaceos emplastrum *Alph.* 160 (cf. ib. 196: †yre ulycera, i. salix; inde †~yceos vel ~yteos).

~lacca [*lac*]: utatur .. ~lacca .. que confort[et] nervos *Quaest. Salern.* L 2; ~lacca GILB. V 215. 2. ~lignum aloes [*lignaloes*]: ~lignum aloes simplex et lignum aloes .., quia ~lignum aloes compositum est magnum et magis calidum GAD. 68v. 1. †~logon [f. l.]: hernia ventosa curatur cum consumptivis ventositatis .. dando †~logon [? l. ~galan(ga)], ~ciminum GAD. 130. 1 (cf. ib. 34v. 2).

~malvatum [*mallow*]: †dymalvatum GILB. I 18. 1. ~marathrum [*fennel* (μάραθρον)]: ~maratrum .. celeriter purgat *Ib.* V 228. 1. ~margariton [*pearls*] *Ib.* VII 351v. 1; **1253** pro v lib. ~margar', xv s. *KRAc* 349/10; **1322** p[ulvis] ~margariton, libra j et quarter' j.. p[ulvis] elect' de perlys, libre ij, precium xiij s. iiij d. *War. Issue* 482; ~margariton magistrale .. valet in omni cardiaca GAD. 68v. 1. ~marte [*marciaton*]: unguentem ~marte vel marciaton, quod idem est GAD. 39v. 1. ~mastix [*mastich*] *Ib.* 76v. 2. ~meconis [*poppy* (μήκων)]: ~miconis GILB. IV 187. 2; ~miconium, i. electuarium de micone *Alph.* 50. ~melon [*quince* (μῆλον)]: ~milon GILB. V 208. 2. ~mentha [*mint*]: ~menta GAD. 76v. 2. ~moron [*mulberry or sim.*], *berigdrenc ÆLF. Gl.*; succum mororum vel ~moron GILB. VII 348. 2; batus, i. morus rubi .. secundum Nich[olaum] in ~moron *Alph.* 20. ~muscum [*musk*]: **1322** p[ulvis] ~musco, libra s[emis] et quarter' j, precium vj s. *War. Issue* 482; oportet uti confortativis, sicut .. ~musco GAD. 66. 2.

~nardinum [*spikenard*]: ~nardinum, quod fit de pulvere spice nardi et de spodio GILB. VI 239v. 2. ~nenupharatum [*water-lily*]: dyanenufaratum GILB. I 18.1; ~nenufaratum et ~cicoreatum, que duo fiunt de floribus cicoree et nenufare GAD. 7v. 1.

~olibanum [*frankincense*]: utatur tyriaca, ~olibano et athanasia ad confortationem nervorum *Quaest. Salern.* L 2; ~olibanum GILB. II 97v. 7 (cf. GAD. 58v. 1: composita calida .. ~olibanum infusum [etc.]). ~orobon [*chick-pea* (ὄροβος)]: rupto apostemate .. offeratur .. ~orob' GILB. VI 240v. 1.

~palma [*palm oil (in plaster)*]: **1414** dya palma, v uncie, ij d. (*EschF* 1066/1) *Invent. Med.* 73. ~papaver [*poppy*]: pro siti dentur electuaria ~papavera GILB. I 19v. 1; insompnietas, inquietatio et ira accidunt .. ex fumis melancolicis ascendentibus ad cerebrum .. et confert huic dispositioni dyapapaver BACON IX 25; ~papaver valet ad provocandum somnum. .. error est dare ~papaver nisi fiat de papavere assato GAD. 6v. 1; ~conidon, ~papaveris idem *SB* 18. ~peganum [*rue* (πήγανον)]: electuaria calidiora ut .. †dyapigamum GILB. IV 188. 2. ~penidium [*barley-sugar*]: per diapēnidia tenuis salvatur usīa GARL. *Mor. Scol.* 595 (*gl.*: electuaria que fiunt ex penidiis, que sunt confectiones sive pilule restaurative; a *dia*, 'de', et *peni*, 'confectio'); apotecarii .. habent †~pendion, quod gratum est †consumis [? l. consumi] *Id. Dict.* 129; dentur electuaria ut ~penidion GILB. II 107. 2; versus: 'si tibi tussis adest, diapēnidion tibi prodest' GAD. 54. 2; **1534** ~pendeon *Rec. Nott.* III 192. ~pente [*five ingredients* (πέντε)]: ~pente valet asmaticis: recipe storacis optimi, mirre, dragaganti, galbani, opii ana ℨ balsami aut olei nardi, mellis quantum sufficit; detur in modum avellane GILB. IV 189v. 1. ~phoenicon [*dates* (φοινίκων)]: **1414** dya ffenicon j lib., ij s. (*EschF* 1066/1) *Invent. Med.* 25. ~prasium [*white horehound* (πράσιον)]: **a1089** mitto tibi dioprasium magnum, quod ad hanc infirmitatem valde utile esse medici perhibent, de quo in modum sylvestris nucis tertia semper die accipies LANFR. *Ep.* 46. (21); ~prasium GILB. IV 183. 2; BACON IX 24 (v. ~iris); **1322** p[ulvis] ~prassin', quarter' j et s[emis], precium ij s. iij d.

War. Issue 482; ~prassium est optimum, quia est amarum GAD. 54. 2; prassio albo utimur in electuariis . ., [unde] ~prassium electuarium *Alph.* 138. ~prunis [*plums*]: febris ut immunis sis efficiet diaprunis GARL. *Mor. Scol.* 599 (*gl.*: purgatrix [? ad] coleram; sc. electuarium quod fit de prunis Damascenis); dyaprunis GILB. I 19v. 1; electuaria sicut . . pro colera ~prunis et diareubarbarum GAD. 7. 1. ~pyrethrum [*pyrethrum*]: dyapiretrum valens asmaticis GILB. IV 189. 2. ~reubarb' [*rhubarb*]: electuarium de succo ro[sarum], dyareubarb' [etc.] GILB. VI 236v. 2; tunc est ~reubarbaratum medicamen speciale GAD. 7. 2. ~rhodon [*roses* (ῥοδῶν)]: dyarodon abbatis valet yctericis [etc.] GILB. IV 197 v. 2 (cf. ib. 199v. 2: si est nobilis, detur dyarodon Julii, quod . . specialissime confert); ~roddon abbatis, vj lib. pro v s., prec' lib. x d. (*KRAc* 350/1) *Nott. Med. Studies* III 40; **1322** Tratessi ~rodon *War. Issue* 482; si colera sit intra, tunc plus debet dari de triasandalis vel ~rodon GAD. 15. 2; rodon, rosa idem; inde dyarrodon *Alph.* 154; **1414** trussa dyarodian ij uncie, ij d. (*EschF* 1066/1) *Invent. Med.* 15. ~satirion [? *orchis* (σατύριον) *or herb savory* (*Satureia*)] : diabolus ~satirion luxurie, calidum electuarium, . . cuilibet offert O. CHERITON *Par.* 130; confortativa . . ut ~satirion et vinum aromaticum GILB. II 125. 1; ~satirion acuitum cum causa †stinchorum [1. scinchorum] GAD. 76v. 2; **1414** dya saturian dim. quartron', ij d. (*EschF* 1066/1) *Invent. Med.* 22; ~satyrion est confectio Venerem excitans *LC*. ~sene [*senna*]: digeratur . . materia cum ~sene GILB. I 48. 1; electuaria sicut . . ~scene in melancolico GAD. 7. 1. ~spermaton [(? *various*) *seeds* (σπερμάτων)]: ~spermaton faciens ad . . vertiginem GILB. V 209v. 2; propter ventositatem . . utatur . . ~spermaton GAD. 69. 2; sperma, i. semen; inde ~spermaton, i. de seminibus *Alph.* 168. ~stomaticon [*medicines for mouth* (στοματικῶν)]: **1322** p[ulvis] ~stomatic' confort' libre iij *War. Issue* 482. ~strobilon [*pine-seeds* (στροβίλων)]: strobile vel strobilia, i. pynee; inde dyastrobilion *Alph.* 177. ~sulphuris [*sulphur*] GAD. 54. 2. ~tarascos [*sort of plaster*]: **1307** ~trascos (v. ceroneum b); **1322** ~tarascos (*KRAc* 379/3) *Cal. Scot.* III 142. ~tesseron (*four ingredients* (τεσσάρων)]: tyriaca dyatesseron GILB. IV 202. 1 (v. et. ceroneum b); fiat emplastrum vel cerotum ~tesseron GAD. 40. 2; tyriaca ~tessaron, quia fit de iiij speciebus tantum *SB* 42. ~tragacanthum [*tragacanth*]: cum . . ~dragaganto frigido GILB. I 23. 2; **1253** pro iij lib. ~dragant' frigidi, ij s. *KRAc* 349/10; **1322** p[ulvis] ~dragant' frigid', libre ij, precium iij s. iiij d. *War. Issue* 482; triasandali, ~dragantum frigidum, çuccarum ros[aceum] GAD. 5v. 1. ~trion pipereon [*three kinds of pepper* (τριῶν πιπερέων)]: electuaria calidiora, ut . . dyatrionpipereon GILB. IV 188. 2; potest digeri materia cum oximelle . . et ~trionpipereon GAD. 14v. 1 (cf. ib. 6. 2: ~triton pipereon). ~turbith [*turpeth*]: electuaria sicut . . ~turbith pro flegmate *Ib.* 6v. 2. ~violis [*violet*]: trocisci dyavi[olis], a viol[is] alias dicti: recipe foliorum violarum viridium [etc.] GILB. IV 201. 2. ~zinziberis [*ginger*]: electuaria . . ut ~zimziber', . . ~zinziber Alexandrinum *Ib.* I 47v. 2; **1252** pro vij lib. ~zinziberios, iij s. viij d. *KRAc* 349/10 (cf. ib.: ~zinziberis); **1265** ~zinziberos . . , vj lib. x d. (*Ib.* 350/1) *Nott. Med. Stud.* III 40; **1288** pro diversis pulveribus emptis ad faciend' d lib. ros[arum] novell[arum], ~zinziberios [etc.] (*AcWardr*) *TRBk* 201 p. 18.

2 through (w. ref. to lines of latitude).

medium primi climatis est ubi . . elevatur polus mundi supra circulum emisperii 16 gradibus, et dicitur clima ~meroes SACROB. *Sph.* 111 (cf. ib. 111–12: ~syenes . ., †dialexandrios [? 1. ~ias]. ., ~rhodos . ., ~romes . ., ~boristenes [i.e. ~borysthenes] . ., ~ripheos); qua ratione in climate ~meroes et †~senes rarissime nubes fiant, jam pridem innuimus *Ps.*-GROS. *Summa* 620.

3 (by misinterp.) two (*cf. GlC* D 259: *dialectica, dualis dictio*).

BACON *Maj.* II 460 (v. diaphanus c; cf. diaphonus); ROB. ANGL. (II) 145 (v. 1 diameter 2a).

2 dia v. dius. **diaaloes**, ~basilicon v. 1 dia 1.

diabetes, ~e [LL < διαβήτης], (med.) diabetes.

passio est ~e proveniens ex calore et ex defectione virtutis contentive, cum renes eam quam habent humiditatem retinere non possunt W. CANT. *Mir. Thom.* II 83; urina magis vel minus redditur colorata ex . . diuturnitate . . in ipsa decoctione, ut in quartana et ~e GILB. I 58. 2; diabetica passio est immoderatus fluxus vel exitus urine per renes cum vehementia sitis; et vocatur A. *caudepise*; et dicitur a ~es, quod interpretatur 'dissolvens renes' GAD. 99. 2; †~os [v. l. ~es] est urine continua emissio *Alph.* 51.

diabeticus (dya-), diabetic; **b** (as sb. m.). **c** (as sb. f. *sc. passio*) diabetes.

GAD. 99. 2 (v. diabetes); ~a passio dicitur immoderata urine effusio, vel dicitur *chaudepisse SB* 17. **b** ex acumine caloris solent apparere tales [resolutiones in urina] in ~is GILB. I 68v. 2; ~i raro generant GAD. 76v. 1. **c** ut in ~a, ubi trahitur sanguis ab epate continue antequam digeratur GAD. 30v. 2.

diaboleus, diabolic.

ad gentes pervenerunt felices in Britanniae limitibus commorantes, quae nuncupantur Anglisaxones, etiam nunc compeditas nexibus zabuleis turificantesque daemonum simulacris LANTFR. *Swith. pref.*.

diabolice, diabolically.

potestates que finguntur a papa . . sunt ficte et ad seducendum subditos ~e introducte (*Concl. J. Wycliff* I 28) *Conc.* III 340b; **1588** (v. fascinatrix).

diabolicus [LL < διαβολικός] **(dya-)**, diabolical, devilish, caused by (or worthy of) the Devil; **b** (w. ref. to illusion or sim.). **c** belonging to or concerned w. the Devil.

nec enumerans patriae portenta . . ~a GILDAS *EB* 4; **c625** a ~ae captivitatis nexibus . . absoluti (*Lit. Papae*) BEDE *HE* II 10; zabulicum magisterium despiciens FELIX *Guthl.* 30; **786** ~o instinctu ALCUIN *Ep.* 3 p. 26; **853** ~a temeritate instigatus *CS* 467; quicquid . . per ~am expugnationem exstiterat commissum OSB. *V. Dunst.* 19; rex . . ~e fortitudini non humane virtuti [factum] attribuit W. MALM. *GP* II 95; **c1236** nefandum est . . locum Deo dicatum ~is adinventionibus execrare GROS. *Ep.* 32; si . . spiritu ~o plenus superbire . . elegerit *Cust. Westm.* 205; *Ziz.* 362 (v. ars 5); **s1454** quicquid contra ipsos sive ~e sive humane moliuntur adversitates *Reg. Whet.* I 137; **1456** Turchi . . putaverunt se castrum obtinere cum eorum ~is instrumentis et ingeniis BEKYNTON II 155; **1573** instigacione diobolica *Pat* 1106 m. 24. **b** zabolica illusio GILDAS *EB* 67; ab errore ~ae deceptionis . . liberari BEDE *Hom.* II 6. 234; **842** (14c) ~a fraude deceptus *CS* 438; per . . ~am fallaciam LANFR. *Corp. & Sang.* 409A; illusione ~a (KYN.) *Ziz.* 51; nec ~e fraudis ignarus BLAKMAN *Hen. VI* 8. **c** si mulier incantationes vel divinationes ~as fecerit THEOD. *Pen.* I 15. 4; **717** ~is rapti manibus BONIF. *Ep.* 9; **1019** (15c) cum zabulicis Gehennarum parasitis *CD* 730; quidam operarii ~i, nomine dumtaxat clerici H. BOS. *Thom.* III 22; nec verecundantur homines ~i . . damnare omne genus sapientie eis incognitum BACON *CSPhil.* 417; non videntur verba hominum sed flatus ~i [ME: *þeos Deoveles bles*] et voces ipsius *AncrR* 22; **1365** (v. conjuratio 3); **s1379** ~a visio sive species apparuit inter eos WALS. *HA* I 422; ex dignitate presumpta papali fides catholica est sopita et fides ~a introducta WYCL. *Chr. & Antichr.* 676; **1456** de . . bombardis magni ~i Turchi BEKYNTON II 157.

diabolinus, diabolical.

a devylle, . . diabolus . . zabulon, zabulus; [*adj.*] zabulinus, demoniacus, diabolicus *CathA*.

diaboliticus [cf. LL diabolicus], diabolical, devilish.

c1000 miseriae, instigante zabolitico conatu, perpetratae sunt (*Lit. Episc.*) *Conc. Syn.* 231.

diabolus [LL < διάβολος] **(dya-)**

1 devil, the Devil, Satan; **b** (in role of tempter); **c** (w. ref. to demonic possession); **d** (in physical manifestation); **e** (invoked in curse); **f** (pl.).

exhibentur membra arma iniquitatis peccato ac ~o, quae oportuerat . . exhiberi arma justitiae Deo. . . auscultantur . . non Dei laudes . ., sed propriae, . . ita ut vas Dei . . vertatur in zabuli organum GILDAS *EB* 34; ubi nuper expulsa ~i tyrannide Christus jam regnare coeperat BEDE *HE* IV 14 p. 233; non est Deus quem colis sed ~us ALCUIN *WillP* I 11; quomodo . . bellum virile gessit cum zabulo BYRHT. *V. Osw.* 457; ne miseri tristem zabuli trudantur in aedem (*Vers.*) HERM. ARCH. *prol*; in cujus potestate est infernus aut ~us? ANSELM (*CurD*) II 54; sit homo ~i! *G. Ric. I* 84 (v. discrete 2); est aquilo zabulus, est Sanctus Spiritus auster [cf. *Cant.* iv 16] H. AVR. *Hugh* 940; [Lucifer] ad yma ruit . ., propter quod dyabolus, i. 'deorsum fluens', a sanctis est dictus BART. ANGL. II 19; immanitatem satellitum ~i AD. MARSH *Ep.* 226; **s1256** (v. damnare 3c); ego . . non comedi neque bibi . . propter quod lex Dei deprimi debeat, lexque ~i exaltari (*Juramentum*) *Fleta* 51; Lucifer . . factus est ex angelo ~us [ME: *deovel*] *AncrR* 12; istud Ricardus [I] rex Anglie referre solebat, asserens non esse mirandum si de tali genere procedentes mutuo sese infestent, tanquam de ~o venientes et ad ~um ituri HIGD. VII 21 pp. 32–4; homo . . potest vendere animam suam ~o WYCL. *Apost.* 38. **b** **c597** suggestio fit per ~um, delectatio per carnem, consensus per spiritum (*Lit. Papae*) BEDE *HE* I 27 p. 61; invida pestis / corda ducis zabuli praestrinxit, hospitis apti FRITH. 939; **995** (12c) instigante humani generis perversissimo temptatore ~o *CD* 692; **c1160** multiformes laqueos zabuli precavere OSB. CLAR. *Ep.* 41; O. CHERITON *Par.* 67 (v. cucumerarium a); **s1265** agente zabulo pacis inimico et zizanniam superseminante [cf. *Matth.* xiii 25] *Flor. Hist.* III 2; sicut lutum figuli factus sum a Deo / et per fraudem zabuli subjectus ab eo PECKHAM *Def. Mend.* 26; **c1370** 'sed Satan antiquus', id est ~us, 'semper amicus bellorum'; . . notandum est quod ~us semper excitat homines ad bella, quia . . ~us est amicus bellorum (J. BRIDL.) *Pol. Poems* I 203. **c** si homo vexatus est a diabolo et nescit aliquid nisi ubique discurrere et occidit semetipsum THEOD. *Pen.* II 10. 1; BEDE *HE* III 11 (v. arripere 2a); majoribus tormentis possessum corpus ~us agitare OSB. *Mir. Dunst.* 19 p. 148; notandum . . his nostris diebus energumenam fuisse a ~o possessam GIR *IK* I 12; OCKHAM *Pol.* I 164 (v. exorcismus a). **d** OSB. *V. Dunst.* 21 (v. deprehendere 3a); **s1100** multis . . Normannis ~us in horribili specie se . . ostendens plura cum eis de rege . . locutus est FL. WORC. II 46 (cf. W. MALM. *GR* IV 331); **s1138** quomodo zabulus . . in puerili forma monachus sit factus J. WORC. 46 *rub.*; **1225** pre timore quem habuit cum solus esset in gaola de ~o, qui ei apparuit in forma . . ni[gri mo]nachi scabiosi *CurR* XII 1055; quidam pictor ~um cum cornibus et acutis dentibus ita turpem et orribilem ut potuit depincxit. . . ~us vero iratus accedens ad pictorem quesivit . . cur ipsum turpiter . . depinxisset O. CHERITON *Par.* 73; **1337** convenit . . quod . . Johannes vendidit . . Roberto ~um ligatum in quodam ligamine pro iij d. et uno ob.; et super hoc . . Robertus tradidit Johanni quemdam obolum in *earles* [*earnest money*], per quod proprietas dicti ~i commoratur in persona . . Roberti, ad habendam deliberacionem dicti ~i infra quartum diem proximum sequentem *CourtR Hatfield, Yorks* (*Transcr. in Surrey R. O.*); **s1513** in . . similitudine †eavis [1. canis] nigerimi aperuit (*sic*) ~us in Essex *Reg. Butley* 31. **e** †**845** (13c) sciat se in aeterna dampnatione dampnandum cum diabulo et angelis ejus *CS* 450; de episcopo qui sacerdotem animam parochiani sui ~o commendantem pro xx s. de debita . . pena laxavit GIR. *GE* II 27 p. 303; **s1252** (v. commendare 4b); cum porcus . . diverteretur, iratus homo clamavit: "~us te habeat!" *Latin Stories* 70. **f** coram illo . . duo zabuli humano habitu se obtulerunt FELIX *Guthl.* 30; quam grave malum sit . . pati tormentum aeternum in societate ~orum ANSELM (*Ep.* 297) IV 217; papa . . a multis ~is assidue est temptatus WYCL. *Chr. & Antichr.* 677.

2 devil (as term of abuse).

O.: "cum qua domina, ~e?" N.: "certe, immo tu ~e, cum domina mea formosa Biblide" MAP *NC* IV 16 f. 58v.; "tu", inquid, "fili sordide meretricis, tu latro, tu traditor, tu ~e!" DEVIZES 40 (cf. ib.: iste Judeus ~us est); *NLA* II 218 (v. corrigia 1a).

3 (w. *morsus*) devil's-bit scabious (*Succisa pratensis*).

gracia Dei similis est ypericon in foliis, sed major. quidam dicunt quod est herba que dicitur morsus ~i *SB* 23; morsus ~i principalem habet radicem incisam et similis est denti leonis; valet contra tercianam; G. †*recopre* [v. l. *recopee*]; A. *deve*[*le*]*sbite Alph.* 120.

diaboragin', ~**borr-** v. 1 dia 1. **diaboresis** v. diabrosis. **diaboristenes** v. 1 dia 2.

diabrosis [διάβρωσις], ulceration.

fluxus sanguinis a naribus aut fit per †dyaboresim, i. per corrosionem ex acumine humoris, aut per rixim, i. per ejus subtilitatem GILB. III 152v. 1.

diabul- v. diabol-. **diabutirum, diaca-, diace-, diach-, diaci-** v. 1 dia 1. **diachonus** v. diaconus.

diacinnum [cf. διακίνησις], slight movement.

quedam [prostitute] solummodo signis et ~is commovent *Quaest. Salern.* B 12.

diaco, ~on [LL], deacon; **b** (w. *cardinalis*). *V. et. diaconus.*

THEOD. *Pen.* II 2. 14 (v. collectio 3d); *Hist. Abb. Jarrow* 26 (v. cereus 2a); **c720** sicut [Deus] . . misit Philippum, unum de septem ~onibus, ad eunuchum [cf. *Acts* viii 26–7] (EANGYTH) *Ep. Bonif.* 14; praeclarae indolis ~onibus HUGEB. *Will. prol.*; **c798** dicunt ab episcopis interdictum esse presbyteris et ~onibus praedicare in ecclesiis ALCUIN *Ep.* 136 p. 209; **803** haec sunt nomina . . episcoporum et . . abbatum et praesbyterorum et ~onum qui . . subscripserunt (*Clovesho*) *CS* 312; **858** (12c) presbyteris, ~onibus, et omni clero consentientibus *CS* 495; ~on *CS* 648 (v. dupliter); **1138** neque ad infirmos nisi per sacerdotem vel ~onem . . [corpus Christi] deportetur (*Conc. Westm.*) GERV. CANT. *Chr.* 107; **c1250** (v. 2 clavis 1d); **1357** ~onibus et noviciis *Ac. Obed. Abingd.* 13; *a dekyn*, diaconus, ~ones, ~on, levita *CathA*. **b** **1289** ~onibus cardinalibus *RGasc* II 466n.

diacocus v. diadochus. **diacodion** v. 1 dia 1. **diacon** v. diaco.

diacona [LL], deaconess. *V. et. diaconissa.*

astruunt . . Paulum apostolum [*1 Tim.* iii 8–11] . . precepisse feminas debere fieri ~as, quia eas commemorat post diaconos (SIG. GEMBLOUX) M. PAR. *Maj.* I 237.

diaconalis [LL], diaconal, of a deacon. **b** (as sb. n.) diaconal vestment.

c1080 vj sacerdotalia vestimenta et vij ~ia (*Invent.*) *Lib. Eli.* II 114; medie [hierarchie] primus [ordo consistens] in pontificalibus [hominibus], secundus in sacerdotalibus, tertius in ~ibus AD. MARSH *Ep.* 246 (*bis*) cap. 1 p. 417; **1400** te Willelmum . ., diaconum pretensum, in habitu et apparatu ~i indutum . ., hereticum et relapsum . ., ab ordine ~i degradamus et deponimus . . ac omni et omnimodo honore ~i privamus *Conc.* III 259b. **b** cantet aliquis . . qui audientes edificet ~ibus indutus (*Ord. Gilb.*) *HBS* LIX 11.

diaconatus [LL]

1 diaconate, office or rank of deacon; **b** (w. *ordo*).

Praxapostolon [*Acts* vi 3] totidem [i.e. vij] viros ~us officio functos et primitivae dispensatores ecclesiae probat ALDH. *Met.* 2; nono decimo vitae meae anno ~um . . suscepi BEDE *HE* V 24 p. 357; **a738** *Ep. Bonif.* 39 (v. diaconium); subdiaconus quatuor annis fit et sic ad benedictionem ~us, si meretur, accedat (*Sermo Innocentii Papae*) EGB. *Pont.* 18; **a1087** ~um ei [clerico uxorato] auferte LANFR. *Ep.* 21 (43); **s1096** [G. episc. Heref.] ordinavit eos . ., ad ~um et presbyteratum unum et alium ad presbyteratum EADMER *HN* 84; ~ui annexa sunt mense

ministerium et annuntiatio verbi Dei P. Blois *Ep.* 140. 421D; *a dekenry*, ~us *CathA.* **b** a**1087** Lanfr. *Ep.* 21 (43) (v. caste); **1191** cum .. commonachis vestris, qui ad ordines subdiaconatus et ~us .. per manuum ignoti episcopi impositionem accessissent, suscepti ordinis non permitteretur administratio (*Lit. Papae*) *Reg. Malm.* I 376; hoc [predicationis] officium spectat ad ordinem presbyteratus et ~us Hales *Qu.* 517; frater A., cum diu in ordine ~us fuisset minister Anglie, noluit promoveri in sacerdotem Eccleston *Adv. Min.* 97; **1448** in sacris subdiaconatus et ~us ordinibus *Eng. Clergy* 223.

2 (by conf.) rural deanery. *Cf. decanatus* 2.

1275 taxaciones .. beneficiorum .. infra ~um de Fiff Sanctiandree diocesis *Conc. Scot.* I cccv; **1450** lego cuilibet ecclesie infra deaconatum de Ros [*Heref*] xij d. *MunAcOx* 606.

diacones v. diaco. **diaconidon (~codion)** v. 1 dia 1. **diaconios** v. diatomos.

diaconissa [LL], deaconess; *v. et. diacona.* **b** deacon's wife.

benedictio episcopalis in ordinatione ~ae: omnipotens Deus intercedentibus sanctis virginibus suis vos dignetur benedicere, qui de antiquo hoste etiam per feminas voluit triumphare Egb. *Pont.* 94 (cf. ib. 19). **b** ~a, quam diaconus habuit *Gl. Leid.* 39. 23.

diaconium [LL], diaconate.

a**738** recitatis supplicatoriis nobis allatis litteris de diaconatu electi fratris mei M. et, quamvis posterius ordinaliter constituto tempore eis venisset qui presbiterii et ~ii ordinem fuerant adepti, non distulimus eum (Dan. Wint.) *Ep. Bonif.* 39; Indrachtus .. erat .. ~ii ordine insignitus *Pass. Indracti* 100; de clerico qui ordinem ~ii .. furtive .. surripuit Gir. *GE* I 51 p. 147.

diaconus [LL]

1 deacon; **b** (attached to higher cleric); **c** (cardinal); **d** ('cardinal' in non-technical sense).

antiqui patres xii [sc. annos] presbitero et vii diacono poenitentiae statuere Gildas *Pen.* 5; in ordinatione presbiteri sive ~i oportet episcopum missas celebrare Theod. *Pen.* II 3. 2; [Cedd], accepto gradu episcopatus, presbyteros et ~os ordinavit Bede *HE* III 22; [Christus] ~us fuit quando confregit v panes in v milia hominum ..; ~us namque oportet ministrare ad altare et evangelium legere in aecclesia, baptizare et communicare in vice presbiteri, peregrinorum pedes lavare et mortuorum corpora sepelire Egb. *Pont.* 10; **786** nullus episcoporum presbiterum aut ~um ordinare praesumat nisi probatae vitae fuerint Alcuin *Ep.* 3 p. 22; **838** signum manus Eadberhti ~i *CS* 421; ~us vel levita, *diacon* Ælf. *Gl.*; ad majorem missam ~us et subdiaconus casulis sint induti Lanfr. *Const.* 91; in eadem villa est quidam ~us habens xxx acras et quartam partem ecclesiae *DB* I 93v.; **1125** (v. archidiaconus); hos [levitas] etiam ecclesia ~os, id est 'ministros', nuncupat, quia sacerdotibus ministrant; horum officium est in ecclesia evangelium [legere], sacrificium in altari componere, sanguinem Domini distribuere, licentiam populo abeundi dare et, si necesse est, predicare et baptizare Gir. *PI* I 19 p. 112; officium .. ~i est oblationes .. disponere in altari et vinum infundere Hales *Sent.* IV 409; Bracton 124 (v. apostatare b); **1376** in solucione .. pro salario diachoni et subdiachoni ministrancium in dicta ecclesia *ExchScot* 337; prelati, sacerdotes vel ~i [ME: *dekenis*] non habebunt officia secularia *Concl. Loll. XXXVII* 742; diaconus [*gl.: decone*], subdiaconus, exorsista, benedictus (*Vers.*) *WW*. **b** [Gregorius] cum ~o suo Petro conloquens Bede *HE* I 1 p. 74; Bercthun, ~us quondam ejus [Johannis episcopi] *Ib.* V 2 (cf. Folc. *V. J. Bev.* 11: Sigga ejus [J. episcopi] ~us); sextus [gradus aecclesiasticus est] ~us, id est 'minister', qui ministrat presbytero ..; nam sacerdos sine ~o nomen habet, sed officium non habet Ælf. *Ep.* 2. **c** **1142** (v. cardinalis 3a); s**1176** Hugo Petrileonis, S. Angeli ~us cardinalis et apostolice sedis legatus .., infaustа navigatione transvectus in Anglia .., receptus est Wintonie Diceto *YH* I 402; s**1191** Jacinctus inter ~os ecclesie Romane primus .. se fieri papam .. consensit *Ib.* II 89; ~i cardinales habentur ibidem [Rome] xviij preter subdiaconos et acolytos in capella domini papae quam plurimos Gir. *Spec.* IV 6; **1345** domini G. de Mota, tituli S. Lucie in Cilicia, .. sacrosancte Romane ecclesie ~i cardinalis *MunAcOx* 149. **d** Egb. *Pont.* 120, *GAS* 549 (v. cardinalis 3b).

2 (Sc.) 'deacon', (president) of incorporated craft.

1569 collectorem aut magistrum hospitalitatis annuatim per ministrum et seniores .. nostri burgi [*Perth*] tempore electionis eorum seniorum et deaconorum nominandum et eligendum *Scot. Grey Friars* II 208.

3 (by conf.) rural dean. *Cf. decanus* 8.

1273 subicio me .. jurisdiccioni episcoporum Sanctiandree et Glasguensis et eorum officialium, archidiac[on]orum et ~orum *Cart. Coldstream* 9.

diacostum, ~cridium (~grydium) v. 1 dia 1.

diacrisis [διάκρισις *or* (?) διάχρισις], (? erron. for διατύπωσις) imagery, vivid representation.

illi per ~im, quam nos illustrationem sive picturationem possumus appellare, cum rudem materiam historie aut argumenti aut fabule aliamve quamlibet suscepissent, eam tanta disciplinarum copia et tanta compositionis et condimenti gratia excolebant ut opus consummatum omnium artium quodammodo videretur imago J. Sal. *Met.* 854B.

diacu- (cf. diachylon), diacy- v. 1 dia 1. **diadamas** v. diamas.

diadema [CL < διάδημα]

1 diadem, royal head-dress (usu. identified w. crown); **b** (fig., as emblem of royal authority); **c** (in name of book).

[Constantinus] induit eam clamidem suam et ~a auro obrizo gemmisque purpureis ornatum posuit super caput ejus Aldh. *VirgP* 25; deadema, vit[t]a regalis capitis *GlC* D 98; **956** (12c) imperiali Anglo Saxonum ~ate infulatus *CS* 932; ~a, *kynegerd* .., corona, ~a, *cynehelm* .., ~a, *bend agimmed and gesmiðed* Ælf. *Gl.*; s**973** regem, cujus sceptrigera gloria tunc lucidius refulsit et ~a aurea resplenduit Byrht. *V. Osw.* 436 (cf. ib. 437: rex .. deponendo ~am de capite); caput .., quod semper fuerat insigne regali ~ate Abbo *Edm.* 10; [Dunuallo Molmutius], cum totam insulam subjugasset, fecit sibi ~a ex auro G. Mon. II 17; s**1120** Anglorum regina, tuos, Adelina, decores / ipsa referre parans Musa stupore riget. / quid diadema tibi pulcherrima? quid tibi gemme? / pallet gemma tibi, nec diadema nitet (*Vers.*) H. Hunt. *HA* VII 33; reginam decuit vultus .., / prefulgens vestis et diadema decens Neckam *DS* V 300; corona regia aut dyadema capiti ejusdem [regis] apponatur *Lib. Regal.* 33v.; regalibus infulis trabeatus ~ateque regio coronatus Blakman *Hen. VI* 4; hec dyadema, A. *crowne WW*. **b** Elfredo tradens proprio diademata nato Alcuin *SS Ebor* 575; **1048** (13c) cunctitonantis almifluo altithroni †clangente [l. cogente] diathemate *Ch. Burton* 38; adjecit hoc de pristina dignitate ~atis regum Francorum fore ut exsules .. regum et regni pace .. fruantur H. Bos. *Thom.* IV 7; dum prefatus rex Dacie ~a Anglie usurpasset *V. Har.* 1 f. 3b; **1580** recipio me regiae nostrae majestati .. fidem .. perpetuo praestiturum et .. defensurum .. omnimodas jurisdictiones .. et authoritates .. imperiali hujus regni ~ati conjunctas et annexas *StatOx* 416. **c** **14**.. liber Smaragdi qui dicitur ~a Monachorum *Catal. Durh.* 65 (cf. *EHR* III 124).

2 (? by conf. w. *diamas* or *diadochus*) precious stone.

hoc ~a, lapis preciosus *WW*.

diademare [CL *p. ppl. only*], to crown; **b** (fig.).

s**1121** ad Pentecosten [Henricus] fuit ~atus cum regina sua nova apud Londoniam H. Hunt. *HA* VII 33 (cf. ib. VIII 1). **b** seva superbia, livor edax ibi non diademant / principis imperium D. Bec. 348.

diadematizare, to crown.

ad Anglicum provehitur regimen Edelredus, anno sub eodem honorifice ~atus Herm. Arch. 1; s**1135** regis .. corpus, cujus cervix ~ata auro .. quasi Dei splendore vernaverat H. Hunt. *HA* VIII 2.

diademocraticus [cf. CL diadema + -κρατικός], designating rule by one wearing a diadem, monarchic or (?) *f. l.*

leges clx que sunt dyademocratice [v. l. adimocratice, ? l. democratice], †oblig'atice [? l. oligarchice], aristocratice, et tirannice W. Burley *Vit. Phil.* 250.

diadisnia v. 1 dia 1.

diadochus [CL < διάδοχος], sort of gem.

si inveneris sigillum in †diacoco sculptum, virum magnum et rectum, et tenet in una manu diabolum et in alia serpentem .. *Sculp. Lap.* 453.

diadragagantum, ~dragantum (~tragacanthum) v. 1 dia 1. **diaecesis** v. dioecesis 1a.

diaeresis [LL < διαίρεσις], diaeresis, separation.

conjunctionem etiam solutionemque syllabarum, quam Graeci episynalipham et ~im vocant, ubi necesse est, licitam scire metricum decet Bede *AM* 122; dirisis, i. divisio *Alph.* 50.

diaeta [CL < δίαιτα; *infl. by* dies]

1 rule of life, regimen, (habitual or prescribed) diet (med.). **b** dietary, book on diet. **c** (regulated) diet (penitential, ascetic, or mon.). **d** (daily) allowance of food (mon. or sim.). **e** (penal) starvation diet, *peine forte et dure*; *cf. poena.* **f** (festive) meal. **g** (eccl.) the Host.

hec vultus varios, varias notat illa dietas Nig. *Mir. BVM* f. 23; insomnes oculi, mens pervigil, arcta dieta / attenuant corpus Gir. *Symb.* II 65; offeratur ~a congrua, ut lactuca, portulaca, cucurbita .. Gilb. V 216. 2; Bacon XV 206 (v. conservatio 1a); s**1294** rex ait: "omnia in necessitate debent esse communia et omnes unam et similem ~am paciemur" W. Guisb. 252; c**1300** cum [Hibernia] sit frigida et humida et ~a ejus ut in †pluries [? l. pluribus] sit frigida Malachy *Ven.* 22v.; sicut persona hominis variatur in corpore et ~a, sic oportet eam variari in observancia legis Dei Wycl. *Ver.* III 241; hec ~a est cibus moderatus *WW*. **b** hoc [cerebrum] a Galieno dicitur esse frigide complexionis, ab Aristotele calide, quod uterque validis astruebat documentis, sicut in ~is universalibus legitur Ric. Med. *Anat.* 213; garus †quod sic [v. l.: quid sit] dicitur [sub] ~as particulares *Alph.* 70 (cf. ib. 155: ut in ~is particularibus); ~e universales, .. ~e particulares *Libr. Cant. Dov.* 57. **c** s**1174** [rex] utens tenui ~a, pane sc. et aqua, .. quousque vota orationum apud Thomam martyrem .. persolveret Diceto *YH* I 383; per continuum frigidioris ~e usum .. internas .. corporis vires attriverat Ad. Eyns. *Hug.* III 13 p. 126; **1234** precipimus ut in hoc monasterio ~a et jejunium observentur prout in regula S. Benedicti continetur (*Vis. S. Edm.*) *EHR* XXVII 733; sic ad salutem pristinam, per quietem et ~am, et solacium .. redire *Obs. Barnwell* 206. **d** **1214** j m. quam abbas R. dedit ad emendationem ~e monachorum prima die minutionum (*Confirm. Consuetudinum*) *Chr. Evesham* 213n.; **1486** (v. diatim b); **1542** solvendo .. E. W. nuper priori .. c s. pro ~is suis et cuilibet duorum monachorum secum commorantium iij li. vj s. viij d. pro ~is suis durante vita naturali predicti E. W. (*MinAc*) *Cart. Glam.* 1929. **e** necuere Rogerum / damna, pudor, carcer, ira, dieta, dolor Garl. *Tri. Eccl.* 80; si [appellatus] aliud nolit dicere pro defensione .., gaole committetur sub ~a salvo custodiendus. .. condicio vero erit talis quod unico indumento indutus et discalceatus in nuda terra quadrantalem panem ordeaceum tantum pro ij diebus habeat ad victum, non tamen quod quolibet die comedat, set altero tantum, nec quod singulis diebus bibat, set die quo non comederit aquam bibat tantum. et hec ~a omnibus legem refutantibus injungatur *Fleta* 51; **1290** David Walensis captus et imprisonatus pro felonia .. se ipsum ponere in aliquam inquisicionem instanter renuebat; unde preceptum fuit quod infligeretur per ~am. .. et postea fecit finem pro ~a remittenda *PlRChester* 6 r. 5; **1373** tanquam †inobedienc' [? l. inobediens] legi positus fuit ad ~am .. in prisona *RCoron* 218 r. 56; **1384** pro eo quod .. ad allocucionem suam .. noluit loqui nec respondere, .. justiciarii .. ipsum ad ~am suam poni adjudicarunt .., in qua ~a tamdiu vixit quod videtur miraculum qualiter vivendo posset illam taliter perdurare *Pat* 317 m. 28. **f** s**1356** princeps .. ibi moratus est per dies Jovis, Veneris, et Sabbati, in quibus fecerunt homines principis pulchras ~as *Eul. Hist.* III 221. **g** quadam die, cum ipse altario presens cepte misse officio insisteret et post evangelium, ~a offerenda, in manus panem et calicem .. sumeret Eadmer *V. Osw.* 7.

2 day's journey; **b** (as a measure of distance); **c** (w. *rationabilis*); **d** (w. ref. to canonical rule *de duabus ~is* or sim.); **e** (fig.) stage or term. **f** goal, journey's end.

perreximus duas ~as ad Thebas Sæwulf 834; ~a, diei itineratio Osb. Glouc. *Deriv.* 172; at si defuerit [conductus], longas protende dietas / contineatque pedes publica strata tuos J. Sal. *Enth. Pol.* 381D; viam .. aggressa, milliarium unum prima die perfecit, secunda quatuor, et secundum numerum dierum faciens augmentum ~arum donec .. se Cantuarie sanam .. exhiberet W. Cant. *Mir. Thom.* III 8; propter crastine ~e longitudinem et vie difficultatem .. in crastino summo diluculo arripuit iter H. Bos. *Thom.* IV 5; postquam bissenas confecerat ergo dietas Nig. *SS* 717; Vac. *Lib. Paup.* 268 (v. diploma 1b); s**1200** cum .. corpus ad †detumulandum .. portaretur, accidit quod, [cum] cerei in exitu civitatis ante corpus fuissent accensi, per iiij ~as jugiter arserunt Oxnead *Chr.* 112; testudo .. parum incedit et parvam ~am facit O. Cheriton *Fab.* 48; faciens unam ~am a Dovera in Londonias *Flor. Hist.* II 452; si quis confratrum aut plures .. extra burgum de vita .. fuerint calumpniati .., probi viri duo .. de gilda laborabunt cum eo duas ~as recedendo super expensas gilde *Stat. Gild. Berw.* 92; que cum sero vel mane ~am sibi deliberantes proponerent "ibi vel ibi pernoctabimus" .., sine impedimento .. illuc sero pervenerunt *NLA* (*Ursula*) II 488; s**1341** summonitus ad parliamentum .., continuatis ~is suis per maneria archiepiscopatus, tandem venit apud Lambeth Birchington *Arch. Cant.* 38; *jurney*, ~a *PP*; *a day jornay*, ~a *CathA*. **b** Athene .. distat duas ~as a latere Corinthie Sæwulf 834; Etna mons frequenter ignes suos in immensum circumquaque diffundit, et adhuc per spatium ~e unius undique combusta .. est .. facies regionis P. Blois *Ep.* 46. 135A; in aere raptus est [clericus] .. et die quarta tribus inde ~is inter rupes .. inventus Map *NC* II 29 f. 33v.; juxta oppidum de Notingham, non longe a Lincolnia, sed quasi per ~am distans unam Gir. *GE* II 18; Kambria .. cc milia passuum in longum, circiter vero c milia in latum habet: longitudo namque .. quasi per viij ~as extenditur; latitudo vero .. quasi per iiij ~as expanditur *Id. DK* I 1; [Britannia] in longum tenditur dccc milliaribus, in latum cc; vicenis itaque millibus passuum pro ~a computandis, ut aliqui a recentioribus pretendunt, in longum †xj [l. xl] ~is et in latum x; verum antiquiores a capite Cornubie usque ad finem Scotie xxxij ~as computaverunt Gerv. Tilb. II 6; de magnitudine .. et altitudine celorum et stellarum, ut homo sciat in milliaribus, et per consequens in ~is, quantum est in omnibus his Bacon *Min.* 319; **1435** si in Anglia vel prope ad tres ~as me mori contigerit *Wills N. Country* 42. **c** **1214** mandamus vobis quod .. ducatis dominam reginam usque Berghamstede .. per rationabiles ~as, sicut melius videritis expedire *Cl* 177a; **1217** iter arripiet eundi versus S. Jacobum ad instans Pascha et per rectas ~as et rationabiles illuc ibit *Pat* 108; vicinum dici poterit mercatum et nocumentum injuriosum, .. ut si novum mercatum levatum sit infra sex leucas et dim. et tertiam partem dimidie. et est ratio secundum dicta seniorum quia omnis rationabilis ~a constat ex xx milliaribus. dividatur ~a in tres partes: prima pars matutina detur euntibus versus mercatum; secunda vero detur ad emendum et vendendum ..; tertia vero pars relinquitur redeuntibus de mercato ad propria Bracton 235b; a domo

sua proficiscatur [essoniatus] per racionabiles ~as sine aliqua mora *Fleta* 392. **d 1181** testes qui fuerint nominati, si se . . subtraxerint, compellantur veritati testimonium perhibere, non obstante constitutione de ij ~is edita in concilio generali, dummodo ultra tertiam vel quartam †arias [l. dietas] extra suam diocesim auctoritate presentium ad judicium non traha[n]tur (*Lit. Papae*) ELMH. *Cant.* 448; **1223** ultra ij ~as extra suam diocesim ad judicium trahebantur contra statuta concilii generalis *Melrose* 308; **1232** renuntiamus . . exceptioni constitutionis de ij ~is edite in concilio generali *Pat* 514; **1279** non obstante constitutione de ij ~is *Reg. Heref.* 234; **1356** in casibus qui judicialem requirunt indaginem per iij, iiij, v pluresve ~as a fine nostre diocesis *Reg. Exon.* II 1186; **1445** nullus extra suam civitatem . . nisi in certis . . casibus, et in illis ultra unam ~am a fine diocesis, . . evocetur (*Lit. Papae*) *Reg. Brechin* 102. **e** figimus hic [sc. in ultima linea libri] metam primam faciendo dietam R. CANT. *Malch.* I 453; Moyses docuit filios Israel illas tres ~as corporales per quas venerunt ad illum locum ubi corporaliter Domino sacrificabant [*Exod.* viii 27]; vos autem . . Benedictus istas tres ~as spirituales docet et viam per quam poteritis istas ~as perficere satis aperte ostendit AILR. *Serm.* 242B; sibi debilis etas / spondet completas viteque vieque dietas NIG. *Paul.* 47. 225; affectus mundos suprema perunctio signat, / ut celum redeat (*sic*) mundi completa dieta GARL. *Myst. Eccl.* 115; de prece surrexit surgendoque se cruce texit / et tunc quam letas incepit adire dietas GOWER *CT* III 157. **f** fecit rex eis compatiens in galeis transportari et navibus usque ad destinatas ~as *Itin. Ric.* IV 14.

3 day's work or working day (esp. man.). **b** day labour, (payment at) daily rate. **c** (as measure of land) 'day-work', 'darg'; *cf. daiwerca, daiwercata.*

rectificatque / curvum [sc. claudum quendam] que rectos solet incurvare dieta H. AVR. *Hugh* 845 (cf. M. PAR. *Maj.* II 470); **1254** de tercia parte unius ~e messionis xiiij hominum in autumpno (*JustIt* 1181 r. 1) *Cal. Scot.* I 368; **c1280** si custodierit porcos et tempestas in autumpno evenerit, opus illius ~i (*sic*) non computetur (*Cust.*) *Crawley* 235; sint cum carucis ballivus, prepositus et messor per totam ~am donec aruras suas . . compleverint, quantum viz. ad unum diem pertinebit *Fleta* 161 (cf. ib. 164: cum cariatoribus presens existat prepositus tota die, ut sine ficticia ~am finiant et laborent; et secundum laborem illius ~e debet futurus labor expediri); **a1300** qualibet septimana anni, quando venerunt de Berwic', fecit quelibet terra unam ~am de opere sibi injuncto; . . et in autumpno, quando non iverunt apud Berwic', fecerit tres ~as *Kelso* II 456 (cf. ib.: reddit sex ~as in autumno); **1342** vadia . . ultra id quod [homines ad arma etc.] . . recipere tenentur, computatis ~is quibus . . in . . obsequio nostro steterunt *RScot* 622b (cf. ib.: computatis diebus [etc.]); **s†1353** [recte **1351**] fiebant statuta popularium, viz. quod servientes operariique ac artifices . . et laborarii . . imposterum pro ~is et terminis anni plus mercedis vel stipendii quam solebant ante annum pestilencie ullo modo non recipiant J. READING 164 (cf. *RParl* II 233b); **1434** (v. commutare 1f). **b 1275** (v. 1 cumba c); **1284** que [precarie] valent per levem extensionem xiiij s., si extendatur opus unius in ij d. per ~am *Reg. Wint.* 674; **1323** in stipendiis diversorum operariorum pro . . calcetis exaltandis, straminandis, et reparandis, per ~am ij li. . . *Sacr. Ely* II 27; **s1326** ejecistis dominam nostram reginam de terris per dominum regem sibi datis et assignatis, quam [? sc. reginam] ordinastis et posuistis ad sua vadia per ~as, contra statum et excellenciam tante domine (*Sententia in Dispensatores*) *G. Ed. II Bridl.* 89 (? *misinterp. of* KNIGHTON I 440: *feistez ouster ma dame la roigne de sa terre, que luy fuist done et assigne par nostre seignour le roy, la meytee dez terres pur son certayne douerment a la journe, contre lestate de sa noblesse*; cf. diatim b); **1353** W. . . carucarius non vult servire nisi per ~as et ad mensem (*JustIt*) *Enf. Stat. Lab.* 196*; **1396** in vadiis diversorum hominum †labore [? l. laborancium] per ~am in quarera *DocCOx* 308; **1442** in vadiis . . laborariorum conductorum, tam per ~as quem in grosso, ad operand' . . listas . . (*Ac. Foreign*) *Analog. Cant. Pilg.* 25; **1583** vadium, stipendium, ~am sive sallarium vj solidorum . . per diem *Pat* 1235 m. 28. **c c1210** dedi . . ecclesiam de W. cum l ~is terre arabilis *Reg. S. Thom. Dublin* 87; **1233** predicti homines debent . . arare unam ~am terre ante Natale et aliam in Quadragesima *CurR* XV 137; **12..** ij ~as blesture (v. blestatura); **1317** sursum reddidit . . j cotagium continens j dayetam terre *CourtR* (*Essex*) 62/786 m. 1; **1358** dedimus . . omnes illas ~as terre cum haiiciis, fossatis, arboribus et aliis suis pertinenciis que (*sic*) habuimus in W. [*Worcs*] *AncD* C 3727; **1401** parcellam terre continentem vij ~as arure *FormA* 328; **1532** una pecia sive una ~a prati vulgariter nuncupata *ane dawarg of medow Form. S. Andr.* II 40.

4 day's expenses. **b** day's entry in account.

clericum eorumdem officiorum, qui de expensis ~e, viz. panis, vini et cervisie, picheriorum, cophorum . . et hujusmodi respondebit *Fleta* 78; **1358** summa totalis utriusque partis ~e et forinsec[arum] per dictos viij dies (*Ac. Univ. Ox.*) *EHR* XXIV 737; **c1367** in expensis factis circa facturam nove coquine . . ut patet per rotulum continentem ~as *Ac. Durh.* 569; **1373** computat in . . diversis aliis expensis . ., ut patet per ~as in papiro computantis *ExchScot* 445; **1450** per vendicionem v lastarum coriorum martarum intratarum in libris ~arum et receptarum per computantem *Ib.* 395. **b 1464** expense . . intrate in libris domicilii, ut patet in ~a quarti Julii . . *Ib.* 274.

5 (eccl.) daily office.

in noctibus . . dierum qui non sunt solempnes, xij psalmi, quos vulgus ~am vocamus, cum sex antiphonis cantantur BELETH *RDO* 22. 34C.

6 'diet', day's sample of metal taken at mint for assay. *Cf. pyxis.*

p1280 aut examinabitur argentum antequam extra manus custodis . . ipsi denarii in usus alios convertantur aut post, certo termino, facta una pixide de una sola ~a vel pluribus, quam vel quas sub illo termino contigerit fabricari (*Tract. Nov. Mon.*) *RBExch* 1004.

7 a 'diet', (daily) session of court. **b** diet, assembly, conference.

a 1286 hujus[modi] visus [franci plegii] bis tenere debet . . coram vicecomite; et ipse inquirere debet de latronibus . . et aliis pluribus capitulis unde proficuus predictarum diettarum de jure communi spectat ad dominum regem *PQW* 671a. **b 1395** ad expensas suas faciendas ad unam ~am trugarum in Marchiis tenendam . ., que ~a non fuit tenta *ExchScot* 371; **1399** dantes vobis plenariam potestatem ad tractandum . . tam super aliquo certo loco et certo die in Marchiis regni nostri tenendo . . quam de numero, statu, et qualitate personarum, ambassatorum, et commissariorum pro ~a hujusmodi deputandorum *RScot* 153a. **1441** cum . . Robertum B. . . in nostram . . ambassiatam ad ~am Maguncie deleg[av]issemus BEKYNTON I 88; **1451** quod alia ~a pro causarum et negociorum in articulis predictis contentorum prosecucione et terminacione . . tenenda instituatur *Cl* 301 m. 4*od.*; **1487** cum nuper certa ~a fuerit . . ordinata teneri in villa Calesie (*DipDocE* 591) *Foed.* XII 320a.

diaetare

1 to diet, treat w. a regimen (med.): **a** (person; also fig.); **b** (ailment).

a 1171 ceteri . . curam carnis propensius agunt; circumspectius se ~ant P. BLOIS *Ep.* 27. 94C; mentem / evocet os, rectrix pena dietet eam GARL. *Epith.* III 384; ~andi sunt ergo homines modo cum grossiori dieta quam antiquitus GAD. 10. 2; **1374** si racionabiliter te regules et ~es in comedendo, bibendo, laborando et dormiendo . ., continue servis Deo. et hoc est contra multos, qui . . irracionabiliter se regulant et ~ant jejunando, vigilando, et laborando ultra quam possunt pati corpore suo BRINTON *Serm.* 33 p. 136; in [diete] administracione hominis ~andi tria particularia plus aliis precipue attendentur, viz. parcium disposicio, corporis complexio atque composicio KYMER 3; *to diet*, ~are *CathA*. **b** si [melencolia] ~aretur vel curaretur ut tertiana, maximus esset error et periculum GILB. I 8. 1.

2 to sojourn, stay.

ubi [ad portum de Barbefleoth] cum aliquot dies . . moraremur et preter voluntatem nostram, ventorum cogente intemperie, ~are cogeremur (*Relatio Lamberti Abbatis*) SAMSON *Mir. Edm.* II 7; *to sojourne*, perhendinare . ., ~are *CathA*.

3 *f. l.*

1380 de . . prebenda prout tenor litterarum . . predecessoris nostri †dietavit [? l. dictavit] concedere *Dip. Corr. Ric. II* 11.

diaetarium, dietary (book prescribing diet or rule of living).

in quarum [trium particularum] prima sunt auctoritates ad dissuasionem amissionis temporis et persuasionem utilis occupacionis in omni hora, que potest dici ~ium J. WALEYS *V. Relig. prol.* f. 217v.; ~ium de sanitatis custodia KYMER (*tit*).

diaetum v. diaeta 3a. **diaf-** v. et. diaph-. **diaffenicon** v. 1 dia 1. **diafonus** v. diaphanus. **diaforestare** v. deafforestare. **diafragmen, diaframa** v. diaphragma. **diagalanga, ~gariofil' (~caryophyll'), ~glitis** v. 1 dia 1. **diagnatus** v. cognatus c.

diagonalis [CL; cf. διαγώνιος], diagonal: **a** (adj.); **b** (sb.).

a quadratum descriptum juxta ~em lineam xvj pedum NECKAM *NR* II 173. **b** rectarum linearum species sunt sex: cathetus, basis, ypotenusa, coraustus, ~is, diametrum ADEL. *Alch.* 15.

diagonicum, diagonal (sb.).

~um lateri numero partium commensurari non posse BALSH. *AD rec.* 2 170.

diagradyon, ~gredium (~grydium), ~hermis, ~hyssopus, ~iris, ~isopus, ~iteon, ~lacca v. 1 dia 1. **dialateca** v. dialecticus c. **diale** v. 2 dialis.

dialectice [CL], dialectically.

disputant scholares, quidam demonstrative, ~e alii W. FITZST. *Thom. prol.* 9.

dialecticus [CL< διαλεκτικός], dialectical. **b** (as sb. m.) dialectician. **c** (as sb. f., *sc. ars*) dialectic.

dialectica dogmata rerum ALDH. *VirgV* 1260; **800** in ~is subtilitatibus ALCUIN *Ep.* 204; bis ternae que sint normae dialecticae, inqui *Altercatio* 71; crudam materiam . . minus dialeticis et rethoricis enigmatibus compositam *G. Herw.* 320; omnia ~e artis argumenta quasi murum cocti lateris validissimis rationibus debellando AILR. *Serm.* 496D (cf. coquere 3c); ~e discipline subtilitate jactanter elatus GIR. *GE* I 51 p. 150; [syllogismus] ~us est ex probabilibus faciens opinionem (SHIRWOOD) *GLA* III 16; *Ib.* 19 (v. disputatio 1); [argumentum] dialeticum movet intellectum speculativum ad debilem notitiam veritatis, sc. ad opinionem, non ad scientiam BACON *Mor. Phil.* 250; *Ps.-*GROS. *Summa* 300 (v. demonstrativus d); **1384** juvenes monachi, ad artem dioleticam in primiciis eorum deputati, circa logicam et philosophiam per octo annos . . insistent *Cant. Coll. Ox.* III 174; **1395** libros gramadicales, civiles, ~os . . scolarium . . furati fuerunt *Pat* 342 m. 27. **b** relictis ~orum disciplinis ALDH. *VirgP* 35; ~us, ipse qui disputat *GlC* D 251; ~i aliter scribunt de vocibus secundum quod sunt significativae, aliter eis utuntur loquendo secundum quod sunt appellativae ANSELM (*Gram.* 18) I 164; magna eruditione litterarum inter dicaces philosophos in scholis grammaticorum et ~orum enituit ORD. VIT. XI 33 p. 280; optimus ~us est cum quo disseritur omnium argumentorum locus, qui loco non clauditur GIR. *PI* II 7; **c1430** aliquid dicere . . quod . . penes dialeticum . . amplius sophistice quam propter quid potissime demonstraret *Reg. Whet.* II 439; hic dioleticus, *a arcister WW*. **c** ~a, dualis dictio *GlC* D 259; **9..** ~a, *wordlocum WW*; illi nostri temporis dialectici, immo ~ae haeretici, qui non nisi flatum vocis putant universales esse substantias ANSELM (*Incarn.* B 1) II 9; **s1119** (v. collocutio b); J. SAL. *Met.* 928C (v. apodicticus b); in illis ~e gyris atque meandris GIR. *IK pref.* p. 4; ~a docet discernere verum a falso NECKAM *NR* II 173 p. 284; quod moderni investigant magis pertinet †dyaletico [? l. ~e] quam rationi, cum nihil juvaminis nobis in medicando largiatur GILB. VI 271. 1; **1390** omnes libros meos gramatice et ~e (*Test. J. Douglas*) *Bannatyne Misc.* II 107; **1498** scola dialatece alta quarta *Cart. Osney* III 278.

dialesis v. dialysis. **dialeton** v. dialyton. **dialexandrios** v. 1 dia 2.

dialexis [LL < διάλεξις], discussion.

~is, disputationis *GlC* D 295.

dialignum v. 1 dia 1.

dialippon [LL < διαλείπων], **~ides,** intermittent fever.

diliponta est cotidiana vel tertiana vel quartana *Gloss. Poems* 103; †lipochomia [λιποθυμία] . ., i. defectus motus cordis, in ~ides sive ~on idem quod defectus *Alph.* 100.

1 dialis [CL]

1 (w. *flamen*) priest of Jupiter at Rome.

GlC F 242, OSB. GLOUC. *Deriv.* 240 (v. flamen a).

2 heavenly. *Cf. dealis.*

c750 ut armata angelicis / vallata legionibus / dextro ac levo latere / dialique majestate (*Vers.*) (BERTHGYTH) *Ep. Bonif.* 148.

2 dialis, revolving daily, (as sb. n.) dial.

1325 expense orologii: . . in pictura ~is interioris et tabule sub ~i exteriori, ix d.; . . item in magno lamine ad ~e, iiij li. vij s. (*Comp. Norw.*) *Arch. J.* XII 176; dividatur rota pro ponderibus ~is in 72 dentes WALLINGF. (*Hor.*) I 472; *Ib.* 474 (v. caliga 2); hujus abbatis [T., ob. **1396**] sumptibus . . artificio magistri L. de S. horologiarii precipui . ., superius ~e et rota †fortuna [l. fortune] . . nobiliter sunt perfecta *G. S. Alb.* III 385.

dialiton v. dialyton

dialogice, in dialogue.

visus est ei . . rex [Malcolmus IV] veste candida amictus . . sibi assistere ac ~e ad queque . . interrogata . . sic metrice respondere . . FORDUN *Cont.* VIII 11.

dialogisticus [διαλογιστικός], dialectical.

idem [Athanasius] in Libello Fidei Suae, quem ~o sermone contra haereticas pravitates exarandum esse optimum censuit . . ALCUIN (*Adv. Elipandum*) *Dogm.* 281B.

dialogizare [cf. διαλογίζεσθαι], to write in dialogue form.

Anselmus 'cur Deus homo' . . vicesimo quarto ~ans sic scribit . . BRADW. *CD* 384B.

dialogon v. 1 dia 1.

dialogus [CL < διάλογος], discussion, dialogue; **b** (dramatic).

~us, liber disputationis *GlC* D 251; [Gregorius] libros . . ~orum iiij fecit BEDE *HE* II 1. p. 76; ~us, locutio duorum OSB. GLOUC. *Deriv.* 175; mementote narrationis in ~o [ME: *dialoge*], quomodo sanctus [Job] consuevit dicere maligno serpenti . . *AncrR* 84. **b** contigit ut . . larvatorum . . et verbis et actu fieret representatio dominice resurrectionis. . . adolescentuli quidam . . murales ascendebant basilice testudines . . ut . . personarum . . ~os auditu faciliori adverterent *Mir. J. Bev. C* 328.

dialtea, ~ia (~althaea) v. 1 dia 1.

dialysis [CL < διάλυσις], (in etym. gl.) resolution.

GERV. MELKLEY *AV* 37 (v. dialyton).

dialyton [LL < διάλυτον], asyndeton.

~on vel asyndeton est figura . . carens conjunctionibus BEDE *ST* 151; hic color scemati dialeton equipollet adeo quod fidelissima interpretatione dialesis [v. l. dialisis] est dissolutio, dialeton [v. l. dialiton] dissolutum GERV. MELKLEY *AV* 37.

diamalvatum, diamar- v. 1 dia 1.

diamandus, ~ans, ~as [OF *diamant* < dia + adamas], diamond.

1205 j baculum cum xxviij ~ant' *Pat* 55a; **1215** cum xxviij ~and' *Ib.* 150b; **1224** xv anulos cum ~andis *Cl* 602a; **1300** anulus auri cum quadam (*sic*) dyamando *AcWardr* p. 348; **1352** j nouch' auri . . cum ij deamant' a latere ejus et vj perulis in iij troch' cum iij deamant' in medio *Reg. Black Pr.* IV f. 43*d*.; ~as *SB* 28 (v. adamas a); **1401** ij boni anuli auri cum dyamantis *Ac. Durh.* 451; adamas est lapis qui et diadamas *Alph.* 110; *a diamant,* ~ans *CathA*.

diamastix, diambra (~ambra) v. 1 dia 1. **diamecon** v. 1 dia 1. **diamedia** v. Dynamidia. **diamelon** v. 1 dia 1. **diamenta (diamentha)** v. 1 dia 1. **diameroes** v. 1 dia 2. **diametare** v. diametrare.

1 diameter, ~rus [CL < διάμετρος]

1 diagonal (adj.).

si ducatur linea ~ra vel a cono ad conum, tunc diameter erit equalis coste BACON XIII 327 (v. et. 2c infra).

2 (as sb. m. or n.) diameter (of circle or sphere). **b** (w. *ex*) in diametrical opposition, contrariwise. **c** diagonal of square.

†deamentro, quod per †modum [? l. medium] fit *GlC* D 119; ad ~rum caeli, quod quintam decimam lunam tenere nemo [est] qui dubitet BEDE *TR* 17; cum . . totius terre latitudo . . minimi puncti proportionem quantum ad celi infinitum fere ~rum obtinere possit ADEL. *QN* 25; quid centrum, quid ~rum, quid rotundum . . contemplans *Id. ED* 29; describatur . . semicirculus et ducatur ~er ab uno terminali puncto ad aliud punctum terminale J. BLUND *An.* 105 (cf. ib. 91: ~er secans oculum et transiens per ejus centrum); ex hiis juxta circuli et ~ri regulam ~er terre sic inveniri poterit SACROB. *Sph.* 85; differencia est inter ~rum et axem, quoniam ~er est circuli in plano et dicitur a *dia*, quod est 'duo', et *metros*, 'mensura', sed axis dicitur esse in corpore rotundo, ut in spera ROB. ANGL. (II) 145; ~er [celi] fixa axis vocatur Latine, Hebraice quidem *magual* GROS. 13 (cf. ib.: in spherico motu circa ~rum immobilem); si sphera sit in loco orbiculari, ~er sphere est ~er orbis continentis PECKHAM *QA* 122; fiat circulus *ABD* super centrum *O* et protrahatur ~er *AC* super quam cadat perpendiculariter *BD* super punctum *E* WALLINGF. (*Quad.*) I 26. **b** 'adhaerere Deo bonum est' [*Psalm* lxxii 28]; qua in re ex ~ro conjectatur non ei famulari non bonum est O. CANT. *Pref. Frith.* 20; si Christi facta consideramus . ., reperiemus . . omnia cum his ex dyametro pugnare quae . . sibi vendicat episcopus Romanus GARDINER *VO* 132; institutis ecclesiae sanctae ex ~ro repugnat CHAUNCY *Passio* 92. **c** umbra in se ipsam ducenda erit atque inde producto cxliiij addenda sunt, totiusque summe *elgidher*, id est quadrati latus, notabitur, eritque hoc *elgidher* hujus ipsius umbre ~ros ADEL. *Elk.* 28a; in duo †quadratum [? l. quadrati] partita diametrus HANV. III 155 (cf. 1 costa 5); illud Aristotelicum . ., 'si ~er est coste symmeter, erunt abundantia equalia perfectis' NECKAM *NR* II 173; nos componimus ista impossibilia, ut †dixametrum esse symetrum BACON XIII 284; *Ib.* 327 (v. 1 supra).

3 direct line (through).

unde [fumus] diffunditur secundum omnes dyamet[ros] ad pectus et dyafragma GILB. II 90v. 2; tunc bonum est quod [sanguis] trahatur secundum omnes opposiciones et secundum diversiones vel ~ros GAD. 27. 2; illam [caracam] . ., que versus Lesclus recto ~ro properavit *G. Hen. V* 24; dux . ., †ville [l. villa] perrerrata ~ro, usque illuc citatis cursibus se divertit *Ps.*-ELMH. *Hen. V* 44 p. 112.

2 diameter v. dimeter.

diametrabilis, diametrical.

ubi iste ecentricus dividit lineam ~em *DB* ponantur puncta *D, B* WALLINGF. (*Alb.*) I 320.

diametralis [LL], diametrical.

cum umbra solis ceciderit super lineam ~em circuli ROB. ANGL. (II) 181; luna . . in oppositione sua ~i ad solem *Ps.*-GROS. *Summa* 572; in tribus . . assimulantur mundus et homo: in dimensione ~i; in disposicione naturali; in operacione virtuali HIGD. II 1 p. 176; si fuerit ~is interposicio terre inter solem et lunam, causatur eclipsis lune WYCL. *Log.* I 27.

diametraliter, diametrically. **b** directly; *cf.* 1 *diameter* 3.

cum . . sol fuerit in opposita parte ~er SACROB. *Sph.* 115*n.*; solum id quod ~er oculo opponitur per se videtur *Ps.*-GROS. *Summa* 501; cum concluditur lunam eclipsari ~er oppositam soli per umbram terre interposite KILWARDBY *OS* 497. **b** illa lamina facit ascendere calorem ~er CUTCL. *LL* 10.

diametrare

1 to provide w. a diameter.

fiat circulus meridianus, qui diamet[r]etur duabus diametris *AL, MB* WALLINGF. (*Quad.*) I 114; tabula quadrata, dyametrata duabus dyametris orthogonaliter se secantibus in quodam puncto *Turquet* 370.

2 to pierce right through (fig.).

dolores dyametrant cor patrum suorum PECKHAM *Def. Mend.* 55.

diametricalis, diametrical.

per eclipses solis et lune, que sunt per conjunctionem seu oppositionem ~em solis et lune BACON VI 146.

diametrus v. 1 diameter, dimeter. **diamicon' (~meconis)** v. dia 1. **diamiffragia** v. drimyphagia. **diamilon (~melon)** v. 1 dia 1.

diamnes [cf. CL amnis], involuntary urination.

diampnes est involuntaria urine emissio et eductio per vesicam, quemadmodum diabetes per renes GILB. VI 279v. 2; dyaprunis †vel [? l. pro] dyampnis †pro [? l. vel] calida gutta virilium membrorum *Ib.* VII 314v. 1; dicendum est de ~e, que est passio vesice in qua urina egreditur involuntarie . .; et dicitur ~es quasi 'duorum damnum', sc. renum et vesice GAD. 99v. 2; **s1451** ut omnes . . dictum patrem [Johannem W.], quamvis . . multifaria, viz. colicam et calculum, diampnem et nephresim, senectam et senium . . pro se in suam excusacionem opponentem . . nihilominus rursus eligerent *Reg. Whet.* I 9.

diamneticus, (w. *passio*) involuntary urination.

dyampnetica passio est involuntaria urine emissio *SB* 18.

diamon [cf. διά + μνήμων], (in etym. gl.) omniscient being.

demones, . . dicti quasi ~ones, id est omnia scientes, utpote nuntii dei ALB. LOND. *DG* 2. 1.

diamoron, ~muscum v. 1 dia 1. **diampn-** v. diamn-. **diana-, diane-** v. 1 dia 1. **dianicalabon** v. iatrolabon. **dianison, ~um (~anisum), dianthos (~anthos), diao-, diapalma, ~papaveris** v. 1 dia 1.

diapason [CL < διὰ πασῶν (χορδῶν)], (mus.) diapason, interval of entire octave (partly fig.).

nobis dic pueris, sophiae rudibus documentis, / quid diatesseron, diapente sit ac diapason *Altercatio* 79; chorus . . virorum et puerorum gratissimam consonantiam ~on reddentium, dum modo junctis modulis concinerent, modo distinctis organis parvuli viris responderent GOSC. *Transl. Aug.* 35A; [Ptolomeus] de diatessaron et ~on unam effici consonantiam ostendit ADEL. *ED* 6; predictas quatuor . . virtutes . ., quasi diatessaron diapente conjungens et ex eis ~on componens AD. SCOT *TGC* 802C; conjunctis diapente et diatessaron resultat ~on NECKAM *NR* I 15; *Transl. Edm. Rich.* 1852 (v. 2 diatessaron); musica modulatio numerorum nominibus advocatur. . . octo ad sex et ix ad xij comparati sesquitertiam proportionem reddunt et simul faciunt dyatesseron consonantiam . . sex vero ad ix et viij ad xij comparati reddunt sesqu[i]alteram proportionem et dyapente efficiunt symphoniam. duodecim vero ad vij considerati duplicem . . reddunt proportionem, sc. ~on simphoniam cantant BART. ANGL. XIX 142; contingit consonantiam esse in secundo et tercio, in quarto et in quinto, in discantu et organo, et hoc ad modum dyapente, que consistit in v vocibus, vel ad similitudinem dyatessaron, que consistit in iiij vocibus, vel ad similitudinem dyapason, que est consonantia consistens in pluribus—comprehendit enim dyapente et †dyatassaron GARL. *PP* 164.

diapeganum, ~pendeon, ~penion, ~penidion, 1 **diapente** v. 1 dia 1.

2 diapente [CL < διάπεντε (χορδῶν)], (mus.) interval of a fifth.

Altercatio 79, AD. SCOT *TGC* 802 (v. diapason); vellent me [sc. asinum] psallere sursum / et geminare meos in diapente tonos NIG. *SS* 2082; GIR. *TH* III 11 (v. 2 diatessaron); BART. ANGL. XIX 142 (v. diapason); ~e est conjunctio v vocum et dispositio trium tonorum cum additione unius semitonii aut in principio aut in medio aut in fine GARL. *Mus.* 165; *Id. PP* 164 (v. diapason); ut diatessaron est sexquitercia proporcio in sonis, ~e est sexqualtera proporcio in sonis et sic de aliis *Ps.*-GROS. *Gram.* 13; rotunda B sonat . . in superioribus cum C tonum, cum D sonat ditonum, cum F ~e TUNST. 215a.

diaphaneitas, transparency; **b** (fig.).

per 'faciem abissi' voluit insinuare diaphonitatem, hoc est perspicuitatem GROS. *Hexaem.* I 18; secundum quod [elementa] plus vel minus participant in materiam et formam, ~atem vel corpulentiam *Comm. Sph.* 276; sunt ista media diversarum diaphanaitatum, ut quando unum densius est et aliud rarius BART. ANGL. III 17; non arbitrantes dyafanitatem, que est puri aeris et celi et aque, esse principium coloris quem ignis habet in natura GILB. VI 259. 1; sunt xx alia sensibilia, sc. . . corporeitas . ., ~as, spissitudo, umbra, obscuritas . . BACON *Maj.* II 6; anguli fraccionis diversificantur secundum diversitatem declinacionis et differenciam ~atis secundi medii PECKHAM *Persp.* III 1; videntur astra per nebulam et omnia visibilia que videntur per media diafaneitatum notabiliter diversarum WYCL. *Dom. Div.* 187. **b** tandem [consecrandi] . ., ut jam †dyaphinitate perspicui et lucis alicujus capaces a perspicacibus ministris censeantur, tunc sacerdotibus offeruntur COLET *Eccl. Hier.* 252.

diaphania [διαφάνεια], transparency.

aer / . . / subtilis, levis, obtusus lenisque fovensque / transparens; sed idem diafanīa facit NECKAM *DS* IV 20.

diaphanus (diaf-) [cf. διαφανής], diaphanous, transparent. **b** (as sb. n., *sc. corpus*) transparent medium.

iste humor ~us et translucens est, ut sit susceptibilis omnium formarum *Ps.*-RIC. *Anat.* 26; cum illi vapores sint corpus ~um, disgregant radios nostros visuales SACROB. *Sph.* 81; opagum infimum, †diafonum medium, et luminosa, ut ignis et stelle, sursum sunt FISHACRE *Quaest.* 50; lumen est qualitas a corpore lucido in corpore ~o derelicta GILB. III 127. 1; corpora rara et pervia et diaphāna (penultima producta (*sic*) que scribitur per A; at dyaphŏna penultima correpta, que scribitur per O) ac perspicua et translucentia et lucida, luce transeunte BACON II 24 (cf. id. 460: ~um idem est quod duplicis apparitionis, sc. in superficie et in profundo, nam *phano* Grece idem est quod 'appareo' Latine, et *dia* idem est quod 'duo'); hec [pars oculi] . . est valde ~a, ut multitudo tunicarum ejus non impediat transitum specierum rerum visibilium *Id. Maj.* II 16. **b** GROS. 74 (v. contiguitas a); ad rem visam per plura †diafona diversorum generum DOCKING (*Deut.*) 115; inter specula et ~a hec est differencia, quum in speculis generatur ignis inter speculum et solem, in ~is autem econverso ipsum ~um interponitur PECKHAM *Persp.* III 17; non enim aqua secundum quod aqua, neque aer secundum quod aer, ~um est BRADW. *CD* 159A; sicut sol, celum et omnia ~a perennis luciditatis NETTER *DAF* II 92.

diaphinitas v. diaphaneitas b. **diaphoenicon** v. 1 dia 1.

diaphonia (diaf-) [LL < διαφωνία], (mus.): **a** discord. **b** diaphony, two-part harmony.

a unde ista diversitas et veluti inconveniens ~ia nascatur ALDH. *PR* 135; ~ia, dissonantia *GlC* D 248; ~ia, *ungeswege sang* ÆLF *Gl.*; cui [eufonie] contraria est ~ia, idem 'vox dissonans' BART. ANGL. XIX 128; *a discording of voices,* ~ia *CathA* (cf. *WW*: †diaphosia, *sunvoys*, vel melius *soun of voys*). **b** ~ia est concors discordia inferiorum vocum cum superioribus ODINGTON 127.

diaphonitas v. diaphaneitas.

diaphonus [διάφωνος], diaphonic.

BACON II 24 (v. diaphanus a); *phonos* est 'sonus', unde ~um quasi 'duplicis sonoritatis', tam sc. in imo quam in summo *Id. Maj.* II 461 (cf. diaphanus c).

diaphoresis (diaf-) [LL < διαφόρησις]

1 diaphoresis, opening of the pores, (induced) perspiration.

vino non utimur in ~im faciendo exterius, sicut in emplastris GILB. I 43. 1; *Ib.* IV 199. 2 (v. diaphoreticus); ~is dicitur pororum apercio *SB* 18.

2 (?) doubt, perplexity.

~is, per quam fit differentia personarum *Gl. Leid.* 28. 80.

diaphoreticus (diaf-) [LL < διαφορητικός], diaphoretic, sudorific.

[saphirus] et cardiacum et ~um fluorem reprimit et sudorem BART. ANGL. XVI 85; passio ~a vocatur quoniam ipsam diaforesis, id est apertio pororum, comitatur GILB. IV 199. 2 (cf. ib. 178. 1: utendum est . . extra emplastris . . et ~is intra gargarismis); propter sudorem ~um vel propter vomitum continuum GAD. 98v. 2; ~i i. cardiaci, vel sic: ~i dicuntur qui sudorem incongruum paciuntur . .; ~a passio fit ex nimia pororum apercione *SB* 18; sordicies que in balneis colligitur, que nominatur 'glio', virtutem calidam gerit, malagticam et ~am *Alph.* 176.

diaphosia v. diaphonia a.

diaphragma (diaf-) [LL < διάφραγμα], diaphragm, midriff.

est matrix membrum organicum . ., folliculos habens in fundo, qui tendit prope ~a RIC. MED. *Anat.* 231; ~a est quedam pellicula dividens regionem vitalium a regione nutritivorum; unde dicitur ~a, quasi 'in duo frangens' *Ps.*-RIC. *Anat.* 41; semen unius ponitur in superiori †dyaframato matricis BACON VIII 134; **1300** a gradu . . cecidit et fregit viscera sua et deafragma *RCoron Lond.* A 12 (cf. *Cal.* p. 12); sicut ~a dividit inter spiritualia et nutritiva, ita sifac inter intestina et nutritiva et generativa GAD. 129. 2; sicut monstrum quod est homo geminus et a ~ate versus superius habet hominem ejus partem WYCL. *Incarn.* 212; antiqui ante tempus Platonis vocabant 'frenes' quod nos hodie dicimus '~a' *Alph.* 65; ~a, *myddereffe* . ., diafragmen, A. *the mydryf WW*.

diapigamum (~peganum), ~piretrum (~pyrethrum) v. 1 dia 1. **diapr-** v. 1 dia 1, diasp-.

diapsalma [LL < διάψαλμα], 'diapsalm', pause or interlude in text. **b** division (of text) into sections.

~a, sermonum rupta continuatio *GlC Int.* 87. **b** hujus operis . . secundum [librum] collegi et . . quarundam causarum necessaria capitula . . subjunxi, quod in v libellorum ~ate titulavi, sicut antiqua patrum disciplina praedocuit (*Quad. Arg.*) *GAS* 535; ~a, divisio psalmi OSB. GLOUC. *Deriv.* 175 (cf. ib. 179: ~a, medietas psalmi).

diapton v. dryopteris. **diapyrethrum** v. 1 dia 1. **diaquilon, ~iloti (~chylon)** v. 1 dia 1.

diarcha [cf. δίαρχος], joint ruler (one of two).

praecepit Edgarus ~a totius regni sui concilium celebrari Osb. *V. Dunst.* 29; Archelaus filius .. fit ~a Judee annis ix R. Niger *Chr. II* 108; conregnabant ipse [Merwaldus] .. et frater ejus Wlferus ..; fratres enim erant filii Pende regis [Mercie], cui mortuo successerunt quasi ~e regni *NLA* (*Milburga*) II 188.

diare [ME *dien, deien*], to dye.

1434 queritur de T. Stretton .., *dyer*, quod .. concordavit cum predicto Thoma quod .. diet sive listet vel tingeret .. unum *pakke* panni lanei *Rec. Nott.* II 146.

diareubarbar, ~rhodon v. 1 dia 1. **diarhodos** v. 1 dia 2. **1 diaria** v. daieria c.

2 diaria [cf. ME *dier, deier* = *dyer*], 'dyery', dye-house.

1455 tenementum .. in quo .. modo Willelmus Newman, *dyer*, deyeriam suam tenet *Rent. Glouc.* 64.

3 diaria, ~icus v. diarr-. **diaripheos** v. 1 dia 2. **diaris (~iris)** v. 1 dia 1.

diarium [CL], daily allowance.

~ium, pensum, *dægwine* Ælf. *Gl.*; ~ium, diei precium Osb. Glouc. *Deriv.* 172; quidam nobilis .. [tempore .. abbatis Pauli, ob. **1093**] .. constituit quedam ~ia dari scriptoribus de elemosina fratrum et cellarii [v. l. cellario] quia prompta fuerant ad edendum, ne scriptores impedirentur *G. S. Alb.* I 57; s**1250** susceperunt .. eos Sarraceni et fame deficientes diarriis sufficientibus aluerunt applaudentes M. Par. *Maj.* V 107.

diaroddon, ~rodian, ~rodon (~rhodon), ~roma (~aroma) v. 1 dia 1. **diaromes** v. 1 dia 2.

diarria [LL < διάρροια], diarrhoea. **b** falling out (of hair); *cf. 2 fluxus* 4.

~ia, *utsiht* Ælf. *Gl.*; s**1136** Guiribecci, quia inconditis post contaminationem sacrorum eduliis intemperanter usi sunt, justo Dei judicio pene omnes ventris fluxu egrotaverunt fluentique ~ia satis anxii feda vestigia obiter reliquerunt Ord. Vit. XIII 26 p. 73; diaria, continuus ventris dolor Osb. Glouc. *Deriv.* 176; Bart. Angl. V 21 (v. dysenteria); egestio .. mollis quasi dyaria Gilb. VI 240v. 2; diaria est fluxus ventris simplex humorum vel ciborum sine ventris excoriacione Gad. 56. 1; ~ia dicitur ingens cursus ventris cum vomitu *SB* 17; *þe flix*, diaria, discentaria, lientaria, fluxus *CathA*. **b** ex hujusmodi signis est sputum fetens, .. dyarria capillorum Gilb. I 71.1.

diarricus [LL < διαρροικός], diarrhoeic.

fluxus diaricus vel aquosus moderatus est salubris, immoderatus vel magnus est mortalis Gad. 32. 1.

diarris (~iris), ~rrodon v. 1 dia 1. **dias** v. dyas. **diasatirion, ~saturian** v. 1 dia 1. **diascema** v. diastema. **diascene** v. 1 dia 1.

diaschisma [LL < διάσχισμα], (mus.) eighth-tone.

quod diesis est semitonium minus et quod comma deest illud, ergo semitonium minus, et quod schisma est dimidium commatis, et ~a est dimidium diesis Tunst. 216.

diasene v. 1 dia 1. **diasenes (~syenes)** v. 1 dia 2. **diasentetica, ~testica** v. diasynthetica. **diasi-** v. et. diasy-. **diasirtica** v. diasynthetica, diasyrticus. **diasistole** v. diastole. **diaspaltum** v. 1 dia 1. **diasperatus** v. diaspratus. **diaspermaton** v. 1 dia 1. **diaspin-** v. diaspri-. **diaspiter** v. Diespiter.

diaspratus [cf. diasprus], diapered: **a** (of cloth); **b** (of metalwork).

a iste abbas [R. ob. **1229**] acquisivit tres capas bonas, unam de albo serico ~eratam et auro stragulatam *Chr. Evesham* 263*n.*; **1295** sandalia cum caligis de rubeo sameto ~erato *Vis. S. Paul.* 315b; **1315** casula .. de *morre* ~erata *Invent. Ch. Ch.* 51; s**1322** [capa] preciosior .., cujus campus aureus est et deasperatus J. Glast. 261; **1340** culcitra .. diaprata cum *scochons* de armis regis *KRAc* 389/4 m. 2; **1349** ij pannos diaspynett' (*Ib.* 391/15) *Arch.* XXXI 85; **1358** j pannus viridis diaspinet' debilis (*Ib.* 333/29) *CalExch* III 237; *Ib.* 236 (v. colponatus); **1368** tunica et dalmatica unius secte de uno panno de aspinet' *Invent. Norw.* 80 (cf. ib. 133: una alba cum amita de deaspineto); **1418** mappam .. diapretam cum manutergio *Reg. Cant.* II 197; **1429** lintheamina .. de opere diapreto (*Invent.*) Amund. I app. 449. **b** **1317** cuppam .. de argento deauratam et deasperatam *PIRCP* 285 *Deeds enr.* r. 1d.

diasprinus [cf. diasprus], diapered (of cloth).

s**1536** empta .. peristromata aulae collegii cubiculi custodis, et interioris ejusdem camerae sunt, cum aliis mensae communis ornamentis et instratis diaperinis (Caius *Ann.*) *Camb. Antiq. Soc.* 8° S. XL 6.

diasprus [Byz. δίασπρος = *pure white*], diaper (adj.). **b** (as sb. f. or n.) fabric w. diaper pattern.

1553 de .. iiij longis mappis diapris, A. *fower longe diaper table clothes Pat* 852 m. 28. **b** **1204** tunicam de dyaspro albo *RChart* 134a; **1225** pannus unus de serico albo ~ero *Reg. S. Osm.* II 131; **1245** capa .. de albo deaspero *Invent. S. Paul.* 477; **1250** quod .. preciosam casulam regis de samito liniri faciat de ~era *Cl* 292; **1260** albam de alba ~ra *Cl* 246; pallas .. de ~re Domerh. *Glast.* 316; **1303** j tunica et dalmatica de rubio ~ro *Ac. Exec. Ep. Lond.* 48; **1345** j pannus albus de ~ero deputatus altari B. Virginis *Sacr. Lichf.* 112; de .. xij pannis j quarterio dyaspin' *Miss. Westm.* II 676*n.*

diastasis [LL < διάστασις], disagreement.

a discordynge of wylle, ~is *CathA*.

diastema [CL < διάστημα = *space, distance*], degree, distinctiveness. **b** (mus.) 'diastem'.

sunt .. quedam specialia [officia], que variantur secundum diversitates temporum et distantiam sollempnitatum: .. secundum distantiam [PL *reads*: pro ~ate seu distantia] sollempnitatum .., in Pascha tres lectiones leguntur, in Natali novem Beleth *RDO* 18. 31. **b** ad melodiam aut armoniam faciendam requiruntur †dyascema, dyesis, tonus .. et suavis vox. .. †dyascema dicitur 'vocis spatium ex duobus vel pluribus sonis aptatum' [Isid. *Etym.* III 20. 5] Bart. Angl. XIX 128.

diastole, ~es [LL < διαστολή], **a** (gram.) mark indicating separation of words. **b** (anat.) dilation (of heart).

a †diastile, separatio *GlC Int.* 94; ~e Graece, Latine interdictum: est autem nota ad pedem litterae posita quae male conjuncta separet Bede *Orth.* 22. **b** Ric. Med. *Anat.* 226 (v. arsis b); est .. pulsus secundum dyastolem et sistolem, id est secundum dilationem et constrictionem cordis Bart. Angl. III 23; major reperitur dilatatio quam constrictio et velocior ~e quam sistole Gilb. I 14. 1 (cf. ib. III 157v. 2: sistole et †diasistole cordis); accidit in ea [sc. quartana] multocies ~es inequalis et sistoles vehementis velocitatis Gad. 16. 1.

diastolice, analytically, by drawing distinctions.

aliquando procedant [predicatores] .. ~e, i.e. separatorie Garl. *Dict.* 133.

diastomaticon v. 1 dia 1. **diastrobilon, ~sulphuris** v. 1 dia 1. **diasuros** v. diasyrtos. **diasya** v. dasia. **diasyenes** v. 1 dia 2.

diasynthetica [cf. συνθετικός; (?) *infl. by* σύνταξις], syntax.

grammaticam sequitur †diasirtica, synthesis illam, / lexis eam, rhesis posteriore gradu J. Sal. *Enth. Phil.* 359; similiter scientialia .., ut 'grammatica' .., 'orthographia', '~a', 'prosodia' Bacon *CSPhil.* 444; deinde oportet ut sciat pronuncians recte pronunciatas conjungere prout exigit diversa complexionis accepcio, et hec est diasintetica, quasi de construccione *Ps.*-Gros. *Gram.* 67; antiquorum grammaticorum orthographiam, prosodiam, etymologiam ac †dyasenteticam [v. l. †diasintasim] .. consideravimus R. Bury *Phil.* 12. 176; grammatice perfeccionem, que ex ethimoligia, ortographia, prosodia et †diasentestica [v. l. diasyntasia] .. profluit Fortescue *LLA* 8; †diasinaxis, bonum opus oracionis dicte *WW*.

diasyrticus [LL < διασυρτικός], mocking, ironic.

'eamdem habentes remunerationem' diasirtica locutione Lanfr. *Comment. Paul.* (2 *Cor.* vi 13) 236.

diasyrtos [cf. διασυρμός, διασυρτικός], deliberate absurdity, paradox. (*Cf.* Isid. *Etym.* II 21. 42).

unus [*Gen.* i 1] dicit Deum Patrem fuisse in Filio; alter [*John* i 1] protestatur Filium fuisse in Patre. .. cum dicitur quia 'in principio creavit Deus celum et terram', perinde est ac si dicatur, 'Deus pater eternaliter existens in Filio, qui est principium de principio, in Filio creavit celum et terram', ut subsit diasirtos [vv. ll. diasuros, diasircos] sub hoc intellectu Neckam *NR* I 1 p. 4.

diatage [διαταγή], arrangement.

Democritus et .. Leucippus .. posuerunt omnia fieri ex corporibus indivisibilibus, sed concurrentibus differenter secundum †risutos [l. rismos, sc. ῥυσμός], †diatigi [l. diatagi], et tropi [sc. τροπή], i.e. secundum figuram, ordinem, et posicionem Bradw. *CD* 261d.

diatapsalon v. 2 diatessaron. **diatarascos** v. 1 dia 1. **1 diatessaron** v. 1 dia 1.

2 diatessaron [LL < διὰ τεσσάρων], **~eron,** (mus.) interval of a fourth.

~eron *Altercatio* 79, ~aron Adel. *ED* 6 etc. (v. diapason); iiij .. timpanistrie timpanizantes ~eron celeste *Lib. Eli.* II 148; seu ~eron seu diapente chorde concrepent, semper tamen a B molli incipiunt Gir. *TH* III 11; **1248** alii tono, alii semitono, alii diapente, alii per †diatapsalon, alii vero usque ad diapason voces Salvatoris laudantium clementiam extollebant *Transl. Edm. Rich.* 1852; ~eron est conjunctio iiij vocum et dispositio duorum tonorum cum additione unius semitonii Garl. *Mus.* 164; quod ~aron sit prima non probatur, sed supponitur, quia sensu habetur duabus cordis eque sonantibus; deinde altera magis protensa prima consonancia quam invenies post dissonanciam erit proporcio sexquitercia, secunda sex[qui]altera et sic deinceps *Ps.*-Gros. *Gram.* 13 (cf. diapente); permiscet singulis ~eron mellifluam melodiam *Miss. Westm.* II 1093.

diatetragrammaton [cf. τετραγράμματον], tetragram (figure of four lines).

diatetragramaton figura est plana Bart. Angl. XIX 124.

diathece [LL *gl.* < διαθήκη], testament.

~e, testamentum *GlC* D 254.

diathema v. diadema b. **diatigi** v. diatage.

diatim [LL], daily: **a** from day to day (continuously); **b** every day (repeatedly); **c** for a day at a time.

a properans agiliter ad novam vitam, lacrymas serendo ~im Byrht. *V. Osw.* 415 (cf. ib.: faciem humectare .. lacrymis non desinens); ne .. regnum ~im adnihila[re]tur renovata contentione *Enc. Emmae* II 14; gaudium meum ~im crescit H. Bos. *LM* 1334a; scalam virtutum haud segniter ~im conscendens Ad. Eyns. *Hug.* I 12 p. 38; s**1241** (v. 1 clima 1c); de hiis que a diebus pertransitis in dies succedentes .. in regno Anglie .. ~im emerserunt Knighton *pref.* p. 1; **1442** scolares .. confluxere et dietim confluere non desistunt Bekynton I 123; **1448** per insolentem et sinistram gubernacionem pastorum ibidem ~im existencium *Reg. Whet.* I 38; s**1474** cum dietim vicinius ac vicinius hostium limitibus appropinquant *Croyl. Cont. C* 558; *from day to day*, die in diem, in dies, dietim *CathA*. **b** †c**1043** (11c) conditoris clementia .. ~im nos ammonere dignatus est *CD* 769; **820** servi Dei .. debent ~im .. officium implere (*Lit. Papae*) W. Malm. *Glast.* 66; *Id. GP* II †91 [l. 94] (v. annuatim); s**1137** ~im horis decantatis .. missam .. audire solebat in illius [B. Virginis] honore J. Worc. 41; **1288** retroactis temporibus receperunt et dietim recipiunt affluenter pro rebus hujusmodi *AncC* LV 10; s**1324** terre et castella .. regine in manibus regis fuerant .. seisita, certis stipendiis ~im dicte regine ex bursa regia †parte [? l. parce; cf. Baker f. 103] concessis Blaneford 151 (= Wals. *HA* I 175: dietim; cf. diaeta 3b); **1413** Marcus habeat ~im vadia sua .., viz. ij s. per diem *BB Winchester* 17; **1486** satisfacere .. magistro A. .. de porcione †dieti [? dietim] donec .. *Reg. Aberbr.* II 245 (cf. ib. supra: una cum cotidiana porcione sicut conventus cotidie recipit); **1543** salva .. parte emolumentorum .. antea annuatim seu ebdomidatim aut dietim .. solvi solitorum *Form. S. Andr.* II 222. **c** rex .. et majores exercitus .. precedunt classem in galeis et per civitates maritimas dietim hospitantes .. Messanam applicuerunt Devizes 29.

diatomos, (of moon) first quarter, half-moon (also fig.). (*Cf.* Martianus capella VII 738, VIII 864: διχότομος, v. l. †διάτομος). *Cf. dichotomos.*

sicut .. in astrologia Martiani luna .. dicitur in augmento cum jam ad medium crevit ~os, .. sic Dei ecclesia .. in tempore prophetarum ~os .. poterat .. nuncupari P. Blois *Ep.* 8. 22a; luna .. dicitur .. in majori incremento †diaconios Gerv. Tilb. I 6 (v. amphicyrtos).

diatonicus [LL < διατονικός], (mus.) diatonic.

Byrht. *V. Osw.* 442 (v. chromaticus 1a); chromaticum genus cantilene pre ~o et enharmonico .. viriles animos fere effeminat Neckam *NR* I 20; primum [genus harmonie] vocatur ~um Bacon *Tert.* 296.

diatragacanthum v. 1 dia 1. **diatrascos (~tarascos)** v. 1 dia 1.

diatriba [CL < διατριβή], school for rhetoric. **b** 'diatribe', critical dissertation.

†diatripas, conflictus, proprium nomen loci ubi discunt dis[ci]puli *Gl. Leid.* 30. 26. **b** †diatrifas, conflictus *GlC* D 263; ~as, dissensiones vel disputationes *Gl. Leid.* 29. 71; dominus J. .. aliquot ex junioribus fratribus domi in ~is non segniter scholasticis exercuit Ferr. *Kinloss* 80.

diatrion [διὰ τριῶν (ἡμερῶν)], **~ium,** period of three days.

~ium, i. spacium trium dierum *SB* 18; †diatricum, i. custos (*sic*) duarum dierum *Alph.* 50.

diatrion pipereon, diatriton pipereon v. 1 dia 1. **diatripa** v. diatriba. **diaturbith** v. 1 dia 1.

diatyposis [LL < διατύπωσις], description.

diatiposis, latine expressio dicitur ubi rebus personisve subjectis et formae ipsae et habitus exprimuntur *Gl. Leid.* 28. 88.

diaviolis, ~yceos (~iteon), ~yris, ~ysopus (~hyssopus), ~zinziberios, ~beros v. 1 dia 1.

dica [cf. CL dica < δίκη = *lawsuit*]

1 tally, account. **b** tally of assignment; *cf. assignare* 1b. **c** (tally recording) gratuity. **d** record of offences (also fig.).

c**1115** si voluero capere aliquam villam, ut dem vel mutuem alicui militi prout Gullielmus instauravit, ita accipiam quod dabo sibi quantum alius dederit vel ponam sibi in ~a sua (*Cart. Comitum Warw.*) *Med. E. Anglia* app. 254; s**1095** Uticenses monachi .. coacti ~am per totam terram suam, que hactenus a malis consuetudinibus libera fuerat, fecerunt et lx li. Cenomannensium de censu pagensium Redberto dederunt ne monasterium .. ulterius vexare[t] Ord. Vit. VIII 24 p. 424; magister marscallus .. debet habere ~as de donis et liberationibus que fiunt de thesauro regis et de sua camera; et debet habere ~as contra

omnes officiales regis ut testis per omnia *Domus Reg.* 134; institutum est ut diligenter per ~am notetur quantum ex omni genere bladi vel leguminis expendatur in semine *Inst. Sempr.* *xli (cf. ib.: ~a illa dividatur (*sic*) in duo, et una pars deputabitur custodie fratris .. et altera grangiario); notator / discretus brevia, cartas formare, receptas, / expensas rerumque dicas D. BEC. 1144; **1182** hoc est de mangno debito quod debet domino meo ..; et inde feci ei unam ~am *Starrs* I 118; **1200** profert ~as ei factas de illa solucione *CurR RC* II 207; **1204** assisum est quod miles et clericus et baillivi cujuslibet portus faciant inter se ~as et cirographa de receptis suis et nominibus .. mercatorum de quibus aliquid receperint et de diebus in quibus aliquid receperint *Pat* 42b; **1221** [castellani] fecerunt ~as suas et nichilominus ceperunt eodem loco cervisiam *PlCrGlouc* 108 (cf. ib.: quamdiu ipsa femina haberet talliam, non possent plus capere de cervisia); c**1300** per ~am inter .. manucaptores et .. custodem gaole factam manifestum .. fuit quod .. receperunt xxxvj averia (*Chanc. Misc.* 96/1) *EE County Court* 157; hec ~a, *a tayle WW*; *a tayle*, acopa .., ~a, caucio *CathA*. **b** s**1248** sic diffamamur et depauperamur, quia [mercatores alienigene] de rege nihil nisi ~as et nugas reportant M. PAR. *Maj.* V 6. **c** **1301** item pro ~a vicemonitoris, ij d. ..; item liberat' ad ~am S. Nicholai, vj d. (*Ac. Coll. Merton*) *Educ. Ch.* 218. **d** consciencia .. est ~a iniquitatis. .. sicut puero datur ~a in qua sua signantur delicta, ut pro eis verberetur .., ita homini datur consciencia, in qua sua peccata veraciter sunt descripta BRINTON *Serm.* 21 p. 85.

2 writ.

~am e summo tribunali ei comparavi [*Eng.*: *I have gotten wryte for him out of the chauncery*] WHITTINGTON *Vulg.* 100.

dicacitas [CL], mockery, gibe.

a**690** jocistae scurraeque ritu ~ate temeraria loquentium fraternae †hironia dilectionis obtentu cavillabatur ALDH. *Ep.* 5; ~atis nec audiende existimaverim .. [animas brutorum] †non [? *omit*] negare demum perituras PULL. *Sent.* 739D; utuntur veteri illa triviali ~ate W. FITZST. *Thom. prol.* 9; homo ~atis amare qui .. nunquam monachos mordere quievit DEVIZES 40v.

dicaciter [LL], mockingly.

paupertatis incommodum juveni ~iter improperans GIR. *DK* I 14; nos tamen nec acerbe aut ~iter agemus JEWEL *Apol.* A 6v.

dicaculus [cf. CL dicax], ready-tongued.

quidam eorum non modice ~us W. MALM. *Mir. Mariae* 139; latrat Judaicum vulgus rabidulum, / delirum, fatuum, tamen dicaculum WALT. WIMB. *Carm.* 98.

dicagium [cf. ME *dic, dich*], duty payable on wool (?) stored on dike.

1462 Boston' [*Lincs*]: officium tronagii, peisagii et ~ii. .. nec respondet de ij partibus [*blank in MS*] proveniencium de ~io *sarplers* lane, que faciunt *lastes*. et memorandum quod x *sarplers* faciunt j *laste*. et dominus nuper habuit de quolibet lasto adjacente super *le stathe* domini exopposito manerii iiij d. *DL MinAc* 639/10376; **1485** officium tronagii, peisagii cum decagio *Ib.* 10378.

1 dicare [CL], to dedicate, consecrate; **b** (as nun). **c** to ordain (as priest). **d** to confirm (as Christian). **e** to join in wedlock. **f** (w. *finem*) to ordain, declare. **g** to assign, devote.

mentem Deo ~atam ALDH. *VirgP* 33; antiquo dilubrum more dicatum *Id. VirgV* 1519; †dicit, consecrat .., ~atur, consecratur *GlC* D 229, 276; BEDE *Sam.* 562 (v. compunctivus); *Id. TR* 8 (v. dies 5a); **9..** ~emus vel consecremus, *utan halgian WW*; eoam / Uuintoniae ad portam Micahelis honore dicatam WULF. *Swith.* I 574; qui diis templa dicant, qui dii sint, hoc mihi dicant SERLO WILT. 2. 29. **b** virgo dicata Deo ALDH. *VirgV* 1975; vovit quia .. filiam suam Domino sacra virginitate ~andam offerret BEDE *HE* III 24; una [ecclesia] .. virgineo Deo ~atarum choro .. ornabatur G. MON. IX 12. **c** ministeria quae usurpato nomine sacerdotis non ~atus .. peregit EGB. *Dial.* 4. **d** vir sanctus credit puerum debere dicari / descenditque pedes. sic scilicet obligat illum / summa ministerii reverentia pontificalis / ut nullum confirmet eques H. AVR. *Hugh* 767; *to conferme*, confirmare, cathezizare, ~are *CathA*. **e** *to cuppille*, conjungere, copulare, ~are, maritare *Ib.* **f** in tanti fine regis finem libro ~abimus H. HUNT. *HA* VII 44. **g** ex his iiij caesuris ij primae ad legem scandendorum versuum sunt ~atae BONIF. *Met.* 110; ~abo, i. donabo, addicam, durabo *GlH* D 437.

2 dicare [cf. dica], to enter on a tally.

talyin or †storyn [l. *scoryn*] *on a taly*, talio, -as, dico, -as *PP*.

1 dicatio [CL], dedication, consecration.

~o, consecratio *GlC* D 228; perfecta domu, ad diem ~onis ejus .. totius .. dignitatis personae .. convenerunt EDDI 17.

2 dicatio v. ditatio b.

1 dicator [CL], hallower.

Jesu, ~or quadragenarie abstinentiae [AS: *halgiend*] *Exp. Hymn.* 57. 1.

2 dicator v. praedicator.

dicax [CL], witty. **b** ready-tongued.

~a[ce]m, *quedol*, ~a[ce]s, *quedole GlC* D 318–9; ~ax, i. facundus, qui verbis jocatur in quamlibet rem, vel *cwedel GlH* D 439; sales .. subtiles et ~aces emittunt GIR. *DK* I 14. **b** plurima Hildeberti carmina Romam transferuntur, que ~acium scholis et didascalis Quiritum admiranda censentur ORD. VIT. X 7 p. 42; ~aces philosophos *Ib.* XI 33 (v. dialecticus b).

dicdelvum [ME *dicdelve*], ditch.

1208 si tota valla illius marisci [*Broomhill, Suss*] vel aliqua ejus pars per forinsecam vallam a mari defensa fuerit, tunc michi .. illius valle medietas cum ~o intus et extra remanebit, remanente alia medietate cum ~o intus et extra predictis sociis *CurR* V 203.

dicella [cf. dica], legal bond.

ave mater .. / que captivos a dicella / servitutis liberas WALT. WIMB. *Virgo* 62.

dicena, ~um v. decena.

dicentia, speech.

hic secundum Anshelmum in de Similitudinibus [cf. *Simil. Anselmi* 130] omnis peccator est mendax, vel propter duplicitatem inter verbum oris aut operis ad verbum mentis vel propter discrepanciam ~ie naturalis ad vitam WYCL. *Dom. Div.* 100.

dicentissimus v. decere 4. **1 dicere** v. 1 dicare.

2 dicere [CL]

1 to say, speak: **a** (w. dir. speech); **b** (w. indir. qu., or acc. & inf. or compl.; *cf. infra* 3); **c** (w. *quod* or *quia*); **d** (w. obj. & *quod*); **e** (w. sb. or pron. as obj.); **f** (absol.); **g** (w. document or abstr. as subj.). **h** (1st pers. sg. in parenthesis) I mean, (w. neg.) I do not say.

a vero sacerdoti ~itur: "tu es Petrus" [*Matth.* xvi 18] GILDAS *EB* 109; ut numquam dicant gentes: "ubi est Deus eorum?" ALDH. *VirgV* 1924; ~ebant ad illos .. "quid hic sedetis?" BEDE *HE* V 14; c**760** (12c) vocem aeterni judicis .. ~entis ad impios: "discedite a me .." [*Matth.* xxv 41] *CS* 194; ut aliquis sic secum tacitus ~at: " .. estne credendum ..?" ANSELM (*Mon.* 1) I 14; cum ~ente, "non video colorem ibi" non est disputandum; sed ~endum sibi, "tu indiges sensu" DUNS *PW* 142. **b** sorores / sex alias nothas non dicimus annumerandas ALDH. *Aen.* 30 (*Elementum*) 2; dic ergo utrum arsis an thesis .. promerebitur! *Id. PR* 131; ~ebant hanc esse consuetudinem eorum BEDE *HE* III 23; s**565** ecclesia [S. Niniae] habetur apud Huuiterne ubi etiam sepultus ~itur *AS Chr.*; ~it patrem suum se posse vertere ubi voluerit *DB* I 10; **1231** (v. discipulatus 2a); s**1326** una cum aliis quos .. dixerunt regi .. adherentes AD. MUR. *Chr.* 48 (cf. ib.: quos dixerunt regi adherere); s**1339** ~it se verum heredem .. Karoli *Ib.* 101; quod ~eretur de eis per mundum .. eos degenerasse *G. Hen. V* 9 p. 64. **c** ~ens quod ipse eum dignum esse episcopatu judicaret BEDE *HE* III 7; ~ens quia ipse quoque delectaretur manducare *Ib.* V 5; **838** a quibusdam ~tum est quia cum recto (*sic*) libertate facta non esset, quia in fugatu ejus .. concessa fuit *CS* 421; ego ~o [AS: *ic secge*] quod utilis sum .. omni populo ÆLF. *Coll.* 96; de hoc ~it nepos Herberti quod episcopus .. concessit .. *DB* I 1; prepositus .. ~it quia valet quater xx li. *Ib.* 2b; **1200** ipse †decit quod non potest perdere terram illam, quia .. *CurR* I 233; **1211** quesitus .. si clamor levatus fuit, ~it quod non *Ib.* VI 138. **d** que .. non poterunt ~i quod sint in tali villa BRACTON 434 (v. denominatio 1a). **e** ~ito exempla ALDH. *PR* 123; bis dicere puppup *Id. VirgV pref.* 20; praecepit eum sententias longiores ~ere BEDE *HE* V 2 (cf. ib. V 14: fratrem .. cujus .. nomen .. ~ere possem); plana et communia compositionum verba ~ebat HUGEB. *Wynn.* 6; quid ~imus [AS: *secgaþ we*] de coco? ÆLF. *Coll.* 98; his ~tis lux cum loquente disparuit AILR. *Ed. Conf.* 753C; quoties falsum coram ipso ab aliquo ~ebatur GIR. *IK* I 51. **f** mittuntur equuli legati, scissis, ut ~itur, vestibus GILDAS *EB* 17; ut poeta de profeta ~it ALDH. *VirgP* 36; **679** cum omnibus .. campis .., ut ~tum est, ad eandem terram pertinentia (*sic*) *CS* 45; legat ipsum de quo dixi libellum BEDE *HE* III 19; intelligatur 'disserere' velut ab oratorio genere ~endi et poetico separatum BALSH. *AD rec.* 2 10; M. RIEVAULX (*Ep.*) 74 (v. falsarius 1); c**1325** (v. falcio). **g** historica relatione ~ente 'septies vindicabitur de Cain ..' [*Gen.* iv 24] ALDH. *Met.* 2; sicut alia ~it editio (*Ep. Ceolfridi*) BEDE *HE* V 21 p. 339; **1219** ~it carta .. quod J. dedit dim. m. .. Roberto *CurR* VIII 14; secundum opinionem ~entem potestatem laicalem supremam tenere temporalia .. a summo pontifice OCKHAM *Pol.* I 93. **h** ut ita dicam GILDAS *EB* 3; a**1110** qui modica non despicit, non ~o paulatim, sed efficaciter proficit ANSELM (*Ep.* 450) V 398; animalia alia .. molli quadam .. materia educantur, lacte ~o ADEL. *QN* 10; H. BOS. *LM* 1361D (v. contemplari d); s**1191** elongavit, non ~o fugiens DICETO *YH* II 99; NECKAM *Ut.* 116 (v. elementum 3b); sepultus, ~o, est sed non cum honore KNIGHTON II 201; s**1455** vestris non ~o .. adversariis, immo verius cognatis *Reg. Whet.* I 176 (v. compatriota a).

2 (p. ppl.) the said, aforementioned; **b** (as sb. m.). **c** (as sb. n.) thing said, saying. **d** (abl. w. *citius*) quicker than speech, no sooner said than done. **e** (supine abl.) to say; *cf. dictus* 1. **f** (inf. as sb.) saying, speech.

ex supra ~tis speciebus ALDH. *Met.* 10 (cf. supradictus); sepultum est .. in saepe ~to monasterio BEDE *HE* II 2 (cf. saepedictus); **957** (14c) ejusdem ~ti protogenis ampla .. pullulante prosapia *CS* 995; tristis et esuriens dictam veniebat ad aulam *V. Merl.* 573; c**1283** valet cariagium cujuslibet ambre ij d.; et habebit pro ~to cariagio xv panes nigros *Cust. Battle* 4; s**1300** precepit predictis ministris ut ~tos monachos catenis ferreis onerarent *G. Durh.* 47; libros .. donamus .. communitati scholarium in aula N. Oxoniensi degencium .., ut .. ~te ville scholaribus .. commodentur R. BURY *Phil.* 19. 237; **1438** dissidiis .. inter ~tas jam partes .. pendentibus BEKYNTON I 199 (cf. jamdictus). **b** s**1457** copia quorundam articulorum in quibus ~us hereticavit contra fidem *Reg. Whet.* I 285 *rub.* **c** prophetarum .. / dicta retexebat ALDH. *VirgV* 1630 (cf. ib. 2302: dictis parere nefandis / rennuit); in patrum praecedentium factis sive ~tis BEDE *HE* IV 3; **798** (12c) neglectis .. archiepiscopi C. ~tis et factis (*Clovesho*) *CS* 291; si .. sic exponimus divina ~ta .. ANSELM (*CurD* I 18) II 82; ut grammatica de dictionibus et in dictionibus .., sic ista [dialectica] de ~tis et in ~tis est J. SAL. *Met.* 860C. **d** ALDH. *VirgV* 1100 (v. cito 2a); ~to citius, *hraður þonne ic mæge an word gecweþan WW*; ~to cicius recessit rex pro die illa FAVENT 16. **e** heu dolendum ~tu! ALDH. *VirgP* 22; quod ~tu mirum est *V. Cuthb.* IV 17; **9..** ~tu, *gesægene WW*; diversa ~tu sunt 'aliquid fieri' et 'aliquid esse quod fit' BALSH. *AD rec.* 2 145; 'sanctificetur nomen tuum': hoc est ~tu 'confirma nomen tuum' *Spec. Eccl.* 80; s**1403** 'procede, signifer!', quod est ~tu '*anavant, baner!*' *Eul. Hist. Cont.* III 397. **f** **1382** propter meum dicere nemo sit iratus (*Contra religiosos* 213) *Mon. Francisc.* I 598.

3 (w. compl.) to call, name; *cf.* 1b *supra*; **b** (w. ref. to spec. language).

urbs est quam vulgo Bizanti nomine dicunt ALDH. *VirgV* 634; *Id. Aen.* 28. 5 (v. cognomen b); s**448** Hengest et Horsa Bryttaniam .. in loco qui ~itur Hypwinesflieot advehuntur *AS Chr.*; c**693** (8c) ad augmentum monasterii tui quae (*sic*) ~itur Beddanhaam *CS* 81; **875** in illo loco ubi ab incolis ~tum est *æt Hamme CS* 539; G. MON. III 19 (v. deus 5c); presumptuosus ~ar an providus? GIR. *TH intr.* p. 5; palpo .. / .. / dicitur os aurum WALT. WIMB. *Van.* 118; R. BOCKING *Ric. Cic.* I 51 (v. bria); apozima ~itur quando decoquuntur alique herbe .. in aqua .. *SB* 11. **b** *spix* ~itur Graece crabro ALDH. *Met.* 10; vocatur locus ille lingua Anglorum Hefenfelth, quod ~i potest Latine 'caelestis campus' BEDE *HE* III 2; **836** a difficultate illa quam nos Saxonice *faestingmenn* ~imus *CS* 416; *CS* 834 (v. Anglice); **948** vj mansas, quod Cantigenae ~unt *syx sulunga CS* 869; GIR. *DK* I 7 (v. Cambricus).

4 **a** to report (an event). **b** to specify. **c** to promise, undertake.

a de quo plura virtutum miracula .. ~ere solent BEDE *HE* V 2; egressum suum ~et subpriori *Obs. Barnwell* 54 (v. demandare 4a). **b** **1293** emit quendam pannum furatum .. et noluit ~ere warrantum suum de quo emit *Leet Norw.* 44. **c** quae dixerat .. perfecit BEDE *HE* V 21.

5 (eccl.) to say, recite ceremonially: **a** prayer or sim.; **b** mass, psalm or sim.

a Christo .. / grates dicamus dulciter (ALDH.) *Carm. Aldh.* 1. 195; ~ta super me oratione BEDE *HE* V 6 (cf. ib. III 11: ~ebat presbyter exorcismos); donec veniat sacerdos et ~at orationem dominicam super eum DICETO *Chr.* 14; **1297** ivit ~endo preces et oraciones suas *SelCCoron* 89; c**1340** in graciis in mensa ~endis *Deeds Balliol* 297; **1395** prior .. unam oracionem .. pro anima nostra .. solempniter ~et *Lit. Cant.* III 38. **b** eos qui missas familiares debebant suam pro anima fratris missam ~ere faciebat EADMER *V. Anselmi* I 10 p. 19; **12..** ad missas cotidie cum cantu et nota ~endas *Reg. Aberd.* II 46; c**1293** exequias et missam cum singulis psalteriis .. ~ere teneantur *StatOx* 103; **1344** ~atur non post majorem missam *Eng. Clergy* 285; **1380** pueris .. ~entibus psalterium pro anima mea *Test. Karl.* 130; **1509** ~ant psalmum .. cum collecta speciali *StatOx* 324.

6 (leg.): **a** (of jurors) to declare, pronounce (as verdict). **b** (p. ppl. as sb. n.) verdict. **c** assertion, plea, or testimony. **d** (w. *simplex*) 'nude parole'.

a si quidam eorum [juratorum] dixerint pro uno, quidam pro alio litigantium GLANV. II 17; **1200** omnes hoc dixerunt preter Humfredum de M., qui solus contradixit ceteris *CurR* I 334; **1220** vicecomes dixit quod fecit inquisitionem et inquisitio ~it quod sunt de malo retto *Ib.* VIII 270; **1203** xij juratores ~unt in veredicto suo ut scriptum eorum testatur et ore ~unt quod non fuit utlagatus *SelPlCrown* 28; **1221** omnes juratores tam de villa quam de hundredo ~unt precise quod K. non est culpabilis *Ib.* 104; **1225** predicti juratores et villate veniunt et ~unt super sacramentum suum [quod] omnes isti .. sunt culpabiles *Ib.* 116. **b** **1202** juratoribus qui super sacramentum suum ~tum suum dixerunt *SelPlCrown* 16. **c** **1130** (v. dirationare 1b); **1182** r. c. de ix li. pro falso ~to *Pipe* 137; c**1228** ex ~tis suis nichil certum potuit perpendi *Feod. Durh.* 259. **d** **1236** simplex ~tum non debet ei nocere quin ei respondeat *CurR* XV 1887; **1242** nullam sectam producit nec aliquam editionem ostendit .. nisi simplex ~tum suum tantum *Ib.* XVI 2200.

7 to pronounce (an award), decide. **b** (p. ppl. as sb. n.) award, decision.

1267 ~imus et providimus quod .. rex Anglie .. regiam potestatem .. libere exerceat (*Dictum of Kenilworth*)

StRealm I 12; **1268** promiserunt . . quod de . . contencionibus . . stabunt dicto . . Roberti. . . et hoc dictum debet ∼i citra festum S. Petri *Cl* 530; **1279** hec . . nos arbitri . . pronunciamus, ∼imus et ordinamus *RGasc* II 60. **b** **1199** dum . . ∼tum veridicorum de predictis convencionibus in respectum positum fuerit *RChart* 31b; **1253** ∼tum et arbitrium supra se recipiant *RGasc* I 285 (= *CalPat* 254); **s1263** rex Francie . . protulit ∼tum suum et sentenciam sollempniter pro rege Anglie contra barones *Flor. Hist.* II 486; **1266** de . . aliis terris . . posuerunt se in ∼tum . . regis *Cl* 249; **1268** (v. 7a supra).

8 to tell, instruct, command. **b** (p. ppl. as sb. n.) command.

c**597** cui non est ∼tum ut Christum negaret (*Lit. Papae*) BEDE *HE* I 27 p. 51; **1226** ∼tum est episcopo Exon' quod teneat in manu sua beneficium Johannis *LTRMem* 8 r. 2 (1); **1230** dic eis quod sint . . coram baronibus de Scaccario *Ib.* 11 r. 10; **1269** ∼atur ei quod sit intendens capitali plegio suo *CBaron* 77; **1405** ∼tum fuit . . Elizabethe quod interim prosequeretur penes nos *Cl* 254 m. 20. **b** †∼ta [? l. ∼to] parens, praecepto obediens *GlC* D 288.

9 (theol.) to utter the 'Word'; *cf. dictio* 1b. **b** to utter as preliminary to creation.

sicut tres sunt loquentes, ita et tres '∼entes'. sed . ., si tres sunt ∼entes . ., ita erunt tria verba. respondeo: 'dicere' ∼itur multipliciter. . . quando dicitur 'Pater ∼it se', hic ponitur essentialiter . . HALES *Qu.* 88–9; [∼ere] quandoque idem est quod creare, ut cum dicitur 'Pater ∼it creaturam'. . . vel videtur '∼ere' idem quod 'generare' *Id. Sent.* I 129; 'intelligere', quod est operatio Patris, et '∼ere', quod est 'producere' Patris DUNS *Ord.* II 315 (cf. ib.: ∼ere vel Verbum). **b** ANSELM I 26 (v. dissimilitudo a).

10 to signify, mean, imply.

Ps.-GROS. *Gram.* 46 (v. dicibilis); dampnificacio . . ∼it privacionem boni actualis quod punitus, subducta obice, naturaliter habuisset WYCL. *Innoc.* 477; *Id. Log.* II 124 (v. commodifer); *Ziz.* 163 (v. comestio a).

dicerium v. dicterium. **dicerpere** v. discerpere. **diche** v. 2 chirographarius a.

dichotomos [LL < διχότομος], divided in half, (of moon) first quarter, half-moon. *Cf. diatomos.*

cum [luna] monoides est aut dicotomos aut tricotomos, minus accensa videtur NECKAM *NR* I 13 p. 50; primis . . vij diebus usque ad medietatem velud divisi orbis excrescit [luna] et dicotomos tunc vocatur GROS. *Hexaem.* IX 10 p. 282; antequam [luna] sit dycothomos, id est semiplena BACON VI 71.

dichronus [CL < δίχρονος], (of vowels) potentially either long or short.

nisi forte finalis sillaba in ∼o terminata secundum rationem ∼arum producatur, ut 'lectito' . . ALDH. *PR* 122; nostrae omnes vocales sunt ∼ae, hoc est et brevibus syllabis habiles et longis BEDE *AM* 83; accipe, quas dicronas partes in carmine ponas, / que confusa sono distincta vocabula pono SERLO WILT. 2. 5.

dicia, ∼iae v. divitiae.

dicibilis [LL], speakable, expressible in words.

∼e, †sive [l. sc.] vocatur quod dici potest *GlH* D 444; J. SAL. *Met.* 904AB (v. dictio 1c); patet quod significare cum generibus, modis et temporibus dicit tria consequencia verbi, vel perfectiva vel perfectivum perfecti, quod est de altero ∼e, ∼e quidem ad [noticiam] adicit *Ps.*-GROS. *Gram.* 46; Deus habet esse non signatum in loco nec ∼e verbo BACON I 24; actu universale cognoscitur sub tanta indifferencia sub quanta ipsum sic cognitum est simul ∼e de omnibus singularibus in quibus salvatur DUNS *PW* 143; a**1345** (v. coordinatio b); secunda [proposicio sc., 'Socrates non dicit verum sicut est'] est falsa, cum impossibile sit quicquid dicere nisi dicatur necessitas eterna sequens ad omne ∼e WYCL. *Log.* II 215.

dicidium v. discidium 2a. **dicimentum** v. documentum 1.

dicio (ditio) [CL]

1 authority, lordship.

omnipotens genitor mundum dicione gubernans ALDH. *VirgV* 1; ita ut . . omnes Brittaniae fines . . sub ∼one acciperet BEDE *HE* II 9; **790** [Sclavos] suae subegit ∼oni ALCUIN *Ep.* 7; **838** (9c) populi Christiani eorum seculari ∼oni subjecti *CS* 421; †∼o [? l. ∼one], i. arbitrio, judicio vel ratione, lege vel *dihte GlH* D 433; corporis quoque sui ∼onem protinus homo [i.e. Adam] amisit G. CRISPIN *Serm.* 114; indignum ferentes tot . . preclaros ∼oni senatuique paucorum subjacere OSB. BAWDSEY clxxvii; [Henricus I] mulierum ∼oni . . continue subjacebat H. HUNT. *HA* VIII 1; W. NEWB. *HA* V 14 (v. consequenter a); **1381** (v. curare 5d).

2 domain.

1126 qua curia dulcius, quo sub rege honorabilius, quam in propria ∼one vitam ducere? *Ep. Anselm. Bur.* 96; [monachus] a . . terre sue optimatibus ad regimen relicte ∼onis repetitur MAP *NC* IV 7 f. 50v.; **1451** nomina personarum infra Pruciam et ∼onem Hanze *Cl* 301 m. 40*d.*; **1579** lucis detrimentum omnes nostrae ∼ones sentient *StatOx* 342.

3 submission or (?) *f. l.*

s**1223** tota regio . . eosdem [maleficos] . . ad dicionem [? l. dedicionem] violenter compulerunt (*sic*) *Flor. Hist.* II 179.

dicior v. dives.

Diclux [*anagram of numeral* dclxvj], name of Antichrist. (*Cf. Rev.* xiii 18).

[Antichristus] latine vocabitur ∼x, quia dicit se lucem . . nomen Latinum est ∼x et significat idem [sc. dclxvj] HARCLAY *Adv.* 80.

dicotomos v. dichotomos. **dicra** v. dacra. **dicronos** v. dichronos.

dictamen [LL]

1 a written copy, draft. **b** literary work. **c** (art or practice of) literary composition. **d** literary style, elegance.

a reparat Anselmus aliud de eadem materia ∼en in aliis tabulis EADMER *V. Anselmi* I 19; nec erubescebant . . tenorem tocius ∼inis de libris . . monasterii de verbo in verbum extrahere ELMH. *Cant.* 224. **b** de vestro ∼ine et metrico et prosaico mittite mihi H. LOS. *Ep.* 20 (cf. ib. 39: meis †indictaminibus [l. in ∼inibus] pedes quaeritis); judices importuni, qui nesciant quod secundum mores gentium varientur modi ∼inum W. MALM. *GP* V 196; est ∼en litteralis editio, clausulis distincta, verborum et sententiarum coloribus adornata GARL. *PP* 98 (cf. ib. 4: exemplum prosayci ∼inis); *an enditynge*, dictura, ∼en *CathA*. **c** **1103** in ∼ine, et plus in prosa quam in versibus, te exerce ANSELM (*Ep.* 290) IV 210; hec Robertus . . se sic in libris veteribus Anglicis descripta invenisse retulit, cujus etiam genus ∼inis in moderne lingue modulatione rhythmico pedis metro decurrit R. COLD. *Osw.* 50; in cantilenis ritmicis et ∼ine . . subtiles inveniuntur GIR. *DK* I 12; expliciunt xv gaudia B. Virginis edita ritmice ex ∼ine Johannis de H. J. HOWD. *Gaudia postscr.* p. 7; **1364** quoddam ∼inis compendium scribere dignum duxi *FormOx* 365. **d** **990** talis excellentiae dignitatem . . justum videretur . . moderni faminis venustate pulchraeque capacitatis adire ∼ine, ni . . B. *Ep.* 386; neglecta venustate ∼inis *Enc. Emmae prol.*; scholastico ∼ine scripta W. JUM. IV 20; ne id quod tantus scriba [sc. Gildas] tanto stilo paravit . . videar viliori ∼ine maculare G. MON. I 17; si cui vilitas forte et abjectio ∼inis sorduerit *V. Thom. A* 2; s**1307** cujus [Ed.I] bonitatis magnitudinem . . quidam eleganti ∼ine ad metros breviter sic comprehendit *Flor. Hist.* III 138; c**1370** modus scribendi . . prosaicus, qui consistit in plano ∼ine, sicut litere scribuntur et epistole (J. BRIDL. *gl.*) *Pol. Poems* I 130.

2 motto.

1378 garteria . . cum litteris de serico plunkett' de ∼ine *hony soit qi mal y pense* ordinata et broudata *KRAc* 400/4 m. 12; **1406** cum una corona de panno blank' . . operata in brouderia et scissor' cum isto ∼ine *soveraigne* (*Ib.* 406/10) *Arch.* LXVII 176; c**1421** super opere . . j coopertorii . . pro bargea regis superoperati in broudera cum istis ∼inibus *une sanz pluis* et *humblement le requier Ib.* 407/5 m. 3.

3 a utterance. **b** dictate, bidding (fig., w. subj. gen. of abstr.).

a post multa precum ∼ina *Croyl.* 75. **b** qui laqueare studet alios dictamine fraudis WALT. ANGL. *Fab.* 43. 23; ubi hec . . dominantur, . . fas locum non habet, nature ∼en perit . . BACON *Maj.* III 3; ex ∼ine juris naturalis OCKHAM *Dial.* 550 (cf. ib. 551: secundum jura et ∼en recte racionis); c**1433** ille videtur . . rectum racionis ∼en flectere in obliquum (*Replic. Abbatis*) AMUND. I 342; **1445** ∼ine sancte regule nostre obligamur BEKYNTON I 260; lex humana est quoddam ∼en racionis practice J. BURY *Glad. Sal.* 591.

4 indictment. *V. et. dictamentum* a.

1275 ballivus . . cepit j summam avene de T. D. et hoc injuste . . sine ∼ine patrie *Hund.* I 478; **1276** vic. defamavit Petrum . . quod debuit ad concensionem fuisse de morte . . Roberti . . injuste et sine ∼ine patrie *Ib.* II 176.

dictamentum, indictment; *v. et. dictamen* 4, *indictamentum.* **b** (Sc.) (?) impeachment.

1243 attachiatus fuit per ∼um Walteri de B. latronis *JustIt* 756 r. 14*d.*; **1281** ad quem diem vic. retorn' ∼um suum *Gaol Del.* 35/2 r. 40*d.* **b** **1266** (17c) per finem Simonis L., quem fecit pro ∼o hominum senescalli in Kyll *ExchScot* 28.

dictamnus, ∼um [CL < δίκταμνον] **∼ia**, dittany (*Origanum Dictamnus*) or sim.

herba ∼us *Leechdoms* I 28; diptamnus vel bibulcos, *wilde næp* ÆLF. *Gl.*; item a 'dico' . . hoc dictannum, ∼ni, i. quedam herba OSB. GLOUC. *Deriv.* 158; diptannus, piretrum, piper, allia, salvia, ruta D. BEC. 2657; ditanum [*gl. ditayne*] NECKAM *Ut.* 102 (v. 2 costus); diptannus est herba medicinalis. . . hanc quidam pulegium Mar[t]is vocant, quia habet †cella eiciendi †bellicam potestatem BART. ANGL. XVII 49 (= Isid. *Etym.* XVII 9. 29: propter belli tela excutienda); hec †dictamus [MS: dictamis], *ditain Gl. AN Glasg.* f. 19; **12..** diptannum, *ditaundere WW*; res que . . eas confortent, ut terra sigillata et radix diptani BACON IX 108; digerent[es] melancoliam . . herbe sunt . . saturegia, arthemisia, diphthamus GAD. 15. 2; diptannum multi dicunt pulegium agreste. folia habet lanosa . ., sed nec semen nec florem habet. creditur quod sit pilocella *Alph.* 51; diptania, A. *dytayne* . ., hic ditamnus, *detane WW.*

dictare [CL]

1 to dictate (to writer or scribe).

673 quam sententiam definitionis nostrae Titillo notario scribendam ∼avi (*Conc. Hertf.*) BEDE *HE* IV 5; Adamnan . . scripsit . . librum . . cujus auctor erat docendo et ∼ando . . Arculfus *Ib.* V 15; totum illum diem docebat et hilariter ∼abat CUTHB. *Ob. Baedae* clxii; [vitam S. Guthlaci], prout a ∼antibus idoneis testibus . . audivi, . . depinxi FELIX *Guthl. prol.*; non . . nisi ab ipso audita et ex illius ore ∼ata perscripsimus HUGEB. *Will.* 6.

2 to compose; **b** (charter or sim.); *v. et. dictitare* 2; **c** (judgement).

fateor . . quod hoc opusculum . . ita perniciter ut sategistis ∼are nequiverim, quia . . morosam ∼andi intercapidinem . . ecclesiastici regiminis sollicitudo denegabat ALDH. *VirgP* 59; dictanti titulum mihi te sancte oro sacerdos / succurras precibus semper ubique piis *Epigr. Milredi* 810; **792** hoc dolens ∼avi ALCUIN *Ep.* 13; i liber . . / nitere, sub pullis quamvis dictate cucullis R. CANT. *Malch. pref.* 25; c**1105** ∼are cotidie assuesce, et maxime in prosa. et ne multum ames difficile ∼are, sed plane et rationabiliter ANSELM (*Ep.* 328) V 260; Greci involute, Romani splendide, Angli pompatice ∼are solent W. MALM. *GP* V 196; **1245** liberate . . magistro Henrico versificatori x m. pro servicio suo quod nobis impendit ∼ando vitas beatorum Edwardi et Georgii *Liberate* 21 m. 10; materia [opusculi] est ars ∼andi, metricandi, rithmicandi GARL. *PP* 2; **1432** artes scribendi et ∼andi loquendique Gallicanum ydioma . . magis grammatice et rhetorice quam aliis . . facultatibus . . appropinquant *StatOx* 240. **b** †**701** (12c) ego W. hanc donationem ∼ans subscripsi *CS* 103; **956** (14c) ego O. episcopus ∼avi *CS* 935; **956** (14c) ego D. jubente rege hanc singrapham ∼avi *CS* 941; **1001** (14c) cum ego hoc [privilegium] . . pro . . generali salute ∼averim *CD* 706; a**1070** concessi . . archiepiscopo ∼are privilegium ad omnes illas terras quae adjacent ad aecclesiam S. Johannis de B. (*Breve Will. I*) *E. Ch. Yorks* I 88 (cf. F. E. Harmer *Anglo-Saxon Writs* p. 432); **11..** hanc cartam ∼avit S. Dunstanus *CS* 88*d*. **c** debent episcopi cum seculi judicibus judicia ∼are [AS: *domas dihtan*], ne permittant . . ut aliquid injustum illuc pullulet (*Quad.*) *GAS* 478.

3 a to rule, govern. **b** (w. document or abstr. as subj.) to dictate, enjoin. **c** (p. ppl. as sb. n.) dictate, command.

a s**1106** rex [Hen. I] subegit sibi totam Normanniam et secundum suam voluntatem ∼avit FL. WORC. II 55. **b** ∼ante fidei devotione BEDE *HE* III 2; juret sicut causa ∼abit (*Leg. Hen.* 66. 9a) *GAS* 586; non quid . . justa retributio ∼et attendit MAP *NC* III 2 f. 38; natura ∼ante GIR. *TH* I 14; c**1300** statutum ∼ans causas in universitate . . sine scriptis debere ventilari *MunAcOx* 72; non enim intellectus moderate sive medio modo ∼at actum, ita quod ∼are circumstancionetur hac circumstancia mediocriter, sed . . ∼at secundum ultimum potencie sue DUNS *Ord.* I 235; ubi jus naturale . . ∼at excipiendum OCKHAM *Dial.* 568; **1380** (v. diaetare 3). **c** secundum anterioris ∼atum [AS p. 448: *æfter ðæs arran dihte*] *RegulC* 69 *epil.*

dictatio [CL], **a** dictation (to writer). **b** draft (of document).

a nobis referente de ori (*sic*) sui ∼one HUGEB. *Will. prol.* **b** **1228** treugam puram, firmam et rectam secundum ∼onem rationabilem parati sumus firmare vobiscum *Pat* 213.

dictativus, directive, authoritative.

quicunque . . intellectus non potest habere aliquam talem cognicionem ∼am de operando DUNS *Ord.* VI 304; potest distingui de practica, quia quedam est ∼a et quedam tantum ostensiva; prima est illa que determinate dictat, aliquid esse faciendum vel non faciendum (OCKHAM *Sent. prol.*) *GLA* III 331 *n.* 741.

dictator [CL]

1 a dictator (official). **b** director.

a ∼orem, *aldur*; ∼or, princeps vel praeceptor v annis †tenet [? l. tenens] potentiam *GlC* D 256–7; urbs Romulea . . demum regi statuit per ∼ores GIR. *PI* I 1 p. 8. **b** ∼or, i. dictor, relator, praeceptor, imperator, *dihtnere*, ordinator, prescriptor *GlH* D 420; praestantissimus artificum magister templique spectabilis ∼or Blitherus GOSC. *Transl. Aug.* 17C.

2 composer (of document or literary work). **b** secretary, clerk. **c** informant.

talia sed timidus dictator tela pavescat ALDH. *VirgV* 2849 (cf. ib. 2855: neu timeat scriptor . .); ∼or consideret quam circumstanciam notet preposicio GARL. *PP* 112; o dictatores, quorum stilus aureus aulas / exercet *Id. Hon. Vit.* 279; s**1278** J. de Pecham . . in Cant' archiepiscopum consecratus . ., qui . . erat . . carminum ∼or egregius TREVET *Ann.* 300; **1340** serenitas regia imponere nobis pro sue litere ∼oris malevola voluntate videtur quod . . (*Lit. Archiep. Cant.*) *Conc.* II 667b; sacrorum canonum ∼ores viri acutissimi in sciencia . . morali . . fuerunt OCKHAM *Dial.* 401; c**1390** quantum simplici ∼ori talis libri prodesset inspeccio, cum sit plenus stilorum elegancia *FormOx* 238; potest ∼or de duobus monosillabis facere bisillabum *Dictamen* 336; *an endyter*, ∼or, indictator *CathA*. **b** ut . .

ipse mihi ∼or simul, notarius et librarius existerem BEDE *Luke prol.*; fui in cancellaria ejus ∼or; in capella, eo celebrante, subdiaconus W. FITZST. *Thom. prol.* 1; MILEMETE *Nob.* 70 (v. 1 dependere 3a); **1468** domino R. R., ∼ori rotulorum, pro feodo suo *ExchScot* 591. **c** non ambigo illos ∼ores non omnia facta illius potuisse cognoscere FELIX *Guthl. prol.* (cf. dictare 1).

3 arbiter (of truce).

1194 rex Francie duos elegit ∼ores et rex Anglie similiter duos, quorum arbitrio . ., si alter regum adversus alterum vel aliquis hominum suorum inter se interciperet, emendatio hinc inde fieret (*Lit. de Treugis*) R. HOWD. III 259; **1228** interceptio facta [in treugis] nunciabitur ∼oribus hinc inde constitutis *Pat* 193; **1262** mandavimus ∼oribus treugarum predictarum pro parte nostra deputatis quod . . sint ad vadum de M. pro emendacione intercepcionum . . contra formam earundem *Cl* 128.

dictatorius [CL = *of a dictator*], concerned w. literary composition.

c**1380** licet me inter dictatores reputem minimum, . . quasdam regulas pueriles artis ∼ie compilare presumo *FormOx* 338*n*; ars ∼ia, id est lepida diccionum congeries *Dictamen* 333.

dictatrix [CL], directress (fig.).

hec [sc. animi sollercia] tibi dictatrix operum . . / invigilet HANV. VIII 164 p. 364.

dictatura [CL], dictatorship, governance. **b** writing, composition.

∼a honor est supra †consulatio [l. consulatum] *GlC* D 325; monarchia post Franciae cum puero monarcha ipsius consiliosissimi viri tutelae, ∼ae atque administrationi cessit W. POIT. I 22; in hujus jure sunt ∼e, consulatus, magistratus ADEL. *ED* 8; ∼a, quasi prefectura OSB. GLOUC. *Deriv.* 172. **b** ∼a, A. *dytynge WW*.

dictatus [LL]

1 literary work.

c**803** ea quae referre videbatur . . ∼u admodo compendioso titulo vitae . . Richarii aptavimus ALCUIN *Ep.* 306; Fulcardus plures ∼us memoria dignos edidit ORD. VIT. XI 23 p. 282.

2 decision, command.

misit . . ad congregandas facultates suas quas . . spontaneo liberoque ∼u disponeret B. *V. Dunst.* 20.

dicterium [CL], joke, witticism.

∼ium, . . i. verbum jocose dictum; unde Macrobius de Saturnalibus jocos non raro ∼ia nominat OSB. GLOUC. *Deriv.* 158; *a bowrdeworde* [v. l. *bowdword*], †dicerium, dictorium *CathA*.

dicticos [LL < δεικτικός], deictic, (?) demonstrative.

primum [genus sermonis] est dragmaticon vel ∼on, id est imitativum vel interrogativum GARL. *PP* 98.

dictio [CL]

1 saying, utterance. **b** (theol.) utterance of the 'Word'; *cf. dicere* 9a. **c** (log.) statement. **d** (med.) aphorism.

GlC C 890 (v. crionason); ∼o, elogium, *saga* ÆLF. *Gl.*; innocens sum actionis et ∼onis [AS: *ge dæde ge dihtes*] ab ea compellatione (*Quad.*) *GAS* 399; **1230** r. c. de dim. m. pro †falso ∼one *Pipe* 219. **b** [Pater] produccione sive ∼one producit, sicut aliquid calefaccione calefacit DUNS *Ord.* II 321; omnis talis numerus est eterna sapiencia vel ∼o qua Deus eternaliter dicit omnia in Verbo WYCL. *Innoc.* 486. **c** est . . enuntiatio veri vel falsi ∼o ut ad disserendum BALSH. *AD* 11; in omni enuntiatione spectanda sunt tria, ∼o, dicibile, et res. est autem res de quo aliquid, dicibile quod de aliquo, ∼o quo dicitur hoc de illo. interdum tamen ∼onem rem esse contingit, cum idem sermo ad agendum de se assumitur. . . porro res, ut in pluribus, et dicibilia pertinent ad naturam, ∼o vero ex hominum pendet arbitrio J. SAL. *Met.* 904AB; cum arguitur: 'eque nobiles sunt, ergo tot', figura ∼onis est, commutando 'quid' vel 'quale' in 'quot' DUNS *Ord.* II 341. **d** ∼ones particulares . . magistrorum . . in opere medicationis expertissimas GILB. I 1. 1.

2 decision, command.

sit secundum ∼onem ejus [AS: *be his dihte*] pecunia recte divisa (*Quad.*) *GAS* 357 (= *Inst. Cnuti*: secundum ordinationem suam; *Cons. Cnuti*: ex dispositione illius); J. rex . . ecclesiam Anglicanam novis . . exactionibus urgebat, suis ∼onibus jus ecclesiasticum subjiciens *Meaux* I 326.

3 word. **b** (w. *probatoria*) word of text (usu. first word of second folio) cited to identify volume in catalogue.

iv habens ∼o breves in heroico poni non aliter poterat ALDH. *PR* 133; G. MON. I 1 (v. ampullosus 2b); J. SAL. *Met.* 860C (v. dicere 2c); artis principium simplex censent elementum; / syllaba subsequitur; dictio deinde subit NECKAM *DS* X 48; quod quidam sic intelligunt quod in una lingua licet ex una ∼one aliam formare, ut ex hac ∼one 'saxum' formare hanc ∼onem 'saxior' VINSAUF *AV* II 3. 141; si qua sit hic rara tibi dictio, sit tibi cara GARL. *Mor. Scol.* 7 (*gl.*: quoniam preter curialitatem possumus etiam multas ∼ones diversas inusitatas addicere); 'non vult' potest esse ∼o una composita HALES *Sent.* I 458; ∼o est vox significativa cujus nulla pars per se est significativa, preter formam vero composicionis quam habet ∼o a formis parcium et sillabarum *Ps.*-GROS. *Gram.* 32; BACON *Maj.* I 374 (v. Cathaius); faciant apochas solventibus de receptis cum ∼onibus aperte scriptis, non cum litteris numeralibus *Lib. Mem. Bernewelle* 208; **1412** ∼onem 'octo' de quadam billa sua . . abradi et deleri et ∼onem 'novem' loco ejusdem ∼onis 'octo' . . scribi fecit et imponi *Cl* 261 m. 15*d*. **b** **1389** primo loco ponitur figura numeralis pandens quotus sit liber ille in ordine gradus sui; secundo adjungitur nomen voluminis; tercio numeralis locus probacionis; quarto ∼ones probatorie (J. WHYTEFELD *Pref. Catal.*) *Libr. Cant. Dov.* 409.

dictionalis, verbal, concerned w. words.

sicut elementarius est Predicamentorum, Periermeniarum vero sillabicus, ita et Topicorum liber quodammodo ∼is est J. SAL. *Met.* 904B; necessitas . . ∼is seu consequencialis et complexa est necessitas alicujus dicti et enunciacionis composite . ., et hec . . est tanta necessitas quod ejus oppositum contradiccionem formaliter implicat BRADW. *CD* 722E.

dictionalitas, wordiness.

O. CANT. *Pref. Frith.* 44 (v. 1 epithema b).

dictionaliter, in the form of a (single) word.

aggregatum ex substantia infinita et verbo per participium significatur, set non orationaliter set ∼er BACON XV 63.

dictionarius, (*sc. liber*) word-book, dictionary.

∼ius dicitur libellus iste a dictionibus magis necessariis, quas tenetur quilibet scolaris non tantum in scrinio de lignis facto sed in cordis armariolo . . retinere GARL. *Dict.* 120; **1396** excerpta Ambrosii de Officiis; ∼ius; et alia (*Invent.*) *Meaux* III xcix; **1439** item prima pars ∼ii; secundo folio 'similia' (*Invent.*) *MunAcOx* 759; **1501** item prima pars dixionarii; secundo folio 'amici' (*Invent.*) *Cant. Coll. Ox.* I 18; nec ∼ium aliquem praeter Hesychium ac Dioscoridem MORE *Ut.* 216.

dictitare [CL]

1 to say (repeatedly).

∼at, frequenter dicit *GlC* D 322; ∼o, dico, dicto *GlH* D 432; ∼are, frequenter di[c]tare OSB. GLOUC. *Deriv.* 172; *to say* aire . ., dicere, dictare, ∼are . . *CathA*.

2 to draft, compose (charter or sim.). *V. et. dictare* 2b.

†**680** (10c) ego A. scolasticus archiepiscopi T. hanc cartulam ∼ans . . scribere jussi *CS* 50; †**949** (10c) ego Dunstan hanc domino meo hereditariam kartulam ∼ando conposui et propriis digitorum articulis perscripsi (DUNST.) *CS* 880; **1033** ego Cnut rex . . hanc scedulam †ducitare promisi *CD* 749.

dictor [LL], speaker, utterer. **b** informant. **c** writer.

fator, ∼or *GlC* F 5; non varius dictor rumorum sis necque (*sic*) fictor D. BEC. 1460. **b** dum relatori, si forte secundum ∼ores suos mentiatur, difficilis sit regressus ad veniam W. MALM. *GR* III 248. **c** quod ∼or advertat se consuere materiam intentam ex dactilis et spondeis *Dictamen* 335; hic ∼or, *a endyter WW*.

dictorium v. dicterium.

dictrix, eloquent (f.).

a**705** notus propter alburnum ∼icis Romaniae decorem (CELLANUS) *Ep. Aldh.* III (9).

dictura, literary composition or (?) *f. l.*

an enditynge, dictura [? l. dictatura], dictamen *CathA*.

dicturire [LL], to wish to speak.

∼io, meditor dicere *GlH* D 426; plura . . dicerem, nisi . . suspicio mee adulationis . . ∼ientem cohiberet W. MALM. *GR* V 449; ∼ire, dictare desiderare OSB. GLOUC. *Deriv.* 172.

dictus [CL]

1 saying, speech. *Cf. dicere* 2e.

quo dictu matris turgescunt viscera fetu ALDH. *VirgV* 1707 (= *CE* 1. 2. 29); quid sit hoc ∼u non discutimus modo nisi hoc tantum quod . . GROS. *Quaest. Theol.* 203.

2 (abl.) by name.

venit ad ignotam . . regionem ∼u Galliae [v. l. dictam Galliam] B. *V. Dunst.* 23.

dicum [cf. Fr. *digue*, OF vb. *dicquier*], dike (C. I.). *Cf. diketta.*

1154 concedo . . abbatie . . quicquid habeo in ecclesia et in maresco et in ∼o ipsius Ansleville *CartINorm* 292.

didascalare, to teach.

to teche, catezizare, docere . ., didasculare *CathA*.

didascalatus, office of teacher, doctorate.

798 (12c) piissimo prosatori atque in didasculatus sullimissimo ordine amantissimo Æ. archiepiscopo (*Professio D. Episcopi*) *CS* 292.

didascalicus [CL < διδασκαλικός], didactic (style of discourse). **b** (as sb. n.) title of book by Hugh of St. Victor.

Gl. Leid. 39. 64 (v. doctoralis); tria genera loquendi, sc. ∼on, id est doctrinale, dragmaticon, id est interrogativum, hermeneticon, id est interpretativum GARL. *Dict.* 134; tercium [genus sermonis] . . dicitur ∼on, idest doctrinale *Id. PP* 100. **b** **1396** ∼on Hugonis (*Invent.*) *Meaux* III app. xcvi; **1510** †didasculum Hugonis (*Invent.*) *Cant. Coll. Ox.* I 47.

didascalus [LL < διδάσκαλος], teacher.

ad famulam Christi scripsit dēdasculus idem ALDH. *VirgV* 2154 (cf. id. *VirgP* 36: pedagogis et ∼is); †dedasculum, magistrorum . ., didasculus, doctor *GlC* D 53, 308; magis jam dedasculus quam discipulus esse poterat HUGEB. *Wynn.* 2; noster ∼us B. Gregorius EGB. *Dial.* 16; **956** (11c) Alfwald didasculus *CS* 937; †**974** (14c) piscatorum didasculus *CS* 1310 p. 636; ORD. VIT. X 7 (v. dicax b); corrector simul his dīdascalus atque magister GARL. *Syn.* 382. 1584C; **1284** vestri collegii [*Merton*] institutor . . decrevit inter vos grammatice discipulos sub grammaticali didasculo confoveri PECKHAM *Ep.* 589 p. 813; **1440** didascolus (v. barridus).

didascul- v. didascal-.

didere [CL], to spread abroad.

∼itur, devulgatur *GlC* D 277.

didimus v. didymus, 2 dindymus. **1 didiscere** v. 2 dediscere. **2 didiscere** v. 1 discere.

didrachma [LL < δίδραχμον], didrachm (*cf. Matth.* xvii 23).

dedragmae, duae mensurae *GlC* D 149; **10.** . didragma, due dragma *WW*; ∼a, obolus OSB. GLOUC. *Deriv.* 175; Petrus . . piscem extraxit, in cujus ore didragma invenit J. FURNESS *Kentig.* 36; a Christo solo census [cf. *Matth.* xxii 17] sive ∼a petebatur OCKHAM *Disp.* 17; **1381** [Christus] solvit didragma stateris / et Cesari que Cesaris / cuncta persolvi precipit (*In Lollardos* 15) *Pol. Poems* I 236; [mysterium] solutionis didragmatis GARDINER *VO* 156.

diduc- v. deduc-.

didymus [LL < δίδυμος]

1 twin.

∼us, quod est geminus vel gemellus BACON *Gram. Gk.* 62.

2 (anat.; sts. conf. w. 2 *dindymus*) 'didymis', testicle, or epididymis.

est quidam nervus bifurcatus, utrique testiculo colligatus; . . et vocatur didimus, id est dubius [cf. 3 infra] an magis ab intestinis aut magis a testiculis originem trahat, et dubium cui magis deserviat RIC. MED. *Anat.* 230; didimus, qui est nervus per quem materiam spermaticam mittit natura ad testiculos GAD. 129v. 1 (cf. ib. 75. 2: vel forte illud in viro est in paralesi dindimorum vel virge); dindimus est †rimus [? l. rivus] per quem natura mittit materiam spermatis ad testiculos *SB* 18; *an hole in a mannys ȝerde*, dindimus *CathA*.

3 (as adj.) doubting, doubtful. (*Cf. John* xx 25).

dowtfulle, . . dubius, . . crep[er]us, ∼us, dubitans; . . *untrewe*, . . ∼us, incredulus *CathA*.

diecula [CL], (brief) day.

nomina ad peonem secundum pertinentia: . . sororcula, ∼a . . ALDH. *PR* 133; ∼a, parva dies OSB. GLOUC. *Deriv.* 172; **1166** ad deliberandum unius ∼e posset indutias impetrare J. SAL. *Ep.* 193 (187); sic . . vertitur . . / meror in canticum, nox in dieculam WALT. WIMB. *Carm.* 38; *a day*, dies, ∼a . . *CathA*.

diennium [LL *gl.*], period of two years.

twa days (sic) *space* [v. l. *twaȝere*], biennium, ∼ium *CathA*.

dieperdulum [cf. It. *perdigiorni*], heron.

ardea, *hragra* et ∼um *GlC* A 729 (cf. *Gl. Leid.* 47. 64: perdulum, *hragra*).

diere v. diescere a.

1 dies [CL]

1 day, (period of) daylight. **b** period of 12 hours centred on noon. **c** (fig.) night. **d** (fig.) ideal brightness. **e** 'light', pane (of window).

diebus ac noctibus GILDAS *EB* 19; hic famulabantur jugiter noctesque diesque ALDH. *VirgV* 1395; ductor dierum Lucifer (*Id.*) *Carm. Aldh.* 1. 66; dies est aer sole illustratus, nomen inde sumens 'quod tenebras disjungat ac dividat'. . . vulgus enim omne diem solis praesentiam super terras appellat. . . diem vulgarem Dominus sententia . . definivit, dicens: 'nonne duodecim horae sunt diei?' [*John* xi 9] BEDE *TR* 5 pp. 186, 189; vernalis dies, *lenctenlic dæg* ÆLF. *Sup.*; lucescente die, ita ut pueri . . sine laternis

possint exire LANFR. *Const.* 105 (cf. ib. 90: clarescente die); **c1200** stertit in dies medios (v. cyrius b); **1233** in crastino de magna die recesserunt *CurR* XV 214; ante diem *Ib.* (v. contra 7a); absentem diem lux agebat emula W. MALM. *GP* III 101; dies usualis vel artificialis GERV. TILB. I 5 (v. artificialis 2a); dicitur dies artificialis equari sue nocti tantum in equinoctiis. .. dicitur eciam aliquando dies continere xiij horas et nox xj, et dies alia longior esse xiiij et nox x, et dies longissima in climate septimo xvj horas habere, nox octo BACON VI 46; *Ib.* XIII 424 (v. discontinuatio 1); **1285** (v. de 4a); **1341** tempestas per totum diem artificialem W. MERLE 6; **1344** absenciam .. prepositi ultra diem artificialem *Eng. Clergy* 282; **1442** Anglici .. istud .. fecerunt in clara die (*DipDoc E* 427) *Bronnen* 1251/2. **b** sciendum est .. deceptos esse quamplurimos .. dum opinantur omnes dies naturales esse equales. .. sed certo certius est quod dies artificialis brumalis eque habet xij horas sicut et estivalis NECKAM *NR* I 10; sunt omni die artificiali sex hore ante meridiem et sex post meridiem BACON VI 47. **c** dum Phebi roscidus orbis / crescit in occasu sublataque redditur astris / flamma suusque dies HANV. III 302 p. 285. **d** ALDH. *VirgP* 19 (v. aurora b). **e** **1367** solut' Waltero le Maceon pro j *fourme* pro j fenestra iij dierum pro boreali parte *del freitour KRAc* 544/20 m. 2; **1409** j fenestra trium dierum (*Will*) *OED* (s. v. *day sb.* 4).

2 day of 24 hours (*cf. J. Soc. Archiv.* II 87–9). **b** (w. *in* or *per*) daily. **c** (w. *per*) one day ahead.

flagitat indutias septem sufferre dierum ALDH. *VirgV* 1270; **705** ante paucos dies hoc placitum communi consensione condixerunt WEALDHERE *Ep.* 22; proprie dies xxiiij horis, id est circuitu solis totum orbem illustrantis, completur BEDE *TR* 5; multa circa idem varie estimata aut estimabilia, ut an dies sit tempus a mane usque ad mane, ut Babilonii dixerunt, an ab occasu usque ad occasum, ut Attici, an a meridie ad meridiem, ut veteres Umbri, an a media nocte ad mediam noctem, ut Romani decreverunt, an quodlibet spatium xxiiij horarum undecumque inchoatum BALSH. *AD rec. 2* 176; vendicat ergo dies horas sibi bis duodenas, / ut claudat luci nox sociata diem NECKAM *NR* I 11; opus prime diei, id est spacii xxiiij horarum S. LANGTON *Gl. Hist. Schol.* 41; cum dies naturalis sit una revolutio firmamenti et insuper ascensio ejus quam describet sol in celo interim motu suo proprio et durante una revolutione plus aut minus describit sol quam sequenti revolutione, manifestum est quod, quantum est de ista causa, erunt dies naturales inequales. preterea .., etiam si sol uniformiter moveretur in celo, contingeret inequalitas dierum naturalium .. GROS. 22–3; BRACTON 264 (v. artificialis 2b); **1258** quilibet .. militum .. debet capere quolibet die xl dierum .. iiij s. .., dum stant in servicio domini regis per dictos xl dies *SelPlMan* 62; dominus J. .. de cujus exitu de die in diem metuitur AD. MARSH *Ep.* 33 (cf. de 3b); **1338** die in diem (v. custodia 4b); **s1338** contra horam diei terciam venit imperator .. AD. MUR. *Chr.* 84*n.*; **1377** requisitus si vellet regnum Anglie abjurare, dicebat quod non adhuc usque ad quadragesimum diem *SelCCoron* 86; dicto cicius recessit rex pro die illa FAVENT 16; alium respectum habere possumus ad diem naturalem, qui continet xxiiij horas et sic incipit media nocte et terminatur media nocte LYNDW. 24 (23 f). **b** clericus thesaurarii .. v denarios habet in die *Dial. Scac.* I 3 F; **1242** rex concessit Philippo .. ij denarios in die de elemosina constituta *Cl* 518; **c1283** percipiet per diem .. ij panes .. et dim. *Cust. Battle* 5; **1430** habebunt cibum semel in die *Feod. Durh.* 11. **c** **c1325** ordinavit quod de cetero nullus articulus .. in plena congregacione .. pertractetur, nisi seorsum .. saltem per diem articulus hujuscemodi inter artistas .. proponatur tractandus *StatOx* 128 (*gl.* ib. [**1344**]: interpretacio istius termini 'saltem per diem', id est in aliqua parte diei precedentis).

3 (usu. pl.) time, times (indefinite). **b** (w. *per* or *in*) continually, in course of time. **c** (gen. pl. w. *Liber*) *Chronicles* (bibl.); **d** (fig.).

ad hanc diem BEDE *HE* I 7 (v. ad 3a); post dies venit ad insulam rex *Ib.* I 25; **s1137** uno dierum, stante populo ad celebrationem misse, lux quedam infulserat J. WORC. 43; nec in die bonorum immemor fuit malorum AILR. *Ed. Conf.* 749D; his diebus AD. MARSH *Ep.* 48 (v. desolatio 1b); dierum damna *Ib.* 51 (v. desperare e); **1342** dierum invalescens malicia, qua mundus in deteriora jugiter labitur *Conc.* II 709b (*gl.* LYNDW. 97 y: dies ipsi de se mali non sunt, sed dicuntur mali propter malicias hominum que in eis committuntur; propterea dicit apostolus: '.. quia dies mali sunt' [*Ephes.* v 16]); **1430** debent .. j sexterium cervisie, quod non reddunt istis diebus *Feod. Durh.* 17. **b** crescente molestia per dies BEDE *CuthbP* 31; multi per dies locum frequentare illum .. coeperunt *Id. HE* III 10; divitiis indies temporalibus augebantur AILR. *SS Hex* 11 p. 193; majora merebatur indies odia MAP *NC* V 5 f. 65v.; **1283** ad partes vobis viciniores, cum de domino rege fuerimus expediti, iter arripiemus indies veniendi *Conc. Syn.* 948; **s1304** jussit rex indies impleri fossata cum ramis W. GUISB. 357; **1380** in dies (v. consuetudinarie). **c** audiat .. librum Paralipomenon, qui et Liber Dierum dicitur ab Ebreis NECKAM *Sac.* (*extr.*) 375; in Regum Dierumque Libris BEKINSAU 737. **d** ab anno Domini mcccv, quo ego tante eram etatis quod facta precipua ponderavi et ea scripsi breviter modo meo ex libro dierum meorum AD. MUR. *Chr. prol.* 4.

4 **a** (sg. or pl.) life-time, span. **b** reign or term of office. **c** (last) day, day of death.

a ante dies .. mihi .. / .. / deficiet .. quam ALDH. *VirgV* 2781; hoc .. multo ante horum .. qui nunc supersunt gestum est dies *V. Greg.* p. 90; senex ac plenus dierum juxta scripturas [*Job* xlii 16] patrum viam secutus est BEDE *HE* II 20; **c695** (11c) ut post diem ejus terra ista .. ad Uu. ecclesiam .. sit donata *CS* 76; **c800** in diebus meis vel successorum meorum *CS* 201*d.*; **804** (11c) quando mihi contingat exitus mei diei *CS* 313; **899** terram .. dies ij hominum .. concedo *CS* 580; **981** telluris particulam .. meo fideli largior Æ. utenti nomine, duorum sc. addendo diebus hominum *CD* 631; **1184** auctorem justitie Salahadin .., cujus dies Deus augeat (*Lit. Saladini*) DICETO *YH* II 26; *Meaux* I 407 (v. deducere 8b); **1309** cum dierum longitudine [cf. *Psalm* xc 16 etc.] *Deeds Balliol* 336; **1325** utinam antequam hec eveniant transeant dies mei! *Lit. Cant.* I 152; **1411** hoc .. sacramentum cui nonnulli diebus nostris .. obviant *Ib.* III 123; in diebus meis UPTON 256 (v. declaratio 1b). **b** dixerunt fuisse in die regis E. sicut nunc est *DB* I 373v.; **c1228** boscum .. quod idem H. [episcopus] habuit diebus suis *Feod. Durh.* 239; postea, diebus Willelmi Rufi ELMH. *Cant.* 167. **c** diem obiit, *asualt GlC* D 249; BEDE *HE* III 19 etc. (v. claudere 8a); die quo rex E. fuit vivus et mortuus *DB* I 45; sicut pater eorum fuit in die mortis et vite sue (*Leg. Hen.* 70. 18) *GAS* 589; **a1200** die illa qua pater meus R. fuit vivus et mortuus *FormA* 50; usque ad diem sibi peremptorie prefixum *Chr. Rams.* 106; **1285** die quo in fata decessit *CBaron* 119.

5 day of the week. **b** (Sunday). **c** (Monday). **d** (Tuesday). **e** (Wednesday). **f** (Thursday). **g** (Friday). **h** (Saturday).

gentiles hanc [sc. hebdomadam] in laudem suorum deflexere deorum, primam viz. diem Soli, secundam Lunae, tertiam Marti, quartam Mercurio, quintam Jovi, sextam Veneri, septimam Saturno dicantes, eisdem utique monstris suos dies quibus et errantia sidera consecrantes BEDE *TR* 8; accidit .. ut unusquisque planeta diei unius dominium sortiatur in hebdomade septem dierum. dies igitur Solis dicitur feria prima, quia prime hore preest sol. unde oportet ut secunde ferie prima hora lune assignetur NECKAM *NR* I 10; quidam antiqui philosophi putaverunt singulos planetas per ordinem dominari et quemlibet planetam habere infra 7 dies semel suum dominium in prima hora alicujus illorum et ideo .. voluerunt .. denominari unumquemque diem .. ab illo planeta qui in prima hora diei dominatur BACON VI 48 (cf. id. *Maj.* I 382). **b** die Dominico GILDAS *Pen.* 1; surrexit mane prima †subbati [l. Sabbati], quae nunc dies Dominica vocatur BEDE *Hom.* II 7. 134; Dominicus dies [AS: *sunnandæg*] est ÆLF. *Coll.* 92; **c1086** W. rege tenente curiam et placitum una Dominica die a mane usque ad vesperam *Regesta* p. 127; Dominici dies [AS: *ælces Sunnandæges freolsunge*], a precedentis Sabbati hora nona usque ad lucem sequentis ferie secunde feriantur (*Inst. Cnuti*) *GAS* 295; **s1200** [Eustacius abbas de Flaiz] Lundoniis et in aliis locis multis per Angliam predicatione sua effecit quod de cetero in diebus Dominicis forum rerum venalium nequaquam exercere presument R. HOWD. IV 124 (cf. ib. 167); fingamus nos esse in die Dominica, quam philosophi dicunt esse diem Solis NECKAM *NR* I 10; unam diem vocaverunt [quidam philosophi] diem Solis, que congrue dies Domini dicitur, quia ipse sol justitie .. dedicavit eam sua resurrectione BACON VI 48; ut incipiat sol dominari in prima hora diei Dominici *Id. Maj.* I 382; **1281** obligatio ad feriandum in Sabbato legali secundum formam Veteris Testamenti expiravit omnino cum ceteris in Lege cerimoniis et successit in Novo Testamento modus vacandi cultui divino diebus Dominicis et ceteris diebus solempnibus *Conc. Syn.* 902 (*gl.* LYNDW. 56 p: 'diebus Dominicis', i.e. feria prima, que ideo dicitur Dominicus dies quia illo die Dominus resurrexit .. et quicquid insigne a Domino constitutum est illo die factum est .. et, ut dicit canon, die Dominica nihil aliud agendum est nisi Deo vacandum); **14..** nulli alii dies observandi sunt de mandato ecclesie nisi dies Veneris sancta [etc.] .. et dies Dominicales *Conc. Scot.* II 75; **1585** usque diem Solis proximo ante festum S. Mich. *Pat* 1270 m. 1. **c** a nona hora Sabbati usque ad diem Lunis (*sic*) *DB* I 263; sollenne diei Dominice conservetur ab hora nona Sabbati usque ad lucidum diei Lunae [AS: *Monandæges lihtinge*] (*Quad.*) *GAS* 199; debet omni die Lune [AS: *ælce Mondæge*] .. operari domino suo (*Quad., Rect.*) *Ib.* 445; in die Sabbati ab hora nona usque in diem Lune mane (*Mir. Brit.*) DICETO *Chr.* 13; **c1185** die Lune perjurata [? *Hock Monday*] j ward' d[enarium] et alias consuetudines .. faciet *Rec. Templars* 9 (cf. ib. 153 [**12..**]: dabit ij *wardpanies* ad *Hokedai*; *Ib.* 155: dabit .. die *Ropmoneday* ij d. de *wardpanies*); **1286** sunt ibidem ij lundinarii, qui operabuntur quolibet die Lune per annum *IPM* 45/2 r. 9; **s1356** hec in die Lune in crastino sanctissimi festi paschalis .. principi [Edwardo] .. in principio sue male fortune acciderunt. qui postea .. hunc diem Lune paschalem *Blac Monunday* .. vocavit *Plusc.* IX 43 (= FORDUN *Cont.* XIV 17: hucusque in Anglia feria secunda Pasche *Blak-mononday* .. nuncupatur). **d** in privatis diebus, viz. Dominica, die Martis, die Jovis ac Sabbatis W. MALM. *Glast.* 118; nec .. rationi dissonum si Martis potissimum die martia negotia sint completa GIR. *EH* II 7; **1199** (v. cinis 2b); **s1281** officialis testes .. examinavit, sed publicare usque in diem Martis proximum protelavit GRAYSTANES 17; **1377** mane die Martis (*Epitaph. Ed. III*) *Pol. Poems* I 220. **e** †**844** (13c) ut omnes fratres et sorores nostri ad unamquamque ecclesiam omni ebdomada Mercoris die, id est *Wodnesday*, .. cantent l psalmos .. *CS* 447; erant abnepotes illius antiquissimi Woden, .. quem .. gentes Anglorum deum esse delirantes ei quartum diem septimane et sextum uxori sue Free perpetuo ad hoc tempus consecraverunt sacrilegio W. MALM. *GR* I 5; Frithowald, de quo Woden ortus est, a quo Angli feriam sextam (*sic*) Wodenis diem nuncupant ORD. VIT. VII 3; ab isto Sem genealogia ducitur usque ad Woden, qui fuit tante auctoritatis apud suos ut feriam quartam, quam gentiles Romani diem Mercurii appellabant, ejus nomini consecrarent, que consuetudo ab Anglis hodie servatur; vocant enim eumdem diem *Wodnesdei*, id est 'diem Woden' AD. SCOT *TT* 716B (cf. *Plusc.* VI 1); **1199** die Mercurii infra Pascha *CurR* I 113. **f** qui furatur .. in sancto die Jovis [AS: *on ðone halgan Þunresdæg*] in Ascensione Domini (*Quad.*) *GAS* 53; det su[um] *heorþpenig* in sancto die Jovis [AS: *on halgan Ðunresdæg*] (*Quad., Rect.*) *Ib.* 446; **s1177** (v. absolvere 9e); **1207** (v. absolutio 5b); **1246** die Jovis proxima post nativitatem BMV *Reg. Paisley* 25; **s1344** solempnitas duravit diebus Dominica, Lune, Martis, et Mercurii. .. mane, hoc est die Jovis, superveniente .., fecit se rex solempniter parari .. AD. MUR. *Chr.* 231; *Thursday*, dies Jovis, feria quinta *CathA.* **g** pisces per dies Veneris *DB* I 149; decantetur omni die Veneris [AS: *ælc Frigdæge*] .. unum quinquagenarium pro rege (*Quad.*) *GAS* 169; **c1144** totam terram .. sicut .. circuivimus die Veneris crastino Ascensionis Domini *E. Ch. Scot.* 141; **s1238** dies Veneris .. sancta (v. antonomastice b); **s1305** (v. bonus 3d); **14..** dies Veneris sancta, viz. dies proprius Passionis *Conc. Scot.* II 75; *Fryday*, dies Veneris, feria sexta *CathA.* **h** paratus esto die Sabbati hinc nobiscum Romam transire OSB. *V. Dunst.* 41; mercatum .. sedet die Sabbati *DB* II 379; **1196** die Sabbati ante Purificationem *CurR* I 25; **1246** (15c) actum .. die Saboti prima post festum S. Nicholai *Inchaffray* 62; **1391** assueta est emere .. gallinas .. in mercato diebus Sabbati et ea diebus Dominicis vendere *Leet Norw.* 72; **1434** diebus †Sabativis [l. Sabatinis] *Reg. Heref.* 177; **1584** ante septimam horam meridianam diei Saturni .. precedentis .. tempus electionis *StatOx* 436.

6 day of the month: **a** reckoned backwards from calends, ides, or nones. **b** reckoned forwards from first day. **c** reckoned in latter half (*mense exeunte*) backwards from end. **d** unlucky day (*cf. OED s. v.* dismal). **e** (w. *mensis*) month's mind (commemoration of death after one month).

a **601** (v. dare 13a); **675** (15c) sub die Kalendarum Aprilis *CS* 36; die quarto Nonarum Februariarum BEDE *HE* II 7; peracto Pascha, hoc est vij^a Iduum Maiarum [v. l. Idus Mai] die *Ib.* V 23; **993** die xvj Kalendarum Augustarum *CD* 684; dies Kalendarum LANFR. *Const.* 89; **s1344** die Januarii xix et xiiij Kalendas Februarii AD. MUR. *Chr.* 155. **b** **s664** facta est eclipsis solis die tertio mensis Maii BEDE *HE* III 27; **s1095** etc. (v. dare 13b). **c** **1268** die tercia exeunte Madio *AncC* III 122; **1292** sexta die exeunte mense Decembri (*Instrumentum*) *Anglo-Scot. Rel.* 63 (cf. ib. 70 [**1296**]: quinta die intrante mense Aprili); die undecimo exeunte mense Junio GRAYSTANES 26. **d** *Itin. Ric.* II 5 (v. conjecturare 1a); W. NEWB. *HA* IV 1, GILB. I 74. 1 (v. Aegyptiacus b); **s1249** quidam .. illo die non regem sed militem facere voluerunt, dicentes quia dies Egyptiacus est FORDUN *Cont.* X 1; Pharios .. dies GARL. *Tri. Eccl.* 88 (v. digitare c). **e** **1412** lego pro .. distribucionibus faciendis inter pauperes die obitus mei .. item in die mensis obitus mei *Reg. Cant.* II 33; **1417** volo quod .. omnes capellani .. pannis nigris vestientur in die mensis mei *Ib.* 132.

7 day of (solar) year. **b** year's mind, anniversary (usu. of death). **c** day of Christian calendar.

anni vertente quoque die EDDI 3; sol annuum caeli ambitum .. non in ccclxv diebus sed superadditis sex horis adimplere cognoscitur BEDE *TR* 38; **s1242** etc. (v. canicularis c); BRACTON 359b (v. bissextus a); BACON *Tert.* 275 (v. annus 1b); **1307** exceptis .. diebus saltatis *IPM* 129/17. **b** **c1220** etc. (v. anniversarius 1c); **1335** diem anniversarium Willelmi patris ipsius W. et Matillis matris sue *Eng. Clergy* 259; **s1459** (v. annalis 6a). **c** ALDH. *VirgV* 1605 (v. coste); unde mos obtinuit ecclesiasticus ut dies beatorum martyrum sive confessorum Christi quibus de saeculo transierunt natales vocitemus eorumque sollemnia non funebria sed natalitia dicantur BEDE *Hom.* II 13. 157 (cf. LYNDW. 104 s.v. depositio 3b); die sancto Paschae *Id. HE* III 6; usque ad diem Ascensionis dominicae CUTHB. *Ob. Baedae* clx; die paschali HERM. ARCH. 17; OSB. *V. Dunst.* 41 (v. ascensio 1d); in xij diebus Nativitatis *DB* I 262v.; omnibus liberis hominibus dies isti condonati sunt ..: xij dies in sancto Natali Domini [AS: *xij dagas on Gehhol*] .. (*Quad.*) *GAS* 79; Sancti Martini die [AS: *on Martinus mæssedæg*] (*Quad., Rect.*) *Ib.* 446; **1198** a die S. Michaelis in j mensem *CurR* I 41; *Cust. Westm.* 90 etc. (v. cena 2b); **1268** etc. (v. cinis 2b); *Obs. Barnwell* 150 (v. anima 5f); **1303** die de *la Hok'* [*Hockday*] *CourtR* 192/59 *rot. ult.*; **1412** pro pauperibus scolaribus in die S. Nicholai depascendis *StatOx* 215; 'ante Annunciacionem', i. diem quo celebratur festum Annunciacionis B. Marie; et supple 'diem finitum' LYNDW. 23 f (cf. *Conc. Syn.* II 82*n.* 3).

8 (eccl. or acad.): **a** day dist. as festal or ferial ('private'). **b** fast-day. **c** day of penance. **d** day on which sermon is preached. **e** day appointed for lecture or disputation.

a dies festos celebrant GILDAS *EB* 12; nempe die festo laxantur frena rigoris! ALDH. *VirgV* 1591; cum gaudio spiritali venerabilium patrum nostrorum festivos celebrare dies ALCUIN *WillP* I 31; missa matutinalis de Dominica, major de vigilia. alia vero die, sicut privatis diebus, signa pulsentur LANFR. *Const.* 92; in die festo S. Martini *DB* I

174; aderat dies pro diei illius recordatione festivus AILR. *Ed. Conf.* 748C; in diebus ferialibus, quando de feria agitur *Offic. Sal.* 14 (cf. ib. 36: tam in festis quam in profestis diebus); **1283** die festiva vel non festiva *RGasc* II 204; SWAFHAM 111 (v. cappa 5d); **1342** communibus diebus (v. communis 9b); c**1360** j vestimentum .. pro diebus festivis; j vestimentum .. pro diebus ferialibus *Fabr. York* 279; *Ib.* 123 (v. duplex 4a). **b** jejuniorum diebus 'gloria in excelsis Deo' non canitur *RegulC* 59; ad sanos jejunialis abstinentie dies GIR. *Spec.* II 24 p. 69; **1257** etc. (v. caro 1b); c**1260** tribus diebus quarti jejunii [*ember days*] in ebdomada Pentecostes statim post capitulum ibunt in dormitorium *Cust. Norw.* 123; **1268** (v. 1 carnalis 1b); **1268** duo fercula de coquina tam diebus carnalibus quam diebus piscinis *Fines* 251/21/25; **1283** diebus .. quibus jejunatur *Cust. Westm.* 63; **1307** diebus piscium una fercula piscium precii oboli *Year Bk. I Ed. II* 5; **1370** in Epiphania .. in die comedunt in refectorio si contigerit in die piscium *Cust. Norw.* 239; c**1472** (v. abstinentia 1); **1493** solut' xx servientibus infra abbathiam capientibus in diebus piscium pro eorum *soulsilver* per totum annum extra Quadragesimam iiij li. *Ac. Durh.* 652. **c 680** non prius .. quam xl dierum spatia in penitendo peragere compellantur ALDH. *Ep.* 4; vij dies in pane et aqua, lxx sine pinguedine peniteat THEOD. *Pen.* I 1. 6; R. Cicestr' episcopus [ob. **1123**] .. eas [reliquias] .. annuatim requirentibus vij dies de penitentia indulsit *Chr. Battle* f. 48; ecclesia dedicata est in honore S. Andree die Translacionis S. Benedicti. eodem die xxx dies veniales [*of indulgence for those hearing mass*] *Vis. S. Paul.* 11; **1279** omnibus parochianis nostris .. xl dies de injuncta sibi penitencia relaxamus *Reg. Ebor.* 22; s**1340** archiepiscopus indulsit Christicolis cunctis [etc.] ac eciam omnibus qui predicacionem audierunt, de peccatis suis vere penitentibus et confessis, concessit xl dies BIRCHINGTON *Arch. Cant.* 23 (cf. ib.: confitentibus peccata indulgenciam xx dierum concessit). **d** c**1340** cum .. fuerit .. statutum ut diebus singulis in ordine predicabilibus sermones .. habeantur *FormOx* 308; **1526** Dominicis et sermonum diebus (*Vis. Thame*) *EHR* III 714; duas .. sellas .. quibus cantor et succentor chori diebus sermonum insiderent FERR. *Kinloss* 74. **e** a**1350** statuit universitas vesperias .. posse .. teneri in die quolibet apud arcistas legibili ..; incepciones vero non nisi die disputabili vel saltim apud arcistas festine legibili celebrentur *StatOx* 36; **1458** bacallarius [collegii S. Andree] omni die legibili in theologia legere [teneatur] *Mon. Hib. & Scot.* 408b; **1549** ut theologus .. omni die legibili, saltem in unaquaque hebdomada, in sacris litteris publice legat et interpretetur *Conc. Scot.* II 100.

9 (theol.): **a** day of Creation. **b** Doomsday.

a qualiter hunc mundum summi prudentia Patris / tempore praesentem tunc per bis terna dierum / fecerit ALDH. *VirgV* 673; si dies illi, in quibus Moyses istum mundum non simul esse factum videtur dicere, aliter sunt intelligendi quam sicut videmus istos dies in quibus vivimus, intelligere nequeo quomodo facti sint angeli in illo integro numero ANSELM (*CurD* I 18) II 77; creatio lucis proprie dicta est opus prime diei S. LANGTON *Gl. Hist. Schol.* 41; prima die creavit celum et terram. sed ante lucem non erat dies ..; ergo simul facta est lux et dies primus et que fiunt in primo die. dicendum quod equivoce sumitur dies, sc. pro naturali et artificiali HALES *Sent.* II 116–7. **b** in die judicii GILDAS *EB* 28; dies munerum, punitio reorum *GlC* D 263; **679** in die judicii rationem reddet Deo in anima sua *CS* 45; **815** sciat se a Deo in die magno .. ejectum *CS* 353; **845** diem tremendum *CS* 450; **858** in die magni aexaminis, quando celum et terra moventur *CS* 496; **933** novissima ac magna examinationis die classica archangeli clangente salpice, bustis sponte patentibus somata jam rediviva propellentibus *CS* 694; tunc tantam lugentis populi videres confusionem .. ut diem judicii adesse .. putares OSB. *V. Dunst.* 42; s**992** architectoris [Elphegi] .. exuvie deposite diem extremum operiuntur resumende *Chr. Rams.* 107; **1170** ne .. una vobiscum in die judicii dampnationis sententia involvamur (*Lit. Papae*) DICETO *YH* I 340; hic liber ad indigenis *Domesdei* nuncupatur, id est 'dies judicii' per metaphoram *Dial. Scac.* II 16 B; cessa, caro, lascivire, / quia dies instat ire P. BLOIS *Caro & Spir.* 1130A; ut separatus sit a consorcio aliorum, tradatur Sathane in interitum carnis, ut spiritus salvus fiat in die judicii *Cust. Westm.* 206; si quis cogitaret districti judicii diem [ME: *dom of domes dei*] *AncrR* 35; quod anime purgate non vident facialiter Deum ante diem judicii OCKHAM *Dial.* 740.

10 a market or fair day. **b** working day or day's work (esp. man.). **c** day on which free food is supplied; *cf. cibus* c. **d** day as measure of farm or food-rent. **e** day's rent or profit.

a c**1150** ferie iiij dierum quam episcopus habebat alios quatuor dies ferie .. in prebendam concedo (*Ch. Comitis*) *Reg. Heref. 1283–1327* 48; **1263** concessi .. in quolibet die nundinarum suarum j pipam vini *BBC* (*Agardsley*) 129; **1283** si bos .. vendatur per extraneum ad diem mercati, dabit venditor nobis j d. pro leuda (*Liber B*) *Foed.* II 262b (cf. ib.: dabit venditor extraneus in die fori pro leuda .. ij d.); **1315** pro pondere j hominis rerum predictarum solvetur obolus in diebus fori et in diebus nundinarum j d. *RGasc* IV 1626 p. 474; diebus fori *Quon. Attach.* 48. 14 (v. comitatus 6e); **13..** quod nullus bladarius nec alius emat bladum .. antequam aperte expectaverint .. per tres dies mercatus *MGL* I 454; c**1525** ad faciendam publicam proclamationem .. duobus diebus mercatoriis infra ij dies proxim' post deliberationem .. brevium *Entries* 592b. **b** secabant in pratis domini sui .. unam diem *DB* I 174v.; **1185** pro j tofto [reddit] ij s. .. et iiij dies operis et *le present Rec. Templars* 86; **1226** quod faciet nobis singulis diebus operabilibus c quarellos *Cl* 92a; **1275** cum predictis bobus et caruca per quemlibet diem operabilem arravit *Hund.* I 67; **1283** si die operali festivitas evenerit, dabunt alium diem in septimana *Cart. Blyth* 420; c**1283** debent operari tota die excepta hora comedendi *Cust. Battle* 28; **1353** solut' Johanni le Redere operanti super dormitorium per xxxij dies operabiles *Sacr. Ely* II 154. **c 1279** (v. companagium). **d** Beddinges .. reddebat unum diem de firma *DB* I 28; dimidiam diem firmae reddidit in omnibus rebus *Ib.* 38v.; inter totum reddidit per annum .. dim. diem ad firmam regis in frumento et melle et aliis rebus ad firmam pertinentibus *Ib.* 209; reddebat dimidium diem mellis et consuetudinem mellis *Ib.* II 110; c**1182** (v. cotlanda a). **e 1241** (v. annus 4b).

11 (leg.): **a** day appointed for appearance in court, hearing of judgement, *etc.* **b** day for amicable settlement. **c** day available for court business. **d** day's session of court ('law-day' or sim.). **e** formal colloquy or parley.

a si in eodem comitatu sit, inde ad vij dies terminum habeat; si in alia scira sit, xv dierum terminus ponatur (*Leg. Hen.* 41. 1a-1b) *GAS* 567–8; s**1170** instabat peremptorius dies, ut sententia ulterius differri non posset J. SAL. *Thom.* 20; si [summonitus] non venit .., adversarius ejus .. coram justiciis appareat et se adversus eum liti offerat et ita in curia per tres dies expectabit. si vero nec quarta die venerit .., iterum per aliud breve summonebitur per intervalla xv dierum GLANV. I 7 (cf. ib.: si ad terciam summonitionem venerit et premissas summonitiones recognoverit, statim amittit saisinam nisi dies salvare possit per dominum regem guarantum); **1196** etc. (v. audire 3c); **1196** ipse V. non venit nec se essoniavit; et receperat diem in Banco. judicium: .. ipsi eant sine die *CurR* I 19; **1206** ad diem sibi datum comparuit in curia et postea essoniavit se eo die de malo veniendi; et quoniam non servavit diem suum remanet in misericordia *Ib.* IV 216; **1224** (v. diffundere 5b); **1230** pone eis diem in crastino Trinitatis, quod sint coram baronibus de Scaccario nostro *LTRMem* 11 r. 6d.; **1260** (v. brevis 1b); **1284** (v. adjornare a); **1287** R. B. habet diem legis sue [sc. vadiande] ad diem leg' unde sum[monebatur] *CourtR* (*Highworth*) 170/57 r. 4; dies communes HENGHAM *Magna* 6 (v. communis 9b); cum in patriam .. se posuisset .., Willelmus contra ipsum dies de gracia concessit ac si fuisset in placito dotis *State Tri. Ed. I* 19. **b** BRAKELOND 137v. (v. concordia 2c); **1219** recepta die pacis inter eos reformande *Leg. Ant. Linc.* III 653; **1230** etc. (v. amor 5b); **1260** (v. concordare 2e); **1282** prece parcium datus est dies amoris inter R. .. et N. .. concordandi citra proximam curiam *CourtR Hales* 203; s**1328** abbas .. cum .. comite diem sumsit amoris, in quo post multas altercaciones concordarunt in hunc modum .. WHITTLESEY *Cont.* 228; **1410** (v. amabilis c). **c** †**1307** (recte **1305**) ad primam diem judicialem post festum Penthecostes (v. adjornare a); ad alium diem legitimum *APScot* app. 275 (v. adjornare c); est summonicio certi diei et loci exhibicio, partibus facta ad diem legalem. est autem dies legalis in predictis placitis quaterdenus et unus dies sive xv dies *Quon. Attach.* 2 (cf. ib. 60: quod dies in quo datur judicium sit legalis et non festivus); **1321** sitis coram nobis tercio die juridico post festum Translacionis B. Thome .. venturo *Lit. Cant.* I 51; **1593** in proximo die juridico non legibili *StatOx* 450; in curiis illis, ad †quod [? l. quas] omni die placitabili confluunt studentes in legibus illis, quasi in scolis pupplicis leges ille leguntur et docentur FORTESCUE *LLA* 48 (cf. *CurR* XV 1567). **d** s**1245** rex [Francorum] cepit diem parliamenti cum domino papa M. PAR. *Maj.* IV 484; **1290** cum .. Thomam .. ad diem baronum jam instantem in parliamento Parysius transmittamus *RGasc* II 552; **1291** consuetudo Wallie .. talis est quod in casibus ubi contenciones emerserunt inter magnates Wallie qui tenent de rege in capite quod (*sic*), antequam querela fiat in curia regis .., capi debet quidam dies amoris sive parliamenti, qui quidem dies vocatur 'dies marchie'; et ibi per vicinos et amicos communes, qui sunt quasi justiciarii, debent hujusmodi querele proponi et per cons[uetudinem] marchie emendari (*CoramR* 127 r. 26d.) *Abbr. Plac.* 226 (cf. *Arch. Cambr.* 4th s. IX 244); **1359** ad quandam diem marchie apud Belymire [*Scot.*] tentam *IMisc* 178/23 r. 2; s**1378** WALS. *HA* I 373 (v. consuetudinaliter); **1423** nec ad dies treugarum seu marchiarum vel curias forenses .. ipsos compellatis laborare *Melrose* II 507. **e 1354** que quidem obstupacio ad duos dies lete .. presentata fuit (*Anc. Indict.*) *Pub. Works* I 188; **1375** sunt ibi [*Fairford, Glos*] due (*sic*) legales dies, viz. ad Hokeday et S. Michaelis *IPM* 253 r. 1.

2 Dies v. Dios.

diescere [LL *gl.*], to dawn; **b** (fig.).

mane, non tamen statim ut ~it sed sole recens orto GIR. *TH* II 7; dum ecce aurora albescente .. ~ebat *Hist. Meriadoci* 370; s**1381** cum lumine cere antequam ~eret viam .. peregit KNIGHTON *Cont.* II 144; *to day .., to daw*, diere, ~ere *CathA*. **b** mors mihi nunc abiit; mihi nunc in mente diescit *Babio* 73; nuda humeros, exerta sinus, totoque diescit / ore J. EXON. *BT* II 608; me noctescente diescat / hic liber HANV. IX 479 p. 392; gemmis diadema diescens GARL. *Epith.* VI 327; hinc pluvie crescunt nec tempora certa diescunt [*gl.*: clarescunt] *Id. Mor. Scol.* 536; cum ipse qui est vita vestra ~et [ME: *edeawet*] post noctis tenebras *AncrR* 136; Amor, sputo linita facie / qua diescunt celi delicie J. HOWD. *CA* 107; s**1429** advesperascente anno xviij, ~ente xix AMUND. II 203.

diesis [CL < δίεσις], (mus.) quarter-tone.

diesses, spatia de uno in alterum sonum vergentia OSB. GLOUC. *Deriv.* 172; quis assignare presumet quare †luna [l. lima, i.e. limma] potius dominetur in connexione anime et corporis quam ~is? NECKAM *NR* II 173 p. 299 (cf. id. *DS* X 127: quid diesis, quid lima docet, cantus †moderatur [? l. moderator] / organa cum citharis psalterioque regit); BART. ANGL. XIX 128 (v. diastema b); TUNST. 216 (v. diaschisma).

Diespiter [CL *var. of* Juppiter], day-star.

hic diaspiter, *a daysterre WW*.

diet- v. et. diaet-. **dietim** v. diatim.

diezeugmenon [(τετράχορδον) διεζευγμένων], (as sb. n., mus.) disjunct tetrachord.

nete ~on [sc. νήτη διεζευγμένων], i.e. ultima disjunctarum. .. ~on, i.e. disjuncte, quia hoc est tetrachordum disjunctum ODINGTON 81; ~on .. et synemmenon creant reliqua tetrachorda, sc. meson et hypaton *Ib.* 83.

dif- v. et. def-, diff-. **diferri** v. 1 deferre. **diferverare** v. diverberare. **diff-** v. et. def-.

diffacere [OF *desfacier* < *disfaciare, cf. It. *sfacciare*; *conf. w.* facere], **a** to disfigure, mutilate (persons). **b** to deface (artefacts); *cf. defieri* b, *dispactus*. **c** to undo (acts).

a si tunc dominus velit eum disfacere [AS: *mid woh fordon*], disrationet se .. in conventu publico (*Quad.*) *GAS* 169; qui murdrum fecerit, si capiatur, debet reddi justitie regis—et [si sit] talis de quo justitia fieri possit, non viz. occisus aut ~tus (*Leg. Hen.* 92. 3) *Ib.* 607; diffecerit *Ib.* 609 (v. excoriare 1e); **1130** fullones Wintonie r. c. de j m. auri ne disfaciant utlagos *Pipe* 37 (cf. ib. 42: Brand monetarius r. c. de xx li. ne esset disfactus cum aliis monetariis); **1155** pro disfaciendo falso monetario vj s. et viij d. .. et pro disfaciendo homine victo in duello v s. *Pipe* 4; **1167** in custamento v juisiorum et j duelli, et ij hominibus disfactis et j suspenso *Pipe* 1; **1168** in ij juisis et in vj hominibus ~iendis *Pipe* 2; s**1211** obsides duo .. ~iuntur et pre dolore moriuntur *Ann. Margan* 31. **b** ibi juxta fuit quidam vicus; fuit ~tus quando rex fecit facere suum fossatum *Lib. Wint.* 5b; si vero non compareat carta, set ab illo qui [eum] inservire vult disfacta sit, weregildum ejus componet (*Leg. Hen.* 89. 2b) *GAS* 605; **1290** sigilia, quibus ciste .. consignabantur, defaciebantur, et frangebantur *KRAc* 231/14. **c 1262** R. .. dicit .. quod habuit [gildam] .. per consensum forewardmannorum. nolunt defacere quod predecessores eorum fecerunt (*Andover*) *Gild Merch.* II 4; **1268** omne quod actum fuit inter duo bella [de Lewes] totum defactum [(?) defectum; MS: def'cm] est *JustIt* 618 r. 15*d*.

diffactio, disfigurement, mutilation. *Cf. diffractio.*

in furto et murdro et proditione et incendio et domus infractione et eis que ad ~onem pertinent (*Leg. Hen.* 64. 2) *GAS* 584; corporalis ~o (*Ib.* 82. 9) *Ib.* 599.

diffalta v. defalta.

diffamare [CL]

1 to publish abroad, make widely known; *v. et. defamare* 3; **b** (impers. pass. usu. w. acc. & inf.).

quibus patefactis ac ~atis longe lateque miraculis BEDE *HE* III 10; increbruit, ~atus [est] *GlC* I 156; longe lateque ~atum *Ib.* V 14; **9..** ~averunt, *gewidmærsan WW*. **b** adminiculum est .. iste vir ex Scotorum libello sciscitasse quod ~atum est THEOD. *Pen. pref.*; s**1212** rege volente .. invadere Walenses, subito ~atum est apud Cestriam comites et barones conspirasse in eum *Flor. Hist.* II 142.

2 to defame, slander, denounce. **b** to disgrace, dishonour. *V. et. defamare* 1.

~atus, i. traductus, accussatus *GlH* D 474; a**1078** si .. didicissem qua infamia ~aretur caritas vestra .. ANSELM (*Ep.* 63) III 178; me nothum degeneremque .. indicavit et hostiliter ~avit ORD. VIT. VII 15 p. 231; cum allegat burse rethor / .. / cedit quicquid diffamabat, / defembat et fedebat WALT. WIMB. *Van.* 18; **1269** ~avit vilibus verbis majorem et ballivos *Rec. Leic.* I 109; **1290** ipsum male ~avit pupplico asserendo ipsum falsum fore hominem plenum fraudibus *SelPlMan* 36; cum multos criminosos cernamus qui alios, eciam quibus inimicantur, non ~ant OCKHAM *Dial.* 598. **b** facias .. fidem .. quia non ~abis ossa mea *Ghost Stories* 416.

3 to accuse (of): **a** (w. *de*); **b** (w. *super*). **c** (p. ppl. as sb.) accused person. *V. et. defamare* 2.

a 1324 de perjuria, sacrilegio, furto .. vel incontinentia super lapsu carnis notorie ~atur *Stat. Mich. Cantab.* 642; **1342** ~ati de criminibus .. et de eis purgare se volentes *Conc.* II 700b (cf. LYNDW. 313 r). **b 1262** cum L. de F. clericus .. ~atus esset super crimine roberie et in prisona .. detentus *Cl* 23. **c** si ~atus non instituerit actionem seu causam diffamationis *Praxis* 118.

diffamatio [LL = *publication*], defamation, slander. **b** accusation. *V. et. defamatio.*

1231 si implacitavit eum in curia Cristianitatis, hoc fuit de quadam ~one *BNB* II 479; s**1240** imperator se .. accingens ad ultionem super ~one .. qua nomen suum

dominus papa .. denigraverat *Flor. Hist.* II 237; **1381** sic horum predicacio / est vilis diffamacio / probrosumque convicium (*In Lollardos* 42) *Pol. Poems* I 245; **s1434** (v. 2 causa 1a); **1559** (v. convicium). **b** **s1194** processerunt ad ~onem ipsius archiepiscopi et accusationem R. Howd. III 230; quoniam per accusationem factam in curia nostra de morte illa satis habetur suspectus et per talem ~onem et indictamentum nihil aliud restat nisi quod .. admittatur purgatio Bracton 124; H. de E. .. graciam ab eo [rege Hen.] obtinuit ut posset ponere se super patriam de illa ~one *Meaux* I 316; *Praxis* 118 (v. diffamare 3c).

diffamator, defamer, slanderer. *V. et. defamator.*

criminatores, ~ores, falsorum criminum impositores Ockham *Dial.* 595.

diffamatorie, defamatorily.

hoc calumniose et ~ie additur Ockham *Pol.* II 635.

diffamatorius, defamatory. *V. et. defamatorius.*

1334 in quibus [Johannis XXIV constitucionibus] quamplura hereticalia .., fantastica, insana et ~ia .. inveni Ockham *Pol.* III 6; **1418** codicillos ~ios nostri sanguinis Bekynton II 132; **1431** omnes .. qui invenerint seu legerint .. billas quascumque ~ias, sediciosas seu pacis nostre perturbatorias *Cl* 281 m. 6*d.*; **1450** libellos ~ios, 'famosos' vulgariter nuncupatos (*Cl*) *Foed.* XI 268a; si diffamans et diffamatus post prolationem verborum ~iorum .. simul se invicem familiariter gesserint *Praxis* 118.

diffamatrix, defamer, slanderer (f.).

1519 Margaret F. est communis ~ix suorum vicinorum *Vis. Linc.* I 80.

diffarreatio [CL], divorce.

~o, dissolutio inter virum et feminam Osb. Glouc. *Deriv.* 175.

diffat-, diffen- v. def-. **diffencio** v. defensio 6.

differenter [LL], differently. **b** (compar.) more distinctly. **c** more excellently.

sic ergo asseremus gladium spiritualem exercendum viro ecclesiastico ut nullatenus ad eum pertinere fateamur materialem? nequaquam; utriusque siquidem usus per ipsum est agendus, sed ~er Ad. Marsh *Ep.* 246 c. 10 p. 436; sic similiter genus et differentia sunt principia eorum [accidentium], set ~er Bacon VII 21; periodus dicitur .. ubi sententia perfecte terminatur .. et non debet fieri ante perfectam sententiam. sed reliqua duo [sc. comma et colon] fiunt ante eam, ~er tamen *Id. Tert.* 248; *dyversyly, diverse,* ~er .. *CathA.* **b** ad ~ius principiorum genera internoscendum, distantius de quibus enuntiari contingit distinguendum Balsh. *AD* 22. **c** *GlH* D 448 (v. eminenter a); vigiliis .. orationibus et elemosinis jugiter insistebat et, sicut ~ius ceteris obtinebat militie Christiane titulos, ita quibuslibet religiosis .. sanctitatis gratia preeminebat P. Blois (*Passio Reginaldi*) *Opusc.* 965c; Salomon .. de aliorum laboribus jocundatur. Edwardus vero, de propriis .. adeptis .. exultans, quanto ~ius triumphator nanciscens .. quam successor sabatizans .., tanto gloriosius poterit commendari J. Lond. *Commend. Ed. I* 13; Plato .. 'in hoc', inquit, 'manifestus est philosophus, si absolvit animam a corporis communione ~ius aliis hominibus' R. Bury *Phil.* 15. 193 (cf. Plato *Phaedo* 64e: διαφερόντως τῶν ἄλλων ἀνθρώπων).

differentia [CL]

1 difference, dissimilarity. **b** (math.) difference (in quantity). **c** difference of opinion, disagreement.

si quis pro morte heretici missam ordinavit .., quia multum jejunavit et nescit deferentiam catholicae fidei Theod. *Pen.* I 5. 13; cum nunquam .. de tonsurae ~ia legatur aliqua fuisse controversia (*Ep. Ceolfridi*) Bede *HE* V 21 p. 342; **9..** ~ia, *toberennes WW*; rerum quarumlibet tam similium ~ias quam differentium similitudines distinctius ab invicem mens non incauta discernit Gir. *TH* I 17; 'distinctio' .. est ipsarum personarum inter se ~ia. '~ia' autem communiter se habet ad distinctionem et diversitatem.. . si [~ia est] in situ, dicitur 'non simul'; si in qualitate, 'dissimilitudo'; si in quantitate, 'inequalitas' Hales *Sent.* I 227; ~ia .. duorum modorum ponendi supernaturalitatem noticie revelate patet separando unum ab alio Duns *Ord.* I 40; nec causatur sensibilis ~ia ex diametro solis exeuntis in auge vel in ejus opposito Wallingf. (*Alb.*) I 290. **b** in simplicii divisione sine ~iis .. divisor .. superducatur ei [sc. dividendo] Thurkill *Abac.* 57v.; cum superfluum inter partes, vel partium ~ia, sit 10 praeter 2 res .. Rob. Angl. *Alg. add.* 150; ~ia inter diluvium et nativitatem Christi fuit 3101 anni cum quartis annorum et 318 dies Ashenden *AM* 5v. 1. **c** **1458** mature .. consideravimus hujusmodi varietates, contraversias et ~ias que fuerunt certo tempore inter .. R. ducissam Eboraci .. et alios .. ex una parte ac .. A. ducissam Somercetrie .. et alios .. ex alia parte (*Pat*) *Reg. Whet.* I 299.

2 differentiation, distinction. **b** (w. *ad*) in contradistinction.

tripertitam sillabarum ~iam Aldh. *Met.* 6 (cf. ib. 9: duos metaplasmos .. quos talis discretionis ~ia dirimit); **s1321** rex .. omnes regni primores .. sine ~ia discrecionis .. delere studebat *Flor. Hist.* III 200; **1430** quod clerus ubique infra regnum nostrum .. non in disparitate et ~ia set uno jure unoque privilegio et libertate generali .. gaudeat *Conc. Scot.* I cccvii; **s1445** mors, que cuncta rapit vivencia .. absque personarum ~ia *Plusc.* XI 7; **1490** quasi omnes quercus .. sine ~ia prosterni .. fecisti *Conc.* III 633a. **b** Trojana agmina .., que a puerulis hastiledia, ad ~iam hastiludiorum, dici solent Neckam *NR* I 26; sic .. dicitur usus nudus, 'nudus' additur ad ~iam ususfructus Ockham *Pol.* I 302; **c1380** carta est scriptum sigillatum de re immobili data .. sine condicione adjuncta. .. quare dicitur 're immobili'? ad ~iam †convencione [? l. convencionis], que potest fieri de re mobili. .. quare dicitur 'sine condicione'? ad ~iam cirographi, qui fit cum condicione *Reg. Rough* 209.

3 (log.) differentia, distinctive feature, specific difference.

nec ullis ~iis vel accidentibus intelligi potest esse mutabilis Anselm (*Mon.* 27) I 45; internosci poterunt eorum que interrogantur genera duo .. et ~iis et nominibus discernenda Balsh. *AD rec. 2* 126; unamquamque rem informans specifica ~ia aut ab eo est per quem facta sunt omnia aut omnino nichil est J. Sal. *Met.* 836a; in intellectu .., in quo genera et species, ~ias, propria et accidentia .. planum est invenire *Id. Pol.* 438d; Bacon II 50 (v. divisivus b); est medium inter accidentale et essentiale, ut contrahens, sicut ~ia contrahit genus Duns *Ord.* II 374; ~ia ultima dicitur quia non habet ~iam, quia non resolvitur in conceptum quiditativum et qualitativum, determinabilem et determinatum, sed est tantum conceptus ejus qualitativus, sicut ultimum genus tantum quiditativum habet conceptum *Ib.* III 81.

4 (her.) 'difference', distinctive mark.

1387 vidit .. dominum Henricum le Scrope .. recipere ordinem militis in dictis armis cum uno labello de argento et *goules gobone*.. . et postea vidit dictum H. armari in dictis armis cum ~ia predicta ad bellum de Halydonhill' *Scrope v. Grosvenor* 240; sunt eciam labelle in armis quorundam, et ille semper sunt ~ie signorum Bad. Aur. 134; sunt insuper diversi nobiles qui portant lingulas sive labellas ..; pro quibus est sciendum quod .. non dicuntur proprie signa set ~ie signorum; ut, quando .. aliquis habet plures filios legitimos, tunc primus filius .. portabit integra arma sui patris cum aliqua modica ~ia .., cui specialiter attribuitur luna crescens .. vel aliqua alia parva ~ia, ut modica macula vel crux parva cruciata, vel aliqua consimilis ~ia Upton 255; **1532** cum signis et differenciis in eisdem sigillis sculpi consuetis *KRMem* 311 *rec. Pasch.* r. 3.

5 distinct kind or category. **b** section (of book). **c** (math.) column in decimal notation. **d** (mus.) mode (of antiphon).

'animam viventem' .. dividit [sc. Deus] in iij speciales ~ias, jumentorum viz., reptilium, et bestiarum Gros. *Hexaem.* VII 2; de aquis et ejus (*sic*) ~iis et ornatu, sc. de piscibus Bart. Angl. *proem.* **b** Albumazar .. 6 majoris introductorii, ~ia prima, dicit .. Bradw. *CD* 73a. **c** ferunt unitatem in prima ~ia, denarium in secunda, centenarium in tertia, millenarium in quarta, sic in infinitum his tribus ultimis progressione facta, principium possidere. .. verbi gratia, prima [figura] in prima ~ia unitatem, secunda binarium, sic in ordine naturali ultima novenarium significat; et idem in ceteris fiat Adel. *Alch.* 18. **d** principalis rector chori ab initio in vesperis antiphonam super psalmum et †psalmum intonat [v. l. psalmi intonationem] et ~iam a cantore querat, et in quo gradu debeat incipi *Offic. Sal.* 23; ad secundam ~iam primi toni pertinet una sola variacio *Tonale Sal.* iii.

differentialis

1 illustrative of difference (between homonyms); *cf.* Serlo Wilt. *Poem.* 2 (*versus de differentia*).

clericos qui de elemosina pascuntur .. debet .. elemosinarius .. sub virga tenere .., ut sciant .. versus ~es cordetenus repetere *Obs. Barnwell* 174.

2 (log.) differential, distinguished by specific difference.

per idem, si genus posset plures formas ~es vel specificas suscipere, ipsum de tanto esset vacuum, quia formis sibi possibilibus semiplenum Wycl. *Dom. Div.* 45.

differentiare, to differentiate, distinguish.

ignis clarificat spiritus alienos et facit proporciones, ad colores juvans ut sue †speciei [? l. species] cum †irradicacione [l. irradiacione] luminis extranei per medium dyafanum sensibiliter †~iuntur [? l. ~ientur] Wycl. *Log.* III 84.

1 differre v. 1 deferre.

2 differre [CL]

1 to disperse. **b** (pass.) to be 'carried away', distraught, misguided.

~t, dispergit *GlC* D 235 (cf. ib. D 258: †dilotis [l. dilatis], *todældum*); ~t, i. .. dividit *GlH* D 446 (cf. ib. D 500: dilatis, divisis). **b** si quis minister altaris hominem occidat aut in aliis (vel malis) actibus supra modum ~atur [AS: *to swyðe manweorc gewyrce*], ordine .. privetur (*Quad.*) *GAS* 341 (= *Cons. Cnuti* ib.: aliud criminale peccatum pat[ra]verit).

2 to pass, spend (time).

tribuat vobis Dominus dona perennia, ut post tempora feliciter dilata percipiatis gaudia sempiterna Egb. *Pont.* 72.

3 to defer, delay, put off; **b** (w. *de*); **c** (w. inf.); **d** (w. *quin*); **e** (w. pers. obj.); **f** (absol.).

diu .. conversationis gratiam distuli *V. Greg.* p. 75; qui .. ~re tempus paenitentiae .. timerent Bede *HE* V 13 (cf. ib. 14: ad agendam et non ~endam scelerum suorum paenitudinem); distulit, i. moram fecit, tardavit .., *ylde, elcode GlH* D 715; thesaurus assumendus .. in noctem ~tur Gosc. *Transl. Aug.* 36d; festivitas in crastinum ~atur Lanfr. *Const.* 91; sit inde judicium an in presenti finiendum an ad terminum ~endum sit (*Leg. Hen.* 61. 18b) *GAS* 582; Pull. *Sent.* 844b (v. catechizare b); **1168** ut placitum .. ~atur usque ad Scaccarium *Pipe* 197; **s1170** (v. dies 11a); sepe nimirum quod ~tur aufertur Gir. *GE* I 13; **1199** ne assisa posset deferri *CurR RC* I 384; **1252** redditum suum .. tribuant et non ulterius deferant *BBC* (*Weymouth*) 57; **1377** ne .. via concordie .. diucius deferatur *FormOx* 381. **b** **1224** quod deferatis ei de regardo faciendo .. usque in tres annos *Cl* 648b. **c** nostram commonitionem non distulimus conferre Bede *HE* II 11; quod enim gratis excepimus, gratis impendere non ~amus O. Cant. *Const.* 3; qui ~t in futuram, et forsitan non futuram, aetatem vitam suam corrigere Anselm (*Ep.* 101) III 234; [signum] dare non distulit G. Mon. I 9; rex audire sitit, hic differt dicere, causam Walt. Angl. *Fab.* 58. 17; **1303** vos rogamus quatinus usque ad festum S. Petri .. ad execuciones .. procedere deferatis (*Lit. Episc. Lond.*) *Chr. Rams.* app. 381; **1326** vicarium .. instituere .. non curastis, quinpocius recusastis seu plus debito detulistis *Lit. Cant.* I 177. **d** nec distulit .. quin continuo polliceretur .. se secuturum doctrinam illius Bede *HE* II 12; *Ib.* V 10 (v. concipere 3d). **e** te fugit hoc quod amas? tu discis Tantalus esse? / non vis differri; facis hoc properando necesse Nig. *Paul.* 48v. 412; **1397** parochiani .. dilati sunt usque ad diem Dominicam proxime futuram (*Vis. Heref.*) *EHR* XLIV 281. **f** qua excusante se propter visionum incertas varietates .. distulisse, .. ait ille .. Ad. Eyns. *Visio* 23.

4 to lay aside, abandon. **b** (w. *ab*) to refrain (from), abstain.

s1295 ipse ad tempus iram ~ens usque Scociam properavit *Flor. Hist.* III 96; inierunt tractatum cum rege ut, si ~re dignaretur assultum et parceret plagis premencium lapidum, ei redderent villam *G. Hen. V* 8. **b** Cassibalan .. ab obsidione distulit *Eul. Hist.* II 254 (= G. Mon. IV 9: deseruit obsidionem); **1388** ab illo tempore usque in annum .. Ed. III .. regis .. primum a quocumque exennio pissium .. omnino destulerunt *IMisc* 239/2 r. 2.

5 to differ; **b** (w. *ab*). **c** (impers. w. *inter*) there is a difference. **d** (pr. ppl.) different. **e** (pr. ppl. as sb., gram.) ? exception. **f** (compar.) more excellent.

quomodo virginitas, castitas, jugalitas .. separatim ~ant Aldh. *VirgP* 19; Pater et Filius non ~ant in unitate deitatis Anselm (*Proc. Sp.* 9) II 202; ~unt sic iste definitiones: prima respicit ad rem hujus nominis 'persona'; secunda ad rationem nominis Hales *Sent.* I 226; isti duo ~unt specie Duns *Ord.* III 21. **b** 'lavo' .. ~t a 'labo', quod est 'nuto' Aldh. *PR* 113; sex sunt differentiae Patris et Filii et Spiritus Sancti. .. harum .. singulus quisque habet unam propriam qua ~t ab aliis duobus Anselm (*Proc. Sp.* 16) II 216; ~t ab equivocatione indistinctio, quod illa ex diversorum est eadem nominatione, hec ex unius indistincte variata Balsh. *AD* 63; Siccav. *PN* 106 (v. dissimilitudo a); ~unt cause per se .. ordinate a causis per accidens .. ordinatis in tribus Duns *Ord.* II 154. **c** plurimum ~t inter .. Fariseorum traditiones et .. sacrae scripturae diffinitionem Aldh. *VirgP* 54. **d** deferentes, desimiles *GlC* D 142; Filius est non ~ens essentia de Patris essentia Anselm (*Mon.* 45) I 62; si rerum solo numero ~entium substantialem similitudinem quis mente pertractet, speciem tenet J. Sal. *Pol.* 439a; prima divisio unius comparati ad aliud est per conveniens et ~ens. ~ens autem est aut in substantia aut in quantitate vel qualitate vel situ Hales *Sent.* I 227. **e** si penultima [sillaba] fuerit corepta naturaliter, ultima corepta aut producta, antepenultima est acuenda, exceptis barbaris et apocopatis et ~entibus et diccionibus prepositis *Ps.*-Gros. *Gram.* 34. **f** 'angelis' .., volens probare ~entius prae angelis Christum habere nomen Lanfr. *Comment. Paul* (*Heb.* ii 5) 379.

6 (pass.) to be distinguished, differ.

ei nomen Latinum, ut 'Melsa' Latine diceretur, commutans imponebat, eo quod a civitate Gallie dicta 'Meldis' nomine tenus ~retur *Meaux* I 78.

differte [cf. CL differtus], in close formation.

sagittariis in circuitu ~issime ordinatis *G. Steph.* II 94.

diffesantia v. defesantia.

diffessio [cf. diffiteri], denial, refusal.

1193 J. clericus debet viij s. quia fecit contra defessionem justic[iariorum] *Pipe* 111; **1432** absque nostra licencia .., qui dominus tue congregacionis, ut aliarum, absque defessione aliquali esse comprobamur *FormOx* 439.

diffibulare [CL], to unclasp (fig.). **b** to loosen, release, dissolve.

1430 in amicicie clamide, quam locorum distancia ~at

Reg. Whet. II app. 453. **b** senos diffibulat urbem / murus in egressus J. Exon. *BT* V 131; sacra ligabo / federa, que nulla caveas diffibulet etas Hanv. IX 296 p. 386; dicamus 'nebulas diffibulat aer'; hoc enim verbum '~at' proprie de homine [dicitur] . ., quia, quando removet a se pallium, †dicamus [? l. dicimus] quod ~at pallium; similiter et de aere dicimus quod '~at nebulas' Vinsauf *AV* II 3. 13 (cf. *Id. PN* 545); nigra supercilii se linea curvat in arcum, / non patiens errare pilos, arcusque gemellos / alba superfusi diffibulat area lactis H. Avr. *Hugh* 177; quo sol vernus nubes diffibulat J. Howd. *Ph.* 875; donec . . serenior aura tante perturbacionis nebulas ~aret J. Glast. 190.

difficax, difficult.

harde, ~ax, deficilis *CathA*.

difficere v. deficere, diffacere.

difficile [CL], w. difficulty.

~e, *wearnwislice GlC* D 291; aegre, ~e *Gl. Leid.* 42. 19; ~e, *earfoplice GlM* 60. 19; haec questio non ~e solvitur Anselm (*Mon.* 61) I 71; Ailr. *Serm.* 411b (v. 2 dediscere); cum illa armatura . . ~e descenditur, ~ius ascenditur, ~lime cum opus est pedibus itur Gir. *EH* II 38; quanto est universalior, tanto ~ius potest intellectus diu sistere in tali conceptu Duns *Ord.* III 118; *Alph.* 138 (v. contegere a).

difficilis [CL]

1 difficult. **b** (as sb. n. w. *ex* or *de*) w. difficulty.

671 ~lima rerum argumenta . . repperi Aldh. *Ep.* 1; liquet quod artissima sit violentia et ~lima rerum condicio ut homo . ., spretis naturae legibus, . . angelicae castitatis comes existere cogatur *Id. VirgP* 18; **705** in adversis et in ~ibus rerum eventibus Wealdhere *Ep.* 22; **8..** dificilia, *earfoðu WW*; ~iore, i. graviore, *earfeðran GlH* D 468; primum . . unde hujusmodi comperire ~e, deinde qualiter facile, ostendemus Balsh. *AD* 49 (cf. ib. 55: sine ~i labore); ut dictu ~limum sit quantis laboribus . . maximam diei partem protraxerint Osb. Bawdsey clxxvi; ~limum est ea ex creaturis concludere Duns *Ord.* III 41; **1342** unum portiforium . . cujus litera est nimis tenuis et ~is ad legendum (*Vis. Totnes*) *EHR* XXVI 120; **1405** (v. 1 artare 2b). **b** ex ~i curatur Gad. 81. 1 (v. dislocare 1a); de ~iori Wycl. *Act.* 71 (v. difficultare a); **1382** funis triplex de ~i rumpitur *Conc.* III 172; *Ps.*-Elmh. *Hen.V* 25 (v. 1 discere 2c); **s1455** [dux] magis incaluit in animo magisque de ~i remittere sibi volebat *Reg. Whet.* I 160; vitare debetis . . commestionem . . omnium dedifficili digestibilium Kymer 3.

2 (of persons) obstructive, reluctant.

discolis i. ~is, discordator, discors contrarius, *wiþercora ungeþwæra GlH* D 587; **1312** in solucionibus vj^c^ . . librarum . . reddidistis vos ~es *RGasc* IV 744; mirum est quod te reddis in hoc ~em Trevet *Troades* 21; **1411** quia religiosi reddunt se deficiles in solucionibus suis . ., deponatur summa solida in cista (*Test.*) *Reg. Durh.* I 158; **s1435** satis ~em reddebat se cancellarius . . ad scribendum pro capcione corporis Amund. II 81.

difficilitas, difficulty.

difficultas, i. ~as, dubietas, labor *GlH* D 454; accepi quod . . sermonum ~as eorum animos sepe perturbat Ric. Armagh *Serm.* 31; **1440** ex causa generalitatis et obscuritatis, ~atis et difficultatis verborum et terminorum predictorum (*Ch. Regis*) Amund. II 224 (cf. *Reg. Whet.* I 29).

difficilius, ~illime v. difficile.

difficiliter [CL], w. difficulty.

difficulter, i. tarde, ~iter *GlH* D 453.

difficultare, to make difficult, obstruct. **b** to raise objections, quibble; **c** (w. indir. qu.).

sic alia agencia possunt ~ari quantum ad acciones quas possunt facere, sic quod una vice de difficiliori possunt facere quam alia Wycl. *Act.* 71; lex scripture . ., que non ~atur sed facilitatur ex multitudine servorum *Id. Ver.* II 150; ritus adjecti secundum tradiciones humanas . . peccatum sapiunt, cum Dei legem ~ant et impediunt cursum sermonis sui *Id. Sim.* 51; **1412** [quod] papa nec angelus de celo habet potestatem ~andi media que Christus instituit viatoribus ad beatitudinem promerendam (*Haereses J. Wycl.* 28) *Conc.* III 341a. **b** hinc volo extraneare . . diffiniendo quod hoc sacramentum sit panis materialis, substancia panis, vel quocumque alio nomine nominatur quo supra fidem scripture ecclesia ~are poterit Wycl. *Conf.* 508. **c** quomodo panis ille potuit a Christo frangi ~ant increduli Netter *DAF* II 69.

difficultas [CL]

1 difficulty: **a** (of task or action); **b** (of situation or sim.); **c** (intellectual or log.); **d** (as literary device).

a victus operis ~ate Aldh. *Met.* 10; dicimus nos non posse aliquid, non quia nobis est impossibile, sed quia illud sine ~ate non possumus. haec autem ~as non perimit voluntatis libertatem Anselm (*Lib. Arb.* 1) I 218; ~as anhelitus Gad. 46. 2; ~as hanelandi *SB* 12; **1421** cum magna ~ate et duritate (*R. Gildh. K's Lynn*) *EHR* XLII 586 (cf. camera 4b). **b** **c1105** tota ~as causae inter regem et me . . in hoc . . videtur consistere Anselm (*Ep.* 389) V 333; **s1140** ~as monete tanta erat ut interdum ex x . . s. vix xij d. reciperentur W. Malm. *HN* 483; loca . . hostibus invia reddens, naturalem ~atem industria plurimum et arte munivit Gir. *EH* I 5. **c** superet attentionis industria ~atem; afferat superata ~as propositi utilitatem Balsh. *AD* 29; videtur remanere ~as argumentorum Averrois Duns *Ord.* II 329 (cf. ib. IV 89: in ista questione videntur due ~ates). **d** septem sunt que ~atem operantur ornatam. primum est ponere significans pro significato Vinsauf *AV* II 3. 4.

2 obstruction, obstructiveness.

671 quia . . obstaculis retardati . . illud perficere nequivimus, idcirco ~atis veniam . . impendite Aldh. *Ep.* 1; facta ~ate tumulandi Bede *HE* IV 11; Ludovicus . ., rempublicam regere disponens nonnullas . . tam a liberis quam a regni tyrannis ~ates patiebatur R. Niger *Chr. II* 151; **1216** sine dilacione et ~ate aliqua . . medietatem eidem G. integre habere faciatis *Cl* 8; ut . . fratris W. . . copia secundum presentiam personalem . . sine ~atis gravamine exhibeatur . . regine Ad. Marsh *Ep.* 185; **s1381** cui [Carolo] sine ~ate populus regionis illius [sc. Neapolis], tanquam domino suo, se tradidit *V. Ric. II* 34.

3 burdensome custom.

a716 (11c) ab omnibus ~atibus secularium servitutis . . liberas (*sic*) eos esse . . statuimus *CS* 91; **805** [eandem terram] ab universis terrenis ~atibus ac tributis et ab omni opere puplico aedificiorum perpetualiter liberam esse concedimus *CS* 321; **822** hanc . . terram libero . . ab omnibus laboribus, operibus, et oneribus sive ~atibus *CS* 370; **836** praedicta loca . . liberabo . . a ~ate illa quam nos Saxonice *faestingmenn* dicimus *CS* 416; **c1080** praecipio ut terrae et homines sint ab omni opere castelli liberi et ab omnibus placitis, querelis et ~atibus *Regesta* p. 124.

difficultatio, obstruction, objection.

ipsam privatam religionem necessario consequitur personarum accepcio, ad observanciam consiliorum Cristi ~o et tradicionum infundabilium oneracio Wycl. *Blasph.* 247.

difficulter [CL], w. difficulty.

[frater infirmus ad locum] ~er a ministro deductus *V. Cuthb.* IV 16; cum hoc tarde et ~er impetraremus Bede *HE* V 4; ~er, tarde *GlC* D 231; **9..** ~er, *earfoplice WW*; qui anteacte vite infamia sorduit, is ~er promovetur Pull. *Sent.* 927b; naturalibus existentibus integris, [homo] hoc [sc. vitare peccatum] potuit faciliter, in natura vero lapsa ~er R. Marston *QD* 200; Wycl. *Dom. Div.* 85 (v. elongatio 4b).

diffidamentum [cf. OF *desfiement*], 'defiance', renunciation of amity, aggression.

1360 promittimus . . burgensibus . . Rupelle [*Gasc*] . . quod (*sic*), si contingat eorum aliquem deffidari vel aliter per viam facti gravari . ., ipsos . ., prout dominus fideles suos subditos tenetur, defendere . . et deffyamentum seu dampnum quod ipsis infligetur . . capere et ad finem debitum . . ducere pro eisdem (*TreatyR* 41 m. 4) *Foed.* VI 218a.

diffidare, ~iare, ~ere [cf. OF *desfier*, CL fidere], to 'defy', renounce fealty to or amity with (as preliminary to rebellion or war). **b** (w. *ab*) to exclude by 'defiance'. **c** (sts. w. *ad*) to challenge (to battle). *Cf. diffiduciare.*

s1138 fama . . volitabat quod comes Gloecestre . . in proximo partes sororis foret adjuturus, rege tantum modo ante ~iato W. Malm. *HN* 467 (cf. ib.: regi more majorum amicitiam et fidem interdixit, homagio etiam abdicato); **c1150** non potest . . impedire corpus comitis Leecestrie, nisi eum defidaverit xv dies ante (*Conventio*) *Eng. Feudalism* 287; **s1188** rex . . Francorum, ferens indigne quod comes Pictavorum Ricardus regnum suum hostiliter impugnaverat, eo non ~ato nec certiorato Diceto *YH* II 55; **s1195** rex Francie calumniatur te de fide lesa . . quia . . fidem dedisti quod venires hodie ad colloquium . . et non venisti; et ideo te defidat R. Howd. III 304; **1201** comes Augi nos defidavit . . non ob culpam nostram †et [l. set] ob culpam suam et superbiam *Pat* 2a; **s1213** ipsum ~ens (v. curia 3a); **s1215** barones Anglie regem suum ~ant et ei homagia sua resignant Coggesh. *Chr.* 112b (cf. Gerv. Cant. *GR Cont.* 109: facta est discordia . . inter J. regem . . et barones . ., ita quod, illis adinvicem ~atis, guerra mota est); **s1233** rex . . marescallum ~avit . . et . . jussit contra eum arma movere Wend. III 55 (cf. ib. 65: quod ego essem extra homagium suum et ~atus ab eo; = M. Par. *Maj.* III 258: diffiduciatus); **1264** cum . . appareat manifeste quod fidelitatem nostram nobis non observatis . ., eo quod . . fideles nostros . . pro posse vestro gravare proponitis . ., de vestra fidelitate non curamus nec amore, et eorum inimicos ~amus (*Lit. Regis*) Rish. 23 (cf. diffiduciatio); **1296** quia . . ~avimus dominum nostrum regem Anglie et posuimus nos extra fidem et homagium suum (*Lit. J. Regis Scotiae*) Trevet *Ann.* 348 (= *Anglo-Scot. Rel.* 73: *defier nostre seignor*; v. et. dirimere 1b); **s1320** quilibet istorum Hugonem [Despenser] ~at, quia contra singulos . . deliquerat *V. Ed. II* 255; **1345** Philippum ut violatorem . . treugarum . . et regni nostri fraude occupatorem injustum . . ~amus (*Lit. Regis*) Ad. Mur. *Chr.* 168; **1360** deffidari (v. diffidamentum); **s1399** sibi . . cujuscunque obediencie juramentum et fidelitatem totaliter reddiderunt, ipsum ~endo nec pro rege . . de cetero eundem habituri Ad. Usk 32; *to breke conande*, depacisci, ~are *CathA*. **b** **1220** comes [Marchie] . . nos ab omnibus feodis suis ~avit (*Lit. Majoris et Communie de Niort*, *AncC* IV 110) *RL* I 140; **s1296** rex Scocie literas minatorias regi Anglie transmisit, ipsum . . ab omni servicio, fidelitate et homagio ~endo *Eul. Hist.* III 160. **c** **s1264** R. comes Cornubie . ., qui ante paucos dies ~arat barones ad bellum, . . perterritus fugit in molendinum *Chr. Melrose* 196; Colibrandus ~ebat eum [Gydonem de Warwyk]; Gydo vero percussit Colibrandum de una magna lancea Knighton I 26.

diffidatio [cf. fidatio], 'defiance', renunciation of fealty or amity. *Cf. diffiduciatio.*

s1233 aperte didici quod [rex] nullam pacem voluit mihi [comiti marescallo] observare. . . unde homo suus non fui, sed ab ipsius homagio per ipsum absolutus cum ad primam ~onem redirem Wend. III 66; **1264** ex litteris vestris . . accepimus nos esse diffidatos a vobis, licet hujusmodi verbalis ~o satis fuerit in nos realiter ante manu hostili . . probata (*Lit. Ric. Regis Romanorum*) Rish. 24; **1301** per litteras . . regis [Scocie] verba offensionum exprimentes et . . verba ~onis continentes (*Lit. Regis Angliae*) *Ib.* 206 (= *Ann. Lond.* 119: per verba effectum diffidencie exprimencia); **1345** si nobis qui . . nutrire pacem debemus inter cunctos Christicolas . ., scribi debuit ~o supradicta (*Lit. Papae ad Regem Angliae*) Ad. Mur. *Chr.* 186.

diffidens v. defendere, diffidere.

1 diffidentia [CL]

1 a diffidence (lack of self-confidence), misgiving. **b** mistrust.

a ~ia, disperantia, *ortreownes GlH* D 467; nobiles . . ausus nihil eque impedit ut ~ia; omnes appetendi conatus perit ex desperatione consequendi Gir. *TH intr.* p. 5; **s1254** in abissum desperationis, ~ie et desolationis Franci precipitati . . significabant . . regi Francorum . . ut . . redire properaret M. Par. *Maj.* V 433. **b** **1253** (v. cataclysmus b); timor . . humanus junctus ~ie, qua unus Christianus diffideret de alio Ockham *Dial.* 735; divine pietatis ~ia R. Bury *Phil.* 6. 92 (v. climax 1b).

2 lack of (religious) faith, 'disobedience' (*cf. Eph.* ii 2, v 6).

qui . . a filiis discordiae, superbiae, ~iae . . migrat ad filios pacis Lanfr. *Ep.* 60. 550a; **1177** ipse iniquus, qui misterium jam operatur iniquitatis in filios ~ie (*Lit. Comitis Tolosae*) Gerv. Cant. *Chr.* 270; ut universitas hominum nullam sciret in eo [Constantino] de fide Christi †dissidenciam [? l. diffidenciam] *Eul. Hist. Cont.* I 338.

2 diffidentia [cf. OF *desfiance*], 'defiance', renunciation of fealty or amity.

s1301 *Ann. Lond.* 119 (v. diffidatio); **1389** litteras suas ~ie omnibus subditis nostris apud Dantz existentibus despectuose mandavit guerrarum turbinem comminantes *Dip. Corr. Ric. II* 69; **s1401** Scoti . . cum Anglicis . . treugam tractare detestantes, ~iam et guerram Anglicis decreverant . . fore inducendae Ad. Usk 71.

3 diffidentia v. 2 dissidentia. **1 diffidere** v. diffidare.

2 diffidere [CL], to be mistrustful, despair (of), lack confidence (in); **b** (trans.). **c** to lack (religious) faith. **d** (w. acc. & inf. or compl.) to doubt. **e** to suspect.

armis diffisus Aldh. *VirgV* 2080; defisus, †desperavit [? l. desperans] *GlC* D 197; in suis consiliis ~ens *Ep. Bonif.* 14 (v. confidere 1d); langor eum vite †diffigere [? l. diffidere] coegit Gosc. *Wulsin* 24; ut nullus vestrum de premio capiendi celi ~at Osb. *V. Dunst.* 43; sit confessio nostra . . fidelis, ne de indulgentia ~amus Ad. Scot *TT* 772d; de proprio robore ~it et de superno . . adjutorio confidit *Id. Serm.* 381b; non tua diffidat [*gl.*: i.e. desperet] mens de bonitate superna D. Bec. 30; Ockham *Dial.* 735 (v. 1 diffidentia 1b); ~endo de Dei auxilio Paul. Angl. *ASP* 1554. **b** tanto remedium super his salutare ~imus quanto semper gravioribus graviora succedere circumspicimus (*Quad., Dedic.*) *GAS* 532. **c** inter credentes, qui Christum corde fatentur, / et diffidentes, qui Christum fraude refutant Aldh. *VirgV* 1544; ~it, i. . . non credet *GlH* D 455. **d** nec ~endum est nostra etiam aetate fieri potuisse quod . . aliquoties factum . . historiae narrant Bede *HE* IV 17; †c700 ut . . Bedam . . ad nostrae mediocritatis conspectum non moreris dirigere, quem . . non ~as propere ad te redire (? *Lit. Papae*) W. Malm. *GR* I 58; **1082** a summo retributore sibi nequaquam ~imus remunerari *Regesta* p. 122; quod per Sanctum non difido factum esse Spiritum Hil. Ronce. 1. 40. **e** has sequentes paginulas . . fidelium attestatione purgabo, si qua propria temeritate effigiata insignia in hiis me conseruisse ~as B. *V. Dunst.* 1.

diffidiare v. diffidare.

diffiduciare [cf. CL fiduciare], (w. pers. obj.) to 'defy', renounce fealty to or amity with. **b** (p. ppl.) declared in 'defiance'. *Cf. diffidare.*

ille quem reducere non potuit ~iatum dimisit et debitam domino . . suo reverentiam non exhibuit W. Cant. *V. Thom.* I 33; *Ib.* II 37 (v. deprehendere 3c); **s1188** destinatur ab imperatore nuncius cum litteris . . ad Salahadinum, ut vel Christianorum universitati . . satisfaciat in plenum vel ~iatus se preparet ad congressum *Itin. Ric.* I 18; **1202** sciatis vic[ecomitem] Toarc' [*Thouars, Poitou*], culpa sua nos ~iasse; et ideo vobis mandamus quatinus fidelitatem vestram juretis coram H. . . et J. . ., quia decetero non eritis in manu ipsius vic. . . set in manu nostra eritis *Pat* 19a;

s**1215** [barones] regem ~iantes per internuncios et homi-nia sua reddentes W. COVENTR. II 219; s**1233** M. PAR. *Maj.* III 258 (v. diffidare a); s**1378** [cardinales] ad ~iandum .. papam hanc epistolam .. transmiserunt WALS. *HA* I 382; s**1381** nunciaverunt .. ad ~iandum abbatem faldas quas fecerat .. esse frangendas ipsa nocte *G. S. Alb.* III 301. **b** GIR. *PI* III 16 (v. 1 despicari 2).

diffiduciatio, 'defiance'. *Cf. diffidatio.*

s**1188** quia imperialis majestas neminem citra ~onem impetit, hostibus suis bella semper indicit *Itin. Ric.* I 18 (cf. diffiduciare a); in minas et ~onem superbe nimis proprumpentem *V. II Off.* 2; s**1264** rex ad bellum .. inardescit, rescribens eis hanc litteram ~onis RISH. 23 (cf. diffidare a).

diffiduciator, herald proclaiming 'defiance'.

NECKAM *NR* II 173 *gl.* (v. clarigator b).

diffigere v. 2 diffidere a, diffugere 2b. **diffigium** v. diffugium 2.

diffigurare [cf. OF *desfigurer*], to disguise. **b** to disfigure, deform.

s**1215** rex .. predis piraticis vacabat inter nautas et piscatores .., ~atus sub divo M. PAR. *Min.* II 161; s**1217** Eustachium, qui se defiguraverat, .. quem .. in sentina invenerunt latitantem .., decollaverunt *Id. Maj.* III 29; s**1387** M. atte Pole .. mutato habitu et rasa barba .. fugit Calesiam ad fratrem suum. sed ille .. nunciavit domino W. B. .. de adventu .. fratris .., asserens res .. non stare recte cum eo qui tali modo se disfigurasset *Chr. Angl.* 386; s**1388** Robertus [Tressylyan] .. disfiguraverat seipsum, fingens se pauperem debilem in tunica hispida. .. adeo disfigura-tus fuerat quod nullus eum agnovit nisi ex sola loquela KNIGHTON *Cont.* II 293; s**1392** rex Francie .. disfiguratus in sylvestrem hominem, habens strictum vestimentum resina piceque linitum WALS. *HA* II 212; s**1415** papa occulte ~atus fugit cum duce Austrie in terram suam *Chr. S. Alb.* 85. **b 1244** alii morbo fistule enormiter deturpati, alii a tumore horribili .. defigurati (*Lit. Abbatis Pontiniaci*) M. PAR. *Maj.* IV 325; s**1334** [episcopus] contulit archi-diaconatum Almarico .. nepoti suo, torto et defigurato GRAYSTANES 43.

diffigurate, in a misshapen form.

pictor .. parietibus, cortinis, fenestris vitreis ipsum [Morpheum] defiguratissime pingebat et fidissime MAP *NC* IV 6 f. 48v.

diffiguratio, disguising, tricking out.

multitudo arcium non necessariarum homini in nostra ecclesia multum peccatum nutrit in superflua curiositate et ~one [ME: *disgysing*] hominum per vestes curiosas *Concl. Loll. XII* 304.

diffindere [CL]

1 to split.

H. HUNT. *HA* VIII 14 (v. cuneus 2a); *to cleve*, scindere, findere, con-, dif- *CathA.*

2 to put off, postpone. **b** (p. ppl. *diffisus*, of time) protracted or distant (in future). *Cf. diffundere* 5a.

c**1103** videte quam periculosum sit .. in tali re †diffindere [MSS: †diffidere] correctionem ANSELM (*Ep.* 297) IV 217. **b** c**1186** si .. aliqui parrochianorum tuorum a tuo .. judicio appellaverint et tempus diffisum prefixerint (*Lit. Papae*) *Reg. Glasg.* 47.

diffini- v. defini-. **diffisus** v. diffidere, diffindere.

diffiteri [CL]

1 to deny; **b** (w. acc. & inf. or compl.); **c** (w. *quia*, or *quin*).

forsitan aliquis dicat: non ita omnes .. mali sunt. quod nec vehementer et nos ~emur GILDAS *EB* 69; deffitentur, negant .., ~eor, nego .., †deficitur, negat *GlC* D 42, 299, 309; **9..** ~emur, *we wiðsacað WW*; ne super his quisquam dubitet vel diffiteatur NIG. *Laur.* 39v. 2; primam hominis generationem ~eri non audes GIR. *TH* I 15; ut verum non ~ear AD. SCOT *QEC prol.* 801A; comparentibus plegiis in curia, aut confitentur suam plegiationem aut ~entur eam *RegiamM* III 1. 8 (= GLANV. X 5: negant); **1342** eidem C. pro una pecia panni radiati, cujus receptum clericus Gardrobe ~etur *ExchScot* 507. **b** sicut ipsum veracem esse necesse est confiteri, ita nihil quod in illis [libris] continetur verum esse potest aliquis ~eri ANSELM (*CurD* II 22) II 133; PULL. *Sent.* 725A (v. consecutive a); c**1158** [Radulfus apostata] abicit nomen infame et se .. Radulfum Barathri ~etur J. SAL. *Ep.* 75 (34); non me .. debitorem defeteor, si dicendi subesset peritia. totum me illi debeo SERLO GRAM. *Mon. Font.* 117; **1420** quos quidem articulos .. ~ebatur se predicasse .. animo defendendi eosdem *Reg. Cant.* III 160. **c 1165** non ~eor quin ecclesie .. fidem servaverim J. SAL. *Ep.* 139 (138); scimus equidem, nec possumus ~eri, quia 'vie Domini pulchre ..' [*Prov.* iii 17] P. BLOIS *Serm.* 563B.

2 a to belie, disavow. **b** to belie the name of.

a fidem, quam profitemur verbis, operibus ~emur P. BLOIS *Serm.* 627A. **b 1191** H. Coventrensem episcopum, quem sollemniter excommunicavimus, .. quia verbo et opere episcopum ~etur (*Lit. W. Legati*) *G. Ric. I* 224; P. BLOIS *Ep.* 217 (v. descire).

difflorare v. deflorare.

diffluere [CL], to flow in different directions. **b** to be dispersed. **c** to radiate outwards. **d** (of language) to flow.

videres ceras liquentes supra lapidem hac et illac excurrendo ~ere R. COLD. *Cuthb.* 45. **b** ut meminerimus facta et cogitationes nostras non in ventum ~ere [v. l. defluere], sed ad examen summi judicis cuncta servari BEDE *HE* V 13. **c** videt orbem .., cujus procreatio ~ebat a .. lucis mirabili solo BYRHT. *HR* 5; defluebant .. diversoria M. PAR. *Min.* I 127 (v. claustralis 3a). **d** J. HERD *Hist. IV Regum* 5 (v. dissolvere 3e).

2 (trans.) to distribute.

licet in casu quilibet teneatur omnia ~ere pauperibus S. LANGTON *Quaest.* f. 171v.

diffluus, hanging loose. **b** (?) loosely wrapped, untidy.

de barba illius ~um conspicit dependere pilum R. COLD. *Godr.* 249. **b** tu et tui consimiles .., qui ecclesie limina mente incomposita et cervice tumida et erecta, collo distento, turgente, jactabundo ac ~o, introire presumitis *Id. Cuthb.* 114 (cf. ib.: velud stola aurea collum undique orbicularíter circumtexerat, que ad inferiora .. productius dependebat).

diffodere v. defodere.

diffoederare [cf. CL foederare], to unknit, disunite.

[Venus] amplexum in planctus solvit, defederat urbes, / arces frangit J. EXON. *BT* II 436; [vir] suavi suadaque facundia ~erare prevalens conjunctissima GIR. *TH* III 52; inter electores ipsos schismata plerumque creantur et .. in partes varias et ad invicem discordes disgregantur penitus et ~erantur *Id. Spec.* IV 37.

difforestare [cf. forestare], to disafforest, remove (land) from forest status. *V. et. deafforestare, deforestare, disafforestare.*

1583 ~atam forestam de D. *Pat* 1234 m. 6.

difforestatio [cf. afforestatio], disafforestation. *V. et. deafforestatio, deforestatio, disafforestatio.*

1224 loquendum de xl m. de hominibus de com. Huntedon' pro ~one comitatus *KRMem* 6 r. 12; **1307** ad disforestacionem foreste de Blakemor' de novo afforestate expediendam per finem .. pro eadem deafforestacione facienda *Cart. Glast.* I 184.

difformare, to reshape (for the worse), warp. *Cf. deformare* 2a.

sicut creatura racionalis debilis, quantum est de sui natura, potest libere confirmare aut ~are se suo debili judicio racionis et sic mereri atque peccare BRADW. *CD* 527D; gracia est confirmacio; et conformiter ymaginandum est de eadem lege eterna quod homo †sit [? l. sic] premiatus non potest ~are volucionem suam ab illo quod Deus voluerit ipsum velle WYCL. *Act.* 78.

difformis, dissimilar, diverse.

duo gemelli .. sortiuntur diversitatem complexionis, ut postea .. sequantur artes diversas et occupationes ~es BACON *Maj.* I 138; [religiosus] diformem conversacioni mundane et quasi angelicum conversacione celica se ostendat J. WALEYS *V. Relig.* 11. 252; **1299** comperimus ipsum hospitale per .. habitus ex toto ~es .. a statu congruo .. eductum *Reg. Cant.* 827; ubicunque est intensio motus localis uniformis, est motus localis uniformiter ~is RIC. SWYN. *Mot.* 245; c**1358** honestum est .., quibus Deus ultra laicos in ornamentis intrinsecus tribuit prerogativam, eciam extrinsecus laicis in habitu sint ~es *StatOx* 158; WYCL. *Log.* III 193 (v. difformitas); infortunatus Tresilian, solito ~is, miro repertus est .., pocius apparens .. mendicus quam justiciarius regis FAVENT 17; **1444** (v. additio 1a).

difformitas, dissimilarity of form, variation.

quanta sit ei defectionis ~as ad desiderabilem illius hominis virtutem AD. MARSH *Ep.* 242; in curva [linea] est angulus, qui facit dispersionem [radiorum] et ~atem et repugnat unitati BACON *Maj.* I 120 (cf. ib. II 143: propter hanc ~atem in partibus aeris accidit quod una pars habet vicem speculi et alia non); lux lunaris propter sui ~atem significat statum vidualem PECKHAM *QA* 160; nulla ~as perpetuatur nisi in virtute alicujus permanentis DUNS *PW* 3 p. 43; infinita sunt quorum nullum potest esse per tempus vel instans. illud .. patet .. de talibus, 'iste motus est difformis quo ad tempus alio gradu usque ad *B*', et ita de ~ate motus WYCL. *Log.* III 193; 'justum' est denominacio absoluta respiciens conformitatem ad simpliciter per se justum; et 'injustum' contrarie dicit ~atem ad primam voluntatem *Id. Ente Praed.* 109.

difformiter, dissimilarly, at variance.

solum agens quod agit secundum libertatem voluntatis et per deliberationem potest agere ~er a parte sua BACON *Maj.* II 417; ipse [archiepiscopus] calumpniabatur factum .. archidiaconorum sede vacante; placatus tamen muneribus non ~er aliis ordinavit GRAYSTANES 10; nullus meretur nec peccat nisi libere faciendo, quantum in eo est, conformiter aut ~er voluntati divine BRADW. *CD* 642D; *Ziz.* 482 (v. disparitas).

diffortiamentum [cf. OF *desforcement*]

1 'deforcement', withholding by force. **b** (w. *recens*, Sc.) 'fresh force', recent dispossession; *cf. fortia frisca*. **c** (Sc.) obstruction of official. *V. et. diffortiatio* 1.

1188 debent j m. pro ~o terre contra assisam *Pipe* 79; **1191** debet dim. m. pro disforciamento contra assisam *Ib.* 7; **1198** consideratum est quod A. et G. .. habeant saisinam .. de terra prefata; et Robertus .. in misericordia pro deforciamento *CurR* I 33; **1236** quicunque eis [viduis] deforciaverit dotes suas .. et ipse .. postea .. recuperaverint, ipsi qui de injusto deforciamento convicti fuerint reddant .. viduis .. dampna sua (*Prov. Merton*) *StRealm* I 1; cum quis conqueritur domino regi de feudo vel terra sua quam quis ab eo detinet per deforciamentum [v. l. forciamentum] *RegiamM* I 6. 1; c**1320** nec tenens .. sit calumpniatus sicut indefendens nec amerciatus quamdiu defendat .. deforciamentum .. et jus demandantis ante exitum illorum de curia *Reg. Aberbr.* I 256. **b** placitum recentis deforciamenti tangit liberum tenementum, feodum et possessionem .., quia recens deforciacio idem est quod recens spoliacio vel recens intrusio (*Fragm. Coll.*) *APScot* I app. 358; **1459** x li. .. que pendebant a diu de uno brevi de recenti deforciamento *ExchScot* 508. **c 1349** processus .. in quo continebatur deforciamentum grave et notorium super ministros .. episcopi officia sua exequentes per eundem W. .. factum fuisse *Reg. Aberd.* I 80.

2 violation (of woman), rape.

1289 ut de .. delacione armorum, fraccione itinerum, deforciamento mulierum .. et aliis que de ascensa preposi-ture nostre Baione excipiuntur .. respondeatis *RGasc* II 355.

diffortiare [cf. OF *desforcier*]

1 a to deny (justice or jurisdiction). **b** to 'deforce', withhold or appropriate (land, payment *etc.*) wrongfully. **c** to dispossess. **d** (pr. ppl. as sb.) 'deforciant', party (allegedly) withholding land *etc.*, (usu. defendant in action leading to final concord); *v. et. diffortiator* 1. **e** (p. ppl.) or (?) *f. l.*

a si quis Dei rectitudines aliquas ~iat [AS: *forwyrne*] (*Quad.*) *GAS* 133; ne quisquam rectum disfortiet alicui [AS: *dæt nan man oðrum ryhtes ne wyrne*] (*Ib.*) *Ib.* 143; (*Leg. Hen.*) *Ib.* 566 (v. concriminatio); si forte aliquis disfortiaret domino regi rectitudinem suam, archiepiscopi, episcopi, et archidiaconi debent justiciare, ut domino regi satisfaciat *Const. Clar.* 13 (cf. 3a infra). **b 1166** comes Gloucestrie .. debet servitium ij militum, quod fecit usque ad extremum exercitum Wallie, sed postea deforciavit *RBExch* 188 (= *BBExch* 51: difforciavit); c**1187** ita quod .. viridarii comitis .. hanc consuetudinem nullo modo ~iare possint vel impedire *Act. Hen. II* II 294; de x carrucatis terre .. quas clamat tenere de te per liberum servicium .., quas Rodbertus .. ei deforciat (*Breve de Recto*) GLANV. XII 3; **1188** de dim. m. de Willelmo et Burnello, quia disforciaverunt Alizie jus suum *Pipe* 97; **1196** abbas .. conqueritur quod A. Dacus ei deforciat presentacionem super ecclesiam de W. *CurR* I 19; **1221** deforciavit ei fenum ad valenciam x s. de quodam prato quod tenuit de eo ad firmam *PlCrGlouc* 25; **1236** (v. diffortiamentum 1a); satis .. ~eat qui possessorem uti seisina non permiserit omnino vel minus commode impediat presentando, appellando, impetrando BRACTON 238; **1275** dicta averia eisdem garcionibus deforciaverunt *Hund.* I 164b; dominus W. .. opturat et deforciat quamdam viam communem hominibus ped[itibus] per medium boscum suum *Ib.* 201a; **1279** quas piscarias dominus J. .. eidem abbati vi et potestate deforciavit *Ib.* II 656a; **1342** nihil hic de warda et maritagio heredis Godfredi .. et Isabelle sponse sue racione dicte sponse, quia ~iantur per eundem G. *ExchScot* 504. **c** s**1296** posuimus nos extra fidem et homagium suum [sc. regis Anglie], stabilientes gentes armatas .. ad defendendam terram contra eum et deforciandum eum de feodo suo (*Lit. J. Regis Scotiae*) TREVET *Ann.* 349 (= *Anglo-Scot. Rel.* 74: *por son fili deforcer*; *Foed.* II 719a: ad feodum suum deforciandum); *APScot* I 357 (v. diffortiatio 1c); **1406** queritur quod predictus J. ei (*sic*) deforciat de uno mesuagio *CourtR Banstead.* **d 1200** loquela inter Y. viduam et Ricardum .. ~iantes *CurR* I 192; **1220** finalis concordia .. inter P. thesaurarium .. S. Pauli .. querentem et Anselmum .. deforciantem .., unde idem thesaurarius questus fuit quod idem A. .. deforciabat ei servicium .. terre .., sc. v s. per annum *E. Ch. S. Paul.* 155; **1227** Theobaldus .. attornavit Robertum .. et Henricum .. contra Willelmum .. et multos alios deforciantes de consuetudine etc. ad molendinum suum *Cl* 87; **1236** (v. diffortiator); **1239** contentio .. inter probos homines nostros de M. querentes et probos homines de Suhampton' deforciantes de tellonio *BBC* (*Marlborough*) 257; **1267** finalis concordia .. inter Radulfum P. querentem et W. abbatem .. deforciantem de advocacione tercie partis ecclesie de C. *Reg. S. Thom. Dublin* 117; *APScot* I 357 (v. diffortiatio 1c); **1488** finalis concordia .. inter Morganum .. et Philippum .. querentes et Thomam .. et Johannam uxorem ejus deforcientes (*sic*) de manerio de C. K. *Cart. Glam.* 1739. **e** †**1263** (? **1243**) abbas de †Derbia [l. Derl'] conquestus est †et [? l. de] A. de F. †deforciatus [? l. difforciante] de placito cujusdam chimini *MonA* VI 360a (cf. *Cart. Darley* 553, 559).

2 to defend, maintain (accused person) by force.

si [culpabilis] aliquis hominum sit qui omnino populo sit incredibilis, .. prepositus regis .. mittat eum sub plegio ut ad rectum perducatur. .. si quis eum ~iet [AS: *hine forenne forstande*], sint ambo unius recti digni (*Quad.*) *GAS* 221.

3 to 'deforce', obstruct, prevent (esp. an official): **a** (w. inf.); **b** (w. *quod non* or sim.); **c** (w. obj. only).

a si quisquam de proceribus regni defortiaverit archiepiscopo vel episcopo vel archidiacono de se vel de suis justitiam exhibere, dominus rex debet justitiare *Const. Clar.* 13 (cf. 1a supra). **b** **1220** deforciaverunt ei quod preceptum domini regis facere non potuit *CurR* IX 110; **1221** burgenses de B. queruntur quod burgenses Salopie .. contra libertatem suam deforciant eis quod non possunt in villa de S. emere coria recencia .. sicut solent *SelPlCrown* 113; **1241** deforciavit ne vic. possit distringere (v. communa 5b); **a1242** juravit .. quod tenementum .. non includet versus se nec ~iabit quod non sit S. Paulo et vicario de H. distringibile *E. Ch. S. Paul.* 253; **1269** serviens de C. deforciat tenentes domini quod non possint piscari in Charwelle *CBaron* 72; **1293** deforciat communem populum civitatis N., ita quod non possint defalcare quandam insulam .. et herbas ibidem coligere *Leet Norw.* 45. **c** **1468** de amerciamento in quo adjudicatus erat .. ex eo quod deforciavit serjandum *ExchScot* 565.

4 to violate, rape (a woman).

1242 Matilda, que appellavit Rogerum .. de rapo, non venit; .. et convictum est .. quod deforciavit eam *AssizeR Durh* 20; **1309** rectatus est de eo quod rapuit uxorem Guillelmi M. et eam deforciavit contra pacem et coronam domini regis *S. Jers.* XVIII 175.

5 (?) to enforce.

a1350 est .. advertendum statuta .. consciencias magistrorum .. ea .. jurancium sic ligare ut nullis .. impune liceat ea scienter transgredi [*gl.* (? **14**..): de statutis magistrorum deforciandis] *StatOx* 18 & *n.*

diffortiatio

1 **a** denial (of justice). **b** 'deforcement', withholding by force. **c** (w. *recens*, Sc.) 'fresh force'. *V. et. diffortiamentum* 1.

a sepe ex i[n]scitia placitantium cause transeunt in jus aliorum .. ~one recti, miscravatione .., tarditate (*Leg. Hen.* 22. 1) *GAS* 561. **b** **1188** Reginaldus .. r. c. de c s. pro disforciatione terre contra assisam *Pipe* 192. **c** statuit Robertus rex primus super deforciacione recenti in burgo quod, si aliquis conqueratur .. quod injuste deforciatur de tali terra .. vel tali annuo reddditu, deforcians citabitur .. incontinenti quod compareat .. parti conquerenti responsurus (*Fragm. Coll.*) *APScot* I 357; *Ib.* 358 (v. diffortiamentum 1b).

2 (?) (goods seized in) distraint.

1247 facere debent omnia attachiamenta et omnes summoniciones et omnes deforciaciones que accidunt in burgo *BBC* (*Farnham*) 173; **1279** quod quilibet justiciarius, vicecomes vel ballivus nos et heredes .. nostros distringere possint per bona nostra mobilia et immobilia .. et ~onem tenere quousque dicto J. et heredibus .. suis plenarie fuerit satisfactum *Ambrosden* I 414.

diffortiator [cf. OF *desforceor*]

1 'deforcer', 'deforciant'. *V. et. diffortiare* 1d.

1199 habeat brevia super deforcitores *CurR RC* II 38; **1205** inter quem deforciatorem et R. .. petentem assisa ultime presentationis .. summonita est *CurR* III 352; **1230** ad assisam mortis antecessoris capiendam quam J. filia Walteri .. habet aramiare versus quosdam deforciatores de terra in Th. *Cl* 446; **1236** et nichilominus ipsi deforciatores sint in misericordia regis (*Prov. Merton*) *StRealm* I 1 (= *Cl* 337: deforciantes; cf. diffortiamentum 1a); jacent duo [essonia] de servitiis et consuetudinibus postquam deforciator responderit BRACTON 347; **1267** in placito .. communi de custodiis, si ad magnam districcionem non venerint deforciantes, tunc bis vel ter iteretur breve .., nisi prius inventus fuerit deforciator (*Marlb.* 7) *StRealm* I 21; [assisa] nove disseisine .. inter Martinum .. petentem et .. priorem deforciatorem de uno mesuagio *State Tri. Ed. I* 62; **1349** quod dicti deforciatores eos [pisces] capiunt contra eorum voluntatem *Lib. Kilken.* 13; **c1497** non habetur tenens liberi tenementi unde supponitur reditus predictus provenire, neque perceptor neque deforciator reditus illius *Entries* 73b.

2 violator, ravisher (of woman).

omnes raptores de roboria et deforciatores mulierum et murdratores hominum .. comparebunt .. coram justiciario regis (*Leg. Malc.*) *APScot* I app. 347.

diffortunium v. dysfortunium.

diffractio [cf. CL diffractus *p. ppl. of* diffringere], breaking (in pieces). *Cf. diffactio.*

si vulnus eveniat alicui, sive menbri truncatione vel debilitatione vel ~one [vv. ll. defractione, diffactione] (*Leg. Hen.* 93. 1) *GAS* 609; **1387** super defraccione et pertricione salpetre (v. carbo 1f).

diffrodiare v. exfridiare.

diffugare [cf. CL fugare], to pursue.

dispalatum, ~atum *GlC* D 293; *to chase*, fugo .., con-, dif- *CathA.*

diffugere [CL]

1 to flee (in different directions), scatter. **b** (of one person) to flee. *V. et. defugere.*

morbi diffugiunt, ydros et ater abit (*Hymn*) BEDE *HE* IV 18; in denso tanquam vulpes .. ~iunt GIR. *TH* I 24. **b** rex a .. congressione .. ignominiose ~erat *G. Steph.* II 75.

2 to avoid, shun: **a** (w. obj.); **b** (w. inf.); **c** (w. *quin*). **d** to quit (a place).

a ~iebant .. ipsum velut belue ferocem leonem G. MON. X 11; **s1185** noli ~ere quod preparavit tibi Deus et predestinavit *G. Hen. II* I 257; **1280** ut .. Amanevus judicium inde, quantum in ipso est, ~iat, et in judices competentes .. nolit .. consentire *RGasc* II 117; **1333** non solvendo regi .. set ~iendo solucionem inde *LTRMem* 105 r. 51. **b** **s1120** ad regem Francorum venire ~it H. CANTOR 22v.; sit ei mors illa omnium delictorum suorum .. ablutio, dum hoc modo eam recipere non ~erit G. MON. IX 4 (= *Eul. Hist.* II 312: †diffigerit); **s1233** si [rex] hec emendare ~eret WEND. III 49; **1400** [quidam] perfidi et perversi de diocesi in diocesim se transferunt et coram .. diocesanis comparere ~iunt *Conc.* III 252b; contigit .. quod rex Dacorum .. tributum .. reddere ~eret CANTLOW *Orig. Cantab.* 262. **c** **s1223** rex ~ere non potuit quin hoc faceret WEND. II 269. **d** **1384** asserentibus se .. villam ~ituros *IMisc* 230/9 r. 2.

3 **a** (trans.) to scatter, disperse. **b** to demolish, refute (an argument).

a quod pastor greges non ~erit *Fleta* 167 (v. circinare 2b). **b** hec autem principalis falsigraphia non ~it argumentum BRADW. *CD* 766A.

diffugium [CL]

1 (taking) flight, escape, refuge.

memorabat ille abesse ~ium, in terra sc. hostes et a litore longe remotas pupes *Enc. Emmae* II 6; **1157** quid facerem? insulam egredi imaginem videbatur habere ~ii J. SAL. *Ep.* 96 (31); querere diffugium domino veniente, caponem / audax accipiter dum videt, inquit ei: / "quid fugis?" WALT. ANGL. *Fab.* 56. 1; **s1205** quere ~ium si potes, quia abbas querit animam tuam *Chr. Evesham* 145.

2 evasion, subterfuge.

1153 quoniam .. Henricus plus causa ~ii quam alicujus gravaminis ad sedem apostolicam appellavit (*Lit. Papae*) *Lib. Eli.* III 110; manifeste [episcopus Londoniensis] Saresberiensem .. adjutorem in omnibus molitionum et appellationum ~iis habuit *V. Thom. B* 31; quia onus probandi denuntiationes suas subire .. cum impudentiori ~io feralis insanie .. recusarunt AD. MARSH *Ep.* 30 p. 126; **c1267** rogamus quatenus nobis istud sine ~io intimetis (*AncC* IV 54) *RL* II 318; **1275** in hoc negocio post multa †diffigia in tantum processit .. *SelCKB* I 14; **1301** sine more ~io *Reg. Cant.* 744; **1338** absque dilacionis ~io *RScot* 556a; cum appellacionibus xvj contra interpositis successive—non propter confugia que tu, Veritas, concessisti, sed propter ~ia que tu, Veritas, †notuisti [? l. noluisti] RIC. ARMAGH. *AP* 20; **a1440** nec aliter de nobis concipiatis, quesumus, quod ~ia solucionis querimus aut ambages *Reg. Whet.* II app. 410.

diffulcire [cf. CL fulcire], to support.

bine .. bases singulis tabulis per duos angulos subjiciebantur, ut bene diffultis angulis tota recte et indeclinabiliter posset tabula consistere AD. SCOT *TT* 639C (cf. *Exod.* xxvi 19–25).

diffundere [CL]

1 to pour out, shed (also fig.); *v. et. defundere* 1b. **b** to pour into.

diffudit silva cohortes G. AMIENS *Hast.* 363; non .. est ullius ducis victoria, set illorum qui pro eo sanguinem suum pugnando ~unt G. MON. IV 9. **b** ~itur, immittitur *GlH* D 452.

2 to diffuse, disperse, spread (sts. refl.): **a** (of fluid or sim.); **b** (of troops or sim.); **c** (of abstr.); **d** (intr.). **e** (impers. pass.) to be spread abroad.

a sol .. / limpida quadrato diffundens lumina templo ALDH. *CE* 3. 68; **8**.. ~et, *togiot WW*; cholera .. ~itur ADEL. *CA* 12 (v. 1 cera 3); venenum suum ~ere jam preparavit GIR. *EH* I 7; BART. ANGL. II 8 (v. ebullire 1a). **b** [apes] densos .. turmarum exercitus per .. campos gregatim ~unt ALDH. *VirgP* 3; exercitus .. sese .. ~ens *G. Steph.* I 66 (v. circumquaque a); ORD. VIT. IV 5 p. 191 (v. egredi 1b). **c** caritas .. diffusa est in corde suo *V. Greg.* p. 108; virtus summe activa summe se ~it DUNS *Ord.* II 276 (cf. ib. 278: oporteret probare quod possibile esset aliquid ~i sive communicari in unitate nature). **d** humiditas copiose ~it ad exteriora *Quaest. Salern.* B 63; **c1340** J. .. menestrallus, quem .. in .. sceleribus participem extitisse .. detractorum lingua, invidia circumquaque ~ente, notavit *FormOx* 142. **e** **1297** (v. conscribere 3b).

3 to spread out, extend. **b** (pass., of territory). **c** to extend in influence or power.

unde .. verborum vimina patulis defusa ramusculis succreverunt ALDH. *Met.* 4; rumusculus, qui passim per Europam .. ~itur *Id. VirgP* 49; cum ea, quae toto orbe diffusa est, ecclesia Christi BEDE *HE* II 4; aut ~et se [Deus] in creaturis sub esse spirituali, sc. in ydeas, aut [in] creaturis sub esse reali BACON XIII 375; Oxonia .. tanquam vitis .. palmites suas circumquaque ~it *Dictamen* 350. **b** **s1172** (v. dominatio 3a); in cxx milia passuum .. latitudinem Hibernia ~i describitur GIR. *TH* I 3. **c** **1362** nos .., sperantes .. paternum solium .. condecenter ~ere et firmius stabilire *Lit. Cant.* II 425.

4 (p. ppl. *diffusus*): **a** extensive. **b** lavish.

a [Britannia] defusioris, †langioris [? l. longioris *or* largioris] *GlC* D 158; religiosus ex fure ~iorem corporis molem jejuniis .. attenuans W. MALM. *Mir. Mariae* 205; ~ior bibitorum numerus *Ib.* 226; succincte medio solee diffusior ante / et retro forma sedet HANV. II 94 p. 261. **b** **s1326** abbas .. ~as fecit expensas pro .. falso clamore sedando *Chr. Rams.* app. 351.

5 (p. ppl. *diffusus*, of time) protracted or distant (in future); *cf. diffindere* 2. **b** time-consuming, tedious.

1209 credebatis terminum, qui erat usque ad Assumptionem B. Virginis, ad consummationem negotii satis esse ~um (*Lit. Episcoporum*) *Chr. Rams.* II app. civ; **1224** datus fuit ei dies ~us ad cartam suam habendam *CurR* XI 2533; **1228** cum ulterius sine periculo more ~ioris non posset inquisitio deferri *Conc.* I 562b; **1237** (v. devolvere 5d); **1258** predictum diem ita ~um .. vobis assignamus ne ulteriorem dilacionem querere possitis *Cl* 463; **1284** supplicantes .. quatinus ~iorem diem .. concedatis *AncC* XLVII 186; loquela .. respectuabitur sine die vel ad diem ~um *Fleta* 310. **b** **s1403** cum ~um fuerit visitare omnia loca indulgencie in ecclesia S. Petri AD. USK 83.

diffungi v. defungi.

diffusculus, somewhat protracted.

s1267 rex .. Londoniis .. morabatur et, difusculis .. tractatibus de regni moderatione pertractans, nihil memorabile .. gessit WYKES 207.

diffuse [CL], **a** widely. **b** abundantly. **c** (of writing or argument) copiously, at length.

a [cum] sequentis testamenti luminaria .. in triquadro terrarum ambitu ~ius spargerentur ALDH. *VirgP* 22; ~ius, i. .. latius, planius *GlH* D 451. **b** ~ius, i. habundantius, .. largius *Ib.*; quo [Romana ecclesia] preesset aliis et prodesset ~ius H. READING (II) *Cel.* 29. **c** ad haec omnia .. vellem aliquanto ~ius scribere ANSELM (*Ep.* 101) III 233; ea quae ab ipsis [chronicis] ~e nimis et inordinate .. congesta fuerant GIR. *TH intr.* p. 8; consideremus qualiter velimus eam [materiam] tractare, sc. an breviter an ~e VINSAUF *AV* II 3. 154; [Augustinus] pertractat ibi ~e DUNS *Ord.* I 81; que .. ~issime probare conantur OCKHAM *Pol.* I 65.

diffusio [CL]

1 diffusion, expansion (esp. phil.).

in fumo vini tibi se diffusio debet, / aer NECKAM *DS* IV 800; ex essentia Primi fluxerunt omnia, non per viam nature solius .. sed potius per viam effusionis seu ~onis T. YORK *Sap.* II 1; omnis emanatio vel diffusio facta ab alico diminuit ipsum a quo fit BACON VII 62; ~o radii vel speciei non tam est operatio quam instrumentum operandi PECKHAM *QA* 149.

2 **a** spread, extent (in space). **b** outpouring (also fig.). **c** (of writing) copiousness, prolixity.

a montes .. erant .. arboribus cooperti habentibus congruam altitudinem staturae, ~onem ramorum, opacitatem foliorum BEDE *Gen.* (ii 5) 40; tanta est ~o et oportunitas fundorum W. MALM. *GP* II 91. **b** studium non est philosophicum sine ~one sumptuum et multarum expensarum BACON XI 173; **1331** de caritatis ~one, pro qua instanter laboramus ut inter fratres continuetur *Lit. Cant.* I 417. **c** W. MALM. *GP* IV 164 (v. defloratio 2); quibus omnibus rationabili ~one distinctius emensis AD. MARSH *Ep.* 30 p. 126; in qualibet arte ~o fastidium generat .. et memoriam perturbat J. MIRFIELD *Brev.* 50.

diffusivus, (phil.) diffusive, expansive.

[anima sensibilis] per singulas partes corporis est sue virtutis ~a [v. l. distributiva vel ~a] BART. ANGL. III 12; continuitas est in celo quoad lumen, quod continuum [est] et ~um et multiplicativum per omnes orbes *Comm. Sph.* 282; omne quod est suiipsius difussivum maxime est largum BACON VII 61; si [lux] summe est sui multiplicativa et spheraliter ~a *Ps.*-GROS. *Summa* 536; bonum est sui ~um PECKHAM *QA* 4; quod summe activum est summe ~um sui DUNS *Ord.* II 278.

dific- v. diffic-. **difid-** v. diffid-. **difin-** v. defin-. **difixisti** v. defigere. **diform-** v. difform-. **difortium** v. divortium 2a. **diga** v. daga.

digamia [LL < διγαμία], second marriage.

non fit ut homicida aut digamus .. in ecclesia promoveatur .., non quod post veniam peccati aut ~iam conjugii minus pertineat ad salutem, verum [? sc. ad] sacramenti dignitatem PULL. *Sent.* 927A.

digamma [CL < δίγαμμα], digamma (Greek character).

†digammos, duplex littera *GlC Int.* 95; F littera in speciem figurata est cujusdam litterae quae ~a nominatur, quia duos apices ex gamma littera habere videatur. ad hujus soni similitudinem V consonantem loco eius nostri posuerunt, ut votum virgo: ~a enim oportuit poni, Fotum Firgo ALCUIN *Orth.* 2335; ~a, i. vau vel F *GlH* D 486; vos Angli . ., qui pro Θ frequentius Þ scribitis . . sicut pro ~a Ƿ ABBO *QG* 12 (28); digama NECKAM *Ut.* 117 (v. delta); BACON *Gram. Gk.* 50 (v. F 1).

digamus [LL < δίγαμος], (one) twice married. *V. et. bigamus* b.

~us peniteat j annum iv^ta feria et vj^ta; . . non dimittat tamen uxorem THEOD. *Pen.* I 14. 2; maritus si seipsum in furtu aut fornicatione servum facit . ., mulier, si prius non habuit conjugium, habet potestatem post annum alterum accipere virum; ~o [sc. mulieri] non licet *Ib.* II 12. 8; ~us, secunde uxoris vir *GlH* D 487; PULL. *Sent.* 927A (v. digamia); quum peto sacratae sublimes sedis honores, / tunc, quod sim digamus, mihi mystes denegat illos J. HERD *Hist. IV Regum* 12.

digara v. diger. **digena** v. indigena.

diger [ON *digr*], stout, fat.

Siwardus dux Northumbrorum Dan[ic]a lingua 'digara', hoc est fortis, nuncupatus *V. Ed. Conf.* 42v.; sub rege Cnuto vir predives Osgotus cognomine ~era, Danus natione, partem terre . . sue possessioni . . moliebatur adjungere *V. Kenelmi B* f. 82; nervosus lacertis, thorosus pectore, robustus et procerus toto corpore, filius Siwardi . . comitis, quem ~era Danico vocabulo, id est fortem, cognominabant W. MALM. *GR* III 253; Hugoni †Dirganae, id est grosso ORD. VIT. X 6 (cf. *Heimskringla*: *Hugi digri*).

digerere [CL]

1 a to digest, assimilate (food) or promote digestion; **b** (w. ref. to plants); **c** (fig.).

a digesti, i. soluti, *gemette GlM* 14. 1; ADEL. *QN* 20 (v. decoctio 2a); digesto calore vini W. MALM. *GR* III 255; caseus insulsus bene digerit et bene nutrit D. BEC. 2751; [eruca], cum cibus efficitur, digeret ipsa cibos NECKAM *DS* VII 198; BART. ANGL. IV 7 (v. coquere 4a); M. SCOT *Phys.* 39 (v. dirigere 7); cibaria que sui natura generant bonos humores, si non bene ~antur, generabunt malos humores BACON IX 132; nunquam calidi secundum quod hujusmodi, . . fomenta ossium optetice, carnis vero et similium epsetice disgerere SICCAV. *PN* 187; GAD. 30V. 1 (v. chylus); *to defy*, . . degerere *CathA.* **b** J. SAL. *Pol.* 427D (v. decoctio 2b); queritur . . de opere ~endi in cibo, que qualitas debet ei attribui BACON XI 193 (cf. cibatio b). **c** hic panis [Christus] digerit et non digeritur WALT. WIMB. *Carm.* 123.

2 a (alch.) to 'digest', calcine or sim.; *cf. decoquere* 4. **b** to mature (wine); **c** (fig.). **d** (p. ppl. *digestus*) mature.

a ignis in eo [sc. auro] agens omnes malos humores consumit in corporibus egris existentes; sed hoc argentum facere non potest, quia . . tantum non est digestum *Correct. Alch.* 14; mitte in furno philosophorum in stufa sicca ad ~endum, prout quidam volunt nominare, licet alii dicunt 'ad calcinandum', 'ad ignem lentum de carbonibus factum CUTCL. *CL* 3. **b** degesto, sereno vel praeclaro *GlC* D 114; degesta, i. . . clarificata, serena, praeclara *GlH* D 91 (cf. ib. D 476: digesti, i. sereni, levi, . . *gelihte*); cum vinum actu ~itur, in 3 partes dividitur et separatur, sc. in subtiliorem . . et in mediocrem . . et in grossiorem. . . unde . . mercatores vini . ., ut melius . . vinum cognoscant, gustant de vino in ista triplici parte BACON VIII 203; *Ib.* 204 (v. digestio 2b). **c** c**1435** non est res perfecta . . donec, interne caritatis degerente calore, deduci poterit ad maturum *FormOx* 445; in hac materia bene et matura deliberacione degesta *Plusc.* VIII 2. **d** **1401** assensu ac avisacione nostri saniorís et ~i consilii (*TreatyR*) *Foed.* VIII 215a; **1403** super hoc ~a meditacione prehabita (*Lit. Papae*) AD. USK 81; s**1422** in quo [codice canonis] si glosam cum textu ~o stomacho discusseris . . reperies . . AMUND. I 96; **1434** (v. communicatio 3c); **1466** matura et degesta deliberacione prehabita *Reg. Paisley* 150.

3 to set out in order, dispose. **b** to expound, compose. **c** to count. **d** (p. ppl. *digestus* as sb. f., m., or n.) Digest (compilation of civil law).

expositis enigmatum propositionibus et degesta metrorum melodia ALDH. *PR* 112; haec . . prout . . scire potui . . digessi Baeda BEDE *HE* V 24 p. 357; degesto, *geraedit GlC* D 186; digessimus, congrecavimus, ordinavimus *Gl. Leid.* 2. 47; *De libero arbitrio* 14 (v. 1 erus 2); †**809** (13c) coram his testibus, quorum infra nomina caraxata digesta sunt *CS* 328; [Oswaldi] gesta vario diversorum stilo digesta EADMER *V. Osw. prol.*; quanto compendiosius potui . . digessi GIR. *TH intr.* p. 8. **b** diserto digessit famine librum ALDH. *VirgV* 738; †degetit, conscribit . ., digessit, disputavit *GlC* D 165, 215; digesta, i. . . composita, enarrata, descripta, *geendebyrde*, dicta *GlH* D 477; o nox . . / digere lamentum Malchi Malchaeque dolentum R. CANT. *Malch.* III 102. **c** o quia digestos volui numerare colores, / nec potui, numero copia major erat GOWER *VC* I 59; *to cownte*, calculare . ., numerare, degerere *CathA.* **d** [Justinianus] singulorum magistratuum . . leges . . intra l librorum numerum redegit eumque codicem ~orum sive Pandectarum vocabulo nuncupavit R. NIGER *Chr. II* 189; [abbas B., ob. **1193**] plurimos libros scribere fecit, quorum nomina subnotantur: . . Institutiones Justiniani cum Autenticis et Infortiato, ~um Vetus, tres partes cum ~o Novo SWAFHAM 99; c**1250** magister Henricus leget ~um Vetus (*Lit. W. de Bernham*) *FormOx* 481; **1337** liber qui dicitur ~a Vetus *Lit. Cant.* II 151; a**1350** inceptururus in jure civili libellum Institucionum, ~um Novum et Inforciatum legisse tenetur *StatOx* 44; **1438** ~um forciatum *Reg. Cant.* II 562; *Ib.* 38 (v. 1 codex 2b); **1451** liber vocatus ~us Forciati *MunAcOx* II 610.

digestibilis [LL], **a** (of food) digestible. **b** digestive.

a carnis ~ioris BART. ANGL. XII 1 (v. convertibilis 3b); in febribus interpolatis . . meliora sunt nutrientia in die quietis, ea que ~ia sunt laudabilis substantie, sicut pulli, galline . ., pisces parvi . ., quia convertibiles sunt GILB. I 25V. 2; qui in senio sunt positi . . nutrientibus bonis . . et facile ~ibus sunt alendi BACON IX 91; utantur facile ~ibus GAD. 40V. 2; *a defiynge*, digestio; †digestilis [v. l. degestibilis] participium *CathA.* **b** operatio ~is . . melius compleur in membro carnoso *Ps.*-RIC. *Anat.* 15.

digestim [LL], in order.

~im, ordinatim, *endebyrdlice GlP* 555.

digestio [CL]

1 digestion (of food); **b** (w. ref. to plants). **c** matter digested or in process of digestion; **d** (fig.).

pisis est cibi et potus ~o *Gloss. Poems* 103; in animalibus triplex perficitur ~o *Quaest. Salern.* B 168; cum urina spissior plene ~onis tempus nuntiaverit P. BLOIS *Ep.* 43. 127A; caro pavonis . . ~oni inobedientissima est NECKAM *NR* I 39; *Id. DS* VII 45 (v. celeber 1f); nutrimentum recipitur in corpore nutriendo; ita ejus tota materia facta ~one eicitur J. BLUND *An.* 54 (cf. ib. 231: celebrata ~one); hoc triplici calore concurrente operatur stomachus primam ~onem et dissolvendo et liquefaciendo ciborum grossitiem RIC. MED. *Anat.* 223; secunde ~onis . . principale fundamentum est epar *Ib.* 225 (cf. ib. 226: sic celebratur secunda ~o, in qua . . formantur quatuor humores); ypostasis est superfluitas tercie ~onis, et sic dicitur quasi 'substans' *SB* 25; pepsis interpretatur 'degestio' et ponitur similiter pro prima ~one . . *Alph.* 144 (cf. anadosis, anapepticus); rex cum post primam degestionem media nocte vigilet *Plusc.* VII 19. **b** BACON XI 193 (v. cibatio b). **c** epar secundam obtinet ~onem ALF. ANGL. *Cor* 3. 1. **d** ypocriosa cauterisacio stilo ferreo in superfluitate ~onis modo ultra debitum excrescente [cf. *Jer.* xvii 1; *1 Tim.* iv 2] WYCL. *Sim.* 27.

2 a (alch.) 'digestion', (matter in process of) refining or sim. **b** maturation.

a ~o, i. perfinitio, egestio *GlH* D 480; quarta operacio est ut ~onem predictam in urinali ponas clauso in balneo CUTCL. *CL* 4 (cf. *LC*: ~o est operatio chymica . ., alludens ad stomachi humani ~onem, in quo et per quem materia decoquitur in separationem puri ab impuro). **b** dum celebratur ~o in vino, maximus fit motus; et propter hoc, si apponatur aliquid digestivum in vino ut fermentum vel ponatur prope ignem, citius digeritur BACON VIII 204; sudor superveniens febricitanti ante signa ~onis malum J. MIRFIELD *Brev.* 60.

3 digest, summary.

illa diversa confusaque degestio regularum illarum cum statutis THEOD. *Pen. pref.*

digestivus, digestive. **b** (as sb. f., *sc. virtus*) digestion. **c** causing maturation or fermentation.

aurum . . in cibariis sumptum virtuti cooperatur ~e NECKAM *NR* II 53; [struthionis] exuperat ferrum vis digestiva potenter *Id. DS* II 491; naturalis virtutis due sunt species: nutritiva sc. quadripartita . . in appetitivam, retentivam, ~am, et expulsivam; est et alia naturalis quedam generativa RIC. MED. *Anat.* 229; H. AVR. *Poem.* 2. 239 (v. cruor d); virtuti ~e due obsequuntur, id est immutativa cibi ultimi ad proximam dispositionem membri similis et informativa *Ps.*-GROS. *Summa* 469; potus ~us potest dari post primum somnum GAD. 43. 2; que non habent virtutem ~am equalem, non debent recipere alimentum equale OCKHAM *Dial.* 790. **b** [pirorum] durities digestive nocet NECKAM *DS* VIII 97; corruptis virtutibus corrumpitur nutrimentum. ~am igitur corrumpit . . et perturbat GILB. II 104. **c** vinum naturaliter calidum est et siccum et idcirco causa est ebullitionis et evaporationis et ideo maxime ~um BACON VIII 203.

1 digestus v. digerere 2d, 3d.

2 digestus [LL], digestion.

fleubotomĭa / . . / . . oculorum curat aquosos / cursus, invitat digestum, sana ministrat D. BEC. 2691.

digitabulum [CL], finger-stall, thimble.

a themelle, digitale, ~um, parcipollex . . *CathA.*

digitalis [CL], **a** measuring a finger's breadth. **b** (?) fitting the finger, w. ref. to foxglove (*Digitalis*) or sim. (? *cf.* Virgil *Ecl.* IV 18–19). **c** (as sb. n.) finger-stall or thimble. **d** (?) ring-holder, holder for precious stones. **e** (as sb. m. or f.) (?) glove or mitten.

a longitudinis ferme ~is os educit W. CANT. *Mir. Thom.* III 16. **b** ~ium musculorum [*Erf.*: munusculorum], *fingir-doccana GlC* D 294. **c** ~e, A. *a themyl WW*; *a fyngyr stalle*, ~e *CathA* (v. et. digitabulum). **d** **1328** capella : . . apparatus pro cirothecis, duo ~ia (*Invent.*) *Reg. Exon. 1307–26* app. 562. **e** da mihi duas manicas, i. ~es ÆLF. BATA 4. 16 p. 41; emo cutes et pelles et praeparo eas . . et facio . . peras et marsupia atque ~es, stropheos, et capitia *Ib.* 6 p. 89.

digitaliter, w. the finger, by pointing.

sicut dicit [scriptura], 'Johannes non est propheta', cum hoc quod nunc ~er ostendit Messiam, ad quem sunt prophecie (WYCL.) *Ziz.* app. 462.

digitare [CL digitatus = *having toes*], **a** to finger, handle. **b** to 'finger', point a finger at. **c** (?) to reckon, count (on fingers).

a consilium tractare cave, nummos digitare,/ dum resides cenans D. BEC. 1410; *Ib.* 1038 (v. addigitare); sic honor ex onere non est; nam fulget honore / †corpore [? l. corpus], set corpus non digitabit onus GOWER *VC* III 1004. **b** conjunctis digitis genibus digitos reprimendo / non sedeas fatue, ne pro fatuo digiteris D. BEC. 1216; *to finger*, ~are *CathA.* **c** sed Pharios digitare dies didicere, putantes / pravum temporibus omen inesse bonis GARL. *Tri. Eccl.* 88 (cf. dies 6d).

digitata, ~us, finger's breadth.

1246 vulneraverunt M. forestarium . . cum . . sagitta in brachio sinistro ad profunditatem duorum ~um *SelPlForest* 80; **1247** debent . . de qualibet domo duas gallinas, et non debent refutari si habeant tres ~as caude (*Inq. Guerns.*) *Cl* 546.

digitatio, pointing the finger (of scorn).

1426 ~one dignus (v. curiositas 2b).

digitorium, thimble.

1558 ~ium argenti vocatum *a thymble of silver Pat* 932 m. 26.

digitulus [CL], (tiny) finger.

cum Prisciani . . xviij volumina . . propriis palmarum ~is calce tenus digesta describeret ALDH. *PR* 143 p. 203; invenit super altare quod posuit ut ~i auricularis particulam sanguilenti *V. Greg.* p. 94; **790** tempus amabile, quo collum caritatis vestrae desideriorum meorum ~is amplecter ALCUIN *Ep.* 10; si . . demonstranti ~o corrigentis indicetur . . B. *V. Dunst.* 1; **1093** virgam, caeteris ~is pertinaciter occlusis, pollici atque indici cruderliter impactam ANSELM (*Ep.* 149) IV 7; nanum miserum cujus laterculi / vix grossitudinem habent digituli WALT. WIMB. *Palpo* 101.

1 digitus [CL]

1 finger; **b** (dist. individually); **c** (used for gesturing or counting); **d** (fig.). **e** thumb. **f** toe.

GILDAS *EB* 1 (v. demonstrare 1a); ALDH. *Aen.* 80. 6 (v. comprehendere 1a); dactulus, ~us *GlC* D 7; ~i, *fingras* ÆLF. *Gl.*; **949** (v. dictitare 2); mirum quod in tanta tam precipiti ~orum rapacitate musica servatur proportio GIR. *TH* III 11; s**1326** ut nullus caperet . . valorem trium d. sub poena mutilacionis ~i WALS. *HA* I 181; **1439** pro emendacione degetorum imaginis S. Thome *Ac. Churchw. Bath* 48; est manuum digitus, articulusque pedum (*Vers.*) *WW*. **b** secundus ~us nominatur index sive demonstratorius . .; tertius ~us . . nominatur impudicus . .; quartus anularis . .; quintus auricularis *Text. Roff.* f. 76 p. 40; W. CANT. *Mir. Thom.* II 36 (v. anularis 2); T. MON. *Will.* I 5 (v. auricularis 2a); **1266** cepit ~um qui vocatur index juxta policem in manu dextra et morsit dictum ~um *SelCCoron* 2; **1271** alium ~um juxta dictum [auricularem] ~um, qui vocatur medicus *Ib.* 22; vene . . in manibus inter minimum ~um et sibi proximum *SB* 38. **c** Johannes ~o Christum ostendit AD. DORE *Pictor* 154; aliis quam pluribus ad ~um rationibus ostensis N. DUNSTABLE *Chr.* 8; s**1242** signum ad ~um in subsannationem *Flor. Hist.* II 258. **d** affectum . . asinae . . quae . . angelum . . ~o quodammodo . . demonstravit [cf. *Num.* xxii] GILDAS *EB* 1. **e** folia similia ~o majori et obrotunda *Alph.* 138. **f** quendam hominem . . habuisse plantas duorum non amplius ~orum comperimus *Lib. Monstr.* I 25; inter singulos ~os pedis et manus RIC. MED. *Anat.* 229; *Canon. G. Sempr.* 141V. (v. excoriare 1b).

2 finger's breadth, inch.

neque in tantae mole magnitudinis . . unum ~um tantum addere vel demere crediderim BEDE *TR* 32 (cf. id. *HE* IV 11: mensura iiij ~orum); virga virilis . . longitudinem naturalem inter vj ~os habet *Ps.*-RIC. *Anat.* 40; *Ib.* 35 (v. duodenus 6).

3 (math.) digit.

considera . . utrum . . numerus . . ex caracterum duplatione confectus ~us sit an articulus THURKILL *Abac.* 56; ADEL. *ED* 11 etc. (v. articulus 2); quadruplex multiplicatio, sc. articuli cum articulo, et ~i cum articulo, deinde articuli cum ~o et quarto ~i cum ~o ROB. ANGL. *Alg.* 136; ordines numerorum sive limites a primis numeris, qui ~i

vocantur et sunt ix, per decuplos in infinitum procedunt OCREATUS *Helceph* 132; BART. ANGL. XIX 121 (v. componere 5b).

4 (?) holder for precious stones; *cf. digitalis* 1d.

1281 lapides subscriptos, viz. ix balesios quadratos, v in uno ∼o et iiij in alio et in quodam alio ∼o iiij balesios grossiores *Pat* 100 m. 26.

2 digitus [? *by conf. of* OF *dois* < discus *w. dois* < digitus], dais, high table. *Cf. discus* 4a.

invenire in Quadragesima panes xij denariorum deportandos ad ∼um ad elemosinam *Reg. Pri. Worc.* 106b; si .. ebdomadarius sederit ad ∼um *Ib.* 126b (cf. ib. 131b: minister ∼i); in refectorio cum sederit ad ∼um *Lib. Evesham* 6; curtarius .. allocabit unum panem pro frang[mentis] que portantur ad ∼um in die Nativitatis S. J. Baptiste *Cust. Swith.* 23.

digladiabilis [LL], **∼alis,** murderous, savage.

Kedwalla .., ∼abile odium in Cantuaritas spirans W. MALM. *GR* I 14; quod .. ∼abili odio impetierint Wilfridum *Id. GP* III 107 (cf. ib. IV 142: qui ∼abili dissidebant odio); **s1264** signo regis, quod draconem vocant, ∼ale mortis judicium pretendente *Flor. Hist.* II 495.

digladiari [CL], **∼are,** to fight, wound w. sword; **b** (fig.).

degladiati, persecuti sunt *GlC* D 63(cf. ib. D 320: ∼iati, occisi); ∼ior, pugno, *ic feohte* ÆLF. *Gl.*; ∼iare, discindere, †exoccare [l. exossare], exartuare OSB. GLOUC. *Deriv.* 177; sic imperiosa virago / degladiata ruit J. EXON. *BT* VI 649; qui viciosos .. corripuerunt / dilaniando, digladiando disparuerunt WALT. WIMB. *Scel.* 131; hic mors carnem solam digladiat, / dum majestas intacta radiat J. HOWD. *Ph.* 454. **b** GARL. *Tri. Eccl.* 95 (v. cor 2a); cor revera sacrum plus laniat / quam cum rosam grando digladiat J. HOWD. *CA* 105.

diglutio v. deglluttitio.

digma [LL < δεῖγμα], (badge of) honour, decoration.

wyrshipe, honor .., decor .., dignitas, ∼a, fasses *CathA*.

dignanter [LL], graciously, w. condescension.

super hunc famulum tuum, Domine, ∼er intende EGB. *Pont.* 106; **c798** iste, supplico, ∼er ac diligenter inspicite ALCUIN *Ep.* 132; **949** (13c) cujus donum ∼er imo corde collaudat *Ch. Burton* 9; [Ælfgiva] orat eundem [regem] ut .. prandium quod sibi paraverat ∼er suscipiat OSB. *V. Dunst.* 15 (cf. ib. 38: postulationi ∼er annuens); [Will. I] exterarum nationum homines ∼er ad amicitiam admisit W. MALM. *GR* III 278; sompnum .. quo Dominus .. eventus hujus veritatem mihi .. ∼er preostendere curavit T. MON. *Will.* I 14; M. PAR. *Maj.* I 522 (v. digne); **1246** Deo auctore et gratia vestra liberali nobis ∼er assensum prebentibus *Ch. Sal.* 303; **1401** hec vestra .. sanctitatis clemencia ∼er, si placet, et benigne consideret *FormOx* 201.

dignare v. dinare b.

dignari [CL], **a** (w. abl.) to think worthy of. **b** (w. inf.) to think fit, deign; **c** (*s. pass.*).

a W. MALM. *GP* V 215 (v. erroneus 3b); gratias Deo retulit quod .. tanto eam solatio ∼atus esset GIR. *TH* II 19. **b** de qua nos salvare Deus dignetur ab arce! ALDH. *VirgV* 2665; **705** obsecro ut mihi innotescere ∼eris quid de hac re agere debeam WEALDHERE *Ep.* 22; non me ∼eris derelinquere, Domine EGB. *Pont.* 134; **795** de aliis rebus quas mihi injungere ∼ans fuisti *Ep. Alcuin.* 46; **836** ut .. Deus .. a cunctis me emundare ∼etur *CS* 416; lectos cernere qui dignaris, corrige versus OSW. *Vers.* 17; de infirmitate mea, de qua vestra excellentia †dignorata est requirere H. LOS. *Ep.* 25; GIR. *TH* II 54 (v. dignatio a); **c1233** mandamus .. quatinus .. sententiam nostram .. latam executioni demandare ∼emini *Reg. Paisley* 168; **c1340** scire ∼etur regia celsitudo quod .. *Couch. Furness* II 698. **c** grata quies vulgo Martisque remissius ardens / dignatur consulta furor J. EXON. *BT VI* 108.

dignarium, ∼ius v. dinarium.

dignatio [CL], graciousness, condescension. **b** (as title) grace.

maxima conditoris et redemptoris nostri ∼o, qui .. incarnari pro nobis .. voluit BEDE *Hom.* I 6. 336; ∼o nature W. MALM. *GR* II 156 (v. colludium b); **s1163** ut .. si vultum pretenderet hilarem .., tante ∼oni sue gratias agerent G. COLD. *Durh.* 4; non satis elucet utrum unus ille fuerit de celestibus an majori ∼one ipse .. Christus J. FORD *Wulf.* 20; divina indignatione, seu verius ∼one, que .. sanctorum suorum injuriam vindicare dignatur GIR. *TH* II 54; per illuminationem celice ∼onis AD. MARSH *Ep.* 74; ECCLESTON *Adv. Min.* 113 (v. dignificare 1a). **b c1078** quotiens litteras ∼onis vestrae suscepero ANSELM (*Ep.* 57) III 172; **1188** quid .. super hoc vestre placuerit majestati .. vestra nobis significare velit ∼o (*Lit. Regis Anglie ad Imp.*) DICETO *YH* II 52; clementissime sublimitatis vestre [sc. archiep. Cantuar.] ∼oni .. assurgo gratiarum actibus AD. MARSH *Ep.* 1; **1339** non prius a vestra ∼one .. credulitas illi detur quam .. (*Lit. E. Regis ad Papam*) AD. MUR. *Chr.* 98; **s1458** si regie placeat ∼oni *Reg. Whet.* I 318.

digne [CL], **∼iter,** worthily, fittingly. **b** (w. abl.) in a manner worthy of.

dum cruor insontis cum sontis sanguine fuso / ulciscebatur digne pro talibus ausis ALDH. *VirgV* 1841; **955** (13c) ni prius in hoc seculo ∼e castigetur *CS* 903; rex regum .. permisit eum sepelire, non tam ∼iter tunc sicut postea fieri concedere dignatus est BYRHT. *V. Osw.* 450; vatis gloria stat rectori maxima digne OSW. *Vers.* 20; si quid ∼e dici potest ANSELM (*Mon.* 27) I 45; **s1052** Eadgitham reginam ∼iter rex recepit FL. WORC. I 210 (= M. PAR. *Maj.* I 522: dignanter); Odo corpus B. Wilfridi .. in editiore entheca .. ∼iter collocaverat EADMER *Rel. S. Audoeni* 7; **1427** in nulla facultate .. quisquam magistrali censetur ∼e potiri honore nisi .. *StatOx* 234. **b** statuit decanum, thesaurarium, cantorem, dans cuique ∼e et ecclesie et suo et personarum honore H. CANTOR 3v.

dignerium v. dinarium.

dignificantia, (theol.) making worthy. *V. et dignificatio.*

beatificatio creature preexigit propriam ∼iam ad eam WYCL. *Dom. Div.* 230.

dignificare [LL]

1 to make or deem worthy (esp. theol.): **a** (w. abl.); **b** (w. *ad*); **c** (w. inf. or *ut*).

a dubitare nefas est quin impleatur officium sacre pastionis duplici honore divinitus ∼andum si forma pastoris, quam prerogat infallibilis certitudo, suscipiatur AD. MARSH *Ep.* 100; o immensa dignatione ∼atos qui tot et talium personarum .. potuerunt consiliis dirigi in dubiis! ECCLESTON *Adv. Min.* 113. **b c1241** laudemus Deum .., qui in hoc fecit nobiscum misericordiam suam, ∼ans nos ad sui imitationem GROS. *Ep.* 94 p. 292; peccatum amoris inordinati temporalium ∼at eos ad paciendum ablaciones temporalium WYCL. *Ver.* III 56; *Id. Dom. Div.* 230 (v. dignificatio). **c** cum accusabit se de quocunque furto, ∼abit se suspendi *Id. Log.* II 27; Deum .. habere beatum quem non ∼at ut sit talis *Id. Dom. Div.* 230.

2 to dignify, elevate (esp. theol.).

dignificatur, magnificatur, qui scelus ungit WALT. WIMB. *Scel.* 128; in hoc magis ∼atur natura quam si suprema sibi possibilis speculacio poneretur illa naturalis DUNS *Ord.* I 46; **c1393** pietas compassio veraque cordis, / dignificans animum, vos probat esse probum R. MAIDSTONE *Conc.* 295; eleccio .. Dei gentem sanctificat ac ∼at PAUL. ANGL. *ASP* 1530.

dignificatio, (theol.) making worthy.

pocius talis per ∼onem suam, tanquam per meritum dignum preciumque condignum, emit a Patre ut veniat ad Christum BRADW. *CD* 605A; illud ergo previe requisitum ad ∼onem, .. edocet quod nulla creatura potest recipere beatitudinem nisi prius se ipsam dignificet ad eandem WYCL. *Dom. Div.* 230.

digniosus v. dignitosus. **dignitalibus** v. dignitas 2b.

dignitas [CL] **(dingn-)**

1 dignity, worth, honour, importance. **b** (of language or appearance) stateliness. **c** (as title of addressee) honour or sim.

in altiore ∼ate positis .. debitum .. honorem GILDAS *EB* 4; ut [Benedictus] .. aliter .. vivere nequiret quam propriae appellationis ∼as .. permitteret ALDH. *VirgP* 30; ut ob regiam ejus et animi et vultus et meritorum ∼atem ab omnibus diligeretur BEDE *HE* III 14; ibi [*Naples*] est sedis (*sic*) archiepiscopi et magna ∼as ejus illic habetur HUGEB. *Will.* 4; ∼as i. honestas, excellentia, fastigium, *weorþscipe* vel *geþungennes GlH* D 481; **990** (v. dictamen 1d); rerum naturas .. sentit non .. omnes contineri una ∼atis paritate ANSELM (*Mon.* 4) I 16; tanti sacramenti ∼atem minus attendere videntur GIR. *GE* I 50 p. 138; exceptis in missa que est 'requiem' pro anniversario secunde ∼atis et infra *Cust. Cant. Abbr.* 318; **c1456** in quibus respondentis probitas aut ejus sciencie ∼as dilucidari .. nequeat *StatOx* 276. **b** neque possunt carmina .. ex alia in aliam linguam ad verbum sine detrimento sui decoris et ∼atis transferri BEDE *HE* IV 22 p. 260; mutilata frondibus arbor .. tam ∼ate minuitur quam decore GIR. *TH* III 53. **c 722** notum facimus Deo dilectae tuae ∼ati .. fratrem Bonifatium (*Lit. Papae ad Karolum Ducem*) *Ep. Bonif.* 20; **c1160** notum sit ∼ati vestre .. (*Petitio ad Regem*) *Couch. Kirkstall* 189; **s1157** Deum celi vestramque regalem testor ∼atem *Chr. Battle* f. 74v.; **c1210** noverit ∼as vestra .. (*Lit. Prelati ad Prelatum*) *FormOx* 274.

2 (dignity or status of) office, rank, or sim.: **a** (royal); **b** (eccl.); **c** (var.). **d** symbol of dignity or status.

a habuit Osuiu .. consortem regiae ∼atis BEDE *HE* III 14; **1026** (12c) ut .. possideat praedictam donationem secundum meam regalem ∼atem *CD* 743; **c1070** cum omnibus aliis consuetudinibus et legibus que ad meam regiam ∼atem pertinent *Regesta* p. 120; **1237** (v. communis 7a); **c1280** in prejudicium regie ∼atis (*DipDocE* 1576) *DocExch* 369. **b** rapto tantum sacerdotali nomine nec tamen tenore, vel apostolica ∼ate accepta sed qui nondum .. sunt .. idonei GILDAS *EB* 66; pontificali ∼ate decoratus ALDH. *VirgP* 27 (cf. ib. 54: primus summi sacerdotii ∼ate subnixus); probitas est in O. preter solam etatem et pontificalem ∼atem tota pene reperta EADMER *V. Osw.* 11; **1216** hec omnia observentur de custodiis .. episcopatuum .. ecclesiarum et ∼atum vacantium *Magna Carta* 5; **1242** conferat .. Guidoni primam prebendam vacantem .. sive in ecclesia prebendali sive alia, excepta ∼ate *RGasc* I 131 (= *CalPat* 377); clavis data est ministris ecclesie habentibus ordinem et habentibus ∼atem. est enim ∼as supereminentia ordinis, sicut in alia facultate ∼as est supereminens propositio quam quisque probat auditam HALES *Qu.* 1216 (cf. 5 infra); **1255** ordinando decanatui, cantorie, cancellarie, et thesaurarie omnes decimas garbarum de R. et de C. inter ∼ates ipsas equaliter dividendas (*Lit. Papae ad Ep. Rossensem*) *Mon. Hib. & Scot.* 69b (cf. ib. 70a: statuisti quod .. nullus ad aliquam quatuor ∼atum admittatur .. nisi sacerdos existat); **1294** proventus ecclesiarum, personatuum, et †∼atuum (*Lit. Papae*) B. COTTON 262 (cf. ib.: ecclesie, personatus, ∼ates); prius suis nepotibus .. ecclesiasticas ∼ates anticipant quam nature successu .. maturescant R. BURY *Phil.* 9. 155; **1372** (v. beneficium 3a); **1377** ecclesiasticas personas .. in †dignitalibus [? l. ∼atibus] constitutos (*sic*) *Mon. Hib. & Scot.* 358b; **a1450** in .. ecclesia Lincolniensi post episcopum xiij sunt ∼ates: decanatus, precentoria, cancellaria, thesauraria, subdecanatus, archidiaconatus Lincoln', archidiaconatus Northampton' [etc.] *Stat. Linc.* II 272 (cf. ib. 273: ∼as episcopi, cujus ordo pocius dici debeat ∼atis culmen quam ∼as). **c** multi sunt qui ampliora a te beneficia quam ego et majores accipiunt ∼ates BEDE *HE* II 13; censor, ∼as judic[i]alis *GlC* C270; **798** convocans .. episcopos nostros, duces et abbates et cujuscunque ∼ates (*sic*) viros ad sinodale concilium (*Clovesho*) *CS* 291; **948** (12c) universis regni nostri principibus, tam ecclesiarum praesulibus quam palatinarum procuratoribus ∼atum *CS* 860 (cf. ib.: si quis cujuslibet sexus, ordinis vel ∼atis .. hoc memoriale meum corrumpere temptaverit); emendetur infractio pacis ecclesie .. secundum ∼atem singulorum (*Leg. Hen.* 79. 5a) *GAS* 595; dignum esset, si Deus permitteret, cives pristine ∼ati restitu[e]re G. MON. XII 6; propter cupiditatem ∼atum aut divitiarum HALES *Sent.* IV 306; inhabilis .. ad quecunque ∼ates et officia obtinenda OCKHAM *Pol.* I 293; **1579** presentari ad doctoralem ∼atem *StatOx* 413. **d** fasces, ∼as *GlC* F 13; toga, ∼as, *Gl. Leid.* 27. 20 (cf. ib. 39. 65: infulas, ∼ates); *CathA* (v. digma).

3 **a** person of high rank or office, dignitary. **b** (collect.) nobility, (persons of) high rank.

a 747 (12c) cum ex diversis Britanniae provintiis sacri ordinis .. praesules cum minoris ordinis ∼atibus convenissent (*Clovesho*) *CS* 174; *Ib.* 177 (v. actionarius a); **1005** (12c) rex .. omnibus aecclesiasticae pietatis ordinibus seu saecularis potentiae ∼atibus *CD* 714; **13..** excepto quod inferiores persone decano et ∼ates tunc temporis exercent officia per ordinem *Stat. Linc.* I 382; **1507** deducentibus eum [episcopum] duabus ∼atibus majoribus residencium in ecclesia per navim .. ad cathedram *Ib.* II 554. **b** EDDI 17 (v. 1 dicatio); cum quo speciosi duces et omnis Anglorum ∼as gloriose fulserunt BYRHT. *V. Osw.* 438; ne ∼as gentis .. deleretur G. MON. IV 9.

4 'liberty', privilege, authority: **a** (eccl. or mon.); **b** (civil). **c** area within which such 'liberty' is exercised.

a 1091 ∼as decani est et omnium canonicorum ut episcopo in nullo respondeant nisi in capitulo. .. habent etiam .. ∼atem archidiaconi ubicumque prebende assignate fuerint in parochia nostra. .. quando vero aliquis constituitur canonicus debet .. jurare .. se ∼ates et consuetudines Sar' ecclesie .. observaturum (*Stat. Sal.*) *Stat. Linc.* II 8–9; **a1166** hoc nostri statuti decretum, hanc nostre dispositionis ∼atem totus conventus studeat observare et superius positam ∼atem de dispositione prebendarii firmiter .. retineat *DC Wells* (*Ch. Roberti Episcopi*); ea que contra ∼ates Cantuariensis ecclesie .. erant .. peremptoria esse precepta sunt *Chr. Battle* f. 77v. **b 1088** dedi .. monachis omnes ∼ates quas habebam in eadem villa sc. *soc* et *sac*, *tol* et *them*, .. ferrum et fossam et furcas cum aliis libertatibus uti tunc temporis tenebam de rege *Cart. Blyth* I 208; **1103** ut socna .. pleniter monasterio S. Edmundi adjaceat .. cum omnibus libertatibus et ∼atibus et forisfacturis ad coronam regis pertinentibus *CalCh* II 258 (cf. *EHR* XXIV 425); qui injuste judicabit .. ∼atem judicandi perdat (*Leg. Hen.* 13. 4) *GAS* 558; **c1170** huic .. elemosine mee cum ceteris ∼atibus suis has libertates concedo .., sc. *sac* et *soc* [etc.] *Reg. Paisley* 6; facta est predictarum consuetudinum et ∼atum regiarum recordatio ab archiepiscopis .. apud Clarendunam H. BOS. *CE* 1416B; **1513** cum per ∼atem gladii nostri Cestrie .. nullus qui in advocarias nostras .. se posuit ad sectam alicujus attachiari debeat (*Breve Regis*) *EHR* XXIX 52. **c c1218** salvis mihi advocariis qui sponte ad me venerint et aliis qui pro transgressu aliunde ad ∼atem meam venerint (*Ch. Comitis Cestrie*) *Ib.* 44.

5 self-evident proposition, axiom (ἀξίωμα). *Cf. GLA* III 86 *n.*40.

HALES *Qu.* 1216 (v. 2b supra); tria sunt in scientia, subjectum, passio, et ∼as BACON XIII 94; ∼ates sunt propositiones communes et per se note, quibus utitur logicus quando facit suas probationes *Ib.* XV 194.

6 (astr.) 'dignity', (position of) heightened 'influence'.

1184 effectum quinque vagantium .. per domos et ∼ates suas se moventium (*Lit. Pharamel Cordub.*) R. HOWD. II 297; D. MORLEY 37 (v. dejectio 2c); sunt in signis predictis quedam fortitudines, que planetis attribuuntur, que dicuntur potestates vel ∼ates seu testimonia GROS. 42; sunt v

prerogative virtutum que vocantur ~ates planetarum; et sunt nomina earum significativa per similitudinem sumpta a potestatibus regis et ~atibus et que dicuntur domus, exaltatio, triplicitas, facies, terminus BACON V 20 (cf. ib.: ~as domus continet quinquies ~atem termini); satis racionabile videretur quod .. Deus .. mota celestia in locis, ~atibus, aspectibus et ceteris talibus ordinasset BRADW. *CD* 113C; caput et pes sex linearum sequencium declarant .. dominos triplicitatum, quarum tres prime demonstrant de quolibet gradu ceteras ~ates essenciales quas ibi habent planete ELVEDEN *Cal.* 5.

7 dais, high table (at Winchester). *Cf. dignus* 5.

si aliquis ospes .. fuerit invitatus a prelato et comederit in ~ate, eciam administrabitur ei de omnibus sicut uni de conventu *Cust. Swith.* 24.

dignitatus v. dignitas 2b. **digniter** v. digne.

dignitosus [CL], meritorious.

propter ~am innocentiae palmam ALDH. *VirgP* 54; ~a, *meodomlice GlC* D 333; ~a, i. mediocriter, *medomlice GlH* D482; ~us, dignus OSB. GLOUC. *Deriv.* 173; dignosus, A. *worthy WW*; *worthy*, .. dignus, digniciosus vel digniosus .. *CathA*.

dignorari v. dignari b. **dignoscere** v. dinoscere. **dignosus** v. dignitosus.

dignus [CL]

1 merited, due, appropriate. **b** (w. *ducere*) to think fit, approve.

solamina digna petentes ALDH. *VirgV* 1589; ~o a cunctis honore venerantur BEDE *HE* III 6 (cf. ib.: ~um fuit ut tantus praecessor talem haberet .. heredem); **853** nisi prius ~a satisque placavili factione Deo .. emendare voluerit *CS* 467; nisi ~a satisfactione peniteat (*Leg. Hen.* 66. 1) *GAS* 585; BRADW. *CD* 605A (v. dignificatio). **b** ~um ducens aliqua de gestis Æthelwoldi memoriae .. commendare ÆLF. *Æthelwold* 1; **1031** ego B. episcopus ~um duxi *CD* 744; **1163** ~um duxi redditum istum assignare *Cart. Rams.* II 197.

2 **a** of (great) worth, precious. **b** exalted (in rank).

a 8.. ~as res, *medeme ðinc WW*; non noscitur ~ior essentia quam spiritus aut corpus, et ex his spiritus ~ior est quam corpus ANSELM (*Mon.* 27) I 45. **b** te nunc sancte speculator, / verbi Dei digne dator, / Hæddi, pie presul, precor THEOD. *Pen.* (*Vers. epil.*); **c1190** donec ~ior persona que in capitulo fuerit dicat 'benedicite' *Stat. Lich.* 13.

3 worthy, deserving (of): **a** (w. abl. or gen. or *ad*); **b** (w. dat.); **c** (w. inf. or rel. cl.).

virum .. laude ~issimum BEDE *HE* III 25 p. 187; quae memoria ~a videbantur *Ib. pref.* p. 6; dua [v. l. duo] opuscula memoriae [v. l. memoria] ~a .. facere studuit CUTHB. *Ob. Baedae* clxii; aliquid memoriae ~um lectoris legendi manibus inponere me libet HUGEB. *Will. prol.*; furtum probatum et morte ~um (*Leg. Hen.* 13. 1) *GAS* 558; itineris nostri .. que .. relatu ~a fuerint .. manifestabimus OSB. BAWDSEY cxliv; memoratu ~am .. historiam GIR. *TH intr.* p. 8; **s1239** (v. distractio 2); de eo qui nondum imperat vel laudatur, sed ad hoc ~us est, dicendum, 'iste est ~us imperio vel laude'; de eo vero qui jam imperat vel laudatur dicendum, 'iste est ~us imperii vel laudis' *Ps.*-GROS. *Gram.* 65. **b c597** ~um se congregationi fratrum aestimare non debet (*Lit. Papae*) BEDE *HE* I 27 p. 57; abbas si habuerit monachum ~um aepiscopatui THEOD. *Pen.* II 6. 10; si ~um aliquid vestrae lectioni confecero *V. Cuthb.* I 1 (= EDDI *pref.*: †electioni); nobilium honori personarum .. ~i [AS: *þegenrihtes wyrþe*] habeantur (*Paraph.*) *GAS* 249 (cf. ib. 255: ut corporis et sanguinis participationi .. ~i .. efficiantur); vidit per somnium .. Petrum .. ~um tante majestati habitum preferentem AILR. *Ed. Conf.* 743B; **a1235** est Thome signum Virgo: fac hunc tibi dignum (*legend on counterseal*) *AncD* AS 302. **c** quem solum .. ~issimum ratus est cui Constantinam .. nuptiali dote subarraret ALDH. *VirgP* 48; non ~a est haec gens talem habere rectorem BEDE *HE* III 14; monachus .. ~us per omnia cui Dominus specialiter sua revelaret arcana *Ib.* IV 3; nos ~os qui eas scribamus efficiat AILR. *Nin. prol.*; digna perire peri WALT. ANGL. *Fab.* 38. 16; cui via danda fuit libera, dignus eram *Ib.* 42. 8; **s1223** ~us est .. conculcari qui .. suos .. conculcat M. PAR. *Min.* II 257; ~a dividi BACON XV 334 (v. compositio 1c); **1294** non ~us fuit manere in villa *SelPlMan* 116.

4 (leg.) 'worthy of', *i. e.* entitled to.

838 suae libertatis electione absque omni obstaculo .. ~i habeantur *CS* 421; **1067** volo quod sitis omni lege illa ~i [AS: *ealra þoera laga weorðe*] qua fuistis Edwardi diebus regis (*Breve Will. I*) *MGL* II 247 (cf. *Eng. Roy. Writs* pl. xiv); **a1097** ut non cogatis homines Sancti ire ad schiras .. nisi illos qui tantum terre habent unde ~i fuissent T. R. E. ire ad schiras (*Ch. Will. II*) *Regesta* p. 135; homines imperatoris .. bonarum legum ~i tenebantur (*Quad.*) *GAS* 234; volo ut omnis homo sit venatione sua ~us [AS: *his huntnoðes wyrðe*] .. in dominio suo (*Ib.*) *Ib.* 367.

5 (as sb. n. or m.) dais, high table (at Winchester). *Cf. dignitas* 7, *2 digitus*.

camerarius debet invenire .. unam novam mappam ad ~um et ad ceteras mensas pannos de canobio *Cust. Swith.* 17 (cf. ib. 18: coquinarius .. sedebit in ~o); **1390** in vino empto et misso ad ~um in refectorio *Comp. Swith.* 417.

1 digredi v. degredi.

2 digredi [CL]

1 to go different ways, separate (also fig.). **b** to depart. **c** to travel, pass (to or through). **d** to shamble. *V. et. degredi* 2.

postquam ab invicem digressi fuerimus BEDE *CuthbP* 28 (= *Id. HE* IV 27); ratio loci et ratio temporis hic ab invicem ~ientes disputationem videntur diversis quasi fugere anfractibus ANSELM (*Mon.* 21) I 36; ~iuntur ergo legati, ~iuntur reges, ~iuntur proceres G. MON. IX 20; digrediuntur ab invicem J. SAL. *Anselm* 1022A (= GERV. CANT. *AP* 372: disgrediuntur); regibus .. ~ientibus, singuli suas revertuntur in partes DEVIZES 29 p. 16. **b** digreditur cupiens panem deferre calentem BEDE *CuthbV* 196 (cf. *GlM* 7. 10: ~itur *he framcyrde*); postquam a te .. digressus sum ABBO *Edm. pref.*; quia Pylato visum est quod tantus propheta non sic disgrederetur de sua regnacione nisi rex foret alibi WYCL. *Civ. Dom.* III 68. **c** festinabat singulas regionis ~i civitates OSB. *V. Dunst.* 34; quidam pauper ei per officinas ministeriorum ~ienti occurreret R. COLD. *Cuthb.* 107. **d** *to schayle*, .. ~i *CathA*.

2 to stray from the subject, digress.

redeam nunc ad id de quo digressus sum NEN. *HB* 162; ut ad id unde digressus sum redeam .. expedire procurabo ASSER *Alf.* 73; nunc redi ad id unde digressi sumus ANSELM (*CurD* 18) II 84; deinde revertor / unde prius digressus eram VINSAUF *PN* 536; hucusque in solutione tertie questionis digressi sumus KILWARDBY *OS* 191; parum disgrediendo a proposito OCKHAM *Dial.* 641; ut supradicta magis appareant, oportet parumper disgredi WYCL. *Innoc.* 475.

digressare v. disgregare 2c.

digressio [CL], digression.

ad haec .. investiganda, .. ~onem .. cogamur interserere ANSELM *Misc.* 342; ipsa omnia possemus vobis aperte in scripturis ostendere; sed faceremus nimis magnam ~onem AILR. *Serm.* 312A; facta est voluptuosa ~o, non sine re tamen GIR. *TH* III 12; fit ~o duobus modis: .. unus modus ~onis est quando digredimur in materia ad aliam partem materie; alius modus quando digredimur a materia ad aliud extra materiam VINSAUF *AV* II 2. 17; est etiam quedam digressio quando propinqua / transeo, quod procul est premittens ordine verso *Id. PN* 532; disgressio *Ps.*-GROS. *Gram.* 74 (v. epanalepsis 2).

digressive, by way of digression.

s1207 his .. ~e digestis, jam propositum nostrum prosecuturi ad Cantuar' electum stilum vertamus GERV. CANT. II app. lxi; hoc ~e de predictis nuncupacionibus apud Latinos dictum sit KILWARDBY *Jejun.* 166.

digressivus [LL], digressive.

s1252 per hanc igitur recapitulationem ~am patet quare comes R. non doluit .. de regis .. perturbatione M. PAR. *Maj.* V 294.

digressus [CL], withdrawal.

lunae status idem eademque sit pro variante solis ~u conversio BEDE *TR* 25.

diiambus [CL < δiίαμβος], double iamb.

nomina seu verba ~o mancipata acuuntur quidem ut dispondeus, sed .. ~us .. in antepaenultima acutum habebit accentum, cetera gravabuntur ALDH. *PR* 127; partimur in aequo hos: .. ~um ⏑– | ⏑– BONIF. *Met.* 109; ~us est pes constans ex brevi et longa et brevi et longa et sex temporibus, ut 'prŏpīnquĭtās' GARL. *PP* 218.

dijudicare [CL]

1 to discern, discriminate; **b** (w. *ab*); **c** (w. *inter*).

discerne, i. ~a, divide, *toscead* segrega *GlH* D 570; dum anima queque corporalia ~at, sensum sibi inesse .. manifestat PULL. *Sent.* 736B; in hujusmodi intelligere quam ~are prius esse temptandum non sit immemor qui attendet BALSH. *AD* 79; eucharistiam sacram qui totiens conficiunt et consumunt .., corpus dominicum non plena discretione ~antes [cf. *1 Cor.* xi 29] GIR. *GE* I 50 p. 138. **b** PULL. *Sent.* 912B (v. 2 disparare 1a). **c** cujus mens obscura est ad ~andum inter asinum suum et colorem ejus ANSELM (*Incarn. A* 4) I 285.

2 to judge, decide (esp. leg.): **a** (w. matter as obj.); **b** (w. pers. obj.). *V. et. dejudicare* 1.

a audita et ~ata causa .. utriusque partis BEDE *HE* V 19; secundum eos [libros Augustini] opusculum meum ~et ANSELM (*Mon. prol.*) I 8; propter aliquam dubitationem que emergit in comitatu super loquela ipsa, quam comitatus nesciat ~are GLANV. VI 8; **c1239** ex verbis Exodi [xviii 22, 26] .. planissimum est quod tantummodo minora et faciliora possunt illi ~are, .. qui .. GROS. *Ep.* 127 p. 362. **b** qui [sc. Deus] genus humanum dijudicat omne per ignem WULF. *Swith.* I 1359; deinde contemptibiliores eliguntur, ut horum ab insania flendus juvenis ~etur *Enc. Emmae* III 6; ergo nostrum quisque, semet ipsum districte ~ans, divina consideret judicia OSB. BAWDSEY clxxxi; **c1239** cum minor non possit majorem ~are nec ut judex corrigere seu punire GROS. *Ep.* 127 p. 363.

3 to decide, determine, decree: **a** (w. inf.); **b** (w. acc. & inf.); **c** (w. *quod*). **d** (of jurors, w. acc. & inf.) to declare (that). *V. et. dejudicare* 2.

a 812 terram donare ~averat *CS* 341; **933** libertatem episcopatui .. perdonare ~avi *CS* 694. **b 1129** ~avit rex et ejus curia .. monachis remanere marescum quietum et liberum *Norm. Inst.* 91. **c 824** ab illa [synodo] ~atum [est] quod justum fieret ut .. *CS* 378. **d** ~averunt homines hundreti Ranulfum esse saisitum *DB* II 424; mansura regis .. modo iterum ~ata est esse teglanda *Dom. Exon.* 478b.

4 **a** (w. pers. obj.) to condemn. **b** to vilify. *V. et. dejudicare* 3.

a 1093 debet esse ut ab illis ~er [cf. *1 Cor.* iv 3: judicarer] ANSELM (*Ep.* 148) IV 4; **s1337** omnes .. qui .. in conflictu cum E. de Balliolo fuerunt .. divine majestatis judicio ~ati, in vinculis fuerunt *Plusc.* IX 35; clientes ejus [J. de Veteri Castro] .. quidam ~abantur suspendio et ignibus et quidam solo supendio *G. Hen. V* 1. **b** episcopos .. et omnem clerum ecclesie Dei .. non amavi .., sed vituperavi eos et detraxi atque ~avi ALCUIN (*In Psalm.*) *Liturg.* 499D; abbas ira commotus .. capitulum nostrum .. intravit atque .. minando atque spernendo me ~avit *Chr. Battle* f. 77v.

5 (astr.) to use as basis of prognostication.

quandoque [astrologie professores] 'genethliaci' [vocantur], quia generaciones hominum ~ant et per constellationem nativitatis tocius vite eventus ordinare volunt KILWARDBY *OS* 71.

dijudicatio [CL], discrimination.

'sine prejudicio' .., ~one, id est discretione LANFR. *Comment. Paul.* (*1 Tim.* v 21) 357; PULL. *Sent.* 912B (v. 2 disparare 1a); omne quod diximus precessit cogitatio et quedam interius ratiocinatio vel ~o AILR. *An.* I 20 f. 7; racio cognoscendi est nocior re cognita, sicut principium ~onis est nocius cognicione PECKHAM *QA* 63.

dijudicativus, discriminative.

anima .. est naturaliter boni et mali, veri et falsi ~a BART. ANGL. III 13; hec pupilla omnium colorum et figurarum rerum superficiem exprimentium est distinctiva et ~a *Ib.* V 7.

dijudicator [cf. CL dijudicatrix], regulator of proceedings.

s1128 jurant .. per ordinem episcopi, Rogero Saereberiensi presule ~ore omnium existente J. WORC. 27 (cf. ib.: ~or exclamat: "abbates procedant! juramentum faciant!").

dijuriare, to wrong.

to do wronge, ~iare, injuriare *CathA*.

†dijuvare, *f. l.*

ipse [sanguis] est quasi spiritus subtiliatus pulmonem †dijuvans [? l. adjuvans] magis in suo motu *Ps.*-RIC. *Anat.* 25.

dikera v. dacra.

diketta [cf. ME *dik*], little dike or ditch (Yorks). *Cf. dicum.*

1241 concessit .. cursum aque et fossatum a Flaxeleyker usque in ~am *AncD* A 11128.

1 dilabi v. delabi.

2 dilabi [CL], to fall apart, disperse. **b** (of information) to leak out. **c** (fig.) to grow weak, decay.

optentum est .. ut non ~eretur exercitus donec a Salahadino postularentur indutie DEVIZES 41. **b** ne tanti doloris arcanum ~eretur ad hostes *Ib.* **c** nos tenues, rebus dilapsis, pluris egemus *V. Ed. Conf.* 38; concordia res parve crescunt; discordia maxime ~untur OSB. BAWDSEY clxi.

dilacer, torn.

armorum compages gemescebant ~e *Ps.*-ELMH. *Hen.V* 45 p. 110; me miseram miserans intuearis; / .. / vestes dilaceras consue clemens (*Vers.*) *Ib.* 130.

dilacerare [CL], to tear apart, mangle. **b** to wreck, ravage. **c** (w. *de*) to tear off. *V. et. delacerare.*

carnem .. delaceratam [v. l. ~atam] a bestiis THEOD. *Pen.* I 7. 6; exquisitis poenarum machinamentis .. viventis hostiae artus .. ~ant ALDH. *VirgP* 33; FELIX *Guthl.* 31 (v. compago a); juvene .. frustatim securibus ~ato GIR. *EH* II 1; **1255** duo mastini .. inventi fuerunt .. ~antes unum brokettum *SelPlForest intr.* xxv; **1362** [homo] in parte ~atus cum canibus *SelCCoron* 39; **1294** verberavit Ricardum .. et tunicam suam †delitaverit [MS: dilaceravit] *CourtR Ramsey* 213; **s1381** statuta et libros eorum et munimenta ibidem reposita aliqua ~abant et aliqua comburebant *V. Ric. II* 26; *G. Hen. V* 24 (v. distendere 2a); *Entries* 7 (v. dilaceratio a). **b** cum .. provincias .. quasi tyrannus saeviens .. tragica caede ~aret BEDE *HE* III 1. **c 1384** quandam loricam .. de corpore suo violenter ~averunt *Pat* 317 m. 11d.

dilaceratio [LL], tearing, mangling, butchery (also fig.). **b** splitting, riving. **c** severance, estrangement.

subjectos cives tam atroci ~oni ex imminenti captivitate liberavit GILDAS *EB* 15 (cf. *Ann. Ang. & Scot.* 375 [**s1296**]: omnes [Scotos] a finibus depulit atque plebem suam a tam atroci ~one liberavit); membrorum crudelis ~o ALDH. *VirgP* 41; **c1275** pelles: in ~one canum et volucrum, vj *Ac. Beaulieu* 169; scriptum .. integrum et minime fractum neque dilaceratum .. deliberavit . . . dicit quod in nullo est culpabilis de fraccione neque ~one scripti illius *Entries* 7. **b** **1473** pro ~one et exasperacione iiij *stakez Ac. Durh.* 94 (cf. ib.: pro *le ryvyng* et *sharpyng .. del stakes*). **c** in via [i. e. *earthly pilgrimage*], ubi tanta varietas, tanta diversitas et adversitas, tanta distractio, tanta ~o est H. BOS. *LM* 1348A.

dilaceratrix, tearer down (f.).

1499 Margareta Smyth junior est communis dilaseratrix sepium *CourtR* (*N. Leigh, Oxon*) 197/54.

dilactare v. 2 dilatare 1a. **dilaectissimis** v. diligere. **dilanatio** v. dilaniatio.

dilancinare [LL], to tear apart, mangle.

'dis' praepositio interdum 's' litteram in compositione perdit, ut .. ~o, ~atus, ALDH. *PR* 140 p. 198; ~ata, *cwale GlP* 729; ~are, dilaniare OSB. GLOUC. *Deriv.* 177.

dilanguidus v. delanguidus.

dilaniare [CL], to tear apart, mangle. **b** to wreck, ravage.

toto corpore .. sagittis horridus et .. asperitate tormentorum ~iatus ABBO *Edm.* 11; congredientur dracones et alter alterum ~iabit (*Proph. Merl.*) G. MON. VII 4; **1126** una ovis .. morsibus raptorum ~iata *Ep. Anselm. Bur.* 97; adhuc proponis Dominum ~iare deterius in membris suis MAP *NC* V 6 f. 67; NECKAM *NR* I 64 (v. deplumare a). **b** sed mortis princeps jam tantum regnat in orbem; / totum delaniet mortificetque sibi GARL. *Epith.* I 650; pontis .., ampla ~iati ruptura, prepediebant suffragia *Ps.*-ELMH. *Hen. V* 59.

dilaniatio [LL], mangling.

coronacio spinea et vulneracio . ., flagellacio, et dilanacio crudelissima UHTRED *Medit.* 197.

dilaniator, butcher.

1457 alioquin pauperum eris occisor, inopum dislaniator (*Lit. Soldani ad Papam*) *Reg. Whet.* I 272.

dilanio, butcher; **b** (fig.).

item inhonestum puta si clericus sit ~o, carnifex aut publicus faber J. BURGH *PO* VII 10. **b** [burgenses] non sunt cives gentibus sed †delamones [l. delaniones] (*Divers. Ord.* 173) *Ps.*-MAP 234.

dilapidare [CL]

1 to stone, hit w. stones. **b** to hurl (? stones).

Cesaris ira potest .. corpora dilapidare NIG. *Laur.* 31v. 1; fundit funda David lapidem quo fronte Goliam / dilapidat; lapidem funda Maria parit GARL. *Epith.* VII 300. **b** ~at, projecit *GlC* D 247.

2 a to ruin (building) by removal of stones or sim. **b** to ruin, impoverish. **c** to waste, squander; **d** (?) (dep.).

a si episcopus, rector sive vicarius ~averit .. ecclesias .., vel alia aedificia .., tunc proximus successor agere potest contra predecessorem suum in causa dilapidationis dicti episcopatus, rectoriae vel vicariae *Praxis* 122. **b** non est veri simile quod vellem redditus peramplos relinquere .. propter pauperem cathedram depilatam undique et ~atam GIR. *Invect.* I 13. **c** **s1023** [Emma], que .. thesauros ~abat sanctitate prodiga W. MALM. *GR* II 181; **1163** constat .. patrem meum in irrogatione damnorum memorate ecclesie bona thesauri in cappis et textis, et hujusmodi plurimum delapidasse *Cart. Rams.* II 197; **s1239** [P. de Rupibus] thesaurum ecclesie [Winton'] ~ando .. soli regi placere cupiebat M. PAR. *Maj.* III 622; **1328** bona .. sua .. manus temerarie delapidant et consumunt *Lit. Cant.* I 269; **1552** res et bona ecclesiarum .. alienantur, ~antur et profligantur *Conc. Scot.* II 134. **d** **1399** hi sunt inflati, pro nummis infatuati, / querunt ditari, pro gazis delapidari (*In Adventum Ducis Lanc.*) *Pol. Poems* I 366.

dilapidatio [LL], ruin (of buildings), dilapidation. **b** waste, squandering, wastefulness.

s1381 Jekke Lister .. multa horrenda fecit, specialiter in ~one domorum et locorum CAPGR. *Hen.* 171; **1396** quamplura vasta et estreppamenta .., ~ones .. et defectus infra villam et castra nostra Berewici .. facta existunt *RScot* 131b; **1440** prioratus .. reddituum suorum diminucionem ac edificiorum ~onem passus fuit et ruinam BEKYNTON I 121; **1446** rector notatur super ~one mansi rectorie sue *Eng. Clergy* 233; *Praxis* 122 (v. dilapidare 2a). **b** **1202** cum .. de vita ipsius R. .. inquisiisses, de ~one, incontinentia et turpi ejus conversatione *Ep. Innoc. III* 15; **s1213** quod [abbas] propter ~onem vel collusionem vel insufficientiam debuit deponi *Chr. Evesham* 243; **s1248** rex .. reprehensus est de .. thesauri regii .. dispersione et rerum ~one M. PAR. *Min.* III 33; **1326** nec est hereditatis alienacio sponsam dotare, nec eciam bonorum delapidacio filios locupletare *Lit. Cant.* I 190; si imperator committit crimen ~onis vel destruccionis imperii OCKHAM *Pol.* I 84; **s1367** ne illud in ~onem seu prejudicium jurium ecclesie sue .. facere viderentur *Meaux* III 119.

dilapidator [LL], waster, squanderer.

s1179 priores .. nisi pro .. rationabili causa non mutentur, viz. si ~ores fuerint, si incontinenter vixerint .. (*Decr. Papae*) *G. Hen. II* I 231; dilapidatori, meretrici vel nebuloni / fraudibus imbuto que dantur sunt data vento D. BEC. 2338; GIR. *JS* 7 (v. dilatator); domus sue ~or N. DUNSTABLE *Chr.* 8; ex tot et ex opibus tantis a patre relictis / dilapidator opum non habet quo tegmine velet / pauperiem VINSAUF *PN* 1539; **s1213** manifestus possessionum hujus ecclesie ~or est abbas noster *Chr. Evesham* 242 (cf. *Ann. Dunstable* 109); **s1252** regni ~or (v. depauperator); **s1415** J. papam simoniacum .., jurium .. ecclesiarum et plurium aliorum piorum ~orem notorium WALS. *HA* II 304.

dilapidatorie, wastefully.

~ie, sparsim, vastatorie OSB. GLOUC. *Deriv.* 177.

dilapidatrix, squanderer (f.).

s1023 [Emma], que in talibus thesaurorum ~ix erat sua prodiga largitate M. PAR. *Maj.* I 505 (cf. dilapidare 2c).

dilapsus v. delapsus.

dilargiri [CL], to give (lavishly).

to gife, .. donare, .. delargiri .. *CathA.*

dilargus [LL], lavish, munificent.

~us, multum donans *GlC* D 304; ~us, i. multum donans, largus *GlH* D 505; ~us, valde largus OSB. GLOUC. *Deriv.* 180.

dilaseratrix v. dilaceratrix.

dilatabilis, dilatable, expansible.

animalium spermata .. oportuit loco .. capaci et cum crescentibus ~i concludi ALF. ANGL. *Cor* 12. 2; nervus est membrum mediocre in duritia et ~e et extensibile *Ps.*-RIC. *Anat.* 42; parvissimum radii corpus in oculo muris erit juxta hoc prolongabile usque in centrum et ~e usque ad mediam quantitatem celi *Ps.*-GROS. *Summa* 505; quia orificium matricis non est ~e ad exitum fetus GAD. 76v. 1.

1 dilatare v. 1 delatare 2.

2 dilatare [CL]

1 to enlarge, expand, spread; **b** (w. abstr. obj.). **c** to open. **d** to dilate (heart or sim.; partly fig.). **e** to deploy (troops). **f** (intr.) to widen, grow broader.

quasi metallum feriendo ~atum BEDE *Tab.* 419; quando evenerit .. ut .. ignis [montis Ethnae] ~are se voluerit super regionem HUGEB. *Will.* 4; paludibus ~atis stagnorum ABBO *Edm.* 2; ~ant, *tobrædaþ GlH* D 504; GIR. *TH* I 3 (v. caput 14b); **s1244** episcopus .., quem .. hydropisis undique ~averat M. PAR. *Maj.* IV 330; **s1245** fratres Minores Oxonie .. ceperunt delatare terminos suos et nova edificia construere WYKES 93; humiditas .. humectat et †dilactat et facit fluxum materie. . . calor .. movet materiam in suas extremitates et ~at GILB. I 6v. 1; †dilitatur humor BACON V 85*n.* (v. distensivus); res ~antes sanguinem et spargentes ipsum ad exteriora sunt multe *Ib.* IX 71; fossatum in solo nostro proprio conficitur .., ut .., si quando .. mundari debeat seu ~ari, in solo nostro proprio pro dicto fossato ~ando perfod[i]amus *Meaux* I 80; **1318** ad actus pacificos manus extendimus ~atas *FormOx* 45; **1336** in canevacio veteri empto .. ad ponendum super *hacches* .. galee .. et in pice et bitum[ine] et lymo emptis .. ad dictum canevacium cum eisdem ponendum et †tylatandum (*sic*) *KRAc* 19/31 m. 5; ne nimis epistolam ~arem LUTTERELL *Vis. Beat.* f. 95. **b** [Dominus] catervis credentium regni sui gloriam ~at BEDE *Hom.* I 25. 109; [Osuald] ecclesiam Christi in regno suo .. ~are curavit *Id. HE* III 3; †**741** (8c) ad ~andum (*sic*) et augendam vitam Christi sacerdotum *CS* 160; FOLC. *V. Bot.* 2 (v. devincire 1b); GOSC. *Werb.* 2 (v. Christianitas 1a); ut [ecclesia] et vestro merito et exemplo proficiat et amplius in ipso ~etur H. READING (II) *Cel.* 29; **s1327** rumorem .. ~at (v. circumgyrare 2c); pro fide catholica ~anda OCKHAM *Dial.* 566; conatus est .. ut celeste et subceleste coartasset imperium ut proprium ~aret *G. Hen. V* 1 p. 10. **c** ~averunt, i. aperuerunt, *hi geopenadon GlH* D 506. **d** BEDE *Sam.* 603 (v. coangustare 1a); †dilato [? l. ~ato] sinu mentis oculus interior .. usque Ephesiorum civitatem .. porrexit AILR. *Ed. Conf.* 768A; **1184** magnificentiam tuam .. duximus exorandam, immo ~atis precordiis .. pulsandam, quatenus .. (*Lit. Papae*) *G. Hen. II* I 332; musculi orificia sinistri et medii cordis claudentes .. inter ipsa orificia tenduntur, ut alterutro ~ato alterum claudi sit necesse ALF. ANGL. *Cor* 6. 1; dum [cor] ~atur vel elevatur, aerem attrahit et inspirat RIC. MED. *Anat.* 219; **s1274** non habeo in quo irascendo ~are cor meum possum GRAYSTANES 16; potest esse cordis dilatatio vehementi gaudio existente, quod [? l. quo] cor ultra modum ~abitur J. BLUND *An.* 380; animus per caritatem ~atus BRINTON *Serm.* II 29. **e** [armatorum cunei] per arvorum largas planicies ~ati *Ps.*-ELMH. *Hen. V* 75. **f** **1155** terra .. que .. tendit obliquando et ~ando versus occidentem *Feod. Durh.* 121*n.*

2 (w. ref. to persons): **a** to magnify, exalt. **b** (pass.) to be puffed up (*cf. Deut.* xxxii 15). **c** (refl.) to spread oneself, devote one's energies.

a an non istud est quo nihil pium presulem honorat excellentius .. et abundantius ~at? AD. MARSH *Ep.* 36. **b** clerici Eboracenses multum jam exaltati et ~ati AILR. *SS Hex* 15; **1422** etsi .. incrassatus impinguatusque .. immoderanter in tuis diffugiis ~eris (*Lit. Abbatis*) AMUND. I 93. **c** circa tales casus .. minime te ~es OCKHAM *Dial.* 451.

3 to delay, to put off. *Cf.* 3 *dilatio.*

~are, differre OSB. GLOUC. *Deriv.* 179; **1241** episcopus est ultra mare et, per hoc quod prior vocat ipsum ad warantum, posset loquela ista diu ~ari *CurR* XVI 1659; brevia .. ~avit pro donis que ab adversis partibus recepit *State Tri. Ed. I* 11; **1571** conveiancie .. contrivate de malicia .. ad ~and', retardand' vel defraudand' creditores *Entries* 207b.

dilatate, at large.

1346 humane memorie nimis arcta capacitas in variis paginis †queque †dilate [? l. ~ate] conspersa infra limites sui sinus *Conc.* II 729a; hiis expositis vel effusis delatatius COLET *In 1 Cor.* 223.

dilatatio [CL]

1 enlargement, expansion, spread; **b** (of abstr.). **c** dilation (of heart; partly fig.). **d** deployment (of troops).

latus .. componitur .. ~o OSB. GLOUC. *Deriv.* 316; **1192** quod habeat .. iiij acras .. ad ~onem et emendationem curie sue *Reg. S. Osm.* I 264; **s1250** maris insolita ~o M. PAR. *Abbr.* 317 (= *Id. Min.* III 91: ascensus .. insolitus); dedit nobis .. unum sellionem ad ~onem curtis grangie .. †includendam [? l. includendum] *Meaux* II 10; per expansionem et ~onem ejus [sc. sanguinis] BACON IX 70; motus a medio ~one fit, motus ad medium constrictione *Ps.*-GROS. *Gram.* 20; **1385** in ~one altaris *Ac. Durh.* 265. **b** **796** pro ~one Christiani nominis ALCUIN *Ep.* 104; **1236** ad .. libertatis ecclesiastice ~onem GROS. *Ep.* 29; ad ~onem Christiane religionis AD. MARSH *Ep.* 8; **1309** ad ~onem sancte fidei (*Lit. Baronum*) *Reg. Heref.* 474 (= *Ann. Lond.* 164: †dilationem); intencio ejus [Luce] primitive ecclesie statum discribere et .. ~onem ejus per orbem factam .. notificare CAPGR. *Acts* 222. **c** eorum [cordis thalamorum] orificia ~one et constrictione alterna mutuas vicissitudines .. observant ALF. ANGL. *Cor* 5. 3; J. BLUND *An.* 376 (v. constrictio a); BACON III 279 (v. cor 1); **s1274** nec electuaria .. preciosa tam mihi conferre poterunt .. ad ~onem vel purgacionem cordis mei GRAYSTANES 16. **d** [Franci] sonipedum impetuosis cursibus .. †initis [*ed.*: immitis] sue ~onis [v. l. delatacionis] perficere temptabant effectum *Ps.*-ELMH. *Hen. V* 75.

2 (by conf. w. 3 *dilatio*) delay.

1348 si .. solverit .. xi li. .. argenti sine omni fraude et ulteriori ~one *Mem. Ripon* I 280; **1389** quod .. Johannem [Bradborne] sine †dilitacione arestari .. faciatis (*Cl*) *Peasants' Rising* 43.

dilatativus, dilative (of heart).

Ps.-RIC. *Anat.* 42 (v. cibalis); ista virtus per virtutem ~am cordis et constrictivam anhelitum in animali operatur, qui movet pectus BART. ANGL. III 15.

dilatator [LL], **a** expander, increaser. **b** spreader (of faith), propagator.

a sit rerum ecclesiasticarum dispensator non dissipator, .. ~or non dilapidator GIR. *JS* 7 p. 366. **b** Wlferus .. Christianae fidei .. amator et ~or GOSC. *Werb.* 102C; ut [rex] ecclesie catholice sit defensor, fidei Christiane ~or *Lib. Regal.* 3.

dilate v. dilatate.

dilatescere, to be widespread.

1435 paterni honoris gloria tunc ~it in orbe *EpAcOx* 120.

1 dilatio v. delatio 4.

2 dilatio v. dilatatio 1b.

3 dilatio [CL], delay. **b** adjournment, respite.

famis .. multos eorum .. compulit praedonibus sine ~one victas dare manus GILDAS *EB* 20; epistolarum .. debita vicissitudo quasi quodam ~onis obstaculo tricabatur ALDH. *VirgP* 59; ~o, *aelding GlC* D 265; **1163** festinantiam .. vestram nullum retardet negotium ..; omnis procul amoveatur ~o (*Lit. Regis*) *Ep. G. Foliot* 143; *Chr. Battle* f. 47v. (v. chrisma 1a); accepta .. spe .. sibi non abfuturum auxilium, .. delationem .. patientissime sustinuit *Transl. Ecgwini* 35; sine omni ulteriori ~one *FormMan* 11; GAD. 92. 2 (v. dilativus 2); 'nichil moror', id est non faciam ~onem TREVET *Troades* 71; *a delay*, delacio, prolongacio *CathA.* **b** **1169** (v. delusio); **1226** nec debet judicium poni in ~onem quin fiat infra predictum terminum *Pat* 82; **s1242** etc. (v. capere 15b); **s1255** tandem ~onem sumpsit negotium hoc usque ad festum S. Mich. M. PAR. *Abbr.* 344; si [absens fuerit] extra regnum .., ~onem habebit xl dierum et duorum *floz* [v. l. flodorum] et unius ebbe BRACTON 163; quibus ~onibus potest tenens litem differre HENGHAM *Magna intr.*; **1348** cepisse debuit .. iiij m. argenti in ~onem accionis ipsius J. *SelCKB* VI 66.

dilativus

1 productive of delay.

1408 .. omnibus .. unionis .. delativis (v. disturbativus).

2 (med.) 'dilative', promoting diffusion (of food).

[potus] delativus [debet accipi] post prandium, facta delatione, et postquam descenderit cibus de stomaco, vel in descendendo GAD. 92. 2.

dilator [CL], delayer, postponer.

juris et justitie ~or GIR. *EH* I 46.

dilatorie, by dilatory procedure (esp. leg.).

quare [mulier] dotem habere non debeat peremptorie, vel quare ad tempus differ[r]i debet actio et dotis exactio ~ie BRACTON 301b; **s1281** ego .. procurator .. abbatis et conventus de B. .. contra eundem W. .. excipiendo ~ie propono quod .. littere provisorie dicti W. .. carent effectu *Chr. Peterb.* 48; **c1430** nec amicabiliter sciveritis honestum quicquam petere, in quo licebit nobis negatorie aut ~ie seu quomodolibet excusatorie respondere *Reg. Whet.* II app. 454; **s1176** ~ie longos terminos dare *Plusc.* VI 30.

dilatorius [CL], dilatory, causing delay (esp. leg.). **b** (as sb. n. or f.) dilatory plea or exception.

ad .. ~ium laudabilis ausus impedimentum GIR. *EH* II 29; exceptionum alie perpetue et peremptorie, alie temporales et ~ie. .. ~ie tantum in principio opponi possunt et non postea RIC. ANGL. *Summa* 38; **1208** ad omnes exceptiones ~ias preponendas *Melrose* 101; est quedam [exceptio] peremptoria quantum ad personam unius et ~ia judicii BRACTON 187b; videtur [quod non debet] de cetero admitti ad aliquam responsionem ~iam *State Tri. Ed. I* 76; **c1410** [causa] solis fictis ac ~iis verbis et fabulis tam diu impudenter atteritur *FormOx* 206. **b 1281** solempnitas per quam totum jus deciditur non debet per errorem factum in ~ia adnichilari *SelCKB* I 89; **1310** procurator .. archiepiscopi .. ponit ~ias *Reg. Cant.* 1182; **1311** in quibus causis non licet ~ia proponere *Conc.* II 411b (*rub.*).

dilatrix, causing delay (f.).

segnities, .. / .. dilatrix operum, dissuada laborum HANV. I 8 p. 240.

dilatus v. deferre, differre, dilatare. **dileberare** v. 1 deliberare. **dilactabilis, ~are, ~atio** v. delect-. **dilect-** v. et. delect-.

dilectator, lover.

multi fuerunt sancti reges .. qui justitiam dilexerunt ..; aliter omnes reges .. extitissent delectatores iniquitatis OCKHAM *Dial.* 907.

1 dilectio v. deletio.

2 dilectio [LL]

1 love, affection (towards person). **b** sexual love. **c** (as title of addressee) amiability or sim.

ut virtutem ~onis et pacis ad invicem .. servarent BEDE *HE* IV 22 p. 261; affectui, *megsibbe* vel ~one *GlC* A 371; **784** amicitia fraternae ~onis .. olim inter nos .. specialiter verbis est conjuncta pacifica ALCUIN *Ep.* 24; **838** quomodo pax et unianimitas ecclesiarum .. ~onis vinculo servari potuisset (*Conc. Kingston*) *CS* 421; **c1075** majorem .. ~onem puto quod a me nemo valet exigere quam ut velim eum tamquam me ipsum diligere ANSELM (*Ep.* 44) III 157; MAP *NC* IV 16 (v. commonitio); sit Deus in primis super omnia corde colendus; / inde comes vera dilectio proximitatis D. BEC. 21; Goriorilla .. numina celi testata est ipsum [Leir] majori ~oni esse quam animam que in corpore suo degebat G. MON. II 11; GROS. *Ep.* 76 (v. desiderabilis 1a); cum in aliquo offenderint .., corripi .. debent .. spirituali ~one *Cust. Westm.* 188; DUNS *Ord.* II 57 (v. delectatio); **1463** cupientes .. sibi pro tanta dilexione vicem reddere *Cant. Coll. Ox.* III 107; **1527** [episcopus] singulos accipiet per manum dexteram, ad ~onis oscula admittendo *Stat. Linc.* II 554. **b c597** qui .. huic nefando conjugio dicuntur admixti ad fidem venientes admonendi sunt ut se abstineant .., ne pro carnali ~one [v. l. delectatione] tormenta aeterni cruciatus incurrant (*Lit. Papae*) BEDE *HE* I 27 p. 51; injecit juvenis ille oculos in cujusdam formose virginis faciem et eam cepit juvenali ~one concupiscere KETEL *J. Bev.* 282. **c 601** haec ~onem tuam praedicto fratri necesse est dicere (*Lit. Papae ad M. Abbatem*) BEDE *HE* I 30; **c750** notum tuae sit sanctitatis ~oni quia .. BONIF. *Ep.* 96 (*ad L. Abbatissam*); **c800** saepius vestrae probatissimae caritati scriberem, si occasionem mihi vestra ~o daret ALCUIN *Ep.* 204 (*ad virginem nobilem*); **1138** significavit nobis paternitatis vestre ~o (*Lit. Archiep. Ebor. ad Papam*) DICETO *YH* I 250; **c1205** dilecto sibi in Christo magistro Ade Rufo: .. rogavit me dulciflua ~o tua quatenus scriberem tibi .. GROS. *Ep.* 1; **c1377** amice predilecte. .. vestram ~onem ob librorum defectum .. eclipsim pati nolentes, x libras .. destinamus presencium cum latore *FormOx* 384.

2 love of God: **a** (as subj.); **b** (as obj.). **c** love as personified in Christ.

a quod dominici pectoris accubitor .. specialem divinae ~onis praerogativam ac privatam amoris munificentiam .. promeruerit ALDH. *VirgP* 7; bone Domine, .. satiet eam ~o tua ANSELM (*Med.* 3) III 91. **b** larga .. differentia inter divinae ~onis munificentiam et infimi amoris diligentiam ALDH. *VirgP* 17; redemptionem totius mundi .. completa fide ac ~one colere (*Ep. Ceolfridi*) BEDE *HE* V 21 p. 341; **a792** floreas, fili, .. sancta ~one ad Deum et bona fide ad hominem ALCUIN *Ep.* 11; decem .. sunt precepta, quorum tria pertinent ad ~onem Dei HALES *Sent.* II 366; jocunditas in ~one Dei ROLLE *IA* 170; WYCL. *Mand. Div.* 106 (v. diligibilis). **c** quoniam Christus, dilectio sancta, / incipit in mundo GARL. *Myst. Eccl.* 248.

3 (feud. or sim.): **a** favour (to an inferior). **b** devotion, loyalty, allegiance (to a superior). **c** (opp. to *pretium*) 'love or money'.

a rex [Eadwig] .. ignaros quosque sibi consimiles studio ~onis adsciscens B. *V. Dunst.* 24; **1122** virum .. vobis utilem .. in primum ~onis vestre gradum et in officium sibi injunctum .. revocate (*Lit. Archiep. Cant.*) EADMER *HN* 353 (= *E. Ch. Scot.* 42); **1270** dabit domino abbati pro ~one sua habenda xx s. *CourtR Hales* 18; **1335** sincera domini ~o et grata devocio subditorum suos communicant sic affectus ut .. ad auxilia mutua sint parati *RScot* 340b. **b** [Brennius] profusus erat in dandis cibis. .. tractis ergo quibusque in ~onem suam .. G. MON. III 7; episcopus [H., ob. **1195**] .. venientes ad se monachos honorifice .. excipiebat et dominos vocabat, quo eorum ~onem non mediocriter obtinebat G. COLD. *Durh.* 4; **s1257** magnates Alemannie .. dixerunt domino suo regi Ricardo: "domine, nos gratuita ~one te in dominum et regem .. elegimus" OXNEAD *Chr.* 211; **1270** vobis mandamus in fide, homagio et ~one quibus nobis tenemini .. quatinus .. (*Breve Regis*) *Leg. Ant. Lond.* 128. **c** ~one aut pretio (*Inst. Cnuti*) *GAS* 614 (v. aisia).

4 a love of (hallowed) place. **b** love of abstr. **c** love (miscalled) of temporal things.

a aliquod .. monumentum, quo et devocio mea cresceret ad Deum et ~o perseveraret ad locum *Croyl.* 75. **b** homines .. ab amore scelerum abstrahere, ad ~onem vero et solertiam bonae actionis excitare curabat BEDE *HE* IV 22 p. 261; cupiditas glorie superetur ~one justitie J. SAL. *Pol.* 722A; in iste praxi que est ~o finis ut pertinet ad theologiam DUNS *Ord.* I 186. **c** que [temporalium] ~o vocatur contemptum vel odium (WYCL.) *Ziz.* app. 487 (cf. distanter b).

dilector [CL]

1 lover (of person); **b** (sexual).

c1075 dilecto ~ori dilectus ~or Gondulfo frater Anselmus ANSELM (*Ep.* 16) III 121; **1166** Thomas .. Cantuariensis ecclesie minister humilis dilecto et ~ori amico suo R. .. preposito (*Ep. Herberti in persona Thomae Cantuar.*) H. BOS. *Ep.* 11. 1435B (= *Ep. Becket* 171). **b** illa [muliercula] statim ~ori suo adventum ejus intimavit ORD. VIT. III 3 p. 44.

2 a lover of God. **b** lover, as epithet of Christ.

a "me ipsum," inquit, "manifestabo ~oribus meis" [cf. *John* xiv 21] BEDE *Hom.* I 2. 30 (cf. AD. SCOT *Serm.* 235A: ~oribus suis ostendet se ipsum); ~or tuus et unice matris tue .., Domine meus AILR. *Ed. Conf.* 747B; verus ~or nec ad mundum dirigit oculum nec pro Deo pati metuit omne .. durum ROLLE *IA* 172. **b** latus lucis limatum lancea, / dilectoris cor fractum framea J. HOWD. *Ph.* 484.

3 lover: **a** (of abstr.); **b** (of the world); **c** (of books).

a 1107 cunctis ecclesie catholice filiis et ~oribus *CalCh* II 490 (= *Regesta* II 847); **1191** virum illum .., quem novistis ecclesie vestre ferventissimum ~orem *Ep. Cant.* 381; vere vite et eterne glorie ~ores *Latin Stories* 8. **b** 'Egyptii' sunt ~ores mundi, seculares et vitiosi AILR. *Serm.* 213C; mundi non desertores sed ~ores GIR. *GE* II 8 p. 199. **c** socialem communionem .. cum .. librorum ~oribus R. BURY *Phil.* 8. 117.

dilectrix, lover (f.) of God (w. ref. to Mary Magdalene).

electa ~ix et dilecta electrix Dei ANSELM (*Or.* 16) III 65; de osse brachii beatissime Christi ~icis M. Magdalene duo mordicitus excussit frustra (*sic*) AD. EYNS. *Hug.* V 13 p. 169; **c1480** in honorem Dei .. et beate ~icis sue (*Chr. Tewkesb.*) *MonA* II 60b.

dilectus [CL], **a** muster (of troops). **b** choice. **c** discrimination, discernment.

a ~um, *meniu*, exercitum *GlC* D 290; **1560** delectus bellicos (v. conscribere 3a). **b** delectum, *cyri* vel electio *GlC* D 126. ~us, electio OSB. GLOUC. *Deriv.* 178. **c** proscriptos addixit exsilio sine ~u dignitatis aut ordinis J. SAL. *Thom.* 19; non sine delectu promissis credere fas est WALT. ANGL. *Fab.* 20. 13; avibus istis [bernacis] .. viri religiosi jejuniorum tempore sine delectu vesci solent GIR. *TH* I 15; [mustela] tantum habet herbarum medicinalium delectum ut fetus suos reanimare .. putetur NECKAM *NR* II 123; **1297** sine †deletu personarum *Conc. Syn.* 1154; **1440** sine delectu cujuscunque persone *Stat. Linc.* II 354.

dilemma [LL < δίλημμα], dilemma; **b** (log.).

ut quasi sub bipenni ~ate .. concludam: anima benevola talia non exquirit, in malevolam vero animam sapientia non introibit GIR. *TH* I 13; ex vehementia animi subticet efficatiam ~atis, scilicet hoc: 'si miles, duc, si comes, sequere' GERV. MELKLEY *AV* 29. **b** nullo decipitur bursa sophismate, / nullis arguciis, nullo dilemate WALT. WIMB. *Sim.* 55.

dilexio v. 2 dilectio 1a. **dilibatus** v. delibuere. **diliber-** v. deliber-. **dilic-** v. et. delic-, diluc-. **dilictus** v. delinquere 1d, diligere 1c. **diligare** v. deligare.

diligenter [CL], attentively, earnestly.

ni .. prodigiorum gesta .. ~er didicerit ALDH. *VirgP* 43; causam, quam nesciebam, ~issime investigabam BEDE *HE* II 1 p. 77; **738** (12c) tam ~er postulavi ab archiepiscopo N. et rege Æ. .. ut ipsi manu sua hanc donationem corroborassent *CS* 159; ut unusquisque artem suam ~er [AS: *geornlice*] exerceat ÆLF. *Coll.* 100; ~er, *willendlice GlH* D 526; quanto .. ~ius consideratur DOMINIC *V. Ecgwini prol.*; cepit ~er deliberare GIR. *EH* I 37; EDMUND *Spec. Relig.* 10 (v. diligere 2a); **1251** ~er examinatus *SelPlForest* 97; **s1327** cum requirerent ~er quod renunciaret dignitati regie AD. MUR. *Chr.* 51.

diligentia [CL], care, zeal, diligence. **b** (?) backing, approval. **c** effort.

ALDH. *VirgP* 17 (v. 2 dilectio 2b); quasi subito sublatum eum quaesierit cum omni ~ia BEDE *HE* IV 21 p. 256; ne afferat docendi ~ia dicendi odiosam prolixitatem BALSH. *AD* 60; ut desidiam ~ia, .. ignaviam strenuitate dediscant GIR. *TH* I 12; **1239** (v. 1 apponere 5); ~ia est generalis habitus in omni virtute, et ipsa consistit in 'precavendis insidiis' HALES. *Sent.* III 389; maxime credendum est .. illis .. que communitas famosa et honesta cum maxima ~ia precepit approbanda DUNS *Ord.* I 69. **b** concede ut ad aliarum terrarum nationes cum ~ia tua abscedant G. MON. I 4. **c 1371** noluit facere ~iam suam pro uno bercario querendo ad communitatem ville *Hal. Durh.* 109; **1447** domino R. L. pro laboribus et magnis ~iis suis factis .. in negociis regis *ExchScot* 276; **1460** mandavit .. apparitori .. ut ~iam faceret *Conc.* III 578.

diligere [CL]

1 to love (person); **b** (sexually). **c** (p. ppl. *dilectus*) beloved, dear.

hic [Constantinus] sobolem sanctam miro dilexit amore ALDH. *VirgV* 2062; cuidam virginum .., quae illam immenso amore ~ebat BEDE *HE* IV 21; quam benigno ~ebat affectu studiosos .. fratres WULF. *Æthelwold* 37; GOSC. *Mir. Iv.* lxxxii (v. commilito c); **c1093** ~ende frater Normanne H. LOS. *Ep.* 1; ego dilexi te semper ut patrem G. MON. II 11; eum cepit deligere T. MON. *Will.* VII 13 (v. despicabiliter a); cum .. ea .. de quibus dicitur transposite et internexe sibi annecti licet, hoc modo: .. 'alicui odio habent quos diligunt' BALSH. *AD* 100; queritur unde fit quod parentes magis ~unt filios quam filii parentes *Quaest. Salern.* B 161; quod caritati deberetur aureola, cum difficillimum sit ~ere inimicum HALES *Qu.* 1138. **b** qui ~it feminam mente veniam petat THEOD. *Pen.* I 2. 22; [presbyter] volebat .. amicis suis incognitum esse quod eam ~eret ORD. VIT. III 3 p. 44; **1287** (v. conjugalis a); *Arthur & Gorlagon* 7 (v. dominus 1e); GAD. 132. 1 (v. amor 1b). **c 673** ~issimi fratres (*Conc. Hertf.*) BEDE *HE* IV 5; **a705** ~issimae atque amantissimae sorori et mihi sincero caritatis affectu venerandae ALDH. *Ep.* 6 (8); **838** (10c) cum consensu dilaectissimi filii nostri Æ. *CS* 418; **8..** mi ~e, *eala ðu min gecorena WW*; **1258** H. rex Anglie .. ~o sibi in Christo abbati Rames' (*Breve Regis*) *SelPlMan* 59; **1289** †dilicta in Christo filia Margareta, nata .. E. Norwegie regis (*Lit. Papae*) *Doc. Scot.* I 112; **1520** delectis filiis tam ecclesiasticis quam secularibus (*Lit. Papae*) *Let. Ch. Ch.* xlv.

2 to love (spiritually): **a** (w. divine subj.); **b** (w. divine obj.); **c** (p. ppl. *dilectus*) beloved (of God).

a quoniam omnino idipsum est quod amat vel amatur in Patre et quod in Filio, necesse est ut pari amore uterque ~at se et alterum ANSELM (*Mon.* 51) I 65; consideranda sunt .. diligenter Dei beneficia, ut ipsum ~as quia prior dilexit te [cf. *1 John* iv 10] EDMUND *Spec. Relig.* 10 (cf. 2b infra). **b** Lucia, quae Dominum dilexit sedula Christum ALDH. *VirgV* 1783; intentione pia Deum dilexerunt BEDE *HE* III 23; **a785** (12c) habeat beatam communionem in praesenti cum ~entibus Deum *CS* 260; EDMUND *Spec. Relig.* 10 (v. 2a supra); **c1301** (v. diligibilis); cogitate quod debetis inclinari faciliter ad ~endum [ME: *to luvien*] regem glorie *AncrR* 159. **c** Salamon ecclesiastes .. est ~us Domini *GlC Int.* 301; illos Dei famulos ac Deo ~os esse non nego BEDE *HE* III 25 p. 187; Johannes .. ~us Domini [cf. *John* xiii 23] OSB. *V. Dunst.* 31; sanctissimus, Deoque ~issimus Dunstanus *Ib.* 41; ANSELM (*Or.* 16) III 65 (v. dilectrix); Christo dilecte Johannes GARL. *Hon. Vit.* 287; sic sollicitus .. est [Dominus noster] ut amorem suum accendat in corde sue ~e [ME: *in his leoves heorte*] *AncrR* 159.

3 (feud. or sim.): **a** to favour, look kindly on (an inferior or protégé). **b** to be loyally devoted to (a superior).

a 1204 rex .. dilecto et fideli suo G. .. comiti Essex *Cl* 7b; **s1213** juravit rex .. quod sanctam ecclesiam ejusque ordinatos ~eret, defenderet et manuteneret WEND. II 81; potest equidem dominus aliquis curie, si voluerit, ex gracia sua per litteras suas patentes scribere domino regi quod remisit ei curiam suam, si tamen ~at petentem HENGHAM *Magna* 3. **b c1087** precipio ut nullus vestrum de illis terris .. amplius se, si me ~itis, intromittat *Regesta* p. 130; **1256** sicut ipsum dominum regem ~itis (*AncC* VI 180) *RL* II 117.

4 to love, like, desire: **a** (material obj. or place); **b** (abstr.); **c** (w. inf. or *quod*).

a fructiferas .. quercus / diligo ALDH. *Aen.* 54 (*Scrofa*) 9; sanctam, / quae mortale nihil vano dilexit amore *Id. VirgV* 2011; dilectaque rura, *and þa lufwende eardas* vel *leofe GlH* D 531; nota dilectae solitudinis secreta .. repetit ABBO *Edm.* 13; **1267** sicut vitam et membra ~erent *SelPlJews* 37; **1289** ad memoriam revocans †delictam terram Agenn' *AncC* XIV 140; codices plus dileximus quam florenos R. BURY *Phil.* 8. 123. **b** quod caelibatus castimoniam .. medullitus dilexerit ALDH. *VirgP* 25; cum eis qui canonica patrum statuta ~erent BEDE *HE* IV 5; prima causa ab intellectu practico ipsius intelligentie per se ~itur, quia est optimum et ita delectissimum BACON VII 120; unum [cognoscendi genus] secundum quod cognoscimus res prout exeunt a suis causis, ut habeamus verum .., et hec cognicio .. est contemplacionis gracia, ut ~amus; alterum secundum quod cognoscimus res ut tendunt in suam causam, ut bonum habeamus, et hec cognicio .. est accionis gracia, ut ~amus *Ps.*-GROS. *Gram.* 11; oportet eam [justiciam] ~ere volicione efficaci, qua videlicet volens eligeret ipsam in se tamquam vite sue regulam observare DUNS *Ord.* III 123. **c** ipse plus Lindisfarnensi ecclesiae .. dilexit praefici BEDE *HE* IV 26 p. 273; illum denique ipsemet [Aman] honorare compulsus est, quem morti ignominiose tradere super vitam quodam modo gloriosam dilexit AD. SCOT *OP* 599B; **c1218** laicis inhibeatur .. ne testamenta sua faciant sine presentia sacerdotis, sicut ~unt quod voluntates eorum ultime adimpleantur *Conc. Syn.* 91.

5 (pr. ppl.) diligent, attentive, earnest: **a** (of person); **b** (of abstr.).

a †sodolus [l. sedulus], ~ens *GlC* S 413; cepi ~ens scrutator eruere .. que gentis origo, qui mores GIR. *TH pref.* p. 20; **s1258** custos .. ~entissimus (v. custos 4c); **1264** custos .. minus ~ens (v. custodia 9a). **b** exemplorum que posuimus ~enti ad similia accommodatione BALSH. *AD rec. 2* 104; homagium faciendum precedere debet ~ens examinatio BRACTON 80; **s1372** operam .. ~entem (v. doma 2b); **1416** (v. 2 discussio 1); **1449** proviso .. quod .. circa indempnitatem .. bonorum supradictorum .. custodiam adhibeat ~entem *Test. Ebor.* II 150.

diligiatus v. delegiatus.

diligibilis [LL], lovable, desirable.

diligibillime, i. dilectissime scolastice! ÆLF. BATA 5. 11; **c1301** si diligit Deum in speciali ~em intelligit Deum ut ~em in speciali *Quaest. Ox.* 349 (cf. ib.: ascendere ad summum ~e); voluntas infinita est recta; ergo diligit ~e quantum est ~e DUNS *Ord.* II 229; illud pro fides .. predicaretur lucidius ~ius debet esse fideli R. BURY *Phil.* 2. 33; nullus effectus peccati est propter se ~is RIC. ARMAGH *Def. Cur.* 1405 (*recte* 1305); omne finaliter ex se ~e est magis ~e quam aliud quod solum est ~e in ordine ad dileccionem prioris ut finem. sed Deus est finaliter ~is ex seipso et quodlibet aliud in ordine ad dileccionem Dei WYCL. *Mand. Div.* 106.

diligibilitas, lovability, desirability.

alias esset aliqua racio ~atis in una persona [Trinitatis] que non esset in alia, quod est falsum, quia tunc nulla beatificaretur in se ipsa DUNS *Ord.* I 210; major racio complacencie, delectacionis et ~atis est in entitate et bonitate perfecta quam in entitate imperfecta W. ALNWICK *QD* 151.

diliponta v. dialipides. **dilir-** v. delir-. **dilitare, ~atio** v. dilat-. **dilitere, ~iscere** v. delitescere. **dilitus** v. delere 1a.

dilla, dock (*Rumex*). *Cf. paratella* (*paradilla*).

~a vel acrocorium, *docce* ÆLF. *Gl.*; in viridario vestro .. crescit .. ~a [*gl.*: *docce*] ÆLF. BATA 6 p. 99; ~a, *docc Gl. Durh.*

diloricare [CL], to pull apart, strip off (breastplate; also fig.).

cum ab eis captus et ~atus juberetur ensem reddere W. MALM. *GR* IV 388; OSB. GLOUC. *Deriv.* 181 (v. depuvire); eum .. pro voto susciperet qui ingenio quolibet compedum triplici catena firmatas ~aret habenas *Ep. ad amicum* 6 (cf. ib. 10: prior .. ~avit iniquitatis sue scrutinium); cum [mors] nexus phisicos delorícaverit WALT. WIMB. *Sim.* 137.

dilotus v. 2 differre 1a. **dilubrum** v. delubrum.

dilucēre, ~escere [CL], to dawn.

usque ad aurore ~entis exordium R. COLD. *Cuthb.* 56 (cf. ib. 112: crastino altius ~escente).

dilucidare [LL], to elucidate, make clear, explain; **b** (absol.); **c** (w. indir. qu. or *quod*).

in eo lectionis .. divine lampas hoc lucissime agendum ~avit *V. Greg.* p. 104; Beato Lucae moris est .. quae ab eis [sc. aliis] omissa vel breviter cognoverit attacta ~are sollertius BEDE *Luke* 417; [Anselmus] obscuras sacre scripture sententias .. strenue verbis aut scriptis ~avit ORD. VIT. IV 10 p. 245; delector dum dilectionis divitias verbis ~o GIR. *Symb.* I 9 p. 231; quadam / cum gravitate tamen dilucidat omnia plane VINSAUF *PN* 1240; hujus verbi ['scire'] obscuritas mihi videtur ~ata differentiam fati et providentie intelligentibus GROS. 186; **s1254** re delucidata certificatus M. PAR. *Maj.* V 435; scimus quod veritas divina sit complete revelata jam a mccl annis, que omnino perficit philosophiam et ~at et certificat BACON I 6; ad fidem delucidandum NETTER *DAF* I 121. **b** visio hec interior ignis est .., quia videndo ~at PULL. *Sent.* 736A; **s1247** sicut sermo subsequens plenius auditoribus ~abit *Flor. Hist.* II 338 (= M. PAR. *Maj.* IV 628: declarabit). **c** quomodo illud et quam mirabiliter contigerit, clarius in sequentibus ~abimus *G. Steph.* I 56; **c1380** reverencie vestre delucidans per presentes quod corporis gaudeo .. sanitate *FormOx* 321.

dilucidatio [LL], elucidation, clarification.

ad ~onem priscae lectionis BEDE *TR* 65; **s1217** major hujus rei ~o M. PAR. *Maj.* III 28*n. marg.*; **1285** ad ~onem juris patronatus (*Pat*) *MonA* VI 88b; magis callide dicunt modo scripturam sacram esse falsissimam .., non ad sensum quem ipsi dicunt Deum intendere .., sed ad sensum quem apostoli .. et doctores tam doctrina vite quam verborum ~one †relinquerant [l. reliquerant] WYCL. *Ver.* III 107; **1425** ad veritatis delucidacionem *EpAcOx* 16 (= *Reg. Cant.* III 132); **1431** continenciam scripturali delucidacione declarare .. volentes *Reg. Heref.* 127.

dilucide [CL], lucidly, clearly.

discipuli .. adeo carnales adhuc erant ut .. nec ipsam ignorantiam suam intellegerent, putantes simpliciter et ~e prolata quae non intellegentibus proverbia erant BEDE *Hom.* II 12. 167; apparet ~e in divina scriptura quid sit .. ÆLF. *Ep.* 2a.1; subtrahe fundamentum fidei; jam teipsum in sacra scriptura non videbis ~e NECKAM *NR* II 154; de verbis .. minus ~e intellectis GROS. 185; **1452** lecta fuit per .. fratrem J. ... constitucio concilii generalis .. per eundemque J. exposita .. satisque delucide declarata *Reg. Whet.* I 15; quod in ejus [racionis speculi] claritate ~e videam primi angeli casum CHAUNDLER *Apol.* 15b.

dilucidus [CL], (visually) clear, bright. **b** (intellectually) clear, lucid; **c** (w. ref. to peace of mind or sanity). **d** (as sb. n.) lucidity (of speech or thought).

~us, valde clarus OSB. GLOUC. *Deriv.* 180; quasi speculo quodam ~o GIR. *TH intr.* p. 7; lapis epistiten rubicundus et ~us *Alph.* 92. **b** ~a brevitate sunt hec explanata GIR. *TH* II 3. **c** in ~is intervallis imperialis majestas nonnunquam sono cithare David vexationem, in Saule a spiritu perturbante factam, amotam sentit aut emollitam GERV. TILB. *pref.*; **1286** compos mentis .. non existit, quamquam aliquando dillucidis gaudeat intervallis *Reg. Heref.* 116; **1422** [prior de B.] quasi continuo laborabat furore, pauca habens vel nulla ~a intervalla *Doc. Eng. Black Monks* II 147. **d** contra ~um ex parte vocis sunt hec tria vicia: inusitatum, defectus, dubium, que appellantur acirologia, eclipsis, amphibologia. similiter ex parte sentencie tria vicia contra ~um, quando inusitata utitur sentencia .., aut diminute .., aut dubie perturbando sentenciam per transposicionem diccionum *Ps.*-GROS. *Gram.* 69.

dilucifluus, clear-flowing.

clere, clarus .., lucidus, ~us .. *CathA*.

dilucior v. 1 deluere 1b.

diluculum [CL], daybreak, dawn.

tempus ~i exortum .. gratiae .. demonstrat BEDE *Hom.* I 25. 106; incipiente ~i *Id. HE* III 2; una die valde ~o unus intrabit (*sic*) in aecclesiam missam facere HUGEB. *Wynn.* 10; exeo ~o [AS: *on dægræd*] minando boves ad campum ÆLF. *Coll.* 90; vermis ascensu ~i arefacit hederam super caput Ione AD. DORE *Pictor* 155; revertente ~o ibidem .. mane conspicitur GIR. *TH* I 24; ante ~um et infra conticinia noctis *G. Hen. V* 3; hoc diluculum, *a mornyng WW*.

1 diludium v. deludium.

2 diludium [CL], intermission in games.

~ium, diversus ludus ab alio OSB. GLOUC. *Deriv.* 177.

diluere [CL]

1 to wash away. **b** to dissolve, dilute. **c** (p. ppl.) washed out, dilute. *V. et. deluere* 1.

quod .. fons .. totam provinciam illam .. simul ~eret et deleret GIR. *TH* II 9. **b** diluit, i. .. permisceat, .. admiscet, solvit *GlH* D 513. **c** dilutas, i. dissolutas *Ib.* 512.

2 to bathe, wash, cleanse.

salutiferum mundus baptista Tonantem / diluit aequoreis mergens in gurgite limphis ALDH. *VirgV* 410; licet omnes intra unam fidem contineantur eodemque baptismate ~antur BEDE *Gen.* 87; cum .. elevanda essent ossa de sepulchro .. ipsa autem abbatissa intus .. ossa elatura et ~tura intrasset *Id. HE* IV 17 p. 245; GOSC. *Mir. Aug.* 549 (v. arsura 2d).

3 (fig.): **a** to wash away, wipe out (guilt or crime). **b** to clear, discharge (debt). *V. et. deluere* 2.

a nanctus rudimenta fidei, / flagitium sceleris baptismi diluit unda ALDH. *VirgV* 1136; credendum est quia talis mors viri religiosi .. talem culpam ~erit BEDE *HE* III 22; si crimina inlata et aliquas minus honestas suspiciones injectas ~emus ALCUIN *Rhet.* 20; **c1000** per illa sancta / te rogamus vulnera / quae mundi cuncta / diluerunt crimina *Anal. Hymn.* LI i. 107. 3; penitentes .. peregrinationis sue conversionem utcumque inceptam inundatione lacrymarum ~entes OSB. BAWDSEY cxlv; bursa quanto plus inflata / tanto semper ad peccata / diluenda forcior WALT. WIMB. *Van.* 72. **b** debita solvendo non esto sodalis avari, / pollicitis vacuis qui diluit illa petenti D. BEC. 2458.

dilumentum, bath, washing. *V. et. delumentum.*

~um, lavatio, dilutio, ablutio OSB. GLOUC. *Deriv.* 180.

dilusorius v. delusorius.

dilutio, washing, cleansing.

OSB. GLOUC. *Deriv.* 180 (v. dilumentum).

diluviosus, swollen by flood, torrential.

quia tanta tamque ~a Sequane fluenta .. regales bipercieba[n]t exercitus *Ps.*-ELMH. *Hen. V* 96.

diluvium [CL], **~ius** [LL], flood, deluge. **b** Noah's flood. **c** Deucalion's flood. **d** deluge (fig.).

oceani flustra et spumantis cataclismi caerula cum proprios egrederentur terminos et quasi divinae potestatis censura ~ii irruptionem minaretur ALDH. *VirgP* 29; cataclismus, ~ium, *brym* vel *holm GlH* C 511; ~ium, *flod* ÆLF. *Sup.*; perpaucis diebus evolutis, aquarum illarum ~ium preteriit R. COLD. *Godr.* 98; **s1175** ~ius fit per Hoilondiam *Chr. Peterb.* 4; **14..** deluvius, A. *a floode WW*. **b** sicut .. venit ~ium et tulit omnia quae extra eam [arcam] erant, sic, ubi omnes qui praeordinati sunt ad vitam †aeternum [l. aeternam] ecclesiam intraverint, veniet finis mundi et peribunt omnes qui extra ecclesiam fuerint inventi BEDE *Gen.* 85 (cf. ib. 86: ~ium aquam baptismi, qua ipsa ecclesia .. abluitur, .. significat); aque ~ii levant archam AD. DORE *Pictor* 156; a tempore primi terre istius post ~ium incole GIR. *TH* I 7; **s1227** precipio vobis .. in nomine ejus qui vos .. in arca Noe ab aquis ~ii liberavit (*Sermo*) WEND. II 331; **s1358** aquarum pluvialium inundaciones .., qualis nunquam visa fuit a ~io Noe *Plusc.* IX 44. **c** Deucalionem, nomen regis sub [quo] ~ium factum est, non †generare [l. generale] *Gl. Leid.* 38. 22. **d** tanto ~io paganorum .. Augustinianum vestibulum .. manebat intactum GOSC. *Transl. Aug.* 18A; pro quo mori mei est amantium / et dulcoris dulce diluvium J. HOWD. *Ph.* 762; **1357** numerum annorum a diluvio aque, qui (*sic*) erat tempore Noe, usque ad ~ium ignis futurum (ASHENDEN) *Wycl. & Ox.* 103*n*.

dimaceratio v. demaceratio. **dimed-** v. dimid-. **dimembr-** v. dismembr-.

dimensio [CL], measuring, measurement, extent. **b** (geom.) dimension.

rythmus, i. e. modulatio, quae certa ~one temporum terminatur BONIF. *Met.* 110; **948** (12c) magnitudo illius terrae tanta esse asseritur quantum bis quinas (*sic*) mansarum spatium equa demensione fore cernitur *CS* 866; **998** (12c) (v. distributio 2); nocte illa suis ~onibus terminata EADMER *V. Osw.* 34; ~o, numeratio OSB. GLOUC. *Deriv.* 180; **s870** in omni corporis ~one simul et proceritate incomparabilis (*V. Edm.*) M. PAR. *Maj.* I 396. confidentem [me] letificat, quam ~o non excludit distantiarum, presens benigni spiritus vestri consolatio AD. MARSH *Ep.* 94; **1286** quintus [articulus damnatus] est identitatem fuisse numeralem corporis Christi mortui cum ejus corpore vivo tantummodo propter identitatem materie et ~onum interminatarum et habitudinis ipsarum ad animam intellectivam PECKHAM *Ep.* 661 (= *Conc.* II 124a); HIGD. I 5 (v. compendiosus 2a); **s1465** trabes ipsa sua ~one murorum equabat quadrum *Croyl. Cont. B* 541. **b** hic simplex corpus reddit dimensio trina NECKAM *DS* V 903; in corpore inveniuntur tres ~ones: prima est longitudo ..; secunda est latitudo, in qua due ~ones intelliguntur ..; tertia ~o est soliditas, in qua tres intelliguntur HALES *Sent.* I 363; anima in corpore regendo non per ~onem et loci spatium in corpore extenditur BART. ANGL. III 3; vacuum non est nisi trina demensio geometrica, secundum longum, latum et profundum BACON *Tert.* 154; *Ib.* III 164 (v. 1 compati 4a); littere [P, T, K] diversificantur secundum triplicem ~onem, sc. longitudinis, latitudinis et spissitudinis *Ps.*-GROS. *Gram.* 22; ~o non est aliud quam superficies KILWARDBY *OS* 193; corpus .. non potest figurari in plano, quia habet tres ~ones: longitudinem, latitudinem, et profunditatem ODINGTON 45.

dimensionabilis, spatially measurable.

species lucis et soni est ~is alico modo; distat enim pars lucis in medio ab alia BACON XIV 117; figura spherica capacissima est isoperimentrorum (*sic*), i. figurarum equaliter ~ium PECKHAM *Persp.* I 29.

dimensionalis, dimensional, spatially measurable.

ipsam [materiam primam] per se nusquam esse nec temporalem esse, per accidens autem .. et localem et temporalem existere sensibilemque ac ~em *Ps.*-GROS. *Summa* 321; in ipsis substanciis spiritualibus est diversitas parcium materie substancialium, licet non sit diversitas parcium ~ium PECKHAM *QA* 188; magister [J. Wyclyff] recitavit .. tres opiniones de multiplicacione corporis [Christi], viz. ~em, diffinitivam, et virtualem *Ziz.* 107.

dimensionaliter, dimensionally, in spatial measurement.

sic philosophi intellexerunt aliquam substantiam extendi in infinitum ~er sine quantitate BACON XIII 145; nimis

leviter sapiunt qui dicunt rem nullicubi esse, eo quod nullicubi est ~er WYCL. *Ente Praed.* 150; sicut corpus Christi extensum est ille panis, sed ipsum corpus non est extense vel ~er ille panis (WYCL. *Conf.*) *Ziz.* 115; **1412** corpus Christi non est substancialiter in sacramento altaris attendendo ad corpus Christi secundum naturam suam, sed est ibi substancialiter, corporaliter et demencionaliter attendendo ad modum hostie secundum naturam suam (*Errores J. Wycliff abstracti*) *Conc.* III 349b.

dimensionare, to measure spatially.

duo corpora non possunt esse simul, cum sint undique ~ata *Comm. Sph.* 4 p. 284; omne ~atum a parte ea qua non est ~atum compatitur secum aliquid BACON *Tert.* 143; nec tamen secundum hanc diffusionis sue rationem posse ~ari magis [lucem] quam materiam primam, cujus nulle sunt dimensiones *Ps.*-GROS. *Summa* 537; dimensiones habent motus et tempus, sed per accidens, sc. per magnitudinem que per se ~atur KILWARDBY *OS* 102; lumen requirit subjectum ~atum in quo existat, sicut et albedo SICCAV. *PN* 116; color que (*sic*) est in sacramento altaris est unum ~atum et una dimensio terminata, et ita sapor, et ita de aliis ~atis *Ps.*-OCKHAM *Princ. Theol.* 111; materialis .. essencia, ut ~ata dimensionibus interminatis NETTER *DAF* II 121.

dimensitas, spatial extension.

lux .. ratione expressionis sue ~atis res est quantitatis continue *Ps.*-GROS. *Summa* 536.

dimensive, dimensionally, by spatial extension.

lumen, quia medium est inter pure incorporalia et corporalia, .. habet .. naturam replendi [locum] ~e et replendi spiritualiter HALES *Qu.* 766; [in sacramento eucharistie] sunt 23 miracula: .. quinto, quia dimensionatum est ibi non ~e PECKHAM *QR* 99; aliter oporteret concedere quod esse substancialiter sit esse accidentaliter .. et esse ~e sit esse multiplicative (WYCL. *Conf.*) *Ziz.* 124.

dimensivus, dimensional, (spatially) measurable.

quantitas ~a est habens positionem T. SUTTON *Quodl.* 141; nec est bene intelligible aliquod esse quantum ~um quin sit signare in toto ordinem hujus partis ad illam secundum quantitatem interjacentem OCKHAM *Sacr. Alt.* 334; non semper agens est simul cum passo simultaneitate mathematica vel ~a *Ps.*-OCKHAM *Princ. Theol.* 141.

dimensor [LL], measurer, surveyor.

cur .. nostri non erunt laude digni orbis quadrifidi ~ores, quadriviales [v. l. quadrivialis] historie descriptores HIGD. I 1 *prol.* p. 6.

dimentiri v. dementiri. **dimergere, dimers-** v. demer-.

dimeter, ~rus [LL < δίμετρος], (metr.) dimeter.

v genera versuum .. in dactilico exametro .. : exameter, pentameter, tetrameter, trimeter, ~er ALDH. *Met.* 10; dimetron, duorum pedum *GlC Int.* 96 (cf. ib. D 119: †diametro, duplici mensura); dici .. monometrum, ~um, vel trimetrum versum in iambicis BONIF. *Met.* 113; versus herilis / tardus hic est; demeter cursitat ille cito GARL. *PP* 216. 1882; †diametrus, *a duble metre WW.*

dimetiri [CL], **~ire,** to measure. **b** to equal in measurement. **c** (p. ppl.) having elapsed.

demensus [est], mensuravit *GlC* D 160; erat .. insula .. latis locorum dimensa sinibus B. *V. Dunst.* 3; in infinita annorum .. spatia stellarum motus dimensi sunt ADEL. *Elk.* 3; si modum nesciat amor aut nequeat ~iri J. GODARD *Ep.* 220; sepulcrum cui, si quis †accederit [v. l. accesserit] et se demetierit, inveniet mensure sue quantitatem (*Mir. Britanniae*) *Eul. Hist.* II 142 (cf. DICETO *Chr.* 13). **b** [carcannus] undique colli superiora et inferiora ~iendo et percurrendo circumvolvens R. COLD. *Cuthb.* 20 (cf. ib.: pars [carcanni] inferior .. parietem ~ierat). **c** **1299** demensis jam trium annorum curriculis *Reg. Cant.* 336.

dimettum v. dimitum.

dimicare [CL]

1 to fight, contend (with). **b** (trans.) to defeat. **c** (w. acc. & inf.) to maintain.

lacertosis viribus ~andum est ALDH. *VirgP* 11; pro patria ~ans BEDE *HE* III 9; **s455** hic Hengest et Horsa contra Britones ~ant *AS Chr.*; ~antibus illis prevaluit Eneas G. MON. I 3; ibi venenis ~atur, hic viribus GIR. *TH* I 37; **s1244** cum seipso ~avit (v. domesticus 3a); **s1250** (v. conglomerare a); *AncrR* 102 (v. compugil). **b** **1301** Adelstanus .. Scotos rebellantes ei ~avit [OF: *venqui*] (*Lit. Ed. I*) *Anglo-Scot. Rel.* 99. **c** **941** (15c) in illis terminis quibus periti coloni ipsius regionis nomen proprium antiquo proposito esse dim[i]cant Stoke *CS* 769.

2 (? by assoc. w. *mica*) to cut to bits.

1305 Willelmum de H., vicecomitem de Lanarke, .. interfecit et postea .. interfectum frustatim ~avit *Ann. Lond.* 140.

dimicatio [CL], fight, contest.

ipso certamine beatus es, laurea tandem ~onis triumphante donandus PULL. *Sent.* 915D; ~one fortissima detentus aliquandiu MAP *NC* II 12 f. 27; inter elephantes et dracones perpetua est ~o BART. ANGL. XVIII 37.

dimidiare [LL; CL *p. ppl. only*]

1 to halve; **b** (absol.). **c** to diminish by half (partly fig.). **d** to divide, separate, or (?) *f. l.*

extremi quoque duo septentrionales, axem caeli ipsius dnms [? l. dimidiantes] *Gl. Leid.* 44. 29; sextus erat egritudinis, duodecimus etatis annus ..; ~iaverantque dies puelle salus et incommoditas W. MALM. *GP* V 273; navem dissolutam et pene .. fluctibus ~iatam R. COLD. *Cuthb.* 23; ad illius .. pontificis [S. Martini] opus exemplare .., qui, cum nihil preter chlamidem .. haberet, cum paupere tamen nudo illam ~iat H. BOS. *Thom.* III 6 p. 197; **1198** totam terram inter se ~iabunt *CurR RC* I 196; **1206** si aliquod comodum placitorum .. emerserit, ballivus .. abbatis †dividiabit cum predictis W. et R. *Kal. Samson* 105; **1237** (v. dimidiatio 1); cum pia sobole parentem crucient / ne piam impie matrem dimidient WALT. WIMB. *Carm.* 600; *to halfe*, mediare, ~iare *CathA.* **b** multiplicant et dimidiant; addunt sibi; nobis / subtraxisse volunt GARL. *Tri. Eccl.* 88. **c** **c1220** mirabile fuit .. vos nomen cancellarii in literis vestris nobis destinatis suppressisse. .. quia quid me ~iant? integer esse volo (*AncC* VI 23) *RL* I 180; **c1370** mors faciet gyrum per terras undique dirum; / non consummabit carnem sed dimidiabit [*gl.*: pestilencia .. accipiet unam medietatem hominum] (J. BRIDL.) *Pol. Poems* I 206–7. **d** **c1220** cum terra que sita est .. inter aquam et semitam que †~iat dominicum ab illa terra *Reg. Malm.* II 25 (cf. ib. 26: que dividit dominicum ab illa terra).

2 **a** to half-complete, live out the half (or the residue) of (w. ref. to *Psalm* liv 24); *cf. dimidiatio* 2. **b** to half-purchase, equal half the value of. **c** (p. ppl.) mixed half-and-half. **d** (w. *grano*) half-dyed in grain.

a **956** (13c) sin autem .. [hoc decretum] aliquis mutare voluerit, dies ejus non ~iaverit *CS* 921 (cf. ib. 970: ut non ~iet dies suos); corruet in fine fallax, mendax, nec ei spes / genti pro speculo dimidiare dies WALT. ANGL. *Fab.* 46. 22; **s1182** Arnulfus .. perrexit Parisius, suos dies ~iaturus apud S. Victorem TORIGNI *Chr.* 298; **1307** [Ricardus I] non ~ians dies suos J. LOND. *Commend. Ed. I* 15. **b** libertas .. inestimabilis res est; / hanc precium nullum dimidiare potest WALT. ANGL. *Fab.* 51. 26. **c** panis ejus nunquam purus fuerat, sed semper cinere ~iatus R. COLD. *Godr.* 69; **c1180** habebit v acras ~iatas frumenti et avene *Reg. Malm.* II 318; **s1465** licet spuriosi ~iatique sanguinis fuerit habueritque patrem qui de privata muliere procreamen sumpsit *Reg. Whet.* I 165. **d** **c1410** pannos .. / tam grano plenos quam grano dimidiatos (*Vers. Exch.*) *EHR* XXXVI 59.

dimidiatim, half-way.

fluenta aquarum quercuum altitudines pene ~im operiendo alluerant R. COLD. *Godr.* 98.

dimidiatio [LL]

1 halving, division into halves.

1237 fructus medii temporis inter abbatem et archidiaconum dimidiabuntur ..; simul etiam erit ~o sequestrorum *CalCh* I 239; quis ignorat duplacionem et ~onem, duplum et dimidium, ibi esse? BRADW. *CD* 132E; quantum poterit de sanguine recolligat in calicem quia ~o sacramenti non poterit absque grandi sacrilegio provenire MIRK *Man.* f. 39.

2 living out the half (or the residue). *Cf. dimidiare* 2a.

'viri sanguinum non dimidiabunt dies suos' [*Psalm* liv 24]. inchoatio tamen vere penitentie quasi ~o dierum est, quia 'melior est dies una in atriis tuis' [*Ib.* lxxxiii 11] et penitentis 'super millia' existentis in peccato GIR. *GE* II 8 p. 204.

dimidiator, halver, equal sharer.

cenans convivis sis potus dimidiator D. BEC. 2356.

dimidietas [LL], half, half-share, moiety. **b** (w. *linguae*) jury equally representative of two communities.

1159 dimidiam feriam que est in Maio apud Salmurum .. cum omnibus redditibus pertinentibus ad ~atem ferie predicte *Act. Hen. II* I 230; **1199** confirmasse .. canonicis .. de Lanton' .. ex dono Walteri .. ~atem de Berington' cum ecclesia .., ex dono Rogeri .. aliam ~atem Berington' *RChart* 7b; **c1200** reddendo annuatim, .. pro unaquaque dimidia *davach* ij s., ~atem ad Pentecostem et ~atem ad festum S. Martini *Reg. Moray* 12; **1282** posuerunt super nos omnes satellites de Anglicis, quod nunquam fuit nisi ~as *Ep. Peckham* 348; **c1350** de dimedietate tocius terre *Melrose* 466; *Conc. Scot.* II 66 (v. detector). **1472** pro colleccione .. decime seu ~atis ejusdem (*Breve Regis*) *Reg. Whet.* II 139. **b** **1585** ~as linguae (*Dyer's Rep.* III 304a) *SHR* XXV 171.

dimidius [CL]

1 half. **b** half the service or profit of. **c** holding half a unit of land. **d** having half the quality or status of. **e** (w. *prima*) 'half-prime' (? half-way between lauds and prime).

post annum et dimedium GILDAS *Pen.* 1; sicut emisperium semispera Latina lingua intelligitur, id est ~ia pars poli ALDH. *Met.* 10 p. 95; transacto quasi ~iae horae spatio BEDE *HE* IV 3; **811** duas possessiunculas et tertiam dimediam, id est in nostra loquella *ðridda half haga CS* 335; **812** demediam partem unius mansiunculae *Ib.* 341; ~ia terra est regis *DB* I 1; *Ib.* II 182 (v. commendatio 3); reddat sex †~iam marcam [AS: *vj healfmarc*] (*Quad.*) *GAS* 232; **1198** ~ium hundredum de Wiham *CurR RC* I 207; **c1225** nos dedisse .. tres ~ias acras terre *Cart. Osney* IV 341; **12..** valorem dimedie marce *Conc. Scot.* II 45; **1266** meremium ad reparationem unius gurgitis et ~ii *Cl* 367; **1393** proditorie tondebat monetam nostram, viz. nobilia, ~ia nobilia, quadrantes de auro, grossos, ~ios grossos et denarios de argento *Pat* 338 m. 17; **1464** (v. denarius 4b). **b** *DB* I 218 (v. bos 1a); in dominio est una car[uca] et iiij villani integri et vj ~ii *Ib.* 252; in eadem j presbyter integer et ij dim[idii] *Ib.* II 196; in T. xiiij liberi homines; ex istis habuit S. Edmundus commendationem super iiij integros et iiij ~ios *Ib.* 284v. (cf. ib. 285v.: ij ~ii liberi homines); in W. j bor[darius] et dim[idius] *Ib.* 286; *Ib.* I 206, *RDomin* 42 (v. carruca 3a); †**1092** (12c) R. comes [Norhunbrensis] .. clamavit .. episcopo .. omnes praedictas calumnias .. quietas, sc. has, ~ium latronem et ~ium fracture pacis .. (*Ch. Will. II*) *Feod. Durh.* p. lxxxii (cf. 2 infra). **c** **a1190** servicium .. quantum pertinet ad feudum ~ii militis *Ch. Gilb.* 17; **1223** de feodo ~ii militis *Pat* 416; **1234** Hereman .. tenet ~iam virgatam terre .. et debet habere ghestum ad Natale sicut ~ius virgatarius *Cust. Glast.* 127; **1278** liberavi eidem homag[ia], viz. .. Cecilium .. et Johannem .., ~ios virgatarios ..; item Willelmum .. et Walterum .. tenentes quartam partem j virgate terre, cum eorum serviciis *AncD* A 13636; **1300** ij virgatarii, xxiij ~ii virgatarii *IPM* 95/7; **1325** sunt ibidem v ~ii ferdellarii ..; et unusquisque illorum debet facere .. medietatem servicii j ferdellarii *IPM* 81/20. **d** *DB* II 106 (v. blancus 1b); ad magnum munus prefulsit amiculus unus [*in gl.*: '.. ego nullum habeo amicum, set adhuc credo habere ~ium amicum'] GARL. *Mor. Scol.* 609; **s1312** .. rex .. domino †Thoma [l. Thome] .. filio suo ex secunda regina genito, fratri regis hujus ~io, comitatum .. donavit WALS. *HA* I 131. **e** **1344** nullus exponat blada vendicioni apud Ripam Regine nec Billyngesgate ante ~iam primam (*LBLond.* F f. 81) *MGL* I 693; **1385** Martinus .. circa ~iam primam conti[n]gebat ambulare per grangiam *IMisc* 234/5.

2 (as sb. n.) a half.

si reddere vult .. pecuniam .. levior erit penitentia, i. e. ~io spatii THEOD. *Pen.* I 4. 1; conditum est .. corpus in sarcofago .., quod primum toto Dei famuli corpori quasi dimedium pedis brevius inventum est ALCUIN *WillP* 25; **803** (11c) archiepiscopus Deneberhtum rogabat dimedia sibi hujus praestare *CS* 309; sic tamen es sine omni spatio ut nec medium nec ~ium nec ulla pars sit in te ANSELM (*Prosl.* 21) I 116; he adjectiones, dum ~ium diei aut eo minus, non computantur, eritque annus cccliiij dierum ADEL. *Elk.* 1; **1296** de Johanne le Cartere, quia emit et vendit cum catallis Johannis .. capellani ad ~ium lucri et ea advocat tanquam sua propria *Leet Norw.* 48; **13..** sub pena dimedii marce *Conc. Scot.* II 67; **1435** quam summam [xij nobilium] solverunt .. in xxiiij ~iis *ExchScot* 641; **1460** duabus ulnis cum dimedio *Ib.* 36; **1476** de firmis dimedie (*sic*) de Drumcors *Ib.* 333; **1467** sigilletur super preceptum ~ium sigilli *MunAcOx* 726.

diminiculum, diminution, omission.

cum puer leccionem sine libro proferre cogeretur, non solum quod magister ejus tradiderat absque obstaculo et ~o reddidit, verum eciam illud quod preceptor ejus traditurus fuerat *NLA* (*Erkenwald*) I 403.

diminitivus v. diminutivus 1b. **diminium** v. 2 dominium 3c.

diminuere [CL], **~are**

1 to break in pieces, shatter, crush. **b** (p. ppl.) finely divided, minute.

c625 hos, quos eatenus materiae conpage vobis deos fabricastis, confringendos ~endosque procurate (*Lit. Papae*) BEDE *HE* II 10; ~it, confregit *GlC* D 225; colores suos .. ~unt R. COLD. *Cuthb.* 75 (v. 3 color 1d). **b** ad interioris materie ~tiora fragmenta *Ib.* 21.

2 to diminish, reduce (in size or amount). **b** (w. abstr. obj.) to lessen, weaken, impair. **c** (log.) to restrict in meaning. **d** (p. ppl. as sb. n.) diminution; *cf. diminutivus* 2c. *V. et. deminuere.*

quemadmodum in numeris integris multiplicatur, ita etiam in numeris ~tis, hoc est in fractionibus ROB. ANGL. *Alg.* 98 (cf. 3d infra); dum ~atur, ex ~ata materia ~atum generabitur animal *Quaest. Salern.* N 57; **1191** tam subtractione virorum [? l. vivorum] quam amissione ibidem mortuorum exercitus .. Christianitatis multum erat ~tus (*Lit. Episc. Sar.*) DICETO *YH* II 88; M. SCOT *Phys.* 15 (v. concavare b); **1263** illa [summa] .. penitus insufficiens et ~ta videbatur *Cl* 283; **s1314** expense regis cotidiane in x li. sunt ~te *V. Ed. II* 209; **1341** nolentes quod elemosina nostra aliqualiter subtrahatur vel ~atur *RScot* 608a; **s1406** relique [naves] .. venerunt salve Burdegaliam, sed numero ~to *Chr. S. Alb.* 9; [nota] larga perfecta ex omnibus perfectis ~i potest per longam precedentem HAUBOYS 407. **b** **941** (15c) (v. 1 conversatio 3b); **12..** quod nulli permittatur violare aut ~ere libertates .. et consuetudines rationabiles rerum aut personarum ecclesiasticarum *Conc. Scot.* II 19; **13..** ne divinus cultus nostris ~atur temporibus *Ib.* 66; **1265** devocionem populi nostri ~ere *Cl* 119; **1269** si franchisa bene fuerit servata et per quem fuerit

~ata *CBaron* 71; fletus .. ~it dolorem TREVET *Troades* 56; **s1066** ne justam causam bellandi temeraria presumpcio ~eret *Eul. Hist.* II 198 (= W. MALM. *GR* III 238: decoloraret). **c** univocacionem completam dico quando est similitudo in forma et modo essendi forme; ~tam dico quando est similitudo in forma licet habeat alium modum essendi, quo modo domus extra est a domo in mente artificis DUNS *Ord.* I 236; quia respectu tercii 'lapis' ~itur per 'esse in cognicione', ideo non sequitur quod 'lapis' dicitur univoce nec unitate numerali de lapide in esse cognito et de lapide in effectu W. ALNWICK *QD* 20 (v. et. distrahere 6b). **d** ex ea parte qua virtus ab homine est suscipit superfluum et ~tum GROS. *Templ.* 11. 1; **1423** quadam excepcione de ~to contra dictum processum per partem dictorum T. P. et aliorum coram eisdem commissariis .. proposita ac pendente *Pat* 412 m. 19.

3 a to draw off, let (blood). **b** to take away, subtract; **c** (absol.). **d** (p. ppl. w. *numerus*) number exceeding the sum of its aliquot parts.

a contigit ut .. [matrona] fleubotomata dies ~ti sanguinis sollicitius observaret R. COLD. *Cuthb.* 115. **b c1070** nolo ut aliquis aliquid de illo auferat aut ~at *Regesta* p. 120; ex qua medietatem radicum 2½ ~as [v. l. subtrahas] ROB. ANGL. *Alg.* 72*n.* 2; quorum [Hebreorum etc.] recte dicta recipiens, aspera complanavit [Grecia], superflua resecavit, ~ta supplevit et errata delevit R. BURY *Phil.* 10. 160. **c** ut .. neque astutia .. inferat fraudem .. aut ~at ex eo quod contulimus BYRHT. *V. Ecgwini* 381; possessio propriorum non necessario ~it de caritate, licet possit esse occasio diminucionis caritatis vel diminucionis actus caritatis; necessario tamen de paupertate ~it OCKHAM *Pol.* II 455; **1442** quod .. apellacionem suam possit .. emendare, eidem addere et ~ere .., prout viderit oportunum *FormOx* 469. **d** numerus .. ~tus est cujus partes multiplicative reddunt summam minorem toto, ut octonarius NECKAM *NR* I 173 p. 295; ~ti sunt numeri qui partibus suis computati [? l. computatis] minorem summam efficiunt BART. ANGL. XIX 121.

diminuibilis, (as sb. n.) something susceptible of diminution.

sunt in ea [caritate] plures gradus actualitatis in potentia, et ita ~is est MIDDLETON *Sent.* I 168; ad illud de II De Anima, patet quod [Aristoteles] loquitur de quantitate augmentabilis et deminuibilis DUNS *Ord.* VII 327.

diminute

1 finely, in small pieces.

lapides .. cinerescunt et ~e se in similitudinem calculorum .. dissolvunt R. COLD. *Cuthb.* 21.

2 defectively, inadequately.

1256 oportebit colligere legata et alias subventiones crucis ab Hiberniensibus... que etenim satis ~e congregant, multum inordinate consumunt (*AncC* XLVIII 60) *RL* II 118; Arabes in tabulis et canonibus computant ~e et deficiunt in omni lunatione per tria secunda et xv tertia et xliiij quarta BACON *Maj.* I 197; *Ps.*-GROS. *Gram.* 69 (v. dilucidus d); theologie vero quamvis nihil addiderit [Aristoteles], nichil tamen de ea ~e determinavit J. WALEYS *Compend.* 5. 6 f. 166 (cf. ib.: nihil ~e tradens seu tractans de ea sed multa adiciens ex sua solertia); qui .. in premissis aliqua ~e, confuse, vel obscure prolata repererit .. brevitati temporis et ingenii mei tenuitati tanquam discretus lector ascribat OCKHAM *Pol.* II 858; Deus igitur seipsum cognoscit, et non imperfecte et ~e BRADW. *CD* 6c; malens tantum mysterium tacere quam de eo loqui ~ius COLET *Sacr. Eccl.* 54.

3 (log.) in restricted sense.

quia objectum est causa proxima respectu noticie et univoca, licet ~e, sequitur quod distinccio formalis objectorum .. necessario concludat distinccionem formalem noticiarum DUNS *Ord.* I 237.

diminutellus, (gram.) diminutive.

hoc †'cerobellum' .. ~um est de 'cerebrum' GARL. *Mor. Scol.* 591–2 (*gl.*).

diminutio

1 diminution, lessening (in size or amount); **b** (gram.). **c** (of abstr.) weakening, impairment.

quia mundus cottidie in se naturaliter sui detrimentum ~onis .. patitur WILLIB. *Bonif.* 8; **a1080** quatinus res suas quae injuste ei ablatae sunt sine ~one adquirat LANFR. *Ep.* 30 (25); Griphinus, plus animo dives quam auro, ob hereditatis .. ~onem nihil unquam animositatis .. imminuens GIR. *IK* I 2 p. 34; ~o [corporis] non fluit ab aliqua vi, immo exit in effectum per inpotentiam et virtutis nutritive debilitatem J. BLUND *An.* 51; Pater .. generando totam substantiam suam ei [Filio] dedit sine divisione et tamen totam retinuit sine ~one BART. ANGL. I 2; P, T, K ~one propter soni sui gracilitatem ab aliis [litteris] differunt *Ps.*-GROS. *Gram.* 22; sicut .. corpori naturali est certus terminus in augmentacione, sic et in ~one KILWARDBY *OS* 181; **1361** de falsacione seu ~one monetarum, balanciarum seu ponderum (*Pat*) *Foed.* VI 308a. **b** diminutivum est quod rem sui primitivi cum ~one quantitatis aut qualitatis significat, ut 'homuncio' *Ps.*-GROS *Gram.* 38; dicitur per ~onem a 'signo' 'sigillum' ELMH. *Cant.* 119. **c** ne .. augmentum suscepti honoris ~o praeteritae videretur fuisse virtutis OSB. *V. Dunst.* 32; **1235** ut hec ordinacio nostra et taxacio sine quacumque ~one vel incremento in perpetuum permaneat *Reg. S. Thom. Dublin* 292; conjunctiones [stellarum] que faciunt ad augmentum naturalium et ~onem innaturalium BACON *Maj.* I 387; **1301** quatinus .. dominum nostrum regem .. jura sua et libertates et consuetudines ac leges .. absque ~one et inquietudine .. possidere .. permittatis (*Lit. Baronum ad Papam*) *Ann. Lond.* 125; malas observancias tangentes ad ~onem status studencium [Oxon'] BIRCHINGTON *Arch. Cant.* 12; **1539** in divini cultus ~onem *Form. S. Andr.* II 116.

2 a drawing off, letting (of blood). **b** cutting off (of limbs), mutilation. **c** subtraction. **d** amount by which a number exceeds the sum of its aliquot parts.

a quippiam .. quo .. aggravata matrona quietem ~onis .. in vehementiam acerrime tribulationis, turbato toto cordis sanguine, commutaret R. COLD. *Cuthb.* 115; Andresia .., ubi ipse rex Willelmus senior et sanguinis ~one et antidoti perceptione se recreare solebat *Chr. Abingd.* II 49; eligitur .. ~o sanguinis .. luna existente in signo igneo vel aereo M. SCOT *Intr.* 289; in duabus noctibus sequentibus post ~onem in chorum ad matutinas non intrent *Cust. Cant.* 306; **1510** in ~one sanguinis diversorum equorum *Ac. Durh.* 661. **b** episcopi .. debent interesse judiciis curie regis cum baronibus usque perveniatur .. ad ~onem membrorum vel ad mortem *Const. Clar.* 11; **c1230** judicium aque vel ferri vel ~onis sive capitis dampnationis vel alterius mortis *Ch. Coupar Angus* I 80. **c** in ~one quoque unusquisque ponendus est in propria statione, et minor de majore auferendus est vel minor minuendus ADEL. *Alch.* 20; hoc caput solum adjectione simul et ~one indiget ROB. ANGL. *Alg.* 74. **d 798** perfectus numerus est qui partibus suis impletur, nec ~one frangitur nec multiplicatione partium superabundat, ut senarius numerus ALCUIN *Ep.* 133.

diminutium v. diminutivus.

diminutive, a (gram.) in a diminutive sense. **b** (log.) in a restrictive sense.

a 'scalprum', a quo ~e 'scalpellum' ALDH. *PR* 116; femella, ~e femina *GlC* F 146. **b** quidam dicunt optationem esse voluntatem, aut ~e voluntatem imperfectam GROS. 247; hec dictio 'preter' aliquando tenetur exceptive, aliquando ~e OCKHAM *Summa* II 18 p. 307.

diminutivus [CL]

1 (as sb. n.) diminutive: **a** (gram.); **b** (her.).

a 'rumusculus', quod est 'rumoris' ~um ALDH. *PR* 132 (cf. ib.: ~a ~orum inveniuntur, ut .. 'agnus, agniculus, agnicellus'); quasi ~a, origine tamen carentia, ut 'tabula', 'ferula' BONIF. *AG* 16; 'avunculus' per duo U, quia ab 'avo' ~um est, -vo- syllaba in '-vun-' conversa ALCUIN *Orth.* 2329; per hoc .. quod ~um [sc. sarcinulas] ponit, notat quod cum omnia bene fecerimus sc. dicamus 'servi inutiles sumus' S. LANGTON *Ruth* 102; *Ps.*-GROS. *Gram.* 38 (v. diminutio 1b). **b** crux cruciata .. multociens portatur in ~is, hoc est in parvis crucibus cruciatis. .. quando tales cruces ponuntur in †diminitivis et sine numero certo, tunc vocantur in Gallico *crosselettis* UPTON 215.

2 a diminutive, causing diminution. **b** (gram.) depreciative. **c** (?) designed to procure diminution (of sum due); *cf. diminuere* 2d. **d** (math.) subtractive, negative.

a vis augmentativa et vis illa a quo fluit diminutio, sc. vis ~a J. BLUND *An.* 49. **b** 'aut', si semel subicitur, deminutiva est et gradum habet ad inferiora tendentem, ut cum dicimus, 'librum volo, aut pretium', ut, si liber quem volo minime reddatur, tum quod secundum est vel pretium reddatur BONIF. *AG* 541. **c 1310** executores .. ab onere administracionis .., †salvis [? l. salva] tamen cuilibet creditorio et legatario qui .. inventarium arguere †voluerint [? l. voluerit] †diminutium [? l. ~iva], si quam obtinet, †accionem [? l. accione], absolvimus *Reg. Cant.* 1240. **d** quotquot [v. l. quidquid] fuerit in multiplicatione adjectum seu diminutum semper in lance consimili apponitur, id est, si unum fuerit adjectivum, alterum erit ~um ROB. ANGL. *Alg.* 96*n.*; *Ib.* 90 (v. adjectivus 1a).

diminutor, diminisher, injurer. **b** understater.

c1087 infractores seu ~ores hujus meae elemosinae *FormA* 240; infractores earum [possessionum] vel invasores aut ~ores aut dispersores AILR. *Ed. Conf.* 759D. **b** dum confiteris, non sis fraudulentus ~or W. RAMSEY *Cant.* f. 188vb.

dimisse v. demisse.

1 dimissibilis, (leg.) demisable. *V. et. dimittabilis.*

tenementa .. ~ia *Entries* 231b (v. custumarius 1a).

2 dimissibilis v. divisibilis 1d.

dimissio [CL]

1 sending forth, dispatch (fig.).

non multum citra corde ~onem arcum traxit. o quam amara erit teli ~o *Medit. Farne* 21.

2 a discharge (of executors). **b** release or acquittal. **c** dismissal (of appeal).

a 1418 emanavit ~o pro executoribus testamenti domini S. P. *Reg. Cant.* II 137. **b** de irrepleggiabilium ~onibus per plevinam (*Cap. Coronae*) *Fleta* 28; **a1553** ad laborandum penes .. constabularium pro exoneracione et ~one predictorum A. et B. de impeticione predicta habenda et obtinenda *Entries* 203. **c 1311** si .. pars appellans sit absens et certificatorium appareat presente parte appellata, non fiat ~o citra diem tercium a tempore quo lecta fuit suggestio in judicio *Conc.* II 412a.

3 a abandonment (of liegeman). **b** (fine for) neglect of military service. **c** surrender (of claim). **d** surrender, resignation (of benefice or office).

a pensandum erit omni domino .. ut ita suum hominem manuteneat ne dampnum pro defensione vel pro dimissione [v. l. dimissione] incurrat (*Leg. Hen.* 57. 8) *GAS* 576. **b** in lege Danorum habet rex .. ~onem belli, quod Angli dicunt *ferdwite*, fractionem pacis [etc.] (*Inst. Cnuti*) *Ib.* 319. **c 1145** ut de clericis suis mitteret qui prefate calumpnie ~onem audirent et capellarum concessionem *Act. Hen. II* I 9 (cf. ib.: calumpniam illam penitus dimisit); **1284** noverit universitas nos .. dimisisse, concessisse, et quietum clamasse Johanni .. filio Willelmi .. totum jus et clamium quod habuimus .. in vj solidatis annui redditus. .. pro hac autem ~one, concessione, et quieta clamacione quietum clamavit nobis predictus W. iiij s. annui redditus .. *Deeds Balliol* 4. **d 1284** cogitetis de beneficiis que sine juris titulo retinetis, in quorum ~one serenetis conscienciam vestram .. PECKHAM *Ep.* 407; **1412** si capellanus qui pro tempore fuerit .. officium hujusmodi dimittere velit .., teneatur .. de ~one hujusmodi cancellarium .. premunire *StatOx* 217; **1421** ad scolariam non presbiteralem .. vacantem per ~onem Roberti Cole *Reg. Cant.* I 199; **1472** commisimus .. custodiam .. temporalium .. monasterii .. de Oseney .. jam vacantis per ~onem magistri J. W. ultimi abbatis ibidem, qui in archiepiscopatum Dublinensem .. electus .. existit *FineR* 281 m. 6; **1483** rector .. ecclesie parochialis de B. .. resignacionem et ~onem simul in scriptis redactas .. fecit, legit, et interposuit dictamque ecclesiam .. resignavit et dimisit *Reg. Whet.* II 275.

4 remission (of sin, debt or sim.).

hanc beatitudinem nulli dari debere nisi illi cui penitus dimissa sunt peccata nec hanc ~onem fieri nisi debito reddito ANSELM (*CurD* 24) II 94; questio est de ~one injurie: primo si licet alicui petere vindictam; quid est dimittere proximo ..; si potest judex penam dimittere HALES *Qu.* 1549; maximum divine pietatis .. sacramentum declarat culpe ~onem CHAUNDLER *Apol.* 11a.

5 permission.

673 ut ipsi monachi non migrent de loco ad locum .. nisi per ~onem proprii abbatis (*Conc. Hertf.*) BEDE *HE* IV 5.

6 demise (release and grant): **a** of land or sim.; **b** of goods, rent or sim.

a 1199 kartam ipsius Matillidis habet, que testatur quod ipsa dedit et dimisit Willelmo et Christiane illam terram ..; et .. Ernaldus .. et Willelmus .., qui testes sunt in eadem carta, [dicunt] quod nunquam interfuerunt concessioni et ~oni *CurR RC* II 72; **1202** quod teneatis .. omnes divisas et ~ones que fient Bonis Hominibus Grand' Montis de la Berliere [*Norm*] *Pat* 16a; **1203** defendit ~onem patris sui de terra illa et concessionem illius terre *CurR* III 25; **1221** sciatis nos ratam et gratam habere ~onem quam .. Philippus .. fecit Galfrido .. de dominico nostro in Rudes [*Wilts*] .. excolendo ad medietatem fructuum *Pat* 286; **1225** ad audiendum .. si idem A. de terris suis .. se velit demittere et cui illam (*sic*) velit assignare per demissionem suam *Cl* 83a; postea .. ipse xij bovate terre in D. in ~ones tenentibus de D. sunt divise *Meaux* I 164; si quis demiserit quod tenuerit ad vitam suam tantum et seisinam propriam post terminum sue ~onis repecierit *Fleta* 365; **1322** [inquiras] de nominibus .. ipsorum qui hujusmodi †escaetis [l. escaetas] tenent et per quorum ~ones illas receperunt *Lit. Cant.* I 87; **1368** ad arentandum .. vacuas placeas .. pro certa firma nobis .. reddenda .. dimittendi et concedendi tibi committimus potestatem, ita quod per arentacionem et ~onem hujusmodi nobis .. incommodum non eveniat *RScot* 922b. **b 1338** in camera sacriste sunt .. ij panni aurei viridis coloris; item j pannus aureus indici coloris pro tumba domini A. ex ~one ejusdem *Ac. Durh.* 375; **1384** capitulum ecclesie .. R... ad firmam dimisit J... vicario de N. decimam garbarum .. de N... usque ad terminum sex annorum ..; prefatus insuper .. J. .. concedit .. quod, si contingat ipsum vicariam de N. .. quocumque modo dimittere, quod (*sic*) tunc bene liceat dicto capitulo de predicta decima .. libere diffinire .., presenti ~one in aliquo non obstante *Mem. Ripon* I 299.

dimissor, lessor.

1279 in brevi de ingressu de dimissione facta ad terminum qui preteriit, sive ~or haberet feodum aut liberum tenementum aut haberet tantum terminum, bene jacet visus *SelCKB* I 53; dimitti poterit terra pro voluntate ~oris tenenda de termino in terminum et anno in annum *Fleta* 193; **13..** qualiter tenentes ad voluntatem facient premunicionem ~oribus suis *MGL* I 178 (= ib. 221: *ferrount garnissementz al lessour*); **14..** quando ~or ingreditur tenementa .. infra terminum *Reg. Brev. Orig.* 97*n. marg.*

dimissorialis, (w. *litterae*) letters dimissory.

1408 duo homines coram .. archiepiscopo, qui ei [sc. nativo prioris] litteras ~es ad omnes sacros ordines contulit, jurati fuerunt *Lit. Cant.* III 108; **1518** dantes .. nostris

vicariis generalibus .. potestatem .. litteras commendatorias et ~es ad sacros ordines .. concedendi *Form. S. Andr.* I 21; **1529** nullus episcopus .. quempiam aliene diocesis .. ad sacros ordines .. admittat .. nec .. liceat extraneos .. ordinare eciamsi .. literas episcoporum suorum ~es habuerint .. *Conc.* III 718b.

dimissorius [LL], (w. *litterae* or as sb. f. pl.) letters dimissory: **a** (authorising departure from religious house or law-court). **b** (recommending for ordination or sim.). **c** (granting conditional pardon).

a s1207 quum [monachus] ab abbate impetrasset quod daret ei literas ~ias *Chr. Evesham* 224; **1221** R. pauper presbiter .. ab abbate ac fratribus .. licenciatus exinde cum eorum litteris ~iis non facta professione recessit *Mon. Hib. & Scot.* 20b; **1467** concedimus [W. monacho de Wymondham] .. licenciam inter nos de cetero conventualiter conversari, dummodo litteras ~ias simul et commendatorias nobis pro parte vestra [sc. abbatis de W.] .. exhibuerit *Reg. Whet.* II 65; **s1284** prefixus est dies in curia proximus juridicus post festum J. Baptiste oblateque sunt procuratori archiepiscopi litere ~ie, sed non curavit; procurator vero prioris et capituli benigne recepit Graystanes 19. **b 1294** dyaconi: .. Ph. de Camera, per litteras ~ias domini episcopi Glasguensis, ad titulum vj m. de camera Rogeri de K. percipiendarum *Reg. Carl.* I 12; **1301** quod .. vos [sc. Lincolniensis episcopus] .. ad ordines quos ipsius cura beneficii requirit ipsum [rectorem de M.] admittere et sibi sacras manus vestras imponere aut saltim litteras ~ias, quarum optentu possit ab alio episcopo catholico ordinari, concedere recusastis *Reg. Cant.* 780 (cf. ib. 779 *rub.*: quod concedat sibi ~ias); **1322** ordinati in Hibernia, Wallia vel Scocia, maxime sine literis sui diocesani et nostris commendatoriis seu ~iis, non admittantur ad ordinis sic suscepti execucionem in episcopatu nostro (*Const. Cant.*) *Conc.* II 512a (*gl.* Lyndw. 47 i: he [littere ~ie] dicuntur per quas aliquis dimittitur a jurisdiccione sive potestate sui prelati ..; et dicuntur quandoque licenciales, quando viz. licencia datur ad aliquid faciendum, utputa ordines ab alieno episcopo suscipiendos); **13..** quod nullus alterius diocesis, presertim alienigena, admittatur ad celebrandum divina nisi habeat litteras sufficientes tam ordinum suorum quam dimissori[as] et que per nos aut officialem nostrum .. approbate fuerint *Conc. Scot.* II 65; **1386** vobis .. litteras dimmissorias .. conferendi .. committimus vices nostras *Reg. Heref.* 101; **1408** vos .. ordinamus nostrum in spiritualibus vicarium generalem ad .. litteras ~ias pro ordinibus a quibuscumque episcopis catholicis infra Angliam intitulatis tam regularibus quam secularibus clericis concedendum (*Reg. Ebor.*) *Eng. Clergy* 189; **1419** W. R. .. per litteras ~ias sui diocesani ad titulum beneficii sui *Reg. Cant.* I 193. **c s1294** ad augmentandum .. rex exercitum suum pacem profligatis suis et profugis nunciavit, si ipsi in prima velificacione cum regis fidelibus transmigrarent. confluebant quidem mox ad regem multa milia de talibus .. et post pusillum .. recalcitrando discesserunt. .. tactus ergo rex dolore cordis .., juravit ex eo tempore nunquam hujuscemodi litteras ~ias talibus concedere sceleratis *Flor. Hist.* III 89.

dimissus, demise, lease. *Cf. dimissio* 5, *dimittere* 7g.

idem r. c. de v li. et xiij s. de A. de N. receptis pro demissu unius virgate terre *FormMan* 13.

dimisum v. 2 dimittere 7g.

dimittabilis, demisable. *V. et.* 1 *dimissibilis.*

1557 viginti boni (*sic*) et ~ia (*sic*) vaccas *Pat* 924 m. 28.

1 dimittere v. 1 demittere.

2 dimittere [CL]

1 to send (away), let go, release: **a** (inanim. obj.); **b** (animal); **c** (person); **d** (husband or wife). **e** (refl.) to discharge oneself (of), part (with); *cf.* 7e *infra*. **f** to lose, forfeit, give up. **g** (w. abstr. obj.) to reject, dismiss.

a velut sagitta ab arcu demissa [v. l. dimissa] Felix *Guthl.* 45; aperit .. aqueductum omnemque aquam a stagno ~it Coggesh. *Visio* 33; ~it .. custos cuilibet custodi .. officinarum .. que de officinis suis sibi superhabundant sub preciis in tabulis .. contentis *Ac. Beaulieu* 271. **b** ne quis ~at [v. l. vendat; AS: *sylle*] equum ultra mare, nisi velit eum dare (*Quad.*) *GAS* 159; nobilis quidam .. nisum ad predam a manu sua dimisit et amisit W. Cant. *Mir. Thom.* VI 109; cum [girfalcus] post quinque grues vel alias quaslibet aves in aiere volantes fuerit dimissus Upton 187; **1270** dimiserunt .. quinque de canibus suis, quos B. [parcarius] cepit *SelPlForest* 56; **1293** ridemanny conqueruntur quod ponunt ibi [in parco fracto] districciones et statim ~untur per defaltam *SelPlMan* 72; **1311** hominibus regis querentibus animalia ejusdem dimissa *Ac. Durh.* 508. **c** Petrum offendisti, Romam destruxisti, Gregorium dimisisti *V. Greg.* p. 86; ut .. nullum a se ~at qui inculpatus sit in manupasto ejus antequam publicum rectum .. fecerit (*Quad.*) *GAS* 395; Eadmer *HN* 350 (v. contestari 3a); **s1172** rex .. dimisit regem filium suum .. in Normanniam *G. Hen. II* I 35; **c1200** [appellatus] non ~itur ei [officiali episcopi] quietus, set ei committitur, ita quod illum habeat in adventu justiciariorum *SelPlCrown* 79; **1202** tunc dimisit eum liberatum sine plevina *Ib.* 19; non fuit in tali statu quando dimissus fuit plegiis, ut Ricardus .., qui eum dimisit, et alii testantur *Ib.*; **1209** per .. forestarium dimissus sub plevina *SelPlForest* 5; captus fuit et inprisonatus et dimissus per plevinam decenne de W. et villate *PlCrGlouc* 36; **c1225** burgensis captus a baillivo ~atur per vadia et plegios (*Ch. Haverfordwest*) *EHR* XV 518; **s1228** G. de B. laicus .. adjicit quod unum eorum [latronum] dimisit ipse propria manu in polam *Feod. Durh.* 270; **s1289** (v. comparitio b); dimisit eos de villa versus interiores partes Francie quo vellent *G. Hen. V* 8. **d** si cujus uxor fornicata fuerit, licet ~ere eam et aliam accipere. .. mulieri non licet virum ~ere, licet sit fornicator Theod. *Pen.* II 12. 5–6; alii si habeurunt uxores dimiserunt Ælf. *Ep.* 2. 67; **1122** nec vir uxorem suam, aut uxor virum, ut alii nubat ~ere legaliter potest (*Ep.*) Eadmer *HN* 351; dicitur quod patriarchis plures concesse fuerint uxores .. et quod multis de causis ~ebantur Pull. *Sent.* 668A. **e 1200** demisit se de tota terra sua et ipsum E. heredem constituit *CurR* I 363; **1203** petit .. xiiij virgatas terre .. sicut jus suum et unde Ph. avus suus se dimisit in vita sua in curia Walteri .. et illam concessit J. filio suo *Ib.* III 25; **1218** demisit se coram nobis .. de toto honore .. de Bremble *Pat* 165; **1218** ipsa nunquam dimisit se de terra illa, set revera dimisisset se si auderet *Eyre Yorks* 9; **1219** Ricardus .. presentavit ultimam personam, sc. Philippum ..; set postea .. predictus Ph. demisit se de ecclesia illa et recepit vicariam *CurR* VIII 118; **1243** quod, postquam extiterit senescallus Wasconie per unum annum plene completum, .. poterit se ~ere de senescalcia illa si voluerit *RGasc* I 153 (= *CalPat* 396); **1404** dimisit se de regimine regni *Cl* 252 m. 19. **f** ipsa [anima] ab illa celesti harmonia ad inferiora transmissa, dum dimisse jocunditatis ac felicitatis reminiscitur .. *Quaest. Salern.* B 16; **s1236** quia .. papa parti .. favit .. Mediolanensium, quorum fama super multis heresibus, usuris et symoniis laboravit, multorum fidelium diatim dimisit [v. l. amisit] devotionem *Flor. Hist.* II 218; **1297** non habet unde possit vivere .., immo oportet quod ~at libros suos *RGasc* III cxc; **1298** si .. secularis minister domus ea .. fecerit, per octo dies sequentes corrodium suum ~at *Reg. Cant.* 823. **g** omnes tenemur ~ere rancorem ex corde, mortalem scilicet, et affectum rancoris Hales *Qu.* 1585 (cf. 5c infra); Wycl. *Civ. Dom. III* 110 (v. ditabilis).

2 to leave (behind), abandon (sts. in a specified condition): **a** (place or sim., not necessarily visited); **b** (thing, incl. land or building); **c** (person or community); **d** (as successor or representative); **e** (w. inanim. subj.).

a aethereas dimittens furcifer auras / .. / corruit Aldh. *CE* 4. 1. 30; venerunt .. in insulam .. Choo et demittebant Chorintheos in sinistra parte Hugeb. *Will.* 4; de †bursensibus qui manserunt in burgo de Norwic' abierunt xxij .. et dimiserunt burgum *DB* II 117v.; **s457** reliqui [virorum] Cantiam penitus dimisere [*AS Chr.*: *forletan*] Fl. Worc. I 5; **s1100** [Anselmus] dismissa curia in pace ad sua secessit Eadmer *HN* 137; **s1191** tunc ~ende sunt insule ille in dextera parte navis *G. Ric. I* 204. **b** dimissis [v. l. dismisis] ordinate omnibus navigavit Galliam Bede *HE* III 19 p. 168; manicas suas illic obliviscendo se dimissuse aiebat Felix *Guthl.* 40; **1121** precipio quod cito deliberetis terram abbatis de R. .. et quod ibi invenistis ~atis (*Breve Regis*) *Chr. Rams.* 231 (= *Regesta* 1293); in tegula recenter facta posita ad solem vel ad ignem, quod si diutius ~atur, .. sal destruitur *Quaest. Salern.* Ba 108; **1209** idem r. c. de xx s. .. pro plevina hominum qui fuerunt in cippo .. et de xx s. de H. preposito pro clav[e] ~end[a] *Pipe Wint.* 50 (= *Crawley* 189); **1223** quod ipsa penitus vastavit boscum, ita quod .. non dimisit ibi nisi tantum xxx quercus *BNB* III 483; **1242** iter arripuimus versus Berbizillum [*Gasc*], in villa de Ponte .. sufficientem ~entes munitionem *Cl* 531; **1289** concedimus .. licenciam .. construendi .. piscarium .. in nostro flumine .., ~endo tamen competentem viam seu iter .. necessarium navigantibus *RGasc* II 447; **1298** nisi .. ostia quandoque ~antur aperta *Reg. Cant.* 823; **1324** (v. derelinquere 2a); **1379** messuagium .. reparatum sustentabunt et in fine terminorum suorum in adeo bono statu vel melius ~ent *Deeds Balliol* 30; inter unamquamque fossatam terra ~ebatur integra ad latitudinem unius cubiti pro unius solius hominis introitu vel exitu *G. Hen. V* 3; **1460** [terre] assedabantur Willelmo S. et ipse dimisit eas vastas *ExchScot* 13. **c 706** quid de vobis dicetur si pontificem .. in exilio solum dimiseritis? Aldh. *Ep.* 9 (12); mirum quare nolueris ut aliquos nostrum, qui tibi ministrarent, hic ~eremus abeuntes Bede *CuthbP* 37; quos ante insalutatos ~ebat, iterum salutaribus praeceptis commendare disposuit Felix *Guthl.* 26; non licet clerico ~ere ecclesiam suam .. et migrare ad alteram .. quia ecclesia est ejus uxor spiritaliter Ælf. *Ep.* 2. 194; illi [sc. magi] repatrient, oblato munere, / ego puerulum nolo dimittere Walt. Wimb. *Carm.* 217; **1266** cum .. reginam .. in castro .. de Windesor' post nos ~amus faciendam moram ibidem *Cl* 187; **1266** ipsam fere mortuam dimiserunt *SelCCoron* 16; ~ere eos in sua libertate Bacon *Maj.* II 377 (v. Christianus 1a); **1332** (v. desolare d); rex, nolens .. ~ere imperatorem solum absque pari presencia in terra sua *G. Hen. V* 20. **d s796** [Offa] Egfertum filium, ante mortem suam in regem inunctum, successorem dimisit W. Malm. *GR* I 94; **1236** dum .. Isabella .. ipsum Rogonem loco suo dimisit ad finem cum .. rege faciendum *CurR* XV 1961; **1303** dimisit in capitulo magistrum W. .. clericum suum *DCCant. Reg.* Q f. 29b; **1451** vicarius provincialis, quando .. sic infirmatur quod non possit capitulo provinciali interesse, ~at commissarium de consilio discretorum (*Abbr. Stat. Francisc.*) *Mon. Francisc.* II 112. **e** Ælf. *Coll.* 100 (v. 3b infra); uno momento eadem quae illum dimiserat infirmitate percussus est Osb. *Mir. Dunst.* 4.

3 a resign, surrender (office or tenure). **b** to abandon, desist from (practice, activity, purpose, opinion). **c** to relinquish (claim). **d** (?) to give up (disease) as incurable. **e** (absol.) to leave off. **f** to die. **g** (w. inf.) to cease.

a dixit non eum episcopatum ~ere debere Bede *HE* IV 2; **1122** nec me juste potuisse episcopatum ~ere Eadmer (*Ep.*) *HN* 351; **1266** compotum .. justiciarii Laudonie .. de lucris .. adquisitis post ultimum computum usque in diem quo dictam balliam dimisit *ExchScot* 9; **1362** cum alter eorum cesserit loco suo .. sive ipsum demiserit .., ad locum sic vacantem .. nominabimus idoneum sacerdotem *Lit. Cant.* II 426; **1375** quod illi tenentes qui demiserunt tenementa sua quod (*sic*) faciant eos metere cum domino *Hal. Durh.* 127; **1412** (v. dimissio 3d); **1449** Bekynton I 265 (v. compatibilis). **b** demissa [v. l. dimissa] intentione bellorum Bede *HE* III 14; qui artem suam dimiserit [AS: *forlæt*] ipse ~atur [AS: *byþ forlætan*] ab arte Ælf. *Coll.* 100 (v. et. 2e supra); Arrius .. noluit ~ere suam heresim *Id. Ep.* 2. 54; dimisso signo [*ed.* '*when the bell stops*'], omnes simul tres orationes faciant Lanfr. *Const.* 87; ritum .. Anglorum, qui pro sternutatione et somnio vetularum ~unt iter suum seu negotium Ord. Vit. X 14 p. 87; **s1172** [rex] juravit quod consuetudines que inducte sunt contra ecclesias terre sue in tempore suo penitus ~eret *G. Hen. II* I 33; non propter istam racionem ~atur opinio Duns *Ord.* III 37; **s1383** nostri dimissa obsidione .. recesserunt *V. Ric. II* 47. **c 1284** (v. dimissio 3c); **1301** (v. clamor 4a). **d** quandoque .. sentitur gravitas ad caput ascendere .. et cetera que diximus, et vertigo est durabilis et omnino ~itur Gilb. II 99v. 1. **e** si sacerdos, prius quam inceperit canonem [misse], incurrerit [infirmitatem] .., sedeat donec convaluerit et postea incipiat ubi dimisit *Cust. Westm.* 222; cum in diebus paribus febris dimiserit, reverti consuevit Bacon IX 203. **f** Austraberta pia ternas dimiserat [v. l. pausaverat] idus *Kal. M. A.* I 399. **g 790** obsecro .. ne me umquam consolatoriis ~as reficere litteris Alcuin *Ep.* 9; ~amus .. loqui de dubitante Ockham *Dial.* 440.

4 to leave out, omit; **b** (w. inf.); **c** (w. *quin*).

psalmo 'Domine, quid multiplicati sunt' dimisso [AS p. 426: *for lætenum*] *RegulC* 50; tunc processio ex toto ~itur Lanfr. *Const.* 126; per confessionem est absolutum quicquid aut per .. negligentiam dimissum aut per diabolicam expugnationem exstiterat commissum Osb. *Mir. Dunst.* 19 p. 148; non ~et hostelarius vesperas nec matutinos in dupplici festo propter hospites *Cust. Cant. Abbr.* 257; **1288** magistri .. lecciones suas omnino ~ent quousque a dicta balliva idem R. totaliter sit amotus *MunAcOx* 45. **b** cum sacerdoti .. aliquid .. evenerit propter quod ipsa die missam celebrare non debeat .., non ~at quicquam facere de officio suo nisi missam et benedictionem in refectorio .. Lanfr. *Const.* 160; eciam pro morte vitanda non debet quis ~ere corrigere delinquentem si .. Ockham *Dial.* 544. **c 1253** mandatum est .. quod pro nulla re mundana ~ant quin regi mittant .. xxx quintillas [MS: quintallas] fili de Hispania [etc.] *Cl* 178.

5 to remit: **a** (offence); **b** (debt); **c** (penalty or exaction); **d** (impers. pass.).

a omnia peccata ~untur, sicut in baptismo Theod. *Pen.* II 3. 3; quod .. factas ab eis injurias mox obsecrantibus placida mente ~eret Bede *HE* III 22; quasi diceret: "O Judaei, vos putatis quod Christus gentibus plus dimiserit; sed quibusdam vestrum plus ~it, quos praevaricatores legis invenit" Lanfr. *Comment. Paul.* (*Rom.* v 20) 123; **1184** concedo eisdem [abbati et monachis] eandem auctoritatem et potestatem puniendi et ~endi commissa delinquencium .. quam mea dominica curia habet *Cart. Glast.* I 187; si [sacerdos] fuerit in caritate, digne ~it peccata; si tamen non fuerit, nihilominus remittit Hales *Qu.* 1223 (cf. ib.: 'remittere est debitam penam temperare et in parte relaxare', ut dicit Hugo [recte Ricardus] de S. Victore [*Pot. Lig. et Solv.* 24] .., '~ere vero est ex toto indulgere'); **s1297** quod [rex] omnem offensam comitibus et eorum confederatis ~at Trevet *Ann.* 367; **s1455** confiteor .. abbati J. .. me contra ipsum peccasse graviter. .. ideo precor te .. mediare taliter pro me ut velit mihi ~ere omnia hujusmodi peccata mea *Reg. Whet.* I 157. **b** cum orare debemus ut ~antur debita [*Matth.* vi 12] oramus ut dimittantur peccata Anselm. *Misc.* 349; queritur an peccet qui hoc ['~e nobis debita nostra'] dicit et non ~it Hales *Sent.* III 363; **1360** procurator gratanter et ex corde universum debitum dimisit eidem *MunAcOx* 224. **c 749** (12c) cunctas tribulationes quae nocere vel impedire possunt in domo Dei omnibus principibus sub ejus potestate degentibus demittere et auferre praecepit *CS* 178; obsecro te .. ut ~as quod conscientia metuit et adicias quod oratio non praesumit Alch. *Or.* 144; de omni homicidio .. et omnibus incendiis .. totum ~atur [AS: *man eall onweig læte*], et nemo .. emendationem exigat (*Quad.*) *GAS* 224; debemus ~ere penam nobis debitam pro injuria, penam dico quam voluntas nostra .. inordinata dicat nobis inferendam; non tenemur autem ~ere penam debitam et ordinatam et rationabilem Hales *Qu.* 1585 (cf. 1g supra). **d c1283** de horsgabulo non ~itur pro aliquo opere nisi quando fiunt averagia *Cust. Battle* 77.

6 to permit; **b** (w. inf.).

si virtus dimiserit, postea erit ei nutriens sufficiens panis cum ptisana donec omnis febris declinaverit Gilb. I 64. 2; **1269** paratus fuit .. processisse per eundem attornatum, si hoc lex et consuetudo Anglie dimisisset *Cl* 109. **b 793** si .. Deus .. habitator est cordis nostri, numquam inimicos suos tacere ~it quae sua sunt Alcuin *Ep.* 19 p. 55; **836** ut

elemosinam quam .. datam habeo .. stare demittetis *CS* 416; in vere ~o [AS: *ic læte*] eos [accipitres] avolare ad silvam ÆLF. *Coll.* 96 (cf. 1b supra); laxatis nodis ~untur [tauri] per atrium proludere W. MALM. *GP* III 110; **1220** eum .. recedere ~ant (v. 2 clericus 1a); **1224** ~imus eis tenere terram quam .. comes habet in insula *Pat* 431; aperiunt bursam et ~ant aquam fluere GILB. VI 255v. 1; **c1310** (v. 2 coppare); aliquando oportuit fideles ~ere per plures annos vacare apostolicam sedem OCKHAM *Dial.* 866.

7 a to commit, entrust, deposit (for safe-keeping or sim.). **b** to demise, or bequeath; *cf. dividere* 9b. **c** (w. abstr. obj.) to transmit, pass on. **d** to refer (for decision). **e** to demise, grant (land *etc.* usu. for a term). **f** (w. *ad firmam* or sim.). **g** (p. ppl. as sb. n.) demise; *cf. dimissio* 6, *dimissus*.

a sciscitabatur .. cui pastorum oves Christi .. ~eret BEDE *HE* II 6; quadam nocte, dum fessa membra solitae quieti ~eret FELIX *Guthl.* 18; **790** (v. commutatio 2b); **1219** (v. anulus 2a); **1220** ballivus .. dicit .. quod comes ejus [Alicie] custodiam non dimiserat Johanni .. set maritagium Alicie ei dimiserat tantum *CurR* IX 67; **1220** ut ei custodiendus ~atur (v. 2 clericus 1a); **1253** quod .. custodiam terrarum .. heredis nomine regis ~at Petro *Cl* 178; **1269** rex dimisit eidem P. custodiam foreste .. reddendo per annum regi .. xl s. *SelPlForest* 46; **1275** convenit .. quod .. ~eret eis nomine vadii ij equos *SelPlMan* 150; **1321** (v. custodia 3c); demittere *Quadr. Reg. Spec.* 32 (v. dispendere 1a); **s1399** thesaurum .. et alia jocalia viz. bona regni, que ab antiquo dimissa fuerant in archivis regni *V. Ric. II* 197. **b** tainus vel miles regis dominicus moriens pro relevamento ~ebat regi omnia arma sua et equum *DB* I 56v.; dux .. Willelmus .. transnavigavit ut regnum Anglie sibi a suo consanguineo rege Edwardo dimissum de manu Haraldi .. abstraheret *Chr. Battle* f. 22; **s1181** (v. distributor a); **1386** volo quod .. dicti duo equi oblentur die sepulture mee .. et sint demissi [sc. domui hospitali] cum ecclesia (*Test.*) *FormA* 429; **1556** ex fructibus rectoriarum per .. reges dimissarum et universitati appropriatarum *StatOx* 367. **c** ne corpus tuum extinctum putetur vitalem in te flatum ~am COGGESH. *Visio* 6; **1299** licet predecessores nostri .. injuncciones salubres vestre religionis honestati congruentes dimisissent a vobis .. firmiter observandas *Reg. Cant.* 848. **d** O. episcopus tenet in dominio B... de episcopatu suo, ut dicit; .. unde judicium non dixerunt, set ante regem, ut judicet, dimiserunt *DB* I 58v.; clamores .. ~untur in judicio regis *Ib.* 377v. **e** aliam medietatem Uluuardo in vita sua tantum ita dimisit quatinus post obitum suum .. rediret ad monasterium *Ib.* 43v.; **c1150** me .. quicquid a .. rege H. in ecclesia W... mihi datum et a vobis concessum fuerat ipsi [episcopo] absque omni reclamatione in perpetuum dimississe *Ch. Sal.* 17; **1199** (v. dimissio 6a); **1271** volumus quod .. terre et tenementa illa Christianis qui sibi [sc. Judeis] ea dimiserint, remaneant ..; hac adjecta condicione ut, si Christiani illi incontinenter inde satisfacere non possint, liceat Judeis predictis tenementa illa aliis ~ere, donec [etc.] (*Lit. Regis*) *Leg. Ant. Lond.* app. 236; **1275** Hugo .. dimisit et tradidit Willelmo Fabro dim. acram prati .. ad terminum xix annorum *SelPlMan* 28; **1285** Willelmus .. petit versus Walterum j mesuagium et iij acras terre ut jus suum in quod .. Walterus non habet ingressum nisi per Herveum .. patrem .. Willelmi, qui illud tenementum dimisit .. Waltero ad terminum qui preteriit *CBaron* 119; **1364** pro uno messuagio et dim. virgata terre .. sibi dimissis .. usque finem v annorum *Banstead* 338; **1402** de puteo de R. dimisso pro quarterio anni *Ac. Durh.* 603. **f 1220** dicit quod idem Ph. dimisit manerium illud ei ad firmam ad terminum xviij annorum, reddendo [inde] annuatim ei et heredibus suis xv li. *CurR* VIII 297; **a1250** A. dimisit ad feodi firmam .. G. fratri suo medietatem domus .. tenendam et habendam .. G. et heredibus .. reddendo .. iiij s. argenti ad duos anni terminos *Deeds Newcastle* 31; **s1250** Rogerus .. crucesignatus .. partem suam in silvis et aliis redditibus .. priori et conventui [de Coventre] .. pro magna summa pecunie, ut sibi in viaticis provideret, ad feudofirmam dimisit M. PAR. *Maj.* V 98; **1292** rex .. quod illam [villam] dimisit burgensibus .. ad firmam *PQW* 121a; **s1399** rex R. commisit et ad firmum (*sic*) dimisit regnum Anglie .. comiti Wilton' [et al.] *Croyl. Cont. B* 493; **1457** (v. arrentare a); **1539** me .. ad feodifirmam seu emphiteosim .. ~ere .. Johanni T. .. terras nostras .. in dominio de Lauderdaill *Kelso* I pref. p. liv. **g c1095** remiserunt michi totum illud dimisum (v. destaurare).

8 (?) to submit, render (account).

1327 status hostillar[ie] dimissus per fratrem J. de H. hostillar[ium] *Ac. Durh.* 114.

3 †dimittere, *f. l.*

terram in quatuor †dimiserunt [? l. diviserunt] partes *DB* II 104; **1300** vota sua in quatuor †dimiserunt [? l. diviserunt] *Reg. Cant.* 632.

dimitum [cf. δίμιτον], cloth woven w. two threads, dimity.

1300 pro xxviij peciis de dimett' .. emptis pro uno cubito de plum' faciendo *AcWardr* p. 57.

dimmissorius v. dimissorius.

dimovēre [CL], to part (fig.), deter.

ab observatione justitie Dei .. terrores vestri non me ~ere poterunt W. FITZST. *Thom.* 135; ~eo i. advertere OSB. GLOUC. *Deriv.* 333.

dimpnia v. dyspnoea.

dimulgare [cf. promulgare], to divulge, publish. *Cf. divulgare.*

s1300 quibus coram populo demulgatis *Flor. Hist.* III 303; non est consuetudo ecclesie quod omnes constituciones pape noviter edite priusquam obligent per episcopos ~entur OCKHAM *Dial.* 660 (cf. ib.: constitucionem .. publice promulgatam).

dimulgatio, announcement, publication. *Cf. divulgatio.*

prima solennis ~o sufficit ad hoc quod constitucio pape obliget universos. .. ergo simpliciter ~o facta per superiorem non minus obligat quam ~o facta per inferiorem [etc.] OCKHAM *Dial.* 660.

dimultiplicare, to multiply.

ita intelligamus .. Jesum unum ~atum esse ut quam plurimi in ipso uniantur COLET *Eccl. Hier.* 227.

dinaldis, dinamis v. dynamis.

dinare [AN *diner*, OF *disner* < disjejunare], to dine. **b** (inf. as sb.) dinner.

datur eis panis conventualis quantum sufficit, et tercia die ~ant et recedunt *Ac. Beaulieu* 271. **b** laborantes in lardario habeant ad dignare panem dispensabilem *Reg. Pri. Worc.* 123b.

dinarium, ~ius [OF *disner*], dinner.

errans dignĕrium, quisquis sit, si petat a te, / sit plus sitve minus, quod habes des fronte faceto D. BEC. 2386; **1204** invenite .. quandam sellam bonam ad sumerium †disuar' [l. disnarii] nostri cum toto harnas[io] *Cl* 4a; **1204** invenite .. ad hernesium sumarii de disnerio nostro xiiij s. vj d. *Liberate* 80; **1206** pro v pariis buscellorum ad disnarium regis *Pipe* 47; **1207** facias nobis habere .. duos panerios ad dignerium nostrum *Cl* 86b; **1212** per servicium ferendi dingnerium domini regis in Wichewude *Fees* 103; illud tenementum tenet .. burgensis .. de A. de S. .. faciendo ei j dinnarium cum se tercio annuatim vel xij d. *Ib.* 196; **1214** ij buttas et ij butell' ad dinnierium nostrum *Cl* 141b; **1222** educet x plaustra de fimo post Pascha et habebit dignerium de domino *Dom. S. Paul.* 62; **1226** sicut ipse et frater suus fuerunt in domo Willelmi Pistoris .. ad dignarium suum *CurR* XII 1967; **1233** quia predictus H. denegavit cuidam .. venatori domini regis dinnerium suum, venit dominus rex et disseisivit H. *BNB* II 587; **1241** rex perdonavit magistro J. de S. coco de ~io regis unam scultellam argenteam .., quam casu fortuito amisit in dedicatione ecclesie S. Pauli Lond' *Cl* 295; **c1250** ubicunque operatus fuerit infra villam, veniet ad ~ium suum et post ~ium redibit ad opus suum *Cart. Rams.* I 399; **1257** percepit .. sextarium vini pro digneriis et soperis suis *Cl* 144; **c1260** debet falcare in pratis domini per v dies, et debet habere iiij dygnarios, sc. panem et caseum *Cust. Glast.* 203; **1265** tota familia comitis in dinerio existente *Manners* 15; **c1350** comedent ad mensam abbatis et habebunt ad dignarium duo et duo j panem et caseum *Reg. S. Aug.* 79.

dindrare v. drindrare.

1 dindymus (dindimus) v. didymus.

2 dindymus, -on [CL Dindymon < Δίνδυμα], holy mountain, sanctuary (also fig.; *cf.* Virgil *Aen.* X 252). **b** (adj.) secret, mysterious. **c** angels' seat. **d** high seat, dais.

macharii penetrant rutilantia dindima Petri FRITH. 1137; vasta palus, piscosa nimis, sua dindima pandit ABBO *QG prol.* 3; ingressi †dindinma [*gl.*: clandestina] cordium vestrorum caelotenus suspendite et pro reatibus vestris .. superni arbitris (*sic*) munificentiam .. precamini ÆLF. BATA 5. 5; postquam .. pietas divinae majestatis .. ~a [*gl.*: secreta] celsi poli [Odoni] concessit cernere BYRHT. *V. Osw.* 410; [Dominus] qui poli regit dindima *Offic. Kentig.* p. c; *an hille*, Alpes, collis, dindimus, mons *CathA.* **b** †nec [? l. nunc] solent casto corde caelum caelique factorem ~a [*gl.*: secreta] contemplatione conspicere BYRHT. *V. Osw.* 42; dindima priscae legis mysteria .. intellexit [Baeda] eaque .. tyrunculis aecclesiae .. propinavit *Id. Man. epil.* 244. **c** *angell setis*, dindima .., *a sete of angellis*, dindimus *CathA.* **d** *deece of hy benche*, subcellium, †didimus, orcestra *PP.*

dinerium v. dinarium. **dinexus** v. devexus 1d. **dingia** v. dungia. **dingn-** v. dign-, din-. **dingus** v. thainus.

dinmulta [cf. Gael. *dionag* = *lamb*, *mult* (< OF *multon*) = *sheep*], (Sc.) 'dinmont', ewe after first shearing.

1202 reddendo .. duas melas Scoticanas farine ordeicee et unam pernam et unam dinmult' ad festum S. Martini (*Indent.*) *Scot. R. O.* RH 6/16.

dinnarium, ~erium, ~ierrium v. dinarium.

dinoscentia [LL], distinguishing, discerning.

si medicus .. appellaret eundem cibum ~ie boni et mali et †sanitas [MS: sanitatis] et inbescillitatis eo quod per ipsum homo cum egrotare cepisset experiendo dinosceret GROS. *Hexaem.* XI 4 p. 309.

dinoscere [CL]

1 to distinguish, discern. **b** (med.) to diagnose. **c** to determine, decide. **d** to mark as distinct.

inter bonum ~entes et malum BEDE *Luke* 403; egressi dignoscere quid esset, viderunt lucem .. permaximam *Id. HE* III 8; quid sit de quo sic enuntietur ~i non facile BALSH. *AD* 35; D. BEC 729 (v. contestari 3a). **b** propter dispositionem egritudinis vel egroti sic dignoscitur prolixitas vel brevitas egritudinis RIC. MED. *Signa* 38. **c** ad ~endum si .. *GAS* 554 (v. decania 1). **d** ternarius numerus hujus substantie unam ostendit radicem, que viz. substantia novenario ~itur numero ROB. ANGL. *Alg.* 72; appellativa interioris hominis est facies ad denoscendum ipsum in merito et similiter ad aliis KILWARDBY *Jejun.* 170.

2 (pass. w. inf.) to be known (to). **b** (p. ppl.) well known.

[Helias] generali mortis debito caruisse ~itur ALDH. *VirgP* 20; denoscimur *Id. Met.* 4 (v. 1 conciliare 1a); **796** ruina altioris loci periculosior esse ~itur ALCUIN *Ep.* 114 p. 168; **957** (14c) cum omnibus quae ad ipsum locum pertinere ~untur *CS* 988; **c1043** quam ignominiosum .. esse ~itur ut malum nomen .. post se quis derelinquat *CD* 769; de castello .., cujus custodia ad hereditatem Nicholae .. spectare ~itur DEVIZES 33; **c1218** (v. cura 5); quanto eamdem [pietatem vestram] et virtutis strenuitas et circumspectio prudentie .. commendare dignoscuntur eminentius AD. MARSH *Ep.* 85; **1343** devocione sincera quam ad Deum .. gerere dignosceris (*Lit. Papae*) AD. MUR. *Chr.* 150; disnoscitur *FormOx* 415 (v. corditer b); **s1399** regalitati .., cui pocius largitatis affluencia convenire denoscitur AD. USK 39; **1408** (v. 2 dangerium 3b). **b** ante introitum in religionem fuit magnus armiger et denotus in boria Anglie GASCOIGNE *Loci* 170.

dinoscibiliter, w. a discerning eye.

ille .. nullam penitus feminarum ~iter intueri solebat AD. EYNS. *Hug.* IV 12 p. 55.

dinotio, discernment, perception.

c1100 celitus .. inspirata sibi ~one, [cecus] caput hominis esse persentit *Pass. Æthelb.* 13.

dintellus v. duitellus.

dinumerabilis [LL], numerable, countable.

partes planetarum et domos et exaltationes .. vix ~ia GROS. *Hexaem.* V 9.

dinumerare [CL], to number, count, reckon.

ALDH. *VirgP* 35 (v. computare 1a); xij mancusas volo .. ~are in manu tua ÆLF. BATA 4. 26 p. 50; **†1066** (12c) praeparavi et ~avi expensas necessarias itineri *CD* 824; dinumeres guttas equoris, astra poli NECKAM *DS* V 628; nec unum ex membris ejus [B. Virginis] pretermisit quin denumeraret omnia *Latin Stories* 66; **s1387** multa plura, que ~are longum foret *V. Ric. II* 82.

dinumeratio [CL], numbering, counting.

1397 pro ~one pellium per tempus compoti *ExchScot* 407.

dinumerator [LL], numberer, counter.

1398 denumeratori pellium .. vj s. viij d. *ExchScot* 442; **1410** precipitur Johanni C. .., ~ori pellium, quod .. *Ib.* 114.

diobol- v. et. diabol-.

diobolaris [CL], priced at two obols, cheap.

~es, merces duobus obolis emtae OSB. GLOUC. *Deriv.* 175; ganea .. diovalari relicta [viciosa uxore], vir validus est prospere reversus ad patriam *Collect. Stories* 229.

diobolariter, cheaply.

malui .. pecunialiter dampnificari quam filiam meam pati quodam modo diovolariter meretricari *Collect. Stories* 206.

dioc- v. et. dioec-. **diocesenarius** v. dioecesanus 2a. **diocesa** v. dioecesis.

dioecesanus (dioc-) [LL]

1 diocesan, belonging to a diocese; **b** (w. *episcopus* or *praesul*).

~i magnates illius provincie [Eboracensis] J. FURNESS *Walth.* 29; **s1202** episcopus Wigorn' .. indulgentiam a domino papa .. impetravit, viz. ut liceret sibi ecclesias ~a lege sibi subjectas, appellatione remota, visitare *Chr. Evesham* 109; **c1239** episcopus .. jure ~o sibi subjectos et ab ipso non exemptos absque anime sue discrimine non potest non visitare GROS. *Ep.* 127 p. 371; **s1240** ut, si ecclesia cathedralis per menses sex vacaret viduata pastore, per archiepiscopum ~um sibi provideretur *Flor. Hist.* II 237 (= M. PAR. *Maj.* IV 14: per archiepiscopum loci); custodie carceris dyocesani *Conc. Scot.* II 19 (v. commendare 3b); **1295** quatenus possumus ex potestate ~a *Reg. Carl.* I 40. **b** monitu sani consilii Ælfwini praesulis diocesiani HERM. ARCH. 17; **1142** ecclesiastica sacramenta a ~o suscipietis episcopo, si quidem catholicus fuerit (*Lit. Papae*) *Reg. Malm.* I 346; **s1175** O. prior Cantuar', electus in abbatem S. Martini de Bello, bellum statim .. indixit episcopo diocesiano DICETO *YH* I 403; cujus [decime

magne] duas partes ecclesie sue baptismali, tertiam vero episcopo ~o dare solent GIR. *DK* I 18; **1201** episcopo dyocesiano *CurR* II 85; **1234** illum prisonem qui habet tonsuram clericalem liberari faciat episcopo diocesiano *Cl* 461; **c1350** ex concessione episcoporum dioscesanorum *Melrose* 466; religiosis . . a ~is episcopis admissis in forma juris (CROMPE) *Ziz.* 351.

2 (as sb. m.): **a** a diocesan, bishop of diocese. **b** resident of diocese.

a **1181** donec . . cum litteris dyocesani rei veritatem continentibus apostolico se conspectui representet (*Lit. Papae*) *Reg. Newbattle* 257; **c1220** de consensu . . Willelmi episcopi S. Andree, loci ~i et patroni ecclesie de D. *Reg. Dunferm.* 111; **a1225** ut in singulis vicariis . . presentatio libera ~o facienda abbati et conventui S. Thome . . reservetur *Reg. S. Thom. Dublin* 319; **12..** quicumque oriundi extra regnum Scotie nullatenus admittantur ad deserviendum . . nisi eorum diutina conversatio honesta fuerit probata per ~um vel ejus archidiaconum [et] ~is fuerint presentati *Conc. Scot.* II 50; **s1253** excommunicaverunt omnes qui . . manus violentas in . . clericos injecerunt . ., nisi . . ad emendationem veniant et secundum arbitrium loci †~iorum satisfacerint *Leg. Ant. Lond.* 123; dummodo dyocisani [*corr. from* dyocisiani] voluntas ad id accesserit *FormMan* 24; **1354** per eundem dominum et patrem, †diocesenarium nostrum *DocCOx* 261; **1388** pro eo quod ejusdem loci ~us . . scismaticus ac nostri inimicus . . existit *RScot* 93b. **b** mandando pervenit ad abbatiam regis mandatum; indicit priori fratribusque personatis cum loci diocesianis curiam fore †petendum [? l. petendam] HERM. ARCH. 22; presbyter ipse qui vobis preest . . peccatum commisit. . . H. diocesianus ejus hujusmodi delicti tenetur reus W. CANT. *Mir. Thom.* II 38; nullum . . excommunicare potuit nisi diocesianum suum ROB. FLAMB. *Pen.* 150; **1248** a vero ipsius [ecclesie] patrono . ., episcopo S. Andree, cujus ~us existis, canonice presentatus *Mon. Hib. & Scot.* 50a; **1549** quod in condendis testamentis . . Orcadenses ~i eisdem legi et consuetudini subjaceant quibus ceteri in aliis . . Scotiae . . dioecesibus *Conc. Scot.* II 111.

dioeceseus [*adj. or ? gen.* διοικήσεως], of a diocese.

dioceseus episcopus . . vocabatur Adulfus HERM. ARCH. 1.

dioecesianus v. dioecesanus.

dioecesis [CL < διοίκησις], **(dioc-)** [LL], **~a,**

1 (eccl.) diocese, bishopric. **b** province.

quia latiora sunt spatia locorum quae ad gubernacula tuae ~is pertinent quam ut solus per omnia discurrere . . sufficias BEDE *Egb.* 5; **747** statuimus quod . . unusquisque episcopus, si quid in sua ~i corrigere . . nequiverit, id item in sinodo coram archiepiscopo et palam omnibus ad corrigendum insinuet BONIF. *Ep.* 78; in diocesi, in parrochia *Gl. Leid.* 39. 54; ~is episcopi . . uxor est quam non licet ei dimittere ÆLF. *Ep.* 2. 196; diaecesis vel parochia, *bisceopscir* vel *biscopric Id. Gl.*; **9..** diocessin, *biscopscir WW*; **c1022** (12c) hujus pacti summi testes affuerunt archiepiscopus Æ. Cantuar' et archiepiscopus Ebor' W. et ~eos pontifex Æðelricus *CD* 733; **s942** additus est sextus [episcopus], qui haberet sedem in Ramesberia, ~im in Wiltensi [v. l. Wiltonensi] pago W. MALM. *GP* I 14; **c1200** possessiones in nostra ~i [de Stradern] prefato loco [sc. Insule Missarum] assignatas . . hic duximus annotare *Inchaffray* 10; [episcopus Menevensis] qui tam ecclesie quam ~is sue rarus tantum visitator fieret GIR. *JS* 2 p. 161; quo proficiscentem sua quando dioecesis ipsum / primo suscepit H. AVR. *Hugh* 714; **1224** H. Heref' episcopus reddidit nobis . . xx li. de carucagio nobis . . concesso de dominicis . . in ~y sua *Pat* 466; **1237** in Londoniensi ~a *E. Ch. S. Paul.* 73; **1255** que sic de plano . . corrigi non poterunt . . diocesanis denuncient episcopis, viz. que in suis ~ibus, et, si negligentes in hoc extiterint, archiepiscopo Tuamensi . . que in ipsis episcopis et in ejusdem archiepiscopi ~i . . corrigenda fuerint *Mon. Hib. & Scot.* 68b; **1347** acta . . et jurata fuerunt hec . . in campis prope Calesium, Morinensis ~eos (*Treugae*) AVESB. 119; ita est de episcopis absentantibus a suis dyocesibus J. SHEPPEY *Fab.* 71; **1438** Constanciensis ecclesia, de et in cujus ~a prefatus . . R. exitit oriundus BEKYNTON I 21; **1529** presentibus magistris J. W. [et al.] . ., Exoniensis . ., Eboracensis, et Londoniensis ~um *Deeds Balliol* 128. **b** praeceperat Theodoro . . domnus apostolicus ut in ~i sua provideret et daret ei [Hadriano] locum BEDE *HE* IV 1; **s797** [Kenulfus] quantum nefas in mutilatione Cantuariensis ~is antecessor ejus Offa rex commisisset edoctus M. PAR. *Maj.* I 364; **s1268** archiepiscopus Ebor', qui contra dignitatem Cantuariensis archiepiscopi in ~i sua fecit portare crucem ante se, que ~is durat per omnia loca a fluvio de Humbre usque mare versus austrum *Leg. Ant. Lond.* 108.

2 governance. **b** (w. *perpetua* or *sempiterna*) ecclesiastical possession.

diocisa, gubernatio *GlC* D 261; ad fratres sub suae ~eon [vv. ll. ~eos, ~ion, ~im] gubernationis constitutos . . migravit WILLIB. *Bonif.* 6 p. 36. **b** **936** (17c) omne territorium episcopatus . . liberum restituo et in †diocesi [l. ~im] perpetuam liberter offero *Reg. Plympton* 170; **937** (18c) M. . . dedit Sancto Heldeno Lanlovern [*Lanlawren, Cornw*] in ~im sempiternum (*MS Phillipps* 4810 p. 119) *Cornish Studies* VII 43; **c957** (12c) mansas v . . reddere procurat imperialis nostra potestas et in ~im perpetuam eidem praefatae aecclesiae denuo immolat *CS* 936.

diocis- v. dioeces-.

Diogeneus, Diogenic, Cynical.

nemo adeo est Diogineus quem quandoque infirmitatem naturalem consolari non oporteat W. DONC. *Aph. Phil.* 3. 8.

dioleticus v. dialecticus.

Diomedeus [CL < Διομήδειος], **~ita,** (w. *avis* or as sb. f.) kind of bird, var. identified as heron, egret, or swan. *Cf. avis* 2c & d, erodios 1. (Cf. Pliny *HN* X 126: prob. Cory's Shearwater [*Calonectris diomedea*]).

10.. ~ia Gr., vel herodios, *swan WW*; ~ite aves sunt . ., quas Greci herodies appellant. magnitudinis enim sunt cigni, coloris candidi, oculos habent igneos, ora dentata, gregatim volant UPTON 186.

dionymus [LL < διώνυμος], two-named.

Africanus . . pro Mathat posuit Melchi, quia fortasse . . in historia in qua haec didicerat eundem Mathat invenit esse dyonimum BEDE *Luke* 362.

dionysiacus [διονυσιακός], dionysiac.

de objurgacionibus ~is [vv. ll. dionysaticis, dionysiaticis, dyonisicis] librum unum W. BURLEY *Vit. Phil.* 250.

dionysias [CL < Διονυσίας], **~ia, ~ius, a** sort of gem. **b** chicory (*Cichorium*) or sim.

a dionisius lapis est niger vel fuscus rubentibus venis [cf. Isid. *Etym.* XVI 4. 7, 11. 8] BART. ANGL. XVI 33. **b** NECKAM *NR* II 58 (v. cichorea); dionisia, flos cicoree *SB* 18 (cf. *Alph.* 50).

dionysium [CL *only pl.*], festival in honour of Dionysus. **b** (transf.) devotion or guild of devotees.

~a, festa Bacchi OSB. GLOUC. *Deriv.* 173. **b** isti sunt fratres et sorores ~orum S. Anselmi (*MS BL Cotton Nero* C IX f. 22) *Med. & R. Stud.* I 13*n*.

dioprasium v. 1 dia 1.

diopros, (rhet.) type of syzygy.

sinzigiae replicationes . .: proxilius, diprolius, ~os, trampus. . . ~os et trampus reciproca duarum sillabarum alternatione variantur, utpote ‒ ‒ ⏑ ⏑ ⏑ ⏑ et iterum ⏑ ⏑ ‒ ‒ ‒ ‒ ALDH. *PR* 141 (142).

diorisma [LL diorismos < διορισμός], definition, argument.

exhinc convaluere nimis diorismata fortis / athletae pereuntque mali sophismata civis FRITH. 1293.

Dios [LL < Δῖος], Macedonian month.

vocatur apud eos [Graecos] . . November Dios BEDE *TR* 14; [†Februarium] evocitant Ebrii Graecique per Tios *Kal. M. A.* 399; [November] Grece †dies *Miss. R. Jum.* 19.

dioscesanus v. dioecesanus 1b. **diosculatorius** v. deosculatorius. **diosios** v. dusius.

diota [CL < δίωτος], two-handled jar.

dyota, vas vinarium OSB. GLOUC. *Deriv.* 173.

dioval-, diovol- v. diobol-. **diphthamus** v. dictamnus.

diphthongus [CL < δίφθογγος], diphthong.

vocalium . . duarum conjunctione, quod diptongon vocant BEDE *AM* 86 (cf. ib. 87: in Latinis non invenitur haec diptongus); 'aeger' animo, 'aegrotus' corpore, utrumque per ~on scribitur ALCUIN *Orth.* 2327; sciat [notarius] . . ubi virgula representans diptongon scribi debeat NECKAM *Ut.* 117; ~us apud Grecos est conjunctio duarum vocalium sonum unius vocalis habentium BACON *Maj.* III 92; AE et OE diptongi non sunt nisi scripto tantum *Ps.-*GROS. *Gram.* 30.

diplodea, diploega, diploida v. diplois.

diplois [CL < διπλοΐς ; *infl. by* duplus], doublet; **b** worn as armour; **c** (w. ref. to *Psalm* cviii 29). *Cf. dublettus* 1, *duplicium, dupliteca.*

~is, *twifeld hrægel* ÆLF. *Gl.*; ~is, duplex vestimentum OSB. GLOUC. *Deriv.* 175; dipplois D. BEC. 1198 (v. cappa 1a); quod . . conducticii gwerrarum unusquisque in sola sua ~ide . . exiret STRECCHE *Hen. V* 174; **1427** lego J. coco nostro duploidem de *wirsted* (*Test.*) *Mem. Ripon* I 330; **1440** unum antiquum deploidem de fustianno *Pat* 446 m. 13; **1442** in villa de Lynnen . . duo Anglici sibi incogniti in strata publica sibi extraxerunt de corpore suo ~idem suam, quia novam (*DipDocE* 427) *Bronnen* 1251(2); **1445** item pro corpore unum ~idem de albo *carassay MunAcOx* 545; **1451** item una ~is russetica *Ib.* 612; ~is . ., ~ydis, *dobelat WW*; **1460** plures hujusmodi presbyteri utuntur . . coleriis duploidorum suorum ex scarleto vel alia fulgida veste ultra modum supra togas seu jupas suas publice extendentibus ad modum illorum qui nominantur galantes *Reg. Cant.* 92; **1481** pro una deploide sive tunica *DC S. Paul.* (*HMC*) 25a; **1506** pro emendacione diplodee *DCCant.* C 11 f. 112a; **1507** pro faccione diploege *Ib.* 115a; **1508** pro emendacione diploide *Ib.* 116a; **1524** vestram beatitudinem . . rogatam facimus . . [ut episcopus Morav'] vestem possit episcopalem, rochetam lineam albam, inducere atque . . sui [sc. Cluniacensis] ordinis signum scapulare subtus togam prope deploidem gestet (*Lit. Regis Scotiae*) *Mon. Hib. & Scot.* 539a. **b** **s1396** ut . . altera pars eligeret . . xxx personas adversus xxx de parte contraria, gladiis tantum, arcubus et sagittis absque deploidibus vel armaturis aliis preter bipennes FORDUN *Cont.* XV 3; **1426** etc. (v. defensivus 1b); **1514** pro cxviij ulnis panni linei pro linthiaminibus ex hoc quod . . expendebatur in ~idibus pro guerra hoc anno *Ac. Durh.* 160. **c** **1293** ecclesia Cantuar' . . pro pallio laudis disploide induta meroris *Reg. Wint.* I 34; **s1321** quibus indumentis, sicut disploide, confusione sua, in judiciis suis sunt induti TROKELOWE 109; **1375** habitu meroris abjecto, felici leticie †duplonmide circumamictus THORNE 2151; **1378** non, sicut scribitis, . . Romane ecclesie cardinalibus, immo . . lupis rapacissimis, . . non salutem sed languorem, non gaudium sed merorem et indui, sicut ~ide, confusione vestra (*Lit. Episcoporum*) WALS. *HA* I 385; **c1430** si spiritu diffidencie operiatur sicut ~ide *Reg. Whet.* II 453.

diploma [CL < δίπλωμα]

1 official document (esp. papal letter of appointment); **b** (fig., w. ref. to *diploma* authorizing travel) 'post haste'). **c** (w. *felix*) favourable auspices. **d** (fig.) peaceful negotiation, diplomacy.

diplo[m]a, duplicatio *GlC* D 252; obtulit expressum patribus diploma legendum FRITH. 759; ~a, *bod on cine* ÆLF. *Gl.*; **1512** ut omnia sacerdocia, quorum reditus quadragenas libras excederent, pape pensionem decimarum ac ~atum nomine numerarent (*Syn. Edinb.*) *Conc.* III 658b; **1537** is primum transmisit Romam pro hujus loci a Kynlos ~atibus, cum antea abbates eligerentur canonice per monachorum suffragia FERR. *Kinloss* 34; **1565** a sanctitate tua . . petimus ut istam cessionem admittere ac ~ata desuper necessaria concedere . . dignetur (*Lit. Reginae Scotiae*) *Inchaffray* app. 161. **b** accelera gressus, cauto duplomate pergens / ad mare J. SAL. *Enth. Pol.* p. 5; **1163** quos ego continuato duplomate usque ad idem castrum prosecutus . . (*Lit. J. Episc. Pictav.*) *Becket Mat.* V 40; **1169** nos properamus ad . . regem Francorum et dupplomate, ut vos videamus, utimur (*Lit. Mag. Viviani*) *Ib.* VII 152; **s1172** incedens tanquam duplomate venit ad Porcestre DICETO *YH* I 351; **1178** ego ~ate eum e vestigio sequor P. BLOIS *Ep.* 52. 159B; accelerans igitur, usus duplomate, longum / abbreviabis iter NIG. *SS* 627; duploma dicitur tempus duplicatum, cum quis faciat de †duobus [? duabus] dietis unam VAC. *Lib. Paup.* 268 (cf. diaeta 2); R. BURY *Phil.* 9. 155 (v. dispendiosus a). **c** **1295** felici duplomate . . in sancta Romana curia post creacionem summi pontificis . . nostra negocia prosperantes . ., subsequenter . . fastiditi . . in regno applicuimus Anglicano *Reg. Cant.* 12. **d** [leo] in venatoris obvius arma ruit; / sed, cum luminibus sese subduxerit hostis, / utile jam censet esse duploma sibi NECKAM *DS* IX 30.

2 (infl. by *duplus*) 'doubler' (napkin or tablecloth). *Cf. duplarius* 1.

in omnibus festis que celebrantur in cappis et in precipuis anniversariis debent mappe duplomata tabulis superponi. . . refectorarius . . inveniet in refectorio scyphos, obbas, mappas, pelves, duplomata, candelabra, manutergia, salina *Obed. Abingd.* 402.

dipondius v. dupondius. **dipplois** v. diplois.

diprolius, (rhet.) type of syzygy.

~ius . . ex tribus brevibus et tribus longis constat, tali figura ⏑ ⏑ ⏑ ‒ ‒ ‒ ALDH. *PR* 141 (142).

dipsacus [CL < δίψακος], teasel.

~us frutex est spinosa, virgam habens longam spinis plenam et †foliis [? l. folia] in circuitu similia lactuce *Alph.* 51*n.*; ~os, *called in Latin* Labrum Veneris, *is called in English wilde tasel* TURNER *Herb Names* C8.

dipsas [CL < διψάς], **~a,** kind of snake (said to provoke thirst by its bite); **b** (fig.). *V. et. gypsa.*

sunt plurimi adhuc serpentini generis angues, ut ~ades *Lib. Monstr.* III 24; ~as genus serpentis est intollerabilis; quando percusserit hominem, siti moritur ipse homo . . *GlC* D 292; placaris ut ~as, cui sol incanduit a Cancro MAP *NC* IV 3 f. 45v.; quem ledit dipsas, estuat igne novo NECKAM *DS* IX 294; ~a . ., serpens modicus, cujus venenum ante extinguit quam sentiatur GIR. *TH* I 36; ~as BART. ANGL. XVIII 36 (*quoting* Isid. *Etym.* XII 4. 13); †disperas est genus serpentis, cui morsus facit hominem intollerabiliter sitire *Alph.* 50. **b** **c1346** intrat in eclipse fines ejus David ipse; / virus dans dipse, frustrabitur apocalipse. / Brus, serpens dipsas, faciens guerras bibit ipsas (*Neville's Cross*) *Pol. Poems* I 46.

diptam-, diptan- v. dictamn-. **diptarius, diptericus** v. dryopteris. **diptongus** v. diphthongus.

diptoton [LL < δίπτωτον], (gram.) noun having only two cases.

[nomina] ~a sunt quae duos casus diversos habent, ut †'sors' a 'sorte' [? l. 'fors', abl. 'forte'] ALCUIN *Gram.* 869C; *sume naman syndon* ~a *gecwedene, þa habbað twegen mislice* casus *and na ma* . .: veru, . . veribus, tabi . . *and* tabo ÆLF. *Gram.* 89; ~a, nomen in singulari duos casus habens, ut Jupiter, Jovis OSB. GLOUC. *Deriv.* 176.

diptycha, ~ia [LL diptychum < δίπτυχον, diptychium], diptych, double-leaved (writing) tablet; **b** (recording names of martyrs).

scribe mihi unum exemplar in una scedula .. sive in una dyptica ÆLF. BATA *Coll.* 4. 26; hec diptícha, .. i. tabula manualis, que et pugillaris dicitur OSB. GLOUC. *Deriv.* 158; quanta nobilis materiei jactura erat, si .. putrescat speciosissima arbor ista [sc. pirus], ex qua diptice tot possent excidi quod totius Anglie sive Gallie studiis scolasticis quivissent sufficere AD. EYNS. *Hug.* V 18 p. 209; vos, o beatuli diptice geruli, / sursum me rapite de ceno seculi WALT. WIMB. *Palpo* 197; *handtabye*, pugillaris, diptica *PP*; hec diptica, *a smale tabyle WW*. **b** eos qui injuste condemnati sunt revocaverunt post mortem et in sacris diptichiis scripserunt BART. EXON. *Pen.* 19.

dipundius v. dupondius.

diradiare [cf. CL radiare], to irradiate.

prima .. illa hierarchia secundam sub se et proximam ~iat, ut illustrata illuminet tertiam COLET *Cel. Hier.* 184.

diragamen v. dirigamen. **diratiatio** v. dirationatio.

diratio, deraignment, proof, (procedure for) establishment of title (to).

c**1120** R. abbas .. dirationavit quoddam vini dolium quod fuerat apud B. werecatum.. huic vero ultimi ~oni .. testes fuerunt presentes R. filius Walteri tunc vicecomes [et al.] *Cart. Rams.* I 149; si de .. quibusdam illorum [appellantium] male contigerit, illi qui superstites fuerint ad disrationem faciendam admittuntur BRACTON 138.

diratiocinamentum, deraignment.

a**1122** volo .. quod .. ij hide .. sint ita quiete de .. geldis burgi H. sicut comitatus intravit inde in ~um adversus burgenses et in burgensibus defecit *Cart. Antiq.* I no. 241 (= *CalCh* IV 10: disrationamentum).

diratiocinare, ~ari [cf. ratiocinare], to deraign, claim or establish title (to); **b** (w. acc. & inf.). *V. et. dereinare* 1, *dirationare* 1.

~avit illud [manerium] Lanfrancus archiepiscopus contra Baiocensem episcopum *DB* I 5v.; homines de S. deratiocinati fuerunt unam hagam et theloneum ejus ad firmam de C. *Ib.* 32; supersunt ibi ij hidae quae sunt ~atae in dominio regis *Ib.* 158v.; Doddus tenet [S.] ..; Eldredus ~atus est a B. filio ejus *Ib.* 173v.; homines de wapent[ac] deratiocinaverunt eas [terras] ad opus regis *Ib.* 375; **1109** quas omnes consuetudines et earum calumpnias ~avit adversus illos R. episcopus *CalCh* V 454 (cf. ib. 455 [c**1157**]: disraciocinavit); si quis de propria causa tractaret, que ad feodum suum disratiocinandum pertineret (*Leg. Hen.* 61. 13) *GAS* 582; s**1166** 'ita quod saisinam non amittat qui prius inde saisiatus fuerit' donec per placitum disratiocinatum fuerit (*Add. to Const. Clar.* 9) H. BOS. *CE* 1415A; **1169** dixit se disratiocinasse totam terram suam per duellum *Pipe* 36; a**1183** disratiocinati sunt .. decimas terre quam R. Latimarius .. tenuit *Cart. Glam.* 125; partem prebende .. in laicali .. curia .. diratiocinari et evinci vidistis GIR. *Symb.* I 31 p. 318; **1234** de manerio de C., quod idem E. †disratiocionavit (*sic* MS) coram nobis *Cl* 467. **b** a**1086** de xv hidis in Hantona, unde episcopus ~avit socam .. et expeditionem et cetera mea servitia ad suum *hundred* .. pertinere *Pl. Anglo-Norm.* 19 (= *Regesta* 230); qui in civitate terram alterius saisibat et non poterat ~are suam esse, xl s. emendabat *DB* I 262v.; *Ib.* 102v. (v. dereinare b).

diratiocinatio, deraignment. *V. et. dirationatio* a.

c**1110** precipio vobis ut nullo modo intretis placitum neque in aliquam ~onem de terra de S. ante quam veniat ante me *E. Ch. Scot.* 27; in ~one feudi precedere debet feudatus testem suum ad bellum vel aliam legem (*Leg. Hen.* 48. 12) *GAS* 572; c**1170** si contigerit quod plures milites quam quinque inveniantur in feodo vel per disratiocinationem vel per recognitionem (*Ch. Com. Cestr.*) *Eng. Feudalism* app. 257; c**1180** per †disrationtinationem suorum hominum et recognitionem meorum reddidi .. ecclesie de E. predictam pasturam *Cart. Eynsham* I 107; s**1230** disratiocinatio burgi de A. contra abbatem de T. *Chr. Peterb.* 11 *rub.*

diratiocinium, deraignment.

c**1125** notificari nobis .. utile duximus ~ium hujus terre et concordiam calumnie de istis divisis *Cart. Rams.* I 143 (cf. *Chr. Rams.* 255); s**1090** recordum sive ~ium predictum confirmant Henricus rex primus, Stephanus, Johannes THORNE 1793.

dirationabilis, unreasonable.

si maritagia fuerint disrationabilia, vel per justiciam vel per amicos fient rationabilia *Cust. Norm.* 14. 2.

dirationamentum [cf. OF *deraisnement*], deraignment.

a**1132** abbas .. dirationavit in curia sua .. coram justitia mea .. terram de S. et G. .. et hoc ~um warantizo et per cartam meam confirmo *Cart. Rams.* I 239 (= *Regesta* 1751); **1132** abbas .. S. Augustini Cantorb' per ~um regni mei et curie habet prebendam unam de me in ecclesia S. Martini de Dovera (*Ch. Hen. I*) ELMH. *Cant.* 357 (= *Regesta* 1736); *CalCh* IV 10 (v. diratiocinamentum); **1321** quoad articulum .. quod ipsi de placitis ad coronam regis pertinentibus se possint disracionare .. dictum est eis per justiciarios quod declarent curie modum et formam hujusmodi disracionamenti *MGL* II 321 (= *PQW* 451b).

dirationare, ~ari [cf. rationare]

1 to deraign, establish a title to (land, payment or sim.). **b** to establish or maintain (claim, right, covenant or sim.); **c** (absol. or (?) impers. pass.); **d** (w. acc. & inf., indir. qu. or *quod*). *V. et. dereinare* 1, *diratiocinare*.

a**1083** alias terras quas ipse abbas ~avit coram multis baronibus meis *Regesta* p. 125; Frakenaham tenuit O. teinus Heroldi .. et postea derotionatus (*sic*) est Lanfrancus jussu regis in episcopatum Rovensem *DB* II 381; c**1100** Stockes quod Goduuinus .. tenuit .. et Lanfrancus .. disrationavit eum (*sic*) contra episcopum Baiocensem *Text. Roff.* p. 211; **1130** pro terra quam dirrationavit contra Willelmum Lond' *Pipe* 3; idem R. ~avit terram illam in curia mea per recognitionem GLANV. II 20; in Danelahe ponatur res in manu equali donec ~etur [*de ici qu'il seit derehdned*] (*Leis. Will.*) *GAS* 509; c**1200** octo acras terre .. quas deratiovavit a domino abbate *FormA* 12; c**1200** illam sc. partem quam disrationavi de eisdem monachis ad assisas *Couch. Kirkstall* 129; c**1200** alios homines, qui naturales sunt ad terras predictas, quos episcopus non ~avit, adquiret .. comes .. ad prefatas terras inhabitandas *Reg. Moray* 12; a**1218** ~avit terram contra R. fratrem suum *Cart. Glam.* 220; **1223** licet .. debita sua per sectam legalium virorum ~are et probare *BBC* (*Carlow*) 187; **1285** si advocacio disracionetur infra tempus semestre (2 *Westm.* 5) *StRealm* I 77; **1292** Rogerus nichil aliud dicit per quod [Margeria] ipsas cc m. disracionare non debet *RParl* I 108a (= *Doc. Scot.* I 381); pro .. manerio de K. cum distracionatum fuisset *Tri. W. Langton* 306; s**1333** si contigerit aliquam piscariarum predictarum extra manus nostras .. poni et disracionari *RScot* I 257a. **b** id .. Baldwinus .. discussit, discutiendo necnon derationando firmiter conquisivit, conquisitum .. confirmavit HERM. ARCH. 45; si .. fecerit aliquis clamorem .. quod .. injuste jacet inter latrones et si dixerit quod velit illud ~ari, det vadimonium et plegios (*Leg. Ed.*) *GAS* 666; si voluerit quis conventionem terre tenende adversus dominum suum disracionare [OF: *derehdner cuvenant de terre vers sun seinur*] (*Leis Will.*) *Ib.* 511; **1130** A. presbyter .. r. c. de x m. argenti pro dicto suo, quod non potuit dirrationare *Pipe* 85; per hoc jus suum ~abit heres propinquior GLANV. II 6 (cf. ib. IV 6: 'habeo probos homines qui hoc viderunt et audierunt et qui parati sunt hoc ~are secundum considerationem curie'); **1196** hoc offert disracionare .. per corpus suum prout curia considerav[er]it *CurR* I 20; s**1196** ut electis hinc inde v militibus, disracionaretur jus utriusque regis per eos TREVET *Ann.* 156; **1221** contra possessionem juris nostri, quam per judicium curie nostre contra ipsos disrationavimus *Pat* 311; s**1242** infitiabatur sibi scelus impositum, offerens corpus suum ad disrationandum judicialiter coram rege et curia sua innocentiam ejus contra quemcunque armis et viribus prepotentem M. PAR. *Maj.* IV 201; s**1249** paramur judicialiter duello super eos veritatem, Deo judice, discutere et disrationare *Ib.* V 56; **1292** petit quod dicant quid attendant disracionare per breve istud (*AssizeR Northumb*) *Doc. Scot.* I 366. **c** c**1080** volo .. quod .. Wido abbas de S. Augustino et fratres ejusdem .. terram illam .. habeant .. quam (*sic*) ita ~atum est inter homines .. et .. coram justicia mea *MonA* I 143b; A. .. calumniatur unam virgam terre ..; et ipse ~avit coram regina *DB* I 48v.; per plegium dimittatur ad diem ~andi [v. l. disratiocinandi] vel emendandi (*Leg. Hen.* 29. 2a) *GAS* 563; si isti decem et octo velint deraționari cum illo qui prius fecerat clamorem (*Leg. Ed.*) *Ib.* 666; c**1150** sicut .. ~averunt apud B. et juraverunt apud A. *E. Ch. Scot.* 223; **1211** dies data erat eidem Aliz ad disracionandum cum xij et alio (*sic*) cum xxxvj ad defendendum *CurR* VI 118; quia appellans non disrationavit secundum quod se ad hoc appellavit BRACTON 142. **d** antequam G. de rationaret ea [maneria] pertinere suo feudo *DB* II 61; †**1109** quamquam ipse T. Ebor' archiepiscopus et Eboracensis ecclesia .. parati essent ~are quod facere non deberet (*Ch. Hen. I*) H. CANTOR 7v. (= *Regesta* 916); a**1135** sciatis me reddidisse .. xij bovatas terre quas R. B. disrationavit esse in dominio meo *MonA* VI 1274; T. Ebor' archiepiscopus [ob. **1140**] .. ~avit quod a medio impetu ipsius fluminis incipit pax .. ecclesie RIC. HEX. *Hist. Hex.* II 14; cum ~averis versus eos hoc esse jus tuum BRAKELOND 136v.; **1218** quod terra illa ei debet descendere offert ~are prout curia consideraverit *BNB* II 7; **1281** quousque coram vobis disrationetur ad quem eadem ecclesia de jure debeat pertinere PECKHAM *Ep.* I app. p. 392 *k*.

2 to uphold, justify: **a** (a writ); **b** (oneself).

a appellator semper debet probare et disracionare [v. l. defendere] dictum suum HENGHAM *Judic. Esson.* 124; **1315** Th. .. et Ph. deracionaverunt hoc breve tanquam participes *Year Bk. 8 Ed. II* 120. **b** disrationet se [AS: *berecce hine*] (*Quad.*) *GAS* 169 (cf. diffacere a); quia vadimonium dedit ad se disrationandum et non potuit (*Leg. Ed.*) *Ib.* 668; c**1132** si quis civium de placitis corone implacitatus fuerit, per sacramentum quod judicatum fuerit in civitate se disrationet homo London' (*Ch. Hen. I*) *Ib.* 525; **1156** de quocunque in placito ponentur se disrationabunt secundum leges .. civium London' *BBC* (*Oxford*) 13; **1204** W. de Burgo obtulit se coram nobis ad standum recto in curia nostra Hibernie .. de appellis unde appellatus est ..; et per hoc ei reddidimus .. terram suam .., ita quod obsides sui remaneant .. quousque se de predictis .. disrationaverit *Pat* 46a; **1313** qualiter .. burgenses de Lenne se disracionare debeant *MunCOx* 23.

3 to exclude, deprive (person) judicially.

s**1306** Robertus [Bruys] jus regie corone ad se ipsum pertinere jure hereditarie successionis exponebat, quamvis rex Anglie ipsum a suo regno ~aret *Meaux* III 276.

dirationatio, deraignment, proof (of title or sim.); *v. et. diratiocinatio.* **b** criminal proceedings, trial.

a**1190** precipio quod monachi de B. habeant .. rectas divisas suas .. sicut monstrare poteritis quod fuerunt tempore regis H. avi mei .. et quod vos eos juste adjuvetis ad hanc ~onem faciendam *FormA* 295; in ejus [domini petentis] voluntate erit aut se ad ~onem petentis tenere .. aut per se jus suum versus alium dirationare GLANV. III 8; **1201** quia R. non nominavit in narratione sua annum et diem quo rex [H.] avus fuit vivus et mortuus et de incerto termino non fit aliqua disrationatio *CurR* II 12; **1208** habet litteras de protectione .. pro disrationatione facienda pro .. senescallo inter ipsum et Rogerum .. de terra de M. *Pat* 85b; si [appellans] victus sit in campo, aliud erit, quia non stat per ipsum quin faciat disrationationem BRACTON 142; **1292** predicta tenementa fuerunt .. escaeta .. regis ita disracionata quod secundum .. consuetudinem Wallie licuit .. regi H. .. predictos M. et alios de tenementis illis ejecisse et illa sibi .. tenuisse .. nulla facta disracionacione inde in aliqua curia *PQW* 686b. **b** **1304** disracionacio facta apud Neugate *Gaol Del.* 38/5 r. 4d.; disraci[on]acionem FORTESCUE *LLA* 53 (v. arrettamentum).

dirationator [cf. OF *deraisneor*], **a** deraigner. **b** disseisor or (?) *f. l.*

a c**1200** si aliquis disrationaverit adversus me unam virgatam .. et disrationator reddiderit de illa virgata minus quam v s., ego perficiam v s. et quietus ero de redditu illius virgate *Reg. Malm.* I 439. **b** disracionator erit in forisfacto regis pro sua transgressione et dissaisina (*Stat. Rob. III* 15) *RegiamM* II f. 66v. (= *Leg. IV Burg.* 99: dejector).

diravatus v. derivare 1a. **dircea** v. circaea.

dire, dreadfully, sorely, harshly.

aecclesiae puppis vexatur dirĕ procellis FRITH. 1046; Dunstanus .. fugientem beluam ~issime caedit OSB. *V. Dunst.* 26; s**978** Elfrida de illo regali supercilio inclinata ~e penituit, adeo ut .. carnem .. cilicio convolveret W. MALM. *GR* II 162; s**1197** unde rex Anglie terras suas .. in acquisitione pecunie ~issime aggravavit GERV. CANT. *GR* 84; c**1347** Scocia servire non vult nec querit amari; / dire servire semper vult et dominari (*Neville's Cross*) *Pol. Poems* I 51.

directaneus [LL], continuous, without pause (for response; *cf. Regula S. Benedicti* 17). *Cf. directe* e, *dirigere* 2d.

~ei, *fortrihte GlH* D 553; conventus, dicto a noviciis .. 'gloria Patri', addant 'sicut erat in principio' etc., cum pausa, puncto et modo quo prius .., et postea 'Kyrieleyson', 'Christeleyson', 'Kyrieleyson', puncto ~eo, ut est moris *Cust. Cant.* 425.

directe [CL], straight, in a straight line (partly fig.). **b** upright. **c** diametrically, in direct confrontation (partly fig.). **d** directly, without intermediary. **e** continually, without pause; *cf. directaneus, dirigere* 2e. **f** (?) expressly.

s**878** si vincendi in futuro fuissent, penderet [vexillum] ~e nihil movens *Chr. S. Neoti*; ADEL. *QN* 12 (v. discretive); GROS. 74 (v. discontinuitas); c**1242** ~ius (v. consiliatio a); per ipsam [sc. sophisticam] non pervenitur ad scienciam ~e sed magis per illam deviatur a sciencia KILWARDBY *OS* 586; in bonis perfectis infusio gratie comparatur luci ~e incidenti BACON *Maj.* I 216; **1272** ab inferiori angulo terre arabilis ~e sequendo divisas usque ad superiorem campum de W. *Cart. Chester* 386; meliores homines de omnibus terris veniebant ~e ad commorandum cum eo [sc. rege Arthuro] *Eul. Hist. Annot.* II 319; tractus ascendens super semibrevem ~e HAUBOYS 427a. **b** s**1231** in multis regni perturbationibus stans ~e .., nec declinans ad dextram vel sinistram M. PAR. *Maj.* III 206. **c** voluit ultra domos et rupes .. et omnia que ~e ante se invenit transire *Latin Stories* 123; in ipsam partem que se regalibus ~ius oppositam hospiciis exhibebat *Ps.-*ELMH. *Hen. V* 45; s**1174** W. rex Scotorum .., non acquiescens consilio procerum .., ~e contra Salomonem dicentem: 'qui sapiens est audit consilia' [*Prov.* xii 15] *Plusc.* VI 27; **1526** tu nunquam fecisti compotum inter fratres tuos, ~e contra decreta patrum et institucionem religionis (*Vis. Thame*) *EHR* III 706; **1549** si reus petat articulos ~e contrarios *Conc. Scot.* II 125. **d** c**1245** non .. conamur ~e seu indirecte inter imperium vestrum et sacerdotium dissonantiam procurare GROS. *Ep.* 124; cum talis donatio ~e fieri non possit a viro uxori vel e contrario .., si fiat indirecte, ita quod vir dederit extraneo ut extraneus .. rem datam det uxori vel e contrario .. BRACTON 29; **1343** quod dicti reges se interponere non habeant per se vel per alium, ~e vel indirecte (*Treugae*) AD. MUR. *Chr.* 132 (cf. WALS. *HA* I 251); **13..** ne quis .. clericus .. beneficium habens ecclesiasticum ipsum .. laicis assedare vel ad firmam presumat concedere ~e vel indirecte *Conc. Scot.* II 67; **1456** (v. directorie). **e** versus 'haec dies' ~e [AS p.429: *forþrihte*] a puero prolato *RegulC* 53. **f** **1235** defendit quod numquam ~e tenuit placitum

in curia Christianitatis de aliqua terra ad [terminum data] *CurR* XV 1462.

directio [CL]

1 movement in a straight line. **b** (astr.) direction.

ex diversis accidentibus radiorum, cujusmodi sunt ~o, fractio, refluxio, conversio KILWARDBY *OS* 77. **b** arcus epicicli superior inter duas stationes interceptus dicitur ~o, et quando planeta est in illo dicitur directus SACROB. *Sph.* 115.

2 dispatch (of a document).

s**1173** carta ~onis cujusdam carte ad summum pontificem causa confirmandi *Ch. Sal. rub.* 37 (cf. ib.: cujus transactionis rescriptum .. duximus dirigendum paternitati vestre).

3 **a** guidance (of a journey). **b** guidance (fig.), direction, instruction; **c** (w. subj. gen.); **d** (w. obj. gen.).

a s**1305** Deus pro ~one prosperi itineris .. collaudatur FORDUN *Cont.* XII 7. **b** s**1183** [filii Henrici II] cum moderatione justitie virgam ~onis [cf. *Psalm* xliv 7] assumere strenuis repromittunt operibus DICETO *YH* II 17; comiti Simoni [de Monte Forti], precor, in verbis vite consiliorum ~ones impendere studeatis AD. MARSH *Ep.* 227; ad hoc quod recte agat [voluntas] circa finem particulariter ostensum requiritur ~o DUNS *Ord.* I 185; in multis imperator debet recipere ~onem a papa .., sc. in causis divinis OCKHAM *Dial.* 896. **c** **719** humiliter te submittens ejus ~oni (*Lit. Papae*) *Ep. Bonif.* 12; c**1520** sint .. rectores [et al.] .. intra ecclesiam .. parati ad processionem gradatim incedentes .. juxta ~ones decanorum eis tradendas *Conc. Scot.* I cclxx. **d** c**1108** ~o ecclesiarum .. pendet ex auctoritate paternitatis vestrae ANSELM (*Ep.* 451) V 398; honori et ~oni .. scholastice professionis .. providebitur AD. MARSH *Ep.* 16; de recto theologico sermo nobis est, cujus due sunt regule, una circa cordis ~onem, altera versatur circa exteriorum rectificacionem *AncrR* 5; **1358** pro uno breve (*sic*) in Scaccario pro ~one Johannis L. vicecomitis ad supersedendum de xv li. argenti de assisa cervisie (*Ac. Univ. Ox.*) *EHR* XXIV 742; suppono quod, sicut conservacio creature est ejus servacio in esse naturali a nichilo, sic ejus gubernacio est creature ~o sine Dei mercede sive pro nichilo WYCL. *Dom. Div.* 11; ~onem et gubernacionem morum humanorum a scripturis sanctis diripiens J. BURY *Glad. Sal.* 576.

4 (?) dressing (of meat). *Cf. directorium, dressor.*

1395 una mensa pro ~one; tres mense in despensa *Test. Ebor.* III 7.

directivare, to direct along a particular course (fig.), give a slant to.

non potest mens humana ~are quod sapiencia divina dictat WYCL. *Civ. Dom.* III 118.

directivus, directive, indicating or determining a course. **b** (as sb. n.) directive, direction, guidance.

illud septemplicis indiculi memoriale quod judicii in exemplaribus ~um constituimus—'que, cui, a quo, qualiter, qua occasione, quo proposito, qua spe dicantur' BALSH. *AD rec.* 2 164; ars est notitia bonorum operum in effectu, et prudentia est habitus ~us horum [operum] BACON *Maj.* II 258; intelligentie planetis presidentes †actiones [v. l. actionis] eorum in completionem specificam et finem proprie sunt ~e *Ps.*-GROS. *Summa* 562; cum cognicio finis sit ~a in actibus circa ea que sunt ad finem DUNS *Ord.* I 187; baculus pastoralis in summitate est allectivus, ut desides alliciat evagantes; in medio ~us, ut debiles sustineat titubantes; in immo pungitivus, ut rebelles corrigat et errantes BRINTON *Serm.* 23 p. 95; sic .. omnis scriptura foret a quotlibet hominibus .. adversabilis, nullus virtutis ~e vel honoris et per consequens nullius autoritatis WYCL. *Ver.* I 111; **1456** regunt .. se domini potentes potenter magis quam prudenter aut alicujus concilio juridice ~o *Reg. Whet.* I 222. **b** non requiritur ~um nisi ubi potest esse error DUNS *Ord.* I 184; unum .. ~um intrinsecum, quod in archivis presentis monasterii reperi, habeo .., cui in tanto tucius arbitror adherendum quanto papalibus ac regalibus munimentis .. perpenditur roboratum ELMH. *Cant.* 309; hoc ~um .. in principiati conquestus continuacionem felicissimam alte mentis regalis concepit discrecio, viz. ut .. persone .. volentes devenire sui homines ligei deberent ad hoc .. invitari *Ps.*-ELMH. *Hen. V* 47; non esset ei opus alicujus ~i supra legem naturalem aut humanam J. BURY *Glad. Sal.* 592.

director [LL], director, guide, overseer.

11.. [Dunstanus] erat archangelus, quia aliorum similium angelorum ~or et dux (*Sermo*) *Mem. Dunst.* 457; s**1253** R. Lincoln' episcopus .., prelatorum correptor .., presbiterorum ~or, clericorum instructor M. PAR. *Min.* III 146; oportet quod inter ipsos sint quidam qui sunt quasi duces, ~ores et capita aliorum OCKHAM *Dial.* 736; **1465** prior presidens et ceteri monachi .. magistros J. G. [et alios] .. eleccionis negocii ~ores .. deputaverunt *Reg. Whet.* II 31; **1549** ut uniuscujusque monasterii magistri fabricae et operum ~ores .. [ad] loca ecclesiastica ipsis .. annexata pro defectuum correctione visitanda mittantur *Conc. Scot.* II 114.

directorie, (?) by giving directions (to agents).

1456 pars senciens se aggravatam ab ultima .. congregacionum .. immediate ad sedem apostolicam .. directe vel ~ie .. appellare valeat *StatOx* 277.

directorium [LL]

1 **a** (?) 'dresser', place for dressing meat; *cf. dressorium.* **b** (*sc. planetarum*) astronomical instrument (v. WALLINGF. II 259*n.*).

a **1301** in parietibus domus poletr[ie] et director[ii] de daubura emendandis *MinAc* (*Bungay, Suff*) 991/25. **b** (J. WHET. *Gran.*) WALLINGF. III 114 (v. cylindrus 1b).

2 **a** guide, directive (for behaviour). **b** (eccl.) directory, rule-book for procedure at time of moveable feasts.

a **1381** sacrum dat hoc eloquium, / alius per judicium / vita nostra nunc regitur. / .. / ex hoc plane †committitur [? l. convincitur], / sacerdos instituitur / ut fiat directorium (*In Lollardos* 27) *Pol. Poems* I 240. **b** **1497** liber presens ~ium sacerdotum, quem 'pica' Sarum vulgo vocitat clerus (R. PYNSON) *OED* s. v. *pica*; **1555** cum ordinali .. quod dicitur 'pica' sive ~ium sacerdotum in tempore paschali (*Brev. Sar.*) *Ib.*

directrix, guide or guiding (f.).

quod punctuaciones previe, in concordiam ~ices, per personalem regis presenciam finalem sortirentur effectum *Ps.*-ELMH. *Hen. V* 91 p. 251 (cf. ib. 107: regis Anglorum .. prudencia ~ice); Grecia .., scienciarum inventrix .., milicie et armorum flos et ~ix *Plusc.* VII 14.

directura, right, jurisdiction (Gasc.). *V. et. dreitura.*

1219 vos .. scitis quod vexationes et mala sustinuimus pro dominio et ~is conservandis regis Anglie (*AncC* I 58) *RL* I 65.

diregere v. dirigere.

diremptio [CL], separation.

inde colligendum quod ab aequinoctio ad aequinoctium dimidium anni computare debeamus .., maxime cum hanc aequissimam anni inter †aequinoctiorum [v. l. aequinoctia] ~onem .. Aristoboli verbis astruat BEDE *Wict.* 6; s**1053** altero contra alterum potiorem sibi partem [marisci] vendicante .., tandem vicini abbates .. per fideles homines .. ~onis terminos posuerunt *Chr. Rams.* 166.

direptio [CL]

1 plunder, spoliation. **b** spoil.

quod .. tam crebris ~onibus vacuaretur omnis regio totius cibi baculo GILDAS *EB* 19; ~o, i. abstractio *GlH* D 551; per earundem [rerum ecclesiasticarum] ~onem incurrere sacrilegium *G. Steph.* II 79; curia illa celestis apparuit .. in ~onem data et tanquam hostibus ad mactandum exposita GIR. *EH* II 30; **1322** per terrarum suarum destruccionem et bonorum derepcionem *FormOx* 77. **b** Anglia .. fuerat earum [terrarum] ~o et preda MAP *NC* V 3 f. 60v.

2 pulling down.

1465 in opere latamorum, cum ~one et deposicione antique trabis *Ac. Durh.* 154.

direptor [CL], plunderer, spoiler.

rerum ecclesiasticarum ~ores *G. Steph.* II 78; patrocinia protectoris cujus potentie nulla reniti poterit violenta depredatio ~oris R. COLD. *Cuthb.* 55.

direptrix [LL = *thieving*], (fig.) thief (f.).

non mundialis amicitie ~ix mors formidatur AILR. *Comp. Spec. Car.* I 1. 621B.

direvestire [cf. revestire], to disrobe.

finita missa, redire debet ministri cum sacerdote in revestiarium .. et ab eo non debent .. recedere quousque sacerdos disrevestitus ipsos precedat *Obs. Barnwell* 118; cum [sacerdos] derevestitus fuerit, debet redire in chorum *Cust. Cant.* 382.

dirgana v. diger. **diribare** v. derivare 4.

diribere [CL], to count out.

~ere, denumerare *GlC* D 284; diripere, i. dinumerare *GlH* D 537.

diribitorium [CL], place of assembly (for counting votes *etc.*).

dirivitorium, locus contuberni[i] *GlC* D 176, 338.

dirictus v. diruere a.

dirigamen, channel.

c**930** (14c) termini per descensum rivuli in Hodder, ipso ~ine in Ribbel, et sic in illo flumine .. in mare *E. Ch. Yorks* I 1 (= *MonA* VI 1176b: †diragamine).

dirigere [CL]

1 **a** to align, set straight. **b** (p. ppl. *directus*) direct, straight, **c** (astr.) 'direct'. **d** direct, immediate (of feudal tenure).

a sub potencia faciendi domum comprehenditur potencia .. parandi et ~endi parietes R. ORFORD *Reprob.* 76. **b** quattuor infindens directo tramite sulcos ALDH. *VirgV* 645; ~i callis, *rihtes sipfœtes GlH* D 556; quomodo melius probatur trinitas personarum per incessum lucis ~um BACON *Maj.* I 217 (cf. directe a). **c** SACROB. *Sph.* 115 (v. directio 1b). **d** **1301** vacante regno Scocie .., nobiles et communitates .. Scocie ad nos tanquam ad .. dominum capitalem ejusdem regni .. jus nostrum .. ac possessionem superioris et ~i dominii in regno eodem .. recognoverunt *Anglo-Scot Rel.* 104 (cf. ib: prestitis nobis .. tanquam superiori et ~o domino Scocie .. fidelitatum juramentis); s**1286** rex cujusdam regni .., regnum ipsum a quodam alio rege ut superiori et ~o domino ejusdem regni pro homagio tenens in feodum FORDUN *Cont.* XI 4.

2 (p. ppl. *directus* as sb. n.): **a** (w. *ab*) at right angles. **b** (w. *ex* or *in* & abl.) in direct alignment. **c** (w. *ex* or *in* & abl.) directly, immediately. **d** (w. *in* & acc., mus.) continuously, without pause; *cf. directaneus, directe* e. **e** (w. *in* & abl. or acc.) straight, in a direct line. **f** obverse (of quilt).

a denticulus egredietur a medio meridiani lateris basilice a ~o linee meridiane *Turquet* 371. **b** saphirus specialis est in antrace, si ducatur in circuitu et post ex ~o teneatur GILB. III 173v. 1; in unoquoque circulo ponam testimonia planete in ~o signi in quo reperiuntur GROS. 49; si fuerit caput Arietis mobilis in equatore diei †indirecto [l. in ~o] Arietis fixi BACON IV 456; vide si argumentum planete concordat aliquo numero in ~o ejus posito WALLINGF. (*EPT*) I 212. **c** regi pertinet temporalia, sede prelatorum vacante, sua ipsis ad suum libitum conferre prelatis; ergo et ab eisdem aufferre †in hoc in ~o seu legitima causa emergente WYCL. *Compl.* 91; s**1453** abbas .. conclusit melius esse ad tempus silere quam e ~o in inquisicione procedere *Reg. Whet.* I 119. **d** in ~um capitula canonici cursus dicantur *RegulC* 38; in quinta feria in alto cantantur ymni, intonantur psalmi, cantantur antiphonae; in his vero duobus diebus haec omnia in silentio et in ~um dicuntur LANFR. *Const.* 114; c**1190** (v. 8b infra). **e** de Trechenholt in ~um per immensam paludem ad Derevorde H. ALBUS 11; aliud .. maris brachium Hiberniam in ~um versus boream preterlabitur GIR. *TH* I 2; s**1305** constitutis a tergo tortoribus .. flagellantibus incurvantes [in chorea] et pungentibus ut incederent †indirectum *Flor. Hist.* III 321 (= RISH. 226: in ~um); tractus descendens in ~o seu obliquo HAUBOYS 427a. **f** **1285** (v. cubitare 2b); **1286** pro ~o bordure cujusdam culcitre facte de ij pannis de cangio radiato, ij sindones virides; pro indirecto ejusdem culcitre, xxxvj ulne card' (*KRAc* 91/7) *Arch.* LXX 56.

3 to direct, aim: **a** (missile); **b** (steps or course); **c** (pen, in writing); **d** (eyes); **e** (prayer); **f** (light); **g** (p. ppl. *directus*) intent, directed to an end.

a alius .. sagittarum spicula .. ad destinatum .. ~it locum ALDH. *VirgP* 2 (cf. id. *VirgV* 576: ferrea scripturae direxit spicula miles); "~e" inquit "sagittam in avem" *V. Greg.* p. 88; **1246** malefactores .. in forestarios sagittas suas direxerunt *SelPlForest* 80. **b** cursus ad dulcia fluviorum freta ~unt *Lib. Monstr.* II *pref.*; a**1078** praemoneo ut .. quocumque iter vestrum Deus direxerit regulariter sub abbatis oboedientia .. vivatis ANSELM (*Ep.* 38) III 148; direxerunt inde gressus ad majorem montem G. MON. X 3; s**1336** rex Anglie .. versus Scociam iter suum †~iens *Meaux* II 379; **1440** ab hoc seculo ad Dominum direxit gressus suos *Pri. Cold.* 110. **c** ad praefatae cursum locutionis ~ere stilum ÆTHELW. I 1 p. 3. **d** ~ens ad caelum oculos (*Passio Albani*) BEDE *HE* I 7 p. 20; ad divini luminis intuitum .. oculos ~ere interiores GIR. *TH* I 13. **e** ut et nostra vobis supplicantibus .. oratio ~atur, sicut incensum [cf. *Psalm* cxl 2] in conspectu divinae majestatis turificatur ALDH. *VirgP* 60; sicut patet de orante unam personam [Trinitatis] oracione que non ~itur actualiter alteri persone DUNS *Ord.* II 45. **f** perrupit densitatem carceris lucerna superne directa W. MALM. *GP* III 101. **g** omnes dies vitae suae illic degere ~a [*gl.*: i.e. intenta] mente devoverat FELIX *Guthl.* 25; marinae tempestatis procella nostris servit remigiis nec removet a proposito ~ae intentionis ABBO *Edm.* 7.

4 to direct, address, dispatch: **a** (letter or sim.); **b** (gift or sim.).

a **680** ut ad vestrae pietatis praesentiam litterarum apices diregerem ALDH. *Ep.* 4; cum epistulis quas .. regi .. direxit BEDE *HE* II 4; **784** has vobis litteras ~ere praesumpsi ALCUIN *Ep.* 11; **1173** (v. directio 2); **1214** tulit breve domini regis eis directum *CurR* VII 169; c**1228** occasione cujusdam mandati episcopi vicecomiti suo directi *Feod. Durh.* 263; **1377** quia breve domini regis venit directum majori et ballivis *Mem. York* I 30; **1410** per evidenciam ejusdem Johannis auditori super hunc compotum directam *Crawley* 299. **b** litteras in quibus significat se ei pallium direxisse BEDE *HE* I 29; pensantem plurime discum / pondera cum dapibus statim direxit egenis ALCUIN *SS Ebor* 298; *Id. Ep.* 226 (v. 1 cancellus 1a); mater ejus largius solatia munerum eis direxit WULF. *Æthelwold* 11; oblatis muneribus que sanctorum ecclesiis rex sanctus direxerat AILR. *Ed. Conf.* 752A.

5 to send, appoint (person); **b** (w. inf.).

ecclesia .. doctores .. celebrare non cessat, quos .. ad se directos .. congaudet *V. Greg.* p. 75; per praedicatores quos huc direxit BEDE *HE* II 1 p. 78; **790** nec ego renuo si

me, indignum digne pretium pacis, ⁓ere velint ALCUIN *Ep.* 9; quod .. abbas A. Osgarum monachum trans mare direxerit WULF. *Æthelwold* 14; ⁓itur [v. l. deligitur] ad patriarchatum Cantuariensis ecclesiae B. Dorsatensium episcopus OSB. *V. Dunst.* 32; nisi tales †⁓entur [v. l. ⁓erentur] obsides quibus securius applicare quivisset G. MON. IV 9; W. MALM. *GR* I 58 (v. 2 diffidere 1d); de Cantuariensibus archiepiscopis ab ecclesia Romana directis vel a synodo propria consecratis DICETO (*De Praelatis*) II 181; **s940** Edmundus exercitum colligens copiosum contra eos direxit SILGRAVE 53; **1319** apud Doveriam, ad portum maris .., qui portus vulgariter directorum a monasterio S. Albani pro itinere versus curiam Romanam .. reputatur *G. S. Alb.* II 139. **b** legatos ultra mare ad Galliam magistros acquirere direxit ASSER *Alf.* 78.

6 to direct, guide. **b** (p. ppl. as sb. n.) direction, instruction.

farus, cenaculum altum juxta mare .. per quot ⁓untur errantes naves *GlC* F 114; **a1103** ecclesia .. vestro consilio directa et auctoritate roborata ANSELM (*Ep.* 272) IV 187; non potest animus noster ad invisibilium contemplationem ascendere nisi per visibilium considerationem ⁓atur BART. ANGL. *proem.*; ECCLESTON *Adv. Min.* 113 (v. dignificare 1a); ubicumque contingit in praxi errare et recte agere, ibi est noticia practica necessaria ad ⁓endum DUNS *Ord.* I 186 (cf. ib. II 176: ipsum primum efficiens ⁓it effectum suum ad finem); illius [sacre scripture] sciencie proprium officium est fundare omnem gubernacionem et actum ⁓entes homines in obsequium Dei J. BURY *Glad. Sal.* 577. **b** **1236** ad plenius respondendum secundum tenorem mandati nostri tibi de predictis prius directis *KRMem* 14 r. 13*d*.

7 to set right, correct, mend.

alienigene, si concubitus suos ⁓ere [AS: *heora hæmed rihten*] nolint, extra patria recedant (*Quad.*) *GAS* 349 (= *Cons. Cnuti* ib.: suam Venerem corrigere); **c1185** si .. mercator aliquod inconveniens in villa fecerit .., coram justitia supradicta illud ⁓at *BBC* (*Coventry*) 198; caseus malus est in cibo tam dulcis quam salitus; tamen utilis est dulcis post reliquos cibos, quia tunc assumptus facit ⁓ere [? l. digerere] M. SCOT *Phys.* 39; **1294** ita quod ea que de bonis predictis per putrefaccionem vel viam aliam sint in periculo, .. displicentur, ⁓antur, et exsiccentur *RGasc* III 249; **1295** (v. domus 15b).

8 a (inf.) opening of collect. **b** (imp. sg. as sb.), antiphon at matins in office for the dead, dirge (*cf. Psalm* v 9).

a ⁓ere et sanctificare [et regere dignare, Domine Deus] *RegulC* 21 (cf. *Brev. Sal.* II 55). **b** **c1190** anima defuncti absolvetur et ⁓e in directum juxta morem decantabitur *Cart. Rams.* II 252 (cf. 2d supra); contigit diem anniversarium R. abbatis recitari in capitulo et decretum fuit ut placebo et ⁓e cantarentur sollempnius solito BRAKELOND 147; **1219** capellanus .. commendationem dicet pro anima ipsius defuncti et post vesperas placebo et ⁓e *Conc. Syn.* 53 (cf. ib. 54: episcopus .. animam absolvet et cum commendatione et placebo et ⁓e missam pro defunctis personaliter pro anima ipsius cantabit); **1343** item j missale cum placebo et ⁓e et aliis *Ac. Durh.* 205; **1415** ad tenendum v torteras circa corpus meum ad exequias et ad ⁓e *Reg. Cant.* II 31; **1471** unum derige cum nota *Reg. Glasg.* 419.

dirigescere v. derigescere.

dirigibilis, that can be guided. **b** able to guide.

si noticia que de se esset directiva in praxi, dato quod potencia rectificans vel practicans in sciente esset ⁓is in agendo, sit practica ex hoc solo quod sic esset directiva, vel non practica ex hoc quod potencia practicans in sciente non est ⁓is DUNS *Ord.* I 217. **b** pura oracio continet secundum septem appetibilia septem ⁓ia et septem detestabilia. .. septem appetibilia sunt septem dona Spiritus Sancti. septem ⁓ia sunt septem virtutes ab istis manantes, per quas possumus a septem detestabilibus nos tueri WYCL. *Mand. Div.* 270; quare sufficienter in sacra scriptura omnium actuum ⁓ium in Deum sufficiens fundacio reperitur J. BURY *Glad. Sal.* 578.

dirimere [CL]

1 a to divide, separate. **b** to shatter, destroy. **c** to dissolve (relationship).

a duplici dirimuntur tramite causae ALDH. *VirgV* 2662; aequinoctia veris et autumni aequis spatiis dixit esse dirempta BEDE *Wict.* 6; **c745** (v. 1 clima 1b); **9**.. ⁓entes, *todælende WW*; **956** (13c) praefatam rus nullis certis terminis ⁓itur, set jugera adjacent jugeribus *CS* 925; partes in geminas dirimit genuina potestas *De libero arbitrio* 25; gentibus Arcturi quae vertice sidera cernunt, / moribus, eloquiis †habito [l. habitu] varioque diremptae WULF. *Swith. prol.* 559; non in nocte spolia ⁓unt *Enc. Emmae* II 11; **s628** cum uterque exercitus, fuga abjurata, invincibiliter persisterent, solis occidentis gratia diremptі sunt H. HUNT. *HA* II 31; R. COLD. *Cuthb.* 42 (v. disseparare). **b** diremptam, vastatam vel *genumenan GlH* D 555; ⁓e et dirumpe impietatis fasciculos A. TEWK. *Ep.* 10; **s1296** domini nostri fidem et dominium ac fidelitatem infrenate ⁓entes (*Lit. J. Regis Scotiae*) FORDUN *Cont.* XI 26 (= *Anglo-Scot. Rel.* 73: *defier nostre seignor .. e nous metre hors de son homage e sa foy*; cf. RISH. 226; v. et. diffidare 1a); **1323** (v. dissensio); R. BURY *Phil.* 11 (v. desuetudo); **s1215** rex concessit castrum Malmesburie ad ⁓endum cuidam abbati ejusdem loci *Eul. Hist.* III 108 (cf. ib.: leges .. quas S. Edwardus ordinaverat omnino ⁓ebat). **c** si post contractum matrimonium sectus fuerit, non ideo ⁓itur matrimonium ROB. FLAMB. *Pen.* 13.

2 to resolve (a dispute).

ut dirimant odii crudelia jurgia prisci FRITH. 1222; ad causas mediante justicia decidendas et lites ⁓endas GLANV. *prol.*; ut hanc ambiguitatis contentionem certitudo ⁓eret GIR. *TH* II 12; **1289** quicquid iidem electi [ad sedandam discordiam] .. ⁓erint (*sic*) et diffinierint *RGasc* II 415; **1303** debent seneschalli .. absque strepitu judiciali et figura judicii mox totam ⁓ere questionem (*Resp. Archiepiscopi*) THORNE 2001; judices ⁓entes litigia pacem faciunt et conservant OCKHAM *Pol.* II 809; **1443** (v. controversia); ut †⁓at [? l. ⁓atur] lis, sub equo judice optat contendere CHAUNDLER *Laud.* 104.

3 to distinguish.

volucrum .. voces .. ⁓ere ALDH. *PR* 131 (v. 1 discretio 2a).

1 diripere v. diribere.

2 diripere [CL]

1 to tear apart. **b** to tear off. **c** to tear down (fig.).

gemini serpentes .. duos .. parvulos .. venenosis ⁓uerunt morsibus *Lib. Monstr.* III 10; **10**.. direptas, divisas *WW*. **13**.. tempestas .. naves preclaras dispersit et eas ⁓uit *Mem. S. Edm. I* app. 368. **b** a pecore direpta tergora PULL. *Sent.* 692C (v. 2 dissilire 1b). **c** ut coepit tua saeva feritas, post famulos regem solio ⁓iat ABBO *Edm.* 9.

2 to seize, steal, appropriate by force; *v. et. deripere*; **b** (w. abstr. obj.).

actutum scaevis reddunt direpta rapinis ALDH. *VirgV* 1492; vasa ejus quae nos fuimus .. ⁓iebat *V. Greg.* p. 80; **9**. . . ., diri[pi]et, *gegripeð* .., direpta, *þa genumenan WW*; **c957** (12c) quicumque .. hoc [donum] ⁓ere .. temptaverit, anathema sit *CS* 936; **s1097** (v. cursitor); evenit ut juvenis quidam .. [corvorum] pullos direpturus tecta ecclesie .. conscenderet R. COLD. *Cuthb.* 68; **s1191** (v. clitella 1); **s1524** (v. deprimere 3a). **b** **s1152** inclusis [in castello] escarum illationem et liberum progressum ⁓iebat *Meaux* I 132 (= H. HUNT. *HA* VIII 32: prohibuit); J. BURY *Glad. Sal.* 576 (v. directio 3d).

dirisis v. diaeresis. **dirisorie** v. derisorie. **dirivare** v. derivare. **dirivitorium** v. diribitorium. **dirmare, ⁓atia** v. derivare. **dirnum** v. durnum. **dirob-** v. derob-.

†dirocheum [? *for* dittocheum < διττός + ὀχή], (title of work by Prudentius, said to mean) twofold nourishment (*i. e.* temporal and spiritual). (*Cf. EHR* LVIII 199*n.*).

c970 praecipio ut succedentium temporum episcopi .. gregem dyrocheo, id est duplici pastu, nutriant monachorum *CS* 1159; **981** abbas .. gregem sibi commissum ⁓eo, id est duplici pastu, foveat *CD* 629.

dirogatorius v. derogatorius. **dironomon** v. creanomon. **dirrachium** v. Dyrrachium. **dirrationare** v. dirationare. **dirrigescere** v. derigescere. **dirritio** v. duritio.

†dirritum, *s. dub.*

1274 Robertus de B. debet vj d. pro ⁓o [MS *clearly not* dominico] r[egis]; Johannes le B. debet vj d. de dominico; Petrus L. debet vj d. de dominico r[egis] *S. Jers.* II 32.

diruere [CL], to tear down, demolish; **b** (w. abstr. obj.). *V. et. deruere.*

ne nunc quidem, ut antea, civitates patriae inhabitantur; desertae ⁓taeque hactenus squalent GILDAS *EB* 26; excelsum forti compage sacellum / .. / diruit ad fundum sternens molimina prisca ALDH. *VirgV* 1326; ⁓ta ab hostibus moenia BEDE *Ezra* 883; ⁓te, *GlH* D 236 (cf. ib. D 560: dirutus, i. erutus, *ahryred*); castris .. ⁓tis GIR. *EH* II 3; **s1253** vic. Myddelsex .. fecit dirrui omnes gurgites stantes per totam Tamisiam versus occidentem *Leg. Ant. Lond.* 20; **1279** qui pons penitus †dirictus est et per quem locus non est transitus ad carectas *Law Merch.* III 141; **1285** regie strate .. per frequentem transitum carectarum .. †discute [? l. disrute] sunt et profunde (*Breve Regis*) *Ann. Dunstable* 322; **1297** in meremio cariando .. usque ad molendinum .. †dirictum per decursum aque *Ac. Cornw.* II 193; **1337** una .. prisona .. debilis et fere disruta [MS: disurta] *Capt. Seis. Cornw.* 1; 'tot urbes sparse', id est ⁓ute TREVET *Troades* 20; **1426** (v. 1 ejectio 3a). **b** daemonis ut regnum necnon et sceptra tyranni / diruat ALDH. *VirgV* 315; **†676** (12c) cum nobis evangelica .. dogmata .. fuissent delata et omnia simulacrorum figmenta ridiculosa funditus ⁓ta *CS* 43.

dirumpere [CL], to break, shatter, disrupt; **b** (w. abstr. obj.). **c** (intr.) to break off, be detached. **d** (p. ppl.) ruptured (med.). **e** (of utterance) interrupted, jerky. *Cf. indiruptus.*

terrae glebas cum stirpibus imis / nisu virtutis validae disrumpo feraces ALDH. *Aen.* 83 (*Juvencus*) 4; BEDE *Kings* 735 (v. clusor); **9**.. disrupta, *tobrocene WW*; disrumpitur ille, / qui secuit ventris vitalia, ferreus orbis WULF. *Swith.* II 286; A. TEWK. *Ep.* 10 (v. dirimere 1b); ut cito ejus jugum ⁓at GIR. *GE* I 19; **1241** potestatem .. firmandi castrum, quod diruptum fuerat *CurR* XVI 1611; **1336** ad veteres muros castri †disrupiendos [MS app.: disrupend'; (?) l. disrumpendos] (*KRAc* 19/40) *Cal. Scot.* III app. 366; **s1388** exercitum ducens ad Novum Castrum, omnia ⁓endo et inflammando *Plusc.* X 9 (= FORDUN *Cont.* XIV 53: vastando). **b** disrumpit foedera ALDH. *VirgV* 2628 (v. copulare 3a); disrupto rerum ordine (*Id.*) *Carm. Aldh.* 1. 62; **690** (13c) quisquis hanc donationem .. disrumpere temptaverit *CS* 35; propositi tui ortonomias disrumpere nolumus FELIX *Guthl.* 30; **s1306** [bulla], excommunicando jusjurandum illud observare volentes, ⁓entes vero illud approbat et absolvit *Flor. Hist.* III 130. **c** de deodando de quadam parte cujusdam pontis, que quidem pars disrupit cum T. de H. eundem pontem transire voluit *JustIt* 573 r. 26. **d** **1326** moriebatur habens corpus infra diruptum et nullam habens plagam *SelCCoron* 68. **e** cujus vox est dirupta, alta et placabilis M. SCOT *Phys.* 72.

diruptio [CL], **a** breakdown. **b** breaking, disruption. **c** (?) injury. **d** (of sound) outburst.

a **1380** inquisicio capta .. super ⁓one et confraccione duorum poncium *IMisc* 222/14. **b** omnes justi .. exultant ⁓one captivitatis suae ANSELM (*Or.* 7) III 21. **c** **s1337** moleste ferens graves ⁓ones per Scocie nobiles Anglorum gentibus ad se pro subsidio venientibus *Plusc.* IX 36. **d** insonat clamor hinc et inde fitque ⁓o vocum laudationis divine EADMER *V. Osw.* 36.

diruptivus, destructive, diruptive. *Cf. dirutivus.*

ab oris ignivomi faucibus sulphureis ⁓i parietum evomuntur lapides *Ps.*-ELMH. *Hen. V* 42.

dirus [CL], dire, dreadful: **a** (of place, thing, or animal); **b** (of person); **c** (of utterance, act, or event); **d** (of emotion).

a diro sub carcere ALDH. *VirgV* 385; dirorum contra morsus rictusque luporum *Ib.* 1038; quando profectus fueram / usque diram Domnoniam / per carentem Cornubiam (*Id.*) *Carm. Aldh.* 1. 9; **723** (10c) sub ⁓is dentibus salamandri *CS* 144; sicut carnales ejusdem populi oppressores Aegyptii ⁓iora nequitiae spiritalis arma designant BEDE *Hom.* II 7. 138; flagris ⁓issimis diutissime vexatur ABBO *Edm.* 10; tam ⁓um virus ut .. doloris sensum mors anticipet GIR. *TH* I 36; sepe columbinum vultum vestit leo dirus WALT. WIMB. *Scel.* 150. **b** diri tortores ALDH. *VirgV* 2223; dum tollunt dirae librorum lumina Parcae *Id. Aen.* 89 (*Arca Libraria*) 5; ⁓e Parce, i. contrarii doctores, vel *repre, wylfenne GlH* D 554; fortibus erat ⁓us, humilibus erat mitis DOMINIC *V. Ecgwini* I 4. **c** dirae post funera stragis ALDH. *VirgV* 1358; ⁓a antistitis praesagia .. impleta sunt BEDE *HE* III 14; **933** ⁓is obscenae horrendaeque mortalitatis circumsepta latratibus *CS* 694; ⁓a clade WULF. *Æthelwold* 29; DEVIZES 37v. (v. durus 3a); **s1225** ⁓issimo conflictu inter partes confecto WEND. II 285; ⁓a Dei passio [ME: *Godes stronge passiun*] *AncrR* 111; est inter vos conflictus ⁓us, ⁓e contrariarum opinionum .. collisiones CHAUNDLER *Apol.* 28. **d** ringitur et consul dira Pascasius ira ALDH. *VirgV* 1815.

dirutio [CL], ruin.

1261 damna .. illata in ⁓one et combustione domorum et repariorum (*AncC* IV 13) *RL* II 181; **s1360** cum villa de Ravensere Odd atque capella ipsius ville .. ⁓onem [per inundaciones maris] paterentur *Meaux* III 120.

dirutivus, destructive. *Cf. diruptivus.*

jacientes magnos, omnium obviorum ⁓os lapides *Ps.*-ELMH. *Hen. V* 94.

1 dis v. dives.

2 dis- [CL *prefix*]

1 (in new comp., expr.): **a** (dispersal, removal, or separation) *v. diffractio, disannectere, discontinuare, disjacere, dispennare, dispersare, dissyllabare*; **b** (divergence) *v. difformis, ⁓itas, ⁓iter, discantare, ⁓us, discoire, discoloritas, discontiguare, distonatio, distonare*; **c** (reversal of action) *v. disauthenticare, diffoederare, difforestare, ⁓atio, direvestire, disafforestare, ⁓atio, disbanniamentum, ⁓ire, discarcare, ⁓atio, disclaudere, discopulare, dishereditare, ⁓atio, dishonorare, ⁓atio, diskippagium, dispaccare, disparcare, dispropriare, disquietare, dissaisina, ⁓ire, dissuadus, distroppare, distrussare, diswarennare, divadiare* 1, *⁓atio* 1, *divadimoniare*; **d** (refusal) *v. diffiduciare, ⁓atio, disadvocare, disallocabilis, ⁓are*; **e** (negation) *v. discalceate, discaligatus, discohaerentia, ⁓ere, discordia, disconformis, ⁓itas, discredentia, dishabilis, disparantia, disquietare, disseminare* 2, *dissolere, diswarnitus*; **f** (badness, pejoration, or deformation) *v. diffacere, ⁓tio, diffigurare, ⁓ate, ⁓atio, difformare, diffortunium, disparagare, ⁓atio*; **g** (intensification) *v. diffugare, diffulcire, diradiare, diratio, diratiocinare, ⁓atio, dirationare, disconficere, disperquirere, dispissitudo,* 1 *distingere, distuppare, divadiare* 2, *⁓atio* 2. *V. et. de* 17.

2 (conf. w. *de-*): **a** (from CL or LL) *v. diffamare, ~atio, ~ator, ~atorius, differre, digredi, dijudicare, dilacerare, diluere, diminuere, dimittere, diripere, diruere, discissio, 2 distringere, diverberare, 1 diversari, diversorium, divertere, diverticulum, divestire*; **b** (from OF *des- < de-, di-, dis-*) *v. diffacere, diffidamentum, ~are, 2 diffidentia, diffigurare, diffortiamentum, ~iare, ~iator, dirationamentum, ~ator, disaccordare, disallocare, discaetus, disclamare, discomputare, disemparare, disgerbigator, dismembrare, dispersonare, 1 disporta, dissacaria, dissaisonare. V. et. de* 18. (*Cf. Year Bk.* XXV Selden Soc. 81 p. cxxiv).

c798 secunda .. interrogatio fuit inter 'de', 'dis': an debuisset esse 'dispexeris' sive 'despexeris'. sed 'dispexeris' esse non potest propter sequentem 'S', quae exigit 'dis', ut Priscianus vult ALCUIN *Ep.* 162; sunt quedam prepositiones que non separatim construuntur cum casibus sed per compositionem semper, ut 'dis', 'con', 're', 'se', 'an'. 'dis' vero dicit separationem duorum vel plurium, 'con' contrarium *Ps.*-GROS. *Gram.* 56.

disabilis v. dishabilis.

disaccordare [cf. accordare, AN *disacorder*, OF *desacorder*], to disagree.

quid si rotulus unius coronatoris discordet a rotulis aliorum cum plures fuerint? standum erit pluralitati. si autem non nisi duo coronatores [sint] et ~ent, tunc stabitur rotulo ipsius cum quo concordat rotulus vicecomitis BRACTON 140b.

disadvocare [cf. CL advocare, OF *desavoer*], to disavow, disclaim, disown: **a** feudal lord; **b** legal representative; **c** document; **d** statement; **e** (responsibility for) action by servant. **f** (w. *quod* and neg.) to deny. *V. et. deadvocare, devocare* 3.

a cum .. ipse reus dedicat in pleno comitatu ipsi petenti hujusmodi servicia petita et ipsum ~et pro domino HENGHAM *Magna* 4 p. 12. **b 1352** Agnes, presens in curia, instanter ~at placitatores suos qui superius pro ea placitaverunt et placitum illud omnino recusat *SelCKB* VI 85 (cf. *Gild Merch.* II 7 [**1263**]: idem A. *desawoa* suum narratorem); **1439** quod decanus .. attornatus seu procuratores hujusmodi per se solum absque capituli communione et consensu in curia aliqua .. revocare seu ~are non presumat *Stat. Linc.* II 221. **c 1411** postea .. Johannes .. disavocavit et revocavit bullam predictam .. et peciit inde misericordiam *BB Winchester* 28. **d 1334** quod ipsi .. pro veredicto prius dixerunt omnino ~verunt *SelCKB* V 76. **e 1278** nolentes .. quod, si aliquis de familia .. regis transgressionem vel forisfactum aliquod .. fecerit, hoc .. regi imputetur, dummodo ille ~averit *Foed.* II 117b (cf. *CalPat* 268). **f 1275** ~avit quod nunquam ipsum appellavit *Hund.* I 448; **1310** Edmundus .. in curia hic ~at quod ipse nullam licenciam ei dedit ad blada .. trituranda *Doc. Ir.* 517.

disafforestare [cf. 1 afforestare, OF *desafforester*], to disafforest, remove (land) from forest status. *V. et. deafforestare, deforestare, difforestare.*

1201 exceptis terris quas disaforestavimus *Pat* 3b; †**a1215** concedo ut omnes forestas quas pater meus et frater meus et ego †afforestavimus [v. l. afforestaveramus] desafforesto (*sic*) (? *Ch. J. Regis*) *EHR* VIII 291 (cf. ib. IX 328); **1298** ut manerium de D. desafforestetur et quod .. habeat parcos suos inclusos in eodem manerio *PQW* 124b; **1304** rex vult quod [locus ille] ~atus sit, set quod sit ibi warenna *RParl* I 161a.

disafforestatio [cf. afforestatio], disafforestation. *V. et. deafforestatio, deforestatio, difforestatio.*

s**1227** [M. abbas] pacavit ad Scaccarium de debito domini A. abbatis pro disaforestatione Nassiburgi l m. *Chr. Peterb.* 9; **1307** reddendo ad Scaccarium .. Novi Castri pro ~one foreste iiij s. v d. per annum *IPM* 125/17.

disagreare [cf. agreare, OF *disagreer*], (refl.) to disagree, dissociate oneself.

a**1540** eadem M. ad dimissionem predict' omnia se ~eando tenementa predicta re[li]quit et occupare cessavit *Entries* 690.

disais- v. dissais-.

disallocabilis [cf. allocabilis], disallowable.

tercio die apparente petente, reus essonietur: procul dubio essonium illud ~e est, quia reus non potest essonium gaudere donec salvetur prima defalta postquam terra sua capta fuit HENGHAM *Magna* 9.

disallocare [cf. allocare, AN *disalouer*, OF *desaloer*], to disallow: **a** (item in account); *v. et. deallocare* a, *dislocare* 2; **b** (petition).

a 1341 in denariis liberatis eisdem superius sibi ~atis et hic allocatis ex precepto regis *MinAc* 1120/11 r. 19; **1362** ad audiendum compotum .. et eorum [ballivorum etc.] cuilibet allocandum et ~andum juxta formam .. vobis .. committimus potestatem *Reg. Heref.* 7; **1368** de diversis superoneratis et ~atis (*Ac. Man. Hutton*) *EHR* XXVI 336*n.*; **1393** petit allocacionem de mij^c iiij^xx gr[ossis] sibi ~atis ut in mij^c iiij^xx fr[ancis] oneratis ad iij s. iiij d., ut patet in compoto ipsius computantis, quos idem computans solvit *le franc* ad iij s. *Ac. H. Derby* 291; **1408** littere patentes, tallie, assignaciones in contrarium ordinacionis predicte imposterum faciende coram thesaurario et baronibus nostris de Scaccario omnino ~entur (*Pat*) *Foed.* VIII 510b; **1410** allocantur eidem iij s. de stipendiis famulorum superius ~atis; et .. lxiij s. quad. de diversis superon[eratis] et disall[ocatis] (*ed.*: superon[eracionibus] et disall[ocacionibus]) (*Pipe Wint.*) *Crawley* 299; **1445** de diversis expensis et liberacionibus eis similiter injuste ~atis et respectuatis *Law Merch.* II 108. **b 1456** quod .. peticio .. comitis quoad eum per pares suos .. deducendum, triandum seu judicandum eidem comiti ~etur *Entries* 50.

disamis, a logical mood.

BACON XV 301 (v. bocardo a); quod .. consequens sit falsum patet et quod antecedens sit verum probatur ... consquencia patet in ~is LAVENHAM 56.

disana v. decena 3a.

disannectere [cf. CL annectere], (p. ppl. *disannexus*) disannexed, detached.

1587 [officia] deinceps imperpetuum separata, devisa et ~a ab officio senescalli .. foreste nostre de Shirwood *Pat* 1303 m. 14.

disappropriare (disapr-) [cf. 2 appropriare], to disappropriate. *V. et. dispropriare.*

1290 quia presentatum est .. quod R. le V. .., dum fuit justiciarius Cestr' apropriavit sibi quandam magnam placeam terre .., preceptum est Galfrido [et al.] quod .. inquirerent .. si predicta occupacio fuisset disapropriata *Eyre Chester* 12 r. 11; **1576** damus .. potestatem .. rectoriam predictam disappropriandi et ad eandem presentandi de tempore in tempus .. clericos idoneos .. et quod .. licite possint amortizare .. advocacionem .. predicte rectorie cum fuerit disappropriata *Pat* 1150 m. 32.

disappropriatio, disappropriation.

1380 priore et monachis per ~onem prioratus [S. Nicholai, Arundel] .. depositis penitus et amotis *MonA* VI 1378b (cf. *CalPat* 494); **1434** de rectore ecclesie de S. eadem pensio habetur, ~one non obstante *Reg. Roff.* 572 (= *MonA* I 183b).

disarmare [cf. AN *desarmer*], (p. ppl.) disarmed, unarmed. *V. et. dearmare* a.

s**1388** comes de Douglas .. cum aliis .. militibus et nobilibus ~ati induerunt se stolis et talaribus robis FORDUN *Cont.* XIV 53.

disarrestare [cf. OF *disarester*], to 'disarrest', release (seized property) from arrest. *V. et. dearrestare* b.

1294 eadem debita .. esse asserunt arestata .., quamquam nos predictos mercatores et omnia bona eorum disarestari mandavimus jam est diu *Bronnen* I 42 (= *CalPat* 102); **1327** precipimus quod dictam navem disarestari et .. liberari facias *KRMem* 103 r. 244.

disauthenticare [cf. authenticare], to 'disauthenticate', invalidate.

1400 [sigillum] disautenticatum, dampnatum, et annullatum *Reg. Exon.* I f. 51 (*Cal.* p. 97).

disauthenticatio, invalidation.

1400 disautenticacio sigilli domus S. Nicholai Exon' *Reg. Exon.* I f. 51 (*Cal.* p. 97).

disavocare v. disadvocare. **disawarrenare** v. diswarrenare.

disbannimentum [cf. bannimentum], release from 'ban' or sequestration (Gasc.).

1289 instrumentum publicum super †disberaniamento [MS: disbanniamento] bonorum magistri B. jurati nove bastide de Colome ad requisicionem bajuli dicte bastide pro rege Francie *TRBk* 187 p. 183.

disbannire [cf. bannire], to release from 'ban' or sequestration (Gasc.).

1285 quod .. bajuli .. ambo .. ~iant et recredant homines et pignora capta .. et pignora in uno loco communi .. reponant *RGasc* II 271.

disbrigare [cf. brigare], to disencumber, protect from claims or disputes (Sc.).

1391 Laurencius .. recognovit .. se .. alienasse in .. dominum R. .. et assignatos suos imperpetuum j m. .. percipiendam annuatim de terris de Fothil .., promittens .. ipsi domino R. .. litem vel controversiam ullo nunquam tempore non inferre .. sed ipsam marcam .. ipsi domino R. .. ab omni homine et universitate †legittima [l. legittime] defendere et ~are *Reg. Aberd.* I 189; **1543** A. B. .. vendidit domino N. unum equum .., promittens ipsi emptori .. dictum equum sibi ab omni homine et universitate .. legittime defendere, auctorizare, et ~are *Form. S. Andr.* II 303.

disca v. discus.

discaëtus [cf. AN *dechaet*, OF *decheoit*], decayed, ruined. *V. et. decadere* 1b.

1297 pro quodam columbar' ~o de novo faciendo *MinAc* 1090/4 r. D 16; **1315** (v. cumulus 6).

discalaciare [cf. scalaciare (OF *eschalacier*)], to clear (vineyard) of vine-stakes.

1235 in vinea discalcianda, provignianda, fodienda, howanda et scalettanda (*Ac. Man. Northfleet*) *Arch. Cant.* XLVI 141*n.*; **1274** in †vineus [l. vineis] discalciandis et compostandis et eisdem fodiendis et cindendis, ligandis, rebinendis et reparandis (*Ac. Man. Teynham*) *Ib.* 144*n.*

discalceare, ~iare [LL; CL *p. ppl. only*; cf. AN *deschalcer*, OF *deschaucier*]

1 to unshoe, take off footwear: **a** (refl.); **b** (w. wearer as obj.); **c** (w. footwear as obj.); **d** (absol.).

a coactus est .. se ~iare suosque pedes .. ad abluendum praebere BEDE *CuthbP* 17; facto .. capitulo, ~ient se [AS p. 413: *unsceogien hi*] fratres et intrantes ecclesiam .. lavent pavimenta ecclesiae *RegulC* 40; ~iens (*sic*) se in hospitio suo, nudis perrexit pedibus ad .. Athelwoldi praesentiam BYRHT. *V. Osw.* 446; crura manu teneas dum se discalceat hospes D. BEC. 33; ecce hic quod homo iste ~iabat se S. LANGTON *Ruth* 123; s**1243** rex .. majori Wintonie .. injunxit ne .. episcopum Wintoniam intrare permitteret. quo audito, episcopus civitati adveniens et .. se ~ians cum magna humilitate ad unam portarum .. advenit *Ann. Wav.* 331. **b c1100** vigilans vel dormiens, monachus vix discingitur aut ~eatur HAM. S. ALB. 1455; **1101** sponse contemptor a futuro sponso ~iari mandatur [cf. *Deut.* xxv 10] (*Lit. Papae*) EADMER *HN* 148; monachum .. in scamno sedere fecit et, ~iato eo, coram ipso genibus orabat flexis, pedem illum nudum inter manus habens MAP *NC* II 4 f. 24v.; abbas .., faciens se ~iari, intra portam nudipes susceptus est BRAKELOND 127; mulier ~iabat eum ut legitur in Deuteronomio xxx° capitulo S. LANGTON *Ruth* 123. **c** exuit Osbertus arma militaria et, cum caligas ferreas ~earet, unam sanguine coagulato videt inpletam GERV. TILB. III 59; quorum [noviciorum] eciam incumbit officio .. botas domni abbatis .. reverenter cum genuflexione ~iare *Cust. Westm.* 118; s**1356** 'veni huc .. decalciare .. botas meas!' *Plusc* IX 43 (= FORDUN *Cont.* XIV 17: abstrahe). **d** violenter quidam Latino vel Graeco nomini Hebraeam quaerentes aethimologiam dicunt, Petrum 'dissolventem' sive '†disculciantem' vel 'agnoscentem' interpretari BEDE *Luke* 397 (cf. WYCL. *Chr. & Antichr.* 664: Petrus dicitur 'agnoscens' sive '~ians'); si festum ix leccionum contingat .., non ~iant fratres *Obs. Barnwell* 148.

2 (p. ppl.) unshod: **a** (of person); **b** (of feet); **c** (fig.). **d** (as sb. m.) Barefoot Friar, Franciscan.

a venientes ad primam, ~iati [AS p. 416: *unsceode*] omnes incedant quousque crux adoretur *RegulC* 43; vir .. pannosus et miser, omni tempore exercens nudipedalia, unde et cognomento vocabatur '~eatus', Girardus nomine proprio H. BOS. *Thom.* IV 16; **1231** [sacerdos] descendit et venit ad eum ~iatus pedes *Reg. S. Osm.* II 23; †discalcinatus .. usque ad extrema vite sue tempora semper pergebat STUDLEY 5 p. 371; [milites] inveniunt eum in lecto, sicut decet taliter essoniatum, ~iatum [v. l. decalceatum] et sine braccis et discinctum [v. l. decinctum] vel forte nudum BRACTON 356b; s**1274** [episcopus Lond'] .. decalciatus perexit usque ad ecclesiam S. Pauli et ibidem .. intronizatus est *Leg. Ant. Lond.* 164; s**1304** exiverunt [ex castro de Strywelin] ~eati, funes in collis habentes et misericordiam postulantes AD. MUR. *Chr.* 7; s**1429** in die Cinerum conventus non fuit ~eatus in processione pro asperitate nimis [? l. nivis] et frigore *Chr. S. Alb.* 33. **b** mane adveniente .. ~iatis pedibus perrexi .. ad locum BYRHT. *V. Ecgwini* 375; s**1099** Christiani .., manibus a cede ablutis, multi pedibus ~iatis, gaudentes .. ad sanctum S. Salvatoris sepulcrum deosculandum catervatim properaverunt ORD. VIT. IX 15 p. 611; s**1170** [rex] didicit humiliari et .. Cantuariam celerius adiit ~iatisque pedibus .. sepulchrum beati martyris petiit *Chr. Battle* f. 109; in omnibus feriis quartis et sextis per totam Quadragesimam debet conventus pedibus ~iatis facere processionem circa claustrum *Obs. Barnwell* 148; dormire pedibus non ~iatis GAD. 110v. 2. **c** res publica .. est quasi ~iata quando injuriis exponitur J. SAL. *Pol.* 619B. **d** Beseleel interpretatur 'umbra Dei'. Beseleel igitur est .. Fr. Dominicus quoad Predicatores, Fr. Franciscus quoad ~eatos O. CHERITON *Cant. extr.* 68.

discalceate, barefoot.

infecciones .. in tibiis pauperum et consumptorum ~iate sedencium juxta ignem GAD. 40v. 2.

1 discalciare v. discalaciare.

2 discalciare, discalcinare v. discalceare.

discaligatus [cf. 1 caligare 2], not wearing hose.

s**1381** cancellarius .. et .. thesaurarius .. restiterunt talia suadentibus, dicentes nequaquam debere regem adire tales ~os ribaldos WALS. *HA* I 456; nudipedes et ~i sacrum hominis Dei revisere spondent habitaculum *Mir. Hen. VI* I 23.

discantare [cf. CL cantare], to sing descant. **b** to outsing (fig.).

de modo psallendi et modulandi, ~andi, aut organizandi (*Ord. Exon.*) *HBS* XXXVII 19. **b** ad vos .. in brevi veniam, ea vobis, que de me falsis suggestionibus cantata sunt, veris .. assertionibus ~are paratus Gir. *JS* 3 p. 206.

discantus, descant.

organum et decentum, fausetum et *pipeth* omnibus nostris .. in divino officio .. prohibemus *Inst. Sempr.* *xlii; ~us est aliquorum diversorum cantuum consonantia secundum modum et secundum equipollentis equipollentiam Garl. *Mus.* 106; aliud est genus [cantus organici] in quo attenditur consonancia vocum et mensuracionum in duplici aut triplici [aut] quadruplici; et dicitur ~us, quasi duorum cantuum ad minus Odington 138; mensurabilis [musica] simpliciter est ~us, eo quod in omni parte sua tempore mensuratur. partim mensurabilis dicitur organum Tunst. 255a; **1415** decanus .. debeat compellere .. clericos .. ad cantandum planum cantum et ~um (*Stat. Stoke*) *MonA* VI 1420a; **1461** (v. 2 cantus 2b); quamvis species sive consonancie ~us infinite sint, tamen in presenciarum communiter novem utende reperiuntur Hothby *Contrap. Fa* 101 (cf. ib. 102: sed quoniam per Anglicos iste modus canendi vocatur ~us visibilis); ~uum alius simplex prolatus, alius truncatus, qui hoketus dicitur, alius copulatus, †quia [? l. qui] copula nuncupatur Hauboys 404b; **1504** quintus capellanus .. erit organista ac .. scolam cantationis docebit, dietim pueros inibi in cantu Gregoriano punctuato sive precato et descantu .. erudiendo *Reg. Glasg.* 509.

discare [cf. CL discus], to make dishes.

~o, *to make dyshys WW.*

discarcagium [cf. 1 carcagium], (payment for) unloading.

1242 cum .. †discartagio, **1298** †discarragium (v. 1 carcagium); **1272** in cariagio vij doliorum vini ab aqua Thamisie usque ad castrum nostrum [de Windelesor'] et †discariagio eorundem *Liberate* 48 m. 11; **1387** pro extraccione xxj doliorum vini de diversis celariis .. ac carcagio et ~io super et de diversis carrectis et imposicione eorundem in diversis batellis *KRAc* 183/12 f. 21.

discarcare [cf. carcare]

1 to unload, discharge: **a** (ship or boat); **b** (cart); **c** (absol.). *V. et. decarcare, dischargiare.*

a 1224 quod illis qui navem predictam carcatam waida versus Angliam ducent nullam faciatis .. molestiam .. et, cum ipsa ~ata fuerit, .. ad partes suas platam nostram relire permittatis *Pat* 458; **1234** *Cl* 552 (v. carcare 1a); **1265** mandamus quod predictum Petrum navem predictam coreis suis .. in villa vestra ~are .. permittatis *Cl* 25; **s1287** batelli .. †cartati et †discartati solebant venire apud H. *MonA* II 572a; **1378** in tantum quod quedam navis carcata cum bosco .. ibidem non potuit ~ari *Mem. York* I 27. **b 1266** carecta in exitu suo extra villam, si fuerit †discariata, dabit ij d. *MGL* II 279. **c 1201** ponit se .. super juratam patrie †quam [MS *perh.* q'm; ? l. quod] melius potuerunt carcare et ~are apud W. quam apud J. *CurR* I 449; **1204** assisum est .. quod .. mercatores .. waranta reportabunt quod in loco ad quem ire proposuerunt applicuerint et ~averint *Pat* 42b; **1232** de nulla navi .. prisam capiat .. nisi ibidem applicat et discarket *Pat* 505; **1335** quedam magna navis .. armaturis et aliis mercandisis .. onerata .. apud castrum [de Dumbretayne] in auxilium .. inimicorum nostrorum .. applicuit et ibidem discar[ca]vit *RScot* 320b.

2 to unload, discharge (goods).

preter ~atam lanam et dissutum unctum (*Quad.*) *GAS* 234; **1196** pro vinis regis carriandis et ~andis et in cellariis reponendis *Pipe* 18; **1198** pro vinis regis descarcandis *RScacNorm* II 461 (cf. *EHR* XXXVII 48n.); **1215** sal quod †discariatum fuit apud Sandwic' de ij navibus de Gipeswich' *Cl* 228a; **1236** ad ij pulinos faciendos ad ~anda vina regis *Cl* 394 (= *OED* s. v. *puleyn*: †discarocanda); c**1290** (v. carcare 2); **1306** omnia mercandise et mercimonia .. infra portum .. ~entur *BBC* (*Yarmouth*) 245.

3 (?) to dismantle.

1239 in predictis castris [ligneis] ~andis et cooperiendis in castro Cestr' *Liberate* 13 m. 14.

discarcatio [cf. carcatio], unloading, discharge: **a** (of ships); **b** (of goods).

a 1212 (v. custos 4d); **1290** ~ones navium de mercandisis *RParl* I 27; **1387** laborantibus .. super ~one naviculaum *KRAc* 183/12 f. 21. **b 1253** pro altari et †discariatione petre de Came, xiiij s. *Ac. Build. Hen. III* 232; **1254** vij li. .. quas posuit .. circa ingenia nostra carianda usque Burdegalam .. et pro ~one eorundem ibidem *Cl* 257; **1338** ipsi litteras patentes .. duccionem et ~onem victualium illorum .. et que et cujusmodi victualia .. ibidem sic discarcata fuerint testificantes vobis reportabunt *RScot* 536b; **1339** (v. cubatio 3a).

discarg- v. discharg-. **discari-** v. et. discarc-.

discarius [cf. discus 2], dish-bearer, sewer. *Cf. discifer.*

ocius abjectas discarius efferat illas [sc. conchas ovorum] D. Bec. 2620; **1265** magistro W. salsario nostro et W. Hagman ~io nostro *Liberate* 41 m. 7 (*Cal.* p. 158); **12..** isti sunt servientes per omnes †officias [? l. officinas]: .. claviger .., ~ius .., focarius (*Lib. Alb. S. Edm.*) *MonA* III 159a; **1335** familia que est utilis in coquina conventus: .. item potagiarius et ~ius habentes unum garcionem; .. *Lit. Cant.* II 94.

discark-, discaroc-, discarr-, discart- v. discarc-.

discata [cf. CL discus], dishful (measure of barley). *V. et. discus* 3a.

1328 vj discat' ordei, [unde] xvj discat' faciunt bussellum de manerio *DCNorwich* (*Ac. Man. Hindolveston*).

discator, ~orius, dish-bearer.

presbyter qui .. nescit ministerium suum .. caecus ~or est Ælf. *Ep.* 2. 158; **1335** cum ~orio (v. coltonarius).

1 discedere [CL]

1 to depart, withdraw; **b** (from a condition or practice); **c** (from a feudal lord); **d** (from a contract). **e** to be dislocated. **f** to vanish. **g** (p. ppl. *discessus, s. act.*). *V. et.* 1 *decedere* 1.

675 ~ens a Cantia Aldh. *Ep.* 2; ibi .. [Wilfrithus] mansit, ~ente ab eo .. duce sicut a Paulo Barnabas .. recessit Eddi 3; [Furseus] ab ipsa quoque insula patria discessit Bede *HE* III 19; **9..** discessurus, *from gewitende WW*; **s871** Saxones cum .. paganis, ea condicione ut ab eis ~erent, pacem pepigerunt Asser *Alf.* 43; **a1078** unigenitus Patris ita in mundum venit ut tamen a Paterno sinu nunquam ~eret Lanfr. *Ep.* 50 (46); ~it a curia G. Crispin *Herl.* 90; incarceraverat .. tres viros quod ab expeditione Hybernica clam discessissent W. Cant. *Mir. Thom.* III 19. **b** si quis a fide Dei discesserit .. vij annos paeniteat Theod. *Pen.* I 5. 14; si a cultu nostrae religionis ~ere temtas (*Passio Albani*) Bede *HE* I 7 p. 19; stultos ut a malo ~erent [cf. *Eccles.* vii 2] verberibus corrigendo Wulf. *Æthelwold* 27. **c** non poterat ~ere a domino suo *DB* I 177; iiij homines tenuerunt, sed ~ere non potuerunt, quia soca hujus terrae pertinet ad Waredone *Ib.* 227. **d 1301** (v. 2 contractus 2a). **e** [excidio], eversio, a cadendo, a ~endo *GlC* E 323; Gilb. IV 180v. 1 (v. disjungere 2e). **f** ni .. / .. fragilis tenues flatus discedat in auras Aldh. *Aen.* 62 (*Famfaluca*) 5; fatiscit, i. evanescit .., ~it .., *fordwinþ GlH* F 108. **g** apostata, ~us a fide *GlC* A 692; id tempus annum vocant dum luna a sole ~a duodecies eum consecuta est Adel. *Elk.* 1.

2 to diverge, differ.

his verbis nec addatis quicquam nec minuatis quod ab hac sententia ~at Anselm (*Ep.* 314) V 242.

3 to decease. *V. et.* 2 *cedere* 2, *concedere* 1b, 1 *decedere* 2.

11.. si iste B. ab hac luce sine herede discesserit *Feod. Durh.* 128n.; **s1168** dum in fata ~eret B. Cotton 75 (= Diceto *YH* I 332: concederet); **1220** si predictus F. ante solutionem .. pecunie .. in fata ~at *CurR* IX 347; **1314** ubi fratres .. malis multiplicibus lacessiti aut cito †~ent [v. l. ~unt] aut .. privantur .. valitudine residuo vite sue (*Instr. Publicum*) *Flor. Hist.* III 163 (cf. *EHR* V 109); **s1347** ex morbo disenterico .. discesserunt *Meaux* III 65; **s1349** discessit eadem pestilencia frater S. .. abbas Westm' J. Reading 160.

2 discedere v. dissidere a. **discena** v. decena 1. **discenarius** v. decenarius. **discendere, ~sus** v. descen-. **discens-** v. dissens-. **discenter-** v. dysenter-.

discentia [LL], (activity of) learning.

sicut unus discit librum solo visu in quantum ipsum cognoscit, alius discendo distincte literas et silibas, alius discendo legere, alius cognoscendo signatum scripture secundum sensum literalem aut alium, que ~ie [v. l. distancie] possunt secundum gradus quotlibet variari, sic longe proprius addiscitur liber vite Wycl. *Ente* (*Sum.*) 109.

disceptare [CL], **~ari**

1 to argue, dispute; **b** (w. indir. qu.).

si qua liberius de his .. non tam ~avero quam deflevero Gildas 26; nos de .. vitiorum radicibus .. ea potissimum causa ~are et disputare coegit Aldh. *VirgP* 13; ~ant, *flitat GlC* D 271 (cf. ib. D 298: ~avero, *sciro*); †**974** (13c) (v. cuneus 2c); ~ant, i. contendunt, *flitaþ*, disputant, dijudicant, litigant *GlH* D 563; **s1125** ~ati sunt W. Cantuar' et T. Ebor' archipresules de primatu M. Par. *Maj.* II 152 (= *Id. Min.* I 235: deceptaverunt); **s1254** ceperunt pueri inter se deceptare de hereditate *Ib.* V 435; **1309** quidam .. canonicus monasterii .. de placitis secularibus circa negocia aliena .., quasi secularitеr vivens, deceptans *Reg. Cant.* II 1106; quia de materia ista .. sufficienter puto me desceptasse Fortescue *LLA* 9. **b 1225** sepe .. in Anglia fuerat deceptatum an homines terre regem in Pictaviam prosequi tenerentur, et post deceptationem .. negaverunt omnino prosecutionem ipsam fieri debere (*Quer. Falcasii*) W. Coventr. II 269.

2 (trans.) to discuss or (?) conclude.

pro quinquenali treuga componenda apud Calesiam .. litteras regias regi Francie .. clandestine miserunt hoc modo, sc. quod noster rex Anglie ad deceptandum dictam fraudolosam treugam ibidem interesset Favent 6 (cf. ib.: priusquam finem litis in ipso N. B. †decetassent [v. l. deceptassent]).

disceptatio [CL], argument, dispute, debate; **b** (acad.).

759 (15c) longa deceptatio inter familias duorum monasteriorum orta est *CS* 186; quaestio est constitutio in qua causae ~o, constat hoc modo : 'non jure fecisti,' 'jure feci' Alcuin *Rhet.* 10; *Id. Ep.* 245 (v. confrater d); hec [dialectica] certis divisionibus omnem deceptationem locutionis excludens, nodos sophisticos aperit Adel. *ED* 21 (cf. ib. 19: quicquid sub civilem ~onem (*sic*) cadere potest); *Lib. Eli.* II 132 (v. 1 constituere 4b); **s1234** ad talem finem multis pervenerunt ~onibus [v. l. deceptationibus] M. Par. *Maj.* III 290; **s1327** rex antiquus .. ignominiose peremptus est. de cujus meritis, an inter sanctos annumerandus sit, frequens in vulgo .. adhuc ~o est Higd. VII 44 p. 324; Ockham *Dial.* 804 (v. consiliatio a); **1404** ita quod ex deceptacionibus et anfractibus eorumdem [commissariorum] occasio dubitacionum et discordiarum .. inter predicta regna .. auferatur *RScot* 170b (= *Foed.* VIII 332). **b 1542** de ~onibus et exercitamentis scholasticorum *Deeds Balliol* 323.

disceptator [LL; CL = *arbitrator*], **a** arguer, investigator. **b** pleader.

a 680 fortasse quilibet strofosus librorum lector ac sagax scripturarum ~or tali se excusationis clipeo defendat Aldh. *Ep.* 4; ~or, examinator, inquisitor *GlC* D 211; ~or, i. .. judex *GlH* D 562. **b** *motar or pletare*, discept[at]or vel deceptator, placitator *PP*.

disceptio v. deceptio. **disceptorius** v. discerptorius. **disceptum** v. dissaepire 1c.

1 discere [CL]

1 to learn (an art or sim.); **b** (absol.); **c** (w. inf.). **d** (pr. ppl.) learner, pupil.

ut puer indolis librorum disceret artes Aldh. *VirgV* 1127; linguam Scottorum jam plene didicerat Bede *HE* III 3; ut regularis observantiae mores .. ~eret Wulf. *Æthelwold* 5; logica pre omnibus ~enda est Kilwardby *OS* 639; **1363** ut .. prius humiliter addisceret .., postquam (*sic*) quod sic didiscerint (*sic*) aliis .. revelarent *Lit. Cant.* II 443. **b a690** Hiberniae rus ~entium opulans .. numerositate lectorum Aldh. *Ep.* 5; vultis flagellari in ~endo [AS: *on leornunge*]? Ælf. *Coll.* 89; quid est audire Spiritui Sancto nisi quasi ~ere, et quid est ~ere nisi scientiam accipere? Anselm (*Proc. Sp.* 6) II 197; ~ere est motus ab ignorantia in scientiam Hales *Sent.* III 139. **c** et didicere truces praedam servare leones Aldh. *VirgV* 1443; ecclesiae regulas .. amare didicerat Bede *HE* V 19 p. 325; vellem interim ~ere [AS: *leornian*] sermocinari Latina lingua Ælf. *Coll.* 90; W. Cant. *Thom.* II 31 (v. cauterium 2b); disce pati famis acre jugum, vel disce labori / cedere Walt. Angl. *Fab.* 52. 5. **d** cum fuerit discens transgressus in erudiendo, / non caput, immo latus, doctoris sentiat ictus D. Bec. 1720; ex ~entium consensu Balsh. *AD rec.* 2 126.

2 to learn (a fact or sim.), ascertain; **b** (absol.); **c** (w. acc. & inf. or indir. qu. or *quod*).

705 ut postquam hoc dedicerim liberius consentissem (*sic*) Wealdhere *Ep.* 23; quae non ab illis qui viderunt et audierunt per ore didicimus vulgata tantum habemus *V. Greg.* p. 107; obitum proxime suum, quem revelatione didicerat, non celavit esse futurum Bede *HE* III 8; comperit, i. .. cognovit, invenit, didicit, *onfunde GlH* C 1293; quam [causam] cum a camerario didicisset, "tace" inquit Ailr. *Ed. Conf.* 746d; **s1178** fluctuabat utrum sub silentio preteriret an aliis que in visu vel potius, ut presumebat, re corporaliter gesta, didicerat revelaret Wend. I 111 (= M. Par. *Min.* I 405: didiscerat). **b** ut dudum angelico discit virguncula fatu Aldh. *VirgV* 1694; **765** (12c) sicut celesti magisterio adhortante didicimus *CS* 260; **1216** sicut pro certo didiscimus *Cl* 282b; cum de nece filii didicisset *Eul. Hist.* II 234 (= G. Mon. II 16: certitudinem habuisset). **c** ubi gentem Nordanhymbrorum .. ad fidem .. Christi .. conversam esse didicit Bede *HE* II 17; quando eadem prima Sabbati .. veniret, minime didicerant *Ib.* III 4; **798** omnem .. hominem proximum esse exemplo .. Samaritani [*Luke* x 29–37] ~amus Alcuin *Ep.* 19; **1166** (v. comminatorius c); c**1192** si .. didicerit .. illos pauperes .. non exhiberi *Ch. Sal.* 46; cum didicisset quod .. de difficili ultra .. fluminis .. alveum sibi .. transitus securus pareret *Ps.*-Elmh. *Hen. V* 25.

3 to teach.

qui alienis didicisti misereri semper et parcere tibi servientibus Ailr. *Ed. Conf.* 785d.

2 discere v. ducere 1a.

discernere [CL]

1 to divide, separate. **b** to distinguish (by forming or marking difference). **c** (her.) to blazon.

materiam mundi discernens ordine recto Aldh. *VirgV* 742; insula .. non magno ab ea [sc. Brittania] freto discreta Bede *HE* III 3; *GlH* D 567 (v. discerpere a); discriminalia, unde ~untur crines de auro, vel argento vel aere *Gl. Leid.* 13. 7; ypodiastile .. male coherentia descernit et separat per notam que est quasi pars dextra circuli Bacon *CSPhil.* 517; *to departe*, .. dirimere .., †disternere [l. discernere], discriminare, distingere, distinguere .. *CathA*. **b 680** ut sacerdotes Veteris et Novi Testamenti in tonsura et habitu ~erentur Aldh. *Ep.* 4; tempus .. invisibilia ~ens *Id. PR*

140; tribus graduum ordinibus quibus credentium multitudo ~itur *Id. VirgP* 19; J. SAL. *Met.* 883B (v. 1 discretio 2a); BALSH. *AD rec. 2* 166 (v. coaptatio c); S. Trinitas .. secundum personales proprietates est discreta BART. ANGL. I 2; cum diccionis accentus ~atur per sillabam finalem *Ps.*-GROS. *Gram.* 33. **c** qui portat arma inbatellata sic Gallice debet ~i, ut hic in scuto: *il port d'ore et sable enbatelle* BAD. AUR. 128; in armis ~endis est semper incipiendum a cono, si conus fuerit unius coloris UPTON 210.

2 (p. ppl. *discretus*) discrete, distinct, discontinuous; **b** (w. ref. to sound); **c** (math.); **d** (log.). **e** (as sb. n.) discontinuous entity. **f** distinguished, outstanding.

triquadrum discreto limite mundum ALDH. *VirgV* 1040; quanquam sacramentorum genere ~o, sicut una eademque fide, Pascha celebrare possemus (*Ep. Ceolfridi*) BEDE *HE* V 21 p. 337; **c745** [liber] clare ~is et absolutis litteris scriptus BONIF. *Ep.* 63; **9..** ~as, *todælede WW*; ~e sunt servitutes ductus aque et haustus BRACTON 233; *Ib.* 9 (v. accessio 2a); **s1300** pecierunt ut .. afforestaciones, quibus plebs angariebatur, .. fierent ~e *Flor. Hist.* III 108 (cf. ib. app. 303 s. v. deafforestatio). **b** cithara .. melodiam acutissima simul ac ~issima modulatione personuit OSB. *V. Dunst.* 10; oratio .. est vox composita ex dictionibus, que est ~a quia dictiones ~e sunt, et dictiones componuntur ex sillabis ~is, et sillaba ex litteris BACON III 155; in sono est multiplex motus: unus continuus, a continuitate parcium motarum et movencium sibi continuas; alter motus ~us, a numero redicionum parcium violencia motarum et expulsarum a sua naturali continuitate ad ipsam *Ps.*-GROS. *Gram.* 26; summa .. super musicam continuam et ~am HAUBOYS 403 *tit.* **c** BART. ANGL. XIX 123 (v. continere 3e); [astrologia speculativa] speculatur quantitates omnium que sunt in celestibus et omnia que ad quantitatem reducuntur, tam ~am quam continuam quantitatem BACON *Maj.* I 109; KILWARDBY *OS* 207 (v. continuus 3). **d** universalia et res dicuntur esse et plerumque simpliciter esse; sed non ob hoc aut moles corporum aut subtilitas spirituum aut singularium ~a essentia in eis attendenda est J. SAL. *Met.* 879A (cf. ib. 884B: quantumlibet conformia sint opera Dei, omnia singularia sunt vicissimque ~a); [suppositio] est .. quedam ~a, que fit per terminum ~um, ut 'Socrates currit' (SHIRWOOD) *GLA* III 18 (cf. communis 2c); terminus ~us est triplex. unus qui significat unam solam rem, ita quod sue significacioni repugnat significare quamlibet diversarum rerum sine nova imposicione vel demonstracione. alio modo dicitur terminus ~us qui supponit vel significat quamlibet diversarum rerum quibus illa res singularis est eadem, verbi gracia 'hec essencia divina'. tercio modo dicitur terminus ~us ut iste terminus 'Sequana', quia nunc significat aquam que nunc est et postea significabit aquam que postea erit .., tamen iste aque habent vel habuerunt vel habebunt aliquam unionem ad invicem propter continuam successionem (DUNS *Quaest. Anal. Pri.*) *Ib.* 289B. **e** non dicimus spatium et motum .. componi ex continuo et ~o; ergo nec tempus in proposito BACON III 155. **f** hominis persona erat decentissima, ~ae proceritatis, capillis et barba canitie insignis lactea *V. Ed. Conf.* 40 (cf. W. MALM. *GR* II 220); **s1350** ad novum Francie regem Johannem, utique statura magnum et ~um AVESB. 121b.

3 to distinguish (by perceiving or drawing difference), discern, discriminate; **b** (w. *ab*); **c** (absol., incl. use of inf. as sb.); **d** (intr. w. *inter*); **e** (w. indir. qu. or *quod*).

cum .. fletum hominum et risum daemoniorum clare ~ere nequirem BEDE *HE* V 12; cum tam innumerabilia bona sint, quorum diversitatem et sensibus corporeis experimur et ratione mentis ~imus ANSELM (*Mon.* 1) I 14; BALSH. *AD rec. 2* 126 (v. differentia 3); *Itin. Ric.* I 24 (v. complangere b); in prima [cellula cerebri] forma a sensibus apprehensa in phantasia sive ymaginatione recolligitur; deinde ad mediam transmissa ~itur; tandem post judicium rationis ad ventriculum puppis transmittitur et memorie commendatur BART. ANGL. V 3; formas .. in materia .. intellectus ~it KILWARDBY *OS* 201. **b** Ambrosius, ~ens sacramentum Christianorum a sacramento Judeorum, .. ait .. LANFR. *Corp. & Sang.* 430D; non est aliud esse rationalem quam posse ~ere .. verum a non vero .., magis bonum a minus bono ANSELM (*Mon.* 68) I 78; W. NEWB. *HA* I 3 (v. cervicida); GIR. *TH* I 17 (v. differentia 1a); GILB. II 76 (v. discretio 2a); dicit illam stellam †dissertam ab aliis fuisse in splendore ita .. quod lux diei lucem ejus non impediret *Eul. Hist.* I 72. **c** **c597** sancti mysterii gratia .. viventibus atque ~entibus cum magna discretione providenda est (*Lit. Papae*) BEDE *HE* I 27 p. 54; vivit et vegetatur animal, sentit et movetur, ~it et intelligit ALF. ANGL. *Cor* 1. 2; homo .. in se totius mundi representat imaginem, habens esse cum lapidibus, vivere cum arboribus, sentire cum animalibus, ~ere cum angelis GERV. TILB. I 1. **d** sufficienter inter duas veritates orationis discrevisti ANSELM (*Ver.* 2) I 179; ADEL. *QN* 13 (v. discretivus 2); quantum ad secundum actum, qui est ~ere inter delectabile et tristabile, est gustus de bene esse BACON XI 186. **e** si .. intellectus non posset ~ere que materia habet simul, esset mendacium KILWARDBY *OS* 200; mortis .. lima / .. / .. / quem obtruncet non discernit WALT. WIMB. *Van.* 138; WYCL. *Ver.* I 368 (v. conjugare 1b).

4 (p. ppl. *discretus s. act.*; *cf.* 1 *discretio* 5), possessing discernment or discretion, discerning, discreet, prudent: **a** (of quality or act); **b** (of person); **c** (as qualification for office). **d** (as sb. m.) provincial official in Franciscan order.

a †**c625** qua mentis deceptione eos deos .. colentes sequimini judicio ~o repperire non possumus (*Lit. Papae*) BEDE *HE* II 8; **788** (12c) in ~o Dei judicio *Ch. Roff.* 12; invento utili et ~o consilio ASSER *Alf.* 104; **c1074** de magnitudinis vestrae .. circa omne hominum genus ~issima aequitate LANFR. *Ep.* 38 (10); quatinus [aurifex] aptam formam ex lammina formet, nunc eam suo instrumento leniter premit et percutit, nunc ~o levamine lenius levat et format EADMER *V. Anselmi* I 22. **b** erat rex ille in exequendis judiciis, sicut in ceteris aliis omnibus rebus, ~issimus indagator ASSER *Alf.* 106; ~us, i. modestus, *gesceadwis GlH* D 655; **1044** (12c) rex regum .. suae creationis ~issimus dispositor *CD* 775; erat .. in loquendo ~us EADMER *V. Osw.* 5; virum ~um .. seque suosque tam magnis .. exponere periculis non debere GIR. *RG* I 5; ita quod infra breve tempus, tum librorum inspectione, tum causarum exercitio, judex ~us haberetur BRAKELOND 129v.; **1265** quoniam Midensis ecclesia ~os consuevit habere prelatos, visitacio omnium ecclesiarum parochialium dicte dyocesis relinquetur .. discrecioni episcopi *Reg. S. Thom. Dublin* 81; in ambiguis .. causis decidendis .. decretissimus legislator J. LOND. *Commend. Ed. I* 6; ~orum interest predicare, simplicium vero per auditum sacri eloquii .. se cibare R. BURY *Phil.* 6. 95; **s1355** ad locum .. per ~os in armis .. milites .. eligendum AVESB. 126b. **c** **1203** vic. apponat sex legales homines de villa S. Botulfi qui ~i sint et qui rei veritatem sciant *CurR* II 222 (cf. ib. 265*n.* 3); **c1215** (v. custodia 4d); **1293** assumptis tecum uno vel duobus de discrescioribus universitatis (*CoramR*) *MunCOx* 292; **1346** mandamus quod aliquem ~um hominem .. ad sumptus et expensas .. tam pro prisonibus .. quam pro ductoribus eorundem .. solvend' .. deputetis *RScot* 676a; **1401** legavit .. tenementa sua .. per rectorem .. et tres ~issimos parochianos .. ad disponend' pecuniam .. in .. usibus pietatis *FormA* 406; **1549** ut hujusmodi elemosinarum dispensatio viris fidelibus et ~is ac honestis committatur *Conc. Scot.* II 114. **d** **1451** ego, talis vicarius vel custos seu ~us talis vel talis provincie (*Abbr. Stat.*) *Mon. Francisc.* II 107 (cf. ib.: in eleccione vocem habeant vicarii provinciales et custodes, ubi habentur, et ~i ~orum).

5 (infl. by *decernere*) to decide; **b** (w. acc. & inf. or compl.); **c** (w. indir. qu.).

a690 aequa veritatis censura trutinante ~am ALDH. *Ep.* 5; ibat ad judicium, praetor quod maximus omni / egredienti animae discernit sedibus altis ÆTHELWULF *Abb.* 338; quid nunc tibi placet? quid vis? quid ~is? AILR. *Ed. Conf.* 781B. **b** quicquid discreveris faciendum BACON V 57; **s896** Stephanus papa Formosum papam defunctum persequebatur inique, omnes ordinaciones ejus irritas ~endo OCKHAM *Dial.* 475; **13..** panis (*sic*) extra Lond' factus et in civitate Lond' ad vendendum deportatus ~imus esse adulterinum (*Halimot. Pistorum*) *MGL* I 358; **1431** si contrarium quoquomodo attemptetur, ipsam dispensacionem vigorem ~imus non habere *StatOx* 238. **c** in furia non ~itur quid sit faciendum TREVET *Troades* 23; **s1324** donec rex ~eret quando .. responderet (v. 2 deliberare 3a).

discernibilis [LL], distinguishable.

formam monete .. ~em *RBExch* 992 (v. cuditio).

discerniculum [CL]

1 hair-pin.

~um, ornamentum capitis virginalis ex auro *GlC* D 313.

2 distinction.

hunc pedem [sc. coriambum] quibus divisionum speciebus partimur? aequis temporum ~is ut antespastum ALDH. *PR* 130.

discerpere [CL], to tear to pieces, mangle; **b** (absol.). **c** (fig.) to rack, torment.

sicut agni a lanionibus, ita deflendi cives ab inimicis ~untur GILDAS *EB* 19 (= G. MON. VI 3: plebs .. decerpitur [v. l. discerpitur]); quamvis squamigeros discerpam dira colobros ALDH. *Aen.* 31 (*Ciconia*) 4; se ipsum crudeli vesania decerpit FELIX *Guthl.* 41; **935** (12c) si quis .. hoc nostrum decretum mutare satagerit (*sic*), terribile spectaculum inter rabidis rictibus (*sic*) crudeliter ~atur *CS* 707; ~it, i. devorat, carpit, lacerat, *toslit, ploccap*, discernit *GlH* D 567; **s1067** (v. discorporare a); pedibus discerptus equorum NIG. *Poems* 420; **12..** avem .. dicerpserunt (v. bernaca); **s1254** vestes et capillos ~ere M. PAR. *Maj.* V 471; dum lupos cerneres oves decerp[s]isse *Latin Stories* 157. **b** mox vulnerum hiatus vel carnis frustratim (*sic*) morsus ~sisse videres R. COLD. *Cuthb.* 48. **c** puer subitis doloribus ~tus exspiravit W. CANT. *Mir. Thom.* VI 90; qui nondum senciunt carnis incendia, / quos nondum Veneris discerpit lamia WALT. WIMB. *Palpo* 166; **s1255** (v. 2 dissecare 1d).

discerpsio v. disceptio.

†discerptare, *f. l.*

†discerptantibus [? l. disceptantibus] *Hist. Meriadoci* 358 (v. discerptio b).

discerptim [LL], separately.

~im, carptim, minutim OSB. GLOUC. *Deriv.* 172.

discerptio [LL], tearing to pieces, laceration; **b** (fig).

inaudita membrorum ~one lacerati GILDAS *EB* 11; interemerunt .. Nigellum .. horrenda membrorum omnium ~one BEDE *HE* V 10. **b** inter eos causarum discerpsiones et controversiarum oriuntur litigia. at, ubi †discerptantibus [? l. disceptantibus] finis esse non potuit, res parum suorum procerum .. committitur *Hist. Meriadoci* 358.

discerptorius, rending, lacerative.

quicquid .. digitis corripere prevaluit, .. unguibus †disceptoriis dilaniare .. consuevit R. COLD. *Godr.* 587.

discertatio v. decertatio.

discessio [CL], departure. **b** falling away (*cf.* 2 *Thess.* ii 3). **c** decease; *v. et. decessio* 2.

c1098 partim fuimus tristes, partim laeti, de ~one vestra (*Lit. M. Episc. Waterf.*) *Ep. Anselmi* (207) IV 101. **b** excidium, eversio, .. vel ~o *GlC* E 526; **s1253** consilium dederunt .. pape ut omnia hec .. sub dissimulatione transire permitteret .., maxime propter hoc quia scitur quod quandoque ~o est ventura M. PAR. *Maj.* V 393. **c** **941** (12c) quatenus .. vite post sue disscessionem ab hujus caducitate mundi donum ipsius firmiter .. permaneat *CS* 941; jam illi [virgini] formidatur quod Christianorum est egressurae animae †discussio [? l. discessio] GOSC. *Mir. Iv.* lxii.

1 discessus v. descensus 5.

2 discessus [CL], departure. *V. et. decessus* 1. **b** decease. *V. et. decessus* 2a.

601 post ~um congregationis nostrae, quae tecum est (*Lit. Papae*) BEDE *HE* I 30; **s1138** rex inde ~um egit J. WORC. 51; **1166** erat nobis solacio quod post ~um vestrum .. fama divulgante pervenit vos .. paupertatis onus cum modestia sustinere (*Lit. Cleri ad T. Archiep.*) *Ep. G. Foliot* 167; **1168** in ~u exercitus de Ruelent [*Rhuddlan, Wales*] *Pipe* 199; multas .. sacerdoti .. in ~u gratias referebat GIR. *TH* II 19; hoc .. donarium .. contulit in suo ~u [ME: *in his departunge*] suis discipulis *AncrR* 92. **b** **c1268** post ~um .. Helene *Starrs* I 52; **1353** racionabilem partem .. terrarum .. et redditum qui predicte M. hereditarie acciderint post ~um Hamonis *Reg. Rough* 40; **1421** tenementa .. que habuimus post ~um Simonis *FormA* 206.

discgregatio v. disgregatio.

dischargia, ~ium [AN *discharge*, OF *descharge*], discharge (of debt).

1514 exoneracionem vel aliquam ~iam campsorum thesauri nostri (*DipDocE* 758) *Foed.* XIII 461a (cf. ib. 462b: non obstante .. quod littere exoneracionis et ~ii non fuerint levate).

dischargiare [AN *dischargier*, OF *deschargier* < discarcare], to discharge, unload: **a** (ship or boat); **b** (goods). *V. et. decarcare, discarcare* 1, 2.

a **1245** in j batello locando ad lanam, vj d.; in eodem discharg[iando], iij d. *Pipe Wint.* 159287 r. 9; **c1300** quod nulla navis discargiata sit de aliqua mercandisa quousque fuerit custumata (*Dublin Chain Bk.*) *Doc. Ir.* 233; **1317** discharkyand' [*two barges*] *Fabr. Exon.* 83. **b** si .. summa illa non fuerit discargiata de equo vel de carecta, celerarius vel emtores sui summam integram ement BRAKELOND 150; **c1300** quod nullus mercator Cestrie vendat sal in navi, sed discargetur et hospitetur priusque vendatur (*Dublin Chain Bk.*) *Doc. Ir.* 235.

discibilis [LL], learnable, easy to learn.

duo .. sunt sensus ~es, sc. visus et auditus R. ORFORD *Sciendum* 182; unde stat quod una credulitas ~is sit sciencia et alia credulitas ejusdem intensior sit nonsciencia propter formidinem oppositi WYCL. *Log.* I 179.

discibilitas, learnability.

ex ~ate veritatis, que satis presto est cuilibet indaganti, et ex mocione doctrinali prime veritatis evenit cuicunque quod scrutando invenit veritatem aliquam quam prius ignorans diucius fuerat perscrutatus WYCL. *Log.* II 227.

discibiliter, w. ease of learning.

que nominatim distinguntur ~ius et memorabilius innotescunt quam que non BALSH. *AD rec. 2* 131.

discicio v. discissio. **discidere** v. 2 decidere, dissidere.

discidium [CL]

1 **a** separation, divorce. **b** division, disruption. **c** (eccl.) schism.

a ~ium, i. separatio, divisio *GlH* D 638 (cf. ib. D 737: divortium, i. ~ium, divisio conjugiorum, *hiwgedal*); cum propter fornicationem carnis dissidium Deus permiserit et non propter aliud PULL. *Sent.* 668D. **b** ~ium, i. .. ruina *GlH* D 638; **s1066** quod regni ~ium vere quaedam prognosticaverat cometes HERM. ARCH. 22; qui cunctis preminens mira scientia / predixit Baltasar regni discidia HIL. RONCE. 15. 212. **c** Hildebrandus .. contra H. imperatorem quia ~ium procurabat in ecclesia invehitur CAPGR. *Hen.* 31.

2 dissension, strife. **b** enmity.

s1051 orto inter illum [Godwinum] et regem gravi ~io EADMER *HN* 6; **s1138** hoc dissidium gravissimum .. omni

patrie intulit excidium FL. WORC. *Cont. A* 111; discordia commune inter eos [Walenses] ~ium operante *G. Steph.* I 11; **c1180** in dicidiis et appellacionibus ad nos .. faciendis (*Ch. Ep. Bath*) *Cart. Glast.* I 2 (= *MonA* I 29); **s1232** secutum est in regno Anglorum inter regem et barones miserabile dissidium WEND. III 42; **1318** de contencionibus .. et antiquis desidiis inter vos et fratres Predicatores motis *FormOx* 41; **s1381** ortum est decidium civile rusticorum *Chr. Kirkstall* 124; **1422** post .. guerrarum .. erumnas et decidia (*TreatyR*) *Foed.* X 168a. **b** me tam irate despexit, angelico vultu mutato in tam intolerabilem horrorem, in tam ineffabile dissidium .. MAP *NC* V 6 f. 67.

3 (?) fall (infl. by 1 *decidere*) or injury.

s1298 [quod], cum rex noster per plateas [de Gaunt] incederet, immensam cathenam ex transverso protensam, sonipede calcaribus exacuato, valido congressu protriverit, tam suum quam equi sui parvipendens ~ium *Chr. S. Edm.* 69.

discifer, dish-bearer, sewer. *V. et. discarius, discophorus.*

discifer ut dudum momenti tempore vates / angelico raptu lustrabat Cheldea regna [cf. *Dan.* xiv 35] ALDH. *VirgV* 1475; **926** (12c) ego Wulfhelm ~fer regis *CS* 659 (cf. ib. 785, 941); ~fer vel discoforus, *discþen* ÆLF. *Gl.*; **9..** ~fer, *discberend WW.*

disciliabulum, (facet.) self-contradictory council.

1164 comes Suessionensis .. omnes articulos Londoniensis, nescio conciliabuli aut ~i dicam, .. seriatim exposuit J. SAL. *Ep.* 134 (136) (= *Becket Mat.* V p. 97).

discinctus v. decingere, discingere, distinguere 1b.

discindere [CL; *conf. w.* 2 decidere]

1 to tear apart, pull down; **b** (fig.). **c** to divide.

factum est ut in passione Domini pontifex Judaeorum sua ipse vestimenta desciderit BEDE *Mark* 281; discissis [v. l. discisis] viculis .. advexit .. congeriem trabium *Id. HE* III 16; **s1163** in die Palmarum orta est .. tempestas valida, que tentorium, quod .. pro .. solemnitate diei erectum est, solo tenus decissum est et dissipatum GERV. CANT. *Chr.* 173; **1229** si .. telas .. descindat (v. 2 decidere 1a). **b 797** ut ecclesiae unitas, quae partim discissa est, .. adunetur ALCUIN *Ep.* 128; animam meam discissam vulneribus daemonum ANSELM (*Or.* 9) III 32; desperationis discissa nube SAMSON *Mir. Edm.* II 3. **c** regnum Judaeae .. Augustus per tetrarchias ~ere curavit BEDE *Luke* 351; *Conc. HS* 542 (v. discissio 1c).

2 to separate (seed) in the act of generation. *Cf.* 2 decidere 3.

et tunc materia eorum que generantur per descisionem non venit in unam rem cum efficiente, quia quod descinditur non est talis rei materia nisi post descisionem, sc. quando est actuale semen KILWARDBY *SP* f. 28rb.

3 (? by conf. w. *dissidere*) to quarrel. *Cf. discissio* 2.

ut vix .. alter alteri assensum .. prebuerit, invicem ~entes OSB. BAWDSEY clxxvii; **1318** corda ~encium .. ad vere caritatis dulcedinem .. revocanda *FormOx* 45.

discinere, to sing descant.

hic succinit, ille ~it; alter supercinit, alter medias quasdam notas dividit et incidit AILR. *Spec. Car.* II 23. 571B; cum canentium et decinentium .. modulationes audieris J. SAL. *Pol.* 402C; videbatur illi chorus multorum concinentium, subcinentium seu etiam ~entium prose alicujus ordinem prosequenter imitari R. COLD. *Cuthb.* 38; melus, qui medullitus subcinit, affectus et opus ipsius est qui interius et subtilius ~it *Ib.* 81.

discingere [CL], to ungird, unbelt; *v. et. decingere*; **b** (w. ref. to *1 Kings* xx 11). **c** to unseal (letter). **d** (p. ppl.) undisciplined.

discinxit se gladio suo BEDE *HE* III 14; **c1100** (v. discalceare 1b); discinctus sub veste et pedetentim incedens transegit W. CANT. *Mir. Thom.* VI 59; non coram domino discinctus eas famulando D. BEC. 1174; BRACTON 356b (v. discalceare 2a); **s1323** discinctus est balteo militari WALS. *HA* I 169 (v. calcar 1d). **b** 'discinctus', qui cingulum nuper deposuit, verbi gratia balneum intraturus BEDE *Kings* 727; accinctus in prelio sed discinctus in triumpho BALD. CANT. *Tract.* 11. 526B. **c** nulla manus cartam discingat, ni tua, praesul ALCUIN *Carm.* 29. 2. 1 (cf. ib. 83. 2. 1); **801** fratri vestro has litteras .. clausa cartula, sicut est, deprecor ut dirigas, quia, si discincta veniat in praesentiam illius, vilescit apud eum *Id. Ep.* 221. **d** vox teneris discincta jocis, mens ardua, fusi / artus Locrensis titulos Ajacis opimant J. EXON. *BT* IV 116.

disciplina [CL]

1 a (branch of) study, science, or art. **b** doctrine.

a Origenes .., qui .. omnes propemodum philosophorum ~as, hoc est arithmeticam, geometricam, musicam, astronomiam, astrologiam, et mechanicam in pubertatis principio perfecte consummavit ALDH. *VirgP* 59; ita ut etiam metricae artis, astronomiae, arithmeticae ecclesiasticae ~am .. suis auditoribus contraderent BEDE *HE* IV 2; **798** quam jocunda est et utilis arithmeticae ~ae cognitio ALCUIN *Ep.* 143; ex his intelligatur sine hujus [artis disserendi] cognitione singularum que secundum philosophiam sunt ~arum notitiam necesse deesse BALSH. *AD* 10; omnis doctrina et omnis ~a sumit ortum a cognitione sensitiva J. BLUND *An.* 2 (cf. ib. 67: medicina una et eadem est ~a sani et egri). **b** [Plato] se ad Pithagore contulit ~am J. SAL. *Pol.* 644D.

2 discipline, tuition, regulation (esp. moral); **b** (mon.).

tres .. puerulos quos .. sub ~ae paedagogio regulariter instruendos acceperat ALDH. *VirgP* 33; juxta apostolicam ~am BEDE *HE* III 5; quidam clericus .. qui sub ~is ipsius caste Deo vivere proposuit FELIX *Guthl.* 35; nobis ad propositum accedentibus est discentibus utilem quam [? i. e. potius quam] inaudita fastidientibus jocundam aut inexperta horrentibus gratam tradere ~am BALSH. *AD rec.* 2 136; videtur quod ~a spontanea pluris sit quam injuncta NECKAM *NR* II 69; ~a tendit ad hoc ut sit homo perfectus HALES *Qu.* 354; cum congruum sit ante verum ~a et usu *Ps.*-GROS. *Gram.* 34. **b** monasticae conversationis ~a ALDH. *VirgP* 6; curavit locum monasterii .. construere ac regularibus instituere ~is BEDE *HE* III 19; **803** ea regula et observantia ~ae sua monastica jura studeant observare (*Clovesho*) *Conc. HS* 546 (= *CS* 312); **813** (17c) juxta regulam monasterialis ~ae *CS* 342; rudis adhuc in ~is regularibus erat EADMER *V. Osw.* 10; **1300** cum .. in religiosis viris abbate et conventu de D. ~e regularis et perfeccioris ad Dei laudem et proximorum informacionem fervor vigeat caritatis *Reg. Dunferm.* 121.

3 chastisement, correction; **b** (eccl. or mon., sts. w. ref. to scourging); **c** (mon. as part of funeral service).

1341 nos, ad ~am et correccionem hujusmodi nostrorum officialium mentis aciem dirigentes .., quosdam ex eis .. a suis fecimus officiis .. amoveri, alios .. sub tuta custodia detineri (*Lit. Regis*) AD. MUR. *Chr.* 333; **s1401** rex .. scripsit fratri suo .. ut dux Rothsaiensis .. custodie deputaretur, donec virga ~e castigatus seipsum melius cognosceret FORDUN *Cont.* XV 12. **b** si frater .. culpam gravem commiserit .., corporalem ~am acriter patiatur LANFR. *Const.* 164; ceteri fratres .. ~as sumant, si que sumende fuerint *Inst. Sempr.* *lx; ipse sepe ~am secretam, nudato ad flagella dorso, recipiebat W. FITZST. *Thom.* 12; unus pro Christi amore se jejuniis, vigiliis, ~is a pueritia usque in senectutem continue maceravit P. BLOIS *Serm.* 623A; **s1217** [Falcasius] humiliter intravit capitulum et spoliatus tenens virgam disciplinam accepit a quolibet fratre M. PAR. *Min.* II 205; **1233** non fuit eis inflicta [coram decano et officiali] aliqua pena pecuniaria, immo quod ~as haberent in diebus festivis *BNB* II 585; **1238** si .. horis canonicis .. defuerit, pro qualibet hujusmodi .. hora unam ~am a subdecano eodem die in capitulo prostratus recipiet *Reg. Moray* 104; injunctum fuit cuidam ut quotiens rideret in choro vel in mensa tot reciperet ~as ECCLESTON *Adv. Min.* 32; **s1329** quidam R. de H..., qui .. [episcopum] cum cultello percussit, unde nudus et discalciatus processionem antecedens ~am a penitenciario in medio ecclesie accepit *Ann. Paul.* 345; **1526** sub pena regularis ~e domino sacriste infligend' (*Vis. Thame*) *EHR* III 713. **c** absolvitur anima [fratris defuncti] ante generalem ~e satisfactionem et post *Cust. Cant. Abbr.* 253; in capitulo .. abbas .. debet .. pronunciare decessum fratris defuncti et rogare Deum ut dimittat ei sua peccata. .. [postea] sedeat et capiat ~am a priore .. et recipiet vij percussiones. .. postea surgat totus conventus et capiat ~am .. et unusquisque recipiet vij percussiones *Cust. Cant.* 355.

disciplinabilis [LL], amenable to discipline, teachable. **b** concerned w. discipline, disciplinary.

sola animalia audientia sunt ~ia GILB. IV 175v. 2; omnia animalia memoriam juxta auditum habentia ~ia sunt BACON VIII 122 (cf. KILWARDBY *OS* 8); **1344** (v. corrigibilis); veritas que lucet in libris omni se ~i sensui manifestare desiderat R. BURY *Phil.* 1. 23; **c1430** (v. disciplatio). **b** canonici sub rigida et ~i regula ecclesiasticis excubiis .. mancipati *V. Har.* 3 f. 6b; pono itaque *A* Deum, *B* et *C* duo dicta Dei ~ia vel duas res suppositas sub eternis revelationibus GROS. 191.

disciplinabilitas, amenability to discipline.

nulli .. dubium est quin aquatilia sint .. minoris ~atis quam animalia terrestria GROS. *Hexaem.* VI 9; providere debet princeps ut in se et suis militibus sit debita et recta ~as, cohercendo sc. carnis lascivias .., discordias, presumpciones, inobediencias J. WALEYS *Commun.* f. 30v.

disciplinabiliter [LL = *learnedly*], in a disciplined manner, submissively.

inclinate suppliciter ad almas aras et state ~er [AS: *þeawlice*] ÆLF. *Coll.* 103.

disciplinalis [LL]

1 scholarly, technical, concerned w. a science or art. **b** (as sb. n.) title of book.

advertatur .. interrogationum .. genera duo .. internoscenda esse, alterum ~e, alterum electivum; horum tamen apud veteres primum 'percunctatio', secundum .. 'interrogatio' appellabatur, et est harum appellationum prima ~ibus ex equo etiam nunc aptabilis, secunda vero jam utrimque communis BALSH. *AD rec.* 2 127; circa communia communibus .. uti verbis obtinui, ne ~ia rudimenta novitas insueta turbaret *Dial. Scac.* I 8 A; quod si diceret aliquis ~es propositiones non esse veras antequam res essent create, saltem concederet tales habuisse veritatem sine initio: 'diameter ducenda per medium circuli erit omnium maxima' .. GROS. 190; auditu et visu, qui .. sensus ~es nuncupantur FISHACRE *Sent. Prol.* 81; hec mathematica dicitur doctrinalis vel ~is, quia omnes alie scientie per hanc docentur et sine illa non possunt doceri BACON V 3; instructis .. in ~ibus mathematicis satis constat .. WALLINGF. (*Rect.*) I 414. **b 13..** Doctrinale sive ~e magistri H. de S. Victore (*Catal. Librorum*) *Chr. Rams.* app. 357.

2 a orderly, prescribed by discipline (mon.). **b** instituted for the sake of discipline.

a ut labore manuum cottidiano et ~i officiorum administratione .. secundum .. Benedicti rectae constitutionis formam insisteret WILLIB. *Bonif.* 2. **b c1180** ~ia sunt hec et quodam exercitio scholaris militie ad cautelam majoris observantie introducta P. BLOIS *Ep.* 115. 344A.

3 disciplinary, castigatory.

verberibus ~ibus .. dorsum nudum exponebat W. FITZST. *Thom.* 26; talis .. excommunicatio coercio erat quedam ~is H. BOS. *Thom.* IV 17 p. 389; [rex] coram martyris sepultura .. singulis fratrum virge ~is percussiones singulas .. accepit *Id. LM* 1316B; preter virgas ~es quas subelemosinarius providet *Cust. Westm.* 49.

disciplinaliter [LL = *wisely*], **a** in the course of instruction. **b** by the exercise of discipline.

a quoniam disputatio prior est disciplina, prius est disserendum de his que ~er interrogantur quam de his que elective BALSH. *AD rec.* 2 129. **b 941** (15c) misericors Auctor .. alios in superiori gradu constituit .. reges, qui .. subditorum causam displinaliter (*sic*) modo misericorditer procurarent *CS* 769; populum ~er eruditum J. SAL. *Pol.* 611A (v. collutatio b); principem anathematizare non est principi maledicere .., sed principem tanquam ecclesie filium ~er coercere H. BOS. *Thom.* IV 17 p. 389.

disciplinare [LL]

1 to teach. **b** (p. ppl.; also as sb.) educated (person). **c** disciplined, orderly.

to teche, catezizare .., didasculare, ~are, discipulare *CathA.* **b** [Wlstan] inter ~atos viros et litterarum curam .. adolevit W. MALM. *GP* IV 137; **s1130** substituit loco ejus [A. prioris Hagustaldensis] T. archiepiscopus .. camerarium ejusdem loci Robertum Biseth, litteratum et ~atum J. HEX. *HR Cont.* 284; ~ati hominis est certitudinem querere R. BURY *Phil.* 2. 30; in quo differunt ~ati ab indisciplinatis? W. BURLEY *Vit. Phil.* 242; **s1415** archiepiscopus Senonensis, vir verbosus et arrogans, sed parum ~atus WALS. *HA* II 305; Henricus iste, germanus Lodewici [VI] regis Francie, .. monachatur et apud Clarevallem cum bono magistro ~atus discipulus mansit CAPGR. *Hen.* 159. **c** ut .. inconvulsa (*sic*) .. pontificalis haec (*sic*) ~atae institutionis ordo permaneret WILLIB. *Bonif.* 6 p. 30; mansit .. apud inferiorem, ubi conversi morantur, habitationem diebus aliquot, ut .. ex eorum colloquiis et moribus ~atis epularetur AD. EYNS. *Hug.* V 14 p. 166; **s1217** cum ordinem eorum [sc. hostium] ~atum et numerum contemplati fuissent M. PAR. *Min.* II 210; ille [abbas] studuit ~atam domum habere BRAKELOND 132.

2 to chastise, correct; **b** (eccl. or mon., sts. w. ref. to scourging).

c1239 numquid idem paterfamilias injuriatur filio suo, si filium filii ~et .., corrigat, et reformet? GROS. *Ep.* 127 p. 407; **s1334** tamdiu fame et frigore eum .. ~avit ut .. fidem regi D. fecit FORDUN *Cont.* XIII 33; **s1356** voluit .. castigare, †~are [? l. disciplina] militari omnes habitatores ducatus Aquitannie .. rebelles AVESB. 134. **b** optabam sepius confessionem repetere et pluries ~ari AD. EYNS. *Visio* 12; culpe famulorum .. corrigi possunt verbis .. aut verbere gracilis baculi, ita ut ~atus prostratus jaceat vestitus *Cust. Cant.* 125; **1447** nudus circuibit omnia loca mercati ville Huntingdonie .. tempore publici mercati .., decano .. cum virga in manu sua ipsum R. insequente et in locis consuetis ~ante cum virga hujusmodi (*Court Bk. Linc.*) *Eng. Clergy* 217; *scoryn with a balyes*, verbero, .. ~o *PP.*

disciplinaris, a educated. **b** scholarly, educational.

a quod inanimata sit [extima sphera] dicere non vulgarem sed ~em pudeat hominem ADEL. *QN* 76. **b** omne ~e opus non artificis sui verum tamen alienum exspectat judicium *Id. ED* 3 (cf. ib. 33: lectiones .. ~es); *techynge*, doctrina .., informacio, disciplina; [*adj.*] ~is *CathA.*

disciplinariter, in good order: **a** (mil.); **b** (mon.).

a in anteriores nostros balistarii ipsorum [Grecorum] jacula mittere satagebant, sed nec sic acies nostre ~iter coherentes se sustinebant dissipari *Itin. Ric.* II 38. **b 1425** prior .. advertat ad regimen fratrum .., quatenus hii ibidem regulariter ~iterque conversentur (*Ordin. Abbatis*) AMUND. I 217.

disciplinate [LL], w. good discipline (mon.).

magistrum H. suppriorem .., qui .. xiiij annis claustrum ~e rexerat BRAKELOND 158v.

disciplinatio, a (scholastic) discipline, tuition. b (eccl. or mon.) chastisement (sts. w. ref. to scourging). *Cf. indisciplinatio.*

a c1430 domino Lichefeld' episcopo .. sue ~onis discipulus J. de S. Albano abbas *Reg. Whet.* II app. 436; **1437** quod concluderent quis haberet ~onem choristarum infra eorum domum *Stat. Linc.* II 426. **b 1476** admittimus .. personam vestram .. in consorcium nostre fraternacionis .. in vigiliis, jejuniis, in inclinacionibus, prostracionibus, et ~onibus (*Ch. Abbatis S. Alb.*) *FormA* 366 (= *MonA* II 244b); **1509** a curato virgam post eum deferente recipiat ~onem *Reg. Heref.* 111.

disciplinatus [LL], discipline, regulation. **b** tuition. **c** study.

†**1039** (12c) ut nullus .. episcoporum aut aliqua (*sic*) secundi ordinis eorum ~ui adherentium personarum audens .. hujus nostrae constitutionis violare judicium praesumat *CD* 761 p. 63; quandiu aliquid .. de possessis retinent, summi .. magisterii medullitus inherere ~ui nullatenus valent Ad. Scot *OP* 520D; totus mundus, sicut debet militare sub ~u Cristi .. Wycl. *Ver.* II 43. **b** Joseph ab Arimathea B. Philippi apostoli ~ui se tradidit et .. ab ipso .. baptisatus est J. Glast. I 51; rex Oswyus tradidit filiam ~ui Hilde abbatisse Elmh. *Cant.* 187; *techynge*, doctrina .., disciplina .., ~us *CathA*. **c** quia .. ad legum Anglie ~um mihi jam conspicio sufficienter esse suasum Fortescue *LLA* 54.

2 discipleship. *V. et. discipulatus* 2.

talia que in ~um Christi prepediunt, si occasione adjacencie temporalium clericis molestant, tunc sunt temporalia ipsa per manum laicam a clericis subtrahenda Wycl. *Civ. Dom.* I 269.

1 discipula v. decipula a.

2 discipula [CL], pupil, novice (f.).

monasterium .. in quo .. regis filia primo ~a vitae regularis .. extitit Bede *HE* III 24.

discipulare [LL], to teach.

to teche, catezizare, disciplinare, ~are, doctrinare .. *CathA*.

discipularis, belonging to a pupil.

alios sub ~e [v. l. ~i] habitu sollertis [v. l. sollertibus] litterarum studiis inherendo Hugeb. *Will. prol.*

discipulariter, a by virtue of discipleship. **b** like (Christ's) disciples.

a non est color in isto argumento .. [quod] non debemus eos [autores sancte scripture] imitari in logica vel eloquencia. .. habemus enim graciam non solum temporaliter sed ~iter subsequentem Wycl. *Ver.* I 4. **b c1430** contenti stetis in ea vocacione qua vocati estis, nullatenus quis vestrum mitior videatur esse aut superior ~iter contendentes [cf. *Matth.* xx 24–6] *Reg. Whet.* II 462.

discipulatio, (scholastic) discipline, education.

c1430 ad vestre ~onis scolam .. unum de nostris professis fratribus, virum, ut credimus, disciplinabilem et habilem in moribus jam transmittimus *Reg. Whet.* II app. 400.

discipulatus [LL]

1 (collect.) following, company of disciples; **b** (of Christ).

erant magistri sinagogae de ~u legis latoris Bede *Sam.* 682; quicunque .. de ~u ipsius [Dunstani] necem subierant inevitabilem B. *V. Dunst.* 15; cernimus et vatum cum Musis discipulatum R. Cant. *Malch.* IV 338; Pehtelmus .. Aldelmi ~ui interesse meruerat W. Malm. *GP* III 118 p. 257; Wilfridus junior, de clero et ~u [v. l. disciplinatu] B. Johannis *Chr. Pont. Ebor. A* 329; **1400** sic ex istorum ~u electi fuerunt plurimi qui multa loca per Angliam celebria reddiderunt Amund. II app. 301. **b** duo evangelistae ~ui Salvatoris in carne praedicantis .. adhaerebant Bede *Tab.* 403 (cf. id. *Hom.* II 13. 154); Deo fideliter studuit finetenus placere, ut .. cum electo magistro suo .. in electionem ~us Christi permaneret Folc. *V. J. Bev.* 2.

2 discipleship; **b** (of Christ); *v. et. disciplinatus* 2; **c** (as title).

ut et tu de nostro ~u et nos de tuo magisterio gloriemur Anselm (*Or.* 15 *ad S. Benedictum*) III 64; **1231** dixistis .. me virum auctoritate et scientie claritate preditum, cum adhuc ad ~um viri auctentici me sentiam minus idoneum Gros. *Ep.* 4 p. 32. **b 796** aliter [Petrus] in domo Caiaphae pro confessione ~us Christi ancillae respondit [cf. *John* xviii 17] Alcuin *Ep.* 113; merito .. qui ejus pro terra reliquit ~um [cf. *Luke* xiv 33] .. terram quam optavit .. perdidit Ad. Eyns *Hug.* IV 6 p. 31; [apostoli] non reliquerunt omnia quoad dominium quando ad ~um vocati fuerunt Ockham *Pol.* II 742; apostate .. a ~u Christi (Herford) *Ziz.* 303. **c a690** tuum affabilem ~um .. efflagito Aldh. *Ep.* 5 (cf. id. *Ep.* 3).

3 tuition. **b** place for scholar, scholarship.

hujus [Boisil] ~ui Cudberct humiliter subditus et scientiam ab eo scripturarum et bonorum operum sumsit exempla Bede *HE* IV 25 p. 269; ab eis qui illo (*sic*) [sc. Wynnebaldo] in ~u et ministerio subditi fuerant Hugeb. *Wynn.* 10; Atheluuoldus .. Dunstani abbatis .. ~ui se tradidit Ælf. *Æthelwold* 6; ~us, *lareowdom* vel *leornung* *GlH* D 646. **b 1572** ordinamus .. quod de cetero sint .. in collegio de Brasen Nose [Oxon] .. ultra antiquum .. numerum ~uum et discipulorum .. sex ~us seu loca pro discipulis perpetuo duratur' *Pat* 1082 m. 23.

discipulus [CL]

1 pupil.

Aldh. *VirgV* 1264 (v. astus 1b); supersunt de eorum [Theodori et Hadriani] ~is qui Latinam Graecamque linguam aeque ut propriam .. norunt Bede *HE* IV 2; ~us vel mathites, *leorning-cniht* Ælf. *Gl.*; **971** (12c) ego Ætheluuard ~us *CS* 1270; tractatus .. facti sunt per interrogationem et responsionem, et persona interrogantis nomine notatur '~i', respondentis vero nomine 'magistri' Anselm (*Ver. praef.*) I 173; formam / indue discipuli, si meus esse cupis Neckam *DS* V 32; fiunt magistri illorum quorum debent esse ~i [ME: *ancre*] *AncrR* 16; **1408** nec permittant scholares suos sive ~os de fide catholica .. disputare *Educ. Ch.* 394 (= *Conc.* III 317).

2 disciple, follower, adherent; **b** (of Christ, esp. w. ref. to 12 apostles).

quis eorum carissimum ~um .. ut Helisaeus .. multavit? Gildas *EB* 72; discipulus Pauli Aldh. *VirgV* 520; Pauli enim per se, Petri per se, ~i cenabant, dedignantes alterutrum Lanfr. *Comment. Paul.* (*1 Cor.* xi 18) 194; sectam .. Peripatheticam condidit, sic .. dictam quod deambulans disputare consueverat, plurimosque ~os .. vivo adhuc preceptore in suam heresin congregavit J. Sal. *Pol.* 647D; **1178** factus es ~us non Epicuri sed Christi P. Blois *Ep.* 15. 57B; **s1381** Johannes Ball, unus .. de Johannis Wyclyff ~is, .. erat captus *V. Ric. II* 33. **b** audistis .., Domino sciscitante quem se esse putarent ~i, Petrum respondisse "tu es Christus" Gildas *EB* 109; **680** salvator .. ~orum pedes abluens [cf. *John* xiii 16] Aldh. *Ep.* 4; unus qui fertur de septuaginta fuisse / discipulis Domini *Id. CE* 5. 3; evangelista Johannes, ~us specialiter Domino dilectus Bede *HE* III 25 p. 184; omnes xij apostoli et lxxij ~i Christi .. in castitate vixerunt Ælf. *Ep.* 2. 12; gradibus quibus itur ad aram / discipuli Christi signantur Garl. *Myst. Eccl.* 68; **1383** de trono ubi sedebat Jesus cum xij ~is *Ac. Durh.* 435.

discíscere v. desciscere. **discisio** v. 2 decisio.

discissere [*backformed from* discissum, *p. ppl. of* discindere], to tear apart.

navis .. ad quendam sabuli acervum propellitur, ubi tabulati junctura omnis disploditur, asser ab assere ~itur Ciren. I 372 (cf. *Mem. S. Edm.* I 368).

discissio [LL]

1 tearing open, gash. **b** cutting (of cloth). **c** division. **d** separation. *Cf.* 2 *decisio* 1, 2.

Christus plagas virgarum vulnerumque ~ones .. sensit Lanfr. *Ep.* 50 (46). **b a1272** discicionem pannorum (v. extraneus 2a). **c 803** Offa rex .. honorem et unitatem sedis S. Augustini .. dividere et discindere praesumsit; et Æ. archiepiscopus .. ~onem injuste factam archiepiscopalis sedis narravit (*Clovesho*) *Conc. HS* 543 (= *CS* 310). **d** nulla hic recipi [inter Christum et Deum] separatio potest, nulla ~o Alcuin (*Adv. Felicem*) *Dogm.* 180D.

2 dissension.

1121 papa .. precepit quatenus uterque [archiepiscopus] revertatur ad propria et, collectis in unum majoribus natu tam episcopis quam nobilibus Britannie, illorum memoria .. tanta ~o terminetur (*Lit. Archiep. Cant.*) *Conc.* I 401b.

disclamare [AN *disclamer*, OF *desclamer* < declamare]

1 to disclaim, renounce (a right or sim.); **b** (w. inf.). *V. et. declamare* 3.

1309 quo ad exempcionem de terris suis etc. disclam[at] *S. Jers.* XVIII 42; **1321** prior, quoad hoc quod clam[at] habere *thol* et *them* [etc.], clamium suum .. relinquit et omnino ~at *PQW* 461a; pratum nostrum cum ceteris .. calumniatis integre ab eis ~atum recepimus *Croyl.* 77; circa hec [Ed. II] tempora quidam G. S. .. mariscum quendam .. in plena curia .. ~avit Thorne 2027; **1442** decernimus quod .. magister J. faciet omnes illos statum vel terminum habentes .. in .. terris et tenementis in R. .. predicta terras et tenementa .. dicto abbati .. et successoribus suis .. finaliter et sufficienter ~are Amund. II app. 283. **b c1320** major et communitas modo ~ant ponere aliquem in exigenda in hustengo .. nisi auctoritate brevium domini regis (*Eyre*) *Lond. Ed. I & II* II 188.

2 to disclaim, renounce (obligation or sim.), refuse to acknowledge; **b** (w. inf.).

1380 vos dominum A. et curiam vestram ~avimus et dominum nostrum regem acclamavimus *Reg. Moray* 184; **s1397** si quis ~averit homagium regis (*Act. Parl.*) *V. Ric. II* 143 (cf. *RParl* I 351b: *chescun qui .. purpose .. de susrendre son homage liege*); **1484** si contingat predictos J. et R. .. feloniam committere aut dominum ~are *Cart. Glam.* 1728. **b 1424** contra suos dominos erexerunt calcaneum ~averuntque tenere de ipsis quemadmodum tenuerunt patres eorum Amund. I 190; *Entries* 224 (v. deadvocare h).

disclamatio, disclaimer, renunciation: **a** (of right); **b** (of obligation).

a 1442 decernimus quod .. infra j mensem .. post sursumreddicionem, relaxacionem vel ~onem predictam dimittent prefatis personis .. predictas terras Amund. II app. 286. **b** *Entries* 224 (v. deadvocare h).

disclamium, disclaimer, renunciation: **a** (of right); **b** (of obligation).

a 1330 dicit quod predictus T. contra disclam[ium] suum predictum usus est habere mercatum et feriam in manerio suo *PQW* 502b; **1352** eorum ballivus .. dixit quod ipsi nichil .. clamaverunt in tenementis predictis; .. unde eadem Agnes nunc petit judicium si .. contra ~ium suum proprium assisam versus eam .. habere debeant *SelCKB* VI 85. **b 1295** per ~ium .. Rogeri idem R. .. priori omnino est extraneatus *PlRCP* 109 m. 11.

disclaudere [cf. 2 claudĕre], **a** to unlock. **b** to open or leave open (a well). **c** (p. ppl.) unenclosed (of land); *v. et. declausus* a. *Cf. discludere* 2.

a a1195 vidit s[eruram] que potuit manu intus ~i et fores clave firmari *CurR PR* 104. **b** si quis puteum vel cisternam fodiat vel factam ~at (*Leg. Hen.* 90. 3) *GAS* 605 (cf. ib. 35 (*Quad.*); *Exod.* xxi 33–4). **c** rustici curtillum debet esse clausum estate simul et hieme. si disclausum [AS: *untyned*] sit .. (*Quad.*) *Ib.* 107.

disclavare [cf. LL clavare, OF *desclaver*, *descloer*], to unnail (from the cross).

disclavatur a crucis cornibus / corpus sanctum sanctorum manibus J. Howd. *Ph.* 976 (cf. id. *Sal.* 38: ave, videns natum / ligno disclavatum / expallescere).

discludere [CL]

1 to divide. **b** to detach.

disclusum, divisum *GlC* D 335; ~o, *ic todæle* Ælf. *Gl.* **b** nullus valuit .. / a Christi cultu mentes discludere fixas Aldh. *VirgV* 2270; **9..** ~ere, *aweg alucan oððe asceadan WW*.

2 to open. **b** to unwall. **c** (p. ppl.) unenclosed. *V. et. decludere. Cf. disclaudere.*

c1430 quatinus .. possemus nos vestris, cum accesserint, portas alias claudendas ultro ~ere *Reg. Whet.* II app. 401. **b 1328** hospicium meum London' .. adeo per eosdem interius est destructum, disclusum, et per particulas asportatum quod honestius .. tuciusque crederem me in nemoris solitudine pernoctare *Conc.* II 551a. **c 1233** dicit quod semper tempore patris ipsius W. fuit parcus ille disclusus *CurR* XV 568; **1313** quidam maliciose permisit clausum suum esse disclusum [v. l. exclusum], ut sic imparcaret avera vicinorum *Eyre Kent* I 91.

3 to disclose, declare.

non nostrum facinus metro discludere tantum Frith. 188.

discoagulare [cf. CL coagulare, OF *descaillier*], to free from clots, liquefy.

in viscosis humoribus et frigidis conferunt diuretica et inunctiones calide, et danda sunt que ~ant, ut ea que conveniunt lapidi Gilb. VI 275. 1; pro experimento accipiatur pars una psilii .. et ponatur in dolio duorum modiorum .. ita quod coagulet vinum et gutta non exibit; et si post ponatur una quarta .. vini calidi, totum ~abitur et effluet Gad. 14. 1.

discoagulatio, liquefaction.

~o [in epate] Gilb. VI 247v. 1 (v. coagulatio c).

discoforus v. discophorus.

discohaerentia [cf. CL cohaerentia], **a** incongruity, inconsistency. **b** disagreement, dissension.

a si 'equus' dicatur 'patronomicus' .., junctura incompetens est, prepediente quidem rationem intelligendi principali significatione verborum, non aliqua ~ia accidentium J. Sal. *Met.* 842D. **b 1284** ut gravamina ecclesie, que ~ia fratrum aggravat omni die, .. minuantur Peckham *Ep.* 501.

discohaerēre [cf. CL cohaerēre], to be incongruous, inconsistent.

omnes vie sciencie, quibus homo potest comprehendere .. principia ad vias omnium methodorum et scire raciones adductas super eas que racionabiliter adherent rebus disputabilibus et que ~ent ab eis Bradw. *CD* 71E.

discoire [cf. CL coire], to part, move apart.

discoeunt, coeunt, alternant vulnera Garl. *Epith.* III 545.

discol- v. et. dyscol-.

discolor [CL], **a** differently coloured, of changing colour. **b** particoloured, variegated (also fig.). **c** deprived of colour, colourless.

a disc[ol]or, dissimilis *GlC* D 222; ~or, *mislic bleo* Ælf. *Gl.*; Pull. *Sent.* 681A (v. concolor a); quid est quod vultus dubios gero et alterno cursu sanguinis, nunc in ruborem,

nunc ecce in oppositum pallorem, ~or facies immutatur? CHAUNDLER *Apol.* 17b. **b** quid tu .., pardo similis moribus et nequitiis ~or, .. Vortipori? GILDAS *EB* 31; pardus est fera rapax et toto corpore ~or *Lib. Monstr.* II 6; discolor in curvis conversor quadripes antris ALDH. *Aen.* 82 (*Mustela*) 1; ~or, varius, *fah* ÆLF. *Gl.*; discolor ornat eam [plectam] vestis NECKAM *DS* III 437. **c** BART. ANGL. IV 1 (v. discolorativus).

discolorare [LL]

1 to discolour, deprive of colour; *v. et decolorare* a; **b** (p. ppl.). **c** (fig.) to blacken, denigrate; *v. et. decolorare* b. **d** (fig.) to brighten, illuminate.

cadit appetitus et ~atur mulier GAD. 83v. 2 (cf. ib. 80v. 1: quando mulier incipit esse ~ata). **b** queritur [quare] cuminum reddit homines pallidos? .. humores quasi mortificantur, unde cutis ~ata redditur *Quaest. Salern.* P 2; [Gwydo de Warwyke] multum erat debilitatus et ~atus anxietateque minoratus KNIGHTON I 23; **s1485** [rex Ricardus] faciem magis ~atam et mortiferam pre se tulit *Croyl. Cont. C* 574. **c** ubi ex dispensacione sua [sc. papali] ~aretur status universalis ecclesie PAUL. ANGL. *ASP* 1557. **d** ut deinde tercia [hierarchia] opacos homines pulchre ~et faciatque ut aliquatenus divinam pulchritudinem imitantes referant COLET *Cel. Hier.* 184.

2 to depict distinctively.

animal rationale quod cernis, secundum quod in universitate definitionis substantialis intelligitur, homo judicatur; in eo vero quod singularitate descriptionis ~atur, Socrates appellatur ADEL. *ED* 18.

3 (p. ppl.) variegated, mottled.

leporarius .. virgea varietate ~atus GIR. *IK* I 7; [urina] ab humore melancolico apparet in diebus quietis ~ata, in die paroxismi subpallida GILB. I 52v. 1.

discoloratio, discoloration, loss of colour.

cum fiat defectus naturalis caloris in epate, sequitur urine ~o *Quaest. Salern.* B 318; aliqu[ando] .. humores naturales veniunt ad cutem et fit color naturalis, et aliqu[ando] innaturales humores et fit color innaturalis, et aliqu[ando] †ex [? *omit*] penuria etiam provenit humorum et fit ~o GILB. III 169v. 1; sine lesione matricis et corporis et sine ~one GAD. 76. 1.

discolorativus, causing discoloration.

[caliditas] accidentaliter est ~a, quia per caliditatem poros aperientem exalant humores et spiritus evanescunt, ex quorum presentia fiebat coloratio, eorum absentia color discolor generatur, sicut est videre de rosa que ex fumo sulphuris albescit BART. ANGL. IV 1.

discoloritas, difference of colour.

certior habet opinio quod potius ex parentibus naturaliter hec proveniat [nisorum] ~as GIR. *TH* I 12.

discolus v. dyscolus. **discomfitura** v. disconfitura.

discommunicare [cf. CL communicare], to 'discommune', exclude from intercourse.

a1380 ordinatum est .. ne quis scolaris vel laicus serviens .. cum eis [subversoribus pacis etc.] .. emendo vel vendendo .. communicare presumat *StatOx* 181 (cf. ib. 180 *in marg.* [? **14.**]: hic potest commissarius accipere formam †discominicandi impugnantes privilegia etc.).

discomputare [cf. CL computare, OF *desconter*], to discount, deduct (C.I.).

1270 de predictis redditibus prior S. Clementis quolibet anno deducet seu ~abit dicto Ph. .. tres cabotellos frumenti *CartINorm* 140; **c1327** quicquid in his impenderitis .. gratanter .. vobis discumputabimus *Ib.* 109.

disconcordia [cf. CL concordia], disagreement, dissension or (?) *f. l.*

1489 super controversiam et disconcordiam [? l. discordiam] illam *Rec. Leic.* II 327.

disconficere [cf. conficere 6, AN *descomfiter*], to discomfit, defeat.

homo cruce signatus diabolum ~it ALEX. BATH *Mor.* IV 38 p. 134; **1251** soldanus Halapie fuit .. ~tus in capite versus Babyloniam ab eisdem Babylonicis (*Lit. Patriarchae Jerus.*) *Ann. Burton* 296; **s1403** armati inter se acriter confligentes ex parte dicti H. Percy †disconflicti, mediante laudabiliter acie principis, dorsa verterunt *Dieul.* f. 147.

disconfitura [cf. AN *discunfiture*, OF *desconfiture*], discomfiture, defeat.

1202 ante discomfituram de Mirabel *AssizeR Northants* 91; **1223** unde ipse W. fuit seisitus post ~am [v. l. discumfituram] Lincoln' *CurR* XI 808; **1226** post ~am Francorum in mari *Cl* 142b; **s1239** discumfitura facta est in terra Sancta contra Christianos per superbiam militum Francie *Ann. Tewk.* 114; **s1265** in †discumfutura Kelingwrth' contra ipsum dominum regem capti *JustIt* 618 r. 14; duello eventum victorie seu discumfiture non assecuto *Meaux* II 101*n.*; **1276** usque †disconfitam [MS: disconfituram] de Northampton' *Hund.* II 129; **1295** prisones captos in discumfitura facta super Maddok (*MiscR Exch. Rec.*) *EHR* XXXIX 8; **s1298** quia [non] venit ad pacem post desconfecturam apud le Faukyrke *Pri. Cold.* app. xci (cf. ib.: post disconfecturam); **s1332** facta discomfitura de fugacione revertentes, .. ubi fuerat prelium convenerunt *G. Ed. III Bridl.* 107 (cf. ib. 148).

disconflictus v. disconficere.

disconformis [cf. conformis], unconformable.

1363 quidam tam froccis quam cucullis in colore adeo vario variatis ab habitu aliorum quod .. eciam in eodem claustro videntur quasi in professione ~es *Doc. Eng. Black Monks* II 66 (= *G. S. Alb.* II 451); **s1382** quidam canonicus Leycestrie hoc solum eis [sc. canonicis sui ordinis] deesse ad gradum perfeccionis asseruit quod in habitu essent secularibus ~es WALS. *HA* II 57; **1426** plerisque .. cenobiis ideo exempcionis privilegia indulta supponimus ut quiecius in eisdem fratres vivant et non ab aliis .. ~es fiant (*Ordin. Abbatis*) AMUND. I 214.

disconformitas [cf. conformitas], disconformity, disagreement.

lux solaris delectat habentes oculos sanos, oculos infirmos habentes cruciat, nec hoc propter solis varietatem set propter objecti ~atem H. HARTLEPOOL 198; *a debate*, .. discordia, ~as, discrepancia *CathA.*

disconfortare [cf. LL confortare, AN *discunforter*, OF *desconforter*], to discomfort, vex.

1403 ne aliqui ligei nostri pro aliquibus novitatibus sibi .. reportandis se aliqualiter affraient seu ~ent (*Cl*) *Foed.* VIII 314b; **s1428** tempus brumale fuerat siccum, a vigilia Cene Domini valde pluviosum .., plebem communem multum ~ans, formidantes (*sic*) quidem de caristia *Chr. S. Alb.* 22.

disconsulere [cf. CL consulere], to advise against, dissuade.

s1205 rex .., prohibente et ~ente [*corr. from* consulente] sibi Cantuariensi archiepiscopo, .. navium multitudinem .. coadunari fecit M. PAR. *Min.* II 103.

discontiguare [cf. contiguare], to separate, cause to slip.

hastula de manibus statim discontiguatur (*Vers. Fridesw.*) *MS Bodl. Rawl.* C 558 f. 154v.

discontinuare [cf. CL continuare]

1 (phil.) to separate, interrupt, make discontinuous.

ergo rarum habet partes ~atas, set nichil ~at eas nisi pori vacui BACON III 214; queritur utrum ipsum 'nunc' sit in tempore, et videtur quod non: in nullo continuo necessario est aliquid ponere, et est causa discontinuitatis; set tempus est quid continuum, 'nunc' autem dividens est et ita ~ans *Id.* VIII 223; SICCAV. *PN* 99 (v. discontinue); ex quo sequitur †quo [? l. quod] talis quies compatitur secum tempus; ymo sequitur ad esse temporis, nec ~at tempora ad invicem WYCL. *Log.* III 218; *Id. Sim.* 61 (v. continuare 2c).

2 (leg.) to discontinue (proceedings), bring to an end.

s1316 xij processus et amplius in casu predicto perierant et ~abantur *MGL* II 171; *Ib.* 336 (v. continuatio 2); **1331** qualiter .. abbas ~avit retornum brevium *PQW* 16b; **s1437** abbas .. totum hunc suum processum, licet pars adversa pro viribus obstiterit .., ~ari fecit AMUND. II 153; **14..** loquela .. per non-sectam ipsius B. jam est ~ata *Reg. Brev. Orig.* 13; *Praxis* 117 (v. circumducere 3).

discontinuatio [cf. CL continuatio]

1 (phil.) interruption, discontinuity; *v. et. decontinuatio*; **b** (med., *cf. continuitas* 1b).

ut in contiguitate duorum diaphanorum non sit completa radii ~o GROS. 74; dies appellatur uno modo presentia solis in emisperio nostro .. et sic loquendo .. cadit inter duos dies distinctio vel ~o BACON XIII 424; non possunt [tabule plane circulares] ab invicem elevari sub eadem figuratione et equali distantia partium undique, quia tunc sequeretur quod esset ~o nature in partibus universi *Id. Tert.* 166; aqua per ~onem corrupta per recontinuacionem eadem numero generatur BRADW. *CD* 868A; **1359** (v. departire 1c); posito quod *A* et *B* essent discontinuata, visu percipiente ~onem eorum, essent diverse visiones presumpte ad percepcionem ~onis WYCL. *Act.* 15; nec quelibet adquisicio situs est motus, cum stat †aliquod [? l. aliquid] subito adquirere vel deperdere situm per continuacionem vel ~onem partis quantitative, ut patet de augmentato vel diminuto *Id. Log.* III 27. **b** cum dolor sensus sit rei nocive contingens ex partium ~one, res inferens dolorem membro maxime ledit tactum BART. ANGL. III 21.

2 (leg.): **a** interruption or (?) discontinuance (of proceedings). **b** breach of succession.

a 1385 talem processum .. qualem fecissetis si dies in dictis brevibus contenti absque ~one aut dilacione tenerentur *CoramR* 497 r. 36. **b 1436** si Alienora .. aliqua alienacionem, feoffamentum seu ~onem de predicto manerio .. fecerit in feodo simplici, feodo talliato vel termino vite *Cl* 287 m. 24*d.*; **14..** si aliqua persona de .. terris .. expulsa sit .. vel aliquod feoffamentum vel ~o inde post talem ingressum pro jure possessoris defraudando .. fiat *Reg. Brev. Orig.* 289 (cf. *StRealm* II 244 [**1429**]: *diverses douns, feoffementz et discontinuances*).

discontinuativus, interruptive.

universaliter .. oppilationi [epatis] debetur aperitivum. sed tale .. est extenuativum multitudinis aut subtiliativum et resolutivum grossitudinis aut incisivum, adherentium partium ~um et separativum ab adjuncto et rarefaciens GILB. VI 237v. 2.

discontinue, discontinuously, w. breaks.

discretio .. magnitudinis non discontinuat eam [sc. oracionem], partes autem oracionis distincte et ~e proferuntur SICCAV. *PN* 99.

discontinuitas, discontinuity.

medium inter plenam continuitatem et completam ~atem non potest esse nisi punctus unius contingens duas partes non directe sed angulariter GROS. 74; BACON VIII 223 (v. discontinuare 1); fatigatio vel ~as operationis potest dupliciter causari *Id.* XI 203; videtur quod .. illud non probet ~atem in motu recto *Id.* XIII 423; *Id. Maj.* II 516 (v. discontinuus a).

discontinuus, discontinuous, interrupted; **b** (as sb. n.).

talis motus ~us est et non unus, eo quod quies intercidit media BACON XIII 424; theologi querunt .. an orbes celestes sint continui vel ~i *Id. Maj.* I 181; sunt species diverse et ~e propter diversitatem et discontinuitatem subjectorum et mediorum *Ib.* II 516; talia successiva tempore ~a secundum partes frequenter †desiniunt [? l. desinunt] et incipiunt sicut continua WYCL. *Log.* III 116; **1455** per unum integrum mensem continuum vel ~um *Reg. Heref.* 28. **b** continuum et ~um [sunt] contraria, set contraria simul non sunt in eodem BACON VIII 223.

disconvenientia [LL], **a** disagreement (between persons), quarrel. **b** (gram.) disagreement. **c** disconformity, incongruity.

a 1217 orta est quedam ~ia inter ipsum G. et Ricardum, ita quod Ricardus appelavit ipsum G. de felonia *BNB* III 322. **b** quia solecismus est tam in discrepancia vocis quam in ~ia parcium et earum accidencium *Ps.*-GROS. *Gram.* 73. **c** tunc nec in hospitiis nec in ecclesiis ~ia notabitur ulla GIR. *JS* 1 p. 144; BART. ANGL. V 7 (v. 2 contristare); morbi .. cum ~ia particularium magis perniciosi et cum convenientia particularium citius terminantur BACON IX app. 190; ~ia particularium est materialis et formalis: in febri flegmatica diurna est ~ia materialis et non formalis; e contrario est de nocturna GAD. 12. 1; **1399** dissenciones propter ~iam conversacionis regularium et secularium .. oriuntur (*Pat*) *MonA* VI 308a.

disconvenire [CL], to disagree, be discordant or unsuitable: **a** (of persons); **b** (of things or abstr.); **c** (pr. ppl. as sb. n.).

a [Paule et Jesu], licet plenitudine miserationis non convenientes, intentione tamen non ~ientes ANSELM (*Or.* 10) III 40; si silueris dum personaliter unito mihi te disjunxeris, 'assimilabor descendentibus in lacum' [*Psalm* xxvii 1] .. ut non ~iam in pena quibus convenerim in culpa PULL. *Sent.* 714A. **b** cum nihil unum possit fieri ex affectu et conceptu, cum simpliciter ~iant et †repugnant [? l. repugnent] BACON XV 95; conveniens aptitudinaliter est quod convenit alicui ex se ..; et tale convenit actualiter omni ei in cujus potestate non est quod ei actualiter aliquid conveniat vel ~iat DUNS *Ord.* II 106; absit regem delectari vel assuesci viciosis et vilibus operibus ~ientibus sue dignitati! MILEMETE *Nob.* 87; **1453** ipsi .. per .. loca suspecta, nostro ordini ~iencia, .. insolenter vagantur et discurrunt *Pri. Cold.* 178. **c** si .. ~iens statim ut percipitur offendit, cur nullus intellectus ab intelligibili infinito naturaliter refugit, sicut a non conveniente .. ? DUNS *Ord.* II 208; **1333** si .. intollerabilia ~iencia sequerentur, sc. quod .. prior cancellariam suam propriam habere .. et monetam facere posset, quod esset absurdum .. *PQW* 74a.

discooperare v. discooperire 4c. **discooperator** v. discoopertor.

discooperire [LL]

1 a to remove (a covering; also fig.). **b** to bare, expose, unveil; *v. et. decooperire.* **c** to uncover ritually. **d** (med.) to lay bare (arrow in wound). **e** to clear of earth. **f** to clear of vegetation or weeds.

a ~to vultus indumento, monstraverunt mihi .. vulnus .. curatum BEDE *HE* IV 17 p. 245; Paulus docuit eos ~ire a parte pedum pallium S. LANGTON *Ruth* 111; ~uit velamen de mortui facie *VSH* (*Declan* 37) II 57. **b 9..** ~iens, *onwreonde WW*; laesus jam dictus brachium ~it timidus HERM. ARCH. 48; palpebre .. superiores non possunt .. conjungi cum inferioribus, unde pars illa quam ipsa cooperiri deberet ~itur *Quaest. Salern.* B 36; si [vir] impudice ~uerit [mulierem] et se super eam posuerit BRACTON 148b; ascendent mensas [in refectorio] et, quando incipitur leccio, ~ient panes *Cust. Cant.* 7; si alius peccet, et si non actu cum [faciem] ~iente, tamen affectu cum illa vel cum alia, [illa], nisi peniteat, pro alterius crimine punietur *AncrR* 14; **13..** rex .. venit ad corpus recubantis et manu propria faciem discooparuit *Chr. Holyrood* 18; **s1370** interfectus est .. cum incaute caput suum ~uisset WALS. *HA* I 312. **c** ad secretarii officium pertinet .. in festivis octavis altare ~ire LANFR. *Const.* 149; ut calix in sacrificando non ~iatur propter .. quasdam ..

incommoditates Anselm (*Sacr.*) II 242; in unam partem trahendo ridellum .. altare ~iet *Cust. Westm.* 54; **1389** nec princeps debet unum altare ~ire ad cooperiendum aliud *Reg. Heref.* 78. **d** Gilb. V 234. 1 (v. barbellatus). **e** **1253** liberate fuerunt Roberto de Turri ad quarriam ~iendam viij li. *Ac. Build. Hen. III* 216; **1289** in .. stanstardo ~iendo et recooperiendo de terra *Ac. Man. Cant.* (*Agney*). **f** **1241** quod permittat constabularium de Notingham .. querere quareram et ~ire terram .., ubi non est vestita quercu, ad operationes ejusdem *Cl* 297; **1282** in gardino fodiendo et pomario ~iendo in yeme *Ib.* (*Merstham*).

2 (p. ppl.) uncovered. **b** bare, unclad, unveiled. **c** (as sb. n.) exposed part of body. **d** (of horse) unbarded. **e** (of bowl) lacking a lid; *cf.* 2 *cooperire* 5e. **f** (as sb. n.) unwooded country. **g** disclosed, displayed to view; **h** (fig.).

quam cito fons .. ~tus relinqueretur Gir. *TH* II 9; fluvium .. Saraceni .. cooperuerant ne videretur, quatenus .. nostri incidentes periclitarentur. sed .. conservavit nos Deus et ex eodem fluvio ~to nostri biberunt *Itin. Ric.* IV 14. **b** feminam que capite ~to incedit infelicem crede J. Sal. *Pol.* 413A; s**1189** [rex] jacebat habens vultum ~tum *G. Hen. II* II 71; Bacon IX 19 (v. 2 cooperire 1a); s**1455** ut tam discinctus in corpore quam ~tus in capite [dux] ad regem accederet *Reg. Whet.* I 162. **c** si plaga in ~to [OF *en descuvert*] faciei fuerit (*Leis Will.*) *GAS* 501 (v. et. 2 cooperire 1c). **d** **1288** inveniendo unum equum ~tum *Cal. CourtR Chester* 111; **1289** quilibet armigerorum et servientum cum equis coopertis cepit per diem xij d. .. et unus armiger cum equo ~to cepit per diem vj d. (*Pipe*) *MinAc W. Wales* I 40; **1297** alii tenentes habeant hobinos et alios equos ~tos *StatIr* I 200; **1300** pro vadiis hobelariorum cum equis ~tis *AcWardr* p. 245. **e** **1466** lego .. Johanni N. .. unam crateram argenteam ~tam *Test. Ebor.* III 157. **f** **1238** quod habeant communem pasturam .. ad omnia animalia sua .. exceptis capris in .. Nova Foresta tam in cooperto quam in ~to *ChartR* 115 m. 24; **1448** communiam pasture .. ad animalia sua .. tam in cooperto quam in ~to *Ib.* 190 m. 35. **g** **1315** cum saphiro .. ~to (v. crampo b); s**1321** per totam Angliam equitarunt cum vexillo domini regis ~to *Ann. Paul.* 293; **1347** armis suis propriis ~tis (*CoramR*) *Collect. Staffs* XIV 71; **1363** armis ~tis armati (*Pat*) *EHR* XXVII 236. **h** unde et novus quidam homo, quem .. pro tempore veteris hominis habitu opertum magis quam oppressum a veteri diximus, ~tus mox totum se exserit H. Bos. *Thom.* III 6.

3 to unroof.

ipsa [aecclesia] vasta est et ita ~ta ut pene corruat *DB* I 65; **1222** domos castri .. de Walingeford', que ~te sunt per ventum et tempestatem *Cl* 527a; **1243** domos .. abbacie de Evesham sustentari .. faciant, ne decidant vel ~iantur *Cl* 186; s**1273** illa magna coquina .. est tota discoperta in summitate sua, ut omnimodus fumus possit exire *Leg. Ant. Lond.* 173; **1307** in grangia ordei ~ta watulanda *Crawley* 253; **1327** domos .. ~uit et mmm tegularum pro x s. vendidit *KRMem* 103 r. 259d.; **1450** in cooperiendo et ~iendo campanile *DocCOx* 326.

4 to discover, disclose, reveal: **a** (fugitive in hiding); **b** (unknown lands); **c** (secret intention or decision); *cf. discuperare.*

a s**1484** dux [Bukynghamie] in .. pauperis tugurio .. ~tus capitur *Croyl. Cont. C* 568. **b** **1496** dedimus .. Johanni Cabotto .. potestatem navigandi .. ad inveniendum, ~iendum et investigandum quascumque insulas, patrias, regiones sive provincias gentilium et infidelium .. que Christianis omnibus ante hec tempora fuerunt incognite (*TreatyR* 176) *Foed.* XII 595; **1501** ad inveniend', recuperand', ~iend' et investigand' insulas, patrias [etc.] *Pat* 587 m. 20 (7). **c** retectum, ~um, *unwrigene GlP* 66; **1218** Simon hoc audivit quod ipse [Willelmus] ~uit consilium suum, venit ad domum Willelmi .. et occidit eum *Eyre Yorks* 378; **1351** unus juratorum .. ~iebat et puplicabat consilium domini regis et veredictum sociorum suorum *Proc. J. P.* 65; **1395** (v. discoopertura 2); s**1455** (v. dissimulatio 1); a**1470** inquiratur si aliquis proprius in aliqua juratura seu inquisicione juratus in curia admirallitatis detexit seu ~uit consilium regis et sociorum suorum *BBAdm* I 221; **1551** quod nullus capitalis plegius hujus lete ~abit (*sic*) consilium nostrum *Leet Norw.* 86.

discoopertio, unroofing.

1273 per ~onem ecclesie (v. corrositas).

discoopertor, spy.

s**1339** capti sunt quidam discooperatores Francorum .. et medio tempore quidam de nostris discooperatoribus capti sunt, inter quos miles quidam de Almanya qui arrayamentum .. Anglorum .. Francis per ordinem retulit Knighton II 12.

discoopertura

1 a laying bare, clearing of earth. **b** unroofing.

a **1415** in ~a ij rodarum ejusdem quarere *Fabr. York* 34. **b** **1315** magna aula .. deteriorata fuit in cumulo et ~a *IMisc* 75/21; **1470** super ~a et nova tectura capelle de B. *Ac. Durh.* 642.

2 disclosure (of secret).

1395 consilium domini regis .. de veredicto .. falso et deceptorie narravit et discooperuit, per quod iidem xj juratores socii sui .. propter ~am et narracionem predictam infra civitatem London' pro timore mortis venire non audent (*Anc. Indict.*) *Pub. Works* II 62.

discophorus [LL < δισκοφόρος], dish-bearer, sewer.

~for[u]m, discum portantem *Gl. Leid.* 16. 6; Ælf. *Gl.* (v. discifer); ~forus, discifer vel *stiweard GlH* D 586; Habacuc, cocti pulmenti ~phorum [cf. *Dan.* xiv 32], non pensatis R. Bury *Phil.* 6. 91; *a dische berer*, ~forus .., *a sewer at the mete*, depositor .., ~forus *CathA.*

discopulare [cf. copulare 1a, AN *descopler*] to uncouple, unleash (hounds, partly fig.); *v. et. decopulare.* **b** to take apart, dismantle.

curraces discopulat inque repertum / venator stimulat voce sonoque canes L. Durh. *Dial.* II 71; ~atis canibus .. hunc [cervum] insequuntur R. Cold. *Godr.* 347; ~atis canibus J. Furness *Kentig.* 36 p. 223; s**1239** [legatus] miserat ad curiam Romanam unum legistarum suorum, quorum magnam catervam retinuit, quasi venator canes venaticos, super electores prelatorum ~andos M. Par. *Maj.* III 531; **1255** in eo [bosco] ~avit duos brachettos de mota sua *SelPlForest* 99; **1293** requisiti si .. predicti leporarii discupulate (*sic*) fuerunt in chacia *Reg. Cant.* 319. **b** **1322** de j springald' .., ij ingeniis veteribus ~atis *MinAc* 1145/21 m. 34; *to departe*, .. dirimere, ~a[re], .. disjungere .. *CathA.*

discoragium [cf. OF vb. *descoragier*], discouragement (C.I.).

1454 inhabitantes [Insularum] .. tanquam alienigenas pertractantes in maximum ~ium et dampnum que unquam eis .. citra .. Conquestum evenerunt *Pat* 479 m. 10.

discordanter, diversely, discordantly.

dyversly, diverse, differenter .., ~er .. *CathA.*

discordantia, a disagreement. **b** (mus.) discord.

a de .. ~ia .. sapientum de colore .. non est mirandum Bacon IX 62; *a discordance*, ~ia, desonancia, discrepancia *CathA.* **b** c**1400** duo libri tonarii vocati sunt valde necessarii pro choro .., quia librorum hujusmodi defectus in tonizacione psalmodie inter psallentes in choro frequenter ~ias disseminant inhonestas (*Vis.*) *Fabr. York* 244 (cf. ib. 245).

discordare [CL]

1 to disagree, differ, be discordant; **b** (of persons or communities); **c** (? mus.). **d** to be at variance w. oneself, inconsistent.

680 illud quam valde a fide catholica discrepat et ab evangelica traditione ~at ..! Aldh. *Ep.* 4; distat, i. .. discrepat, ~at, interest, *tostent GlH* D 677 (cf. ib. 691: dissona, i. ~antia, incongrua, *ungeswega* vel *gehleoþre* vel *ungerade*); Bracton 140b (v. disaccordare); s**1362** dictum est .. quod ordinaciones Clementine et Innocentine ~arunt *Meaux* III 154. **b** provinciae, quae eatenus ab invicem ~abant, in unam sunt pacem .. conpaginatae Bede *HE* III 6; a**1105** (v. concordare 1b); S. Durh. *HR* 51 (v. comprovincialis 1b); [reprobi] discordiam habebunt cum omni creatura et omnis creatura ~abit ab aliis Eadmer *Beat.* 600D; non ~abit a communi opinione Duns *Ord.* III 159; si tota ecclesia .. ab evangelio ~aret, non isti ecclesie sed evangelio esset fides .. adhibenda Ockham *Pol.* III 66. **c** ventum est [in missa] ad illum versum tractus 'scitote .. [*Psalm* cix 3]'; in quibus verbis cum ~aret puer presbiteri, sacerdos concitatiori voce respondit .. 'ipse fecit nos ..' *NLA* (*Narratio*) II 370. **d** nec mirandum est si ab aliis .. dissentire probaris, dum tibi ipsi per vices ~are videris Alcuin (*Adv. Felicem*) *Dogm.* 189A; a seipsis .. verborum conflictu .. ~ant J. Sal. *Pol.* 476B.

2 to set at odds, sow dissension among. **b** (pass.) to be at odds, at variance. **c** (p. ppl.) variable, irregular.

1412 hec .. heresis .. ponit zizania ad catholicos in fide catholica ~andum [? l. ~andos] (*Lit. Univ. Ox.*) *Conc.* III 345b. **b** s**1123** rex mare transiit et ~atus est ei comes de Mellent R. Niger *Chr. II* 179; hic [papa] fecit concordiam inter regem Ethelredum et R. comitem Normannie, qui longo tempore ~ati erant *Eul. Hist.* III 25. **c** cujus passus fiunt ampli et ~ati viam rectam non tenentes significant simplicem .. ac sagacem in malo M. Scot *Phys.* 98.

discordatio, rupture.

ne videretur inter eos personarum accepcio aut universitatis cordium effectualis ~o Wycl. *Civ. Dom.* III 79.

discordator, trouble-maker.

†discolis [l. dyscolus], i. .. ~or, discors, .. *wiþercora*, *ungeþwæra GlH* D 587.

discordia [CL], discord, disagreement, dissension. **b** (mus.) discord.

Aldh. *VirgV* 2627 (v. ciere 1d); ante .. quam .. graviorem cum eis .. cogeretur habere ~iam Bede *HE* V 15; **8..** ~ias, *undwernesse* .., *twirednesse WW*; s**1135** maxima ~ia fuit inter Britones et Francos *Ann. Cambr.* 39; dicitur '~ia maximum peccatum est'; .. dicendum quod uno modo ~ia est major et alio modo superbia Hales *Sent.* II 408; **1261** (v. divadiare 2); dea ~ie pomum aureum in fontem projecit Trevet *Troades* 9. **b** quacumque consona ~ia convenit Adel. *ED* 27; cum ~ia in sono .. faciliter offendat auditum Duns *Ord.* II 208; concordia sequens tollit offensionem ~ie prioris Odington 127.

discorditer [LL], discordantly, without agreement; **b** (mus.).

Anselm II 240 (v. concorditer a); **1339** Ludovicum de Bavaria, ~iter in regem Romanorum electum (*Lit. Papae*) Wals. *HA* I 209; s**1366** vacante sede Cantuar' .., conventus ejusdem loci in priorem illorum dominum W. Wynton' episcopum [et al.] .. ~iter consenserunt J. Reading 190b; **1423** sicut sub Christi capite unum corpus existitis, sic .. providere necesse est ne vestra membra abinvicem ~iter separetis *Reg. Cant.* III 520. **b** [cantor], si aliquos percipiat .. aliter quam decet .., segniter viz. aut ~iter cantare aut psalmodizare, usque ante eos humiliter incedet .., signum eis .. faciens ut .. conveniencius psallant *Cust. Westm.* 26 (cf. *Cust. Cant.* 96).

discoriare [LL], to skin, lay bare; *v. et. decoriare* a; **b** (fig.); *v. et. decoriare* c. **c** to bark; *cf. decorticare* a.

~iat, *hyldeþ GlH* D 591; variole .. flegmatice .. cum prurire incipiunt ~iantur, et emittuntur putredines inde eruginose Gad. 41. 1. **b** **949** (10c) disscoriatis coram Christo Jhesu meritis (Dunst.) *CS* 880. **c** **1357** in vadiis v hominum et j garcionis ~iancium quercus per iij dies mensis Junii *MinAc* (*Essex*) 846/21 (= *MFG*: †discoriarium).

discoronare [cf. coronare 2, OF *descoroner*], to discrown. *V. et. decoronare* a.

s**1399** adierunt regem R. et eum de solio regali deposuerunt, et sic per triduum mansit ~atus (*BL MS Harl.* 3600 f. 232v.) *JRL Bull.* XIV 157.

discorporare [cf. CL corporare], **a** (?) to disembody, kill (based on *f. l.*). **b** to 'discorporate', dissolve (a corporate body).

a s**1067** ut, quos gladius non prostravit, hos ~et horribilis asperitas prerupti montis Wals. *YN* 67 (= W. Jum. VII 39: discerperet). **b** **1550** episcopatum Westm' corpusque suum .. ac nomen episcopi Westm' .. dissolvimus .., corpus ~atum †dissolutum [MS: dissolutumque] declaramus .., et successionem suam .. dissolutam .. declaramus (*Pat*) *Foed.* XV 224a.

discors [CL], discordant, disagreeing; **b** (mus.).

9.. ~des, *ungetwære WW*; quid ibi faciunt illae tres ~des res? Anselm (*Incarn. A*) I 290; sibi ipsi quisquis eorum ~s videri potest Vac. *Mat.* 275. **b** Gir. *TH* III 11 (v. concordia 1c).

discrasia, ~iari v. dyscras-.

discredentia [cf. credentia], disbelief.

ex sinistro intellectu scripture et ex ejus ~ia oriuntur multa mala Wycl. *Ver.* I 156; ~ia, A. *mysbyleve WW.*

discredere [LL]

1 to disbelieve: **a** (w. acc. & inf. or compl.); **b** (w. *quod*); **c** (w. *quin*); **d** (w. dat. of person); **e** (w. dat. of statement); **f** (w. acc. of statement); **g** (absol.). **h** (pr. ppl.) unbelieving, unbeliever. *V. et. decredere.*

a [Joseph] non ~ebat in ea [Maria] prophetiam .. fuisse completam Bede *Hom.* I 5. 32; quorum nomina scribere .. refugio, quia barbarum quiddam stridunt, non quod eos sanctos vel ~am vel diffitear W. Malm. *GP* IV 186; num .. sententiam hanc veram esse ~is? Ad. Scot *OP* 585B; Augustinum .. quandoque dormitasse ~i non debet Gir. *Spec.* II 23. **b** cum Judei dubitarent, imo, quod pejus est, ~erent, quod humanitas .. relaxare facinora posset Pull. *Sent.* 803C; nephas est ~ere quod Verbum Dei .. sic alternat .. verba sua Wycl. *Conf.* 508. **c** quin .. iret comes G. .. nullo modo ~ens, .. curiam ivit G. Crispin *Herl.* 90; non dubitavit quin auderet interrogare quod vellet, nec ~idit quin .. ei responderetur Ad. Scot *Serm.* 304B. **d** nec adhuc eis estimas ~endum, qui me .. tuum vocant proditorem Ailr. *Ed. Conf.* 767A; s**1263** res mane regi refertur; sed ipse ~it narrantibus Rish. 15; posteriores non potuerunt eos [priores] per racionem improbare et noluerunt eis ~ere nisi .. Duns *Ord.* I 64; numquam .. vel raro ~itur doctoribus ab ecclesia approbatis Ockham *Dial.* 844. **e** irrideant .. aut nimium litterati aut parum creduli: illi sillabas captent et cavillent; isti sentenciis derogent et ~ant Ad. Eyns. *Hug.* I 14 p. 43; s**1399** ne forte ~as verbis, audi quid (*sic*) sequitur operibus cum effectu *V. Ric. II* 151. **f** c**1240** hec omnia non ~imus, sed talibus omnimodam fidem adhibemus (*AncC* IV 118) *RL* II 19. **g** ab eis qui Christianae paci ~endo resisterent Bede *Sam.* 641. **h** *un trewe*, infidelis, infidus qui fide caret, descre[d]ens, hereticus, paganus *CathA.*

2 to discredit.

1563 si aliqua persona .. committeret perjurium .., tunc .. foret ~it[us] et dishabilitat[us] in perpetuum jurari (*sic*) in aliqua curia *Entries* 481b (cf. *StRealm* IV 437).

discredibilis, incredible.

quod quidem verisimile minusque ~e videri potest, quia tam favorabilis hic [Cisterciensis] ordo est apud curiam Romanam GIR. *Spec.* III 12 p. 204.

discrepantia [CL], discrepancy, disparity, lack of correspondence.

volens ~iam ostendere inter manna Judaeorum et sacrificium Christianorum LANFR. *Corp. & Sang.* 419D; cepit scrutari omnia, ut videret an †si [*marked for omission*] revelatio Cadwaladri inscriptis oraculis concordaret. et, cum nullam ~iam reperisset.. G. MON. XII 18; quid.. est proprias oves vocare nominatim nisi singulos subditorum.. per studia suarum occupacionum, per ~ias suarum fortunarum.. distinctius designare AD. MARSH *Ep.* 247 cap. 8 p. 445; *Ps.*-GROS. *Gram.* 73 (v. disconvenientia b); propter ~iam dicencie naturalis ad vitam WYCL. *Dom. Div.* 100 (v. dicentia); ~iam.. ab originalibus.. codicellis ELMH. *Cant.* 237 (v. codicillus 1b).

discrepare [CL]

1 to disagree, differ, be inconsistent; **b** (w. *ab*); **c** (w. dat.).

ALDH. *VirgP* 60 (v. 1 altrinsecus b); illam quoque [editionem].., quoties ~are videbatur, inserui, ut legens quisque simul utrumque conspiciat BEDE *TR pref.*; non ~ante materia GIR. *EH intr.* p. 212; GARL. *PP* 124 (v. commutatio 2c); **1406** unanimiter et concorditer, nemine ~ante (*Instr. Conclavis*) *Chr. S. Alb.* 5. **b** ALDH. *Ep.* 4 (v. discordare 1a); quia [Christus].. mortalibus veritate naturae concordabat, sed ab eisdem impeccantiae virtute ~abat BEDE *Sam.* 613; asstans habet.. naturam convenientem cum natura pugnantis et ~at a natura alterius *Quaest. Salern.* B 209; si vere vita sit tanta fugacitas / in nullo discrepat ab umbra veritas WALT. WIMB. *Sim.* 178; non ~ant ab invicem illa duo dicta secundum veritatem KILWARDBY *OS* 489. **c** quae in subjunctivo modo posuimus huic regulae participiorum ~ant ALDH. *PR* 136.

2 to separate, distinguish, discriminate.

~ent, distant, *tosceadaþ GlH* D 651; **9..** ~antes, *todælende*, .. ~ent, *scandaþ WW*.

discrepatio [LL]

1 disagreement, dissension, dispute.

a**1062** qui in aliqua fraude vel ~one.. istud [donum] frangere aut minuere temptaverit *CS* 1006; nec Cantuariensem ecclesiam in ~onem trahere H. CANTOR 6v.

2 discrimination.

discrimen et periculum significat et ~onem *GlC* D 227; **9..** ~o, *þridung WW*.

discresc-, **~cress-** v. et. discernere, discretio 5a.

discrescere [cf. crescere 2b], to wane. *V. et. decrescere* 1b.

to wayne, ~ere, redundare *CathA*.

†discressivus, *f. l.*

si vis †discressiva [? l. discursiva *or* discretiva] potest ferri super signandum ambiguo, discurrendo utrum possit esse an non, patet quod contingit intelligere ante discrecionem †ut [? l. aut] judicium †tam [*ed.*: tamquam] quod potest esse WYCL. *Ente* 71.

discrete [LL]

1 discretely, separately, distinctively. *Cf. discernere* 2.

ponamus fontem de quo nascatur et fluat rivus, qui postea colligatur in lacum; sitque nomen ejus Nilus. sic itaque ~e dicimus fontem, rivum et lacum ut fontem non dicamus 'rivum' aut 'lacum', nec rivum aut 'fontem' aut 'lacum' [etc.] ANSELM (*Incarn. B* 13) II 31 (cf. ib. 5 p. 18: propria ~e intelliguntur a communibus et communia a discretis); si [cera] ex utrisque, duritia sc. atque mollitie, ~e habens sigillo inprimitur EADMER *V. Anselmi* I 11; proprietates personarum [Trinitatis] vocabula quedam designant ~e, alia confuse: ~e singulas, confuse autem binas vel ternas PULL. *Sent.* 683A.

2 discreetly, w. discrimination or discernment, in moderation. *Cf. discernere* 4.

~e et moderanter illorum [judicum] imperitiam et insipientiam redarguens ASSER *Alf.* 106; O. CANT. *Pref. Frith.* (v. compaginare 1c); sicut.. iste materialis panis ~e sumptus humanam carnem nutrit LANFR. *Corp. & Sang.* 438D; s**1184** respondit archiepiscopus minus ~e quam deberet, dicens: "si ipse homo Dei esse non vult, sit homo diaboli!" *G. Ric. I* 84; GLANV. VII 9 (v. aetas 2a); c**1218** si [sacerdos] invenerit laicum ~e et in forma ecclesie baptizasse.., approbet factum *Conc. Syn.* 69; debet.. paulatim et ~e ejus carnis superbiam dominare BACON *Maj.* I 186; **1423** procurator.. asseverat quod in visitando monasteria.. invenit.. singula ~issime ordinata *Doc. Eng. Black Monks* II 144 (= *Conc.* III 423a).

discretilis, discernible.

nec tamen [indumenta sancti] sue texture genus ~e cuique prebent R. COLD. *Cuthb.* 41.

discretinus v. discretivus 3b.

1 discretio [CL]

1 separation, interval, discontinuity. **b** division, apportionment.

erat inter naves et processiones earum tali ~one indictum nautis spatium quod de uno ordine ad alterum vox tube.. audiri potuit DEVIZES 33 p. 35; per quietem interjacentem duas accessiones talis fit ~o temporum RIC. MED. *Signa* 33; dupplex est ~o: quedam est absque ordine naturali et consequentia, et hec est que causatur ex divisione continui..; alia est que conservat naturalem ordinem et consequentiam, et hec est ratio numeralis BACON VIII 10; cum in omni numero sint duo, sc. ~o partium et unitas congregationis earum *Id. Maj.* I 222 (cf. ib. II 6: sunt.. xx alia sensibilia, sc... continuatio, ~o vel separatio, numerus..); in quolibet continuo invenitur ~o, sed non e converso; omne enim bicubitum est bis monocubitum SICCAV. *PN* 98; DUNS *Metaph.* IV 2 p. 165 (v. disparatio); **1506** primum pulsum [campanarum] pro majori missa intonabit per equales durationes et temporum ~ones *Reg. Aberd.* II 102. **b** s**1191** carta.. de ~one membrorum prebende *Ch. Sal.* 52 *rub.*; c**1430** in ~one operis duplicem.. laboris speciem assumpsistis, unam quidem corpoream, que est de capelle fabrica, alteram vero incorpoream, que restat de scolarium disciplina *Reg. Whet.* II 416.

2 distinction, (indication of) difference; **b** (exegetical). **c** (her.) difference, blazon.

ob differentiam vocum et ~onem sonorum non absurdum arbitror quadrupedum et volucrum.. voces.. dirimere ALDH. *PR* 131; 'fero' verbum ~onis causa per syncopen adjicit I in secunda et tertia persona propter 'ferio' verbum, quod.. 'feris, ferit' facit ALCUIN *Gram.* 884B; materie concreta est forma.., ita tamen ut, sicut ~onis forme, ita privilegium existendi materie relinquatur. quodam enim modo per materiam existit forma, sicut discernitur materia ipsa per formam J. SAL. *Met.* 883B (cf. concrescere 2a); unaqueque ampullarum ~onis titulum super se habeat scriptum, prima 'oleum infirmorum' [etc.] *Offic. Sal.* 103; generatio pilorum necessaria est propter.. sexus ~onem.. ut sexus a sexu discerneretur, unde ad sexus ~onem barbas in viris creavit natura GILB. II 74. 1 (*recte* 76. 1); quid est barba? sexus ~o (*Dictum Secundi*) *Leg. Ant. Lond.* app. 185; sunt tales [declinaciones] 5. hoc autem est ad ~onem parcium et ad confusionem vitandam *Ps.*-GROS. *Gram.* 42. **b** de quadrimoda tabernaculorum ~one et potentia R. COLD. *Cuthb.* 5 *tit.* **c** BAD. AUR. 124 (v. conalis 2); audivi quosdam in ~one predictorum armorum [de campo nigro maculato cum albo] aperte errasse, dicentes quod *il port ermenee* UPTON 116.

3 a differentiation, difference of treatment or conduct. **b** (w. *ultima*) separation of the saved from the damned (*cf. Matth.* xxv 32–3), last judgement. **c** classification, assignment to different groups.

a justa ~onis lance ALDH. *VirgP* 22; per ventilabrum.. ~o justi examinis.. figuratur BEDE *Luke* (iii 17) 356 (cf. cribrum 1d); ut.. patres simul cum conjugibus ac.. liberis.. absque ~one trucidati sint J. SAL. *Pol.* 420D; **1231** sicut in hac vita est nobis ~o operum, sic erit in illa gloria.. ~o dignitatum GROS. *Ep.* 6; s**1321** (v. differentia 2a); sequetur.. quod circumcisionem, ~onem ciborum et alia cerimonialia.. Veteris Legis deberet ecclesia imitari OCKHAM *Pol.* I 49; quod inter apostolos erat ~o potestatis *Id. Dial.* 860; bella carencia racionis judicio.. sine differencia ~onis progressa vasa destruunt racionis R. BURY *Phil.* 7. 101. **b** hi.. tempore ultimae ~onis inanes totius beatitudinis dimittuntur a Domino BEDE *Hom.* I 4. 20; **793** in die ultimae ~onis magno judici rationem reddituri sunt ALCUIN *Ep.* 17. **c** hac tripertita ~onis normula omnis heroici exametri versificatio.. principaliter constat ALDH. *Met.* 9; c**793** hanc duarum partium orationis ~onem.. consideravi ALCUIN *Ep.* 162; [adverbiorum] ordo et ~o sub qualitate [comprehenduntur] *Ps.*-GROS. *Gram.* 58.

4 discrimination, perception of difference.

sensus et sensuum ~o non idem sunt; sensus enim in corpore et circa corpora sunt, ~o vero quarumlibet rerum.. non nisi in anima esse potest ADEL. *QN* 13; Bernardus abbas Clarevallensis.. propter magnam abstinenciam.. ciborum ~onem amiserat, ita.. ut oleum pro vino.. aliquando sumeret HIGD. VII 20 p. 16; tertium [lingue juvamentum] est ~o gustus *Ps.*-RIC. *Anat.* 29; ~o pertinet ad visum, distinctio ad tactum; sed accipiuntur hic per translationem, et accipitur ~o quoad visum spiritualem HALES *Sent.* I 227 (cf. ib. IV 412: ad ~onem mundi et immundi); quod de tua gloria.. credimus, hoc de Filio tuo, hoc de Spiritu Sancto, sine differencia ~onis sentimus *Ord. Sal.* 8.

5 discretion, discernment, prudence, intelligence; **b** (w. *secundum* or equivalent prep.); **c** (w. ref. to age); **d** (personified).

[Gregorius] patefecit.. qua ~one [pastores] singulas.. audientium instruere personas.. debeant BEDE *HE* II 1 p. 76; **796** doctor populi Dei.. debet.. sagacissima ~onis intellegentia pollere ALCUIN *Ep.* 113; ~o, i... *gesceadwisnes GlH* D 653; quam pie ~onis et discrete pietatis in omnes fuerit EADMER *V. Anselmi* I 22; ADEL. *ED* 3 (v. dealbare 1b); o singulare in virtutibus et operibus ~onis officium! H. BOS. *Thom.* II 9; queritur, cum.. animalia quadrupedia naturaliter natent, quare homo qui ~onem habet et discretior est sine arte id facere non valet? *Quaest. Salern.* B 75; **1218** spem certam gerentes de fidelitate et ~one.. camerarii nostri *Pat* 152; **1325** de discressione et zeli fervore.. confidentes *Reg. Heref.* 339; in sale signatur prudens discrecio justi, / ut discretus homo condiat inde suos GOWER *VC* III 201; **1480** de vestris discrescione, circumspeccione et industria.. confidentes *Reg. Whet.* II 219. **b** hoc posse.. inutile illi est.. nisi quod discernit, amet, aut reprobet secundum verae ~onis judicium ANSELM (*Mon.* 68) I 78 (cf. discernere 3b); **1219** relinquimus discretioni vestre hunc ordinem.. observandum.., ut.. secundum ~ones et consciencias vestras.. procedatis *Pat* 186 (v. et. 6 infra); c**1283** habebit.. prepositus de consuetudine j acram de frumento.. per liberacionem et ~onem servientis *Cust. Battle* 66; **1313** ex ~one capitalis justiciarii.. ad omnia placita.. terminand' *PQW* 333a; **1314** ut ipsi super premissis.. juxta ~onem eis a Deo datam arbitrentur (*Pat*) *Collect. Ox.* II 266; **1392** secundum eorum descrescionem *IMisc* 252/12 r. 3; **1457** commissionarii.. deliberent ballivis.. vel aliis.. sufficientibus personis.. per ~ones suas scripta [etc.] *Lit. Cant.* III 228; **1569** ad ipsorum ~onem *Scot. Grey Friars* II 209. **c** BRAKELOND 151v. (v. annus 3); **1220** usque heredes sui pervenerint ad annos ~onis (*AncC* IV 107) *RL* I 95; *Chr. Wallingf.* 29 (v. consepelire b); †**1189** (14c) quia talis [sc. puer tenere etatis] non habet ~onem quod sciat agere vel defendere in aliquo placito *MGL* I 330; BRACTON 86b (v. aetas 2a); furtum.. puerorum ante annos ~onis RIC. ARMAGH *Def. Cur.* 1398 (*recte* 1298). **d** qui gratia ~onis, quae virtutum mater est,.. probabatur inbutus BEDE *HE* III 5; a**800** ~o.., quae inter monachos mater virtutum esse dicitur, Salomone attestante [*Prov.* iv 25] 'palpebrae praecedant gressus tuos', id est, ~o actus tuos ALCUIN *Ep.* 209 (cf. ORD. VIT. XIII 13 p. 30); †a**1253** ~o virtutum omnium parens pariter et regina (*Lit. ad Regem Natalicium*) *Collect. Ox.* I 44.

6 discretion (as title, of addressee, sts. collect.).

precor ~onem vestram ut.. ANSELM (*Ep.* 143) III 289; c**1166** erat.. genus hominum [sc. archidiaconorum].. quibus vestra ~o omnem salutis viam querebatur esse preclusam (*Ad N. Archidiac. Hunt.*) J. SAL. *Ep.* 166 (140); vestram, venerande presul W., prudentissimam deprecor ~onem ut libellum presentem.. diligenti percurratis animadversione T. MON. *Will. prol.* p. 8; **1196** W. Rothomag' archiepiscopus R. decano Lundon': ~oni vestre satis innotuit.. DICETO *YH* II 148; c**1200** universis sancte matris ecclesie fidelibus:.. noverit vestra ~o *Reg. S. Thom. Dublin* 38; **1203** ~oni vestre gratiarum actiones referimus (*Ad Archiep. Burdegal.*) *Pat* 27b; **1219** (v. 5b supra); **1231** volo ~onem vestram non latere.. (*Decano Linc' et Concanonicis*) GROS. *Ep.* 3; **1448** sciat prenobilis vestra ~o.. (*Cancellario Oxon'*) *MunAcOx* 584.

7 decision.

1297 petunt ~onem utrum.. Thomas obiit sesyitus de.. manerio an non *IPM* 79/9; **1309** petit super hoc ~onem majoris et aldermannorum *MGL* I 339.

2 discretio v. indiscretio.

discretive [LL], separately, distinctly, as (consisting of) distinct objects.

cum aliquid videre volueris directe, supercilia stringis, ut collectus non vagetur visus sed percipienda ~e pertingat ADEL. *QN* 12; de quibus [Levitis] etiam ~e subjungit [Dominus], dicens: 'eruntque Levite mei' [*Num.* iii 12] GROS. *Ep.* 72* p. 216; quidquid eadem necessitate representat aliqua qua necessitate continet illa, si representat illa ~e, continet illa ~e... cum ergo essencia divina representet ~e †alia [? l. aliqua], sequitur quod contineat †alia [? l. aliqua] ~e et non unitive W. ALNWICK 404; sic opinans concedit quod nullum infinitum ~e est WYCL. *Ente* 64.

discretivus [LL]

1 a (gram.) separative. **b** distinctive, indicative or constitutive of difference.

a [adverbia] alia ~a, ut 'seorsum', 'secus', 'separatim' ALCUIN *Gram.* 888A; ~a *synd syndrigendlice*: separatim.., secrete.., singillatim sedet ÆLF. *Gram.* 229; pronomen 'ipse' ~um est et exclusivum comparticipis in dictione GROS. *Hexaem.* II 1. **b** nos antiquitus populi decepti dixere semideos aut semideas, pro forma corporis assumpti vel apparitionis nomina ponentes ~a sexus MAP *NC* IV 6 f. 48; de differenciis febrium generalibus et signis ~is febrium putridarum ad alias GILB. I 13v. 1 *rub.*; tempus est hujusmodi [sc. quantitas discreta], quia ibi est ponere 'ipsum nunc', quod est ~um et distinctivum partium temporis BACON VIII 229; quoniam tam corpus quam anima Christi est in triduo vere pars Christi, sed nec qualitativa nec quantitativa, cum non tunc componuntur ad idem, sed est pars ~a WYCL. *Incarn.* 46.

2 discriminative.

canis.., cum utriusque [bestie] odorem occupet, inter easdem discernit... in illa igitur differentia notanda non parva judicii ~i subtilitas est ADEL. *QN* 13; animam vim habere constat ~am PULL. *Sent.* 737B; c**1239** ad caput pertinet de toto residui corporis per virtutem ~am judicium GROS. *Ep.* 127 p. 363; visus est sensus colorum, figurarum, et formarum et proprietatum exteriorum susceptivus et ~us BART. ANGL. III 17; virtus ~a et separativa differunt, ut dicit Aver[roes]... ~a est ista que cognoscit omnes species cibi [etc.] GAD. 31. 1; justicia est virtus animi ~a, inter partes conquerentes recte judicans, unicuique quod suum est discernens et tribuens MILEMETE *Nob.* 104; *Ib.* 43 (v. discurrere 3a); inspiremus ei [sc. homini] sensum racionis, amorem, / vim discretivam, quid

sit et unde venit Gower *VC* VII 516; **c1430** habitum mentis, qui est boni et mali ~us *Reg. Whet.* II 464.

3 a (?) expressive of discretion. **b** discreet, prudent.

a inquiens in fratres .. verba probrosa, non usus ~a sed voce fellita Herm. Arch. 24 (cf. ib.: usus voce corvina). **b** †discretinus, A. *skylful WW*; *wyse*, .. astutus .., disertus, ~us, dolosus, discretus .. *CathA*.

discretor [LL]

1 a distinguisher. **b** discerner (w. ref. to *Heb.* iv 12). **c** decider.

a ~or, i. divisor, *tosceadend GlH* D 650; gallus discretor temporis esse solet Neckam *DS* III 62. **b** verbum gladius est bisacutus .., ~or etiam cogitationum J. Sal. *Pol.* 475A; qui absconditorum cognitor et intentionum est ~or Ad. Scot *TT* 786D (cf. id. *Serm.* 158B: ille †districtor [? l. discretor] cogitationum); qui scrutator est cordium et cognitor atque ~or occultorum Gir. *Invect.* I 13 p. 123. **c** †**948** (12c) (v. 1 constituere 3b).

2 sorter (of wool).

1481 per infidelitatem diversarum personarum misteram sive occupacionem supervisoris sive ~oris lanarum infra villam nostram Cales', vulgariter vocat' *wolpakkers*, .. excercencium *Pat* 548 m. 11.

1 **discretus** v. discernere.

2 discretus, difference, distinction.

de his sermo ad ortum prorumpit quae leviore ~u ab humano genere distant *Lib. Monstr.* I *pref.*

3 **discretus** v. dyscritus. **discribere** v. describere.

discrimen [CL]

1 separation. **b** parting (of hair, crown of head).

~en, separatio *GlC* D 223; **9..** ~ine, *todælednesse WW*; quorundam animalium fumositas licet consolidetur in ungulas, quoniam .. humiditatem subtilem sibi habet admixtam, valet siccitas eam consumendo partis facere discretionem vel ~en *Quaest. Salern.* B 80. **b** in fronte nitent capilli, qui dependent undique circa ~en Garl. *Dict.* 121; ~en .. et frons inungantur olio ro[sato], viol[ato] .. Gilb. II 94v. 1; hoc ~en A. *the sced of the hede*; 'sit tibi discrimen, divisio, glabra, periclum' *WW*.

2 discrimination. **b** difference.

GlC D 227 (v. discrepatio 2). **b** est .. multum ~inis inter elixir et medicinam Ripley 114.

3 test, crisis, hazard. **b** death, martyrdom.

barbari, veluti militibus et magna .. ~ina pro bonis hospitibus subituris Gildas *EB* 23; ira succensus quod se ille .. ~ini dare praesumsisset Bede *HE* I 7; ~en, i. periculum, dampnum, *orleahter GlH* D 594; †**1026** (12c) cum mundi cursus vario incertoque ~ine tendat ad calcem *CD* 763; notus in auro / dux timet et vite discrimina ditia gestans, / cum vellet latuisse, perit J. Exon. *BT* IV 391; **1218** litteras .. istas dupplicavimus propter ~ina viarum *Pat* 181; **c1239** absque anime .. ~ine (v. dioecesanus 1a); cur blando pasceris sirene carmine / quo nemo pascitur sine discrimine? Walt. Wimb. *Palpo* 121; ignota maris querere ~ina *G. Hen. V* 25. **b** militibus Christi mortis discrimina patrans Aldh. *VirgV* 2351; tu, Petronella pia, finis discrimine mensem *Kal. M. A.* I 406.

discriminalis [LL]

1 (w. *vena*) (?) vein on crown of head. **b** (as sb. n. pl.) parting (of hair).

[in obtalmia] precipua est inscissio vene ~is Gilb. III 136v. 2. **b** ungatur caput per ~ia cum sapone camphorato *Ib.* 159. 2.

2 (as sb. n.) hair-pin.

[virgines] ~ia capitum .. ad stipem mancis .. contulerunt Aldh. *VirgP* 52; *Gl. Leid.* 13. 7 (v. discernere 1a); ~e, *uplegen* vel *cæfing GlH* D 595; **9..** ~ia, *heafodfrætennesse* .., *gegirelan WW*; ~ia, *uplegene* vel *feaxpreonas* Ælf. *Gl.*

discriminare [CL]

1 to separate. **b** to part (hair). **c** to cleave, plough (the sea) or (?) to hazard, brave.

~are, i. disjungere, discernere, *tosceadan*, i. dividere *GlH* D 596. **b** capilli a vertice usque ad frontem ~antur Bald. Cant. *Tract.* 8. 483A; in modum dentium instrumenti illius quo crines ~antur, quod et pecten dicitur Neckam *NR* II 40; preloti capitis discriminet ordine crines / pectinis officium Vinsauf *PN* 978. **c** ignotas peregrinationis vias probare volebat .. atque inmanissimas maris ~are decreverat aequoras (*sic*) Hugeb. *Will.* 3.

2 to discriminate, distinguish.

quo pacto longae et breves syllabae .. sagaciter ~entur Aldh. *Met.* 8; virginibus .. / quas, licet inferior sexus discriminet ordo, / non tamen inferior virtutum cardo sequestrat *Id. VirgV* 1301; ~atis, distinctis, variis, *mislicum GlP* 463; si Deus atque caro duo sunt que discriminari / .. non possunt Nig. *Laur.* 38v. 2.

3 to quash (a charge).

crimen discriminat omne Nig. *Mir. BVM* 10. 2.

discriminatim [CL], separately, disconnectedly.

ut quaeque phantasiae et memoriae sese offerunt ~im sine ordine a nobis referuntur André *Hen. VII* 20.

discriminatio [LL], **a** separation (in time), interval. **b** decision.

a s871 (v. applicatus a). **b 1196** per ~onem sentencie [in curia Cristiana] dedit ei duas acras terre *CurR* I 21.

discriminose [LL], dangerously.

1339 in laboribus illis nuper currentibus ad nostre .. salutis occasum consulcius venimus in occursum, ne contra nos forte ~e procederent (*Lit. Regis*) Ad. Mur. *Chr.* 96.

discriminosus [LL], critical, dangerous.

inter tot occupationum urgentias et tam ~a regiminis ecclesiastici negotia Ad. Marsh *Ep.* 6; **1285** longa et ~a viarum spacia *Mon. Hib. & Scot.* 132a; **1339** istis .. ~is temporibus *Lit. Cant.* II 214; talis plenitudo potestatis in summo pontifice .. esset periculosa multis imperfectis [subditis], quibus eciam ad obedienciam perfectissimam obligari ~um esse videtur Ockham *Dial.* I 38; istis ~is immoderati coitus incommodis preattentis Kymer 19; **1437** utinam non ab ista tam varia tamque ~a decertacione superveniant gregi Christi illa tempora periculosa .. juxta presagium Salvatoris [*Matth.* xxiv 21] Bekynton II 41.

1 **discriptio** v. descriptio.

2 discriptio [CL], arrangement, disposition.

~o, adfixio *GlH* D 597.

discritus v. dyscritus.

discruciare [CL], to torment, (p. ppl.) (?) sinner.

tercia causa quare moderni tam modice intendunt legi evangelii est spiritualitas premii intendentis, cujus valor non percipitur a ~iatis intendentibus voluptuose aut infantiliter sensibilibus (Wycl. *Ente*) *Wycl. & Ox.* 164.

discubitus [CL = *taking one's place at table*], dinner-party, group of guests.

diversi convivantium ~us diversos per orbem conventus ecclesiarum .. designant Bede *Luke* (ix 14) 450; facie hilari .. abstinentiam obumbrabat, quo et totum jocundabat ~um et .. abstinentia, propter simul discumbentes civili .. dissimulatione velata, vix etiam notari valuisset H. Bos. *Thom.* III 16 p. 232.

discuc- v. discuss-.

disculcare [cf. CL deculcare], to tread, trample (on). *V. et. decalcare, deculcare.*

omnes [imagines] prorsus aculeis ~atas W. Malm. *Mir. Mariae* 229.

disculciare v. discalceare. **disculus** v. dyscolus d.

discumbere [CL], to take one's place at table, to dine. **b** (pr. ppl. as sb.) dinner guest.

rex .. preparato .. convivio .. omnes .. faciet simul ~ere *Simil. Anselmi* 46; descendit sedeque locata ante regem discubuit *Arthur & Gorlagon* 3; non membrum scalpe discumbens de vice talpe *Doctus dicetur* 26. **b** H. Bos. *Thom.* III 16 (v. discubitus); stante mensa coramque ~entibus Map *NC* III 2 f. 36; facto a rege convivio, dum ~entes gauderent, ipse rex non gaudebat *Latin Stories* 92; **s1388** induerunt se .. talaribus robis .., cenatum se disponentes. ~entibus igitur illis supervenit quidam Scotus Fordun *Cont.* XIV 53.

discumfitura, ~futura v. disconfitura. **discumportans** v. discus 3e. **discumputare** v. discomputare.

discuperare [cf. AN *descuverir* < discooperire], to disclose, reveal.

1352 quod ipse commune consilum .. ville ~avit contra juramentum suum *Lib. Kilken.* 14.

discupulare v. discopulare a.

discurrere [CL]

1 to run (about), roam, stray: **a** (of person); **b** (of animal); **c** (of water); **d** (med.); **e** (astr.). **f** (trans.) to traverse.

a Gildas *EB* 22 (v. 1 comparare 2c); **673** ut nullus clericorum, relinquens proprium episcopum, passim quolibet ~at (*Conc. Hertf.*) Bede *HE* IV 5; ~ere per cuncta .. loca .. pedum incessu vectus .. solebat *Ib.* III 5; peccatum unius [monachi] .. per exteriora negotia ~entis Gir. *Spec.* III 16 p. 236; **c1300** ceroferarii qui ministrant ad majus altare .. intrent chorum et tunc redeant ad officium prestinum (*sic*), nec ~ant invicem vel cum aliis .. confabulando *Vis. Ely* 13; **s1355** (v. dementia a); **1453** (v. disconvenire b). **b** garrula nigriferas noctis discurro per umbras Hwætberht *Aen.* 58 (*Noctua*) 1; Byrht. *V. Osw.* 432 (v. capreola a); absentia freni facit equum ~ere Anselm (*Casus Diab.* 26) I 274; Gir. *Invect.* I 9 (v. 2 catulus 1c); **1294** oves .. vagantes per patriam ~ebant huc et illuc *SelPlMan* 168. **c** fluvius Nilus qui in septem ostia ~ens in mari Turrheno absumitur *Lib. Monstr.* II 21. **d** multi spiritus generantur qui ~entes per nervos et arterias replent eas *Quaest. Salern.* P 126. **e** Janus .. /. ./ lunaticis denis discurrens terque diebus *Kal. M. A.* I 397; videnda est via per quam ~unt [sol et luna], que est in zodiaco circulo Walcher *Drac.* 87; *Ib.* (v. draco 5b). **f** vario discurritur aer / alite Hanv. IV 278 p. 301.

2 to circulate: **a** (of cups at banquet); **b** (of letters); **c** (of money). **d** (of seal) to be current. **e** to fly or flash about.

a s883 consumptis ferculis poculisque ~entibus M. Par. *Maj.* I 416 (= W. Malm. *GP* V 240: procedentibus). **b 1223** iste Bartholomeus [Albigensis 'papa'] in litterarum suarum undique ~entium tenore (*Lit. Episc. Portuensis*) M. Par. *Maj.* III 78 (cf. Coggesh. *Chr.* 121: in literis suis ubique ~entibus). **c s1279** facta est mutatio monete in Anglia .., nec tamen adhuc pristina racionabilis moneta inter novam ~ere prohibetur Fl. Worc. *Cont. C* 222 (= B. Cotton 159). **d s1218** factum est regi H. sigillum autenticum et cepit ~ere in Novembri *Ann. Tewk.* 64. **e** letus se posse cum tanto viro, gladiis ~entibus, prelium commiscere M. Par. *Maj.* I 72 (cf. G. Mon. IV 3); Boece 70v. (v. cyparissias 1).

3 a (log.) to range (discursively). **b** (w. *per*) to range, run through (mus.). **c** to consider in turn. **d** (w. *pro*) to treat for. **e** (trans.) to treat discursively, discuss.

a [logica] docet raciocinari .. per comparacionem ad id quod in rebus invenitur... et hoc facit .. in rebus omnibus per condiciones entis generales .., super quas ~it sua consideracio componens et dividens Kilwardby *OS* 578; intellectus beatorum non ~et, et ita non habebunt scienciam quantum ad istam .. condicionem sciencie Duns *Ord.* I 142 *prol.*; si congnoscitur Deus per creaturam, oportet aliquem conceptum prehabere de Deo ad quem ~itur, quia discursus presupponit aliquem conceptum de termino ad quem est *Ib.* III 67; W. Alnwick *QD* 578 (v. discursivus 2); sapiencia est habitus animi discretivus per quem descurrit universaliter et cognoscitur effectus per suas causas Milemete *Nob.* 43. **b** ponamus notas vel voces que possunt fieri per octavam super vj cordas per quas omnes cantus cantilenarum ~unt Hothby *Contrap. FL* 64. **c** revolvens bibliotecam .. et per singula capitula ~ens, probavi traditum vetustatem Senatus *Ep. Conc.* xlvii; **s1303** prior .. recuperavit contra eum [episcopum] moram de B.. . et in multis aliis, de quibus prolixum esset ~ere per singula Graystanes 26; ~endo per singula jura quibus temporalia possidentur, in multis rebus [viri ecclesiastici] nullum jus habent preter dominium Ockham *Pol.* I 307; ~e per objecciones quas feci *Id. Dial.* 445. **d 1229** ut possent ~ere pro pace vel treuga optinenda (*Lit. Patr. Jerusalem*) M. Par. *Maj.* III 180. **e** rebus universalibus scientificis, quas considerant philosophi qui theses ~unt Kilwardby *Quomodo Deus* 120; cum diversas et adversas asserciones fueris discursurus Ockham *Dial.* 398; **s1408** super hoc potest allegari d[istinccio] xiiij, que hanc materiam ~it *Chr. S. Alb.* 37.

4 (eccl.) to proceed, be conducted. *Cf. currere* 10.

in anniversariis episcoporum Sar' ecclesie totum servitium ~it sicut in duplici festo S. J. Baptiste... quando vero fit servitium pro corpore presente, pro non-canonico, omnes antiphone preter v principales in secunda forma ~unt *Offic. Sal.* 104.

discursanter v. discursim.

discursare [CL], to roam, prowl.

est .. noctis umbra .. data .. ut .. bestiis .. ~andi ubique ac victum quaeritandi copia suppeteret Bede *TR* 7; cum barbarica ubique Dani ~arent petulantia W. Malm. *GP* II 88; ubi clam esset etiam frequenti et ~anti populo *Id. Mir. Mariae* 141.

discursim [LL], in a rush. **b** dispersedly.

~im, discursanter, discursiliter Osb. Glouc. *Deriv.* 181. **b** ~im, adv., i. passim, sparsim *Ib.* 92.

discursio [LL], running. **b** gadding about, bustle. **c** raid.

~o, cursus *GlH* D 701. **b** ne vel ipse vel quispiam ex monastica professione foris vagaretur, inepta rei secularis ~one B. *V. Dunst.* 18; tanta .. et tam confusa .. erat equitum peditumque ~o ut crederes .. eruptionem fieri ab inferno P. Blois *Ep.* 14. 49B. **c** egressus Northguici ad similem ~onem Radulfus de G. invasit Ord. Vit. IV 5 p. 191.

discursitatio, gadding about.

occupantur multi inutiliter ammittendo tempus in numerosa [? l. innumerosa] diversitate ~onum J. Waleys *V. Relig.* f. 223 [recte 224].

discursivus

1 migratory (of fever).

immoderatus calor elementaris ~am [v. l. discrasiva] febrilem [v. l. febrile] inter innumeras febrium varietates teste Avicenna causare videtur *Ps.*-Gros. *Summa* 522.

2 (log.) discursive, inferred by rational discourse.

si cognicio [Dei] habeatur per creaturam, ita quod cognicio ~a incipiat a creatura, quero in quo termino sistitur ista cognicio DUNS *Ord.* III 7; in videndo essenciam divinam et alia in essencia non erunt cogitaciones ~e, discurrendo a cognicione unius ad cognicionem alterius, quia beatus immediate per essenciam divinam intelligit omnia in Verbo, non per discursum W. ALNWICK *QD* 578; qualitercunque Deus cognoscit *A* [sc. possibile non existens] esse cognitum, ab eodem taliter cognoscit *A*; sed intuitive Deus cognoscit *A*. consequencia patet ex forma ~a (KYN.) *Ziz.* 32.

discursor

1 **a** raider. **b** gadabout monk.

a s1098 invenerunt [principes nostri in Antiochia] unum .. tabernaculum .., a cujus medio .. defluebant .. diversoria .. in quibus spatiose possent duo hominum milia considere et illud per aliquod tempus a ~oribus defendere M. PAR. *Min.* I 127. **b** vidimus monachos, et maxime cellullarum priores perque negotia domorum exteriora ~ores, .. [rebus] mundanam pompam redolentibus .. passim abutentes GIR. *Spec.* II 30 p. 98 (cf. ib. III 16 p. 236: quatinus cuilibet ~ori tali sive monacho seu canonico, frater domus ejusdem fidelis et cautus .. comes .. et coadjutor adjungatur); si [succentor] vagus reperiatur aut ~or, ab oracionibus, horis, missis se negligenter absentans *Cust. Westm.* 42.

2 investigator, judge. *Cf. discussor* 1.

~or, i. interpretator, inquisitor, investigator, arbiter, judex *GlH* D 699.

discursorius, inferred by rational discourse, syllogistic.

c1370 duplex est consequencia bona et formalis: una, ut est consequencia syllogistica seu ~ia; secunda, sicut est enthymematica (RIC. FERIBRIG.) *GLA* IV 56 *n.* 206.

discursus [CL]

1 running about, movement, straying: **a** (of persons); **b** (of bees).

a 'pes' sunt dicti tales [amici inemendabiles] propter ministerium ~usque in nostris usibus accommodos BEDE *Mark* (ix 45) 227; GOSC. *Wulfh.* 2 (v. conclamare 1f); hospitalarii liberum ~um habent et tempore hostilitatis et pacis *Cart. Worc.* 256; 1234 ut transitus et ~us secularium presente conventu a claustro arceantur (*Vis. Bury*) *EHR* XXVII 731; angelis .. pictorum licencia pennas fingit, ut eorum ~um celerem significent BART. ANGL. II 18. **b** nulla ex immensa [apum] multitudine fugitivis ~ibus et passivis volatibus per aethera vagatur ALDH. *VirgP* 6.

2 (of fluids) flow, stream. **b** (med.) diffusion, dispersal. **c** (of garment) undulation.

pergo per innumera flexis discursibus arva HWÆTBERHT *Aen.* 34 (*Flumen*) 1; quia liberiorem .. ~um sive fluendo sive refluendo oceanus habet GIR. *TH* II 3; ista dieta ingrossat sanguinem et reddit eum ineptum ad ~um GILB. VII 311. 1. **b** ex repletione fiant [febrientes] vigorosi et intensi, unde cessante ~u spirituum fiunt debiles *Quaest. Salern.* P 126. **c** tunice ~us HANV. II 118 p. 262 (v. castigare 4b).

3 course: **a** (of sun or moon); **b** (of time).

a ob varium lunae ~um, a qua menses computant Hebraei BEDE *Luke* 310; W. DONC. *Aph. Phil.* 3. 37 (v. 1 eclipticus 2). **b** 1321 dignitatis regie sublimitas .. universitatem vestram Oxon' utriusque temporis ~u, belli utique et pacis, .. continens sub quiete plena *FormOx* 68.

4 (log.) rational discourse.

omnis veritas causata in intellectu nostro per aliquid prius naturaliter notum causatur per ~um, quia ~us non requirit successionem temporis .. sed ordinem nature, viz. quod principium ~us sit prius naturaliter notum et ut sic sit causativum alterius extremi ~us DUNS *Ord.* I 143 *prol.*; *Ib.* III 67 (v. discurrere 3a); cecus .. exclamat: "licet visu caream, auditus tamen et ~us in me sunt intensiores" *Latin Stories* 78; consequencia patet per ~um (KYN.) *Ziz.* 80 (cf. discursivus 2).

discus [CL < δίσκος], **~a**

1 discus, quoit.

discus erat lignum, rota parva, volubile signum, / orbe suo mundum similans, lĕve, lēve, rotundum R. CANT. *Malch.* II 150.

2 dish, bowl; **b** (of spec. material); **c** (shaped like ship); **d** fire-pan. **e** vessel (fig.).

in ~o caput occisi protulit [cf. *Mark* vi 28] BEDE *Hom.* II 23. 240; 9.. ~us, *disc WW*; cum Romanus pontifex esset, .. eundem scyphum et ~um sibi et mihi .. faciebat .. esse communem J. SAL. *Met.* 945C; pulmentum comedens, digitos non excute disco. / non tibi sorbenti pulmentum palma reservet / discum, nec lesca panis circumrotet illud D. BEC. 1044–6 (cf. ib. 2549: in mensa disci nimis ampli sive profundi / non apponantur); in primo ferculo sex ova in ~o sibi et filio deferri procuravit GIR. *GE* II 37 p. 350; in coquina sint .. ~us [*gl.*: *quele*], scutella [*gl.*: idem] NECKAM *Ut.* 97; heres .. habebit .. patellam .., ~um, perapsidem .. *Leg. IV Burg.* 116; c1382 nec vult ciphum socii sed proprium portare [v. l. †potare]; / et, ni discus plenus sit, hic vult †minitare [v. l. †murmurare] (*Contra Religiosos* 154) *Mon. Francisc.* I 597 (cf. *Pol. Poems* I 258); instituit .. rex quod per elemosinarium .. quidam ~us v Christi vulnerum .. representativus mense sue .. ante omnia alia fercula poneretur BLAKMAN *Hen. VI* 13. **b** cum .. positus esset in mensa coram eo ~us argenteus regalibus epulis refertus BEDE *HE* III 6 (cf. ALCUIN *SS Ebor* 297: rex .. / argenti .. pensantem plurima discum / pondera cum dapibus statim direxit egenis); †841 (17c) dederunt .. magnum ~um optime ex argento fabricatum in cxx mancusis auri puri *CS* 435; [presbyter] debet habere .. calicem et ~um de incorruptibili materia, id est de auro vel de argento sive stagno vel vitro ÆLF. *Ep.* 2. 141; 1288 una ~a argenti ad elemos[inam] *KRAc* 231/26 m. 12; 1332 j duodenam ~orum de *puetre LTRMem* 105 r. 22; 1374 j duodenum de vetere ~o de stanno (*Invent.*) *Pri. Cold.* app. p. lxxvi; 1390 super officio scutellarie .. pro ij duodenis viij ~orum ligneorum *Ac. H. Derby* 9; 1390 lego .. j duodenam ~orum argenteorum ponderancium xxj lib. xviij s. (*Test. J. Douglas*) *Bannatyne Misc.* II 107; 1423 j ~us de *tyn* pro coclearibus imponendis *Ac. Obed. Abingd.* 94. **c** s1386 quoddam jocale argenteum et deauratum formatum ad modum navis, vocatum ~us elemosinarum, longitudinis trium pedum *Chr. Westm.* 154; 1421 liberavit .. j ~um elimosinar' ad modum navis (*Lib. Mem. Cam.*) *CalExch* II 102; 1427 (v. currere 3a). **d** 1563 portabat ignem in ~o contra ordinem (*CourtR Auburn*) *Yorks Arch. J.* X 73. **e** Guthlaci .. vitam sacrosanctam S. Felicis .. humili ~o in vestri dictaminis auream craterem transferentes (? *Lit. Abbatis*) *Croyl. Cont. A* 108.

3 dish or bowl as measure: **a** of grain or sim. (usu. $\frac{1}{10}$ to $\frac{1}{8}$ bushel); **b** of salt; **c** of ale (unauthorized); **d** of ore (usu. $\frac{1}{9}$ 'load'). **e** (w. *portans*), judge in mining court, 'bar-master'.

a c1182 ad festum S. Martini de *chireset* queque virgata [reddet] x mensuras, que vocatur '~us', de frumento mundo *RB Worc.* 353; 1234 debet triturare .. de avena iij *hops* et debet habere j ~um de eodem blado *Cust. Glast.* 145; 1298 conventus capit de granario abbatis .. singulis diebus vij ~os pisarum, de quibus viij ~i faciunt j esk[eppam] (*White Bk. Peterb.*) *BL MS Cotton Vesp.* E XXII f. 36b; 1334 pro xxvij ~is farine xiij d. ob. *Surv. Denb.* 223; 1352 per servicium xvij ~orum plenorum ordei palmalis, quorum x faciunt bussellum *Reg. S. Aug.* 331; 13.. vij ~i cumulati de †*wouk*' [? l. *wonk*'] faciunt parvam mensuram rasam; que mensura sexies impleta et rasata facit j mensuram cumulatam; que mensura sic mensurata continet j communem ringam de Huntingd' *Cart. Rams.* III 159 (cf. ib. I 487: †*twougkecorne*; v. et. *Eng. Weights* 33); c1375 J. de A. molendinarius non ostendit aliquas mensuras preter j ~um falsum *Ac. Durh.* 328; 1512 J. T. est communis molendinarius ..; in misericordia quia non protulit ~um sue tolonie *CourtR Lygh* II f. 9v. **b** 12.. falcabunt ix opera .. et habebunt vj panes et vj d. et plenum ~um salis (*Temple Cressing, Essex*) *Rec. Templars* 154; c1270 pro carectata salis dabitur j ~us salis, qui continere debet j *tolhop* (*Cust. Gt. Faringdon, Berks*) *OED* s. v. *toll sb.* 1 (3). **c** 1361 vendiderunt cervisiam per ~os et non per mensuras sigillatas *Proc. J. P.* 367; 1372 testatores cervisie dicunt quod .. braciatores vendunt cervisiam per ~os et siphos et non per mensuras legales *DL CourtR* (*Derb*) 44/517; 1375 braciatrix .. vendi[dit] cervisiam suam .. in domo sua .., et hoc per ~os et ciphos, ad voluntatem suam *SessPLincs* 22 (cf. ib. 211: vendiderunt cervisiam suam per ~os non sigillatos per sigillum domini regis nec per sigillum domini de franciplegio .. ville); 1396 sunt communes *tipelers* et vendunt infra domos suas cum ~is et ciphis contra assisam *Rec. Nott.* I 314. **d** 1243 de exitibus manerie plumbi cxlij s., unde recepit tercium decimum ~um; et est summa ladi lx. xviij *MinAc* (*Derb*) 825/16 m. 7; 1278 ~us debet esse tam magni ponderis et tante mensure quod contineat tantam minam quantam unus homo fortis poterit elevare de terra *JustIt* (*Cumb*) 132 r. 34*d.*; 1292 rex debet percipere quemlibet nonum ~um mine quem fodiunt minatores; et sciendum quod ~us debet esse tam magni ponderis [etc., ut supra] *Ib.* 135 r. 26 *d.*; 1288 (v. dominium 6); 1300 idem r. c. de mmccclxix ladis et dim. ~o tam albe quam nigre mine .., lada continente ix ~os *Pipe* 145 (*Devon*); 1301 (v. albus 5c); 1322 pro xiij ~o mine nomine lot' domino regi pertinent' *MinAc* (*Derb*) 1146/11 m. 12; 1406 reddendo .. pro quolibet *loode* de *byngoore* vj s. viij d., quolibet *loode* continente ix ~os, et pro quolibet *loode* de *watreoore* v s. (*Flint*) *Enr. Chester* 78 r. 6; 1451 (v. 1 bolla 2e). **e** 1517 unacum officio ~um portantis (v. delia).

4 (*cf.* It. *desco etc.*): **a** high table or dais; *cf. deisium*, 2 *digitus*. **b** writing table or desk, also used as book-case; **c** (dist. as 'movable' (? revolving) or 'hanging', *i. e.* w. lid suspended by chains; *cf. Arch. Hist. Camb.* III 419). **d** (eccl.) lectern or sim. **e** reckoning-board. **f** tablecloth.

a sedens cum priore .. in ~o principali GIR. *RG* II 5; 1206 qui sederit ad ~um [percipiet] j ciphum ad cibum et alium ad vesperam (*Cust.*) *Chr. Evesham* 218*n.* (cf. ib. 270: [T. abbas, ob. 1236] tintinnabulum in refectorio ad ~um .. cum catena ferrea appendit); abbas alienus ad ~um nostrum nil faciet nisi benedictionem dare ad lectionem et lectionem terminare *Cust. Cant. Abbr.* 253; 1251 descum in eadem aula ligneum de franco plastro fieri facias *Liberate* 28 m. 17 (*Cal.* p. 11); c1300 in .. summo desco, formis et aliis necessariis faciendis in eadem [aula] *MinAc* 863/8 (cf. ib.: in gabulo ultra *le hautdeis*); J. S. [fl. c1303] .. dedit .. ciphum argenteum ad descum in refectorio *MonA* III 326a; s1317 mulier .. equum ascensa .. aulam [Westm'] intravit, mensas .. circuivit, ad descum per gradus ascendit, mense regie appropinquavit TROKELOWE 98; [sacrista inveniet] mattulas in capitulo ad ~um et ad scanna *Cust. Cant.* 107 (cf. ib. 162: viso .. signo consueto a fratre qui stat cum presidente ad ~um); 1426 pro viij ulnis panni viridis de ~o *ExchScot* 405; a1440 ubicunque abbas comederit, ad descum, vel in oriolo vel alibi AMUND. II app. 320. **b** 1294 descam (v. carola 1a); 1305 cum .. in .. aula descos et banca apponi fecerit, proponens per se personaliter ordinarie et per alios baccalaureos cursorie legere in eisdem *Cart. Osney* I 111; 1326 j deskam [pro libris, val' j d.] *Cal. RCoron Lond.* 148; 1336 littera .. est in desca camere plumbate, viz. in pixide ubi sunt testamenta [archiepiscoporum] *Lit. Cant.* II 125; 1339 tenentes vesperias .. habeant coram se et secum in eodem scanno considentibus unam descam vel duas descas in qua vel quibus libros suos reponant, si voluerint *StatOx* 142; c1320 ne quis .. frangat .. descos vel formulas in scolis *FormOx* 169; 1432 magistri regentes facultatis arcium disputantes bachalariis sedendo in cathedra disputent, bachalariis eorumdem ad descam stantibus eis in respondendo *StatOx* 247; 1450 in xvj seris pro descis librarie et ij clavibus *Arch. Hist. Camb.* I 12*n.*; c1470 (v. cristatio); 1472 pro reparacione dixtorum in scola juris canonici *Arch. Ox.* II 305; c1495 in superiori parte primi dextus (*Library List xiii All Souls Oxon*) *Ox. Bibliog. Soc.* 1971 p. 35 (cf. ib.: subtus eodem dextu). **c** 1405 in studio unum descum versatile .. cum alio desco pendente in parvo oratorio (*Test.*) *Chap. Linc. Act Bks.* A 2. 29 f. 20. **d** 1317 bolto ferreo ad descam decani in choro emendendo *Fabr. Exon.* 79; 1325 ad vicarios pertinet: pixis pro conservando corporis Christi ..; item formule in cancello cum deschis *Stat. Ebor.* 131; 1391 in factura duarum descarum in capella *Ac. Durh.* 267; 1400 in emendacione dexti, j d. *Ac. Churchw. Bath* 16; 1416 deski in choro .., ubi saltem capellanus parochialis et clericus parochialis sedere usi sunt, nimis deformes [sunt] et indigent reparacione (*Vis.*) *Fabr. York* 248; 1446 executores .. Johannis H. fecerunt fieri pro anime sue memoriali .. pavimentum chori cum descis inferiorum grad[u]um (*Reg. Peterhouse*) *Arch. Hist. Camb.* I 58*n.*; s1446 super reparatura ~orum et stallorum in cancello ecclesie .. controversia .. est exorta *Croyl. Cont. B* 521; hic ~us, *a leyterne WW*; *a lettron*, ambo, ~us, lectrinum .. *CathA*. **e** *a burde*, abacus, ~us, mensa ..; versus 'rex sedet in disco tendens sua brachia discus;' 'in disco disco discens mea dogmata disco' *Ib.* **f** *a burdecloth*, ~us .., mappa .., mensale .. *Ib.*

discusitus [OF *descousu* < *disconsutus], unstitched.

ad instar sachi ~i M. SCOT *Intr.* f. 114 (v. bussulus).

1 discussio v. discessio c.

2 discussio [LL < CL = *shaking*]

1 threshing out (fig.), investigation, discussion.

nec sine ~one praetereundum est quare Dominus .. noster tertia die resurgere voluit BEDE *Hom.* II 10. 152C; a1087 quatenus .. ea quae ad Christianae religionis notitiam prodesse possunt sine interpellatione vel ~one aliqua a vobis audirent LANFR. *Ep.* 27 (30); dudum in ~onem venerat an mari an terra potius tanta belli moles incederet *Itin. Ric.* I 19; fiet ~o per parentelam servi [se liberum dicentis] productam, tam ex parte domini quam ipsius servi BRACTON 25; 1261 ut tunc de die in diem procedatur in discucione negotii *Cl* 465; s1292 Scoti .. tradiderunt regi E. regnum Scocie .. quousque .. debita ~one habita, de legitimo constaret herede RISH. 128; 1328 residuum debiti pendet .. in ~one inter executores testamenti .. regine .. et vos *Lit. Cant.* I 275; 1416 ~one et examinacione .. super hiis que processum eleccionis .. tangebant habita diligenti *Reg. Cant.* I 32.

2 (leg.) judicial proceedings, trial; **b** (w. ref. to Last Judgement). **c** (w. subj. gen.) inquisition (conducted by). **d** (right of) trial, jurisdiction.

†821 (14c) in cunctis rerum eventibus et discucionibus causarum abbatis .. decreto subiciantur *CalCh* IV 373; mandamus quod ~oni predicte querele coram vobis supersedeatis *State Tri. Ed. I* 77; s1320 apud Turrim .. itinerantes justiciarii .. consederunt, .. in cujus itineris discucione plus viguit iniquitatis quam equitatis *Flor. Hist.* III 195; 14.. quia ~o hujusmodi donacionis .. in curia nostra et non alibi tractari et fieri debet *Reg. Brev. Orig.* 39. **b** jam illi [virgini] formidatur quod Christianorum est egressurae animae ~o GOSC. *Mir. Iv.* lxii; pastoris officium operibus adimplebat .., semper habens pre oculis ~onem futuram pecorum et pastoris SERLO GRAM. *Mon. Font.* 108. **c** s1273 apud Norwycum [inundacio] tante fuit violencie quod nec insulanorum rapine nec regalium ibidem nuper facta ~o eidem vix possent equiparari infortunio OXNEAD *Chr.* 243. **d** †1077 cuncta quae idem monasterium .. obtinebit sint omnino libera .., redditus, servitia debita .., causarum ~ones, emendationes .. *Cart. Rams.* II 97 (= *Regesta* I 95); 1133 causarum .. ~ones habeat et jura causarum de omni placito quod in terra sua evenerit *MonA* VI 296a (= *Regesta* II 1761); s1260 dicens omnes alios barones et comites sibi [domino Edwardo] de jure non esse pares nec suas in eum exercere ~ones *Flor. Hist.* II 448; s1287 abbas de Ramsie .. clamat habere discuciones extra banleucam *MonA* II 572b.

3 affray.

s1292 facta est magna ~o in mari inter Anglos et Normannos, sed Normanni triumphabant *Eul. Hist.* III 157; *Ib.* 234 (v. conflictio).

discussivus, decisive, determinative.

1277 sinistre relacioni fides certa non est adhibenda quousque inde audiatur relacio veri ~a (*Lit. Abbatis*) THORNE 1924.

discussor [LL]

1 investigator, judge. *Cf. discursor* 2.

~or, inquisitor, interpretator OSB. GLOUC. *Deriv.* 181; quod pro manifesto falso a ~oribus asserebatur *Cust. Westm.* 24; cum negaverit [Christus] se esse judicem et ~orem temporalium rerum [? cf. *Luke* xii 14: judicem aut divisorem] OCKHAM *Err. Papae* 969; **1456** utinam tam tui justus censor et ~or quam nunc mei fueris injustus reprehensor BEKYNTON II 161.

2 disperser.

~or Moysaicarum tenebrarum Jesus Christus COLET *Rom. Enarr.* 212.

discutere [CL]

1 a to shake violently, shake out, ransack. **b** to shake apart (fig.), discompose. **c** to shake off, repel. **d** to shake free, release.

a ~iens, .. *swengende GlH* D 698; **a1079** dicit se .. exspoliatum vestesque suas, si quid forte in eis quod tolli posset inveniretur, discussas ANSELM (*Ep.* 55) III 170. **b** †**c1093** resarcire concupivi quod male scissum fuerat et ad unitatem vere caritatis revocare quod diu discussum [? l. discissum] sub discordia manserat *Regesta* I p. 134; si quis a sompno excitetur subito, natura ~itur BART. ANGL. III 24. **c** **a690** limato .. grammatico dente .. rebelles falanges ~it ALDH. *Ep.* 5; agnus qui suae mortis signum frontibus nostris ad ~ienda tela mortiferi hostis inposuit BEDE *Hom.* II 7. 138; discusso torpore concupiscentiae mundalis *Id. Gen.* 181; A. TEWK. *Ep.* 10 (v. deforis 1c). **d** **s1231** regnum Anglie .. de jugo tributi, quo tenebatur, ~ere *Flor. Hist.* II 202; nil juvat .. / .. / .. genus inclitum / cum mors discuciat a limo spiritum WALT. WIMB. *Sim.* 123.

2 to dispel, disperse, dissipate.

~ite .. tenebrosam atramque cordis vestri caliginem teporis GILDAS *EB* 74; arbiter horrendas discussit carceris umbras ALDH. *VirgV* 1949 (cf. ib. 2089: discusso turbine belli); flammas a domo discussit ALCUIN *Vedast.* 424; per aures [fetus leonum] .. motus [parentis rugientis] ingreditur, unde humores ipsi ~iuntur et spiritibus via paratur, et sic vivificantur *Quaest. Salern.* B 58.

3 a to thresh out (fig.), discuss, elucidate. **b** to examine, scrutinize. **c** (w. pers. obj.) to examine (acad.).

a ut librum .. Job, magnis involutum obscuritatibus, mystica interpretatione ~eret BEDE *HE* II 1 p. 75; ne quis, antequam sit idoneus, altissimas quaestiones praesumat ~ere ANSELM (*Incarn. A* 4) I 285; hujusmodi .. dubitabilibus nec omnino intactis .. nec plene hic discussis BALSH. *AD rec.* 2 144; officium logice est quod recte formatum est in intellectu secundum tripartitam rationem sui quale sit judicare et †~are [l. ~ere] GROS. 1; philosophi qui theses ~iunt KILWARDBY *OS* 495; vix sufficiunt successores priorum comperta ~ere atque ea .. captare .. que antiqui .. effoderunt R. BURY *Phil.* 9. 145; *Ziz.* 479 (v. custodia 10b); per *techel* et *mane, phares* discussaque plane [cf. *Dan.* v 25] (J. BRIDL.) *Pol. Poems* I 164 (*gl.* ib. 165: per ista verba 'discussa plane', i. clare exposita). **b** ~iens, .. investigans, .. querens *GlH* D 698; omnia .. tuo examini ~ienda exhibeo FOLC. *V. Bot. pref.* 374; diligenter discussa apparet mihi aut peccatum aut sterilitas fere tota vita mea ANSELM (*Medit.* 3) III 76; ~e vitam tuam et inquire utrum inter quotidiana sint illa unde quereris in inter damnabilia PULL. *Sent.* 969D; eorum [regum] facta ab inferioribus ~ienda vel condempnanda non sunt *Dial. Scac. pref.* A; [angeli] singulorum merita et demerita ~iunt, mensurant et ponderant BART. ANGL. II 4; libros debet armarius .. frequenter ~ere, emendare et punctare, ne fratres in cotidiano officio ecclesie .. aliquem errorem vel impedimentum inveniant *Obs. Barnwell* 64. **c** **1296** docendi regendique .. facultas ad quam soliti rigoris examine discussi in .. universitate assumpti fuerint *Reg. Linc.* V 126.

4 (leg.) to try (cases or sim.); **b** (w. ref. to Last Judgement). **c** to examine, question (persons). **d** (w. indir. qu.) to consider, decide. **e** (intr. w. *inter*) to decide between.

~iens, i. judicans *GlH* D 698; HERM. ARCH. 45 (v. dirationare 1b); [ut rex], causa recenti examinatione discussa, supremam .. in eum mox judicii sententiam invehi juberet EADMER *HN* 68; Lanfrancus .. maluit pro successoribus laborare quam eis inposterum indiscussam hanc tantam calumniam ~iendam reservare W. MALM. *GP* I 25; **c1200** cum causa .. nobis .. commissa esset ~ienda et fine canonico terminanda *Reg. S. Thom. Dublin* 478; **s1249** veritatem .. ~ere (v. diratioare 1b); **1253** quod per xxiiij juratos .. omnia placita essent discussa et determinata *Rec. Leic.* I 42; principes fora statuerunt in quibus proponerentur questiones civiles .. et racionibus ~erentur KILWARDBY *OS* 587; **s1264** orta fuit dissensio .. que .. in curia Romana terminabatur et †dusciebatur *Ann. Cambr.* 102; **1378** inquisicio originalis missa fuit coram rege discuscienda *IMisc* 213/4 r. 3*d*.; **1421** ad .. probaciones de et super veritate ejusdem [testamenti] recipiendas et ~iendas *Reg. Cant.* II 227. **b** perversus .. jure judicium ~ientis Domini pertimescit BEDE *Hom.* I 24. 97; arbiter .. qui discutit orbis / totius factum GODEMAN 7. **c** **s1190** incole, cum propter hoc ~erentur a regiis, in peregrinos .. factum refuderunt W. NEWB. *HA* IV 7. **d** †**1189** (14c) ita quod per visum predictorum xij virorum discussum sit si tales fovee rationabiliter facte sint an non (*Assisa Aedific.*) *MGL* I 324; **1192** ut secundum eorum [canonicorum] judicium ~iatur utrum in integrum percepturi sint communam vel quantum eis debeat detrahi (*Stat. S. Paul*) DICETO II app. lxxii; **1200** qui tenet terram teneat donec ~iatur cui cedere debeat *CurR RC* II 263; donec discussum fuerit apud barones Scaccarii ad cujus presentationem .. ecclesia pertineat GIR. *Symb.* I 22 p. 264; **1246** (v. covata); **1280** coram officiali nostro .. ~iatur qui (*sic*) eundem calicem debeat acquitare *Reg. Heref.* 238; **1285** quousque discussum fuisset in curia .. regis si .. secta debebatur ad hundredum .. vel non *PQW* 239b. **e** **s1291** rex .. E. ad ~iendum inter dictos magnates .. statuit parliamentum suum super Twedam *Meaux* II 252.

discutus v. diruere a.

disemparare [cf. OF *desemparer*, Prov. *desamparar*, emparare], to cede, resign, relinquish possession (of) (Gasc.).

1289 dedit, cessit, dezamperavit, reliquit, et divisit .. regi .. medietatem pro indiviso loci vocati M. V. *RGasc* II 313 (cf. ib. 317: omnia .. data, cessa, desamparata, relicta .. et concessa); **1310** non solvit per vj annos .. xxx s. tur. .. quia deseruit et desenparavit seu reliquit .. salinas in manu magistri G. *Reg. Gasc. A* I 62.

disemparatio, cession, resignation (Gasc.).

1289 donaciones, cessiones, desamparaciones, seu reliquimenta *RGasc* II 316.

diseptus v. dissaepire 1a. **disertare** v. dissertare.

diserte [CL], eloquently, cogently.

1417 necessariam domini regis subvencionem .. faciendam satis deliberate et ~e in vulgari eloquio declaravit *Reg. Cant.* III 40.

disertio v. desertio a.

disertitudo [LL], eloquence, command of language.

Basilius .. Cappadox .., mira eloquentiae ~ine fretus ALDH. *VirgP* 27; dissertitudo, astutia, *gleawnes GlH* D 610; erat [H. de Losinga] ~inis et litterarum copia nec minus secularium rerum peritia Romane celsitudini suspitiendus W. MALM. *GP* II 74 (= *Id. GR* IV 339); apud .. paternitatis vestre ~inem AD. MARSH *Ep.* 4; nescis .. unde sit faminis / gurges et copia disertitudinis WALT. WIMB. *Carm.* 148; *a discrecion*, discreccio, desertitudo .., *an eloquence*, desertudo, eloquencia .., *wysdome*, discrecio .., dissertitudo .., sapiencia .. *CathA*.

1 disertus v. deserere 1a.

2 disertus [CL], eloquent, fluent: **a** (of person); **b** (of speech). *Cf.* 2 *disserere* 2.

a ~issimi oratores ALDH. *VirgP* 35; dīsertos [v. l. dissertos] arte sophistas *Id. VirgV* 619; **9..** dissertas, *getinge* .., desertissimi, *swa swa þa glaewestan WW*; ~issimae et verae Christi ancillae .. Mahtildi ÆTHELW. *prol.*; disputans acute .. cum literatis et ~is GIR. *IK* I 12; **1293** ex assertiva relacione .. fidelium nostrorum juris et facti experiencia desertorum *RGasc* III 72; *CathA* (v. discretivus 3b). **b** dīserto [v. l. disserto] digessit famine librum ALDH. *VirgV* 738.

disf- v. diff-. **disgarnitus** v. diswarnitus.

disgerbigator [cf. OF *desgarber*], 'tedder', haymaker.

~or, A. *a teddere WW*.

disgerere v. digerere 1a.

disglobare [cf. CL globare], to disintegrate, dissolve.

nulla pinguedo adeo grossa est in corpore sicut pinguedo renum et, si a remotis partibus esset, in via ~aretur GILB. I 68. 2.

disgredi v. 2 digredi.

disgregabilis, (as sb. n.) separable entity.

albedo non solum comparatur ad subjectum ut ad album, sed ad objectum ut ad ~e R. ORFORD *Reprob.* 172.

disgregare [LL]

1 to separate (people), disperse (crowds).

~ati .. Romani partim devia .. carpebant, partim civitates G. MON. X 12; ~atis singulis capitibus, nihilominus est unus grex J. CORNW. *Eul.* 18 p. 293; turbam Griffonum prosternens ~avit *Itin. Ric.* II 30; GIR. *Spec.* IV 37 (v. diffoederare); quid si [sorores] ~entur, id est, si non fuerint in una villa? HENGHAM *Magna* 9 p. 30; **s1298** statim ~ati Scoti ceciderunt, equites ducenti, pedites vero xl milia et amplius *Flor. Hist.* III 104; **s1322** rex .. supervenit et illorum cuneos ~avit *G. Ed. II Bridl.* 74; catervam .. nequaquam ~are potuit *Eul. Hist.* II 352 (= G. MON. X 9: disjungere).

2 to disintegrate, break up, dissolve. **b** to diffuse (light rays). **c** (w. *visum* or sim.) to dissipate, dazzle.

~ato, disjuncto *GlH* D 726; aqua partes habet ~atas et expansas ALF. ANGL. *Plant.* II 6; cum calor in partibus ~ans sit, calidum naturale facit constare ~ata humida suscipientia materiales dispositiones GILB. I 6v. 2; omnes .. radii .. concurrunt ad punctum unum ad aerem ~andum et inflamandum PECKHAM *Persp.* II 55; calor ~ans, naturalis cum sit, constare facit ~ata SICCAV. *PN* 186; BRADW. *CD* 531C (v. calefactivus); UPTON 99 (v. calidus c). **b** SACROB. *Sph.* 81 (v. diaphanus a); radii [visuales] reflexi a convexo magis ~antur quam a plano BACON *Maj.* II 136. **c** disgregat et visum candor NECKAM *DS* IX 417; *Id. NR* II 153 (v. disgregatio d); albedo .. †incensa [v. l. intensa] visum †digressat [v. l. disgregat, *gl.*: *dejunct*] et maxime †nimium obtinctum [v. l. nervum obticum] obtenebrat et obnervat *Id. Ut.* 117 (168); visu quasi ~ato H. BOS. *LM* 1385C; libera frons et plana, nitens et candida, visum / disgregat H. AVR. *Hugh* 174; quedam .. dicuntur videri in umbra eo quod videantur in aere non illuminato luce extrinseca sed intrinseca, unde adveniente luce extrinseca ~atur visus GILB. III 127v. 2; *Ps.*-RIC. *Anat.* 26, GAD. 110v. 2 (v. congregare 2e); albedo ~at visum [ME: *awilgeð þe echnen*] *AncrR* 105.

disgregatio [LL], **a** separation. **b** solvent action. **c** diffusion (of light rays). **d** dissipation (of 'visual spirit'), dazzle.

a **1050** sit separatus a Christo ipsiusque sanctis discgregatione perpetuae anathematis fiat (*Ch. Regis*) *Conc. Syn.* 531 (= *CD* 791: †dissegregatione). **b** quedam pars spermatis ex ~one caloris ponitur grossior, quedam liquidior GILB. I 66. 2. **c** sicut patet de denario projecto in fundo aque limpide, qui propter .. ~onem radiorum apparet majoris quam sue vere quantitatis SACROB. *Sph.* 81; BRADW. *CD* 469C (v. congregatio 3d). **d** pro aeris claritate .., cooperante oculorum albedine, ad ~onem visibilis spiritus .. facile disgregatus dispergitur NECKAM *NR* II 153 (cf. ib. 237: solem diu conspicere non valemus pro spirituum nimia ~one); divisio erit propria passio quantitatis, sicut ~o albedinis BACON XIII 169.

disgregativus [LL], **a** distinctive. **b** dissipative, diffusive (of vision). *Cf.* διακριτικός.

a homo et opera .. bonorum et malorum .. ~a sunt et discretiva; opera .. illorum secuntur illos STUDLEY 1. **b** 'albedo' .. ipsam significat qualitatem, viz. coloris speciem ~am J. SAL. *Met.* 893B; omnia predicta [humores et tunice] in compositione oculi erant alba et clara et spiritus visibilis ~a BART. ANGL. V 4 (cf. congregativus 2); ratio albedinis est color ~us visus BACON XV 209; alia distinccio .. est in intellectu, concipiendo duobus actibus duo objecta formalia, et hoc sive illis correspondeat diverse res, ut intelligendo 'hominem' et 'asinum', sive una res extra, ut intelligendo 'colorem' et '~um' DUNS *Ord.* II 351; nigredo temperat nigredinis ~am claritatem UPTON 113.

disgregator, disperser, dissipator.

GIR. *JS* 7 (v. congregator b).

disgressio v. digressio.

disgrex [LL *gl.*], distinct, unlike, separate.

~ges, dissimiles, diverse *GlH* D 727; ~ges, segreges, divisi, separati OSB. GLOUC. *Deriv.* 181.

dishabilis, disabled, disqualified.

stabit disabilis .. in perpetuum .. portare officium vicecomitis infra aliquem com. Anglie *Entries* 206b (cf. *StRealm* II 334 [**1445**]: *destoier disable perpetuelment .. destre ou porter loffice de viscount*).

dishabilitare, to disable, disqualify.

1477 non potuit placitasse ad ~and' personam querentis postquam sua possessio fuit extincta *Entries* 288b; **1563** (v. discredere 2).

dishabilitatio, disablement, disqualification.

1477 defend[ens] non habens alium statum nisi nudam dimissionem ad voluntatem aliorum in manerio .. ad placitandum in ~onem persone querentis *Entries* 288b.

disherbergatus [cf. OF *desherberger*], deprived of shelter, unfit for habitation.

1331 principalis turris castri [Oxon'] vacuus (*sic*), dirrutus et disherbigatus est (*IMisc* 115/21) *OHS* LXXX 293.

dishereditare [cf. AN *disheriter*, OF *deseriter*, LL hereditare], to disinherit. *V. et. dehereditare, exheredare, exhereditare.*

1201 magnum pudorem .. deberet habere quando patiebatur alios barones vestros injuste deshereditare vos *RChart* 102b; **13..** mea voluntas non est aliquem meorum consanguineorum in aliquo dishereдare (*Test. Alfredi regis*) *CS* 555 p. 186 (= *Ib.* 554 [**a888**]: *þæt ic mine mægcild .. mid wo fordemde*); **1573** de regali statu .. ~are (v. compassare).

dishereditatio, disherison, dispossession (of inheritance). *V. et. dehereditatio, exhereditatio.*

1278 unum lignum de quercu .. asportavit ad deseritacionem Johannis *Hund. Highworth* 76; in evitand' dolores, vexaciones, et ~ones que de die in diem contingunt pluribus ligeis regis per escaetores *Entries* 315 (cf. *StRealm* II 252 [**1429**]: *dolours, grevances, e disheretisons*).

dishoner- v. dishonor-, disoner-.

dishonorare [cf. AN *deshonurer, disonurer*, OF *desonorer*], to dishonour, disgrace; **b** (w. cognate acc.).

quando portans arma debet ~ari propter prodicionem, fugam vel fidem ruptam, tunc arma sua sunt pingenda per traversum BAD. AUR. 143. **b** **s1460** si et quatenus nil mali contra personam regis vellent intendere aut regium regis honorem in aliquo ~are *Reg. Whet.* I 371.

dishonoratio, dishonour (but *cf. disonerare* 2).

1468 quilibet confrater .. qui reprobat .. aliquem confratrem suum per aliqua verba per que dictus confrater .. dampnum incurrit .. vel per aliqua alia verba in sonum dishoneracionis dicti confratris *Doc. Bev.* 126.

dishypatus [δισύπατος], twice consul.

hoc monasterium construxit Studius †tisipatus et senator et primus palacii magni Constantini et nobilissimus Romae *Descr. Constant.* 262.

disicere [CL], **a** to cast loose, unfasten. **b** to disperse, dissolve (partly fig.).

a Petrus .. / dissicit ignavae torquentia lora senectae FRITH. 297; a metropolitano .. †dissictis ansulis in apertura tunice et camisie .. manus principis .. inungantur *Lib. Regal.* 11b. **b** dissice, disperge *GlC* D 289; disjectas, dispersas *GlH* D 725; dissice placatus nostri genus omne reatus R. CANT. *Malch.* VI 48 (cf. ib. I 247); hec meditanti fides occurrens dubietatis nebulas dissicit W. MALM. *GP* IV *prol.*; hic panis anime dolores dissicit WALT. WIMB. *Carm.* 125.

disicio v. desitio. **disilire** v. 2 dissilire. **disillabus** v. disyllabus. **disinere** v. desinere 1b. **disipere** v. desipere. **disis** v. dysis. **disitus** v. 3 disserere b.

disjacēre, (pr. ppl.) lying separately, detached.

1002 (12c) quandam possessionis propriae tellurem xxiij mansarum .. tribus in locis ~entem *CD* 1295.

disjugare [LL], (p. ppl.) unmarried.

[Paulus, *1 Cor.* vii 7] suadet .. ~atis, tum viduis tum virginibus, soluti et libri maneant Deo COLET *Sacr. Eccl.* 75.

disjugatio, unyoking.

1312 pro opere in die ab hora matutina usque disjungacionem carucarum (*Cust. Tolleshunt Tresgoz*) *Essex RO* D/DC 21/12.

disjuncte [CL], disconnectedly; **b** (log.).

ADEL. *QN* 64 (v. abolescere). **b** accidit interrogari et alia multiplicia, ut 'an mundus sit rationalis vel irrationalis an non'; hujusmodi autem ~e multiplicia appellari poterunt BALSH. *AD rec. 2* 170; *Ib.* 172 (v. cohaerenter).

disjunctim [CL], (gram.) disjunctively.

cum apostolus dicit se desiderare dissolvi et esse cum Christo [*Philip.* i 23], aut intelligit ~im hanc vocem .. aut conjunctim S. LANGTON *Quaest.* 149; BRACTON 205 (v. conjunctim c).

disjunctio [CL]

1 parting, separation (of persons). **b** divorce.

ALCUIN *Rhet.* 34 (v. conqueri 2e); tu habes ex ipsa nostra ~one praesentem alterum ANSELM (*Ep.* 84) III 209. **b** **1223** dolens .. super ~one sororis sue et Olavi *Chr. Man* 86.

2 taking to pieces, dismantling.

1313 circa distraccionem et ~onem magni ingenii *KRAc* 468/20 p. 2.

3 disjunction: **a** (gram.) (conjunction expressing) contrast. **b** (log.) disjunction, alternative.

a [sophistica sunt principia] ex ~one, cum an ut unius enuntiationis unum sit principium an ut plurium plura dubitabile est, hoc modo: 'diem vel noctem esse semper est verum'; dubitabile enim an de eo quod est 'diem esse vel noctem esse', ut sic unum sit enuntiandi principium, an de eo quod est 'diem esse' an de eo quod est 'noctem esse', ut sic plura enuntiandi principia ~one intelligantur BALSH. *AD* 92; hee prepositiones [non separatim constructe cum casibus] non dicunt comparationes casuales; sed consequentia quedam, ~o et conjunctio, sive sit secundum tempus sive secundum locum, post causas sunt *Ps.*-GROS. *Gram.* 56; hic, volens recitare sententiam constitucionis 'cum inter', quoad unam partem ejus mutat notam copulacionis in notam ~onis OCKHAM *Pol.* II 651. **b** **1312** (v. disjunctivus 1c); **1318** oblata eis per nos ~one, alteram partem .. preoptabant *FormOx* 45 (cf. ib. 42: primam viarum hujusmodi a secunda vobis sub ~one duximus offerendam).

disjunctive [LL], disjunctively, alternatively. **b** separately.

tres rationes in contrarium procedentes altero sensu ~e concedantur BACON VII 103; *Fleta* 241 (v. copulative); **1312** cum dicit quod est fallacia consequentis in disjunctivis arguere ad alteram partem, respondetur quod factum narratur ~e nulla illacione facta, sine qua impossibile est esse fallacia[m] consequentis *Collect. Ox.* II 258; **1325** non petit simpliciter et absolute, sed condicionaliter et ~e, quod possit ad hujusmodi habitum et ordinem transvolare *Lit. Cant.* I 161; predicta capitula loquuntur ~e vel equipollenter de jure poli et de jure fori OCKHAM *Pol.* II 579; statutum concilii generalis solum obligat parochianos ~e, sc. ad confitendum semel in anno proprio sacerdoti vel alteri de licencia proprii sacerdotis CONWAY *Def. Mend.* 1422 (*recte* 1322). **b** **s1377** dux [Lancastrie] .. peciit .. ~e dari regi duas decimas uno anno *Chr. Angl.* 112.

disjunctivus [CL]

1 a (gram.) disjunctive, expressing contrast. **b** (log.) disjunctive, involving alternatives. **c** (as sb. f.) disjunctive proposition; *v. et. disjungere* 4e.

a ALDH. *PR* 133 (v. conjunctio 2c); potestas conjunctionum in v species dividitur: sunt enim copulativae, ~ae .. BONIF. *AG* 537; [conjunctiones] ~ae sunt quae, quamvis dictiones jungant, sensus tamen disjungunt, et unum e duobus esse significant, ut: 'vel', '-ve', '†ne [? l. neu]', 'nec' .. ALCUIN *Gram.* 895B; [conjunctiones] ~e sunt que significant ea inter que distingunt simul non esse *Ps.*-GROS. *Gram.* 58. **b** est cognoscenda differencia inter proposicionem ~am et de disjuncto extremo OCKHAM *Dial.* 802; preceptum statuti super confessione parochianorum semel in anno facienda est ~um, sc. quod fiat proprio sacerdoti vel alteri de licencia proprii sacerdotis CONWAY *Def. Mend.* 1415 (*recte* 1314). **c** sicut non est dandum quod sit per se essencia vel per se non-essencia, ita nec alterum membrum illius ~e cum 'que est' in sensu composicionis DUNS *Ord.* II 372; **1312** respondetur quod hoc ponitur sub disjunccione quod legerit sentencias vel sit bachellarius, et ~a est vera cujus pars altera est vera *Collect. Ox.* II 258; contradictorium ~e debet dari per unam conjunctivam factam ex contradictoriis parcium LAVENHAM *Log* c. 11 p. 58; **c1430** quodsi .. ~e vobis proposite preeligitis partem primam *Reg. Whet.* II 426.

2 separative.

frigiditas .., quamvis sit naturaliter conjunctiva, tamen accidentaliter dissolutiva et partium ~a BART. ANGL. IV 2.

disjunctura, dislocation.

de ~a ossis juguli GILB. IV 180v. 1 *rub.* (cf. disjungere 2e).

disjungatio v. disjugatio.

disjungere [CL]

1 to unyoke.

~it [AS: *unscenþ*] ÆLF. *Coll.* 91 (v. bubulcus a); **1223** (v. carruca 2a); **1285** ab illa hora quando boves junguntur [*ed.*: †merguntur] quousque ~antur [*ed.*: †dismergantur] (*Slyndon*) *Cust. Suss.* II 3; [ballivus] carucas dominicas adeat .., prospiciens quod antequam dietam suam plene paraverint minime ~entur *Fleta* 161 (cf. dieta 3a).

2 a to dismantle. **b** to cleave asunder. **c** (pass.) to come to pieces. **d** to be held apart. **e** (anat.) to be dislocated.

a **1211** in molendino de vento ~endo, effodiendo, sternendo *Pipe Wint.* 131; **1241** quando vidit quod ipsi reliquerunt domos suas desertas et quod domus ille cadebant, ipse fecit ~ere meremium et inde abducere *CurR* XVI 1822; **1313** (v. caciator 2); **1345** in magno ingenio .. ~endo et .. tractando usque *le watergate* (*Pipe* 198) *EHR* XXVI 689. **b** fortuna ei [Corineo] bipennem a[d]ministraverat, cum qua †quamcumque [v. l. quemcumque] attingebat a summo usque ad imum ~ebat G. MON. I 12. **c** **1337** una parva capella, quarum parietes sunt de maheremio et plaustro et maheremium inde fere ~itur (*Surv. Launceston*) *N. & Q.* V 249; **1345** daeria: .. in veteribus stoppis et tynis disjunctis religandis *Comp. Swith.* 148; **1417** *Ib.* 366 (v. cuvella). **d** ut inferius labium, dissoluta penitus mandibula, a labro ~eretur superiore LANTFR. *Swith.* 33. **e** si os juguli a proprio loco discedat et collum ~atur GILB. IV 180v. 1; si .. pes a suo loco ~atur, modo hac modo illac modo versus plantam modo versus calcaneum jungatur *Ib.* VII 385. 2.

3 to separate: **a** (people); **b** (things or abstr.); **c** (gram. or rhet.); **d** (mus.).

a **c597** ut ipsi sibi episcopi longo intervallo minime ~antur (*Lit. Papae*) BEDE *HE* I 27 p. 52; omnes homines natura aequales genuit, sed varietate meritorum ~ebantur HUGEB. *Wynn.* 5; **a1089** eos .. quos .. caritas jungit corporalis absentia .. minime ~it LANFR. *Ep.* 10 (23); PULL. *Sent.* 714A (v. disconvenire a). **b** hoc sirenarum et Scyllae ~it naturam *Lib. Monstr.* I 14; quicquid toto junxit natura favore / disjungit [mens] ADEL. (*Vers.*) *ED* 7; J. SAL. *Pol.* 437C (v. conjungere 2a); R. COLD. *Cuthb.* 42 (v. disseparare); ambitio, fraterna paulatim ~ens federa GIR. *TH* III 7; **1321** vires quas prosperitatis hora pigritantes disjunxit *FormOx* 74. **c** disjunctum est quando orationes ~untur ita quod quelibet illarum suum respiciat verbum, verbi gratia: 'exhilarant frondes silvam; vacat imbribus aer; / murmure ludit aqua; flore superbit ager' VINSAUF *CR* 324. **d** optimum est notas jungibiles jungere ~ereque non jungibiles HAUDLO 398.

4 (p. ppl. *disjunctus*) separate, disjunct. **b** (geom.) involving section of only one side of triangle; *cf. conjungere* 2c. **c** (as sb. n.) asyndeton. **d** (log.) disjunctive. **e** (as sb. f. or n.) disjunctive proposition, dilemma; *v. et. disjunctivus* 1c.

GlH D 726 (v. disgregare 2a); **a1070** propter nimis ~am conversationem nullis .. colloquiis ipsum de vobis cor meum potestis percipere ANSELM (*Ep.* 2) III 99. **b** WALLINGF. (*Quad.*) I 154 (v. 2 cata). **c** VINSAUF *CR* 324 (v. 3c supra). **d** altera pars predicati ~i DUNS *Ord.* I 53. **e** ne suspicionibus agamus, audi brevem ~am et conclude in summam W. MALM. *Mir. Mariae* 125; *Id. GP* V 276 (v. convenire 2e); sicut passio simplex convertibilis includitur primo in subjecto, sic et ~a; ergo in subjecto includitur primo quod aliqua pars ~e alicui enti conveniat DUNS *Ord.* III 9; possibile est quod proposicio cathegorica de ~o extremo, in qua subjiciuntur termino discreto contento sub aliquo termino communi, sit necessaria, et tamen quod ~a correspondens cum modo necessitatis sit falsa OCKHAM *Dial.* 802.

diskippagium [cf. skippagium], disembarkation.

1290 pro restauro unius runcini ferr[andi] quem amisit in .. itinere per ~ium de navi (*AcWardr*) *Chanc. Misc.* 4/5 f. 3*d.*; **1332** diversis hominibus de Kaleys pro ~io, pontagio, portagio, et batillagio diversorum hominum et equorum (*KRAc* 386/7) *Arch.* LXXVII 126 (cf. ib. 132: pro .. skippagio equorum); **1393** pro ~io equorum ibidem [apud Dover'], x s. vj d.; item pro ~io militum, scutiferorum et aliorum ibidem, ij s. *Ac. H. Derby* 255.

dislaniator v. dilaniator.

disligare [LL]

1 to unbind, release; **b** (w. ref. to sheaves). *V. et.* 2 *deligare* 1a.

~o, i. resolvo *GlH* D 709; disligere, solvere, quod et ~are dicitur OSB. GLOUC. *Deriv.* 181; Christus .. peccatorem .. adhuc ligatum assignat sacerdotibus ~andum vera absolucione CONWAY *Def. Mend.* 1416 (*recte* 1316); **1403** quod bona Anglicorum, arrestata in Sclusa †debentur [MS: debent] integraliter conservari .. et non desligari (*DipDocE* 358) *Foed.* VIII 327b. **b** **1345** in avena domini ~anda, vertenda et iterum liganda et tassanda propter tempus pluviosum (*Pipe Wint.*) *Econ. HR* NS XII 399.

2 (p. ppl., w. ref. to book) disbound, without binding.

1365 portiforium est defectivum et ~atum (*Vis.*) *Fabr. York* 243.

dislocare [cf. CL locare, OF *desloer*]

1 (pass.): **a** (anat.) to be dislocated; **b** (fig.).

a si ~atur pes, statim ponatur in aqua frigidissima GILB. VII 358. 1; cum videris juncturam non moveri, judica quod ~ata est integre GAD. 127v. 2 (cf. ib. 81. 1: si matrix steterit ~ata et maxime si exiverit ad exteriora, ex difficili .. curatur); in .. mundo, dum membrum fuerit extra locum suum .., fit .. perturbacio ..; sic quoque in corpore humano, quando membra ~antur .., fit dolor et morbus HIGD. II *prol.* p. 180; *oute of lyth*, ~atus, luxus *CathA.* **b** anima .. leprose tumescens superbia extra statum debitum ~ata deficiet a recepcione naturalis influencie lucis prime WYCL. *Innoc.* 488.

2 to disallow (item in account). *V. et deallocare* a, *disallocare* a.

1380 damus eis .. potestatem ad allocandum, seu ~andum et omnia alia faciendum .. que ad auditorum officium pertinere noscuntur *Reg. Heref.* 20.

3 to cancel lease of.

1426 ad .. fructus, redditus .. et emolumenta ad eundem P. .. pertinencia .. locandum, ~andum et ad firmam seu annuam pensionem dandum et concedendum *Reg. Cant.* I 238.

dislocatio, **a** (anat.) dislocation. **b** displacement, dispersal.

a si ~o [pedis] non sit maxima .., stupa canabina .. applicetur GILB. VII 358. 2; ~o est egressio vel separacio juncturarum a loco suo ..; et, quando non est integra, tunc vocatur ~o proprie GAD. 127v. 1 (cf. ib. 65v. 1: si paralesis veniat ex ~one aut contraccione mala nervorum); *Alph.* 61 (v. exarthrema). **b** in mixto terrestri est parum ignis .., dum natura paucos igniculos spargit cum multo terreo. nec oportet quodlibet elementum in mixto continuari cum alio sue speciei; nec obest tali ~oni quod corpuscula distancia constituant unam substanciam corpoream WYCL. *Log.* III 67.

disma v. dyspnoea.

dismantacompanionum [cf. CL dis- + ML mantum + OF *compagnon* < LL *companio; cf.

OED s.v. *dismantle*], one who steals his fellows' cloaks.

maledicte, filius maledicti, dismantaconpagnum, non eris papa! Boso *V. Pont.* 398.

dismaritare [cf. CL maritare, AN *dismarier*, OF *desmarier*], (p. ppl.) unmarried.

1295 fuit idem Willelmus iterato ~atus, eo quod uxor ejus obiit *PlRCP* 107 m. 79*d*.

dismembrare [cf. OF *desmembrer* < LL demembrare], to mutilate (person). **b** to dismember (body). **c** to break up (estate) or detach (appurtenance). *V. et. demembrare.*

1250 serjantia [*in Guildford*] .. pro qua debuit esse marescallus in hospicio domini regis et ~are malefactores in hospicio domini regis adjudicatos *Fees* 1235; **1404** manerium [*Shorfield, Hants*] de nobis [tenetur] per magnam serjanciam, viz. per servicium essendi marescallus de meretricibus et ~andi malefactores adjudicatos *Cl* 278 m. 28. **b** [David princeps Wallie] v judiciis mortalibus torquebatur: suis namque meritis exigentibus detractus, suspensus, decollatus, ~atus fuit et combustus *Fleta* 16. **c** **1308** perpendens quod, si idem R. eadem maneria .. judicialiter recuperasset, quod (*sic*) baronia predicta ~aretur et quod hoc in prejudicium domini sui cederet *SelCKB* IV 10; **1454** si .. prioratus de Pluscardyn .., qui membrum dependens de prioratu .. Valliscaulium .. existit .., a dicto prioratu V. penitus ~aretur et separaretur *Mon. Hib. & Scot.* 392a; **1473** de bonis .. prioratus de Coldingham ab illo [Patritio] dimembrandis *Ib.* 473a; **1491** Glasguensem .. et Lismorensem ecclesias, civitates et dioceses a provincia .. ecclesie S. Andree .. separamus, dividimus et ~amus (*Lit. Papae*) *Reg. Glasg.* 471; **1532** quatenus dictas xxiiij merchas monete Scotie .. de integris fructibus .. dicte parochialis ecclesie .. deducendas .. dimembrare illasque .. dicte collegiate ecclesie .. unire .. dignemini *Form. S. Andr.* II 10.

dismembratio, detachment (of appurtenance).

1532 dimembrationi summe xxiiij mercharum .. monete regni Scotie ex integris fructibus .. rectorie dicte parochialis ecclesie .. deducendarum et extrahendarum .. consentimus *Form. S. Andr.* II 9; **1543** separatio seu dimembratio .. ecclesiarum [a matrice parochiali ecclesia] *Ib.* 292.

dismergere v. disjungere 1. **dismittere** v. 2 dimittere. **dismarium, ~erium** v. dinarium. **disnia** v. dyspnoea.

disnodare [cf. OF *desnoer*, denodare], to untie.

~ans filum de pollice dextre mee (*Visio Caroli*) W. MALM. *GR* II 111.

disnoicus v. dyspnoicus. **disnoscere** v. dinoscere 2a.

disoboedientia [cf. CL oboedientia, OF *desobeissance*], (act of) disobedience.

s1478 littera suspencionis .. dompni J. .. nuper prioris de Tynemutha .. propter suas contumacias et ~ias factas domino J. .. et domino N. .. ad prioratum .. visitandum .. missis *Reg. Whet.* II 186 *rub.*; **1498** quilibet contributor .. qui premunitus fuerit per senescallum ad veniendum ad duos *prime gyldes* in anno, et non vult venire, solvet aldermanno .. vj d. pro sua ~ia *Doc. Bev.* 113.

disoboedire [cf. CL oboedire, OF *desobeir*], (w. dat. or absol.) to disobey.

1448 nec unquam paruit monicionibus canonice sibi factis de utendo tonsura et vestibus clericalibus sed .. tociens ~ivit pertinaciter (*Court Bk. Linc.*) *Eng. Clergy* app. 225; **1487** urgente .. rumore insurreccionis .. per quosdam regi ~ientes *Reg. Merton* 98.

disobstruere [cf. CL obstruere], to clear of obstruction, open up. *V. et. deobstruere* a.

1291 consuetudo ville talis est quod, si domini seldarum seldas obstruxerint, quod (*sic*) postquam domini requisiti fuerint de predictis seldis aperiendis et hoc recusaverint, licitum est ballivis comitis seldas illas ~ere *CoramR* 122 r. 13.

disobstuppare [cf. obstuppare], to clear, free from obstruction. *V. et. deobstuppare.*

1387 juratores .. dicunt quod quedam via .. obstructa est et obstupata per levacionem fossatorum. .. ideo consideratum est quod via predicta disobstupetur et quod fossate predicte .. deleantur *Pub. Works* I 51.

disoculare [cf. LL oculare], to blind. *V. et. deoculare, exoculare.*

s1435 dominus de Dernley captus fuit ab Anglis in conflictu de C. .. et uno lumine ~atus FORDUN *Cont.* XVI 25.

disolvere v. dissolvere.

disonerare [cf. CL onerare]

1 to discharge, relieve (of debt or duty); *cf. deonerare*; **b** (impers. pass.). **c** to discharge, release (suit of court). **d** (w. *gaolam*) to deliver gaol; *cf.* 2 *deliberare* 2c.

1292 [tallagium] .. condonatur per majorem et communitatem, unde collectores dishonerantur *Rec. Leic.* I 221; dixit .. Pecok 'papa Dionisius ~avit episcopos ab onere predicandi' GASCOIGNE *Loci* 208. **b** hucusque carcatur eis redditus in Astret Oweyn injuste. ideo de cetero oportet ibi ~ari ibidem de ij s. per annum *Surv. Denb.* 39. **c** **1390** exacti .. fuerunt ad sectam faciendam ad hundredum .. de anno in annum, quousque predictus J. C. ~avit et relaxavit predictam sectam Willelmo G. *IMisc* 244/5. **d** **1336** dictum est senescallo .. quod .. sequatur recordum etc. ad gaolam .. dishonerandam *Gaol Del.* 64/3 r.5.

2 to discharge (from status or privilege).

1434 si aliquis burgensis .. rebellis inventus fuerit contra aliquam ordinacionem .. et illam .. recusaverit, quod extunc .. ~atur de libertate sua imperpetuum *Doc. Bev.* 47; **1492** quisquis frater .. artis [carnificum] .. exiet extra villam et patriam in discepcione populi domini regis, quod expellet et pro perpetuo ~abitur de dicta confraternitate et vestura *Ib.* 127.

disoneratio, discharge (from debt or duty), exemption. *V. et. deoneratio.*

1433 custodes petunt allocari pro diversis expensis, vacacionibus et aliis desoneracionibus *Leet Coventry* 149; in scriptura sacra .. non lego .. ~ones eorum [episcoporum] ab .. actu predicandi GASCOIGNE *Loci* 16.

disordinare, (p. ppl.) inordinate, excessive. *V. et. deordinare* 1b.

ne .. ~ata mora eveniat pronunciandi leccionem *Cust. Westm.* 28; MORE *Chr. Ed. II* 299 (v. deordinare 1b).

dispaccare [cf. paccare], to unpack.

1399 mercimonia in .. portu [de Lenne] .. paccata et paccanda ac ~ata et ~anda *Pat* 351 m. 17.

dispactus [cf. CL pactus, *p. ppl. of* paciscere], uncoordinated.

dum [mulier] nullatenus cibum posset capere solidum nec intelligibile ullum exprimere verbum, quoniam utrobique ~um habebat vocis artificium LANTFR. *Swith.* 33.

dispalari [CL], to be scattered, spread out.

~atum, diffugatum *GlC* D 293; Britones ~ati haud sine strage eos sunt persequuti BOECE 32v.

dispalatim, dispersedly.

Scoti ~im in regionibus agentes BOECE 19v.

dispar [CL], unlike, different. **b** (as sb. n. abl. sg.) separately.

vultus [militum] non catulorum leonis in acie magnopere ~pares visebantur GILDAS *EB* 33; par labor ambarum, dispar fortuna duarum ALDH. *Aen.* 66 (*Mola*) 3; dum calles gemini dispāri tramite tendunt *Id. VirgV* 763; sunt .. qui, etsi signa non faciunt, signa tamen facientibus ~pares non sunt *V. Greg.* p. 78; ~parem utriusque [S. J. Baptistae et Christi] qualitatem ~par modus passionis insinuat BEDE *Hom.* II 23. 241; **9..** ~pari, *ungelice WW*; tam ~pari paritate GIR. *TH* III 2; ~pares mores ~paria studia sequuntur *Id. IK pref.* p. 3; carpens alios sit dispar aliis WALT. WIMB. *Palpo* 188. **b** *sunderly*, separatim .., ~pari, divisim .. *CathA.*

disparagare, ~iare [cf. OF *desparagier*], to 'disparage', degrade by unequal marriage.

1194 pro maritando herede ubi non sit ~iatus *Pipe* 238; **1199** pro filiabus suis maritandis ubi voluerit, ita quod non sint ~iate *Pipe* 28; **1218** neque domina neque heres maritetur ubi ~etur, set per graciam et assensum generis sui maritetur (*Ch. Comitis Cestr.*) *Pat* 120 m. 22; **s1234** [P. Winton' episcopus et P. de Rivallis] habent sub potestate sua .. plures puellas nobiles et mulieres cum wardis et maritagiis, quas dant suis et ~ant WEND. III 77; **1236** de dominis qui maritaverint illos quos habent in custodia villanis vel aliis, sicut burgensibus, ubi ~entur, si talis heres fuerit infra xiij annos et talis etatis quod consentire non possit, tunc, si parentes conquerantur, dominus ille amittat custodiam (*Merton* 6) *StRealm* I 3; **1243** licebit nobis distringere viduas .. ad .. viros capiendos .., dummodo non disperagantur *Cl* 60; cum heres minor .. extiterit sub custodia domini, masculus vel femina .., ipsum maritare potuerit quando voluerit et ubi, dum tamen non ~etur BRACTON 89; **1290** cum rex dedisset maritagium herēdis Johannis de N. Thome de W. sine disparagacione, conqueruntur amici sui quod ~atur in filia ipsius Thome, cui maritatur postquam catalla sua forisfacta fuerunt regi *RParl* I 52a; *Quon. Attach.* 91 (v. disparsonare).

disparagatio, 'disparagement', marriage to an inferior.

1215 heredes maritentur absque ~one *Magna Carta* 6; **1227** concessimus .. Philippo .. custodiam terre et heredum Willelmi .. et maritagium eorundem heredum, ita tamen quod maritentur absque ~one *Pat* 117; **1290** (v. disparagare); **1292** concessimus W. S. Andree episcopo .. maritagium .. Amabille que fuit uxor Petri de M. habendum absque ~one, ita quod ille cui debet maritari nobis et regno Scocie fidelis existat *RScot* 7a; **1309** absque dispergacione (*Pat*) *Foed.* III 136b; **1500** absque desperagatione *Entries* 90.

disparantia, disparity. *V. et. disparatio.*

equalitas et similitudo sunt relaciones equiparancie, †personali autem proprietate [v. l. personales autem proprietates] sunt relaciones ~ie LUTTERELL *Occam* 271; affirmacio de positivo fundatur in paritate vel equiparancia .. ; affirmacio vero de comparativo gradu fundatur .. super inequalitatem vel ~iam WYCL. *Log.* I 221.

1 disparare v. desperare.

2 disparare [CL]

1 to separate. **b** (pass.) to be distant. **c** (p. ppl., assoc. w. *dispar*) disparate, incongruous.

putant ecclesie prelatos id ex potestate habere, ut ecclesie membris integra a putridis dijudicent, dijudicatione facta ab aliis alia ~are satagant PULL. *Sent.* 912B; si ita est, rerum ordo transpositus est; nam et contraria conjunguntur et similia ~antur ADEL. *QN* 74 (cf. ib.: si [ignis interior] peremptorius esset, jampridem suum suppositum ~asset). **b** villa .. non longe a Remesia, sed quasi vij millibus passuum, ~atur GOSC. *V. Iv.* 90A; vicus xij milliariis ab Exonia ~atus W. CANT. *Mir. Thom.* II 36. **c** principia secundum essentiam non sunt opposita set ~ata BACON VIII 25; materia prima .. formarum summe contrariarum sibique ~atarum in genere substancie est receptiva *Ps.*-GROS. *Summa* 310 (cf. ib. 318: duo ~atissima conjungere); intellectus in diversis recipit diversa et ~ata penitus PECKHAM *QA* 48; potencie distincte habent objecta omnino distincta, quia nulla earum, ex quo sunt ~ate, est per se operativa circa objectum circa quod alia. tales sunt .. visus et auditus DUNS *Ord.* III 108 (cf. ib. 314: lignum .. est receptivum qualitatum ~atarum et contrariarum eciam); **1326** cum dantis et recipientis inspectis qualitatibus personarum neque donum sit in se magnum neque alienacio ~ata, et que subest causa sit legitima *DC Cant.* (*HMC*) 272; quedam sunt vicia penitus ~ata. qui autem habet unum ~atorum, non propter hoc dignoscitur habere reliquum OCKHAM *Dial.* 591; **c1370** pertinentes [termini] sunt duplices. vel sunt ~ati, quod nullus de altero potest vere affirmative predicari .., vel sunt pertinentes sequela .. (STRODE *Conseq.*) *GLA* IV 50 n.182; quae sunt ~ata, i. e. natura et specie discreta GARDINER *CC* 622.

2 to strip of ornament.

Circumcisio celebretur sicut una de tribus superioribus festivitatibus, excepto quod aula monasterii non ornatur, quae quinta Dominicae Nativitatis die ~ari debet LANFR. *Const.* 95.

disparatio [LL < CL = *separation*], disparity. *V. et. disparantia.*

non est ~o vera opposicio sed distancia quedam eorum que nulla contrarietate vel aliqua alia opposicionis specie sibi adversantur *Ps.*-GROS. *Summa* 347; non obstat ~o quin natura divina et humana possint convenire in una persona PECKHAM *QA* II 158; aliquarum rerum est ~o atque diversitas .., aliquarum autem convenientia KILWARDBY *Quomodo Deus* (*extr.*) 118; Aristoteles dicit illa [unum et multa] opponi .. ut contraria, ut extenditur contrarietas ad ~onem, nec talem que est inter diversas species sed quasi inter individua, que proprie dicitur 'discrecio' DUNS *Metaph.* IV 2 p. 165.

disparcare [cf. parcare], to dispark, remove from status of park.

1550 [pro custodia] perci dispercati de Oveston' [*Northants*] *CalPat* III 408; **1584** infra nuper ~atum parcum de Belgraves *Pat* 1252 m. 9.

disparēre [LL], to disappear, vanish: **a** (of supernatural apparition or unspec.); **b** (of visible object or visual image); **c** (of abstr.).

a omnis praestigiarum scena .. ut fumus evanescens ~uit ALDH. *VirgP* 43; repente ductor meus ~uit ac me solum .. reliquit BEDE *HE* V 12 p. 305; ~uit, *ungesene wearð GlC* D 273; subito nitidus disparuit hospes ALCUIN *SS Ebor* 1613; ~uit, i. evanuit, *gedwan GlH* D 663; **9..** ~uit, *forswealt, ætiewde WW*; OSB. *V. Dunst.* 42 (v. confestim a); [Virgo] cum .. valefactione ~uit DOMINIC *V. Ecgwini* I 8; AILR. *Ed. Conf.* 753 (v. dicere 1e); vetula statim ~uit, que nec prius nec postea visa fuit R. BURY *Phil.* 3. 42. **b** amicis .. quasi in occulto ~entibus GIR. *EH* I 5; non semper ~ebit imago dextra oculo sinistro clauso BACON *Maj.* II 97; multa sunt que .. luci exposita ~ent PECKHAM *Persp.* I 9; 'cum celsa Yde .. latitabit longe', id est ~ebit propter elongacionem navigancium TREVET *Troades* 74. **c** ad coruscum veritatis ~ebit vanitas G. HOYLAND *Ascet.* 260D; nos hic bona que summitate digitorum tangimus refuga fallunt et quasi jam obtenta ~ent utilitas MAP *NC* V 7 f. 71v.; omnis honor temporalis | .. | disparere cernitur WALT. WIMB. *Van.* 2.

dispargere v. dispergere.

disparilis [CL], dissimilar.

~e, dispar *GlC* D 242; ~ile, dissimile OSB. GLOUC. *Deriv.* 181; disparilis causa manet et mors una duobus GOWER *VC* I 1061 (cf. ib. VII 975).

disparilitas [CL], dissimilarity, inequality.

unius mensurae et operis duo cherubim [cf. *1 Kings* vi 25], quia ~as voluntatum sive cogitatuum in superna patria nulla est BEDE *Templ.* 765; videbitis pro ~ate trahentium aratrum non recte procedere W. MALM. *GP* I 48; nulla est personarum acceptio. .. sola necessitas parit

diversitatem, sola infirmitas ~atem AILR. *Spec. Car.* II 17. 43. 563; confusam ~atem atque promiscuam .. in unum corpus digerere R. NIGER *Chr. II pref.* p. 105.

dispariliter [CL], unequally.

[Deus] conversum et subversum tam hominem quam angelum diligit; sed aut pariliter aut ~er; si ~er, magis bonum [diligit], minus malum PULL. *Sent.* 693B.

disparitas [LL], disparity, inequality.

Meldontis musam Corydonis musa secuta / disparitate styli, morbi redolentis odorem GIR. *Symb.* II 43. 9; cives celestes sua mulcet musica; mentes / pascit concordi disparitate modi GARL. *Tri. Eccl.* 142; **s1293** sicut in eis fuerat ~as animorum, sic et eodem die contingit maxima inequalitas elementorum W. GUISB. 241; si objicitur quod ipse [papa] vivit difformiter a Christo et suis apostolis .., [respondetur] quod illorum [impugnancium] est interpretare scripturam sacram pro illa ~ate allegandam (WYCL.) *Ziz.* 482 (cf. WYCL. *Ver.* I 152); **1430** quod clerus ubique infra regnum nostrum .. non in ~ate et differencia [? sc. vivat] set uno jure unoque privilegio .. gaudeat (*Lit. Regis Scotiae*) *Conc. Scot.* I cccvii; coloribus .. vestimentorum .. transmutatis secundum differenciam et ~atem festorum W. SAY *Lib. Reg. Cap.* 58.

dispariter [LL], differently, unequally.

1253 cum .. hec duo genera peccatorum, licet ~er, sunt pessima GROS. *Ep.* 128 p. 435; prima [beatitudo] est Deus, qua ipsemet et beati beatificantur .., licet ~er BRADW. *CD* 456B; non est repugnancia si Spiritus Sanctus simul dixit utraque, licet ~er et equivoce .., quia utrobique est eadem sentencia WYCL. *Conf.* 509; *Id. Log.* III 77 (v. calcinatio); **s1381** doluit .. abbas ..; doluerunt villani, sed ~er WALS. *HA* II 29; etsi de viciis et virtutibus in philosophia morali humana et in philosophia morali divina mencio fiat, ~er tamen J. BURY. *Glad. Sal.* 582.

dispartire v. dispertire.

dispectare [LL *gl.*], to look down on, despise. *V. et. despectare.*

~are, dispicere *GlC* D 216.

dispectere [cf. CL pectere], **~inare,** (?) to comb out.

ut pecto, ~o (id est pectino, ~ino), pendo, dispendo ALDH. *PR* 140.

dispectibilis, ~io, ~or, ~us, v. desp-.

dispellere [CL], to drive out. **b** to ward off.

Dominus .. dispulit negotiatores injustos [cf. *John* ii 15] BEDE *Hom.* II 1. 115. **b** **s1036** Godwinus .., qui .. resistentes umbone nominis sui aliquamdiu dispulit W. MALM. *GR* II 188.

dispendere [CL]

1 to spend, distribute, manage. **b** to administer (sacrament).

c1230 qui porcionem substancie sue cum filio prodigo et cum meretricibus ~entes scolas umbratice frequentant *FormOx* 348; **c1370** non vivit sane qui dispendit sacra vane [*gl.* : hoc dicit propter papam, qui sacra et bona ecclesie quibus adjuvit regem Francie contra regem Anglie vane expendidit et male] (J. BRIDL.) *Pol. Poems* I 164–5; rex .. debet .. providere virum fidelem .., cui debet demittere res pupplicas ~endas *Quadr. Reg. Spec.* 32. **b** spiritualia vocant illa que religioni Christiane sunt propria .., sicut que pertinent ad sacramenta ecclesiastica ~enda OCKHAM *Dial.* 513.

2 (p. ppl. *dispensus* as sb. f.): **a** expense. **b** 'spence', store-room or office of steward; *v. et. expendere* 5b, *spensa.*

a **a1185** si in exercitum summonuero burgenses meos .., ibunt cum ~a sua *BBC* (*Swansea*) 89; **s1337** plures eorum [nautarum] naves suas vendebant pro ~is et victualibus suis *Ann. Paul.* 366; ~a, A. *a spense*, vel A. *spendynge WW.* **b** has claves mulier debet sub cura sua custodire, sc. ~ae suae [AS: *hyre hordern*] et arcae et scrinii (*Inst. Cnuti*) *GAS* 363 (cf. BRACTON 151b); **c1174** (v. buticularia); **c1180** [panetarius] habeat omnibus diebus .. liberationem, sc. in despensa mea iiij denariatas panis .. et in coquina mea iiij fercula, unum ex magnis et duo ex †militibus [? l. militaribus] et unum dispensabile .., et ipse .. debet invenire panem in curia mea et talliare cum dispensariis meis *Act. Hen. II* II 329; **s1191** [obiit] Radulfus clericus de ~a regis *G. Ric. I* 149; NECKAM *Ut.* 98 (v. dispensatorius 3); **1204** expulit eum de domo sua et ibi cepit .. bladum flagellatum quod inventum fuit in ~a *CurR* III 97; **1234** (v. butellaria 2); **1395** tres mense in despensa parve cum *tristiles Test. Ebor.* III 7; **c1400** ~am hospicii [Fratrum] cum cameris versus infirmariam procuravit frater R. Knotte *Mon. Francisc.* I 511.

dispendialis, expensive, wasteful.

s1265 cum ibi moram fecissent fere per sex hebdomadas cum xx equis ~em, dominus rex pro quolibet milite xl m. exegit RISH. 42.

dispendiose, expensively, to one's cost.

[verba auctorum] ~ius ignorantur, cum ad urgendum aut resistendum potentissima sint J. SAL. *Met.* 900A; qua patientia et .. ~e .. omnia sustinuerim D. LOND. *Ep.* 13; **1300** morabar in confinibus Scocie .., securioris progressus ad regem oportunitatem non tam ~e quam anxie expectando *Reg. Cant.* 572 (= *Ann. Lond.* 107); **1309** commodis et honoribus regiis ~e detrahitur *Ib.* 1035; **1435** remediis premissis ~e contemptis *Mon. Hib. & Scot.* 374a.

dispendiosus [CL], expensive, detrimental, time-wasting; **b** (of persons). **c** prolix.

vacare ~um, operari autem in tanta festivitate arbitror periculosum AILR. *Ed. Conf.* 783C; hec .. apponere .. ~a quorundam subterfugia compulerunt *Dial. Scac.* II 1 D; dicere .. instancias .. eorum per singula difficile esset, ~issimum et parum utile *Ps.*-GROS. *Gram.* 27; **1265** (v. captivatio b); **1282** ~a solucionis retardacio *Reg. Ebor.* 43; **s1319** post longam et ~am in curia Romana moram *G. S. Alb.* II 140; itinera ~o compendio damnosoque diplomate transmeantes R. BURY *Phil.* 9. 155; **1450** ne quid ~um, grave vel prejudiciale contra et adversus nos .. fieri .. videretur *Pri. Cold.* 167. **b** rex Henricus II .. ~us est in suorum negotiis, unde fit ut antequam negotia eorum consequantur multi moriantur MAP *NC* V 6 f. 69; **1235** qualiter P. Winton' episcopus .. ~us nobis et subditis nostris extiterit onerosus *TreatyR* I 15 (cf. ib.: quot et qualia .. dispendia nobis attulerit). **c** **c1400** cedulas antiquas .. collegi .., in quibus .. ~a in breviorem stilum converti *Meaux* I *pref.*

dispendium [CL]

1 expenditure, loss, detriment: **a** (absol. or w. gen. of sufferer); **b** (w. gen. of thing lost); **c** (w. gen. of cause or description). *V. et. expendium* 1.

a qui Sodomitanum pereuntis feminae ~ium [cf. *Gen.* xix 26] minime pertimesceret ALDH. *VirgP* 31; ~ium, *wom GlC* D 234; ~ium vel damnum vel detrimentum, *hynð*, vel *lyre*, vel *hearm* ÆLF. *Gl.*; presbyter .., verens ~ium in utraque parte BYRHT. *V. Osw.* 409; quamquam compaterentur ~io fraterno GOSC. *V. Iv.* 86A; res monasterii posse pati ~ium *Chr. Battle* f. 114; G. COLD. *Durh.* 3 (v. dispersio 2); **a1250** in grave ~ium animarum predecessorum meorum *Feod. Durh.* 129*n.*; in verbi Dei ~ium R. BURY *Phil.* 6. 92; **1435** ad meum ~ium cum pudore *FormOx* 444; **1492** (v. deperdere 1e). **b** quippe qui commune bonorum ~ium malorumque cumulum .. defleam GILDAS *EB* 1; sine .. ~io castitatis ALDH. *VirgP* 7; **798** qui terrarum ~io .. laboraverunt (*Clovesho*) *CS* 291; ~ium pacis AILR. *Ed. Conf.* 751C; incurrunt ~ium vitae BALD. CANT. *Sacr. Alt.* 729C; ubi ecclesiastice libertatis ~ium vertitur H. BOS. *Thom.* IV 11 p. 353; AD. EYNS. *Hug.* IV 7 (v. compendium 1). **c** cum .. gurgitum maris evasisset ~ium WILLIB. *Bonif.* 5 p. 18; ~ium tanti dedecoris minime quibat perpeti LANTFR. *Swith.* 25; **s1066** Haroldus graviter vulneratus mortis ~ium evadebat *Meaux* I 153; **c1230** sine more ~io *Melrose* I 263; **s1399** dummodo regnum .. non esset guerrarum ~iis oneratum *V. Ric. II* 192; hec unica menda .. [civitatem Rotomagensem] lumine privat et in cecitatis ~ia introducit *Ps.*-ELMH. *Hen. V* 64 p. 178 (cf. ib. 92: in desperacionis ~ia).

2 **a** delay, detour. **b** prolixity.

a epistolas illi [sc. Ceolfrido] dedit [rex Hilpericus] ut .. ei quispiam ~ium itineris facere praesumeret *Hist. Abb. Jarrow* 32; itineris tanti ~io res necessarias accuravit *Hist. Meriadoci* 366 (cf. ib: terra marique multis trajectis ~iis); M. PAR. *Maj.* V 447 (v. compendium 2a). **b** non nihil est .. ex aliorum ~iis compendiosum aliquid elicere GIR. *GE proem.* p. 6; **1346** pacificus, mitis, linquens dispendia litis, / sordibus attritis vixit (*Epitaph*) *Hist. Durh.* 2.

dispennare [cf. pennare], to deprive of feathers.

preter alas effigiem habens ardee ~ate J. YONGE *Vis. Purg. Pat.* 6.

dispensa v. dispendere 2.

dispensabilis [cf. AN *dispensable*, OF *despensable*]

1 for ordinary use. *V. et. expensabilis.*

c1180 [ferculum] ~e (v. dispendere 2b); **1205** faciatis venire .. vj tonellos vini .., tres sc. ad opus nostrum et tres ~es *Cl* 45b (cf. ib. 57b: iiij dolia vini, sc. iij de vino ~i et iiij^{tum} ad os nostrum); **1214** mitti faciatis .. j dolium boni vini et aliud ~e *Ib.* 177b; *Fees* 342 (v. 3 butta); ex .. candela despensabili *Cust. Cant.* 371 (v. candela 1c); **c1363** magister cementarius .. habeat quolibet die unum panem ~em et alterum de pane avene *Pri. Cold.* 37.

2 susceptible of dispensation.

c1218 dictas irregularitates de cetero ordinandos precipimus ante susceptionem ordinum .. attendere et .. dispensationis beneficium, si ~is sit irregularitas, postulare *Conc. Syn.* 60 (= *Ch. Sal.* 129); crimen notorium, intolerabile, / data pecunia, fit dispensabile (*De Cruce Denarii* 29) *Ps.*-MAP 226; argumentum videtur innuere quod hec ordinacio Christi fit irracionabilis, vel saltem quod fuit ~e cum ipso vel suo opposito WYCL. *Civ. Dom.* IV 381; illa [vota] ~ia non sunt que dignam compensacionem habere non possunt, ut votum Christiane religionis quod emittitur in baptismo. .. alia vero fiunt supererogacione, id est ad majus bonum agendum; et talia sunt ~ia PAUL. ANGL. *ASP* 1558.

dispensamen, provision, regulation.

hac sola occasione ~ina B. Cuthberti possumus annichilando attenuare R. COLD. *Cuthb.* 107.

dispensanter, economically, to advantage.

nobis .. nichil emolumenti provenit, si dampna pensentur; nichil ~er agimus MAP *NC* IV 13 f. 54v. (cf. ib. III 3 f. 39: ~er et provide ministrat).

1 dispensare v. desponsare 1d.

2 dispensare [CL]

1 to distribute. **b** to spend. **c** to administer (sacrament). **d** to deliver (sermon).

790 misi .. aliquid de oleo .., ut ~ares per loca necessaria ALCUIN *Ep.* 7; confluebat ad eum tanta multitudo militum ut ei quod ~aret deficeret G. MON. IX 1; ebria tellus / plus equo potavit aquas et prodigus imber / dispensavit eas temere VINSAUF *PN* 867; PAUL. ANGL. *ASP* (v. commensuratio 2b). **b** ea .. quae sibi .. donaria pecuniarum largiebantur .. ad redemtionem eorum qui injuste fuerant venditi ~abat BEDE *HE* III 5; cum .. tributis que in publica regni commoda .. ~ari debuerant GIR. *EH* II 36; **c1215** l s. et ij s. .. in usus pauperum scolarium ~andos *Reg. Ant. Linc.* II 63 (= *Stat. Linc.* II lxvii). **c** **1219** certa forma prescribatur per quam ecclesiastica sacramenta .. rite tractentur et recte ~entur *Conc. Syn.* 59; si ex hoc erretur circa sacramentum penitencie, dicendo illud posse a quocumque non sacerdote ~ari DUNS *Ord.* I 61. **d** episcopus .. post evangelium .. populo sermonem ~at GOSC. *Transl. Aug.* 19B.

2 to manage, administer, regulate; **b** (pr. ppl. in abl. abs. w. *Deo* or sim.; *cf. disponere* 2b).

episcopus ~at causas pauperum usque ad l solidos, rex vero si plus est THEOD. *Pen.* II 2. 4; saecularium negotia, quae contemptibilibus ecclesiae apostolus ~anda praecipit [cf. *1 Cor.* vi 4] ALDH. *VirgP* 59; natura Dei .. / omnia regnando dispensat saecula simplex *Id. VirgV* 44; nec, si terrestris dispenset pondera curae, / grandia dona ferens cessabat reddere Christo ÆTHELWULF *Abb.* 586; **804** (17c) ego B. ad suscipiendam ac ~andam aecclesiam Rofensis [v. l. Rofensem] electus (*Professio episcopi*) *CS* 315 (cf. ib. 375); **s1070** (v. Christianitas 2a); **1346** sit tua mens pura, stricte responsa datura / cum quali cura dispensasti mea jura (*In Franciam*) *Pol. Poems* I 35. **b** **a700** (11c) Deo ~ante *CS* 76; adfuit superno ~ante judicio tempus BEDE *HE* IV 3; Domino ~ante HUGEB. *Wynn.* 2; W. dux Northmannorum, Deo ~ante eruditionem plebis suae, in regem transiit Anglorum GOSC. *Transl. Aug.* 34A.

3 (esp. eccl.) to allow by special dispensation: **a** (trans.); **b** (w. *ut* or *quod*, usu. w. *cum* in ref. to person); **c** (intr. w. *cum* in ref. to person); **d** (w. *cum* in ref. to rule); **e** (w. *cum* in ref. to breach of rule); **f** (w. var. preps. or absol.).

a **1107** cetera que in regno illo pro necessitate temporis ~anda sunt juxta gentis barbariem juxta ecclesie opportunitates sapientie et religionis tue sollicitudo ~et (*Lit. Papae*) EADMER *HN* 220; diximus que sunt in quibus dispensatio pastoralis admittitur, que non possunt omnibus penitentibus imponi omnia sed ex multiplici rationis consideratione sunt ~anda BART. EXON. *Pen.* 22. **b** Dominus non omnia revelavit expositoribus Sacre Scripture et etiam ~avit quod [v. l. ut] ipsi aliquid relinquerent S. LANGTON *Ruth* 106; vel Judei debent esse homines S. Ædmundi vel de villa sunt eiciendi. .. quod tamen .. ~atum est per justiciarios regis, sc. ut, si Judei venerint .. ad exigendum debita sua .., sub hac occasione poterunt ij diebus .. hospitari in villa BRAKELOND 133; **c1238** nisi fuerit ob causam rationabilem ut in ecclesiis suis non resideant cum eis [rectoribus] ~atum GROS. *Ep.* 52* p. 161; **s1272** ego [episcopus] ~abo cum senioribus .. ut ipsi veniant in habitu GRAYSTANES 9; **1295** ut ab ecclesia tua .. per triennium .. te absentare valeas .. tibi licenciam concedimus specialem, tecum ~antes ut interim .. non vexeris *Reg. Carl.* I 13; **1412** ne inclemens artacio residendi .. faciat lassescere, universitas ex abundanti ~avit quod in magna vacacione mensem habebit [custos librarie] ab onere liberum *StatOx* 219; **s1412** papa .. ~avit cum .. Thoma filio regis ut duceret in uxorem uxorem patrui sui *Eul. Hist. Cont.* III 420. **c** **1191** licet nobis aliquando .. cum personis religiosis rigore postposito misericorditer ~are (*Lit. Papae*) *Reg. Malm.* I 375; **s1218** generaliter .. quos irregularitatem in ordinis susceptione .. constat contraxisse, nisi cum eis expresse ~atum fuerit ab eo qui cum eis ~are potuit, ab officii sui executione suspensos denuntiamus *Conc. Syn.* 60; **s1237** dominus Otho .. cardinalis venit legatus in Angliam .., habens potestatem ~andi cum non legitimis *Ann. Tewk.* 105; **1238** non existimet abbas .. quod super habenda proprietate possit cum aliquo monacho ~are (*Stat. Ord. S. Bened.*) M. PAR. *Maj.* III 508; si convincatur .. quod id fecit [sc. alium interfecit] per infortunium vel se defendendo .., [rex] graciose ~abit cum tali *Fleta* 34; **1317** (v. dispensatorius 2b); WYCL. *Sim.* 68 (v. 3e infra); **a1350** solent .. regentes .. graciose cum personis aliquibus .. contra statuta .. ~are *StatOx* 18; dum ab alio admonetur, uti .. multa prohibeat, maxime talia quae ne fiant in rem sit populi; post pecunia cum illis ~et quorum commodis obstat interdictum MORE *Ut.* 90. **d** papa cum regula cujuscumque secte private potest despensare, ~avit et de facto despensat; sed cum norma apostolica ~are non potest WYCL. *Compl.* 89; **1400** placeat congregacioni .. cum .. statutis ad .. eleccionem et officium cancellarii spectantibus .. ~are, quatinus .. abbas de Pratis Leicestrie .. ad predictum officium .. sit vocatus *StatOx* 190; **1509** nullo pacto licebit minori congregacioni ~are cum aliquo articulo vel articulis pro hac cista factis vel faciendis *Ib.* 324. **e** alii sunt actus principiati de lege

nature cum quibus Deus non potest ~are Wycl. *Act.* 23; sicut Petrus non potuit ~are cum levi veniali peccato .., sic nullus papa sequens .. potest ~are cum aliquo de quantumcumque levi peccato nisi de quanto Deus prius ~at et ipse .. promulgat conformiter voluntati divine *Id. Sim.* 68 (cf. 3c supra); **s1378** rex non potest ~are cum minima concupiscencia rei aliene contra mandatum Dei *Eul. Hist. Cont.* III 346. **f** de talibus [clericis uxoratis] absque difficultate curia Romana ~at, quia et de subdiaconibus quibusdam audivimus a domino papa ~atum Gir. *GE* II 5; **1220** ita tamen quod circa sublimes et litteratas personas possit super hoc per sedem apostolicam ~ari *Mon. Hib. & Scot.* 18b; ut dispensetur super hoc modo Roma petetur [*gl.*: dispensatio est relaxatio rigoris juris] Garl. *Mor. Scol.* 479; **s1248** bulla quod abbas potest ~are super statutis Gregorii Elmh. *Cant.* 46; **1316** (v. curare 5b); Christus .. potuit .. contra statuta ab ipso [papa] edita ~are Ockham *Pol.* I 56; nulli licet venire contra verba alicujus precepti, nisi qui habet potestatem ~andi circa tale preceptum *Id. Dial.* 811; **a1350** ista forma ita stricte servabitur quod cancellarius contra ipsam sine universitate non poterit ~are *StatOx* 30; **s1383** accepta inaudita potestate a papa .. ~andi in casibus curie reservatis Wals. *YN* 337 (= *Chr. Angl.* 355); pia .. mater illa in quam plurimis dispensat que fieri ipsa non concedit Fortescue *LLA* 39; **s1518** legatus Henrici ad Leonem pontificem, a quo impetravit ut liceret legato Angliae solvere legibus quos vellet ad commodum eorum qui nexu aliquo legum tenentur, id quod vulgo dicitur '~are' P. Verg. *Camd.* 256.

dispensaria, office or service of 'dispenser', stewardship. *Cf. dispendere* 2b.

tenuit per serjanteriam ~ie *RDomin* 36; **1198** per servicium dispenserie *Fees* 11; **1219** T. le Despenser tenet c sol. terre de domino rege per serganteriam ~ie domini regis *Ib.* 252; **1214** habere faciatis .. duo collaria ad carretam ~ie nostre; item .. unam sellam ad sumarium ~ie nostre *Cl* 160b; **1243** Hugoni .. vadletto de ~ia regis *Cl* 47.

dispensarius

1 'dispenser', store-keeper or steward (developing into surname). *V. et. dispensator, expensarius.*

c1130 W. comes de Warenna Osmundo ~io (*Breve Comitis*) *Eng. Feudalism* 269 (cf. ib. 77); **c1180** (v. dispendere 2b); **1219** hiis testibus: .. Constantino dapifero, Thebaldo ~io meo (*Ch. Comitis*) *Inchaffray* 34; **1227** testibus: .. Hugone Despenserio .. *Cart. Osney* IV 410; **1255** L. Bolman, ~ius dicti vicarii, dictas scapulas et colla [bestiarum] ad opus domini sui recepit *SelPlForest* 37; senescalli officium est .. de expensis hospicii cum emptore, marescallo, coco, ~io et officiariis computare *Fleta* 161; **s1326** Londonienses .. dictos ~ios odio habentes Avesb. 77b (cf. ib.: dominus Hugo le Spenser junior et dominus Hugo le Spenser senior).

2 beneficiary of dispensation.

dispensacio non est nisi licenciacio ad insistendum occupacioni vel operi meliori, qua licenciacione intercidente remaneret ~ius ad occupacionem graviorem vel opus abjeccius obligatus Wycl. *Civ. Dom.* III 333.

dispensatio [CL]

1 distribution, apportionment. **b** (w. *verbi*) preaching, propagation.

[princeps] honorum distributor est et .. penes eum est perpetua ~o munerum J. Sal. *Pol.* 630B; Paul. Angl. *ASP* 1555 (v. commensuratio 2b); **1549** ut .. elemosinarum ~o viris .. honestis committatur *Conc. Scot.* II 114. **b** **719** ut ad ~onem verbi divini .. te comministro utamur (*Lit. Papae*) *Ep. Bonif.* 12.

2 management, administration, regulation. **b** procedure, behaviour. **c** (divine) governance, dispensation.

summus ecclesiasticae ~onis auctor Aldh. *Met.* 2 p. 67 (cf. *PR* 143 p. 203: mundanae ~onis curis .. fatigatus); tempus est ut expleta ~one assumptae mortalitatis .. revertar ad patrem Bede *Hom.* II 13. 155; ita transire praesentis vitae ~onem ut .. proveniatis ad peccatorum .. remissionem Egb. *Pont.* 61; ~o, *dihtnung, brytnung, scir, gedal* vel *diht GlH* D 575; communis .. causa commodi provida ~one statutum est ut .. (*Leg. Hen.* 8. 2) *GAS* 554; **c1190** cum ex officio ~onis nobis credite omnes teneamur ad opus caritatis invitare *Reg. S. Thom. Dublin* 338; pia dispensatio jura / temperat et mollit Vinsauf *PN* 858; si quid residuum fuerit, in ~one executorum meorum dispono (*Test.*) *FormMan* 17; *Obed. Abingd.* 349 (v. curiarius). **b** laudabilis hec et digna memoria ~o Gir. *PI* I 10; convivantibus et convescentibus secum honestissima se ~one conformabat Ad. Eyns. *Hug.* III 13 p. 125. **c** **716** gratias agere non cesso ~oni superni examinis .. quod te .. electionis vas regimini totius aecclesiae praeficere dignata est Hwætberht *Ep.*; mira divinae ~o provisionis erat quod .. in Pascha transivit de hoc mundo Bede *HE* V 22; **c756** (10c) ego Æ. rex .. populorum quibus me divina ~o .. praeesse voluit *CS* 181; Dei ~one coactus Alcuin *WillP* I 6; non .. dignum videri debet ut divinitas .. tantum opus sine causa atque magna ~one efficere voluerit *Eccl. & Synag.* 57; placuit supernae ~oni illum .. revelari Wulf. *Æthelwold* 42; mira Dei pietas et dispensatio mira Nig. *Mir. BVM* 16v. 1.

3 dispensation, relaxation of rule: **a** (eccl., var.); **b** (papal); **c** (mon.); **d** (civil); **e** (acad.).

a annon tibi videntur quedam Laban idola .. tulisse [cf. *Gen.* xxxi 19] .. qui antique observancie regulas novellis ~onibus temperant? G. Hoyland *Ascet.* 286C; Bart. Exon. *Pen.* 22 (v. dispensare 3a); presulis assensus et dispensatio cleri / queritur, ut liceat lege coire thori Nig. *Mir. BVM* 21. 1; deinde .. pauci diaconi qui etate et moribus exigentibus in superiori gradu tolerantur ex ~one *Offic. Sal.* 12; **1214** sacerdotes .. de non legitimo matrimonio natos et absque ~one episcoporum suorum promotos *Conc. Syn.* 25; **1236** legitimatio quam vis matrimonii efficit .. est legitimatio naturalis .. et non est ex gratia ~onis Gros. *Ep.* 23 p. 78; notatur quid sit ~o, quis possit dispensare, quibus de causis fiat ~o Hales *Sent.* IV 348; ipsi de gratia et ~one poterunt eam [ecclesiam] in proprios usus retinere Bracton 53. **b** **s1173** postquam .. filia ejus filio regis fuerit desponsata vel per legitimam etatem vel per Romane ecclesie ~onem *G. Hen. II* I 39; **c1186** alioquin hujusmodi absolutio et ~o quoad non professos .. nullius penitus sint valoris (*Lit. Papae*) Elmh. *Cant.* 473; **1227** ducemus in uxorem Yolentam .. quam cito poterimus ~onem impetrare a domino papa *Pat* 153; Garl. *Mor. Scol.* 479 *gl.* (v. dispensare 3f); **1279** absque sedis apostolice despensatione (v. commendatio 1c); **1317** fecit papa unam constitucionem .. per quam cassavit omnes ~ones super pluralitate beneficiorum per quoscunque predecessores suos concessas Ad. Mur. *Chr.* 28; **c1477** obtinuit .. bullam ~onis a papa de esu carnium in Septuagesima *Croyl. Cont. C* 560. **c** [monachi] nigri habent regulam quod vilissimos induant sue provincie pannos, et ex ~one pellicias agninas tantum Map *NC* I 25 f. 18; tam monachi quam canonici normas relinquentes Benedicti et Augustini sectas fratrum tamquam perfecciores sine ~one amplexantur Wycl. *Compl.* 89. **d** si per hujusmodi legem .. fuerit quis convictus, ex regie ~onis beneficio tam vite quam membrorum suorum ejus pendet judicium Glanv. XIV 1; **1203** meruit mortem, sed per ~onem eruantur ei occuli *SelPlCrown* 34. **e** **1409** istud statutum .. ita stricte observetur quod sine cancellarii et singulorum regencium consensu nulla super hoc ~o concedatur *StatOx* 202; **1431** si contrarium quoquomodo attemptetur, ipsam ~onem vigorem discernimus non habere *Ib.* 238.

4 (?) suspension from office.

1259 quod clerici arma portantes in ipso conflictu .. ad tempus suspendantur ab officio et, decurso tempore ~onis, possint ad officium restitui *Leg. Ant. Lond.* 66.

dispensative

1 **a** administratively, as a steward. **b** diplomatically, in a spirit of compromise.

a quando ecclesia pastore vacaverit, licet priori aliquem monachari .. et abbatis vice .. omnia negotia domus ~e pertractare *Obed. Abingd.* 359. **b** **1167** si aliquid in causa quam contra regem Anglie habetis ~e diximus .., ut .. quasi placida manu eum ad pacem traheremus id fecimus (*Lit. J. Cardinalis*) *Becket Mat.* VI 169; quoniam purum Walensem eligere non ausus fuerat, quasi ~e mixtum et ex utraque gente oriundum Giraldum elegit Gir. *JS* 1 p. 120.

2 by way of dispensation, as a special case.

1191 ecclesiam .. in proprios usus convertere .. ~e vobis indulgemus (*Lit. Papae*) *Reg. Malm.* I 360; quatenus divina potentia ~e permisit Gerv. Tilb. III 103; [Cluniacenses] mulieres vivas inter septa domorum suarum non recipiunt .. preter illas solum, quasi ~e sed cupide revera magis et lucrative, .. quas regina pecunia .. introducit Gir. *Spec.* III 12 p. 200; forsan pro nobis oraret, et eriperemur / dispensative fato quod jure subimus H. Avr. *Hugh* 659; **1236** prolem naturaliter et non ~e legitimatam Gros. *Ep.* 23 p. 86; **1238** si .. alibi nequiverint commode collocari .., recipiantur in eisdem monasteriis ~e (*Stat. Ord. S. Bened.*) M. Par. *Maj.* III 512; **1280** ~e permittimus ut .. Willelmus .. canoniam .. retineat Peckham *Ep.* 114; nec alicui, ingruente necessitate, ~e petenti debet renui *Obed. Abingd.* 396; precepta .. de observancia paupertatis .. nunquam nisi ~e ad tempus relaxata fuerunt Ockham *Pol.* I 352; despensative laxavit apostolus virginitatis frena, quod consulere noluit [cf. *1 Cor.* vii 38] Fortescue *LLA* 39.

dispensativus

1 administrative, regulative.

~a sapientia cunctipotentis P. Blois *Euch.* 24; dispensativum jus, dispensatio justa, / lege rigens pietas, lex pietate tepens H. Avr. *Poems* 27. 7; Dominus Exercituum, ~am majestatis sue clementiam .. depromens Ad. Marsh *Ep.* 143 p. 271; ethica tres habet partes: sc. moralem specialiter dictam .. seu solitariam ..; economicam seu ~am seu privatam, per quam homo sciat familiam regere; politicam .. vel civilem Kilwardby *OS* 658.

2 exercising special dispensation, permissive.

[ecclesia] Orientalis, que [de presbyteris desponsandis] Pauli potius ~e adhesit indulgentie Gir. *GE* II 6 p. 187; **s1316** presulatuum dignitatibus suis pastoribus sic viduatis prefecit dominus papa magistrum T. de Cobeham .. ac sic deliberacio ~a summi pontificis insolenciarum regis acerbitatem .. in cinerem sufflavit *Flor. Hist.* III 177; quam ~us est dominus papa cum mendacio quoad multitudinem personarum, tam ~us est cum mendacio quoad genus Wycl. *Ver.* II 57.

dispensator [CL]

1 distributor, disburser. **b** dispenser of sacrament or teaching (*cf. 1 Cor.* iv 1).

episcopus [Æthericus, ob. **1034**] .. singulis [baronum] duas residui auri marcas largifluus tribuens ~or, .. gratitudinem eorum .. sibi federavit *Chr. Rams.* 139; Gir. *GE* II 34 (v. dissipator b); Paul. Angl. *ASP* 1555 (v. commensuratio 2b); **s1451** non dissipator prodigus, immo verius ~or fidelis et prudens .. bonorum ecclesie *Reg. Whet.* I 6. **b** **747** ut presbyteri .. reminiscant .. quod Dei .. ministros (*sic*) et ~ores mysteriorum Christi vocantur (*Clovesho* 8) *Conc. HS* 365; quatinus verbum vite .. predicaret .. fidelis ac prudens ~or misteriorum Dei Boso *V. Pont.* 388; erat egregius ~or divini dogmatis *VSH* (*Abban* 9) I 8.

2 steward, bursar or sim.: **a** (unspec. or private; developing into surname); **b** (eccl., mon., or acad.); **c** (royal). **d** (naut.) purser. *Cf. dapifer. V. et. dispensarius* 1.

a ~or, *dihtnere* Ælf. *Gl.*; de hoc manerio tenet Willelmus ~or j *solin DB* I 3; **a1190** testes sunt: .. Willelmus ~or Thome de Salebi .. *Danelaw* 97; **1242** Willelmus filius Ricardi †disponsatoris *Pipe* 180; **s1322** factus fuit comes Wyntonie dominus H. ~or pater Ad. Mur. *Chr.* 37; **c1370** rex adhesit duobus ~oribus Hugoni patri et filio ejusdem nominis (J. Bridl. *gl.*) *Pol. Poems* I 133. **b** Aldh. *Met.* 2 (v. diaconatus 1a); praecepit ~ori cenobii, E. sacerdoti, ut .. omnia que monachi indigent .. construeret Byrht. *V. Osw.* 430; *DB* II 372 (v. cervisiarius 3b); de episcopo ~ori precipiente quatinus elemosinas pauperibus via qua regem venturum audierat largius daret Gir. *GE* II 27 p. 297; **1535** stipendia .. trium bursariorum vel ~orum .. collegii [Novi, Oxon.] *Val. Eccl.* II 264. **c** dispensator ei fuit obvius ecce repente / regius Wulf. *Swith.* II 533; **s1040** [Heardecanutus] Edricum ~orem .. et alios magne dignitatis viros Londoniam misit Fl. Worc. I 194; Azor ~or regis E. tenuit *DB* I 62; **1087** teste .. Eudone dapifero et Rotberto ~ore *Regesta* p. 130 (cf. ib. p. xxvii); **1105** x hidas .. quas tenet .. Hugo [filius] Turstini, curie mee ~or *Regesta* II 683; de ~oribus panis... de ~oribus lardarii... de buteleria: .. magister ~or butilerie [debet habere] sicut magister ~or panis et vini. .; ~ores butilarie qui per vicem serviunt sicut ~ores expense qui per vicem serviunt *Domus Reg.* 130–2; **a1154** Ethelredo ~ori domus regis L. Durh. *Ep.* 263 (cf. *Regesta Scot.* I p. 32); **1198** per servicium esse ~or regis *Fees* 11; **1221** Thurstanus Despenser tenet c solidatas terre per serjantiam quod sit ~or domus regis *PlCrGlouc* 50. **d** **1560** (v. bursarius 6).

3 administrator, regulator; **b** (as divine epithet). **c** (w. *privati sigilli*) keeper of Privy Seal.

Clemens .. secundus Romanae ecclesiae ~or Aldh. *VirgP* 25; **862** (10c) omnia regna hujus labentis vite regnorumque ~ores .. ceciderunt *Ch. Roff.* 25; contigit unum ex prebendis ecclesie Lincoln', decessu canonici qui eam possederat vacantem, novum expectare ~orem Ad. Eyns. *Hug.* III 9. **b** **948** (12c) omnipotens factor atque monarchus ~or *CS* 870; optimi ~oris providentia Gir. *TH* I 27. **c** magister Roderam .., episcopus Roffensis et ~or privati sigilli domini regis Herrison *Abbr. Chr.* 10.

4 granter of special dispensation.

si dispensatio fuerit illegitima propter ordinem juris omissum .., tunc ipse ~or non poterit hoc revocare J. Burgh *PO* VII 9 f. 119.

dispensatorie [LL]

1 **a** by (divine) dispensation. **b** as an agent. **c** for practical reasons, prudently.

a ubi primum ecclesiae celebratum est baptisma, ~ie pietas divina .. numerum collegit animarum Bede *Acts* 950D; Ad. Scot *Serm.* 362C (v. demeritorie). **b** armiger ab milite ~ie directus et creditori Judeo bene cognitus T. Mon. *Will.* II 14 p. 100. **c** **s1066** navium parte maxima ~ie jam combusta, ne sc. repatriandi spe aliquid forsitan negligentius ceptis instarent *Chr. Battle* f. 9.

2 by (special) dispensation, as a special case.

seu constringat seu relaxet seu ~ie aliquid, interveniente causa aliqua rationabili, agat .., totum ad caritatis integritatem transferat Ad. Scot *TT* 615D.

dispensatorius [LL]

1 executing (divine) dispensation.

fit ut .. sit ei ~ius iste tentationis tactus, acutus quidam cultellus, quo .. universa .. carnalis inhonestas abscidatur Ad. Scot *Serm.* 381B; qui manu proprie actionis non habuit gladium iniquitatis, ~ium ab ipsis membris diaboli suscepit gladium mortis [cf. *1 Sam.* xvii 51] *Ib.* 389C; *Ib.* 426B (v. disponere 2c); videbis post paululum quod exspectatio hec ~ia fuerit preparatio Domini in diem crastinum J. Ford *Wulf.* 98 (cf. ib. 30: ~ia quadam avaritia et ambitione religiosa).

2 concerned w. (special) dispensation (from rule); **b** (w. *litterae*).

si tale quid exprimo: 'jura / mollescunt,' vel 'jura rigent', nondum bene lucet / .. / dic igitur melius: 'dispensatoria jura / mollescunt, districta rigent' Vinsauf *PN* 855;

supponitur .. quod secunda pars [statuti] .. sit ∼ia super prima parte, que alias obtinet vim precepti CONWAY *Def. Mend.* 1413 (*recte* 1313). **b** **1317** visis litteris ∼iis .. domini R. nuper Heref' episcopi de triennio concesso .. rectori de E. ad vacandum scolasticis disciplinis, dispensavit pater A. .. cum eodem per unum annum .. post .. triennium *Reg. Heref.* 34; **1523** litteras apostolicas ∼ias absolutorias et declaratorias debite executioni per .. vicarium generalem judicem in hac parte et executorem a .. sede apostolica .. deputatum demandari *Form. S. Andr.* I 110.

3 (as sb. n. or f.) 'spence', store-room.

in dispensa sive in ∼io sint gausape, mantile, manutergium NECKAM *Ut.* 98; **1251** apud Guldeford .. ∼ium et butellarium cooperiri et in utroque unam novam fenestram fieri .. faciatis (*AncC* II 116) *RL* II 66; **1311** in gumfis et vertevellis ad fenestram contra ostium ∼ii *MinAc* 856/17 m. 2; **1380** una aula cum dispensat' bene cooperta cum *sclattes Cart. Osney* I 45; **1435** omnia .. hustilamenta, ornamenta, utensilia .. ad meum domicilium pertinencia, sc. pro aula, camera, ∼ia, coquina et aliis officiis hospicii mei *Reg. Cant.* II 519.

dispensatrix [LL], dispenser (f.), manageress (partly fig.).

796 saluta quoque ill[am] dominam et ∼icem domus regiae [i.e. reginam] ALCUIN *Ep.* 101; anima corporum ∼ix ADEL. *ED* 32; omnis persona Dei .. ∼ix est clementie .. sue J. SAL. *Pol.* 814A; natura ∼ix P. BLOIS *Ep.* 238 (v. disponere 6a).

dispenser- v. dispensar-.

dispensio, dispensation or (?) *f. l.*

s**1129** R. de Carun .. dedit S. Neoto .. crucem et v imagines de dispensione [? l. dispensatione *or* suspensione] (passionis [*interl.*]) Domini *MonA* III 473b; **1338** abbas .. qui dispensioni [? l. dispensacioni] negociorum .. abbaciam suam .. contingencium .. personaliter vacare non potest *Reg. Brev. Orig.* 22.

dispensorium [cf. dispensatorius 3], 'spence', store-room.

hoc ∼ium, *a spens WW.*

disperabilis v. desperabilis. **disperagare** v. disparagare. **disperantia, ∼are, ∼atio** v. desper-. **disperas** v. dipsas. **dispercare** v. disparcare. **dispercio** v. dispersio. **dispercionare** v. dispersonare.

disperdere [CL], to waste, ruin, destroy; **b** (w. pers. obj.).

regnum illud .. reges dubii vel externi ∼iderunt BEDE *HE* IV 24 p. 268; prepositus .., comes vel villanus qui hoc facere nolet aut ∼et emendet cxx s. (*Quad.*) *GAS* 191; rex Saul reservat predam de Amalech quam ∼ere debuerat AD. DORE *Pictor* 155; Ulixes .. precipit suis ∼ere tumulum Hectoris TREVET *Troades* 48. **b** **967** (11c) si quis .. hanc .. donationem .. infringere temptaverit, ∼et eum Deus, nisi resipiscat *CS* 1201; fere sunt innocentes quos .. tanquam appositos tibi fructus dilanias, devoras, et ∼is MAP *NC* V 6 f. 67.

disperditio, ruin.

ne brevi ad ∼onem ruat respublica REDMAN *Hen. V* 22.

dispergatio v. disparagatio.

dispergere [CL]

1 to scatter, disperse: **a** (things); **b** (people); **c** (abstr.). **d** to break up (a siege). **e** (pass., of information) to be found in separate places, occur sporadically. **f** (p. ppl. as sb. n. abl.) sporadically.

a nubes .. / .. quas rapidis dispergunt flamina ventis ALDH. *CE* 4. 12. 17; diffusa, i. sparsa, dispersa, *tobrædde GlH* D 450; si non aeris .. ventositas minuta [apium] corpuscula .. ∼eret GIR. *TH* I 6; ut ossa [Hectoris] .. in mari ∼antur TREVET *Troades* 48; **13..** (v. diripere 1a). **b** contigit ut .. municipes .. vagabundis meatibus passim ∼entur [v. l. †dispargerentur] ALDH. *VirgP* 52; [Britanni] relictis civitatibus fugiunt, ∼untur BEDE *HE* I 12; [clerici maligni] per diversas Anglorum provincias huc illucque dispersi sunt WULF. *Æthelwold* 19; **1152** (v. congregatio 2b); **1231** habent Judei .. ex Dei justitia ut per diversas nationes vagi et profugi ∼antur GROS. *Ep.* 5 p. 35; ∼entur captive .. in navibus Grecorum TREVET *Troades* 73; quidam ea tempestate dispersi in lateribus Anglie .. requierunt in anchoris *G. Hen. V* 25; **1461** (v. cursualiter). **c** plurima frugiferis dispergens semina verbis ALDH. *CE* 4. 2. 3; Pelagius .. venena suae perfidiae longe lateque dispersit BEDE *HE* I 10; s**1186** dispargitur rumor in civitate .. de adventu archiepiscopi GERV. CANT. *Chr.* 342; BRADW. *CD* 150C (v. congregatrix). **d** obsidione dispersa ad propria singuli sunt reversi GIR. *IK* I 12. **e** que .. erit tam confuse dispersorum ad disciplinalem cognitionis modum coartatio? BALSH. *AD rec. 2* 155; naturas rerum et proprietates per sanctorum libros .. dispersas BART. ANGL. *proem.*; hoc in parte determinata hujus libri invenietur quod in locis dispargitur infinitis BACON *CSTheol.* 36. **f** epistole vario et disperso [v. l. diverso] per scedulas collecte corpus rediguntur in unum A. TEWK. *Prol. Thom.* 300.

2 **a** to divide, distribute. **b** to dissipate, squander.

a hoc ∼ere ac dare pauperibus curabat BEDE *HE* II 1 p. 77; thesauros et facultates aecclesiae dispersit deditque pauperibus WULF. *Æthelwold* 29; cibus in ∼entis fit manus [AS: *mete gæþ on †banan* [? l. *bryttan*] *hand*] *Prov. Durh.* 34; s**1181** (v. distributor a). **b** nec dispersa revocare nec pauca .. retenta colere GIR. *JS* 1 p. 146; **1228** cum [ecclesia] sub umbra pastorum prodigos habuerit dispersores, qui non solum .. dispersa colligere non curarunt sed .. pelles .. ovium rapiebant (*Lit. Papae*) *Reg. S. Osm.* II 90; Turstinus [Glastoniae abbas, ob. c**1101**] ecclesie possessiones per aliquot tempus ∼endo longe a monasterio expiravit *Eul. Hist.* I 417.

3 to spread (hay or manure).

c**1230** ∼ere debet fena *Doc. Bec* 64; **1234** Golliva .. ∼et pratum ante (*sic*) falcationem et erit ad pratum levandum cum rastillo suo *Cust. Glast.* 79; *Ib.* 68 (v. compostum a); faciant .. ante .. festum [nativitatis S. J. Baptiste] .. prata falcari, dispargi, desiccari *Fleta* 170.

dispergibilis, liable to be dissipated, evanescent.

laus secularis ∼is est more spume W. LEIC. *Sim.* 76.

disperire [CL], **a** to be destroyed. **b** to be overcome, surrender.

a excitant Dominum discipuli ne eo dormiente fluctuum feritate ∼eant BEDE *Mark* 174; ne animae pro quibus Dominus passus est in aeterna poena ∼eant ÆLF. *EC* 37; nec pro levi re ∼eat [AS: *forspille* (*man*)] opus manuum Dei (*Quad.*) *GAS* 311 (cf. deterere d); **1346** ∼iunt (v. desipere a). **b** cogitavi .. aliqualem ostendere responsionem et redarguentibus omnino non ∼ire ROLLE *IA* 233.

dispernere v. despernere.

disperquirere [cf. CL perquirere], to seek; **b** (w. indir. qu.).

c**1410** alter alterius mortem .. callide ∼unt *FormOx* 424; s**1412** dux Aurelianensis .. †dispersiquivit media per que regem Anglie .. in affectum sibi posset allicere WALS. *HA* II 287 (= *Id. YN* 434: disperquisivit). **b** s**1309** rex remansit tristis .., ∼ens omni studio qualiter ipsum [Petrum de Gavestone] posset ab exilio revocare *Ib.* I 124.

dispersare, to scatter, spread out.

to departe, .. disjungere, dispergere, ∼are, dispescere .., *to sprede oute*, dilatare .., dispergere, ∼are, displicare *CathA.*

disperse [CL], dispersedly, sporadically.

a pluribus ∼e de arte quedam, a nullo totam artem ordine explicatam contingit inveniri BALSH. *AD* 7; H. HUNT. *HA* VIII 8 (v. dissolute).

dispersim [CL], dispersedly.

quod stupidis .. hominibus et juris ignaris ∼imque degentibus .. persuaserit ALB. LOND. *DG* 8. 20; **1414** vicarii hospicia sua in diversis habitacionibus ∼im et non in communi tenent (*Pat*) *Mem. Ripon* I 123.

dispersio [LL]

1 dispersal, dispersion (of people). **b** dispersion (of Jews), diaspora. **c** dispersion (of light).

GILDAS *EB* 19 (v. desperabilis); †**948** (14c) duo [monachi] a ∼one regressi *CS* 872 p. 20; s**1202** alii .., timentes .. fratrum ∼onem, querebant ut pax fieret in diebus suis *Chr. Evesham* 110. **b** **680** duodecim tribubus in ∼one constitutis [cf. *James* i 1] ALDH. *Ep.* 4; cognovi totius mee gentis ∼onem ex omnibus mundi partibus iterum colligendam *Eccl. & Synag.* 77. **c** ∼o speciei secundum omnes diametros in omni parte medii BACON *Maj.* II 520.

2 dissipation, squandering.

lucrorum suorum ∼onis amissionem R. COLD. *Cuthb.* 32; [H. episcopus, ob. **1194**] in edificiis eandem habebat instantiam, nec in qualibet rerum pensabat erogatione sive ∼one dispendium G. COLD. *Durh.* 7 (cf. *Hist. Durh.* 3 p. 138); M. PAR. *Min.* III 33 (v. dilapidatio b); s**1256** secundum quod dicimus omnia esse principis, ac si diceretur 'defensione, non ∼one' *Id. Maj.* V 540.

3 **a** spreading (of hay or manure). **b** breaking up (of mole-hills).

a c**1308** in falcacione tocius prati ad tascham, cum ∼one et levacione tocius feni *LTRAc* 19 r. 41; **1439** pro ∼one, levacione et lucracione feni *Ac. Durh.* 72; **1532** pro dispercione fimi *Househ. Bk. Durh.* 76. **b** **1493** pro dispercione *del moldhillez Ac. Durh.* 652.

4 (by conf. w. *disperdere*) perdition.

a700 (11c) [donationem] minuentibus vel contradicentibus ∼o perveniat sempiterna! *CS* 76; **855** (18c) aeterna ultio vel ∼o super illos perveniat! *CS* 490.

dispersiquire v. disperquirere.

dispersonare [cf. OF *despersoner*], to 'disperson', disgrace, insult. *V. et. depersonare.*

s**1170** [pater meus] non est ∼atus, degradatus, minoratus vel degeneratus si mihi ministret M. PAR. *Min.* I 353 (cf. depersonare); si aliquis ∼averit prepositum in plena curia, oportet eum .. ut deneget aperto ore *Leg. IV Burg.* 100; si quis ∼averit ballivum in curia domini sui seu maledixerit ei *Quon. Attach.* 40; si dominus ei offert racionabile maritagium, ubi non alias disparagetur vel ∼etur *Ib.* 91; si aliquis ribaldus ∼averit aliquem virum vel mulierem de valore, imprisonetur per xl dies *Chain Bk. Dublin* 235; **1305** vadit emendas domino quia ∼avit .. priorem in plena curia *CourtR Hales* 511; **1328** quod frangeret brachia et tibias hominum ville de A. .. et eos dispercionaret (*Andover*) *Gild Merch.* II 318 (cf. ib. 328); **1424** (v. dispersonatio).

dispersonatio, insult.

1424 ordinatum est .. quod, si aliquis civis vel indigena .. civitatis injuste dispersonaverit, vilependerit vel scandelizaverit majorem .. vel aliquem de ballivis .. civitatis, si idem dispersonatus .. producat .. duos cives .. qui illam ∼onem vel scandelum audierunt .., quod (*sic*) .. idem dispersonator et scandelizator habeatur attinctus *BB Winchester* 61.

dispersonator, insulter.

1424 (v. dispersonatio).

dispersor [LL], dissipator, squanderer.

AILR. *Ed. Conf.* 759D (v. diminutor); **1228** (v. dispergere 2b); tam ∼ores quam redintegratores, ut utrique dignam remunerationem .. consequantur, .. commendabimus *Chr. Evesham* 76; s**1253** cum non haberet rex predictam ad manum pecuniam, quia consuevit esse undecunque rapte ∼or M. PAR. *Maj.* V 364.

dispertire [CL], **a** to divide, apportion. **b** to separate, cut off.

a †**765** (13c) haec terra ∼itur *CS* 197; eleemosynae circa domos uberrime pauperibus ∼iebantur ALCUIN *Vedast.* 423; ∼iens, *brytniende GlH* D 584; **9..** ∼itus, *todæled WW*; [haec terra] erat ∼ita in tribus locis *DB* I 10v.; hanc terram tribus filiis suis ∼ivit *Ib.* 32; res .. transitorie minuuntur ∼ite, caritas autem quanto plus spargitur tanto magis amplificatur ALEX. CANT. *Dicta* 14 p. 160; dispertiri (*sic*), dare, donare, dispungere, praebere, tribuere OSB. GLOUC. *Deriv.* 178; fluvius .. iste quadrifarie dispartitur GROS. *Hexaem.* XI 23. **b** **847** sit a consortio Christi ecclesiae et a collegio sanctorum hic et in futuro dispartitus *CS* 451; dispartire, *tostenc GlH* D 666.

dispescere [CL], to divide.

dispe[s]cit, secernit *GlC* D 315; dispi[s]catis, divisis *Gl. Leid.* 4. 30 (cf. ib. 35. 134: dispi[s]catis, disruptis); ∼ere, separare OSB. GLOUC. *Deriv.* 178; *CathA* (v. dispersare); Scotus populus in tres ordines ∼itur LESLEY *RGScot* 66.

dispicabilis v. despicabilis. **dispicare** v. dispescere.

1 dispicere v. 1 despicere.

2 dispicere [CL], **a** to consider. **b** (w. acc. & inf.) to perceive.

a ∼iamus ne a via veritatis recedamus BYRHT. *Man.* 226; cum quidquid aliud est, si singula ∼iantur, aut sit melius quam non ipsum aut non ipsum in aliquo sit melius quam ipsum ANSELM (*Mon.* 15) I 29. **b** mihi locum despicio aeternae perditionis esse praeparatum BEDE *HE* V 14 p. 314.

dispiscat v. desipiscere.

dispissitudo [cf. CL spissitudo], thickness, density.

exteriorum cooperatio requiritur [ad auditum], ut non sit magnum intermedium, et dico vel vie longitudine vel interpositi ∼ine GILB. III 145. 1.

displicare [CL = *disperse*; cf. OF *desploiier*]

1 **a** to unfold. **b** to 'display', unfurl. **c** to unpack.

nulli .. licitum est .. pannum lineum suo lecto habere appensum et ∼atum .., nisi brevi tempore dum .. pannus ille siccatur *Cust. Westm.* 147 (cf. *Cust. Cant.* 194); *to sprede oute*, dilatare, distendere .., ∼are, ex- .. *CathA.* **b** **1265** venerunt cum magno exercitu et baneriis desplicatis ad civitatem Hereford' *IMisc* 12/11; s**1356** princeps .. ∼avit vexilla sua *Eul. Hist.* III 216 (cf. ib. 312 [s**1359**]: rex .. vexilla ∼uit super Franciam); s**1378** Henricum [de Percy], qui primo tunc suum vexillum ∼uit WALS. *HA* I 388; s**1381** venit .. R. de Walingforde .., deferens ante eum vexillum sive pencellum ∼atum de armis S. Georgii juxta morem illorum qui Londoniis tot scelera perpetrarunt *G. S. Alb.* III 304; ∼atus, A. *displayd WW*; **1571** bellum crudele, contra .. reginam Mariam vexillis erectis et †displacitis .. paraverunt *Entries* 643b (cf. ib. 413: vexillis ∼atis). **c** **1294** (v. dirigere 7).

2 **a** to open (eyes). **b** (w. *sinum*) to open arms (in sign of welcome).

a per biduum jacet †examinis [l. exanimis]; tunc egra sopore / lumina displicuit *V. Ed. Conf. Metr.* I 444. **b** s**1367** portum verrinum sic intravere marinum; / cives ad dominum displicuere sinum [MS: †suum] W. PETERB. *Bell. Hisp.* 112.

displicenter, w. displeasure.

1327 sicut ∼er audivimus *Reg. Heref.* 235; si quis bene .. facit, .. invidi .. connivent oculis .., si quid sit ibi quod

reprehendant vel ~er [ME: *ladliche*] se habeant *AncrR* 75; imperator multum ~er tulit frustracionem laborum suorum pro eis *G. Hen. V* 25 p. 174; **1440** quod ~er et egre .. audimus et ferimus Bekynton I 190.

displicentia [CL], displeasure.

nichil .. in displicientie signum .. metuis? Andr. S. Vict. *Comm.* 273; hec voluntas ei naturalis est, sc. quod per se velit id quod in se est indifferens et non habens relationem ad Dei placentiam vel ~iam Gros. 224; **1263** certe non levem suscitat hoc in nobis ~ie spiritum (*Lit. R. Regis Romanorum*) *Foed.* I 769; s**1297** villam .. depredati sunt, in magnam ~iam regis nostri Rish. 177; s**1316** nunquam verbum murmuris vel ~ie hoc .. est auditum de ore ejus Graystanes 37; **1418** quandam mulierem .. rapuerunt in Dei ~iam non modicam et offensam *RNorm* 366; **1517** non absque gravi animi ~ia *Form. S. Andr.* I 12.

displicēre [CL], to displease. **b** (inf. as sb.) displeasure.

omnia quae ~uerunt Deo et quae placuerunt aequali .. lance pendebantur si non gratiora fuissent ~entia Gildas *EB* 22; quantum pro industria exteriori regi placens, tantum pro interna suimet neglegentia ~ens Bede *HE* V 13; c**1074** inter multa quae placent relata nobis sunt quaedam quae ~ent Lanfr. *Ep.* 38 (10); omnia que Deo placebant et ~ebant equali lance .. pendebant G. Mon. XII 6; displicet imprudens quando placere putat Walt. Angl. *Fab.* 17. 16; jus civile mihi displicuisse neges Neckam *DS* X 338; cujus [mulieris] nates desplicent viro religioso Garl. *Dict.* 121; ~eo, A. *to dysplese WW*. **b** nunquam feci tuum ~ere O. Cheriton *Fab.* 59A.

displicibilis, displeasing, disagreeable.

tristatus de adventu alicujus rei nocive seu ~is Duns *Sent.* I 13. 1. 12 (= *Id. Ord.* V 90: de eventu alicujus rei nocive sive disconvenientis); s**1317** eos ~iores esse novimus regi pacifico *Mon. Hib. & Scot.* 192a; **1343** pertulit .. ad nos rumor ~is et infestivus quod .. (*Lit. Papae*) Ad. Mur. *Chr.* 151.

displicibiliter, disagreeably.

s**1308** defecerat ibi specularis dispositio convivii regibus assueta. .. missa in ecclesia .. et prandium de nocte ~ius finita *Ann. Paul.* 261.

displicientia v. displicentia. **displinaliter** v. disciplinaliter.

displodere [CL], to break apart, shatter; **b** (fig.). **c** to blurt out. **d** to elide.

~ere, delere, concutere Osb. Glouc. *Deriv.* 173 (cf. ib. 181: displosus, distractus); Ciren. I 372 (v. discissere); c**1370** Gallorum porte displodentur sibi sorte [*gl.*: aperientur .. per fortunam] (J. Bridl.) *Pol. Poems* I 153, 155; *to †bacon* [l. *baten*], dissplodere, .. *departyd*, .. displosus .. *CathA*. **b** male complosa displosit R. Cant. *Malch.* V 430 (v. complodere d). **c** ne quid displodat [v. l. resonet] inepti / lingua tenax justi Frith. 7. **d** terminalem genetivi sillabam ~it, dicens '.. bellor(um) incendia ..' Aldh. *Met.* 9.

displois v. diplois c. **dispnia** v. dyspnoea. **dispol-** v. despol-. **dispondaicus** v. dispondeus. **dispondere** v. despondere.

dispondeus [LL < διϲπόνδειος], **~aicus,** composed of double spondees. **b** (as sb. m., *sc. pes*) double spondee.

circa rithmum ~eum sunt iiij differentie Garl. *PP* 180; si rithmus est ~aicus .., potest esse iambica differentia in tertio vel in quarto vel in quinto .. 'o Mārīā, / māter pīā, / hīīs sūccūrrē mīsērīs'. .. differentia iambica cadit hic in tertio loco *Ib.* 190–2. **b** nomina ad ~eum rite congruentia: 'sērvātōrēs ..' Aldh. *PR* 126. partimur ergo in aequo hos: spondeum - -, .. ~eum - - - - Bonif. *Met.* 109.

dispondius v. dupondius.

disponere [CL]

1 to place, set. **b** to arrange, set in order. **c** to draw up, marshal (troops or chess pieces). **d** (p. ppl. *dispositus*) properly arranged.

Hales *Sent.* IV 409 (v. diaconus 1a). **b** ~o, *ic geendebyrde* vel *gafadige* vel *todæle GlH* D 707; hi .. quatuor numeri sic ~untur ut eorum primus .. ultimo .. opponatur Rob. Angl. *Alg.* 120; planius est sic esse ut in complexione ~untur singula quam quidlibet ad alterius locum transferre Balsh. *AD* 95; materie quantum ad essentiam non opponitur aliquid, sc. materie non disposite contrariis dispositionibus ..; set ipsi quantum ad esse, sc. in quantum est disposita contrariis dispositionibus ad aliquam formam, sic illa forma est ei opposita Bacon VIII 26. **c** Arturus .. precepit .. eis .. exercitum promissum ~ere G. Mon. IX 20; Neckam *NR* II 184 (v. dispositio 1a); dispositis .. catervis M. Par. *Maj.* I 18 (cf. G. Mon. I 8); s**1234** dispositis aciebus ad pugnam Wend. III 83; s**1264** (v. congressio a); s**1332** (v. collateralis 2a); s**1383** dispositus est regalis exercitus ad pergendum illuc *V. Ric.* II 48. **d** †degesta [l. digesta], ~a *GlC* D 94; cum loqui incipimus, proponimus pauca loqui et verba ~a [ME: *for to speoke lutel & wel isette wordes*] *AncrR* 18.

2 to contrive, manage, settle, regulate; **b** (absol.); **c** (w. ref. to divine providence or nature; *cf. dispensare* 2b); **d** (astr.).

furibus invisis, vastant qui farris acervos,/ insidiis tacite dispono scandala mortis Aldh. *Aen.* 65 (*Muriceps*) 5; nec vacabat eum semper gubernandis ~endisque monasterii curis implicari *Hist. Abb. Jarrow* 12; quae in Galliis bene disposita vidit Bede *HE* III 18; ecclesiarum .. sollicitudinem strenuus gerebat et earum causas, que ad eum .. quotidie ferebantur, ~ebat Eadmer *V. Dunst.* 28; mulier nichil potest ~ere circa dotem suam in vita sui mariti Glanv. VI 3; Map *NC* V 3 (v. composite a); s**1264** transfretaverunt .. pro pace ~enda et confirmanda *Leg. Ant. Lond.* 69; potestate quadam speciali vendicandi rem aliquam temporalem et defendendi ac tenendi et ~endi Ockham *Pol.* I 305; s**1383** ~ere bellum (v. consodalis); s**1399** [comes] vj carucatas per [Rogerum de] Walden versus castrum de Saltwod pro tutamine dispositas .. abstulit Ad. Usk 38. **b** corpora distemperata .. male comedunt nec curant bibere; male digerunt et ~unt M. Scot *Phys.* 32. **c** summi prudentia Patris, / .. / .. aeterno disponens saecula nutu Aldh. *VirgV* 674; divina gratia ~ente ut .. ad vitam raperetur aeternam Bede *HE* V 15; †**730** (12c) Domino .. jura imperiorum ~enti *CS* 155 (cf. *Chr. Abingd.* I 38: †impiorum dissonenti); **875** in nomine Domini .. ~entis ubique omnia *CS* 539; **957** (12c) omni creantis ~ente clementia *CS* 994; mundanas variare vices natura stupebit / cunctaque disponens proprias laxabit habenas *Altercatio* 12; a**1089** [Deus] non .. te in hoc seculo tantis flagellis attereret, nisi post hoc seculum sine flagello te esse ~eret Lanfr. *Ep.* 46 (21); aliquid .. illi quidem dispensatorium, nobis autem necessarium, ipsa [gratia] .. ~ente circa nos Ad. Scot *Serm.* 426B; natura ~ente Gir. *TH* I 4; [Meilduf] cogitans ubi Deus pro eo ~eret *Eul. Hist.* I 225 (cf. W. Malm. *GP* V 189); **1545** ~ente altissimo *Conc. Scot.* I cclxii. **d** cum sol in anno gratie **1249** mense Julii fuerit in Leone et sic in domo sua, erit Mars tempore eodem in primo decano Arietis et sic in domo et facie sua. ~et ergo tempus illud in calido et sicco superflue Gros. 50 (cf. ib. [Saturnus] ~et tunc 5 hiemes continuas).

3 to dispose, incline. **b** (w. acc. & compl.) to dispose to become. **c** (pr. ppl. w. *causa*) disponent cause. **d** (refl.) to dispose oneself, be disposed. **e** (p. ppl. *dispositus*) disposed, esp. well disposed; *cf. benedispositus*.

s**991** ex ictu belli morti dispositus, testamentum faciens, unam hidam nobis dedit *Chr. Rams.* 117; per essentiam non differunt a materia rarum et densum; unde non sunt principia, set sunt conditiones vel dispositiones ~entes ad agendum Bacon VIII 17; quidam [lapides preciosi], etsi non agant in spiritum, tamen ~unt ad effectus spirituales, et hoc naturaliter Peckham *QR* 81; hec racio .. arguit contra proprie removens [prohibens], non contra ~ens passum ad recipiendum Duns *Ord.* III 220; si in communitate fidelium fuerint plures judices summi .., sequitur .. quod eadem communitas .. semper erit disposita discordiis, dissensionibus .. et guerris Ockham *Dial.* 950; [diabolus] ducit ipse suos discipulos in errorem mendacii, secundum quod ipsos percipit plus ~i Wycl. *Versut.* 102. **b** fit .. denigratio, quare fumo et spiritu superiora petentibus pauca emissa cum urina ~unt substantiam urine tenuem et obscuram Gilb. I 22v. 2 (cf. denigratio 1a). **c** salvatio et damnatio consequuntur ad motum liberi arbitrii meritorium vel demeritorium, que sunt ex nostra causa .. [sc.] ~ente, non faciente Hales *Sent.* I 461; cause putrefactionis .. sunt caliditas et humiditas; humiditas autem est causa ~ens, †quum [? l. quoniam] .. facit fluxum materie .. et introducit dispositionem passibilem in ea Gilb. I 6v. 1; Bacon VIII 16 (v. conferre 1c). **d** si nesciat [agens] quomodo .. finis acquiratur, nesciet qualiter ad consecucionem ipsius se ~et Duns *Ord.* I 12; s**1384** nec est aliquis jam qui ~at se exurgere et stare ex adverso pro ecclesia Dei *Chr. Westm.* 41; s**1398** (v. 5d infra). **e** natura clementissima parens omnium et ~issima moderatrix .. hominem privilegio rationis extulit .., id agens .. lege ~issima ut homo .. ad alta conscendat J. Sal. *Met.* 825C; si animal non nutritur cibo isto, efficitur macilentum et male ~um [v. l. dispositionis] Bart. Angl. IV 7; [Brennius] erat in armis furens, in pace tranquillus, in membris bene ~us M. Par. *Maj.* I 57 (cf. G. Mon. III 6); circa quamcumque [proposicionem] potest potencia indisposita errare, sicut patet in somniis; ergo ad hoc ut aliqua cognoscatur per se esse nota, oportet quod possit cognosci quando potencia est ~a et quando non Duns *Ord.* III 156; Bradw. *CD* 564C (v. dispositivus 2c); sic manet eadem persona Cristo propinquior .. et .. ut prosit ecclesie ~ior. nam sancti in celo coronati .. sunt ~iores ad juvandam ecclesiam militantem quam forent in seculo conversantes Wycl. *Ver.* I 324; s**1454** volumus .. loqui pro eo ad confratres nostros experirique quomodo ipsi, hiis auditis, sint ~i super recepcione ipsius *Reg. Whet.* I 139; **1455** per infideles et male ~as personas (*Breve Regis*) *Ib.* 181.

4 (intr.): **a** (w. *de*) to dispose of, deal with. **b** (w. dat. or *pro*, or *ut* or *quod*) to arrange, provide (for).

a **1179** si omnes .. neglexerint, metropolitanus de episcopis secundum Deum absque illorum contradictione ~at (*Conc. Lateran.*) *G. Hen. II* I 234; **1192** quod non possit civitas de terris illis sicut de aliis ~ere *BBC* (*Dublin*) 35; **1262** (v. de 6a); freneticus erat et in tali statu quod de bonis suis ~ere non potuit *State Tri. Ed. I* 71; nec a se abdicaverunt [Romani] omnem potestatem causaliter ~endi de imperio Ockham *Pol.* I 150; **1420** de tercia parte .. consueverunt executores ~ere pro exequiis *Conc. Scot.* II 78; **1495** residuum .. bonorum .. lego [executoribus meis] .., ut ipsi inde ~ant prout eis melius videbitur expedire *Deeds Balliol* 335. **b** **1187** [ut] subprior .. de conventus consilio rebus vestris libere ~ere possit (*Lit. Papae*) *Cant. Cath. Pri.* 37; qui bene vult ~ere familie sue .. et rebus suis, primo provideat sibi in utensilibus Neckam *Ut.* 96; **1219** sue .. domui .. ~ere (v. desolatio 2b); decenter ~ere pro lecto regis et ut camere .. ornentur, et quod ignes sufficienter fiant *Fleta* 70 (v. camerarius 2a); **1400** ministros .. qui pararent et ~erent pro necessariis premisimus *Lit. Cant.* III 73; **1421** deputentur .. magistri .. ad ~endum pro caucionibus ante .. pestilenciam incistatis *StatOx* 229; **1437** fiat unus provisor novarum scholarum, qui .. ~at et solvat pro operariis et materia .. operis *Ib.* 257.

5 to undertake, intend, decide (on); **b** (w. acc. & inf. or compl.); **c** (w. *ut* or *quod*); **d** (w. indir. qu.); **e** (w. inf.). **f** (w. *pro*) to intend, destine (for).

fecit ut animo disposuerat Bede *HE* IV 29 p. 278; eum id quod mente disposuerat perficere suadebant *Ib.* V 19 p. 323; temtavit iter dispositum incipere *Ib.* 9; **1400** iter .. disposuimus (v. deputare 3c). **b** qui .. magis prosperantur in omnibus quae agenda vel adquirenda ~unt Bede *HE* II 13; ter denosque duces totidem deducere turmas / disposuit Alcuin *SS Ebor* 522; **1340** quam quidem collacionem [terre etc.] .. confirmo et apud eosdem magistrum et scolares manere imperpetuum ~o *Deeds Balliol* 287; s**1387** Deus omnipotens dictos xij .. tam fortiter accedere disposuit ita ut .. Ad. Usk 5. **c** dispositum est ut .. synodus fieri .. deberet Bede *HE* III 25 p. 183; disponit ut illi / in Parthos vertant Martia signa crucis Garl. *Tri. Eccl.* 64; **1340** ~o quod eleccio magistri .. secundum formam inferius annotatam celebretur *Deeds Balliol* 283. **d** **1253** quod redditus, fructus, terras et tenementa sua .. colligi faciat et salvo custodiri donec rex disposuerit quid inde facturus sit *Cl* 172; s**1398** ~e quid acturus sis et ego me disponam *Eul. Hist.* III 379 (v. et. 3d supra); **1431** pro toto anno futuro ~ant que persone quibusque Dominicis debeant predicare *StatOx* 238. **e** quid tu nugando mutire ~is? Gildas *EB* 1; abbas B. Romam ire disposuit *Hist. Abb. Jarrow* 9; in unaquaque regione in qua ~ebant manere Eddi 41; ~ebat .. condere casulam Bede *CuthbP* 21; **798** sollicitus fui .. audire .. quomodo dispositum habuisses facere secundum Dei voluntatem Alcuin *Ep.* 157; a**1086** aliquam accipere medicinam disposui Lanfr. *Ep.* 18 (44); **1102** (v. defensio 8); proficisci foris disposui Hil. Ronce. 12. 9; **1231** disposueram .. statim post Epiphaniam iter peregrinationis arripuisse Gros. *Ep.* 4; **1327** in animo suo disposuit amaritudines nostras .. temperare *Lit. Cant.* I 260; **1435** sanam .. doctrinam .. ~it .. Christianis distribuere *FormOx* 450. **f** s**1404** ecclesiam Herfordensem vacantem pro presencium compilatore papa disposuit Ad. Usk 85.

6 to grant, assign, bequeath, spend (usu. for spec. purpose). **b** (Sc.) to depone.

intempesto noctis silentio, quod animantibus ad quietem disposuit natura dispensatrix P. Blois *Ep.* 238. 542A; Elmh. *Cant.* 93 (v. conamen); **1425** ~it fabrice .. ecclesie pro sepultura sua in eadem xl s. *Reg. Cant.* II 326 (cf. ib.: vult quod .. lx li. eidem disposite ~antur in cooperturam .. capelle); **1426** (v. definitor b); **1495** volo quod [x m.] ~antur circa edificacionem .. capelle *Deeds Balliol* 335; **1502** que pecunia .. ad utilitatem universitatis .. per discrecionem .. cancellarii .. ~atur *StatOx* 305. **b** **1549** usque ad vacationem beneficiorum ad praemissum effectum ~endorum *Conc. Scot.* II 101; **1559** potestas ~endi et conferendi *Ib.* 166.

disponibilis, that can be disposed or executed.

oportet ponere voluciones Dei eternas de genere respectivorum; et sic non possunt de potencia Dei per se esse set ~e facere racione sui subjecti, quod est Deus Wycl. *Ente* 133.

dispons- v. despons-.

1 disporta, ~um, ~us [cf. AN *disport*, OF *desport*]

1 exemption, remission of penalty. **b** (mon.) relaxation of rule (or room in which it is enjoyed).

1211 de ij s. de Roberto de S. pro ~a habenda *Pipe Wint.* 84; **1275** cepit de R. vicario S. Clementis xvj s. pro ~u habendo, eo quod equus suus percussit quendam puerum, qui mortuus fuit, in cimiterio S. Clementis *Hund.* I 457; **1406** dant domino de fine pro ~a secte curie usque festum S. Mich. *CourtR Banstead*. **b** quando aliquis sociorum est minutus, omnes ad instanciam ipsius habebunt aliquod solacium. sciendum tamen quod in tempore quando tenetur ~um [novicii] non capient solacium nisi feria quarta et sexta *Cust. Cant.* 11; liberentur fratri qui custodit ~um duo cerei *Ib.* 372.

2 diversion, enjoyment, sport.

1415 reservatis .. loco competenti pro focali suo ac ~u gardini et libertate hauriendi aquam ad puteum *AncD* A 10958; **1438** quod durantibus treugis .. gentes unius partis vel alterius non ingredriantur terras, boscos, nemora, forestas, warennas, loca vel dominia alicujus subditi alterius regum predictorum causa venandi, piscandi, aucupandi, ~um aut solacium aliquod in eisdem exercendi *RScot* 309b (cf. *Foed.* XI 251); **1450** per solucionem factam domino regi et regine et eorum servitoribus .. ad ludos et ~us suos *ExchScot* 396.

2 disporta v. 2 dispositus.

disportare [cf. AN *disporter*, OF *desporter*], to relieve, exempt.

1276 si quod tallagium assisum fuit per quod pauperes gravati fuerunt et divites desportati (*EyreR*) *Lond. Ed. I & II* II 136; **1336** nec .. unquam virtute carte predicte inde ∼ati fuerunt seu quieti (*DL Couch.* 298b) *N. Riding Rec. Soc.* III 106.

disportatio, exemption, remission.

a1300 concessi .. Ade .. et heredibus suis .. [terram] tenendam de me et de heredibus meis .., ita viz. quod .. ex decena imperpetuum permaneant. .. pro hac autem .. concessione .. et hoc excambio et pro ∼one pro se et heredibus .. suis habendo (*sic*), dedit mihi dictus A. x s. *AncD* C 146; **1412** pro ∼one secte curie *CourtR Banstead.*

disportum, ∼us, v. 1 disporta, 2 dispositus.

disposite [CL], in order, in an orderly fashion.

subter et supra ∼e educuntur domicilia memoriis apostolorum, martyrum, ac virginum consecranda *V. Ed. Conf.* 49.

dispositio [CL]

1 (act of) disposition, arrangement, situation; **b** (rhet.); **c** (log.); **d** (math.).

molitionibus, ∼onibus, .. molimen, ∼o *GlC* M 282, 286; pedites in una linea disponuntur, reliquis secundum varias ∼ones varia loca sortientibus NECKAM *NR* II 184; contra meridionales plagas eisque ∼one conterminas GIR. *TH* I 40; existens in ∼one sibi naturali in ea quiescit, ut ponderosum existens in centro terre J. BLUND *An.* 4; auguriorum quedam fiunt ante, quedam post, quedam dextre, quedam †sinister [l. sinistre]; et, cum diverse sint in sua ∼one, quodlibet illorum proprie nominantur (*sic*) M. SCOT *Phys.* 56. **b** ∼o est rerum inventarum in ordinem distributio ALCUIN *Rhet.* 4; inventio, ∼o, elocutio, memoria, et pronuntiatio partes sunt rhetorice oracionis KILWARDBY *OS* 598. **c** ex hujusmodi adjunctorum ∼one [est] principium sophisticum BALSH. *AD* 87; oportet in syllogismo .. judicare .. de modo, qui consistit in ∼one propositionum KILWARDBY *OS* 505. **d** considerat aliquando geometria magnitudines discretas ab invicem numerali ∼one ac proporcione *Ib.* 154.

2 a (usu. w. obj. gen.) management, regulation, ordinance. **b** (w. subj. gen. or possessive adj.) authority, decision, disposal. **c** (divine) governance or ordinance; *cf. dispensatio* 2c. **d** (astr.) 'disposition'.

a 956 (13c) ego Eadwig ∼one gentis Angligenae .. industrius rex *Ch. Burton* 16; **1184** talis est ∼o ad subveniendum terre Jerusalem a .. Ph. rege Francie et H. rege Anglie .. approbata *MGL* II 653; mihi incumbit tamquam patri et summo custodi ∼o monasterii BRAKELOND 146v.; **s1199** [episcopus] literas a sede apostolica impetraverat, quarum auctoritate officialium monachorum ac rerum ∼onem cum jure abbatis exigeret G. COLD. *Durh.* 15; quamvis ∼o earum [rerum] arbitrio relinquatur executorum *Fleta* 430; **s1308** (v. displicibiliter); **1443** habebitis ∼onem m ducatorum BEKYNTON I 186. **b 601** ei [Eburacae episcopo] .. pallium tribuere .. disponimus, quem tamen tuae fraternitatis volumus ∼oni subjacere (*Lit. Papae*) BEDE *HE* I 29; **1072** quod Eboracensis ecclesia .. debeat .. archiepiscopi [Cantuar'] .. ∼onibus in iis quae ad Christianam religionem pertinent .. oboedire *Lit. Cant.* III app. 351; invasit .. timor .. rectorem navis .., quam relicto remige ∼oni fortune permisit G. MON. XII 4; in regis ∼one contradito castello *G. Steph.* II 94; non est mirum si .. mulieris .. res .. omnes plene intelligantur esse in ∼one ipsius viri GLANV. VI 3; **s1244** (v. 1 censura 1a); **1279** in manu et desposicione .. prioris *PQW* 347a; **1429** residuum .. lego dicto E. et sue ∼oni (*Test. Ad. Usk*) *EHR* XVIII 316; **1549** ut in his sacrorum canonum ∼o ad unguem servetur *Conc. Scot.* II 106. **c** quanta sunt maledictione digni qui prohibent nubere et ∼onem caelestis decreti quasi a diabolo repertam condemnant BEDE *Gen.* (i 28) 31; *CD* 633 (v. dispositor 1b); ad nutum supernae †depositionis GOSC. *Transl. Aug.* 22C; **a1075** quotiens ejus [Dei] ∼onibus in nullo dissonamus ANSELM (*Ep.* 9) III 112; **s1212** an talia [incendia] in detestationem impietatis humane .. divina providerit ∼o, quis ambigat? *Ann. S. Edm.* 24; Deus, cujus providentia in sui ∼one non fallitur GIR. *Invect.* VI 2; **1340** cum .. regnum Francie ∼one divina .. sit ad nos jure serenissimo devolutum (*Lit. Regis Angliae*) AVESB. 88. **d** cum ∼onem aeris ad aliquem certum terminum prognosticare volueris, oportet te primum .. uniuscujusque planete locum .. invenire GROS. 49; R. BURY *Phil.* 18. 234 (v. complexio 4d).

3 disposition, balance of ingredients, tendency (esp. log.). **b** (w. ref. to persons) temperament, inclination, bent. **c** (gram.) modification.

non sequitur sicut effectus ad suam causam efficientem, sed sicut finis ad suam ∼onem precedentem HALES *Sent.* I 461; RIC. MED. *Signa* 38 (v. dinoscere 1b); GILB. I 6v.1 (v. disponere 3c); in omni animali bone ∼onis est sanguis mediocris BART. ANGL. IV 7; BACON V 120 (v. complexionari b); *Id.* VIII 17 (v. disponere 3a); 'armi-' [*in* 'armiger'] est per se significativum forme que materialis ∼o est partis materie in qua est ∼o *Ps.*-GROS. *Gram.* 32; ∼o que est secundum quod contentum dicitur habere continens .. constituit predicamentum per se, quod vocamus 'habitum'. ∼o autem que est secundum quod continens dicitur habere contentum non est de isto predicamento SICCAV. *PN* 109; in oculo bene disposito recipitur aliqua species ejusdem racionis cum illa que est in medio, ex hoc quod ipsum organum est similis ∼onis cum medio, propter perspicuitatem utriusque DUNS *Ord.* III 284; BRADW. *CD* 564C (v. dispositivus 2c); stupor est ∼o mentis quando instrumenta sensuum ad sensum parata animalem sensu privantur *SB* 41; quod non videtur [color] in tenebris non est ex defectu coloris, set pocius ex defectu a parte recipientis, eo quod non habet ∼onem quam oportet ipsum habere UPTON 99. **b** in anima constituitur ∼o quedam que est intellectus formalis et similitudo rei, et illa ∼o non est anime innata, immo est adquisita J. BLUND *An.* 342 (cf. ib. 335: secundum ∼ones quibus afficitur homo cum accidit ei confusio aut erubescentia aut risus aut aliquid consimilium); PECKHAM *QA* 127 (v. complexionalis); in moralibus sunt quedam ∼ones ad plures actus virtutum vel viciorum naturaliter inclinantes OCKHAM *Dial.* 592; **1458** (v. agreabilis). **c** 'tunc', cum sit adverbium, est accidens et ∼o verbi BACON XV 134.

4 grant, disposal. **b** (testamentary) disposition or sim. **c** order, command.

c1235 ecclesie datio ad firmam non est ejusdem libera ∼o GROS. *Ep.* 18 (cf. datio 1c); **1426** (v. dispositor 2a); **1559** ut nullus .. assumatur .. ad quodcumque ecclesiasticum beneficium per .. quemcumque .. ad quem .. collatio, provisio seu quevis alia ∼o .. pertinet, nisi .. inveniatur idoneus *Conc. Scot.* II 166. **b 1255** prout in sua ultima ∼one precepit *RGasc* I sup. 9; **1414** Robertum .. episcopum Sar' hujus testamenti .. supervisorem constituo, eidem supplicans devote quatinus ut hec mea ∼o efficaciter exequatur supervidere .. dignetur *Reg. Cant.* II 40; **1559** cum sufficiente cautione de fideli et debita ∼one et administratione bonorum *Conc. Scot.* II 167. **c** decrevit .. ut nullus .. episcopus .. pape .. obedire deberet. ut hanc perniciosam ∼onem posset .. adimplere .. Boso *V. Pont.* 363.

5 (?) dispossession.

1382 que quidem ordinacio, si continuetur, in maximam desolacionem ville .. et ∼onem burgensium ejusdem cederet *Doc. Bev.* 7.

dispositive, a by inducing a disposition or inclination. **b** w. ref. to disposition. **c** in accordance w. disposition.

a introducere formam in materia .. aut effective, et sic duo contraria, sc. forma et privatio, aut ∼e, et sic hujusmodi conditiones vel dispositiones, rarum et densum et hujusmodi BACON VIII 17; forte potuit virtus lapidis ∼e immutando organum, ut cor vel cerebrum, excitare in eo alium affectum .., non agendo in animam sed corpus alterando PECKHAM *QR* 82; OCKHAM *Dial.* 642 (v. causaliter a). **b** [sapphirus] tollit invidiam, expellit timorem .., portantem autem mitem reddit et humilem et benignum, que omnia tamen puto esse dicta ∼e pocius quam effective UPTON 108. **c** [potestatem papae] causative et principaliter non esse ex homine, sed solum ∼e, in quantum eleccionem canonicam, tanquam disposicionem previam, sequitur spiritualis potestas, efficiente Deo PAUL. ANGL. *ASP* 1544.

dispositivus

1 coordinative, directive, regulative.

logica .. sic est sibi et aliis [scienciis] communis quod ipsa est ∼a et ordinativa tam sui quam aliarum KILWARDBY *OS* 581; quero quid intelligis per sapienciam ∼am sive disponentem DUNS *Ord.* VII 5; prudencia est habitus et virtus animi rerum ∼a .., per quam rememorat preterita, deliberat presencia et verisimilia conjectural futura MILEMETE *Nob.* 106; quantumlibet magnum artificiale secundum formam artis ∼am potest esse proposicio WYCL. *Log.* II 20.

2 a dispositive, inducing a disposition. **b** indicative, inducing expectation. **c** attributive, expressive of an attribute.

a stellas benivolas et ∼as ad effectus diversos PECKHAM *QR* 81; hic cum prioribus ad ipsum ∼is status [sc. supremus amor Christi] permanet usque in finem ROLLE *IA* 190. **b** inter alia signa ∼a ad Anticristum videtur michi signum precipuum quod scriptura sacra sit tantum hodie .. parvipensa WYCL. *Ver.* I 383. **c** aut [multa nomina] significant illam [eandem rem] diverso modo et racione diversa; et tunc secundum Averroem [*Metaph.* xii 39] possunt vocari nomina ∼a, eo quod se habent sicut disposicio et dispositum, aut nomina attributalia BRADW. *CD* 564C (cf. attributalis).

3 effecting (testamentary) disposition.

1415 quedam voluntas specialis ∼a rerum mearum *Reg. Cant.* II 86.

dispositor [CL]

1 disposer, manager, regulator; **b** (as divine epithet). **c** (astr.) 'dispositor'. **d** overseer or (?) planner of building operations (*cf. Building in Eng.* 13; *Trans. Birmingham Arch. Soc.* XLVIII 42).

s747 ut presbyteri non sint negotiorum secularium ∼ores W. MALM. *GP* I 5 (cf. *Conc. HS* 360); **c1158** justum est ut qui Cantuariensis ecclesie rector et ∼or est plenam disponendi in omnibus auctoritatem in Doverensi .. obtineat *Doc. Theob.* 83; sicut quilibet in tradicione seu donacione rei sue potest imponere pactum vel legem quam vult et in re propria quilibet est moderator et ∼or et arbiter OCKHAM *Pol.* I 160. **b** omnipotens Deus, honorum dator, ordinum distributor, officiorumque ∼or EGB. *Pont.* 19 (cf. ib. 97: providentiae ∼or); **982** (12c) creaturarum .. inaestimabili ∼ore, qui nativa sua incomprehensibili dispositione cuncta .. regit atque disponit *CD* 633; rerum ∼or Deus *G. Steph.* II 91. **c** qui planeta plura testimonia habuerit, ∼or illius temporis erit GROS. 49. **d 1385** H. de Yevele, quem .. avus noster constituit ∼orem operacionum suarum artem cementariam tangencium in palacio [Westm'] et Turri [London'] predictis *Cl* 225 m.23 (cf. *CalPat 1388–92* 122); **1451** cum .. per litteras nostras patentes concesserimus Simoni C. officium capitalis carpentarii nostri, ∼oris et supervisoris operacionum nostrarum infra palacium nostrum Westm' .. et alibi infra regnum nostrum Anglie *Cl* 302 m. 32.

2 grantor. **b** supervisor of testamentary disposition.

1426 quod .. Prosperus [de Columpna] omnimoda beneficia ecclesiastica infra regnum nostrum Anglie ad collacionem, presentacionem seu aliam disposicionem quorumcumque patronorum .. spectancia, que patroni .. eidem P. conferre, dare seu disponere .. voluerint .. acceptare .. possit, proviso .. quod .. sanctissimus pater .. declaret quod, quandocumque contigerit hujusmodi beneficia .. vacare .., donatores, conferentes, patroni et ∼ores predicti .. beneficia illa .. dare, conferre et ad ea presentare et de eisdem .. disponere .. possint .., quibuscumque aliis disposicionibus .. non obstantibus (*Pat*) *Reg. Cant.* I 234 (= *Foed.* X 354). **b 1424** ipsos facio, ordino, constituo ∼ores bonorum meorum *Ib.* II 298 (cf. ib. 189).

dispositorie, as a manager or administrator.

aliqua dona sunt in potestate .. creature, ut bona fortune et nature; aliqua autem dona sunt soli Deo propria, ut bona gracie. .. omnia quidem ista Deus appropriate donat, creatura ministrat; in dispositoriis antecedit ad ista, ut sacerdos dicit ministratorie verba .. vel ungit personam, et Deus .. superaddit graciam, in cujus dacione ministrans ∼ie non concurrit WYCL. *Civ. Dom.* I 258.

dispositorius, (as sb. n. pl.) administrative matters.

WYCL. *Civ. Dom.* I 258 (v. dispositorie).

dispositrix, (as epithet of divine providence) disposer (f.).

hoc rerum ∼ice Dei actum est providentia *G. Steph.* I 21.

1 dispositus v. disponere.

2 dispositus, (?) area of disposal, dump.

1351 in mundacione .. j fossati circa grangeas et cariagio fimi extra ∼um dictarum grangearum *MinAc* (*Drakelow*) 783/16 (= *Ac. Chamb. Chesh* 197: †disporta).

dispoticus v. despoticus. **dispotus** v. despotes b.

dispropriare [cf. propriare], to disown. *V. et. disappropriare.*

sic magis improprie propriat, propriisque repugnans / dispropriat clerus que dedit acta Deus GOWER *VC* III 680.

dispulverare [CL], to reduce to dust.

tunc cum dispulverat corpus mors effera WALT. WIMB. *Carm.* 642.

dispum- v. despum-. **dispunctor** v. dispungere a.

dispunctuare [cf. OF *despointer*], **a** to discharge, dismiss. **b** to disappoint, deprive.

a 1485 dantes eisdem [commissariis] potestatem generalem et mandatum speciale .. stipendiarios ultra numerum ordinarium .. in dictis villis [Calesii etc.] .. et marchiis .. exonerandi et ∼andi (*TreatyR*) *Foed.* XII 280a. **b 1503** admonitis omnibus sociis .. ut convenirent .. pro electione sociorum facienda, quidam ex senioribus magistris .. venire contempserunt, unde omnes magistri et socii .. sunt .. ∼ati de modo procedendi eorum ad electionem *Reg. Merton* 276.

dispungere [CL], to tick off (as recipient), pay. **b** to strike out, dismiss (from episcopal office).

dispuncta, dispensata .., ∼it, donat, unde et †spumatores [l. dispunctores] dicuntur qui militibus dona erogant *GlC* D 297, 312; OSB. GLOUC. *Deriv.* 178 (v. dispertire a). **b** instabant etenim violento famine agentes, / se pater ut proprio vellet dispungere voto [*gl.*: a dignitate avellere, reicere] FRITH. 1089.

disputabilis, disputable, admissible for disputation. **b** available for disputation (acad.).

1426 recognovit .. quod, licet illa conclusio .. opinabilis esset secundum aliquos doctores et ∼is, tamen, cum .. tanquam erronea et heretica condemnaretur, ipsorum [archiepiscopi et al.] determinacioni esset .. insequendum

Reg. Cant. III 177 (= *Conc.* III 460b). **b a1350** (v. dies 8e); **c1425** consuetudo est quod in medicinis incipientes per xl dies post suam incepcionem in eisdem quolibet die ~i disputent *StatOx* 231.

disputare [CL]

1 to dispute, argue. **b** (trans.) to maintain or discuss in debate; **c** (w. *quod* or *quomodo*).

quatenus cum rege .. reciprocis conflictibus et alternis vicibus ~ans altercaretur ALDH. *VirgP* 33; de primordiale vitae .. Willibaldi prochemio ~are decreveram HUGEB. *Will. prol.*; profundius nobiscum ~as [*þu smeagst*] quam aetas nostra capere possit ÆLF. *Coll.* 101; ~at, i. tractat, estimat, contendit vel *flit GlH* D 683; ut sciatur neminem tunc de regis continentia dubitasse, cum de causa taliter ~averint AILR. *Ed. Conf.* 748C; cum dicitur quoniam ~are est disserere .., hoc .. falsum est; ratio autem est quoniam ~are [est] quoddam disserendi genus BALSH. *AD* 21; tecum ~avi plus quam aliquis Christianus contra aliquem Judeum umquam .. ~averit P. CORNW. *Disp.* 149; de sancta Trinitate nimis acriter et frequenter ~are consueverat GIR. *GE* I 51; non licet eis [theologis] de eadem veritate opinando contrarie ~are OCKHAM *Pol.* III 63; quod post prandium debet [rex] .. aliquam bonam questionem movere et in presencia sua cum clericis ~are *Plusc.* VII 19. **b** HUGEB. *Wynn.* 10 (v. 1 capitulare 1b); si quid ego de firmitate fidei nostrae .. ~avero ANSELM (*Incarn. A* 1) I 281; *Ziz.* 9 (v. concordantia 3b). **c** quod Deus .. simplex sit natura et tres personae .. inexpugnabilibus rationibus ~atum est ANSELM (*Incarn. B* 6) II 20; numquam de hac fide ~abo quomodo non sit *Id.* (*Incarn. A* 4) I 283.

2 (acad.) to 'dispute', debate (intr. or trans.). **b** (pr. ppl. as sb.) disputant.

a1255 tempora et modus legendi et ~andi .. ad ipsos [rectores] pertineant *StatCantab* 205; **1282** inter scolares .. ~etur unum sophisma et determinetur *Deeds Balliol* 279; quis scholas lecturus vel ~aturus ingreditur, qui nostris [sc. librorum] conatibus non fulcitur? R. BURY. *Phil.* 4. 57; **a1350** magistri scolarum gramaticalium teneantur die Veneris gramaticalia .. ~are *StatOx* 23; **a1407** magister ~aturus questionem vel problema *Ib.* 194; **1516** *Ib.* 333 (v. cursorie c). **b 1409** (v. correctio 2b).

disputatio [CL]

1 dispute, argument, discussion.

Judeorum praeceptores .. dira ~onum spicula contra Christi tironem .. torquentes ALDH. *VirgP* 25; cum longa ~one habita .. suas traditiones praeferrent BEDE *HE* II 2; ea ipsa sic B. Augustinus .. suis magnis ~onibus probat ANSELM (*Ep.* 77) III 199; miracula divina sunt admiranda, non in rationem humane ~onis trahenda GIR. *TH* II 19; quatuor sunt genera ~onum, sc. doctrinales sive demonstrative, dyalectice et temptative et sophistice (SHIRWOOD) *GLA* III 19; questio .. civilis quam discutit rhetorica ~o multipliciter nominatur KILWARDBY *OS* 588.

2 (acad. or sim.) disputation.

apud Athenas, qua .. grammaticorum gloria et clandistinum academicae ~onis sofisma pollebant ALDH. *VirgP* 27; que et quot ~onum [sint] genera premonstrandum. sunt enim tria: primum exercitativum, secundum contentiosum, tertium inquisitivum BALSH. *AD* 30; W. FITZST. *Thom. prol.* 9 (v. colluctare b); GIR. *GE* II 37 (v. divinatio); **a1255** ingrediantur scolas singulas aliqua hora lectionum et ~onum, bedello decretistarum et theologorum horis .. debitis .. primam ad eorum ~onem pulsaturo *StatCantab* 207; **1311** (v. determinatio 4a); **1415** (v. concursorius b); **1549** in ~one theologica in theologia baccalaureus magistro artium pro forma responsuro cedere debet et postea suo ordine respondere *StatOx* 358.

disputative [LL], by way of argument.

commentator .. loquitur ~e et recitative et ideo quasi disputando et inquirendo dicit BACONTHORPE *Quaest. Sent.* 3D; postquam ~e quesivimus an expediret mundo uni imperatori subesse OCKHAM *Dial.* 885 (887); recitat 5 opiniones de ipsa [fortuna] .., circa quas ~e procedit BRADW. *CD* 269A; respondebo ad ea que sunt ~e reducta contra me (KYN.) *Ziz* 43.

disputativus [LL], concerned w. logical dispute or argument.

sunt .. dubitabilia principia .. ex ignotis [verbis], ut si illud genus disserendi quod disputatur '~um' appelletur BALSH. *AD rec. 2* 109.

disputator [CL], (acad. or sim.) disputant.

non Filio incarnato necesse est alias quoque personas, sicut ille ~or putat, incarnari ANSELM (*Incarn. B* 9) II 23; Judeus ille ~or .. me provocando adorsus est G. CRISPIN *Jud. & Chr.* 28; nec quelibet sophismatum genera invenire serium [est], nec quelibet non statim dinoscere ~ori erudito dignum BALSH. *AD* 40; **1549** singulis disputationibus quatuor e collegiis .. replicatores aut ~ores adsint *StatOx* 347.

disputatorius [LL], (acad.) concerned w. disputation.

1588 quicunque regionibus transmarinis licentiati degunt, ii .. ab isto ~io munere imunes sint *StatOx* 428.

disquietare, to disquiet, disturb.

s1423 non .. preintellexit quomodo [presules] ecclesias gravant, monasteria ~ant, clericorum subvertunt ordinem AMUND. I 75.

disquiparantia [cf. aequiparantia], disquiparancy, relation between dissimilar correlates.

hic, sc. in assimilante [et assimilato], illud in quo fundatur relacio activi est relacio equiparancie, et tale nomen importat duas relaciones tales, unam communem et aliam ~ie. DUNS *Ord.* V 279; patet quod ordo importet relacionem ~ie in comparacione ad aliquod principium determinatum; unde patet quod ordo est relacio ~ie plurium diversimode sese respiciencium in comparacione ad determinatum principium W. ALNWICK *QD* 252.

disquiparare [cf. CL aequiparare], (pass.) to stand in a relation of disquiparancy. *Cf. aequiparare* d.

si [una proposicio supponitur alteri secundum modum] secundum, sic est causalis, ut dicendo: 'quia Deus wlt me esse, ergo sum'. in nulla enim ypothetica tantum relucet et tam clare ~atur secundum modum respectivum sensus ad sensum quam in causalitate sensus ad sensum WYCL. *Quaest. Log.* 242.

disquiparativus, expressing relation of disquiparancy.

WYCL. *Quaest. Log.* 242 (v. aequiparativus).

disquirere [CL], to inquire, investigate. **b** to seek out, devise. **c** (p. ppl. as sb. n.) matter under investigation.

~ite, quaerite *GlH* D 712; **1122** de istis epistolari brevitate ~i commode non valet EADMER (*Lit. ad Regem Scotiae*) *HN* 351; cum fratres de sanctorum reliquiis diligenter ~erent, reperiunt schedulam et evolvunt AILR. *Ed. Conf.* 761B; hoc [utrum providentia mundum regat] apud nostros ut ambiguum ~i jam est ociosum, fide facta veri BALSH. *AD rec. 2* 133; **a1160** cum dominus Norwic' utrum eadem ecclesia vacaret diligenter disquisisset J. SAL. *Ep.* 16 (81); ~etur per visnetum qui eorum eidem sunt proximiores, et secundum hoc judicabitur GLANV. V 4; *Ib.* II 6 (v. decurrere 1b); **c1242** (v. collatio 3a). **b s1364** commenta .. disquisivit (v. commodarius). **c** [sunt dubitabilia principia] ex disquisito, ut est quod 'argumentum' appellari putant alii id ex quo sequitur quod probatur, nostri rationem qua id [sequitur] ex eo—disquisitum dico quod inquisitionis diductione a diversis diverse estimatur BALSH. *AD rec. 2* 109.

disquisitio [CL], investigation.

advertantur que hic dicimus juxta consuetum quendam loquendi usum, ut ad disciplinam, tamen non ad ~onem, hic dicta BALSH. *AD rec. 2* 16; accidit et in predictis tribus [dubitabilibus] ex ~one varie aliquid existimari *Ib.* 109 (cf. disquirere c); in ipsa ~one consilii tam in civilibus quam in criminalibus causis ad examinandas probationes instrumentorum ratio habenda est J. SAL. *Pol.* 574D; cepti qui finem preterit errat, / turpius admittens quam qui non inchoat: illud / accusat levitas; hoc disquisitio recti / excusare potest HANV. VIII 193 p. 365.

disquisitor, scrutineer.

1451 [in eleccione vicarii generalis] vicarius provincialis, ubi sit capitulum, ~ores instituat .., qui singulorum vota .. perquirant (*Abbr. Stat.*) *Mon. Francisc.* II 107.

disr- v. et. dir-. **disraisn-, disrein-, disrem-, disreni-, disresn-** v. derein-.

disripatio [cf. OF *vb. desriver* < *disripare], overflowing (of water over bank).

s1287 lacus qui vocatur Houghton Lake factus fuit per ~onem aque de magna ripa per quem lacum aqua de magna riperia diminuitur *Tract. Peterb. & Ramsey* 179 (= *MonA* II 572a; cf. *CalPat* 270).

disrob- v. derob-.

dissacaria [cf. OF *vb. dessachier*], tearing up, demolition.

1301 de finibus diversorum pro ~ia vel distraccione facta de rebus applicatis et projectis ad terram de wrecco maris *Pipe* 146 r. 31 (2).

dissaepire [CL]

1 to fence off, partition. **b** to shut away. **c** (p. ppl. as sb. n.) diaphragm.

deseptus .., diseptus, divisus *GlC* D 174, 226. **b** regnator Olimphi / .. / dissepsit varios eliso principe lurcos [v. l. varias .. larvas] FRITH. 14. **c** disseptum, *midrif* ÆLF. *Gl.*; **10..** de membris hominum: .. omentum, *midhriðre*; disceptum, i. reticulum, *nette WW*.

2 to disenclose.

to close, .. sepire .. ; *to unclose*, ~ire, discludere *CathA*.

dissaisiat- v. dissaisit-.

dissaisina [cf. AN *disseisine*, OF *dessaisine*], disseisin, dispossession. **b** (w. *nova* or sim.) novel disseisin, recent dispossession. **c** assize of novel disseisin. **d** amercement for disseisin. **e** (*s. dub.*).

1166 r. c. de xx s. pro ~a injusta *Pipe* 4; pro disseisina *Ib.* 65 (v. assisa 6c); **1167** pro ~a super breve regis *Ib.* 48; **1176** justitie .. regis faciant fieri recognitionem de ~is factis super assisam (*Assize Northampt.*) R. HOWD. II 90 (= *SelCh* 180); **s1224** rex .. justiciarios assignavit coram quibus fieret recognitio de conquerentium disseisina M. PAR. *Maj.* III 88; **1267** illi qui pro iterata disseysina capti fuerint et detenti non deliberentur sine speciali precepto regis (*Marlb.* 6) *StRealm* I 21; est disseisina de redditu in omni casu cum tenementum aliquod alicui obligatur in aliquo redditu, sive de eo teneatur sive de alio, et districcio recusetur vel replegietur HENGHAM *Parva* 7. **b** de illa recognitione que appellatur de nova ~a restat dicendum. cum quis .. infra assisam domini regis, id est infra tempus a domino rege de consilio procerum ad hoc constitutum .., alium injuste et sine judicio desaisierit de libero tenemento suo, desaisito hujus constitutionis beneficio subvenitur et tale breve habebit: breve de nova desaisina .. GLANV. XIII 32; **1196** etc. (v. assisa 6c); **1199** etc. (v. arramare a); **1215** recognitiones de nova ~a .. non capiantur nisi in suis comitatibus *Magna Carta* 18; **s1223** [justiciarii] qui tenebant placita regis de nova ~a WEND. II 278; cum disseisitus ita negligens fuerit .. quod nolit vel non possit disseisitorem suum reicere, .. succurritur ei per recognitionem assise nove disseisine, .. inventam recuperande possessionis gratia quam disseisitus injuste amisit et sine judicio BRACTON 164b; **1267** [heres] dampna sua recuperet sicut in actione nove disseysine (*Marlb.* 16) *StRealm* I 24; **1318** quod de cetero, si plures dissaisitores faciant unam ~am et principalis dissaisitor moriatur antequam dissaisitus habuerit statum suum recuperatum, propter hoc non perdat dissaisitus recuperacionem suam per breve de nova ~a quamdiu invenire poterit tenentem in vita aut dissaisitorem qui fuit ad ~am factam (*Stat. Rob. I*) *APScot* I 110 (= *Reg. Aberbr.* I 254 *rub.*: breve de dissasyna); **1319** si assysa de †dissasisa .. deberet procedere vel admitti *Reg. Dunferm.* 352; **1338** placitum assise nove disseisine per billam de frisca forcia .. tentum coram majore *MunCOx* 95; **13..** de assisis nove disseisine vocatis *fresshforce MGL* I 173 (cf. ib. 195: *les assises de novelle disseisine appellez fresheforce*). **c 1205** judicium suum de quadam nova ~a quam idem H. tulerat versus eum in itinere justiciariorum *CurR* III 318. **d 1275** de bobus de dissesina provenientibus (*Concordia*) DOMERH. *Glast.* 558. **e** nec .. sustineat [prepositus] quod aliquis alicui officio deputatus .. ferias, mercatos, disseysinas, vigilias, luctas adeat vel tabernas *Fleta* 171.

dissaisio, disseisin or (?) *f. l.*

1200 recognitores nove disseisionis [v. l. assise nove disseisine, ? l. dissaisitionis] *CurR* I 274.

dissaisire, ~iare [cf. AN *disseisir*, OF *dessaisir*]

1 to disseise, dispossess; **b** (w. *de* or abl. alone). **c** (p. ppl. as sb. m.) disseisee.

Ældredus .. dicit se eam [terram] tenuisse .; et disaisitus fuit postquam rex W. mare transiit *DB* I 48v.; ipse N. inde saisitus fuit ..; sed Radulfus eum disaisivit *Ib.* 214; hund[retum] testatur se nescisse S. E[dmundum] postea fuisse †dasaisitum (*sic*) *Ib.* II 360v.; **1104** si [rex] me ~ierit, ut nostrae res non sint in mea potestate, dicite ei quia ego nullas inducias accipio, sed ita me habebo sicut episcopus ~itus sine judicio quo episcopus ~iri debeat ANSELM (*Ep.* 316) V 244; ne disseisiatus vel inplegiatus vel illegiatus .. judicetur (*Leg. Hen.* 5. 3) *GAS* 548; postquam aliquis ~itus legem vel rectum domino suo vadiaverit .., saisitus esse debet (*Ib.* 53. 6) *Ib.* 574; **s1139** rex .. revestiat episcopos de rebus suis; alioquin jure gentium ~iti non placitabunt W. MALM. *HN* 474; **1169** r. c. de xx m., quia ~ivit Jordanum F. super assisam *Pipe* 156; **1215** nullus liber homo .. ~iatur .. nisi per legale judicium parium suorum *Magna Carta* 39; **1280** ita quod .. rex .. vel heredes sui predictum A. .. non dissesirent vel dissesiri permitterent antequam racionabile excambium .. fecissent *MS PRO* C. 266/2/38; *to disseise*, disseisire *CathA*. **b** Walerannus .. desaisivit quendam hominem .. de una domo *DB* I 30; **a1087** de illis hominibus Frodonis, de quibus homines comitis E. eundem Frodonem disseisierunt in B., .. eum resaisiatis *Regesta* p. 129; **a1098** facito abbatem Ramesiae juste resaisiri de dim. hida .. unde H. Larderarius eum desaisivit *Ib.* 413; **s1090** pro terra matris sue, qua rex eundem .. ~iverat ORD. VIT. VIII 15 p. 350; **s1095** ut illum pontificatu ~iret [rex] impossibile sibi videbat EADMER *HN* 75; **s1119** decrevit rex .. de archiepiscopatu eum [Turstinum] dissaisire H. CANTOR 18v.; **1130** ne sit ~itus de terra sua *Pipe* 110; comitissa fuit ~ita terra sua *RDomin* 6; GLANV. XIII 32 (v. dissaisina b); **a1231** quod nullus ~itus sit de burgagio suo .. sine judicio *BBC* (*Haverfordwest*) 104; **1233** disseisivit Philippum .. de quadam pastura *Cl* 177 (= *RL* I 524: †dessaisavit); **1284** si fuit dicta rebus disseisitus *RGasc* II 232; **1286** desseiserunt (*sic*) Walterum .. de communa pasture sue *Reg. Heref.* 115; **1307** disseisivit eos de una camera et de quodam corodio *Year Bk. 1 Ed. II* 4. **c** GLANV. XIII 32, BRACTON 164b, *APScot* I 110 (v. dissaisina b); **1236** si quis fuerit disseisitus de libero tenemento suo et .. seisinam suam recuperaverit per assisam nove disseisine .. et ipse disseisitus per vicecomitem seisinam suam habuerit .. (*Merton* 3) *StRealm* I 2 (*cf. Cl* 338).

2 to seize or (?) *f. l.*

1444 'nisi prius' prosecutum ad instanciam domini prioris .. pro bonis cujusdam felonis .. super eundem priorem injuriose disseisatis [? l. disseisati] *Ac. Durh.* 185.

dissaisiscere, to disseise (Norm.).

1080 episcopos inde non disaisiscant donec in curia regis monstratum sit quod episcopi inde habere non debeant (*Conc. Illebon.*) ORD. VIT. V 5 p. 323.

dissaisitio, disseisin.

nemo dissaisiatus placitet, nisi in ipsa dissaisiatione agatur (*Leg. Hen.* 53. 5) *GAS* 574; **1122** cum .. †his [? l. hic] vester habitus circa me et ~o qua me his rebus ad pontificatum pertinentibus sine lege et judicio spoliastis attestarentur, necessario dimisi quod ablatum retinere non potui EADMER (*Lit. ad Regem Scotiae*) *HN* 351.

dissaisitor, disseisor, dispossessor.

1199 dissaisiatores de libero tenemento ipsius R. *CurR RC* I 370; **1200** assisa de nova disseisina inter Robertum de B. et Eulariam T. †disseisitores [v. l. Yllariam uxorem suam petentes] et Ricardum de B. ~orem *CurR* I 229; **1218** persona habeat seisinam suam et disseisiator in misericordia *Eyre Lincs* 28; **1236** si iidem disseisiatores .. iterum eundem conquerentem disseisiverunt et inde convicti fuerint, statim capiantur (*Merton* 3) *StRealm* I 2 (cf. *Cl* 338); BRACTON 164b, *APScot* I 110 (v. dissaisina b); **1331** [abbas clamat habere] pro qualibet disseisina facta in domina sua de disseisitoribus unum bovem vel v s. et iiij d. *PQW* 70a; *a disseiser*, disseisitor *CathA*.

dissaisitrix, disseisoress.

quo casu habebitur uxor pro disseysitrice *Fleta* 240.

dissaisonare [cf. OF *dessaisoner*], to cultivate out of season or sequence.

1261 ipse disseysonavit predictam terram, eo quod seminavit bonam terram que jacuisse deberet ad warect' *JustIt* (*Oxon*) 701 r. 8; **1302** Robertus disseyonavit (*sic*) in hoc anno, arrando tres diurnas terre que debuissent [esse] ad warectam in anno presenti *CourtR Hales* 453 (cf. ib. 455: dysseonavit tres diurnas terre .. et seminavit illam terram de vessis).

dissas- v. dissais-. **dissc-** v. disc-.

1 dissecare v. 1 desecare b.

2 dissecare [CL]

1 to cut in pieces; **b** (fig.). **c** to mangle, lacerate; **d** (fig.).

H. HUNT. *HA* IX 23 (v. compaginare 1a); eum .. percussum [bipenni] a summo usque ad imum in ambas partes ~uit G. MON. I 13; parietes multis ~uit distrahendo foraminibus R. COLD. *Cuthb.* 68; **s1283** membra .. desecta (v. debellator b). **b** fluctuum implicamenta ~ando divisit R. COLD. *Cuthb.* 23. **c** sub immenso murmure lugentium populorum .., facies suas ~antium, palmis sese ferientium OSB. *V. Dunst.* 45; cum suspiceres .. carnem de carne tua ab impiis crudeliter ~ari ANSELM (*Or.* 2) III 8; desecti .. corporis *V. Har.* 17 (v. denigrare 1a); dissecat illa genas, nudum ferit altera pectus J. HERD *Hist. IV Regum* 160. **d** caram justitiamque Dei mox †dissico [v. l. disseco] demens BONIF. *Aen.* 2 (*Iracundia*) 4; **s799** Romani inter se ~abantur et magnam dissensionem habebant BYRHT. *HR* 61; ne discipline series intersertis ~etur BALSH. *AD rec.* 2 144; sepe laxo frigidus, flebili rebellis, / ipse se dissecuit pius versipellis *Poem. S. Thom.* 78; **s838** tot .. rumoribus sinistris reges cum subjectis cordibus ~antes M. PAR. *Maj.* I 378 (cf. H. HUNT. *HA* V *prol.*: tot rumorum .. plaga percussi rex et populus manibus et corde dissolvebantur); **s1255** rex .. curis et sollicitudinibus discerpitur et ~atur *Ib.* V 510.

2 to cut off. **b** (fig.) to detach, wrest.

alii caput ictu truncat, alteri crura ~at G. MON. I 13. **b** **s1318** villam de Berewyk .. a manibus regis Anglie .. ~uit et sub dicione regis R. ceteris membris compaginavit *Flor. Hist.* III 183.

dissectio, quartering. **b** (anat.) dissection.

s1238 David frater Liwelini .. corporis detraccioni, combustioni, atque membrorum adjudicatus est ~oni OXNEAD *Chr.* 262. **b** inferior venter ..—hinc enim humani corporis incipere ~onem oportet D. EDW. *Anat.* A3.

dissector, (anat.) dissector.

hoc jejuni nomen corporum ~ores intestino dederunt D. EDW. *Anat.* A4v.

dissegregatio v. disgregatio a. **disseis-** v. dissais-.

disseminare [CL]

1 to sow (fig.), broadcast, disseminate. **b** (intr.) to spread. **c** to fill by scattering, infest.

deseminat, dispargit *GlC* D 154; peragrata insula tota .., rectum vivendi ordinem .. per omnia .. ~abat BEDE *HE* IV 2; **8..** ~abunt, *tosawað WW*; W. MALM. *GR* II 165 (v. disseminator); [doctores] vobis sepe verba vite ~ant S. LANGTON *Serm.* 2. 1; **c1400** librorum hujusmodi [tonariorum] defectus in tonizacione psalmodie inter psallentes in choro frequenter discordancias ~ant inhonestas (*Vis.*) *Fabr. York* 244. **b** hoc malum dissolutionis .. inchoans a pedibus per omnia membra deseminavit [v. l. ~atum est] *V. Cuthb.* IV 17. **c** si [Christiani] terras suas ~atas jam ubique terrarum heresibus, symoniis .. ac aliis viciis .. innumerabilibus .. neglexerint expurgare OCKHAM *Dial.* 505.

2 (p. ppl.) unsown.

13.. quod due culture .. Thome, que singulis annis pro voluntate sua seminari solebant, cum aliis .. adjacentibus dehinc seminarentur et cum eisdem jacerent ~ate *Meaux* II 219.

disseminatio [CL], sowing (fig.), spread.

s1098 hec fame ~o (WILL. TYR.) M. PAR. *Maj.* II 75; **1440** ut viris credantur .. qui .. sanctimonia vite gregem sibi commissum illustrare queant et ~one verbi Dei fructum facere BEKYNTON I 16 (cf. ib. 28).

disseminator [LL], sower (fig.), broadcaster.

s1166 quidam pravi dogmatis ~ores tracti sunt in judicium apud Oxenefordiam DICETO *YH* I 318; **s1003** erat [Eadricus] .. bilinguis, versutus, secreti ~or *Flor. Hist.* I 528 (cf. W. MALM. *GR* II 165: consilia regis .. ut proditor disseminabat).

dissenarius v. decenarius.

dissensio [CL], disagreement, dissension, dispute.

705 ecclesiastici .. in hanc ~onem .. implicantur WEALDHERE *Ep.* 22; orta inter ipsum regem .. et Uilfridum ~one BEDE *HE* IV 12; dissentio, discordia vel *geter GlH* D 605 (cf. ib. E 260: emulatio, i. ~o, *anhering*); BYRHT. *HR* 61 (v. 2 dissecare 1d); si dissentionum excluderet placationem pertinacium improbitas AD. MARSH *Ep.* 30 p. 127; **1323** dissenciones que pacis unitatem dirimunt *Lit. Cant.* I 98; suborta .. discensio inter regem et barones MILEMETE *Nob.* 34; **1330** pro pace .. super discordiis, discencionibus et querelis .. procuranda *PQW* 565b; **1387** suscitata fuit magna †distensio [l. discensio] inter .. regem R. et coherentes sibi ex una parte et T. ducem Glovernie et alios multos .. ex altera *Dieul.* 143v.; **1411** verior causa dessensionis hujusmodi *FormOx* 189; **1427** discensiones, lites, et controversias (v. continuare 3a); **1455** lis et †distencio [l. discencio] *FormA* 103.

dissensor [LL *gl.*], dissenter.

discensor, *ungedyre GlC* D 283; ~or, discordator *GlH* D 602.

dissensus [CL], dissension, dissent.

urbs Acronensis capitur probitate potentum / regum; dissensum sed nova palma parit. / ortus adhuc durat dissensus; bella sequuntur GARL. *Tri. Eccl.* 142; **1291** ~u priori mutato in consensum *Reg. Linc.* III 176.

dissentar-, dissenter-, dissentir- v. dysenter-. **dissentio** v. dissensio.

dissentire [CL]

1 to disagree, dissent; **b** (w. dat. or *ab*). **c** (impers. w. *quod*) to be at variance.

~iat, i. discrepat, discordat, ~it *GlH* D 603; **9..** ~it, *geunþwærað WW*; ~ire, contradicere OSB. GLOUC. *Deriv.* 180; utrum potius parentibus obediendum an legibus, si ~iant KILWARDBY *OS* 564; equitati .. naturali, que est inter homines pronos ad ~iendum et male agendum OCKHAM *Pol.* II 669; *to discorde*, .. discordare, ~ire, -ri, discrepare .. *CathA*. **b** **a1078** ceteri .. religionis doctores .. ab horum sententia .. minime dissenserunt LANFR. *Ep.* 50 (46); **1291** quod .. archidiaconus nominacioni de se facte omnino dissenserat *Reg. Linc.* III 176; si .. omnem actum ejus precedat cognicio practica, ab intellectu determinabitur [voluntas divina] ad primum actum, quia non potest ei ~ire; tunc enim posset peccare DUNS *Ord.* I 212 (cf. ib. 214: licet [voluntas divina] non posset ~ire a noticia recta et priore praxi). **c** quamvis apertos celos [cf. *Mark* i 10] mystice intelligamus, non tamen a vero ~it quod ita eos corporales oculi dissiluisse conspexerint PULL. *Sent.* 851B.

2 (w. acc. & inf.) to maintain in mutual disagreement.

deum quidam esse perhibent, alii vero idipsum negant; qui vero asserunt, alii materiam, alii formam, alii mundum, quidam aplanon, quidam solem deum esse ~iunt ADEL. *QN* 76.

disseparare [LL], to separate.

quedam intextura .., que hac et illac illarum imagines ~ando dirimit et distinguendo disjungit R. COLD. *Cuthb.* 42.

dissepire, ~tum v. dissaepire.

disserare [CL], to unlock.

to opyn, ~are .. *CathA*.

1 disserere v. deserere.

2 disserere [CL]

1 to utter, declare. **b** (intr.) to discourse. **c** to demonstrate.

disseruit verax sermone futura ALDH. *VirgV* 334; **c690** limpida discipulis dogmata disseruit (*Epitaph. Theodori*) BEDE *HE* V 8; videtur opportunum de sollemnitate adhuc hodierna breviter aliqua ~ere *Id. Hom.* II 17. 193; **9..** ~uit, *sæde* .., †dissire, *gerece* .., ~entis, *secgende WW*. **b** dogmatistae doctrina de integritatis dono ~entis ALDH. *VirgP* 46; est .. ad duo ars ~endi: ad quod ex initio manifestum, et ad que ~endo dicuntur intelligendi facultatem BALSH. *AD* 10; ego et qui mecum ~ebat Judeus, Petrus et Symon P. CORNW. *Disp.* 155; satis exquisite .. de pietate nobis ~uit GIR. *EH* I 15; amodo de unitate materie in his que fiunt ex se invicem ~amus SICCAV. *PN* 92; si eum ~entem audieris, putes te doctissimorum philosophorum gignasiis interesse (CHAUNDLER) BEKYNTON II *app.* 285 p. 324. **c** ~o, i. .. interpreto, manifesto, .. expono *GlH* D 613; **c1127** videns .. quod nullo modo posset hec ~ere (*Cart. Thorney*) *Eng. Justice* 140; quoniam tractatu exigente anni terminos introduximus, ejusdem divisio ~enda est ADEL. *Elk.* 2.

2 to make eloquent. *Cf. disertus.*

hoc .. dentes mundificat .., desserit [*gl.*: facit disertam] linguam, clarificat loquelam BACON V 69.

3 (w. *bellum*) to join battle. *Cf.* 1 *conserere* 2a.

s1217 ardens desiderium bellum cum excommunicatis †~ere Francigenis OXNEAD *Chr.* 139 (= WEND. II 212: conserere).

3 disserere [CL], to separate. **b** (p. ppl.) scattered, lying far apart.

deseruit, separavit *GlC* D 163; vis tua .. umbrarum seras disseruit J. HOWD. *Ph.* 1026. **b** disita, separata *GlH* D 629; dissitus, separatus, divisus OSB. GLOUC. *Deriv.* 179; inter se ac finitimas sed procul etiam dissitas gentes terra marique commercia MORE *Ut.* 31.

dissertare [CL], to discourse, orate.

disertans, †perornans [? l. perorans] *GlC* D 303; disertans, i. perorans *GlH* D 607; *to speke wysely*, disserere, desertare *CathA*.

dissertatio v. indiscretio.

dissertio [CL], discourse, dissertation.

de eis disputatio alias omnes ~ones et intellectus subtilitate et sermonis difficultate precellit ADEL. *QN* 76.

dissertitudo v. disertitudo.

dissertor [LL], expositor, interpreter.

~or, interpres *GlH* D 609.

dissertus v. discernere 3b, 2 disertus. **disses** v. deses. **disses-, dissey-, disseys-** v. dissais-, disseis-. **dissicare** v. 2 dissecare. **dissicere** v. disicere. **dissictus** v. 1 dissuere 1c.

1 dissidentia v. 1 diffidentia 2.

2 dissidentia [CL], **a** disagreement, discrepancy. **b** dissension, dispute.

a Plato .. ipsam [philosophiam] non posse constare credidit nisi limitum, qui utrimque .. ab unitate profluxerant, ~iam .. uniret J. SAL. *Pol.* 401C. **b** dum .. opportunitatem quando ~iam excitarent prestolarentur *G. Steph.* I 12; DEVIZES 33v. (v. compromissio b); contra ~ias jurgiorum AD. MARSH *Ep.* 30 p. 126; sedandis formidabilis †diffidentie [? l. dissidentie] seditionibus tam dudum excitatis *Ib.* 191.

dissidēre [CL], to be at variance; **b** (w. dat., *ab* or *de*).

Scottorum Pictorumque greges, moribus ex parte ~entes GILDAS *EB* 19; desidebat, *unsibbade GlC* D 48 (cf. ib. D 268: ~ebat, discordabat); **a1077** nos sepe alterutrum monuisse esse multos .. qui semper velint nos invicem ~ere LANFR. *Ep.* 17 (41); mali .. in discordia tanta persistent ut eorum corpus et anima semper ~eant *Simil. Anselmi* 63; W. MALM. *GP* IV 142 (v. digladiabilis); **c1320** universitatis .. membra .. nuper discidencia .. invicem .. coherent vinculo caritatis *FormOx* 58 (cf. ib. 75: discedentibus ipsis ad invicem). **b** AD. SCOT *TT pref.* (v. coaptare 1a); [aves] ab eadem specialitate longe ~entes GIR. *TH* I 17; nec quemquam repperi qui non in aliquo michi ~eret usque ad te MAP *NC* IV 11 f. 58v.; in desercione discipulorum et a fide discidencium *AncrR* 33; **1360** quod tamen pars adversa, de communitate ~ens, patenter recusavit *MunAcOx* 222.

dissidium v. discidium. **dissiduus** v. 2 desiduus.

dissigillare [CL; cf. OF *desseeler*], to unseal.

1290 cistas et coffinos .. desigillasse *KRAc* 231/14; **1290** nunquam .. bagge vel scripta per ipsum desigillabantur vel de cistis capiebantur (*Pet. Parl.*) *DocExch* 60; **1301** jocalia .. nomine pignoris .. tradidimus .. in domo Fratrum Minorum deponenda .. sub hac condicione quod, si predicta summa .. persoluta non fuerit .., pignora licite possint ~are, vendere et obligare *RGasc* III 402; **s1221** ~atum est illud vas saxeum super .. altare in quo continebatur (*sic*) caput et majora ossa [B. Augustini] THORNE 1877.

dissignare [cf. LL dissignator], to unseal.

s1156 sepulto patre, testamentum designatum [v. l. dissignatum] est W. NEWB. *HA* II 7.

dissillibare v. dissyllabare.

1 dissilire v. 1 desilire.

2 dissilire [CL]

1 to leap or spring apart, burst asunder. **b** to fly about. **c** to depart (from purpose). **d** to dissent.

~iunt, *toscutan GlH* D 637; ~it, *tosprang GlP* 783; vas vitreum quod in multas particulas ~uit pristine sanitati restituit HON. *Spec. Eccl.* 835B; PULL. *Sent.* 851B (v. dissentire 1c); ex temperamento subtilissimorum elementorum fit sensus; que cum ob instrumentorum defectum ab invicem ~uerint, desinit esse sensus AILR. *An.* III 55 f. 124; vir ille, qui in mare dimersus fuerat, .. fluctibus jactatus .. a navis confinio longius disiluit R. COLD. *Cuthb.* 32; spicula ~ientia *Ib.* 102 (v. cervical a); o terra stupida .. / cur non Judaicum scelus increpitas? / quare non dissilis, quare non oscitas? WALT. WIMB. *Carm.* 488. **b** sepe videmus post a pecore direpta tergora hinc inde particulas ~ire PULL. *Sent.* 692C (cf. dissultus). **c** **1268** ut .. deliberarent an .. communitas appellationem .. prosequi vellet vel a proposito desilire *Conc. Syn.* 746. **d** in eo magna mentis ammiratione distrahor .. quod [phisici] a seipsis tanto verborum conflictu et collisione rationum ~iunt et discordant J. SAL. *Pol.* 476B.

2 to be dissolved (fig.), fail.

omne robur tam carri quam boum ~uit R. COLD. *Godr.* 593.

dissillabus v. disyllabus. **dissimila-** v. dissimula-.

dissimilis [CL], unlike, different; **b** (w. dat.).

oves unius ovilis ~es GILDAS *EB* 1; tramite dissimili tendens ad praemia vitae ALDH. *VirgV* 2275; deferentes, desimiles *GlC* D 142; **8**.. ~e, *ungelic WW*; sanccitum est .. eum judicare debere qui nec munere impar sit nec jure ~is (*Leg. Hen.* 5. 7) *GAS* 549; erant ambo optime litterati et .. eloquentes, sed ~ibus studiis J. SAL. *Hist. Pont.* 12; BALSH. *AD rec. 2* 52 (v. contrarie 2); accipitres et nisi, quantitate magis ~es quam qualitate GIR. *TH* I 12; in relacionibus proporcionum vel proporcionalitatum et non-similitudinum .. prima extrema sunt maxime ~ia DUNS *Ord.* II 12. **b** ALDH. *Aen.* 28. 1 (v. biformis); aliud quoque non multum huic ~e miraculum BEDE *HE* V 4; MAP *NC* III 4 (v. curare 1d).

dissimiliter [CL], differently.

quia non consideras quam ~er significent sc. nomen hominis ea ex quibus constat homo ANSELM (*Gram.* 12) I 156; BALSH. *AD* 64 (v. consignificare 1a); sic patet qualiter ~er inest potentia illi materie corporali et isti KILWARDBY *OS* 263.

dissimilitudo [CL], unlikeness, difference. **b** (w. *regio*) estrangement from God (*cf.* Augustine *Conf.* VII 10. 16 and *Med. Stud.* IX 108–130).

parabolas Dominus aut secundum similitudinem aliquem ponit, sicut de homine qui habebat duos filios .., minorem in longinquo luxoriantem [*Luke* xv 13], aut ex ipsa ~ine aliquid probat, veluti est illud [*Matth.* vi 30] BEDE *Luke* 550 (cf. ib. 551: hic iniquus judex non ex similitudine sed ex ~ine adhibitus est); quamvis summam substantiam constet prius in se quasi dixisse cunctam creaturam quam eam .. conderet, quemadmodum faber prius mente concipit quod postea .. opere perficit, multam tamen in hac similitudine intueor .. ~inem ANSELM (*Mon.* 9) I 26; dum rerum similitudines et ~ines colligit J. SAL. *Pol.* 438C; HALES *Sent.* I 227 (v. differentia 1a); KILWARDBY *OS* 19 (v. diversitas a); relaciones dicte secundum ~inem differunt secundum diversitatem ipsarum qualitatum SICCAV. *PN* 106. **b** imperiosus amor dominandi quendam .. archilevitam adeo traxerat in regionem ~inis ut lucernam virtutum .. non poterat intueri *V. Will.* 271; per sensus exteriores itur in regionem ~inis cum filio prodigo J. GODARD *Ep.* 237; patrem satagit emulari, qui filium de regione ~inis revertentem .. gratia magnifici honoris ampliavit AD. MARSH *Ep.* 71; *Ib.* 221 (v. apostatice).

dissimulanter [CL], w. dissimulation.

rem ~er secretam tenuit *V. Neot. A* 18; **s1432** contra ipsos .. choleram indignacionis concepit. pertransiit tamen ~er, nec adhuc contra ejus [prioris] stoliditatem ad id tempus elocutus fuit AMUND. I 301.

dissimulare [CL]

1 to disguise, dissemble; **b** (feelings or sim.); **c** (absol.).

680 aut veritatem ignorando aut falsitatem ~ando obmutescunt ALDH. *Ep.* 4; ~at, *miðið GlC* D 272; **9**.. dissimilat, *miðeþ* .., ~ato, *bemiðenum WW*; ~ato dampno W. MALM. *GR* 205; [discretio] qua plerumque non minus sapienter quam scienter ~atur quod agitur et agi putatur quod non agitur H. BOS. *Thom.* II 9. **b** dum .. ardens mentis desiderium ~are nequeant ALDH. *VirgP* 14; NECKAM *DS* IX 25 (v. concipere 3a); **s1213** rex Anglie, indignatus .. in Angliam .. rediens .., dissimilando indignacionem aliquantulum permansit *Plusc.* VI 43. **c** ~are cautus, fingere paratus W. MALM. *GR* II 165.

2 to ignore, disregard; **b** (w. acc. & inf.). **c** to concede by waiving claim.

c597 ecclesia .. quaedam per considerationem ~at, .. ut saepe .. malum quod adversatur .. ~ando conpescat (*Lit. Papae*) BEDE *HE* I 27 p. 51; propter .. protervorum insolentiam .., qui malunt neglegenter ~ari quam clementer increpari ALDH. *VirgP* 58; **a798** sunt consulentes .. adjuvandi, resistentes .. obviandi, dubii vero vel rationabiliter adtrahaendi (*sic*) vel circumspecte ~andi ALCUIN *Ep.* 132; quorum [hostium] monita ~ans mori pro Christo non timuit *Itin. Ric.* I 2; **a1273** pericula hec et majora .. si negligenter ~averimus (*Lit. Prioris*) *Ann. Durh.* app. 117; **1325** (v. dissolutio 4b); rex audiens et sciens hec omnia ~abat, tanquam collectam multitudinem parvi penderet *V. Ric. II* 98; injuriam ad tempus dissimilare .. et stulti stulticiam .. ignorare *Quadr. Reg. Spec.* 32. **b** ista .. testimonia .. fuisse premissa tu forsitan non recolebas aut certe ~abas *Eccl. & Synag.* 84; hec .. qui omnipotentem peregisse ~at ÆLNOTH *Cnut* 4. **c** quoniam quandoque onerosa est custodia castri vel capitalis mesuagii sine tenente heredi, cum uxor dotata sit de tali manerio sine excepcione, ~atur quandoque uxori seisina castri propter onus, dum tamen restituatur regi tempore guerre vel alterius necessitatis BRACTON 93b.

3 (w. inf.) to forbear, neglect. **b** (w. *ad*) to refrain from (? compelling).

a690 illud .. nequaquam promens ~o propalare ALDH. *Ep.* 5; **s1050** Goduuinus, nolens destruere comitatum suum, ~avit ire illuc *AS Chr.*; nec parcant vel ~ent [AS: *wandiað*] pro aliqua re populi rectum .. recitare (*Quad*) *GAS* 139; qui furem dimittet vel ad capiendum eum adjuvare ~abit (*In*) *Ib.* 395; nova monasteria quot et quanta fecerit [Ethelstanus] scribere ~o W. MALM. *GR* II 131; qua .. fronte .. curam adhibere pastoralem .. per inscitiam .. ~abit? GIR. *JS* 7 p. 362; si ipsos .. castigare ~ent *Cust. Westm.* 11; **s1281** archiepiscopus ~avit .. execucioni suam sentenciam demandare *Flor. Hist.* III 55; **1313** coram prefato J. .. venire ~avit *Cl* 95 m. 12 (= *Cal.* p. 514: †dissumalavit). **b** **1233** ~atum est de vic. Kanc' ad reddendum compotum suum de anno xvij donec habuerit mandatum *KRMem* 13 r. 11d.

4 to simulate, feign.

Dei judicio ficta debilitas facta est ei efficacissima... tum vero .. vera necessitate cum insito gemitu flagitavit quod antea ~averat, quatinus eum sancti .. virtus jam probatissima in pristinum vigorem restituat GOSC. *Mir. Iv.* lxx; ~o, A. *to lykeny or feyne or myslykene WW*.

5 to disfigure.

caput [faunorum] .. curvata naribus cornua ~ant *Lib. Monstr.* I 5; **1221** nasus ei fuit abscissus et unum ex labris et facies ejus ~ata *PlCrGlouc* 106.

dissimulatio [LL]

1 dissimulation, concealment.

ut tibi in lucem prodeant quae verborum velata sunt ~one, pauca .. dignum duxi denudare NIG. *Ep.* 17; sunt quatuor ale [cf. *Dan.* vii 6] quibus vehitur hypocrita: jactantia de bono manifesto, excusatio de malo manifesto, simulatio boni occulti, ~o mali occulti HALES *Sent.* IV 303; **s1455** mox ille odii sintillulas sub dissimilacionis cineribus coopertas .. discooperuit *Reg. Whet.* I 163.

2 a disregard, (seeming) neglect. **b** negligence or connivence.

a dormire dicitur [Deus] et oblivisci propter injurie dissimilationem et vindicte retardationem BART. ANGL. I 20; **s1253** (v. discessio b). **b** generale .. prelatorum malum fuit neglectus officii suscepti, .. oneris ~o AD. EYNS. *Visio* 35; **1254** si tam festinam [excommunicationis] tulissetis sententiam in illos .. vispiliones .. qui abbaciam nostram de Silva Majori [*Gasc*] .. depredati sunt .., forte multa alia remansissent que per ~onem vestram perpetrata sunt *Cl* 246; si .. intrasset monasterium ante etatem legittimam et cum ~one parentum per annum et diem stetisset in monasterio, omnino ei regredi non liceret PECKHAM *Puer Obl.* 433; **1284** non .. potest se majestas regia excusare in hiis que sub ~onis vestre pallio proveneruntt *Id. Ep.* 558; obstabit petenti excepcio per negligenciam et ~onem suam *Fleta* 111; **1306** ne .. nos per ~ones hujusmodi videamur ipsius injurie consentire *Lit. Cant.* I 31.

dissimulative, by way of dissimulation, as a cloak.

s1332 rex [Anglie], congregato exercitu valido, partes Scocie intrare conatus est, misso tamen prius signifero suo ad custodem, dissimilative negocia fingendo, ut actus et statum ejus exploraret *Plusc.* IX 25.

dissimulativus, meant to dissemble.

homicidium quandoque committitur precepto .., quandoque facto, et hoc multipliciter .., quandoque turbativo, quandoque ~o .., quandoque instigativo J. BURGH *PO* VII 8 f. 114.

dissimulator [CL], dissembler.

rerum omnium simulator varius et ~or GIR. *TH* III 52.

dissimulatorius, dissembling, affecting disregard.

quidam ~io vultu palliant ad tempus injurias et abscondunt P. BLOIS *Ep.* 12. 38C.

dissimulatrix, dissembler (f.).

[discretio] auriga virtutum, ~ix operum oculis intentionum H. BOS. *Thom.* II 9; [mustela] injuriarum pro loco ~ix et ultrix GIR. *TH* I 27.

dissimultas [cf. simultas], grievance, dissension.

705 ut .. omnium ~atum causae determinarentur WEALDHERE *Ep.* 22.

dissinter- v. dysenter-.

dissipantia, enervation.

tales novitates in subsanando, lacerando et blasfemando scripturam sacram .. introduxerunt ~iam legis Dei WYCL. *Ver.* I 277.

dissipare [CL]

1 to scatter; **b** (intr. *s. pass.*); **c** to separate, part. **d** to spread. **e** to squander.

~o, i. spargo *GlH* D 623; adversi venti .. naves ~ant G. MON. III 2; *Itin. Ric.* II 38 (v. disciplinariter a); [equites] ~arunt et †precurrerunt [v. l. percurrerunt] staciones Anglorum per medium *G. Hen. V* 16. **b** diminuta fuerat eorum [demonum] potestas, adeo quidem ut a facie ipsius undique diffugerint et ~averint GIR. *IK* I 12. **c** antiquos sceve lacerando dissipo amicos BONIF. *Aen.* 2 (*Iracundia*) 3. **d** agricola coacervat stercora, custodit, per agrum ~at PULL. *Sent.* 944A. **e** ~o, i. .. erogo *GlH* D 623; **a1092** nec ~avit 'substantiam suam cum meretricibus' [*Luke* xv 30] ANSELM (*Ep.* 140) III 286; **s1524** bona ~avere (v. deprimere 3a).

2 to undo, bring to nothing (bibl.). **b** (*s. pass.*) to come to nothing, fail. **c** to demolish, dismantle, ruin.

post .. ~atas fanaticae gentilitatis caeremonias ALDH. *VirgP* 30; ut superbiam eorum ~et et conturbet audaciam BEDE *HE* IV 3; sic Dei virtute ~atum est malignum consilium clericorum WULF. *Æthelwold* 19; vocem hanc .. celitus emissam audivit: '~asti ecclesiam meam ..' GIR. *IK* II 14; AD. MARSH *Ep.* 202 (v. conculcabiliter); cum sic .. ~ata esset fortitudo gencium et finita duricies belli *G. Hen. V* 13. **b** fatiscit, i. evanescit .., *ateorade*, ~at, deficit, *fordwinþ GlH* F 108. **c** ad domum .. pervenerunt, ~antes parietes ejus *V. Cuthb.* II 6; ecclesia vasta est et ~ata *DB* I 65; si quando [inimicus] illud [molendinum] vacuum invenerit, aut arenam statim ibi proicit que illud ~at, aut picem que conglutinat *Simil. Anselmi* 41; **s1163** tentorium .. ~atum (v. discindere 1a); ~abant Levite tabernaculum [cf. *Num.* ix 21] AD. SCOT *TT* 670C.

dissipatio [CL], **a** undoing, ruin. **b** dismantling.

a nullus .. adherencium papae, qui imperii ~onem affectant OCKHAM *Dial.* 928; **s1524** ad nostrae religionis obprobrium, scandalum, dessipacionem et ruinam *Reg. Butley* 47. **b** quia nimis laboriosum videbatur in ~one tabernaculi cortinas singulas .. disjungere [cf. *Exod.* xxxvi] AD. SCOT *TT* 644C.

dissipativus, annihilative.

quando persone vel communitates ad tantum offendunt Deum .. quod legi Dei repugnat injurias inpunitas cumulari, necesse est vindictam ejus ~am injurie ad servandum statum ecclesie distillari WYCL. *Civ. Dom.* I 218.

dissipator [LL], **a** scatterer. **b** squanderer, ruiner. **c** demolisher.

a **c935** rex [Adelstane] gloriose, .. exaltator ecclesiae .., ~or hostium (*Lit. Radbodi Prioris*) W. MALM. *GP* V 249. **b** prodigus, ~or substantiae *GlC* P 747; hunc [Thomam] .. aulica cupiditate et voracitate quadam lupina totius gregis ~orem potius et voratorem quam pastorem .. presumendum H. BOS. *Thom.* III 2; pastores nostri qui non .. querunt .. dispensatores esse sed ~ores GIR. *GE* II 34 p. 333; **s1321** ~or substancie sibi relicte WALS. *HA* I 158; **1330** non prodigus nec bonorum communium ~or *Lit. Cant.* I 309; **s1451** (v. dispensator 1a). **c** ~or urbium .., ecclesias Dei cum praesulibus despiciens EDDI 33; **c790** ipsi structores .. fiunt destructores et edificatores ~ores ALCUIN *Ep.* 67.

dissipatrix, undoer (f.).

superbie vanitas est .. humilitatis ~ix AD. SCOT *Serm.* 382A.

dissipere, ~ientia v. desip-. **dissire** v. 2 disserere 1a. **dissitus** v. 3 disserere b, 1 dissuere 1b.

dissociabilis [CL], uncompanionable.

~e, i. separabile, insociabile, *ungeferlices GlH* D 693.

dissociantia v. dissonantia 2b.

dissociare [CL], to separate, part, break up. **b** to exclude, oust. **c** to restrain, stop. **d** (p. ppl.) disunited, at variance.

~iari, *beon unge[ferlæht] GlM* 27. 5 (cf. ib. 28. 251: ~iata, *todæledu*); sin ab invicem ~iari eligant, viri est idoneum locum uxori providere ubi quod opus est nec anime desit nec corpori PULL. *Sent.* 950A; ~iata locis in coitu convenire non possunt J. SAL. *Pol.* 440D; ille [canis] suo nostrum latratu fundit amorem;/ ille bonum pacis dissociare cupit WALT. ANGL. *Fab.* 57. 6; sic fera dissociat mors quos Deus associavit, / et moriente morans viduatur conjuge conjux H. AVR. *Hugh* 59; facilius partes rupisset continuas quam palpebras ~iasset conclusas *Mir. J. Bev. C* 333. **b** **c1185** Jordanus de Ros, dicens se esse personam illius ejusdem [advocationis] medietatis, scitatus ad Scaccarium quia videbatur ~iare inde abbatem, advocavit inde abbatem (*Nig. Reg. S. Ædm.*) MS Camb. Univ. Lib. Mm 4. 19 f. 123. **c** [diabolus] volens eum .. perterrere et ab

opere satis sibi contrario dolositatis industria .. ~iare B. *V. Dunst.* 16. **d** cum pastore lupus sociabile fedus inivit,/ interius totus dissociatus ei WALT. ANGL. *Fab.* 57. 2.

dissolatio v. desolatio 2a.

dissolēre [cf. CL solere], to be unaccustomed.

to be un wonte, dessuere .., ~ere, absolere *CathA*.

dissologia [LL *gl.* < διssολογία], prevarication, double talk. **b** dialogue.

non igitur coeptum dissolvit dexia votum,/ pichria neve tulit, seu dissōlōgia [*gl.*: bifaria locutio] rupit FRITH. 457; ~ia, *twigspræc* ÆLF. *Sup.* **b** ~ia, sermo duorum OSB. GLOUC. *Deriv.* 175.

dissolubilis [CL], dissoluble, disintegrable. **b** (of objection) able to be resolved.

non negabit se intelligere quia, si esset aliquid quod nec actu nec intellectu dissolvi posset, majus esset quam quod vel intellectu esset ~e ANSELM (*Incarn. A* 10) I 289; pira naturaliter sunt ~ia sicque naturali dissolutione veniunt ad maturitatem *Quaest. Salern.* C 29; est ergo omne causatum aliqualiter compositum et omne compositum natura ~e SICCAV. *PN* 122. **b** monstravimus quod praescientiam Dei et liberum arbitrium simul esse .. non sit impossibile neque possit aliquid obici quod non sit ~e ANSELM (*Praesc.* II 1) II 260.

dissolute [CL], dissolutely, without restraint.

s1138 jam finem loquendi conferunt hostes inordinate prorumpentes et proruentes atque †dissute [? l. dissolute] M. PAR. *Min.* I 259 (= H. HUNT. *HA* VIII 8: hostis inordinate proruens et .. disperse confluens); **1300** ut extra domum suam et precipue tam ~e non vagetur *Reg. Cant.* 721 (cf. ib.: indecenter .. ac eciam ~issime .. se gerit).

dissolutio [CL]

1 dissolution, breaking in pieces, crumbling. **b** (of body) decay. **c** physical death. **d** ripping (of dress).

c625 hos quos .. materiae conpage vobis deos fabricastis confringendos .. procurate. ipsa enim eorum ~o corruptioque .. vobis patenter insinuet quam nihil erat quod eatenus colebatis (*Lit. Papae*) BEDE *HE* II 10; ~o, *towesnes* vel *tolesednes*, †dispar [MS: dispersio] *GlH* D 696; fit ut, quia continua est ~o, continuo fiat reparatio ADEL. *QN* 45; *Itin. Ric.* IV 34 (v. distemperare 1b); *Quaest. Salern.* C 29 (v. dissolubilis a); cadunt epileptici frequentius in .. foro aut teatro ex ~one materie .. et hanelitu hominum GILB. II 111. 1. **b** malum ~onis [v. l. desolutionis] *V. Cuthb.* IV 17 (v. disseminare 1b); sanatam se ab illa corporis ~one sentiens BEDE *HE* III 9; paralisin, ~o membrorum *GlC* P 127; *Chr. Wallingf.* 59 (v. cachexia). **c 951** (12c) quatenus .. possideat quandiu vitalis spiritus aluerit corpus, cum autem ~onis suae dies advenerit cuicumque voluerit heredi derelinquat *CS* 892; **956** (12c) cum vero ~onis suae tempus accesserit *Ib.* 963. **d 1575** pro ~one et iterum nova factura [*for ryppyng and making up againe of a gowne*] *Ac. LChamb.* 66 f. 9v.

2 scattering, distintegration (of community). **b** dissolution, break up (of religious house).

1105 non decet ut .. incipiam vos dispergere... non sine magno scandalo aut sine magna ~one fieri possit ANSELM (*Ep.* 355) V 296. **b 1538** decimas .. nuper monasterio de Holme Cultran .. spectantes .., que in occupacione propria nuper abbatis dicti nuper monasterii tempore ~onis inde reservate fuerunt *Augm. Bk.* 211 f. 12*d.*; **1553** pretextu ~onis dicti nuper monasterii de Glaston' *Pat* 852 m. 23 (v. et. dissolvere 2d); **1586** (v. deventio a).

3 untying (fig.). **b** loose connection.

[sacerdotes nostri] clavibus suis de valde possibili errantibus, nec solvunt nec ligant subditos suos quo ad Deum, sed intricant se ipsos fingentes superficie tenus nodos vel ~ones nodorum WYCL. *Blasph.* 37. **b** animalium aures, quia non sic [ut hominum] adherent sed in altum tendunt, possunt moveri ex ~one quam habent *Quaest. Salern.* P 131.

4 relaxation, slackening (of order). **b** (act of) dissoluteness, licentiousness.

1179 (1270) sciatis moniales de Ambresbyria circiter xxx propter vite turpitudinem et ordinis sui ~onem et infamiam que devulgabatur pupplice .. a monasterio suo fuisse amotas et in aliis monasteriis collocatas *CalCh* II 157; **1405** in magnas ~ones bone discipline, honestatis victus et aliorum viciorum intollerabilium *Cl* 254 m. 2. **b** si districtionem .. odit .., se vitiosum esse et ~onem diligere demonstrat ANSELM (*Ep.* 286) IV 206; **1234** qui in refectorio necessitatem habuerint bibere, sic desolutionem caveant .. ut in potatione teneant moderantiam et freno silentii non laxent habenam (*Vis. Bury*) *EHR* XXVII 732 (cf. ib. 730: cum confessio .. sit potissima debellatrix ~onis); **1245** ut de suis [sc. imperatoris] nephariis ~onibus sileamus (*Sententia Papae*) M. PAR. *Maj.* IV 454; jocis, nugis, trufis, ociis ~onibusque vacantes *Obs. Barnwell* 32; **1325** religiosos quorum ~ones intolerabiles conniventibus oculis dissimulantur *Lit. Cant.* I 150; **1526** seculares personas cum fratribus chorum intrantes, una cum ipsis ibidem sedentes, confabulantes, ~ones moventes (*Vis. Thame*) *EHR* III 713.

5 a resolution, settlement (of dispute). **b** resolution, solution (of problem).

a 1559 ad querelarum et controversiarum, quae inter diversos ecclesiae ordines nasci assolent, ~onem *Conc. Scot.* II 141. **b** ~o tercie difficultatis SICCAV. *PN* 124 *rub.*

dissolutivus [LL], solvent (esp. med.).

BART. ANGL. IV 2 (v. disjunctivus 2); si apostema sit valde durum, tunc oportebit uti calidis valde ~is GILB. I 65. 1 (cf. ib. II 107v. 2: [medicine] attractive .. virtutis, phlegmatis et melancolie ~e et comsumptive); balneari in aquis sulphureis et salsis et ~is et calidissimis BACON V 95; eo quod calor solis .. vaporis sit magis ~us *Ps.*-GROS. *Summa* 585; cum medicina mollificativa et ~a, igitur non repercussiva GAD. 27. 2; tapsus barbatus .. cum sulphure et aliis ~is valet contra scrofulas *Alph.* 182.

dissolutorius, assoc. w. melting.

in hieme fractiva audiuntur tonitrua, in estate vero ~ia ADEL. *QN* 64.

dissolvere [CL]

1 to decompose, dissolve or melt; **b** (fig.). **c** to fracture. **d** to take to bits, break up, dismantle. **e** to shake loose, spread out. **f** (p. ppl. *dissolutus* as sb. n.) asyndeton.

cadaver nudum vermibus et putredine desolvendum limus suscepit ALCH. *Ep.* 299; fatiscit, i. evanescit, ~itur .., *mylt GlH* F 108; *GAS* 234 (v. 1 dissuere 1d); opus quod fit secundum aliquam artem, non solum quando fit verum et antequam fiat et postquam ~itur ANSELM (*Mon.* 34) I 53; interiora nostra ab illis exterioribus ~antur necessario fit ADEL. *QN* 45; RIC. MED. *Anat.* 223 (v. digestio 1a); nix .. ibi .. non potest ~i *Quaest. Salern.* Ba 116; humores disgregantur .. et ~unt materiam corruptam GILB. II 111. 1; ut partes materie constent et non ~antur a calido SICCAV. *PN* 190. **b** omnis praestigiarum scena .. ut umbra fatescens dicto citius ~ebatur ALDH. *VirgP* 43. **c** confracta sunt crura et brachia, omnibusque membris desolutis ultima spiramina trahens jacebat EDDI 23; dissolutam .. emicranii juncturam componere BEDE *HE* V 6. **d** R. COLD. *Cuthb.* 52 (v. compago a); in illa [veteri] navi custodienda antequam possit ~i super ripam *Ac. Build. Hen. III* 70; tam cito vestrum aliqua a cemento recedens ~etur [ME: *sone se ai unlimeð hire*], cito corruet .. sicut lapis a cemento solutus proicitur *AncrR* 83; edificia .. vel .. corruerunt .. vel saltem dissolutis compagibus enormiter ledebantur *G. Hen. V* 6 (cf. ib.: ad intra muros dissolutos); **1432** [pro] uno carpentario ad ~end' et deponend' domum predictam conducto *KRAc* 478/13. **e** stat formatus homo, miratur seque suosque / gestus. .. / .. / artus distendit, dissolvit brachia GOWER *VC* VII 549. **f** quando proferuntur plures clausule sine conjunctione media, color est que appellatur .. ~um; ~um enim est color quando dissolute sunt clausule, id est quando non ligantur vinculo conjunctionis VINSAUF *AV* II 2. 36.

2 a to disband (troops). **b** to raise (a siege). **c** to dissolve (council or parliament). **d** to dissolve (religious house or sim.). **e** to dissolve (alliance). **f** to break (vow).

a dissolutis agminibus ORD. VIT. VIII 5 p. 299. **b s1217** ut .. obsidionem castri Lincoln' ~ere laborarent WEND. II 212; **s1314** [rex] ad obsidionem castri de Strivelin ~endam gressus suos .. maturavit TROKELOWE 83; **s1405** soldarii Calisie ~i fecerunt obsidionem OTTERB. 252. **c 1312** concilium non ~entes sed continuantes *Conc. Syn.* 1366; **s1387** querebatur ab eis numquid rex, quandocumque sibi placuerit, poterit ~ere parliamentum *Eul. Hist. Cont.* III 362; **1399** quod potestas parliamenti .. remaneret apud quasdam certas personas ad terminandas, dissoluto parliamento, certas peticiones in eodem parliamento porrectas *RParl* III 418b; **s1415** magnates regni nuper ad parliamentum modo tamen desolutum per regis exitum congregati *Ps.*-ELMH. *Hen. V* 8; **1549** in concilio Tridentino nondum dissoluto *Conc. Scot.* II 113. **d s1524** (v. deprimere 3a); **1538** scitum nuper prioratus de Haverholme .. modo dissoluti *Augm. Bk.* 211 f. 12*d.*; **1553** pretextu dicti actus de diversis cantariis, collegiis, gildis, fraternitatibus ~endis et determinandis .. aut .. pretextu separalium dissolucionum dictorum nuper prioratuum *Pat* 853 m. 25. **e** fortuna .. / .. / dissolvit fedus que fecit pridie WALT. WIMB. *Carm.* 346; **1288** confederaciones .. ~imus (v. colligatio c). **f** FRITH. 456 (v. dissologia).

3 to loosen or open. **b** to unleash (hounds). **c** (naut.) to cast off. **d** to release, set free. **e** (p. ppl.) freed from restrictions of metre.

~e secundum prophetam [*Is.* lii 2] vincula colli tui GILDAS 29; arida spumosis dissolvens faucibus ora ALDH. *Aen.* 83 (*Juvencus*) 1; sic sator arcitenens dissolvit competa clausa *Id. VirgV* 1538; desolutus, *onsaelid* .., disolverat, †*ascaeltte* [l. aslaecte] *GlC* D 29, 336; desolvit, *arafaþ GlH* D 307; mercator .. trussellum deferens, si absque licencia .. ~erit eum *DB* I 263; **c1157** quod ~ant sine licentia trussellos suos et eant ad .. mercata *Act. Hen. II* I 174; dissoluta sunt vincula *NLA* II app. 653 (v. comprobare 1c). **b** aspexit cervum .. / dissolvitque canes *V. Merl.* 398. **c** ~it naves et portum cum impetu dereliquid *V. Ric. II* 76 (= WALS. *HA* II 151). **d** desolutus, i. liberatus, *onlesed GlH* D 305; quedam femina, que hoc tenuit T. R. E., vult ferre judicium quod [hoc] dissolutum est a vadimonio; hoc tenet Siwardus in vadimonio *DB* II 137; a corpore mortis hujus liberari ~ique cupiunt et esse cum Christo [cf. *Rom.* vii 24, *Philip.* i 23] GIR. *TH* I 19; **s1087** incarceratos omnes ~i precepit *Eul. Hist.* III 44 (= W. MALM. *GR* III 282: vinctos solvi). **e** ut quae versibus constricta sunt .. altius in memoriae penetralia infigantur quam quae dissoluto orationis genere diffluunt J. HERD *Hist. IV Regum* 5.

4 a to relax, weaken (w. abstr. obj.). **b** to relax, unbend (a person). **c** to weaken (physically or emotionally). **d** to deprave.

a prudens monachus ejus [antiqui serpentis] callidas persuasiones ~at et annihilat ANSELM (*Ep.* 37) III 147; **1285** vident dissolutum esse nervum pristine consuetudinis ecclesiastice discipline *Conc. Syn.* 970; bellum quod ~it legem et destruit civitates *Quadr. Reg. Spec.* 33. **b** subito rex, vultu hilarior et erectior oculis, in risum modicum .. ~itur AILR. *Ed. Conf.* 749A. **c** [puer] paene cunctis membris mortifactis dissolutus jacebat *V. Cuthb.* IV 17; hic per multos annos .. omnium membrorum paralysi dissolutus fuerat OSB. *Mir. Dunst.* 4; **a1108** de .. sancto viro qui, paralysi toto corpore dissolutus, .. feminis traditus est ANSELM (*Ep.* 425) V 371; H. HUNT. *HA* V *prol.* (v. 2 dissecare 1d). **d** nisi segnitia et torpore ~eretur GILDAS *EB* 18; luxuriae ~entis sordidiora genera (*Quad. Dedic.*) *GAS* 529; in annis puellaribus .., non dissoluta otio nec onerosa fastidio, legere aut operari manibus consuevit AILR. *Ed. Conf.* 747D.

5 to resolve: **a** (dispute or disagreement); **b** (problem); **c** (false syllogism).

a revellit [l. repellit], ~it *GlC* R 161; ~amus [AS: *uton towurpon*] citius has contentiones et sit pax et concordia inter nos ÆLF. *Coll.* 100; nunc discordiam quae inter praedestinationem et liberum arbitrium videtur esse aggrediamur ~ere ANSELM (*Praesc.* II 1) II 260. **b** cum multis [somnium suum] aperuisset nec esset qui ~eret J. FORD *Wulf.* 11. **c** dic quomodo tu ~eres hunc syllogismum ANSELM (*Gram.* 6) I 150.

dissonantia [LL]

1 (mus.) dissonance, discord; **b** (of languages).

diafonia, ~ia *GlC* D 248; tanquam ex variarum vocum ~iis mulcens auditum coaptatur symphonia *Itin. Ric.* III 2; altera magis protensa prima consonancia quam invenies post ~iam erit proporcio sexquitercia *Ps.*-GROS. *Gram.* 13; contrapunctus semper debet incipi et finiri per consonancias, tamen penultima debet esse ~ia HOTHBY *Contrap.* FL 63. **b** ut per talis consonantiam devotionis omnis ammoneatur ecclesia .. ad illam in futuro patriam festinare in qua .. nulla est ~ia linguarum BEDE *Hom.* II 16. 185.

2 a disagreement, discrepancy. **b** dissension, dispute.

a multi seducti ab hereticis .. ubi ~iam dogmatis eorum cognovere .. reversi sunt BEDE *Sam.* (*1 Sam.* xvi 21) 588; haec ~ia paschalis observantiae .. patienter .. tolerabatur *Id. HE* III 25 p. 182; viderit lector quomodo hanc ~iam componat W. MALM. *GR* I 9; velle illos ~iam facere, ut aratrum sancte ecclesie .., ove vetula cum tauro indomito jugata, distorqueatur a recto *Id. GP* I 48; si in verborum tenore ~ia est *Dial. Scac.* II 1 C; alia .., que palam cum sacris canonum constitutionibus ~iam resonabant W. FITZST. *Thom.* 35; DICETO *Chr. prol.* 19 (v. annus 2a); est et alius inter compotistas et cronicarum scriptores error et ~ia GERV. CANT. *Chr. prol.* 88; inter illa est ~ia in tempore BACON VII 17; *CathA* (v. discordantia). **b 825** multae discordiae et innumerabiles ~iae [v. l. †dissociantiae] extollebantur (*Clovesho*) *Conc. HS* 606; GROS. *Ep.* 124 (v. directe 1d).

dissonare [CL]

1 to be discordant (mus., fig.).

nisi quod in musica hac una vocum dumtaxat ~abat H. BOS. *Thom.* III 24 p. 273.

2 to disagree, be discrepant. **b** (of persons) to be at variance.

desonuit, †dissentit [? l. dissensit] *GlC* D 86; ratio et auctoritas divinorum scriptorum, quamvis ~are videantur, unum idemque sunt W. MALM. *GR* IV 334; cum dissonant cor et locucio / sermo concipitur ex adulterio WALT. WIMB. *Palpo* 53; quecunque tempore ~ant, non est necessario si unum corrumpitur quod alterum BACON VII 16; racioni ~at ipsum A. in curia hic .. ulterius detineri *Entries* 190. **b** quotiens ejus dispositionibus in nullo ~amus, tum maxime placamus misericordem Dominum ANSELM (*Ep.* 9) III 112; **1187** potestate opprimimur contra quam mutire nefas est et, cum sepe pium sit dissentire, ~are non licet *Ep. Cant.* 100; dissonat ingenuo genitus de sanguine pravo D. BEC. 104; *Ib.* 1350 (v. cliens 1a); quia geometra et naturalis [philosophus] considerant magnitudinem, ad eorum consideracionem spectat infinitum. sed quid est tunc quod ita ~ant circa ipsum? KILWARDBY *OS* 181.

dissonere v. disponere 2c.

dissonus [CL]

1 (mus.) dissonant, discordant.

canticum in nullo absonum, in nullo ~um H. BOS. *LM* 1299B; est citharista rudis quem dissona corda fatigat D. BEC. 1779.

2 disagreeing, discrepant, at variance; **b** (of persons).

psalmistae .. oracula praefatae supputationi non desonam pertulere sententiam ALDH. *Met.* 2; Susannam cum fabricatores .. ∼a sermonum procacitate .. insimulare machinarentur *Id. VirgP* 44; omne genus pestis superat mens dissona verbis WALT. ANGL. *Fab.* 3. 3; eventus varios dissona vota tenent NIG. *SS* 1056; rationi ∼um GIR. *EH* II 7 (v. dies 5d); gens .. / .. fidei dissona, cedis amans GARL. *Tri. Eccl.* 110; regem, si loquitur duo dissona, palpo tuetur WALT. WIMB. *Scel.* 136; nihil dixerunt ∼um a prioribus DUNS *Ord.* I 64; animadvertam an sit consona vel ∼a veritati OCKHAM *Dial.* 614. **b** s**1066** etiam benevoli et veritati, ut videtur, non ∼i dicere presumunt quod rex religiosus de genere proditoris heredes .. noluerit procreare *Flor. Hist.* I 589.

disspellire v. desepelire. **dissplod-** v. displod-.

dissuadēre [CL], to advise against, discourage.

ne .. utilia persuadenti vulgus acquiescat, incommodis quibusque propositis ∼endo insistunt ÆLNOTH *Cnut* 41; antistes .. in quantum potuit truculentam recalcitrationem dissuasit ORD. VIT. VIII 11; desuadent tamen indigine certaminis ausum H. AVR. *Guthl.* f. 66. 18; nulli imponitur ut locum [sc. purgatorium S. Patricii] intret, sed potius in principio ∼etur ingressus. quod si omnino intrare voluerit, accedit primo ad episcopum loci, qui pro ingressu ∼et *Meaux* I 139 (cf. M. PAR. *Maj.* II 194); OCKHAM *Pol.* II 809 (v. dissuasibilis).

dissuadus [cf. CL suadus], dissuasive.

dissuada laborum HANV. I 8 (v. dilatrix).

dissuasibilis, that can be discouraged.

omne justum est bonum; nullum autem bonum est ∼e, sed magis suasibile. multa autem sunt litigia justa; ergo non omnia litigia dissuadet apostolus OCKHAM *Pol.* II 809.

dissuasio [CL], dissuasion, discouragement.

de Radulfo .. qui contra ∼onem regis Henrici II .. Parasceue ante Pascha die .. venationi indulgeri presumpsit GIR. *GE* I 54; pluribus exemplis bellum dissuasio damnat,/ sit nisi legitimum GARL. *Tri. Eccl.* 3; s**1066** [Willelmus] rogavit .. regem Francie, qui per ∼onem suorum ei auxilium denegavit SILGRAVE 74.

dissuasor [CL], dissuader, discourager.

suasor concordie, ∼or discordie et prorsus ad quod intenderet pro viribus eloquentie persuasor W. MALM. *GR* V 407; GARL. *Tri. Eccl.* 13 (v. consultor).

1 dissuĕre [CL]

1 to unstitch. **b** to unknit (fig.). **c** (?) to dislodge. **d** *f. l.*

ementem / calciamenta virum .., / ut postquam dissuta forent usuque forata / illa †resartiret [l. resarciret] *V. Merl.* 517; virgo .. fibulam pallii .. ∼tam resarciebat W. CANT. *Mir. Thom.* II 36; tegmine [*gl.*: pro 'roba mea'] dissuto [*gl.*: *decouse*] non tardatus michi nuto GARL. *Mor. Scol.* 208; c**1250** cum casula de panno serico .. ∼ta anterius, alias sufficiente *Vis. S. Paul.* 17. **b** **1167** ne .. vestem Christi scindi, inconsutilem ejus tunicam [cf. *John* xix 23] male ∼i .. sineremus *Ep. G. Foliot* 182; virtus est quam nihil vincit, nemo ∼it; tunica enim est Domini inconsutilis H. BOS. *LM* 1388B; federe dissuto plebs conculcata tributo H. AVR. *Poems* 93. 24; quos .. natura texuit / nexos armonicos in hora dissuit WALT. WIMB. *Sim.* 136; s**1311** Isabella .. †dissitum [? l. dissutum] regnum affectans .. suis precibus resarciri *Flor. Hist.* III 148; tam ∼ta omnia unum decenter compingere FERR. *Kinloss* 10. **c** culmina dissuto violabant trabe palumbes FRITH. 439; saxa saxorum ictibus scematibus desuta corruunt *Ps.*-ELMH. *Hen. V* 123. **d** preter discarcatam lanam, †dissutum [? l. dissolutum] unctum (*Quad.*) *GAS* 234.

2 (?) to open mouth, gape. **b** (pass. *s. act.*) to burst (into).

hec ille [demon in specie canis] deforis audiens stridulis vocibus infremendo ∼it R. COLD. *Cuthb.* 17 p. 37. **b** longo post tempore muta [sc. Hecuba] / "heu" iterat repetitque "meus", sic sepe diuque / in voces dissuta breves J. EXON. *BT* VI 816.

2 dissuĕre, ∼escere, ∼etudo v. desue-.

dissultus, leaping about. *Cf.* 2 *dissilire* 1b.

cedatur animal .. in multas partes; angelica agilitate [cf. *Dan.* xiv 35] †deportetur [? l. deportentur] per orbis climata; tanto intervallo disjuncte, haud secus ac conjuncte, ∼u anime presentiam evincent PULL. *Sent.* 692C.

†dissumptio, ? *f. l.*

s**1337** ita ut in †dissumpcione [? l. disrupcione *or* dissolucione] gelicidii multi pontes caderent *Dieul.* 131 *n.*4.

dissumulare v. dissimulare. **dissuria** v. dysuria. **dissute** v. dissolute. **dissyl-, dissyll-** v. et. disyll-.

dissyllabare [cf. CL syllaba], to divide by syllables.

in fine linee .. potest diccio dissillibari, sed sillaba nullo modo separatur *Orthog. Gall.* 23.

dista v. dextans.

distabescere [CL], **distabēre** [LL], to melt away.

∼uerunt, *asundun GlC* D 275; cum .. arido in corpore vires ∼erent [vv. ll. ∼uerunt, ∼uerent] FELIX *Guthl.* 41; ∼ui, tabefactus *Gl. Leid.* 48. 44; ∼uit, *aswand GlH* D 680.

distaedere [CL], to be tired (of).

∼et, valde tedet OSB. GLOUC. *Deriv.* 179.

distainiatus v. desteiniare.

distanter [LL], at a distance, far apart: **a** (in space); **b** (in quality or degree).

a rarum est quod habet partes ∼er jacentes BACON *Maj.* II 479. **b** de quibus [ille liber] dicat primo in quatuor, deinde ∼ius distinximus BALSH. *AD* 56; *Ib.* 22 (v. differenter b); lex Christi docet Deum esse bonum supra omnia diligendum, secundo proximum ut seipsum, et tercio †infinitum [v. l. in infinitum] ∼er temporalia (WYCL.) *Ziz.* app. 487.

distantia [CL]

1 distance: **a** (in space); **b** (in time); **c** (in quality or degree).

a certi estote quia nulla locorum ∼ia .. dulcedinem amoris vestri .. a corde meo poterit separare ANSELM (*Ep.* 166) IV 41; posita est in hoc volumine .. examinatio planetarum .. secundum medium locum terre dictum Arin, a quo .. ad quatuor mundi terminos equalis habetur ∼ia ADEL. Elk. *pref.*; hi .. ∼ia pedum composita magnum spatium latere altero pretenso [in glacie] perlabuntur W. FITZST. *Thom. prol.* 17; quanto linee .. extense ab oculo magis distant ab oculo, tantum major est ∼ia ipsarum ad invicem J. BLUND *An.* 93; AD. MARSH *Ep.* 94 (v. dimensio a); in maxima ∼ia, ut ab oriente ad occidens BACON *Maj.* II 528; c**1262** (v. distemperantia a); ut ipsa .. ecclesia .., notabili ∼ia a retro existens .., perceptibiliter quateretur *Ps.*-ELMH. *Hen. V* 42; regina .. regem in ∼ia decenti humili vultu sequitur W. SAY *Lib. Reg. Cap.* 65. **b** si per ∼iam temporis factum fuerit [vulnus] et frigida sint intestina GILB. V 234v. 1; dico 'esse formale' ipsam ∼iam vel extensionem quam habet [tempus] inter duo 'nunc' BACON VIII 231; *Ib.* 250 (v. distare 1b). **c** multa est ∼ia peccandi inter eos qui ita Dei mandata contempnunt ut aliquos inter se justi aemulatores .. habeant et inter eos qui .. unanimo consensu mandatis caelestibus contradicunt BEDE *Gen.* (xi 6) 125; qui notitiam metricae artis habere desiderat, primo necesse est ∼iam litterarum syllabarumque .. discat *Id. AM* 82; inter peccatum et crimen ∼ia est ÆLF. *EC* 34; BELETH *RDO* 18 (v. diastema a); Deus distat in infinitum a creatura .. non propter aliquam ∼iam mediam inter extrema sed propter infinitatem unius extremi DUNS *Ord.* II 200; oportet videre que conversacio fuit homini debita ex institucione primaria, et secundum accessum ad illam vel ab illa ∼iam debent aliorum justicie vel injusticie mensurari WYCL. *Innoc.* 475.

2 **a** discrepancy, disagreement. **b** dissension.

a in hoc loco lxx interpretes unam generationem plusquam Hebraica veritas posuere .. verum chronographi Grecorum, hac comperta ∼ia, generationum .. seriem .. emendarunt BEDE *Gen.* (xi 12) 132. **b** si modo esset inter eum et archiepiscopum suum ∼ia, non esse culpam regis W. FITZST. *Thom.* 64 (cf. ib. 98: qui .. neque presentiam archiepiscopi comitabatur .. neque regis et ejus ∼ie se immiscebat); s**1205** ob ∼iam monachorum in eleccione discordancium *Meaux* I 341 (cf. HIGD. VII 33: dissensio in ecclesia); **1361** (v. distare 2).

3 distinction, classification.

tripertitam humani generis ∼iam orthodoxae fidei cultricem catholica recipit ecclesia ALDH. *VirgP* 19 (cf. id. *VirgV* 84: humani generis triplex distantia).

distantialis, remotely analogous.

dicit [J. Damascenus] ipsa [panem et vinum] non esse typum corporis Christi, hoc est .. figuram distancialem .., sed ipsummet corpus Christi et figuram ejus presencialem WYCL. *Apost.* 52.

distare [CL]

1 to be distant, parted, remote, to differ: **a** (in space); **b** (in time); **c** (in quality or degree). **d** (pr. ppl.) remote, different.

a tantum inter virginitatis flores et jugalitatis mores distare dicimus quantum ∼at oriens ab occasu [cf. *Psalm* cii 12] ALDH. *VirgP* 8 (v. et. 1c infra); ∼ant inter se monasteria haec xiij ferme milibus passuum BEDE *HE* IV 21; cum aliquis .. consideret quantum sol et luna ∼ent a terra *Simil. Anselmi* 29; **1126** cum presumant subjecti prelatis loco ∼antibus suas mentes litteris pandere *Ep. Anselm. Bur.* 96; J. BLUND *An.* 93 (v. distantia 1a); s**1248** per pedes hinc inde ∼antes a trabibus suspenditur M. PAR. *Maj.* V 34; **1285** sunt duo saltoria ad nocumentum foreste, de eo quod unum non ∼at a foresta .. per unam leucam et aliud ∼at fere per unam leucam et dim. *SelPlForest* cxxvii (cf. ib. *n.* [**1364**]: parcus non ∼at a foresta tres leucas); **1452** (v. de 1a). **b** si tempus mensurat distantiam, quod ∼at mensurabit BACON VIII 250; mors a qua [Heccuba] minimum ∼at TREVET *Troades* 67. **c** quam longe a meritis ejus [Christi] ∼etis GILDAS *EB* 108; de his [monstris] .. quae .. ab humano genere ∼ant *Lib. Monstr.* I *pref.*; ALDH. *VirgP* 8 (v. 1a supra); debetis scire .. quid ∼at inter vetus et novum testamentum ÆLF. *Ep.* 2. 92; quid pars a specie distet, te posco, profari *Altercatio* 73; si nostra scientia tam longe superatur ab illis [creatis substantiis] quantum earum similitudo ∼at ab earum essentia ANSELM (*Mon.* 36) I 55; vel verum vel a vero parum ∼ans BALSH. *AD* 37; AD. EYNS. *Hug.* III 6 (v. cycnus 1a); nulla .. creatura a quacumque alia tantum potest ∼are quantum Creator et creatura; immo in infinitum ∼ant FISHACRE *Sent. Prol.* 94; T. YORK *Sap.* II 19 *rub.* (v. communitas 1b); DUNS *Ord.* II 200 (v. distantia 1c). **d** ut sic sit mendax a veritate ∼antior WYCL. *Ver.* II 94; omnes alios inferiores illuminans ∼antissimus a profundo abissi maximaque loci securitate gaudens CHAUNDLER *Apol.* 12.

2 to quarrel.

1361 distancia movebat inter .. Johannem F. et Matildam uxorem ejus .., ita quod .. Johannes traxit cultellum suum in defensionem suam ..; et in ∼ando .. Matilda currebat super cultellum viri sui *RCoron* 18 r. 57.

distas v. dextans.

distemperamentum, mixing.

[cellararius] ad ∼um incausti de meliori cervisia prebebit cantori *Obed. Abingd.* 397.

distemperantia [LL], disproportion: **a** of temperature (climatic); **b** of elements or 'humours' (med.). **c** 'distemper', physical or mental disturbance (attributed to such disproportion). **d** ill-will, resentment.

a abolita foret estatis et hiemis injocunda ∼ia; qua excessione caloris et frigoris eliminata, vigeret mortalis respublica ADEL. *QN* 71; aeris ∼ia P. BLOIS *Ep.* 46 (v. distemperatio b); c**1262** invitus illuc laboravi, tum propter loci distantiam, tum propter ∼iam aeris mee complexioni valde discordantem (*AncC* VII 142) *RL* II 222. **b** sicut medicamentum discrasie, id est ∼ie, debet esse proportionale GIR. *GE* I 5 p. 19; ceteris ∼iis in alimento superfluentibus, [cerebrum] pro eorum affectionibus disponitur ALF. ANGL. *Cor* 15. 4; ∼ia caloris naturalis [in senectute] fit duobus modis: per resolutionem naturalis humiditatis et augmentum extranee BACON IX 9; calefaccio epatis dicitur discrasia, ∼ia in caliditate, sc. lapsus a colore suo naturali GAD. 72. 2. **c** cum aliquid extrinsecus adhibetur, cujus aliqua qualitas instrumentorum [sc. sensuum] temperantiam excedit, similis subjecti passio in ∼iam convertit instrumentum ADEL. *QN* 31; dicuntur Therapeute a θεραπεύω, quod est 'sano', eo quod animas accedentium ad ipsos .. a malitia passionum quasi ab egritudinum ∼ia sanant GROS. *Ep.* 57 p. 176; aliquando sunt propria vitia in substantia lingue, sicut complexio mala ex qua est sensibilis ∼ia ex nimio calore vel frigiditate vel humiditate vel siccitate BART. ANGL. V 21; quandoque he ∼ie [membrorum] sunt naturales, ut frigiditas stomachi et calida discrasia epatis GILB. VI 238. 1; s**1270** miles .., ingravescente dolore vulnerum, febrilem incurrens ∼iam .., exspiravit WYKES 235; s**1423** in mee nondum plene sopite nuperrima ∼ia infirmitatis AMUND. I 151; s**1455** incidente .. rege in hujusmodi ∼iam distraccionemque infirmitatis ut sensu .. careret et memoria *Reg. Whet.* I 163. **d** s**1458** de qua [latronum] evasione abbas audiens non parvam inde ∼iam contra custodem gaole conceperat *Ib.* 290.

distemperare [LL]

1 to temper, mix, steep. **b** to soak.

illum filicis accipite ramum et aqua ∼atum benedicta michi bibendum tradite T. MON. *Will.* II 6; sumens hanc [herbam] ∼a et repone tibi in scypho W. CANT. *Mir. Thom.* II 4; aliatam fortem, vino .. ∼atam NECKAM *Ut.* 102; GILB. III 146v. 2 (v. crocodes); **1296** in ovis et *glayr* pro orpymento ∼ando *KRAc* 5/20 m. 4; tutia .. alba cum aqua rosarum vel saltem cum aqua simplici ∼ata valet hiis qui habent oculos rubeos *SB* 42. **b** tanta exorta est tempestas .. ut .. equi .. nimietate aquarum perirent; et pars maxima victualium, panis biscoctus, ∼abatur in dissolutionem *Itin. Ric.* IV 34.

2 to 'distemper', affect by disproportionate mixture: **a** (climate); **b** (human body or sim.); **c** (fig.).

a quando sol venit ad oppositum augis comburit terram ..; et hoc est quando sol est in Sagittario et Capricorno et Scorpione. nam oppositum augis est in Sagittario, et in locis propinquis ei comburit similiter et ∼at; et ideo sol ∼abit Libram et Arietem BACON *Maj.* I 137; iste mansiones [lune] distinguuntur, quia quedam sunt temperate, quedam ∼ate in sicco, frigido, calido vel humido *Ib.* 384; s**1349** illic [apud Avinionem] aque servari non possunt ad horam estivo tempore pre nimio et ∼ato colore *G. S. Alb.* II 386; **b** [clericus] dysenteria ∼atus W. CANT. *Mir. Thom.* VI 39; s**1190** quosdam [apud Aconem invenimus] aeris inclementia ∼atos GIR. *IK* II 14; si forte colera menstrua ∼et ALF. ANGL. *Cor* 15. 4; cum sperma leprosi sit ∼atum et .. mutatum in id quod est preter naturam *Quaest. Salern.* B 33; jam tres humores unus distemperat humor H. AVR. *Hugh* 1142; corpora ∼ata et male sana in omni sunt dissimilia corporibus temperatis et bene sanis M. SCOT *Phys.* 32; [quedam medicina] ideo temperate calefacit quia est temperate calida .. et ideo sanat quia est sana; .. et cum est ∼ata ∼at et convertit corpus ad dispositionem suam propter similitudinem quam habet cum corpore humano BACON IX 58; BRINTON *Serm.* 16 (v. 2c infra). **c** res monstruosa est philosophus curialis .., eo quod curia philosophiam excludit... non tamen ad omnem

curiam comparatio transit, sed ad illam dumtaxat que insipientis ~atur arbitrio J. SAL. *Pol.* 567A; hyemalis intemperies que omnia hec terrena ~at, que frigida mortalium corda viciis .. durat AILR. *Nin.* 11; ~abatur in eo [sc. Adam] spiritus ex aere .. ~ato *Quaest. Salern.* B 216 (cf. 2a supra); sicut moriens naturaliter primo distemperatur, secundo infirmatur, tercio moritur .., sic anima moriens spiritualiter ~atur per temptacionem, infirmatur per delectacionem, moritur per consensum et operacionem BRINTON *Serm.* 16 p. 63 (v. et. 2b supra).

distemperatio [LL = *disproportion*], **a** slaking (of lime). **b** mixing, compounding (of poison).

a **1221** in ~one calcis, sc. cl summarum in tassca *Ac. Build. Hen. III* 40. **b** **c1173** ipsam [Siciliam] abominabilem mihi reddunt aeris distemperantia et veneni ~o frequens P. BLOIS *Ep.* 46. 134A.

distendere [CL]

1 to distend (also fig.). **b** to cram. **c** to stretch. **d** (pass.) to extend (intr.). **e** to pad, extend (a text). **f** to expand, extend (meaning).

[fatuus] audientium rictus cachinno ~ens W. MALM. *GR* V 439; neque sola spiritus quantitate ~itur [cor], sed pro majori parte vaporis ex aere admisso generati. is igitur cor ~ens, qua ingressus est, erumpit ALF. ANGL. *Cor* 11. 21 (cf. ib. 12. 2: animalium spermata .. spumosa spirituque distenta); infirmitas .. miningas cerebri ~it, quam distensionem subsequitur dolor *Quaest. Salern.* B 28; *A* in calidissima parte gutturis ~endo formatur *Ps.*-GROS. *Gram.* 21; hec [superbia] cor tumoribus / distendens vacuat cunctis virtutibus WALT. WIMB. *Carm.* 319. **b** ~unt, replent *GlC* D 246 (cf. ib. D 340: distentis, *adegen*); cibo ac potu supra metas etiam necessitatis ~ebar AILR. *Spec. Car.* II 17. 562C; distentos agmine vicos / et concursantes vidi per moenia cives J. HERD *Hist. IV Regum* 71. **c** o arcus extentus nec jam ultra ~endus J. FORD *Serm.* 53. 7; artus distendit GOWER *VC* VII 549 (v. dissolvere 1e). **d** aedificium situ pene rotundum, a muro usque ad murum mensura iiij ferme sive v perticarum distentum BEDE *CuthbP* 17; distenta, i. extenta, *apened, tobræd GlH* D 667; *GAS* 638 (v. cheminum c); AD. EYNS. *Hug.* III 1 (v. comitatus 5a); ab anima est vegetatio in totum corpus procedens et distensa per totum, non tamen ipsa anima distensionem habet J. BLUND *An.* 309 (cf. ib. 310: quod anima sensibilis et anima vegetabilis sunt corporee et ~untur per totum corpus vegetatum). **e** ne nimio epistola ~atur excursu *Ep. ad amicum* 140. **f** *GAS* 654 (v. dominus 2a).

2 to spread (cloth), pitch (tent). **b** (fig.) to set (snares).

impositus est cilicio humi distento ALEX. CANT. *Mir.* 48 (I) p. 256; **1233** quod auxilium ad eos [papiliones] tendendos et ~endos [*Cal.* p. 209: †extendendos] ei [papilionario regis] habere faciat *Liberate* 10 m. 7; in omnibus [missis] .. que de Quadragesima dicuntur ipsa cortina debet esse distenta *Rit. Gilb.* 24; ventus .. tentorium capelle regis distentum in planicie ante castrum .. dilaceravit ad medium *G. Hen. V* 24. **b** tu, antiquissime seductor, .. haud mirum si .. in hominem Dei insidiarum machinas ~as! ÆLNOTH *Cnut* 46.

distensio v. dissensio, 2 distentio.

distensivus, spreading, extensive.

humor colericus naturalis .. est .. corporis secundum dimensionem longitudinis at altitudinis ~us BART. ANGL. IV 10; apostematum signa accipiuntur ex tumore, dolore, colore. .. dolor .. ~us [est] ex flegmate GILB. IV 203. 1; quando multum extenditur et †dilitatur [? l. dilatatur] humor, quia flegma est fluidum et ~um BACON V 85*n.*

distentare [LL], to spread, extend.

~at, *tobrœde GlH* D 668; *to sprede oute*, dilatare, distendere .., ~are *CathA.*

1 distentio v. dissensio.

2 distentio [CL], **~sio** [LL], distension. **b** stretching. **c** extension, enlargement.

~sionem *Quaest. Salern.* B 28 (v. distendere 1a); ruptura .. venarum .. aliquando est interior, aliquando exterior, et exterior fit vel ex vulneribus vel ~sionibus GILB. IV 194V. 2. **b** **s1389** sequebatur membrorum ~sio, et juvenis exilire cepit WALS. *HA* II 184. **c** summae veritatis .., quae nullam penitus localis vel temporalis ~tionis magnitudinem suscipit vel parvitatem ANSELM (*Mon.* 22) I 40; ~sione J. SAL. *Pol.* 444D (v. contractio 1b); ~sione R. COLD. *Osw.* 51 p. 380 (v. demisse); oportet quod ipse ymagines rerum .. habeant aliquam dimensionem, ut, si mensuraret in longum, est ibi porrectio; si in latum, est ibi in duas partes ~tio J. BLUND *An.* 300; ~sionem *Ib.* 309 (v. distendere 1d); sic [ut aranea] anima in centro cordis residens sine sui ~sione totum corpus vivificat BART. ANGL. III 3; cum [materia prima] sit .. fundamentum situs et cujuscunque ~sionis corporee WYCL. *Compos. Hom.* 13.

3 distentio [LL; cf. CL distinēre], distraction, preoccupation.

monachum .., regni, auri, argenti et .. propriae voluntatis ~onibus ruptis, perpetuo [te] vovisti GILDAS *EB* 34; diversarum rerum ~onibus fessae mentis cervicem .. deprimentibus ALDH. *VirgP* 59; **a739** postposita nobis ~one et sua deposita pertinatia .., tandem consentaneus effectus est (DAN. WINT.) *Ep. Bonif.* 39; abice nunc onerosas curas et postpone laboriosas ~ones tuas ANSELM (*Prosl.* 1) I 97.

dister- v. et. distr-.

disterminare [CL]

1 to form boundary between, separate, divide; **b** (fig.). **c** to distinguish.

in vicinia freti quod Anglorum terras Pictorumque ~at BEDE *HE* IV 24 p. 267; **s957** (v. definitio 4a); ad Humbram .. fluvium, qui Meridianas et Boreales Anglorum gentes interluvio ~at GOSC. *Aug. Maj.* 60B; ad mare quod Galliam Angliamque ~at W. MALM. *GP* V 222; [flumina] insulam per partes longis excursibus ~ant et distinguunt GIR. *TH* I 7. **b** quod si medii interruptione spatii .. nisus noster ab accessu loci illius [paradisi] ~atur PULL. *Sent.* 747A. **c** supponitur hec differentia 'modo nature consentaneus' habitus coactos a diffinitione virtutis ~ans W. DONC. *Aph. Phil.* 3. 3.

2 to put an end to, kill.

to slaa, cedere .., mortificare ..; versus: 'interemit, .. / .. / mortificat, truncat, disterminat exanimatque' *CathA.*

disterminatio [LL], end, death.

[Dominus regem] alium cita ~one preoccupat, ne populus suus nimia tyrannide oppressus non respiret H. HUNT. *HA* IV 20.

disternere v. desternere, discernere 1a.

disticare, to squeak. *Cf. denticare.*

to cry, .. soricum [est] ~are *CathA.*

distichon, ~ia, ~ium [CL < δίστιχος, ~ία], **a** double row. **b** distich, couplet (metr.). **c** poem in elegiac couplets.

a ut sibi disticiis acies vicina propinquis / et campo propiore stetit J. EXON. *BT* V 230. **b** ut Vergilium disticon fecisse commentaria declarant .. ALDH. *PR* 115; poesis est opus multorum librorum, .. ~on duorum versuum BONIF. *Met.* 112; cartula, percurrens colles camposque liquentes, / disticon hoc cantet semper in ore suo ALCUIN *Carm.* 74. 26 (cf. id. *Ep.* 171); *sticos* 'versus', unde ~ium duorum versuum carmen J. SAL. *Met.* 843D. **c** ad divum Cuthbertum ~on Johannis Alti missum .. priori ecclesie .. Dunelmensis A.D. 1502 (*MS BL Harl.* 4843 f. 253v.) C. Eyre *History of St. Cuthbert* ed. 3 (1887) p. 300.

distignere v. distinguere 1a. **distill-** v. destill-. **distinare** v. destinare.

1 distincte [CL], w. clear distinction of parts. **b** distinctly, w. distinct articulation.

computus Paschae .. ~ius in ordinem conpositus (*Ep. Ceolfridi*) BEDE *HE* V 21 p. 341; si eadem natura sit tota in singulis temporibus aut simul aut ~e per singula tempora ANSELM (*Mon.* 21) I 37; ex locis .. incolatus vel permissis officiis ~ius appellamur MAP *NC* IV 6 f. 48; AD. MARSH *Ep.* 30 (v. diffusio 2c); si intellectus non potest ~e ostendere [in Trinitate] essenciam sine persona vel personam sine persona, igitur nec voluntas poterit ~e frui DUNS *Ord.* II 25 (cf. distinctive). **b** ex parte Dei ~e vos adjuro .. ut non communicetis .. secreta RIPLEY 182; **1502** hanc nostram fundacionem .. de verbo in verbum ~e leget *StatOx* 307.

2 distincte v. 1 distinctus.

distinctim [LL], **a** distinctively. **b** separately.

a cui parvulo mox ~im haec proprietatis nomina imposuit ALCUIN (*Adv. Elipand.*) *Dogm.* 277A. **b** Trojanus mos est ut solemnibus diebus mares cum maribus, mulieres cum mulieribus, discumbant seorsim atque ~im GERV. TILB. II 17 p. 937 (cf. G. MON. IX 13).

distinctio [CL]

1 division, separation. **b** boundary. **c** line, cloison. **d** punctuation mark. **e** break, pause (mus.).

1228 cum fere nulla ibi inveniatur †districtio [MS: distinctio] inter monachos et mulieres de civitate (*AncC* VI 97) *RL* I 341; **1241** facias fieri apenticium, .. in quo per distrinctionem (*sic*) fiant due camere *Liberate* 15 m. 8; BACON XIII 424 (v. discontinuatio 1). **b** **1466** in quadam causa debate seu controversie penes ~ones diocesis [? l. diocesium] S. et B. *Reg. Brechin* I 191. **c** cernitur in ea [cruce] quedam dominice crucis portio .., Salvatoris nostri ymaginem habens de ebore .. sculptam et aureis ~onibus mirabiliter decoratam AILR. *Gen. Regum* 350. **d** mec [μέση], media ~o *GlC Int.* 219; **799** punctorum ~ones vel subdistinctiones licet ornatum faciant pulcherrimum in sententiis, tamen usus illorum propter rusticitatem paene recessit a scriptoribus ALCUIN *Ep.* 172; *se forma prica on þam ferse is gehaten* media ~o ..; *se oðer hatte* subdistinctio ..; *se þridde hatte* ~o *oððe* periodus ÆLF. *Gram.* 291; est punctus cum virgula inferius ducta, .. et talis ~o vocatur finitiva *Dictamen* 337. **e** ~o est congrua respiracio sive repausacio, sc. ubi nostra vox inter cantus modulacionem convenienter respirare videtur TUNST. 234; **s1423** in omni psalmodia .. fiat pausa aliqualis in medio versus; nec discurrant fratres de cetero precipitanter, dum dicunt, et absque spiritu ~onis AMUND. I 103.

2 a division, section (of book). **b** clause; *cf. clausula* 2b. **c** division of Carmelite province (*cf. EHR* XXXIV 208). **d** book case, compartment (in library). **e** shape, mould. **f** segment, growth-ring (in horn). **g** rank (in hierarchy).

a ~ones capitulorum ex tractatu B. Hieronimi excerptas BEDE *HE* V 24; quidam testantur psalterium apud Hebraeos in v ~ones dividi GOSC. *Mir. Iv.* lxv; sicut supra in prima hujus opusculi ~one retulimus *Chr. Rams.* 53; volo in hac secunda ~one ostendere .. BACON *Maj.* III 36; in hac [parte] sunt ~ones [ME: *chapitres*] quinque *AncrR* 9; presidens .. tres primos articulos positos supra eadem [regule S. Benedicti] ~one, capitulo primo, .. inquiret *Cust. Cant.* 404; **c1370** ista prophecia primo dividitur in tres ~ones .. quelibet istarum trium ~onum habet capitula in principio sui designata (J. BRIDL. *preamb.*) *Pol. Poems* 127–8; in lege papali .. xxxij destinccione, capitulo 'nullus †audeat [l. audiat]' WYCL. *Compl.* 92. **b** **a1400** omnis clausula vel ~o epistolaris dictaminis in trissillabam vel tetrasillabam terminatur (T. MERKE) *Salter Essays* 81; cadencia nichil aliud esse poterit nisi ~onis vel scissure et precipue diccionum finalis clausura *Dictamen* 334. **c** **1396** [*the province of England has been divided into*] iiij ~ones [*corresponding to*] iiij plagas [Anglie] *Cal. Papal Letters* V 1 (cf. ib. 19). **d** **a1331** tituli librorum de libraria .. et contenta in eisdem libris ..: prima demonstracio. ~o prima: Augustinus super Genesim [etc.] *Libr. Cant. Dov.* 13 (cf. ib. 82: incipit secunda demonstracio cum contentis. ~o prima); **c1452** A ~o: liber continens Universalia S. Thome [etc.]. B ~o: Thomas super libros Phisicorum [etc.]. C ~o: Vita Plinii [etc.] (*Catal. Librorum*) *Arch. Hist. Camb.* I 537 *n.* 3. **e** accendantur .. tres cerei de xxv lib. in ~one sua facti super tria majora candelabra *Cust. Cant. Abbr.* 269. **f** in ~onibus cornuum pecorum anni ipsorum numerari solent NECKAM *NR* II 121. **g** singulas ecclesiasticorum graduum ~ones AD. MARSH *Ep.* 8 p. 90.

3 distinction, difference. **b** (log. & exegetical). **c** drawing distinction, differentiation. **d** distinct articulation.

patriarchae habitabant in tentoriis, sed hoc velut peregrini ad ~onem eorum qui in .. dominibus quasi terrae cives habitare solebant BEDE *Gen.* (iv 20) 74; ea ~one ut .. unus Niger Heuuald, alter Albus Heuuald diceretur *Id. HE* V 10; nec in se recipit [summa natura] ~ones locorum aut temporum ANSELM (*Mon.* 22) I 41; jam .. non est ~o virtutis et vitii MAP *NC* IV 2 p. 141; HALES *Sent.* I 227 (v. differentia 1a); cum proprietates rerum sequantur substantias secundum ~onem et ordinem substantiarum BART. ANGL. *proem.* **b** verbi [sc. tabernaculum] diversarum significationum ~ones annotavimus P. CORNW. *Panth. Prol.* 40; [duo conceptus] comparati secundum analogiam aut secundum similitudinem vel ~onem DUNS *Ord.* III 20; ~o realis est ista qua aliqua distinguuntur ut existunt in naturis propriis in reali existencia. ~o intencionalis est qua aliqua distinguuntur in esse representativo, cum aliquid diversimode representatur. ~o vero racionis est ista qua aliqua distinguuntur solum per operacionem intellectus W. ALNWICK *QD* 7 (cf. ib. 180: consequens est distinguendum secundum quod potest esse formalitas ~onis et ~o formalitatis). **c** separatius .. distingui hec .. inutile; sunt enim quibus minus est ad doctrinam multiplicem quam nullam fieri ~onem BALSH. *AD* 81; respondent huic sillogismo per ~onem majoris et interempcionem minoris DOCKING (*1 Tim.* vi) (*extr.*) 111; voluntas non potest habere actum distinctum ex parte objecti nisi ponatur ~o ex parte objecti vel secundum racionem DUNS *Ord.* II 25 (cf. ib. 34: non oportet ad ~onem racionis quod intellectus habeat illa sicut objecta distincta, sed sufficit quod in primo objecto concipiat illa). **d** **c1218** precipimus quod cum .. reverentia magna celebretur hoc baptismi sacramentum et magna cautela, maxime in ~one et prolatione verborum, in quibus tota vis consistit sacramenti *Conc. Syn.* 68.

distinctionalis, divided into clauses.

de exemplaribus ~ibus non modicum lucide pertractavi *Dictamen* 340.

distinctionaliter, by clauses.

[sententias] diffinire luculencius intendo, scissuraliter et ~iter, ut in exemplis precedentibus *Dictamen* 337.

distinctive [LL], distinctively.

1236 si judicant per nativitatem solam .., unde nominabitur proles spuria et illegitima ~e immunda? GROS. *Ep.* 23 p. 88; intellectus non ~e comprehendit vel non distincte apprehendit hoc et illud; ergo non distinguit hoc et illud DUNS *Ord.* II 25; alique sunt proprietates perfeccionales primi agentis ad quas distincte concipiendas non oportet intellectum ~e facere per comparacionem ad essencias ad extra WYCL. *Quaest. Log.* 285.

distinctivus

1 a (gram.) disjunctive. **b** (phil.) distinctive, constituting or indicating a difference. **c** (as sb. n.) distinguishing feature. **d** indicative of a boundary.

a inveniuntur saepe conjunctiones in aliarum conjunctionum potestatem transire, ut 'vel' ~a conjunctio pro copulativa ponitur ALCUIN *Gram.* 895D. **b** omne habens distinctionis vel discretionis causam est quantitas discreta; tempus est hujusmodi, quia ibi est ponere 'ipsum nunc'

quod est discretivum et ~um partium temporis BACON VIII 229; iste [relaciones] in proprietatibus diversis trium hypostasum ~is radicate sunt *Ps.*-GROS. *Summa* 392; cum generacio sit assimilativa quatenus eadem natura communicatur, ~a quatenus est geniti distincti a generante distincto DUNS *Ord.* IV 128. **c** per talem speciem non habetur sufficiens ~um quando representat se ut se vel ut objectum, et ita nec sufficiens ~um veri a falso *Ib.* III 130. **d** **1538** marchias seu lapidea aut alia signa ~a et divisiva *Form. S. Andr.* II 57.

2 discriminative.

BART. ANGL. V 7 (v. dijudicativus); auctores perspective virtuti ~e mediante visu ascribunt judicia facienda de xx speciebus visibilium BACON *Maj.* II 4; ad omnia ista [sensibilia] concurrit virtus ~a vel sensus communis, eliciens diversos actus de istis secundum modum presentandi speciei per se sensibilis WYCL. *Log.* II 177.

distinctorius [cf. distingere], colorative.

1342 pro aqua ~ia et aliis coloribus pro eisdem armis *KRAc* 389/14 m. 4.

1 distinctus [CL = *distinctive character*], (?) section or separate place.

798 lunaris saltus supputationes, quas in alterius cartulae †~e [*ed.*: ~u] notavi ALCUIN *Ep.* 145.

2 distinctus v. 1 distingere.

3 distinctus v. distinguere.

distinere [CL], to hold or keep apart.

interim tamen quaecumque nos locorum vel propinquitas contineat vel longinquitas ~eat, caritas semper unum de duobus nobis animum conficiat ANSELM (*Ep.* 13) III 118.

1 distingere [cf. CL tingere], to distain, dye or (?) embroider. *Cf. desteiniare.*

1427 unum frontale et contrafrontale de panno lineo distincto *Reg. Cant.* II 391.

2 distingere v. distinguere.

distinguere [CL]

1 to separate. **b** (p. ppl.) separate.

ut Severus receptam Brittaniae partem vallo a cetera distinxerit BEDE *HE* I 5 *rub.* (cf. Orosius *Hist.* VII 17); R. COLD. *Cuthb.* 42 (v. disseparare); cancelli debitis †distignantur [v. l. destinguantur; *gl.*: distent] proportionibus NECKAM *Ut.* 104. **b** per distincta loca BEDE *HE* I 1; prorarum puppes rumpuntur concussu et cum armatis quos continent †discincte [l. distincte] a navium corporibus in maria submerguntur *Ps.*-ELMH. *Hen. V* 37.

2 to divide, split up: **a** (land or building); **b** (book or sim.). **c** to articulate (sound). **d** to punctuate. **e** to diversify.

a GIR *TH* I 7 (v. disterminare 1a); carceres debitis mansionibus distingti [*gl.*: divisi] NECKAM *Ut.* 105; **1289** [terram nostram] certis limitibus †distringatis [*sic* MS] ab aliis terris .., ita quod clare .. pateat quid ad nos .. pertinebit *RGasc* II 371; FORTESCUE *LLA* 24 (v. comitatus 5a). **b** librum de orthographia, alfabeti ordine distinctum BEDE *HE* V 24 p. 359 (cf. ib. II 1 p. 76: omelias .. quas in duobus codicibus aequa sorte distinxit); quod [opus], secundum materiam de qua editum est, 'Cur Deus homo' nominavi et in duos libellos distinxi ANSELM (*CurD prol.*) II 42; AD. SCOT *TT* 792C (v. congruentia b); in quarto folio 'De origine Psalmorum', in cujus fine ~it psalterium in v libros ELMH. *Cant.* 98. **c** insueta labia [hippocentaurorum] humanae locutioni nullam vocem in verba ~unt *Lib. Monstr.* I 7. **d** grammaticorum periodos colo et commate sequestratim distinctas ALDH. *VirgP* 32; potest et ita ~i ut 'causa' nominativus casus sit LANFR. *Comment. Paul.* (*Heb.* v 9) 387. **e** sapientis est proprium .. fastidiosa quelibet alterna delectatione ~ere GIR. *TH intr.* p. 8.

3 to distinguish, mark a distinction between or within. **b** (pr. ppl.) distinctive, (as sb. n.) distinctive element. **c** (p. ppl. *distinctus*) distinct, different, (as sb. n.) distinct element. **d** (p. ppl.) distinguished, outstanding, notorious.

si quis intendat rerum naturas, .. sentit .. quasdam earum ~i graduum imparitate ANSELM (*Mon.* 4) I 16; essentia [divina] nec ~itur, sed sole persone [Trinitatis] ab invicem ~untur BART. ANGL. I 4; vestigium representat aliquid confuse .., imago perfecte .., sicut per vestigium ~itur equus a bove .., non autem ~itur hic equus ab illo; sed imago ~it, quia imago Jovis non representat Christum DUNS *Ord.* III 175 (cf. ib. IV 73: quomodo relacio possit esse ~ens personam et essenciam non ~ens); concilia generalia symbola condiderunt articulos [fidei] distinguencia OCKHAM *Dial.* 459; *Id. Pol.* I 14 (v. cadere 3b). **b** si dicatur quod ibi est ~ens in divinis sicut proprietas, distinctum ut persona, distinguibile [ut] essencia, ergo oportet quod apud Grecos sit *usiosis* ~ens, apud nos vero subsistentia ~ens HALES *Qu.* 16; BACON VII 114 (v. distinguibilis). **c** has ~as colorum varietates .. rimamini ALDH. *VirgP* 15; hujusmodi principia et infinita sunt et ~iora quam ut demonstratorum distinctionibus conveniant BALSH. *AD* 19; HALES *Qu.* 16 (v. 3b supra); DUNS *Ord.* II 34 (v. distinctio 3c). **d** militum Christi .. x milia sub ~o [v. l. districto] Juliani regimine conversantes ALDH. *VirgP* 36.

4 **a** to discriminate, recognize or treat as different, classify. **b** to distinguish (intr.), perceive or draw a distinction; **c** (w. indir. qu. or *quod*). **d** to particularize, draw a distinction within. **e** (p. ppl. *distinctus*) involving distinct perception, clear.

a quae tripliciter dirimuntur, angelo hoc modo alternatim ~ente ALDH. *VirgP* 19; *Ib.* 35 (v. categoria 1b); nisi omnia .. sophismatum genera distinximus BALSH. *AD* 40; BACON *Mor. Phil.* 21 (v. cacodaemon); ~itur habitus speculativus in mathematicam, physicam, et metaphysicam DUNS *Ord.* I 6; *Ib.* II 25 (v. distinctive); W. ALNWICK *QD* 180 (v. distinctio 3a); OCKHAM *Pol.* I 306 (v. de 1e); secundum quod reges contra alias potestates publicas ~untur *Ib.* III 12; *Id. Dial.* 489 (v. contra 5). **b** fautores episcoporum sic forte †distringunt [? l. distinguunt] ut clericorum casas visitent episcopi, ecclesias autem archidiaconi GIR. *JS* 1 p. 144; distingunt BART. ANGL. II 3 (v. dividere 7e); Boethius ~it .. inter dialecticam et rhetoricam penes illas [sc. thesim et hypothesim] KILWARDBY *OS* 478. **c** BALSH. *AD* 56 (v. distanter b); ~o ulterius quod 'potencia denominative sumpta' aliquando sumitur pro suo fundamento precise, aliquando autem [etc.] DUNS *Ord.* IV 120; declarata sic distinccione qua ~itur quod quedam hereses contrariantur veritatibus que [explicite, quedam veritatibus que] implicite sunt credende OCKHAM *Pol.* III 50. **d** c**1228** de eo quod dixerat de necessariis capiendis in foresta, dictum suum sic ~it quod est ibi foresta .. juxta L. versus occidentem in qua nulli licet aliquid capere .. absque licentia .., a L. autem versus orientem .. monachi capiunt sine .. licentia *Feod. Durh.* 268. **e** actus [videndi] .. ~ior WYCL. *Act.* 14 (v. conjunctio 1c).

distinguibilis, distinguishable, (as sb. n.) distinguishable element.

HALES *Qu.* 16 (v. distinguere 3b); primum exemplum, sc. prime cause, est distinguens, non distinctum, quia componeretur ex distinguente et ~i BACON VII 114; c**1301** in illo [Deo] videntur esse ~es intenciones, que sunt in genere *Quaest. Ox.* 318.

distinguibilitas, distinguishability.

sicut est duplex ~as ad propositum, viz. 'tocius essencialis' in partes essenciales et 'tocius universalis' in partes subjectivas, ita est duplex indistinccio duplicis predicti 'tocius' ad suas partes DUNS *Ord.* III 49.

distirbatio, distirp- v. disturbatio. **distitu-** v. destitu-.

distonatio [cf. LL tonatio], discord, dissonance (mus., fig.).

1426 [inquisivit abbas] nunquid in concordi claustralium cithara aliqua fuerit lupina cordula que non convenit cum ceteris, immo in choro concordie causare solet .. ~ones AMUND. I 208.

distoppare v. distuppare.

distornare [cf. OF *destorner*], to 'disturn', divert: **a** (watercourse); **b** (dower).

a in aquis ~atis a recto cursu *RegiamM* II 74. 1 (= *APScot* I 258: trestornatis, *as in* GLANV. IX 11). **b** **1315** [Robertus] destornavit ei [Amabille] dotem suam *CourtR Wakefield* III 69.

distorquēre [CL], to turn, twist, wrench. **b** (fig.) to wrest, distort, pervert. **c** to change.

cingulum illud ~endo dissiluit R. COLD. *Cuthb.* 94; que vis distorqueat axes / sideris errantis HANV. III 141 p. 280; in distorta .. via H. BOS. *Thom.* III 30 (v. deviare 1b); nec ~eas aspectus tuos vel ad momentum vel ad aliquod aliud J. GODARD *Ep.* 240; sicut in aqua commota et turbulenta apparent ymagines distorte, sic in sanguine commoto et turbulento apparent fantasmata distorta BACON VIII 106; haec dicens commovit caput ac distorsit labrum MORE *Ut.* 71. **b** distortum, .. perversum, obliquum, .. *misbroden* *GlH* D 728; *GAS* 331 (v. compellatio b); W. MALM. *GP* I 48 (v. dissonantia 2a); quasi violenter exponendo ~ebitur quidquid adversari cernetur PULL. *Sent.* 726A; mutatione aspirationis in S, ut distortis a Greco in Latinum fieri solet, dicta est Sabrina GIR. *DK* I 5 (cf. Cambricus); si non ~eatur auctoritas .. ad alium intellectum, quem non sonant verba DUNS *Ord.* II 54; alius intellectus ipsorum [verborum], nisi patenter ~eantur .., haberi non potest OCKHAM *Dial.* 851. **c** T. THURKILL *Abac.* 57v. (v. denominatio 3a).

distorte [LL], **a** distortedly (also fig.). **b** by extortion, wrongfully.

a nervi a cerebro usque ad caudam [canis] recta linea protenduntur .. nervi vero qui ad pedes veniunt ~e protenduntur *Quaest. Salern.* P 91; inde est quod pueri ~e, indiscrete et confusse apprehendunt BACON VIII 106. **b** **961** (12c) ruris .. particulam .. pridem †indepte ~eque a B. Petri .. oraculis ablatam *CS* 1073.

distortio [CL], distortion; **b** (fig.). **b** extortion.

passus est insensibilitatem et ~onem labii *Quaest. Salern.* Ba 91. **b** quod non .. absurditate quorundam fraudulenta distorsione dici consuevit R. MELUN *Sent.* II 35. **c** *an extorcion*, ~o ex injuria *CathA.*

distortor [LL], distorter.

nec textus esse doctorem .. sed impudentem ~orem R. MELUN *Sent.* I 17.

distractio [CL]

1 tearing apart, separation.

reliquos .. in ergastula deputavit, separatos ab invicem ~one miseranda W. POIT. I 3.

2 'drawing' (dragging of criminal to execution).

s**1239** non tantum .. suspendio, sed eum [H. de Burgo] dignum ~one asserebat M. PAR. *Maj.* III 619; s**1329** [R. de Mortuo Mari] .. ~oni et suspensioni addictus est *Meaux* II 360; s**1382** judicatus est traditor [J. Balle] ~oni, suspensioni, et quarterizacioni *Ziz.* 273; **1415** due pene predicte, viz. †districcionis [*sic* MS] et suspensionis, eidem Thome Gray relaxantur *RParl* IV 66a.

3 forcible seizure, dispersal, waste. **b** withholding.

1221 (v. distrahere 3a); s**1232** de ~one bladi de W. violenta WEND. III 19 *rub.* (cf. distrahere 3a); **1262** quod interim non fiat vastum seu ~o de rebus seu possessionibus ad .. prioratum pertinentibus *Cl* 41 (cf. ib. 51: sine ulla ~one inde facienda); **1311** bona .. restituere compellantur per capcionem personarum aliorumque bonorum eorum; et, si in dicta compulsione et bonorum ~one necesse fuerit [etc.] *RGasc* IV 562; **1380** cum .. comes .. navem .. cepisset et in salvam et securam custodiam absque diminucione seu ~one aliqua bonorum .. custodiendam .. committere voluisset *RScot* 25a. **b** c**1430** rogo .. ut id quod noster attornatus in vestrum alumnum exercuerit in ~one sui juris non displiceat paternitati vestre *Reg. Whet.* II app. 424.

4 disposal, selling off, sale.

fit rerum repentina ~o ALDH. *VirgP* 42; **9..** †distratio, *bibycgong WW*; ~o, *ceap* ÆLF. *Sup.* 180; s**794** dinumerata pro ~one patronum pecunia *V. II Off.* 29 (= M. PAR. *Maj.* I 359: innumerata soluta); quandam villam .. e regione monasterii A. sitam ipsi abbati [Adelelmo, ob. **1084**] pretio accepto, distraxit; in qua ~one et calix .. expensus est *Chr. Abingd.* II 9; propter dictas tam spiritualium quam temporalium ~ones, tam simoniacas sc. emptiones quam Gieziticas venditiones GIR. *JS* 1 p. 146; **1380** quantum ad mutuacionem pecunie et ~onem pignorum *StatOx* 76.

5 (mental) distraction, absence of mind.

propter ~onem cordis per ipsa sensata exteriora [ME: *eaver se þeos wittes beoð mare ibreinde utwardes*], per quam ~onem privatur delectacione spirituali *AncrR* 26; que .. inordinate prolata comperierit, non malicie sed impericie mee aut .. ~oni mentis .. aut inadvertencie .. ascribat OCKHAM *Pol.* I 217; s**1455** (v. distemperantia c).

distractivus, (gram.) disjunctive, separative.

species .. significacionis conjunccionis .. continuative, contiguative sive copulative et disjunctive sive ~e *Ps.*-GROS. *Gram.* 57.

distractor [LL], one who tears apart. **b** seizer, stealer.

s**991** in subeundo portum .. navi et oneri propter tabulatorum ~ores memineris providendum *Chr. Rams.* 100 (cf. carinula b). **b** plag[i]arius, mancipiorum vel pecodum alienorum ~or *GlC* P 476; **1143** pervasores harum rerum et ~ores .. dampnandos esse denunciamus *Cart. Osney* I 5; c**1265** ad prosequendas causas nostras contra quoscunque ~ores, invasores, receptores seu detentores bonorum ecclesiarum de H. et E. et emendas .. recipiendas ab eisdem *Ann. Durh.* app. 168.

distractrix, distractive (f.).

1261 lites sunt .. vexatrices corporum et mentium ~ices *Stat. Linc.* I 311 (= *Conc.* I 756).

distraere v. distrahere.

distrahenter, analytically.

pueri nesciunt intelligere falsum ~er, modo quo methaphisicus dicit falsum esse quod Deus non est WYCL. *Ver.* I 193.

distrahere [CL]

1 to pull apart, tear to pieces, mangle. **b** to break up (fig.).

distraxit, i. discidit, dividit; distractus, i. disjectus, elongatus, tractus *GlH* D 675–6; pars eorum [dictorum] transscripta, pars distracta est ALEX. CANT. *Dicta prol.*; quem cum in terram distractis crinibus, distortis brachiis .. procumbentem aspicio *Ep. ad amicum* 115; non ad ~enda vel divaricanda .. testis Christi membra .. fuerat invitatus SAMSON *Mir. Edm.* 8 p. 134; **1280** distractus .. per goggos (v. 2 cogga). **b** peccata mea, quomodo discerpendo ~itis, ~endo corroditis .. praecordia mea! ANSELM (*Or.* 5) III 14; qui eloquentie preceptionem a studiis philosophie eliminat .. societatis humane fedus ~it J. SAL. *Met.* 827C; quanquam [Hibernenses] .. a fide quantocius resilire non formident, a fidei tamen et fidelitatis vinculo non solvuntur. in contrahendo quippe liberi sunt contractus hujusmodi, non in ~endo GIR. *EH* II 6; ~it animum meum TREVET *Troades* 48.

2 to 'draw' (drag a criminal to execution). *V. et. detrahere* 2a. *Cf. detrectare* 4.

s**1196** equis distractus ac deinde patibulo appensus est W. Newb. *HA* V 20; s**1242** a Westmonasterio usque ad turrim Londoniarum et illam penalem machinam que vulgariter gibbetus dicitur distractus M. Par. *Maj.* IV 196; s**1255** per plateatum diverticula, calculos et saxos, ligna et lapides, distractus *Ann. Burton* 345; **1330** distractus fuit a Neugate usque collistrigium et ibidem positus fuit *MGL* III 421; s**1331** [R. de Mortuo Mari] judicio Parliamenti distractus et suspensus est Higd. VII 44 p. 328; **1415** ~atur a .. porta vocata la Watergate usque .. portam vocatam la Northgate et ibidem solomodo decapitetur et non suspendatur *RParl* IV 66b.

3 to seize, pillage, disperse. **b** (w. abl.) to strip, deprive.

1221 cum .. quedam ibi inventa a servientibus meis distracta fuissent .., promisimus quod .. plenam .. distractorum faciemus restitutionem in pecunia numerata .. conservanda, rebus in eo statu manentibus quo erant cum cepit distractio fieri *Ch. Sal.* 110–111; s**1232** distracta sunt horrea de W. .. ditissima .. a paucis armatis servientibus Wend. III 19 (cf. ib. 20: distractis omnibus); **1261** ballenam .. distraxerunt et asportaverunt *Cl* 459 (cf. ib.: qui porcionem ad nos inde pertinentem distraxerunt); **1280** procurator .. curam apponet .. ut pecunia distracta colligatur, quam procurabit reponi in cista *MunAcOx* 782. **b** s**886** Aurelianis perveniunt captamque urbem auro ~unt W. Jum. I 7 (cf. depilare 2a).

4 to alienate, dispose of, sell.

distraxit, vendidit *GlC* D 274 (cf. ib. U 66: ven[did]it, distractus est); viri cujusdam servula olim furata fuerat .. atque deducta ab avidis mangonibus ad urbem .. et distracta cuipiam viro praefatae civitatis urbano Lantfr. *Swith.* 20; J. Sal. *Pol.* 423D (v. drachma 1a); W. Cant. *Mir. Thom.* III 11 (v. caedere 2a); ascriptitii .. licite venduntur vel quomodolibet ~untur *Dial. Scac.* I 11 C; s**1178** comes de Marchia .. patrimonium suum .. Anglorum regi distraxit Diceto *YH* I 425; *Itin. Ric* VI 14 (v. condicionaliter a); **1285** si pensionem nostram .. emere volueritis, pro cc m. eam distraere vobis proponimus *Reg. Ant. Linc.* III 179; **1324** terre .. tempore antiquo sunt distracte et in manibus extraneis collate (*Reg. Spalding*) *Terr. Fleet* lviii *n.*; c**1357** frater W. Scharshille, quondam justiciarius regis .., distractis omnibus temporalibus intravit ordinem *Mon. Francisc.* I 541; **1549** post novendium ea [pignora] ~antur *StatOx* 349.

5 **a** to twist, slant. **b** to divert, distract (mentally), perplex; *cf. detrahere* 3b.

a ut quid ipse zodiacus ita distractus sit queritur. potuit nempe per medium duci recta linea hemispherium Adel. *QN* 71; s**1455** ut [rex] .. distracta taliter et eciam sequestrata haberet pene omnia .. sua membra quod nec valeret pedibus pergere nec sursum erigere verticem *Reg. Whet.* I 163. **b** J. Sal. *Pol.* 476B (v. 2 dissilire 1d); virtuose viventes .. non ~untur per concupiscencias Kilwardby *OS* 643; quociens molestiis domesticarum necessitatum ~imur Siccav. *PN* 110; Rolle *IA* 150 (v. cupere b).

6 (log. or gram.) to distinguish, analyse; **b** (pr. or p. ppl. as sb.n.).

J. Sal. *Pol.* 437C (v. conjungere 2a); genus ~itur in species et differentias Gilb. I iv. 1; 'vivere est viventibus esse': .. 'esse' sumptum in sui communitate non sumitur in diffinitione vite nisi per comparationem ad hanc differentiam 'vivens', per quam ~itur Bacon XI 180; *Id.* XV 13 (v. contrahere 2c); qualitas est ex parte significati prout ipsum ~i potest in numerum aut fuerit distinctum et numeratum *Ps.*-Gros. *Gram.* 32 (cf. ib. 52: distraitur persona racione numeri, ut sint in unoquoque [verbo] 3 persone). **b** sicut distractum respectu ~entis non est distractum, sed distractum acceptum sub ~ente respectu tercii est distractum, sic diminutum respectu determinacionis diminuentis non est diminutum, sed ut determinatur per determinacionem diminuentem respectu tercii est diminutum W. Alnwick *QD* 19.

7 to injure or (?) *f. l.*

si eveniret ut ordinatus vel alienigena distraheretur [v. l. disturbaretur; AS: *man* .. *gederede*] alicubi verbis vel operibus (*Quad.*) *GAS* 459 (= *Inst. Cnuti* ib.: aliquem nocuisse ordinato).

8 to distrain or (?) *f. l.*

s**1279** Amabilia .. fecit defaltam; et preceptum fuit quod distraheretur [? l. distringeretur] per terras etc. *Reg. Malm.* I 251.

9 (p. ppl. as sb. f.) estreat or (?) *f. l.*

1267 de finibus et amerciamentis quorum distractas [? l. extractas] .. J[ohannes] le Breton' .. liberabit *Liberate* 43 m. 7.

distrarius v. dextrarius a. **distrasia** v. dyscrasia. **distratio** v. distractio 4. **distrationare** v. dirationare.

distribuere [CL]

1 to distribute, apportion. **b** to divide into units (for assessment).

eadem egenis .. ~i .. non sinimus Gildas *EB* 42; tertiam [portionem] .. pauperibus ~it Bede *HE* V 12; adduc presbiteros .. ut et ego munuscula .. illis ~am Cuthb. *Ob. Baedae* clxiii; ~antur ipsae palmae Ælf. *EC* 7; cum .. populo Dei vivificum panem ~endo porrigeret Osb. *V. Dunst.* 33; in infirmitate qua et mortuus est inter caetera sua quae commendavit et ~it *Text. Roff.* 201v.; s**1181** precipiens quod universa que .. archiepiscopus in infirmitate sua ~erat confiscarentur *G. Hen. II* I 283; Gir. *PI* I 19 p. 112 (v. diaconus 1a); [rex] elemosinarium largiciones et erogaciones in propria persona destribuere precipiat *Plusc.* VII 18. **b** regale manerium fuit, sed non fuit per hidas ~tum *DB* (*Hants*) I 39v. (cf. ib. 39: nunquam geldum dedit nec hida ibi ~ta fuit).

2 (log.) to 'distribute', apply generally. **b** (p. ppl.) general.

nec oportet aliquid dicere de his dictionibus 'quilibet, quisque', que ejusdem potestatis fere sunt cum hac dictione 'omnis', secundum quod ~unt pro partibus secundum numerum (Shirwood) *GLA* III 10 *n.*68; quod signum non ~it subjectum in comparatione ad predicatum (Kilwardby *Err. Log.*) *Ib.* 186 *n.*21; quia termini primorum principiorum sunt communissimi, igitur, quando ~untur, ~untur pro omnibus conceptibus inferioribus; accipiuntur autem tales termini universaliter in primis principiis, et ita extendunt se ad omnes conceptus particulares Duns *Ord.* I 8 (cf. ib. 51: quando termini subjecti, quia ~ti, accipiuntur pro omnibus); Wycl. *Univ.* 87 (v. distribuibilis a). **b** omnes mortales essent servi summorum pontificum secundum ~tissimam accepcionem vocabuli 'servi' Ockham *Pol.* I 285.

3 to render tributary.

Ecgfrithus .. regem [Merciae] fugavit regnumque ejus sub tributo ~it Eddi 20.

distribuibilis, (log.) capable of 'distribution' (general application); **b** (as sb. n.).

hoc medium [sc. genus generalissimum substancie] non distribuitur pro aliqua speciali substancia .. sed solum pro substancia generalissima; nec est ille terminus 'genus generalissimum' ~is, sicud nec ille terminus 'Sor' [i. e. Socrates] Wycl. *Univ.* 87. **b** sic concedunt eruditi in logica quod hoc signum 'totus' includit suum ~e, ut equivaleat isti 'quelibet pars' quando sumitur syncategorematice, unde illa 'totus Socrates est minor Socrate' equivalet illi 'quelibet pars Socratis est minor Socrate' (Ockham *Summa*) *GLA* III 364 *n.*829.

distributim [LL], severally.

1357 (v. communiter 1a).

distributio [CL]

1 distribution, apportionment; **b** (gram.). **c** gift or allowance distributed; **d** (w. gen. of recipient).

dic utrum arsis an thesis in temporum ~one palmam victoriae promerebitur Aldh. *PR* 131; c**980** (12c) haec est ultima commendatio sive rerum suarum pro Deo ~o (*Test.*) *Text. Roff.* 145v.; nobilis, quam ~o non minuit, possessione Gir. *PI pref.* 1 p. lxvii; in hoc [medio cordis thalamo] fit ~o altrinsecus genitorum quantum debetur altrinsecus Alf. Angl. *Cor* 5. 3; [Christus] est multiplex in .. donorum ~one Bart. Angl. I 21; **1281** ne [religiosi] .. ~oni hujusmodi [bonorum defuncti] se inmisceant *Conc. Syn.* 914; Andromacha deplorans hanc ~onem captivarum Trevet *Troades* 70. **b** si plures fuerint conjunctiones .. ~o resultabit Gerv. Melkley *AV* 193. **c** c**1250** (v. cotidie b); c**1250** nocturnam ~onem, cum presentes fuerint ad matutinas, percipient sicud alii canonici *Stat. Heref.* 60; **1437** capiendo omni anno quotidianas ~ones et alia residencie emolumenta *Ib.* 367; **1542** reservatis .. communiis seu ~onibus *Form. S. Andr.* II 192; **1560** (v. dividentia). **d** **1340** in fabis emptis pro ~one pauperum *Ac. Durh.* 202.

2 (?) demarcation.

998 (12c) quoddam ruris .. territorium, cujus circuitus ambitum et ~onis funiculum patria dimensione *syx sulunga* provinciales solent appellare *CD* 700.

3 assignment, arrangement.

12.. defunctus non moveatur de loco ubi moritur nisi de licencia proprii sacerdotis per cujus ~onem exequie fuerint omnino ecclesie *Conc. Scot.* II 44.

4 (log.) 'distribution', general application.

Bacon XV 333 (v. collectio 5); in hoc signo 'nullus' includitur negacio et ~o; ergo, cum ~o precise respiciat supposita talis nature, negacio erit pro eisdem Duns *Ord.* IV 7 (cf. ib. I 53: semper predicatum universalis affirmative stat confuse tantum, sive sint ibi due ~ones in subjecto sive una); consequencia .. patet per regulam sciencie topicalis, qua dicitur quod a superiori cum ~one ad inferius consequencia tenet Ockham *Dial.* 729; raciones quibus argueretur a minus communi ad magis commune sine ~one peccant per fallaciam consequentis *Id. Pol.* II 773.

distributive, (gram.) distributively. **b** (log.) in a general sense.

~e, ut hic: dum rex, dum proceres, dum starent Pergama, Troja / et decus et species et caput orbis erat Gerv. Melkley *AV* 194. **b** [propositio] confusa et distributiva sive modalis est quando signum universale affirmativum ibi adjungitur termino communi inmediate et casus et numeri, vel quando signum universale negativum vel negacio negans precedit terminum communem sive mediate sive inmediate, ut 'omnis homo currit, †nullius [l. nullus] asinus', tam *li* 'homo' quam *li* 'asinus' stat confuse et ~e Bacon XV 269; dubitatur de ista 'totus Socrates est minor Socrate', et dicitur quod est universalis capiendo hoc signum 'totus' ~e (Duns *Anal. Post.*) *GLA* III 226 *n.*183; cum negativa confuse neget et ~e Fortescue *NLN* II 57.

distributivus [LL], (gram. & log.) distributive, used in a general sense.

assisa [ultime presentationis] facit .. tam pro non nominato in brevi quam pro nominato, propter virtutem hujus dictionis 'quis', que ~a est et certas personas non complectitur Bracton 248b; Bacon XV 269 (v. distributive b); quedam nominum .. ab actu imponuntur, ut interrogativa, redditiva, ~a, ficticia, numeralia *Ps.*-Gros. *Gram.* 37; divisivum sive ~um .., ut 'singuli', 'bini' Linacre *Emend. Lat.* f. 4.

distributor [LL], distributor, dispenser; **b** (as divine epithet or sim.).

s**900** erat ille rex Alfredus .. largissimus ~or elemosinarum *Chr. S. Neoti*; J. Sal. *Pol.* 630B (v. dispensatio 1a); s**1181** [R. archiepiscopus] moriturus .. partem aliquam [thesaurorum] dispersit in pauperes .., partem etiam familiaribus .. serus ~or legato dimisit W. Newb. *HA* III 5; s**1251** redditus vacantes .. alienis distribuuntur, de quorum moribus .. nihil constat ~oribus M. Par. *Maj.* V 221; **1281** nonnulli religionis habitum deferentes, licet non sint executores, tamen ~ores efficiuntur bonorum defuncti *Conc. Syn.* 913; **1291** facient .. distribucionem mccc pauperibus de vj li. x s. .., et ~ores dictorum denariorum habeant .. v s. pro eorum labore et expensis *Reg. Newbattle* 174. **b** mons Oliveti, id est summus spiritalium ~or gratiarum Bede *Luke* 567; Deus, honorum dator, ordinum ~or Egb. *Pont.* 19; **1002** (12c) omnium ~ori dignitatum *CD* 1295; partes quas potuit sibi a ~ore bonorum [anima] vendicavit J. Sal. *Pol.* 478A; **1297** auctor et ~or omnium graciarum *Reg. Cant.* 527; **1477** universi fons et boni ~or, luminum pater ipse *Reg. Whet.* II 172.

distributrix [LL], distributor, dispenser (f.).

1451 sedes apostolica .., liberalitatis honeste circumspecta ~ix *Mon. Hib. & Scot.* 383a.

districta v. 2 distringere 7b.

districte [CL], **a** strictly (w. ref. to injunction, investigation or sim.). **b** attentively (w. ref. to observance or sim.). **c** carefully, w. concentration. **d** straitly.

a ne forte nos .. ad perpetuam perditionem ~ius examinans tollat Bede *HE* IV 23 p. 266; ~e temetipsam semper examina Elmer Cant. *Record.* 715C; s**1187** statutum est .. singulorum omnium rerum habitudinem ~ius inquiri G. Cold. *Durh.* 8; **1189** precipimus ~e quod .. *BBC* (*Exeter*) 186; **1204** vos ~e summonemus *Pat* 45b (cf. ib.: †distrincte precipimus); c**1218** prohibemus ~e ne .. *Conc. Syn.* 65; s**1232** rex .. sciscitabatur ~ius ab eo si ita fuisset M. Par. *Maj.* III 232; ex precepto Judicis qui ~e precipiat [ME: *þe heterliche hatte*] *AncrR* 116; **1441** in visceribus Jesu Christi ~ius exhortamur Bekynton I 138. **b** ut silentium suum ~e teneant Lanfr. *Sermo* 638C; in monasterio ubi minima ~e custodiuntur, ibi .. rigor .. permanet Anselm (*Ep.* 231) IV 137; **1300** silencium ab omnibus .. ~ius observari precipimus *Vis. Ely* 12; **1412** cujus donum frequencius inspicitur, ejus memoria ~ius retinetur *StatOx* 221. **c** s**1208** ceperunt ~e cogitare ad cujus principis sinum aliquod refugium possent invenire *Flor. Hist.* II 137. **d** ipsum in eadem turri ~e obsedit Boso *V. Pont.* 362.

1 districtio v. distinctio 1a.

2 districtio v. distractio 2.

3 districtio [LL]

1 **a** constriction, compression. **b** press, confined space. **c** (w. *maris*) strait. **d** configuration, confines. **e** confinement, restriction; **f** (fig.); **g** (of time). **h** (mus.) degree, step.

a s**1384** imponentes super ventrem ejus lapidem tante ponderositatis qui .. torqueret eum per ~onem verendorum Wals. *HA* II 114; **1428** (v. compes a). **b** s**1198** rex Anglorum .. eum [regem Francorum] .. in tanta ~one posuit in portam Gisortii quod pons fractus est sub illo Diceto *YH* II 164. **c** transivimus inter duas insulas [Sardiniam et Corsicam] .. ibi est magna maris ~o *Itin. Ric.* II 10. **d** in domo habitans quilibet, si materiam ejus et .. quantitatem .. sive ~onem ignoret, tali hospicio dignus non est. .. de mundo igitur ejusque ~one .. subscribam Adel. *Astr.* 29. **e** in artissime eum custodie ~onem retrusit *G. Steph.* I 75. **f** licentiam hanc isti non suscipientes, antique ~onem semite [cf. *Jer.* vi 16] servant, ut ab esu carnium sint alieni Map *NC* I 24 f. 16v. **g** s**1346** cum exercitu quem collegerant Anglicorum prout poterant in tanto temporis ~one Wals. *HA* I 270. **h** omnis antiphona octavi toni que incipit in gesolreut et per ~onem descendit in elami *Tonale Sal.* lvii.

2 hardship, austerity; **b** (mon.).

quae quidem illi [Adamnano] ~o vitae artioris .. procedente tempore necessitatem in consuetudinem verterat

BEDE *HE* IV 23 p. 263; solitaria se ipsum mancipavit ~one ALCUIN *WillP* I 1; ~o, rigor, *stræc GlH* D 718; MAP *NC* III 4 (v. conficere 6); in victus parsimonia post susceptum pontificatus laborem solito minorem visus est tenuisse ~onem AD. EYNS. *Hug.* III 13; propter imitacionem vite Salvatoris in via ~onis .. apostolis commendate PECKHAM *QR* 118. **b** in monachica ~one vitam non sibi solummodo sed et multis utilem .. duxit BEDE *HE* IV 24 p. 267; fastidientes ~onem tantae observantiae ÆLF. *Regul. Mon.* 175; ceteri fratres frustra metuentes se plus solito regulari destrictione coartari SERLO GRAM. *Mon. Font.* 23; si eum qui ~onem monasterii non fert fugam meditari agnoverit *Cust. Cant.* 253.

3 severity, sternness.

apparuit ei apostolorum princeps et .. sciscitabatur apostolica ~one quare gregem relinqueret BEDE *HE* II 6; **802** providendum ne aut ~o rigida aut pietas sit remissa ALCUIN *Ep.* 245; c**961** sit in te et boni pastoris dulcedo, sit et judicis severa ~o (*Lit. Papae*) EADMER *HN* 326; aliud est ~o, aliud misericordia PULL. *Sent.* 689A; c**1085** precor .. sanctitatem vestram ut non tam consideret ~o vestra quod ille fecit peccando quam penset pietas vestra quod facit humiliter paenitendo ANSELM (*Ep.* 105) III 238; ex tota cordis affectione, ex tota anime ~one AD. MARSH *Ep.* 141.

4 constraint, rigour, authority: **a** (divine); **b** (eccl.); **c** (secular); **d** (unlawful).

a quando [Deus] .. cum judiciaria ~one quaeret operum perfectionem ab eis .. BEDE *Hom.* I 24. 96; ubi reprobis civibus judicium ultimae ~onis incubuit *Id. Gen.* 149; **811** justum arbitrorum judicium subire cogetur, ibique juste ~ones accipiat sentiatque satisfactionem *CS* 332; divine ~onis manum experti miserabiliter decesserunt G. COLD. *Durh.* 3; in die terrifica sempiterne ~onis AD. MARSH *Ep.* 1 p. 81; extremi judicii ~o [ME: *þe sterke dom of domes dei*] *AncrR* 46. **b** s**1108** [Anselmus] eadem sententia archidiaconos et canonicos omnes complectebatur .. de ~one censure, si statuta transgressi fuissent EADMER *HN* 232; s**1170** [archiepiscopus a Romano pontifice] ad coercendos episcopos magne ~onis literas impetravit W. NEWB. *HA* II 25; **1179** sub anathematis ~one severius prohibemus ne .. (*Lit. Papae*) *G. Hen. II* I 235; s**1200** ~one apostolica (v. crux 9a); **1215** alioquin .. curabimus de idoneo vos presule providere, contradictores .. per ~onem canonicam graviter punituri *Ep. Innoc. III* 81 (= *Cl* 269a); s**1252** ut nulla auctoritate papali vel alia compulsi ~one .. conferrent subsidium pecuniare M. PAR. *Min.* III 125; quando non est aliquis judex secularis qui contemnentem pro peccato commisso plectat, digne potest papa ipsum per ~onem ecclesiasticam coercere OCKHAM *Dial.* 916. **c** necessaria [est] justitia et ~o secularis in divinis plerumque legibus et secularibus institutis (*Leg. Hen.* 11. 16) *GAS* 557; **1188** injungentes quatenus .. regem Scotie ~one regali qua ei preemines, compellas ut .. (*Lit. Papae*) *G. Hen. II* II 57. **d** **1198** inquisicionem fecit .. utrum dederit .. episcopo per ~onem prisone iij virgatas terre *CurR* I 193; **1218** dixit quod hoc factum fuit per ~onem imprisonamenti *Eyre Yorks* 137; **1229** hoc fecit per ~onem et per metum, sicut illa que fuit in potestate sua *BNB* II 284.

5 (leg.) 'distress', distraint. **b** (w. *magna*) grand distress (involving all available chattels). **c** property seized (or available for seizure) by way of distraint. *V. et. destrescia.*

si ad hujusmodi auxilia reddenda possit aliquis dominus tenentes suos ita distringere, multo forcius ~onem eo modo licite poterit facere pro ipso rellevio suo GLANV. IX 8; **1198** factis racionabilibus summonicionibus et ~onibus non [venit] *CurR* I 58; **1242** si distrinctio aliqua facta fuerit per terras et catalla ipsius pro hujusmodi debito, distrinctionem relaxari faciant *Cl* 504; detentio namii pro ~one facienda pertinet ad coronam domini regis BRACTON 155b; **1259** Johannes .. districtus per unam vaccam non venit; ideo per meliorem ~onem distringatur *CourtR Ramsey* 57; **1269** obligo me et heredes meos et omnia bona nostra .. cohercioni et ~oni baronum de Scaccario *Deeds Balliol* 327; ~onum quedam sunt personales et quedam reales. de realibus non fit ~o nisi per capcionem rei petite. de personalibus fit ~o per personas, et hoc multipliciter .. *Fleta* 141; si vicinus super vicinum faciat ~onem sine consideracione curie regis .., puniatur .. secundum quantitatem delicti (*Fragm. Collecta*) *APScot* I 374; **1457** quod .. ballivi .. habeant auctoritatem .. ad compellendum per ~ones at aliter .. omnimodas personas infra eadem .. loca ad contribucionem invencionis .. sagittariorum .. (*Commissio Regis*) *Lit. Cant.* III 228; *a stresse*, ~o *CathA*. **b** **1267** in placito communi de custodiis, si ad magnam ~onem non venerint deforciantes, tunc bis vel ter iteretur breve (*Marlb.* 7) *StRealm* I 21; **1285** quamcito hujusmodi tenens in dominico habens medium inter ipsum et capitalem dominum distringitur, statim perquirat sibi tenens breve de medio; et, si medius habens terram in eodem comitatu defugerit usque ad magnam ~onem, detur querenti in brevi suo de magna ~one talis dies .. et precipiatur vicecomiti quod distringat medium per magnam ~onem prout in brevi continetur (2 *Westm.* 9) *Ib.* 78 (cf. *Fleta* 107); **1332** fit execucio per breve de magna ~one returnabile *LTRMem* 105 r. 7*d*.; **1359** omnes alii in misericordia quia venerunt per magnam ~onem etc. *Pub. Works* I 252. **c** **1263** si contingat me .. in solucione .. deficere .., bene licebit predicto R. et heredibus suis me .. per .. manerium meum de D. distringere et ~onem quo voluerint fugare *Cl* 280; **1267** nullus ducat ~ones extra comitatum (*Marlb.* 4) *StRealm* I 20; c**1282** licebit .. abbati .. ad voluntatem suam distringere et ~ones captas tenere quousque .. *Couch. Furness* I 6; **1293** de villa E., quia non fecerunt parcum domini fractum, unde ridemanny conqueruntur quod ponunt ibi ~ones et statim dimittuntur per defaltam predictam *SelPlMan* 72; **1293** asportavit ~onem sub sigillis eorum signatam ad valenciam v s., sc. in pane (*St. Ives*) *Law Merch.* I 60; c**1300** fugabit oves ad aquam et ~ones ad tondendum *Pri. Cold.* app. p. lxxxviii; **1336** quia medietas illa jacuit vacua et nulla ~o inveniri potuit in eadem (*KRAc* 331/21) *Cal. Scot.* III 317; **1394** quod extunc bene liceat .. Johanni .., heredibus vel assignatis suis in predicto mesuagio .. distringere et ~ones sic captas .. retinere quousque .. eisdem plenarie fuerit satisfactum; et, si sufficiens ~o .. inveniri non poterit .. *Deeds Balliol* 61; **1444** licebit .. distringere et ~ones sic captas asportare, effugare et retinere quousque .. *MunCOx* 208.

6 area of jurisdiction (w. ref. to distraint). *V. et. districtus* 1.

15.. qui .. tenementa in eodem comitatu [Cestr'] aut alibi infra ~onem vestram non habent per que per ballivos .. ad warranciam aliquam faciend' distringi possunt *Reg. Brev. Orig.* 6b.

1 **districtor** v. discretor 1b.

2 districtor, distrainer.

[essonium hujusmodi] locum non habebit in persona disseisitoris vel redisseisitoris vel district[oris] contra vadium et pleg[ios] venientis *Fleta* 384; s**1298** littera conservatoria directa abbati de W. contra ~ores bonorum ecclesie ELMH. *Cant.* 57 *rub.*

districtualis

1 (person) resident in a district (or subject to jurisdiction).

1393 amicicie fedus quod inter vos [regem Aragonie] et nos ac nostros ~es hincinde viguit *Dip. Corr. Ric. II* 120 (cf. ib. 146); **1478** an eadem Margarita regina [Scocie] .. ab omnibus presertim incolis loci .. et aliis ~ibus et convicinis pro optima et bona muliere reputata fuerit *Mon. Hib. & Scot.* 500b.

2 (It.) civic magistrate (*distrettuale*).

1370 ad faciendum .. concordiam .. et amicicias .. cum duce, communitate et ~ibus Janu[ensibus] (*Pat*) *Foed.* VI 670a; **1371** ducem ac communitatem et ~es totumque populum civitatis, territorii et districtus Januensis (*Ib.*) *Ib.* 679a.

districtus [LL]

1 (area of) jurisdiction or authority: **a** (Continental); **b** (Eng. or Sc., royal); **c** (civic); **d** (eccl.). *V. et.* 2 *distringere* 7.

a **1244** sub ~u alicujus potestatis alterius non ita burgenses seu rustici nobilibus dominantur sicut in istis partibus [Gasconie] que vestro dominio sunt subjecte (*AncC* II 130) *RL* II 34; **1253** non permittat feiditos a civitate Vast' [*Gasc.*] villam illam vel ~um ejusdem ville ingredi *Cl* 190; **1258** in Medulco et alibi in ~u nostro Vasconie *CalCh* II 13; **1264** rogamus quatinus alienigenas regnum nostrum per potestatem aut ~um vestrum [sc. regis Francie] ingredi .. nullatenus permittatis *Cl* 396; **1294** in recuperacione .. terrarum .. regis Anglie sui dominii et ~us per reges Francie occupatarum (*Lit. Regis Romanorum*) B. COTTON 241; **1306** ad portus seu terram sub ~u et honore comitis [Bolonie] ubilibet existentes *Lit. Cant.* III 388; **1423** venientibus .. ad sacrum generale concilium celebrandum in nostra civitate Senarum seu ad ipsam civitatem ejusque comitatum, territorium, ~um (*Lit. Salvi Conductus*) AMUND. I 140; **1441** per quoscumque passus, portus, pontes, terras, dominia, ~us, civitates .. et quelibet alia loca vestra (*Lit. Salvi Conductus Regis Romanorum*) BEKYNTON II 103. **b** **1242** quod [custos regni] capiat in manum regis omnia bona eorum [mercatorum de Florencia] que in ~u regis poterunt inveniri *RGasc* I 115 (= *CalPat* 365); **1314** vobis [ballivis et fidelibus nostris] mandamus quod eidem A. aut hominibus secum .. existentibus, cum per ~us vestros ipsos transire contigerit, non inferatis .. impedimentum aliquod seu gravamen *RScot* 125a; **1336** vobis [vicecomitibus, ballivis etc.] .. mandamus .. quod ei .. salvum et securum conductum cum per ~um vestrorum loca transitum fecerit habere faciatis *Ib.* 449b; **1529** in .. regno et ~ibus Scotie *Form. S. Andr.* I 316. **c** **1268** concessit .. burgensibus suis de R. .. burgum predictum .. cum omnibus .. pertinentiis .. cum omni jure et ~u dicti burgi *BBC* (*Richmond*) 318. **d** **1283** in singulis ecclesiis existentibus sub vestro [sc. episcopi Wigorn'] ~u PECKHAM *Ep.* II app. p. 755; **1301** vobis [archidiacono Linc'] .. mandamus quatinus omnibus beneficiatis sub ~u vestro .. premissa .. exponentes .. ad levacionem .. subsidii .. procedere non tardetis *Reg. Carl.* I 144; **1304** omnes illos quos sub ~u vestro [sc. archidiaconi Oxon'] compereritis culpabiles *FormOx* 8.

2 property seized by way of distraint. *V. et.* 2 *distringere* 6b.

1382 fecit rescussum .. de quodam distrinctu capto pro expensis militum *SessPCambs* 54.

distriggere v. 2 distringere.

distrigiare [cf. CL strigare], to stride.

~io, A. *to stryde WW*; *to stryde*, ~iare *CathA*.

distrinct- v. district-, distinctio 1a.

1 **distringere** v. distinguere 2a, 4b.

2 distringere [CL]

1 to stretch out. **b** to draw or (?) wield (a weapon).

Macrobius .. ait illos radiis rotarum pendere districtos [*cf.* Virgil *Aen.* VI 617] ALB. LOND. *DG* 6. 6. **b** barbarus advena districto ense veteribus nostri regni colonis imminet ABBO *Edm.* 8; baculo districto R. COLD. *Godr.* 329 (cf. ib. 168: districtis ensibus).

2 to constrict, narrow, squeeze. **b** (p. ppl. *districtus*) narrow; **c** limited; **d** (as sb. f. pl.) straits. **e** (as sb. n.) narrow pass, defile. **f** tight corner (fig.), awkward situation.

1278 distrixerunt (*sic*) iter regale versus ecclesiam *Hund. Highworth* 103 (cf. ib. 108: in misericordia pro via districta); **1279** totum iter .. distriggitur (*sic*) per arraturam *Ib.* 123; **1534** disterrinxit (*sic*) collum suum *AncIndict* 531/136. **b** **1261** si .. comes Sabaudie ~a passagia sue terre a vobis in homagium .. recipiat (*AncC* III 78) *RL* II 200. **c** s**1004** exercitus sub tam ~o tempore congregari non potuit *ASChr.* **d** s**1190** venerunt ad ~as Africe et transierunt per medium ~arum Africe . . . et ibi incipit Mediterraneum mare R. HOWD. III 47; s**1191** via navium est .. stricta inter insulam illam et Romaniam; .. et dicuntur ~e de insula de Cuverfu *G. Ric. I* 204. **e** s**1282** inter montium ~um (v. deprimere 3a). **f** s**1154** quod abbas, in ~o positus, etsi minus canonice, benigne concessit *G. S. Alb.* I 124.

3 to discipline, restrain. **b** (p. ppl. *districtus*) strict (of metrical caesura). **c** strict, disciplined, austere. **d** strict, severe, pressing (of abstr.); **e** (of person, esp. of God as judge).

ut vagantes anime et superbe severiori regula ~antur [cf. Gratian XII 1. 1] PECKHAM *Puer. Obl.* 426. **b** quis est versus ~us? qui in scansione pedum numquam orationem accomodat integram. . . praebet Arator [I 871] exemplum: morta/lisque si/bi studi/um pro/ponat o/rigo ALDH. *Met.* 10 p. 92. **c** ~iore continentiae sudore BEDE *Ezra* 857 (v. eluere b); theoricam solus vitam districtus agebat ALCUIN *SS Ebor* 1024 (cf. ib. 1096: intrans ergo locum districtis usibus aptum). **d** c**692** (14c) sciat se in ~o omnipotentis Dei judicio poenam .. incurrere *CS* 78; ~ior, i. rigidior, *stiþlicor GlH* D 719; c**1074** contra pravos ~a severitate LANFR. *Ep.* 38 (10); s**1093** [Anselmus] ~a interpellatione ab H. Cestrensi comite .. coactus, Angliam ingressus est DICETO *Chr.* 217; ~iori justitia RIC. HEX. *Stand.* 37 (v. deprimere 3b); **1146** in extremo examine ~e ultioni subjaceat (*Lit. Papae*) ELMH. *Cant.* 396; naturalemque negabat / humane menti districta lege quietam *V. Merl.* 1166; ~o jure in nullo negocio debuerunt fideles .. eis [philosophis] indubitatam credulitatem .. adhibere OCKHAM *Dial.* 591. **e** in examine ~i judicis BEDE *Gen.* 128; **948** ante tribunal ~i judicis *CS* 869; c**1090** ut .. intra cor tuum assistens coram ~o judice .. pertractes .. consilium meum ANSELM (*Ep.* 137) III 281; ad magistrum in schola discipulorum tam ~um H. BOS. *Thom.* III 18 p. 248; timendum ne forte .. audierit ex sententia ~i judicis quod sepius vertebatur in ore .. ipsius sui preconis AD. EYNS. *Hug.* IV 5 p. 26.

4 to constrain, compel (unlawfully).

1200 ipse H. .. ei tradidit quendam runcinum suum et distrinxit eum ad illum equitandum *CurR* I 255.

5 (leg.) to distrain, compel by distraint (w. pers. obj. or absol.); **b** (w. *ad*); **c** (w. *ut* or *quod*); **d** (w. inf.); **e** (2nd pers. sg. pres. subj. as sb.) name of writ ordering distraint. *V. et. destringere* 1.

1183 ut sit quietus de plevina .. et ne ~atur pro ipsa plevina *Pipe* 97; in tali placito .. potest quis ~i per feodum suum vel per plegiorum attachiamentum GLANV. X 3; **1241** (v. communa 5b); **1259** (v. 3 districtio 5a); s**1280** si contingat tenentes .. in solucione .. redditus .. cessare, licitum erit .. monachis .. illud [tenementum] ingredi et tenentes .. ~ere per omnia bona .. infra tenementum illud inventa donec sibi plenarie fuerit satisfactum *Reg. S. Bees* 363. **b** possunt autem domini tenentes suos ad .. rationabilia auxilia reddenda etiam suo jure .. ~ere per catalla que in ipsis feodis suis invenerint vel per ipsa feoda GLANV. IX 8; **1208** quod curia ~at eum ad perficiendam istam convencionem *CurR* V 245; nullus ~atur ad faciendum majus servitium de feodo militis nec de alio libero tenemento quam inde debetur *Magna Carta* 16; **1221** vendunt de tenementis illis Hospitalariis .. et iterum ea resumunt tenenda de eis; unde non possunt ~i ad faciendum quod facere debent sicut alii tenentes *PlCrGlouc* 12; **1378** preceptum est ipsum ~ere ad faciendum citra festum S. Mich. *Banstead* 357. **c** potest heres .. ~i quod ad curiam veniat per feodum suum GLANV. VI 10; **1200** terra Radulfi capiatur in manum domini regis et sic ~atur quod veniat *CurR* I 148; **1257** ~untur episcopi per baronias suas ut .. clericos compellant de suis beneficiis solvere condempnationem (*Artic. Episc.*) M. PAR. *Maj.* VI 357; **1269** preceptum est quod ~eretur ut veniret facturus finem *CBaron* 72. **d** **1200** catalla ejus ceperunt, ut sic ~erent eum debitum solvere *CurR* I 221; nec villa nec homo ~atur facere pontes ad riparias nisi qui ab antiquo et de jure facere debent *Magna Carta* 23. **e** s**1380** pergunt latenter .. et occulte aliud breve, quod '~as' dicitur, .. petunt et accipiunt *Chr. Angl.* 260.

6 (leg.) to distrain (property), seize by way of distraint; *v. et. destringere* 2. **b** (p. ppl. as sb. n.) property so seized; *v. et. districtus* 2. **c** to recover by distraint.

1216 cum quedam corredia que usibus monachorum .. debuerant deputari et quedam officia per eosdem concessa sunt illicite ac districta (*Lit. Papae*) *Reg. Malm.* II 7; **1228** mandatum est vic. Norhamt' quod non ~at dominica abbatis de Burgo ad parcum .. regis .. claudendum *Cl* 19; **1228** episcopus [Lond'] .. ~it .. terram pro secta quam W. ei debet *CurR* XIII 426 (= *BNB* II 229: destringit); **1352** (v. coveragium a); **1369** quod dictos dominos seu tenentes earumdem terrarum et omnia bona mobilia et immobilia .., quanto strictius poterunt compellant et ~ant (*Breve Regis Scot.*) *Mon. Hib. & Scot.* 334b; **s1399** dominus .. Cantuar' .. peciit a Parliamento quod posset bona .. Rogeri, ubicumque inventa, .. ~ere et sic sua debita exigere AD. USK 37; **1454** obligo .. terras meas .. et eciam bona mea quecunque fore namanda et ~enda ad voluntatem .. abbatis *Inchaffray* 146; **1483** manerium nostrum .. districtum erat per officiarios .. comitis pro c s. *Reg. Merton* 19. **b 1558** comes [de Clanrycarde] .. et major pro tempore existens in dicta villa [de Galvia] ~ent et sufficientia districta sive pignora capient pro solutione et satisfactione .. rerum que per .. commissionarios erunt decreta *ActPCIr* 60. **c 1237** preceptum est vic. .. quod ~at debita .. baronum, ita quod ea habeat super arreragia sua *KRMem* 15 r. 9.

7 (p. ppl. *districtus* as sb. n. or f.) area of jurisdiction or authority; **b** (w. ref. to powers of distraint). *V. et. districtus* 1.

1254 dominus debet dare ei .. securitatem in toto ~o suo *RGasc* I 546 (= *CalPat* 357); **s1412** [capellanus] adversa maris tempestate infra ~a soldani Babilonie propulsus AD. USK 102. **b 1270** obligasse .. omnes terras .. dicte Matillis .. una cum catallis et bonis in dictis terris .. existentibus cohercioni et districcioni .. vicecomitum et ballivorum .. regis et aliorum magnatum .. in quorum ~a terre et .. bona predicta consistunt *Cl* 285.

distringibilis, liable to distraint: **a** (of person); **b** (of land or goods).

a 1275 ubi dictus Rogerus fuit ~is domino regi extra dictam socam *Hund.* I 389a; ut [vic.] .. tales plegios recipiat qui sibi sint ~es et sufficientes ad misericordiam regis solvendam, si querens forte se retraxerit *Fleta* 222. **b a1242** (v. diffortiare 3b); **1277** obligavit xiij acras terre sue .., quicunque eas in posterum tenuerint .., nobis et successoribus nostris inperpetuum fore ~es *Reg. S. Aug.* 570; **1291** terram .. ita sustinebunt in edificiis quod ad dictam firmam levandam singulis annis inperpetuum michi et heredibus .. meis sufficiencia ~ia inveniantur *Deeds Newcastle* 107; si .. illud tenementum sit vacuum et non ~e *Quon. Attach.* 46. 1; **1444** cum .. Philippus nichil habeat destringibile et sit eciam mortuus *ExchScot* 174.

Distrios v. Dystros.

distroppare [cf. stroppare], to unstrap.

1333 pro bermannagio eorundem [doleorum] trahendorum ad terram et ~andorum *KRAc* 78/11 m. 4.

Distros v. Dystros. **distruere, distruct-** v. destr-.

distrussare [AN *destrusser*, OF *destrosser*], to unload, unpack. **b** to 'distruss', plunder, carry off.

1286 pro .. garcionibus conductis laborantibus pro trussando et ~ando sepius illam pecuniam, viij d. *Rec. Wardr.* 871. **b 1275** quidam latrones venerunt noctanter ad villam Norht' et ~averunt quoddam hernesium ad domum fratrum de Monte Carmelo *Hund.* II 5.

distrusus, expulsion (of official).

1191 monachi, sed falsi, sunt arctiori sed claustrali custodie mancipati, sed in brevi in aliis cenobiis excessus et falsos ~us expiaturi *Ep. Cant.* 354.

distulisse v. deferre, differre.

distuppare [cf. AN *destuper*, OF *destoupper*], to stop up, block. *V. et. deastuppare.*

1223 (v. deastuppare); **1279** quedam fons communis .. est distoppata per H. le Mercer (*Hund.*) *Lond. Ed. I & II* II 153.

disturbamentum [cf. AN *desturbement*, OF *destorbement*], disturbance, injury.

c1190 unde .. monachi aliquid de predicto tenemento perdant et ~um habeant *Cart. Wardon* f. 19.

disturbare [CL]

1 to disturb, molest, interfere with: **a** (person); **b** (grant or property).

a 1091 nulli licuit peregrinum ~are pro aliquo anteriori forisfacto (*Consuet. Norm.*) *EHR* XXIII 508; **c1136** super hoc nemo eos inde ~et injuste *Regesta* 754 (= *EHR* XXIV 429: desturbet); **1218** prohibemus ne quis eos [burgenses de Kaermerdin] injuste ~et *Pat* 159; ecce ~or, avellor, et concutior sicut in cribro AD. MARSH *Ep.* 83; **1331** nec eos .. pro consuetudine aliqua desturbet de rebus suis *PQW* 32b. **b a1190** quicunque hanc donationem desturbare presumpserit, noscat se excommunicatum *Reg. S. Thom. Dublin* 248; **c1215** vic. civitatis pecuniam alicujus retinere vel ~are non presumat (*Mun. Lond.*) *EHR* XVII 714.

2 a to deflect, parry (a blow). **b** to interrupt, obstruct (a road). **c** to hinder (an action). **d** (w. *ne*) to prevent.

a c1266 sicut ipsa predictum ictum ~are voluerit *IMisc* 13/36. **b 1279** communis via est desturbata et adnichilata de ecclesia S. Joh. Sakar' usque ad portam de Aldresgate; nescimus per quem (*Eyre*) *Lond. Ed. I & II* II 153. **c** 'vade retro me..' [*Mark* viii 33], id est .. 'noli ~are passionem meam' BELETH *RDO* 123. 130D. **d 1170** inquiratur si vicecomites .. pacem aliquam cum hominibus fecerint postquam audierunt adventum domini regis, pro ~are ne ante regem vel justitias querimonia veniret (*Inq. Vicecom.*) GERV. CANT. *Chr.* 218.

disturbatio [CL], disturbance, molestation, interference; **b** (w. subj. gen.); **c** (w. gen. of injury inflicted).

a1100 concedo ut capiant de boscis suis ad necessarios usus suos sine aliqua ~one *Regesta* I p. 138; **a1107** sine omni impedimento et ~one *Chr. Abingd.* II 78 (= *Regesta* II 855); **s1135** ubique locorum per Angliam et Normanniam dirupto pacis federe plurima fit distirbatio J. WORC. 40; **c1139** ministris meis precipio quatenus marcam istam dictis monachis sine ~one habere faciant *E. Ch. Scot.* 123 (= *MonA* III 584); publice strate ~o GIR. *IK* II 13; **1396** nec paciemur fieri .. molestiam, arrestacionem .. nec ~onem ullo modo per tempus nostre convencionis (*Juramentum Regis Franc.*) WALS. *YN* 371. **b** donec venirent eo quo minime ~onem Romanorum timuissent G. MON. X 4 (= *Eul. Hist.* II 345: distirpationem); **1227** quod .. liceat eis sine ~one .. ballivorum nostrorum et aliorum ponere se in seisinam de predictis catallis *Cl* 177a; **c1240** omnia predicta in pace .. habeant sine ~one mei et heredum meorum *Cart. Sallay* 450. **c a1350** quicquid vulneratus per ~onem plage sue poterit probare quod perdidit, alius ei reddet (*Cust. Preston*) *EHR* XV 498.

disturbativus, causing disturbance, disruptive.

1408 proposito .. cardinalium .. censemus .. inherendum .. omnibusque aliis ipsius unionis impeditivis et ~is sive delativis .. resistendum *Conc.* III 313b.

disturbator [LL], disturber.

s1066 Haroldus .. suis .. precepit ministris fures, raptores, regni ~ores comprehendere FL. WORC. I 224; **1222** tranquillitatem vestram in Hibernia .. per predictum ~orem .. confundi (*AncC* XLVII 30) *RL* I 184; **1383** insultum fecit .. servientibus contra pacem sicut communis ~or pacis *SessPCambs* 52; **1433** consolacionis et gaudii ~or BEKYNTON II 145.

disturberium [cf. AN *desturber*, OF *destorbier*], disturbance.

1214 per .. conculcationem et ~ium †wannagii [? l. wainiagii] deterioratus est *CurR* VII 216.

disturbium, ~ia, ~um [cf. AN *desturbe*, OF *destorbe*], disturbance; **b** (w. subj. gen.).

1284 si presensissemus .. inde nullum nobis remedium affuturum, sed plerumque ~ium unde presidium sperabatur PECKHAM *Ep.* 592; **s1252** de mutacione consiliariorum regis et de ~ia in regno FORDUN *Cont.* X 5 *rub.*; **s1402** Gwelforum et Gyblynorum parcialitate ferro et flamma vibrantur ~ia AD. USK 76; **1412** si aliqua persona .. rebellat contra .. regem .. aut deputatos suos vel eos impediat vel eis ~um faciat (*DipDocE* 377) *Foed.* VIII 741b; **1416** nec .. fieri permittant alicui ipsorum impedimentum, molestiam, desturbium sive dampnum in corporibus vel in bonis (*TreatyR*) *Ib.* IX 393a; **1447** concedimus .. salvum conductum .. cancellario Scocie .. per .. dominia nostra .. transeundi .. ac .. redeundi pacifice, quiete, absque ~io sive impedimento quocumque *RScot* 332a. **b 1219** debent habere .. sine ~io ipsorum R. et A. tantum de instauramento .. *Cart. Ciren.* I 193.

disuarium v. dinarium. **disuria** v. dysuria. **disubitatio** v. desubitatio.

disunire [cf. CL unire], to sever.

mors immitis, que compacta / solvit et disuneat WALT. WIMB. *Virgo* 84.

disvad-, disvag-, diswag- v. divad-. **disvest-** v. divest-.

diswarennare [cf. warennare], to diswarren, remove (land) from warren status. *V. et. deawarennare, dewarennare.*

1275 dominus H. rex deforestavit et deswarennavit de Lond' usque ad pontem de Stanes *Hund.* I 417; **1289** dedimus potestatem .. constabulario .. Burdegale diswarennandi warrennam nostram Xanctonie *RGasc* II 376; **1331** quod predicta warenna ~ata remaneat *PQW* 41b.

diswarnitus [cf. warnire], unarmed, unprotected.

1313 quamdiu [gentes armorum] vadunt ita inforciate cum equis et armis per patriam et capiunt suas gentes de una die in alteram, ipsi non proponunt ire disgarniti *Tract. Ed. II* 9.

disyllabus [CL < δισύλλαβος], disyllabic. **b** (as sb. n.) disyllable.

hic dactilus totidem locis inseritur excepto ultimo pede, quem necesse est disillabum esse, ne sillabarum amplior numerus crescat ALDH. *Met.* 10 p. 88; A ante L est brevis quando diccio est dissillaba *Ps.*-GROS. *Gram.* 26; homo est dissylaba vox LUTTERELL *Occam* 46. **b** [praepositiones] corripiuntur cum crescendo ~a reddunt, ut 'ădit', 'ŏbit' BEDE *AM* 95; 'vos' si pronomen monosyllabum, per U; si ~um erit, prior syllaba ab U, sequens a B incipit, ut 'vobis'; si animal significat, monosyllabum per B; si ~um, prior syllaba a B, sequens ab U incipit, ut 'bos, bovis' ALCUIN *Orth.* 2348; dissyllabum hoc 'Deus' †par [? l. pars] orationis non est PULL. *Sent.* 675B.

ditabilis, concerned w. riches.

dominus [Ric.] Ardmachanus, dimittens has proprias terminorum significaciones, capit secundum usum vulgarem paupertatem pro carencia temporalium in natura ~i WYCL. *Civ. Dom.* III 110.

ditalis, bountiful.

972 (12c) ita ut ab omni mundiali censu perpetualiter ~i munificatione collocetur *CS* 1285 (cf. *Ch. Burton* 34 [**1011** (13c)]).

ditanum v. dictamnus.

ditare [CL], to enrich; **b** (fig.).

dicebant 'benedictus Dominus et ~ati sumus' [cf. *Zech.* iii 5] GILDAS *EB* 88; ecclesiam .. diversis donis ~avit BEDE *HE* I 33; conlocopletatus, ~atus *GlC* C 555; **875** cuius [Domini] .. largitate ~atus ego E. dabo .. aliquam partem terrae juris mei *CS* 539; quibus donariis ~abis hominem qui Aurelium .. interficiet? G. MON. VIII 14; AILR. *Ed. Conf.* 771C etc. (v. dotare 2a); **1200** (v. ditatio a); apud quosdam philosophos melius est philosophari quam ~ari M. SCOT *Phys.* 1; **1247** (v. depauperatio a); **s1312** sperabat unum de filiis suis .. rex Philippus ~andum .. prediis destruendorum militum Templi Dei BAKER 100. **b** in giro volvens jugiter non vergo deorsum./ .. / hac gaza ditor quoniam sum proximus axi ALDH. *Aen.* 53 (*Arcturus*) 5; ~or, *gefyrðro GlC* D 266; pauperiem ditat pax opulenta michi WALT. ANGL. *Fab.* 12. 26; te ditant Salomon, Cicero, Cato pectore, lingua / moribus SERLO WILT. 23. 6; *Spec. Laic.* 84 (v. ditificare).

ditatio, enrichment. **b** (?) endowment.

1200 homines de Winchelessey et de Rya .. jam in tantum ditati sunt quod ~o eorum est ad nocumentum ville nostre de Hasting' *RChart* 62a; **1291** culpabilis .. de proprietatis alicujus adquisicione seu parentum vel amicorum ~one *Reg. Cant.* 836; ~o, que est habitus, bona est et Deo amabilis, cum ipse summe sit dives; ergo paupertas, que ~onem privat, est mala RIC. ARMAGH *Def. Cur.* 1405 (*recte* 1305); omnes tales ~ones generis clericorum .. fiunt ex turpi lucro WYCL. *Ver.* III 84; **1459** (v. drachma 1c). **b** quis [Londoniis] tantam populositatem crederet .. sic omni mundana copia fluere, sic sanctorum monasteriorum ac illustrium canonicorum copiosa †dicatione [v. l. ditatione] regularitateque gaudere? GERV. TILB. II 17 p. 932.

ditativus, eristic or (?) *f. l.*

sophistice, quam Aristotiles ditativam [? l. litativam; cf. Arist. *Soph. El.* 11: ἐριστικήν], nos circumventoriam vel cavillatoriam dicere possumus J. SAL. *Met.* 932C (cf. cavillatorius b).

ditator [LL], enricher.

s1136 corpus ejus [Henrici I] .. apud Radingum in monasterio, cujus ipse devotus fundator largusque ~or exstiterat, sepultum est W. NEWB. *HA* I 3; **s1249** abbas [de Burgo], consanguineorum suorum in dampnum ecclesie sue amator et ~or, .. de dilapidatione .. convictus depositus est M. PAR. *Min.* II 62; **s1458** rex Henricus II tam largus et largifluus ~or ac eciam dotator illius [ecclesie Cluniacensis] fertur fuisse ut dicatur .. precipuus noster fundator *Reg. Whet.* I 318.

ditescere [CL], to grow rich (also fig.). **b** to become (or count as) luxurious. **c** to enrich.

infelix monachus .. nulla bonorum operum ubertate ~it ANSELM (*Ep.* 37) III 146; occasione pauperum vobis ~ere non est bonum P. BLOIS *Serm.* 743D; nunquam voluit beneficiorum pluralitate ~ere R. BOCKING *Ric. Cic.* I 52. **b** victus ditescit pauper, amatur / vilis, blanditur asper, dulcescit amarus; / nam raras capiunt epulas H. AVR. *Hugh* 299. **c** [Deus] invigilat summo studio ditescere terram GOWER *VC* II 607; distribuens sortes, ditescat ut inde cohortes *Id. CT* III 119.

dithyrambus [CL < διθύραμβος], dithyramb, chorus.

sunt alii [pueri] qui .. mordacius dente rodunt Theonino audacibus dithirambis [cf. Horace *Ep.* I 18. 82; *Carm.* IV 2. 10] W. FITZST. *Thom. prol.* 9.

ditiae v. divitiae.

ditificare [LL], to enrich (fig.).

timor .. primo hominem gratificat, .. secundo gratificatum ~at, .. tertio ditatum ad operandum excitat, .. quarto excitatum beatificat *Spec. Laic.* 84.

ditio v. dicio. **ditior, ~issimus** v. dives.

ditissime [CL], most richly.

camera regine ~e ac honestissime debet preparari W. SAY *Lib. Reg. Cap.* 72.

ditonice, (mus.) in ditone.

ditonice canerem bellum, nisi bella timerem GARL. *Tri. Eccl.* 89.

ditonicus, (as sb. f.) music based on ditone, martial.

GARL. *Tri. Eccl.* 100 (v. chromaticus b).

ditonus [LL < δίτονος], (mus.) ditone, major third.

~us est conjunctio trium vocum et dispositio duorum (*sic*) sine aliquo semitonio; et ~us a 'dya', quod est 'de' (*sic*), quasi duo toni et integri GARL. *Mus.* 163–4; si duos copulaveris tonos, statim ex eis oritur ~us, eo quod duos tonos habet; 'dia' enim Grece Latine dicitur 'duo' TUNST. 212b (cf. ib. 227b: dytonus est spatium sive intervallum inter duas voces, continens duos tonos); **s1439** sit tibi lausque, decus ..; / sit ditonusque tonus, sint organa, neumata, psalmus (*Vers.*) AMUND. II 186.

ditrochaeus [CL < διτρόχαιος], (metr.) double trochee.

da formulas exemplorum, quibus ~ei regula competenter clarescat. 'cārtĭlāgŏ, cāntīlēnă ..' ALDH. *PR* 128; partimur ergo in aequo hos: .. ~eum ‒⏑‒⏑ BONIF. *Met.* 109; ~eus est pes constans ex longa et brevi et longa et brevi .., ut Cāthēlīnă GARL. *PP* 220.

dittocheum v. dirocheum.

diu [CL]

1 long, for a long time. **b** (w. *est quod*) it is long since. **c** (w. *est* in parenthesis) long since, for a long time (*cf.* Fr. *il y a longtemps*).

stante diu arca prope glareas testamenti in medio Jordanis canali [cf. *Josh.* iii 17] GILDAS *EB* 11; perfecit opus diu desideratum BEDE *HE* II 1 p. 81; †faniticus [l. fanaticus], qui templum diu deser[v]it *GlC* F 76; potestis quidem per aliquod spatium sine arte mea vitam ducere, sed non diu [AS: *na lancge*] nec adeo bene ÆLF. *Coll.* 98; reddit de firma xl li.; sed diu non potest pati *DB* I 40v.; non loquatur vir cum muliere sepe aut diu [ME: *ofte ne longe*] *AncrR* 17; DUNS *Ord.* III 118 (v. difficile); **1407** determinatores minus diu starent *StatOx* 197. **b** **a1078** diu est quod nostris nos invicem litteris non visitamus ANSELM (*Ep.* 69) III 189; diu est quod rumor insonuit et publice jam crebrescit P. BLOIS *Ep.* 10. 27B. **c** **1250** cum vobis diu est dictos denarios persolvisem *FormOx* 483; **1289** domum .. quam construximus, non est diu, in ingressu ville *RGasc* II 320; prior .. Martino de dampnis .. adjudicatis diu est satisfecit *State Tri. Ed. I* 67; **1304** nullus justiciariorum .. diu est venit ibidem *RParl* I 161a; **1341** prout in capitulo nostro, non est diu, ad plenum fuistis .. informati *Lit. Cant.* II 247; **1438** diu est animus nobis erat nostros ambassiatores misisse BEKYNTON II 78.

2 (w. *jam*) long ago; **b** (w. *est* in parenthesis).

ubi .. episcopatus jam diu cessaverat BEDE *HE* IV 2. **b** **1269** cum .. iter vestrum in com. Ebor' jam diu inchoatum non dum terminaveritis nec iter vestrum jam diu est in com. Norhumbr' .. sumonitum inceperitis *Cl* 39; **1276** in curia .. moram faciunt his diebus et jam diu est fecerunt *TreatyR* I 56; **1294** (v. disarrestare); **1310** proximior parens dicti R... nunc existo et pacifice exstiti jam est diu *Reg. Carl.* II 20; **1315** quousque predicta bastida jam non est diu fundata fuit *RGasc* IV 1401.

3 (w. prep. *a*) long ago, for a long time past; **b** (w. *jam*); **c** (w. *est* in parenthesis).

AD. MUR. app. 252 (v. a, ab 2e); **1356** super possessionem regni .. Scocie .. a diu fuimus et adhuc sumus .. impediti (*Ch. E. Balliol*) AVESB. 132; **s1400** Bohemie rege a diu imperium occupante AD. USK 55; **1419** in qua quidem .. excommunicacionis sentencia adiu perseveravit et perseverat *Reg. Cant.* I 189; **1421** qui non a diu .. gratissima vestre .. humanitatis solacia est expertus *Lit. Cant.* III 141; **1461** in solucione .. porcionis .. negligentes adiu extiterunt *Eng. Clergy* 114. **b** **1321** magnates .. a jamdiu nobis inobedientes et rebelles *Conc.* II 511; **1333** (v. a, ab 2e); **1337** hostium .. navigium quod jam a diu mare lustravit *Lit. Cant.* II 518; **1433** domino regi in regno suo Francie a jam diu obsequiosum se incessanter exhibuit *RParl* IV 443a. **c** **1309** licet inobedienciam hujusmodi potuissemus a diu est canonice punivisse *Lit. Cant.* I 34; **1309** jurati presentant quod quidam Odo le Clerk suspensus fuit adiu est *S. Jers.* XVIII 255; **1380** (v. a, ab 2e); **1413** cum .. possessionem suam inde .. adiu est adeptus fuerit et optineat in presenti *FineR* 219 m. 1.

4 (w. *ex*) for a long time past.

1458 inimicorum nostrorum, qui ex diu .. gavisi sunt in divisione inter nostros subditos *Reg. Whet.* I 301.

5 (?) late.

1271 circa horam cubacionis .. ceperunt equos et perrexerunt in campum de B. ad querendum unam carettam bladi, eo quod diu fuit et noctanter *RCoron* 1 r. 6d.

diureticus [LL < διουρητικός], diuretic, promoting urination. **b** (w. *granum*) gromwell (*Lithospermum*).

quotienscumque necessitas urine poscebat debita sua, solvere non potuit. .. eger .. ~a cibo vel potui non admiscuit W. CANT. *Mir. Thom.* II 65; asserunt illi cibis abstinendum, ~is utendum *Mir. Fridesw.* 106; GILB. VI 275. 1 (v. discoagulare); cum sirupo ~o sapido BACON IX 102; cum medicinis ~is et urinam provocantibus, sicut est spica et cassis GAD. 32v.2. **b** granum ~um, A. *lichewal* *Alph.* 72.

diurnalis [LL *gl.*], **a** (w. *opus*) day's work. **b** (as sb. m. measure of land). **c** worn by day, (as sb. n. pl.) day-time shoes or clothes. **d** celebrated or sung by day. **e** (as sb. n.) 'journal', service-book of day-hours; *cf. jornalis.*

a [cotsetla] apud quosdam operatur per totum Augustum omni die et unam acram avene metit pro ~i opere (*Quad.*, *Rect.*) *GAS* 446. **b** x jugera vinearum, x jugeres vel ~ales (cf. *Is.* v 10) *Gl. Leid.* 13. 15. **c** tunc [hora secunda] facto signo eant [fratres] et se ~ibus [AS p. 383: *middægþernum*] induant calceamentis *RegulC* 20; antequam sonet signum ad apparatum terciae, nullus calciet se ~ibus suis LANFR. *Const.* 87; **1293** cum surgitis ad vigilias .., calciatis ~ibus .. incipiatis antiphonam 'salve regina ..' (*Obs. Cantariae de Otringham*) *Meaux* II 197; [camerarius inveniet] Sabbato in Ramis Palmarum cuilibet fratri unum par sotularium ~ium *Cust. Cant.* 196; surgentes fratres vestiti ~ibus *Ord. Ebor.* I 49. **d** qualiter ~e sive nocturnale officium hebdomada Pentecostes agatur *RegulC* 58 *rub.*; in fine ejusdem psalterii sunt ympni tam nocturnales quam ~es ELMH. *Cant.* 97. **e** ambo [capellani abbatis] .. psalterium et ~e semper secum habeant *Cust. Cant.* 52; **1337** deficiunt libri, psalterium Johannis de W., ~e Johannis P... *Lit. Cant.* II 148; **1519** precentori pro uno ordinale et pro uno ~e et uno mortuario *DCCant.* C 11 f. 131a.

diurnalitas, duration of a day, transience.

lignum vite non habuit ex sua virtute naturali dare homini perpetuitatem vivendi. quia cum esset res creata virtus sua finita fuit in †duralitate [? l. diurnalitate] HOLCOT *Wisd.* 108.

diurnaliter, daily.

magna (*sic*) mentis conamine ~er desudans ut illos .. ad meliora provexit HUGEB. *Wynn.* 5.

diurnatim [cf. LL diurne], from day to day.

coherebat exercitus, ~im [v. l. diatimque] receptis pugnandi viribus pugnare *V. Neot. A* 13.

diurnia v. insigne.

diurnitas

1 day's work (as measure of land).

1531 soluti eisdem pro falcacione xxxiiij ~atum et dim. in S. ad vj d., xvij s. iij d. *Househ. Bk. Durh.* 11; **1537** pro falcacione xxxv ~atum prati in una clausura vocata S. *Ac. Durh.* 696.

2 duration or (?) *f. l.*

ex quo more diurnitates [? l. diuturnitates] longeve a labili humanorum memoria presencia fataliter absorbeant FAVENT 1.

diurnus [CL], **~ius**

1 belonging to day (as dist. from night). **b** (w. *nutrix*) day-nurse. **c** (as sb. n. abl.) by day.

ALDH. *VirgV* 1512 (v. centies); ~i luminis fulgorem BEDE *HE* IV 7; qualiter ~a sive nocturna laus paschali festivitate agatur *RegulC* 48 *rub.*; contra seu fures nocturnos seu latrones ~os DOMINIC *V. Ecgwini* I 4; ad ortum ~e lucis jussit nocturnam deponi W. CANT. *Mir. Thom.* VI 146; non amo nocturnum panem plus pane diurno WALT. ANGL. *Fab.* 22. 7; **a1260** archidiaconi .. provideant .. quod .. ordo Londoniensis ecclesie in officio nocturno et ~o observetur *Conc. Syn.* 649; **1308** (v. divagatio); in febri .. ~a GAD. 12. 1 (v. disconvenientia c). **b** **1423** dilecta nobis M. F. nutrix nostra ~ia *War. Issue* 27 *April.* **c** atro liquore cordis lingue calamus intinctus presentes pinxit characteres nocturnus; ~o quippe non vacavit AD. MARSH *Ep.* 191.

2 daily. **b** pertaining to a (single) day. **c** (w. *operarius*) day-worker, journeyman. **d** (as sb. m. or f.) day's work. **e** (as sb. f.) 'day-work' (measure of land; *cf. daiwerca, diawercata, diaeta*).

~ae orationis HUGEB. *Will.* 1 (v. crux 7a); ~e psalmodie, *þas dæglican sealmsanges*; ~ae aesce [i.e. escae], *dæghryne mettas* *GlH* D 762–3; ~a vita ~e refectioni debetur BALD. CANT. *Sacr. Alt.* 680B; presidente .. R. Glanvillensi ~am adepta est Anglia diuturnamque letitiam GIR. *EH* I 45; **c1300** recipiunt denarium ~ium pro denario (*sic*) operis (*Cust.*) *Rec. Norw.* I 189. **b** ~um, i. unius diei *GlH* D 761; [hystoria] ~a, de gestis unius diei vel supra, ita quod infra mensem, ut de Judith S. LANGTON *Gl. Hist. Schol.* 39. **c** **c1355** R. Legat, operarius ~us *JustIt* 312 r. 1. **d** **c1250** totus ille ~us pro uno opere sibi allocabitur *Cart. Rams.* I 461; **c1283** habebit arruram sue carruce ..; et, si impedimentum fuerit .., computabitur sibi illud impedimentum pro ~o arrure *Cust. Battle* 66 (cf. ib. 74: debent extraere fimos, sc. qui habet carectam cum j curtana; et qui non, inveniet j hominem per ~um quousque extrahentur); **1285** non fecit ipsum attachiari in honore de W., unde amisit ~am caruce sue *Hund. Highworth* 298; **c1300** quia plures servientes operantes cum diversis hominibus de civitate .. unum denarium pro ~o [? recipiunt] *Rec. Norw.* I 189; **1380** R. P... cepit excessive de W. S. xx d. pro unico ~o et dim. contra statutum *SessPWarw* 49; **1380** [stabulum] sic remanet discoopertum preter duos ~os unius hominis parcellam .. stabuli cum stramine cooperientis, viz. die confecionis presencium et proximo die preterito *IMisc* 221/1. **e** **1302** (v. dissaisonare).

dius [CL]

1 divine, holy, sacred. *Cf. divus* 3a.

11.. mater Virgo pia, titulo domus ista, Maria, / est tua dos propria; sua sis rectrix ope dia (R. ESK) *Couch. Furness* I 22; te postibus uti / credo, quibus fulcis edem, sapientia dulcis, / per tristega tria disponens dogmata dya M. RIEVAULX (*Vers.*) 29. 17; solvere principia methodorum principe dia M. CORNW. *Hen.* 9; ave virgo, casa dia WALT. WIMB. *Virgo* 81; karismata dia (*Vers.*) BACON VI 115 (v. angaria 1c).

2 (as sb. n.) sky, open air. *Cf. divus* 1a.

noctu sub dio quiescentes GOSC. *Aug. Maj.* 46.

diuscule [LL], for a longish time. *V. et. diutiuscule.*

cum ~e se contineret, tandem .. cum juvencula fornicatus est ALEX. CANT. *Mir.* 22 p. 200; **s1169** ipse [rex H.] et rex Francorum, cum jam ~e fuissent discordes .., pacis iterum inter se jura firmarunt W. NEWB. *HA* II 24;

diusculus, longish (of time).

1266 rex .. ~am in obsidione [Londonie] .. sed frivolam et inutilem moram traxit WYKES 204.

diusius v. dusius.

†diutile, *f. l.*

s1100 rex .. [cervum] †diutile [v. l. diutine, ? l. diutule] adhuc fugitantem vivacitate oculorum prosecutus W. MALM. *GR* IV 333.

diutine [CL], for a long time.

Eduardi tercii .., cujus tempora .. serenare dignetur Altissimus ~e et tranquille R. BURY *Phil.* 8. 118.

diutinus [CL], long (of time).

~um, longinquum *GlC* D 241 (cf. ib. D 183: deutinum, diuturnum); ~ae orationis dulcedine instructus BEDE *Hom.* I 9. 48; **801** tam ~o tempore ALCUIN *Ep.* 218; ex crebris belli ~i conflictibus GIR. *EH* II 38; **1236** ex possessione ~a ac consuetudine *Cart. Worc.* 323; AD. MARSH *Ep.* 97 (v. decursus 2b); **c1380** vobis concedat Altissimus ~is temporibus prosperare *FormOx* 323.

diutior, lasting longer.

ut sit de his .. disciplina certior, memoria ~ior, differentia patentior BALSH. *AD* 103; **1257** oportet nos duciorem moram trahere in partibus illis quam credebamus *Liberate* 34A m. 5; **1411** voluerunt inter se †deliberari [? l. deliberare], captata maturitate ~iori, si in aliquo juvare possent *Conc.* III 334b.

diutius [CL], longer, for a longer time. **b** longest.

lichinum sub modio coruscantem [cf. *Matth.* v 15] clam ~ius delitescere non patitur ALDH. *VirgP* 44; cum ibidem ~ius .. oraret, nihilo tardius meruit exaudiri BEDE *HE* IV 10; PULL. *Sent.* 927C (v. degradatio 1b); nec senatui subjectionem voluit [Arviragus] tenere ~ius G. MON. IV 16; **1167** imperator .. egressus est, letus quod ei fata concesserant Italiam perdere, quam demereraturt ~ius [v. l. divitus] retinere J. SAL. *Ep.* 244 (= *Becket Mat.* VI 405). **b** **1335** unam clavem penes .. custodem et alteram penes subcustodem et terciam penes illum qui ~ius fuerit .. in collegio volumus .. remanere *Eng. Clergy* 265.

diutiuscule, for a longish time. *V. et. diuscule.*

s1340 rex Anglie .. borealem partem Francie vastavit, urbem munitissimam ~e [*ed.*: diuscule] obsedit AD. MUR. *Cont. A* 173.

diutule [CL], for some time.

~e, aliquandiu OSB. GLOUC. *Deriv.* 181.

diuturnare, to spend the day.

1274 quantus quidem nocturnus et diuturnus labor ei e medio quidem ~are usque ad solis occasum impransus, modo vero et nocturnare quasi totaliter pervigil (*Lit. Praelatorum de Graecia*) *Flor. Hist.* III 40.

diuturne [CL], for a long time.

cum nuper a parte orientali venires, qua causa studii ~e steteras ADEL. *QN* 32; clades furoris diabolici .. gravius ac ~ius aliis sevit in ecclesiam ORD. VIT. V 8 p. 333; tutius esse mori reor in cruce quam diuturne / vivere GARL. *Tri. Eccl.* 140.

diuturnitas [CL], (long) duration, extent.

rotante prolixi temporis ~ate ALDH. *Met.* 4; **795** temporum ~as ALCUIN *Ep.* 38; **930** (10c) aliena gemendae peregrinationis ~ate exulans *CS* 1343 (cf. ib. 669); **c1084** quia .. virorum illustrium devota institutio ~atis senio frequentius aboletur *Ch. Durh.* 4; **c1107** ut omnes boni .. vitae vestrae ~atem desiderent ANSELM (*Ep.* 427) V 373; quid est vite ~as nisi quedam mortis prolixitas? NECKAM *NR* II 155 p. 241; **c1200** de generibus morborum et ~ate .. inquiratis *Canon. G. Sempr.* 115v.; ut non langueat .. alicujus spacii seu temporis ~ate BART. ANGL. II 16.

diuturnus [CL], long-lasting.

~o temporis intervallo ALDH. *VirgP* 36; famam suae malitiae posteris ~am [v. l. diurnam] relinquens BEDE *HE* I 14; si sibi .. ~ior vita concederetur G. MON. I 8; ut .. dicere possit: .. 'talium [stellarum conjunccio facit] mortem ~am' KILWARDBY *OS* 99; quia secundum regnum ~ius est quam primum W. BURLEY *Pol.* 280; *G. Hen. V* 21 (v. delenire c).

diva v. divus, duva.

divadiare [cf. vadiare, OF *desgagier*]

1 to disengage, redeem from pledge. **b** (w. *duellum*) to quash a wager of battle. **c** to 'break custom' (?).

hanc terram disvadiavit Hernald .. antequam Wido fuit saisitus de terra Offram; et post habuit semper Wido servitium *DB* I (*Lincs*) 367 (cf. ib.: socam .. terrae quam Offram in vadimonio habuit, et post devadiata fuit); **1108** illam terram .. quam Hugo abbas disvadiavit de Wyberto in Taenet (*Ch. Hen. I*) ELMH. *Cant.* 360 (= *Regesta* 873); **c1130** molendinum .. quod monachi emerunt de Waltero C. et diswagiaverunt de Adelicia .. l solid[is] *Regesta* p. 382 (cf. *Eng. Feudalism* 278: disvagimoniaverunt); **c1130** si quis prestitit suam pecuniam alicui .. et non poterit eam habere .., accipiet namiam pro ea. si autem vadimonium habuerit .. et debitor illud deguajare sive deliberare †voluerit [l. noluerit] .., vendet vadimonium .. quantum potuerit et inde suam pecuniam capiet *Doc. Bury* 113 (= *BBC* 166: †degniare; cf. *Kal. Samson* 1 p. 76); **s1155** dimisit idem R. .. feudum infirmarie quod abbas disvadiavit ab eo (*Cart. Mont St. Michel*) TORIGNI app. 334; **1179** vic. r. c. de lij s. quos Robertus .. optulit pro disvadianda terra sua Thome .. et ille renuit *Pipe* 83; **1200** terram .. invadiaveramus Judeis pro tanta pecunia quod eam disvadiare nequivimus *RNorm* 19. **b** **1212** consideratum est quod duellum sit devadiatum, eo quod nullus testatus fuit quod captus fuit cum vacca *CurR* VI 215; **1220** duellum vadiatum inter comitatum et Willelmum .. per consilium domini regis devadiatum est, ita quod campiones recedant inde quieti *Ib.* VIII 223; **1233** quia curia cognoscit quod duellum vadiatum fuit de predicto R. de alteris catallis [quam] suis .., consideratum est quod curia falsum judicium et quod duellum devadietur *Ib.* XV 905; [in causa civili], etiam si per imperitiam esset inter eos duellum vadiatum, deberet devadiari per judicium BRACTON 102. **c** *to breke custom*, deguadiare *CathA.*

2 (w. pers. obj.) to attach by gage.

pro una quaque harum forisfacturarum, solvet regi c s.; et, si abierit domum non apprehensus vel ~iatus, tamen minister regis eum sequetur et c s. emendabit. de *gribrige* vero, siquis eam fecerit et calumniatus in calle aut ~iatus fuerit, viij li. regi emendabit *DB* I (*Kent*) 1; si quis ubi forisfecerit retentus aut ~iatus sit, plene componat (*Leg. Hen.* 41. 1c) *GAS* 567; *Ib.* 596 (v. cravare); **1188** debet xx s. quia, cum non esset forestarius, devadiavit homines in foresta *Pipe* 183 (cf. *CurR* I 180); **c1215** concessit quod .. nullus burgensis .. in aliqua subscriptarum viarum pro viridi devadietur ..; si vero aliquis alibi infra nemus .. inveniatur, ~ietur veniendi ad curiam ibi standi judicio *BBC* (*Corbridge*) 57; **1230** perrexerunt carri et carrette .. abbatis et equi per foreram illam; et aliquando [? homines abbatis] fuerunt devadiati, aliquando non *CurR* XIV 167; respondere poterit quod nullam habuit [seisinam] pacificam, quia numquam ibi ingressum habuit quin esset devadiatus et quin faceret emendas pro transgressione BRACTON 266b; **1261** quia .. Robertus venit ad vesperam ad devadiandum .. Jacobum, quasi vellet movere discordiam et alio modo quam debuit venisse ad namia capienda (*JustIt*) *SelCWW* 120; **1274** cum Philippus .. et socii sui pascerent pratum Thome .. vj equis suis, messor dicti Thome hoc videns †noluit [? l. voluit] degagiare .. Philippum et alios *Hund.* II 101; **1279** Willelmus .. abbatem †communicandum [? l. communicando] et .. estoveria †capienda [? l. capiendo] impedivit et devadiavit ad dampnum .. abbatis *Couch. Furness* II 440; **1290** ballivi .. exigunt ab eodem E. theloneum pro mercandisis suis .. et ipsum ea occasione .. devadiaverunt .. et vadia sua injuste adhuc detinent (*Plac.*) *Chr. Peterb.* 128; **1304** venit warennarius .. Johannis .. et ipsos devadiavit et vadium adhuc tenet sine aliqua transgressione facienda eidem J. (*CoramR* 178) *SelPlForest* cxxxi.

divadiatio [cf. vadiatio]

1 disengagement, redemption (from pledge).

1195 de ~one vadii quod Willelmus .. habuit de Michaele .. de ~one terre quam Willemus .. habebat in vad' de eodem *RScacNorm* 196 (cf. ib. 170: de divadicione terre sue).

2 attachment by gage.

si quis blodwitam .. et hujusmodi forisfaciat et inde veniat sine div[a]diatione vel calumpnia, placitum domini sui est (*Leg. Hen.* 23. 1) *GAS* 561; si sanguinem .. faciat et recedat sine cravatione et ~one, ..; si autem retineatur vel divadietur vel implegietur, .. (*Ib.* 94. 2d) *Ib.* 611; **1287** per devadiaciones et averiorum capciones et alia impedimentorum genera *Cal. CourtR Chester* 68.

3 wager of law or (?) *f. l.*

contra quorum testimonium [tenens] dedicere non poterit summonicionem per legis sue devadiationem [? l. vadiationem] *Fleta* 376.

divadimoniare, ~izare, to disengage, redeem from pledge.

v libras denariorum dedit presbyter abbati [Rainaldo, ob. **a1100**], quibus quandam situlam argenteam devadimonizavit, que invadimoniata fuerat pro c s. *Chr. Abingd.* II 29; **c1130** disvagimoniaverunt idem molendinum a domina Aelizia .. l solidis *Eng. Feudalism* 278 (cf. *Regesta* p. 382: diswagiaverunt).

divaditio v. divadiatio.

divagari [LL], to wander about.

1215 [oves] veri pastoris destitute sollicitudine .. extra loca pascue devagantur errabunde (*Lit. Prioris Dunelm.*) *RChart* 208a; **1298** quamplures monachi ecclesie Elyensis .. per diversas patrias, ipsius monasterii sumptibus, .. nequiter devagantur *Reg. Cant.* 259; **1335** nullus .. sacerdotum .. in locis exteris devagetur (*Stat. Cantar. Sibthorpe*) *Eng. Clergy* 271.

divagatio [LL], wandering about.

1300 scandalum vehemens quod ex devagacione et prosecucione tam notabilis persone [R. monachi Elyensis] undique oriretur est .. evitandum *Reg. Cant.* 722; **1308** quod omnes moniales monasterii vestri presentes .. ad officium divinum tam diurnum quam nocturnum simul conveniant absque devagacione qualibet *Ib.* 1308; **1327** licet frater H. .. monasterium exiit et statim rediit sine ~one majore *Lit. Cant.* I 240.

divalis [LL], divine.

~e, divino *GlC* D 278; ~is, dius, divinus OSB. GLOUC. *Deriv.* 181.

divaricare [CL]

1 to spread (legs) apart, straddle; **b** (intr.).

devaricare, separare *GlC* D 90; rex [Dacie] .. pedes et crura sinuose ~ans, dum incautius unum pedem extendisset, e prora labitur AILR. *Ed. Conf.* 749B; femora separando ~averat R. COLD. *Cuthb.* 20; SAMSON *Mir. Edm.* 8 (v. distrahere 1a); tam mulieres quam mares ~atis cruribus .. equitare solent GIR. *TH* III 26; *to cruke*, curvare .., ~are .., repandere *CathA.* **b** tumoris multitudo pedes illi ~antes confederare conjungendo minime permittebat R. COLD. *Cuthb.* 103.

2 (? by assoc. w. *varius*) to vary, alter, diversify.

~are, diversum facere OSB. GLOUC. *Deriv.* 178; **s1205** ingressus sum civitatem, occulte tamen, vestibus ~atis; et tamen in ipso ingressu .. a quibusdam .. cognitus sum *Chr. Evesham* 144; **s1266** venit in Angliam dux de Brundewico, cum magna familia variisque indumentis ~ata *Ann. Lond.* 76; conditor orbis .. / .. / res animare novas, varias formare figuras / et speciebus eas divăricare parat GOWER *VC* II 612 (cf. ib. VII 474: hec quoque nec perstant que nos elementa vocamus; / immo gerunt varias divăricata vices).

divaricatio, straddling.

[puella] falso Minerve peplo velavit Affroditem, et sub tue pretextu repulse in suam alii ~onem appulerunt MAP *NC* IV 11 f. 52v.

divastare v. devastare a.

divellere [CL], **a** to tear apart, separate. **b** to tear to bits, crumble.

a divulsum, separatum *GlC* D 243; ut .. nulla labentium rerum contrarietate terrente .. a fidei firmitate ~amur BEDE *Hom.* I 16. 261; quid mirum si Christus, divulsis partibus hominis, totus homo erat? J. CORNW. *Eul.* 18 p. 293. **b** devellunt, discerpunt *GlC* D 214; sic rerum creator regnum et vitam in Deo suo perjurantis .. scindens destruat et consumens in favillam devellat EDDI 27.

divendicatio v. divindicatio.

diventilare [LL], to spread (news) abroad.

postquam certum fuit et in omnium notitia manifeste ~atum militum eum globum .. adduxisse *G. Steph.* II 107.

diverberare [CL]

1 a to cleave. *V. et. deverberare* 2.

a diferverat, intervenit, separat *GlC* D 238; aerem virga ~ans, quam manu gerebat W. CANT. *Mir. Thom.* I 14.

2 to strike, beat soundly. *V. et. deverberare* 1.

mulieres .. propriis manibus crines lacerant, pectus ~ant AILR. *SS Hex* 2; [egrotum] nunc videres precipitem, nunc renitentem et invitum ex adverso ~ari R. COLD. *Cuthb.* 48.

3 to thresh out (fig.).

1291 ~ato negocio hinc et inde (*Reg. Linc.* III 176) *EHR* XXVI 505.

divergere [CL = *to diverge*], (?) to take a wrong turn (fig.).

s1387 in Turri .., quem locum putabat optime se posse tueri, si quid sinistri ~eret ea vice *Chr. Angl.* 387 (= WALS. *HA* I 170: emergeret).

diverium v. deverium a.

1 diversari [CL *usu.* de-], **a** to reside. **b** to be occupied, engaged.

a quod ambos .. in curia ejus .. familiariter ~atos vidissent W. MALM. *GR* III 271; qui [reges Anglorum] magis ad austrum quam ad aquilonem ~ati noscuntur *Id. GP* II 99; **1526** (v. castigate). **b** dum ~amur in hac provintia W. MALM. *GP* III 116 p. 254; **c1450** cum tua voluntas omnis in bene agendo bonis studentibus ~etur *Let. Ch. Ch.* 16.

2 diversari [LL ~are, (pass.) to differ, be distinguished; **b** (act.). **c** (intr.) to differ.

cutis ~atur in raritate et spissitudine *Ps.*-RIC. *Anat.* 16; ista cura ~atur ab aliis GILB. I 61. 1; res .. scibiles penes modos apprehendendi differentes ~antur in eo quod scibiles sunt BACON VIII 111; secundum hoc leges hominum ~antur *Id. CSPhil.* 421. **b** que causa diversitatis temporis numeralis? si dixerint quod diversitas motuum celestium, et que causa diversitatis numeralis istorum? et sic continue ascendendum donec perveniatur ad primum hujusmodi ~atum BRADW. *CD* 868C; diversat fratres tantummodo vestis eorum GOWER *VC* 1183. **c** ~are, variare OSB. GLOUC. *Deriv.* 179; **1309** habent .. consuetudines in hac insula [*Jersey*] .. ~antes .. a legibus Normannorum *PQW* 835a; *to discorde*, absonare .., variare, differre, ~are, diversificare *CathA.*

diversarium v. diversorium.

diversatorium, (?) by-way.

taurus .. leonem .. percutiet, expellet eum per regni ~ia (*Proph. Merlini*) G. MON. VII 4 p. 394.

diverse [CL], **a** differently. **b** in various ways, on various occasions.

a BALSH. *AD* 64 (v. consignificatio). **b** TATWINE *Aen. prol.* (v. 1 conserere 1b); **1249** Willelmus fatue gerebat se, ~e dicendo probra et enormia verba de eis (*JustIt* 776) *SelCWW* 72.

diversiclinis [LL], (as sb. n.) heteroclite, irregularly declined word.

heteros 'diversum', unde 'heteroclita', id est '~ia' NECKAM *NR* II 173 p. 291.

diversiclinium, branch road or road-fork.

variarum viarum ~ia, que se citius fugitantibus obiciebant, subeuntes, per plurima diverticula .. sua expetierunt *G. Steph.* I 62; ~ium, diverticulum, .. diversitas viarum OSB. GLOUC. *Deriv.* 181; *a gateschadylle*, bivium, ~ium *CathA.*

diversicolor [LL], variously coloured.

in ~oribus picturis W. MALM. *GP* I 43 (v. ars 1a).

diversificare [cf. LL diversificus]

1 to differentiate, distinguish. **b** (intr.) to differ. **c** to diversify, 'embroider' (a story).

est idem subjecto intellectus materialis et intellectus in effectu. ~antur autem in comparatione J. BLUND *An.* 340; propter diversitatem patientis ~antur effectus GROS. 60; Platonici .. ~ati sunt in sectas multas post mortem magistri sui BACON *Maj.* II 267; hec [concava et convexa] specialiter ~ant actionem specierum venientium ad ea propter diversitatem suarum specierum *Ib.* 466; si [sermocinans] sententiam ~at contra communitatem, utitur ethimologia sapientis *Ps.*-GROS. *Gram.* 67; **s1338** rex .. epistolam .. pape .. destinavit et .. consimilem epistolam, verbis salutatoriis dumtaxat ~atis, .. cardinalium collegio .. transmisit *G. Ed. III Bridl.* 139; istud non ~at necessitatem et non-necessitatem, sed tantum facit intensiorem et minus intensum actum DUNS *Ord.* II 93; hec omnia [cantare, legere etc.] .. sunt spiritualia per accidens .., quia ~ant species ad spiritus seu anime perfeccionem accidentalem PAUL. ANGL. *ASP* 1550; multociens .. bendule ~antur UPTON 235. **b** **s1292** interrogati, si .. leges Anglie et Scocie in hoc casu ~ent invicem et repugnent, per quas leges .. debent judicari *Ann. Scot.* 258. **c** talia [regis vitia] vulgus liberum ~abat H. HUNT. *HA* VIII 1.

2 (intr. w. *inter*) to draw a distinction.

c1236 convincetur (*sic*) ~ans inter sacerdotes Levitici generis et judices illius temporis [cf. *Deut.* xvii 7–9] GROS. *Ep.* 72* p. 221.

3 to disagree, to be variance: **a** (pass.); **b** (act.).

a quomodo aut in quibus regionibus assignentur signa et planete difficile est certificare; nam auctores ~antur BACON *Maj.* I 381; **s1452** cum .. per hunc modum starent ~ati coram principe nec forent omnes concordes, immo magis contrarii in opinione *Reg. Whet.* I 19. **b** cum he [tres forme] .., ut diverse sint persone, Deus non sint—idem enim se non posset ~are PULL. *Sent.* 677D; in principiis magistrorum, quando scolares ~ant se, portant enim in capite signum crucis sed in corpore portant dyabolum portando vestes histrionum (PECKHAM *Serm.*)

Med. Cult. 70*n*. (cf. *Powicke Studies* 277*n*.); **1309** justiciarii una cum illis xij debent recordum illud facere; sed, si ~ent inter eos .. *PQW* 826a.

diversificatio, differentiation, variation.

hee et alie aves prede recipiunt in predando div[e]rsificationem BART. ANGL. XII 1; maxime non possunt [affirmatio et negatio] esse simul in eodem instanti, quoniam major est divisibilitas et ~o temporis penes partes et esse quam instantis BACON III 251; idem manens idem, in quantum est de se, semper natum est facere idem; tamen est ~o solum ex parte materie *Id.* XIII 108; declinacio est vocis in parte ~o regularis, ipsius rei quam significat habitudines diversas pretendens *Ps.*-GROS. *Gram.* 34; **1309** rex non percipit hic plusquam iij s. [loco xiij^mi^ den.] de vendicione, licet non specificetur illa ~o in predicta cedula communitatis [Jereseye] *PQW* 835b; ad omnem punctum mundi est summa ~o; que cum sit contraria ydemptificacioni, videtur quod tollit ydemptificacionem pro eodem tempore et subjecto WYCL. *Euch.* 192.

diversimode [LL], **a** in different ways. **b** in various ways. *V. et. diversimodus* 2.

a ut diversimode rem significabit eandem / edocet equivocis opus hoc GARL. *Syn.* 14. 1577A; totum Hieronymi quod habemus in antiquis bibliis et in originali, hec ~e hinc inde aliquotiens transtulerat BACON *Min.* 347; ostensum est quomodo ~e ponunt [geometra et naturalis] et quomodo similiter KILWARDBY *OS* 191; **s1285** .. obiit A. rex Scottorum, de cujus morte diversi ~e senciebant WYKES 305; **1391** diversi ~e sunt opinati *Reg. Heref.* 336. **b** arteriis .. ~e bifurcatis transfunditur spiritus vitalis per totum corpus BART. ANGL. III 22; si cogitatio sua [sc. anime] sit per corporales ymaginationes ~e dispersa *Spec. Eccl.* 127; **s1243** postquam [J. prior Winton'] illam nobilem ecclesiam ~e .. turbaverat *Flor. Hist.* II 266; [res incorporales] quarum possessio ~e transfertur de persona in personam BRACTON 13b; **c1339** aliis diversis officiis quibus prefuit .. eundem novimus [priorem] ~e profuisse *Pri. Cold.* 24; R. BURY *Phil.* 18. 234 (v. complexio 4d); unde hoc pervenit quod potestas regum tam ~e variatur FORTESCUE *LLA* 13.

diversimodus

1 a of a different kind, different. **b** of various kinds.

a translatio quelibet debet habere sua propria verba sed ~e habent diversa verba BACON *Min.* 348; hujusmodi ~e accepcionis exemplum sumitur a B. Augustino (KYN.) *Ziz.* 30. **b** **s1212** ignis .. maximam partem civitatis [Norwici] cum ipsis civibus et .. possessionibus et supellectili ~a devoravit *Ann. S. Edm.* 23; **s1260** domos eorum clam intrarunt et bona ~a abinde asportaverunt *Flor. Hist.* II 458; **1266** de capcione deversimoda ad opus domini Edmundi *Rec. Leic.* I 124; **1326** ad combustionem monasterii de D. et ejus ~as destrucciones oculos dirigentes *Dryburgh* 247; **1333** pro pannis de *velvet* .. et aliis rebus ~is *LTRMem* 105 r. 110; **1341** una vobiscum et aliis prelatis .. Anglie ac pro vobis ~as .. obligaciones fecimus (*Lit. J. Archiep.*) BIRCHINGTON *Arch. Cant.* 30; **1346** causis ~is ad hoc ductus (*Lit. Confessoris Regis*) AD. MUR. *Chr.* 212.

2 (as sb. n. abl.): **a** in different ways. **b** in various ways. *V. et. diversimode.*

a **1232** secundum quod de scuto ~o capietur pro diversis exercitibus *CalCh* I 165; **1325** diversi ~o senciunt *Lit. Cant.* I 136. **b** quod ipse .. ad Simonem .. accederet et diligenter ac ~o secum tractaret ad videndum utrum esset compos mentis sue necne *State Tri. Ed. I* 74; considerantes monasterium .. ere alieno ~o depressum *Cust. Cant.* 24; **1416** oneribus quibus clerus .. ~o pregravatur *Reg. Cant.* III 7; **1461** dicit quod in recordo et processu predictis .. ~o est erratum *Law Merch.* II 119.

diversio [LL], diversion, deflexion, turning aside.

1222 de ~one cursus cujusdem aque .. ad nocumentum .. archidiaconi *Pat* 342; quod .. capiatur aqua in manum domini simpliciter et sine aliqua .. ~one BRACTON 181; quod [medicina] figet se in loco suo firmiter et divertet se ad viam quam intendimus sua ~one BACON IX 106; GAD. 27. 2 (v. diameter 3); **c1400** divertit cursum aque illius usque ad molendinum cujusdam J., ante quam quidem ~onem .. molendinum .. comitis molere potuit quolibet die .. x quar. frumenti et x quar. brasii *Entries* 441.

diversitas [CL], **a** difference. **b** diversity, variety.

a **680** quando singulis quibusque pro meritorum ~ate dispar retributio .. trutinabitur ALDH. *Ep.* 4; de Paschae vel fidei ~ate conflictus (*Ep. Ceolfridi*) BEDE *HE* V 21 p. 342; ubi pluralitas, ibi ~as; at, ubi ~as est, non est perfecta concordia ANSELM (*Incarn. B* 15) II 33; de regibus et tyrannis eorumque ~atibus ab invicem et differentiis GIR. *PI* I 17; arcus inter hec duo loca [verum et apparentem] comprehensus vocatur ~as aspectus lune GROS. 30; HALES *Sent.* I 227 (v. differentia 1a); BACON *Maj.* I 138 (v. difformis); *Ib.* II 516 (v. discontinuus a); duo sunt in littera, ~as nature ipsarum litterarum et earum diversa figuracio, que forte a ~ate nature egreditur ipsarum litterarum *Ps.*-GROS. *Gram.* 19; motum .. celi .. qui .. per dissimilitudinem et ~atem motuum aliorum orbium stellarum erraticarum causa [est] contrarietatis KILWARDBY *OS* 19; SICCAV. *PN* 106 (v. dissimilitudo a); ex hoc non sequitur ~as et non-identitas realis substancie et relacionis DUNS *Ord.* II 361. **b** rami hujus arboris dogmatum sunt ~ates in quibus animae castae .. nidificare .. gaudent BEDE *Luke* (xiii 19) 507; patriam egressus .. transitis terris periculorum ~atibus plenis Romam pervenit EADMER *V. Osw.* 22; cum .. his .. modis superbia operari consideretur, vij ~atibus eam posse dividi videtur ALEX. CANT. *Dicta* 2 p. 118; de proprietatibus anime rationalis quo ad nature sue simplicitatem et quo ad virium suarum ~atem BART. ANGL. *proem.*

diversivocus [LL], heteronymous, having different names.

multivoca et ~a, que Boetius adicit, magis ad gramaticam pertinent.. ~a [sunt] que sensu et voce diversa sunt, ut 'homo', 'lapis' J. SAL. *Met.* 895A.

diversorium [CL *usu.* de-]

1 inn, guest-house. **b** (private) apartment, compartment (esp. eccl. or mon.). **c** partition. **d** privy. **e** 'day' (division of mullioned window); *cf.* 1 *daia*.

panis .. non erat in ~io, nisi .. micas .. super mensam constituit *V. Cuthb.* II 2; quum .. in ~io fuisset remisit post eum agmen BYRHT. *V. Ecgwini* 383; ~ium, *tocirhus* vel *cumenhus* ÆLF. *Gl.*; **9..** ~ium, *gestærn WW*; **1212** (v. coquina 1d); in una domo sine pariete que dicitur ~ium a divertendo; nam illic homines divertebantur pro pluvia et aliis tempestatibus *Spec. Eccl.* 93; hoc ~ium, *a hyn WW*; *ostel or in or herborwe*, hospicium, ~ium *PP*; **c1545** juxta ~ium vocatum *the George Cart. Osney* III 288; **1587** totum illud hospicium sive ~ium suum vocatum *le Bell* infra Neugate London' *Pat* 1303 m. 2. **b** cum .. [hominem] non inventum primum in capella deinde per aulam et ~ia cuncta quesissent GIR. *EH* I 40; edificaverunt certatim etiam absentes canonici circa ecclesiam [Coventrensem] ampla et excelsa ~ia, ad usus forte proprios, si vel semel in vita locum visitandi causam casus offerret DEVIZES 40; [B. abbas, ob.**1193**] erexit .. magnam aulam cum omnibus ~iis suis SWAFHAM 101; **c1228** fuit in ~io camere episcopi .. et vidit monachos Dunelm' .. venientes ab episcopo *Feod. Durh.* 242; refectorario tunc temporis locus non erat in diversario *Cust. Westm.* 134; **1321** cum .. intelleximus quod vos xviij nova ~ia in loco studentibus oportuno fecistis parari, .. mandamus quod prefato lectori vestro locus competens ad studendum in hujusmodi novis ~iis assignetur *Lit. Cant.* I 46; **1440** j aulam .. simul cum uno stabulo sive ~io infra clausum domus *Cl* 290 m. 11*d*. **c** **1300** ne frequens accessus secularium et maxime mulierum contemplacionem inpediat monachorum, .. ordinamus quod inter altare B. Virginis et vestiarium ~ium statim erigatur *Ord. Ely* 23. **d** [incarcerati] non habebant ~ia, sed ubi accubabant ibi ventres purgabant W. CANT. *Mir. Thom.* III 19; **e** **1348** faciet eciam in .. capite orientali unam fenestram tria ~ia, que *dayes* dicuntur, habentem (*Contract.*) *Arch. J.* LXXXVII 22.

2 (pl.) recesses. **b** wilds, backwoods.

per angulorum basilice ~ia R. COLD. *Osw.* 49 p. 377. **b** cum in ~iis montium et silvarum eos [Walenses] persequi non posset H. HUNT. *HA* VII 4; illic [*Copeland, Cumb*] miles quidam, suis contentus ~iis, .. habebat quoque predia in Anglie partibus orientalis SAMSON *Mir. Edm.* 12; **s1400** [Scoti] ex hujusmodi absconditis sepius exeuntes, in desertis deviis ac ~iis nostratum quam plures interfecerunt AD. USK 47.

divertere [CL; *not dist. here from* devertere]

1 to divert, deflect, turn aside: **a** (watercourse); **b** (ship); **c** (journey, route); **d** (stationary object); **e** (fig., pen); **f** (intr.).

a niveus senex .. fluvium Perironis ~et .. et molendinum super ipsum metabitur (*Proph. Merlini*) G. MON. VII 3; **1199** si .. injuste et sine judicio ~erunt cursum aque molendini Johannis .. ad nocumentum liberi tenementi sui *CurR RC* II 60; **1221** A. le Macecrer ~it cursum aque de Fulebroc ad nocumentum abbatie *PlCrGlouc* 109; non posset ille cujus fundus esset .. aquam ~ere vel diminuere, quo minus cursum debitum haberet BRACTON 181; **c1400** (v. diversio); **1493** ripam fossati fregit et aquam .. a recto et antiquo cursu ~it *Entries* 291b. **b** **1217** quod .. sub omni festinatione .. veniatis cum toto navigio vestro .. in servicium nostrum in Tamisiam nec aliquam alibi navium vestrarum .. ~ere presumatis *Pat* 89. **c** cum illuc iter ~issent, in quadam insula haud procul a Crugland noctem duxerunt FELIX *Guthl.* 41; ALCUIN *WillV* 15. 9 (v. delusor). **d** si movendo aut evertendo voluerint quid a suo statu quomodocumque ~ere EADMER *Beat.* 3. **e** ad disserendum gesta .. regis E. tercii .. stilum amodo ~amus *G. Ed. III Bridl.* 93. **f** ORD. VIT. XII 34 (v. declinare 6a); dum [dux] ad partem alteram inflecteret vectorem suum, animal pontificis de recto ~entem tramitem per devia sequeretur AD. EYNS. *Hug.* V 17 p.202.

2 a to divert (property), alienate. **b** to remove (a plea). **c** to separate.

a isdem W. tenet Begestan. Edric tenuit de episcopo .. et non poterat ab eo ~ere, quia de victu suo erat *DB* I 257 (cf. ib. 181: Rogerus .. ~it illas [hidas] ad Glouuecestresire); **1446** super alienacione .. meremii .., quod rector .. defunctus emebat ad reparacionem rectorie, quod .. Thomas ~ebat ad usum edificiorum tenementorum .. ville *Eng. Clergy* 220. **b** sic ante aliquem ingressum litis in curiam baronis vel comitatu[m] potest hujusmodi placitum ~i primo die ad majorem curiam domini regis HENGHAM *Magna* 3. **c** *GlC* D 172 (v. divortium 2a).

3 to depart, betake oneself, resort: **a** (refl.); **b** (pass.); **c** (intr.); **d** (pass. or intr., w. ref. to board or lodging; *cf. diversorium* 1a). **e** (fig.) to turn away, desist (from).

a ille [pontifex] ~ens se ab altare, stans in gradu suo EGB. *Pont.* 120; BACON IX 106 (v. diversio); **s1307** cum .. thesaurarius versus Westmonasterium se ~eret, ut ordinaret regiam sepulturam *Ann. Paul.* 257; **1314** cum .. licenciatus existat se ad propria ~endi *RGasc* IV 1261; **1416** (v. devillare a); *Ps.*-ELMH. *Hen. V* 44 (v. 1 diameter 3); **1439** injunxit Ade K., *lodisman* navis predicte, quod ipse se ~eret ad navem predictam cum omnimoda festinacione ad conducendam dictam navem *Pat* 444 m. 3; **1468** proviso .. quod .. usque hoc regnum .. infra quinquennium .. se corporaliter ~at *Lit. Cant.* III 244. **b** saepius ibidem ~i ac manere .. consueverat BEDE *HE* III 17. **c** licentiam poscebant ut [v. l. ut in] aliam viam .. devertissent [v. l. ~ere possent] FELIX *Guthl.* 43 (cf. ib.: in alteram viam devertisse); unde diverterunt [v. l. de-] ad provinciam Occidentalium Saxonum BEDE *HE* III 28; ~unt ab invicem pontifices maerentes pro invicem OSB. *V. Dunst.* 38; quid mihi faciendum sit, quo ~endum AILR. *Ed. Conf.* 776C; **s1154** Lodovicus, quia regina Alienor contristaverat eum .. simulata fuga, ~it ab ea R. NIGER *Chr. I* 92 (cf. R. HOWD. I 214: fecit divortium fieri); ecclesia de gentibus non venit donec Dominus ~it ad dormiendum S. LANGTON *Ruth* 111; **s1226** prelati .. ~entes seorsum ad colloquendum WEND. II 296; **1243** non permittendo .. marinellos .. alias ~ere quam Lond' cum .. navibus *Cl* 51 (= *RGasc* I 205: †~ire); dedi etc. P. de C. et heredibus suis .. liberos esse in omnibus molendinis meis super terram meam ubicunque devertant ab omni exaccione (*Ch.*) *FormMan* 4; **s1399** [leporarius] cum eo [rege] semper lateri suo ubicumque ~eret, staret sive jaceret .., semper assistebat AD. USK 41; ab his studiosis monachis qui ad ea loca saepenumero ~unt FERR. *Kinloss* 3. **d** illuc, si placet, ~unt et se pro modo suo singuli reficiunt W. FITZST. *Thom. prol.* 10; de hospita ipsius Londonie .., ad cujus semper hospitium solus .. ~ere consuevit GIR. *Symb.* I 1 p. 208; *Spec. Eccl.* 93 (v. diversorium 1a). **e** a via pacis ~entes .. in evangelicum scandalum inciderunt ÆLNOTH *Cnut* 63; si a proposito vestro ~entes cum Grecis commanere volueritis G. MON. I 11.

4 (intr.) to turn round, rotate. **b** (trans.) to change, turn into (something else).

1473 pro redditu capitis molendini bladiferi, super quo *le eaxeltre* jacet et ~it *DCCant. Ac. Prioris* xvii 12. **b** **1313** de omnibus pheliparii quia dubbant et ~unt pannos, faciendo scelerem falsitatem in opere *Leet Norw.* 55 (cf. ib. xciv).

5 (p. ppl. *diversus*): **a** diverse, different. **b** divers, various, sundry. **c** (as sb. n. pl.) sundries.

a quis .. alii ~o funere occubanti .. proficiet? GILDAS *EB* 72; hoc .. uno et non ~o temporis ordine geri conperimus BEDE *HE* III 25 p. 184; cum [tales naturae] aequales esse non possint per ~a quaedam sed per idem aliquid ANSELM (*Mon.* 4) I 17; alii eum [Henricum I] tribus .. irradiasse splendoribus asserebant ..; alii autem ~o studio tribus eum vitiis inficiebant H. HUNT. *HA* VIII 1; ~orum ~is institutionibus plurima de arte ad disciplinam edisseri accidit BALSH. *AD* 5; **1237** ~us a nostro (v. dualitas 1b); res ~e sequuntur complexiones ~orum signorum BACON *Maj.* I 381; WYCL. *Act.* 15 (v. discontinuatio 1); CAPGR. *Hen.* 102 (v. depositio 7b). **b** pauca .. de sanctis martyribus, de ~is haeresibus, de tyrannis .. dicere conamur GILDAS *EB* 2; [aves] quae .. / .. creatorem diversa voce fatentur ALDH. *VirgV* 16; **c705** ut .. tanto .. eloquii divini profundissimos .. sensus facilius .. intelligas quanto illius rationis qua contexitur ~issimas regulas plenius ante didiceris *Id. Ep.* 8 (11); calciamenta ~i generis [AS: *mistlices cynnes*] ÆLF. *Coll.* 97; **957** (14c) dicti protogenis ampla .. per ~a v †tonarum [? l. zonarum] liniamenta pullulante prosapia *CS* 995; **1231** (v. dispergere 1b); **s1307** accepto super hoc ~orum consilio TROKELOWE 67; **1341** per plures nuncios et ~as literas (*Lit. Regis*) AVESB. 95b; **1466** in certis pannis .. ~orum colorum *ExchScot* 424; **1502** venerunt ad pacem S. Johannis Bev' pro ~is causis concernentibus securitatem corporis sui *Sanct. Bev.* 220. **c** **1335** pro ~is (v. cuva 1b); **1494** in ~is emptis ad predictum opus *Lit. Cant.* III 331.

6 (p. ppl. *diversus* as sb. n.): **a** (w. *a, de, e*, or (?) abl. only) from or on the opposite side or sides. **b** (fig. w. *e*) in direct opposition, on the other hand, to contrary effect. **c** (*in ~a*) all about, in various directions.

a perge .. ad quadrangulam a ~o positam *Alea Evang.* 175; **1147** de ~o (v. avironatus); agnus et lupus sitientes ad rivulum †et [? l. e] ~o venerunt J. SHEPPEY *Fab.* 1. **b** audiebam 'multi ab oriente et occidente venirent ..' et e ~o .. 'discedite a me' GILDAS *EB* 1; nonnumquam rationabilis creatura irrationabilium gestu .. utitur et e ~o irrationabilis .. intellectualium gestu .. fungitur ALDH. *Met.* 7; frontis pallor .. et ediverso quorundam .. genarum rubor *Id. VirgP* 32; **704** (8c) si quis .. hanc .. munificentiam augere maluerit ..; si quis e ~o .. infringere temptaverit ..

CS 111; dicentur separate multiplicia illa ad que solis affirmationibus respondetur, sed et hujusmodi omnia ad que e ~o affirmative responderi potest etsi interdum etiam negative BALSH. *AD rec. 2* 175; Beda .. dicit eam [Hiberniam] vinearum expertem non esse; Solinus vero et Ysidorus apibus eam carere asserunt. sed .. circumspectius e ~o scripsissent GIR. *EH* I 6. **c** uxor .. coepit vexari .. brachia vel caetera sui corporis membra in ~a raptando BEDE *CuthbP* 15.

diverticulum [CL *usu.* de-]

1 branch road, by-road; **b** (fig.). **c** backwater. **d** distraction. **e** digression. **f** (w. *verbi*) turn of speech.

deverticulum, de altera via in alteram flexio *GlC* D 37; ÆLF. *Gl.* (v. divortium 1); ~um, *wegtwiflung Id. Sup.*; dum regales .. viarum circa civitatem ~a, ne quid escarum interius ingereretur, curiosissime observarent *G. Steph.* I 65; puella .. divertentes eos per privata ~a a longe secuta est T. MON. *Will.* I 5; *G. Ric. I* 204 (v. circumanfractus); habebat jugiter ante se equitem, equum suum precedentem et callium ~a que sequeretur meatu proprio premonstrantem AD. EYNS. *Hug.* V 17 p. 202; **s1255** (v. distrahere 2); platearum ~a et callium secreta compendia rimantur, si forte quem persequebantur comprehendere possent *NLA* (*Osyth*) II 235; **s1387** non sunt secuti fugientem [ducem Hibernie] servi procerum, eo maxime quod ~a patrie nesciebant *V. Ric. II* 96. **b c675** per lubrica dumosi ruris ~a, immo per discolos philosophorum anfractus, iter carpere ALDH. *Ep.* 3; **798** per apostolicae doctrinae publicam pergite stratam, nec per ~a cujuslibet novitatis in dexteram vel sinistram a via regia declinate ALCUIN *Ep.* 137; hoc in historia exigitur, ut nullo erroris .. ~o a recto veritatis tramite declinetur *Enc. Emmae prol.*; per multiplicia sophismatum ~a incauta levitate discurrens ANSELM (*Incarn. A*) I 285. **c** quivis piscator fluminis libens redit ad ~um, in quo .. retia laxaverit ad capturam *Collect. Stories* 216; comparat se magister rivulo qui, licet ~a que secus alveum invenit repleat, cursum tamen solitum non dimittit S. LANGTON *Gl. Hist. Schol.* 43. **d** in quo casu confessorem et medicum .. ad eam [monialem] permittimus habere accessum, ita tamen ut .. omni alio ~o denegato .. celeriter redeat sic ingressus PECKHAM *Ep.* 70 p. 84. **e** genealogiam comitum Andegavensium .. transcurram, prefata ~i venia W. MALM. *GR* III 235; a ~o materia repetatur W. DONC. *Aph. Phil.* 6. 11; in cursu sermonis .. statum se transtulit ad orationes; quibus expletis, a ~o repetiit orationem GIR. *IK* I 2; nunc a ~o redeuntes materiam continuemus *G. S. Alb.* I 87 (cf. declinare 4e); longum a proposito meo ~um CAPGR. *Hen.* 123; unde longiori fortassis ~o .. digressi sumus BOECE 119v. **f** per ambages multas .. in aliquo demum verbi ~o, qui responsum solerter observat, quod petit accipiet enucleatum GIR. *DK* I 16 p. 195.

2 evasive movement, dodge. **b** (fig.) evasion, trick.

quilibet venatus formam videre cupiens .. ibi cuncta potest ferarum ~a perspicere R. COLD. *Godr.* 50. **b** ut acumen ingenii tui experiar, eo ~o me protego, herbas a terra nullum habere nutrimentum ADEL. *QN* 3; **s1169** alia et enormia querens ~a, [rex] novas pravitates in Angliam misit GERV. CANT. *Chr.* 214; cum justitia pauperis multis posset ~is prorogari, felici celerique judicio consecutus est eam MAP *NC* V 7 p. 253; quid melius per vulpem quam dolositas accipitur? hec quidem .. foveas habet et multa fraudium ~a NECKAM *NR* II 125; **s1239** vulpina ~a regis M. PAR. *Maj.* III 531.

3 recess, compartment. **b** (place of) refuge, shelter. **c** inn; *cf. diversorium* 1a.

s1238 festinus quesivit eum per plura thalami ~a M. PAR. *Maj.* III 497; *Ib.* IV 627 (v. conclave 1a); **s1277** Wallenses .. ad solita ~a Snoudonie confugerunt *Flor. Hist.* III 49; fortalicium .. armatum .. interius meremio, terra et tignis excisis in antris et ~is pro recepcione hostium et hostilium *G. Hen. V* 4 (cf. ib. 1 p. 6: conspirans in antris et ~is cum suis comitibus); uterque in sue papilionis ~a se promovit *Ps.*-ELMH. *Hen. V* 77. **b** cadit imbrium spissitudo .. intrant ad ~a, si forte facies caeli sit ei[s] propitia HERM. ARCH. 39; **s1139** rex comitem persequitur. nil autem certi audiens de eo—quedam enim ~a ad tempus ille petierat—expeditionem movit J. WORC. 56; quo se verteret? .. Dacus a tergo perurget; ~a nulla patescunt SAMSON *Mir. Edm.* 5 p. 121; **s1382** ut pene fugerent universi, ~a querentes et latebras WALS. *HA* II 67; **s1434** (v. contutari 1a). **c** ~a, .. hospitium *GlH* D 733; hoc sinodogium, hoc ~um, i. diversorium *WW*.

dives [CL]

1 rich (or rich man), richly endowed (partly fig.). **b** plentifully supplied.

sceleratos ~ites .. sicut caelestes angelos venerantes GILDAS *EB* 66; Hædi, pie presul, precor, / pontificum ditum decor, / .. THEOD. *Pen. epil.*; ut simul offerrent dites patrimonia Christo ALDH. *VirgV* 1807; quamvis innumeris esset ditissimus heros / virtutum donis *Ib.* 299; ita ut .. nullus ibi ~es, nullus esset egens BEDE *HE* IV 21 p. 254; tanto quis ~itior elatus .., tanto austerior .. jura rectitudinis exercere non formidavit HUGEB. *Wynn.* 5; utilis sum .. et ~itibus [AS: *weligum*] et omni populo ÆLF. *Coll.* 96 (cf. ib. 103: non sum tam ~es [AS: *spedig*] ut possim emere mihi vinum); ditior est liber mendicus divite servo WALT. ANGL. *Fab.* 51. 17; ~es omnis .. aut iniquus est aut heres iniqui GIR. *GE* II 20; **1252** isti sic electi sint ~ites, sive regentes sive non-regentes *StatOx* 84; **s1272** habebunt potestatem predictam terram .. ad firmam dare alicui ditiori vel potentiori *Reg. Paisley* 52; ~es mercator [ME: *þe riche mercer*] sine tumultu procedit *AncrR* 49; post hec expercior in secularibus / fit cito dicior suis comparibus *Planct. Univ. Ox.* 28; possunt ~es et pauper subdividi in ~item et pauperem in Deum, ~item et pauperem quoad mundum WYCL. *Civ. Dom.* III 108; **s1381** (v. curare 5d); *a ryche man* dis, ~es *CathA*. **b** ~es lactis et mellis insula [Hiberniae] BEDE *HE* I 1; vinis non vineis ~es est insula GIR. *TH* I 6; ~ibus mensis NECKAM *DS* III 429 (v. conger a); **s1232** horrea ditissima (v. distrahere 3a).

2 rich, costly, precious.

plurima dum felix ditis patrimonia gazae / possidet ALDH. *VirgV* 2181; omni possessione ditius lumen oculorum amisit GOSC. *Wulsin* 16; **s943** (v. divestire 1); **s1126** ~iti apparatu (v. curia 3e); J. EXON. *BT* IV 391 (v. discrimen 2); **1432** capis ditissimis (v. curare 5d).

divestire [CL de-]

1 to undress, disrobe (esp. eccl.); **b** (refl.); **c** (intr.).

s943 cujus [ducis W.] corpus .. cum devestirent, argenteam clavim in ejus strophio reperiunt dependentem, satis ditissimum thesaurum sub se habentem, stamineam sc. et cucullam monachilem W. JUM. III 12; exeat sacerdos .. et qui in choro albis vel cappis induti fuerunt; quibus disvestitis .., cantent matutinas laudes LANFR. *Const.* 94 (cf. ib. 140: disvestitis fratribus); **s1285** T. episcopus missam .. celebravit, conventu disvestito et in froccis suis .. in choro stante et canente *Ann. Durh.* 64. **b 1108** T. archiepiscopus .. surrexit et dicesit a choro ac vestiarium ingrediens se ~ivit (*Lit. Capituli Ebor.*) H. CANTOR 4v.; abbas ~iat se *Miss. Sarum* 554. **c** si quis .. audito signo hore nondum collo suo stolam imposuerit, disvestire debet et in chorum ad horam ire *Obs. Barnwell* 86; in vestiendo et disvestiendo juvabit sacerdotem *Ord. Ebor.* I 112.

2 to divest, deprive; **b** (refl.).

1061 ut nullus rex .. praesumat .. te .. de bonis .. divestire (*Lit. Papae*) *Conc. Syn.* 549; **s1119** papa .. inquit .. "de archiepiscopatu non eum ~ivi" .. H. CANTOR 19v.; *Cust. Norm.* 22. 1 (v. divestitus); **1438** a doctoratu non devestivimus eundem *EpAcOx* 167. **b c1250** dedi .. jus .. advocacionis .. quod habui .. in ecclesia de W. .., investiendo .. episcopum et successores suos de dicta advocacione et devestiendo me et heredes meos in perpetuum (*Ch.*) *Reg. Heref. 1344–60* 48; **1560** de jure et actione dictarum terrarum se ~iendo *Scot. Grey Friars* II 247.

divestitus, deprivation.

de [de]vestitu facto sine judicio: nullus ausus sit aliquem de aliqua re devestire nisi ordine judiciario *Cust. Norm.* 22. 1.

divexatio [cf. CL divexare], vexation, harassment.

ut sine turba et ~one Deo et Christo inservire possint COLET *Rom. Exp.* 200; **s1525** obiit dominus Patricius post varias ~ones FERR. *Kinloss* 33.

divexus v. devexus. **divia** v. duva. **divictus** v. devincere 1b.

dividentia, apportionment, supplement to prebend or sim. (eccl.).

1482 compotus ministrorum collegii [de Otery]. .. in pensionibus et aliis expensis: .. summa ~ie cuilibet per se ij li. viij s. viij d. ob. quad. *Mon. Exon.* 283b; **1535** pro porcione prepositi ibidem [*Penryn, Cornw*] pro tempore existentis, viz. pro corpore prebende sue xxiiij li., pro obit[ibus] ij s. ij d., et devidencia sua viij li. xvj s. v d. *Val. Eccl.* II 392; **1546** confrater noster M. B. .. vult et concedit quod tota devidencia [sua] .. pecunie ex communia ecclesie nostre collegiate proveniens, que solet sibi et aliis residenciariis ejusdem ecclesie pro canonicali residencia facienda .. persolvi, .. pro spacio trium annorum .. in .. reparaciones .. ecclesie incumbentes .. applicetur *Mem. Ripon* I 305; **1560** dedimus .. Georgio Carewe .. decanatum collegii sive capelle nostre regie infra castrum nostrum de Wyndesour .. cum omnibus juribus .., libertatibus, privilegiis, titulis, quotidianis distribucionibus, ~iis, excrescenciis (*Pat*) *Foed.* XV 580a; **1573** communas, vina, ~ias, distribuciones ac alia quequumque (*sic*) emolumenta canonico residenciario .. debita *Stat. Linc.* II 599.

dividere [CL]

1 to cut or break in pieces, cut through. **b** (w. *contra se*) to disrupt (*cf. Luke* xi 17). **c** (pr. ppl. as sb.) app. diviner practising a form of sortilege.

macellarius in macello carnes ~it *Gl. Leid.* 45. 19; **9..** fressa, i. molita, fracta, divisa, *gegrunden WW*; gallina .. membratim divisa NECKAM *Ut.* 102; aratro terram ~ente BACON *Maj.* II 209; potencia motiva in manu potest uti cultello .. ad ~endum .. corpus DUNS *Ord.* III 296. **b** si universitas mortalium habendo plures principes nequaquam uni subjectos fuerit per discordiam contra se divisa, desolacionem incurret OCKHAM *Dial.* 873. **c** sortilegi sunt qui sub nomine ficte religionis superstitiosa quadam observatione rerum pollicentur eventus, quod genus sortes apostolorum et prophetarum et dividentium J. SAL. *Pol.* 409A.

2 (p. ppl. *divisus*): **a** designating verse in which division into words coincides w. that into metrical feet. **b** (w. *cantus*) prick-song. **c** (bot.) segmented.

a quis est ~us versus? qui in scandendo partes orationis separatas habet, id est ut, quot pedes habet, tot et orationis [partes habeat], ut puta: 'dic mihi, Clio, quisnam primus fingere versus' ALDH. *Met.* 10 p. 93; ~a, scansio *MS Univ. Libr. Camb.* Gg. 5. 35 f. 419. **b 1519** (v. 2 cantus 2b). **c** *gyth* .. viridem habet stipitem .. foliis circumdatum, in extremitate ~um [v. l. divisiones habens] *Alph.* 2.

3 (gdv. as sb. f., *sc. charta*) indenture (written in duplicate and divided).

1297 facta fuit hec ~enda inter .. Johannem .. et Humfridum .. super diversis arreragiis vadiorum *RGasc* III p. cliv; **1300** in cujus rei testimonium huic ~ende predicti Robertus et Rogerus sigilla sua alternatim apposuerunt *LTRMem* 72 r. 30 *sched.*; **1301** prout continetur in quadam ~enda inter ipsum regem et cancellarium facta et cujus una pars penes cancellarium remanet *RParl* I 145a; **1327** de lanis diversorum annotatis in quadam ~enda facta de lanis .. inter R. de Sandwico .. ex una parte et Johannem A. *KRMem* 81 r. 165.

4 to divide (into parts); **b** (math., incl. pr. ppl. and gdv. as sbs. m., *sc.* factor and dividend); **c** (w. ref. to books). **d** (w. *talliam*) to divide (sum specified in) tally so as to cover separate payments (*cf. Arch.* LXXIV 300–2). **e** to split into smaller groups.

ex intervallo, i. e. diviso tempore *GlC* E 511; scande, ~e verba vel versum *Ib.* S 208; omnem quam possederat substantiam in tres divisit portiones BEDE *HE* V 12 p. 304; **8..** ~unt, *todeleð WW*; haec terra nunquam per hidas divisa fuit *DB* I 77; **s1159** rex illud *cantref* secundum ei [Reso] in diversis baronum terris divisum dedit *Ann. Cambr.* 47; **1311** oportet quod .. subboscus ~atur in xij partibus ad prostrandum *Cust. Battle* 138. **b 796** si septem in duo ~eris (*sic*), id est in iij et in iiij ALCUIN *Ep.* 113; in simplici .. divisione divisuro posito caractere .. THURKILL *Abac.* 60; ponatur talis numerus super primam ~entis qui per ultimam ejusdem demat ultimam vel ultimas ~endi ADEL. *Alch.* 1 p. 20; [numerum] pariter imparem intelligens qui primo loco quidem in equa ~itur, ~entia vero mox indivisibilia reperiuntur *Id. ED* 24; si radicem numeri novenarii in [v. l. per] radicem quaternarii ~ere volueris ROB. ANGL. *Alg.* 100; errare .. videtur naturalis ponens lineam ~i posse in infinitum KILWARDBY *OS* 181; potest magnitudo ~i secundum unumquodque signum; non tamen possibile est quod stet ejus divisio nec ad puncta nec ad corpora indivisibilia; immo ipsa ~itur in semper divisibilia, et possibilitas signandi quodlibet signum in linea et ~endi eam secundum unumquodque signum non potest reduci ad actum eciam a divisore infinite potencie SICCAV. *PN* 100. **c** GOSC. *Mir. Iv.* lxv (v. distinctio 2a); ~itur istud opusculum in v libellis *Eul. Hist. proem.* I 3. **d 1253** quod tallie quas .. habet de solucione inde facta ad Scaccarium nostrum secundum consuetudinem ejusdem Scaccarii ~antur et .. coexcaetoribus suis super compotum eorum .. allocentur *Pat* 64 m. 12; **1284** camerarii non faciant de cetero vicecomitibus seu aliis quibuscumque ballivis tallias ~endas, nisi receptis prius ab eis particulis summas et occasiones debitorum et nomina ea solvencium continentibus, in quas quidem particulas velint hujusmodi ~endas partiri, quibus sub sigillis eorum receptis non licet eas in alias particulas aliquatenus immutare (*Rhuddlan*) *StRealm* I 70. **e** in tribus cohortibus praefati regis [Ælfredi] satellites .. ~ebantur ASSER *Alf.* 100; Gallorum nobilitas .. diviserunt se in tres turmas *G. Hen. V* 13.

5 to divide (notionally), analyse, classify (incl. pr. ppl. as sb. n., *sc.* category); **b** (refl.).

~untur haec in iiij, sc. in tonos, in tempora, in respirationes, in passiones ALDH. *PR* 141; dubitabilium genera rursum aliter ~emus BALSH. *AD* 57; J. BLUND *An.* 252 (v. componere 2a); oportet habere artem componendi terminos et ~endi KILWARDBY *OS* 517; *Ib.* 195 (v. divisibilis 1a); quando ens ~itur per opposita, alterum ~encium est perfeccionis in ente, alterum imperfeccionis DUNS *Ord.* II 271; usus sic dictus ~i potest in nudum usum et in usumfructum OCKHAM *Pol.* I 301 (cf. ib. II 674: iste modus [dicendi] in multis ~itur); WYCL. *Quaest. Log.* 293 (v. divisibilitas). **b** summam naturam .., quae nec in plures substantias ~it se nec cum alia aliqua .. se colligit ANSELM (*Mon.* 27) I 45.

6 to separate, detach; **b** (refl.). **c** to estrange. **d** to separate in thought, regard as distinct. **e** (w. *contra* or *versus*) to distinguish (from).

cum .. primi tres pedes concatenati inter se a reliquis tribus sequentibus divisi separatique sunt ALDH. *Met.* 10 p. 93; eas [reliquias] singulis imponendo buxis pannis partim ~ens sigillo suo signavit *V. Greg.* p. 95; hostis antiquus adhuc longe divisus .. transfigitur providentia *Simil. Anselmi* app. 193 p. 102; super utraque littora maris quod Lodoneiam ~it et Scotiam TURGOT *Marg.* 9; unum [maris brachium] Galliam ~it et Britanniam GIR. *TH* I 2. mors fratres dividit WALT. WIMB. *Sim.* 66. **b s1175** Galwidienses, se a regno Scocie ~entes, contiguas sibi terras inquietaverunt FORDUN *Cont.* VIII 25. **c** divisi ab

invicem sunt mater et filius EADMER *HN* 17; H. LOS. *Ep.* 10 (v. condescendere 2a). **d** nec hominem ~imus a deitate, sed unum et eundem dogmatizamus ALCUIN (*Adv. Felicem*) *Dogm.* 94C. **e** ex divisione probabili potest vulgus ~i in oppositum versus sapientes BACON *NM* 543 (cf. conceptio 3a); alio modo [logica] est sciencia racionalis et sic est una trivialis sciencia divisa contra grammaticam et rhetoricam KILWARDBY *OS* 492; usus juris non ~itur contra jus utendi, cum usus juris sit jus utendi rebus alienis OCKHAM *Pol.* II 515.

7 a (refl.) to march together, form a boundary. **b** (trans.) to impose or form a boundary within or between. **c** (intr. w. *inter*) to form a boundary (between). **d** to make a division (between). **e** to discriminate (between).

a **c1250** sic sequendo dictum divisum forreste et mete de R. se ~unt usque ad W. (*Ch. Lanc.*) *OED s. v. pike sb.* 2 (v. et. 8a infra). **b** quis .. terminos .. sicut .. Finees .. et Jesus sagaciter divisere ostendit? GILDAS *EB* 70; cujus virgae medietas est regis, sicut via eam ~it *DB* I 249; BRACTON 180 (v. 8a infra). **c** **1241** usque ad viam Flandrensem, que ~it inter terram monachorum et terram Madoci B. *CurR* XVI 1846; **14..** juxta viam que ~it inter parochiam S. Egydii [London'] et S. Andree *Mon. Francisc.* I 511. **d** o quam grandi distantia divisit Deus inter lucem et tenebras [cf. *Gen.* i 4] BEDE *HE* V 14; **1268** quando peccata nostra ~unt inter nos et Deum nostrum *Conc. Syn.* 781. **e** nares eis [angelis] pictores attribuunt .., quia vitia velud fetida refugiunt sed virtutes .. diligunt et inter munda et immunda .. sagacissime .. ~unt et distingunt BART. ANGL. II 3.

8 (p. ppl. *divisus* as sb. f. or n.) boundary. **b** boundary-strip, free-board, balk. **c** (pl.) marches, march-lands. **d** quarter, ward (of city). **e** boundary-mark. **f** (leg.) court held at boundary; *v. et. divisio* 6c.

926 (13c) secuntur ~ae et metae hujus terrae *Ch. Burton* 3; †**1087** do .. villam de H. .. cum .. omnibus rectis ~is ejus *Hist. Durh.* app. p. xxi (= *Regesta* 286); si [murdrum] in ~is accidat, utrimque pertranseat (*Leg. Hen.* 91. 4) *GAS* 607; **1144** dedisse .. terram de D. per terminos et rectas ~as suas *E. Ch. Scot.* 141; quod juste et sine dilatione facias rationabiles ~as inter terram R. .. et terram A. (*Breve*) GLANV. IX 14; **a1195** (v. crux 7d); **1198** de placito perambulationis et ~arum *CurR* I 51; **1235** (v. 2 bunda 1a); **1246** cresta fossati est ~a inter eos, eo quod ea cresta erecta fuit super antiquam ~am *SelPlMan* 9; **c1250** ~um (v. 7a supra); multiplex poterit esse ~a inter vicinos, que dividit dominia et distinguit fines agrorum BRACTON 180b (v. et. 7b supra); **1268** memorandum de ~is montanis de K. inter abbatem .. et dominum R. *Reg. S. Thom. Dublin* 2; **1298** tenent .. terram de Stelden per certas suas ~as *Hexham* II 113 (= *MonA* VI 183a: per †cartas ~as); **1380** duo maneria sunt ita contigua quod plures vie et semite a toto tempore supradicto extiterunt mete et ~e inter maneria predicta *G. S. Alb.* III 263. **b** **a1121** ut faciat ibi rectum monachis Winton' de terra quam preoccupat super eos et ~am (*Ch. Hen. I*) *EHR* XXXV 393; **1240** levavit quoddam fossatum circa bercariam suam in terra sua, ita quod extra fossatum illud et terram Radulfi restat adhuc quedam devisa *JustIt* 3 r. 5; **1246** J. B. in misericordia quia preocupavit super ~am juxta terram suam *SelPlMan* 12; **c1250** [quod habeant] liberam ~am [ij pedum extra dictum] fossatum *Cart. Harrold* 30; **1269** (v. amputare 2c); **1306** (v. caput 14h); **1344** duo crofta mea .. cum sepibus, fossatis, ~is, vivariis, *fraunburd* ad utrumque croftum spectantibus *Doc. Coll. Wint.* (*A. Chacedeu, Cranfield*); **1549** sursum reddidit .. dim. acram terre jacentem apud *Blackmyle furlong* inter duas ~as vocatas *balks* (*CourtR*) *Kingsthorpiana* 30. **c** **1180** concessimus ad invicem quod de .. omnibus .. rebus quas modo habemus alter adversus alterum nihil amodo petet .. exceptis minutis feodis et ~is terrarum nostrarum de Berri (*Tractatus*) *Foed.* I 53b. **d** **1157** quod .. omnes homines .. qui infra iiij ~as civitatis manent et mercatum deducunt sint ad gildas *BBC* (*Lincoln*) 108 (cf. ib. [**c1160**]: infra iiij ~as que pertinent civitati Linc'). **e** **1195** de Cecilia de V., v s. pro ~a eruta *RScacNorm* I 244 (cf. ib. 189: de Gervasio E., v s. pro devis[a] eradicat[a]). **f** si quis latronem .. ceperit .., dabit x s. de *hen[g]wite* et ad primam ~am [OF: *a la primere devise*] faciet de eo justiciam (*Leis Will.*) *GAS* 497; omnis causa terminatur vel hundreto vel comitatu vel halimoto socam habentium vel dominorum curiis vel ~is parium (*Leg. Hen.* 9. 4) *Ib.* 555; si inter compares vicinos utrimque sint querele, conveniant ad ~as terrarum suarum et qui prior querimoniam fecerit prior reatum habeat (*Ib.* 57. 1) *Ib.* 576 (cf. ib. 57. 8: in ~is vel [m]erchimotis).

9 a to share, apportion, distribute. **b** to devise, bequeath; *v. et. divisare* 2a, *cf. dimittere* 7b. **c** (p. ppl. *divisus* as sb. f. or n.) 'devise', grant, bequest.

a dividimus mundum communi lege quadratum ALDH. *Aen.* 79 (*Sol et Luna*) 7; discum confringi et eisdem [pauperibus] ~i praecepit BEDE *HE* III 6 (cf. ib. IV 12: subreguli regnum .. divisum inter se tenuerunt); statuunt inter se ~ere victores alienigenae insulam ABBO *Edm.* 1 (cf. ib. 7: ut cum eo .. paternas divitias .. ~as); praebendae .. modo sunt divisae per singulos per episcopum *DB* I 1v.; *Ib.* II 107 (v. communis 1b); **1100** uxor sua sive liberi .. eam [pecuniam] pro anima ejus ~ant, sicut eis melius visum fuerit (*Ch. Hen. I*) *GAS* 522; si ceorli habeant herbagium in communi vel aliam compascualem vel divisam [v. l. divisionis] terram [AS: *gamænne oððe ȝedālland* (*Quad.*) *GAS* 107; inter puellas drachmam sic ~o ut unicuique earum equalis particula rei contingat ROB. ANGL. *Alg.* 118; GROS. *Ep.* 6 (v. comparticeps); actiones, sicut negotiorum gestorum, tutele, communi ~undo BRACTON 100b (cf. Cicero *Fam.* 7. 12. 2 etc.); **1281** postea devidebatur baronia .. inter v sorores *PQW* 426a; **1417** (v. dublettus 1a); **1588** tenementa .. devisa (v. divisabilis). **b** si quis morte praeventus non divisisset quae sua erant, rex habebit omnem ejus pecuniam *DB* I 179; **c1190** quam terram nobis divisit A. filius S. *AncD* A 2441; **c1205** testamentum ij acrarum terre .., quas pater meus divisit eis *Ib.* 2557. **c** quidam .. frater singulis annis xxx s. .. ad opus matris sue .. solebat accipere. huic quadam vice solidi v de illis—nam ~e per temporum vices conferebantur—ex precepto ejus dati sunt EADMER *HN* 17; **c1162** fuerunt ad ~am comitis R. et audierunt quod .. comes .. dedit .. abbatie .. xx solidatas terre *FormA* 2; **1170** debet lx m. de catallis Reginaldi, qui obiit in domum suam sine ~a *Pipe* 46; **1176** heredes .. catalla sua habeant, unde faciant ~am defuncti (*Assisa Clar.*) *G. Hen. II* I 109; **s1181** tota ~a quam ipse [archiepiscopus Ebor'] fecerat per preceptum regis ad nichilum redacta est; dicebat enim rex quod .. archiepiscopus judicium fecerat quod .. non liceret alicui viro ecclesiastico ~am facere nisi prius quam egrotare inciperet *Ib.* 283; **c1180** precipio .. quod teneatis .. omnes ~ias et divisiones que fient Bonis Hominibus Grandimontis de B. et inde non disturbetis eos .. sed easdem ~ias et divisiones absque vexatione .. habere faciatis *Act. Hen. II* II 252; **1182** feci ~am meam de quadam parte pecunie mee in hunc modum (*Test. Hen. II*) *FormA* 422; quod juste et sine dilatione facias stare rationabilem ~am N., sicut rationabiliter monstrari poterit quod eam fecerit et quod ipsa stare debeat GLANV. VII 7; **1215** si aliquis .. burgensium moriatur et ~am suam fecerit de rebus suis *BBC* (*Eynsham*) 74; **1588** aliquod .. ~um (v. divisare 2a).

10 to devise, arrange, design; *v. et. divisare* 2b. **b** (p. ppl. as sb. f.) device, badge.

1182 constituta est pax et concordia .. et .. in manum cepi ad efficiendum ut secundum quod divisa est procedat (*Lit. Regis*) GIR. *PI* II 16; quando dividimus serena per oscula pacem,/ exoramus ut hanc possimus habere tenacem GARL. *Myst. Eccl.* (*versio B*) p. 151; **1255** fieri facias quoddam novum stabulum .., prout vobis divisimus *Liberate* 31 m. 6. **b** [cives] omnes juxta eorum artificia certas habuerunt divisas culciores, que unumquodque artificium notabiliter ab alio distinguebant *G. Hen. V* 15; **1440** quem [nuncium vestrum] .. non parum recommendatum habuimus atque devisa seu liberata nostra de collera facimus insigniri (*Lit. Regis ad Papam*) BEKYNTON I 39.

dividia [CL], vexation, distress.

~ias, tristitia *GlH* D 746; ~ia, tristitia, molestia, maestitia OSB. GLOUC. *Deriv.* 181 (cf. ib. 176: ~a, discordia, Bellona).

dividiare v. dimidiare 1a.

dividuus [CL], **a** divisible, partible (also as sb. n.). **b** divisive, cleaving.

a ~a, i. divisa *GlH* D 744; que queruntur de eodem et diverso .., de numero et oratione .., de ~o et individuo, de substantia et forma vocis J. SAL. *Pol.* 640C (cf. ib. 401C: ex substantia ~a et individua); docentur inquirere .. de eodem et de diverso, de diviso, de ~o et individuo P. BLOIS *Ep.* 101. 313A; proprietas in personis adoratur, non aliqua tamen que sit tribus personis communis—tunc enim jam non esset proprietas sed communio—sed singularum personarum sua proprietas et ~a H. BOS. *LM* 1363C. **b** *sume synd* ~a, *þa getacniað todal mid edlesendre spræce*: uterque .., quisque .., singuli ÆLF. *Gram.* 13; **s1097** erat Hugonis lancea quasi fulmen advolans, gladius Anselmi quasi flamma ~a H. HUNT. *HA* VII 7.

divinaculum [LL], oracle. **b** oracular response.

~um, locus divinationis OSB. GLOUC. *Deriv.* 173. **b** *an answere of goddis*, fatum, ~um, oraculum *CathA*.

divinaliter [cf. LL divinalis], in a spirit of godliness.

pudicam continentiae vitam ~er ducendo HUGEB. *Wynn.* 4.

divinare [CL]

1 to practise divination.

Cosan, ~ans, *GlC* C 680 (cf. *Luke* iii 28); hos [aruspices] in extis animalium ~are predictum est J. SAL. *Pol.* 461C; per stellarum inspeccionem .. putat ~ando predicere futura KILWARDBY *OS* 69; quidam .. ~abat per os demoniaci et multa abscondita manifestabat *Latin Stories* 17.

2 (trans.) to predict or detect by divination. **b** to determine, ascertain.

inter xij [zodiaci] signa, unde mathematici fatum, fortunam vel genesim .. se ~are et praenoscere posse .. arbitrabantur ALDH. *Met.* 3. **b** ecce subitus ei vir astat .. multa feditate faciei terribilis, .. suavi tamen .. ipsum confidere jubet alloquio mentisque sue sibi ~at angustias MAP *NC* IV 6 f. 47v; si .. scripserit Jeronimus alia nomina pro hiis, fateor quod illa ~are nescio GROS. *Hexaem. proem.* 61.

divinatio [CL], divination, fortune-telling.

si mulier incantationes vel ~ones diabolicas fecerit, j annum .. peniteat THEOD. *Pen.* I 15. 4; futura profeticae ~onis oracula ALDH. *VirgP* 29; alii aruspicia observantes, alii ~ones demonium (*sic*) dicentes HUGEB. *Wynn.* 7; **8..** ~o, *wilung WW*; ~o, prophetia, divinitas, *halsung GlH* D 740; lege libros, nusquam fere in bona significatione ~onem invenies J. SAL. *Pol.* 466C; quasi in ~ones, que ad levandum noctis hiemalis .. tedium .. excogitari solent .., verse sunt hodie disputationes GIR. *GE* II 37 p. 356; principes [Tartarorum] .. regunt populum per ~ones et scientias que instruunt homines in futuris BACON *Maj.* I 368; domina, rogo vos ut aliquam ~onem mihi dicatis *Latin Stories* 111; ~o, A. *wychcraft WW*; **1510** (v. conjuratio 3).

divinativus, divinatory.

ubi inquirit [Averroes] causam somniorum ~orum sive propheticorum de futuris BRADW. *CD* 222D.

divinator [LL], diviner, fortune-teller, soothsayer.

deus, .. unde divinitus adv., et .. inde verbalia ~or, divinatio OSB. GLOUC. *Deriv.* 164; prophetas reprobos ~ores non prophetas esse scriptura commemorat J. SAL. *Pol.* 466C; de ~oribus in hac gente et quasi arreptitiis GIR. *DK* I 16 *rub.*; **c1358** [R. episcopus Ossoriensis], viris catholicis .. coram eo citatis .., si .. aliqua verba .. incaute emiserant, ipsos ~ores, sortilegos et hereticos statim fore pronunciavit *Reg. North.* 404; **1406** datum est nobis intelligi quod .. magici .., nigromantici, †divinitores, arioli .. infra diocesim vestram [Linc'] existunt, qui diversa horribilia .. indies perpetrant (*Pat*) *Foed.* VIII 427a; *a divine* [v. l. *divinour*], auspex .., ~or, ~orius participium, carminator .. *CathA*; **1514** ad .. quoscumque subditos .. ~ores, sortilegos aut in fide nostra male sapientes et devios sive errantes incarcerandum (*Reg. Ebor.*) *Eng. Clergy* 198.

divinatorius, divinatory.

multa sunt mathesi doctrinali et ~ie mathesi communia J. SAL. *Pol.* 440B; *CathA* (v. divinator).

divinatrix [LL], diviner, fortune-teller (f.).

'matĕsis' media corepta et sine aspiratione est divinatio sive ars divinandi, qua[m] Manto ~ix adinvenit BACON V 3; a phytio Apolline dicitur phyton .. et phytonissa ~ix *Id. Gram. Gk.* 67; de vetula ~ice *Latin Stories* 111 *rub.*

divinculatus, (prisoner) held in fetters.

pro summa hujusmodi ~os cum eorum creditoribus componendo fecit piissime liberari AYLWARD 290.

divindicatio, claim.

omne emolumentum .. quod de maneriis coquine assignatis progreditur coquinario deputatur, exclusa abbatis divendicacione vel reclamacione *Obed. Abingd.* 392.

divine [CL], divinely.

mistice, †sacrae [l. sacre], ~e *GlC* M 206.

divinificare, to make divine.

[imperatores] qui post mortem ~ari censentur GERV. MELKLEY *AV* 176.

divinitas [CL], divinity, godhead (Christian); **b** (personified); **c** (not spec. Christian). **d** divine possession, ecstasy.

799 Christus .., ~ate consubstantialis Patri, humanitate consubstantialis matri ALCUIN *Ep.* 166 p. 272; incarnatum Verbum adorare admonendi erant angeli; in ipsa ~ate admonitionis non indigebant LANFR. *Comment. Paul.* (*Heb.* i 6) 377; sicut dicimus potestatem aut divinam potestatem sive potentem ~atem, cum in ~ate non sit aliud potestas quam ~as ANSELM (*Ver.* 12) I 196; sic ei [homini] est et via in humanitate, ut perditus redimatur, et vita in ~ate, ut redemptus beatificetur AD. SCOT *TT* 628C; quidam dicebant essentiam ~atem, a qua essent persone tres HALES *Qu.* 38. **b** quia .. virtus ei divinae cognitionis infunditur, ejusdem ~atis terrore refrenatur BEDE *HE* II 1 p. 78; ~atis sibi affuturum inscius exspectabat auxilium ÆLNOTH *Cnut* 18; **1152** adjutrice ~ate (*Lit. H. Episc. Wint.*) DICETO *YH* I 296; **1195** illis qui pro ~atis amore laborem hujus profectionis [in Terram Sanctam] assumere .. studuerint (*Lit. Papae*) *Ib.* II 134; seu se ~as .. hoc lumine vestitam suis in terra voluit ostendi cultoribus MAP *NC* IV 9 f. 51v.; ~ate propitia AD. MARSH *Ep.* 1 p. 78 (cf. *Chr. Rams.* 370). **c** sciscitabatur .. qualis sibi doctrina haec eatenus inaudita et novus ~atis, qui praedicabatur, cultus videbatur BEDE *HE* II 13; numinis, ~atis *Gl. Leid.* 35. 232. **d** **10..** extaseos, ~atem *WW* (cf. ib. s. v. divinatio).

divinitor v. divinator.

divinitus [CL], by or from God.

706 perpendite .. creaturarum ordinem eique ~us insitam naturam ALDH. *Ep.* 9 (12); consiliarii ~us admoniti BEDE *HE* II 13; mortalibus gratiam ~us collatam GIR. *TH* I 37; de matris utero / homo divinitus / natus humiliter LEDREDE *Carm.* 16. 9; **1456** hac consideracione mota et ~us inspirata *StatOx* 279.

divinus [CL]

1 divine, concerned w. the gods (Classical).

te sacre assument acies divinaque bella J. Exon. *BT* I 57; Vesta dea ignis, sc. ~i, in collegio deorum annumerabatur *Deorum Imag.* 17.

2 (as sb. m.) diviner, magician.

c**738** ~os vel sortilegos, sacrificia mortuorum seu lucorum vel fontium auguria .. respuentes (*Lit. Papae*) *Ep. Bonif.* 43; **747** prohibens .. paganas observationes, id est ~os, sortilegos, auguria .. sive omnes spurcitias impiorum *Clovesho* 364 (cf. Bonif. *Ep.* 78); ariolus, ~us *GlC* A 800; ~os, *uuitgan Ib.* D 337; legimus in historiis veterum ~orum tres fuisse philosophos quorum unusquisque Hermes vocabatur Rob. Angl. *Alch. pref.* 509.

3 divine, belonging to or emanating from God (Christian or Jewish). **b** (of persons) inspired by God.

Britannia insula .. ~a .. ponderatrice librata Gildas *EB* 3; Lucas .., / lucida divino qui scripsit dogmata libro Aldh. *VirgV* 504; ~a se juvante gratia Bede *HE* IV 13; *Ib.* I 25 (v. daemonicus 1); **a758** (12c) ad ~am pervenire clementiam *CS* 260; **859** in nomine almo trino ~o *CS* 497; ut pareatis ~is disciplinis [AS: *godcundum larum*] Ælf. *Coll.* 103; sicut eidem .. postmodum ~a revelatione innotuit Osb. *V. Dunst.* 3; ~am naturam .. asserimus impassibilem Anselm (*CurD* 8) II 59; in ~is legibus et secularibus institutis (*Leg. Hen. proem.* 1) *GAS* 547; omnia intelligibilia actu intellectus ~i habent 'esse intelligibile' Duns *Ord.* III 160; **1343** miseracione ~a (*Lit. Cardinalium*) Ad. Mur. *Chr.* 129 (cf. ib.: ~a providencia). **b** s**946** ~us Dunstanus in remotioribus constitutus .., spiritum sibi solito influentem hauriens, regis obitum intellexit *Chr. Rams.* 18; cum ~issimo legislatore .. vices ascendendi in montem et descendendi ad planitiem .. frequentans Ad. Marsh *Ep.* 8 p. 89 (cf. ib. 172: ~um Moysen); ~issimus Moyses fontem originalem in paradiso terrestri erupisse .. testatur *Ps.*-Gros. *Summa* 621.

4 directed or offered to God. **b** (as sb. n. pl.) divine service. **c** (of persons) consecrated, devoted to God, ecclesiastical. **d** (as sb. m.) bishop or priest.

ad tantum .. ~ae contemplationis culmen .. surrexit Aldh. *VirgP* 22; virguncluae ~o servitio subjugatae *Ib.* 52; cotidie psalterium totum in memoriam ~ae laudis decantaret Bede *HE* III 26; **948** ~ae servitutis officio mancipatus *CS* 869; in his sanctis diebus Quadragesimae aliquid nobis augendum ~ae servituti [AS p. 406: *godcundum þeowdome*] .. censuimus *RegulC* 35; s**1214** ~a mysteria (v. celebrare 4a); **1226** servitii ~i honorem quem Deo devotus impendit M. Par. *Maj.* III 113; sacerdotes .. et Levite .. horis statutis et debitis eo convenerunt, ut ~is vacarent obsequiis *Mir. J. Bev. C* 346; **1333** volentes ~a officia in ecclesia domus monialium .. frequentari *RScot* 257a; dum naves Anglice, ~is tamen serviciis prius, prout maria sinebant, perfectis .., in bellum navale se prepararent *Ps.*-Elmh. *Hen. V* 32; **1545** horarum ~arum solemnia *Conc. Scot.* I ccxciv. **b** s**1132** ecclesiam hanc interdicimus et monachos in ea commorantes .. suspendimus a ~is Serlo Gram. *Mon. Font.* 9; **1207** concesserunt ei .. capellam in curia sua et ibi audire ~a cum ibi venerint *Kelso* I 207; **1252** ut .. Deo laudabili[u]s officiari valeant in ~is Gros. *Ep.* 131; *EHR* XXVI 731 (v. celebrare 4a); s**1378** statim monachi cessaverunt a ~is *Eul. Hist. Cont.* III 342; **1448** monitus est quod decetero .. ecclesie sue deserviat in ~is *Eng. Clergy* 231; **1526** inhibemus quod .. seculares sive laici cantores .. tempore ~orum ab ipso choro conventuali excludantur (*Vis. Thame*) *EHR* III 713. **c 858** ego E. rex cum consensu .. meorum secularium optimatum ~orumque personarum *CS* 496; **956** ego Æ. Uuintaniensis aecclesiae ~us speculator proprium sigillum impressi *CS* 961; Ord. Vit. XII 25 (v. 2 cultor 2a). **d 956** (14c) ego Æ. Wintaniensis aecclesiae ~us proprium sigillum impressi *CS* 958; a**1165** testibus .. magistro Radulpho ~o *Cart. Godstow* f. 189.

5 godlike.

consistit felicitas in operacione nobilissime et ~ioris potencie quam habemus R. Bury *Phil.* 2. 35.

6 theological. **b** (as sb. n. pl.; acad.) theology, divinity.

unam diximus esse scienciam ~am meliorem philosophia Kilwardby *OS* 16; **1358** fiunt .. facultatis ~e plurimi professores indigni, quam nequaquam pro posse pedetentim pertranseunt *MunAcOx* 208; **1549** ~arum litterarum professor *Conc. Scot.* II 83. **b** ut .. solito sollic[ic]ius .. ~orum studiis valeat invigilare Ad. Marsh *Ep.* 214; si .. papa asserit non esse in ~is tres personas distinctas Ockham *Dial.* 535; quis .. dubitat hanc esse heresim pessimam: 'Filius in ~is non est genitus de Patre ..?' Conway *Def. Mend.* 1425 (*recte* 1325); **1438** lego .. domino J. T. .. xx m. ad scolatizandum apud Cantibrigg' in ~is per iiij annos *Reg. Cant.* II 563.

Divionensis v. Dunio. **divis** v. dives 2a. **divisa** v. dividere 8, 9c, 10b.

divisabilis [cf. divisare 2a], 'devisable'. *V. et. divisibilis* 2.

1408 omnia tenementa in eadem civitate [*Exeter*] fuerunt et sunt ~ia et legabilia *Cl* 258 m. 30; **1431** omnia tenementa in eisdem burgo et civitate fuerunt et adhuc existunt per testamenta legabilia et ~ia *Cl* 282 m. 15.

divisamentum [LL = *divided part*], **a** device, badge; *cf. dividere* 10b. **b** device, contrivance.

a 1436 liberatam nostram .. devisamenti (v. 2 collare 3d). **b 1571** per .. fraudulenta devisamenta (v. covinosus).

divisare [cf. OF *diviser*]

1 to divide, demarcate, form a boundary.

1197 dedit .. terram que jacet inter cheminum regium et portam que fuit Ricardi D., sicut due sepes Roberti M. devisant (*Fine*) *Pipe* 167.

2 a to 'devise', bequeath; *v. et. dividere* 9. **b** to devise, contrive, plan; *v. et. dividere* 10.

a 1588 cui .. aliquod hujusmodi divisum seu aliqua hujusmodi devisa forent legata seu devisata a tempore mortis alicujus hujusmodi persone sic legantis seu devisantis terras seu tenementa sua *Entries* 431. **b 1554** prout consiliarii eorundem H. et F. in lege eruditi devisarent *Pat* 872 m. 19; **1564** omnimodos rationabiles actus et acta rem et res, quales devisati seu advisati forent per eruditum consilium *Entries* 691b; **1571** *Entries* 207b (v. contrivare); **1573** (v. compassare).

divisatio, 'devise', bequest.

idem J. eundem R. ad dictam devisacionem messuagiorum sive tenementorum .. in curia Christianitatis indebite probandam .. machinabatur *Entries* 486b.

divisia v. dividere 9c.

divisibilis [LL]

1 divisible; **b** (as sb. n.). **c** separable. **d** (leg.) partible.

impossibile est ut [illa substantia] qualibet sectione sit ~is Anselm (*Mon.* 27) I 45; Gros. 2 (v. divisibilitas); J. Blund *An.* 332 (v. componere 4e); Hales *Qu.* 230 (v. 1 dolor 1); Bacon *Tert.* 170 (v. commetiri b); cum ipsi [abstrahentes] per intellectum dividant que secundum rem non sunt divisa nec eciam ~ia Kilwardby *OS* 195; in quacumque mensura ~i potest aliqua virtus aliquid facere, potest major virtus facere in minore Duns *Ord.* VII 383; quod idem sit caro Christi et panis secundum speciem, et sic secundum substanciam indivisibilis, secundum speciem ~is (Tyss.) *Ziz.* 152. **b** natura indivisibilis spiritualis nullam comparationem nec proportionem habebit ad indivisibile vel ~e in quanto corporali Bacon *Tert.* 173; ~e non habet entitatem actualissimam sive existenciam actualissimam Duns *Ord.* II 376. **c** passio est vox passibilis conjuncta et unita et ~ia discernens Aldh. *PR* 141. **d** quod corporale est et de natura sui ~e inter coheredes et participes, de communi consensu eorum remanere poterit indivisum Bracton 208; querunt metaphisici si dominium istud sit †dimissibile [? l. divissibile] vel †indimissibile Wycl. *Versut.* 100 (cf. ib.: istud totale dominium seculare est partitum).

2 devisable. *V. et. divisabilis, cf. dividere* 9.

1588 omnia terre et tenementa in .. civitate [*London*] sunt .. devisibilia et devisa, legabilia et legata per testamentum *Entries* 431 (cf. ib. 143: ~ia ac divisa).

3 dividing, (w. *murus*) party-wall.

1300 cementarius juratus est justam consideracionem facere omnibus hominibus .., de muris lapideis inter vicinos, ~ibus et indivisibilibus, ruinosis *MGL* II 100.

divisibilitas, divisibility.

est motus divisibilis ~ate temporis, et secundum hanc ~atem dicitur motus duplus ad alium qui duplo mensuratur tempore Gros. 2; materia radix est ~atis et partibilitatis Bacon VIII 40; Kilwardby *OS* 518 (v. componibilitas b); punctus .. constituit substanciam continui et non retinet suum formale in eo, sc. indivisibilitatem, propter hoc quod suum contrarium, sc. ~as, est essenciale continuo Siccav. *PN* 99; in ipsa [eternitate] nulla ~as, nulla majoritas, nulla minoritas .. Bradw. *CD* 826b; ~as seu divisio, quod idem est .., alia est qua terminus dividitur in sua significata, alia qua totum integrale dividitur in suas partes integrales, et tercia qua totum dividitur in suas partes subjectivas Wycl. *Quaest. Log.* 293.

divisim [LL], separately, severally; **b** (w. ref. to strips in open field). **c** (gram. or log.) disjunctively. **d** alternatively.

in omnibus furtis aut solus compella[tu]s est aut plures, servi vel liberi, ~im vel permixtim (*Leg. Hen.* 59. 22) *GAS* 580; **1225** iter arripiatis ad hec perficienda .. conjunctim vel ~im, prout expedire videritis *Pat* 568; c**1242** (v. collatio 3a); hec nomina predicantur de omnibus personis [Trinitatis] simul et ~im, singulariter et non pluraliter Bart. Angl. I 6; **1258** presentibus cirographis sigilla sua ~im apposuerunt *Cart. Bath A* 71; Bacon XV 342 (v. conjunctim c); *Cust. Cant.* 161 (v. conjunctim a); c**1340** seipsos conjunctim et quemlibet eorum in solidum et ~im *FormOx* 123; **1440** ea que ipsis, ~im aut communiter, vertere possunt in promocionem Bekynton I 85. **b 1430** tenent .. j bovatam terre, viz. xij acras terre, jacentes ~im in xij culturis *Feod. Durh.* 22; **1431** sex acras et dim. ~im jacentes in campis de Peterburgh *Cl* 282 m. 21*d.*; **1485** illas .. v acras .. terre cum suis pertinenciis ~im jacentes .. in campo vocato Upton Feld' (*Ch. West Ham*) *EHR* III 320. **c** cum apostolus dicit se desiderare dissolvi et esse cum Christo, aut intelligit ~im hanc vocem .. aut conjunctim; si ~im .. S. Langton *Quaest.* 149; si plures condiciones ascripte sint donationi conjunctim, ut si dicatur 'si illud et illud factum sit', omnibus est parendum; si ~im .., cuilibet vel alteri eorum satis est obtemperare Bracton 19; *Ib.* 205 (v. conjunctim c); 'si intelligere ipsum est alicujus, ergo et velle ejusdem' non sequitur, sed tantummodo sequitur quia est velle, quod quidem velle est aliquid ejusdem, quia intelligendum est 'ejusdem' ita quod ~im inferri potest, non conjunctim propter accidens Duns *Ord.* II 187; ita usus facti potest separari ab utroque dominio ~im, non tamen ab utroque conjunctim Ockham *Pol.* I 332; dicendo hec omnia debere intellegi in sensu composicionis semper conjunctim, non in sensu divisionis sive ~im Bradw. *CD* 757e. **d 1429** lego Thome W. .. gladium meum .. vel togam meam .. per ipsum ~im eligendam *Reg. Cant.* II 387.

divisio [CL]

1 cutting in pieces.

Ric. Med. *Anat.* 212, *Alph.* 187 (v. anatomia).

2 division (into parts); **b** (math.); **c** (rhet.); **d** (metr. or sim.); **e** (mus.).

8 .. ~ones, *todal WW*; Anselm I 36 (v. compositio 2a); unicuique composito respondet sua ~o, quoniam quecumque erit componere erit resolvere J. Blund *An.* 332; proprie loquendo non est ~o nisi ubi fuerit multitudo substantiarum Hales *Sent.* I 204; quarum [arteriarum] nulla est ~o, et .. per earum continuitatem fumositas .. diffunditur *Quaest. Salern.* C 26; dum dividis lineam per equalia, remanet potencia ~onis in partibus diversis .. et hec ~o in infinitum procedit Kilwardby *OS* 172. **b** Adel. *Alch.* 2 p. 21 (v. duplatio); erit radix substantie 6, unam ~onis partem numeri decem exprimens Rob. Angl. *Alg.* 104; capitulum 2^m de multiplicacione, ~one et radicum extraccione Killingworth *Alg.* 714. **c** partitio est rerum ad causam ipsam pertinentium ~o Alcuin *Rhet.* 23; [raciocinacio rhetorica] habet sex partes, sc. proemium .., narracionem, particionem sive ~onem, confirmacionem, confutacionem .., conclusionem Kilwardby *OS* 589. **d** hypodiastoli est ~o compositarum litterarum propter ambiguitates Aldh. *PR* 141; quodsi .. scandendi ratio et caesurarum ~o per cola et commata sequestrare compulerit *Ib.* 113. **e** due breves igitur inequales manent, nisi per ~onem modi aliter distinguatur Hauboys 420; punctus ~onis dividit longas imperficiendo maximas, semibreves imperficiendo breves, minimas imperficiendo semibreves Hothby *Cant. Fig.* 331.

3 section, part: **a** (of book); **b** (of human body). **c** (bot.) segment.

a s**1059** in Decretis conscribitur, ~one II *Eul. Hist.* I 382 (= Higd. VI 27: distinccione). **b** [Ricardi I] brachia productiora .., nihilominus tibiarum longa ~o totiusque corporis dispositione congrua species digna imperio *Itin. Ric.* II 5. **c** *Alph.* 2 (v. dividere 2c).

4 distinction, analysis, classification.

qua ~onis specie idem pes sequestratur? amphimacrum sescupla ~one partimur Aldh. *PR* 122; Bacon XV 178 (v. collectio 5); [modi] ad diffinitionum vel ~onum assignationes in per se disserendo expeditiores Balsh. *AD rec.* 2 122; qualiter hec [virtutum] ~o trimembris et illa [vitiorum] septimembris est? Hales *Sent.* II 407; cum motus secundum quid sit consonancium causa, patet consequens ~o in liquidas et mutas *Ps.*-Gros. *Gram.* 20; Rob. Angl. (II) *Sph.* 13 (v. 1 clima 1a); modus omnis sciencie in tribus consistit, .. sc. in definicione, ~one, et colleccione Kilwardby *OS* 649; a philosophis intellectus ponitur potencia distincta a potenciis sensitivis .. propter composicionem et ~onem Duns *Ord.* III 209; Wycl. *Quaest. Log.* 293 (v. divisibilitas).

5 separation, parting. **b** estrangement, dissension, disunion.

c**802** festinat hora ~onis inter fratres, separationis inter amicos Alcuin *Ep.* 252; unum cum sponso suo mater est ecclesia et membra sua non ~oni sed unitati parit Lanfr. *Cel. Conf.* 632c; unitas est rei in se indivisio et ab aliis ~o, numerus autem unitatum colleccio Kilwardby *OS* 271. **b 1255** ~ones et dissensiones in civitatibus .. Wasconie existentes, quas pacificare .. volumus *RGasc* I sup. 40; s**1300** facta est ~o in conventu Graystanes 23; quando ex questione fidei oriuntur ~ones, secte et schismata Ockham *Dial.* 619; s**1406** ad redintegrandam ecclesie ~onem *Chr. S. Alb.* 3; s**1451** quod pulex est in aure .. hoc ~o seu discordia fertur esse inter fratres in eleccione *Reg. Whet.* I 8.

6 a delimitation. **b** boundary. **c** (leg.) court held at boundary; *v. et. dividere* 8f.

a 1108 si amodo exurgat placitum de ~one terrarum vel de preoccupatione *Regesta* 892; s**1276** facta est contencio .. inter regem A. Scocie et regem E. Anglie pro ~one marchiarum Scocie *Plusc.* VII 29 (= Fordun *Cont.* X 36: super diversis marchiis utriusque regni). **b** a**1130** dedit .. omnem terram quam .. habebat .. a fossato quod est juxta domum O. fabri—et vadit in directo usque ad majorem aquam ~o—omnem illam terram sc. .. a .. fossato usque ad ~ones de K. (*Conventio*) *Chr. Rams.* 264; c**1180** usque ad ~ones et metas que posite sunt inter pratum predictorum W. .. et R. .. et pratum monachorum

Act. Hen. II II 153; **c1230** ij bovatas terre .. cum metis et ~onibus et aisiamentis cum quibus .. Hugo eas tenuit *FormA* 193; **1305** balleucam ville de B. .. et ejusdem balleuce metas et ~ones *RGasc* III 478. **c** ~ones sciranum regis proprie cum judicio iiij chiminorum regalium sunt ~ones hundredorum .. comitibus [et] vicecomitibus cum judicio comitatus (*Leg. Ed.*) *GAS* 640.

7 **a** sharing out, apportionment (of land). **b** (allotted) portion (of land).

a erat inde seisitus quando facta est ~o terrarum inter regem et comitem *DB* II 150; *GAS* 107 (v. dividere 9a). **b** Hugo de M. tenet de episcopo j *solin* vacuae terrae extra ~onem suam, et adjacuit N. m[anerio] quod habet intra suam ~onem *DB* I 11v.; haec ~o [extendit] a mari usque Jernesmua *Ib.* II 371v.; qui ~onem habet juxta terram regis claudat contra regem .. (*Inst. Cnuti*) *GAS* 614 (v. aisia); **c1180** (v. dividere 9c).

divisios- v. divitios-.

divisive, analytically, w. ref. to particulars.

ista proposicio 'possibile est continuum dividi secundum quodlibet signum' .. posset distingui secundum quod signum posset distribuere ~e vel collective DUNS *Ord.* VII 313; iste terminus 'omnis' distribuit quandoque pro speciebus, quandoque pro individuis, quandoque stat collective, quandoque ~e; sed iste terminus 'singularis' distribuit semper ~e pro individuis WYCL. *Log.* I 86.

divisivus [LL], **a** (?) solvent. **b** distinctive, analytical, classificatory. **c** delimitative.

a digeratur .. materia cum oximelle †~o vel diuretico prius, post squillitico vel rafanino GILB. II 111. 1 (cf. ib. VI 281. 2: pellem arietinam .. coque †~am [? l. divisam] in frusta). **b** opposita .. sunt genera corpus et spiritus, opposite et eorum species homo et anima; opposite ergo erunt eorum differentie generum .. ~e, specierum .. constitutive PULL. *Sent.* 737D; si vegetabile esset differentia ~a anime, tunc esset aliqua anima in corpore que non vegetaret corpus .. J. BLUND *An.* 39; differentie ~e generum separant species essentialiter differentes BACON II 50; ex genere primo et una aliqua contrariarum differenciarum ~arum speciem quodammodo .. constitui planum est *Ps.*-GROS. *Summa* 311; sermo .. ~us primus est secundum construccionem; unde, cum dico animalium aliud racionale, aliud irracionale, ab actu dividendi dependet tota construccio et perfectus est sermo ab inclinacione dividendi *Ps.*-GROS. *Gram.* 61; KILWARDBY *OS* 529 (v. collectivus); BRADW. *CD* 221A (v. compositivus b); voliciones generum et specierum causantur ex volicionibus diffinicionum et ~arum parcium WYCL. *Dom. Div.* 171; LINACRE *Emend. Lat.* f. 4 (v. distributivus). **c** **1538** marchias seu lapidea aut alia signa distinctiva et ~a vetera inter terras nostras de R. .. et terras de L. .. infixa et statuta .. furtive evulserunt *Form. S. Andr.* II 57.

divisor [CL]

1 divider. **b** (math.) divisor. **c** boundary.

~or, *dælere* ÆLF. *Gl.*; SICCAV. *PN* 100 (v. dividere 4b). **b** ultima ~oris sub ultima dividendi ponitur, si minor vel equalis fuerit numerus ADEL. *Alch.* 1 p. 20; cum constet quod, multiplicato illo quod provenit ex divisione cum ~ore, redeat census tuus ROB. ANGL. *Alg.* 152. **c** Loagrie Tameris divisor Cornubieque NECKAM *DS* III 905.

2 (w. ref. to *Luke* xii 14): **a** apportioner. **b** disrupter, separator.

a auditis aperte Christum in temporalibus nec judicem nec ~orem constitutum OCKHAM *Disp.* 14. **b** negat se Dominus hominum esse ~orem, ad quos .. secum .. pacificandos venerat. .. solus autem fraternitatis ~or et auctor dissensionis est ille de quo supra [*Luke* xi 23] dicitur BEDE *Luke* 491.

3 'deviser', architect or sim.

1540 devisor (*Ac. Sandgate*) *Med. Mason* 192 (cf. ib. 147).

divisum v. dividere 8a, 9c.

divisura [CL], breach, cleft. **b** segmentation.

fissura, scissura, ~a *Gl. Leid.* 13. 4. **b** falangion .. habet .. flores albos similes lilio cum multa ~a *Alph.* 61.

divitas, godhead or (?) *f.l.*

the Godhede, deitas, ~as [?l. divinitas], numen, majestas *CathA.*

divitiae, ditiae [CL], **~ia,** riches, wealth; **b** (fig.).

laudantes deos suos, i. e. sensus, extollentes ~ias GILDAS *EB* 71; ALDH. *VirgV* 1742 (v. conculcare 1c); vitam .. monachicam cunctis regni ~iis et honoribus praeferens BEDE *HE* IV 11; **8..** ~ias, *weolan WW*; donis innumerabilibus in omni genere terrestris ~iae ASSER *Alf.* 81; **948** (12c) transitorias largiri Christo ~ias *CS* 860; de felicitate .. locuti sunt, et dico de vera, non de voluptate Epicurea neque de ditiis neque de honoribus BACON I 14; regni principes, qui dono ipsius [E. Confessoris] .. et tot dicia[s] et predia se gloriantur habere CIREN. II 319; **s1405** (v. depauperatio 1a). **b** GIR. *Symb.* I 9 (v. dilucidare a); **1231** de ~iis aule celestis erit rerum pretiosissima lux nullis admixta tenebris GROS. *Ep.* 6.

divitiositas, riches.

ryches, copia .., divicie, †divisiositas .. *CathA.*

divitiosus, rich.

riche, copiosus .., dives, †divisiosus [v. l. diciosus] .. *CathA.*

divitus v. diutius. **divolvere** v. devolvere 6. **divorium** v. deverium b.

divortiare [LL], to divorce, dissolve marriage: **a** (intr. or w. *matrimonium*); **b** (w. pers. obj.).

a proposuit rex [Hen. II] hanc puellam [Rosamundam] duxisse, qua de causa H. cardinalem ad ~iandum inter ipsum et reginam A. invitavit HIGD. VII 23; **s1200** solemniter ~iatum est inter regem J. et uxorem suam *Ib.* 32 (= *Meaux* I 338: ~iatum est matrimonium). **b** hic [W. de Douglas, ob. **1353**] reliquit .. unicam filiam .., que nupsit Reginaldo Mure ..; sed postea per quasdam causas exquisitas ~iata fuit ab eodem FORDUN *GA* 170*n.*; **s1461** ut sufficeret uxorem ad tempus ~iatam restituere nobis iterum *Reg. Whet.* I 394; **1526** consistorii officialis .. Robertum et Matildam ab invicem separavit et devorciavit *Reg. Heref.* 179; **1533** principem Hen. VIII et .. dominam Katherinam .. ab invicem seperamus et ~iamus (*Decr. Archiep. Cant.*) *Foed.* XIV 464a; non licet personis .. nec propter adulterium nec propter saevitiam ~iatis aut separatis ad secundas convolare nuptias viventibus prioribus maritis vel conjugibus *Praxis* 113.

divortiatorius, effective of divorce.

1460 sentencie ~ie prius late .., ex fictis causis habite .., annullentur *Reg. Cant.* 91.

divortio [LL], separation.

c1260 admirans qua consciencia .. prior noster a consorcio vestro et fratrum vobiscum commorancium, quod michi est amara .. et fere inconsolabilis ~o, .. conatus est .. [me] separare *Ann. Durh.* app. 105.

divortium [CL]

1 by-road, devious route, out-of-the-way place.

~ia, diverticula, *mistlice woge wegas* ÆLF. *Gl.*; invinit consilium .., se velle sc. per quedam ~ia in eadem nocte egredi et infra nemus .. usque ad diem delitere G. MON. I 15; **s796** rex Merce .. regem eorum [Centensium] .. per latibula et ~ia delitescentem comprehendit H. HUNT. *HA* IV 27; **1163** comitem Flandrensem non inveni, et in eo querendo ~ia facere mihi periculosum et vobis non expedire credebam (*Lit. Anon.*) *Becket Mat.* V 58; facta per ~ium via T. MON. *Will.* II 14 (cf. deflectere 1b); **s1386** Londonienses .., meticulosi ut mures .., requirunt ~ia, scrutantur latebras *V. Ric. II* 73.

2 divorce. **b** (fig.) separation. **c** partition (of territory).

cum uxor sua displicuit fecit sibi ab ea .. ~ium *V. Greg.* p. 97; si non obstinatus conjugis animus ~ium negaret BEDE *HE* IV 11; difortium, deflexio, a devertendo; inde inter viros et feminas defortia dicuntur quando divertuntur *GlC* D 172 (cf. ib. 233); **s1154** (v. divertere 3c); **1160** cum ex apostolico rescripto fuerit ~ium celebratum J. SAL. *Ep.* 89 (131 p. 229); **s1200** factum est ~ium inter J. regem Anglie et Hawis uxorem suam R. HOWD. IV 119; **s1231** (v. celebrare 2b); ~ium et repudium in hoc conveniunt quod separatio est ab uxore HALES *Qu.* 1167; BRACTON 298b (v. compaternitas); **1445** commissio ad cognoscend' in causa matrimoniali et ~ii *Stat. Linc.* II 489. **b** huc sponsum sponsa non sequitur; celebratoque locali ~io, consortes orationum non effecti, in hac parte jam ad imparia judicantur GIR. *TH* II 4; o quoties .. sanguinolentum ~ium ipsam interrumpit desponsationem! *Ib.* III 22; **c1381** sic corpus Christi varium / membrorumque divortium (*In Lollardos* 31) *Pol. Poems* I 241; **1450** de ultimo corporis et anime ~io *Regim. Princ.* 93. **c** lampades martyrum .., quorum nunc .. passionum loca, si non lugubri ~io barbarorum quam plurima .. civibus adimerentur, .. intuentium mentibus ardorem divinae caritatis incuterent GILDAS *EB* 10.

divulgare [CL], to divulge, announce, disseminate, publish; **b** (w. indir. qu.). **c** (p. ppl.) renowned. *V. et. evulgare. Cf. dimulgare.*

plurimus idcirco devulgans semina famae / virtutum rumor ALDH. *VirgV* 466; **1024** his vero vocabulis ~ari videntur termini agrorum viz. praedictorum *CD* 741; **1166** fama ~ante (v. 2 discessus a); **1179** (v. dissolutio 4a); maxime insanit qui ostentat et tanquam portentum suam scientiam nititur devulgare BACON *Maj.* III 23; nunc est sic ~atum [ME: *se wide ibrocht forð*] per alios quod ego hoc negare non possum *AncrR* 24; OCKHAM *Dial.* 450 (v. divulgatio). **b** **1401** in gilda aula .. devulgatum fuit coram communitate tunc congregata qualiter magister et fratres hospitalis S. Leonardi fecerunt seperalitatem de communi pastura *Mem. York* I 179. **c** (ÆTHELWALD) *Carm. Aldh.* 2. 21 (v. cunctamen); te .. ob enormitatem ~atae peritiae .. secernam B. *V. Dunst.* 1; devulgatissimum, i. opinatissimum, *þone hlisfulestan GlH* D 364.

divulgatio [LL], announcement, publication. *V. et. evulgatio. Cf. dimulgatio.*

nonne .. offendiculum faciam .. audientibus .. nominis mei ~onem, quod episcopi vocabulo .. nuncupabar? EDDI 47; **s758** [Cuthbertus] precepit ne aliqua ~o infirmitatis ejus vel mortis fieret .. donec corpus ipsius sepulture traditum esset GERV. CANT. *AP* 345; hec veritas 'ecclesia universalis non potest errare' non est apud omnes Christianos .. divulgata. .. si hec racio procederet, videretur quod ~o apud Christianos esset majoris auctoritatis quam divina scriptura OCKHAM *Dial.* 450; **s1381** se .. ante ~onem charte .. hec .. obtinuisse WALS. *HA* I 482.

divus [CL]

1 (as sb. n.) sky, open air; *cf. dius* 2. **b** radiance.

stabant ad orandum mulieres .. sub ~o vel, si tempestas non sinebat, proxima .. tecta subibant BEDE *Kings* 729; sub ~o, sub caelo puro *GlC* S 673; **10..** sub ~o, *under lyfte WW*; sub aquis indifferenter et sub ~o tria hec animalium genera spiritum trahunt GIR. *IK* II 3. **b** recubat monachus sub martyre, martyr vero sub ~o luciflue columne CIREN. I 358 (cf. SAMSON *Mir. Edm.* 120: Christus exhibet martyri suo polo radiante luminis officium).

2 (Classical) divine (being), god; **b** (as title of emperor).

~o, deo *GlC* D 245; ~i, i. dii *GlH* D 743; **10..** ~i, *godes WW*; divos / presago jubet ore sequi J. EXON. *BT* IV 302 (cf. ib. II 369: hic edita partu / divum pandit iter); quos immortales colis, Alexandria, divos / mors eterna tenet NIG. *Paul.* f. 48. 383. **b** ~us, imperator qui post mortem quasi deus factus est *GlC* D 305; facti sunt ~i indigetes aut .. heroes, quos nec etiam humana sorte dignos Romanorum perfidia reputavit J. SAL. *Pol.* 496A; ~us etiam imperator dici solet, quasi divinus, eo quod in tribus diis quoque similis esse debeat, pietate sc. et patientia et beneficiorum largitione GIR. *PI* I 19 p. 103.

3 (Christian), divine, holy, sacred; *cf. dius* 1. **b** (applied to Christian ruler). **c** blessed, saint.

B. *V. Dunst.* 1 (v. 1 despicere 2d); pre ceteris piissimus ille et Christianissimus ~e recordationis rex Francorum Ludovicus H. BOS. *LM* 1309C; mixtura sanguinis / agne divique numinis LEDREDE *Carm.* 29. 6; **1381** plebs crismate diva (v. dux 2a); **1499** monachis ~e Cantuariensis ecclesie *Cant. Coll. Ox.* II 228. **b** tractum est hinc nomen quo principes virtutum titulis et vere fidei luce presignes se ~os audeant, nedum gaudeant, appellari, veteri quidem consuetudine etiam in vitio et adversus fidem catholicam obtinente J. SAL. *Pol.* 496A (cf. 2b supra); **s1487** Henrici cano Septimi triumphos,/ divi principis (*Vers.*) ANDRÉ *Hen. VII* 53. **c** non enim, cum ~us Paulus Athenienses alloqueretur, unius Dei auctoritatem probare intendit, sed mediis philosophicis .. deorum multitudinem improbavit *Ps.*-GROS. *Summa* 287 (cf. ib.: supradictus ~issimus Paulus); ~o Thome Cantuariensi vota persolvens ANDRÉ *Hen. VII* 60; **1506** missa ~e Virginis Marie celebrata *Reg. Aberd.* II 102; [coenobium] regulae ~i Benedicti professorum FERR. *Kinloss* 15; divi Petri P. VERG. IV 90 (v. denarius 5a); quis nescit ~um Stephanum? JEWEL *Apol.* A3v. (*recte* A2v.); viri [sc. Aldelmi] tamen memoria permanet, utpote qui in ~os relatus CAMD. *Br.* 210.

diwerca v. daiwerca a. **dixameter** v. diameter 2c. **dixionarius** v. dictionarius. **dixtus** v. discus 4b. **dizena** v. decena 3a.

doageria [OF *doagiere*], dowager.

1518 dabunt donacionem propter nuptias sive doarium .. qualem et quantam .. Maria .. regis Anglie soror et Francie ~ia .. possidet (*DipDocE* 817) *Foed.* XIII 635a.

doaressa, doweress, dowager.

1520 Annam dominam Roos, dowaressam et executricem testamenti .. Georgii Mannours, militis, nuper domini Roos *Rutland MSS View Ac. Bailiffs Yorks* p. 4.

doarium, ~ia [OF *doaire* < dotarium], dower, marriage portion. *V. et. dotarium* 1.

c1160 confirmasse .. donationes que .. date sunt ecclesie .. de Fulcardimonte [*Norm.*]: .. ex dono Radulfi R. et B. uxoris ejus .. ~ium uxoris Enguerranni de S. ad campartum solum *Act. Hen. II* I 307; **a1166** servicium totius dowarii quod Jordanus frater suus dedit uxori sue (*Fine*) *Eng. Feudalism* 262; **1176** Willelmus .. r. c. de xl s. ut noverca sua non habeat ~ium nisi rationabile *Pipe* 111; **1177** quia nostra dignum est celsitudine ut tam nobile .. conjugium decenti dodario debeat honorari .., damus et in dodarium concedimus .. uxori nostre .. in demanio civitatem Montis S. Angeli (*Ch. W. Regis Siciliae*) *G. Hen. II* I 170; **c1180** terram que dicitur terra duarii *Melrose* 154 (cf. ib. 287 [**c1250**]: terram quam .. tenuit in ~ium); **c1200** ego Emma .. uxor Eudonis .. dedi .. unum toftum in N. quod est de duaria mea *Reg. Ant. Linc.* IV 196; **c1200** ego Editha .. concilio et voluntate R. mariti mei, de duario meo de W. dedi fratribus in O. .. viventibus dominium illud *MonA* V 404b; **1332** cum .. procuratores .. comitis [Gelrie] .. sorori nostre nomine donacionis propter nupcias dotem seu duariam assignassent (*Pat*) *Foed.* IV 509a; **1525** de dicti dotalicii, douarii, sive donacionis propter nuptias possessione (*DipDocE* 903) *Ib.* XIV 84a.

dobare, ~atio, ~ator, ~iare v. daub-. **doberius** v. daubarius. **doblettus** v. dublettus 4.

docēre [CL]

1 to teach, inform (w. person taught in acc. or unspec.); **b** (w. *scholam*); **c** (w. indir. qu. or acc. & inf.); **d** (w. abstr. subj.); **e** (w. *de*); **f** (absol.).

videamus quid Dominus .. ad .. sacerdotes .. non bene populum .. ~entes .. loquatur GILDAS *EB* 76; Hēlēna docens regem sermone futura ALDH. *VirgV* 613; ea que ad fidem .. pertinent et verbo cunctos ~ebat et opere BEDE *HE* III 26; cum .. corda hominum ea quae nec per se nec per aliam creaturam sciunt ~entur ANSELM (*Orig. Pecc.* 11) II 153; sunt quedam verba transitiva que regunt accusativum virtute cause sine apposicione preposicionis simul cum accusativo transitivo, ut '~eo te grammaticam' *Ps.*-GROS. *Gram.* 64; **1431** ita quod nulle sciencie prohibite ~eantur *StatOx* 236. **b** **1504** scolam cantationis ~ebit dietim, pueros inibi in cantu Gregoriano .. erudiendo *Reg. Glasg.* 509. **c** vis .. ~eam te quomodo cureris? BEDE *HE* III 12; quidam [tumorem] abscidendum esse ~ebant *Ib.* IV 30 p. 279; ~tus ab eodem qualiter petitionem facere debeat LANFR. *Const.* 168; R. CANT. *Malch.* II 376 (v. cura 2a); **1219** (v. documentum 2a); angelus .. docet qualiter / fetari debeat WALT. WIMB. *Carm.* 102; ~ens [ME: *teacheð*] quomodo homo debeat in exterioribus conversari *AncrR* 5; s**1381** (v. curare 5d). **d** ALDH. *VirgV* 132 (v. duplus 1a); quibus et qualiter sit miserendum, eum [judicem] ~eant merita vel demerita personarum BRACTON 107b; **1410** (v. confluentia d). **e** s**1324** citavit papa ducem Bavarie, in imperatorem electum, ut .. veniret ad curiam et de eleccione et de jure suo ~eret [v. l. diceret] AD. MUR. *Chr.* 42. **f** ut ecclesiastica ~et historia BEDE *HE* III 25 p. 186; qui dedit prava consilia .. vel qui prave ~uit HALES *Sent.* IV 260; verbum caro factum est, angelo docente LEDREDE *Carm.* 59. 5.

2 to teach (how), instruct: **a** (w. inf.); **b** (w. *ad* & gd. or gdv.). **c** (w. *ad*) to show the way (to).

a barbara qui docuit doctrinis agmina sacris / credere ALDH. *CE* 4. 8. 3; ~uit eos piscando victum quaerere BEDE *HE* IV 13; ut ~eas [AS: *þu tæce*] nos loqui Latialiter recte ÆLF. *Coll.* 89; suum [fratris ad suscipiendos hospites deputati] est .. ~ere eos [novicios] priorem petitionem facere LANFR. *Const.* 154; c**1180** qui de se amplius quam oportuit confidebat, ~etur in se humiliari A. TEWK. *Ep.* 5; sic olim dominus vigil in verbere, / doctus conterere doctusque tundere WALT. WIMB. *Carm.* 35; BACON IX 88 (v. curativus a); non ~et determinare utrum .. KILWARDBY *OS* 507. **b** **1284** (v. 1 copare b); **1396** [Christus] ~uit homines ad diligendum inimicos .. et non ad occidendum eos *Conc.* III 222b. **c** **1219** cognoscens se esse latronem, appellat Walterum .. de societate, sc. quod ipse .. ~uit eum ad domum .. Hugonis .. et dixit quod ibi potuit lucrari *CurR* VIII 180.

3 to teach (w. dependent cl. and dat. of person).

quemadmodum vestimenta pontificalia sacerdotibus .. ornamenta quoque fieri famulo tuo Moysi per xl dies ~uisti EGB. *Pont.* 43; quantum differtur terre promotio sancte / hereticis claudis carmina clauda docent GARL. *Tri. Eccl.* 6.

4 (p. ppl.) learned, skilled. **b** (as sb. n. pl.) things taught, doctrines.

sacerdotes habet Britannia .. in flexibus mundialium negotiorum mendacibus ~tissimos GILDAS *EB* 66; doctus in horrenda sceleratorum arte magorum ALDH. *VirgV* 1855; multis ~tioribus viris praesentibus BEDE *HE* IV 22 p. 260; [aquila] in stipulam docto dirigit ore facem WALT. ANGL. *Fab.* 13. 6; nostrorum ~tissimus poetarum [Virgilius] J. SAL. *Met.* 858A; ab omni pagina quam bajulaverit recedit ~tior MAP *NC* III 3 f. 41; hominem .. in dolis ~tum, in dissimulatione ~tissimum DEVIZES 42v.; noster doctor, doctior inter doctiores,/ est inter discipulos mitis mitiores GARL. *PP* 190. 1273. **b** est pietatis opus indoctos docta docere, / ut vigilent docte doctis mentes adhibere D. BEC. 83.

docibilis [LL], teachable, apt at learning. **b** (as sb.) disciple. **c** apt at teaching, instructive.

667 hominem .. ~em et in omnibus ornatum .. minime valuimus nunc repperire (*Lit. Papae*) BEDE *HE* III 29; dicentes virum esse .. prudentem .., ~em et bene docentem sermone puro et aperto EDDI 9; nec facile erat quempiam auditorum ejus non esse ~em, propterea quod tanta illi .. inerat .. dicendi facultas OSB. *V. Dunst.* 34; nunc ~is, in provectiori etate capax doctrine non eris P. BLOIS *Ep.* 9. 25A; c**1180** sic qui facile fuit .. effrenis dabit manum correctioni et fiet ~is A. TEWK. *Ep.* 5; **1262** ad .. sustentationem .. xx pauperum ~ium scolarium *Ch. Sal.* 335; licet hic laici homines fuerimus, / illic docibiles et docti erimus (*Vers.*) *G. Ed. II Bridl. prol.* 26; sitis boni pueri, mites et ~es BLAKMAN *Hen. VI* 12. **b** ut secundum prophetam omnes Dei ~es essent [cf. *Is.* liv 13; *John* vi 45] EDDI 2. **c** *techeabylle*, ~is, qui faciliter docet alios; docilis qui faciliter docetur; versus: 'esto puer docilis, liber atque docibilis esto' *CathA*.

docibilitas [LL], teachability.

de ~ate et sagacis mentis ipsius ingenio discendarum artium FELIX *Guthl.* 13 *tit.* p. 66.

docilis [CL], teachable, docile. **b** easily learnt, instructive.

~is, ingeniosus *GlC* D 354; ~is, i. docibilis, qui facile discit *GlH* D 804; ~es discipuli epistolas typicosque sermones ejus scripto retinuerunt ORD. VIT. IV 10; ergo [? l. Argo] sequi docilis, quas nondum noverat, undas / Thetios in gremium migrat prerepta Diane / pinus J. EXON. *BT* I 78; ea que de principibus exempla posuimus ad .. privatos quoque ~es et bonos erudiendum referri possunt GIR. *PI* I 20 p. 142. **b** mihi sententiarum tuarum desiderium subrepet: sunt enim .. auditu ~es ADEL. *QN* 42.

docilitas [CL], readiness to learn, docility.

qua ratione .. auditores in benevolentiam, ~atem, attentionem .. ducendi sunt ADEL. *ED* 21; ~as est naturalis aptitudo doctrinam animadvertendi unicuique innata W. DONC. *Aph. Phil.* 3. 19.

docillus v. 2 dola, duciculus. **docinna** v. decena 1a. **docma, ~matizo** v. dogm-.

docmen [cf. CL documen], teaching, doctrine. *Cf. dogmen.*

enervi trutinans exotica docmina plectro FRITH. 1392.

docte [CL], skilfully.

fabre, ingeniose, ~e *GlC* F 9; D. BEC. 83 (v. docere 4b); tulerat contra scelus ensem, / quo factum temere posset docte cohibere *V. Anselmi Epit.* 62; ille [accipiter] silet; doctius illa [philomena] canit WALT. ANGL. *Fab.* 46. 6; adverbium .. construccionem habet cum casu duplicem, sc. de natura comparacionis, ut '~ius illo facit', '~issime illorum facit' *Ps.*-GROS. *Gram.* 66.

doctificare, to make learned.

ingeniosis ars hec paret, nescia mismet, / .. / doctilogorum [*gl.*: doctorum] nam socium dat doctificando [*gl.*: doctum faciendo] OSW. *Vers.* 8.

doctificus [LL], making learned.

~us, A. *makyng wys WW*.

doctilogus, learned in words (also as sb.). *Cf. doctiloquus.*

OSW. *Vers.* 8 (v. doctificare); pneumate doctilogo cordis secreta rigante *Trop. Wint.* 14; ~os philosophos te, Paule, Christus dat vincere sua voce (*Commem. S. Pauli*) *Miss. Westm.* II 854.

doctiloquus [CL], skilful in speech. *Cf. doctilogus.*

quae profetae, apostoli / doctiloqui oraculi / indiderunt pergaminae / almo inflati flamine (ÆTHELWALD) *Carm. Aldh.* 2. 114 (cf. ib. 12: doctiloquus Sedulius); talia doctiloquo retulerunt fata magistro FRITH. 750. ~us, docte loquens *GlH* D 810; doctus componitur ~us OSB. GLOUC. *Deriv.* 168; duplicavit lingua ~a pro sibi palma futura supera *Miss. Ebor.* II 302.

doctisonus [LL], skilful in melody.

Delia doctisono [? *supply* tangat] grammatica plectro ALCUIN *Carm.* 12. 7.

doctitare [LL], to teach regularly.

alia [verba frequentativa] frequenter inveniuntur, ut .. 'lectito', '~o' *Ps.*-GROS. *Gram.* 52.

doctor [CL]

1 teacher, instructor; **b** (w. gen. of subject taught); **c** (w. gen. of pupil).

veluti conspicuo ac summo ~ori talis cura committitur GILDAS *EB* 1; ~or vel imbutor vel eruditor, *lareow* ÆLF. *Gl.*; dilige doctrinam, doctores dilige doctos D. BEC. 74; possibile est Deo .. quemlibet salvare .. sine omni [fide] acquisita, si ~or desit DUNS *Ord.* I 34. **b** Joseph et ipse castitatis .. ceterarumque virtutum exsecutor ac ~or eximius BEDE *HE* V 21 p. 342 (cf. ib. 9: primus ~or fidei Christianae .. Pictis); ~oribus veritatis .. [adolescentem] tradidit imbuendum AILR. *Nin.* 2. **c** Amphibalus .. B. Albani ~or GIR. *IK* I 5; **1301** J. de N. clericus et ~or puerorum .. ivit post prandium ad querendum virgas pro pueris .. castigandis (*Inq. Coron.*) *DocCOx* 161.

2 doctor of the church, theologian, scholar, sage; **b** doctor of Jewish law, rabbi; **c** (dist. by personal epithet; *cf.* P. Lehmann *Erforschung des Mittelalters* I 140–8).

Paulus, qui omni ecclesiastico ~ori imitandus est GILDAS *EB* 97; sacrum jugiter doctorem dogma docentem / .. / discipulus fidis devotus passibus aequat ALDH. *VirgV* 531; **680** omnis probabilium catholicae ecclesiae ~orum chorus (*Conc. Hatfield*) BEDE *HE* IV 15; Augustinus convocavit ad suum colloquium episcopos sive ~ores .. Brettonum *Ib.* II 2 (cf. ib. 19: Sarano ceterisque ~oribus seu abbatibus Scottis); c**743** dicam .. quod ex operibus antiquorum excerpsi ~orum (DAN. WINT.) *Ep. Bonif.* 64; catholicus doctor, caelestia dona ministrans / gentibus aequoreis ALCUIN *SSEbor* 139; quamvis post apostolos sancti patres et ~ores nostri multi tot et tanta de fidei ratione dicant ad confutandum insipientiam ANSELM (*CurD Commend.*) II 39; H. BOS. *Thom.* IV 11 p. 350 (v. confoederatio 1a); sic ~ores beneficio doctrine tenebras ignorantie excludunt et discipulos cibo spirituali reficiunt NECKAM *NR* II 163; ~ores dicuntur prophete [cf. *1 Cor.* xiv 3] HALES *Qu.* 322; [ecclesie] turres doctores sunt; summa gallus in arce / pervigil est doctor GARL. *Myst. Eccl.* 23–4; prelati, judices et ~ores .. pre aliis vasis sapiencie zelum debent R. BURY *Phil.* 14. 186; a**1350** ut heresis illic aliquociens pululantis memoria non existat, quam in sui ortu non occiderit catholicorum ~orum solercia *StatOx* 17; s**1381** festa iiij ~orum, Ambrosii, Gregorii, Augustini, et Hieronymi *Chr. Pont. Ebor. C* 423 (cf. duplex 4b); **1444** in festis iiij ~orum ecclesie *Stat. King's Cantab.* 561. **b** Moyses, quem tu et legis latorem et maximum ~em te habere gloriaris *Eccl. & Synag.* 70. **c** **1457** Celestis ~oris Jeronymi (v. caelestis 4a); s**1274** cum sapiencie ejus [T. de Aquino] tam publica sint monumenta ut ~or Communis a viris scholasticis nuncupetur TREVET *Ann.* 287; Egidius ~or Declarativus CAPGR. *Hen.* 179 (v. declarativus b); ~or Egregius Augustinus GASCOIGNE *Loci* 75; utinam vellent credere quod ~or Evangelicus [J. Wyclyf] dicit .. quod panis materialis est habitudinaliter corpus Christi R. DYMMOK 89 (= *Conc. Loll. XII* 4); Augustinus, ~or Eximius GASCOIGNE *Loci* 66; c**800** de quo ~or Gentium [Paulus] ait .. ALCUIN *Ep.* 281; ~or Invincibilis [W. Ockham] WYCL. *Ver.* I 348n.; frater Alexander Hales .., ~or Irrefragabilis *Mon. Francisc.* I 542; ut .. allegat ~or Profundus [T. Bradwardine] WYCL. *Act.* 92; iste [Henricus de Gandavo] ad summam laudem [dictus est] ~or Solemnis CAPGR. *Hen.* 180; una opinio que imponitur ~ori Subtili [J. Duns Scoto] (OCKHAM *Sent.*) *GLA* III 353 *n.* 799.

3 (pl.) king's advisers (AS *witan*).

969 ego Eadgar rex Anglorum cum consensu ~orum meorum .. roboravi *CS* 1229; c**1043** propter haec et his similia a ~oribus ammonitus ego Eadwardus .. Æþelredo .. quandam ruris portiunculam .. impertior *CD* 769.

4 doctor (acad.); **b** (w. gen. of faculty); **c** (w. *in*).

a**1360** sequitur absurditas .. quod in casu magistrorum arcium, si alios excedant in numero, possent cancellarium et procuratores ~oresque .. expellere *StatOx* 127; **1412** quod archiepiscopus et successores sui .. habeant visitacionem .. omnium ~orum, magistrorum regencium et non-regencium ac scolarium .. universitatis [Oxonie] *RParl* III 652a; **1458** quod [dominus J. D.] presentetur a ~ore nunc presente vel a ~ore pro tunc ordinario *MunAcOx* 753. **b** **1304** G. .. et J. .. ordinarii legum ~ores *RGasc* III p. clxxvi; **1305** juris utrius ~orem *Ib.* 449; s**1345** J. de S., ~or legum, advocatus et miles de concilio regis AD. MUR. *Chr.* 171 (cf. *EHR* XI 668); a**1350** (v. decernere 5c); roba longa .. cum capicio penulato .. et desuper collobio cum duobus labellulis qualiter uti solent ~ores legum in universitatibus quibusdam FORTESCUE *LLA* 51; **1433** quod quidam ~or juris in ordinario suo suis retulisset scolaribus quod .. *StatOx* 255; **1549** magister artium, quinquennium rei medicae dans operam, postquam bis in eadem facultate responderit totiesque disputaverit, publice poterit fieri ~or medicinae *Ib.* 346. **c** **1293** R. de Wynchelese, ~orem in theologia *DCCant. Reg.* Q f. 17; **1311** per .. cancellarium Oxonie, venerabilesque ~ores in sacra pagina tunc regentes *MunAcOx* 88; a**1350** ~ores in decretis *StatOx* 44; s**1348** obiit .. Simon de Eye, .. ~or in jure canonico *Chr. Rams.* 349; **1481** per liberam resignacionem magistri J. C., in legibus ~oris *Reg. Whet.* II 244.

5 medical doctor, physician.

o doctor Cincy, medicorum qui quasi sol es M. CORNW. *Mansel* 3; de speciebus [valent ad fecunditatem] zinziber conditum, yringi conditi, .. semen malve, cum aliis communiter positis per ~ores KYMER 19; **1430** magistro J. Somerseth, magistro in medicina et ~ori regis *ActPC* IV 30.

doctoralis [LL], belonging to a doctor, doctoral (usu. acad.). *V. et. doctorilis.*

didascal[ic]um, ~e *Gl. Leid.* 39. 64; prout ventilatur [sapientia] in studio, occcupationibus studii ~is utilibus et magnificis in omni facultate legendo et disputando BACON *CSPhil.* 395; cum dixerat palam in scholis, in ~i cathedra .. (HERFORD) *Ziz.* 306; **1427** quousque pura exeat liquide veritatis intencio ~is NETTER *DAF* II 32; **1448** (v. doctorare b); **1453** memini tui olim laboris studiosissimi ac in civili jure ~is preeminencie BEKYNTON I 275; *StatOx* 272, 413 (v. apex 1b, dignitas 2c).

doctorare, to doctor (acad.), confer a doctorate on; **b** (refl.) to take a doctorate.

1311 cum aliquis debet in sacra theologia ~ari *Collect. Ox.* II 222; c**1340** nonnullos .. universitatis magistros ~atos et approbatos *FormOx* 169; s**1372** P. Repyngdone .. baccalaureus existens humillimus .. apparuit. .. sed, ~atus in termino estatis, in prima sua leccione incepit magnificare Wyccleff *Ziz.* 297; s**1377** frater R. Lambourne .. primo bachillarius in theologia .., prius in ordine S. Benedicti ~atus, ordinem B. Francisci .. intravit *Mon. Francisc.* I 543; **1458** vir .. in facultate sacre theologie ~atus *Reg. Whet.* I 318. **b** **1448** te, qui .. in studio S. Andree in decretis longo tempore studuisti et ab illius universitate licenciam te in decretis ~andi obtinuisti, tenore presencium decretorum doctorem facimus ac doctoralibus insigniis decoramus *Mon. Hib. & Scot.* 379b; **1543** domino A. tanquam sufficienti et ydoneo in ipso [civili] jure gradum et insignia hujusmodi recipiendi et se in ipso jure ~andi quandocunque sibi placuerit *Form. S. Andr.* II 311.

doctoratus, (acad.) doctorate, degree or status of doctor.

s**1274** Thomas de Aquino ~us gradum merito est adeptus RISH. 82; **1311** ne .. minus sufficientes et indigni ~us gradum .. adscenderent *Collect. Ox.* II 222; c**1318** qui

. . facultatis juris civilis . . profunde scrutatus in eadem ad ~us apicem . . est assumptus *FormOx* 30; procedere per debita media, veluti per viam ad terminum . ., per disciplinam ad ~um . . BRADW. *CD* 732D; **1358** ordinatum fuit . . quod nunquam exerceret actum ~us in universitate Oxon' nisi habita licencia cancellarii et singulorum doctorum in theologia *MunAcOx* 209; **1381** nec doctoratum vendicat,/ nisi quum judex applicat / et prebet normam thematis (*In Lollardos* 9) *Pol. Poems* I 234; **1421** incepturi in facultate sacre theologie, completa eorum forma in eadem facultate usque ad ~um *Reg. Cant.* III 71; **1438** visum est . . propter . . suam contumaciam . . fratrem W. insigniis ~us ad tempus privari *EpAcOx* 163; FORTESCUE *LLA* 47 (v. bachelariatus); **1451** in hiis que ad magisterii seu ~us honorem . . requiruntur *Mon. Hib. & Scot.* 383b.

doctorilis, doctoral. *V. et. doctoralis.*

1389 aureola ~is indifferenter omnibus desuper non paratur nec officium predicandi aliis quam vocatis . . conceditur *Reg. Heref.* 234.

doctrina [CL]

1 (act of) teaching instruction. **b** doctrine, that which is taught; **c** (Christian).

antistes cujus ~a ac ministerio gens . . Anglorum dominicae fidei . . disceret BEDE *HE* III 3; sacerdotes . . Mercios genere eruditos . . quorum omnium ~a et sapientia regis . . desiderium crescebat ASSER *Alf.* 77; exortatio, i. monitio, ~a, vel *trymnes GlH* E 688. **b** India tum sacris colivit simulacra nefandis / doctrinis veterum stolidis instructa parentum ALDH. *CE* 4. 6. 17; etas doctrinam credere prisca solet; / doctrinam loquitur sapiens prolixior etas WALT. ANGL. *Fab.* 29. 14–15. **c** periculosa . . sacerdotibus ~a est quae pravis operibus obfuscatur GILDAS *EB* 96; scriberet ut soboli doctrinam rite supernam ALDH. *VirgV* 2191; **680** nos pie atque orthodoxe, juxta divinitus inspiratam ~am eorum [discipulorum etc.], professi credimus . . (*Conc. Hatfield*) BEDE *HE* IV 15; Romam prius propter ~am ecclesiasticam adierat *Ib.* III 25 p. 182; ecce quomodo in gaudium Domini sui intravit qui in commissa sibi ~e pecunia fidelis erogator exstitit [cf. *Matth.* xxv 21] OSB. *V. Dunst.* 44; in nonnullis angulis . . multi sunt . . ad quos . . fidei nunquam ~a pervenit GIR. *TH* III 26; de necessitate ~e revelate: . . queritur utrum homini pro statu isto sit necessarium aliquam ~am specialem supernaturaliter inspirari, ad quam viz. non posset attingere lumine naturali intellectus DUNS *Ord.* I 1; pabulo sacre ~e [ME: *fode of hali lore*] *AncrR* 7.

2 (act of) learning. **b** learning, branch of knowledge.

precipua . . sunt ad totius philosophie et virtutis exercitium lectio, ~a, meditatio, et assiduitas operis. lectio vero scriptorum prejacentem habet materiam; ~a et scriptis plerumque incumbit et interdum ad non scripta progreditur J. SAL. *Met.* 853A; D. BEC. 74 (v. doctor 1a); HALES *Qu.* 304 (v. agnitio a); J. BLUND *An.* 2 (v. disciplina 1a); T. YORK *Sap.* I 30 (v. cognitio 1a). **b** imbuit hos pariter saecli doctrina medelam / necnon divina praestavit gratia gratis ALDH. *VirgV* 1080; carius est nobis flagellari pro ~a [AS: *for lare*] quam nescire ÆLF. *Coll.* 90; tribus his causis adquiritur scientia: ~a sc., experimento, ratione. ~a percipitur lectione et auditu; experimento autem per hoc quod quisque experitur, quod satis omnibus notum est; ratione vero naturali, quam habet quisque a Deo secundum gratiam sibi datam ANSELM *Misc.* 306; grammatica forma ~e est, et homo id in quod ~a transit *Ps.*-GROS. *Gram.* 64.

doctrinabilitas, teachability.

omnis proprietas proprie dicta . . potest sumi principaliter a quolibet iiij generum causarum substancie, ut corruptibilitas, †doctrinibilitas, univoca generabilitas et felicitabilitas insunt homini ex ejus iiij causis WYCL. *Ente* (*Sum.*) 59.

doctrinalis [LL], pertaining to teaching. **b** instructive, demonstrative, theoretical. **c** (of person) didactic, scholarly. **d** (as sb. n., title of book; also fig.).

ordinis . . ~is magna confusio est et discipline intolerabilis perturbatio secundarium principali adequare R. MELUN *Sent. pref.* I 9. **b** J. SAL. *Pol.* 440A (v. divinatorius); *GLA* III 19 (v. disputatio 1); **s1304** quod facio nunc [sc. post castellum redditum] non est destruccio, sed post me bellancium . . hostilium castrorum ~is quassacio *Flor. Hist.* III 120; cujus [Edwardi I] et suorum frequens armatorum exercitatio, quid aliud nisi, post ejus exitum de Egypto, paganorum et infidelium expugnacio ~is? J. LOND. *Commend. Ed. I* 8; licet modus hujusmodi respondendi simpliciter forsitan caucior videatur, alius tamen modus respondendi per definiciones premissas aut alias meliores ~ior comprobatur BRADW. *CD* 734A; **1431** publica et ~ia singillatim gingnasia pertranseat philosophorum *StatOx* 234. **c** os cujus fuerit parva . . aperitio significat hominem pacificum, timidum, fidelem . ., verecundum, ~em M. SCOT *Phys.* 67 (cf. ib. 83: manus . . longe significant hominem . . ex facili timidum . ., discretum, servicialem domestice conversacionis et ~em). **d** Doctrinalis editor sicque producebat / cucumer in medio *Qui majora cernitis* 189; novum morum doctrinale / nove vite formula WALT. WIMB. *Virgo* 111; [Brito] uno modo inducit ~e pro auctore. . . magnus error est, quia nunquam fuit dignus auctoritate, licet pueris sit utilis in aliquibus, sicut ait: 'scribere clericulis paro Doctrinale novellis' BACON *CSPhil.* 477; **1281** liberantur eidem . . unus liber Prisciani . ., unum ~e Magnum, precii ij d. . . *SelPlJews* 114; **1396** Magnum ~e (*Invent.*) *Meaux* III app. xcvii; **1417** lego . . j ~e rubium *Reg. Cant.* II 119; doctor Thomas Walden in suo ~i . . testatur . . GASCOIGNE *Loci* 2.

doctrinaliter, instructively, systematically.

ut, quod antea ~er edocuimus per precepta, de cetero declaremus per exempla GIR. *PI* I 17; modus tamen et ordo tractandi, ob quorumdam in eo [priore tractatu] contentorum inordinatam replicacionem, non videtur ~er ordinatus J. BURGH *PO proem.* f. 2; **1409** se . . disputando, arguendo et respondendo ~er exercentes *StatOx* 200.

doctrinamentum, instruction.

†430 (12c) ecclesiam construxerant . . per ~um beati archangeli Gabrielis (*Ch. Patricii*) W. MALM. *Glast.* 9 (= *CS* 1).

doctrinare, to instruct.

providendum est . . prelato qualiter quem fratrem ~are et tractare . . debeat ANSELM *Misc.* 316; quoad hunc actum [sc. discursum] logica est prior, et ita prior inquantum ad doctrinam, quia per discursum ~amur (DUNS *Anal. Post.*) *GLA* III 209 *n.* 108; **c1382** factum est cum monachis simul concordarent / atque falsas fabulas fratres predicarent, / et doctores ordinum scholas doctrinarent (*Contra Religiosos* 195) *Mon. Francisc.* I 598 (= *Pol. Poems* I 259: scholis doctrinarent); rex debet . . transmittere juvenes habiles ad ~andum in partibus extraneis *Plusc.* VII 19; *to teche*, . . docere . ., discipulare, ~are, dogmatizare *CathA*.

doctrinatio, teaching, instruction, learning.

quod bono animo fieri nequit, sicut est . . veritatis damnacio, heresium ~o, diffamacio innocencium OCKHAM *I. & P.* 31; WYCL. *Ver.* II 131 (v. exercitatio 4b); **1426** utrum juvenes omnes . . vacent jugiter studio et assidue exerceant ~onem (*Quaestiones Abbatis*) AMUND. I 209; **s1451** nec claustrum convertit in forum . ., immo obloquium pocius in silencium . . ociumque et pigriciam in leccionem, diligenciam et ~onem *Reg. Whet.* I 6; **1458** in tanto duo vestra munuscula fuerunt nobis acceptiora de quanto illorum unum invitat ad bonum, alterum vero [sc. tractatulus pro ordine . . domini regis et suorum nobilium] instruit ad mores et dat ~onem (*Lit. Abbatis*) *Ib.* 321.

doctrinibilitas v. doctrinabilitas.

doctrix [LL], teacher (f.); **b** (fig.).

ut . . ordine praepostero ~icem propriam ad martirii palmam praecederent ALDH. *VirgP* 47. **b** **797** sicut praedecessores vestri . . ex . . aecclesia fontem veritatis auriebant . ., ita et vestra excellentia protectricem et ~icem prorsus utens usque tenus amplectere et tenere habebit (*Lit. Papae*) *Ep. Alcuin.* 127; quia sapientia est mater et ~ix omnium virtutum AILR. *Serm.* 19. 320A; lingua Greca . . omnium gencium est ~ix *Ord. Ebor.* II 287; **1430** contra ecclesie honestatem, que caritatis et pacis ~ix est et magistra *Reg. Durh.* III no. 870; FORTESCUE *NLN* I 44 (v. electrix).

docturire, to wish to teach.

[verba] alia [desiderativa] . . frequenter inveniuntur, ut 'lecturio,' '~io' *Ps.*-GROS. *Gram.* 52.

documentum [CL]

1 example, model.

sic caro, mirandum fatu, putrescere nescit,/ ut referunt nobis veterum documenta virorum ALDH. *VirgV* 232; inter alia vivendi ~a saluberrimum . . continentiae clericis exemplum reliquit BEDE *HE* III 5; †dicimenta, *tacne* . ., ~um, exemplum *GlC* D 330, 360; ~um vel specimen, *larbysn* ÆLF. *Gl.*; **c800** plenae sunt scripturae ~is oboedientiae; plenus est mundus exemplis quid cui ex humilitate oboedientiae evenisset ALCUIN *Ep.* 281; tot sacrilegiorum exemplaria, tot rerum malarum ~a GIR. *TH* III 24.

2 teaching, instruction, doctrine; **b** (leading to salvation).

virgo veterum sprevit documenta librorum / et sequitur Christi quadratis dogmata biblis ALDH. *VirgV* 1182; si quis voluerit scire hanc aleam plene, illi ante omnia hujus disciplinae ~a haec vij scire animo necesse est *Alea Evang.* 173; dicebat se potius . . pecorum balatus . . quam eloquia vel ~a humana cognoscere R. COLD. *Cuthb.* 114; urbanis pueros documentis instrue parvos D. BEC. 2419; miserunt eos [pueros] parentes ad Salomonem regem Armoricanorum Britonum, ut in domo sua ~a militie ceterarumque curialium consuetudinum addiscerent G. MON. XII 1; **1219** misit cum eo . . unam feminam, ut doceret eum quo loco deberet frangere domum; . . et ipse et socii sui per ~um ejusdem femine fregit (*sic*) domum *CurR* VIII 180; **s1220** mirabilis artifex, cujus ~o omnia tractabantur M. PAR. *Maj.* III 59; de quibusdam specialibus ~is noviciorum post eorum ingressum *Cust. Cant.* 406 *rub.*; **1381** nonnulli . . quasdam hereses innovant et . . publice dogmatizant, duo inter alia sua ~a pestifera asserentes (*Sententia Cancellarii Oxon.*) *Ziz.* 110. **b** disceret ut magno fidei documenta magistro ALCUIN *WillV* XI 3; sufficiebat ovans cunctis documenta salutis FRITH. 243; Christus inter caetera sua ~a clamabat, dicens [etc.] ÆLF. *Ep.* 2. 16; **s899** divinis . . ~is imbutus ÆTHELW. IV 3; viam quae ducit ad vera Jesu Christi ovilia exemplo pariter et ~o monstravit B. *V. Dunst.* 25; **1324** per divini cultus obsequium et scripture sacre ~um juxta sancciones canonicas *Stat. Mich. Cantab.* 640.

3 written evidence, certificate, document.

†syntasma [l. syntagma], ~um, †syntasmata [l. syntagmata], ~a *GlC* S 723–4; **803** (11c) ea . . pro evitando (*sic*) futuri temporis ambiguetate fidelissimis scripturis et ~is sunt commendata *CS* 308; **c1075** si quae ad domos . . reficiendas necessaria vobis fuerint, inde [de bosco prioris de Herleia] praecipio ut vobis necessaria prioris vel suorum ~o habeatis *FormA* 290 (= *MonA* III 434a); **1252** sententiam . . redigi fecimus in publica ~a *Mon. Hib. & Scot.* 55a; petitis pro parte regis per legitima ~a que intitulantur in codice recordorum *G. Hen. V* 20; **1552** defectu legitimorum ~orum natalibus . . temporibus *Conc. Scot.* II 135; **1559** dummodo per hujusmodi coqueta sive ~a evidenter constet eisdem quod . . (*TR Scots Doc.* 100/121) *Foed.* XV 525a.

docutio, teaching, instruction, or (?) *f. l.*

1467 pro diligenti labore . . in erudicione et ~one [sic MS; *but* ? l. elocucione] grammatice dilectis fratribus . . regine (*TRBk*) *JRL Bull.* L 471.

dodarium v. doarium.

dodda, doddocus [ME *dodde*], measure(s) of grain or sim.

1222 singule hide debent . . flagellare xxiiij ~as, sc. xxvij quar. de †Colocestr', unam partem de frumento, aliam partem de fabis, terciam partem siliginis et ordei, quartam de avena, sc. duas mensuras pro una, . . et dare domino de propria avena ij ~as, que continent iiij summas frumenti de Colcestr' *Dom. S. Paul.* 47; **c1290** quantum reddat de . . †deddis vel minis avene *Ib.* 154*; **1299** debet x ~ocos avene per annum; . . et illa mensura semper restat in custodia episcopi; et continet de frumento ij estricas et dim.; et continet de ordeo dim. quarterium, et tantum de avena *RB Worc.* 296 (cf. ib. 297: debet . . vj *doddoks* frumenti, ij *doddoks* avene; *Vac. Roll Durh.* 1148/18 [**1334**] *ap. Cust. Rents* 29: de redditu vocato *dodcor*[*n*]).

dodecaëdrum [δωδεκαέδρον], dodecahedron.

duodecedron, quod est corpus ex duodecim basibus pentagonalibus BACON IV 340; tantum erit una figura corporalis ex pentagonis superficiebus; et oportet quod habeat duodecim superficies pentagonas . .; et hoc vocatur ~um, id est figura corporalis duodecim basium pentagonarum equilaterarum *Id. Maj.* I 161; omne corpus hujusmodi est pyramis, cubus, octoedron, duodecaedron, icosaedron vel sphera BRADW. *CD* 120C.

dodecatemorium [CL < δωδεκατημόριον], twelfth part (of zodiacal sign).

in eclipticae ~iorum notis DEE *Monas pref.* 181 (cf. ib. 194: ~ii Arietis omnibus est notissima . . figura ista).

dodrans [CL], **~a,**

1 three quarters (of *as*), nine ounces. **b** three quarters of year.

~ans sive doras: ix uncie. . . si [aliquod temporis spatium] in quattuor [partiri vis], quarta pars quadrantis nomen, residuae tres ~antis accipiunt BEDE *TR* 4 pp. 184–5; THURKILL *Abac.* 61v. (v. deunx); quadrans quartam partem uncie ponderat et ~ans dicitur in Ebraico (*sic*) ciclus in Latino (*sic*) [cf. Isid. *Etym.* XVI 24. 17] BART. ANGL. XIX 127. **b** Philippicus [711–13] regnavit quadram cum anno; Anastasius [713–15] regnavit ~am cum anno (*Imp. Romani*) DICETO II 215.

2 (? by assoc. w. third quarter of the moon) flood or (?) neap tide, or eagre (tidal bore).

a690 caerula trans ponti glauca [v. l. glauci] inormesque ~antium glareas atque spumiferas limphae obstirpationes circili carina procellosum sulcante salum ALDH. *Ep.* 5; oceanus cum molibus / atque diris dodrantibus / pulsabat promontoria (*Id.*) *Carm. Aldh.* 1. 108; ~ans, *egur GlC* D 343; ~ans, i. malina, *egur*, ~ante, *dreariende GlH* D 811–2; †**10.** . †detrans, *egor WW*.

doela v. douella 2. **doemon** v. daemon 2. **doetus** v. duitus.

doga [cf. DuC], wainscot.

1472 in nave Rolandi Petrif' de Aernemude j centenarium ~arum, sc. *waghenscot* (*KRAc* 129/1) *Bronnen* no. 1684.

doggera [ME *dogger*], dogger (sort of fishing vessel).

1417 Robertus Andre magister ~e vocate *Petre* de Whitby *RNorm* I 326.

doggetum [ME *dokked*], 'dogget', docket, summary.

1459 ~um compoti domini Johannis Eden *Ac. Durh.* 638; **1507** dogettum Briani Bradford sessionis Lanc' tente ibidem *PLDocketR* 6 (*PRO Ind.* 4670) r. 22; **1647** doggetum . . prothonotarii et clerici corone . . de Magna Sessione (*Brecon Doggett Bk. MS National Library of Wales, Great Sessions*) *Ind.* 17542 f. 1.

dogma [CL < δόγμα], dogma, (religious) doctrine.

saepe salutifero correxit dogmate pagos ALDH. *VirgV* 687; **†676** (12c) cum nobis evangelica et apostolica ~ata fuissent delata *CS* 43; **724** per intervalla nostris, id est

Christianis, hujuscemodi conparande sunt ~atibus superstitiones (DAN. WINT.) *Ep. Bonif.* 23; [Gregorius] probavit hoc [Eutycii] ~a orthodoxae fidei omnimodis esse contrarium BEDE *HE* II 1 p. 75; **800** secundum quod ~atibus sanctorum patrum informamur ALCUIN *Ep.* 199; sincero docmate fretus FRITH. 965 (cf. ib. 1291: Uuilfridi dogma); **9..** ~a, *lare*; ~atum, *haligra lara WW*; **a975** Eadgaro, uranei terrenique ~atis fastu .. pollenti (*Ep. ad Eadgarum*) *Mem. Dunst.* 366; libros perversi ~atis LANFR. *Corp. & Sang.* 409B; faciam me monachum .. omni ~ate eruditum G. MON. VIII 14; D. BEC. 75 (v. dedocere b); ut legatus ei dogmata sacra ferat GARL. *Tri. Eccl.* 72; veridico ~ate et assercione simplici affirmando OCKHAM *Pol.* I 264; WYCL. *Ver.* I 160 (v. dogmatizare 1d); **c1400** (v. catholicus 2b); **1431** heresibus, erroribus falsisque ~atibus perverse favere *Cl* 281 m. 6*d*.

dogmaticus [LL < δογματικός], doctrinal, scholarly (also as sb. m.).

GlC D 358 (v. consultivus); ~us, sophisticus, doctus, sagax, prudens, instructus OSB. GLOUC. *Deriv.* 175; **c1427** hinc, miser, adverte docearis tuncque docere / presumas. .. / desine plus sapere quam dogmatici sapuere (*Vers. Abbatis in Lollardiam*) AMUND. I 231; *wyse*, .. doctus, ~us, disertus .. *CathA*.

dogmatistes [LL < δογματιστής], **~a**, doctor (of the church), propounder of doctrine.

~istae sententiis et doctoris sermonibus credula praecordia pando ALDH. *Met.* 10 p. 88; egregius agonista et divini sermonis ~a [S. Paulus] *Id. VirgP* 2; **956** (11c) Dunstan ~a *CS* 937; quem [Origenem] utinam tam catholicum suscepissemus ~en quam fidum admiramur interpretem H. BOS. *Ep.* 1. 1419B; ubi [in Boemia] .. magnus archiepiscopus, novus eorum tyro et fortis ~a, contra Christi ecclesiam decertat NETTER *DAF* II 7.

dogmatizare [LL < δογματίζειν]

1 to propound, proclaim (doctrine, esp. religious): **a** (trans.); **b** (w. acc. & inf. or compl.); **c** (w. *quod*); **d** (absol.).

a damnatur haeresis Origenis, qui revolutiones saeculorum infinitorum eodem ordine semper currentium ~are praesumsit BEDE *Gen.* 109; Manes .. duo principia ~avit, unum bonum et alterum malum R. NIGER *Chr. I* 31; **1334** ea que a nonnullis perversis .. religiosis .. contra constituciones nostras super hoc editas ~antur et eciam predicantur *Mon. Hib. & Scot.* 261b; errores .. assertos et ~atos OCKHAM *Err. Pap.* 961; non enim homo hereticus quia dicit opinionem hereticam; sed prius naturaliter est eum ipsum dogmatisare hereticam scienciam quam ipsum esse hereticum WYCL. *Ente Praed.* 55; primo dicet de prelatis illis qui Cristi scolam ~ant et ejus contrarium operantur GOWER *VC* III 1 *tit.*; **1420** juravit quod ab illa hora in antea non tenebit, predicabit, docebit, ~abit vel aliquo modo pertinaciter defendet .. aliam opinionem errorem vel heresim sapientem *Reg. Cant.* III 85; **1539** ne .. libros .. dogmata falsa .. continentes legere, studere seu interpretari aut ~are praesumant *Form. S. Andr.* II 106. **b** ~abat corpus nostrum in illa resurrectionis gloria inpalpabile .. esse futurum BEDE *HE* II 1 p. 75; ALCUIN *Dogm.* 94C (v. dividere 6d); datur intelligi quosdam fuisse qui ~arent peccatum non esse escis et voluptatibus affluere LANFR. *Comment. Paul.* (*Heb.* xiii 9) 406; objiciunt illis qui essentialiter Deum hominem ~ant H. BOS. *LM* 1379A; mundum .. in Marcio factum ~at ecclesia *Eul. Hist.* I 8; ille qui docmatisat per bullas tali inhabili esse beneficium ecclesiasticum conferendum WYCL. *Sim.* 25. **c** errat aperte ~ando quod res usu consumptibiles erant communes illis credentibus OCKHAM *Pol.* I 357. **d** instantia quae ~ando conferat lepidinis adesse peritiam B. *Ep.* 386; contra hereticos secus quam catholica fides habeat ~antes (J. KELSO *Ep.*) AD. SCOT *TT* 624D; sicut de columba ~ant, quam ex corpore aerio sumtam in idem dicunt rediisse GERV. TILB. I 5; sicut Aristoteles verissime ~at R. BURY *Phil.* 13. 180; est dogma actus vel habitus ~antis WYCL. *Ver.* I 160.

2 to teach (w. acc. or dat. of person).

mus genuit murem, dogmatizavit eundem [? l. eandem]: / 'filia pulchra mihi, dogmata disce patris' WALT. ANGL. *Fab.* 63. 1; **1310** frater B. [de ordine Templi] ~abat eum quod Jesus Christus non erat verus Deus et verus homo *Conc.* II 383b (cf. *Ann. Lond.* 180 [**s1311**]: [Templarii] dicebant et ~abant illis .. Christum non esse vere Deum).

dogmatizatio, proclamation, preaching. **b** doctrine.

si ex dogmatisacione alicujus assercionis magnum scandalum esset OCKHAM *Dial.* 433; sicut Machometus per tradicionem legis contrarie legi Dei diminuit Christianismum .., sic post dotacionem ecclesie multiplicacio, ~o et appropriacio tradicionis humane .. diminuit de vera religione populi Christiani WYCL. *Ver.* II 130; **1414** universitati vestre [Parisiensi], quam pro ~one salubrium negociorum et profuturorum promocione .. fervidam scimus zelatricem BEKYNTON II 123. **b 1415** an .. in dicto libello contenta .. pro veris .. dictis et ~onibus habuit et reputavit *Reg. Cant.* IV 134; **1425** de et super iniqua, perversa et erronea doctrina, predicacione, assercione et ~one suis *Ib.* III 122; **1540** causantibus suis manifestis, perversis, iniquis et damnatis heresibus, doctrinis, instructionibus, predicationibus et ~onibus ac heresum predictarum .. divulgationibus *Form S. Andr.* II 226.

dogmatizator, preacher, propounder.

idem Dei ~or adgregatum coenobium .. divini verbi coepit fomento nutrire B. *V. Dunst.* 15; frater S. .. istius heresis precipuus est ~or *Remonstr. Ir.* 920.

dogmatorium, book of dogma or (?) *f. l.*

ave, sporta pane plena, / Christi ciclas, Christi lena, / Christi dogmatorium [v. l. dormitorium] WALT. WIMB. *Virgo* 16.

dogmen [cf. CL dogma], teaching, doctrine. *Cf. docmen.*

vir clarus, bonitate dogmine gnarus *V. Neot. A* 21.

dogmittatio v. deguttatio.

doinus [cf. ME *don*], (of ox or horse) dun (sts. combined w. *badius*).

1279 ij boviculos, unum nigrum et unum *doynne Hund. Highworth* 130; **1312** de uno somero *duyn KRAc* 99/8; **1313** G. de Punsonby .. habet j runcinum doign' [*corr. from* sorum] cum musello albo *Ib.* 14/15 r. 6; T. de Veraton' habet j equum don' [*corr. from* faugh'] cum nigra lista *Ib.* r. 4; **1313** pro restauro unius equi badii doyni *Cl* 130 m. 12; **1317** pro restauro .. unius equi sui doyn' badii cum stella *RGasc* IV 1749.

doit- v. duit-.

1 dola v. dala.

2 dola, 'dossil', spigot. *Cf. duciculus.*

~a, i. docillus, A. *a dosel WW*.

dolabella [CL = *axe*], **~ellula, ~ellum,** broad axe. **b** gimlet or sim.

~ella, *bradacus Gl. Leid.* 47. 47. **b** *a wymbylle*, dolabra, ~ellula [v. l. ~brella], ~ellum, terebrum *CathA*.

dolabilis, fit to be hewn. *V. et. dolatilis.*

Ps.-GROS. *Summa* 632 (v. comminuibilis); regula edificacionum Lesbie mutatur ad edificia, cum lapides non sint ibi ad rectam lineam ~es SICCAV. *PN* 195.

dolabilitas, susceptibility to hewing.

accidentia lapidum famosiora sunt durities et mollities, ~as et polibilitas et eorum contraria *Ps.*-GROS. *Summa* 629.

dolabra [CL], **~um** [LL], pick or sim. **b** axe, blade, or sim.; **c** (fig.). **d** (?) pair of tongs.

~a, ascia lapidaria *GlC* D 355. **b** bovina cornua alba ac in una tenuiter ~is erasa non minus vitreo vasculo elucent ASSER *Alf.* 104; ~um, *bradæx* ÆLF. *Gl.*; ~a, securi seu bipenni assumpta egrediebatur foras R. COLD. *Godr.* 73; minister economi regis Scotorum, assuetus ~o W. CANT. *Mir. Thom.* VI 81; **s1194** cubicularius .., ad hoc coactus, dum ipse dux [Austrie] ~um manu propria tibie apponeret, malleo vibrato vix trina percussione pedem ejus abscidit W. NEWB. *HA* V 8 (= W. COVENTR. II 81: †dolarium .. apposuit); **s1382** hec [imago S. Katerine] nova martiria dolabro pacietur et igne (*Vers.*) KNIGHTON II 184; **1471** pro emendacione unius ~i pertinentis ad fabricam *Fabr. York* 75; hoc †dolubrum, *a brodax* .., hoc †dolebrum, *a brodehax WW*; **1566** cum una ~a vocata *a fellyng axe Pat* 1019 m. 7. **c** caelestis disciplinae ~o tortitudinem veteris vitae deponunt ANSELM *Misc.* 313; ex utroque parentum, ~o generationis, origo nostri exterioris hominis recisa traducitur PULL. *Sent.* 729A; feci .. quod potui duce carens ..; de intacta namque rudi silva regiis edificiis missa securi ligna secui prudentioris architecti ~o complananda *Dial. Scac.* II 28 B. **d** †delebra, *tang GlH* D 152.

dolabratio, hewing or trimming.

1387 laborantibus .. super amputacione, dolebracione, aptacione et scapulacione maeremii regis *KRAc* 183/12 f. 23; **1466** Galfrido Carpenter pro †dolobracione stipidum ulmorum *Ac. Churchw. Bath.* 64.

dolare [CL], to hew, trim, whittle; **b** (absol.); **c** (fig.).

~antur lapides pretiosi [cf. *I Sam.* v 18] cum electi quique .. sanctorum .. quicquid in se habent .. inane relinquunt atque .. solam insitae justitiae regulam quasi stabilem quadraturae formam ostendunt BEDE *Templ.* 744; ~antes .. lapidem in quantum valebant *Id. HE* IV 11; ~atum, *gesniden GlC* D 342; ~atum, i. incisum, planum, *hywyt GlH* D 764; lignum quoddam in sudis morem ~ando preacuunt R. COLD. *Cuthb.* 17; **1241** cindulas .. bene escapulatas et ~atas *Liberate* 15 m. 19; prostravit .. boscum et vendidit et assumpsit sibi duos carpentarios ad ~andum lignum *Lib. Mem. Bernewelle* 145; [W. episc. S. Andree, ob.**1328**] magne ecclesie trabes tabulis ~atis et celaturis .. ornavit FORDUN *Cont.* VI 44; **1460** *hewers* ~ancium mdccc *corfes* [carbonis] (*MinAc Eccl. Comm.*) *VCH Durh.* II 324. **b 1269** Willelmus tenens .. cultellum in manu sua .. (?) dol[a]vit [*Cal.*: †deluit] in quadam virga *IMisc* 15/20; nullus debet in choro .. ungues scindere, scribere, ridere vel ~are *Obs. Barnwell* 80. **c** tam ~atos ex illis [noviciis] tradidit ut eorum quidam adhuc .. superstites illius predicabilem industriam .. morum suavitate .. affirment W. DAN. *Ailred* 14; Virgo, David orta progenie, / dola linguam hanc imperitie / in sonantis lyram placencie J. HOWD. *Ph.* 3 (cf. ib. 394: qui doloris dolatur gladio).

dolarium v. dolabra b.

dolatilis [LL], fit to be hewn. *V. et. dolabilis.*

s1053 plenam .. fodiendi tam ~es quam communis structure lapides mercatus libertatem *Chr. Rams.* 166.

dolatio [LL], hewing, shaping.

[abbas T., ob. **1396**] solvit .. pro factura fenestrarum .. xx li. preter expensas pro lapidibus volte et ejus ~one *G. S. Alb. cont.* III 385; **1407** pro sarracione et ~one unius *cartbody Ambrosden* II 213; **1417** pro quadracione et ~one cxxij pedum pro *le aloure* et watertabula .., cxxxj pedum de *ascheler* .. et iiij^{xx}v pedum de *le crest Rect. Adderbury* 18; **1434** pro ~one lignorum in castro de Strivelyne *ExchScot* 593; **1454** in j pare molarum .. et in ~one earundem ad molendinum *Ac. Durh.* 191.

dolatura [LL], hewing, shaping. **b** chip, shaving (of wood).

ligna saxeam duritiem contrahunt et in .. effigiem per quamvis ~am vel celaturam fuerint transformata GERV. TILB. III 4; **1286** W. .. et D. .. capti pro suspicione .. pro eo quod subtiles sunt in sculpturis et ~is, pretextu cujus suspicabatur versus eos quod sciebant contrafacere claves de ligno *Gaol Del.* 36/1 r. 32. **b** pulvillulus .. non ex plumis vel bombice .. sed solummodo tenuissimis lignorum ~is HERM. ARCH. 20; **s1116** de theca pulvinaris ejus [S. Eadmundi] et de ~is de buxu unde plenum fuit *Chr. Abingd.* II 157.

2 broad axe.

~a, *braadlastaecus GlC* D 346; ~a, i. lata securis, *bradæx GlH* D 765.

doleator v. doliator. **doleatum** v. dolium 2a. **dolebr-** v. dolabr-.

dolenter [CL], grievously.

egre, i. graviter, ~er, *earfoþlice GlH* E 156; nunc modice tactus ita ~er succlamat EADMER *Beat.* 5; ut .. sis meretrix diaboli confusibiliter et ~er [ME: *sorchfullich*] *AncrR* 158; ~er hac sepe cogitavi GASCOIGNE *Loci* 14.

doleratus, *s. dub. Cf. cultellus* 1d.

1242 (v. cnipulus a).

dolēre [CL]

1 to feel pain, ache; **b** (w. acc. of part affected).

sentit .. quasi magnam .. manum caput sibi in parte qua ~ebat tetigisse BEDE *HE* IV 29; an dices fragilem carnem .. acuto ferro penetratam non debuisse ~ere? ANSELM (*Ver.* 8) I 187; si dolori medicamentum vult adhibere ubi ~eat, expedit ut ostendat ei quem scit .. posse mederi EADMER *Beat.* 15; cogitans de dolore non afficitur, sed ~ens *Ps.*-GROS. *Gram.* 59; liniatur super dentem ~entem GAD. 119. 1. **b** homines infirmi capitis jejuni ~ent caput, refecti cibis alleviantur *Quaest. Salern.* B 28.

2 to feel sorrow, be grieved; **b** (w. inf. or acc. & inf); **c** (w. *quod*). **d** (pr. ppl.) sorrowful. **e** (trans.) to deplore.

[Judith] pro contribulibus ~itura ALDH. *VirgP* 57; episcopus gravissime de casu meo .. ~ebat BEDE *HE* V 6; ANSELM *Ep.* 168 (v. concutere 1b); ut .. lucis beneficio ~eant destituti GIR. *TH* III 35; licet invidus ~eat de bono proximi, delectatur tamen in malo proximi HALES *Sent.* IV 217; de quo valde ~eo [ME: *wa is me*] *AncrR* 24. **b a1073** ut .. ~eam .. me usque ad haec tempora perventum LANFR. *Ep.* 1; cum .. intelligit se malum esse, oportet ut si bonus fieri vult, ~eat se malum esse EADMER *Beat.* 15; trux Amalec Josue doluit succumbere [cf. *Exod.* xvii 13] GARL. *Tri. Eccl.* 13; ~ens in sanctuario Dei fieri picturarum ineptias AD. DORE *Pictor* 142; si vana gloria dominetur, que ex invidia nascitur, ut ideo ~eat quis esse secundus quia desiderat esse prior ELMH. *Cant.* 87. **c 1072** quod .. rite non potuimus satisfacere valde ~uimus LANFR. *Ep.* 6; **c1093** quod exaudire me noluit [Deus] ~eo ANSELM (*Ep.* 165) IV 38. **d** Job, ~ens *GlC* I 473; quam ~ens et tristis erit anima mea ANSELM (*Ep.* 120) III 260; anxius et ~ens [ME: *sari*] sum quod debeo hoc dicere *AncrR* 24; ~entior [ME: *sorechfulre*] potest esse peccator .. *Ib.* 117. **e** heu ~endum dictu! ALDH. *VirgP* 22; debilitatem populi nostri ~eo G. MON. XII 5; mortis discrimina non ~enda GIR. *TH* I 19.

3 (pass.) to be troubled, molested.

quod, quantacunque sanctitate quis polleat, per Theodorum videri et ~eri poterit ELMH. *Cant.* 276.

doleum, ~eus v. dolium. **dolfinus** v. delphin-.

doliare, to pack in tuns.

1440 (v. barellare); **1449** mercandisarum .. ~iatarum *Cl* 299 m. 16*d*.

doliata, ton (measure). **b** (naut.) 'ton-tight' (measure of burden). *V. et. dolium* 2.

1444 pro iij ~is ferri *EEC* 635. **b 1388** frettagium cujuslibet batell' xxij dol', prec' doliat' xij d. *KRAc* 473/2 m. 8; **1449** in quadam batello portagii decem ~arum (*KRMem*) *Bronnen* 1342; *le Mary and John* ponderis 900 ~arum constabat sibi .. 4000 m. W. WORC. *Itin.* 132.

doliator, cooper.

1561 Gelius de Jongh, doleator (*SPDom Eliz.*) *Hug. Soc.* X 274.

dolichuros [δολιχόουρος], (of verse) having a redundant syllable.

pathos in dactilico exametro inserta . . sunt numero sex: acefalos, procefalos, lagaros, procilios, ~os, miuros vel spicodis ALDH. *Met.* 10 p. 94.

doliolum [CL], little cask.

crescebat . . moles limphatica et ad instar ~i tumescebat alvus egroti *Mir. Cuthb. Farne* 5.

dolium, ~eum [CL]

1 tun, cask; **b** (fig.). **c** salt-pan.

dŏlium deferre poposcit ALDH. *VirgV* 1494; ~eus, *byden GlC Int.* 88; ~ium, *cyf* ÆLF. *Gl.*; **10..** ~eum, *wæterbyden WW*; videamus quomodo prudens cellerarius soleat ordinare ~ia in cella vinaria *Simil. Anselmi* 194; **1173** pro ducendis vj tonellis vini ad Sandwicum et reparandis eisdem ~eis *Pipe* 81; videns . . ~ium illud ex magna parte vacuatum W. CANT. *Mir. Thom.* VI 107; quotiens temptationis ardore caro efferbuit, aperto ~ii ore corpus suum totum . . ingessit GIR. *GE* II 10 p. 214; dolia plena tua fecundent pocula leta D. BEC. 2216; ~ea [*gl.*: *tunneus*] NECKAM *Ut.* 98 (v. 1 cadus); **1196** etc. (v. circulus 5a); **1224** etc. (v. circulare 3a); **s1250** ~ia vacua per pavimenta rotaverunt, que sonitum terribilem emittentia equos aufugarunt M. PAR. *Maj.* V 145; BACON VIII 199 (v. clepsydra c); ipsi . . lignis . . et ~iis plenis terra, fimo, arena vel lapidibus . . muros . . rearmarunt *G. Hen. V* 6 p. 38; **1462** pro expensis . . iij piparum . . j ~ii . . ad conservandum martas *ExchScot* 127; hoc ~ium, A. *townne WW*. **b** immensus capitur ventrali dolio. / o quam mirabilis ventris dimencio WALT. WIMB. *Carm.* 110; R. BURY *Phil.* 8. 134 (v. defaecare 1a). **c** †**972** (10c) ad usum conficiendi salis duobus in locis xviij ~iorum situs *on Middelwic CS* 1282.

2 tun, ton (measure): **a** (of fluids); **b** (of dry goods); **c** (of building materials, coal, or munitions). **d** (naut.) 'ton-tight' (measure of burden). *V. et. doliata.*

a 1217 pro . . duobus ~eis vini *Cl* 346b; **1234** mandatum est ballivis domini regis Suhampton' quod de primis vinis que ventura sunt apud S. retineant ad opus domini regis xx ~ea vini Wasconie et v ~ia vini Andegavie *Cl* 414; **1258** taxatur amerciamentum . . ad duo ~ia vini *Rec. Leic.* I 81; **c1263** cum . . ij ~iis vini succo nigri hellebori . . delibuti FORDUN *Cont.* X 17; de vinorum contra rectam assisam venditoribus et quot ~ea [v. l. doleata] (*Cap. Corone*) *Fleta* 24; **1302** (v. custuma 6b); **c1330** ~ium vini de Moysun continet communiter cxlii justas cervisie; justa cervisie continet j lagenam et dim. secundum standardum regis (*Canterbury*) *Eng. Weights* 31. **b 1290** pro j ~eo farrine frumenti pro stauro . . navis (*Chanc. Misc.* 4/5) *DocScot* I 141; **c1300** de quolibet ~eo de *wayde Reg. S. Aug.* 138; **1329** de . . ij ~iis et xviij bollis pisarum . ., quolibet ~io continente xiij bollas *ExchScot* 200; **1334** in ~eis pisc[is] sals[i] *Ac. Durh.* 21. **c 1336** iiij ~ia sagittarum longitudinis j ulne *RScot* 457b; **1369** pro xvj pond[eribus] dol[iorum] libre petre . . pro quolibet pond[ere] dol[ii] x s. (*KRAc* 479/30) *Arch. Cant.* II 112; **1371** in viij ~iis lapidum cariandis de Tadcastre usque Ebor' *Fabr. York* 6 (cf. ib. 50 [**1433**]: in iiij ~eis plastri); **1378** (v. carbo 1f); **1480** pro ij ~iis de *Folkestone stone* . .; pro vij ~iis de *le boldyr* . .; pro j ~io et dim. silicis *Ac. Chamb. Cant.* 137; **1508** x ~ea meremii *Reg. Merton* 362; **1533** operario fodenti xij ~ia calcis apud montem *Comp. Swith.* 218. **d 1309** quod . . quandam . . navem ccc ~iorum vini fieri faciat ad opus nostrum *RGasc* IV 238; **1327** aliquas naves pondus xxx ~iorum vini portantes *KRMem* 103 r. 83; **1327** in conduccione trium shoutarum . . pro cariagio . . meremii . ., viz. duabus de dictis shoutis cariantibus . . pondus xl ~iorum vini *LTRMem* 99 r. 140d.; **1337** ad arestandum omnes . . naves xl ~ia et ultra portantes *RScot* 490b; **s1514** facta est regia navis vocata *Herry the Gracidew* continens xviij[c] ~ia *Reg. Butley* 32 (cf. ib. 28).

3 a barrel or sim. for sheathing mill-stone. **b** 'tun', chimney pot. **c** 'tun', prison.

a 1282 in j ~eo faciendo ad circulandum molare *Ac. Man. Cant.* (*Cliffe*). **b 1507** ij lathomis versantibus circa facturam verticis et ~ii camini camere . . diruti impetu venti *Cant. Coll. Ox.* 249. **c 1347** quod ipsi unum ~ium pro prisonibus infra villam . . de novo facere . . possint et tenere . . ad imprisonandum in eodem . . malefactores et pacis nostre perturbatores, si quos ibidem de nocte vagantes inveniri contigerit, eodem modo et prout in civitate nostra London' est usitatum (*Ch.*) *Bristol Rec. Soc.* I 108 (cf. S. Seyer *Hist. Bristol* 36–7); **s1382** [Londonienses] captas [in fornicacione] mulieres in prisona, que vocatur '~ium' apud eos, primo seclusas incarcerarunt WALS. *HA* II 65; hec sunt Londonis: . . / Chepp, stupha, Cok Lana, Dolium, Leo, verbaque vana *Staura Civ.* 2.

dolo [CL < δόλων], **~um**.

1 short spear or dagger (or sheath for same). **b** axe.

~ones, *hunsporan GlC* D 356; ~ones, *stæfsweord* ÆLF. *Gl.*; in vaginis mucrones et pugiones in ~onibus [*gl.*: *gaines*] BALSH. *Ut.* 49; praeliaria tela ac ~ones gestantes BOECE 69v. **b 1502** unum ~um vocatum *an ax* (v. contrafacere 4).

2 small sail.

dalum, *lytel segel* ÆLF. *Gl.*; dalum, *se lesta segl Id. Sup.*

dolobratio v. dolabratio.

1 dolor [CL]

1 pain, ache.

Colossus . . in †quem [v.l. quam, sc. undam Thybridis] se ~ore marcescens moriturum jactavit *Lib. Monstr.* I 3; BEDE *HE* V 3 (v. ardere 2c); emigraneum, i. ~or timporum, *þunwonga sar GlH* E 247; telum, i. ~or lateris, *sticwærc, sticadl* ÆLF. *Gl.*; EADMER *Beat.* 15 (v. dolere 1a); in statu innocencie . . caro ejus [Ade] habuit continuitatem. . . hec autem continuitas divisibilis fuit. sed ad hanc divisionem sequeretur distantia partium vel solutio. sed hec est causa ~oris; ~or enim est distantia partium vel solutio, vel sensus hujus distantie HALES *Qu.* 230; ~or sensibilis *Id. Sent.* IV 217 (v. 2a infra); [vinum cum succo mandragore mixtum] solet dari hominibus qui sunt propter infirmitatem secandi, ut possint sine ~ore secari FORDUN *Cont.* X 17. ~or dentium prosternit virtutem GAD. 119. 1; *SB* 10 (v. anodynus).

2 sorrow, grief; **b** (in interj. w. *pro*).

silui, fateor, cum inmenso cordis ~ore GILDAS *EB* 1; virgo Christum pulsabat corde benignum / ut sibi dignetur vulnus sanare doloris ALDH. *VirgV* 2039; BEDE *HE* IV 23 (v. conscientia 3a); **s1108** (v. dejectio 2a); cum . . gravi cordis ~ore GIR. *TH* I 32; ~or est passio de aliquo tristabili, ut de malo habito vel bono amisso HALES *Sent.* II 318; [ad medicinam peccati] semper requiritur ~or rationalis sive spiritualis, aliquando etiam ~or sensibilis *Ib.* IV 217 (v. et. 1 supra); ~or et gaudium sunt oppposita. . . ~or est id quod putatur esse nocivum J. BLUND *An.* 81; *Ib.* 376 (v. constrictio a); ~or est affectus presentis inconvenientis, timor futuri inconvenientis *Ps.*-GROS. *Gram.* 60; nonne hoc ~or ingens [ME: *muche sore3e*]? *AncrR* 37. **b** heu pro ~or! BEDE *HE* II 1 p. 80; proh ~or! eo [dolore] amoto, alius infestior . . eum arripuit ASSER *Alf.* 74; proh ~or! *Enc. Emmae* II 12; proch ~or BACON XV 103 (v. 2 eclipticus); **1335** proch ~or! *Reg. Glasg.* 25; prothdolor! [ME: *weilawei*] *AncrR* 45.

2 dolor v. 2 dolus a.

dolorifer [LL], grievous.

1291 dicitur hoc infortunium ~ferum per Hospitalariorum et Templariorum discordiam contigisse *Ann. Dunstable* 366.

dolorose, a painfully. **b** grievously.

a lacerti extendentur ~e GAD. 128. 1. **b s1068** igne . . qui . . totam civitatem [Eboracum] . . ~e consumpsit W. GUISB. 6 (cf. R. HOWD. I 118).

dolorosus [LL]

1 painful, aching.

ex dente ~o GAD. 120. 1.

2 grievous. **b** expressing sorrow, plaintive. **c** (of persons) sorrowful.

G. MON. XI 2 (v. describere 3a); **1188** trenis . . producimus [dies] ~os et noctes insomnes, flentes vobiscum et gementes *Ep. Cant.* 206; MAP *NC* IV 11 (v. dolosus); **s1334** transiit annus iste . . Scotis lamentabilis et ~us WALS. *HA* II app. 377; **s1339** guerra continua et ~a . . inter reges Francie et Anglie exordium tediosum †sortitum [*ed.*: sortita] est *Meaux* II 380; conclusio ~a [ME: *sorwful*] auditu *Concl. Loll. XII* 297; **s1454** (v. dedecorosus). **b** cum ~is [ME: *sorchfule*] suspiriis . . clamet ad Deum *AncrR* 106; **1440** patris B. . . ~am nuper querimoniam . . recepimus BEKYNTON I 32. **c c1370** de Gallis mestis [*gl.*: qui sc. fuerant mesti et ~i propter cedem . . quam ab Anglicis paciebantur] (J. BRIDL.) *Pol. Poems* I 163–4; **s1455** legatus . . pape . . officium non exercuit, sed ~us ultraquam credi potest recessit *Plusc.* XI 7.

dolose [CL], guilefully.

1077 ut ~e semper alicui tentent aliquid auferre ANSELM (*Ep.* 80) III 204; quia alios circumvenire ~e attentabat, et ille dolo circumventus . . interiit *G. Steph.* I 51; a viris sanguinum et dolosis tam ~e et inique funditur sanguis GIR. *TH* III 22; aurum inventum sub lecto quod . . Ulixes ~e ibi absconderat TREVET *Troades* 55; nulli ~e egerat, aut falsum aliquod cuiquam proferre solebat BLAKMAN *Hen. VI* 4.

dolositas [LL], guile, trickery, deceitfulness. **b** trick, deceit.

B. *V. Dunst.* 16 (v. dissociare c); Edricus consiliis pollens, sed tamen ~ate versipell[is] *Enc. Emmae* II 8; **1183** ne . . mundane fictionis ~as deciperet animam illius P. BLOIS *Ep.* 167. 462B; Moyses . . simplicitatem Jacob [cf. *Gen.* xxv 27], ~atem Esau (*sic*) . . manifestat TORIGNI *Chr. prol.* 61; NECKAM *NR* II 125 (v. diverticulum 2b); GIR. *Invect.* I 9 (v. 2 catulus 1c); **s1210** rex [Johannes] tante erat ~atis ut vix aliquis dictis ejus fidem haberet vel scriptis GERV. CANT. *GR Cont.* 106; **s1368** Franci . ., ut erant semper fraude et ~ate pleni WALS. *HA* I 307; **c1430** fraudium pedice, ~atis . . muscipule *Reg. Whet.* II app. 459; *a falsed*, falsitas . ., dolus, ~as . . *CathA*. **b 1298** propter eorum [Scotorum] malignitatem, nequiciam, ~ates et alia execrabilia facta ipsorum *Anglo-Scot. Rel.* 79.

dolosus [CL], guileful, crafty, deceitful.

Romani regni molimina leaena trucidavit ~a GILDAS *EB* 6; pellax, ~us *GlC* P 274; ex commodis vel incommodis naturae [hominis] conjectura sumenda est . .: memor an obliviosus, ~us an simplex ALCUIN *Rhet.* 25; **8..** ~us testis, *facynful cyðere WW*; ~us, i. insidiosus, fraudulentus, callidus, *inwitful* vel *facenful GlH* D 769; quis dolus dolosior quam in patrem prolis? *Poem S. Thom.* 83; GIR. *TH* III 22 (v. dolose); tam dolorosa quam ~a dispendia MAP *NC* IV 11 f. 52; **s1210** ~as ut vel sic sibi preparatas evitaret insidias GERV. CANT. *GR Cont.* 106; a quorum labiis iniquis et linguis ~is liberabit Deus animam meam ROLLE *IA* 170; **1424** de illo ~issimo proditore . ., qui . . ausus est . . falsa proditoria instimulacione suggerere . . BEKYNTON I 279.

dolphin- v. delphin-.

dolua [LL], (bot.) rocket.

~a, toroc [? l. τορός] *GlH* D 772.

dolubrum v. dolabra a. **dolum** v. dolo.

1 dolus v. dala.

2 dolus [CL < δόλος], guile, fraud, trickery; **b** (leg., as ground of objection).

quid tu . . in throno ~is pleno . ., Vortipori, stupide riges? GILDAS *EB* 31; praestigiae, ~i, insidiae *GlC* P 813; ~us, *facn* ÆLF. *Gl.*; sine ~o fideliter militare *Enc. Emmae* II 15; *G. Steph.* I 51 (v. dolose); *Poem S. Thom.* 83 (v. dolosus); puellarum ~o delusus occubuit GIR. *TH* III 37; ut ex ~o non reportet commodum sed penam HALES *Sent.* IV 552; **1281** moniales quedam . ., cum sint etatis legitime et ~i capaces *Conc. Syn.* 912; OCKHAM *Dial.* 638 (v. delusio); si . . hec desint, non est nisi fraus et ~us [ME: *an truchunge & an fals gile*] *AncrR* 8; quisque dolos fingit GOWER *CT* II 177 (= *Pol. Poems* I 432: †dolor); **s1406** omni ~o, fraude, ac maligna interpretacione cessantibus *Chr. S. Alb.* 5. **b 1276** renuncians . . excepcioni ~i, metus, et in factum *Reg. Heref.* 85; **1289** renunciantes excepcioni non numerate . . pecunie, ~i, et in factum *RGasc* II 302.

doma [LL < δῶμα]

1 house, home; **b** (w. allusion to *Prov.* xxi 9). **c** (mon.) house of religion; *cf. domus* 7.

quorum [presbiterorum] primus . . in proprii ~atis tigillo . . conflagrasse memoratur ALDH. *VirgP* 32; ~atis, *huses GlC* D 352; *CS* 1311 (v. 2 Codrus 2); ut vacuo solus domate pellicanus [cf. *Psalm* ci 7] *V. Ed. Conf.* 53; ut . . potius in domo ejus mortem suscipiendo persolveret quam in suo proprio ~ate finis exitum expectaret R. COLD. *Cuthb.* 134; est domus atque dōma, presepe, domuncula, tectum GARL. *Syn.* 375. 1584D. **b** plus sed ego vatis humili sub domate mirer / pelliculam sanctus fragilem qua texerat anglum BEDE *CuthbV* 897; in cujus ~atis angulo lectisternia patris ministri straverunt W. DAN. *Ep.* 62b; **s1177** sedens cum eis in angulo ~atis *G. Hen. II* I 156; **s1225** ubi in quodam ~atis angulo mattam sub se pro stratu . . supponebat WEND. II 293. **c 1384** jocalia . . ac alia bona . . in custodia ac in ~a (*sic*) vestra [sc. S. Maria, Suthwerk] †existentibus [l. existencia] *IMisc* 233/19 r. 2;

2 roof; **b** (as shelter for ship).

puer duodennis retulit mihi tunc super culmen ~atis se . . ascendisse ORD. VIT. XIII 16 p. 42; verbum curto 'dŏma', longo pro culmine 'dōma' SERLO WILT. 2. 33; tignis usque ad ~a edificii attingentibus NECKAM *Ut.* 109; nicticorax in domicilio [cf. *Psalm* ci 7] significat anachoritam sub ~ate ecclesie [ME: *under chirche evesunge*] *AncrR* 45; debent prelati in suis visitacionibus . . mederi morbos anime, non primo notare defectus ornamentorum codicum, ~atis vel fenestre WYCL. *Blasph.* 97; **1406** in bordis, clavis, latheis . . emptis . . pro . . ~ate . . cooperiendo *Comp. Swith.* 288; *a rufe of a howse*, ~a, domicilium, tectum; *a rufe tre*, festum, ~a *CathA*. **b s1372** rex misit apud Fordwicum unam galeam, ut tuta contra tempestates yemales servaretur, mandans abbati quod pro fossatura et ~a (*sic*) super illa construenda . . operam daret diligentem THORNE 2145.

domabilis [CL], that can be subdued.

turris excellentissima . ., sola fame ~is H. HUNT. *HA* VIII 34; summus stupet Seraph mirabile, / summum videns robur domabile J. HOWD. *Ph.* 51.

domalis, (as sb. n. pl.) household goods or (?) *f. l.*

1415 lego uxori mee . . dimidietatem domalium [? l. domesticalium] et supellectilis domus mee (*Test.*) *Berks R. O.* 453.

domanium v. 2 dominium 5e.

domare [CL]

1 to tame, subdue: **a** (animals); **b** (men or their spirits); **c** (human frailty or impulses). **d** (p. ppl.) submissive, subject.

a cui [sc. Jasono] rex [Aeeta] tauros flammantes ~are . . tribuit *Lib. Monstr.* II 33; cur permittis [accipitres] ~itos [AS: *þa getemedon*] avolare a te? ÆLF. *Coll.* 96; nolite ovi catulos leonum ~andos committere ANSELM (*Ep.* 144) III 291; cum omnia animalia possint ~ari, illud [unicornis] nunquam potest ~ari *Quaest. Salern.* B 161; **1377** pro hominibus ~antibus equos *Ac. Durh.* 585; **13..** de quolibet equo ~ito et equitato in foresta invento capiat forestarius iiij d. (*Leg. Forest.*) *APScot* app. 325. **b s940** [Eadmundus] totam Cumberland, quia gentem provincie illius perfidam et legibus insolitam ad plenum ~are

nequibat, predavit et contrivit H. Hunt. *HA* V 21 (= B. Cotton 23: dominare); sic igne caritatis accensa viscera ferreos olim .. animos ∼ant et .. mansuescere .. compellunt Gir. *TH* I 14; D. Bec. 1969 (v. dominatrix a); s**1400** rex .. iter .. arripuit versus Scociam, ut eorum .. qui pacis inimici extiterant .. insolenciam ∼aret *V. Ric. II* 171; s**1426** parleamentum ∼avit eos [nobiles] valde et timere regem fecit *Plusc.* XI 4. **c** corpus senile inter cotidiana jejunia ∼abat Bede *HE* V 12; necesse habemus vigiliis et jejuniis et labore corporis carnem ∼are Ailr. *Serm.* 17. 306c; omnis superbia fame ∼atur Map *NC* III 4 f. 41v.; Simeon .. cum carnum (*sic*) ∼uit .. sedens in columpna S. Langton *Ruth* 96; Garl. *Tri. Eccl.* 1 (v. caro 7); per hujus fortitudinis virtutem beati et sancti corpus ∼ant, spiritum roborant Chaundler *Apol.* f. 31. **d** [vir] indomitis ∼itus, ∼itis indomitus Gir. *EH* II 16; ut eos teneret insomnes et per consequens ∼iciores [v. l. †dormitiores] in crastino redderet ad vincendum *G. Hen. V* 8.

2 a to soften (flesh), make tender. **b** to card (wool).

a Ethiopes [cf. *Psalm* lxxiii 13–14] .. excitant dracones de cavernis suis .. et equitant super eos .. in aere .., ut ∼etur rigiditas carnium Bacon *Maj.* II 211. **b** pectinibusque dari lanam ferroque domari R. Cant. *Malch.* III 545.

domatio, a (falc.) taming. **b** softening, suppling (of leather), making supple.

a [alietus] primo anno ∼onis parum valet, secundo plus, tercia tamen mutacione aucupat satis bene Upton 189. **b** **1460** pro tannacione et ∼one vj coriorum bovinorum *Ac. Durh.* 90.

domayn-, domen- v. domin-. **domcilla** v. domicella 2a.

domesticalis, (as sb. n. pl.) household goods. *V. et. domalis.*

1423 ne [ministri] victualia aut alia ∼ia per hec [claustralia] loca differant .. nisi cum urget necessitas (*Ord. Abbatis*) Amund. I 109.

domesticare, to domesticate, tame. **b** to adopt into household. **c** (p. ppl.) familiar, intimate.

1174 a quibusdam dicitur Machabeus ∼asse accipitres in avium capturam P. Blois *Ep.* 61. 183a; hic [falco] ad nutum civium .., tanquam [? avis] mansueta et ad hoc ∼ata, anates et alias aves .. persequi solebat et ad terram .. coercere Gir. *TH* II 37; cum .. sic ∼averint eos [dracones] Bacon *Maj.* II 211 (cf. domare 2a); merula ∼ata contra suam naturam carnes comedit Upton 174. **b** antichristianos papas .. caesareos clericos .. filios diaboli et diabolos incarnatos .. non ∼andos in filios Netter *DAF* I 138. **c** s**1390** ad .. ∼atiorem familiaritatem (v. collibertus b).

domesticatim [CL], internally, within the country.

Anglia .. vectigal Romano pontifici pendit ∼im collatum et numi illi .. vocantur denarii Divi Petri P. Verg. IV 90 (v. denarius 5a).

domesticatio, inclusion in household, (assumption of) familiarity.

c**1430** cum .. devocio perficiendi opus jam nos incitaret extranei patris gracie domesticas preces porrigere .., racione ∼onis nos, quesumus, non contemnatis *Reg. Whet.* II 403.

domestice, familiarly.

doctores .. et homines ingeniosos .. apud te invenies et sepe cum multis sermonem facies, coram eis sapienter ac ∼e verba pronuncians M. Scot *Phys. prol.*

domesticitas, willingness to serve.

Christus fuit domesticus suis apostolis, quod .. tunica se succinxit et lavit pedes suorum apostolorum [*John* xiii 5]; sed ubi mansuetudo vel ∼as major posset esse? Wycl. *Chr. & Antichr.* 690.

domesticus [CL]

1 domestic, belonging to household. **b** willing to serve. **c** (as sb. m. or f.) member of household, domestic servant. **d** inmate of religious house.

omissis ∼is levioribusque Gildas *EB* 33; velut Aethiopica nigredine fuscatus, a propriis parasitis et ∼is clientibus non agnoscitur Aldh. *VirgP* 50 (cf. ib. 44: familiaris clientelae ∼a sollicitudo); cujusdam .. ∼i viri filia Wulf. *Æthelwold* 44; s**1142** [rex] castellum in quo cum suis ∼is militibus imperatrix erat obsedit R. Niger *Chr. II* 187; cum [coloni] nocturnas propter ∼as operas agunt vigilias Gerv. Tilb. III 61; 'penates' i. e. dii ∼i Trevet *Troades* 64. **b** Christus fuit summe ∼us, ostendens suam inferioritatem Wycl. *Chr. & Antichr.* 690; *Ib.* (v. domesticitas). **c** lingua patria, quam rex et ∼i ejus non noverant Bede *HE* III 15; **8..** ∼is suis, *hiore gehusan WW*; Gosc. *Transl. Aug.* 18a (v. desiderare 2b); ut .. ∼os fidei apostolica traditione ad bonum opus instrueret Osb. *V. Dunst.* 34; paruit .. Arturus ∼orum suorum consilio G. Mon. IX 2; erat hoc omnibus ignotum .., quia nulli ∼orum ejus sive servorum .. accessibile Gir. *GE* II 10 p. 215; **1235** fuit camerarius ipsius Willelmi et ∼us ejus *CurR* XV 1480; **1480** in zuccero et vino dato ∼e et suis honestis vicinis *Ac. Chamb. Cant.* 135. **d** non domorum culpa est sed ∼orum si .. mali sponte recedant Gir. *Spec.* III 9 p. 175.

2 a (of animals) domesticated, tame. **b** (of plants) cultivated.

a *G. Herw.* 337 (v. congratulari 1b); R. Cold. *Cuthb.* 27 (v. contrectabilis); in tantum secure atque ∼e fuerunt [hirundines] quod ad monitum hominum .. cantare solebant Alex. Cant. *Mir.* 42 (I) p. 242; rex Connacie hircum habebat ∼um album Gir. *TH* II 23; volucrem [sc. nisum] apprehendit et tanquam ∼um domum reportavit W. Cant. *Mir. Thom.* V 22; psittacus .., cum in cavea recluditur, effectus etiam ∼us Neckam *Sac. extr.* 362; *Id. Ut.* 102 (v. auca b); s**1336** nullus audebat volatilia pennata ∼a manducare *Plusc.* IX 39; **1511** summa gallinarum ∼arum xv duodene vj; summa gallinarum muralium viij duodene *Reg. Aberd.* I 364. **b** Bart. Angl. XVII 34, 42 (v. 1 calamentum a, caepa b); plantarum alia ∼a, alia ortensis, alia silvestris Bacon XI 230 *rub.* (cf. ib. 230: non semper dicitur planta silvestris, propter locum, set propter proprietatem silvestris [sc. plante]. .. similiter intelligendum est de ortensibus et ∼is); allium ∼um, tyriaca rusticorum idem. .. A. *garleke Alph.* 5.

3 a internal, native, private. **b** inner, inward-facing.

a augebantur externae clades ∼is motibus Gildas *EB* 19; ∼a scissura, *hiwcuðlic geter GlH* D 775; ne tantum aliorum exemplum sumamus, ecce ∼um Vinsauf *AV* II 3. 52; s**1244** [S. Edmundus] cum seipso dimicavit, ut, ∼o tormento superato corpore, de se triumphum .. adquireret M. Par. *Maj.* IV 329; cessante .. diluvio .. et rivo .. aquis suis ∼is contento *Ps.*-Elmh. *Hen. V* 122. **b** ad partem cruris ∼am *Ps.*-Ric. *Anat.* 44 (cf. ib.: ad partem .. silvestrem); ventosaciones super crura et super calcanea ex parte ∼a, sc. interiori Gad. 9 (cf. ib. 5v. 1: capiatur folium unum cresule majoris et depiletur a parte ∼a).

4 a familiar, intimate. **b** habitual, ingrained.

a in .. consanguineum suum [sc. regis] germanum, H. dominum Lescrop, de sibi magis ∼is et qui secretis regiis vix fuit alicui tercius in regno *G. Hen. V* 2 p. 18. **b** Brettones, quamvis .. ∼o sibi odio gentem Anglorum impugnent Bede *HE* V 23; ita ∼um regibus vitium evicerunt ut nunquam feratur in eorum thalamos nisi legitimas uxores isse W. Malm. *GR* V 400 (cf. id. *GP* II 95: ∼o adequitaverant otio).

domicella [AN *damecelle*, OF *donzele*, *dancele*, *damoisele* < dominicella; *in some exx. MS may read* douncella, daunsella *or sim.*; cf. dangerum, doungerium < domigerium]

1 damsel, young lady; **b** (as title). **c** (w. name of country) princess or sim.

1220 sicut homines domini sui .. duxerunt quandam ∼am .. que fuit in custodia domini sui .., venit Johannes de M. .. *CurR* IX 65; **1241** duas damisellas, filias et heredes Nicolai de W., .. secum abduxerunt *CurR* XVI 1744; **1279** nulla secularis ∼a nubilis etatis inter vos aliquatenus commoretur *Reg. Heref.* 202; si quis rapuerit ∼as infra etatem existentes sponte vel ipsis invitis (*Cap. Itin.*) *Fleta* 27; **1295** super sponsalibus .. contrahendis cum serenissima ∼a nepte vestre seu consanguinea .. (*Lit. Regis Scotiae*) W. Guisb. 268; ∼arum sacratissimarum princeps et magistra *NLA* (*Ursula*) II 471; s**1306** Nigellus de Bruse .. cum pluribus dominabus et ∼is Fordun *GA* 120; s**1344** fuerunt ibidem domina regina Ph.., comitisse, baronisse necnon domine et ∼e Ad. Mur. app. 231; Parce .. tres erant domicele sorores *Deorum Imag.* 314; **1390** de uno pari pelvium .. aymell[atarum] in fundo cum una damisella sedente super uno leone ducente j *wodewose Ac. Foreign* 25G (cf. ib. 25: cum una damaisella); hec damicella, *a damselle WW*; *CathA* (v. dominella a). **b** **1220** damisellam Johannam, sororem domini regis (*AncC* I 77) *RL* I 149; **1235** liberate .. ∼e Margarete Biset xl s. ad expensas suas versus partes suas *Liberate* (*Exch*) 1203 m. 1; **1255** domicille A. de Beles *CalIMisc* I 218; **1265** ad portiforium domiselle Alianore (*RHosp*) *Manners* 9; **1470** honorabilis et provida ∼a M., relicta quondam A. H. *Melrose* 575; **1513** divorcium .. inter nobilem ∼am Agnetem H. sponsam nobilis domini W. domini L. de Calendar actricem .. et dictum dominum W. *Offic. S. Andr.* 3. **c** **1236** in robis regis et regine, et regine Scocie, domicille Britannie, xxvj dominarum, domicillarum et lotricum (*Pipe* 81 r. 13) *Cal. Scot.* I 238 (v. et. 2a infra); **1290** pro facto maritagii inter dominum E. filium regis et ∼am Scocie consummando (*Chanc. Misc.* 4/5 f. 166) *Doc. Scot.* I 142; **1291** Margarete quondam ∼e Norwagie et domine .. regni Scocie *RScot* 5b.

2 a lady-in-waiting; **b** (w. ref. to prostitute).

a **1199** assignasse Beatricie et Aelicie ∼is .. regine sororis nostre xxv li. redditus *RChart* 25b; **1205** pro robis emptis ad opus comitisse Gloecestr' et damisellarum suarum *Pipe* 113; **1216** habere faciat domine regine unam robam de scarletta .. et ∼e ejus unam robam de nigra burnetta *Cl* 274b; **1223** [Johanna que fuit uxor Jordani] committatur alicui legali militi in custodiam, ita quod nulla ∼a cum ea sit que pregnans sit vel alia de qua aliqua suspicio haberi possit alicujus falsitatis faciende *CurR* XI 602; **1231** de Katerina domicilla sororis regis desponsanda *Cl* 502; **1236** (v. 1c supra); **1242** (v. domina 1d); **1259** cum domina Guillelma, domcilla (*sic*) regis, .. senio .. sit confecta *Cl* 397; **1284** habendo domum sibi competentem in eodem castello pro se et uxore sua cum una domicilla et familia sua *IPM* 39/8; **1315** in presencia .. Agnetis de M. †donicelle ejusdem comitisse *RParl* I 334b; in quo loco statuit [H. abbas, ob. c**1136**] tres virgines sacratas, ∼as viz. camere Matildis bone regine Flete *Westm.* 88; s**1405** heredes comitis Marchie .. abducti fuerunt a curia regis per quandam ∼am de camera regine *Eul. Hist. Cont.* III 402; **1460** pro uno equo .. liberato uni ∼e sororis domini regis defuncti *ExchScot* 11. **b** **1284** Willelmus Hoppeshort tenet dim. virgatam terre in eadem villa [*Bockhampton, Berks*] de domino rege per serjanciam custodiendi domino regi sex damisellas, sc. meretrices, ad custum domini regis *JustIt* 48 r. 28d.

domicellula, little damsel.

vultque venire metrum tanquam domicellula, compto / crine, nitente gena Vinsauf *PN* 1859.

domicellum v. domicilium 1a.

domicellus [AN *dommaisel*, OF *donzel*, *dancel*, *damoisel* < dominicellus]

1 'donzel', young gentleman, squire, or sim.; **b** (as title).

GAS 665 (v. adelingus); **1254** dominis et ∼is de Hispania, qui conduxerunt Johannam reginam Castelle ad partes Francie *RGasc* I 532 (= *CalPat* 347); **1296** rex comitibus, vicecomitibus, baronibus, militibus, ∼is, civibus, burgensibus .. (*Commissio Regis*) *Reg. Carl.* I 67; s**1344** post hastiludia ∼orum rex fecit cenam magnam Ad. Mur. *Chr.* 155; s**1356** dominus Ph. .. duos .. milites et duos ∼os misit .. in Angliam Avesb. 135b; ∼us *CathA* (v. dominellus). **b** **1282** inclitum ∼um Alfonsum .., tunc infantem Arragonum *PS* 1679/31; **1358** peticio pro parte .. nobilis viri D. de Berclay ∼i *Mon. Hib. & Scot.* 312b; **1418** J. Lytiltone, domisellus *Reg. Heref.* 49; **1423** Johanni C., ∼o et armigero *Test. Ebor.* III 83; **1440** nobilis et strenuus ∼us, J. Burian .., dominus in Rabenstein ex regno Bohemie Bekynton I 188.

2 squire (in attendance), page; **b** (fig.).

loricatus miles .. sonipedem ascendit dimissoque ∼o campum solus .. ingreditur Gerv. Tilb. III 59; per te leo fit agnellus, / dominator domicellus Walt. Wimb. *Virgo* 129; s**1287** ictus fulminis .. duos ∼os, qui in eorum [regis et regine] presencia stabant, interfecit Rish. 114; **1299** coram Alberto .. et Jacobino .. ∼is .. domini episcopi Vicentini *Doc. Scot.* II 404; **1312** per H. de Cundicote, .. cancellarii [Oxon'] ∼um *Collect. Ox.* II 244; s**1315** assignans eis certum numerum servitorum, viz. cuilibet cardinali unum clericum et duos ∼os Ad. Mur. *Chr.* 23; **1324** cum sitis episcopus et dominus meus et ego vester ∼us portans robas vestras *Proc. A. Kyteler* 5; **1326** (v. 1 cum 1b); s**1046** cuidam Turstino ∼o abbatis Thorne 1748; s**1301** ∼i et servientes monasterii *Ib.* 1980; s**1402** mercatores quendam regis ∼um literas regias .. deferentem .. trucidabant Ad. Usk 62. **b** cujus erat solus nuper catulus domicellus, / en sequitur totus hunc quasi mundus eum Gower *VC* III 1391.

domicialis v. domitialis. **domicila, ∼illa** v. domicella 1a.

domiciliarius, domestic, familiar, ordinary.

13.. aucuparius habeat aves silvestres et agrestes et domesticas.. . capit volucres .. ubi omnes volucres et campestres .. capi possint, ubi †domicilianos [MS: domiciliarios] sive †scingudarios [?l. singularios] (*Nominale*) *Neues Archiv* IV 341.

domicilium [CL]

1 domicile, house, dwelling-place. **b** friary. **c** chapel. **d** (? infl. by *cilium*) eaves.

penates, ∼ia, sacra *GlC* P 361; c**1160** masuram quandam que prope predictum domicellum erat *Ch. & Rec. Heref.* 12; Gir. *TH* I 8 (v. dominator a); **1389** (v. coopertura 6a); **1428** sunt nisi octo inhabitantes ∼ia tenentes in parochia de F. *Aids* I 243. **b** **1290** juxta ∼ium fratrum de Domina *Rec. Norw.* II 15 (cf. *MonA* VI 1611). **c** *V. Ed. Conf.* 49 (v. disposite). **d** ∼ium, A. *ovese WW*.

2 household: **a** (private); **b** (royal). **c** household connection.

a **1435** (v. dispensatorius 3); **1450** xxxj dolia .. vini .. sibi [H. duci Glouc'] pro expensis ∼ii sui missa *Cl* 300 m. 15. **b** a ∼io regis plures officiarios expulerunt Favent 13; **1460** pro vij martis .. liberatis compotorum rotulatori ad expensas ∼ii domini regis *ExchScot* 3 (cf. ib. 8: pro ij pipis vini .. non intratis in libris ∼ii). **c** statutum est quod clericus sit specialiter deputatus per regem non habens aliquam ligam vel ∼ium cum camerario et sit obligatus regi dumtaxat .. (*Fragm. Coll.*) *APScot* I 365.

3 a abode (fig.). **b** (med.) seat. **c** (astr.) 'house'; *cf. domus* 17.

a secedat veritas, nam domicilium / hic nullum meruit Walt. Wimb. *Sim.* 35. **b** cum sinister [cordis] thalamus anime, vite et caloris sit ∼ium Alf. Angl. *Cor* 5 (cf. ib. 16: cerebrum .. spirituum et zoticarum virtutum ∼ium est); virtus vitalis .., cujus fundamentum sive proprium ∼ium est cor Bart. Angl. III 15. **c** adde tantundem supra id cum quo invenisti casam tertiam et per inde coacervatum .. ∼ii quarti principium Adel. *Elk.* 32; omnes [planete] preter solem et lunam .. duobus ∼iis gaudent, naturali sc.

et accidentali J. SAL. *Pol.* 441D; Saturni ~ia sunt Capricornus et Aquarius, Jovis Sagittarius et Pisces, Martis Aries et Scorpio, Veneris Taurus et Libra, Mercurii Gemini et Virgo, Solis Leo, Lune ~ium est Cancer D. MORLEY 37; queri potest utrum necessarium sit bellum aut famem futuram esse si Mars in suo ~io sit et Mercurius et Saturnus sint in eodem hemispherio cum Marte, remotis benevolis planetis NECKAM *NR* II 173 p. 300; BACON IX 192 (v. accidentalis c).

domiciuncula, humble abode. *V. et. domicula, domuncula, domuscula.*

1187 quam cito facte fuerint apud Hakintune alique ~e, non laudarem ut monachi extra septa ecclesie sue aliquam faciant processionem *Ep. Cant.* 76.

domicula, little house. *V. et. domiciuncula, domuncula, domuscula.*

postquam nostram introgressus es ~am, sopor . . recessit ocellis LANTFR. *Swith.* 1.

domiduca [cf. CL Juppiter domiducus], one who brings a bride to her husband's home. **b** bride.

~a, quae ducit in domum *GlH* D 787; Juno . . quae etiam ~a dicebatur quia in domum puellas viratas introducere videbatur OSB. GLOUC. *Deriv.* 161; Juno . . dicitur domoduca, quod ad domos maritorum eas [nubentes puellas] adducat ALB. LOND. *DG* 4. 3. **b** ~a, *a bryde WW.*

domifex, house-builder (as transl. of surname 'Carpenter').

1432 per fabrum sive ~ficem vestrum Johannem, . . urbis [London'] secretarium indignissimum (J. CARPENTER) *MGL* III 464.

domificare, to build a house.

howsyn or make howsys, ~o *PP*; *to make an howse*, ~are, edificare, fundare *CathA.*

domificatio, house-building.

[sciencia] familitica consistit in ~one, in liberorum educacione, in administracione officiorum . . et consimilibus *Ps.*-GROS. *Gram.* 15.

domificativus, pertaining to house-building.

~a [scientia] est de domibus faciendis FISHACRE *Sent. Prol.* 93; ars ~a . . ad omnia se extendit que possunt racionem domus habere R. ORFORD *Sciendum* 115.

domificator, house-builder.

sicut ~ori per artem suam ascribitur domus et non securi BACON *Tert. Sup.* 2.

domiger- v. danger-.

domina [CL]

1 mistress. **b** lady, gentlewoman. **c** heiress or dowager in king's gift. **d** lady-in-waiting. **e** principal (f.) of proxy. **f** (w. *noctis* or sim.) witch.

Joseph, / qui dominam sprevit nectentem retia luxus [cf. *Gen.* xxxix 7–8] ALDH. *VirgV* 2556; Christi famula Torctgyd . . post obitum ~ae [sc. abbatissae] BEDE *HE* IV 9; **10..** ~a, *hlæfdige WW*; ipse [Wilfridus] . . ob amorem dilectissime ~e sue, . . sc. regine [Etheldride] RIC. HEX. *Hist. Hex.* I 2; cum domina dormire viri scelus est scelerosum D. BEC. 1902; GIR. *GE* II 18 (v. dominatrix a); hec regula [exterior] non est nisi ut subserviat alteri [interiori], altera quasi ~a [ME: *alswa lavedi*], hec quasi ancilla *AncrR* 6; **1344** Edwardus P. . . fecit fidelitatem ~e servilem (*CourtR Chatham Hall*) *EHR* XX 482 (cf. ib. 483: posuit filium suum ad scholas sine licencia ~e). **b** rex W. dedit Rogero D[eus] Salvaet ~as iij virgatas *DB* II 21v.; **1255** Johanni de F. et uxori sue faciant habere duas robas militi et ~e convenientes *Cl* 23; multociens nudus gladio cinctus ~as illius patrie visitabat *State Tri. Ed. I* 76; **1294** assignavimus vos . . ad recipiendum fines . . ab . . episcopis . ., viris religiosis, personis ecclesiasticis, ~abus, viduis et aliis mulieribus . . ac eciam ab aliis . . qui fines nobiscum facere voluerint pro servicio quod nobis debent . . in . . expedicione nostri Vasconie (*RGasc*) *Foed.* II 650a; **s1344** congregatis comitibus, baronibus, militibus et quam plurimis ~abus . . fecit rex . . convivium AD. MUR. *Chr.* 155; **s1348** ubi hastiludia prosequebantur, quasi in quolibet loco, ~arum cohors affuit . . in diverso . . apparatu virili ad numerum quandoque quasi xl . . ~arum de speciosioribus et pulcrioribus †non [? l. necnon] melioribus tocius regni KNIGHTON II 57; **s1362** fiebant hastiludia . . presentibus rege, regina, majori milicia Anglie . . aliarumque regionum et excellencioribus ~abus Anglie J. READING 179b. **c** rotulus de ~abus, pueris et puellis de xij comitatibus *RDomin* 65; **c1227** de ~abus dicunt quod Emma de B. F. tenet feodum dim. militis in S. de domino rege . . et est maritanda *Fees* 387 (cf. ib. 392: de ~abus dicunt quod Alicia que fuit uxor Rogeri de Burgo est de donacione domini regis et est maritanda); **1313** de ~abus que sunt de donacione domini regis sive sunt maritate sive maritande (*Artic. Itin.*) *Eyre Kent* I 29 (cf. *Fleta* 24: de viduis quarum domini obierunt seisiti de tenementis que tenuerunt de rege, si sint maritate vel non). **d 1242** ad opus regine, ~arum et domicillarum sibi assistentium *Pipe* 127; **1264** Alienore consorti E. primogeniti regis, ~abus, domicellis et familie sue *Cl* 8; **1268** mandatum est . . emptoribus Garderobe regis quod habere faciant . . ~abus . . consortis filii regis robas suas ut ~abus . . regine *Cl* 7. **e** procurator mulieris agentis potest ad statim petere sumptus litis et alimoniae ~ae suae decerni *Praxis* 31. **f** spiritus malignus . ., qui in quosdam tanta . . licencia debaccatur ut quod in spiritu patiuntur . . credant in corporibus evenire; quale est quod nocticulam quandam vel Herodiadem vel presidem noctis ~am concilia . . de nocte asserunt convocare J. SAL. *Pol.* 436A; que dicebat se cum quibusdam ~abus de nocte super quasdam bestias equitare et multa terrarum spacia una hora pertransire *Latin Stories* 21.

2 lady, dame (as title): **a** (of queen or princess); **b** (var.); **c** (of Dame Fortune).

a c625 ~ae gloriosae filiae Aedilbergae reginae (*Lit. Papae*) BEDE *HE* II 11; **c790** saluta . . domnam reginam et meae parvitatis nomine ALCUIN *Ep.* 62; **900** ego Aþelfled ~a Merciorum *CS* 583; **1141** M. imperatrix regis H. filia et Anglorum ~a *Regesta* 791; **1215** ~e Hibernie (v. ducissa 2a); **1291** ~e . . regni Scocie (v. domicella 1c); **s1312** ~a I. regina Anglie peperit filium suum primogenitum TROKELOWE 79; **s1344** sequebantur ~a regina juvenis et ~a regina mater AD. MUR. app. 232; **1565** virtute brevis ~e regine (*IPM*) *Form. Hist. Doc.* II 73. **b 1231** (v. comitissa 3a); **1235** ~a Roesia de la Rokel *KRMem* 14 r. 5; **1334** terras . . que fuerunt . . Margarete Corbet ~e de Malkerston' *RScot* 274a; **s1363** obiit . . ~a Elizabetha, ducissa Clarencie J. READING 182b; **1520** Annam ~am Roos *Rutland MSS View Ac. Bailiffs Yorks* p. 4; **1566** dilectis nostris consanguineo et consanguinee Davidi domino Drummond et ~e Lilie Ruthvene sue sponse *Inchaffray* 165. **c** me veteres falso dominam vocitare solebant ALDH. *Aen.* 7 (*Fatum*) 3; **s1399** ~a Fortuna . . projecit eum regem quasi subito a summo usque ad yma *V. Ric. II* 149.

3 a (title of) nun. **b** (w. *pauper*) Poor Clare.

a vos, ~a abbatissa, precor ut [etc.] ANSELM (*Ep.* 185) IV 71; **a1160** concedo Deo et B. Marie de Casa Dei et ~abus ibi Deo servientibus (*Ch. A. Comitisse Leic.*) *EHR* XXXII 248; **c1279** sciatis vos monachas vel moniales dicendas esse, non ~as, sicut nec monachi possunt sine ridiculo domini appellari PECKHAM *Ep.* 610 p. 849 (cf. *Conc. Syn.* xxxiii); ~a Mabilia, sanctimonialis de Stodeley *Mir. Montf.* 83; **s1321** quandam ~am Agnetem de L. conventus [de Mallynges] elegit in abbatissam *Hist. Roff.* f. 38; **1392** religiosas ~as Margaretam F. priorissam de Nun Monktone et ejusdem loci conventum *Feod. Durh.* 164; **s1488** ~a Elizabet Gayton priorissa *ObitR Durh.* 275. **b s1227** frater Helias . . contra generalem prohibitionem generalis ministri sine licentia accessit ad loca Pauperum ~arum ECCLESTON *Adv. Min.* 85.

4 (often w. *nostra*) Our Lady, Virgin Mary. **b** image of Virgin.

regina angelorum, ~a mundi, mater ejus qui mundat mundum ANSELM (*Or.* 7) III 18; **c1226** capellanum . . qui missam de ~a . . in perpetuum celebrabit *MonA* VI 1190; **1246** unus [sacerdos] celebrabit pro defunctis, alius missam de ~a cantabit, tertius de die *Ch. Sal.* 303; **1290** fratrum de ~a (v. domicilium 1b); ad secundarium servicium de ~a unus de junioribus cantabit †invictatorium *Obs. Barnwell* 102; **1335** matutine et hore ac vespere de ~a . . ante incepcionem vesperarum et matutinarum diei . . dicantur (*Stat. Cantar. Sibthorpe*) *Eng. Clergy* 273; pictor quidam in partibus Flandrie ~am pro posse venerabatur per omnia *Latin Stories* 34; *Plusc.* VII 19 (v. assumptio 3b); **1515** prepositus ecclesie collegiate Nostre ~e de Campis prope Edinburgh' *Offic. S. Andr.* 5. **b 1352** j nouch' cum j magna ~a posita *Reg. Black Pr.* IV 43d.; **1436** unus mantellus pro nostra ~a borderatus cum *ly velvate Reg. Aberd.* II 142.

5 mistress (fig.). **b** (w. *capillorum*) name of a comet.

mentis monarchia regnet, / ut non insultent animam fantasmata carnis / ne vincat dominam stolido bernacula gestu ALDH. *VirgV* 136; conturbatae gentes contra olim ~am orbis [sc. Romam] *V. Greg.* p. 99; hec . . regina propria est voluntas, omnium inoboedientium ~a *Simil. Anselmi* 37; **13..** [aqua vite] omnium medicinarum mater et ~a *RB Ossory (HMC)* 255; hec est ~a regula. omnes alie ei serviunt *AncrR* 163. **b** commemorat idem Haly stellam de genere cometarum, quam dicit '~am capillorum', que signat mortalitates regum et principum *Ps.*-GROS. *Summa* 587.

dominabilis [LL]

1 lordly, exercising lordship.

utilitas [hujus tractatus] est quia nobilitat addiscentes . . et facit eos . . sedere in aula regia . . actores et reos ordine ~i judicantes vice regis BRACTON *proem.* 1b; **1282** paternitatem vestram et ~em amiciciam . . exoramus quatenus . . ecclesie nostre negocia dignemini habere specialiter commendata PECKHAM *Ep.* (*ad J. Cardinalem*) 225 (cf. *Reg. Cant.* *1294–1313* I 12); **1320** vestre ~i reverencie supplicamus quatinus nostram absenciam . . habere velitis favorabiliter excusatam (*Lit. Episc. Roff. ad Archiep. Cant.*) *Hist. Roff.* 25v.

2 (as sb. n.) susceptibility to lordship, governability.

nec requiritur communicacio ulterior propter ejus [dominii divini] complecionem preter ~e et ipsum dominum, cum non possit esse ~e nisi Deus eo ipso fuerit ejus dominus WYCL. *Dom. Div.* 16; multa sunt dominia civilia hominum civiliter dominancium super temporalibus . ., et ad tale dominium non sufficit ponere dominativum et ~e esse simul *Id. Civ. Dom.* I 6.

dominalis, due to a lord.

1298 quas quidem litteras . . reperimus indecentes nec ~i subjeccioni ullatenus reverentes *Reg. Cant.* 278.

dominanter [LL], **a** w. the authority of a lord. **b** in a lordly fashion.

a rex debet specialiter providere de cunctis spectantibus ad ejus officium, de quanto ad cultum Dei pertinet . .; ergo regum est in nomine Domini exequi ~er illud officium WYCL. *Sim.* 33. **b** vivunt ~ius *Id. Ver.* III 93 (v. curiose 1c).

dominari [CL], **~are** [LL]

1 to rule, be lord or master (partly fig.): **a** (absol. or unspec.); **b** (w. gen.); **c** (w. dat.); **d** (w. *de* or *super*); **e** (w. acc.).

a ut non ~aretur [mulier] in ecclesia THEOD. *Pen.* I 9. 3; [superbia] ~andi monarchiam prae ceteris [vitiis] sibi usurpare dinoscitur ALDH. *VirgP* 11; eas . . insulas jure ~andi possidebant BEDE *HE* I 11; **8..** ~ari, *wealdan WW*; **1082** Romanis in partibus imperiali jure ~ante Henrico *Regesta* 150; ~andi . . appetitum J. SAL. *Pol.* 436A; pro miraculo duci potest quod ubi vina ~antur Venus non regnat GIR. *TH* III 27; possumus loqui istas duas qualitates [calidum et humidum] ~ari in plantis aut materialiter—et sic ~antur in omnibus viventibus—aut formaliter BACON XI 179; OCKHAM *Pol.* I 150 (v. despotice); sacerdotes, levite vel curati non debent seculariter ~ari [ME: *be lordis bi worldli manere*] *Concl. Loll. XXXVII* 1. **b** arsis trium temporum ~atur, thesis duorum ALDH. *PR* 133; P. cognomento Peverel . . duas . . Ramesiensis cenobii villas . . usurpare sibi conatus est, . . affirmans . . ipsarum se justa possessione ~ari debere GOSC. *Mir. Iv.* lxxvii; aiebant . . dedecus esse ipsum totius insule non ~ari G. MON. II 15; ipsi . . servi tui [sc. rationis] sunt, tu vero eorum ~aris AD. SCOT *Sol.* 857D; Pontisera subicitur in manus Anglicorum et ~atur ejus qui oderunt eam [cf. *Psalm* cv 41] *Ps.*-ELMH. *Hen. V* 79. **c** †1081 regnante . . Domino nostro Jesu Christo . . ac ~ante omnibus elementis *Reg. Malm.* I 325 (= *Regesta* 136); **1093** uni vel multis vel omnibus hominibus ~ando ANSELM (*Ep.* 159) IV 27; succurrite angustiis famuli vestri, nec patiamini ei ultra inimicum ~ari GOSC. *Mir. Iv.* lxxiii; **c1116** non toti Cumbrensi regioni ~abatur [David princeps] *Reg. Glasg.* I 7; H. AVR. *Poems* 43. 37 (v. dominatio 4); honoretis eam [sc. animam] nec sinatis carnem infimam ei ~ari [ME: *meistren hire*] nimis *AncrR* 45; dixit Christus: 'reges gencium dominantur eorum' [*Matth.* xx 25], i. e. reges gencium ~antur eis tamquam servis, non tamquam pure liberis OCKHAM *I. & P.* 15; rex Anglie . . principatu . . nedum regali sed et politico . . suo populo ~atur FORTESCUE *LLA* 9. **d** Deus Filius . . in mundo super gentes ~aturus *Eccl. & Synag.* 77; **c1250** qui post ipsum de villa de W. ~abuntur *AncD* A 3212; Deus dicit 'dedit vobis . .', ad denotandum quod homo ~atur super talia, et non bestie WYCL. *Dom. Div.* 5; **1423** Deus non vult voluntate beneplaciti sed permissive solum reges . . ~ari super servos suos *Reg. Cant.* III 169. **e** gentem . . ~are B. COTTON 23 (v. domare 1b); vincas rexque cito; tales dominare nōlito (*Vers.*) *State Tri. Ed. I* app. 99; Romana provincia . . fere totum mundum superabat et ~abatur *Eul. Hist.* II 70 (cf. BART. ANGL. XV 128).

2 (pr. ppl. as sb. m.) lord, master.

967 (11c) rex regum et dominus ~antium *CS* 1201; non sedeat juxta dominantem verna cibando D. BEC. 1394; non scelus est gravius quam sponte suum dominantem / mechari *Ib.* 1893; obruitur cum sole dies, cum lampade splendor,/ cum rectore ratis, cum dominante domus NIG. *Poems* 401; GOWER *CT* II 77 (v. appellare 4d).

dominatio [CL]

1 domination, lordship. **b** exercise of lordship, coercion. **c** (eccl.) patronage or (?) *f. l.* **d** wergeld payable to master.

agnus paschalis . . crucifixus . . nos . . a daemonica ~one redemit BEDE *Hom.* II 3. 121; **825** quod . . archiepiscopus per . . violentiam . . Coenwulfi regis omni ~one propria privatus est . . in his liberis monasteriis *CS* 384; **c1100** non debent principes sponsam Dei . . aestimare sibi datam in hereditariam ~onem, sed a Deo sibi commendatam ANSELM (*Ep.* 249) IV 159; **c1180** totam ~onem quam ego et antecessores mei in predicta [terra] habuimus, sc. in dominico et in franco tenemento et in villenagio *FormA* 274; BART. ANGL. I 19 (v. dominus 10a); OCKHAM *Pol.* I 28 (v. despoticus); **c1488** miles . . multum litigiosus multaque ~one suffultus *Reg. Whet.* I app. 469. **b 858** ut . . penalium rerum principali ~one furisque comprehensione . . [terra] secura et inmunis permaneat *CS* 496 (cf. ib. 438); [Godwinus] recessit ad Boseham et violenta ~one retinuit . . posseditque pacifice MAP *NC* V 3 f. 61. **c** †1141 *Regesta* 115 (v. advocatio 6b; *but* cf. ib. 116: jus advocationis et donationis ecclesie). **d** *Leg. Hen.* 11. 1a (v. cognatio 2b).

2 lordship (as title).

1217 scripsit nobis . . summus pontifex . . sicut audire poteritis . . ex forma litterarum suarum nobis a ~one sua transmissarum *Pat* 46; **1264** cum . . liqueat quod quidam . .

multa de nobis mendacia vestre ~oni suggesserint (*Lit. Baronum ad H. Regem*) *Flor. Hist.* II 492; prior .. patri [sc. episcopo] verbaliter supplicabat †quantinus [l. quatinus] illud, si ~oni sue placeret, .. observaret *G. Durh.* 5; **1316** vestram regiam ~onem conservet Altissimus! *Reg. Carl.* II 117; quedam .. supplicaciones .. cardinalium ~onibus preponentur CONWAY *Def. Mend.* 1411 (*recte* 1311); **1388** metuendissime domine, vestre ~onis excellencie patefacimus .. quod .. *MunAcOx* 795; **1536** vestram reverendissimam paternitatem et ~onem amplissimam veluti .. ecclesie .. Glasguensis archiepiscopum et metropolitanum .. fraternaliter .. exhortamur .. *Conc. Scot.* I ccxlix.

3 (area of) lordship, dominion, domain. **b** demesne.

s1066 hujus vaticinii veritatem nos experimur, quod sc. Anglia exterorum facta est habitatio et alienigenarum ~o W. MALM. *GR* II 227; **s1172** ab ingressu regis in Hyberniam xx continuis ebdomadibus de regno suo vel de aliqua parte ~onis sue, que tam longe lateque diffunditur, ad ipsum rumor aliquis minime penetravit DICETO *YH* I 350; **s1258** W. de Walencia et fratres sui Pictavenses .. coacti sunt repatriare propter tyrannidem quam exercuerant in ~onibus suis *Chr. Clun.* 100; **s1392** dixerunt stultum fore et nimis dampnosum regi et sue corone ut pro comodo unius persone tantas et tam pulcras ~ones [sc. ducatum Normannie et comitatum de Artoys] perpetualiter amitteret *Chr. Westm.* 206; **s1200** salvis omnibus et singulis suis terris, ~onibus, dignitatibus, libertatibus et privilegiis regalibus *Plusc.* VI 38. **b** j aecclesia, xv acrae de quattuor ~onibus *DB* II 417v.

4 'dominion' (order of angels; *cf. Eph.* i 21, *Coloss.* i 16).

a975 adjuro te .. per omnia agmina sanctorum angelorum, thronorum, ~onum, principatuum, potestatum, virtutum, cherubin atque seraphin (*Jud. Dei*) *GAS* 405; PULL. *Sent.* 885B (v. angelus a); AD. SCOT *Serm.* 292B (v. cherub a); post cherubin sequitur dominatio, tertius ordo,/ subjectis qui spiritibus preest et dominatur H. AVR. *Poems* 43. 37; quemadmodum astruit S. Dionysius se a B. Paulo .. didicisse, .. in secunda [trium hierarchiarum] primo ~ones, secundo virtutes, tertio potestates .. collocantur AD. MARSH *Ep.* 246 *bis* cap. 1 p. 416; sicut et illi sancti angelici spiritus in quodam medio ordine constituti qui ~ones dicuntur BRADW. *CD* 676C.

dominative, a despotically. **b** by virtue of lordship.

a pauciora potest imperare principans ministrative sibi subjectis quam principans ~e servis suis OCKHAM *I. & P.* 15. **b** damnat illa duo capitula de immunitate ecclesiarum .., quia statuunt quod domini temporales non exigant ~e tallagia vel decimas ab ecclesiasticis personis (PURVEY) *Ziz.* 395.

dominativus, a despotic. **b** lordly. **c** (as sb. n.) lordship.

a accipiatur 'eleccio' ibi pro liberalitate sive potestate ~a DUNS *Ord.* I 195 (v. elicitio); Christus .. ~um modum regendi a potestatibus seculi observatum apostolis interdixit [cf. *Matth.* xx 20–8] OCKHAM *Pol.* I 36; ille principatus qui .. curam debet habere de sibi subjectis .. non ~us sed ministrativus merito est vocandus *Id. I. & P.* 13; *Ib.* 14 (v. despoticus); 'potestas' dicit potenciam ~am; set Deus non est eternaliter dominus; igitur non habet potestatem super volucione sua, set solum super creaturas WYCL. *Ente* 148; prefeccio ~a hominis super sublunaria *Id. Dom. Div.* 5. **b** **1327** sciat vestra paternitas ~a quod .. *Lit. Cant.* (*ad Archiep.*) I 227. **c** WYCL. *Civ. Dom.* I 6 (v. dominabilis 2).

dominator [CL], lord, master; **b** (as divine epithet).

erat ~or serpens setosus et tam vasta corporis mole ut .. *Lib. Monstr.* III 12; **904** (11c) Æþelred dux et ~or Merciorum *CS* 607; **s1036** dixit [Cnut] mari ascendenti: ".. impero tibi ne in terram meam ascendas, nec vestes nec membra ~oris tui madefacere presumas" H. HUNT. *HA* VI 17; mediamnas .., ubi .. refugii loca propriaque domicilia .. ~ores terrarum metari solent GIR. *TH* I 8; Rogerus viguit illa dominator in urbe [Biterrensi] GARL. *Tri. Eccl.* 68. **b** ~or Christe EGB. *Pont.* 119; nunc, ~or, exaudi orationes nostras *Descr. Constant.* 257; tam terre quam maris ~orem GIR. *TH* II 54; **1188** ecce advenit ~or Dominus! [cf. *Is.* iii 1] *Ep. Cant.* 195; WALT. WIMB. *Virgo* 129 (v. domicellus 2a).

dominatrix [CL], mistress; **b** (as epithet of abstr.).

dominatrix effera servae WULF. *Swith.* II 100; repulsam passus ipsemet per Jezabel ~icem judex fuit in reddendo [cf. *1 Kings* xxi 7] H. BOS. *Thom.* III 14 p. 222; sic domat indomitum dominum domini dominatrix D. BEC. 1969; cum dominam illam et ~icem, ne meretricem dicam, presbyter .. domum reduxerat GIR. *GE* II 18 p. 253; AD. EYNS. *Hug.* IV 5 (v. ancillari a). **b** caeca et temeraria ~ix cupiditas ad se explendam corporis viribus abutebatur ALCUIN *Rhet.* 2; **956** (v. creatrix c); sunt sensus hebetes et ratio ~ix ADEL. *ED* 14.

dominatus [CL], domination, lordship, authority. **b** exercise of lordship, coercion.

post haec non sponte reduxit / praefectus puerum quidam patris in dominatum FRITH. 525; **s870** ut monachi semper haberent ~um super clericos *AS Chr.*; ipsa habuit terram suam separatam et liberam a ~u et potestate Bernulfi mariti sui *DB* I 373; quasi omnia mortua erant, cum amissa congenita dignitate favendi ~ui vel usibus Deum laudantium, ad quod facta erant, .. decolorabantur ab usu idolis servientium ANSELM (*Or.* 7) III 20; a carnis ~u nos prohibet Paulus [cf. *Rom.* vi 12] AILR. *Serm.* 418D; ridiculum videtur .. delicias et ~um [ME: *mestrie and lafdischipe*] querere ampliorem quam in mundo *AncrR* 32; ~us, A. *a lordshyp WW*. **b** violento ~u cunctos opprimere cupiens GIR. *EH* I 8.

dominella, damsel, (young) lady; **b** (as title).

a damesselle, domicella, ~a, nimpha *CathA*. **b** **c1200** hujus rei testes sunt ~a Elena [et al.] *MonA* II 601.

dominellus, esquire.

a squyere, armiger, domicellus, ~us, scutifer *CathA*.

domineum, ~eus v. 2 dominium, ~ius. **Dominica** v. dominicus.

dominicalis [LL]

1 (man.): **a** belonging (or due) to lord. **b** (w. *terra* or sim.) belonging to demesne. **c** (as sb. n. pl.) demesne lands.

a villa [*Shillington, Beds*] .. vallata nemoribus .., curiam spatiosam et penates ~es ad oram nemoris in loco edito habens sitos *Chr. Rams.* 143; **1330** [de omnibus redditibus] tam regalibus quam ~ibus *CalCh* IV 174. **b** **1375** fabricam poncium et *le cause* jacencium ex parte occidentali abathie .. versus terram nostram ~em †le [? l. de] Foulys *Inchaffray* 132; **1434** per firmas .. terrarum, tam ~ium quam aliarum terrarum .. in manibus domini regis *ExchScot* 597; **1452** de custodia parcelle terre ~is et pasture nostre juxta civitatem nostram Karlioli *RScot* 355b; **1467** ~es pasture eidem manerio [*Essendon, Herts*] pertinentes *FormA* 148; **1514** (v. dominium 5e); **1537** pro redditu assise terrarum et tenementorum ac pratorum ~ium *Ac. Durh.* 667. **c** **1526** quicquid pecorum sive animalium in ~ibus nostris .. depascitur (*Vis. Thame*) *EHR* III 709.

2 a (w. *dies*) Lord's day, Sunday. **b** (w. *annus*) year of the Lord. **c** (w. *oratio*) Lord's prayer. **d** (as sb. f., *sc. domus*) Lord's house, church. **e** (w. *evangelia* or as sb. n. pl.) gospels.

a *Conc. Scot.* II 75 (v. dies 5b). **b** HERM. ARCH. 8, DICETO *Chr. prol.* 19 (v. annus 2a). **c** in ferialibus diebus .. ad matutinas, cum dicitur oratio ~is [v. l. dominica] ante lectiones *Offic. Sal.* 18. **d** BELETH *RDO* 2. 15D (v. cyriace). **e** **1396** exposicio super Evangelia ~ia (*Invent.*) *Meaux* III app. xcix; **1501** Parisiensis super ~ia (*Invent.*) *Cant. Coll. Ox* I 19.

3 for use on Sunday. **b** (w. *littera*) dominical letter (indicating dates of Sundays in spec. year). **c** (w. *nummus*) a customary payment.

benedictio ~is cotidianis diebus Dominicis EGB. *Pont.* 58; Sabbato ~is vesperae canatur hymnus: 'Deus creator omnium' *RegulC* 60; abbas Egelricus [ob. **992**] .. dedit .. omnibus altaribus in ecclesia duas casulas, [unam] ~em et alteram principalem *Croyl.* 53; **1393** unum vestimentum ~e cum ij tuniculis *Lit. Cant.* III 22; **1419** lego ecclesie cathedrali Sar' unum par vestimentorum .. ad orandum .. in precibus ~ibus .. singulis diebus Dominicis in navi ecclesie in vulgari dicendis *Reg. Cant.* II 177; **1447** missale cum missis ~ibus et aliis peculiaribus *MunAcOx* 559. **b** **s1187** quinto idus Octobris, D littera dominicalis (*Vers.*) *Expug. Terrae Sanctae* 16b; **s1189** inunctus est R. rex in regem, viz. tertia die Septembris in die Dominica, ~i littera existente A, anno sc. proximo post bissextum *Itin. Ric.* II 5; si tabulam revolvamus .., inveniemus G esse literam ~em in tempore Passionis et G esse in viij calendarum BACON *Maj.* I 206; **s1307** mutacio regis data hoc anno, littera ~is A *Ann. Lond.* 149; ELVEDEN *Cal.* (v. aureus 1g); **1448** hoc anno viz. v idus Septembris, feria ij[a], litera ~is F *Invent. Ch. Ch.* 162. **c** **12..** item de cereo paschali nummus a quolibet habente per se domum vel existente in domo alterius habente peculium; nummus ~is cum candela et pane a quolibet habente per se domum vel valorem dim. m. vel existente in domo alterius *Conc. Scot.* II 45 (cf. ib. 274).

4 Dominican, of the Order of Friars Preachers. *V. et. Dominicanus.*

1567 fratribus ~ibus seu Predicatoribus *Scot. Grey Friars* II 259.

dominicaliter, by the Lord, divinely.

1187 ea .. nulla mundane rationis .. subtilitas .. poterit avertere, quando secundum divine dispositionis seriem suo revertuntur tempore, sibi deputatis atque dispositis ~er terminis et eventibus *Ep. Cant.* 148.

Dominicanus, Dominican, of the Order of Friars Preachers. *V. et. dominicalis* 4.

1536 in templo Fratrum ~orum sive Predicatorum intra oppidum Edinburgense *Conc. Scot.* I cclix; ~i ordinis in Scotia primas FERR. *Kinloss* 80; **s1538** J. Hilsey .., ordinis Praedicatorum et conventus ~i Londinensis praeses .., eundem [conventum] regi in manus tradidit (*Hist. Roff.*) *Anglia Sacra* I 383; coenobium fratribus ~is, unde *Blackfriars* locum nominamus, fundavit Robertus Kilwardby CAMD. *Br.* 370.

1 dominicatus

1 (man.) belonging to demesne.

†969 (12c) ipse de ~is terris meis aliquanta addidi et cartis .. corroboravi *CS* 1264.

2 (?) held on Sunday.

de mercatis et placitis ~is (*Inst. Cnuti rub.*) *GAS* 616 (cf. ib. 295: interdicimus mercatum dierum Dominicorum).

2 dominicatus [LL = *lord's power*], (man.) demesne. *Cf. dominicus* 3, 4.

c1030 (11c) quandam terram dominicam S. Mariae Raculfensis [*Reculver, Kent*] .. in praestariam annuo duobus ministris meis .., ut illam terram habeant non longius quam ipsi placuerit decano ..; ubi vero decano .. visum fuerit ut illam terram possint fructificare ~ui suo, recedant ab ea .., quia dominica est S. Mariae *CD* 754 (= *FormA* p. xxi); rex et barones sui habent in ~u suo xiij hidas et dim. et iij fertinos *Dom. Exon.* 67; ~us regis ad regnum pertinens in Devenescira *Ib. rub.* 83; de aecclesia S. Germani ablatus est j ager terrae qui erat de ~u aecclesiae *Ib.* 507; **c1155** in Foresthill [*Oxon*] duas acras de ~u (*Lit. Papae*) *MonA* II 147a (cf. ib.: villam .. cum decima de ~u); **c1200** possessiones istas .. confirmamus, viz. .. totum ~um de Budifordia [*Bidford, Warw*] .., totum ~um de Nortona .. *FormA* 53.

dominicus [CL]

1 belonging to a lord (esp. man.) or his demesne: **a** (of building or sim.); **b** (of chattel or sim.); **c** (of abstr.); **d** (of person). **e** (as sb. m.) tenant of demesne.

a in Lundon' una masura ~a fuit *DB* I 31v.; *Ib.* 222 (v. aedificium a); *Ib.* II 257v. (v. aula 5b); **c1124, a1135** (v. curia 10a); **1174** in operatione ~e aule abbatie *Pipe* 137. **b** *DB* I 13 (v. carruca 3a); tres hidae que fuerunt de ~o victu monachorum *Ib.* 59; *Ib.* 173v. (v. congregatio 2b); **1101** ne aliquis disturbet .. carreiam S. Mariae de A. nec aliquid aliud quod sit ~um abbatis vel monachorum ejus (*Breve Regis*) *Chr. Abingd.* II 78; *æhteswane*, qui ~um gregem curie [AS: *inheorde*] custodit (*Quad., Rect.*) *GAS* 449; **a1150** porcos ~os .. ecclesie in omnibus nemoribus meis concedo esse quietos de padnagio *E. Ch. Scot.* 153; **a1190** (v. assecurare 2d); **c1205** ne quis in regno meo ab aliquo illorum [burgensium] .. aliquam .. consuetudinem de ~is catallis suis exigat *Regesta Scot.* 462; **1225** (v. carretta 1a); **1236** quod ipse recuperet seisinam suam ad ~a averia sua quantum pertinet ad tenementum suum *CurR* XV 1936; **c1257** (v. bladum 1a); **1289** (v. advocare 7b); **14..** quod permittat B. molere ~um bladum suum de N. ad molendinum ipsius A. .. quietum de multura *Reg. Brev. Orig.* 153b. **c** pratum .. ad ~um opus *DB* I 139v.; **c1130** omnes res .. quas .. affidare †poterint se emere ad ~um opus monachorum et ecclesie *Cart. Bath A* 47; **11..** ~is monachorum .. usibus terram illam deputari *Chr. Abingd.* II 22; **c1250** quod .. monachi mittant se in corporalem et ~am possessionem et saisinam .. mansi mei *FormA* 356; ~a potestas BRACTON 6b (v. cubare 1b); **1328** [quicquid tenuerint in] ~o dominio [et servicio] *Cart. Fount.* II 484. **d** **c1125** quod ~i servientes abbatis C. habeant omnes quietantias suas *BBC* (*Colchester*) 105. **e** **1165** Felix, Herveus, Malgerius, ~i nostri *Kent Archive Off., Ch. Capit.* T 57.

2 belonging to king as lord; **b** (of person holding directly from king or employed in his service).

1108 nolo ut vicecomes meus propter aliquod necessarium suum .. faciat ea [comitatus meos et hundreda] sedere aliter. ego enim, quando voluero, faciam ea satis summonere propter mea ~a necessaria *Regesta* 892; hec sunt ~a placita regis, nec pertinent .. ministris ejus sine diffinitis prelocutionibus (*Leg. Hen.* 10. 4) *GAS* 556 (cf. ib. 13. 5: ~a captalia regis); **a1162** precipimus vobis quod manuteneatis .. abbatiam de M. et omnes possessiones suas sicut meas ~as (*Breve Regis*) *Reg. Malm.* I 332; cum vacaverit .. episcopatus vel abbatia .. de dominio regis, debet esse in manu ejus et exinde percipiet omnes redditus et exitus sicut ~os *Const. Clar.* 12; **1180** alter [rex] .. terram illius qui in peregrinatione erit et homines sicut sua propria ~a .. custodiet (*Tractatus*) *G. Hen. II* I 248; **1214** quod protegatis .. terras et omnes possessiones episcopi E. sicut ~am nostram *Cl* 173b; **1217** de omnibus ~is dominibus nostris ad forestas nostras pertinentibus *Pat* 124; **1241** (v. camera 2a); **1242** pro x saccis .. ad imponendam ~am ferinam [i. e. farinam] regis *Pipe* 282. **b** tainus vel miles regis ~us moriens pro relevamento dimittebat regi omnia arma sua *DB* I 56v.; in Norwic erant .. mcccxx burgenses, quorum unus erat ita ~us regis ut non posset recedere nec homagium facere sine licentia ipsius *Ib.* II 116 (cf. ib. 109: de ~is hominibus regis); **1108** si .. exurgat placitum .. inter ~os barones meos *Regesta* 892; **1164** nullus qui de rege teneat in capite vel aliquis ~orum ministrorum ejus excommunicetur .. nisi .. *Const. Clar.* 8; **s1164** quantacumque rex Anglorum, etsi ~us homo meus [sc. regis Francie] sit, adversus ipsum [T. archiepiscopum] moliatur H. BOS. *Thom.* IV 20; [milites] ~i MAP *NC* IV 6 (v. baro 1a); **1185** ut sit in custodia et protectione regis sicut ~us clericus suus *Pipe* 66; **1199** nos suscepisse in ~um mercatorem nostrum Hugonem Oisel [Flandrensem] et ipsum et homines suos .. in manum et protectionem nostram *RChart* 12b; **1203** *Pipe* 86 (v. 2 clericus 2a); **1205** ~um pistorem nostrum (v. 5 infra).

3 (of land or sim.) held in demesne. **b** (as sb. n.) demesne, tenure by lord for his own use. **c** demesne, land held for lord's use. *V. et 2 dominicatus, dominium* 3.

1082 de ∼is terris S. Ætheldrithe sit abbas saisitus *Regesta* 151; A. [tenet] unum manerium .. de abbatia; et est de ∼a terra *DB* I 42; hoc manerium est unum de xij maneriis ∼is episcopatus Lincoln' *Ib.* 190; **c1105** presbiteri qui tenent ecclesias que sunt super terras ∼as monachorum (*Ch. Wint.*) *EHR* XXXV 391; de hoc denegeldo quieta erit .. omnis terra que de ecclesiis propria et ∼a erat, etiam de ecclesiis parochiarum (*Leg. Ed.*) *GAS* 635; W. Malm. *GP* IV 157 (v. contiguus 1b); **1130** in ∼is carrucatis terre Hamonis dapiferi *Pipe* 67; mesuagium cum orto adjacente .. fuit mansio Beodrici, qui fuit antiquitus dominus istius ville .., cujus campi ∼i nunc sunt in ∼o celerarii Brakelond 150; **1203** ne .. ponantur in placitum de ullo ∼o feodo suo nisi coram rege *Pipe* 197; **1206** fenum levare .. in prato de M. in ∼o prato abbatis de Burgo (*Fine*) *Croyl. Cont. B* 472; **c1280** (v. aripennis); **1302** fecit unam semitam injuste per medium ∼e terre domini *CourtR Hales* 456. **b** omnis terra que in proprio ∼o ecclesie erat (*Leg. Ed. retr.*) *GAS* 635; **c1180** (v. dominatio 1a); ita quod inde fuerit saisitus in ∼o Glanv. VI 1; **a1199** petit inde recognitionem utrum Ricardus debeat eam [terram] tenere de ipsa Juliana vel illa in ∼o *CurR* I 1 (cf. ib. 16 [**1196**]: utrum ipse habet majus jus tenendi de eo quam Gillebertus tenere in †∼a [MS *prob.* ∼o]); feodum .. quod tenebat B. episcopus in die quo obiit in ∼o Gir. *David* 432; **1221** appellatur terra illa *forshard*, eo quod remaneat domino in ∼o in perpetuum pro defectu servitii *MGL* I 63; si dixisset, "do tibi rem talem in †dominio [v. l. dominico] vel in feodo" Bracton 13b; *Ib.* 92 (v. dos 2a); in defectu terre Bernardi tracte in ∼o, iiijs. *Ac. Beaulieu* 64 (cf. ib. 109: in defectu terre Willelmi C. tracte in ∼um); **1345** in defectu redditus terre Bildekay tracte in ∼um, xxij d. *Comp. Swith.* 145; **1372** quod quidem tenementum tenetur in libero ∼o *Reg. S. Bees* 274; **1399** (v. dominium 5a); **1400** (v. dominium 5b). **c** **1115** me dedisse G. episcopo episcopatum Hereford' .., sicut R. episcopus melius habuit, et omnia ∼a que postea extramissa sunt in prebendam et ceteris rebus (*sic*) precipio ut resumat ad ∼um suum *Regesta* 1101; in Denelahe homo liber qui habuerit catallum campestre ad valenciam dim. m. dabit denarium S. Petri; et per denarium domini adquietabuntur omnes qui in ∼o illius manent [OF *en sun demeine*] (*Leis Will.*) *GAS* 505; dicta terra valet annuatim .. sine ∼o xvj li. *RDomin* 2; **1189** de terris suis [regis Scotie] quas habet in Anglia, seu ∼is seu feodis (*Ch. Ric. I*) R. Howd. III 25; **c1200** concessi .. pasturam .. extra portam de *south'* cum liberis ingressu et egressu per ∼um meum ad prefatam pasturam (*Ch. Comitis Leic.*) *Rec. Leic.* I 5; **1211** x acras terre in W. de ∼o Simonis de B., sc. de terra quam ipse colit carucis suis propriis *CurR* VI 54; **1227** inquirat si Willelmus .. dissaisiavit homines de K. de pastura de H. voluntate sua propria an eo quod eadem pastura fuit de ∼o suo, ita quod predicti homines in ea nullam communam habere deberent *Cl* 8; **1242** vicecomes .. habebit †∼am [MS: ∼a] et wardas spectantes ad eadem castra *Pipe* 14; **c1257** blada de ∼o castri ita expendita fuerunt in autumno quod ballivi vix invenerunt unde ∼i (*sic*) possent seminari (*AncC* IV 3) *RL* II 125; est ∼um quod quis habet ad mensam suam et proprie, sicut sunt *bordlandes* Anglice. item dicitur ∼um villenagium quod traditur villanis, quod quis .. resumere poterit pro voluntate sua et revocare. item dici poterit ∼um de quo quis habet liberum tenementum et alius usumfructum... et sciendum quod ∼um dicitur ad differentiam ejus quod tenetur in servitio Bracton 263; **1282** de terris et tenementis que fuerunt domino de Mortuo Mar' de dominio et ∼o intrinseco de Anglicis de Nerberd [*Pembr*] *IPM* 32/7 r. 10 (cf. ib. r. 11: de ∼o forinsceco); **c1300** cum .. omnibus aliis pertinenciis suis ut in ∼is, dominiis, serviciis libere tenencium *Feod. Durh.* 179*n*.; **1306** quia predictum tenementum est de condicione nativorum, est per consequens ∼um domini *CourtR Hales* 550; **1444** infra villam sive ∼um de Aldcambus *Pri. Cold.* 151.

4 (of crown land) held by king in demesne. **b** (as sb. n.) royal demesne. **c** (usu. w. *antiquum*) 'ancient demesne' (held by king at time of Norman Conquest). **d** (as sb. m.) royal demesne or (?) demesne tenant. *V. et. dominium* 4.

Henricus .. tenet in hoc manerio de ∼a terra regis cxx acras terrae et iij acras prati *DB* I 57v.; in ∼a terra regis tenet Rogerius .. j domum et j piscariam in ipsa villa [*Gloucester*]; et est extra manum regis *Ib.* 162; vicecomes .. de ∼is maneriis regis reddit cxxiij li. et iiij s. ad pensum *Ib.* (*Worcs*) 172; hec sunt que ad .. fiscum proprie censentur .. ubicumque .., sive terra ∼a regis et socna sit, sive sit alterius (*Leg. Hen.* 19. 1) *GAS* 559; **1157** rex dedit episcopo Sar' .. xxx libratas terre .. de ∼a terra corone regis *Ch. Sal.* 29; **1217** boscum [regis] ∼um (v. 1 afforestare); **s793** dedit Offa .. beato prothomartyri Albano villam suam ∼am que Wineslawe nuncupatur *V. II Off.* 31; **1255** villate de Herford' et Rypton Regis [*Hunts*] dicunt quod solent et debent habere communam herbagii in Sappel', eo quod dicte villate aliquando fuerunt ∼a maneria regis *SelPlForest* 26; **1321** quot et que maneria ∼a dominus rex habet in manu sua, tam sc. de antiquo ∼o corone quam de escaetis et perquisitis (*Artic. Itin.*) *MGL* II 353 (v. et. 4c infra). **b** **c1127** in Watebergia ∼um regis iiij car[ucate] (*Surv. Leic.*) *Feudal Eng.* 198; **c1128** me dedisse .. unam carrucatam terre de ∼o meo de Rokesburge *E. Ch. Scot.* 83; quando aliquid super dominum regem injuste occupatur, ut in ∼is regis Glanv. IX 11; **s1155** eo quod regia ∼a per mollitiem regis S. ad alios multosque dominos majori ex parte migrassent, [rex] precepit ea .. quibuscunque detentoribus resignari W. Newb. *HA* II 2; **1196** jurata .. venit recognitura que sint ∼a domini regis apud Ailesberi [*Bucks*] et que esse debent *CurR* I 26; **1200** hundredum de Kingeston' [*Surr*] pertinet et semper pertinuit .. ad ∼um illud [domini regis] *Ib.* 252 (= *Ib.* 240: ad †∼am); **s1181** ut tantum honorem .. regis Henrici fultus auxilio ab injusto detentore revocaret suoque ∼o et mense regali .. adjiceret persuadentes Gir. *PI* III 2 p. 229; **s1213** misit rex literas .. ut de singulis ∼orum suorum villis quatuor legales homines cum preposito .. facerent convenire Wend. II 82; **1359** dicta terra fuit de ∼o regis tempore mortis domini R. regis Scocie *ExchScot* 578. **c** **1228** abbas .. dicit quod assisa non debet inde fieri, quia terra illa fuit de ∼o domini regis. .. et R. dicit quod terra illa non est de antiquo ∼o ejusdem manerii *CurR* XIII 1132; **1241** Bensington est de antiquo ∼o regis, ubi nullum breve nove disseisine currit (*JustIt* 695 r. 10d.) *Abbr. Plac.* 117; **1242** de hominibus de Ewell', que fuit anticum ∼um antecessorum regis *Cl* 408; **1258** Petrus .. dicit quod .. homines sui de Wytele [*Suss*] nullam accionem habere possunt versus eum tanquam sokemanni de antiquo ∼o .., quia dicit quod manerium de W. nuncquam fuit ∼um domini regis de corona, immo de baronia del Egle, que aliquando fuit eschaeta domini regis. .. et quod ita sit ponit se super librum qui vocatur *Domesday SelCWW* 91; **1266** cum .. recuperaverimus versus .. homines de Stanleya .., quod est de antiquo ∼o nostro, quasdam consuetudines et quedam servicia de tenuris illorum *Pat* 85 m. 34; sokemannus de antiquo ∼o, licet contra verum dominum vel vicinum de eodem socagio placitare non possit nisi per parvum breve de recto clausum, versus tamen extraneum, si eum eiciat, competit ei remedium per breve nove disseisine Hengham *Parva* 8 p. 65; quo casu succurritur hujusmodi [sokemannis] ejectis per beneficium commune, non obstante antiquarum ∼arum (*sic*) excepcione *Fleta* 4; **1289** Milesinta dicit .. quod .. villa de Houctone est antiquum ∼um corone, ut patet per recordum *del Domesday Ann. Dunstable* 348; **1311** tenentes de antiquo ∼o certa servicia et certas consuetudines tenentur facere, et non ad voluntatem domini (*CoramR* 206) *Villainage in Eng.* 114 (cf. ib. 123); **1321** (v. 4a supra; cf. bassus 2c); †**1324** [recte **1321**] (v. bondemannus; cf. *Eyre Kent* I 34); **1417** cum .. homines de antiquo ∼o corone Anglie quieti sint .. a prestacione theolonii per totum regnum nostrum (*Pat*) *MunCOx* 182. **d** **1277** (1392) quociens dominus rex suos ∼os talliare contigerit, dabunt .. v m. *Cart. Boarstall* 538.

5 fit for a lord, (w. *panis*) 'pain-demaine'.

1184 pro viij tonellis vini ∼i *Pipe* 136; **1194** nos confirmasse W... regi Scottorum .. singulis diebus ex quo venerit ad curiam nostram .. xij de ∼is guastellis nostris et totidem de simenellis nostris ∼is et xij sextercia vini, iiij videlicet de ∼o vino nostro unde nobis servitur et viij sextercia de vino unde domui nostre servitur .. et xl candelas de ∼is candelis unde nobis servitur *Anglo-Scot. Rel.* 9–10; **1205** mittimus ad vos H. dominicum pistorem nostrum ad faciendum ∼um florem ad sequendum filium nostrum *Cl* 31a (cf. ib. 58: habere faciatis W. pistori nostro xij summas frumenti .. ad faciendum ∼um panem nostrum; v. et. 2b supra); **1209** pro flore ad panem ∼um *Misae* 129; **1287** panis ∼us, qui dicitur *demeine*, de obolo ponderabit quantum wastellus de quadrante (*Assisa Panis*) *MGL* I 353; **1330** in pane ∼o et melle, v d. *Ac. Durh.* 17; **1353** in flore ∼o, iij s. iiij d. *Ib.* 553.

6 belonging to the Lord (Christ); **b** (of utterance, also as sb. n.); **c** (of event or its commemoration).

si non lupus callidus ille .. te ab ovili ∼o .. rapuisset Gildas *EB* 34; **680** peccatricem .. ∼os pedes .. tergentem [cf. *Luke* vii 47] Aldh. *Ep.* 4; obitum suum ∼i corporis et sanguinis perceptione munivit Bede *HE* IV 3; innotescit quod vera Christi caro verusque ejus sanguis in mensa ∼a immolatur Lanfr. *Corp. & Sang.* 435C; Osb. *V. Dunst.* 16 (v. corpus 7b); etiam ab angelis Domini sunt abscondita judicia ∼i pectoris Map *NC* IV 6 f. 49v.; **c1220** crux una aurea cum ligno ∼o *Process. Sal.* 169; **1315, 1383** (v. crux 4d); **1327** (v. ager 1c); **1341** ut .. possemus ad meritorum nostrorum cumulum bellis ∼is intendere (*Lit. E. Regis*) Ad. Mur. app. 270; vos estis pastores gregis ∼i R. Bury *Phil.* 4. 49; **1442** numerosi doctores .. et scolares in vinea [cf. *Matth.* xx etc.] et agro ∼is in variis .. scienciis laborantes Bekynton I 123. **b** **713** fateor .. nos vestrum visceraliter juxta praeceptum ∼um [*John* xv 12] .. amorem caepisse (Ælfled) *Ep. Bonif.* 8; **747** ut presbyteri .. symbolum fidei ac ∼am orationem .. exponere posse propria lingua .. discant (*Clovesho*) *Conc. HS* 366; memor ∼ae jussionis [*Matth.* xvii 9] Alcuin *WillP* 18; **793** timenda est illa ∼a sententia [*James* ii 13] *Id. Ep.* 16; pre oculis semper retinens illud ∼um [*Matth.* xx 26] Wulf. *Æthelwold* 9; **a1090** in his verbis ∼is [*Mark* x 11–12; *Luke* xvi 18] luce clarius liquet quia, vivente viro vel uxore, extraneam copulam quaerere nulli eorum licet Lanfr. *Ep.* 10 (23); ∼ae memor promissionis [*Matth.* v 10] Osb. *V. Dunst.* 27; **s1215** completum est illud ∼um [*Luke* xi 17] W. Guisb. 153. **c** in hoc [loco] xl ante ∼um Natale dies .. transigere solebat Bede (*CuthbP* 42) *HE* IV 28; ante ∼ae incarnationis tempus *Ib.* I 2 (v. annus 2a); Lanfr. *Const.* 131 (v. annuntiatio b); in die ∼ae resurrectionis Ailr. *Ed. Conf.* 767C; *Ib.* 786D (v. 3 apparitio 3d); **s1170** [T. archiepiscopus] solus occubuit .., plurimum formam ∼e imitans passionis G. Cold. *Durh.* 5; **s1183** (v. circumcisio 2e); **s1213** (v. ascensio 1d); **s1228** rex .. festum ∼e Nativitatis apud Eboracum solenniter celebravit Wend. II 333; *Cust. Westm.* 176 (v. cena 2b); **1476** a ∼o Natalicio (v. annus 2a).

7 (w. *dies*) Lord's day, Sunday; **b** (as sb. f. or m.).

presbiter .. faciens fornicationem .. paeniteat .. pane sine mensura .. die ∼o Gildas *Pen.* 1; Bede *Hom.* II 7 etc. (v. dies 5b); papa Silvester .. primam quidem diem, qua et lux in principio facta et Christi est resurrectio celebrata, ∼am nuncupavit *Id. TR* 8; **798** inquirendo .. cur Septuagesima et Sexagesima necnon et Quinquagesima in ordine per dies ∼os ante Quadragesimam dicatur vel scribatur Alcuin *Ep.* 144; dies illuxerat alma, / Dōminicam vocitare solent quam quique fideles Wulf. *Swith.* I 849; in hoc manerio est mercatum in die ∼o *DB* I 120v.; **1236** secundo (*sic*) die ∼a Quadragesime *CurR* XV 1967; **s1283** quo die solemnitas S. Oswaldi episcopi contigit, cujus dies .. in .. episcopatu Wygorniensi solemnis est ut ∼us Graystanes 19; **1339** citra diem ∼am in Ramis Palmarum *RScot* 558a; die ∼a proxima post diem ∼am Reliquiarum [*Sunday after 7 July*] *Entries* 154. **b** in ∼o Graeci et Romani navigant et aequitant, panem non faciunt, neque in curru pergunt nisi ad aecclesiam tantum, nec balneant se. Graeci in ∼a non scribunt puplice Theod. *Pen.* II 8. 1–2; Paulinus .., qui tam facile signum Dei sui sapientiae quadam ut reor ∼a dicitur dedisse *V. Greg.* p. 88; sequente ∼a Bede *HE* V 2; si vigilia ∼ae Nativitatis in ∼a die evenerit, duo fratres invitatorium de ∼a in albis dicant, primum et secundum nocturnum de ipsa ∼a fiant, tercium et matutinae laudes de vigilia Lanfr. *Const.* 92; imperator .. ∼a illa que vocatur Quinquagesima venatum pergens W. Malm. *GR* II 175; in prima ∼a Adventus, in ∼a Palmarum *Offic. Sal.* 2; Gros. *Comp.* 266 etc. (v. adventus 3c); *Conc. Syn.* 323 etc. (v. albus 8d); **1252** diem emendationis treugarum .. que assignata est .. ∼a in Passione Domini [*5th Sunday in Lent*] (*AncC* V 55) *RL* II 81; **1256** datum Rome ∼a qua cantatur 'letare Jerusalem' [*4th Sunday in Lent*] (*AncC* VI 180) *Ib.* II 117; **1267** a primo ∼o temporis quadragesimalis *Cart. Osney* IV 268; **1446** per quatuor primos ∼os Quadragesime *Eng. Clergy* 229; **1493** ∼a proxima post festum Purificacionis B. M. V., viz. in Septuagesima . .; ∼a in Sexagesima . .; ∼a in Quinquagesima . .; ∼a prima Quadragesime .. *Comp. Swith.* 318–20.

8 having the nature of the Lord, divine.

sicut Augustinus in libro Retractacionum suarum vellet vocare Cristum hominem ∼um, si auctoritatem habuerit ex scriptura Wycl. *Chr. & Antichr.* 661.

dominigerium v. dangerum 3a.

dominio [cf. OF *dominion*], dominion, territory; **b** (fig.).

1573 ubicumque .. erimus .. infra regnum nostrum Anglie vel ∼ones nostras (*Comm. Gaol Del.*) *Foed.* XV 718. **b** orandum est ut imperet ventis et mari is in cujus manu cor regis est, sicut ∼ones aquarum, ut post tempestatem .. faciat tranquillitatem Ad. Marsh *Ep.* 226.

1 dominium v. dominicus 3b.

2 dominium [CL; cf. OF *demaine*]

1 dominion, lordship, authority: **a** (proprietorial or feud.); **b** (political); **c** (eccl. or mon.); **d** (divine). **e** self-mastery. **f** mastery over persons. **g** (w. *bonum*) patronage, favour. **h** mastery over animals.

a *Dial. Scac.* II 4 C (v. dominus 3a); numquam circa ejus personam concurrerunt ista duo jura, sc. jus hereditarium et ∼ium Glanv. VII 1 p. 74; cum nuda traditio ∼ium non transferat Vac. *Lib. Paup.* 110; **c1215** quod dominus de Castello Bainardi deberet optinere ∼ium aque ut signifer domini regis .. usque ad pontem de Stanes (*Mun. Lond.*) *EHR* XVII 486; **c1220** in .. terram [canonicorum] sive eorum catalla manum mittere vel aliquid ∼ium exercere .. nec poterimus nec debemus *Reg. S. Thom. Dublin* 9; nec pro solo ∼io fiunt homagia nisi soli regi vel principi sine tenemento vel servitio Bracton 79b (cf. Glanv. IX 2); **s1272** (v. communa 5b); **s1291** Willelmus de L. dedit S. abbati Cestrie totum ∼ium quod habuit in aqueductu de L. tam ad piscandum quam ad stagna levanda *Cart. Chester* 445; **1314** quietum clamavi eisdem [monialibus] quodlibet ∼ium distringendi easdem .. causis supradictis *FormA* 386; quod ille res erant effecte communes quoad ∼ium et proprietatem Ockham *Pol.* I 367; R. Bury *Phil.* 4. 72 (v. devolvere 5b); omne ∼ium dependet a possesso serviente ..; sed nulla potestas sic dependet; ergo nullum ∼ium est potestas Wycl. *Dom. Div.* 9. **b** Franci multi, Frisones, Galli, pagani, Britones, et Scotti, Armorici sponte se suo ∼o subdiderunt Asser *Alf.* 76; **s1000** predixit eis [Anglicis] quidam vir Dei .. insperatum a Francia adventurum ∼ium H. Hunt. *HA* VI 1; Gir. *EH* I 9 (v. devolvere 5a); **s1199** plerique barbari indignantes, ∼ium ex animi virtute .. resistere decernebant G. Cold. *Durh.* 15; **1293** Johannes Masun a .. juris denegacione per vos [J. regem Scocie] sibi facta ad nos ut ad superiorem ipsius regni Scocie dominum appellavit, petens .. per nos in vestri defectum sibi justiciam exhiberi, juxta quod racione superioris ∼ii quod in eodem regno habemus ad nos dinoscitur pertinere *RScot* 17b; **1294** (v. de 12c); **1301** directi ∼ii (v. dirigere 1d); **1321** potestatem et ∼ium sibi usurpantes in lesionem corone regie (*Eyre Lond.*) *MGL* II 332; impugnatores [istius constitucionis] .. ∼ium strictissime sumptum tali modo diffiniunt: '∼ium est potestas humana principalis rem temporalem in judicio vendicandi et omni modo qui non est a jure naturali prohibitus pertractandi' Ockham *Pol.* I 308; ∼ii politici aliud est ∼ium monasticum, aliud civile, et aliud est regale

—monasticum respectu unius domus sive familie, civile respectu civitatis vel communitatis amplioris familia, et regale respectu regni sive imperii WYCL. *Dom. Div.* 16; **1397** quousque ipse per altum ~ium occasione deafforestacionis predicte absque debito legis processu in ea parte facto inde [sc. de balliva forestarie] ammotus fuisset *Pat* 347 m. 20; regnum Anglie, quod ex Bruti comitiva Trojanorum . . in ~ium politicum et regale prorupit FORTESCUE *LLA* 13. **c** Adamnan pene omnes qui ab Hiensium ~io erant liberi . . ad unitatem reduxit catholicam BEDE *HE* V 15; **838** familiae liberorum monasteriorum, qui (*sic*) . . sub jure ~ioque abbatum abbatissarumque constituti fuerint *CS* 421. **d** ~ium divinum, tanquam metrum et principium simplicissimum, omnium aliorum obtinet principatum WYCL. *Dom. Div.* 16; licet dacio Dei non infert super ipso ~ium, tamen ex speciali ~io Dei super donatorium vere infert ejus ~ium super alia *Ib.* 214. **e** hoc nomen '~ium' sepe in philosophia morali accipitur pro potestate qua quis libere potest in actus contrarios; et sic dicunt quod homo est dominus et habet ~ium actuum suorum OCKHAM *Pol.* I 305. **f** Aristotelem, cui in orbis dominum [sc. Alexandrum] . . Deus ipse commisit ~ium R. BURY *Phil.* 7. 103. **g** **1388** quedam exennia . . constabulario castri Dovorr' . . pro bono ~io, favore et auxilio ipsius . . versus . . abbatem habendis in hac parte transmiserunt *IMisc* 239/2 r. 1 (cf. ib. r. 2: pro bono ~eo). **h** societas ei [sc. homini] ~ium omnium animalium dedit J. WALEYS *Commun.* I 1 f. 6v.

2 predominance (of component). **b** (astr.) dominance, ascendancy (of planet); *cf. dominus* 9.

sunt quatuor [elementorum qualitates] prime et principales, sc. caliditas et frigiditas, siccitas et humiditas. . . harum . . due sunt active, sc. caliditas et frigiditas, alie vero due . . passive; unde ab istarum qualitatum prevalencia et ~io dicuntur elementa activa vel passiva BART. ANGL. IV 1; sunt inter albedinem et nigredinem multi gradus intermedii secundum intencionem ~ii tam qualitatum activarum quam passivarum UPTON 104. **b** Mars, cum habuerit ~ium anni, . . boreales yemes mitigat, australem exasperat WALLINGF. (*EPT*) I 232.

3 (of land or sim.): **a** freehold. **b** demesne, tenure by lord for his own use. **c** demesne, land held for lord's use. *V. et.* 2 *dominicatus, dominicus* 3.

a **681** (12c) dono . . monasterio vestro manentes xx . ., ut habeatis jure ~ioque vestro *CS* 57; **690** (13c) terram . . Æbbae abbatissae jure ecclesiastico ac monasteriali et quibuscunque successoribus ipsa voluerit derelinquere tantum in ~[i]o in sempiternum possidendam perdonamus *CS* 42; **704** (9c) agri partem . . episcopo in ~io donare decrevimus *CS* 111; **924** (10c) postea revertatur [terra] in ~[i]um aecclesiae Christi *CS* 638; quaerit . . supergressionem cujusdam manerii . . quod habet . . noster sanctus, dicendo rogans inreverenter id sibi concedi pro suorum equorum pabulo quod servitores sancti tenebant in suo ~io HERM. ARCH. 39. **b** **1085** quam terram . . episcopus in proprio ~io ad victum aecclesiae et sui tenebat (*Ch.*) *EHR* XLIV 372; **c1090** concedo monasterio . . elemosinam quam Willelmus . . dedit, mansionem viz. que E. nominatur, quantum ipse in ~io suo inde tenebat *Regesta* p. 132; quedam puella . . est heres de dim. hida terre . . [sed] non habet in ~io nisi j virgatam *RDomin* 43; **1194** inquiretur . . quantus sit assisus redditus per singula maneria in demenio (*Cap. Coronae*) R. HOWD. III 265; **1209** in defectu gabuli terre Strong' tracte in ~ium, ij s. *Pipe Wint.* 50 (= *Crawley* 188); **1328** (v. dominicus 1c). **c** **a1070** precipio ut ~ia S. Edmundi sint quieta ab omnibus scottis et geldis *Regesta* p.118; ibi sunt in ~io iij carucae, et x villani et v bordarii cum xij carucis *DB* I 179v.; *Ib.* 283 (v. aula 5a); modo tenet R. in ~io halle *Ib.* II 449; decimae reddantur . . tam de ~io liberalis hominis [AS: *of þegnes inlande*] quam de terra villanorum . ., sicut carruca perarat (*Inst. Cnuti*) *GAS* 197; volo ut omnis homo sit venatione sua dignus in nemore et in campo in ~io suo [AS: *on his agenan*] (*Quad.*) *Ib.* 367; **c1126** sit una cultura et una firma in ~io aule de H. (*Cart. S. Benet Hulme*) *Med. E. Anglia* 245; **c1140** dedi . . totam demeniam meam que est in manu mea (*Ch.*) *Eng. Feudalism* 274; **c1150** (v. balcus 1); **c1155** dedisse . . duas bovatas . ., alteram . . de terra rusticorum . ., alteram de demenio nostro *Danelaw* 185; **1167** debet vij s. qui remanent super ~ium Willelmi de B. *Pipe* 161; noveris ~ia cujuslibet hec dici que propriis sumptibus vel laboribus excoluntur et item que ab ascriptitiis suis suo nomine possidentur; quia enim ascriptitii a dominis suis . . licite venduntur, merito tam ipsi quam terre quas excolunt ut dominis suis serviant ~ia reputantur *Dial. Scac.* I 11 B; **1181** remiserunt . . monachis decimas de antiquo ~io de Shepeley et decimas R. venatoris quas antiquitus habeurunt (*Concord.*) *Rec. Templars* 230; *Ib.* 41, 44 (v. 2 assidere 4); **a1190** j bovatam terre quam excepi de meo domenio *Ch. Gilb.* 62; **c1220** duas mansuras de diminio halle . . et ix bovetas terre de diminio meo . . tenendum (*sic*) . . de me . . liberas . . sicuti de meo diminio *FormA* 185; **1309** si aliqui de hujusmodi custumariis exierint de ~io et noluerint plus trahere moram ibidem, solebant venire in curiam et sursum reddere in manum domini tenuram suam bondagii (*Inq.*) *Antiq. Warw.* 639.

4 royal demesne (Eng.). *V. et. dominicus* 4.

901 illius terrae . . quae prius erat foras concessa in ~ium regale *CS* 587; **967** hanc terrae dimidiam partem quidam laicus . . per puplicum perdidit latrocinium et sic reputata est regis in ~ium *CS* 1198; rex W. . . tenet Windesores in ~io *DB* I 56v.; supersunt ibi ij hidae quae sunt diratiocinatae in ~io regis *Ib.* 158v.; omnium terrarum quas rex in ~io suo habet socnam pariter habet (*Leg. Hen.* 19. 2) *GAS* 559; **1169** de aux[ilio] ~iorum regis de Oxenefordscira ad maritandam filiam ejus *Pipe* 85; **1202** totum manerium illud fuit ~ium domini regis *CurR* II 111.

5 domain (in wider sense than demesne), dominion, lordship, territory: **a** (Eng.); **b** (W.); **c** (Ir.); **d** (Sc.); **e** (Continental).

a BRACTON 180b (v. dividere 8a); **1316** exceptis . . honore et ~io . . T. comitis Lancastrie *RScot* 160a; **1330** Ricardus pro domino rege . . dicit quod *infangthef* est quedam jurisdiccio regalis . . attribuens potestatem judicare furem . . cum manuopere deprehensum infra ~ium illius domini cui libertas illa per regem conceditur; et non habetur extendere ad †furca [l. furta] . . extra idem ~ium alicubi perpetrata *PQW* 519a; **1366** nichil habuit in ~io isto set infra civitatem London' *SelCCoron* 55; **c1380** in factura unius pillorii et furcarum in ~io de Hemyngburgh' *Ac. Durh.* 181; **1399** [? tam] in ducatu nostro Lancastrie quam in . . aliis comitatibus, honoribus, castris, maneriis, feodis, possessionibus et ~iis nobis ante adepcionem dignitatis nostre regie . . jure hereditario in dominico, servicio vel reversione . . descensis (*Ch. Hen. IV*) *MGL* II 487; **1399, 1449** (v. 1 chevagium 1e); **1583** infra parochias sive ~ia de Shenston' et Alderiche [*Staffs*] *Pat* 1234 m. 18. **b** **1221** recepturi emendationes . . de injuriis nobis . . illatis et terras et demania nostra (*Lit. Ll. Princ. Norwallie, AncC* IV 18) *RL* I 177; **1400** tenuit in dominico suo . . terras ac ~ium de Gower ac manerium et ~ium de Kylvey (*IPM*) *Cart. Glam.* 1435; **1421** (v. dominus 2b); **c1555** quod patria sive ~ium de Wales . . continuaret incorporat', unit', et annex' ad et cum hoc regno Angl' *Entries* 186. **c** **s1186** inter proceres regis Anglorum qui erant in Hibernia, Hugo de Lascy . . prepollens habebatur; cui idem rex . . amplissimas ibidem possessiones contulerat et suorum ~iorum administrationem commiserat W. NEWB. *HA* III 9; **a1225** quod . . canonici omnia supranominata et cetera quecumque in nostro habent ~io . . in pace . . teneant *Reg. S. Thom. Dublin* 4; **1226** cum castra quedam Hibernie ad demanium . . regis Anglie . . pertinencia contra voluntatem detineantur ejusdem *Mon. Hib. & Scot.* 26b; **s1398** comitatus Marcie . . de comitatu Ultonie et ~io de Connach in Hibernia . . gaudet . . augmentatus AD. USK 23. **d** **c1120** donavi . . totum ~ium meum de Malros *E. Ch. Scot.* 35; **c1150** rex A. . . concessit . . capelle decimas ~iorum suorum in soca de Struelin que eadem die fuerunt ~ia sua, sive accreverunt sive decreverunt *Ib.* 182; **1200** nec conferemus . . terram aliquam vel possessionem alicui nisi salvis eis [canonicis] de eadem terra et possessione omnibus rectitudinibus que eis dum nostro erant ~io exinde debebantur *Inchaffray* 17; **1356** dedimus . . domino E. [regi Anglie] regnum et coronam Scocie una cum . . omnimodis regalitatibus nostris, ~iis, homagiis et serviciis . . (*Ch. E. Balliol*) AVESB. 132b. **e** **1177** in demanio (v. doarium); **1239** hos [homines] fatetur imperator se ad demania sua revocasse secundum formam generalis constitutionis regni, per quam etiam comites et barones et omnes de regno homines de demaniis revocant ubicunque eos invenerint (*Lit. Nuntiorum Papae*) M. PAR. *Maj.* III 554; **1292** potestatem . . in personas alias transferendi omnia illa que inveneritis in manu seu tenura et domanio nostro non posse commode remanere *RGasc* III 48; R. BURY *Phil.* 8. 124 (v. ambasciatus); **s1354** rex E. rehaberet omnes terras et ~ia ducatui Aquitanie ab antiquo pertinencia et per reges Francie hactenus usurpata J. READING 164b; **1507** sub obediencia et jurisdiccione ~ii sive seniorie Veneciarum (*Pat*) *Foed.* XIII 161a; **1514** damus . . villam et gubernamentum Rupelle [*Gasc.*] una cum domaynio sive terris dominicalibus dictorum locorum (*DipDocE* 758) *Ib.* 460a.

6 royalty, payment to king as landlord.

1288 de minera lucrata in hujusmodi opere in feodo domini regis, . . rex habebit pro ~io suo tertium decimum discum, qui dicitur *le loth IMisc* 47/1 (cf. *VCH Derb* II 326).

dominius, belonging to a lord (esp. man.) or his demesne. *V. et. dominicus* 1, 3.

j car[ucata] terrae Hugonis, quae fuit de ~io manerio soca regis T. R. E. *DB* II 409v.; **c1120** terram . . que collateraliter . . prope ad propriam illam terram que sua fuit ~ia jacet (*Venditio*) *Chr. Rams.* 249; **1189** (1290) tam ipsos [canonicos] quam que eorum sunt sicut res proprias et ~eas in manu nostra . . retinemus *CalCh* II 377; **12. .** pasnagium ad demainios porcos suos *Reg. S. Thom. Dubin* 86; **c1347** cum libertate molendini primo post nostrum demanium bladum *Reg. Dunferm.* 384.

dominus [CL; *form* domnus (dompnus), *freq. in address or as eccl. title*, v. 6, 8 infra]

1 master, lord: **a** (of household or servants); **b** (of slave or serf); **c** (of apprentice); **d** (of self). **e** husband. **f** client, principal (of attorney *etc.*). **g** owner (naut.). **h** master (fig.).

a susceptus a ~is domus, resedit et ipse ad convivium BEDE *HE* III 10; sint hilares famuli domino relegente jocosa D. BEC. 1320; *Ib.* 1350 (v. cliens 1a); **1283** (v. ad 7d). **b** **748** servos tonsuratos, qui fugerunt ~is suis (*Lit. Papae*) *Ep. Bonif.* 80 p. 175; non est tam aspera hiems ut audeam latere domi pro timore ~i mei [AS: *hlafordes mines*] ÆLF. *Coll.* 90; si servus operetur die Dominica per preceptum ~i sui [AS: *his hlafordes*], sit liber et ~us emendet xxx s. ad witam (*Quad.*) *GAS* 91; si ~us suus [sc. nativi], volens eum ad libertatem perduci a villenagio suo quo ei tenetur obnoxius, et a se et heredibus suis quietum clamaverit, vel si eum ad liberandum alicui donaverit vel vendiderit GLANV. V 5; si verus ~us opposuerit exceptionem servitutis servo sub potestate constituto, sufficit si probet illum esse servum suum per parentes vel per assisam BRACTON 190b; **1296** in plena curia confitetur se nativum ~i; et est reseisitus terra sua et ponit omnino se in misericordiam ~i *SelPlMan* 46; *Quon. Attach.* 56 (v. bondagium d); ita posset papa . . privare . . reges . . regnis suis et facere eos aratores, immo servos rusticorum suorum, et imponere eis quecumque opera servilia que potest aliquis ~us imponere servis suis OCKHAM *Pol.* III 262; *Ib.* I 197 (v. despotes a). **c** **1300, s1383** (v. apprenticius). **d** OCKHAM *Pol.* I 305 (v. dominium 1f). **e** **1142** si ~us meus comes Andegavie et ego voluerimus (*Ch. M. Imp.*) *Mandeville* 167; **1172** confirmavi ei [Milesenti] quicquid ~us et vir suus Hugo emerit *Act. Hen. II* I 472; MAP *NC* III 2 (v. donum 1a); habuit ipsa iij ~os *RDomin* 53; [regina] diligebat quendam juvenem, . . cujus amorem amori sui ~i preferens operam . . dederat ut suum conjugem . . discriminis traderet *Arthur & Gorlagon* 7; *Fleta* 24 (v. domina 1c). **f** aut advocatus errat presente ~o aut absente W. DROGHEDA *SA* 52; attornati sui dixerunt in plena curia quod ~us eorum mortuus fuit *State Tri. Ed. I* 22; procuratorium . . est potestas seu mandatum quod datur procuratori a ~o suo *Praxis* 19. **g** navis proprietas . . quam ~us ejus . . dicit se . . emisse VAC. *Assumpt.* 28; **1328** quod omnes ~os et magistros navium tam de villa predicta [Suthampton'] quam de membris ejusdem . . injungatis quod . . naves suas . . ad eosdem portus . . reduci faciant *Cl* 147 m. 22d. **h** nasus cum fuerit subtilis, ejus ~us est valde iracundus BACON V 168; nummus est dominus et princeps omnium WALT. WIMB. *Sim.* 35.

2 lord, ruler, governor. **b** (w. *marchians*) marcher lord. **c** (w. *deputatus*) lord deputy.

tanta insania in ~os debacchatus est ut duos imperatores legitimos . . pelleret GILDAS *EB* 13; *greve* nomen est potestatis; Latinorum lingua nichil expressius sonat quam 'prefectura', quoniam hoc vocabulum adeo multipliciter distenditur quod de scira, de wapentagiis . ., de hundretis, de burgis, de villis etiam *greve* vocetur, in quo idem sonare videtur et significare quod '~us' (*Leg. Ed. Retr.*) *GAS* 654; **1074** W. rex Anglorum et Normannorum ~us *Regesta* 76; **1192** Johannes ~us Hybernie, comes Moretonii (*Ch.*) *MSS Ir.* 65; **1200** carta nostra, quam . . fecimus dum essemus tantum ~us Hybernie *RChart* 69a; **1200** postquam pax ~i regis tunc ducis Normannie et ~i Anglie fuit jurata *CurR* I 255; **1215** Johannes Dei gratia rex Anglie, ~us Hybernie, dux Normannie et Aquitannie *Magna Carta preamble*; **1375** A. de Valencia, comes Pembrochie, ~us Weysefordie et Monciniaci (*Ch.*) *EHR* XVI 102; **1434** de illo anulo dico quem a ~o Venetorum habui *Reg. Cant.* II 540. **b** **1421** adeo plene et libere sicut aliqui ~orum marchiancium in dominiis et marcheis suis Wallie habent et utuntur (*RNorm*) *Foed.* X 132b. **c** **1556, 1558** (v. deputare 6e).

3 lord (feud. or sim.). **b** lord of Parliament, peer (Eng. or Ir.). **c** Lord of (king's) Council (Eng. or Sc.). **d** lord, nobleman.

c980 (12c) primum naturali ~o suo regi armillam auream (*Test.*) *CS* 1133; **a1082** concedente Hugone de G., qui ~us feodi erat *Regesta* p. 124; quietus erit erga regem, non erga ~um cujus homo fuerit *DB* I 1; **s1099** ad ducem Normannorum accessit, satellitiumque suum ei, utpote naturali ~o, fideliter obtulit ORD. VIT. IX 15 p. 598; illi Deus est fidus qui suo ~o [AS: *his hlaforde*] recte est fidus (*Cons. Cnuti*) *GAS* 301; *Ib.* 293 (v. caput 20c); hic [Lotharius II, ob. **1138**] legem feudorum primus instituit, sanciens ut nullus feudum . . audeat . . alienare sine permissione majoris ~i ad quem feudum spectare dignoscitur GERV. TILB. II 19 p. 942; **1176** si heres [franci tenentis] fuerit infra etatem, ~us feodi recipiat homagium suum et habeat in custodia illum quamdiu debuerit; alii ~i, si plures fuerint, homagium ejus recipiant, et ipse faciat eis quod facere debuerit (*Assize Clar.* 4) R. HOWD. II 90; si ~us ejus, qui vulgo ligius dicitur, hoc est, cui soli ratione dominii sic tenetur ut contra ipsum nihil alii debeat, rege dumtaxat excepto, vocaverit ipsum *Dial. Scac.* II 4 C; GLANV. VII 10 etc. (v. capitalis 7b); **1230** veni ad fidem et servicium ~i mei H. regis Anglie . . et homagium ei feci de jure meo quod de eo tenere debeo; et . . juravi quod fideliter decetero ei serviam contra omnes homines, salvo ~is meis feodalibus servicio suo eis debito *Pat* (*Gasc.*) 409; BRACTON 81 (v. deadvocare a); **c1280** de terris et feodis ubi ~i capitales mediati et inmediati sunt laici (*DipDocE* 1576) *DocExch* 362; **1293** superiorem ~um (v. dominium 1b); **1301** prelati, comites, nobiles et communitates regni Scocie quos ad pacem nostram regiam suscepimus . . homagia et fidelitates nobis tanquam immediato et proprio ~o ejusdem regni . . fecerunt (*Lit. Regis Angliae*) *Anglo-Scot. Rel.* 108; directo ~o *Ib.* 104 (v. dirigere 1d). **b** **1387** certi articuli limitati per regem, super quibus ~i et communes regni in eodem parliamento procedere debeant *RParl* 233b; **s1387** (v. communis 11d); **1398** (*Ir.*) (v. communitas 9b); **s1397** statuunt quod . . omnes ~i jurarent se totis viribus statuta hujus parliamenti observare . . et quod omnes heredes et successores ~orum tam spiritualium quam temporalium prestabunt idem juramentum omnibus futuris temporibus, quando eis liberabuntur hereditates et possessiones in faciendo homagia et fidelitates sua *Eul. Hist. Cont.* III 377; **1412** filii . . ~orum qui in parliamento regio sedem habent, cum quibus ex gracia speciali ingrediendi [in librariam] faculta-

tem universitas ordinavit *StatOx* 218. **c 1376** pro ~is de consilio regis (*IssueR*) *EHR* XXI 16; **1423** de mandato ~orum de consilio *SelCExchCh* 26; **1460** super quo consulendi sunt ~i de consilio *ExchScot* 12; **1566** ordinamus .. ~os nostri consilii et sessionis *Inchaffray* app. 169. **d s1399** occurrerunt sibi plures ~i et valentes cum suis retinenciis OTTERB. 203; **1454** j par lintheaminum, unum novum boni panni et subtilis texture pro ~is recipiendis *Ac. Durh.* 149; **1487** ne quis presbiter .., filiis ~orum ac viris in aliqua dignitate ecclesiastica constitutis vel aliter notabiliter beneficiatis dumtaxat exceptis, capucium .. cum corneto .. gerat *Reg. Bath* f. 142.

4 lord (man.), landlord (not necessarily noble).

istud manerium habet .. consuetudinem in silva regis de Wochinges; hoc est quod ~us ville hujus potest habere in ipsa silva cxx porcos sine pasnagio *DB* I 31; has terras tenuerunt v teini ..; nec poterant recedere a ~o manerii *Ib.* 172; ille eat landesrico [AS: *landrican*], id est terre ~o, ad ordalium vel reddat [ei] duplum (*Quad.*) *GAS* 230; in cujuscumque terra fur cum furto invenitur, ~us terre [OF: *li seinur de la terre*] et uxor furis habebunt medietatem omnium bonorum furis (*Leis Will.*) *Ib.* 511; tempore Willelmi Painel, qui fuit ~us, .. fuit Berton posita ad firmam *RDomin* 20; GLANV. IX 8 (v. districtio 5a); **1195**, **1392** (v. bederipa); **1230** ipsi principales ~i sunt de Burtona *CurR* XIV 528; **1246** Simon .. levavit quandam sepem super terram ~i *SelPlMan* 6; **1259** (v. curia 6a); *FormMan* 11 (v. computus 2a); **1304** qui tenent ad voluntatem ~i istius manerii *IPM* 97/34; **1317** scire facias omnibus .. ~is libertatum quod ipsi in libertatibus suis .. eandem assisam cervisie custodiri faciant (*Breve Regis*) TROKELOWE 97; **1326** (v. conducere 3b); **1559** baronibus et aliis terrarum ~is *Conc. Scot.* II 155.

5 a bishop or archbishop. **b** person of (scholarly) authority, doctor (esp. of law). **c** (w. *scholarum*, acad.) master of the schools.

a c805 si .. pertingat ut aliquis ex heredibus ejus .. Ferhnham vendere mavellet, tunc primum nostrae aecclesiae ~o innotescatur *CS* 324; **838** [monasteria] spiritales ~os, id est episcopos .., propria voluntate .. habeurunt *CS* 421; **987** (11c) ea conditione ut .. suus heres veram amicitiam habeat cum ~o aecclesiae *CD* 661; **c1199** non similia .. in ecclesia Dei perpetrata, exceptis his que in ~o Cantuariensi leguntur impleta G. COLD. *Durh.* 16; **1200** inquisitio inter ~um Cantuariensem et dominum regem *CurR* I 279; **1219** commissus fuit magistro J.., officiali ~i Londoniensis *Ib.* VIII 95; **1255** taxatio .. per ~um Norwicensem facta *Val. Norw.* 209. **b** ne omnino non audiar, omnes meas sententias ~us quidam invenit, non ego ADEL. *QN intr.* p.1; **a1190** ut legis doctores appellarentur ~i, indigne ferentes appellari doctores vel magistri R. NIGER *MR* 19 p. 250; hoc modo procedit dictum ~orum de Rota in conclusione lxiij LYNDW. 78 h; ~us legum, A. *a man of lawe WW*. **c 1546** de pecuniis per illum [scribam universitatis] collectis ~us scholarum sibi et ceteris servientibus academie pro stipendiis satisfaciet *StatOx* 340.

6 (voc.) sir.

o, mi ~e [AS: *eala, leof hlaford*] ÆLF. *Coll.* 90; at vereor rursus dicere: "domne, jube" R. PARTES (*Fratri suo*) 227; domne, sedeto prior *Babio* 140; lector .. benedictionem, tanquam licentiam legendi, petit dicens: "jube, dompne, benedicere" .. sed nota quod hic dicit "dompne", non "~e", .. quoniam ad hominem loquitur, qui semiplenus et inperfectus est dominus respectu Domini, et ideo utitur sincopato vocabulo, quod observant monachi dicentes "domnus abbas", non "dominus abbas" BELETH *RDO* 25. 37D; ~e [ME: *sire*], hoc peccatum commisi sic et hoc modo *AncrR* 122.

7 (as honorific title of layman) lord: **a** (of emperor, king, or prince); **b** (of nobleman or royal minister). **c** (of knight) sir.

a 680 ~o gloriosissimo .. Geruntio regi ALDH. *Ep.* 4; **796** domnus rex (v. demandare 5b); **a1160** concordia .. facta .. in curia ~i regis (*Fine*) *Cart. Rams.* I 257; illic residet capitalis ~i regis justitia *Dial. Scac.* I 4 B; GLANV. I 1 (v. criminalis 1a); **1225** Henricus Lupus de Groningen, mercator de terra ~i imperatoris *Pat* 536; **s1238** misit ~us rex Anglie militare presidium ad ~um imperatorem juvandum contra rebelles suos in partes Ytalicas M. PAR. *Maj.* III 485; **1266** in expensis factis circa vina ~i regis *ExchScot* 3; **s1302** ~us rex Francie (v. 7b infra); **s1355** mirabatur quod ~us rex Anglie habuit ibidem tantam potenciam ex quo ~us princeps Wallie .. tam magnum exercitum habuit in Vasconia AVESB. 126; **1438** ~us imperator Romanorum (v. despotes b). **b c1165** in curia ~i comitis Willelmi [de Derbeia] (*Fine*) *Eng. Feudalism* 262; **s1302** transfretarunt nuncii regis Anglie ad parliamentum Francie .., viz. ~i comites Sabaudie, Lincolnie et Pembroke. .. et misit dominus rex Francie ad partes Flandrie .. ~os comites de Artoys, Bononie, et S. Pauli *Ann. Lond.* 128 (v. et. 7a supra); **s1312** ~us H. de Sandale, Anglie thesaurarius, et ~us I. de Warle garderobe regis custos TROKELOWE 79; **1409** ~o comiti Orcadie *ExchScot* 102; **1442** decretum sive arbitrium illustris principis ~i Humfridi Glowcestrie Ducis AMUND. II 278. **c 1247** dixit se esse cum ~o Henrico de Drayton', milite *SelPlForest* 85; **s1290** ~us Radulphus de Sandwyco, miles, custos Londoniarum *Ann. Lond.* 99; **1459** nobilis et potens ~us Patricius ~us le Grahame, miles *Conc. Scot.* II 79; miles quidam honorandus, ~us Ricardus Tunstall BLAKMAN *Hen. VI* 15.

8 (as honorific title, eccl. or mon.): **a** (of pope); **b** (of archbishop or bishop); **c** (of abbot or prior). **d** (of monk, esp. Benedictine) dom, dan. **e** (of priest) sir.

a praeceperat Theodoro .. domnus apostolicus BEDE *HE* IV 1; **824** (11c) Noðhelm praeco a domno Eugenio papa *CS* 379; **s1138** Albericus Ostiensis episcopus predicti domni pape in Angliam et Scottiam legatus J. WORC. 53; a ~o papa munere consecrationis suscepto AILR. *Ed. Conf.* 758A; **a1191** sciatis quod domnus apostolicus Rome .. precepit decimas omnium rerum que renovantur in singulis annis .. persolvi .. sancte ecclesie *Reg. S. Thom. Dublin* 304; **s1213** ex parte Pandulphi subdiaconi ac ~i pape familiaris WEND. II 68. **b 671** ~o reverendissimo [Leutherio episcopo] ALDH. *Ep.* 1; **930** (? 11c) fratribus .. qui in antefato ergasterio Deo, aeclesiae, domno praelato .. obtemperare voluerit *CS* 1343; **964** (11c) venationis sepem ~i episcopi ultronei ad edificandum repperiantur suaque, quandocumque ~o episcopo libuerit, venabula destinent venatum *CS* 1136; **1200** loquela .. inter cives Lond' et ~um G. Wintoniensem episcopum *CurR* I 277; **1281** (v. archiepiscopus); **1298** dompni Ricardi .. predecessoris nostri [sc. episcopi] *FormA* 10; **c1300** reverendissimo .. patri et ~o ~o .. Dei gratia Cantuariensi archiepiscopo *Lit. Cant.* I 14; **1307** cum exhennio misso ~o archiepiscopo Ebor' *Ac. Durh.* 2; hic mutet dompnus metropolitanus vocem suam *Lib. Regal.* 11; **1546** a reverendissimo in Christo patre ac ~o ~o Johanne Longland episcopo Lincolniensi *StatOx* 340. **c** abbatizans erat apud Sanctum [Eadmundum] domnus Baldewinus HERM. ARCH. 24; super quae [tapetia] prosternantur primum domnus abbas et induti LANFR. *Const.* 115 (cf. ib. 93: incipiat ~us abbas 'te Deum laudamus'); **s1137** non secus agentem novimus domnum priorem Wigorniensem J. WORC. 41; BELETH *RDO* 25 (v. 6 supra); dompnus abbas ei fugam obicit et vidue raptum MAP *NC* IV 6 f. 49; tacui, domnum abbatem .. nec volens condempnare, nec volens excusare BRAKELOND 144; accessit .. ad ~um R. de H. priorem ecclesie Dunelm' *G. Durh.* 2; **1335** dompnum J. abbatem de Cuper *RScot* 390b. **d** episcopus [Hugo, ob. **1195**] .. venientes ad se monachos honorifice semper excipiebat et ~os vocabat, quo eorum dilectionem non mediocriter obtinebat G. COLD. *Durh.* 4; sic cupit in vino dampnus adesse Deo GOWER *VC* IV 34 (cf. ib. 323: non dompni set et hii domini nomen sibi querunt); **1417** lego dompno J. Wotton monacho cognato meo xl s. *Reg. Cant.* II 131; **c1430** lettera composita per dompnum Hugonem, monachum S. Albani, magistrum nostrum *FormOx* 435; **1498** in solucione facta ~is suppriori, terrario, bursario, senescallo, capellano, cancellario, confessori ~i prioris, presentori et granatori, offic[ialibus] ~i prioris, cuilibet eorum x s. *Ac. Durh.* 655; **1518** deliveravi dampno Johanni Crambroke ij s. *DC Cant.* DE 63. **e 1200** eam [insulam] custodie et dispensationi domni Malisii presbiteri et heremite committimus *Inchaffray* 7; ~us Andreas, rector de Kevelston' *Mir. Montf.* 73; **13..** (**s1188**) illi duo [fratres] et ~us presbyter ville et duo de legalioribus parochianis elemosinam .. colligant (*Ord. de Subsidio Terrae Sanctae*) *MGL* II 654 (cf. R. HOWD. II 335: colligatur pecunia .. presente presbytero parochie et archipresbytero).

9 (astr.): **a** 'dominator', planet in the ascendant. **b** (w. *Aschone*) name of a comet.

a cognito ~o anni adequatione tabularum de Tolleto, scimus quod futurum est in rebus M. SCOT *Part.* 294n.; caput et pes sex linearum sequencium declarant naturam signorum et de die ac nocte ~os triplicitatum ELVEDEN *Cal.* 5; oportet te scire extrahere ~um anni, mensis, et hore et scire potestates eorum WALLINGF. (*EPT*) I 228 (cf. ib. 234: ~us hore est planeta †que [? l. qui] accidit in illa hora diei secundum denominacionem diei et successionem planetarum, ut Sol in prima hora diei Dominice, Venus in secunda hora ..). **b** ~us Aschone ex complexione est Mercurii et est ceruleus parvus sed cauda ejus longa. .. vidimus nuper ~um Aschone ante bellum quo comes de Monte Forte .. occubuit anno gratie 1264 *Ps.*-GROS. *Summa* 586–7.

10 (theol.) the Lord; **b** (w. spec. ref. to Christ).

paenitentiae tabulam .. exquirit ut avertatur furor ~i a vobis GILDAS *EB* 110; **596** (v. auxiliari a); qui Dominum lucis tenebroso corde negabant ALDH. *VirgV* 851; BEDE *HE* II 9 (v. adjuvare b); **841** (11c) agio et alto ~o Deo Saboth *CS* 435; Patricii .. veneratione .., qui .. ibidem [apud Glastoniam] in ~o quievisse perhibetur OSB. *V. Dunst.* 6; **s991** (v. dormire 3c); **s1165** congratulabuntur tibi in ~o quod illesus evasisti A. TEWK. *Add. Thom.* 17; **s1171** episcopus [Wint'] .. migravit ad ~um DICETO *YH* I 347; BELETH *RDO* 25 (v. 6 supra); sextum nomen [Dei] est Adonai, id est ~us, quia ejus dominationi subicitur totus mundus BART. ANGL. I 19; cum sit angelus ~i Exercituum in scala Jacob AD. MARSH *Ep.* 8 p. 89; **1269** ~o concedente *Cl* 78; **1334** remedium adhibuit ~us ulcionum *Conc.* II 575; creatorem .., qui est rex et ~us [ME: *king and keiser*] celi et terre *AncrR* 44; **s1370** est justus Dominus; hic justicias adamavit (J. BRIDL.) *Pol. Poems* I 152. **b** attendite verba ~i ad apostolos et turbas GILDAS *EB* 95; **679** etc. (v. Christus 2b); credula si Domino pandant praecordia Christo ALDH. *VirgV* 2393; **s874** etc. (v. adventus 3b); LANFR. *Const.* 107 (v. corpus 7b); in matrem ~i salvatoris EADMER *V. Osw.* 20; ~us ac salvator noster .. quosdam voluit esse perfectos [cf. *Matth.* v 48] AILR. *Ed. Conf.* 737B; a Dominica passionis ~i *RDomin* 61; **s1213** etc. (v. ascensio 1d); **1315** (v. crux 4d); **1409** ad festa Nativitatis ~i et Pasche *Comp. Swith.* 213.

domisell- v. domicell-.

†**domistrare**, to house.

howsyn, or puttyn yn an hows, ~o *PP*.

domitare [CL], to tame, break in.

in vere dimitto eos [accipitres] avolare ad silvam, et capio mihi pullos in autumno et ~o eos [AS: *temiȝe hiȝ*] ÆLF. *Coll.* 95; **c1330** in ij frenis emptis pro pullanis ~andis *Ac. Durh.* 518; *to tame*, domare .., ~are *CathA*.

domitator [cf. CL domitor], subduer, conqueror.

Jabim [cf. *Jud.* iv 2] .. / .. hic in Asor dum domitator erat GARL. *Epith.* I 492.

domitialis [cf. LL doma]

1 built in to a house, fixed.

1290 v mense cum trestellis, j mensa domitialis [*but* ? l. dormiens] *Reg. Wint.* II 705.

2 pertaining to a roof.

impertinentibus additis celaturis nugatoriis et .. sumptuosis, antequam medium operis in tabulatum ~em exurgeret, .. languit opus *G. S. Alb.* I 219.

domitor [CL], subduer, conqueror.

flammarum domitor, qui mundi comprimis ignes FOLC. *Carm.* 26; **c1168** quare .. qui tot .. urbium ~or est intemperantiam hanc domare non potest? J. SAL. *Ep.* 233 (239); venit Hercules monstrorum ~or, qui ipsum [leonem] interfecit ALB. LOND. *DG* 15. 5.

domitrix [CL], subduer, conqueror (f.).

o domitrix mundi GARL. *Epith.* I 351.

domn- v. domin-, damnum 4. **domoduca** v. domiduca.

domorsum [cf. dextrorsum etc.], homewards.

1424 pro transitu ~um xx d. (*Ac. J. Arundel*) *Poole Essays* 422; **1439** de viij s. solutis .. pro *pylys* Johanni Bole .. et de ij s. ad portand' ~um dicto J. *Stewards' Bk. Southampt.* II 76 (cf. ib. 86: pro centum de pilis et de iiij s. ad portand' ~um a Crakenhorde usque Watergate ville Suthampton').

dompn- v. domin-, damnum 3.

domuitas, essential nature of house.

~as non componitur ex forma fundamenti et forma parietis et tecti, sed est forma egrediens ab ordinacione illarum parcium habencium tales formas. quamvis ergo paries sit pars domus, non est tamen parietas pars ~atis *Ps.*-GROS. *Gram.* 32.

domum v. 1 domus, donum 1.

domuncula [CL], **~us, ~um**

1 little structure, house or cell (esp. mon.); *v. et. domiciuncula, domicula, domuscula*. **b** shed, sheepcote. **c** cage. **d** coffin.

vidit equum capud sursum elevantem ad tecta ~i [v. l. ~ae] *V. Cuthb.* I 6 (cf. ib. III 1: faciens ibi ~as de quibus nisi sursum caelum videre nihil potuit); est locus idem sepulchri tumba lignea in modum ~i facta coopertus BEDE *HE* IV 3 (cf. ib. 23 p. 265: ~ae .. ad orandum vel legendum factae); **738** Bernhardus operarius sit et edificet ~a nostra BONIF. *Ep.* 40; praetoriola, ~a in nave *GlC* P 665; **801** (v. 2 cloca 1a); properemus .. in armarium, i. ~us codicelli, nostrum ÆLF. BATA 5. 10; ~am [sc. capellam ligneam] succedenti tempore vepres obtexerant W. MALM. *GP* II 74 p. 153; **1127** ~as sibi propter naves advectantes ibidem fecerunt (*Plac. Sandwic.*) *Eng. Justice* 116; **1173** de bosco et ~is venditis *Pipe* 89; videns ~am quandam per postem deforis a muro dependentem GIR. *EH* I 16; **c1250** Mabilia .. tenet unum ~um pro iiij d. *Cart. Rams.* II 46; **1341** in structura j ~e lapidee supra *le Welleheved Ac. Durh.* 539; *a cottage*, contagium, ~us *CathA*. **b** caulas, ~as *GlC* C 131; **1205** j mansuram in capite .. ville, ad faciendam ibi ~am [MS: domc'lam] ovibus suis *RChart* 143b. **c** ut, cum in cavea recluditur [psittacus], .. ex virgis ferreis ~a ejus contexatur NECKAM *NR* I 38; **s1306** [comitissa de Bokan] in ~a quadam lignea super murum castri Berewici posita est TREVET 408 (= RISH. 229; cf. cagia b). **d** si aliquis .. moriatur in equore .., si terram non videant, fiat ei ~a de lignis, si possint haberi, et proiciatur in mari BELETH *RDO* 159. 158A.

2 little room.

747 per interiora monasterii ~a (*Clovesho*) *Conc. HS* 369; **c1250** capellanus habet .. unum mansum cum tribus ~is *Vis. S. Paul.* 5.

1 domus [CL]

1 home. **b** (locative or dat. for acc.) homewards, (to) home.

revertuntur .. Hiberni ~os GILDAS *EB* 21; ductus ad ~um suam ALDH. *VirgP* 50; remanere ~i passus est BEDE *HE* V 9; non est tam aspera hiems ut audeam latere ~i [AS: *æt ham*] ÆLF. *Coll.* 90; indignum ferentes tot .. ~i militieque preclaros ditioni .. paucorum subjacere OSB. BAWDSEY clxxvij; **s1390** (v. collibertus b). **b s891** alter ~i vertitur ÆTHELW. IV 3; precepit eis quod irent ~ibus *State Tri. Ed. I* I 19 (cf. ib. 38); **1326** ita quod ~i possit redire *Lit. Cant.* I 203; **s1355** domino R. .. ~i dimisso AVESB. 125b.

2 house, dwelling place; **b** (w. ref. to 'hamesucken'); **c** (royal). **d** fortified house, guard-house, barracks or sim. **e** app. manor. **f** receptacle or container (partly fig.). **g** 'sacrament house' (repository for reserved sacrament).

qui .. in domus suas hujusmodi homines introducunt in exquirendis aliquam artem maleficiorum .. quinquennio paeniteant THEOD. *Pen.* I 15. 4; accenso grandi igne in medio, contigit volantibus .. scintillis culmen ∼us, quod erat virgis contextum ac foeno tectum, subitaneis flammis impleri BEDE *HE* III 10; quis vestrum non utitur arte mea [sc. lignarii], cum ∼os [AS: *hus*] .. fabrico ÆLF. *Coll.* 100; corruit et mulier .. / eque domu mandat pellacem vertere gressus ÆTHELWULF *Abb.* 356; *DB* I 205 (v. curia 10b); eat omne cyricsceattum ad matrem ecclesiam de omni libera ∼o [AS: *be ælcum frigan heorðe*] (*Quad.*) *GAS* 197; **a1200** reddendo .. de unaquaque ∼o hominum illorum qui de eis tenet j ob. per annum, qui vocatur *halideisilver*, salvo capitali masuagio prenominati G. et heredum suorum; ita ut, si plures fuerint dom[us], ad numerum ∼orum crescet numerus obolorum *Kal. Samson* 106; **1204** per servicium, sc. ut idem R. de †quolibet [MS: qualibet] ∼o hominum suorum de K. haberet j gallinam per annum *CurR* III 150; si ∼us ejus in burgo .. fuerit constituta, prosternatur et extra villam deportata in media die comburatur *Cust. Norm.* 37. 2; †**1189** (14c) si aliquis habeat proprium murum lapideum .. altitudinis xvj pedum, vicinus ejus debet facere stillicidum sub severunda ∼us que sita est super murum illum et in illo aquam stillantem de dicta ∼o recipere (*Assis. Aedif.*) *MGL* I 323; non debent .. plures cohabitare quam possit ∼us distincte capere *Ps.*-GROS. *Gram.* 40; *Conc. Scot.* II 45 (v. dominicalis 3c); **1300** extraneos secum habuit ad potandum et ad manducandum sicut ad tabernam in quodam loco distanti a ∼o focali *IMisc* 59/28; **1305** quod dicta aula cum ∼ibus adjacentibus .. pro ∼ibus habitabilibus et non pro scolis .. habeantur *Cart. Osney* I 111; **1322** Sarra ospitata fuit in una ∼o debili et ruinosa et .. ∼us noctanter cecidit super eam .. ligna et lapides prostrate appreciantur ad xij d. *SelCCoron* 77; **1397** nulli mercenarii .. infra villam N. portent †pactas [l. paccas] suas nec mercandizas de ostio ad ostium .. seu ∼o ad ∼um ad mercandizas suas vendendas *Lib. Cust. Northampt.* 73. **b** *CD* 756 (v. assultus 2b); †**1060** (12c) ∼us assultum [AS: *hamsocne*] et pacis infractionem *CD* 888; *hamsocne*, hoc est invasio in propria ∼o aut infra curiam causa alicujus mali (*Inst. Cnuti*) *GAS* 317; **c1160** habeant .. *hamsoch* et *gridbrich* et pacis fracturam et pugnam in ∼o factam et ∼us vel curie invasionem *CalCh* II 369. **c** incipit Alea Evangelii, quam D. episcopus Bennchorensis detulit a rege Anglorum, i. e. a ∼u Adalstani regis *Alea Evang.* 173; *Leg. Hen.* 80. 7a (v. curia 3b); dispensator .., si extra ∼um regis commederit *Domus Reg.* 130; **1254** ∼uum regalium (v. aedificatio 1b). **d** *DB* I 184v. (v. defensabilis 3a); **s1071** rex .. insulam [Ely] obsedit, pontem paravit, ∼um belli artificiose construxit, que usque hodie perstat H. HUNT. *HA* VI 33; **1284** pro factura unius longe ∼us apud Caernarvan ad pedites cum rege existentes intus hospitandos *KRAc* 351/9 m. 13; **1304** (v. 1 carnellus a); **1313** quandam ∼um fortem de petris, lignis, et fossatis facere *RGasc* IV 921 (cf. ib. **1161** [**1314**]: quandam ∼um fortem seu fortalicium). **e** de defectibus implementorum ∼orum episcopatus *Hist. Roff.* f. 43. **f** domus est constructa mihi de tergore secto ALDH. *Aen.* 61 (*Pugio*) 6; in merothece, in ∼o ung[u]entorum *GlC* I 142; in .. cordis atrio .. sibi edificavit ∼um Spiritus Sanctus DOMINIC *V. Ecgwini* I 2; mens labis inhospita nevo, / munda domus cordis HANV. IX 397 p. 389; superior [venter] est ∼us cordis et pulmonis ..; inferior vero venter ∼us est organorum in quibus assimilatur nutrimentum *Ps.*-RIC. *Anat.* 24; ave, cujus ventris promus / et matricis sacre domus / Deo gaudent hospite WALT. WIMB. *Virgo* 27; ipsa [anima] hic est in extraneo intrusa carcere [sc. corpore] in ∼o mortis [ME: *in an qualm hus*] *AncrR* 45. **g** **15..** ornamenta summi altaris: .. velamen unacum sustentaculis ligneis .. et baculis .. cum .. clavibus ferreis ad dirigendum hujusmodi sustentacula ∼us sacramenti *Reg. Aberd.* II 192 (cf. ib. 196: *þe sacrament hous*).

3 household; **b** (royal; *cf. hospitium*). **c** 'house', lineage; (*cf. Luke* ii 4). **d** (?) house-community (E. Anglia; *cf. Econ. HR* X 192–3).

praefectum .. cum ∼u sua convertit ad Dominum BEDE *HE* II 16; ve[r]na, in ∼o natus *GlC* U 138; tota ∼us tres erant: ipse laboriosus, uxor erumnosa, filia morbosa W. CANT. *Mir. Thom.* III 11. **b** hec est constitutio ∼us regis *Domus Reg.* 129; in primitivo regni statu post Conquisitionem, regibus de fundis suis .. sola victualia solvebantur, ex quibus in usus cotidianos ∼us regie necessaria ministrabantur *Dial. Scac.* I 7 A; magna parte ∼us regie comitante W. SAY *Lib. Reg. Cap.* 59; Liber Niger ∼us regis Anglie, id est, ∼us regie sive aule Anglie regis *Househ. Ed. IV* 74 *rub.* **c** inclitissime ∼us Francie .. reconciliacionem BEKYNTON II 123 (v. effectualis a). **d** **c1105** apud Suthstede ∼um Elfgari cum carrucata terre; .. et apud Ouby abstulit ipse S. ∼um Leofchildi et dim. possessionem ejus *Reg. S. Ben. Holme* I 169; **1275** Ricardus ad Grenam, ∼us Aylward, ∼us Fraunceys in Runhal subtraxerunt se de leta de Runhal spectante ad hundredum *Hund.* I 527a (cf. ib. 529b: una secta subtrahitur de ∼o Walteri de M.).

4 **a** prison-house. **b** workhouse.

a [Henricus II] reginam, ut liberius stupris vacaret, in ∼o carceris inclusit R. NIGER *Chr. II* 168; *Dial. Scac.* II 21 A (v. carceralis b). **b** **1553** eosdem ruffianos, ganeones, vagabundos et mendicos .. in ∼um occupacionum et Bridewell committere *Pat* 863 m. 13.

5 **a** court-house. **b** council-house. **c** house of Parliament. **d** house of Convocation (eccl.).

a praetorium, ∼us judic[i]aria *GlC* P 622; **1297** in .. stramine pro ∼o placiti [MS: pl'i], muris turris cooperiendis, stipendio coopertorum *Ac. Cornw.* II 162; **s1327** (v. communis 4a); **1414** ipsum arestavit et detinuit in ∼o placitorum ejusdem curie (*Northwich*) *Law Merch.* I 115. **b** ∼us consilii *GlC* C 925; *GlH* C 2194 (v. curia 1a); **1388** Lamkino Lokyer .. pro ij ceruris, viz. j *spryngelok*' et j *stoklok*, factis pro ostio ∼us consilii (*Westm.*) *KRAc* 473/2 m. 20. **c** **s1397** sagittarii regis .. circumvallantes ∼um parliementi in medio paviamenti palacii ex hoc capite tantum †factum [? l. factam], credentes fuisse in dicta ∼o aliquam rixam aut pugnam AD. USK 11; **s1453** inferebant quamplures billas suas in ∼um inferiorem inter Communes *Reg. Whet.* I 92 (cf. ib. 93: ut procuraret .. ipsam [billam] apportari ad ∼um superiorem ac ibidem tam per dominum regem quam eciam per singulos dominos alios approbari). **d** **1439** cedula .. post .. communicacionem habitam .. inter .. episcopos et prelatos .. de ∼o superiori, tandem ipsis de clero ∼us inferioris pro avisamento et deliberacione .. capiendis extitit liberata *Reg. Cant.* III 285 (= *Conc.* III 535a).

6 (usu. w. *Domini* or *Dei*; *cf.* 7c, 18 *infra*) church (building or institution); **b** (w. *orationis*; *cf. Luke* xix 46).

∼um Domino .. fundavit, cujus profunditatem in terra cum ∼ibus mire politis lapidibus fundatam et super terram multiplicem ∼um columnis variis .. suffultam .. non est meae parvitatis .. explicare EDDI 22; perfecta ∼u *Ib.* 17 (v. 1 dicatio); vasa sancta aliaque hujusmodi quae ad ornatum ∼us Dei pertinent BEDE *HE* V 20; qualiter ∼us Dei consecrandus (*sic*) est EGB. *Pont.* 26 *rub.*; **749** (12c) cunctas tribulationes quae nocere .. in ∼o Dei possunt .. auferre praecipit *CS* 178; prior .. honorabilior est reliquis ministris ∼us Dei LANFR. *Const.* 143; in manibus nefariorum principum .. et ingredientium pompatice ∼um Domini [cf. *Amos* vi 1] AD. MARSH. *Ep.* 244. **b** **795** (v. convocare 2); **1390** in ecclesia, que ∼us orationis existit *Stat. Linc.* II 248.

7 (mon.) house of religion or sim.; **b** (dist. as mother or daughter house). **c** (w. *Dei*; *cf.* 6a *supra*) *maison Dieu*, hospital. **d** almshouse.

nos sumus filii ejus [Benedicti Biscop], quos in hanc monachiae ∼um pius provisor induxit BEDE *Hom.* I 13. 227; †**1093** (12c) damus priori .. ut habeat .. facultatem plenariam cum consilio capituli sui ordinandi ∼um suam in interioribus et exterioribus agendis suis *Ch. Durh.* 7. p. 55; **1171** ∼um Templi, que Londoniis super Tamensem fluvium sita est *Rec. Templars* 163; **c1188** has terras .. licebit .. archidiacono dare, vendere vel invadiare unicuique hominum voluerit preterquam ∼ibus religiosis ac Judeis *Ch. Sal.* 45; **1200** quidam canonicus .. dixit quod pro ∼o †suo [MS: sua] venerat ad respondendum *CurR* I 307; GIR. *Spec.* III 19 (v. abbatia c); **s1233** (v. convertere 7c); **1242** ∼ui S. Mathei de B. et sororibus infirmis ejusdem ∼us *Pipe* 343; **1255** (v. canonicus 6a); **1362** fundator ∼us hospitalis .. de Droheda [*Ir.*] (*Pat*) *MonA* VI 1139b; **1420** fratribus minoribus de Dunde .., uno fratre dicte ∼us fatente receptum .. iij li. *ExchScot* 329; **1537** burgagium ∼us sive hospitalis de G. *Ac. Durh.* 674. **b** **c1239** patres abbates Cisterciensis ordinis possunt suas filias ∼os visitare GROS. *Ep.* 127; **s1275** cum .. priores cellarum [senio confractos] .., tanquam milites emeritos, ad matricem ∼um morandi causa vocari contingat *G. S. Alb.* I 452; **1319** frater W... de Holmcoltram in Anglia, que est ∼us filialis de Meuros in Scocia *RScot* 193a; **1426** (v. capitalis 8b). **c** **1176** pro plumbo ad opus ∼us Dei de Grantmonte *Pipe* 141; **1267** confirmasse Deo et B. Marie et ∼ui Dei de B. liberum introitum *Reg. Brechin* I 7; **1279** de proventibus et redditibus leprosiarum, ∼orum Dei et hospitalium pauperum qui in usum infirmorum et pauperum convertuntur (*Lit. Papae*) *EHR* XXXII 86; **1335** custos ∼us Dei de Berewico *RScot* 383a; **1421** hospitale sive ∼us Dei de Villaribus (*RNorm*) *Foed.* X 111a. **d** **1201** quatenus .. nuntios ∼us elemosinarie S. Antonii .. benigne admittatis *Pat* 3b; **s1207** incepimus ∼um elemosinariam in Martio et ante festum S. Luce fuit consummata *Ann. Dunstable* 30; **1272** ∼um elemosinarum apud T. .. construxisse *Reg. Aberd.* I 30; magister sive custos collegii ∼us eleemosinarie S. Trin. de C. *Entries* 246.

8 (mon.) building, room or office (spec.).

813 (17c) ∼um refectionis et dormitorium communiter frequentent *CS* 342; dum senserit se nimia invalitudine praegravari .., ingrediatur ∼um infirmorum [AS p. 442: *on hus untrumra*] *RegulC* 65; nec quicquam ex omnibus monasterii officinis incombustum remansit praeter duas ∼os sine quibus monachi remanere non possent, dormitorium sc. et refectorium OSB. *Mir. Dunst.* 16 (cf. ib. 19: ut transferri deberent corpora sanctorum .. in ∼um quandam refectorii); frater qui ad suscipiendos hospites deputatus est in ipsa hospitum ∼o haec praeparata habere debet: lectos, sedilia [etc.] LANFR. *Const.* 153 (cf. ib. 169: ducat eum [novitium] .. magister suus in cellam camerarii vel in aliam ∼um); in ∼o hospitum et alibi ubicunque comedebant extra refectorium vescebantur carnibus SWAFHAM 110; **a1237** etc. (v. capitularis 4b); permittimus quod fratres nostri pondus officii portantes .. in infirmitorio, in mensa communi ac in ∼o misericordiarum ibidem, cum hoc justa necessitas vel eciam pia utilitas exigerit (*sic*), carnibus recreentur *Cust. Cant.* 40; **1369** pro diversis operariis comedentibus in parvo (*sic*) ∼o bursar[ie] *Ac. Durh.* 575; **1382** in ∼o capituli (v. 1 capitulare 2); **c1530** quod .. mulieres suspectas in ∼o officii tui, viz. *le Cheker*, .. tecum conversantes habuisti (*Vis. Leic.*) *EHR* IV 308.

9 **a** (acad.) house (of scholars), college. **b** school-house.

a **1264** ad fundationem ∼us quam dici volo .. ∼um scholarium de Merton' *Stat. Coll. Ox.* I (*Merton*) 6 (cf. custos 9a); BACON *Maj.* III 96 (v. corrector 1a); **1274** (v. collegium 2); **1287** per consilium .. rectorum ∼us [scholarium de B.] *Deeds Balliol* 283; **1292** omni anno .. fiat missa pro omnibus benefactoribus ∼us *MunAcOx* 59; **1313** quia nomina delinquencium per principales ∼uum .. melius †poterint esse nota *StatOx* 110; **a1350** a procuratoribus eligentur duo procuratores ∼orum universitatis .. ut ∼os tempore vacationis possint reparare *Ib.* 70. **b** ECCLESTON *Adv. Min.* 8 (v. camera 2a); **c1330** reparacio .. ∼us scolarum grammaticalium in villa S. Albani *Educ. Ch.* 296; **1384** quandam ∼um scolarum in quadam placea sua continenti duas acras terre .. in Wotton Underegge de novo construere pro inhabitacione sive fundacione unius magistri et duorum pauperum scolarium artis gramatice *Pat* 317 m. 2.

10 **a** guild. **b** (w. ref. to 'guild-house', ale-house); **c** (w. ref. to brothel).

a **1262** Robertus .. intrat in gildam mercatoriam per uxorem suam; faciat que facere debet ∼ui, et habeat (*Andover*) *Gild Merch.* II 4 (cf. ib. I 196). **b** ad ∼um in hora nemoris magnam delatus est, quales Anglici in singulis singulas habebant diocesibus bibitorias, *ghildhus* Anglice dictas MAP *NC* II 12 f. 27; aiebat se aliquando ∼um potationis ingressum vidisse hujusmodi demones in specie simiarum singulos potatoribus singulis in scapula sedentes W. NEWB. II 21; **1475** in clavis emptis pro ∼o scotale hoc anno *Ac. Churchw. Sal.* 17 (cf. *OED* s. v. *scotale*); **1542** (v. cervisianus); **1549** ∼us tabernarie *CalPat* III 95; **1661** custodit communem ∼um tipulatoriam, A. *a common alehouse* (*Quarter Sess.*) *Surrey Rec. Soc.* XIII 102. **c** in prostibulo, in ∼o fornicaria *GlC* I 143; **1321** de quadam ∼o .. que lupanar vilium mulierum existebat (*Pat*) *Foed.* III 880a; **1541** B. H. custodit unam lupanem (*sic*) sive ∼um lupanariam *Augm. Bk.* 134 f. 40v.; **1553** suspiciosas ∼os (v. aleatorium).

11 building (var.). **b** (w. *forinseca*) outhouse. **c** 'summerhouse', shieling. **d** (w. *rotunda*) round-house (pavilion on ship). **e** (w. *Scoticana*) app. building in Highland style.

[minotaurus] inclusus laberinto .. ∼um illam Cretae egredi non potuit *Lib. Monstr.* I 50; cum .. mansionem angustam circumvallante aggere et in ea necessarias .. construxisset BEDE *HE* IV 26 p. 271; **1155** in reparatione ∼orum de Scaccario *Pipe* 4; **c1160** (v. curia 10b); **1222** (v. discooperire 3); **1228** (v. camera 2a); BACON *CSTheol.* 47 (v. cooperimentum a); **1270** habuit .. quandam ∼um vocatam piscalem *IMisc* (*Great Yarmouth*) 24/16; **1306** (v. dressor b); **1309** (v. cultilis); **1318** manerium cum omnibus ∼ibus, viz. grang', bovar' et columbar', in bono statu *Ac. Durh.* 374; **1323** (v. conflator); **1342** una cum defectubus in ∼ibus rectorie .. imminentibus (*Vis. Totnes*) *EHR* XXVI 111; **1373** injunctum est tenentibus dominicorum quod reparari faciant ∼us manerii *Hal. Durh.* 118; **1471** pro nova tectura j parve ∼us supra fontem in orto abbathie *Ac. Durh.* 643; **1627** j ∼um fontalem, A. *a welhouse* *KB ContrR* 276 r. 74. **b** **1221** caro j vacce furate inventa fuit in ∼o sua forinseca *SelPlCrown* 111; **1235** Brianus .. fuit in curia in quadam ∼o forinseca in quodam stabulo *CurR* XV 1438. **c** *Cart. Bilsington* 15n. (v. aestivalis d); **14..** tenentes mittent ad curiam .. ad terminum Nativitatis S. Joh. .. xx d. pro ∼o estatis et *bereard* *Ib.* 191; **1521** Jonet habebit .. ∼um lapideam .. cum ∼o ad montanas tempore estivali ..; set .. debet edificare aliam ∼um estivalem [cf. W. *hafod, hafdy*] pro .. sorore sua *AncD* (*Wales*) C 5233. **d** **1342** circa facturam .. j magne ∼us rotunde de *carde ynde* extra et virid' infra poste de xxij pedibus longitudine florettat' cum tela lin[ea] extra *KRAc* 389/14 m. 3. **e** **1266** expense pro constructione j ∼us Scoticane infra castrum de Invernes .. cum constructione j garderobe *ExchScot* 14.

12 administrative office: **a** toll-house; **b** weigh-house; **c** custom-house; **d** counting-house; **e** registry.

a statutum est ut homines celerarii venirent ad ∼um thelonei cum aliis .. et ibi darent prefecto denarium qui dicitur *borthselver* BRAKELOND 150. **b** **1338** pro cariagio [lanarum] usque ∼um ponder' *KRAc* 457/7; **1593** ad edificandum pretorium, carcerem, ∼umque ponderum [Scots: *weyhous*] et telonium .. ad publicos usus .. burgi *RMSScot* 817b. **c** **1358** pro firma ∼us custume per tempus hujus compoti *ExchScot* 595. **d** **1403** etc. (v. computus 2e). **e** in ∼o registri ad Nettelham comparuit (*Court Bk. Linc.*) *Eng. Clergy* 220.

13 privy. *Cf. camera* 3.

s1016 [Edmundus rex] ivit nocte quadam in ∼um evacuationis ad requisita nature H. HUNT. *HA* VI 14; **s1016** [Edricus] sub purgatoria ∼o sese occultans, regem ad requisita nature nudatum .. percussit AILR. *Gen. Regum* 365; erat ibi a parte australi ecclesie ∼us purgatoria in proximo posita, que .. omnibus erat advenientibus pro officiis necessariis promptissime semper aperta R. COLD. *Godr.* 321; **1141** recepit .. j privatam ∼um juxta cameram et aliam in curia *Dom. S. Paul.* 136; intrantes ∼um necessariam .. abscondant vultus suos in caputiis *Inst.*

Sempr. *lv; vidit lumen in ~o necessaria, candelam sc., paratam cadere super stramen BRAKELOND 129; longitudo ~us necessariorum [constat ex] lxiiij ulnis *Cust. Cant.* 32; **1377** de factura cloacarum circa pontem London': .. conquestum fuit quod ~us necessaria, viz. garderoba, confracta erat *Pl. Mem. Lond.* A 22 m. 4b; [J. abbas, ob. **1401**] construxit .. ~um secessui necessariam, secretum sive privatum dormitorium vulgariter nuncupatum, qua nulla pulchrior aut sumptuosior poterit .. reperiri, cameram quoque in fine dicte ~us .. pro domino abbate *G. S. Alb.* III 443; **1497** (v. aisiamentum 2c).

14 a pig-sty, cow-shed, or sheepcote. **b** rabbit-hutch. **c** henhouse. **d** (falc.) aviary. **e** bee-hive.

a Golenus *bard*, qui de ~o porcorum festucam unam retulit sine alicujus grunnitu MAP *NC* II 23 f. 31v.; **1321** J. Piscator levavit unam ~um porcorum in communa *CBaron* 134; **1286** cum quadam ~o *byer'* [*Kent*] *CalCl* 467; **1335** j parvulam ~um ad vitulos (*Dimiss. S. Paul.*) *Camd. Misc.* IX intr. p. xvi; **1341** pro .. ~o vaccarum (v. crucka); **1553** barcarias sive ~us oviles *CalPat* I 213. **b** **1281** (v. cunicularium). **c** c**1160** ~us gallinacee (v. daieria a); **1297** carpentariis facientibus .. porcherium et ~um gallinarum et *le cartehous* (*MinAc*) *Econ. Condit.* app. 35; **1350** j ~um pro gallis et gallinis (*MinAc*) *Surv. Durh. Hatf.* 219; **1362** ad cooperiend' .. ~um gallin' discoopertam turbine venti superflui *MinAc* 840/23 m. 2. **d** **1202** (v. avis 1b); **1391** pro j magna ~o pro *les faucons* domini *Ac. H. Derby* 65. **e** si aliquibus ~ibus apum erectis alie ponantur secundum alium situm .., vacuum spatium relinquitur BACON *Maj.* I 164.

15 a storehouse. **b** workshop, kiln, mill-house, or sim. **c** blowing-house (for tin-smelting).

a **1221** ad ~um cooperiendam inter bracinum et ~um turbe *Ac. Build. Hen. III* 36; **1271** in muris ~us lane *MinAc* 1078/13 r. 3; **1297** pro .. ~o palee (*MinAc*) *Econ. Condit.* app. 6; **1299** pro ~o farine apud Wardeley *Ac. Durh.* 500; *FormMan* 21 (v. carrettivus a); **1309** corneriam cujusdam ~us carectarum *Cl* 126 m. 8*d.*; **1310** ~us ad carectas *MinAc* 992/8; **1350** carpentario elargeanti bovariam pro j ~o pro feno de novo facienda (*MinAc*) *Surv. Durh. Hatf.* 219; **1365** *le thresshewold* .. ~us toralis et ~us turbarum *DLMinAc* 242/3888 m. 3; **1387** (v. couchatio); **1404** in ~o olei *Ac. Durh.* 397; **1421** ~us carbonum (v. carbo 2c); **1430** (v. alleciarius); **1462** ~um plaustralem *CourtR Lygh* f. 1v.; **1627** j ~um lacteam, A. *a milkehouse*, j camerum (*sic*) supra eandem ~um lacteam vocatum *a cheselofte KB ContrR* 276 r. 74. **b** sutrina ~us, *sutera hus* ÆLF. *Sup.*; **1091** nulli licuit in Normannia monetam facere extra ~os monetarias Rothomagi et Baiocarum (*Consuet. Norm.*) *EHR* XXIII 508; **1232** in virgis ad walduram et pro ~o molendini cooperanda *Pipe Wint.* 159283 r. 11; **1279** ad ~um que dicitur *le pressurhous* erigendam *MinAc* 840/2; **1295** pro ~o pressorie de postis dirigend' et trabis ad eosdem ligand' *Ib.* 840/8; **1300** ad ~os bracine (v. bracinum 1); **1303** (v. braciatricius); **1320** ~us cementar' (v. astellaria); **1365** ~us toralis (v. 15a supra); **1376** ~us tegulat' *MinAc* 900/12 (cf. *CalPat* I 116 [**1547**]: ~us tegularis, [vulgariter vocata] *a tyle kylle*); **1388** in ~o laboris caruce .. cum toto apparatu *Augm. Bk.* 52 f. 48; **1404** (v. cereus 1f); **1409** factura ~us forgei (*Aud. Durh.*) *EHR* XIV 517; **1415** in ~o rasure *Ac. Durh* 268 (cf. ib. 272: in ~o rasture); s**1423** combusta fuit ~us pandoxatoria Johannis H., carpentarii *Chr. S. Alb.* 3; **1435** in fabrica ~us artillerie quedam due incudes .. et tres pares follium (*Invent. Rouen*) *Collect. W. Worc.* 568; **1437** j homini locato pro *le stubel* vocato *helmebought*, falcando hoc pro .. ~o pistrine cooperienda *Ac. Churchw. Som* 178; **1450** concessimus ei omnes ~us artificiales armature infra Turrim nostram Lond' *Pat* 470 m. 3. **c** **1508** possessoribus ~orum sufflaticarum, vocatarum *bloweinge houses* in com. Cornub' (*Pat*) *Rec. Stan.* 31; **1618** proprietarii ~orum flaticorum (*sic*) infra stannariam .. in misericordia quia non certificabant curiae de nominibus flatorum suorum *Ib.* 72.

16 room (esp. main room); **b** (dist. as upper and lower). **c** chamber cut out of rock.

1212 omnia intus claustra .. deponantur, ita quod non remaneat nisi simpliciter ~us et thalamus *MGL* II 86; **1267** transcendebat muros, fregit portas, ostia et fenestra et seruras et quesivit ~um ubi G. jacuit. ~ui huic fecit insultum cum sequela sua .. et ab illa ~o asportaverunt lintheamina *Rec. Norw.* I 212. **b** **1280** consideratum est .. quod Thomas .. erit pincerna de ~o superiori (*Andover*) *Gild Merch.* II 293; **1330** pincerne de ~ibus inferiori et superiori *Ib.* 326. **c** locus ubi Christus natus est .. nunc est quadrangulus (*sic*) ~us in petra excisum (*sic*) HUGEB. *Will.* 4.

17 (astr.) 'house'. *Cf. domicilium* 3c.

de aequatione xij ~orum ADEL. *Elk.* 36; ROB. ANGL. *Jud.* (v. coaequatio a); **1184** (v. dignitas 6); ~us planete dicitur signum in quo erat creatus in mundi origine. est ergo Leo ~us solis, Cancer lune, Virgo Mercurii, Libra Veneris, Aries Martis, Sagittarius Jovis, Capricornus Saturni GROS. 43; quilibet planeta habet de numero signorum duas ~os preter solem et lunam; unde Saturnus habet Capricornum et Aquarium [etc.] BACON V 22; '~us' .. dicitur equivoce, quoniam iste ~us vocantur essentiales et naturales, priores vocantur accidentales et situales *Id. Maj.* I 258; xij sunt ~us in zodiaco .. sicut signa continue movuntur, sic eciam mutantur de ~o in ~um, .. alie autem sunt ~us secundum quod planete habent quedam signa pro ~ibus ROB. ANGL. (II) 168.

18 (w. *Dei*, representing ME *Domesdai*) Domesday Book. **b** name of a register at Salisbury.

c**1320** transcriptum libri qui dicitur ~us Dei regis (*Invent.*) *MS BL Cott. Galba* E IV f. 30. **b** **1306** in .. registro quod cives ipsi apud se '~us Dei' appellant *Pat* 251 m. 6.

2 domus v. tomus.

domuscula [CL], little house (w. ref. to beaver's lodge).

sunt [castorum] ~e bicamerate vel tricamerate, que quasi per tria tabulata seu solaria sunt distincte BART. ANGL. XVIII 28.

dona v. 1 duna a.

donabilis [LL < CL = *worthy to receive*], (theol.) that can be given.

donum ~e fieri potest quamvis non sit cui donetur; quod donum, id est Spiritus Sanctus, non ex tempore sed ab aeternitate procedit ALCUIN (*Trin.* II 20) *Dogm.* 36c; WYCL. *Dom. Div.* 208 (v. donabilitas).

donabilitas, (theol.) capacity to be given.

videtur quod Spiritus Sanctus, sicut eternaliter donatur Filio, sic eternaliter est donatus, quia indubie ~as qua est donabilis creature non est formaliter qua tercia persona refertur ad suum principium, sed voluntaria dacio que, ut sic, est donacio qua absolute necessario adintra datur Filio WYCL. *Dom. Div.* 208.

donamen, gift.

multa magnanima / producebant donamina / Christi sponsae, ecclesiae (ÆTHELWALD) *Carm. Aldh.* 2. 178; *Ib.* 104 (v. 1 charisma a).

donantia, act of giving.

si Deus alicui noviter donat quicquam, tunc facit donatorium sub nova racione habere Deum beneficum; et per consequens, juxta descripcionem ~ie, ipsemet principaliter est donatus WYCL. *Dom. Div.* 214.

1 donare [CL]

1 to present (with). **b** (pass.) to be gifted, endowed (fig.).

[Agnes] peplis ~atur dominicis ALDH. *VirgP* 45; multis ab ea muneribus ~atus patriam remissus est BEDE *HE* V 15; Haroldus .. filie .. desponsione et totius patrimonii amplitudine ~atus W. MALM. *GR* II 228; s**1119** etc. (v. cingulum 2); LIV. *Hen. V* 6a (v. corona 7a). **b** qui fuit .. donatus mente sagaci ALDH. *VirgV* 1129.

2 to give, grant, pay (partly fig.); **b** (absol. or impers. pass.); **c** (theol.). **d** (w. *sententiam*) to pass sentence. **e** (pr. ppl. as sb.) donor. **f** (p. ppl. as sb. n.) gift.

victoria .. Dei nutu ~ata est GILDAS *EB* 2; **697** decrevi dare aliquid omnia mihi ~anti *CS* 97; substantiis .. pro Deo ~atis EDDI 24 (v. defraudare a); cuncta quae sibi a regibus .. ~abantur BEDE *HE* III 5; †**823** (12c) hanc libertatem .. aecclesiae ~abi [i. e. ~avi] *CS* 395; **859** hanc casam .. ~abo sibi abendum (*sic*) et possidendum *CS* 497; absque firma ~ante (*sic*) *DB* I 86v. (v. absque 1c); cuilibet .. potest quis quandam partem sui liberi tenementi ~are in remunerationem servicii vel loco religioso in elemosinam, ita quod, si donationem ipsam saisina fuerit secuta, perpetuo remanebit illi cui ~ata fuerit terra illa et heredibus suis, si jure hereditario fuerit eis concessa GLANV. VII 1; D. BEC. 2197 (v. dator a); ~ari non poterit res que possideri non potest, sicut res sacra vel religiosa vel quasi BRACTON 14. **b** ~are potest omnis qui a lege vel jure non prohibetur *Ib.* 11b (cf. ib. 12b: ~ari potest tam servo quam libero). **c** ALCUIN *Dogm.* 36c (v. donabilis); AD. EYNS. *Hug.* IV 9 p. 47 (v. conjugare 1c); WYCL. *Dom. Div.* 208 (v. donabilitas). **d** ut, si in nos et ipsos sententiam dare presumpseritis, et ipsi non minus audacter in vos .. sententiam ~ent GIR. *RG* I 6. **e** **1315** (v. donatarius). **f** **855** (11c) gesta est hujus libertatis †~atum [v. l. ~atio] *CS* 487; ÆLF. *Gl.* (v. dare 1g).

3 (w. pers. obj.) to give: **a** (villein); **b** (woman in marriage). **c** (refl.) to devote (oneself). **d** to restore (to health). **e** (p. ppl. as sb. m.) oblate.

a GLANV. V 5 (v. dominus 1b); **b** s**1189** rex Francie petiit A. sororem suam, quam rex Anglie in custodia habuit, ~ari Ricardo comiti Pictavensi in uxorem *G. Hen. II* II 66. **c** hoc opus offero legendum parvulis / quando post seria se donant ludulis WALT. WIMB. *Palpo* 156. **d** juvenculus .. in vesaniam versus .. ad eum deductus .. incolomitati pristinae ~atur ALDH. *VirgP* 37; nihil in pede quod .. doleret inveniens, sensit se per B. Edwardum perfecte sanitati ~atum AILR. *Ed. Conf.* 790A. **e** **1199** quod .. monachi [de Cadomo], ~ati, pastores et homines eorum habeant predictas .. libertates *RChart* 6b; **1338** Johanni B. ~ato ibidem pro robis et necessariis suis *Hosp. in Eng.* 44; **1375** omnibus .. fratribus, sororibus, et ~atis .. in dicta bajulia constitutis .. precipimus .. ut vobis tamquam eorum .. preceptori .. obediant (*Bulla Magistri Hospitalis S. Joh.*) *Cl* 214 m. 20.

4 to grant, permit; **b** (w. *ut* or inf.).

Domino ~ante .. victi sunt BEDE *HE* IV 16 p. 242; **838** gratia Dei ~ante *CS* 421; tua gratia ~ante *Rit. Durh.* 117; [Fernham] T. R. E. et modo se defendit pro xx hidis. tamen sunt numero xxx hidae; sed rex E. ita ~avit causa Wichingarum, quia super mare *DB* (*Hants*) I 40v. **b** si mihi divina gratia .. ~averit ut .. vivere queam BEDE *HE* IV 26 p. 271; cui propitius ~asti verba tua scientiae .. haurire *Ib.* V 24; huic familiae .. ~a salutem adquirere EGB. *Pont.* 87; **749** (12c) Æ. rex .. famulis Dei .. libertatem in fructibus silvarum agrorumque habere ~avit *CS* 178; ~a mihi ut ab hac .. molestia .. citius liberer ALEX. CANT. *Mir.* 41 (I) p. 239; figura arboris .. videtur suas frondes effundere, sub quibus .. animalium sculptiles texture ~antur exsurgere R. COLD. *Cuthb.* 42; post transitum vite nostre terrene / frui donet eterno munere LEDREDE *Carm.* 30. 20.

5 to condone, forgive.

Petro .. abjuratio sua, .. Paulo .. immanitas sua, .. M. Magdalene peccata sua, et multis aliis multa quae sciuntur jam ~ata crimina sua EADMER *Beat.* 8.

2 donare, (sb.) gift (to church). *Cf. donarium* 2.

hic [quartus pastor] cellam multis donaribus auxit ÆTHELWULF *Abb.* 432.

donarium [CL]

1 temple treasury (also fig.).

~ium, i. locus in quo collocantur oblata vel quo dona reponuntur quae in templis offeruntur *GlH* D 795; si multum non valeam cum Zacheo, saltem minutum vel unum cum vidua inferam in ~iis Domini P. CORNW. *Panth. prol.* 39.

2 a (eccl.) endowment, votive offering. **b** gift, contribution; **c** (given as birthday present). **d** spiritual gift or treasure.

a Judas .. loculos compilabat; vos ecclesiae ~ia .. vastatis GILDAS *EB* 107; recte principes patrum ~ia ad construendum domum Dei sponte obtulisse BEDE *Ezra* 822; *Id. HE* III 19 (v. adornare a); diaconus .. crucem auream .. cum aliis ~iis ecclesiae .. non horruit rapere furtu ALCUIN *WillP* 30; ~ia sancta, i. sacrificia, *halige gife GlH* D 798; **1005** (12c) rura .. quae ad usus monachorum .. aeterno concessit ~io *CD* 714; s**1140** ecclesiam terris, possessionibus et ~iis magnis auctam J. HEX. *HR Cont.* 304; ad sanctam crucem Waltamensem .. ~ia obtulit preciosa *V. Har.* 2 f. 4b. **b** [Aedan] quae sibi a divitibus ~ia pecuniarum largiebatur .. in usus pauperum .. dispergebat BEDE *HE* III 5; Oswi .., multa ~ia auri et argenti Cadwalloni .. donans, pacem ejus adeptus est G. MON. XII 11; ab omnibus era et ~ia .. exigere *G. Steph.* II 111; s**1173** gaze multiplices .. ~iorum multiplicitate possent exinaniri, ni .. DICETO *YH* I 353; quosdam ex ipsis [Kambrensibus] .. ~iis alliciat, tam premissis quam promissis GIR. *DK* II 8; s**1344** his [histrionibus] dantur mutatoria; his abundabant ~ia AD. MUR. app. 231; jus, quod est proxima racio utendi ~io, cum precedit omnem usum .., a solo Deo donatur WYCL. *Civ. Dom.* I 29 (cf. id. *Dom. Div.* 211: secundum racionem ~ii); licet .. in gradum doctoratus erecti .. ~ia .. erogent, non tamen .. ~ia sumptuse faciunt hiis [serviencium] expensis similia FORTESCUE *LLA* 50. **c** mos erat regi singulis natalicii sui diebus singula regine ~ia pro voto conferre MAP *NC* III 2 f. 36. **d** quo [judice] adveniente, non incurratis supplicium aeternum, sed remuneremini ~iis sempiternis EGB. *Pont.* 82; hoc [cf. *John* xiv 27] fuit ~ium [ME: *his driwerie*] quod .. contulit in suo discessu suis discipulis *AncrR* 92; sed hoc Lollardus minime / curat, dum struat pessime / de hoc sacro donario [sc. sacramento mystico] (*In Lollardos* 46) *Pol. Poems* I 246.

3 (? facet.) horse-dung.

an horse turde, ~ium *CathA*.

donatarius, donatary, donee, recipient.

Constantinopolitanus imperator .. ~ium suum summum pontificem non evocat in adjutorium GERV. TILB. I 18; presentatur belua [sc. lupus aquaticus] ante oculos ~ii .. adhuc cauda .. palpitante J. GODARD *Ep.* 223; in .. prejudicium donatorii *Id. Ap.* 250 (v. captiosus); si donatio .. fuerit .. coartata, ita quod ~ius rem sibi datam dare vel vendere non possit certis personis BRACTON 11b; **1315** volumus .. quod .. burgenses dicte bastide .. possint suas possessiones libere vendere, dare .. vel legare .., dum tamen receptores .. faciant .. illud .. deverium quod vendens vel donans .. faciebat; et dominus rex seu gentes sue .. dictos donaterios vel emptores seu receptores de predictis investiant *RGasc* IV 1626 p. 472a; **1330** omnia ista transeunt de possessione donatoris in possessionem donatorii sub nomine honoris cum pertinenciis *PQW* 659a; ~ius .. tenetur recognoscere rem donatam a donatore tanquam ab illo a quo habuit ipsam, non tanquam ab illo a quo tenet eam, quia sepe ~ius non tenet terram vel aliam rem donatam a donatore OCKHAM *Pol.* I 151; donatorium WYCL. *Dom. Div.* 214 (v. donantia); si ~ius sobole caruerit masculino, terra donatori .. revertetur .. non nisi masculina donatorii proles terram .. possidebit FORTESCUE *NLN* II 10; **1516** Alexandrum G. ~ium .. bonorum .. et debitorum quondam magistri Johannis G. *Offic. S. Andr.* 118.

donatio [CL]

1 gift (esp. of land or sim.); **b** (w. *propter nuptias*); **c** (w. *inter vivos*, Fr.). **d** (w. *forma*)

formedon; *v. et. forma doni.* **e** deed or charter attesting gift.

679 quisquis contra hanc ~onem venire temptaverit *CS* 45 (cf. ib.: manentem hanc ~onis chartulam in sua .. firmitate); monasterium .. postea .. regum nobiliumque ~one in majus auctum est *Hist. Abb. Jarrow* 7; promissa non parva pecuniarum ~one BEDE *HE* IV 5; **836** factum (*sic*) est haec ~o in Craeft *CS* 416; *Ib.* 487 (v. 1 donare 2f); **867** hanc .. †dotionem [? l. donationem; cf. ib.: anc meam donationem] .. donabo (v. concedere 4a); †**1070** (v. contraire a); ut ipse de ea [terra] nec ~onem nec venditionem facere .. posset *DB* I 373; **c1144** ~ones .. patris mei .. confirmavit in perpetuum possidendas *E. Ch. Scot.* 164; GLANV. VII 1 (v. 1 donare 2a); ~onum quedam libera et pura et quedam sub condicione vel sub modo suspensa BRACTON 11b. **b** **1186** compositio .. tam super .. [terris] quas petebam nomine maritagii .. quam super aliis que nomine ~onis propter nuptias petebam in Normannia vel in Anglia *Act. Hen. II* II 275; fit ~o propter nuptias, quod (*sic*) sponsus dat sponse ad ostium ecclesie et de qua hic agitur die desponsationis. et hoc proprie dicitur dos mulieris secundum consuetudinem Anglicanam BRACTON 92b; **1278** (v. dosculum); **1285** (v. dotalicius 1c); **1332** etc. (v. doarium). **c** dedimus in escambium .. ecclesie [*St. Josse au Bois, Ponthieu*] ~one inter vivos .. quandam peciam nemoris *Pat* 100 m. 22; **1316** Fulconem filium suum emancipaverat duasque partes ipsius partis que ipsum in dictis bonis contingebat Fulconi filio dederat post emancipationem ~one pura et simplici inter vivos *RGasc* IV 1542. **d** **1285** quod C. dedit [tale manerium] tali viro in liberum maritagium cum tali muliere et quod post mortem predictorum viri et mulieris .. B. filio predictorum .. descendere debet per formam ~onis (*1 Westm.*) *StRealm* I 72. **e** **836** (9c) ego Ælfred rex .. hanc meam †danationem cum signo .. †crucrucis Christi *CS* 426; ~o, *landbec GlH* D 794; ~onem super altare adhuc sacrosancta consecratione madidum deposuit ORD. VIT. V 13 p. 407; **1136** hanc .. ~onem .. super altare posui, patrocinia .. apostolorum .. in adjutorium meum .. implorans *Cart. Bath A* 57.

2 a (right of) presentation (to benefice). **b** (right of) giving (ward) in marriage. **c** (right of) giving lordship (of land *etc.*).

a **1142** *Regesta* 116 (v. dominatio 1c); **a1160** reservata ~one ecclesie ejusdem nobis et successoribus nostris *Cart. Rams.* II 268; **1230** [ecclesie] que sunt de ~one dictorum monachorum *Feod. Durh.* 216; **1252** ecclesia de Ryptone Abbatis est in ~one abbatis et conventus Rameseie *Cart. Rams.* I 320 (cf. ib. 330: ecclesia de B., cujus advocatio et ~o spectant ad abbatem et conventum de R.); nescitur ex cujus ~one dictus Ph. habuit dictam ecclesiam, sed pater ejus habuit illam ex ~one Walteri de E. *RDomin* 19; **1291** habet litteras de presentacione ad ecclesiam .. ad †donatorem [? l. ~onem] regis spectantem *RScot* 1b; **1426** proviso .. quod ipsi quibus hujusmodi ~ones, collaciones, seu presentaciones fient beneficia illa libere recipere et acceptare possint *Reg. Cant.* I 235. **b** uxor Everardi de Ros .. est de ~one domini regis *RDomin* 1; **1198** r. c. de lxxij li. .. quia pater ejus dedit quandam feminam que erat de ~one regis sine licentia *Pipe* 19; **a1210** nullus .. habeat custodiam vel ~onem seu filiorum vel filiarum aut viduarum eorum *BBC 1216–1307* (*Kilkenny*) 98; **1218** desponsavit sine licencia Adam .., que ad nostram spectat ~onem *Pat* 165. **c** **c1250** de omnibus que sunt de ~one regis; que sunt et qui illas habeant .. et quantum terre illarum valeant (*Artic. Itin.*) *MGL* I 117.

3 spiritual gift.

etsi ~ones habent electi secundum gratiam que data est illis differentes BEDE *Tab.* 427.

1 Donatista, Donatist (heretic or heresy).

heresis .. ~a, que minorem Patri Filium dixit; hec fere totam corrupit Africam R. NIGER *Chr. II* 129; sicut .. Arriani, Sabelliani, ~e et alii heretici quamplurimi OCKHAM *Dial.* 760; omnia opera Petiliani episcopi ~arum GASCOIGNE *Loci* 78.

2 Donatista, grammarian, student of Latin grammar. *Cf. Donatus.*

~a, doctor *GlH* D 796; ipse [M. Walterus] .., de tenebrosis et confusis Prisciani tractatibus educens lucem, .. ipsius veterem et antiquum ~am compescuit et apostatam reformavit P. BLOIS *Ep.* 175. 470B; *a Donnett lerner*, ~a *CathA.*

donatiuncula, little gift.

979 ut nemo .. hanc nostram floccipendat ~am *CD* 623.

donativus [CL *sb. n. only*]

1 (as sb. n.) gift of money from ruler to troops. **b** gift. **c** (as sb. f.) donative, right of presentation (to benefice).

Roberto filio suo de thesauro .. lx m. li. jussit accipere famulisque suis atque stipendiariis militibus mercedes et ~a erogare ORD. VIT. XIII 19; ~um, -i, i. stipendium; unde et in vita sancti Martini dicitur 'quum coepit imperator ~um erogare militibus' OSB. GLOUC. *Deriv.* 163. **b** **680** (14c) peto ut nullus .. hoc ~um in irritum facere praesumat *CS* 47; **840** (11c) tunc illis terra sua reddita est cum pace et simul etiam ille episcopus hanc (*sic*) ~um regem (*sic*) predonavit *CS* 430; **1121** imprecati sunt in illum iram furoris Domini, quicunque tam liberale .. regis [Kenulfi] ~um .. pervertere presumpsissent *Cart. Bath A* 49; **s1141** votum Deo persolvite, tanto ~um majus a Deo accepturi quanto fidelius .. pro rege vestro .. contra infidos .. pugnaveritis H. HUNT. *HA* VIII 17; **s1248** (v. donum 3a); **s1249** rex illud ecclesie contulit Westmonasterii .. nobile ~um M. PAR. *Maj.* V 82; ~um, *waresun WW.* **c** **1588** omnes illas ecclesias et rectorias nostras et liberas ~as nostras SS. Johannis et Laurencii de Ilketsale [*Suff*] *Pat* 1319 m. 40.

2 (as adj.): **a** concerned w. making (or eliciting) gifts. **b** inclined to give. **c** (?) freely given.

a propter .. artem monachorum ~am pariter et corruptivam, cujus efficacia quantumlibet injuriose quesita retinere solent GIR. *Spec.* III 15 p. 230. **b** WYCL. *Dom. Div.* 216 (v. acceptivus). **c** **1044** (12c) si quispiam .. hoc meum ~um donum infringere .. voluerit *CD* 775.

donator [CL], donor. **b** (?) *f. l.*

679 signum manus Hlothari regis ~oris *CS* 45; ~orem laudavit archiepiscopum MAP *NC* V 3 f. 61; **1205** secundum cartas .. ~orum vel venditorum vel eschambitorum suorum *RChart* 148b; in .. prejudicium .. ~oris J. GODARD *Ap.* 250 (v. captiosus); si ita incepta fuerit [donatio], sed traditio in vita ~oris non subsecuta BRACTON 11b; **1330** (v. donatarius); **s1427** propter defectum sigilli ~oris in inactitacione composicionis AMUND. I 233. **b** **1291** (v. donatio 2a).

donatorius v. donatarius.

donatrix [LL], donor (f.).

nota de ~ice, que post donum suum remansit in seisina usque ad mortem et in seisina obiit. filius suus donatarius post mortem ~icis ejectus, recuperavit per assisam *BNB* III 262 *n. marg.*

Donatus, Latin primer (not necessarily that of Donatus).

dono, .. inde verbalia et hic ~us, ~i, pro nomine libri OSB. GLOUC. *Deriv.* 163; *Ac. Durh.* 565 (v. 3 carda); **1401** pro ~is emptis London' et datis confratribus *Ib.* 216; *a donett*, ~us *CathA.*

Donaus v. 2 Danus.

dondania [OF *dondaine*], 'dondaine' (sort of firearm).

1435 v milliaria fustorum †dondamarum, .. item v milliaria vij^c fustorum †semidendamarum, .. item in ij coffris v †fustra †semidondamarum impennatis *Collect. W. Worc.* 571.

donec [CL]

1 until: **a** (actual event, usu. w. indic.); **b** (expected or intended event, w. subj.).

a non quievit accensus ~ec .. oceanum .. delamberet GILDAS *EB* 24 (v. delambere); neque caelorum culmina / carent nocturna nebula, / .. / donec nimbo ac nubibus / torve teguntur trucibus (ALDH.) *Carm. Aldh.* 1. 59; donēc †sūpernam [v. l. suppremam] claudebat tempore vitam *Id. VirgV* 593 (cf. ib. 2159: sic .. degit lectissima virgo, / donēc supremam clausissent saecula metam); lux caelestis apparuit ~ec .. vicini abstulerunt corpus BEDE *HE* I 33 (cf. ib. IV 24 p. 268: regnum .. reges externi disperdiderunt, ~ec legitimus rex .. gentem suam .. liberaret); donēc ipse fidem concepit pectore toto ALCUIN *SS Ebor* 166; ~ec .. direxerat *Id. WillP* 22 (v. depellere a); donēc absterserat omnem / lux solis limpham ÆTHELWULF *Abb.* 242; Uluuard tenuit .. ~ec mortuus fuit *DB* I 43v.; ~ec opus integre compleretur *G. Hen. V* 6 p. 42. **b** supremis donec solvantur saecula flammis ALDH. *VirgV* 1656; manere illos .., ~ec videret quid eis faceret, jussit BEDE *HE* I 25; ~ec sciam quid de me fieri Deus velit *Ib.* V 19 p. 329; **9..** ~ec transeat, *oð þæt þe gewiteþ WW*; non cibus utilis est donec stomachus vacuetur D. BEC. 2776; consideret ~ec certior fiat .. cognitio BALSH. *AD rec.* 2 48; **1219** (v. deducere 1a); ~ec .. steterit SACROB. *Sph.* 85 (v. cosmometra); **1289** ~ec cognitum fuerit (v. condemnatio 2); non dimittit eum in pace ~ec [ME: *ear þenne*] omnia petita concesserit *AncrR* 90.

2 while, as long as.

~ec, quamdiu *GlC* D 344; **9..** ~ec, i. dum, *þa hwile WW*; ut sibi ~ec viveret necessaria vitae inde donaret *DB* I 59; oportet ut aqua fluat a sedibus suis ~ec durat hujusmodi ebullitio vaporum BACON *Maj.* I 140; WYCL. *Ver.* I 187 (v. convertibiliter).

donerettum v. doverettum. **dongerium** v. dangerium. **donicella** v. domicella 2a.

doniferus, bringer of gifts.

a gift berer, ~us, munifer *CathA.*

donjo, ~ona v. dunjo.

donsorire, to void excrement.

facio stercus [*gl.*: *tourde*], / donsorio [*gl.*: idem], cacco [*gl.*: idem], fedo [? l. pedo], feteo, †cumo [l. cunio, *gl.*: *shyte*], mingo STANBR. *Vulg.* 9.

donum [CL]

1 gift. **b** bribe or sim. **c** bride gift. **d** right of giving in marriage. **e** deed or charter attesting gift.

prohibens Dominus sacrificia et ~a sibi a talibus [iniquis regibus] offerri GILDAS *EB* 42; ut .. regi litteras et ~a miserit BEDE *HE* I 32; **749** ego Bercul patricius his ~is consentiens subscripsi *CS* 178; **966** ego Aþelwold .. †domum consensi *CS* 1176; ÆLF. *Gl.* (v. dare 1g); rex habet de isto manerio pro novo ~o episcopi quod valet x d. *DB* I 6; hos liberos homines reclamat de ~o regis *DB* II 151; **1158** in ~is et terris datis Engelgero de B. *Pipe* 149; [regina] optinet a domino suo pro donario sine nomine [i. e. *unspecified*] ~um MAP *NC* III 2 f. 36; **1220** (v. de 10b); **1259** omnibus qui .. tenent aliquid per ~um, per escambium vel per venditionem .. aut alio simili modo *TreatyR* I 39 (= *Foed.* I 677b: per †domum); **1330** menestrallis de ~o xx s. *Ac. Durh.* 532; **1412** (v. districte b). **b** argenti spondendo plura talenta / nititur intactam donorum fallere visco ALDH. *VirgV* 1936; de ballivis qui ceperunt ~a vel denarios pro recognitoribus removendis de juratis BRACTON 117; **1275** ballivi hujus hundredi .. ceperunt ~a a pluribus pro officiis suis exercendis *Hund.* I 529b; qui ~a vel lucra receperint pro officiis suis exercendis vel non exercendis (*Cap. Itin.*) *Fleta* 29. **c** si quis emat feminam et ~um non compleatur [AS: *sio gyft forð ne cume*], reddat ipsam pecuniam (*Quad.*) *GAS* 103. **d** **1221** due filie Jacobi .. sunt de ~o regis *PlCrGlouc* 33. **e** **855** (11c) ego B. rex hoc meum ~um cruce Christi munio *CS* 488; hanc terram donavit quidam U. .. aecclesiae de E. et posuit ~um super altare quando filius ejus A. factus est ibi monachus *DB* I 177v.

2 spiritual or God-sent gift. **b** (w. *Dei*) God's giving.

candida virtutum concedens dona sacrorum ALDH. *VirgV* 494 (cf. ib. 413: baptismi dona capessunt); in quo tunc monasterio nonnulla caelestis gratiae ~a specialiter ostensa fuisse perhibentur BEDE *HE* IV 14 p. 232; spiritalia ~a ALCUIN *Ep.* 298 (v. demandare 5d); †**948** (12c) apostolus Spiritus Sancti ~o afflatus *CS* 860; est ~um interius et exterius, interius majus est quam exterius HALES *Qu.* 1245 (cf. id. *Sent.* II 322: infirmitas .. respectu ~i fortitudinis, ut timor qui est in aggressione arduorum); per exorcismum et catechismum consequitur quis graciam ~i spiritualis OCKHAM *Pol.* I 164; ~um supernaturale *Id. Dial.* 471 (v. confirmare 2b). **b** premissa [temptacio] est ex ~o Dei [ME: *of Godes sonde*] *AncrR* 62; **s1340** Anglici, ventum habentes ~o Dei prosperum, illico redierunt AVESB. 89b.

3 a 'gift' or impost payable to crown, sts. as supplement to scutage (*cf. EHR* VI 633–8). **b** payment to forest officer. **c** payment to sheriff; *cf. auxilium* 4d. **d** payment (var.).

a **1071** ut [ecclesia S. Olavi] libera sit ab omni consuetudine terrene servitutis .. et ab omni geldo et scoto et auxilio et ~o et denegeldo (*MonA* III 377a) *Regesta* 58; **1130** r. c. de lviij li. .. de ~o militum episcopatus [Dunelm'] *Pipe* 132; **1156** vic. r. c. de xl li. de auxilio civitatis Eboraci; .. et idem vic. r. c. de de ccc et xxxiiij li. .. de ~o comitatus et civitatis *Pipe* 27 (cf. ib. 44: de ~o burgi de Salopesberia); **1160** vic. r. c. de xxix li. de veteri ~o civitatis [Danecastr'] *Pipe* 15 (cf. ib. 58: de veteri ~o comitatus); **1230** intitulatur illud scutagium [de anno 1159] 'de ~o' ea quidem ratione, ut credo, quod non solum prelati qui tenentur ad servitia militaria sed etiam alii .. dederunt auxilium *RBExch* 6; **1248** rex .. a civibus Londoniarum .. donativa die Circumcisionis a quolibet exegit singillatim primitiva, que vulgares nova ~a novi anni .. solent appellare M. PAR. *Maj.* V 47; **1332** (v. arrentare b). **b** **c1160** B. est regardator .. mearum forestarum habens tantum in ~is et liberationibus regardi et pasnagii quantum unus ex magistris regardatoribus et pasnagatoribus meis per totam Normanniam *Act. Hen. II* I 349; **1267** in don' forestar' in mense defenc[ionis] j quar. frumenti; de cetero non allocabitur *MinAc* (*I. of W.*) 984/1 r. 1d. **c** **1234** homines petierunt inducias de ~o vicecomitis, sc. de qualibet virgata iij d. *Cust. Glast.* 167. **d** de ~o reginae et de feno x li. et v oras *DB* I 219 (*Northants*); **1258** rec[epte] in com. Dors': ~um S. Martini: in primis de hundredo de Bruneshull de ~o S.Martini xij s. *LTR MiscR* 6/5 r. 2 (cf. austagium); **1283** de quadam certa consuetudine in manerio de Northbourn' [*Kent*] que vocatur ~um boum *Pipe* 127 *r. comp. 2d.*; **1356** recepcio de Drayton': de ~o yemali viij li. *Ac. Obed. Abingd.* 6 (cf. ib. 101); **1397** agni: .. in ~o S. Anton', j (v. 1 agnus 1d);

donus v. doinus. **doracus** v. deaurare 3. **doras** v. dodrans 1.

dorcas [CL < δορκάς = *gazelle*], roe deer, doe.

~ades, genus quadripedum *GlC* D 357; vallis Seboim, id est caprearum sive dammarum, .. rationabilem mentis intuitum figurate denuntiat. namque haec animalia oculorum acie perhibentur excellere, unde et a Graecis ab acute cernendo ~ades appellantur nec frustra .. sub Christi et ecclesiae laude repetuntur [cf. *Cant.* ii 9 etc. (capreae)] BEDE *Sam.* (*1 Sam.* xiii 18) 582; ÆLF. *Gl.* (v. caprea); hec ~as, A. *a rabuke WW* (cf. ib.: ~e, i. capre).

dorcerium v. dorsarium 3a.

dorcium [cf. δορκάδιον], sweetheart.

a lufe, amasio .., amasiolus, ~ium, filorcium *CathA.*

dorcus, crooked.

cruked, aduncus .., curvus, ~us .., sinuus, tortus .. *CathA.*

dorea, ~eta [OF *doree* < deaurata], dory (kind of fish). *Cf. deaurare* 3.

gustum doree, que nomen sumpsit ab auro, / Crasso †quia [? l. quam] Parthis plus placuisse reor NECKAM *DS* III 561; hec ~a, *doree Gl. AN Glasg.* f. 21; **1265** pro ij ~etis ponendis in pane *Manners* 50; **1266** (1324) exceptis magnis piscibus, viz. congris, dorreis, *rayes* (*Inq.*) *MGL* II 279 (= *CalIMisc* I p. 103: *doreys*).

dorignum v. dorycnium.

dormantus, 'dormant tree' (horizontal beam).

1313 concessit . . unum ~um jacentem in predicto muro lapideo . . pacifice requiescere in futurum sicud nunc jacet *RR K's Lynn* I 70.

dormentarium v. dormitorium. **dormentille** v. tormentilla.

dormire [CL]

1 to sleep; **b** (w. internal acc.). **c** (w. *cum*) to sleep with (sexually; *cf. Gen.* xix 32). **d** (pr. ppl. as sb. pl.) Seven Sleepers of Ephesus (or of Tours). **e** (pass. impers.).

qui voluntate obsceno liquore maculatus fuerit ~iendo . . stando vigilet GILDAS *Pen.* 22; dormio nam patulis, non claudens lumina, gemmis ALDH. *Aen.* 39 (*Leo*) 6; exsurgens . . a somno, cuncta quae ~iens cantaverat memoriter retenuit BEDE *HE* IV 22 p. 260; ~ivimus [AS: *we . . slepon*] et iterum surreximus ÆLF. *Coll.* 101; si aliquem ~ientem repperit, evigilato in chorum . . reverti praecipiat LANFR. *Const.* 89; T. MON. *Will.* III 10 (v. caecutire c); ~ire dicitur [Deus] et oblivisci BART. ANGL. I 20; **1301** (v. cubare 1a). **b** corpora temperata . . bene ~iunt suos somnos M. SCOT *Phys.* 31. **c** maritus qui cum uxore sua ~ierit lavet se antequam intret aecclesiam THEOD. *Pen.* II 12. 29; D. BEC. 1903 (v. domina 1a). **d** in illum locum ubi septem ~ientes requiescent (*sic*) HUGEB. *Will.* 4; ibi erat sepulta S. Maria juxta septem ~ientes *Descr. Constant.* 249; oculus interior . . radios usque Ephesiorum civitatem porrexit et . . sanctorum septem ~ientium quiescentium in spelunca proprietatem vultuum . . contemplatus est AILR. *Ed. Conf.* 768A (cf. *G. S. Alb.* I 47); suscitationem . . illorum septem ~ientium [Turonensium] qui fuerant consobrini S. Martini AD. EYNS. *Hug.* V 19 p. 223. **e** nocte dolis instructus abit, dormitur ab Argis *Brutus* 255.

2 to be spiritually asleep.

qui non expergiscitur . . ad tantum tonitruum [diei judicii] non ~it, sed mortuus est ANSELM (*Medit.* 1) III 77; quisquis somniorum sequitur vanitatem, parum in lege Dei vigilans est, et dum fidei facit dispendium, perniciosissime ~it J. SAL. *Pol.* 433D; talis habens cum virtutibus vitia nequaquam profunde ~it, sed quasi dormitat H. BOS. *Thom.* II 6 (cf. dormitatio e).

3 (euphem.) to die, be dead (*cf. 1 Cor.* xv 6); **b** (w. *cum patribus*; *cf. 1 Kings* ii 10 *etc.*); **c** (w. *in Domino*; *cf. 1 Cor.* xv 18: *in Christo*). **d** (w. *in pace*).

c1080 multi alii seniores et nobiles, quorum major pars jam ~iunt *MonA* I 602a. **b** cum ~ieris cum patribus tuis sepultus in senectute bona AILR. *Ed. Conf.* 743C; **s924** ~ivit . . cum patribus suis rex Edwardus FORDUN *Cont.* VI 13. **c** ex quibus [fratribus] aliquanti jam ~ierunt in Domino BEDE *HE* V 11; **s991** quidam in Domino ~ierunt *Chr. Rams.* 94. **d** corpore ~it in pace [cf. *Psalm* iv 9] a quo est resuscitandus in gloriam *V. Greg.* p. 110.

4 to be in abeyance; **b** (of legal action or dispute); **c** (of law-court). **d** (pr. ppl.) decried (of coinage).

omnia †que [? l. qui] vici, me vincunt omnia: dormit / vis mea; dormit honor; dormit honoris onus WALT. ANGL. *Fab.* 16. 7; modo dormit veritas WALT. WIMB. *Van.* 114. **b s1364** facta fuit finalis concordia . ., ita . . quod illud negocium ~iret pro perpetuo sine aliqua continuacione *Reg. Malm.* II 421; **1549** ne . . causas ultra per collusionem inter se ~ire patiantur *Conc. Scot.* II 123. **c 1552** profic[ua] de defaltis lib[erorum] sect[atorum] in ij hundredis predictis cur[ia] ~ient[e] *MS PRO LR* 2/189 f. 111. **d** W. GUISB. 333 (v. crocardus).

5 a (of table) 'dormant' (fixed). **b** (w. *liber*) coucher.

a c1160 in aula fuerunt duo bancha tornatilia et una mensa ~iens *Dom. S. Paul.* 137; cum tabula grandis fuerit et spissa et firmiter etiam, sicut solent mense ~ientes, et immobiliter defixa GIR. *Rem.* 27; **1254** tabula ~iente *Pipe Wint.* (*High Clere*) 159296; **1431** unam mappam pro tabula *dormaunt Reg. Cant.* II 450. **b** dicentibus in ecclesia ad librum ~ientem media nocte matutinas candelas . . dare consuevit *Obs. Barnwell* 78.

dormiscere [LL], to sleep; **b** (fig.).

~o, dormio *GlH* D 789; *to slepe*, dormire . ., ~ere, dormitare . . *CathA*. **b** insidiae veteres dormiscant otius omnes FRITH. 1196.

dormitare [CL]

1 to nap, doze. **b** to be inattentive or negligent. **c** to be spiritually half asleep.

8. . paululum ~abis, *gehwede hneppast WW*; ~avit, dormit *GlH* D 790; T. MON. *Will.* III 10 (v. caecutire c); medius illorum [noviciorum], qui propior erat demoni, dormivit; alter autem ~avit P. CORNW. *Rev.* II 893; **s1263** (v. dulcorare 1a); ~at, *nappyt WW*. **b** si mihi dormites, tibimet vigilare memor sis D. BEC. 2148; negligenter agimus et ~amus GIR. *GE* II 9; *Id. Spec.* II 23 (v. discredere 1a); **1228** super hoc negotio non ~abimus *Reg. S. Osm.* II 89; desuescit deses et iners dormitat in arte GARL. *Syn.* 584. **c** quid ad haec ~antibus animae oculis aspicitis? GILDAS *EB* 74; quid ~as, anima tepida et digna evomi, quid ~as? ANSELM (*Medit.* 1) III 77; J. SAL. *Pol.* 433D (v. conjectorius); H. BOS. *Thom.* II 6 (v. dormire 2).

2 (of jurisdiction) to be in abeyance.

c1204 eo quod per appellationem interpositam excommunicantis videtur jurisdictio ~asse *Ep. Innoc. III* 22 p. 73; **1306** ecclesia Cant' caruit regimine . . archiepiscopatus . . et ~avit jurisdiccio spiritual' et disposicio temporal' cessavit *DC Cant. Reg.* Q f. 31v. (cf. *Reg. Cant. 1294–1313* I xxv); **1326** jurisdiccio archidiaconalis vacare non potest nec eciam ~are, quia cedente vel decedente archidiacono, statim ipsius jurisdiccio redit ad †suum [*ed.*: cum] †totum a quo sumpsit originem *Lit. Cant.* I 180.

dormitarium v. dormitorium a.

dormitatio [LL], nap, (light) sleep. **b** loss of consciousness, coma. **c** 'sleep' (numbness in limb). **d** inattention, connivance. **e** spiritual drowsiness.

8. . ~o, *rest WW*; ~o, *hnappung GlH* D 791; nocentia memorie: . . ~o multa in meridie et proprie post repletionem BACON IX 74n.; *a nappynge*, ~o *CathA*. **b** puer . . egrotavit et eo usque ductus est ut mortuus putaretur. . . [pater] rediens invenit eum a ~one sua jam duos dies habentem W. CANT. *Mir. Thom.* VI 29. **c** quandoque digiti minores . . paciuntur frigus et ~onem et quasi sensus privacionem GAD. 46. 1; in cujus corpore sepe acciderit ~o membrorum pronosticat ipsum mori subito J. MIRFIELD *Brev.* 72. **d 1423** si in ea parte debitam absque ~one feceritis diligenciam (*Lit. Abbatis*) AMUND. I 145; **14.** . ut . . ~oni committeret mille nocendi palpebras [cf. *Psalm* cxxxi 4] et nos . . quiescere sineret tempore medio in cubili pacis *Reg. Whet.* II app. 408. **e** modo . . illo revolvitur, vicissim inclinans caput, jamjam . ., nisi Domino manum suam apponente fortius traheretur, post ~onem quasi lethargicus nimis profunde dormiturus H. BOS. *Thom.* II 6 (cf. dormire 2).

dormitio [CL]

1 sleep. **b** numbness in limb. **c** swoon or sim.

sicut comestio, ~o, ambulatio, ita quoque concubitus actus naturales sunt PULL. *Sent.* 948D; rex vitam illorum [vij Dormientium] . . et ~onis modum exposuit AILR. *Ed. Conf.* 768C; dextrum requiescat / paulisper latus; hinc alio dormitio fiat D. BEC. 2770; Booz in ~one sua ventilavit aream S. LANGTON *Ruth* 112; quamquam et dormienti corpore mentis nunquam ~onem subrepere credidisses AD. EYNS. *Hug.* II 9 p. 75; vapores ad capud ascendentes tempore ~onis a stomacho BACON V 69; juvenis . . cepit dormire et in ~one illa perseveravit per totam noctem *Mir. Montf.* 71; dolor . . cum alienacione vel somnietate nimia sine ~one vigilativa GAD. 70. 2; **1323** occasione cujus potus . . custodes talem ~onem sumpserunt quod vigilias suas . . facere non potuerunt *Abbr. Plac.* 343. **b** stupor vulgariter appellatur ~o membri, sicut cum aliquis tenuit tibiam super aliam tunc non sentit nec bene potest movere donec aliquantulum steterit *SB* 41. **c** stupor sive extasis, i. ~o ymaginacionis vel sic *Ib.*

2 (euphem.) 'dormition', death.

s100 ~o Johannis evangelistae *AS Chr.*; cum beatis collegis suis a die ~onis est conditus GOSC. *Transl. Aug.* 18B; ~o dicitur mors sanctorum quasi quies BELETH *RDO* 4. 18A; instat dies ~onis ipsius [abbatis] P. CORNW. *Rev.* I 205 p. 199; **1423** ut ultima fratrum cum pietate ~o sanctam ac repositam habeat graciam (*Ord. Abb.*) AMUND. I 115.

dormitior v. domare 1d.

dormitor [CL], sleeper.

contra accidiosos et ~ores [ME: *slauwe and sleperes*] est . . manifesta ejus matutina resurreccio *AncrR* 95.

dormitorium [CL]

1 dormitory, dorter (esp. mon.). **b** bed. **c** (euphem.) tomb.

haec, in ~io sororum pausans, audivit . . campanae sonum BEDE *HE* IV 21 p. 257; in dormiturio ALCUIN *Carm.* 96 *tit.*; *CS* 342 (v. domus 8); ubi dormis? in ~io [AS: *on slæpern*] cum fratribus ÆLF. *Coll.* 103; unus eorum [circumitorum] in ~io debet circumire lectos omnium . ., ne forte aliquis frater dormiens ibi remanserit LANFR. *Const.* 146; in dormitario *Inst. Sempr.* *xlv (v. dortorarius); ~ia et refectoria, . . sine quibus cultores religionis ecclesie deservire non possunt BRACTON 207b; **1294** dormiant omnes fratres simul in uno ~io, ita quod nullus frater habeat cameram seperatam *MonA* VI 610b; **s1380** hic prior . . lectulo dormentarii in sua juventute sibi a suo priore assignato . . quamdiu advixerit usus fuit *Chr. Kirkstall* 123; privatum ~ium *G. S. Alb.* III 443 (v. domus 13); ~ium, A. *a doortur WW*. **b** *a bedde*, . . ~ium, grabatum *CathA*. **c** vocatur . . diversis nominibus . . sepulcrum, mausoleum, ~ium, tumulus, monumentum . . BELETH *RDO* 159. 156D.

2 sleeping draught.

c1400 ~ium magistri Johannis Wyke: recipe opii vel se[minis] pappaveris [etc.] *MS Pembroke Coll. Ox.* 2 f. 298.

dormiturire, to be sleepy, drowse.

videmus . . imagines earum rerum obversare ante oculos ~ientibus FERR. *Kinloss* 16.

dormiturium v. dormitorium 1a.

dormitus, sleep.

dormitus brevitas reficit post prandia corpus D. BEC. 2771; **1554** tempore aditus ad ~um *Midlothian* 221.

dormundus v. dromo. **dornedies** v. durnedies.

doronicum, (?) leopard's bane (*Doronicum*). *Cf. deronica.*

[cordialia] calida sunt sicut . . crocus, melissa, ~um, cassia lignea GAD. 68. 2.

dorrea v. dorea.

dorsalis [LL < CL dorsualis]

1 portable on back.

1327 concessionem . . de duobus fassis [*Cal.*: †tassis] ~ibus cotidianis ramorum grossorum bosci sui *ChartR* 114 m. 24; **1330** concessit . . duos fassos ~es ramorum grossorum (*Cl*) *MonA* VI 372.

2 (w. *pars* or as sb. n.) back of vestment. *V. et. dorsarium* 2.

1295 casula Radulfi de Diceto de rubeo sameto cum ~i puri aurifrigei vineat' *Vis. S. Paul.* 322; **1316** capa . . de *inde* cum floribus aureis de *liz* et dorsal[i] de ymaginibus *Invent. Ch. Ch. Cant.* 54; **1477** unum vestimentum de rubio *worsted* habens in sua orfra ex parte ~i unum crucifixum et duas literas R. et E. *Fabr. York* 280.

3 (as sb. n. or m.) 'dossal', hanging, esp. for back of altar; **b** (used as carpet). **c** (?) wooden panel. *V. et. dorsarium* 3.

997 (12c) ego Ælfgyva Ymma regina . . contuli . . aecclesiae Christi . . duo ~ia de pallio et duas capas de pallio *CD* 697; LANFR. *Const.* 103 etc. (v. cortina 3a); pro . . duobus ~iis (*sic*) de pallio *Lib. Eli.* II 36; **1080** hec sunt que invenit Eudo dapifer . . in ecclesia S. Æðeldreðe: . . xxx cortinas, xx ~ia lanea . ., ij tapetas ad altare *Ib.* 114; **a1100** iiij tapeta; xxxij †dosseta lanea *Ib.* 139; quidam prior . ., Alfricus nomine [temp. Will. I], qui fecit dorsellos capituli *Chr. Evesham* 91; Willelmus [I] . . Hrofensem ecclesiam . . in tantum dilexit ut . . ei . . ~e unum cum feretro deargentato dimitteret *Text. Roff.* 210v.; abbas F. [ob. **1116**] contulit ad ornatum ecclesie . . pallia per ecclesiam pendentia, xiiij cortinas, vij tapetia, vj dossalia, vj banchalia *Chr. Abingd.* II app. 151; [abbas R., ob. **1119**] dedit dossale unum sive tapecium in quo passio S. Albani figuratur *G. S. Alb.* I 70; ornatus chori consistit in ~ibus et tapetis substratoriis BELETH *RDO* 85. 89D; **1222** dossella ij pendentia in choro . .; item dossellum unum ultra vestiarium, quod 'Arca Noe' appellatur; item dossellum unum ultra novum hostium quod 'Abraham' appellatur *Reg. S. Osm.* II 135 (= *Process. Sal.* 176); revestiarii officium est capas et albas . . cum pannis sericis, cortinis et ~ibus, calices et corporalia ceteraque altaris indumenta et ecclesie ornamenta . . in sua . . habere custodia *Cust. Westm.* 58; **1303** c s. de uno dossali ad aulam *Ac. Exec. Ep. Lond.* 57; **1374** in aula j ~is, j *bangwer*, j xij de *qwyssenys Pri. Cold.* app. p. lxxv; **1395** (v. bordura 2a); **s1426** flamma consumpsit ~ia in minori camera abbatis *Chr. S. Alb.* 9. **b** item dossella ij que dominus H. episcopus dedit ad conducendum episcopum ad altare *Reg. S. Osm.* II 135 (cf. 3a supra). **c 1513** in dolacione pro ~i novo in aula estivali *Ac. Durh.* 160.

dorsamentum

1 back panel or cover (of altar). *V. et. dorsalis* 3, *dorsarium* 3.

1396 in ecclesia ad magnum altare tabule et imagines (cum toto ~o [*interl.*]) decenter picte (*Invent.*) *Meaux* III app. lxxxii.

2 endorsement (of document).

1389 sicut continetur in ~o cujusdam brevis regis quod est in ligula brevium *LTR AcExch* 10 r. 2(2); **s1437** prout in eodem scripto obligatorio et in ~o [? l. indorsamento] ejusdem plenius continetur AMUND. II 135.

1 dorsare

1 to back, cover the back of.

1368 j pulvinar dosatum cum serico *Invent. Norw.* 8.

2 to endorse (a document).

c1285 illa brevia non sunt dossata nec in thesaur[aria] posita *KRAc* 234/19 m. 1; **1344** cum . . ipse vic. mandasset curie . . brevia illa sub sigillo suo non ~ata, responsione aliqua ad eadem . . nullatenus facta *PlRExch* 70 r. 16d.

3 a (?) to pound or knead. **b** to plaster, pug (*cf. Suss. Arch. Coll.* XLIX 11).

a qui crustis alia pistant [*gl.*: *pestelent, chansent*; dossunt; 'indossat panem ne panem sumat inanem'] GARL.

Mor. Scol. 392. **b** **1285** in aula dossenda de terra ad tascam, xiiij d. *MinAc* (*Pevensey, Suss*) 1027/17 r. 3; **1286** in australi latere grangie tegendo per totum et dossando *Ib.* r. 4; **1290** in aula et camera domine regine dossandis de mortar[io] et terra *KRAc* (*Pevensey*) 479/15 r. 1 (cf. ib. r. 2: in columbar' dossando).

2 dorsare v. dorsarium 3a.

dorsarium, ~ia [cf. AN *dosser*, OF *dossier*, *dossiere*]

1 a back-band, ridge-band (of cart-horse). **b** 'dorser', 'dosser', pannier (or pannier-load).

a **1200** duas carrettas novas et octo collaria et octo ~ias *Liberate RC* 9; **1213** pro .. duobus dossariis (v. avalaria); **1220** habere faciatis .. ad carectam butellarie nostre .. tria paria tractuum, unam dorseram, unam culariam, unam bridam .. *Cl* 440b; **1242** pro ~iis (v. croparium); **1265** pro .. j dosserio (v. attillum b); **1301** in coler[iis], cruperiis, dosser[iis] et aliis hernas[iis] carect[arum] emptis *Ac. Durh.* 502; **1316** pro emendacione dorcer[ii] ejusdem currus *KRAc* 99/21 m. 1. **b** de dosseris cum gallinis j gallina telonei et de uno dossero cum ovis v ova telonei, si veniant ad mercatum (*Quad.*) *GAS* 234; **1279** in ij dosser' ad caseum, ix d. *Ac. Man. Cant.* (*Lydden*); **1315** de mensuracione dosseriorum piscis *LBLond.* E f. 29 (= *MGL* I 689: amensuracio dossariorum; cf. ib. 468: de scrutinio .. de .. paneriis piscium que non continent j bussellum avene); **13..** navis que ducit piscem dossoriis: serviens capiet de quolibet dossorio j piscem. .. item eodem modo de dossoriis qui veniunt per terram, et de equo obolum, qui debent consuetudinem *MGL* I 375; **14..** de quolibet dosserio piscis ven[alis] j d. *EEC* 216; **1460** pro xxj dosseris et dimidio helme emptis pro tenemento Johannis W. . ., precium *le* dosserum iiijd. *Ac. Churchw. Bath* 55.

2 back of vestment. *V. et. dorsalis* 2.

1315 vestimentum integrum .. cum casula viridi de velvetto cum ~io brudato de armis regis Anglie *Invent. Ch. Ch.* 67; **1442** lego .. ecclesie de W. . . j vestimentum *cheker* coloris cum dorsorio et frontellis ejusdem operis *Test. Ebor.* II 88.

3 'dosser', 'dossal', hanging, esp. for back of altar or bed; **b** (used as carpet). **c** wooden bed-head or panel. *V. et. dorsalis* 3.

dedit etiam ij magna dossaria que pendent in choro in precipuis festivitatibus, unum de x virginibus, alterum de historia Job *Chr. Abingd.* II app. 151 (cf. dorsalis 3a); **1328** de .. supellectilibus, dosseriis et canabo *SelCKB* V 34 (cf. ib. 39: de .. coverlectis, *dosers*, canobio); **1329** (v. Begina 2); **1368** j culcitra, j dorsorium, j novum missale *Invent. Norw.* 40; **1369** in j dorsorio de novo empto pro *le botyvand* [i. e. *chimney*] infra aulam *Ac. Durh.* 129; **1378** queritur de Ricardo T. *webster* in placito convencionis, viz. dorsorium sibi fecit non idoneum *Rec. Leic.* II 177; [T. episcopus, ob. **1381**] dedit .. unum magnum dorsare pro aula, operis de Arrace *Hist. Durh.* 3 (cf. Atrebatensis); **1385** salaria de *peutre*, veru (*sic*) ferrea, doseras, ciphos de mazero .. et alia ornamenta capelle *CoramR* 497 r. 6*d.*; **1390** dorceriorum et costerarum de Arraz *CalPat* 251; **1395** (v. cuissaria b); **1401** j lectum de *worstede* .., j vetus dorsorium de *worstede* pauliatum de albo, nigro, rubeo et viridi *Cl* 247 m. 8; **1406** in ij dorsoriis de linea tela .. pendentibus in scaccario hordarie *Comp. Swith.* 288; **1406** ad ij dorsoria cum ij celuris et curtinis de *carde blu* facienda .. et pendenda cum corda fili .. pro pilis, robis et lectis domine regine erga transitum .. versus partes [Dacie] (*KRAc* 406/10) *Arch.* LXVII 180; hoc ~ium, A. *dosur WW*; *a dorsur*, dorsorium *CathA*. **b** venientibus (*sic*) coram altari .. statim capient longam veniam super dorserium ibidem positum *Cust. Cant.* 14 (cf. ib. 49: procedet [abbas], ut est pontificaliter indutus, .. ad altare, stratis ubique ~iis sub ipso usque ad gradus altaris, sc. ob reverenciam sandaliorum); **1411** lego .. dorsorium largum .. ad sternendum coram summo altari *Reg. Exon.* I 403*n.* **c** **1366** pro xij de regalbord' emptis pro uno ~io inde faciendo ac capud lecti domini regis *KRAc* 476/11 m. 2; **1512** pro dorsoriis ligneis in capella sive insula, xxxix s. *Midlothian* 163.

4 (?) walling or plastering. *Cf.* 1 *dorsare* 3b.

1345 cuidam cementario .. facienti dosseriam trium caminorum per iij dies *MinAc* (*Bucks*) 1120/12 r. 2(2).

dorsarius [LL], one who carries a load on his back.

1252 chiminagium ad custumarios suos caretarios et dossarios *IMisc* 7/2 r. a.

dorsata [cf. OF *dossee*], blow on back.

quidam de paganis .. eum super dorsum percussit. .. Robertus vero comes .. dixit: "magis sum letus de ista ~a, quam mihi dedit, quam si mihi magnam pecuniam dedisset" *BR Will. I* 3.

dorsatim, back to back.

s**1281** apparuerunt octo semicirculi circa solem, ~im conjuncti RISH. 99 (= *Flor. Hist.* III 53).

dorsellus v. dorsalis. **dorser-** v. dorsarium.

dorsiculum, little back.

nunc genas osculans, nunc os, nunc collulum,/ manus, brachiola, pectus, †dorsiolum [v. l. dorsiculum] WALT. WIMB. *Carm.* 229; *a bakke*, dorsum, ~um *CathA*.

dorsilis, backward, reversed.

ordine dorsīli ne fercula ponat in aula D. BEC. 1156.

dorsilollum [cf. lolidodium], cart-saddle.

hoc ~um .., hoc dorsolallium, *a cartsadylle WW*.

dorsiolum v. dorsiculum. **dorsor-** v. dorsarium.

dorsum [CL]

1 back: **a** (human or unspec.); **b** (animal). **c** hide or fur of animal's back.

a ~um versant et non faciem GILDAS *EB* 62; tergiversator, ~i versator *GlC* T 51; ~um, *hricg* ÆLF. *Gl.*; dorsis ad dorsum versis, flet uterque seorsum R. CANT. *Malch.* III 115; **1297** verberavit eum cum .. baculo per scapulas et ~um et renes *SelCCoron* 89; proprium est mendicancium ferre saccum in ~o [ME: *on backe*] *AncrR* 55; confidentes in Deo non debent se in ~is [? sc. vestiendis] vel birris vel calciamentis induendis .. onerare WYCL. *Pol.* 370; s**1403** ~a verterunt (v. disconficere); s**1459** (v. dare 11a). **b** quod homines .. in ~o supradicti generis beluarum vecti .. fuissent *Lib. Monstr.* II 32; non equorum ~o sed pedum incessu vectus BEDE *HE* III 5; qui caballum ita onerabat ut ~um frangeret *DB* I 268; [Elfredus] feram [mustelam] .. cum catulis reperit. .. ~um pellicule manu blandiente complanavit R. COLD. *Cuthb.* 26; [martinete] albo ventre nigroque ~o GIR. *TH* I 18. **c** **1252** ~a bovina *DC Cant. Reg.* H f. 172a; de ix s. et vj d. de xxxviij coriis vitulorum venditis ..; et de ij s. viij d. de ij ~is coriorum majorum venditis *Ac. Beaulieu* 209; **1316** pro ij fururis de *strallyng*', j capucio de *menuver*, lx ~is de *strallyng* .. felonice furatis *SessP Northants* 78; **1374** octo ~a de *grys*, precii xij d. *IMisc* 204/15.

2 ridge; *cf. condorsum* a. **b** back, outer or upper surface (of finger).

Bethleem .. in ~o sita est (*De Locis Sanctis*) BEDE *HE* V 16; 'summa juga', i. e., ~a moncium TREVET *Troades* 15. **b** interiora pollicis lateri vel ~o indicis superduces BEDE *TR* 1 p. 180.

3 back, dorse (of membrane or document).

1198 alibi est in ~o *CurR* I 49; **1203** vic. .. mandavit in ~o brevis quod .. *Ib.* III 27; **1219** continetur in ~o rotuli *Pat* 187; c**1320** presentatur .. in prima presentacione in ~o rotuli (*AssizeR*) *Lond. Ed. I & II* II 158; **1332** inseritur in ~o ultimi rotuli *LTRMem* 105 r. 8.

4 a back (of building). **b** reredos. **c** rear (of army).

a **1427** lego .. corpus meum ad sepeliendum ad ~um presbiterarii in ecclesia B. Marie de Arcubus *Reg. Cant.* II 402. **b** s**1510** obitus .. Roberti S. .., qui ~um altaris B. Virginis fieri fecit *Mon. Francisc.* II 132. **c** erant .. post has [turmas] quatuor a ~o statute G. MON. V 6; s**1367** (v. 2 cauda 4a); rex noster se movere decrevit versus eos, mittens pro evectionibus exercitus ut essent ad ~um prelii *G. Hen. V* 12 p. 84.

dorsus v. darsus.

dortorarius, (mon.) official in charge of dorter.

c**1162** testibus .. laicis istis .., Godrico portario, Willelmo †dortario *DC S. Paul.* (*HMC*) 12a; sint .. duo paria [sotularium] .. in dormitario a ~io equitaturis tradenda *Inst. Sempr.* *xlv.

dortoria [AN *dortour*, OF *dortoir*], dorter, dormitory (eccl.).

1349 coopertura aule, firmarie, ~ie vicariorum *IMisc* 163/4.

dorwardus [ME *dorward*], 'doorward', janitor.

j messuagium .. quondam Simonis Hostiarii vel Simonis ~i *Surv. Durh. Hatf.* 23.

dorycnium [CL < δορύκνιον], (?) species of solanaceous plant. *Cf. halicaccabus.*

†corignum [v. l. dorignum], quod alii cacabum dicunt, folia habet in colore similia olive .., florem album et semen orobi *Alph.* 51.

dos [CL]

1 dowry (given by or with bride); **b** (fig.).

in alia acceptione accipitur dos secundum leges Romanas, secundum quod proprie appellatur dos id quod cum muliere datur viro, quod vulgariter dicitur maritagium GLANV. VII 1; cum dos proprie dicatur quod datur viro a sponsa, hic accipitur e contrario HALES *Sent.* IV 479; BRACTON 92 (v. adventicius 1b); **1332** cum .. procuratores .. comitis [Gelrie] .. de recipiendo nomine dotis a nobis de certa quantitate pecunie .. convenissent (*Pat*) *Foed.* IV 509a. **b** dos datur a nupta: vigil observantia recti, / casta quies lingue HANV. IX 393 p. 389; optima dos est uxoris pudicitia W. DONC. *Aph. Phil.* 10. 18 (cf. Ausonius *Sept. Sap.* I, *Bias* 4).

2 dower (given to bride or unspec.), marriage portion; **b** (held or claimed by widow); **c** (claimed by widow alleging she has received no part of it); **d** (fig.).

si mallent omnes consortes esse procorum / nobilium, pulchra fungentes dote virorum ALDH. *VirgV* 2205; dos, *wituma* vel *wetma GlC* D 347; dos, *morgengifu* ÆLF. *Gl.*; si quis aliquem interfecerit intra curiam vel domum suam, corpus ejus et omnis substantia sunt in potestate regis preter dotem uxoris ejus, si dotatam habuerit *DB* I 154v.; dos dicitur vulgariter id quod aliquis liber homo dat sponse sue ad hostium ecclesie tempore desponsationis sue. . . cum quis sponsam suam dotat, aut nominat dotem aut non. . . minus tercia parte tenementi potest quis dare in dotem, plus vero tercia parte non GLANV. VI 1; *Ib.* VI 3 (v. disponere 2a); scio quod a viro mulieri datur dos, viro maritagium ab illo qui dat uxorem ALEX. BATH *Mor.* II 1 p. 130; **1200** ad recognoscendum utrum terra illa data fuerat in maritagium vel in dotem *CurR* I 281; dos est id quod liber homo dat sponse sue ad ostium ecclesie propter onus matrimonii et nuptias futuras ad sustentationem uxoris et educationem liberorum, cum fuerint procreati, si vir premoriatur. rationabilis autem dos est cujuslibet mulieris .. tertia pars omnium terrarum et tenementorum que vir suus tenuit in dominico suo et ita in feodo quod eam inde dotare poterit die quo eam desponsavit [v. l. desponsaverit] BRACTON 92; **1324** Alicia .. absque cohercione ex assensu mariti sui .. remittit .. Randulfo totum jus quod habet in dicto mesuagio ut in dotem ad totam vitam suam *CBaron* 138. **b** hanc [Guincestram] regina tenet regis de dote prioris / Hetguardi G. AMIENS *Hast.* 627; Eldredus .. [tenet] j hidam et dim.; uxor ejus tenuit in dote *DB* I 42v.; quodsi [vidua] infra annum virum eligat, amittet dotem [AS: *þære morgengyfe*] et omnia quae possidet per priorem virum (*Cons. Cnuti*) *GAS* 361; **1100** mortuo marito, uxor .. dotem suam et maritationem habebit (*Ch. Hen. I*) *Ib.* 521; Sibilla .. habet ij filios ..; sed non sunt heredes de dote ejus, sed Ricardus B., qui fuit de prima uxore viri sui *RDomin* 24; clamabit mulier ipsa dotem suam tamquam nominatam aut rationabilem dotem suam non nominatam GLANV. VI 17; **1199** (v. desponsatio 1a); **1218** Alicia .. petit .. terciam partem ij bovatarum terre .. ut †dotem [MS: dotem] suam *Eyre Yorks* 21; s**1246** adjudicatum fuit .. quod mulier certa et specificata dote dotata non potest nec debet amplius habere de catallis viri sui defuncti quam .. dotem sibi assignatam, nisi de voluntate viri sui *Leg. Ant. Lond.* 12; **1258** (v. 2 bancus 4); **1268** Willelmus remisit .. Ermetrude omnia blada in terris .. Christianam [filiam ipsius E.] .. jure hereditario contingentibus et in dote sua seminata *Cl* 546; **1333** rex .. commisit .. custodiam omnium terrarum et tenementorum que Agnes .. tenuit in dotem *LTRMem* 105 r. 39. **c** **1256** nulla brevia nostra currant infra libertatem .. ville nisi breve de recto, breve de nova disseisina et breve de dote unde nihil fiet *BBC* (*Southampton*) 195; s**1260** provisum fuit .. [quod] omnia placita mota per breve de dote unde mulieres nichil habent .. placitarentur illo die quo placita communia tenentur *Leg. Ant. Lond.* 45; **1267** in placito dotis quod dicitur 'unde nichil habet' (*Marlb.*) *StRealm* I 23; accio dotis ubi mulier nichil habet alibi quam in curia regis non potest terminari. .. si autem aliquam partem habuerit mulier de dote, tunc non habet locum illud breve, sed breve de recto de dote *Fleta* 346. **d** sponsam potius spondebat se fore Christi, / .. / qui se vite subarravit cum dote fidei ALDH. *VirgV* 1944; deficit huic tumulo dos forme, gratia laudis D. BEC. 351; sapiens .., quanto magis sapientie dote prefulget, tanto libidini datus .. modestiam minus observat GIR. *TH* I 22; bona pauca / paucis sufficiunt dosque modesta Dei GARL. *Tri. Eccl.* 15; non quodcumque donum datum tunc sponse a sponso nomine dotis censetur, sed quod est primum et precipuum; unde proprie dos est donum quod datur sponse spirituali a sponso spirituali in traductione in amplexum primum et precipuum, quod respicit primas potentias corporis et anime HALES *Qu.* 1320; ista est dos [ME: *marech3eve*] quam dixi inclusas pre ceteris habituras *AncrR* 27.

3 (eccl.) endowment.

c**1070** habeant manerium .. sicut .. rex [Eadwardus] ad dedicationem illius ecclesiae in dotem perpetuam eternaliter eandem hereditavit ecclesiam *Regesta* p. 120; a**1160** ecclesie .. Dunfermelin .. omnia subscripta concedo .., cum omnibus rebus .. pertinentibus, sicut date fuerunt predicte ecclesie in dotem ab avo meo rege D. die qua dedicata fuit *Regesta Scot.* 118; s**1239** quod .. imperator .. dotes ecclesie hostiliter invadens eas sibi .. manciparet *Flor. Hist.* II 233; **1268** commodum gardini valet communibus annis preter dotes x solidos (*Extenta*) *Cart. Glouc.* III 46; c**1280** tenet vij acras terre .. pertinentes ad dotem ecclesie *Suff. Hund.* 9; **1315** predicta toftum et terra non sunt de dote ecclesie de H. *IMisc* 75/5; **1354** que .. dabo .. in partem dotis perpetue dicte cantarie *Lit. Cant.* II 323; **1441** ad ordinacionem .. dotis et porcionis quam in dicta ecclesia vicarius .. et successores sui .. percipient *Reg. Cant.* I 315; LYNDW. 254 b etc. (v. gleba 3).

dosare v. 1 dorsare 1. **dosca** v. doxa a.

dosculum, dowry.

1278 potestatem .. acceptandi nomine nostro et dicte filie nostre assignacionem dotalicii seu doscli vel donacionis propter nupcias (*DipDocE* 12) *Foed.* II 115.

doscus, doseus v. dosinus. **dosen-** v. dozena. **dosera** v. dorsarium 3a. **dosillus** v. duciculus.

dosinus [LL], **dosius,** dun. *Cf. doinus.*

~inus vel cinereus, *assedun* ÆLF. *Gl.*; equos ~ios vel ~inos [*gl*: *redoys*, asinini coloris], cinereos, quos dignius equiferos quam equos dixerim BALSH. *Ut.* 46; unum equum badium .. et unum ~inum *FormMan* 17; c**1428** j pullus ~ei coloris (*CourtR Elton*) *BL Add. Roll* 34370 m. 6*d.*; **1445** j equum ~ium *Cl* 295 m. 9*d.*; **1447** una vacca †dosca [? l. dosea] *MinAc Essex* (*Hatfield*); **1456** equus ~ii coloris *Ib.* (*Wimbish*).

dosis [LL < δόσις], (med.) dose; **b** (fig.).

crocus .. proprie in vino coctus, et ~is ejus ʒ j BACON IX 71; nisi medicina detur ultra ~im debitam GAD. 68v. 2; **13**.. ~is ejus in potu est a ʒ j usque ad ʒ ij *RB Ossory* (*HMC*) 254; ~is, i. dacio sive distribucio *Alph*. 51; **s1436** (v. 2 crisis). **b** devote mentes .. / antidotum spondent efficiuntque sibi; / firma fides sociata spei, dilectio fervens, / ad dŏsym veniunt, pondere pensa pari GARL. *Tri. Eccl.* 93.

dosius v. dosinus.

dossa [cf. AN *dosse*, OF *dousse*], clove (of garlic).

due ~e allii filo ducto per medium imponantur et fiat minutio de sophena interiori GILB. VII 293v. 1 (cf. ib.: ~a allii ligata superponatur); si mulier fuerit corrupta supponatur sibi †de dersa [? l. dossa] allii quando vadit dormitum; si sentiat odorem allii .. parata est ad concepcionem GAD. 75 v. 2.

dossale, ~ellum, ~etum v. dorsalis 3a. **dossar-, dosser-, dossor-** v. dorsar-. **dossena** v. dozena a. **dosys** v. dosis. **dota** v. dos 2b.

dotabilis, entitled to dower.

1441 dotabunt .. M. uxorem meam de et in omnibus illis terris et tenementis .. de quibus illa secundum legem Anglie ~is erit *Reg. Cant.* II 614; predicti T. et J. petierunt .. tertiam partem manerii de S. ut dotem ipsius J. ex dotatione .. O. quondam viri sui .., cum eadem J. de eodem manerio ~is non fuit *Entries* 2.

dotalicius [LL]

1 dotal, derived from dowry or dower. **b** (as sb. n.) dowry (given by or w. bride). **c** dower (given to bride), marriage portion; **d** (fig.).

s1110 Andegavia .. ~iis incrementis multo felicius terminos dilatavit quam cedibus DICETO *Chr.* 239. **b** **1175** nulli liceat ecclesiam nomine ~ii [v. l. †dotalitatis] ad aliquem transferre (*Conc. Westm.*) *G. Hen. II* I 87 (= *Conc. Syn.* 987; v. et. dotalis); **s1269** rex [Alemannie] .. nobilem quandam filiam .. domini T. de Falkemonte, non ambitu ~ii sed incomparabilis forme ipsius captus illecebra, .. solemni sibi connubio copulavit WYKES 224; **s1423** rex J. .. intravit terram Scocie, ducens secum Johannam sponsam suam. .. de c millibus mercarum premissis pro ~io remittitur regi medietas FORDUN *Cont.* XVI 2. **c** **1008** (12c) quidam miles .. quandam injuste adquisivit villam .. deditque conjugi suae .. sub hereditario †datalicii dono *CD* 1305; †**c1050** (12c) regina .. insulam pro ~io possedit *CD* 907; **1173** concessisse .. Milesenti de G. totum ~ium suum, quod vir ejus .. ei dedit *Act. Hen. II* I 471; **s1190** donavi .. sponse mee medietatem ville de W. in ~ium *FormA* 297; **1215** (v. detentor 2a); **1217** rogantes quatinus .. reginam [matrem meam] .. dote sua .. gaudere permittatis, ut .. [? ipsa] suo gavisa ~io .. digna retribucione respici debeamini *Pat* 113; **1278** (v. dosculum); **1285** quod .. A. rex Scocie .. concessit quod, si .. superviveres .. primogenito [suo], .. annuatim .. mccc m. .. in ~ium seu donacionem propter nupcias perciperes .. *Mon. Hib. & Scot.* 134b; **1298** ut .. rex Anglie .. sororem .. regis Francie .. ducere cum ~io xv^{m} li. Turonensium assignando per ipsum regem Anglie in locis competentibus .. in uxorem .. teneatur (*Lit. Papae*) *Foed.* II 820a; **1402** ad concordandum .. de et super summa dotis, ~iorum ac donacionis propter nupcias necnon de arris et sponsaliciis .. et ceteris in hac parte constituendis *RScot* 162a. **d** in eorum [Eormenredi et Erconbyrhti, ob. **664**] natali .. gavisa est telluris sublimitas, se ornari sentiens duplicis doni gratia .. gratulatur insuper et mater sancta ecclesia, dum sui tanto sponsi illustratur ~io BYRHT. *HR* 2.

2 (eccl.) pertaining to endowment. **b** (as sb. n.) endowment.

1309 ad hec pietatis opera exercenda [progenitores nostri] .. bona ~ia et alia concesserunt (*Lit. Baronum*) *Ann. Lond.* 164; **1338** me in pura viduitate mea .. dedisse .. monasterio de N. .. jus patronatus .. ecclesie mee de C. jure hereditario me contingentis .. in liberam .. elemosinam cum terra ~ia et universis pertinenciis suis *Reg. Newbattle* app. 292. **b** †**974** (13c) quaecunque aliae personae in ~ium ejusdem ecclesiae et jus hereditatis perseverabile .. indulserant *CS* 1310; †**1066** posui in ~ium et in perpetuum hereditatem super altare varia ornamentorum genera *CD* 824; **c1070** dedi .. ecclesiae .. terram Ædwardi de W. .. in ~ium *FormA* 239 (cf. ib. 38).

dotalis [CL], dotal, concerned w. dowry or dower.

innuba sed voluit dotales linquere pompas ALDH. *VirgV* 2184; ab inferioribus militibus .. licet contrahere matrimonium sine solempnitate omni, i. e. sine ~ibus instrumentis. ab illo vero usque ad illustres non nisi ~ia conficiantur instrumenta VAC. *Lib. Paup.* 176; **1313** comes [Fuxensis] promisit dare sufficientes cauciones .., qui (*sic*) se obligabunt .. de solvendis dc li. Turonensium annuatim, quamdiu dicta domina vixerit, sine diminucione dotis et post ejus vitam donec m marche ~es fuerint .. persolute *RGasc* IV 977 (= *Foed.* III 421a); 'nomine †dotalitatis' [v. dotalicius 1b] .. alio modo potest intelligi quod jus patronatus alicujus ecclesie transferatur in maritum cum fundo ~i LYNDW. 281 e.

dotalitas v. dotalicius 1b.

dotalium, (text of) dower (given to bride).

primo legitur ~ium, deinde detur femine (*MS Trin. Coll. Camb.* B. 11. 10 f. 112v.) *HBS* XXXIX 222; **a1218** me [Amabilem uxorem Normanni] .. confirmasse .. ecclesie .. de C. .. ~ium meum de terra de S. *Cart. Coldstream* 5.

dotare [CL]

1 to dower (a bride); **b** (fig.).

DB I 154v. (v. dos 2a); **s1183** (v. dotarium); mulier .. jus suum in hec verba proponet: 'peto terram istam sicut pertinentiam illius terre .. unde maritus meus ~avit me ad hostium ecclesie die quo me desponsavit' GLANV. VI 8; **1199** (v. desponsatio 1a); **1236** Matillis .. petit .. maneria .. ut dotem suam, unde .. R. quondam vir suus eam nominatim ~avit ad hostium ecclesie, quando eam desponsavit, per cartam suam *CurR* XV 1855; **1241** (v. 2 bancus 4); **1294** de quo redditu ~ata fuit post mortem .. mariti sui *SelPlMan* 83; **1475** (v. assieta 2); **1559** ne qui prelati .. filias suas baronibus .. de patrimonio Christi ~ent aut in matrimonio collocent *Conc. Scot.* II 155. **b** ~ata, *gewelgod GlP* 612; anima mea, .. candidata caelesti lavacro, ~ata Spiritu Sancto ANSELM (*Medit.* 2) III 80; animam sibi desponsat et fide sue incarnationis ~at ALEX. CANT. *Dicta* 20 p. 190.

2 to endow: **a** (eccl.); **b** (acad.); **c** (civic).

a sustinet ecclesiam / quam pater ille pius .. / .. / fundavit, struxit, dotavit, et inde sacravit WULF. *Swith. pref.* 61; possessiones quibus illud oratorium et ~aretur et ornaretur et ditaretur AILR. *Ed. Conf.* 771C; **c1164** cum terra .. de qua prefata ecclesia ~ata est *Regesta Scot.* 239; quam cito [monachi] in immensum ditari ceperant et ~ari GIR. *IK* I 3; **1327** reges .. ecclesiam .. de regia munificentia ~averunt *Lit. Cant.* I 219; cum ecclesie et collegia alia ex donacione fidelium sint ditata et dotata, potuerunt fideles ditando et ~ando ecclesias talem legem imponere quod a nullo vivente .. tollerentur bona collata ecclesiis .. absque causa .. manifesta OCKHAM *Pol.* II 627; **1345** cum dominus W. .. cantariam .. faciendam ~averit, fundaverit et in scriptis ordinaverit *Mem. Ripon* I 154; **1378** ad ~andum unum monachum, qui habitabit in eadem cella *FormA* 267; **1424** licet .. cantariam .. in certis redditibus .. ~asset *Ib.* 68. **b** **1284** cum nobilis mulier .. domum .. variis proventibus .. ~averit atque ditaverit *Deeds Balliol* 281; **1412** cum .. absurdum .. foret eum [custodem librarie] minori prerogativa ~ari quem major ordinis dignitas perillustret *StatOx* 218. **c** Johannes fuit primus rex Anglie qui umquam ~avit Quinque Portus Anglie de libertatibus et consuetudinibus quas usque ad moderna tempora clamant tenere KNIGHTON I 198.

3 (p. ppl.) endowed (fig.), gifted.

Zebedeus, ~atus *GlC Int.* 337; qui in fortes columnas ecclesie poterant excrevisse, subtilis ingenii capacitate ~ati, studiorum gymnasia derelinquunt R. BURY *Phil. prol.* 6.

dotaria, dowager.

1559 principis Mariae .., reginae ~iae ac regentis *Conc. Scot.* II 152.

dotarium, dower, marriage portion. *V. et. doarium.*

s1183 [rex] misit in Angliam nuncios suos, mandans quod Alienor regina .. libera exiret et †iret [? l. viveret; cf. DEVIZES 28v. p. 14] per ~ium suum *G. Hen. II* I 305 (cf. ib.: affirmabat .. rex Anglie quod ipse dotaverat reginam A. eodem ~io quod rex Francie exigebat reddi sorori sue); **1221** sponse nostre .. concessimus in ~ium has terras subscriptas *Pat* 309.

2 pledge (for fulfilment of promise).

que pignora vir ille grantater accepit et domum rediens ~ia protulit R. COLD. *Godr.* 511.

dotarius v. datorius.

dotatio

1 provision of dower, marriage settlement.

1203 Willelmus .. petit versus Simonem .. xiiij virgatas terre .. ut jus suum .., ita quod [pater suus] inde dotavit uxorem suam Hermegardam, quam dotem adhuc .. possidet. econtra Simon defendit .. ~onem Ermegarde per patrem Willelmi *CurR* III 25; **1353** Thomas .. et Emma uxor ejus .. pecierunt .. terciam partem unius mesuagii .. ut dotem ipsius E. ex ~one Ricardi .. quondam viri [sui] *MGL* I 411; **14**.. warrantizavit maneria .. ut dotem Matilde ex ~one H. .. quondam viri ipsius M., qui .. ad ostium ecclesie eam inde dotavit *Reg. Brev. Jud.* 15b;

2 endowment: **a** (eccl.); **b** (acad.); **c** (civic).

a de fundatione, ~one et privilegiatione monasterii *G. S. Alb.* I 4 *rub.*; comes Robertus [Leycestrensis, ob. **1163**] .., preter primam ~onem abbathie, dedit illis [canonicis] .. manerium de Stocton KNIGHTON I 147; **1367** vicarius .. juxta antiquam ~onem .. percipiet .. altilagium .. cum decimis [etc.] *Reg. Heref.* 42; ~o cleri ex stulticia Cesaris ad magnum malum ecclesie inolevit WYCL. *Pol.* 94; ecclesia Christi posset regulari prospere et quiete sine tali papa, ut patet de tempore ab Ascensione usque ad ~onem ecclesie *Id. Chr. & Antichr.* 676 (cf. ib.: sicut magister istius ~onis [sc. dyabolus] est mendax, sic et ista ~o est ficticia et plena mendacio); **1381** jam horum est opinio, / defensio, dotacio / catholice ecclesie, / necnon Silvestri dicio / ac Sancti Thome passio / sint species insanie (*In Lollardos* 35) *Pol. Poems* I 242; nec sine misterio sunt tanta et talia primitiva nostre ~onis insignia contemplanda ELMH. *Cant.* 100; **1419** rogo .. quod .. tenementa .. aut certe advocaciones ecclesiarum .. perquirantur et †appropriantur [? l. approprientur] in ~onem cantarie mee *Wills N. Country* 27; **1429** (v. crescentia 1b). **b** **1554** et muneribus donentur regii officiarii quorum opera et studio regine ~o ad effectum producebatur *StatOx* 362. **c** causa cujus ~onis adhunc clamant [V Portus] liberiores esse pre ceteris portubus omnibus regni Anglie KNIGHTON I 198 (cf. dotare 2c).

dotator, (eccl.) endower.

~or non solum se ipsum inficit, sed suos elemosinarios, quibus bona Domini sic partitur WYCL. *Pol.* 246; omnes fundatores abbatiarum et ~ores episcopatuum, prioratuum, et cantariarum deberent emendare hoc peccatum .. auferendo ab eis [simoniacis] secularia dominia (PURVEY) *Ziz.* 394; *Reg. Whet.* I 318 (v. ditator).

dotatrix

1 (eccl.) endower (f.).

1243 a tempore .. Matildis Anglorum regine fundatricis et ~icis domus nostre (*AncC* XI 91) *RL* II 30.

2 dowager.

1536 assignata fuerunt Katherine, ~ici nuper .. principis Arthuri principis Wallie *Rutland MSS Ac. Receiver* 27–8 *Hen. VIII* r. 1.

doterellus, dotterel (bird).

morinellum .. nostri etiam ~um vocant, quasi stultitia delirantem dicant CAIUS *Anim.* 21.

dotice [CL < δοτική], (gram.) dative case.

~e, dativus *GlC Int.* 91.

dotio v. donatio 1a.

dotissa, dowager.

1544 compotus .. receptoris generalis domine E. comitisse ~e Rutland' .. possessionum .. T. nuper comitis *Rutland MSS Ac. Receiver* 35–6 *Hen. VIII* r. 1; **1549** (v. exsecutrix 2a).

douarium v. doarium. **doub-** v. et. daub-. **doubla** v. duplus 3b. **doublett-** v. dublettus. **doubura** v. daubatura.

douella, ~um [cf. OF *douelle*]

1 barrel stave.

1290 pro .. duellis (v. cantera a); **1300** pro circulis et ~is emptis pro quibusdam doliis ligandis *AcWardr* p.356; **1313** pro .. circulis, ~is, et aliis rebus necessariis emptis pro debilibus doleis reparandis *KRAc* 375/8 f. 46d.; **1327** pro c circulis et vij ~is emptis et positis super dicta dolia .. xj s. x d., pro circulo j d., pro ~o vj d. *Ib.* 78/2 m. 6.

2 dowel, peg (for cart-wheel).

1297 in ij novis rotis ligandis ad dictum carrum, iij s.; in eisdem rotis ligandis cum ligatura veterum rotarum una cum novis dulis et groppis emptis ad idem, xiiij d. *Ac. Cornw* I 62; **1299** in j ligatura ad dictas rotas ferro ligandas cum duel' ad idem emptis *Ac. Man. Wint.* (*Alton Priors*); **1309** in xxv doelis pro eodem [pari rotarum] emptis, vj d. *Ib.* (*Alton*); **1322** in x doul' ad eandem carectam, ij d. *MinAc* (*Salop*) 965/5.

3 *s. dub.*

1228 pro ccc bordis de fagina ad cyntros et duvell' et pro xix fustibus [etc.] ad cyntros et vias faciendas .. hottoribus *KRAc* 462/10 (= *Ac. Build. Hen. III* 78: duvellis; *Building in Eng.* 249: †durnell').

douellare, to fit w. dowels.

1305 carette: in ij axibus imponendis cum ij mod[iis] perforandis et dulandis *MinAc* (*Essex*) 840/12.

douellegia, dowel or 'duledge' (for cart-wheels).

1285 in clavis, clipp[is] et douleg' et aliis emendis j carette sals[arie] *KRAc* 351/18 m. 2; **1335** [pro] dulegiis (*Ac. Man. Hinderclay, Suff*) *Mod. Philol.* XXXIV 60; **1351** custus carectarum: idem computat .. in ij wynekis et dewleggis emptis, v d.; et in ferramentis j paris rotarum de rebus precomputatis et xij dewilleggis emptis de fabro pro eodem, ij s. (*MinAc*) *Econ. Condit.* app. 61 (cf. ib. 56 [**1324**]: pro *dyvelegges*).

doukera [ME *doukere*], 'ducker', diver or loon (kind of bird).

Aristoteles urinatricis [sc. κολυμβίδος] unum tantum genus commemorat; ego tamen tria urinatricum genera vidi. horum primum .. nautae nostrates 'lounam' nominant, alii '~am' TURNER *Av.* I 8v.

doul- v. douell-. **douna** v. 1 duna b. **douncella** v. domicella. **doungerium** v. dangerium.

doverans, (officer) receiving *dofreth*. *Cf. doverettum.*

c1205 [*abbot's land acquitted*] de satellitibus ~antibus (*Ch. Haghmon*) *Antiq. Salop* X 73 (cf. ib. XI 3).

doverettum [W. *dofreth*], payment for maintenance of foresters or other officers.

1219 relaxavi etiam dovereth' servientium, si quos ego vel heredes mei habuerimus in partibus illis [de Boreton'] *Cart. Worc.* 158; **1227** sciatis nos concessisse .. quod, si aliquo tempore constituti fuerint servientes in com. eodem [*Salop*] qui vocantur *grith serganz doveranz* [*ChartR* 18 m. 1: *gridserjanz doverant*] ad communem pacem servandam, ipsi abbas .. et monachi et homines sui quieti sint imperpetuum de *doverette* [*ChartR*: doveretto] predictorum servientium, ita quod in terra .. abbatis et monachorum sive in terra hominum suorum nullum de cetero capient ~um (*Ch.*) *Hist. Shrewsb.* II 112; **1230** quod teneat conventionem factam .. de quietantia †doneretti forestariorum per totam terram S. Milburge que est circa Clivas [*Clee, Salop*] *CurR* XIV 436; **1290** de lxv quar. .. avene de *dovereth* venditis *MinAc W. Wales* I app. 462; **1306** de quodam annuo redditu dicto *hildoverith*' per communitatem .. commoti .. solvendo *Ib.* 438; **1327** quidam redditus de avenis qui vocatur *deverith IPM* (*Wales*) 5/2.

dovetum v. duvetum. **dowar-** v. doar-. **dowb-** v. daub-.

doxa [LL *gl.* < δόξα], glory: **a** (celestial); **b** (worldly).

a a**690** (v. cyrius b); doxa Deo ingenito! (ALDH.) *Carm. Aldh.* 1. 197; **940** in aeterna dosca laetetur *CS* 761; *CS* 780 (v. compos 1b); a**975** gaudia sanctorum ut capias cum stemmate doxae (*Vers.*) (*Ep. ad Eadgarum*) *Mem. Dunst.* 368 (cf. ib. 366); ad glorificandum .. Dominum, cui honor .., ~a, majestas paxque tripudium per immortalia saecula saeculorum LANTFR. *Swith.* 10; c**1000** laus sit tonanti Domino; / doxa sit tibi filio / Christo *Anal. Hymn.* LI 1 70; cum deveniens ejus manifesta videres / signa, decus, doxam (*Vers.*) ÆLNOTH *Cnut* 44; **1391** valeatis in Marie Filio, qui ~am preparavit universo mundo *FormOx* 413. **b** rusticitatis notam cavens et urbanitatis ~am captans, inter urbaniores etiam primus haberi semper enisus est *V. Thom. B* 3; equos et phaleras et doxas aulicas WALT. WIMB. *Palpo* 7; *joy*, .. delectamen, ~a, doxula .., felicitas .. gloria .. *CathA*.

doy- v. et. doi-. **doyt-** v. duit-.

dozena, ~um [OF *dozaine*], dozen, set of twelve; **b** (w. ref. to jury).

1226 pro xxj duzenna (*sic*) costarum de If ad balistas faciendas .., pro qualibet duzenna iiij s. *Cl* 119a; **1265** pro viij ducenis bullarum nigellarum ad cameram *Manners* 10; **1402** pro x dossenis panni lati in j fardello *EEC* 559; **1421** pro .. v dossenis pellium ovinarum .., v dossenis forpicium et xviij cornuum *Ib.* 470; **1428** de quolibet doseno capuciorum (*Ch. muragii*) *Lib. Kilken.* 159; **1432** lego .. unum doss[enum] cocliarium argenti *Test. Ebor.* II 22; **1446** in coquina .. ij ~e parapsidum stanneorum vasorum, ij ~e discorum, ij ~e acetabulorum *Feod. Durh.* 191; **1504** pro uno dussen' et dim. *cusshyns EEC* 649. **b** **1299** fuerunt de dosena jurata ad ultimam curiam *CourtR Hales* 392.

dracaena [LL < δράκαινα]

1 serpent or dragon (f.).

predictis nepa conjungatur et anguis / atque dracena, draco GARL. *Syn.* 657; *a dragon*, draco, †dracona *CathA*.

2 rudder or sim.

s**1217** perrexerunt .. audacter, obliquando tamen ~am, id est *loof*, acsi vellent adire Calesiam M. PAR. III 29; s**1405** quarum [navium] una, ventis pro voto fruens, disposuit supernavigasse navem in qua filius regis erat; sed providencia probitateque naucleri, obliquantis ~am subito navemque girantis, navis regia vaste ratis declinavit impetum OTTERB. 253.

dracantea v. 2 dracontia.

†dracca, *f. l.*

s**1247** cum xxx acris prati juxta dictum novum locum ex parte occidentali in †dracca [? l. cloaca] juxta fossatum de Redeclos jacentibus *Croyl. Cont. B* 479.

drach- v. et. drasca.

drachma [CL < δραχμή; (?) *infl. by* δράγμα]

1 drachma, dirhem, or bezant (coin); **b** (w. ref to *Luke* xv 8–9); **c** (w. ref. to *Neh.* vii 70–2). **d** silver penny, sterling. **e** (?) noble or mark.

dedragma ij dragmae sunt *Gl. Leid.* 33. 5; **10..** (v. didrachma); [obsessi in Hierusalem] de quisquiliis collectis parvissimum pondus dragmis quattuor distrahebant J. SAL. *Pol.* 423D; dragma vel aureus, †uma [l. mna], besantius atque talentum; / sed dragmam proprie specimen dic ponderis esse GARL. *Syn.* 291–2. 1583A (v. et. 2a infra); in ea [Alexandria] .. perpera, que non est purum aurum, xij [Venetos grossos valet] et dragma j et duo carub S. SIM. *Itin.* 38; *besaunt*, dragma *PP*. **b** dragmam perditam quaesitura ALDH. *VirgP* 7; ut .. tam diu .. querant quousque dragmam perditam reperiant AD. SCOT *Serm.* 210C; supra caput iconis scribitur hic titulus: 'genus humanum, quod est ~a decima' *Id. TT* 703C; ut dictum ~a perdita inventa novem ~is jungeretur HALES *Sent.* IV 3; dragma letaris decima relucente, / que te querente perdita repperirir J. HOWD. *Cant.* 323. **c** **1459** pro vobis, Christianissime princeps, qui dragmas auri et argenti in nostram dudum intulistis Jerusalem, in non parvam ditacionem exigui templi nostri *Reg. Whet.* I 326. **d** interim [temp. S. regis] .. numisma et es et commercii formam quisque apud se transformavit, inminuit et adulteravit .. preter dragmam de Ely, quod (*sic*) integrum servabatur ex argento electo *Lib. Eli.* III 73 (cf. ib. II 111: dolo nummulariorum dragma fraudata). **e** **1565** quicunque abesse illum professor deprehenderit, eidem ~ae mulctam statim pendito *StatOx* 391; dependat dragman (*sic*) *Ib.* 414 (v. 2 dependere 1).

2 drachm (weight), one eighth of one twelfth of a *libra*, one ninety-sixth. **b** (math.) unit.

dragma pondus est denarii argentei quod pensat siliquas xviij *Gl. Leid.* 32. 1; dragma THURKILL *Abac.* 61v. (v. deunx); pulvis magnetis in quantitate duorum dragmatum valet contra ydropisim BART. ANGL. XVI 61; dragma ponderabit ij denarios et obolum, hoc est iiij^{xx} grana frumenti *Cust. Cant.* 33; GARL. *Syn.* 292 (v. 1a supra); *Ib.* 295–6 (v. 2 drama); **1357** in ij dragmis diagridii, iiijd. *Ac. Obed. Abingd.* 14; trocisscus [pondus] unius dragme. dragma habet pondus trium scrupulorum. .. [*Vers.*] 'in dragmam scrupulus surgit ter multiplicatus' *Alph.* 188; *drame, qwyte*, drama, dragma *PP*; hec dragma est octava pars uncie *WW*. **b** substantia et 10 radices 39 coequantur dragmatibus ROB. ANGL. *Alg.* 70.

draco [CL < δράκων]

1 serpent. **b** dragon (partly fig.). **c** (w. ref. to *Deut.* xxxii 33).

pugnas exercens dira cum gente draconum ALDH. *Aen.* 82 (*Mustela*) 2; **9..** ~onum, *nædrena WW*. **b** [Silvester] squamigerum vinxit virtute draconem, / .. / qui prius e crypta funesto flamine spirans / Romani regni vexabat jure catervas ALDH. *VirgV* 545; de ~one (*tit.*): horridus horriferas speluncae cumbo latebras, / concitus aethereis volitans miscebor et auris HWÆTBERHT 42; trux ero valde draconi *Ib.* 44 (*de Panthera*) 2; *AS Inscr.* 105 (v. 1 deserere 3c); exurget in illum [gigantem] ~o Wigornie (*Proph. Merlini*) G. MON. VII 4 p. 394; [Hibernia] caret serpentibus et colubris; .. caret et ~onibus GIR. *TH* I 28; S. SIM. *Itin.* 41 (v. cocatrix a); hic drago, *a dragon WW*. **c** **747** sit furor ~onum vinum eorum BONIF. *Ep.* 75.

2 image of dragon. **b** figurehead of warship. **c** (eccl.) processional banner, streamer or sim. **d** ensign, standard.

†**833** (15c) cyphum .. deauratum et per totam partem exteriorem barbaris victoribus ad ~ones pugnantibus celatum *CS* 409; puer timet sculptum ~onem aperto ore ANSELM (*Ver.* 6) I 183; si [artifex] .. faciat ymaginem ~onis J. BLUND *An.* 96; **1303** cyphus argenti deauratus .. cum opere elevato de equitibus et ~onibus (*KRAc* 363/6) *DocExch* 282. **b** aureus puppi leo prominet; aequora prore / celse pennato perterret corpore drāco *V. Ed. Conf.* 40v. **c** ~o, qui per triduum illud [Rogationum] deportatur cum longa cauda et inflata duobus diebus primis ante crucem et vexilla et post ultimo die retro vadit, significat diabolum BELETH *RDO* 123. 130A (cf. 3 infra); c**1250** v vexilla et unus ~o *Vis. S. Paul.* 11; **1322** pro ~one portando et capella tempore Rogacionum *Sacr. Ely* II 31 (cf. 2 capella 5); **1327** quesitus .. quid voluit fecisse de rotulis predictis [de particulis custume], dicit quod voluit fecisse inde ~ones *LTRMem* 99 r. 39*d.*; **1440** in salario j hominis portantis ~onem per tres dies Rogacionum cum processione et in festo Ascensionis Domini *Mem. Ripon* III 234; in Rogacionibus .. in principio processionis deferatur ~o, iij vexillis rubeis precedentibus, secundo loco leo, tercio loco cetera vexilla *Process. Sal.* 92 (cf. ib. 93: in die Ascensionis Domini .. ultimo loco procedat ~onis vexillum). **d** s**752** Edelhun precedens Westsexenses regis insigne, ~onem sc. aureum, gerens H. HUNT. *HA* IV 19 (cf. ib. VI 13 [s**1016**]: loco regio relicto .. inter ~onem et insigne quod vocatur *standard*); jussit fabricari duos ~ones ex auro ad similitudinem ~onis quem ad radium stelle inspexerat .. ab illo tempore vocatus fuit Utherpendragon, quod Britannica lingua 'caput ~onis' sonamus G. MON. VIII 17; signa ipsa minus pregnantia vento / mentitas laxant animas moriturague tardis / flatibus inclinant faciles languere dracones J. EXON. *BT* VI 7; s**1191** cum .. rex Anglie fixisset signum suum in medio et tradidisset ~onem suum Petro de Pratellis ad portandum R. HOWD. III 129; s**1257** vexillum suum regale explicans, quasi ~onem, qui nemini novit parcere M. PAR. *Maj.* V 648; s**1264** rex .. cum suis mox progreditur vexillis explicatis, precedente eum signo regio indicium mortis pretendente, quod '~onem' vocant RISH. 26; s**1264** rex Anglie .. precedente ~one rubeo, qui mortem generalem adversariorum portendebat *Chr. Battle* 376.

3 Satan.

veteris ructantur fauce draconis / atra venena sacra Christi torquentia turmas ALDH. *VirgV* 1308 (cf. ib. 1421: strofa stimulante draconis); †**676** (12c) ubi truculentus et nefandus prius ~o errorum deceptionibus serviebat *CS* 43; *GAS* 425 (v. basiliscus b); ipse [diabolus] ~o est et leo. ~o modo est, quia homines non ita aperte sed latenter seducit. leo erit in tempore Antichristi, quia tunc .. deseviet. ~o fuit, quando Christum supra pinnaculum templi .. latenter fallere voluit [cf. *Matth.* iv] BELETH *RDO* 123. 130B; [Lucifer] dicitur serpens vel ~o propter ejus virulentam astutiam BART. ANGL. II 19.

4 (fig.) leader in war (*cf.* W. *draig, dragon*).

tu, insularis ~o, multorum tyrannorum depulsor .., Maglocune GILDAS *EB* 33; ex hiis gestabant ter tres diadema dracones *V. Merl.* 629.

5 a (astr.) Draco, constellation. **b** 'dragon' (part of lunar orbit south of ecliptic). **c** 'firedrake' (comet, meteor, or sim.).

a R. CANT. *Malch.* V 44 (v. cycnus 2). **b** inter vij planetas per zodiacum circumeuntes discurrit etiam ~o, sed contrario motu WALCHER *Drac.* 87; **1126** liber iste septem planetarum et ~onis statum continet ADEL. *Elk. pref.*; J. WORC. 37 etc. (v. caput 5e); excentricus lune .. secat eclipticam in duobus punctis oppositis; vocaturque punctus per quem transit luna a parte australi eclyptice in partem septentrionalem 'caput ~onis', et punctus oppositus 'cauda ~onis'. conjunctio enim duorum circulorum, eo quod facit figuram tortuosam, vocatur '~o lune' GROS. 29; figura intersectionis appellatur '~o', quoniam lata est in medio et angustior versus finem SACROB. *Sph.* 114. **c** apparuit stella mire magnitudinis et claritatis, uno radio contenta. ad radium vero erat globus igneus in similitudinem ~onis extensus G. MON. VIII 14; s**1239** apparuit .. stella maxima .., relinquens ignem et fumum post se cum moveretur; .. censebatur autem ~o vel cometa M. PAR. *Min.* II 424; stella .. sive cometa vel ~o major .. Lucifero *Id. Maj.* III 566; s**1248** volavit .. flamma .. usque ad castrum regis .. ad instar ~onis ignivomi mappam post se trahentis *Ib.* V 35; multa .. luminosa .. [in aere] apparent in diversis figuris .., ut sunt ~ones ardentes .. et columpne BACON V 10; **1343** in secunda septimana videbatur in Lyndesay ardens ~o circa solis occasum vel ante, qui futuram tunc siccitatem significavit W. MERLE *Temp.* 9.

6 waterspout.

in gulfo .. Satalie videtur .. quod ~o magnus niger in nubibus veniat ..; et ~o ille .. attrahit ad se undas. .. quidam dicunt quod hoc non est ~o sed sol, qui attrahit aquas maris ad se *G. Ric. I* 196–7.

7 (alch.) 'dragon'.

os vasis diligenter claudatur et coque ad ignem donec totum vertatur deorsum. tunc ~o alas suas comedit et diversos emittit colores DASTIN *Ros.* 17; ~o chymicus est materia lapidis philosophorum *LC*.

8 dragon-tree (*Dracaena draco*). **b** (w. *sanguis*) 'dragon's blood', gum derived from dragontree.

illic arborea sanguis de fronde draconis / sudat GARL. *Epith.* IV 319. **b** anthera .. valet summe per se .. vel cum sanguine ~onis .. vel cum mastice GAD. 6. 2.

dracoma (~onea), ~omaticus v. trachom-. **dracona** v. dracaena 1, draconiculus.

draconarius [LL], bearer of dragon standard. *Cf. draco* 2d.

~ius, i. vexillarius, signifer, *segnbora GlH* D 814; *a banerer*, vexillifer, .. ~ius, antesignarius *CathA*.

draconiculus [cf. CL dracunculus], dragonet.

a dragon, draco, dracona, ~us *CathA*.

draconinus, serpentine.

[chimera] in posterioribus ~a est, quoniam post peractionem libidinis aculeus penitentie mentem pungit W. DONC. *Aph. Phil.* 7. 6.

draconitis [CL], 'dragon-stone'.

†~itas, gemma ex cerebro †serpentes *GlC* D 365; †dracontides, lapis a dracone vocatur *GlH* D 815; ~ites .. gemma est, quae fit e cerebro draconum *LC*.

1 dracontia [cf. CL dracontias < δρακοντίας], 'dragon-stone'.

~a (*tit.*): me caput horrentis fertur genuisse draconis ALDH. *Aen.* 24; auri obriza lammina .. sine .. rubicunda gemmarum gloria vel sucini ~ia .. vilescere videbitur *Id. VirgP* 15; ~ia, *gimrodr GlC* D 364.

2 dracontia [cf. CL dracontion < δρακόντιον], 'dragons', dragonwort (*Dracunculus*).

~ia, herba in modum .. serp[entis] *GlC* D 368; dracantea, *dracentia Gl. Durh.*; herba ~ea, *þæt ys dracentse Leechdoms* I 12; draguncia BART. ANGL. XVII 50 (v. coluber a); dracundeam *Ib.* XVIII 34 (v. dammula a); radix serpentarie, i. draguntee, idem facit GILB. V 229.2; hec dragantia, *dragonce Gl. AN Glasg.* f. 19; succus radicum aliarum herbarum preparatus sicut dragea [*some MSS omit*], dragantia, viticella etc. ..; hec omnia albificant .. faciem BACON IX 122; si sit dolor in causa frigida .., cinamomum, peonia, coriandrum valent pre ceteris, maxime si cum his apponitur dragontea GAD. 6. 1; ~ia, proserpinale *SB* 18; draguncea *Alph.* 48 (v. colubrinus a); *dragaunce, herbe*, dragancia *PP*; *dragence or nedder grysse* [v. l. *gresse*], dragancia, basilisca, herba serpentaria vel serpentina *CathA*.

dracontides v. draconitis.

dracontinus, serpentine.

Erictonius cum pedibus ~is HIGD. II 18 p. 364.

dracontopes [cf. δρακοντόπους], serpent-tailed giant.

de ~edibus: ferunt fabulae Graecorum homines inmensis corporibus fuisse et in tanta mole tamen humano generi similes, nisi quod draconum caudas habuerunt, unde et Graece ~edes dicebantur *Lib. Monstr.* I 49.

dracunculus [CL], dragonwort.

dracontia Latine ~us .. dicitur, A. *dragon* TURNER *Herb.* A 4v.

dracundea v. 2 dracontia.

dracus, a dragon. **b** water-sprite.

a 10. .. ~us, *draca WW.* **b** ~os .. perhibent in cavernis fluviorum mansionem habere, et nunc in specie annulorum aureorum supernatantium .. mulieres allicere et pueros in ripis fluminum balneantes. .. nec plus hoc contingere dicunt quam feminis lactantibus, quas ~i rapiunt ut prolem suam infelicem nutriant; et nonnunquam post exactum septennium remunerate ad hoc nostrum redeunt hemispherium. .. vidimus equidem hujuscemodi feminam raptam dum in ripa fluminis Rhodani panniculos abluebat GERV. TILB. III 85.

dradgetum v. 2 dragetum. **draenerum** v. drainerum.

draga [ME *dragge*], 'drag': **a** sledge; *cf. draia.* **b** drag-net. **c** *s. dub.*

a 1248 in carucis et herciis et ~is faciendis, vj d. *Ac. Man. Wint.* (*Portland, Dorset*); **c1314** de j caruca .., j hercia, j dragga *LTRAc* (*Templ.*) 19 r. 41*d.* **b 1276** habent ~as et alia retia i[t]a contra assisam quod destruunt ripariam *Hund.* I 198. **c** custos sutorie liberat .. subcell[er]ario corium ad draggas *Ac. Beaulieu* 208.

dragagant- v. tragacanth-. **dragant-** v. 2 dracontia, tragacanth-.

1 dragea [ME, AN *dragge*], drag, grappling hook.

1286 in ij bussellis carbonis maris emptis ad faciend' quarell' et j ~eam ad puteum *KRAc* 462/11; **1311** in stipendium j hominis cum affro suo et ~ea tractantis iiij bargeatas petrarum *Fabr. Exon.* 54 (cf. ib. 57: draggeam).

2 †dragea, (?) kind of herb. *Cf.* 2 *dragetum.*

BACON IX 122 (v. 2 dracontia).

1 dragetum, ~ium [OF *dragee*, (?) < τράγημα], 'dredge', sweetmeat, comfit.

1317 in albo pulvere et ~eto, x d. *Rec. Leic.* I 303; **1328** in .. j bala gingiberis .., l lib. de ~eto, *ExchScot* 119; **1342** in diversis confeccionibus et ~iis *Sacr. Ely* II 115; **c1375** in .. iij *cofyns* diversarum confeccionum cum li. (*sic*) de ~eto empt' in grosso, v s. *Ac. Durh.* 129; de nominibus specierum: .. hoc ~etum, *drage WW; a dragie,* ~etum *CathA.*

2 dragetum, ~eum, ~ia [*etym. dub.*; (?) cf. drasca, drauca], 'dredge', mixed corn (barley and oats).

1227 in manerio de K. .. seminate sunt xij acre cum ~eo, sc. de vj quar. *LTRMem* 9 r. 6 (*sched.*); **1234** triturabit ij bus. frumenti vel ordei et de avenis vel ~eto iiij bus. †cumilatos *Cust. Glast.* 63; **1270** ordeum: .. in mixtione ad ~iam ut inferius vj quar. .. ~ia: idem respondet de ordeo ut supra vj quar. et de avena ut inferius vj quar. .. avena: .. in mixtione ad ~iam ut supra vj quar. *Ac. Stratton* 34 (cf. ib. 37: in .. xxix acris ~ie metendis); **1283** opus avene facit j quar. peccum, et tantum de ~eto et ordeo *Cust. Battle* 98; **c1285** cum ~eo (v. 1 cum 3a); **1297** ~etum: idem r. c. de xix quar. vj bus. ~eti de toto exitu grangie hoc anno; et de iiij quar. j bus. ordei receptis ad semen; et de ij quar. avene receptis ad idem. .. inde in semine super xij acras et j rodam terre vj quar. j bus., sc. super acram dim. quar. *Ac. Cornw* I 22; draggetum *Ib.* 66 (v. drauca); **1343** ~ium et avena domini ligata et cariata domi fuerunt non in tempore congruo *Cuxham* 684; **1343** districtus est per ix thravos et dim. ~eti *CourtR* (*Breedon, Leic*) 183/51 m. 1; **1350** ~etta: et de j quar. j bus. ~ette inventis in pallea (*MinAc*) *Surv. Durh. Hatf.* 235; **1421** j acram .. occupavit et illam seminavit cum dradgeto *CourtR Banstead*; avena / et brasium, vicia, dragetum [*gl.*: *dragge*] mixtilioque (*Vers.*) *WW.*

dragg- v. drag-. **dragia** v. 2 dragetum, draia, drasca. **dragium** v. 1 & 2 dragetum, drasca a. **dragla** v. draila. **dragma** v. drachma, 2 drama. **dragmaticon** v. dramaticus. **drago** v. draco 1b. **dragont-, dragunt-** v. dracont-.

draia [ME *draie*], 'dray', wheelless cart; *cf. draga* a. **b** dray-load.

1256 habeant .. annuatim meremium ad unam drayam faciendam (*Fine*) *Reg. Exon.* III 1586; **1312** in stipendio ejusdem [carpentarii] facientis ij drayas pro magnis petris ad molendinum de Hadl' [*Essex*] cariandis ad siccam terram, ubi carette non potuerunt se carcare propter profunditatem marisci *MinAc* 843/3 (cf. ib.: pro petris ponendis super ij drayas ad molendinum ad car[iandum] usque siccam terram pro fluminibus, quousque carette possent advenire quando tempus siccabatur); **1370** in calce empta, xij d.; in una dreia empta, xiiij d.; in rastris, vj d. ob. *Ac. Obed. Abingd.* 17. **b c1235** prosternet et congregabit v dragias clausture pro j operatione (*S. Weald*) *MFG.*

draila [ME **draile*], drail (notched iron projecting from plough-beam).

1280 custus carucarum: .. in vj dreylis, vj d. *Ac. Man. Cant.* (*Milton, Essex*); **1284** in iiij draglis emptis, iiij d. *MinAc* (*Cowick, Essex*) 839/30; **1285** in ij draylis emptis, iij d. ob. *Ib.* (*Hallingbury, Essex*) 843/26; **1361** in vj draill' emptis pro carucis, xviij d. *Ib.* (*Eastwood, Essex*) 840/22 m. 2.

drainerum [Eng. *drainer*], drain.

1575 avertit cursum communis draeneri (*CourtR Peterb.*) *Northants Rec. S.* XVIII 80 (cf. ib.: non escuravit partem suam communis draeneri).

drainetta [ME *drai net*], drag-net.

1290 duas .. batellas cum duabus draynettis et sex stalnettis *PlRChester* 6 r. 2*d.*

draituria v. dreitura.
1 drama v. drachma 2a.

2 drama [LL < δρᾶμα], drama (dialogue, song, or interrogation).

qui sceptrum regni Solimis erexit in arvis, / personam Christi sponsali dramate sumens ALDH. *VirgV* 2141; ~atis, †motatio [l. mutatio] personarum vel introductio *GlC* D 366; **10.** .. ~ate, *þy brydelican gewrite* .., mutatio personarum, ut est Cantica Canticorum *WW*; est neutrum dragma tibi, 'dragmatis' est genitivus; / questio dramaticum dicas genus esse loquendi; / dragma melos †pondus [? l. ponas], sic 'dragmatis' est genitivus; / sed, [si] sit †genitivus [? *omit*] 'dragme', pondus tibi denotat esse GARL. *Syn.* 293–6. 1583A (cf. drachma 2a); *a melody,* dragma, melodia, melos .., *a question,* questio, interrogacio, ~a *CathA.*

dramaticus [LL < δραματικός], dramatic.

GARL. *Syn.* 294 (v. 2 drama); dragmaticon, *Id. PP* 98 (v. dicticos); *Id. Dict.* 134 (v. didascalicus).

drameda v. dromas. **drana** v. drova. **drangagium** v. drengagium.

drapa, ~is [OF *drap* < LL drapus], cloth.

1336 ordinatum est .. quod nullus de cetero siccat lanas, pelle[s], drappas lineas neque lanutas neque aliqua alia bona ibi inponit (*Andover*) *Gild Merch.* II 331; **1402** ordinatum est .. quod nullus civis nec aliquis alius pannarius infra libertatem civitatis W. commorans .. mittet extra libertatem .. alicui textori vel fullario aliquam ~em texandam (*sic*) vel fullandam sub pena .. forisfaciendi ij s. de qualibet ~e *BB Winchester* 9.

drapacismus v. dropacismus.

drapale [cf. OF *drapel*], piece of cloth.

1278 furtive asportavit de domo sua tapet', bratt' et juncta drappal[ia] *Gaol Del.* 35/2 r. 53*d.*

draparia, ~ium [cf. OF *draperie*]

1 cloth market or fair, drapers' quarter.

c1220 seldam quam Radulfus P. de me tenuit in draperia Oxonefordie in parrochia S. Martini *Cart. Osney* II 46 (cf. ib. II 68: shopam situatam in veteri draperia); **1223** quod non permittant feriam et draperiam Wigorn' teneri in festo Nativitatis B. M. alibi quam in eo loco quo teneri solebant tempore domini Johannis regis *Cl* 555a; **1242** mandatum est majori et ballivis Winton' quod (*sic*), †quia [? l. quia non] sine magno dispendio civitatis regis ammota est .. draperia a loco illo in quo esse consuevit .., quatinus draperiam illam esse faciant in magno vico, in loco eodem in quo esse consuevit *Cl* 449; **1257** in foro draperie Lincolnie *CalCh* I 467; **1275** viam .. que extendebat se a draperia Norhamt' usque ad viam de Layre *Hund.* II 3; **1282** de draperia apud Burdegalam .. facienda *RGasc* II 167; **1319** [apprenticius] in draperia London *Cal. IPM* VI 191.

2 cloth (collect.).

1257 quod mercatores Leycestrie qui cum draperia accesserint ad nundinas Stanford .. tenebunt illas schopas ibidem que solite sunt teneri *Rec. Leic.* I 74; **1284** ultra .. custumam capit lestagium de .. trosetis de draperio *Law Merch.* III 149; **1302** Johannes dicit se dictum equum in alia forma non vendidisse nisi pro vj m. argenti vel pro vj marcatis ~ie *Ib.* I 88; **c1300** de falsa draperia et de falsis ponderibus fiat idem *Chain Bk. Dublin* 233; **1400** ad melioracionem pannorum et ~ie ibidem conficiendorum et venalium *Mem. York* I 242.

draparius [cf. AN *draper*, OF *drapier*]

1 draper, seller of (woollen) cloth. **b** (w. *lineus*) linen-draper.

1191 Lambertus ~ius debet iiij m. *Pipe* 16; **1240** confirmavi Thome filio Thome filii Ricardi draperii sex domos et gardinum *E. Ch. S. Paul.* 274; **1242** burgus de Suwerc exceptis ~iis et vinitariis r. c. de c s. de fine ante judicium *Pipe* 134 (cf. ib. 203 etc.); **s1270** J. Adrian ~ius Londoniarum major *Ann. Lond.* 80; **1275** reliquerunt fullones, textores, tinctores, ~ii .. et alii hujusmodi menestralli villam Norhamt' *Hund.* II 3 (cf. chirothecarius a); **1302** versus R. de Welburne, civem et ~ium de Norwyco *Law Merch.* I 86 (cf. ib. 87: R. de Welburne, civis et pannarius Norwyci); **s1327** mediam fenestram [nove ecclesie] et magnam supra magnum altare vitrari[i] fecerunt in suis expensis communibus pannarii vel draperii civitatis London' *Mon. Francisc.* I 516; **1447** Ricardus C. draperius civitatis London' .. Johanni S. drapero *Cl* 298 m. 35*d.* **b 1192** David lineo drapero *CurR RC* I cvi; **1260** selda Payn exterius proxima versus aquilonarem; lineus draperius respondet; J. de Abendone manet (*Rental*) *Cart. Osney* III 103.

2 standard-bearer (of Hospitallers).

s1250 vicemagister Hospitalis .. occubuit cum ~io Hospitalis in conflictu ultimo M. PAR. *Maj.* VI 197.

drapeletus [OF *drapelet*], little cloth.

c1258 in ij pannis vel ~is ad caseum et ad lac emptis, iij d. *FormMan Shorwell.*

draper- v. drapar-. **drapis** v. drapa. **drapp-** v. drap-. **draptismus** v. dropacismus.

drasca, ~us, ~um [cf. OF *drasche*]

1 draff, malt dregs; **b** (as food for animals).

audivi .. alium fratrem reprobatum .. quia impeditioris lingue fuerat; de quo dicebatur quod habebat pastum vel draschium in ore suo cum loqui deberet BRAKELOND 124v.; idem est ~a in cervisia quod vinacia in vino O. CHERITON *Fab.* 30a; **1265** pro busca empta ad braciandum apud hospitale [*Dover*] ..; et ~us dimissus fuit in domo ejusdem *Manners* 58; **1289** in expensis braciatorum et coadjuvancium ad brac[iandum], ij s. vj d.; in stipendiis eorundem xvj d. qui pervenerunt de drachia et non cadunt in summam *Ac. Swinfield* 32; **1322** de quolibet bracerio integro ij *tinees* de drasc'. .. de quolibet quarto bracerio integro j *tine* de fec[e]' *DCCant. Reg.* J f. 509; *draffe,* segisterium, ~um *PP*; hoc dragium, A. *draf WW.* **b 1194** de ~o (v. cribrum 2); **1209** in ~o ad equos molindini *Pipe Wint.* 60; **1211** in draschia ad opus equorum *Ib.* 155; lupus invenit in via porcam commedentem ~am O. CHERITON *Fab.* 30a; **s1257** vidimus eos [mendicantes] .. more porcorum devorare dragiam porcis expositam *Lanercost* 65; drache *Ac. Beaulieu* 179 (v. civera d); **1272** in vij summis drachei emptis in ieme ad vij porcos sustinendos *MinAc* (*Norf*) 935/3 m. 2; officium prepositi .. braseum ad braciandum .. pistori deliberari et exitum .., viz. .. draschiam, .. custodi carucarum .. liberare *Fleta* 171; **1312** in drachea pro sustentacione porcorum *LTRAc* (*Templ.*) 19 r. 32*d.*; **1319** in v quar. drachii emptis pro porcis sustinendis *Cuxham* 337.

2 dregs of dye.

1200 non licet tinctoribus pannos suos proprios tingere nisi tantum in waido vel illos vendere nisi waido tinctos vel albos, eo quod, si facerent, proprios pannos tingerent in prima tinctura et meliori, pannos aliorum in ~a *CurR* I 260.

drauca [cf. ME *drauk*, W. *drewg*], (?) wild oats (dist. from 2 *dragetum*).

1297 frumentum: .. summa cxlij quar. j. bus.; inde in semine super cvj acras xxv quar. frumenti, viz. super quamlibet acram ij bus. cum †drenca [l. dreuca] seminata minus in toto de dim. quar. .. †drenca: idem r. c. de ij quar. †drence receptis de toto predicto exitu grangie *Ac. Cornw* I 65–6 (cf. ib. 66: draggetum: idem r. c. de xiij quar. j bus. draggeti ..); **1328** mixtura et *tolcoryn*: .. idem respondet de ij summis v bus. curall' frumenti de supra mixtura ..; et de x summis drauek' receptis de firma molendini *MinAc* (*Kent*) 892/23*d.*; **1339** drauek' .. et aven' empt' pro porcis *BL Add. Roll* (*Suss*) 32136; *drawke, wede*: ~a *PP.*

draul- v. traul-. **drav-, draw-** v. drov-. **dray-** v. drai-. **dregemundus** v. dromo b. **dreia** v. draia. **dreinus** v. drengus.

dreitura [AN *dreiture*, OF *droiture* < directura], right, jurisdiction. *V. et. directura.*

1250 non ememus seu in pignus vel donum recipiemus a vicecomite de Franciaco .. seu et aliis quibuscumque justiciam, ~am seu aliud quicquam ibidem habentibus *V. Montf.* app. 308; **1255** redditus cum exitibus et draituriis *RGasc* I *Sup.* 36.

drenca v. drauca.

drengagium [cf. drengus], drengage service, tenure, or land (N. Eng.).

1179 in quietancia terre Walteri .. xxxij d. de ~io pro vj s., quas annuatim reddit *Pipe* (*Westmorland*) 25; facit quartam partem j dringagii, sc. quod arat iiij acras .. et facit iiij precationes in autumno .. et custodit canem et equum .. et facit *utware* .. *Boldon Bk.* 18; **a1189** faciendo michi .. servicium idem ~ii quod predictus Æ. faciebat *Feod. Durh.* 140*n.*; **1205** inquiri facias .. que serganterie et theynnagia et drengacia et alia servicia et terre que ad nos pertinent fuerint alienata de honore Lanc' post primam coronacionem regis H. patris nostri *Cl* 55a; **1224** de domino rege tenet in capite terram suam [in Northumb'] in drangagio *Ib.* 626b; **c1209** W. de Buterwic tenet B. [*Durh*] hereditarie in drangagium de antiquo tenemento *Fees* 31; **c1211** S. de M. [tenet] unam villam in drennagium (*Northumb*) *RBExch* 564; **1278** R. .. tenuit .. villas de Fenwyk et Matfen [*Northumb*] de .. O. de Insula .. in ~io, quod est certum servicium et non servicium militare; et postea, per convencionem inter predictos R. et O. factam, per servicium c s. per annum et per quoddam servicium forinsecum, viz. cornagium et finem curie, que sunt certa servicia et non servicium militare, pro omnibus aliis serviciis *CoramR* 37 r. 14*d.*; **1307** tenuerunt manerium de Grendon [*Northumb*] de A. quondam rege Scocie .. in dringagio *RParl* I 210a; **1365** faciet alia servicia .. episcopo more ~ii (*IPM Durh*) *EHR* XLI 17; **1517** dicunt juratores .. quod .. servicium drangagii est servicium socagii *JustIt* 129 r. 12.

drengus [AS *dreng*, ON *drengr*], dreng, free tenant (N. Eng. or Scot.; *cf. EHR* XLI 1–42).

hujus manerii [*Newton in Makerfield, Lancs*] aliam terram xv homines quos *drenchs* vocabant pro xv maneriis tenebant; sed hujus manerii bereuuich[i] erant; et inter omnes xxx s. reddebant *DB* I 269v. (cf. ib.: vj *drenghs*); **c1117** David comes .. omnibus suis fidelibus tegnis et ∼is de Lodeneio et Tevegetedale (*Ch. Comitis David*) *E. Ch. Scot.* 30; **1128** dedisse .. terram que fuit Gamel .. et Glassam .. drengnorum meorum reddendo inde michi .. de servicio gabulum animalium sicut alii liberi homines .. qui de me tenent in capite in Cumberlanda *Regesta* 1560; **1130** de tainis et dreinis et smalemannis de inter Tinam et Teisam et de Norhamscira *Pipe* 129; **c1165** Cospatricius comes omnibus probis hominibus theinis et ∼is *Cart. Coldstream* 6; **1169** vic. [*Northumb*] r. c. de lxxj m. de auxilio theinorum et ∼orum *Pipe* 131; **a1171** barones mei et vavassores et milites et *drenges* (*Ch. Conani Com. Richm.*) *MonA* III 550 (cf. *CalPat 1313–17* 556); **1172** honor comitis Conani: .. de firmis maneriorum et de servitio ∼orum *Pipe* 5; ∼us pascit canem et equum quantum ad medietatem dringagii pertinet et vadit in magna caza .. et sequitur placita et vadit in legationibus *Boldon Bk.* 37 (cf. ib. 26: Elstanus ∼us tenuit iiij bovatas); **1188** quia .. non erant adhuc tempore regis Willelmi milites in Anglia, sed *threnges*, precepit rex ut de eis mulites fierent ad terram defendendam. fecit .. Lanfrancus threngos suos milites *Ep. Cant.* 243; **1201** xvij ∼i de Westmeriland' dant domino regi l m. ut remaneant ne transfretent *RObl* 127; **1229** magister S. r. c... de ccccv li. v s. vj d. de tallagio ∼orum, theinorum et villanorum episcopatus [Dunelm'] *Pipe* 73 r. 1a; **1271** (v. bracinagium).

drennagium v. drengagium.

drensare [CL], (of swan) to cry.

to cry, .. olerum †densare *CathA*.

drensitare [cf. drensare], (of swan) to cry.

cicni †desistant .., olores ∼ant ALDH. *PR* 131.

dressare, ∼ere [OF *dresser* < *directiare], to 'dress', set in order, put to rights. **b** (absol.) to prepare food.

1269 in bord[is] in butelria drescend[is] *MinAc* (*Suff*) 994/27; **1388** in vomeribus et cultris ∼andis *Ac. Man. Cant.* (*Lawling, Essex*). **b** **c1310** in panetria: .. j me[n]sa ad ∼andum *LTRAc* (*Templ.*) 19 r. 42*d*.

dressor, ∼orium, ∼erium, ∼ura [OF *dressoir*], dresser: **a** a table for 'dressing' or serving food; **b** room for the same; *cf. directorium* 1a.

a **1289** in j ∼or' et j penticia faciendis ante hostium aule versus coquinam et ante hostium lardar' *Ac. Swinfield* 34 (cf. ib. 124 [**1290**]: in .. bordis ad ∼er'); **1297** magistro [carpentario] emendanti ∼orium constabularii *Ac. Cornw* I 133; **1307** mandavimus per vos provideri .. *bordes* pro drestrariis (*sic*) et aliis pro officio .. J. [scutellarii] necessariis *Cl* 125 m. 12; **1309** in tabulis, trestellis, †∼oris faciendis, xxxiiij s. (*Ac.*) THORNE 2011; **1360** in j cultello empto pro ∼ore in coquina *Sacr. Ely* II 190; **1456** solut' pro uno novo ∼ore in *le slaghows* vij d. ob. *DCCant. Ac. Cellarer* 9/5. **b** **1287** in uno muro inter capellam et ∼uram per partes cooperiendam et emendandam *MinAc* (*Suff*) 991/21; **1289** in una verina reficienda vitri de stauro in ∼io regis *KRAc* 467/20 m. 4; **1304** in splent' emptis ad pariet' †drestur' nov[e] ..; in *brodnail* emptis pro lacchet' tachiand' super dictam domum novam *MinAc* (*Suff*) 999/3; *Ib.* 991/27 (v. cubare 3b); **1306** ad domum dreszure et salsarie de novo faciendam *Ib.* 28; **1338** in iiij bordis emptis pro fenestris ∼ure faciendis (*MinAc*) *Surv. Durh. Hatf.* 203; **1388** in vadiis j tegulatoris operantis super coopertura de novo cujusdam ∼orii et unius gradus per ignem cremat' *KRAc* 473/2 m. 3; **1416** pro bono .. servicio quod dilectus servitor noster J. C. supervisor ad ∼orium nobis impendit *Pat* 399 m. 36.

dreuca v. drauca. **drey-** v. drai-, drei-, dri-. **Drias** v. Dryas.

dribarellus [ME *dri barel*] 'dry-fat', cask for dry goods.

1465 pro custuma unius dreyebarelli mur[velli], j d. (*CourtR Gt. Yarmouth*) *Bronnen* 1550.

drigabulum [ME *dri gabul*], rent, (?) dry-gavel. *Cf. OED s.v.* 'rent-seck'.

1535 villa Oxon': .. redditus resolutus ballivis ville ibidem, pro †langlabull' [l. langabul'] et drigabul' per annum, viij s. vj d. *Val. Eccl.* II 250.

drilingus, drimulvellus [ME *dri ling, dri mulvel*], dried ling and dried cod.

1493 in drylyngis .., in fungiis .., in allecibus et congris recentibus .., in drymillewellis .. *Comp. Swith.* 307.

drimyphagia [LL < δριμυφαγία], acrid diet.

†diamiffragia, id est †accumina *Alph.* 50 (v. acrumen b).

drimys [δριμύς], harsh, acrid (wine).

†dromus, A. *sharp wyn WW*.

drindrare [CL], (of weasel) to cry.

mustelae †dindrant ALDH. *PR* 131; *to cry*, .. mustelarum [est] †drivorare *CathA*.

dringagium v. drengagium. **drion** v. thryon. **drivorare** v. drindrare.

Drocensis, coin of Dreux.

Ascelinus .. dominum suum Guillelmum Bretoliensem bello victum comprehendit. .. mille libras ∼ium ab illo pro redemptione .. extorsit ORD. VIT. V 20 p. 469; *Ib.* V 13 (v. concessio 1a).

drof- v. drove-. **dromad-** v. dromed-.

dromas, dromeda [LL < δρομάς], **∼edus,** dromedary. *V. et. dromedarius* 1b.

dromidus, *afyred olbenda*; dromidarius, *se eorodmon GlC* D 361–2; ∼a, camelus, *olfend ÆLF. Gl.*; sternite cursores, dromedas cursu citiores R. CANT. *Malch.* V 89; dromedarius est ∼edorum vel dramedarum custos BART. ANGL. XVIII 35 (cf. Isid. *Etym.* XII 1. 36); nec mulus Yspanie .. nec ∼edus Arabie .. hoc asino nostro apcior Anglie RIC. ARMAGH *Serm.* (*extr.*) 37; reges Saba et Arabum / Jesu .. / et multitudo dromedum / te querunt, natum puerum LEDREDE *Carm.* 38. 5; *CathA* (v. dromedarius a).

dromedarius [LL; cf. CL dromadarius]

1 a rider or keeper of dromedaries. **b** dromedary; *v. et. dromas*.

a dromidarius *GlC* D 361, BART. ANGL. XVIII 35 (v. dromas); *a dromydary*, dromedus; ∼ius est custos dromedorum et ponitur pro ipso animali *CathA*. **b** dromedariae, castrati cameli, ∼ius unus *Gl. Leid.* 13. 60; est .. ∼ius animal minus camelo, et tamen velocius BELETH *RDO* 73. 79C (cf. M. PAR. *Maj.* I 85); *Itin. Ric.* VI 5 (v. cursorius 2a); vidi .. camelos et ∼ios [v. l. dromadarios] per pascua spaciantes GARL. *Dict* 136; **s1099** †admiravisus, super ∼ium positus, rapido cursu ejus evasit M. PAR. *Maj.* I 106 (cf. WILL. TYR. IX 12); animalia velocissima utpote ∼ios BACON V 154; hic ∼ius, A. *drowmondere WW*.

2 dromond. *Cf. dromo* b.

s1321 [venerunt] duo ∼ii de longinquis partibus versus Angliam cum diversis mercimoniis; et, cum .. Hugo le Despenser exulatus esset a regno Anglie .., contigit quod ipse cum sua ingenti classe dictis dromodariis obviavit .. et dictas naves .. depredavit *Ann. Paul.* 300 (cf. *V. Ed. II* 261: dromonem).

dromedus v. dromas. **dromid-** v. dromas, dromed-.

dromo, ∼on, ∼undus [LL < δρόμων], **a** long ship, light naval vessel. **b** dromond (transport ship); *cf. dromedarius* 2.

a [Hengest et Horsa] advecti sunt cum tribus ∼onibus ÆTHELW. I 3 (cf. cyula); **s875** exiit .. obviam ei [Ælfred] barbara classis, ∼ones ardui numero septem [*AS Chr.*:*vij sciphlæsta*]; pugna init; Dani fugae dant undas; capitur unus ∼on a rege *Ib.* IV 3; ∼o, *æsc* vel *barð* ÆLF. *Sup.*; ∼o, longa navis OSB. GLOUC. *Deriv.* 174. **b** ex navibus .. maximis quarum quaedam dormundi, quaedam .. gulafri .. vocantur, omnibus oneratis .. mercimoniis SÆWULF 838; erant in nostro ∼undo .. cc virorum *Ib.* 852; **s1165** cum cardinales .., ∼onem Hospitalis Jerosolymitani ingressi, dominum papam .. exspectarent, contingit ∼onem a .. classe piratica infestari W. NEWB. *HA* II 17; **s1184** venerunt infinite galee [Saracenorum]. .. ad Ulixibonam et duxerunt unam navem que dicitur *dromund* .. sed .. quidam in aqua se ∼undo subposuit eamque perforavit et perforatam submersit DICETO *YH* II 30; **s1191** rex [Ricardus] .. sponsam suam premisit prima fronte in navibus quas vulgo dicunt ∼ones. .. sunt autem hujusmodi generis naves ex sui gravitate ceteris pigriores, fabrica firmiori *Itin. Ric.* II 26; **s1191** in secundo ordine [classis Ricardi] erant inter naves et buceas et ∼undos xiij (*sic*) DEVIZES 33 p. 35; [Ricardus] ∼undum Saladini .. per galeas .. expugnare .. non cessavit GIR. *PI* III 8 (cf. *Itin. Ric.* II 42); GARL. *Tri. Eccl.* 49 (v. carvanna 1a; cf. *EHR* V 321); **s1291** patriarcha .. et minister Hospitalis, letaliter vulnerati, tracti a suis in ∼undum, .. perierunt RISH. 122; **1321** veniente.. apud *les Dunes* juxta portum de Sandwyco .. Jakemino .. mercatore de Janua cum quadam magna nave vulgariter ∼onda nuncupata, quidam Berengarius, custos quarundam navium .. regis Francie, .. et alii malefactores .. navem predictam .. vi armata ceperunt (*Cl*) *Foed* III 894a; **s1321** Hugo [Despenser] filius .. in grandem navem Januensem, quam vulgo appellant ∼onem, invasit *V. Ed. II* 261 (cf. *Ann. Paul.* 300: dromodariis); ita ut .. Hugo .. ∼ondos cum mercandisis versus Angliam tendentes .. per mare captos spoliaret *Meaux* II 338; **1457** tu habes galeas, nos hissiros, tu classes, nos †dregemundos, tu naves, nos hicticos (*Lit. Soldani*) *Reg. Whet.* I 270; ∼o, A. *a dromond* .., hic †∼edus, *a dromund WW*.

dromod- v. dromed-. **dromundus** v. dromo. **dromus** v. drimys.

dropacismus [LL < δρωπακισμός], (application of) pitch-plaster.

dropax vel †draptismus [v. l. drapacismus], ruptorium idem *Alph.* 51.

dropax [LL < δρῶπαξ], pitch-plaster.

unge tubera cum †∼ate [l. ∼ace] vel unguento de Tartaro GILB. VII 343. 2; cura allopicie: .. due scapule inscindantur et †dropano apposito rumpantur et postea similiter unguantur *Ib.* 344. 1; ∼ax, ruptorium idem *SB* 18.

drova [ME *drave, drove*], drove, drove-way.

c1170 precipio ne vicecomites nec castellani de Notingehama vexent .. monachos in dravis boum *CalCh* III 317 (cf. *RChart* 56a); **c1200** dedit .. terram .. et dravam sub molendino *MonA* (*Mottisfont, Hants*) VI 482b; **1201** inter croftam .. et †dranam [l. dravam] que extendit de P. I. usque ad croftam que vocatur H. *Fines Norf & Suff* 1; **1234** R. filius E. [tenet] unam †foruhtham in campo occidentali, †qui [? l. que] quondam fuit †drana domini *Cust. Glast.* 67; **1260** W. W. tenet j ferlingum .. et fugat drowam *Ib.* 182; **1312** de viij d. novi redditus per annum pro quadam ∼a dimissa *Ac. Man. Cant.* (*Bocking, Essex*); **a1280** abbuctat super mariscum .. et super dravam meam propriam *Terr. Fleet* 77; **1316** idem R. habet liberum introitum et exitum per mediam drawam juxta mesuagium suum ad latitudinem xviij pedum *Ib.* 51; **1375** fecit quandam †dranam vocatam Hasthevedland separalem, quod (*sic*) debet .. esse commune ad homines villatarum de Holbeche et Quappelade [*Lincs*] cum equis, carectis et peditibus, ad nocumentum omnium hominum ibidem transeuncium *Pub. Works* I 275; **1442** abuttantes .. super comunem dravam *Cl* 292 m. 4*d*. (= *Cal.* p. 77: †dranam).

drovedenna, ∼um [ME *droveden*], droveden, 'denn' (*cf.* 1 *denna*) into which beasts were driven for pasturage (Kent).

11.. (14c) concessi .. forestario meo quandam partem terre mee in dravedenna mea que vocatur nemus Evenoth' *AncD* C 2179; **1309** arbores in predictis terris .. crescentes una cum proficuo pannagii racione drovedenn[e] sunt ipsius archiepiscopi (*PlR Ed. II*) *OED* s. v. *droveden*; **1353** remisimus .. omnimodas .. demandas quas .. habuimus racione cujuscunque transgressionis in boscis seu ∼is nostris in villa de Hedecrone *Lit. Cant.* II 316; **1356** dedimus .. manerium nostrum de Heriettesham cum reddit' de Walda, proficuis drofdennarum et omnibus aliis pertinenciis suis *AncD* AS 71.

drovemannus [ME *droveman*], 'droveman', drover (*cf. Cust. Rents* 79).

1285 B. .. tenet circa x acras de *droflond*; et debet cum ij aliis drofmannis fugare omnes districciones factas .. pro aliquo tangente .. archiepiscopum apud Southmallyng ..; et debet fugare animalia que proveniunt de herietto; et debet fugare .. porcos de consuetudine de parroco *Cust. Suss.* II 35 (cf. ib. 79).

droviare [cf. ME *drover* sb.], to act as drover, drive beasts.

1234 Willelmus F. tenet j mesuagium cum curtillagio; .. et debet ∼iare semel in anno versus Glaston' et apud Boclande .. quando opus fuerit *Cust. Glast.* 92.

drowa v. drova.

druchemannus [Ar. *turjumān*], dragoman, interpreter.

1292 lib[erat]' Danesio turchemanno pro ejus servicio [apud Trapesund'] c asper' *KRAc* 308/13 m. 3; ipsius [Soldani] ∼is, id est interpretibus, mediantibus, .. optinuimus liberum aditum .. ad sepulcrum Domini S. SIM. *Itin.* 77; solvimus magno drugemanno pro quolibet homine iiij ducata ..; item j alio drugemanno usque ad civitatem Kaire vj ducata ex omnibus BRYGG *Itin.* 387.

Druides [CL], Druids.

ecclesiae duces, *durcergliis* prisca Scotorum lingua appellatos, qui minoribus sacerdotibus preessent, Romani scriptores ∼es, ut peregrinum vocabulum inflexionem caperet Latinam, appellant BOECE 23.

Dryas [CL < Δρυάς], dryad, wood sprite.

∼ades, *wuduelfen* ÆLF. *Sup.*; cetus Driadum MAP *NC* II 12 (v. alaris a).

drylyngus v. drilingus.

dryopteris [CL < δρυοπτερίς], oak-fern.

exemplum de †diptario, que est herba acerrima, qua gustata attendit os et ferrum a vulnere extrahit, ut dicit Plinius [*HN*] l. xxvij c. xlviij *Spec. Laic.* 19; †briocteris nascitur in locis algosis; radix est ei aspera et stricta, gustu dulcis *Alph.* 27; †diapton, pallipodium idem. G. *polipodie*, A. *†oefarn* [? l. *ocfarn*] *Ib.* 50; †diptericus, quem multi polirizon dicunt, herba est sine flore et sine hasta et sine semine; folia sunt in uno copulo (*sic*) divisa partibus, gustu stiptica; nascitur in locis saxosis et asperis *Ib.* 51*n*.

drys [LL < δρῦς], oak.

sideritis .. folia habet .. oblonga sicut elilifagus aut †ynos [= Diosc. IV 33: δρυός] *Alph.* 170.

dua v. duo.

dualis [CL], relating to two. **b** (gram.) dual. **c** (w. *dentes*) middle incisor teeth. **d** (as sb.) 'doubler' (large dish).

dialectica, ∼is dictio *GlC* D 259. **b** numeri pronominum sunt duo: singularis, ut 'hic'; pluralis, ut 'hii'; item ∼is secundum quosdam, ut 'duo, uterque, ambo' BONIF. *AG* 492; dividunt numerum in tres partes Greci, in

singularem, ~em et [pluralem] numerum, tribus inflexionibus utentes *Ps.*-GROS. *Gram.* 40. **c** supra sunt duo dentes qui vocantur '~es'; et correspondent duo oppositi inferius; et ex utraque parte sunt duo qui vocantur quadrupli; et sunt omnes isti incisivi GAD. 118v. 1. **d** *a dublar*, ~is et cetera, ubi *a dische CathA.*

dualitas [LL]

1 duality, 'twoness'; **b** (theol.); **c** (mus.).

ad unitatem addita unitas [? l. unitate] ~as procreatur BART. ANGL. XIX 113; ~as ab unitate descendit BACON *Maj.* II 411; quantitas discreta, sc. unitas et ~as *Ps.*-GROS. *Summa* 311; principiare necessario et principiare contingenter sunt oppositi modi principiandi; et tamen hec ~as reducitur ad unitatem DUNS *Ord.* II 311; impossibile est duas ~ates esse aliquorum duorum simul; essent enim quatuor SICCAV. *PN* 117; postquam multiplicatur facies in ~atem in eadem intelligentia non est inconveniens multiplicare trinitatem BACONTHORPE *Quaest. Sent.* 6E. **b** ne dicatur ~as majestatis in Christo, in quo est unitas individuae personae ALCUIN (*Adv. Felicem*) *Dogm.* 181B; **1237** si ~atis sensum circa eucaristie sacramentum vester diversus a nostro ritus inducit (*Lit. Papae*) M. PAR. *Maj.* III 468; tantum esset imago ~atis, non trinitatis DUNS *Ord.* III 342. **c** de brevibus imperfectis, si tres semibreves vel plures, ita quod unitas transit ~atem, inveniatur .. semibrevis subsequens brevem ad eam pertinet HAUBOYS 432a.

2 (?) two thirds.

1546 vendidit .. terras ~atis unius caruce, vulgariter *the twa pairt of ane pleuch* de ly Northtoun de Ardwyne *RMS Scot* 3267.

duar- v. doarium. **dubarius** v. dubbarius.

dubbare [ME *dubben*], to 'dub', dress (cloth or hide).

in lana ~anda, v s. *Ac. Beaulieu* 166; **1288** Alanus de R. habet truncos fullonis et ~at pannos *Leet Norw.* 12 (= *Rec. Norw.* I 360*n.*); **1300** de tannatoribus, quia faciunt falsitatem in opere, viz. ~ant coria bovina in fraudem .. populi .. *Ib.* 50; **1313** (v. divertere 4b).

dubbaria, dubbing (of cloth).

de hiis qui duobus utuntur officiis, viz. sutorie et tannerie vel tannerie et carnificis vel officio scissoris et dubberie *Fleta* 113.

dubbarius [ME *dubber*], dubber (of cloth).

c1200 his testibus: .. Salomone dubario *AncD* A 7826.

dubbatio, dubbing (of cloth).

in ~one gardus' non habet dubbator nisi unum pagium *Ac. Beaulieu* 163.

dubbator, dubber (of cloth or hides).

hanc liberacionem ~or lane dum lanam nostram preparat cotidie solet recipere *Ac. Beaulieu* 295; **1288** omnes ~ores de correo vaccino faciunt falsitatem in opere suo *Leet Norw.* 13.

dubberia v. dubbaria. **dubbl-** v. dupl-.

dubie [CL], doubtfully, ambiguously.

suspensi, ~ie cogitantes *GlC* S 606; est de talibus ~ie disputare contingens BALSH. *AD* 46; *Ps.*-GROS. *Gram.* 69 (v. dilucidus d); aliter dicitur quod sunt duo conceptus propinqui, tamen et propter istam propinquitatem videntur esse unus conceptus, et videtur certus de 'uno', hoc est de illis duobus [conceptibus] ~ie conceptis, dubius autem de illis duobus distincte conceptis DUNS *Ord.* IV 179.

dubietas [LL], doubt, uncertainty; **b** (w. gen. of matter in doubt). **c** moot point, question at issue.

testimonia .. vera ac sine scrupulo ~atis suscipienda BEDE *Mark* 134; [Christus] qui ab eorum [discipulorum] pectoribus adtactu sui corporis vulnus amputavit ~atis EGB. *Pont.* 67; ut nulla te de credendis hiis quae audisti ~as attingat OSB. *V. Dunst.* 17; **c1090** infrunitum est .. quod supra firmam petram .. fundatum est in nutantium quaestionum revocare ~atem ANSELM (*Ep.* 136) III 280; nulla de his ~ate fluctuare permittimur EADMER *Wilf.* 57; ad hec credenda .. veneranda illius vita ad omnem ~atis caliginem detergendam proficit DOMINIC *V. Ecgwini* II 52; **1285** ne de premissis possit ~as suboriri *RGasc* II 250; **1341** nolentes .. negocium propter hujusmodi ~ates taliter retardari *Mem. Ripon* I 220; **1400** omnes et singulas †dubitates [MS: dubietates], ambiguitates et obscuritates in quibusdam treugis (*TreatyR*) *Foed.* VIII 132b. **b** **s1049** propter ~atem eventus, litem .. periculosum arbitratus est .. publice contestari *Chr. Rams.* 170; **c1218** ad episcopum semper referatur omnis matrimonii ~as *Conc. Syn.* 85. **c** **1369** propter ~atem inter .. abbatem .. et dominum J. .. decidendam .. super .. concessiones regis eis factas *ExchScot* 324.

dubiosus [CL], involved in doubt.

s1461 Martis ut eventum fore scire sic dubiosum (*Vers.*) *Reg. Whet.* I 395.

dubitabilis [CL], open to doubt.

vera loquor, quamvis fatum dubitabile fingam TATWINE *Aen.* 37 (*De seminante*) 1; indecens esse reputans de beata matre Dei quid ~e in laudem ejus recitari EADMER *Excell. B. M.* 560B; quare moriantur homines mihi ~e est ADEL. *QN* 43; sunt ~ia sapienti que nec fidei nec sensus aut rationis manifeste persuadet auctoritas J. SAL. *Pol.* 640B; an ut de utroque separatim an ut de duobus simul .. sic enuntietur ~e est BALSH. *AD* 47; quandoque ~e fuit utrum venirent .. P. BLOIS *Ep.* 101. 312C; jam oportet dicere aliqua ~ia et ea determinare KILWARDBY *OS* 79; questio ~is est propositio ut 'curritne Socrates vel non?' BACON XV 195.

dubitalis, open to doubt.

dubiorum vel ~ium judicia que frequenter emergunt sub una tractatus serie comprehendi non valent *Dial. Scac.* I 4 C.

dubitamen, doubt.

magnum cum sit dubitamen in actu H. AVR. *Poems* 2. 82.

dubitare [CL]

1 to doubt; **b** (w. acc. & inf. or *quod*); **c** (w. indir. qu.); **d** (w. *quin*).

quicunque de baptismo suo ~averit baptizetur THEOD. *Pen.* II 9. 3; vir de amara morte nihil ~ans .. vocavit .. S. Cuðberhtum *V. Cuthb.* II 8; ut .. lectoribus hujus historiae occasionem ~andi subtraham BEDE *HE pref.* p. 6; **796** ~antium (v. confortatio 2); de talibus .. nichil scire quam ~are contingentius [est], ~are quam statim scire putare eruditius BALSH. *AD* 27; **1213** de quibus ne possit in posterum †debutar [l. dubitari] .. presentem cartam nostram facimus sigillari *RChart* 195a; ignorantes an sit, incipimus ~are. habito quidem quod sit per dubitacionem, admiramur propter quid et querimus causam *Ps.*-GROS. *Gram.* 59; an omnis qui dicit opinando vel ~ando heresim .. sit statim hereticus reputandus OCKHAM *Pol.* III 51; *Ib.* 57 (v. dubitatio b). **b** quos ipse sanctos esse non ~ans, .. eorum .. disciplinam sequi non desisto BEDE *HE* III 25 p. 187; nec .. ~andum est quod [divina clementia] .. animarum nostrarum egrotationes .. exaudire non cessat ALCUIN *WillP* 30; PULL. *Sent.* 803C (v. discredere 1b); W. CANT. *Mir. Thom.* II 38 (v. collocutio a); Deum esse vix insipiens ~at BART. ANGL. I 5. **c** ~avit .. quis ille esset G. MON. XII 7; **1219** (v. deducere 2a); ~abit aliquis quomodo dicatur quod [grammatica] docet congrue significare KILWARDBY *OS* 486; ~o utrum sit determinate hoc ens .. vel illud ens DUNS *Ord.* IV 184; ~antibus cunctis an ad Lesclus vel quorsum alias [caraca] proras verteret *G. Hen. V* 24. **d** de quo ~andum non crediderim quin .. sit .. retentus BEDE *HE* III 23; si .. Romam adire volueris, non ~o quin triumpho potiamur G. MON. IX 17; AD. SCOT *Serm.* 304B (v. discredere 1c); AD. MARSH *Ep.* 100 (v. dignificare 1a).

2 (p. ppl.): **a** doubted, held to be a matter of doubt. **b** doubtful, troubled by doubt.

a error tali veritati contrarius prius assertus, opinatus vel eciam ~atus est verbis expressis .. negandus et revocandus OCKHAM *Pol.* III 69. **b** nunc id, nunc aliud, dubitata mente revolvi GOWER *VC* 1561.

3 (w. inf.) to hesitate.

non ~avit promittere quin .. responderet BEDE *HE* II 12; ~avit Occa resistere G. MON. VIII 8; ut vivat, dubitat perdere nemo fidem *Babio* 308; **1184** rex .. precepit bene forestariis suis .. quod .. non ~ent in eos [clericos] manum ponere (Ass. Forestae) *G. Hen. II* II clxiii.

4 to fear: **a** (trans.); **b** (w. inf.). **c** (w. acc. & inf. or *quod*, sts. refl.) to fear or suspect (that). **d** (w. *de*) to have fear or suspicion of.

a **1169** (v. appretiare 2c); **1241** [dominus] R. de Ros, quando wlt, currit in foresta regis cum canibus propriis et .. adducit secum plur[es] de malefactoribus prenominatis .., unde forestarii minus ~antur a transgressoribus foreste in omnibus *CurR* XVI 1487; [Saxones] usi arborum auxilio tela Britonum minus ~abant *Eul. Hist.* II 311 (= G. MON. IX 3: tela .. vitabant); **s1210** monachi, maliciam regis ~antes .., in partibus transmarinis aufugerunt *Ib.* III 97; **s1402** hoc fecerunt ~antes revelacionem dicte suggestionis *Plusc.* X 17. **b** ~abat sensu privari *Mir. Montf.* 93; **s1212** rex regnum amittere ~ans *Eul. Hist.* III 101; pars rectoris .., ~ans in posterum forcius posse ledi et gravari *FormOx* 469. **c** **1209** (v. deperdere 1a); Alicia .. inflaturam sustinens, per quam ~abatur eam morte subitanea extingui *Mir. Montf.* 89; **1293** ~avit quod .. Douenaldus vellet ire contra regem ad guerram *RParl Ined.* 36; **1411** Johannes et Reginaldus se ~ant quod .. prior .. eis inpugnare .. voluerit *FineR* 216 m. 9; **1418** cum .. tu ~es provisionem .. ecclesie .. fuisse disposicioni apostolice reservatam (*Lit. Papae*) *Reg. Cant.* I 54. **d** **1308** ~atur de fraude inter eos prelocuta *Year Bk. I Ed. II* 14; **1321** ~avit de attachiamento corporis sui (*Inq. Coron.*) *DocCOx* 171; **s1342** (v. consequentia 2a).

dubitas v. dubietas a.

dubitatio [CL], doubt, uncertainty; **b** (theol.); **c** (rhet.).

legebam .. legislatorem ob unius verbi ~onem terram desiderabilem non introiisse GILDAS *EB* 1; sine ~onis scrupulo ALDH. *Met.* 10 p. 84; **770** absque ~one constat *CS* 203; ANSELM I 25 (v. deducere 5a); qualiter rerum istarum .. memoria .. retenta fuerit .. non indignum videtur ~one GIR. *TH* III 1; **1213** si super ceteris capitulis fuerint †debitatores [l. ~ones] suborte de quibus merito valeat dubitari *RChart* 193b; est ~o circa contrarie opposita et est ~o circa proposita non accidencia *Ps.*-GROS. *Gram.* 57; tunc est ~o quo objecto peccans mortaliter fruitur, sc. an actu suo an objecto sui actus DUNS *Ord.* II 117 (cf. ib. III 92: de nullo .. simpliciter simplici conceptu potest esse certitudo secundum aliquid ejus et ~o secundum aliud); **1579** cujus [questionis] ambigua et ~ones dum .. enucleaverint .. *StatOx* 345. **b** [est] triplex ~o vel nescientia .. infidelitatis, que fuit in Judeis; vel tarditatis, que fuit in discipulis euntibus in Emmaus .. [cf. *Luke* xxiv 25]; vel amoris sive pietatis [cf. ib. vii 19 seqq.] HALES *Sent.* III 307; forte dicet aliquis quod nulli catholico licet dubitare de aliquo spectante ad fidem, quia certitudo et ~o de eodem se non possunt compati in eodem OCKHAM *Pol.* III 57. **c** ~o est quando dubitamus de duobus utrum vel de pluribus quid eorum velimus dicere, ut hic: 'tu mihi te confers, homo—quo te nomine dicam? / nescio: si dicam "spurcissime", non erit equum ..' VINSAUF *CR* 324.

dubitative [LL], doubtfully, tentatively.

quod dominus vineae ~e et deliberativo modo loqui dicitur BEDE *Luke* (xx 13) 576; clarebat circumquaque .. fulgor .., monstrans de eo nil ~e quem Deus sic munificaret celico lumine HERM. ARCH. 1; non est certum ex intencione Philosophi quod posuerit aliquam aliam vitam, quia in diversis locis .. videtur loqui ~e DUNS *Metaph.* II 3. 103; glossa .. ~e loquitur, dicens: 'forte Valerius cessit administracioni Augustini' OCKHAM *Dial.* 815; **1428** objectis eidem .. articulis diversis, ad quos omnes ficte et †dubitive ac semper quasi ridendo .. respondebat *Reg. Cant.* III 188 (= *Conc.* III 493b: dubitative).

dubitativus [LL], **a** (gram.) expressive of doubt. **b** doubtful, hesitant.

'aut' conjunctio ~am, si geminetur, habet potestatem; qui dicit 'aut librum volo aut pretium' utrumque ex aequo desiderare significat BONIF. *AG* 541; sunt quoque conjunctiones ~ae, ut 'ne', '†nec' [? l. necne], 'anne' ALCUIN *Gram.* 896A; quando ad neutram partem magis inclinatur, ut 'dubito an Socrates currat', aufert quidem inclinacionem a verbo ~o, et ob hoc verbis subjunctivis apponuntur ~a *Ps.*-GROS. *Gram.* 57; ~ae [sc. conjunctiones] sunt quas ibi adhibemus ubi de duobus dubitamus, ut 'ne', 'an', 'anne', 'num' LINACRE *Emend. Lat.* 34. **b** **c1430** cujus causacionis motivum eo magis arguitive ~a patris opinio formaverat in alumnum quo .. *Reg. Whet.* II app. 453; *dowtfulle*, ambiguus .., dubius .., dubitans, ~us, hesitativus .. *CathA.*

dubitator, doubter or (?) *f. l.*

absque †dubitatoris [? l. dubitacionis] scrupulo ad imperatorem .. videtur causa matrimonialis .. pertinere OCKHAM *Pol.* I 280.

dubitive v. dubitative.

dubius [CL]

1 (of person or mind) doubtful, hesitant.

quamvis .. / .. fidem dubio gestaret corde sinistram ALDH. *CE* 4. 6. 6; **a798** (v. dissimulare 2a); **a1075** de hac .. ~ius fui LANFR. *Ep.* 3; solum verum vel falsum ~ium qui dubitat ~ius [est] BALSH. *AD* 52 (v. et. 3 infra); omnis intellectus certus de uno conceptu et ~ius de diversis habet conceptum de quo est certus alium a conceptibus de quibus est ~ius DUNS *Ord.* III 18; *Ib.* IV 179 (v. dubie); ne foret ultra dubius /—resurexit Dominus—/ Thomas .. / palpavit Christi vulnera LEDREDE *Carm.* 20. 27.

2 of doubtful authority, questionable.

cujus ordinem miraculi non quilibet ~ius relator sed fidelissimus mihi .. presbyter .. narravit BEDE *HE* III 15; regnum illud .. reges ~ii vel externi disperdiderunt *Ib.* IV 24 p. 268;

3 (of concept or proposition) doubtful. **b** (w. *haud* or *non* in parenthesis) no doubt, doubtless.

fide non ~ia GILDAS *EB* 70; ut nulli esset ~ium quin ipsa lux .. locum .. monstraret BEDE *HE* IV 7; si falsa et ~ia hoc modo intelliguntur ANSELM (*Resp. Ed.* 6) I 136; BALSH. *AD* 52 (v. 1 supra); *Dial. Scac.* I 4 C (v. dubitalis); de conceptu uno certo et duobus ~iis DUNS *Ord.* IV 178. **b** ipse erat, haud dubium, presul venerabilis ipse / tempore nocturno tibi qui comparuit WULF. *Swith.* II 1035; **1391** vestra nobilis discrecio, non ~ium, satis novit quod .. *Pri. Cold.* 68.

4 (as sb. n.) doubt, uncertainty; **b** (w. prep.).

animalia coitu hominum pulluta occiduntur ..; ubi autem ~ium est, non occidantur THEOD. *Pen.* II 11. 9; *Ps.*-GROS. *Gram.* 69 (v. dilucidus d); non .. determinavit Petrus supradicta ~ia circa fidem de plenitudine potestatis OCKHAM *Dial.* 847; remanet adhuc apud quosdam unum magnum ~ium in differencia inter istam crucem fimbriatam .. et crucem umbratam UPTON 221 (cf. ib.: tunc nullum est ~ium); **1556** illum benigne audiant, difficultatibusque et ~iis sibi motis respondeant *StatOx* 374. **b** procul ~io mortuo Deo, vitiis vero viventi GILDAS *EB* 72; palmam .. quam procul ~io .. percipere merebitur ALDH. *VirgP* 18; sine ~io credendum est quod .. CUTHB. *Ob. Baedae* clxvi; **948** se proculdubio ante tribunal .. rationem redditurum *CS* 869; **956** hus fugitivis et sine ~io transitoriis possessiunculis *Ib.* 978; absque ~io vult ANSELM (*Lib. Arb.* 8) I 220; **c1170** etc. in ~ium (v. devocare 2a); **1325** in ~ium vertitur apud multos si .. ordinem suum .. mutare desiderat ex pura devocione .. vel alia quavis occasione *Lit. Cant.* I 161; **s1460** dum populus fluctuaret taliter sub ~io *Reg. Whet.* I 376.

dubl- v. et. dupl-. **dublera, ~um** v. duplarius.

dublettus, ~a, ~um [AN *dublet*, OF *doblet*; cf. duplus]

1 doublet (garment); **b** (worn as armour). *Cf. diplois, duplicium, dupliteca.*

1349 ad faciend' ij doublettos pro rege de panno viridi longo frettat' cum *rubanttz* stuffat' cum tela de Reyns (*KRAc* 391/15) *Arch.* XXXI 44 (cf. ib. 45: ij doublettos frounciatos); **1398** detinuit unum dubletum precii viij s. et unam togam longam precii xx s. *Reg. Burgh Aberd.* I 371; **1417** lego omnes alias togas et ~as, ut inter servientes meos .. dividantur *Reg. Cant.* II 125; **s1419** stipendiarii tam castri quam civitatis permissi sunt abire in suis ~is *Chr. S. Alb.* 122. **b 1336** ~a cum platis (v. armatura b); **1406** ad numerum x personarum modo guerrino arraiatarum et armatarum, viz. loricis, palettis, doublettis de defenso .. *Pat* 375 m. 27; **1442** volo quod dupletum meum †de fensi [l. defensi] vendatur *Test. Ebor.* II 85.

2 'doublet' (counterfeit jewel; but *cf. Building in Eng.* 167).

1245 ubi fuit kamacu [sc. in morsu cape] appositus est modo lapis rubeus ~us *Invent. S. Paul.* 478 (cf. ib. 479: dubletus rubeus); **1300** justa argenti deaurat' nigell' cum ~is *AcWardr* p. 342 (cf. ib. p. 344: zona magna de serico cum apparatu et lapid' dublett'); **1355** magistro Hugoni pro lx doublett' emptis pro ymag[inibus] B. Marie *KRAc* 502/17.

3 cask of double size. *Cf. duplarius* 2a.

1300 pro lxvij doliis, ij ~is et xix pipis vacuis emptis ad farinam imponendam *AcWardr* p. 110 (cf. ib. 115: r. c. .. de lvij doleis, ij duplectis et xxj pipis floris receptis); **1332** (v. 2 casta).

4 due paid by tin-miners (Cornw).

1296 stagnaria: .. de xj s. viij d. doublett' de Kerrier *Ac. Cornw* II 248; **1298** r. c. de cviij s. de fine stagminis per annum et de xj s. viij d. de dobletto de Kerr' per annum *MinAc* 811/1 m. 2.

duca [LL *gl.*], form, mould.

moolde, forme, ~a *PP*; ~a, A. *a leste or a molde WW*; *a form*, forma .., formella, ~a .. *a mulde to cast in*, ~a, formula, †effegies .. *CathA.*

ducalis [LL]

1 a belonging to a ruler or commander. **b** belonging to a duke, ducal.

a denique collectim censura urgente ducali / synodus astruitur FRITH. 1065; adeo belli cupidus .. ut, militi dux prefectus, ~i plerumque deserta constantia, ducem exuens et militem induens, .. impetuosus et preceps .. victoriam amisisse videretur GIR. *EH* II 18. **b s1053** crebrescente fama Arcensis victorie .. non leve incrementum accessit ~is [sc. Willelmi] glorie W. MALM. *GR* III 232; **1385** pro statu suo ~i decencius sustinendo *RParl* III 205b; **1423** privilegiis .. a quibuscunque personis .., eciamsi pontificali, imperiali, ~i aut alia quacumque .. prefulgeant dignitate, concessis vel concedendis, non obstantibus (*Ord. Concilii Senensis*) AMUND. I 167; **s1460** [dux Eboracensis] ostiis apertis, more regio pocius quam ~i, hospitabatur .. ibidem *Reg. Whet.* I 377; **1486** (v. comitalis).

2 (as sb. n.) leading rein.

~e, *latteh* ÆLF. *Sup.*

ducamen

1 guidance. *V. et. ductamen.*

visus maxime destituebatur officio et ab horis vespertinis indigebat ~ine G. CRISPIN *Herl.* 104.

2 duchy.

non reddetur Rainerius [dux Hainaucensis] tibi .., nisi .. mihi .. dederis quicquid auri est et argenti sui ~inis W. JUM. II 8 (cf. ib.: vectigal illius ~inis).

3 moulding, kneading. *Cf. duca.*

mooldyng of paste, pistura, ~en *PP.*

1 ducata, duchess.

s1297 Margareta filia regis Anglie et ~a Brabancie *Chr. S. Edm.* 64.

2 ducata v. 2 ducatus a.

ducator [LL < CL = *pilot*], guide.

presbyter qui .. nescit ministerium suum .. caecus ~or est ÆLF. *Ep.* 2. 158.

1 ducatus [CL]

1 guidance (in travelling); **b** (of infirm or blind). **c** escort or safe-conduct; **d** (under compulsion). **e** aid to movement, vehicle.

deos sibi fieri, qui eremitice eis vie ~um preberent, exposcunt [cf. *Exod.* xxxii 1] ÆLNOTH *Cnut* 32; [stella] magos .. novo et inaudito ~u perduxit J. SAL. *Pol.* 409A; duces .. fatuitatis argumentabatur .., quod instante nocte se sic inter hostes ingererent absque ~u et cujuscunque tuitione *Itin. Ric.* VI 31; **s1238** ~u eorum qui vada secretiora noverunt .. amnem .. transivit M. PAR. *Maj.* III 483. **b** alieno fulta ducatu, / non proprio veni NIG. *SS* 3349; cum .. unus precedens oculis viris [cecis] septem ~um prestaret AILR. *Ed. Conf.* 777A; SAMSON *Mir. Edm.* I 1 (v. 1 credere 1c); elemosinario decani .. ~um ei [mulieri cece] prebente GIR. *Hug.* III 3. **c 1158** ~um vobis dantes a mare usque ad regem (*Lit. Archiep. Cant.*) *Ep. J. Sal.* 101 (38); **s1179** (v. conducere 1d); **s1213** (v. 2 conductus 1c); **1244** ita quod [heres] sub ~u ejusdem W... regi mittatur *Cl* 177; quod .. sui novicii .. non debeant .. absque illius [magistri] ~u aut noticia .. a claustro egredi *Cust. Westm.* 94. **d 1472** ne abbas .. permittat quod aliquis ipsius professus ballivi vel forestarii officium .. vel eciam arestacionem vel ~um secularium .. exerceat *Melrose* II 577. **e** cum humor ille non nutrimentum sit corporis, sed tantum modo ~us cibi ADEL. *QN* 10.

2 guidance (in conduct or belief); **b** (afforded by abstr. guide).

praevium populis ~um praebens, portam domini Dei .. ipse .. aperuit WILLIB. *Bonif.* 3 p. 11; a cujus [demonii] dominatione et ~u citius interibit nisi .. ALEX. CANT. *Mir.* 19 p. 218; quidam homines [Galwadie] .., si fuerint in domo quavis regulari constituti, redduntur admodum religiosi, aliorum tamen consilio et ~u W. DAN. *Ailred* 38; sacerdos etiam dicitur 'sacer dux', quia verbo et exemplo ~um ad vitam populo prebere debet GIR. *PI* I 19 p. 112; pastor debet singulis prebere ~um sciencia .., similiter et vite sanctitate OCKHAM *Dial.* 798; [prelatus] facillime peccare poterit in ~u hujusmodi gregis sui WYCL. *Apost.* 18; **1438** quid est quod mulier [sc. ecclesia] vestre custodie deputata non parit .. nisi quia ducibus indoctis commissa ~um perdidit? *Conc.* III 530a. **b** [vir bonus] natam bonitatem accumulat, scientia scripturarum per omnia prestante ~um PULL. *Sent.* 854C (cf. ib. 865C: absque ~u rationis); nature ~u ALF. ANGL. *Cor* 7. 2; benignus est spiritus sapientie, cui et verborum nostrorum et sensuum ~um committimus J. FORD *Serm.* 3. 1; PECKHAM *QR* 47 (v. coexsistentia); propitius sit mihi celestis consilii ~us AD. MARSH *Ep.* 12.

3 leadership, command, governance; **b** (divine). **c** (astr.) 'influence'.

sicut Moyses ad ~um Israheliticae plebis ab ipso Domino electus *Hist. Abb. Jarrow* 6; Neemias .. ita in ~u vivebat ut 'annonas quae ducibus debebantur ipsi non comederent' [*Nehem.* v 14; cf. ib. 18] BEDE *Ezra* 900; rex Orientalium Saxonum, qui .. eidem suae genti ~um praebebat *Id. HE* II 5; **10..** ~um, *ladscipe WW*; tres .. †civile [vv. ll. cuille, chiule, i.e. cyule] .., quibus .. Horsus et Hengistus ~um †prerabant [v. l. prestabant] G. MON. VI 10; **s1237** rex .. destinavit .. comitem Cornubie .. cum quibusdam aliis magnatibus .. sub ~u .. archiepiscopi Ebor' et episcopi Elyensis M. PAR. *Maj.* III 393; cum [talis] ad regimen plebis et ~um populi preficiatur, timendum est ne relicta Terra Promissionis .. in Egiptum revertatur *V. Ed. II* 253. **b** [Andreas] perfecte conditoris sui ~um sequitur, qui etiam proximi [Simonis] .. habere comitatum nititur BEDE *Hom.* I 16. 258; quam strenue pugnat hic miles Christi sub tuo ~u ANSELM (*Or.* 15) III 63. **c** coagulata et compressa pro ~u Saturni materia, sistitur spiritus. .. Martis vero ~us fluxa consolidat. sol suo ~u formarum essentias .. imprimit ALF. ANGL. *Cor* 13. 2.

4 (Continental): **a** dukedom. **b** duchy.

a s1026 dux Normannorum .. Ricardus tertius .. primo anno ~us sui mortuus est DICETO *Chr.* 173; **s1199** [comes Johannes] accinctus est gladio ~us Normannie in matrici ecclesia per manum W. Rothomagensis archiepiscopi R. HOWD. IV 87 (cf. circulus 4d); dum .. [Johannes] intra sacra missarum solemnia ~us susciperet insignia, cum .. ei daret archiepiscopus lanceam in manus, vexillum preferentem quo duces Neustrie honoris sui investituram solebant percipere AD. EYNS. *Hug.* V 11 p. 144; **1200** ecclesiam Rothom' super omnes alias Norm' venerari debemus .., sicut illam unde ~us nostri honorem accepimus *RChart* 69b. **b s927** (v. dux 3b); **s1016** [uxor Edelredi] fuerat filia Ricardi [II] comitis Normannie .., qui .. lij annis illi ~ui prefuit W. MALM. *GR* II 165; **1131** me Henrico in Anglia regnante et Normanorum ~um tenente *Regesta* 1698; **s1012** mortuo Ottone duce Lotharingie, datur ~us comiti Godefrido R. NIGER *Chr. I* 81; hec est causa quare Willielmus Bastardus jus hereditarium ~us Brittanie Minoris sibi competere dicebat *Id. Chr. II* 153; **s1183** [Henricus II] Ricardo filio in administrando ~u Aquitannico suas vices commiserat W. NEWB. *HA* III 7; principes et barones .. populum subjectum confundunt bellis et exactionibus .., quibus nititur (*sic*) aliena rapere, etiam ~us et regna BACON *CSPhil.* 399; regina [Margareta] cum subole sua .. in ~u Barrenni [*Bar*] .. morabantur (*sic*) FORTESCUE *LLA intr.*; **1489** in oppido Antwerpensi parcium ~us Brabancie *Reg. Brechin* app. 131.

5 (Eng.): **a** (pre-Conquest) office or territory of *ealdorman* or sim. **b** (post-Conquest) earldom. **c** (post-Conquest) duchy.

a 812 ut .. [terra] ab omni opere puplico aedificiorum aut in quolibet ~u perenniter libera frueretur *CS* 341; ~us, *ealdordom* ÆLF. *Sup.*; **c1000** cum [Ælfric] in ~u suo contra me .. reus existeret *CD* 1312; antequam idem dux [Tostinus] ejusdem regionis ~u ex dono regis potiretur *V. Ed. Conf.* 51; Cassibellanus .. urbem Trinovantum cum ~u Cantie largitus est Androgeo, ~um vero Cornubie †Tenuancie [v. l. Tenuancio] G. MON. III 20; **s1016** audiens dux Eadricus sese a ~u Merciorum spoliatum M. PAR. *Maj.* I 500. **b s1153** obiit .. Ranulfus II .. comes Cestrie, cui successit .. Hugo II, qui prefuit in ~u illo xxix annis HIGD. VII 20 p. 20. **c s1337** rex primogenitum suum E. ducem Cornubie nominavit eidemque ~um Cornubie dedit *G. Ed. III Bridl.* 129; **1397** patruum nostrum .. in ducem ereximus, eidem ~us Gloucestr' titulum assignantes et nomen *RParl* III 206a; **1399** in ~u nostro Lancastrie .. talia .. libertates, jura regalia .. et franchesie .. in perpetuum .. continuentur (*Ch. Regis*) *MGL* II 487; **1415** arbitrio Johannis W. ~us Lancastrie cancellarii *Croyl. Cont. B* 506.

2 ducatus, ~um [It. *ducato*], ducat (gold coin); **b** (of papal camera).

1392 pro naulo xvj ~a apud Alexandriam BRYGG *Itin.* 387; **1419** legavit A. H. clerico suo .. c ~os solvendos .. in Florencia *Reg. Cant.* II 181; **1426** de modica illa provisione, viz. xx †~arum per annum *Conc.* III 475b; **1443** solus habebitis disposicionem m ~orum et ad priscos ccc ~os jam adjecti sunt in banco Alexandri de P. alii ccc ~i in idem negocium, si opus fuerit, exponendi BEKYNTON I 186; **1514** x ~os majores, quorum quilibet valet x ~os usuales *Scot. Grey Friars* II 225; marcha .. apud Anglos tres valet aureos numos, quos vulgo ~os vocant P. VERG. X 166. **b 1432** (v. camera 7c); **1466** habuit a me xix ~os papales *Pri. Cold.* 209.

ducella, little duchess.

a duches, ducissa, ~ella diminutivum *CathA.*

ducellus v. duciculus. **ducena** v. dozena a.

ducenarius [LL], prefect.

~ius, praeses *GlC* D 371; ducennarium, presidem *Gl. Leid.* 35. 282.

ducendandum v. ducere 8a.

ducentenarius, lasting 200 years.

1150 ~iam possessionem ecclesie nostre, viz. Stevechewrðe, .. sibi vendicare non veritus (*Lit. ad Papam*) *Lib. Eli.* III 97.

ducentenus [CL *distributive only*], **a** (pl.) two hundred. **b** two-hundredth. **c** (as sb. (?) f.) two hundredweight.

a GARL. *Tri. Eccl.* 134 (v. connumerare 2a); **s1346** Franci .. gregatim per centenos et ~os inter Anglicos .. inciderunt *Meaux* III 59; **s1399** in ejus [Henrici] exercitu ultra ~a milia universorum plures pravorum quam bonorum fuisse referuntur *Dieul.* 144v.; **s1435** numero plusquam ~a millia armatorum *Plusc.* XI 7 (= FORDUN *Cont.* XVI 26: ducenta milia). **b s1270** anno milleno Domini cum septuageno / atque ducenteno, Carolo sub rege sereno (*Vers.*) *Flor. Hist.* III 22. **c 1222** faciatis habere N. de C. servienti nostro ducent[enam] cere ad opus nostrum *Cl* 485b.

ducentesimus [CL], two-hundredth.

s731 anno adventus Anglorum in Brittaniam circiter ~o octogesimo quinto BEDE *HE* V 23; olimpiade, i. .. ~a sexagesima septima *GlN* 1. 3036; **1299** anno gracie [millesimo] ~o nonogesimo nono *Deeds Balliol* 104.

ducenti [CL], two hundred.

Britannia insula .. milium ~orum in lato spatium .. tenens GILDAS *EB* 3; servos et ancillas ~os [v. l. ~as] quinquaginta BEDE *HE* IV 13; si andras in primo arcu statuatur .. significat .. duo, si in secundo .. xx, si in tertio .. ~a, .. si in nono .. ducenties mille milia THURKILL *Abac.* 56; centum dūcenti cedunt quadrupe dūcenti SERLO WILT. 2. 32; **s1252** rex ipsos [Wintonienses] ad ~as marcas in brevi persolvendas obligavit M. PAR. *Maj.* V 359 (= OXNEAD *Chr.* 193: †decentas).

ducenties [CL], two hundred times.

THURKILL *Abac.* 56 (v. ducenti).

ducentuplus, two-hundredth (? *recte* two-hundredfold).

twa-hundrethe, ducenti, ~us *CathA.*

ducere [CL]

1 (w. pers. obj.) to guide, bring, escort; **b** (under compulsion, esp. leg.). **c** to 'draw' (criminal to execution). **d** to lead, command (mil. or fig.). **e** to lead (fig.), induce.

si quis laicus de monasterio monachum duxerit furtim, .. intret in monasterio Deo servire THEOD. *Pen.* I 3. 1; angelicis turmis ad caeli culmina ductus ALDH. *CE* 3. 15; quasi contra ortum solis brumalem me ~ere coepit BEDE *HE* V 12; aut unum hominem secum ~ebat pro honore v hidarum *DB* I 64v.; docto crede dūci, si vis ab eo bene dūci SERLO WILT. 2. 28; *Ib.* 32 (v. ducenti); **1168** in liberatione Algari de L. probatoris et in apparatu ejus pro eo †discendo [*sic* MS] *Pipe* 36 (cf. ib. 174: pro ipso [probatore] ~endo et reducendo); ipsam [mulierem cecam] ad manum trahens secum in hospitium duxit GIR. *Hug.* III 3; *Hist. Roff.* 59v. (v. chorea 4); **1381** (v. conscientia 2c). **b** Ignatius Antiochiae .. episcopus .. cum ad passionem ~eretur GILDAS *EB* 74; si in captivitatem ~ta fuerit, vir ejus v annos expectet THEOD. *Pen.* II 12. 21; sorores / diri tortores ducunt e carcere caeco ALDH. *VirgV* 2223; si quis latronem

.. ceperit et captum ultra duxerit .. (*Leis Will.*) *GAS* 497; **1219** positus fuit .. in prisona et fuit ~tus in pleno comitatu *CurR* VIII 142; **1313** in ferris ~tus fuit ad barram *Eyre Kent* I 81; opto quod nulla Trojana ~atur illuc captiva TREVET *Troades* 61. **c** **1378** habeat judicium claye et ~atur a Guyhalda per Chepe *MGL* III 425. **d** Theodbald .. cum omni illo, quem ipse ~ebat, exercitu peremtus est BEDE *HE* I 34; ille qui ex parte *AM* ~et omnes suos homines qui sunt in *Φ* per paginas *ΦT Ludus Angl.* 161. **e** Christianae pietatis, quae ad regnum perenne ~it, devotione BEDE *HE* IV 14; pio ~tus amore *Ib.* V 7; **798** (12c) rex .. sera ~tus penitentia *CS* 291; auditores in benevolentiam .. ~endi ADEL. *ED* 21 (v. docilitas); **11..** monachi ~ti misericordia *Feod. Durh.* 127*n.*; BACON *Tert.* 187 (v. 2 confricare c); conscientia ~tus balliviam suam dimisit *Latin Stories* 124.

2 to marry: **a** (wife); **b** (husband).

a si quis presbiter .. uxorem extraneam duxerit, .. deponatur THEOD. *Pen.* I 9. 4; mallet si ditem ducere sponsam ALDH. *VirgV* 1269; uxores quas illicite duxerunt WULF. *Æthewold* 16; *DB* II 232 (v. 1 amare 1b); fratres .. fratrum defunctorum uxores, non dico ~unt, sed traducunt, immo verius seducunt GIR. *TH* III 19; **1217** ita quod .. filiam Eustacii .. ~at in uxorem *Pat* 49; **1247** Willelmus I. dat dim. m. pro habenda saisina masuagii quod Willelmus le P. tenuit et pro ~enda relicta ipsius Willelmi *SelPlMan* 11; HIGD. VII 23 (v. divortiare a); cum vir noviter duxerit uxorem [ME: *haveð ilead wif ham*] .., benigne aspicit ejus speciem *AncrR* 78. **b** **1130** Willelmus filius Ricardi .. r. c. de xj li. et xiij s. et iiij d. ut mater sua ~eret virum ad electum suum *Pipe* 92.

3 a to drive (animals). **b** to lead (hounds).

a ego ~o [AS: *ic læde*] eos [boves] ad pascua ÆLF. *Coll.* 91; **1279** ~et ad aulam domini sui omnes oves quas habet a festo S. Mich. usque ad Natale Domini *Hund.* II 461a; **1283** debent ~ere et reducere porcos domini ad nemus *Cust. Battle* 30. **b** †**845** (11c) liberata .. ab hospitorum (*sic*) refectione vel venatorum .. et puerorum qui ~unt canes *CS* 450; **c1175** (v. currere 2a); **1246** invenit .. messorem villate de B. ~entem duos mastinos contra defensum forestariorum *SelPlForest* 83; **1255** homines .. equites .. transierunt per landam de B. ~entes leporarios *Ib.* 31.

4 (naut.): **a** to tow. **b** to pilot or command (a ship). **c** (of light-house) to guide seafarers. **d** (w. ship as subj.) to convey.

a **1296** (v. cabula d). **b** **1205** probos marinellos ad eas [galeas] ~endas *Pat* 52b; **1217** navem quam Thomas V. ~it *Pat* 68. **c** errantes fluctibus actos / arcibus ex celsis signans ad litora duco ALDH. *Aen.* 92 (*Farus*) 8. **d** **1336** in fretto navis conducte ad ducend' *stokfissh* de S. Botholfo usque ad Novum Castrum *Ac. Durh.* 532; **1435** magistro navicule que duxit ambaxiatores Francie versus Franciam *ExchScot* 610.

5 to carry, cart (things); **b** (farm produce, esp. man.); **c** (w. cart as subj.).

Thaddeus .. / quem duxisse ferunt Christi cum grammate scedam / Abgaro ALDH. *CE* 4. 12. 3; carrum in quo eadem ossa ~ebantur BEDE *HE* III 11; **1173** (v. dolium 1a); **c1228** meremium .. ad ~endum per aquam ad maneria sua *Feod. Durh.* 236 (cf. ib. 279: cum ipse aliquando precederet ~entes meremium, forestarii arestaverunt ipsos ~entes cum meremio); **1267** (v. districtio 5c); **1278** nullus qui ~it wysdam mensurat eam, sed ille qui ad hoc juratus fuerit (*LBLond.* A f. 130) *MGL* I 725; **1335** in expensis .. euncium Londonias .. pro .. cc libris ibidem ~endis *Comp. Swith.* 240; **1340** lanas .. ~i fecerunt (v. cokettare). **b** †**c1100** (14c) ~et fimum et vigilabit circa faudam (*Ext. Binham*) *Med. E. Anglia* 267; **a1128** (v. apparare 1a); **a1197** invenire debet viam ad ~endum fenum per terram suam (*Ch. Marg. de Bohun*) *Camd. Misc.* I 74; **1222** faciat (*sic*) iij quar. brasii et ~et inter duas aquas; et erit quietus de ij operationibus, nisi duxerit super diem festivum (*Ext. Ely*) *Med. E. Anglia* 260; **c1283** debent facere quantum facit dim. hida, sc. sarculando, falcando, fenum vel bladum ~endo .. *Cust. Battle* 29. **c** **1269** forestarius .. cepit de qualibet carecta ~ente buscam vel meremium .. iiij d. *SelPlForest* 51; **s1323** ad preparand' viam carecte episcopi ~entis harnesia de Thamisia apud hospicium episcopi *Hist. Roff.* f. 43.

6 a to emit. **b** to draw, lead (fluid). **c** (med.) to draw out; *cf. educere* 4c.

a ~ta crebro suspiria ALDH. *VirgP* 48; spissa statim spiramina / duelli ducunt agmina (*Id.*) *Carm. Aldh.* 1. 30. **b** siccis nam laticum duxisti cautibus amnes *Id. Aen. pref.* 32; quanquam ambigant medici utrum in mediam cordis cellulam respiratio aerem continuo tractu ~at aut .. ALF. ANGL. *Cor* 6. 4; **c1228** requisitus de aque ductu, dicit quod vidit .. aquam ~i ad monasterium per terram episcopi *Feod. Durh.* 264; BRACTON 221b (v. continue 1a); nec penetrativum ~et secum grossum .. nec stans retardabit currentem BACON IX 116. **c** scoria argenti .. miscetur medicaminibus per emplasticam et cicatricem ~entibus *Alph.* 178; quare uncia mirobalanorum si distemperetur in aqua frigida plus ~it quam uncia et semis si distemperetur cum aqua calida *Quaest. Salern.* R 34.

7 a to derive. **b** (w. *in consuetudinem*) to turn into a custom, make a habit of. **c** to lead, point (to a conclusion). **d** to effect, bring (to a condition).

a nomina de verno ducentes tempore prisca ALDH. *Aen.* 8 (*Pliades*) 5; genus a proavis .. nobile .. ~ens BEDE *HE* II 1 p. 73; *Correct. Alch.* 5 (v. ductibilis 2). **b** **a1200** si quis silentium non tenere in consuetudinem duxerit (*Cap. Ord. Arroac.*) *EHR* LII 270. **c** si ab effectibus arguatur ad causam, magis deducunt in oppositum et in errorem. .. proprietas istius nature ad extra est contingenter causare; et ad oppositum hujus magis effectus ~unt, in errorem. .. de proprietatibus eciam aliarum substanciarum patet idem, quia effectus magis ~unt in .. necessitatem earum quam in contingenciam DUNS *Ord.* I 24–5. **d** si limetur scissura [in tintinabulo] et ad equalitatem ~atur, fiet sonus clarus *Quaest. Salern.* Ba 1; **c1240** consideravit quod si totam severitatem expenderet forsan legatus pape .. in irritum ~eret HIGD. VII 35; si paciatur fluxum ventris restringatur .., quia citissime ~eret eum ad mortem J. MIRFIELD *Brev.* 86.

8 a to direct, guide the movement of. **b** to draw (a thread). **c** to draw compasses or (?) a circle. **d** to draw or trace a line (also fig.); *cf.* 7a *supra*. **e** (w. *in se ipsum*) to erect a square on (a line). **f** (math.) to multiply, (w. *in se ipsum*) to square.

a ALDH. *VirgV* 2640 (v. contus a); a sinistra primum ad dexteram ~ebant stilum BONIF. *Met.* 112; obliquum cultrum a fronte victime usque ad caudam ante immolationem ~ere consueverant ALB. LOND. *DG* 6. 32; **1329** pro iiij hamis ferreis pro dicta rama post appensionem ejusdem inde ~enda *KRAc* 467/6 (1) m. 6 (= *Building in Eng.* 328: †ducendandum). **b** filo ~to per medium GILB. VII 293v. 1 (v. dossa). **c** ~as compassum DASTIN *Ros.* 12 (v. 1 compassus 1a). **d** ~ta ex puncto *E* linea perpendiculari *ET* ROB. ANGL. *Alg.* 82; ADEL. *QN* 71 (v. distrahere 5a); variarum gentium originalem a puncto lineam ~ere GIR. *TH intr.* p. 7; lineam rectam ~ere BACON VIII 89 (v. curvus 1a); PECKHAM *QA* 121, BRADW. *CD* 36E (v. contingentia 1). **e** in omni triangulo rectangulo, quadratum quod a latere recto angulo opposito in se ipsum ~to describitur equum est duobus quadratis que ex duobus reliquis lateribus conscribuntur ADEL. *Euclid* 155. **f** longitudo cortinorum viginti octo erat cubitorum, qui est numerus quaternarius septies ~tus BEDE *Tab.* 427; BYRHT. *Man.* 3 (v. duodecies); omnis integer, si ~atur in aliquam fractionem, ex genere illius fractionis efficitur ADEL. *Alch.* 21 (cf. ib. 25: radix .. est cujuslibet numeri numerus qui in se ipsum ~tus ipsum efficiet); nunc dicendum est qui [numerus] proveniat exductu [l. ex ductu] cujuslibet terminorum primi ordinis ~ti in semetipsum aut ex quolibet uno in quemlibet alium ejusdem limitis ~to OCREATUS *Helceph* 133; de ratione denarii bis ~ti ad productionem millenarii AD. MARSH *Ep.* 180; [novenarius numerus] si in se ~atur, 81 producit *Mus. Mens.* (*Anon. VI*) 399.

9 to lead (direct the course of) a road. **b** (w. road or sim. as subj.) to lead, run (also fig.); **c** (refl.).

†**680** (10c) haec sunt territoria ad P. pertinentia: .. ab occidente U. per illum portum ad locum qui dicitur H. .. et sic ~itur in Lang Port *CS* 50; **1313** quidam regiam viam duxit ex obliquo propter proficuum suum *Eyre Kent* I 91; **1430** ad aliam stratam que ~itur versus capellam (*Ch.*) *Med. Bor. Snowd.* 298. **b** per latam diversorum vitiorum morti proclive ~entem .. discurrebant viam GILDAS *EB* 22; B. *V. Dunst.* 25 (v. documentum 2b); viam quae ~it Cantuariam arripuit OSB. *Mir. Dunst.* 22; **1263** habeant unam largam viam .. que ~it de B. usque tenementum R. carectarii *BBC* (*Agardsley*) 377; 'iter cecum' .. quod ~it ad infernum TREVET *Troades* 53; **s1330** THORNE 2056 (v. gardinum 1b); **c1350** usque ad altam viam que ~it de E. ad S. *Dryburgh* 231; **1420** quoddam venellum ~ens ad le Slyke *Feod. Durh.* 24*n*. **c** quo se trames ~ebat FELIX *Guthl.* 37; **c1300** in illo viculo qui se ~it versus .. portam de W. *Reg. Malm.* I 117; **1349** cheminum quod se ~it a mari usque Ludam *Pub. Works* I 226.

10 a to lead (life). **b** to spend (time).

a vitam sine crimine ducens ALDH. *VirgV* 828; usque ad diem Ascensionis .. vitam ~ebat CUTHB. *Ob. Baedae* clx; si sine te possimus vitam ~ere [AS: *adreogan*] ÆLF. *Coll.* 98; **1290** cum .. ordinaverimus quod .. [Judei] per negociaciones et labores suos ~erent vitam suam (*Stat. Jud.*) *SelPlJews* xl; B. Virgo Maria, nonne solitariam vitam duxit [ME: *ledde*]? *AncrR* 52; 'degere evum', i. e. ~ere vitam TREVET *Troades* 19; **1439** quamdiu .. vitam duxerit in humanis *StatOx* 261. **b** ab illis abbas ubi moram hesternae diei duxerint sciscitabatur FELIX *Guthl.* 43; noctem ~ebat pervigilem BEDE *HE* V 6; **790** laetum duc diem ALCUIN *Ep.* 8; o utinam laetos, pueri, feliciter annos / ducatis FRITH. 634; pro ineptissima vanitate noctes ~imus insomnes AILR. *Spec. Car.* II 24. 72. 573D; vigiles lunas et duros ducere soles J. EXON. *BT* VI 38; plurimas noctes ~ebam insompnes P. CORNW. *Rev.* I 205 p. 198.

11 to conduct: **a** (battle); **b** (dance); **c** (affair, proceedings). **d** (?) to convene (court).

a **720** (v. duellum 1a); **1169** (v. consideratio 3). **b** R. COLD. *Cuthb.* 136 etc. (v. chorea 1a). **c** intelligens placitum non ~i per rectitudinem *DB* I 32; **1285** teneatur assistere .. Johanni in causa .. vel eciam ipsam causam incipere et ~ere, si necesse fuerit *RGasc* II 256; **1300** quod .. inter vos et ipsum hoc ita secrete .. ~atur quod .. inter alios nulla mencio habeatur *Ib.* III 400. **d** **1225** ballivi .. non permittunt eos [coronatores] hundredum ~ere .. ut inquisiciones faciant *SelPlCrown* 117.

12 to reckon, consider: **a** (w. *pro*); **b** (w. gdv.); **c** (w. other compl.).

a **803** si .. hoc nostrum mandatum .. spreverint et pro nihilo ~unt (*Clovesho*) *CS* 312; **956** (12c) nisi anathema fieri pro minimo ~at *CS* 957; omnem gloriam mundi pro nihilo duxit AILR. *Serm.* 19. 318C; pro miraculo ~i GIR. *TH* III 27 (v. dominari 1a). **b** nec putei laticem spernendum ducimus altum ALDH. *VirgV* 218; **1093** possessiones priori et conventui concessas .. propriis duximus exprimendas vocabulis *Ch. Durh.* *7 p. 56; **c1190** eam [confirmacionem] .. sigilli nostri apposicione duximus corroborandam *Cart. Osney* IV 45; **1222** presenti scripto sigillum nostrum duximus apponendum *Cart. Boarstall* 6; **1255** rex tunc habebit consilium †quod [MS: quid] de assarto illo duxerit faciendum *Cl* 53; **1376** quousque dominus de eodem aliud duxerit disponendum *Hal. Durh.* 137. **c** nos .. nullius momenti ~as GILDAS *EB* 36; personas .. ad formam virginalis materiae congruentes praeterire incommodum duxi ALDH. *VirgP* 45; BEDE *HE* V 2 (v. commodus 1); ÆLF. *Æthelwold* 1 etc. (v. dignus 1b); de conviciis .., que si mihi .. dicta fuissent, semimortuum me ~erem H. HUNT. *CM* 1; quos nominare superfluum duxi H. ALBUS 89; ea .. non inutile duxi in unum congerere GIR. *TH pref.* p. 21.

13 to think fit, resolve: **a** (w. inf.); **b** (w. acc. & inf. pass.).

a ea duximus summatim adjicere A. TEWK. *Addit. Thom.* 1; **s1189** de .. nominibus episcoporum duximus supersedere DICETO *YH* II 68; **a1198** cartam sigilli nostri testimonio duximus roborare *Reg. Malm.* II 13; **1226** nuntii quos ad predicandum .. in Anglia [Hospitalarii] duxerint destinare *Pat* 47; **s1316** pauca .. huic scripto duxi inserere TROKELOWE 95; **1335** forma commissionis .. valitura quousque duxerimus eam revocare *Lit. Cant.* II 111; KYMER 3 (v. curare 4a). **b** ADEL. *QN* 37 (v. cavatura b); **1257** in hujus rei fidem et testimonium presentibus sigillum nostrum duximus apponi (*Lit. Episc. Sar.*) *SelPlForest* lxxxix; **1448** huic .. scripto .. sigillum nostrum duximus apponi *Reg. Whet.* I 50.

duceria, 'dukery', duchy.

1504 dim. acra .. juxta .. terram ducherie Lancastr' ex parte occid[entali] *AncD* A 10058.

duchissa v. ducissa 2a.

ducibilis [LL], that can be guided or directed.

omnis volicio Dei adintra est immobilis et per consequens non est trahibilis .., regibilis, ~is, gubernabilis .. WYCL. *Dom. Div.* 149 (cf. annullabilis).

duciculus, ducillus [cf. AN *dusil*, OF *doisil*], 'dossil', spigot. *Cf.* 2 *dola*.

cucurrit ad patrem, serraculum, quod ~iculum vocant, manu deferens *NLA* (*Columbanus*) I 209; **c1240** tres galones de cervisia conventus de eodem doleo et dosillo quo conventus habet in die *Cart. Glouc.* III 280; **13..** vinitarius [MS: vinetarius] .. habeat .. intonellaria, clepsedres sive dusellos, costrellos (*Nominale*) *Neues Archiv* IV 339; *claret of a tune*, ductilium .., *dotel, stoppyng of a vessel*, ~illus vel ductileus .., *stoppel of a vessel, botel or oþer lyke*, ~illus, ductilis, docillus, ductileus *PP* (cf. clepsydra c); docillus, A. *a dussel* .., hic ~ellus, A. *dosylle WW*; evulso .. cultello, velut alter ~illi rivus rubeus cruor ilico cepit effluere *Mir. Hen. VI* I 26 (cf. ib. II 44: liquoris rivulum veluti apposito docillo .. compescuit).

ducifer v. lucifer. **ducillus** v. duciculus. **ducior** v. diutior.

ducissa

1 leader (f.).

quia ipsa ~a eorum, inter omnes qui aderant nobilissima, Scota dicebatur, ipsam partem terre .. Scociam vocaverunt FORDUN *Chr.* I 18.

2 duchess: **a** (Continental); **b** (Eng. or unspec.); **c** (Scot.).

a **s1182** Henricus dux Saxonum .., veniens in Normanniam ad socerum suum, habens secum ~am [sc. Matildem filiam regis Anglorum] DICETO *YH* II 13; ut .. Guillelmus [dux Normannie] Heraldi sororem in conjugem juraret et ~am GERV. TILB. II 20; **1215** nos dedisse .. uxori nostre Isabelle .. regine Anglie, domine Hibernie, ~e Norm[annie] et Aquit[annie] .. *RChart* 213b; **a1290** Alianora regina Anglie, duxissa Aquitannie (*Ch. Reginae*) *MGL* III 430; **s1342** prope litus Britannie, juxta castrum [*Brest*] .. in quo fuit duchissa cum liberis suis AD. MUR. *Chr.* 126; **s1377** Blanchia de Turri Britonumque ducissa Maria (*Epitaph. Ed. III*) *Pol. Poems* I 220; **1425** Margareta ~a Turonie, comitissa de Douglas (*Ch. Dumfries*) *Scot. Grey Friars* II 101; Maria Burgundie duxissa Austrie ANDRÉ *Hen. VII* 12. **b** **s1363** ~a Clarencie (v. domina 2b); **s1396** commendata est regina ducisse Lankastrie et Glovernie WALS. *HA* II 221; **s1464** duxit rex E. in uxorem Elizabetham filiam domini de R. et ~e Bedfordie *Compilatio* 180; hec ~a, *a duches* .., hec ducissa, *a dukes WW*. **c** **1403** domine M. ~e de Rothesay in partem solucionis pensionis sibi debite ex conjuncta infeodacione facta quondam D. duci Rothesaye et sibi *ExchScot* 566; **s1423**

translatus est dux [Albanie] ad castrum de C. et ~a ad T. FORDUN *Cont.* XVI 9; **1497** super vendicionem unius tenementi Margarete C. ~e Montis Rosarum *Reg. Brechin* 214.

ducitare v. dictitare 2. **ducius** v. dusius.

ductamen, guidance. *V. et. ducamen* 1.

surgens et caelestis medici ~ine perfruens ad monasterium .. tendit ADEL. BLANDIN. *Dunst.* 2.

ductare [CL], to lead repeatedly. **b** to lead (to war).

~at, ducit frequenter *GlC* D 372. duco, .. inde .. et ~o, ~as, verbum frequentativum OSB. GLOUC. *Deriv.* 160. **b** Vulferius rex Mertiorum [ob. **674**] in eosdem [Pictos] efferatus ~avit exercitum suum W. MALM. *GP* III 100 p. 218.

ductator, escort.

s1170 ad mare Flandrie vadit archiepiscopus, solo ~ore comitatus decano Saresberiensi W. FITZST. *Thom.* 114 (cf. ib. 113: itineris sui ducem decanum S. accepit).

ductellus, little watercourse. *V. et. ductulus, duitellus.*

c1270 concessit .. terram .. a divisis de N. usque ad ~um qui descendit de habitaculo sanctemonialium (*AncD* L 20) *MonA* IV 329b.

ductibilis [cf. ducibilis]

1 that can be led.

13.. per equos, boves, oves vel alias quascunque bestias que sunt res ~es seu fugabiles *Little RB Bristol* I 73.

2 ductile (also fig.). *V. et.* 2 *ductilis* 1a.

artifex .. excogitavit vitri temperamentum, ut flexibile esset et ~e M. PAR. *Maj.* I 92 (= Isid. *Etym.* XVI 16. 6: ductile); sunt ~ia omnia liquabilia metalla que originem ducunt ex Mercurio *Correct. Alch.* 5; rex ut est figulus, palpo ductibile / lutum WALT. WIMB. *Palpo* 73; sic habet et aurum in se virtutem omnium lapidum ~ium DASTIN *Ros.* 3.

ductibilitas, ductility.

stannum .. admixtum ceteris metallis .. aufert ab eis .. ~atem *Ps.*-GROS. *Summa* 540.

ducticius, ~ia [cf. conducticius], drudge.

dryvyl, servaunt, ~ius, ~ia *PP.*

1 ductilis, ~eus v. duciculus.

2 ductilis [CL]

1 (of metal or metal artefact) ductile, malleable; *v. et. ductibilis* 2. **b** (w. *tuba* or sim.; *cf. Psalm* xcvii 6). **c** (w. *opus*) metalwork. **d** (of water) easily channelled.

stipes [candelabri] obrizo ~i .. fabrefactus [cf. *Exod.* xxv 31] ALDH. *Met.* 2; hos [libros] conspicui praevelat ductilis auri / lamina ÆTHELWULF *Abb.* 639; ~i, levi, fusili, vel *astrenged GlH* D 827; virgas ferreas ~es ad clavos navium regis *DB* I 162. **b** ut cornibus [vel] tubis ~ibus singuli contenti essent ABBO *Edm.* 12; canere eductui, canere receptui, in lituis suis ~ibus W. FITZST. *Thom.* 23; **s1191** ~ium clangor tubarum WEND. I 196; **s1327** cum ferro plumbarii, incense ignito trans tubam ~em ad egestionis partes secretas applicatam membra spiritualia .. combusserunt BAKER 107b; solve tuam vocem sicut tuba ductilis altam GOWER *VC* III 1091. **c** vasa .. ~i aurificum opere .. celata *G. Steph.* I 46; peritus .. tam in opere plumali quam in opere ~i NECKAM *Ut.* 118. **d** mobilis, humidus est aqueus liquor insipidusque, / ductilis et fluidus *Id. DS* IV 233/4.

2 (of thread) that can be drawn. *Cf. ducere* 8b.

manus superior .. appensa est ad colum .., inferior affixa est ad fusum; in medio autem stupentibus brachiis protendebatur ~e filum GOSC. *Wulsin* 15.

3 (?) passable (of road).

que via salva fuit, furit ignibus impetuosa, / quo longum castrum ductile nescit iter GOWER *VC* I 930.

4 (of person) amenable, tractable.

palpo sententias magnorum sequitur / aqua ductilior, quo placet ducitur WALT WIMB. *Palpo* 79; **s1288** [Nicholaus IV] pre nimia .. benignitate sua ~is fuit, ita quod pro voluntate cardinalium regebatur *Meaux* II 240; coguntur inclusi fieri ~es in tractatum et .. reddebant in manus regias opidum *Ps.*-ELMH. *Hen. V* 87 (cf. ib. 103: quanquam regalis nobilitas .. non fuerit de facili ad desideriorum suorum complementa ~is).

ductilium v. duciculus. **ductilus** v. ductulus.

ductio [CL]

1 a towing or haulage. **b** carriage, transport. **c** cartage, leading in (man.).

a 1329 pro ~one magne navis domini regis ab aqua in rivulum juxta manerium [de Cardros] *ExchScot* 126. **b 1338** ~onem .. victualium (v. discarcatio b). **c 1433** ad ~onem feni et glebarum venient sicut ceteri husbandi *Reg. Aberbr.* II 62; **1435** consueverunt servire episcopis quolibet anno .. de una dieta in ~one bladi, et .. quil[i]bet eorum solebat servire sibi cum plaustro suo in ~one feni et per unam dietam cum plaustris in ~one turbarum *Reg. Brechin* I 84; **1539** pro ~one et lucracione feni prati de R. *Rent. S. Andr.* 31.

2 a escorting (of prisoners). **b** (spiritual) uplift; *cf. anagoge* b.

a 1299 de custagiis circa eorum [prisonum] ~onem imponendis *MGL* II 135; **1340** clamat habere .. capcionem prisonum seu indictatorum .. et custodiam eorundem, ~onem eorum et reduccionem coram .. justiciarios *SessPCambs* 6. **b** 'ana' quod est 'sursum' et 'goge' quod est '~o'; unde 'anagoge' quasi sursum ~o S. LANGTON *Gl. Hist. Schol.* 43.

3 marriage.

hic ~one magis quam commixtione carnis consistere videtur tam conjugium quam ejus sacramentum VAC. *Matr.* 279.

4 (mus.) length of time during which note is held.

[gradus] mihi non videtur necessarius nec regularis propter ~ones ternarii superius declaratas *Mus. Mens. (Anon. VI)* 401.

ductitare [CL], to lead (troops).

militum stipatus frequentia, quasi ad subveniendum regi eos ~aret *G. Steph.* I 34.

ductivus, a inducive, conducive. **b** leading, offering a way.

a regimen ~um ad Dei similitudinem BART. ANGL. II 13; intentio rei, elicita .. in phantasia vel estimativa, ~a est memorie in imaginem apud imaginationem respectu preteriti *Ps.*-GROS. *Summa* 481 (cf. ib. 636: est .. calidum .. quasi instrumentum et ~um ad finem et formam); similitudinem convenit ostendere dupliciter, vel secundum esse quod habet in anima vel secundum quod est ~um in cognicionem rei (DUNS *Periherm.*) *GLA* III 215 *n.* 127; angelus .. potest circa bonum sufficienter ostensum per aliquod tempus ociari in voluntate et per aliud illud velle .. quid magis necessitat angelicam voluntatem ad perpetualiter continuandum liberum actum suum quam ad ipsum, post liberam vacacionem ~am, temporaliter producendum? BRADW. *CD* 523A. **b** Karolus .. satagebat exquisitis mediis introitus ad unionem ~os obstruere *Ps.*-ELMH. *Hen. V* 78.

ductor [CL], guide, (partly fig.); **b** (of blind person). **c** escort (of prisoner). **d** one who leads (dog). **e** (?) councillor.

ut populum Domini .. / ferret ad aeterni ductor vestigia regni ALDH. *VirgV* 847; quo cum perductus essem, repente ~or meus disparuit BEDE *HE* V 12; eorum [noviciorum] ~or .. solus cum illis remaneat LANFR. *Const.* 154; ad vitam ~ore previo B. Cuthberto redierat R. COLD. *Cuthb.* 63; necessarius est ~or alicui viatori ne deviet a via recta *Regim. Princ.* 109. **b** caecus .. / cum puero ductore citim properabat ad ipsum WULF. *Swith.* II 709; dum haberet praevium ~orem, sicut oculis privati habere solent LANTFR. *Swith.* 18; redit domum absque ~ore que ceca advenerat *Lib. Eli.* III 117. **c 1267** quod .. prisonem .. a ~oribus ejusdem recipiat et .. custodiat *Cl* 332. **d** sint .. duo homines colloquentes, assit canis veniens cum altero eorum; .. cum recedit ~or ipsius [canis], ducem sequitur cum quo venit S. LANGTON *Serm.* 2. 6. **e s1331** ~ores regis ordinarunt quod quilibet eorum in propria patria capitanius justiciarius foret *Hist. Roff.* 58.

2 leader, commander. *Cf. campiductor.* **b** (w. ref. to animal).

divino comites potabat fonte fideles, / .. / gratia quos tanti servat ductoris opima FRITH. 1131; *GAS* 656 (v. 2 constabularius 1); Moyses ~or et legislator BALD. CANT. *Sacr. Alt.* 708C; **c1370** perdent Flandrenses ductorem [*gl.*: i. comitem seu ducem eorum] nocte per enses (J. BRIDL.) *Pol. Poems* I 149–50; **s1379** (v. campiductor a); **s1381** ululatus factus est: "~or noster [sc. Watte Tyler] mortuus est!" KNIGHTON II 137; **s1435** (v. cateranus). **b 706** si .. creatura [ratione] carens [sc. apis] .. ~oris praecepto paret ALDH. *Ep.* 9 (12); taurus ingens, ~or armenti TREVET *Troades* 41.

3 (naut.): **a** captain. **b** pilot.

a 1224 cum .. Willelmo ~ore ejusdem navis et marinellis suis *Pat* 444; **1434** Petro Vens, ~ori cujusdam navis, pro quibusdam doliis vini *ExchScot* 575. **b 1338** navis .. fuit deperdita super quoddam sabulum in Selandia pro defectu cujusdam ~oris, qui wlgaliter vocatur *lodman*, qui eam ibidem adduxit, qui quidem ~or conductus .. fuit per .. magistrum dicte navis *IMisc* 136/4.

4 carrier, transporter.

1336 quod .. pelles lanutas .. nullatenus transire permittatis antequam ~ores eorundem sufficientem securitatem vobis in portu .. invenerint quod lanas illas .. ad partes que non sunt de amicicia nostra non ducent seu duci facient *RScot* 464b; **s1311** ad numerum ccc millium armatorum, nudis sequacibus ac mercatoribus cum .. victualium ~oribus omnino exceptis *Plusc.* IX 12.

ductrix [LL], guide or leader (f.).

Filargiria producit tertia bellum. / .. / haec ductrix pugnae stipatur milite denso ALDH. *VirgV* 2573; muta .. regebat .. caecam, quae pro ~ice .. requirebat .. semitam LANTFR. *Swith.* 21; muta regit caecam, quae pro ductrice viantes / explorat WULF. *Swith.* II 212; quedam clauda, .. sui fratris ceci ~ix *G. Walth.* 134; **1346** (v. caduce); usque Beverlacum, devocione ~ice, peregre profectum est *Ps.*-ELMH. *Hen. V* 115 (cf. ib. 130: semita ~ice).

ductulus, little watercourse, brook. *V. et. ductellus, duitellus.*

a1187 in marisco juxta ductilum aque *Danelaw* 156; **1226** per ~um qui vocatur Mercbroc et qui cadit in Sculebroc [*Derb*] *CurR* XII 1642.

ductus [CL]

1 guidance, leading.

deambulans sibi sine ~u alterius *V. Cuthb.* IV 16; designavit .. in cinctione alterius [cf. *John* xxi 18] quod vinciendus a persecutore in ~u quo non vellet .. tormenta .. esset passurus BEDE *Hom.* I 9. 45; **c1170** divine ~u pietatis .. renunciavit juri .. in ecclesia S. Cadoci *Cart. Glouc.* II 13; cum hominum universum genus ipso naturae ~u .. sit appetens veritatis JEWEL *Apol.* A3v. (*recte* A2v.).

2 drawing: **a** (of air); **b** (of line).

a hoc orificium clauditur fiente ~u [aeris], illud emissione ALF. ANGL. *Cor* 6. 2. **b** ~ibus, figuris *GlH* D 830; incipiens a columna illa juxta quam Aaron .. intrat in circuitu .. uno ~u usque ad columnam que est contra Moysen [cf. *Exod.* xxviii & xxxviii] AD. SCOT *TT* 706C

3 watercourse, mill-lade or sim. *V. et. aquaeductus, duitus.*

a1150 concedo .. unam croftam in H. inter †duttam et fossam canonicorum *Cart. Harrold* 47 (= *MonA* VI 330b); **c1170** a fonte inter ecclesiam de H. usque in ~um [v. l. usque indoitum] qui cadit de vivario in magnam aquam *E. Ch. Yorks.* VI 159; **1173** cum .. omnibus consuetudinibus terre et fluminis a Rupe C. usque ad ~um, a ~o (*sic*) .. usque ad vallem .. *Act. Hen. II* II 65 (cf. ib. 66: in flumine Ligeris ~um unum cum piscaria .. et molendinis duobus); [apud Kaerleon] reperies ubique .. edificia subterranea, aquarum ~us hypogeosque meatus GIR. *IK* I 5; **c1228** requisitus de ~u aque versus H. *Feod. Durh.* 247; **1248** debent .. exclusas et ~us curare et reparare .., molas ducere et meremium cariare ad molendina reparanda *CalIMisc* (*C. I.*) I p. 16; **c1270** a ~u aque currentis inter T. et H., qui ~us descendit in Bolyn *Cart. Chester* 332; **1514** pro factura j *le gutter* pro ~u aque de *le stepled* subter pontem ligneum *Ac. Durh.* 161.

4 duct, proboscis.

subtilis explica ductus [sc. culicis] itinera WALT. WIMB. *Carm.* 394.

5 chase, hunting. *V. et.* 2 *deductus* 2a.

1215 concessimus Waltero de Lascy quod habeat quandam fabricam in foresta nostra de Den', ita tamen quod non sit ad nocumentum ~us nostri *Cl* 191a.

duculus, dukeling. *V. et. dukettus.*

~us, parvus dux OSB. GLOUC. *Deriv.* 173.

dudda [ME *dudde*], (pl.) duds, garments of coarse cloth.

1307 in xcvij ulnis russeti et xxvj ~is emptis ad pauperes (*ReceiptR*) *Boldon Bk.* app. xxxvii; **1335** in donis eisdem [carectariis etc.] pro eorum ~is, v s. *Comp. Swith.* 238.

dudum [CL], some time ago or before, formerly; **b** (w. *jam*). **c** (w. *quam*) some time before.

~um summitates montium conspicantes, nunc recte ad aethera GILDAS *EB* 67; Paulus, ~um Saulus ALDH. *VirgP* 24; ~um, paulo ante *GlC* D 382; se .. perditas ~um vires recepisse sentiens BEDE *HE* V 4; archiepiscopus tenet Petchinges.. . ~um fuit ad xx li., sed non potuit pati *DB* I (*Kent*) 16v.; talia .. mihi ~um proponenti diuque in animo .. volventi GIR. *TH intr.* p. 5; **1278** (v. congregatio 1c); **s1397** (v. dukettus); controversiam illam motam ~um, inde intermissam et jam denuo resuscitatam *G. Hen. V* 9; **1441** cum ~um, nondum exactus est annus, .. Robertum B... deleg[av]issemus BEKYNTON I 88. **b** principibus .., / quorum descripsi jam bina vocabula dudum ALDH. *CE* 3. 34; protoplaustus .. / .. / jamdudum cecidit prostratus fraude gulosa *Id. VirgV* 2497; jamdudum, pridem *GlC* I 2; conversis jam ~um ad fidem veritatis .. ecclesiis BEDE *HE* II 1 p. 73; jamdudum .. sacramenti Christianae fidei imbutus est *Ib.* II 15; **1280** (v. convalescentia d). **c** quod, dudumquam nascatur de viscere matris,/ sanctificaretur praestanti munere virgo ALDH. *VirgV* 311.

1 duella v. douella 1.

2 duella [LL], one third of an *uncia*, one thirty-sixth.

THURKILL *Abac.* 61v. (v. deunx); luna .. in nostris regulis invenitur post xiij gradus, trientem, et ~am et emisesclam WALCHER *Drac.* 93.

duellare [LL], **~ari,** to fight a duel.

OSB. GLOUC. *Deriv.* 177 (v. duellio a); *cumbatre*, ~are *Gl. AN Ox.* f. 154; **1314** salvo in casu alte justicie quod

infra subicitur de corpore condempnati et quod consuetum est de guagio ~ar[i] *RGasc* IV 1539; **s1391** miles cum quodam Anglie milite ~abat *Plusc.* X 11; **s1397** cum [duces] ~are cepissent, rex .. pacem statim proclamabat *Dieul.* 144; **s1398** dux Herefordie .. de prodicione .. ducem Norfolkie appellavit; unde rex assignavit eis crastinum Exaltacionis S. Crucis ad ~andum AD. USK 23; requiritur quod partes ~are volentes .. sint jurate .. ad pugnandum usque ad certum punctum per .. judicem eisdem assignandum UPTON 73 (cf. ib. 76: ex .. causis honestis ~antes debent sicut volunt optimis .. indui armaturis, tubicinantibus et aliis instrumentis musicis ministrallis ludentibus); **s1508** hic [comes Hemertoniae, sc. *Hamilton*] est ille qui cum illo strenuo milite de Labastide in Scotia .. strenuissime ~atus est ANDRÉ *Hen. VII* 105.

duellaris, concerned w. (or taking the form of) a duel.

1438 ab ulteriori .. processu circa dictum ~e negocium BEKYNTON I 200 (cf. ib. 198: super ~i quodam .. certamine); **s1508** ad ~es ludos conspiciendos, quos dominus H. Bukkynghamiae et .. dominus comes Kantiae cum suis commilitonibus .. inierunt ANDRÉ *Hen. VII* 111.

duellator, (victorious) duellist.

~or, gemine pugne victor OSB. GLOUC. *Deriv.* 175; *Ib.* 177 (v. duellio a).

duellicus, decided by duel.

lite tandem deducta, partes in ~a restiterunt determinacione *NLA* (*Bertellinus*) I 165.

duellio [LL], duellist, champion, warrior. **b** war.

~o, rebellis *GlH* D 838; ~o, duelli victor, qui et duellator dicitur vel duellans OSB. GLOUC. *Deriv.* 177; juvenes ludentes exercentur .. parmis ~onum W. FITZST. *Thom. prol.* 16; statua .. gigantea, que .. ferebat velut ~o securim magnam in dextra *G. Hen. V* 15 p. 102. **b** ~onis, bellum *Gl. Leid.* 29. 37.

duellis [LL], warrior. **b** war.

~es, bellatores *GlH* D 837. **b** ~is, bellum *Gl. Leid.* 4. 40.

duellum [CL], **~ium** [LL *gl.*]

1 conflict (other than single combat); **b** (fig., of chess game).

duelli agmina (ALDH.) *Carm. Aldh.* 1. 30 (v. ducere 6a); ~ium bellum dixerunt, qui[a] ex utraque parte geritur *GlC* D 375; **c720** cum x milibus adversus xx milia [cf. *Luke* xiv 31] ~ium ducturae (EANGYTH) *Ep. Bonif.* 14; gens pigra Britonum, / .. fere continuis Pictorum pressa duellis ALCUIN *SS Ebor* 42; **9..** ~i, *gefeohtes WW*; ergo petens diri praefixum scamma duelli / accepit socium FRITH. 197; **s1137** communi principum consilio statuitur dies quo inter Romanos et Apulienses ~ium fiat et Deus omnipotens judex omnium cui disposuerit victoriam tribuat J. WORC. 44; *bataille*, hoc ~um *Gl. AN Glasg.* f. 19. **b** it pedes ad bellum; prior incipit ille duellum (*Vers. Corpus*) *Hist. Chess* 519.

2 single combat, duel; **b** (chivalrous); **c** (in war, as substitute for general engagement).

~um, duorum bellum quod et ~ium dicitur OSB. GLOUC. *Deriv.* 177; monomachia interpretatur ~um .., quasi pugna unius ad †altera [v. l. alterum] *Alph.* 120; in questione quid sit ~um, respondit Joh. de Lyniano dicens quod '~um est pugna corporalis deliberata hinc inde duorum ad purgacionem, gloriam vel odii aggregacionem' .. in ~o est utriusque deliberacio. dixit doctor 'duorum' quia inde ~um vocatur adherendo ethimologie vocabuli. .. 'corporalis' dixit ad differenciam pugne judiciarie .. UPTON 72. **b** [Raimundus (ob. **1105**) filius comitis Tolose], in quodam ~io altero lumine privatus, .. insigne calamitatis pre se ferens .. gloriabatur ultro specimen nobilis militie ostentans W. MALM. *GR* IV 388; **s1163** Henricus de Exexia victus in ~o exheredatus est DICETO *YH cap.* I 269 (cf. id. *YH* I 310: certamine singulari; TORIGNI *Chr.* 218: bellum Roberti de Monte Forti cum Henrico de Essessa pro fuga prelii contra Gualenses); jam non quid comitas aut justa retributio dictet attendit, sed .. ictu consummare temptat unico ~um MAP *NC* III 2 f. 38; **s1377** preparaverat se quidam miles, dominus Johannes cognomento Dymmok, qui clamabat se habere jus ad defendendum jura regis illo [coronacionis] die et †eciamsi [? l. eciam, si] opus esset, ~o confligendum, si aliquis presumeret affirmare regem non habere jus in regno Anglie WALS. *HA* I 337; **s1395** fuit ~um inter T. S. Anglicum invasorem et W. I. defensorem Scotum, milites, ubi Anglicus occisus est, presentibus custodibus Marchiarum pro judicibus FORDUN *Cont.* XV 3; **s1406** hastiludia bellica: .. Scotis bella vel ~a vendicantibus, pugnavit Londoniis coram rege comes Cancie contra comitem de Marryk .. et quidam Anglici impetiti contra ceteros, et verberaverunt Scotos *Chr. S. Alb.* 1. **c** **s1016** dixerunt inter se proceres: "cur insensati necis periculum totiens incurrimus? pugnent singulariter qui regnare student singulariter!" .. positi ergo reges in Olanie ~um inceperunt H. HUNT. *HA* VI 13 (cf. MAP *NC* V 4 f. 61v.: ut non totius exercitus sed unius hominis attemptetur obitus fiatque pro bello ~um); Frollo mandavit .. Arturo ut ipsi soli ~ium inissent et cui victoria proveniret alterius regnum optineret G. MON. IX 11; ut sic pax fiat, sua jura petit sine bello, / aut solum solo rure duella dare ELMH. *Metr. Hen. V* 370 (cf. *G. Hen. V* 9: invitans .. responsum .. ut .. controversiam .. sine alia .. sparsione fraterni sanguinis inter se ipsos persona ad personam per ~um terminarent).

3 duel (leg.), judicial combat: **a** (Continental); **b** (Eng.); **c** (Sc.); **d** (Ir.); **e** (W.); **f** (fought w. dog). *Cf. bellum* 4.

a **1129** unde justicia mea placitaverat et ~um tenuerat de combustione in curia mea [Normannie] *Regesta* 1579; **1151** (v. conducticius 1d); **1182** si contentio fuerit inter homines abbatie unde ~um surgat, judicabitur apud Fontem Ebraudi *Act. Hen. II* II 228; **1185** *Ib.* 263 (v. curia 4b); **1438** super .. dissidiis inter dictas jam partes olim pendentibus que occasionem seu causam ~o ejusmodi dare possent (*Lit. ad Infantem Arragonie*) BEKYNTON I 199. **b** **s1096** (v. delator 1); (*Jud. Dei*) *GAS* 418 (v. defensor 4a); **a1115** ubicumque sit ~um Ebor', juramenta debent fieri super textum vel super reliquias ecclesie S. Petri et, facto ~o, victor arma victi ad ecclesiam S. Petri offerat *Regesta* 1083*; **1167** M. clericus r. c. de c s. quia fecit bina ~a fieri ab uno homine una die *Pipe* 84; **1168** (v. concordia 2a); GLANV. II 3 (v. 1 assisa 6b, campio a); **1200** etc. (v. armare 3); **1212** etc. (v. divadiare 1b); **1229** (v. adjudicare 1a); **s1249** (v. dirationare 1b); **1253** duo nepotes .. quoddam vadiaverunt ~ium pro quadam terra unde placitum ortum fuit inter eos et pugnaverunt ab hora prima usque ad horam nonam *Rec. Leic.* I 41; si .. per corpus suum intret in defensionem .., statim vadietur inter eos ~um, si omnia rite concurrant et principalia maxime appellum facientia et que jungunt ~um BRACTON 137; **1279** inrotulata fuit .. sententia scripti istius .. ipsis justitiariis sedentibus in area ~i in parte percussi et retractis utrimque campionibus pacificati[s] *AncD* L 465*d*. (cf. *Reg. S. Bees* 439*n*.); ~um [est] singularis pugna inter duos ad probandum veritatem litis, et qui vicerit probasse intelligitur *Fleta* 50; **1368** apud Totehull' venerunt tam predictus probator quam predictus W. .. per marescallum ducti prout moris est arraiati; et ~o ibidem inter eos percusso prefatus probator devicit prefatum W. .. ideo ipse suspendatur *Pat* 278 m. 17; **s1398** dux Albemarlie .. appellatus fuit de morte ducis Glouc' .. precipue per dominum le Fizwauter, qui ad ~um inde probandum capucium suum jecit coram rege publice in Parliamento OTTERB. 222. **c** **1124** me dedisse ecclesie .. de Scon .. suam propriam curiam, sc. in ~o, in ferro, in fossa et in omnibus aliis libertatibus ad curiam pertinentibus *E. Ch. Scot.* 49; **a1150** examen ~i, aque, et ferri calidi quantum ad ecclesiasticam dignitatem pertinet *Ib.* 153; **c1200** si quis appellat aliquem de furto in curia regis .., fit in libitum appellati utrum velit ~um vel purgacionem xij fidelium hominum (*Ass. David I*) *APScot* I 317; locum non habet ~um ad probandum vel reprobandum alicujus hominis libertatem *RegiamM* II 11. 16; **1364** pro meremio recepto .. ad clausuram palicii pro ~o *ExchScot* 129. **d** **1391** defendens in hoc casu [raptu mulieris] ad ~um minime recipiatur, ymmo rei veritas per inquisicionem patrie trietur *StatIr* I 496. **e** **1284** placita de terris in partibus istis non habent terminari per ~um neque per magnam assisam (*Walliae* 8) *StRealm* I 65. **f** judicatum est ~o rei certitudinem experiri. in campo itaque constitutis .. hinc inde cane dentibus armato, illinc baculo cubitali milite munito, tandem cane victore victus homicida succubuit GIR. *IK* I 7.

4 (w. ref. to animals) duel (or pair of duellists).

rana studet mergi, set mus emergit et obstat / naufragio; vires subtrahit ipse timor. / milvus adest miserumque truci rapit ungue duellum WALT. ANGL. *Fab.* 3. 13; [mustela] cum colubro plerumque ~o congreditur GIR. *TH* I 27.

duernio [cf. duo], binion, gathering of two bifolia, quarto signature. *Cf. quaternio, ternio.*

regestrum operis. A. B. C. [etc.] CC. DD. omnes ~ones, EE. ternio (*printer's note*) LINACRE *Emend. Lat.* f. ii v.

duillus, duellist. (*Cf.* Quintilian I 4. 15).

antiqui, teste Quintilliano, bellos dicebant quos modo ~os appellamus; et sine orbis et urbis periculo vincat alteruter ~orum, quem Deus sc. approbaverit aut victorem esse permiserit J. SAL. *Pol.* 810D.

duitelettus [OF *duitelet*], little watercourse.

1292 de Ricardo .. submerso in quodam doyteletto *JustIt* (*Lancs*) 413 r. 12*d*.

duitellus [OF *duitel* < ductellus], little watercourse, brook. *V. et. ductellus, ductulus.*

c1200 terram de Scrogges .. per has divisas sc. a †dintello de Westerdene *desus* Homeldon' usque ad aquam de Line et deorsum de Westerden' *entravers* usque ad sursum †dintelli Gilleminesden' *Reg. Glasg.* I 74 (cf. ib. 75); **1248** inventus fuit submersus in quodam doytello *JustIt* (*Essex*) 232 r. 4*d* (cf. ib.: in .. duytello); **1282** a Bitewod †dintellus qui vocatur Sandbrok venit de molendino de Staverden' *Cart. Glast.* I 177.

duitus [OF *duit* < ductus], watercourse (stream or mill-lade). *V. et. ductus* 3.

c1160 a ~o ultra Rempestunam usque ad aquam de Radeford *Rec. Nott.* I 1; **c1210** per ~um qui cadit de lacu illo usque ad G. *E. Ch. Northants* 53; **a1220** incipiendo .. ad tres quercus .. et sic descendendo doetum et sicut sepes .. circuit .. *Cart. Chester* 418; **1235** descendendo usque ad doitum de Heleyburn' *Fines* (*Northumb*) 180/4/63; **1271** jecit ipsam in aquam in uno doyto *SelCCoron* 15; **1347** unam placiam .. turbarie .. que extendit se .. de doito molendini usque tenementum Thome de B. *AncD* (*Staffs*) C 4442.

dukettus, dukeling. *V. et. duculus.*

s1397 volens rex magnificare personas quas dudum nominibus ducum, marchionis vel comitum honoraverat, quos vulgares derisorie vocabant non duces sed ~os a diminutivo *Ann. Ric. II* 223.

1 dula, ~are v. douell-.

2 dula [δούλη], slave (f.), maidservant.

~a, ancilla, serva, abra, *wyln*, ÆLF. *Sup.*

dulcare [LL], to sweeten.

9.. ~avit, *geswette WW*.

dulcarius [cf. CL dulciarius], confectioner. *V. et. dulcorarius* a.

plane [Vegetius] .. piscatores, ~ios, linteones, et omnes qui aliquid tractasse videbuntur ad genecia pertinens, a militari officio .. repellit J. SAL. *Pol.* 593C.

dulcarnon [Ar. *dhū 'l-qarnayn = possessor of two horns*], Pythagoras' theorem.

probat Pythagore ~on, quadratum descriptum juxta diametrum esse duplum ad quadratum descriptum juxta costam NECKAM *NR* II 173 p. 295 (*gl.*: ~on nomen est figure sed et theorematis quod ponitur in primo libro Euclidis; et dicitur a dulia, id est a servitute carnis, tauri sc. quem immolavit Jovi ob inventionem dicte speculationis); necessario erit mihi nota linea *OD* per ~on, que est penultima primi, quia, si quadravero *ED* et *EO* et conjungam utrumque numerum, illius radix est quantitas linee *OD* WALLINGF. (*Quad.*) I 38.

dulce v. dulcis 2c.

dulcedo [CL]

1 sweetness (to taste). **b** (med.) sweet taste (in mouth). **c** freshness (of water or air).

quae superant mellis mulsum dulcedine gustum / flaventisque favi ALDH. *VirgV* 2771; ~o, *werednes GlH* D 821; **9..** *swetnesse WW*; numquid montes illi stillabunt ~inem? [cf. *Amos* ix 13] GIR. *TH intr.* p. 6; radix [centauree] .. habet .. amaritudinem cum ~ine BART. ANGL. XVII 47; claretum .. a melle ~inem mutuatur et saporem *Ib.* XIX 54; ut in pomis, que cum maturitate acquirunt ~inem GILB. I 41v. 2; **s1263** (v. dulcorare 1a). **b** adest dolor capitis .., oris ~o, eructuationes fetide GILB. I 42. 1. **c** [aqua] cujus nos magnam suavitatem ~inis .. degustantes .. probavimus *V. Cuthb.* III 3; **s1175** ~inem nativi aeris vestri Anglici P. BLOIS *Ep.* 46; quod [lignum] in ~inem eas [aquas Mara; cf. *Exod.* xv 25] convertit AD. DORE *Pictor* 161; fluvius qui illabitur [in sinum de Archelo] innate ~inis saporem retinet illibatum GIR. *TH* II 2.

2 (fig.) sweetness, pleasantness: **a** (to senses); **b** (to spirit). **c** (source of) joy.

a ut .. universam mundanae suavitatis ~inem .. superet ALDH. *VirgP* 6; didicit mellifluam metrice rationi[s] ~inem .. WULF. *Æthelwold* 9; missa .. mirabili ~ine .. decantatur DOMINIC *V. Ecgwini* II 52. **b** [Ambrosii] mellifluum dogmatum ~inem ALDH. *VirgP* 26; semper sanctuario pectoris nostri .. evangelicae laudationis ~o sancta resonet BEDE *Hom.* II 25. 433; [Caedmon] de .. ~ine regni caelestis multa carmina faciebat *Id. HE* IV 22 p. 261; **933** ad nanciscendam mellifluae ~inis misericordiam *CS* 694; **948** audivi a sapientibus .. hanc mellitam ~inem sermocinationis seriem quod bona voluntas .. pro bono opere reputabitur *Ib.* 869 (cf. ib. 917); amaritudinem sequitur ~o [ME: *swotnesse*] quam amaritudo emit *AncrR* 147. **c** eas [leges Moysis] legere sancte contemplacionis ~o est FORTESCUE *LLA* 2.

3 (of persons) sweetness of character, gentleness; **b** (as title). **c** affection.

c961 boni pastoris ~o (v. 3 districtio 3); celestem celica virgo dulcedine / procum illaqueat WALT. WIMB. *Carm.* 26. **b** **990** si placet ~ini vestrae B. *Ep.* 388. **c** **1080** paterna me ~ine reprehendere studuistis LANFR. *Ep.* 8 (38); **1424** BEKYNTON I 280 (v. amaricare b).

dulcescere [CL], **dulcēre,** to be, become, or make sweet (also fig.).

dulcia mulsorum portendit verba favorum, / e quibus affatim dulcescunt pectora plebis ALDH. *VirgV* 669; **934** fastidiunt jam infima, ~escunt superna *CS* 702; quia mellito dulcescit nectare gutur FRITH. 49; extorres statuunt agio incassum palinodo / quos sacer electis gradibus formaret adelphos / dulsos coenosi lichinos †audititidestos [? l. auditu et idestos; cf. *ALMA* XXV 86] *Ib.* 1118; OSB. *Mir. Dunst.* 19 (v. efficere 1b); ab hoc nomine, quod est 'dulcis', ~eo, ~es, quod non est in usu OSB. GLOUC. *Deriv.* 165; nullo rerum eventu tantum amaricatus est animus meus quin statim eloquii tui melle †~eretur [? l. ~oretur; cf. dulcorare 3a] GIR. *Symb.* I 9 p. 233; dulcia sunt porrecta malis falerata venena; / nil dulcescit eis; omnis amara quies WALT. ANGL. *Fab.* 8. 10; lectio dulcescit, sed juvat illa [sc. oratio] magis NECKAM *DS* V 140; sic pena ~escit [ME: *þe schal þunche swa swote*] *AncrR* 43; *to make* [v. l. *be*] *swete*, ~ere *CathA*.

dulchorarius v. dulcorarius.

dulciamen [LL], (pl.) sweetmeats.

placentas, ~ina *GlC* P 457.

dulcibilis, sweet (fig.), pleasant.

erat .. consuetudo ut omni anno ad locum ~em properassent, quia nimio cultu locum ipsum et habitatores dilexerant BYRHT. *V. Osw.* 447 (cf. ib. 458: audivit dulcissimum hymnum †~e [? l. ~is] jubilationis).

dulcicanus, sweet-singing.

obvius est sponsus sponse, sponsique phalanges / reginam stipant dulcicanique levant GARL. *Epith.* X 72.

dulciculus [CL], (dim.) sweet little. **b** (? as sb. m.).

nascuntur haec diminutiva .. de disillabis, ut 'ensis, ensiculus', 'dulcis, ~us' ALDH. *PR* 133; ~us, aliquantulum dulcis OSB. GLOUC. *Deriv.* 173; palpo dulciculus lingua mellicula / potentes pellicit WALT. WIMB. *Palpo* 103. **b** momentis singulis ventris dulciculi / per dies singulos fiunt majusculi *Id. Carm.* 19.

dulcido v. dulcitudo.

dulcifer [CL], sweet (partly fig.).

dulcifero pia nos genetrix ditavit honore TATWINE *Aen.* 4 (*Litterae*) 1; huc conviva tuum fidus transmitte ministrum, / si vis dulciferum, dulcis amice, merum ALCUIN *Carm.* 55. 6. 2 (cf. ib. 7. 4: victu / dulcifero).

dulcificare [LL] to 'dulcify', sweeten.

nisi fermentetur compositum confortativum, non confortabit simplicia debilitantia membra, nec calidum temperabitur a frigido .. aut dulce ~abit amarum BACON IX 116.

dulcificatio, (alch.) 'dulcification', reduction of acidity by washing out soluble salts.

capitulum ~onis M. SCOT *Alch.* (*tit.*) 156.

dulciflue, sweetly.

swetly, dulciter, ~e .. *CathA.*

dulcifluus [LL]

1 a sweetly flowing. **b** exuding or emitting sweetness, fragrant (partly fig.).

a ipsum mausoleum scatet unda ~a GOSC. *V. Iv.* 89B (= W. MALM. *GP* IV 181: manat .. fons dulcis potui). **b** filius ejus [ducis W.] .., velut surculus ex ~a abscissus arbore, .. coepit odoriferos gratissimae pueritiae flosculos emittere W. JUM. IV 1; **s1034** florem .. nectareum, cujus .. ~is perfundebamur odoribus .., Aethericum episcopum *Chr. Rams.* 147; balsama dulcifluo vincit odore locus NIG. *Mir. BVM* f. 17. 1.

2 sweet (to hear), dulcet, melodious. **b** (fig.) heard w. pleasure.

~o modulaminis genere .. alleluia concinere R. COLD. *Cuthb.* 38; intra se sonus celicus resonat melosque ~um solitarium jocundat ROLLE *IA* 181. **b s1066** sermo ducis ~us .. mirabiliter in suorum majorum exemplis diutius peroravit TORIGNI *Access. Sig.* 36; ~um beati martiris .. nomen T. MON. *Will.* VI 17; inde petuntur / dulcifluis precibus presentis commoda vite GARL. *Myst. Eccl.* 610.

3 (of abstr.) bountiful in sweetness (fig.), delightful.

tu me dulcifluo semper amore foves L. DURH. *Hypog.* III 8 p. 71; suaviis et ~is obligationibus ad earum alliciunt amplexus *Quaest. Salern.* B 12; **c1205** (v. 2 dilectio 1c); ut amaram humane malignitatis acrimoniam ~a divine bonitatis consideratio temperet AD. MARSH *Ep.* 105; **c1290** ex ~a vestre sanctitatis clemencia (*Lit. ad Archiep. Cant.*) *Ann. Durh.* app. 138; puerulus .. ~o luminum risu vultuque sereno J. FURNESS *Walth.* 22.

dulciloquium, sweet or welcome speech.

c1183 precordia / venantur omnium / jocunditas / et dulciloquium (*Mors Henrici*) *EHR* V 316; **c1380** voluistis .. vestrum subsidium et ~ium cum sanissimo concilio vestro michi benigniter impartiri *FormOx* 326.

dulciloquus [CL], sweetly speaking.

'dulcis' componitur .. ~us OSB. GLOUC. *Deriv.* 165.

dulcimode, sweetly, melodiously.

cunctis qui aderant .. Deum una ~e laudantibus DOMINIC *V. Ecgwini* II 51.

dulcimodus [LL], sweet (to hear), melodious.

cum ~is laudum organis GOSC. *Transl. Aug.* 38A (cf. ib. 34D: cum ~o virginum choro); laudes ~as in beati honore Cuthberti sollempni vocis officio decantando persolvit R. COLD. *Cuthb.* 73.

dulcis [CL]

1 sweet (to taste); **b** (of wine). **c** tasty. **d** sweet-smelling. **e** (as sb. n. pl.) 'doucets', sweets.

dulcior in palato quam lenti nectaris haustus ALDH. *Aen.* 100. 31; *Ib.* 80. 8 (v. basium); *Id. VirgV* 342 (v. alimentum); **c1230** ad vesperam habebunt panem et florem et lac ~e et sal' *Cust. Waltham* f. 210; BACON IX 116 (v. dulcificare); *Id.* XIV 80 (v. amarus a); ficus que suo ~i [ME: *swete*] fructu .. pascere deberet Dominum celi *AncrR* 48; *SB* 10 (v. cyminum 2a). **b** quantum distat ~is sapa a merulento temeto ALDH. *VirgP* 60; ~is sapa, *caerin* *GlC* D 369 (cf. caroenum); **9..** †dulcisapa, *cyren odde awylled win* *WW*; **1264** quedam vina ~ia mercatorum .. comitis [Pictavie] *Cl* 393; **1365** omnes taberne in quibus ~ia vina venduntur in civitate nostra London' .. in manibus majoris et camerarii .. capiantur (*Cl*) *Foed.* (4th ed.) III ii 768 (cf. ib. 781 [**1366**]: intencionis nostre non .. existit quod vina de Osye, de Algarbe vel aliunde de Ispannia vina ~ia dici seu reputari debeant); **1377** cum J. Pecche .. impetitus fuisset de eo quod ij s. iiij d. de quolibet vase vini ~is in civitate nostra London' venditi .. per extorsionem recepit *Pat* 296 m. 21; **1482** pro vino ~i, viz. malvesino, j lagena et j laguncula, ij s. *Ac. Chamb. Cant.* 136b. **c** quis hominum ~ibus [AS: *þurhwerodum*] perfruitur cibis sine sapore salis? ÆLF. *Coll.* 98; caro ferina aliis carnibus est carior et ~ior *AncrR* 67. **d c1022** ubi .. ~issima odoramina flagrantia rosarum a justis .. capiuntur naribus *CD* 736. **e** ~ia, A. *ducettus* (*sic*) *WW*.

2 fresh, salt-free: **a** (of water); **b** (of water-meadow). **c** (acc. sg. n. as adv.) freshly, w. fresh water.

a cursus ad ~ia fluviorum freta dirigunt *Lib. Monstr.* II *pref.*; aperuit dulces in salsis rupibus amnes FRITH. 662; dulcia piscosae flumina traxit aquae WULF. *Swith. pref.* 38; W. MALM. *GP* IV 181 (v. dulcifluus 1a); NECKAM *NR* II 1 (v. depuratio 1a); **c1200** invenient .. hominem qui me debeat cariare per navem .. quam longe aqua ~is cursum suum protendit *Danelaw* 358; **1290** pisces aque †~e (v. aqua 1a); **1319** ubi salmunculi .. seu fria alterius generis piscium maris vel aque ~is descendunt (*Stat. Rob. I*) *APScot* I 109; **1447** eedem treuge .. tam per terram et aquas ~es quam per mare .. durabunt *Cl* 298 m. 26d. **b 1296** ix acre prati .. in pratis salsis et ~ibus versus solem *Cl* 113 m. 9d. **c 1459** manerium ipsiusque membra .. adjacent aque de Usa, que tam salse quam ~e fluit et refluit (*Pat*) *Eng. Clergy* 113.

3 sweet (to hear), dulcet, melodious. **b** (of speech) heard w. pleasure, honeyed.

ut .. ~em melodiam ymnista modulaturus proclamet ALDH. *VirgP* 18; melo[p]s, ~is sonus; melopoeum, ~e compositum *GlC* M 173–4; cuncta quae audiendo discere poterat .. in carmen ~issimum convertebat BEDE *HE* IV 22 p. 260; *Ib.* V 12 (v. cantilena 2); dulcia Daviticis resonantes organa psalmis WULF. *Swith.* II 37; GIR. *TH* I 21 (v. 2 cantus 3c); **c1190** (v. feriari 1a). **b** rithmus, ~is sermo *GlC* R 180; dulcia post modicum rex mitis protulit ora FRITH. 288; alloquio dulci pariter haec dicere et illi / "dormisne an vigilas?" WULF. *Swith.* I 242; bene loquentes et male cogitantes, ~ibus [AS: *swæsum*] verbis dediti ÆLF. *Coll.* 101.

4 sweet (fig.), pleasant, lovable: **a** (of thing or abstr.); **b** (of person or character); **c** (as surname).

a nec ~ior mors quae infertur a bono .. homine quam malo GILDAS *EB* 110; **706** secura ~is patriae otia ALDH. *Ep.* 9 (12); virginitatis amor .. / dulcia mundanae sprevit consortia vitae *Id. VirgV* 1980; semper aut discere aut docere aut scribere ~e habui BEDE *HE* V 24; ~e erat ei adolescentes .. docere ÆLF. *Æthelwold* 20; J. SAL. *Pol.* 386A (v. amarescere b); SERLO WILT. 19. 18 (v. acidus b); tam ~is et saluber mentium nexus GIR. *Symb.* I 9 p. 229; **s1254** quod pro amore .. Dei .. ~e regnum Francie deseruit M. PAR. *Maj.* V 425; peccatum aliquando videbatur ~e [ME: *swete*] *AncrR* 117. **b c800** sanctissima mater [abbatissa] et ~issima Dei ancilla ALCUIN *Ep.* 297; *Id. Carm.* 55. 6. 2 (v. dulcifer); **990** aedituum .. dempsit .. ~issimum amarissima leti conditio B. *Ep.* 387; **a1135** pro Dei dilectione et vestra ~issima nobilitate *Feod. Durh.* 151*n.*; Dei .. ~em benignitatem [ME: *milde milce*] *AncrR* 71. **c 1170** Alanus ~is *Pipe* 45.

5 (of iron) lacking rigidity, 'soft'.

frangitur calebs. ferrum ~ius est, ideo non frangitur, sed penetrat *Quaest. Salern.* B 206.

dulcisapa v. dulcis 1b.

dulcisapus, sweet-tasting. **b** (of speech) 'honeyed'.

~us, quod dulce sapit OSB. GLOUC. *Deriv.* 173; Maria decoquit panem salvificum, / panem dulcisapum WALT. WIMB. *Carm.* 118. **b** si studes animum placare regium, / verbis dulcissapis indulca labium *Id. Palpo* 22; non has [Parcas] propiciat munus aut munium, / sermo dulcisapus aut blandiloquium *Id. Sim.* 180.

dulcisone, melodiously.

incipiat mediocri voce ~e [AS p. 427: *werudlice*] cantare *RegulC* 51; dulcesone, i. blanda (*sic*), *weredre* vel *wynsumre*, melleflue *GlH* D 817.

dulcisonus [LL], sweet-sounding, melodious; **b** (fig.).

~is melodie concentibus ALDH. *VirgP* 7; et nova dulcisono modularis carmina plectro (*Hymn*) BEDE *HE* IV 18; **c790** caritas .. de qua ~us decantavit psalta [cf. *Cant.* viii 7] ALCUIN *Ep.* 60; **931** (13c) dulcissonas modulationes psalteriorum *CS* 671; organa cum tibiis resonant dulcīsona pulchris (*Vers.*) ÆLNOTH *Cnut* 44; si tibi dulcisona sit vox, modulatio cantus, / cantes D. BEC. 1774; ~am .. sonoritatem GIR. *IK* I 2. **b** aurea dulcisonae restaurat munera mentis ÆTHELWULF *Abb.* 498; o anima mea, .. lauda Dominum; laudando sencias dulcissona et canendo degustes mellita ROLLE *IA* 169.

dulciter [CL]

1 sweetly: **a** (of taste); **b** (of scent); **c** (of sound).

a ~ius sapiebant R. COLD. *Cuthb.* 118 (v. desuescere 1a). **b** cum .. flores .. suavi odoris flagrantia ~ius redoleant ALDH. *VirgP* 9. **c** grates dicamus dulciter / manenti immortaliter (*Id.*) *Carm. Aldh.* 1. 195; cantantes Domino psalmorum dulciter ymnos WULF. *Swith.* I 891; qui eam [nolam] audit ~iter sonare *Simil. Anselmi* 14.

2 pleasantly, agreeably. **b** dearly.

795 [nuntius] nos .. magna salutatione vestrae dilectionis ~iter reficiebat ALCUIN *Ep.* 41; hanc adolescens ~iter convenit et verbis allicit *V. Kentig.* 2; hinc addiscant prelati .. subditos suos ~iter tractare NECKAM *NR* I 54; principium temporis coitus, sc. in quo sperma ~iter exit M. SCOT *Phys.* 2; ego remaneo, visurus qualiter / jocatur parvulus cum matre dulciter WALT. WIMB. *Carm.* 222. **b** eam ~iter [ME: *sweteliche*] diligit *AncrR* 78.

dulcitudo [CL], sweetness (fig.), delight.

earum [legum humanarum] studia non vacant a ~ine consolacionis sancte FORTESCUE *LLA* 3; *swetnes*, .. dulcedo in gustu, ~o [v. l. dulcido] in anima [v. l. animo], suavitas *CathA.*

dulcivomus, sweetly gushing.

una cum veritate et justitia et pacis ~a consolatione *Quaest. Salern.* B 1.

dulcor [LL]

1 sweetness (of taste); **b** (fig.). **c** melody (fig.).

H. CANTOR 222 (v. amarescere a); dulcedo que omnem mellis ac favi ~orem excederet R. COLD. *Godr.* 41. **b** gusta bonitatem redemptoris tui .., gluti salubrem ~orem ANSELM (*Medit.* 3) III 84; cum aliorum opera non tantus comitetur fructus ~oris, eos quasi tediosos devitant *Quaest. Salern.* B 12; cujus [sapiencie] ~ore .. amarescunt gustui mel et manna R. BURY *Phil.* 1. 14; **c1430** (v. cithara b). **c** ipse fuit jubar in oculis et dulcor in aure VINSAUF *PN* 390.

2 sweetness (fig.), delight.

FRITH. 6 (v. antrum 1d); *Ib.* 1312 (v. cyclicus b); est mihi dulcori mors hec NIG. *Laur.* 37v. 2; tam sapidi ~oris .. affectus GIR. *Symb.* I 9 p. 229; Domine, .. / tui salutaris ostende dulcorem J. HOWD. *Cant.* 203; **1335** latex gracie .. que vestram universitatem .. subvencionis ~ore .. irrigavit *FormOx* 88.

dulcorare [LL]

1 to sweeten (in taste); **b** (fig.). **c** (*s. pass.*) to be sweetened (fig.).

mulsum est vinum melle ~atum BEDE *Ezra* 905; **8..** ~atur, *bið geweorðleht* *WW*; tale qui cor habuit pravum et rebelle / nunquam gustet pocula dulcorata melle GIR. *Symb.* II 44. 10; addatur mel ut ~etur GILB. I 35. 1; **s1263** vinum ex dulcedine †factum [v. l. fructuum] .. elebori ~atum egregie potantes, .. inebriati .. dormitaverunt *Plusc.* VII 23; *to swete*, delinire, ~are *CathA.* **b** fides .. dilectionis melle ~ata BEDE *Luke* 540; non perpendens .. venenum melle ~atum .., verba captancia decepcionis blandiciis illita extitisse *Hist. Meriadoci* 391; hec [caritas librorum] .. peregrinacionum absinthia quasi quedam pigmentaria pocio ~avit R. BURY *Phil.* 8. 125. **c 990** si .., jam jamque ~ante saporis nectarei fauce, forte quidam .. diriperet .. miseris vivendi victum optabilem B. *Ep.* 386.

2 (w. ref. to salt water) to freshen; **b** (fig., w. ref. to *Exod.* xv 25).

quare aqua marina cum sit .. salsa, transiens per cavernas terre ~atur? *Quaest. Salern.* Ba 117. **b** his [aquis] salsuginem earum absorbuit lignum Crucis et ~avit eas J. SAL. *Pol.* 777B; hec est virga que ~avit aquas Marath P. BLOIS *Serm.* 609D; lex datur in Syna, set aquam sale vasque farina/ dulcoravit Hely M. RIEVAULX (*Vers.*) 46. 10.

3 to sweeten (fig.), refresh. **b** to bribe.

s1191 (v. amaricare b); GIR. *Symb.* I 9 (v. dulcescere); Hugo .. / .. [matrem Sion] egram / sanat, anum renovat, acrem dulcorat, egenam / fecundat H. AVR. *Hugh* 852; tuus nos recreet suavis aspectus / et tali cor nostrum odore dulcoret J. HOWD. *Cant.* 317. **b s1225** quid .. faciendum est tibi tali viro nisi .. ejus amaritudinem beneficiis ~are regalibus? W. COVENTR. II 273.

dulcorarius, confectioner; *v. et. dulcarius.* **b** (fig.) purveyor of honeyed words.

regis curiam sequuntur assidue .. aleatores, ~ii, caupones .. P. BLOIS *Ep.* 14. 49A. **b** dulchorarii mendaces, histriones vani .. et .. concentores inanium fabularum J. SAL. *Pol.* 765B (cf. concentor).

dulcoratio, sweetening.

ab hoc nomine, quod est 'dulcis' .. ~o Osb. Glouc. *Deriv.* 165; addatur zuccarum aut mel ad ~onem Gilb. VII 336v. 1; *swetnes*, .. dulcor, dulcoratus, ~o .. *CathA.*

dulcorosus [LL], pleasant.

attrahit ad finem dulcorosum bona vita / et male finire pessima vita facit Walt. Angl. *Fab.* 46. 19.

dulegia v. douellegia.

Dulheia [Ar. *Dhū 'l-Ḥijja*], an Islamic month.

est hic annus Arabum xij menses in se continens ..; ultimus .. ~a, cum ex sua positione xxviiij dierum sit, .. ipse etiam xxx dierum nonnunquam supportatur Adel. *Elk.* 1.

dulia [LL *gl.* < δουλεία], service.

[in Graeca lingua] 'servitus' duobus modis ac diversa significatione solet appellari: dicitur enim λατρεία, dicitur et δουλεία sed δουλεία intellegitur servitus communis. .. λατρεία autem vocatur servitus illa quae soli divinitatis cultui debita .. est Bede *Luke* (iv 8) 368; in aula veritas est pestilencia / et assentantium dolus est dulia [*gl.*: servitus exhibenda homini] Walt. Wimb. *Palpo* 38; s**725** si creatori latriam, creature post Deum ~iam debemus Higd. V 24 p. 210; respondebis fortassis dicendo quod sic et non aliter istos deos honoras cultumque ~ie non latrie eis prebes Bradw. *CD* 17c; nulla talis [sc. complexa] veritas est Deus vel creatura; unde venerari debeat, nescio an sibi competeret ~ia vel latria, credo tamen pocius quod esset idolatria (Kyn.) *Ziz.* 65; prohibuit Johannem angelus [cf. *Rev.* xxii 9] seipsum vel ~ia adorare Wycl. *Incarn.* 35; honor vocatus ~ia debetur homini et angelo *Concl. Loll. XII* 8; *a service*, .. ~ia, latria; versus: 'dic dūlīam gentis; latriam, omnipo[te]ntis' *CathA.*

dulsus v. dulcescere.

dulus [δοῦλος], slave, servant.

δουλεία .., a qua etiam servus, id est δοῦλος, Graece nomen accipit Bede *Luke* 368 (cf. dulia); a**988** praeclui D. archipraesuli L. .. infimus ~orum (*Ep. ad Dunst.*) *Mem. Dunst.* 376; ~us, servus, *þeowa* Ælf. *Sup.*; exaudique dūlos, alme Birine, tuos Wulf. *Poems* XLVIII 2. 48; *a servande*, .. clientulus, ~us .., famulus .., manceps .. *CathA.*

dum [CL]

1 (adv.) yet.

1398 inter .. quod .. non est dum levatum *ExchScot* 457.

2 (conj.) while, (during or at the time) when, (for as long) as: **a** (w. ind., esp. pres., or unspec.); **b** (w. subj.). *V. et. dummodo.*

a cum clanget classica salpix, / ultima dum prisci labuntur tempora saeclis Aldh. *CE* 4. 5. 19; aurora in fulvis dum luxit lutea bigis *Id. VirgV* 1363; pro aliis .. qui, ejus interitum cognoscentes, differre tempus paenitentiae, dum vacat, timerent Bede *HE* V 13; ex contrariis saepe legibus nascitur quaestio, dum de una re alia lex aliter cavet, aliter et altera Alcuin *Rhet.* 9; **9**.. dum non perturbant, *þa whyle þa na gedrefaþ WW*; bello .. vulneratus, dum medetur emoritur Gosc. *Transl. Aug.* 36b; 'cum' dicit conjunccionem consequentem, 'dum' simul adjuncta *Ps.*-Gros. *Gram.* 57; avis .. dum sedet [ME: *þe hwile hit sit*] in terra non est secura *AncrR* 41. **b** quondam dum parvulus esset, / magna futurarum meruit spectacula rerum Aldh. *VirgV* 655; qui semper, dum viveret, .. pauperibus .. opem ferre non cessabat Bede *HE* III 9; quae omnia erant in firma regis E. dum viveret *DB* I 2v.; est imago S. Mariae .. quam pinxit Lucas evangelista dum adhuc viveret ipsa Dei genitrix *Descr. Constant.* 259; pater dum .. sacrum mysterium administraret, corpus dominicum .. apparuit Eadmer *V. Osw.* 3; illam rapuerat Eadwinus .. dum .. per provintias Britonum deseviret G. Mon. XII 7; dum Maro Cartaginis jocaretur hospitium, amantium vota conciliare nescivit, nisi .. J. Sal. *Pol.* 391a; T. Mon. *Will.* II 9 (v. deintus 1a); non possum credere sorti, / saltem dumque Deus sit super omne potens Gower *VC* II 88.

3 when, after, as soon as: **a** (w. ind.); **b** (w. subj.).

a c**710** quam rem dum ad effectum tua perduxerit benivolentia .. gratiarum actiones habebis (Berhtwald) *Ep. Bonif.* 7; c**792** dum plenum perficitur [pacis] vestimentum, mox ad induendum vestrae dirigetur fraternitati Alcuin *Ep.* 14; dum .. quieverit ista passio, crastino die, Deo auctore, apparebo A. Tewk. *Add. Thom.* 8. **b** quies cum fessos occupat artus, / dulcia dum famulae cecinissent carmina Christo Aldh. *VirgV* 2232; dum .. ad mensam consedissent, subito .. mentem ad spiritualia contemplanda contulit Bede *CuthbP* 34; quod dum factum esset, episcopatum .. anno uno servabat .. Uilfrid *Id. HE* IV 27 p. 275; Lotharius, dum .. duodecim annis regnasset, .. emoritur Gosc. *Transl. Aug.* 36b; dum .. promisisset se .. consuetudines .. observaturum, ad mentem sedulo revocavit quanta ex his potuerint .. oriri dispendia A. Tewk. *Add. Thom.* 3.

4 (esp. w. *usque*) till: **a** (w. ind. or unspec.); **b** (w. subj.).

a dum, donec *GlC* D 380; curam .. suscepit ac tenuit usque dum et ipse .. ad caelestia regna .. ascendit Bede *HE* II 20; haec, usquedum ad ejus visionem pervenire meruit, intemerata servavit *Ib.* IV 21 p. 252; meos convivas .. usquedum rediero letificate *Arthur & Gorlagon* 2. **b** cujus in hac aula sacra conservabitur ara, / dum polus et tellus ac ponti flustra fatescant Aldh. *CE* 4. 11. 6; ipse .. presbyteros .., usquedum archiepiscopus perveniret, ordinabat Bede *HE* IV 2; nolunt accipere legem .. usque dum diffiniatur per regem *DB* I 44v.; de electo in abbatem, qualiter se geret usquedum confirmetur *Cust. Cant. rub.* 69.

5 whereas, seeing that, in that, since: **a** (w. ind.); **b** (w. subj.).

a quod illi [Jeremiae; cf. *Lam.* iv 7-8] .. ad cumulum doloris crescebat, dum .. eosdem statu prospero viventes egregios luxerat Gildas *EB* 1; **671** ut sententiam B. Hieronimi, dum se occasio obtulit, depromam Aldh. *Ep.* 1; qui, dum .. Sunamitis sobolem .. suscitaverat [cf. *2 Kings* iv 35], redemptorem signat genus humanum .. vivificantem *Id. Met.* 2; sed secus evenit, / praefatus lector dum fraudem prodidit atram *Id. VirgV.* 1006; **749** (12c) dum mihi omnipotens Deus .. sceptra regiminis .. largitus est, ideo ei libenter .. ex eo quod accepi iterum retribuo *CS* 178; **793** quid de aliis estimandum est locis, dum huic sanctissimo loco judicium non pepercit divinum? Alcuin *Ep.* 16; dum .. mores in eo imitabantur dignitatem pontificis, ratus est B. Dunstanus .. mores illius jure sullimandos dignitate pontificis Eadmer *V. Osw.* 12. **b** heu! frustra factor confinxit corpus inorme, / totis membrorum dum frauder sensibus intus Aldh. *Aen.* 72 (*Colossus*) 8; optatam senserunt saecla salutem, / dum Deus ad Herebi vagas descenderit umbras *Id. VirgV* 455; dum illum [lapidem] .. nullo conatu .. movere valerent, adjuncti sunt eis alii et alii viri Eadmer *V. Osw.* 20; s**1205** orte sunt in ecclesia Cantuariensi dissentiones .. super electione archiepiscopi, dum monachi priorem electionem, quam de suppriore suo fecerant, .. relinquerent G. Cold. *Durh.* 17.

6 although (w. subj.).

quod utrum de se an de alio aliquo diceret nobis manet incertum, dum tamen hoc quod tantus vir dixit, quia verum sit, esse non possit incertum Bede *HE* IV 3.

7 so long as, on condition that, provided that (w. subj.); *cf. dummodo*; **b** (? w. *cum*). **c** so that, in order that. **d** (repeated, w. pr. ppl.) whether .. or.

promittens me elimosynas .. dare, dum ille domum comitis pransurus .. intraret Bede *HE* V 4; **1255** mandavit .. senescallo foreste quod .. ipsos deliberaret, dum tamen non essent capti cum venacione *SelPlForest* 31; **1267** quod .. habeant .. liberam warennam .. in omnibus dominicis terris suis .., dum tamen terre ille non sint infra metas forreste nostre (*Ch. Regis*) *Ib.* cxxiv (cf. *CalCh* II 80); parum curo de illis dum tamen hec [amoris regula] care servetur *AncrR* 163; **1437** dumtamen (v. 1 cunagium 2b). **b** c**1200** liberum erit eis .. ij m. .. recipere sicut antiquitus solebant, dum †cum nec dolus nec necgligentia eorum in aliquo possit deprehendi *Dryburgh* 67. **c** censebis ficta fuisse / que de me dixit, dum silvas possit adire *V. Merl.* 327. **d** c**800** vera est sapientia ut quisque se ipsum considerans dum volens dum nolens aeternus erit, ut (*sic*) aeternam sibi ex hoc brevi labore comparet requiem Alcuin *Ep.* 297.

duma v. 1 dumus a.

dumalis [LL], thorny.

~ibus, spinetis *GlH* D 834; ~is, dumis plenus Osb. Glouc. *Deriv.* 176.

dumare, to beset w. briers.

to thorne, ~are, spinare .. *CathA.*

dumescere [LL], **dumēre,** to be overgrown w. briers or weeds; **b** (fig.). **c** to grow bushy (w. hair).

to thorne .., ~ere .., ~escere *CathA.* **b** **1423** apud istos .. religionis frumentum ~escit in lolium (*Sermo*) Amund. I 78. **c** dumescente pilis facie radioque juvente / obscuris pallente genis Hanv. I 216 p. 247; multi dumescunt mento qui mente virescunt Walt. Wimb. *App.* 2. 4.

dumetum [CL], brier-patch, thicket.

~um, spinetum *GlH* D 835; [Edmundi] caput a corpore .. divisum ~a, Danis proicientibus, occuluerant W. Malm. *GP* II 74 p. 153; sylvas et ~a peragrabat W. Cant. *Mir. Thom.* V 22; hic mihi sit requies inter dumeta sub hortis *Babio* 323; pisces .. vi ventorum intra ~a projectos Gir. *IK* I 13; **1252** traxit illam [damam mortuam] in quendam (sic) ~um *SelPlForest* 106.

dummodo [CL; al. div.]

1 so long as, provided that: **a** (w. subj.); **b** (w. fut. perf. ind.).

a promittens se multum illi esse placatum, dum modo ille .. tristitiam deponeret Bede *HE* III 14; promisit se ei .. donaria .. largiturum .., ~o ille domum rediret *Ib.* III 24; utrum proprietarii sint non curant, ~o .. possessores efficiantur Neckam *NR* II 187; Map *NC* III 4 (v. curare 1d); licet [schismatici] aliqua jura ecclesiastica †possunt [? l. possint] habere, ~o non †sunt [? l. sint] heretici Ockham *Dial.* 945; **1559** quod nulli .. liceat aliquos alterius partis subditos navigantes, ~o .. evidenter constet .. quod alterius partis subditi naves .. sint, .. a licita navigatione impedire (*TR ScotDoc* 101/121) *Foed.* XV 525a. **b** **1467** ~o litteras dimissorias .. exhibuerit (v. dimissorius a).

2 until (w. ind.).

1311 debet invenire j equum .. ad fima .. extrahenda ..; et valet opus per diem ij d. et non plus, quia dominus inveniet pastura[m] ad animalia ~o fecerint opus *Cust. Battle* 156; cujus [ducis Hibernie] stolida precordia .. spes pascebat inanis, ~o de .. ejus .. rabie .. appellantes in punctu temporis cerciorati extiterant Favent 11; **1459** summi regis clemencia .. pacem .. vestris concedat temporibus, ~o reges et principes .. habebunt laudare regem regum *Reg. Whet.* I 327.

3 while (w. subj.).

s**1319** Scotti .., ~o Angli in .. obsidione [Berwici] residerent, .. subito venerunt in comitatum Ebor' *Meaux* II 336; **1464** ego Johannes de M. .., ~o sic ut premittitur agerentur .., presens interfui *Reg. Glasg.* 418.

dumosus [CL], overgrown w. briers, thorny; **b** (fig.).

Aldh. *Ep.* 3 (v. diverticulum 1b); (Æthelwald) *Carm. Aldh.* 2. 62 (v. devius 1a); in .. saltibus ~is Bede *Egb.* 7; festinabant per adversa et prospera, per plana et ~a Gosc. *Aug. Maj.* 56a; **1388** j acram bosci ~i *IMisc* 332/37; **1550** unam domum ~am vocatam *le storehouse CalPat* III 383. **b** vir Dei ab hac [natione] vipereum pereuntis lolii germen .. exstirpavit, ut ~i ruris rudera .. pullulare prohiberet B. *V. Dunst.* 2.

†dumpedare, to 'wince', kick back.

to wynche, calcitrare, re-, repercutere, repedare, ~are *CathA.*

dumtaxat [CL]

1 a no less (than), at least. **b** no more (than), at most, only.

a primus occurrit .. Samuel .., denuntiando primo regi apud Hebraeos ~at Sauli Gildas *EB* 38; †**676** (12c) ad augmentum catholicae .. fidei pontificalem ~at erigentes cathedram .. construere censuimus *CS* 43; praetorum filias .. ad .. coronam castitatis .. instigavit, ita ~at ut unamquamque .. caelestis sponsi amplexus .. satagere .. suspiria faterentur Aldh. *VirgP* 48; tabernaculum perfectam fidelium vitam in hoc ~at saeculo commorantium typice denuntiat Bede *Tab.* 456; huic responsioni obviandum est, primum ratione .., deinde auctoritate, non qualibet sed divina ~at Fridug. 126; **964** (11c) ita ~at ut semper aecclesiae servitia .. persolvantur *CS* 1136; validissimam pubem, totius duntaxat Anglie florem *G. Steph.* I 16; nisi duntaxat gracie regalis benignum favorem perpenderint *Ps.*-Elmh. *Hen. V* 69. **b** **706** apum .. cohortes rapido volatu ad aethera glomerant, exceptis ~at antiquarum sedium servatricibus Aldh. *Ep.* 9 (12); ~at, tantummodo *GlC* D 370; ut nihil aspicerem, excepta ~at specie .. ejus qui me ducebat Bede *HE* V 12; tota septimana non apparent [aves] excepto Sabbato ~at et die dominica Alex. Cant. *Mir.* 36 (I) p. 233; J. Sal. *Met.* 869b (v. 2 dediscere); *Ib.* 920c (v. demonstrativus d); [accipiter] avolavit .., ut non oculos omnium duntaxat evaderet sed et redeundi spem penitus auferret W. Cant. *Mir. Thom.* VI 66; H. Bos. *LM* 1301a (v. chorda 2b); **1298** (v. delineare).

2 (as conj. w. subj.) provided that.

1305 admittenda est probacio cujuslibet testamenti, duntaxat testes deposuerint de ultima voluntate testatoris *MGL* I 120.

1 dumus [CL], brier or thicket; **b** (prov.).

Gildas *EB* 20 (v. 1 conserere 1d); in Nitriae frondosis accola dumis Aldh. *VirgV* 1456; ~us, *þyrne*; ~is, spinis *GlC* D 373-4; ~us, i. spina, spineta, *þyrne*; .. †~as, spinas vel *græfe GlH* D 831, 833; ~orum asperitatem W. Malm. *GP* I 14 (v. eluctari a); *Ib.* IV 186 (v. condensitas); locum ~orum et veprium densitate inaccessibilem R. Cold. *Godr.* 347; prosilit a dumo perdix Walt. Angl. *Fab.* 58. 11; cum bestiola .. fetus teneros .. extra ~os in planitiem eduxisset Gir. *IK* I 12; **1249** usque ad quendam ~um extra boscum *IMisc* 3/26 (= *Cal.* 2063: †dunum); **1316** cum bosco, ~is, sepibus et divisis omnibus *ChartR* 102 m. 10. **b** excussi dumos; aucupat alter aves *Babio* 184 (cf. J. Blund *An.* 164: excutit hic dumos; occupat alter aves); vulgari proverbio dicitur Gallice: 'avis que ad quemlibet ~um [OF *ib.*: *a tuz buysuns*] resistit, tarde veniet ad bonum arboris subclinatorium' J. Godard *Ep.* 237.

2 dumus [cf. OF *dumet*], down (of chicks). *Cf. duvetum.*

~o abjecto et caude pennis ordine perfectis Adel. *CA* 9.

1 duna [AS *dun*], down. **b** high ground (in marsh).

unam virgam terrae et pascuam quam vocant ~am *DB* (*Hants*) I 39v.; c**1230** debet habere omnes oves in pastura sequendo [v. l. sequentes] vestigia ovium domini super donam .. et grossa animalia habere †debent [? l. debet] .. a †Natale [? l. Natali] usque ad autumpnum super donam continue (*Cust. Quarley, Hants*) *Doc. Bec* 59; c**1283** debent communare cum abbate de Begeham et nobiscum in pastura de ~a de Teletun' [*Suss*] *Cust. Battle* 32; **1285** si cariat buscam, descendendo ~am habebit vj d. quilibet pro stipendio *Cust. Suss* II 25 (cf. ib. 135 [**1306**]: super

dounam). **b** **1194** de una dunna vocata Cnocke in Oxenell' et alia dunna vocata Wokele et dim. †denna [v. l. dunna] in Idunne et de quarta parte unius dunne que vocatur Fugelebroc *Doc. Robertsbr.* 44 (cf. *Kent Arch. Soc.* XV p. cxxiv); **1250** super dounam que jacet inter terram R. de W. et veterem fordam [*Hackney, Middx*] *AncD* A 2634; **12..** dedi . . j acram terre arabilis jacentem super ~am inter terram ecclesie dicte ville [*Soham, Cambs*] et terram meam *Ib.* 6062; **12..** [vj acras terre jacentes super] duna [*Lambeth, Surr*] *Cart. S. Thom. Hosp.* no. 551.

2 duna v. duva.

dungia [AS *dung*], dung.

pastoris ovium rectum est ut habeat dingiam [v. l. dungiam] xij noctium [AS: *twelf nihta dingan*] in Natali Domini (*Quad., Rect.*) *GAS* 451.

dungio, dungo v. dunjo.

†Dunio, *f. l.*

nec denarios invenerunt preter octo †Duniones [? l. Divionenses, i.e. *coins of Dijon*], qui sterlingos duos non valebant GIR. *JS* 5 p. 293.

dunjo, ~ona [AN *dungun*, OF *donjon*, *danjon* < dominionem], dungeon, keep.

rex habet . . in villa . . castellum quoddam, supra castellum autem unum dungionem; . . tanta . . securitas est in dungione ut, si quis illuc poterit ascendere, numquam eum inde libeat redire *Simil. Anselmi* 76; dangionem regis apud Ebroas funditus dejecerunt ORD. VIT. X 33 p. 279 (cf. ib. XII 37 p. 451: munio regii dangionis); **1233** de convencione inter nos et dominos vestros facta, quibus commisimus ~onem castri nostri Divisarum (*Pat*) *Foed.* (4th *ed.*) I 210; **1238** quod pontem dungone castri nostri Cestr' . . reparari faciatis *Liberate* 13 m. 23; **1269** novum turrellum donjone castri nostri Winton' . . de novo fieri . . *Ib.* 45 m. 4; **1339** in quodam homine locato ad petendum bokettum de magno puteo infra donjonem [castri Dovorr'], xij d. *KRAc* 462/15 m. 5; **1348** pro coopertura camere et garderobe domini regis infra ~onem [castri Dovorr'] *Ib.* 462/16 f. 9.

dunna v. 1 duna b. **duntaxat** v. dumtaxat. **dunus** v. 1 dumus a.

duo [CL], two.

quos jussit construere inter duo maria trans insulam murum GILDAS *EB* 15; ALDH. *Aen.* 66. 3 (v. 1 ambo a); 'duorum' rationis est, 'duum' eufoniae *GlC* D 378–9; [cepi] duos [AS: *twegen*] heortas et unum aprum ÆLF. *Coll.* 93; †**1083** tradidi . . duo Pittindunas *Ch. Durh.* *3; in his duabus Meltunis *DB* (*Norf*) II 204v.; ut non sint duo sed unus spiritus ANSELM (*Mon.* 29) I 48; non sequitur 'ergo Christus est duo', cum 'duo' dicit collectionem duorum quorum utrumque est [unum] numero HALES *Sent.* III 85; 'duo' numerus non est, sed necessitas ad numerum, quia unitas non est numeri principium nisi postquam ipsam replicatam intellexeris *Ps.*-GROS. *Gram.* 40; †dua inveniet luminaria *Cust. Cant.* 102; [sacerdos] potest imponere . . duo pater noster [ME: *twa pater nosteres*], x ave *AncrR* 134; c**1350** duo et duo (v. dinarium).

duodecades v. decas a. **duodecedron, -decaedron** v. dodecaëdrum. **duodecem** v. duodecim.

duodecennis [LL], twelve years old. *V. et. duodennis* a.

quod ipse ~is [v. l. duodennis] in templo sedit in medio doctorum [*cf. Luke* ii 46] BEDE *Hom.* I 19. 64; ~is, duodennis, xij annorum OSB. GLOUC. *Deriv.* 181.

duodecies [CL], twelve times.

~es quinquagenis expeditionum milibus [cf. *Exod.* xii 37] ALDH. *VirgP* 12; **9..** ~es quinquagies millia, *twelfsiþum fiftig þusenda WW*; decem horae . . ~es ductae centum viginti reddunt horarum BYRHT. *Man.* 3; *GAS* 593 (v. centenus 1d); **12..** hoc sigillum in anulo aureo pondere sigilli ~es exequato ponas *Sculp. Lap.* 452.

duodecim [CL], **~em,** twelve.

680 ~im tribubus in dispersione constitutis [cf. *James* i 1] ALDH. *Ep.* 4; ~im apostolorum ministerio BEDE *Luke* 348; si eum intra ~im menses [AS: *on twelf monþum*] non redemerint (*Quad.*) *GAS* 101; c**1160** perdonavimus ~em denarios de viginti sex denariis *Lit. Cant.* III app. 379; hic sunt sex ova; proba ergo quod hic sunt ~im GIR. *GE* II 37; BACON *Maj.* I 161 (v. dodecaëdrum).

duodecimhyndus [AS *twelfhynde*], (man) having wergeld of 1200 *solidi.*

si *twelfhind* [v. l. duodecimhindus; AS: *twelfhynde*] sit, quotquot interfuerint cxx sol. reddant (*Quad.*) *GAS* 65 (cf. ib. 97: debet esse medietas jurantium per †hulsgengas [AS: *huslgengum*], id est ~os).

duodecimus [CL]

1 twelfth. **b** (every) twelfth, one out of twelve. **c** (as sb. f.) tax of one twelfth. **d** (mus.) twelve-tone scale.

rex Hyglacus . . quem equus a ~o aetatis anno portare non potuit *Lib. Monstr.* I 2; ~um [sidus] Piscium . . finitur in medio Martii BEDE *TR* 16; accipiat undecim et ipse sit ~us [AS: *beo sylf twelfta*] et ita se purget (*Inst. Cnuti*) *GAS* 345; ~a manu BRACTON 310 (v. compurgator b); cum se ~o *Quon. Attach.* 24 (v. acquietatio 3c). **b** s**1295** clerus decimum, cives sextum, populus ~um denarium regi contulerunt W. GUISB. 258. **c** **1296** racione ~e nobis a laicis regni . . concesse *RGasc* III 346; **1299** petit . . viij d. pro taxacione illarum vaccarum taxatarum ad ~am domini regis *CourtR Hales* 398; **1319** breve majori . . ad recipiendos rotulos pro xij^{ma} in civitate . . assessa (*LBLond.* E f. 93) *MGL* I 595. **d** secuntur regule v alie universales per ~am HOTHBY *Contrap.* FL 66; expliciunt regule per ~am *Ib.* 67.

2 (abl. sg. m. or n.) in the twelfth place, twelfthly.

1282 ~o petimus ut [Wallenses] . . ad cor redeant penitentes PECKHAM *Ep.* 340; ~o potest quis convinci pertinax . . si de veritate damnabiliter renuit informari OCKHAM *Dial.* 465.

duodecuplus, (abl. sg. m. or n.) in twelve-fold quantity, twelve-fold.

~o reddat . . *GAS* 91 (v. cyricsceattum).

duodena v. 2 duodenus 4 & 5.

duodenarius [CL]

1 (w. *numerus* or as sb. m.) number twelve or set of twelve, dozen; **b** (w. ref. to twelve apostles).

~io numero, qui multiplicatis inter se invicem septenarii partibus constat BEDE *Luke* 348; [numerus] cujus partes multiplicative reddunt summam majorem toto, ut ~ius NECKAM *NR* II 173 p. 295 (cf. 2 abundare 4b); numero . . fratrum ~io presidens *Cust. Cant.* 166; **1465** lego . . unum ~ium paropsidum de stagno *MunAcOx* 712; *twelfe*, duodecim . . , ~ius *CathA.* **b** noluit Dominus ~ium in undenario consistere numero; ideo Mathias in solio duodeno residere permittitur BYRHT. *Man.* 220; factum est ut post paucorum excursum mensium [discipuli Oswaldi] numerum excederent †sacroduodenarium [? l. sacrum ~ium] *Id. V. Osw.* 424 (cf. EADMER *V. Osw.* 15: collecti fratres ~ii numeri summam complent).

2 (every) twelfth, one out of twelve.

s**1296** concessus est ei [sc. regi] a civibus et burgensibus octonarius denarius; a ceteris ~ius est extortus *Flor. Hist.* III 98 (cf. duodecimus 1b).

duodennis [LL], twelve years old; *v. et. duodecennis.* **b** lasting twelve years.

[evangelista] eundem [Jesum] . . ~em in templo doctorum choris insert BEDE *Luke* (ii 42) 348; Ethelfridus . . habuerat [tempore exitus] . . filios duos, Oswaldum ~em et Oswium quadriennem W. MALM. *GR* I 47; puer ~is ORD. VIT. XIII 16 (v. doma 2a); juvenis erat duodecim annorum quum patrem ipsius rex Edwindus et Redwaldus peremerant. ita ~is effectus exul a patria R. COLD. *Osw.* 40; s**1175** Philippus . . tunc temporis †duodenus [? l. duodennis] existens GIR. *PI* III 25 p. 289; s**1212** multitudo [puerorum] . ., quorum nullus ~e [? l. ~i] major erat *Chr. Peterb.* 6; s**1236** puellam . . etate fere duodenem M. PAR. *Min.* II 386. **b** post bellum diutinum et ~e discrimen tandem . . Troie nobilis secuta ruina est GIR. *JS* 3 p. 205.

duodennium [cf. LL duodecennium], period of twelve years.

Macedonem Alexandrum . . ~io illicita tyrannide fastigatum . . parvissima urna . . excepit *Chr. Rams.* 33; sic fere ~ium michi elapsum est diversis studiis occupato J. SAL. *Met.* 869A; **1199** nobis jam plusquam per ~ium continuis tempestatibus fatigatis *Ep. Cant.* 523.

1 duodenus v. duodennis a.

2 duodenus [CL]

1 (pl.): **a** twelve each. **b** twelve.

a communium annorum menses ~os explicabant BEDE *TR* 45; s**1188** posuerant prefecti scelerum homines de villis archiepiscopi denos et ~os et vicenos . . in curiam monachorum GERV. CANT. *Chr.* 401. **b** ~os Judeorum preceptores . . disputationum spicula . . torquentes ALDH. *VirgP* 25; FRITH. 741 (v. dyas); ter quater fiunt ~i BYRHT. *Man.* 224; ~os pedes extendit R. COLD. *Cuthb.* 92 (v. circumambire).

2 **a** twelve-fold. **b** (w. *numerus*) number twelve.

a ~us apex, *twelffeald geþungennes GlH* D 845; stat duodena cohors multis stipata columnis FRITH. 344; cibum turbe duodene / se dat manu propria LEDREDE *Carm.* 21. 5. **b** s**1309** elegerunt ex se in ~o numero quatuor episcopos, quatuor comites et quatuor barones *Flor. Hist.* III 146; **1324** de numero ~o quinque personas . . modo recepi *Lit. Cant.* I 129.

3 twelfth.

~o †folio [MS: solio], *twelffealdum setle GlH* D 843 (cf. duodenarius 1b); undecimum . . numerum smaragdus adimplet; / huic quoque chrysoprasus fert duodenus opem G. AMIENS *Hast.* 774; ut . . alter eorum juraret cum manu ~a vicinorum *MunAcOx* 632; s**1460** anno milleno centum quater x quoque seno, / ter denoque die duodeno mense Decembre (*Vers.*) *Reg. Whet.* I 383.

4 (as sb. f. or n.) set of twelve, dozen; **b** (dist. as long dozen, *i. e.* thirteen, or short; *cf. Arch.* LXIV 154 *n.*).

ut [mercator], si [pannos] fuscotinctos attulerit, non minus ~a simul vendat (*Lib. Lond.*) *GAS* 674; **1214** (v. coifa 1a); **1281** (v. cochlear 1b); **1303** in v ~is parcameni emptis *DCWestm.* 72/12 335; **1332** etc. (v. discus 2b); **1334** in xx ~is carbonum . . precium ~e iij s. x d. (*MinAc Kent*) *Arch.* LXIV 158; **1335** in j ~o salmonum empto, xij s. *Comp. Swith.* 246; **1374** j ~um de vetere disco de stanno *Pri. Cold.* app. p. lxxvi; **1388** (v. birretum); **1393** (v. chorda 4a); **1409** in lucracione . . liij petre minere ferri, ~a continente iij *fothers* (*Aud. Durh.*) *EHR* XIV 518; ~a carbonis *Ib.* 519 (v. comburere 3b); **1409** item xj ~e [? sc. librarum] cere et iiij lib. *Ac. Durh.* 607 (cf. ib.: iiij ~e *rasyng* de Coreyns); **1432** ~as . . panni (v. crudus 3b); **1434** (v. chirotheca 1a); **1460** (v. centenarius 2b); **1511** gallinarum . . xv ~e (v. domesticus 2a). **b** **1462** pro tribus magnis ~is vasorum stanneorum *ExchScot* 147 (cf. ib. 149: pro duabus parvis ~is perapsidum); **1466** pro . . una magna ~a vasorum stanneorum *Ib.* 401.

5 (as sb. f.) body of twelve men (esp. inquest jury).

1276 libere tenentes de Alvertonschire solebant respondere cum ~a de Brudeford *Hund.* (*Yorks*) I 123a; **1279** unus villanus de homagio Radulfi . . et unus villanus de homagio Roberti . . ibunt ad duos turnos pro tito feoudo . ., ita quod de homagio . . Radulfi erit tastor servisie et de feodo Roberti . . erit alius tastor, et . . Radulfus et Robertus habent suas ~as *Ib.* (*Cambs*) II 461b; ad placita corone de qualibet ~a xx †denarios [v. l. denarii] tantum capiantur *Fleta* 88; per presentacionem †~orum [MS: ~e] de hundredo de S. *State Tri. Ed. I* 70; **1291** statutum fuit quod, si aliqua ~a sit attincta per iij prebendas viciniores de fracto sacramento, quod (*sic*) illi qui fuerint in juramento amerciabuntur *Stat. Ebor.* 119; **1300** maledixit ~am taxantem talliagium *Rec. Leic.* I 230; **1322** abbatem et commonachos . . in abbathia . . obsederunt . ., quousque . . concessissent eis certas libertates . ., viz. fieri burgenses et habendum (*sic*) ~am de seipsis, ubi solebant cum forinsecis de libertate . . abbatis adjungi (*Verdict*) *G. S. Alb.* II 230; c**1325** breve quod ~e existentes cotidie coram justiciariis itinerantibus haberent racionabiles expensas (*LBLond.*E 125) *MGL* I 672; WALS. *HA* II 24 (v. 2 edicere 3b); s**1402** justiciarius audita ~a tulit sentenciam, dicens "tu traheris . . super claiam usque ad Tyburn' . ." *Eul. Hist. Cont.* III 390; **1434** (v. concurrere 5a); **14..** de . . malis procuratoribus ~arum, inquisicionum, assisarum et juratarum *Reg. Brev. Orig.* 186b; *quest*, ~a *PP*; *an inqwest*, inquesicio, ~a *CathA.*

6 (as sb. n., anat.) duodenum.

ad proximum intestinum, quod ~um dicitur, quia habet duodecim pollices ejus cujus est, et etiam porta stomachi inferior judicatur RIC. MED. *Anat.* 224; primum intestinum . . ~um appellatur, quia continet xij digitos *Ps.*-RIC. *Anat.* 35; notandum sex esse intestina, tria gracilia, sc. ~um, †jejunium [? l. jejunum] et yleon . . GILB. V 225v. 1; assurgit supra haec intestina omnia ~um . . Graecis δωδεκαδάκτυλον vocatur a duodecim digitorum mensura D. EDW. *Anat.* A4v.

7 (as sb. m.) penny (Scot.).

in plerisque Scotiae locis duobus ~is magnum salmonem recentem habebis, in aliis autem uno solido MAJOR I 6.

duodetricenarius, (w. *numerus*) twenty-eight.

est et aliud in ~io numero sacramentum aeque ad septenarium pertinens BEDE *Tab.* 427.

duodetricesimus [CL], twenty-eighth.

agitur nunc annus ~us ex quo Mercensibus preesse ceperat *Pass. Æthelb.* 3.

duodevicesimus [CL], eighteenth.

ut plane dicitur Matthei [capitulo] ~o et Johannis vicesimo WYCL. *Chr. & Antichr.* 666.

duodeviginti [CL], eighteen.

in gravi egritudine ~i menses transigebat W. CANT. *Mir. Thom.* V 6; hec vox annorum '~i' est una vox composita et significat idem quod 'octodecim' et est adjectivum ejus quod est 'annorum'; . . et est nomen compositum ex corruptis et integris, quia idem est quod 'duobus demptis a viginti' BACON XV 185; *aghten*, decemocto, duodeviginta (*sic*) *CathA.*

duodigitalis, (of pigs, w. ref. to the thickness of the fat) measuring two finger-breadths.

si pasnagium capiatur de porcis, de tridigitali tertius, de ~i quartus [AS: *æt twyfingrum þæt feorðe*], de þimelo quintus (*Quad.*) *GAS* 111.

dupl- v. et dubl-.

duplare [CL]

1 to double (math.).

cum census radicem, sive notam sive surdam, ~are volueris, multiplica duo cum duobus et cum producto multiplica censum ROB. ANGL. *Alg. add.* 140; si duplicationem probare voluerimus, que ~averamus novenario dividamus, reliquumque ~atum itidemque divisum no-

tam note integri ~ati eademque divisi similem ostendit ADEL. *Alch.* 1 p. 20; ergo si relationes iste haberent essentias preter essentias extremitatum, unico nato et unico addito numero rerum, ~abitur et triplabitur vel forte multiplicabitur numerus rerum GROS. 192; c**1267** fructum .. in conspectu missi agricole .. ostendit, qui ~ato et utinam de superna pietate mansuro talento suspirat in requiem (*Lit. O. Cardinalis*) *EHR* XV 111; ~abitur ei [priori] sua porcio .. in prandio et in cena *Cust. Cant.* 137; c**1410** quod pro 2ª vice eandem summam, ad quam tenebitur in prima vice, ~are, pro tercia triplare astringatur *StatOx* 206; primi fructus episcopatuum ~antur et precio majori quam duplo solvuntur GASCOIGNE *Loci* 153; *to dowbylle*, ~are, duplicare, binare .., *to dubylle*, .. ~are, duplicare, geminare .. *CathA.*

2 a to duplicate (document). **b** (leg.) to make a 'duply' (rejoinder).

a a**1347** in qua cista reponantur .. rotuli continentes .. munimenta et cartas; et similiter ponantur ibi carte, si sint ~ate *StatOx* 148; **1384** dat' clerico nostro pro labore suo circa .. scripcionem compoti nostri ~ati, xx d. *Ac. Obed. Abingd.* 46. **b** **1487** procuratores .. ad .. opponendum, respondendum, accipiendum, repliandum, ~andum, triplandum .. *Conc.* III 621.

3 to bend, crook (fingers).

~are, duplicare vel curvare OSB. GLOUC. *Deriv.* 181; ut patet in gelu .., quia homo non potest digitos ~are GAD. 64v. 2.

4 (p. ppl.): **a** (?) double-leaved (of gate). **b** lined (of gown).

a muro urbis alto et magno ~atis heptapyle portis intercontinuante, turrito ab aquilone per intercapedines W. FITZST. *Thom. prol.* 5. **b** toga .. / simplex, duplata [*gl.*: *lyned*], pellita; pallium adde STANBR. *Vulg.* 8.

duplarius [LL; cf. AN *dubler*, OF *doblier*]

1 (w. *mappa* or as sb. n.) 'doubler' (napkin or table cloth). *Cf. diploma* 2.

1191 robavit ei .. iiij dubler' et octo lintheamina *CurR RC* II 121; c**1195** dedit nobis .. unum dublarium de viginti ulnis *Rec. Eton* XXVI (*Cottesford*) no. 1; **1204** pro iiij doliis vini et dub'lariis et linea tela, que emit ad opus nostrum *Cl* 12b; **1218** habere faciatis .. servienti nostro tres dubleras mappas ad opus nostrum proprium, quarum quelibet habeat xx ulnas in longitudine, .. et c ulnas linei panni ad mappas faciendas ad opus familie nostre *Ib.* 370a; **1212** reddendo inde annuatim .. j dublerum et j manutergium *Fees* 80; **1231** legat .. Andree filio ejus culcitram suam et dublarium *Cart. Osney* I 136 (= *EHR* XX 292).

2 (as sb. n.) **a** 'doubler' (measure of wine; sts. = tun). **b** double measure of food or drink. **c** (?) plate, dish.

a **1212** computate .. tres pipas et unum dublerum de musco *Cl* 124a; **1237** pro xj tresell' et xx ~iis vini Francie *Pipe* 81 r. 15; **1242** vj li. j m. pro v ~iis vini Gallici, viz. pro quolibet dolio ij m. *Liberate* 16 m. 12 (*Cal.* p. 101). **b** non sunt nisi duo servitores ad discum, quorum ille qui ~ium abbatis portat sonitum faciet nole ad primum generale... prior alienus .. habebit ~ium ad omnia fercula sua... et ipse [qui ad discum sedet] in dublario mittet priori externo *Cust. Cant. Abbr.* 254; ministretur eis cum dubblario tam de potagio quam de ferculis *Reg. Pri. Worc.* 130a. **c** **1250** disci vj, dublar' vj, cyphi vj, sausar' vj *MinAc* (*Ramsey*) 766/20d.

duplatio [CL], doubling, multiplication (by two).

THURKILL *Abac.* 56 (v. 1 digitus 3); si ~onem radicis numeri novem habere volueris, dicas: "bis duo procreant 4, que cum novenario multiplicata ad 36 excrescet multitudo.." ROB. ANGL. *Alg.* 98; de integrorum multiplicatione, additione, diminutione, ~one, mediatione, et divisione compendiose diximus ADEL. *Alch.* 2 p. 21; BRADW. *CD* 132E (v. dimidiatio 1); capitulum primum de addicione, subtraccione, ~one, et mediacione KILLINGWORTH *Alg.* 713 *tit.*

duplator, twister.

1561 ~or fili (*SPDom. Eliz.* 17/33) *Hug. Soc.* X 277.

duplatura, lining (of gown).

duplatura [*gl.*: *lynynge*], sinus †sinnosus [l. sinuosus] plicaque ruga STANBR. *Vulg.* 8.

duplectus v. dublettus.

dupleitas, doubleness.

sciencia, que est habitus, est proximum fundamentum relacionis, sicut quaternarius in genere quantitatis et ~as in genere relacionis DUNS *Metaph.* V 13 p. 299; ~as est tota in toto duplo, et nec ~as nec aliqua pars ejus est in parte dupli respectu ejusdem dimidii OCKHAM *Sacr. Alt.* 18.

duplex [CL]

1 twofold, having two components or aspects. **b** comprising two kinds. **c** double, paired. **d** 'double' in speech or dealing, deceitful.

materia duplici .. plasmabar ALDH. *Aen.* 52 (*Candela*) 1; in loco qui dicitur Adtuifyrdi, quod significat 'ad ~ex vadum' BEDE *HE* IV 26 p. 272; **8..** ~icibus, *of twifealdum WW*; D. BEC. 1123 (v. 1d infra); manualis spiritualem / fabrica designat fabricam duplexque refulget / ecclesie facies, duplici decorata paratu H. AVR. *Hugh* 948–9; Momoniam ~icem, borealem et australem GIR. *TH* I 7; GILB. I 22v. 1, BACON *CSPhil.* 502 (v. duplicitas 1a); construccionem .. ~icem *Ps.*-GROS. *Gram.* 66 (v. docte); contra ~ex [ME: *twafald*] malum quod hic paciuntur ~ex gaudium [cf. *Is.* lxi 7] *AncrR* 139; functus .. ~i sedicione, in regem et universalem ecclesiam *G. Hen. V* 1; **1568** (v. bombardus). **b** ab his .. que equivoce dicuntur, quoniam in eis ~ex designatio BALSH. *AD* 80; pulcrum in te [Maria] fecit zeuma / cum univit verbo pneuma / dupplicem substantiam WALT. WIMB. *Virgo* 31; rosa ~ex est, alba sc. et rubea *SB* 36. **c** *Lib. Monstr.* II 34 (v. duplicitas 1a); procedunt duplices in Martii tempore pisces *Kal. M. A.* I 402; aqua .. coletur per arenam limpidam recentem aut .. sublimetur per ~icia vasa, sc. per alembicum ad nobiles GILB. VII 362v. 2. **d** duplicis officii duplex non esto minister D. BEC. 1123 (v. et. 1a supra); quorum lingua ~ex et dolosa FORDUN *Cont.* X 6.

2 double (in quantity or duration); **b** (math.); **c** (mus.).

vij car[ucatae] terrae ad geldum ..; terra arabilis ~ex *DB* I (*Lincs*) 351 (cf. *EHR* VII 533); *Domus Reg.* 133 (v. cibus c); †**1091** decanus .. et cancellarius ~icem percipiunt communam; reliqui canonici simplicem (*Inst. S. Osm.*) *Stat. Linc.* II 9; **1212** quod W. thesaurarius Ebor' instanter peteret dupplicem sibi assignari communiam *Stat. Ebor.* 107. **b** drachmam et medium ita in duo divido ut major pars ~ex minori habeatur ROB. ANGL. *Alg.* 118. **c** ~ex longa valet sex tempora HAUDLO 384; longarum ~icium quedam sunt ~ices longe que recte vocantur et quedam sunt ~ices longe que altere nominantur HAUBOYS 410.

3 (of documents) duplicate (adj. or sb.).

carte .. scribantur dupplices *Inst. Sempr.* xxi (*xxxiii) (v. chirographum 2a); **13..** Prescianus constructus, cum dupplici et notulis (*Catal. Libr.*) *Chr. Rams.* app. 365.

4 (w. *festum* or sim.) double festival; **b** (dist. as 'greater' and 'lesser'). *V. et. duplicare* 5. (*Cf. Linc. Rec. Soc.* XIII pp. 155–9).

tres sequentes festivitates, id est B. Stephani, Joannis apostoli, SS. Innocentium, uno et eodem modo celebrentur. .. pulsentur signa, accendantur luminaria, agantur caetera omnia sicut in aliis ~icibus et secundae dignitatis festivitatibus LANFR. *Const.* 94; omni ~ici festo .. [decanus] tenetur exequi officium *Offic. Sal.* 2 p. 4; c**1250** hec sunt festa ~icia in ecclesia Salusbur', dies Natalis Domini et quatuor sequentes, dies Circumcisionis Domini [etc.] *Conc. Syn.* 323; in omnibus ~icibus festis anni que ex antiquitate coluntur, in quibus sc. iiij aut v fratres ad invitatorium in tabula ponuntur *Cust. Westm.* 51 (cf. ib. 183: in ~icibus et festis principalibus); s**1344** abbas [W.] festa SS. Jamberti, Nothelmi, Brytwaldi, et Tatwyni sub ~ici festo .. statuit celebrari THORNE 2081; **1371** per lxviij dies .., unde xvj dies ~ices et xviij dies ix leccionum *Fabr. York* 123; s**1416** peregit .. solemnia S. Georgii .., cujus festum prius impetraverat .. more ~icis festi .. celebrari *G. Hen. V* 18; **1437** exceptis principalibus et ~icibus festis *Reg. Cant.* II 555. **b** c**1280** sunt quedam festa in ecclesia H. que dicunt minus dupplitia, sc. quando iij intabulantur ad invitatorium .. dicimus autem illa festa dupplicia quando iiij intabulantur ad invitatorium *Stat. Heref.* 65; **1335** omnibus majoribus dupplicibus festis (*Ord. Cantar. Sibthorpe*) *Eng. Clergy* 257; ad vesperas festorum majorum ~icium *Cust. Cant.* 47 (cf. ib. 11: de festis principalibus et paribus principalibus, ~icibus et altis ~icibus); **1340** in aliis festis ix leccionum et ~icibus .., nisi magis ~ex festum fuerit, post primam collectam specialem dicat [capellanus] et in suo memento pro nobis specialiter .. exoret (*Stat.*) *Deeds Balliol* 295; s**1381** ordinatum fuit .. quod festa iiij evangelistarum et iiij doctorum .. ut festa ~ia de minoribus celebrarentur *Chr. Pont. Ebor. C* 423 (cf. doctor 2a).

5 (of garment) lined; **b** (her.). **c** (as sb.) lined garment, cloth of double thickness (*cf. Prov.* xxxi 21).

coniferas galeas, duplicem thoraca, trilices / loricas laxant GARL. *Epith.* I 577; s**1237** in .. vestimentis mollibus et ~icibus M. PAR. *Maj.* III 412; **1326** lintheamina ~icia *Ac. Durh.* 114; a**1350** (v. casura 2); **1375** furata fuit .. unum *cloce* ~icem *Leet Norw.* 66; **1431** lego .. unam togam ~icem *Reg. Cant.* II 451; **1434** (v. chirotheca 1a). **b** sunt nobiles qui portant arma ~icia ad modum unius ~icis tunice, ut si quis forte habens unam tunicam de colore aureo duplicatam cum rubio vult jaggare .. superiorem partem .. UPTON 248. **c** **1170** nisi .. quispiam credat Deum in extremo examine glorificaturum illos qui ~icibus induti sunt J. SAL. *Ep.* 296 (300 p. 704).

duplicamentum, duplicate (of document).

transumptum episcopi [Cycestr'] ..; datum anno Domini mcclvij; ~um *FormA* 7 (*endorsement*).

duplicare [CL]

1 to bend (double).

non est possibile infirmo ut ~et brachium GAD. 128v. 1.

2 to double; **b** (math.). **c** to compose of two elements. **d** (w. *arma*, her.) to bear double arms (paternal and maternal). **e** (p. ppl.) twofold. **f** (p. ppl., of flower) double.

ut commissa tibi duplicata talenta reportans, / introeas Domini gaudia vera tui WULF. *Swith. pref.* 317; oppidani .. egressi cladem que dabatur dupplicabant G. MON. I 9; inter modorum numeros continuo progressu distantias ~are BALSH. *AD rec. 2* 168; quare aliquis magis debilitatur in ~ato coitu quam in emissione unius libre sanguinis *Quaest. Salern.* B 40; causa quare cetera officia ecclesiastica in sua simplicitate .. maneant et non ~entur et istud solum [sc. officium misse] contra institutionem suam ~etur, constat quod oblatio [sc. est], que ad hoc affertur et non ad illa GIR. *GE* II 26 p. 290 (cf. duplifaciare); cum .. ex duplici putrefactione unus fiat paroxismus fortior et ~etur virtute caloris intensi GILB. I 22v. 1; **1254** ut .. luminarium quantitas .. ~etur *Ch. Sal.* 323; ~abo tibi omnem pecuniam quam mihi tradidisti *Latin Stories* 117; **1468** (v. cursus 6a). **b** ita centenarius numerus ~atur et triplicatur sicut denarius numerus ROB. ANGL. *Alg.* 66; sume .. adjunctum de temporibus horarum et ~a illud ADEL. *Elk.* 32. **c** duplicat ars geminis mihi nomen rite figuris; / nam partem tenebrae retinent partemque volucres ALDH. *Aen.* 35 (*Nycticorax*) 1; in ventre virginis simplex se duplicat WALT. WIMB. *Carm.* 90 [*w. play on sense* 1]. **d** sunt et alii qui habent arma ~ata... et nota quod quis potest ~are .. arma sua secundum quod sibi placuerit BAD. AUR. 136. **e** [proceleumaticus] ~atum revolutionis officium et recapitulationis seriem continet ALDH. *PR* 125. **f** **12..** reddendo .. unam rosam dupplicatam ad Nativitatem S. J. Baptiste *AncD* A 10395.

3 to duplicate (document), prepare in duplicate. **b** (p. ppl. as sb.) (?) duplicate.

1218 dupplicavimus (v. discrimen 3a); **1275** receptis ad ipso prius litteris suis patentibus et carta de cartulario dupplicatis *RGasc* II 6; **1292** breve .. ~atum (v. brevis 10b); **1316** articulus in forma littere patentis sigillo regis signatus et ~atus *MGL* II 176; **1331** vellemus .. quod hujusmodi littere dimissorie dupplicarentur propter eventus inopinatos *Lit. Cant.* I 390; **1338** vellemus commissionem originalem et litteras dupplicatas habere *Ib.* II 197; chartas .. Edgari .. et aliorum regum Anglorum .., que partim ~ate tam Gallicana manu quam Saxonica scribebantur *Croyl.* 85; **1406** scribenti rotulum et ~anti, x d. *Ac. Obed. Abingd.* 73. **b** **1353** solut' pro graciis xxxv monachorum et †~atorum [? l. ~atis], cuilibet eorum iij s. *Sacr. Ely* II 155 (cf. ib. 167: pro graciis xlj sociorum cum sex duplic' de conventu, cuilibet iij s.).

4 (leg.) to make a 'duply' (rejoinder). **b** (p. ppl. as sb. n.) 'duply'.

1392 dictus J. C. ordinavit Thomam G. procuratorem suum .. ad ulterius .. respondendum sive ~andum *SelPlAdm* I 6 (cf. ib. 7: de qua replicacione pars dicti J. C. petebat copiam et diem ad ~andum, si voluerit); **1559** quicumque procurator .. frivolam excepcionem replicandam, ~andam, triplicandam, quadruplicandam .. exhibuerit .. tercia [vice] suspendatur *Conc. Scot.* II 171. **b** **1549** statuatur terminus ad pronunciandum in principali causa, in omnibus tamen hic salvis .. parcium defensionibus, replicatis, ~atis ex arbitrio boni judicis necessariis *Ib.* 125.

5 (eccl.; p. ppl.) 'double' (of feast). *V. et. duplex* 4.

c**1220** solvendo .. annuatim dim. m. .., sc. in festo S. Katerine ad .. peticionem predicti Radulfi [capellani] dupplicato sicut in festo S. Mich. ij s. vj d. ad pitanciam canonicorum tunc presencium augendam, et in festo S. Marie Magdalene similiter .. dupplicato ij s. vj d. ad [dictam] pitanciam .. augendam, et xx d. ad subsidium cerei ardentis ante altare B. Pauli *E. Ch. S. Paul.* 245; [G. abbas, ob. **1321**] dedit .. sex tapeta pro gradibus ante magnum altare in principalibus et ~atis festis cooperiendis WHITTLESEY 19.

6 to line: **a** garment or curtain; **b** (naut.) sail; **c** shelf. **d** (p. ppl. w. *arma*, her.) showing a lining of another colour.

a **1315** casula dupplicata de viridi et indico sindone palliata intus et extra *Invent. Ch. Ch.* 66; **1317** cum tunica et dalmatica ~atis, viz. de rubea sindone ex parte una et de sindone de india ex alia *Reg. Heref.* 42; **1345** pro .. sex paribus robarum liniarum pro rege faciendis, frounciandis et dupplicandis de novo modo (*KRAc* 390/5) *Arch.* XXXI 6; **1371** dupplicata (v. 2 cloca 2); **1385** unum mantellum .. ~atum cum viridi taffata *MonA* VI 1366b; FORTESCUE *LLA* 51 (v. 2 caputium 2e); **1516** (v. conopeum 1b). **b** **1337** in lx ulnis canevac' emptis ad dictum velum ~andum (*KRAc* 19/31 m. 5) *Sea Terms* II 73. **c** **1472** j armariolum cum sex *stagys* ~atis pro cartis et munimentis conservandis *Ac. Durh.* 245 (cf. *OED* s. v. *stage* 1f). **d** sunt arma argentea ~ata de nigro .., et G. sic: *il port d'argent decoppee sus sable* UPTON 249; *Ib.* 248 (v. duplicatura).

duplicarius [CL = *recipient of double rations*]

1 a one lame in both legs. **b** double dealer.

a *an halter*, claudicarius; ~ius, qui ex utraque parte claudicat *CathA.* **b** ~ius, ille qui duabus favet partibus OSB. GLOUC. *Deriv.* 176; *a faverer*, fautor; ~ius, qui favet utrique parti *CathA.*

2 dwale, deadly nightshade (*Atropa belladonna*).

†*dowle, herbe*, ~ius *PP*.

duplicatio [CL]

1 doubling; **b** (anat.); **c** (math.); **d** (gram.).

1254 per .. cc lib. [cere] .. thesaurarius .. ~onem [luminarium] supplebit *Ch. Sal.* 323; **a1300** heres ejus per dupplicacionem sui redditus .. relevabit (*Cust. Headington*) *Pat* 247 m. 15; **1356** onerat se .. de ij lib. piperis per dupplicacionem firme de P., que reddit j lib. piperis per annum *ExchScot* 589; **1460** per ~onem albe firme *Ib.* 633. **b** propter reflexionem et ~onem nervorum ibidem [i. e. in subascellis et plantis pedum] fit major sensibilitas *Quaest. Salern.* P 64. **c** numerus qui ab .. caracteris ~one surrexerit .. THURKILL *Abac.* 56v.; fiunt ex ejus [denarii numeri] ~one 20; et triplicatione 30 ROB. ANGL. *Alg.* 16. **d** est figura alia quando diccio geminatur, ut 'quisquis'. .. per ~onem istam intelligitur †summa [? l. summe] multiplicacio, unde geminacio dicitur *Ps.*-GROS. *Gram.* 41.

2 duplication (of document), copying.

1441 allocantur ei xx d. pro factura et scriptura hujus compoti et ~one alterius *Cant. Coll. Ox.* II 162.

3 (leg.) 'duply', rejoinder.

contra replicacionem datur ~o et contra ipsam rursum triplicacio et sic deinceps in infinitum *Fleta* 428; **1295** si quando .. replicacionem directe contrariam excepcioni aut ~onem replicacioni seu deinceps proponi contigerit *Conc.* II 209b; **1392** pars dicti J. C. quandam ~onem in scriptis redactam curie porrexit *SelPlAdm* I 7.

4 lining (of garment).

1378 ij uln' et dim. de *blanket* pro ~one tunice prioris *Ac. Durh.* 586; **1391** pro xxxvj ulnis de *blanket* .. pro ~one juparum domini *Ac. H. Derby* 89.

duplicatura, lining (of garment).

1408 in ~a ij caparum *Ac. Durh.* 401; **1458** pro ix ulnis de fustina pro una casula ad capellam domini regis, factura et ~a ejusdem *ExchScot* 385; in istis armis sunt iij pecie ad modum barrarum ablate de superiori parte tunice duplicate .., per quarum quidem peciarum foramina aperte .. ostenditur ~a, vel saltem color ejus UPTON 248; *Ib.* 249 (v. duplicare 6d); **15..** iiij pulvinaria cum ~a ex viridi bisso *Reg. Aberd.* II 192.

duplicitas [LL]

1 doubleness. **b** doubling, duplication.

quoddam genus duplicibus fertur fuisse caudis, quae ~as ad sex pedum mensuram patebat *Lib. Monstr.* II 34; duplex febris non dicitur a ~ate materie .. sed a ~ate febris GILB. I 22v. 1; 'ix' est duplex consonans ..; et ejus ~as percipitur per casum genitivum, quia aliquando valet quantum hec litera G et S ut 'grex, gregis' .. BACON *CSPhil.* 502; *a dubylnes*, biplicitas, ~as *CathA*. **b** preter .. ~ates missarum .. invenit cupiditas novitatem missarum GIR. *GE* I 49 p. 137 (cf. duplifaciare).

2 **a** ambiguity. **b** discrepancy.

a principiis sophisticis uti, si non ex hujusmodi sophismatibus [*rec. 2*: ~ate] disputatio instituatur, nulli contempnendum BALSH. *AD* 61. **b** in operum inconstantia [Ph. episcopi, ob. **1208**] oris et anime plurima inesse videbatur ~as G. COLD. *Durh.* 15; WYCL. *Dom. Div.* 100 (v. dicentia).

3 duplicity, double-dealing.

Nathanahel .., cui .. doli ~as nulla inesse probatur BEDE *Hom.* I 17. 93; **s1102** habebis re ipsa iis que dicimus nihil ~atis inesse EADMER *HN* 161; hypocrisis ~atem AD. SCOT *Serm.* 137A; se .. asserens pupillo fore tutorem fidelissimum .. auferrique de medio scandalum et ~atem MAP *NC* II 18 f. 30; **1231** non crederetis me habere ad circumveniendum vos rugam ~atis et fucum simulate voluntatis GROS. *Ep.* 4; de mundi duplicitate / .. canere propono WALT. WIMB. *Scel.* 1; *Cust. Westm.* 190 (v. contrarietas 1a); ~as temerarii consensus WYCL. *Sim.* 106; sub velamine verborum et multis ~atibus multos deceperant (HERFORD) *Ziz.* 326; robur polliciti duplicitate ruit ELMH. *Metr. Hen. V* 820.

dupliciter [CL], **a** in double quantity or at double rate. **b** in two ways or senses.

a pecunia ecclesiis furata .. reddatur quadruplum, saecularibus ~er THEOD. *Pen.* I 3. 2; dupliciter rutulat piscis in tempore Martis *Kal. M. A.* I 401; in R. habet Rolf xiij bovatas terrae et dim. .. ad geldum; terra ~er ad arandum *DB* I (*Lincs*) 365; quando aliquis homo inculpatur quod .. furtum fecerit .., tunc debet per lx hidas—id est per sex homines—abnegare ipsum furtum. .. si vero Anglicus in furto compellabitur, neget ~er [AS: *be twyfealdum*]; si autem sit Waliscus, non sit jusjurandum eo amplius (*Quad.*) *GAS* 111. **b** ~er peccavit, quia et quod jussus est facere non fecit et quod praeceptum est ne faceret fecit ANSELM (*CurD* I 24) II 92; ~er est scientia Dei causa futurorum, sc. antecedens vel conjuncta GROS. *Quaest. Theol.* 201; potest .. nomen stare pro voce et pro re; et pro voce ~er .. SICCAV. *PN* 78; forma in creaturis habet aliquid imperfectionis ~er, sc. quia est forma informans aliquid et quia pars compositi DUNS *Ord.* IV 271; hoc nomen 'usuarius' ~er accipi potest OCKHAM *Pol.* 303; WYCL. *Ver.* III 124 (v. durative).

duplicium, doublet; **b** (worn as armour). *Cf. diplois, dublettus, dupliteca.*

1457 exceptis una toga de panno nigro, una gallera, uno ~io, et omnibus vestibus laneis et lineis corpori meo paratis *Cl* 307 m. 9*d*. **b 1419** unum ~ium de *defence* .. ad opus .. prioris [Hospitalis S. Joh. in Anglia] *Cl* 269 m. 9.

duplifaciare, to provide (mass) w. double preface. *Cf. cauda* 5c.

ex ejusdem venalitatis vitio provenit .. quod, cum duas integre missas pre pudore quidam sex timore celebrare non audeant, unam ~iant (sic) vel trifacient vel etiam multifacient, id est multarum facierum celebrent GIR. *GE* II 26 p. 290.

duplifestarius, celebrant (chorister) of double festival. *Cf. duplex* 4.

a1450 eligantur per canonicos .. tam ipsi vicarii [sc. chorales] quam ceteri ministri chori in ~ios in vigilia Omnium Sanctorum *Stat. Linc.* II 353.

dupliteca, doublet. *Cf. diplois, duplicium, dublettus* 1.

1454 [lego] filio meo tres .. togas .. et duas optimas ~as meas *Test. Ebor.* II 183; hec ~a *a doplyt WW*.

dupliter, (?) a second time, likewise.

933 (10c) Wigferð diacon; Eadhelm diacon ~er *CS* 648.

duplois, ~oidus v. diplois. **duploma** v. diploma. **duplonmis** v. diplois.

duplula, little (double) bell.

squilla pulsatur in triclinio, i.e. in refectorio, cymbalum in claustro, nola in choro, nolula vel ~a in horologio, campana in campanili, signa in turribus BELETH *RDO* 86. 90B.

duplus [CL]

1 twofold (having two components or aspects); **b** (w. *crux* .. *partita*, her.) cross double parted. **c** (pl.) two.

spiritus ac castae conjungant foedera carnis, / dum divina docet duplam sententia vitam ALDH. *VirgV* 132; **798** qui numerus .. significat simplam mortem Dei Christi ad ~am nostram; quia nos duabus mortibus fuimus obnoxii, id est animae et carnis ALCUIN *Ep.* 143; vestibus ornantur famuli, quas ordine duplo / ejus in activis fert operosa manus GOWER *VC* V 305. **b** que quidem crux ideo ~a partita appellatur quia, si esset secundum longum aut secundum latum partita .., adhuc remaneret ibi una crux ~a. .. variatur autem .. aliquando ..; et tunc vocatur crux ~a partita florida UPTON 219 (cf. BAD. AUR. 127). **c** gemellos / edidit in mundo sortitos nomina dupla [sc. Cosmam et Damianum] ALDH. *VirgV* 1078; patet quod adhuc sufficio durare per ~a instancia WYCL. *Log.* II 158.

2 double (w. ref. to size or number). **b** (as sb. n.) double amount.

[peon primus] sescupla divisione dirimitur, quia caret aequa divisionis regula et ~a et tripla ALDH. *PR* 133; utrum quadratum quadrato ~um sit, ut Plato docuit, an non, ut numerorum ratio exigere videtur BALSH. *AD rec. 2* 133; motus ~us ad alium GROS. 2 (v. divisibilitas); ~a proportio *Ib.* 53; quaternarius est ~us ad binarium DUNS *Ord.* I 52. **b** bidentum numerus .. in ~um restitutus [cf. *Job* xlii 12] ALDH. *Met.* 2; ipsum scambium valet ~um *DB* I 84v.; terra arabilis ad ~um *Ib.* 351v. (cf. *EHR* VII 533); radix ducentorum subtractis 10 addita ad ~um subtracti, sc. ad 20 ROB. ANGL. *Alg.* 142; ~o fere angustiore spatio mare coarctatur GIR. *TH* I 1; quando prosa vel psalmus 'benedictus' sive 'magnificat' solemniter in ~um cantatur *Cust. Westm.* 32; habemus .. idem et diversum, ~um et dimidium SICCAV. *PN* 101; **s1322** ad furcas in ~o furcis communibus alciores .. tracti et suspensi fuerunt AVESB. 77; **1448** causant eas (*sic*) sc. pisces magis ~o carius vendi *MunAcOx* 590.

3 **a** (as sb. n.) double payment (for maintenance of sea-wall). **b** (as sb. f.) coin of double value.

a 1239 computus de ~o walle, quod vocatur *twysket* (*Ac. Man. Cant., Aldington*) *Gavelkind* 29; **1295** de .. ~o walliarum maris, viz., quando dominus reficit wallias maris propriis custibus ob defectum tenencium, capiet custus eosdem in ~o de eisdem tenentibus per predictum tempus (*Ac. Wingham, Kent*) *Pipe* 141 r. 28*d*. **b** in ea [Alexandria] .. doubla de auro [valet] xxviij [Venetos grossos] S. SIM. *Itin.* 38.

dupondius [CL], sum of two *asses* (or pounds).

dipondio BEDE *TR* 4 (v. cantio b) (cf. ib. 52: dipundius); dipondius, *twegra pundra gewiht* ÆLF. *Gl.*; indeclinabile pondus; / illinc est natus dispondius, as geminatus GARL. *Syn.* 165. 1580D.

duppl- v. dupl-.

dupulsare [cf. duplus, pulsare], to ring two bells.

in tota septuagesima in profestis diebus non debet prepulsari nec conpulsari nec ~ari, sed simpulsari, i.e. simpliciter pulsari ad horas vel ad matutinas BELETH *RDO* 86. 90B.

durabilis [CL], durable, lasting.

quorum generatio protrahitur ad annum vel plus ut elefantes, unde eorum vita ~ior efficitur *Quaest. Salern.* N 11; causa quare invenitur forma ~is et perpetua est quia ex planetis ~ibus et perpetuis est BACON V 159; quod violentum est non est ~e. .. 'durant', i. e. ~ia sunt TREVET *Troades* 22; tunc .. Deus non posset scire in qua proporcione unum est ~ius reliquo WYCL. *Log.* II 158; de .. lapide satis ~i *G. S. Alb.* III 447 (v. cristare 2).

durabilitas [LL], durability, persistence. **b** longevity.

dico quod hoc verum est, nisi forma contradiceret materie imperfecta, unde propter imperfectionem forme non addit ad ~atem subjecti GILB. VII 303v. 2; frigora et calores summa providencia .. stabilivit ad generationem, propagationem, et ~atem rerum temporalium et naturalium BACON V 54; perdurat prelium quamdiu durat perseverancia in spe superandi partem quamlibet utriusque. sit ergo conatus tuus .. in ~ate, in perseverancia tui *Ib.* 152; motus .. uno modo recipit continuationem sue extensionis et expansionis, et sic a mobili; alio modo sue permanentie et ~atis, et sic a motore *Ib.* VIII 145; nec aliquod tale posset tamdiu durare sicut posset. nec esset dare maximam ~atem mei WYCL. *Log.* II 158. **b** sanitas et ~as in hiis modis duobus [sc. caliditate et humiditate] consistit BACON V 89.

durabiliter [LL], durably, lastingly.

nec suscipit [forma] in se corruptionem .., quia .. recedit per corruptionem .. materie deferentis ipsam .. et informatio ~er perseverat BACON V 159.

duracinus [CL = *hard-berried*], **~um,** 'stire apple' (crab or sim.).

a sturtre, ~acenus, ~acenum fructus ejus *CathA*.

duralitas v. diurnalitas

duramen [CL = *that which hardens*], endurance.

mater Dei, vivus rivus GARL. *SM* 7 (*gl.*: 'vivus' per ~en, propter septem dona Spiritus Sancti que habuit B. Virgo).

durare [CL]

1 to harden. **b** to be hard.

ferrum accensum igni, nisi ~etur ictibus, corrumpitur NECKAM *NR* I 54; *to make harde*, ~are, con-, in-, ob- .. *CathA*. **b s1309** [gelu] ~avit (v. chorea 1a).

2 to endure, last, survive: **a** (of inanim. things); **b** (of living beings). **c** (of persons or institutions) to continue, persist (in a spec. state or activity).

a *Cust. Westm.* 274 (v. calepugnus); si terra semel abscondatur, si sulphurea sit, nunquam postea extinguitur sed ibi perpetuo ~ans flammam emittit *Quaest. Salern.* P 56; WYCL. *Log.* II 158 (v. durabilitas). **b** [aquile] per tot secula ~ant ut .. cum ipsa videantur perennitate contendere GIR. *TH* I 13; a .. pisce qui tantum per unum diem .. ~at S. LANGTON *Gl. Hist. Schol.* 44; si aliquis homo esset semper ~ans et immortalis J. BLUND *An.* 293; magister J. .. non diu vixit .. et in episcopatu Glascuensi sibi successit .. Willelmus T. [ob. **1454**] .., qui similiter non diu ~avit *Plusc.* XI 7. **c** usque ad diem mortis in .. contritione ~avit BEDE *HE* V 12; languores curat, patiens sub verbere durat *V. Anselmi Epit.* 138; **s1202** (v. confratria 1b); nullus predo vel latro ipsius [Edgari] tempore ~are potuit quin secundum excessum suum statim puniretur SILGRAVE 55; **s1188** factus est Henricus .. major Londoniarum .. et ~avit majorem (*sic*) usque ad finem vite sue *Leg. Ant. Lond.* 1.

3 (of abstr.) to last, continue. **b** to remain valid, in force.

1103 non diu ~abit [duritia presbyterorum] ANSELM (*Ep.* 254) IV 166; patet quam .. frustra nominis nostri famam incole provinciarum appetamus, cum nec ipsarum .. provinciarum nomina ~are possint H. HUNT. *HA* I 4; si sunt animata que tempus non sentiunt .., sentiunt in se passionem semper, quamdiu ~at, quasi novam HALES *Sent.* II 423; dum fervor ~avit [ME: *leste*] *AncrR* 36; persona ecclesie .. ~ante predicto tempore obiit *State Tri. Ed. I* 17; non est necesse operacionem angeli ~are cum instanti temporis nostri; igitur nec illa duracio erit racio quietis in termino transitus subiti DUNS *Ord.* VII 378; de aliquo officio ~ante per ebdomadam *Cust. Cant.* 99; **1367** cum .. numerum monachorum .. perpetuis temporibus ~aturis .. ordinarunt *Reg. Paisley* 32; **1406** ex .. scismate quod tantis .. temporibus .. perduravit et ~at *Chr. S. Alb.* 4 (cf. ib. 1: ~ante parliamento); **1552** quod nulla venalia ~ante sacro exponantur .. prope limites ecclesiarum *Conc. Scot.* II 132. **b** ne per librariorum .. antiquitatem vel negligentiam confuse vitiose lex illa ~aret quam .. Deus .. mandavit THEOD. *Pen. pref.*; **1216** habet litteras de conductu ~aturas a die Mercurii .. usque ad diem Dominicam .. *Pat* 3 (cf. ib.: litteras de conductu ~aturo [*sic* MS]); **1343** quod ~antibus dictis treugis nulle .. mesprisie fiunt ab una parte contra aliam (*Treugae*) AD. MUR. *Chr.* 132.

4 to continue (in space), extend. **b** (of army) to be deployed.

ibi incipit .. palus .. que per miliaria sexaginta .. ~at H. ALBUS 5; **a1187** unum .. selionem qui vadit versus *le west*

quantum quarentana ~at *Danelaw* 152; **c1200** in quantum pratum ~at (v. dala); **c1205** piscariam meam, que ~at a Crag .. quantum terra mea tenditur versus occidentem *Reg. Aberbr.* I 35; **c1215** quod libertas aque de Tamisia a castello Bainardi usque ad pontem de Stanes ~at (*Mun. Lond.*) *EHR* XVII 486; **c1260** quamdiu ~at boscus versus B. (Ch. Warton) *Ib.* 294; **12..** terram que .. ~at in longum a magno vico usque ad vicum qui dicitur Crokerestrete *Reg. S. Thom. Dublin* 469; **1300** (v. aquilo c); [commentum] quod ~at per duo maxima folia Baconthorpe *Quaest. Sent.* 3D; **1421** capiendo .. iiij pedes et iiij pollices in latitudine ~ante longitudine xx pedum *AncD* A 1995; **1461** mesuagium a paviamento .. versus boriam ~ante longitudine lx pedum continet in latitudine xxiiij pedes *Cl* 313 m. 17*d*. **b s1356** ~avit .. exercitus .. in latitudine fere per xx leucas Avesb. 133b.

durascere v. durescere.

duratio

1 hardening; **b** (fig.).

1397 pro iiij^{xx}xiiij lib. aceris de Spayne emptis et expenditis circa ~onem securium et aliorum instrumentorum cement[arie] *KRAc* 479/23 (cf. *Building in Eng.* 288). **b** divicie sunt causa ~onis anime *Quadr. Reg. Spec.* 32.

2 duration, (period of) continuance. **b** (period of) validity.

non .. reduci potest ~o nisi ad predicamentum quantitatis et ad speciem continui Hales *Sent.* I 115; ne species deficiat .., eo quod minoris ~onis sunt modo singularia quam prius fuerunt, natura plus et plus multiplicat singularia J. Blund *An.* 293; semper movere dicitur .. tertio [modo] quod in omni tempore movet, id est, per equalitatem ~onis temporis Bacon VII 28; motus quantecumque ~onis non est perfectior effectus quam motus unius diei Duns *Ord.* II 190; 'secula', i. e. ~ones rerum Trevet *Troades* 31; tunc foret eterogenia composita ex ~onibus disparium specierum .. et per consequens partis mundi corrupcio variaret mundi ~onem et per consequens suum esse (Wycl. *Temp.*) *Wycl. & Ox.* 157 *n.* 2; **1456** ut ineternum (*sic*) pro ~one presentis seculi talis Christi .. victoria .. de ore omnium Christianorum .. nunquam cesset Bekynton II 156. **b 1416** infra tempus ~onis presentis nostri salvi conductus *RScot* 219a.

durative, lastingly, w. ref. to duration.

pro quantiscunque bonis delectabilibus intensive aut extensive vel etiam ~e lucrandis Bradw. *CD* 111A; forme dicuntur dupliciter contrarie, sc. active et ~e: .. †contraria [? l. contrarie] sunt forme que non possunt simul subjecto et tempore inesse eidem Wycl. *Ver.* III 124.

durativus, having duration, existing or persisting in time.

Deus, dans ei [sc. angelo] quantitatem ~am perpetuam .., dat ei semper uniformiter quo extendatur toti tempori Duns *Ord.* VII 179; in eternitate nulla est prioritas aut posterioritas ~a nec ulla successio hinc in illud Bradw. *CD.* 835E; omnis actus sensitivus est essencialiter ~us Wycl. *Act.* 12; oportet quod [fortitudo] sit constans et ~a Brinton *Serm.* 11. 42.

dure [CL]

1 hard, severely, w. force. **b** rudely. *V. et. duriter.*

flante .. vento Euroaustro ~e Eddi 13; quo malis praesentibus ~ius deprimebatur Bede *HE* II 1 p. 77; ~e, i. pertinaciter, pessime, *heardlice GlH* D 847; cum diutius penitendo se ~ius afflixisset, raptus est in visione P. Cornw. *Rev.* I 200; ut ~ius atque efficacius corpus affligeret Gir. *GE* II 10; clericorum plurimos in pungnis et fustibus ~e visitaverunt Map *NC* V 5 f. 65; tam ~e eum [canem Inferni] percute quod odiat odorem cibi sumere *AncrR* 125; **c1400** super pollices ipsius .. quoddam instrumentum vocatum *pyrewinkes* .. stricte et ~e posuerunt (*Cart. S. Edm.*) *OED* s. v. *pilliwinks*. **b** [ancilla latro] magistre, si audet, ~ius respondet *Simil. Anselmi* 88.

2 hardly, with (or so as to cause) difficulty.

quod tanto nunc ~ius tolero quanto me ei imparem sentiens *V. Greg.* p. 76; quid improbabiliter .., quid ~e, quid his contrarie dici soleat Balsh. *AD* 8; **s1214** non video pure; mihi nil sapit; audio dure (*Vers.*) *G. S. Alb.* I 247; bucca ~e movetur M. Scot *Phys.* 73 (v. custodiosus); **s1407** ~e ferens quod illic tempus inane trivisset *Chr. S. Alb.* 10.

durescere [CL], **durēre** [LL], to be or become hard; **b** (fig.). **c** to stiffen.

sanguis .. coagulatus in pessimum apostema ~uerat Ailr. *Ed. Conf.* 788C; projectis tribus in fornacem juvenibus [cf. *Dan.* iii], cessit suo juri natura, cum vel caro durasceret ne sentiret incendium aut ignis frigesceret *Id. An.* III 21; queritur [quare] ferrum candens in aqua ~escit *Quaest. Salern.* P 63; *to be harde*, callere .., ~ere, ~escere etc. *CathA.* **b** quae in virginitatis perseverantia inflexibili mentis rigore .. ~uerunt Aldh. *VirgP* 39; **9..** ~uerunt, *þurhwunedan WW*; riget, ~escit, *stearcode GlP* 1013; angeli illi qui steterunt cadentibus aliis .. ex aquis sue mutabilitatis in crystallum eterne stabilitatis ~uerunt H. Reading (I) *Haeret.* 1261D; Dominus in principio parcit debilibus. .. cum viderit eos ~escere [ME: *harden*], .. docet eos .. penuriam pati *AncrR* 79. **c** [Sciapodae] singula .. habent in pedibus crura et eorum genua inflexibili compagine ~escunt *Lib. Monstr.* I 17; ~escit, regescit *GlH* D 848.

duribuccus, ~ius, 'dasybeard', block-head.

dastard or dullard, ~buxius .., ~buccius, agrestis *PP*; hic †~buctus, *a dasyberd WW*; *a dasyberd*, ~buccus *CathA.*

duricordia [LL], hardness of heart.

1166 neque .. ~iam archiepiscopi .. quisquam familiarius accedens .. arguere poterit. sed quis .. nostratum et veterum amicorum de gente duricordium non convincitur esse? J. Sal. *Ep.* 168 (167).

duricorium [CL duricorius = *hard-skinned*], 'holleke' (scallion or sim.).

9.. de herbis terrae .. ~ium, *holleac WW.*

duricors [LL], hard-hearted; **b** (w. play on *Durocortorum*; *cf.* J. Sal. *Ep.* (*ed.* 1979), p. 100*n.*).

ubi erat sanctitas verbi Christi, quod nec Phariseos convertit nec discipulos ~des in fide sacramenti corporis et sanguinis sanctos fecit? Netter *DAF* II 163. **b 1166** nec tantum .. pro me, licet apud ~des habitem, quantum pro amicis sollicitor ... si nescitis, Belgica secunda, que modo Remorum dicitur, in antiquis historiis provincia ~dium appellatur J. Sal. *Ep.* 168 (167) (cf. duricordia).

durificare, to harden.

to make harde, durare .., ~are *CathA.*

duritas [CL], difficulty.

1421 (v. camera 4b).

duriter [CL]

1 severely, harshly. *V. et. dure.*

716 maligni spiritus in omnibus consonantes vitiis accussando et ~er testificando Bonif. *Ep.* p. 10; aliquando magister meus excitat me ~er [AS: *stiplice*] cum virga Ælf. *Coll.* 103; ~er eos increpans Dominic *V. Ecgwini* I 4; hec est hominis vox .. castigati ~er et stupidi Map *NC* III 2 f. 37; mors .. / .. / regem a solio dejectum duriter / rodendum vermibus commendat Walt. Wimb. *Sim.* 107.

2 hardly, w. difficulty.

si .. multus esset spiritus [in tertia cellula cerebri] multo motu induresceret, unde ~er retineret *Quaest. Salern.* P 49; **1557** secreto se subducere et sic ~er evadendo castellum vacuum relinquere *ActPCIr* 40.

duritia [CL]

1 hardness. **b** (med.) hardening.

rigentis cippi ~ia .. ad nihilum redigitur Aldh. *VirgP* 35; hunc rigorem per ~iam lapidis insinuat [cf. *Luke* xi 11] Bede *Hom.* II 14. 172; cum latus inferius tori ~ia lassari .. ceperit Gir. *DK* I 10; lapis .. secundum ~iam in quantum durus esset bonus Duns *Ord.* III 198. **b** hepatis ~ia, quam physici sclirosim appellant Ben. Pet. *Mir. Thom.* I 15; confluunt humores frigidi et .. indurantur et in sclirosim, id est ~iam, sepius commutantur Bart. Angl. IV 4; lilium .., cujus vires possunt remollire ~ias nervorum *Alph.* 98.

2 harshness (of weather).

1225 in bobus sustinendis propter ~iam hiemis (*Pipe Wint.*) *Econ. HR* 2nd S., XII 366; **1255** in porcis sustinendis propter ~iam temporis in hieme (*Ib.*) *Ib.* 372.

3 hardness of heart (spiritual insensitivity), cruelty.

ostensa sua ~ia caecitatis, majores gratias illos suo redemptori .. reddere monent Bede *Gen.* 113; feritas, i. crudelitas .., inclementia, ~ia, *repnes GlH* F 225; vae mirabilis ~ia, ad quam confringendam leves sunt tam graves mallei Anselm (*Medit.* 1) III 78; ut .. cordium eorum ~iam emolliret Gir. *RG* II 18; **1545** Pharaonis ~iam [cf. *Exod.* vii 13 etc.] imitando *Conc. Scot.* I cclxv.

4 **a** hardship. **b** harsh treatment, duress. **c** (w. ref. to imprisonment).

a ~iis .. affligi carnem eligunt Gir. *TH* I 12; spine sunt ~ie [ME: *þe hardschipes*] de quibus supra locutus sum *AncrR* 148; **1316** civibus ~ia periculumque maximum videbatur imminere *MGL* II 170. **b 1290** tantam ~iam fecit Reginaldo .. quod terras suas extentas ei tradere noluit .. ; tantas ~ias fecit episcopo de L. quod .. (*Pet. Parl.*) *DocExch* 62; **1384** Johannem .. copiam quorundam mandatorum ipsius episcopi comedere per non modicam ~iam coegerunt *Pat* 317 m. 11*d.*; **14..** si ballivus .. forte aliam ~iam eis facere voluerit *Reg. S. Aug.* 151. **c 1275** obiit ob ~iam prisonis *Hund.* I 481; **1298** Ricardo .. alleviacionem de ferris quibus detinetur et eciam de ~ia prisone habere facias *Cl* 115 m. 8; **1303** (v. dirritio); **1453** cum .. me .. in eisdem fortaliciis in magna ~ia custodivissent *Cl* 304 m. 30*d.*

durities [CL]

1 hardness. **b** hard mass (of metal). **c** (med.) hardening, callosity.

duritiem ferri quadrata fronte polibo Aldh. *Aen.* 27 (*Coticula*) 2; Neckam *DS* VIII 97 (v. digestivus b); due pellicule .., que cerebri molliciem .. impacientem ~iei ab asperitate defendunt cranei Ric. Med. *Anat.* 213; saxeam ~iem Gerv. Tilb. III 4 (v. dolatura 1a); non omnis resistentia est a ~ie, et est ipsum resistere aeris ei loco ~iei J. Blund *An.* 174; *Ps.*-Gros. *Summa* 629 (v. dolabilitas). **b** scopaturas .. torridis fluentis abluebant conflatamque ~iem duro lapide comminuebant Gosc. *Mir. Aug.* 16. **c** interdum .. humor cadens super oculum indurat et aliquando infra residens induratur et reddit oculum durum et vocatur ~ies Gilb. III 130v. 2; apostolicon valet .. in omnibus ~iebus, unde ista nodositas est quasi gutta innodata Gad. 29. 1; *Ib.* (v. chorda 6a); emfraxis aliquando dicitur ~ies et aliquando opilacio viarum urinalium *SB* 19; †neutrorocos [? l. neurotrotos], id est nervi ~ies *Alph.* 125; hec ~ies, *hardnes of the hande WW.*

2 hardship.

cum sic .. dissipata esset fortitudo gencium et finita ~ies belli *G. Hen. V* 13 p. 92.

duritio, duress. *V. et. duritia* 4b.

1303 cognovit confessionem suam, sed dixit quod eam fecit rigore et †dirricione [l. duricione] quam sustinuit in prisona *Year Bk. 30–1 Ed. I* app. p. 543 (cf. ib.: ne esse in prisona talem duriciam .. ? .. propter duriciam prisone).

duriuscule, somewhat harshly.

loro ceperat verberari ~e J. Sal. *Pol.* 531A; **s1215** cum per internuncios ~e eis rex respondisset W. Coventr. II 219.

durnedies [ME *dorne dai*], 'durn-day' (app. day on which burgage rents were payable under pain of sealing tenants' doors; hence borough court held on that day). *Cf. consignare* 1b.

1388 curia dornediei ibidem tenta (*Rec. Bridgwater*) *Som Rec. Soc.* LIII no. 434 (cf. ib. no. 322 [**1378**]: *durneday*, xxx s. vj d.; perquisitorum istius curie cum *pipoudre*, ix s. vij d.; v. et. ib. p. xviii).

durnella v. douella 3.

durnum [ME *durne, dirne*], durn, door-post.

1408 unum hostium cum dirnis de chelario *Rec. Nott.* II 58 (cf. *OED* s. v. *durn*); **c1450** in iiij novis gumfis pro -o ostii ecclesie *Ac. Churchw. Glast.* 285.

durus [CL]

1 hard, firm. **b** (of mus. note) not 'softened'. **c** (anat. w. *mater*) *dura mater*, outer cerebral membrane. **d** (of land) firm, dry (also as sb. n.). **e** (of fish) hardened by drying.

durior aut ferro, tostis sed mollior extis Aldh. *Aen.* 100. 44; germina / dura atque tenerrima (Æthelwald) *Carm. Aldh.* 4. 46; tellus ~issima et saxosa Bede *HE* IV 26 p. 271; **9..** ~as, rigidas, *hearde WW*; ~a carne Ric. Med. *Anat.* 219; in lapide agapis qui est ~issimus, qui .. aut vix aut nunquam potest frangi *Quaest. Salern.* B 147; **1222** (v. bladum a); Gilb. III 130v. 2 (v. durities 1c); [pulsus] ~us est quando cum quadam asperitate et duritia resistere videtur Bart. Angl. III 23; **1258** in xxxvj bobus sustinendis .., quia diu araverunt ad sementem ordei et habuerunt ~am terram *Crawley* 226; **1297** (v. caseus b); propter incompossibilitatem unius corporis ~i ad aliud corpus ~um quod non cedit ei Duns *Ord.* VII 531; *SB* 15 (v. cataplasma a). **b** Tunst. 222b (v. B 2a). **c** cerebrum primo et proximo loco obvolvunt due pellicule, que dicuntur pia mater et ~a mater, et quasi materno amplexu alteram altera amplectitur et utraque cerebrum Ric. Med. *Anat.* 213; ~e matris lesio cognoscitur dolore capitis, rubore faciei [etc.] Gilb. II 84v. 2; ~a mater, que adheret concavitati ossis capitis Bacon *Maj.* II 4. **d c1200** dedisse .. Edrikescroft .. sicut rivus descendit ad M. .., tam ~um quam molle usque ad fontem *Couch. Furness* II 524; **a1314** donacionem .. de tota gaira sua .. tam in prato ~o quam in marisco *ChartR* (*Lincs*) 101 m. 15. **e 1285** in ccc de *stocfis*, xxij s. vj d.; in c de ~is piscibus xxxviij s. (*KRAc* 91/4) *Arch.* LXX 25; **1329** de .. ~is murvellis receptis *ExchScot* 148; **1334** iiij milia de *stokfish* et *screyfish* et alio pisce ~o *RScot* 296a; **1350** dim. centum ~i piscis de *stocfish*, viz. *coursfish*, percipiet *Reg. Winchcombe* 264 (cf. *OED* s. v. *stockfish*); **1358** in salso pisce et ~o (*Ac. Univ. Ox.*) *EHR* XXIV 740.

2 harsh, strenuous, disagreeable; **b** (of weather).

quos [episcopos] me .. ~is verborum cantibus .. necesse est lapidare Gildas *EB* 65; genus versificationis .. ~um et horrens Aldh. *Met.* 10; duro vitam sustento labore *Id. Aen.* 56 (*Castor*) 3; dura quidem jugiter virtutes bella facessunt *Id. VirgV* 2537; ~a dictu Bede *ST* 616 (v. charientismos); **716** ut nihil tam odibile, nihil tam ~um foetorem evaporans .. videret Bonif. *Ep.* 10; pronuntientur ei [novitio] ~a et aspera quae in hoc ordine perferunt qui .. regulariter vivere volunt; item ~iora et asperiora quae, si indisciplinate se habeat, sibi poterunt evenire Lanfr. *Const.* 168; numquam desistat [anachorita] ~a pati exterius [ME: *neaver slakien to dreȝen hard widuten*] *AncrR* 42; si adhuc post omnia hec mala absque ~iori duricia belli .. posset pax inclita resarciri *G. Hen. V.* 20 p. 140. **b** frigora dura viros sternant, ni forte resistam Aldh. *Aen.* 45

(*Fusum*) 7; **1271** quando annus ita ~us venerit quod pro defectu foragii . . oporteat eos averia sua . . de bosco de G. juvare *Cart. Chester* 423.

3 (of person or character): **a** hardy, resolute. **b** hardened, inured. **c** insensitive, dull. **d** hard-hearted, ruthless. *Cf. cervix* b, c, *cervicosus*.

a ut ad thalami taedas et . . ferreos juvenculi affectus, immo adamante ~iores, inclinarent ALDH. *VirgP* 36; cum duro patitur tormenta Crisanto *Id. VirgV* 1228; erat . . ~us in praedicatione contra eos qui in vitiis jacebant BYRHT. *V. Ecgwini* 357; fit dira inter ~os decertatio DEVIZES 37v. p. 54. **b** utinam [clerici Hiberni] post longa jejunia tam sobrii fuerint quam seri . ., tam puri quam ~i GIR. *TH* III 27; infortuniorum frequentia ~us sum MAP *NC* V 5 f. 65v. **c** homines indomabiles et ~ae ac barbarae mentis BEDE *HE* III 5; ~us intellector BALSH. *AD rec. 2* 105 (v. compertor); Orpheus . . homines . . rhetorica dulcedine ex feris et immanibus mites reddidit et mansuetos et ex vagis ~isque composuit ALB. LOND. *DG* 8. 20; intellectus ~us et obliviosus BART. ANGL. IV 2. **d** ~a cervix illa, multis . . peccaminum fascibus onerata, . . de imis ad inferiora curvatur GILDAS *EB* 35; ferus, i. crudelis, immitis, ~us, *reþe GlH* F 202; nec cessit duri spolians capitolia furis FRITH. 427; ipsa [domina] . . non curans et sic . . ~a corde [ME: *hard-iheorted*] *AncrR* 153.

4 difficult, intractable.

quare, cum colera sit ~ior ad purgandum quam fleuma, tertiana citius resolvitur quam cotidiana *Quaest. Salern.* N 19.

dusciebatur v. discutere 4a. **dusellus** v. duciculus.

dusius [LL < Gall.], kind of demon, goblin.

maxime quando vel viris in specie feminea vel in virili habitu feminis apparentes, quos daemones Galli ~ios [v. l. diosios] vocant, infando miraculo spiritus incorporei corporis humani concubitum petere se ac patrare confingunt BEDE *Luke* 438; a 'duco' hic ~ius, ~sii, i. demon qui homines educit a sensu OSB. GLOUC. *Deriv.* 161; Sylvanos et Panes, quos incubos nominant, Galli vero ~ios [v. l. †diusios] dicunt GERV. TILB. III 86 (cf. ib. Vol. II p. 782); *bugge or boglarde*, †mavirus, †bucius . ., *thyrce, wykkyd spyryt*, ducius *PP*; *a devylle* . ., demon, diabolus, ducius . . *CathA*.

dussenum v. dozena. **dussinator** v. decenator. **dutta** v. ductus 3.

duumvir [CL = *municipal officer or sim.*], sheriff (of London).

s1508 alter ~vir . . [*gap in text*] ANDRÉ *Hen. VII* 105.

duva [OF *dove*], bank of ditch or moat.

1227 concessimus . . fratribus . . de platia nostra . . partem illam quam incluserunt quodam fossato . . usque ad †dunam fossati civitatis Ebor' *Cl* 11 (cf. *CalCh* I 70); **1241** H. de Holdernes habuit vij domos super duwam fossati *IMisc* 1/10; **1243** ita quod . . mete ille et divise sint ubique ad †divam fossati [castri Wint'] latitudinis xij pedum *Liberate* 20 m. 20; **1291** illud stagnum aque dicte placie adjacens cum ambabus †diviis . . et unum fossatum quod vocatur Milnecroftdik' habentem (*sic*) . . in latitudine inter ~as iiij pedes *ChartR* 77 m. 4.

duvella v. douella 3.

duvetum [OF *duvet*], down (for stuffing pillows). *Cf. 2 dumus*.

1342 pro dovet' ad ij auricularia pro altari, vj d. *KRAc* 389/14 m. 3.

dux [CL]

1 guide; **b** (appl. to thing or abstr.).

ut . . episcopum ducem sibi itineris fieri . . rogaret BEDE *HE* IV 5; **8..** ducem, *lateau WW*; SERLO WILT. 2. 28 (v. ducere 1a); duce carens *Dial. Scac.* II 28 B (v. dolabra c); statim ad hostes se transferendo exploratores in nos et vice versa vie duces sunt effecti GIR. *EH* II 36 p. 390; *Itin. Ric.* VI 31 (v. 1 ducatus 1a); **1290** cuidam puero duci hominis ceci *Ac. Swinfield* 155; **1438** (v. 1 ducatus 2a). **b** morituros vivere vidi / spe duce WALT. ANGL. *Fab.* 28. 14; oleo vel aqua duce M. SCOT *Lumen* 266 (v. 1 cerare b).

2 leader, commander; **b** (fig.).

miserrimi cives . ., duce Ambrosio Aureliano . ., vires capessunt GILDAS *EB* 25; salvatrix superni ducis nativitas ALDH. *VirgP* 21; Laurentius cum ipso duce Augustino primus venit GOSC. *Transl. Aug.* 20B; ad pecorum transvolat illa ducem WALT. ANGL. *Fab.* 43. 12; tantis belli ducibus que regna resisterent? GIR. *TH* III 53; dux superatur Averni GARL. *Tri. Eccl.* 1; querenti populo [cf. *Judges* i 1] quis dux [ME: *hare duc*] fieret *AncrR* 114; **s1312** [magnates] . . Thomam Lancastrie comitem . . in ducem sibi et capitaneum . . statuerunt TROKELOWE 70; **1381** ne duce Stramineo pereat plebs crismate diva (*Mors Simonis*) *Pol. Poems* I 228; **s1381** (c1400) vulgaris populus in regem sub duce Jak Straw / consurgitur necat (*Mem. Vers.*) *Ib.* 455. **b** principalium bis quaternos vitiorum duces . . vincere laboremus ALDH. *VirgP* 12 (cf. id. *VirgV* 2471: contra bellantes studeat certare catervas / octenosque duces).

3 duke: **a** (unspec.); **b** (Continental).

a dux, *heretoga, heorl* ÆLF. *Gl.*; hec [cf. *Matth.* xvi 18] . . dicta accipimus . . vicario B. Petri et per ipsum ceteris episcopis . ., non alicui regi, non duci, non comiti EADMER *HN* 65; dux dicitur a ducendo, quoniam alios ducere debet GIR. *PI* I 19 p. 105; cum unus homo dux sit et episcopus, dux est episcopus, nec unum dicitur ad alterum HALES *Sent.* I 245; dux, *duke WW*; dux et comes, olim officii tantum, at summe nunc dignitatis vocabula P. VERG. *Camd.* 336; dux primus est post principem dignitatis titulus. hoc primum nomen erat officii et non honoris CAMD. *Br.* 143. **b 722** etc. (v. 1 comes 2); **742** Carlomannus dux Francorum BONIF. *Ep.* 50; **s927** Rollo dux Normanniae . . de ducatus sui dispositione . . deliberabat W. JUM. II 22; dux Normannorum cum Gallis atque Britannis / invasit terram G. AMIENS *Hast.* 159; **1122** H. rex Anglorum duxque Normannorum *Regesta* p. 345; AD. EYNS. *Hug.* V 11 (v. ducatus 4a); minor Britannia, que Armorica dicitur . ., nunc duces habuit, nunc reges, secundum vicarias temporum GERV. TILB. II 10 p. 916; **s1213** illustris dux Burgundie et reliqui magnates WEND. II 90; **1225** rex . . amico carissimo duci Austrie *Pat* 558; **s1266** dux de Brundewico (v. divaricare 2); **1395** in oblationibus domini . . cum duce [*doge*] Venis *Ac. H. Derby* 276; **1443** domino Philippo Marie, duci Mediolani BEKYNTON I 164.

4 a (pre-Conquest Eng.) *ealdorman, eorl*, or sim.; *cf. 1 comes* 3. **b** (post-Conquest Eng.) earl.

a 705 ad conventum Coenredi regis episcoporumque ejus et ducum reliquorum . . non veni WEALDHERE *Ep.* 23; **s698** Berctred dux regius Nordanhymbrorum a Pictis interfectus BEDE *HE* V 24; **736** agrum . . quem ego Edilbalt rex Suutanglorum fidele duce (*sic*) atque comite meo Cyniberhttae . . donavi *CS* 154; *CS* 177 (v. actionarius a); **749** (12c) hii testes adfuerunt, et nostri magistratus, optimates et duces fidelissimique amici consenserunt et scripserunt *CS* 178; **770** fideli meo ministro Æ., viz. filio Ingeldi qui fuit dux et praefectus Æðelbaldi regis Merciorum *CS* 203; **836** ego Sigred dux hanc donationem signo crucis Christi confirmavi *CS* 416 (cf. ib.: Sigrede *aldormenn*); **904** *CS* 607 (v. dominator a); **c970** (11c) cum voluntate Ælfhere Merciorum finium ducis *CS* 1139; **s887** dux Eðelhelm . . adiit Romam ÆTHELW. IV 3; utilis sum et regi et ducibus [AS: *ealdormannum*] . . et omni populo ÆLF. *Coll.* 96; Alfwold frater Æthelwoldi principis Orientalium Anglorum tantae potestatis auctoritate erat sublimatus ut dux fieri dedignaretur BYRHT. *V. Osw.* 429; **1012** (12c) quae habebat germanum . . vocabulo Leofsinum, quem de satrapis nomine tuli, ad celsioris apicem dignitatis dignum duxi promovere ducem constituendo *CD* 719; *V. Ed. Conf.* 38v. (v. bajulus 6a). **b** opusculo meo, Roberte dux Claudiocestrie [*Gloucester*], faveas G. MON. I 1.

5 duke (as title): **a** (Eng.); **b** (Sc.); **c** (Ir.).

a 1337 [Edwardo] filio nostro nomen et honorem ducis Cornub' . . in . . parliamento nostro . . dedimus ipsumque in ducem Cornub' prefecimus et gladio cinximus sicut decet (*ChartR* 124 m. 28) *Dign. Peer* V 35; **s1337** etc. (v. ducatus 5c); **1340** teste E. duce Cornubie et comite Cestrie (*Lit. Regis E.*) AVESB. 90; **s1397** (v. dukettus); de ipsius ducis [Clarencie] gestis perpetue memorie commendandis *Ps.*-ELMH. *Hen. V* 55; solet unusquisque servientium hujusmodi tempore creacionis sue dare cuilibet principi, duci et archiepiscopo in solempnitate illa presenti . . anulum ad valorem octo scutorum FORTESCUE *LLA* 50. **b 1398** factus fuit dux de Rothezay dominus David primogenitus regis comes de Carryc, et dominus Robertus germanus regis comes de Fyf et de Menteth factus fuit dux Albanie *ExchScot* 460; **s1398** rex R. . . filium suum primogenitum D. Stewart de comite de Carrik in ducem Rothsaiensem et dominum R. fratrem suum . . de comite de Fife et Meneteth fecit ducem Albanie; ante quem nullus legitur dux fuisse post decessum Fulgencii, qui . . interfecit . . imperatorem Severum FORDUN *Cont.* XV 4; **s1398** volebat rex creasse dominum Archibaldum Nigrum comitem de Douglas in ducem, sed ipse noluit . .; et, quando herraldi clamaverunt super eum "*Schir Duk, Schir Duk*", ipse eis respondens [dicebat], "*Schir Drak, Schir Drak*" *Plusc.* X 11. **c 1386** ipsum [Robertum] de nomine ducis Hibernie . . investimus et ducem Hibernie preficimus (*ChartR* 161 m. 1) *Dign. Peer* V 79; **s1386** dominus rex . . dominum Robertum de Veer, quandoque comitem Oxonie sed nuper . . creatum marchionem Dublinie, ducem fecit Hibernie, facturus expost de duce regem, si fortuna faveret WALS. *HA* II 148.

6 (as playing-piece in board game) rook (in chess).

si quis voluerit scire hanc aleam . . scire animo necesse est: duces sc. et comites, propugnatores et impugnatores *Alea Evang.* 173; in ludo †scatorum [l. scacorum] . . quidam dicuntur reges, quidam milites, quidam duces, quidam pedones O. CHERITON *Fab.* 36B.

duxissa v. ducissa 2. **duzenna** v. dozena. **duy-** v. et. doi-. **duytellus** v. duitellus.

1 dya- v. dia-.

2 dya v. dius 1. **dyaceos (diaiteon)** v. 1 dia 1. **dyaris (diairis)** v. 1 dia 1.

dyas [CL < δυάς], two.

edictum posuit, patrium sintagma gregavit, / atque quater duodena patrum, nectente diade, / agmina conduxit FRITH. 741; dyas Grece, duo Latine OSB. GLOUC. *Deriv.* 169.

dycenum v. decena 1a. **dycothomos** v. dichotomos. **dygnarius** v. dinarium.

Dynamidia [LL *pl.*], healing property. **b** (title of book by Galen).

~ia, potestas herbarum, vel locus ubi medicina reconditur OSB. GLOUC. *Deriv.* 175. **b** [B. abbas, ob. **1193**] plurimos libros conscribere fecit, quorum nomina subnotantur: . . Liber Dinamidiorum et aliorum multorum in uno volumine SWAFHAM 99; Gal[enus] in Dyamediis GILB. VI 235v. 1; secundum quod G. in libro Dinamidiarum docet BACON IX 165.

dynamis [LL < δύναμις], power. **b** potentiality.

he ealneg sceal / boethia *biddan georne* / . . / *þæt him Drihten gyfe* dinams *on eorðan*, / fortis actor (*Aldhelm*) *ASPR* VI 98; imprudens mulier, / . . / siste, capesse fidem: dinami capieris eadem: / otius amisso mutaberis ipsa marito FRITH. 686; **c970** (11c) magnifica poliarchis Christi allubescente dinami *CS* 1139; **1011** (13c) Deum . . qui suae incircumscripte †diuamia majestatis circumscripta quaeque quasi pugillo continet cherali *Ch. Burton* 33; BACON *Gram. Gk.* 62 (v. dynastia a). **b** numquid minus perfectus es logicus, etsi nescias . . que predicatio fiat secundum †dinaldim, que secundum energiam? NECKAM *NR* II 174 p. 311.

dynastia [LL < δυναστεία], supreme power. **b** dynasty.

dynamis virtus vel potentia, et ~ia summa potestas BACON *Gram. Gk.* 62. **b** variate . . sunt ~ie per diversa regum genera usque ad hunc regem Cambysem GERV. TILB. II 15.

dyo- v. dio-. **dyptica** v. diptycha. **dyrocheum** v. dirocheum.

Dyrrachium [CL < Δυρράχιον (*place-name*)], (scene of) civil strife.

intestina pater postquam dirrachia planxit, / ad vicina redit lentis habitacula plantis FRITH. 1152.

dyscolare, to grudge, be perverse. **b** (p. ppl.) perverse.

cum titulus a Cristo traditus non sufficit clericis sic discolantibus ad vendicandum vel vite necessaria WYCL. *Ver.* III 61. **b** discolis, i. . . discordibus vel discolatis mor[t]alibus *GlH* D 588.

dyscolatus, 'truandise'.

trowantysy, trutannia, discolatus *PP*.

dyscolia [δυσκολία], disaffection, perversity.

ad discernendam discoliam oportet quod sacra scriptura et eorum opera ei conformia indicent veritatem WYCL. *Ver.* I 340.

dyscolicus, perverse.

WYCL. *Ver.* I 344 (v. argutio a).

dyscolus (dis-) [LL < δύσκολος], contumacious, unruly, perverse. **b** (w. ref. to *1 Pet.* ii 18) 'froward'. **c** (appl. to abstr.) arduous, tangled. **d** (as sb. m.) 'truant', vagabond.

†discolis, i. . . discors, contrarius, . . *ungeþwæra GlH* D 587; erat terribilis ut leo inoboedientibus seu ~is, mitibus vero et humilibus mitior columba ÆLF. *Æthelwold* 19; edicimus . . ut ~i [AS: *wiðersacan*] et exleges [AS: *utlagan*] Dei et hominum a patria discedant (*Cons. Cnuti*) *GAS* 311; ~is vero et jocosis nebulonibus . . suum consortium . . denegabat ORD. VIT. V 19 p. 448; rex . . totum in hoc direxit animum ut paci rebellantes et ~os multiplici subversione contereret *Dial. Scac.* II 2 D; elegi potius loquendo ridiculus quam tacendo ~us inveniri GIR. *RG* II 2; Micheas discolus cornicans fatua WALT. WIMB. *Palpo* 40; sunt ~i et contentiosi et litigiosi et turbant . . inquisitionem veritatis BACON *CSPhil.* 409; **c1314** quosdam ~os, lupi rapacis seviciam sub vestibus ovium in grege nostro palliantes *FormOx* 11; **1401** nunc flent discreti, rident ~i BEKYNTON I 152 (= AD. USK 66). **b c803** si etiam ~is, quanto magis sapientissimo principi . . debemus . . oboedire! ALCUIN *Ep.* 265; crede michi, satrapas non est offendere tutum; / magnus honoretur discolus atque bonus WALT. ANGL. *Fab.* 48. 16; eciam ~i possunt esse veri domini OCKHAM *Dial.* 898; Petrus honorem culminis / jubet impendi dominis / modestis atque discolis (*In Lollardos*) *Pol. Poems* I 236. **c c675** (v. diverticulum 1b). **d** *trowant*, trutannus, ~us *PP*; hic disculus, *a trowean WW*; *a trowan*, ~us, trutannus *CathA*.

dyscrasia (dis-) [LL < δυσκρασία], (med.) 'dyscrasy', distemper; **b** (fig.).

si aliquid horum [elementorum] fuerit in causa ~ie, recurrendum est ad consimile ADEL. *Alch.* 17n.; multe particule frigide . . cum cerebri cellulam petant ipsius reprimunt ~iam *Quaest. Salern.* B 51; GIR. *GE* I 5 (v. distemperantia b); **s1238** ingruente ~ia, non se meminit aliquis tot vidisse in uno anno quartenarios M. PAR. *Maj.* III 522; ~ia purgetur cum theodoricon euper[iston] vel anacardino GILB. I 52v. 2; animarum mediatrix, / delet vite renodatrix / febriles discrasias GARL. *SM* 117; signa ~ie future in vulnere sunt . . dolor, rubor, et tumor GAD.

124. 1; **1423** ne nimie evagacionis egressibus ullas paciamini aut cordis aut corporis ∿ias (*Lit. Abbatis*) AMUND. I app. 413. **b** necesse est ut, corde appropinquante morti politice, . . ∿ia suboriatur in toto corpore policie WYCL. *Blasph.* 64; omnes contenciones . . ecclesie, omnes †distrasie ab observancia legis ewangelice . ., a cupiditate temporalium . . sumpserant originem *Id. Civ. Dom.* I 160; nec debet . . credi appetitui infirmorum, qui propter †distrasiam amplexati sunt stercora sensus scripture *Id. Sim.* 38.

dyscrasiari (dis-), to be distempered; **b** (fig.); **c** (alch.).

moriente corpore . . corpus distemperatur et ∿iatur HOLCOT *Wisd.* 43. **b** mercenarii civile dominium ecclesiasticorum indignantes . . ∿iantur in moribus et effrenes facti . . dissipant bona regni WYCL. *Civ. Dom.* II 14; debent juvare partes plus nobiles ∿iatas febre vel alio morbo pestifero *Id. Ver.* III 60. **c** quia indigestus nimium incaluit omnino ∿iatus virtute defecit DASTIN *Visio* 325.

dyscritus [δύσκριτος], (of fever) lacking an obvious crisis. *Cf. eucritus.*

brevis erit egritudo et discrita GILB. I 29v. 1; sequitur [cardiaca passio] . . febres vel egritudines longas discritas, ut quartana *Ib.* IV 200. 2; que in paribus [diebus] judicantur, discreta sunt et amica conversioni: rursus febricitantem, cum in diebus paribus febris dimiserit, reverti consuevit BACON IX app. 203.

dysenteria [CL < δυσεντερία], dysentery, diarrhoea; **b** (fig.).

leporem licet comedere et bonum est pro desintiria THEOD. *Pen.* II 11. 5; fratrem . . desyntirie languore infirmantem *V. Cuthb.* IV 12; dissenteria, *blodig utsiht* ÆLF. *Gl.*; [milites] dyssenteria languentes W. POIT. II 27; confitebatur se Deum precari ut vel dissinteria vel febri urgente moveretur W. MALM. *GP* I 44; inducit diarriam vel dissinteriam, id est fluxum ventris BART. ANGL. V 21;

dysentria, fluxus BACON *Gram. Gk.* 62; **s1285** Ph. rex Francie . . incurrit dissentiriam et obiit *Ann. Dunstable* 318; dissinteria est fluxus ventris humoralis cum excoriacione vel solucione continuitatis intestinorum et est utplurimum cum sanguine GAD. 56. 2; rubus . . valet contra discenteriam [v. l. dissinteriam] *Alph.* 157; *skytte or flux*, †henteria [l. lienteria], dissentaria *PP.* **b** quicquid fetet et fedatur / fetida luxuria, / . . / totum potest emundare / burse dissenteria WALT. WIMB. *Van.* 52.

dysentericus [CL < δυσεντερικός], (one) afflicted w. dysentery. **b** (w. *morbus*) dysentery.

ad dissentericos, *to utsichte GlM* 73b 3; quidam puerulus diu †dissenteriatus [? l. ∿icus] effectus R. COLD. *Cuthb.* 125 *rub.*; dat dissintericis gratum paratella juvamen NECKAM *DS* VII 279; dissinterici melius curantur secundum viam cibi constrictivi GILB. V 220v. 2. **b** ambobus fratribus his morbo ∿o interemptis H. BOS. *Thom.* IV 30 p. 461; **s1216** rex Johannes . . obiit . . morbo ∿o HIGD. VII 33 (= *Meaux* I 397: discenterico); **s1316** morbus dissentericus ex corruptis cibis conceptus fere omnes maculavit TROKELOWE 94.

dysenum v. decena 1a.

dysfortunium [δυσ- + fortunium], misfortune. *Cf. eufortunium.*

eufortunium et diffortunium proprie sunt differentie fortune et sic [ali]quando accidunt preter intentionem agentis BACON XIII 121; fortuna invenitur tantum in eis in quibus potest contingere bonitas et malitia; eufortunium autem vel diffortunium est cum magnitudinem habentia sunt SICCAV. *PN* 199; hominem . . a demonio vel manifesto diffortunio . . liberatum *Mir. Hen. VI* I 1 p. 16.

dysis [LL < δύσις], sunset, west.

in disis loco, qui est occidens BYRHT. *V. Ecgwini* 382; arctos . . ∿is, anathole, mesembria dicuntur oriens et occidens, aquilo et meridies ANSELM *Misc.* 318; fluenta . .

novi Jordanis, qui de capite novi martyris emergens derivatur in disim W. CANT. *Mir. Thom.* II 56 (cf. 1 arctus b).

dyspnoea [CL < δύσπνοια], shortness of breath.

asma et dispnia et †orthomia [? l. orthopnia] hanelitus . . difficultates sunt hanelandi GILB. IV 198. 1; hanc crisim precedunt plurima signa: dolor colli vel cervicis, precordiorum intensio, dispnia . . BACON IX app. 202; disnia est difficultas anhelitus in trahendo aerem GAD. 54. 2; †dimpnia est difficultas hanelandi sine sonitu *SB* 18; †disma *Ib.* (v. asthma).

dyspnoicus [CL < δυσπνοϊκός], short of breath.

∿us, suspiriosus, qui plus recipit quam remittit OSB. GLOUC. *Deriv.* 177; abrotanum . . / disnoicis dat opem NECKAM *DS* VII 32.

dyssenteria v. dysenteria. **dysseonare** v. dissaisonare.

Dystros [LL < Δύστρος], Greek (or Macedonian) month.

vocatur apud eos [Graecos] . . Martius Distros BEDE *TR* 14 (cf. *Miss. Jum.* 11); Ebrus Adar Martium Graecus et nomine Distrios *Kal. M. A.* I 401.

dysuria [LL < δυσουρία], dysury, difficulty in urination.

disuria, aride urine digestio OSB. GLOUC. *Deriv.* 175; dyapiretrum . . dissuriam et stranguriam solvit GILB. IV 189. 2; si appetit mingere . . sed non potest nisi per horas certas et cum difficultate . ., tunc vocatur dissuria GAD. 98v. 1; dissuria dicitur involuntaria retencio urine; vel dicitur difficultas mingendi, viz. qui sepe et in multa quantitate mingit *SB* 17.

dytenum v. decena 1a. **dytonus** v. ditonus. **dyus** v. dius. **dzifta** v. sifta.

E

1 E [CL]

1 E (letter of alphabet). **b** (w. *brevis* or *pente*) epsilon, fifth letter of Greek alphabet; **c** numeral (= 5).

cum E littera adsumitur et in sequenti pro I ponitur E, [Aelli] *all* vocatur, quod in nostra lingua 'omnes' absolute indicat *V. Greg.* p. 87; 'accedit' per E ab ambulando, 'accidit' per I ab eventu BEDE *Orth.* 12; cum additur E ad A, sonat E, ut 'caelum' sonat 'celum'; et, cum additur E ad O, sonat E, ut 'coepit' sonat 'cepit' BACON *CSPhil.* 507; E in confinio gutturis et oris, gutture aliquantulum protenso et ore aliquantulum rotundo, profertur *Ps.*-GROS. *Gram.* 21. **b** E brevis, 'E', ε, v *Runica Manuscripta* 351; E pente BACON *Maj.* I 75 (v. delta a); *Id. Gram. Gk.* (v. eta a); nomen Grecum .. 'Antemos' habet vij litteras, quarum .. quarta .. est E brevis et significat v HARCLAY *Adv.* 80. **c** *Runica Manuscripta* 351, HARCLAY *Adv.* 80 (v. 1b supra).

2 musical note.

rotunda B .. cum E inferioribus nullam dat consonantiam .. nec in superioribus cum E resonat TUNST. 215a.

2 e (prep.) v. ex.

eadem [CL], likewise.

cujus pater .., cum ∼em sobolem suam liberalibus sofismatum disciplinis imbueret .. ALDH. *VirgP* 47.

ealdormannus v. aldermannus 1.

eale [CL], African animal, yale. (*Cf. Arch. J.* LXVII 173–202).

bestia que dicitur ∼e, magnus ut equus, cauda elephanti *Best.* 25 f. 16b (cf. Solinus 55).

eapropter [CL, al. div.], **a** therefore, for that reason. **b** thereby, by that means.

a ∼er opera B. Cuthberti non reticenda existunt, eo quod ipsa se virtutum novitatibus innotescunt R. COLD. *Cuthb.* 47; non premisit apostolus 'nemo sumit sibi honorem', nisi subjungeret, 'sed qui vocatur a Deo ..' [*Heb.* v 4]; .. ∼er .. vos admoneo .. ut .. fiducialiter ducatim militie celestis subeatis AD. MARSH *Ep.* 100; **1347** ea propter .. tractatores infrascripti .. ad infrascriptas treugas .. concordaverunt (*Treugae*) AVESB. 116b; **1434** ea propter, nolens hujusmodi officium bedellorum .. minui .. sed pocius volens augeri, [congregacio] ordinavit .. hujusmodi feoda bedellorum .. persolvenda StatOx 257. **b** huic [Ceolwulfo] Beda scripsit historiam Anglorum, ut ∼er imperium roboraret et populi ingenium emendaret SILGRAVE 29.

easiamentum v. aisiamentum 1a.

Eastanglus [AS *East Engle* (*pl.*)], East Angle.

679 imperantibus dominis .. Ecgfrido rege Humbronensium .. et Alduulfo rege Estranglorum (*Lit. synodalis*) BEDE *HE* IV 15 p. 239; de ortu regum ∼orum NEN. *HB* 203 (cf. ib. 208: Onnam regem Esteranglorum); post Danicam cladem in qua beatus Estanglorum rex Edmundus .. occubuit ORD. VIT. XI 33 p. 281; **s910** Edwardus rex .. constituit inducias cum Estanglis et Nordhumbris apud Itingforde H. HUNT. *HA* V 15.

Eastsexanus, **∼ensis** [AS *East Seaxe* (*pl.*)], East Saxon.

693 provincia ∼orum CS 81; **s904** frater regis .. duxit navigium .. in Estsexe; et Estsexenses .. subditi sunt H. HUNT. *HA* V 14.

eatenus [CL]

1 so far, to such an extent; **b** (w. *ut*).

R. NIGER *Mil.* IV 24 (v. elongare 4a); intellectus divinus continet istas veritates quasi liber. .. et ∼us posset dici intellectus noster videre veritates in luce eterna, hoc est in libro illo sicut in continente objectum DUNS *Ord.* III 161; †eetenus .. imperator insignivit ipsam cum milicie laurea *Wager* f. 43a. **b** **s1141** (v. 1 communio 4c); nec tamen ∼us superbiam vitet ut incidat in contemptum J. SAL. *Pol.* 528A.

2 till then, hitherto.

affectum .. intellegibilis asinae ∼us elinguis [cf. *Num.* xxii 28] non refugio GILDAS *EB* 1; insulam Vectam, quae ∼us erat tota idolatriae dedita BEDE *HE* IV 14 p. 237; ∼us, *oð ðaet* GlC E 2; ∼us vel eotenus, *oð þæt* ÆLF. *Sup.*; eotenus, i. decreto [MS: eo decreto] ordine, †thus [MS: huc] usque, vel *forþy* GlH E 295; ostendens locum ∼us inconvulsum OSB. *V. Dunst.* 17; relictis canonicis, quorum conversatione ∼us usus fuerat EADMER *V. Osw.* 5; rex

Philippus .. eas [litteras] .. Ricardo, qui in exercitu patris existens ∼us eidem .. fideliter adheserat, destinavit GIR. *PI* III 2.

3 (w. *ut*) to the end, in order (that).

†**854** (12c) v mansiones donavi .. familiae Maldubiensi, eotenus ut ipsi .. orent pro nobis *CS* 481; **939** concedo cuidam .. Christi ancille .., eatinus ut mei memoriam suis .. orationibus .. habeat, xv mansas agelluli *CS* 734; **a1122** eotenus (v. deservire 3a).

eaudere v. evadere.

†**eavis**, *f. l.*

s1513 †eavis [l. canis] (v. diabolus 1d).

ebalatio v. avalatio. **eban-** v. heben-.

ebba [AS *ebba*], ebb.

1151 expectabunt unum fluctum et unam ∼am; et, si navis inde [*from Dowgate, London*] ablata non fuerit, .. cives Rothomagi .. eam .. inde depellant *Regesta* 729; si extra regnum [fuerit] .., dilationem habebit xl dierum et duorum *floz* [v. l. flodorum] et unius ∼e BRACTON 163 (cf. ib. 338).

ebbingwera [ME *ebbing wer*], 'ebbing-weir' (for catching fish on ebb-tide).

1547 contra formam .. statuti [12 *Ed. IV* 7] .. provisi de .. gurgitibus, stagnis, pilis, lokkis .., gutteris, seweris, hebbyngweris .. *Pat Sup.* 64 m. 1.

ebbullire v. ebullire 3. **ebd-** v. hebd-.

ebel, hebel [Ar. *abhul*], savin, dried tops of *Juniperus sabina*. *V. et. alhel*.

ebel, i. *savin SB* 18; hebel, i. savina vel juniperus *SB* 23.

eben- v. heben-.

1 ebes v. abies a. **2 ebes** v. hebes. **ebet-** v. hebet-. **ebibatus** v. epibata 3.

ebibere [CL], to drink up, consume, absorb; **b** (fig.). **c** to drink (intr.).

fontis Siloe recessus .. calor solis ∼erat W. MALM. *GR* IV 369; exhibitus GILB. VII 344v. 1 (v. decorticare d). **b** quas [artes] ita ∼it [Gerbertus] ut inferiores ingenio suo ostenderet W. MALM. *GR* II 167; sagitte ejus [Domini] infixe sunt tibi [cf. *Psalm* xxxvii 3], quarum indignatio ∼it spiritum tuum [cf. *Job* vi 4] AILR. *Serm.* 450C; totam recipit in cor ∼itque pestilentem malitiam, qua totus deperit MAP *NC* IV 12 f. 54; **c1390** (v. compunctio b). **c** amici cornua habuerunt et ∼erunt ÆLF. BATA 4. 11 p. 36.

ebiculum v. hebidus. **ebiglotum** v. epiglottis. **ebilare** v. evirare.

Ebionita [cf. 'Εβιωναῖος], Ebionite heretic.

Simon Samaritanus, qui .. ∼as, i. e. pauperes in intelligentia, seduxit, ut dicerent Christum natum ex viro et femina et postea natum ex Spiritu Sancto et femina, et non fuisse Deum ante secula R. NIGER *Chr.* I 24 (cf. id. *Chr. II* 115).

ebiscus v. hibiscus. **ebitare** v. hebetare. **ebitis** v. hebes. **ebolus** v. 1 ebulus. **ebor** v. ebur.

Eboracensis, **∼acus**, of York. **b** Yorkist.

Ulfrido administrante episcopatum ∼ensis ecclesiae BEDE *HE* IV 3 p. 206; **1229** profert literas ∼ensis archiepscopi *CurR* XII 1609 (= *BNB* II 271 Eboriensis); **s992** Adulphus .. factus est archiepiscopus ecclesie ∼ensis WHITTLESEY f. 27 p. 161; Eborac' capitulum, kekus, porcus, fimus Eborecus *Staura Civ.* 4. **b** flagrantibus inter Lancastrenses et ∼enses funestis dissidiis CAMD. *Br.* 174.

Eboralis, of or near York or (?) *f. l.*

1244 dies datus est .. coram domino rege si sit citra partes Northamton'; et, si sit versus partes Eborales [? l. boreales *or* Eboracenses], tunc sit loquela coram justiciariis de Banco *CurR* XVIII 905.

Eborecus, Eboriensis v. Eboracensis. **eborneus** v. 2 eburneus.

†**ebraia** [? cf. bracium, braisis], (?) malt.

1203 et iij quart[eriis] ∼e, quos recepit de catallis ejusdem .. ad mensuram Cadomi .. ; et ij boiss[ellis] fabarum et iij quart[eriis] ibraie *RScacNorm* II 569.

Ebraicus, Ebreus v. Hebr-. **ebredio** v. radius.

ebriare [CL], to inebriate, intoxicate (fig.).

huic .. fideli, quem Dominus .. de fonte voluntatis sue .. potaverat, immo ∼averat STUDLEY 5 p. 372.

ebriatio, drinking bout.

1434 delicaciis et aliis carnis illecibris (*sic*) et †ebricacionibus *Reg. Heref.* 177.

ebrietas [CL], drunkenness, intoxication; **b** (fig. or jocular).

pastores .. ∼ate .. quasi vino madidi torpebant GILDAS *EB* 21; si monachus pro ∼ate vomitum facit, xxx dies paeniteat THEOD. *Pen.* I 1. 2; ebrietas animos solet enervare virorum ALDH. *VirgV* 2501; cum diutius epulis atque ∼ati vacarent BEDE *HE* III 10 p. 147; †**747** fertur in parrochiis vestris ∼atis malum nimis adsuetum esse, ut .. episcopi .. ipsi nimis bibentes inebrientur BONIF. *Ep.* 78 p. 170n.; ebrietas nil est nisi demonis ignis adurens D. BEC. 965; detur semen caulis .., quod optimum est contra ∼atem GAD. 135. 7. **b** tam vehementi sacrilegiorum caecitate et ineffabili ∼ate propheta conterritus [est] GILDAS *EB* 49; si [delectat] ∼as, 'inebriabuntur ab ubertate domus' Dei [cf. *Psalm* xxxv 9] ANSELM (*Prosl.* 25) I 118; ob miram ipsius potus [sc. anagoges] dulcedinem ebrius erit illa .. ∼ate ad quam sponsus electos suos invitat in Canticis *Simil. Anselmi* 194; explicit Refectorium Salutis editum ab opulentissima ∼ate et deliciis pleno ipso viro Dei Ricardo Methley METHLEY *Tract.* 70v.

ebriolus [CL], tipsy.

∼us, .. i. aliquantulum ebrius OSB. GLOUC. *Deriv.* 190.

ebriositas [CL], drunkenness.

747 caveant .. ne aliqua pravae conversationis exempla .. praebeant .., vel in ∼ate vel turpis lucri gratia (*Clovesho* 9) *Conc. HS* 366; .. Angli olim tam militia quam literatura laudabiles fuere; nunc vero propter luxuriam et ∼atem in neutra prestantes inveniuntur GIR. *GE* II 36.

ebriosus [CL], addicted to drink, (as sb.) drunkard. **b** intoxicating (fig.).

evenit saepe ut .. qui ∼um condemnant virus invidiae quo exeduntur ipsi non videant BEDE *Hom.* I 25. 108; **742** inveniuntur quidam inter eos episcopi qui .. sunt ∼i .. vel venatores BONIF. *Ep.* 50 p. 83; **747** ut .. ante canonicam horam .. potationibus ∼orum more non serviant (*Clovesho* 21) *Conc. HS* 369; temulentus, ∼us GlC T 58; H. LOS. *Ep.* 3 (v. acediosus); divinum judicium contra .. ∼um [ME: *be druncwile*] AncrR 77; R. MARSTON *QD* 188 (v. ebrius 1a); da ∼o cinerem irundinum combustarum et nunquam inebriabitur GAD. 135. 1. **b** hujus seculi quasi amaritudinum ∼a voluptate delitescentium R. COLD. *Cuthb.* 50.

ebrius [CL]

1 drunk; **b** (fig.). **c** addicted to drink, drunkard.

nonne sator soboles stupro cognovit adultas / ebrius? [cf. *Gen.* xix 33] ALDH. *VirgV* 2522; [convivae] ∼ii nec erigere se valentes G. *Herw.* 328; non vidi ∼ium aut vesanum tante memorie MAP *NC* IV 16 f.58v.; ebrius exclamat: "quis sum? vir nonne potens sum?" D. BEC. 969; nutat ut ∼ius [ME: *fordrunken mon*] AncrR 77; sicut probat Augustinus, ponens exemplum de quodam non tantum ebrioso sed actualiter ∼io R. MARSTON *QD* 188. **b** *Simil. Anselmi* 194 (v. ebrietas b); mater doloribus nutans et ebria WALT. WIMB. *Carm.* 290. **c** inceperat percutere conservos suos, manducans et bibens cum ∼iis GILDAS *EB* 96; **1549** curent prelati ut tales in eorum familiares .. teneant qui non .. scortatores publici, ∼ii, pugnaces .. aut .. divini nominis blasphematores .. reputentur *Conc. Scot.* II 91.

2 steeped.

[indumentum] fili delicatissimi, quod conchiliorum sucis ∼ium rapuerit colorem coccineum W. MALM. (*V. Aldh.*) *GP* V 218.

Ebul v. Elul. **ebula** v. 1 ebulus.

ebulinus [cf. CL ebulus], made of danewort (*Sambucus ebulus*).

coquantur [folia ebuli] in aqua diu .. ; erit unguentum optimum in causa frigida, et vocatur unguentum ∼um GAD. 39v. 2.

ebulire, **∼itio** v. ebullire, ∼itio.

ebullare, to boil (trans.). *V. et. ebullire* 3.

1296 cum ollis terre ad eamdem *cole* ∼andam cum ovis ad *glayr* et sepo ad roellas unguendas *Ac. Galley Newcastle* 182.

ebullatio [LL], bubbling up, gushing forth. *V. et. ebullitio.*

s1466 de ~one sanguinis a tumba [comitis Lancastrie] .. et de aliis miraculis HERRISON *Abbr. Chr.* 10.

ebulliaria, boiler. *V. et. 2 bullaria.*

s1518 coquina nova .. cum iij focis in uno camino et cum ij fornacibus et ~iis *Reg. Butley* 35.

ebullio, boiling or bubbling up. *V. et. ebullitio.*

c**1130** ebullivit aqua undique... non tantum pro ~one multimoda .. mirabantur stupefacti *Lib. Landav.* 85 (= *MonA* VI 1220b); capita .. in ferventi liquamine .. eminebant ex vi ~onis [v. l. bullionis] COGGESH. *Visio* 28.

ebullire [CL]

1 (intr.) to boil or bubble up, gush forth, break out: **a** (of fluid, fire or odour); **b** (of dust or worms); **c** (of abstr.).

a flagrantia suavitatis ab imis ~ivit BEDE *HE* III 8 (cf. ib. V 12: fetor .. cum .. vaporibus ~iens); nec etiam a fonte, qui ibi ~iebat, aquam haurire .. praesummebat ALCUIN *WillP* 10; **8.** .. ~it, *wapolað WW*; pyriflegitonta, ignis ~iens *Gl. Leid.* 38. 24; ingens vapor inexpertae suavitatis ~iens GOSC. *Transl. Aug.* 21C; per fontem intelligitur aqua de abysso ~iens ANSELM (*Proc. Sp.* 9) II 205; aliquando delectantur simul .. auditus et olfactus, ut cum aliquem bibendi aviditate delectat auscultare mustum ~iens .. et ejus odorem naribus attrahere *Simil. Anselmi* 15; c**1130** (v. ebullio); queritur quare .. sanguis ex vulnere occisi ~iat *Quaest. Salern.* B 269; illud quod ~it caloris vehementia undique se jactitat et diffundit BART. ANGL. II 8; **1377** in vadiis viij hominum .. mundancium fundamentum .. fontis in castro [de Corff'], ut aqua in eadem fonte possit ~ire *KRAc* 461/7 (cf. *Building in Eng.* 277). **b** cum de sepulcri tumba pulvis ~iat et .. in superficie antri .. scaturiat ALDH. *VirgP* 23; rupta cute cum sanie vermes ~iunt AILR. *Ed. Conf.* 762A; vermes ~ebant ab eo [Simeone] S. LANGTON *Ruth* 96. **c** ex uno superbae elationis fonte pene diversarum origo sectarum ~ivit ALCUIN (*Adv. Elipand.*) *Dogm.* 285C; **1188** nunc tanta monachorum ~ivit insania .. *Ep. Cant.* 182; sub .. Trajano tertius impetus persequutionis ~ivit R. NIGER *Chr. I* 24; ebulivit hec heresis in magis blasfemum mendacium WYCL. *Blasph.* 139.

2 (trans.) to exude, generate.

ubi fetida damnatorum cadavera .. horrida vermium examina ~iebant ALDH. *VirgP* 36; has ranas Egypti fluvius ~it S. LANGTON *Serm.* 1. 3; agri .. et nemora tanta fecunditate germina ~iunt FORTESCUE *LLA* 29.

3 (trans.) to boil; *v. et. ebullare.* **b** (p. ppl.) invecked (her.).

1256 Angnes .., ebulliendo plenum plumbum de bertisa [? l. bercisa; cf. bersisa], cecidit in plumbum et excaturicata fuit *AssizeR Northumb* 69. **b** incisiones tantum marginės symboli afficiunt et earum .. sunt .. nuperiores ~ite SPELMAN *Asp.* 108.

ebullitio [LL], boiling or bubbling up, gushing forth; *v. et. ebullatio.* **b** source. **c** scum.

semine [in matrice] locato, incipiet virtus digestiva .. per ~onem inspissare *Quaest. Salern.* B 24; facta est .. ~o pelagi MAP *NC* IV 12 f. 54; maris .. absorptio vicissim et ~o GIR. *TH* II 3; ex calore .. sanguis in coleram convertitur et per eundem aqua per fortem ~onem subtiliores partes aereas consummantem, terrestribus manentibus, salis in substantiam transmutatur BART. ANGL. IV 1; est iterum putredo ~o sive perturbatio nature moventis localiter et permiscentis GILB. I 5. 2; BACON VIII 203 (v. digestivus c); *Id. Maj.* I 140 (v. donec 2); J. ROUS *Hist. Reg. Angl.* 104 (v. 1 ebulus). **b 1293** dedisse .. unam perticam terre .. cum marisco et ~one fontis de Pukeleshale *PQW* (*Kent*) 357b. **c** coclear quo spume et ebulitiones [v. l. ~o, *gl.*: *bullium, bulluiz*] possint castigari NECKAM *Ut.* 97.

1 ebulus, ~um [CL], **~a,** wallwort, danewort, dwarf elder (*Sambucus ebulus*). *Cf. chamaeacte, eriphion.*

sambucus, in silva putris dum fronde virescit / est mihi par foliis .. ALDH. *Aen.* 94 (*Ebulus*); ~um, *walhwyrt GlC* E 11; ebullus est †fructus [? l. frutex] sive herba in foliis .. sambuco arbori similis BART. ANGL. XVII 60; cathaplasma eb[u]li sive ell[ebor]i superpositum diminuit scrop[h]ulas GILB. III 175. 1; **12.** .. ~um, i. *eble*, i. *walwurt WW*; potest fieri vomitus levis .. cum modico succi sambuci vel ~i GAD. 5. 1; ~us vel ~a, G. *eble*, A. *welleuort* vel *licheuurt Alph.* 51; hic ebolus, *walwortte*.., hec ~a, A. *a wallewurte WW*; herbam ~i, id est *walwort* .., que ex ebullicione sanguinis humani .. originem trahit J. ROUS *Hist. Reg. Angl.* 104.

2 ebulus v. kebulus.

ebur [CL], ivory; **b** (fig.). **c** (w. *ustum* or *combustum*) calcined ivory or bone-ash.

ebor, *elpendbaan GlC* E 3; [adduco vobis] .. ebur [AS: *ylpesban*] et auricalcum, aes et stagnum ÆLF. *Coll.* 96; ymaginem de ebore AILR. *Gen. Regum* 350 (v. distinctio 1c); ~or, ut aiunt, os elephantis est BALD. CANT. *Tract.* 16. 568A; feretris auro et ebore distinctis GIR. *PI* III 30 p. 323. **b** sobrietatis ebur, pastor pie, pacis amator M. RIEVAULX (*Vers.*) 4. **c** spodium dicunt quidam esse ebur combustum. .. sed spondium est fuligo quedam que invenitur in domibus ubi funduntur metalla... nos tamen utimur pro eo ebore usto *Alph.* 178.

1 eburneus v. alburneus.

2 eburneus [CL], made of ivory. **b** white as ivory.

9. .. ~eus dens, *elpend toþ WW*; [portam] ~eam J. SAL. *Pol.* 428D (v. corneus 1a); dentes .. tanquam ~eos GIR. *DK* I 11 (v. confricatio a); **1245** baculus cantoris est totus de peciis eborneis cum circulis argenteis deauratis *Invent. S. Paul.* 473; c**1250** teca yburnea *Vis. S. Paul.* 15; **1383** (v. crucifigere 2b); ~ea, *everey WW*. **b** planities / .. / purpurata cum rosetis, / quibus inter eburnea / lilia lucent linea (ÆTHELWALD) *Carm. Aldh.* 2. 155; ALCUIN *Ep.* 26 (v. elephantinus 1); venter eburneus, venter mirificus WALT. WIMB. *Carm.* 46.

eburninus, made of ivory.

collum ut turris eminet eburnina [*cf. Cant.* vii 4] J. HOWD. *Cant.* 642.

eburnus [CL], made of ivory.

~a, ex ebure *GlH* E 9; ex ~a, *of ylpebane GlM* 25. 6; ~a, *ylpenbaenum GlP* 369.

ebursare, to expend, disburse. *V. et. debursare.*

c**1365** tota pecunie summa .. penitus ~ata *FormOx* 365; totam pecunie summam .. totaliter ~avi *Dictamen* 369; **1441** de pecuniis quas mei gracia in bullas ~averis BEKYNTON I 227; **1477** inhibeo .. nequid nomine meo .. vanas aut immoderatas expensas .. ~ari faciat *Test. Ebor.* III 230.

ebutyrare [cf. butyratus], (p. ppl. w. *lac*) buttermilk.

lac vaccinum quod est ebutiratum GAD. 73. 1.

ecambium v. excambium 1b. **ecariare** v. excarriare.

ecce [CL], behold! mark! **b** (w. nom.); **c** (w. indir. qu.).

ecce, casae cacumina / cadebant ad fundamina (ALDH.) *Carm. Aldh.* 1. 167; "hic est ecce meus dilectus filius!" inquit [cf. *Matth.* iii 17] *Id. VirgV* 431; ecce sacerdotis pandam praeconia lauti *Ib.* 1619; cum .. laudes decantarent, ~e subito lux emissa caelitus .. venit super omnes BEDE *HE* IV 7; huic aliud simili successit in ordine signum. / ecce! comes quidam venerandum jure Johannem / advocat ALCUIN *SS Ebor* 1136; o monache, qui mihi locutus es, ~e [AS: *efne*], probavi te habere bonos socios ÆLF. *Coll.* 99; patet ~e rationi via, si disciplinalia .. distinguere conemur BALSH. *AD rec. 2* 156; [adverbia] demonstrandi, .. ortandi, prohibendi .., ut '~e', 'eya', 'ne' .. *Ps.-*GROS. *Gram.* 59. **b** 'per fidem operationis Dei', quam operatus est in Christo — ~e operatio LANFR. *Comment. Paul.* (*Coloss.* ii 12) 326; conveniunt omnes barones .. ; et ~e Thomas de H... clamans senescaldiam BRAKELOND 128; ~e [ME: *lo*] racio subtilis et clara *AncrR* 73; sic se [Christus] ostendit vobis ac si diceret: "~e ego hic [ME: *lour ich her*]! quid wltis?" *Ib.* 97. **c 1385** ostendit illi pecuniam predictam, dicendo sibi: "~e quid inveni hic!" *IMisc* 234/5; ~e quam patenter explanatur .. quod T. non dedit istam abbatiam Benedicto ..! ELMH. *Cant.* 204.

eccec- v. excaec-.

†eccensus, *f. l.*

1253 quatinus .. excommunicatos denuntietis .., candelis †eccensis [l. accensis] et pulsatis campanis *Reg. Gasc. A* II 397.

eccentricitas, eccentricity (geom.).

~as circuli solis SACROB. *Sph.* 101; ostenditur per solis excentricitatem quod regio inter eclipticam et parallelum australem est inhabitabilis GROS. 25; si ~as solis sit prout mathematici ponunt, impossibile est pure temperatum esse sub equinoctiali BACON *Maj.* I 137; PECKHAM *Persp.* I 30 (v. concentricitas); [Albategni] discordat a sequacibus Ptolomei in equacionibus ecentricorum et epiciclorum, quia discordat ab eis in longitudine ecentricitatum WALLINGF. (*Alb.*) I 260.

eccentricus [cf. LL eccentrus < ἔκκεντρος], eccentric (geom.); **b** (as sb. m., *sc. circulus*).

planete circulus respectu terre excentricus invenitur ADEL. *Elk.* 33; septem terra vagis excentrica subjacet astris, / quam tamen ut centrum maximus orbis habet J. SAL. *Enth. Phil.* 1071; NECKAM *DS* I 489, GROS. 28 (v. aux a); necesse est quod, si fuerit orbis habens utriusque superficiem †encentricam, nec sit supremus .. nec infimus, .. set intermedius tantum; si autem fuerit ecentricus quantum ad concavitatem tantum, non poterit esse infimus BACON IV 435; theologi disputant .. de figura eorum [celorum] et de circulis ~is et epicyclicis *Id. Tert.* 200. **b** ~us dicitur omnis circulus .. qui dividens terram in partes equales non habet centrum suum cum centro terre sed extra SACROB. *Sph.* 113; circulus solis vocatur excentricus solis, eo quod centrum ejus egressum est a centro terre GROS. 22; *Ib.* 29 (v. draco 5b); BACON IV 420 (v. concentricus a); WALLINGF. (*Alb.*) I 294 (v. concentricus b); *Ib.* 356 (v. aux a).

eccentris, eccentric (geom.).

circulus ecentris egressa cuspide mundum / non figit medium.. / .. / volvitur ecentri brevior epiciclus in orbe HANV. IX 97, 100 p. 380 (cf. concentris).

eccheud[rum] v. caldaria 2b. **eccho** v. echo.

ecclesia [CL < ἐκκλησία]

1 (in etymological sense) calling forth or out. **b** assembly.

~ia, evocatio *GlC Int.* 113. **b** sinagoga, ~ia *Ib.* 300; *Ib.* C 841, 846 (v. contio a); ~a .. 'convocatio' interpretatur S. LANGTON *Chron.* 143.

2 (organized) community of (all) Christians; **b** personified as 'mother' or as 'bride of Christ'; **c** described as universal; **d** dist. as militant or sojourning (on earth) or triumphant (in heaven). **e** dist. as primitive or modern. **f** body of worshippers, congregation. **g** clergy.

ut .. ad .. caelorum regna .. tota festinaret ~ia GILDAS *EB* 9; peonis primi .. exempla, ut 'ēcclēsĭā' .. ALDH. *PR* 133; ecclēsia laetatur clerus in urbe *Id. CE* 3. 27; crescere Pippinus dum viderat .. / ecclēsiam Christi ALCUIN *WillV* 3. 2; aecclēsiae puppis FRITH. 1046 (v. dire); ecclēsieque foro presunt sublimia jura NECKAM *DS* I 139; ecclēsia triplex divisio: corpus / terram sortitur, homo nubes, spiritus astra H. AVR. *Hugh* 920; triplex est status ~ie, quoad initium, quoad progressum, quoad consummationem HALES *Sent.* II 278*n.*; debetis .. credere quod quicquid sancta ~ia [ME: *hali chirche*] facit, legit aut cantat et omnia ipsius sacramenta vos spiritualiter roborant *AncrR* 99; OCKHAM *Pol.* III 191 (v. congregatio 2a); c**1370** 'tristi', i.e. †regis [? l. regi] Anglie, qui fuit tristis quando vidit ~iam contra eum (J. BRIDL. *gl.*) *Pol. Poems* I 165. **b** omnes exultant filii gremio ac si matris ~iae confoti GILDAS *EB* 12; **1017** (17c) tellus libera ab omni .. servitute .. exceptis sanctae matris ~iae necessitatibus *CD* 1313; a**1100** a liminibus sanctae matris ~iae sequestramus illos malefactores (*Excom.*) *GAS* 440; c**1102** mater nostra, ~ia Dei, quam Deus pulchram amicam et dilectam sponsam suam vocat [cf. *Cant.* iv 7–8 etc.] ANSELM (*Ep.* 262) IV 177; Jesus, qui est .. ~ie sponsus ORD. VIT. III 3 p. 52; **1311** ad .. sacrosancte matris ~ie exaltacionem *MunAcOx* 87; R. BURY. *Phil. prol.* 8 (v. abortire b); **1407** vos .. hortamur in Christo et per eam quam de immaculate sponse sue ~ie laceracione feda compassionem geritis obtestamur BEKYNTON II 129. **c 680** etc. (v. catholicus 2a); numquid universali quae per orbem est ~iae Christi eorum est paucitas .. praeferenda? BEDE *HE* III 25 p. 188; **1271** ad honorem Dei et universalis ~ie (*Lit. Regis de Judeis*) *Leg. Ant. Lond.* app. 235; **1343** (v. 3c infra). **d** ecclesia partim in terris peregrinatur a Domino, partim cum Domino regnat in caelis BEDE *Hom.* II 1. 119; 'caelestia' vocat praesentem Christi ~iam, cujus pars est in caelis, pars secutura adhuc peregrinatur in terris LANFR. *Comment. Paul.* (*Heb.* viii 4–5) 394; ~ia militans in multis decipitur, triumphans vero non irridetur GIR. *TH* III 31; in fide ~ie militantis et triumphantis fit divisio HALES *Sent.* IV 76; non magis est solus Christus fundamentum ~ie militantis quam triumphantis OCKHAM *Dial.* 861. **e** apostolo ministro membrisque illius primitivae ~iae Dominus non pepercit cum a recto tramite deviarint GILDAS *EB* 1; ne [Scotti] paucitatem suam .. sapientiorem antiquis sive modernis, quae per orbem erant, Christi ~iis aestimarent BEDE *HE* II 19; in primitiva ~ia prohibitum erat ne quis loqueretur linguis nisi esset qui interpretaretur... quid .. in nostris temporibus est agendum? BELETH *RDO proem.* 14; cetera que sequuntur induci possunt ad commendationem ~ie primitive et blasphemiam moderne GIR. *GE* II 31 p. 316; in primitiva ~ia non erant hujusmodi nomina, sed pullulantibus heresibus a catholicis sunt inventa HALES *Sent.* I 339. **f** cum omnia perambulantes multam Domino ~iam congregassent BEDE *HE* III 22. **g** vos [clerici] antonomatice ipsa ~ia Dei dicimini, quasi laici non sint ecclesiastici nuncupandi R. BURY *Phil.* 4. 48; extra cleri ~iam WYCL. *Sim.* 5 (v. clerus 2c).

3 Christian community or congregation (national or sim.): **a** (general); **b** (Eastern or Greek); **c** (Western or Roman); **d** (Fr.); **e** (Eng.); **f** (Sc.); **g** (Ir.).

a c**800** (v. congregatio 2a); **838** pax et unianimitas ~iarum Dei totiusque populi Christiani *CS* 421; quae est ~ia, quae vel per amplitudinem unius regni dilatetur, cui non liceat aliquid secundum rectam fidem constituere quod in conventu populi .. cantetur? ANSELM (*Proc. Sp.* 13) II 212; **1172** licet plures sint ~ie, sic tamen in unius compagem corporis uniuntur ut .. unius ~ie desolatio in commune gemitum convertatur P. BLOIS *Ep.* 28. 97A. **b** tales [heretici] .. fidem Constantinopolitanae ~iae multum conturbaverunt BEDE *HE* IV 16; quaeritur quare hoc Graecorum ~iae consensu factum non est ANSELM (*Proc. Sp.* 13) II 212; [copulam conjugalem sacerdotibus prohibere] persuasum clero occidentalis ~ie fuit, non autem orientalis GIR. *GE* II 6 p. 187; hoc elegit sibi ~ia occidentalis ut manentes conjugati non possent promoveri ad sacros ordines, orientalis autem non HALES *Sent.* IV 555; s**609** Phocas imperator statuit ut ~ia Romana caput esset omnium ~iarum et magistra; nam antea ~ia Constantinopolitana primam sese scribebat omnium ~iarum M. PAR. *Maj.* I 263; s**1237** erigitur Greca ~ia contra Romanam *Ib.* III 446; **1256** quod recessus ~ie Grecorum ab ~ia Romana fuit a Spiritu Sancto (*Errores*

Joachim Abbatis) *Ib.* VI 336; cum episcopi habeant uxores in ~ia orientali Ockham *Pol.* II 823; **1440** circa Grecorum reduccionem orientalisque ac occidentalis ~ie redintegracionem Bekynton I 134. **c** Ignatius .. in epistola quam ad Romanam ~iam misit Gildas *EB* 74; **680** ut .. non .. traditionem ~iae Romanae .. arroganter aspernemini Aldh. *Ep.* 4; secundum Romanam ~iam mos est monachos .. defunctos aecclesiam portare .. ibique pro eis missas celebrare Theod. *Pen.* II 5. 1; **753** Bonifatius .. legatus vel missus Germanicus catholicae et apostolicae Romanae ~iae Bonif. *Ep.* 109; †**1093** (12c) ponimus priorem et conventum Dunelmi .. et omnes .. possessiones suas in perpetua protectione sancte Romane ~ie *Ch. Durh.* 7 p. 56; s**1175** (v. 1 concilium 2a); ~ia occidentalis Gir. *GE* II 6 etc. (v. 3b supra); multi Greci et Chaldei et Armeni et Syrii et Arabes et aliarum linguarum nationes subjiciuntur ~ie Latinorum Bacon *Maj.* I 95; **1343** attenta devocione sincera quam ad sacrosanctam Romanam ~iam, matrem tuam, gerere dignosceris, sicut .. progenitores tui, reges Anglie, gesserunt (*Lit. Papae*) Ad. Mur. *Chr.* 150 (cf. ib. 143: sacrosancte Romane ac universalis ~ie .. pontifici). **d** c**597** mihi placet ut, sive in Romana sive in Galliarum seu in qualibet ~ia aliquid invenisti quod plus .. Deo possit placere, sollicite eligas et in Anglorum ~ia .. institutione precipua quae de multis ~iis colligere potuisti infundas (*Lit. Papae*) Bede *HE* I 27 p. 49; **1169** audivit ~ia Gallicana vos in causa ~ie Anglorum mutasse sententiam Becket *Ep.* 541; de Lanfranco, qui .. ivit ad concilium ad convincendum Berengarium, quia tunc fides quoad quemdam articulum periclitabatur in Gallicana ~ia Hales *Sent.* IV 346. **e** c**597** (v. 3d supra); Theodorus .. primus erat in archiepiscopis cui omnis Anglorum ~ia manus dare consentiret Bede *HE* IV 2; **1174** quod ~ia Scot' talem subjeccionem faciet ~ie Angl' quam illi facere debet et solebat tempore regum Anglorum predecessorum nostrorum *Anglo-Scot. Rel.* 2; s**1176** episcopi Scotie .. miserunt legatos .. ad summum pontificem, postulantes ut eos .. tutaret a subjectione illa quam ~ia Anglicana ab eis exigebat *G. Hen. II* I 112 (cf. ib. 111: ad faciendam subjectionem ~ie Anglie); H. Bos. *Thom.* III 2 etc. (v. Anglicanus b). **f** **1174** (v. 3e supra); **1218** cum Scoticana ~ia sedi apostolice, sicut filia specialis, nullo medio sit subjecta (*Lit. Papae*) *Anglo-Scot. Rel.* 15; s**1176** R. Cantuar' archiepiscopus nitebatur quod ~ia Scottica Cantuariensi subjiceretur ~ie R. Howd. II 92 (cf. Fordun *Cont.* VIII 26: quidam clericus Scotus .., cum illorum Scoticane subjeccionis ~ie conatum perceperat); **1403** secundum ~ie Scoticane generalia statuta *Reg. Glasg.* 295; **1454** (v. computatio 1). **g** **1216** concessimus .. quod Hybernicana ~ia libera sit *StatIr* 6.

4 church (local institution, often incl. appurtenances): **a** cathedral or collegiate; **b** monastic; **c** parochial or sim., esp. w. ref. to advowson (*cf. advocatio* 6b, *beneficium* 3a); **d** (w. *mater, matrix*, or sim., usu. dist. from chapel).

a Hrofensis ~iae episcopus Bede *HE* II 8; **799** terram xliiij aratrorum ad metrapolitanam Salvatoris ~iam [Dorovernensem] .. reddo *CS* 293; a**1087** noveritis Walkelinum .. concessisse Willelmo terram .. in A. de victu monachorum episcopalis ~ie (*Ch. Wint.*) *EHR* XXXV 387; s**1093** cum diceretur " .. hec Dorobernensis ~ia, totius Britannie metropolitana ..", [archiepiscopus Ebor'] subintulit, dicens: ".. si totius Britannie metropolitana, ~ia Eboracensis, que metropolitana esse scitur, metropolitana non est" Eadmer *HN* 49; **1106** mater ~ia .. episcopatus (v. caput 19a); *GAS* 493 etc. (v. cathedralis 2a); magistratum .. ~ie Ord. Vit. III 13 (v. 1 castellanus 1a); sunt quedam foreste de quibus decime constitutorum censuum ~iis majoribus solvuntur, sicut de Wiltescira et Hantescira ~ie Saresberiensi *Dial. Scac.* II 11; **1193** majores ~ie thesauros ab antiquis congestos temporibus, ~ie parochiales argenteos calices premiserunt Diceto *YH* II 110; **1225** etc. (v. collegiatus a); **1266** statuimus .. quod ~ia B. Marie et B. Machorii una sit ~ia et cathedralis, baptismalis et parochialis, libera ab omni exactione temporali *Reg. Aberd.* I 28; **1277** magistri R. de L., archidiaconi Exessie in ~ia Londoniensi (*Comp. Collect. Apostol.*) *EHR* XXXII 75; **1295** ~iis et precipue episcopalibus viduatis *Reg. Cant.* 513; **1317** (v. archiepiscopalis a); ~ie cathedralis officiarii injungunt .. ut solvant .. matrici ~ie aliquid Gascoigne *Loci* 1; **1496** Johanni .. priori ~ie metropolitane Sanctiandree *Reg. Aberbr.* II 303. **b** a fratribus ~iae Lindisfarnensis Bede *HE pref.* p. 7; W. prior Malvernensis ~ia Walcher *Drac.* 87; a**1130** ~ia Ramesiensis (v. caput 19a); **1179** etc. (v. conventualis a); s**1186** juxta monachalem ~iam Higd. VII 28 p. 126; Domerh. *Glast.* 343 (v. coenobialis a); c**1260** situs loci monasterialis ~ie de Coldingham *Ann. Durh.* app. 112; **1281** plures invenimus .. domos ordinis S. Augustini que .. olim quibusdam matricibus ~iis ultramarinis adheserant *Conc. Syn.* 911 (*gl.*: Lyndw. 213 l: sic dictis quia ab eis tamquam filie a matribus procedebant, aliter dicitur matrix ~ia illa que est major et baptismalis); **1470** in ~iis parochialibus et monasterialibus *Melrose* 575. **c** aecclesiam hujus manerii tenent duo clerici cum ij hidis *DB* I 56v. (cf. ib. 4: ibi aecclesia, in qua jacent de hac terra ij hidae et una virga); *GAS* 277 etc. (v. cyricsceattum a); s**1105** omnes ~ie que parochias habebant sub debito posite sunt et unaqueque indicta pecunie quantitate per personam que in ea Deo serviebat redimi jussa est Eadmer *HN* 203; a**1123** dedit .. B. scriptori in elemosina omnes ~ias terre sue .. cum terris et decimis et omnibus rebus ~iis pertinentibus (*Ch. B. Scriptoris*) *EHR* XIV 419; a**1128** W. presbyter tenet aecclesiam ville cum j bovata terrae *Chr. Peterb.* app. 160; de ~iis parochiarum *GAS* 635 (v. dominicus 3a); c**1150** de ~ia parochiali (v. 2 capella 7); a**1160** (v. donatio 2a); a**1161** miles quidam ~iam .. eis [monachis] molitur auferre sub pretextu advocationis quam adversus ~iam Dei laici apud nos perniciosissime vendicant (*Lit. archiep. Cant.*) *Ep. J. Sal.* 125 (85); **1175** (v. dotalicius 1b); post mortem mariti habebit mulier liberam inde presentationem, ita quod clerico cuilibet idoneo poterit ~iam ipsam concedere si vacaverit Glanv. VI 17; **1194** de ~iis que sunt de donatione domini regis (*Cap. Coronae*) R. Howd. III 263; c**1194** ~ia .. ville (v. decimus 4b); hoc in minoribus ~iis dico et parochialibus atque capellis; nam in majoribus et cathedralibus vel conventualibus .. nihil unquam tale fieri presumitur Gir. *GE* I 48; **1200** ipse R. quandam ~iam dederat cuidam nepoti ejusdem H. *CurR* I 256; **1222** diffinimus ut in singulis parochialibus ~iis quarum parochia est diffusa duo sint vel tres presbiteri *Conc. Syn.* 113; Hales *Sent.* IV 260 (v. cura 4e); **1344** (v. commensalis 2); [in] perpetua pensione soluta episcopo Wigorn' .. pro peculiari jurisdiccione ~ie de Bybury *Val. Eccl.* II 220b. **d** venientes ad ~iam quo eunt iterum agant orationem et post .. preces et orationem .. revertantur ad matrem ~iam [AS: p. 405 *to meder cyrcean*] *RegulC* 34; hujus manerii aecclesiam tenet Richerius cum ij aliis aecclesiis juxta Hantone, quae ad hanc aecclesiam matrem pertin[ent] *DB* I 41v.; antiquis ~iis *GAS* 197 (v. antiquus 3c); matrix ~ia *Ib.* 493 etc. (v. 2 capella 7); c**1150** salvis decimis ad matricem ~iam pertinentibus *Reg. Newbattle* 6; **1194** de placito separacionis capelle de C. de matrice ~ia de H. *CurR RC* I 132; **1199** capella est pertinens ad ~iam de A., que mater ~ia est *CurR* I 112; c**1200** concessisse leprosis S. M. Magdalene de Rathowa cimiterium suum, observata in omnibus indempnitate matricis ~ie de Rathowa *Reg. S. Thom. Dublin* 53; Gir. *RG* I 3, **1214, 1252** (v. baptismalis); S. Langton *Quaest.* f. 340v. (v. curialis 3d); Lyndw. 213 l (v. 4b supra).

5 church (building); **b** (as place of sanctuary); **c** (in surname). **d** image of church.

renovant ~ias ad solum usque destructas Gildas *EB* 12; aecclesiam licet ponere in alium locum, si necesse sit, et non debet iterum sanctificare; tantum presbiter aqua aspergere debet et in loco altaris crux debet conponi. .. ligna aecclesiae non debent ad aliud opus jungi nisi ad aecclesiam aliam Theod. *Pen.* II 1. 1–3; [rex Aedwini] baptizatus est Eburaci .. in ~ia .. quam ibidem ipse de ligno .. construxit Bede *HE* II 14; in qua [Lindocolina] civitate .. ~iam operis egregii de lapide fecit *Ib.* II 16; *Ib.* III 25 (v. cooperire 6d); [Osuald] extruit ecclesias donisque exornat opimis Alcuin *SS Ebor* 275; cum auscultaveritis ~iae campanas [AS: *cyrcean bellas*] Ælf. *Coll.* 103; ~ia lignea *DB* I 320v.; s**1107** (v. cancellus 3a); s**1120** etc. (v. 2 altare 2a); a**1127** de hominibus qui fregerunt ~iam suam de Winton' noctu et armis *Regesta* 1538; ~ia sic edificanda est. parato loco fundamenti primo episcopus debet ibi aspergere aquam benedictam Beleth *RDO* 2. 16B; Gerv. Cant. I 8 etc. (v. ala 4a); [B. abbas, ob. **1193**] edificavit totam navem ~ie opere lapideo et ligneo a turre chori usque ad frontem Swafham 99; instauramenta ~ie sunt hec: lavacrum sive fons, mariolum, crusifixum et alie ymagines, pulpitum sive anologium .., cathedra .., sacrarium, vestibulum .., altare .. Neckam *Ut.* 119; **1229** (v. dedicare 1a); **1234** (v. berefredum 2); **1259** quod veterem fabricam ~ie Westm' prosterni faciant .. et eandem ~iam .. relevari faciant prout alia fabrica ibidem incepta requirit *Cl* 390; **1260** etc. (v. chorus 4); **1270** etc. (v. campanarium); s**1275** sub terra inventi fuerunt muri cujusdam veteris ~ie rotunde, que quidem multo latior fuit quam capella et ita constructa quod altare capelle quasi in medio ejus fuerat *Chr. Bury Cont. A* 162v.; **1368** (v. butericius a). **b** *GAS* 91 (v. cyricsocna); cujuscunque criminis reus ad ~iam [OF: *a seinte iglise*] confugerit, pacem habeat vite et membrorum (*Leis Will.*) *Ib.* 493 (cf. R. Howd. II 220); **1106** si quis homicida vel fur vel criminator vel exul fugerit ad ~iam S. Petri pro defensione vite sue et membrorum suorum, per spacium xxx dierum ibi pacem habebit *Mem. Ripon* I 34; †**11..** (17c) si homicida vel fur aut traditor vel quilibet reus mortis inimicis fugiens ad ~iam venerit, debet cum humanitate suscipi et xxx diebus ac noctibus in pace ~ie morari (*Lib. Bev.* 7) *Sanct. Bev.* p. 100; **1195** etc. (v. abjurare 4a); **1221** (v. abducere 1a); **1258** (v. abjuratio 3); **1308** cum quidam ad ~iam nostram .. pro immunitate habenda confugerit, vos .. quedam circa fugitivum ipsum in nostri prejudicium nitimini attemptare *Mem. Bev.* I 217; **1477** W. R. .. et W. N. .. convolarunt ad ~iam cathedralem S. Cuthberti Dunelm', ubi .. pro felonia per eosdem commissa .. pecierunt .. immunitatem ~ie .. et per pulsacionem unius campane, ut est moris, .. obtinuerunt *Sanct. Durh.* 5; **1503** (v. capere 8b). **c** **11..** in Toucestre .. Wybertus ad ~iam [tenet] vj virgatas (*Surv. Northants*) *VCH Northants* I 373; **1251** Hugonem ad Portam ~ie (*ChartR* 44 m. 25) *EHR* XVII 290; **1286** Johanni filio Ricardi ad ~iam *CourtR Wakefield* I 218. **d** **1295** duo turribula argentea exterius totaliter deaurata, cum opere gravato et levato, cum ~iis et turribus. .. item duo turribula argentea .. cum ~iis et thurellis rotundis *Vis. S. Paul.* 311.

ecclesialis, of the church.

salve sancte pater, salve lux ecclēsialis R. Cant. *Poems* 12. 5; sint in amore tuo decus et decor ecclĕsialis D. Bec. 137.

ecclesiarches [ἐκκλησιάρχης], church ruler, bishop.

980 (11c) ego Osuald Christi dapsilitate aecclesiarches *CD* 625; **1017** ego Wulfstan in humilitate ~es *CD* 1313.

ecclesiastes [LL < ἐκκλησιαστής], preacher; **b** (name of book of Old Testament).

Carliolensis episcopus ex illis verbis 'magister adest et vocat te [*John* xi 28]', ~en egit *Conc.* III 273. **b** Parabolae Salomonis et ~es, quae in sua lingua .. metro constat esse conscripta Bede *AM* 140; **802** opusculum in ~en Salomonis Alcuin *Ep.* 254; a**957** (12c) cum aecclesiastes noster non solum parabolis verum etiam evidenti et perspicua re omnia mundialia frivola esse .. ostenderit *CS* 936; ut testatur sapiens ~es R. Bury *Phil.* 8. 116.

ecclesiastice [LL], in accordance w. canon law.

Paschalis secundum Deum ~e est electus Anselm (*Ep.* 378) V 322; c**1105** [G. archiep. Ebor.] mendatio suo sedem apostolicam infecit, dicens regi quod, si se in aliis ~e ageret, investituras ecclesiarum ab eo fieri equanimiter papa toleraret W. Malm. *GP* III 118 p. 259.

ecclesiasticus [LL < ἐκκλησιαστικός]

1 ecclesiastical, belonging to, or concerned w. the (or a) church, w. ref. to: **a** offices, ranks or dignities; **b** buildings, possessions, privileges *etc.*; **c** court or legal matters; **d** procedures, observances or practices; **e** doctrine; **f** abstr. var.

a ~os .. gradus propensius quam regna caelorum ambientes Gildas *EB* 66; **676** (12c) ~us ordo in clero conversantium *CS* 43; ab ~o clericatus gradu discedens Aldh. *VirgP* 38; **796** quatinus .. aecclesia septiformi aecclesiasticorum graduum distinctione fulgeat Alcuin *Ep.* 114; ut hii quos jam ~us ordo admiserat de virtute contenderat Osb. *V. Dunst.* 34; R. Bury *Phil.* 9. 155 (v. dignitas 2b); **1432** personis in dignitatibus ~is constitutis *StatOx* 239. **b** **732** in universis ~is terris quae in .. Cantia esse noscuntur *CS* 148; **736** aliquam terrae particulam .. in possessionem aecclesiasticam .. trado *CS* 154 (cf. ib.: in jus ~am (*sic*) donavi); **774** quam terram Oshere .. Dunnan famulae Dei, ut esset juris ~ici, tradidit *CS* 217; **946** (14c) ut .. omne sacrificium quod nos dicimus munus ~um et opus ~um et munus rogificum ab omni familia illius terrae reddatur *CS* 816; **967** etc. (v. census 3c); **987** (11c) possessor terrae illius reddat tributum aecclesiasticum quod *circ-sceat* dicitur *CD* 661; tenet j presbiter Algar xliij acras ~ae terrae *DB* II 195v.; Eadmer *HN* 231 etc. (v. beneficium 3a); **1136** distributionem bonorum ~orum in manu episcoporum perhibeo et confirmo *Regesta* 271; **1182** (v. elemosina 4a); falco .. qui ~e turris summitati insidere consueverat Gir. *TH* II 37; **1253** transgressores libertatum ~arum *MGL* II 43; **1255** cum .. appellacione 'proventuum ~orum' intelligantur proventus maneriorum includi *Reg. Roff.* 62; Augustinus [*commenting on John* xiii 29] .. dicit quod 'tunc primum ~e pecunie forma est instituta', ex quo '~e' videtur concludi quod, cum prelati ecclesie habeant aliquale dominium pecunie, Christus tunc habuit aliquale dominium illius pecunie Ockham *Pol.* II 712. **c** episcopi aecclesiasticam habeant correctionem et Christianam dominationem super omnes quos debent docere (*Inst. Cnuti*) *GAS* 615 (cf. ib. 614: omnis aecclesiastica et secularis emendatio communis erat regi et episcopo); (*Leg. Ed.*) *Ib.* 630 (v. curia 5g); Eadmer *HN* 25 (v. 2 causa 1a); H. Bos. *Thom.* III 37 etc. (v. 1 censura 1b); **1199** sine omni exceptione ~e vel secularis justicie *CurR RC* II 7; **1228** Th. de M. capellanus sufficienter se purgavit in foro ~o de crimine homicidii unde rectatus fuit coram justiciariis qui ultimo itineraverunt in com. Buk' *Cl* 24; **1549** jus .. ~um (v. civilis 2d); ~i juris Camd. *Br.* 144 (v. curia 5g); poterit puniri propter pacem violatam per judices seculares et per judicem ecclesiasticum pro contemptu judicis et jurisdictionis ~ae *Praxis* 61 (v. et. 2a infra). **d** auscultantur .. non .. ~ae melodiae Gildas *EB* 34; ~o exorcismo catacizatus Aldh. *VirgP* 43; regulis servandis semper de ~is observationibus Bede *Hom.* I 13. 228; proposuit animo venire Romam et qui ad sedem apostolicam ritus ~i sive monasteriales servarentur videre *Id. HE* V 19; ~a electio Ord. Vit. IV 7 (v. astipulatio a); s**1198** clerus et religiosi processionibus, hymnis et canticis ~is .. Deum .. collaudabant Fordun *Cont.* VIII 59; **1234** ea que .. de ~o servitio corde tenus scire tenentur (*Vis. Bury*) *EHR* XXVII 731; **1267** habuit jura sua ~a et tunc obiit *SelCCoron* 5; miles .., mortem metuens supervenientem, omnia jura ~a festinanter sibi dari praecepit *Mir. Montf.* 106 (cf. ib. 77: Agnes .., usque ad mortem infirmata, .. omnibus sacramentis ~is inuncta); **1431** lego .. corpus meum ~e sepulture, viz. infra cancellum ecclesie mee *Reg. Cant.* II 450; de tropis ~is Hauboys 403. **e** quadriformis ~ae traditionis normulis Aldh. *VirgP* 4; regulam ~ae veritatis edoctus Bede *HE* III 25 p. 181; *Ib.* p. 182 (v. doctrina 1c); ~is dogmatis (*sic*), *ciriclicre* doctrinis *GlH* E 28. **f** quantae .. sanctorum patientiae fuere ~a historia narrat Gildas *EB* 9; relucente gratia ~ae societatis et pacis Bede *HE* V 22; abit in nihilum vigor ecclēsiasticus Nig. *Mir. BVM* f. 18. 2; superborum colla jugo ~o subjecisse R. Bury *Phil. prol.* 10; **1440** pro ~a unitate .. decertare Bekynton I 95.

2 (of persons) ecclesiastical, clerical. **b** (as sb. m.) ecclesiastic, churchman.

Gildas *EB* 97 (v. doctor 2a); J. diaconum .., virum .. ~um et sanctum Bede *HE* II 20; **786** convenerunt omnes principes regionis, tam ~i quam seculares Alcuin *Ep.* 21; c**956** (12c) viris ~is .. operam impendere curabo *CS* 936; **1136** ~arum personarum et omnium clericorum et rerum eorum justiciam et potestatem .. confirmo *Regesta* 271; viri qui ~a gaudent immunitate et quos viros ~os vocant, quanquam laici et uxorati .., in signum protectionis

pontificali impositione amplas in capite coronas habent GIR. *TH* III 26; **1301** dilectis filiis ~is (*Lit. Papae*) *MGL* II 159; **1322** moram traxit apud Oxon' pacifice et honeste, ut decet homini ~o *IMisc* 87/18; quod prelati et viri ~i habent dominium rerum ~arum OCKHAM *Pol.* I 306; ut illum [Augustinum] statueret sue metropolis ~um presidem ELMH. *Cant.* 79; *Praxis* 61 (v. 1c supra). **b** reges, publici, privati, sacerdotes, ~i suum quique ordinem servarunt GILDAS *EB* 26; ~orum sub dicione pontificali in clero degentium ALDH. *VirgP* 58; **705** ~i etiam in hanc.. dissensionem .. inplicantur WEALDHERE *Ep.* 22; **786** ut nullus ex ~is cibum in secreto sumere audeat ALCUIN *Ep.* 21; sive ~i sive mundani sint, omnia posse volunt J. SAL. *Pol.* 778D; *Ps.*-GROS. *Summa* 301 (v. canonicus 1d); R. BURY *Phil.* 4. 48 (v. ecclesia 2g); **s1419** si Henricus Katherinam uxorem duceret .., nobiles, ~i, plebeii et municipes .. in Henrici imperio .. acquiescerent REDMAN *Hen. V* 57; **1543** prelatum et ~um beneficiatum *Conc. Scot.* I cclv; ~os, hoc est verbi Dei ministros et altari servientes BEKINSAU 739.

3 'spiritual' (as dist. from temporal).

estimatio bonorum ~orum et temporalium abbatis *Val. Norw.* 520; **1273** dedit Anglicana ecclesia .. E. regi decimam omnium proventuum tam temporalium quam ~orum *Ann. Osney* 256.

4 Ecclesiasticus (book of Old Testament Apocrypha).

ut legitur in ~o, vicesimo capitulo BRACTON 106b; auctoritas ~i superius allegata OCKHAM *Dial.* 885; **1396** secunda pars Biblie, in qua .. Ecclesiastes, Cantica Canticorum, liber Sapiencie, ~us, liber Job .. (*Invent.*) *Meaux* III lxxxiv.

ecclesiatim, church by church.

Lib. Landav. 281 (v. decanatim).

ecclesiola [LL], little church, chapel.

753 Colonensis episcopus illam sedem .. sibi usurpat .. propter fundamenta cujusdam destructae a paganis ~ae, quam Uuilbordus derutam usque ad solum in castello Trajecto repperit BONIF. *Ep.* 109; extra hanc [aecclesiam de Rouecestre] sunt adhuc ibi iij aecclesiolae *DB* I 2v.; ibi est ~a ad quam pertinent viij acrae de decima *Ib.* 38v.; **s1095** [Anselmus] absolvit eos [episcopos] in quadam ~a, que se nobis obtulit ambulantibus EADMER *HN* 82; **s701** locum illum [Eveshamum] .., incultum antea et spinetis horridum, sed aecclesiolam ab antiquo habentem, ex opere forsitan Britannorum W. MALM. *GP* IV 160; **c1150** in provincia Merciorum lignea antiquitus fabricata est ~a OSB. CLAR. *Ep.* 33; non movebat vestra deploranda capitivitas episcopos .. ut vos [Blesenses] ad aliquam ~am qualem qualem .. admitterent P. BLOIS *Ep.* 78. 240C; **1302** cum ~a de Knapwelle .. vestri patronatus .. vacet rectore legittimo destituta *Reg. Cant.* 443 (= *Chr. Rams.* 377: ecclesia seu ~a); **1453** declarat concilium [Cashellense] antiquas ecclesias, ~as in possessione immunitatis existentes, et que habent insignia sanctitatis, immunitate gaudere ecclesiastica debere *Conc.* III 568a; ad ortum juxta portam [*Silchester*] praedium et ~a est recentior CAMD. *Br.* 239.

ecco, ~onizare v. ech-.

eccum [CL], behold him!

eccum! securus praeda mortemque daturus, / ut leo frendebat R. CANT. *Malch.* V 173.

ecentr- v. eccentr-. **ecere** v. eicere 1b.

echenais [CL < ἐχενηΐς], remora, sucking-fish (conf. w. *echinus*).

de †ocenao pisce. / forma manet tenui, cum semipedalis imago est; / et tamen inmensas solus retinebo liburnas HWÆTBERHT *Aen.* 54 (*tit.*); semipedalis echinus / herens cui fuerit fixam quasi litore navem / detinet *V. Merl.* 836; que est hominum fortitudo .. quorum plenam navim echinus in mari retentat? *Simil. Anselmi* 52; echinus piscis est navis retinens OSB. GLOUC. *Deriv.* 195;

1 echinus v. echenais.

2 echinus [CL < ἐχῖνος]

1 sea-urchin, conf. w. crab, shell-fish, urchin (hedgehog). *Cf. echenais, ericius.*

~us, piscis vel *scel GlC* E 15; ~us, i. piscis, cancer vel *scel GlH* E 25; vincis, echine, favum mellis dulcedine magna; / .. / libramen certi ponderis ore geris NECKAM *DS* III 459; †elchinus, ericius, erinacius idem, animal est spinosum cujus due sunt species s[c]. aquaticus et terrenus, que nobilior est .. ; G. *hirison*, A. *hirichoun Alph.* 54 (cf. ib. 59: †erinansius [v. l. erinacius], †eschinius idem; G. *hirichon*); **1429** in magno stagno apud Churchegate .. cepit ~os et murices *MinAc Essex* (*Fyfield*).

2 tench.

hic ~us, hic †ectinus, *a tenche WW.*

echios [CL < ἔχιον], (?) viper's bugloss (*Echium*).

10.. eicios, *haranspeccel WW*; herba acios, *wiþ nædrena slitas Leechdoms* I 60; ecios, *haransveccel Gl. Durh.*

echites [CL < ἐχίτης], sort of gem. (*Cf.* Pliny *HN* XXXVII 187).

de efficacia lapidis qui ~es dicitur... versus de ~e ALEX. BATH *Mor.* III 83 p. 136; *perdycle, precyows ston,* ~ites *PP.*

echo [CL < ἠχώ], echo.

~o, *wudumer GlC* E 12; velut in eccho resultu ab ictu fecundavit vi oppressam *V. Kentig.* 2; hec [laus] resonet virtuti recte, tanquam ~o voci, tanquam imago exemplari W. FITZST. *Thom.* 29; ~o nihil aliud est quam quedam resultatio aeris informati repercussione vocis prolate NECKAM *NR* I 20; per reverberationem soni fit eccho J. BLUND *An.* 48; non nimis multiplicabilis est aer qui per nares exit, magis tamen in N quam in M, quia N minus frangitur et generatur hecco post fraccionem N, quo magis auditur *Ps.*-GROS. *Gram.* 29; saxivoma .. sonis terrificis .. in reboaciones valles, in ecco predia .. coegerunt *Ps.*-ELMH. *Hen. V* 20; hic (*sic*) †ecto, vox in †aera [? aere] respondens *WW.*

echonizare, to re-echo.

ecconizant nubes lituorum mugitibus *Ps.*-ELMH. *Hen. V* 110.

eciam v. etiam.

eciare [ME *echen*], to 'eche', enlarge.

1508 solut' .. facientibus foveam .., viz. querendo *le whikkes*, plantando, fodiendo foveam et eciando ad profunditatem iij quar., latitudinem in alto v vel vj quar. et in fundo ij quar. amplius *Ac. Durh.* 660.

ecios v. echios. **eclaratio** v. declaratio 1c.

eclıgma [CL < ἔκλειγμα], electuary.

semen atriplicis .. bulliant in aqua et eligma inde expressum propinetur GILB. V 212. 1; eligma, i. medicina calida per os sumpta *SB* 19.

eclipsalis, concerned w. eclipse.

quare multitudo omnium instancium preteritorum simpliciter equaretur multitudini instancium equinoccialium, ~ium, annalium et myriadalium inchoancium sc. seu terminancium eclipses BRADW. *CD* 184D.

eclipsare, to eclipse, (pass.) to suffer eclipse; **b** (pr. ppl. *s. pass.*); **c** (fig.).

s1179 visa est luna †eclipsimari xv kal. Sept. TORIGNI 301; suumque / eclipsata sitit rediturum Cynthia Phebum HANV. I 171 p. 246; stelle inferiores ~ant superiores .. quando cadunt inferiores inter solem et superiores BACON *Maj.* I 127; si quis dicit quod ipso balneante sol ~atus est a casu .., derisio est SICCAV. *PN* 203; KILWARDBY *OS* 497 (v. diametraliter a); frequencius lapis cadens frangit caput quam luna †~etur DUNS *Ord.* II 326 (cf. ib. III 143: quod luna frequenter ~atur); **s1339** fuit eclipsis solis .. et duravit per duas horas; ~abatur enim usque ad quartam partem WALS. *HA* II app. 381 (= *Chr. Angl.* 9: eclipticabatur). **b** **s1133** rex Henricus iiij kal. Augusti sole ~ante in Normanniam transfretavit BROMPTON 1020. **c** scribe solem pupille nobilis / frontis fixum celo mirabilis / eclipsatum J. HOWD. *Ph.* 729; **1257** ne per ministros indignos claritas sua [sc. ecclesie Sar'] .. ~etur *Conc. Syn.* 553; hec responsio lumen beatorum ~at BRADW. *CD* 764C; regalis preclara nobilitas, quam nulla infidelitatis tenebra ~are .. valebat *Ps.*-ELMH. *Hen. V* 73; **1470** en lux pastorum .. / nunc eclipsatur, marcescit, et incineratur (*Vers.*) *Croyl. Cont. B* 544.

eclipsatio, eclipse (fig.), obfuscation.

[Antichristus] secundum leges quas invenit palliat et tegit eclypsacione dampnabili legem Christi WYCL. *Apost.* 77.

eclipsimari v. eclipsare.

1 eclipsis [CL < ἔκλειψις], (astr.) eclipse; **b** (fig.).

philosophi dicunt .. acuminatis instar pyramidum tenebris lunam .. aliquando .. obscurari, nullumque aliud sidus taliter ~im, hoc est defectum sui luminis, pati BEDE *TR* 7; **s664** anno praefatae eclypsis et mox sequentis pestilentiae *HE* IV 1; ~is, defectio solis *GlC* E 14; **s879** ~is solis inter nonam et vesperam .. facta est ASSER *Alf.* 59; ~is, i. solis vel lunae defectio, *onsprungennes GlH* E 18; **s1179** circa trinenium temporis ejusdem tres solis ~es contigerunt, non generales tamen sed partiales GIR. *EH* II 20; cum luna lumen non habeat nisi a sole, in rei veritate deficit a lumine et est ~is generalis SACROB. *Sph.* 115; **s1256** sol passus est ~im particularem, Toleti vero universalem M. PAR. *Maj.* V 539; duplex est consideratio ~is: aut quantum ad situm solis et lune et stellarum in signis, et sic pertinet consideratio ~is astronomis; aut quantum ad obscuritatem et impedimentum lucis secundum quod subtrahitur beneficium lucis a mundo inferiori, et sic pertinet ~ium consideratio ad hanc scientiam experimentalem BACON V 11; **s1484** in die magne ~is solis .. obiit Anna regina *Croyl. Cont. C* 572; hic (*sic*) clipsis, *the clyppes of the sunne WW.* **b** hic vivens lux urbis erat, defunctus eclipsis (*Epitaph.*) ORD. VIT. X 1 p. 2; in sene deliro sensus patiuntur eclipsim NIG. *SS* 3091; eclipsim patior, homo dudum, nunc homo nullus D. BEC. 1658; neque in occasu hujus sideris ruinam vel ~im patitur exercitus, sicut Saul, sed victoriam J. LOND. *Commend. Ed. I* 18; **c1370** ne opus propter auctorem eclypsim paciatur, sub silencio nominis mei .. me occultavi (J. BRIDL. *pref.*) *Pol. Poems* I 124; pluribus expensis patitur thesaurus eclipsim GOWER *VC* VI 297; *Ps.*-ELMH. *Hen. V* 76 (v. depauperativus).

2 eclipsis [cf. ἔλλειψις], (gram. & rhet.) ellipsis, omission. **b** deficiency.

dicit Priscianus .. quod nominativus nominis non potest proferri sine verbo actu expresso ejusdem persone et numeri nisi per ~im BACON XV 110; in ~i potest esse figura cum dicitur 'hec secum' et subticetur 'loquebatur' *Ps.*-GROS. *Gram.* 73; ~is *Ib.* 69 (v. dilucidus d); ut devocius sit et plenius est cantandum sine scincopa vel ~i *Ord. Exon.* I 19; Graeca ~is est et quum in citandis authoribus ablativo utimur sine .. praepositione LINACRE *Emend. Lat.* lxxii v. **b** ut loquar uberius, adsit michi virgo Maria; / suppleat eclipsim [OF: *mon deffaut*] Filius ipse suus WALT. ANGL. *Fab. prol.* 14; non est ibi carnis eclipsis, / immo copia M. CORNW. *Hen.* 228; **1297** modicum aut nullum ex hujusmodi ~i [sc. xxx personarum ex debito numero monachorum] quoad sumptus vestros annuatim sentire vos credimus *Lit. Cant.* I 24.

3 eclipsis v. ecthlipsis.

eclipticare, to eclipse; **b** (fig.). **c** (intr.) to suffer eclipse (fig.).

luna .. que ex umbra terre ~atur GARL. *Mor. Scol.* 267 *gl.*; **s1399** (v. eclipsare a); *to make clippys,* ~are *CathA.* **b** laudis eclipticat astrum / livor HANV. III 343 p. 287; ista luna [i. e. vis argenti] .. / .. / solem enim equitatis / .. / tegit et eclipticat WALT. WIMB. *Van.* 49. **c** **1188** nisi status universalis ecclesie, qui terribiliter †ecliptitare videbatur, .. feliciter respirasset *Ep. Cant.* 195.

ecliptice [cf. LL ellipticos], elliptically, in abbreviated form. *V. et. eclipticos. Cf. 2 eclipsis, 2 eclipticus.*

omnes alii versiculi tribus noctibus ~e, i.e. defective, et non plene sunt pronuntiandi *Rit. Gilb.* 31.

eclipticos [cf. LL ellipticos < ἐλλειπτικῶς], elliptically. *V. et. ecliptice. Cf. 2 eclipsis, 2 eclipticus.*

a990 ut ~os loquar (*Lit. F. Abb. S. Vedasti*) *Mem. Dunst.* 384.

1 eclipticus [CL < ἐκλειπτικός]

1 involving or affected by eclipse; **b** (fig.).

cur [luna] ~am patiatur obscuritatem ADEL. *QN* 70; Phebus .., ~a diu vicissitudine varius factus est frequenter sui egenus luminis, quo totus egebat mundus MAP *NC* IV 3 f.45. **b** **c1200** mundane varietatis ~a vicissitudo *Ep. Glasg.* 309; agnus salubris misticus, / .. / splendor nusquam eclipticus J. HOWD. *Cyth.* 4. 12.

2 (w. *linea* or as sb. f.) ecliptic.

in flexuoso solis circa lineam eclypticam discursu W. DONC. *Aph. Phil.* 3. 37; linea dividens zodiacum in circuitu .. dicitur linea ~a, quoniam, quando sol et luna sunt linealiter sub illa, contingit eclipsis solis aut lune. sol quidem semper decurrit sub ~a SACROB. *Sph.* 88–9; capita Cancri et Capricorni moventur progrediendo et regrediendo in superficie ~e zodiaci immobilis BACON *Maj.* I 192; nodos .. orbis noni existentes in ~a apud equatorem et tropicos WALLINGF. *Rect. prol.* 407.

2 eclipticus [cf. 2 eclipsis], elliptical; *cf. ecliptice, eclipticos.* **b** defective.

geminabat, "Thomas! Thomas! mortuum! mortuum!", ~o sermone designans planam letitiam, non plenum generans intellectum W. CANT. *Mir. Thom.* II 47; cum dicitur "proch dolor" .. manet oratio ~a propter .. necessitatem exprimendi sententiam BACON XV 103. **b** erit .. in communibus ecliptica opusculi hujus traditio [*in marg.*: eclypsis i.e. defectus. inde ~us defectivus] GERV. MELKLEY *AV* 1n.

ecliptitare v. eclipticare c.

ecloga [CL < ἐκλογή], eclogue, pastoral poem or sim.

Vergilius prima ~a infit ALDH. *Met.* 10 p. 96; eglogae, cantationes in theatris *GlC* E 104 (cf. ib. H 2: haec egloga et haec eglogae (*sic*) cantationes in carminibus sunt); egloga, sermo de capris, nam aegos capra dicitur OSB. GLOUC. *Deriv.* 193.

2 (? by assoc. w. αἴξ) lewd language.

a foule speche, †eglota [v. l. egloga], turpiloquium *CathA.*

eclyp- v. eclip-. **eco** v. eggon. **econom-** v. oeconom-.

econtra [LL; al. div.]

1 a on the opposite side, in confrontation. **b** in the opposite direction.

a canes perduxerunt eum [aprum] ad me et ego ~a [AS: *þær toȝeanes*] stans .. jugulavi eum ÆLF. *Coll.* 93; **c1022** (12c) ad hujus aquae medietatem in longitudine est locus e contra in palude .. ubi australis est terminus *CD* 733; **s1066** e contra Willelmus .. inter primos discurrebat M. PAR. *Maj.* I 542 (= W. MALM. *GR* III 244: item); anima ejus ante tribunal .. adducta est; cumque maligni spiritus eam .. accusarent et .. ejus peccata proferrent, .. angeli e contra librum quem .. scripserat ostentabant ORD. VIT. III 3 p. 49; episcopus .. cum turba suorum pedes accessit. archidiaconus e contra sacerdotes .. de ecclesia exeuntes in

faciem procedere jussit GIR. *RG* I 6 p. 36; laqueo suspenduntur; suspensos autem pueros ipsi [tortores] ∼a . . observantes residebant *Hist. Meriadoci* 347. **b 1291** indigent quod fiat iter per quod possit iri . . de . . bastida apud N. et ∼a *RGasc* III 23; debent . . carectas e contra venientes . . seorsum divertere vel . . arestare *Obs. Barnwell* 170; motus unus naturalis, quo moventur orbes inferiores ab occidente in orientem, et alius violentus, quo rapiuntur ∼a . . ab oriente in occidentem HIGD. II 1 p. 184.

2 a on the contrary, on the other hand, in rejoinder. **b** on the other part, in return. **c** contrariwise, in a contrary manner. **d** conversely.

a cornua saepe in scripturis solent eminentiam designare virtutum . ., sicut e contra non numquam bella vitiorum . . cornuum nomine solent indicari BEDE *Tab.* 488; dum rex . . postulante episcopo laetitiam reciperet, coepit e contra episcopus tristis . . effici *Id. HE* III 14; unda tuo jussu pelagi fit pervia justis, / terra sed econtra vindex fit gurges iniquis ALCUIN *SS Ebor* 1380; renuunt dictis illi; e contra tali sermone responsa dant amicis ÆTHELW. II 18; cum illum omnes honorare . . satagerent . ., ille e contra nihil in se dignum honore . . judicabat EADMER *V. Dunst.* 3; **1203** (v. dotatio 1); **s1215** (v. conductivus 1a); **c1318** processus festinus discordie finalis . . incentivus et ∼a dilacio bona . . tranquillitatis poterit esse . . inductiva *FormOx* 39. **b a1130** abbas . . dedit ei . . idem. hidam apud S. . . ipse autem dedit abbati e contra xx m. argenti *Chr. Rams.* 252. **c 1236** loca sancta ab usibus humanis . . abstracta sunt . . et in usus divinos conversa; et qui e [*some MSS omit*] contra presumunt de . . loco orationis speluncam latronum faciunt [cf. *Matth.* xxi 13] *Conc. Syn.* 204; si [detractores] aperirent [peccata] ipsis qui peccant et operirent aliis, bene facerent. nunc faciunt omnino ∼a [v. l. econtrario] *AncrR* 24; humiles non aliorum mala sed sua considerant; . . reprobi vero ∼a faciunt, quia magis aliena peccata quam sua respiciunt ROLLE *IA* 219; firmabo tecum †quam [? l. quod] plus lucrabor per mendacium quam tu per veritatem. respondit: "et ego ∼a" J. SHEPPEY *Fab.* 30; supplicans . . quod . . justum judicium adhibeatur, ut, si fratrum raciones fuerint forciores, sim ego punitus, si vero ∼a, ipsi fratres . . puniantur RIC. ARMAGH *Def. Cur.* 1392 (*recte* 1292); sic luxuries fatuis sua dona refundit / vertit et econtra quicquid ab ante tulit GOWER *VP* 160. **d 797** filius sapiens gloria est patris [cf. *Prov.* x 1], et ∼a filius stultus ignominia est magistri ALCUIN *Ep.* 124; qui se humiliat exaltabitur et ∼a [cf. *Luke* xiv 11] *Eul. Hist.* I 187; videtur quod omnis symoniacus est hereticus et ∼a WYCL. *Sim.* 15.

econtrariari, to oppose.

1449 nos . . eosdem . . nostros vicarios generales et speciales, ipsa quod generalitas specialitati non deroget nec ∼ietur, . . constituisse *Reg. Heref.* 1.

econtrario v. contrarius 2e. **econverso** v. convertere 3c. **ecponere** v. exponere 2.

ecquando [CL], whether at any time, ever.

∼o, aliquando *GlH* E 19.

ecquis [CL], is there anyone that . .?

∼em, aliquem . ., ∼is, aliquis; ∼id, aliquid; eccui, alicui *GlC* E 14, 20–22; ∼id, pro enquid, interjectio increpantis *GlH* E 22; ∼em hominum illa . . simulata simplicitas . . inter initia non deciperet? GIR. *Symb.* I 31 p. 322.

1 ecstasis (ext-) [LL < ἔκστασις], **a** ecstasy, (visionary) trance. **b** swoon, loss of consciousness. **c** stupor, amazement.

a [S. Johannes] spectacula plura / crevit in extāsi caelesti numine fretus ALDH. *CE* 4. 5. 15 (cf. id. *VirgP* 7: raptus in oromate ∼eos); ista per extāsin [*gl.*: excessum mentis] scalpello luminas unco FRITH. 692; **9** . . in ∼i, *in modes heannesse, on gastlicre gesihðe WW*; ecce inter somnolentiam vel exstasim . . vidit eminus caelum apertum GOSC. *Transl. Aug.* 19C; 'sive in corpore sive extra corpus' sc. in exstasi LANFR. *Comment. Paul* (*2 Cor.* xii 2) 258; sacerdos qui tam mirabilem . . ∼im induerat . . palam omnibus . . quae viderat absolvit OSB. *V. Dunst.* 42; dum in ∼i supra me raptus obstupescerem, ecce . . ORD. VIT. X 14 p. 83; AILR. *Serm.* 369D (v. consopire a); in ∼im raptus putabat se pro foribus splendidissimi habitaculi assistere *NLA (Ithamar)* II 83; A ante S breviatur in primitivis, ut 'extāsis'. BACON *Tert.* 260; ut sibi stat saxum non mobile, sic stat et ipse, / nec movet a visu, qui velut extāsis est GOWER *VC* V 138; **s1468** ipse in extisi raptus miranda vidit HERRISON *Abbr. Chr.* 13. **b** puella, agnito fratre, pene in ∼i collapsa est, timens ne . . ab hostibus caperetur G. MON. XII 7; **s1183** cum ad notitiam ejus [Hen. II] venisset quod rex filius suus exspirasset, semel et secundo et tertio in ∼im cecidit G. *Hen.* II I 301; debilis pre lassitudine cecidi, passus aliquamdiu suavem ad pedes ejus ∼im MAP *NC* III 2 f.36; mirum de avibus istis . . quas hiemali exilio nature rigor relegare solet, quod interim . . in ∼im diuturnam et statum quemdam inter mortem et vitam . . rapi videntur GIR. *TH* I 20; videas . . homines . . subito in terram corruere et primo tanquam in ∼im ductos et quietos, deinde statim tanquam in phrenesim raptos exsilientes *Id. IK* I 2 p. 32; **s1224** cum [Falcasius] de suspendio fratris sui . . certificaretur, corruit in terram in ∼im M. PAR. *Min.* II 265; novies fuit in ∼i propter illam angustiam et in statu mortis *State Tri. Ed. I* 51; *SB* 41 (v. dormitio 1c); **s1405** sepcies ∼i positus extenditur pro mortuo AD. USK 100; rex Francie [L. ob. 1270] . . tribus diebus sine

2 ecstasis (ext-) v. ectasis.

ecstaticus (ext-) [ἐκστατικός], ecstatic: **a** causing ecstasy. **b** experiencing ecstasy, overcome w. emotion.

a ave, cujus cor a cunis / consecratum erat prunis / amoris extatici WALT. WIMB. *Virgo* 26; hic amor ∼us tam potenter nos rapuit ut . . acquirendorum librorum solummodo flagraremus affectu R. BURY *Phil. prol.* 11; **1381** amorem dat extaticum / cum sacramentum mysticum / in cibum nobis contulit (*In Lollardos* 44) *Pol. Poems* I 245. **b** sicque micat facies juvenum tam in his quam in illis / fiat ut extaticus intime respiciens R. MAIDSTONE *Conc.* 293 (cf. ib. 295: inde crucifixi Christi stat sculpta figura, / discipuli flentis matris et extatice); oculos suos ad celum attollere consueverat, quasi celicola quidam aut raptus . ., quasi esset homo ∼us BLAKMAN *Hen. VI* 16.

ectasis [LL < ἔκτασις], ectasis, lengthening of vowel.

nomina ad proceleumaticum pertinentia . .; miseria, memoria, Italia, quamvis per ∼in [v. l. extasin] producatur, apicula . . ALDH. *PR* 125; ∼is, productio syllabae *GlC* E 18; addicio quidem [macrologus] dicitur, corepcio sive subtraccio microl[ogus], transmutacio extasis quasi extrastatum, immutacio sistole quasi commissio *Ps.-Gros. Gram.* 70.

ecthesis [LL < ἔκθεσις], exposition, interpretation.

649 impiissimam ∼in, quae . . facta est ab Heraclio quondam imperatore adversus orthodoxam fidem (*Conc. Lateran.*) *Conc. HS* 150.

ecthlipsis [LL < ἔκθλιψις], (gram.) ecthlipsis (squeezing out).

Vergilius . . in uno versu geminas, sinalipham et ∼in [v. l. eclipsin], comprehendit ita: 'nunc repeto: Anchises fatorum arcana reliquit'. . . si prior vocalis exploditur, sinalipha; si posterior fuerit explosa, ectlipsis est [v. l. eclipsis] ALDH. *Met.* 9; edidit librum hec continentem capitula: . . de sinalimpha; de scansione et eclipsi versuum . . W. MALM. (*V. Aldh.*) *GP* V 196.

ectinus v. 2 echinus 2. **ecto** v. echo.

1 eculeus v. aculeus 2a.

2 eculeus, equuleus [CL], ∼ius

1 young or small horse.

quid si his omnibus habitis, tale haberes gaudium quale is habet qui cum ad ∼eum ducitur, repente in itinere ad regnum rapitur? HON. *Eluc.* 1170C; honorificos viros diligens habere et non pueros, equos pro vectura, non equulos *Hist. Durh.* 137.

2 rack (instrument of torture) or sim. **b** gibbet.

∼ei tormento vexatos et gabuli patibulo suspensos ALDH. *VirgP* 34; in ∼eis, in ferreis ligno infixis et curbis in terra positis *GlC* I 85; ∼eus, *unhela prepel* ÆLF. *Gl.*; ∼eus vel catasta, *wearhrod* vel *prypeluf Id. Sup.*; seminecem . . avellit . . avulsumque . ., ac si raptum ∼eo . ., jubet caput extendere ABBO *Edm.* 10; **s1215** in ∼eo extensus est et duo canes hinc inde suspensi *Ann. Dunstable* 95; in ∼iis extenduntur, quo eorum rumpuntur nervi FORTESCUE *LLA* 22. **b** seditionum auctoris cadaver in equleo suspendi jubet, ut manifestetur in mortuo quod male vixerit MAP *NC* III 3 f. 41; **s1306** non est tractus, sed ascenso equo in ∼eo quinquaginta pedum suspensus est *Flor. Hist.* III 135; **s1381** quorum capita amputata in villa de Bury super ∼ium horribiliter sunt affixa *Chr. Kirkstall* 124 (cf. ib.: capita . . super ∼ia confusibiliter suspendentes); *a gibett,* aculeus, ∼eus, †patubilum *CathA*.

ecumen- v. oecumen-. **ecuriare** v. excarriare. **eda** v. hodus.

edacitas [CL], gluttony, voracity; **b** (fig.).

dentes tui non fuerunt ∼ate assueti HON. *Sig.* 511D; dentes strident [cf. *Matth.* viii 12 etc.] qui hic de ∼ate gaudebant PULL. *Sent.* 999B; fornicatio vitium est, cujus regio est ∼as, semolentia, otium . . AILR. *Serm.* 8. 392A; ∼as cibos terit sed oculos vorat J. SAL. *Pol.* 727C; qui quos [morsus berbitonum] inexplebilem gehennalium ∼atem vermium me . . spero evasurum AD. EYNS. *Hug.* IV 12 p. 58. **b** curarum ∼atem 'sollicitudo omnium ecclesiarum' in Apostolo pariebat [cf. *2 Cor.* xi 28] PULL. *Sent.* 914B; scalpe unguibus . . temporum saperchium, quia ibi sentio quasi cujusdam mordentis ∼atem R. COLD. *Godr.* 193.

edaciter, voraciously.

ab edo . . ∼er, edacius, edacissime, adverbia OSB. GLOUC. *Deriv.* 184; edere . . nimis ∼er [ME: *to frehliche*] *AncrR* 72 (v. deliciose a).

edaculus, (somewhat) voracious.

∼us, . . i, aliquantulum vorax OSB. GLOUC. *Deriv.* 184; etyng, edax, ∼us, edens . ., *gredy,* edax, ∼us, avidus, gulosus *CathA*.

edax [CL], gluttonous, voracious; **b** (fig., esp. of flame).

edax, commedens *GlC* E 34; valde edax [AS: *waxgeorn*] es cum omnia manducas quae tibi apponuntur ÆLF. *Coll.* 102; edax vel glutto, *frettol Id. Sup.*; ut . . / seminecem . . virum . . / proiceret canibus rabidis exactor edendum, / nocturnisque avibus, corvis et edacibus WULF. *Swith.* II 451; dentes tui non erant cibi delicati edaces HON. *Sig.* 506A; vermes edacissimos AD. EYNS. *Hug.* IV 12 (v. berbicio); quando canes edaces stant ante mensam, nonne opus est virga? *AncrR* 124. **b** licia . ., / quae mox ignis edax flammis combussit acerbis ALDH. *VirgV* 1429; labes edax BEDE *CuthbP* 42 (v. deponere 3b); **933** edacibus . . tormentorum flammis *CS* 694; ignis edax sotii subeat ne culmina tecti FRITH. 40; tanti caloris edatior flamma . . intestina succenderat R. COLD. *Cuthb.* 119; cultelli nitidi mense ponantur edaces D. BEC. 2543; edax . . mors AD. SCOT *Serm.* 267A (v. consumptrix).

edecimatus [CL], selected.

inter edecumatos litterarum sectatores (*Ep. Waleramni prol.*) *Ep. Anselmi* II 233; edecumatus, excerptus OSB. GLOUC. *Deriv.* 193; symposia ex cecis ignorantie abducta et edecumata latibulis R. NIGER *Chr. II* 106.

edelingus v. adelingus.

edelingus v. adelingus.

edentare [CL], to knock out teeth. **b** (p. ppl.) deprived of teeth.

∼at, dentes excutit *GlC* E 45; ∼are, dentes excutere OSB. GLOUC. *Deriv.* 197. **b** ∼atus, dentibus [abdicatus] *GlC* E 46 (cf. *GlH* E 36); ∼atus, edentulus, dentifragus OSB. GLOUC. *Deriv.* 197; *tutheles for age,* indentulus, ∼atus, indentatus; unde versus: 'qui dentes habuit nec habet nec habebit / est edentatus; edentulus est modo natus' *CathA*.

edentator, extractor of teeth.

∼or, A. *a tothdrawere WW*.

edentulus [CL], toothless; **b** (fig.).

∼us, i. senex sine dentibus *GlH* E 37; ∼arum, *topleasera GlP* 449; *Poem S. Thom.* 75 (v. 2 anus); si sit anus sterilis, edentula D. BEC. 2017; ne dum duriora sumunt ∼i, prius intereant quam pascantur *Spec. Laic. prol.*; *tutheles for yonge,* ∼us *CathA* (cf. edentare b). **b** assentacio dulcis edentula WALT. WIMB. *Palpo* 123.

edepol, pol [CL], oath of affirmation (by Pollux).

edepul, jusjurandum *GlC* E 47 (cf. ib. P 550: pol, jusjurandum per Policem); sunt adverbiorum 8 species speciales, ut . . jurandi, ut . . ∼pol *Ps.-Gros. Gram.* 59.

1 edera [ME *eder* < AS *eodor* = *hedge, fence*], edder, osier.

c1230 claudet j perticam bona sepe cum ∼a *Cust. Waltham* f. 218.

2 edera, ∼inus, ∼osus v. heder-.

ederare [ME *ederen*], to 'edder', interlace w. osiers.

c1230 claudet sepem ∼atam, iij rodas pro j operatione *Cust. Waltham* f. 201; haia ∼ata *Ib.*

1 ēdere [CL]

1 to bring forth, produce; **b** (offspring, also fig.). **c** to give rise to, cause. **d** to perform.

edat, proferat *GlC* E 29; **c960** (12c) cum omnibus utensilibus quae Deus in ipsa telluris superficie mirabiliter edidit *CS* 1319. **b** Roma sacerdotem Clementem tempore prisco / edidit ALDH. *VirgV* 525; **759** nos tres germani, uno patre editi *CS* 187; **9** . . editus, *acenned WW*; matrona fidelis, / edita nobilium clara de stirpe parentum WULF. *Swith.* II 821; egregio marito edidit utriusque sexus optatam sobolem ORD. VIT. IV 5 p. 188. **c** ritmi melodiam quot possunt edere tantam? *Altercatio* 81. **d** describere . . quos habuit mores . . quos edidit actus DOMINIC *V. Ecgwini* I *prol.*.

2 to emit, utter (sound); **b** (speech). **c** to relate, declare, state; **d** (w. indir. qu.).

dulcisonos cantus . . ediderunt ORD. VIT. IV 10 p. 247; melodiam . . ediderunt *Chr. Rams.* 90 (v. cochlea 3). **b** R. COLD. *Cuthb.* 20 (v. consolamen); ELF. *Gl.* (v. 1 esse). **c** sunt innumerabilia quae, si quis ad exploranda pennis volare posset, edita rumoroso sermone . . ficta probaret *Lib. Monstr. prol.* (cf. ib. I 25: manus in hujus normae mensuram editae describuntur); edidit, dixit, . . indicavit *GlH* E 48. **d** unde est / hoc nomen tractum? cujus generis siet ede *Altercatio* 30 (cf. ib. 76: commune quid ede?).

3 to compose, publish. **b** to promulgate, enact (decree or statute).

qui nobis unum facundo famine biblum / edidit ALDH. *CE* 4. 12. 11; *Id. VirgV* 2151 (v. bargina); historiam . .

quam nuper edideram BEDE *HE pref.* p. 5; **9..** edidit, *awrat oððe asægde WW*; epitaphium .. a Ricardo .. canonico editum est ORD. VIT. IV 2 p. 169; incipit liber Restaurationis et Oppositionis Numeri, quem aedidit Mahomet filius Mosi Algaurizin ROB. ANGL. *Alg.* 66; novis quibusdam et que vel nullis hactenus edita sunt vel perpaucis enucleata GIR. *TH intr.* p. 7. **b** edidit extemplo leti decreta resurgens ALDH. *VirgV* 1419; **1314** ex statuto universitatis .. a duobus annis citra edito *Collect. Ox.* II 270; **1338** (v. editio 3b); **1348** juxta formam statuti .. pro mercatoribus †edicti *SelCCoron* 112 (cf. ib. 118: contra statutum pro operariis editum); **1422** ponderabat novo pondere per statutum domini regis noviter editum *Ac. Durh.* 228.

4 (p. ppl. *editus*): **a** elevated, lofty. **b** (as sb. n.) height. **c** (of person or abstr.) exalted, distinguished.

a ut ~i montis civitas vertice constituta GILDAS *EB* 93; oppido frequens oratio quasi arx ~issima .. fore creditur ALDH. *VirgP* 60; quoniam ipsa domus Domini in ~iore loco constructa erat BEDE *Kings* 728; **9..** ~iorem, *hearan WW*; castellum .. ~issimo aggere sublatum *G. Steph.* I 16; fossam contra murum ~ioris castri effodere incipiunt OSB. BAWDSEY clxx. **b** statuitur .. in ~o arcis acies GILDAS *EB* 19; pyram strue stipitum in ~o constructam ALDH. *VirgP* 29; promotus in ~um W. MALM. *GP* I 53; *Ib.* II 73 (v. crypta 2). **c** te cunctis .. Brittanniae ducibus tam regno fecit quam status liniamento ~iorem GILDAS *EB* 33; ~a pudicitiae proceritas ALDH. *VirgP* 22; Cnuth .. / regibus innumeris viribus editior G. WINT. *Epigr. Hist.* 1. 2; quicquid est editum mors facit humile WALT. WIMB. *Sim.* 139.

2 ēdere v. 1 esse. **edes** v. aedes, ethees.

edia [cf. CL inedia; *app. infl. by* OF *eise or* ME *ēse*], sufficiency of food, comfort, ease. **b** (by conf.) lack of food.

melius est infirmum ire ad celum quam sanum in infernum, ad amenitatem cum inedia quam ad dolorem cum edia [ME: *eise*] *AncrR* 64; **1351** sic in cibis et potibus laucius procurantur quod carcer pro eorum flagiciis non cedit ad penam .. ; et propterea .. plures .. per tantam ediam ingrassati .. ab hujusmodi custodia .. recedunt *Conc.* III 14a; a luce media ad solicidium / abs quavis edia committunt prelium *Planct. Univ. Ox.* 76; edia, A. *ese WW*; *an ese*, edia, ocium .., *an hele*, columitas, edia .., sanitas .. *CathA.* **b** edia, i. famis *GlH* E 47.

edibilis [LL], edible. *V. et.* 2 *edilis, edulis.*

herbas non ~es *Eul. Hist.* III 120 (v. 2 cardo 1a).

1 edicere v. 1 edere 3b.

2 edicere [CL]

1 to utter, pronounce, recount. **b** (w. indir. qu. or acc. & inf.).

GILDAS *EB* 1 (v. condelectare c); clarorum vitam .. / sanctis aggrediar studiis edicere pauper ALDH. *VirgV pref.* 35; ~it, narrat, exponit *GlC* E 31; post alii septem, quos nunc edicere promptum est / carmine versifico WULF. *Swith. pref.* 71; quales ~is rumores? W. DAN. *Ep.* f. 62a; **1299** nisi .. oracionem dominicam cum .. 'ave Maria' et simbolum 'credo' .. sciat .. ~ere distinctius et aperte *Reg. Cant.* 828. **b** edixit [sc. se] priscum nullo frustramine foedus / vellere FRITH. 1111; ingredere et quis sis, unde venias, quid videris ~ito ANSELM *Misc.* 357; quantus .. fuit dolor .. supersedemus dicere quia non possumus ~ere DOMINIC *V. Ecgwini* I 17.

2 to ordain, decree; **b** (w. *ut*). **c** (p. ppl. as sb. n.) edict, proclamation, decree. **d** resolution.

omnes Dei rectitudines pacificentur .. per witam quam sapientes ~ent [v. l. addicent] (*Quad.*) *GAS* 131; callidus hec pridem nobis edixerat arma / serpens antiquus GARL. *Epith.* I 403. **b** rursumque edixit ut idem / iret ad examen WULF. *Swith.* II 319; hunc pete et ut tibi indicet quod inde noverit mea ex parte ~ito *Arthur & Gorlagon* 3. **c** GILDAS *EB* 12 (v. emarcescere 2); ~it, foris dicit, unde ~ta dicuntur quasi foras dicta *GlC* E 44; **749** (12c) quae .. ~to regis facienda jubentur *CS* 178; **9..** ~ta, *gebodo* .., ~tis, *gebennum, gescrifum WW*; Suriani, ordine spreto et ~to militum neglecto, .. ceperunt .. fugere ORD. VIT. IX 12 p. 574; **s1164** ex ~to regio regni pontifices .. et proceres .. convocantur H. BOS. *Thom.* III 32; **s1196** (recte **1197**) exiit ~tum a rege R. ut omnium rerum venalium commercia .. unius mensure, ponderis et pretii fierent *Ann. Cambr.* 60 (cf. R. HOWD. IV 33); **s1213** vocati fuimus ~to peremptorio ut compareremus apud Eboracum *Chr. Evesham* 231; GIR. *JS* 4 p. 213 (v. editio 2c); **c1224** in matrimonio contrahendo .. quasi tribus ~tis perquirat sacerdos .. de legitimitate sponsi et sponse *Conc. Syn.* 146; **1549** quod beneficia patronata non conferantur nisi previo ~to *Conc. Scot.* II 114. **d** Lotharius dux Saxonum generali plebis ~to intronizatus accessit ORD. VIT. XII 43 p. 467.

3 (w. pers. obj.): **a** to command; *cf. edictus.* **b** to indict.

a cum [rex] in Walis pergere vellet, vicecomes qui ab eo ~tus non pergebat xl s. de forisfactura dabat *DB* I 252. **b** **s1381** miles convocata duodena de villanis, onerat ut .. ~ant quoscunque reos sciverint. .. in crastino autem .. vocavit viros duodene ad cameram suam, ut sciret quos indictassent WALS. *HA* II 24 (cf. ib. 35).

4 (intr.) to speak.

stans in cancellis dat cunctis sperma salutis, / regibus edixit, repetitaque rura recepit FRITH. 469.

edictalis [CL], appropriate to, or embodied in, an edict.

cessionis actionum formam sequi .. parati sumus ~em *Collect. Stories* 205; Constantinus .. legem ~em promulgavit de solo Deo Christianorum adorando R. NIGER *Chr. I* 33; data ~i lege evangeliorum per apostolos *Id. Mil.* III 5.

edictio v. editio 2c.

edictus, command. *Cf. edicere* 3a.

quando rex in hostem pergit, siquis ~u ejus vocatus remanserit .., est in misericordia regis *DB* I 172.

edifi- v. aedifi-.

1 edilis v. aedilis.

2 edilis, edible. *V. et. edibilis, edulis.*

cum .. herbarum ~ium tantummodo alimentis vitam sustentarent *Eul. Hist.* I 301; *eteabylle*, comessibilis, ~is *CathA.*

edilitas, edibility.

~as, *ætnes GlH* E 52.

edilium v. edulium 1a. **ediosmus** v. hedyosmon.

ediosus [cf. edia], easy.

esy, ~us .., levis et suavis *CathA.*

ediscere [CL], to learn (thoroughly); **b** (w. inf.); **c** (w. *quod*).

Ceolfriðus .. cupiens sui gradus officium .. ~ere *Hist. Abb. Jarrow* 10; ab ipso .. rationem fidei ~ere BEDE *HE* II 9; nemo .. quivit .. elementorum sacras recitando scedulas ~ere LANTFR. *Swith. pref.*; nec sacris elementa legens ediscere libris WULF. *Swith. pref.* 577; ut monachus fieret et monachilem normam ~eret ORD. VIT. IV 6 p. 204. **b** rigorem Cluniacensium experiri .. ferventer edidicit *Ib.* III 5 p. 86. **c** missis exploratoribus, edidicit quod rex ille delicatissime viveret MAP *NC* V 2 f. 59v.

edisertare v. edissertare.

edissecare [LL], to divide.

~atur, i. †dividit [MS: dividitur] *GlH* E 60; ~are, dividere, discindere, digladiare OSB. GLOUC. *Deriv.* 197.

edisserere [CL], to expound, explain; **b** (w. indir. qu.).

restat ut .. tempora epitrito quarto congruentia regulariter ~as ALDH. *PR* 140; edissere[re], *asaecgan GlC* E 36; ~it, i. explanat, enarrat, exponit .., vel *arecþ GlH* E 56; ut brevius ~am ANSELM I 285 (v. 1 designare 2a); de fine .. ejus latius in sequentibus ~am ORD. VIT. III 2 p. 28; BALSH. *AD* 5 (v. divertere 5a); de duabus sedibus istis .. quod mihi videtur .. paucis ~am GIR. *IK* II 1. **b** ut .. regulariter ~as quot species in carminibus Vergilii .. deprehendi queant ALDH. *Met.* 10 p. 90; ~e, si potes, qua ratione herbe contrarie eodem in loco vivere possint ADEL. *QN* 3; artem ea inveniendi .. et ad quid utilis sophismatum inventio .. ~emus BALSH. *AD* 57.

edissertare [CL], to expound thoroughly.

edisertandi, disputandi *GlH* E 47; ei cum .. laborem .. itineris, Gallicanam elegantiam, pompam Romanam .. ~aret, libenter est auditus W. MALM. *GP* III 100 p. 214; ~are, disserere OSB. GLOUC. *Deriv.* 197.

edissertio [LL], exposition.

supra linguam sunt in quorum ~one elinguis est quamlibet eloquens G. HOYLAND *Ascet.* 268B.

editicius [CL], nominated by plaintiff.

edi[ti]cius judex, quem una pars elegit *GlC* E 41.

editio [CL]

1 procreation, birth; **b** (fig.).

filium genuerunt, de cujus ~one magnam gaudii materiam habuerunt S. FOUGÈRES *Vitalis* 358. **b** [musica] disciplina siquidem liberalis est et, sive Pictagoram sive Moysen .. ~onis sue laudat auctorem, ingenuum habet ortum J. SAL. *Pol.* 401A; **1278** ecclesia, dum ad ~onem spiritualis patris, filii sponsique votivam enititur, parturientis partes experiens (*Lit. Papae*) *Reg. Heref.* I 57.

2 statement. **b** declaration of war. **c** statement of claim (leg., esp. eccl.).

affirmavit ~o Grecorum hunc eundem extitisse gallum qui .. ter cantando Petrum arguit negantem *Judas Story* 70. **b** **s1188** continebatur .. in epistola [Fretherici] diffidatio et ~o belli *Flor. Hist.* II 100. **c** archidiaconus .., ad secundum edictum et peremptorium primum, ubi et inserta fuit ~o grandem pecunie summam .. complectens .., procuratorem misit GIR. *JS* 4 p. 213; **1225** R. .. defendit quod nunquam traxit eum in placitum nisi de decimis mi[n]utis .. : et inde profert literas domini pape et ~onem suam *CurR* XII 948; **1231** thesaurarius [S. Pauli, Lond'] profert ~ones sigillatas sigillis .. judicum [in curia Christianitatis] *Ib.* XIV 1767 (cf. ib. XV 1165, 1580; v. et. dicere 6d); **1236** causa que vertitur .. super jure dyocesano ecclesiarum de D. et de F. .. et aliis in ~one episcopi M. contentis *Reg. Moray* 101; **12..** petitis copiis omnium †edictionum et aliorum instrumentorum quibus in judicio contra eos uti nitebamur *Meaux* II 38; si rectus ordo proponendi exceptiones servetur, primo oportet proponere illas que petunt super jurisdictione judicis et postea confirmare personas partium et alias que dilatorie sunt .. et tunc super ~one facienda BRACTON 376.

3 edition, publication (or published work). **b** promulgation, enactment (of statute). **c** authorship.

in Genesi scriptum est .., vel, sicut alia dicit ~o .. BEDE *HE* V 21 p. 339; ~ones, †duplicationes *GlC* E 25 (cf. *Gl. Leid.* 35. 23: ~onis, puplicationis); dicit Boethius in secunda ~one super Porphirium .. J. BLUND *An.* 87; ~o vulgata, que fuit septuaginta interpretum BACON *Min.* 336. **b** **1313** ad ~onem duorum statutorum .. consenciebant tantum magistri arcium cum [uno] medico .. ; obtemperant tamen statutis sic editis theologi et alii *Collect. Ox.* II 218; **1338** cum .. papa .. quedam statuta ediderit et ordinaciones fecerit .., ut .. persistat †sanctimonie fortitudo ~onum et ordinacionum suarum in Cantuar' et Ebor' provinciis .. *Doc. Eng. Black Monks* II 6 (= *Conc.* II 626a); **1555** tempore ~onis et confectionis predicti statuti *Entries* 187. **c** *Ziz.* 313 (v. compilatio 1a).

editiuncula, (little) edition or publication (*i. e.* published work).

a706 [ut] omnem tibi .. mearum litterarum ~am primum pandens propalarem (ÆTHELWALD) *Ep. Aldh.* II (7); **s1268** bene memini de eo [S. de Monte Forti] in ~a de bello Lawensi facta *Chr. Melrose* 203.

editiusculus [cf. 1 edere 4a], slightly elevated.

ex ~o loco tum rem divinam faciebat BOECE 314.

editor [LL], publisher (*i. e.* one who makes known), writer, author.

quid ad haec respondeat ~or ipsius libelli? ANSELM (*Resp. Ed.*) I 130; ut .. occidentalia .. nostro tandem labore .. inveniant ~orem GIR. *TH* II *pref.* p. 74; *Qui majora cernitis* 189 (v. doctrinalis c); **c1240** lapides fundamentales vos in fundamento ponitis et disponitis cum .. libros [Prophetarum et Apostolorum] secundum mentem ~orum auditoribus exponitis GROS. *Ep.* 123; Paulus .. in epistola ad Hebreos .. tacet nomen suum usque in finem .., ubi .. se ipsum expresse explicat illius epistole ~orem WYCL. *Ver.* I 246.

1 editus v. 1 edere 4.

2 editus [CL], dung.

querenti cuidam quare noluit intrare in domum que erat lita ~u boum, respondit: "non sum crabo, ut intrarem in ~um boum" VINSAUF *AV* II 3. 24.

edituus v. aedituus. **ediverso** v. divertere 6b.

1 edo [CL], glutton.

hic †ego, *a gluton WW.*

2 edo v. medo.

edocare, ~atio v. educ-.

edocēre [CL]

1 to teach (thoroughly), inform, impart knowledge (of): **a** (w. person taught in acc. or unspec.); **b** (w. inf.); **c** (w. indir. qu. or *quod*); **d** (w. person taught in dat.).

a sacerdos considerare debet personam, in qua aetate vel quomodo ~tus THEOD. *Pen.* I 15. 5; gentem Anglorum .. per se [Gregorium] .. ~tam *V. Greg.* p. 80; Nynia .. qui erat Romae regulariter fidem et mysteria veritatis ~tus BEDE *HE* III 4 p. 133; †~it, bene †docit *GlC* E 37; quod A. verbis ~uit, hoc Suuithinus miraculis .. decoravit ÆLF. *Æthelwold* 18; erga Deum emendet sedulo, sicut ~ebitur [AS: *swa swa man him tæce*] (*Quad.*) *GAS* 343; non dederunt eam patres corrumpendam moribus, / sed dederunt †edocendo [? l. edocendam] in divinis artibus HIL. RONCE. I 32; GIR. *PI* I 17 (v. doctrinaliter); M. PAR. *Maj.* V 401 (v. eligere 1g); audientes asserciones hujusmodi a magnis doctoribus ~eri OCKHAM *Dial.* 431. **b** quem Deus edocuit mundum servare pudorem ALDH. *VirgV* 714; dum [B. Edmundus] eos [scholares suos] missas audire sic ~uit HIGD. VII 35 p. 220; **1457** (v. 1 compati 2d). **c** quod septinarius numerus .. interdum priscae legis imaginem praetulerit, sacra auctoritate ~emur ALDH. *Met.* 2; quid erga eum agere rex promisisset, ~uit BEDE *HE* II 12; ~tus quibus tormentis affligendus erat nisi faceret que jubebantur .., respondit .. G. MON. I 11; ELVEDEN *Cal.* 5 (v. 2 infra). **d** **s870** advocatis suis strenuus dux et somnium *Chr. S. Neoti*; S. Patricius eis [Hibernicis] fidem Christi ~uit *Eul. Hist.* II 124.

2 to teach, impart knowledge (of, w. abstr. or inanim. subj.).

sicut Exodi sequentia patenter ~ent (*Ep. Ceolfridi*) BEDE *HE* V 21 p. 335; nisi sicut affectus ~et *Ps.*-GROS. *Gram.* 59; novum lumen .. / natum regem edocuit / et magos antecessit LEDREDE *Carm.* 39. 5; tercius [libellus] .. quasdam narraciones monstruosas ~et *Eul. Hist. proem.* I 3;

secunda [linea kalendarii] ~et quantum *clok* percuciet vicinius ortui solis ELVEDEN *Cal.* 5.

3 (p. ppl.) learned, skilled (in).

601 Augustinus episcopus in monasterii regula ~tus (*Lit. Papae*) BEDE *HE* I 32; Basilius .. rethoricis sofismatum ~tus disciplinis ALDH. *VirgP* 27; fuit .. deductus ad medicos ~tos cenobii nostri *V. Cuthb.* IV 17; gens .. usu pariter et exercitio sagittis et armis paulatim ~ta et assueta GIR. *EH* II 34.

edocte, skilfully.

puer .. omnibus in domum patris sui venientibus .. ~e ministravit EDDI 2.

edomare [CL]

1 to tame, subdue: **a** animals; **b** men (or their natures); **c** 'the flesh'; **d** the elements.

a c**750** accipitres .. qui .. ad .. artem [grues captandi] animo agiles ac bellicosi educantur et ~antur ac doceantur (*sic*) (*Lit. Æ. regis Cantiae*) *Ep. Bonif.* 105; pro .. novis ferruris affrorum primo ~itorum *Ac. Beaulieu* 264. **b** **1108** expectavimus .. ut ferocia gentis illius [Teutonicae] ~aretur (*Lit. Papae*) *Ep. Anselmi* (452) V 400; barbare nationis feritatem .. ~itam GIR. *EH pref.* p. 224; s**1213** homines .. ~are (v. clericaster); gens [Suecie] cujus potentia .. totius fere Asie et Europe partem maximam multis temporibus ~avit BART. ANGL. XV 153. **c** BEDE *Tab.* 483 (v. concupiscibilis 2a); abstinentia semet ipsum ~ans ÆLF. *Æthelwold* 6; R. COLD. *Cuthb.* 91 (v. curiositas 3); quot crucibus corporee afflictionis carnis sue incentiva ~averit *Chr. Rams.* 23; AD. EYNS. *Hug.* II 2 (v. contritio 1c); **1283** (v. crucifixio c). **d** oceanus ejusque barbaros motus, quos terreni principes ~are ferro nequiverant BEDE *HE* II 1 p. 78.

2 (p. ppl.) tamed. **b** (by conf.) untamed.

9.. ~iti, *pæs atemedan WW*; ~itis, *getaccodon GlP* 1022. **b** ~itus, *untemed, wilde GlH* E 69.

edomatio [LL], subdual, subjection.

~one passionum interiorum et redactionem [? l. redactione] earundem sub lege racionis fuit moderatus J. WALEYS *Compend.* f. 161v.

edomitor, subjugator.

s**1219** W. Marescallus .. fuit Hibernicis nocivus ~or, Anglis honor et gloria M. PAR. *Maj.* III 43.

edonare v. enodare 2.

edormire [CL], to fall asleep (euphem. for death). **b** (by conf.) to wake up.

[H. Episc. Senon.] vitam suam .. concludens †edormuit [l. ~ivit] in Domino CAPGR. *Hen.* 160. **b** ~ire, evigilare *GlH* E 70; ~ire, vigilare, noctare OSB. GLOUC. *Deriv.* 198.

edorsare [cf. CL exdorsuare], to gall, chafe.

equus ~atus, *cheval †redois* [MS: *redois devant*] *Gl. AN Glasg.* f. 21; *gallyn or make gallyd*, strumo, ~o *PP*.

edrius v. hedraeus.

edubitare [cf. CL dubitare], to call in doubt.

hoc etiam, quoniam ~ari potest, querendum est ADEL. *QN* 33.

educamen, ~entum, nourishment. **b** 'team', brood (of poultry).

~en, nutrimen, fomen, fomentum, nutrimentum, alimentum, alimonia, nutricamen OSB. GLOUC. *Deriv.* 199. **b** ~en, A. *a teme of checonn*; ~entum, A. *brodyng WW*.

educare [CL]

1 to nurture, bring up, educate: **a** (animals or unspec.); **b** (children).

a cum .. sit .. naturae .. ibicum caricibus ~ari et vesci ALDH. *PR* 114 (cf. ib. 117: ~o, quod est nutrio); **798** quid [valet] inter leones agniculus in pace nutritus, edocatus [v. l. educatus]? ALCUIN *Ep.* 145; foverat, i. ~averat, *gehyrte GlH* F 620; ADEL. *QN* 10 (v. dicere 1h); NECKAM *NR* II 157 (v. educator). **b** frater .. qui .. erat in monasterio ac magisterio illius ~atus BEDE *HE* IV 3; datus sum ~andus .. abbati Benedicto *Ib.* V 24 p. 357; c**1150** nos, qui a puero in ipsa patria ~ati fuimus *Ch. Durh.* 36a; in curia B. Cuthberti ~atus erat R. COLD. *Cuthb.* 53; **1240** (v. conjugare 1c); s**1383** (v. deliciose a); mater .. Chironi centauro Achillem ~andum commendaverat TREVET *Troades* 60.

2 to mellow, refine.

nonnullos regio composita malos ~at GIR. *PI pref.* (v. componere 1e).

3 to govern.

quibus nobiliter instructus, et regni fastigium sagaciter valeas ~are et hostium jacula triumphaliter defringere (*Benedictio Regis*) EGB. *Pont.* 96; quomodo populum Deus suum .. paterno affectu ~averit *Eccl. & Synag.* 55; dux .. comissum .. sibi populum ut dulcis patricius ~avit ORD. VIT. IX 11 p. 570; †Ebrancus [l. Ebraucus] .. regnum suscepit et xl annos in summa pace ~avit *Eul. Hist.* II 224 (= G. MON. II 7: regimen .. tenuit).

educatio [CL]

1 upbringing, education.

722 ut .., si quos .. a recte fidei tramite destitisse cognoverit .., corrigat atque sui edocatione ad portum reportet salutis (*Lit. Papae*) *Ep. Bonif.* 17; **802** de nido paternae edocationis educti, ad publicas evolastis auras ALCUIN *Ep.* 245; in filiorum ~one et filiarum quanta sollicitudo; quos ut promoveat, illas vero pompose nuptui tradat, quid est quod abhorreat? GIR. *GE* II 23 (cf. ib.: puerorum sumptus, ~ones et promotiones); BRACTON 92 (v. dos 2a); *Ps.*-GROS. *Gram.* 15 (v. domificatio).

2 rearing (of game). *Cf. deductus* 2a, *ductus* 5.

consecratas aedes pro ~one ferarum derelictas Dominus sibi displicere .. ostendit ORD. VIT. X 14 p. 83.

educator [CL], nurturer, trainer.

miles quidam canem nobilem .. studio diligenti educavit, qui adultus tanquam fidelis ~oris sui custos .. super pedes domini sui jacere consuevit NECKAM *NR* II 157 p. 253.

educatrix [CL], breeder, nurse, fomenter (f., also fig.).

~ix, nutrix *GlH* E 67; [invidia] rixarum et discordie ~ix nimis sedula NECKAM *NR* II 189 p. 339.

educere [CL]

1 (w. pers. obj.) to lead (out), convey. **b** (mil. or sim.).

caeci ~ti a caecis pariter in inferni foveam cadetis [cf. *Matth.* xv 14] GILDAS *EB* 68; dicitur .. se obtinuisse ut in cratere occultatus ~eretur *V. Greg.* p. 82; populum de Aegypto .. per Rubrum Mare ~tum BEDE *Hom.* I 1. 23; ALCUIN *Ep.* 245 (v. educatio 1); si cognatio ejus nolit eum [de carcere] ~ere [AS: *útniman*] (*Quad.*) *GAS* 183; abbates .. suas ~unt cohortes *Itin. Ric.* I 61 (v. clerus 2c); de quodam milite .. per tres dies .. ~tus a corpore COGGESH. *Visio* 3. **b** ~it Gaufredus copias .. equestres et pedestres W. POIT. I 18; lx millia equitum contra hostiles cuneos secum eduxit ORD. VIT. IV 12 p. 257; s**1391** resistendo eorum [nobilium] rapinis de Angusia ~tis *Plusc.* X 11.

2 **a** to lead out, cart. **b** to carry away, export.

a c**1350** curtenas ad ~endum fimum (v. curtana 2a). **b** **1303** de quolibet sacco lane quem dicti mercatores .. de regno nostro ~ent aut ~i facient solvent xl d. de incremento ultra antiquam custumam (*Stat. Regis*) *MGL* II 209; **1341** lane .. quas extra portus .. ~i contigerit (v. cokettare); **1342** onerant se de viij li. vij s. ix d. receptis per contribucionem impositam ~entibus pecuniam de regno *ExchScot* 496; **1347** (v. clewa); **1359** diversas .. prisas de rebus et victualibus ad .. civitatem per terram ductis et exinde ~tis (*Breve Regis*) *MGL* I 45; *Cust. Fordwich* 23 p. 257 (v. custumabilis 2b).

3 **a** to draw (sword, partly fig.). **b** to tear out (eyes). **c** to knock out (pegs).

a **1108** B. Petri gladium, quem jam ~ere cepimus (*Lit. Papae*) *Ep. Anselmi* (452) V 400; hic est .. cujus gladius ~tus ut proderet non est reversus inanis *Fleta proem.*; erant .. eorum plus quam lx milia ~encium gladium *G. Hen. V* 14 p. 94. **b** ~antur ei [AS: *do man ut*] oculi et truncetur ei nasus (*Quad.*) *GAS* 333 (= *Inst. Cnuti, ib.*: eruantur). **c** **1350** magistro A. fabro .. pro j poncona ferri vocata *drivel* empta pro cavillis ligneis ~endis *KRAc* 471/2 m. 3 (cf. *Building in Eng.* 345).

4 **a** to extract (metal). **b** to draw out (thread). **c** to draw off, drain (water). **d** to draw out (bodily fluid or sim.).

a BART. ANGL. IV 1 (v. deductivus). **b** textrix .. filum subtiliter ~et NECKAM *NR* II 171. **c** **12..** ad faciendum unum fossatum .. ad ~endum aquam de .. petaria sua *Cart. Newm.* 33. **d** tumbam .. lacrimarum fluentis, quas ejus eduxit .. devotio, .. irrigavit GIR. *Hug.* III 3; infans qui, etiam dum lac ~ere non curat ab ubere, papillam .. lambit J. GODARD *Ep.* 223; scammonea coleram ~it ALF. ANGL. *Cor* 13. 2; aer .. inflat et vomitum facit et ~it *Quaest. Salern.* B 156; medicina .. ~ens co[leram] *SB* 16 (v. cholagogus b).

5 to bring forth, give birth to. **b** (?) to facilitate childbirth.

Cuthbertus .. de styrpe regia satis ~itur ut merito flos et gemma pontificum predicetur *Cuthb. Hib.* 1; queritur cum genitum in septimo mense ~atur salubre est ..? .. si fetus in eo mense ~atur salubre est quia per naturalem fortitudinem atque matricis confortationem emittitur *Quaest. Salern.* B 118. **b** nepta .. valet ad concipiendum et inde ~it *Alph.* 125.

6 **a** to produce, publish (literary work). **b** to elicit (abstr., var.). **c** (phil.) to educe. **d** to divert (from).

a 'Itinerarium' ~ens, laboriosam viri sancti legationem sub ignorantie tenebris perire non permisi GIR. *DK* I *pref.* p. 155. **b** nos nunquam quiescimus agere perverse, ne quiescat Deus de malis nostris sua ~ere bona PULL. *Sent.* 811C; erit experto compertum verba quedam .. translatius ad artes docendas quam in sermone loquendi licentia ab usu ~i posse BALSH. *AD* 44; tua .. justa simplicitas .. eduxit 'quasi lumen justiciam tuam' [*Psalm* xxxvi 6] AILR. *Ed. Conf.* 781A; qualis ex cithara nudata, aura leniter impulsa, melodia solet ~i GIR. *IK* I 2. **c** BACON VII 25 (v. concausatio); de potentia .. materie ~itur forma *Id.* VIII 42; consideravi quomodo [res] ~itur in esse, an per generationem de potentia materie, an per exitum ab agente, an per impressionem, sicut sigillum agit in ceram *Id. Tert.* 108; MIDDLETON *Sent.* II 163 (*recte* 153) (v. educibilis); R. MARSTON *QD* 409 (v. eductio 4). **d** **1299** hospitale .. a statu congruo ~tum (v. difformis).

7 to deduct.

c**1250** de bonis ejus ecclesiasticis tanta portio ~atur que sufficiat ad reparandum hec *Reg. Aberd.* II 30 (= *Conc. Scot.* II 36).

8 to lay out or extend (buildings).

~untur domicilia *V. Ed. Conf.* 49 (v. disposite).

9 ? *f. l.*

si equum .. de furfure fabisque †educi [?l. educari] faciatque nutriri *Fleta* 164.

educibilis, (phil.) that can be educed.

educi potest forma ~is de potencia materie MIDDLETON *Sent.* II 163 (*recte* 153); forma serpentis vel vini, vel quecumque alia de potencia materie ~is WYCL. *Form.* 188.

eductio [CL]

1 leading out or away (of persons).

magna .. multitudo .. vel corporali .. praeventa morte vel hostili ~one captivata est WILLIB. *Bonif.* 6 p. 32; ab ~one Israel de Egypto R. NIGER *Chr. II* 107; festivitas S. Petri ad Vincula, que celebratur in memoriam ~onis illius J. FURNESS *Walth.* 89; interrogabant eum .. quenam sub tanta mora sue ~onis vidisset COGGESH. *Visio* 8; decentius esset ut ad ~onem penitencium [ab archidiacono abbati] .. sequens caneretur responsorium *Miss. Westm.* II 555*n*.

2 **a** leading out (of plough on Plough Monday). **b** carrying away (of goods), export.

a **1378** (v. carruca 2g). **b** †**1053** (14c) concedo eis [abbati et fratribus Ramesiae] mercatum de Dunham per aquam et terram, cum inductione et ~one *CD* 853; **1303** iidem mercatores concesserunt dare nobis .. iij d. de qualibet libra argenti in ~one quarumcunque .. mercandisarum hujusmodi emptarum in regno et potestate nostra .. ultra custumas antiquas (*Stat. Regis*) *MGL* II 210; **1338** quoddam sigillum .. pro ~one lanarum ad partes exteras .. de novo fabricatum *RScot* 547a.

3 drawing out: **a** of thread; **b** of fluid (esp. med.). **c** of breath.

a in carpendo lanam et quandoque in fili ~one succurret leva sorori [sc. dextre] NECKAM *NR* II 171 (cf. ib. 113: Arachne .. mutatur in araneam et artem exercet inutilem, sibi ipsi in materie cassium ~one operatrix perniciosa). **b** quando per frigiditatem constringentem multa fit humiditatis oppresse ~o BART. ANGL. IV 2; in .. dolore capitis ex calida causa .. laborandum est cum expressivis et alterativis .. et non ad dissolutionem vel ~onem GILB. II 94. 1; *Ib.* VI 279v. 2 (v. diamnes); accipit eradicacionem pro remocione omni[s] materie de loco suo absque ~one extra corpus GAD. 38v. 2; rascacio est aspera sputi ~o vel expulsio *SB* 36. **c** ~one singultum *Dictamen* 358.

4 (phil.) eduction.

~o forme substantialis rei naturalis non est a virtute finita set ab infinita BACON VII 128; oportet .. quod per viam impressionis fiat species aut quod (*sic*) per naturalem immutationem et ~onem de potentia materie patientis *Id. Maj.* II 432 (cf. ib. III 152); nec habet [anima] multiplicacionem naturalem rei permanentis, sicut cum candela illuminatur a candela, quia talis multiplicacio est generacio et ~o de potencia materie PECKHAM *QA* 8; ~o potencie ad actum non attribuitur tantum illi a quo semen descinditur sed ei quod fovet ipsum SICCAV. *PN* 181; species qua formaliter homo cognoscit per intellectum aut fit in anima per creacionem .. aut per ~onem de ipso intellectu; et hoc non potest esse, cum sole forme materiales de potencia materie educantur R. MARSTON *QD* 409.

eductivus, able to draw out, eductive: **a** (med.); **b** (phil.).

a GILB. VI 254. 2 (v. ejectivus). **b** spiritus creati in loco sunt quidem definitivo, per modum tamen non corporalem .. sed spiritualem, cum eorum virtus alicujus sit operationis in loco exercende ~a et causativa *Ps.*-GROS. *Summa* 452.

eductor, (phil.) one who, or that which educes.

[formarum] ~ores T. YORK *Sap.* II 28 *rub.* (v. datio 1f).

eductus, leading out (mil.).

canere ~ui W. FITZST. *Thom.* 23 (v. 2 ductilis 1b); eductus bene dispositos tutosque receptus / advertit NECKAM *DS* III 377.

edulia v. edulium, eudulia. **edulion** v. idyllium.

edulis [CL], edible. *V. et. edibilis, 2 edilis.*

versatur questio .. / .. que terra feras effundat edules HANV. II 186 p. 264.

edulitas, food supply.

1192 desevit morbus pestilens et ~as invalescit P. BLOIS *Ep.* 143. 430C.

edulium [CL]

1 food; **b** (spiritual). **c** bait (fig.).

~ia, alimenta, . . ~ia, apta ad mandu[candum] *GlC* E 43, 51 (cf. ib. 330: †eudolia, victualia); **9..** ~ium, *æt* . ., ~io, *mete WW*; in prandio . ., multa ~ii parte consumpta W. MALM. *GP* I 6; omne genus ~ii in castellum ingerere *G. Steph.* I 15; grossa cliens . . det edulia primus opima GARL. *Mor. Scol.* 175 [*gl.*: ~ium dicitur omnis cibus preter panem, unde G. *companage*]; **1307** ne quisquam fratrum de †edilio suo quicquam extra refectorium mittere . . presumat *Ord. Ely* 34; **1314** nullus fratrum de cibariis et de annona sibi apposita quicquam det vel subtrahat . .; si quis autem in premissis deliquerit . ., simili ~io . . privetur *Ib.* 37; hoc ~ium, A. *sowle WW*. **b** sic . . nectareo contemplativae dulcedinis ~io saginantur ALDH. *VirgP* 14; dum caput Cantiae civitatis caelesti ~io pascitatur, membra festivius terrestri esu replentur BYRHT. *V. Osw.* 407; misericordia [Domini] . ., sine qua nemo salvandorum potietur ~io spiritualis intelligentiae HERM. ARCH. *prol.*; M. RIEVAULX (*Ep.*) 56 (v. depascere 2d); apocrypha deliramenta producunt, non ad refocillativum animarum ~ium, sed ad pruritum pocius aurium auditorum R. BURY *Phil.* 6. 88. **c** **s1252** (v. concupiscibilis 1a).

2 (w. obj. gen.) eating.

sub tyrannica Antiochi monarchia suellum scrofarum contempserunt ~ium ALDH. *Met.* 2; in . . mandatis et hoc erat ut de lignis paradisi concessis vescerentur . .; per horum ~ium . . immortalitatis dona conservarent BEDE *Gen.* 32; **10..** edylio, esu *WW*; **1004** (11c) generis humani parentem . . fraudulenti seduxit ~io pomi *CD* 710; ut ab omnium animantium temperasse credatur [Pithagoras] ~io J. SAL. *Pol.* 643B; Esau pro ~io lentis primogenita dedit [cf. *Gen.* xxv 34] P. BLOIS *Serm.* 737A; ferias tres in aque et solius panis ~io . . transigere consuevit AD. EYNS. *Hug.* I 12; **1283** si . . oporteat eos . . carnis ~io . . recreari PECKHAM *Ep.* 488.

edulus v. haedulus.

edurus [CL], thoroughly hard.

~um, satis durum *GlC* E 50; ~us, valde durus, predurus, quamdurus OSB. GLOUC. *Deriv.* 198.

edus v. haedus. **edylium** v. edulium 2. **eetenus** v. eatenus. **efario** v. pharus. **efax** v. 2 evax. **efectus** v. 1 effectus 2a. **efer-** v. effer-.

1 effabilis v. affabilis.

2 effabilis [CL], **a** utterable. **b** eloquent.

a *spekabylle*, ~is *CathA*. **b** adjutor benignus caris / doctor effabilis fonis (*Vers.*) NEN. *HB* 144.

effaecare [LL *p. ppl. only*]

1 to purify (from dregs). *V. et. defaecare* 1a.

~atus, purus, limpidus OSB. GLOUC. *Deriv.* 194; ~o, . . i. purgare quasi fecem extra ponere, et inde ~atus *Ib.* 230; *to clense*, . . diluere, ~are, ellimare . . *CathA*.

2 to drain to the dregs.

Anglorum . . more servato . ., sub . . clangore bucine . . inhiabat calicibus ~andis DEVIZES 41.

effamen [LL], utterance.

~ina, loquela *GlH* E 81; carpit onus itineris, . . martyris ~ine fisus HERM. ARCH. 6 (cf. ib.: aliquod affamen); talia effundens ~ina DOMINIC *Mir. Virg.* f. 145b; ~ina, loquelae, verba, famina OSB. GLOUC. *Deriv.* 198; *a speche*, . . loquela, famen, ~en . . *CathA*.

effaminare [cf. faminare], to speak.

~are, narrare *GlH* E 78; *CathA* (v. faminare).

effari [CL], to utter. **b** (p. ppl. *s. pass.*) mentioned.

ad rapaces judices sententiam dirigens ita ~atur, "principes tui infideles . ." GILDAS *EB* 43; quis ubertim angusto stili textu ~ari valeat quanta . . Julianus . . perpessus sit? ALDH. *VirgP* 36; quae effari sublimiter / odes hujus . . / . . prolixitas / refragat (ÆTHELWALD) *Carm. Aldh.* 4. 71; **796** nullula cartula sufficit caritatis ~ari dulcedinem ALCUIN *Ep.* 95; de cujus caritate . ., quamvis dignum aliquid vix quisquam ~ari queat AD. EYNS. *Hug.* IV 9 p. 47; quod nefas videtur ~atu R. BURY *Phil.* 4. 64. **b** **c675** (15c) ego Uu. presbiter, qui hanc cartulam rogante supra ~ato abbate scripsi et subscripsi *CS* 107.

effascinare [CL], to bewitch, enchant.

homo existens in perversa societate . . ~atur. . . ~ati . . sunt antiqua societate HOLCOT *Wisd.* 182–3.

effati v. effutire. **effatum** v. efficere 3d.

1 effatus v. effari.

2 effatus [CL], utterance.

~u, locutione *GlH* E 75.

effebus v. 2 ephebus. **effecio** v. effectio 1.

effectare

1 to effect. *V. et. effectuare, efficere.*

casus est causa ~ans preter ejus intentum contingens aliquid in minori WYCL. *Log.* I 172.

2 (?) to affect, assume. *V. et. affectare* 2.

s1214 ille [legatus pape], ~ata felicitate simplicior, . . justam eorum [monachorum] esse petitionem dicebat . ., sed tamen in omnibus regi deferendum G. COLD. *Durh.* 21.

effectibilis, that can be effected (produced by an efficient cause).

prima conclusio . . est ista, quod aliquod effectivum sit simpliciter primum, ita quod nec sit ~e nec virtute alterius a se effectivum DUNS *Ord.* II 151; aliqua [natura] est ~is; ergo aliqua est effectiva *Id. Prim. Princ.* 655.

effectibilitas, capacity to be effected.

~as independens potest inesse alicui nature, et illa simpliciter est prima; ergo ~as simpliciter prima est possibilis DUNS *Ord.* II 159.

effectio [CL]

1 effecting, (production of) effect.

[Martha] quod bene voluit tandem efficit; sed voluntati minus respondet ~o, et turbatur [cf. *Luke* x 41] PULL. *Sent.* 936D; oportet ipsum [mundum] processisse in ~onem per creacionem a Deo in primo instanti temporis WYCL. *Form.* 192; considerare potes quomodo opera illorum sorciuntur effe[c]ciones a finibus FAVENT 19.

2 affection. *V. et. affectio* 1b.

1587 paterni amoris et ~onis *Pat* 1298 m. 10.

effective [LL], **a** (phil.) w. ref. to effect produced by efficient cause. **b** effectively.

'ab aliquo' vel 'ex aliquo' est multipliciter: aut ordinaliter, ut 'ex nocte fit dies'; aut materialiter, ut 'ex ferro fit cultellus'; aut ~e, ut 'ex patre fit filius' BACON *Tert.* 197; motus in celo diversi non proveniunt ex defectu sed ex efficiente causa et ideo non possunt esse nisi ex diversis causis ~e loquendo PECKHAM *QA* 34; quomodo igitur forent hec verba Christi in nobis ~e sacramenti altaris vel panis tam mirabiliter conversiva WYCL. *Conf.* 505; quilibet . . titulus beneficialis institutus est ~e et finaliter propter aliquod officium vel ministerium ecclesiasticum PAUL. ANGL. *ASP* 1535. **b** omnis potestas regis referri debet ad bonum regni sui, quod ~e consistit in defencione ejusdem ab exterorum incursibus et in tuicione regnicolarum FORTESCUE *LLA* 37.

effectivitas, ability to effect.

apud eam [voluntatem] specialiter residet ~as . . omnia que voluerit causare *Ps.*-GROS. *Summa* 393; dieta sana ab efficiencia vel ~ate sanitatis WYCL. *Ente Praed.* 113.

effectivus [CL]

1 effective, productive (of effect); **b** (w. obj. gen.); **c** (phil.); **d** (gram.). **e** (as sb. n.) effective power.

de ~a lunae potentia BEDE *TR* 28; **c798** si . . aqua et sal . . unius sunt naturae, infunde carnem recentem aqua et aliam sale consperge. videbis cito si unam aqua et sal habuerint ~am potentiam ALCUIN *Ep.* 137 p. 212; **12..** quo pio inchoata sunt principio, piissimum est ut fine compleantur ~o *Reg. S. Thom. Dublin* 290; **c1380** quod exorare teneor precibus ~is *FormOx* 314; **1406** nec responsum congruum reportavimus nec verbum . . ~um (*Lit. Cardinalium*) *Conc.* III 289a. **b** effectiva boni bona simpliciter reor esse R. PARTES 230; hec . . organa alicujus operationis [ad] animalis integritatem . . sunt ~a ALF. ANGL. *Cor* 13. 4; si planete fuerint contrariarum qualitatum †~e [? l. ~i] sicut et signa BACON IX app. 193; non videtur aliqua racio quare calor est calefactivus nisi quia calor est calor; et ita videtur quod hec sit immediata 'calor est caloris ~a' DUNS *Ord.* IV 138. **c** *Ib.* II 151 (v. effectibilis). **d** [conjuncciones] causales sunt ut 'quia' . ., 'enim'. dicunt enim hec comparacionem cause ad effectum; quedam ut †'quam' [? l. quare], 'ideo' et consimilia comparacionem effectus ad causam, et has appellant quidam ~as *Ps.*-GROS. *Gram.* 57; dicciones terminantes motus effectus construuntur cum verbis racione effectus sive adquisicionis; et huic construccioni proprius est dativus, et appellatur construccio ~a sive adquisitiva . ., construiturque ex hac virtute tam id quod adquiritur quam id cui adquiritur aliquid, ut 'vivo tibi honori' *Ib.* 63. **e** si cui . . difficultatem subducens contigerit facultas . ., illaborato judicio non contentus, superate difficultatis non solum effectum sed et ~um debite circumspiciat BALSH. *AD rec.* 2 124.

2 produced as effect, resultant.

a . . stellarum calore ipsum mare calefieri necesse est, ex quo et ejus caloris ~am salsuginem accipere consequens est ADEL. *QN* 51; unde et †~um [? l. effectum] est ut, qui modo cum filiis vivere non poterat, sine filiis vivere jam recusaret GIR. *PI* II 10.

effector [CL], causer, author, agent.

Sancte Spiritus . ., esto solus et suggestor et ~or judiciorum nostrorum EGB. *Pont.* add. 98; nullus peccatorum conscius aliorum in tantum timendus est quantum ille qui ipsorum malorum ~or est ALEX. CANT. *Dicta* 7 p. 143; alii autumant consensum utriusque, quoniam is est conjugii ~or, prevalere sponsioni, quamvis juramento confirmate PULL. *Sent.* 954C; tam amica operatione unius virtutis ~ores existunt R. COLD. *Cuthb.* 108; tanti ~orem miraculi *Id. Godr.* 126.

effectorius [LL], effective, operative.

illa ~ia vis vacare non potest quin id quod ab ea factum est tueatur et specie carere non sinat BRADW. *CD* 148A.

effectrix [CL], causer (f.), cause.

lux . . diei perstat ~ix propria GROS. *Hexaem.* V 6.

effectualis

1 effectual, having (intended) effect. **b** (leg.) effectual, valid. **c** (as sb. n.) valid plea.

ramus impegit ejus in oculo, sancti videlicet ~is ultio HERM. ARCH. 26; **1414** negocia que . . concernunt Romani imperii augmentum nec non . . domus Francie et regni omnimodam et ~em reconciliacionem et exaltacionem BEKYNTON II 123; qui in provisione simoniaca, ad ~em ipsius consummacionem habendam, sua servicia impendunt PAUL. ANGL. *ASP* 1552; **1457** pro bona et ~i expedicione ejusdem [provisionis sagittariorum] *Lit. Cant.* III 227; ea que ad ostensionem ~em veritatis rei gerende sufficere videntur *Plusc. prol.* p. 4. **b** **1371** potestatem . . realem et ~em dicte sentencie execucionem fieri petendi *Lit. Cant.* II 505; **1378** licet non sit persona capax nominata, tamen legatum sit ~e *MGL* I 685 (= *LB Lond.* H f. 96 *rub.*: legatum capiat effectum; cf. capax 2c); **1408** concedens quod eedem littere quoad dictas xl personas valide sint et ~es in forma supradicta *RScot* 187b; **1428** nihil ~e (v. deducere 5d); **c1488** impetravit . . litteras apostolicas ~es *Reg. Whet.* I app. 460. **c** **c1315** si quod ~e pro se habeant quare sentencie et decretum predicta non debeant execucioni debite demandari *RGasc* IV 1407; **c1340** si . . ~e non proposuerit quare . . excommunicacionis sentencia exequi contra eum non debeat *FormOx* 129.

2 (phil.) occurring by way of effect.

necessitas sequens causalis seu ~is potest dici, a causa vel ab effectu; et videtur esse illa necessitas consecutiva inter causam non impedibilem et suum effectum BRADW. *CD* 723E; prima delectacio Dei respectu creature est ydealis et secunda contingens ~is, ut patet de objectis [sc. creaturis] ad que principaliter terminatur WYCL. *Dom. Div.* 34.

effectualiter

1 effectually, so as to produce (intended) effect. **b** in set terms, w. full legal effect.

jam nunc viget veridici ~er sententia Pauli [*Rom.* i 20] docens Romanos Dei invisibilia . . cognosci HERM. ARCH. 7; **†1086** (14c) chartam . . in omnibus ~er observari praecipio *Regesta* 222 (= *Croyl.* 85); **1259** pacem cum ipso rege [Francie] ~er inivimus *Cl* 260; **1285** ad . . negocium ~er decidendum *Reg. Heref.* 88; **1303** quod . . promissionem vestram . . cum omni . . celeritate ~er adimplere curetis (*Breve Regis*) *BBC* (*Oxford*) 102; **s1321** quod . . ipsum [regem] ~er inducerent ut exilium amborum Dispensariorum . . confirmaret *Flor. Hist.* III 197; **1435** quod unum altare fiat bene et ~er de tabulis *Test. Ebor.* II 53; **s1452** indisposicio ad procedendum ~er in ulla operacione laudabili *Reg. Whet.* I 22. **b** **1329** de dubio utrum comes M. vesturam suam . . pro se habuit vel ex liberacione Willelmi de A., ~er est protestatus *ExchScot* 236; **1340** vestras . . recepi litteras ~er continentes quod . . *Lit. Cant.* II 239; **1345** que litere ~er continebat quod . . (*Lit. Papae*) AD. MUR. *Chr.* 177; **14..** cum religiosi viri . . domum suam . . et bona sua licite et ~er nuper obligassent . . *Reg. Brev. Orig.* 51b.

2 intensely, w. sincere feeling. *V. et. affectualiter.*

hoc . . notificato . ., ~er omnibus placet ut . . [miles] alteretur habitu religionis HERM. ARCH. 37; **1381** quod T. . . ep. Dunelm' . . domos religiosas . . relevare . . ~er cupiebat (*Stat. Eccl. Cath.*) *Hist. Durh.* 3; **1384** coexecutores . . ipsum ~er rogarunt quod . . residuum . . una cum eis . . administrare voluisset *PlRCP* 495 r. 492; **1447** vestre devocionis affeccionem quam ad . . S. Cuthbertum . . hactenus habuistis . ., prout in nostris agendis ~er experimur *Pri. Cold.* 158; **1452** placeat . . paternitati vestre . . ad memoriam ~er revocare quanta dileccionis insignia inter vos et . . dominum J. O. fuerant *Ib.* 176.

effectuare

1 to effectuate, bring about. *V. et. effectare* 1.

multe sunt voluciones et bone et male que numquam implentur. si ergo Deus has volendo causaret, faceret et vellet volucionem fieri in aliquid volutum quam nollet ~ari, immo vellet non ~ari BRADW. *CD* 568A.

2 *f. l.*

possunt . . viri ecclesiastici et bene et male vocare se dominos: male, . . usurpando sibi civile dominium; et bene, †effectuantur [? l. effectualiter] domando rebelles regule Christiane WYCL. *Civ. Dom.* I 79.

effectuose

1 effectually, so as to produce (intended) effect. **b** w. effect, conclusively.

1202 quatinus .., quanto citius paci nostre et tranquillitati vestre mederi desideratis, tanto largitionis vestre munificentiam ∼ius maturare satagatis *Pat* 18b; **1259** mihi responderunt quod partes suas circa expeditionem negotiorum vestrorum cum festinatione qua poterunt ∼e intromittent (*AncC* VI 177) *RL* II 135; illa [beatitudo] est .. filiis regni pro tempore legis gracie ∼ius preparata Wycl. *Ver.* III 154. **b** jam ∼e patebit quod aegrotus potius visione vidit quam somno somniaverit Herm. Arch. 41; cur tunc tam ∼e fuerit electus, nunc autem, cum longe dignior extiterit .., non .. ad dignitatis honorem .. †vocatur [v. l. vocatus], satis admirari non possum Gir. *JS* 1 p. 120.

2 earnestly, w. sincere feeling. *Cf. affectuose.*

s1162 Thomas .., ipso rege ∼e pro ipso petente .., electus est in archiepiscopum Cantuar' M. Par. *Min.* I 316; **1229** ea agere que regie placeant serenitati .. ∼e cupientes *Reg. S. Osm.* II 99; **1229** †∼e supplicantes *Foed.* I 308b (= *Cl* 234: affectuose); nonne .. solus Deus .. ∼issime est amandus Bradw. *CD* 64A; **1434** omnes et singulos .. ∼e rogamus et exhortamur .. *Pri. Cold.* 108.

effectuosus, earnest, heart-felt. *V. et. affectuosus.*

benignitatem regiam .. flectere allectivis precibus et ∼is incepere alloquiis *Ps.*-Elmh. *Hen. V* 63 p. 175.

1 effectus [CL]

1 fulfilment, accomplishment. **b** (phil.) actualization. **c** (w. *cum*) effectively; *v. et.* 5b *infra, effectualiter.*

barbari .. testantur se cuncta insulae .. depopulaturos. nec mora, minas ∼ibus prosequuntur Gildas *EB* 23; sancti doctores numquam ab invicem vel in assertione veritatis vel in ∼u dilectionis discrepant Bede *Tab.* 412; ∼um piae postulationis consecutus est *Id. HE* I 4; genitrix .. praesagium futuri ∼us .. vidit Ælf. *Æthelwold* 2; ∼ibus, i. operibus, monitionibus vel *dædum GlH* E 104; constantis viri affectum, sapientis animi ∼um, optimi consilii profectum laudare .. debemus G. Mon. IX 17; ut iniquitatis affectum facilius perduxerint ad ∼um Gir. *TH* III 21; puto quod .. minister Anglie .. poterit .. quod voluerit sanctitatis vestre consideratio ∼ui desiderato mancipare Ad. Marsh *Ep.* 8 p. 91; **c1270** etc. (v. capere 15d); **s1307** (v. demandare 1c); **1347** considerantes quod negocia ipsa .. nequaquam ad presens poterant optatum sortiri ∼um (*Treugae*) Avesb. 116b; **1473** per egregia beneficia in ∼u posita *Lit. Cant.* III 270; **1554** ad ∼um producebatur (v. dotatio 2b). **b** visus exiens in ∼um est visus formalis in visu materiali exiens J. Blund *An.* 59. **c** **1269** Willelmo .. annuas xx m. .. persolvent donec eidem W. .. in beneficio .. Robertus .. providerit cum ∼u *Cl* 93; **1276** supplicamus quatinus dictas villas .. ecclesie nostre velitis restituere cum ∼u *Reg. Heref.* I 30; **1412** judices causas .. infra tres dies .. terminent et finiant cum ∼u *StatOx* 215; **1543** quilibet .. persolvat realiter et cum ∼u sub pena excommunicationis *Conc. Scot.* I cclvi.

2 purport, gist. **b** (w. *in*) to all intents, virtually.

1319 ∼us verborum *Conc.* II 496a; **c1400** dixi .. tunc plura alia verba hujusmodi. sed iste quodammodo efectus illius diei Wyche *Ep.* 532; **s1400** sequitur tenor ∼us literarum .. regis Francie Ad. Usk 51; **1442** juxta vim, formam, et ∼um statutorum *MunAcOx* 529. **b** si sint diverse anime, contingit hominem habere tres animas in ∼u J. Blund *An.* 37; **1345** quod .. ipse te per verba protrahens nihil voluit facere in ∼u (*Lit. Papae*) Ad. Mur. *Chr.* 177; **1482** (v. 1 cornagium a).

3 (w. *ad*) on purpose, to the end (that).

1335 citacionem .. mandavimus fieri .. publice .., ad ∼um ut in lucem .. veritas deducatur *Lit. Cant.* II 81; **1412** ad ∼um quod custodes .. defendant stacionarium .. et ad ∼um quod non fiat decepcio *StatOx* 216; **1458** ubi diversi milites .. et alii .. fuerant obligati .. alicui dictorum consanguineorum nostrorum .. ad ∼um ad standum ipsorum regimini *Reg. Whet.* I 305.

4 effect, result, consequence. *V. et. efficere* 3d.

Anselm I 22, J. Sal. *SS* 960C (v. 2 causa 4a); oculus videns ∼um credit se videre causam illius ∼us J. Blund *An.* 110; possunt in memoria simul reponi ymagines duorum contrariorum; nec tamen .. contrarie sunt, quoniam ipsi non sunt immediati ∼us contrariorum, immo valde remoti ∼us *Ib.* 291; effectus cessat causa cessante H. Avr. *Hugh* 457; sunt quatuor prime et principales [elementorum proprietates], sc. caliditas, frigiditas, siccitas, humiditas. .. dicuntur etiam principales quia ab eis omnes secundarii ∼us oriuntur Bart. Angl. IV 1; **s1252** causa .. adventus sui multos latuit in principio, sed ∼us per opera causam postea patefecit M. Par. *Maj.* V 346; posita causa proxima et immediata, ponitur ∼us Bacon VII 84; quoad cognicionem virtutum stellarum quas influunt in inferiora mundi et ∼uum inde causatorum in eisdem Kilwardby *OS* 73.

5 emotion, feeling, disposition, frame (of mind); *v. et. affectus* 1b. **b** (w. *cum*) earnestly; *v. et.* 1c *supra, affectuose.*

in amorem et ∼um [v. l. affectum] Judae traditoris sponte corruistis Gildas *EB* 108; devotae mentis ∼um [*edd.*: affectum] ostendens Aldh. *PR* 143; **801** si paternae valetudinis ∼um scire curam habetis .. Alcuin *Ep.* 228; Osb. Bawdsey clxxiii (v. conversio 4a). **b** **1228** pro qua [concordia] .. laborare proponit cum ∼u *Pat* 213; oro cum ∼u Ad. Marsh *Ep.* 207 (v. consolatorie); **s1272** Edwardus a rege Francie terras que sibi .. competebant peciit cum ∼u *Flor. Hist.* III 31; **1291** presenciam ipsius domini regis Anglie peto cum ∼u *Anglo-Scot. Rel.* 47 (cf. ib. 45 *n.* 4); **a1350** quod pene commisse ad augmentum ciste communis .. per regentes sine dilacione cum ∼u petantur *StatOx* 68.

2 effectus v. efficere. **effegies** v. effigies 4.

effeminare [CL], to unman, make effeminate (partly fig.). **b** (p. ppl., sts. as sb. m.) effeminate, weak.

∼at, evirat *GlC* E 64; ∼avit, *fylde GlP* 393; quod laudi alius duceret illum pro auro velle ∼are W. Malm. *Mir. Mariae* 139; quem, queso, .. magis ∼avit lascivia? P. Blois *Serm.* 759C; ∼atos a feminis viros debita virilitate femine depredantur Gir. *TH* I 12; qui transvehit ipsum animus ad omnes victorias a seipso ∼atur; sed infeminatur, quoniam in femineam transit impotentiam Map *NC* III 5 f. 42v.; aspicio .. ∼antes blandimentorum mollities Ad. Marsh *Ep.* 38; **c1430** (v. effeminatio); Kymer 19 (v. ereos). **b** ∼atus, exinanitus *GlC* E 56; **9..** ∼ati, molles *oðde bædlingas WW*; W. Malm. *GR* V 393 (v. curia 3b); **s1298** tua inercia et ∼ata ignavia me .. provocant ad tue juris patrie liberacionem Fordun *Cont.* XI 34; ∼ati sunt qui habent mores femineos .. et sunt inepti ad generandum Gad. 37v. 1.

effeminate [CL], effeminately, weakly.

∼ate, i. molliter *GlH* E 100; omnis bonus tanto alacrius resurgit quanto se a veritate ∼ius exorbitasse recognoscit H. Los. *Ep.* 12; quicquid viriliter incepit ∼e reliquit H. Hunt. *HA* VIII 17.

effeminatio [CL], effeminacy, enervation.

s1298 Scotti .. per xxx annos .. Anglos .. sepe protriverunt; quod quidem infortunium dolo et ∼oni Anglorum multi deputarunt Higd. VII 40; **c1430** cum talis ∼onis invasionisque sit vis vigorque libidinis, fugiatis, consulimus, omne consorcium effeminans *Reg. Whet.* II app. 461.

effeminativus, that makes effeminate, weak, or unmanly.

[voluptas carnalis] est ∼a vigoris potencie militaris Holcot *Wisd.* 79.

efferare [CL], **a** to brutalize, barbarize. **b** to enrage. **c** (p. ppl.) savage, ferocious.

a silvescunt [homines] et ∼antur inopia discipline R. Niger *Mil.* II 41. **b** W. Malm. *GP* III 100 (v. ductare b); affuerunt .. plurimi qui .. dicerent ipsum regem pacificum et non scelerum ultorem et quecunque possent eum ∼are Map *NC* V 6 f. 69v. **c** ∼atiores suave Christi jugum suscipiunt Gosc. *Aug. Maj.* 86; ∼atus, sevitia elatus Osb. Glouc. *Deriv.* 202; ∼atis animis in edes Albani irruunt W. S. Alb. *V. Alb. & Amphib.* 11; **s1307** erat .. Edwardus [II] .. adversus hostes suos infortunatus, in domesticos ∼atus Higd. VII 41 p. 298.

efferatio [LL], brutalization.

quia .. in tanto populo non †omnis [? l. omnes] occupat ∼o, suggerit justitie ratio ut electi de populo .. mittantur explorare promisse terre merita [cf. *Jos.* ii] R. Niger *Mil.* II 42; ferus componitur efferus .. et inde .. ∼o Osb. Glouc. *Deriv.* 209.

efferbere v. effervere. **efferiateuli** v. ferituale.

efferre [CL]

1 to carry out, bring away.

Alexander Macedo paucos de valle .. lapidum extulit *Lib. Monstr.* III 11; ita ut .. non posset de cubiculo .. foras ∼ri Bede *HE* V 4; **9..** ∼ri, *beran WW*; vix potuit fato pastorem efferre locello Frith. 415; leaena catulos ∼t, locum abscedendo trepidis offert Hon. *Spec. Eccl.* 897A; mox inde sese jussit ∼i Ord. Vit. III 3 p. 52.

2 a to emit (sound), uplift (voice). **b** to utter, pronounce. **c** to express (gram.). **d** to make known, publish, spread abroad.

a elata in altum voce Bede *HE* III 2; synodus elata respondit voce beata Frith. 295; vox cum quodam impetu ∼tur *Quaest. Salern.* B 272; bellica tuba .. musicam ∼t consonantiam Gir. *TH* III 12. **b** nisi tam leviter tum ∼tur [littera U] ut vix sentiri queat Bede *AM* 84. **c** dictio qua tempus rei gerendae significatur, si veluti ad quaestionem 'quamdiu?' redditum ponitur, .. per accusativum vel ablativum ∼ri potest Linacre *Emend. Lat.* 262. **d** ut in proverbium et derisum longe lateque ∼retur quod Britanni nec in bello fortes sint nec in pace fideles Gildas *EB* 6; **1103** quod [privilegium] ita mitto vobis ut illud nec in publicum ∼atis nec transcribi faciatis Anselm (*Ep.* 307) IV 230; J. Sal. *Pol.* 545C (v. cyriadoxa); cum prima meos [sc. Veneris] lux extulit ortus, / fovi hominem J. Exon. *BT* II 466.

3 to lift up; **b** (w. *calcaneus*; *cf. John* xiii 18). **c** to carry aloft. **d** (p. ppl. *elatus*) lofty, prominent.

viderat .. animam sanctam .. ad coelum ∼ri *V. Cuthb.* I 5; cum .. abbatissa intus .. ossa elatura et dilutura intrasset Bede *HE* IV 17 p. 245; ut corpus virgineum levaretur et altius ∼retur W. Malm. *GR* II 218; regum .. occisorum quorum cadavera elata sunt et in rogis combusta Trevet *Troades* 13. **b** J. Sal. *Pol.* 465D, **1174** (v. calcaneus 2c). **c** **s1244** M. Par. *Maj.* IV 393 (v. crucifer 2b). **d** qui quolibet ∼iorem gigante nanum ictu fecit unico Map *NC* III 2 f. 37; naso mediocriter ∼o Gir. *EH* II 8; *Ps.*-Elmh. *Hen. V* 6 (v. brevitas a).

4 to exalt (in status); **b** (refl.). **c** (p. ppl. *elatus*) puffed up (w. pride), haughty.

a690 cur .. Hibernia .. ineffabili quodam privilegio ∼atur? Aldh. *Ep.* 5; **706** si pontificem, qui vos nutrivit et extulit, in exilio solum dimiseritis *Ib.* 9 (12); J. Sal. *Met.* 825C (v. disponere 3e); in his avibus .., degenerante masculorum privilegio, virilius .. feminei sexus ∼untur Gir. *TH* I 12. **b** diabolus .. adversus Deum se extulit G. Crispin *Serm.* 113; nobiles .. admonendi sunt ne se ∼rant aut inaniter glorientur de sua nobilitate J. Waleys *Commun.* III 3. 1. **c** onagri .. ∼a exultantes fortitudine saxa de montibus evellunt *Lib. Monstr.* II 3; maluit elatum regis differre tumorem Frith. 1055; **a1075** hoc .. ignorantia magis quam spiritus ∼i pertinatia agebat Lanfr. *Ep.* (3); elatus, livens, irascens, segnis, avarus, / ventrosus, petulans in sua damna ruunt Garl. *Tri. Eccl.* 10; dux Hibernie, ∼us de honoribus quos .. rex impendebat eidem *V. Ric. II* 84; o mens elata, presumpcio dira Gower *VC* III 729; **s1455** (v. elevare 2d).

5 to extol.

a690 domino venerabili, praeconio ∼endo et sanctorum meritis .. honorando Aldh. *Ep.* 5; altum ingenium, / .. / quod idcirco non effero / laude quavis nec reffero / quia .. (Æthelwald) *Carm. Aldh.* 5. 63; omnes praesidem ∼unt Augustinum Gosc. *Transl. Aug.* 25A; hos .. perspicax Beda laudibus extulit Ord. Vit. IV 6 p. 207; si veris cupias efferri laudibus, / non eas compares ab assentantibus Walt. Wimb. *Palpo* 50.

efferus [CL], savage, untamed.

∼a fluctuum ferocitas Aldh. *VirgP* 34; effera stans inimica mea sustollitur alta Hwætberht 27 (*Humilitas et Superbia*) 3; ∼us, i. †sevreus [MS: severus], ferox, †mansuetus [MS: immansuetus], *reþa*, contrarius *GlH* E 91; edes / nisibus †efferis verruncare parabant Frith. 1115; Wulf. *Swith.* II 100 (v. dominatrix a); ut ∼e temeritatis haberent auctoritatem *V. Ed. Conf.* 50v.; gens occidentalis, audax et ∼a, diuturnam unius populi dedignatur dominationem W. Malm. *GR* IV 360; familie / timentes effere dant locum manie Walt. Wimb. *Carm.* 529; *Ib.* 642 (v. dispulverare).

effervēre, ∼vĕre [CL]

1 to be intensely hot, to boil over. **b** to rage, erupt (of anger, strife, or sim.); **c** (of desire); **d** (fig.).

eferbuit, incanduit *GlH* E 106; †efferre, ∼vere, calfacere, ebullire Osb. Glouc. *Deriv.* 194; divine fervorem caritatis meridiem appellaverim, cum sol ea hora luxerit et ∼buerit in virtute sua J. Ford *Serm.* 58. 12. **b** cujus crudelitas .. super miseras plebes nimium ∼buit Ord. Vit. III 3 p. 47; ∼buit illo in tempore .. persecutio *V. G. Sempr.* *xvii; **s1321** quo et acrius regis rigor erga peregrinos ∼buit Knighton I 426; postquam .. utrimque ∼buisset duricies belli *G. Hen. V* 16 (cf. ib. 21: cum .. ∼buisset bellancium feritas); judicis ira / efferbet; nunc tela pluet; nunc fulmina mittet *V. Ed. Conf. Metr.* I 452. **c** spiritu vehementiori ∼bui quo aliqua .. digna relatu adiscere concupivi *Cuthb. Hib. pref.*; caro ∼buit Gir. *GE* II 10 (v. dolium 1a); cum cognovissem quod ex interiori solummodo ∼buisset [fervor] et non esset a carne illud incendium Rolle *IA* 145 (cf. ib. 239: non ∼buit cor meum in concupiscenciam corporalem). **d** quantus et quam dulcis tunc ∼buit odor suavitatis Herm. Arch. 20.

2 (of persons) to rage. **b** (trans.) to keep (anger) on the boil.

[comes Glaornie] in regales crudelissime ∼vebat *G. Steph.* II 87. **b** **s1254** a curia indignanter recessit, indignationem suam pro loco et tempore ∼biturus M. Par. *Maj.* V 436.

effeta v. ephphetha.

effetus [CL], worn out, exhausted (also as sb.).

∼a voluntate Aldh. *VirgP* 50 (v. efficere 2b); ∼a mulier, frequenti partu fatigata *GlC* E 69; ∼um, †*ontudri* [? l. *ortudri*] *Ib.* 73; **798** Entellus [cf. Virgil *Aen.* V 387–484] .. ∼o corpore .. caestus deposuit suos Alcuin *Ep.* 145; ∼o, i. sine foetu, ebetato, debilitato, evacuato, exinanito, *ortydre GlH* E 95; quod ∼us de ∼a potest generare contra naturam est R. Melun *Paul.* 79; effeta senectus H. Avr. *CG* f. 8. 15 (v. ephphetha).

effevus v. 2 ephoebus. **effibulare** v. exfibulare.

efficacia [CL]

1 (of persons or their actions) efficiency, ability.

nolite scrutari scrutinia, ne deficiatis in ∼ia vestra Alcuin (*Adv. Elipand.*) *Dogm.* 294D; Mauritius .., quam-

vis in quibusdam minus prospere fame, predicabilis tamen ~ie W. MALM. *GP* II 73; nec ~iam, qua sublimitas ejus [Creatoris] .. a nobis enarrari possit, habemus ORD. VIT. III *prol.* p. 1; **1310** (v. commentariensis b); **1336** vobis .. mandamus quod .. diligenciam .. apponatis et ad hoc cum ~ia laboretis *RScot* 403b.

2 (of things) efficacy, potency; **b** (spiritual). **c** intensity. **d** force, validity (log.); **e** (leg.).

venenum .. omnem malignitatis ~iam prorsus amittit GIR. *TH* I 29; sinape Phitagoras inter ea que habent virtutis ~iam laudat *Alph.* 172. **b** Spiritus Sanctus duobus modis in ea [B.V.M.] divinae duae potentiae ~iam ostendit BEDE *Hom.* I 3. 12; que verbis dicebat, mirabili signorum ~ia in ipsorum [audientium] oculis sic esse comprobabat EADMER *Wilf.* 52; **c1218** quod .. efficacior sit et utilior nunc baptismus quam olim circumcisio apparet; nam de ~ia circumcisionis dicitur: .. 'cujus prepucii caro ..' [cf. *Gen.* xvii 14]. .. de virtute autem et ~ia baptismi dicitur: 'qui renatus fuerit ..' [cf. *John* iii 5] *Conc. Syn.* 67; hujusmodi vie ~iam .. innuit Salvator [cf. *John* v 36] DUNS *Ord.* I 83; **1329** vehemens .. est in eisdem regibus hujusmodi ~ia unccionis *Mon. Hib. & Scot.* 244b; de eis [oracionibus] jam dixi iiij magnas ~ias [ME: *efficaces*] quare sunt diligende *AncrR* 91. **c** est pallii [mei] viriditas ad quantitatem major, smaragdi vero ad ~iam ADEL. *QN* 2. **d** tua interrogatio facit me suspectum, ne forte in illis aliqua lateat ~ia ANSELM (*Gram.* 4) I 149; si rationum non contradicitur ~iis AD. MARSH *Ep.* 59. **e** **1306** volentes omnimodas occupaciones, extorsiones et exacciones .. nullius ~ie de cetero haberi *BBC* (*Swansea*) 15; **1447** quod idem ingressus .. adeo validus et efficax ac talis vigoris, ~ie et valoris in lege existat prout esset una liberacio generalis aut specialis *Cl* 297 m. 16; **1569** quam .. declaracionem volumus tante esse fortitudinis et ~ie ac si .. *Scot. Grey Friars* II 208.

3 putting into effect, fulfilment.

~ia, perfectio *GlC* E 57; **s1139** ille [rex] .., malorum .. preventus consiliis, nullam bonarum promissionum exhibuit ~iam W. MALM. *HN* 477; rege Willelmo [I] pluribus .. intento .., voti pretaxati ~iam .. diutius .. intermisit *Chr. Battle* f. 12.

efficaciter [CL], effectually, so as to produce (intended) effect. **b** intensely, perceptibly. **c** w. full legal effect.

~iter, *fromlice GlC* E 88; **c750** quod .. alio .. in tempore melius ~iusque adimplere me posse non arbitror quam modo nunc (ÆTHELBERT) *Ep. Bonif.* 105; ~iter, i. †velociter [MS: velociter], *caflice, scearplice GlH* E 115; animos ~ius ut provocet GIR. *TH* I 12; *Id. GE* II 10 (v. dure 1); **c1242** (v. consiliatio a); ut ~ius inducatur auditor ad operacionem eorum que hic persuadentur DUNS *Ord.* I 231. **b** ut .. tanto magis amor confessionis .. dulcesceret .. quanto virtutis istius sublimitas ~ius appareret OSB. *Mir. Dunst.* 19; sunt .. omnes herbe .. magis .. quantitativе frigide, earumdem quedam magis ~iter calide ADEL. *QN* 2; per innumerabilium animarum salutem, quas Deo lucratus est, ~issime in sancta ecclesia claruit RIC. HEX. *Hist. Hex.* I 3; ut quemadmodum Petrus ita ille [Cornelius] ~iter placeret Deo J. BURY *Glad. Sal.* 597. **c** **1238** manucepimus ~iter quod .. mitti facient cartam .. in hec verba *Reg. Paisley* 26.

efficativus, that effects or brings about.

duas [cruces] usque in presens miraculorum ~as extruxit J. FURNESS *Kentig.* 41 p. 233.

efficax [CL]

1 (of person or unspec.) efficient, effective, active.

~ax, *from GlC* E 89; ~ax, i. citus, expeditus, .., peritus, *arud* .., *hwæt GlH* E 113; da mihi .. veracem mentem et ~acem ANSELM (*Or.* 1) III 5; [Hen. I] in sermone verax, in promissis ~ax RIC. HEX. *Stand.* f. 37.

2 a efficacious, having (desired) effect; **b** (w. gen.). **c** real, actual. **d** valid (log.); **e** (leg.).

a ~aci oratione .. pii regis Ezechiae .. clxxxv milia exercitus Assyriorum .. prostrata sunt GILDAS *EB* 72; ~aces, expedientes omnia *GlC* E 82; [disciplinalia] assecutiva .., quorum usus ~acior et multiplicior BALSH. *AD rec.* 2 144; contra serpentum .. morsus .. ~ax remedium ferre solent GIR. *TH* I 31; multas .. sacerdoti .. gratias .. referebat, promittens ~aciores multo se gratias ei se relaturum si .. *Ib.* II 19 p. 103; **c1218** (v. efficacia 2b); in radio non est ita ~ax potencia calefaciendi sicut et illuminandi R. MARSTON *QD* 351; oportet eam [justiciam] diligere volicione ~aci DUNS *Ord.* III 123; OCKHAM *Pol.* III 16 (v. delere 2a); ~ax signum *Ziz.* 105 (v. consecrare 2b). **b** remotis etiam .. ad potandum ~ax sanitatis defertur aqua G. FONT. *Inf. S. Edm.* 39. **c** Dei judicio ficta debilitas facta est ei ~acissima GOSC. *Mir. Iv.* lxx. **d** illud argumentum videtur ~ax DUNS *Ord.* III 353. **e** **1447** (v. efficacia 2e).

efficere [CL]

1 to make. **b** to compose.

sacramentum altaris .. non ~it corpus Christi .. sed efficit in homine quod figurat in homine, sc. unitatem ecclesie S. LANGTON *Quaest.* 370 (v. et. 2b infra). **b** hymnos post Numam primum Emmia Timote effecit in Apollinem et musas BONIF. *Met.* 112.

2 to finish, complete. **b** to fulfil, accomplish, put into effect.

quod scriptum est de Aphorismo tecum affer. .. quantum potes de textu primum ~e, deinde .. de glosis ANSELM (*Ep.* 43) III 155. **b** non effecta sed effeta voluntate egreditur ALDH. *VirgP* 50; **801** quod tu ipse non vis facere, alios non permittas propter cupiditatem .. ~ere ALCUIN *Ep.* 217; quamvis multi sint qui hoc melius me possint ~ere [etc.] ANSELM (*Proc. Sp.* 1) II 177; PULL. *Sent.* 936D (v. effectio 1); S. LANGTON *Quaest.* 370 (v. 1a supra); **s1270** idem predecessor noster quod promiserat .. ad effectum perducere nequivit nec successores ejusdem .. id ~ere curarunt *Feod. Durh.* 183*n*.

3 to produce (as effect), bring about; **b** (w. *ut* or *ne*). **c** (pr. ppl. w. *causa* or as sb. n.) efficient cause. **d** (p. ppl. *effectus* as sb. n.) act, effect; *v. et. effectus* 4.

~it, i. perficit, facit, *he gefremeþ* vel *gewyrcþ GlH* E 118; ADEL. *Alch.* 25 (v. ducere 8f); Hibernici in duobus .. instrumentis .. jucundam ~iunt harmoniam BROMPTON 1075 (cf. GIR. *TH* III 11: completur melodia). **b** Aðelstanus .., quem .. nullo modo excitare nec ut homo fieret poteram ~ere WULF. *Æthelwold* 39; quanto saepius .. prioris meae indignitatis recordaris, tanto magis ut .. meo dilectori majores grates rependam .. ~is *Eccl. & Synag.* 54; diabolus .. ~ere vult ut Deus non sit .., in quo sunt omnia G. CRISPIN *Serm.* 113; multi sunt in populo Dei qui .. aliis conjuncti proficiunt, sive ne noceatur ab aliis ~iunt R. NIGER *Mil.* II 7; cave .. ne id intelligendo ~ias ut minus intelligere videaris GIR. *TH* I 13; non id efficient ne dies finiant WALT. WIMB. *Sim.* 84. **c** quod dicitur esse per aliquid videtur esse aut per ~iens aut per materiam aut per aliquod aliud adjumentum ANSELM (*Mon.* 6) I 19; ADEL. *QN* 69 etc. (v. 2 causa 5a); de differentia causarum ~ientium inter primum ~iens et ultimum effectum GROS. 123; BACON XV 206 (v. conservatio 1a); res omnis que fit in hoc mundo exit in esse per ~iens et materiale principium ex quo producitur per virtutem ~ientis *Id. Tert.* 107. **d** nec mora, dicta ~a secuta sunt FELIX *Guthl.* 52; ~um, *deid GlC* E 90; †effatum [l. effectum], *dæd GlH* E 76; illud .. fuit causa, istud est ~um ANSELM (*Orig. Pecc.* 26) II 169; actus ~i est ab efficiente GROS. 120; *Ib.* 123 (v. 3c supra).

4 to cause to be something or of some kind, make, render: **a** (w. acc. & compl.); **b** (w. acc. & inf.). *Cf.* 6 *infra.*

a **749** (12c) ut eam [animam meam] bonis operibus liberam ~erem ab omnibus vinculis piaculorum *CS* 178; **801** [sapientia] potentem gloriosum ~it ALCUIN *Ep.* 229; sinchrisis est cum causam suam quis adversariis nititur ~ere meliorem *Gl. Leid.* 28. 70; [perversi] .. solent eos [rectos] .. in operatione sancta tardiores ~ere ORD. VIT. III 3 p. 51 (cf. ib. IV 4 p. 178: aura hiemalis mare sevissimum ~iebat); **1217** de statu nostro .. vos ~iet cerciores *Pat* 107 (cf. certus 4); **1269** (v. collegiatus a); confessio .. nos filios Dei ~it [ME: *makeð*] *AncrR* 113; **1418** (v. elixir). **b** ut, que in disserendo .. difficile fieri comperiebamus, ea artificiosa facilitate fieri posse ~eremus BALSH. *AD rec.* 2 124; spes refovet multos; spes firma beatius iri / efficit WALT. ANGL. *Fab.* 28. 16.

5 to constitute, make up, (math.) to equal.

ij libre ij ~iunt marcas et insuper j ex ij medietatibus constitutam. ij ergo libre iij constituunt marcas THURKILL *Li.*; duo et tria ~iunt quinque LINACRE *Emend. Lat.* xiii.

6 (pass.) to be made, become: **a** (of persons); **b** (w. ref. to office or status); **c** (of things or abstr.). **d** (w. *in* & acc.) to be made into.

a Saulus .. / credulus efficitur mutato nomine Paulus ALDH. *CE* 4. 2. 2; fratres .. / effecti nimium tristes ALCUIN *WillV* 25. 5; ut .. omnes .. subito velut oves ex lupis ~erentur WULF. *Æthelwold* 40; de stulta protinus ~itur insana L. DURH. *Brig.* 4; de malorum fine certus effectus AILR. *Ed. Conf.* 743D; vidue .. ~iuntur livide et reumatice M. SCOT *Phys.* 6; J. GODARD *Ep.* 220 (v. effrons a); [diabolus], assumpta humana speciei figura, juvenis quidam ~itur *Latin Stories* 85. **b** qui postmodum archiepiscopus in Cantia effectus est ÆLF. *Æthelwold* 16; effectus est monachus in S. Mariae Stou *DB* I 345; modo effectus est unus de villanis *Ib.* II 1; W. MALM. *GP* V 189 (v. 2 conventus 3a); ecclesiarum specialis tutor effectus H. READING (II) *Cel.* 30; **s1214** effectus est major Serlo le Mercer *Leg. Ant. Lond.* 4; [Lanfrancus] effectus est abbas Cadomensis et postmodum presul Cantuariensis HIGD. VII 6. **c** regius morbus, corporis color ~itur sicut pedes accipitur [l. accipitris] *GlC* R 32; crescebat morbus .. et .. gravior effectus est BEDE *HE* IV 29 p. 278; ex genere illius .. ~itur ADEL. *Alch.* 21 (v. ducere 8f); **1293** status ipsius ~itur deterior *SelPlMan* 171; **1359** mercimonia ibidem ducta indies ~iuntur cariora *MGL* I 415; **1365** cor paternum ~itur multipliciter tediosum *FormOx* 367; *Alph.* 126 (v. efflorescere a). **d** 9. . nec patiaris ab †illa [? l. illo] inpune bajulari sed .. aefficiaris ei in conbustionem [AS: *ðu sie gifremmed him on byrne*] (*Adjuratio Ferri, Jud. Dei*) *GAS* 412; **s1452** quomodo lapis ille .. sit reductus effectusque in caput anguli [cf. *Psalm* cxvii 22] *Reg. Whet.* I 20.

7 a to affect; *v. et. afficere* 1a. **b** (w. inf.) to strive; *v. et. afficere* 2b.

a **1270** tedio non mediocriter ~imur *Cl* 290. **b** doce nos quid agamus, quo gradiamur; ostende quid ~iamus operari EGB. *Pont.* 98.

efficialiter, effectively. *Cf. officialiter.*

1425 partem ipsam sic petentem ~er exaudire et justiciam .. impendere non curastis *Reg. Heref.* 63; **14..** constitucio in consilio .. Lond' contra impedientes ecclesiarum rectores quominus decimas .. cariare poterunt impedientes hujusmodi ~er arctavit *Reg. Brev. Orig.* 46b.

efficiatus v. officiare.

efficienter [CL], effectively, as efficient cause.

unde actus meritorii et demeritorii denominant homines ~er esse bonos vel malos WYCL. *Act.* 42.

efficientia [CL], efficient power, production of effect.

~iam, i. operationem, effectum *GlH* E 117; 'veritas' pro manifestatione in sacris saepe litteris reperitur .., quamvis .. quidam exponant hoc in loco esse carnis ac sanguinis 'veritatem' ipsam eorumdem ~iam, id est, peccatorum remissionem LANFR. *Corp. & Sang.* 436C; anima propter diversas suas ~ias diversa sortitur vocabula ROB. BRIDL. *Dial.* 31; **c1301** racio ~ie in Deo prior est racioni exemplari *Quaest. Ox.* 336; conservancia Dei respectu talis [creacionis etc.] convertitur cum ejus ~ia WYCL. *Ente Praed.* 131.

effictio [CL], imaginative creation, devising.

primis et summis hominibus apertiores sunt visiones ac in mentes eorum irradiatio simplicior deitatis. reliquis deinde crassioribus per signa commode indicantur omnia, et morum ~o et Dei excultio et veritatis expectatio COLET *Cel. Hier.* 174 (cf. ib. 169: [theologia] ~onibus poeticis divinarum rerum statum .. discribens).

effigere [cf. CL figere], to fix in place, stake out.

1505 secundum metas ligneas .. per dictum militem effixas *Scot. Grey Friars* II 225.

effigialis, represented in effigy.

1432 apud conductum ecclesie S. Pauli vicinum indivisibilis Trinitatis splendor ~is in .. throno residebat (J. CARPENTER) *MGL* III 462.

effigiare [CL]

1 to shape, model, fashion (an image); **b** (in wax, esp. as votive offering); **c** (fig.).

~iat, pulchre format *GlC* E 55; [abbas Abbendoniae] ejus [S. Letardi] et .. reginae Bertae .. imagines enormi magnitudine ac decore ~iavit GOSC. *Transl. Aug.* 46C; solebant antiquitus Gratiarum simulachra ~iari nuda J. SAL. *Pol.* 488B; **s1377** [Londonienses] in dedecus persone [justiciarii] ~iaverunt simile sibi caput .., quod .. evomeret ore vinum *Chr. Angl.* 153. **b** cera instar lancee illius [qua vulneratus erat] ~iata, .. formam illam .. ad sepulcrum obtulit R. COLD. *Cuthb.* 128; stetit vir ad tumbam martyris, habens pre manibus ceram quam in columbe speciem ~iaverat W. CANT. *Mir. Thom.* V 25; formam brachii curati de cera expressam et ~iatam .. obtulit GIR. *Hug.* III 5; accedens beati regis Henrici sepulcrum, tum presencia sua corporali, tum in cera ~iata, tum muneribus honoravit *Mir. Hen. VI* IV 148 p. 273. **c** [Albinus et Aldelmus] scriptis laudabilia virtutum suarum monimenta posteritati ~iaverunt ORD. VIT. IV 6 p. 207; ut manus Deo consecrate, et que paulo ante .. mundi Salvatoris in altari ~iaverunt imaginem, nunc post tergum ligate publicum latronem effigient H. BOS. *Thom.* III 24 p. 269 (v. et. 2c infra); latrantis Scylle gula in me monstrum sepius ~iat dum me tempus refectionis anticipare compellit J. GODARD *Ep.* 222; voluminis hujus .. connexio .. statue illius simulacrum, ut olim in Daniele [ii 32–3], .. videbitur ~iare *Croyl. Cont. B* 545.

2 to portray, represent, typify: **a** (by visual image); **b** (by language); **c** (by appearance or actions); **d** (by miming); **e** (by symbolism of name).

a figura arboris sic [in lodice] formabiliter ~iate .. videtur suas frondes, quamvis minutas, effundere R. COLD. *Cuthb.* 42; **s1216** multi .. eandem orationem .. picturis ~iarunt hoc modo M. PAR. *Maj.* III 7; **s1234** apparuit ei Dominus .. crucifixus, sicut manibus artificum solet insculptus ~iari *Ib.* 291. **b** cujus [Faritii] laudes ~iare quia successit animo .., Petri monachi versus apponam W. MALM. *GP* II 88; fertur de isto [Joachim abbate] quod quasi prophetice ~iavit mores, actus et numerum omnium virorum apostolicorum qui futuri forent in ecclesia HIGD. VII 22. **c** H. BOS. *Thom.* III 24 (v. 1c supra); jacet ille soporem / effigians mortis H. AVR. *Hugh* 1095. **d** formant voce sues effigiantque grues GARL. *Tri. Eccl.* 122; quemadmodum psittacus idiota auditas voces ~iat R. BURY *Phil.* 6. 96 (= *MunAcOx* 208: †citatus [l. citacus]). **e** effigians mundum, nomen geris, Odo, rotundum [*gl.*: rotundum, id est circulare, quod patet si retro sillabicetur 'Odo'] GARL. *Mor. Scol.* 39.

3 to portray in imagination, imagine. **b** (w. compl.) to picture, represent (as).

~are, imaginare OSB. GLOUC. *Deriv.* 199; cum lego .. 'diliges proximum tuum' [*Luke* x 27] .., proximum absentem spiritu ~io per figuram imaginabilem, sed per formam intelligibilem AD. MARSH *Ep.* 247 cap. 14 p. 456; intelligentia creata .., increata imagine et similitudine ei supersplendente eamque quasi ~iante, formas omnium creatorum per modum idealem .. intelligit *Ps.*-GROS. *Summa* 391; tamquam vobis omnibus ibi presentibus,

vultibus vestris ~iatis valedicens *Croyl. Cont. A* 109. **b** ipsius [regis] .. mores subditorum speculum ~ians W. Malm. *GP* I 18.

4 to disguise.

s**1099** ferebatur Wibertus imaginem ejus [Anselmi] in tabula pingi fecisse, ut, quocumque se habitu ~iaret, non lateret W. Malm. *GP* I 55; s**1295** vallatus quatuor tortoribus larvatis et ~iatis in serabaris et pelliciis *Flor. Hist.* III 282 (cf. ib. 95).

5 to imagine, invent, devise. **b** (w. inf.) to plan.

~iata insignia .. conseruisse B. *V. Dunst.* 1 (v. 2 diffidere e). **b** effigiare cave vitam tibi tollere prave R. Cant. *Malch.* III 306.

effigiatim, in the form of an image, symbolically.

unitas hec militaris unitatis illius triumphalis .. similitudo est ~im expressa H. Bos. *LM* 1390B.

effigiatio, imaginative construction.

agitur vita sensus in susceptione specierum sensibilium vita spiritus in ~one figurarum imaginabilium, vita intellectus in apprehensione formarum intelligibilium Ad. Marsh *Ep.* 247 cap. 14 p. 455.

effigies [CL]

1 effigy, image, portrait: **a** (in sculpture or sim.); **b** (in embroidery or sim.); **c** (in language).

a falsas effigies, quas glauco marmore sculpunt, / .. / .. veterum .. deorum Aldh. *VirgV* 1340; tertium signum est imago Colosei, quam quidam .. Rome ~iem dicunt Greg. *Mir. Romae* 6; s**1415** in cujus [gigantis] dextro latere stetit ~ies, non multum minoris magnitudinis, muliebris *G. Hen. V* 15 p. 102; ~iem antilupi *Ib.* p. 104 (v. antilops); **1432** septem deifice virtutes in puellaribus ~iebus (J. Carpenter) *MGL* III 459; **1447** quod .. ponat supra sepulcrum meum .. lapidem marmoreum cum ~ie et insignibus doctoris legum *MunAcOx* 557. **b** fit eadem malorum punicorum ~ies ex hyacintho et purpura [cf. *Exod.* xxviii 33] Bede *Tab.* 476; fabrica intextilis .. et tam florum quam bestiolarum inserta ~ies R. Cold. *Cuthb.* 42. **c** Protei poetice commentatam ~iem H. Bos. *LM* 1373C.

2 likeness, appearance, visible form. **b** imitation, parody.

bella puella, / quam prius effigies turpabat torva senectae Aldh. *VirgV* 605; qui ~iem .. Paulini referre esset solitus, quod esset vir longae staturae, .. facie macilenta Bede *HE* II 16; haec indumenta sanctitatis ~iem ostendentia .. sanctificare facias Egb. *Pont.* 114; **9..** ~iae, *on hiwe WW*; egestio carbonis ~iem preferebat W. Cant. *Mir. Thom.* II 64; in unoquoque folliculo [matricis] .. dicunt medici inpressam formulam humane ~iei Ric. Med. *Anat.* 231; angeli .. ~iem mutare possunt *Quaest. Salern.* B 24 (cf. ib. 175: si .. spermata temperate conveniant, fetus utriusque protendit ~iem, partim patris, partim matris); nullam in .. habitatione terrena repertam cujusvis animantis ~iem cujus similitudinem non liceat in piscibus .. ab umbilico superius speculari Gerv. Tilb. III 63; quomodo angeli in ~ie corporali depingantur Bart. Angl. II 3 *tit.*; [corpus regium] in currum .. imponitur, posita alia ymagine portante sani regis ~iem super corpus .. inclusum W. Say *Lib. Reg. Cap.* 114. **b 1448** matrimonium, quinverius ~iem matrimonii (*Court Bk. Linc.*) *Eng. Clergy* 223.

3 (?) phantom.

Anglia demones quosdam habet — demones, inquam, nescio dixerim an secretas et ignote generationis ~ies — quos Galli Neptunos, Angli Portunos nominant Gerv. Tilb. III 61.

4 mould.

a mulde to cast in, duca, dormula, †effegies, patrona *CathA.*

effimatus v. ophiomachus. **effimericus** v. ephemericus. **effimerum** v. ephemerus.

†effimoleus [? cf. ἐπιμελής], (?) guardian angel.

dicat hoc nomen in aure suspecti: "recede demon vel exi, quia ~ei tibi precipiunt!" Gad. 61. 2.

effingere [CL], to imagine, picture.

cum secundum vocem tantum auditam rem prorsus ignotam sibi conatur animus ~ere Anselm (*Resp. Insip.* 5) I 128.

efflagitare [CL], to demand, beseech (urgently); **b** (w. *ut* or inf.); **c** (w. abstr. subj.).

~at, petit *GlC* E 86; reminiscatur [lector], ~o, quia regnum Dei non in verborum facundia .. persistit Felix *Guthl. prol.* (cf. ib. 43: ~ata licentia); apostolicus .. quidquid potest .. religiosorum virorum in opus evangelii ~are .. undique .. genti certat delegare Gosc. *Aug. Min.* 752D; **1105** responsionem, si placet, per eosdem ~o Anselm (*Ep.* 388) V 332; quo in loco .. Dei clementiam piis precibus ~es .., donec .. F. Malm. *V. Aldh.* 81D; quando quis voluit intendere interdictum, debuit ~are a pretore Vac. *Lib. Paup.* 246. **b 680** vestram fraternitatem adjurantes suppliciter ~amus ut .. decreta B. Petri .. non abominemini Aldh. *Ep.* 4; **1063** praecordialiter ~o ut vos .. hujus .. discordiae malum .. abolere festinetis (*Lit. W. presbyteri*) Ord. Vit. III 7 p. 98; c**1077** quidquid .. vestro placuerit judicio, ut mihi .. notum fieri jubeatis ~o Anselm (*Ep.* 72) III 194; vobis ~o .. me habere .. excusatum *Dictamen* 368. **c** jam promissus rerum ordo ~at ut .. pedum regulas .. propalare non abnuas Aldh. *PR* 112; **1167** cum nostra seu nostrorum necessitas ~at amicorum, confidenter ad vos ingredimur G. Foliot *Ep.* 189; hujus modus sermonis jam finem ~at J. Ford *Serm.* 15. 10.

efflare [CL]

1 to breathe out. **b** to gasp out (words). **c** (w. *spiritum* or sim., or absol.) to give up the ghost, die.

quidam spirituum .. de ore ac naribus ignem putidum ~antes angebant Bede *HE* V 12 p. 306; teterrimi spiritus ab illo abysso †mmergebant [l. emergebant], putidum ignem de ore et naribus ~antes Hon. *Spec. Eccl.* 898A. **b** multa in hunc modum verba doloris ~averat Devizes 33v. **c** expertus calloso corpore lepram / .. efflavit flamen in auras Aldh. *VirgV* 2425; ~abant, mortui sunt *GlC* E 62; illa [Eadgitha] predicta die citra juvente terminum ~avit W. Malm. *GR* II 218; cum .. spiritum ~aret *Id. GP* II 94; cum hic ad extrema veniret et ultimum spiritum jam ~are crederetur P. Cornw. *Rev.* II 892; ipso [fratre] .. †afflante spiritum, oculi ejus claudentur *Obs. Barnwell* 216; in uno .. cruce pendeant / ut simul animas efflare valeant Walt. Wimb. *Carm.* 596.

2 to blow out (fig.), extinguish. **b** to blow away (fig.).

s**1227** summam tam ardui negotii .. ad nihilum redactam ~avit consilium malignantium *Flor. Hist.* II 188; c**1430** ne ventosi folles oris tociens in amoris faculas exerceant suas vires ut tandem .. incipiant ~ate deficere, ut carbones *Reg. Whet.* II app. 413. **b** at pia ventilabro Christi sententia justo / efflavit paleas Frith. 1120.

efflatio [LL], (w. *spiritus*) last gasp, death.

ad ~onem spiritus perductus est W. Cant. *Mir. Thom.* IV 5.

efflator, one who breathes out or utters.

non abstinuit [Elsinus] quin furias mente confotas evomeret. .. sed illo exacto die, cum rabiei ~or cubili se dedisset .. W. Malm. *GP* I 17; inter ceteros trivialium tramitum protritores ac sesquipedalium verborum ~ores Higd. I *prol.* p. 6.

efflictim [CL], agonizingly, in torment.

~im, cruciabiliter Osb. Glouc. *Deriv.* 202.

effloratus v. deflorare 2c.

efflorescere [CL], **efflorēre** [LL], to flower, to blossom (to the full). **b** to finish flowering (fig.). **c** to flourish; **d** (w. abstr. subj.).

nimphea .. semen habet in medio croceum; sed, cum ~uerit, rotundum efficitur *Alph.* 126. **b** ~uisti plane; evacuati sunt flores tui et non sunt reservati ad messem G. Hoyland *Ascet.* 278A; s**1306** timeto .. nequando, tanquam flos agri qui 'hodie est .. ' [*Matth.* vi 30], sic ~eas *Flor. Hist.* III 130. **c 798** gratum habeo laicos .. ad evangelicas ~uisse inquisitiones Alcuin *Ep.* 136 p. 205; [R. de Monte Gomerici] inter maximos optimates maxime ~uit Ord. Vit. IV 7 p. 221. **d** nihil .. tam bene tractatur quod per te non posset luculentius ~ere Adel. *QN intr.* p. 2; c**1450** nil in materia reperiens .. honestis obvium moribus, quin pocius .. contemplancium quies ~eret *Reg. Whet.* I 151.

effluenter, copiously, lavishly. *V. et. affluenter.*

s**1306** siclades auro texte ~issime (v. 1 cyclas 1a); ut .. ad regem venirent, de sua garderoba cuncta militaria ornamenta ~issime admissuri J. Lond. *Commend. Ed. I* 16.

effluentia [LL], outpouring (of bounty).

uberes dotes ejus [Ed. I] .. qui trahit ~ia largitatis ut adamas *Fleta prol.*

effluere [CL]

1 to flow out or ebb; **b** (fig.). **c** to derive, descend. **d** (phil.) to emanate. **e** (of garment) to slip off.

ut ~eret noxius umor qui inerat Bede *HE* IV 17 p. 245; quare in quibusdam provinciis mare ~at et refluat et in quibusdam non? *Quaest. Salern.* N 58; quolibet unda die refluit bis et effluit illic Garl. *Tri. Eccl.* 65; venas capitales, ex quibus ab ejus capite acutis spinis coronato sanguis ~xit [ME: *þet bledden on his heaved*] *AncrR* 95. **b** omnium bonorum copia plenis ~ebat cornibus W. Malm. *GP* I 18; lapis fluens percusso latere / petre latus presignat libere, / quo fluenta sciunt effluere / et nos aqua viva reficere J. Howd. *Ph.* 936. **c** ex Woden .. Elle originaliter ~xit R. Cold. *Osw.* 1 p. 339. **d** liquet eum [Creatorem] in singulorum creatione venerabilis exempli normam secutum. .. hec in ipso ab ipso non discrepat; ~ens intelligentiam perficit; derivata intellectus fit forma. .. ~entem materie inhabilitate non percipimus; derivatam pauci admodum et laboriose .. assequuntur Alf. Angl. *Cor* 15. 1–2; forme .. vel species mentis angelice .. ~unt ab essencia divina W. Macclesfield *Quaestione* f. 6v. **e** si tantum idonee lorica corpori coaptetur ligaturis suis, ne ~at R. Niger *Mil.* I 5.

2 (of persons): **a** (w. p. ppl. *s. act.*) having burst out. **b** to be voluble (in speech). **c** to be lavish (in bounty). **d** to wander at large.

a s**1202** Arthurus .. totus ~xus in lacrymas et .. querimonias Oxnead *Chr.* 114. **b** Lanfrancus .. gesta scripto excepit .. modeste .., ut nec scienda pretermitteret nec dicendo ~eret W. Malm. *GP* I 42; macte Paris — quid enim numerandis improba veris / effluo et in titulos suspiro prodiga J. Exon. *BT* II 406; vir .. mollito super oleum ~ens sermone Gir. *TH* III 52; inter varios quibus ~unt sermones *Id. DK* I 16 p. 195. **c** in .. largitione .. longe pre ceteris ~ebat *Id. GE* II 27 p. 297. **d** quasi indomitus et effrenis per seculi devia excurri, †~i [? l. effluxi], erravi in invio H. Bos. *Thom.* IV 13 p. 367.

3 a (of time) to flow by, elapse; **b** (p. ppl. *s. act.*). **c** (of events) to slip (of memory).

a jam agenti in tenebris tertius ~xerat annus Ailr. *Ed. Conf.* 763D; nulla fere dies ~ebat ei qua non ipse aliqua magna largiretur donaria W. Fitzst. *Thom.* 12; si due [consonantes] precedunt vocalem et tercia sequatur (*sic*), necesse unum ad minus tempus in prolacione illarum ~ere *Ps.*-Gros. *Gram.* 26; non multum tempus ~xerat *Arthur & Gorlagon* 10. **b 1293** post terminum .. peremptorium completum totaliter et ~xum *DCCant. Reg.* Q f. 53a; **1302** de primo anno jam ~xo *MGL* II 232; **1325** tempus .. archiepiscopi, infra quod ecclesiam debuit contulisse, totaliter est ~xum *Lit. Cant.* I 136; c**1350** infra certum peremptorie terminum competentem jam ~xum *MunAcOx* 170; **1458** (v. curriculum 3); **1474** tricesimo die mensis Julii ultimo ~xo *RScot* 444b. **c** s**1470** quum ea que multis jam retroactis ~xere seculis .. ad agnicionem modernorum minime pervenerunt *Croyl. Cont. B* 545.

effluxio [LL], a flood, flowing in (of tide). **b** lapse (of time).

a J. Sal. *Pol.* 640C (v. defluxio a); si ab occidente prior et velocior fiat ~o, multitudinem aquarum ad orientem impellit *Quaest. Salern.* N 58; c**1350** cum unus ager .. eidem [ecclesie] decimabilis .. per aquas maris inundatus exsisterat (*sic*) .., octo annis ultra ultimo (*sic*) effluxionem .. ballivus .. archiepiscopi, asserens decimas .. ad ecclesiam cathedralem tanquam de novale (*sic*) pertinere debere, .. eas .. occupavit *Reg. Rough* 267. **b 1393** corruptela .. inolevit, cui nulla dierum ~o nullaque revolucio .. temporum .. poterit suffragari *Conc.* III 219a.

effluxus [cf. CL fluxus], efflux, flowing out (phil.).

non secundum motum qui est ab uno termino in alterum sed secundum ~um qui est ab agente in factum R. Orford *Sciendum* 56.

†effocale [cf. focale], fuel or (?) *f. l.*

1304 cum duabus carectatis †effocal[is, ? l. de focali] contra hyemem *AncD* C 5273.

1 effodere [CL]

1 to dig up, out, or for (partly fig.). **b** to excavate. **c** to dig through (w. ref. to *Ezek.* viii 8–9).

belvis effossum funesto corpus ab antro Aldh. *VirgV* 1570; **8..** ~iant, *up adelfað WW*; sociis .. volentibus eum jam circum obrutum ~ere W. Cant. *Mir. Thom.* III 1; veteres celestis depositi thesauros libet ~ere R. Cold. *Osw.* 1 p. 338; terram ab aliis effossam .. pedibus complectentes Gir. *TH* I 25; hunc ignem ~it Nehemias quam Jeremias infoderat [cf. *2 Macc.* i 20] P. Blois *Serm.* 725A (cf. ib.: ignem quem N. inquisivit et ~it, sed non invenit); quidquid auri ~ere poterimus .. inferemus in thesauro ipsius [domini] J. Ford *Serm.* 13. 1; p**1300** ubi .. minera .. ~itur (v. conflatio 1); fecit .. terram effossam .. ad intra proici *G. Hen. V* 6 p. 42; **1476** (v. demolire b). **b** s**1052** cum .. tumulum .. ~isset (v. conscius 1b); taxus .. scrobes subterraneos .. ~iens Gir. *TH* I 25; ~i fecit fossam bone profunditatis et latitudinis inter eum et hostes *G. Hen. V* 6 p. 42 (cf. ib. p. 36: cotidie ~erunt). **c 1239** manibus propriis effosso suarum abominationum pariete (*Lit. Papae*) M. Par. *Maj.* III 606.

2 to tear out.

effosis, *ahlocadum GlC* E 65; effossis, i. †evulsi [MS: evulsis], *ut aneddum*, subversis *GlH* E 124.

2 effodere v. effutire.

effoditio, digging out. *Cf. effossio* 1.

placita habuit [T. abbas, ob. **1399**] .. cum tegulatoribus Beverlaci pro ~one soli nostri *Meaux* III 274.

effontire v. effutire.

efformare [LL], to shape, fashion.

cujus [Ricardi Foxe, ob. **1528**] imago summo cum artificio in lapide ~ata ibidem [apud Wintoniam] conspicitur *Hist. Durh.* 11.

effortialiter, vigorously. *V. et. effortiate.*

1254 alii episcopi et abbates Anglie .. promiserunt quod ~er vobis subvenirent de pecunia sua contra .. regem Castelle (*Lit. R. Com. Cornub.*) M. PAR. *Maj.* VI 283 (= *Foed.* I 499a).

effortiamentum [cf. AN *efforcement*, OF *esforcement*]

1 a fortification. **b** reinforcement.

a 1175 in operatione et ~o castri de Toppecliva *Pipe* 165; **1203** in excambium illius aque quam nos eis abstulimus pro ~o ville nostre de Rupella [*Gasc*] *Pat* 32a; **1254** si castrum .., dum fuerit in manu nostra, emendaverimus vel efforciaverimus, emendacio vel ~um illud ab eodem E. non exigetur *RGasc* I 336 (cf. *CalPat* 289); **1272** ita quod illud [castrum de Kaerfili] in eodem statu quo tunc fuit, ut in muris, fossatis vel alio afforciamento seu municione, remaneret *Cl* 546; **1275** aforciamenta (v. barbacana). **b 1336** pro majori et potenciori afforciamento nostri et fidelium nostrorum in obsequio nostro in partibus Scocie *RScot* 462a (cf. ib. 809b [**1357**]: quod tres magnates de Scocia in afforciamentum .. obsidum alternatim se intrabunt in prisona nostra pro certo tempore moraturi).

2 (leg.) 'afforcement': **a** (of court or judgement); **b** (of distraint). *Cf. effortiare* 4.

a 1212 tenet manerium de Faddecote [*Devon*] .. per servicium sequendi curiam de F. pro ~o judicii *Fees* 99; **1231** solebat facere sectam ad curiam de Ferenduna [*Berks*], quando latro ibi esset judicandus et quando breve regis ibi esset de recto, pro afforciamento curie *BNB* II 502; **1239** quia pauci magnates presentes fuerunt in curia, qui in se non fuerunt ausi assumere de faciendo judicio, ideo pro afforciamento curie datus est dies .. de audiendo judicio .. *Ib.* III 282; **c1240** veniet .. ad ~um curie de Heybrug [*Essex*] cum summonitus fuerit *E. Ch. S. Paul.* 253; **a1246** nullus burgensium sequatur hundredum nisi .. pro ~o judicii vel [si] in placito fuerit *BBC* (*Saltash*) 196; sunt .. servitia que pertinent ad regem, sicut secte ad justitiam faciendam per breve de recto et ad pacem, sicut de latrone judicando, et pro aforciamento curie in predictis BRACTON 35; **1280** omnes sectatores curie summoneantur per †assorem [MS: afforc'] curie *CourtR Hales* 158; **a1300** recognovit sectam ad hundredum .. per se vel per .. attornatum suum .. quocienscumque judicium positum fuerit super afforciamentum curie *Reg. Malm.* II 178; **1330** de tribus virgatis terre .. quietis de sectis curie de adventibus et afforciamentis (*Pat*) *MonA* VI 1564b. **b** ad quem [tertium comitatum in com. Lanc'] si [tenens] non venerit, capiatur magnum namium de eadem terra, sc. averia et catalla in duplum pro afforciamento districtionis BRACTON 330.

effortiare, ~ire [cf. AN *efforcier*, OF *esforcier*]

1 (mil.). to strengthen, fortify (castle or sim., by defence works, provisions *etc.*).

1142 sciatis me reddidisse .. comiti G. Essexe .. turrim Lund[on]' cum castello quod subtus est ad firmandum et ~iandum ad voluntatem suam (*Ch. M. Imp.*) *Mandeville* 167; **s1183** Ricardus .., veniens in Pictaviam .., castella nova firmavit et vetera ~iavit R. HOWD. II 274; **1193** pro civitate Roffensi esforcianda muro et fossato *Pipe* 166; **1198** pro esforcanda gaiola et reparanda *RScacNorm* II 368; **1202** capere meremium ad ~iendum civitatem Rothom' [*Norm*] *Pat* 10b; **1221** ballivi mei voluerunt .. partem bladi mei de manerio meo de Exeminstre .. adducere per mare usque castrum meum de Plimton' ad ipsum muniendum et ~iandum (*AncC* I 69) *RL* I 173; **1253** ~iari faciat warnisionem de Ryuns [*Gasc*] ita quod dominus rex securus sit de castro illo *Cl* 168; **1254** cujus [recluse] domum rex evelli fecit ad afforciandum burgum suum de Brugeraco *RGasc* I sup. lxxvii; **1270** intelleximus quod vos insulam de Portelaund' de die et nocte firmare et alio modo afforciare facitis *Cl* 292; **1308** (v. assecurare 3a).

2 to strengthen, reinforce: **a** (masonry or woodwork); **b** (metalwork); **c** (woven fabric).

a 1240 quod possint libere .. sustinere et afforciare stagnum suum [super Derewentam] *Cart. Darley* II 486; **1336** iiij hominibus .. ad afforciandum fundum fontis [castri de Edenburgh'] (*KRAc* 19/24) *Cal. Scot.* III app. 359; **1424** in stipendio j carpentarii afforcientis .. porcarium *Ac. Man. Wint.* (*Chilbolton*); **1449** in stipendio j carpentarii .. facientis necnon afforciantis et emendantis *lez rakkes* in .. bercaria *Crawley* 479. **b 1245** candelabra .. argentea .. cupro pedibus inclavato ad ~iandum *Invent. S. Paul.* 468. **c 1225** de .. cendalo .. ~iato (v. cendalum); **1245** contra instans Pascha sepulcrum ex quodam panno serico tenui vel sindallo ~iato .. fieri faciat *Cl* 294; **1257** vexillum de rube[o] scendalo aforciato *Cl* 68; **1286** in selda sua ceperunt iiij ulnas de rayo afforsato (*PlRCP*) *Gild Merch.* II 179; **1286** de quolibet panno de serico sine auro et *chef* de cendallo afforciato, j quad. *Pat* 105 m. 14 (= *Cal. Ir.* IV no. 226).

3 to reinforce, support (persons).

1202 mandamus vobis quod totum servicium quod nobis debetis habeatis promtum ad faciendum id quod .. H. de Burgo .. vobis dic[et] ex parte nostra et insuper nos ita ~ietis quod vobis grates scire debeamus *Pat* 9b; **1293** quidam serviens .. comitis .. interfectus fuit in predicta chacia .. per malefactores, propter quod .. ~iavit custodem chacie per homines .. armatos *Reg. Cant.* 319; licet homines simplicis qualitatis fuissent, attamen in premissis prodicionibus cum predictis potestatibus prout participes ambo afforciebantur FAVENT 19.

4 (leg.) to 'afforce': **a** (court or assize by increasing number of jurors or sim.); **b** (pledges). *Cf. effortiamentum* 2.

a 1217 dominus .., ut bene provideret sibi, ~iavit curiam suam semel, iterum et tercio *BNB* III 306; **1218** petunt respectum faciendi recordum usque comitatus afforcietur *Eyre Yorks* 276; **1229** si .. pro defectu consilii positum fuerit aliquid (*sic*) judicium in .. curia in respectum, tunc poterit prior alios in capite tenentes ad sequendum curiam summonere pro aforcianda curia sua (*Breve Regis*) *Ann. Dunstable* 120; **1240** Henricus .. dat domino regi dim. m. per sic quod assisa ~ietur *JustIt* 3 r. 5d. (= *Beds Rec. Soc.* IX no. 111); **1251** si .. velimus .. curiam nostram afforciare, veniet ipse R. et heredes sui, quando in tali casu summoniti fuerint, ad curiam nostram S. Augustini ad ~iandum ipsam curiam *Reg. S. Aug.* 422; contingit multotiens quod juratores in veritate dicenda sunt sibi contrarii ..; quo casu de consilio curie afforcietur assisa, ita quod apponantur alii juxta numerum majoris partis que dissenserit, vel saltem quatuor vel sex BRACTON 185b; si juratores sibi invicem fuerint contrarii .., in eleccione justiciariorum erit vel de consilio curie assisam afforciare per alios *Fleta* 230. **b** tunc .. plegii considerandi sunt in misericordia domini regis et super capitali placito plegii etiam afforciabuntur [v. l. plegios .. afforciabunt] GLANV. I 31; **1198** Robertus S. ~iet plegios suos *CurR RC* I 207.

5 to supplement or (?) strengthen (allowance of ale).

1251 r. c. de ij justis, de quibus in donis domino pape j justam; et alia justa fuit liberata ad afortiandam aliam justam *Pipe* 95 r. 7d.; in omnibus festis principalibus prime dignitatis cellerarius providebit conventui per iiij dies panem dominicum et cervisiam afforciatam *Obs. Barnwell* 186.

6 a to force, constrain. **b** to violate, rape.

a 1205 ita quod per regem non ~ietur ad se maritandam *Pipe* 33; **1300** nullus ballivus de Ripa Regine afforciat aliquem mercatorem de libertate civitatis neque extraneum de ipso capiendo j ciphe (*sic*) salis ad opus suum *MGL* I 244. **b** ?**1198** (14c) exceptis iiij querelis que ad coronam meam pertinent, sc. de roberia, de *murdir*, de combustione et de femina ~iata *Regesta Scot.* II 400; **1375** rapuit Sarram .. et illam aforciavit contra voluntatem suam *Proc. J. P.* 119.

7 (? infl. by *farcire*) to 'force', season (food). (*Cf. OED s.v.* force *v.*3 1).

1514 in legumine afforciato, vij d. *Comp. Swith.* 332.

effortiate, in force, w. vigorous reinforcement. *V. et. effortialiter.*

1208 dominus autem rex, secundum quod ego honorifice et ~e venero ad servitium suum, mihi retornabit de custo meo quod posuero in veniendo ad ipsum *Pat* 82b; **1212** quod .. eatis .. cum equis et armis et toto posse ville vestre .. et tam ~e hoc faciatis ut vobis inde grates scire debeamus *Cl* 122b; **1213** videas quod tu ita ~e venias cum equis et armis et hec ita exequaris ne inde ad corpus tuum nos capere debeamus (*Breve Regis*) WEND. II 67.

effortiatio, fortification.

1308 in .. afforciacione ville et pontis (v. assecurare 3a).

effortire v. effortiare.

effortium [cf. AN *efforce*, OF *esforz*], force (mil.).

1372 ad .. defensionem .. regni .. progredi nos disponimus cum eo quod habemus ~io de presenti *Reg. Exon.* I 187 (= *Conc.* III 92b).

effossare [cf. fossare], to dig (up).

~o, A. *to dygge up WW*; *to dike*, fodere, ef-, fossare, ef- *CathA*.

effossio [LL]

1 digging up. **b** hole (dug). **c** digging through (w. ref. to *Ezek.* viii 8–9). *Cf. effoditio.*

1292 cum .. cimiteria .. porcis .. et aliis animalibus .. conculcentur et sanctorum quoque corpora .. execrabili ~one fedentur *Conc. Syn.* 1115; morte filii et ~one Hectoris TREVET *Troades* 48. **b s1052** sanguis recens ex ~one [sc. Edgari tumulo] visus est distillare KNIGHTON I 5. **c c1430** prophete paries, in quo post ~onem pessime scelerum .. apparuerant abominaciones *Reg. Whet.* II app. 385.

2 tearing out, mutilation.

1100 Deo gratias quia .. non tyrannorum violentia .., non incensione ignis, non ~one manus, a veritatis annunciatione desistis (*Lit. Papae*) *Conc.* I 379b; quidam .. publica manu addicente oculorum ~one punitus est J. FORD *Wulf.* 73.

effossor, sapper.

s1189 rex Francie turrim obsedit et tum per ~ores suos tum per machinarum suarum insultus .. dedita est turris R. HOWD. II 364.

effractarius [CL], house-breaker, burglar.

hujus abbatis [F., ob. **1077**] tempore .. ubique ~ii, passim raptores vagabantur *G. S. Alb.* I 42; **s1255** precepit rex ut sui ~ii, licet contradicerent monachi, a cistis .. pecuniam .. tollerent M. PAR. *Maj.* V 508 (cf. ib. 343, 594).

effractio, a breaking, rupture. **b** house-breaking, burglary. **c** breaking open (of door in defiance of mon. rule). **d** prison-breaking.

a per fraccionem claustrorum absque seminis effusione non efficiuntur vir et mulier una caro; ideo per talem .. ~onem .. non provenit affinitas J. BURGH *PO* VIII 10 A f. 134v. **b s1249** domorum ~ones (v. confractio 1e). **c 1277** precipimus .. quod ~ones ostiorum .. quorundam monachorum per priorem .. corrigantur (*Ord. Archiep. Ebor.*) *MonA* IV 625a. **d 1426** ut .. ~onis carcerum et fuge processum continuaret *Reg. Cant.* III 139.

effractor [CL]

1 a breaker (of seal). **b** house-breaker. **c** church-breaker, violator of church property. **d** prison-breaker.

a unius sigillorum cautus ~or ex brevi incluso se in brevi agnoscit capitali dandum supplicio *V. Har.* 1 f. 3b. **b 9..** (v. clasmatorius); tempus discernit predonem a fure vel ~orem et furem diurnum a nocturno BRACTON 105. **c s1140** legatus .. omnes ~ores cimiteriorum et violatores ecclesiarum .. excommunicavit W. MALM. *HN* 483; [episcopus] gladium ecclesiastice precisionis in ~ores [ecclesie de G.] exseruit W. CANT. *Mir. Thom.* VI 92; **1188** institimus ut in murorum ~ores et eos qui bona ecclesie diripuerunt excommunicationis ferret sententiam *Ep. Cant.* 209; **c1240** incendiarii aut ecclesiarum ~ores *Conc. Syn.* 373; **1377** ecclesiarum ~ores .. excommunicatos .. nuncietis *Mon. Hib. & Scot.* 359a. **d 1426** carcerum publicum ~orem *Reg. Cant.* III 144.

2 disturber (of peace). **b** violator (of truce).

~ores pacis J. FURNESS *Kentig.* 44 p. 240. **b 1451** si eorum .. aliqui .. contrafecerint tanquam ~ores et violatores treugarum *RScot* 354a.

effrahura v. effraiura. **effraia** v. effraium.

effraiamentum [cf. OF *esfreement*], affray, disturbance.

1388 turbaciones, rumores et affrayamenta de die in diem suborta et perpetrata fuerunt in civitate [London'] et suburbiis (*CoramR* 507 *Rex* r. 39) *Peasants' Rising* 38; **1392** Johannes M. .. cum aliis ignotis .. Emmam uxorem .. Willelmi [et alios] .. vi et armis ceperunt et eos detinuerunt .. in affrayamentum populi .. domini regis .., per quodquidem affraiamentum dicta Emma .. moriebatur *KB ContrR* 39 r. 6.

effraiare [AN *effraer*, *affraier*, OF *esfreer* < exfridiare], to disturb (violently), startle, alarm; *v. et. exfridiare.* **b** (refl.) to be alarmed. **c** (intr.) to make an affray, brawl.

1308 †lacitavit [l. latitavit] se in domibus et gardino .. Johannis ipsum Johannem ad affrayandum et insultandum *CourtR Ramsey* 246; **1354** affraiando damas (v. dammicula); **1378** unde non modicum fuerat affraiatus [comes de Buk(enham)] *LBLond* H f. 101b; **1446** Thomas M. .. uxorem .. Willelmi in nocte vocavit et ipsam male affraiavit *DL CourtR* 126/1885–6 m. 2. **b 1403** ne .. se aliqualiter affraient (v. disconfortare). **c 1539** Petrus E. affraiavit super Matheum W. contra pacem domini regis. .. Matheus .. affraiavit et traxit sanguinem super corpus Petri *CourtR* 173/46 r. 13 (cf. ib. r. 18: insultum fecit et affraiavit cum Johanne).

effraiator [cf. OF *esfreor*], disturber, brawler.

1371 est communis .. affraiator pacis et communis noctivagax contra pacem *SessPLincs* 182; **1375** capellanus est communis affreiator et pertorbator pacis *Ib.* 210.

effraium, ~a [AN *effrai*, OF *esfroi*], affray, brawl. **b** (w. gen.) disturbance, alarm.

1232 omnes affraie, tractationes sanguinum, transgressiones .. terminentur .. coram ministris domini regis et non alibi *Pat* 484; **1345** de finibus pro affraio et sanguine extracto *MGL* I 391; **13..** quod inquisiciones officii †capti [? l. capte] pro affraiis non erunt contradicte per novas inquisiciones *Ib.* 178 (= *Ib.* 223: *les enquestes doffice qe sount prys .. denquerer des affrayes et bateries*); **1391** Rogerus S. noctanter vi et armis insultum fecit super Johannem M. capellanum in regia via in affraiam. .. Johannes T. cum quodam baculo et *dagger* intravit domum Roberti B. noctanter in *hamsok* et magnam affraiam *Leet Norw.* 69; **1391** Thomas fregit arestum et affrayam fecit *Lib. Kilken.* 48; **a1470** inquiratur .. qui .. percussit, verberavit vel sanguinem traxit vel aliquam affraiam fecit *BBAdm* I 230. **b 1293** ubi commodius et ad minus ~um cervorum .. foreste fieri poterit *Cl* 110 m. 7; **1326** in affrayum civitatis (v. custos 5b).

effraiura, disturbance, alarm.

1366 jurati presentant effraihuram ignis ad domum W. Basset in civitate *CourtR Winchester*; **1375** preceptum est attachiare J. Gardener pro effrahura facta cum cornu noctanter *Ib.*

effrangere v. effringere.

effrenare [CL], (p. pl.) unbridled, unrestrained: **a** (of person); **b** of abstr.).

a ~atus, abruptus [? l. arreptus], immoderatus *GlC* E 59; ad omnes illicitum ~ati, quicquid flagitii mente [v. l. menti] occurrebat promptissime peragebant *G. Steph.* I 1; **s1245** Wallenses ~ati iterum insurrexerunt in regem W. GUISB. 182; **s1381** quod .. domini cum armata manu in Canciam .. ad sedandum .. populum taliter ~atum transirent *V. Ric. II* 32. **b** ALDH. *VirgP* 35 (v. cachinnus); per ~atam loquendi licentiam BALD. CANT. *Tract.* 1. 414A; ne ~ata libertate luxurient GIR. *GE* II 8; **1306** (v. collatio 6b).

effrenate [CL], unrestrainedly.

~e, *amidludes GlH* E 121; ~e in eum ingerebantur *G. Steph.* I 42; BLAKMAN *Hen. VI* 7 (v. commanere 2c).

effrenatio [CL], giving rein to (speech). **b** unbridled passion.

1284 fractio silencii et cum loqui licet ~o garrula [MS: garule] vel clamor insolens .. PECKHAM *Ep.* 583 p. 803. **b** alterum consulit ratio; alterum impellit turbata ~o PULL. *Sent.* 880B.

effrendēre [cf. CL frendere], to gnash one's teeth (fig.), chafe.

pro obsidione .. tam obstinate intenta non minimum ~uerunt *G. Steph.* I 19.

effrene, without restraint.

quia callidus posset capere ~e evidenciam ad injuste decipiendum proximum WYCL. *Ver.* II 34.

effrenescere [cf. CL effrenare], to become unrestrained.

~ens Tiberius Cesar indignacione, quam plures .. trucidavit *Eul. Hist.* I 139.

effrenis, ~us [CL], unbridled, unrestrained: **a** (of person or unspec.); **b** (of abstr.).

a illorum qui gentili diu libertate ~es .. ad fidei .. sunt gratiam conversi BEDE *Hom.* II 3. 123; ~us, *unmidled* vel *unsæled GlH* E 120; ambos in rebus commissis strenuos sed ~es W. MALM. *GP* III 132; A. TEWK. *Ep.* 5 (v. docibilis a); similis .. omnium quos avara cupiditas fecit ~os MAP *NC* II 23 f. 31v.; quicquid ~is audet *Fleta proem.*; WYCL. *Civ. Dom.* II 14 (v. dyscrasiari b); **s1381** qualiter populus tam ~is posset sedari *V. Ric. II* 32. **b** ut illam ~em et ingenitam Romanorum cupiditatem cohiberet W. MALM. *GR* V 435; lingua fit effrenis, nullo moderata tenore NIG. *Laur.* 40. 2; ~es semper et luxuriantes incommodis animos GIR. *EH* I 14; ~es .. impetus *Id. PI* I 10 (v. demembratio a); ecclesiarum multiplicacionem avidam et ~em PECKHAM *Ep.* 41.

effrigere [LL], to turn cold (fig.).

post illos [filios Wihtredi] nobile germen regum exaruit, generosus sanguis ~uit W. MALM. *GR* I 15 (cf. ELMH. *Cant.* 337: sanguis Cantie ~uit generosus).

effringere [CL]

1 to break (partly fig.). **b** to break into.

~o, frango *GlH* E 129; ideo chorde rupte sunt et cithara effracta est P. BLOIS *Serm.* 633A; effractis claustris eolicis et convulsis maris ructibus GIR. *EH* I 36; jamque effractas rapiebat harenas / in pelagus classis J. EXON. *BT* III 186. **b** si quis furtum capitale comiserit, i.e. .. domos effregerit EGB. *Pen.* 10. 3; qui per noctem ~ebat civitatem c sol. emendabat regi *DB* I 56v.; si quis alicujus curiam vel domum violenter effregerit vel intraverit *Ib.* I 154v.; baronum castella .. ~entes *G. Steph.* I 9.

2 (pass., of person) to be worn out, weakened.

Dunstanus longo senio et magnis ecclesiae laboribus effractus OSB. *V. Dunst.* 36; licet tenear causa breviterque coarcter, / non tamen effranger ipsa dolore meo NIG. *SS* 444; (cf. ib. 3496: viribus atque vigore / corporis effractus diceris esse senex); **s1189** minis tandem et blanditiis effracti, monachi concesserunt ut .. GERV. CANT. *Chr.* 461; FORDUN *Cont.* XV 17 (v. confringere 2a).

3 (w. abstr. obj.): **a** to beat down (price). **b** to break (peace). **c** to crush (liberty).

a cum gnarus folia [libri] volveret, pretium ~eret, barbari eum .. convitiis aggrediuntur W. MALM. (*V. Aldh.*) *GP* V 224; homo [Will. II] qui nesciret cujuscunque rei ~ere pretium vel estimare commercium *Id. GR* IV 313. **b** **1226** retraxit se de appello de pace regis effracta *LTRMem* 8 r. 11. **c** conculcantur jura nostra, libertates ~untur OCKHAM *Disp.* 13.

effronia v. officina.

effronite, shamelessly. *Cf. effrons, effrunitus, infrunitus.*

1222 ab illis qui fidelitatem erga vos pretendunt et contra .. hostem vestrum vobis .. ~e [*sic* MS] defecerunt .. injuriis aggravamur (*AncC* XLVII 30) *RL* I 184.

effrons [LL], shameless: **a** (of person); **b** (of abstr.).

a cum amittit homo verecundiam, ut tanquam ~s .. ad illicita .. ruat R. NIGER *Mil.* I 38; ~tes et effrenati demones MAP *NC* I 15 f. 13; ~s adulator NECKAM *NR* II 180; **s1237** facta est filia Syon quasi meretrix ~s, non habens ruborem M. PAR. *Maj.* III 389; ad cujus [amoris] imperium verecundus et ~s efficior J. GODARD *Ep.* 220; est hostis legis indoctus, perfidus, effrons, / hostis munificus, hostis et ipse sibi GARL. *Hon. Vit.* 215; **1282** velut ~s et furiosus *Reg. North.* 61 (= *Conc.* II 43); isti [mendicantes] .. clerum et populum importune velut ~tes ubilibet onerantes RIC. ARMAGH *Def. Cur.* 1399 (*recte* 1299); *unschameful-le*, inpudens .., inverecundus, ~s .. *CathA* (s.v. *schameful-le*). **b** mira impudentia et ~ti audacia GIR. *Invect.* I 6; impudens et ~s esse .. solet nimie egestatis anxietas *Id. SD* 14.

effronter, shamelessly, w. effrontery.

1281 visitationem et auctoritatem nostram metropoliticam ~er et contumaciter subterfugit et evitat *Reg. North.* 65; **1349** ostia ipsa mandarunt et preceperunt ~er et impetuose frangi .. et disrumpi *Ib.* 398; adhuc fortasse aliquis tam ~er proterviet ut dicat graciam .. esse liberum arbitrium homini gratis datum BRADW. *CD* 474B.

effrotum v. aphrotum.

effrunitus [cf. CL infrunitus], impetuous.

ille, juvenili fervore fervens, effrenis et ~us, .. Deum et homines non reveretur T. MON. *Will.* VI 9 p. 233.

effucitare v. effutire.

effugare [LL]

1 (absol.) to flee, escape.

Petrus apostolus .. efugavit W. MALM. *Mir. Mariae* 164.

2 to drive out (person or unspec.), banish, put to flight. **b** (p. ppl. as sb.) refugee.

quod Dominus .. sublatus est .. in Aegyptum significat electos .. suis ~andos sedibus vel etiam exilio damnandos BEDE *Hom.* I 10. 51B; ~entur, *syn afligde GlH* E 138; fuit David rex .. bis ab Anglia ignominiose ~atus *G. Steph.* I 64; [Gregorius VI], basilicam B. Petri preoccupans, raptores oblationum vel extinxit vel ~avit W. MALM. *GR* II 201; Turcos omnes a facie sua rex ~avit *Itin. Ric.* IV 14; **s1250** quidam .. Armenii, exterminio Tartarorum ~ati, venerunt in Angliam M. PAR. *Maj.* V 116; **1341** nostra .. existit intencio vos de regno nostro ejicere et ~are (*Lit. Regis Franciae*) WALS. *HA* I 230. **b** dum .. quotidie ex ~atis .. et ab exhereditatis manum suam .. crescere cerneret *G. Herw.* 328b.

3 to drive off (animals, esp. those seized in distraint).

vultur .. niger dejecit albos impetu subito et ~avit MAP *NC* IV 15 f. 56; **1250** boves suos ~averunt usque ad P. *CurR* XIX 1686; **c1266** cum per me et homines meos ablata fuissent de bonis domini J. de B. c m. .. sterlingorum .. cum ix pull[anis] de parco suo .. ~atis *Deeds Balliol* 327; **c1300** si .. averia .. Johannis .. infra terras predictas pro defectu clausture invenientur, predicto J. .. quiete liberentur et sine impedimento .. ~entur *Reg. Malm.* II 268; **1351** vaccas ~andas ad inparcandum .. rescussit *SessP Essex* 131; **1444** (v. 3 districtio 5c).

4 to rout, banish, expel (devil or his instruments).

taceo quam mire daemones ~avit *V. Cuthb.* I 7; timent immundi spiritus et viribus nostris ~ata eorum tentatio repellitur BEDE *Ezra* 902; ut ante sonitum ejus [tintinnabuli] longius ~entur ignita jacula inimici EGB. *Pont.* 119; hostis ille antiquus a Dei imagine hac ~atur et fugit H. BOS. *Thom.* IV 13 p. 361; crisolitus .. demones ~at R. NIGER *Mil.* II 10.

5 to dispel; **b** (w. abstr. obj.).

prima creator saeculi / die tenebras effugans BEDE *Hymn* 1. 3; ut .. fetorem .. ~aret .. hujus suavitas odoris *Id. HE* V 12; ad ~andas .. erroris nebulas et peccatorum tenebras OSB. *V. Dunst.* 19; pro .. pestilentiis ~andis R. NIGER *Chr. I* 49; quasi sol oriens nocturnas effugat umbras GARL. *Tri. Eccl.* 13; *Ps.*-ELMH. *Hen. V* 19 (v. 1 elatio 2b). **b** crucis Christi signaculum hostilem .. ~avit insaniam *V. Greg.* p. 97; ocio penitus ~ato R. BURY *Phil.* 15. 192.

effugatio [LL], driving off, banishment, rout.

purgatio atque ~o daemonum ex hominibus ALCUIN (*Proc. Spir.*) *Dogm.* 67A; **s1251** ne videretur [rex H.] .. Caursinorum ~one ipsum papam aliquatenus provocasse M. PAR. *Min.* III 104; **1336** ad destruccionem foreste .. et detrimentum et ~onem ferarum nostrarum a receptamentis suis *Cl* 157 m. 23*d.*; **1457** in evasionem et ~onem .. gravium periculorum animarum *Reg. Whet.* I 287.

effugere [CL], to flee, take flight. **b** to escape (trans.). **c** to elude (fig.), avoid.

ut procul effugeret facies larvata nefandi ALDH. *VirgV* 2252; prosternat aereas potestates dextera tuae virtutis, ut hoc audientes tintinnabulum tremescant ~iantque ante sanctae crucis vexillum EGB. *Pont.* 118; **8..** ~iet, *forflioh* .., *afliot WW*; linquere ut examen tantum digneris, et iste / effugiat vivus WULF. *Swith.* II 326; **1255** percipiens ille equitans dictos forestarios ~it *SelPlForest* 114. **b** hic non effugiet manuum tormenta mearum WULF. *Swith.* I 552; fere, cum canes e vestigio sequentes nullatenus ~ere se posse presentiunt, .. ad locum istum quantocius transferuntur GIR. *TH* II 40; **s1197** ignorabant [monachi] quod licet oppressis onus ab humeris excutere quociens oppressoris manum constiterit ~isse G. COLD. *Durh.* 12; **1279** aliter, mox ut eum tetigero, appellacionis alis falsidice rete meum ~iet PECKHAM *Ep.* 41; non potes .. absque meo adjutorio eorum manus ~ere [ME: *edfleon*] *AncrR* 153. **c** **798** in qua assertione [haeretica] nullatenus ~ere poterit duas personas in Christo ALCUIN *ad Beatum* 319; ANSELM I 36 (v. compositio 2a).

effugium [CL], **a** flight. **b** escape. **c** line of retreat.

a reliquos in ~ium coegerunt ORD. VIT. IV 5 p. 191; ~ium, fuga, diffugium OSB. GLOUC. *Deriv.* 199. **b** colliria .. demoniace invasionis impetus .. non conterunt nec ~ii subsidio esse possunt R. COLD. *Cuthb.* 17. **c** locum belli .. explorat, situm sc. loci, optimum in illo adventum, stationem, ~ium MAP *NC* IV 15 f. 57v.

effugus v. effundere 2b.

effulcire [CL *p. ppl.* effultus], to support, hold up.

celsa duci Priamo late surgentibus armis / effulcit [v. l. †effulsit] roseum cervix caput J. EXON. *BT* IV 44.

effulgentia [LL], radiance (fig.).

quod Filius ~ia aeterna luminis est aeterni [cf. *Heb.* i 2] ALCUIN (*Trin.*) *Dogm.* 18A.

1 effulgere v. effulcire.

2 effulgēre [CL], to shine, grow clear or bright; **b** (fig.).

obsecrat et dicto citius sub fronte [sc. caeci] gemellae / effulgent acies WULF. *Swith.* I 1587 (cf. ib. 1608: mox ergo virorum / vultibus effulgent oculi). **b** qualibus in mundo signis effulserit almus ALDH. *VirgV* 767; cum venerabilis Domini famulus .. magnis virtutum signis ~eret BEDE *HE* IV 25 p. 270; **798** desiderata vestrae bonitatis litterarum facies subito effulsit ALCUIN *Ep.* 145; dum Uticensis ecclesia .. in bonis operibus aucta coram Deo et hominibus ~eret ORD. VIT. III 3 p. 51; venerabilis vir .. sacre scripture intelligentia non mediocriter effulsit *Chr. Witham* 505; [miles] victoriose quibus[cun]que prevalens effulsit MAP *NC* II 16 f. 28.

effulminare [cf. CL fulminare], to strike w. a thunderbolt.

audacter provocando Dominum non subito ~atus, excisus vel ad inferos detractus est GOSC. *Mir. Iv.* lxx.

effumigare [LL], to smoke out.

s1138 castellina fossa .. [congerie lignorum] impletur. ignis succenditur; fumus in altum se levat. omnes infumigat et exfumigat J. WORC. 51.

effundare, to make (a road) founderous. *Cf. funderare.*

1383 regia via .. ~ata, inundata et ruinosa extitit (*CoramR*) *Pub. Works* II 76 (cf. ib. 78: viam .. que inundatur et ~atur).

effundere [CL]

1 to pour out (liquid or powder). **b** to spill (container or contents); **c** (w. container as subj.). **d** to discharge (missiles, fig.). **e** (w. ref. to crowd).

rursus in obliquum latices effuderat antrum ALDH. *VirgV* 787; sicca pruinosam crebris effundo fenestris / candentemque nivem *Id. Aen.* 67 (*Cribellus*) 1; cum mundi crimina diluvio quondam expiarentur †effusa [? l. effuso], .. columba .. pacem terris redditam nuntiavit EGB. *Pont.* 121; pueri mensis discos digitare laborant, / .. cuppis effundere potus D. BEC. 2418; si oleum ~atur [ME: *sched*] a vase, aliquid liquoris remanebit in eo; .. sed, si aqua, totum simul ~itur *AncrR* 123; super cujus [sc. regine] verticem ~etur oleum sanctum W. SAY *Lib. Reg. Cap.* 97. **b** nummolariorum quos expulerat aes et mensas subvertit [cf. *Mark* xi 15] BEDE *Hom.* II 1. 117; unam illarum [ampullarum] nolens effudi W. CANT. *Mir. Thom.* VI 43 (cf. ib.: vas effusum). **c** dum [urna] ~eret sortes immissas TREVET *Troades* 69. **d** ~it aculeos J. SAL. *Pol.* 574B (v. consulte). **e** ecce per effusas denso tamen agmine turmas FRITH. 494.

2 to shed: **a** (tears); **b** (blood *etc.*). **c** (w. *animam* or *spiritum*) to give up the ghost.

a questus e pectore promit / salsaque palpebris effundit flumina luctus ALDH. *VirgV* 1906; lacrimas effudit amaras WULF. *Swith.* I 1563; effusis lacrimis, fletibus ora rigas G. AMIENS *Hast.* 61; lacryme effuse sunt ORD. VIT. III 14 p. 144. **b** effuso rubuerunt sanguine lances ALDH. *VirgV* 446; ubi regis Osualdi sanguis fuerat effusus BEDE *HE* III 10; habent .. sanguinem, si ibi ~itur *DB* I 56 (cf. effusio 2a); **1274** percussit .. Robertum juxta capitis, ita quod cerebrum effudit *SelCCoron* 32; **1285** emendas de sanguine †effugo [MS: effuso] (*JustIt* 242 r. 53) *PQW* 236b; Deus .., parcens effusioni sanguinis, qui in assultu murorum verisimiliter ~i debuit *G. Hen. V* 8. **c** "tandem," ait, "pessime senex, vivacem animam effudisti .." W. MALM. *GP* I 17; Eorpwaldus inviolatum spiritum Deo effudit, a Ricberto gentili innocenter peremptus *Id. GR* I 97.

3 a to cast (metal artefact). **b** to smelt (metal).

a [T. abbas, cess. **1399**] considerans metallum esse derelictum .. pro tribus campanis exinde effu[n]dendis *Meaux* III 240. **b 1447** in esculentis et poculis datis .. plumbariis et aliis operariis tempore quo ∼ebant cineres plumbi *Fabr. York* 63; **1449** j furnellum pro argento ∼endo *KRAc* 294/6.

4 a to bring forth (offspring). **b** to put forth (leaves).

a non est auditum ut aliqua somniando ∼eret partum W. MALM. *Mir. Mariae* 219; ut .. conceptum fetum .. cogeretur ∼ere *Mir. Hen. VI* III 125. **b** frondes .. ∼ere R. COLD. *Cuthb.* 42 (v. effigiare 2a).

5 to emit (odour). **b** to cause to blow.

odoris flagrantia miri .. de loco ∼ebatur BEDE *HE* V 12 p. 307; nullus inde [ex cadavere] fetor vivorum naribus ∼i moleste poterat ORD. VIT. III 5 p. 74. **b s1267** hoc anno †effuditus est ventus tempestuose ita quod domos .. prostravit *Chr. Clun.* 104 f. 31v.

6 to utter; **b** (prayer). **c** (w. *cor* or *animam*) to pour out one's heart or soul (fig.). **d** (p. ppl. *s. act.*) having burst (fig.).

∼o *GlH* E 136 (v. effutire). **b** ut Soteris populum in biblo potuisset / sanctificare, Deoque preces effundere sacras GODEMAN 17; effusis precibus fidei virtute resolvit FRITH. 1316. **c** si firma fide et confessione vera cum lacrimis ∼imus .. corda [cf. *Psalm* lxi 9] ALCUIN *WillP* 30; ∼am animam meam et quae intra me sunt ante ipsum ANSELM (*Or.* 14) III 55; sic ∼e [ME: *schet*] cor tuum [cf. *Lam.* ii 19], id est totum malum quod est in corde tuo *AncrR* 123. **d** Arturus, in nimiam effusus letitiam, reginam .. amplexatus est *Arthur & Gorlagon* 1.

7 a to pour out (abstr.) in profusion, lavish. **b** (p. ppl.) profuse, diffuse. **c** to expend (money). **d** to use up, consume, destroy.

a ut .. ∼i videretur contemptio super principes GILDAS *EB* 21; ut .. benedictionis suae gratiam .. ∼at EGB. *Pont.* 19 (v. consecratio 2b); [monachi trutanni] magistri prius effecti quam discipuli .. et antequam conche ad colligendum facti canales ad ∼endum GIR. *Spec.* III 9. **b** non convenit ut in prefatiuncula nimis simus effusi *Cuthb. Hib. pref.*; letitia effusiore MAP *NC* IV 3 (v. deliquare). **c 1279** pecuniam effusurus PECKHAM *Ep.* 41; **1436** pro expensis effusis circa solucionem j decime *Cant. Coll. Ox.* II 149. **d** ∼ere, interficere *GlC* E 79; ∼e, i. .. sparge, .. interfice *GlH* E 131.

8 to throw or drag down.

∼e, i. .. trahe, *ateoh* *GlH* E 131 (cf. ib. 139: effusus, prostratus).

effunerarius, funerary attendant.

medicum animarum querimus, non ∼ium GIR. *Symb.* I 28 p. 306.

effungia [dub.], cocket bread.

cokett, †iffungia [v. l. effungia], est quidam panis *CathA*.

effusare [cf. CL fusus], to wind a spindle.

to wyndd spyndylle, infusare [v. l. effusare] *CathA*.

effuse [CL], profusely.

Gl. Leid. 28. 64 (v. epitrocasmos); ignis .. volucres flammas ∼ius dilatabat R. COLD. *Cuthb.* 45; cum praesertim Gaufredus multa ∼issime de Arthuro litteris mandaverit P. VERG. *Camd.* 199.

effusio [CL]

1 pouring out, downpour. **b** spilling. **c** leakage. **d** (phil.) emanation.

si .. ∼o pluvie .. descenderit *Fleta* 163. **b** de casu micarum vel .. ∼one potus [ME: *of schede .. ale*] *AncrR* 132. **c 1300** in fraccione et ∼one apud castrum de D. de nocte pro gelu, j doleum (*Pipe*) *MinAc. W. Wales* 166. **d** T. YORK *Sap.* II 1 (v. diffusio 1a).

2 a scattering, shedding; **b** (w. *sanguinis*) bloodshed (or amercement therefor). **c** emission (of urine or semen). **d** spawn (of fish).

a ∼one, *on todale* *GlH* E 141; legimus de triplici aque ∼one per Cristum facta ALEX. BATH *Mor.* IV 2 p. 130; fit lacrimarum ∼o *Quaest. Salern.* N 56. **b 801** ne inter altare et sepulchrum .. confessoris .. sanguinis ∼o sit ALCUIN *Ep.* 246; **1104** non timeo sanguinis ∼onem ANSELM (*Ep.* 311) V 236; **c1160** habeant [canonici] soccam et sacam .. et pacis fracturam .. et sanguinis ∼onem .. et omnia forisfacta in suo jure facta *CalCh* II 369; **s1188** teneant .. in mercato, in theoloneo .., in furis apprehensione et evasione, in sanguinis ∼one, infra burgum et extra *Ib.* 333; tam cruente conquisitionis, plurima quippe sanguinis ∼one .. fedate GIR. *EH* II 9; **1269** omnis violenta ∼o sanguinis in patria debet presentari in hundredo *CBaron* 88; *blodwyte*, quietanciam misericordie pro sanguinis ∼one *Fleta* 63; *SB* 12 (v. apoplexia); **1382** de quadam *fray* in campo de W. per homines de T. ad ∼onem sanguinis *Hal. Durh.* 172; si poterit carnes scindere sine sanguinis ∼one, statim mittat manum in eum *Latin Stories* 120. **c** ex utriusque spermatis ∼one *Quaest. Salern.* B 11; urine ∼o *SB* 17 (v. diabeticus a); absque seminis ∼one J. BURGH *PO* VIII 10 A (v. effractio d). **d** piscarias .. discretus .. perchiis fecit instaurare, set non de lupis aquaticis .., qui ∼onem piscium †intuitur [v. l. nituntur] devorare *Fleta* 164.

3 a casting (of metal artefact). **b** smelting or melting down (of metal).

a 1387 super factura et ∼one novorum gunnorum *KRAc* 183/12 f. 31. **b 1443** in mercede .. Willelmi [Plumber] in ∼one lxxx petrarum plumbi *Fabr. York* 58; **1460** Willelmo Potter pro ∼one j patelle erie continentis iiij den. et ij lib. *Ac. Durh.* 88; **1480** pro ∼one et nova factura j mortarii *Ib.* 96; **1533** ∼one xxj †centenis plumbi unacum fixura ejusdem super tecturam infirmarie *Comp. Swith.* 220.

4 expenditure.

1164 ∼o pecunie J. SAL. *Ep.* 134 (136 p.8); ne bonorum suorum vastam videat .. ∼onem MAP *NC* IV 16 f. 58v.; **s1256** dampnificavit eum rex in multe pecunie .. ∼one M. PAR. *Maj.* V 555; **1437** subtrahuntur ab ipso expense per eum facte pascendo *ly folcfeste* in ultimo Natali, quod .. rogatus fecit cum promisso sibi facto de ∼one expensarum *Stat. Linc.* II 388.

effusivus, profusely generative, lavish. **b** (as sb. f.) power to diffuse or generate.

splendoresque serit alios fecundula florum / Flora, perhennantis jubar effusiva diei HANV. VIII 295 p. 369. **b** tripliciter res habent se: uno modo in se, et sic a potentia ..; secundo modo in ordine, et sic a sapientia ..; tertio modo .. in decore et ∼a, et sic a bonitate, quia bonum est diffusivum BACON VII 85.

effusor [LL], (w. *sanguinis*) shedder of blood.

sanguinis effusor humani sanguine pallet WALT. ANGL. *Fab.* 58. 27; virtus effusi sanguinis ipsos suos ∼ores .. tetigit H. BOS. *LM* 1303C; **c1334** sanguinis effusor, mutulator quando fuisti (*Vers.*) *FormOx* 110; sanguinis effusor .. / .. templum non valet esse Dei GOWER *VC* III 429.

effutilis [LL], vain, worthless.

†effutalis, i. inanis, instabilis *GlH* E 135.

effutire [CL], to utter foolishly.

†effati[re], †vaniloquium [? l. vane loqui] sine effectu .., †effontire, †venenose [? l. vane] loqui .., †effodit, vane loquitur *GlC* E 71, 74, 76; ∼io, .. effundo *GlH* E 136; futio componitur ∼io OSB. GLOUC. *Deriv.* 237; *to speke in wayn'*, .. vanaloqui .., †effucitare, ∼ire *CathA*.

eflux- v. efflux-. **efortunium** v. eufortunium. **eftafolium, eftafylon** v. heptaphyllum. **efug-** v. effug-.

egama [Ar. *ḥijāma*], cupping glass or vessel used in distilling.

egem BACON IX 157 (v. attrenum); *a ventosynge boxe*, guma, gumis, ventosa *CathA*.

egeator v. hegetor.

egellus [*dim. of* egenus], needy.

subitur mendax veraci, dives egello H. AVR. *Guthl.* 63v.

egem v. egama.

egene, sparingly.

interea presul [Odo] .. miracula non ∼e facere W. MALM. *GP* I 17.

egentia [LL], need, neediness.

nondum suscipit in se aliorum defectus et ∼ias suplendas GROS. *Hexaem.* I 18; Deus .. a sua creatura ipsum [donum] graciose accipit tamquam suum .., non ad sui ∼iam sed ad fortificandum .. creature sue .. titulum WYCL. *Dom. Div.* 218; [panis quotidianus] ad commemorandum nostram quotidianam ∼iam signanter petitur hodie nobis dari *Id. Apost.* 90.

egenus [CL], needy, (as sb.) pauper. **b** poor in spirit. **c** deficient. **d** (w. gen.) having need of, lacking. **e** lacking in substance, jejune.

eadem ∼is et paene nihil habentibus distribui .. non sinimus GILDAS *EB* 42; dum [Martinus] .. peplum ferret egenis ALDH. *VirgV* 682; ∼us, *wædla* ÆLF. *Sup.*; emptis cibis sustentavit .. multitudinem ∼orum WULF. *Æthelwold* 29; ∼is fratribus suis .. subvenire volens ORD. VIT. III 3 p. 57; J. SAL. *Enth. Pol.* 384C (v. egestas); convenit regie majestati populum regimini ejus commissum, divites et †egerios, .. defendere *Quad. Reg. Spec.* 39. **b** quem cernimus et in divitiis ∼um et in deliciis sobrium AILR. *Ed. Conf.* 740D. **c** fuit vir quidam Romae dives in rebus sed ∼us in religione *V. Greg.* p. 97. **d** ∼us luminis MAP *NC* IV 3 (v. 1 eclipticus 1a). **e 1072** [archiepiscopus Ebor'] vertit se ad alia ∼a atque infirma argumenta, quae .. paucis sunt objectionibus abolita LANFR. *Ep.* 3 (4).

eger v. aeger.

egēre [CL]

1 (absol.) to be needy, in want. **b** (pr. ppl.) needy, (as sb.) pauper, beggar.

8.. ∼ebit, *he wedlað* .., **9..** ∼et, *beþearf* *WW*; is etenim largas, quamvis devotus egeret, / inpensas eleis palmis fundebat apertis FRITH. 1132; coepit .. ∼ere et ex sua paupertate .. vilis haberi ALEX. CANT. *Mir.* 32 (I) p. 221; NIG. *Laur.* 32v. 2 (v. coegenus); semper avarus eget, semper formidat egenus D. BEC. 1612; priusquam pauperem unum enormiter egere conspicerent GIR. *IK* I 3; pauper pauper erit et egenus semper egebit WALT. WIMB. *Scel.* 98. **b** farcit egens jugiter fulvo nummismate saccum ALDH. *VirgV* 2618 (cf. ib. 1764: clemens defensor egentum); BEDE *HE* IV 21 p. 254 (v. dives 1a); egentum *þyrfendra* *GlH* E 148; [W. archiepscopus, ob. **1340**] corpora defunctorum omnium, quamvis ostiatim egencium, .. ad absolvendum sibi oblata .. prompta absolvebat devotione T. STUBBS *Chr.* 416; **1367** (v. derogamen).

2 to have need (of), lack: **a** (w. abl.); **b** (w. gen.); **c** (w. *de*); **d** (w. inf.).

a vulnus .. quod .. ignis medicamine eget GILDAS *EB* 108; **671** cum astrologicae artis peritia .. elucubrata doctoris indagatione egeat ALDH. *Ep.* 1; Deus .. ad explendum onus suum non eguit mora temporum BEDE *Gen.* 13; *Id. Hom.* II 9 (v. desipere a); *GAS* 577 (v. definire 4a); **1147** si .. domus illa aliquibus eguerit que nobis .. exuberent (*Ch. Prioris*) *Rec. Barts.* 491; neminem volebat egere justicia vel pace MAP *NC* V 6 f. 67v.; BRADW. *CD* 567B (v. coefficientia). **b** pluris egemus *V. Ed. Conf.* 38 (v. 2 dilabi c); alterius rei non multum egebat ALEX. CANT. *Mir.* 32 (II) p. 221. **c 1324** de eisdem [equis] ulterius non egebit *Lit. Cant.* I 118. **d** egent sane populi .. audire GILDAS *EB* 96; si egeat ostendi (GROS.) *GLA* III 89 (v. definitio 2a).

egerere [CL], to carry out or away (esp. refuse). **b** to excrete. **c** to discharge (fig.), exercise (power).

∼ere, *ascrepan*, .. egesta, *ascrepen* *GlC* E 95, 98; erat .. ostium in pariete altaris unde .. carbones et cineres possent ∼i BEDE *Tab.* 454; verisimile videtur quia porta sterquilinii [*Neh.* iii 13–14] vocetur illa per quam sordes et immunditiae consuessent ∼i *Id. Ezra* 890; **9..** egessit, *ut apyde* *WW*; †egere [MS: ∼ere], *ascrepen* *GlH* E 146 (cf. ib. 152: egesta, i. ablata, deducta, translata). **b** Arrius infaustus, ventris dum viscera foeda / turpiter egesit ruptis extalibus ani ALDH. *VirgV* 977; jussus est a lege [cf. *Deut.* xxiii 13] secedens ad requisita nature palo humo fossa egesta recondere NECKAM *NR* II 180; misit Saturno lapidem .. quem pulveratum devoravit. deinde egestus et formatus est in speciem humanam et vivificatus ALB. LOND. *DG* 15. 10; **s1016** Eadricus quendam in loco stercoris abscondit, qui regem [Eadmundum] egesturum veru confoderet DICETO *Chr.* 169; J. FORD *Wulf.* 21 (v. cellula 3c); sordes quod fuderat resorbet iterum / et rursus egerit virus pestiferum WALT. WIMB. *Sim.* 14; tenasmon est appetitus et voluntas nimia ∼endi cum modico aut nullo effectu *SB* 41. **c** vigorem pontificalem in eum egessit [vv. ll. egesset, ingessit] *Eul. Hist.* III 18.

egeries [LL], excrement.

lynces egestum liquorem .. contegunt, invidia sc. ne talis ∼ies transeat in nostrum usum NECKAM *NR* II 138; revixit proditor qui quondam crepuit / cujus egerie Judea sorduit WALT. WIMB. *Sim.* 13.

egerius v. egenus a.

egersimon [LL < ἐγέρσιμον], alert (sb.), rousing call.

hec tritonia, i. e. trina notio, nuncupatur, quia humano animo sapientia illustrato †engerimion, i. e. surrectionis, liber aperitur, in quo ab humanis ad divina surgere septem septenis eruditur J. SAL. *SS* 948AB.

eges v. aegis.

egestare, ∼itare [*backformed from* egestus *p. ppl. of* egerere], to excrete.

to schyte, cacare, egerere, ∼are, ∼itare *CathA*.

egestas [CL], need, destitution.

∼as, paupertas *GlC* E 96; non dolor aut gemitus veniet, .. / non sitis, esuries, .. / .. mors, casus, egestas BEDE *Hymn* 14. 134; **800** populus in aegestate, .. ecclesia in sollicitudine ALCUIN *Ep.* 193; **8..** ∼atem, *wedle* *WW*; nescit egestatem dives, egenus opes J. SAL. *Enth. Pol.* 384C; perditus usus opum manifestat quid sit egestas D. BEC. 2156; una tamen felix miseria, ultima sc. ∼ate MAP *NC* IV 11 f. 52; in hujus amore patire, propter quam cuncta dampna, contumelias, ∼ates, abjecciones nequaquam formidare .. debes CHAUNDLER *Apol.* 34a.

egestio [LL < CL = *clearing away*], excretion or excrement; **b** (fig.).

∼o, degestio *GlC* E 93; eum quem luxurie Charybdis absorbuit, carnis sue colluvione, quasi proprii stercoris ∼one, asserens esse corruptum AILR. *Spec. Car.* I 26. 529C; miles .. per ∼onis fenestram vitulum edidit GIR. *IK* I 2; ad emissionem spermatis .. omnes spiritus cooperantur ... in expulsione vero ∼onis sola virtus expulsiva operatur *Quaest. Salern.* P 145; separatio quedam purioris liquoris et subtilioris a quadam inpuriori et feculentiori massa ac grossiori superfluitate, que dicitur ∼o RIC. MED. *Anat.* 224; sicut in urina et aliis ∼onibus BACON XIV 83; odor fetidus in ∼one et ∼o virulenta et aquosa et pinguis GAD. 57v. 1; BAKER 107b (v. 2 ductilis 1b). **b** fimus qui de ventre porcis (*sic*) egeritur, sunt immundi et luxuriosi altaris ministri .. qui ventrem matris ecclesie onerant, quos per mortis ∼onem demones, ut porci, devorant HON. *Eluc.* 1129A.

egestitare v. egestare.

egestura, (?) agistment (payment for pasturage) or manure. *Cf. agistare, egestio.*

1572 quod reddat ei iij s. iiij d. pro ~a unius equi et diversarum bestiarum (*CourtR E. Witton*) *Arch. Soc. Yorks J.* X 419.

egetea v. gentiana.

eggon [LL = *parsnip*], rustic priest.

~ones, sacerdotes rustici *GlC* E 97; *cherlyche preyste*, ego, eco *PP*.

egilopa v. aegilops. **egipsum** v. gypsum. **egis** v. aegis.

eglentia [cf. AN *eglent*, OF *aiglent*], eglantine, briar rose.

GAD. 120. 2 (v. bedegar).

egloceron v. aegoceros. **egloga, eglota** v. ecloga.

1 ego v. 2 edo.

2 ego v. eggon.

3 ego [CL], I; **b** (w. emph. *-met*); *cf. ipse*; **c** (acc. *meme*); **d** (gen. *mis*); **e** (gen. *mei* in preference to CL *meus*); **f** (dat. *michi*); **g** (abl. w. *-cum*).

ista ego et multa alia .. intuens GILDAS *EB* 1; quos ego virgineo descripsi carmine metri ALDH. *VirgV* 2829; auctor .. / mi dedit in mundo tam victrix nomen habendum *Id. Aen.* 91 (*Palma*) 2; ea quae .. per me ipse cognoscere potui BEDE *HE pref.* p. 8; at ego, aperiens oculos, aio: "*itam*" *Ib.* V 6; **749** (12c) hanc donationem me vivente concedo *CS* 178; **867** ego Edelred rex .. concedo .. W. presbytero unam sedem .. mihhi ad elemosynam *CS* 516; scribo tibi tuus ego, / ne[c] me pudet dicere, / nec me tuum esse nego, / quem emisti munere HIL. RONCE. 3. 5; 'ego sum qui sum' [*Exod.* iii 14]: hoc pronomen 'ego' sumitur hic essentialiter HALES *Sent.* I 99; hec diccio 'ego' substancie infinite inponitur, sed ab actu loquendi de se ad alium *Ps.*-GROS. *Gram.* 44; carissima mi electa MAP *NC* IV 16 (v. elegere 6b). **b** malleus in primo memet formabat et incus ALDH. *Aen.* 54 (*Cocuma duplex*) 7; mihimet sciscitanti .. an ita esset BEDE *HE* IV 17 p. 243; memet *CD* 715 (v. debriare 1b); **a1087** (15c) rectum facite monachis meis sicut michimet *Regesta* p. 68; **c1150** aut dominis meis aut michimetipsi *Danelaw* 232; cum .. considero apud memetipsum ROLLE *IA* 217. **c** quoniam meme putat esse peremptum ALCUIN *SS Ebor* 814; *Ib.* 1347 (v. captare 1c). **d** [pronomina] sic declinantur: 'ego, tu, mei, tui' vel 'mis, tis' BONIF. *AG* 493; terror .. / qui linguam verbaque demit / mis reminiscentis haec R. CANT. *Malch.* VI 512; me prohibens a ve, mis memor, eia, fave PECKHAM *Poems* 598. **e** **1291** propositum mei (v. decretalis 2c); **13..** de statu mei *FormOx* 321 (cf. ib. 323: mei sine merito); nec esset dare maximam durabilitatem mei WYCL. *Log.* II 158. **f** **856** (12c) cuidam michi oppido fideli .. ministro *CS* 491; **a1200** reddendo inde annuatim michi et heredibus vj d. *Danelaw* 305 (cf. ib.: dederunt .. mihi .. iiij m.); **1322** michi vestras litteras destinare *Lit. Cant.* I 81; **s1455** phisici nec Phebi placuit michi nec Galieni (*Vers.*) *Reg. Whet.* I 157. **g** **798** (12c) ego A. .. archiepiscopus et C. primicerius mecum *CS* 291; **838** (9c) spiritales dominos, id est episcopos, mecum constituti (*sic*) .. mecum habuerunt *Ib.* 421; **1397** (v. 1 cum 1a).

egoceros v. aegoceros. **egre** v. aegre.

ēgredi [CL]

1 (of persons) to come or go out, depart. **b** to disembark. **c** (mon.) to leave one's order. **d** (euphem.) to die. **e** (of heir) to issue; *cf. exire* 3a.

egreditur tandem infelix gurgustia linquens ALDH. *VirgV* 2241; ipsam de qua egressi eramus insulam BEDE *HE* V 1; ~imini [AS: *gaþ ut*] .. in claustrum ÆLF. *Coll.* 103; egressus Lundonia, rex .. in propinquo loco .. morabatur ORD. VIT. IV 1 p. 165; ~iebatur foras R. COLD. *Godr.* 73 (v. dolabra b); a claustro ~i *Cust. Westm.* 94 (v. 1 ducatus 1c). **b** **s1069** [Dani] nacti opportunitatem ~iendi apud Gepesvicum in predam diffusi sunt ORD. VIT. IV 5 p. 191. **c** **c1218** quoniam quidam apostate .. de ordine suo ~i .., abjecto religionis habitu, non verentur *Conc. Syn.* 93. **d** hunc cum dies mortis ~i e corpore cogeret BEDE *HE* III 17; egredienti anime ÆTHELWULF *Abb.* 338 (v. discernere 5a); GOSC. *Mir. Iv.* lxii (v. discussio 2b); **1326** senciens me viam universe carnis fore †egressurum [? l. ingressurum] *Deeds Balliol* 53; jam egressure anime salus eterna regem sollicitat *Ps.*-ELMH. *Hen. V* 127. **e** **c1250** heredibus suis de se legitime ~ientibus *FormA* 398.

2 (trans.) to leave, quit. **b** (w. abstr. obj.) to depart from, decline to follow. **c** (w. *se*) to take leave of one's senses.

cum ~eretur .. praetorium ALDH. *VirgP* 47 (cf. ib. 4: examen [apum] .. alvearii vestibula .. egressum); [Minotaurus] domum illam Cretae [sc. laberintum] ~i non potuit *Lib. Monstr.* I 50; W. MALM. *GR* IV 336 (v. claustrum 3b); papilionem ~itur MAP *NC* II 17 f. 29; **1292** electo egresso capitulum *DCCant. Reg.* Q f. 47. **b** natura suam ~itur temperantiam et .. non sibi similia appetit *Quaest. Salern.* B 161; **1243** quia Annora .. consanguinea Fulconis .. egressa est consilium ipsius F. *Cl* 12. **c** mentes Thesifone pulsat, Erinis agit. / egressi tectum sese simul egrediuntur / armaque corripiunt in furiale nephas H. AVR. *Poems* 27. 205.

3 a (of things) to issue. **b** to rise, project. **c** (of abstr.) to arise, emanate. **d** to come off. **e** (p. ppl.) distant, separate.

a tanquam de igne fulgur ~iens GIR. *TH* III 49. **b** **1445** cum cuspide ~iente de latere (v. cuspis 1c); **1447** una crux .. de argento undique deaurato cum ymaginibus .. foliisque de lateribus crucis et sub ymaginibus supradictis copiose ~ientibus *DC S. Paul.* (*HMC*) 54b. **c** forma ~iens ab ordinacione *Ps.*-GROS. *Gram.* 32 (v. domuitas). **d** membra [sc. digiti] graciliantur, quare anulus melius ~itur *Quaest. Salern.* B 271. **e** HANV. IX 97 (v. eccentris); NECKAM *NR* I 13, GROS. 22 (v. cuspis 2).

egreferens v. aegre b.

egregie [CL], outstandingly.

~ie nimis et valde miraculose gesta GIR. *TH* II *pref.* p. 74; ~ie locutus *Id. RG* II 2 (v. consistorium 1c); milites ~ie induti apparentes *Latin Stories* 112; **s1263** ~ie potantes (v. dulcorare 1a).

egregius [CL], outstanding: **a** (of person or unspec.); **b** (of thing or abstr.).

a persolvo debitum .. amicale .. ~iis Christi tironibus GILDAS *EB* 1; linqueret egregius cum carnis vincula miles ALDH. *VirgV* 1501; viri .. per omnia mente et opere ~ii BEDE *HE* IV 17 p. 243; **956** (v. Anglosaxo); **9..** ~ius, *æmirce* *WW*; ~ii juvenes Edwinus et Morcarus ORD. VIT. IV 4 p. 182. **b** nequis me ~iam vitam .. carpere putet GILDAS *EB* 26; condidit egregiam divino dogmate legem ALDH. *VirgV* 731; auri laminae cedrinis .. tabulis adfixae vel abiegnis vel certe de lignis olivarum paratis [cf. *1 Kings* vi], quae omnia ligna esse ~ia constat BEDE *Hom.* II 1. 119; aegregia virtutum opera *Id. HA* 15; rex augustissimus ~o vocabulo Edmundus O. CANT. *Ep.* 66; ~ium aliquod mundo memoriale relinquere GIR. *TH intr.* p. 3.

egrescere v. aegrescere.

egressibilis, a permitting egress, escapable. **b** (geom.) capable of issuing or being produced.

a vix ~es rei publice labyrinthos R. BURY *Phil.* 8. 125. **b** etsi puncto daretur virtus intelligendi, in effectu se tantum intelligendo in relatione lineari infinities multiplicabili omnes lineas a se ~es unite et tamen distincte intelligeret *Ps.*-GROS. *Summa* 391.

egressio [CL]

1 (of persons) coming or going out, departure, exodus. **b** (euphem.) death.

790 Saraceni .., de quorum ~one .. scripsi ALCUIN *Ep.* 7; **s911** Edwardus .. in ~one Merce vicit eos [Dacos] gloriose H. HUNT. *HA* V 32; cccc secundo anno ~onis Israel de Egypto R. NIGER *Chr. I* 6; **s1290** de tota .. Judeorum [exilio damnatorum] turba, certo ~onis die statuto, non remansit unus qui .. ad fidem converteretur Christianam OXNEAD *Chr.* 277. **b** post ~onem ejus [Augustini] de corpore ELMH. *Cant.* 117.

2 (of things) emergence, exit, detachment. **b** (of Nile) overflow, flood.

solis ~o super terram .. manifestationem ultimi designat examinis BEDE *Gen.* (xix 23) 177; causali .. illius caloris ~one .. nimia pororum apercio fit ADEL. *QN* 20; additis in eo [horologio] totidem [xij] equitibus, qui per totidem fenestras horis expletis exibant et impulsu ~onis totidem fenestras aperiebant R. NIGER *Chr. II* 150; ~o .. juncturarum GAD. 127v. 1 (v. dislocatio a). **b** secundum cujus [Nili] ~ones stat Egyptiaca fertilitas vel negatur BACON *Maj.* I 321.

egressor, runaway, fugitive (mon.).

s1454 efficiat .. id pietas in vobis .. ut, quos in transgressores pios esse oportet .. impios in ~ores nulla in vobis voluntaria disposicio .. fore permittat *Reg. Whet.* I 141.

egressus [CL], departure, exodus. **b** (right of) egress; **c** (in board game). **d** (euphem.) death.

canebat .. de ~u Israel ex Aegypto BEDE *HE* IV 22 p. 261; HERM. ARCH. 40 (v. consessus 1a); Noemi vendidit agrum in ~u suo tali pacto ut rediens redimeret S. LANGTON *Ruth* 120. **b** **1285** dummodo tenentes ipsi haberent sufficientem pasturam ad tenementa sua cum libero ingressu et ~u ad eandem (2 *Westm.* 46) *StRealm* I 94; **1292** communitas habet libere ingressum et †ekressum ad tentorium *Rec. Leic.* I 218; naute .. observabant introitus et exitus ut nulli omnino pateret ~us *V. Ed. II* 242. **c** punctum *G* nodare impediet ~um adversarii sui *Ludus Angl.* 162. **d** cui aegressui victoriosissimo psalmus .. testimonium dat BEDE *HA* 14; ne justo tuo judicio habeam quod valde timeo, ~um lamentabilem UHTRED *Medit.* 196.

egretarius v. aegrotare a.

egrex, outcast from herd.

hinnulus ut cervae si matris sique catervae / egrex cervorum sit factus forte suorum R. CANT. *Malch.* IV 615.

egri-, egrot- v. aegr-. **egromonia** v. agrimonia.

egtendalum [ME *eighten dēl*], 'eightendeal', eighth part (dry measure).

1199 dedit .. j m. argenti et j egtendal' de *mesteilun* *Fines RC* (*Cambs*) I 268 (cf. *Ac. Durh.* 606 [**1406**]: in iij *aghtyndell* anguill[arum] sals[arum]).

eheu [CL], exclamation of grief, 'wellaway!'. *V. et. heu.*

9.. eheu, *wa la wa* *WW*; heheu! quam cecos habet Alexandria cives NIG. *Paul.* f. 48 l. 357; eu! mammona iniquitatis indignos levat in prelatos J. READING f. 191.

ehtemannus [AS *æhte man*], bondman, serf.

omnibus ~is [AS: *æhtemannum*] jure competit natalis firma et paschalis (*Quad. Rect.*) *GAS* 450 (cf. ib. 222 *Quad.*: si eahta men occidantur, pertineat infractio pacis intra curiam vel adjacentias ejus. *eahta men* persolvantur plena wera (= *Leg. Hen.* 70. 7a; ib. 588: *athemen*).

ei v. hei.

1 eia [ME *ei* < AS *ieg*], island (in marsh). *V. et. eilondus.*

c1230 [j acr' dim.' terre] tam .. extra foveam quam infra usque in mediam per eyam que vocatur Broynstan, [que] capitant ad watergangam *Doc. Robertsbr.* 88 (cf. *Chr. Rams.* 9: Ramesia .. dici potest a duobus nominibus Anglicis, *ram* quod est 'aries' et *eie* quod insulam sonat).

2 eia v. heia.

eicere (ejic-) [CL]

1 (w. pers. obj.): **a** to drive out, eject, throw off. **b** to oust (from possession of land or sim.). **c** to exile. **d** to release, deliver.

a quis vestrum, .. ejectus de consilio impiorum .. toto corde Trinitati gratias egit? GILDAS *EB* 73; operarios fraudulentos .. Dominus .. ejecit de Templo [cf. *Mark* xi 15] BEDE *Hom.* II 1. 117; **1248** serviens .. ejecit eam de equo suo et abstulit ab ea xx s. *SelCWW* 70; **s1252** ~ite rusticum hunc! ~ite et ejectum excludite! M. PAR. *Maj.* V 332; si quis [leprosus] casualiter ingressus fuerit [limina portarum burgi], per servientes burgi .. statim ~iatur *Stat. Gild. Berw.* 18 p. 92*; **1341** (v. effugare 2a); **1375** [Walterus] Robertum .. ejecit de domo sua vi et armis per tres noctes continuas *Leet Norw.* 67. **b** a .. possessiunculis suis ejecti BEDE *HE* I 12; offitio .. sedulus, hereditate tamen eitiendus PULL. *CM* 219; **1255** fuerunt in seysina [commune] donec .. senescallus foreste .. ipsos ejecit *SelPlForest* 26; fit disseisina non solum cum quis presens .., vel familia qui nomine suo fuerint (*sic*) in seisina, violenter, injuste et sine judicio de tenemento suo qualicumque ejecti fuerint BRACTON 161b (cf. ib. 168: [assisa] non competit ei qui de nave sua ejectus fuerit quasi de libero tenemento suo; ib. 220: si quis ~iatur de usufructu [etc.]); *Ib.* 7 (v. consuetudo 3a); **1269** inde [sc. de manerio] non †eciatur quousque .. *Cl* 57; HENGHAM *Parva* 8 (v. dominicus 4c). **c** **1276** de regno .. ejectus (v. deputare 5a). **d** **s692** Withredo et Suihardo .., qui religione simul et industria gentem suam ab extranea invasione ejecerunt M. PAR. *Maj.* I 311 (= BEDE *HE* IV 24: donec .. Wictred .. liberaret).

2 to cast out (devils).

sacerdotes qui per exorcismi gratiam daemones ~ere norunt BEDE *Luke* 438; *Id. Hom.* II 11. 160 (v. daemonium 1b); EGB. *Pont.* 10 (v. exorcista b); [diabolus], adjuratus quomodo [ea] curari posset, dixit quod .. episcopus eum ~eret GIR. *GE* I 18; nummus mutum / eicit demonium WALT. WIMB. *Van.* 42.

3 to throw out or away. **b** to excrete. **c** to emit, release (air or fluid). **d** (naut.) to jettison. **e** to take away, remove, release.

aedituus ipsius sanc[t]um corpus de ecclesia ejecit in coemeterium GOSC. *Transl. Aug.* 44A; W. MALM. *GP* V 274 (v. decimare 6a); *RBOssory* 254 (v. destillatorius); **12..** ita quod .. liceret nobis terram ~ere super terram suam ubicunque abbuttat super .. fossatum *Meaux* II 37; vidua volens domum .. mundare colligit primo grossiora et expellit; postmodum revertitur et dimissa cumulat ac .. ~it [ME: *schuveð hit þenne ut*] *AncrR* 119; evolavit cum ejulatu magno quasi spacium lapidis †entcardi [MS: eiiciendi] *Ghost Stories* 415. **b** J. BLUND *An.* 54 (v. digestio 1a). **c** sunt tria necessaria, semen quod emittitur, calor qui in homine accendat et semen ~iat, .. spiritus [qui] virgam erigat et semen expellat *Quaest. Salern.* B 6; vesica inflata vento non .. mergitur in aqua, sed punctura acus ~it [ME: *warpeð .. ut*] totum ventum *AncrR* 105; **1324** per quod .. tassum ordei non potuit ~ere humores et erat putrefactum *CBaron* 137. **d** ut earum rerum que in tempestate maris levande navis causa ~iuntur non amittatur dominium GIR. *PI* I 20 p. 120; **1285** omnia alia bona .. debent appreciari in auxilium restitucionis vinorum et aliorum bonorum sic in navi extra navem per hujusmodi tempestatem ejectorum (*Pat*) *Foed.* II 298b. **e** **1266** quod xxxvj dolia vini, que captor vinorum nostrorum cepit ad opus nostrum apud Lenn', a manibus mercatorum ibidem ~i et acquietari .. facias *Cl* 205; **1272** quod .. ceram .. a manibus mercatorum, a quibus eam ceperint, ~i .. et in garderoba nostra liberari faciant *Liberate* 48 m. 4.

4 (leg.) to remove (land) from (forest status).

1209 quod .. capiat terram Thome de C. et boscum suum, qui per falsam juratam ejectus [MS: †ejecit] fuit de foresta *SelPlForest* 10.

eicios v. echios. **eignec-,** v. aesnec-.

eilondus [ME *eilond, heland*], island. *V. et.* 1 *eia.*

dedi .. ij carucatas terre in insula ex australi parte, et iiij heilandos proximos ipsi terre cum piscariis *MonA* VI 1130 (*Wexford*).

einesc- v. aesnec. **eir[arius]** v. 2 aerarius.

eirenarcha [εἰρηνάρχης], justice of the peace. (*Cf.* W. Lambard *'Eirenarcha' or the Office of the Justices of Peace* London, 1581).

assisae .. in quibus duo assisarum justitiarii ad hoc deputati cum ~is, sive pacis justitiariis, comitati et de civilibus et de criminalibus cognoscunt CAMD. *Br.* 143.

eirare, ~iare v. 3 errare.

eirum [AN *eire*, OF *erre, oirre*; cf. 3 errare], (leg.) eyre, circuit. *Cf. iter.*

1285 dant dim. m. pro licencia concordandi .. de placito terre, et habent eyrum (*Eyre*) *DocCOx* 225 (cf. ib. 228: et habent oyrum).

eis- v. ais-. **ejactare** v. ejectare.

ejaculari [CL], to hurl, fling; **b** (*s. pass.*, of utterance).

quas procul oceanus absorbet gurgite vasto, / illuc retrogradas ejaculatur aquas GARL. *Tri. Eccl.* 65. **b** alii tenentes istam doctrinam, per quos fallacia accidentis et figure diccionis in scholis tam diu ~antur LUTTERELL *Occam* 158.

ejaculatio, shooting, bombardment.

propter assiduam castri ~onem .. fuerant disturbati LESLEY *RGScot* 473.

ejectare [CL], to throw out. **b** to discharge from the body.

1339 in terra circa *standard* fodienda et ~anda in grosso pro novo *standard* inponendo *Ac. Man. Cant.* (*Milton*); *to caste owte*, eicere, ejactare .. *CathA.* **b** ~at, i. ructat, emittit *GlH* E 165.

1 ejectio [CL]

1 driving out (of person), expulsion. **b** (leg.) ousting, ejectment (from).

in principium Genesis usque ad .. ~onem Ismahelis, libros iiij BEDE *HE* V 25 p. 357; *Chr. Battle* f. 103 (v. elephantiosus); **s1296** de ~one Anglorum beneficiatorum de regno Scocie FORDUN *Cont.* XI 21 *tit.*; **c1400** non legavit .. dilectis scolaribus .. secularia desideria sed .. affliccio-nes, flagellaciones, ~ones a populo [cf. *Matth.* x 17] WYCHE *Ep.* 542. **b s1196** monachi canonicos ad causam vocaverant et usque ad ~onem eorum .. institerant G. COLD. *Durh.* 12; **1292** pro dampnis sibi adjudicatis pro ~one manerii de T. *Manners* 133; **1348** sine aliquo impedimento, ~one et calumpnia cujuscumque *Mem. Ripon* I 279; **14..** de ~one firme *Reg. Brev. Orig.* 227b *rub.*; **1573** cum Ricardus W. .. in curia nostra coram justiciariis nostris de Banco .. implacitasset Johannem R. .. de quibusdam transgressione et ~one firme eidem R. per predictum J. illatis *Pat* 1105 m. 31.

2 casting out (of devils).

cum .. signorum illis faciendorum potestatem delegaret, daemonum ~onem, linguarum novitatem [cf. *Mark* xvi 14] OSB. *V. Dunst.* 42.

3 a throwing out, discharge (of cannon-balls). **b** excretion. **c** release (of heat). **d** (naut.) jettison.

a 1426 navis .. per ~onem petrarum canonum diruta fuit et confracta *Pat* 420 m. 16. **b** futura est sordium ~o et ideo descendens feculentia ALF. ANGL. *Cor* 14. 6. **c** caloris superflui ~onem secuta temperies *Ib.* 13. 12. **d 1277** pro ~onibus vinorum et aliarum mercium, que periculis in[ter]venientibus frequenter contingunt in mari (*Pat* 96 m. 14*d*.) *Law & Cust. Sea* I 51; **c1280** quod, cum .. oportet .. propter tempestatem mare supervenientem facere ~onem pro navi .. salvanda .., usitatum sit et .. baronibus [V Portuum] concessum quod navis .. quieta esse debeat de omnimodo auxilio prediecte ~oni faciendo .. *MGL* I 490; **1285** navis in †quo [l. qua] mercimonia .. fuerint, .. victualia nautarum, utensilia ad prandia sua facienda .. erunt quieta de auxilio prestando ad ~onem maris (*Pat*) *SelCKB* I 156 (= *Foed.* II 298); **1300** (v. contributio a).

2 ejectio v. electio 1b.

ejectivus, 'ejective' (med.), expulsive.

medicinam ~am et eductivam humoris nocentis GILB. VI 254. 2; effectus superbie sunt xij: .. secundo celis ~a, .. octavo mundane dignitatis ~a *Spec. Laic.* 82.

ejector, one who drives out. **b** (leg.) ejector, dispossessor.

~ores [Dunstani] B. *V. Dunst.* 22 (v. conscribere 2b). **b** cum neuter jus habeat, melior est causa possidentis; et ideo, si ille qui jus non habeat talem eiciat, ~or contra eum exceptionem non habebit BRACTON 161.

ejectus

1 outcast.

13.. rex [Hen. I] fundavit .. hospitale super x leprosis .. ; et dicunt quod dicti leprosi erunt de ejectibus [? l. ejectis] civitatis Lincolnie (*Inq.*) *MonA* VI 627a.

2 (naut.) jetsam.

rex Ædwardus .. Ringstede cum libertate adjacente et omni maris ~u, qui *wrech* dicitur, .. largitus est *Chr. Rams.* 160 (cf. *CD* 853 [†c1053]: *scipbryce and ðа sæ upwarp .. æt Ringstyde*); †**1077** (13c) concedo .. Bramcestre cum .. omni maris ~u quod (*sic*) nos *wrec* nominamus *Cart. Rams.* II 93 (= *Regesta* I 95); **1226** de navi .. periclitata .. catalla .. tunc nostra sint et heredum nostrorum nomine †ejecti [? l. wrecci] '*Ch. Hen. III*' ap. *DuC* s. v. 2 ejectus (cf. *ChartR* 29 m. 4: wrecci).

ejulare [CL], to wail, lament (intr.); **b** (fig., w. inanim. subj.). **c** (of foxes) to howl. **d** (gdv.) lamentable.

716 spiritus .. hejulantes cecidisse in puteos BONIF. *Ep.* 10; [homo lubricus] lacrymans et ~ans veniam poscit GOSC. *Aug. Maj.* 86B; mater .. pueri nimio dolore constricta †evilando [l. ejulando] clamare cepit ANSELM BURY *Mir. Virg.* 19; inspexit .. anum flentem et ~antem G. MON. X 3; illum excitantes .., quare sic in quietis silentio ~aret, fleret et voces emitteret explorarunt R. COLD. *Godr.* 267; flens et ~ans [ME: *graninde*] *AncrR* 126. **b 1163** non ~abit clamans terra tua post te, quoe doctrine fluentis .. irrigabitur G. FOLIOT *Ep.* 147. **c** vulpes ~ant ALDH. *PR* 131. **d** †**680** (12c) fortuna fallentis saeculi procax .., fellita ~andae corruptionis amaritudine odibilis *CS* 54 (= W. MALM. *GP* V 201); **934** fellita hejulandae corruptionis amaritudine *CS* 702.

ejulatio [CL], wailing, lamentation.

audita est per totam noctem vox doloris et ~o planctus miserabilis fere per omnes civitatis partes OSB. BAWDSEY clxix; talis lamentatio, / talis ejulatio, / non est necessaria HIL. RONCE. 11. 53; gemituum suspiriis et ~onum lamentis R. COLD. *Cuthb.* 20.

ejulatorius, wailful.

verbis ~iis deflentes peccamina *NLA* (*J. Bridl.*) II 73.

ejulatus [CL], wail, lament.

~us, planctus, ploratus *GlH* E 162; infans .. ut major esset hejulatus trucidabatur ABBO *Edm.* 5; magno ~u flevit HON. *Spec. Eccl.* 881D; lacrime cum ~u proruperunt ORD. VIT. IV 13 p. 267; in tot suspiriis atque ~uum meroribus R. COLD. *Godr.* 125; mulier quedam cum magno ~u plangebat MAP *NC* II 5 f. 24v.; **a1268** sicut †egretarius [? l. egrotantis] passio, incessanti dolore concuciens, successivis †ejulantibus [? l. ~atibus] cedere nescit (*Lit. O. Cardinalis*) *EHR* XV 116; **1311** (v. complodere a).

ejurare [CL], to abjure. *V. et. abjurare* 4.

1198 R. de M. debet v m. ut posset ~are forestam quando fugerat in ecclesiam pro venatione *Pipe* 223; **1201** ut possit ~are forestam *Pipe* 27; **1204** Johannes le Stiward fugit in ecclesiam et cognovit quod receptor fuit malefactorum et socius eorum; et ~avit regnum *CurR* III 145; **1221** Nicholaus G. occidit Ricardum A. et fugit in ecclesiam .. et ~avit regnum. N. non fuit in franco plegio, quia infra etatem, sc. x vel xj annorum; et ideo loquendum qualiter ~avit regnum. et T. .. et W. .., servientes abbatis Cirencestrie, cognoverunt quod fecerunt eum ~are regnum sine coronatoribus et sine vicecomite; et ideo in misericordia *PlCrGlouc* 41.

ejusmodi [CL], (things) of that kind, the like. *Cf. hujusmodi. V. et. modus.*

in omnibus ~i praeteritis ABBO *QG* 13 (31) (v. antecrescere); haec natura quae talis est, aut sola est aut plures ~i et aequales sunt ANSELM (*Mon.* 4) I 17; ut et in ipsis et in ~i ex ipsis facile sit exercitium BALSH. *AD* 8; **1438** duello ~i (v. duellum 3a).

ekressus v. egressus b. **ela** v. 1 ala 4a.

elabi [CL]

1 to slip out or away, escape: **a** (of person); **b** (of bird); **c** (w. inanim. subj.); **d** (fig., of possession); **e** (of abstr.).

a †~e [l. ~i], i. evadere, effugere *GlH* E 173; ipsi .. qui in tanto periculo superfuerant vix †elaxi [v. l. elapsi] .. tellurem scandunt G. MON. IV 7; ego te .. quodam modo fugitantem et ~entem votive deosculor G. HOYLAND *Ascet.* 255D; cunctos .. milites preter duos fuga elapsos mactaverunt ORD. VIT. IV 5 p. 187; omnibus evigilantibus .., elapsa est illa [hospita] et disparuit GIR. *GE* II 11; hiis dictis inter manus volentis eum comprehendere elapsus disparuit P. CORNW. *Rev.* I 205 p. 199. **b** [passer] mox .. in hiemem regrediens tuis oculis ~itur BEDE *HE* II 13. **c** lana ostri elabitur / vermiculo, cum vertitur (ÆTHELWALD) *Carm. Aldh.* 2. 141; aerea humiditas ratione expressionis ~itur circa interiora teste *Quaest. Salern.* B 146; si contingat quod .. cellule [cerebri] nimis fiat .. fluida, forme impresse cito ~untur *Ib.* N 43. **d s1255** nunquam illum archiepiscopatum antea in manu tenui; ideo cavendum est ne nimis cito ~atur M. PAR. *Maj.* V 516. **e** quando amor Dei et timor pariter ab eo [milite] turpiter ~untur R. NIGER *Mil.* I 34 (cf. ib. 78: frequenter iterantur mandata .., ne .. ~atur ab homine quod habeat facere); qualiter pro elapsis a memoria satisfaciemus? ALEX. BATH *Mor.* III 16 p. 162; laus que depromitur verbo volatili / statim elabitur cum verbo labili WALT. WIMB. *Carm.* 201.

2 (p. ppl. *elapsus*) having elapsed. **b** (in abl. absol.) after (the lapse of). **c** (in abl. absol. or sim. phr.) before, ago.

1236 predicte l m. debebantur pro fructibus autumni proximo ~i GROS. *Ep.* 26; **1395** pro .. annua pensione trium annorum ultimo ~orum *Lit. Cant.* III 48; **1455** solutum abbatisse .. pro anno ~o *Cant. Coll. Ox.* II 176; **1516** post tres dies immediate ~os a deputatione judicum *StatOx* 332; **1549** in mense Augusti ultimo ~i *Conc. Scot.* II 86. **b** non multo post haec ~o tempore BEDE *HE* IV 6; quoniam .. tanto tempore ~o calumniae ansam non pretendistis OSB. *V. Dunst.* 36; ~is dictis tribus diebus (*Assisa David* 22) *APScot* I 10; **1220** ~is tribus annis .., volumus .. quod consuetudo predicta cesset *Pat* 242; presentatus fuit ad ecclesiam .. ij annis ~is postquam breve ei venit *State Tri. Ed. I* 18; **1407** tempore non longo ~o, Godekynus .. viam arripuit .. *Lit. Cant.* III 100. **c 1222** L. dicit quod octo annis ~is fuit inde persona; set littere sue recentes sunt et cera recens est *CurR* X 277; **c1228** vidit .. usque ad circiter duos annos ~os .. parochianos de K. S. sequi capitulum episcopi de A. *Feod. Durh.* 251; **1235** Walterus, multo tempore ~o antequam R. .. filius suus dedit J. regi manerium de W. in escambium, dedit advocationem .. abbatie .. *CurR* XV 1950; **1241** idem M. venit in eadem curia in festo S. Hil. proximo preterito, fuerunt duo anni ~i, et recognovit .. *Ib.* XVI 1789; **1309** Clemencia de B. suspensa fuit ab octo annis ~is *S. Jers.* XVIII 267; **13..** xxvj annis ~is .. rector .. fuit seisitus de decima *Meaux* II 289; de hac questione .. ad xxvj ~os annos fuit maxime .. controversum *Praxis* 269.

elaborare [CL]

1 to accomplish laboriously. **b** (p. ppl.) elaborate.

tantis lucubrationibus ~andum mihi onus arripui GIR. *TH intr.* p. 5; dejectionem .. ~avi *Id. Symb. pref.* (v. dejectio 2a); **1439** coram consilio nostro apud villam Calesie pro arduis negociis nostris jam ~at[is] *Cl* 289 m. 14. **b** planum est non ~ate cujusdam fictionis sed communis .. cognitionis esse BALSH. *AD rec.* 2 130.

2 to labour, strive; **b** (w. *ut*); **c** (w. inf.).

†desidans [l. desudans], ~ans *GlC* D 89; explicare .. quantum in structura monasterii ~aret WULF. *Æthelwold* 37; si me viderent alii homines onustum paxillis et funibus .. ~are circa montem Olympum ad confirmandum illum .. ANSELM (*Incarn. A* 1) I 281. **b 1024** nobis ~andum .. extat .. ut .. theoricae vitae amoenissima consequi mereamur contubernia *CD* 741; ut diutius haec memoria perseveraret ~avit GOSC. *Transl. Aug.* 46B; Gundulfus .. ~avit ut pacis vincula .. nectere posset *V. Gund.* 35; ut optineas profectum in illa [gratia Dei] studiosius ~a J. SAL. *Ep.* 250 (148); W. CANT. *V. Thom.* I 3 (v. collateralis 2c). **c** nunc scies quem ~averis ante destituere quam cognoscere GOSC. *Transl. Aug.* 44A; cum .. fornacem .. succendi omnimodis ~asset DOMINIC *V. Ecgwini* I *prol.*; validos ictus .. inferre ~abant G. MON. X 4; **s1157** libertates .. jure mihi concessas a majestate regali demere ~as *Chr. Battle* f. 74v.; **1166** quanto melius .. intimares ei et persuadere modis omnibus ~ares BECKET *Ep.* 224.

elaborate, elaborately.

hanc eandem conclusionem ferventi spiritu ~issime demonstravit BRADW. *CD* 549E.

elaboratio [CL], elaboration; **b** (alch.).

contingit leges humanas multum proficere, de quanto sunt implicite in scriptura; sed in ~one et appropriacione istarum jacet periculum WYCL. *Sim.* 51. **b** tam arte quam natura cognoscitur ex partibus mixtorum elementa resultare, ut in dissolucionibus lapidum .. et idem patet ex ~onibus olei de minutis seminibus *Id. Log.* III 77; ~o est operatio manuaria qua res in substantia .. mutata elaboratur *LC.*

elaborator, one who works out, puts into effect. **b** (w. *terrarum*) land-worker, tiller.

c1400 adjutor sibi et ~or fuit in multis frater J. M., prior monasterii AMUND. II app. 305. **b 1559** per locationem terrarum ecclesiae spectantium .. aliis personis quam antiquis nativis tenentibus, possessoribus et ~oribus terrarum *Conc. Scot.* II 168.

elaborus v. helleborus. **elactar-** v. et. elater-.

elactare [cf. CL lactare], to 'spane', wean. **b** to suckle (fig.).

~are, a lacte tollere *GlC* E 126; *to spayn*, ablactare, ~are .. *CathA.* **b** ~asti ignorantiam meam uberibus rationis ADEL. *QN* 69.

elacter- v. elater-. **elafion** v. elaphoboscon.

elami, (mus.) note E on which la and mi are sung.

GARL. *Mus.* 160 (v. descendere 5b); *Tonale Sal.* lvii (v. 3 districtio 1h).

elanceatus [cf. CL lanx], (?) weighed in the balance (fig.).

975 (12c) hoc ei .. meritorum repensator Deus ~o repensamine reddat *CS* 1314.

elanguescere [CL], **~ēre** [LL], to ail, pine, be or grow faint.

emarcuit, †~et [l. ~it] *GlC* E 146; †~et [l. ~it], *ablacode GlH* E 166; ordo clericorum .., mundi blandimento succumbens .., ~it ORD. VIT. III 1 p. 6; non dolore tabescas .., non pavore ~eas H. BOS. *Thom.* IV 13 p. 364; talibus insudans olei librique lucerna / tabidus illanguet [v. l. elanguet] HANV. III 188 p. 281; segni ~isse per mensem inhercia MAP *NC* II 25 f. 32v.; en fauces elanguent stridore clamoris J. HOWD. *Cant.* 386 (cf. id. *Ph.* 169: et elanguet flos frontis regie); c**1430** quatinus .. cordis et corporis expendatis impensas ad consolacionem proximi ~entis *Reg. Whet.* II app. 378.

elaphoboscon [CL < ἐλαφόβοσκον], wild parsnip, ragwort. **b** (?) sow fennel (*Peucedanum*).

ragworte, elephebascum LEVINS *Manip.* 173. **b** elophaboscos .. elafion *Alph.* 54 (v. cervaria).

elapidare [CL = *to clear of stones*], to deprive by stoning.

si secus hinc teneo, pulmonibus elapidari / debeo L. DURH. *Dial.* III 283.

elapsus, a lapse (of time). **b** 'falling out', quarrel.

a 1239 si ipsa moriatur ante ~um .. termini *CurR* XVI 775. **b** reversiones tot et ~us H. BOS. *LM* 1369D (v. avolatio a).

elaqueare [LL], to disentangle (fig.).

~eatis morarum retibus W. MALM. *GR* III 293.

elargare, ~eare, ~iare, ~ire [OF *enlargier, enlargir, eslargier, eslargir*]

1 to widen.

[humiditate augmentata] arbor .. confortatur et ipsius pori ~antur *Quaest. Salern.* B 198; **1243** ~ari faciant fossata circa castrum [de Windlesor'] *Cl* 24; GILB. III 154. 1 (v. elargatio 1); **1266** quod portam suam per medium muri ville nostre Sallop', que nimis arcta est, .. ~are possint *Mon. Francisc.* I app. 618 (= *CalPat* 113); quod vie regales a villis mercatoriis usque ad villas mercatorias se extendentes ~entur *Fleta* 35 (= *StRealm* I 97 [**1285**]: *qe les hauz chemins .. seient enlargiz*); **1342** trencheas .. ~are (v. deobstruere a).

2 to enlarge, extend: **a** (area); **b** (building); **c** (abstr.).

a 1237 videri faciat in quibus boscis .. possint ~ari dominica regis per purpresturas et assarta in eisdem facienda *Cl* 519; **1263** quod .. viculum .. includere possint ad ~andam curiam suam (*Breve Regis*) *MonA* III 223b; **1281** Petrus .. non ~avit warennam suam in G. *PQW* 422b; ~iavit gardinum et inclusit cum novo muro WHITTLESEY 164. **b 1243** quoddam appenticium camere nostre de longitudine x pedum .. eslargiri facias *Liberate* 14 m. 5; **1331** ad .. muros .. ~iandos *IMisc* 114/9; **1350** cuidam carpentario ~eanti bovarium pro j domo pro feno de novo facienda (*MinAc*) *Surv. Durh. Hatf.* 219; **1429** cum .. convenerit .. domum sive hospitale ac mansum ejusdem .. ~are et ampliare (*Pat*) AMUND. II 163 (= *CalPat* 517); **1476** si .. persona voluerit facere illam insulam [ecclesie] de novo et eam ~are per ix pedes *Test. Ebor.* III 220. **c** possunt dari, si oportet ~are dietam, .. carnes minorum avium GILB. I 36. 1; **1455** ad ~andum fidem nostram et ligianciam erga metuendissimam personam vestram (*Lit. Ducis Ebor.*) *Reg. Whet.* I 184.

3 to set at large, release.

1402 ~iti (v. elargimentum); **1440** nisi .. intellexissent personam nostram .. ad tempus .. ~andam sive laxandam esse a prisona (*DipDocE* 456) *Foed.* X 778b; **1453** comes de Menteth, unus obsidum in regno nostro Anglie .. infra castrum [de Pountfret] existens, ~abitur *RScot* 368a.

elargatio

1 widening.

nares elargentur et tunc ferrum candens .. immittatur .. vel .. post ~onem cum spatulo (*sic*) .. usque ad radicem incidatur GILB. III 154. 1; **1267** ad ~onem fossati *Cl* 414; **1433** quod .. propter ~onem .. vie regie .. barre .. ammoveantur et vicinius .. pasture a .. via regia per spacium xxx pedum ponantur *Rec. Leic.* II 251; **14..** per ~onem .. aque de H. *Reg. Brev. Orig.* 250b.

2 enlargement: **a** (of area); **b** (of building or other artefact); **c** (of angle); **d** (of abstr.).

a 1268 concedere quandam placeam nostram in civitate Ebor' contiguam placee .. archiepiscopi .. ad ~onem placee sue predicte *Reg. North.* 19 (= *CalPat* 261); **1281** quoad ~onem warenne *PQW* 395b (cf. *SelPlForest* cxxv *n.*); **1296** concessimus .. priori et fratribus ordinis .. de Monte Carmeli de Berewico .. iiij placeas terre .. ad ~onem aree sue *RScot* 34b; **1353** dederunt .. j acram .. in ~onem .. cimiterii, mansi et claustri *FormA* 165; **1386** quod .. tria tofta dare possint .. magistro et scolaribus in ~onem mansi sui .. et .. quod ipsi [magister et scolares] tria tofta .. recipere possint in †elongacionem mansi sui predicti *Deeds Balliol* 71; c**1470** in augmentacionem, ampliacionem et ~onem dominii terrarum de S. perquisivit duas parcellas terre *Reg. Whet.* I 428. **b 1306** quod possint includere quandam placeam .. ad ~onem domus sue *RParl* I 196b; s**1438** in ~one studii abbatis AMUND. II 199 (= *Reg. Whet.* I 456: elargicione); **1441** super empcione j pecie veluti rubei .. pro ~one unius frontalis et subfrontalis ex utroque latere et utroque fine pro altari principali Dunelmensi *Reg. Cant.* II 580. **c** ex elargicione anguli piramidis radialis WYCL. *Civ. Dom.* I 377. **d 1354** ad ordinandum super refusione damnorum eis [magistris et scholaribus universitatis Oxon'] .. illatorum ac super ~one privilegiorum *Conc.* III 34.

3 setting at large, release.

1440 ut liberius .. dux Aurelianensis pro procuranda pace laborare posset, regia majestas ipsius elargiacioni .. consensit BEKYNTON II 74.

elargeare v. elargare. **elargiare** v. elargare, 2 elargire. **elargiatio** v. elargatio.

elargimentum, setting at large, release.

1402 si .. capti .. elargiti a carceribus exierint seu ab eorum ~o recesserint, a .. carcerum et cujuslibet aresti aut ~i infraccione .. quitti (*sic*) permaneant (*DipDocE* 355) *Foed.* VIII 275a.

1 elargire v. elargare.

2 elargiri [CL], **~ire,** to bestow freely.

de mercatore quodam pauperibus omnia sua ~iente *Spec. Laic.* 31; **1346** vobis .. plenam .. licenciam .. ~imur (*Lit. Papae*) *Scot. Grey Friars* II 149; **1350** sed dies indulgencie .. a vobis .. petimus ~iri *Conc.* III 3b; **1520** facultates .. concedimus et ~imur *Form. S. Andr.* I 176; **15..** preter pluries ~itas elemosynas (*Necrol.*) *Mon. Francisc.* II 132; **1551** super aliis x li. ~iandis pauperibus *Reg. Aberd.* I 455.

1 elargitio v. elargatio.

2 elargitio, bestowal, expenditure.

1312 nullus .. ministrorum nostrorum .. subditos nostros per immoderatam sumptuum ~onem vel apposicionem .. gravare presumat *Conc.* II 417a; **1541** litteras questoribus pro elimosinarum requisitione et ~one *Form. S. Andr.* II 127.

elate [CL], magnificently.

regina .. suffulta ~ius ceteris matronis BYRHT. *V. Osw.* 438.

elateriatus, compounded of wild cucumber.

fiant .. inunctiones de unguento mixto ex sex unguentis, ca[lamento], euforbito, scamoneato vel elacteriato, sinapizato, piperato GILB. II 119. 1.

elaterium, ~is [CL < ἐλατήριον, *conf. w.* λαθυρίς (*spurge*)], wild cucumber (*Ecballium elaterium*) or spurge (*Euphorbia lathyris*).

recipe .. sinapis ℥ unam, centauree, mi[conis], elactarii ana ʒ v GILB. II 119. 1; recipe .. cinamomi, elacteridum, croc[i] ana ℥ ij *Ib.* V 212. 1; elactarium est succus cucumeris asinini. elacteris est cucumer agrestis. elacterides secundum quosdam sunt cucumeres, tam fructus eorum quam ipsa herba. elacterides, ut quidam volunt, sunt catapucie *SB* 18; elacterium, succus cucurbite agrestis idem; sed electerides [v. l. elacterides] sunt cucumeres agrestes ..; item lacterides sunt cathapucie *Alph.* 53.

elatine [CL < ἐλατίνη], (?) fluellin (*Kickxia elatine*).

†elatmo folia habet similia elixine sed minora ..; nascitur in locis cultis et in agris *Alph.* 54.

1 elatio [CL]

1 (ceremonial) carrying out.

sperasse se .. aliquod alleviamentum .. pro tot ~onibus funerum W. MALM. *GR* III 293.

2 elevation, height. **b** ocean swell, billow (*cf. Psalm* xcii 4).

GIR. *TH* II 23 (v. cornu 1a); arenosa loca .. in .. aggeres .. levata et iterum .. de montuosis ~onibus Eoli commotivis agitacionibus in valles repressa *Ps.*-ELMH. *Hen. V* 59 p. 151. **b** c**1170** [Christus] qui comprimit ~ones maris J. SAL. *Ep.* 295 (297); s**1174** maris sevitiam, fluctuum ~onem, procellarum fragores .. expavit DICETO *YH* I 388; **1199** gratie vestre, que .. maris ~onibus mirabilis se objecit (*Lit. ad Papam*) *Ep. Cant.* 522; s**1343** per maris ~ones mirabiles fluctusque procellosos .. agitati AVESB. 101b; maris hec elacio mira, / imber, grando silent ELMH. *Metr. Hen. V* 1034; montanis ~onibus effugatis, a ponto mansueti pelagi aura favorabilis ipsas classes .. invitabat *Ps.*-ELMH. *Hen. V* 19.

3 pride.

ni pro contribulibus .. mori optasset .. inconsideratam cordis ~onem propria morte piaret GILDAS *EB* 39; tumido ~onis supercilio inflati ALDH. *VirgP* 10; ALCUIN *Dogm.* 285C (v. ebullire 1c); **939** si quis .. hanc nostram difinitionem ~onis habitu incedens .. infringere temptaverit *CS* 734; clerici, ~one et insolentia ac luxuria praeventi ÆLF. *Æthelwold* 12; si gaudium inflatur in ~onem, opponit ei justitia humilitatem R. NIGER *Mil.* II 12; s**1269** cum archiepiscopus Ebor', adhuc in ~one sua perseverans, fecisset ante se crucem suam portare *Leg. Ant. Lond.* 117; ut deploret transactas ~ones vanissimas R. BURY *Phil.* 20. 248; nec inanis ~onis tumorem concipit *Ps.*-ELMH. *Hen. V* 45.

2 elatio v. eleatio. **elatmo** v. elatine.

elator, exalter, upholder.

amicus pauperum et ~or animarum *Canon. Edm. Rich* 192; **1347** qui .. justiciam .. diligunt tuique honoris ~ores exsistunt (*Lit. Papae ad Ed. III*) AVESB. 111b.

elatus v. efferre. **elaxus** v. elabi 1a. **elb-** v. helv-. **elchinus** v. 2 echinus 1.

eldefader [ME *ēldefader*], 'eldfather', ancestor.

1263 Adam de F. petit gildam que fuit ~eri sui super Johannem W. (*Andover*) *Gild Merch.* II 7.

eleare [ME **ēlen* < AS *ǣlan*], **a** to calcine (iron ore). **b** to anneal, bake (tiles); *v. et.* 1 *anelare* b. (*Cf.* L. F. Salzman *Med. Eng. Industry* 178; *VCH Kent* III 393).

a 1330 in eisdem [blomis ferri] elend[is], iij s. vj d., pro c ij s. *MinAc* (*S. Frith, Kent*) 890/22 (= *Arch.* LXIV 156). **b 1370** solut' pro factura vij furnorum de tegulis et illis eleandis cum bosco domini, iiij li. xviij s., viz. pro quolibet furno facto et †eleando [? l. elevando] xviij s. *MinAc* (*Wye, Kent*) 899/23; **1374** pro factura tegularum et eleand' ad dictos v furnos *Ib.* 900/8.

eleatio, annealing (of tiles).

1373 pro factura et elacione tegularum de furnis predictis cum bosco domini *MinAc* 900/6.

eleborum, ~orus, ~brus, v. helleborus.

elecebra [CL], prostitute. (*Cf.* Plautus *Men.* 377).

~a, meretrix, ab eliciendo OSB. GLOUC. *Deriv.* 194.

electare [CL], to elicit (information).

~are, elicere OSB. GLOUC. *Deriv.* 194.

electeris v. elaterium.

electio [CL]

1 selection, choice. **b** (leg.) choice (by party) of procedure; *cf. eligere* 1e. **c** (astr.) 'election', choice of favourable conjunction; *cf. eligere* 1f. **d** (phil.) deliberate choice, free will (sts. = προαίρεσις); *cf. elicitio*.

si dignum aliquid vestrae ~oni confecero EDDI pref. (= *V. Cuthb. prol.*: lectioni); *GlC* D 126 (v. dilectus b); quid est ~o, nisi quedam de diversis pro libito facta portionis assumptio? PULL. *Sent.* 714C; cum [Corineus] .. pre omnibus .. ~onem provintiarum posset habere G. MON. I 16; elegantium verborum .. ~o GIR. *EH intr.* p. 213; c**1242** in .. ~one vie (v. consiliatio a); *Fleta* 230 (v. effortiare 4a); **1326** tenentes de T. metere debent per ij dies .. vel dabunt pro opere ij d. pro ~one domini *BB St. Davids* 50; **1457** *MunAcOx* 673 (v. 1 capsula d). **b** in ~one accusati erit vel probationem ipsius mulieris [accusantis] sustinere contra se vel se per Dei judicium ab imposito crimine purgare GLANV. XIV 3; **1202** fiat lex, et in ~one sit appellati portare ferrum [calidum] vel ut A. [appellans] illud portet (*Eyre*) *SelPlCrown* 10; quo casu appellatus .. amisit ~onem defendendi se per corpus suum vel ponendi se super patriam BRACTON 133b; appellatus .. per utlagariam amitteret excepciones et ~ones [v. l. †ejecciones] *Fleta* 45; **1285** cum debitum fuerit recuperatum vel in curia regis recognitum .., sit .. in ~one illius qui sequitur pro hujusmodi debito .. sequi breve, quod vic. fieri faciat de terris et catallis, vel quod vic. liberet ei omnia catalla debitoris .. quousque debitum fuerit levatum (2 *Westm.* 18) *StRealm* I 82 (cf. *State Tri. Ed. I* 37: secundum quod hujus[?modi] ~o concedatur per ultimum statutum Westm'). **c** BACON *Tert.* 107 (v. constellatio). **d** singuli quique libero voluntatis arbitrio dediti et ~onis examine praediti ALDH. *VirgP* 18; nec aliquid facit vis necessitatis ubi operatur ~o sola voluntatis ANSELM (*Praesc.* 6) II 257; heresis Grece, ~o Latine M. PAR. *Maj.* V 401 (cf. eligere 1g); DUNS *Ord.* I 189 (v. consiliativus); ~o est cum racione et intellectu BRADW. *CD* 465B.

2 election (to office): **a** (imperial or royal); **b** (papal); **c** (episcopal); **d** (mon.); **e** (acad.); **f** (mun.); **g** (parliamentary or sim.).

a s**1257** hi sunt maximi in Alemannia ad quorum nutum pendet ~o ipsius regni, quod est quasi arra imperii Romanorum M. PAR. *Maj.* V 604 (cf. ib. 617); s**1324** (v. docere 1e); nonnullis apparet quod ~o imperatoris debet nunc presentari summo pontifici, per quem tamen minime est confirmandus; presentabatur eciam ~o summi pontificis imperatori, non ut imperator confirmaret eandem ~onem sed ut .. examinaret eandem OCKHAM *Dial.* 928; de novi regis .. ~one *Lib. Regal.* 4 (v. consecrare 3f); s**1403** electores .., ipso [Wynceslao] amoto, ad alterius ~onem .. procedere disposuerunt .. et te .. Bavarie ducem .. in regem Romanorum et futurum imperatorem .. eligerunt

(*Lit. Papae*) AD. USK 81; prelati et nobiles regni .. tractaturi de novi regis consecracione et ~one W. SAY *Lib. Reg. Cap.* 76. **b** **s1159** scisma de ~one duorum paparum DICETO *YH* I 303; **s1272** cardinales .. dominum Thealdum .., qui commorabatur in transmarinis partibus .. elegerunt; qui, de sua ~one auditis rumoribus, ad curiam properavit *Flor. Hist.* III 29; **s1312** rex Francie .. peticiones proposuit et fecit; inter quas .. quod ipse rex et successores sui vocem trium cardinalium haberent in omni ~one papali AD. MUR. *Chr.* 17; WYCL. *Ver.* III 74 (v. 5a infra); **s1378** schisma in Romana ecclesia oritur et continuatur usque ~onem Martini V FORDUN *Cont.* XIV 43; **1378**, **s1404** (v. conclave 1d). **c** adsumpserunt cum ~one et consensu .. ecclesiae gentis Anglorum virum .. aptum episcopatu BEDE *HE* III 29; **742** ut .. cum consilio servorum Dei de ista [successoris mei] ~one faciam quod nobis .. optimum esse videatur BONIF. *Ep.* 50; ORD. VIT. IV 7 (v. astipulatio a); *Const. Clar.* 12 (v. consulere 3a); **1173** H. rex Anglorum .. monachis Guintoniensis ecclesie, salutem. mando vobis ut liberam ~onem habeatis; et tamen nolo ut aliquem accipiatis nisi R. clericum meum *Act. Hen. II* I 587; loco istorum successit canonica ~o, cum sc. Deo auctore magis literatum et honestum eligit ecclesia ministerio. .. hodie vero loco canonice ~onis in plerisque partibus successit intrusio principis GIR. *GE* II 34 p. 338; **s1214** legatus .., regiis favens voluntatibus, in ecclesiis vacantibus prelatos minus sufficientes posuerat intrusione magis quam canonica ~one WEND. II 97; **s1226** (v. compromittere 4b); **1228** (v. eligere 2c); **s1239** (v. celebrare 2d); **s1283** (v. compromissio c); **s1316** (v. canonicus 2a). **d** sicut Graeci solent in ~one abbatis agere THEOD. *Pen.* II 3. 2; EGB. *Pont.* 105 (v. eligere 2d); abbatissarum ~o [AS p. 372: *cyre*] *RegulC proem.* 9; in [abbatis] ~onem LANFR. *Const.* 140 (v. abbas 1a); **1239** quod episcopi non compellantur respondere coram seculari judice de officio suo, viz. quare talem ~onem factam de tali in abbatem non confirmavit *Conc. Syn.* 281; **c1240** (v. abbatissa a); **s1273** (v. compromittere 4a); **1291** inquisicio de forma et modo ~onis: .. quesitum fuit si celebrata fuit ~o infra tempus a canone diffinitum, sc. infra tres menses a tempore vacacionis *G. S. Alb.* II 9; **s1309** die ~onis celebrande statuto, convocatis omnibus et singulis qui .. ~oni debuerunt, voluerunt et potuerunt commode interesse .., quedam [MS: †quasdam] moniciones .. facte erant per priorem *Cust. Cant.* 19; **s1399** dominus T. B., vi et potencia .. ducis Gloucestrie .. fundatoris nostri monasterii, .. ab ~one tam activa quam passiva omnes nostri monasterii religiosos penitus excludebat *Meaux* III 269; **1415** placuit nobis .. per formam scrutinii in negocio ~onis procedere et .. ecclesie nostre, monasterio sive prioratui de futura priorissa providere canonice per viam scrutinii *Reg. Cant.* III 363; **1426** compertum est evidenter ipsam [abbatis] ~onem fuisse et esse concorditer per viam quasi Spiritus Sancti celebratam *Ib.* I 102. **e** **a1350** fiat ejus [cancellarii] ~o per scrutinium sub hac forma *StatCantab* app. 313; **a1350** cancellarius et procuratores in eorum cujuslibet ~one coram universitate sacramentum prestent .. corporale quod ad ejus defensionem fidelem diligenciam adhibebunt *StatOx* 63; **1400** presupposita discordia de vocum collacione inter scrutatores ~onum .. et magistros voces conferentes *Ib.* 189; **1433** iiij magistros arcium ad intrinsecam ~onem officii inferioris bedelli utriusque juris .. nominatos *Ib.* 254; **1450** ut .. singula supposita universitatis in ecclesia cathedrali .. post finem .. misse usque ad ~onem rectoris permaneant *Mun. Univ. Glasg.* II 5. **f** **a1175** concessi eis [burgensibus] ut propriam ~onem habeant prepositi *BBC* (*Bradninch*) 243; **a1183** quod ipsi burgenses forent ballivi et cachepolli burgi illius quotienscunque ad hoc electi fuerint .. per ~onem communitatis burgi .. de anno in annum *Ib.* (*Tewkesbury*); **1279**, **1330** (v. 1 coronator 2b); **1375** de ~one camerariorum *Mem. York* I 16 *tit.* (cf. ib. supra: *a la eleccion del maier de la dite citee*); **1419** in ~onibus majorum et vicecomitum, quia solebat antiquitus ad Gildhalle confluere multa turba .., solebant major et aldermanni per aliquos dies ante diem ~onis .. insimul tractare qualiter ~o talis pacifice fieret *MGL* I 18. **g** **1265** primi tres electores seu nominatores in ~one seu nominatione consiliariorum [regis] (*Ch. Regis*) *MGL* II 664; **1413** quod .. nomina hominum [sc. militum et burgensium .. in parliamento nostro] sic eligendorum in quibusdam indenturis inter te et illos qui hujusmodi ~oni interfuerint inde conficiendis .. inseri .. facias (*Cl*) *Dign. Peer* IV 826; **c1555** pro ~one militum, civium et burgensium ad veniendum ad parliamentum *Entries* 186.

3 (leg.): **a** selection of oath-helpers (*cf. Leg. Hen.* ed. Downer 374, 430–5). **b** (by misinterp. of AS *unceases aþ* = 'oath of non-enmity') choice. **c** selection of jurors (esp. for grand assize).

a unde accusatus cum una decima se purgaret per ~onem et sortem, [ni]si ad judicium ferri calidi vadat (*Leg. Hen.* 64. 1g) *GAS* 584; in Denelaga [habendi sunt] xlviii [consacramentales] electi, et sorte potius quam ~one juraturi (*Ib.* 66. 10) *Ib.* 586. **b** qui furem occiderit .., parentibus ipsius occisi juret *unceases aþ*, id est sacramentum sine ~one (*Quad.*) *GAS* 105. **c** summone .. iiij legales milites .. ad eligendum .. xij milites .. ad recognoscendum .. quis .. majus jus habeat in terra ..; et summone .. R. qui terram illam tenet quod tunc sit ibi auditurus illam ~onem (*Breve*) GLANV. II 11; **1200** dies datus est Willelmo .. et Ade .. ad audiendum ~onem xij militum ad faciendum magnam assisam *CurR* I 220 (cf. ib. 183: de placito audiendi †electorem [? l. ~onem] xij militum); **1219** dies datus est Thome .. et Aveline .. de audienda ~one de servitio j virgate terre .. pro defectu electorum, quia nullus venit *Ib.* VIII 166 (cf. ib. 367: magna assisa venit recognitura inter T. .. et A. .. de servitio quod idem T. exigit ab ea de una virgata terre).

4 (mil.) recruitment, enlistment.

1332 (v. arraiatio a); **1338** ita quod pro defectu ~onis et arraiacionis hujusmodi passagium nostrum .. nullatenus differatur *TreatyR* II 145 (= *Foed.* V 7b).

5 (theol.): **a** divine appointment. **b** election for salvation (*cf. Rom.* xi 5 *etc.*). **c** (collect.) company of the elect. **d** (w. *vas*) 'chosen vessel' (*cf. Acts* ix 15); *cf. eligere* 5c.

a exemplum sanctorum quoque apostolorum, ~one vel judicio Christi non propria voluntate sortiti GILDAS *EB* 108; spiritalem Dei ~onem praedestinatam .. didicit *V. Cuthb.* I 3; **s1077** Gundulfus [episcopus] .., qui putatus sit divina potissimum ~one hunc honorem meruisse W. MALM. *GP* I 72 p. 137; non est tantum sacramentum in istis humana ~o quin quecunque persona promulgaverit ~onem Dei WYCL. *Ver.* III 74 (cf. 2b supra). **b** **c1070** qui .. se de 'paucis' [cf. *Matth.* xx 16] esse jam judicat, non statim de securitate ~onis confidat ANSELM (*Ep.* 2) III 100; est ~o eterna nihil aliud quam previsio ad graciam et gloriam; ~o vero temporalis est collacio gracie in presenti HALES *Sent.* I 357. **c** **814** (9c) a communione .. corporis .. Christi .. et ab ~one omnium sanctorum esse separatum *CS* 348; in ~onem discipulatus Christi FOLC. *V. J. Bev.* 2 (v. discipulatus 1b). **d** vas ~onis magisterque gentium electus [sc. S. Paulus] GILDAS *EB* 73; **680** praedicator egregius et vas ~onis ALDH. *Ep.* 4; [archiepiscopus], eo quo afflatus est Dei spiritu vas ~onis illum [Dunstanum] futurum praenoscens OSB. *V. Dunst.* 9.

6 (alch.) elective attraction, affinity.

~o ejus [stanni] est .. quod trahit ad albedinem mixtam cum croceo colore et quod non strideat BACON *Min.* 382.

elective [LL], **a** (log.) so as to allow for choice, disjunctively. **b** by election.

a cavendum .. ne quis ~e perquirendorum certificatione excludenda frustra conquirere conetur ut, prequisito an mundus ex aliquo factus sit et certificato quoniam non, exclusum est et queri ineptum ex quo factus sit mundus BALSH. *AD rec. 2* 165 (cf. ib. 166: est .. ~e interrogabilium aliud simplex .., aliud multiplex). **b** successive .. et post patres filii ecclesias obtinent, non ~e, hereditate possidentes et polluentes sanctuarium Dei GIR. *DK* II 6; viderat quosdam episcopus .. potestative potius quam ~e translatos *Id. JS* 1 p. 135.

electivus [LL]

1 a (phil.) concerned w. choice. **b** (gram. & log.) allowing for choice, disjunctive. **c** (?) freely chosen.

a in creatura .. inter voluntatem naturalem et ~am vere distinguitur *Ps.*-GROS. *Summa* 382. **b** fiunt et ~ae [conjunctiones], quando ex diversis rebus aliquid eligitur ALCUIN *Gram.* 896A; est .. interrogatio ~a .. cum queritur 'an vox sit corpus', ut Stoicis visum est, 'an non', ut Platoni BALSH. *AD rec. 2* 133; *Ib.* 127 (v. disciplinalis 1a); 'quam' ~a subjunctivo jungitur LINACRE *Emend. Lat.* xix. **c** **1450** gracia addiscendi veniunt ad ~am matrem sciencie et virtutis *EpAcOx* 292.

2 (eccl.): **a** elective, appointed by election. **b** disposable by election.

a **1293** priores cathedralium ecclesiarum et abbates non exemptos ac omnes priores perpetuos et ~os plenum conventum habentes *DCCant. Reg.* Q f. 52a; **1320** invenimus quod .. v monachi dum taxat .. in dicto prioratu residebant, nec priorem ~um invenimus †perfectum [? l. prefectum] aliquo tempore in eodem *Reg. Heref.* 192 (cf. ib. 191: priorem .. dativum a dicto abbate se dicente[m] prefectum); **s1380** asseverabant .. priorem [de Wymundham] ~um esse et ideo deponi nec posse nec debere *Chr. Angl.* 260. **b** **1414** hospitale [S. Katerine] .. non est ~um set ex primeva fundacione beneficium perpetuum *Reg. Bath* 173; **1454** proventus .. prioratuum, qui conventuales, curati et ~i .. fore noscuntur *Mon. Hib. & Scot.* 391b; **1459** rex .. erat in possessione .. presentandi ad .. vacancia beneficia, quovismodo vacantibus sedibus, ad ecclesiasticum patronum .. pertinencia .., donec ad temporalitatem episcopi admittantur, et ad ~a secularia, eciam si majora, post pontificales, et ad alia .. qualitercumque reservata *Conc. Scot.* II 80 (= *Conc.* III 577a).

1 elector v. electio 3c.

2 elector [LL]

1 chooser, decider.

quanto appetibilius ab aliis eligi quam bonus aliorum ~or videri GIR. *EH intr.* p. 213; [Godwinus] strenuus in agendis .., dubiorum ~or velox MAP *NC* V 3 f. 60v.

2 elector: **a** (imperial); **b** (eccl. or mon.); **c** (acad.); **d** (parliamentary or sim.).

a **s1248** coronatio [Willelmi de Holandia] a multis nulla reputabatur, quia omnes ~ores non erant ibi presentes nec etiam consentientes M. PAR. *Maj.* V 26; **1414** Ludowicus comes palatinus Reni et Bavarie dux .., princeps ~or (*DipDocE* 1065/1) *Foed.* IX 176a; **1416** si .. serenissimus princeps [Sigismundus] .. per ~ores Imperii .. easdem alligancias pari forma ratificare .. procuraverit *RParl* IV 99a; **s1486** (v. archiprinceps). **b** **878** eum [sc. Grimbaldum] ad vos mittendum cum suis ~oribus (*Lit. Archiep. Remorum*) *Conc. Syn.* 11; electis tribus .. elegerunt [vij alios] .. ut essent ~ores [abbatis] N. DUNSTABLE *Chr.* 8; **s1238** archiepiscopus electionem [prioris Cantuar'] .. cassavit; totum conventum, precipue electum et ~ores, .. anathematis vinculis innodavit M. PAR. *Maj.* III 493; ~ores prelatorum *Ib.* 531 (v. discopulare a); in ordinacione prioris, cum abbas presens fuerit in capitulo, precentor .. nominabit primum ~orem *Cust. Cant.* 73. **c** **a1350** ~oribus injungatur quod virtute sacramenti prestiti fideliter eligant cancellarium *StatOx* 63. **d** **1265** (v. electio 2g); per indenturas .. inter .. vicecomitem et .. ~ores .. conficiendas *Entries* 446.

3 selector: **a** (of jurors); **b** (of royal workmen).

a **1220** dies datus est .. petentibus .. de audienda electione de sex bovatis terre .. unde .. tenens .. posuit se in magnam assisam .. pro defectu ~orum, eo quod omnes obierunt. et ideo iiij de novo summoneantur *CurR* VIII 373; exigendi sunt .. iiij milites ~ores vel xij milites ad faciendam magnam assisam electi BRACTON 351b; **1285** isti remanent coronatores in suburbio Oxon', viz. .., juratores .., ~ores .. *DocCOx* 223. **b** **1354** ~oribus carpentariorum (v. captor 2b).

electoralis, electoral, carrying the status of (imperial) elector.

1414 omnia jura .. que ad ipsum [ducem Bavarie] et suum principatum ~em .. pertinent (*DipDocE* 1065/1) *Foed.* IX 176b.

electorium, (phil.) principle of choice.

consciencia semper inest racioni, quia est ejus naturale judicatorium; igitur eciam liberum arbitrium voluntati, quod est ejus liberale ~ium WYCL. *Quaest. Log.* 247.

electorum v. electrum 1b.

electrarius, worker in pewter or sim.

1492 nullus mercator .. neque ~ius presumat aliquod stannum fundere in vasa sive aliqua vasa de stanno puro extra hoc regnum nostrum traducenda fundere *Pat* 572 m. 29; **1508** ~io de Rychemond pro dim. *garneshe* vasorum electr' *Ac. Durh.* 104.

electreus, **~ius**, made of pewter or sim.

c1436 vasa enea, erea et ~ia *Entries* 646b; **1492** subsidium pro vasis ~eis extra hoc regnum nostrum traducendis nobis solvatur in forma sequenti *Pat* 572 m. 29.

electria v. electrum.

electricus, rich in amber.

Plinius [cf. *HN* XXXVII 35] .. dicit quod [electrum] colligitur in insulis Glosaphis inter Germaniam et Angliam, que ~e vocantur propter abundantiam electri BACON *Min.* 387.

electrim v. electrum.

electrinus [LL < ἠλέκτρινος]

1 made of amber.

1605 unam armillam rosarii ~i, A. *a bracelett of tenn amber beades and of one glasse beade* (*Mun. Stratford on Avon*) *HMC Rep.* IX app. 1 293a.

2 made of pewter or sim.

Croyl. 98 (v. cupreus a); **1387** unum barellum vasorum ~orum et ligneorum *Cl* 227 m. 4; **1394** xij duodenas vasorum ~orum in portu civitatis .. London' .. in navibus carcare *RScot* 124b; **1396** ornamenta ecclesie: .. candelabra ferrea iiij et j candelabrum ~um pendens in medio chori *Meaux* III app. lxxxii; **1460** pro ij *merkyngiryns* pro vasis ~is signandis *Ac. Durh.* 88; **1485** in conduccione de ij *garnesshis* discorum ~orum *Comp. Swith.* 382.

electrius v. electreus.

electrix [LL], chooser (f., partly fig.).

eletrix, ~ix *Gl. Leid.* 11. 8; ~ix Dei ANSELM (*Or.* 16) III 65 (v. dilectrix); doctrix ipsa [lex divina] est discipline Dei et ~ix operum illius FORTESCUE *NLN* I 44.

electrum [CL < ἤλεκτρον]

1 amber; **b** (identified w. lyncury or sim.); **c** jet.

~um, *smylting* vel *glær* .., succinum vel ~um, *sap*, *smelting* ÆLF. *Gl.*; **9..** ~i, *eolhsandes WW*; ~um, i. sucus arboris *GlH* E 174; ex pino in insulis Germanie gignitur lacrima sive gutta que defluens .. induruscit et gemmam facit et dicitur ~um [cf. Isid. *Etym.* XVII 7. 31] BART. ANGL. XVII 120; triplex est species †~ia [? l. ~i]. .. secundum genus .. fit ex succo arboris pinee distillante ex ea in mare BACON *Min.* 387. **b** †flestria [? l. electrum], *gim þe bið on coches micga* ÆLF. *Gl.*; ligurius ~o similiter placat dolorem stomachi R. NIGER *Mil.* II 9; locium linchis .. lapis fit quem multi †electorum vocant; dolorem stomachi compescit *Alph.* 105. **c** *geate*, ~um LEVINS *Manip.* 212.

2 alloy of gold and silver or other bright metal; **b** (w. ref. to *Ezek.* i 4: 'amber' *AV*, 'brass' *NEB*);

c mercury. **d** gold-leaf. **e** brass. **f** pewter or sim.

auri obriza lammina, quod cetera argenti et ~i stagnique metalla praecellit ALDH. *VirgP* 15; ~um, *elotr* .., ~um, aurum et argentum mixtum *GlC* E 116, 118; **823** vas ~i, auri et argenti *CS* 373; B. *V. Dunst.* 1 (v. chrysendetus b); dotem auro et ~o cariorem W. POIT. I 58; **1176** cum ~um sit genus metalli temperatissimum, significat correctionis suavissimum blandimentum P. BLOIS *Ep.* 100. 310B; [angeli] nunc aurum, nunc argentum, nunc ~um nominantur, quia splendorem habent purum BART. ANGL. II 5; triplex est species †~ia [? l. ~i] .. una .. est de commixtione quarundam partium argenti et auri BACON *Min.* 387; ~um aliud artificiale ex argento et auro simul mixtis; aliud naturale et minerale, quod est omni metallo carius habetque proprietates argenti et auri sicut et colorem eorum pariter mixtorum [cf. Isid. *Etym.* XVI 24] *Ps.*-GROS. *Summa* 643. **b** viderunt sancti Deum per ignem, angelum, nubem, ~um BEDE *Hom.* I 2. 29. **c** ~um, i. .., *cwicselfer GlH* E 174; splendor solis ~o Mercurii languebit et erit horror inspicientibus (*Proph. Merlini*) G. MON. VII 4. **d** †electum, A. *a lefe of goolde WW*. **e** ~um, i. .. *mæstling GlH* E 174; quedam regiones ponunt tuciam in cupro ut habeant ~um, quedam tamen calaminam .. et, quia ~um fit cum follibus, ideo impetu follium exspirat multum de tucia et cetera, unde quod subtile est exit, et remanet materia dura que indurat ~um; et ideo durius est quam orichalcum, quod fit sine follibus. et licet sic fiat ~um communiter, potest fieri pulchrius longe et nobilius per quedam alia opposita tucie et calamine, ut sunt radices urusci et ficus et alia quedam BACON *Min.* 386 (cf. id. *CSPhil* 442: ~um, quod est *laton*). **f 1393** pro .. discis de ~o (v. bolstera a); **1449** officia .. paccacionis vasorum de ~o *Cl* 299 m. 16*d.*; **1471** custus plumbi: .. Johanni E. .. pro xxxviij petris xj lib. plumbi, xv s. ij d.; eidem J. pro ix lib. ~i, xxij d. ob. *Fabr. York* 76; hoc ~um, A. *pewtyre WW*; *pewder*, ~um *CathA*.

3 (bot.): **a** (?) lupin (*Lupinus*); **b** (?) figwort (*Scrophularia*; cf. AS *brunwyrt*).

a nomina herbarum: .. ~um, *elehtre ÆLF. Gl.*; †eleotrum, †*eleotre Gl. Durh.*; **10..** ~um, *electre WW*; ~um multos habet stipites, folia viridia et flores croceos *Alph.* 54. **b** hanc poete †~im vocant, phisici boricam, Angli sua lingua nigram herbam dicunt; cujus ramus quadrangulus est ad modum eliceferis, folia vero foliis magne urtice similia; in summitate vero ramorum quasi racemi quidam nascuntur ADEL. *CA* 12 (v. borith).

electuarium [LL], electuary, medicine meant to dissolve in mouth; *cf.* 1 *dia* 1; **b** (fig.).

~ium, quod morbo sorbeatur *GlH* E 175; **1171** in speciebus et ~iis per Joseph medicum *Pipe* 86; carvanne custodes .. camelos cum sarcinis offerebant .. et mulos .. portantes .. species pretiosas .., preterea .. ~ia plurima et medicinas *Itin. Ric.* VI 4 p. 390; non ~iis electis nec medicinis artificiose confectis GIR. *Spec.* III 9; **c1250** qui vobis .. diversa transmisit letuaria W. BERNHAM *Ep.* 15; *Fleta* 73 (v. apothecarius b); apothecarii accipiunt citonia .. et medullam eorum coquunt in aqua et addunt succum et pistant simul in modum ~ii GAD. 87v. 2; **1307** (v. confortativus a); libra subtilis conceditur specietariis pro labore eorum in omnibus que teruntur †pistelle [? l. pistello], ut in pulveribus et ~iis *Cust. Cant.* 33; ~ium dicitur eo quod fit de electis speciebus *Alph.* 54; *lettwary*, ~ium *CathA*. **b** diabolus diasatirion luxurie, calidum ~ium avaricie .. cuilibet offert O. CHERITON *Par.* 130; morbosis sanitatis / es electuarium WALT. WIMB. *Virgo* 67; digne letaris nimium, / cum panem cibas civium / lactis electuario J. HOWD. *Gaudia* 5; tot habet pixides maledictus medicus infernalis plenas ~iis [ME: *letewaries*] *AncrR* 82.

electuarius, taking the form of an electuary.

reubarbarum .. administratur .. aliquando in ~ia substancia GAD. 134v. 1.

electum v. electrum.

1 electus [CL], choice.

1130 ut .. duceret virum ad ~um suum (v. ducere 2b).

2 electus v. eligere. **eleemosyn-** v. elemosyn-. **elefan-** v. elephan-.

elegans [CL]

1 good-looking, fine: **a** (of person); **b** (of animal).

a virgo .. pulchra et satis ~ti forma ALDH. *VirgP* 35; ~s, i. speciosus, gratus, pulcher, *wynsum, wlitig GlH* E 177; ~tem et multa laude dignam ediderunt sobolem ORD. VIT. IV 4 p. 183; **s1138** attollite igitur animos, viri ~tes, et adversus hostem .. exsurgite H. HUNT. *HA* VIII 8; **s1177** interfuerunt quatuor viri ~tes, quos fideles appellabant *G. Hen. II* I 145; persona ~s SAMSON *Mir. Edm.* 11; ~s corpore M. PAR. *Maj.* V 464. **b** P. CORNW. *Rev.* I 205 p. 199 (v. dextrarius a).

2 a (of person) elegant, well-spoken, refined. **b** (of writing or sim.) elegant, well-phrased.

a cum habueris praeceptorem paene totius Britanniae magistrum ~tem GILDAS *EB* 36; ~s [*gl.*: loquax], *smicre GlC* E 141 (cf. ib. F 35: facetus, ~s); clerico .. ~ti et plurima scientia pollenti H. CANTOR 1; vir .. ellegans et affabilis, doctus omnium se conformare moribus AILR. *SS Hex.* 11. **b** ~ti prosae sententia ALDH. *VirgP* 58; **9..** ~ti, *gecorenlice WW*; ~tiora queque presenti volumine .. digessi GIR. *TH intr.* p. 8.

1 eleganter [CL], **a** decorously, judiciously. **b** elegantly, in well-chosen language.

a ~ius, i. aptius, onestius *GlH* E 179; vos hortatur vester eruditor ut .. observetis vosmet ~er [AS: *ænlice*] ubique locorum ÆLF. *Coll.* 103; amiciri ~ius W. MALM. *GR* V 400 (v. amicire a); [femine] venusto habitu ~er culte, lineo tantum MAP *NC* II 12 f. 27; non est de racione libertatis simpliciter posse velle et non velle, sed solum modo affectanter et quasi eliganter velle T. SUTTON *Quodl.* 365. **b 680** sicut praedicator egregius .. ~er attestatur ALDH. *Ep.* 4; ASSER *Alf.* 77 (v. elucubratim); quem Guillelmus .. Gemmeticensis coenobita secutus ~er abbreviavit ORD. VIT. III *prol.* p. 3; illud ~er pertractat .. Anselmus R. MARSTON *QD* 441.

2 eleganter v. elongate.

elegantia [CL], elegance, beauty: **a** (human); **b** (literary); **c** (arch.).

a matrone .. ~ia et ingenuitate spectabiles ORD. VIT. IV 8 p. 224; laudat eam .. ab ~ia corporis et faciei MAP *NC* III 2 f. 34v. **b** cum metrica leporis ~ia ALDH. *VirgP* 60. **c** arcus .. super sanctorum corpora Romana ~ia solemniter aedificatos GOSC. *Transl. Aug.* 30C; mirae .. magnitudinis et ~ie basilicam cepit ORD. VIT. IV 10 p. 247; **s1254** rex Anglie .. consideravit ~iam domorum que de gipso .. fiunt in civitate Parisiaca M. PAR. *Maj.* V 481.

elegare v. eligere. **elegatio** v. legatio. **elegebiliter** v. eligibiliter. **elegere** v. eligere.

elegia [CL < ἐλεγεία = *elegiac poetry*], tragedy, lamentable fate. **b** (w. *linguae*) harsh speech.

gaudia sunt parta Parthis, ēlĕgīa mestis / Christicolis GARL. *Tri. Eccl.* 52 (cf. ib. 141: natis prima suis ēlĕgīa fluxit ab Eva). **b** vulnerat oppositas acies ēlĕgīa lingue *Ib.* 41.

elegiace, in elegiac verse. **b** in elegiac style.

sic dictum est ~e: 'quis mihi det fontem, quid enim potius, lacrimarum? / et lacrimer patrie gesta nefanda mee' H. HUNT. *HA* VIII 12; cepit [abbas] concinere ~e sub hiis metris: 'inter carmineas ..' (*Vers.*) AMUND. II 221. **b s1422** ubi pro nunc .. concantas satyrice .., renovatus pro tunc cum Psalmista recenseres ~e: 'heu mei .. ' [*Psalm* cxix (cxx) 5] *Ib.* I 93.

elegiacus [LL < ἐλεγειακός], elegiac.

~o versu subjunxit ALDH. *Met.* 9; BEDE *AM* 110 (v. 2 elegus); librum epigrammatum heroico metro sive ~o *Id. HE* V 24 p. 359; secundo adjeci sermoni hele[g]iacum carmen ALCUIN *WillP pref.*; planctus ~us de eo quod propria bona paucis sufficiunt et ideo vindicant aliena GARL. *Tri. Eccl.* 15n. *marg.*

elegius v. 2 elegus. **elegoos** v. elenchus a.

1 elegus [CL *pl.* < ἔλεγος], elegy.

movere precatur / cum digitis chordas elegosque sonare priores *V. Merl.* 203; lyra mutat, †elogus [v. l. elegos] dulci plaudens sono *Poem S. Thom.* 90.

2 elegus, ~ius [cf. ἔλεγος, ἐλεγεῖος], miserable.

hoc et superius metrum ubi juncta fuerint, elegiacum carmen vocatur; '~ios' namque miseros appellant philosophi BEDE *AM* 110; largas .. / inpensas elegis [*corr. from* eleis] palmis fundebat apertis FRITH. 1133; ad catenatam accessit mulierculam, dulcibus affaminibus interrogans quid haberet ~am LANTFR. *Swith.* 20; percunctabatur et idem / praedulci sermone elegam quid haberet WULF. *Swith.* II 115; sors mea, sors elegi, quid ego miserabilis egi? R. CANT. *Malch.* III 153; contemptis ~i supplicationibus, ipsum .. per fenestram .. precipitavit ORD. VIT. VIII 15 p. 356; hic locus est elegis, ēlĕgīa quos mihi vertit / tempore de vario fluctivagoque mari GARL. *Tri. Eccl.* 27; ave, pelta peccatorum / et asilum elegorum [*gl.*: i. e. miserorum], / immo refectorium WALT. WIMB. *Virgo* 15; grex occurrit scholarium ~orum, quin pocius electorum R. BURY *Phil. prol.* 5.

eleison, the hymn Κύριε ἐλέησον. *V. et. cyrieleison.*

ecclesiastica vocabula [Greca] sunt .. ecclesia, eleyson [etc.] BACON *CSPhil.* 444; **1346** Anglorum primas docet nos eleyson et ymas; / Scotorum primas sedes deduxit ad imas (*Neville's Cross*) *Pol. Poems* I 44.

elelisphacus [CL < ἐλελίσφακος], kind of sage (*Salvia*). *Cf. facus.*

lilifagus, salvia agrestis idem *SB* 28; elilifagus sive lilifagus aut fagnon frutex est oblonga ..; salvia agrestis idem, A. *wyldesauge Alph.* 54.

elemasina v. elemosina 3.

elementalis, elemental: **a** consisting of a single element. **b** existing in its natural form. **c** basic, fundamental.

a quia [ventus] est de materia ~i, recipit compositionem M. SCOT *Part.* 296; aqua .. rosacea vel ardens non est aqua ~is; ergo in ipsa non potest quis baptizari OCKHAM *Pol.* III 239 (cf. elementaris 1c). **b** quum .. monachus flumen .. transmeasset, in tantum sanctum suum clarificavit Omnipotens ut .. veluti per fluctuantes segetes .. equitatum isset; ita a natura ~is aque discriminatus appareret DOMINIC *V. Ecgwini* II p. 59. **c** nota hoc quod dicit [Aristoteles] ibi sc. quod forma non generatur, quod hoc intendit de primis formis, sc. de ~ibus, que communicantur BACON VII 7.

elementaris

1 elemental or corporeal, composed of or involving the elements; **b** (w. ref. to weather). **c** consisting of a single element.

pulchritudo .., valetudo .. et quicquid ~em universitatem letificat ADEL. *ED* 9 (cf. ib. 10: fex illa ~is); ~i conjunctione *Id. QN* 14 (v. componere 5a); in hac ~i aula *Ib.* 65 (v. collatio a); da formas elementares, da tam levitatem / †supprime [? l. supreme] cause quam gravitatis onus NECKAM *DS* IV 756; ~is [regio], alterationi continue pervia, in quatuor dividitur: est enim terra .. in medio omnium sita, circa quam aqua, circa aquam aer, circa aerem ignis est .. orbem lune attingens SACROB. *Sph.* 78; ~es qualitates HALES *Qu.* 1308 (v. corpus 3b); utrum proprietates prime ~es sint sensibiles et elementa sensibilia per ipsas J. BLUND *An.* 226; ~es proprietates GROS. 11 (v. 2 essentia 2c); BART. ANGL. IV 1 (v. 1 caliditas b); [in argento] ignis non vincit alias qualitates ~es sicut in auro *Correct. Alch.* 14; hanc [materiam primam] subjectum esse omnis transmutationis ~is ostendit ipsa resolutio *Ps.*-GROS. *Summa* 314; celum et corpus ~e sunt unum in corpore, sed differunt differentiis specificis, que sunt celeste et non celeste BACON *Tert.* 129; quando erit mundus inferior ~is in disposicione naturalissima, in figura, in locacione, in circumdacione elementorum ab invicem spherica et equali ac disposicionibus aliis, nisi motu celi cessante? BRADW. *CD* 144B. **b** effectus elementares perstringere, ventos / bis senos libuit claudere lege metri NECKAM *DS* III 13. **c** J. BLUND *An.* 325 (v. corpus 11b); sole aque ~es, non aqua rosea vel ardens OCKHAM *Pol.* III 239 (cf. elementalis a); [calor ille] ita inflammat animam meam ac si ignis ~is ibi arderet R. ROLLE *IA* 145.

2 elementary, concerned w. rudiments.

1155 vos circa litteram et syllabam et circa hujusmodi ~es doctrine primitias vestrum adhuc ingenium exercetis P. BLOIS *Ep.* 6. 18A; quia ad hunc ~em librum magis ~em quodam modo scripsit Porphirius, eum ante Aristotilem esse credidit antiquitas prelegendum J. SAL. *Met.* 873D.

elementaritas, elemental composition.

terra nomen est informis materie ~ate communi disposite *Ps.*-GROS. *Summa* 314.

elementariter, elementally, of the elements.

hic visibilis spiritus omnibus ~er compositis .. subtilius elimatus est ADEL. *QN* 25.

elementarius [CL]

1 elemental, composed of, or involving, the elements.

anima .., ut universum ~ium regeret, insita est .. ADEL. *ED* 16 (cf. ib.: hanc ipsam fecem ~iam); illud .. longe ab omni ~ie prolis generatione alienum affirmo D. MORLEY 14; elementa, mediantibus et cooperantibus ~iis qualitatibus, transeunt *Quaest. Salern.* C 28; mortis simulacrum est sine dubio / elementaria reciprocacio WALT. WIMB. *Sim.* 160.

2 elementary, concerned w. rudiments (also as sb. m.). **b** (sc. *liber*) elementary treatise.

J. SAL. *Met.* 904B (v. dictionalis); literas, quarum notitiam copiose satis habuerat, denuo mendicantem tanquam ~ium senem GIR. *TH* III 34; hic abbas didicit esse novicius, / magister maximus elementarius WALT. WIMB. *Carm.* 41. **b** ~ius, qui de elimentis tractat *GlC* E 136; [J.] Damascenus in ~io, cap. v .. DUNS *Ord.* VII 422; ex verbis Papie in suo ~io in *M* littera W. SAY *Lib. Reg. Cap.* 106.

elementatio, (?) composition from elements.

in ista latitudine amoris est dare duplicem ordinem, sc. ~onis et fundacionis. primus ordo est imperfeccionis, quo ascenditur ab inferiori vel natura imperfecciori ad suum perfeccius tanquam finem, ut a minus communibus ad magis communia. in secundo vero ordine econtra descenditur a communioribus usque ad personam amantem; et sic in ordine ~onis omnis caritas hominis incipit a seipso WYCL. *Mand. Div.* 120.

elementativus, belonging to an element.

asserit Averroes nullam qualitatem ~am competere celestibus nisi raritatem et densitatem *Ps.*-GROS. *Summa* 542.

elementatus, composed of (the four) elements. **b** (as sb. n.) body composed of elements.

quidam volunt ipsum [ignem visibilem] esse .. ~um, id est, ex omnibus quattuor elementis compositum, quamvis in eo alia tria igneum superet elementum AILR. *An.* II 56 f. 39; fortior est caliditas in igne quam sit in re ~a, ut in homine J. BLUND *An.* 228; quicquid ~um est virtute iiij elementorum factum esse necesse est RIPLEY 102. **b** quid

prodest homini elementorum aut ~orum nosse naturam .. et sui ipsius esse ignarum? J. SAL. *Met.* 943C; dicimus ~a ex elementis constare D. MORLEY 19; placet Aristoteli ut nec leve nec ponderosum sit celum, sed neque calidum neque frigidum; hujusmodi enim proprietates ~is conveniunt NECKAM *NR* I 6; BART. ANGL. IV 3 (v. corpus 11b). utrum hec sensibilis terra vel aqua itemque aer et ignis vere sint elementa an magis, sicut estimavit Empedocles, vere sint ~a ex quattuor vel saltem ex duobus aut tribus elementis composita, merito queri poterit *Ps.*-GROS. *Summa* 598; elementum e[s]t prius naturaliter quam ~um ex eo compositum; e contra autem ~um est prius dignitate vel perfeccione suo elemento WYCL. *Form.* 214.

elementicus, one who studies the elements.

nullus est itaque particularis sciens precise, puta ~us, sive lapidicus seu planticus, nisi qui precise confusam noticiam subjecti accipit ex sensu DUNS *Metaph.* VI 1 p. 317.

elementum [CL]

1 element (esp. one of the four); **b** (w. ref. to human body); **c** (w. ref. to weather).

liquentis ~i qualitatem ALDH. *VirgP* 32; quibus .. qualitatibus .. ipsa quoque mundi ~a constat esse distincta: terra namque sicca et frigida, aqua frigida et humida, aer humidus et calidus, ignis est calidus et siccus BEDE *TR* 35; *CS* 1215 (v. constare 1c); ylimento [AS: *giscæfte*] huic .. virtutem tuae benedictionis effunde (*Benedictio aquae*) *Rit. Durh.* 121 (cf. EGB. *Pont.* 35: elemento); ADEL. *QN* 1 (v. commixtura); sunt ~a corpora simplicia, que in partes diversarum formarum minime dividi possunt SACROB. *Sph.* 78; ignis .. ~orum dignissimum GIR. *TH* II 12; in his que non ex sui generis semine sed ex ~is coeuntibus sumunt originem ALF. ANGL. *Cor* 12. 7; cum duo sint ~a, ignis et aqua, in quibus dominantur qualitates active, per hec fit purgatio HALES *Sent.* IV 454; J. BLUND *An.* 226 (v. elementaris 1a); *Ps.*-GROS. *Summa* 598 (v. elementatus); olementum, A. *the element WW*. **b** quia .. homo quatuor ~is constat, id est, igne, aere, aqua, et terra EGB. *Dial.* 16; **930** (13c) tuba perstrepente archangeli .., zomata diu corrupta relinquentibus ~is omnium creaturarum pavefactis *CS* 669 (cf. ib. 677); **957** (14c) Adam .. ex informi materia creatus .., sine alicujus ~i perturbatione feliciter collocatus *CS* 995; nec post reversionem corporis humani in ejus ~a dicetur corpus humanum esse J. BLUND *An.* 325; est itaque corpus hominis compositum ex quatuor ~is .., quorum quodlibet habet proprias qualitates BART. ANGL. IV 1. **c** quotiens [mare] ingressus et repulsus, tamquam Deo per ~a sua ipsi in facto hoc †resistenti [v. l. resistente] H. BOS. *Thom.* III 31 p. 293; injuriam martyris ~a testantur ..; namque .. terram ros aut pluvia non infudit W. S. ALB. *V. Alb. & Amphib.* 25 (*recte* 15); fluctuat infelix elementorumque vereri / cogitur insidias H. AVR. *Hugh* 629; remigando furentibus ~is .. reluctari nitebantur (*Mir. Edm.*) CIREN. I 375.

2 (pl.): **a** components (of diet or sim.); **b** basic principles; **c** elementary stages (of education).

a [oratio] pro emendatione cervisae et aliorum ~orum [epulae], si mus aut mustela mergitur intus EGB. *Pont.* 127; aqua deest et nemus longe est. .. absque his duobus ~is monachi esse non possunt ORD. VIT. III 2 p. 17. **b** qui prima totius philosophie ~a posteris tradere curaverunt J. SAL. *Pol.* 479C; constitutiones justitie et ejus ~a sunt sacra principatus R. NIGER *Mil.* II 57. **c** **675** dum post prima ~a iterum apud vos essem ALDH. *Ep.* 2.

3 letter of alphabet. **b** sound represented by letter.

9.. elimentum, *stæfrof WW*; membrana .. ~is Anglicis erat conscripta W. MALM. *GP* IV 156; artis principium simplex censent elementum; / syllaba subsequitur NECKAM *DS* X 47. **b** ut ea [transumptio] qua ~orum nomen ad litteras transumitur BALSH. *AD rec.* 2 44; ipse sonus quo litteram ipsam voce proferimus dicitur ~um BACON *Gram. Gk.* 29.

elemona, ~**ia** v. elemosina 3a.

elemosina [LL < ἐλεημοσύνη; *form* eleemosyna *seldom found in medieval MSS*]

1 alms, alms-giving. **b** (mon. or sim.); **c** (royal); **d** (fig.).

~as largiter dantes GILDAS *EB* 27; promittens me elimosynas in alimoniam inopum dare BEDE *HE* V 4; **747** ~a .. nomen et opus est misericordiae (*Clovesho* 26) *Conc. HS* 371; **787** sit tibi manus in ~is aperta ALCUIN *Ep.* 4; **847** si quid in elemoxsinarum largitate .. expenderet *CS* 451; ~a, agape, *ælmesse* ÆLF. *Gl.*; adolescens .. curvatus somate .. Wintoniam accessit quadam die ut ~am acciperet pro Christi nomine LANTFR. *Swith.* 37; GOSC. *Wulfh.* 5 (v. dexter 2a); ~a sufficit sine jejunio; jejunium non sufficit sine ~a (*Leg. Hen.* 72. 3) *GAS* 590; **s1144** [W. Albemarlensis] largis crebrisque ~is in pauperes expensis .. expiavit excessum W. NEWB. *HA* I 12; **c1180** parochiani .. venient ad suam matrem ecclesiam .. cum ~is suis et oblationibus tribus festivis diebus per annum *Cart. Boarstall* 128 (= *Ambrosden* II 283); nobiles largas faciunt ~as [ME: *relef*] *AncrR* 55 (cf. ib. 81: si .. possem eos juvare et ~am [ME: *almes*] facere); certum est quod dare ~as temporales est [Christiano] via certa, dare autem ~as perpetuas est via ambigua WYCL. *Eccl.* 203; **s1401** in die Parasceues, quem maximus ~is, penitenciis .. et aliis devocionibus .. colere solebat [comes Warwyci] AD. USK 61; **1565** scholares .. pretextu paupertatis de ~is collegiorum seipsos .. sustentantes *StatOx* 392. **b** [feria sexta] cibi fratrum coquantur in coquina sicut ceteris diebus et inde portentur ad ~am LANFR. *Const.* 117; [R. abbas, ob. **1166**] cuidam porrigenti manum ad ~am, argenteum a sistarchio volens extrahere, extraxit aureum *G. S. Alb.* I 180; *Mir. J. Bev. A* 312 (v. acquisitor b); [S. abbas] carnes voluit sibi anteferri sedens ad mensam, ad augmentum sc. ~e BRAKELOND 131v.; [monachi Wintonie] factum suum sic colorant, quod propter ~am .. augmentandam tanta in ordine ipsorum inventa .. est ferculorum numerositas GIR. *RG* II 5; dixit .. quod non peccaret frater si per manum suam dispensaret pecuniam alienam in ~a ECCLESTON *Adv. Min.* 129; *Cust. Westm.* 178 (v. elemosinarius 3b); [R. episcopus, ob. **1345**], si plures supervenirent post distribucionem dicte ~e, contulit singulo obolum *Hist. Durh.* 1; sic viget in claustris ēlēmōsina ficta sinistris, / dum monachus genitis dat sua dona suis GOWER *VC* IV 263; **1549** hortatur haec conventio .. abbates, priores [etc.] quatenus ~as per ipsos pauperibus mendicantibus erogari solitas renovandas et continuandas curent *Conc. Scot.* II 114. **c** multitudo pauperum .. postulans aliquid elimosynae a rege BEDE *HE* III 6; **836** supplico ut ~am, quam in altitudinem caeli culminis datam habeo, communiter pro me et pro totum (*sic*) gentem Merciorum .. multiplicare dignemini *CS* 416; post quem [Hen. I] non surrexit princeps alius qui sic .. pauperes et inopes sumptuosis ~is foveret RIC. HEX. *Stand.* 37b; **s1199** etc. (v. elemosinarius 4b); **1334** quod .. solvatis de ~a nostra fratribus in .. villa de Berewico commorantibus victualia subscripta *RScot* 263b. **d** porrige animae pauperis servi .. vitalem ~am ANSELM (*Or.* 12) III 45.

2 established (endowed) alms; **b** (royal). **c** Peter-pence; *cf. denarius* 5a. **d** plough alms.

a1128 summa in ~a constituta in die de lazaris et ~a monachorum ..; et preter hoc constituta ~a E. abbatis *Chr. Peterb.* app. 168; **1259** cum leprosi hospitalis .. Wintonie percipere consueverint singulis annis xxx li. de ~a statuta, mandatum est .. custodi episcopatus .. quod .. eisdem leprosis de exitibus .. episcopatus solvat .. redditus quos nomine ~e .. percipere consueverunt *Cl* 383; quicumque fundaverit ~am ecclesie corporalem, habebit in se et suis heredibus curam ut condicio illius racionalis compleatur WYCL. *Sim.* 34. **b** **1131** xij li. in firma nostra de A. .. et lx s. et x d. de teloneo meo de O., que dederunt pater meus et mater mea ecclesie Sagiensi [*Norm.*] ad victum canonicorum duorum, quod antiquitus in ~a statutum fuerat (*Regesta* 1698) *EHR* XXIV 223; **1169** etc. (v. constituere 4b); **1261** denarium illum quem R. quondam venator regis percipere consuevit de firma ville regis Wintonie de ~a regis antiquitus constituta *Cl* 389; **1284** in quibus quidem remanentibus [firmarum] allocentur liberaciones et ~e constitute et alie allocaciones, si quas vicecomites habuerint de exitibus ballive sue (*Rhuddlan*) *StRealm* I 69; **1464** abbati et conventui .. ex ~a regis antiqua *ExchScot* 306. **c** **s880** Beocca princeps Romam detulit ~am [*AS Chr.*: *ælmessan*] regis Elfredi BYRHT. *HR* 80; quoniam ille [S. Petri] denarius ~a regis est (*Leg. Ed.*) *GAS* 634; **1118** super B. Petri ~a colligenda segnius vos hactenus egisse cognovimus (*Lit. Papae*) EADMER *HN* 295. **d** †**1031** ut .. omnia debita que Deo secundum legem antiquam debemus sint persoluta, sc. ~e pro aratris [etc.] (*Lit. Canuti*) FL. WORC. I 189; *GAS* 253 (v. aratralis a); *Ib.* 290 (v. carruca 2f); **1194** (v. ceragium); **c1235** (v. 1 carrucatus).

3 almoign or frank-almoign (freehold tenure, eccl. or mon.); **b** (w. *libera*, *pura*, or sim.). **c** grant in frank-almoign. **d** tenure by layman dispensing alms for king.

c†**700** (11c) ut terra ista .. ad Uegernensem ecclesiam in jus episcopalis sedis sit donata .. in ~am sempiternam *CS* 76*d*.; **838** in sempiternam aelemosynam *CS* 421; horum ij maneriorum aecclesias et presbyteros et decimas et duos villanos tenet S. Maria de C. in ~a de rege *DB* I 179v.; in Colecestra est quedam ecclesie (*sic*) S. Petri quam tenuit (*sic*) ij presbiteri T. R. E. in elemasina (*sic*) regis, cui adjacent ij hidae terrae. .. de hac ~a reclamat Robertus .. iij partes *DB* II 107v.; hec [Etheldrida] .. S. Wilfrido .., jam existenti Eboracensi episcopo, predictam villam .. in perpetuam ~am dedit, ut eam episcopali cathedra sullimaret RIC. HEX. *Hist. Hex.* I 1; **c1120** sciatis me concessisse monachis de Daventre quicquid tenent de meo feudo in terris et decimis et in aliis rebus, sc. in ~a *E. Ch. Scot.* 51 (cf. ib. 59 [**a1130**]: concessisse .. in perpetuum in ~am); **a1123** dedit B. scriptori in ~a omnes ecclesias terre sue que fuit Brictrici Walensis (*Ch. B. Scriptoris*) *EHR* XIV 419; **a1147** concessisse .. ecclesie .. de Kelchou .. in perpetuam ~am Treverlen cum suis rectis divisis *Regesta Scot.* I 29; **1161** dedisse .. in permanentem ~am *Ib.* 182; **a1200** octo bovatas terre .. in perpetuam elemoniam [*corr. from* elemonam] concessimus *Danelaw* 311; **1300** ita quod .. episcopus dictum manerium .. non possit alienare vel in ~am dare sine assensu .. regis *Reg. Carl.* I 140. **b** †**1046** (14c) haec dedi dictis monachis in puram et perpetuam ~am *CD* 1335; **c1155** concessisse .. sanctimonialibus .. in liberam et quietam ~am *Danelaw* 62; **c1160** concessisse .. monachis .. in liberam, puram, et perpetuam ~am quicquid habent de feudo nostro .. *Ib.* 150; **11**.. dedisse .. R. capellano .. ecclesiam de Mune et carrucatam terre quam eidem ecclesie dedi .., tenendam et habendam libere et quiete .. in francam et perpetuam ~am *Reg. S. Thom. Dublin* 199; nec [fieri debet homagium] de feodo in liberam ~am dato GLANV. IX 2; **1196** in lib[e]ram ~am *CurR* I 22; **1212** abbas Eboraci habet in franca ~a .. x bovatas terre *Fees* 195; **1230** villam de C., quam princeps Henricus .. nobis et successoribus nostris imperpetuum in liberam, puram, et perpetuam ~am .. dederat *BBC* (*Cashel*) 309; tenementum datum in liberam ~am rectoribus ecclesiarum, que pura est et libera, et magis libera et pura BRACTON 207; *Ib.* 286b (v. baronia 2); **1316** dedisse .. x m. sterlingorum in liberam et perpetuam ~am percipiendas monachis [de Lesmachu] .. inperpetuum de molendinis nostris de C. *RMS Scot* 75. **c** **a1137** si quis huic ~e contradicere vel largitionem infirmare temptaverit *Cart. Bath A* 36. **d** **1212** Randulfus [et al.] .. tenent .. dim. hydam terre in ~am distribuendi .. j cuvatam cervisie die Omnium SS. pro anima domini regis *Fees* 68.

4 land *etc.* held in almoign; **b** (w. *libera* or *pura*).

preter j hidam quae jacuit in aecclesia S. Pauli in ~a T. R. E. ..; sed R. episcopus posuit eam extra ~am aecclesiae S. Pauli injuste *DB* I 209; infra hanc metam continetur ~a pauperum *Ib.* 316v.; habet rex medietatem ~ae trium festorum S. Mariae, quae jacet ad Wackefeld *Ib.* 373v.; aecclesiae hujus villae l acrae de libera terra pertinent pro ~a *Ib.* II 361v.; **c1090** concedo monasterio .. ~am quam Willelmus de W. predicte congregationi dedit, mansionem, viz. quae Erceham nominatur *Regesta* p. 131; **1127** precipio quod tota terra et homines canonicorum .. sint quieti .. de sciris [etc.] .. et prohibeo quod nullus eis .. contumeliam faciat, quia ipsi sunt de propria ~a mea *Cart. Osney* IV 8; **a1135** nolo quod mercatum ~e mee [sc. de Monteborc, Norm.] per occasionem destruatur *Regesta* 1950; **c1150** villa ~a illius benedicti regis est *BBC* (*St Andrews*) 243; **1157** terram G. fratris sacerdotis, que est de ~a *Act. Hen. II* I 136; si calumnia emerserit .. de ullo tenemento quod clericus velit ad ~am attrahere, laicus vero ad laicum feudum .. *Const. Clar.* 9; **a1182** hanc ecclesiam et omnia ad illam pertinentia .. dedi .. E. filio E. sacerdotis libere et quiete tenere, sicut decet ecclesiasticam ~am *MonA* VI 270b; due sorores in P. manent in helemosina domini regis et debent pascere j pauperem propter dominum regem *RDomin* 83; **s1306** rex [Ed. I dixit]: " .. ita posset papa conferre quamlibet abbathiam in Anglia secularibus, et destrueretur ~a nostra et progenitorum nostrorum" GRAYSTANES 27; **1354** quod nullus vicecomes .. seu alia persona .. infra ~as suas homines capere, verberare, ligare .. audeat (*Ch. Regis*) *MonA* VI 980b; **1377** domini temporales potestatem habent subtrahendi suas ~as collatas ecclesie, ipsa illis ~is abutente (WYCL. *Libellus*) *Ziz.* 249. **b** **c1130** donamus .. molendinum de A. solutum et quietum de omnibus rebus sicut liberam helemosinam *Eng. Feudalism* 278; **c1160** ad tenendum ita bene et libere ut ipsi tenent suas alias elimosinas, sicut elimosine libere teneri debent *Regesta Scot.* I 193 (cf. ib. 202 [**c1163**]: ut liberam ~am tenere ipsam ecclesiam); si fuerit placitum inter duos clericos de aliquo tenemento quod sit de libera ~a feodi ecclesiastici GLANV. XII 25; **1199** assisa de recognoscendum utrum j virgata terre .. sit laicum feodum Willelmi .. an libera ~a Simonis *CurR* I 82; **a1257** sint quieti de omni tallagio, sicut pura ~a antecessorum nostrorum *BBC* (*Bodmin*) 107; liberorum [tenementorum] aliud libera et perpetua ~a, aliud pura et libera et perpetua, que quidem sunt tam in bonis hominis quam bonis Dei, quia dantur non solum Deo et tali ecclesie sed abbatibus et prioribus ibidem Deo servientibus BRACTON 207.

5 almonry: **a** (eccl.); **b** (royal). *V. et.* 2 *elemosinaria*.

a **1272** nisi sit quod .. magister [domus elemosinarie], capellani, pauperes vel eorum homines infra dictam ~am aliquem .. manifestum malefactorem retineant *Reg. Aberd.* I 32. **b** **1217** uni sumetario butellarie nostre et uni sumetario ~e nostre *Cl* 345b.

elemosinalis, eleemosynary, of alms. **b** (w. *feodum*) almoign. **c** (w. *scutella*) alms-bowl.

miserendo anime sue .., quod primum et precipuum est genus ~e [v. l. elemosine] AD. EYNS. *Visio* 26. **b** **a1182** concessisse .. ecclesie S. Brigide .. villam nomine Apeltun [*Cumb*] .. et omnia ipsi ville adjacentia in ~i feodo *MonA* VI 270b. **c** **1237** in grosso argento .. ad faciendam scutellam ~em *Pipe* 81 r. 15.

elemosinanter, by way of alms.

1412 non videtur magna prudencia ~er dare eleemosynam diuturniorem quam sit tempus quod Deus ei donaverat ad merendum (*Lit. Univ. Ox.*) *Conc.* III 349b.

elemosinare, ~**ari**

1 to give alms.

vetat dari pauperibus quicquam boni nisi noverint ~antes rectitudinem status eorum, ne forte sint presciti NETTER *DAF* I 400; **1456** in hoc congaudeo quod plurimas .. cotidie elemosinas facis. .. sed .., si ~ari te delectet, de propriis facito BEKYNTON II 158.

2 to grant in almoign. **b** to convert into almoign.

1190 nulla fiet recognitio in foro seculari super possessione quam viri religiosi vel quecunque persone xx annis vel amplius possederint .. [nec] si carta vel alio modo ~atam esse possessionem probare poterint (*Artic. Cleri Norm.*) DICETO *YH* II 87; **1225** super c s. annui redditus monete currentis quos .. W. [archiepiscopus Rotom'] illis ~averat *Foed.* X 243b; **c1235** abbas Oseneie tenet Stanhale et nichil inde solvit, quia ~atur *Fees* 544; **1244** [exceptis] terris ~atis ad araturam iiij carrucarum *CalIMisc* 19; **1255**

quot feoda tenentur de eo [sc. rege] in capite .. et quid inde sit ~atum (*Artic. Itin.*) *Ann. Burton* 339; **12..** dedi in puram et perpetuam elemosinam, sicut aliqua terra purius potest ~ari *DL Cart. Misc.* II 138; **12..** raptores bonorum ecclesiasticorum seu in terris ~atis nonnulla vi .. capientes *Conc. Scot.* II 6; **1343** quod .. abbas non solvit domino regi nonam nec quintamdecimam pro manerio de C., quod non est ~atum, toto tempore domini regis nunc *Couch. Kirkstall* 311; quis dubitat quin ex perpetuacione elemosinarum fundantur lites et bella, per que .. originantur utrimque superbia et cetera vicia, in tantum quod elemosinarius insurgit .. contra ~antem? WYCL. *Eccl.* 203; **1378** quod dicta pars terre .. tanquam terra ~ata ab omni .. servicio seculari remaneat libera *RMS Scot* 655. **b 1276** prior de Kenylworth tenet villam de B., que solet esse geldabilis et modo ~atur per predictum priorem *Hund.* I 45; **1281** dicit .. abbas quod predecessores sui perquisierunt illas [bovatas terre] .. de antecessoribus .. Henrici ..; set, quia solebant esse geldabiles et modo ~antur, ponitur ad judicium *PQW* 391b.

1 elemosinaria, alms-giver (f.); **b** (mon.) almoner.

regina .. religiosa valde et ~ia maxima *NLA* (*Ursula*) II 481. **b 1159** ex parte sanctimonialium [S. Marie de Caritate Andegavensis] H. abbatissa, O. sacrista, Rustica ~ia *Act. Hen. II* I 239.

2 elemosinaria, ~ium [cf. AN *almoignerie*, OF *aumosnerie*], alms-house, almonry (office or place for dispensing alms): **a** (eccl. or mon.); **b** (royal); **c** (for specified charity). **d** (*episcopus elemosinariae*) boy bishop (from St. Nicholas' Day to Holy Innocents' Day).

a [abbas P., ob. **1093**] cetum sanctimonialium quibusdam regulis sanctis et honestis coartavit, in ~ia vel locis illi propinquis collocando *G. S. Alb.* I 59; **c1150** ecclesiam de W. .. elemosinario Rameseie ad pauperum sustentationem concedimus .., ita tamen quod N. de Sigillis eandem nomine ~ie quamdiu vixerit .. possidebit *Cart. Rams.* II 171 (= *Chr. Rams.* 302: nomine ~ii); **a1160** concedimus ecclesiam M. .. sacristarie et ~ie monasterii T. (*Cart. Tavistock*) *EHR* LXII 358; **c1190** in domo ~ie pernoctabunt (*Lib. Elemos. Dunelm.*) *Educ. Ch.* 124; facta est ~ia nostra lapidea, que prius erat debilis et lignea BRAKELOND 148; **1214** ad ~iam pertinent duo furni in E. *Chr. Evesham* 214; **1261** rex contulit W. de C., servienti suo, officium almarie conventus S. Swithuni Winton' *Cl* 335; **1271** (15c) capellano divina celebranti in ~io de Insula Missarum *Inchaffray* 91; **1330** clericos in ~ia nostra degentes *Lit. Cant.* I 309; **1339** modus vivendi pauperum scolarium in ~ia *Reg. Whet.* II app. 315; **s1427** pro tempore campanam elimosinarie supra prisbiterium suspenderunt *Chr. S. Alb.* 12; **1511** domino J. de ambria, iij s. iiij d. *DCCant.* C 11 f. 121a. **b 1185** in operatione ~ie [de Windlesores] *Pipe* 25; **1209** in almosneria domini regis, v s. *Misae* 126; **1213** ad ponendum in almoneria domini regis, v s. *Ib.* 239 (cf. ib. 257: in elmoneria domini regis); **1231** habere faciat J. elemosinario regis tres quercus .. ad ~iam regis de Clarendon' emendandam *Cl* 486; **1232** ad quandam ~iam ibidem [apud Westm'] levandam ad opus regis *Cl* 114; **s1236** Willelmo de Bello Campo officium ~ie [in coronatione] consummante M. PAR. *Maj.* III 338; **1251** [apud Guldeford] murus inter .. thalamum et ~ium crestetur (*AncC* II 116) *RL* II 67; **1262** nos .. concessisse Henrico Prat regie ~ie servienti unam liberacionem in victu et vestitu *Cl* 102; dominus N. de Bello Campo .., qui ab antiquo ~ie regie officium habet W. SAY *Lib. Reg. Cap.* 77. **c 1387** de elemosinis ibidem pertranseuncium per ~iam pro ponte .. faciendo: .. diversi petentes elemosinas de sic pertranseuntibus pontem .. fecerunt et reparaverunt *Pub. Works* I 153. **d 1356** etc. (v. episcopus 3).

3 elemosinaria, ~ium [cf. OF *aumosniere*], 'almoner', alms-bag, wallet.

elemosinariam / mihi mittas eciam / pariter cum versibus HIL. RONCE. 4. 46; **1212** ei robavit j anulum .. cum toto almererio (*sic*) in quo fuit *CurR* VI 209; **1225** Willelmus de Raleg' [clericus] habet breve in almonera *Ib.* XII 908 (cf. ib. 1574: W. de R. habet cyrographum in almonera sua); **1247** robavit ab eo .. unam zonam et unum amenerium precii xij d. *JustIt* 455 r. 3*d.* (cf. ib. r. 7: abstulerunt ab eo .. unam zonam argenteam cum uno aumenerio pleno speciebus); **1261** casu perdidit quandam aumoneram zone sue atachiatam, in qua depositum fuit signum suum *KRMem* 34 r. 8*d.*; quia non habet ~ium preparatum, in libris dimittit reliquias fragmentorum [fructus et casei] R. BURY *Phil.* 17. 220.

elemosinariatus, (mon.) office of almoner.

1327 statuimus .. Robertum T. commonachum nostri loci in officium elimosinariatus nostre domus de D. *Reg. Dunferm.* 370.

elemosinare, by way of (giving or seeking) alms.

[Knud rex] in partibus transmarinis multum aurum ~ie transmisit *Eul. Hist.* III 29 (cf. W. MALM. *GR* II 186); **c1363** licet pape .. exigere a subditis supra titulum vicarie ministrandi vel ~ie mendicandi bona ecclesie *Ziz.* app. 488.

elemosinarium v. 2, 3 elemosinaria, elemosinarius.

elemosinarius [LL]

1 bountiful in alms-giving.

clementissimum animum .. et ~ias manus in pauperes .. quis digne memoret? GOSC. *Wulfh.* 5; **s472** Hyllarius Arelatensis ecclesie presul, vir ~ius et paupertatis amator (ADO) M. PAR. *Maj.* I 217.

2 granted in almoign.

1159 terra ~ia xxx s. v d. *Pipe* 3; **c1160** concessisse .. illam carucatam terre .. quam D. O. abbati .. in perpetuum elemosinam dedit .., tenendam libere et quiete sicut aliqua terra ~ia liberius et quietius tenetur et possidetur in regno nostro *Regesta Scot.* I 110; sicut aliqua terra ~ia in regno Scotie ab aliquo liberius, quietius, plenarius, et honorificentius tenetur *Ch. Beauly* 74; **1477** infeodatio elimosinaria de xx m. *Scot. Grey Friars* II 4.

3 eleemosynary, used (or suitable) for, or concerned with, alms-giving. **b** (w. *domus*) alms-house, almonry.

repperit opus .. ~ium eum fecisse paganum *V. Greg.* p. 105; cum ei de panibus proprii unum .. rex misisset, ipse .. in regio conspectu ~ia panem in frusta concidit et elemosynarum more primo remotius exposita, deinde singulatim retracta, comedit universa GIR. *IK* II 12; **1254** aula ~ia et magna aula domini regis .. indigent coopertorio *CalIMisc* I 205; **1431** lego priori prioratus .. Norwici .. unum discum ~ium argenteum *Reg. Cant.* II 438; **1445** incarceratus est et punitus pena pecuniaria et ~ia *MunAcOx* 543; loca ~ia *Plusc.* VII 18 (v. 4b infra). **b 1180** ecclesiam .. de N. .. domui vestre ~ie .. confirmamus (*Lit. Papae*) ELMH. *Cant.* 449; **1201** (v. domus 7d); faciet .. subelemosinarius .. bis in omni ebdomada .. omnibus egenis ad domum ~iam inferius adventantibus generalem elemosine erogationem *Cust. Westm.* 178 (cf. ib. 179: domus prelibata .., que a plebeis patrie ydiomate *dolhus* vocitatur); **1327** in domo nostra ~ia extra portam *Reg. Dunferm.* 370; rex .. et communes possunt invenire .. c domos ~ias pro decumbentibus (PURVEY) *Ziz.* 393; **1415** volo quod illa terre et tenementa .. existencia .. ad usum et proficuum domus ~ie in Arundell' amortizentur domui [Hospitalis S. Joh. in Anglia] *Reg. Cant.* II 75; in domo ~ia vocata Seynt Johns prope collegium *Val. Eccl.* II 273.

4 (as sb. m.) almoner: **a** (eccl. or mon.); **b** (royal); **c** (mun.).

a ~ius .. perquirat .. ubi egri et debiles jaceant LANFR. *Const.* 154 (cf. ib. 107: ducente eos fratre ~io); ordinate itaque illi vos, domne prior, de elemosina, non per servientes .. sed per monachum ~ium .., quatenus .. nullam duram patiatur indigentiam ANSELM (*Ep.* 380) V 323; **c1135** carectarii habent .. singulis diebus unum panem de †orto [? l. ordeo]; †avelenum [MS: ab elemosinario] vero habent xxxij d. per annum *MonA* IV 43; frater noster W. medicus, tunc temporis ~ius BRAKELOND 148; **1222** statuimus .. ut prelati singuli ~ios honestos habeant *Conc. Syn.* 108; **1234** omnes reliquie tam cibi quam potus per ~ium integre pauperibus erogentur (*Vis. Bury*) *EHR* XXVII 731; ~ius debet esse caritate fervidus, misericordia diffusus, pietate dotatus, orphanorum adjutor, inopum pater, pauperum recreator *Obed. Abingd.* 404; **c1300** ~ius .. diligenter observet ut diebus statutis distribuat elemosinas secundum modum per illos ordinatum qui ad hoc ipsum redditus elemosinarie contulerint. pauperes eciam mendicantes, quos in cimiterio vel deprope mori contigerit, faciat gratis .. in majori cimiterio tumulari. habeat insuper continuo secum octo pueros .. quos .. ad ministerium ecclesie .. faciat informari *Reg. S. Paul.* 74; **s1429** juramenta prestitere de vero dicendo de annua pensione xxx s. officio ~ii spectante *Chr. S. Alb.* 36; **1583** decimas .. que per elimozinarium ejusdem nuper monasterii .. collecte fuerunt *Pat* 1234 m. 23. **b s1177** rex .. fratrem Templi nomine Rogerum .. constituit domus sue ~ium *G. Hen. II* I 169; **s1199** [rex Ricardus] abbatem de Pinu .. secum .. retinuit, ~ium suum illum constituens ut de elemosinis regiis et de pauperibus .. curam gereret COGGESH. *Chr.* 98; **1232** de blado regis .. faciat habere ~iis regis xxvij quar. .., distribuenda fratribus S. Margarete .. et aliis hospitalibus *Cl* 44; **s1319** J. de Jargolio procurator regine et ipsius ~ius *Hist. Roff.* 5v.; officium .. ~ii est fragmenta diligenter colligere et ea distribuere .. egenis; egrotos, leprosos .., viduas .. vagosque in †prisona [v. l. patria] commorantes caritative visitare; item pecuniam .. et alia ad elemosinam largita recipere et .. distribuere. debet eciam regem super elemosine largicione .. stimulare *Fleta* 81; reliqua pars [panni] tota extra ecclesiam distribuetur pauperibus per manus .. elimosinarii *Lib. Regal.* 30; [rex] ~ium suum magnum providum virum faciat et discretum, et omnia loca ~ia regni sui reformari et ad verum statum pristinum sue primeve fundacionis reduci faciat, ac elemosinarum largiciones et erogaciones in propria presencia destribuere precipiat *Plusc.* VII 18 (v. et. 3a supra); instituit idem rex quod per ~ium suum quidam discus v Christi vulnerum .. representativus mense sue .. poneretur BLAKMAN *Hen. VI* 13; **1491** magistri Christofori Ursewyk decani ecclesie Ebor', magni ~ii nostri *RScot* 497a. **c 1162** michi .. concesserunt [burgenses Salmuri] quod, quando elemosinas suas dividerent, darent lessam de testamento suo ad pontem faciendum .. ad consilium sacerdotis sui et ~iorum suorum *Act. Hen. II* I 366; **1461** dicunt .. quod ~ius burgi non mundat communem seweram (*Leet Peterb.*) *EHR* XIX 528.

5 **a** supported by alms. **b** (as sb.) recipient of alms, almsman. **c** tenant (?) holding as almsman or (?) by service as almoner; *cf. elemosina* 3d.

a 1221 liberate .. xl s. ad faciendum fieri quandam domum in prioratu in Kintun' ad opus ij puellarum ~iarum, que ibidem commorabuntur quamdiu nobis placuerit *Cl* 479a; quelibet femina ~ia habuit xl d. W. WORC. *Itin.* 356. **b 1287** A. receptavit meretrices; .. condonatur quia ~ius *Law Merch.* I 16; primo .. argumentum [quod dari potest dominium in perpetuum] patet ex hoc quod ~ii .. 'effluentem mensuram dabunt in sinum' benefactorum [cf. *Luke* vi 38] WYCL. *Civ. Dom.* I 249; *Id. Pol.* 246 (v. dotator). **c** j Francigena, ~ius regis *DB* I 132v.; prefecti regis et bedelli et ~ii *Ib.* 209a; abbas [S. Eadmundi] tenuit ad victum monachorum c et xviij homines, et potuerunt dare et vendere terram suam; et sub eis lij bord[arios] .., liiij liberos satis inopes, xliij elemosin[arios]; quisque eorum habet j bord[arium] *Ib.* II 372.

elemosinatio, a alms-giving. **b** grant in almoign.

a cum Christus docuit nos dare temporalem elemosinam et non sic perpetuam, sequitur quod temporalis ~o sit magis autentica WYCL. *Eccl.* 277. **b c1152** predictas cartas et omnes donationes et ~ones .. confirmavi in pura et libera elemosina *Act. Hen. II* I 48.

elemosinator, (generous) alms-giver.

egregius ~or et devotus Dei cultor, Ethelricus GOSC. *Mir. Iv.* lx; **s1132** [abbas H.] bonus ~or omnibus diebus fuit et ideo .. bonum finem fecit H. ALBUS 104; de quodam ~ore, Petro .. theloneario COGGESH. *Visio* 15; **1456** audio quod plurimas .. cotidie elemosinas facis; fructum operum tuorum pauperes senciunt, quorum vocibus eciam in remotis partibus famaris ~or egregius BEKYNTON II 158.

elemosyn-, elemoxsin- v. elemosin-. **elempnium** v. helenium. **elena** v. helenium, inula.

elenchice, a (log.) by way of refutation. **b** preventively, preclusively.

a oportet correspondenter ~e intelligere et exponere illum librum [Augustini, de Libero Arbitrio] BRADW. *CD* 728D; correspondenter et ~e eandem [necessitatem] negat *Ib.* 733B. **b** viam .. custodit sic quod nullus potest in Egiptum de terra Inda descendere nec inde absque sua licencia remeare; et hoc satis ~e sive cautelose S. SIM. *Itin.* 87.

elenchicus [cf. LL elencticus < ἐλεγκτικός], refutative, (as sb. n.) refutation.

Aristoteles dicit quod medium ~um arguendi contra eos est querere ab illis quid terminus signet, ne equivocent in signacionibus terminorum WYCL. *Act.* 112; **a1400** hic [abbas Louperticus], nimis nimius in suis oculis, / mentem non adhibet Patrum sentenciis, / set, suis jugiter utens elenchicis, / signum insinuat elati criminis TRYVYTLAM *Laus Ox.* 411.

elenchus (elencus) [CL < ἔλεγχος], (log.) 'elench', refutation. **b** (pl.) Aristotle's *Elenchi.*

†elegoos, castigatio *GlC* E 145; J. SAL. *Met.* 930A (v. eluctatorius); logice .. / portio quarta suis sese concessit elenchis; / utitur hac studiis parte sophista suis NECKAM *DS* X 67; [medici] nunc per artem topicorum et ~orum multiplicant questiones accidentales infinitas BACON IX 154; cum infertur ulterius 'ergo quiescit et non quiescit', ibi est ignorancia ~i et fallacia secundum quid et simpliciter DUNS *Ord.* VII 272; peccat graviter, eo quod ignorat ~um BRADW. *CD* 370A. **b** audiat .. Aristotelis .. librum Periarmonias et librum ~orum (NECKAM *Sac.*) *Med. Sci.* 373; secundum Aristotelem in ~is GILB. III 144v. 1; B. Edmundus Cantuar' archiepiscopus primus legit Oxonie librum ~orum temporibus meis BACON *CSTheol.* 34; **1268** bachilarii .. determinaturi .. de nova logica librum Priorum, Topicorum, ~orum bis, librum autem Posteriorum saltem una vice jurent se audivisse *StatOx* 26; **c1390** Egidius super libros ~orum (*Catal.*) *FormOx* 243; **1443** textus ~orum priorum (*Catal.*) *Cant. Coll. Ox.* I 6.

1 elencus v. elenchus.

2 †elencus, *f. l.*

frater †elencus [? l. elegus] sanctum sepe requirit *NLA* (*Edmund*) II 634.

eleotrum v. electrum 3a.

elepannus [ME *elepan*], wall-plate of an 'ell', eyling, lean-to (*cf. Building in Eng.* 204).

1341 pro xij elepostibus et viij ~is, xl tignis et alio maeremio necessario pro reparacione domus vaccarum apud vaccariam de Stapelock' *MinAc* (*Yorks*) 1091/6, K4 (cf. ib. 1147/23 [**1325**] m. 11: in stipendio j sclatoris removentis sclat' super magnum stabulum, ad vacuandum locum ibi pro emendacione unius *elepan* fracti).

elephans v. elephas.

elephantia [CL], 'elephancy', elephantiasis or sim.

ut [mulieres] ex eadem copula ~ie ducant maculam ADEL. *QN* 42; percussus ~ia et propterea facie et membris reliquis deformatus W. CANT. *Mir. Thom.* VI 58; at lepre

species superest elephantia tales, / horribilis cholere filia nigra nigre NECKAM *DS* IV 856; lepra cedit leonina; / sua victa medicina, / cedit elephancia GARL. *SM* 14. 306; lepre .. species .. quarta dicitur ~ia propter tuberositatem et grossitiem innaturalem similem elephanti GAD. 45. 2; **1468** (v. alopecia a); *a lepyr*, lepra, elefancia, missella *CathA*.

elephantiacus [LL < ἐλεφαντιακός], elephantiac.

elefantiacus, morbus magnus *GlH* E 182.

elephanticus [LL], elephantiac, (w. *morbus*) 'elephancy'.

nec leprosos vel ~os exhorruit, sed quasi fratres amplexabatur ALCUIN (*Rich.*) *Hag.* 685; ÆLF. *Gl.* (v. 1 arcuare 2c); ~o morbo correptus W. CANT. *Mir. Thom.* II 52; in ~o perfecta fit secunda et tertia digestio *Quaest. Salern.* B 254; ut leprosi et ~i ex hac conceptione nascantur ROB. FLAMB. *Pen.* 288.

elephantinosus v. elephantiosus.

elephantinus [CL < ἐλεφάντινος], elephantine.

794 mirum animal [sc. pecten], duo habens capita et dentes lx, non elefantinae magnitudinis sed eburneae pulchritudinis ALCUIN *Ep.* 26; genu .. more ~o incurvum reclinari .. non potuit R. COLD. *Cuthb.* 48.

2 elephantiac, (w. *morbus* or sim.) 'elephancy'.

Sirorum .. princeps, quem lurida leprae spurcitia .. elefantino tabo contexerat [cf. *2 Sam.* v] ALDH. *Met.* 2 (cf. id. *VirgP* 52: elefantina cutis callositate); tanquam ~o perculsa incommodo T. MON. *Will.* III 15; ~a peste deformiter laboro *NLA* (*Ethelbert*) I 418; morbo ~o .. percussi *Ib.* (*Kenelm*) II 113; **s1321** sevicia [Judeorum et Agarenorum] .. multos per diversa mundi climata conventus ~orum .. copulavit, ut ipsi leprosi .. pilas conficerent .. intoxicatas *Flor. Hist.* III 195.

elephantiosus (elef-) [LL], elephantiac, (of skin) scabrous, (w. *morbus*) 'elephancy'.

[Constantini] elefantiosa corporis incommoditas ALDH. *VirgP* 25; quomodo leprosus quidam elephantuosus ad corpus viri Dei damno mundatus est *Mir. Nin.* cap. 11 *tit.*; elefantinosa, i. maxime *þare* [MS: *þære*] *unsmeþan GlH* E 181; **9..** elephantinosa, *sio hreoflice WW*; R. dux Normannorum .. compassionem semper habebat de his quos ~us morbus vexabat, ita ut ipsi ~i sepe [eum] fratrem vocarent *BR Will.* I 1; cur, ad mulierem sanam si vir ~us accedat, .. qui eam deinde primus cognoverit morbum sustinebit ADEL. *QN* 41; [elephantis] cutis adeo ulcerosa est ut ab ipsa dicatur lepra morbus ~us NECKAM *NR* II 143; leprosorum .. et ~orum ab hominibus ejectioni compatiens *Chr. Battle* f. 103; Hugo [ep. Dunelm', ob. **1195**] .. hospitale .. construxit et elefantiosos in episcopatu suo circumquaque collectos ibidem instituit G. COLD. *Durh.* 7 (= *MonA* VI 669a: elefantuosos).

elephas ~ans, ~antus [CL < ἐλέφας], elephant; **b** (fig.). **c** elephant-house in Tower of London (used as place of custody for Jews).

belliger impugnans elefantes vulnere sterno ALDH. *Aen.* 60 (*Monocerus*) 5; ~anti .. cognitis majores sunt animantibus *Lib. Monstr.* II 2; ~ans, *ylp* ÆLF. *Gl.*; medicina de ~anto *Leechdoms* I 368; dentem .. ~antis et ungulam gryphis .. exegit ORD. VIT. III 3 p. 60; ~anto .. mus terribilis esse perhibetur GIR. *TH* I 27; artus non flectit elephas; hinc casus ei .. / .. perniciosus erit NECKAM *DS* IX 47; eque vivens est embrio et adolescens, ~as et formica ALF. ANGL. *Cor* 1. 3; **s1255** missus est in Angliam quidam ~as, quem .. rex Francie .. dedit .. regi Anglorum. nec credimus quod unquam aliquis ~as visus est in Anglia .. preter illum M. PAR. *Maj.* V 489; E ante F breviatur, ut 'elefas' BACON *Tert.* 260; ~antes .., animalia monstruosa nimis et non in aspectu graciosa S. SIM. *Itin.* 59; **1425** [cancellarius] assignavit multa bona ex sano consilio provenire .., desiderans quemlibet consulentem in tribus ~anti proprietatibus comparari. ~ans enim est sine felle, inflexibilis et immense memorie *RParl* IV 261a; ~as ab *elphio* Grece, quod est 'mens' (*sic*) Latine UPTON 160 (cf. Isid. *Etym.* XII 2. 14: Graece .. mons λόφος dicitur); hic olefans, *a olefaunt WW*. **b** ingens ~as terrae .. captus est triumphaliter apostolica sagena GOSC. *Aug. Maj.* 64B. **c** **1277** de quadam muliere in elefant', viij s. *KRAc* 249/22 (cf. ib.: de una Judea in *olifant*).

elephebascum v. elaphoboscon.

elepostis [ME **elepost*], post of an 'ell' or lean-to.

1341 (v. elepannus).

elere v. eleare a. **eleus** v. 2 elegus. **eleutropia** v. heliotropium.

elevabilis, that can be lifted, (w. *pons*) drawbridge. **b** that can be exalted (intellectually or spiritually).

s1420 ex utraque parte turris [de Charentone] est pons ~is et tractabilis, sic quod nullus accedere potest ad turrim si isti pontes fuerunt elevati WALS. *HA* II 334. **b** [anima intellectiva] poterit per naturam suam habere proporcionem ad quecunque immaterialia, et hoc saltem de aliqua potencia absoluta, ita quod aliquo modo sit ~is ad ea, si Deus vellet BACONTHORPE *Quaest. Sent.* I 10a.

elevare [CL]

1 to lift, raise; **b** (astr.); **c** (w. ref. to baptism); **d** (w. ref. to elevation of Host). **e** (anat.) to swell, dilate. **f** to raise (punctuation mark). **g** (p. ppl.) embossed, in relief. **h** (p. ppl.) high.

vidit equum capud sursum ~antem ad tecta *V. Cuthb.* I 6; ~atis ad caelum oculis manibusque BEDE *HE* III 16; **8..** ~at, *up ahefð WW*; antequam ossa ejus ~arentur de tumulo ÆLF. *Æthelwold* 26; W. FITZST. *Thom. prol.* 11 (v. contradictorius 1c); humores .. altius ~ati .. nubes vocantur GIR. *TH* I 6; aquile .. alcius se ~ant in aere quam alia volatilia BART. ANGL. III 17; **1296** (v. calcaneus 2c); flatus venti .. te ~aret [ME: *schulde beore þe upwart*] versus celi gaudia *AncrR* 37; **s1420** (v. elevabilis a); duo duces .. debent molliter atque humiliter ~are reginam de lecto W. SAY *Lib. Reg. Cap.* 72. **b** quanto polus mundi ~atur supra orizontem, tanto majores sunt dies estatis SACROB. *Sph.* 103. **c** **735** (v. baptisma a); **c798** tertio ~atus de fonte per gratiam resurgat ad vitam ALCUIN *Ep.* 137 (cf. elevatio 1c); quem Ælfred rex .. de fonte sacro baptismatis ~avit ASSER *Alf.* 56. **d** GERV. TILB. III 24 (v. consecratorius); **c1239** sacerdos .. doceat plebem suam ut, cum in celebratione missarum ~atur hostia salutaris, se reverenter inclinet *Conc. Syn.* 268; **c1250** caveant sibi sacerdotes ne ~ent hostiam .. quousque protulerint hec verba: 'hoc est corpus meum' *Ib.* 641. **e** [sanguis] subtiliatur, dilatatur et arteriam ~at, quam elevationem 'pulsum' vulgus vocat ALF. ANGL. *Cor* 11. 11; RIC. MED. *Anat.* 219 (v. 2 dilatare 1d). **f** punctus ~atus [sc. ;] debet fieri quando non est suspensio absoluta, sed sententia imperfecta, que immediate perficitur per id quod sequitur. .. aliquando non est nisi una sententia perficienda et quia absoluta est, ideo ~atur punctatio BACON *Tert.* 250. **g** **1232** j cuppam magnam cum imaginibus ~atis; item xxviij cuppas argent' deaur' et operatas de opere ~ato *Pat* 43 m. 8; **1235** dedit .. j cuppam deauratam et operatam cum opere ~ato cum ymaginibus hominum et bestiarum *Chanc. Misc.* 3/4d.; **1303** (v. draco 2a); **1445** una pulcra tabula pro osculo pacis ornata cum argento deaurato operis †elmate [? l. elevati] per totum cum imagine B. Marie *Invent. S. Paul.* 521. **h** radius B A, qui est ~atior, reflectitur ad E, quod est superius in re visa BACON *Maj.* II 140; demonstracio est .. sub ~acioribus radiis visa ~aciora apparere PECKHAM *Persp.* II 50.

2 a to elevate (in rank or status). **b** to exalt (spiritually). **c** to puff up (w. pride or presumption). **d** (p. ppl.) overweening.

a divini est judicii cujus sors ~ata palmam teneat BEDE *Prov.* 989; ut ~arent mensem ad debitum primitiarum statum BACON *Tert.* 219; fuit Hester ~ata [ME: *ihechȝet*] in reginam de paupere puella *AncrR* 58. **b** **801** [Johannes] longe a tribus superioribus evangelistis sublimius ~atus est ALCUIN *Ep.* 213; R. NIGER *Mil.* III 67 (v. 4a infra). **c** **601** ne .. infirmus animus in sui praesumtione se ~et (*Lit. Papae*) BEDE *HE* I 31; quem charitas inflammat, non potestas ~at AD. SCOT *OP* 571C; elatio deicit .., quia, cum caro recalcitrat et ~atur .., eripitur humilitas R. NIGER *Mil.* I 28; **1198** (v. constantia 1a); modo vexaris timore, modo ~aris falsa spe *Spec. Eccl.* 8; quicumque .. a Deo avertitur .. superbia ~atur OCKHAM *Dial.* 593. **d** **s1455** elacior in multo ~aciorque in se factus, satis alta presumpsit .. agere *Reg. Whet.* I 203.

3 a to raise (sound) in volume or pitch. **b** to increase in amount. **c** to price highly.

a ~ata in altum voce BEDE *HE* IV 26 p. 273; ad cantoris .. arbitrium quilibet cantus in choro incipietur, ~abitur aut remittetur *Cust. Westm.* 28; *Ib.* 29 (v. deprimere 2a); BACON *Tert.* 248 (v. 2 colon); **s1455** ~antes in altum suas voces *Reg. Whet.* I 179. **b** si ceapgildum .. ~emus [AS: *arærað*] *GAS* 177 (v. ceapgildum); **s1399** regnum non rexisti sed spoliasti, theolonea notabiliter ~ando, tallagia annuatim extorquendo *Eul. Hist. Cont.* III 382. **c** **a1250** si .. predictas acras terre .. vendere voluerit .. predictis fratribus .., pro precio legali vendet et .. non de eis ~abit *DL Cart. Misc.* III 66 (e).

4 to erect, put up: **a** (building, furnace, or sim.); **b** (quintain). **c** to set up, establish (market). **d** (w. abstr. obj.) to institute, bring about, promote.

a ~andi sunt papiliones et figenda temptoria, ut eleventur conversationes singulorum R. NIGER *Mil.* III 67 (v. et. 2b supra); **12..** turris culmen .. ex optima materia bene conjuncta constructum et ~atum est *G. S. Alb.* I 280; **1292** quod nullus eorum [burgensium] infra iiij portas ville nullum furnum ~abit *BBC* (*Knutsford*) 127; **1370** (v. eleare b); **1371** pro quolibet furno ~ando *MinAc* (*Wye, Kent*) 900/1. **b** **s1253** (v. aries 2c). **c** si elevacio unius [mercati] sit ad nocumentum alterius, tunc videndum erit quod ipsorum prius fuerit ~atum *Fleta* 273. **d** ~etur inter eos pax regis (*Leg. Hen.* 76. 1b) *GAS* 593; **a1158** remotis omnibus pravis consuetudinibus post avum meum ibi ~atis (*Ch. Hen. II*) *MGL* II 667; utrum .. hujusmodi occasio eatenus ~etur .., ego non judico R. NIGER *Mil.* IV 58; rempublicam salvabit indempnem, per quod ~et comodum subditorum MILEMETE *Nob.* 30.

5 to lift, carry off ('meadow', *i. e.* hay).

1312 in prato bis falcato et ~ato, xx d. *Comp. Swith.* 399; **1394** debet falcare et ~are unam acram prati *CourtR Tooting Beck* 2.

elevate [LL], aloft, at a height.

oportet quod res appareat propinquius et ~ius versus oculum ubi est concursus radii visualis cum catheto BACON *Maj.* II 155; refectorarius .. coclear abbatis manu ~e dextra feret *Obed. Abingd.* 400 (cf. cochleatorium).

elevatio [LL]

1 lifting, raising; **b** (astr.); **c** (w. ref. to baptism). **d** elevation (of Host). **e** (anat.) dilation. **f** swelling. **g** elevation, height.

incensum .. turificatur, quod porrectarum ~oni manuum simulatur ALDH. *VirgP* 60; cum in singulorum [sanctorum] ~one [a tumulo] merita singulorum superna prodiderit fragrantia GOSC. *Transl. Aug.* 41A; **1261** pontes in ~one sua (v. bretescha a); BACON *Maj.* II 432 (v. depressio 1a); himnus .. in ~one regis in solium suum a .. choro .. decantabatur W. SAY *Lib. Reg. Cap.* 98. **b** ipse [sol] .. earum [planetarum] stationes, cursus et recursus, sed et ~ones et depressiones sua vi variare ab astrologis comprobatur ALB. LOND. *DG* 8. 19; quanta est ~o poli mundi supra orizontem, tanta est distantia zenith ab equinoctiali SACROB. *Sph.* 91; DUNS *Sent.* II 14. 2. 6 (v. depressio 1b). **c** **c798** possunt tres noctes [cf. *Matth.* xii 40] tres mersiones et tres dies tres ~ones designare ALCUIN *Ep.* 137; **c1258** ad ~onem pueri de .. fonte (v. compaternitas). **d** **c1218** quando post ~onem hostia sacra dimittitur *Conc. Syn.* 79; *Ib.* 143 (v. consecratio 1b); ~o eorum [accidencium sacramenti] significat ~onem in cruce (TYSS.) *Ziz.* 164; **1394** ad duos cereos pro ~one sacramenti *Ac. Churchw. Bath* 15; **1397** (v. corpus 7b); **1415** in ~one eukaristie *Reg. Cant.* II 372. **e** ALF. ANGL. *Cor* 11. 11 (v. elevare 1e); [cordis] ~o et depressio RIC. MED. *Anat.* 226 (v. arsis b). **f** cum [apes] pungunt, venenum habent .. et faciunt ~ones nigras GILB. VII 356v. 1. **g** **s1460** turmis .. ipsam [fossam circumvallacionis] non multum prompte propter ~onem verticis .. ascendere valentibus *Reg. Whet.* I 374.

2 a elevation (in rank). **b** (spiritual) exaltation. **c** pride, presumption.

a ambo, sc. nomen Hester et ejus ~o [ME: *hechȝunge*] probant que dixi *AncrR* 58 (cf. elevare 2a); **c1370** ad filii sui ~onem [ad regnum] (v. 1 depositio 7b). **b** quantum ad ordinem quam [res] habent in ~one et approximatione ad ipsum creantem BACON VIII 92. **c** quibus mors intravit per fenestras ~onis GILDAS *Ep.* 2; causa formalis [peccati primi angeli] erat ~o HALES *Sent.* II 19.

3 a (of sound) raising in volume or pitch. **b** levying or (?) increase in amount.

a ALDH. *PR* 112, BART. ANGL. XIX 128 (v. arsis a); *Offic. Sal.* 3 (v. depressio 2); dictio que est gravis in fine, in qua finitur interrogatio, acuenda est; et fit una ~o et unus punctus BACON *Tert.* 255; aspere sonat quando partes [sonorum] ordinantur secundum ~onem et depressionem non recte *Ps.*-GROS. *Gram.* 27; *Obs. Barnwell* 58 (v. 1 depositio 1b). **b** **s1405** depauperacio mercatorum .. per excessivas ~ones theoloneorum et custumarum *Eul. Hist. Cont.* III 405.

4 a erection (of building or sim.) or object erected; **b** (of quintain). **c** setting up, establishment (of market).

a **1231** ad ~onem castrorum meorum (*AncC* IV 139) *RL* I 390; abbas [W., ob. **1235**] turrim .. retegi fecit, .. collateralibus additis ornamentis, viz. octo linearibus ~onibus, a tholo usque ad murale extensis, ut octogona turris manifestius appareret *G. S. Alb.* I 280; **1292** per ~onem paxerie *RGasc* III 54. **b** **1236** precipimus ut .. prohibeatis .. arietum supra ligna et rotas ~ones *Conc. Syn.* 204 (= GROS. *Ep.* 22); **c** *Fleta* 273 (v. elevare 4c).

5 a taking away. **b** lifting, carrying off (of hay from meadow).

a de bonis ipsius A. per executores suos nulla fiat .. administracio seu per aliquos alios ~o antequam eidem W. plenarie fuerit satisfactum *FormMan* 10. **b** **1394** inveniet j hominem in ~one feni sine sibo *CourtR Tooting Beck* 6.

elevativus, elevatory, uplifting; **b** (spiritually).

est hec caliditas suorum subjectorum a centro ad circumferentiam ~a BART. ANGL. IV 1. **b** oracione, que est ~a mentis in Deum, per prorupcionem in laudem oramus WYCL. *Ente* 116.

eleyson v. eleison.

elfarius [ME *el fare*], elver (or 'eel-fare').

1290 in pisce aque dulcis, ij s. v d.; in elfar' xij d. .. in menus', xv d.; in elfar', xij d. *Ac. Swinfield* 61.

elfimerus v. ephemerus.

1 †elia, (?) *f. l.*

ad .. verba sanctorum a mundi principio mutabantur jura nature et obediebant †elia et bruta alia† [? l. elementa et bruta animalia] BACON *Maj.* III 123.

2 elia v. ilia. **eliacus** v. heliacus. **eliceferis** v. helix.

elicere [CL]

1 to lure, summon. **b** (gram.) to elicit.

lacte et sanguine ad tumulum animas ~iebant ALB. LOND. *DG* 6. 26. **b** sunt alia [verba] .. quae .. imperativo

.. iambum, non spondeum, ~iunt, ut făveo, fāvi, fāvē ALDH. *PR* 114.

2 to bring forward. **b** to produce.

mari retrahente, nostri in arena conveniunt, ut machinam muro pedibus solum quatuor adjicerent, ut sic facilius pontem ~erent. cum pontem .. emissum viderent, .. arma deponunt OSB. BAWDSEY clxxvi. **b** VINSAUF *PN* 818 (v. 1 cassis 1a).

3 to extract, draw out; **b** (w. ref. to fire); **c** (fig.); **d** (math.). **e** to tease wool.

8.. ~it, *ut atiohð* .., **9..** ~uit, *gerænte oððe ut ateah* *WW*; in torculari uvae premuntur ut ex eis vini sapor ~iatur *Eccl. & Synag.* 119; qui fortiter premit ubera ~it butirem ANSELM *Misc.* 307; elices, fontes que ex se aquam ~iunt OSB. GLOUC. *Deriv.* 193; *SB* 14 (v. cadmia). **b** [virgo] tonitrua .. concitans simulque igniferas fulminum coruscationes ~iens ALDH. *VirgP* 47; queritur quare ex crystallo posita ad solem ~iatur ignis *Quaest. Salern.* B 176; ~itur scintilla ignis ex aquosa (*sic*) cristallo per virtutem solis oppositi AD. DORE *Pictor* 151; ignem silice ~iunt *Hist. Meriadoci* 350. **c** [Hieronymus] priscae legis patefecit abyssum. / .. / insuper elicuit tractatus jure stupendos ALDH. *VirgV* 1628; o si umquam merebor de caritate Stephani oleum precibus ~ere ANSELM (*Or.* 13) III 53; psalterium didicit, ex quo, spiritu sancto ~iente, spirituali .. nutriebatur adipe DOMINIC *V. Ecgwini* I 1. **d** hinc ~e radicem quadratam ROB. ANGL. *Alg.* 148. **e** *to tese wolle*, carpere, ~ere *CathA*.

4 to extract (by discarding other material). **b** to elicit, ascertain (by research).

ex aliorum dispendiis compendiosum aliquid ~ere GIR. *GE proem.* p. 6 (v. dispendium 2b); quando granum, id est spiritualis intellectus, a palea littere ~itur S. LANGTON *Ruth* 110; **1319** quosdam articulos a litteris predictis ~i .. fecimus (*Pat*) *MGL* II 268. **b 9..** ~uit, .. *asmeade* *WW*; ut quicquid .. opifici propositum fuerit, omni errore abjecto, facilius ~i queat ROB. ANGL. *Alg.* 108; inquisitio diligens .. paulatim ~it radices heresis R. NIGER *Mil.* III 69; ut nihil in libello apposuerim cujus veritatem .. cum summa diligentia non ~uerim GIR. *TH* II *pref.* p. 74; *Ps.*-GROS. *Summa* 481 (v. ductivus a).

5 to evoke (emotional or spiritual response).

aliquam .. superni amoris dulcedinem michi ~io *V. Gund.* 33; an non sufficiunt ad ~iendum sanguinem et medullas in lacrimas? ANSELM (*Medit.* 1) III 78; clavi qui filii corpus afficiunt / .. / de matre gurgites salsos eliciunt WALT. WIMB. *Carm.* 615.

6 a (log.) to educe, infer. **b** (phil.) to elicit (from potentiality), actualize (esp. w. ref. to 'elicit' acts evolved from something inherent in the will).

a rhetorica, licet ejus officium sit ex dialecticis et propriis locis argumenta probationis ~ere, quod maxime attendit est affectum movere GROS. 2; sicut ex verbis Augustini .. ~i potest OCKHAM *Pol.* I 307; WYCL. *Civ. Dom.* I 441 (v. 2 computabilis 1); **1442** (v. colligere 8); ut, utraque legum experiencia doctus, que earum tibi eligibilior sit ex earum effectibus ~ere valeas FORTESCUE *LLA* 35. **b** de desiderio, quod est actus ~itus a voluntate DUNS *Metaph.* I 2 p. 44 (cf. ib. 42: de velle ~ito, non de velle naturali); eleccio, ex qua generatur liberalitas vel que ~itur ex liberalitate *Id. Ord.* I 192; quando principium elicitivum non necessario ~it, habens illud principium non necessario agit; neque principium elicitivum, eodem modo se habens, quod prius ~iebat contingenter modo ~it necessario. .. voluntas autem, habens eandem caritatem quam modo habet, prius contingenter ~iebat actum fruendi; ergo modo non necessario ~it actum illum *Ib.* II 91; WYCL. *Ente Praed.* 115 (v. elicitio).

elicibilis, a (log.) that can be inferred. **b** (phil.) that can be 'elicited'; *cf. elicere* 6b.

a sit Petrus politicus juste judicans cujus judicium non sit ~e ex scriptura WYCL. *Mand. Div.* 22; ex istis .. potest fidelis colligere quod omnes privati ordines, qui non habent aliud fundamentum quam determinacionem papalem, cessare debeant; et per idem omnes determinaciones Romani pontificis que non sunt patenter ~es ex scriptura *Id. Blasph.* 46; **1423** nunquam negavi .. merita aut sanctorum suffragia .. tam vivis quam mortuis .. proficere, quia hoc est ~e ex scriptura .. et ex consona racione (W. TAYLOUR) *Reg. Cant.* III 164 (= *Conc.* III 408). **b** amare et desiderare objectum cognitum .. est vere praxis, nec naturaliter consequens apprehensionem sed libere — recte et non recte ~is DUNS *Ord.* I 197.

elicitio, (phil.) 'elicitation', actualization.

vel accipiatur 'eleccio' ibi [Arist. *Eth. Nic.* 1139a] pro liberalitate sive potestate dominativa vel accipiatur 'eleccio' pro ~one actus volendi, qui non est eleccio vel volicio aliqua DUNS *Ord.* I 195 (cf. WYCL. *Ente Praed.* 115: eleccio actus cujuscumque creature dicit .. ejus mutabilitatem et actualem motum, cum homo non elicit actum de novo nisi moveatur ab objecto ex extrinseco).

elicitive, (phil.) by 'elicitation'.

illa potencia cujus est usus ~e dicitur duo in se habere R. ORFORD *Reprob.* 52; per quod cognoscitur actus super quem reflectimus? .. primum quidem est per voluntatem; et secundum eciam est per vestigium derelictum ab actu .. : illo ergo derelicto, per illud ~e potest haberi actus reflexus, voluntate imperante, et potest non haberi, voluntate imperante aliam intelleccionem DUNS *Ord.* III 270.

elicitivus, (phil.) tending to 'elicit'.

emanatio creaturarum a Deo magis appropriatur summe bonitati .. quam omnipotentie que est principium creationis ~um MIDDLETON *Sent.* I 58a; omni potencie apprehensive correspondet propria appetitiva ~a actus appetendi, non solum appetitus naturalis DUNS *Metaph.* I 2 p. 44; philosophus .. loquitur de intellectu secundum quod cum voluntate constituit unum principium respectu artificialium et non ut est naturaliter ~us sue operacionis *Id. Ord.* II 335; *Ib.* 91 (v. elicere 6b); cum nullo modo magis est sensus receptivus quam ~us, sequitur quod pro quolibet instanti natus est elicere actum WYCL. *Act.* 11.

elicus v. eliquus, elix.

elidere [CL]

1 to strike, knock, crush; **b** (fig.).

Hercules geminos †augues [l. angues] .. in manu premens eliserat *Lib. Monstr.* III 20; ~eret, i. offenderet, *ascrencte*, ~untur, i. percutiuntur *GlH* E 193–4; W. MALM. *GP* IV 183 (v. contraniti); caudam suam servant, ut muscas abigant et ~ant NIG. *Ep.* 18; factus est strepitus .. et collisio tanta ut .. navis .. putaretur ~i W. CANT. *Mir. Thom.* VI 145; terra .. sperica est ex omni parte habens partes elisas et equaliter depressas *Quaest. Salern.* N 58; frater .., terre elisus .., sentit ex impetu casus collisionem humeri sinistri *NLA* (*Edmund*) II 634; **c1276** ~avit (*sic*) pede [? l. pedem] et cecidit super cultellum suum *IMisc* 34/61. **b** grassator .., / qui genus humanum strofis elidere certat ALDH. *VirgV* 922; elisa mens vel dejecta, *forscrenct* ÆLF. *Gl.*; artibus elisis demonis orat opem NIG. *Mir. BVM* 20v. 1; facilius .. a presidiis exterius obsidiones ~untur quam ipsa expugnentur presidia R. NIGER *Mil.* III 56.

2 to force out, emit.

licet pauca .. rear fieri tonitrua ex quibus non ~antur fulmina ADEL. *QN* 66 (cf. ib.: quandoque aer tantum inde ~etur).

3 a (w. ref. to prosody) to elide. **b** to invalidate, quash.

a Vergilius .. sillabam elisit, dicens: 'dur(um) iter ..' ALDH. *PR* 9. **b** ut .. viri Dei praeconium falsis suspicionum argumentis .. ~eret *Id. VirgP* 32; lancee [etc.] .. quibus assultus assidencium ~antur [*gl.*: *seyent bleces*] et enerventur NECKAM *Ut.* 104; sic elidetur objectio que levitatem / intendit primam solvere *Id. DS* IV 722; **1200** dies dat' .. ad ~endum electionem xij de placito servicii *CurR RC* II 276; **1214** nec .. machinabimini .. quod .. episcopi jurisdictio ~atur *MunAcOx* 2; **c1250** miror de vestris ordinariis .. quod tales alegaciones non ellidunt ipsis auditis W. BERNHAM *Ep.* 2; prefati rectoris errorem .. in diversis operibus reprobaverunt .. fundamentaque suorum sequacium eliserunt OCKHAM *Dial.* 761.

eliforus v. helleborus. **eliganter** v. 1 eleganter.

eligentia, deliberate choice. *Cf. electio* 1d.

~ia est voluntas consiliata HALES *Sent.* III 396.

eligere [CL]

1 a to pick out. **b** to select, choose (esp. a course of action); **c** (w. inf. or acc. & inf.); **d** (w. *quod*). **e** (leg.) to choose procedure (esp. w. ref. to writ of *elegit*); *cf. electio* 1b. **f** (astr.) to choose favourable conjunction; *cf. electio* 1c. **g** to choose heretically (w. ref. to etym. of *haeresis*).

a tanquam marinas inter arenas gemmas ~ens GIR. *TH intr.* p. 8. **b 705** elego quae elegeris, rennuo quae rennueris WEALDHERE *Ep.* 23; equum .. quem tibi specialiter possidendum elegi BEDE *HE* III 14; ALCUIN *Gram.* 896A (v. electivus 1b); **798** (12c) hoc .. elegimus, ut .. abbatissa a me percipiet .. coenobium *CS* 291; **804** (11c) sit [mater mea] libera cum libris et ruris (*sic*) ad †elegandam [v. l. ~endum] patrocinium ubi placitum sibi fuerit *CS* 313; **933** (10c) superna ad instar pretiosorum monilium eli[g]ens, animum sempiternis in gaudiis fi[g]ens *CS* 694; in quorum [cenobiorum] uno sibi et in altero conjugi sue sepulturam elegerat ORD. VIT. IV 1 p. 163; curandum est .. quatinus sub lege quam elegerint .. vivant R. NIGER *Mil.* II 33; **1221** abjuravit regnum et elegit portum de Doberna *PlCrGlouc* 79; **1283** debet arare et herciare j acram .. vel dare iij gallinas et j gallum .., prout dominus ~ere voluerit *Cust. Battle* 60; vos anachorite partem Marie [cf. *Luke* x 42] elegistis [ME: *beoð inumen ow*] *AncrR* 166; **1537** in expensis Roberti W. in Novo Castro pro vino ~endo *Ac. Durh.* 696. **c 800** illorum juditio .. quorum dilectione singulariter me laborare elegi ALCUIN *Ep.* 200; **803** Deo soli servire .. ~am *Ib.* 239; elegit magis in domo Domini abjectus manere quam in tabernaculis peccatorum .. florere [cf. *Psalm* lxxxiii 11] ORD. VIT. III 2 p. 40; elegi .. ridiculus .. inveniri GIR. *RG* II 2 (v. dyscolus a); **1203** ipse elegit portare ferrum *SelPlCrown* 30; **s1231** elegimus .. resistere quam eorum [Romanorum] oppressionibus .. de cetero subjacere WEND. III 18; **s1302** ~entes .. liberaliter mori quam serviliter diutius vivere *Flor. Hist.* III 111; tali .. loco ipsum [Quadragesime] tempus sacrum ~ebat deducere *Ps.*-ELMH. *Hen. V* 55. **d 1202** ipse elegit quod Astinus [ferrum] portet *SelPlCrown* 10. **e s1326** peticio pro habendo brevi quod dicitur 'elegit' *Lit. Cant.* I 198; **1369** execucio per elegit super recognicione facta in camera (*Cal. LBLond.* C 238) *MGL* I 610; **14..** terris .. per breve nostrum de elegit liberatis *Reg. Brev. Orig.* 75 (cf. ib. 277b: pro eo quod prefatus R. elegit sibi liberari .. catalla ipsius J. .. ac medietatem terre sue tenend' juxta formam statuti .. quousque prefato R. de .. x li. fuerit satisfactum). **f** M. SCOT *Intr.* 289 (v. diminutio 2a). **g** aliquas .. auctoritates evangelii, eas dumtaxat quas ipsi [heretici] elegerint, admittunt et alias omnes infrunite abiciunt R. NIGER *Mil.* III 66; **s1253** subjunxit episcopus [Linc'] fideli interpretatione Greci idiomatis in Latinum: 'heresis est sententia humano sensu electa scripture sacre contraria, palam edocta, pertinaciter defensa' M. PAR. *Maj.* V 401 (cf. electio 1d).

2 to choose, elect (person, esp. to office; often w. *ad*, *in*, or compl.): **a** (imperial or royal); **b** (papal, p. ppl.) pope elect; **c** (episcopal, p. ppl.) archbishop or bishop elect; **d** (mon. or sim., p. ppl.) abbot or sim. elect; **e** (acad.); **f** (mun. or man.); **g** (parliamentary or sim.); **h** (unspec. & var.). *Cf. erigere* 6.

a ut [Picti] .. magis de feminea regum prosapia quam de masculina regem sibi ~erent BEDE *HE* I 1; **s1066** subregulus Haroldus .., quem rex ante suam decessionem regni successorem elegerat, a totius Anglie primatibus ad regale culmen electus, .. in regem est .. consecratus FL. WORC. I 224; quomodo necdum natus in regem fuerat electus AILR. *Ed. Conf.* 741C; **s1272** principes Teutonie .. Radulfum de Assio .. elegerunt in imperatorem Romanorum TREVET *Ann.* 283; OCKHAM *Pol.* I 188 (v. consequi 2d); **1403** (v. electio 2a). **b** Johannes [IV] .., cum adhuc esset electus in pontificatum BEDE *HE* II 19; **s1130** hos utrosque [Innocentium et Anacletum] Romani bipartiti elegerant H. HUNT. *HA* VII 41; **s1159** R. cancellarius .. in papam ~itur et vocatus est Alexander III. electus est ab aliquibus cardinalibus Octavianus .., qui se vocari fecit Victorem III TREVET *Ann.* 48; **s1272** (v. electio 2b); **1289** cum sedes apostolica ante consecracionem et benediccionem electi in summum pontificem cum defectiva bulla, electi nomen nullatenus exprimente, bullare litteras suas consueverit (*Lit. Papae*) *Foed.* II 427b; si tibi diceretur quod homo quem maxime diligis miraculose .. esset electus in papam [ME: *were icoren to pape*] *AncrR* 89; OCKHAM *Dial.* 799 (v. aristocratice). **c** ad episcopatum nostrae aecclesiae Lindisfarnensium electus est *V. Cuthb.* IV 1; Tatfrid .. electus est antistes BEDE *HE* IV 21; **804** (17c) ego B. electus [Roff'] hanc paginam .. subscribo (*Professio*) *CS* 315 (cf. ib. 333 [a811]: .. ego E. electus Lundoniae); **s1093** T. archiepiscopus [Ebor'] .. interdixit ei [archiepiscopo Cantuar'] .. ne Robertum B., Lincolniensis ecclesie electum, Lincolniensem ordinaret episcopum H. CANTOR 2v.; **s1174** R. Cantuar' electus Romam veniens archiepiscopus, primas, apostolice sedis legatus institutus est DICETO *YH* I 274 (cf. ib. 381–90); **c1205** Florentius Dei gratia Glasguensis electus *Dryburgh* 38; **s1207** (v. contradicere 4c); **1218** mandatum est .. capitulo [Osserensi] quod .. magistrum P. sicut electum suum admittant *Pat* 182; **1228** defuncto episcopo Dunelm', prior et capitulum convenerunt ad ~endum sibi pastorem. .. et priore nominante magistrum W. .. dixerunt omnes: "placet, quia bonus est". unde prior .. dixit: "et ego .. ~o magistrum W. .. in episcopum et pastorem Dunelm' ecclesie", et post eum unusquisque, sicut erat ordo eorum. quod due forme concilii, sc. scrutinium vel compromissum, non fuerunt attemptate patet. item .. ista eleccio non fuit facta communiter ab omnibus, set singulariter, unde non quasi per inspiracionem; et ideo eam irritamus (*Pronuntiatio Papae*) *Ann. Durh.* 3 (cf. ib. 53); **s1332** (v. compromittere 4b); **1417** dominum J. C. .. in suum [Sar'] presulem et pastorem, nullo contradicente ipso electo dumtaxat excepto, per viam Spiritus Sancti .. concorditer elegerunt *Reg. Cant.* I 38. **d** fratres ~ant sibi abbatem de ipsis THEOD. *Pen.* II 6. 1; consecratio abbatis sive abbatissae: concede, quaesumus, Omnipotens Deus, ut famulum tuum N., quem ad regimen animarum elegimus, gratiae tuae dono prosequare, ut .. cum ipsa tibi electione placeamus EGB. *Pont.* 105; LANFR. *Const.* 140 (v. abbas 1a); Uticenses Rodbertum .. sibi elegerunt abbatem ORD. VIT. III 5 p. 68; **1163** cum .. fratres .. episcopum .. requisissent ut R. .. electum suum benediceret in abbatem (*Lit. Papae*) *Reg. Malm.* I 372; **s1191** (v. contradere 1a); **1220** sciatis nos electioni facte de Cecilia de D., moniali S. Marie de Pratis extra Norhamton', in abbatissam ejusdem loci regium adhibuisse assensum et favorem. et ideo vobis mandamus quod predicte electe tanquam domine vestre .. intendentes sitis *Pat* 270; **12..** (v. compromissarius 2a); **1221**, **s1321** (v. 2 conventus 3b); **s1257** (v. compromissio c); **1370** quod, si .. confratres [collegii de Russcheworth] infra tres menses a tempore vacacionis magistrum non eligerint (*sic*), .. provisio illa vice de magistro ad episcopum devolvatur *Lit. Cant.* II 500; **1425** fratrem T. K. .. in priorem ejusdem prioratus per viam scrutinii elegerunt *Reg. Cant.* I 95; **a1455** [episcopus Exon'] dicit quod abbas .. electurus (*sic*) fuit et electus per priorem abbacie et ceteros canonicos *Entries* 496. **e a1350** quod nominatores electorum cancellarii per scrutinium ~antur, sicut infra in eleccione procuratorem expressius continetur *StatOx* 64; **a1380** nullus in bedellum .. elegetur nisi prius congregacioni regencium presentetur *Ib.* 68; **s1387** (v. 2 coetus d); **1450** quod .. ~atur dominus rector universitatis per formam quam supposita ejusdem duxerint in suis nacionibus et per suos procuratores intimaverint servandam et presertim per formam compromissi fiendi in quatuor intrantes per qua-

tuor naciones .. statuendos *Mun. Univ. Glasg.* II 6. **f** **1181** quemlibet ex semetipsis pro me ~ant qui sub me super eos justitia sit *BBC (Coventry)* 242; **1200** quod .. burgenses nostri de N. per commune consilium villate sue ~ant duos de legalioribus et discretioribus burgensibus ville sue et presentent eos vicecomiti Norhamtonscir' *Ib. (Northampton)* 244; **1215** concessisse baronibus nostris de civitate nostra L. quod ~ant sibi majorem de se ipsis singulis annis *Ib. (London)* 247; c**1283** dominus potest .. quem voluerit .. ~ere in prepositum *Cust. Battle* 66; **1290** tota villa .. in misericordia, quia ~erunt (*sic*) sibi communem messorem et non presentaverunt illum ballivo loci, prout moris est *SelPlMan* 36; **1319** (v. aldermannus 2a); **1326** (v. colonus a); **1337** (v. conventionarius 1b); **1362** (v. consul 1c); s**1382** (v. apothecarius b); s**1392** rex .. constituit duos vicecomites Londonie .. steteruntque .. in officiis eorum usque in finem anni et tunc electi fuerunt de novo per Londonienses *Chr. Westm.* 273; **1413** (v. constabulus c). **g** **1283** vobis mandamus quod duos de sapiencioribus et apcioribus civibus .. civitatis [London'] ~i faciatis et eos ad nos mittatis, ita quod sint ad nos .. nobiscum super hoc et aliis locuturi (*WelshR*) *Dign. Peer* III 50; **1295** quod de com. Norht' duos milites et de quolibet burgo duos burgenses de discrecioribus et ad laborandum potencioribus .. ~i et eos ad nos .. venire facias (*Cl*) *Ib.* 66; s**1430** cum in statuto .. ordinatum fuisset .. quod milites com. infra regnum Anglie ~endi ad veniendum ad parliamentum regis .. essent electi .. per gentes commorantes .. in eodem com. .. *Entries* 446. **h** [Dalfinus] sibi illum [Wilfridum] in adoptivum filium ~ere voluit EDDI 4; s**876** cui [Alfredo] ille exercitus electos obsides, quantos ille nominavit, .. dedit FL. WORC. I 93; quodsi [vidua] virum ~at *GAS* 361 (v. dos 2b); ANSELM I 5 (v. consultor); [filius] qui solus potens est sibi coheredes ~ere R. NIGER *Mil.* III 3; GIR. *EH intr.* (v. 2 elector 1); decanus [capelle] .. habens .. potestatem ~endi, examinandi et inducendi cantores W. SAY *Lib. Reg. Cap.* 57.

3 (leg.) to select: **a** (body of oath-helpers or sim.); **b** (jurors, esp. for grand assize); **c** (justices); **d** (*jurats*, Gasc.).

a incredibili ~atur [AS: *ceose man*] simplex lada in tribus hundretis (*Quad.*) *GAS* 325 (= *Cons. Cnuti* ib.: infideli ~antur juramenta hominum in tribus centenariis); in quibusdam locis utrimque ~itur judicium, medietas ab eis quorum est negotium, et ibi testes nominati et electi sunt habendi (*Leg. Hen.* 31. 8) *Ib.* 564; *Ib.* 586 (v. electio 3a). **b** GLANV. II 11 (v. electio 3c); **1200** tunc veniant iiij milites ad ~endum xij *CurR* I 187; **1221** xij juratores dicunt quod culpabilis est .. et xxiiij milites alii a predictis xij ad hoc electi idem dicunt *SelPlCrown* I 99; juratores de consensu parcium electi *State Tri. Ed. I* 15. **c** **1219** quia nos ~istis (*sic*), non nos ~imus nos ipsos .., decens videretur .. quod non tam cito .. de nobis sinistra crederetis (*AncC* I 54) *RL* I 21; **1242** ad .. judices ~endum (v. consentire 3a); **1244** ~antur duo justitiarii (v. 2 bancus 3a). **d** **1315** sint sex jurati de ipsa comunia, qui eliguntur per alios juratos singulis annis *RGasc* IV 1626 p. 473a.

4 (mil.) to recruit, enlist.

s**1257** (v. 1 constabularia 2a); **1258** omnes milites et libere tenentes de curia de B. elegerunt dominum B. le Moyne [et al.] .. ad servicium iiij militum ad presens faciendum domino regi pro domino abbate Rames' et communa curie versus Walliam *SelPlMan* 61 (cf. ib. 77 [**1294**]: electi fuerunt .. ad faciendum modo corporale servicium in exercitu domini regis); **1322** R. filius W. .. et J. filius R. .. fuerunt electi ad serviendum domino regi contra Scotos ..; et viando .. invenerunt J. [filium S.] qui eos elegit, ita quod lis mota est inter eos *SelCCoron* 75; **1338** assignavimus vos .. ad ~endum in com. Leyc' .. lx sagittarios de melioribus .. hominibus *TreatyR* II 123; s**1351** Francigeni .. miserunt multa milia electorum .. Vasconicis in occursum AVESB. 121; **1356** (v. arraiare 1a).

5 (theol.) to choose, w. God as subj. (*cf. 1 Sam.* xiii 14, xvi 10). **b** (p. ppl. *electus*) chosen for salvation, elect (*cf. Rom.* viii 33, *Eph.* i 4, *etc.*). **c** (w. *vas*) chosen vessel; *cf. electio* 5d.

Deus .. ~it virum secundum cor suum, quem regem statuat R. NIGER *Mil.* II 71; David, Dei electus [ME: *Godes a3e deorling*] *AncrR* 13. **b** sic sator electis .. / aurea caelestis largitur praemia regni ALDH. *VirgV* 2004; BEDE *HE* IV 14 p. 234 (v. agmen b); **745** (12c) ut in plenitudinem ~orum Dei collocatus sim *CS* 170; **801** patri T. et omni Deo ~ae etiam et benedictae familiae ALCUIN *Ep.* 223; non in minori numero erunt homines electi quam sunt angeli reprobi ANSELM (*CurD* I 18) II 76; de vera post mortem perpetuaque ~orum vita GIR. *TH* II 5; hec .. gloria .. differtur donec completus fuerit numerus ~orum HALES *Sent.* II 109; quando / hec [crux] electorum frontibus alta patet GARL. *Tri. Eccl.* 46; a**1290** utrum omnes ~i in suo optimo decedunt, non obstante casu per peccatum *Quaest. Ox.* 108; tria sunt genera hominum ~orum [ME: *icorene*] Dei vivencium super terram *AncrR* 135. **c** Paulus, apostolico numeratus in ordine doctor, / vas sophiae electum ALCUIN *Carm.* 109. 17. 3.

6 (p. ppl. *electus*) choice, excellent; **b** (of person).

electos scripturae carpere fructus ALDH. *VirgV* 2774; **955** sex pondus ~i argenti *Ch. Roff.* 29; **1174** pro v ulnis de ~o viridi ..; pro j ~a sabel[lina] ad opus filie regis Francie *Pipe* 147; argentum ~um [ME: *hwit seolver*] *AncrR* 49; s**1348** procedebant in ~is dextrariis vel aliis equis bene comptis KNIGHTON II 58; **1354** in dim. lib. zinzebr' ~i *Ac. Durh.* 554; *Alph.* 54 (v. electuarium a); in ciborum varietatibus seu vinis ~issimis *Ps.*-ELMH. *Hen. V* 31. **b** quod .. de ~is juvenibus Normannie aliquos ei cito mitterent ORD. VIT. III 3 p. 54; imperatores ~i GIR. *TH intr.* p. 4 (v. desistere c); carissima mi ~a et super animam meam dilecta MAP *NC* IV 16 f. 58.

eligibilis [LL], worthy to be chosen, eligible; **b** (of person).

sapiencia causa sui ipsius et gracia sciendi, non gracia eveniencium ~is est MIDDLETON *Sent.* I 8; quod aristocracia .. est ~ior et melior quam regnum OCKHAM *Dial.* 792; in gymnasticis exerciciis premium est melius et ~ius illo pro quo datur R. BURY *Phil.* 2. 23; pro confessione parochianorum .. facienda ~ior est parochialis ecclesia quam Fratrum oratorium RIC. ARMAGH *Def. Cur.* 1392 (*recte* 1292); [nemo] dubitat quin simpliciter ~ius est esse felicem quam esse hominem WYCL. *Act.* 125; **1412** hec verba 'accipiam te in uxorem' ~iora sunt .. quam ista 'ego te accipio ..' *Conc.* III 345a; ~ius erit virum Christi pauperem in apostolica navi esse .. quam .. occupare thronum in atrio Cayphe NETTER *DAF* I 517; FORTESCUE *LLA* 35 (v. elicere 6a). **b** nullus hereticus est ~is in summum pontificem OCKHAM *Dial.* 683; WYCL. *Ver.* III 75 (v. consumptivus a).

eligibilitas, worthiness to be chosen, eligibility.

talis innocencia, libertas et immunitas a peccato .. videtur bonitatis et ~atis simpliciter infinite BRADW. *CD* 455D.

eligibiliter, by choice, electively.

tales .. in eminencia pontificatus ac in cathedra prelacie debent elegebiliter presidere *Regim. Princ.* 155.

eligius v. elinguis. **eligma** v. ecligma. **eliguere** v. eligere 3d. **elilifagus** v. elelisphacos.

1 elimare [CL], to polish (by filing); **b** (fig.). **c** (p. ppl., of speech or style) polished. **d** to produce by striking.

~at, *gesuirbet GlC* E 144; ~at, i. mundat, †expulit, .. †excludit [? l. expolit, .. excudit], †*forsweorfed* [MS: *forsweorfeð*] .., ornat *GlH* E 183; ~are, purgare, eruderare OSB. GLOUC. *Deriv.* 195. **b** qui itinerarium Petri .. luce clarius ~avit ALDH. *VirgP* 25; **9..** ~avit, *gerihte WW*; ADEL. *QN* 25 (v. elementariter); elimasse laborat / pressius Euclidis numeros HANV. III 151 p. 280 (cf. ib. 156: nunc ad miracula limam / rethorice flectit reserans); malus socius in conversatione communi .. quos persequitur ~at et purgat BALD. CANT. *Tract.* 5. 447B; se .. a vitiorum tinea purgant et ~ant GIR. *TH* I 18; *Id. EH* II 29 (v. conscientia 3a); trux natura, quod tunc non potuit, / nunc elimat, nunc telum acuit J. HOWD. *Ph.* 429; ut primos arcium fundatores omnem ruditatem ~asse dicamus R. BURY *Phil.* 10. 158. **c** in rebus forensibus acer et ~atus W. MALM. *GP* I 72 p. 137; sermonis .. minus ~ati rusticitatem *V. Har. prol.* f. 1b. **d** si ictus major fuerit, lapis enititur; si maximus, ignis ~atur ADEL. *QN* 66.

2 elimare v. eliminare 2.

elimate [LL], in a polished manner, brightly. **b** (fig.) clearly.

~e, purgate et enucleate OSB. GLOUC. *Deriv.* 195; lima pernecessaria in officina fabrorum, eradens rubiginem ferri ut ~ius splendeat BALD. CANT. *Tract.* 5. 447B. **b** ut minus ~e verbera labiorum verba proferrent W. CANT. *Mir. Thom.* IV 40.

eliment- v. element-.

eliminare [CL]

1 to drive out, banish: **a** (person or unspec.); **b** (abstr.).

a **705** ut exules ~arentur a nobis WEALDHERE *Ep.* 22; ~at, *adytið GlC* E 142; ~o, i. distruo limitem, foras eicio .., expello, .. *ic ut anyde* vel *drife* vel *adyde GlH* E 192; **985** (12c) ~atis priscis Paradisi accolis *CD* 650; Dominus .. de templo ~avit peccatores [cf. *Matth.* xxi 12]. .. timete sacris ecclesiae ~ari liminibus H. LOS. *Serm.* 5 p. 124; multi a patria ~ati EADMER *Wilf. prol.*; et a nobis hostes eliminat J. HOWD. *Ph.* 911. **b** ni [vitia] virtute Dei procul ēliminata fatescant ALDH. *VirgV* 2452; in quo [Pantheo] ipse [Bonifatius IV], ~ata omni spurcitia, fecit ecclesiam BEDE *HE* II 4; excessione caloris et frigoris ~ata ADEL. *QN* 71; J. SAL. *Met.* 827C (v. distrahere 1b); avaritiam .. a se .. tam longe projiciens .. ut ipsam a domo sua penitus ~aret H. BOS. *Thom.* III 14 p. 223; BEN. PET. *Mir. Thom.* II 41 (v. 2 contractus 1a); **1188** erubescentiam consuevit ~are paupertas *Ep. Cant.* 279; **1226** ad ~andam heresim de terra Albigensium (*Lit. Papae*) *RL* I app. 546; possumus hunc errorem ~are BACON *Tert.* 121.

2 to evacuate (from body).

non fetent stercora boum aut bestiarum propter imperfectam digestionem partem assumptorum ~antem nec omnino nutribile a superfluitate sequestrantem GILB. VII 303V. 1; *Ib.* (v. elongabilis).

elimos v. elymos. **elimosin-, elimosyn-, elimozin-** v. elemosin-.

elingere [CL], to lick up.

eripuisti animam meam de inferno inferiori, in quo elinxi quamdam dulcedinis tue stillam AILR. *Spec. Car.* II 11. 555D.

elinguis [CL], speechless, tongue-tied, inarticulate; **b** (w. abstr. subj.).

GILDAS *EB* 1 (v. eatenus 2); ~is, muti, Graece †adalos [i.e. ἄλαλος], *dumbes GlP* 288 (cf. ib. 694: ~ia, *spæclease* vel *dume*); quis .. non obstupescat et .. ~is .. fiat? EADMER *Excell. B. M.* 578C; **1159** recte dicor ~is aut mutus J. SAL. *Ep.* 60 (110); non solum scribendi rudem .. aut illiteratum sed etiam ~em AILR. *Spec. Car. pref.* 2. 503D; G. HOYLAND *Ascet.* 268B (v. edissertio); quos et pudor ipse parentum / fecerat elingues NIG. *SS* 1830; ille qui .. linguas angelorum erudit .. infantiam simplicem et ~em elegit P. BLOIS *Serm.* 575D; inconsultus et †eligius, cui verba negantur GARL. *Syn.* 666. 1589D; *Id. Tri. Eccl.* 15 (v. bilinguis). **b** elingues siluere huc usque dolores J. EXON. *BT* VI 823.

elio- v. helio-.

eliquare [CL]

1 to purify (by crushing or straining); **b** (fig.); **c** (p. ppl.) pure.

~at, i. exprimit .., minuit .. vel *grint GlH* E 191; qui [calor] .., si ibidem [in cerebro] humorem talem reperit, naturaliter ~at et per exitum suum expellit ADEL. *QN* 33; posset .. argentum .. purgatum corrumpi per scoriam, sicut et oleum purissime ~atum per amurcam H. BOS. *LM* 1395A; ~atur .. humor in epate generatus .. et deducitur ad renes *Quaest. Salern.* B 16; aquosa .. substantia sanguinis .. ad renum deportata .. regionem .. colatur et ad modum seri ~ati depuratur BART. ANGL. V 45. **b** ostendit se necdum vitiorum fetibus [v. l. faecibus] ~atum BEDE *Prov.* 999D; vinum proprie voluntatis ~atum est et expressum in torculari inobedientie BALD. CANT. *Tract.* 16. 565A. **c** ~ata, purgata *GlC* E 140; ex subtilioribus elementis jam purgatioribus et ~atioribus AILR. *An.* II 54 f. 38.

2 **a** to liquefy, melt, smelt (also fig). **b** to drain, pour out. **c** (intr.) to flow out. **d** (fig.).

a duo sunt genera [carnis] liquide: alia enim artificio liquida, ut ~ata per frixuram sc. sagimen, alia est liquida naturaliter BELETH *RDO* 80. 85; abbas G. [ob. c**1146**] .. fecit casulas .. v, quarum una .. postea .. igne concremata est, ut aurum, quo nimis .. onerabatur, ~aretur *G. S. Alb.* I 93; c**1184** de duobus in camino caritatis vehementi amoris igne ~atis *Ep. J. Exon.*; s**1193** picem ~atam .. et alia immunda in obsidentes effundebant GERV. CANT. *Chr.* 516; s**1213** (v. conflatilis b); vidi quosdam homines ~are gemmas, de cujus liquore albe morphee lote .. curate sunt BACON IX 17. **b** vinum post vinum ~at uva pressius calcata BALD. CANT. *Sacr. Alt.* 674A; Mars ubi sevus agit, gladius necis eliquat imbres HANV. V 347 p. 319; s**1097** gladium immergit et .. / ~ato copioso sanguine, mortem [urso] ingerit reluctanti M. PAR. *Min.* I 96; cibus in stomaco decoquitur, a quo per venas meseraicas liquor ~atur ad epar GARL. *Dict.* 122. **c** s**1203** cepit uberius oleum a predicta imagine stillatim ~are *Flor. Hist.* II 127. **d** **1317** quatinus .. de profunda pelagi bonitatis vestre .. rorem salutiferum favoris .. senciat ~are *FormOx* 30.

eliquatio [LL], draining off.

a**1400** molendinum .., cujus fossa jam siccatur per ~onem aque *G. S. Alb.* II 412.

eliquefacere, to dissolve.

puella .. buccellam panis ore ~ta[m] deglutire parat GOSC. *Mir. Iv.* lxii.

eliquescere [CL], to dissolve (intr.).

omne durum dissiliens ~escit R. COLD. *Cuthb.* 47.

eliquus, pure, refined.

~us, purus OSB. GLOUC. *Deriv.* 194; ne pro auro elico [v. l. †elito; *gl.*: purgato; *cler or*] emat auricalcum NECKAM *Ut.* 119; *clene rynynge*, ~us *CathA*.

elisio [CL = *forcing out*], parrying, nullifying. **b** defeat, dejection.

exceptio est actionis ~o per quam actio perimitur vel differtur BRACTON 399b. **b** ~o, i. abjectio *GlH* E 198; **1167** sine .. virtutis ~one J. SAL. *Ep.* 204 (214).

Elisius v. Elysius.

†elitridium, gum of a tree (? poplar; *cf. Collectio Salernitana, s. v. elidrinum*).

†elitridium gumi arboris est *Alph.* 55.

†elitrodamum, (?) varnish used for turning hair gold (*cf.* Alex. Trall., ed. Puschmann, I 457).

†elitrodamum, matris silva idem, ut in Alexandro *Alph.* 55.

elitrop- v. heliotrop-. **elitus** v. eliquus. **Eliudianus** v. Helvidianus.

elix [CL], drainage channel.

elices dicuntur sulci majores ad siccandos agros ducti ALDH. *PR* 114; elix, sulcus major *GlC* E 119; *water fore in lond*, elicus, sulcus *PP*; *a watir fure*, elix *CathA*.

elixabilis, boilable.

aqua, etsi frigiditate coaguletur, nullo tamen modo est calore ∼is *Ps.*-GROS. *Summa* 639.

elixare [LL], to boil, scald. **b** to smelt or (?) produce by means of elixir.

∼are, coquere in aqua OSB. GLOUC. *Deriv.* 194; HANV. VII 380 (v. exassare); vulgo dicitur quod ∼atus aquam timet H. BOS. *Thom.* IV 26 p. 247; dum vasis cibis ∼andis necessariis indigent *Hist. Meriadoci* 350 (cf. elixus); allium ∼atum cum butyro GILB. VII 353v. 1; secundum Aristotelem IV Metaphisice .., assata interius sunt humida et ∼ata interius sunt sicca BACON V 89*n.*; tapsus barbatus .. ∼atus in vino rubeo *Alph.* 182. **b** tale argentum est illud quod fit de magisterio cum †∼itur BACON *Min.* 378 (cf. ib.: illud quod est cum ∼atur est magis frigidum quam illud quod non fit sic; cf. elixis).

elixatio, a boiling. **b** decoction.

a gelatinia est piscium sive carnium quedam muscillago coagulata, que nascitur de illis post †alexaconnum [v. l. elixacionem] *Alph.* 74. **b** hic ponitur jus pro ∼one carnis que G. *bru* dicitur J. BATH 282; acetum .. conveniens est in salsis et ∼onibus carnium GILB. I 36. 2.

elixatura [LL], decoction.

∼a, decoctio OSB. GLOUC. *Deriv.* 195; jus quandoque dicitur pro ∼a carnis, quod Anglice †*brob* [? l. *broo* vel *broð*] vocatur *Ib.* 281; semen urtice vel ejus ∼a multum valet caliginibus oculorum GILB. III 142v. 1; quitissos frutex est. .. ∼a ejus urinam provocat *Alph.* 152.

†elixemum, (?) oil of iris (*cf.* Alex. Trall., ed. Puschmann, I 475: ἔλαιον ἴπινον).

†elixemum, i. lilium, ut in Alexandro de dolore capitis *Alph.* 55.

elixer v. elixir. **elixerium** v. elixirium. **elixine** v. helxine.

elixir [Ar. *al-iksīr* < ξήριον], (alch.) elixir.

vas predictum fornaci sue semper immobiliter adhereat, donec totum tempus fermentationis auri compleatur .. quod quum post 20 noctes extractum sit, deinde bene desiccatum fuerit. Arabice hoc †vexir nuncupatur ROB. ANGL. *Alch.* 517a; ∼ir quoque .. debet projici taliter ut, si de albo corpore partem ei projeceris, de ∼ir partes undecim projicias *Ib.* 518b; signa infallibilia completi ∼iris narrabimus sermone claro M. SCOT *Sol* 720; sic ex corpore et spiritu fit una aqua mineralis que dicitur ∼ir, id est 'fermentum' *Correct. Alch.* 11; medicinam perfectam, quam philosophi vocant ∼ir BACON *Min.* 314; preparato alicxir, quod est medicina laxativa et transmutativa *Id. Tert. sup.* 13; *Spec. Alch.* 384 (v. citrinare); artificio per ∼ir es redit ad argentum et plumbum ad aurum et ferrum etiam ad argentum *Ps.*-GROS. *Summa* 637; magis valet aurum, quoniam est fermentum ∼iris, sine quo nequaquam peragitur DASTIN *Ros.* 3; **1418** ut ipse ibidem per posse suum quemdam pulverem vocatum ∼er facere posset, qui quidem pulvis est talis nature et condicionis quod, si aliqua inde parcella quandocumque modice projciatur super aliquod metallum rubium liquefactum, ut cuprum, ereum, auricalcum, illud metallum efficeret coloratum simile et appariens aurum; et, si effusus fuerit super aliquod metallum album, ut plumbum, stagnum, illud erit simile et appariens argentum *CoramR* 629 r. 18*d.*; ∼er, *a mater of metall in alcomye WW*; ut ∼iria haberi possint ad transmutacionem corporum metallorum RIPLEY 157.

elixirare, (alch.) to concoct an elixir.

modus .. ∼andi cum hoc igne contra naturam est triplex RIPLEY 141.

elixiratio, (alch.) concocting an elixir.

hic est unus modus ∼onis RIPLEY 140.

elixirium, (alch.) retort.

1337 quoddam elixerium suum ac quedam alia instrumenta sua, per que argentum hujusmodi fecit, secum deportare fecerunt *Pat* 189 m. 20*d.*

elixis, (alch.) smelting or (?) use of elixir.

alia [species argenti] est per magisterium, elixum idem per transmutationem cupri liquati in argento. .. naturale est magis frigidum quam illud quod est de magisterio et per ∼im BACON *Min.* 378 (cf. elixare b).

elixus [CL], boiled.

∼us cibus, *gesoden mæt on wætere* ÆLF. *Gl.*; sic carnes ejus [Domini], aut ∼as in lebetibus aut assas in verubus, essent comesuri LANFR. *Corp. & Sang.* 422B; pulli gallique, capones / elixi D. BEC. 2644; GIR. *IK* I 11 (v. armus a); gallina .. cimino condiatur, si ∼a [*gl.*: *quist*] fuerit NECKAM *Ut.* 102; H. AVR. *Poems* 2. 221 (v. assare a); carnes ∼andas in minori [fossa] collocant. .. hoc .. tam diu fit donec sufficienter ∼a caro extrahatur *Hist. Meriadoci* 350.

ellam [CL], there she is!

Malchus adest: "ellam!" sibi dicunt. "sume puellam!" R. CANT. *Malch.* I 29.

ellegans v. elegans. **ellid-** v. elid-. **ellip-** v. eclip-. **elmate** v. 2 elevare 1e. **elmoneria** v. 2 elemosinaria b. **elmus** v. helmus, ulmus.

elocare [CL = *to hire out*], to secure, establish. **b** to dower, settle (in marriage).

∼are, collocare *Gl. Leid.* 38. 3. **b s1559** de non ∼andis filiabus prelatorum et ecclesiasticorum baronibus de patrimonio Christi *Conc. Scot.* II 155 *rub.*

elocericus v. holosericus.

elocutio [CL], a speech, address. **b** (w. obj. gen.) utterance. **c** elocution, (cultivation of) literary style.

a ut pax mundi stet inter Æthelredum regem et .. populum ejus et .. exercitum post ∼ones [AS: *ðam formalan*] quas S. archiepiscopus et Æ. aldremannus .. fecerunt (*Quad.*) *GAS* 220. **b 1235** non est .. in mea correptione reprehensibilis aut mendacii insinuatio aut reticende veritatis ∼o GROS. *Ep.* 11. **c** ∼o est idoneorum verborum ad inventionem accommodatio ALCUIN *Rhet.* 4; difficilis, quatinus tam verbis quam sententiis scintillet oratio, ornati sermonis ∼o GIR. *EH intr.* p. 213; cum rhetorica .. tractet .. de invencione, eciam disposicione, ∼one, memoria, et pronunciacione KILWARDBY *OS* 593.

elocutus v. eloqui, eluctari.

†eloftina, *f. l.*

13.. concessi .. de bosco meo de Spicwyk necessaria ad domos et ad faldas et ad ignem suum et †eloftinam [? l. closturam; cf. clausura 4b] *CatAncD* C 5479.

eloges v. helops.

elogiare [LL], to indicate, pronounce.

[feria quarta post Pentecosten] almiphona jam gaudia. Alleluya. celi rutilant per climata. ∼iantur †cuncti [? l. cunctis] bona *Miss. Westm.* I 367.

1 elogium [CL]

1 elegy, poem (esp. eulogistic). *Cf.* 1 *eulogia* 1.

∼io, *geddi GlC* E 109; ∼ium, i. .. carmen .. vel *gyd GlH* E 213; **10**.. eologium, *gedd WW*.

2 (additional clause in) testament. *Cf.* 1 *eulogia* 5.

∼ium testamentum dicitur *GlC* E 129; ∼ium, i. .. testamentum *GlH* E 213.

3 word. **b** speech, utterance, pronouncement. **c** reproach, stigma.

∼iis, verbis *GlC* E 138; ∼ium, i. .. verbum *GlH* E 213. **b** ex ipsius ∼io conjecturam capesso ALDH. *VirgP* 27; declinat parvi pendens epithalamii ∼ium *Ib.* 35; ∼ium, dictio, *saga* ÆLF. *Gl.*; cum infami eulogio, *mid þy unæþelan gydde* vel *unweorþlican GlH* C 2173; quis .. / elogio archontes queat infamare maligno? FRITH. 1213; hoc [templum] suum [sc. Mariae] sacrarium; hoc, secundum Anglicum ∼ium, suum vestiarium GOSC. *Transl. Aug.* 33A; amicitiae confidentis ∼io reddam tibi novellae plantationis nostrae votiva primordia (*Quad., dedic.*) *GAS* 532; **1166** prescisionis ∼ium in eum jam dicendum fore proponitis (*Lit. Suffraganeorum*) DICETO *YH* I 322; Jerosolimitana .. peregrinatio .. Salomonis oratione et ∼io roboratur R. NIGER *Mil.* I *prol.* **c** ∼ium, i. .. crimen *GlH* E 213; parvipendens loripedis ∼ium W. CANT. *Mir. Thom.* II 23 (cf. ib. III 6: sterilitatis abstulit ∼ium et matrem fecit); **s1171** dolebat rex de modo martyrii .., ne proditoris ∼io .. notaretur GERV. CANT. *Chr.* 233; **s1323** ut falso per nimia supplicionum genera se ipsos .. faterentur proditores ac .. tanti criminis ∼io famam aliorum .. macularent *Flor. Hist.* III 215.

2 elogium v. 1 eulogia. **elogizare** v. eulogiare. **elogus** v. 1 elegus.

Elohim [Heb.], divine title.

in Hebreo habetur ∼im, quod idem sonat quod 'dii' HALES *Sent.* I 229; [feria quinta post Pentecosten] Alleluya. Eloym Eloe Adonay sabaothia *Miss. Westm.* I 373.

elongabilis, removable.

[egestionum fetores] proveniunt a bonitate nature bene digerentis et non nisi ultimatum et †elimatum [? l. eliminatum] sequestrantis, quod a natura ∼e est nullo modo incorruptibile GILB. VII 303v. 1.

elongantia, prolongation.

1361 tractatus habitus .. super .. ∼ia terminorum solucionis financie regis Francie (*LTRMem*) *CalExch* I 199.

elongare [LL]

1 to lengthen (in space), elongate. **b** (refl. or intr.) to become longer.

s1180 ∼ati sunt .. pilarii novi longitudine pedum fere duodecim GERV. CANT. *Combust.* 27; RIC. MED. *Anat.* 221 (v. accurtare a); cum rustici volunt cucurbitas magis ∼ari ponunt vas plenum aqua inferius *Quaest. Salern.* Ba 104; **1256** quod licentiam eis concederemus ∼andi ecclesiam suam versus orientem (*CalPat* 506) *MonA* VI 1278; **c1275** frater T. M. istud [vestibulum] ∼avit et .. adornavit armariis ECCLESTON *Adv. Min.* app. 162; **1278** in j corda ad cordam karre ∼andam *Ac. Stratton* 213; **1287** in fusillo molendini .. reparando et ∼ando *Ac. Man. Cant.* (*Adisham*); **1312** (v. cantera b). **b** electio ejus [stanni] est .., cum percutias, quod se ∼et. .. natura ferri est calida et sicca; et siccitas sua major est omnibus illis que se ∼ant per malleationem BACON *Min.* 382; per latus et gracilem videt elongare staturam, / linea nec recta reccior astat ea GOWER *VC* V 99.

2 a to prolong (in time), protract. **b** to postpone.

a prolongo, ∼o, *ic ylde GlH* E 217; **1218** rex ∼avit nundinas S. Botulfi, duraturas a die S. Joh. .. in octo dies *Pat* 157; **1224** latro .., ut vitam suam ∼aret, appellavit principales homines de societate *Cl* 620a; **1236** voluit ei pocius tradere terram illam et terminum ∼are quam alicui alii *BNB* III 160; *Ib.* 189 (v. accrescere 3a); ut per illud ∼etur vita hominis BACON IX 3; **s1272** videntes nichil proficere ad illud negocium ∼andum *Leg. Ant. Lond.* 151; cumque dies fuerant Ezechie morientis / sic elongati, mors quoque cessit ei GOWER *VC* II 308. **b s1187** convenerunt .. reges in unum, sed dissidentibus ipsis pax .. ∼ata est GERV. CANT. *Chr.* 356; his signis .. supervenientibus, ad plus usque ad c dies poterit ∼ari GILB. II 84v. 2; **1458** morarum dilacionibus, que solent actus hodiernos usque in crastinum ∼are *Reg. Whet.* I 315.

3 a to remove, put at a distance, send away. **b** (pass.) to be remote. **c** (refl.) to remove or absent oneself; *cf.* 5c *infra*. **d** (intr.) to withdraw, retire.

a ut [luna] .. non plus cotidiano progressu a sole quam quaternis punctis .. ∼etur BEDE *TR* 18 (cf. ALCUIN *Ep.* 155); magna .. adjuratio, que demonia ∼at [AS: *afyrsad*] et in fugam convertit (*Cons. Cnuti*) *GAS* 285; **1199** ∼abunt animalia (v. aerea); [abbas] magnates abbacie, tam laicos quam litteratos, .. a privato suo ∼avit consilio BRAKELOND 128 (cf. ib. 132v.: quos infideles probavit, a se ∼avit); [Hostis antiquus] desideratam mihi presentiam vestram .. ∼avit GIR. *Symb.* I 16; **s1235** [episcopus] jussit .. eos [Caursinos] a civitate Londoniarum .. ∼ari M. PAR. *Maj.* III 332; descensus .. in sepulchro, qui nedum ostendit corpus vere mortuum, anima ab eo ∼ata WYCL. *Incarn.* 34. **b 1095** ego a Cantuarberia ∼ari nullatenus audeo ANSELM (*Ep.* 191) IV 77; ∼atis principibus a terra in peregrinatione .., [heretici] citatim publice predicabunt errores suos R. NIGER *Mil.* III 81; quasi per mille passus a Londoniis ∼atus GIR. *JS* 6 p. 323; quanto res magis ∼atur ab oculo, tanto minor videtur J. BLUND *An.* 102; corde [sithare] .. non tantum a medio ∼antur ut prius *Ps.*-GROS. *Gram.* 18 (cf. ib.: minus .. removentur a medio); dum .. ∼ati essent a civitate per duo miliaria *Latin Stories* 100; **1321** a .. vestra presencia multarum terrarum distancia ∼ati (R. BURY *Ep.*) *FormOx* 75; **s1452** tempus illud per quod a vinea istius ecclesie aliqualiter ∼ati perstetimus et absentes *Reg. Whet.* I 23. **c** impium fore judicabat, si se a rege .. propter episcopatum ∼aret EADMER *V. Dunst.* 12; ut, cum draco .. audierit .. voces clamantium, ∼et se ab eis *G. Ric. I* 197; cum ad penitiorem pomerii pervenissent [monachus et puella], dixit illa: "satis nos jam ∼avimus, quia nemo nos hic videt preter Deum" GIR. *GE* II 11 p. 225; **1249** invenit plegios .. quod non ∼abit se a terra domini *SelPlMan* 22; **s1269** illi qui .. ∼averunt se a civitate metu amittendi vitam vel membra *Leg. Ant. Lond.* 119; **1272** prope nos se tenebant nec a nobis se ∼are potuerunt *Cl* 585; **1303** vos exhortamur .. quatinus dictum hereticum abiciatis et penitus ∼atis (*sic*) vos ab ipso *Reg. Carl.* II 54; **s1357** per totam noctem equitando et per xl leucas ante diem se ∼are a dicto loco putando *Plusc.* IX 44; **1378** quilibet frater [gilde] .. dabit .. xvj d. .. ad iiij anni terminos ..; et, si quis ad aliquem .. terminum fraudulenter se ∼averit, dabit ij lib. cere *Gild. Camb.* 93. **d** David .. elegit non modo ∼are et fugere sed et in solitudine manere [cf. *Psalm* liv 8] AD. SCOT *Serm.* 423B; **s1191** (v. conterere 1d).

4 a to remove, separate (spiritually); **b** (refl.). **c** to divert, distract. **d** to estrange. **e** (pass.) to be set apart, alien. **f** (p. ppl.) remote (fig.), immune.

a heu me miserum, unum de aliis miseris filiis Evae ∼atis a Deo ANSELM (*Prosl.* 1) I 99; quanto homo .. accedendo ascendere ad Deum nititur, tanto Deus .. exaltando ∼ari conspicitur DOMINIC *V. Ecgwini* I *prol.*; quandiu nobis [rebus mundialibus] immoraris, tandiu ab eo [Deo] ∼aris AD. SCOT *TGC* 803B; in tuto .. ponitur quatenus ∼atur a seculo, quoniam eatenus appropinquat celo R. NIGER *Mil.* IV 24; **1231** absit ut eam [pacem] .. a me sponte ∼em GROS. *Ep.* 4 p. 28; volens Dei auribus suam linguam approximare, ipsam ∼et [ME: *firsi*] a mundo *AncrR* 19; auctoritas pontificalis in Nova Lege spiritualior est et magis a terrenis negociis ∼ata OCKHAM *Pol.* I 49. **b s1103** [Anselmus] Lugduni resedit .., ne ad horam quidem ab iis que Dei sunt verbo se vel actu ∼ans EADMER *HN* 184; **1338** que ut interiori contemplacioni liberius serviant, se ab exteriorum occupacionum tumultibus ∼arunt *FormOx* 102. **c** ab illis bonis sum ∼atus, in his malis occupatus ANSELM (*Or.* 14) III 58; nec multum a proposito ∼abor W. MALM. *GR* I 67; avaritia .. a celestibus sectatores suos .. removet et ∼at J. SAL. *Pol.* 674B; corporalis exercitatio .. ∼at hominem a peccato suo R. NIGER *Mil.* I *prol.*; que forma predicandi non tenetur a vulgo theologorum, sed sunt ∼ati ab ea his diebus BACON *Tert.* 309; **1333** nonnulli vestrates .., dileccionis solite

semitis ~ati *RScot* 233b. **d** deprehendit archipresul .. cor regis ~atum ab eo H. Bos. *Thom.* III 31 p. 294; **1198** nec distantia longa terrarum vestre puritatem devotionis ab ecclesia Cantuar' potuit ~are *Ep. Cant.* 488; **s1234** quod apparet in marescallo .., quem per mendacia interseminata a vobis ~antes perverterunt M. PAR. *Maj.* III 269; **s1312** perpendentes regni proceres ab eis regis animum ~atum *G. Ed. II Bridl.* 42; ~atur amicus et proximus [cf. *Psalm* lxxxvii 19] R. BURY *Phil.* 4. 53. **e** vita earum [plantarum] occulta est et a nobis ~atur BACON VIII 129; magis ~atur natura accidentis a substantia quam planta a planta *Id.* XI 248; **1431** questiones .. movendo solummodo literales absque digressione a mente textus ~ata *StatOx* 236. **f** [Abraham] surrexit de nocte [cf. *Gen.* xxii 36], ut opus suum foret occulcius et a distraccione ~acius WYCL. *Ver.* II 36.

5 a to abduct (wife). **b** to 'eloign' (heir from custody or sim.). **c** to entice away (servant). **d** (refl.) to abscond, withdraw or absent oneself (from custody or service); *cf.* 3c *supra.*

a Walterus ~avit de Roberto .. uxorem dicti R. per tres †vices [? l. dies] cum bonis et catallis suis *Leet Norw.* 67. **b 1234** de placito quare ~averunt eundem [W.] de eodem H., cujus [W.] custodia ad ipsum [H.] pertinet *CurR* XV 999; **s1282** fecit .. abbas seisire in manus suas terras .. et omnia pertinencia ad wardam et maritagium heredis .. domini P. sed heres ille ~atus fuit multo tempore per dominam M. *Chr. Peterb.* 61; **1285** quod si .. minores ~ati sint, quo minus personaliter sequi possint, propinquiores amici admittantur ad sequendum pro eis (2 *Westm.* 15) *StRealm* I 82; **1308** Margeria, post mortem R. primi viri [etc.], ~avit quemdam R. filium et heredem predicti R. *Year Bk. 17 Ed. II* 25; **1321** de vallectis et puellis qui sunt et esse debent in custodia domini regis; qui sunt et qui illos habent .. et per quem fuerunt ~ati (*Artic. Itin.*) *MGL* II 347; **1332** Egidia ~ata est a custodia et maritagio domini regis .. per Margeriam .. et maritata est Willelmo C. *IPM* 31/2. **c 1350** Gilbertum a servicio .. Andree ~avit, ad dampnum dicti A. de xxx s. *CourtR Winchester*; **1368** in domum .. Henrici intravit et ibidem servientem suum ~avit *Ib.* **d 1287** ~avit se, ita quod .. Johannes nullum servicium de eo habuit *Law Merch.* I 13; Simon freneticus .. et in tali statu quod de bonis suis disponere non potuit .. se a custodia .. Roberti [filii sui] et fratrum suorum ~avit *State Tri. Ed. I* 71; **1375** a servicio .. Simonis recesserunt et a servicio suo se ~averunt (*CoramR*) *Enf. Stat. Lab.* 462*; **1382** de Johanne C., quia ~avit se de servicio Ade J. †pro [? l. per] xv dies .., vj d. *Hal. Durh.* 175.

6 a to remove, take away, carry off (goods *etc.*). **b** to appropriate or alienate (land or sim.).

a 1275 duos equos .. ~averunt et pecuniam pro eisdem receptam detinuerunt *SelPlMan* 150; **1285** ~averunt et extraxerunt bona et catalla sua extra domum .., ne distringerentur (*Eyre*) *DocCOx* 226; **1297** ne quis bona .. in fraudem decime .. distrahat vel ~et *Reg. Cant.* I 212; **1341** ad premuniendum instaurarium .. de ~ando instauro per metum invasionis Scottorum *Ac. Durh.* 539; **1361** felonice interfecerunt Ricardum .. et corpus ejus ~averunt in secreto *SelCCoron* 115; **1362** licite disponere .. de .. catallis .. et sic illa in testamentis suis legare vel alio modo ~are *Lit. Cant.* II 412; **1441** absque hoc quod .. capellanus dicta bona .. alienabit, ~abit, impignorabitur aut ullo modo onerabit seu pejorabit *Mon. Exon.* 405b. **b 1258** ita quod nec ego nec aliquis pro me .. aliquid de predictis bonis meis .., terris vel tenementis dare, vendere vel aliquo modo alio a .. domino J. ~are poterimus *Deeds Balliol* 325; ecclesiam de H., quam olim abbas D. .. impetraverat, sed per rectorum introductionem ~ata fuerat, ipse [abbas A., ob. 1268] .. in usum pauperum reimpetravit OXNEAD *S. Ben. Holme* 299; **c1300** Petrus predictam terram .. nunquam alienabit nec aliquo modo ~abit a predicto Ada *Reg. S. Bees* 311.

7 to oust, dispossess. **b** (w. *a vita*) to kill.

1184 non querent artem vel ingenium unde ego aut heres meus a feudo nostro ~emur *Eng. Feudalism* 276; **1200** Simon dicit quod [Willelmus] .. reliquit terram illam, ut sic ~aret eum a jure suo *CurR* I 167; si quis fuerit disseisitus vel ~atus per nos sine legali judicio parium suorum de terris, castellis, libertatibus vel jure suo, statim ea ei restituemus *Magna Carta* 52; **1219** nec de predictis terris ~abuntur *Reg. S. Thom. Dublin* 171; **1221** si .. homines [priorisse] emerint .. mercandisam ubi *ernes* dederint, nullus .. a mercandisa sua eos ~abit *SelPlCrown* 98; **1232** fecit .. quandam cartam quod nichil dare potuit vel alienare de terra propter quod .. Ricardus esset ~atus post diem suum *BNB* II 525; **s1249** recuperaverunt cives .. duas species libertatum unde ~ati fuerant per plures annos *Leg. Ant. Lond.* 16; **1291** atachiamentum factum erat .. per collusionem, ut .. Willelmus ~aretur de catallis suis *Law Merch.* I 44. **b 1220** defendit .. quod .. non .. eum per gurgitem cepit .. nec per eum fuit morti appropiatus nec a vita ~atus *CurR* IX 168.

elongate, in (spiritual) detachment.

fratres .. qui vocantur religiosi mendicantes .. debent reliquis religiosis humilius, simplicius, et a mundo †elegancius [l. elongacius; ME: *furþere fro þe world*] vivere *Concl. Loll. XXXVII* 28.

elongatio [LL]

1 lengthening (in space), extension.

in .. extensionis ~one ADEL. *QN* 30 (v. deterere a); **1280** in ~one fusilli .. molendini confracti cum ferro empto *Ac. Man. Cant.* (*Meopham*); **1386** (v. elargatio 2a).

2 prolongation (in time).

s1298 quedam ~ones treugarum inter reges affirmantur .. per duos annos firme durature *Chr. S. Edm.* 68.

3 a removal to a distance, withdrawal. **b** remoteness. **c** (period of) absence, exile.

a decrescit angulus sub quo videtur circulus per ~onem ipsius ab oculo NECKAM *NR* II 153 p. 235 (= J. BLUND *An.* 103); quanto major est [oculi] appropinquatio ad unum terminum [diametri], tanto est major ~o ab alio termino J. BLUND *An.* 107; paucos archidiaconos .. videmus qui non potius episcoporum suorum quererent .. ~onem GIR. *RG* II 22; **s1203** rex Francorum, jam ex absentia et ~one regis J. factus erectior M. PAR. *Min.* II 99; variantur operationes eorum [planetarum] secundum appropinquationem eorum ad zenith capitis et ~onem GROS. 49; quod accidit in eorum [corporum celestium] motu de diversitate virtutis alterative respectu inferiorum per ~onem et appropiacionem, conjunccionem, et separacionem KILWARDBY *OS* 102. **b** quoniam in quibusdam [partibus corporis] non posset [pulsus] bene discerni propter earum a centro cordis ~onem BART. ANGL. III 23; **1262** propter ~onem nostram a partibus illis laboribus et expensis ipsarum [monialium] parcere volumus *Cl* 162; remittitur eorum [orbium inferiorum] motus secundum ~onem et remotionem majorem quam habent ab illo primo orbe BACON VII 75; aliarum .. stellarum virtus est debilis propter earum ~onem a terra *Id. Maj.* I 141. **c** in ~one aut fuga AD. SCOT *QEC* 7. 812D; **1377** erumpnosa ~o [S. Thome] a solo proprie nativitatis BRINTON *Serm.* 10 p. 35.

4 a spiritual withdrawal, estrangement. **b** remoteness (in character), difference.

a 1253 hoc esset sue [sc. sedis apostolice] .. potestatis .. vel defectio vel corruptio vel abusio et a throno glorie Jesu Christi summa ~o GROS. *Ep.* 128 (= M. PAR. *Maj.* V 391: omnimoda ~o); primum [necessarium religiosis] est a negociacionibus secularibus et tumultibus mundanis ~o et quieta in claustro habitacio J. WALEYS *Commun.* VI 5. 1 f. 126v. **b** virtus finita et infinita .. habent proportionem .. secundum quid, non tamen simpliciter, quia quantum ad operationem est ~o in infinitum BACON XIII 335; prima veritas est cognoscibilis maxime difficulter .. racione excellencie et ~onis a noticia sensitiva WYCL. *Dom. Div.* 85.

5 'eloignment' (of heir).

1314 Maria, que fuit uxor Alexandri Comyn, .. allocuta fuit .. de ~one primogenite filie .. Edmundi .. et asseruit quod dicta filia elongata fuit in absencia dicta Marie, ipsa penitus ignorante *Cl* 132 m. 32*d*.

6 taking away, carrying off (of goods).

1254 vic. .. non permittat quod .. executores testamenti .. Willelmi faciant aliquam ~onem seu distractionem de bonis que fuerunt predicti W. *Cl* 285; **1336** ad inquirendum .. qui consilium vel assensum ad subtraccionem et ~onem navium predictarum prebuerunt *RScot* 451b.

elongator, alienator, separator, enticer (of servants from employment).

1362 communis ~or in autumno de famulis hominum *Proc. J. P.* 343.

elopare v. alopare d. **elophaboscos** v. elaphoboscon.

eloquenter [CL], eloquently.

~er, *getynglice GlH* E 219; actus trium ducum [Normannie] Dudo .. ~er enarravit ORD. VIT. III *prol.* p. 2.

eloquentia [CL]

1 eloquence, effective speech.

ALDH. *VirgP* 27 (v. disertitudo); Appius Secundus adversus Pyrrum Latinum [? l. Latinam] orationem prius exercuit. jam exhinc ceteri prosae ~ia contenderunt BONIF. *Met.* 111 (cf. Isid. *Etym.* I 38. 2); ~ia, peritia, *getingnes GlH* E 218; **9..** facundia, i. ~ia, *woþ WW*; Athene, quando incolumes florebant .., Lanfranco in omni genere eloquentie aut disciplinarum assurgerent ORD. VIT. IV 6 p. 211; J. SAL. *Met.* 827C (v. distrahere 1b); hec est virtus ~ie ut nihil tam exile quod non extollat GIR. *TH intr.* p. 6.

2 language, tongue.

omnia nomina quibus Latina utitur ~ia v declinationibus inflectuntur ÆLF. *Gram.* 21.

eloqui [CL]

1 a (trans.) to utter, express in words; **b** (fig.). **c** (intr.) to speak (out). **d** (pr. ppl.) eloquent.

a [gloriam Dei] ~i BEDE *Hom.* II 16 (v. enarrare 1); GIR. *Symb.* I 9 (v. condelectare b); quomodo he 8 partes oracionis ad invicem conjungi possunt ad ~endum omne genus complexionum conceptum *Ps.*-GROS. *Gram.* 60. **b** videamus quid evangelica tuba .. inordinatis sacerdotibus ~atur GILDAS *EB* 92; si hii tacuerint .. Dei magnalia pictus quodammodo paries ~atur AD. DORE *Pictor* 143. **c** de his [credendis] primum ~ar *Lib. Monstr. prol.*; de hospitalitate Beccensium sufficienter ~i nequeo ORD. VIT. VI 10 p. 246; **s1432** AMUND. I 301 (v. dissimulanter). **d** Rodbertum ~entem .. aliosque milites et plebeios .. invitavit ORD. VIT. III 10 p. 115; [verba] tam inter ~entes arida quam inter scientes usitata GIR. *TH intr.* p. 6; princeps ~entissimus *Id. EH* I 46; non eris eloquens nisi potaveris WALT. WIMB. *Carm.* 149; **s1323** cujus .. [Roberti Bruce] dominacioni rex Anglorum nuncios ~entes .. destinavit *Flor. Hist.* III 215.

2 (p. ppl. *s. pass.*): **a** uttered. **b** (?) formally worded.

a 1583 occasione nonnullorum contumeliosorum verborum .. ad tunc et ibidem elocutorum *Pat* 1235 m. 27. **b 1272** non †elocutum [MS *indistinct*] apellum formavit nec dixit *SelCCoron* 26.

eloquium [CL], speech, utterance; **b** (w. obj. gen.). **c** (w. *divinum* or sim.) word of God, holy writ. **d** (vernacular) language.

oppida .. / illius [Andreae] eloquio quae fana profana friabant ALDH. *CE* 4. 3. 11; elegi potius rusticano ~io amicorum meorum voto concurrere quam urbano silentio eos contemnendo .. offendere EADMER *V. Osw. prol.*; ampullata gentilium ~ia parvipendens W. MALM. *GP* I 24; T. abbas .., ~io suavis .., sacris litteris eruditus ORD. VIT. III 3 p. 42; ~ia .. humana R. COLD. *Cuthb.* 114 (v. documentum 2a); multi .. in populo plus possunt ~io quam sensu suo R. NIGER *Mil.* II 8; cum torrentis ~ii prius extitisset .., sermonis cujuslibet usum .. amisit GIR. *TH* III 34; confortetur paciens cum bono ~io et mitigetur timor ejus GAD. 110v. 1; veridica semper exercuerat ~ia BLAKMAN *Hen. VI* 4. **b** ubi ficta sed honesta tractatur sentencia, naturalis vel historialis veritas indagatur sub ~io typice ficcionis R. BURY *Phil.* 13. 178. **c 634** ut ipsa vos dominici ~ii promissa in futuro respiciant (*Lit. Papae*) BEDE *HE* II 18; eloquium Domini quaecunque volumina fundunt *Epigr. Milredi* 819; impetentes eos jaculis divinorum ~iorum LANFR. *Ep.* 50 (46); gressus .. tuos dirigas secundum ~ium Dei R. NIGER *Mil.* I 2; **12..** inter opera caritatis .. que imitanda nobis auctoritate sacri ~ii precipiuntur *Reg. Aberbr.* I 326; **1381** sacrum .. ~ium (v. directorium 2a). **d 1023** (12c) praefatae limites terrae Anglico notantur hic ~io *CD* 739; **1417** in vulgari ~io (v. diserte); **s1458** miles quidam .., Johannes Cheyne ~io vulgari nominatus *Reg. Whet.* I 308.

Eloym v. Elohim.

†elpha, ~ion [dub.], (bot.) fane, white iris.

~a vel elpheon, G. *elphone*, A. *fone*, crescit in locis aquosis *Alph.* 54; ~ion, i. elfa *Ib.* 55; folium ~ion, ~a, G. *elphone*, A. *fane Ib.* 68.

elphius v. elephas a.

elpis [? cf. ἕλκυσμα], silver dross.

scoria argenti, quam multi ~im dicunt *Alph.* 178; ~is est scoria argenti *LC.*

elubio v. eluvio a. **elucabratim** v. elucubratim.

elucēre [CL], to shine (out), let through light; **b** (fig.).

bovina cornua .. ~ent ASSER *Alf.* 104 (v. dolabra a); qui magis elucet ter denis atque diebus *Kal. M. A.* I 409; cum in crepusculo aurora dies eluxerit ÆLF. *EC* 2; sole super horizontem ~ente GIR. *TH* II 7; lux noctescit ut nox eluceat J. HOWD. *Ph.* 318. **b 798** magna dubitanti animo de vobis requies .. eluxit ALCUIN *Ep.* 159.

elucescere [LL], to shine out (partly fig.). **b** to be illustrious. **c** to be clear, manifest.

1187 quia post noctem hujus tribulationis ~et vobis dies letitie *Ep. Cant.* 106; sapientie lucernam, ut omnibus in commune deducta pulchrius ~at, palam exponunt [cf. *Matth.* v 15] GIR. *TH* III *intr.* p. 139; **1332** ut .. [veritatis lucerna] omnibus .. ~at *FormA* 12. **b** †**1065** (13c) S. Aldhelmi .., cujus corpus gloriosum .. multis patratis miraculis ~it *CD* 817; gloria beati martyris Thome per se satis ~it ubique terrarum A. TEWK. *Prol. Thom.* 299; **1359** ut ingressus, progressus et egressus martiris ~ant *Lit. Cant.* II 381. **c** ut quod intendo clarius ~at W. MALM. *GR* I 1; ut nobis injurie species enucleatius ~ant W. DONC. *Aph. Phil.* 6. 10; sunt due [sciencie] de octo [rebus] precipuis naturalibus, ut inferius ~et BACON *Maj.* III 41; **s1295** quod .. in autentico scripto .. legentibus clarius ~it *Flor. Hist.* III 95; **1428** ut veritas rei geste eluscescat *Reg. Heref.* 109; quid in hoc veritas habeat utique ~et PAUL. ANGL. *ASP* 1541.

elucidare [LL], to throw light on, make clear, elucidate. **b** to clarify (of colour).

fidei rudimenta .. apostolorum ministerio revelanda et ~anda per orbem BEDE *Luke* (ii 42) 348; Asserus .., qui librum Boetii .. planioribus verbis ~avit W. MALM. *GP* II 80; ne rerum gestarum copia plenius ~ata nimietatem congerat prolixitatis H. HUNT. *HA* VIII 34; *Ib.* IV 31 (v. commixtio 1d); de proprietatibus .. rerum .. ~are aliqua cupientes BART. ANGL. I *prol.*; [scientia perspectiva] ceteras scientias ~at et declarat BACON *Maj.* II 159; **1322** amiciciam firmam temptacionis tempus ~at amplius quam quietis (R. BURY *Ep.*) *FormOx* 77; imponunt heresim fidelibus qui ~ant istam fidem (WYCL. *Conf.*) *Ziz.* 131. **b** potest hec generatio colorum diversificari ..,

quoniam, quanto dominatur siccitas, tanto forte cum majori difficultate subtiliatur et rarefit et ~atur et fit perspicuum BACON XIV 67.

elucidarium, (title of a book by Honorius Augustodunensis).

~ium sive dialogus de summa totius Christiane theologie HON. *Eluc. tit.* 1109; **c1300** ~ium (*Catal.*) *Chr. Rams.* xci; **1396** ~ium (*Catal.*) *Meaux* III app. xcvii; **1501** ~ium sacre scripture (*Invent.*) *Cant. Coll. Ox.* I 41 no. 56 (cf. ib. p. 104).

elucidate, clearly.

ut istud ~ius declaretur, parum alcius ordiendum BRADW. *CD* 655B.

elucidatio, elucidation, explanation.

de regno Westsexe hec ~o adhibeatur H. HUNT. *HA* V 32 *rub.*; **c1240** ubi secundum sanctorum ~ones tribus modis veritas caritatis per pastores ecclesie communicanda precipitur [cf. *John* xxi 15–17] AD. MARSH *Ep.* 77; **1346** ecclesiarum prelatis quibus pro ipsius [veritatis] ~one vita eterna promittitur [cf. *Ecclus.* xxiv 31] *Reg. Heref.* 35; ut materia .. ~onem recipiat clariorem, fingo per dialogum Petrum et Paulum invicem disputantes PAUL. ANGL. *ASP* 1527.

elucide, clearly, lucidly.

s1184 qui postea .. successerunt in regnum, ut in subsequentibus ~ius dicetur *G. Hen. II* I 331.

elucrari [cf. CL lucrari], to gain.

c1430 ut cum apostolo [*1 Cor.* ix 22] 'omnia fiat omnibus', quatinus omnes in Christo ~ari queat *Reg. Whet.* II app. 376; **s1438** quod una [mna] non tantum duas quinimmo decem alias ~ata esset per sollicitudinem sue negociacionis [cf. *Luke* xix 15] AMUND. II 159.

elucratio [cf. LL lucratio], gain, profit.

s1454 studebas .. ad cumulandum pecunias ad exercendumque facta et pacta prohibite ~onis *Reg. Whet.* I 130.

eluctari [CL], to struggle out of, surmount. **b** (w. inf.) to strive.

enisus, †elocutus [l. ~atus] *GlC* E 200; FRITH. 274 (v. chelydrus c); sicut ortu suo dumorum asperitatem ~atur rosa W. MALM. *GP* I 14; in scolari palestra id ~ari puerili stilo conatus sum J. CORNW. *Merl. pref.* **b** clerici prorsus ~abantur omne .. mandatum H. archiepiscopi dissimulare J. HEX. *HR Cont.* 328; follibus eluctans vigiles excire caminos HANV. IX 306 p. 386.

eluctatorius, (log.) refutatory.

sicut dialecticus elencho quem nos ~ium [v. l. reluctatorium] dicimus sillogismum, eo quod contradictionis est, sic et ista [sophistica] sophistico elencho utitur J. SAL. *Met.* 930A.

elucubrare [CL]

1 to 'burn the midnight oil' over, compose laboriously.

671 cum .. perplexa oroscopi computatio ~ata doctoris indagatione egeat ALDH. *Ep.* 1; volumina / .. / multimodis et mysticis / elucubrata normulis (ÆTHELWALD) *Carm. Aldh.* 2. 110; ~atum, evigilatum *GlC* E 112; quod ego admirans pro argumento habui quo tandem ad sancti regis gesta ~anda certior accessi ABBO *Edm. pref.*; ~are, vigilare OSB. GLOUC. *Deriv.* 199; quicquid elucubrans exsculpo studio / detur infantibus WALT. WIMB. *Palpo* 168.

2 to ignite.

~atum, .. accensum *GlH* E 206; fragor armorum multus erat et ab ereis cassidibus ~atus ignis scintillabat ORD. VIT. IX 9 p. 527.

3 (infl. by *elucidare*) to make clear.

tibi .. ~abo et in veritate tibi omnia satagam NEN. *HB* 184; ~atum, i. meditatum, lucidum .., purum, *hlutter GlH* E 206; **9..** ~ate, *ahlutredan WW.*

elucubratim, laboriously, painstakingly.

libros .. in Saxonicam linguam .. †elucabratim et elegantissime interpretatus est ASSER *Alf.* 77 (cf. ib. 97: mala doctrina a malis doctoribus .. ~im exposita); **975** (12c) quorum inferius nomina ~im carraxari videntur *CS* 1314.

elucubratio [LL], laborious exercise.

930 (? 10c) que .. ea que infra sunt .. sempiternaliter manenti ~one voluntatis inestimabiliter .. rimatur *CS* 1343 (cf. ib. 669).

elucubratiuncula [LL *gl.*], laborious little composition.

hanc brevem ~am spero quod mirabitur et .. hunc laborem nostrum .. collaudabit *Croyl.* 80.

eluculenter [cf. CL luculenter], excellently.

librum .. Gaufridi Arturi .., ubi predicta satis prolixe et ~er tractata reperies H. HUNT. *Ep. ad Warinum* 75.

elucus [CL], half-asleep, lethargic.

~us, semisomnis vel languidus OSB. GLOUC. *Deriv.* 194.

eludere [CL], to elude, frustrate, trick. **b** to mock.

~eret, *auuaegde GlC* E 111; frustratus est, elusit, fefellit *Ib.* F 3; habitans in homine Deus .. eum .. insidias, quas astuti hostes excogitare poterant, mirabili prudentia semper ~entem monstravit BEDE *Hom.* I 25. 109; ~it, i. decipit, *beswicþ, awægþ GlH* E 210; hic leporem prendit; fauces lepus exit inhermes; / elusum domini verberat ira canem WALT. ANGL. *Fab.* 27. 6; Deus omnes ejus [sensus spurii] deceptiones ~it et .. in bonum nostrum convertit R. NIGER *Mil.* II 56; J. FORD *Wulf.* 88 (v. delusor); 'quis deus ~at', i. e. ~endo impediat TREVET *Troades* 15. **b** [prelati] frequenter claustrum habent pro derelicto, dum inutilibus occupationibus tempus ~ant R. NIGER *Mil.* IV 25.

eludium, a trick, wile; *cf. deludium* 1. **b** jest.

a ~ia, i. deceptiones *GlH* E 209; Paradisi terrestris primicola viperina minus praesensit ~ia O. CANT. *Pref. Frith.* 11; **s1049** contrarie partis conatus callido fallens ~io *Chr. Rams.* 170. **b** rex .. alludens, in hoc prorupit ~ium: "si invenissem emptorem, Londoniam vendidissem" DEVIZES 27.

eluere [CL], **a** to cleanse. **b** to wash away (partly fig.).

a ~itur, purgatur *GlC* E 110; *Ib.* 114 (v. eluvies); ~ere, unguere .. ~ens, lavans *GlH* E 203, 205; scutellas .. quas .. illotas .. reperisset .. gaudebat ~ere AD. EYNS. *Hug.* IV 10 p. 50. **b** infectum scelus .. districtiore continentiae sudore ~endum est BEDE *Ezra* 857; W. CANT. *Mir. Thom.* II 4 (v. argilla); maris violentia, semper excrescentis et terram amplius ~entis GIR. *EH* I 36.

elugere [CL], to mourn. **b** to complete a period of mourning.

dum immoderatas delicias conquerendo obtenebratis jam propriis oculis nullatenus eluxisti *Dictamen* 372. **b** eluxit, i. luctum deposuit *GlH* E 211.

eluis v. eluvies.

Elul [Heb.], a Jewish month.

sextus [Hebraeorum mensis] Elul Septembri .. comparatur BEDE *TR* 11 (cf. *Miss. Jum.* 17); †Ebul, i. mensis Octobris *SB* 19.

elumbire, to enervate, weaken.

insita doctrina pueris elumbit iniqua D. BEC. 2432.

elumbis [CL], enervated, feeble.

~em, i. enervem, *aswunden GlH* E 208; ~e, i. luxuriosum, *mægenleas GlP* 585; milvus et columbes ut amant commune palumbes R. CANT. *Malch.* III 120; ~is, debilis vel luxuriosus, mollis OSB. GLOUC. *Deriv.* 195; argumentum .. similis est genii cum homine, hoc est, ~e FERR. *Kinloss* 52.

elumin- v. illumin-. **eluscescere** v. elucescere c.

elusio [LL], evasion, frustration (by trickery). **b** cheating, trickery.

de insidiis obiciendis edificatoribus et ~onibus eorum R. NIGER *Mil.* III 8; **1254** si .. prior et canonici .. in ~onem nostram ad eleccionem [episcopi] .. processerint *Cl* 314; **1262** in fraudem et ~onem juris *Cl* 173; **1266** in contemptum .. episcopi .. et ~onem libertatis .. ecclesie *Pat* 84 m. 9d.; **1295** qui inventus fuerit taliter frustratorie .. appellasse gravius .. propter ~onem ipsius curie puniatur *Conc.* II 211b; **c1307** quidam indigene .. in ~onem privilegiorum .. in nos .. proruperunt *Bury St. E.* 176. **b** **1324** nec in fraudem seu ~onem catholicorum aliud predicare seu exponere *Fabr. York* 158*n.*; **1494** si sit ~o, vix possunt continuari miracula ultra xl dies *Conc.* III 636a.

elusor [cf. CL lusor], gambler, one who takes a chance.

qui divertit iter, qua se via publica monstrat, / mox perit infelix elusor luce secunda ALCUIN *WillV* 15. 8.

eluvies [CL], washing away. **b** washing water; *cf. eluvio* b. **c** scourings. **d** diarrhoea, dysentery.

~ies, i. .. lavatio *GlH* E 204; *wastynge* .., haustus .., ~ies, ~is, †elinis .. *CathA.* **b** †eluis, liquor quo aliquid eluetur *GlC* E 114. **c** ~ies, macula, sordes, colluvia OSB. GLOUC. *Deriv.* 194. **d** Vespasianus .. obiit .. ventris ~ie R. NIGER *Chr. II* 113.

eluvio [CL], inundation, flood (also fig.). **b** drain.

elubio, diluvium *GlC* E 131; quod caumate perit, quod involvit ~o, quod aer corr[um]pit MAP *NC* I 25 f. 19; dici potest longe post diluvium .. et tanquam per ~onem insulas natas fuisse GIR. *TH* II 16; ~o oblivionis non delet penitus de memoria nisi que gessimus in infantia GROS. *Hexaem.* VIII 30 p. 253. **b** [Londonia] habet .. ~ones [v. l. eluvies] et aqueductus in vicis W. FITZST. *Thom. prol.* 12.

eluxi v. elucere, elugere. **elyacus** v. heliacus.

elymos [? ἔλυμος = *millet or sim.*], linseed.

10.. elimos, lini semen, *linsæd WW.*

Elysius [CL < Ἠλύσιος], Elysian, (as sb. m. or n.) Elysium. **b** Hell.

Eliseum, *sunfeld, þæt is neorxna wong WW*; mundus suos habet Elisios J. SAL. *Pol.* 492A (cf. ib. 493D: hi jam in suis gaudent Elisiis); hic est .. alter Elisius viris summo Paradiso destinatis ab eterno provisus *Chr. Rams.* 38. **b** carceris offa nigri rapitur, captiva tiranni / Elisii, clibani preda cibusque regi GARL. *Epith.* I 142.

em [CL], there you are! look at that!

em, admiratio *GlC* E 165.

ema [cf. ME *mai*], whitethorn, hawthorn (*Crataegus*).

hec ema, i. alba spina *WW.*

emaceratio [cf. CL maceratio], debilitation, wastage.

s1453 nihil crassitudinis sive fertilitatis in ipsis [compotis] relinquis; immo verius ~onem, depauperacionem .., inopiam *Reg. Whet.* I 103.

emach v. haema. **emachites** v. haematites.

emacitas [CL], acquisitiveness.

~as, emend[i] †abitas [l. aviditas] *GlC* E 182.

emaculare [CL], to cleanse, heal.

diaconus velut decoctus, facie contracta in rugam [v. l. rugas] tota cute penas excepit temeritatis... sanctus Dei .. accitum ad se tactu ~at dextere FOLC. *V. J. Bev.* 11.

emadēre [cf. CL madere, emadescere], to drip, be imbrued.

sanguinis haustu / emadet humani GARL. *Tri. Eccl.* 110.

emagnus [cf. CL magnus], very great.

1451 vestre .. affeccionis integritas .. nobis ~am et constantem tribuit probitatem *Pri. Cold.* 173.

emagogum, ~agum v. haemagogus. **emal-** v. esmal-.

emanare [CL]

1 to flow out, emanate (partly fig.). **b** to originate, come into being. **c** (trans.) to pour out, give rise to.

scientiae salutaris cotidie flumina irrigandis eorum cordibus ~abant BEDE *HE* IV 2; sin [calcaria spiritualia] a cupiditate .. ~averint R. NIGER *Mil.* I 1; a quo quicquid est .. intellectus, tanquam a fonte rivulus, originaliter ~at GIR. *TH* I 13; duo nobis mandata caritatis de fonte caritatis eterne ~asse cognoscimus J. FORD *Serm.* 14. 1; ex quo [martyr] lignea illa elatus est theca .., inusitati mox odoris fragrantia ~avit SAMSON *Mir. Edm.* I 8 p. 133; **1301** percussit eum .. de .. baculo a parte ante, ita quod cerebrum ~avit *SelCCoron* 69; sicut hee emanaciones produccionesve eedem sunt cum hiis a quibus .. emanunt (*sic*) .., sed quia per eas ~antia illa diversimode effundunt vires suas, nomina diversa .. sortiuntur FORTESCUE *NLN* I 36; tres .. flumina orientes et emanentes de tribus fontibus in patria Scocie W. WORC. *Itin.* 4. **b** **s1361** circa ista tempora ~avit una comitiva vocata Alba Comitiva AD. MUR. *Cont. A* 195 (cf. comitiva 2e). **c** fides .. passionis Christi, cui dextrum latus foratum in cruce nobis ~avit sacramenta BEDE *Hom.* II 1. 120; **a795** hujus latus lancea perforatum tuae sanguinem redemptionis ~avit ALCUIN *Ep.* 34; ubi fonticuli per occultas fistulas aquas .. calefactas ex abstrusis terre visceribus .. ~ant *G. Steph.* I 28.

2 (of document or sim.) to issue; **b** (trans.).

1200 breve illud nunquam ~avit a curia *CurR* I 129; **c1210** citatio quandoque ~at a judice ordinario *FormOx* 276; **c1230** mandatum apostolicum .. ad omnes prelatos Anglie generaliter ~avit (*Lit. Nuncii Papalis*) *Reg. Malm.* I 409; **1268** (v. conscientia 2c); **s1307** de mandato .. pape, bulle ~arunt quod .. Templarii .. caperentur *Meaux* II 248; PAUL. ANGL. *ASP* 1544 (v. epistola 4b); **1418** (v. dimissio 2a); **1446** commissarius commisit administracionem .. bonorum .. defuncti .. Thome .., unde ~avit commissio in forma consueta *Eng. Clergy* 220. **b** **1283** commissionibus et mandatis hactenus a nostra curia ~atis *RGasc* II 173; **1455** de relevio .. terrarum de G., regi debito per hujusmodi saisinam ~atam *ExchScot* 100; **1542** collationes .. debere sortiri effectus .. ac si a nobis .. ~atae fuissent *Form. S. Andr.* II 205; **c1545** (v. denuntiatorius).

emanatio [LL]

1 flowing out, emanation. **b** that which emanates.

sanguinis ejus de latere ~o figuratur LANFR. *Corp. & Sang.* 424A; succedente Jovis ducatu ad forme membrorum susceptionem apparatur materia calidi et humidi ~one ALF. ANGL. *Cor* 13. 2; BACON VII 62 (v. diffusio 1); vires [anime] .. et proprietates naturales quarum ortum et ~onem ab ipsa essentia anime secundum ordinem sic possumus intelligere KNAPWELL *Not.* 191; quod .. radices sue [sc. sciencie] pullulationis emineant sueque scaturiginis ~o luceat R. BURY *Phil.* 9. 171. **b** insplendeat .. mundi cordis pio pectori ~o illa omnipotentis Dei sincera AD. MARSH *Ep.* 37; distinccio perfeccionum attributalium est fundamentum respectu distinccionis ~onum, sed distinccio ~onum est realis DUNS *Ord.* IV 246; ad quid assignant ipsi ordinem attributorum, quasi essencia sit

fundamentum, et quedam sint propinquiora essencie et quedam propinquiora ~onibus? *Ib.* 268; FORTESCUE *NLN* I 36 (v. emanare 1a).

2 (of document or sim.) issue.

ante ~onem dicti brevis *Entries* 204.

emancare [CL], to maim, mutilate.

s1245 domini pape quidam ostiarius, dum secus quam decuit cuidam volenti ingredi .. respondisset, ~abatur *Flor. Hist.* II 287 (cf. M. PAR. *Maj.* IV 418: dum .. introitum .. postulanti .. denegaret .. civis manum .. amputavit).

emancipare [CL]

1 to set free. **b** to release (son) from father's authority.

~at, manummittit *GlC* E 177; ~ent, manum mittent *Gl. Leid.* 1. 50; ~are, i. liberare, e manu tradere *GlH* E 226; qui regi velint perpauci sunt, cum quisque ut ~etur a jugo rectoris .. querat J. SAL. *Pol.* 680C; servos et ancillas ~averunt *Id. Ep.* 284 (271); consuevit [rex Indorum] .. reos de carceribus ~are BACON V 49. **b** duo filii ~ari voluerunt, suis familiis provisuri NECKAM *NR* II 40; **1313** cum idem Fulco per .. patrem suum dudum ~atus fuisset et post emancipationem illam .. certa pars bonorum dicti patris sui eidem Fulconi donata fuisset *RGasc* IV 1008.

2 to exempt (eccl.).

c1170 ecclesiam .. ab omni seculari servicio penitus ~atam *FormA* 4; **s793** de monasterio .. constituendo et ab omni episcoporum subjectione ~ando .. curiam consulit *V. II Off.* 29.

emancipatio [CL]

1 emancipation. **b** release from father's authority.

~o, *freodom* ÆLF. *Sup.* 188; hi qui efferente superbia .. ~ones querunt, a cervice sua jugum Christi .. si fieri posset, excuterent J. SAL. *Pol.* 680D; ubi servorum generalis ~o *Id. Ep.* 284 (271). **b** **1313** (v. emancipare 1b).

2 exemption (eccl.).

s1179 (v. chirotheca 2b).

emandare [cf. CL mandare], (w. *exsecutio*) to put into execution.

s1477 qua rigorosa justicia ubilibet ~ata executioni publica latrocinia jam diu postea quieverunt *Croyl. Cont. C* 559.

emanere v. emanare.

emansor [CL], deserter.

c1182 leges imperiales in eum qui desertor est vel transfuga vel ~or penam ordinariam .. dictaverunt P. BLOIS *Ep.* 69. 215B.

†**emao** [dub.], one who produces deceptive appearances, magician, actor.

†emaones, *scinneras GlC* E 170.

emarcescere [CL], **emarcēre** [LL]

1 to grow lean or wizened (also fig.). **b** to dry up. **c** (abstr.) to fade, weaken.

credo .. brachium longo tempore ~uatum (*sic*) in eo lavacro .. posse sanari EDDI 66; **9..** ~uit, *forwisnode WW*; ~uit cor meum ÆLF. BATA 4. 31 p. 63; **s988** statim leta elementorum faties ~uit, pax .. superventu Danorum evanuit W. MALM. *GP* I 19; ipsi [homines] .. carne ~uerunt PULL. *Sent.* 759A; compago †numerorum [v. l. nervorum] in .. corpore ejus pene tota ~uit et dissoluta fuit J. FURNESS *Kentig.* 42; langor in anima perseverat donec dederis quod tanto ardore desideravi, cujus amore ~uit caro mea ROLLE *IA* 247. **b** cur emarcet manna magnificum?/ cur marcescit vitae viaticum? J. HOWD. *Ph.* 781; oblatio crebra / non datur, emarcet pascua, languet ovis GARL. *Tri. Eccl.* 36; *to be or wex dry*, .. mercare (*sic*), e- *CathA*. **c** ~uit, †elanguet [l. elanguit] *GlC* E 146; ~uit, elanguit, *ablacode GlH* E 220; recedente a cancro .. sole primo herbida ~escit viriditas ADEL. *QN* 74; spes .. ex improviso ~uit eventu H. HUNT. *HA* VIII 35; ver emarcet ut marcor vireat J. HOWD. *Ph.* 318; GARL. *Tri. Eccl.* 17 (v. cadere 6b).

2 to vanish, be null.

~escentibus nece suorum auctorum nefariis edictis GILDAS *EB* 12; omnis praestigiarum scena .. ut cera liquescens ~uit ALDH. *VirgP* 43.

3 (trans.) to cause to waste away.

Deus .. auxit nostris potenciam quam prius debilitaverat et ~uerat victualium penuria *G. Hen. V* 13.

emarcidus [cf. CL marcidus], faded, withered (also fig.).

respuens .. carnalem omnem atque inutilem consolationem quasi florem foeni ~um et poma putrida J. FORD *Serm.* 40. 2; **c1407** quoniam dudum ~us regni status .. sub vestro felici regimine refloreat *FormOx* 190; **1425** pro hiis ~is operibus reflorescet inter vos fructus Spiritus (*Sermo Abbatis*) AMUND. I 209; **1458** ramusculos, jam pene ~os *Reg. Whet.* I 313.

emarcuatus v. emarcescere 1a. **emath-** v. haema-, haemo-. **emathoicus** v. haemoptysis. **ematicus** v. emeticus.

emature [cf. CL mature], soberly.

~e, *gepungenlice GlH* E 223.

emax [CL], fond of buying. **b** buyable. **c** (by conf. w. CL *emaciare*) thin.

nomina quae iambicis legibus concurrunt, .. ut .. emax ALDH. *PR* 114; emax, emptor *GlC* E 150; emax, qui amat emere aliquid *Ib.* 172 (cf. *GlH* E 221: emax, i. emptor, .. qui amat emere aliquid). **b** emax, quod cito emitur OSB. GLOUC. *Deriv.* 192. **c** emax, macer, tenuis *GlC* E 159 (cf. *GlH* E 221: emax, .., macer, tenuis ..).

embadum [CL < ἐμβαδόν], area of a plane figure.

quid interest nostra multimodas figuras et areas podismo, radio, lituo, et ~o scire dividere? J. SAL. *SS* 949C.

embamma [CL < ἔμβαμμα], sauce.

embamata interpretatur †incisiones [? l. intinctiones vel infusiones], i. sal[sa]menta ut in Alexandro *Alph.* 56.

embass- v. ambasc-. **embiginatio** v. erubiginatio. **embipedum** v. epipedon.

emblema [CL < ἔμβλημα]

1 inlaid pavement, mosaic.

nec minus approperant opicizi emblemata [*gl.*: prospiciones, varietas pavimenti] proni FRITH. 448; ~ata, pavimenti varietates et pro copia dicitur OSB. GLOUC. *Deriv.* 195.

2 bowl, case, or cover decorated w. inlaid or appliqué work.

~a, *fothr GlC* E 160 (cf. ib. 186: ~a, obscuritas); ~a, *fodor Gl. Leid.* 43. 30; ~ata, varietates, vasa varie sculpta, *græftas GlN* 50. 26.

emblicus [Ar. *amlaj* < Pers.], emblic (*Emblica officinalis*).

GILB. II 96. 2 (v. bellíricus 1); in vere et in estate debet uti unguento scesarino confecto de sandel et emleg BACON V 97; *Id.* IX 47, GAD. 6v. 1, *Alph.* 111 (v. bellíricus 1).

embola [LL < ἐμβολή], addition, increase.

embolismalis, superexcrescens inde inventus ~a S. LANGTON *Gl. Hist. Schol.* 42; **c1296** gens Anglorum .. felici ~a personarum excrescencium et rerum copiosis affluenciis redundabat *Reg. Cant.* 144.

embolesmus v. embolismus.

embolim, in addition.

803 de inquisitionibus quas ~im habuit ex persona carissimorum .. discipulorum ALCUIN *Ep.* 265.

embolismalis, ~aris [LL], pertaining to embolism, intercalary: **a** (w. ref. to year); **b** (w. ref. to cycle of common and embolismic years).

a si tamen hoc spatium tibi sex et quinque dierum / crescis ter denis embōlismalibus annis (*Ps.*-BEDE *Hymn.*) *PL* XCIV 620C; est ~aris annus qui habet dies trecentos octuaginta quinque sibi BYRHT. *Man.* 18; annus .. ~alis, id est superexcrescens, qui ccclxxx dies excedit, habens xiij lunationes GERV. TILB. I 6; est embolismus excrementum anni solaris ad lunarem et dicitur ille annus ~alis in quo cadit et recolligitur una lunacio xxx dierum BART. ANGL. IX 4; hic annus habet xiij menses et dicitur ~alis, id est superexcrescens BACON *Tert.* 219; BRADW. *CD* 141D (v. bissextilis). **b** quando circulus ~alis adimpletur continens annos xij communes et vij embolismales BART. ANGL. IX 4.

embolismus [LL < ἐμβολισμός]

1 intercalary: **a** (of month); **b** (of year).

a tertio vel secundo ubi decebat anno, tertiumdecimum in fine anni mensem xxx dierum apponebant ~um BEDE *TR* 45. **b** hinc annorum diversantur longae latitudines, / quorum quidam embolismi, quidam fiunt communes (*Ps.*-BEDE *Hymn.*) *PL* XCIV 605C; saepe in circulo decennovenali duo erunt duobus annis, sicut circulus ipsius demonstrat, quo scriptum est 'communis, communis, ~us' BYRHT. *Man.* 18.

2 (as sb. m.): **a** intercalation. **b** intercalated day or month. **c** year containing intercalated day or month.

a ~us, superaugmentum *GlC* E 168; BART. ANGL. IX 4 (v. embolismalis a). **b** juxta lunarem Ebraeorum calculationem ccccxc [sc. anni] adjectis quadrantibus et ~orum incrementis ALDH. *Met.* 2; Romani, qui dispares habent menses, non unoquolibet in loco ~os computando interponere voluerunt, sed potius ubilibet mediis anni temporibus vacuum .. inter kalendas locum invenire potuissent BEDE *TR* 45; **797** in annis ~orum x et viiij diebus .. quartadecima luna paschalis transponitur prioris anni quartaedecimae; .. quatenus ~us hujus anni xxx habeat dies secundum rationem ~orum ALCUIN *Ep.* 126; tertius embolesmus pridiis inceditur almis *Kal. M. A.* I 401; voco passiones hic primationes, lunationes, et ~os, et hujusmodi que in computo et kalendario considerantur BACON *Tert.* 212; in tertio anno cycli apponitur unus mensis lunaris et vocatur ~us *Ib.* 283. **c** dividitur circulus idem in ~os annosque communes BEDE *TR* 45; **797** uti detrimentum communium annorum ~is suppleatur et fiat aequalis numerus dierum in xix solaribus et in xix lunaribus annis ALCUIN *Ep.* 126; ~us, magnus annus OSB. GLOUC. *Deriv.* 199.

3 prayer inserted after canon of the mass between Lord's prayer and prayer for peace.

quarta [pars canonis] usque ad ~um, id est orationem illam sc. 'libera nos ab omnibus malis', .. ideo dicitur ~us quasi superaccrescens GIR. *GE* II 20 p. 267.

emboss- v. imboss-.

embotum [OF *embot*], funnel.

fumo anguillarum .. recepto per ~um GILB. V 224. 2; fumigetur lapdano et storace .. aut aliquibus aro[maticis] per ~um aut alio instrumento aptato *Ib.* VII 297v. 1; fiat suffumigium per ~um GAD. 54. 2; ~um est instrumentum factum ad modum tube *SB* 19; samida, i. ~um, G. *tonour*, vel vas sine fundo *Alph.* 160.

embraciator v. imbraciator. **embraud-** v. embroud-. **embreoca** v. embrocha. **embrio** v. embryo.

embrocha (embroca) [LL < ἐμβροχή], liniment, lotion.

in hieme fiat ~ca talis: recipe foliorum viol', malve [etc.] GILB. II 85. 1; ~ca idem est quod emplastrum liquidum. ~ca ut quidam dicunt est quelibet madida infusio *SB* 19; embreoca [v. l. ~ca] interpretatur infusio quam nos fomentum dicimus *Alph.* 56; hec ~ca, A. *maythe WW*.

embrochare (embroc-) [LL], to embrocate.

~cetur et frequenter iteretur calefaciendo GILB. V 227. 1; cum manu caput tangatur et quasi fomentetur, hoc est ~care, sed non diu moretur GAD. 50v. 2 (cf. ib. 128. 2: cum oleo .. liniatur in balneo ~cando embrocatione plurima).

embrochatio (embroc-), embrocation, embrocating. **b** liniment, lotion.

GAD. 128. 2 (v. embrochare); ~catio dicitur cum membrum ponitur in aqua calida, sive simplici sive decoccionis herbarum, et illa super membrum cadit ab alto, quod nos fomentum dicimus *SB* 19. **b** ~catio decoctionis viol. [etc.] GILB. V 226v. 1; fiat ~catio post ex ordeo et violis et camomilla decoctis in aqua calida GAD. 50v. 2.

embroudatus [AN *embroude*, OF *embrosde*], embroidered: **a** (of design); **b** (of cloth). *V. et. broudare.*

a **c1370** dedit .. ecclesie Wellensi .. unam casulam, unam tunicam cum dalmatica rubea, compositas cum ymaginibus †enbrordatis de auro unius secte *Hist. Wells* 56; abbas [T., ob. **1396**] .. contulit .. frontale .. cum armis principis in quodam rosario aureo ~ato *G. S. Alb.* III 380; **1402** unus pannus aureus .. de rubeo velveto cum diversis armis inbroudatis *Invent. S. Paul.* 508; **1430** cum armis .. enbroditis (v. 1 aula 7); **c1500** vestimentum .. habet aurifrigiaturam ante et retro cum coronis inbrudatis *Invent. Ch. Ch.* 127. **b** **1378** j sella de nigro panno imbroidata cum rosis et avibus *IMisc* 213/6 m. 2; [abbas J., ob. **1379**] acquisivit aliud par vestimentorum de blodio velvetto aureo opere enbrowdato cum margaritis, videlicet *peerlus Chr. Evesham* 302; **1402** ij frontalia .. quorum unum .. est enbroudatum cum iij ymaginibus *Invent. S. Paul.* 508; **1415** de .. j coopertorio de rubeo *worsted* embraudato cum uno castro albo .. j coster de rubeo *worsted* embraudato cum albis litteris (*LTRAc*) *Arch.* LXX 91; **1415** quod dentur .. ecclesie una capa .. cum rosis .. florata cum orphreis enbroudata nobiliter cum imaginibus (*Test. H. le Scrop*) *Foed.* IX 273a (cf. ib. 274b: capam albam inbroudatam cum stellis de auro); **1415** lego .. aulam embrowdeatam cum hominibus (*Test.*) *Reg. Exon.* 413; **1419** iiij togas de coloribus viridi et rubeo bipertitas et embrodat' *Cl* 269 m. 9; **1421** pro iij lectis de sargia ~ata cum celoris et curtinis *EEC* 463; **1487** unum par vestimentorum de .. serico cum *le orfray* de blodio *saten* imbraudat' cum ymaginibus aureis (*Test.*) *Cart. Boarstall* app. p. 288; **14..** item j capa de *busteyne* albo inbrodato cum rosis rubiis *Invent. Norw.* 20.

embroudatio, embroidery, embroidering.

1432 singule .. mistere per se cum diversis signis et inbroudacionibus de serico .. artes suas exprimentibus .. sunt †distincti [l. distincte] (J. CARPENTER) *MGL* III app. 458; **1441** remitto eisdem expensas per me factas super empcione unius pecie veluti rubei una cum enbraudacione pecie predicte *Reg. Cant.* II 580.

embryo (embrio) [LL *cf.* < ἔμβρυον], embryo.

a generatione .. animatus est ~io, successusque temporis actu fit animal ALF. ANGL. *Cor* 13. 14; substantia que nondum fetus sed ~ion appellatur .. expellitur *Quaest. Salern.* B 308; M. SCOT *Phys.* 1 (v. concipere 2b); prius tamen ex semine fit ~yo, verumtamen ~yo intenditur propter hominem et est via in hominem et generatur ~yo ex semine a ministrante ei, quod complet homo GROS. 128; hic magnus parvulus servus fit dominus / .. / antīquus embrio WALT. WIMB. *Carm.* 47; eadem res est ~yo, puer,

et vir, et vadit de incompleto esse ad complementum BACON *Min.* 365; superfluitas aquosa que est in ~ione quando est in corpore matris GAD. 31. 2; FORTESCUE *LLA* 13 (v. corpus 6a).

emcio v. emptio. **emdroma** v. endromis. **emdula** v. scindula.

emedullare [CL], to deprive of medulla or pith (fig.).

dotes virtutum .. Rector seculorum contulerat que per etatem mundi jam senescentis, lassatis veluti seminibus ~ate, parum aliquid in hoc tempore in quibusdam .. mirandum ostentant ac memorabile *Itin. Ric.* II 5.

emell- v. esmall-.

emembris [LL *gl.*], maimed, limbless.

~is, debilis OSB. GLOUC. *Deriv.* 195 (cf. ib. 351: ~is, extra membra); *with oute membyr*, ~is *CathA*.

ememorare [cf. CL memorare], to be reminded (of).

804 (11c) ~avi pristinae libertatis mei *CS* 313.

emenda [OF *emende, amende*]

1 correction (of fault).

Christiani domini, si velint habere ~am de malediccione et blasphemia nominis Dei, debent subtrahere temporalia sua a mundanis clericis (PURVEY) *Ziz.* 394.

2 restoration, making good (of deficiency).

attendamus etiam circa quietudinis ~am et circa census ~am (*Cons. Cnuti*) *GAS* 315; **c1336** in expensis bursarii .. hoc anno pro providencia facienda et ~a de garderoba et aliis necessariis .. iiij li. xvj s. vj d. ob. quad. *Ac. Durh.* 532 (cf. ib.: in expensis terrar' .. ad nundinas de Derlington ad emend' lardar' x s. v d. ob.).

3 amends, compensation.

1223 mercatores .. qui venerint in Angliam, petentes ~am sibi faciendam de dampnis eis illatis in terra nostra *Pat* 387; **1236** W. .. optulit ei ~as et ipse eas recusavit *CurR* XV 1916; **c1281** Poncio .. damus .. nomine .. salarii iiij^xx li. et robam .. et ~as equitaturarum suarum *RGasc* II 135; **1283** pro ~is ij equorum, quos amiserat in servitio .. l li. morlanorum *Foed.* II 237a; **s1298** proposuerunt Flandrenses ad excusacionem .. se multas ab Anglicis passos injurias .. et quia equales ~as fieri non sperabant ideo armata manu processerunt W. GUISB. 323; potuit apostolus .. confidere [*Heb.* vi 9] in istis sub specie future ~e NETTER *DAF* II 26; **a1564** (v. cranarium).

4 fine, mulct; **b** (for offence against person); **c** (for theft); **d** (for breach of assize); **e** (for trespass).

si vero calumniatus ibi fuerit .. tunc habet rex ~am *DB* I 30; **1136** hujus .. sacrilegii emendatio sub nullo judicio erat .. set apud Anglos *botolos*, hoc est sine ~a, vocabatur *Regesta* 975; he ~e nichil ad archiepiscopum nisi ipse presens in villa fuerit dum hujusmodi forisfacture contigerint RIC. HEX. *Hist. Hex.* II 14; **a1200** si in amendam ceciderit per vj d. quietus sit *BBC* (*Lostwithiel*) 154; **c1229** de illis qui fuerunt contra .. senescallum nostrum in perturbatione predicta nullas ~as capiemus *Pat* 240; **1269** ~a capcionis cuniculorum in foresta pertinent (*sic*) ad dominum regem et non ad ipsum P. *SelPlForest* 49; **c1283** sunt prata de gavelmed in defenso, et .. possunt ibidem inparcare et secundum delictum ~as capere *Cust. Battle* 51; **1292** quod nullas evasiones nec ~as exhibeant de animalibus predictorum .. infra metas de Werington' *BBC* (*Warrington*) 383; **1302** R. N. acculpatus .. quod .. permisit filios suos lavare pelles lanutas; qui non sunt jurati contra consideracionem gylde: qui noluit respondere nec vadiare ~as.. postea vadiavit unam cuvatam cervisie *Rec. Leic.* I 239; **1320** vicecomites vel ballivus capiunt ~as, que cedunt in auxilium firme civitatis (*Breve Regis*) *MGL* II 402. **b** de adulterio .. habent ipsi ~am in suis domibus *DB* I 56v.; emendet tam cognacionis quam hominis ~am plenam (*Cons. Cnuti*) *GAS* 283; si quis ordinatum liget .. episcopo ~am altaris [AS: *wefodbote*] solvat juxta ordinis dignitatem (*Ib.*) *Ib.* 343; non simul habenda est blodwita et fihtwita, due sc. ~e de una culpa (*Leg. Hen.* 94. 1b) *Ib.* 610; **1240** cum burgenses Oxonie in ~am et satisfactionem cujusdam insultus publici facti in scolares .. quandam peccunie summam solvissent *StatOx* 74; **1347** ~as fusi sanguinis *Couch. Furness* II 18 *rub.*; *BB St. Davids* 11 (v. corruptio 3b). **c** de .. latrocinio habent ipsi ~am in suis domibus *DB* I 56v. **d** **1221** si cervisia sit contra racionem priorissa habebit ~as *SelPlCrown* I 97; **1279** nullam clamat emendacionem panis set clamat emend' assise cervisie ibidem *PQW* 186b; **s1280** (v. assisa 4a); **1330** inquiratur .. si predictus A. et predecessores sui habuerunt ~as predictas [assise panis etc.] et a quo tempore .. et xij jur' dicunt .. quod .. A. et omnes predecessores sui .. habuerunt amendas predictas de tenentibus suis in M. *PQW* 611a; **1348** habuerunt .. ~as assise panis et cervisie fracte *Reg. S. Aug.* 284; **14..** si .. habere possit .. ~as assise panis et cervisie per eosdem homines et tenentes ibidem fracte *Reg. Brev. Orig.* 254. **e** BRACTON 226b (v. divadiare 2); quando aliquis hominum .. fullabat pannos suos alibi .., ipse H. nomine ipsius abbatis [R., ob. **1290**] de hujusmodi transgressione ~as cepit *G. S. Alb.* I 417.

emendabilis [CL = *that can be corrected*], involving fine or compensation.

a1087 praecipio ut abbatia habeat .. omnes alias forisfacturas quae ~es sunt in terra sua super suos homines (*Breve Regis*) *Lib. Eli.* II 117; de nulla ~i re [AS: *botwyrðum gylte*] forisfaciat homo plus quam weram suam (*Quad.*) *GAS* 201; qualitas causarum multa est, ~ium et non ~ium (*Leg. Hen.* 9. 1) *Ib.* 554; **1129** volo .. ut jura mercati et ferie et cause ~es sint Herveo episcopo *CalCh* IV 434; **s1251** promisit .. abbas S. Albani ut quicquid ~e foret laudabiliter ante adventum eorum declararetur et ipse .. processu temporis omnia emendanda emendaret M. PAR. *Maj.* V 258.

emendamentum, repair.

1306 in ~um serure ad eandem .. portam j d. *MinAc* 856/15 m. 2.

emendare [CL]

1 to correct (fault). **b** to reform (person). **c** (p. ppl.) reformed.

V. Greg. p. 88 (v. catechuminium); ex necessitate ~andae suae pravitatis BEDE *HE* IV 23 p. 263; nec agitur in iram, nisi quando perniciosa .. opera execrando ~are non poterat HUGEB. *Wynn.* 6; si frater peccans peccatum suum defendere potius quam cognoscere et ~are voluerit LANFR. *Const.* 166. **b** haec patiuntur qui verbis tantum subjectos et non condigna ultione ~ant GILDAS *EB* 76; unusquisque per doctrinam ejus bene ~atus .. domum suam reversi sunt (*sic*) *V. Cuthb.* II 6; nequaquam Finanum ~are potuit BEDE *HE* III 25 p. 181; quem jure predestinavit, si in flagitiis nondum ~atum mors preriperet .. in inferno exsularet PULL. *Sent.* 700C; criminosi aut ~ati sunt a crimine aut non sunt ~ati de crimine OCKHAM *Dial.* 596. **c** ~atioris vite viam aggredi satagit ORD. VIT. IV 15 p. 269; certe inter eos quorum fuerint ~ati mores, vita composita, ordinati affectus, nec istam [amicitiam] arbitror repudiandam AILR. *Spir. Amicit.* III 12. 680D; ~atiorem vitam promittentes W. CANT. *Mir. Thom.* IV 15.

2 to emend, make corrections to (text). **b** to revise, amend (statute).

nec tamen emendant titubantis gramma poetae ALDH. *VirgV* 2843; librum .. male de Greco translatum et pejus a quodam inperito ~atum .. correxi BEDE *HE* V 24 p. 359; ita ut mihi tempus relegendi vel ~andi non fuit idoneum, vestrae charitatis contentus tantummodo lectione et emendatione ALCUIN (*Adv. Elipand.*) *Dogm.* 234C; bonum .. est ut cum alicujus consilium in placito redditur, cum emendatione dicendum predicatur, ut, si forte perorator vel superadjecerit aliquid vel omiserit, ~are [v. l. ~ari] liceat ei (*Leg. Hen.* 46. 5) *GAS* 570; menda, macula, maxime illa que solet esse in libris nondum ~atis OSB. GLOUC. *Deriv.* 360; **1199** ad ~endum (*sic*) chirographum suum *CurR RC* I 417; **1442** (v. diminuere 3c). **b** ?**1072** episcopales leges quae non .. secundum sanctorum canonum praecepta .. fuerunt .. ~andas judicavi (*Ch. Regis*) *GAS* 485.

3 to mend, repair. **b** to restore, renew.

c1250 debent afferre .. materiem ad ~andum domos *Reg. S. Aug.* 27; **1269** de pontibus et calcatis fractis et cheminis ~andis *CBaron* 72; **c1283** debent in communi ad festum S. Thome xj d. ad hlosam domini ~andam *Cust. Battle* 37; **1308** in duabus patellis ~andis vij d.; in cribris .. reparandis iiij d. *Ac. Durh.* 5; **1309** ad ~endum (*sic*) murum suum *DCSal.* (*HMC*) 344; **1325** in stipendio iiij hominum .. cursum aque ~encium (*sic*) *Ac. Man. Cant.* (*Merstham*); **1375** injunctum est .. tenentibus .. quod ~ari faciant viam in .. H. *Hal. Durh.* 130; **1449** (v. effortiare 2a). **b** vigor .. nature per hominem depravatur, per Deum ~atur .. exspectans consummari in resurrectione ubi corpus mirifice ~atum animam non aggravabit PULL. *Sent.* 721B.

4 to improve; *cf. emundare* 4. **b** (pass.) to benefit; **c** (refl.).

[Guilelmus I] coenobia .. multum ~avit, multimodisque gazis .. ditavit ORD. VIT. IV 1 p. 163; **1215** terras illas ~ent edificiis et aliis prout expediens erit *BBC* (*Limerick*) 44; **1296** J. de M. cepit unam placeam vasti ad unam salinam suam ~endam (*sic*) et dabit ad gersumam xij d. *Hal. Durh.* 2. **b** **1221** milites de comitatu dicunt quod comitatus ~aretur ad opus domini regis si [servientes Hugonis P.] amoverentur *SelPlCrown* 110. **c** **1188** quilibet eorum possit se ~are quantum poterit in edificiis faciendis *BBC* (*Bristol*) 50.

5 to amend, settle, make reparation for; **b** (absol.; *cf. emundare* 3a). **c** to pay as compensation or fine.

†**604** (12c) nisi ~averit ante ejus transitum quod inique gessit *CS* 3; **836** scriptum est 'peccatum ibi ~a ubi nascitur' *CS* 416; ?**1072** qui vocatus ad justitiam episcopi venire noluerit, pro unaquaque vocatione legem episcopalem ~abit (*Ch. Regis*) *GAS* 485; **1097** ipse ~abit mihi fracturam pacis mee *Regesta* p. 135; (*Quad.*) *GAS* 353 (v. Danelaga); que placita ~ari debeant ex hiis placitis quedam ~antur c s., .. quedam non possunt ~ari (*Leg. Hen.* 12) *Ib.* 558 (cf. ib. 566: si quid in eos vel in suos peccabitur, animus hic et honoribus pro modo singulorum ~etur); (*Ib.* 66. 7) *Ib.* 586 (v. emundare 3a); vicecomites et aldermanni .. illud domino regi graviter ~are debent (*Leg. Ed. Conf. Lond.*) *Ib.* 656; **1186** si aliquis extraneus mercator aliquod inconveniens in villa fecerit in *portimanimot* coram justicia supradicta sine causa illud ~et *CalCh* II 88; **c1216** si quid .. eis .. fuerit forisfactum, id eis .. ~ari faciatis *Pat* 16; **1221** K. venit et queritur de eodem et petit hoc sibi ~ari *PlCrGlouc* 63; M. PAR. *Maj.* V 258 (v. emendabilis); donec damnum suum ei esset amendatum BRACTON 158 (cf. ib.: ipse querens noluit damnum ~are). **b** si postea inventus fuerit aut superbus aut inoboediens .. deponatur .. aut satisfactione ~averit THEOD. *Pen.* II 6. 13; **725** (10c) sciat se .. coram Christo rationem reddere nisi ante satisfactione ~averit *CS* 144; **868** nisi ante .. aemendare voluerit *CS* 519; **940** (14c) (v. corporeus 1); **c1072** (v. detinere 2c); per c s. ~abit *DB* I 1; sanguinem fundens ~at per vij s. et iiij d. *Ib.* 26; **1100** secundum modum forisfacti ita ~abit, sicut ~asset retro a tempore patris mei ..; quod si perfidiae .. convictus fuerit sicut erit culpa, sic ~et (*Ch. Hen. I*) *GAS* 522; sortilege .. dispereant omnino nisi cessent et profundius ~ent [AS: *deoppor gebetan*] (*Quad.*) *Ib.* 135; jubeo ut .. ab hujusmodi precibus cesset et quoniam me jam sepe vexavit, prout judicabitur mihi ~et EADMER *HN* 92; **s1214** (v. continuare 5); **a1246** ~abit vel releviabit burgensis de dimidio burgagio sicut burgensis de pleno burgagio *BBC* (*Saltash*) 96; **c1270** quod nullus .. presumat infra limina gilde .. cultellum .. portare; quod si fecerit ~et gilde in xij denariis *Stat. Gild. Berw.* *91. **c** quod si quis ire jussus non iret ~abat regi xl s. *DB* I 179; qui ante archiepiscopum pugnaverit aut arma extraxerit xl s. ~et [AS: *gebete*] (*Inst. Cnuti*) *GAS* 59; (*Leg. Hen.* 10. 1 & 15) *Ib.* 556, 559 (v. Danegeldum); si .. aliquis .. guerram movere praesumpserit in absentia nostra .. et ad justitiam se non offert, primo excommunicetur, et post excommunicationem nisi infra xl dies forisfactum suum ~averit, decernimus ut [etc.] (*Tract.*) DICETO *YH* II 74; **c1230** redditus .. terrarum suarum quos .. per guerram nostram amittet .. eidem ~abimus in denariis vel in terra *Pat* 392; judicaverunt .. ut Lefsius episcopo .. dampnum .. suppleret .., de rapina vero regi forisfacturam ~aret *Lib. Eli.* II 11.

6 (pass., of person) to be fined or punished.

si quis tinxerit manum in aliquo cybo liquido et non idonea manu, c palmadas [v. l. palmitis] ~etur EGB. *Pen.* 13. 9; **1227** si aliquis serviens .. contra jura et libertates burgi agere et venire voluerit ~abitur *BBC* (*Chesterfield*) 371; **c1277** J. le Pee levavit unum fossatum injuste iccirco ~etur *SelPlMan* 23.

7 (?) *f. l.*

hec terra ~ata [? l. commendata] est in manu Turstini abbatis de c et xxviij lib. *Dom. Exon.* f. 173; mortuum .. sepeliunt .. emmendantes [? l. commendantes] Domino animam altissimo ANSELM BURY *Mir. Virg.* 35.

emendates, (pl.) amends, fines. *V. et. emenda* 3, 4, *emendatis* 6.

1276 omnes isti .. sunt aquitati de murdro et .. capiunt ~es de braciatoribus ... W. de H. clamat libertatem in villa de H. de antiquitate et capit ~es de braciatoribus *Hund.* II 177.

emendatio [CL]

1 improvement, removal of physical defect. **b** correction, removal of fault, moral reformation; *cf. emundatio* 3.

RIC. MED. *Signa* 36 (v. enaeoristicus). **b** ut per ~onem morum .. habeas veram vitam GILDAS *EB* 32; nec omnia evangelia tangimus .. sed illa .. quibus speramus sufficere posse simplicibus ad animarum ~onem ÆLF. *CH I pref.* 2; hoc modo tractetur quoadusque humilitate et patientia et ~onis promissione adjunctis fratrum precibus misericordiam consequatur LANFR. *Const.* 165; nonnullos grammatice artis peritos in schola Christi ~onem vite .. docuit ORD. VIT. III 2 p. 20; correctio .. que specialiter tendit ad ~onem fratris delinquentis per simplicem ammonitionem OCKHAM *Dial.* 543.

2 emendation, correction (of text). **b** amendment (of statute); **c** (of verdict). **d** amended version.

ALCUIN *Dogm.* 234C, (*Leg. Hen.* 46. 5) *GAS* 570 (v. emendare 2a). **b** hoc est ~o Willelmi regis in legibus Anglicis (*Quad. pref.*) *Ib.* 543; lagam regis Eadwardi .. beati patris ejus ~onibus roboratam propriis institutionibus honestavit (*Quad. arg.*) *Ib.* 535; decreta domini regis Willelmi bastardi et ~ones quas posuit in Anglia (*Will. I artic. Lond. retr.*) *Ib.* 489; **1549** statutis illis .. haec paucula, seu interpretationes seu ~ones, .. adjicienda praecipimus *StatOx* 358. **c** **1212** ipsi adjudicaverunt duellum inter eos per ~onem. [l. eos. per ~onem] consideratum est quod duellum sit devadiatum *CurR* VI 215. **d** psalmos, quos prius secundum Hieronymi ~onem legerat, more Romanorum juxta quintam editionem †memoraliter transmetuit [v. l. memorialiter transmutavit] EDDI 3.

3 repair: **a** (of roads or structures or their parts); **b** (w. ref. to *brigbote* or *burhbote*); **c** (of small artifacts).

a pasnagium .. et ignem et domorum ~onem inde accipit episcopus *DB* I 173; **1152** de bosco quod opus fuerit ad ~onem domorum et sepium *Cart. Boarstall* 100; **1221** dicunt quod .. abbas et .. predecessores ceperunt consuetudinem illam [i.e. ad pontem de A.] jam per xx annos et nullam ~onem apposuerunt *SelPlCrown* 114; **c1228** elemosinas .. ad ~onem ecclesie sue *Pat* 233; **1236** ad sustentationem pontis et ad ~onem portus de A. *BBC*

(*Ayr*) 333; **1257** (v. coopertorium 6c); **1289** in cooperacione et hemendacione haragerie *DCDurh.* (*Ac. Wardley, sched.*); **1378** cives electi pro ~one murorum, fossatorum, conductus Thamisie et Walbrook ordinanda (*LB Lond.* H f. 97) *MGL* I 581; **1379** pro ~one vie juxta N. xij s. x d. *Ac. Durh.* 588; **1446** pro reparacione et ~one de *le waterwall* ac rote exterioris molendini de S., xv s. *Ib.* 630; **1533** in .. ~one de *lez pyllars* in ecclesia *Comp. Swith.* 221. **b** †**680** (v. arx 2b); **866** (11c) praeter .. ~onem pontis et arcis *CS* 514; **956** praeter expeditionem et ~onem pontis et arcis *CS* 937; (*Inst. Cnuti*) *GAS* 353 (v. civitas 1b); (*Quad.*) *Ib.* (v. burhbota). **c** **1300** pro ~one unius ciste *KRAc* 233/12 m. 3; **1398** ~onem mitre *Invent. Ch. Ch.* 104; **1417** pro ~one vestimentorum et .. missalis *Ac. Durh.* 225; **1419** in factura ij candelabrorum et ~one aliorum vj s. viij d. *Ib.* 227; **1499** pro ~one vasorum (v. cuvarius); **1532** soluti eidem pro ~one iij serarum cum factura ij clavium vj d. *Househ. Bk. Durh.* 70.

4 improvement (of place). **b** benefit, enrichment.

c1195 R. de proprio suo augmentavit cellarium .. et alias amendationes plurimas fecit *Cart. Osney* II 283; frater bonus husebondus est: quod probatur ex .. edificiis et ~onibus quas fecit BRAKELOND 124; **1220** si [tenentes] .. in terra illa posuerint ~onem ad valenciam vj marcarum vel infra, idem R. vel heredes sui .. eandem ~onem per estimacionem legalium hominum restituent *CurR* IX 387; cui etiam [sc. domui] sumptuosam [abbas W., ob. **1235**] addidit ~onem *G. S. Alb.* I 290; **1244** assise civitatis in Hustengo provise .. ad ~onem civitatis *MGL* I 241; **1341** ecclesiam nostram et filios spirituales, domuum et agrorum nostrorum ~onem et culturam reliquimus atque curam (*Excus. Archiep.*) BIRCHINGTON *Arch. Cant.* 33; **1382** pro j purprestura facta capiendo *gravell* pro ~one terre sue .. ij s. *Hal. Durh.* 173. **b** **c1180** comes Flandrie .. recognovit quod nil juris sibi vindicat in terra illa .. nisi tantummodo vadium et suppositionem quam misit in ~onem terre illius (*Lit. Regis*) GIR. *PI* II 16; **a1188** quoscumque mercatores secum ad ville ~onem aduxerint pacem habeant *CalCh* II 88; **1198** (v. 3 burgus 3a); **1214** (v. diaeta 1d).

5 amends, reparation. *Cf. emundatio* 4.

705 condixerunt ut .. unusquisque convictus sit offendisse alio recta ~one satisfaciat WEALDHERE *Ep.* 22; **1136** (v. emenda 4a); "regis ministrum dehonestavi .." inquit, "sed plenam pro maledicto polliceor ~onem" GRIM *Thom.* 24; **s1253** (v. dioecesanus 2a); **1268** si aliquis .. querimoniam faceret .. seneschallus ipsius J. secundum consuetudinem legum burgi inde faceret ~ones *BBC* (*Richmond*) 178; **s1272** villici postulaverunt ~onem de viris occisis *Flor. Hist.* III 25; **1300** si .. super hoc sint convicti .. quod .. facient ~onem secundum quantitatem delicti *MGL* II 94; **s1175** restitucionem et ~onem humiliter offerens *Plusc.* VI 29; **c1516** postquam aliquis convictus fuerit ut pacis perturbator .. super satisfactione aut emmendatione partis lese facienda .. possit appellatio *StatOx* 333.

6 fine, mulct; **b** (for offence against person); **c** (for theft); **d** (for breach of assize).

si quis eam [sc. treuuam] infregisset, inde praepositus regis accipiebat communem ~onem *DB* I 1; quotienscunque preceperit propositus monasterii ire et omnem rei ~onem persolvere (*Inq. Eli.* f. 211b) *Inq. Cantab.* 193; antiqua consuetudo fuit ut omnis ecclesiastica et secularis ~o communis erat regi et episcopo (*Inst. Cnuti*) *GAS* 614; (*Quad.*) *Ib.* 299 (v. contingere 8b); (*Leg. Hen.* 21) *Ib.* 560 (v. 2 causa 1b); **a1150** si aliquis super hoc aliquid presumpserit, ego capiam ~onem quam comes R. instituit *Act. Hen. II* I 13; **1203** idem vicecomes reddit compotum de x li. de ~one maneriorum *Pipe* 59. **b** si quis aliquem ordinatum ligaverit aut ceciderit .. emendet .. episcopo altaris ~onem [AS: *weofodbote*] (*Inst. Cnuti*) *GAS* 343; de omni homicidio et omni robaria et omnibus incendiis, que facta sunt antequam pax fuerat instituta, totum dimittatur, et nemo vindictam vel ~onem [AS: *bote*] exigat (*Quad.*) *Ib.* 224; (*Leg. Hen.* 11. 1a) *Ib.* 556 (v. cognatio 2b). **c** **1100** si quis aliquid de meo .. cepit, totum cito reddatur absque ~one, et si quis inde aliquid retinuerit, ille super quem inventum fuerit graviter michi emendabit (*Ch. Hen. I*) *GAS* 522. **d** **1233** ad nos spectant .. ~o panni, panis, et cervisie *Cart. Osney* IV 345; **1230** consuetudines et ~ones de bracinis et falso pane et falso galone et falso pondere et falsa mensura .. remanebunt monachis Dunelm. *Feod. Durh.* 216; **1279** (v. emenda 4d); **1321** qui clamant .. alias libertates regias, ut furcas, ~ones assise panis et cervisie, et alia que ad coronam pertinent *MGL* II 354; **1388** dominus habet ibidem furcas, pilloriam, trebuchettum, judicialia, ~onem panis et cervicie *IMisc* 240/13.

7 payment (in exchange).

habuit vj hidas .. quas abbas W. deliberavit ei in ~one Waletone *DB* I 35; ?**a1250** tenemur etiam solvere .. Ricardo .. v s. .. in ~onem escambii, pro omnibus rebus *Reg. Malm.* II 188.

emendator [CL = *corrector*], (w. *treugae*) supervisor of truce.

1215 rex ~oribus et pacificatoribus treugarum captarum inter regem Francie et ipsum .. salutem *Pat* 179a (cf. ib: rex dictatoribus et ~oribus treuge); **1254** cum de ipsis [sc. dampnis] ad interceptionem treugarum pertinentibus ad ~ores treugarum cognitio pertineat (*Pat*) *RGasc* I 543.

emendatorius [LL], reformatory, chastening. **b** corrective, emendatory.

in eo quod corripit et aliqua ~ia poena plectit BEDE *Luke* (xi 4) 484; archano Dei examine et ~io verbere traditus est ad tempus Sathane GOSC. *Mir. Iv.* lxxiii; factum est ut pena hominem susciperet ~ia potius †quem [l. quam] interemptoria OSB. BAWDSEY clxii; quod ad arbitrium prelati pertineat ut convictus .. ~iam vindictam subeat ROB. BRIDL. *Dial.* 144. **b** hic prejudicant Grecorum volumina libris Hebraicis; ~ia enim sunt. Gamaliel .. puncta transmutando omnia corrupit quum per puncta Hebraica discernatur scriptura R. NIGER *Chr. II* 107.

emendicare [CL], to obtain by begging; (*cf. Codex Justin.* IX 2. 14); **b** (fig.). **c** (pr. ppl.) beggar. **d** (p. ppl.) wrongfully appropriated, fabricated (infl. by *mendacium*).

verebantur .. populorum ~are suffragia *V. Kenelmi B* f. 83v. 2; si ille insurgit .., ad ~ata sacramentorum suffragia .. frustra decurritur J. SAL. *Pol.* 537B; **1173** [ecclesia] orbata patre aliunde jamdiu sibi ~avit suffragia G. FOLIOT *Ep.* 223; canonum observavit censuram ut ~atis aliunde suffragiis uteretur BRAKELOND 160v. **b** ~ata exempla J. SAL. *Pol.* 518D (v. decurrere 1b). **c** R. NIGER *Mil.* IV 42 (v. emendicatio). **d** Elwardus, dum tinnula et ~ata verba venatur, miserabiliter impegit W. MALM. *GR prol.* (cf. ib. V 394: omnes .. optimates .. transfuge fuere, quidam nullis extantibus causis, quidam levibus occasiunculis ~atis); **1150** ~atis instrumentis suffultus (*Lit. ad Papam*) *Lib. Eli.* III 97; ~ata carmina R. HOWD. III 143 (v. carmen 1a).

emendicatio [cf. CL mendicatio], mendicancy.

sicut .. otium non admittit justitia ita nec ~onem acceptat. .. justitia .. in penam tribuit otiosos .. et emendicantes validos R. NIGER *Mil.* IV 42; quid de pauperum peregrinatione sentietur que de sola ~one negotietur? *Ib.* 60.

emensio [LL], lapse (of time).

s1042 Hardecnut demptis de ~one biennii post sumptum principatum diebus decem .. mortem gustavit immaturam *Chr. Rams.* 154.

emenserant v. emergere 6a. **emensus** v. emetiri. **ementalatio** v. ementulatio.

ementare [cf. LL dementare], to dement. *V. et. amentare, dementare* a.

mox ut illorum quidam .. lapillos cupivit pretiosos trahere e feretro, amisso lumine divina ultione .. cecidit in pavimentum. tunc ~ati hostes ceteri omnia .. fecerunt relinqui F. MALM. *V. Aldh.* 77B.

ementiri [CL], to say or vow falsely, belie. **b** (w. acc. & inf.) to misrepresent (as), pretend that. **c** (absol. or intr.) to lie. **d** to simulate.

si quis ad alterutrum cogatur injuste .., rectius est hoc ~iri [AS: *to aleoganne*] quam implere (*Quad.*) *GAS* 47. **b** quanti preceperat emptas [caligas] ~itus est W. MALM. *GR* IV 313. **c** ~itur, valde mentitur *GlC* E 179. **d** quid .. estimabitur .. de ypocritis qui utinam plures essent saltem ad superficiem boni specietenus ~iendam ne religio obsolescat in desuetudinem? R. NIGER *Mil.* IV 27 (cf. ib. 29: lapides pretiosos adulterant, quoniam suppositis vitro coloribus variis quos volunt lapides ~iuntur. similiter et alia metalla variis artibus obducunt et transferunt et †emerciuntur [l. ~iuntur] colorem aut modum prout volunt ad proximi deceptionem).

ementorium, booth, stall. *Cf. emptorium* b.

1287 seldas et ~ia singulis annis tempore nundinarum illarum .. construere possint in placea illa. .. ita tamen quod statim, finitis nundinis illis predicte selde et ~ia constructa sic .. penitus amoveantur *MonA* II 389 (cf. *Cal. CourtR Chester* p. 123).

ementulare [cf. CL mentula], to emasculate (man); **b** (animal). **c** (p. ppl. as sb. n.) eunuch.

H. HUNT. *HA* VII 36 (v. dexter 2a); **s1180** Haraldus excecavit eum [Magnum] et ~avit *G. Hen. II* I 266; **1202** nequiter fecit ~are R. nepotem suum, unde ipse obiit *SelPlCrown* 26; **1221** Thomas devictus est et obcecatus et ~atus *PlCrGlouc* 22; **1234** A. de R. .. ~atus fuit et oculos amisit propter roberiam *Cl* 493; **1249** pro latrocinio excecatus fuit et ~atus *Cl* 161; quosdam contigit vel ementulari / vel perimi *Ps.*-MAP (*Contra Avaros* 91) p. 155. **b** fratribus [sc. porcis] ~atis solus inveniri non potuit W. CANT. *Mir. Thom.* IV 47. **c** **1160** vicecomes r. c. de xx s. pro ~ato *Pipe* 35; in effusione ~ati *Quaest. Salern.* B 12.

ementulatio, emasculation.

epar ericii assatum dicitur eos [leprosos tyriacos] juvare .. ~o etiam valet GILB. VII 343v. 1; **1252** sciatis me reddidisse Wydoni filio Tece terram suam unde disseysitus fuit pro ementalacione Alani Walensis *CurR* 146 m. 1.

emeraldus v. esmeraldus. **emeraudes** v. haemorrhois. **emercare** v. emarcescere.

emercari [LL < CL = *to bribe*], to purchase; **b** (p. ppl. *s. pass.*).

c1146 redditus sex librarum quas predictus W. archiepiscopus ~atus est de ipsis heredibus *Reg. Cant.* 1503–32 f. 136; (cf. *RChart* 148b [**1205**]: mercatus); sciens .. quod indulta suis beneficia nominis sui gloriam immortalis fame titulis ~antur *Dial. Scac.* I 13. **b** **s1384** ~ata treuga qua patria pro tanta anni parte non indiguit reversus est *Chr. Angl.* 360 (cf. WALS. *HA* II 115: reversus est .. postquam expendisset l^{m} marcarum argenti).

emercere v. ementiri. **emerciamentum** v. admerciamentum.

emĕre [CL]

1 to buy, purchase: **a** (goods); **b** (person; partly fig.); **c** (land); **d** (office); **e** (w. gdv.); **f** (w. *in retallium* or sim.); **g** (w. *sanguis*, to pay merchet); **h** (absol.).

a boves et oves et columbae .. emebantur [cf. *John* ii 12–22] BEDE *Hom.* II 1. 115; *GlC* E 172 (v. emax a); tabernum, domus ubi vinum emitur *Ib.* T 18; **c1140** me dedisse .. dim. carucatam terre .. ad lumen emendum in capitulum pro salute anime mee *Ch. Durh.* 29; **s1191** (v. cambire 1b); **1285** (v. contracingulum); **1301** capellanus parochialis misit J. clericum suum ad domum J. le S. ad emendam sibi candelam sc. j d. *SelCCoron* 69; **1343** in expensis factis pro .. parochianis ementibus decimas *Ac. Durh.* 170; paucos libros .. pro lxxij^{m} sesterciis .. emit R. BURY *Phil.* 3. 40. **b** quatenus .. frater Anselmus, quem jam possidetis amicum, in servum a vobis ematur ANSELM (*Ep.* 36) III 144; puer .. a mercatore emptus *Quaest. Salern.* N 6. **c** **c700** (11c) locus .. ecclesiae pecunia emitur a rege (*Ch.*) GOSC. *Milb.* 202; **1002** (12c) donabo libertatem .. quia tanti pretii emtum [v. l. emptum, (?) l. empta] est suprascripta terra *CS* 1295; comes .. emit illud [manerium] de duobus hominibus qui eum tenebant de episcopo *DB* I 5v.; *Ib.* 46b (v. conventio 2b); †**1084** (v. cambire 1b); **a1233** totam villam de B. quem emimus de Rogero *Feod. Durh.* 149n.; **12..** si H. et I... messuagium .. alicui velint vendere seu alienare, ego J. et heredes mei ad ea emenda omnibus aliis erimus propinquiores *Ib.* 73n.; **1250** quod non permittat quod .. viri religiosi ingrediantur manerium de C. ad emendum in eo vel possidendum aliquam terram *Cl* 286; si .. ecclesia emerit agrum OCKHAM *Disp.* 17. **d** a tyrannis et a patre eorum diabolo .. emunt sacerdotia GILDAS *EB* 67; emit pretio ab eo sedem Lundoniae civitatis BEDE *HE* III 7; W. MALM. *GR* IV 345 (v. canonia 1a); empto presulatu DICETO *Chr.* 219; Gregorius VI .. emit papatum *Eul. Hist.* III 294. **e** eum pecunia sua emere occidendum quaerebat *V. Greg.* p. 90. **f** **c1340** jurare .. quod non emant aliqua victualia ad retallium *FormOx* 171; **c1349** non emant aliqua victualia ad retallium *StatOx* 153; **1451** quod nullus alienigena emat in retallia sive in grosso *Gild Merch.* II 61; **c1492** emendo pannos ad revendendum et retalandum *Doc. Bev.* 75. **g** **1279** de sanguine suo emendo *Hund.* II 321. **h** ex eo [templo] vendentes et ementes ejecit [Jesus] *V. Greg.* p. 106; *GAS* 221 (v. cambire 1a); BRACTON 235b (v. diaeta 2c); **1288** A. G. manens in Pottergate emit per majorem et vendit per minorem *Leet Norw.* 13.

2 to gain, procure (also fig.). **b** to obtain (by entreaty).

emptus Christo concelebrans cane carmina mundus ALDH. *Met.* 10 p. 87; hactenus excolicum quanto sudore sacellum / emerit exposui FRITH. 1310; empta iniquitas sic ad emptorem transit ut nequaquam a venditore recedat J. SAL. *Pol.* 569A; thalamos qui vendit ementem / fallit et emptorem mox penitet empta voluntas HANV. IX 326 p. 387; empta fides GARL. *Tri. Eccl.* 13 (v. 1 cum 5). **b** "hic rex subjectos non regit, immo vorat." / ille refert "emptum longa prece ferte magistrum" WALT. ANGL. *Fab.* 19. 19; taydis est, quod ēmo corpus prece, fletibus ēmo SERLO WILT. II 34.

3 (p. ppl. as sb. n.) buying, purchasing. *Cf. emptio* 1a.

c1130 xiiij solidatos pratorum quos monachi prius habuerunt ex empto *Cart. Glouc.* I 340; **1200** assisa utrum Edwardus .. habeat majus jus .. de j virgata terre .. an Reynilda .. ex empto Willelmi quondam viri predicte R. et ex suo empto ponitur in adventu justiciariorum *CurR* I 306; **1213** inquiri facias si aliqui in feodo .. Linc. episcopi .. absque assensu .. ipsius vel ex empto vel ex vadio .. se miserint *Cl* 154a.

emerēre, ~ēri [CL]

1 **a** to complete (a term of military service). **b** to finish (a task or course). **c** (p. ppl. as sb. m.) veteran.

a ~itos Christi milites .. prosternunt ALDH. *VirgV* 13; in senectute .. ~itus miles permanserit BYRHT. *V. Ecgwini* 353; miles ~itus clipeum veneratur et arma R. BURY *Phil.* 4. 73; milites Romani post lx^{um} aetatis annum non cogebantur militare sed dabatur illis villa .. et tunc vocabatur miles ~itus vel ~ite militie quasi positus extra meritum militie HIGD. I 25 p. 247. **b** ~itus, i. .. *gepungen*, perfectus *GlH* E 229; **1169** eatenus jam profecit per Dei gratiam industria pauperis .. ut in his emerendis [v. l. emendis] ij^{m} marcarum antecessorem suum .. expensurum fuisse non dubitem J. SAL. *Ep.* 303 (293); cum omnes planete cum stellis etiam stabunt quasi ~iti, stabilis erit status noster NECKAM *NR* I 14 p. 54. **c** ~itus, i. veteranus miles *GlH* E 229; ~iti, qui sola quiete domi potiuntur OSB. GLOUC. *Deriv.* 469; de senum et ~itorum comitativa in expeditione peregrinationis onus habetur et interdum consilium, raro vero aliud adjutorium R. NIGER *Mil.* IV 61.

2 to earn, merit. **b** (p. ppl.) meritorious. **c** (by conf. w. *immeritus*) unrewarded.

hec collocutio hunc finem ~uit W. MALM. *GR* V 406; **s1147** qui .. in ministerio Henrici Wintonie episcopi plurimum glorie pretium ~uit J. HEX. *HR Cont.* 321. **b** bonis et ~itis actibus se subdidit BYRHT. *V. Ecgwini* 384; sprevisti emeritas Petri de culmine cartas FRITH. 914; **1325** attendentes .. laborem ~itum ac fructuosam solicitudinem *Reg. Roff. Ep.* 113. **c** *unrewarded*, ~itus *CathA*.

3 to conciliate, be pleasing.

~eor, complaceo *GlH* E 231.

emergator [cf. CL mergus], diving bird.

a dowker, ~or *CathA*.

emergĕre [CL]

1 to emerge, arise (from water); **b** (astr.) to rise, appear above the horizon. **c** (refl.) to extend upwards.

Rufina et Secunda .. sospites a thermis emersisse leguntur ALDH. *VirgP* 51; ~ere, exire *GlC* E 147; relatum est a quodam .. antiquissimo vaticinatum dum pontis illius arcus ~erent [sc. e mari] destructionem gentium .. in Hispania imminere OSB. BAWDSEY cxlvi; dum mergunt ~untque [aves] pede natatili in aquis se gubernant GIR. *TH* I 7; *Ib.* II 12 (v. cumulus 1a); *to bolt up*, ~ere *CathA*. **b** **a690** ~ente axe tenus aequore Titane ALDH. *Ep.* 5 p. 490; SACROB. *Sph.* 3 p. 96 (v. chronicus 3b). **c** alia [sc. extremitas arcus] protensa ultra stratam ~ebat se in vicina edificia quasi connasceretur ex eis *G. Hen. V* 15.

2 to emerge (from concealment), appear. **b** to come to light. **c** to get clear, escape.

~unt certatim de curucis .. quasi .. de .. caverniculis .. vermiculorum cunei GILDAS *EB* 19; **706** examina apum .. ex alvearíis .. certatim ~unt ALDH. *Ep.* 9 (12); BEDE *HE* I 16 (v. abdere 1); septentrionalibus adversariis ex improviso ~entibus ORD. VIT. III 14 p. 143; merge .. in ima viscerum / ne mersus servulus emergat iterum WALT. WIMB. *Carm.* 153. **b** **985** (12c) anathematis antiquis cartulis ita ut nichil valeant ultra, etiam si iterum ~ant *CD* 652. **c** si ab inferis ~eret [Homerus] ALDH. *VirgP* 29; HON. *Spec. Eccl.* 898A (v. efflare 1a); Sabinus .. et qui cum ipso erant natabundi de periculo emerserunt TORIGNI *Access. Sig.* 18.

3 (of fluid) to gush, spring forth; **b** (p. ppl. *s. act.*).

in assumptione .. almifluae glebae .. fons sacer emersit *V. Kenelmi B* 81v. 2; **c1289** super mare et infra quoscumque rivos, aquas, seu rivulos maris usque ad primum pontem ~entes *BBAdm.* I 226. **b** [flumina] ex terrae penetralibus .. emersa GIR. *TH* I 7.

4 (trans., by conf. w. *immergere*) to flood, submerge. **b** to drown.

1378 (v. cretina); **1398** in iij hominibus cond[uctis] pro ripar[ia] falc[anda] .. ne pratum domini ~eretur *Ac. Coll. Wint.*; **1433** aque .. redundant .. super dictum Mawrymedow et illud nimium ~unt *Rec. Leic.* II 251. **b** **14..** omnes qui condempnati sunt .. debent duci .. ad quendam locum vocatum Thefeswelle .. et vivi †festinantur [l. festinanter] depelli et ~i ibidem *Cust. Fordwich* 30 p. 272; *to drowne*, mergere, .. e- *CathA*.

5 to sprout (fig.), originate, come into being; **b** (of storm or sim.).

cultus et ecclesiae fucatur sanctio priscae, / ni coquat emersas calor ecclesiasticus herbas FRITH. 744; unde ~unt concurrentes paucis diximus verbis BYRHT. *Man.* 48; culpa .. vipereum est semen unde tota dolorum seges emerserit PULL. *Sent.* 760A; annum ~entem GERV. TILB. I 6 (v. annus 1b); **1219** quesita unde fides illa emerserit, dicit quod [etc.] *CurR* VIII 53; **c1236** anno quo guerra fuit .. ~ebat obolus qui dicitur *foxalpeni* de v jugis *Cust. Battle* 125; in medio lectionis quando corde placet ~it [ME: *kimeð up*] devocio prevalens multis orationibus *AncrR* 108. **b** **c678** contra gelida brumarum flabra e climate olim septentrionali ~entia ALDH. *Ep.* 3; ut malus abscindi possit tempestate ~ente NECKAM *Ut.* 114.

6 (w. abstr. sb.) to arise, crop up; **b** (pass. *s. act.*); **c** (pr. ppl. as sb. n. pl.).

1164 si calumnia emerserit inter clericum et laicum .. de ullo tenemento *Const. Clar.* 9; GIR. *TH* II *pref.* p. 76 (v. demordere b); [scriptor] incidentium eorum sc. que temporibus suis finitimis regionibus †emenserant [l. emerserant] S. LANGTON *Gl. Hist. Schol.* 39; **1237** (v. determinatio 3a); **c1267** omnia placita .. que emerserunt postquam justiciarii .. ultimo itineraverunt in partibus illis *Cl* 493; **1338** (v. custodia 4b); judicium de difficilibus et obscuris que circa fidem ~unt OCKHAM *Dial.* 496; WALS. *HA* I 170 (v. divergere); *Ps.*-ELMH. *Hen. V* 70 (v. castigativus). **b** **1269** placita foreste .. que post ultima placita foreste sunt emersa et nondum terminata *Cl* 118; **c1298** tam in negociis quam in causis emersis *Reg. Cant.* 247; pro .. scandalis .. que .. ~i solent *MGL* I 357 (v. compistor); quamvis Christiani .. ex causa de novo ~enda [v. l. emergente] servituti possint subjugari OCKHAM *Pol.* I 29; **1448** placitis et querelis .. infra .. libertatem .. emergentibus sive ex nunc ~endis *Reg. Whet.* I 39; **1455** omnimoda escapia .. et transgressiones .. infra .. regnum .. emersa *Ib.* 196. **c** **1295** ~encium nuper necessitas nos inducit confratres .. conlocare *Reg. Cant.* 31; **1318** nisi .. eos ex aliquibus ~entibus impediri contingat (R. BURY *Ep.*) *FormOx* 39; **1325** petit procurator .. fieri in premissis et ea contingentibus, ~entibus, et dependentibus ab eisdem *Lit. Cant.* I 155; **1406** (v. 1 dependere 4c); **1419** quod .. nec cives extra libertatem de ~entibus infra eandem civitatem trahant *MGL* I 160; **1423** singula loci illius emolumenta una cum dependentibus, oneribus, et ~entibus (*Lit. Abbatis*) *Reg. Whet.* II 391; **1429** fuerit et sit ad curiam Cantuariensem cum suis incidenciis, ~enciis, et dependenciis (*Sent.*) AMUND. I 235.

7 (of capital or interest) to accrue; **b** (p. ppl. *s. act.*).

1253 in tam parvo tempore de ix^{xx} li. ~ere non potuerunt cccc li. *SelPlJews* 20; **1280** de xx s. redditus ~entibus de libero tenemento suo *JustIt* 763 m. 5*d.*; **1315** episcopus habebit omnia .. proficua quecumque de corona ~entia *RParl* I 152a. **b** **1253** quod .. de usuris que inde emerse sunt .. ipsos quietos esse faciant *Cl* 198.

emeriatio [cf. AN *emerer* = *to purify, refine*], (?) to clean, polish.

1397 pro pictura, ~one, et vernacione diversorum pavys' *LTR AcWardr* 5 r. 7*d*.

emerite [cf. LL merite], duly, deservedly.

isto modo tironi tradens ensem eques sit factus ~e *G. Herw.* 328b.

emeritio, thanks.

a thanke, meritum, ~io, emericium *CathA*.

emeritus v. emerere.

emerlio [AN *emerlion*, OF *esmerillon*], merlin. *V. et. esmerillunus, merillio.*

1275 inventus erat quidam nidus emerlion' in Bynsrode et presentatus principali forestario *CourtR Wakefield* I 73; **1334** H. H. et W. M. euntibus cum ~onibus ad com. Warenn .. xj d. *Ac. Durh.* 525.

emeroida, emeroyda v. haemorrhois. **emeroidus** v. esmeraldus. **emeroissus** v. haemorrhoicus.

emersio [LL], emergence. **b** outflow. **c** emergency, event, affair.

in baptismo .. trinam mersionem ~o comitatur PULL. *Sent.* 843D. **b** **c1195** concessimus .. fontem .. cum omnibus .. ~onibus suis *Cart. Clerkenwell* 43. **c** dummodo de negotiis suis in eorum ~onibus .. sibi nuntiaretur *Chr. Battle* f. 114v.; **s1302** propter inopinatas ~ones nove guerre *Flor. Hist.* III 309.

emesranda v. esmeraldus.

emeticus [LL < ἐμετικός], emetic.

bulbus ematicus *Alph.* 123 (v. 1 bulbus).

emetiri [CL]

1 a to measure, traverse (a space). **b** to fulfil (a period of time).

a maxima permodica emensus mox caerula lintre / attigit .. litus ALDH. *VirgV* 2805; **778** in longum vallis et sic emenso spatio stratae in quoddam petrosum clivum *CS* 225; Ptolemeus epicyclos .. planetarum figuris et numeris ~itur R. BURY *Phil.* 8. 127. **b** quadrigam Phebo attribuunt .. quod quaternaria sui diversitate diei spatium ~iatur ALB. LOND. *DG* 8. 6.

2 (p. ppl. *emensus s. pass.*): **a** (of a journey) completed. **b** (of a period of time) fulfilled. **c** dealt with.

a adiit, ~a navigatione, Galliae terras *Hist. Abb. Jarrow* 32; itinere .. prolixo .. ~o G. FONT. *Inf. S. Edm.* 2; trium dierum .. ~o itinere GIR. *EH* II 17. **b** ~o unius quadragesimalis circulo ALDH. *VirgP* 13; ~o triennio *Ib.* 52; post ~um temporis sui spatium B. *V. Dunst.* 18A; ~is quippe puerilibus annis AILR. *Ed. Conf.* 766A. **c** ~a sollemnitate paschali BEDE *HE* I 20; ~a, i. transacta, magna consummata *GlH* E 236; AD. MARSH *Ep.* 30 (v. diffusio 2c).

emfimenia v. amphisbaena. **emfr-** v. emphr-. **emi-** v. et. hemi-.

emibilis, buyable; **b** (as sb. n.).

patet quod jus .. vendi non poterit; nullum tale est pecunia ~e WYCL. *Civ. Dom.* I 28; nec videtur aliquid ~e per se pecunia *Id. Sim.* 15. **b** homo .. potest vendere animam suam dyabolo .. sed Deus cum gracia et aliis sibi propriis caret racione ~is *Id. Apost.* 38.

1 emīcare [CL]

1 to dart or spurt out, spring forward; **b** (w. ref. to action of the heart); **c** (w. abstr. subj.).

Carm. Aldh. 3. 34 (v. afflare a); ~at, exilit *GlC* E 175; ~em, exiliam, *þæt ic geleore, gewite GlP* 34; regales exuvias ferro temeravit, unde sanguis undatim ~ans astantium corda pavore concussit W. MALM. *GR* II 160; H. AVR. *CG* f. 9 p. 18 (v. 2 emicare). **b** sequitur nimia cordis calefactio, spiritus corruptio .. non ~at igitur ALF. ANGL. *Cor* 11. 16; [vapor] cor distendens, qua ingressus est, erumpit; spiritus aliorsum exhalat, cum quo etiam virtus ~at *Ib.* 11. 21. **c** universorum conditor mundo suo originales indidit causas quibus confluentibus naturalium rerum progressio ~aret PULL. *Sent.* 729D.

2 (of light) to shine or flash forth (also fig.).

~at, .. elucet *GlC* E 175; in matre praecursoris [sc. J. Baptistae] lux doni caelestis ~uit BEDE *Hom.* I 4. 17; FRITH. 528 (v. crepitaculum); luna .. / emīcat in quadris denis atque kalendis *Kal. M. A.* I 407.

3 to stand out, be conspicuous; **b** (w. pers. subj.); **c** (w. abstr. subj.).

inter globos flammantis incendii incolume tabernaculum .. ~uit BEDE *HE* I 19; haec .. domus .. / .. / emicat egregiis laquearibus atque fenestris ALCUIN *SS Ebor* 1510. **b** Philibertus .. apud Gemmeticum ~uit ORD. VIT. III 1; H. Cantuariensis archiepiscopus .. alter sol in nostro ~at occidente H. READING (II) *Cel.* 30. **c** quanta virtus divina ~uit DOMINIC *V. Ecgwini* I *prol.*; caritas nimirum vestra .. ~ans fructificatione pii operis R. COLD. *Osw.* pref. p. 327; GIR. *IK* I 2 (v. cornicatio).

2 emīcare [cf. CL mica], to crumble.

emīcat panes postquam mus emīcat antris H. AVR. *CG* f. 9 p. 18.

emicatim [LL], brilliantly, in a flash.

~im, resplendenter OSB. GLOUC. *Deriv.* 197; ~im prosiliens W. CANT. *Mir. Thom.* V 1.

emicatio [CL], springing forth, flashing out.

si caloris ~one fit spiritus, necesse est tractu temporis fieri ut prius proxima, deinde remotiora calefiant ALF. ANGL. *Cor* 11. 7; influxa .. lucis et caloris ~one et actu dilatari et permutari non posse *Ib.* 11. 9; aperto .. orificio simul fit ~o ad totum, ut sol oriens .. in remota radios jacit *Ib.* 11. 12.

emicidium, emicidus, emiculum, emicyclum v. hemicyclium. **emigran-** v. hemicran-.

emigrare [CL]

1 to move out or away. **b** (euphem.) to die.

ex ea [sc. Roma] ~ando *V. Greg.* p. 104; ~abit, *ut asceadeþ GlH* E 249; lumina .. que .. radiarant .. vidi .. transferri .. eo transire cupiebam quo lumina ~abant AD. EYNS. *Visio* 12. **b** cum emigro, da clarum vespere J. HOWD. *Ph.* 943.

2 to remove.

ut .. de mundi calamitate translatos se corporis ergastulo ~are inhianter gestiant ALDH. *VirgP* 14; quem Deus .. / .. in furvas emigret luce latebras *Id. VirgV* 2866.

emigratio [LL], emigration; **b** (mon.).

erit tunc .. egressio [anime de corpore], sed ignoratur penitus quo ~o AD. SCOT *QEC* 19. 833C. **b** **s1454** subtraxerunt se ab obediencia abbatis ..; impetraverunt sibi libertatem ~onis ..; imprimis .. frater E. .. vigore bulle papalis de ~one *Reg. Whet.* I 146.

emilianus v. aemilianus. **emina** v. hemina.

†eminamen [? cf. εὐ + μνήμη], commemoration, favourable notice, or (?) *f. l.*

†teto [l. peto] Petri pastoris praesidia, .. alti clari Jacobi eminamina [? l. munimina], multi mundi Mathei merita ..; me defendunt Philippi vocamina *Cerne* 162.

eminare [LL], to drive out.

minet, ~et *GlC* M 211; ~are, .. †prodire [l. perdere] OSB. GLOUC. *Deriv.* 200; dux emīnet [*gl.*: *hors mit*] oves quia fur non emīnet arvis H. AVR. *CG* f. 9. 22.

eminenter [LL], notably, excellently. **b** (log.) in an eminent degree.

†defferentius [MS: differentius], i. ~ius, *todæledlicor* vel *rum[licor] GlH* D 448; **1235** suppetit vobis non mediocriter sed ~er ars edificatoria GROS. *Ep.* 16; AD. MARSH *Ep.* 85 (v. dinoscere 2a); **1337** licet in illis [theologicis et philosophicis] ~er fructificent .. rei tamen familiaris penuriam paciuntur *FormOx* 89. **b** hec noticia obscura et in illa clara includitur ~er DUNS *Ord.* I 39; de cognicione Dei sub racionibus communibus convenientibus sibi et creature que cognita perfeccius et ~ius sunt in Deo quam in aliis *Ib.* II 145; queratur de tercia causa respectu secunde vel respectu prime: .. si respectu secunde sequitur secundam ~er continere perfeccionem totalem que est formaliter in tercia *Ib.* 196.

eminentia [CL]

1 a high place or position. **b** protuberance (on body).

a arce, ~ia *GlC* A 792; **c1230** sex [cereos] in ~ia coram reliquiis .. ibi constitutis *Offic. Sal.* 5; flammarum globi de gurgite marino .. in terrarum ~ias exilire cernuntur AD. MARSH *Ep.* 48. **b** pro naso .. nullam ~iam habens GIR. *TH* II 21; quadrupedia ex quadam pectoris ~ia et aliarum partium concavitate .. ad natandum redduntur habilia *Quaest. Salern.* B 75; fuit ei [Samsoni] quedam ~ia in qua crines .. poris radicitus erant infixi *Ib.* P 125; signando ~iam cum encaustro, faciendo circulum ro[tundum] qui comprehendat totam ~iam GAD. 130. 2.

2 distinction, excellence: **a** (divine); **b** (of person; moral or spiritual); **c** (w. ref. to status); **d** (acad.).

a divinae potestatis ~iam agnoscere BEDE *Gen.* 160B; quanta divine fuit ~ia glorie DOMINIC *V. Ecgwini* I *prol.* **b** laetabatur .. episcopus .. in adventu nepotis considerans in illo .. totius honestatis ~iam OSB. *V. Dunst.* 9; quem plurime meritorum laudabilium commendant ~ie AD. MARSH *Ep.* 167; fideles putant talia a Deo concessa propter ~iam vite *AncrR* 31. **c** **1012** (12c) (v. 2 censorius b); dum ~iam querit fallaciter intumescit J. SAL. *Pol.* 776B. **d** **c1432** nisi racione ~ie gradus magistralis excellencieve sanguinis aut magnitudinis in promocione *StatOx* 239.

3 (as title): **a** (papal); **b** (of cardinal); **c** (royal or unspec.).

a **1095** quod me non egisse rogo ne aegre ferat sancta ~ia vestra ANSELM (*Ep.* 193) IV 82; **1184** placuit Deo et ~ie vestre (*Lit. Prioris ad Papam*) DICETO *YH* II 24. **b** **1338** vestre dominacionis ~iam *FormOx* 100. **c** noverit clarissima reginalis ~ie serenitas quod [etc.] AD. MARSH *Ep.* 154; **1282** monentes .. canonice vestros cujuscunque sint ~ie subditos [etc.] PECKHAM *Ep.* 254.

4 (phil.) eminent quality.

ordo ~ie: primo modo prius dicitur eminens et posterius excessum. et .. quidquid est nobilius et perfeccius secundum essenciam est sic prius DUNS *Prim. Princ.* I 4–5; tres gradus cognoscendi Deum — per ~iam, causalitatem, et abnegacionem *Id. Ord.* IV 172.

eminēre [CL]

1 **a** to protrude, rise, be in a high position. **b** (of person) to stand out, tower. **c** (pr. ppl., also as sb. n.) high (place). **d** (pr. ppl.) protruding.

a ~et, altum est *GlC* E 180; scaurus, cujus calces retro ~ent *Ib.* S 148; oleum .. partibus aque .. cedentibus et aerea .. substantia ad superiora impellente, ~et et supernatat *Quaest. Salern.* W 3; capita .. in .. liquamine nunc sursum ~ebant ex vi ebullionis, nunc deorsum ruebant COGGESH. *Visio* 28; dicitur .. anima 'mens' quia tanquam caput ~et BART. ANGL. III 5; **s1178** in hac planitie duo colliculi ~ebant WEND. I 110; **s1298** (v. castrensis 2a); ex medio .. castri .. ~ebat porta pulcherrima *G. Hen. V* 15. **b** tres virgines .. apparuere quarum .. media ~ebat precelsior DOMINIC *V. Ecgwini* I 8; R. CANT. *Malch.* II 75 (v. cuneus 4). **c** lustrant axis ignifluam / molem mundo minacibus / eminentem cum arcibus (ÆTHELWALD) *Carm. Aldh.* 4. 22; ~enti loco .. stare coeperunt *V. Greg.* p. 97; prom[on]turium, ~ens locus in mare *GlC* P 802; arbores in ~enti positas GIR. *TH* I 6; ad ~entem .. se conferens locum *Id. IK* II 3; preparetur ei [sc. regine] .. solium, solio regis aliquantulum ~enciore existente W. SAY *Lib. Reg. Cap.* 96. **d** [puteus] ferri aculeos ~entes habebat ALEX. CANT. *Mir.* 46 (I) p. 252 (cf. ib. (II): ferri clavos ~entes ad se invicem habebat); sunt in ovibus quibusdam duo dentes ~entiores inter octo ALB. LOND. *DG* 6. 32; oculus ~ens est parvi visus et non videbit bene a remotis BART. ANGL. III 17.

2 to transcend, rise above (fig.).

rebus omnibus quae volvuntur ~ebat *V. Greg.* p. 75 (= BEDE *HE* II 1).

3 to emerge, be revealed. **b** to be imminent; *cf. imminere.*

~uit, apparuit *GlH* E 246; [Februus] eminet at numero bis denis octo diebus *Kal. M. A.* I 399; "ecce solus qui tollit peccata mundi"; nec impetu levitatis hoc creditum ~uit PULL. *Sent.* 780C; H. AVR. *CG* f. 9. 22 (v. eminare). **b** moenia scissa ruunt. / casibus a multis ex omni parte ruina / eminet G. AMIENS *Hast.* 702; **12..** tales perjuri non absolvantur .. nisi mortis periculo ~ente *Conc. Scot.* II 59; **s1402** stella cometa .. quam ipsemet princeps judicavit mortem principis ~entem *Plusc.* X 17.

4 to excel, be preeminent. **b** (pr. ppl.) excellent; **c** (phil.).

cumque tam conspicuis in Christo et aecclesia ~eret et bonorum actuum ornamentis ABBO *Edm.* 4; [sol dicitur] princeps quia ~et BYRHT. *Man.* 16; si rationalis creatura .. sic ~et in omnibus creaturis .. nisi quod supereminet in omnibus naturis ANSELM (*Mon.* 70) I 80; ne si crescat homo et non angelus, ~eat homo PULL. *Sent.* 744D; qui .. divitiis et potestate inter Normannie proceres ~ebat ORD. VIT. III 9 p. 109. **b** his .. cedit omnis continentium ~ens magnitudo ALDH. *VirgP* 14; pollens, ~ens ubique *GlC* P 551; ~entius est locorum misteria credere quam ea videre et eorum misteria non intelligere R. NIGER *Mil.* IV 53; quanto vita ~encior [ME: *herre*] tanto hostis temptacio forcior *AncrR* 59. **c** DUNS *Prim. Princ.* I 4–5 (v. eminentia 4); primum efficiens est ~entissimum *Id. Ord.* II 169; potest intelligi aliquid unum formaliter continens omnem perfeccionem modo ~entissimo, quo possibile est omnes in uno contineri *Ib.* IV 265.

emingere [cf. LL mingere], to urinate.

per illud virgule virilis membrum .. ~ebat sanguinem T. MON. *Will.* III 13.

eminisci [CL], to remember.

~itur, recordatus est *GlC* E 153.

eminoda, (?) clary.

Alph. 132 (v. aurigalis).

eminulus [CL], projecting, slightly protruding.

~is, modice eminentibus *GlC* E 171.

eminus [CL]

1 **a** (mil.) at long range; *cf. comminus* a. **b** (w. vb. of seeing) from a distance, from afar (partly fig.).

a ut sic ~us jactu lapidum .. provocatio fieret OSB. BAWDSEY clxiv; *Ib.* clxx, GARL. *Tri. Eccl.* 13 (v. comminus a); funda et arcu et sagittis ~us expugnandus est hostis magnus veluti Goliath R. NIGER *Mil.* I 16. **b** vidit ~us ex orientis coeli climatibus prorumpentem niveam columbam B. *V. Dunst.* 11; GOSC. *Transl. Aug.* 19C (v. 1 ecstasis 1); ADEL. *ED* 13 (v. cottanum); R. COLD. *Cuthb.* 17 (v. comminus b); propugnacula .. sagittariis ~us observantibus GIR. *EH* I 3; finis memor esse memento; / eminus inspecto fine beatus eris WALT. ANGL. *Fab.* 21. 10; sursum oculos deflectens conspicatur ~us virum .. ad se .. properantem COGGESH. *Visio* 5.

2 far away. **b** apart, aloof. **c** (?) impartially.

ut propulit eminus hostes / monstrabat liquidis salvandos tinguere limphis / .. / nomine [Trinitatis] FRITH. 489; **1390** faciatis ministrari necessaria sua juxta evidentem necessitatem, omni superfluitate ~us profugata *FormOx* 236. **b** vidit .. magos .. ~us stantes altius a ceteris *V. Greg.* p. 98; Odo, ~us a pugna stans, lumina ac manus in celum tetendit EADMER *V. Osw.* 1; ~us .. relictis sociis ipse interius processit DOMINIC *V. Ecgwini* I 8. **c** bene licet tibi [J. ob. **1214**] de substancia ecclesie alicujus pauperis perituri paupertatem relevare. et illud est eleemosyna, ~us assero, irreprehensibilis *G. S. Alb.* I 253.

3 prominently. *Cf. eminenter.*

~us, in promptu, in aperto, palam, in propatulo, coram OSB. GLOUC. *Deriv.* 200; **s1236** quicquid mundus potuit effundere voluptatis et glorie ~us ibi demonstrabat M. PAR. *Maj.* III 339; **s1247** *Ib.* IV 600 (v. credentia 2a).

4 near or (?) *f. l.*

eminus [? l. comminus], prope *GlC* E 164.

emisarius v. emissarius.

emissarium [CL], drain, sluice.

a sluce, emissorium LEVINS *Manip.* 182.

emissarius [CL]

1 emissary, agent. **b** assassin, robber (*cf. Ezek.* vii 22).

emisarii, ministri *GlC* E 148; regis emissarios spernit Matthatias W. COMBE 193; ut singuli crearentur ~ii .. quod (*sic*) fures .. viarumque obsessores proquererent BOECE 26. **b** ~ius, percussor *GlC* E 156; militones, .. ~ii, grassatores, satellites OSB. GLOUC. *Deriv.* 366.

2 stallion; **b** (as adj. w. *equus*; also fig.; *cf. Ecclus.* xxxiii 6); **c** (w. *cervus*).

ascendens ~ium regis pergebat ad idola [destruenda] BEDE *HE* II 13; **9..** emissarius, *steda WW*; †faussarius [l. emissarius], *steda* ÆLF. *Gl.*; **s1014** Suanus .. de ~io cui insederat decidit FL. WORC. I 168; equi fortes ~ii dicuntur, Gallice *estaluns* NECKAM *Sac.* 363; est sonipes .. / istis quadrupedes simul emissarius addes GARL. *Syn.* 398. **1585A**; in .. instauro equarum, ~iorum, cygnorum, et apium quisque [ballivus] studeat instaurare *Fleta* 164; hic ~ius, A. *stalon, stalan WW*. **b** rogavit sibi regem arma dare et equum ~ium BEDE *HE* II 13; equus ~ius, qui mittitur ad jumenta *Gl. Leid.* 12. 35; **a987** (12c) dominae suae reginae .. unum equum ~ium eo pacto ut adjuvaret eum apud regem *CS* 1133; **1174** electus ille, aut potius equus ~ius, .. fluit semine et hinnit in feminas J. SAL. *Ep.* 310 (322 p. 790); si .. arrideat prosperitas ei .. habeat agasonem et mulionem et .. ~ium equum [v. l. admissarium; *gl.*: *stalun*] NECKAM *Ut.* 112; tanquam equus ~ius ad omne jumentum hinniens GIR. *Spec.* II 29; **s1014** tam milites bellatores quam equos ~ios expectabat M. PAR. *Maj.* I 491. **c** jumentum .. cervo ~io pregnans effectum GIR. *IK* I 2 p. 28.

3 (w. *hircus*) scapegoat. (Cf. *Lev.* xvi 8–26).

hircus ~ius portans peccata populi vadit in desertum AD. DORE *Pictor* 163.

emissicius [CL], sent out.

~ius, qui sepe emittitur OSB. GLOUC. *Deriv.* 196.

emissio [CL]

1 dispatch, sending forth.

cibum a Deo praedestinatum per ~onem angeli *V. Cuthb.* I 6; citationum ~o *Dial. Scac.* I 5 N.

2 discharge (of missile).

de cavendis ~onibus et minutorum missilium et tormentorum R. NIGER *Mil.* I 17.

3 (w. ref to *uthleap*) letting out, setting free.

c1075 cum saca et socna et *toll* et *team* et latrone et ~one et hamsocna et *foresteal Regesta* p. 123; *pundbreche* fit pluribus modis, ~one, evocatione, receptione, excussione (*Leg. Hen.* 40. 2) *GAS* 567.

4 (anat.) discharge, emission; **b** (w. ref. to vascular system).

corpore debilitato a sanguinis ~one *Quaest. Salern.* B 96; ~o urine ex voluntario motu provenit .., ~o vero spermatis naturalis est et .. non potest cohiberi *Ib.* 185; [pisces] post ~onem ovorum macrescunt *Ib.* N 20; ALF. ANGL. *Cor* 6. 2 (v. ductus 2a); *SB* 18 (v. diamneticus). **b** saltuosa .. sanguinis ~o spiritus subito generati motu concitato efficitur ALF. ANGL. *Cor* 11. 16.

5 emission (of light or heat).

dum .. lapis cum lapide fortiter .. colliditur, aer interclusus .. accensus flammam emittit, ex cujus ~one utraque substantia ignitur *Quaest. Salern.* B 87; neque aliqua fit lucis ~o sed virtutis ALF. ANGL. *Cor* 11. 12.

6 utterance (of sound).

cujus vocis ~one equus cui insidebat percussus interiit OSB. *V. Dunst.* 24; nunquam hostis ille antiquus .. adeo ecclesiam Dei circumvenit sicut in voti illius ~one GIR. *GE* II 5; sacerdotes propter voti ~onem conjugati esse non possent *Id. Symb.* I 21; **1253** post habitus susceptionem ante professionis ~onem *Cap. Aug.* 32.

7 off-shoot, branch (also fig.; *cf. Cant.* iv 13).

796 ut [sint] .. in Turonica ~ones paradisi cum pomorum fructibus ALCUIN *Ep.* 121; quenam ~ones tue, nisi locutiones et actiones tue, gestus et incessus tui .. et he tue ~ones paradisus sint AD. SCOT *OP* 492AB.

8 extension (in space).

804 (12c) ab occidente et ab austro murus civitatis a statu ecclesiae protenditur in aquilonem ~one virgarum circiter .. xv *CS* 317.

emissivus, emissive, that emits.

omne .. habens lumen intrinsecum est ~um ipsius *Ps.-GROS. Summa* 504.

emissor [LL], one who conjures up.

~ores tempestatum vij annos paeniteant EGB. *Pen.* 4. 14.

emissorium v. emissarium. **emita** v. amita. **emitritheus** v. hemitriteus. **emitrida** v. omotribes.

emittere [CL]

1 to dispatch, send. **b** to send out, dart (glance).

benedixit Deum qui tales hospites .. emiserat ei *V. Cuthb.* IV 3; promittens .. eis .. pretium .. si .. caput ejus [sc. Wilfrithi] occisi sibi emisisset EDDI 27; pluribus emisit sotiis fretum FRITH. 95; de hirco appoponpeio in desertum ~endo R. NIGER *Mil.* II 28; **1220** mater .. filiam suam emiserat per quandam fenestram *CurR* IX 336. **b** quum hac illac sollicitos ~eret visus BYRHT. *V. Ecgwini* 375.

2 **a** to discharge (missile). **b** to shower down. **c** to shed.

a miles sagittam .. emisit ORD. VIT. X 13 (v. catapulta b); sagitte vel lapides in cassum ~untur quando [etc.] R. NIGER *Mil.* I 37. **b** emiserunt ei argenti folia rotunda .. ac vinum ex canellis et fistulis aqueductus; .. emiserunt in caput regis subgredientis minas aureas *G. Hen. V* 15. **c** emissis superfluis pilis [cervi] incipiunt alia crescere *Quaest. Salern.* Ba 11.

3 to release, set free.

portus .. undas .. quas jam recepit ~it et amittit GIR. *TH* II 2; latro de carcere liber emittitur WALT. WIMB. *Carm.* 566; emiserunt cum rex per eos venerat passeres *G. Hen. V* 15.

4 (anat.) to discharge (also internally). **b** to drain, empty.

~ere se sensit .. calculum a virga virili BEN. PET. *Mir. Thom.* IV 98; licet .. sanguis ~atur in multa quantitate *Quaest. Salern.* B 40; queritur quare cum quis sompniet se ~ere sperma, semen ~at, cum licet sompniet ~ere urinam, non ~at *Ib.* 185; splen pultis .. per nares ~itur *SB* 40; **s1450** (v. devenustare a). **b** fissuras ~ere non desiit R. COLD. *Cuthb.* 138 (v. curamen).

5 to emit, give off; **b** (w. abstr. obj.).

lux emissa caelitus BEDE *HE* IV 7; si queratur 'an ad utendum visu aliquid per oculos ~atur', ut ait Plato, 'an intus suscipiatur' BALSH. *AD rec.* 2 175; *Quaest. Salern.* B 87 (v. emissio 5); **s1301** isto anno cometes apparuit, radios versus celum ~ens *Feud. Man.* 118. **b** ~unt Pater et Filius pariter tantum bonum ANSELM (*Mon.* 54) I 66; nullum alium sudorem ~es nisi vitium solum P. CORNW. *Rev.* I 183.

6 (of sound): **a** to emit, give forth. **b** to utter. **c** to raise (key).

a *GlC* B 34 (v. barrire); quam .. vocem .. clamosus anser ~et? GIR *TH intr.* p. 6; quare cygnus imminente morte delectabilem vocem ~it? *Quaest. Salern.* R 7; M. PAR. *Maj.* V 145 (v. dolium 1a). **b** si .. millenos sonos ferrea lingua contra naturam ~erem B. *V. Dunst.* 29; **1304**

cum . . invenerimus fratrem R. . . professionem regularem monasticam nullatenus emisisse *Reg. Cant.* 792; odas ~it ROLLE *IA* 238; c**1358** verba . . emiserant (v. divinator); PAUL. ANGL. *ASP* 1558 (v. dispensabilis 2). **c** cantor omnem cantum . . poterit ~ere et submittere. si quis submisse †inciperit [l. inceperit], pro voto suo ~et *Obed. Abingd.* 370.

7 (w. spiritum) to give up the ghost, die. (*Cf. Matth.* xxvii 50).

Dominus . . nona hora spiritum emisit THEOD. *Pen.* II 5. 5; sine ullo sensu doloris emisit spiritum BEDE *HE* IV 11; BYRHT. *HR* 46 (v. clericatus 1a); s**1312** febre vexatus spiritum emisit TROKELOWE 72; aliqui asserunt Platonem spiritum emisisse quia non solvebat questionem nautarum *Eul. Hist.* I 425.

8 (of plant) to put forth (shoots; also fig.).

vinea Domini . . laborantibus colonis sparsim suas propagines emisit ORD. VIT. III 1 p. 4; W. JUM. IV 1 (v. dulcifluus 1b).

9 to send into. *V. et. immittere.*

petamus . . Deum . . ut animam hujus pueri [mortui] in corpus ~at et vivat EDDI 23.

emleg v. emblicus. **emmend-** v. emend-. **emmologare** v. homologare. **emodosis** v. haematosis. **emol-** v. et. esmall-. **emola** v. aëneola. **emolare** v. emolere, esmallare.

emolere [CL], to grind, whet, sharpen; **b** (fig.). **c** (p. ppl.) sharp-edged.

quam [sc. cultelli laminam] perfectam cum vellet ~ere BEN. PET. *Mir. Thom.* IV 69; **1188** pro iij molis ad esmolendas operationes regis . . xij s. et j d. *Pipe* 14; **1229** mandamus vobis quod habere facias Willelmo le Favre . . quendam lapidem ad emolend[os] quarellos quos fabricat *Liberate* 8 m. 11; **1234** Johannes Faber . . debet emolare falces omnium falcatorum domini *Cust. Glast.* 59. **b** aperto corde decurrit non ut ~at aut lucretur, et in emolumentum et lucrum incautus illabitur MAP *NC* V 3 f. 60. **c** **1251** siccum quod jacuit per terram quod colligere possent manibus suis sine armis ~itis *IMisc* 5 m. 24; fecit . . plagam mortalem . . quodam gladio vel aliquo genere armorum ~itorum *Fleta* 48; **1283** gladium emolutum *RGasc* II 210.

emoliment- v. emolument-. **emolitus, ~utus** v. emolere.

emollescere [LL], to become soft (fig.). **b** to become effeminate.

emollescas, mens licet aspera J. HOWD. *Ph.* 197. **b** a domesticis curis castratus ~it MAP *NC* III 5 f. 42v.

emolog- v. homolog-. **emoloment-** v. emolument-.

emollire [CL]

1 to soften; **b** (med.).

emolli saxea WALT. WIMB. *Carm.* 74. **b** curabant medici hunc [tumorem] adpositis pigmentorum fomentis ~ire BEDE *HE* IV 30 p. 279.

2 (fig.): **a** (w. ref. to heart or mind) to soften, mellow. **b** to weaken. **c** to relax.

a obstinata mens nullis terroribus ~ita ALCUIN (*Adv. Felicem*) *Dogm.* 199D; ut . . predicatione . . populi duritiam ~iant R. NIGER *Mil.* II 46; GERV. TILB. *pref.* (v. dilucidus c); animum . . sic ~uit et mitigavit GIR. *Spec.* II 1; *Id. RG* II 18 (v. duritia 3). **b** ejus ~ire constantiam BEDE *HE* I 7. **c** illud quod in regula sequitur . . rigori deputatur, qui prelati dispensatione possit ~iri ROB. BRIDL. *Dial.* 164.

3 to refine (a sound).

eorlas . . nomine ~ito *earles* CAMD. *Br.* 135 (v. 1 comes 4a).

emolumentarium, money-chest (for multure).

a multer arke, emolimentarium *CathA*.

emolumentum [CL]

1 grinding.

molares . . dentes . . ad ciborum ~a . . capaciores R. COLD. *Osw.* 51 p. 380.

2 advantage, benefit. **b** emolument, profit, due (esp. multure). **c** (spiritual) recompense, reward.

malens scripturarum ~o litterarum carnalis vitae nutrimenta . . adipisci ALDH. *Met.* (*Allocutio*) 4; vertens . . / in ficus spinas et in emolumenta ruinas *V. Anselmi Epit.* 97; [expulsi clerici] gule et libidini . . deserviebant et secularibus ~is ORD. VIT. III 2 p. 22; tres dicuntur persone non temporis ~o discrete H. READING (I) *Fid. Cath.* 1327A; WALS. *HA* II 145 (v. confluentia d). **b** ~um, *lean, fultum*; emolomentum, lucrum, †mercis [l. merces] labo[ris] *GlC* E 154–5; cum sodalibus . . quibus suppeteret amplitudo terrae ad regnandi ~um ABBO *Edm.* 1; ne . . ad ~um mercimoniale cupidos mortalium animos ipsa provocaret abundantia GIR. *TH* II 40; c**1250** liceat . . priori et conventui . . ~a medietatis molendini in suos usus convertere *Cart. Blyth* 130; **1308** in aliquo . . tuto loco una ponatur archa vel truncus . . in quo elemosine et emolimentum . . recondantur (*Lit. Papae*) *Reg. Carl.* II 46; **1309** de . . emulumento ipsius scribanie . .; ad dictam scribaniam, ~um, et custodiam rotulorum *RGasc* IV 282; **1337** A. petit integram restitucionem de . . animalibus . . unacum restitucione ~orum de totis catallis *ExchScot* 436; proventus . . et emolimenta racione sui officii ad decanum pertinencia . . sunt ista W. SAY *Lib. Reg. Cap.* 61; ~um, A. *tolle*; hoc emolumentum, *a meltyre WW*; *a multer*, emolimentum, multura *CathA*; **1546** alios omnes redditus, proficuos, et ~a . . academie . . proveniencia *StatOx* 340. **c** beatae perennis vitae felicitas, quae singulis . . meritorum ~is recompensabitur ALDH. *Met.* 2; a**690** quid . . prosunt bonorum operum ~a si extra catholicam gerantur ecclesiam? *Id. Ep.* 4; **963** (12c) semper mansura supernae patriae emulumenta adipiscentes *CS* 1124; quale est amoris ~um? ANSELM (*Mon.* 70) I 80.

emop- v. haemop-. **emor-** v. et. haemorrh-.

emordēre [cf. CL mordēre], to gnaw away (fig.)

1461 gens boree, gens vipere pellis generisque / mordet et emordet, rodit, corrodit, et urget / matris ad interitum (*Vers.*) *Reg. Whet.* I 400.

emori [CL], to die, perish. **b** (w. abstr. subj.) to die away, die out. **c** (p. ppl. *emortuus*) dead (also fig.). **d** atrophied, paralysed.

velut ~iens sensum . . omnem perdidi BEDE *HE* V 6; GOSC. *Transl. Aug.* 36B (v. dum 2a, 3b); res in tantum patrem pueri contristaverat ut mallet ~i quam filium . . non vindicare ALEX. CANT. *Mir.* 29 p. 217; Eduinus . . ~i quam vivere peroptavit ORD. VIT. IV 7 p. 216; si piscis unius ad . . lacum alterius deferatur . ., ~itur GIR. *TH* I 10. **b** divinitas . . ~i sivit LANTFR. *Swith. pref.*; carnalis concupiscentia contemta ~itur ALB. LOND. *DG* 11. 9; ibi fides ~itur H. READING (I) *Dial.* 1199; in te prava radix hec [amaritudinis] ~itur G. HOYLAND *Ascet.* 277A; hoc . . miraculo . . revivixit memoria que . . fere funditus jam fuerat emortua T. MON. *Will.* II 7 p. 84; caritas, si non ~itur, certe . . languidior fit J. FORD *Serm.* 7. 1. **c** cum Judaeorum populo ~a membra peccati conversae ad Deum gentilitatis ostendit BEDE *Sam.* (*1 Sam.* xviii 27) 633; **801** corpore propemodum ~o vivida caritatis virtus vivit in pectore ALCUIN *Ep.* 218; nec consideravit corpus suum ~um nec vulvam Sare ~am R. MELUN *Paul.* 79; corpus ~um vulneraverunt NECKAM *NR* II 176; ut possit ~um recreare spiritum G. HOYLAND *Ascet.* 283A; os frigidum, os ~um, et os aridum J. FORD *Serm.* 53. 9; **1306** boscum ~um ad ardendum *BBC* (*Swansea*) 68. **d** enervum, ~um *GlC* E 207; ~us, ex parte mortuus, . . enervus, i. sine virtute, *aswunden*, ~us *GlH* E 255, 268; ita a puero debilitatus ut a lumbis ac deorsum per totum ~us duobus inniteretur bacillis OSB. *Mir. Dunst.* 13; inferioris corporis partibus ~is . . tibiarum ad pedum ~a vis *Mir. Fridesw.* 94; [paralysis reddit] corporis totum stupidum torpens et quasi ~um *V. Har.* 2 f. 4b.

emotride v. omotribes.

emovēre [CL], to remove, displace.

emota, i. separata, conversa *GlH* E 254; emotus, semotus, amotus, divisus, segregatus, sepositus OSB. GLOUC. *Deriv.* 200.

emoviare [cf. emovere], ? to remove.

cedulam . . ab auditorio . . cardinalium . . ~iatam de eorumque voluntate et mandato in audiencia . . pape positam atque lectam *Canon. S. Osm.* 11.

emparantia [OF *emparance*], protection, possession, seisin (Gasc.).

1289 senescallus . . Xanctonie posuit ipsos in ~a castrorum et villarum de C. et de M. *RGasc* II 355; **1313** eidem . . promittimus firmam guirenciam et amparanciam *Ib.* IV 973; **1437** possessiones que pro nunc existunt sub gubernacione et imparencia ipsius comitis *Arch. Gironde* XVI 246.

emparare [OF *emparer*], to take possession of, seize (Gasc.).

1242 ratione dictorum defectuum dictos homines ~avimus et tenemus in manu nostra (*Pat*) *RGasc* I 166; **1279** ad . . requirendum deliberari surprisa, sasita, vel alias amparata per vos *Ib.* II 82.

emparatio, possession, seisin (Gasc.).

1289 seisinam seu ~onem quam poni feceramus in . . molendinis . . amovimus *RGasc* II 334.

emparator [cf. OF *empareur*], possessor, occupier (Gasc.).

1289 promittimus . . Hodino . . portare bonam et firmam perpetuo guarantiam ab omnibus ~oribus tam proprietatis quam dominii *RGasc* II 473.

empatica v. hepatica. **empaust-** v. empost-. **empema** v. empyema. **emper-** v. empir-, empyr-. **emperiscon, emperiston** v. euporistus.

emphasis [CL < ἔμφασις], (rhet.) emphasis, stress. **b** implication of more than is stated explicitly. **c** metonymy.

~is, i. e. exaggeratio, quod gradatim crescit *Gl. Leid.* 28. 69; Paulus: 'revelatur enim ira Dei de coelo . . super omnem . . injustitiam (~is) eorum' LANFR. *Comment. Paul.* (*Rom.* i 18) 109; ~is Grece idem est quod expressio Latine VINSAUF *AV* II 2. 34. **b** plurima perstringat paucis expressa locutrix / emphasis VINSAUF *PN* 694; ~is est quedam figura que longam seriem verborum curtat eleganter *Id. AV* II 2. 32. **c** alius modus ~eos quando . . rem appellamus nomine sue proprietatis *Ib.*; circuitio in coloribus idem est quod ~is in figuris *Id. CR* 325; 'vivax senectus' ~is est, i. e. vivax senex TREVET *Troades* 7.

emphatice [cf. LL emphaticos < ἐμφατικῶς], pointedly, emphatically.

~e dictum est ut id quod vanitas dicitur vanum esse intelligatur NECKAM *Eccles.* f. 74; si . . ponantur duo nomina, . . alterum ~e, reliquum . . sine emphasi GERV. MELKLEY *AV* 72.

emphaticus [LL < ἐμφατικός], affirmative, emphatic, forceful. **b** implying more than is stated explicitly, pregnant.

per ~as locutiones, per clausulas non internexas, vinculo copulative conjunctionis conglutinanda est sententia VINSAUF *AV* II 2. 31; emphatice lucis provecta caterva relinquit / solem pallentem, sol quia sole latet / a quo lumen habet sol noster GARL. *Epith.* VII 65. **b** 'Filius est essencia de essencia'. . . ad primum dicendum quod talia verba significativa sunt et ~a, hoc est expressiva, ut in Filio per nomen essencie intelligatur veritas paterne substancie, unde sensus est 'essencia est de essencia', i. e. Filius qui est essencia est de Patre qui est essencia PECKHAM *QR* 26.

empheria v. empiria. **emphiot-, emphit-** v. emphyt-.

emphracticus [LL < ἐμφρακτικός], (med.) obstructive, causing obstruction.

quando [sincopis] est ex distensione matricis, decoquantur . . petro[selinum], †apii [l. apium], et alia †eufratica in aqua et intingatur filtrum et superponatur GILB. IV 202. 1; fiat stupha cum herbis †eufraticis ut ebulo, sambuco [etc.] *Ib.* 254v. 1; fiat stupha cum herbis calidis †eufracticis diureticis *Ib.* 263v. 2; emfraxis interpretatur opilacio, inde emfracticum, i. opilativum, et exemfracticum *Alph.* 56.

emphraxis [LL < ἔμφραξις], (med.) obstruction.

~em, ut pulmones †coangustare [l. coangustati] †cepere [l. capere] spiritus non sufficiant et quasi †concitus [l. concisos] emitta[n]t *GlC* E 181; enfraxim fecerunt, i. e. opilationem et obstruxionem *Quaest. Salern.* Ba 35; enfraxis epatis GILB. I 51v. 1; dolor ex enfraxi humorum oppilantium *Ib.* II 94. 2; valet . . paralisi omnium membrorum; maxime capitis †enfraxini [l. enfraxim] epatis et splenis . . solvit *Ib.* 119. 2; enfrasis quelibet in epate *Ib.* VI 239v. 1; emfraxis aliquando dicitur duricies et aliquando opilacio viarum urinalium *SB* 19; emfraxis *Alph.* 56 (v. emphractus).

emphyteusis [LL < ἐμφύτευσις], emphyteusis, (tenure of) hereditary leasehold.

laborant quod terras quascunque seu precario seu commodato locationis, conductionis, ~eoseos, vel alio quocunque titulo semel ipsos possidere contigerit . . easdem tanquem proprias . . sibi . . vindicabunt GIR. *DK* II 4; a quibus [sacerdotibus] sepe more secularium prediorum aliis atque aliis relinquuntur ad firmam quod emphitosim nuncupant AD. EYNS. *Hug.* V 3 p. 87; **1258** (1311) retinemus omnes possessiones que de . . ecclesia tenentur in emphiteozim *Reg. Gasc. A* I 158; **1276** concessionem, tradicionem, seu dimissionem in feodum immediatum seu emphiteosim quas . . Lucas . . fecit Guillelmo . . de . . placea *RGasc* II 29; **1281** molendinum . . tenendum a nobis . . in emphitesim *Ib.* 137; **1283** concedere . . forestam . . ad puram et perpetuam enfitheosim *Ib.* 213; **1287** ut . . [res immobiles] in perpetuum emphiteosim concedere nullo modo presumant *Conc. Syn.* 1024; **1306** concedimus . . Johanni . . in feodum seu emphitheosim perpetuam unam virgatam terre *FormA* 280; **1335** ut . . porciones prebendales . . in emphiteosim licite concedere valeas *Reg. Exon.* II 778; **13..** in modicis et stirilibus permittitur contractus ~eosis *Reg. Aberd.* I 152; aut est emphitiosis ecclesie et ecclesia potest repetere a fisco . . aut est emphitiosis alterius privati; si . . est talis emphitiosis que forte ex conventione transiret in alium extraneum heredem tunc transibit in fiscum UPTON 51; in evidentem . . utilitatem in emphiteosim seu in firmam perpetuam . . tradere . . intendunt (*Ch. Episc. Wigorn.*) *MonA* IV 453a; **1539** (v. dimittere 7f); **1559** (v. arrentare 1a); **1556** ad feudifirmam seu emphiteosim hereditarie dimisisse *Reg. Brechin* II 206.

emphyteuta [LL < ἐμφυτευτής], lessee, tenant in em-phyteusis.

1277 [deveria] que alii feodarii seu emphiteote facere debent . . dominis suis pro feodis que ab eis tenent *RGasc* II 30; **1433** (v. affeuatus); hec obligacio personalis prosequitur possessorem: secus est in alio emphiteota UPTON 51; **1479** (v. 1 censarius 2c); **1533** nobiles et alii emphiteote et fanaterii ex perditione jurium nostrum recusant nobis satisfacere de redditibus *Reg. Heref.* 274.

emphyteutarius, held by emphyteusis.

1549 ut nullae fiant infeudationes seu emphiteutariae locationes . . terrarum ecclesiasticarum *Conc. Scot.* II 94.

emphyteuticarius [LL], lessee, tenant in emphyteusis.

si ager vectigalis i. e. emphiteotecarius petatur (*tit.*) VAC. *Lib. Paup.* 86; ordinarium est quod emphiteotecarius perpetuo possideat et heredes ejus *Ib.*; creditor et superficiarius jus habent in re et emphitethecar' *Ib.* 157; **1285** omnibus baronibus nostris, castellanis, vavassoribus, vassallis, feodataris, emphiteotecariis *RGasc* II 246.

emphyteuticus [LL], emphyteutic. **b** (as sb. m.) lessee, tenant in emphyteusis.

monachi . . ecclesiam . . parochialem . . emphioteticis ad firmam pactionibus a persona suscipere . . apposuerunt GIR. *Spec.* III 1 p. 135; quid de feudo emphitiotico an publicatis bonis feudatarii transeat feudum in fiscum UPTON 51; **1591** instrumentum saisinae illius tenementi emphiteotici quondam Jacobi C. *Reg. Brechin* II 228. **b** **1546** si . . premissa facere recusaverit . . ut bonus emphiteoticus facere debeat, . . cadet . . a jure hujusmodi infeodationis *Reg. Aberd.* I 431.

empi- v. et. empy-. **empiala** v. empyema. **empic-, empisc-** v. empyic-. **empima, empina** v. empyema. **empipedum** v. epipedon.

empiria [LL *gl.* < ἐμπειρία], experience.

empheria, experientia multorum *GlC* E 161 (cf. ib. 239: ephyria, experientia); ∼ia, *manegra embesmeagunga* ÆLF. *Gl.*.

1 empiricus [CL < ἐμπειροικός], empirical, known by experience; **b** (med., also fig.). **c** (as sb. n.) empirical remedy.

secunda pars [astronomie] est de qualitate et modo cognoscendi motum firmamenti, ortum signorum super rebus empericis antequam fiant sub firmamento lune BACON V 62. **b** theodorico emperico GILB. III 139. 1; consistit in duobus modis operandi, sc. artificiali et emperico GAD. 126. 1; ecce tiriaca emperica contra subrepentem superbiam WYCL. *Dom. Div.* 18. **c** nota emperica in hac egritudine multum juvare GILB. II 111. 1; pes lupinus collo suspensus colices juvat; empericum est *Ib.* V 227v. 1; emperica . . juvant in hac infirmitate *Ib.* VI 269v. 2; empericum est hoc medicis LEDREDE *Carm.* 29. 16.

2 empiricus v. empyricus.

empirus [ἔμπειρος], (as sb. m.) expert, experienced man.

†lempiris crutton empiris et utique lillo [? l. ἔμπειρος κρύπτων ἐμπείροις et utique (κ)ίλλο(ς) i. e. *an expert concealing (his knowledge) from experts, and assuredly an ass*] *Altercatio* 96.

empitostonos v. emprosthotonos.

emplastrare [LL < CL = *to bud, graft* (*a tree*)]

1 (med.) to plaster. **b** to apply as a plaster.

utantur dieta frigidissima . . et ∼etur epar frigidis GILB. I 24. 2. **b** *Reg. Malm.* II *pref.* lvii (v. anthrax); GAD. 5v. 2 (v. atriplex a); tapsus barbatus . . pistatus . . et ∼atus circa manus ab intrante, domo ejus inimicus exiet *Alph.* 182.

2 (arch.) to plaster.

1240 mandatum est Edwardo filio Odonis quod . . faciat . . cameram privatam [regis] ∼ari *Cl* 172; c**1280** de vadiis implastratorum . . Willelmo le Daubour . . et ministris suis facientibus et implastrantibus domos, astelerias, et ceteras mansiones *KRAc* 85/22 m. 3.

emplastratio [CL]

1 (agr.) budding, grafting.

caseus sit et ∼io pomis *Brev. Sal.* I June.

2 (med.) applying a plaster (also fig.). **b** plaster.

s**1457** (v. chirurgicus c). **b** ∼ones fiant super epar ex rebus vere infrigidativis GAD. 8v. 2.

3 (arch.) plastering. **b** plasterwork.

c**1266** in ∼one aule, cum serruris emptis ad turrim *ExchScot* 20. **b** **1534** J. tegulatori emendanti implastrationem cubiculi . . presidentis *Arch. Hist. Camb.* II 31*n.*

emplastrator, plasterer.

c**1280** (v. emplastrare 2); **1354** Ricardo Waltham implastrat[ori] operanti super reparacione coster' gradus camere senescalli *KRAc* 471/6 m. 17.

emplastria, plaster (arch.).

1277 v hominibus ducentibus ∼iam de Wirhale usque Rodolanum ad construccionem camere regine *KRAc* 3/15 m. 2.

emplastrum [CL < ἔμπλαστρον]

1 (med.) plaster, poultice; **b** (for animal); **c** (fig.).

debilia corpora recipiunt cataplasma et ∼a cum antidoto sanitatis BYRHT. *V. Osw.* 422; multis potionibus, pillulis . . ∼is, et unguentis usus W. CANT. *Mir. Thom.* II 32; malagma genus est ad ∼um et epithema BELETH *RDO* 55. 62; tumorem ex morsu aranee provenientem sedat ∼um de muscis factum loco doloris superpositum NECKAM *NR* II 113; non potuit sustinere quod . . aliquis . . emplaustrum apponeret *Mir. Montf.* 94; **1288** pro oleo, melle, et aliis implastris (*AcWardr*) *TR Bk.* 201 p. 28; **1290** cum implaster[is] et aliis medicinalibus (*Ib.*) *Chanc. Misc.* 4/5 f. 5; cum implastar[is] et aliis emptis medicinis *Ib.* f. 9v.; **1322** ad officium suum drogereis emptis pro implastro et aliis medicinalibus (*KRAc* 379/3) *Cal. Scot.* III 766; *SB* 15 (v. cerotum b); *Alph.* 19 (v. basilicon 1); **1414** ∼um †restrativum j li. viij d., ∼um de granis laurei vj unc' iiij d. *Invent. Med.* 71–2. **b** **1312** stalones: . . in unct' empt' pro implastr[o] fac[iendo] *MinAc* 843/3. **c** his in tormentis deerant emplastra medentis *V. Anselmi Epit.* 49; diabolus facit ∼um de congerie rerum temporalium et proicit in oculos prelatorum O. CHERITON *Fab.* 29; c**1430** (v. chirurgicus c).

2 (arch.) plaster. **b** plasterwork.

1311 implastrum emptum: Johanni le Marmer pro implastro ab eo empto per regem (*AcWardr*) *MS BL Cotton Nero* C VIII f. 57; **1313** pro implastr[o] deonerand[o] extra naves. . . in stipendio j carpentarii facientis *pynnes* et perforantis *les laces* . . camere pro implastr[o] melius tenendo *MinAc* 843/4. **b** **1335** (v. 1 caminus 1a).

†**emplatin,** *s. dub.*

nonne venies in numerum legistarum . . nisi scias quid ∼in, que res parafernales? NECKAM *NR* II 174.

emplaustrum v. emplastrum.

emploiare [AN *emploier*, OF *emploiier*], to employ, use. *Cf. implicare.*

1452 canones et ancoras . . tali modo ∼andas prout rex sibi agere mandavit *Ac. Foreign* 86 r. G.

†**emponenth** [? cf. OF *en ponant*], form of good omen.

M. SCOT *Phys.* 57 (v. confert).

emporiolum, small market.

Padstow ∼um habet CAMD. *Br.* 157; Lidston, ∼um tenue *Ib.* 161.

emporium [CL < ἐμπόριον], market.

∼ium, locus super mare ubi negotiant[ur] homines *GlC* E 162; Lundonia . . multorum ∼ium [v. l. emptorium] populorum terra marique venientium BEDE *HE* II 3; c**1104** hoc facite proclamari in vestre vicinitatis circumjacentibus impuriis H. LOS. *Ep.* 7; empurium, emtorium, ubi aliquid emitur OSB. GLOUC. *Deriv.* 192; insane proditor, . . / . . irrita stultum commercium / et Jhesum iterum duc ad emporium WALT. WIMB. *Carm.* 462.

†**empostaticos** [cf. empostatus; ? cf. ὑποστατικός], stable, enduring.

hoc . . verbum sufficiens / . . / est enim stabile, manens non transiens, / sed empostatocon et indeficiens WALT. WIMB. *Carm.* 200.

†**empostatus** [? cf. ἐμπαύομαι *conf. w.* ὑπόστατος *misinterp. as* εὐ-], stable, enduring.

perfectum et ∼um, i. e. subsistens WALT. WIMB. *Elem.* f. 13v. (cf. ib. f. 24: Dei verbum ex seipso genitum non secundum verbum nostrum ampostaton, i. e. subsistens, sed empaustaton, i. e. subsistens).

empriza v. imprisa.

empromptum [AN *emprompt*, OF *emprunt*], loan.

1195 de remanenti emprunti facti . . per Johannem *RScacNorm* I 208; de †empructo facto . . per Robertum *Ib.* 209; emprumtum ville de Ponte Audemer *Ib.* 210; **1198** de empromto facto *Ib.* II 294; **1199** de empromtis liiij li. vj s. x d. *DCCant.* D4 f. 2a; **1201** empromtum cc li. xlvj s. iiij d. *Ib.* f. 9a; **1207** de enprunto c li. *Ib.* V.M.A. f. 59; **1214** de emprunto xxxiiij li. *Ib.* f. 54; c**1214** de emprunto sc. de magistro *Lit. Cant.* II *intr.* xlv; **1223** de emprumpto *DCCant. Ac. Thes.* I 67b.

emprosthotonos [LL < ἐμπροσθότονος], (med.) drawn forward.

dividitur [spasmus] . . secundum locum, quare alius †epitostonos [l. opisthotonos], alius protostonos vel emprotostonos, alius thetanus; quod [opi]tostonos interpretatur, quasi supra elevatus, cum nervi posteriores contrahuntur et digiti in pugnum deducuntur; protostonos sive emprotostonos in se tenens sive inclinatus interpretatur, cum nervi anteriores contrahuntur et caput incurvatur et coacti digiti extenduntur et aperiuntur; et thetanus equaliter tenens, nervi enim anteriores et posteriores equaliter contrahuntur GILB. II 122v. 1; spasmus . . est ante et dicitur †empitostonus GAD. 102. 1.

emprumptum, emprumtum, empruntum v. empromptum.

emptare [*backformed from* emptus, *p. ppl. of* emere], to buy.

1230 ad carbonem ∼andum et ponendum in castro *Pipe* 111.

empticius [CL]

1 obtained by purchase, bought: **a** (of servant, *cf. Gen.* xvii 12, *Exod.* xii 44); **b** (of thing); **c** (W., of land, *tir pryn* 'bought land', held by payment of *twnc*); **d** (of abstr.).

a nos servi ejus ∼ii sumus R. MELUN *Paul.* 17; servus ∼ius, advena et mercenarius BALD. CANT. *Sacr. Alt.* 740D. **b** libros non paucos vel . . emptos vel amicorum dono largitos retulit. rediens . . ∼ios ibi, quos apud amicos commendaverat, recepit BEDE *HA* 4; quisquis inde portaret sal vel proprium vel ∼ium dabat theloneum *DB* I 268 (cf. ib: quicunque emptum sal carro portabat). **c** **1334** medietas terre eorum est terra emptica a tempore principum propter quam nullum reddunt pastum *Surv. Denb.* 58 (cf. ib. 124: terra emptica a principe). **d** ccc m. . . abbas [V. ob. c**1129**] dedit regi in confirmatione sue libertatis ne si forte . . homines hundredi et mercatus libertatem . . quasi suum proprium sibi vendicarent emptiticium *Chr. Abingd.* II 164; he sunt laudes ∼ie conducti vulgi, quibus extollebant ad astra Galonem MAP *NC* III 2 f. 37.

2 (as sb.): **a** (m.) purchased servant. **b** (n. pl.) purchased property.

a ∼ius, *ceapcneht GlC* E 151; ∼ius, *geboht þeowa* ÆLF. *Sup.*; **9..** ∼ius, *hæftincel WW*; 'non estis vestri', quia servi Christi estis vel ∼ii . . 'empti enim estis pretio magno' LANFR. *Comment. Paul.* (*1 Cor.* vi 20) 175. **b** **1151** quod terras et ∼ia sua et teneuras et vadimonia sua in pace teneant *Regesta* 729.

3 (?) buyer, merchant.

∼ius, i. emptor, venditor, *cepemon GlH* E 251.

emptimema v. enthymema.

emptio [CL]

1 buying, purchasing; *cf. emere* 3. **b** office of caterer, purchasing department. **c** (w. *vidua*) payment for widow's right to remarry.

haec terra est de ∼one *DB* I 133v.; haec mater aecclesia medietatem sepulture . . habuit per ∼onem *DB* II 281v.; contraditum pro testimonio . . ∼onum quibus ipsa monasterio suo plures adquisivit possessiones GOSC. *Milb.* 201; in ∼one prospicitur ne ultra justi pretii dimidium homo †circumveniantur [l. circumveniatur] R. NIGER *Mil.* IV 30; **1290** per . . vendiciones sive ∼ones terrarum *StRealm* I 106. **b** **1385** Willelmus Hicche, unus valettorum nostrorum officii ∼onis hospicii nostri *Pat* 320 m. 38; **1397** serviens officii ∼onis hospicii nostri *Pat* 346 m. 27. **c** **1204** quieti sint de murdro . . et de *scotele* et de ∼one viduarum *BBC* (*Marlborough*) 151.

2 a purchase, purchased property.

1141 sciatis me reddidisse et concessisse . . omnes terras et tenementa . . in feoudis, in firmis, in ministeriis, in vadiis, in ∼onibus et hereditatibus *Regesta* 634; c**1255** (v. contingere 1d); **1263** ad emciones regis in instantibus nundinis Stamf' inde acquietandas *Cl* 216.

emptiticius v. empticius.

emptor [CL], buyer, purchaser; **b** (fig.). **c** caterer.

8.. ∼or, *beccen WW*; vasa sancta . ., quia domi invenire non potuit, de transmarinis regionibus advectare religiosus ∼or curabat BEDE *HA* 5; *GlH* E 251 (v. empticius 3); venditores . . ita et ∼ores [liberorum] tam enormi delicto juga servitutis . . meruisse GIR. *EH* I 18; c**1255** (v. contingere 1d); **1290** ∼ores terrarum . . de feodis magnatum . . in prejudicium [eorundem] . . feodis suis sunt ingressi *StRealm* I 106; **1371** (v. conqueri 1a); hic ∼or, *a byer WW*. **b** sic in altero veritatis venditor esse probatur, in altero vero ejusdem veritatis ∼or fuisse asseritur ALEX. CANT. *Mir.* 46 (I) p. 251; J. SAL. *Pol.* 569A, HANV. IX 326 (v. emere 2a); in sacra virginis taberna pocio / non eris emitur sed morum precio; / emptoris sufficit digna condicio / sine pecunia, sine denario WALT. WIMB. *Carm.* 137. **c** **1264** Hugoni . . et Roberto . . ∼oribus garderobe [sc. regis] *Cl* 3; *Fleta* 80 (v. 2 clericus 2a); **1336** item cuidam ∼ori domine regine viij s. x d. *Ac. Durh.* 528.

emptoria, office of caterer, purchasing department.

1502 Edmundus Sharpe valettus ∼ie nostre *Pat* 590 m. 30(7); **1529** Thome Hordey clerico ∼ie nostre *DL Misc. Bk.* 22 f. 104.

emptorium, market. **b** booth, stall.

BEDE *HE* II 3 (v. emporium); ∼ium, i. mercatus, *ceapstow GlH* E 252; emtorium OSB. GLOUC. *Deriv.* 192 (v. emporium); ∼ium, *buying-place PP*. **b** *a buthe*, ∼ium, cadurcum, tenterium, meritorium, opella, staciuncula *CathA*.

emptorius [LL], (of place) having a market. **b** acquired by purchase.

s**716** Ethelbaldus . . dedit ecclesiae . . Hamptone juxta Wictium ∼ium *Chr. Evesham* 72; †**717** (12c) ego Æðelbaldus unam portionem mansionis in wico ∼io salis quem nos Saltwich vocamus . . ad ecclesiam donabo *CS* 138. **b** dicitur titulus omnis causa acquirendi dominium, ut titulus pro ∼io, pro donato [etc.] PAUL. ANGL. *ASP* 1528.

empurium v. emporium.

empyema [LL < ἐμπύημα], abscess, gathering of pus.

empima est sceratus saniei cum infectione pulmonis GILB. IV 195. 2 (cf. ib. 196. 1: in pleuresi et peripleumonia, †epimate et ptisi); sic lippiaria vel †empiala opilat GAD. 12. 2; circa febrem flegmaticam de flegmate vitreo, que est †empiala vel liparia, oportet sic procedere *Ib.* 14v. 1 (cf. ib. 52. 1: de ptisi, tussi, et epimate, i. sputo saniei et emoptoica passione); ex empimate cadit patiens in ptisim J. MIRFIELD *Brev.* 74; empima, i. sputum saniosum ex pulmonis infeccione proveniens *SB* 19; †empina, i. sputum saniosum, inde empicus et empiscus, quasi habens uulcus [v. l. vulnus] saniosum in pulmone *Alph.* 56; ex infirmitate empematis, i. e. tussis et *le murra DCCant.* (*HMC*) 127b.

empyicus [LL < ἐμπυϊκός], (one) suffering empyema.

trifera magna .. peripleuronicis, empicis, et cardiacis probata GILB. I 35v. 1; pillule constrictive empicorum, probate empicis et qui tussiebant ex reumate *Ib.* IV 196. 1; sanies arguit empicum frequenter et non ptisicum GAD. 52v. 1; *Alph.* 56 (v. empyema).

empyricus, empyrean, pertaining to the highest heaven. **b** (alch.) fiery.

ipse [sc. S. Paulus] in raptu suo ~o interiora thalami ingressus fuerat H. BOS. *LM* 1397D. **b** secunda est virtus empirica sive mineralis et hec triplex: alia est lapidificativa, alia metallica, alia inter has media *Ps.*-GROS. *Summa* 594.

empyrius [LL < ἐμπύριος], empyrean, pertaining to the highest heaven; **b** (fig.). **c** fiery. **d** (as sb. n.) the empyrean, heaven.

celum empireum aquis superius erat NECKAM *NR* I 2; ~eum celum mundum dixerim propter sui munditiam, a πῦρ Greco, quod est ignis, quasi eminens super celum igneum sive sidereum GERV. TILB. I 1; ad celum empireum in quadam vitrea S. LANGTON *Gl. Hist. Schol.* 41; humani generis hostis antiquus .. ab empireo fuit celo dejectus GIR. *Spec.* III *intr.* p. 118; si possunt spiritus avium sua corpora non gloriosa elevare in celum aereum, quare non anima Christi corpus levius in celum empireum? FISHACRE *Quaest.* 45; chaos implens totam vacuitatem celi ~ei PECKHAM *QA* 8; HALES *Qu.* 1351 (v. 2 caelum 1a); illac tronos, celum simulantes emperium, .. fulgore mirabili radiare stuperes *Ps.*-ELMH. *Hen. V* 110. **b** s**1252** fercula culta dabas; emperea vina pluebas; / amodo sit Christus cibus et esca tibi (*Epitaph.*) M. PAR. *Maj.* V 320. **c** ~ius, igneus OSB. GLOUC. *Deriv.* 197. **d** Christus .. gerens pulchrum profunda mente ~ium LANTFR. *Swith. pref.*; per celum aereum .. ut tandem perveniant in empirium BELETH *RDO* 4. 17; sub ~eo celum est sidereum GERV. TILB. I 1; oculorum acie per fenestram illam ad ~eum usque transpenetrante GIR. *EH* II 30; primum celum a theologis dicitur ~eum, non ab ardore sed a splendore *Comm. Sph.* 283; [celum decimum] quod est empireum, circumdans .. omnia visibilia BACON *Maj.* II 64*n.*; ut sublevarer supra altitudinem omnem visibilium et ab ~io accensus et illuminatus ad laudandum Deum ROLLE *IA* 239.

empyus [LL < ἔμπυος], abscess, swelling.

enpus, *ingeswel* ÆLF. *Gl.*.

emtio v. emptio. **emtorium** v. emptorium. **emtus** v. emere. **emul-** v. et. aemul-. **emula** v. inula.

emulgēre [CL], to milk or squeeze out. **b** (anat.) to draw off.

8.. qui .. ~et, *se ðe melcð WW*; sic [vacca] ab eo emulsa quo decebat abivit R. COLD. *Godr.* 113; nec olei liquor purissimus prelo ~ente eliquatus educitur *Id. Osw.* 8. **b** quod a matre eadem genitura ~et eodem modo dissociatum asserimus PULL. *Sent.* 726D; his ~entibus venis natura utitur ad deferendam sanguinis aquositatem et bilem a jecore ad renes D. EDW. *Anat.* B 2v.

emulumentum v. emolumentum.

emunctio [CL]

1 emptying, blowing, wiping (of nose, also fig.).

tussis et suspirium et ~o non sunt actus contrarii ROB. FLAMB. *Pen.* 85; **1283** dissimulare credimus esse tutius quam forti ~one sanguinem elicere indigestum PECKHAM *Ep.* 438.

2 squeezing out (of money from purse).

seu publica cambitione seu domestica marsupii familiaris ~one *Chr. Rams.* 44; s**1228** marescalli .. non modicam pecuniam extorserunt. .. consimilem ~onem annuatim vel frequentius iterabant M. PAR. *Abbr.* 256; s**1232** Londoniensis episcopus .. post multos labores et spoliationem obiter et ~onem loculorum in curia domum remeavit *Id. Maj.* III 240; s**1213** alios subrogavit qui jure populum tractarent .. et non crumenarum ~one sed paci comprovincialium et quieti inhiarent W. COVENTR. II 215; s**1326** cives .. in amissione libertatum et ~one pecunie .. sunt puniti WALS. *HA* I 182.

emunctivus, extortionate.

transiit annus [**1244**] .. regno .. Anglie .. pecunie ~us, Francis periculosus M. PAR. *Min.* II 498.

emunctor

1 one who blows or wipes his nose.

naribus emunctor nec rusticus ore screator / sis cenans D. BEC. 1047.

2 one who trims or extinguishes lights; **b** (fig.).

in templo erant ~ores luminum, qui luminaria accendebant et extinguebant BELETH *RDO* 13. 27. **b** pia quandoque desiderantis voluntas et manum imitatur ~oris et inpressionis suae violentia .. minimam .. desideratae scientiae dulcedinem parat WILLIB. *Bonif. pref.* p. 2.

emunctorium [LL]

1 handkerchief. **b** sanitary towel.

nec prius se dignatur ~io tergere quam subjectum librum madefecerit turpi rore R. BURY *Phil.* 17. 219. **b** mulieres habent proprium ~ium per quod mundificant a superfluitatibus matricem per quam mundantur menstrua GAD. 37v. 2.

2 forceps (for trimming a wick or extinguishing a light; also fig. *Cf. Exod.* xxv 38).

~ia, *candeltuist GlC* E 166; ~ium, *candelsnytels* ÆLF. *Gl.*; OSB. GLOUC. *Deriv.* 195 (v. emungere 2a); ~ia, forcipes quibus lucina emungebantur, ut melius lucerent AD. SCOT *TT* 660A; fiant et ~ia quoniam lichini nostre mortalitatis semper habent aliqua emungenda correctione R. NIGER *Mil.* I 57; fuit .. tribulationum immensitas tanquam ~ium hujus lucerne S. LANGTON *Serm.* 4. 38; *a candyl schers*, ~ium; .. *a snytynge yren*', ~ium *CathA.*

3 (anat.) drainage channel (var.).

[nasi est] tertium juvamentum ut sit unum ~ium superfluitatum cerebri *Ps.*-RIC. *Anat.* 28; in cerebro frigiditate aliqua compresso .. humiditas in eo retenta exprimitur, dilabitur, et per diversa cerebri ~ia dispertitur BART. ANGL. IV 2; cum urina .. intret vesicum .. inter duos panniculos profluens per duo colla vel ~ia GILB. II 118. 2; apostemate ~iorum nobilium membrorum, sicut inguinum epatis, titillicorum vel assellarum cordis, radicum aurium cerebri GAD. 20. 1; inguines sunt partes .. ubi .. nascuntur bubones inferiores que sunt ~ia epatis sicut subasselle cordis *SB* 26.

4 grate.

1478 solutum .. lathamo .. ad reparandum ~ium in quadrato xviiij d. *Cant. Coll. Ox.* II 205; **1507** pro duobus ~iis ferreis, que vernacula lingua *grattis* appellantur, ad propulsanda ossa ceteraque hujusmodi, que si in cannalem .. intrarent, impedirent aque inpetum *Ib.* 249.

emunctorius, that cleanses by draining (med.).

[fistula] nascitur aliquando in locis carnosis .. et aliquando in locis .. ~iis cerebri et cordis et epatis et renum GILB. III 143v. 2.

emundare [CL]

1 to wash, clean thoroughly. **b** to clear (ground); **c** (absol.); **d** (fig.).

eorundem agatur mandatum; qui tamen fratres prius pedes suos diligenter ~ent [AS p. 415: *clænsian*] *RegulC* 42; aquam adportans et vasa denuo ~ans ÆLF. *Æthelwold* 10; vomerem .. negotiosum .. usus clarificat et ~at SICCAV. *PN prol.* **b** spinis alii agrum ~abant G. CRISPIN *Herl.* 93; locum .. ~avit DOMINIC *V. Ecgwini* I 8; AILR. *Spec. Car.* II 21. 570B (v. evacuare 3a); primum ~anda est area quam edificetur in ea R. NIGER *Mil.* IV 45. **c** c**1245** singulis Sabbatis .. ~andum est subtus mensas refectorii sicut subtus formas in choro *Cust. Cant. Abbr.* 255. **d** radius solis, quasi scopa lutosi / aeris, emundat celum VINSAUF *PN* 810; sic ~atus elementis, purificatus / belligeram vitam taurus ducet redimitam (J. BRIDL.) *Pol. Poems* I 192 (cf. ib. 193: ~atus, i. purificatus; elementis, i. tribulacionibus omnium elementorum).

2 to purge, cleanse from defilement: **a** (person); **b** (temple or church); **c** (fault or sin).

a ALDH. *VirgV* 77 (v. calculus 1b); lavacro baptismi a peccatis ~ari BEDE *Hom.* II 8. 146; Domine, populum tuum .. ab omnibus peccatis .. ~a [AS: *giclænsig*] *Rit. Durh.* 8; ~abat ergo ecclesiasticus orator prius conscientiam [cf. *Heb.* ix 14] W. MALM. *GR* I 59; H. READING (I) *Dial.* 5. 1203A (v. contactus b); filios ut castiget et ~et GIR. *PI pref.* 1; ut a maculis quas ex contagione peccatorum contraxerant per purgantis incendii adustionem ~ari possent COGGESH. *Visio* 13. **b** Judas Machabeus .. templum ab idolorum imaginibus ~ans nova .. altaria .. dedicavit BEDE *Hom.* II 24. 248; s**1174** accessit .. non ut ecclesiam .. viderit .. sed potius ut eam ~aret a sordibus DICETO *YH* I 380. **c** vaesania .. voluit emendari [v. l. ~ari] BEDE *HE* I 10; haec hostia, Domine, quaesumus, ~et nostra delicta EGB. *Pont.* 5; ad quaeque inutiliter succrescentia falce caeli resecanda et studiosius ~anda commissa vitae FOLC. *V. Bot.* 9; volo ut recta lex erigatur et omnis injustitia ~etur et eradicetur [AS: *þæt man aweodige ond awyrtwalige æghwylc unriht*] (*Const. Cnuti*) *GAS* 309; sordes qui purificat / emundans omnia LEDREDE *Carm.* 32. 38.

3 a (intr.) to make amends; *cf. emendare* 5b. **b** (refl.) to clear (oneself of a charge).

a 867 nisi .. digno satisfactione Deo et omnibus ~are voluerit *CS* 516; si manupastum alicujus accusetur de furto, solus paterfamilias ~are [MSS: emendare] potest, si velit, fracta lege, sine praejurante (*Leg. Hen.* 66. 7) *GAS* 586; si compellatio sit et in ~ando miseveniat [AS: *gif hit tihte sig ond lad forberste*], sit in episcopi potestate (*Quad.*) *Ib.* 349. **b 779** pretio se ~et a delicto commisso *CS* 230; ~et se, quod nec velle nec posse .. ejus extiterit (*Leg. Hen.* 87. 2a) *GAS* 601.

4 (?) to make prosperous. *Cf. emendare* 4a.

iste terminus, 'fortunare' idem significat quod 'fecundare', 'prosperum facere', vel '~are' (J. BRIDL.) *Pol. Poems* I 207.

emundatio [LL]

1 washing, cleaning (also fig.). **b** clearing (site). **c** (w. ref. to recovery of lead from ashes).

cum certum sit .. prophetas qui vasa .. dilui .. jusserunt non in hoc materialium rerum ~onem sed mentium potius .. castigationem .. nobis mandare BEDE *Mark* (vii 3) 199; lebetes ~onum cinerum nostre mortalitatis asportande extra castra (cf. *Exod.* xxxviii 3) R. NIGER *Mil.* I 66; **1375** (v. 2 censura); post ~onem elementorum taurus ducet vitam belligeram et virtuosam (J. BRIDL.) *Pol. Poems* I 193. **b 1511** in expensis j nove domus noviter edificate in tenemento Willelmi W. .. que funditus coruit . . . in primis sol. Roberto T. et Rogero M. pro ~one prefate domus operantibus per duos dies *Ac. Durh.* 291. **c 1420** Tho. Plumber pro ~one cinerum vij s.; pro *charcoyll* empt' pro ~one cinerum xj d. *Ib.* 270.

2 (anat.) menstruation.

hoc ix diebus facto, post ~onem menstruorum fiat scarificacio post tybias GILB. VII 302. 1.

3 cleansing (from sin), purification. *Cf. emendatio* 1b.

sacramenta habent eadem in ~onem peccatorum et perceptionem vitae caelestis BEDE *Tab.* 458; **801** usque ad ~onem .. delictorum meorum ALCUIN *Ep.* 218; tua patientia post illam ~onem baptismi in aliis peccatorum sordibus .. toleravit ANSELM (*Or.* 2) III 7; utraque [sc. disciplina et compunctio] quadripartitum in ~onis remedio habet effectum AD. SCOT *Serm.* 387D; **1237** satagit astutia humani generis inimici ut sanctitatem et ~onem .. destruat *Conc. Syn.* 245; quod Christus Deus et homo, qui potest in ~onem infinitorum peccatorum, noverit peccata infinita W. ALNWICK *QD* 601.

4 (leg.) exculpation, purgation (of offence). *Cf. emendatio* 5.

si compellatio sit et in ~one miseveniat [AS: *gif .. æt lade mistide*; *Cons. Cnuti*: inficianti purgamine] (*Quad.*) *GAS* 349; ut sicut omnium una est inculpatio una ~o vel emendatio sit (*Leg. Hen.* 71. 1b) *Ib.* 590; triplex vero lade vel ~o sit (*Ib.* 92. 19a) *Ib.* 609.

emundativus, purificative.

confessio est anime peccatricis ~a *Spec. Laic.* 20.

emundator [LL], cleaner, **b** cleanser, purifier.

si quelibet arma politori vel ~ori conmissa sint ad purgandum (*Leg. Hen.* 87. 3) *GAS* 601. **b** ad agendas salvatori et ~ori [sc. de lepra] suo gratias BEDE *Luke* (xvii 19) 544; labiorum nostrorum mitte tactorem / et emundatorem a labe reatus J. HOWD. *Cant.* 10.

emundura [cf. AN *emunder*, OF *esmonder*], (collect.) trimmings of wood (*Cf.* DuC *s. v. emunda*).

1223 cleias .. de .. esmundura (v. cleta 1c).

emungere [CL]

1 to blow or wipe one's nose (sts. w. ref. to *Prov.* xxx 33); **b** (fig., trans.). **c** (p. ppl., fig.) refined.

~o, purgo, emundo *GlH* E 265; ~ere, purgare, sicut nasum facimus OSB. GLOUC. *Deriv.* 195; s**1231** qui nimis ~it elicit sanguinem WEND. III 17; nolite .. nimis ~ere OCKHAM *Pol.* III 17. **b** videtur multis .. quod dyabolus numquam ~eret [v. l. iniungeret] hunc errorem, nisi ut placeatur hominibus et attendatur superbia in prelatis WYCL. *Chr. & Antichr.* 665. **c** emunctus, A. *aqueynte WW.*

2 to clean, trim (a candle-wick; also fig.). **b** to extinguish.

emunctorium, ferrum unde candelam ~imus OSB. GLOUC. *Deriv.* 195; AD. SCOT *TT* 660A, R. NIGER *Mil.* I 57 (v. emunctorium 2); hanc etiam lucernam emunxit cum martyrem suum exilio diuturno .. et injuriis innumeris affligi permisit S. LANGTON *Serm.* 4. 38. **b** ~o, A. *to quenche.*

3 to put (extorting) pressure (on), to squeeze. **b** to extort, to squeeze out (usu. money).

quos timore potestatis vel ~endos suscipiunt, toto splendore popine propitiantur MAP *NC* I 25 f. 20; GIR. *GE* II 32 (v. bursa 2b); Ranulpho .. Dunelmensi episcopo [ob.**1128**] .. regnum .. opprimente et ad ipsum sanguinem ~ente *Croyl. Cont. A* 110. **b** alumpnos / equoris emungi

Thetis dolet J. Exon. *BT* I 252; s**1166** denarios quatuor a singulis marcatis ~ens Diceto *YH* I 329; s**1167** vir doctus pecuniam ~endi *Flor. Hist.* II 81; s**1238** [Simon de Montfort] ab uno cive Legrecestrie .. quingentas marcas emunxerat M. Par. *Maj.* III 479; s**1240** collecta .. Petri .. quam a Scotorum finibus emunxit, hanc summam creditur dupplicasse *Flor. Hist.* II 240; Yvo .. abbatem in foveam cadere compulit et .. monasterii .. pecunias ~ere in manus hostiles coegit *Croyl. Cont. A* 125.

emunire [CL], to protect (absol., fig.).

1168 gratius .. fieri solet accipienti postulatum dum offertur, quam cum ab invito judicii calculus ~it [v. l. emungit], et utinam necessitatem faciendi voluntas antecedat, et coherciorem mera liberalitas preveniat G. Foliot *Ep.* 188.

emunitas v. immunitas.

emurmurare [cf. CL murmurare], to grumble, complain.

s**1469** insurreccio .. communitatum patrie .. que se taxis .. graviter oppressos ~abant *Croyl. Cont. B* 542.

emus [οἶμος], song, speech.

Serlo Wilt. II 34 (v. emere 2b). emus, i. sermo *WW*.

emutescere [cf. LL mutescere], to become dumb (also fig.).

Zacharias pater ejus .. ~uit quia jam .. ~escere oportebat sacrificia eorum quae pro peccatis populi offerebantur Bede *Luke* (i 24) 314.

emutilatio [cf. LL mutilatio], mutilation.

1311 in .. perpetua incarceracione .. citra mortem et membrorum ~one puniantur *RGasc* IV 562.

emutuare [cf. CL mutuari], to lend.

1278 petiit plane debita que ~avit communitati *Rec. Leic.* I 188.

emy- v. hemi-. **emyr** v. admirallus 1a.

en [CL], see! behold! **b** (introductory or parenthetic to complete sentence); **c** (w. *ut*).

Frith. 1204 (v. agalma); Stephane, inquam, Stephane, en locus pietatis, en tempus misericordiae, en utique occasio exhibendae caritatis Anselm (*Or.* 13) III 51. **b** en, primus occurrit nobis Samuel Gildas *EB* 38; en, inquam, noctis horrida / nunc apparent spectacula (Aldh.) *Carm. Aldh.* 1. 165; **1044** cum omnibus ad se rite pertinentibus campis, pascuis, .. sillvis, en in suo vivere cum prosperitate semper istum exenium obtineat *CD* 770; *G. Herw.* 322 (v. continuus 2d); en veraciter a me descripta est offensa [etc.] Ord. Vit. IV 13 p. 265; Neckam *DS* V 764 (v. commensurare 2). **c** sub quorum umbra peccati rex egenus mittitur; en ut regnum .. plaga magna percutitur Favent 2; magna quantocius altercacio inter regem et dictos dominos appellantes en ut insurrexit priusquam .. confabularentur *Ib.* 12.

enact- v. inact-.

enaeorema [LL < ἐναιώρημα], matter suspended in urine.

fiunt .. crinoyde resolutiones ex sanguine adusto et ita grossam materiam: et si †everroima fuerint, ventositatem et materie cruditatem significant, quare longa erit egritudo Gilb. I 69. 2; ut urina tincta cum nube alba, †eneoratio alba, vel ypostasi alba Ric. Med. *Signa* 34; per mediam autem regionem urine quam medici †eneormiam dicunt de media regione corporis, id est de corde et sibi adjacentibus indicamus Bart. Angl. V 45.

enaeoristicus, (?) cloudy w. suspended matter.

quod si post appareat cum emendatione coloris et rubee vel eneoristice bonarum differentiarum Ric. Med. *Signa* 36.

enallage [LL < ἐναλλαγή], (gram.) enallage, exchange of form.

~e Graeca est et cum praesens pro futuro accipitur, ut .. 'quid ago?' Linacre *Emend. Lat.* lxxv v.

enamellare [cf. AN *enamelle*, OF *enamaillie*], to enamel. *V. et. esmallare.*

dedit .. [Radulphus ep. Bathon., ob. **1363**] tres capas cum morsu magno argenteo deaurato et anemelato *Hist. Wells* 56; acquisit [abbas J., ob. **1379**] unum pacis osculatorium argenteum deauratum et ~atum *Chr. Evesham* 301; **1397** Alicia B. .. legavit .. unam ollam enamelatam .. rectori (*Vis. Heref.*) *EHR* XLV 456; **13..** una cupa cristallina .. cum pede, argentea deaurata et enamayllata capite S. Pauli (*Invent.*) *Hist. S. Paul.* 337a; **1402** bacini enameliati (v. engrelatus); **1409** anamelatis (v. columbinus 2c); **1414** cum gaudiis de auro puro anamellatis cum albo in forma capitis S. Johannis Baptiste *Reg. Cant.* II 20; **1416** colerum inamelatum (v. 2 collare 3b); **1426** lego eidem ecclesie duas pelves de argento deaurato cum Nativitate Domini et Annunciacione B. Marie anamillatas in medio *Reg. Cant.* II 358; **1426** j crux argenti deaurati .. in cujus quatuor angulis sunt quatuor evangeliste annameliati *DC S. Paul.* (*HMC*) 54b; **1429** tria coleria aurea, quorum duo sunt anamelata cum albo *Foed.* X 433b; **1436** magnum tabulatum .. pretiose et solemniter anemelatum Amund. II 190; **1464** calicem .. cum nodo deaurato et annamelato (*Test.*) *MunAcOx* 707; **1488** pelves argenteas que scuta habent S. Albani anemelata in suis fundis *Reg. Whet.* I 453; c**1500** olla argentea deaurata cum scutis Anglie enamelatis *Fabr. York* 216.

enamellatura, enamel-work. *V. et. esmallatio.*

1447 erigitur .. crux super basem perpulcram ramis vitisque foliis cum splendidis enamulaturis *Invent. S. Paul.* 520.

enancium v. oenanthe. **enarmon-** v. enharmon-.

enarrare [CL]

1 to describe or relate fully; **b** (w. indir. qu.). **c** to recite.

terriginae gloriam Dei narrare possunt; non autem hanc ~are nisi caeli cives sufficiunt, qui quo hanc vicinius vident eo certius valent eloqui Bede *Hom.* II 16. 186; a**1075** epistolam .. in qua .. totius negotii gestionem breviter .. ~avit Lanfr. *Ep.* (3); Ord. Vit. III *prol.* p. 1 (v. efficacia 1); patres nostri .. ~averunt filiis suis .. que tunc historialiter contigerant P. Cornw. *Disp.* 156; dicitur .. breve quia rem de qua agitur .. paucis verbis et breviter ennarat Bracton 112; cum omnia que sibi contigerant per ordinem enarasset .. *Latin Stories* 31. **b** is .. quantum profeticae dignitatis gratia enituerit .. quis .. ~are sufficiat? Aldh. *VirgP* 20. **c** usque ad sextam .. et ultra procul generationem memoriter et prompte genus ~at Gir. *DK* I 17.

2 to expound, interpret.

GlH E 56 (v. edisserere a); a**1089** cur hoc facere velit rationabilem causam ~at Lanfr. *Ep.* 56 (54); sensum mei visionis / .. / enarrare si potestis Hil. Ronce. 15. 58; **1549** mathematices professor si cosmographiam docet, Melam, Plinium, Strabonem aut Ptolomeum ~et *StatOx* 344.

enarratio [CL], full description, recital.

de his in subsequentibus .. manifesta posteris ~o res gestas enodabit Ord. Vit. VI 5 p. 32; generationem linealiter producunt, sed .. tam longinqua, tam remotissima generis ~o .. trutanica .. esse videretur Gir. *DK* I 3.

enarrativus [LL], recitative.

[poematos genus] exegematicon est vel ~um, in quo poeta ipse loquitur sine ullius interpositione personae Bede *AM* 140.

enarrator [CL], expositor, interpreter.

secretorum scrutator et ~or et propheta recte dicitur quia profatur .. futura Bede *Sam.* (*1 Sam.* ix 9) 556.

enasci [CL], to be born (fig.), to issue.

humana laus ex tribus generibus bonorum ~itur *Incept. Ox.* 175.

enatare [CL], to swim (away; also fig.). **b** to escape by swimming (fig.). **c** to float up (fig.). **d** (trans.) to swim across.

alii per aque alveos ~abant R. Cold. *Cuthb.* 65; piscis aquis pene solo tenus arentibus ~avit *Id. Godr.* 121; ut in .. sacre scripture pelago sine .. periculo erroris ~averim R. Niger *Mil.* I *prol.*; huic natura pedem digitis armavit aduncis; / se civem spondens enatat alter aquis Neckam *DS* II 688; s**1250** ad naves fugientes ~ando submersi sunt *Chr. Man* 106. **b** si munus penitentie ad ~andum non dirigitur, profundo criminum absorbetur H. Reading (I) *Dial.* V 1198D; sicut .., eo nolente, non contingeret peccare, ita, eo volente, a malo contingit ~are Pull. *Sent.* 699A. **c** R. Cold. *Cuthb.* 112 (v. cellula 2a). **d** fluvio qui interer at evadato seu potius ~ato, festinum comiti contulit auxilium Ord. Vit. IX 6 p. 495 (cf. ib. 9 p. 531: fluvium .. vix aliquis poterat ~are); non tibi sit cura tanta ~are maria, tanta terrarum perambulare spacia *NLA* (*Winwaloe*) II 565.

enavigare [CL]

1 to sail forth (also fig.). **b** to disembark (fig.).

saecularem gloriam fugiens clam et occulte abscedens ~avit .. et ad hanc insulam .. advenit *V. Cuthb.* III 1; qui maris tumidi crispat flucticulum / ad nos enavigat per ventris lembulum Walt. Wimb. *Carm.* 63. **b** **1165** Deo auctore sedabitur hec procella et nos feliciter ad optatum ~abimus portum J. Sal. *Ep.* 140 (152); c**1168** ne eos .. peniteat cum ~antes Christi discipulos in litore viderint exultare *Ib.* 269 (282).

2 (trans.) to sail through, steer clear of (partly fig.).

1153 lividorum latratuum Scillas .. audimus; omnes aura Sancti Spiritus flante prospere ~abitis G. Foliot *Ep.* 103; **1188** cum .. [ecclesia] universa ~asse pericula et jam portum tranquillitatis crederetur adepta, irruit super eam .. inundatio *Ep. Cant.* 284.

enavigatio

1 sailing about or away (fig.).

ut ad id unde digressus sum redeam, ne diuturna ~one portum optatae quietis omittere cogar Asser *Alf.* 73.

2 disembarking.

s**1186** regina cum rege transfretavit eadem in navi. sub ~one rex Wintoniensem episcopum visitavit apud Merewelle Diceto *YH* II 40.

enb- v. et. amb-, emb-, imb-. **enbraud-, enbrod-, enbrord-, enbroud-, enbrowd-** v. embroud-. **enca** v. enta.

1 encaenia [LL *n. pl.* < τὰ ἐγκαίνια], **~ium,** (eccl.) festival of dedication.

~ia vocabantur sollemnia dedicationis templi Bede *Hom.* II 24. 243; ~ia, initia vel dedicationes *GlC* E 213; **9..** ~ia, *niwecirchalgung* Ælf. *Gl.*; coenobium, / cujus nuper erant encenia rite peracta Wulf. *Swith. pref.* 209; **10..** encenie (*sic*), nove dedicationis *WW*; in hyeme .. celebrant enchenia, id est dedicationem templi Beleth *RDO* 131. 135; in ~iis, quorum meministi, mentibus prudentium sunt exhibita celitus et incentiva desiderii celestis et mundani contemptus argumenta Ad. Marsh *Ep.* 82; ~ium dedicatio ecclesie et hujusmodi Bacon *CSPhil.* 444; ~ia, id est innovationes, ut nova festa et dedicationes ecclesiarum *Id. Maj.* III 110; encenia, *chyrche holy PP*; *a dedicacion*, dedicacio, encennia *CathA*.

2 (by conf. w. *exenia*) gift.

quos nec auri copia / ne divitum encennia / trahunt a rigore (*De Judicibus*) *Pol. Songs* 224; R. Bury *Phil.* 8. 119 (v. exenium a); *sonde or 3eft ysend*, encennium *PP*; *3ereseffe*, encennium *PP*.

encaeniare [LL], to dedicate or renew (a church or part of one).

Plegmund enceniavit .. arduam turrim Æthelw. IV 3; ~iare, sollempnizare, celebrare, dedicare Osb. Glouc. *Deriv.* 199; *to do on newe*, encenniare *CathA*.

encantator v. incantator.

encathisma [LL < ἐγκάθισμα], hip-bath, sitz-bath.

fiat stupha vel †eucatisma ex herbis Gilb. I 39. 1; curatur encatismate facto ex aqua decoctionis [etc.] *Ib.* V 229v. 2; stringit multo fortius si fiat enchatisma, i. particulare balneum, scilicet ad umbilicum vel modicum supra Gad. 59v. 1; *SB* 20 (v. balneum a); encatisma interpretatur balneum particulare in quo sedetur usque ad umbilicum vel circiter *Alph.* 57.

encausterium, ink-horn.

c**1452** unum pennare .. cum incausterio de opere Parisiensi *MunAcOx* 647; *CathA* (v. atramentarium a); incaustorium, A. *an ynkehorn WW*.

encaustum [LL < ἔγκαυστον], ink; **b** (fig.). **c** (?) dye.

Ælf. *Gl.*, *PP* (v. atramentum 1a); quicquid .. contra orthographiae normam .. repereris .. pinnicula profluentis incausti in melius ab errore reformatum emendare praecipias B. *V. Dunst.* 1; cantor vero procurare sibi [sc. novitio] debet membranam et incaustum et scriptorem si nescit scribere Lanfr. *Const.* 171; c**1148** (v. calefactorius 2a); penna riget, cultellus hebet, michi dextra ligatur, / effluit inchaustum, scedula nulla datur R. Partes 238; debet invenire precentor incaustum [= *MonA* II 28: †incoustram] omnibus scriptoribus monasterii, et colores ad illuminandum (*Cust.*) *Chr. Evesham* 210; diversitas incausti et atramenti, ut si in una pars scribatur incausto nigro et altera pars incausto rubro, non atramento Bracton 398b (cf. ib. 415b: si [breve] corrigatur .., eadem erit actio que prius et idem breve .., licet aliud pergamenum et aliud incaustum); in xx li. duri ~i emptis iiij s. iiij d. *Ac. Beaulieu* 196; **1299** ad brevia regis sigillanda .. per diversos comitatus .. portanda, canevacio et pochiis et saccis, bursis, pergameno et incaustro .. et aliis diversis .. rebus emptis *Pipe* (*Chanc.*) 92 m. 7*d.*; signando eminentiam cum encaustro Gad. 130. 2 (v. eminentia 1b); **1351** (v. certus 1c); [rescriptum] suspectum propter rasuras .. tam de alia manu quam de diverso incausto Thorne 2065; **1456** pro pergamino, incasto et filo ad rotulos scaccarii, xxv s. *ExchScot* 291; vinum lacte lava, oleum liquore fabarum, / encaustum vino; cetera mundat aqua *Reg. Whet.* II 297; **1552** pro pergameno, papyro, et enchasto *CourtR* (*Warw*) 207/82 m. 2. **b** scribe mihi .. ex tui cordis incausto et lingue et tuarum manuum calamo quidquid vis H. Los. *Ep.* 42. **c** **1201** ceperunt in domo sua dim. m. et ob. in denariis, et in lino et †in casto [? l. incasto] catalla ad valenciam v s. *Pl. K. or J.* 345; vas plenum cineribus .. potest recipere de aqua quantum cineris .. et .. vas habens lanam recipit incaustum quantum sine lana Bacon III 219.

encen-, encenn- v. encaen-. **encentricus** v. eccentricus 1a. **encha** v. 1 enchia.

encharisma [cf. ἐγχαρίζειν], free gift, favour. *Cf. charisma.*

958 (14c) si quis hoc nostrum icarisma aliqua machinacione infringere conatus fuerit *CS* 1033 (cf. ib. 960 [**956** (12c)]: in incarisma; 1138 [**964** (14c)]: ikarisma).

enchastum v. encaustum. **enchatisma** v. encathisma.

enchelondus [ME *enche* + *lond*], small-holder. *V. et.* 1 *enchia* 2.

1299 ~i: Johannes le Enche tenet j virgatam terre per servitium vj s. per annum *RB Worc.* 100; ~i: .. Petrus le Enche tenet j mesuagium et xvj acras terre. .. summa

redditus assisi dictorum ∼orum per annum xxiij s. iiij d. *Ib.* 156–7; ∼i de Blockleye . ., cottmanni de Blockeleye *Ib.* 306–7; faciet in omnibus de servitiis et consuetudinibus ut predicti sex acremanni ∼i *Ib.* 344.

enchenia v. encaenia. **encher-** v. enchir-.

enchetourus [ME *enchētour*], escheator.

1434 in expensis factis super ∼o domini regis per Johannem Estwell fact' tempore quo major fuit apud S. Jacobum *Stewards' Bk. Southampt.* I 60.

1 enchia [ME *enche* < AS *ynce* < uncia]

1 inch.

1335 gesture . . erunt vij ∼iarum. . . stanciones . . erunt ix ∼iarum, et panni xiij ∼iarum et vij ∼iarum *DCEbor.* (*Reg. K*).

2 small-holder. *V. et. enchelondus.*

c1182 Willelmus Encha [tenet] v acras *RB Worc.* 407; **12..** item de cottariis et limariis et ∼iis et de eorum servitiis et operibus *Reg. Pri. Worc.* 25b.

2 enchia v. euexia.

enchiridion [LL < ἐγχειρίδιον]

1 handbook, manual. **b** title of work by St. Augustine. **c** title of King Alfred's commonplace book.

796 ad cujus libri [sc. B. Gregorii] lectionem te . . remitto, obsecrans ut illum saepius quasi ∼ion habeas in manibus Alcuin *Ep.* 113; **c800** de quibus [psalmis] . . breves expositiunculas quasi quoddam ∼ion, id est manualem librum, fieri flagitastis *Ib.* 243; egregio ∼ione monitos . . ad veritatis reduxerat viam F. Malm. *V. Aldh.* 71B; ∼ion, manuale Bacon *CSPhil.* 442. **b** Augustinus in ∼ion . . allegat . . Ockham *Pol.* II 721; **1390** Encheridion et questiones ad Orosium . . in uno volumine. Encheridion . . cum multis aliis libris B. Augustini in uno volumine (*Catal. Librorum*) *FormOx* 241; **1396** Augustinus de ∼ion [MS: Encherideon] (*Catal. Librorum*) *Meaux* III lxxxviii; **p1440** Augustinus in suo Encherideon (*Catal. Librorum*) *JRL Bull.* XVI 470; **14..** uno volumine in quo etiam continentur hii libri: . . Encheridion de bono conjugii Augustini et Augustinus de bono virginitatis (*Cart. Reading*) *EHR* III 121. **c** quem ∼ion suum, id est manualem librum, nominari voluit [Aelfred] Asser *Alf.* 89; liber proprius quem patria lingua Encheridion [v. l. *Handboc*], i. e. manualem librum, appellavit [Elfredus] W. Malm. *GR* II 123.

2 (fig. in apposition, or (?) as adj.) held or led by the hand.

801 direxi hoc animal, vitulum ∼ion meum, ut adjuves illi et eripias eum de manibus inimicorum suorum . . . misi . . in †ora [l. ore] pueri hujus, quamvis vitulus contra naturam rationale sit animal, quod ipse in auribus sanctitatis vestrae habet mugire Alcuin *Ep.* 248.

enchymus [ἔγχυμος], sapid.

Aristoteles non dicit nisi quod siccum patitur ab humido hencimo, quod vocat saporabile sive aqueum Bacon XIV 99.

enclisis [LL < ἔγκλισις], bowing, inclination. **b** (gram.) throwing back (of accent).

a bowynge, inclinacio, ∼is *CathA.* **b** in dictionibus precedentibus partes que habent vim enclesis [v. l. ∼is], ut δέδωκάς μοι, i. e. dedisti mihi, ultima hujus dictionis δέδωκας est gravis naturaliter, sed acuitur propter encliticam dictionem Bacon *Tert.* 240; de mutacione accentus . . . primus [casus] est propter enclesim *Id. Gram. Gk.* 144.

encliticare, to bow down, incline.

encleticat vultus in fumum, nec mihi vultum / obscurum fusca noscere nube licet Garl. *Epith.* IV 425 f. 26 [*ed. Saiani omits*]; encletico, *to bowe WW.*

encliticus [LL < ἐγκλιτικός], inclining down. **b** (gram.) enclitic. **c** (as sb. m. or f.) bedridden person.

encletice [*gl.*: inclinative] lucis mundus splendore diescens, / non inprovisa nocte soporat eam Garl. *Epith.* VII 579 f. 46v. **b** *sume synd gehatene encleticae on Grecisc, þæt is on Leden* inclinativae . ., *forðan ðe hi . . gebigað heora sweg to ðam stæfgefege þe him ætforan stent* Ælf. *Gram.* 264; in omni dictione trissyllaba vel plurium syllabarum, ubi encletica conjunctio est in fine, syllaba que precedit . . debet elevari accentuando Vinsauf *AV* II 3. 174; antepenultima [syllaba] est acuenda exceptis . . conjunccionibus encleticis, que sunt 'que', 've', 'ne' *Ps.*-Gros. *Gram.* 34; dictio ∼a inclinat accentum suum super syllabam precedentem . ., ut 'que', 've', 'ne' Bacon *Tert.* 239; *Ib.* 240 (v. enclisis b). **c** hic encleticus morti contiguus triduo in agonia positus . . in verba prorumpens . . pandit astantibus Herm. Arch. 7 (cf. ib. 18: accubat encletica nocte eadem in ecclesia); ∼us iste mori differebat quoniam Edmundus nondum superbiam hostis conterebat Ciren. I 355.

encomiasticus [ἐγκωμιαστικός], encomiastic, panegyrical.

item orationum ∼arum de sanctis lib. 1 Ferr. *Kinloss* 45.

encratia [ἐγκράτεια], mastery.

etiam nusquam / *ne sceal ladigan* labor quam tenet / encratea, *ac he ealneg sceal* / boethia *biddan georne* (*Aldhelm*) *ASPR* VI 97.

encraticus v. eucraticus. **encre** v. viridis. **encrochiare** v. incrochiare. **encumb-** v. incumb-. **encusa** v. anchusa.

encyclius [CL < ἐγκύκλιος], general, ordinary, common.

Arist. etiam primo de Coelo 110 multas istarum racionum . . breviter comprehendens, sic ait; in †enkidiis [l. enkicliis] philosophismatibus circa divina multocies declaratum est racionibus, quod divinum intransmutabile necessarium esse omne primum et summum Bradw. *CD* 175E (cf. ib. 462B: in †eucycliis [l. encycliis] philosophismatibus).

encytula [cf. CL encytus < ἔγχυτος], (?) crust.

ex calore agente in materiam illam . . [i. e. testam ovi] materia quedam veluti ∼a operitur, et temporis continuitate eadem ∼a propter ipsum calorem . . desiccatur et petrificatur *Quaest. Salern.* C 1.

endecas v. hendecas.

†endele, *s. dub.*

cum W. . . dormiret nocte quadam audivit vocem de celo . . dicentem sibi "vade et dic Henrico regi Anglie 'in nomine Christi prodele [v. l. perdele], †∼e [? l. en dele]' ", . . sed rex nihil illorum intellegens, cum non esset qui interpretaretur ei visionem, nullam inde curam egit R. Howd. II 272.

endelechia, endelichia v. entelechia.

endemotum [ME *ende* + *mōt*], (service at) county court (Cumb).

a1179 faciemus pro monachis omne forense et terrenum servicium, quodcumque ad dominum regem pertinet, scilicet de noutegeld' et endemot [= *MonA* V 609b: ondemot] (*Ch.*) *VCH Cumb* I 321 (cf. *Reg. Holm Cultram* 18).

endentura v. indentura. **endias** v. hendias. **endic-, endit-** v. indict-.

endivia [LL < CL intibum], endive, chicory.

decoctionis solatri, ∼ie [etc.] Gilb. I 23. 2; **12..** andivia, i. letrun, i. *þugeþistel WW*; Gad. 71. 1, 73v. 1, *SB* 10 (v. altaraxacon); ∼ia, alio nomine scariola, simile est lactuce agresti sed habet pilos in dorso foliorum; G. et A. *endyve Alph.* 57; hec ∼a, A. *endywe WW*; ∼ia qua pharmacopole nostrae aetatis utuntur non est ∼ia qua veteres olim usi sunt; hec enim qua hodie utuntur nihil aliud est quam lactuca agrestis. intybus sive intybum, quod vulgus hodie vocat *suckery*, veterum erat ∼ia. scandix divinantibus aliquot doctis est vulgaris ∼ia Turner *Herb.* B i.

endromis [CL < ἐνδρομίς], thick wrap or fur cloak.

†endromadis, duplex pallium vel palla vilosa Osb. Glouc. *Deriv.* 196; vestes que fuerint de solis pellibus hec sunt: / pellicium, reno, quibus †endromade socientur Garl. *Syn.* 1588A; *slaveyn, garmente*, †enndromades, -dis . . vel †emdroma, -dis *PP.*

enec- v. et. aesnec-.

enecare [CL], to kill, slay. **b** to drown. **c** (w. abstr. obj. or absol.) to destroy.

Mattheus et Bartholomeus decollati, Jacobus, Simon et Thadeus ∼ati Hon. *GA* 578A; mulieres quoque pregnantes sevo ense dissectis visceribus ∼abant Ord. Vit. XIII 37 p. 111; de his qui vim apertam patiuntur, unde ∼entur non quero Adel. *QN* 43; ceteris animalibus ∼tis, pestis eam penitus non attigit W. Cant. *Mir. Thom.* V 26 (cf. ib. 38: bos ∼atus); sunt qui asserunt eum [sc. Saturnum] . . frigidum nuncupari quod sua . . constellatione contraria homines ∼et Alb. Lond. *DG* 1. 4. **b** alios ingressa per rimas aqua ∼abat W. Malm. *GR* V 419 p. 497; aliquando prestabant cunctis usum equi in paludibus ∼ti Ord. Vit. IV 5 p. 198; ∼tus, in aqua occisus Osb. Glouc. *Deriv.* 202. **c** quis ergo est qui charitatem interdum non vulneret, aut potius ∼et, quoniam . . nullus est . . ratio cujus semper pravitati resistat Pull. *Sent.* 861A; quod [sc. vocum exponere significationes] utinam facerent potius quam austero vini sapore ∼arent R. Melun *Sent.* I 41.

enectere [cf. CL nectere], to disentangle (fig.), elucidate.

rogavit idem . . Dei virum quatinus sibi visionis suae somnia solvendo enexuisset B. *V. Dunst.* 32.

enector [cf. LL nector], murderer.

sicarii, multatores, ∼ores [*gl.*: *ocsur de gens*], antropocedi Neckam *Ut.* 105.

enectus v. enecare. **enela** v. helenium.

enema [LL < ἔνεμα], injection, enema.

∼a interpretatur injeccio vel relaxacio *Alph.* 57.

eneor- v. enaeor-. **enerbare** v. enervare.

energia [LL < ἐνέργεια], energy, power, strength; **b** (w. ref. to Jerome *Ep.* 3). **c** (phil.) actuality.

∼ia, . . enfaticus [i. e. ἐμφατικῶς] *GlC* E 219; ad illud . . quod de ∼ia nobis obloqui videtur dicimus quia . . quod auribus doctrinaliter ingeritur suo in transitu efficacius instruit et vehementius . . suos imbuit auditores Gir. *GE proem.* p. 4; quacunque calamitatis ∼ia desolatis [v. l. desolatos] . . munimen protectionis impendit *Mon. Francisc.* II app. 268; cooperire caput muliebris pudicicia vult, nescio qua ∼ia Fortescue *NLN* II 56; *a strenght*, conamen, conatus, ∼ia, fortitudo *CathA.* **b** sermo vester, immo Dei potius, cujus supra fuistis organum, vivus . . non parum in me ∼ie habuit H. Bos. *Thom.* IV 13 p. 368; nescio quid latentis ∼ie, id est interioris operationis, habet in se viva vox Neckam *NR* I 20 p. 66; vivas vocis ∼ias conserere non permittit locorum distantia Ad. Marsh *Ep.* 212; **1440** experiri volentes quantum ∼ie habere queat vive vocis actus Bekynton I 82; **1526** tum quidem pro mutis illis literis tuis quas utcunque degustavi, vivi tui pectoris ∼iam preceptorem habiturus (Gardiner) *Ep. Erasmi* VI 1669. **c** Neckam *NR* II 174 (v. dynamis b).

energomenus v. energumenus.

energumenare, to rave.

quicquid Eboracensium magnifica vanitas et malus semper invidie livor inerguminet (*Quad.*) *GAS* 546.

energumenus [LL < ἐνεργούμενος], possessed by an evil spirit; **b** (as sb. m. or f.).

filium consulis inerguminum . . curavit Aldh. *VirgP* 52; ∼us, *gewitseoc* Ælf. *Gl.*; in villa S. . . mulier ∼a custodiebatur a multis. inter quos et mulierem aliam spiritus arripuit W. Cant. *Mir. Thom.* III 51; in curia regis Hildeberti comitem ∼um curavit *NLA* (*Sampson*) II 354; *wode*, arepticius . . †euarguminus *CathA.* **b** inerguminos et scotomaticos meritorum gratia refocilando Aldh. *VirgP* 34; Bede *CuthbP* 41 (v. daemon 2b); habeto potestatem imponendi manum super inerguminum, sive baptizatum sive cataecuminum Egb. *Pont.* 13; exorcista . . invocat super inerguminos Ælf. *Ep.* 2. 118; frater Egelwinus hortetur . . ut talis ∼us ad tumbam martyris deportetur Herm. Arch. 21; Gir. *IK* I 12 (v. diabolus 1c); ut ∼i . . inunguntur oleo . . consecrato S. Langton *Quaest.* 367; sunt . . energomeni qui secundum lunam moventur. . . dicitur ab *en* quod est 'in' et *ergos* 'labor', et *mene* 'defectus'; laborat enim in defectu lune Gilb. II 103. 2; ut sunt ∼i, epileptici et frenetici Hales *Sent.* IV 435.

enervare [CL]

1 to hamstring, cut sinews of (horse). **b** (p. ppl.) lame.

s1257 Wallenses latibulis suis prorumpentes, equos pretiosos ∼antes et eviscerantes M. Par. *Maj.* V 656; **s1234** comes marescallus . . percussus est . . de quodam *anelaz*, equo suo ∼ato Oxnead *Chr.* 163 (cf. Wend. III 85: equum . . exsanguem fecerunt . . et . . pedes . . equi cum securibus preciderunt). **b 9..** ∼atus, debilis, *lame* Ælf. *Gl.*

2 to weaken, enervate: **a** (physically); **b** (w. ref. to authority); **c** (morally).

a effeta, ene[r]bata, *asuond*, languida; . . enervat[a], *asuond GlC* E 66, 192; ∼ata, *asleacod*, *asionad GlH* E 270; adde quod assuant pulvillos . . ne armorum duritiam sentiat caro. adeo enim ∼ata est militaris conditio ut jam sit delicatior quam muliebris teneritudo R. Niger *Mil.* IV 50; cum sit opus varios robusti ferre labores / non innervati studiis Veneris neque Bachi D. Bec. 2266; luxuria . . illud [sc. corpus] ∼at, hanc [sc. animam] perpetuo damnat Gir. *GE* II 23. **b** **1167** ut [Deus] vos . . roboret et adversarios vestros extenuet et ∼et J. Sal. *Ep.* 200 (235); **s1301** (v. curialis 4b). **c** ebrietas animos solet enervare virorum Aldh. *VirgV* 2501; bellica seditio . . in cultu Dei consistentes territat, . . et quid agant pre timore nescientes ∼at Ord. Vit. XII 21 p. 380; o ceca mundi sapientia supina nimis et crassa ∼ans omnem fortitudinem fidei H. Bos. *Ep.* 4. 1429B; aures obducimus ne subintret quod animam . . ledat vel ∼at R. Niger *Mil.* I 6.

3 to wipe out, destroy.

illos in decimo quarto die radicitus confestim a facie terre ∼are mandant *G. Herw.* 326; volumus . . quod magister . . omnes scholas adulterinas infra . . jurisdiccionem nostram compescat, ∼et, destruat et evellat (*Lit. Abbatis*) *Reg. Whet.* II 307.

4 (w. abstr. obj., esp. w. ref. to law, privilege, or sim.) to weaken effect of, bring to nothing.

munia . . sibi commissa non ∼avit sed viriliter complevit Byrht. *V. Ecgwini* 354; perquiramus simul . . recta . . Christianitatis propensius erigi, quicquid injustum est sollertius ∼are (*Quad.*) *GAS* 317 (cf. *Cons. Cnuti, Ib.*: deicere); debent omnes amici Dei injusticiam ∼are [AS: *alecgan*] (*Quad.*) *GAS* 478; **1158** nostre constitutionis robur ∼are *Lit. Cant.* III 371; **1245** ut hec omnia . . rata permaneant nos . . omnimodis inpetracionibus que illa possint ∼are renunciamus in perpetuum *Reg. Aberbr.* I 205; **1302** ad impediendum et finaliter ∼andum execucionem [mandati] *Reg. Cant.* 620; si concedas quod pro quocumque peccato sit inquirendum de papa, totam istam assercionem ∼as que dicit quod papa in nullo habet superiorem in terris Ockham *Dial.* 570; **1351** vi usurpando ad ∼andum regale gubernaculum domini regis Anglie in perturbacionem pacis et enervacionem legis sue *SelCKB* VI 76; profecit coram Deo et hominibus errores multorum ∼ando Cantlow *Orig. Cantab.* 275.

enervate [LL], feebly, weakly.

~ius, i. debilius, *slaeclice, þweorlice GlH* E 271.

enervatio [LL]

1 weakening, enervation. **b** weakness, paralysis; **c** (spiritual).

~o, i. exinanitio *GlH* E 269; [abbas A., ob. **1339**] ~onem virium sui corporis tolerabat *Meaux* II 313*n*. **b 8**. . ~o, *awordenes WW*; membrorum ~onem quam Greco vocabulo paralysin dicunt F. MALM. *V. Aldh.* 78D. **c** ~o, i. . . pigritia *GlH* E 269; 'magna velut mare contritio tua', contritio spiritualis et ~o cordis ad nullam stabilitatem virtutis reducibilis PECKHAM *Exp. Thren.* II 28; **c1432** in lamentabilem virtutum et scienciarum . . et studii ~onem *StatOx* 238.

2 weakening, impairment (of abstr., esp. law, privilege, or status). **b** detriment (of person).

respondit nil rationis posse afferri ad ~onem rationis Anselmi EADMER *HN* 71; **1261** domum illam . . deforciavit in nostri dedecus et contemptum et prefate collacionis nostre prejudicium et ~onem *Cl* 479; **1270** licet aliqui . . ad ipsius statuti [sc. de Judeis] ~onem conentur, prelati ad ejusdem observationem laborabunt (*Lit. Archiep. Ebor.*) *Leg. Ant. Lond.* 235; **1305** (v. annullatio 1); ?**1334** ad maximum damnum parcium conquerencium et . . ~onem judicii supradicti (*Breve Regis*) *MGL* I 409; **1340** in ~onem pacis . . studencium *FormOx* 158; **1377** super . . erroribus . . proposicionum . . ad ~onem tocius ecclesiastici status tendencium . . (*Lit. Papae*) WALS. *HA* I 347; **a1380** in ~onem privilegiorum et libertatum, pacis et tranquillitatis studii *StatOx* 181. **b 1392** in enervacionem et exheredacionem domini regis et dictorum tenencium *IMisc* 253/1.

enervativus, tending to weaken.

item occiositas est anime quoad suam †potestativam [? l. potestatem] ~a et in desidiam resolutiva J. WALEYS *V. Relig.* I 1. 219v.; sequitur 'non des requiem tibi' in fletu paulatim tepescendo; 'requiem' inquit meroris ~am, vel interruptivam PECKHAM *Exp. Thren.* II 38.

enervatrix, enervator (f.).

[epilensia] et sensuum omnium ~ix est et mortis quedam imago *Mir. Hen. VI* II 47.

enervescere [LL], to become weak, lose vigour.

post cessationem . . typi, et calore jam per aliquantum ~ente, fiant provocativa sudoris ut fomentationes circa pedes GILB. I 18v. 2.

enervis, ~us [CL], nerveless, weak, paralysed; **b** (of abstr.). **c** (of physical obj.) slack, limp, feeble.

~um, emortuum *GlC* E 207; ~is, sine virtute *Ib.* 210 (cf. ib. 350: eviratus, ~is); elumbem, i. ~em, *aswunden GlH* E 208; quem contracto poplite . . ~em atque imbecillem sanitati restituit GIR. *GE* I 23; **s1147** legimus olim numerosissimum Domini exercitum unius hominis . . peccantis scelere ita inquinatum . . ut ~is et languidus appareret W. NEWB. *HA* I 20. **b** longa est fabula, verba insulsa et ~ia GOSC. *Lib. Confort.* 26; argumentum . . ~um ac debile BEKINSAU 748. **c** FRITH. 1392 (v. docmen).

enerviter [LL], feebly, weakly, in unmanly fashion.

Samson . . ~er deceptus illecebrosis lenocinii nexibus ALDH. *VirgP* 53; propositum continentiae nequaquam ~er et fluxa mente custodiunt BEDE *Tab.* 480; B. *Ep.* 386 (v. dagma); non ~er sed viriliter cuncta pergessit, ardens et lucens in domo Domini BYRHT. *V. Osw.* 405; a carnis illecebris ~er superatur R. COLD. *Godr.* 233; terrenis ~er incumbere, que in imo sunt querere . . similitudinem pecorinam induere est AD. SCOT *Serm.* 100C; cur enim non magis fortiter patiuntur injurias . . quam matris sue libertatem . . tam ~er violari permittant GROS. *Ep.* 72* p. 219; **s1322** [ducem Lanc.] tempore . . certandi usque ad mortem pro justicia defensanda ~er fugere debere sanctum censeri *Meaux* II 344.

ene- v. aene-. **enes-** v. aesnec-. **enexia** v. euexia. **enfit-** v. emphyt-. **enfortunium** v. eufortunium. **enfr-** v. emphr-. **engaignum, engania** v. ingenium. **engaranare** v. inwarennare. **engerimion** v. egersimon. **engia, engium** v. engya. **enginator** v. ingeniator. **enginum** v. ingenium. **Engl-** v. Angl-.

engrelatus [cf. AN *engreler*, OF *engresler*], (her.) engrailed.

1390 de . . j godet' argent' . . signat' in fundo cum cruce ~ata *Ac. Foreign* 25 Gd.; **1402** ij bacini argentei enameliati . . cum armis quorum campus est rubeus engreilatus cum uno griffone aureo rapace *Invent. S. Paul.* 513.

engya [ἐγγύα], (pl.) mortgage.

11. . totum tenementum quod M. de S. . . dedit in feudo et hereditate et in engiis *Danelaw* 353; **1310** tenetur in engiis cum Sibilla filia sua in magno cursu averiorum ad festum nativitatis S. Johannis Baptiste *Cornw RO Mount Edgcumbe MSS M. T. D.* 16/10 (*Cornw*).

enharmonicus [cf. LL enarmonius < ἐναρμόνιος], (mus.) enharmonic. **b** (as sb. f.) enharmonic melody.

BYRHT. *V. Osw.* 442 (v. chromaticus 1a); NECKAM *NR* I 20 (v. diatonicus); primum [genus harmonie] vocatur diatonicum, secundum . . chromaticum, tertium dicitur ~um BACON *Tert.* 296. **b** GARL. *Tri. Eccl.* 100 (v. chromaticus 1b).

enhydris [CL < ἐνυδρίς], kind of water snake. (*Cf.* Isid. *Etym.* XII 4. 21).

enydris, serpens in aqua OSB. GLOUC. *Deriv.* 195; est et alia bestia nomine enidrus spinis repleta velut ericius HON. *Spec. Eccl.* 938A; enidris, serpens aquatilis, a quo percussi obturgescunt in ydropisim BART. ANGL. XVIII 9.

enhydrus [LL < ἔνυδρος], sort of gem that exudes water. (*Cf.* Isid. *Etym.* XVI 13. 9).

perpetuo tales alter lacrimatur enydros, / gaudet fons vene divitis esse lapis NECKAM *DS* VI 299; enidros parvus lapis est et modicus: perpetuis distillat guttis BART. ANGL. XVI 40 (cf. ib. 99: ydachites . . quidam dicunt hunc esse lapidem qui dicitur enidros).

enichmus [? cf. ἐνικμος], sort of precious stone. *Cf. enhydrus, onychinus*.

1245 in cujus [crucis] patibulo superiori est ~us in quo sculpitur ymago hominis *Invent. S. Paul.* 471.

enicia v. aesnecius. **enicopare** v. syncopare. **enidium** v. oenidium. **enidr-** v. enhydr-. **enigm-** v. aenigm-.

enim [CL]

1 (inceptive) well now.

canonico . . talibus verbis alloquitur: "~m," inquid, "scio quod per longum tempus me dilexisti" O. CHERITON *Fab.* A21.

2 (confirmative or causal) for; **b** (ellipt.).

†**693** (14c) ~m sunt nomina testium *CS* 121; **c705** te . . exhortari non piget. hoc ~m ideo agimus quia 'karitas Christi . . urget nos' ALDH. *Ep.* 8 (11); supra se . . habet urbem Alcluith, quod . . significat petram Cluith; est ~m juxta fluvium nominis illius BEDE *HE* I 12 p. 26; intravit cubiculum quo dormire disponebat; erat ~m prima hora noctis *Ib.* II 12 p. 108; **749** (12c) dum ~m mihi omnipotens . . sceptra regni largitus est ideo . . ex eo quod dedit retribuo *CS* 140; **s1190** R. HOWD. III 72 (v. corrosio 1a); non solum vox tua sonet laudes Dei . . cum ~m voce cantaveris, silebis aliquando vita. . . si ~m ore clamas et fraudem cogitas, siluisti a Deo, . . cum ~m laudatur Deus de bono opere tuo, laudas Deum GIR. *GE* II 18; confirmative sive adjunctive [sc. conjuncciones] sunt hec 'quod', '~m', 'cum', 'dum', . . [etc.] . . causales vero sunt ut 'quia', 'quamobrem', 'quapropter', '~m' *Ps.*-GROS. *Gram.* 57. **b** quid huc venisti? non ~m mihi aliquid . . salutis potes ultra conferre BEDE *HE* V 13 p. 311.

3 contrastive: **a** nonetheless; **b** however.

a equus niger et superbe hinniens . . videbatur uncis ferreis protuberantibus, super quos misera imposita mox ab oculis intuentium . . disparuit; audiebantur ~m clamores per quatuor fere miliaria *Eul. Hist.* I 402 (= W. MALM. *GR* II 204: tamen). **b** priores [i. e. Christi tirones] . . cum lacrimis forte, quae ex Dei caritate profluunt, alii ~m [i. e. apostatae] atque cum tristitia, sed quae de indignatione . . deprehensae conscientiae extorquetur, illud [? debitum] excipient GILDAS *EB* 1; membra sua propria . . laniavit. non solum ~m seipsum . . decerpebat, quin etiam omnes . . morsibus lacerabat FELIX *Guthl.* 41; [ea terra] ad curiam regis pertinet juste. Godricus ~m occupavit injuste *DB* I 57v.; gens fortis et animosa, vita et moribus conveniens cum Germanicis; non ~m ita inhiat spoliis et rapinis ut gens Germanica *Eul. Hist.* II 60 (cf. BART. ANGL. XV 125).

enimvero [CL], moreover, indeed.

~o, certe, quia, autem *GlH* E 277; emergit septenarius felicissimus numerus, qui sese . . copulat cum quoadusque perveniat ad thronum summi Dei. demonstrat ~o plenitudinem temporis BYRHT. *Man.* 210; ~o quamdiu unus de illo numero defuerit, seculi consummatio . . minime fieri poterit ALEX. CANT. *Dicta* 4 p. 124; Ciceronis exemplo retardari non potui. . . mihi ~o ea mens est [etc.] GIR. *TH intr.* p. 5; terrarum ~o remotissimarum . . qualitates . . a longe speculari . . studiosis animis non ultima laus est *Ib.* 7.

eniola v. aeneola.

†enistus, *f. l.*

†enistus [? l. ethnicus], *erþling GlH* E 281.

enisus [LL], zeal. **b** effort, travail.

hunc . . locum Domini . . adolescens toto mentis ~u amplexatus est *V. Neot. A* 2. **b** ADEL. *QN* 66 (v. ceraunius 1).

enitēre, ~escere [CL], (of light) to shine forth; **b** (w. abstr. subj., fig.); **c** (w. pers. subj.).

~escit, sp[l]endescit *GlC* E 218; flammivomis lampas radiis praesaga futuri / caelitus enituit FRITH. 38; lux supercelestis circa eum ~uit *Latin Stories* 102. **b 676** (12c) nunc cum gratia superna . . profusius ~esceret *CS* 43; †**948** (v. 1 condicio 1a); enituitque bonum praestantis praesulis omen FRITH. 1107; **a1074** vera virtus . . pulchrius ~escit LANFR. *Ep.* 37 (9); virilis in eo animus et virtus ~ebat egregia claritate W. POIT. I 4; tempus . . quo viri virtus digne valuerit ~ere GIR. *TH* III 49; species pulchritudinis ejus . . amantium oculis ~escit J. FORD *Serm.* 35. 5. **c** ALDH. *VirgP* 20 (v. enarrare 1b); Edilbertus rex Cantuariorum . . baptismo dealbatus cum sua ~uit natione *V. Greg.* p. 86; qualiter . . Egcwynus . . ~uerit in pueritia BYRHT. *V. Ecgwini* 353; sanctus sanctorum adhuc puer tanta charitate ~uit ut . . in ea nihil accreverit PULL. *Sent.* 798A; sicut variis virtutibus in vita mortali electi ~uerunt COGGESH. *Visio* 35.

eniti [CL]

1 to strive, struggle; **b** (w. inf. or gd.). **c** (p. ppl. *enixus*) earnest, assiduous.

~or, conor *GlC* E 197; ~endo, conando *Ib.* 215; ad hoc propensius ~endum GIR. *TH intr.* p. 6; quis unquam picturam vidit ad omnes pictoris artes ~i? numquid . . olla figulo sue dicet "quare me superius arctam, amplam inferius compegisti?" *Ib.* I 13; piscibus contra fluctus mos est ~i *Ib.* II 42. **b** condecet eniti poenis Acherontis adusti / exemptas justis mentes miscere saluberrimis FRITH. 289; qui . . in mortali . . peccato vincitur . . ~atur exire et peregrinari Jerosolimam R. NIGER *Mil.* I *prol.*; veniam optinere ~itur DOMINIC *V. Ecgwini* I 18; ob hoc ego sum enisus ad audendum talia HIL. RONCE. 5. 14. **c** cum palatii vestibulum caccabatus irrumpere ~o conamine niteretur ALDH. *VirgP* 50 (cf. ib. 52: Eugenius . . flaminem ~a prece poposcit ut . .).

2 to bring forth, give birth to (partly fig.); **b** (*s. pass.*).

c600 si itaque enixam mulierem prohibemus ecclesiam intrare (*Lit. Papae*) BEDE *HE* I 27 p. 54; baptizare autem vel enixam mulierem vel hoc quod genuerit . . nullo modo prohibetur *Ib.*; quos materna simul matrix enixa gemellos / edidit in mundo ALDH. *VirgV* 1077; enixa, *beorende GlC* E 214; ante ostium domus qua sancta puerpera . . infantulum enixa est FELIX *Guthl.* 5; octavis felix enixa puerpera Christum *Kal. M. A.* I 420; hoc enititur quod †preconciperat [l. preconceperat] / hoc fundit mulier quod vir infuderat WALT. WIMB. *Palpo* 59. **b** enixus, creatus *GlC* E 217; ADEL. *QN* 66 (v. 1 elimare d).

enitus v. evitus.

†enium, membrane, gut, or (?) *f. l.*

dicitur hernia quasi rumpens †enia [? l. entera], i. intestina; vel †enia sunt panniculi et membra nervosa GAD. 129v. 1.

enius v. aeneus.

enixe [CL], earnestly, assiduously.

divina priscorum prophetarum oracula . . ~ius investigando ALDH. *VirgP* 4; ~ius, i. diligentius . . districtius *GlH* E 280; ut commissa ~ius . . scelerum confessione poeniterent BYRHT. *V. Ecgwini* 356; Deum ~ius obsecrans *Ib.* 376; cujus [sc. Mariae] ~ius implorabo interventionem ANSELM (*Or.* 6) III 15; ~e supplicavit *G. Steph.* I 61.

enka, ~um v. inka. **enkidium** v. encyclius. **enkumbrare** v. incumbrare. **enndromades** v. endromis.

ennea [LL < ἐννέα], nine.

FRITH. 1311 (v. cyclicus b).

enneacaidecaëteris [LL < ἐννεακαιδεκαετηρίς], cycle of nineteen years.

~ida, decennovalem *GlC* E 201.

ennicius v. aesnecius.

ennosigaeus [CL < Ἐννοσίγαιος *conf. w.* ἐνναίειν], earth-shaker, misinterp. as dweller in Sigaeum.

ennos ut Grecis placet 'habitator' est . . sic et Neptunum ~um eo quod Sigeum inhabitet J. SAL. *Pol.* 817A; Neptunus dicitur ~us, quasi habitator illius promontorii NECKAM *SS* II 25. 4.

ennulliare v. inolere. **eno-** v. et. oeno-.

enodabilis [LL], explicable. **b** (by misinterp.) inexplicable.

enodabil[i]s, solubilis, extricabilis, explicabilis, . . interpretabilis, intelligibilis, . . scibilis OSB. GLOUC. *Deriv.* 200. **b** ~e, quod solvi non potest *GlC* E 221.

enodare [CL]

1 to loosen, untie (also fig.); *v. et. denodare* 1. **b** to unwrap. **c** to free (prisoner, partly fig.). **d** (w. abstr. subj.) to liberate, unleash.

dira vinculorum ligamina . . ~antur ALDH. *VirgP* 35; ante litem enodetur / judicique demonstretur / pera feta cominus WALT. WIMB. *Van.* 25; mors quicquid artifex natura construit / solvit, effibulat, enodat, dissuit *Id. Sim.* 104. **b** cito ~atum [sc. os in panniculo ligatum] illud idem quod . . amiserat esse cognovit BEN. PET. *Mir. Thom.* VI 4. **c** cum carnalis ergastuli vinculis ~aretur ALDH. *VirgP* 37; Æthelstanus [abbas, ob. **1043**] eum [percussorem suum] a vinculis . . flagitans ~ari . . terminavit vitam *Chr. Rams.* 156. **d** sepius enodat animos opulentia pravos, / sepius immanes paupertas conserat iras D. BEC. 652.

2 to elucidate; **b** (absol.). *V. et. denodare* 2.

precor hoc lucidius exponi et clarius ~ari ALDH. *Met.* 10 p. 84; **a690** ~antes bibliothecae problemata *Id. Ep.* 5; virtutum tramitem ~abo *V. Cuthb.* II 1; mittit etiam praefatarum ~atas et explanatas interrogationum quaestiones quas in Historia Bedae lector reperiet GOSC. *Aug. Min.* 753A; ORD. VIT. VI 5 p. 32 (v. enarratio); obscurissimum prophete locum sicut potuimus ~avimus AILR. *Serm.* 471B; rerum .. tam naturas quam defectus ~are GIR. *TH intr.* p. 7; ad .. nodosa subtiliter atque efficaciter ~andum *Id. GE* II 37; antequam ~emus ista dicamus .. SICCAV. *PN* 178; *to scheve* .. denodare, †edonare, monstrare *CathA.* **b** omnium facta .. puniet justissimus vindex, ut palam omnibus ~at Dei .. lex ORD. VIT. IV 5 p. 196.

enodatio [CL]

1 untying, loosening (also fig.).

inter vincula corporis egri tutare animam; post ~onem ad te anhelantem non abigas W. MALM. *Mir. Mariae* 235; gens barbara .. que navigantibus .. ventum vendere solent, quasi sub nodis fili inclusum quorum ~one ventus augebitur HIGD. I 31.

2 elucidation.

ut ad aliorum transeamus ~onem ALB. LOND. *DG* 1. 5; cum .. emergit ambiguitas ex determinacione Romani pontificis, .. cujus dubitacionis ~onem nescit dubitans per scripturas sacras .., ad apostolicam sedem debet recurrere OCKHAM *Pol.* III 264.

enodis [CL], free from knots. **b** smooth. **c** explained, intelligible.

~is, sine nodo *GlC* E 196; ramusculi .. ab ipso stipite deciderunt; ipse vero medius vectis planus et ~is in gestantis ulnis permansit AD. EYNS. *Hug.* V 18 p. 210. **b** donec .. / obvius enodis uteri tumor erigat arcum HANV. II 25 p. 259. **c** Dominus .. hanc questionem duobus preceptis absolvit et ~em reddidit W. MALM. *GP* I 49.

enormare [cf. CL normare], to disorder, defile. **b** (p. ppl.) disordered, irregular.

mundatur totus infans baptismate lotus, / quamvis forte nothus sit patris crimine notus; / quod pater enormat [*gl.*: deturpat in generando per peccatum] baptismi forma reformat GARL. *Mor. Scol.* 477. **b** quomodo .. tam irregularis, tam ~ata regula, et tam fallax sufficit homini ad ipsum in omnibus dirigendum? BRADW. *CD* 64A; **1427** in primo capitulo unius libelli penes vos reperti inter alia frivola et †enormata [l. enormala] dicta, expresse scribitur quomodo .. (*Ordinatio Synodi*) AMUND. I 226.

enormis [CL], **~us,**

1 a (w. ref. to deed) irregular, outrageous. **b** (w. ref. to words) insulting. **c** (as sb. n.) irregularity, crime.

a ut .. / .. facinus scelerum superans explodat inorme ALDH. *VirgV* 105; **949** (11c) hoc inorme scelus *CS* 880; contigit ut quidam .. clerici .. de maleficiis accusati .. tenerentur in vinculis talibus ut .. solet in regno ~ia patrantibus flagitia H. BOS. *Thom.* III 22; ~ia peccata, sicut adulterium et .. homicidium R. NIGER *Mil.* II 26; **c1230** nolentes tam abusivas enormitates seu tam ~es abusus .. tolerare (*Lit. Papae*) *Couch. Furness* 573; **s1238** (v. consentaneus 2c); **s1239** (v. consentire 2c); **1296** dampna ~a contra nostras libertates *Reg. Carl.* I 68; a crimine maximo et ~issimo OCKHAM *Dial.* 595; in nulla via equitatis .. ad pacem inflecti quivit absque ~i lesione corone Anglie *G. Hen. V* 2. **b 1300** insultavit J. de S. per ~a verba *Rec. Leic.* I 230. **c s1093** rex .. prolongans iniquitatem Anselmum .. ~ia corrigere volentem non pertulit W. NEWB. *HA* I 2; Herodes .. perpetratis .. ~ibus immensis et infinitis .. divinam ultionem non evasit GIR. *PI* I 17; **s1232** multi .. insurrexerunt ei [Huberto de Burgh] .., multa ~ia ei imponentes WEND. III 34; **1288** dicit quod ipsum non defamavit nec alia ~ia ei intulit *SelPlMan* 109; **1315** alia ~ia [etc.] ad grave damnum [etc.] et contra pacem *MGL* I 299; **1365** quod nullus lavet nec alia ~ia ponat nec faciat infra .. Holawpoill et quod reservetur .. pro aquacione averiorum *Hal. Durh.* 38; **1522** viros notabiles .. a .. consilio expelli fecisti aliaque .. quamplurima et inenarrabilia ~ia, impedimenta et extorsiones nobis .. intulisti *Form. S. Andr.* 230.

2 large, huge. **b** numerous. **c** (of abstr.) great.

factor confinxit corpus inorme ALDH. *Aen.* 72 (*Colosus*) 7; codicem protulerunt .. illi perparvum, isti ~em BEDE *HE* V 13; ~is, ingens *GlC* E 202; angeli .. singillatim litteras ~is libri contra singula peccata computabant ORD. VIT. III 3 p. 49. **b** sicut Judas Machabeus .. parva manu populi Dei contra inormem et supra invisibilem hostem .. invasit EDDI 19. **c** gigantes .. inormis alebat magnitudo *Lib. Monstr.* I 54; quidam juvenis .. de pinna inhormae proceritatis elapsus .. cecidit EDDI 23; erga / auctorata volans altaria, liba piarum / fundere jure precum studio satagebat inormi [*altered to* acuto] FRITH. 151; Cedron et alii torrentes ~i estu aruerant ORD. VIT. IX 15 p. 602.

enormitalis, irregular, outrageous, or (?) *f. l.*

ecclesiasticas personas multis molestiis et enormitalibus [? l. enormitatibus et] insolentiis sibi suppeditari volens (*Passio S. Thomae*) *Becket Mat.* IV 432.

enormitas [CL]

1 a seriousness, gravity (of crime). **b** irregularity (of procedure).

a qui ~atem scelerum suorum divini lateris sanguine diffidit preponderandam ÆLNOTH *Cnut* 15; propter excessus ~atem GIR. *TH* II 9; **s1229** inventi sunt .. duo clerici .. magne auctoritatis interfecti .. . hujus .. transgressionis ~as cum ad aures magistrorum universitatis [Parisiensis] pervenisset, convenerunt omnes .. M. PAR. *Maj.* III 168; qui vivi exuri debent non eis verberibus noceatur .. et hoc nisi aliter exigat ~as delicti BRACTON 105; **s1311** puplicate fuerunt attestationes Templariorum super ~ate heresis *Ann. Paul.* 270. **b** pontifices non aperte propter ~atem sed sub .. insinuationis specie .. suadebant ut archipresul .. regis se .. voluntati subjiceret H. BOS. *Thom.* III 36; **1491** tantas ~ates .. amovere cupientes .. concedimus .. quod [etc.] *StatOx* 298.

2 outrage, wicked act; **b** (w. ref. to brothel).

ex quo paradisi .. primicola viperina minus praesensit eludia .. insopibili fere mundialis ~as grassatur parsimonia O. CANT. *Pref. Frith.* 13; a se ipso penas exegit, jejunio .. corpus affligens .. donec .. per condignos penitentie fructus ~atis tante veniam meruisset W. CANT. *V. Thom.* I 18; tam ~atibus quam spurcitiis GIR. *EH* I 34; elegimus .. has potius ~ates sub dissimulatione .. transire quam .. gentem iniquam exasperare *Id. IK* II 4; **s1191** fama .. ~atis hujus [incarcerationis electi Ebor.] velociter discurrens .. W. NEWB. *HA* IV 17; **c1230** (v. enormis 1a); si sacerdos ~atibus se miscuerit OCKHAM *Dial.* 626; **s1402** [rex] majori audacia debriatus ecclesiasticos viros .. molestavit. a quibus et ceteris .. ~atibus illatis .. ut .. desisteret .. archiepiscopus .. rogavit *Chr. Pont. Ebor. C* 431. **b 1485** (v. bordellum 2).

3 a huge size, greatness. **b** large amount.

a draconem .. quoniam tantae inormitatis existat .. armis orationum extinxit ALDH. *VirgP* 29; B. *V. Dunst.* 1 (v. divulgare c). **b 793** alii inormitate vestium laborant, alii frigore pereunt ALCUIN *Ep.* 16; ingentes divitiarum copias trahebant .. ut ~ate gazarum visa cunctis terrori existerent ORD. VIT. X 20 p. 127; copulatio .. interrupta est minis precibusque et auri argentique aliarumque specierum ponderosa ~ate *Ib.* XI 37 p. 294.

enormiter [CL]

1 unsymmetrically, irregularly.

terra .. in colles varios arduosque montes ~er erecta GIR. *TH* I 4.

2 a greatly, excessively. **b** prodigiously. **c** outrageously, heinously, grievously.

a mures .. ~ius quam alibi grana consumunt GIR. *TH* I 27; vix unum invenies qui .. vino .. diurnos labores ~ius quam deceret nocte non redimat *Id. RG* II 14; **1305** pavimentum ville .. ~er est dirutum et confractum *BBC* (*Univ. Ox.*) 374; **1341** erarium nostrum .. est exhaustum et fiscales redditus ~er sunt diminute (*Lit. Regis*) AVESB. 97. **b a690** nonnulli superna noscuntur sofia praediti et arcana luce inormiter referti ALDH. *Ep.* 5; floruit cum caeteris floribus ~er Oswaldus impiger monachus BYRHT. *V. Osw.* 422. **c s1213** [Albigensium] perversitas adeo divinam contempsit severitatem ut .. calices .. in despectum .. sanguinis Christi ~er dehonestarent WEND. II 87; **1248** ipsum verberaverunt et ~er percusserunt *SelPlMan* 18; per bella .. ad patrias peregrinas distrahimur, obtruncamur .. et ~er mutilamur R. BURY *Phil.* 7. 112.

3 unlawfully, wrongfully.

episcopi .. qui in ejus absentia in episcopatum inormiter missi sunt EDDI 32; **1246** ~er destruxit bladum suum super terram suam *SelPlMan* 7; **s1091** Anselmum statuit archiepiscopum Cantuariensem, sed postea ~er persequens eum, usque ad exilium lacessivit *Flor. Hist.* II 24; hic damnetur qui sanctorum ditionem et .. libertatem violare ~er non veretur ELMH. *Cant.* 225.

enormus v. enormis. **enot-** v. innot-. **enoxia** v. euexia. **enphit-** v. emphyt-. **enpruntum** v. empromptum. **enpus** v. empyus.

ens [CL]

1 a being, (living) thing; *v. et. entitas* 1a, 2 *essentia* 1a; **b** (Supreme) Being; *v. et.* 2 *essentia* 1b; **c** (abstr., phil.). **d** (*ens rationis*) subject of logic (sts. dist. from *ens reale*); *v. et. entitas* 1b.

hac scrobe nupserunt, doluerunt et gemuerunt; / hac entes latebra ducunt suspiria crebra R. CANT. *Malch.* III 94; entes non ambidextri .. sed ambisinistri GIR. *GE* II 28 p. 308; vix entis nomen meruit pauper retinere WALT. WIMB. *Scel.* 64; si persone vel hypostases vel entes ponerentur *Ps.*-GROS. *Summa* 384; antiquissimum encium est Deus .. . optimum encium est mundus W. BURLEY *Vit. Phil.* 8. **b** quare est quaedam natura vel substantia vel essentia .. quae est summum bonum, summum magnum, summum ens vel subsistens, i. e. summum omnium quae sunt ANSELM (*Mon.* 4) I 18; trinus /ens in personis, unus in esse Deus GARL. *Epith.* III 108; quoddam ens est quod est ipsum 'esse', sicut Deus, quoddam cui convenit 'esse' sicut omne aliud ens a Deo DUNS *Ord.* III 185–6. **c** Grecorum .. quidam aliquid unum et ens equivoce dici affirmabant, ut Zenonis questionem solverent BALSH. *AD rec.* 2 58; continui .. interpolatum aliquid vel successivum causam esse possibile non est; esset enim et non ens enti quandoque causa ALF. ANGL. *Cor* 16. 14; omne quod est aut est ens actu aut ens potentia, id est aut est in complemento aut non est in complemento, possibile est tamen esse GROS. 126; ens est prima anime impressio, ut dicit Avicenna, unde per se cadit in intellectum, quicquid .. in sensum cadit est ens. quod .. in intellectum cadit, tum est ens tum est non-ens J. BLUND *An.* 85; queritur hic primo utrum de ente separato possit esse scientia BACON VII 1; ad aliud negandum est illud quod assumitur, quod sc. naturaliter cognoscitur ens esse primum objectum intellectus nostri DUNS *Ord.* III 19; sequitur quod ens possit cognosci sub racione entitatis licet non sub ratione veritatis *Ib.* 126; prima causa est illud ad quod omnia encia attribuuntur *Id. Metaph.* I 1 p. 13. **d** ens reale non opponitur enti racionis. item omne ens omni enti comparatum aut est idem aut diversum; idem ergo et diversum sunt contraria immediate circa ens et convertibilia. sed ens racionis est distinctum contra reale et non est passio convertibilis cum ente extra animam *Ib.* 293; non determinatur de vocibus in logica nisi in quantum significant res, ut eis insunt intenciones secunde .. sive ens racionis, et non est aliud intelligendum per ens racionis quam res secunde intencionis (W. BURLEY *Expos. Art. Vet.*) *GLA* III 298 *n.* 579; ens racionis nec est idem cum re nec distinguitur realiter; hoc secundum opinionem que ponit encia racionis objective in anima (OCKHAM *Sent. prol.*) *Ib.* 338 *n.* 765; ens reale aliquando accipitur pro omni vera re existente in rerum natura, et sic ens racionis est ens reale; aliquando accipitur pro ente existente solum extra animam, et sic ens racionis non est ens reale (*Id. Quodl.*) *Ib.* 338 *n.* 766.

2 essence. *V. et. entitas* 2, 2 *esse* 14c, 2 *essentia* 4.

vita est actus fluens ab ente quinto simplici sempiterno BACON VII 57.

3 existence. *V. et. entitas* 3, 2 *esse* 14c, 2 *essentia* 5.

sic sunt ad se invicem essentia et esse et ens, hoc est existens sive subsistens ANSELM (*Mon.* 4) I 20; J. SAL. *Met.* 885D (v. aequivocatio a); tria ista: bonum, ens, et verum, idem sunt; ergo eorum opposita: malum, non ens, falsum. ergo malum est simpliciter non ens HALES *Sent.* I 73; ens est subjectum hujus scientie [i. e. philosophie prime] KILWARDBY *Quomodo Deus* 118.

ensiculus [CL], small sword.

nascuntur haec diminutiva .. de disillabis ut 'ensis', '~us', 'dulcis', 'dulciculus' ALDH. *PR* 133; **1404** quidam feloni .. zonam .. et cultellum .. et unum ensiclium cum manibrio murrato et duabus laminis argenteis fallaratum .. furati fuerunt .. et .. cultellum ac hensiclium .. in quodam dumo .. projecerunt (*CourtR G. Totham*) *Essex R. O.* D/DC 6/3.

ensifer [CL], sword-bearing; **b** (w. ref. to Orion). **c** (as sb. m.) sword-bearer.

~eri, ense[m] ferentes *GlH* E 290; ensifer illi Dei cherubim aditu patefacto / Christicolas intrare modo sinit ense retracto P. BLOIS *Euch.* 1143D; Robertus .. Guillelmus ab ense / longo nomen habens enituere probi. / ensiferum circa Guillelmum sanguis inundat GARL. *Tri. Eccl.* 135. **b** ensiferum videt Oriona severum R. CANT. *Malch.* V 25; Orion ~er dicitur, quia succinctus erat ense ALB. LOND. *DG* 15. 8; ensifer Orion rutilantibus emicat astris NECKAM *DS* I 408. **c s998** officiales sunt vij, quorum nomina sunt ista: iij cancellarii, .. Palatinus dapifer, dux Saxonie ~er, rex Boemie pincerna *Eul. Hist.* I 378 (cf. ib.: dux portitor ensis).

ensis [CL]

1 sword; **b** (ceremonial); **c** (fig.). **d** (w. *placitum*) criminal plea (C. I.).

ut .. instructas peltibus, ~ibus, hastis et ad caedem promptas protenderet manus GILDAS *EB* 18; projecto ~e quem strictum tenuerat BEDE *HE* I 7; ~is, *hiltleas sweord* ÆLF *Gl.*; ~e virorum perierunt ORD. VIT. IV 3 p. 174; †**13**.. (v. dagarius); qui capit ensem / ense perit GARL. *Tri. Eccl.* 17; **1315** tenens in manu sua dextra unum ~em de Colonio tracto (*sic*) de ferro et acero facto de longitudine sex pedum hominis et latitudine juxta hultam quatuor pollicum hominis, precium ~is duorum solidorum *CoramR* 220 r. 105; ~is, *swerde WW*. **b** consuetudo .. orta est quod si quis .. miles fieret, semper nudum ~em super altare .. offerre deberet *G. Herw.* 328b; **11**.. postea ab episcopis ~em accipiat et cum ~e totum regnum sibi .. sciat esse commendatum *Rec. Coronation* 34; Ethelstanus quem .. militem fecerat, donatum chlamyde coccinea, gemmato baltheo, ~e saxonico cum vagina aurea W. MALM. *GR* II 133; **1275** *Cart. Osney* IV 350 (v. creare 3a). **c** qui Dorobernensem tulerat contra scelus ensem *V. Anselmi Epit.* 51. **d 1289** quod [dominus rex] habet visum verecci ibidem piscem regalem cum acciderit .. et totum placitum de ~e *CartINorm* 211.

2 shoulder blade; **b** (used in divination).

in ~e qui suspenditur in furcula ad defensionem oris stomachi *Ps.*-RIC. *Anat.* 2; si vulnera fiant in collo, ~e, vel alio simili .. vulnus suatur GILB. IV 179.1. **b** accidit .. quemdam .. ~is [v. l. ossis] inspectorem .. furtum .. inspiciendo notasse GIR. *IK* I 11; aliquando apparent ymaginarie ut in ungue pueri virginis carminati et in pelvibus et ~ibus BACON V 6.

enta, ~is [OF *ente*], slip, scion, sapling.

1233 idem Johannes scindi fecit et asportari xx fraxinos et ~as eradicavit et asportavit *CurR* XV 77; **1267** in allocatione eidem pro xliij ent' pomorum vij s. ij d., prec' ent' ij d. . pro c ent' pirorum emptis ad plantandum apud Suwerk' xij s. *Pipe Wint.* 159308 r. 33; **1270** ~as emi et eas infra gardinum manerii nostri de Clarendon' plantari . . facias *Liberate* 47 m. 10; **1275** dictum *stubbing* prostravit et asportavit, et etiam †encas [l. entas] in dicto gardino fodit et prostravit injuste *CourtR Wakefield* I 37; **1275** Nicholao le Cuvreur pro ij ~is kaylew', ij s.; cuidam fratri de Ponte pro xij ~is kayl', rewl' et gilefr', xvj s.; pro d †planton' ros[arum], ij s. vj d.; pro j quarterio liliarum, xij d. *KRAc* 467/6 m. 2; Johanni le Fruter pro j ~a kayl', ij s. j d. *Ib.*; **1279** Willelmo Gardinario pro xviij ~is emptis ad gardinum, xiiij s. vij d. ob. *Ib.* m. 7; **1284** posuit ij ~as pomorum in curia sua, que furate fuerunt *Hund. Highworth* 255 (cf. ib. 256: attachiatus est pro ~ibus furatis); **1311** expensa minuta . . in vadio Gilloti gardinarii . . plantantis ~es, iiij s. j d. *Ac. Man. Wint.* (*Michelmersh*); **13.** . in xvj ~is emptis ad plantandum in gardino *Ac. Man. Cant.* (*Rucking*).

entaliare [AN *entalier*, OF *entaillier*], to hew, cut, carve.

1216 cum petris . . intaillatis *Pat* 173a (v. 1 cassa 2); **1253** unum sporum in camera regine nostre bene intalliatum *Liberate* 29 m. 7; **1313** carpentariis operantibus circa cendulas copandas et entall[iandas] *KRAc* 469/16 f. 5; **1318** gobettorum petre . . entelliatorum *Ib.* 1; **1320** cendulis ad eandem coopertura m entalliandis *Ib.*; petras entalliatas *Ib.*

entaliator [cf. OF *entailleor*], stone-carver.

1313 cementario entalliat[ori] penetranti infra batillamenta et ad imponendas dictas hekkas *KRAc* 468/20 f. 3; cem[entario] cub[atori] et ~ori operanti . . ad elarganda batillamenta pro springald' situand' *Ib.* f. 4.

1 entalis, having a particular kind of being.

sicut est denominativa ista 'animal est album', ita 'ens', quod est superius ad 'album', potest denominare 'animal' sive ens particulariter sumptum pro animali; puta, si illud denominativum esset ~e, hec esset vera 'aliquod ens est ~e' DUNS *Ord.* III 99.

2 entalis, (?) powdered alum.

GILB. III 147. 1, VII 342. 2, 345. 2 (v. 2 dentale).

entall- v. ental-. **entarticus** v. antarcticus.

entaticus [LL < ἐντατικός], aphrodisiac, stimulating.

mediousium aut basilion ~um locis asperis nascitur et umbrosis; hastam habet longam, flores majores purpureos et obrotundos, semen minutum, radices longas; virtus est redarguentis *Alph.* 114.

entcardi v. eicere 3a.

entelechia [LL < ἐντελέχεια], (phil.) entelechy, actuality, reality.

[anima] diffinitur a philosopho in li. de Anima sic [Aristotle *An.* 412a27]: anima est endelichia, i. actus primus sive perfectio corporis physici BART. ANGL. III 3; anima est prima endelichia corporis phisici organici, vel anima est perfectio corporis organici phisici endelichie vitam habentis GILB. VI 241v. 2; celos endelichie / federe confederas J. HOWD. *Lira* 1. 3; antequam hylen endelechia induisset [cf. Aristotle *Met.* XI 8. 13] R. BURY *Phil.* 7. 104; Aristoteles in . . De anima sumit essentiam et †quod quid [? l. quidquid] est a forma essenciali: et hanc dicit endelechiam et perfeccionem totius NETTER *DAF* II 120v.

entelliare v. entaliare.

†entenasmon [? cf. ἀνατείνειν, ἐντείνειν], (med.) form of derangement or hallucination.

†~on fit ex ventositate, unde putant se audire melodias et . . in interioribus leditur quandoque ymaginatio quandoque ratio GILB. II 103. 3.

enterlin- v. interlin-.

enteron [LL < ἔντερον], **~ion,** (pl.) guts, intestines.

~ia, intestina, exta, viscera, vitalia OSB. GLOUC. *Deriv.* 194; NECKAM *Ut.* 97 (v. ablutium); ~a, i. intestina *Alph.* 57; *tharme*, intestinum . ., ~ia *CathA.*

entheca [CL < ἐνθήκη], store, supply. **b** furniture. **c** reliquary. **d** coffin.

apothecam et horrea, ~a multiplici referta, videbamus BALSH. *Ut.* 50; *warnstore*, annona, entica, *wernestura* *CathA.* **b** enticam, sublectilem *Gl. Leid.* 34. 4 (cf. ib. 48. 70: †enthetam, subpellectilem); ~a, Graece, suppellex, *ineddisc* vel *inorf* ÆLF. *Gl.* **c** O. CANT. *Pref. Frith.* 36 (v. decusare). **d** solent . . in doliis bituminatis ac †euthecis [v. l. enthecis] corpora mortuorum a longinquis regionibus fluminis Rhodani dimitti GERV. TILB. III 90 (cf. ib.: in thecis).

enthecare [LL], to entomb.

gloriose ut martir intecatus *Chr. Wallingf.* 57 (cf. ib. 60: duos reges et martires . . qui ibidem intechantur).

entheticus [ἐνθετικός], inserted, interpolated.

~us in Policraticum J. SAL. *Pol.* (*tit.*); ~us . . de Dogmate Philosophorum *Id. Enth. Phil.* (*tit.*).

enthim- v. enthym-. **enthron-** v. inthron-.

enthymema [CL < ἐνθύμημα], (log.) enthymeme.

aliquod . . informationis componamus inditium ut saltem per voluntatum existentias in activas rerum utilium propositiones entimemata persolvamus *Ep. ad amicum* 26; quo te concludam, dabit entimema sophisma *Babio* 441; disputant scholares, quidam demonstrative, dialectice alii, hi rotant ~a, hi perfectis melius utuntur syllogismis W. FITZST. *Thom. prol.* 9; [logicus] enthymema tamen jaculi vice mittere novit NECKAM *DS* X 59; sic solecismus est sermo congruus, et sic / entimema nihil curvat in arte sibi GARL. *Tri. Eccl.* 71; argumentationum iiij sunt species, sillogismus, emptimema, inductio, exemplum BACON XV 289; ~a est inperfectus sillogismus, arguit enim ex una propositione actu posita et alia subintellecta sic, 'omnis homo currit, ergo Sor [i. e. Socrates] currit', et dicitur ab *en* quod est 'in' et *mime* quod est 'mens', quasi in mente retinens unam propositionem. ~a vero continetur sub sillogismo *Ib.* 303; Aristoteles . . docet alios modos raciocinacionum que non videntur syllogismi nullam vim raciocinandi habere nisi per syllogismum et per modos predeterminatos ibi, et hoc ostendit de induccione . . instancia et ~ate KILWARDBY *OS* 502; non est formalis consequencia, nec prima, nec secunda consequencia, quia reducuntur in sillogismum, sicut quodlibet enthimema DUNS *Metaph.* IV 3 p. 179; ~a est curtatus syllogismus, habens unicam premissam et unicam conclusionem WYCL. *Log.* I 35.

enthymematice [ἐνθυμηματικῶς], (log.) by means of an enthymeme.

necessario sequitur quicquid Deus vult et prescit fore in esse reali extrinseco naturali sic erit. hoc Deus vult et prescit sic fore: ergo hoc sic erit; vel ~e, si quis velit, Deus vult hoc fore realiter, ergo hoc sic erit, et antecedens est necessarium . ., quare et consequens BRADW. *CD* 823E.

enthymematicus [LL < ἐνθυμηματικός], (log.) enthymematic.

verumptamen est dare aliquas formas substanciales, syllogisticas, entimematicas, et inducciones, quia tenent alique consequencie que vocantur formales, sed non iste vocate materiales WYCL. *Log.* II 187; **c1370** (v. discursorius).

entica v. entheca. **enticon** v. Henoticon. **entim-** v. enthym-.

entitas

1 a being, an entity; *v. et. ens* 1a, *2 essentia* 1a; **b** (*entitas rationis*) subject of logic (sts. dist. from *entitas realis*); *v. et. ens* 1d.

quelibet ~as habet intrinsecum sibi gradum sue perfeccionis DUNS *PW* 75; arguo sic: illud quod est ~as minor quam entitas realis et major quam entitas racionis est ~as media distincta ab utraque, entitate reali scilicet et racionis W. ALNWICK *QD* 5; basis tocius ~atis est substancia vel agencia essencialis WYCL. *Act.* 38. **b** W. ALNWICK *QD* 5 (v. 1a supra).

2 essence. *V. et. ens* 2, *2 esse* 14b, *2 essentia* 4.

uniuscujusque igitur rei ~as est ejus veritas GROS. 130; incomplexa est ipsa rei cujusque ~as, id est indivisio entis et esse *Ps.*-GROS. *Summa* 292; metaphysica considerat ens simpliciter secundum racionem ~atis que est in rebus et proprietates . . entis secundum quod ens in racione ~atis consideratur KILWARDBY *OS* 579; item quod prius presentatur intellectui et novit [intellectus] est ens secundum Avicennam. sed omne prius agnitum est racio cognoscendi postremum. ergo veritas cognoscitur per ~atem PECKHAM *QA* 220; sumo hic ens et unum et hujusmodi pro significatis secundis, scilicet pro re subtracta unitati et ~ati BACON *CSTheol.* 65; quia quidditas rei est ~as per se rei, [philosophia prima] considerat rem secundum suam ~atem (DUNS *Qu. super Elench.*) *GLA* III 204 *n*.89;

3 existence. *V. et. ens* 3, *2 esse* 14c, *2 essentia* 5.

omne quod habet ~atem ab aliquo exemplariter habet simul eam ab eodem effective T. SUTTON *Quodl.* 374; finis est non tantum motus, sed ~atis DUNS *Metaph.* I 1. p. 34; sequitur . . Deum habere ~atem quidditative *Ib.* p. 36; dependencia sequitur ~atem formalem dependentis ab illa a quo dependet *Id. Ord.* II 286; cum in qualibet unitate minore unitate numerali sit dare ~atem positivam (que sit per se racio illius unitatis et repugnancie ad multitudinem oppositam) maxime vel equaliter erit hoc dare in unitate perfectissima que est 'unitas numeralis' *Ib.* VII 417; omne inferius includit per se aliquid quod non includitur in intellectu superioris; . . ergo aliquid per se includitur in racione individui, quod non includitur in racione nature. illud autem 'inclusum' est ~as positiva *Ib.* 465; hec proposicio universalis 'omnis homo est animal' secundum philosophum est perpetue veritatis, quia est necessaria, cujus quelibet singularis est contingens, cujus veritas transit cum sua ~ate CONWAY *Def. Mend.* 1421 (*recte* 1321); dicitur aliquid esse falsum . . quando deficit a summa veritate vel ~ate que Deus est WYCL. *Ver.* I 81.

entole [ἐντολή], command.

a975 o decus imperii certissima spes quoque regni, / aule Dei mentem obducat tibi et entŏle conviet / alluat aethereusque calor . . (*Ep. ad Edgarum*) *Mem. Dunst.* 368.

entractum v. intractum.

entremarta [cf. Gael. *mart*], (Sc.) kind of mart, fattened beast.

1477 et de xxvij li. xv s. de martis dictis entre martis in . . curiis Omnium Sanctorum *ExchScot* 437; **1479** de . . martis . . dictis ~is *Ib.* 588; **1480** pro sex martis dictis entraymartis *Ib.* 34; **1496** summa totalis oneracionis . . lxij iij et dim. quarteris marte dicte *fog* et *fule* et entra marte [etc.] *Ib.* 599.

entubus v. intubus.

enubilare [LL], to free from clouds (fig.), clarify.

[Anselmus] ita pertractavit questionis latera, ita penetravit et ~avit intima ut Latini clamore testarentur gaudium W. MALM. *GP* I 53.

enuch- v. eunuch-.

enucleare [CL]

1 to stone (fruit). **b** to take out (kernel), shell (nut).

aqua decoctionis . . passularum ~atarum GAD. 53v. 2. **b 9..** ~ata, *ascyled*; ~are, *ascilian WW*; testam fregit et de medio nucis nucleum michi ~avit M. RIEVAULX (*Ep.*) 66 p. 78.

2 (fig.) to lay bare. **b** (p. ppl.) clear, pure.

catholici patres spiritalem sermonum medullam ~antes ALDH. *Met.* 4; res a curiosis ~ata patuit ORD. VIT. VIII 23 p. 410; diabolica proposita dictorum proditorum vi proponentes infringere ac eorum fervida corda ferro forciora et indurata celesti nutu enucliando emollire FAVENT 8. **b a690** Hadriano dumtaxat urbanitate ~ata ineffabiliter praedito ALDH. *Ep.* 5 p. 493.

3 to free from obscurity, explain; **b** (w. indir. qu.); **c** (absol.). **d** (p. ppl.) reasoned.

uberiorem exemplorum formulam ~abimus ALDH. *Met.* 8; **804** quaestiones . . a nobis ~andas ALCUIN *Ep.* 308; solius Anselmi gestis ~andis intentus W. MALM. *GP* I 59; hiis qui talia noverint enuclienda [*gl.*: *a demustrer*] vel edisserenda relinguo NECKAM *Ut.* 113; et ut mortis sacrate frameam [sc. crucem] / auditoris dolens enucleam (*sic*) J. HOWD. *Ph.* 177; ut habetur codice de veteri jure enucliando MILEMETE *Nob.* 11; ea que ostensionem . . veritatis rei gerende sufficere videntur . . enucliare, elicere, et explicare *Plusc. prol.* 4; **1579** cujus [sc. questionis] ambigua et dubitationes, dum in utramque partem ~averint, definient determinabuntque *StatOx* 345. **b** mihi patenter ~are precor quid sit quod . . commentator . . inquit ALDH. *PR* 140; nitor palam ~are qualiter . . mutatio nuper ceperit pullulare ORD. VIT. VIII 26 p. 435; quid sibi velit ista descriptio ~emus W. DONC. *Aph. Phil.* 3. 1; quo modo fieri possit enuclea WALT. WIMB. *Carm.* 400. **c 680** ut certius vestra sagacitas animadvertere queat pro quibus causis mea mediocritas scripta direxerit, compendiose et breviter ~abo ALDH. *Ep.* 4; quia . . se offert occasio referendi quid Balduino contigerit, stilus nostre narrationis . . succincte ~abit ORD. VIT. IX 10 p. 563. **d** in octava sua parte juxta vulgarem opinionem, sed juxta ~atiorem sententiam aliquanto prius BEDE *TR* 16.

enucleate [CL], plainly, precisely.

c675 ~e legendo ALDH. *Ep.* 3; si de his singulis ~ius ac latius audire desideras (*Ep. Ceolfridi*) BEDE *HE* V 21 p. 334; **1073** in utrisque [litteris] ~e ostendistis officium vestri ordinis LANFR. *Ep.* 15 (17); ad Karoli Francorum regis . . fortia gesta depromenda ~ius accedamus GIR. *PI* I 18; **1432** quasquidem lecciones . . per nonnullas auctoritates, historias et figuras enucliacius exponendo *RParl* IV 388a.

enucleatim [LL], plainly, precisely.

accingimur vertere stili ultima ~im de eo memorari queque dignissima HERM. ARCH. *prol.*; quis . . conetur omnia . . illa gestorum regalium molimina ~im retexere? W. MALM. *GR* V *prol.*; quibus ex causis huc advenerint ~im expedietur GIR. *TH* III 16; semper manet in latibulo et numquam per . . doctores sinitur aspirare eciam cum ea que sunt de perfecti nominis integritate ~im distinguunt NETTER *DAF* I 120.

enucleatio

1 shelling (of nut).

a crakkynge, nucliacio, enucliacio *CathA.*

2 explanation. **b** description.

subtilis ~o divinarum scripturarum BYRHT. *V. Ecgwini* 353; scrutemini antiquas scripturas et invenietis ~onem cujuscumque rei in hoc libello insertam *Eul. Hist.* I *proem.* 5; consonum videtur pro ~one ulterioris materie videre que sit racio formalis heretici WYCL. *Civ. Dom.* II 58; ad seriem chronicarum . . veritati enucliacionis licet novitas favorabile sit FORDUN *Chr. prol.* liii. **b** ad ~onem virtutum sancti Ecgwini provenere (*Mir. Ecgwini*) *Chr. Evesham* 59.

enucleator [LL], elucidator.

historiarum .. ∼or venio, non impugnator GIR. *TH* III 1; alter ego juris bonus enucleator et ejus: / Hugusius *Vers. S. Alb. L.* 220.

enucli- v. enucle-.

enudare [LL]

1 to denude.

P. BLOIS *Opusc.* 1009 (v. depilate).

2 to lay bare (fig.), explain.

formula .. quam singillatim evolvere et universaliter ∼are taedet ALDH. *PR* 129.

enula v. inula. **enulus** v. hinnulus.

enumerare [CL]

1 to enumerate, reckon, classify among: **a** (persons); **b** (items); **c** (abstr.); **d** (w. indir. qu.). *V. et. connumerare.*

a per Filium tuum .. apostolos sanctos ex sanctis omnibus elegisti; primum Petrum .. et Mathian ejusdem consortem in apostolatum atque cathedram honoris ∼asti EGB. *Pont.* 4. **b** enumerans veterum vulgata volumina patrum ALDH. *VirgV* 1635; huic manerio pertinet Baldereseia beruuita et ∼ata *DB* II 387v.; **a1078** Gelasius .. libros ejus [Hilarii] inter catholicas scripturas ∼at LANFR. *Ep.* 50 (46); quis potest ∼are sacras reliquias sanctorum .. quae sunt in regali urbe? *Descr. Constant.* 245; ∼antur .. porte xij civitatis Jerosolima in Jeremia R. NIGER *Mil.* III 20. **c** nec ∼ans patriae portenta GILDAS *EB* 4; catalogum ∼ando virtutum *V. Greg.* p. 84; ∼atis animi sui virtutibus priscis BEDE *HE* II 1; nullatenus ∼are possum mala que feci ORD. VIT. VII 15 p. 228. **d** ecce capitulum .. ubi .. quot modis tabernaculum in sacro eloquio dicatur ∼avimus P. CORNW. *Panth. prol.* 40.

2 to sum up, recapitulate: **a** (rhet.); **b** (log.).

a te degenerem ab ea, quam modo ∼asti, maiorum nobilitate .. dixisse me non denego *Eccl. & Synag.* 56. **b** videri .. poterit ex primo hic ∼atorum principium sine complexione sophisticum .. BALSH. *AD* 72; omnia facta ab eo [sc. Deo] fuerunt ∼ata in ipso; sed ∼ata sunt distincta et enumeracio non fit sine distinccione W. ALNWICK *QD* 426; non ∼at Philosophus ibi omnia predicata, quia .. DUNS *Ord.* IV 214.

enumeratio [CL]

1 enumeration, list.

catalogus, ∼o *GlC* C 208; 'chathalogo', ∼one S. LANGTON *Gl. Hist. Schol.* 40.

2 (rhet.) summing up, recapitulation.

haec vero [necessaria argumenta] per conplexionem seu per ∼onem .. fiunt. .. per ∼onem, in qua pluribus rebus inductis una (*sic*) necessario confirmatur .. ALCUIN *Rhet.* 28; ∼o conclusionis est per quam res dispersae in unum locum coguntur et reminiscendi causa unum sub aspectum simul subiciuntur *Ib.* 33; *Gl. Leid.* 28. 30 (v. epembasis).

enunctiatio v. enuntiatio. **enund-** v. inund-.

enuntiabilis, (log.) enunciable, utterable.

attendatur .. dubitationis occasio in his que enuntiantur que, etsi quisquam ∼ia appellare nolit, .. expeditiorem obicienti viam prebent, si quis ea que vera sunt omnibus de quibus enuntiari potest suscepta secundum numerum comparatione conferre conetur BALSH. *AD rec. 2* 144; similiter et nomina numeramus et vera vel falsa ∼ia H. BOS. *LM* 1363A; si Sortes [i. e. Socrates] dicit se mentiri et nihil aliud dicit, dicit aliquod ∼e, ergo verum vel falsum NECKAM *NR* II 173 p. 289; 'solus Deus est eternus', sed forsitan quedam fuerunt ab eterno que non sunt eterna ut ∼ia S. LANGTON *Gl. Hist. Schol.* 45; scientia est de ∼ibus veris HALES *Sent.* I 393; per hypothesim igitur omnis ∼is veritas est summa veritas GROS. 132; non .. debet [dici] quod res significate per enunciacionem sunt enunciacio, sed enunciate vel ∼es LUTTERELL *Occam* 40.

enuntiare [CL]

1 divulge, make known, proclaim; **b** (w. compl.).

rectores .. ad ∼ianda plenius vel confirmanda Romani regni molimina GILDAS *EB* 6; *Ib.* 1 (v. desidiosus a); verbum Dei gentibus cotidie praedicavit, ∼ians eis verum Deum Patrem omnipotentem EDDI 26. **b** dicens portitoribus [cartae] "∼iate domino vestro hoc modo me dicentem: [etc.]" *Ib.* 27.

2 (log.) to state, assert. **b** (w. compl.) to represent as.

quando est enuntiatio vera? quando est quod ∼iat, sive affirmando sive negando ANSELM (*Ver.* 2) I 177; est .. enuntiatio veri vel falsi dictio, ut ad disserendum; interrogatio vero quid sit notius est quam ut diffiniri oporteat. quoniam autem non nisi de aliquo aliquid ∼iari .. contingit [etc.] BALSH. *AD* 12; *Ib. rec. 2* 23 (v. designabilis); si queratur an esse insit alicui conceptui quem nos concipimus de Deo, ita quod talis proposicio sit per se nota in qua ∼iatur esse de tali conceptu .. DUNS *Ord.* II 138; LUTTERELL *Occam* 40 (v. enuntiabilis). **b** deinde .. ostenditur quid designamus cum Deum justum, omnipotentem, et similia ∼iamus PULL. *Sent. prol.* 641A.

enuntiatio [CL]

1 statement. **b** (log.) assertion.

nullius ∼onis sentencia capitur cujus pars quantalibet ignoratur R. BURY *Phil.* 12. 175. **b** ANSELM (*Ver.* 2) I 177 (v. enuntiare 2); BALSH. *AD* 11, J. SAL. *Met.* 904A (v. dictio 1c); propositio et ∼o idem sunt secundum rem, licet differant in eo quod ∼o significat absolute, propositio autem significat aliquid in comparatione ad aliud; ideo prius de ∼one agendum (SHIRWOOD) *GLA* III 12; quia composicio et divisio quas facit intellectus debent respicere esse et non esse rerum intellectum, oportet .. in ∼onibus considerare verum et falsum KILWARDBY *OS* 518; LUTTERELL *Occam* (v. enuntiabilis); BRADW. *CD* 722E (v. dictionalis).

2 utterance, pronunciation.

Evander et Evandrus, quorum unum venit ex Graeca ∼one, alterum ex Latina ALDH. *Met.* 10 p. 82; BEDE *AM* 2351 (86) (v. comprehensio 2a); tonus est accuta enunctiatio vocis BART. ANGL. XIX 128.

enuntiativus [CL], (log.) enunciative, predicative.

per conjunctionem ex eadem parte orationis ∼e dictiones adjective nectuntur absque .. vitio R. MELUN *Sent.* II 46; sunt .. disciplinaliter querendorum genera duo: alia enim sunt ad que prima parte locutionis ∼e respondere sufficit, alia ad que secunda BALSH. *AD rec. 2* 146; veritatem orationis ∼e GROS. 134.

enuntiatorius, (log.) enunciatory, declaratory.

non sermone solum indicatorio et ∼io, quomodo nos homines loquimur, sed operatorio et efficaci, ut quia ipse dicit de quo scribitur 'dixit et facta sunt' GARDINER *CC* 34.

enutrida v. omotribes.

enutrire [CL], to nurture; **b** (fig.).

vidua quae ∼ivit eum ab octo annorum usque ad perfectam aetatem *V. Cuthb.* II 7; **a1074** monasticis institutionibus a pueritia ∼itum LANFR. *Ep.* 37 (9); illa .. infantes diligenter ∼ivit ORD. VIT. X 14 p. 82; H. BOS. *Thom.* III 16 p. 234 (v. deliciosus 1b); ne fiam .. causa mortis puero quem ∼ivi MAP *NC* III 3 f. 40. **b** donec paulatim ∼iti verbo Dei [cf. *1 Tim.* iv 6] ad capienda .. sublimiora Dei precepta sufficerent BEDE *HE* III 5; **798** sicut decet filiis lacte ecclesiasticae consolationis ∼itis ALCUIN *Ad Beatum* 318; beatus Ieronymus ab infantia in fundamentis .. scientiarum .. ∼itus OCKHAM *Pol.* III 73; *Reg. Whet.* I 24 (v. complantare a).

envisus [OF *enviesi*], worn-out. *Cf. evitus.*

1213 precium domorum asportatarum et penitus ∼arum *Doc. Interdict* 82.

envius v. invidus. enydr- v. enhydr-.

eocirca [al. div.]

1 therefore.

1297 eo circa *StatIr* I 210 (v. colanum).

2 thereabout.

1218 fuit septennis vel eo circa *Eyre Yorks* 299; **1451** (v. crofta 1e); **1462** acta .. antedicta hora undecima vel ∼a ante meridiem *Inchaffray* 150.

eoiteis v. hutesium. **eolagium** v. oleagium. **eologium** v. 1 elogium. **eolus** v. aeolus. **eon** v. aeon. **eotenus** v. eatenus.

eous [CL < ἠῷος, ἑῷος]

1 of the dawn. **b** (as sb. m.) dawn.

ēoy sideris splendor renascitur WALT. WIMB. *Carm.* 309; pro luce itaque eoi sideris miraculum .. pallii furis unguibus adherentis notetur ELMH. *Cant.* 222. **b** perspicuus quia nondum fulsit ēous / nec rebus certum lux adtulit alma colorem WULF. *Swith.* II 650; *Ib.* I 573 (v. 1 dicare a).

2 eastern. **b** (as sb. m. or f.) the east. **c** easterner.

Didymus .. eoae tripertitas Indiae provincias .. praedicationis lumine illustravit ALDH. *VirgP* 23; trans aequor ēoum ALCUIN *SS Ebor* 1033; eoi magi, *easterne tungelwitegan GlH* E 293; stravi examina turbae, / inclita censurae servans invictus ēoae / famina FRITH. 1099; intravit in portam eoi (*sic*) partis BYRHT. *V. Ecgwini* 383; in eois partibus Christiani contra ethnicos pugnaverunt ORD. VIT. X 5 p. 25; ad eoos tractus celique fervorem GIR. *TH* I 37. **b** oriens, eoo *GlC* E 224; ēoo coiere simul gelida sed et arcto / Scottica plebs et Picta cohors vulgusque Britannum FRITH. 247; nam fundamen ovans a cardine jecit ēoi / porticus ut staret aedificata Deo WULF. *Swith. pref.* 113; **9.** eoae, *eastdaelas WW*; nomen in 'ous' produciter ut eous [*gl.*: orientalis] BACON *Gram. Gk.* 108. **c 9.** eois, *eastfolcum WW.*

eousque [al. div.]

1 to such a point or extent (that): **a** (w. *ut* & subj.); **b** (w. *quod* & ind.).

a non ∼e contendo ut res magnas nullis umquam credam indiciis preveniri J. SAL. *Pol.* 457A; cum .. adversa valetudine .. ∼e deduceretur ut .. judicaretur moriturus W. CANT. *Mir. Thom.* VI 81; eo usque *Ib.* 29 (v. dormitatio b); tandem ∼e ejus processit astutia ut omnes fere regis cognatos .. perturbaret AILR. *Ed. Conf.* 766C; ∼e flagitiorum consuetudo proruperat ut omnes .. ad turpia declinarent *Itin. Ric.* I 1; **s1194** "noli" inquit "sic loqui, imperator, nam ∼e, ut dicitur, res processit ut absque .. filie mee dedecore rescindi non possit" W. NEWB. *HA* IV 32. **b 1188** ∼e in nos .. manum suam extendit .. [cf. *Job* xxiii 2] quod de .. substantiis nihil nobis .. reliquit *Ep. Cant.* 100; eo usque invaluit inimicorum suggestio quod nuntii domini Cant. nec promereurunt a cardinalibus vel in osculo recipi A. TEWK. *Add. Thom.* 18; habebis elixir .. multiplicatum ∼e quod .. multiplicare poteris in infinitum RIPLEY 308.

2 a hitherto. **b** thus far.

a interfuere .. comitatui .. Oswoldus et .. Aethelwinus, nomine tantum sibi ∼e cogniti *Chr. Rams.* 30. **b** accedens Radenouram .. justitiario eo usque comitatus GIR. *IK* I 1; caritas non eo usque se extendit *Id. GE* II 11.

epacmasticus [ἐπακμαστικός], (med.) supervening on the crisis.

febris ista .. rarius epaugmastica [vv. ll. eupaugmastica, opagmastica] NECKAM *NR* II 155; GILB. I 9. 1 (v. acmasticus a).

epacta [LL epactae < ἐπακταὶ (ἡμέραι)]

1 (pl.) epacts, eleven days by which a common solar year exceeds twelve lunations.

inde ∼ae Graeco vocabulo, id est 'adjectiones', dictae, quod per annos singulos xj dierum .. accumulentur augmento BEDE *TR* 50; **797** in communibus annis secundum numerum ∼arum quae singulis annis adcrescunt xj diebus, quarta decima luna paschalis locum prioris quartae decimas xj diebus anticipat ALCUIN *Ep.* 126; ∼arum vero ratio est undecim diebus singulis annis adcrescere *Ib.*; undenis rutulant lunares tempore epactae *Kal. M. A.* I 402; ∼ae quae bis adiciuntur regularibus, duorum annorum inaequalitate solaris sc. et lunaris creantur BYRHT. *Man.* 32; de saltu lune vel epactis defero tractum; / hoc alibi quondam pagina certa docet GARL. *Tri. Eccl.* 89.

2 (number of days in) the age of the moon at the beginning of the year.

primo decennovenalis circuli anno, in quo nullae sunt ∼ae BEDE *TR* 20; **931** indictione quarta ∼a nulla concurrente *CS* 677; **937** (13c) etc. (v. concurrere 5c); transfertur ergo sanctus rex .. millesimo nonagesimo quinto anno Domini .. indictione .. tertia, ∼a duodecima, concurrente .. septimo cyclo decennovenali tertio decimo HERM. ARCH. 46; **1074** m^o^lxx^o^iiij^o^ anno ab incarnatione Domini, indictionis xij, ∼is existentibus j, concurrentibus ij *Regesta* p. 20; indictio .. et era et ∼a in cereo scribuntur .. prius indictiones fuerunt, postea ere. ab es, eris sic dicte ∼am quere BELETH *RDO* 118. 112; cum .. sit error cycli decemnovennalis in singulis annis, sequitur quod .. erit error in cyclis ∼arum. nam xj dies excrescentes in anno solari super annum lunarem dicuntur ∼a sequentis anni solaris, quasi 'epiaucta', hoc est, superaugmentata BACON *Maj.* I 280.

epagomenus [LL < ἐπαγόμενος], epagomenic, intercalary.

quem [mensem Aegyptii] decimo kal. Septembrium die terminantes, residuos quinque dies ∼as vel intercalares sive additos vocant BEDE *TR* 11.

epalliare [cf. LL palliare], to lay hands upon, ordain.

∼io, *to ordayne WW.*

epanalepsis (∼lempsis) [LL < ἐπανάλη(μ)ψις]

1 (rhet.) epanalepsis, repetition after intervening word or phrase.

∼lempsis est sermonis in principio versus positi in ejusdem fine repetitio, ut 'gaudete in Domino semper, iterum dico gaudete' BEDE *ST* 147; ephanalepsis BACON *Gram. Gk.* 135 (v. epanaphora); ∼lepsis .. accidit cum post aliquam multa interposita .. resumimus quod in principio collocavimus LINACRE *Emend. Lat.* lviii v.

2 digression.

∼lempsim aliquantulum protelavi, sed nunc ad propositum nitor opus .. regredi ORD. VIT. VIII 22 p. 405; per plura perlustrans longissimam ∼lempsim protelavi *Ib.* 27 p. 453; juxta macrologiam sumitur epinalensis quod utilis disgressio est *Ps.*-GROS. *Gram.* 74.

epanaphora [LL < ἐπαναφορά], (rhet.) epanaphora.

ephanalepsis, figura barbarismi, similiter ephanaphora, que est repeticio BACON *Gram. Gk.* 135.

epar, epat- v. hepar, hepat-.

epatescere [cf. CL patescere], to become visible.

artificii .. subtilitas in videncium oculis ∼escis *Ars notaria* 439.

epaugmasticus v. epacmasticus. **epdomada** v. hebdomada. **epebus** v. 2 ephebus. **epefania** v. epiphania. **epefiare** v. ephippiare.

epembasis [LL < ἐπέμβασις], (rhet.) repetition.

†epembabis, iteratio enumerationis studio verba repetens *Gl. Leid.* 28. 30.

epemeris v. ephemeris.

ependytes [LL < ἐπενδύτης], garment worn over another.

ependiton, *cop GlC* E 262 (cf. ib. 247: epipendite, scapulare); ependiton, †tonica [l. tunica] vel cocula vel omnis vestis desuper aliis vestibus pendens *Gl. Leid.* 3. 56; ependeton, *cop* vel *hoppada* vel *ufrescrud* ÆLF. *Sup.*; **9..** ependiton, *hacele WW.*

epenthesis [LL < ἐπένθεσις], (gram.) epenthesis, insertion of vowel or syllable within a word; **b** (fig.).

navita, epentesis pro nauta *GlP* 82; si nimis imperat imperator dicet 'induperator', et dicitur hec figura ∼is quasi a supra inposicio *Ps.*-GROS. *Gram.* 70; epentesis .. est figura quod est interpositura BACON *Gram. Gk.* 135; ELMH. *Cant.* 338 (v. apocope a). **b** nec, carnis medie quod epentesis addit, avare / sincopat exertis macies inglora nervis HANV. I 484.

epericum v. hypericon. **epesedium** v. episedium. **epetogium** v. epitogium.

epexegesis [LL < ἐπεξήγησις], (rhet.) epexegesis.

'et' non ponitur .. copulative set expositive vel explanative pro 'id est', et est figura †exefegesis [l. epexegesis] secundum Barbarismum J. GODARD *Ap.* 265; Servius .. vocat .. rationem hanc et cum eclipsi pronominis et citra hanc ∼in, ut 'est locus, Italiam Graii cognomine dicunt' LINACRE *Emend. Lat.* xxix v.

ephan- v. epan-.

1 ephebus [CL < ἔφηβος], ephebe, youth.

effebum puerum .. / suscitat in proprias anima penetrante medullas ALDH. *CE* 4. 2. 14; horresco referens effebi funus acerbum *Ib.* 4. 7. 29; hinc regale decus, ephoeborumque manipli, / turba senum, praesul violento deditus Euro FRITH. 249; ∼us qui jam in adolescentia se illa parte senescere doleret W. MALM. *GP* IV 147; W. FITZST. *Thom. prol.* 14 (v. consul 5a); cum Venus igne suo teneros inflammet ephebos, / te magis excecat, luxuriose senex A. MEAUX *Susanna* 71; epebus *Ib.* 406 (v. 1 ethicus 4a); mors pandis sociat ephebos senibus WALT. WIMB. *Sim.* 131; *ffayr chyld*, ∼us *PP.*

2 ephebus v. 2 ephoebus.

ephemericus [cf. LL ephemerius], lasting one day (of fever). *V. et. ephemerus* 1b.

si habeat famem et vigilias et laborem corporalem .. fit velociter effimericus GAD. 20. 2.

ephemeris [CL < ἐφημερίς]

1 record of daily transactions, day-book. **b** tally.

effimeri[s], cotidiana res *GlC* E 70 (cf. ib. 244, 261: epimeri[s], adbreviatio rerum; epemeris .., breviatio rerum); ∼is, *anes dæges weorc* ÆLF. *Gl.* (cf. ib.: ∼ides, numerus cotidianus, *gerim*). **b** *a nyke of a tayle*, epimeridia; *a score*, epimeridia; *a tayle*, acopa, .. apoca, dica, caucio, epimenda *CathA.*

2 calendar, almanac.

∼is, quam habent mathematici, unde †ligant [l. legunt] dies singulos *GlC* E 245; ∼is, tabula manualis OSB. GLOUC. *Deriv.* 193.

3 ephemeral fever. *V. et. ephemerus* 1b.

quam notat effimerim venarum pulsio velox A. MEAUX *Susanna* 327; denominatur ab ephimere pisce marino qui eodem die quo nascitur moritur; vel ab 'ephimeron' quod est simplex quia fundatur, i. generatur, in substantia simplici; vel ab *e* quod est 'unum' et *fi* quod est 'fervor' et †*meta* [l. *mera*] quod est 'dies' quasi 'fervor unius diei' GILB. I 61v. 1.

4 kind of short-lived fish. *V. et. ephemerus* 2a.

GILB. I 61v. 1 (v. 3 supra).

ephemerus [LL < ἐφήμερος]

1 lasting one day (of fever; also fig.); *v. et. ephemericus.* **b** (as sb. f.) ephemeral fever; *v. et. ephemeris* 3.

cum febris iracundie mentem accendit, vide ut ∼a sit NECKAM *NR* II 191; *Id. DS* III 51 (v. 2b infra); febris .. sic solet dividi, alia effimera, alia ethica, alia putrida GILB. I 3v. 1; [Alexander] dicebat "quia non †fecit [l. feci] bene hodie aliquibus, non regnavi." quod equale est "egroto medice morbo ephimero" propter quod ea die operationes sanorum non facit J. WALEYS *Compend.* 165; a †*mons* [l. *monos*], quod est 'unus', dicitur febris *monoydos*, i. 'unius diei', sc. effimera *Alph.* 120. **b** sunt quedam egritudines quarum est consuetudo ut non prolongentur ultra unum diem, sicut †elfimera, nisi adsit error RIC. MED. *Signa* 37; effimera est febris ex distemperancia spirituum procedens GAD. 20. 1; effi[meram] *Ib.* 11v. 2 (v. amphemerinus).

2 (as sb. f.) short-lived fish, (?) sprat; *v. et. ephemeris* 4. **b** kind of short-lived creature. **c** (as sb. n.) short-lived bird.

diversi [pisces] sunt, utpote mugiles, .. murena, musculus et epimera [*gl.*: *esperling*] NECKAM *Ut.* 97; piscis qui effimera dicitur majoris est etatis unius diei revoluto circulo quam sit piscis transactis vite ipsius annis quamplurimis *Id. NR* I 4; effimera dicitur ab *effimeron* Grece, quod est 'piscis' Latine; iste enim piscis eodem die quo oritur eodem die moritur GAD. 20. 1; **1407** empcio espimar' rub': et in ij cadis espimar' emptis hoc anno .. vj s. viij d. *KRAc* 513 m. 2; *a sperlynge*, ipimera, sperlingus, .. *a sprotte*, epimera, piscis est *CathA*; ephimera, A. *a sperlynge WW*; hic (*sic*) epimora est piscis qui moritur eodem die quo nascitur *WW.* **b** ephemere debet uni se vita diei, / hinc febri nomen historieque datur NECKAM *DS* III 511; caduci plasmatis gens plus quam misera, / nunc es, nunc desines velut effimera (*Humana Miseria*) *EHR* XXXII 403. **c** Aristoteles de volucre ∼o scripsit ... de ephimero autem Aristoteles .. ita scribit... moritur, vita non ultra unum diem protracta, unde ∼um, i. e. diarium appellatum est TURNER *Av.* B 5.

3 (as sb. m.) meadow saffron, autumn crocus (*Colchicum autumnale*). **b** (as sb. n.) lily of the valley (*Convallaria majalis*).

Alph. 45 (v. colchicum). **b** ephimeron est lilium convallium grandius, quod Angli vocant *great parke lyly* TURNER *Herb.* B i.

ephi [LL < Heb.], ephah, dry measure.

de ponderibus secundum Eucherium: .. ∼i sive ofa, iij modii; ∼i idem mensurae (*sic*) habet in aridis et in liquidis *Gl. Leid.* 33. 12; [ephi] .. continet tres modios ..; invenire .. ∼i est invenire fidem Trinitatis S. LANGTON *Ruth* 107.

ephi- v. et. epi-.

ephialtes [LL < ἐφιάλτης]

1 ephialtes, nightmare (imagined as throttling incubus).

in quo genere et ∼em, quo quis .. cum dormiat putatur ab aliquo interim pregravari, connumerandum arbitrantur J. SAL. *Pol.* 429C; differt epilempsia ab ∼e, quoniam ∼es quodammodo est ei contraria: in ea enim privatur motus et non sensus GILB. II 109. 1; incubus sepe veniens sive epilates (*sic*), quod idem est GAD. 61. 2; *nyhtmare*, epialtes .. vel offialtes *PP*; *þe bychdoghter*, epialtis, epialta, noxa *CathA.*

2 witch.

s1382 cum .. quis nominasset S. Mariam de Lincolnia vel S. Mariam de Walsyngham, vocabant [Lollardi] eas epialtes, hoc est in materna lingua *wyche of Lincolne and wyche of Walsyngham* KNIGHTON *Cont.* II 183; s1428 in .. convocatione .. adductus fuit unus clericus de secta Wyklyf et una ∼es †dextris [? l. de exteris] contra fidem *Chr. S. Alb.* 24.

ephilensia v. epilepsia. **ephim-** v. ephem-.

ephippiare [LL *p. ppl. only*], to put on a 'hambargh', to fit w. a horse-collar or harness.

∼are, equum ornare OSB. GLOUC. *Deriv.* 199; epefio, A. *to hamb[urwe]* WW; epyphio, A. *to hamburwe WW.*

ephippiarius [CL], saddler.

1563 ephipiarius *Hug. Soc.* X 290.

ephippium [CL < ἐφίππιον = *saddle-cloth*], **epiphium,** saddle, caparison, horse-collar, harness, trappings.

∼ia, ornatus equorum OSB. GLOUC. *Deriv.* 196; equum cursorem .., cui adherebat puer pedes qui fatigabatur ex itinere, dependens ex epiphiis W. CANT. *Mir. Thom.* II 44; habeat et epiphia [*gl.*: *arneys*] equus tam supra dorsum quam in collo centone multiplici sociata NECKAM *Ut.* 108; carucarii reparant .. epifia [v. l. ephifia] equina [*gl.*: hoc epiphium collarium equorum et dicitur .. et vocant G. *perones*] GARL. *Dict.* 130; hec epiphia, *loreins Gl. AN Glasg.* f. 21; *berewham, horsis colowre*, .. epiphium *PP*; *a bargham*, epiphium *CathA*; epyphium, A. *an hamborowe WW*; de pertinentibus ad equum: epiphium [*gl.*: *sadle*], frenum, habena STANBR. *Vulg.* 12; in mercedem laboris .. facientium piphias MYLN *Dunkeld* 104.

ephod [LL < Heb.], ephod, Jewish priestly vestment. (*Cf. Exod.* xxv 2).

∼d, vestis linea latas manicas habens *GlC* E 233; ∼d, superumerale *Gl. Leid.* 5. 9; sine ∼d, sine theraphin gemebunda resedit [ecclesia] [cf. *Hosea* iii 4] AILR. *SS Hex* 11; ∼t, superindumentum; erat pallium superhumerale ex quattuor coloribus OSB. GLOUC. *Deriv.* 198; succedit soccus ∼t et logion sui largitate .. habet soccus signamentum ∼t et logion quod per partes potentie et sapientie .. determinatur R. NIGER *Mil.* II 3.

1 ephoebus v. 1 ephebus.

2 ephoebus [cf. φοῖβος], clear, brilliant, lucid.

effevum, lucidum *GlH* E 97; ut jubar introiit, jubaris ceu nectar opimi / protulit effevum liquido flavore libellum FRITH. 1161; *clere*, clarus, .. ∼us *CathA.*

ephon v. epimone. **ephot** v. ephod.

ephphetha [LL < Aramaic], (imp.) be opened. (*Cf. Mark* vii 34).

effeta, i. .. aperire *GlH* E 95; hic dat Potens "effeta" loqui non loquenti *Poem. S. Thom.* 92; effēta discludens sonat; est effēta senectus H. AVR. *CG* f. 8. 15.

ephyphania v. epiphania. **ephyria** v. empiria.

epi- [LL < ἐπί]

1 above.

epi Grece, 'supra' Latine... epi componitur hec epistola OSB. GLOUC. *Deriv.* 187; Epyphania ab *epy*, quod est 'supra', et *phanos*, quod est 'apparitio' BELETH *RDO* 73. 79; HIGD. IV 5 p. 334 (v. desursum 1a); *Alph.* 58 (v. epiphora); *Ib.* 78 (v. epiala); FORTESCUE *NLN* I 24 (v. epieikia).

2 (in new comp. expr. 'over') *v. epifemur, epiromanus, episedium.*

epiala [cf. LL epialus < ἠπιάλος], ague.

de ∼a et lipparia... in febri ∼a, in qua putrescit flegma secundum partem sui subtiliorem .. et pars putrefacta calefacit interiora corporis GILB. I 55v. 1–2; ∼a fe[bris] est in qua vitreus humor in exterioribus partibus corporis est *SB* 19; hilon vel hyalon vitrum idem. inde ∼a fe[bris] ab *epi* quod est 'supra', quia vitreus humor in exterioribus corporis partibus est in hac *Alph.* 78.

epialta, ∼es v. ephialtes.

epibata [CL < ἐπιβάτης]

1 soldier on board ship, marine guard. **b** (?) fighting man.

venefica cum naucleris et ∼is anus nuda merensque in littus Normannie exposita est ORD. VIT. X 19 p. 109; feroces ∼e, qui jam in navi sedes nacti turgebant *Ib.* XII 26 p. 412. **b** frugiferis gravida gaudebant horrea glebis, / ēpibatae faciles ausu sprevere latrones, / classica dira silent FRITH. 534 (cf. EDDI 19: pax et gaudium in populis et anni frugiferi victoriaeque in hostes).

2 passenger.

novus .. epipata .. adgressus est navem, nauloque inpenso prospero ventorum flatu pervenit ad Dorstet WILLIB. *Bonif.* 4 p. 16; ∼is, qui pervenient et dant nabulum pro navigatione *Gl. Leid.* 38. 44; ∼a, qui superveniens dato naulo transit OSB. GLOUC. *Deriv.* 195; rector navis cum sociis et ∼is multis, qui pariter Cantuariam venerant orandi causa W. CANT. *Mir. Thom.* II 41.

3 layman.

ebibati, laici *GlC* E 6 (cf. ib. 250: epifati, laici).

epicantorium v. epicaustorium. **epicaris** v. epicharis.

epicaustorium [LL], **∼erium**

1 stove, fireplace (incl. flue or chimney).

ad instar ∼olii GREG. *Mir. Rom.* 25 (v. columna 2a); habeat [scriptor] prunas in ∼erio [v. l. ∼orio; *gl.*: *chemene*], ut citius in tempore nebuloso .. desiccari possit incaustum NECKAM *Ut.* 116; hoc ∼orium, *chimenee Gl. AN Ox.* f. 148; hoc †epicantorium, *cheiminee Gl. AN Glasg.* f. 20; est epicausterium fornax ubi dequoquis ollas. / ast illud longum †que [l. quo] fumus ab ede recedit *WW*; *a chymney*, caminus, epicasterium, fumerium, fumerale; .. *a fornas* caminus, ∼orium, fornax; .. *a tewelle of a chymnay*, ∼erium *CathA.*

2 courtroom, council chamber.

∼erium, *domhus* vel *mothus* ÆLF. *Sup.*

3 scribe's chair, desk.

scriptor habeat ∼orium [*gl.*: talem asserem] multiplici centone coopertum NECKAM *Ut.* 116; dic epicausterium scriptoris esse cathedra *WW*; *a wrytynge chare*, ∼orium *CathA.*

epicedion [CL < ἐπικήδειον], epicedium, funeral ode.

carmen funebre et canticum lamentabile, quod ∼ion et epitaphion vocatur ALDH. *VirgP* 13; †epitathium [l. epitaphium], carmen quod dicitur sepulto corpore; ∼ion, carmen quod dicitur non adhuc sepulto corpore *GlC* E 251–2; ad [l. ab] cujus exequiis epichidion defuit et epitaphion memoriale evanuit BYRHT. *V. Ecgwini* 394; *Id. V. Osw.* 450 (v. concentus a); **9..** ∼ion, *licleoð WW.*

epicharis [ἐπίχαρις = *pleasing*], endowed w. grace.

∼is, supergratiosus OSB. GLOUC. *Deriv.* 193; ad supernam patriam .., ubi non erit sycomachia .., sed locus graciosus et epicaris [*gl.*: i. superna gracia] et deliciosus et eucaris [*gl.*: bona gratia] NECKAM *Ut.* 107; ēpicharis crescas, Bruys, probitate capax (*Neville's Cross*) *Pol. Poems* I 46.

epichenus v. epicoenus. **epichia, ~ima** v. 1 epithema. **epichidion** v. epicedion. **epicicl-** v. epicycl-. **epickaia** v. epieikeia.

epicoenus [CL < ἐπίκοινος], (gram.) epicene, common to either sex.

~i, promiscui sexus masculini et femini[ni] *GlC* E 263; est ~on quod Latine dicitur promiscuum, pariter marem ac feminam significans, in quo nec articulus variatur nec facile sexus deprehenditur, ut hic piscis .. haec aquila BONIF. *AG* 19; de generibus: .. ~a promiscua sunt et sub una voce profertur [MS: proferunt] masculinum et femininum ALCUIN *Gram.* 862A; nam commune duum generum et epicoenomena [v. l. ~on] in participio inveniri .. natura .. prohibet *Ib.* 890B; in illis [nominibus animalium] que sunt sexus promiscui et epicheni .. ut aquila et passere BACON XI 209; *coenos* .. quod est 'communis', a quo 'coenobium' et '~on' scribitur per 'oi' dipthongum *Id. Maj.* III 110; genus .. ex parte nominis participio accidit masculinum, femininum, neutrum, et omne. et hoc a disposicione est que convenit figure generis; commune et ~um non debent ei accidere *Ps.*-GROS. *Gram.* 53.

epicosium v. epicurium.

epicrius [ἐπίκριον], yard-arm.

epar, ~ius, ergastulum BACON *CSPhil.* 442.

Epicureus [CL < Ἐπικούρειος]

1 Epicurean (also as sb.). **b** profligate (also as sb.).

~ei, genus philosophorum *GlC* E 255; **1168** non modo Stoici sed etiam ~ei et omnium philosophantium secte rerum mundialium contemptum predicant J. SAL. *Ep.* 279 (256); omnes inpuri vivunt qui sunt Epicuri / cecati, duri, putres subito morituri [*gl.*: incurrunt epilenciam qui vivunt ad modum ~orum curantes cutem] GARL. *Mor. Scol.* 417. **b** ~ius, voluptarius corporis *Gl. Leid.* 38. 9; Epycuri, qui multorum facultates una lance consumunt, effeminati .., qui .. pecunie fenus exercent, .. qui dampna pupplica malis amplioribus aggravant (*Quad., dedic.*) *GAS* 530; ecce quidam ~us monachus iratus .. motu turpissimo ingrediens W. DAN. *Ep.* 63; cum ille tanta et tam studiose legerit que nos ~a animalia Pelusiote et torpore glires vix perfunctorie transcurrimus H. BOS. *Ep.* 1. 1419A.

2 *f. l.*

9.. †epicurii [? l. empyrei], *up on pæm rodore para steorsceawere WW.*

epicurium [cf. ἐπικούριος], kind of herb, (?) milfoil (*Achillea*).

in nostro viridario .. crescunt .. illa holera quae paene cotidie mandi possunt si erunt cocta: .. betonica, costa, ~ium [*gl.*: *hels*], millefolium ÆLF. BATA 4. 59 (cf. ib. 6. 99: epigurium [*gl.*: *heleswyrt*]; **10**.. ~ium, *halswyrt WW*; †epicosium, †*half vyrt Gl. Durh.*

epicyclicus, (astr.) epicyclic.

BACON *Tert.* 200 (v. eccentricus a).

epicyclus [LL < ἐπίκυκλος], (astr.) epicycle.

HANV. IX 100 (v. eccentris); suppressi prudens epicyclos; abjicit illos / divinum magni pectus Aristotelis NECKAM *DS* II 31; quilibet planeta preter solem habet epiciclum, et est epiciclus circulus parvus per cujus circumferentiam defertur corpus planete, et centrum epicicli defertur in circumferentia deferentis SACROB. *Sph.* 114; GROS. 28 (v. aux a); BACON IX 194 (v. circulus 7c); WALLINGF. (*Alb.*) I 260 (v. eccentricitas); R. BURY *Phil.* 8. 127 (v. emetiri 1a); planetarum cursus erraticos in suis epiciclis *Ps.*-ELMH. *Hen. V* 130.

epidemia [LL n. pl. adj. < ἐπιδήμια; cf. ἐπιδημία], epidemic, plague (esp. w. ref. to Black Death).

Hippo[crates] in libro epid[emiarum] GILB. I 57. 2; **s1349** seviente peste in Anglia .. papa concessit plenam remissionem causa hujus ~ie omnibus vere contritis .. morientibus WALS. *HA* I 274; et postquam viguit hic epidimia / male retinuit catalla nimia *Planct. Univ. Ox.* 31; **1362** propter multiplicacionem doctrine salutaris, que .. per presentem ~iam noscitur plurimum defecisse, concessimus .. archiepiscopo quod .. in universitate Oxonie .. aulam Cantuariensem .. erigere poterit (*Pat*; cf. *CalPat* 139) *Lit. Cant.* II 409; **1363** viros in omni scientia doctos et expertos in epidimiis preteritis plurimum defecisse *Cant. Coll. Ox.* III 4; **c1406** cum decantacione .. specialis collecte pro pace, tranquillitate et hypidemia (*Lit. Archiep.*) *Conc.* III 305a (cf. ib. 304a: tribulaciones varias .. stragem, pestilenciam et hypidimeam ac mortem quasi subitam .. plus solito transmittit in orbem); **s1437** propter ~ie pestem que pro tunc regnabat in civitate Londoniarum AMUND. II 127; **1447** pestilencia et ipidimia *Cart. Boarstall* 170.

epidemialis, epidemial.

aer pestilencialis et epidimialis cito interficit dispositos GAD. 10. 1; WYCL. *Versut.* 102 (v. 1 aura a).

epidemicus, epidemic (adj.).

GIR. *Spec.* III 1 p. 142 (v. caducus 1b).

epidendae [dub.], (pl.) (?) pregnancy.

peractis mensium ~arum cursibus, cum parturiendi tempus inmineret FELIX *Guthl.* 4.

epidim- v. epidem-.

epidiorthosis [LL < ἐπιδιόρθωσις], (rhet.) correction of preceding expression.

nunc utriusque quesiti complacent michi prima. nunc hec displicent, placent fines (†epidiocesis) *Dictamen* 372.

epidromus [LL < ἐπίδρομος = *mizen-sail*], mainsail.

~o, *se medemesta segl* ÆLF. *Sup.*

epieikeia [ἐπιείκεια], equity. (*Cf.* Aristotle *Eth. Nic.* V 14. 1137a31 – 1138a2.)

canones .. exponendi sunt per ~eiam, que est quedam virtus seu equitas naturalis qua discernitur in quo casu leges sunt servande, et in quo non .. ut specialissime de ipso epieikes canones dirigendo dicat quod de ipso in hoc casu canones non debent intelligi OCKHAM *Pol.* I 61; quia ipsas [leges] cognosceret .., si servarentur, in dampnum .. reipublice redundare, utendo ~eia .. contra ipsas licite venire valeret *Ib.* 281; hoc .. videtur unum jus naturale 'nullum apparens malum esse eligendum', cum quo dispensatur in casu, si necesse sit quenquam eligere apparens malum majus vel minus; et hec est ~eia juris naturalis, sicut alia similis est juris positivi legalis BRADW. *CD* 234A; nec dubium .. quin tales casus possent naturaliter contingere, quod .. dominantes deberent ex epikeia communicare sua dominia, quod utique de jure non facerent, si proprietas .. meliorat dominium WYCL. *Dom. Div.* 202; virtus .. docendi quomodo et quando lex humana debet observari et quando non debet observari dicitur epikeya GASCOIGNE *Loci* 94; epickaia dicitur ab επι, quod est 'supra' vel 'laus' et καλα, λ mutato in ι, quasi 'superlaudabilis laxatio rigiditatis' FORTESCUE *NLN* I 24.

epieikes [ἐπιεικής], equitable. **b** (as sb. m.) just man.

quemadmodum .. homo facile transmutabilis malus, et natura que indiget transmutacione; non enim simplex neque ~es BRADW. *CD* 142D. **b** tam diffuse procedit civilis probatio, quia igitur epyeikes supponit quod reus cicius incurreret perjurium pro salute vite sue quam testes extrinseci WYCL. *Ver.* II 85.

epifatus v. epibata.

epifemur [cf. CL femur], armour worn over thigh, 'pauncher'.

epyfemur, A. *breygyrdyl WW*; est bumbicinium vestis, diploydis, epifemur [*gl.*: *panchere*] *WW.*

epifium v. ephippium. **epifora** v. epiphora. **epifugus** v. epistygus.

epigastrion [LL < ἐπιγάστριον], (anat.) epigastrium.

hactenus de ~io et ejus partibus D. EDW. *Anat.* A 3v. (cf. ib. A 3: inferior venter .. a prima cute ad peritoneum Grecis ἐπιγάστριον, barbaris 'mirach' appellatur ..).

epiglottalis, (anat.) epiglottic.

in epiglotali cartilagine *Ps.*-RIC. *Anat.* 2 (cf. ib. 42: quedam est suscipiens et retinens musculos a remotis partibus venientes et dicitur cartillago epiglotalis).

epiglottis [LL < ἐπιγλωττίς], **~ottum,** (anat.) epiglottis.

huic [tracee arterie] superponitur ~otum, id est supra gulam, quasi cooperculum, et clauditur inspirando et aperitur exspirando RIC. MED. *Anat.* 220; intrinseca quatuor, ~otis, meri, canna, intestina *Ps.*-RIC. *Anat.* 17; tumor .. circa ~otum GILB. IV 177v. 1; [guttur] habet .. viam manifestam ad cibum recipiendum et hec duplex via quodam cooperculo quod ~otum dicitur distinguitur BART. ANGL. V 24; naturale [instrumentum] est ut pulmo, guttur, lingua, dentes, palatum, et cetera membra specie alia, sed principaliter forma vocis est ~ottis TUNST. 205; epyglotum, A. *the throtebolle*; hoc ~otum, *a thotegole WW*; ebiglotum, *strowfe of the throte PP.*

epignorare v. expignerare.

epigramma [CL < ἐπίγραμμα]

1 inscription, epitaph.

chronica Eusebii Vergilium .. cecinisse tradunt et ~a, quod epitafium vocatur, ad suprema exequiarum funera composuisse ALDH. *Met.* 10 p. 88; librum ~atum heroico metro BEDE *HE* V 24 p. 359; **9**.. ~atibus, *ofergewritum WW*; prope hoc templum est archus triumphalis Augusti Cesaris in quo hoc epigrama scriptum repperi GREG. *Mir. Rom.* 22; R. BURY *Phil.* 7. 114 (v. camerula b); epigrama, *wryt on a grave ston PP.*

2 epigram, short poem.

item ~a Prosperi triton trocheon protulit ALDH. *Met.* 10 p. 96; sic ternis pedibus properent epigrammata metri! *Id. VirgV* 52; ~a, abreviata scriptura *GlC* E 243; ~ata que satirico modo absolvit W. MALM. *GR* V 444.

3 epigrammatic statement, pithy remark.

Manducator in uno scemate sermonis hec epigramata profert: 'David de optativo jam prosilierat in imperativum, dicens "inclina celos tuos" ' [*Psalm* cxliii 5] M. RIEVAULX (*Ep.*) 74.

epigrammare, to embroider.

to brawde, epigramare *CathA.*

epigrammatice, in the form of an epitaph.

scriptum erat de eo per quendam metristam epigramatice per hunc modum: 'filum fatales quod tres nevere sorores [etc.]' *Reg. Whet.* I 156.

epigrammatista [LL], epigrammatist.

~a, epigrammatis scriptor OSB. GLOUC. *Deriv.* 201.

epigrammator, ~trix, embroiderer, embroideress.

a brawdestere, epigramator, epigramatrix. *CathA.*

epigurium v. epicurium. **epikeia** v. epieikeia. **epilacio** v. oppilatio.

epilacium [cf. ἐπίλακκος], (?) hollowing or cupping of the hand.

hoc ~ium, A. *honde mowle WW.*

epilates v. ephialtes. **epilatum** v. hypelatum. **epilem-, epilen-** v. epilep-. **epilema, epilemma** v. epilimma. **epilencia** v. epilepsia. **epilentiosus, ~ioticus** v. epilepticus.

epilepsia, ~is (epilemps-), [LL < ἐπιληψία, ἐπίληψις], epilepsy.

~lepsia, ÆLF. *Gl.* (v. comitialis 2b); Corporis Christi et sanguinis communio nulli .. pro gravitate morbi .. veluti lepre vel ~lensis denegetur *Inst. Sempr.* *lvi; hec omni die a sua nativitate ex ~lempsia ter tota explosa decubuit R. COLD. *Godr.* 353; ephilensiam W. CANT. *Mir. Thom.* II 87 (v. chronicus 1a); intra has tres cellulas obsessa et inpedita, tam in ~lensia quam in apoplexia, misera cerebro captivatur anima RIC. MED. *Anat.* 214; smaragdus .. / .. / lenit quos pestis epilempseos horrida vexat NECKAM *DS* VI 155; **s622** Machometus crapulatus ~lensia urgente cum veneno interiit M. PAR. *Maj.* I 271; ~lempsia est humor humidus ventriculos cerebri replens .. ~lepsia est spasmus in .. anteriori cerebro .. ~lempsia est oppilatio principalium ventriculorum cerebri GILB. II 108v. 1; *Ib.* II 109. 1 (v. apoplexia, ephialtes 1); medicina que a mari prohicitur .. detur contra sincopim et ~lepsiam BACON IX 54; ~lenciam GARL. *Mor. Scol.* 418 (v. Epicureus 1a); ~lepsiam GAD. 62v. 1 (v. cuculus a); †epileucie *SB* 11, epilencie *Alph.* 10 (v. analepsia); ~lepsia *Alph.* 97 (v. catalepsia); ~lencia *PP* (v. caducus 1b); *the falland evylle*, ~lencia, .. morbus caducus, noxa, gerenoxa, ~lensis; epilenticus qui patitur illam infirmitatem *CathA.*

epilepticus [LL < ἐπιληπτικός]

1 epileptic; **b** (as sb. m.).

de sanctimoniali ~lentica (*tit.*) W. CANT. *Mir. Thom.* II 6; Mahimetus pseudo-propheta ~lenpticus de genere Ismael seduxit reginam Arabum R. NIGER *Chr. II* 142; plures eorum †epilentiotici [v. l. †epilentiosi] effecti horribile spectaculum .. prebuerunt J. FURNESS *Kentig.* 29; morbo .. ~lemtico [v. l. ~lentice] frequenter hec avis [passer] vexatur NECKAM *NR* I 40; Mahumet cepit cadere frequenter ~lentica passione M. PAR. *Maj.* I 270; Hercules .. inciderat in morbum ~lepticum *Eul. Hist.* I 42. **b** nisi quis .. clausis .. orbibus et obtunsis palpebrarum obtutibus velut ~lenticus et scotomaticus contemplabitur arcana legum .. ALDH. *Met.* 2 p. 66; ~lentici die quo morbo suo laboraverint a communione abstineant *Inst. Sempr.* *lvi; quare ~lentici citius cadant ex concursu hominum quam alibi *Quaest. Salern.* B 181; dixerunt alii quod [hec medicina] valet ~lenticis BACON IX 43; si capra excorietur et immediate aliquis nudus induat pellem illam, efficietur ~lepticus GAD. 61. 1; *Alph.* 113 (v. cataphora); *RBOssory* 254 (v. cerebralis).

2 frenzied, maniacal. **b** (as sb. m.) madman.

~lenticus, *woda GlC* E 249; portento simile paradigma gerit vafer atque / .. / babbiger agaffons, epilenticus ac furibundus *Altercatio* 17. **b** **993** si quis .. epylempticus phylargiriae seductus amentia (*Ch. Regis*) *Con. Syn.* 187.

epilimma [CL < ἐπάλειμμα], unguent, plaster.

epilemma, emplaustrum OSB. GLOUC. *Deriv.* 201; *a plaster*, cataplasma, emplastrum, epilema, malagma *CathA*; hoc epilema, -tis, A. *a playster WW.*

epilleolum [cf. CL pilleolus], little cap.

hoc ~um, *aumuce Gl. AN Glasg.* f. 21

epilogare v. epilogizare.

epilogatio, conclusion, summing up. **b** exposition.

isti duo libri sunt ejusdem continuationis sicut patet ex communi prooemio in principio Priorum .. et ex communi epilogo versus finem Posteriorum, ubi ~o brevis fit de utroque libro KILWARDBY *OS* 54; ~o eorum que in duobus proximis capitulis dicta sunt FORTESCUE *NLN* II 20 *tit.* **b** ~o J. CORNW. *Eul.* 5 *n.* 4 (*tit.*; cf. ib. *PL* CXCIX 1056B: ~o proximorum).

epilogium [LL < ἐπιλόγιον], summary narrative. **b** epilogue, peroration. **c** prologue.

epilogi[um], narratio *GlC* E 234; s**734** incipit ~ium de obitu beati atque eximii doctoris Bedae *Chr. S. Neoti*; OSB. GLOUC. *Deriv.* 187 (v. epilogus a); dignum videtur ad historie claritatem ut ejus [R. comitis Normannorum] genealogiam brevi ~io perstringamus M. PAR. *Maj.* I 442; prelibato .. misere desolationis ~io GIR. *PI pref.* 1. **b** ~ium, novissima pars contraversiae *GlC* E 258. **c** proemium, prolocutio, ~ium OSB. GLOUC. *Deriv.* 470.

epilogizare [ἐπιλογίζειν], **epilogare,** to conclude, sum up. **b** to skim over. **c** to compose a prologue.

hic .. reor huic operi supersedendum, breviter epylogizando tot regimina regum quot superius exaravimus post .. Eadmundi martyrium HERM. ARCH. 23; dicit quasi ~ando quod alii sunt modi substancie DUNS *Metaph.* VII 7 p. 374; ~at vel replicat [v. l. explicat] quedam dicta prius, dicens quod .. OCKHAM *Pol.* II 527; ultimo ~at doctor, preter ordinem, quod non videt quin .. (KYN.) *Ziz.* 473; OTTERB. *prol.* 4 (v. chronicare b); sed ad commonitorium .. ~ando me convertam ut alternacio styli delectando proficiat NETTER *DAF* II 270. **b** quod siquis fame et scripture super hoc satis edite magis credat, epyloget sequentia et inveniet .. *Chr. Wallingf.* 40. **c** ~are, proloquium facere OSB. GLOUC. *Deriv.* 201; *Ib.* 187 (v. epilogus).

epilogus [LL < ἐπίλογος], summary narrative. **b** epitaph.

epi componitur hic ~us, .. i. superlocutio alicujus rei, et inde hoc epilogium, .. quod idem significat, et epilogare, i. prologum facere OSB. GLOUC. *Deriv.* 187; vellem ut eorum que dicta sunt summa sub brevi nobis ~o traderetur AILR. *Spir. Amicit.* 327; est .. [sc. Paralipomenon liber] quasi compendiosus ~us Veteris Instrumenti J. SAL. *Hist. Pont.* 1; hec .. summatim et quasi sub ~o commemorantes GIR. *EH* II 18; KILWARDBY *OS* 504 (v. epilogatio a); quod videtur ex ~o sequente DUNS *Metaph.* VII 5 p. 368; **1359** mitto spicas meas .. ut que in quodam epylogo et manipulo sine tropis, seu thomis, vel faleris .. progressus .. martiris elucescant *Lit. Cant.* II 381. **b** versibus hexametris ~um brevem super illo edidi ORD. VIT. XII 32 p. 437.

epiltasia v. epitasis 1. **epima** v. empyema.

epimedium [CL < ἐπιμήδιον], kind of plant. (*Cf.* Pliny *HN* XXVII 16).

~ium sive injecta †hasta [v. l. hastam] habet non majorem edere similem, folia x aut xij, carens flore et semine, radix tenere et nigra cum odore gravi *Alph.* 57.

epimenda v. ephemeris 1.

epimenia [CL < ἐπιμήνια], (n. pl.) rations, provisions; **b** (f. sg.).

GILDAS *EB* 23 (v. contribuere a); ~ia, *nest GlC* E 259; **9..** epimoenia, *fostraþas WW*; dapsilis ast cunctis, dedans (*sic*) †ermenia [v. l. epimenia; *gl.: fornesta*] vitae, / pauperibus largas praebebat sedulus escas FRITH. 226. **b 705** meam adhuc pallentem hebitudinis maciem largissima blandae sponsionis ~ia affluenter refocilabat (ÆTHELWALD) *Ep. Aldh.* 7 p. 496; indignata est Gonorilla .. quia sibi profusior epimonia [v. l. opimonia] non prebebatur G. MON. II 12.

epimer- v. ephemer-.

epimone [LL < ἐπιμονή], (rhet.) elaboration of subject, frequent repetition.

~e, repetitio *Gl. Leid.* 28. 73; juxta tautologiam apostrophe sumitur quod est conversio sermonis, ut magis addat vel exponat .. et cum repetit diversimode dicitur †ephon [? l. epimone] *Ps.*-GROS. *Gram.* 74; si vestrum verecundum ultra loquar, de ira vestra estimo quod sum certus; si silenter hoc teneam, de omissione doctrine sum certior; si calamo hoc conscribam, quod legentes cautos faciam, certissimum me cognosco (~e) *Dictamen* 372.

epimonia v. epimenia. **epimora** v. ephemerus 2a. **epinalensis** v. epanalepsis 1.

†epinasis [? cf. ἐπινεφελίς], (med.) trichiasis, pilimiction.

GILB. I 67. 1 (v. capillositas).

epinguatus [cf. LL pinguefacere], deprived of fat, emaciated.

si unus [geminorum] est masculus et altera femina dextra mam[ill]a est dura et mulier in facie illius partis est macra et colorata et in altera parte est ~ata aliquantulum et pallida vel panniculata M. SCOT *Phys.* 19.

epinicion [CL < ἐπινίκιον], song of victory (also fig.).

assumere mereamur sexagenarium [numerum] vel ~ion, quod nomen palmam sive triumphum possumus appellare BYRHT. *Man.* 230; verum Pascha .. percipiendo, quod est verum ~ion *Id. HR* 19; quid juvat .. / .. fama celebris, quid epinichia, / quod fornix exprimens victoris prelia? WALT. WIMB. *Sim.* 127.

†epinta, kind of herb or (?) *f. l.*

in succo †epinte [? l. nepete] ADEL. *CA* 3 (v. 1 crassula a).

epio v. pteris. **epiousion** v. epiusius. **epipata** v. epibata. **epipatio** v. opipatio.

epipedon [CL < ἐπίπεδον], (geom.) plane figure.

[mensure] genera tria: rectum, planum, solidum .. planum est quod quidam ~on vocant, alii pedes constratos *Eng. Weights* 5; naturalis ponderosi motus ad centrum est; hoc vero cedit embipedum ALF. ANGL. *Cor* 9. 5 (cf. ib. 10. 5: fluit in longum ..; non enim ascendit tantum neque ex se cedit embipedum [v. l. empipedum]).

epipendite v. ependytes. **epiph-** v. et. ephip-.

epiphanes [LL *gl.* < ἐπιφανής], (of god) manifest, apparent.

epyphanes, A. *god schewynge WW*.

epiphania [LL < ἐπιφάνεια]

1 appearance, manifestation. **b** (geom.) plane surface.

ephiphania, †aparatio [l. apparitio] *GlC Int.* 121 (cf. ib. E 230: ephiphania, splendor); ~ia, *ætewung* ÆLF. *Gl.*; ~ia, manifestatio vel superapparitio OSB. GLOUC. *Deriv.* 200; BART. ANGL. XIX 7 (v. 3 apparitio 2a). **b** ad planitiem vero, quam Greci ~iam vocant, mensurandam tali utimur artificio ADEL. *ED* 30.

2 Epiphany of Christ (eccl., sts. dist. as threefold); **b** (as n. pl.).

pervenit ad eos mane in die ~ie Domini ..; dixit autem .. "puto quod aliquid nobis Dominus donaverit ad celebrandum diem in quo magi .. adoraverunt eum et in quo Spiritus Sanctus in specie columbe baptizato [v. l. baptizato eo, ? l. baptizatum] in Jordane super eum descendit, et in quo aquam in Chana Galilaeae vertit in vinum" *V. Cuthb.* II 4; imminentibus sollemniis majoribus, verbi gratia paschae, pentecostes, ~ae BEDE *HE* IV 17 p. 244; post octavas Epyphaniae LANFR. *Const.* 90; W. MALM. *GR* III 285, BELETH *RDO* 73. 79 (v. 3 apparitio 3d); elapso j anno a Piphania *RDomin* 80; **1216** usque ad ~iam Domini *Pat* 15; **1231** disposueram .. statim post ~iam iter peregrinationis arripuisse GROS. *Ep.* 4 p. 28; die Jovis in octavis Epefanie Domini *Lib. Melrose* II 444; s**1462** in aurora Ephiphanie venerunt Scotti .. ad .. Alniwyke *Compilatio* 176; **1511** in vigilia ~ie *Cant. Coll. Ox.* II 254. **b** c**1169** in proximo ~orum die .. ad .. regem supplex accessit J. SAL. *Ep.* 285 (288 p. 636).

Epiphi, an Egyptian month.

Aegyptii .. quorum .. undecimus [mensis] ~i, vij kl. Juliarum .. die sumit exordium BEDE *TR* 11; [vocatur] Aegyp[tice] †Episi *Miss. R. Jum.* 15.

epiphia, ~ium v. ephippium.

epiphonema [CL < ἐπιφώνημα], (rhet.) exclamatory remark in conclusion.

epiphonima, id est adclamatio quae post narratas †rebus [? l. res] breviter cum exclamatione prorumpit *Gl. Leid.* 28. 65; proverbium aliud est ~a GERV. MELKLEY *AV* 182.

epiphora [CL < ἐπιφορά], (med.) epiphora, afflux of fluid. **b** inflammation, sty.

epifora dicitur ab 'epi', quod est supra et 'fero, fers', i. reuma a superioribus descendens *Alph.* 58. **b** hec ~a, .. i. lippido oculorum, quando sc. pellicula superducitur oculo OSB. GLOUC. *Deriv.* 187; epifore oculorum sunt apostemata que nascuntur super oculos *SB* 20.

epiploon [LL < ἐπίπλοον], (anat.) omentum.

epiploten, omentum idem *Alph.* 58 (cf. ib. 129: omentum .. et quando etiam dicitur .. epiplode et pigorontum).

epiraedium [CL < Gall.], cart, barrow; **b** (dist. as handbarrow). **c** thripple.

in stabulo sit .. cenovectorium sive epirodium [*gl.: carette*], capistrum NECKAM *Ut.* 106; c**1312** heres accipiet .. unam mensuram busselli, traham, epiridium, quod interpretatur *barwe Borough Cust.* II 141. **b** *hand barwe*, ~ium *PP*. **c** sunt supra redas partes epyreide dicte GARL. *Syn.* 85; plaustellum, currus, epredia [*gl.: the þerrepyllis*] bigaque, reda *WW*.

epiromanus, designating rule over the Romans.

ad .. xv annum ~i imperii imperatoris Tiberii NEN. *HB* 145.

epirus v. epiurus. **epis** v. pteris. **episciten** v. hephaestites.

episcopalis [LL]

1 (of thing or abstr.) episcopal, belonging or appropriate to a bishop; **b** (w. *cathedra, ecclesia, sedes*); **c** (w. *officium, ministerium*); **d** (w. *dignitas, gradus, ordo*, or sim.); **e** (w. *consuetudo, jus*, or sim.). **f** (as sb. n. pl.) episcopal rights or dues. **g** (as sb. n. pl.) episcopal robes.

.. ~em vitam sive doctrinam .. insito sibi virtutum amore .. exercebat BEDE *HE* V 18 p. 320; crucis vexillum quod .. ante illum beatissimum ~i ritu deferri consueverat OSB. *Mir. Dunst.* 19; o forma jam in necdum episcopo ~is, certe omnibus, sed presertim episcopis, et admiranda et imitanda H. BOS. *Thom.* III 3; H. HUNT. *HA* VI 21 (v. baculus 10a); **1215** unum anulum ~em cum saphiro magno et perlis et granatis *Pat* 147b; s**1247** quod secundum ~e desiderium est completum M. PAR. *Min.* III 15 (cf. id. *Maj.* IV 590: quod secundum .. desiderium suum gaudebat episcopus fuisse completum); s**1428** coram .. domino W. .. Norwicensi episcopo in capella palatii sui ~is *Ziz.* 417; c**1520** si decernere sciant inter casus papales, ~es et sacerdotales *Conc. Scot.* I cclxxv. **b 725** (10c) ad ~em sedem atingens *CS* 144; fecit ecclesiam ~i sedi congruam BEDE *HE* III 25 p. 181; *Ib.* V 12 (v. cathedra 2a); in qua tunc gente sanctus Wilbrordus positus est praedicator sedisque ~is in Traejecto castello delegatus est ALCUIN *WillP* 13; cui .. commendavit ~em cathedram quae sita est in Wigornensi civitate BYRHT. *V. Ecgwini* 355; a**1087**, **1295** (v. ecclesia 4a); BEKYNTON II app. 321 (v. cathedra 2a). **c** omnes loci ipsius [*Lindisfarne*] antistites usque hodie sic ~e exercent officium BEDE *CuthbP* 16; **742** dicunt sibi Romanum pontificem licentiam dedisse ministerium ~e in aecclesia ministrare BONIF. *Ep.* 50; honor episcopalis non parum vilescit dum is ad pontificatum assumitur qui ordinatus quo divertat vel cui per ~e ministerium .. praesideat nescit ANSELM (*Ep.* 435) V 383; c**1239** cogitur episcopus reddere rationem judici seculari de facto suo quod .. pertinet ad officium ~e GROS. *Ep.* 72; cessare ab execucione ~is officii OCKHAM *Dial.* 500. **d 799** non est in Christo divinitatis majestas sicut in quolibet homine ~is dignitas verbi gratia ALCUIN *Ep.* 166; ~em gradum .. accepit et nomen .. Patricius sumpsit NEN. *HB* 195; a**1077** quia ad dedicandam aecclesiam episcopus processurus sacris vestibus ex institutione ~is ordinis debeat esse indutus .. stupui LANFR. *Ep.* 13 (14); ANSELM (*Ep.* 435) V 383 (v. 1c supra); petit populus beatum virum .. ad ~em dignitatem sullimandum DOMINIC *V. Ecgwini* I 3; facta .. est .. inter eos quedam animorum .. contentio, quis eorum videretur major et ad ascensum ~em .. vicinior G. COLD. *Durh.* 2; **1311** W. Coventrensis et Lichfeldensis episcopus in castro .. Eboraci carcerali custodie est addictus in vituperium ~is dignitatis *Conc. Syn.* 1342; **1437** etiamsi .. patriarchali .. et ~i dignitate prefulgeant (*Lit. Papae*) BEKYNTON II 17. **e** si .. aliquis per superbiam elatus ad justiciam ~em venire contempserit (*Leg. Will. I*) *GAS* 485 (cf. ib.: ille .. qui vocatus ad justitiam episcopi venire noluerit, pro unaquaque vocatione legem ~em emendabit); **1096** etc. (v. consuetudo 4b); c**1270** ea que ad ~ia jura pertinent *Reg. Dunferm.* 98. **f 1114** quicquid pertinebat ad ecclesiam Wrdie preter ~ia *CalCh* IV 170 (= *Regesta* 1070); c**1205** .. tenendas .. sicut alie conventuales [ecclesie] parochiales ecclesias suas in episcopatu Glasg' liberius .. tenent salvis ~ibus *Reg. Paisley* 113; c**1211** ecclesiam .. libere .. tenent et possident salvis ~ibus nostris *Inchaffray* 26; **1239** proviso ut .. sacerdoti perpetuo .. porcio assignetur ex qua comode sustentari valeat ac ~ia et alia onera ecclesie supportare (*Lit. Papae*) *Cart. Lindores* 98; c**1300** ut .. abbas .. sit decanus de omnibus ecclesiis que date sunt ecclesie sue .. nec quisquam presumat eum judicare nisi solus episcopus. ~ia reddat vel reddere faciat de ecclesiis decanatus sui (*Ch. Ep. Coventr.*) *MonA* VI 363a. **g** hora .. quarta compositis omnibus preparatoriis, et episcopis suis ~ibus instructis .. electus Thomas progreditur *Becket Mat.* IV 154; **1311** episcopi ~ibus induti, xij presbyteris in sacerdotalibus eis assistentibus, .. penitentes absolverunt (*Acta contra Templarios*) *Conc.* II 389a.

2 (of person) episcopal. **b** (as sb. m.) adherent of bishop.

1077 (v. angaria 1a); **1321** aliquis regalium vel ~ium ministrorum *PQW* 469b; officiarius consiliarius ~is *Entries* 228b. **b** s**1141** ~es .. ex improviso exilientes .. abeuntes insequuntur GERV. CANT. *Chr.* I 121; fugientibus ~ibus omnibus DOMERH. *Glast.* 538; s**1300** illi ~es et quidam falsi fratres appositis manibus extraxerunt Christum Domini de loco suo W. GUISB. 347; videntes ~es et ministri dicti patris quod [etc.] *G. Durh.* 49; querente etiam Papa qua auctoritate episcopus H. de L. prefecisset respondentibusque ~ibus quod per lapsum temporis GRAYSTANES 25.

episcopaliter [LL], episcopally, as befits a bishop.

virum ~er infulatum GOSC. *Mir. Iv.* lxi; [Papa] viri illustris adventum ea qua decuit humanitate suscepit, peregrinationem ~er fovit W. MALM. *GP* V 218; hoc [modo thesaurum Coventreie] Robertus .. episcopus provincie inhians non ~er involavit *Id. GR* IV 341; in vestram .. paternitatem vel in primatum vestrum nec leviter nec ~er deliqui AD. EYNS. *Hug.* V 16 p. 189.

episcopare [LL]

1 to be a bishop; **b** (dep.).

adhuc ~ante Willelmo R. COLD. *Godr.* 208; s**38** Romam venit et ibi annos xxv ~avit *Eul. Hist.* I 164. **b 1168** mentientes quod rex .. Noradini citius sequeretur errores .. quam in ecclesia Cantuariensi Thomam pateretur diutius ~ari J. SAL. *Ep.* 244 (272 p. 560).

2 (trans.) to make a bishop.

1122 nec hec dico quod multum desiderem in regno vestro ~ari (*Ep. ad Regem Scotiae*) EADMER *HN* 351; tu qui in episcopos nunc desevis, cito ~aberis dante Domino P. BLOIS *Ep.* 60; eorum aliqui .. minime renuissent ~ari, si affuisset qui coegisset AD. EYNS. *Hug.* III 1 p. 93 (cf. ib. V 16 p. 192: istum [anulum] dum ~arer digitus noster excepit; istum dum sepeliar dextera hec retinebit); rex Henricus II .. duorum ordinum [sc. Cartusiensium et

Cisterciensium] viris .. ad redimendum sic famam suam quia multos ante indignos ~averat .. sedes dare cathedrales disposuerat GIR. *Rem.* 29; **s1320** juvenem contingit ad regnum sublimari, sed bene non congruit juvenes ~ari *V. Ed. II* 252.

episcopatus [LL]

1 episcopate, office of bishop. **b** period of episcopal office.

†**a699** (11c) pontificis Offtori ego Ecguuine .. successor in ~um existo *CS* 76; sciebat regem invitare eum voluisse ad ~um *V. Cuthb.* III 6; successit Augustino in ~um Laurentius BEDE *HE* II 4; **1071** relicto ~u monachicam vitam petiit LANFR. *Ep.* 2; **s1107** FL. WORC. II 56 (v. baculus 10a); nemo in ea [sc. Anglia] episcopus .. factus est qui non primo fuerit homo regis, ac de manu illius ~us .. investituram .. susceperit EADMER *HN pref.* 2; queritur .. quid sit ordo; .. videtur quod ~us sit ordo: est enim 'signaculum' HALES *Sent.* IV 399; in ~u ostenditur sacerdotium DUNS *Ord.* II 33. **b 813** praesidente .. archipontifice Wlfredo metropolitano .. anno iiij ~us ejusdem archiepiscopi *CS* 342; vixit in ~u xxxiij annis et viij mensibus et xiij diebus FOLC. *V. J. Bev.* 13.

2 bishopric, diocese: **a** (Continental); **b** (British); **c** (Eng.); **d** (Sc.); **e** (Ir.).

a ad castellum Trajectum .. pervenerunt in quo .. sanctus Willibrordus sedem ~us sui habuit ALCUIN *WillP* I 5; **1242** pasturis nostris que habemus in ~ibus predictis [sc. Baione et Aquensi] (*CalPat* 334) *RGasc* I 74. **b** post sacerdotalem ~us vel presbyterii sedem GILDAS *EB* 66; Augustinus invenit eorum [sc. Britonum] provincia vij ~us et archiepiscopatum G. MON. XI 12. **c** ut .. in urbe sedem ~us Augustinus acceperit BEDE *HE* I 26 *rub.*; **933** tantam libertatem ~ui Cridiensis ecclesiae perdonare dijudicavi *CS* 694; **945** (13c) quandam ruris partem de terra ~us sui *CS* 807; cum .. ~um circuire non poterat, suo sacerdoti Wilfrido .. pontificatum commisit Eboracensem FOLC. *V. J. Bev.* 13; **1076** clericus qui apostasiae calumniam habet de ~u tuo recedat LANFR. *Ep.* 24 (40); hoc manerium .. est de ~u Rofensi *DB* I 5v.; **s1108** EADMER *HN* 232 (v. cathedra 2a); regnum Anglie .. habet archiepiscopatus duos, ~um multos [sc. xv], comitatus xxxii (*Leg. Hen.* 6. 1) *GAS* 552; sicut in primo libro Gestorum Regalium regnorum distinxi ordinem, ita hic .. ~us provintiarum distinguam W. MALM. *GP prol.* 4; **s1251** ut aliquis episcopus ad alium ~um ditiorem postulatus transferatur ut una ecclesia alterius pellex habeatur M. PAR. *Maj.* V 228; taxatio omnium ecclesiarum .. per dominum Norwicensem facta in ~u Elyensi *Val. Norw.* 209; **c1440** cuilibet conventui Fratrum infra ~us Ebor' et Dunelmi *FormA* 433. **d c1205** *Reg. Paisley* 113 (v. episcopalis 1f); **12..** fructus toto tempore quo curantur .. accipere debemus: et hoc ipsum inter ~us observetur *Conc. Scot.* II 22; FORDUN *Cont.* VIII 3 (v. demembrare c). **e** dicitur episcopos in terra vestra [sc. Hibernia] passim eligi et sine certo ~us loco constitui ANSELM (*Ep.* 435) V 383; **1227** mandatum est capitulo Midensi et universo clero tam viris religiosis quam aliis de ~u illo [etc.] *Pat* 115.

3 seat of diocese, see, cathedral.

residuam dimidiam carucatam terrae .. habet Sancta Maria de Lincolnia, in qua nunc est ~us *DB* I 336; **1108** canonica auctoritas praecipit ut ecclesia ~us ultra tres menses non maneat sine pastore ANSELM (*Ep.* 443) V 390; principales ecclesie, sicut ~us et abbatie talem emendationem violate pacis .. habere debent: .. v lib. [AS: *heafodmynstres griðbrice*] (*Inst. Cnuti*) *GAS* 283; **1166** pecunia in villis collecta ad ~um deferatur *Act. Hen. II* I 401.

episcopellus, bishoplet.

nuper .. unus ~us dixit GASCOIGNE *Loci* 119.

episcopium [LL < ἐπισκοπεῖον]

1 office of bishop.

injuncto sibi ~io in urbe qui vocatur Trecht WILLIB. *Bonif.* 8 p. 47; **788** (12c) ad ~ium castelli quod nominatur Hrofescester *Ch. Roff.* 12; excedente humanis rebus .. Eata episcopo .. Johannes in ejus successit ~io FOLC. *V. J. Bev.* 3; Nordanimbrorum regem .. cuidam simoniaco ~ium vendidisse W. MALM. *GP* I 29; eo ipso si episcopatum peteret indignum ~io se probaret GIR. *RG* III 3.

2 diocese.

a988 singulis tribubus Jeuuissorum .. aepiscopia constituerunt *Conc. Syn.* 168; pontifici mandans, est qui praelatus in isto / tempore episcopio, quendam quod rexerat ipse WULF. *Swith.* I 47; **s1052** Spearhavoc .. in episcopatum promotus .. ex ~ii pecunia marsupiorum farsisset plurimum receptacula *Chr. Abingd.* I 463; **p1083** senes et prudentiores totius ~ii homines .. sedem illius [Cuthberti] episcopalem in insula Lindisfarnensi fuisse .. responderunt *Ch. Durh.* *3; consideravit in ~io .. Firmini [episc. Ambianensium] quandam villam suis negotiis aptam ALEX. CANT. *Mir.* 31 p. 219; in ~iis duo presules de pontificatu certaverunt ORD. VIT. XI 11 p. 24; [Wilfridus] ab ~io [cf. BEDE *HE* IV 13: a sede episcopatus] pulsus .. Roma petita Britanniam rediit H. HUNT. *HA* III 49; *Chr. Rams.* 136 (v. conscius 1b); ~ia et alia monasteria idem rex [Ethelbertus] .. passim fundare machinatur THORNE 1760; **1386** racione nove creacionis vestre prefate episcopie (*sic*) *AncC* XLIII 1.

3 bishop's palace.

724 Thuringis et Germaniae populo .. scribere non omisimus, inter alia ut construant ~ia et aecclesias condant injungentes (*Lit. Papae*) *Ep. Bonif.* 24; cum .. jam .. civitatis [Doruuernensis] esset pars vastata non minima atque ad ~ium furens se flamma dilataret BEDE *HE* II 7; **s1122** civitas Lincolnie tota incendio consumpta est, excepto tamen monasterio et ~io *Ann. Margan* 11; in villa ~iis ejus ibidem proxima spatiaturus .. resedit ÆLNOTH *Cnut* 40; morabantur interim cum sancto episcopo in ~io suo SERLO GRAM. *Mon. Font.* 30.

episcopus [LL < ἐπίσκοπος]

1 (in etymological sense) overseer. **b** (w. ref. to *1 Pet.* ii 25) guardian.

~us, superspector *GlC Int.* 111 (cf. ib. E 254: ~i autem Graece, Latine speculatores interpretantur); ~us Graece, Latine superinspector, quia omnia prospicere debet vel ordinare EGB. *Pont.* 11; **793** speculator .. est in excelsissimo positus loco: unde et ~us dicitur quasi superspeculator ALCUIN *Ep.* 17. **b** sanctum abbatem elegerunt in pastorem et ~um animarum suarum J. FURNESS *Walth.* 79.

2 (eccl.) bishop: **a** (unspec.); **b** (Continental); **c** (British or W.); **d** (Eng.); **e** (Sc.); **f** (Ir.); **g** (var.).

a ~o licet in campo confirmare si necesse sit THEOD. *Pen.* II 2. 1; ~us cum ordinatur, duo ~i ponant et teneant evangeliorum librum super cervicem ejus et unus fundat super eum benedictionem EGB. *Pont.* 1; Christus .. ~us fuit, quando elevatis manibus benedixit discipulos suos apostolos . . . ~um oportet judicare et interpretari, consecrare et consummare, quin et ordinare, offerre, et baptizare *Ib.* 11; in lege Moysi erat Aaron frater ejus sacerdos Dei, eo ordine quo nunc sunt ~i ÆLF. *Ep.* 2. 93; septimus gradus aecclesiastici ordinis est presbyter sive ~us. . . sed majus officium designatur ~o, id sunt: ordinationes clericorum facere et benedicere sanctum crisma et confirmare infantes et dedicare ecclesias *Ib.* 124, 129; cum magister H. factus fuisset episcopus Meldensis .. dixit "si haberem mortalem inimicum .., orarem quod Deus faceret eum ~um" O. CHERITON *Fab.* 1; **c1239** GROS. *Ep.* 127 (v. dioecesanus 1a); OCKHAM *Dial.* 582 (v. consecrare 3a); **a1450** (v. dignitas 2b). **b 742** Germaniae populis .. correctis tres ordinavimus ~os et provinciam in tres parrochias discrevimus BONIF. *Ep.* 50; ut fuit egregius Wilbrordus episcopus ille / plurima qui populi Fresonum millia Christo / lucratus monitis fuerat caelestibus ALCUIN *SS Ebor* 1036; **789** pio patri Felici ~o [Urgellitano] Alchuinus humilis levita salutem *Id. Ep.* 5; idem [metropolitanus] dum Cenomanensium ~us erat .. apud Uticum .. fuerat honorifice susceptus ORD. VIT. III 3 p. 59. **c** sacerdotes habet Britannia, sed insipientes .. sed forsitan aliquis dicat non ita omnes ~i vel presbyteri GILDAS *EB* 69; THEOD. *Pen.* II 9. 1 (v. catholicus 2c); GIR. *JS* 1 p. 142, *Cart. Glam.* 939 (v. decanatus 2b); GIR. *JS* 2 p. 161 (v. dioecesis 1a). **d** †**604** (12c) cum consilio Laurentii ~i et omnium principum meorum *Ch. Roff.* 1; **673** (*Conc. Hertf.*) BEDE *HE* IV 5 (v. consecratio 2a); **c690** (8c) ego Ercnuualdus ~us consensi *CS* 81; electus .. ad pontificatum .. viros huc Augustinum et Mellitum atque Laurentium direxit .. Augustinum ordinando ~um *V. Greg.* p. 86; BEDE *HE* II 3 etc. (v. archiepiscopus); quomodo ab ~o Headda officium sacerdotale acceperit FELIX *Guthl.* 47 *rub.*; ~us Sarisberiensis *DB* I 56; W. MALM. *GP prol.* p. 3 (v. Christianitas 1c); H. CANTOR 31 (v. crux 5b); in custodia Eliensis ~i *RDomin* 63; **12.., 1333** (v. capitulum 6a); Ricardus de Bury, miseracione divina Dunelmensis ~us R. BURY *Phil. prol.* 1; ostendit de quodam ~o Cantuariensi simoniace exaltando et cito deponendo (J. BRIDL.) *Pol. Poems* I 188; **1438** Thomas Herefordensis ~us jam annosus ac senio .. fractus BEKYNTON I 1. **e 1176** *G. Hen. II* I 112 (v. ecclesia 3e); **c1220** *Reg. Dunferm.* 111 (v. dioecesanus 2a); **c1380** *Conc. Scot.* I p. ccxxxv (v. canum); **1459** Thomas .. ~us Abirdonensis *Ib.* II 79; Turgotum Sanctiandreae ~um *Plusc.* VI 1; **1566** per reverendum patrem Alexandrum ~um Galwidie seu Candidecase *Inchaffray* 165. **f** THEOD. *Pen.* II 9. 1 (v. catholicus 2c); Palladius ad Scottos .. primus mittitur ~us BEDE *HE* I 13; **a1192** M[acrobius], Dei gratia Glindelascensis ~us .. *Reg. S. Thom. Dublin* 337; GIR. *TH* III 17 (v. consecrare 3a); **a1224** Symon Dei gratia Midensis ~us *Reg. S. Thom. Dublin* 319. **g 789** (11c) archiepiscopus simul cum universis provincialibus ~is .. finem composuerunt *CS* 256; †**971** (12c) *CS* 1277 [etc.] (v. comprovincialis 2a); dioceseus ~us HERM. ARCH. 1 (v. dioeceseus); **s1175** ~o diocesiano DICETO *YH* I 403 (v. dioecesanus 1b); cardinales ~os GIR. *Spec.* IV 6 p. 279 (v. cardinalis 3a); **s1254** in cujus [Hugonis ep. Eliensis] obitu flos Nigrorum obiit monachorum; quia sicut abbas abbatum in Anglia extiterat, ita et ~us ~orum choruscavit M. PAR. *Maj.* V 455; **1423** ~orum secularium *Reg. Heref.* 32 (v. 2 caputium 1f).

3 (w. *elemosinariae*, *innocentium*, *juvenum*, *puerorum*, *puerilis*, *S. Nicholai*, or sim.) boy bishop (from St. Nicholas's Day to Holy Innocents' Day).

1356 ~o elemosinar' visitanti amicos suos *Ac. Durh.* 122; **1370** ~o elemosinarie iij s. iiij d. *Ib.* 129; **1441** ~o puerili elemos' ac ~o de Elvett iij s. iiij d. *Ib.* 143; **1245** mitra ~i Innocentum, nullius precii *Invent. S. Paul.* 472; **1321** lego .. officio et statui ~i Innocentium perpetuo remansurum in ecclesia predicta unum anulum cum magno lapide (*Test.*) *Fabr. York* 158; **1396** compotus .. custodis bonorum Johannis de Cave, ~i Innocencium *Camd. Misc.* VII 31 app.; **1327** celerario .. et ~o Juvenum die Innocencium ij s. vj d. *Comp. Swith.* 255; **1533** in servicia .. missa ~o Juvenum die SS. Innocencium *Ib.* 221; **c1200** cenam in octavis Innocentium tenebit, ~um cum pueris et eorum comitiva pascendo *Reg. S. Paul.* 129; **1221** thesaurarius .. inveniet stellas cum omnibus ad illas pertinentibus, preter cirpos quos inveniet ~us puerorum †futurorum [? l. et fatuorum] *Stat. Ebor.* 98; **1295** ~o puerorum facto apud Cestriam in eodem festo [S. Nicolai] ad unam capam chori faciendam pro hujusmodi servicio puerorum episcopali *Prests* 198; **1340** ~o puerorum ecclesie de Andewerp' cantanti coram domino regi in camera sua in festo SS. Innocencium (*AcWardr*) *TRBk* 203 p. 204; **1397** ~us puerorum *Process. Sal.* 54 (v. cruciferarius a); **c1445** ad vesperas post memoriam de S. Stephano eat processio puerorum ad altare Innocencium .. in capis sericis, cum cereis illuminatis .. in manibus, cantando, ~o puerorum pontificalibus induto, executore officii sive ~o presente, incipiente hoc responsorium *Ib.* 52; **1436** ~o puerili elemosinarie xx d. *Ac. Wearmouth* 201; **c1500** una capa de *tyssue* pro ~o puerili *Fabr. York* 229; **1388** paria serotecarum sunt quinque quorum unum par deputatum pro parvulo ~o sancti Nicholai .. [anulus] cupreus deauratus .. deputatus pro ~o sancti Nicholai (*Invent. Westm.*) *Arch.* LII 275; **1418** [xij d.] ~o S. Nicholai (*Rec. Bury St. Edm.*) *HMC* XIV 8. 124; **1526** puero ~o beati Nicholai infra capellam sancti Stephani Westm' *SP Hen. VIII* XXXVII 1939a.

4 (w. *Judaeus* or sim.) Jewish priest. (*Cf. Starrs* II (1932) n. 108 (c)); **b** (as surname transl. Heb. *Cohen*).

1168 ~us Ju[de]us recognovit coram baronibus de Scaccario quod Willelmus de Norwico pers[ol]verat Isaac Judaico dccc m. et iij m. et dim. *Pipe* 222; **1178** in soltis per breve regis Deodato ~o Judeorum *Pipe* 5; **11..** intraverunt forte quidam Judei Londonienses .. inter quos et quidam Judeorum ~us venit *Becket Mat.* IV 153; **1242** Elyas filius Benedicti ~i Judeorum *Pipe* 285. **b 1234** Elyas ~us [Heb.: *cohen*] *Starrs* I 6; **1260** de .. debitis Elie ~i *Cl* 90.

episedium [cf. epi- + sedes], seat of honour.

heybenche, orcestra, .. epesedium *PP.*

episemon [LL < ἐπίσημον], sign, mark.

pro sex interserunt novam figuram hujusmundi ϛ quasi nostrum s incurvatum .. quarum neutra est littera alphabeti sed tamen nota numeri et vocatur epissimon BACON *Gram. Gk.* 80.

Episi v. Epiphi.

epispasticus [LL < ἐπισπαστικός] (med., of drug) epispastic, drawing to itself.

~a sunt medicamina claudentia vulnus *Alph.* 58; virtus est ei [sinapi] calida, leptiutica, epispactica; apoflegmatismis utile est *Ib.* 171.

epissimon v. episemon.

epistasis [ἐπίστασις], attention, observation.

non ēpystăsin capit, extasinque veretur / pagina. lector, have FRITH. 1395.

epistelia v. epistylum.

episteme [ἐπιστήμη], understanding.

Dunstanulus .. a phedia ad ~en erat transiturus *Chr. Wallingf.* 42.

epistes v. hephaestitis.

episticula [cf. CL epistola], short letter. *V. et. epistiuncula.*

mittitur et ~a [v. l. epistola; AS p. 445: *ærend gewrit*] depositionis denuntiatura diem *RegulC* 67.

epistigus v. epistygus. **epistile** v. epistola 4a. **epistilium** v. epystylum. **epistites** v. hephaestitis.

epistiuncula [cf. CL epistola], short letter. *V. et. episticula.*

c740 ut rusticitatem hujus ~ae emendas *Ep. Bonif.* 49; **a780** ceterum .. portitor hujus ~ae viva voce valet enarrare (CYNEHEARD) *Ib.* 114; **a797** scripsi ~as aliquas . . . redde singulis singulas ALCUIN *Ep.* 57.

epistola (~ula) [CL < ἐπιστολή]

1 letter.

Ignatius Antiochiae urbis episcopus .. ait in ~a quam ad Romanam ecclesiam misit 'a Syria' [etc.] GILDAS *EB* 74; **c705** hanc ~am jugiter inter ceteros quos legis libros habere non omittas ALDH. *Ep.* 8 (11); scripsit cum coepiscopis suis exhortatoriam ad eos ~am BEDE *HE* II 4; alia aepistola [regis Hen. I] de intronizatione Girardi ad eundem apostolicum (*Quad., tit.*) *GAS* 544; premittit ~am quam dirigit archiepiscopo Remensi S. LANGTON *Gl. Hist. Schol.* 43; ut .. ~as contexere valeant nobiliores *Dictamen* 334.

2 literary composition in epistolary form; **b** (as preface).

GILDAS *EB* 1 (v. declamare 2a); scrupulosus [lector] .. reminiscatur in primordio ~ae quam tantopere .. protelaveram [etc.] ALDH. *Met.* 4; W. MALM. *GP* I 44 (v.

decretalis 1a). **b** explicit ad domnum specialis epistola patrem / Ælfegum, Uuentam qui regit ecclesiam; / incipit ad cunctos generalis epistola fratres WULF. *Swith. pref.* 329, 331; explicit ad cunctos generalis epistola fratres, / . . / incipit exigui praefatio stricta libelli *Ib.* 393; premittit magister prologum epistolarem, id est ~am loco prologi S. LANGTON *Gl. Hist. Schol.* 39.

3 epistle of New Testament; **b** (w. *canonica*); **c** (liturg.).

iterum ad Corinthios in prima ~a, 'ut sapiens' inquit 'architectus fundamentum posui' GILDAS *EB* 100; specialiter B. Pauli ad Timotheum ~ae, in quibus eum erudire studuit BEDE *HE* I 27 p. 48; **1237** Petrus . . siccine instruit seniores per ~am suam, cum scribat 'seniores qui in vobis sunt' [etc.; *1 Pet.* v 1–4] (*Lit. Archiep. Constant.*) M. PAR. *Maj.* III 453; **1245** finit in ~a Jude *Invent. S. Paul.* 496; **1396** pro magno altari: . . duo . . libri textuum ~arum (*Catal. Librorum*) *Meaux* III lxxxiii. **b** a Dominica tertia usque ad Ascensionem Domini legantur septem canonicae ~ae LANFR. *Const.* 121; **1396** (v. canonicus 3a); **14..** item Beda super canonicas ~as (*Cart. Reading*) *EHR* III 124. **c** subdiaconus . . exuat eam [casulam] dum legit ~am [AS p. 406: *pistel*] *ReglC* 34; videbam . . in visione . . Dunstanum . . missas agentem meque illi in ministerio subdiaconatus servientem. cumque perlecta a me fuisset ~a . . OSB. *Mir. Dunst.* 21; duo subdiaconi . . unus ad prophetiam et alter ad ~am LANFR. *Const.* 93; ejus [precentoris] . . officium est . . mendas legencium corrigere . . in collectis, ~a, evangelio *Obs. Barnwell* 58; **13..** sermones super Evangelia et ~is in Dominicis per annum (*Catal. Librorum*) *Chr. Rams.* 356.

4 letter from pope, bull. **b** (w. *decretalis*) decretal.

exemplar ~ae beatissimi et apostolici papae urbis Romanae ecclesiae Bonifatii directae . . Eduino regi Anglorum BEDE *HE* II 10; **743** secundum tuae . . sanctitatis petitionem et tribus epistolis tuis singulas confirmationis ~as misimus (*Lit. Papae*) *Ep. Bonif.* 51; apperperans ergo, laesus [cunc]tamine nullo, / Alhtfrido regi direxit epistile Petri FRITH. 1271. **b** BRAKELOND 129v., etc. (v. decretalis 2a); sanctionibus vel decretalibus ~is OCKHAM *Dial.* 635; quod . . tot decretales ~e ad diversas partes mundi emanassent PAUL. ANGL. *ASP* 1544.

epistolaris (~ularis) [CL]

1 appropriate to or characteristic of a letter (esp. w. *angustia* or *brevitas*; *cf.* Jerome *Ep.* 36. 1. 4, 53. 6. 1).

a671 ALDH. *Ep.* 1 (v. angustia 1a); **c750** enarrare . . omnia mala quae . . patimur ~is brevitas prohibet BONIF. *Ep.* 91; **798** per . . mentis excessum . . haec locutus sum, non tam ordinate quam ~is postulat angustia ALCUIN *Ep.* 156; **c1075** B. Hieronymus quantis eum . . praeconiis effert ~i brevitate comprehendi non potest LANFR. *Ep.* 50 (46); **c1078** nec ~is angustia poterat . . affectus capere latitudinem ANSELM (*Ep.* 12) III 116; **1189** si mora libera nobis esset non posset ~is brevitas sufficere *Ep. Cant.* 324.

2 in the form of or expressed by a letter, epistolary; **b** (w. *liber*) letter-book, collection of letters; *v. et. epistolarius* 1a; **c** (as manual of style).

sed forte quilibet scrupulosus . . ~em perscrutans rusticitatem perquirat . . ALDH. *Met.* 4; **800** de Bethleem . . ad Romanas arces ~es . . volare cartulas ALCUIN *Ep.* 196; ~is . . dulcedo vestrae magnitudinis mentem nobis hilarem reddit H. BOS. *Ep.* 45. 1474B; minora quedam . . tam ~ia quam metrica . . compegi carmina GIR. *LS* 415; S. LANGTON *Gl. Hist. Schol.* 39 (v. epistola 2b); **1297** (v. 1 affatus b); de ~i [genere prosayci] . . pertractare decrevi *Dictamen* 338. **b** **c798** epistolam . . quam beati Gregorii de simpla mersione dicunt esse conscriptam in ~i suo libro . . non invenimus ALCUIN *Ep.* 137; in eodem ~i libro [Jeronymi] GIR. *GE* II 9. **c** **c1400** Liber ~is Ricardi de Bury (MS *tit.*) *FormOx* 4.

3 (liturg.) concerning (reading of) the Epistle.

postea debent doceri de officio ~i, qualiter se debet habere circa altare *Cust. Cant.* 12; cum verba ~ia sua sunt paris auctoritatis cum evangelio (WYCL.) *Ziz.* 482; **1432** in presentis Dominice ~i officio *FormOx* 437*n*.

4 (as sb. m. or n.) service-book containing Epistles.

10.. missale j, ~em j, 'ad te levavi' et 'aspiciens' (*Invent. Worc.*) *EHR* XXXII 389; **1296** unum manuale, ~e, duo vetera gradalia [etc.] *Ch. Sal.* 369; **1345** ~e cum evangeliis in uno volumine *Sacr. Lichf.* 114; **14..** libri: . . item unum ~e (*Invent.*) AMUND. II app. 360; **14..** capella abbatis graduales ij et unus ~is (*Cart. Reading*) *EHR* III 122.

epistolarius [LL]

1 epistolary, (book) of letters; *v. et. epistolaris* 2b. **b** (as sb. n.) letter-book.

'confidas dictis fictis', i. . . dictis poeticis auctoris, sc. Horatii carmine, i. primo libro ~io ubi versus sequens ponitur: 'quicquid delirant reges' [etc., Horace *Ep.* I 2. 14] (J. BRIDL.) *Pol. Poems* I 181. **b** constat nempe legentibus . . ~ium beati Jeronymi duas esse epistolas intitulatas Jeronymo ad Demetriadem BRADW. *CD* 312C.

2 a (as sb. m.) epistler, letter-writer (mon.). **b** (as sb. ? f.) office of letter-writer.

a Wilton epistolar'. Cristoferus Dyson, ~ius in monasterio predicto, affirmat super sacramentum suum epistol[ariam] predict[am] esse annui valoris in denariis receptis de abbatissa, in precio j robe, in pensione communibus annis . . xlix s. iiij d. *Val. Eccl.* II 99a. **b** *Ib.* (v. 2a supra).

3 (liturg.) for (reading of) the Epistle. **b** (as sb. m. or n.) service-book containing Epistles.

Ernulfus [episc. Roff., ob **1124**] . . fecit fieri . . tunicam ~iam violaciam similem casule principali *Flor. Hist.* II 45. **b** presbyter debet habere . . lectionarium, quod quidam vocant ~ium ÆLF. *Ep.* 2. 137; **1222** item missale unum et gradale unum [et] ~ium unum *Reg. S. Osm.* II 141; **1245** (v. evangelarium); **1368** ij tapeta . . j pistelar', velum quadragesimale *Invent. Norw.* 27; **1432** item ~ium cum evangeliis pro magno altari coopertum coreo albo in volumine magno (*Invent.*) *Reg. Glasg.* II 334; **14..** ~ii duo (*Cart. Reading*) *EHR* III 122 (cf. ib. 123: ~ius cum libro capituli).

epistolator, epistler, letter-writer.

hee terminaciones tribuuntur membris rethoricis que apud ~ores vocantur 'coma', 'colon', et 'periodus' *Dictamen* 336.

epistul- v. epistol-.

epistygus [cf. ἐπιστύγης], odious monster, headless man.

sunt homines in insula Brixontis fluvii qui absque capitibus nascuntur, quos †epifugas [v. l. epistigos] Graeci vocant, et viij pedum altitudinis sunt et tota in pectore capitis officia gerunt, nisi quod oculos in humeris habere dicuntur *Lib. Monstr.* I 24.

epistylium (~stylum) [CL < ἐπιστύλιον, ἐπίστυλον], (arch.) epistyle, architrave (incl. capital); **b** (fig.). **c** cross beam of bridge.

epistelia, capitella *GlC* E 235 (cf. ib. 397: pistilia, capitella); epistilia, Graece, quae super capitella columnarum ponuntur *Gl. Leid.* 1. 49; **9..** epistilia, *headfodlic, ufeweard swer WW*; ~ium, trabs super columpnas posita OSB. GLOUC. *Deriv.* 201; †altilis [l. a stilis] sive epistilis [*gl.*: *de chapitraus*] columpne, tapetum sive tapete dependeant NECKAM *Ut.* 100; *Id. NR* II 172 p. 283 (v. caelatura 2a); quarum [sc. columnarum] debilitas, quamvis in processu operis satis posset adverti per hiatus . . partium, per . . fissuram . . a base usque ad ~um . . *Mir. J. Bev. C* 345; hoc epistilium, *sumet Gl. AN Glasg.* f. 20; preparabimus . . columpnam . . ad supportandum . . instrumentum . . . in ~o . . superemineat . . paxillus WALLINGF. (*Rect.*) I 410; epistilium est supprema pars columne *WW*. **b** quid sunt coxe? epistilii columpnarum (*Dictum Secundi*) *Leg. Ant. Lond.* 185; ex equorum tumultu et equitum collisione . . bases terre, columpnas ejus et epistilia fugam petere autumant et ordinem universi inverti S. SIM. *Itin.* 52. **c** **s1358** Johannes B. . . aqua domum . . invadente . . summitati domus . . innixus transvectus fuit ad pontem . . cui approximans et in ejusdem cacumen secedens ac ~ium fortiter apprehendens, se salvavit FORDUN *Cont.* XIV 21.

episynaloepha [LL < ἐπισυναλοιφή], (gram.) elision.

episynalipha BEDE *AM* 122 (v. diaeresis).

epital- v. epithal-.

epitaphium [CL < ἐπιτάφιον]

1 funeral speech, song, or sim.; **b** (inscribed on tomb).

epitafium ALDH. *Met.* 10 p. 88 (v. epigramma 1); ~ion *Id. VirgP* 13, †epitathium *GlC* E 251, ~ion BYRHT. *V. Ecgwini* 394 (v. epicedion); **10..** ~ion, *byrigleoð WW*; **s1199** de cujus [Ric. I] morte simul et sepultura quidam ~ium edidit in hunc modum . . M. PAR. *Maj.* II 452. **b** scriptum in tumba ipsius [Gregorii] ~ium hujusmodi BEDE *HE* II 1; quam [tumbam] et ~ium . . digniter decoraverat EADMER *V. Osw.* 25 (cf. BEDE *HE* V 19: hoc de illo supra ~ium scriptum); epithaphium hujusmodi repertum 'filius Evandri Pallas . . [etc.] jacet hic' W. MALM. *GR* II 206; obiit [prior Johannes H.] A. D. mccexvj et jacet sepultus sub lapide marmoreo . . eius ~ium 'ecce marmoreus lapis hic tegit ossa Johannis . .' *Hist. Durh.* 5; **1420** unam petram . . cum epithaphio temporis obitus sui scripto in circuitu petre predicte *Reg. Cant.* II 206; **s1445** cujus [Margarete] epithapium sequitur . . quod super ejus tumbam positum fuit *Plusc.* XI 7.

2 hearse, framework over a tomb.

1478 volumus quod collocent in choro . . ~ium coopertum tapeta decenti cum duobus cereis . . quod . . ~ium †thurisitabunt [l. thurificabunt] *Scot. Grey Friars* II 126; **1484** reddendo etiam omni anno . . in die obitus mei . . missam . . cum duabus candelis super epitafium meum *Reg. Brechin* II app. 118.

3 inscription, superscription.

in ~io Domini scriptum est Hebraice, Grece, et Latine BACON *Maj.* III 199; nominativus ponitur absolute . . in epithafiis [a]ut super ymagines, ut 'beatus Nicholaus' 'sancta Maria' *Id.* XV 102; in fortibus Templi hoc ~ium scripserunt: 'Templum pacis in eternum' *Eul. Hist.* I 68.

4 letter-book.

1432 item ephitaphium Senece continens epistolas Pauli ad Senecam (*Catal. Librorum*) *Reg. Glasg.* 339.

epitasis [LL < ἐπίτασις]

1 (med.) stretching, swelling.

fistule, tumorum †epiltasie [? l. epitasis] strangalidesve curantur W. FITZST. *Thom.* 15.

2 (tension of) middle part of play, thickening of plot.

1520 et profecto, si Brixius ut totus est in metaphoris comicis ab epigrammate meo velut ab ~i jubeat hanc auspicari fabulam . ., sui communi more patietur addi suo loco protasim (MORE) *Ep. Erasmi* IV 1087.

epitathium v. epitaphium. **epitegium** v. epitogium. **epitema** v. epithema. **epitertius** v. epitritus. **epiteton** v. epitheton. **epithafium** v. epitaphium.

epithalamicus [cf. CL epithalamium], epithalamic. **b** (as sb. n.) epithalamium, bridal song.

cum hoc ~o carmine admirabilis gratiae GOSC. *Lib. Confort.* 28. **b** de particulari quodam sponsi et sponse ~o melus hic H. BOS. *LM* 1340D; gaude et canta virginitatis ~um, canticum novitatis P. BLOIS *Serm.* 597B; est epithalamicum carmen nuptiale GARL. *Epith.* I *Summa* 61.

epithalamium [CL < ἐπιθαλάμιον], epithalamium, bridal song; **b** (fig.); **c** (w. ref. to *Psalm* or *Cant.*). **d** bridal chamber (fig.); *cf. thalamus*.

declinat parvi pendens ~ii elogium ALDH. *VirgP* 35; epitalamia apud Latinos inventa. hoc genus in scaenis celebratum est primum, postea tantum in nuptiis adhaesit BONIF. *Met.* 112; ymenaeus vel ~ium, *brydsang*, . . ~ium, carmen nubentium, *giftleoð* ÆLF. *Gl.*; ~ium, carmen nuptiale OSB. GLOUC. *Deriv.* 201. **b** novae Dei . . nuptae [sc. monasterii] . . typicum concinamus epitalam[i]um *V. Ed. Conf.* 50; cantare novum cantici ~ium B. Cuthberto possumus quia . . prodigium de novitate . . mirabilium . . videre valemus. . . preclare . . virtutis miraculum quasi cantici ~ium est R. COLD. *Cuthb.* 22. **c** **800** nostrum est . . continuis . . deplorare precibus ut nos suis dignas efficiat conviviis vobiscumque dulcissimum ~ii paradigma decantare: 'introduxit nos rex in cellaria sua . .' [*Cant.* i 3] (*Lit. abbatissae Calensis*) *Ep. Alcuin.* 196; David, cum . . percutiens coram sponso citharam suam . . sacri ~ii carmina . . jubilaret, ait . . 'dilexisti justitiam' [etc. *Psalm* xliv 8] J. FORD *Serm.* 10. 1; edidit Canticum Canticorum in quo . . desponsationis Christi et ecclesie canit ~ium GROS. *Hexaem. proem.* 97. **d** **c795** plura mihi de sanctissimo tui cordis ~io . . protulisti exempla ALCUIN *Ep.* 86.

epithaphium, epithapium v. epitaphium.

1 epithema [CL < ἐπίθεμα], epithem, poultice; **b** (fig.).

BELETH *RDO* 55. 62 (v. emplastrum 1a); dande sunt opiate ut esdra, ut reuma constringant, et ~atibus et emplastris . . est insistendum *Quaest. Salern.* B 205; epithimata et inunctiones fiant frigida [sc. in effimera] GILB. I 54v. 2; quia non observatur latus cordis cum epithimatibus frigidis GAD. 21. 1; epitima est molle emplastrum. epitima . . dicitur quando res pulverizate subtiliter temperantur cum aliquo liquore ad spissitudinem mellis et pecia aliqua ibi intingitur et locus epithimatur. est autem epithima de succis unctio pura *SB*19; †epichia [l. epithima] dicitur supra positum sed †male [l. molle] emplastrum *Alph.* 58. **b** injectae . . deperationis angilogias intrito universalitatis ~ate et ambrosio dictionalitatis collemate indulcabo O. CANT. *Pref. Frith.* 44; dextera virtutis prebens epithēma salutis *V. Anselmi Epit.* 158; velut mordax quoddam ~a a celesti medico super appositia peccatorum nostrorum vulneribus H. BOS. *Thom.* IV 13 p. 362.

2 epithema v. epithymum.

epithemare, to 'epithem', to poultice.

epithimetur venter cum radice bis malve . . et herbis humidis GILB. I 19v. 1; stomachus . . unguatur calidis et epith[im]etur eisdem et mane similiter confortetur *Ib.* V 208. 1; stomachum exterius epithimemus cum mastice *Ib.* 208. 2; GAD. 49. 2 (v. cataplasmare a); *SB* 19 (v. 1 epithema a).

epitheton [CL < ἐπίθετον], (gram.) epithet, adjective used attributively. **b** attribute.

quaedam ~a, quae nominibus copulantur ALDH. *PR* 120; calamistrum, unde dirivatur 'calamistratus' ~um *Ib.* 135; bombicinus (dirivatum nomen ~on a bombicibus, i.e. vermibus) *Ib.* 138; quartae decimae [qualitatis] mediae significationis quae ab aliis ~a dicuntur, ut magnus, fortis BONIF. *AG* 477; epiteton, quando . . dicitur alicujus nomen proprium de aliquo alio cum sua proprietate gracia proprietatis ut 'iste est Plato philosophus' *Ps.-*GROS. *Gram.* 74. **b** sunt epitheta crucis cruciatus, pugna, triumphus, / mens robusta, fides firma, perenne decus GARL. *Tri. Eccl.* 13; talia preludunt epitēta miserrima belli. / cur? quia gesta canens ethicus esse volo *Ib.* 42.

epithim-, epithin-, epithom-, epithum- v. epithem-, epithym-, epitimesis, epitome.

epithyma [cf. CL epithymum], (?) ointment made of thyme flowers. *Cf.* 1 *epithema*.

epithimata [Scheler: epitimata; *gl*.: unguenta facta de timis floribus] NECKAM *Ut*. 110.

epithymium [cf. CL epithymum], (?) thymy field.

ducatum Normannie, antequam in epitimio Senlac contra Heraldum certassem, Roberto filio meo concessi ORD. VIT. VII 15 p. 242; ultra pontem Eguenie in epitimio spatioso tentoria figi precepit *Ib*. X 10 p. 60.

epithymum [CL < ἐπίθυμον], 'epithyme', dodder parasitic on thyme (*Cuscuta epithymum*).

qualiter sene et ~um, qui sunt calidi et sicci, purgant melancoliam *Quaest. Salern*. N 50; epithimum est flos thimi, que est herba cujus tota virtus in flore est, nam solus flos ponitur in medicina BART. ANGL. XVII 59; ~um [sc. deficit] de Babilonia vel de Creta insula BACON IX 177 (cf. ib. 122: turbit associatum zinzibero et †epithema associatum cum pipere); **12..** epitima, i. epithimum, i. *fordboh WW*; si materia melancolica, purgetur cum sene et polipodio et epithimo GAD. 69. 1; epithumi, fila quedam sunt que nascuntur super thimum. nascuntur eciam super alias herbas et frutices, sed eo magis utimur quod super thimum. calidum est et siccum in secundo gradu *SB* 19 (cf. ib. 42: thimus est herba valde aromatica cujus flos dicitur epithimum); †epithinum [v. l. epithimum] appellamus folia que nascuntur super thimum; .. epithimum flos est thimi similis timbre sed capitella levia et rotunda caudas habentia, G. *epytyme Alph*. 57 (cf. Isid. *Etym*. XVII 9. 13).

epitim- v. epithem-, epithym-.

epitimesis [LL < ἐπιτίμησις], castigation, censure.

secunda [species sapientie], que fit per verbum doctrine dicitur epithimim, quod est increpatio, que per verba, non verbera, fit (H. BOS. *Psalt*.) *RTAM* XVIII 40.

epitogium [CL = *garment worn over toga*], **~ius**, coat, cloak. **b** gown.

epytogiis clamidi penulam superducit J. SAL. *Pol*. 760B; tunica, thoga, collobium et ~ium [*gl*.: *surcote*] NECKAM *Ut*. 101; reparant furaturas ~iorum [*gl*.: epythogium Gallice dicitur *surcot*] GARL. *Dict*. 126; **1325** cum .. corpus Domini ad quendam infirmum deferendum sub ~io recepisset *Reg. Heref*. 330; **1330** poterit pro epitegio uti capa clausa rotunda nigri coloris (*Ordinatio*) *Reg. Roff*. 637; **1388** unum *clothsak'*, unum epitegium curtum, unum cornu nigrum cum zona argentea *Cl* 228 m. 15; **1390** item volo quod de uno ~iorum meorum †tularium [l. talarium] de auro fiat vestimentum et donetur ecclesie Sancti D. (*Test. J. Douglas*) *Bannatyne Misc*. II 109; **1396** et de ~io cum capicio *Reg. Aberbr*. II 44; **1415** [lego] Johanni M. nigrum epetogium, Nicholao S. blodium, Willelmo M. unum *dowblet* cum gladio *Reg. Cant*. III 323; hoc ~ium, *A cowrteby WW*. **b 1404** duos torales ~eos precii xx s. *Pat* 371 m. 2; **1442** *1 gown* [~ium] *of scarlet* (*Invent*.) *Rec. Norw*. II 399; ~ium, *a gowne, gowyn WW*.

epitome [CL < ἐπιτομή], **~a** [LL], epitome, abridged version of literary work. **b** (w. *sub*) in abridged form, briefly.

juxta quod testamenti veteris brevis ~a, hoc est Paralipomenon, testatur ALDH. *Met*. 2 p. 65; in ipso illo volumine vel in eo quod de illo .. strictim excerpsimus ~ate BEDE *HE* V 17; ep[it]ome, memoria *GlC* E 232; ~em, memoria[m] vel breviar[i]um *Ib*. 237; ephitomos, breviata, ephitoma, adbreviatio *Ib*. 240–1; ~a, abbreviatio OSB. GLOUC. *Deriv*. 196; c**1443** item, ~um Titi Livii; item, primam partem Titi Livii (*Catal. Librorum*) *MunAcOx* 769. **b** ut verum fatear, sub epithomate / nummus est dominus in omni climate WALT. WIMB. *Sim*. 55.

epitritus [CL < ἐπίτριτος], **a** (math., of a number or quantity) epitrite, having a ratio of 4:3. **b** (mus., of a consonance) comprising a fourth (also as sb. f.). **c** (metr., as sb. m.) foot containing three long and one short syllables.

a [tempus] ~um est quando minus continetur a majore et ejus tertia pars, ut iiij et iij BONIF. *Met*. 109; sesquitertium dicitur numerum esse ad alium quando excedit ipsum secundum ejus tertiam partem tantum, quomodo se habent 4 ad 3, et iste numerus dicitur †epitertius [MS: epitritus] ad illum. ex proportione autem †epitertia [MS: epitrita] nascitur symphonia dyatesseron dicta SICCAV. *PN* 103. **b** dic quid epogdous atque emiolius ast epytritus. / ritmi melodiam quot possunt edere tantam? *Altercatio* 80; nisi limitum .. dissidentiam emioliis, ~is et epogdois uniret J. SAL. *Pol*. 401C; dyatesseron est modulatio, epitryta collatio BART. ANGL. XIX 142; SICCAV. *PN* 103 (v. a supra). **c** correptione ultimae sillabae ~i ALDH. *PR* 126 p. 175; *Ib*. 139 (v. equidem 1); ~us in heroico versu esse non potest BEDE *AM* 126; ~us primus ⏑–––, ~us secundus –⏑––, ~us tertius ––⏑–, ~us quartus –––⏑. sunt igitur ~i iiij BONIF. *Met*. 110.

epitrochasmos [LL < ἐπιτροχασμός], (rhet.) rapid succession of statements.

epitrocasmos idest dicti rotatio cum succincte ea quae sunt effusius dicenda perstringit *Gl. Leid*. 28. 64.

epiurus [LL < ἐπίουρος], wooden peg, pin.

palatium .. ex scindulis non ex lapidibus per succedines vel †epiros [*gl*.: *clou*; Scheler 88: †epitos, *gl*.: *chevruns*, i. clavos, *bord nail*] conjunctum BALSH. *Ut*. 51.

epiusius [LL *gl*. < ἐπιούσιος], ('sufficient for the coming day', interp. as) surpassing all other substance. (*Cf. Matth*. vi 11: *supersubstantialis*; *Luke* xi 3: *quotidianus*).

panem qui de coelo descendit et dat vitam mundo, panem quem Ambrosius et Augustinus eisdem verbis vocant epiousion, id est supersubstantialem LANFR. *Corp. & Sang*. 419A; panem dixit quidem, sed ephiusion, hoc est supersubstantialem (WYNTERTON) *Ziz*. 190.

epizeuxis [LL < ἐπίζευξις], (rhet.) epizeuxis, emphatic repetition.

~is est ejusdem verbi in eodem versu sine aliqua dilatione geminatio, ut 'consolamini, consolamini, populus meus' BEDE *ST* 147; epizeusis, quae Latine conjunctio dicitur, ut est 'dies diei' et 'Deus, Deus meus' *Gl. Leid*. 28. 52; unum membrum scematis epizeusis erit *Qui majora cernitis* 9.

epodos [CL < ἐπῳδός], (metr.) shorter verse of a couplet.

clausula est quam in poemate ~on dicimus, in oratione brevem sententiam BONIF. *Met*. 112.

epogdous [LL < ἐπόγδοος], (mus.) whole tone.

Altercatio 80, J. SAL. *Pol*. 401C (v. epitritus b); viij .. ad ix ipsi contra se medii considerati †epogdonum jungunt qui musica modulatione tonus vo[ca]tur BART. ANGL. XIX 142.

epops [CL < ἔποψ], hoopoe.

avis qui dicitur epopus, quando viderit parentes ejus senuisse .., calefacit eos et renovantur *Best*. 63. 38a.

eportare [cf. CL portare], to carry along, support.

equites .. nonnulli solum se nutabundi vix ~antes W. POIT. I 27.

epotare [CL], to drink up, consume. **b** to drain, empty (also fig.). **c** to engulf (fig.). **d** (intr.) to drink.

tante multitudini, que totas segetes depastura, totos amnes ~atura videretur W. MALM. *GR* IV 357; tunc assimulantur .. illi cui poculum mellis prebetur et post sine fine amarum mare ~are cogetur HON. *Eluc*. 1138B. **b** duae .. flascones, quarum una prandi [v. l. prandii] hora ~ata est, altera in horam cenae reservata est ALCUIN *WillP* 31; **8..** calicibus ~andis, †*drunendum calice* [l. *druncendum calicum*] *WW*; ubi certatur calicibus ~andis, et qui poterit socium vincere laudem meretur ex crimine ROB. BRIDL. *Dial*. 59; ve miseris quibus [? l. qui] calice furoris Domini et furore calicis inebriari imminent, fere nimirum amarissima potanda semper et ~anda numquam, absorbenda jugiter et in eternum non exhaurienda J. FORD *Serm*. 22. 8; calicibus ~andis non codicibus emendandis indulget hodie studium monachorum R. BURY *Phil*. 5. 79. **c** ut .. pertransitor torrente voluntatis divine ~etur et eterne cognitionis plenitudinis satietur H. BOS. *LM* 1338B. **d** ut .. ~arent dulci poculo BYRHT. *V. Ecgwini* 390; permitte eos ad libitum ~are BACON V 51.

epotator, imbiber (fig.).

erat .. vir ille [Aldelmus] .. eruditione multiplex, et .. liberalium artium ~or W. MALM. *GR* I 31.

epredia v. epiraedium. **epse-** v. hepse-. **ept-** v. et. hephth-, hept-. **eptica** v. hectica. **epteris** v. pteris.

epudoratus [cf. LL pudoratus], shameless.

~us, extra pudorem, inpudens, inverecundus OSB. GLOUC. *Deriv*. 199; *unschamefulle*, inpudens, inpudorosus, .. ~us *CathA*.

epulae, ~um [CL], **~a** [LL], feast, banquet (also fig.). **b** food, drink (also fig.); **c** (w. ref. to Eucharist).

vir Deo deditus nec mulsa ~arum sagina superatur ALDH. *VirgP* 35; *Id. VirgV* 1150 (v. culina a); jusserunt eum sedere secum ad ~as BEDE *HE* V 5; a civibus in publico ~o interfectus W. MALM. *GR* III 287; toto in ~is die, in thalami deliciis nocte consumpta GIR. *EH* II 3; s**1404** eodem ludo taberne crapula, sed miserie ~a, cum indomita luxuria .. bestialiter discurrunt Romani AD. USK 95. **b** pro emendatione cervisae et aliorum elementorum si mus aut mustela mergitur intus. Domine .., peto ut digneris .. benedicere ~am istam, sicut benedixisti epulationem Abrahae EGB. *Pont*. 127; a**795** his aepulis animam tuam pasce ALCUIN *Ep*. 39; **8..** †epulos [l. ~as], *wiste WW*; predapifer, positor epularum, providus astet D. BEC. 1155; quum .. defuissent ~e, filium suum Pelopem occisum diis epulandum apposuit ALB. LOND. *DG* 6. 21; mulier .. nunc ~is nunc potibus confovens delicatis, .. inebriare nititur maritum *Latin Stories* 87; hoc ~um, *mete WW*. **c** dum .. secrete cum suis gloriosi agni paschales ~as celebraret BYRHT. *V. Osw*. 406; ad altare rediit, susceptoque vitae aeternae ~o, tam se quam omnes sibi commissos aeterno pastori consignavit OSB. *V. Dunst*. 42; ~a, missa OSB. GLOUC. *Deriv*. 196.

epulari [CL], **~are** [LL], to feast, dine (also fig.); **b** (w. *cum*).

intravit in domum in qua vicani caenantes ~abantur BEDE *HE* III 10; intravit ~aturus domum eius *Ib*. III 23; plebs epulare casam villae tunc venit in unam ALCUIN *SS Ebor* 343; ubi sancti sine fine requiescunt, et ibi aepulentur (*sic*) omnes amici tui *Nunnam*. 81; ~emur, *utan wistfullian* vel *simblian* .. ~entem (*sic*), manducantem *GlH* E 300, 302; volumus modo bene aepulari [*gl*.: *etan*] et alacriter potare ÆLF. BATA 5. 1; tibi si prandere jubetur, / cene consedeas, epuleris D. BEC. 1368; Hercules statuit ut Pinariorum familia tantum ministra esset ~antibus Politiis ALB. LOND. *DG* 13. 7. **b 1236** ut cum vicinis suis ~aret *BNB* III 184; **1251** ~abatur cum eo ad mensam suam *IMisc* 5/25; **1335** in donis datis .. die Dominica proxima post festum Epiphanie, quo die .. episcopus ~abatur cum priore, per visum .. Walteri de S., terrar[ii] *Ac. Durh*. 530.

epulaticius [LL *gl*.], **~icus**, feaster, banqueter, glutton.

~ius, qui epulis dat operam *GlC* E 257; ~us, qui operis [l. epulis] dat operam *GlH* E 303; *a gluton'* .. epulo, ~us qui tota die epulis intendit, epulonus *CathA*.

epulatio [CL], feasting, banqueting. **b** feast, banquet (also fig.).

legalium festivitatum ~o juvat quem fidei pietas non commendat BEDE *Luke* (xiii 27) 509; in tanta .. affluentia nullatenus ipsius in ulla ~onis aviditate .. poterat denotari excessus H. BOS. *Thom*. III 16. **b** EGB. *Pont*. 127 (v. epulae b); non jejunium, sed suavis est magis ~o hujusmodi speculatio [cf. *2 Cor*. iii 18] G. HOYLAND *Ascet*. 253C; quem cum inter paschalis ~onis leta sollemnia Dominus Jesus interrogaret, utrum eum plus ceteris diligeret .. J. FORD *Serm*. 44. 2.

epulatorius [LL], epulary, festive (fig.).

redeamus ab epulis contemplationis ad ubera consolationis .., ab illa mera et ~ia simplicitate ad .. poculum temperatum quod miscuit nobis sapientia G. HOYLAND *Ascet*. 276A.

epulentum, (pl.) victuals.

c**1180** nec [aliqua persona laborans per patriam] hospitetur nisi in locis in quibus poterit habere ~a et poculenta ac pabula equorum pro denariis suis (*Ass. Will*. 42) *APScot* 62.

epulo [CL], feaster, banqueter, glutton.

~o, gluto, quod et epulonus dicitur OSB. GLOUC. *Deriv*. 192; ad purgandam avaritie labem ~ones convocant et parasitos et collegium nugatorum J. SAL. *Pol*. 726A; c**1157** *Id. Ep*. 76 (35) (v. bibo); questio .. / que novitas adjecta cibis epulonis acutum / commendet studium HANV. II 195 p. 264; haustum glutones ducunt, pausant epulones [*gl*.: comestores, Dives ~o fuit] GARL. *Mor. Scol*. 403; *CathA* (v. epulaticius); s**1419** (v. devorator a).

epulonus [CL], feaster, banqueter.

OSB. GLOUC. *Deriv*. 192 (v. epulo); *CathA* (v. epulaticius).

epulos v. epulae b.

epulosus [LL], gluttonous.

~us, mandox, pransor, mandocus, .. dapilentus OSB. GLOUC. *Deriv*. 192; Lazarus mendicus .. Dives ~us *Reg. Whet*. I 129.

epy- v. et. epi-. **epyphiare** v. ephippiare.

equa [CL], mare. **b** (w. *portans*) brood mare. **c** (w. *indomita*, *silvatica*, *silvestris*, or sim.) wild mare (kept only for breeding).

BEDE *HE* II 13 (v. equitare 1c); **1162** de duabus ovibus .. obolus unus; .. de equo aut ~a ad vendendum adductis similiter *Act. Hen. II* I 366; W. FITZST. *Thom. prol*. 11 (v. aratrum a); queritur quare in ~abus diminuatur libido si jube sue come tondeantur *Quaest. Salern*. B 134; ~e .. que ex solo vento concipiunt *Ib*. 175; **1204** j ~a caretaria ceca *RNorm* 128; me perduxit ad has australes partes fama nobilis ~e MAP *NC* II 25 f. 32v.; c**1270** quarto compoto [postquam nati sunt] conjunguntur masculi cum masculis, femelle cum femellis et efficiuntur equi vel ~e *Ac. Beaulieu* 51; uni †stallom [l. stalloni] et quadragenta ~abus *Cart. Dieul*. 329; hec ~a, A. *a mare WW*. **b** c**1230** xxx vaccas portantes et xxiiij ~as portantes cum sequela *Melrose* I 209; **1251** .. dedi .. sufficientem .. pasturam .. ad xx vaccas .. et ad x ~as portantes cum uno stalone cum exitu earum trium annorum *ChartR* 44 m. 24. **c** cui commendavit ~as silvaticas regis custodire *DB* I 36; ~e silvestr[es] *DB* II 206; ibi [*Porbury, Som*] habet episcopus .. ij roncinos et xiiij ~as indomitas et xv animalia *Dom. Exon*. 144 (cf. ib.: lx ~as indomitas); qui aurum furabatur vel ~as silvestres [AS: *goldþeofe ond stodþeofe*] vel apes (*Quad*.) *GAS* 55; c**1150** decimam de omnibus meis silv[est]ribus ~abus de Fif *Reg. Dunferm*. 6 (cf. *E. Ch. Scot*. 209: de meis [silvestribus] ~abus); **1456** nunc occupentur dicte terre cum ~abus silvestribus .. regis *ExchScot* 197.

equa- v. et. aequa-.

equaria [CL], **~ritia,** herd or stud of horses.

1144 medietatem decime carrucarum nostrarum et vaccarum et .. porchariarum et ~riarum de parochia S. Trinitatis *E. Ch. Scot.* 162; **1156** decimam pullorum de ~ria comitis *CalCh* III 379; *an haras of horse*, ~ricia, equicium *CathA*.

equarius [LL], 'equerry', groom. *V. et. equitiarius.*

quidam ~ius regis *DB* I 218v.; c**1120** Edric ~ius et forestarius *Cart. Burton* 20; **1165** in liberatione ~ii et stalon' xliij s. et vj d. et in liberatione venatoris qui duxit canes ad regem v s. *Pipe* 109; **1182** terre Unspac ~ii *Ib.* 138; eques [moritur par] equario WALT. WIMB. *Sim.* 111; hic equiarius, A. *a horsheyrd WW*; *CathA* (v. equitiarius).

equartium v. equitius 2. **eque** v. aeque.

eques [CL]

1 rider. **b** (as adj.) mounted, on horseback.

solum ~item post cuneum .. subsequentem *V. Greg.* p. 97; desiluit ~es BEDE *HE* II 9; ~es, homo equo portatus *GlC* E 269; ~es, i. homo equo portatus, sessor *ridda GlH* E 304; fortuna .. / .. / ex equo detrahit quem fecit equitem; / sic eques iterum redit in peditem WALT. WIMB. *Carm.* 348. **b** terit hic in frena jugales / non longum mansurus eques J. EXON. *BT* I 321; AD. EYNS. *Hug.* V 12 p. 147 (v. compendium 2a); H. AVR. *Hugh* 767 (v. 1 dicare d); **1254** ad conducendum duos fratres minores ~ites usque Lugdunum *Cl* 226; **1268** ~es perrexit apud B. et dicebat se esse infirmum *SelCCoron* 10.

2 mounted soldier, cavalryman. **b** (w. *serviens*) mounted serjeant.

turma, i. xxxij ~ites, *tuu ond ðrittih eorodmonn* ALDR. *Margin.* 56; **1101** comes predictus mille ~ites habebit ad portus suos paratos transfretare in Angliam... et rex .. tot naves mittet quod sufficiant tot militibus, ita ut unusquisque habeat secum tres equos *DipDoc* I 1; plures .. submersi pereunt. ~ites Normanni quantos consectari possunt comprehendunt ORD. VIT. IV 3 p. 175; expediantur .. ad ij^{m} ~itum .., qui non habeant corda in caligis, et j^{m} pedites sagittarii DEVIZES 30v. **b 1239** in iiij servientibus ~itibus deputatis ad eadem maneria et dominica sub .. R. [serviente regis] custodienda *Liberate* 14 m. 25; s**1217** servientes .. ~ites [= WEND. II 212: et ~ites], qui vices poterant ~itum adimplere M. PAR. *Min.* II 209; **1315** duobus servientibus suis ~itibus pro arreragiis vadiorum suorum *RGasc* IV 1449.

3 knight; **b** (w. ref. to knight service); **c** (dist. as *auratus*); **d** (var.). **e** (collect.) gentry.

10.. ut omnis equitandi lex ab eis impleatur quae ad ~ites pertinet *CD* 1287; xij domus ~itum *DB* I 280; dictitabat .. parem comiti Normannorum ~item sive militem sub celo nullum degere W. POIT. I 13; si debitor ille qui solvendo non est militie cingulum semel optinuerit, venditis ceteris, equus tamen ei .. reservabitur, ne qui dignitate factus est ~es pedes cogatur incedere *Dial. Scac.* II 14 B; s**626** interfecto etiam mox ~ite quodam M. PAR. *Maj.* I 273; hic ~es, *a knyght WW*; ~ites qui et milites dicti, .. Anglis solummodo *knights* vocantur CAMD. *Br.* 138. **b** reddit .. xx et iiij li. et unum ~item [= *DB* I 3: militem] *Dom. Cant.* f. 3; **1122** pro servitio dimidii ~itis *Eng. Feudalism* 274. **c** FERR. *Kinloss* 34, etc. (v. auratus c); **1546** nobilem virum J. B. de L. ~item auratum *Form. S. Andr.* II 326. **d 1579** sacrati garterii ordinis ~es *StatOx* 342; baneretti, qui aliis baronetti .., a baronibus secundi erant, quibus inditum nomen a vexillo; concessum enim erat illis militaris virtutis ergo quadrato vexillo perinde ac barones uti, unde et ~ites vexillarii a nonnullis vocantur CAMD. *Br.* 138. **e** effrenis scelus omne licentia pulsat! / laus scelus est; sceleri plebs studet, heret eques L. DURH. *Dial.* I 64.

4 (chess) knight.

tunc equestris apponatur prope ad certamina. / .. / eques equitem, pedestrem pedes prendit pariter (*Vers. Wint.*) *Hist. Chess* 515.

equester (~tris) [CL]

1 (adj.) **a** mounted on a horse; **b** (mil.). **c** (of harness *etc.*) for a horse. **d** knightly.

a Petrus .. venit humiliter, non ~er cum sumptuosa familia, sed pedester WYCL. *Blasph.* 32. **b** consul eram quondam, Romanus miles equester / arbiter imperio dum regni sceptra regebat ALDH. *Aen.* 99 (*Camellus*) 1; chiliarco cum ~ri turma insequente Romam reducuntur *Id. VirgP* 51; in regno Orientalium Saxonum .. hiemavit, ibique ille exercitus maxima ex parte ~er factus est ASSER *Alf.* 21; ~rium exercituum multitudines *Eccl. & Synag.* 87; pars .. statutarum turmarum disponitur ~ris, pars autem altera pedestris G. MON. X 6; sunt .. milites ~res et pedestres utrique in palestra domini R. NIGER *Mil.* I 16; videns ~rem turmam loricis .. insignem GIR. *EH* I 3. **c** donec .. clementiam expeteret et nudis vestigiis ~rem sellam ad satisfaciendum humeris ferret W. JUM. VI 4; dedit insuper .. sellam suam cum omni apparatu ~ri *Chr. Rams.* 84. **d** fratrem qui multa honestate in annis adolescentie et ~ri probitate pollebat ORD. VIT. III 9 p. 10.

2 (as sb.) horseman, rider. **b** cavalryman. **c** (chess) knight.

via peditibus et ~ris perambulatoria *Meaux* II 30; **1440** factis per eundem cum duobus ~ribus secum existentibus laborantibus .. ad Perth pro quibusdam obligacionibus .. regis ibidem obtinendis *ExchScot* 91; ?**1461** sumus nempe ~res pessimi, nec ascensum equi seu descensum scientes *Paston Let.* 655 p. 264. **b** ~er, qui equitat, *rædewiga* vel *cempa GlH* E 305; s**1270** reversi pedestres a cede ceterorum .. ingressi sunt conflictum ~rium et evisceratis quibusdam ex equis .. ascensores eorum in terram corruere compulerunt W. GUISB. 211. **c** (*Vers. Wint.*) *Hist. Chess* 515 (v. eques 4).

equestralis, suitable for horse-riding: **a** (w. *cuculla*) riding-hood; **b** (w. *via*) bridle-path.

a 1476 (v. cuculla 1a). **b** c**1390** quedam via pedestralis et ~is .. a villa S. usque ad villam de M. *Pub. Works* I 185.

equestrare, to provide w. a horse.

sunt xiv anni .. ex quo hyemaverunt barbari in arvis [sc. Orientalium Anglorum] .. et ~ati ÆTHELW. IV 3.

equestrarius, horseman.

c**1175** [*2 bovates .. which*] Reginaldus ~ius [*held*] *Cart. Fount.* II 464.

equi- v. et. aequi-.

equiale [cf. CL equile, LL equale], stable.

~e, domus equorum *GlH* E 312; aequiale, *horsern ÆLF. Gl.* (cf. id. *Sup.*: ~e, *horsern*).

equiarius v. equarius.

equicervus [cf. CL equus + cervus], elk.

hoc animal Norvegia *elend* sive *elke* nominat .., equidem hippelaphum seu ~um cum Aristotele et Alberto Magno dicerem ..; alcem esse non putem CAIUS *Anim.* 11b.

equidem [CL]

1 (w. 1st pers.) I for my part, personally speaking..

~em reor a tertia conjugatione subjunctivo et optativo modo epitritum tertium dirivari ALDH. *PR* 139; ~em, ego quidem *GlC* E 265; ~em memini .. sanctum tuum .. fervorem multis meum precibus postulasse teporem quatenus .. ANSELM (*Ep.* 2) III 99; nos equidem scimus quod ob hoc fit vilis et imus D. BEC. 601; hec ~em quanto frequentius .. intueor .. semper quasi novis obstupeo GIR. *TH* II 38; CAIUS *Anim.* 11b (v. equicervus).

2 certainly, indeed.

~em, *witodlice GlP* 206; ~em ut prelibatum est, aliquando est in sola operatione, aliquando in sola voluntate ALEX. CANT. *Dicta* 2 p. 118; quem ergo odit Deus num diliget homo? ~em de diabolo evangelica dicit auctoritas 'nemo potest duobus dominis servire' [*Matth.* vi 24] PULL. *Sent.* 706A; GERV. TILB. III 85 (v. dracus b); HENGHAM *Magna* 3 (v. diligere 3a).

equiductor, groom.

1526 ipse Cowper quondam ~or tuus erat et quasi nullius reputationis (*Vis. Thame*) *EHR* III 705.

equiferus [CL], **~er, ~era,** horse bred from wild stock. **b** horse, mount.

~eros, dosine (*sic*) de agresti genere orti *GlH* E 313; ~er, *wilde cynnes hors ÆLF. Gl.*; **1318** item ibidem j equs, prec. xlvj s. viij d. item j ~erus, prec. xxv s. *Ac. Durh.* 373; hic ~erus, *a wyld hors*, hec ~era, *a wyld mer WW*. **b** BALSH. *Ut.* 46 (v. dosinus); ~ero igitur suo senex insidens aeris intemperiem caputio exclusit, sed adeo frigoris penetrantis molestiis erat arctatus ut regimini caballi non sufficeret NECKAM *NR* II 129; radii lunaris efficaciam, qui .. pervenit ad ulcus caballi redorsati, mortem ~ero adducit stanti in stabulo *Ib.* 153; s**1252** imposuerunt eum quasi vilissimum mancipium furto deprehensum .. nec permissum est ad ipsum ~erum dirigendum lora retinere M. PAR. *Maj.* V 350; **1340** dominus habebit nomine herioti unum ~erum cum freno, sella, et gladio *CBaron* 104; *hakney, hors*, .. ~erus *PP*.

equilus [cf. CL eculus, equuleus], young or small horse; *v. et.* 2 *eculeus* 1. **b** hackney, nag.

hic pullus, hic equillus, *polein Gl. AN Glasg.* f. 21. **b 1372** Johannes Taylour pro j juvenca et uno ~o ingestat[is] ad pastur[am] domini in estate *CourtR Meltham* (*Yorks*); equillus, A. *an hakeney WW*; hic bladius, A. *hackenay*; hic †equilas [l. equilus], idem est *WW*.

equineus [cf. CL equinus]

1 equine, of a horse.

[spiritus] erant .. ore foetido, dentibus ~eis FELIX *Guthl.* 31.

2 operated by a horse.

1386 una domus molendini ~ii *IMisc* 237/3 m. 1.

equinitas, (phil.) equinity, horseness.

per hoc quod dicit [Avicenna] quod '~as est tantum ~as', non excludit illa que sunt per se de ratione ~atis .. sed excludit illa que sunt passiones entis ut 'unum', 'actus' [etc.] DUNS *Ord.* III 195; ~as non est multa, igitur ~as ex se est una W. ALNWICK *QD* 189; Avisenna .. determinat quod ~as est tantum ~as NETTER *DAF* II 133; quia ut ~as est tantum ~as GASCOIGNE *Loci* 31.

equinocephalus [CL equinus + 1 cephalus], horse-headed monster.

ibi [Seleucia] nascuntur ~i jubas equorum habentes, validissimi immensis dentibus, flammam spirantes GERV. TILB. III 73.

equinus [CL]

1 equine, of a horse. **b** (w. *animal*) horse.

in Perside fingunt esse bestias quas conopenos appellant, quibus sub caninis capitibus ~a dependet per cervices juba *Lib. Monstr.* II 13; s**1251** donec Perusium perveniret, ~is non parcens lateribus iter maturavit M. PAR. *Maj.* V 238; a**1309** lego .. pullos meos ~os *RR K's Lynn* I 4; splen pultis .. est .. superfluitas sanguinea circa cerebrum pulli ~i contenta *SB* 40; **1590** *velvet* de color carnis ~i *Ac. LChamb.* 81/6v. (cf. *Misc. LChamb.* 36 p. 133: *of horseflesh colour*). **b 1430** me .. confirmasse eisdem .. communem pasturam pro sexdecim animalibus bovinis et ~is, et pro centum animalibus ovinis pascendis in magno vasto *FormA* 286.

2 derived from a horse.

1246 invenerunt .. v laqueos de serico ~o quos .. Hugo et Henricus T. illuc posuerunt ad .. lepores capiendos *SelPlForest* 83; Tartari .. lacte ~o abutentes pro potu BACON *Mor. Phil.* 190; **1298** (v. correatio); **1336** (v. correare b); *Ps.*-ELMH. *Hen. V* 68 (v. caro 1a).

3 (used) for a horse: **a** (w. ref. to harness *etc.*); **b** (w. *panis*).

a 1206 pro tribus pariis coopertoriorum ~orum *Pipe* 47; **1282** (v. 1 camus a); pluscularii sunt divites per .. mordacula, per limas et loralia [*gl.*: *brydels*] ~a GARL. *Dict.* 123 (cf. ib. 130: epifia ~a); **1381** sexdecim sellas ~as .. in .. navi .. carcare *RScot* 34a; **1397** unam sarram, unum *mattok* .. unum *billehoke* .. duas ceras ~as *Pat* 348 m. 11 (*Cal.* p. 285); **1404** xl ferramenta ~a *Ac. Durh.* 395; **1457** in ij seris ~is et compedibus ferreis pro equis *Ib.* 241; **1510** tres ceras pendentes ~as cum clavibus eisdem *Rec. Nott.* III 100. **b 1367** pro pane ~o pro equis *Arch. Bridgew.* 161; sic nego quod ille panis in natura est pejor pane ~o vel quacumque materiali substancia vel veneno WYCL. *Conf.* 508; **1384** dictus W. et unus alius hostilarius qui jam inde cessavit, de novo ad panem ~um in domibus suis pinsendum inceperant, ac hujusmodi panem in cistis ne probaret (*sic*) per assisam absconderant *IMisc* 230/9 m. 2; **1446** convictus propter defectum ponderis panis ~i *MunAcOx* II 556; **1487** assignavimus te ad fenum, panes ~os, fabas .. ac omnia alia pro expensis equorum nostrorum necessaria .. providenda *Pat* 567 m. 8 (19).

4 drawn by a horse. **b** (w. *molendinum*) horse-mill, gin. **c** (w. *pondus*) horse-load.

victualia, quae .. ~o gestamine .. ferebant B. *V. Dunst.* 27; **12..** (v. carruca 2b). **b 1426** in toto illo tenemento bracineo una cum molendinis ~is, vasis plumbeis, ligneis et aliis utensilibus necessariis ad officium braciatoris *Cl* 276 m. 7*d.*; **1455** processus destructionis .. cujusdam molendini ~i *Reg. Whet.* I 199; c**1474** unum molendinum ~um cum pertinenciis *FormA* 208; **1587** medietatem manerii de W. cum pertinenciis ac unius molendini ~i in W. *Pat* 1298 m. 39. **c 1526** pro gibsi veteris xx pond[eribus] ~is, ij s. vj d. *Fabr. York* 100; **1528** pro xxx ponderibus ~is gipsi *Ib.* 102.

5 (in plant names).

GAD. 9. 2 etc. (v. cauda 2a); *SB* 17, *Alph.* 49 (v. dens 3b); lappa caprina similis est ~e *Alph.* 94.

equip- v. et. skip-.

equipes, horse-shoe.

1260 reddendo .. unum clavium ~edis pro omnibus .. *Cart. Bilsington* 124.

equisaetum [CL], (bot.) horse-tail (*Equisetum*).

herba ippirus, *þæt is* †aequiseia [l. aequiseta] *Leechdoms* I 22.

equisequelus, henchman.

c**1472** de magistro ~orum regis *BB Househ.* 77.

equistatium, stable.

~ium, stabulum ubi stant equi OSB. GLOUC. *Deriv.* 192; *a sstabylle*, stabulum, ~ium *CathA*.

equitalis, mounted.

nec alaris, -is, i. turma ~is OSB. GLOUC. *Deriv.* 10.

equitare [CL]

1 to ride: **a** (absol.); **b** (dist. from walking); **c** (w. *in* or *super*); **d** (trans., w. *equum* or sim.); **e** (fig.).

a THEOD. *Pen.* II 8. 1 (v. dominicus 7b); c**705** oblectamentis hujus mundi nequaquam te .. subicias .. in ~andi vagatione culpabili ALDH. *Ep.* 8 (11); occasiones ~andi claustrales .. non solum non exquirant, sed nec occurrentes suscipiant ANSELM (*Ep.* 178) IV 62; GIR. *TH* III 26 (v. divaricare 1a); angelus .. qui tenuit nasum obvians superbo luxurioso ~anti [ME: *ridinde*] *AncrR* 77; TREVET *Ann.* 408 (v. currizare); rex .. per mediam civitatem versus palacium .. Westmonasterii in cultu decentissimo ~abit W. SAY *Lib. Reg. Cap.* 75. **b** opus evangelii magis

ambulando per loca quam ~ando perficere BEDE *HE* IV 3; ~ando [AS p. 373: *ridende*] vel pedites iter agendo *RegulC* 11; *Ib.* (v. complere 5a); vadere nec plantis, equitando nec ire valebat WULF. *Swith.* I 102. **c** non licuerat pontificem .. praeter in equa ~are BEDE *HE* II 13; **1248** venit quidam .. ~ans super equm *bay* cum duobus leporariis *SelPlForest* 90; **1377** Willelmus R. super quodam equo ~ans intravit ripam *SelCCoron* 105; **1407** in expensis factis pro j equo super quo ~avit comes de Doglase *Ac. Durh.* 606. **d** baculum .. mendici, quem portavi dum idem ~aret equum meum ALEX. CANT. *Mir.* 21 (II) p. 199; **1200** quod .. runcinum illum non ~avit *CurR* I 255; preter palefridum quem ~abat GIR. *RG* II 21; **1255** vigilantes in foresta obviaverunt tribus hominibus quorum unus ~abat unum equm *SelPlForest* 114; asinus .. non renitendo se submittit; talem asinum ~at Christus et ducit in .. Jerusalem WALT. WIMB. *Elem.* 318; retinuit .. equos et eos ~avit *State Tri. Ed. I* 90; habet potestatem ~andi equum OCKHAM *Pol.* II 378; mulierem inspexit .. mulam ~antem [= W. MALM. *GR* II 205: inequitantem] *Eul. Hist.* I 395. **e** quoniam .. illum tenet [demonium] et tenendo ~at ALEX. CANT. *Mir.* 29 p. 217; parvulis .. / qui .. / .. equitant in arundinibus WALT. WIMB. *Palpo* 180 (cf. Horace *Sat.* II 3. 248).

2 (pr. ppl. as sb. m.) rider; **b** (mil.); **c** (as forest officer); *cf. equitator* 4. **d** (?) courier.

c**1177** pro trossello .. si post tergum ~antis trossatum fuerit, j d. *Act. Hen. II* II 56; **1217** dedit .. salvum .. conductum .. comiti Nivericensi et comiti Britannie et omnibus suis quos secum duxerint, usque ad c ~antes *Pat* 68; **1302** in curialitate ~ancium serviencium famil' sacriste *Sacr. Ely* II 19 (cf. eques 2b). **b** grandis multitudo ~antium pontem .. ascenderunt ORD. VIT. IX 9 p. 531; s**1296** venit exercitus multus a rege Scottorum missus, md ~ancium et xl^m peditum W. GUISB. 278; s**1298** iij^m electorum in equis armatis preter ~antes armatos in equis non armatis *Ib.* 324. **c** s**1300** forestam de F. per certos terminos .. circuibant, et quod in dextera ~ancium remanebat, nomen foreste retinebat *Ann. Worc.* 545; **1461** officium ~antis in foresta nostra de Morff in com... Salop. *Pat* 494 m. 27. **d** de ~antibus qui Gallice vocantur *chivachirs*: sunt autem et post cursores .. alii nuncii qui ~antes appellantur et tales portabunt arma suorum dominorum in humero sinistro et non alibi UPTON 18.

3 (w. *ultra*) to supervise on horseback.

1311 ~are ultra messores *MinAc Essex* (*Hutton*).

4 (feud., w. ref. to escort or cavalry); **b** (trans., w. cognate acc.).

CD 1287 (v. eques 3a); c**1175** servicium suum, sc. ~andi cum eo vel cum uxore sua de uno mansu ad alium mansum (*Middleton MSS*) *HMC Rep.* LXIX 11; **12..** idem Osbertus tenet dim. hidam ut ~et cum sacrista in equo proprio (*MS BL Cotton Vesp.* B XXIV) *VCH Worcs* I 251. **b** ne intermittatur aliquod vestigium .. priusquam omnis homo unam equitationem ~averit qui equum habeat *GAS* 176.

5 (trans., w. *terram* or sim.) to obtain possession (of) by riding over. **b** (mil.) to make a raid.

s**1329** rex Francie .. non admisit homagium pro terris quas pater suus .. ~avit quousque esset sibi satisfactum de dampnis .. et ceteris AD. MUR. *Chr.* 59; s**1359** rex Francie .. obtulit regi Anglie .. Flandriam .. ceterasque terras quas ~averat J. READING 171; s**876** misit Franconem .. ad Rollonem, mandans quod, si Christianus efficeretur, totam terram quam ~averat .. se illi fore daturum *Eul. Hist.* II 190; **1459** quod quociens dicta terra ~ata fuerit cum dicta communi guerra et destructa, tociens fiet .. allocacio .. in firma sua *Reg. Aberbr.* II 113. **b** **1341** dantes eidem comiti .. potestatem marchias Anglie et Scotie defendendi et in terram Scotie de guerra ~andi *RScot* 617b; s**1347** rex Anglorum .. moram traxit ibidem proponens in expeditionem guerre .. ulterius ~are AVESB. 116b; s**1356** rex Anglie incepit in novo regno suo Scocie ulterius ~are *Ib.* 133b; s**1388** capitaneus Cales' .. in Flandriam ~avit, cepit magnam predam bestiarum et rediit Cales'. altera die ~avit in Pycardiam ubi eciam .. predas agebat *Chr. Westm.* 184; prohibemus .. cum ~antes fuerimus quod nullus de excercitu nostro exire audeat sine nostra licencia speciali. .. nullus .. simultationem .. aliquam facere audeat .. ad ~andum de dicto excercitu nostro ad aliquam patriam, villam, vel fortalicium vicinum UPTON 138–139.

6 to include within bounds by riding.

1374 sedente itinere regardum foreste ~atum fuit et per ipsos regardatores villa de Wilton' ~ata fuit infra regardum et infra metas foreste de Grovele *IMisc* 203/27; **1475** quo tempore ipsi ~averunt franchesas et bundas ejusdem *Ac. Chamb. Cant.* 143.

equitarius

1 drawn or operated by a horse.

[abbas] reportatus est ad nos in feretro ~io et devote susceptus BRAKELOND 122v.; **1242** opressus fuit .. per rotam molendini ~ii *AssizeR Durh* 30.

2 (as sb. m.) horseman.

s**1295** asserens comitem de A. affore .. cum nongentis ~iis armatis *Flor. Hist.* III 285; **1342** quod .. nullis angariis, vexacionibus aut injuriis equis aut ~iis regalibus graventur *Conc.* II 712a.

equitatinus v. equitativus.

equitatio [CL]

1 horsemanship, riding.

equitatus, i. ~o *GlH* E 311; videbitis qualiter equitatoris hujus desierit ~o DEVIZES 40v.; tria .. tempora dixit se perdita reputare, viz. tempus comestionis, dormitionis, et ~onis *Canon. Edm. Rich* 188; **1444** (v. cappa 2b).

2 (feud.) escort or cavalry service.

priusquam .. ~onem equitaverit *GAS* 176 (v. equitare 4b); c**1160** libere et quiete de exercitu et warda et scutagio et ~one et opere et omni servitio quod ad militem pertinet (*Ch.*) *Eng. Feudalism* 278; c**1163** nulla .. persona .. aliquid ab hominibus .. et possessionibus .. monasterii exigat, non ~onem seu expeditionem, non .. castrorum edificationem *Act. Hen. II* I 373; **1209** nolumus quod eatis in exercitum vel ~onem pro aliqua summonicione *Pat* 91b; **1214** concessisse Hugoni .. pro homagio et servitio suo id quod habuimus in villa de L., videlicet exercitum, ~onem et tailliam .., faciendo nobis inde .. servicium exercitus et ~onis *RChart* 200a; **1331** quiete .. de †aquitacionibus [MS: equitacionibus] et de exercitibus et de omnibus exactionibus et serviciis terrenis *PQW* 72b (cf. ib. 73b: quieti .. de ~onibus et de exercitibus et de omnibus exaccionibus et serviciis terrenis).

3 (mil.) cavalry raid, foray.

1197 quia dicebatur non fuisse in exercitu regis et in ~onibus suis in Normannia *Pipe* 233; s**1230** comes Cestrensis et alii principes .. cum toto ejus exercitu fecerunt ~onem per Andegaviam .. et villam combusserunt WEND. III 8; exceptis ~onibus [cf. ASSER *Alf.* 42: irruptionibus] multis quas proceres cum populis sibi subjectis fecerant M. PAR. *Maj.* I 406; **1339** habebit restaurum equorum quos ipse et .. homines .. ad arma in ~onibus de guerra .. amittent *RScot* 573a; **1416** [ccxc li.] quas ipse comes asserit se expendisse in diebus treugarum et ~onibus tempore guerre super marchias *ExchScot* 253.

equitativus, for riding.

1422 placet quod concipiatur forma honesta secundum quam uniformiter conformemur tam in cuculliis quam in floccis et capis †equitatinis [l. equitativis] *Conc.* III 417b.

equitator

1 horseman, rider; **b** (as surname); **c** (fig.).

DEVIZES 40v. (v. equitatio 1); c**1270** monachis .. ~oribus, quando in via diriguntur aut pro aliquibus negociis domus foras equitent, singulis ij galon' .. cervisie licet dare *Ac. Beaulieu* 230; s**1307** Petrus .. cardinalis Sabynensis venit Londonias, cui major .. cum multitudine ~orum obviavit *Ann. Lond.* 150; **1488** (v. extendere 3c). **b** assartam .. que fuit Simonis filii Roberti ~oris *Cart. Cockersand* 543 (cf. ib. 544: Simonis filii Roberti Rider). **c** quid est nauta? fluctuum viator, marinus ~or (*Dictum Secundi*) *Leg. Ant. Lond.* app. 185.

2 mounted bandit, highwayman.

1236 Thomas .. et Ricardus .. rettati de societate et receptamento Warini de Derlegh' et aliorum ~orum burgatorum .. ponunt se super patriam *CurR* XV 1678; quia predicta Juliana subtraxit se pro suspicione ~orum Essexie *Ib.* 1857.

3 (?) harvest supervisor. *Cf. equitare* 3.

1268 vj decimatoribus, ij ~oribus, ij tassatoribus, iij quar' *Ac. Wellingb.* 6.

4 (w. *forestae* or sim.) forest officer. *Cf. equitare* 2c.

1270 A. la Z. tunc justiciarius foreste citra Trentam qui habuit sub se A. de S. et A. le B. ~ores in predicta foresta *TR Forest Proc.* 229 m. 9*d.*; **1301** Gilberto de W. ~ori in foresta de Mara percipienti per annum pro stipendiis suis xl s. .. pro dicto servicio equitature *Pipe Chesh* 207; **1386** ~ori foreste de Mara *Enr. Chester* 2/57 m. 4*d.*; **1399** officium supervisoris seu ~oris foreste de la Peek' *Pat* 352 m. 29; **1439** officium ~oris foreste nostre de Waltham cum vadiis vj denariorum per diem *Ib.* 444 m. 8; **1461** officia senescalli et ~oris foreste nostre de Morff *Ib.* 494 m. 26; **1486** officium ~oris foreste nostre de Dene *Ib.* 563 m. 21 (7); **1572** officium ~oris .. foreste et chasee nostre de Dartmore' *Ib.* 1093 m. 3.

equitatorius

1 drawn by a horse.

dicebat quod, si oporteret eum feretro ~io portari, non remaneret BRAKELOND 147v.

2 appropriate to a horseman.

s**1182** eum Alexium .. scapulis suis impositum .. ~io more portavit DICETO *YH* II 12; depositis deinde vestibus ~iis et .. frocco indutus in stallo suo in choro [abbas W., el. **1401**] fuerat introductus *G. S. Alb.* III 493.

equitatrix, skilled in horsemanship (f.).

Anglia luctatrix, equitatrix Gallia GARL. *Tri. Eccl.* 43.

equitatura [cf. CL equitatus]

1 riding; *v. et. equitura*; **b** (feud., w. ref. to escort or cavalry service); **c** (w. *forestae*) forest-riding, survey.

1219 omnia que ad ~am pertinent habeant ordinata *Doc. Eng. Black Monks* 11; **1290** pro duabus sellis ~e, una sella ad somerum (*Chanc. Misc.*) *Doc. Scot.* I 138; capas .. aut sellas et cetera ad ~am pertinencia *Cust. Cant.* 36; nec permittat equos .. per crebras et indebitas ~as .. vexari *Fleta* 162; **1437** lego .. Hugoni G. .. unam togam penulatam pro ~a ordinatam *Test. Ebor.* II 60 (cf. ib. III 13 [**1400**]: j *pilch* de *scrank* et *bys* de j tunica †~a [? l. ~e]. .. pro j tunica de *plunket* †~a [? l. ~e]). **b** a**1220** (v. corpus 5g); **12..** quilibet istorum trium dat per annum †per [? l. pro] ~a iij s. *Reg. Pri. Worc.* 71b. **c** **1301** (v. equitator 4); s**1301** tenuit parliamentum suum .. apud Stanfordiam et movebantur proceres de ~a foreste nondum completa W. GUISB. 334.

2 (mounted) expedition, foray.

1222 fuerunt m milites cruce signati et alii equites v^m cum xl^m peditum. hi omnes fecerunt unam ~am erga terram Babilonis (*Lit. Philippi de Albeneio*) WEND. II 263 (cf. ib.: in illa ~a per tres septimanas .. morati fuerunt); **1402** pro diversis dampnis .. que ipsi .. per Scotos inimicos nostros, videlicet per graves ~as et arsuras per eosdem Scotos, ac graves ~as per homines comitatuum .. versus Scotos .. sustinuerunt (*Pat*) *RParl* III 469a.

3 horse for riding, mount. **b** provision of horse; **c** (as heriot).

in manibus aurea virga qua ~am regebat W. MALM. *GR* II 205; s**1097** ~as habeo, vestes quoque et supellectilem EADMER *HN* 99; **1166** duas amisi ~as J. SAL. *Ep.* 168 (167); si .. violentas manus injecerint aut ipsum de ~a deposuerint *Canon. G. Sempr.* 99; **1238** clerici .. habeant .. habitum convenientem tam sibi quam suis ~is secundum quod determinant sancta concilia GROS. *Ep.* 52; cibavit eum ac potavit, deinde fecit eum equitare ~am BACON V 145; **1314** injunximus .. Gilberto de T. quod .. quasdam sellas pro ~a nostra ad nos .. ducat *RScot* 127b; quod .. dictis confratribus nostris .. ~am et expensas ministretis *Pri. Cold.* 41. **b** **1423** equorum numerus ac reversionis tempus taliter moderentur quod ~a seu alias absencia hujusmodi onerosa non fiat officio *Reg. Cant.* III 521. **c** **1405** dicunt quod accidere deberet .. principi ~a post mortem .. Agnetis racione mortis .. Johannis W. .. de medietate manerii .. pro qua ~a ballivus .. principis cepit .. bovem precii xiij s. iiij d. *Doc. Coll. Wint.* (*Allington, Hants*); **1407** per cujus mortem nihil accidit domine de ~a seu herietto *CourtR Tisbury*.

4 horseman, usu. in attendance on magnate; **b** (collect.).

quin .. in magno .. apparatu revertisset, plus .. quam cum ~is centum repatrians H. BOS. *Thom.* V 5; s**1213** legatus cum septem tantum ~is in Angliam veniens WEND. II 94; **1271** in expensis suis circa custodiam pacis .. equitando aliquando cum xv ~is, aliquando cum xx .. et totidem hominibus peditibus *Liberate* 47 m. 5; s**1290** eodem anno a sede apostolica transmissus est quidam legatus in Angliam .. cum xj ~is, se computato W. NEWB. *HA Cont.* 574; s**1296** cum ~is d et xl^m peditum est regressus *Flor. Hist.* III 97; s**1300** episcopum .. ab ejus episcopatu .. expulsus morabatur cum eo cum ~is vj W. GUISB. 346. **b** s**1253** miles .. collecta sibi manu armata, exemplo Willelmi L. edoctus .., qui consimilem fecerat ~am M. PAR. *Maj.* V 385; s**1355** dux modicam gentem .. secum ducens et nullam habens ~am, rediit in Angliam AVESB. 125b.

equitatus [CL]

1 horsemanship, riding (also fig.).

tales sunt in ~u sanctorum cordium firmissimo qui Deum portat sessorem juxta illud prophetae: 'ascendens super equos tuos et equitatio tua sanitas' [*Hab.* iii 8] BEDE *Ezra* 884; sunt .. quibus .. armatura sit oneri, quibus et .. ~us industria non conveniat R. NIGER *Mil.* I 16; **1382** equus Willelmi A. non fuit mortuus causa ~us uxoris sue *Hal. Durh.* 175; rex .. non in elato supercilio, ~u pompatili seu multitudine gravi, sed in vultu solido, incessu venerando, et paucis comitantibus domesticis .. incedebat *G. Hen. V* 15.

2 (feud.) riding service.

c**1160** liberam et solutam et quietam .. a scutagio, exercitu, ~u tam regis quam comitis *Danelaw* 181; a**1161** .. quietum de .. siris et hundredis, de danegeldis et .. de exercitu et ~u *Act. Hen. II* I 317; **1192** absque venda, telonio .. mensura, excubiis, exercitu, ~u, rivagio (*Ch. Ric. I*) *Thes. Nov. Anecd.* I 649a; a**1200** concessisse .. x acras .. libere .. ab omni servitio regis et exercitu et ~u *Reg. Aberbr.* I 99.

3 (mil.) cavalry raid, foray.

rex Ecgfrithus .. statim ~ui exercitu preparato .. hostem .. invasit EDDI 19; contigit .. capitaneum de H. proposuisse ~um in interiores partes Normannie pro alimentis municipii ampliandis *G. Hen. V* 16; **1221** populum .. admonuit de faciendo ~u super infideles (*Lit. Magistri militum Templi*) WEND. II 261.

4 (collect.) cavalry, knighthood.

'~us' et 'peditatus' ad numerum equitum et peditum pertinebunt ALDH. *PR* 135; ~us, i. .. *ferdwerod* *GlH* E 311; multus ad eum [regem G.] ~us Anglorum convenit ORD. VIT. IV 2 p. 167; Pharao et omnis ~us ejus submergitur [cf. *Exod.* xiv 9] BALD. CANT. *Sacr. Alt.* 707C.

5 equipage.

in ~u .. et familia erat honorificus, viros diligens habere in familia et non pueros, equos pro vectura et non equulos GRAYSTANES 36.

equitiarius [LL], horse-herd, stud-keeper. *V. et. equarius.*

1208 Uctredus ~ius *Fines Northumb & Durh* 32; **c1225** Rogerus ~ius *Cart. Cockersand* 837; **1296** equicium parci de Dynebegh. Adam de Blakeburn ~ius reddit comp' suum de xx jumentis de remanente *DL MinAc* 1/1 r. 1*d*.; **1340** liberarunt .. ~io regis .. xj jumenta, iiij pultras .. de equicio *MinAc* 1120/10 r. 17*d*.; *an horse hyrde*, ~ius, equarius *CathA*.

equitibia, horse's hock.

~ia, A. *a kambrell WW*.

equitius [CL *only as sb. n.*]

1 (of mill) operated by horse.

c1198 in celario molendinum ~ium absque equis et absque lapidibus *Cart. Osney* I 112; **1236** confirmavi .. quod .. nullum .. molendinum aquaticum, ventitium vel ~ium levabimus *Couch. Furness* II 717; *Ann. Dunstable* 402 (v. 2 equus 3d); **1440** molendinum ~ium *Meaux* III 240.

2 (as sb. n.) stud; **b** (royal).

†equartium, *stood* ÆLF. *Gl.*; perrexerat mango .. ad Richemontem, ~ium quod habebat venale distrahere. ad quem, cum versaretur in foro, vir .. accessit rogans sibi pullum vendi W. CANT. *Mir. Thom.* III 40; equus ~io preminet emissarius GIR. *PI* I 1; **a1210** .. ita quod .. habere possint ad pasturam c animalia .. et tot porcos quot eis .. habere placuerit et ~ium similiter *Reg. Aberbr.* I 60; character qui imprimitur in anima, quo discernitur anima baptizati ab anima non baptizati sicut charactere distinguitur pullus in ~io S. LANGTON *Quaest.* 362; **12..** et si ~ium non habuerimus, liceat eis nichilominus xx equas cum sequela sua .. in pastura habere ubicumque ~ium meum .. ire consuevit *Reg. S. Andr.* 125b; **1319** (v. falda 1c); **1446** herbagium .. dividitur inter bursarium et supervisorem ~ii .. prioris (*Invent.*) *Feod. Durh.* 187 (cf. ib. 188: instaurum ~ii ibidem: .. v eque, quarum iiij ambulantes et una trottans; item iiij *coltez* ambulantes; item iij pullani annales masculi); decimas de pannagio .. et de pullanis provenientibus de ~io suo *Reg. Brev. Orig.* 49. **b** **1178** vij s. et vj d. de pullo vendito de ~io regis *Pipe* 17; **1217** mandamus vobis quod .. curam capiatis de ~io nostro .. in Nova Foresta *Pat* 28; **1294** de .. expensis factis circa .. ~ium regis apud Estwode *KRAc* 97/25; **1314** in vadiis j hominis custodientis ~ium regis in parco de Wodestok' *Ib.* 99/16; **1332** dictos parcos pro sustentacione ~ii nostri .. duximus retinendum *LTRMem* 105 m. 8*d*.

3 (?) cavalry raid.

'domini sint tot maledicti, / reges, prepositi, preco, pedester, eques.' / .. / sic ruralis adhuc pugnas et equītia damnat GARL. *Tri. Eccl.* 35.

equitura, riding. *V. et. equitatura.*

expensis variis nummi serventur in archa, / sintque tibi sponse pueris, vestes equiture D. BEC. 2233; **1327** equus vetus stalonus ad equituram [? l. equitaturam *or* equitium] (*KRAc* 239/13) *RIA Proc.* XXVI 372.

equor, equoreus v. aequ-. **equuleus,** ~**ius,** ~**us** v. 2 eculeus.

1 equus v. aequus.

2 equus [CL]

1 horse (for riding or unspec.); **b** (w. *carvannarius* or *emissarius*); **c** (as heriot); **d** (mythical); **e** (fig.).

ALDH. *Aen.* 99. 5 (v. cornipes); rex Hyglacus .., quem ~us .. portare non potuit *Lib. Monstr.* I 2; non ~orum dorso sed pedum incessu vectus BEDE *HE* III 5; qui in burgo vendit ~um dat praeposito nummum *DB* I 26; videtur bonus ~us quia fortis est et per aliud bonus ~us quia velox est ANSELM (*Mon.* I) I 14; **a1161** pro concessione hujus venditionis [habuit] .. Hugo .. unum ~um *Act. Hen. II* I 284; **1242** j bono equu (*sic*) pro habenda uxore *Pipe* 193; nonne est stolidus mercator qui volens emere ~um [ME: *hwen he wule buggen hors*] .. non wlt respicere nisi .. capud? *AncrR* 74. **b** **1300** pro quodam ~o karvannar' (v. carvannarius 1); BEDE *HE* II 13 etc. (v. emissarius 2b). **c** tainus vel miles regis dominicus moriens pro relevamento dimittebat regi omnis arma sua et ~um j cum sella, alium sine sella *DB* (*Berks*) I 56v.; debitum post mortem .. si notus fuerit regi: ij ~os, unus cum sella et alius sine [AS: *ij hors, j gesadelod and oðer ungesadolod*] (*Inst. Cnuti*) *GAS* 359. **d** Protheas caeruleo corpore bipedum ~orum curru per aequora nudus vehi perhibetur *Lib. Monstr.* I 35. **e** quinque ~is [sc. regibus Britanniae] minarum prophetica inclamitent strictim edicere oracula GILDAS *EB* 37.

2 dist. acc.: **a** (colour); **b** (size or speed); **c** (place of origin); **d** (whether wild or broken).

a BALSH. *Ut.* 46 etc. (v. badius); **1248** (v. equitare 1c); **1308, 1312** (v. crinis 1d); **1313** mortuus fuit unus ~us caretti *bronbayard KRAc* 99/11; **1343** j ~us albus pro sella elemosinar' *Ac. Durh.* 205; **1374** in uno ~o nigro, xl s. *Ib.* 580. **b** cursorum .. equorum R. CANT. *Malch.* II 84, etc. (v. cursor 2b); *Croyl.* 38 (v. cursorius 2a); **1290** custodi magnorum ~orum regis (v. cursorius 2b); **1335** cuidam garcioni .. venienti de B. cum grossis ~is *Ac. Durh.* 526; **s1345** in exequiis ejus [R. de Neville] .. habuit sacrista duos ~os magnos portantes corpus ejus in lectica et unum ~um mulum portantem capellam *Hist. Durh.* 1; NECKAM *Ut.* 99 etc. (v. ambulare 2); **1411** (v. carriottarius a). **c** **s1192** (v. Arabicus a); **1237** (v. badius); **1312** de j ~o *powis bauzan* (v. carvanna 2); **1316** unius ~i Powis pro Johanne de C. appreciati vj m. *RGasc* IV 1659; **1463** pro ij ~is Gallicis dictis genatis *ExchScot* 163. **d** **751** fibri atque lepores et ~i silvatici multo amplius [ab esu Christianorum] vitandi (*Lit. Papae*) *Ep. Bonif.* 87; **1161** ut pecora sua redeant singulis noctibus ad proprias terras preter ~os silvestres *Regesta Scot.* 226; ~orum utrumque genus, usuales et indomiti *Dial. Scac.* II 14 A; de homine condempnato ad mortem ..: coronator habebit ~os domitos non ferratos (*Leg. Malcolmi*) *APScot* app. 346; *Quon. Attach.* 48. 10 (v. capitosus 2b).

3 dist. as used for: **a** (baggage); **b** (draught); **c** (farming); **d** (mill); **e** (war or ceremonial); **f** (food).

a sagmarius ~us, *seamhors* ÆLF. *Gl.*; si aequo portabat sal ad vendendum *DB* 268; **1228** habeant .. unum ~um sumericium itinerantem bis in foresta .. ad mortuum boscum et siccum ad focum *Pat* 175; **1232** rex .. concessit monialibus de S. quod .. habeant unum ~um summarium itinerantem .. ad mortuum boscum .. ad focum suum *Cl* 188; M. PAR. *Maj.* IV 419 (v. clitellarius a); ~um summarium ad portandam capellam *Invent. Ch. Ch.* 6. **b** **1155** caretarius ~us *Dom. S. Paul.* 134 etc. (v. carrettarius 1a, b); **1313** ~us caretti (v. 2a supra); **1326** in ~is cariagii (v. carriagium 1b); **1531** expenduntur in prebenda ~orum carectarum *Househ. Bk. Durh.* 26. **c** cum ij ~is et j hercerio *RDomin* 53; *Ib.* 68 etc. (v. carruca 2c); **c1200** apud Bertunam sunt .. due carruce de xvj bobus et unus ~us occarius *Cart. Rams.* III 274; duo ~i occatores, quisque iiij s. *Ib.* 279; *Ac. Beaulieu* 51 (v. equa a). **d** **1264** de corio j ~i molendinar' vendito *Pipe* 108 m. 15; cum .. molendinum .. molere deberet, iiij ~i fortes vix poterant illud movere: et propterea est amotum et vetus molendinum equitium est resumptum *Ann. Dunstable* 402; **1303** de .. ~o carectario pro quodam ~o ad molendinum pretii x s. liberato *Ac. Exec. Ep. Lond.* 94. **e** juvat videre gradarios .. ambulantes ..; hinc ~os qui armigeris magis conveniunt durius incedentes W. FITZST. *Thom. prol.* 11; W. NEWB. *HA* II 11 (v. dextrarius a); *Itin. Ric.* I 67 etc. (v. dextrarius b); M. PAR. *Maj.* VI 373 etc. (v. 2 cooperire 2b); **c1288** preter ~is armaturis (*sic*) *KRAc* 231/26 m. 3 (?2); **1297** accidit quod felones evadunt .. pro eo quod compatriote non habent ~os ad arma ad insequendum eos *StatIr* I 200 (cf. ib.: alii tenentes habeant hobinos et alios ~os discoopertos); **1364** ad omnes ~os de guerra .. quos in portubus de Leverpoll' et Cestr' .. eskippari contigerit more solito appreciandos .. et colorem singulorum ~orum .. imbreviandum *Pat* 270 m. 27; inter viros fortes dirus conflictus invaluit, ~i et ascensores sternuntur *Ps.*-ELMH. *Hen. V* 87; **1573** ~is armatis (v. defensivus 1b). **f** **768** quid pertinet ad rem ut coram hominibus jejunantes .. simulemur, in secretis vero nostris bovem aut ~um glutiamus? *Ep. Alcuin.* 3 p. 23.

4 representation of horse. **b** horse-like object.

de mirabilibus Britannie: .. albus ~us cum pullo suo. mirum est quod in figura ~i sic factus fuit quod .. super ~i formam nunquam herba crescat DICETO *Chr.* 11; ~um ligneum qui plenus erat militibus Grecis TREVET *Troades* 7. **b** ~us vocatur repagulum confirmans laminas intra paxillum WALLINGF. (*Rect.*) I 416; **1435** xij ~i nemorei, quolibet furnito de ij pedibus, deservientes colubrinis, appretiata .. quelibet pecia vij s. vj d. (*Invent.*) *Collect. W. Worc.* 568; avis [sc. buttourus] est .. pigerrima et stolidissima, ut quae in retia ab ~o factitio agi potest facilime TURNER *Av.* C 2.

er- v. et. aer-.

1 era v. 2 aera 2.

2 era, hera [CL]

1 lady, mistress (of house); **b** (fig.).

eleemosyna cui .. ferventer hec hera [i. e. Mathildis] insistebat marito .. succurrebat ORD. VIT. IV 5 p. 189; ut [auce] se ex precepto here sequerentur, clara edixit voce W. MALM. *GP* IV 172; hera, domina OSB. GLOUC. *Deriv.* 275; quicquid .. herus et hera ad quotidianos usus vel esus .. premeditati fuerant GIR. *IK* I 12; me, quam cernis, Æðeldreða, hujus loci era sum *Lib. Eli.* II 133; hec hera, *a lady WW*; abra tenens speculum sese speculatur et hēram [*gl.*: i. dominam] *WW*. **b** utraque [i. e. ira et concupiscentia] modestie limen excedens in heram irreverenter insurgens PULL. *Sent.* 755B.

2 Our Lady, Virgin Mary.

matrem .. Salvatoris .. quam .. omnis creatura heram miratur OSB. *V. Dunst.* 40; ut [BVM] esset imperiosa creature totius hera EADMER *Virt.* 583D; nostra nostrum herum hera / .. / meruisti parere WALT. WIMB. *Virgo* 70.

3 'mistress', concubine.

dico frequenter hēre "michi dic: 'michi noctibus hēre' " SERLO WILT. II 39.

3 era v. hedera.

erad- v. et. heracl-.

eradere [CL]

1 to strip off, scrape away (also fig.). **b** to scrape smooth. **c** to scrape together (fig.).

~e a lingua mea detrahendi consuetudinem *Cerne* 146; cum .. caro circumquaque ~eretur [*altered to* †eradicaretur] .., tenaciter [spina] inhaerebat W. CANT. *Mir. Thom.* V 18; **1317** †eradnand' veteram (*sic*) coperturam plumbi et ponend' eandem cum solduram ejusdem super capellam *Fabr. Exon.* 78. **b** ASSER *Alf.* 104 (v. dolabra b). **c** H. HUNT. *CM* 9 (v. dehereditare).

2 to erase, delete. **b** to wipe out, destroy.

erasa, deleta *GlH* E 354; ut .. mendosos libros .. erasa scriptorum falsitate corrigeret B. *V. Dunst.* 37; omnis .. pecunie memoria de rotulis ~itur *Chr. Battle* f. 89. **b** totum genus Anglorum Brittaniae finibus erasurum se esse deliberans BEDE *HE* II 20.

eradiare [cf. CL radiare], to shine out.

in specie candentis columbe Spiritus Sanctus apparuit, qui .. super caput ipsius .. resplendens resedit, cujus ~ante per queque foramina candore niveo, omnis ecclesia illuxit lumine magno *Chr. Pont. Ebor. A* 328 (cf. FOLC. *V. J. Bev.* 11: irradiat).

eradicare [CL]

1 to uproot (tree *etc.*); **b** (fig.). **c** to remove (post or structure). **d** to pluck (wool from sheep). **e** to dig out (molehills).

~at, exstirpat, *up alucþ GlH* E 352; **1233** (v. enta); **1269** (v. cippus 1a); **1276** ita .. quod non possit alicui de dicto bosco vendere, dare vel irradicare *Reg. Heref.* 89; **1285** in quadam nova trabe ad molendinum erradicanda cum expensis carpentarii *Ac. Man. Cant.* (*Meopham*); **1317** (v. consumptuose); **1334** (v. 1 bruaria a); **1340** in j querco prostrato .. et eredicando *Ac. Man. Cant.* (*Adisham*). **b** **667** ut omnem .. inimici zizaniam .. ex .. insula .. ~et [cf. *Matth.* xiii 25] (*Lit. Papae*) BEDE *HE* III 29; ~atis idolatriae spinis verbum Dei .. serere ALCUIN *WillP* I 12; gramina elationis funditus concupivit ~are .. a cordibus neophytum BYRHT. *V. Ecgwini* 361; sicut zizania .. que tempore messionis a diligenti messore funditus ~abuntur ORD. VIT. III 3 p. 42; cum prophetico sarculo evellens, destruens .. et ~ans quidquid in horto Domini male plantatum repperisset H. BOS. *Thom.* II 31. **c** **1195** (v. dividere 8e); **s1265** quod catene .. et omnes *postes* quibus .. attachiate fuerunt fuissent irradiate *Leg. Ant. Lond.* 78; **1306** irradicavit [*a house*] *CourtR Wakefield* II 54; **1375** quod .. abbas pilos et palos .. de aqua .. irradicat (*sic*) et amoveat *Pub. Works* I 295. **d** **1299** M. .. irradicavit lanam de bidentibus ipsius Andree .. . patria .. dicunt .. quod predicta M. de ista irradicacione non est culpata *Gaol Del.* 37/4 m. 6*d*. **e** **1383** solut' cuidam homini ~anti monticulas talparum *MinAc* 1209/15 m. 6*d*.

2 to eradicate (disease).

pulvis salis .. ~at [scrophulam] GILB. III 175v. 2 (v. cuprosa).

3 (w. living obj.) to banish, exterminate. **b** (pass., w. *vita*) to die.

monstra quae .. per plurimos terrae angulos ~ata funditus et subversa legimus *Lib. Monstr.* I *pref.*; offensa pro qua Guillelmi progenies ~ata sic est de Anglia ut nec passum pedis .. jam nanciscatur in illa [cf. *Job* xxxi 8] ORD. VIT. IV 13 p. 265; ~abo te de terra GIR. *IK* II 14. **b** [papa] Bonefacius .. in cameram rediens infra biduum post vita ~atur humana AD. USK 88 (cf. ib.: post mortem pape).

4 to obliterate (from memory). **b** to quash (statute).

s1263 ira .. de eorum memoria nuncquam .. ~ata delebitur *Plusc.* VII 24; posse omnem perturbacionem †erudicari et exstirpari de mentibus hominum W. BURLEY *Vit. Phil.* 108; **1452** impensa mihi beneficia .. adeo fixe cordi herent ut nullo pacto ~ari queant BEKYNTON I 273. **b** **s1261** magnates .. timentes .. ne rex ita presumeret eorum .. funditus ~are statutum *Flor. Hist.* II 470.

5 (p. ppl.) 'rooted in', *i. e.* native or (?) *f. l.*

1234 naute qui sunt in villa ~i [? l. radicati] et atrium habentes in villa habebunt rectum .. *Eng. Justice* 136 (v. atrium 1d).

eradicatio [LL]

1 uprooting (fig.). **b** removal (of post or structure). **c** plucking (of wool from sheep).

1458 pro ~one radicum rancorum et postposicione discordie (*Breve Regis*) *Reg. Whet.* I 300. **b** **1336** in ~one veteris meremii molendini et aux[ilio] habend[o] ad novum meremium inponendum et rammandum *Ac. Man. Cant.* (*Bocking*); **a1440** in clausuris, aluris, fossuris, piscinis, ~onibus, et in aliis variis reparacionibus AMUND. II app. 262. **c** **1299** (v. eradicare 1d).

2 eradication (of disease, fig.).

1304 ad ~onem .. hujus morbi virosi [supersticionis] *FormOx* 8.

3 banishment, extermination.

1188 nobis, in quorum perniciem et ~onem hinc mundi elementa, hinc regnum et sacerdotium conspiraverunt *Ep. Cant.* 195.

eradicativus, eradicative, tending to root out (disease).

si corpus tertianarii sit bene carnosum, .. flobotomia ~a tibi multo plus valebit GAD. 5. 1; cavendum est .. a flobotomia magna ~a; tamen alterativa et minorativa bene potest *Ib.* 16v. 1 (cf. ib. 33v. 1: cura .. ~a).

eradicator [LL], eradicator, uprooter (fig.).

Anselmus .. errorum strenuissimus ~or *NLA* (*prol.*) I 7.

eradnand' v. eradere 1a. **erare** v. eariare. **erarium** v. aerarium.

erasio, scraping off.

1253 expedit .. in ~one eruginis vas non frangi (*Lit. Papae*) *Conc.* I 702b.

erasti v. eruscum. **erb-** v. et. herb-. **erbicus, erbus** v. ervum. **erchiepiscopus** v. archiepiscopus. **erchimotum, ~miotum** v. merchimotum. **ercia** v. hercia. **ercinos** v. erinos. **ercle** v. hercle.

ercisci (herc-) [CL], to divide (an inheritance).

erciscundae, dividendae *GlC* E 302; familiae erciscundae, *yrfegedal* ÆLF. *Gl.*; herescinda (*sic*), hereditatem scindens OSB. GLOUC. *Deriv.* 275; recte dictatum est judicium familie herciscunde [*gl.*: *her* Grece, 'divisio' Latine, .. inde dicitur in legibus judicium familie herciscunde, i. e. dividunde] NECKAM *NR* II 173; *to departe herytage*, †heretestere *CathA*.

erdescota v. erthescota. **erdibitus** v. redhibere.

Erebeus [CL], **~icus,** infernal.

717 claustra ~ia BONIF. *Ep.* 9 (v. claustrum 1b); **940** (12c) noverit se .. Herebica eterni anatematis macera perforandum *CS* 761 (cf. ib. 782, 801, 875).

Erebus [CL = *underworld*], Hell.

dum Deus ad Herebi vagas descenderit umbras / ferrea .. fracturus limina valvae ALDH. *VirgV* 455; *Ib.* 765 (v. 1 campus 1b); patulis hiatibus igniflua Herebi [v. l. ~i] hostia patescunt FELIX *Guthl.* 31; ~um, *hellescead* ÆLF. *Gl.*; et flammis Herebi cruciantur et igne perhenni *Altercatio* 51; tu Phlaegeton subies, Herebum manesque paveses FRITH. 1094; *RegulC* 31 (v. claustrum 1b); **995** (12c) regnante .. caeli terraeque dispositore ~ique triumphatore *CD* 692; spolians Herebum nobis dedit astra polorum *Mon. Rit.* II 87; grassatur Erinis / cotidieque suos Erebi contrudit in imis ORD. VIT. XI *pref.* p. 160.

erecl- v. heracl-.

†erectare, *f. l.*

1290 †erectatus [l. arrettatus] de morte cujusdam hominis coram S. de R. in itinere Suthamt' *RParl* 56b.

erecticius v. erepticius.

erectio [CL]

1 raising (of part of body); **b** (cosmetic, of eyebrows). **c** erection (sexual).

quippe cui .. acies invicta manuum sola intensa ~o fuerit [cf. *Exod.* xvii 11] GILDAS *EB* 1. **b** superciliorum .. ~one cum humida strictione *AncrR* 69 (v. decapillatio). **c** inflatio virge et ~o *Quaest. Salern.* B 211; priapismus est .. continua virge virilis ~o sine appetitu et desiderio ad coitum *SB* 35.

2 erection, setting up (also fig.).

huic patet in sompnis erectio mistica scale NIG. *Paul.* 46v. 154; ad ~onem .. nostri tabernaculi debemus jugiter intueri R. NIGER *Mil.* II 34; **s1394** abbas T. .. ad ~onem .. crucis .. festinavit *Croyl. Cont. B* 492; **1457** cum xiij d. solut' in posicione primi lapidis et ~one meremii *Ac. Durh.* 241.

3 raising of status: **a** (of person); **b** (of institution).

a a tempore ~onis sue ad episcopatum AYLWARD 289. **b** **1382** quam quidem ~onem in religionem .. rex .. per literas suas patentes recitavit et .. ad supplicacionem .. episcopi eandem ~onem sive transmutacionem de cantaria predicta et ecclesia seculari in religionem ordinis antedicti ut premittitur factam .. approbavit *IMisc* 227/8; **1470** super impetracione bille pro celle dicte in abbathiam ~one *Reg. Whet.* I 150.

4 support, uplifting.

1167 ad ~onem spei, ad tuitionem libertatis, ad virtutis profectum J. SAL. *Ep.* 203 (215); **1237** GROS. *Ep.* 40 (v. excitamentum).

5 (?) erectness.

~o stature in homine .. ac elegantia totius effigiei protendunt .. quod quidquid est in eo ante infusionem intellective ad hoc est .. ut sit instrumentum intellectus SICCAV. *PN* 130.

erectivus, erective, uplifting.

ex defectu virtutis ~e, ut in gibosis et claudis BACON VIII 134; Spiritus Sancti graciam quandoque scriptura ignem quandoque aquam vocat, ostendens quoniam non substancie sunt hec nomina representativa sed accionis; per ignis quidem appellacionem ~um et calidum gracie et consumtivum peccatorum enigmatice insinuat BRADW. *CD* 388D.

erector [LL], uplifter.

nobilium oppressor, humilium ~or GIR. *EH* I 6.

eredicare v. eradicare. **eremagium** v. cremagium.

eremicola (herem-), desert-dweller, eremite (partly fig.).

1171 parricidii crimine suffocato te Britannorum corde, quid valet populus et nos pauperes erimicole, famuli tui? *Ep. Becket* 746; multos habet tales eremus exsilii exiles ~as P. BLOIS *Opusc.* 1016D; scio ~am olim pontificem .. at superinduto pontifice tunicatus latuit eremita *Ib.* 1017B; *an hermett*, anachorita, heremita, ~a *CathA* (cf. ib.: *wyldernes*, .. heremus .. herimicola, que colit heremum); quidam ~a Anglus animas plusculas .. a purgatorio ad celum properantes vidit MAJOR IV 15.

eremin- v. ermin-.

eremio [cf. LL eremus], 'hindberry', raspberry. *V. et. eremius.*

erimio, *hindberge GlC* E 271; **10**. . erimo, *hindberige WW* (cf. ib.: erimigio, *hyndberige*); ermigio, *hind berge Gl. Durh.*

1 eremita (herem-) [LL < ἐρημίτης]

1 desert-dweller.

~a, *westensetla* ÆLF. *Gl.*; palmis puer angelorum / deportatus est duorum / heremite traditus [*gl.*: ~a dicitur cultor heremi] GARL. *SM* 54; secundum Aristotelem .. vir ~a, qui non est pars civitatis sed sibi soli vacat, non est bonus neque malus BACON *Maj.* II 254.

2 eremite, hermit, solitary religious: **a** (Eastern); **b** (Eng.); **c** (Sc.); **d** (W.); **e** (fig.).

a Johannes Niloticae solitudinis ~a ALDH. *VirgP* 29; ~as qui per Egyptum errabant .. impie destruxit R. NIGER *Chr. I* 41; AD. EYNS. *Hug.* V 13 p. 159 (v. 3a infra); vite sanctorum Pauli primi hermite, Antonii, Malchi .. et aliorum (*Catal. Librorum*) *Meaux* III xcviii. **b** hic [in insula Farne] heremita sacer [Cuthbertus] non parvo tempore vixit ALCUIN *SS Ebor* 662; ~a Godricus de Finchala loco .. solitario .. in Domino requievit W. NEWB. *HA* II 20; **1204** Ricardus .. male creditur de morte ~e et ij puerorum occisorum in bosco de Wicchewude *CurR* III 145; **1292** hermitorium S. Hilde in foresta .. cum landa quam Rogerus G. quondam ~a illius loci tenuit *PQW* 130a; **1305** frater Nicholaus de S. ~a de Redefordwath .. per dimissorias capituli Eboraci *Reg. Carl.* I 246; **1328** (v. coeremita); *G. S. Alb.* I 105 (v. eremus 2a); **s1399** venit .. sanctus homo qui dicebatur ~a albus de Anglia FORDUN *Cont.* XV 9; **s1212** erat ea tempestate ~a quidam nomine Petrus, homo Eboracensis, qui .. consueverat predicere futura P. VERG. XV 279. **c** **c1173** me concessisse .. Johanni ~e .. insulam .. in lacu de L. .. et dim. carucatam terre *Regesta Scot.* 142; **†955** (16c) contulit insulam Lochlevine .. Keledeis heremetis ibidem commorantibus *E. Ch. Scot.* 3; **1536** Willelmum J., Willelmum F. et Thomam Duthty ~am, reos *Offic. S. Andr.* 143. **d** vitam S. Caradoci nobilis ~e et confessoris GIR. *Gir. Men.* 399. **e** **s1194** rex vester in comparatione regis Francorum ~a est W. NEWB. *HA* V 3.

3 member of an order of solitary religious: **a** (Carthusian); **b** (Austin hermit).

a ~e .. qui silvarum condensa prosternunt et, erectis monasteriorum et palatiorum excelsis culminibus, ibi tripudiant et gloriam Deo cum dulcedine cantitant ORD. VIT. X 16 p. 92; ~a noster [Hugo], suos cupiens coheremitas invisere, .. nobilem .. heremitarum principem, beatum dico Antonium, .. studuit expetere AD. EYNS. *Hug.* V 13 p. 159. **b** **1249, 1255** (v. Augustinianus); **1371** fratrem Eliarhardum lectorem ordinis fratrum ~arum S. Augustini .. tue fraternitati transmittimus (*Lit. Imp. Lodowici*) AVESB. 97b; **1515** Patritius C. ordinis ~arum S. Augustini (*Lit. Regis*) *Mon. Hib. & Scot.* 516a.

2 eremita (herem-), ermine. *Cf. ermina.*

in Britannia Minori .. mustelam .. incole .. capiunt quam ~am vocant .. [dux Britannie] portat pro armis suis unum scutum de pellibus ~arum earumque caudis nigris consutis UPTON 166–7.

eremitagium (herem-), hermitage; **b** (as place-name). **c** deserted place.

1130 omnia hermitagia in foresta mea de Conchis (*Ch. Hen. I*) *Gall. Christ.* XI 132; **c1160** totam terram que est inter C. et A. .. que est ad occidentem ~ii Theodorici a superiori cilio montium *Cart. Glam.* 131; **1200** concessimus .. monachis de Lenton' .. hermitagium de K. *RChart* 56a; **1376** ~ium vocatum *Le Swannest* prope hospitale S. Katerine juxta Turrim nostram London' *Pat* 294 m. 34; **1399** ad cantariam in ~io de Crepulgate (*LB Lond.* I f. 6) *MGL* I 552; **1415** ~ium de Reculvere .. tibi conferimus .. ac te heremitam ~ii predicti preficimus *Reg. Cant.* I 135; **1445** nos dedisse .. Johanni S. .. ~ium capelle B. Marie foreste de K. .., quod .. ~ium cum iij acris terre .. fuit Hugonis C. heremite dicti ~ii hereditarie *Reg. Brechin* II app. 382; **s1402** per .. Bernam, .. montem Godardi, et ejus cacuminis hermitogium in caruca .. tractus AD. USK 74; **1588** totum illud mesuagium et tenementum nostrum vocatum *the Hermytage* .. ac totum pomarium .. eidem hermitagio adjacens *Pat* 1319 m. 39. **b** **s1296** reddita sunt ei [regi E.] vij castra et ville .. viz. .. castrum quod vocatur Hermitagium de Soules et alia B. COTTON 311. **c** **1237** Robertus de W. .. presentatus ad hermitagium et capellam sanctorum martyrum Stephani et Laurentii. .. vulgariter locus ille a laicis hermitagium nuncupatur propter solitudinem, non quia heremita aliquis .. ibidem solebat conversari *Reg. Linc.* 376.

eremitalis, eremitic.

ad ~em vitam .. electam, derelictis omnibus curis et rebus .., solus profectus est *V. Furs.* 308.

eremitanus (herem-), eremitic. **b** (as sb. m.) eremite.

construxit coenobia duo. alterum .. vocatur Divus Benedictus, ubi loci antea ~um sacellum positum fuerat P. VERG. VII p. 134. **b** **1284** PECKHAM *Ep.* 607 (v. Augustinianus).

eremitare (herem-) [LL = *to make desert, dry up, trans.*], to live as a hermit.

sub eodem tempore quo praefatus vir .. ~are initiavit FELIX *Guthl.* 29; ~andi gratia illo advenit et tamen monachi habitum gessit R. COLD. *Cuthb.* 27; abbas .. quemdam monachum suum .. in loco Everdwic ~are licentiavit *MonA* II 600b.

eremitice (herem-), as a hermit.

mater hujus regis Henrici, vivente priore marito, imperatore sc. Henrico, ~e peregrinante, nupsit altero, sc. Galfrido, de quibus iste rex Henricus processit HIGD. VII 21.

1 eremiticus (herem-) [LL]

1 of the desert. **b** deserted.

Israeliticus populus .. ab Aaron deos sibi fieri, qui ~e eis vie ducatum preberent, exposcunt ÆLNOTH *Cnut* 32. **b** tu, .. cum Norwicum adveneris .., ad meum in silva T. locum ~um venire non differas T. MON. *Will.* IV 10.

2 eremitic.

ad dilectum ~ae conversationis agonem .. remeare curavit BEDE *CuthbP* 36; Eduuoldus frater Edmundi regis et martiris vitam ~am solo pane cibario et aqua trivit W. MALM. *GP* II 84; de excellentia vite solitarie et dignitate professionis ~e *Chr. Witham* 501; GIR. *Ad S. Langton* 401 (v. anachoreticus); non pertinet ad statum tuum, sc. ~um, ludere cum mulieribus ROLLE *IA* 179; **s1335** venit Londonias quidam hereticus .. in habitu ~o, qui prius fuerat de ordine fratrum Minorum et apostatavit *Ann. Paul.* 365; omnes isti .. fuerunt sancti .. in Devonia .. †herecticam vitam ducentes W. WORC. *Itin.* 62.

2 eremiticus, (her.) of ermine; *cf. erminalis.* **b** charged w. ermine.

portat crucem ereminalem sive ermeticam, A. *he berith a croys of armene* BAD. AUR. 192; qui habet ista arma portat unam crucem erminalem sive ~am, et G. sic: *il port ung crois erminee* UPTON 222. **b** portat arma palata de auro et azorio cum quarta ermetica. et G. sic: *il port palee d'or et d'asor ung quart d'ermyn* BAD. AUR. 198.

eremitorius (herem-), serving as a hermitage. **b** (as sb. n.) hermitage; **c** (as place-name).

s1152 concessione G. domini mei .. Radulfus heremita locum herimitorium de M. edificavit *Cart. Boarstall* 295; **s1431** tres fures despoliaverunt locum ~ium de Farley *Chr. S. Alb.* 59. **b** **c1175** hermitorium de M. cum capella .. et cum tota terra sicut eam fossis circumdederunt *Cart. Boarstall* 296; **a1180** dederat .. ~ia de E. et de M. *Cart. Whitby* I 3; **1292** hermitorium (v. eremita 2b); **s1382** [W. Swynderby] ~ium .. in bosco .. ducis petiit KNIGHTON *Cont.* 190; omnes de Croyland qui turbas habere voluerint in marisco abbatis debent .. iij ob. .., unde abbas percipere debet denarios et cellerarius obolos ad stipendia capellanorum de ~iis *Croyl.* 101; **s1410** nondum tetigimus de collegiis, cantoriis, .. nec de glebis aut domibus leprosorum .. nec de ~iis nec de fratribus crucesignatis *Chr. S. Alb.* 55. **c** ad locum quendam solitarium in medio aquarum situm, qui dicitur ~ium et pertinet ad .. congregationem de Simpligeham H. BOS. *Thom.* IV 3.

eremitus [cf. ἐρημίτης], of the desert, eremitic.

anxius et mestus Malchus .. / damnabat vitam penitus jam tunc heremitam R. CANT. *Malch.* IV 4.

eremius [cf. LL eremus], raspberry cane. *V. et. eremio.*

erimius, *hindbrer GlH* E 327.

eremodicium [CL < ἐρημοδίκιον] **(herem-),** (leg.) adverse judgement for default of appearance.

reum contrahere ~ium non dicitur, quia semper fugit. sed actorem contrahere ~ium dicitur VAC. *Lib. Paup.* 70;

major qui ex justa causa abest, si legittime defensus est, restituitur (*sic*) ad appellationem. si non fuerit legittime defensus, restituetur ad ~ium, id est ex integro restituetur ad litigandum, et petet ut audiatur a judice cum ante non fuerit defensus *Ib.* 232; si .. reus abfuerit et similis ejus processerit requisitio .. etiam absente eo ~ium contrahatur RIC. ANGL. *Summa* 41; **1257** judices ~ium contrahere non morantes monachos ab observatione judicii absolutos fore decreverunt (*Reg. Werketone*) *Mon. Francisc.* II app. 271.

eremus (heremus) [LL < ἐρῆμος], **~a**

1 desert, wilderness, waste land; **b** (fig.).

Narcissus .. abstrusam ~i vastitatem petiit ALDH. *VirgP* 32; Crugland .. insula media in palude posita, quae ante paucis propter remotioris ~i solitudinem inculta vix nota habebatur FELIX *Guthl.* 25; locus ipse desertus erat et .. duo soli senes clerici .. in tanta ~o .. Deo .. famulabantur ORD. VIT. III 2 p. 16; **s1257** confinia Wallie in ~um inhabitabilem .. sunt redacta M. PAR. *Maj.* V 660; **1274** forestas .. et alia vasta seu ~a nostra *RGasc* II 4; ex duris Moyse saxis heremique jubente / dum saliunt fluctus GOWER *VC* II 261; *CathA* (v. eremicola). **b** sancti .. per ~um hujus vitae .. caelestem feruntur ad patriam BEDE *Tab.* 490; de gregeque errantes eremi per devia vastae / ad Domini caulas humeris revehebat amicis [cf. *Luke* xv 4–5] ALCUIN *SS Ebor* 1474; [Athelwynus] ~um nostram ingressus in caulas .. sue .. visitationis gratia sanctificatas pusillum gregem introduxit *Chr. Rams.* 40; ave, cujus faber poli / reservavit sibi soli / virginalem heremum WALT. WIMB. *Virgo* 103.

2 solitary place, hermitage. **b** cell or monastery.

~um cum curioso eximiae sollicitudinis animo petere meditabatur FELIX *Guthl.* 24; **s1196** S. Godricus .. heremita cum annos lx in ~o apud Finkehale peregisset OXNEAD 62; imperator Henricus [IV] .. imperium .. reliquit et .. versus Cestriam .. ~um petens .. penitentiam egit GIR. *PI* III 27 p. 300; vivebat in heremio .. porro locus ~i quem colebat .. *G. S. Alb.* I 97; heremita S. cultor ~i in Northaga .. de loco sui ~i ad monasterium S. Albani venire consuevit ad interessendum matutinis, quibus expletis ad eundem (*sic*) redibat ~um *Ib.* 105; hec ~us, A. *armytegke WW.* **b** o Ramesigia cohors, .. / vasta palus, piscosa nimis, sua dyndima pandit, / ut nova sint eremi claustra reperta tibi ABBO *QG prol.* 4; duos bone religionis viros in ~o degentes sibi vicina AD. EYNS. *Hug.* IV 13 p. 64; **c1250** ut nulli .. persone liceat .. monasterium .. instituere seu ~um inclusorum vobis reclamantibus ordinare *Kelso* II 460; [Bruno] relicto seculo ~um Cartusie .. fundavit et rexit vj annis HIGD. VII 4; **s1250** congregati sunt fratres Carmelite de ~is ubi solitariam duxerant vitam ad villas *Meaux* II 122.

3 eremitic life.

pluribus secum ratiocinantibus agebat quid prestaret ~um sectari an monachum W. MALM. *GP* I 45; hic monachus monachos, hic clerum clericus ornat, / hic eremi cives jus eremita docet L. DURH. *Hypog.* 69; mira sub his parcitas potus atque cibi, / sed vetat varietas testium id scribi; / ne nil tamen exequar, se furando sibi / turbis jungit erĕmum; stans hic, degens ibi *Poem. S. Thom.* 79.

erenacia (heren-) [cf. Ir. *airchinneach*], 'herenachy', office of erenach.

1397 quendam ipsius ecclesie vicarium et eo herenacum per eundem primatem de ~ia ejusdem ecclesie .. ad se vocavit *Vis. Derry* 4; cartas seu literas ~iarum, terrarum, possessionum, et officiorum quorumcumque ostensuri *Ib.* 25.

erenacus (heren-) [Ir. *airchinneach*], 'herenach', hereditary warden of church, farmer of church lands.

1397 (v. erenacia); **1426** [*granted to petitioner as principal herenach*] ~o [*in that part, half a charter*] *Reg. Armagh* 47; **1438** *Ib.* 180 (v. comurbanus); **c1592** episcopus debet habere ex qualibet feodi quarta j m., licet ballivi et herenaci .. aliter disposuerunt *Anal. Hib.* II 35; **c1606** Aghdowie Sancti Gromi: rector J. McReady, vicarius D. McReady, .. herrinacus B. McReady *Ib.* XII 81.

Erenis v. Erinys.

ereos (her-) [cf. CL Eros < Ἔρως], (w. *amor* or *passio*) passionate or wanton love. (*Cf. Mod. Philol.* XI (1914) 491–546).

in passione que ~eos dicitur *Quaest. Salern.* N 6; interdum fit [cogitatio] de rebus .. inhonestis, sicut de amore ~eos et carnali concupiscentia GILB. I 63.2; licet mentem nostram librorum amor ~eos possideret a puero R. BURY *Phil.* 11.88; GAD. 132.1 (v. amor 1b); coitus enim talis si continuetur .. morbos nepharios procreat, virum effeminat, amorem ~eos et zelotipiam producit KYMER 19.

ereosus (her-) [cf. ereos], (one) obsessed by passionate love.

commotio accidentium anime ut est ira .. aut angustia spei aut desperationis, sollicitudo, et cogitatio superflua ut in ~is GILB. I 4.2.

erep- v. et. erip-.

ereptibilis, that can be saved, rescuable.

c1239 anime quas occupaverunt vitia seculari potentatu roborata non sunt ~es ab hujusmodi vitiis nisi in manu forti .. ecclesiastice potestatis GROS. *Ep.* 127.

†erepticius, (by conf. w. *arrepticius*) inspired or demented person.

areolus [sc. hariolus], ~ius *GlC* A 778; ~ius, ariolus, divinus *GlH* E 320; hic †erecticius, qui vexatur multis demonibus *WW.*

ereptio [CL]

1 taking away.

796 (11c) concedo .. iij cassatos .. pro ~one peccaminum meorum *CS* 277.

2 rescue, deliverance; **b** (w. *ab*); **c** (spiritual).

ut [discipuli] .. paventes .. ~onis suae miraculum stuperent ac .. ereptori suo gratias referrent BEDE *Mark* (vi 48) 197C; Jesus .. mirabiliter emicuit in ~one suorum comprimendo contrarios conatus ORD. VIT. III 3 p. 52; omnis spei subsidium vel ~onis remedium .. amiserant R. COLD. *Cuthb.* 75; **s1342** rex .. pro sua ~one [de mari] votum construendi aliquod monasterium .. adhibebat *Meaux* III 51; **s1388** novissime decollatus est .. Symon B., quamvis comes de Derby omnes vires apposuisset ejus ~oni *V. Ric. II* 102. **b** ~o ejus a vinculis ORD. VIT. IV 14 p. 266; **1391** ~onem a carcere (v. 2 deliberatio 1a). **c** accensi sunt .. ad offerendas Deo victimas sacrae oblationis pro ~one suorum qui de saeculo migraverant BEDE *HE* IV 20; **c795** terram .. pro ~one animae meae .. concedo *CS* 274; **c945** (14c) pro communi nostrarum ~one animarum et abstercione piaculorum *CS* 817; .. ut qui resurrectionis Dominicae solemnia colimus ~onis [AS: *generenise*] nostrae suscipere laetitiam mereamur *Rit. Durh.* 30.

4 ripping (of garment).

1565 pro iterum ~one ejusdem *Ac. LChamb.* 58 f. 2v. (cf. *Misc. LChamb.* 33 p. 144: *for rippinge the same farthingale*).

ereptor [LL < CL = *robber*], rescuer, deliverer; **b** (spiritual).

BEDE *Mark* 197 (v. ereptio 2a); quiddam .. de spiritu Saulis mente concipiens ~orem suum propugnatoremque strenuissimum dolo perdere cogitavit *V. Har.* 1. 3b; fit ut .. inde foveat tam festina ab eis ereptio et jocunda ~oris mei visio *NLA* (*Milburga*) II 189. **b** omnes quos possunt diaboli manibus eripientes pro ~oris sui pace potius certamen agere BEDE *Sam.* 660.

ereptrix, rescuer, deliverer (f.). **b** (as adj. f.) bringing salvation.

NLA (*Milburga*) II 189 (v. 2 claviger 1a). **b** hostiam agnus immolas ereptricem J. HOWD. *Cant.* 708.

eregium v. arreragium 2a. **eres** v. heres. **eresgieva** v. geresgieva. **ereticus** v. haereticus.

ereuxis [ἔρευξις], vomit.

†orexis, i. vomitus exiens ab ore *SB* 32.

erga [CL]

1 over against, adjoining. **b** towards, in the direction of. **c** (?) around.

~a, juxta *GlC* E 273; de preposicione: .. 'contra' dicit distanciam nature rerum racione loci, '~a' convenienciam *Ps.*-GROS. *Gram.* 54; **1305** quilibet tenens habens terram .. juxta ripariam potest piscari ~a terram suam propriam sine perturbacione *Ext. Hadleigh* 230; **1393** purprestur' jacent' ~a Balisgate *DL CourtR* 68/846 m. 5; **1435** xxiiij alie baliste pendentes ~a fenestras, quarum ij pendent contra parietem retro arcus *Collect. W. Worc.* 569; **1552** grovam nostram jacentem prope regiam viam ducentem a London' versus Croydon' ~a crucem vocatam *le Stone Crosse Pat* 850 m. 48. **b** ille .. erga / auctorata volans altaria FRITH. 149; **c1185** [seilinius] extenditur a porta ejusdem domus ~a mare *Rec. Templars* 240; **s1028** patre ejus ~a Jerusalem proficiscente *Eul. Hist.* III 34. **c** †agga, circa *GlC* A 388.

2 as regards, about, concerning.

ultroneum [apum] .. servitutis affectum quem ~a suorum obsequia principum exercere noscuntur ALDH. *VirgP* 6; mox ut eam aqua benedicta tetigit languentem et quid ~a eam ageretur prorsus ignorantem, ita plenam .. sanitatem recepit BEDE *CuthbP* 29; quae sint gesta ~a fidem Christi .. didicimus *Id. HE pref.* p. 7; quid ~a eum agere rex promisisset edocuit *Ib.* II 12 p. 108; R. BURY *Phil.* 4. 44 (v. 2 clericus 7a); nominatim non dicat illum [quem accuset], licet confessor sciat ~a quem cogitet [ME: *towart hwam hit turne*] *AncrR* 131; **s1297** Scotti miserunt unum de suis in Flandriam, qui gesta ~a .. regem exploraret *Meaux* II 269.

3 **a** (of feeling or acting) towards. **b** in the eyes of. **c** (w. ref. to intercession) 'with'.

a placidam mentem .. ~a omnes Dei famulos gero BEDE *HE* IV 22; dilectionem ~a nos et pietatem monstravit ANSELM (*CurD* 3) II 51; immisericorditer se ~a sub[d]itos habentes GIR. *GE* II 27; per confessionem et alias devociones ~a Deum *Itin. Mand.* 106. **b** **s1207** rex [Johannes] .. ~a .. papam in magnam indignationem incurrebat, dicente papa se non preceptis paternis ecclesiasticis obedire *Eul. Hist.* III 93. **c** rogans quatinus ~a reginam ut mecum mitteretur efficerem GIR. *Symb.* I 1; **1331** instetis ~a .. dominum nostrum Cantuariensim ut .. Johanni purgatio .. favorabiliter judicatur (*sic*) *Lit. Cant.* I 413; cum .. Adam .. coadjuvante eum .. patre .. Bernardo ~a .. papam Eugenium tertium [ob. **1153**] .. negotium .. ad finem perduxisset *Meaux* I 76.

4 to, in relation to (feud. overlord, esp. king).

quietus erit ~a regem, non ~a dominum cujus homo fuerit *DB* I 1; hanc terram deservivit R. ~a G. de Magnavilla *Ib.* II 97v.; (*Quad.*) *GAS* 535 (v. contra 2c); **1217** si .. a fidelitate sua recederem .., concedo quod .. terra mea et hereditas mea ~a ipsum .. regem incurratur *Pat* 107; **1452** remisimus .. punitiones quas .. ~a nos incurrere deberent (*Pat*) *Reg. Whet.* I 90.

5 against; **b** (in war); **c** (in game).

1216 licet .. pater noster .. ~a vos deliquerit *Pat* 4; **1249** per defaltam quam [G.] fecit ~a [v. l. versus] E. *CurR* XIX 572. **b** **s1198** si .. burgenses villam .. defendere possent ~a comitem usque pridie Kal. Octobris, ad succurrendum eis .. die illa veniret DICETO *YH* II 163; **s364** dum ~a Sarmatas debellaret *Eul. Hist.* I 342; rex .. fovet bella ~a terras diversas *Chr. Westm.* 152. **c** **1243** xx m., quas rex amisit ~a .. Walterum per gajuram (*FineR*) *RGasc* I 243; **c1425** (v. collusor).

6 (leg.): **a** before (judge or sim.); **b** (w. *dicere* or sim.); **c** (w. ref. to other party in transaction) 'against'. **d** (in warranty clause).

a qui aliquem ~a justitiam accusabit .. et mendacium denique pernoscatur, linguam perdat (*Leg. Hen.* 34. 7) *GAS* 566; Wilfridus .. ~a regem .. accusatus, ab eodem rege .. ab episcopatu pulsus est M. PAR. *Maj.* I 311; consideratum fuit quod .. Katerina nil caperet per breve suum sed esset in misericordia pro falso clamio suo et sequeretur ~a .. regem, si sibi videretur expedire *Meaux* II 228. **b** **1217** ita quod stet recto in curia nostra, si quis ~a eum inde loqui voluerit *Pat* 60; **1266** ad standum recto .. si nos .. ~a ipsum loqui voluerimus *Cl* 177; Willelmus .. petit ab attornato prioris si aliquid velit dicere ~a eum: et attornatus dicit quod non *State Tri. Ed. I* 63. **c** **c1180** (v. dereinare 1a); **1218** intravit in soltam ~a dominum suum .. de quadam parte illius pecunie *Eyre Yorks* 393; Rogerus ~a ipsos accionem habet et non ~a eum *State Tri. Ed. I* 22; **1314** ut possit per eundem (*sic*) scriptum debitum suum .. ~a predictum Willelmum exigere et recuperare *Deeds Balliol* 53; [tempore abbatis P., ob. **1182**] Willielmus de B. .. directionavit ~a nos pasturam *Meaux* I 175. **d** **c1200** warantizabimus .. ~a omnes homines *BL MS Cotton Claudius* D XI f. 207; **1434** manerium .. heredibus .. suis ~a abbatem de Bylande et successores suos warantizabimus *Cl* 285 m. 14*d*.

7 'against' (time), in preparation for (event).

s1392 imperabant ut ~a diem sequentem comitis consilium premuniret *Croyl. Cont. B* 487; exiit edictum [ut] .. ~a crastinum mane se pararent ad ascensum cum eo *G. Hen. V* 3; **1448** decrevit .. Isabellam .. citandam .. ~a diem Veneris *Eng. Clergy* 224; **1470** quousque competenter .. de singulis necessariis ~a diem installationis provideri posset *Reg. Whet.* I 20; **1507** exoptans .. omnia ~a mortis [diem] providere miseroque cadaveri suo sepulturam .. preparare *Lit. Cant.* III 337; **1533** cuidam homini .. diferenti j *buk* a W. pro judicibus ~a sessiones xij d. *Househ. Bk. Durh.* 143; **1535** Roberto T. pro .. preparatione *le borehede* arga [Nat]ale Domini iij s. iv d. *Ac. Durh.* 112.

ergage [ergo + agere], come now, well then.

~e, fare quicquid decrevisti ÆLF. BATA 5. 10; ~e, ~e! sumamus hoc exordium *Ib.* 5. 13.

ergalabus v. ergolabus.

†ergalum [cf. Fr. *ergot*], rye.

hec siligo, hoc ~um, A. *rye WW.*

ergasterium [CL < ἐργαστήριον]

1 workshop; *v. et. ergastulum* 1a. **b** shop, market.

opificium, ~ium *GlC* O 216; ~ium, *werchus* ÆLF. *Gl.*; ~ium vel operatorium, *weorchus Id. Sup.*; in pinsentium ~io [*Scheler*: ergastio] sive ergastulo molas, cribra .. respeximus BALSH. *Ut.* 51; BELETH *RDO* 117. 121C (v. ergastulum 1a); *trawe of smythy*, ~ium *PP*; hoc argasterium, ubi aliquid opus fit *WW*. **b** †**c1083** nundinalia et argisteria, id est mercatoria loca *Regesta* p. 58; **s1150** ut .. liberum civibus commeatum offerret, terra, lignis, lapidibus comportatis construi super aquas in habitaculis ~ia toleravit DICETO *YH* I 292; VAC. *Lib. Paup.* 165 (v. ergolabus).

2 monastery. *V. et. ergastulum* 1b.

plura monachorum ~ia in .. Antiochiae municipio .. construxere ALDH. *VirgP* 36; ~ium, monasterium *GlC* E 299; **930** (?11c) (v. dominus 8b).

3 tomb.

~ium dicitur ab *erga*, quod est 'labor', et *sterion*, quod est 'statio'. ibi .. requiescunt corpora sanctorum BELETH *RDO* 159. 157.

ergastularis [LL], of a prison.

s**1100** Rannulfo .. tenebris ∼ibus incluso W. MALM. *GR* V 393; capto Eudone .. atque vinculis ∼ibus mancipato W. POIT. I 43.

ergastulator, gaoler (fig.), keeper.

c**1425** episcopus D. cum socio suo G. .. mores anserinos tam indefatigabili pretenderunt auspicio, quod unus auca et alter anas .. sunt effecti. ∼or ovis, sed res mira .. quod cimia [i. e. simia] ovi famulatur *Cant. Coll. Ox.* III 71.

ergastulum [CL]

1 (penal) workshop; *v. et. ergasterium* 1a. **b** cell (of holy man); *v. et. ergasterium* 2.

∼um, locus ubi damnati aut marmora secant aut aliquid operentur (*sic*); ∼um, metallum *GlC* E 276, 285; venerandum est hoc tempus [Paschale] quod omnia ∼a et ergasteria et operatoria .. claudere debemus et nulla venalia exponere BELETH *RDO* 117. 121C. **b** cum .. eum amatorem catholicae fidei .. necnon ∼a confessorum crebro frequentantem comperissent ALDH. *VirgP* 36; Dunstanus nocturnas fugiens tenebras ad suum remeat ∼um. et ecce, dum ostium ecclesiae psallendo praeteriret .. OSB. *V. Dunst.* 16.

2 prison; **b** (fig., w. ref. to earthly life); **c** (w. *carnis, corporis,* or sim.); **d** (w. ref. to Purgatory or Hell).

putidos ∼i squalores libenter laturus ALDH. *VirgP* 23 (cf. id. *VirgV* 1947: pertulit in terris insons ergastula tetra); **9..** ∼a, *nirwþa WW*; testis adest custos, ergastula saeva serenis / inspiciens radiare focis in tempore noctis FRITH. 847; episcopalis ∼o carceris hunc reclusit R. COLD. *Cuthb.* 95; s**1410** pecierunt .. ut clerici convicti .. non traderentur carceribus episcoporum sed regiis ∼is *Chr. S. Alb.* 56; **1447** Johannem imprisonavit ac ibidem sub tam diris carceribus in ∼o tam obscuro et tenebroso .. detinuit *Pat* 464 m. 9. **b** quem Dominus de ∼o hujus saeculi vocare dignatus est *RegulC* 67; quem pietas Salvatoris noluit diutius in ∼o tenere BYRHT. *V. Osw.* 470. **c** (ÆTHELWALD) *Carm. Aldh.* 2. 85 (v. caro 4c); ALDH. *VirgV* 830 (v. carneus 3a); *Id. VirgP* 14, BEDE *HE* IV 3, etc. (v. corpus 2b); **742** BONIF. *Ep.* 50 (v. corporeus 1); ex quo pontificis linquens ergastula carnis / spiritus alta petens scandit super astra polorum ALCUIN *SS Ebor* 678; **1073** quatenus .. Deus aut ad meliorem fructum me perducat aut de ∼o hujus carnis animam meam .. educat LANFR. *Ep.* 43 (18); **1156** ut anima de carnis ∼o letior exeat J. SAL. *Ep.* 102 (8); *to dye,* .. de corporeo spiritus sese relaxavit †argatustulo, vel sic: anima resoluta est ab argastulo carnis *CathA.* **d** ut in caelis nequaquam ascendatis, sed infaustis Tartari ∼is .. decidatis GILDAS *EB* 109; altera [miseria est] in ∼o inferorum quam perditi post mortem patientur ALEX. CANT. *Dicta* 5 p. 128; c**1300** anime defunctorum de purgatorii ∼o .. liberantur *Lit. Cant.* I 13.

3 birdcage.

UPTON 185 (v. catasta 1d).

4 imprisonment.

quosdam longo gravique ∼o .. afflixit ORD. VIT. XI 3; ad mortem perpetuo inclusus ∼o W. MALM. *GR* V 398.

ergata [LL *gl.* < ἐργάτης], worker.

∼a, †operata [? l. operator] *GlC* E 286.

ergis [ἔργις], labour.

∼is .. labor dicitur, sed ergon opus *Alph.* 100.

ergo [CL]

1 (conj.) therefore, accordingly; **b** (log.); **c** (jussive); **d** (in question); **e** (in dialogue); **f** (ellipt.).

705 in adversis .. tuae .. considerationis industriam consulari .. necessitas meam .. parvitatem perurget. inde ∼o, nunc instante necessitatum causa quid agi debeat, tuae benivolentiae ingenium flagitando inquirere opus pretium reor WEALDHERE *Ep.* 22; accersitus est a sanctimoniali .. Æbba. veniens ∼o .. *V. Cuthb.* I 3; **725** (10c) testium ∼o .. signa aeterna demonstrabo *CS* 144; tandem obtinuit ut ad languentem intraret; intravit ∼o BEDE *HE* V 3 p. 286; fletibus .. deposcit opem medicantis. / ergo pater .. / passibus approperat conferre juvamen FRITH. 1355; **963** (11c) ego O. ∼o Christi chrismate presul judicatus *CS* 1105. **b** si .. in Deo tres personas sunt una tantum res .., ∼o Pater et Spiritus Sanctus cum Filio est incarnatus ANSELM (*Incarn. B* 1) II 4; innotescat ∼o ex his que dicta sunt elective interrogatorum quedam simplicia quedam multiplicia esse BALSH. *AD rec. 2* 177; *Ps.*-GROS. *Gram.* 32 (v. domuitas); HALES *Sent.* III 85 (v. duo); WYCL. *Dom. Div.* 9 (v. dominium 1a). **c 836** scitote ∼o nos qui [etc.] *CS* 416; †c**950** (12c) oportet nos ∼o, fratres .., istum contempnere mundum *CS* 894. **d** quid ∼o simile hujus temporis sceleribus? GILDAS *EB* 38; quid ∼o? numquamne dactilus in fine ponitur? ALDH. *Met.* 9 p. 89. **e** 'qualiter accusator vel defensor .. impulsione .. uti debet?' '∼o accusator, cum impulsione aliquid factum esse dicet ..' ALCUIN *Rhet.* 18. **f** numquid .. valles fluent mel et lac? sugamus ∼o mel de petra GIR. *TH intr.* p. 6.

2 (prep., w. gen.) for the sake of, because of.

tumulus .. quem .. lucri ∼o .. adquirendi defodientes scindebant FELIX *Guthl.* 28; ob hoc cernuus omnipotentem deprecor orans / idem quatinus haud omittat criminis ergo / perpetuali infaustum subdi segnitiei OSW. *Vers.* 12; ad quas [reliquias] .. olim fiebat religionis ∼o Christiani populi concursus LESLEY *RGScot* 27; CAMD. *Br.* 138 (v. eques 3d).

ergolabus [CL < ἐργολάβος], contractor.

idem de ergalabis, i. e. laborantibus in ergasteriis .. ergalabi dicuntur qui sunt in ergasteriis, stationibus .. alii dicunt quod illi dicuntur ergalabi qui conducunt mancipia ut carius locent VAC. *Lib. Paup.* 165.

ergon [ἔργον], work.

∼a ta [ex emeron vel] exaemeron, id est opus sex dierum .. edidit ALDH. *VirgP* 27; *Alph.* 100 (v. ergis).

erica, ∼e [CL]

1 heather (prob. *Calluna vulgaris*).

de oleribus ad idem [sc. fecunditatem] valent menta, sparagus, pastinata, ∼a, rapa. .. de speciebus .. zinziber conditum .. semen ∼e, semen mercurialis KYMER 19; *Ib.* (v. eryngion); in planis et locis ∼a consitis .. [galerita] degit TURNER *Av.* E 1.

2 (?) colophony, Greek pitch.

∼e, i. colofonia, quedam gumma *Alph.* 58.

ericetum, heath, moor.

dum esset .. sancta Brigida foris in ∼o juxta gregem ovium monasterii sui *V. Brig.* II 72; recta littus porrigitur, per Purbecke insulam, quam vocant, magna ex parte ∼um, et saltuosam, damis cervisque refertam CAMD. *Br.* 177 (cf. ib. 188: Guilielmum Briewr, quia in ∼o natus, sic denominatum).

ericius [CL], **∼io (her-)**

1 hedgehog; **b** (fig.). **c** porcupine. **d** sea-urchin. *Cf.* 2 *echinus* 1, *erinaceus* 1.

∼ius, *iil GlC* E 303; spiculorum .. aculeis circumfossus .. velut asper ∼ius ABBO *Edm.* 10; rege .. venante .. exsiliit ∼ius .. tanquam tumultu venantium excitatus .. ipse .. ad mare festinabat portans in dorso suo librum intitulatum Actus Apostolorum W. CANT. *V. Thom.* 32; lupus defunctus est: .. ∼ii cereos portaverunt O. CHERITON *Fab.* 43; judicavit de mutacione ventorum per ∼ium, qui certas in se fecit mutaciones ante varietatem ventorum BACON V 10; hic ∼ius, *a hurchyn WW.* **b** fiat, Domine, cor meum ∼ius plenus spinis AILR. *Serm.* 440D. **c** Plinius [*HN* VIII 125] .. et Isidorus .. memorant [hystricem] esse animal in Affrica quod Affri ∼ii genus dicunt W. MALM. *GR* V 409. **d** yricii qui in mari inveniuntur GILB. III 172. 2; erinacius sive ∼ius animal est spinosum cujus due sunt species, sc. aquaticus et terrestris *SB* 20.

2 (in explanation of bibl. usage) porcupine, coney, hare; *cf. choerogryllus* a, *erinaceus* 2. **b** (w. ref. to *Is.* xiv 23) kind of bird. (*Cf. Is.* xxxiv 11).

BACON *CSPhil.* 483 (v. erinaceus 2). **b** in eorum oculis patria nudabatur hostilique depredatione in domos ∼ii redigebatur *G. Steph.* I 61.

3 thistle.

erithius, *brad thistle Gl. Durh.*

4 (mil.) spiked palisade.

1167 pro ∼io claudendo xvij s. iij d. *Pipe* 147; **1173** in operatione j magni fossati circa castellum .. cum heric' et bretesch' *Pipe* 116; a**1180** liberam .. ab opere putei et pontis et britesche et hericeon et ab omni alio opere ad castellum pertinente *Reg. Plympton* 154; **1198** in operationibus domorum et hericonorum et fossatorum de Cultura .. et in operationibus de pontibus et breticis et hericonibus de versus Toenie *RScacNorm* II 309; **1212** in reparacione palitii et ∼io novo xxx s. *Pipe Ir.* 56; **1215** villam de D. claudi faciatis ∼one et palo secundum quod fossatum factum exigit *Cl* 192b; **1231** ad hirucones circa villam Salopie faciendas *Cl* 508; **1235** quiete .. de clausura facienda ad ∼ium de Pikering' *RChart* 28 m. 16; **1264** faciat habere .. hominibus regis de S. usque ad l vel lx carrettatas subbosci ad herisones et alias clausturas faciendas circa villam regis S. .. ad .. defensionem ville *Cl* 340; **1314** pro reparacione ∼onis nihil hoc anno, quia non accidit nisi quolibet tercio anno (*DL MinAc*) *N. Riding Rec. Soc.* II 15 (cf. ib. IV 196 [**1322**]: pro reparacione †hericini circa *barbkambe* castri); **1326** debent facere hirsonas circa domos domini *BB St. Davids* 248.

5 (as adj.) spiky.

abundat capillis .. et pili per loca .. sunt grossi et ∼ii M. SCOT *Phys.* 27 (cf. ib. 33, 38: capilli .. rari sunt in cuti, ac grossi .. et plus ∼ii; .. pilis nigris et ∼iis).

erif- v. eriph-.

erigere [CL]

1 to lift, raise up, direct upwards; **b** (part of body; also fig.); **c** (naut.); **d** (math.). **e** (p. ppl. *erectus*) upright, pointing upwards; **f** (mus.); **g** taut, stiff; **h** (w. ref. to eyes) bright, alert.

princeps / qui sceptrum regni Solimis erexit ALDH. *VirgV* 2140; EGB. *Pont.* 119 (v. 2 cloca 2); sol .. poros ejus [nenufaris] .. aperit et dilatat unde caput ∼ere videtur *Quaest. Salern.* B 221; s**616** erectis vestibus quantis esset verberibus laceratus ostendit M. PAR. *Maj.* I 266 (cf. BEDE *HE* II 6: retecto [v. l. recto] vestimento); **1266** ∼ens .. hachiam (v. Daneschus). **b** erectis ad aethera palmis ALDH. *VirgP* 1; expansis cruribus erecti pedes ad coelos sursum prominebant *V. Cuthb.* I 3; GIR. *TH* III 10 (v. deprimere 1a); Moyses manus non demisisse sed erexisse describitur ut Amalech sterneretur [*Exod.* xvii 10–13] J. SAL. *Ep.* 201 (234); *Quaest. Salern.* B 6 (v. eicere 3c); ∼e sursum [ME: *hold up*] oculos et manus ad celum *AncrR* 109; vidit quasi equum stantem super pedes posteriores, pedibus anterioribus sursum erectis *Ghost Stories* 414. **c** sublimant alii malos; aliique laborant / erectis malis addere vela sua G. AMIENS *Hast.* 83; ventis instantibus erexit vela sua G. MON. IV 7; **1296** in mercede xij marinariorum .. laborancium circa malum ∼endum in galea *Ac. Galley Newcastle* 181; ∼i fecit veli virgam in medium mali ut .. suam promptitudinem velandi ostenderet *G. Hen. V* 3; quidam .. tempestate dispersi .. erecta carbasa tenuerunt *Ib.* 25. **d** dividam .. lineam *DF* equaliter in punctum *G* et ∼am super latus *GD* quadratum *GKMD* ROB. ANGL. *Alg.* 132. **e** queritur quare galli habeant cristas multum ∼as *Quaest. Salern.* B 199; **1307** ne .. crucem suam ∼am per .. diocesim Lond' .. deferre presumat *Lit. Cant.* III 352. **f** si tractum habeat a parte dextra solummodo ascendentem, ∼a longa vocatur HAUDLO 383; *Ib.* 384 (v. brevis 3b). **g** non .. corpus ∼um et rigidum est, sed membra .. motabilia requiescebant *V. Cuthb.* IV 14. **h** ∼ior oculis AILR. *Ed. Conf.* 749A (v. dissolvere 4b).

2 to raise, construct, set up: **a** (building or part); **b** (other structure).

a hoc templum Bugge .. / .. erexit ALDH. *CE* 3. 2; erectis castrorum turribus altis *Id. VirgV* 646; nulla ecclesia, nullum altare in .. Berniciorum gente erectum est BEDE *HE* III 2 p. 130; qui edificium facere vult stabile .. soliditatem prius considerat terre, quo .. parietem ∼ere .. possit *Simil. Anselmi* 98; Geroiano baroni .. castrum S. Serenici .. erexit ORD. VIT. III 2 p. 28; AD. EYNS. *Hug.* III 12 (v. contentiosus 2a); a**1260** (v. aula 4b); **1338** in reparacione medietatis infirmarie .. que fuit erecta a solo *Ac. Durh.* 201. **b** Romani .. erexerunt statuam *Lib. Monstr.* I 3; Osuald signum sanctae crucis erexit BEDE *HE* III 2 p. 128; jussit ut .. machinas ∼erent ORD. VIT. XIII 8 p. 16; OSB. BAWDSEY clxix (v. convictualis 2); gigantes eam [choream] mirabiliter erexerunt GIR. *TH* II 18; **1237** (v. deguttare 1b); **1266** (v. bretescha a); s**1306** erexerunt papiliones et tentoria *Flor. Hist.* III 131; **1359** pro badiis .. errigendis (v. 2 baia); **1411** ut .. pagendam .. ∼erent (v. 2 contractus 2a); habent potestatem .. ∼endi altare, etiam sub divo W. SAY *Lib. Reg. Cap.* 66.

3 to heap up; **b** (fig.). **c** (intr.) to rise, be heaped.

13.. cum una acra et uno fossato erecto de terra Thome *Reg. Malm.* II 295; **1310** terra erecta de eodem fossato *MinAc Essex* (*Birdbrook*). **b** si non tantos .. malitiae episcoporum .. ∼i adversus Deum vidissem montes GILDAS *EB* 65. **c** c**1300** de .. parcella terre jacente [etc.] .. una cum uno itinere in latitudine xvj pedum ad eandem terram juxta .. fossatum ∼entem *Reg. Malm.* II lxxvi.

4 (with ref. to living things, partly fig.): **a** (refl. or pass.) to rise, stand up; **b** (p. ppl. *erectus*). **c** (trans.) to lift, help to stand.

a surculamen incredulitatis .. plantaverat, quod .. venenatis imbribus irrigatum et ad Dei offensam .. se ∼ens parricidii .. crimen producit GILDAS *EB* 28; paraliticus .. / .. / debilis .. ut se / .. nulla ratione valeret / erigere WULF. *Swith.* I 1206; cum Evangelium legeretur ad reverentiam .. misterii sese ∼i fecit *V. Gund.* 46; sic .. [quedam animalia] expeditius ∼untur et celerius *Quaest. Salern.* W 8; terminata .. oracione ∼et se regina et genuflectet W. SAY *Lib. Reg. Cap.* 97. **b** nunc quomodo ferrum inhereat lapidi decumbentes explorant, nunc ∼i se invicem coarctantur ut videant AILR. *Ed. Conf.* 780C; [homo] Grece *antropos,* i. 'sursum ∼us' appellatur BART. ANGL. III 1; teneatis vos ∼as [ME: *up richt*] in firma fide *AncrR* 99. **c** cadaver .. de porta mortis redivivum erexit ad lumina vitae ALDH. *VirgP* 26; memento .. ut, sicut gratia Dei te sic sublimavit, sic misericordia tua ∼at quem culpa sua sic humiliavit ANSELM (*Or.* 8) III 26; fortuna .. prostratum .. spe melius ∼it ORD. VIT. XII 19 p. 364; ubi .. quilibet tenet manum alterius, si aliquis labescat alius eum ∼it [ME: *breit up*] priusquam omnino cadat *AncrR* 93.

5 to raise (spiritually or mentally). **b** (p. ppl. *erectus*) resolute.

erecto ad superna desideria mentis intuitu BEDE *Hom.* I 16. 261; ∼e nos [AS: *ahef usig*] ad consedentem in dextera tua *Rit. Durh.* 35; excita nunc, anima mea, et ∼e totum intellectum tuum ANSELM (*Prosl.* 24) I 117; *Id.* (*Or.* 17) III 70 (v. exigere 6c); EADMER *Excell. B. M.* 578B (v. dejectio 2a). **b 864** (12c) ab omnibus catholicis ∼am fidem colentibus *CS* 410; his auditis nostri .. animis ∼i per dies amplius hostes infestare OSB. BAWDSEY clxviii.

6 to promote, raise up; **b** (w. *in*); **c** (of institution). *Cf. eligere* 2.

rex .. dejectis .. Merciorum .. consulibus .. ex infimis Normannorum clientibus tribunos .. ditissimos erexit ORD. VIT. IV 7 p. 218; Moyses de Egyptiorum tenebrosis sordibus virtutis predicator ∼itur R. COLD. *Osw.* 8; **1480**

ad visitandum prioratum .. necnon .. ad deponendum, ~endum et absolvendum, citandum, suspendendum .. [subditorum] quoscunque *Reg. Whet.* II 213. **b** [Brutus] erectus .. in ducem convocat undique Trojanos et oppida Assaraci munivit G. MON. I 4; **s1040** Hardecnut .. adductum .. in regem erexerunt *Chr. Rams.* 149; Egbertum filium suum ante mortem in regem erectum [= W. MALM. *GR* I 94: inunctum] SILGRAVE 25; **s1016** postquam erectus est in regem [= H. HUNT. *HA* VI 12: electus] B. COTTON 182; Karolum Magnum, qui post obitum patris sui .. in regem ~itur [v. l. eligitur] *Eul. Hist.* II 122; **1385** (v. creare 3b); **s1399** AD. USK 26 (v. contemporarius). **c 1395** parochialem ecclesiam .. in collegiatam ~ere *Lit. Cant.* III 45; **1430** (v. collegium 1c); **1470** ecclesia de W... erecta .. de cella in abbathiam *Reg. Whet.* I 148.

7 (w. abstr. obj.) to institute, uphold, maintain.

primum .. est quod volo, ut recta lex ~atur et omnis injuria dejiciatur .. Deique rectitudo ~atur (*Cons. Cnuti*) *GAS* 309 (= *Quad. Ib.*: ut juste leges ~antur; AS: *þæt man rihte laga upp arære*); si quis .. unlagam ~at vel injustum judicium judicet .. (*Quad.*) *Ib.* 319 (= *Cons. Cnuti*: quicunque .. injusticiam statuerit; AS: *and se ðe inlage rære*); ad officium [advocati] .. pertinet lapsa ~ere, fatigata reparare sue defensionis viribus W. DROGHEDA *SA* 33; **1403** vigilias more pastoris tam corporales quam mentales ~imus, visuri quid gregi .. expediat (*Lit. Papae*) AD. USK 79.

8 **a** (incl. refl.) to rise, exalt (oneself); **b** (w. var. parts of body, fig.) to behave insolently or rebelliously. **c** (p. ppl. *erectus*) cocky, insolent.

a et vos, ac si Lucifer .. de caelo projectus, verbis non potestate ~imini GILDAS *EB* 74; angeli .. creaturam sese inlicitis ~entem examine districtionis premunt BEDE *Gen.* (xi 7) 125; amor sine timore ~it in presumptionem ALEX. BATH *Mor.* I 69 p. 135; **s1202** M. PAR. *Min.* II 95 (v. cervicose). **b** erit .. [vestrum] his .. demisso vultu obedire aut supercilio erecto contraire *Chr. Battle* f. 64v.; ex eis qui contra eum cervicem erexerant de Anglia quosdam exlegavit *G. Walth.* 115; AD. SCOT *OP* 522B (v. cervix c); **1317** ad impugnandum jura regalia et rebellionis calcaneum .. ~endum in regem eundem patenter inducunt *Mon. Hib. & Scot.* 194a; **1350, s1459** (v. calcaneus 2c); **s1415** (v. 2 cauda 1e). **c s1203** rex .. Francorum .. ex .. elongatione regis J. factus ~ior M. PAR. *Min.* II 99.

9 (?) to remove by lifting.

1354 que .. obstupacio ad duos dies lete .. presentata fuit, et preceptum fuit per senescallum .. ~ere, et erecta fuit *Pub. Works* I 188.

10 to upset (moot).

si placitum populi exererit propter extractionem armorum suorum xl sol. solvat comiti (*Inst. Cnuti*) *GAS* 73 (= *Quad. ib.*: si quis *folcgemot*, id est populi placitum, armorum exercione turbabit, emendet .. cxx sol. wite; AS: *gif he folcgemot mid wæpnes bryde arære*).

11 (intr.) to arise, crop up.

1327 contencio erexit inter Willelmum H. .. et Willelmum filium Johannis .. et quilibet eorum alterum vilificavit *Rec. Leic.* II 2.

erigeron [CL < ἠριγέρων], groundsel (*Senecio vulgaris*).

12.. iregerontis, i. *cenesuns*, i. *grundeswilie WW*; sisamus .. folia habet minuta, similia †geronchee *Alph.* 172.

erigibilis, erigible, erectile.

radius declinat ad perpendicularem ~em a puncto casus sui super medium secundum PECKHAM *Persp.* I 15.

erilis (her-) [CL]

1 appropriate or due to a lord, of a lord. **b** of God.

postquam ad proprium pervenit herum, .. metu ~i territus siluit dominoque in timore distulit quod .. amico spopondit LANTFR. *Swith.* 1; qua re dum ~i assisteret obsequio, hujusce rei .. subintulit querimoniam W. MALM. *GP* IV 172; reum esse mortis definitum est, qui sodalibus de morte domini tractantibus consenserit, nec eos pro ~i exitio perculerit ORD. VIT. IV 14 p. 266; assit amor constans, absit timor omnis herilis D. BEC. 808; Resi principis ex sorore nepotibus .. ~i portione, sicut Gualensibus mos est, pro patre dominantibus GIR. *IK* 1 7 (cf. id. *DK* II 9: paternam hereditatem filii inter se .. ~i portione dividere contendunt). **b** herilis at mox buccina / respondit BEDE *Hymn.* 6. 25; **c720** corpora .. in terrae pulvere .. requiescunt, iterum resurrectura in die necessitatis quando ~is tuba concrepat (EANGYTH) *Ep. Bonif.* 14; **1019** (14c) postquam .. protoplaustus .. praeceptum †heriale .. floccipendit *CD* 730; **1048** (13c) ~is promulgando intonat buccina *Ch. Burton* 38; hic agnis Domini / pabula verbi / donat, corporeae / tempore vitae / dispensando fide / pondus herile *Anal. Hymn.* LI 183.

2 noble, lordly. **b** (as sb. m.) nobleman.

moenibus in superis resides patronus herilis WULF. *Poems* 13; matronam ~em *Lib. Eli.* III 60; dat verba canis: "me ditat herilis / gracia, cum domino me cibat ipsa domus" WALT. ANGL. *Fab.* 51. 3; rege propinquante comites glomerantur heriles R. MAIDSTONE *Conc.* 285; ~i, i. nobili; .. ~is, *lordlyche WW*. **b** Anglia .. / .. / fortes, subtiles, claros, agiles dat heriles *Pol. Poems* I 54.

erim- v. et. erem-. **erimigio** v. eremio. **erimola** v. harmala.

erinaceus [cf. CL irenaceus], **~ius (her-)**

1 **a** hedgehog. **b** sea urchin. *Cf. 2 echinus* 1, *ericius* 1.

a 10.. yricius vel ~ius, *il WW*; de invidia: .. exemplum de ~io, qui de urina propria, quam in gravamen emittit aliorum, primitus pergravatur, ut dicit philosophus *Spec. Laic.* 44; **s1402** ad Scotos procedentes arcitenentes Angli ipsos .. ad modum ~ii tanquam cetis et spinis hispidos reddiderunt FORDUN *Cont.* XV 14; hic ~ius, A. *hurchon*, .. *nurchon WW*; .. hic †irmacius, *a hurchyn WW*. **b** *SB* 20 (v. ericius 1d); elchinus, ericius, ~ius idem. animal est spinosum cujus due sunt species, sc. aquaticus et terrenus, que nobilior est *Alph.* 54–55.

2 (in explanation of Bibl. usage) coney or rock badger (Heb. *saphan*, χοιρόγρυλλος), conf. w. porcupine or hare. (*Cf. Lev.* xi 5; *Deut.* xiv 7; *Psalm* ciii 18; *Prov.* xxx 26; and commentary, Jerome *Ep.* 106. 65. 6). *Cf. choerogryllus* a, *ericius* 2a.

~ius, lepus *GlH* E 326; petra refugium et virtus est etiam ~iis ROB. BRIDL. *Dial.* 5; ~ius, lepus vel gens invalida OSB. GLOUC. *Deriv.* 200. BART. ANGL. XVIII 62 (v. choerogryllus a); Hieronymus .. dicit quod *saphan* Hebreum significat leporem, ericium seu ~ium, et chirogryllum BACON *CSPhil.* 483; cum ~iis refugium mihi est humilis petra solide veritatis (KYN.) *Ziz.* 15.

erinos [CL < ἔρινος], plant like basil.

†ercinos nascitur in fluviis et circa puteum, folia habens ozimo similia et divisa in summo, hastas v vel vj duabus palmis longas et flores albos *Alph.* 59.

Erinys [CL < Ἐρινύς], Fury. **b** Valkyrie.

Erenis, *haegtis*, Furia *GlC* E 283; **9..** Erenis, *hægtes WW*; manibus infernis, ut fortis mandat Erinis, / expedit ammisso plebs cara cruore litari FRITH. 377; cur vivo, Domine, dira servatus Herine? R. CANT. *Malch.* III 151 (cf. ib. V 60: serva repentinis hunc febribus artat Herinis); Erinis ORD. VIT. XI *pref.* p. 160 (v. Erebus); **s1440** Erinis AMUND. II 221 (v. exasperare 3a). **b** Eurynis, *Walcyrge GlC* E 351 (cf. ib. H 87: Herinis, *Walcrigge*).

eripere [CL]

1 to pluck out. **b** to wrest away. **c** (?) to deduct.

s1174 precepit ut oculos ei ~erent [v. l. eruerent] *G. Hen. II* I 80. **b** diripio, i. rapio, abstraho, ~io, *ic ætbrede* vel *ic forgripe*, aufero *GlH* D 544; quam [libertatem] si ipsi dii conarentur nobis ~ere .. G. MON. IV 2; non cessavit donec illud [castellum] a manibus illorum .. ~uit GIR. *EH* II 15. **c 1457** pro expensis .. tantum †erepitur de summa supra expensarum quas fecit .. Willelmus in primo compoto suo *ExchScot* 325.

2 to rescue, snatch (from danger or disaster); **b** (spiritual).

s1011 quem .. Ælfegus archiepiscopus ~uit a morte *ASChr.*; ut me .. a quadam ordinis nostri fluctuatione .. ~ere dignemini (*Lit. Abbatis ad Papam*) ORD. VIT. III 7 p. 97; suis puerique sui magnis conatibus ~itur, nec omnino indempnis MAP *NC* II 12 f. 27; M. PAR. *Maj.* V 123 (v. confinium 1c); ut .. supremus judex .. nos .. ~eret de Gallorum gladiis *G. Hen. V* 10. **b** magnas antiquo hosti praedas .. baptizando ~uit BEDE *HE* II 20; ut ipse me pius pastor .. ab inferni tenebris ~iat ALCH. *Or.* 155; de errore quotquot voluit Redemptor ~uit PULL. *Sent.* 743C.

eriphion [LL < ἐρίφιον], (?) 'lithwort', dwarf elder (*Sambucus ebulus*). *Cf. chamaeacte, ebulus.*

10.. erifeon, *liðwyrt*, idem est ostriago *WW*; erifeon, *lith wyrt Gl. Durh.*; †erificium herba est que in summis montibus invenitur, folia habet similia appio, florem violacium intrinsecum, semen recentem (*sic*) *Alph.* 59.

erisima, erismon v. erysimum. **erisip-** v. erysip-. **erithius** v. ericius 3. **eritridanum, eritrodanum** v. erythrodanum. **eritron** v. erythros. **ermenia** v. epimenia. **ermeticus** v. eremiticus 2a. **ermi-** v. et. erem-. **ermigio** v. eremio.

ermina, ~ium, ~us (herm-) [OF *ermine, hermine*], ermine, stoat (*Mustela erminea*). **b** fur of ermine. *Cf. 2 eremiticus.*

insula [Hibernia] .. caret ~is GIR. *TH* I 26; luterium, mustelarum, ~arum .. satis copia est que nunc gravi hieme .. laqueis .. capiuntur *Lib. Eli.* II 105. **b** Kaius dapifer ~io honoratus, mille .. nobilibus comitatus qui omnes ~io induti fercula .. ministrabant G. MON. IX 13; **1138** prohibemus .. sanctimoniales .. marterinis, beverinis pellibus, hereminis, anulis aureis uti (*Conc. Lond.* 14) GERV. CANT. *Chr.* 108; **1200** (v. cisimus); **1205** coopertorium .. urlat' de *ermine Cl* 25a; **1208** j penulam de ermin' pro iiij li. xiij s. et iiij d. *Cl* 88b; **1213** sex penulas de ~a *Cl* 145b; **1251** pallia furrentur de ~o *Cl* 13; **1302** abbas et .. predecessores sui habuerunt wreccum maris .. preterquam aurum, balenam, pannos de scarleto et irmina, cum acciderint *PQW* 110a; **1303** (v. bever); **1331** per unam supertunicam de grosso vario, et unam duodenam de ~o .. xliij s. iiij d. *ExchScot* 365; **s1399** omnes heroes regni in rubio, scarleto et ~io ornanter induti AD. USK 33; mantello aureo desuper furrato cum arimineo W. SAY *Lib. Reg. Cap.* 69.

erminalis, (her.) of ermine. *Cf. 2 eremiticus.*

crucem ereminalem BAD. AUR. 192; crucem ~em UPTON 222 (v. 2 eremiticus a).

ermula v. hermula.

1 erna, ~esium [ME, AN *ernes*, OF *erre* < arra], earnest money, pledge. *V. et. arra.*

11.. si burgensis aliquid forum vel aliquem mercem emerit et hernas dederit *Borough Cust.* I 217; **1221** si .. homines emerint bladum aut aliam mercandisam, ubi *ernes* dederint, nullus inde eos perturbabit *SelPlCrown* 98; **1279** pro qua lana dicti mercatores solverunt .. religiosis in errestum (*sic*) pre manibus mille marcas bonorum sterlingorum *LTRMem* 52 m. 13; **1322** recepit unum denarium racione ~esii super vendicionem *FormA* 91.

2 erna [cf. ἀρήν, acc. ἄρνα], ewe lamb.

hec ~a, A. *a hewlambe WW*.

3 erna [ME *ern*], erne, white-tailed eagle (*Haliaetus*).

pygargus Anglorum lingua, nisi fallar, ~a vocatur TURNER *Av.* B 6.

Ernaldensis v. Arnaldensis. **ernesium** v. 1 erna. **ero-** v. et. erro-. **erobus** v. orobus.

erodius, ~ion, (her-) [LL < ἐρωδιός; cf. CL ardea]

1 (w. ref. to bibl. or CL usage) egret or heron, conf. w. swan. (*Cf. Deut.* xiv 16, *Lev.* xi 9, *Job* xxxix 13, *Psalm* ciii 17; Pliny *HN* X 126).

~ios, Gr., *swan* ÆLF. *Gl.*; **10..** ~ios (v. Diomedeus); quidam boni passeres quorum dux ~ii domus, petra videlicet Christus erat ROB. BRIDL. *Dial.* 4; pennas strucio gestat / hĕrōdii pennis ancipitrisque pares [cf. *Job* xxxix 13] GOWER *VC* IV 1060; herodies UPTON 186 (v. Diomedeus).

2 bird of prey: **a** goshawk or sim.; **b** gerfalcon or sim.; **c** unspec.

a ~ius, *walchhabuc GlC* H 83; ~ion, *walchefuc Gl. Leid.* 19. 35; *goshawke*, ancipiter, .. ~ius *PP*; *a goshauke*, .. ~ius *CathA* (v. accipiter). **b** assit pertica cui insidere possit nisus et capus, ~ius [*gl.*: *merilun, gerfauk*], alietus NECKAM *Ut.* 100; *gerfawcen*, ~ius *PP*; ~ius qui et *girfale*, ut glossa super Leviticum dicit, in loco ubi aves immunde prohibentur, vel girfalcus dicitur. inter omnes autem aves nobiles nobilissima avis est, colore vestita ceruleo UPTON 187 (cf. ib. 188: aliud genus [falconum] est illud quod ~ius vel vulgariter girfalcus dicitur); *a fawcon*, ~ius, falco, .. *a gerfaucon*, ~ius *CathA*. **c** ibi omnis generis volucres maxime que ex rapto vivunt .. ibi milvi, ibi accipitres, ibi lari, ibi ~ii H. BOS. *LM* 1320; dicit Plinius quod ~ius et consimiles aves in die quo audiunt aquilam vix predantur BART. ANGL. XII 2 (cf. ib. 21: ~ius est avis regia prede avida et manu gestantis assueta; est autem avis animosa ad modum accipitris); **c1260** (v. chirotheca 2d).

erogacitas, generosity.

quod sibi filioque reservabat paupercule laudabilis parcitas, tantulum ipsum non deficere laudabilior ~as impetravit P. BLOIS *Opusc.* 1006C.

erogare [CL]

1 to pay. **b** to invest.

sumtuarius, qui ~at sumtos (*sic*) *GlC* S 660; primogenitum meum .. litteris imbuendum .. didascalo mancipavi, eique locum .. inter vernulas Dei apud Uticum .. procuravi; pro quo eulogias benedictionis xxx sc. marcos argenti .. ~avi ORD. VIT. V 14 p. 420; ~are .. impendere OSB. GLOUC. *Deriv.* 193. **b 1167** talentum vobis creditum ~ate [cf. *Matth.* xxv 15–27] J. SAL. *Ep.* 226 (226); ~are, .. prorogare OSB. GLOUC. *Deriv.* 193.

2 to give, bestow as a gift; **b** (alms or sim., esp. to the poor). **c** (pr. ppl.) generous, charitable.

GlC D 312 (v. dispungere a); **s990** (v. cochlea 3); subtiles .. versus .. edidit studioque juniorum, quibus ipsi emendarentur, sine invidia ~avit ORD. VIT. IV 7 p. 218; non margaritas set siliquas collegi quasi pecoribus ~andas *Spec. Laic. prol.*; a Deo hec tria tibi erogata cognosce *NLA* (*Wenefreda*) II 419. **b** pauperculorum .. quos sumptuosa ~atae stipis alimonia sustentabat ALDH. *VirgP* 23; *Ib.* 27 (v. agape a); cuncta quae sibi .. donabantur mox pauperibus .. ~are gaudebat BEDE *HE* III 5; multimoda .. indumentorum genera .. pauperibus ~abat *V. Gund.* 29; **1206** (v. corredium 3a); **1234** (v. elemosinarius 4a); ad ~andum [ME: *dealen*] .. pauperibus bona paterna *AncrR* 81; **s1386** (v. crucesignatio); cum .. nec haberet quod pauperibus erogaret *NLA* (*Piranus*) II 321; **1467** ~avimus Fratribus Minoribus .. xx s. *Arch. Hist. Camb.* II 430*n*. **c** Cantuarie archipresul .. sed pecuniarum .. possessor avidior quam ~antior *G. Steph.* I 4.

3 to grant: **a** (land); **b** (letters patent).

a ut .. terram .. ~aret *Meaux* I 83–4 (v. 1 cangium a). **b 1219** quatenus .. super ea nobis vestras patentes literas dignemini ~are (*AncC* III 58) *RL* I 46.

4 to award.

cui . . licet . . vetustatem juris abrogare vel ei derogare et justis premia ~are et penas malis irrogare? R. Niger *Mil.* II 3.

5 a to administer (sacrament). **b** to spread (gospel).

a 1195 decrevimus . . ut non . . diaconus baptizet vel corpus Christi cuiquam ~et (*Conc. Ebor.*) R. Howd. III 295. **b** Petrus . . divini verbi semina . . ~avit Sæwulf 836; quoniam †episcopus [l. episcopos] vices apostolorum ad ~andum verbum Dei agere scimus Eadmer *V. Dunst.* 13; tuum erat verbum ~are: Dei est bonam vitam exigere erogatorem verbi Gascoigne *Loci* 59.

6 to amplify (statute).

illa capitula non derogant statuto, sed ~ant, unde potest multiplicius adimpleri Conway *Def. Mend.* 1339.

7 to entreat.

1477 monachi . . pro illius anima . . Deum ~are debent *Lit. Cant.* III 294.

erogatio [LL], erogation, distribution, almsgiving. **b** distributed sum, alms.

vestiarium, ~o vestis quod accipit miles *GlC* U 140; G. Cold. *Durh.* 7 (v. dispersio 2); **1192** que unquam ecclesia . . super ~onibus domini Eliensis vel ecclesiarum gravamine verbum ad nos miserat aut querelam? (*Lit. Cleric. Rotomag.*) *G. Ric. I* 243; *Cust. Westm.* 178 (v. elemosinarius 3b); **1467** piis fidelium votis . . et illis presertim que ~ones elemosinarum divinique cultus augmentum . . aspicere dinoscuntur *Reg. Glasg.* 414. **b** inpendium, ~o *GlC* I 398; **1353** eidem [sc. elemosynario] pro errogacione Walteri de W. et Johannis de C. x s. *Sacr. Ely* II 157; **1415** volo . . quod . . pecunia . . per viam vendicionis recepta disponatur pro anima mea . . in celebracionibus missarum, ~onibus pauperum et aliis operibus pietatis *Reg. Cant.* III 405; [elemosinarius regis] elemosinarum largiciones et ~ones . . destribuere precipiat *Plusc.* VII 18.

erogator [LL]

1 investor (fig.).

Osb. *V. Dunst.* 44 (v. doctrina 1c).

2 bestower, distributor. **b** (w. *verbi*) preacher.

quotiens . . largius de bonis ipsis [? l. ipsius] distribuendo erogatur, totiens omnium bonorum ubertas suos ~ores comitatur R. Cold. *Cuthb.* 106; [abbas A., ob. **1077**] erat tam divitibus quam pauperibus ~or largissimus *Chr. Evesham* 93. **b** Gascoigne *Loci* 59 (v. erogare 5b).

erogatrix, generous (f.).

~ix, prodiga, larga *GlH* E 330.

eron- v. erron-. **eros** v. heros.

erotema [LL < ἐρώτημα], (rhet.) question.

~a, interrogatio *GlC* E 280.

erotice [cf. CL eroticus < ἐρωτικός; cf. ἐρωτικῶς], erotically.

aliquando procedat herotice, quod est amatorie [*gl.*: herotice dicitur ab 'heros, -ois', G. *baron*] Garl. *Dict.* 133.

erp- v. herp-, serp-. **err-** v. et. aer-.

errabilis [LL], wandering. **b** errable, (one) liable to error.

~es *huerbende GlC* E 300; ~is, vertibilis, *hwerfende GlH* E 348. **b** authenticissima . . est allegacio prophetarum cum dicunt "hec dicit Dominus"; non autem "hec dicit Priscianus" . . aut quilibet aliorum ~ium Bradw. *CD* 610A; hinc dico . . quod locus a testimonio Augustini non est infallibilis, cum Augustinus sit ~is Wycl. *Ver.* I 35.

errabiliter, erroneously.

nec legatis sic ~er, sed legite distincte Ælf. Bata 5. 4.

errabundus [CL], wandering (also fig.).

errabunda vocans caelorum sidera sontes Aldh. *CE* 4. 12. 21; a recto religionis tramite ~is anfractibus exorbitans *Id. VirgP* 38; **796** non est ovibus . . major damnatio quam pastor ~us Alcuin *Ep.* 117; **1095** quid agam nescio, ~us suspiro, et quem rei finem imponere debeam ignoro Anselm (*Ep.* 193) IV 83; hodie omnes pastores ecclesie domum Dei reedificant, dum oves ~as ad gregem reportant Hon. *Spec. Eccl.* 923A; nocte tota circumeundo . . ~us excubare solebat Gir. *EH* II 8; *Id. IK* II 9 (v. erraticus 1a); **1215** (v. divagari); **1229** ne presbiteri . . ~i sint de nocte per villas *Conc. Syn.* 125.

eradicare v. eradicare.

erramentum [OF *erraments*], (pl., records of) legal proceedings (Cont.). *Cf.* 3 *errare.*

1270 citata fuerat . . ad respondendum eis secundum ~a dicte querele mote ad certam diem competentem *CartINorm* 179; **1312** infra castrum nostrum Burdeg' . . rotuli, papira, et alia arramenta compotum predictum tangencia sub sequestro ponuntur *RGasc* IV 686.

errandus [AN *errant*], wandering, straying.

1307 pro una vacca ~a veniente quasi *weyf Econ. Condit.* app. 21.

erraneus, wandering, straying. **b** erroneous. *V. et. erroneus.*

Dei proles descendens ovem ~eam [*gl.*: i. errantem, *dweliende*] redemptura Aldh. *VirgP* 7; cum ille residens tres velut ~eos [AS p. 427: *worigende*] ac aliquid quaerentes viderit sibi approximare, incipiat . . cantare . . *RegulC* 51. **b** verbum Domini, paganico repulso ritu et ~eo gentilitatis more destructo . . praedicabat Willib. *Bonif.* 8 p. 47.

erranter, erroneously.

necesse est . . declinantes a logica scripture, que est aliis principium, ~er dividi Wycl. *Ver.* II 73.

1 errare v. arare 1b.

2 errare [CL]

1 to wander about, stray (also fig.). **b** (pr. ppl. as sb. m.) wanderer, drifter. **c** vagrant.

ut omnes . . per invios . . scelerum calles ~are faciat Gildas *EB* 93; semita . . / quae non errantes ad caeli culmina vexit Aldh. *Aen.* 59 (*Penna*) 8; erro [*gl.*: *ic hwearlie*] caput circa tenues et tendor in aures *Ib.* 74 (*Fundibalum*) 9; inde sacerdotes . . / . . longis anfractibus errant *Id. VirgV* 1521; freneticus . . dum per cuncta ~ando discurreret Bede *HE* IV 3; **1202** juratores dicunt quod postquam positus fuit in gaola viderunt eum ~antem per patriam *SelPlCrown* 17; H. Avr. *Hugh* 177 (v. diffibulare). **b** occidere consuevit vitulum filio saginatum et proferre primam ~anti stolam [cf. *Luke* xv 15] Gildas *EB* 29; et tamen immensis errantes fluctibus actos / arcibus ex celsis signans ad litora duco Aldh. *Aen.* 92 (*Farus*) 7. **c 1212** Rannulfus est ~ans et nullam habet reseantisam *CurR* VI 307.

2 to move erratically. **b** (pr. ppl.) erratic, unreliable. **c** (w. *sidus* or *stella*) planet; *v. et. erraticus* 1b.

798 [planetae] errantes dicuntur quia certum . . cursum non habere noscuntur; . . sol et luna . . non ~ant Alcuin *Ep.* 149 (v. et. 2c infra); dicitur ~are dum austronotho in sublimi erecto vertix se in summum poli †demergit [l. emergit] *Gl. Leid.* 44. 26; Neckam *NR* I 17 (v. circumvolitare b). **b** manus ~antissima dantis Hanv. VII 47 p. 343. **c 798** hortans seniorem . . stellarum in caelo ~antium vagabundos exponere cursus Alcuin *Ep.* 155; ratione ipsa etiam que dicuntur ~antia torquentur sidera W. Malm. *GR* IV 334; errantes stelle stabunt, / terra curret Walt. Wimb. *Van.* 198.

3 to err (in judgement); **b** (impers.); **c** (dep.); **d** (trans.) to mistake, be mistaken about. **e** to make a mistake (in performing a task).

hypodiastoli est divisio compositarum litterarum propter ambiguitates . . ut non ~et qui leget Aldh. *PR* 41 p. 200; multos ~are fecerunt somnia *V. Greg.* p. 92; nisi fallor, nisi ~o *GlC* N 115; Adel. *QN* 70 (v. erraticus 1b); P. Blois *Ep.* 95 (v. 3 errare a); multos in hac parte graviter ~asse Gir. *TH* I 13; scientia beatorum non est practica, quia beati ~are non possunt Duns *Ord.* I 185. **b** si alter alterius dicatur essentia, non ~atur a veritate Anselm (*Mon.* 44) I 60; non debeat esse promptus ad disputandum . . de illis in quibus non ~atur sine periculo *Id.* (*Incarn. A*) I 290. **c** eo amplius quo incommodius . . est in inquirendis ~ari Balsh. *AD rec.* 2 130. **d** etiam, si id ~as, non Stoicum me sed Bathoniensem dico. quare non Stoicorum errata, sed meum intellectum docere debeo (v. et. 4d infra) Adel. *QN* 28. **e** si quis ~ans commotaverit aliquid de verbis sacris . . triduanum . . faciat Gildas *Pen.* 20; J. Ford *Wulf.* 82 (v. consutura b).

4 to err morally, to sin. **b** to err doctrinally. **c** (pr. ppl. as sb. m.) sinner, heretic. **d** (p. ppl. as sb. n.) error, sin; *v. et. erratus.*

in eo isti . . ~ant, quo non ab apostolis . . sed a tyrannis . . emunt sacerdotia Gildas *EB* 67; cur angelus ~ans non meruit revocari ut homo Pull. *Sent.* 643C; ~assem utique si aliter egissem Rolle *IA* 239. **b** [Scottos] in observatione sancti Paschae ~asse conpererat Bede *HE* II 19; ~ans gens, hereticus, divisus *GlC* E 295; mentaliter contra fidem minime ~ant Ockham *Dial.* 635. **c** viam veritatis praedicabat ~antibus Bede *HE* IV 25 p. 269; Deus ecclesiam suam . . protegit et ~antes corrigit Ord. Vit. III 12 p. 127; preeligens ~antes emendare quam perdere R. Niger *Chr. I* 45; tertius [liber] . . considerat quis ~ans inter hereticos est computandus Ockham *Dial.* 398; mirandum est . . cur non fatentur se hereticos aut ~antes Conway *Def. Mend.* 1337; si quis ausus fuerit affirmare quod quilibet sacerdos possit absolvere a peccato super quo non habet commissam auctoritatem . . et correctus revocare noluerit, tanquam ~ans et subversor carceri mancipetur (*Abbr. Statut.*) *Mon. Francisc.* II 99; **1552** populum recte in fide catholica . . instruere aut ~antes convertere *Conc. Scot.* II 136. **d** sed magis arbitror, quod sic errata rearum / Nitria purgavit Aldh. *VirgV* 1465; ~atis, *gedwolum GlN* 43. 8; monachi . . pietate moti ~ata sua . . ei indulserunt Ord. Vit. III 3 p. 60; Adel. *QN* 28 (v. 3d supra); P. Blois *Ep.* 95 (v. 3 errare a).

3 errare [OF *errer* < iterare], (pr. ppl.): **a** (w. *justitia* or *justitiarius*) justice in eyre. **b** (w. *baillivus*) bailiff errant. **c** (of bird) circling, hovering. **d** (of vehicle) plying, going to and fro. **e** (of forge) moveable, that can be moved. *V. et. iterare, cf. itinerare.*

a ipsos . . justitiarios quos vulgariter ~antes vel itinerantes dicimus, dum errata hominum diligenter explorant, frequenter errare contingit P. Blois *Ep.* 95. 298B; apud proconsules quos nostrates vulgariter dicunt justitias esse ~antes J. Sal. *Pol.* 576C; *Dial. Scac.* I 8 D (v. deambulatorius 1b); **1189** ubicunque summoniti fuerint coram justitiariis nostris ~antibus, licet acquietare eos per quattuor legales homines de ipso burgo [*Colchester*] *CalCh* I 410; **1219** coram justiciariis ~antibus in comitatu Suff' *CurR* VIII 87; per officiales publicos, quos justitiarios ~antes vocant, pena pecuniaria multati fuerunt Gir. *Spec.* III 12; s**1312** Henricus de B. . . fuit manucaptus ad iter justiciariorum eiriantium apud Turrim *Ann. Lond.* 219. **b 1307** (v. baillivus 2c). **c 1333** falcones hominum . . transeuncium ad deductum illum jactatos et eirantes *CoramR* 294 r. 62 (cf. ib.: cum . . idem falco volatum suum ultra ripariam . . eirando cepisset). **d** c**1178** quinque carettas ~antes . . ad ligna deferenda *Act. Hen. II* II 115; **1204** (v. 2 batellus 1d); **1252** (v. 2 biga a); **1349** duas bigas ~antes in bosco meo cotidie bis . . ad capiendum ibi de bosco meo quod eis necessarium fuerit *ChartR* 135 m. 4. **e 1230** quod permittat abbatem de F. habere fabricam suam ~antem in foresta nostra de D. *Cl* 354; **1282** si dominus rex habeat unam forgeam ~antem, predicti operarii invenient ei mineam ad sustentacionem predicte forgee *TR Forest Proc* 31 m. 17.

errarium v. aerarium. **errarius** v. 1 & 2 aerarius.

erratice, by going astray (fig.).

1373 oves . . ~e lapsas ad viam veritatis . . reducere *Reg. Exon.* I 289.

erraticula, little error. *V. et. erratiuncula.*

1463 pro una ~a de novo per eundem [computantem] facta in castro de Dunbar *ExchScot* 179.

erraticus [CL]

1 wandering, not fixed; **b** (astr.). **c** (med.) erratic. *V. et. errativus.*

ob imbelles ~osque latrunculos Romana stigmata . . fatigari Gildas *EB* 18; curia . . temporalis . . est, mutabilis et varia, localis et ~a, nunquam in eodem statu permanens Map *NC* I 1 f. 7; alter [lacus] insulam habet ~am, vi ventorum impellentium ad opposita plerumque lacus partes errabundam Gir. *IK* II 9. **b 798** mirum quomodo ~as illarum [stellarum errantium] semitas ad certum quis valeat reducere ordinem Alcuin *Ep.* 155; cum . . eam [lunam] cum ceteris stellis sex stellam ~am vocent, magis eos quam stellas errare puto Adel. *QN* 70; firmamentum . . jugiter volvitur motu continuo sed non ~o Neckam *NR* I 5; per . . diversitatem motuum aliorum orbium stellarum ~arum Kilwardby *OS* 19; *Ps.*-Elmh. *Hen. V* 130 (v. epicyclus). **c** R. Cold. *Godr.* 421, *Mir. Fridesw.* 53 (v. gutta 2a); sunt preterea febres . . que dicuntur ~e ab inordinato modo affligendi Gilb. I 12. 1; ~a febris inter interpolatas computatur; . . ter in die quandoque typum patiuntur, ad modum tertiane . . quandoque de die in diem diversimode interpolat *Ib.* 54v. 2; caro eorum [gallorum] valet contra arratice febris prolixitatem Bart. Angl. XII 17.

2 (of plant) wild, uncultivated.

herba malfa ~a, *þæt is hocleaf Leechdoms* I 22; Turner *Herb.* B ii (v. dens 3c).

3 vague, unreliable.

ista non apocriforum †venia [v. l. nenia] ~a dissertione relata esse cognoscamus (*sic*), sed sicut illo ipso vidente et nobis referente Hugeb. *Will. prol.*

4 (morally) mistaken, erroneous, sinful.

tempore mortalitatis . . ad ~a idolatriae medicamina concurrebant Bede *CuthbP* 9; scripturas . . sanctas . . ~o ac gentili sensu interpretantes *Id. Ezra* 923; perpera, ~a *GlC* P 277; c**798** cavete vobis venenosum ~ae infectionis fermentum, sed . . sacrae fidei panes comedite et vinum . . bibite Alcuin *Ep.* 138; **1532** Jacobus N. . . et Johannes W. . . se purgarunt de omnibus punctis ~is eis . . impositis *Scot. Grey Friars* II 143.

erratilis [LL], (med.) erratic.

guttam quandam per omnes artus corporis sevissimam habuit et ~em, qua cogente sepius nervorum contractionem percipi consuevit R. Cold. *Godr.* 470.

erratiuncula, little error. *V. et. erraticula.*

pueros delectare solet . . praeceptoris ~am annotare Whittington *Vulg.* 112.

erratius, wandering, not fixed (astr.). **b** (med.) erratic. *V. et. erraticus* 1.

stelle fixe vel ~e Gros. *Com.* 24 (= *ed. Baur* 38: erratice). **b** si [dolor capitis est] de ventositate, est ~us Gad. 69v. 1.

erratus [LL], error, sin. *V. et.* 2 *errare* 4c.

leviores et cotidiani ∼us levioris paenitentiae possunt remedio curari BEDE *Mark* (v 43) 184; pro meis ∼ibus .. Dominum deprecari *Id. HE* IV 23 p. 265; intervenite pro vestris ∼ibus [AS: *synnum*] ÆLF. *Coll.* 102; quis eos quasi non conjuges ab invicem separet, et non potius ab ∼u corripiendo revocaret? PULL. *Sent.* 957D; cum .. veram suorum ∼uum confessionem audirent *G. Steph.* I 4; veniam meis postulabat ∼ibus MAP *NC* III 2 f. 36v. (cf. ib. IV 11 f. 53: veniam petit ∼ui); quod .. infortunium non absque .. Dei judicio .. evenisse arbitrandum est, sive pro regis .. ∼ibus castigandis, sive .. COGGESH. *Chr.* 62.

errebellis [cf. CL rebellis], rebellious.

1379 de H. T. eo quod fuit ∼is in curia in presencia .. prioris xx s. *Hal. Durh.* 153.

errestum v. 1 erna. **erreus** v. 2 aereus. **errigere** v. erigere 2b. **errititus** v. irretire. **errog-** v. erog-.

erronee, erroneously, mistakenly.

Judei adhuc inaniter et ∼ee expectant [Salvatorem mundi] BACON *Tert.* 205; ∼ee determinavit OCKHAM *Pol.* I 297; **c1360** virtute ejusdem statuti .. ∼ee intellecti *MunAcOx* 223; Lollardi sunt zizania / .., / que vastant hortum vinee; / nam pejor pestilencia / non fuit in ecclesia / incedens tam erronee (*In Lollardos*) *Pol. Poems* I 232; illa portio ix solidorum .. ∼ee exigebatur per defectum scriptoris, qui scripsit Rynera pro Ruda *Meaux* III 28.

erroneus [CL]

1 wandering, straying.

Dominus .. nonaginta novem oves electas non deseruit .. etiam cum unam ∼eam quaereret [cf. *Matth.* xviii 12] BEDE *Sam.* (*1 Sam.* xvii 20) 615; Tosticus .. per aequora vagabundus .. ∼eus exul ad tantum laborem tyrannum excivit .. ut .. injuriam expulsionis sue .. ulcisceretur ORD. VIT. III 11 p. 124.

2 erroneous, mistaken, false; **b** (phil. or theol.).

oblitteratis .. ∼eis lxxx et iiij annorum [Paschae] circulis BEDE *HE* V 21 p. 346; hunc fructum mathesis sue horoscopi afferunt et planetis suis magis ∼ei, dum a scientia pietatis exorbitant, .. descendunt in infernum viventes J. SAL. *Pol.* 459; in hac opinione quanquam ∼ea et deceptoria non solum ipse sed et patria fere tota propter circumstantias .. quibus falli poterant, tunc temporis erant GIR. *JS* 7 p. 339; ubi et gentilium error .. propter soli fecunditatem easdem insulas Paradisum esse [putavit], quod quidem ponere est eronium cum predicte insule fortunate sint in occidente BART. ANGL. XV 112; BRADW. *CD* 775D (v. delusorius). **b** videtur quod [diffinitio] sit ∼ea BACON VIII 72; **1314** isti articuli subscripti fuerunt reprobati tanquam ∼ei a magistris theologie universitatis Oxonie *MunAcOx* 100; ∼ea ac heretica .. dicta OCKHAM *Pol.* I 293; **1382** (v. damnare 3d); **1425** (v. defensatio b, dogmatizatio b).

3 morally wrong, misguided, sinful. **b** (as sb. m.) one in error. **c** (as sb. n.) error, wrongdoing.

a1154 sacerdotalis officii est pravorum .. ∼eis conatibus .. contraire (*Lit. Archiep. Cant.*) *Chr. Rams.* 307; **s1104** H. .. Losenga .. empto presulatu Teodfensis ecclesie factus est episcopus. verumtamen ∼eum impetum abolevit penitentia DICETO *Chr.* 219. **b** **722** si quos .. a recte fidei tramite destitisse cognoverit aut astutia diabolica suasos ∼eos reperit, corrigat (*Lit. Papae*) *Ep. Bonif.* 17; sicut illa [Helena] quondam .. Judeos similiter nunc et hec regina convicerat ∼eos TURGOT *Marg.* 8; sententia .. hunc finem habuit: non vi cogendos scismaticos sed rationibus ducendos; .. id quominus fieret, nichil obstare si Aldhelmus .. sua ∼eos ammonitione dignaretur W. MALM. *GP* V 215; **s1160** ∼ei quidam venerunt in Angliam ex eorum .. genere quos vulgo 'Publicanos' vocant W. NEWB. *HA* II 13; credunt hujusmodi ∼ei quia .. DOCKING 114; ut tam feros et ∼eos .. assurgendo inflaret quos potius corrigeret increpando ELMH. *Cant.* 105. **c** **s1189** [Ric. I] ∼ea patris sui .. studuit corrigere *Meaux* I 243.

4 (leg.) unjust, improper.

s1233 malum exemplum darem omnibus .. propter voluntatem ∼eam, contra omnem justitiam WEND. III 68; **1254** ut ab hujusmodi sententiis ironeis .. desistat *Cl* 314; **1285** stet judicium .. quousque per judicium .. regis, tanquam ∼ium, si error inveniatur [cassetur] (*2 Westm.* 5) *StRealm* I 76; **1315** ad .. terminandum .. ∼eas taxaciones, collecciones, injustas exacciones et districciones ballivorum *Bury St. Edm.* 186; **s1321** processus exilii dominorum H. et H. Despenser fuit ∼eus et rex cum concilio suo pronunciarunt illud exilium non tenere AD. MUR. 35; **1345** judicia super placitis .. motis reddita que sic falsa vel ∼ea pretenduntur remanent indiscussa et indeterminata *RScot* 66a; **s1387** an judicium .. contra comitem S. fuit ∼eum et revocabile an non *Chr. Angl.* 382 (cf. ib.: videtur eis quod judicium illud revocabile [est] tamquam ∼eum); **1409** petiit quod .. rex .. factum justiciariorum predictorum .. eronium, precipere [vellet] revocare et emendare *Foed.* VIII 757a (cf. *CalPat* 55); **1470** fateri .. suum ingressum fuisse .. ∼eum *Reg. Whet.* I 206 (cf. ib.: fatebatur .. coram judicibus suum ingressum .. esse injustum); quod predictum judicium tanquam ∼ium adnullaretur et omnino revocaretur *Reg. Brev. Jud.* 60b (cf. ib.: judicium ∼ium in hustengo nostro .. redditum).

erronice, ∼ie, erroneously, in error. **b** unjustly, improperly.

1244 crisma vero ut supra eronice hic scriptum est *MonA* I 39b; **1281** breve illud ∼ice emanavit a curia *Law Merch.* II 38; **1347** ut asseritur .. licet ∼ie *Reg. Heref.* 121; quis nisi ∼ice ductus solveret talibus religiosis taliter adquesita? WYCL. *Compl.* 93. **b** **1327** absque arenamento et responsione idem T. ∼ice et contra legem terre tempore pacis morti extitit adjudicatus *RParl* II 5a; **1388** (v. 1 commotus a); **1396** (v. annullatio 2); literas sub eorum sigillis scriptas ∼ice composuerunt GOWER *CT* I 25 *rub.*

erronicus, erroneous. **b** liable to error, misguided.

ipsa positio secundum se est ∼a. nam tunc esset omnis predicatio equivoca BACON II 107. **b** **s800** Egbritus omnia regna unico quadravit imperio, ut populus animosus et ∼us magis bellum .. movendum quam pacem .. pavere *Cart. Glouc.* I 7.

erronie v. erronice.

error [CL]

1 wandering, roaming (astr.). **b** devious course, maze (of labyrinth). **c** wanderer (astr.), planet.

quoniam de ∼ore stellarum mentionem fecisti, quas Graeci planetas vocant ADEL. *QN* 70; J. SAL. *Pol.* 440B, D. MORLEY 35 (v. aplanes). **b** domum illam [sc. laberintum] Cretae egredi non potuit, quae mille parietibus intextum ∼orem habuit *Lib. Monstr.* I 50. **c** hae omnes stellae, quas ∼ores appellamus, iisdem vagantur spatiis quibus et sol ROBYNS *Com.* 53.

2 error, mistake; **b** (of nature); **c** (textual).

nec error / seduxit vana specie molimina mentis ALDH. *Aen. pref.* 27; ∼ores forte .. locorum distantia reddat veniales GIR. *TH* I 6; .. quod falsum, prout est a fallendo, in effectu est ab humano ∼ore HALES *Sent.* I 474; utroque modo potuit supernaturaliter talis doctrina revelari, sed neutro modo sine ∼ore potuit ab homine tradi primo DUNS *Ord.* I 43; nec est opinio Augustini, sed ∼or Heracliti *Ib.* III 150; **1342** si in receptis .. inveniatur herror, paratus est .. herrorem illum corrigere *ExchScot* 514. **b** .. in hermofroditis, set hoc est ex ∼ore nature BACON XI 210; hoc esset orbare eas propria perfectione, quod esset magnus ∼or in natura BACONTHORPE *Quaest. Sent.* 5a. **c** BACON *Maj.* III 94 (v. correctio 1b).

3 moral error, sin. **b** doctrinal error, heresy.

omittens priscos .. communesque cum omnibus gentibus ∼ores, quibus ante adventum Christi .. omne humanum genus obligabatur astrictum GILDAS *EB* 4; Gregorius .. nostris parentibus ∼orem tetrae gentilitatis abstulit ALDH. *VirgP* 55; porrige dexteram tuam .. plebi .. misericordiam tuam postulanti per quam .. ∼ores [AS: *gidvolo*] declinet humanos *Rit. Durh.* 39; vae .. dolor de aerumnoso ∼ore filiorum Adae ANSELM (*Ep.* 117) III 253; de .. sceleribus et ∼oribus atque illicitis copulationibus DOMINIC *V. Ecgwini* I 4; in hac .. peregrinatione nature fragilis ∼ore plerumque deviatur in tenebras peccatorum R. NIGER *Mil.* I *prol.*; PULL. *Sent.* 743C (v. eripere 2b). **b** ALDH. *VirgV* 2291 (v. anfractus a); BEDE *HE* III 30 (v. corrigere 2a); blasphemus heresiarcha .. discipulis pecunia .. corruptis recens scriptum .. per eosdem peregre transmisit, ut vetus ∼or .. in futuros .. annos porrigeretur ORD. VIT. IV 6 p. 211; resumens fere omnes ∼ores et hereses quos .. ille pseudo-propheta .. J. Wyclif .. ab antiquo paganismo revocaverat *G. Hen. V* 1; **1420** (v. dogmatizare 1a); **1431** (v. dogma).

4 judicial error, miscarriage of justice; **b** (w. *breve*).

s1239 rex .. cum ∼ores non correxerit .., episcopus .. civitatem Londoniarum .. erat interdicto suppositurus M. PAR. *Maj.* III 544; per ∼orem et favorem et manutenementum .. injuriam fecerunt .. justiciarii *State Tri. Ed. I* 2; **1318** assignabimus .. justiciarios itinerantes pro gaola de N. deliberanda et ∼oribus apud S. Martinum Magnum .. corrigendis (*Ch. Regis*) *MGL* II 267; quia in recordo et processu loquele .. ac in redditione judicii ejusdem loquele .. ∼or intervenit manifestus .. *Reg. Brev. Orig* 131. **b** **1292** brevia .. de ∼ore in curia vicecomitum factum corrigendo (*LB Lond C* f. 4) *MGL* I 531; **1315** (v. demanda b); **13..** in brevi de ∼ore corrigendo et de processu ejusdem *MGL* I 172 (cf. ib. 187: *en brief derrour*).

erscha [AS *ersc*], stubble, stubble-field.

1376 .. [blada] inventa in suis hersch' dominicis post ipsos ligata, tunc habeant suas garbas [etc.] *IMisc* 208/4 (cf. ib.: habebunt illos [sc. boves] ubique in hersch' cum bobus domini).

erthendalis [cf. MED s.v. *erthe* 2], (? as equiv. to ME *daies erthe*) ploughland, measure of land ploughed in one day, or (?) *f. l.*

c1200 virgata que est ad opus dat xvj denarios de *heusire* et ij ∼es [? l. egthendales; cf. egtendalum] de avena *Cart. Rams.* III 278.

erthescota [ME *erthe* + *scot*], plough-scot.

1267 [carruce:] j de erdescota, quia dat secundo anno *MinAc* (*Little Hinton, Cambs*).

eruatus v. eruere 4.

erubescentia [LL]

1 blush, blushing; **b** (fig.).

pro peccatis faciem rubore ∼ie tinctam habere debemus ALEX. BATH *Mor.* IV 18 p. 154; **1287** [confessores] habeant oculos .. pronos in terram, non respicientes faciem confitentis, nisi quatenus .. ∼iam, que est maxima pars penitentie, valeant estimare *Conc. Syn.* 992. **b** frons noctis vincitur erubescentia WALT. WIMB. *Carm.* 549.

2 shame, disgrace. **b** shamefacedness.

796 noli ∼iam obponere tibi demittendi quod coepisti. major est ∼ia animam tuam perpetualiter perire quam impios viros .. deserere ALCUIN *Ep.* 109; finiunt in voce confusionis illud in fine cum ∼ia et confusione replicantes .. H. BOS. *LM* 1408C; mira facti confunditur ∼ia GIR. *IK* I 8; J. GODARD *Ep.* 231 (v. complodere d); **1272** ecce .. que solutionem nostram [m marcarum] .. in nostram ∼iam et dedecus quod timemus adeo distulerint *Reg. North.* 45; in confessione ordinario facta est ∼ia amplior quam cum confessio est fratri facta, quoniam quisque amplius erubescit pandere sua peccata illi quem quotidie cernit presentem quam uni extraneo RIC. ARMAGH *Def. Cur.* 1396 (*recte* 1296). **b** omnis .. voluptas libidinis turpis est, ea excepta que excusatur federe conjugali, et indulte licentie beneficio quicquid ∼ie poterat inesse abscondit J. SAL. *Pol.* 749B; **1188** mementote quia sicut non habet legem necessitas sic et ∼iam consuevit eliminare paupertas *Ep. Cant.* 279; secundum [inconveniens est] minoratio ∼ie (CROMPE) *Ziz.* 345; *a schamefastness*, ∼ia, pudorositas *CathA.*

erubescere [CL], **erubēre** [LL]

1 to become red.

∼escant, ignescant *GlH* E 344.

2 to blush for shame (also fig.); **b** (trans.) to blush (at), feel shame (for); **c** (w. gen.); **d** (w. *quia* or *quod*); **e** (w. acc. & inf.).

∼escant, .. *asceamien GlH* E 344; erubuit loetum vita medicante repulsum FRITH. 597; illi [artifices] .. signum et emendationem experti letum †erubere [MS: erubuere] W. MALM. *GP* V 216; sterilisque vetustas / erubeat dum culta venis, dum libera frontem / exeris J. EXON. *BT* I 12; Adam et Eva agnoscunt se nudos et ∼escunt AD. DORE *Pictor* 161; justum est quod ∼escamus [ME: *us scheome*] coram homine *AncrR* 127; quecumque .. in his libellis compilavi, spero quod de eis veritas non ∼escet *Eul. Hist.* I *proem.* p. 4. **b** ORD. VIT. XI 2 p. 168 (v. derisorius a); non armatas in prelia lingue / credideram venisse deas, hac parte loquacem / erubeo sexum J. EXON. *BT* II 326; negacio .. communicacionis cum talibus ipsos ∼escentes peccata sua converteret WYCL. *Sim.* 111; ∼esco nuditatem meam, sed magis a facie potentis Dei contremisco CHAUNDLER *Apol.* 18b. **c** **800** tantum mihi .. laudata est sanctitatis vestrae .. devocio et .. sollicitudo ut ∼esco pene meae pigritiae ALCUIN *Ep.* 207; virginalis palmae impudentium quam propriae tyrannidis cepit ∼ere GOSC. *V. Mild.* 13. **d** nec ∼escam quod spero in vobis hanc pietatem ANSELM (*Or.* 6) III 16; ∼esco quia hoc quaesivi *Id.* (*CurD*) II 108; ille hostilis memor odii primo denegavit, postmodum ∼escens quod in mortuum seviret, concessit ORD. VIT. III 5 p. 73; **1272** ∼escimus et .. desolamur quod impotentiam .. tanto patri .. pretendere compellimur *Reg. North.* 44. **e** sit aliquis forte malus, qui quod est esse ∼escat EADMER *Beat.* 15 p. 288; bonum quod in aliis diligunt minus in se reperiri non ∼escunt GIR. *EH* II 36.

3 (w. inf.) to blush or be ashamed (to).

quod vir Dei .. spoliare se de melote et amiculis ∼esceret ALDH. *VirgP* 37; jam ∼escebat illam olim religiosam tamen a daemonio vexatam indicare *V. Cuthb.* II 8; aures summorum doctorum .. offendere ∼esco GREG. *Mir. Rom. prol.*; erubeo ulteriora loqui J. EXON. *BT* II 431; GERV. CANT. *Chr.* 418 (v. dejerare 2); GIR. *Invect.* I 7 (v. contradictorius 2a).

4 to blush in the presence of, to respect. **b** (w. gen.).

1166 si non vultum Josaphat regis Judae ∼escerem [cf. *2 Kings* iii 14] J. SAL. *Ep.* 228 (182). **b** nonne ∼uisti honestatis et pudicicie? CHAUNDLER *Laud.* 114.

erubescibilis [LL], of which to be ashamed.

si [adulatio] manifestatur, jam vitium ∼e detectum est NECKAM *NR* II 180.

erubiginare [cf. CL rubiginare], to remove rust from, burnish.

to frubische, elimare, ∼are, .. *to score* [v. l. *scowre*], limare, .. ∼are, polire *CathA.*

erubiginatio, removing of rust, burnishing.

1462 pro †embiginacione [l. erubiginacione] vj candelar' de cupro ij s. et in †embiginacione fontis portabilis de cupro pro aqua benedicta x d. *Ac. Churchw. Sal.* 8; **1501** solut' pro ∼one gladii S. Georgii iiij d. *Cart. Osney* II 475.

eruca [CL]

1 (bot.) rocket (*Eruca sativa*), charlock (*Sinapis*), hedge mustard (*Sisymbrium*), or sim. **b** skirret (*Sium*). **c** basil (*Ocymum*).

∼a, *calfwyrt* ÆLF. *Gl.*; eruci, sinapis *Gl. Durh.*; sepius erucam si Birria sumat in esum / ictus quos meruit fit

tolerare potens NECKAM *DS* VII 185; †erutha est herba alba domestica et aliquando silvestris .. p[ar]alisim curat BART. ANGL. XVII 57; ciborum quidam inducunt luxuriam, ut .. ~a sicca ..; sunt etiam quidam cibi quorum comestione castitas conservatur, ut .. ~a viridis M. SCOT *Phys.* 1; hec ~a, *erut Gl. AN Glasg.* f. 19; ~a, sinapis albus, A. *cherloc SB*; ~a multum comesta venerem stimulat *Alph.* 58; ~a, A. *whytpyper*, .. *a schynlock*, .. *a carlok WW*; euzomon Latini ~am nominant vulgus *rocket*; aliqui vocant *whyte pepper* TURNER *Herb.* B 1. **b** ~a tam semen quam herba, A. *skirwhit.* calidus est in secundo gradu, siccus in primo *SB*; ~a, A. .. *skyrwyt WW*; ~a *is an herbe þat men clepe skyrwyt*. .. *it steryth a man to letcherye Agnus Castus* f. 183. **c** ~a, vel ocimi *GlH* E 343.

2 kind of caterpillar.

~ae, modici vermes qui mandunt folia; multos pedes habent *Gl. Leid.* 39. 7; ~a, .. vermis in holera *GlH* E 343; ~a, *mælscæafa* ÆLF. *Gl.*; transgressores legis ab ~a et brucho et locusta et rubigine comesos plangit et hortatur Johel [cf. *Joel* ii 25] ORD. VIT. VIII 15 p. 357; heruca, vermis holera erodens OSB. GLOUC. *Deriv.* 276; **s1193** ut nulla vacaret occasio et residuum ~e locusta .. absumeret [cf. *Joel* i 4], ad vasa sacra ventum est W. NEWB. *HA* IV 38; nomen accepit .. ~a ex oleribus que corrodit P. CORNW. *Disp.* 150; hec ~a, *a coleworm* .. hoc eruga, A. *a wurtwurme WW*; tantus ~arum .. proventus tantaque vis fuit ut omnes fructus arborum herbarumque absumerent, mala, pyra, pruna, quaecunque ad frugem aliquam pervenerant, corrumperent, holera et quaecunque in hortis minores herbae crescunt ad caules usque arroderent BOECE 302.

eructare [CL], **~uare** [LL]

1 to eruct, belch forth. **b** to breathe out; **c** (fig., w. ref. to death). **d** (intr.) to belch.

Aegaeon .. habuit l capita et .. crepitantes ~abat flammas *Lib. Monstr.* I 48; ~uat, i. *bylcetteþ, roccetеþ GlH* E 342; mala eructuatio, quando, sc. ~et acre vel acerbum .. BACON V 68. **b 9**.. ~ant, *forþblawaþ WW*; fatetur .. anxia suspiria ~uasse GOSC. *Mir. Iv.* lxiii. **c** pro qua [necessitate], ni fallor, multi ~abunt animas ORD. VIT. X 20 p. 125; vitam cum sanguine ~avit G. MON. X 5. **d** eructuatio alleviat istos, et semper vellent ~uare propter exitum ventositatis GAD. 34v. 2; feruntur aliqui nunquam risisse .., aliqui nunquam ~asse HIGD. II 1 p. 194.

2 to declare, proclaim, utter. **b** (intr.) to speak.

minus ~are proloquendo sufficiunt quanta ipsi intus dulcedine in abdito vultus Dei reficiantur BEDE *Tab.* 487; **c746** rutilat arbiter .. et melliflua dogmata salutis aeternae †habundet [v. l. abundant, l. abundat], ~uat nimirum laudabilis in arvis *Ep. Bonif.* 85; ~at, a corde emittit [cf. *Psalm* xliv 2] *GlC* E 291; multa declamarem et digna ~uarem convitia H. LOS. *Ep.* 10; [Willelmus II] ante cibum venatu abstinuit seriis negotiis cruditatem indomite mentis ~uans W. MALM. *GR* IV 333; nichil prodest eructare / compta verba Tullii WALT. WIMB. *Van.* 33; Marie virginis laudes eructuo *Id. Carm.* 2; contritus corde meruit esse sine sorde, / eructans vere "Deus, alme, mei miserere" (J. BRIDL.) *Pol. Poems* I 171 (cf. ib. 173 *gl.*: '~ans vere', i. clamans ad Deum in psalmo); **s1178** Anglorum quidam .. clericum, ex eo quod intrepide .. animi motum ~arat .., collaudabant FORDUN *Cont.* VIII 26; *to schewe* .., *CathA.* **b** de cujus [Francie] dulcedine .. cum tempus est non ~are [v. l. ~uare] non possumus. de ipsius dulcedine plenius nunc ~assem [v. l. ~uassem] nisi .. H. BOS. *Thom.* IV 21; ~et in confessione [ME: *culche hit i schrift*] omnino quicumque sicut fecit *AncrR* 73.

3 (w. inanim. subj.) to throw up, emit. **b** (intr.) to gush forth.

centenos .. eructant mea viscera cantus ALDH. *Aen.* 13 (*Barbita*) 3; **716** referebat se .. vidisse igneos puteos horrendam ~antes flammam BONIF. *Ep.* 10 p. 11; puteus putidum qui eructuat ignem / est os inferni ALCUIN *SS Ebor* 990; enorme incendium .. immensos flammarum globos ~avit ORD. VIT. VII 16 p. 251. **b** stagna subito ex terre visceribus ~antia GIR. *TH* III 2; dic nobis de aquis dulcibus quomodo ipse omni tempore ~uant extra terram M. SCOT *Part.* 293 (cf. ib. 294: vellemus .. scire quomodo est .. ignis qui ~uat de terra).

eructatio [CL], **~uatio**

1 eructation, belching.

aqua cui diutius [berillus] infuerit pota .. ~ationibus [v. l. ~uationibus] valet R. NIGER *Mil.* II 10; ~uatio .. est fumi in stomacho cum sonitu per isophagum expulsio *Quaest. Salern.* Ba 29; ~uationes GILB. I 42. 1 (v. dulcedo 1b); *Ib.* V 206v. 2 (v. catatropa); ~uatio BACON V 68 (v. eructare 1a); evigilans habuit .. ~acionem, et fecit vomitum et sic convalescit *Mir. Montf.* 84; anhelitus .. illius qui habet ~uaciones fetidas nocet infirmo GAD. 11. 1.

2 outpouring, utterance.

s1423 sciebat utique ex quo stomacho tam fumosa verborum processit ~acio AMUND. I 79; dignemini .. in ~acionibus talium [sc. susurrancium contra nos] respondere .. quomodo non est vestri moris ut propter satores zizanii .. facem suffocetis in cinere *Reg. Whet.* II 413.

eructativus, that induces belching.

sugat .. dulcia aut comedat semina eructuativa; post vero vomitum, si accederit, accipiat ma[l]a granata acria et dulcia GILB. VII 362. 2.

eructatorium, drug that induces belching.

~ium .. omnem ventositatem stomachi expellit GILB. V 209v. 1.

eructu- v. et. eruct-.

eructus [cf. CL eructare, eructus, *p. ppl. of* erugere], outburst.

missa .. tandem sicut potuit pre lacrymarum abundantia et singultuum crebris ~ibus vix finita H. BOS. *Thom.* III 37 p. 304.

eruderare [CL]

1 to clear (site or sim. of rubbish).

area purgatur rastrisque serenda novatur. / eruderatur humus, tumet agger, in aggere dumus / spinaque figuntur R. CANT. *Malch.* V 516; a puteo mundato et ~ato NECKAM *NR* II 174; putei aquarum viventium, quos Abraham primo fodit, Isaac ~avit R. BURY *Phil.* 1. 27; [abbas J., ob. **1260**] molendinum .. reparavit .. et stagnum adjacens .. ~avit *G. S. Alb.* I 328; abbas [H., ob. **1326**] cemeterium .. derelictum .. totum fecit competenter mundari, ~ari, ac decenti ordine complanari *Ib.* II 125; ~ato monasterio toto .. et de cineribus .. expurgato *Croyl.* 24.

2 a to clear away (rubbish or debris). **b** to dig or hollow out (also fig.).

a ut .. Wilfridi dirutam .. ecclesiam .. conspicatus, ruinis super mausoleum ~atis, reliquias Cantuariam .. transferret W. MALM. *GP* I 15; †erudeare [MS: eruderare], purgare, quasi †rudem [MS: rudera] auferre OSB. GLOUC. *Deriv.* 195. **b** ut .. fundamentis obfirmatio privetur et in ruinam †erudentur [? l. eruderentur] R. NIGER *Mil.* III 69 (cf. ib.: inquisitio que .. elicit radices heresis et ~at fundamenta paulatim erute falsitatis); **s1098** ceciderunt in foveam quam aliis ~averant [cf. *Psalm* vii 16] M. PAR. *Min.* II 124; **s1256** *Id. Maj.* V 600 (v. calamus 2b); ~o, A. *to myne WW.*

3 to strip away.

~ato penitus argento a rota memorata *Chr. Abingd.* I 345; abbas [Ingulfus, ob. **1158**] .. xij thecas ex auro puro et argento coopertas iterum ~avit, utilius dijudicans aurum et argentum pro .. libertate ecclesiastica in fisco regio .. exaggerare quam servitium ejusdem terre .. amittere *Ib.* II 214.

4 to manure.

to mukke, ~are, fimare, pastinare, purgare, stercorare *CathA.*

5 (?) *f. l.*

1252 hic theologi discipulos in pulpitis .. informant, logici .. tyrones Aristotilis eruderant [? l. erudiunt], grammatici balbutientium linguas in analogiam effigiant (*Lit. Magistrorum Tolosan.*) GARL. *Tri. Eccl.* 97.

eruderatio, clearance.

1187 judices delegati .. nimie simplicitatis .. sunt redarguendi, qui murorum constructionem .. pro ecclesia sunt interpretati, vel saltem ad illius loci ~onem et inchoationem oculos deflexissent ubi suum .. archiepiscopus propugnaculum intendit edificare *Ep. Cant.* 39.

erudicare v. eradicare 4a. **erudictio** v. eruditio.

erudire [CL]

1 to instruct, educate: **a** (w. acc. of person taught); **b** (w. acc. & *ad* or inf.); **c** (absol.). **d** (p. ppl. *eruditus*) learned. **e** (leg., w. *consilium*) learned counsel. **f** (as sb. m.) erudit, scholar.

a rector caeli, cum .. adoptivas .. filias .. viderit .. divinis dogmatibus ~iri ALDH. *VirgP* 2; instituit scholam in qua pueri litteris ~irentur BEDE *HE* III 18 (cf. ib. IV 3 p. 210: qui me in scripturis ~iebant); admonemus presbyteros ut .. populum Dei .. doctrina sancta ~iant O. CANT. *Const.* 4; alia lingua nesciunt ~iri quam in qua nati sunt ÆLF. *CH* I *pref.* 1; **a1073** quam studiose eos .. in .. litteris ~ivi LANFR. *Ep.* 1; GIR. *PI* I 20 (v. docilis a); **1504** (v. docere 1b). **b** cum omnibus quos ad correctiorem viam ~ire poterant BEDE *HE* III 25; **a795** qui eos .. ~iunt Deum timere ALCUIN *Ep.* 33; nos a nobis otiositatem depellere ~iunt ORD. VIT. III 5 p. 78; filios .. ad divini pabuli predas paulatim ~iunt GIR. *TH* I 12; rex regum altissimus suos ~iens mites et humiles esse corde .. J. MASON *Ep.* 17; **1365** dicit quod ~ivit .. plures .. pueros ad legendum et cantandum *SelCKB* VI 143. **c** plena est civitas ista doctoribus qui vobis sepe verba vite disseminant et doctrina ~iunt salutari S. LANGTON *Serm.* 2. 1; **s1253** magistrum [Jo]hannem de S. Egidio, in arte peritum medicinali et in theologia lectorem eleganter eruditum et ~ientem M. PAR. *Maj.* V 400. **d** Gregorius .. litteris incomparabiliter ~us ALDH. *VirgP* 27; viris venerabilibus atque ~issimis BEDE *HE pref.* p. 6 (cf. ib. V 15 p. 315: a pluribus qui erant ~iores .. admonitus); erat ei nobilis mulier .. omnibus artibus ~a G. MON. III 13; GIR. *PI pref.* 1 p. lviii (v. componere 1e). **e 1564** per ~um consilium (v. divisare 2b). **f** ut a quibusdam .. ~is illa depravata incorrectaque .. abnegantur THEOD. *Pen. prol.*; facilius est accipitrem ex milvo fieri quam ex rustico subitum ~um G. MON. VI 3; sunt .. ex indistinctione sophismata, velut ex equivocatione que per se, ~o ne insistat contempnenda, velut ex quibus compertis disputatio non seria videtur BALSH. *AD* 61; inter ~os vero Thome eruditissimus preclarus quidam H. BOS. *Thom.* VII 1.

2 to learn.

in tali .. via aperitur homini disciplina et ex malis, que viderit, multa ~itur experientia R. NIGER *Mil.* II 53; **1283** ad ducendum ad partes transmarinas pro ideomate ~iendo *Gaol Del.* 35B m. 37; scholares rudimenta ~ientes in exiguum conventum coaluere *Eul. Hist.* I 225; Sigesbertus .. scholam instituit in qua pueri literas ~ierunt *Ib.* II 159 (cf. BEDE *HE* III 18: in qua pueri litteris ~ientur); nobis miracula cariora sunt .. quovismodo videntur et sacris sunt litteris ~ita *Mir. Hen. VI* I 15 p. 42.

erudite [CL], eruditely, learnedly.

H. BOS. *Thom.* III 16 p. 236 (v. curialiter 1a).

eruditio [CL]

1 instruction, teaching. **b** reproof, chastisement.

symtagmateseon, magister ~onis *GlC* S 726; **798** nostris ~onibus adsuetus et illorum moribus edocatus (*sic*) ALCUIN *Ep.* 156; judicia, non solum ad vindictam malorum sed ad ~onem bonorum facta OSB. BAWDSEY clxxxii; si cui ~onis nostre comperta industria difficultatem subducens contigerit facultas, cavere nitatur ne .. BALSH. *AD rec. 2* 124; rescribit .. commendans .. amorem scientie Scripturarum et discendi eas .. ex magistrorum per vivam vocem erudictione GROS. *Hexaem. proem.* 2; **1370** pro ~one puerorum *Ac. Durh.* 207. **b** GOSC. *Transl. Aug.* 34A (v. dispensare 2b); heretici .. sunt .. subtilioribus ~onibus incidendi, ut in secretioribus emendentur R. NIGER *Mil.* III 80.

2 study, learning.

roboratus sacra instantia ~onis et redimitus praepulcrae sapientiae doctrina BYRHT. *V. Ecgwini* 354; traditus divinarum ~oni litterarum .. psalterium didicit DOMINIC *V. Ecgwini* I 1.

3 erudition, knowledge.

manifestissime declaratur quod tua sagaci ~one non livescam (*Allocutio ad regem*) ALDH. *PR* 42; virum Latina, Graeca, et Saxonica lingua atque ~one multipliciter instructum BEDE *HE* V 8 p. 296; litteras tuae devotae ~onis legi CUTHB. *Ob. Baedae* clx; ~onem legendi et canendi et ipse affatim didicit et aliis .. gratis intimavit ORD. VIT. III 9 p. 110; latet .. sub otio laudabilis plerumque virtus et ~o GIR. *TH intr.* p. 5.

eruditivus, educative, instructive.

dicitur sequens voluntas et concessio .. duplex: hec dispensativa et ~a ad salutem BRADW. *CD* 598B.

eruditor [LL], instructor, tutor; **b** (w. gen. of subject taught).

o probi pueri et venusti mathites, vos hortatur vester ~or ut pareatis divinis disciplinis ÆLF. *Coll.* 103; illico fugatis angoribus puer recepit sanitatem ibidemque .. suscepit ~orem GOSC. *Mir. Iv.* lxix; parentes quippe eo usque superstites pravi solent fieri natorum ~ores PULL. *Sent.* 761C; ~ores nationum, magistri populorum BALD. CANT. *Comment. Fid.* 619D; abbas Westmonasterii .. in hiis principis ~or W. SAY *Lib. Reg. Cap.* 76. **b** quot enim sunt ~ores justitie, tot sunt stelle [cf. *Dan.* xii] P. BLOIS *Serm.* 594C.

eruditorium, school.

†pedagogum [? l. paedagogium], ~ium puerorum *GlC* P 268.

eruere [CL]

1 to pluck or dig out, to remove (also fig.); **b** (eyes); **c** (plant or sim.).

796 agricola uniones ~it de glarie, sed aurum in opus coronae deficit ALCUIN *Ep.* 99; evellit, i. ~et, *alyft GlH* E 380; lapides .. de locis subterraneis ~ti ANSELM *Misc.* 313; paulatim .. subducantur desideria carnis .. et ab eis ~antur bona temporalia R. NIGER *Mil.* III 69; GARL. *Tri. Eccl.* 114 (v. capsa c). **b** (*Inst. Cnuti*) *GAS* 333 (v. educere 3b); **c1157** interdum sibi lesit nasum vel ~it oculum qui salutifero signo faciem munire disponit J. SAL. *Ep.* 51 (96); capto insultas Samsoni .. cui ~ti sunt oculi AILR. *Serm.* 446C; **1203** (v. dispensatio 3d); Philistei ~unt Samsoni ambos oculos ejus AD. DORE *Pictor* 161. **c** ~ta radicibus paganorum cultura, ad fidem catholicam conversus est ALDH. *VirgP* 48; W. MALM. *GR* IV 324 (v. 1 desecare a); ut ~eret virgulas et poneret eas in aquarum fonticulis *Holy Rood-Tree* 44; ipsas potius morborum radices ~ere conemur AILR. *Spec. Car.* II 1. 547C.

2 to 'unearth', dig out (fig.).

798 nobis dirigere .. Plinii libellos .. si forte inde .. aliquid ~ere valeamus ALCUIN *Ep.* 155; R. NIGER *Mil.* III 69 (v. eruderare 2b); GIR. *TH pref.* p. 20 (v. diligere 5a); ut de indefinitis et inextricabilibus paucissima ~amus ALB. LOND. *DG* 6. 8.

3 (w. pers. obj.) to pick up, drag away. **b** to rescue, deliver, protect. **c** to release (from obligation).

Sigberctum .. invitum monasterio ~entes duxerunt in certamen BEDE *HE* III 18 p. 163; regina .. prostrata precatur ut properent ..; ~unt se, properant, ut interficiant innocuum MAP *NC* IV 15 f. 56; zabulum ~entes ..

a terra, projecerunt illud de ripa in flumen *VSH* (*Ciaran de Cluain* 12) I 204. **b** ~e me de manibus inimicorum meorum ALCH. *Or.* 145; inquit "Deiri, de ira ~ti et ad misericordiam Christi vocati" BEDE *HE* II 1; **c780** ~e te de harum carcere tribulationum ALCUIN *Ep.* 1; sit ejus vobis inexpugnabilis clipeus eundo et redeundo, quo mentis et corporis incommoditate ~amini EGB. *Pont.* 98; ~e, i. defende, .. *gener* vel *arede GlH* E 335; cum de manu filiorum alienorum ~ti exultabuntur HON. *Spec. Eccl.* 1074A; **s1188** convenit .. quod .. ~erentur a manibus Saracenorum DICETO *YH* II 56; a limbo / sanctos patres eruis WALT. WIMB. *Virgo* 108; regalis nobilitas .. tales nobiles .. in civitate premiserat qui .. ipsam a predonibus .. ~erent *Ps.*-ELMH. *Hen. V* 69. **c 1361** viros religiosos .. ab omnimodis servitiis .. exemimus, ~imus, liberamus *Reg. Paisley* 68.

4 to reclaim (land). **b** to pluck (hide).

c1155 terram quam de eadem silva ~tam fratribus de L. jam ante concesseret G. FOLIOT *Ep.* 330. **b 1444** certi coriorum molitarii et operarii civitatis predicte [London'] .. se ad suburbia .. diverterunt, moram suam in eisdem .. facientes coriumque vitulinum, ovinum et agninum ex parte pilosa eruatum, rasum, contrafactum et omnibus corio caprino et hedulino simile .. molitantes, parantes et operantes *Pat* 458 m. 6 (cf. ib.: quod nullus .. aliud corium vitulinum, ovinum vel agninum ex parte pilosa eruatum, rasum ..).

5 to raze, destroy.

~ta, i. distructa *GlH* E 340; in cujus regni sunt tempore cuncta / regibus antiquis regnantibus eruta quondam / limina sacrorum reparata monasteriorum WULF. *Swith.* II 1076.

eruga v. eruca 2.

erugare [CL], to free from wrinkles.

~at, planum facit *GlC* E 288.

erugire [cf. CL rugire], to bellow, roar.

subito emulus ejus .. de occultis ~iendo prosiliit R. COLD. *Cuthb.* 67.

eruitio, erutio

1 tearing out.

1355 si de oculorum .. ~tione .. constiterit [cf. *Matth.* v 29] *Mon. Hib. & Scot.* 309b; si faceret sibi maculam vel aliud impedimentum in oculo etiam sine ~itione J. BURGH *PO* f. 113.

2 rescue.

c1239 nostrum est .. omnis vitii .. correctio et anime ab eodem ~itio GROS. *Ep.* 127.

erula, core (of fruit).

~a, A. *the core WW*; *a colke*, ~a, interior pars pomi *CathA*.

erulus [cf. CL erus], lordling.

~i, domini *GlC* E 278; ego .. minimus regis massarum ~us Hibernie, benevolus innocentis exulis *Quadr. Reg. Spec.* 31.

erumn- v. aerumn-.

erumpere [CL]

1 (of person or animal) to spring, burst forth. **b** (mil.) to make a sortie. **c** to break away (from, also fig.).

~ens grex catulorum de cubili leaenae barbarae tribus .. cyulis GILDAS *EB* 23; properavit erumpere portis SERLO BAY. 243; G. MON. X 5 (v. curare 1b). **b** Osricum .. ~ens subito .. inparatum cum toto exercitu delevit BEDE *HE* III 1; erupit ab ea [villa] pars Gallicani exercitus *G. Hen. V* 10. **c** nec .. de sordibus peccatorum surgere potest ~ere ANSELM (*Or.* 9) III 30; GIR. *TH* II 24 (v. carcer 2).

2 (of natural phenomenon) to break out. **b** (of fluid, esp. river or sim., also pass.) to rise or branch out. **c** (of rock) to break (surface), project.

accidit .. validam inundantis pluviae tempestatem ~ere WULF. *Æthelwold* 5; pluvie mira .. inundatio erupit ORD. VIT. XII 5 p. 327; puteus .. flammivomus .. ~ebat secus pedes diaboli COGGESH. *Visio* 13. **b** bini aestus oceani qui circum Britanniam ex infinito oceano septentrionali ~unt BEDE *HE* IV 14; in insula stagni .. de quo Deruuentionis fluvii primordia ~unt *Ib.* 27 p. 274; domina mea .., quos fontes dicam erupisse de pudicissimis oculis? ANSELM (*Or.* 2) III 8; [flumina] subito e stagnis erupta GIR. *TH* I 7; lacte in uberibus ~ente J. FURNESS *Kentig.* 1; erant .. meatus per quos aqua ~ens terram .. dividebat et in .. montes conglobabat *Quaest. Salern.* P 57; *Ps.*-GROS. *Summa* 621 (v. divinus 3b). **c** *V. Cuthb.* III 4 (v. concavare a).

3 (of light) to become visible, to burst into view.

erumpens aurora micat WULF. *Swith.* I 1181; radii solis foras ~ebant *VSH* (*Comgall* 15) II 8.

4 (of plant) to spring up (also fig.). **b** (refl.) to swell.

tyrannorum virgultis crescentibus et in immanem silvam jam jamque ~entibus GILDAS *EB* 13; purpurei passim flores ~unt ALB. LOND. *DG* 8. 7; BART. ANGL. XVII 46 (v. chelidonius 2a); videmus folia ~ere *Regim. Princ.* 98. **b** tandem .. illo tantillo veneni [canis rabidi] sese ~ente et acuto .. tota facies [morsi] inflata est *Quaest. Salern.* Ba 89.

5 (w. ref. to speech or utterance): **a** to speak out, burst forth, shout; **b** (w. *in fletum*, *verba*, or sim.); **c** (trans.).

a alii .. virtutes .. per illum factas .. disputabant, alii in cujus virtute illa quae faciebat dubitantes ~ebant FELIX *Guthl.* 46; turbare in me cor meum! ~e et clama, anima mea! ANSELM (*Or.* 15) III 63. **b** Dei sacerdos .. extemplo erupit in fletum OSB. *V. Dunst.* 38; in vocem laudis .. potentie superne erupit DOMINIC *V. Ecgwini prol.*; vehementi merore tactus mox in lacrimas erupit ORD. VIT. XII 45 p. 482; G. MON. VI 8 (v. 2 contristare); in hujusmodi verba erupit *Chr. Battle* f. 112v. **c** quia causam tanti ploratus narrare non posset, nisi crebro verba interrumpendo et ingeminatos gemitus ~endo ANSELM (*Or.* 76) III 66 (cf. ib 53: dic, beate Stephane, quod intus fovebas, unde mixturam tot suavitatum foras ~ebas).

6 (of abstr.) to break out, burst forth. **b** (of event) to crop up.

~it amantis dulcedo, ut non ~at flentis amaritudo ANSELM (*Or.* 16) III 66; cogor quae conantur ~ere animi reprimere *Id.* (*Ep.* 47) III 160; que [species] de corruptione ~unt, ut vermium quoddam genus PULL. *Sent.* 718C; erupit hostilitas inter angelum et hominem ALEX. BATH *Mor.* IV 53 p. 146; succedit invidia, ~it anxietas R. NIGER *Mil.* III 32 (cf. ib. 66: jam usque ad aliquos potentes, illiteratos tamen, erupit contagio). **b** cum autem cause majores ~ebant, referebantur ad superiores eorum justiciarios (*Leg. Ed. retr.*) *GAS* 652 (cf. ib. *Leg. Ed.*: insurgebant).

7 to break (trans.). *V. et. rumpere.*

W. CANT. *Mir. Thom.* II 30 (v. anguina).

erumptiolum v. eruptiolum.

eruncare [CL], to uproot.

~are, eruere radicitus *GlC* E 287; ~are, i. eradicare *GlH* E 334; ~are, evellere, vellicare OSB. GLOUC. *Deriv.* 199; ~ant .. et evellunt nemus et radicitus a stirpe compellunt in planitiem MAP *NC* I 24 f. 16v.

erund- v. hirund-. **erupere** v. exubere.

eruptio [CL]

1 (mil.) attack, sortie.

799 castigatio est magna [paganorum] ~o .. quia .. vota non servant famuli Dei ALCUIN *Ep.* 184; dum .. ~onem .. propugnatorum .. timeret ORD. VIT. IV 3 p. 174.

2 discharge. **b** eruption.

aeris inclusi et per fenestras occultas sensim exhalantis, subita .. et violenta .. ~o GIR. *IK* I 2; humores commoventur et inde fit ~o sanguinis *Quaest. Salern.* Ba 82. **b** nigrorum apostematum per corpus ~o COGGESH. *Visio* 31.

3 spring (of water).

1375 [Johannis] effodientis et exquirentis .. saltus et ~ones aque dulcis pro uno conductu aque a laco usque in castrum de Q. *KRAc* 545/5.

eruptiolum, skirmish, little sortie.

[erat] erumptiolum bellice cladis. indifferenter decurrunt ad remedium *Collect. Stories* 221.

1 erus (herus) [CL]

1 lord, master (of house).

erus, dominus *GlC* E 279; ille herus agilis .. ditatus erat praerogativa HUGEB. *Wynn.* 2; herum LANTFR. *Swith.* 1 (v. erilis 1a); si vis .. / nobilis inter heros urbanam ducere vitam D. BEC. 2; GIR. *IK* I 12 (v. 2 era 1a); splendide pransus herus vermibus esca datur *Brutus* 536.

2 the Lord, God.

omnipotentis Heri quicquid provincia cernit / actus per varios digerit haec series *De libero arbitrio* 13.

2 erus v. ervum.

eruscum [LL], bramble (*Rubus fruticosus*).

herba erusti, *þæt is bremel Leechdoms* I 34; †erasti, *bremel Gl. Durh.*

erutago [dub.], kind of herb.

item ~inem, acetum, centauream, lapacium [etc.] .. cum modico sale commisce GILB. II 81v. 2.

erutha v. eruca 1. **erutio** v. eruitio.

ervum [CL], **~us,** vetch (*Vicia* [*Ervum*] *ervilia*) or its seed. **b** couch-grass (*Agropyron*) or sim.

si appareant elevationes dure grosse quasi †herbus in brachiis GILB. IV 205. 2; erbus vel erbicus, erus, orobus idem *Alph.* 58; herbum, sive, ut alii dicunt, orobum, nascitur ut lenticula, seritur etiam, cujus aliud est pallidum, aliud subrufum, et aliud album; vires habet acres et dictericas valde *Ib.* 81. **b** habeat ligones quibus tirsos extirpet .. vel ~os [*gl.*: *quichepens, esternuris*], lollia, carduos, avenas steriles NECKAM *Ut.* 111; ~us, A. *quechyn WW*; *quikk*, versus: dic herbas ervos, dicas in corpore nervos *CathA*.

eryngion, ~ium [CL < ἠρύγγιον], **~us,** 'eryngo', sea holly (*Eryngium maritimum*).

herba ~ius, *wiþ þæs migðan astyrunge Leechdoms* I 64; yringi radic. GILB. II 99. 1; yringorum quos Sarraceni secacul vocant *Ib.* V 215 v. 2; recipe radicum feniculi, .. millefol', iringorum, endivie GAD. 66v. 2; yringus, saliunca idem *SB* 25; sanatilis, yringus idem, A. *yringus* [v. l. *yringes*] *Alph.* 160; de speciebus [plus fecundancia sunt] zinziber conditum, yringi conditi, galanga, liquincia, saturien, semen erice KYMER 19; ~ium *is named in Englishe sea hulver or sea holly* TURNER *Herb Names* D 1; ~ium autem laetissimo proventu per litora [Cornwalliae] passim reperitur CAMDEN *Br.* 149.

erysimum [CL < ἐρύσιμον], hedge mustard (*Sisymbrium*) or sim. *Cf. eruca* 1.

recipe .. petre capitis corvi, malle, vij erisi[ma], anisi, viscaginis etc. GILB. II 112v. 2; erismon, quam alii erucam goratinam dicunt, nascitur in muris et in ortis; folia habet et virgam eruce agresti similia, florem nigellum, semen simile cardamamo *Alph.* 59.

erysipelas [CL < ἐρυσίπελας], (med.) erysipelas, 'St. Anthony's fire'.

erysipila, *wilde fyr* ÆLF. *Gl.*; pessimas et mortiferas inducit in corpore passiones sicut herisipilam BART. ANGL. IV 1; [frigida et incisiva] .. in exterioribus posita calidos tumores repercutiunt, ut flegmonem et herisipelam GILB. III 162. 2; *Ib.* IV 204. 2 (v. erysipelatus); si est vincens colera rubea, generatur apostema quod nominatur herisipilla GAD. 24v. 2 (cf. ib. 25. 1: herisipilarum sunt due species: una est herisipila ruboris ..; alia est herisipila formicularis); erisipila interpretatus 'sacer ignis', i. execrabilis; .. herisipila, i. ignis sacer vel acer *SB*; erisipela interpretatur sacer ignis vel acer vel execrabilis .. vel ignis persicus *Alph.* 59.

erysipelatodes [LL < ἐρυσιπελατώδης], (med.) erysipelatoid, of the nature of erysipelas.

si [sanguis fit] subtilis non multum, facit flegmonem †herisipillidem; adhuc si subtilis valde, facit herisipillam flegmonidem GAD. 24v. 2.

erysipelatus, (med.) erysipelatous, afflicted w. erysipelas.

herisipila est apostema factum de ignita colera, unde membrum cui insidet .. comburit. .. fit locus niger, combustus, durus .. et male tractabilis, .. et labia tenuia, et tunc cognoscitur locus ~atus GILB. IV 204. 2.

erythrodanum [CL < ἐρυθρόδανον], madder (*Rubia tinctorum*).

eritridanum vel eritrodanum, rubea major idem, quo utimur tinctores, A. *mader Alph.* 59 (cf. ib. 155: rubea major, G. *warence* vel *wadde*, A. *mader*).

erythros [CL < ἐρυθρός], red.

eritron, i. rubicundum, inde yperitron, i. subrubicundum *Alph.* 59.

es v. aes, 1 esse. **esa** v. esus 1. **esarbera** v. eusarcia. **esart-** v. essart-. **esb-** v. et. exb-. **esborda** v. evesborda. **esbranc-** v. exbranc-.

esbrium, marjoram (*Origanum*).

~ium, saltica, lilifagus, eupatorium idem, licet quidam lilifagum accipiant pro sola agresti salvia; ~ium, secundum quosdam i. majorana *SB*; majorana, ~ium, sansucus [persa] idem, minuta habet folia et plures stipites graciles *Alph.* 107.

esc- v. et. exc-, sc-.

esca [CL]

1 food: **a** (collect.); **b** (pl.); **c** (fig.).

a si quis habet .. matrimonia non licita, tamen licitum est ~am quam habent manducare THEOD. *Pen.* II 12. 31; post insolitam .. aescae potusque parcitatem BEDE *HA* 16; sumo mihi mundos [pisces] in ~am [AS: *mete*] ÆLF. *Coll.* 94; rex quoque quem genuit piscibus esca fuit ORD. VIT. XII 26 p. 417; quasi aves ad ~am clanculo pedetentim advenere OSB. BAWDSEY clxx; *Brutus* 536 (v. 1 erus 1); **c1200** reddendo .. tres preces cum aratro et tres in Augusto cum ~a de domo mea *AncD* A 3023; nonne es vas sordium? numquid eris ~a [ME: *fode*] vermium? *AncrR* 103; **1494** uti poterit arte sua panes, †estiam [l. escam], et serviciam facere *Lib. Kilken.* 98. **b** sic quoque mellifluis escarum pasco saginis ALDH. *Aen.* 10 (*Palma*) 91; de vino et ~arum dapibus HUGEB. *Wynn.* 6; FRITH. 227 (v. epimenia a); mures .. ~as eorum omnes et potiones tam consumunt quam corrumpunt GIR. *IK* II 7; quos ab ~is carnalibus [AS: *giriordum*] precipio abstinere *Rit. Durh.* 16. **c** forestariorum .. officiales .. depredantur pauperes ... pauperes vicecomitum aut nemoralium judicum .. sunt ~a et potus P. BLOIS *Ep.* 95. 298C; jejunum suscepit .. / .. / amplius affectans anime quam corporis escam H. AVR. *Hugh* 980.

2 tinder, fuel (as food for flames).

escha ANSELM *Misc.* 302 (v. exstinguibilitas); aer ignitus inter crystallum et ~as existens ipsius ignis est causa quare ~a ille, sc. aer existens fomentum .. ignis, ignitur *Quaest. Salern.* B 142.

escaat-, escact-, escaett- v. escaere c, escaet-.

escaēre [AN *eschaier*, OF *escheoir* < *excadēre], **a** (intr.) to escheat, revert by escheat, be forfeited. **b** (trans.) to take as escheat, confiscate. **c** (p. ppl. *escaetus*); *cf. escaeta* 1. *V. et. escaetare.*

a **1205** in .. escaetis et aliis que eam contingunt de baronia patris sui quando ~ient *RChart* 150b (cf. ib. 152a: si ipsa [terra] forte per defectum heredis predicti A. nobis ~iat); **1229** rex concessit Thurstano de P. illas duas carucatas terre .. que regi ~ebant per suspensionem Willelmi de B. *Cl* 206; **1249** ita .. quod omnia que ratione predicte terre infra terminum predictum poterunt exchaire .. priori et conventui .. remanebunt *FormA* 135; **1268** si .. contigerit terciam partem terre .. in manibus Galfridi et Matildis permanere vel eschaere *Cl* 381; **1314** quod eidem J. eskaere seu jure hereditario descendere posset *ChartR* 101 r. 13 (cf. *CalCh* III 255). **b** **s1435** cum venisset eskaetor .. regis ad partes, eskaevit locum dictum egitque ut cogeretur abbas ostendere titulum sui juris .. et totus tam eskaetacionis quam responsionis subsequitur hic processus AMUND. II 109. **c** **c1141** dedi ei .. c libratas terre de terris excaatis *Regesta* 276; **1142** dedi Willemo filio Otuel' .. c libratas terre de terris ~is *Mandeville* 169 (cf. ib. 167: eschaetis); **1159** vicecomes r. c. de c solidis de Bercholt, terra escaetta *Pipe* 6; **1168** vicecomes r. c. de xxiij s. iiij d. de feodo militis escaetto de .. eodem auxilio *Ib.* 53; **1173** de c s. de firma de W. terra escacta *Ib.* 108; **1175** vij s. de firma de Merton', terra excacta, de feodo Peverelli *Ib.* 89 (cf. ib. 139: de firma maneriorum et excactarum); **1220** terram .. que excaeta fuit in manu sua de Hugone *CurR* VIII 217; **1224** vicecomes debet xxij s. .. de quadam domo exchaetta in Oxon' *KRMem* 6 m. 8 (cf. *LTRMem* ad loc. (m. 6): domo escheeta); **1239** onerant se .. de v s. iiij d. per quasdam terras ~as infra burgum *ExchScot* 165.

escaëta, ~um [AN *escete, eschaete*, OF *escheoite*; cf. escaetus *p. ppl. of* escaere]

1 escheat. *Cf. excidamentum.*

1163 xiij s. et ij d. .. de escaetta ferie que fuit Willelmi de H. *Pipe* 19; **1169** de propresturis et ~is *Ib.* 2; eschaete vulgo dicuntur que, decedentibus hiis qui de rege tenent in capite, cum non extet ratione sanguinis heres, ad fiscum relabuntur. .. at cum paterfamilias miles vel serviens de rege tenens in capite fati debita solverit relictis tamen liberis quorum primogenitus minor est annis, redditus quidem ejus ad fiscum redeunt, sed hujusmodi non simpliciter '~a' sed '~a cum herede' dicitur. .. item est ut tertium genus excidentium vel ~arum, quod fisco provenit jure perpetuo. cum aliquis de rege tenens in capite perpetrati sceleris sibi conscius .. per fugam vite consulit, vel si super eodem objecto convictus vel confessus terra simul et vita judicatur indignus, omnia que sui juris fuerant mox infiscantur *Dial. Scac.* II 10 B-F; cum quis .. sine certo herede moritur .. solent domini feodorum feoda illa tamquam escheatas in manus suas capere GLANV. VII 17 (cf. ib.: domino remanet hereditas illa eskaeta ad permanentia); **s1189** [Ricardus] rex constituit Johannem fratrem Willemi M. .. custodem et receptorem omnium escaitarum suarum in Anglia *G. Ric. I* 91; **1193** R. M. .. iiij li. .. de escaeta in Stanton' lega *Pipe* 123; **1194** in rotulo exchaetarum *Ib.* 195; **1201** (v. custos 5c); **1205** (v. escaere a); **1212** rex Henricus pater dedit Ricardo Robbe Sterta, quod fuit escheta vigilatorum de Monte Acuto reddendo inde j gruem *Fees* I 79; **1212** tenet dim. carucatam terre in villa de K. de esketo, sc. de feodo Ricardi .., de dono domini regis *Ib.* 177; **1212** Albertus .. habet in B. et F. iiij partem unius militis de feodo Gilberti de Gant de ~o domini regis *Ib.* 187; nonne vides quod abbas dat eschoetas terrarum de dominicis terris conventus? BRAKELOND 151v.; **1225** manerium de C. .. fuit ~um .. regis *CurR* XII 172; **1233** faciemus eidem R. .. competens escambium in wardis et escheatis ad valentiam predicti manerii *Ambrosden* II 286; **1236** quietum clamavi .. redditum xx sol. et regale servitium et wardos et esceitas et cartam et quicquid juris mei .. evenire potuit *FormA* 374; **1239** per omnes terras suas habeat et teneat terras Normannorum que sunt de feodo suo cum exciderint tanquam ascaeta sua *KRMem* 18 m. 12d.; **1243** Roberto de M. faciant habere x libratas terre de primis exkaetis regis, quamcito acciderint *Cl* 23; **c1249** quicquid .. me possit contingere in exchetis, wardis, et ceteris omnibus convencionibus *Cart. Osney* II 127; **1250** cum homagiis, releviis, achaetis et secta ad curiam *Reg. S. Aug.* 488; **1253** in quinquaginta libratis terre in exscaetis (*Pat*; cf. *Cal.* 253) *RGasc* I 283; eschetis et gardiis suos honorare / debet rex *Carm. Lewes* 297; **1275** Wobernefond fuit ~um Norman' per Johannem .. et post decessum dicti J. dominus H. rex .. dedit .. villam .. domino T. de E. *Hund.* I 71b; **1279** nos .. concessisse .. maritagium .. cum omnibus pertinenciis et excahetis ad dictam custodiam pertinentibus *Reg. Heref.* 205; **1279** unam domum .. que fuit acchaeta domini regis propter feloniam et fuit ascheator Walterus Hervi (*Hund.*) *Lond. Ed. I & II* II 146; **1285** tria brevia communia locum tenere debent de perquisitis et eschatis .. regis *PQW* 250a; **1292** (v. dirationatio a); **c1300** de ascheitis scilicet marescallus tenet terram que fuit Walteri *Reg. S. Aug.* 60; **1309** sive .. rex presentet .. racione custodie vel exchaeti *Reg. Cant.* II 1030; **1331** terras de eskaeta in dicto burgo *ExchScot* 358; **1335** confirmavimus .. forestam de S. .. cum .. regalitatibus .. officiis .. ascaetis ac etiam cognitionibus placitorum *RScot* 380a; **1407** de omnibus .. terris .., aquis, piscariis, escheatis et releviis .. in campis de G. *FormA* 329.

2 brash, 'cablish', wood fallen or cut from tree. **b** grain fallen from stalk. **c** material from derelict building. **d** (w. *nubis*) something fallen from clouds.

1175 sciatis .. me dedisse .. duas karectas .. ad trahendam ramillam de landis parci et kaetam de mortuo bosco ad focarium .. monachorum *Cart. Colne* 16v.; **1231** mandatum est Galfrido E. quod .. faciat habere abbatisse Wilton' in bosco suo .. sexties xx quercus ad cheverones faciendos cum ~is earundem quercuum *Cl* 5; **1234** escaettis (v. carbonare 2b); **1243** faciat .. habere .. x bonas quercus .. cum cooperonibus et omnibus excaetis in bosco de C. *Cl* 42; **1244** eschaetas, **1268** ~as (v. cippagium); **1252** de exscaetis lignorum *DCCant. Reg.* H f. 174b; **1263** (v. copero 1); **1300** r. c. de xv s. vj d. receptis de escaet' meremii prostrati *MinAc* 925 (2) m. 3; **1364** de loppis et ~is arborum (*MinAc*) *Econ. Condit.* app. 76; **1369** respondet de xliij s. receptis de ramis arborum, cortic' et aliis ~is arborum provenientibus de .. arboribus prostratis *KRAc* 476/11 m. 1. **b** **1297** frumentum .. in aucis et gallinis de ~is ij buss' (*MinAc*) *Econ. Condit.* app. 10 (cf. ib. 11: in mixtione cum avena de ~is, ix ring'). **c** **1297** debent .. conservare .. parvam grangiam .. cum meremio .. domini et habebunt ~as de veteribus domibus (*Ext. Thorpe-le-Soken*) Essex R. O. D/DHw M. 1 m. 3. **d** bidentes .. per commestum cujusdam nubis ~e, que tunc temporis cadere contingit .., corrumpi poterint et infirmari *Fleta* 169.

3 offal (of carcass).

1238 commodum regis faciendum de eschaetis et exitibus porcorum regis *Liberate* 13 m. 24; (= *Cal.* p. 354: eshcaeta); **1242** quod ~e bestiarum quas capiet ei allocentur sicut ei allocari consueverunt in warderoba nostra *Cl* 442; **1307** de vij ~is porcorum necat' ad lardarium (*Ac. Combe*) *Doc. Bec* 147 (cf. ib. 170 [**1308**]: escheta: .. de x eschaeyttis receptis de porcis necatis); **1344** ~a unius apri, xij d. *KRAc* 390/11 r. 15; **1478** de le *fog lammis* .. et ~is ovium concessis D. C. seniori *ExchScot* 480.

escaëtabilis, escheatable, liable to escheat.

1389 quod terre sue Wallenses forent ~es pro defectu exitus corporum suorum [i. e. tenencium] *Pat* 328 m. 8.

escaëtare [AN *escheter*, OF *escheoiter*], **a** (intr.) to escheat, revert by escheat. **b** (trans.) to take as escheat, confiscate; **c** (p. ppl. *escaetatus*). *V. et. escaere.*

a **1202** venit ad domum .. sicut ad suam propriam que ~avit in manum suam de R. villano suo qui obiit *SelPlCrown* 9; **c1220** que v m. mihi vel heredibus meis debebunt ut de warda eschaetare si .. Walterus .. obierit *Reg. S. Thom. Dublin* 17. **b** **1454** Alexander N. .. cujus bona eschaetabantur *ExchScot* 672; *to enchete*, fiscare .. eschaetare *CathA*; omnia bona Macduff eschaetavit *Extr. Chr. Scot.* 57 (cf. FORDUN *Chr.* VI 54: terras .. et predia .. confiscari mandavit). **c** **1429** de duabus perticatis terre .. eschaetatis propter rebellionem .. domini Johannis *ExchScot* 493; **1479** de bonis eschaetatis cujusdam .. fugitivi *Ib.* 18.

escaëtaria [AN *escheterie*], escheatry, escheatorship.

1248 de bonis .. Stephani de H. levari faciat .. xix li. .. de arreragiis in quibus tenetur regi de officio eschaeterie dum fuit choeschaetor in comitatu illo [Glouc'] *Cl* 53; **1250** Willelmus de S. amotus est ab officio ~ie in comitatu Norf' *Cl* 278; **1265** me .. recepisse iiij m. argenti de eschaetria .. regis per manus magistri Willelmi de B., eschaetoris .. regis in Hibernia *Chanc. Misc.* 35/14 (8); **1290** venit ad Scaccarium coram ipso [thesaurario] et baronibus, set pro nullo debito eschaeterye (*Pet. Parl.*) *DocExch* 59; **1296** commisimus .. Petro de Donewyk officium ~ie *RScot* 27b; **1304** onerantur .. in quodam alio compoto eskaeterie (*Chanc. Misc.*) *Doc. Scot.* II 429; **1320** cives civitatis London' non permiserunt ipsum escaetorem officium suum escaetrie exercere infra eandem civitatem *RParl* I 370a; **c1336** quod major .. officium escaetrie infra civitatem exerceat *MGL* I 145.

escaëtarius, escheator. *V. et. escaetator, escaetor.*

1239 Willelmus filius Ricardi habet diem ad computandum de tempore quo fuit escaetar' *KRMem* 17 m. 11d.; **1246** de eschaetis: .. duo burgagia .. in Preston' sunt escaeta .. regis et posita sunt per eschaetarium .. regis ad dim. m. per annum, et Adam .. ea tenet per predictos ~ios *Fees* 1389; **c1290** super hoc ~ius .. regis nostri inhibuit omnem ministracionem *AncC* XXV 11; **s1290** Henricus de B. capitalis eschaetarius .. regis B. COTTON 175; **1316** Robertus .. camarariis, justiciariis, vicecomitibus, ~iis .. salutem *Cart. Holyrood* 86; **13..** v marcarum per officialem nostrum .. et eschaetorios nostros levand[ar]um *Conc. Scot.* II 65; *an encheter*, fiscator, .. eschatarius, eschaetor *CathA*.

escaëtatio, escheating.

s1435 eskaetacionis (v. escaere b).

escaëtator, escheator. *V. et. escaetarius, escaetor.*

1212 Ricardus de E. et Robertus de B. ~atores r. c. de lxiiij s. de exitu terre Derekin del Acre *Pipe* 58; **1239** rex [manerium] illud commisit .. ~atoribus suis *Cl* 731.

escaeteria v. escaetaria.

escaëtor, ~ator [AN *escaetour, eschetur*, OF *escheoitor*], escheator: **a** (var. & unspec.); **b** (dist. as *citra* or *ultra Trentam*); **c** (dist. by county); **d** (dist. by city or town); **e** (Scot.); **f** (Ir.); **g** (of bishop); **h** (eccl.) receiver. *V. et. escaetarius, escaetator.*

a **1214** ~ores r. c. .. de firma et exitibus terrarum Willelmi de B. *Ib.* 61; **1217** de ~oribus atornatis .. attornavimus Simonem et R. clericum ad custodiendum omnes escaetas *Pat* 66 (cf. ib. 70: de excaetoribus assignatis); **1233** computate Willelmo R. et Bernardo de G. ~oribus nostris, in exitibus escaetarum ccc li. .. per Petrum de R. *Liberate* 10 m. 11; **1234** rex .. Ricardo de la L. et Ade filio Willelmi escaettoribus suis salutem *Cl* 488; **1235** memorandum quod asscheitores regis habuerunt xx s. de villa de Herefeud *Fees* 474; **1243** de tempore quo fuit custos escaetarum nostrarum sub Petro de R. capitali excaetatore nostro *Cl* 52; **1253** habeat libertatem .. quod non eligatur in coronatorem nec fiat vicecomes, exscaetor, viridarius [etc.] (*Pat*; cf. *Cal.* 252) *RGasc* I 281; **1255** (v. 2 claudere 8a); **1275** de escaietoribus et subescaietoribus *Hund.* I 69 (cf. ib. 81: de eschaytoribus; 203: excaitor); **1283** Agnes dicit quod postquam .. rex habuit seisinam predicti manerii ipsa perquisivit breve .. regis eschaetori qui ipsam in seisinam nomine termini predicti posuit *PQW* 706a; **1290** et eschaetor bene cognoscit quod fecit reextendere manerium predictum (*Pet. Parl.*) *Hist. Exch.* 66; **1292** de omnibus bonis depredatis tam per eschettores quam per alios depredatores *RParl* I 72a; **1297** petiit escheator ad opus .. regis cupam et palefridum .. abbatis [Oseneye] defuncti *Ambrosden* I 470; **1313** de escheatoribus vel subescheatoribus in seisina .. regis facientibus vastum vel destructionem in parcis boscis [etc.] *Eyre Kent* I 39; **1331** concessit .. abbati et conventui quod .. habeant omnes fines .. omnium hominum suorum .. sine .. impedimento regis .. ~orum, vicecomitum aut aliorum .. ministrorum *PQW* 23b; **1340** breve ad puniendos ~ores, vicecomites, taxatores, collectores et omnes alios ministros regis (cf. *LB Lond.* F f. 46) *MGL* I 623; **1361** justiciarios, escheatores, vicecomites *Lit. Cant.* II 410; **s1381** voluit [Walterus Tylere] commissionem .. ad decollandum omnes juridicos et ~ores WALS. *HA* I 464; **1427** datum hesceatori domini regis vj s. viij d. (*Ac. Robertsbridge*) *HMC Rep.* LXXVII 168; **s1435** eskaetor (v. escaere b); **1439** aliquis justitiarius vicecomitum, escaitorum aut aliorum quorumcumque ministrorum BEKYNTON I 45; **1450** justiciarios, ~ores, coronatores, aut alios ballivos seu ministros nostros *Lit. Cant.* III 207; **1583** nolentes quod .. per justiciarios, ~ores, vicecomites, ballivos .. nostros .. occasionentur, molestentur .. seu graventur *Pat* 1234 m. 39. **b** **1261** ~ori nostro citra Trentam (v. coescaetor); **1271** hiis testibus: .. Johanne de R., tunc exchatore domini regis ultra Trentam .. *Reg. S. Bees* 377; **1293** ~or .. regis citra Trentam .. feriam illam in manum .. regis seysivit *RParl* I 97b; **1295** rex .. ~ori suo citra Trentam salutem (*Pat*) *Cart. Glam.* 906; **1308** rex .. Gerardo S., ~ori suo ultra Trentam, salutem (*IAQD*) *Mem. Ripon* I 209; **s1319** facta .. fidelitate literas patentes regis habuit ad escheatorem citra Trentam pro liberatione maneriorum *Hist. Roff.* 7v. **c** **1217** rex Waltero de V. et aliis excaetoribus comitatus Linc' *Cl* 311b; **1223** inquirat que .. catalla R. de P. et W. de T., quondam escaettores Cornubie, receperint in terris que fuerunt Willemi de B. *LTRMem* 6 m. 3d.; **1252** rex constituit Willemum R. ~orem suum in comitatu Suff' *Cl* 85; **1257** Radulfo de D., ~ori regis in comitatu Devon' *Cl* 44; **1264** rex eschaetori suo in comitatu Dorset' salutem *Cl* 345; **1334** ut .. velimus eis terras et tenementa .. in comitatu Northumbrie per ~orem nostrum ibidem in manum nostram capta .. restitui jubere *RScot* 261b; **1265** assumpto tecum ~ore nostro ejusdem comitatus [*Surr*] (*Pat*) *MGL* II 278; **s1281** Matheus B. .. regis eschaetor in comitatu Lincolnie, Northamtonie, Cantabrigie, Rotlandie omnia .. abbathie bona in manus regias confiscabat *Croyl. Cont. B* 482; **s1344** rex .. precepit Johanni de C. eschaetori suo in comitatu Middlesexie quod .. FLETE *Westm.* 128. **d** **1344** rex .. fideli suo Waltero de C. ~ori suo in villa Berewici *RScot* 647a; **1396** quod quilibet major .. sit eschaetor noster .. in civitate Ebor' (*ChartR*) *Mem. York* 157. **e** **1296** commisimus .. Petro de D. officium escaetarie nostre citra mare Scotie ... et ideo vobis mandamus quod eidem P. .. tanquam ~ori nostro .. citra mare predictum .. intendentes sitis *RScot* 27b (cf. ib.: commissum est Henrico de R. officium escaetarie regis ultra mare Scotie); **1326** justiciariis, vicecomitibus, ~oribus *Melrose* 361; **1369** justiciariis, vicecomitibus ~oribus et omnibus aliis ministris nostris *RMSScot* 331. **f** **1265** per manus .. Willelmi de B. eschaetoris .. regis in Hibernia (v. escaetaria); **1283** inquisicionem .. inter Petrum le P. et escheatorem Hibernie de quodam debito *AncC* IX 57. **g** episcopus [Dunelmensis] per litteras suas patentes .. constituit unum vicecomitem et unum ~orem .. ad exercendum .. omne id quod ad officia vicecomitis et escaetoris .. regis alibi in Anglie pertinebat faciendum *Langley* app. 248. **h** **1399** decano nostro et eschaetori christianitatis de K. *Melrose* 517; **1403** M. episcopus Glasg. officiali nostro ejusdem curie .. universisque et singulis decanis, exchaetoribus, rectoribus ecclesiarum *Reg. Glasg.* I 294; **1424** prope cameram ~oris ipsius ecclesie *Reg. Cant.* II 299.

escaetria v. escaetaria. **escaettus** v. escaere, escaeta. **escaetum** v. escaeta. **escaf-** v. scaff-. **escaiare** v. escaere. **escaiet-, escait-** v. escaet-. **escalatus** v. scalare.

escaldare [OF *eschauder* < LL excaldare], to scald (person). **b** to scald (carcass, to clean or remove hair).

1219 occiderunt .. hominem et eum escaudaverunt et .. asportaverunt corpus in campum *CurR* VIII 143; **1220** occiderunt .. hominem .. et eum escaudaverunt in domo *Ib.* 270; **1242** quedam garcia scaldata fuit in plumbo Roberti *AssizeR Durh* 12 (cf. ib. 17: quidam Flandrensis ~atus fuit in plumbo R. Tannatoris); **1248** ascaldata fuit in quodam plumbo *JustIt* 232 m. 1 (*Essex*) (cf. ib. m. 2*d*.: ~ata fuit in .. tyna); **1277** Robertus cocus .. cescidit in quodam kymenello pleno aqua calida et scaldatus fuit ita quod obiit *RCoron* 208 m. 1; **1363** Henricus .. etate duorum annorum .. cecidit in .. vase pleno aque boliantis .. et ibidem scaldiatus fuit *SelCCoron* 40. **b 1212** Robertus de S. tenet Bures per sergantiam ~andi porcos regis *Fees* 345; **1454** quilibet carnifex scaldet porcos suos ad communem *scaldynghouse Leet Coventry* 279.

escaldaria [AN *eschauldeure*, OF *eschaudeure*], (service of) scalding. (*Cf. King's Serjeants* 252–4).

1219 Robertus de S. tenet in Bures [*Bowers Gifford, Essex*] per serjantiam de cauderie, et valet terra ejus c s. *Fees* 276; **1227** Willelmus de B. tenet cum uxore sua villam de Bures .. per servitium eschauderie *Ib.* 1350; **1248** Willelmus G. tenet manerium de Bures per serjantiam, et est de scalderia .. regis *Ib.* 1411.

escaldarius, scalder.

1212 terram Hugonis scaldarii in parochia S. Nicholai apud macellum *E. Ch. S. Paul.* 60 (cf. ib. 209: Hugonis *le scaldur*).

escaldus v. alcaldus.

escale [OF *eschale* < Frk.; cf. AS *scealu*], bowl, vessel.

1428 vasorum de electro, ut in ~ibus [= *Foed.* X 392a: estalibus], parapsidibus, discis, sausariis et ollis *Cl* 278 m. 8; *mawnde*, ~e .. *a mete wesselle*, ~e *CathA*.

escalleta v. scarl-. **escamb-** v. excamb-.

escampa [OF *eschampe*], evasion.

a1139 precipio tibi quod sine dilatione et ~a teneas plenum rectum abbati S. Augustini .. de ecclesia de N. *Regesta* 159; **1141** concedo .. castellum de C. sine placito finaliter et sine ~a *Ib.* 634.

escancio [OF *eschancon*]

1 butler.

de ~onibus: quatuor tantum debent servire simul vice sua *Domus Reg.* 132.

2 'butlerage', duty paid on imported wine.

1266 in carriagio xx doliorum vini usque castrum de K. cum windagio et carriagio et cum emendacione dolii et libere ~onis, xxix s. iij d. *ExchScot* 26.

escangiare [AN *escanger*, OF *eschanger*], to exchange. *V. et. cambire* 1a, *excambire* 1a.

c1160 (1268) omnes concessiones et .. fidelium dona, vel .. vendita seu ~iata vel quieta clamata .. confirmo *CalCh* II 97.

escangium [OF *eschange* < excambium], **~ia,** exchange (esp. of property for other property or for money); *v. et. cambium* 1a, 1 *cangium* a, *decambium, excambium* 1a. **b** property given in exchange; *v. et. excambium* 1b.

de terra .. A. non habuit nisi x bovatas de dominico in ~io .. *DB* I 376v.; hanc terram recepit pro ~io (*Norf*) *DB* II 238; mansio [est] de excangiis Willelmi *Dom. Exon.* 475b; **c1140** x acras in excangio pro virgulto meo de C. ... dedi eis in exchangiam Corucroftam vicinam suis aedificiis .. item dedi eis in exchangium *MonA* III 276b; **c1155** ego .. pro exchangio de Hodenoc concessi et donavi Roberto priori .. in elemosinam tres forgias unamquamque pro xx solidis *BM Ch.* xli. **b** R. episcopus tenet .. xxx mansiones .. ita quod G. nichil inde habet, neque scangium neque aliam redditionem *DB* I 336; **c1200** et si non volemus eis guarantizare .. dabimus eis exchangias in predicta villa (*Wratting, Suff*) *Beds R. O.* D.D.L.L.

escariola v. scariola.

escapagium [OF *eschape*], (fine for) straying (of animal). *V. et. escapium* 1, *escapura.*

1178 r. c. de xxj s. de pasnagio et de iij s. de ~io de Beskewuda *Pipe* 88; **1278** si animalia nostra infra procinctum predicte haye inveniantur .. sine imparcacione, scapagio, et omnibus aliis dampnis et exaccionibus curialiter rechacientur *ChartR* 66.

escapelare [OF *escapler, eschapler*], to scapple, dress (timber).

1214 carpentarios .. faciatis prosternere et eskapellare .. mairemium in .. foresta *Cl* 210b (cf. ib.: esckapelandum); **1215** lx cheverones ~atos et de alio maireno quantum opus fuerit ad domum suam .. reedificandam *Cl* 224b; **1228** quod .. prosterni facias c quercus in bosco nostro de Kingeswode et ~ari et inde cariari usque ad acquam Thamisie *Liberate* 7 m. 5; **1230** ad quercus .. prosternendas et escapulandas .. carpentarios inveniat, et quercus illas sufficienter escapulatas cariari faciat usque Dovor' *Ib.* 9 m. 3; **1241** cindulas .. escapulatas (v. dolare a).

escapēre, ~iare [AN *escaper, eschapir*, OF *eschaper*]

1 (of animal) to escape (from confinement). **b** to stray (into enclosed pasture or forest).

13.. si homo, canis, catus seu alia viva bestia extra navem seu batellum viva ~ient *Little RB Bristol* I 67. **b 1279** si averia illorum in bladum vel pratum .. regis eschapiant *Hund.* II 852; **1293** capit de quolibet animali alieno ~iante in terras suas vj d. vel xij d. vel plus vel minus *PQW* 204b (cf. ib. 216a: de quolibet animali .. eschapiato in pastura sua).

2 (of person) to escape (from custody).

1274 N. le Gardiner .. traditus fuit .. Waltero vic. et ab custodia sua exchapiavit per malam vardam *Hund.* I 444; **1315** Thomam atte B. felonum et utlagatum in comitatu Kanc' permiserunt voluntarie ~iare *RParl* I 324b; **1475** Johannes S. et Henricus M. .. ab eadem prisona .. ad largum suum evaserunt et eschapuerunt (*AncIndict*) *Proc. J. P.* 242.

escapia v. escapium.

escapiamentum [OF *eschapement*], escape.

1458 propter ~um .. domini Egremond extra prisonam nostram et [vicecomitum] custodiam (*Lit. Regis*) *Reg. Whet.* I 304.

escapiare v. escapere.

escapium [OF *eschape*]

1 straying (of animal into enclosed pasture or forest). **b** fine for straying. *V. et. escapagium, escapura.*

1185 de placitis foreste de Hantescira ..: Walterus r. c. de lxxvj s. pro ~io *Pipe* 211; **1223** de boscis dicit quod .. nullam communam habere debet nec unquam habuit nisi per octo annos proximo transactos et hoc per ~ium *Cl* 132; si .. herbam paverit per eschapium Bracton 230; **1263** nunquam aliquam communiam habuit in predicto bosco .. nisi tantum aliquando per ~ium, aliquando de gracia *JustIt* 874 r. 6; **1287** quod ~ia averiorum in dominicis haiis vel boscis implacitentur in attachiamentis et emende ibidem capiantur *SelPlForest* 64; tota campania infra metas suas est in defenso .. et si averia .. ibidem venerint per eschapiam, dabitur pro eisdem [etc.] *DL Forest Proc.* 1/5 r. 15*d*.; **1362** si .. averia .. infra hayam predictam per ~ium inveniantur, absque aliquo escapio dando rechacientur *Pat* 265 m. 4 (v. et. 1b infra); **1545** de diversis tenentibus villarum ibidem pro eorum *lez overlepes* sive ~iis cum averiis suis in brueris domini .. xxxiiij s. *Rutland MSS Bailiff's Ac.* (*Notts* etc.) 35–7 *Hen. VIII* m. 5. **b 1202** si porci sui venient sine licencia mea in forestam meam .. dabunt eschapium *BBC* (*Egremont*) 61; **1205** si averia monachorum .. in forestam meam prohibitam venerint .. sine ~io et sine causa mei .. quieta redibunt *Reg. S. Bees* 372 (cf. ib. 373: sine ~is); **a1245** quod nullum eschapium capiatur inter baroniam Valis Anand' et tenementum de T. nisi de tanto, sc. de x averiis j d., de x bidentibus j d., de x capreis j d., de x porcis j d., pro equo ob. *DL Cart. Misc.* III 211; **1269** custos foreste .. appropriavit sibi injuste .. ~ium in parco de R. unde recepit dim. m. *SelPlForest* 47 (cf. ib. 48: cepit de averiis intrantibus boscum .. per ~ium .. aliquando pro uno averio ij s., .. aliquando vj d.); **1270** si .. boves et vacce per aliquos casus fortuitos infra predictas landas .. inveniantur, nolumus quod propter hoc exchapium detur *ChartR* 60 m. 12; **1327** est .. in eisdem boscis quoddam ~ium forinsecarum bestiarum, quod valet per annum ij s. *IPM* 3 (7) m. 5; **1362** (v. 1a supra).

2 escape (of person from gaol). **b** failure to prevent escape or fine for delict (paid by gaoler to king).

1477 ad gradum ecclesie .. confugit, quem parochiani .. custodire tenentur ... qui .. fecit inde ~ium *Cart. Glam.* 1711; occasione ~ie predicti J. [de prisona] *Entries* 583b. **b a1068** sint quieti in civitatibus, burgis .. de omni terreno servitio .. similiter de sectis curie .. et de murdro, et latrocinio, ~io et hamsokne *Couch. Selby* II 19; **1224** habet respectum .. de xxv solidis de eschapio *LTRMem* 6 m. 7 (cf. ib. 7 m. 1 A *d*.: pro exchapio latronis); **1227** debet c s. pro eschapio latronis *Ib.* 10 m. 8*d*.; **1227** perdonavimus Willelmo de V. viij li., quas ab eo exigis .. pro ~io cujusdam latronis *Cl* 11; **1237** de perdonatione eskapii prisonum *Cl* 507; **1260** rex perdonavit Mathie B. ~ium cujusdam mulieris deprehense cum ij panibus furtive ablatis in manerio suo de A., ubi .. pro furto .. imprisonata fuit *Cl* 96; **1261** cum quidam J... fugisset ad ecclesiam .. et inde evasisset .. vicecomes .. ab eisdem hominibus regis .. exigit ~ium .. et mandatum est .. quod .. exaccionem predicti ~ii ponat in respectum usque ad .. *Cl* 350; **1330** non fuit intencionis .. regis Ricardi per illud verbum †*utsak* [MS: *utslath*] proficuum de eschapio latronum alicui concedere, cum sit ignotum et non intelligibile *PQW* 71b (cf. ib.: de evasione latronum); **1342** quod vicecomites Londoniarum pro ~io latronum aliter quam alii vicecomites citra Trentam nullatenus onerentur seu amercientur (*Ch. Regis*) *MGL* I 145; **1354** rex .. perdonavit populo suo .. ~ia latronum, fines, amerciamenta de murdris [etc.] *G. S. Alb.* III 49; **1415** omnia amerciamenta, redemptiones .. necnon omnimoda ~ia felonum de et in villa, terris .. *MonA* VI 33.

escapulare v. escapelare.

escapura, straying (of animal). **b** fine for straying. *V. et. escapagium, escapium* 1.

1226 (1227) nec fiet imparcatura averiorum abbatis in W. si per ascapuram inventa fuerint in .. bosco sive in .. croftis *CalCh* I 49. **b c1200** denarios qui capi solebant de singulis vaccis in defenso meo pro ~a *BBC* (*Leicester*) 94; **1207** dim. m. pro ~a morarum *Pat* 70b; **1298** perquisita wodemoti cum ~is valent per annum xiij s. iij d. *IPM* 81/18; **1330** de xlj s. de eschapuris foreste hoc anno *MinAc* 802/1 r. 2.

escara v. eschara.

escare [LL], to feed, nourish.

to yife mete, ~are *CathA*.

escariare [OF *escharir*], to administer (an oath).

c1155 super quattuor evangelia juravit, Radulfo .. vicecomite jusjurandum ei ~ante *Doc. Theob.* sup. A.

escarinus, meat dish.

hic ~us, *a metdysch WW*.

escarius [CL = *used for food or eating*], (as sb. m.) carver. **b** (as sb. f.) dresser, sideboard. **c** (as sb. n.) manger. **d** (?) food.

kervare before a lorde, ~ius *PP*. **b** hec ~ia, .. i. mensa escis plena Osb. Glouc. *Deriv.* 183; ~ia, A. *dresserbord*, .. hec ~ia, *a mettabylle WW*. **c** *a mawngeur for horse*, ~ium, mansorium *CathA*. **d 1245** confirmasse .. denar' de vitulis et pullis, aucarum, gallinarum, suorum molendinorum, escar' maris, linorum, canab' *DC Chich. Liber Y* f. 153; ~ium, A. *ees WW*.

escarl- v. scarl-. **escart-** v. essart-. **escatare** v. escaere. **escaton** v. hecaton. **escaud-** v. escald-. **escauf-** v. scaff-. **escav-** v. scaw-.

escawardus, 'calver', curd-like, fresh (of salmon). *V. et. calvarius.*

1233 mandatum est ballivis Glouc' quod omnes salmones ~os quos in villa sua invenerint .. ad opus regis appretiari et in panem poni facient et bene attornatos ad regem transmitti *Cl* 349.

esceccor [cf. AN *eschec*], thief, robber.

1292 latrones et eskectores de terra de Morgannon .. intraverunt .. terram de Brakennok' et illam depredati fuerunt *RParl* 72a (cf. ib.: predicti eskettores quandam domum .. combusserunt).

esceccum [AN *eschec*], deceit, theft.

s1240 inquiratur utrum predictus G. et antecessores sui .. habuerunt chaciam illam .. pacifice ut de jure .. vel si habuerint .. illam vi aut permissione predecessorum .. abbatis vel per eskeccum; .. per eskeccum, ut .. abbas dicit M. Par. *Maj.* IV 52; **1250** absque hoc quod predictus R. et alii aliquid in predicto bosco pacifico capere solebant, nisi pro suo dando vel per eskeccum vel quod in eo devadiati fuerunt *CurR* 143 m. 32; **1256** predictus J... nuncquam .. aliquam pacificam seysinam inde habuit nec etiam predicti J., R., et A., nisi per vim et †eskottum *AssizeR Northumb* 21.

esceita v. escaeta. **esceppa** v. skeppa. **escew-** v. scaw-. **escha** v. esca 3. **eschaere** v. escaere. **eschaet-, eschaeyt-** v. escaet-. **eschalent-** v. esculent-. **eschalinga** v. scalinga. **eschamb-** v. excamb-. **eschap-** v. escap-.

eschara [CL < ἐσχάρα], (med.) eschar, scar.

corrosio, cauterizatio, membri mortificatio, escara, et similia Gad. 25v. 1; *Ib.* 29v. 1 (v. cicatrix a); *SB* 20 (v. 2 crusta 1c).

eschat- v. escaet-. **eschaton** v. hecaton. **eschaub-** v. scab-. **eschaud-** v. escald-.

eschaugwaita [OF *eschaugaite* < Frk.], guard-service (Fr.).

1200 quietum clamasse de .. tallagiis et communibus et vigiliis et eschaugwaytis et omnibus aliis exactionibus in villa de C. *RChart* 58a; **1230** sint quieti de exercitu et equitatione et escheweita, quando cives nostri Burdegalenses hujusmodi servicium nobis facere debent *Pat* 391.

eschayt- v. escaet-. **escheat-** v. escaet-. **eschec-** v. scacc-. **escheet-** v. escaere. **escheweita** v. eschaugwaita. **eshcaet-** v. escaet-. **eschetum** v. escaetum.

1 eschina [OF *eschine* < Frk.; cf. AS *scinu*], chine, backbone. **b** (of pork) chine of bacon-pig.

1278 cepit predictam Matillidem et per pedes de grandi in gradum usque ad terram prostrauit, ita quod †estinia ipsius Matillidis disrumpit, unde ipsa statim obiit *SelCKB* I 40; **1301** de eadem securi in capite suo percussit .. inter humeros et fregit ~am dorsi *Ib.* III 109. **b 1235**

de xxxviij eschin' porc' *Pipe Wint.* 159284 r. 7*d.* (cf. ib. r. 8: de ~is eorundem porcorum); **1252** (v. esclenca); **1266** de xviij eschin' porc' receptis de R. lardinario *MinAc* 1087/6 r. 1; **1321** de exitibus c porcorum mactatorum ad lardarium domini in castro .. et de ~is dictorum porcorum venditis, prec' cuj[us]libet j d. *Ib.* 992/11; **1322** habebit de lardar' quartam partem .. de collis et caudis boum et vaccarum de quibus skyne extrahuntur *DCCant.* J p. 509.

2 eschina v. eschiva.

1 eschinum [cf. AN *eskignon*], arm-bone.

s**1165** R. abbas Montis in .. brachio auro [v. l. aureo] .. jussit reponi reliquias S. Laurencii, sc. os brachii quod ~um vocant et .. minora ossa TORIGNI *Chr.* 226; **1234** percussit eum super dextrum humerum et postea super brachium, ita quod fregit unum os, sc. *le esckingnun CurR* XV 1266.

2 eschinum v. eschiva. **eschinius** v. 2 echinus 1. **eschip-, eschipp-** v. skipp-.

eschiva, ~um [OF *eschive*], guard-house, sentry-box.

1180 in facienda †eschina [l. eschiva] castri de Gisortio *RScacNorm* I 72; **1192** et eidem [Rogero constabulario de Tikehell] x m. ad faciendum eschiwas *Pipe* 224; **1209** pro uno eschiwo parando in castello de Sudhanton', xl s. *Ib.* 172; **1212** in nova domo facienda ultra portam apud Karlingford .. et una eschiwa incipienda et aliis edificiis emendandis *Pipe Ir.* 64; **1232** quod ~as castri Matillidis fieri faciat *Liberate* 10 m. 11; **1233** in fenestris .. celarii emendandis et in .. hostio .. celarii obstruendo et in una esciva facienda et ponenda in eodem celario *Ib.* 10 m. 8; **1242** viij m. quas posuit .. in quodam †eschino lapideo facto ante magnam portam castri de Notingeham *Ib.* 17 m. 6.

eschoeta v. escaeta. **esciva** v. eschiva. **esclata** v. sclata. **esclausa** v. excludere. **esclavus** v. sclavus.

esclenca [OF *esclenc, esclenche*], left fore quarter (of animal carcase).

c**1250** noverit .. nos .. concessisse Ingerando .. quartam partem feodi .. coquine nostre .. : colla multonum, et de agnis colla et capita, de spinis porcorum, partem de collo, et gulam et caudam, de bobus colla et caudas, et iiij †schleuchas *MonA* II 484b; **1252** abbas [Malmesbur'] .. concessit Willelmo .. colla et esklencas boum, colla multonum, colla et caudas eschinarum porcorum, capita hakarum [etc.] *Cl* 261 (cf. *Reg. Malm.* II 337: esclenkarum boum).

esclotura [OF *esclotoire* < ex + clausura], flood-gate, water-gate.

1331 debent .. facere caput stanni, quod wlgariter *escluse* nuncupatur, pro conservando aquam pro .. molendino, excepto quod dominus rex debet facere circa excloturam in viciniori parte dicte excloture unam brachiam *S. Jers.* I 8; rex debet invenire excloturam et postes ejusdem et facere unam brachiam capitis stagni in viciniori parte excloture *Ib.* 35.

esclus- v. excludere, excluseta. **escomarium** v. scumarium.

escorcheria [OF *escorcherie*], shambles, abattoir.

12.. de escorgeria *DCCant.* H f. 16 (cf. ib. 5v.: *de lescorcherie*).

escorchiare [OF *escorchier* < excorticare], to bark (tree). *V. et. excorticare* 1a; *cf. excoriare* 3b.

1277 de hussis ~atis *CourtR Wakefield* I 167.

escoriare v. excoriare. **escosus** v. esculentia b.

escotare [OF *escoter*], to pay scot.

unum jugum quod in Hardes ~avit et nunc usque scotum regis non scotavit *DB* I 9v.

escren-, escrin- v. scrin-. **escru-** v. exscru-. **escuagium** v. scutagium. **escuare** v. escurare.

escuilliare [AN *escuillier*, OF *escoillier*], to castrate.

1198 Walterus .. appellat Reginaldum et Radulfum .. quod eum ~averunt *CurR RC* I 208; **1249** R. filius J. le B. per auxilium et vim prenominatorum ambobus testiculis suis quodam rasario excoliavit *CurR* 229 m. 3.

esculentia [LL], food. **b** obesity.

s**1190** hyems .. olim effluens variis ~ie speciebus, sed nunc alterati vices temporis austeriori redimens parcitate *Itin. Ric.* I 66. **b** escosus, -a, -um, i. escis plenus, et esculentus, -a, -um, i. crassus, et inde hec ~ia, .. i. crassitudo OSB. GLOUC. *Deriv.* 183.

esculentus [CL]

1 edible. **b** (as sb. n. pl.) food.

nisi forte ad [v. l. aliquid] ~um et poculentum aliquid offerretur H. BOS. *Thom.* III 14. **b** reges consederunt ad mensam .. regalibus ~is et poculentis refecti *V. II Off.* 24; **1265** (v. communiter 4a); **1313** concessimus .. Rogero .. honestam perhendinacionem in ~is et poculentis, viz. sicut uni de monachis nostris *Reg. Aberbr.* I 291; **1334** in exculent' et poculent' bondorum .. viij s. viij d. *Ac. Durh.* 116; **1376** *coke* pro †excolano [? l. excolento] ad terminum vite xij s. *Ac. Obed. Abingd.* 37; **1412** mandans .. bursemagistro .. ut incarceratis ~a et poculenta custubus suis propriis ministraret *Foed.* VIII 727b; **1539** (v. comestibilis a); in feodis eschalentis et poculentis xviij li. viij s. vij d. MYLN *Dunkeld* 140.

2 gluttonous (person). **b** fat, obese.

quid ~o, temulento, et martyri? non bene conveniunt .. calix vini quod [v. l. quem] potas et calix martirii W. CANT. *V. Thom.* I 41. **b** OSB. GLOUC. *Deriv.* 183 (v. esculentia b).

3 (as sb. n.) place for eating.

a mete place, ~um *CathA*.

escumator v. scumator.

escurare, ~ere, ~iare [OF *escurer* < LL excurare], to scour, clean: **a** (ditch, sewer, or waterway); **b** (armour or tackle); **c** (clothing). *V. et. excurare.*

a 1254 ad scurandum fossata et cariandum clausuram .. castri *RGasc* I sup. 3; **1280** in xxiiij perticatis fosse circa curiam scurandis (*Ac. Milton*) *DCCant.*; a**1335** liberat' .. servienti de Chartham pro fossis scuriandis *DCCant.* D. E. 3 f. 3a; **1372** attachiare Thomam C. ad respondendum quare non ~avit cursum aque *Arch. Bridgw.* 191; **1378** fossata apud P. non est scurata ad nocumentum tocius patrie *Banstead* 359; **1384** in stipendio diversorum operariorum mundancium et scowrancium xxiij acras veteris fossati *DL MinAc* 507/8228 m. 27; c**1390** nullus .. transire potest pro defectu escuracionis et mundacionis fossatarum .. quas .. tenentes manerii predicti a tempore quo non extat memoria ~arunt et mundaverunt *Pub. Works* I 28; p**1394** quod abbas de T. fossatas .. tenetur de jure mundare, scuriare, ac viam .. facere et emendare *Ib.* II 70 (cf. ib.: viam .. fecerunt, mundaverunt et scuriaverunt); **1398** fossatum .. escuare *CoramR* 547 m. 1*d.*; **1412** scurandum (v. clarificare 1a); **1487** omnes cepes, haias, et fossata manerio .. pertinentia ~abit et plantabit *Crawley* 467; **1509** ordinatum est quod quilibet tenens debet sufficienter ~iare .. *le .. broke CourtR* 195/69 m. 5; escurrare *Entries* 263 (v. escuratio a). **b 1286** scurendis (v. croparium); **1291** ad scurenda et emendanda arma in castro *KRAc* 479/15 m. 1; in j quarterio vj bussellis furfuris emptis ad arma scurenda *Ib.* m. 2. **c 1393** in j pellipario conducto per v dies pro furrura robe et capucii domini emendanda et ~anda iij s. vj d. *Ac. Dom. Ep. Wint.*

escuratio [cf. escurare, CL curatio], scouring, cleaning: **a** (of ditch, sewer, or waterway); *v. et. excuratio* a; **b** (of armour or tackle); **c** (of clothing).

a c**1390** (v. escurare a); c**1390** communis via .. est profunda et ruinosa in defectu scuriacionis cujusdam fossati Thome H. *Pub. Works* II 80; **1395** via regia apud Stretham est submersa et profunda ad commune nocumentum defectu scuracionis fossati Johannis Grene *CourtR Tooting Beck* 14; **1404** regia via apud B. est submersa in defectu scuracionis fossati ejusdem Johannis *CourtR Banstead*; c**1460** pro mundacione claustri .. et pro ~one vawte xx d. (*AuditR Eton*) *Arch. Hist. Camb.* I 414*n.*; **1469** J. S. Dykar, pro scuracione et plantacione cum *Whik* lx rod. fossati apud Rilley *Ac. Durh.* 92; **1526** pro ~one communis sueri (v. essewera 2); **1546** viij s. viij d. soluti pro escurac[ione] cujusdam rivoli vocati Foulney *Rutland MSS. MinAc* 35–8 *Hen. VIII* m. 34; quoddam fossatum .. in .. venella .. pro defectu escurrationis et mundationis fimo, verra, zabulo et aliis sordidis .. obstupatur .. quod .. fossatum W. B. ratione tenure sue .. reparare, mundare et escurrare debet *Entries* 263. **b 1377** in vadiis Walteri Mareshall .. et Edwardi Fourbour similiter operancium super syuracione et furbacione divers[arum] armat[uram] bacynett', palett', et ketelhatt' *KRAc* 30/15. **c 1476** pro scuracione j cuculle domini prioris equestralis *DCCant.* D. E. 53.

escurator [OF *escureor*], (mil.) 'scourer', scurrier, scout. *Cf. excurator.*

1387 pro vadiis .. c iiij^{xx}iiij sagittariorum peditum quolibet ad vj d. et quatuor scuratorum quolibet ad xviij d. *KRAc* 183/12 f. 2; **1413** pro vadiis .. c hominum ad arma peditum .. et iiij scuratorum *Ib.* 185/8 f. 4*d.*

escurellum v. curallum. **escurellus, ~eus** v. sciurellus. **escurere, ~iare** v. escurare. **escurr-** v. escur-.

escurtare, ~iare [AN *escurcer, escurcier*, OF *escorcier*], to dock (horse's tail). *V. et. excurtare* a.

1211 j runcinum suum .. ~avit *CurR* VII 187; **1247** equos suos scurciaverunt de caudis suis *JustIt* 455 r. 7.

esdentim [Ar. *'fsntīn* < ἀψινθίον], wormwood. *V. et. apsinthium.*

accipiat ~im et decoquat .. in vino BACON V 84 (cf. ib. 202: afsintin).

esdra [Ar. *afyūn* < ὄπιον *misr. as afdra*], (med.) opium.

Quaest. Salern. B 205 (v. 1 epithema a); dentur muse enee ʒ iiij vel v, aut auree alexandrine, vel utriusque ana ʒ ij cum aqua calida, vel ~a, vel cum vino calido multum limphato GILB. I 35v. 1 (cf. ib. III 147. 2: detur ~ia).

esedum v. essedum. **esemum** v. sesamum. **esertum** v. essartum. **esforcare, ~iare** v. effortiare. **esgarat-** v. esgaret-. **esgard-** v. esward-.

esgaretare [AN *esgareter*, OF *esjareter*], to hamstring.

1221 robaverunt domum et esgarataverunt [v.l. exgartaverunt] duos servientes qui venerunt *PlCrGlouc* 19; **1238** manifesti sunt malefactores in foresta de Chipham, .. qui ~averunt quendam forestarium nostrum et alium male vulneraverunt *Cl* 144; **1254** et ipsum bovem agarectaverunt ita quod bos ille .. obiit *SelCWW* 34.

esgargatare [OF *esguargueter*; cf. gargata], to cut the throat (of).

1198 occiderunt uxorem ejus et famulam et eum ligaverunt et esgargataverunt *CurR RC* I 204.

eshcaeta v. escaeta. **esia** v. aisia. **esiamentum** v. aisiamentum.

esibilis [LL], edible.

c**1275** in oleo ~i empto *Ac. Beaulieu* 309; non comeditur panis vel quodquam ~e, nisi dum dividitur aut teritur in ore vel digeritur in stomacho WYCL. *Civ. Dom.* III 342; mos feminarum est .. in lautis ~ibus et stramentis mollibus delectari *Id. Blasph.* 3.

esicius [cf. CL esocis *gen. of* esox], salmon or sim. *V. et. esox.*

insula .. praecipue issicio abundat BEDE *HE* I 1; isic, *laex GlC* I 490; quid capis in mari? alleces et isicios [AS: *leaxas*] ÆLF. *Coll.* 94; esocius vel salmo, *lex Id. Sup.*; c**1000** (14c) decerno eidem aeclessiae procurari viij isicios *CD* 971; omnes erant paene ejusdem generis pisces praeter unum mirae enormitatis ~ium GOSC. *Mellitus* 39; ysitium qui vulgo salmo dicitur captum .. exhibuit J. FURNESS *Kentig.* 36 p. 225; Loagrie Tameris divisor Cornubieque / indigenas ditat pinguibus isiciis [*gl.*: salmonibus] NECKAM *DS* III 906; ut haberet conventus xxx ~ios, sc. salmones, de Henrico de N. DOMERHAM *Glast.* 319; *a salmon'*, salmon, †isicrus [l. isicius], mugil *CathA.*

1 esitare [CL], to eat (habitually).

~abant, comedebant *GlC* E 306.

2 esitare v. haesitare. **esk-** v. et. esc-, sc-, sk-. **eskaere** v. escaere. **eskaet-** v. escaet-. **eskamb-** v. excamb-. **eskapellare** v. escapelare. **eskapium** v. escapium. **eskecarium** v. scaccarium. **eskeccum** v. esceccum. **eskector, eskettor** v. esceccor. **eskerm-** v. skirm-. **esketum** v. escaeta. **eskipp-, eskipr-** v. skipp-. **esklenka** v. esclenca. **eskottum** v. esceccum. **eslai-** v. allai-. **eslargare** v. elargare. **esled-** v. sled-. **eslingator** v. slingator.

esmale, ~allum [OF *esmal*]

1 enamel.

c**1268** in auro in folio, aimallis, diversis coloribus, et aliis necessariis ad picturas voltarum ecclesie (*Pipe* 113 r. 1*d.*) *Ac. Build. Hen. III* 426 (cf. ib. 428 [**1271**]: admallis; ib. 434 [**1272**]: aymall'); asmal etiam metalli naturam habet *Ps.-*GROS. *Summa* 636.

2 enamel-work. **b** enamel plaque.

1205 duas zonas cum ~allo *Pat* 55a; **1206** cinctorium de aurifrisio cum auro de †adinal *Pat* 58b; c**1220** feretrum unum de ~ali continens reliquias, .. candelabra viiij de ~ali, et ij stagnea et ij ferrea *Process. Sal.* 170; **1240** quod provideat quod [ciphus] intus sit excentellatus aimallo *Cl* 258; c**1250** due cruces in altari portatiles de ~allo *Vis. S. Paul.* 3 (cf. ib. 9: una crux de admallo; ib. 15: .. due pelves de asmallo); **1285** factura .. iiij ciphorum unde .. iij [erant] argentei deaurati cum aemallo *Rec. Wardr.* 520; Ernulfus [episc. Roff., ob. **1124**] .. in tabula argentea ante majus altare accrevit duas lictas de emalo *Flor. Hist.* II 45; **1315** calix aureus ad feretrum, cum viridi amal' in nodo pedis *Invent. Ch. Ch.* 69; c**1322** j par garteriorum factorum de serico ornato argenti (*sic*) et amalo rubio *IMisc* 87/25; **1332** pro j pari cutellorum .. cum manubriis .. amellatis de amello de plyte (*KRAc* 386/7) *Arch.* LXXVII 128; **1451** item unum bassum siphum stantem cum cooperculo de auro operat' cum amell' aplite .. item unum goblettum cum cooperculo de auro voc' amell' aplyte fract' garnesiat' cum quatuor parvis balais *Pat* 473 m. 14. **b 1245** casula .. cum nobili tassello .. breudato Agno Dei cum duobus ~allis magnis et rotundis *Invent. S. Paul.* 482; **1290** cuppam de auro cum scuto in medio partito armis Francie et Navarre .. cum esmaellis (*TRBk* 274 f. 178v.) *Doc. Scot.* I 182; ciphum .. operatum cum esmaellis de armis Francie *Ib.* 183; **1338** unum ciphum argenteum .. cum diversis scuchonibus et aymellis infra et extra (*TreatyR*) *Foed.* V 49b; **1352** j cupa arg' deaur' de opere Paris' cum diversis emall' elevat' in fundo et in cooperculo (*Reg. Black Prince* IV) *TRBk* 278 f. 43.

esmallare, to enamel. *V. et. enamellare.*

1295 crux .. cum pede triphoriato et aymallato cum yconis crucifixi [etc.] *Vis. S. Paul.* 312; **1300** unum par cultellorum cum manicis argenti aymellat', cum uno furchetto *AcWardr* 343 (cf. ib. 348: justa argenti annellata [? l. aimellata]); **1313** duo pecie argentee in fundo aimmallate (*Invent.*) *DC S. Paul.* (*HMC*) 29b; **1315** iij morsi regis Francie amalati (= *Hist. Cath. Cant.* xv: amulati) .. quilibet cum crucifixo a dextris .. amalato *Invent. Ch. Ch.* 74; **1315** baculus .. argenteus anelatus cum floribus de *liz Ib.* 70; **1326** unam cupam argenteam deauratam et esmelat'

per partes *Cl* 144 m. 4; 1332 manubriis .. amellatis (v. cultellus 1b); 1335 unam cuppam argenteam deauratam et annelatam .. liberetis (*Cl*) *Foed.* IV 657b; 1338 item ij pomelli argentei pro capis deaurati et an'i'ati *Ac. Durh.* 376; 1345 firmaculum aumollatum et deauratum *Sacr. Lichf.* 109; 1352 j salar' arg' deaur' .. et emellat' in summitate cooperculi .. j godett' arg' deaur' et emellat' exterius de leopardis .. j tabernaculum arg' deaur' emellat' de ymagine Sancti Daniel' inter ij leones (*Reg. Black Prince* IV) *TRBk* 278 f. 43; 1386 item una ymago S. Pauli argent' deaurat', super cujus basim ammaylantur scuti domini Thome Fog militis (*Invent.*) *Hist. S. Paul.* 337b; 1388 [mitre] bordura amelata est cum rosis albis circumquaque (*Invent. Westm.*) *Arch.* LII 220; abbas J. [ob. 1292] .. contulit .. unam capam .. cum morsu argenteo emalato J. Glast. 251 (cf. ib. 256: morsum emolatum); 1403 lego .. domui de E. unam cupam argenteam deauratam et hamelatam *Test. Ebor.* III 24; 1448 unam ymaginem .. stantem super viride terragium amilasatum (*Test. H. Beaufort*) *MonA* II 280*n*.

esmallatio, enamel-work. *V. et. enamellatura, esmale* 2.

1286 pro reparatura eorundem [pelvium] cum scuticis aureis et aumellacione xx s. (*KRAc* 91/7 m. 3) *Arch.* LXX 42.

esmallum v. esmale. **esmel-** v. esmal-.

esmeraldus [AN *esmeralde*, OF *esmeraude* < CL smaragdus < σμάραγδος], emerald. *V. et. smaragdus.*

a1216 legavit filie sue ∼am suam *FormA* 423; 1216 unum monile assisum in medio de diamandis circumdatis de rubis et de ameraudis *Pat* 173a; 1225 assignavi eidem domui .. unum calicem de auro cum pulcris ∼is et rubetis *Cl* 71a; 1234 habuit de catallis Aaron Judei suspensi j *camehew* et unam emesrandam (*sic*) *CurR* XV 1110; 1275 quartus [annulus] habet lapidem qui vocatur amiradus paulisper fractum *Cart. Glouc.* I 171; 1286 pro octo rubettis balasis, et octo admeraudis pro circulo ad bacinettum S. Georgii *KRAc* 372/11 m. 3; 1300 unus anulus auri cum amerauda *AcWardr* 345 (cf. ib. 347: una crux auri cum rubettis, amaraudis et margaritis); 1303 petraria .. ameraldarum (v. balasius); 1303 cum aymeraldis (v. camahutus); 1303 in lapidibus amarill' de Alexandr' emptis *KRAc* 363/18 m. 10*d.*; 1332 pro xxiiij nucheis firmaculis auri cum rubinis .. emeraldis [etc.] (*KRAc* 386/7) *Arch.* LXXVII 137; 1345 sex rubei, quinque saphiri, quindecim emeroidi *Sacr. Lichf.* 108; 1352 j firmaculum magnum cum iij rub' bal' et emerald' (*Reg. Black Prince IV*) *TRBk* 278 f. 43.

esmerillunus [AN *esmerillun*, OF *esmerillon*], merlin. *V. et. emerlio, merillio.*

1213 item in uno panerio ad rosas siccandas ad opus domini regis, iij d. item in j panerio ad †esmerillimos domini regis ferendos, j d. *Misae* 267.

esmerum [OF *esmeril*], emery.

1420 in .. c li. esmeri *EEC* 514.

esmina v. hemina. **esmolere** v. emolere. **esmum** v. isthmus. **esmund-** v. emund-. **esnacca, esnecca, esnecka** v. snecca. **esnecia, esneseya** v. aesnecia. **esocius** v. esicius. **esophagus, ysophagus** v. oesophagus.

esox [CL], salmon or sim. *V. et. esicius.*

essox, *laex GlC* E 315; †merocem [? l. esocem], nomen piscis *Gl. Leid.* 3. 20; 9.. esox, *leax WW*; 11.. ysox vel isicius, *lax WW Sup.* 205; ut .. piscibus hamum / mittat et esocem hinc trahat inde lupum Nig. *SS* 2792.

espaalt-, espaet- v. espelt-. **espainellus, espanellus, espaniellus** v. hispanellus. **espalt-** v. espelt-. **espane** v. estraia 1c. **espark-** v. esperc-. **esparvarius** v. spervarius.

espaudlera, espaul- [AN *espaudler*, OF *espauler*], shoulder-piece, epaulette. *V. et. spatularia.*

1215 mittat domino regi .. unas lineas quisseras et unas ∼dleras *Cl* 229a; 1224 recepit .. de lineis armaturis, j purpunctum et j ∼leram de nigro cendalo *CurR* XI 1913.

espeatare v. espeltare. **especialiter** v. specialiter. **espedire** v. expedire 7c.

espedor [W. *ysbydwr*; cf. *ysbyd* < hospitem], tenant of Hospitallers (W.).

1284 ∼ores Ospitalis foren[seci] liberi esse consueverunt et quieti de omnibus .. operibus principal' domino et .. non possunt singno singnari absque voluntate dominorum si fuerint villani *IMisc* 43/15 (cf. ib.: quod expedores sui singno Hospitalis singnati solebant esse quieti de exercitu principum, cariagiis, et aliis operibus. et quod hujusmodi expedores non possunt singno singnari absque voluntate dominorum suorum); 1338 bajulia de Halstan in Nort Wallia .. escaeta expedorum ibidem valent per annum vij li. *Hosp. in Eng.* 38; 1344 quod .. prior et fratres Hospitalis Sancti Johannis Jerosolim in Anglia .. habere consueverunt .. omnes homines suos forinsecos qui expedores vocantur liberos et quietos de omnibus servitutibus *Pat* 212 m. 32; c1370 prior [Hospitalis] .. dicit quod omnes tenentes sui et residentes infra dominium suum dicuntur expedores intrinceci, et expedores forinceci sunt illi qui fuerunt aliorum villani *Rec. Caern.* 206–7.

espeium [OF *espee* < CL spatha], sword.

1210 ad furbiandum duo espeia, viij d. *Misae* 151 (cf. ib.: duas spatas).

espelc-, espelk- v. esperc-.

espeltamentum, expeditation, hambling, lawing (of dog). *V. et. expeditamentum, expeditatio* a.

1205 (v. espeltatio); quieti .. de espaltamentis canum Domerh. *Glast.* 493; 1230 quieti .. de ∼is canum et de bobus et denariis dandis pro canibus non expeltatis *Cl* 296; 1236 quod non permittat quod forestarii sui vexent .. abbatem .. pro expeltamento canum *Cl* 261.

espeltare [AN *espeleter* < expeditare], to expeditate, hamble, law (dog). *V. et. expedare, expeditare.*

1171 sint liberi et quieti de .. sectis comitatuum et foreste de canibus suis expeltandis *BBC* (*Maldon*) I 84; 1199 soluta et libera et quieta .. de canibus suis espaetandis *E. Ch. S. Paul.* 37; 1200 libera et quieta .. de canibus suis espeatandis *RChart* 67a (cf. *Ch. Sal.* 179 [1200 (1227)]: †expetendis); 1200 quod canes sui .. non sint espaltati extra reguardum foreste *Peramb. Dartmoor* 285; 1204 canes suos et canes hominum suorum non espetatos *RChart* 114b; 1205 (v. espeltatio); 1208 (v. expedare a); 1227 nullus dominicos canes abbatis et monachorum espaaltare cogat; verum canes hominum suorum intra forestam manentium abbas et monachi espaaltari faciant *ChartR* 18 m. 23; 1230 pro canibus non expeltatis (v. espeltamentum); 1328 nullos dominicos canes abbatis et monachorum [de Reding'] expaaltare cogat, verum canes hominum suorum infra forestam manencium abbas et monachi expaaltari faciant *CoramR* 106.

espeltatio [AN *espeleteisoun* < expeditatio], fine for avoidance of expeditation (of dog). *V. et. expedatio, expeditatio* b, *expeditura.*

1205 ipsum quietum esse permittas de espeltamento canum suorum si nunquam espeltati fuerunt vel ∼onem dare solebant *Cl* 58.

espera v. spera.

espercaria [OF *esperquerie*], place in which congers are cured or sold (C.I.). **b** custom of royal pre-emption of congers. (*Cf.* J. H. LePatourel *Medieval Administration of the Channel Islands* Oxford, 1937, 79 & *nn.*).

1288 piscatores teneantur ad piscacionem congerorum et eorum portacionem ad esperquerias nostras [sc. regis] vel placeas consuetas *AncD* D 389; 1289 teneatur venire ad esperqueriam dictorum religiosorum .. cum congris captis in mari certo tempore, super quibus dicti religiosi habent certam firmam prout rex habet alibi in eadem insula *CartINorm* 192. **b** 1195 pro esperkeria quam Vitalis de Villa habet per cartam regis xxv li. *RScacNorm* 225 (cf. ib. 390 [1198]); c1240 rex .. habet pesquariam piscium, et tenet totam esperqueriam insule totius nomine suo *CartINorm* 398; 1248 spelkeria omnino deperibit, libertates domini regis minorabuntur *Ext. Guern.* 27; 12.. inquiratis si M. de Saumares experqueriam suam de jure et libertate feodi sui habeat et possideat ab antiquo et si in dicta parrochia homines sui sectam ad dictam experqueriam suam inter festum Pasche et festum S. Michaelis debe[a]nt de piscacione congrorum captorum per eosdem piscatores suos quolibet anno et si homines sui piscatores costumam maquerellorum in recompensacionem pro firma experqueriarum nostrarum posuerunt, et si simili modo homines dicti M. piscatores eandem costumam maquerellorum pro recompensacione firme experquerie sue solvant necne (*Pet. Guernsey*) *AncC* LV 4; 1270 cum ad instanciam nostram dilectus nobis dominus N. abbas monasterii de Monte Sancti Michaelis ∼ias suas quascunque insularum dilecto nobis Amato de Contino mercatori nostro speciali ad firmam dimiserit, volumus .. *CartINorm* 190; 1274 dicunt quod diversi ∼ias levaverunt in terris suis sine licentia regis .. et .. incertum extitit utrum hiis esperkerias levare et locatas tenere sine licentia et auctoritate regis liceat *S. Jers.* II 26; 1309 clamat percipere et habere liberam esperkeriam apud †Saynk [l. Sayrk] de piscibus per homines suos captis in aquis domini regis *PQW* 823a; 1319 cum .. custumis maquerellorum, esperqueriarum congruorum *CartINorm* 37; 1331 esperqueria congrorum (v. conger a); 1364 in possessione esperkarie congrorum et custumarum makerellorum *CartINorm* 181.

espercatio, (season for) cure and sale of congers or period of royal pre-emption (C.I.).

1248 omnes .. homines consueverunt .. ferre in Normanniam .. omnes denariatas suas .. ad vendendum, exceptis congris in tempore espelcationis, nihil inde dando. .. tempus espelcationis durare debet .. a Pascha usque ad festum S. Michaelis *Ext. Guern.* 27.

espercator, royal official who preempts congers.

1247 ad festum S. Michaelis .. debent vendere congros suos absque pretio espelcatorum .. si espelcatores †voluerint [? l. noluerint] congros suos emere ad justum forum eis factum, licebit piscatoribus piscem suum custodire per unum retractum maris vel per unam munteiam, et deinde voluntatem suam inde facere *Cl* 547; 1248 fiderunt etiam quando espelkiatores, mercatores, et piscatores in unum non fuissent ad piscem vendendum vel emendum ad justum forum, quod tunc electi essent duo piscatores .. ex una societate et duo alii ex alia societate ad piscem .. juste appretiandum *Ext. Guern.* 27.

esperduta, ∼is [OF *esperduite* < experducta, *p. ppl. of* experducere], 'esperduct', (metal) rod. *Cf. experducere.*

c1160 viij *esperduites* (v. acerum); 1173 pro xxx garb' ferri et cxxv esperd' ferri lxiiij s. *Pipe* 82; 1198 pro .. picoissis et esperduitis ferri *RScacNorm* II 413; 1229 in duobus fabris et in cc ∼is ferry .. ad nos transmissis ad ligones et cisellos et alia utensilia ad rupem scindendam necessaria *Liberate* 8 m. 11; c1262 et iiij^{xx} ∼iis ferri operandis ad utensilia domorum *DL CourtR* 128/1920; 1270 in vj sperdut' grossi ferri ad strakas et ad vomeras *MinAc* 935/2; 1276 levaverunt .. de c sperducibus ferri j d. *Hund.* I 90; 1313 de xxxviij vomeribus, iij exsperducis ferri, ij plaustris et ij rotis ad carectas *MinAc* 1128/4 m. 2; c1350 j esperductam ferream de solu' vij d. *Reg. S. Aug.* 260.

esperes v. hesperis. **esperinum** v. espernerium, espernium. **esperiolus** v. sciurellus. **esperk-** v. esperc-.

espernerium [cf. OF *espargne*, *esperne*], protective cover, net.

c1308 j rete quod dicitur ∼ium ad cooperiendum lectum, precii ij s. (*Ac. Templars*) *LTRAc* 20 r. 3 (cf. ib. 18 r. 7 (14): †esperinum).

espernium [cf. OF *espargne*, *esperne*], (department dealing with) food reserve, surplus. *V. et. sparnum.*

c1267 nec bladum nec brasium retineatur sed si espernum inde facere poterunt in magna domo reponatur *Cart. Glouc.* III 106; 1286 ∼ium *DCWint.* Quire V f. 111; c1330 in solutis ad †esperinum [l. espernium] conventus pro O. hordarii xiij s. iiij d. *Comp. Swith.* 258.

esperqueria v. espercaria. **esperv-** v. sperv-. **espet-** v. espelt-. **espicurnaucia** v. spigurnalcia. **espimara** v. ephemerus 2a.

espletum, ∼a, ∼ia [AN *espleit*, OF *esploit* < explicitus, *p. ppl. of* explicare], 'esplees', produce or revenue from land. *V. et. explectum.*

1156 donum .. concesserunt, viz. paduenciam omnium nemorum suorum atque ∼um et pacherium porcorum [etc.] *Act. Hen. II* I 121; 1196 (v. capere 2b); 1198 capiendo inde ∼ias ad valentiam xx s. et plus *CurR* I 38; c1200 concessi .. servitium R. .. cum omnibus exitibus, redditibus, et esplatis terre in bosco et plano *Couch. Kirkstall* 101; 1201 capiendo inde ∼a ad valenciam v s. et plus *CurR* I 428; 1255 in nemoribus .. espleitum habebit, .. sed illa non poterit vendere nec aliorum usibus deputare *RGasc* I sup. 36b; 1274 omnes ∼e curiarum et aliorum exituum nobis remanserunt *Ann. Dunstable* 264.

esporlum v. sportula. **esporonum** v. spurrum. **espoerum, esporum** v. spera. **esprevus** v. spervarius. **espringaldus** v. springaldus. **espurrum** v. spera. **esquarl-** v. scarl-. **esquarta** v. quarta.

esquieria [AN *esquierye*, OF *escuerie*], office of esquire. *V. et. squieria.*

a1285 nobis facere debuerunt dimidiam ∼iam nomine serjantie *Cart. Glouc.* II 207.

esquierus, ∼ius [AN *esquier*, OF *escuier*], esquire, shield-bearer. *V. et. squierus.*

1216 ∼os et garciones Francos *Pat* 171b; 1282 religiosi concesserunt .. Benedicte .. unum parvum panem album et .. septem panes ∼ii *Cart. Glouc.* I 309; 1301 abbas v ∼ios habeat .. quorum quilibet unum equum habeat *Reg. Cant.* 858.

esquilleria [AN *esquilerie*, OF *escuelerie*], scullery, pots and pans (coll.). *V. et. squilleria.*

1332 uno sacco et una brochia ad cariand' esquillariam domini regis *IPM* 31/36.

esquitifer v. scutifer. **essae-** v. essai-. **essaia** v. 1 essaium, sagum.

essaiamentum [OF *essaiement*], assay, testing: **a** (of metal or coinage); **b** (of bread). *V. et.* 1 *essaium* 1.

a p1280 regule assaiamenti (v. allaiator); 1300 de incremento per numerum per assaimentum [pollardorum] tunc factum *AcWardr* 59. **b** 1330 quociens panis alibi furnatus vendicioni fuit expositus ibidem post assayamentum inde factum per ministros .. abbatis, iidem ministri nullum invenerunt defectum *PQW* 519b.

essaiare [OF *essaiier*], to assay, test: **a** (metal or coinage); **b** (weights or measures); **c** (bread); **d** (fish).

a 1253 denarii non debent .. poni extra manus .. magistrorum quousque essaiator et custodes .. ipsos ∼averint (*Pat*) *RGasc* I 273; a1275 assayare platas (v. essaiator); 1299 moneta de qua habetur suspicio mali statim assaietur per dimidiam unciam *StatIr* I 214; 1369 mandamus quod .. predicta vasa et zonas .. per touchum nostrum, et alias vias et modos, quibus racionabiliter

sciveritis, assaiari faciatis (*Cl*) *Foed.* VI 611b. **b 1320** detulit apud gildaulam mensuras domini regis ad assaiandum per standardum civitatis *MGL* II 382; **1352** pro eisdem tronis assaiandis *Pipe* 197 (*London*). **c 1280** panem illum ponderari et assaiari fecit *RParl Ined.* 9; **1389** idem prior [de Tippetrete] de nobis tenet per servicium portandi die coronacionis nostre ferra in quibus wafre nostre fient et ipsas coram nobis assaiandi *Pat* 328 m. 15. **d 1364** allecia predicta, ne per diutinam detencionem eorundem in navi periissent, per ballivum et quatuor probos homines de mister' piscenariorum assaiari . . fecerit *IMisc* 188/15.

2 to inspect, test (arms).

1399 ad armaturas . . assaiand' et triand' (v. essaiatio).

essaiatio, inspection, testing (of arms).

1387 super factura et effusione novorum gunnorum et assaiacione eorundem *KRAc* 183/12 f. 31; **1399** ad armaturas . . supervidend', inspiciend', assaiand', et triand' et ad eas quas per circumspectam assaiacionem . . vestram . . minus sufficiencia (*sic*) invenire poteritis extra garderobam nostram . . evacuari . . faciend' *Pat* 358 m. 27*d*.

essaiator [cf. OF *essaieor*], assayer: **a** (of mines); **b** (of metal or coinage); **c** (of weights and measures); **d** (of bread).

a 1307 in expensis factis circa quoddam assag[ium] mine factum per L. R. assagiatorem regis in Anglia . . vij d. ob. *KRAc* 260/19 m. 3. **b 1182** in . . conductu W. H. ∼oris Cantuarie a Wintona usque London' *Pipe* 146; **1217** assaiatores ex parte regis Thomas Aurifaber et ex parte archiepiscopi Rannulfus Aurifaber *KRMem* 1 m. 3; **1221** monetarii, custodes, operarii, et essaetores *Pat* 322; **1221** asaiator monete R. de G. *LTRMem* 4 m. 5 (3)*d.*; **1236** W. H. presentavit . . Ernaldum Ruffum, aurifabrum, ∼orem monete Cantuar' loco Roberti le Eschanjor *KRMem* 15 m. 15*d.*; **1253** preposuimus in dicta moneta temptatorem seu esseiatorem nostrum et custodes. . . ∼or debet esse ad sumptus magistrorum (*Pat*) *RGasc* I 273; **1253** (v. 1 computator 1d, essaiare a); **a1273** in cambio erit unus assayator qui debet assayare platas ante quam defera[n]tur ad cuneum, quod sint recti ponderis et de bono argento, et faciet quamlibet assayam de xx platis ponderantibus xx denarios legalis monete *RBExch* III 984; **1398** constituimus dilectum nobis Willelmum Fitz Hugh contrarotulatorem magistri ac camsoris et assaiatoris monete nostre infra Turrim London' *Pat* 350 m. 16. **c 13..** assiator et afforiator mensurarum (v. afforator b). **d** abstrahe medietatem de pondere panis facti per assaiatores *MGL* I 352.

essaimare, ∼iare [OF *essaimer* < exsaginare], (falc.) to 'enseam', rid of superfluous fat. *V. et. exsaginare.*

1219 quod . . moram fecerit apud N. ad ∼iandum Blakemannum girfalconem nostrum et ad faciendum eum volare ter vel quater *Cl* 400b; **1220** vaslettis perendinantibus apud N. . . ad exsiaimiandum Blakeman girefalconem nostrum *Cl* 441b; **1241** quod austurcum quem rex ei liberari fecit . . et alium austurcum qui vocatur Lespagnol . . a muta extrahi et †essainiari faciat, et cum parati et prompti fuerint ad volandum, eos ad regem mittat *Cl* 363; **1254** necessaria ad falcones . . trahendos et esseymiandos ita quod prompti sint ad volandum contra adventum regis in Angliam *Cl* 266 (= *RGasc* I 422: †esseyniandos); **1287** ostriciariis regis morantibus apud Bikenovere ad assemiandum ostorios regis, quolibet percipiente per diem vij d., . . cv s. *KRAc* 351/24 m. 1; **1290** pro vadiis et expensis suis ab viij die Sept', quo die austurci predicti tractati fuerunt de mutis, usque v diem Octobr', ad quem diem austurci fuerunt plenarie assemati *Ib.* 352/20 m. 3; **1290** austurci assemantur (v. essaimatio); **1306** asseymando eundem asturcum *KRAc* 369/11 f. 116*d*.

essaimatio, (falc.) cleansing of superfluous fat.

1284 Johanni de Bykenore militi pro mutacione et assemacione ostor[iorum] regis anni duodecimi, xviij li. (*AcWardr*) *KRAc* 351/11 m. 1; **1286** Johanni de Wik' pro mutacione et †acemone predictorum ostoriorum . . xx li. *Ib.* 351/20 m. 5; **1290** super assemacione austurcorum (*AcWardr*) *Chanc. Misc.* 4/4 f. 55 (cf. ib. f. 60: pro assummacione austurcorum regis . . videlicet pro cibo et potura illorum . . per unum mensem dum austurci assemantur . . tempore assemacionis); **1291** a vij die Octobr', quo die recesserunt de domo dicti Johannis de mutis post assemacionem *KRAc* 352/26 m. 6.

1 essaium, ∼a [AN *essai*, OF *essaie* < LL exagium]

1 assay, testing: **a** (w. ref. to mines); **b** (of metals and coinage); *v. et. essaiamentum, exagium* 1; **c** (of weights and measures); **d** (of bread and ale); *cf. assisa* 4.

a 1307 in factura fornellorum et aliorum ingenitorum (*sic*) pro assag' de mina extracta ibidem faciend' *KRAc* 260/19 m. 1; assag[ium] *Ib.* (v. essaiator a); **1325** de . . j balanc' pro asag' . . alia balancia pro asag' (*Comp. Minere*) *Pipe* 170 r. 53. **b** facto ∼io per quod firma dealbatur *Dial. Scac.* I 5 K; **1229** in primo assaio (v. dealbare 2b); **1236** habet respectum . . ad respondendum de asaia monete cunei sui *KRMem* 14 m. 11; **1248** examinationem [monete] quam assaiam vocant in hunc modum fecerunt . . (*Examinatio Monetae*) *Doc. Eng. Mint* 54; **a1273** faciet . . assayam (v. essaiator b); **1291** assagium monete nostre nove *RGasc* III 19; **c1350** debet hujusmodi assaium auri fieri in igne per iij dies et iij noctes in olla cum cimento de pulvere tegularum bonarum et rubearum et sale de Peyto *RBExch* III 1009; **1408** j par bilanc' pro subtili assaia *AncD* D 708; **1414** facto . . assaio in pondere cum standardo libre Turris London' *Pat* 394 m. 29; **1534** factoque inde assaio per ignem, videlicet per libram subtilem ponderis post scissuram eorundem [denariorum etc.] prout moris est *KRAc* 303/2. **c 1316** habuerunt . . assisam panis et cervisie et custodiam et assaiam mensurarum et ponderum *ChartR* 102 m. 2; **c1345** assaia mensurarum de aldermannia Johannis de Selewode *Arch. Ox.* II 267; **1368** quia assaia mensurarum et ponderum omnisque cognicio et punicio transgressorum . . assise mensurarum et ponderum forstallatorum . . ad vos et officium vestrum pertinerant *RScot* 919a; emendas assise panis . . necnon assaiam mensurarum et ponderum et omnia alia que ad coronam pertinent *Reg. Brev. Orig.* 279b. **d s1258** pistores . . quorum panes non ponderaverunt secundum assagum civitatis . . exaltati fuerunt in tumberella *Leg. Ant. Lond.* 41; **1331** idem E. nunquam usus est facere assayam panis seu cervisie diebus feriarum seu mercatorum preterquam in ultima feria *PQW* 146a; **1366** conservatores de die in diem cum necesse fuerit de cervisia tastum et assaiam facient et secundum valorem dicte cervisie tastate inde ponant assisam *Cl* 204 m. 6a; **1539** †asseisinam (*sic*) et assisam panis, vini, et cervisie fracte ac assisam mensurarum et ponderum *Entries* 425.

2 (monet.) trial plate, standard against which coin is assayed. **b** gold or silver which issues from assay.

1248 facta sunt duo assaia, pondus utriusque x s., quorum unum est de puro argento et aliud de argento ad cujus exemplar debet fieri moneta, que duo assaya quodam quonio impressa, posita sunt in thesauro domini regis *Doc. Eng. Mint* 54–5; comes Cornubie habet unum assaium de puro argento ponderis x s. *Ib.* 106; **1250** quelibet villa ubi faciat cambiam . . debet restituere assaiam suam regi (*LTR Mem*) *Brit. Numism. J.* XXII 105; **1251** de xxvj s. viij d. receptis de assaiis missis per diversas villas Anglie ubi cambium fuit *Pipe* m. 9 r. (*unnumbered*) 6. **b 1198** de quater xx et vj ∼iis que computantur ei pro quater xx li. et lxxvij s. ad redigendum in legalem monetam *Pipe* 172; **1408** j pipa de eneo ad sufflandum ad assaiam . . j assaiam auri cum remedio et aliam assaiam sine remedio *AncD* D 708.

3 revenue from fine for breach of assay.

nec . . abbas nec . . prior extra refectorium prandens aliquid de asseio habere consuevit *Cust. Westm.* 120: (cf. ib. 121: aliquid nomine assaii; cf. ib. 114: de asaio); **1448** concessimus . . abbati et conventui . . quod habeant . . assaiam et assisam panis, vini etc. (*Ch. Regis.*) *Reg. Whet.* I 42.

2 essaium v. sagum.

essartare [OF *essarter*, AN *assarter*], to essart, assart, bring (land) into cultivation; *v. et. exsartare.* **b** to uproot, clear (woodland); **c** to weed (garden); **d** to pull up (crop or sapling).

c1102 concessisse . . lx acras ad ∼andum et hospitandum *Regesta* II p. 307; **c1130** reddidit . . abbati suam terram sartatam et quietam *Chr. Rams.* 253; **a1160** quicquid poterit idem episcopus ∼are in foresta de Dena (*Ch. Regis*) *Reg. Heref.* 96; **a1204** apparabunt . . terram infra istas divisas ubique sartando et colendo sine disturbacione ad opus suum *Kelso* 110; **1205** (v. descensus 4a); **1321** quod . . fratres de omnibus boscis suis quos habent infra metas foreste possint assartare et excolere sine licencia regis *PQW* 464a; arbores . . succidere . . ac commodum suum inde facere et solum illud postmodum assertare et in culturam redigere *Reg. Brev. Orig.* 257. **b a1154** totum episcopo boscum ville . . ∼are concedo (*Ch. Comitis Heref.*) *Reg. Heref. 1283–1317* 48; **1197** Hugo L. et Benedictus A. r. c. de ij s. et vj d. pro licentia sertandi ij parva *riffleis* *Pipe* 44; **1199** (v. bosculus); **1204** *CurR* III 154 (v. brusca 1); **1229** boscus Alani de L. . . non erit ad nocumentum foreste regis si ∼atur *Cl* 262; **1311** si . . grava fuerit assarta (*sic*), pastura valeret in eadem per annum v s. vj d. *Cust. Battle* 139. **c 1245** in quodam homine locando . . assartante gardinum de spinis et eundem plantando et curtill' faciendo *Pipe Wint.* 159287 r. 11. **d c1300** in predictis incitis assartandis et cariandis usque Esserugge *MinAc* 863/8; **1305** tulit avenas in grangia ipsius Thome ligatas de avenis quas . . assartavit de terra ipsius Galfridi *CourtR Hales* 502.

essartarius [cf. OF *essartier*], tenant of assart. *V. et. exsartarius.*

1299 assartarii Willelmus et Simon Dun . . tene[n]t j assartum per servitium v s. vj d. *RBWorc.* 199.

essartatio, 'assart', clearance (usu. to produce arable).

a1195 quod . . monachi hanc villam . . teneant . . salva foresta nostra, quantum ad feras et sartationem, ultra quod predictum est *Feod. Durh.* 182*n.*; **c1200** quod . . monachi habebunt . . communitatem in illa medietate bosci quam . . S. essartare debet, et antequam essartatus (*sic*) fuerit . . et post ∼onem quando bladum in eadem non fuerit *Couch. Kirkstall* 182; **1221** de ∼one facienda (*rub.*): sciatis quod licenciam dedimus Thome C. . . assartare et excolere tres acras de riffletto in Cumb' *Cl* 453a; **1304** pro assartacione interioris ballii castri predicti de quibusdam arboribus et spinis in eo crescentibus . . ij s. viij d. *KRAc* 486/15 m. 2; **1392** de . . assartacione (v. approuatio).

essarticare, to have the right of cutting wood.

uni æsno . . [contingit] esarticare juxta situm terre [AS: *wuduræden be landside*] (*Quad.*) *GAS* 449.

essartulum, small assart.

1226 dissaisivit eum . . de quodam parvo ∼o *JustIt* 229 m. 2*d*.

essartum, ∼a [OF *essart* < exsartum]

1 assart, area reclaimed from woodland; *v. et. exsartum* 1. **b** (dist. as old or new); **c** (as surname).

in eodem manerio sunt lviij acrae terrae [*gl.*: *essarz*] projectae de silva *DB* I 179v.; **1092** ne aliquis vestrum se . . intromittat de nemore . . abbatis de R. nisi de bestiis et de esartis *Chr. Rams.* 210 (= *Regesta* 332); placitum quoque forestarum multiplici satis est incommoditate vallatum: de ∼is, de cesione, de combustione [etc.] (*Leg. Hen.* 17. 1, 2) *GAS* 559; **1115** sartum quod Robertus filius Haimonis dedit ecclesie *Chr. Abingd.* II 110 (= *Regesta* 1092); **1131** do etiam in Anglica terra . . de Roberto de la Barduna de uno escarto et partem decime de salinis (*Ch. Hen. I*) *Gall. Christ.* XI *instr.* 129E; **a1135** ij ∼as et silvulam (v. 2 brecha); **a1159** (1235) me concessisse . . ∼as . . suas, sc. Rahaige [etc.] *CalCh* I 206; **a1160** me dedisse . . omnia esarta sub M. unde G. . . episcopus saisitus fuit die qua primo coronatus fui . . et quicquid poterit . . essartare in foresta de Dena (*Ch. Regis.*) *Reg. Heref.* 96 (cf. ib.: carta de esertis); ∼a vero vulgo dicuntur que apud Isidorum [*Etym.* XVII 2. 4] occationes nominantur, quando scilicet foreste nemora vel dumeta quelibet pascuis et latibulis oportuna succiduntur; quibus succisis et radicitus avulsis terra subvertitur et excolitur *Dial. Scac.* I 12; **c1185** pro iiij bovatis et sarcii (*sic*) et aliis peciis xv s. *Rec. Templars* 97 (cf. ib. 127: Aliz de B. pro sarta quadam, ij s. pro omni servicio); **a1198** assignavimus . . omnes decimas quoque assartorum et novalium *E. Ch. S. Paul.* 218 (cf. ib.: de viij acris de sarto sagum. . . de ix acris ∼orum); **1199** (v. exsartum 1); **c1200** totum assartum integre plenarie . . sicut carta W. de F. quam de eodem sarto habemus nobis testatur *AncD* A 3357; **1357** quidam Johannes de Cotyngham fecit assart' eodem anno de solo suo vastato juxta Desburgh' Wode et inclusit illam, et magnus tumultus erat inter communitatem villate predicte *IPM* 138/8; **1458** unam virgatam terre . . et unum assertum (*Indent.*) *Reg. Whet.* I 309 (cf. ib.: tenente terrarum et esserti predictorum); **1539** dedimus . . †acerta, vasta, moras (*Pat*) *Mon. Exon.* 104b. **b 1189** videnda sunt in rewardo nova ∼a et vetera inbladata post ultimum rewardum R. Howd. IV 65; **1203** abbas et monachi de Becco debet (*sic*) c m. per quas finem fecerunt cum justic' Anglie pro habendis xlviij acris de novo ∼o ad perticam regis et ij acris de veteri ∼o in manerio de W. liberas et quietas de assarto et reguardo et visu forestariorum *Pipe* 135; **1213** de veteri ∼o foreste de T. . . de novo ∼o *Cl* 165b; **1588** omnes illas quadraginta et octo acras . . terre et pasture nostras per estimacionem novi et veteris †assait' cum suis pertinenciis *Pat* 1319 m. 2. **c 1200** Rogerus de Essartis ponit loco suo Ricardum de Essartis versus Godefridum de Cramavill' de placito terre ad lucrandum [etc.] *CurR* I 174.

2 tax on assart. *V. et. exsartum* 2.

1141 rex concessit libertates monachis de B. . . quod ipsi . . sint quieti de placitis . . et omnibus geldis, scotis, et sartis, et parcis claudendis *Regesta* 93; **c1157** me . . concessisse . . xl acras essartorum quietas de ∼is et de placitis . . et assisis ∼orum; et amplius non numerantur inter essarta *Act. Hen. II* I 216; ecclesiam . . liberam et quietam . . esse constituit . . ab . . omnibus auxiliis et lestagiis et sartis et clausuris *Chr. Battle* f. 30v.; **1189** quod sint quieti a thelonio et passagio, et de sartis, et omni consuetudine *BBC* (*Bedford*) 182 (= *PQW* 17a); **1203** (v. 1b supra); **1231** sint quieti . . de guastis, regardis, et de assartis et placitis foreste (*Ch. Regis*) *MGL* II 670; **1287** quiete . . de theloneo . . hidagio et assartis et operacionibus et aliis regalibus prestacionibus *PQW* 14a; **s1286** concessit quod . . prior et homines sui et res sue sint quieti per totam terram . . de theloneo, . . scottis, . . hidagiis, assartis, operacionibus, et aliis regalibus prestacionibus *Ann. Dunstable* 331.

essaticum, kind of barley.

nomina bladorum et arborum: . . hoc ∼um, A. *bere* *WW*.

esscaeta v. escaeta. **esscamb-** v. excamb-. **esscewinga** v. scawagium. **essciamentum** v. aisiamentum. **esscoriatio** v. excoriatio.

1 esse [CL], **ĕdere** [LL], to eat.

natum, / . . / quem coctum laribus crudelis mater edebat Aldh. *CE* 4. 7. 27; dulcior et favo gustantum in faucibus eso Tatwine *Aen.* 1 (*Philosophia*) 7; non sum tam vorax ut omnia genera ciborum in una refectione edere [AS: *etan*] possim Ælf. *Coll.* 102; edendis dapibus, *ætlicum estum* *GlH* E 38; esse, comedere, vesci, cibare, epulari, prandere Osb. Glouc. *Deriv.* 192; cum dape vescor, ēdo; sermonem cum loquor, ēdo Serlo Wilt. 2. 38; ne dicare loquax vel garrulus inter edentes D. Bec. 921; [precursor Domini] magis elegit in eremo locustas et mel silvestre edere quam ineptis divitiis et deliciis affluere M. Rievaulx (*Ep.*) 63; **s1254** (v. 2 cardo 1a); edere *AncrR* 72 (v. deliciose).

2 esse [*as* CL, *but w. freer use of tenses, more extensive use of periphrastic constructions, and non-classical use of inf.* esse *as sb., gd.* essendum, *and inf.* fore.]

1 (absol.) to be, exist: **a** (of person or living thing); **b** (of Supreme Being); **c** (of inanim. object); **d** (of abstr., phil.). *V. et. exsistere* 1, *exstare* 2a.

a **a802** hic semper non erimus, sed in alia quadam vita semper erimus ALCUIN *Ep.* 243 (v. et. 6b infra); absque his .. elementis monachi esse non possunt ORD. VIT. III 2 (v. elementum 2a); Christus .. fuit capud ipsius Abel quando Abel erat. sed post fuit quando non erat, ergo membrum precessit capud S. LANGTON *Quaest.* 134; **1269** devenio homo vester .. ad portandum vobis fidem .. contra omnes qui sunt et mori possunt *CBaron* 78. **b** ANSELM (*Mon.* 4) I 18 (v. ens 1b); **c1170** Deus ens nullo mediante NIG. *Laur.* 39. 2; Deum esse vix insipiens dubitat BART. ANGL. I 5; Jhesu vena dulcedinis, / Proles pudica numinis, / Verbum ens in principio J. HOWD. *Cyth.* 1. 3; DUNS *Ord.* III 185–6 (v. ens 1b); cujus nomen est Qui est LEDREDE *Carm.* 1. 3. **c** de civitatibus .. ubi nunquam ante fuerunt construendis ASSER *Alf.* 91; lapides sunt et non vivunt *Quaest. Salern.* B 23. **d** **1011** cuncta quae sunt ejus [sc. Dei] bonitate bona sunt *Ch. Burton* 33; aut est unum aut sunt plura per quae sunt cuncta quae sunt ANSELM (*Mon.* 3) I 16; GROS. 126 (v. ens 1c); mensura adjacens .. motui diversimode distinguit motum et dicitur mensura sic diversificata: tempus transitum vel preteritum, tempus presens vel ens, tempus futurum vel postremum *Ps.-*GROS. *Gram.* 48; BACON III 262 (v. desitio a); Manicheus .. asseruit duo fore principia, unum boni et lucis, alterum mali et tenebrarum *Eul. Hist.* I 334 (= HIGD. IV 24 p. 96: esse); **c1363** antiquitas .. aliquando accipitur pro vetustate .. rerum entium (WYCL.) *Ziz.* 454; (KYN.) *Ziz.* 9 (v. concordantia 3b).

2 to exist, be found. **b** (impers., indicating passage of time) it is, there are, ago (*cf.* Fr. *il y a*); **c** (w. *diu*).

ferunt genus esse hominum quos Graeci Sciapodas appellant *Lib. Monstr.* I 17; fuit in Mercia moderno tempore quidam .. rex nomine Offa ASSER *Alf.* 14; sunt loca, sunt gentes, quibus est mactare parentes (R. NIGER *Vers.*) GERV. TILB. II 3 (v. et. 5c infra); in regione Bullensi dicunt fore fontem *Eul. Hist.* I 1. **b** nunc sunt iiij anni quod Willelmus manerium amisit *DB* I 129v.; "non" ait "plusquam quindecim anni sunt quod .. lues .. multos monachorum extinxit" W. MALM. *GR* III 293. **c** ANSELM III 189, P. BLOIS *Ep.* 10. 27B, etc. (v. diu 1b, c, 2b, 3c); **1380** (v. a, ab 2e).

3 (of condition, state, or sim.) to exist, remain, be in force. **b** *quid* (*sibi*) *est*? what is the matter (with him)? **c** *quid erit de* ..? what will become of ..? **d** *quid sit inter* ..? what is the difference between ..?

sit [AS: *sy*] pax et concordia inter nos ÆLF. *Coll.* 100; omnes hae consuetudines erant ibi quando rex Willelmus venit in Angliam *DB* I 1; quia calor erat, depositis amictibus in solo renone manebat ALEX. CANT. *Mir.* 29 p. 217; **s1225** ut que foreste remanere ut fuerunt prius .. debeant discernatur (v. deafforestare); cetera omnia et singula .. terminantur: exceptis legibus de burlawis, que per consensum vicinorum erunt *RegiamM* IV 39. **b** interrogatus quid sibi esset *V. Cuthb.* I 3. **c** **p793** quid erit de grege, si pastor oberrat? ALCUIN *Ep.* 282; **1242** loquela illa remanet quousque sciatur quid erit de petitione Walerami *CurR* XVI 2279; quicquid fuerit de Friderico—sive sc. hereticus sive catholicus fuerit OCKHAM *Pol.* I 86. **d** **799** quid sit inter aeternum et sempiternum ..? ALCUIN *Ep.* 163.

4 (impers.) to be the case, to be so; **b** (w. *ita* or *sic*); *cf.* 7d *infra*. **c** (ellipt.) *est qui*, there is someone who; *est quod*, there is something which. **d** *est quod, est ut*, it is the case that. **e** (w. inf.) to be possible. **f** one is, they are (to do something).

quid erit ubi nec pater nec filius .. conspicitur castus? GILDAS *EB* 109; absit ut meam putridam carnem .. incrassare debeam .. esto R. MERTON f. 94; quod non esset WYCL. *Log.* III 104 (v. curvedo). **b** sic fuit, ut verax fatur sermone sacerdos ALDH. *VirgV* 1567; **1221** unde solet ita esse, quod [etc.] (*Quaest. Itineris*) *MGL* I 63; non est sic de aliis DUNS *Sent.* I 2. 3. 6 (v. consignificativus); WYCL. *Act.* 73 (v. consequentia 3). **c** ac si non esset quod timeretur GILDAS *EB* 1; **790** sunt qui dicunt nos pro pace esse in illas partes mittendos ALCUIN *Ep.* 7; **798** sunt qui sibi laudem quaerunt ex alterius reprehensione *Ib.* 149; **1070** judicatum est ut .. querela sic remaneret quousque .. dum esset qui .. querelae responderet *Conc. Syn.* 570; nec est qui .. J. SAL. *Pol.* 811A (v. confurere); nec erat de cetero qui eum .. in causam traheret *Chr. Battle* f. 91v.; qualeque gaudium non est qui noverit, / non est qui pandere sermone poterit WALT. WIMB. *Carm.* 306. **d** inde est quod, licet antiquam pellem mutare non possis, te tamen littere faciunt insanire. .. frequens est ut [ebrii] homines bestias putent J. SAL. *Ep.* 283 (270); esto quod papa posset in casu necessitatis constituere regem, hoc tamen non potest in prejudicium .. illorum .. ad quos spectat institucio regum, presertim .. illis .. inconsultis OCKHAM *Pol.* I 129; CONWAY *Def. Mend.* 1424 (*recte* 1324) (v. consecrare 2b); esto quod tenor sit in C gravi, contrapunctus debet esse in C acuto HOTHBY *Contrap.* Fl 63. **e** quid ergo prodest crudelem Christum invocare, / a Quo non sit misericordiam impetrare? (*Vers.*) OSB. *Mir. Dunst.* 22; in .. antiquis cartis est animadvertere quantum .. verbis abstrusis .. delectentur W. MALM. *GP* V 196 p. 344; tunc videre erat quomodo artus spiritui famulabantur W. FITZST. *Thom.* 142; ut est adhuc cernere, universos continuo revocavit ad pacem H. READING (II) *Cel.* 30; est in fabrorum follibus videre BART. ANGL. III 15; de exemplari est loqui dupliciter BACON VII 113; nec esset dare .. durabilitatem WYCL. *Log.* II 158 (v. durabilitas); quia .. non esset dare gradum eis *Ib.* III 33 (v. descriptibilis b). **f** **1279** sunt recuperare .. vj li. (v. computarium b).

5 (w. dat. or prep.) to be property (of), to belong (to): **a** (of material possession or right); **b** (of physical attribute); **c** (of abstr. quality or condition). **d** *quantum in me est*, as far as in me lies, as much as I am able.

a ipse archiepiscopus tenet T., quod semper fuit in monasterio *DB* I 8; W. episcopus tenuit de rege E. sed non erat de episcopatu suo *Ib.* 43; de his habet archiepiscopus vj carucatas quas possunt arare iij carucae. hae sunt ad firmam aulae suae *Ib.* 298; **c1250** concessi eciam quod forisfactura ligne (*sic*) sit eis in iiij d. (*Ch. Warton*) *EHR* XVII 294; **1378** dicunt quod est ad predictam medietatem ejusdem A. medietas cujusdam scitus manerii .. item dicunt quod sunt ad predictam medietatem predicte A. de manerio predicto lxxiij s. iiij d. ob. de redditibus assise *IMisc* 213/5 m. 2. **b** radices sunt illi .. longe *Alph.* 76 (v. constringere 1c). **c** moris continui erat genti ut .. GILDAS *EB* 21 (v. continuus 2a); o quanta ecclesiae matri laetitia .. foret *Ib.* 34; non est mihi moris ad hanc conditionem habere subjectos ORD. VIT. IV 4 p. 180 (v. et. 10c infra); ei fuit detrimento H. HUNT. *HA* VII 29 (v. detrimentum 2a); (R. NIGER *Vers.*) GERV. TILB. II 3 (v. 2a supra); **s1272** non sunt de substancia professionis (v. bene 5). **d** **a1254** in eam quantum in nobis est tanquam in uxorem legitimam consentimus *Foed.* I 520a.

6 a to be (at a place). **b** (w. local adv.) to be present, located, situated; **c** (w. adverbial phr.). **d** (w. local adv.) to be present, to appear, attend; **e** (w. prep., w. ref. to person or place); **f** (w. *ad*, w. ref. to occasion); **g** (w. dat.); **h** (ellipt.); **i** (of time) to be present. *V. et. exsistere* 2.

a fui Tyntern Abbey tota die W. WORC. *Itin.* 36. **b** ALCUIN *Ep.* 243 (v. 1a supra); nemus longe est ORD. VIT. III 2 (v. elementum 2a); **1220** sumus in veniendo versus Salopesbiry, ita quod ibi erimus .. die lune proxima *Pat* 260 (v. et. 7c infra); si sol eternaliter esset sursum violenter, motus contrarius esset ei possibilis FISHACRE *Quaest.* 51. **c** Scylla monstrum .. in eo freto .. fuisse perhibetur *Lib. Monstr.* I 14; erat .. in eodem loco unica spinosa arbor ASSER *Alf.* 39; omnia regna quae sunt inter mare Tyrrhenum et illum marinum sinum *Ib.* 70; in unaquaque navi erant homines xx et unus *DB* I 1; apostoli .. erant in deserto OCKHAM *Pol.* II 766 (v. deserere 3c). **d** **1332** attachiati fuerunt essendi hic (v. attachiare 3b); **c1335** quod summoneret predictum T. .. essendi hic a die Pasche in unum mensem proxime sequentem *MGL* I 411; **c1377** predictus W. attachiatus est essendi hic ad eundem diem *Ib.* 395. **e** ut .. monstraretur non nisi innoxios .. in dominica domu esse debere GILDAS *EB* 69; ut per sex menses mecum fueris et tantundem in Britannia ASSER *Alf.* 79; qui in collegio fuerit (*Quad.*) *GAS* 103 (v. accredulitare), (*Leg. Hen.* 87. 8) *Ib.* 602 (v. collegium 1a); **c1185** essoniatur de esse ultra mare GLANV. I 25; **1214** habuit quandam hacham in manu sua et fuit extra domum *Ib.* 173; **1229, 1266** (v. ad 2f); **1284** ita quod eo die coram justiciariis .. esse non possit *Reg. Malm.* I 239; **s1316** ubi cum domino Ricardo L. milite fuissent in prandio (*Chr. Abingd.*) *EHR* XXVI 730; **1353** breve ad eligendos duos cives ad essendos coram consilio regis (*LBLond.* G f. 8) *MGL* I 626; **s1382** ei permiserunt intrare cum omni turba secum essencium bellatorum WALS. *HA* II 82; videbatur mihi .. me in regno meo fore consulesque .. pariter assistere (*Visio Æthelberti*) CIREN. II 281; **c1507** liberatus est de essendo coram eisdem superiore et concilio .. ad respondendum superiori et parti pro delicto per eum nequiter commisso *Lib. Kilken.* 132. **f** R. vult probare per illos homines qui ad suas conventiones fuerunt *DB* II 287; **c1162** fuerunt ad divisam (v. dividere 9c); **1212** fuit cum eo ad plura alia latrocinia *CurR* VII 339; **1227** (v. depraedatio b); **1283** quilibet istorum .. debet esse ad fenum colligendum *Cust. Battle* 31; **1318** (v. dissaisina b). **g** **1218** sub sigillis illorum qui vobiscum fuerint mensuracion[i] faciende *Pat* 163. **h** **1218** summoneantur quod sint a die Purificacionis in xv dies ..; fuit summonitus quod esset in crastino octabarum S. Hillarii *Eyre Yorks* 68. **i** 'prope est dies Domini'. si tunc prope erat, quid nunc putabitur? GILDAS *EB* 44.

7 (w. adverbial phr.) to be (in specified condition or situation); **b** (w. abl. of gd.); **c** (w. prep. & abl. of gd.); **d** (w. adv. of manner; *cf.* 4b *supra*). *V. et. exsistere* 5, *exstare* 3b.

qui iram corde multo tempore retinet in morte est GILDAS *Pen.* 17; si .. in consuetudine non erit ei multum bibere .. nihil nocet THEOD. *Pen.* I 1. 4 (v. et. 10e infra); nec ab re est unum .. enarrare BEDE *HE* III 2 (v. a, ab 5d); omnes Angli et Saxones qui .. cum paganis sub captivitate erant .. se subdiderunt ASSER *Alf.* 83; tunc se defendit pro x hid', modo pro viij hid' .. tamen fuit pro xv hid', sed rex E. condonavit pro xj hid' ut dicunt *DB* I 58v.; *DB* I 31, 41, **c1120** (v. de 12b); ut omnis homo liber sit in hundreto et decima (*Quad. rub.*) *GAS* 536; et in hundreto sit et decima (*Leg. Hen.* 8. 2) *Ib.* 554; si quis hominem habeat qui ei nolit esse ad rectum .. (*Ib.* 43. 4) *Ib.* 569; **c1132** de terris .. que erant in calumnia inter nos (v. concordia 2b); in hac opinione .. non solum ipse sed et patria fere tota .. erat GIR. *Invect.* V 15 (v. deceptorius b); **1216** non fuit .. contra nos in hac guerra *Pat* 6; **1225** etc. (v. ad 7d); **1227** (v. 1 assisa 1a); **c1228** (v. controversia); **1235** (v. de 12g); **1242, 1262** (v. ad 2j); **1268** Petrus fuit contra .. regem (v. contra 4b); *State Tri. Ed. I* 54 (v. contra 4c); *Ib.* 64 etc. (v. de 12e); **1290** etc. (v. de 12d); **1294**, OCKHAM *Dial.* 519 (v. de 12c); **1297** in hoc non fuerunt in aliqua negligencia sive culpa *RGasc* III 372; **1326** domicellus qui dixit se esse cum comite Kancie *Lit. Cant.* I 173; OCKHAM *Dial.* 478 (v. caritas 2b); **1337** (v. de 12h). **b** **1242** idem R., sicut fuit veniendo versus curiam, cecidit .. de equo *CurR* XVI 2337. **c** **1214** quesivit candelam ut iret cubitum; sicut fuit in eundo versus lectum .. *CurR* VII 171; **1220** rex Scoccie est in veniendo versus partes istas *Ib.* VIII 361; **1220** (v. 6b supra); **1242** quedam navis est in veniendo de Hyspannia *Cl* 502; **1342** grangia .. excepta, que jam est in corrigendo seu reparando (*Vis. Totnes*) *EHR* XXVI 110; rector .. habet unum scriptorem qui est in scribendo novos [libros] *Ib.* 117; **c1448** toto tempore quo .. scole in construendo fuerint *StatOx* 271. **d** Deo .. possibilius .. videtur quod non est ad esse .. quam quod male est .. emendari PULL. *Sent.* 745A; quia non sunt simul HALES *Sent.* I 259 (v. correlativus b).

8 (w. adverbial phr.): **a** (denoting origin from place); **b** (denoting composition from material); **c** (denoting propagation); **d** (denoting derivation or issue from abstr.).

a ab Hibernia potestne aliquid boni esse? (cf. *John* ii 47) GIR. *TH intr.* p. 6. **b** pars feretri est de argento *Lib. Eli.* III 50 (v. deauratura); **1388** primum par est de rubeo *velvett* (v. custos 10c). **c** quedam vegetabilia sunt per ramos, quedam per semina, quedam nascuntur sine semine BACON V 120. **d** *DB* I 133v., **1228** (v. de 12a); si universitas rerum est ex aliqua materia .. ANSELM (*Mon.* 7) I 21; eam que est a verbis BALSH. *AD* 67 (v. demonstrare 2a); esse est a perfectione rei J. BLUND *An.* 323; in hiis que sunt a casu vel a nobis GROS. 198 (v. a, ab 6f).

9 (w. adj. as compl.) to be (of specified description); **b** (w. adv.); **c** (w. inf. or noun cl. as subj.). *V. et. exsistere* 4, *exstare* 3a.

quid .. deformius .. potest .. esse .. quam Deo timorem .. denegare GILDAS *EB* 4; me .. rogabit ut .. familiaris ei essem ASSER *Alf.* 79; en qui confirmas Christum fore cunctipotentem FRITH. 504; die quo rex fuit vivus et mortuus *DB* I 45; memores estote G. MON X 8; est oblita [*gl.*: tradita oblivioni] Deum meretrix, ens [*gl.*: existens] oblita [*gl.*: *squasse*] sorde [*gl.*: sordida, *englue*] H. AVR. *CG* 7v. 3 (v. et. 13 infra); **a1296** concernentes porcionem ad pauperum sustentacionem .. assignatam nimis fore exilem (*Ch. Abbatis*) *Reg. Malm.* II app. 368; **s1355** rex proclamari fecit .. quod .. sagittarii forent parati apud S. .. ad transfretandum cum eo apud C. AVESB. 125b; putabat enim ipsum rusticum fuisse *Eul. Hist.* I 379; num ignoras hoc nobis naturaliter fore proprium BROMPTON 1045; tales scientes fore simoniacos .. eis in crimine simonie participant PAUL. ANGL. *ASP* 1539; peto quod ex tunc declaretis illas [conclusiones] prout sunt esse veras et rectas PECOCK *Abbr.* 616. **b** sat erat patria expunxisse beatum FRITH. 682; quisquis .. tota mente in peccata migrat, vix est ut redeat R. NIGER *Mil.* III *prol.* **c** non satis foret ut quadro cum cardine mundus / .. / usibus humanis serviret? ALDH. *VirgV* 2689; novi .. multum mihi esse necesse vigiliis .. insistere BEDE *HE* IV 23 p. 265; dolorosum est describere G. MON. XI 2 (v. describere 3a); certo certius est quod .. NECKAM *NR* I 10 (v. certus 2c); **1226** (v. desiccare 1c); non necesse est hoc fieri GROS. *Quaest. Theol.* 197; difficillimum est .. concludere DUNS *Ord.* III 41 (v. difficilis 1a).

10 (w. sb. as compl.); **b** (w. sb. or pron. in agreement as compl.); **c** (w. compl. in gen.); **d** (w. compl. in dat.); **e** (w. inf. or noun cl. as subj.); **f** (w. inf. or noun cl. as compl.). *V. et. exsistere* 5, *exstare* 3c.

1196 canonici .. concesserunt michi et meis fore participes beneficiorum et orationum *AncD* A 2507; **1324** calumniavit jus suum essendi marescallus *MGL* II 297; **1393** concessio unius orphane essende monialis in prioratu de Kylburne (*LB Lond.* H f. 288) *MGL* I 611; **1422** aliis finibus factis de diversis personis ad essendos liberos burgenses in villa *Lib. Kilken.* 87; **1567** concessimus eidem Nicholao Barham officium unius servientium nostrorum ad legem, habendum .. dictum officium, necnon ad essendum unum servientium ad legem quamdiu nobis placuerit (*Auditor's Patent Bk.*) MS PRO E. 404/2452 f. 157d. **b** interdictum apostoli denegantis posse adulteros regni caelestis esse municipes suspicis? GILDAS *EB* 32; E. et A., qui sponsi earum futuri fore credebantur .. impetrant ut .. ALDH. *VirgP* 52; cum .. successorem fore Ceoluulfum decrevisset BEDE *HE* V 23; hanc creaturam N. formatici sive casei sive butyri sive sit quod sit EGB. *Pont.* 132; sive sis [AS: *þu sy*] sacerdos .., seu miles .., esto quod es ÆLF. *Coll.* 100; **a1089** quatinus .. abbatissam esse abbatissam et

priorem esse priorem jubeatis LANFR. *Ep.* 31 (59); grammaticus non est idem quod homo, id est non habent eandem definitionem ANSELM (*Gram.* 5) I 149 (v. et. 11b infra); qui fuerint mores hominis vicinia novit D. BEC. 587; parvus adulator .. / .. / inter magnates magnus fertur fore vates *Ib.* 598; licet .. mediocribus esse poetis non liceat GIR. *TH intr.* p. 4; **1254** hoc idem est de lardario *CallMisc* I 70; **1279** occasione mortis Petri .. de qua se fore culpabilem diffitetur *RGasc* II 84; **1291** eundem fore apostatam .. nullatenus ignorantes (*Compositio*) *Mon. Francisc.* II 35; negat scienciam fore clavem distinctam realiter a clave potencie OCKHAM *Pol.* II 825; Cristi discipulos affirmant se fore fratres GOWER *VC* IV 717; **1446** scientes Thomam .. fore apparitorem (v. apparitor b). **c** moris continui erat GILDAS *EB* 21 (v. continuus 2a); nos, licet vilissimae qualitatis simus *Ib.* 36; [Sciapodes] sunt celerrimae naturae *Lib. Monstr.* I 17; BEDE *HE* V 24 (v. 2 cum 1b); 'duorum' rationis est, 'duum' eufoniae *GlC* D 378–9; **a994** et unde est / hoc nomen tractum? cujus generis siet, ede *Altercatio* 30; **774** (10c) ut esset juris ecclesiastici (v. ecclesiasticus 1b); **s1016** (v. consilium 1d); non est .. moris ORD. VIT. IV 4 p. 180 (v. et. 5c supra); **a1154** sacerdotalis officii est .. (v. erroneus 3a); *Dial. Scac.* I 5 F (v. 1 constabularia d); Domini est corrigere HALES *Qu.* 510 (v. corrigere 3c); a ventre clauditur cujus est claudere WALT. WIMB. *Carm.* 116; **1309** arbores .. sunt ipsius archiepiscopi (v. drovedenna); cujus .. consecraciones .. nullius essent momenti OCKHAM *Dial.* 578 (v. consecratio 2a); **1368** (v. duellum 3b); canum est †baulare [l. baubare] .., boum mugire *CathA*. **d** pastores qui exemplo esse omni plebi debuerint GILDAS *EB* 21; despectui erat EADMER *V. Dunst.* 6 (v. 1 despectus 1a); multos filios .. qui in .. Anglia hostibus in armis magno terrori fuerunt ORD. VIT. III 2 p. 22; quod maximo .. fuit detrimento H. HUNT. *HA* VII 29 (v. detrimentum 2a). **e** THEOD. *Pen.* I 1. 4 (v. 7a supra); cum humanae sit naturae .. caricis nutriri ALDH. *PR* 114; suum .. operari est suum intelligere GROS. *Quaest. Theol.* 194; **1288** (v. contumultuare); **1441** nobis cordi fuit ambassiatores .. direxisse BEKYNTON II 98 (v. cor 2a). **f a1089** non sum quod putas, sed sim quia putas LANFR. *Ep.* 61 (50); ficta ruina mali moneat mala vera caveri. / palma fuisse mihi non erit absque fore *Babio* 302.

11 (expressing equivalence): **a** (of word) to mean; **b** *hoc est, id est,* that is (introducing more accurate or explicit expression).

a esse cum successione .. cadit in circumlocucione presentis et dicitur de re presenti et idem est sic 'amatus sum' quod 'amor'; esse autem cum permanencia est esse ad quod terminatur fieri .. et dicitur de re preterita ut 'amatus sum, es, est' BACON XV 149 (v. et. 13a infra); dicitur apozima ab *apos* quod est 'decoccio' et *zeo* quod est 'ferveo', i. decoccio fervens *SB* 11. **b** in arca [Noe], hoc est nunc ecclesia GILDAS *EB* 69; id est ANSELM (*Gram.* 5) I 149 (v. 10b supra); hoc est *Id.* (*Mon.* 4) I 20 (v. ens 3); duo boves validi .. id est rex et archiepiscopus Cantuariensis W. MALM. *GP* I 48; id est GROS. 126 (v. ens 1c); hoc est embrocare GAD. 50v. 2 (v. embrochare).

12 (w. verbal form as compl.): **a** (fut. ppl.); **b** (pr. ppl.); *v. et. exsistere* 6.

a omnia quae sibi dicta erant recordans indubitata spe .. futura fore credebat FELIX *Guthl.* 52. **b** nos fuimus stantes in culmine muri ALCUIN *SS Ebor* 963; **795** dignans fuisti *Ep. Alcuin.* 46; **c1140** parva mihi commissa domus caret his alimentis / est humana quibus natura fruens elementis OSB. CLAR. *Ep.* 32; herens .. fuerit *V. Merl.* 837 (v. echenais); **1218** ne .. debita nostra .. remaneant insoluta, et ne inde simus perdentes *Pat* 180; **s1223** cum ipso fuerant surgentes primo diluculo et videntes se .. circumseptos .. obstupuerunt *Chr. Man* 88; **1242** ei sint intendentes (v. 2 constabularius 5a); **1242** dum nostri essent .. dormientes (v. 1 credere 5b); **1267** nos per consequens valde inde sumus perdentes *BBC* (*Oxford*) 244; **1294** unusquisque burgensium essoniabit alterum ad curiam sine calumpnia quando fuerint absentes *Ib.* (*Chesterfield*) 202; **s1356** intravit domum ubi erant sedentes AVESB. 135b; a musca carnes tunc servans non fuit olla GOWER *VC* I 607; patrocinium illud patriarchale rex ipse .. fuit .. excipiens ELMH. *Cant.* 79.

13 (as auxiliary vb.): **a** (pres. w. p. ppl. as pres.); **b** (pres. or inf. w. p. ppl. as perf.); **c** (imperf. or perf. w. p. ppl. as perf.); **d** (imperf. w. p. ppl. as pluperfect); **e** (fut. or fut. perf. w. p. ppl. as fut. perf.); **f** (w. fut. ppl.); **g** (gd. or gdv.); **h** (w. inf., infl. by ME grammar). *V. et. exsistere* 7, *exstare* 4.

a idem est .. "amatus sum" quod "amor" BACON XV 149 (v. 11a supra); **c1310** nomina aliquorum sunt scripta (*Lit. Collectorum Apostol.*) *EHR* XLI 353; **s1430** quod milites .. essent electi (v. eligere 2g). **b** H. AVR. *CG* 7v. 3 (v. 9a supra); **1291** domus in qua Johannes queritur predictum ciphum fore captum *Law Merch.* II 51; differencia est inter .. alterari et alteratum esse OCKHAM *Pol.* II 602; **s1400** terra Wallie .. conquesta fore dinoscitur (v. conquaerere 2a). **c** cum .. multa venalia in forum fuissent conlata BEDE *HE* II 1; injustum .. videbatur .. loca in quibus .. coronatus fuerant .. derelinquere, nisi coactus ASSER *Alf.* 79; **1219** positus fuit .. in prisona (v. ducere 1b); **s1264** statutum fuit .. ne aliquis advocatus fuisset essoinator in Hustengo *Leg. Ant. Lond.* 70; cum circumlocucio .. fiat per participium et verbum de preterito, ut "amatus fui", non fit per presens BACON XV 147; **1313** ductus fuit ad barram (v. ducere 1b); **1314** cum .. fuerim pro excommunicato denunciatus (v. condemnatorius); **s1430** cum in statuto .. ordinatum fuisset quod .. (v. eligere 2g). **d** urbes, quae .. ob metum hostium collocatae fuerant, directo librant GILDAS *EB* 18; paucos Britones .. occiderunt; ceteri .. accolae .. ante .. occisi erant ASSER *Alf.* 2. **e** nisi citius .. conversus fueris ad Dominum, ensem in te vibrabit .. rex [cf. *Psalm* vii 13] GILDAS *EB* 30; **a1188** ab omni officio curie ero depositus (v. consentire 2c). **f** indecens .. est si in hoc mundo habuerimus odio quos ibi sumus habituri karissimos ANSELM *Misc.* 298. **g** qui cum ipso nomine certatim delendi erant GILDAS *EB* 27; egenis eleemosynam esse dandam .. praedicantes *Ib.* 66; credendum est quia .. BEDE *HE* III 22; **793** non est .. conversio disperanda ALCUIN *Ep.* 23 (v. desperare a); **1073** omnia .. reseravi quae reseranda esse .. judicavi LANFR. *Ep.* 43 (18); **1345** brevia predictis custodi, fratribus .. ac eciam vicecomiti Ebor' de esse intendenda remaneant affilata inter recorda *Mem. Ripon* I 229; **1433** determinando .. quomodo senciendum esset (v. conceptus 2a); **1433** ambassiatores .. mittendi essent (v. consolitus). **h 1196** debuit esse exhereditari (*sic*) *CurR* I 19.

14 (inf. *esse, fore, fuisse,* or gd. *essendum* as sb. n.): **a** condition, state; *v. et.* 2 *essentia* 3. **b** essence, nature; *v. et. ens* 2, *entitas* 2, 2 *essentia* 4. **c** existence; *v. et. ens* 3, *entitas* 3, 2 *essentia* 5. **d** being present, attendance. **e** (perf. inf. *fuisse*) past. **f** (inf. *fore*) future.

a pro statu vero causarum et esse temporum et modo inplacitatorum (*Leg. Hen.* 49. 2) *GAS* 572; queritis esse meum; querentibus ordine pandam H. HUNT. *HA* XI 169; uno modo contingit loqui quantum ad essentias suas .. alio modo ad esse naturale et transmutationem BACON VIII 35; videtur quod ista .. possint significare diversa esse ejusdem rei specifice *Id.* XIV 76; qui .. vos ad esse clericale creavimus studiorum vestrorum fabricas appellatis R. BURY *Phil.* 4. 70. **b** sors oblita sui stabilis sors desinit esse; / non variando vices deserit esse suum R. PARTES 226; esse viri scire sitiens, non ejus ab hoste / explores quis sit D. BEC. 584; **1187** (v. 1 continentia 3); **c1200** adde quod esse rei cujuslibet assero majus / ipsa re NECKAM *DS* I 111; (cf. ib. 37: esse Dei Deus est). **c 1011** quia a summo bono essendi ceperant formam bona sunt *Ch. Burton* 33; clarum est rationalem creaturam totum suum posse et velle ad memorandum et intelligendum et amandum summum bonum impendere debere, ad quod ipsum esse suum se cognoscit habere ANSELM (*Mon.* 68) I 79; alia [animalia] .. ipsum esse suum fuge levitate conservant ADEL. *QN* 15; [anima] a simplici esse .. multa varietatum .. possibilitate discordat ALF. ANGL. *Cor* 16. 13; res de non esse munus producit ad esse D. BEC. 1545; **a1200** benignitatem autem artificis summi loquuntur conservatio rei in esse et utilitas ejusdem NECKAM *NR* II *prol.*; de non esse Potens produxit in esse potenter *Id. DS* I 57; **c1205** quamdiu domus manet in esse, domus ut formata in esse servetur GROS. *Ep.* 1 p. 5; sic mundi machina in esse ordine debito servaretur BART. ANGL. IV 4 (v. debere 2); ab intelligentia intelligente seipsam, in quantum ipsa habet esse possibile, fluit in eam anima celi .. J. BLUND *An.* 13; esse quod est a creatione est supra esse naturale *Ib.* 17; anima secundum suum esse concretum partim est de physica et partim est de metaphysica *Ib.* 21; anima rationalis .. habens perpetuitatem essendi *Ib.* 38; memento matris tue, cujus viscera te cum angustiis intolerabilibus ad esse perduxerunt M. PAR. *Maj.* I 57 (cf. G. MON. III 7: te in mundum produxit); *Ps.*-GROS. *Summa* 292 (v. entitas 2); non quantum illud esse quod habet per materiam .. set quantum ad esse essentie BACON VIII 70; *Id. Maj.* II 43 (v. corporalis 2b); DUNS *Ord.* III 185–6 (v. ens 1b); **1337** universitas .. temporibus .. vestris condignos flores producens in esse, indies laudabiliter cepit pululare *FormOx* 96; WYCL. *Quaest. Log.* 262 (v. desinentia); si cause essendi simonie ad factum .. concurrunt, non potest Papa naturam rei aliter quam est appellare PAUL. ANGL. *ASP* 1549. **d 1432** quam quidem summam .. ab eis .. pro certis negociis et agendis suis in ultimo esse nostro ibidem mutuatus est *Cl* 282 m. 6. **e** *Babio* 302 (v. 10f supra). **f** *Babio* 302 (v. 10f supra).

15 (gd., gdv. *essendum*).

1332, c1335, c1337 (v. 6d supra); **1353, c1507** (v. 6e supra); **1324, 1393, 1422, 1567** (v. 10a supra); **1011** J. BLUND *An.* 38, PAUL. ANGL. *ASP* 1549 (v. 14c supra).

16 (inf. *fore*): **a** (as pres. inf.); **b** (forming subj. with fut. force, *forem,* ~*s,* ~*t etc.*); **c** (w. p. ppl. as perf. pass. inf.); **d** (inf. as sb.) the future.

a *Eul. Hist.* I 334 (v. 1d supra); *Ib.* I 1 (v. 2a supra); CIREN. II 281 (v. 6e supra); FRITH. 504, **a1296**, BROMPTON 1045 (v. 9a supra); **1196** (v. 10a supra); ALDH. *VirgP* 52, BEDE *HE* V 23, D. BEC. 598, **1279, 1291,** OCKHAM *Pol.* II 825, GOWER *VC* IV 717, **1446** (v. 10b supra). **b** GILDAS *EB* 34 (v. 5c supra); **s1355** (v. 9a supra); ALDH. *VirgV* 2689 (v. 9c supra). **c s1400** (v. 13b supra). **d** *Babio* 302 (v. 10f, 14f supra).

essecambium v. excambium. **esseceppa** v. skeppa.

essedum [CL < Gall.], **~a,** cart, chariot. **b** (astr.) Wain.

~um, vehiculum *GlC* E 312; bida vel basterna vel capsus vel currus vel ~a vel quadriga vel carpentum, *cræt* ÆLF. *Gl.*; ~um, i. currus, vehiculum *GlH* E 355; ~a, vehiculo, *on cræte GlP* 376; esedum, genus curruum OSB. GLOUC. *Deriv.* 196. **b** sidereis stipor turmis in vertice mundi; / esseda famoso gesto cognomina [MSS: cognomine] vulgo ALDH. *Aen.* 53 (*Arcturus*).

esseia- v. essaia-. **esselda** v. selda. **essendum, ~us** v. 2 esse.

1 essentia [cf. 1 esse], eating, consuming, digesting.

ALF. ANGL. *Cor* 15. 4 (v. euthenia a).

2 essentia [CL; cf. 2 esse]

1 a being, living thing; *v. et. ens* 1a, *entitas* 1a, *exsistentia* 1. **b** (Supreme) Being; *v. et. ens* 1b.

ipsa anima, cum incorporea ~ia sit nullique sensui subjacens ADEL. *QN* 18; ut .. anima, natura vigil ~ia, cum ad aures suas aliquid extraneum accedit, de eadem re ad judicium excitatur *Ib.* 21; summas .. ~ias supermundane hierarchie Salvatorem .. docentem ostendit Isaias AD. MARSH *Ep.* 246 (*bis*) p. 417. **b** summa ~ia .. rerum molem .. sola per seipsam produxit ex nihilo ANSELM (*Mon.* 7) I 22; aut ipsa anima habet hoc ipsum quod ipsa est a seipsa, vel a prima ~ia, que summe et maxime est incommutabilis J. BLUND *An.* 322.

2 substance, material; *v. et. exsistentia* 2. **b** essence, extract from substance. **c** (w. *quinta*) quintessence.

~ia, i. .. substantia *GlH* E 356 (cf. *Gl. Leid.* 1. 46); metallum est quedam ~ia que dicitur secunde compositionis, cujus species sunt 7, sc. ferrum, plumbum, [etc.] M. SCOT *Part.* 295; per 'substantiam' [comprehenditur] ~ia et hypostasis; per 'formam' ratio .. insita [etc.] HALES *Sent.* II 26; anima existens in corpore potest intueri ymagines formatas in ipso corpore, non tamen erit presens secundum sui ~iam cum ipsis ymaginibus J. BLUND *An.* 308. **b** ~ia est extractum simplex e rebus tota sua natura perfectis productum. nominatur ~ia quod, in elementariis loculamentis nata et comprehensa, totius substantiae misturae pars sit perfecta, natura et essentiali ratione virtuteque instructa *LC* 240. **c** affirmant corpus celi esse non ex massa hujus substantie corruptibilis sed ex quadam quinta ~ia, que preter quatuor naturas ex nichilo fuit creata D. MORLEY 23; Aristoteles .. / .. / quod stellis sit origo potens essentia quinta / censuit NECKAM *DS* I 301; hec [elementaris regio] a philosophis quinta ~ia nuncupatur, cujus novem sunt spere SACROB. *Sph.* 79; corpus hujus mundi est unum, quod quintam ~iam nominant philosophi, sive ethera, sive corpus celi, et preter elementares proprietates circulariter mobile GROS. 11; ab illo mercurio sublimato .. extrahe spiritum ejus, qui a quibusdam magnis philosophis quinta ~ia clamatur CUTCL. *CL* 191.

3 condition, state, actuality. *V. et.* 2 *esse* 14a.

1002 (11c) praesentis ~iae periculis incubantibus *CD* 1297; nescio quid magis afferebat ei certa spes in futurum regnandi, quam patri suo ipsa ~ia regni, quia patri magnum regnandi spatium jam preterierat, filio vero totum adhuc reservabatur H. HUNT. *CM* 5.

4 essence, nature (phil.); *v. et.* 2 *esse* 14b; **b** (w. *divina*); **c** (w. ref. to Christ); **d** (w. ref. to Trinity).

~ia i. .. natura *GlH* E 356; ~ia, *auuesnis GlM* 72. 1; probare contendis panem vinumque post consecrationem in principalibus permanere ~iis LANFR. *Corp. & Sang.* 417D; *Id. Comment. Paul.* 277 (v. accidentalis 1b); character est sacramentum et ~ia baptismi S. LANGTON *Quaest.* 362; angelica natura .. homine subtilitate ~e .. sublimior GIR. *TH* I 13; eorum [sc. angelorum] ~ia est simplex et inmaterialis, pura distincta seu discreta BART. ANGL. II 2; 'substantia' dicitur quod est, '~ia' quo est, 'natura' quo operatur HALES *Sent.* I 32; intelligentia secundum suam propriam ~iam intelligit ea que intelligit J. BLUND *An.* 31; simplicis ~ie est anima *Ib.* 333; ~ia est rei quiditas nomine absolute BACON VIII 234; quamvis esse sit causatum sicut ~ia, tamen ~ia est causata tamquam participans, esse vero tamquam participatum T. SUTTON *Quodl.* 394; '~ia' dicit rem absolute sine contraccione ad genus aliquod per aliquam formam WYCL. *Form.* 183. **b** quidquid de divina ~ia credi oportet ANSELM (*Resp. Ed.* 10) I 139; nullus tanta amentia ignorantie excecatus est, qui aliquam harum vocum 'essentia', 'est', 'ens', in illa significatione retenta in qua creaturis convenit, Deum vel ~iam divinam significari presumat (R. MELUN) *GLA* II 214; neque divina ~ia neque divina providentia est pars anime J. BLUND *An.* 328; 'precipit et prohibet, permittit, consulit, inplet' .. ista verba significant divinam ~iam GROS. *Quaest. Theol.* 200; ~ia divina non causat in nobis immediate actum credendi sicut causabit in nobis immediate actum videndi DUNS *Ord.* II 43; [heresis] quod omnis sperans aliquod futurum non videt clare divinam ~iam OCKHAM *Dial.* 740. **c** si Hieronymus unam solam in Christo substantiam assereret, id est naturam sive ~iam, non modo aliis catholicis sed et sibi contrarius esset J. CORNW. *Eul.* 12 p. 283; [Monothelite] unam Christo inesse naturam predicant .. Filius Dei de sue divinitatis ~ia dicit 'Ego et Pater unum sumus' M. PAR. *Maj.* I 282. **d 680** sanctae Trinitatis unam ~iam .. confiteor ALDH. *Ep.* 4; aequalitatem atque incommutabilitatem suae [sc. Trinitatis] ~iae .. vestris mentibus infigat EGB. *Pont.* 71; **c1218** confitemur quod unus [est] solus Deus verus .. Pater et Filius et Spiritus Sanctus: tres .. persone sed una ~ia, substantia, seu natura *Conc. Syn.* 61; unum in tribus Abrahe revelatur, / simpla cum sit .. essentia Trinitatis J. HOWD. *Cant.* 597; PECKHAM *QR* 26 (v. emphaticus b).

5 existence; *v. et.* 2 *esse* 14c, *exsistentia* 3. **b** eternal existence, eternity.

~ia, i. . . *wunung GlH* E 356. **b** a**804** quid sit inter substantiam, ~iam, et subsistentiam? . . ~ia proprie de Deo dicitur, qui semper est quod est ALCUIN *Ep.* 268; ~ia, i. aeternitas *GlH* E 356.

6 existence in a place, presence, whereabouts.

qui depredati fratris intelligens angustiam, praedonum quoque signis quibusdam agnoscens ~iam, post ipsos impiger equitat HERM. ARCH. 32; s**1141** se apud Lincolniam exceperunt. quorum ibidem ~iam rex perpendens Lincolniam obsedebat *Meaux* I 124; **1413** (v. dens 1c); **1415** quando ibidem interfui cum domino rege, nunc . . a tempore dicte ~ie mee ibidem (*Test.*) *Reg. Cant.* II 74.

3 essentia v. euthenia.

essentialis [LL]

1 of the essence, essential (esp. phil. & theol.); **b** (dist. from *accidentalis*); **c** (mus.); **d** (astr.).

'Ego et Pater unum sumus' confiteantur nobiscum propter ~em identitatem Patris et Filii ANSELM (*Proc. Sp.* 7) II 199; convertibilis autem [motus] duas habet species, alteram ~em, ut constructio et destructio, sicut de aqua in christallum, et alteram qualitativam ADEL. *Alch.* 17; quod potentia est ~is primo subjecto SICCAV. *PN* 61; actus nocionales fundantur super actus ~es immanentes; sed tantum sunt duo actus ~es manentes intra, qui sunt intelligere et velle DUNS *Ord.* II 287; volens probare ~em unitatem personarum in divinis . . (KYN.) *Ziz.* 6. **b** quod agens est ~e, non accidentale BACON VII 20; beatitudo . . ad actum . . voluntatis . . pertinet . . non quidem accidentalem, tum quia voluntas . . est imaginis per beatitudinem reformande pars ~is KNAPWELL *Not.* 188; specificatur . . nomen per ~ia et per accidentalia; ~ia vero rei sunt aut priora ipsa re aut equalia. sumimus . . ~ia large ad omnia ingrediencia essenciam rei *Ps.*-GROS. *Gram.* 64; *Id. Summa* 463 (v. dependentia 4b); minor eciam secundo assumpta patet ex diffinicione 'quid nominis' ~is cause. nam causa accidentalis rei est causa que non requiritur ad hoc quod data res causetur, et causa ~is, que requiritur WYCL. *Ente* 274. **c** dantur viij regule, quarum iiij dicuntur ~es et iiij accidentales HOTHBY *Contrap.* Fa 101. **d** dignitates ~es ELVEDEN *Cal.* 5 (v. dignitas 6).

2 actual, real. **b** indispensable. **c** (as sb. n.) necessary condition or state.

secundum autem veritatem ~em frons est, ut dicit Constan[s], os semicirculare BART. ANGL. V 10. **b** modus . . operacionis [sc. Creationis] ~is fuit et materialis *Eul. Hist.* I 13. **c** s**1426** utrum . . tria ~ia, obedienciam sc., paupertatem, et continenciam, regulariter observarent AMUND. I 206; dicunt seipsos esse professores ~ium regule sancti doctoris Basilii GASCOIGNE *Loci* 2; si est [sentencia] injusta, sic, sc. quod realiter est excommunicacio, quia excommunicacionis omnia ~ia ponuntur, tunc . . est timenda MAJOR IV 7; **1536** quod illae . . hujusmodi . . domorum religiosarum quas . . dissolvendas esse noluissemus . . permanerent in eisdem suis . . ~ibus, statu, qualitate, conditione (*Pat*) *Foed.* XIV 574b.

3 pertaining to being or existence (also as sb. n.). **b** causing existence.

nomina [Dei] que notificant essentiam dicuntur ~ia, . . que notiones notionalia BART. ANGL. I 6; theologia . . magis proprie est de personalibus quam de ~ibus, quia ~ia plurima possunt cognosci a metaphysico DUNS *Ord.* I 211; *Id. Prim. Princ.* 628 (v. dependentia 4b). **b** sunt . . in animali: vita, nutrimentum, sensus, motus. omnis vero vis . . alicujus operationis proprie est effectiva, ex eo quod hoc aliquid est eamque alterius effectus proximum et ~ale principium esse impossibile est ALF. ANGL. *Cor* 2. 2; nulli rei dum est potest deesse sua causa ~is; sed ~issima causa uniuscujusque Deus; ergo Deus est ubique GROS. *Quaest. Theol.* 205; res temporales . . dupliciter considerantur: primo, inquantum sunt naturales, et naturalium operum productive; vel eciam inquantum sunt ~es cause et effectus inter se PAUL. ANGL. *ASP* 1547.

essentialitas [LL], essentiality.

PECKHAM *QA* 173 (v. causalitas a); iste modus ~atis reducitur ad secundum modum dicendi per se SICCAV. *PN* 135; donec hujusmodi morbus fuerit quasi naturalis et essencialis, ita quod propter naturalitatem et ~atem sit hereditarius GAD. 37. 1.

essentialiter [LL]

1 in essence, essentially (esp. phil. & theol.); **b** (dist. from *accidentaliter* or sim.). **c** basically, fundamentally, in fact.

'quia fecit mihi magna qui potens est . .' [*Luke* i 49]. . . totam suam magnitudinem ad illius donum refert qui ~er potens et magnus existens fideles suos . . fortes facere consuevit BEDE *Hom.* I 4. 18; superius volens astruere panem vinumque altaris inter sacrandum ~er non mutari, duo quaedam pro argumentorum locis assumpsisti LANFR. *Corp. & Sang.* 417B; cum omnis substantia tractetur . . esse universalis, quae pluribus substantiis ~er communis est . . ANSELM (*Mon.* 27) I 45; quoniam . . non est nisi unus Christus, ipseque est non nuncupative sed ~er homo et Deus, constat quod . . PULL. *Sent.* 787A; si corpus Christi sub specie panis ~er corpus Christi est, quanto fortius ipse Christus in propria specie ~er homo est J. CORNW. *Eul.* 9; est . . hoc indicium quod anima . . sit ~er in sanguine quia . . sanguis est nutrimentum totius corporis J. BLUND *An.* 378; stella et sua sphera non sunt uniformes; differunt enim ~er in suis luminibus GROS. 35; dixit Christus . . 'nemo bonus nisi solus Deus' [*Luke* xviii 19], sc. ~er et primo; et tamen angeli boni, et beati in celo atque justi omnes sunt boni OCKHAM *Dial.* 853; non . . audeo dicere quod corpus Christi sit ~er, substancialiter, corporaliter, vel identice ille panis WYCL. *Conf.* 115; *Id. Act.* 12 (v. durativus). **b** pono differentiam in mercurii generatione et sulphuris, quamvis ex utraque parte causent metallum, sc. mercurius ~er et sulphur ex parte accidentali *Correct. Alch.* 9; GROS. 66 (v. accidentaliter b); homo ex hoc quod est rationalis differt ab asino ~er et substantialiter; sed accidentaliter unus homo differt ab alio homine per nomen et figuram et colorem BACON *CSPhil.* 498; quidquid ergo est in aliquo aut est idem sibi ~er aut accidentaliter DUNS *Ord.* II 247. **c** non nomine solum sed et omine, non vocaliter tantum sed ~er et quasi substantialiter primatie sedes Cantuaria foret GIR. *JS* 1 *prol.* p. 113; colera nigra actionibus suis duplex est circa somnum et vigilias quoniam ~er dominatur cerebro, ipsum deprimens ex fumi multitudine GILB. II 104. 1; prebenda . . ~er idem est quod canonia . . et ita canonia et prebenda non differunt ~er sed respectu divini officii . . dicitur canonia, respectu fructuum . . dicitur prebenda PAUL. ANGL. *ASP* 1531.

2 in respect of being, with reference to existence. **b** with reference to permanent existence, eternally.

sicut primum ~er est ubique et virtus simul, sicut celum movetur BACON VII 41; aliquis actus habet primum objectum a quo ~er dependet et habet objectum secundum a quo ~er non dependet sed tendit in illud virtute primi objecti DUNS *Ord.* II 28; *Id. Prim. Princ.* IV 732 (v. causatio 2); *Id. PW* 52 (v. dependentia 4b); actus magis habet denominari ab eo a quo magis et essencialius dependet *Quaest. Ox.* 316. **b** ~er, aeternaliter *GlH* E 357; **942** (13c) perpetua hereditas que in . . Trinitatis Dei theologia . . manet ~er, ultroneis meritorum magnopere est mercimoniis comparanda *Ch. Burton* 5; impossibile est Deum aliqua magis perfecte et alia minus perfecte cognoscere sed omne possibile Deus perfecte cognoscit; ergo ~er intuitive . . cognoscit (KYN.) *Ziz.* 32.

essentiare, ~ificare [cf. 2 esse, 2 essentia], (phil. & theol.) to cause to be, to endow with existence.

appositum se habet ad illud cui apponitur tamquam illud quod posset ~iari de illo BACON XV 54; Deus . . respondit 'Ego sum Qui sum; sic dices filiis Israel, "Qui est misit me ad vos," ' Exod. iij, quasi velit innuere se esse seipsum simpliciter per seipsum, et se eciam esse quodammodo totum ens, ~ificando videlicet alia universa BRADW. *CD* 154E.

essentificatio, (phil. & theol.) causing to be, endowing with existence.

essenciam divinam . . dicimus . . per seipsam vivificacionem (secundum aliam translacionem ~onem) et per seipsam deificacionem BRADW. *CD* 150B.

essennum v. sagena. **essequium** v. exaquia. **essert-** v. essart-.

essewagium [cf. esseware], haulage (of casks) from water. **b** (?) charge for haulage.

1337 in guindagio cxiij doleorum j pipe vini guindand' extra naves ibidem in aquam xviij s. xj d. . . et pro sewagio eorundem ad terram ix s. v d. ob. *KRAc* 78/18 m. 6; pro sewagio predictorum x doleorum vini de recta prisa de navibus a quibus capiebantur ad terram x d., pro doleo j d. *Ib.* m. 8; **1411** mercatores . . solvere consueverunt pro quolibet dolio vini et olei pro cariacione de navibus extra mare usque predictam villam per portum predictum nisi solomodo ij d. viz. pro tawagio cujuslibet dolii j d. et pro sewagio j d. *IMisc* 289/4. **b** **1297** exitus manerii . . de xxvj s. viij d. de passagio et assewag' de Chykeston *Ac. Cornw.* 216.

esseware, ~eare [cf. AN *essiwer*, OF *essavier*, *essevier* < exaquare]

1 to drain, lead water from: **a** (pond); **b** (marsh or land). *V. et. essewerare, exaquare.*

a **1263** vivarium regis de B., quod rex nuper per eos ~iari precepit, sine dilacione mundari faciant *Cl* 215; **1299** pro wayer' sewand' *MinAc* 1079/16 r. 2. **b** **1248** licebit . . assewiare mariscum suum . . usque per medium guttere . . de Babbingflet *Fines Suss* 499; **1271** in xlviij perticatis fossat' . . pro pastura comitisse assueanda *MinAc* 1078/13 r. 1*d.*; **1284** in x acris terre arrandis, herciendis, et reonandis ad ~iandum eandem terram *Ib.* 1027/17 r. 2; **1306** terre brocales, si fuerint competenter assewiate, valebit †qualibet [l. quelibet] acra per annum x d. *Cust. Battle* 18; **1327** mariscum . . assewiatum (v. 1 cultura 1a); **1359** guttera . . debet . . reparari . . per omnes tenentes terrarum et tenementorum que sewantur ad eandem *Pub. Works* I 251; **1373** quedam magna sewera que vocatur Lambwath', per quam diverse ville assuantur *Ib.* II 346; **1382** ubi cursus aque esse solebat . . pro terris adjacentibus seweandis *Pat* 313 m. 37*d.*; **1405** ad fossata . . reparanda et cum indigerit (*sic*) asseuanda *Doc. Bev.* 16.

2 to flood (meadow).

1231 singulis annis inter Ascensionem Domini et Nativitatem [S. Johannis] Baptiste potest . . scindere stagnum [molendini] ad prata sua essewyenda in loco certo de profunditate duorum pedum *CurR* XIV 1094.

esseweator, drainer.

1445 quod ipse . . non fiat neque elegatur major, vicecomes, escaetor, coronator, ballivus, constabularius, vel seweator noster vel heredum nostrorum *Pat* 460 m. 22.

essewera [cf. OF *sewiere*]

1 drain, (domestic) drainage channel. *V. et. exaquia* 1.

1299 levavit quemdam murum juxta Bykynedrane in communi †assewen' longitudine dimidii pertice . . ad nocumentum . . *CourtR Ramsey* 178; **1316** pro j sewar' habend' extra curiam suam j d. *Terr. Fleet* 126; **1336** pro vadiis . . scrutancium fundos muri et sewere (*KRAc* 19/40) *Cal. Scot.* III 366; c**1423** in gardino juxta aulam et seweram j mortarium de petra (*Invent.*) *Test. Ebor.* III 100; **1461** elemosinarius burgi non mundat communem seweram a tenemento Ricardi S. usque parietem Willelmi C. ad grave . . nocumentum communitatis (*Court Leet, Peterborough*) *EHR* XIX 528.

2 ditch, dyke, trench (for draining land). *V. et. essewitium, exaquia* 2.

†**716** (16c) cum aqua vocata Asendick, versus aquilonem, ubi communis sewera est, inter Spaldeling et dictam insulam *CS* 135; **1258** quod omnes terras in marisco custodiantur et salventur contra maris impetum . . per wallas et †essewas [MS: esseweras] *Cl* 307; **1260** per defectum reparacionis walliarum, fossatorum, gutterarum, pontium, et sewerearum . . [*Lincs*] *Cl* 154; **1266** ad faciend' wallias et fossata, gutteras, pontes et sewerrias, ita quod quelibet acra sit par alteri *Pat* 84 m. 31*d.*; **1269** de scutagiis domini regis, sectis curie, omnimodis releviis, fossatis maris et marisci, pontibus, ~is, gutteris *ChartR* 59 m. 17; **1281** per inundacionem maris . . et per defectum reparacionis walliarum, fossatorum, gutterorum, poncium, et seweriarum in . . partibus Hoyland' *PQW* 406b; **1319** justiciarii ad gutteras, seweras, et gurgites . . reparandas (*RParl*) *DocExch* 14; **1375** tenetur mundare et reparare quamdam sueram . . que . . obstupata est ita quod aqua . . non potest habere debitum cursum (*Anc. Indict.*) *Pub. Works* I 280 (cf. ib.: seueram); **1400** processu temporis vetus Hullum obstructum vix sewera valet nuncupari *Meaux* I 169; **1526** pro escuracione communis sueri ibidem vocati *le Moredyk Rutland MSS Receiver's Ac.* 17–18 *Hen.* VIII m. 2; **1535** pro escuracione magni seweri ibidem vocati *le Lordes Dyke* pro salvacione more *Rutland MSS MinAc* 24–7 Hen. VIII p. 186.

3 weir, fishgarth.

1387 habuerunt . . quendam gurgitem in aqua de Severne. . . quiquidem gurges est illa eadem sewera per quam supponitur predictum Ancelmum cursum aque . . obstupasse (*CoramR*) *Pub. Works* I 159; c**1390** est quedam sewera apud Chesilhampton' in aqua vocata Thamestreme facta cum pilis et meremio ita stricte quod aqua ibidem rectum cursum suum habere non potest *Ib.* II 130; c**1396** in aqua de Braynt . . construxit quandam sueram cum pilis, palis, et hirdellis adinvicem positis et aliis ingeniis ad capiendum . . *pyke, fry et brode de rochys, pykes* [etc.] (*Anc. Indict.*) *Ib.* II 10; **1424** concessimus . . monachis . . quandam seweram nostram in aqua Thamisie . . vocatam Petirsamwere (*Pat*) *MonA* VI 32a; **1552** unam placeam sive locum unius suere sive gurgitis una cum piscacione ibidem pro capcione salmonum . . et unam aliam placeam sive locum alterius suere sive gurgitis vocat' *a fisshing were Pat* 848 m. 39.

esseware [cf. essewera], to drain, lead water from. *V. et. esseware* 1, *exaquare.*

1315 riparia aque predicte per quam solebant terras suas sewerare est obstructa per jactus et repulsus maris *RParl* I 319a; **1375** seuwera . . vocata Benwelldyk in Byker que debet seuwerare Helpringham, Hale, et alias villas (*Anc. Indict.*) *Pub. Works* I 253.

esseweria, (office of) drainage.

1439 officium sewarie aquarum in com' Ebor' *Pat* 444 m. 8.

essewitium, ditch, dyke, trench (for draining land). *V. et. essewera* 2.

c**1200** faciendum (*sic*) dimidiam perticatam fossedi maris et dimidiam perticatam sewitii *AncD* A 2994; **1250** semper fuit lis et contencio . . de ~iis et cursibus aquarum diversis versus mare et mariscum *ICrim* 1/8; dedimus . . duas acras terre in marisco . . faciendo fossata et essewycia *MS Camb. Univ. Libr.* E.D.R. G/3/28 f. 333; faciend' fossata et essewicia *Ib.* f. 367.

essewium [cf. exaquium], ditch, dyke, trench (for draining land). *V. et. essewera* 2, *essewitium.*

1289 in x quarenten' ejusdem terre sulcandis propter ~ium faciendum *MinAc* 1027/17 r. 6 (cf. ib. r. 9: in xxij quarent' . . ejusdem terre sulcandis pro ~io).

essewyere v. esseware. **esseymiare, esseyniare** v. essaimare. **essiam** v. etiam 2c. **essiamentum** v. aisiamentum. **essoin-** v. esson-.

essonia, ~ius, ~ium [OF *essone, essoine*]

1 (leg.) essoin, excuse for non-attendance (in court); **b** (dist. by form).

si de nominatis [placitis] terminum susceperat, nisi competens soinus eum detineat, si non venerit, omnium reus sit (*Leg. Hen.* 29. 3) *GAS* 563; **1180** W. B. r. c. de j m. pro falso exonio *Pipe* 27; assisa . . ipsa tot non expectat ~ia, quot duellum GLANV. II 7; **1202** ipsemet A. salvatur de placito per ~ium quod fecit *SelPlCrown* 14; **1211** warantizavit sonium suum contra R. . . de placito terre *CurR* VI 118; **s1258** nullo rationabili summonitione facto vel essoino admisso illa [placita] terminavit *Leg. Ant. Lond.* 40; **1267** nullus habeat necesse jurare pro ~io suo warantizando (*Marlb.* 18) *StRealm* I 24; HENGHAM *Magna* 9 (v. concurrere 4b); **1318** *APScot* 113 (v. allocabilis b). **b** ~ium de infirmitate de reseantisa GLANV. I 18 *rub.*; **1244** ~ie de morte hominis *MGL* I 77; quinque sunt ~ia. primum viz. de ultra mare, secundum de Terra Sancta, . . tertium de malo veniendi . . . quartum est de malo lecti. . . quintum ~ium est de servitio . . regis HENGHAM *Parva* 1; est . . quoddam ~ium anomalum eo quod non sequitur regulas aliorum ~iorum, quod dicitur ~ium de malo ville *Fleta* 394; **1318** ordinatum est . . quod nullus indictatus sit essoniatus . . nisi tantum per servicium regis . . aut pro ~ia que vocatur Gallice *mal de lyt* (*Stat. Rob. I* 6) *APScot* 108 (= *Reg. Aberbr.* I 251: assoniatus . . assonia); de aliis ~iis aliud notandum est sicut de ultra mare, de servitio domini regis, de malo lecti *CBaron* 81; ~ium ratione nundinarum (*rub.*) *RegiamM* I 8. 30; abbas fecit quoddam essonum infra summonicionem, de malo lecti, quo detinebatur apud C. (*Processus*) *Croyl. Cont. B* 469.

2 excuse.

1101 comes R. . . in auxilium regis veniet, nisi pro aliqua harum iiij exoniarum remanserit (*Conventio*) *DipDoc* I p. 2; **1176** nulli liceat . . hospitari aliquem extraneum ultra unam noctem in domo sua . . nisi hospitatus ille exsonium rationabile habuerit (*Assisa Clar.*) R. HOWD. II 89.

essoniabilis, (leg.) entitled to essoin.

1201 assisa spectat ad dominum Norwicensem et dominum Eliensem, ut dicitur, qui non sunt ~es *CurR* II 39; **s1229** si aliquis sit ejus [sc. defendentis] inimicus vel ~is et justam causam ostenderit *MGL* I 92; **1233** apponat alios qui nullo modo sint ~es *CurR* XV 568; precipimus quod . . venire facias xxiiij de legalioribus . . militibus de comitatu tuo . . qui nec predictos C. et D. aliqua affinitate attingant vel qui aliquo modo non sint ~es ad recognoscendum [etc.] BRACTON 111b.

essoniare [OF *essoniier*]

1 (refl. or pass.) to be essoined, to excuse oneself (from appearing at court); **b** (w. *de* and excuse).

cum quis se ~iat, essoniator poterit se ~iare rationabili essonio GLANV. I 22; **1189** potest utraque pars ad diem statutum se assoniare et habebunt diem a die illa in quindenam *MGL* I 326; **1196** (v. dies 11a); **1219** ponitur in respectum usque in octabas S. Trinitatis pro defectu recognitorum, quia . . duo se ~iaverunt *CurR* VIII ix; **1269** (v. comparere 2a); **1275** calumniatur quia nullam facit mencionem de abbate eo quod erat bis contra predictum abbatem assoiniatus *CourtR Hales* 75; **s1293** rex Francie . . regem Anglie . . fecit appellare, qui die prefixo nec comparens nec assoinatus ab ore regis amerciatus est *Eul. Hist.* III 157; **1333** W. P. . . ~iatur in placito debiti (*CourtR*) *EE County Court* 182; **1470** omnes sutatores ~iantur usque capitalem curiam *DL CourtR* 128/1934 m. 3*d*. **b** **1194** ipsa fecerat se ~iari de malo lecti et habuit languorem *CurR RC* I 7; **1206** (v. dies 11a); **1255** mortuus est et ~iatus de morte *SelPlForest* 35; **1269** N. fuit in servicio regis . . et . . ~iatus fuit de eodem servicio *Cl* 106; cum . . participes simul se ~iaverint de malo lecti omnibus poterit languor adjudicari vel omnibus surrectio *Fleta* 393.

2 to essoin (someone else), to act as essoiner (for).

precipio . . quod . . queras per comitatum tuum F., qui falso ~iavit R. versus M. in curia mea GLANV. I 14; **1224** H. de C. assuniat Rogerum G. contra Willelmum de B. de debito pannagii *LTRMem* 6 m. 5(2)*d*.; **1233** inquiras quis sit ille Rannulfus qui illum assoniavit, et illum capias *KRMem* 12 m. 11*d*.; **1294** unusquisque burgensium ~iabit alterum ad curiam sine calumpnia quando fuerint absentes *BBC* (*Chesterfield*) 202.

3 (w. *quod* & cl.) to give as excuse. **b** (w. *dies* as obj.) to make excuse for.

1220 inventi sunt in laico habitu et sine tonsura et ita liberati gaole, et nullus ~iavit ante vadia data quod fuerunt clerici *CurR* VIII 383. **b** **p1224** si . . venerit ad quartum diem . . ad ~iandum dies in quibus fuit absens, sufficit *RegiamM* I 7. 10.

essoniator [cf. OF *essonieor*], (leg.) essoiner, one who offers excuse.

GLANV. I 22 (v. essoniare 1a); **1188** statuit diem ~oribus ad judicia facienda *Pipe* 59; **1233** dies ille datus fuit Rannulfo de Glenteworth' assoniatori suo *KRMem* 12 m. 14*d*.; **s1264** statutum fuit . . ne aliquis advocatus fuisset essoinator in Hustingo neque in aliis curiis civitatis *Leg. Ant. Lond.* 70; **1274** de veredicto . . dicendo utrum assoniator magistri R. satis dixit vel non *CourtR Hales* 58; mittat excusatorem, qui dicitur ~or, qui pretendat excusacionem summoniti esse talem, quod venire non possit *Fleta* 382; **s1297** primo igitur die litis . . comparuit per parcium assoniaciones [? l. essoniatores] prout communis sinebat justicia *G. S. Alb.* I 441; R. sic inculpatus, elapsis essoniis, . . venit et obtulit se ad essonias suas warantizandas et ~oribus presentibus eo warantizavit et querela audita fuit *CBaron* 74.

essoniatus, (leg.) essoin.

1280 iterum in misericordia pro ~u *CourtR Hales* 149; quousque per iiij milites ex parte domini regis missos ad ~um sciatur si . . HENGHAM *Judic. Esson.* 117.

essonium, ~ius, ~um v. essonia. **essox** v. esox.

1 est v. 2 esse.

2 est [ME *ēst*], (in compounds) east, eastern.

c1147 in Estgata (*DC Linc.*) *EHR* XXXV 214; **a1200** xvj perticatas in latitudine que . . buttant in estcapite super Brakenhille et in westcapite super Nortcroftum *Danelaw* 137; quicquid fossatis suis includitur ex estparte porte veteris Dufwudde usque ad Mikelgate et ex westparte ejusdam porte . . usque ad . . [etc.] *Ib.* 138; **c1240** inter terras sanctemonialium de Ormesby . . ex west parte et predicti Philippi ex est parte *DL Cart. Misc.* I 22; **a1250** ex west parte ville quicquid habui super Theny . . ex est parte ville ij perticate . . inter duas vias (*Cart. Kirkstead*) *Free Peasantry* 83; **1315** unum mesuagium . . jacens in parochia de Sothenover' predicta in Estporta *CatAncD* III A 4091.

est- v. et. aest-, east-, exst-, ext-, st-.

estainum [OF *estain* < CL stagnum], tin. *V. et.* 2 *stagnum.*

1198 pro ferro et clavis et acero et plumbo et †estaīmo [? l. estaino] *RScacNorm* II 310; **1290** in vj li. esteini empt' ad idem xij d. *KRAc* 479/15 v. 2.

estale v. escale.

estampeta [OF *estampie*], (mus.) form of dance.

1326 quintus modus constat ex brevibus et omnibus semibrevibus . . . ab hoc siquidem modo proveniunt hoketi omnes, rondelli, ballade, coree, cantifractus, ~e, floriture, et universe note brevium et semibrevium HAUDLO 402.

Estanglus v. Eastanglus. **estantivus** v. stantivus. **estanum** v. 2 stagnum. **estapula** v. stapula. **estas** v. aestas.

estaurinus, gurnard.

~us, A. *a gurnard WW.*

estaurum v. instaurum. **estaverium** v. estoverium. **estcaput** v. 2 est. **esteinum** v. estainum.

estencellare [OF *estenceler* < CL scintillare], to spangle. *V. et. scintillare.*

1233 ita quod campus sit de viridi colore estencelatus stellis aureis *Liberate* 10 m. 8; **1240** excentellatus (v. esmale 2a); **1241** casulam . . panno serico auro extencellato interius lineari faciatis *Cl* 321; **1241** xxiij s. x d. pro aurifrag[iis] fresell[is], bordura, et factura . . casule facte de quodam panno rubeo ~ato de auro *Liberate* 15 m. 10; **1244** columpnas circa lectum regis de novo depingi viridi colore vivo et auro ~ari *Cl* 169; **1258** celuram in eadem [camera] cum viridi colore depingi et auro decenter extencellari et argento *Liberate* 32 m. 10; dedit . . j capam cum ij tunicis bene extensellatis cum parvis rosis aurifragiatis; . . j casulam de Thars', quasi cum bezancio extensellato WHITTLESEY 168; **1349** unum hernes' de bokeram' albo . . extencellato cum argento (*KRAc* 391/15) *Arch.* XXXI 43.

esteneatus v. stainiatus. **estenta** v. extendere 5e. **Esteranglus** v. Eastanglus.

esterius [cf. W. *hestor* < sextarius], measure of grain.

1294 de uno *istor* bladi (*Ext. Anglesey*) *Doc. Aberffraw* 7; **1294** de vj quarteriis vj ~iis mixtil' de blado empto apud Tredyntone et vendito per subcelerarium xlvj s. j d. *Comp. Worc.* 17.

esterlingus v. sterlingus. **esterrateus** v. exsternare. **esteya** v. statha. **estgata** v. 2 est.

esthiomenus [ἐσθιόμενος], (med.; w. *herpes*) devouring herpes.

1170 cum herpes estiomenus qui vulgo lupus dicitur femur ejus enormiter occupasset P. BLOIS *Ep.* 93. 293A; vocatur lupus sive herpes estiomenus, i. se ipsum corrodens GILB. IV 202v. 2; generat aut herpetem aut hestiomenum, qui generatur ex adustione aliorum humorum calidorum GAD. 45. 2; herpes cingulus et hestiomenus, i. seipsum comedens *Ib.* 121v. 1; *yomenum* interpretatus 'seipsum comedens', inde erpes yomenus, i. serpens seipsum comedens, . . idem est estiomenus *SB* 44.

estia v. esca 1a. **estichia** v. stichia. **estika** v. stica. **estim-, extim-,** v. et. aestim-. **estimarium** v. estoverium 3. **estinctum** v. exstinguere. **estinia** v. 1 eschina. **estiomenus** v. esthiomenus.

estiro [OF *estire*], plot (of land; Gasc.).

1276 unum ~onem terre pro orto *RGasc* II 15.

estirpare v. exstirpare. **estivale** v. aestivalis. **estiverium** v. estoverium.

estlandborda [ME *ēst lond bōrd*], timber from eastern (Baltic) region. *V. et. estrichborda.*

1466 pro . . xij tabulis dictis estlandburdis missis versus S. *ExchScot* 425 (cf. 1 borda 1a [**1336**]: iij^m bordarum de Estland).

estmannus v. ostmannus. **estonium** v. estoverium. **estop-** v. stop-.

estor, estrix [cf. CL comestor], eater, glutton.

hic ~or . ., i. vorator, et hec ~rix . ., i. femina gulosa OSB. GLOUC. *Deriv.* 183; *a gluton*, ambro, . . ~or, ~rix *CathA.*

estoverium [AS *estover*, OF *estovoir* < est opera]

1 maintenance, supply of food; **b** (w. ref. to widow or child).

s1201 (14c) nativi . . sint quieti de theloneo . ., viz. . . de omnibus rebus emptis pro suis propriis †estoviis *Gild. Merch.* II 124; **1202** quod . . eis [sc. prisonibus] rationabile estuverium suum usque Londinium habere faciatis *Pat* 16; **1205** in estiverio Andree de Luches dum moram fecit in Kent xx s. . . et in stiverio xv minatorum apud Cant' c s. *Pipe* 112; **1212** in stuverio ij militum *Pipe Ir.* 54; **1229** ballivi nostri spontanea voluntate hominum . . ville emant ab eis ~ium suum *BBC* (*Montgomery*) 112; **1260** capellani . . habere debent ~ia duorum monachorum, quod minime sic est intelligendum quod cotidie pisces edant cum seculares sint, nec possunt ad hoc artari *Ann. Durh.* 116; **1276** ballivi civitatis Ebor' impediunt omnes venientes ad emenda estaveria sua et victualia sua *Hund.* I 126; **c1300** tassator habebit de domino abbate . . stuverium suam dum facit tassos pisarum, stipularum, et feni *Reg. S. Aug.* 119; **1312** molent bladum suum quantum molere voluerint ad astovaria sua *ChartR* 98 m. 1; **c1315** residuum catallorum suorum ultra ~ium suum predictum domino regi remaneat (*Fragm. Collecta*) *APScot* I 374 app.; **c1363** duo capellani . . singulis annis habeant sua ~ia in cibo et potu sicut conventus *Pri. Cold.* 37. **b** **1217** provideatur ei [sc. vidue] domus competens in qua possit honeste morari . . et habeat rationabile estuverium suum interim de communi (*Ch. Regis*) *SelCh* 341; **1227** idem Gaufridus invenit ei [Alicie] ~ia sua per ix ebdomodas *CurR* XIII 171; **1230** uxori et filiis et filiabus et neccessarie familie [Willemi de C.] de bladis que sunt in terra que fuit ipsius Willelmi rationabile ~ium suum ad victum inveniri faciant *Cl* 368; **1243** capiat in manum regis . . tenementa que fuerunt Ricardi . ., salvo . . ~io Egidie, que fuit uxor . . Ricardi, donec . . dos ei fuerit assignata *Cl* 41; **1267** cum . . secundum tenorem magne carte nostre vidue post mortem maritorum . . †racionabilem [MS: racionabile] ~ium suum de communi habere debeant usque ad quadraginta dies *Cl* 414.

2 store (of seed corn); **b** (w. ref. to growing crop).

1238 retento ad opus nostrum de blado nostro de F. . . rationabili ~io wainagii nostri . . una cum ~io autumpni instantis . . *Cl* 42; **1243** vendi faciat . . blada . . salvo rationabili ~io ad terras . . seminandas et excolendas (*FineR*) *RGasc* I 261. **b** **1325** communam habeat ad tot averia quot superannare possunt per ~ium suum proprium crescens in suis dominicis terris et pratis in Poulet (*Indent.*) *Pat* 399 m. 26.

3 'estovers', allowance of wood.

concessi . . in bosco meo . . suum stuverium igni sepibus et domibus parandis et edificandis *Cart. Worc.* 315; **c1212** super quibusdam pasturis, ~iis, aysiamentis et libertatibus infra villam et extra *BBC* (*Corbridge*) 22; **1230** (v. capere 2c); **1231** (v. aisiamentum 1a); **1232** (v. claudere 5e); **c1240** concessi . . eis rationabilem estovariam de bosco de K. ad illam terram . . edificandam *Couch. Furness* II 124; **c1256** homines domini regis . . habeant in predicta foresta ~ia sua de mortobosco et sicco *IMisc* 9/20; BRACTON 222b (v. 1 bruaria a); **1275** ballivus hundredi habuit preceptum . . quod agistaret omnes . . ad auxilium regis . . salvis †estimariis [l. estuvariis] *Hund.* I 448; **1290, c1300** estowarium (v. blesta a); **12..** capiet per visum forestarii dicti prioris et conventus in bosco de H. rationabilia ~ia sua sine wasto ad haias suas claudendas et ad domos et carucas et hercias reparandas *Feod. Durh.* 176*n*.; **1389** cum estaveriis suis de blestur', fuger', turbar' et javun' ad unum focum *AncD* A 8698; **1415** †estoniorum (v. confoederatio 2).

estovium v. estoverium. **estpars, estporta** v. 2 est. **estowarium** v. estoverium. **estraat-** v. estraiare. **estracus** v. strica. **estraet-** v. estraiare. **estrahere** v. extrahere.

estrahura, ~aura [cf. estraia *infl. by* extrahere], stray animal; **b** (gen.); **c** (w. *de*). *V. et. estraia.*

1274 capiunt omnes astrauras que veniunt super terras suas *Hund.* II 119; **1275** clamat habere libertates, sc. . . *weyf* et ~auram *Ib.* I 84; **1279** clamat habere . . *cumeling, weyf*, et astrauras in manerio de W. *PQW* 700a; **1322** dicens ipsum esse furem et quod cepit et appropriavit unam ~auram (*Andover*) *Gild Merch.* II 316; **1330** abbas . . clamat . . *weyf* et strauras in manerio suo *PQW* 583a;

1451 heriettis, escaetis, extrahuris *Cl* 301 m. 21*d*.; **1462** nihil de vagis et extrahuris ibidem accidentibus *Rec. Leic.* II 275; **1540** dedimus .. tolneta, catalla, waviata, extrahuras (*Pat*) *Mon. Exon.* 104b; **1548** †dextrauris [l. de extrauris] venditis vij s. *CourtR* 168/32. **b** **1436** omnes turnos nostros vicecomitum et visus franciplegii .. cum vagis extrahure .. et omnibus aliis proficuis (*CalPat* 507) *Pat* 438 m. 8. **c** **1274** episcopus Bathon' capit et retinet averia de astraura que dicunt *wayf* vel *cumeling Hund.* II 118; **1297** de quodam equo venienti de ∼aura *Ac. Cornw* 235 (cf. ib. 238: r. c. .. de viij d. de una bidente de ∼aura); **1306** de j [vacca] proventa de ∼ahura (*Ac.*) *Crawley* 246; **1366** de j examine apium proveniente de extraur' *MinAc* 992/7; **1378** [decenarius] presentat quod j ovis venit de ∼ahura usque festum Pentecost' *Banstead* I 359; **1466** decenarius .. presentat j multonem album precium vj d. proven[ientem] de extrahura *Crawley* 506; **1475** (v. bidens a).

estrahurare [cf. estrahura, estraiare], (p. ppl. *s. act.*) strayed.

1530 remittimus .. Thomae Cardinali .. felonum attinctorum .. catalla wayviata et extrahurata (*Pat*) *Foed.* XIV 366b.

estraia, ∼aius [AN *estray*, OF *estraier*], estray, stray animal; **b** (in apposition); **c** (w. *de*). *V. et. estrahura.*

†1115 dedi .. decimas cum omnibus strayis, wreckis, et waiviis per totum dominium (*Reg. Bardney*) *MonA* I 629b; **1331** habuerunt in .. manerio suo .. ∼aios et *wayf* venient[es] in eodem manerio *PQW* 148a; habuerunt omnimodo *waiff* et strayas infra honorem .. contingentes *Entries* 682b. **b** **1275** habent averia exstraya in Rokelund ... habet gallon' [et] extraya de tenementis suis in Saxlingham *Hund.* I 471; **1516** de xx d. receptis de Thoma Brayne pro straia †ardente [? l. bidente] hoc anno *Ac. Churchw. Bath* 103. **c** **1311** respondet de vij^{xx}xviij gredling' receptis de remanenti, et de vj^{xx}iij de adjunccione hogettorum post tonsionem, et de j recepto de †espane [? l. estraia], Anglice *cumeling MinAc* 856/17; **1313** receptavit unam aucam venientem de strahie nec liberavit illam ballivis *Leet Norw.* 58; **1391** uxor R. de S. cepit unum agnellum de straio vagantem qui fuit C. B. et illum vendidit pro xij d. in contemptum ballivorum *Ib.* 67.

estraiare [cf. OF *estraier*], (p. ppl. *s. act.*) strayed.

c1245 averia .. †estraeta [MS: estraata] et hominis [MS: homines] †adventii [l. adventicii] .. in W. advenientia †et [MS: vel] inventa .. priori et canonicis remanebunt (*Cart. Castleacre* f. 40) *Med. E. Anglia* 240; **1251** bestias estraatas que vocantur *uaif* (*Surv. Ely*) *Kal. Samson* p. 5*n*.; **1276** ballivus cepit ij s. de villa de Stratford' pro uno pullano estrato *Hund.* II 176; **1277** liberam warennam .. et bestias estratas que vocantur *waif* (*Ext. Ely*) *Med. E. Anglia* 171; habuerunt .. visum franciplegii .. ac bona et catalla waiviata et straiata *Entries* 683.

estraius v. estraia. **Estranglus** v. Eastanglus. **estrat-** v. estraiare. **estraura** v. estrahura. **estrava** v. thrava. **estreca** v. strica.

estreciare [OF *estrecier*]

1 to constrict, narrow: **a** (road); **b** (watercourse).

a **1189** (15c) hec .. assisa non conceditur alicui per quod huseria, introitus, vel exitus, .. ad nocumentum vicini sui extricetur vel arctetur (*Assisa Aedific.*) *MGL* I 322; **1198** de viis domini regis ∼iatis (*PlCrown*) R. HOWD. IV 62; **1201** pro via estresciata *Pipe* 156; **1204** nec potest astreciare chiminum ipsius Roberti .. quin liberum ingressum et regressum habeant ad pasturam suam *Cart. Worc.* 216; **1221** A. persona de S. ∼iavit duas vias ex utraque parte domus sue et levavit quendam murum super viam in exitu earum *PlCrGlouc* 15. **b** **1202** debet dim. m. quia exstreciavit [v. l. ∼iavit] Trente *Pipe* 102.

2 to shrink (cloth).

1202 de residuo de Esseburn' j m. pro pannis ∼iatis *Ib.* 101; **1203** residuum de Esseburn .. de j m. pro pannis estresciatis *Ib.* 170.

estregebordium v. estrichborda.

estrensis, ∼ius [ME *ēstren*], eastern, from eastern Baltic; **b** (as sb. m.) easterner, eastlander.

1266 bordas ∼es (v. 1 borda 1a); **1325** Bercelot' estrensius pro xxxj barellis calibis .. pro xxvi^{c} bordis ∼iis val. xv li. *EEC* 375. **b** **1175** vicecomes r. c. de xx li. pro estresiis qui habuerunt catalla Flandrensium et voluerunt ire in Flandriam *Pipe* 155; **1176** vicecomes debet xvj li. pro estresiis qui habuerunt catalla Flandrensium et voluerunt ire in Flandriam *Ib.* 82; **1325** (v. a supra).

estrepamentum [OF *estrepement* < exstirpamentum], estrepement, devastation, stripping. **b** right of or fine for estrepement. *V. et. exstirpamentum.*

1291 ita quod .. nullum vastum neque strepementum in .. tenementum neque in arboribus crescentibus .. facere possint *Deeds Balliol* 220; **1344** remisimus .. omnimodas acciones .. quas erga eum habere potuerimus racione strepiamenti .. coquine nostre *Lit. Cant.* II 273; **1347** estrippamentum de domibus super terram predictam existentibus fecerunt (*PlRCP*) *Collect. Staffs* XII 63; **1347** si .. aliquam vendicionem districcionem vel strippamentum domorum fecerint (*Scriptum dimissionis*) *G. S. Alb.* II 329; **1395** vasta, estreppementa, exilia, dilapidaciones *Pat* 342 m. 1*d*.; **1396** estreppamenta (v. dilapidatio a); **14..** (v. estrepare). **b** **c1275** seisivit terram .. et cepit inde strepementum *IMisc* 34/17; **1350** terras .. cum pratis, .. redditibus, .. estrepementis *Reg. Rough* 274; **1399** annum, diem, vastum, et †estrepinamentum, et quicquid ad ipsum nuper regem .. pertinere posset de anno, die, vasto, et estreppamento (*Ch. Regis*) *MGL* II 483; **1412** habeant .. terras .. vastum et estreppamentum (*Pat*) *MonA* VI 1413b.

estrepare [OF *estreper* < CL exstirpare], to estrepe, devastate, strip.

1205 quod non permittat quod ipse vel aliquis per eum ∼et illud [gardinum] *CurR* III 329; **1261** rex dedit Elizabethe .. vastum .. terre ..; quequidem Elizabetha dictam terram omnino astrepavit *IMisc* 23/ 30; **1266** nec licebit .. capellano .. domos vel arbores .. strepare vel eradicare *Reg. S. Aug.* 565; **1291** ita quod dictum tenementum .. non poterit aliquo modo alienare aut extrepiare *Cart. Wardon* 101*d*.; septies viginti acre terre jacuerunt .. inculte .. et multe mansiones .. exstrepuntur ubi magnus numerus bidencium nut[rie]batur *Inq. Non.* 12a; **14..** predictus J. vastum et estrepamentum de manerio .. predicto, viz. prosternendo ibidem unam boveriam .. succidendo .. de boscis .. c quercus .. necnon ∼ando .. xl ostia .. et ix fenestras .. pendente placito .. fecit .. contra formam .. statuti *Entries* 317.

estrepinamentum v. estrepamentum.

estrepitus [AN *estrep*], estrepement, devastation, stripping.

1540 amputare maeremium .. sine aliquo stripitu seu vasto ibidem faciendo *MinAc* 2020.

estrepum [AN *estrep*], estrepement, devastation, stripping. **b** (fine for) right of estrepement.

1316 predicti Attehill vastum et extreppam tenementi fecit ipse Alger *Abbr. Plac.* 328a; **1355** non faciet vastum neque streppum in eisdem terris *AssessR Cornw* 1 r. 24. **b** **1274** episcopus London' habet streppum et wastum felonum *Hund.* I 141; **1286** clamat habere .. catalla felonum .., streppum et vastum cum aliis libertatibus *PQW* 293b; **1364** omnia que ad nos pertinere poterant de anno, die et vasto sive streppo et murdris (*Ch. Regis*) *Couch. Furness* II 197; **1408** et quod predictus nuper rex annum, diem, strippum et vastum inde .. habuit et percepit *Cl* 257 m. 27; **1534** annum, diem, streppum, vastum, et deodanda, ac omnia alia que ad nos .. pertinere possent vel deberent (*Pat*) *Foed.* XIV 545b.

estrepura [AN *estrep*], stripping, plucking (of wool from sheep).

1280 A. A. captus .. pro suspicione latrocinii et strepura ovium *Gaol Del.* 71 m. 18.

estresciare v. estreciare. **estresius** v. estrensis. **estrica, ∼icha, ∼ika** v. strica.

estrichalis [ME *ēst riche*], easterner (from Baltic).

s1254 orientales, viz. quos ∼es et Gutlanenses appellamus, idem de maribus orientalibus sunt perpessi M. PAR. *Maj.* V 453.

estrichborda [ME *ēst rich bōrd*], timber from eastern region (Baltic). *V. et. estlandborda.*

1335 in v cent' de estrich' bord' empt' apud Lenne cum cariagio ejusdem, prec' cent' ij li. xviij s. iij d. *Sacr. Ely* II 72; **1352** in iij^{m} .. de estrichebordis, righoltis, waynscotbordis, et aliis *Windsor Castle* I 170; **1355** in j pecia meremii, iiij holmis, iiij ulmis, c loggis, m ∼is emptis et provisis *Ib.* 175; **1377** sunt ibidem xl de estregebordiis *IMisc* 212/8; **1449** de j tabula de estrich' bord' cum j par' de trestill' pro cera facienda *Obed. Abingd.* 126.

estrip- v. estrep-. **estrivus, estriwes** v. strivium. **estrix** v. estor.

estronare [cf. OF *estronchier* < extruncare], to pollard. *V. et. extroniare, extruncare.*

1241 iij acre .. in foresta nostra .. non sunt vestite bosco, nisi quod medietas inde vestita est quercubus †estrovatis [MS: estronatis] *Cl* 273; **1282** residuum chasten[ariorum] sunt (*sic*) extronati et viliter exbrancati et tibie chasten[ariorum] succise *TR Forest Proc.* 31 m. 9 (cf. ib.: quercus et fagi remanentes sunt ∼ati; cf. ib. m. 12: multe quercus ∼ate et viliter exbrancate); **1302** †extrovando [l. extronando] et succidendo et asportando arbores et clausturas *CourtR Hales* 453.

estronatura, (collect.) branches lopped in pollarding. *V. et. estronicium, extroniamentum.*

1330 prostraverunt j carectatam de extronatura querc[uum] precii vj d. *KR Forest Proc.* 2/26.

estronicium, (collect.) branches lopped in pollarding. *V. et. estronatura, extroniamentum.*

1330 attachiament' foreste: .. de Rogero de B. pro j gemell', j ramo xviij d.; de Henrico Ward' pro j estronic' xij d. *KRAc* 131/24 m. 4*d*.

estrov- v. estron-. **estruc-** v. exstruere d.

estructum [OF *estruit* < CL exstructus *p. ppl. of* exstruere], jewel, ornament.

1130 in soltis per breve regis eidem Johanni pro estruct' que rex habuit de eo *Pipe* 147; **1316** pro .. emendacione duorum estrucorum ejusdem selle, vij d. *KRAc* 99/21 m. 1.

estrumelarium [OF *trumeliere*], (pl.) greaves.

1275 tria [paria] ∼iorum .. tradatis *Reg. Heref.* 6.

Estsexensis v. Eastsexanus. **estuar-** v. aestuar-. **estuccia** v. astutia. **estucha** v. stichia. **estuffare** v. stuffare. **estup-** v. stop-, stup-.

estus [AN *estu*, OF *estui*], storeroom, hiding place.

1282 Johannes .. felonice et insultu premeditato stans in estu celarii .. eandem Margeriam transeuntem ex opposito illius celarii .. cepit ac ipsam portavit usque predictum celarium *Gaol Del.* 35B m. 39.

estuverium v. estoverium.

esula, (*bot.*) spurge (*Euphorbia*).

∼a quedam arbor est que a medicis calida dicitur in tercio gradu atque sicca .., cujus multe sunt species, et illarum virtus nunc est in lacte et in humore, nunc in semine, nunc in radice BART. ANGL. XVII 56; acuantur acuminibus compositis ut reubarb' in duplo et ∼a in tertio GILB. I 21. 2; apposuit de ∼a in magna quantitate et minus de scammonia BACON IX 172; accipe radicem titimali, i. ∼e, et decoquatur in vino et cum illo vino colluatur os GAD. 119v. 1; *SB* 42, *PP* (v. anabulla).

esulare, to mix with spurge.

ut cum parte predicti liquoris distemperetur ℥ j benedicte ∼ate et iniciatur per clistere[m] GILB. I 38v. 2.

esuries [LL], hunger; **b** (fig.).

exempla coriambo congruentia: .. ∼ies ALDH. *PR* 130; esuriem dapibus superavit, frigora veste (*Epitaph. S. Greg.*) BEDE *HE* II 1; ut .. leo .. discurrit caecus ∼iei ardore F. MALM. *V. Aldh.* 77A; post longam ∼iem .. immoderatam appetunt refectionem GIR. *DK* II 5; ∼ies est appetitus nutrimenti BACON XI 196; Franci .. / esurie populum vexare sitique studebant ELMH. *Metr. Hen. V* 407. **b** ut .. ∼ies aeternae vitae aepulis satiaretur ALCUIN *Vedast.* 1 p. 416; ille [Adam] ructabat satietate, nos suspiramus ∼ie ANSELM (*Prosl.* 1) I 98; ad scelerum suorum satiandam ∼iem castra suis implet complicibus MAP *NC* IV 6 f. 49v.; GARL. *Tri. Eccl.* 109 (v. cibare 1c).

esurire [CL]

1 to hunger, be hungry.

frequenter ∼ienti [v. l. ∼iente] eo Dominus cibavit eum *V. Cuthb.* II 2; **a1078** Christus .. verus homo .. secundum humanitatem .. ∼ivit, sitivit LANFR. *Ep.* 50 (46); ANSELM (*Ver.* 12) I 193 (v. cibare 1a); GIR. *GE* I 18 (v. continue 1a).

2 (trans.) to hunger for; **b** (fig.); **c** (w. inf.); **d** (fig.).

permissus lambere sum vescentium abjectas uti catellus ∼iens miculas B. *V. Dunst.* 386; 'manducabat' tunc 'homo panem angelorum' quem nunc ∼it ANSELM (*Prosl.* 1) I 98; si ∼ias [ME: *3ef þu art ofhungred efter*] dulce, oportet te prius amarum gustare *AncrR* 147. **b** ∼ire justitiam [cf. *Matth.* v 6] ANSELM *Misc.* 328; dux et comes .. bellum inhianter ∼iebant ORD. VIT. IX 14 p. 590; esuriunt [cleri] mundum semper GOWER *VC* III 295. **c** de carnibus ejusdem statim comedere non mediocriter ∼ivit GIR. *PI* III 30. **d** D. BEC. 2242 (v. crinalis c).

esursum [cf. CL sursum], from above. *V. et. desursum* 1a.

∼um, A. *fro above WW*.

esus [CL]

1 eating; **b** (w. ref. to *Gen.* iii); **c** (w. *agni*, ref. to Passover); **d** (w. *carnium*).

601 ad laudem Dei in esu suo animalia occidant (*Lit. Papae*) BEDE *HE* I 30; nil esu melius visum mihi quam sapor ejus R. CANT. *Poems* 1. 39; J. GODARD *Ep.* 221 (v. collyrida); de meo esu ne quidquam loquaris *Arthur & Gorlagon* 5; convesci renuunt esu domestico / volunt enim †esam de cibo regio TRYVYTLAM *Laus Ox.* 204; **1451** de jure vel consuetudine esus lacticiniorum et butiri (*Lit. Papae*) *Reg. Glasg.* 389. **b** mortiferum ante esum mulier .. credidit esus prohibitionem .. non solum falsam verum etiam invidam PULL. *Sent.* 748B; ut representetur exsulatus Ade et Eve propter esum pomi BELETH *RDO* 89. 92. **c** imminebat Pascha quo sanctificatum quemque ac mundum ad esum agni venire oporteret BEDE *Hom.* II 4. 125; **c1218** sicut filii Israel in esu agni typici renes suos accingebant *Conc. Syn.* 78. **d** minime esu carnium quadrupedum .. usus est ÆLF. *Æthelwold* 20; esui carnium indulgebat W. MALM. *GP* IV 137; omnes [Cistercienses] .. ab adipe et carnium esu abstinent ORD. VIT. VIII 26 p. 444; WALT. ANGL. *Fab.* 47. 4 (v. devorare 7); **1283** PECKHAM *Ep.* 488 (v. camerula a); **14..** in Rogacionibus ab esu carnium saltem abstinere jubemur *Conc. Scot.* II 76.

2 food.

illa animalia .. esu quodam cibis nostris admodum puriore uti debent ADEL. *QN* 75; ad diversos esus condiendos non indigent sagimine ORD. VIT. VIII 26 p. 439; hinc manifestat / discipulis Ihesum proprii dare corporis esum AD. DORE *Pictor* 147; **s1252** ut omni gleba emarcente prata esum omnimodum pecudibus denegaverint M. PAR. *Maj.* V 279; mors .. / .. / in esum vermibus tradit eximios WALT. WIMB. *Sim.* 133.

eswarda, ~um [AN *esward*, OF *esgard*]

1 (leg.) decision, judgement.

a1190 si .. burgenses mei ad exercitum ire debeant salva custodia ville mee per esguardiam ipsorum, eant cum ballivo meo *BBC* (*Pembroke*) 89; **1251** sin autem judicium vel esgardum curie vestre G. .. fieri faciatis (*AncC* IV 183) *RL* II 68; **1261** per sententiam vel esgardium curie senescalli (*Ib.* 13) *Ib.* 182; **s1258** noluerunt stare ad awardum nec jurare, sed .. ab Oxonia discesserunt *Ann. Tewk.* 165; **1275** usque quo esset transgressio ad esguardum curie regis Francie congrue emendata *RGasc* II 9; **1277** judicium curie nostre ad castrum episcopi de hoc, per awardam ipsius curie, ipse M. heredes sui vel assignati sustinebunt *Reg. Heref.* 146; **1279** dat domino xij d. ad habendum evardum curie inter ipsum et Matildam *Court-R Hales* 584; **1315** de dampno satisfaciet domino fundi ad esgardum bajuli et juratorum *RGasc* IV 1626 (cf. ib.: satisfaciendo tamen ad esguardum bajuli et juratorum dicte bastide); **1372** de awardis (v. confinitas b); **1491** per consideracionem, awardam, regulam, vel judicium alicujus predictorum commissionariorum *Pat* 572 m. 5(32)*d.*; (cf. ib.: si .. continuaverit eundem defectum incontrarium dicte agarde, regule, et judicii dictorum commissionariorum).

2 award.

1203 quietus .. ab omnibus querelis .. nisi de ~o terre qui fuit Walteri de Windesor' *Liberate RC* 36.

eswardare [OF *esgarder*; cf. AS *wardian*], (leg.) to award.

1556 quo die judicium pro petente et breve de distr[ictione] agard[atur] *Entries* 231.

eswardum v. eswarda.

et [CL]

1 (beginning a phr.): **a** (*et is* or *et quidem* w. adj.) and .. at that; **b** (*et hoc*).

a legebam .. populum .. et quidem Deo carissimum .. periisse GILDAS *EB* 1; **s1192** populus unus et is parvus numero DEVIZES 41. **b** BEDE *Gen.* 75 (v. deperire 1a); *DB* I 36v. (v. debere 7d); BART. ANGL. VI 5 (v. convertibilitas 2); **1320** (v. dens 1c); **1434** (v. defectivus 3).

2 (beginning a cl. or sentence) and indeed, in fact; **b** (postpositive).

et in India .. pilosum .. genus hominum didicimus *Lib. Monstr.* I 15; os .. speluncae ad mare est, et ecce navis navigabat ad se NEN. *HB* 216; et si a rege illud impetrare non posset, veneno eos necabat ASSER *Alf.* 14; modo appreciatur xl li., et tamen prepositus inde reddit liiij li. *DB* I 1; non habent aliquod testimonium praeter se, et tamen volunt probare omni modo *DB* II 285. **b** postmodum et fato victus pice nigrior exsto ALDH. *Aen.* 44 (*Ignis*) 8; pars cujus inferior Stigia Letheaque palude / fertur et inferni manibus succumbere nigris *Ib.* 53 (*Arcturus*) 9.

3 (copulative) and: **a** (joining words, phrs., cls., or sentences); **b** (repeated); **c** (joining last two items of list); **d** (in compound numbers); **e** (w. other copulatives).

a ista ego et multa alia .. intuens GILDAS *EB* 1; **†604** (12c) in conspectu Dei .. et sanctorum ejus .. cum consilio .. episcopi et omnium principum meorum *CS* 3; **875** habendum aet possidendum *CS* 539; quasi .. nullam aliam intrinsecus et extrinsecus perturbationem pateretur, ita tamen cotidiana et nocturna .. tristitia .. querelaretur ASSER *Alf.* 76; quod mihi et meis utile .. esset *Ib.* 79; saccam et socam *DB* I 1; de quibus .. habebat rex E. duas partes et comes G. terciam *Ib.*; ne domus vacua remaneret et ne rex careret servitio *Ib.* 179; **1308** (v. destinare 2b). **b** appresenta meum clarnum [*gl.*: *sticce*] et meum cultellum et meam legulam et utamle meum ÆLF. BATA 5. 1. **c** vitae, salutis, et beatitudinis aeternae dona BEDE *HE* II 13; iij canonici .. idest Sired, Godric, et Seuuen *DB* I 2; sanctorum martyrum Simplicii, Faustini, et Beatricis ELMH. *Cant.* 99. **d** homines xx et unus *DB* I 1; decem et duo cum decem et uno multiplicanda sunt ROB. ANGL. *Alg.* 90. **e** ALDH. *VirgV* 1556, etc. (v. atque, ac 1a, b); **853** unum aratrum .. avendum et possidendum feliciterque .. perfruendum *CS* 467; nutritus et doctus ac coronatus fueram ASSER *Alf.* 79; in quantum infirmitas et possibilitas atque suppetentia permitteret *Ib.* 103.

4 **a** (w. repetition of same word); **b** (implying distinction); **c** (joining different words implying distinction).

a bino et bino ALDH. *PR* 125 (v. binus 2c); alii et alii EADMER *V. Osw.* 20 (v. dum 5b); plus et plus J. BLUND *An.* 293 (v. duratio 2); *Offic. Sal.* 31 etc. (v. binus 1d); **c1350** duo et duo (v. dinarium); **1313** ad .. solucionem dicte pecunie .. predicti prior et prior *Pri. Cold.* 8; **s1428** per annos et annos AMUND. I 255 (v. clamitatio). **b** **1176** amice, est lenitas et est lenitas; est lenitas necessaria et lenitas dissoluta P. BLOIS *Ep.* 100; erudito lectori multum dissimiliter sapit stilus et stilus LUCIAN *Chester* 54. **c** debemus .. distinguere senium et juventam, opes et inopiam, libertatem et servitudinem (*Cons. Cnuti*) *GAS* 355; **1338** et aliquando plus et aliquando minus (v. confratria 2).

5 **a** (*et maxime, et praecipue*, or sim.) and especially. **b** (adding neg. phr. or cl.) and not, rather than, or sim. **c** (as CL *nec* after neg.). **d** (joining syntactically different phrs.).

a querulas sanctorum prophetarum voces et maxime Hieremiae GILDAS *EB* 1; noscendis priorum gestis sive dictis et maxime nostrae gentis virorum inlustrium BEDE *HE pref.*; insula .. fluviis .. piscosis .. et quidem praecipue issicio abundat *Ib.* I 1. **b** quidam .. officio diaconus et non merito, .. crucem auream .. portare solebat ALCUIN *WillP* 30; **793** esto pastor non mercenarius, .. lux et non tenebrae, .. praedicator et non adolator *Id. Ep.* 17 p. 45; attrahebant funem et non poterant uncum .. avellere W. CANT. *Mir. Thom.* III 44; in estate tantum, et nunquam in hieme GIR. *TH* I 10; quidlibet ut libet agimus, et non est distinctio virtutis et vitii MAP *NC* IV 2 f. 44; M. PAR. *Maj.* IV 633 (v. deturpatio b); **1295** predicta Editha vocatur Eda et non Editha *JustIt* 1306 r. 12; GAD. 12. 1 (v. disconvenientia c); **1339** (v. deponere 7c); **1414** ita quod ad intra remaneant et non distribuantur ad extra *Reg. Cant.* IV 149. **c** ASSER *Alf.* 76 (v. 3a supra). **d** **†604** (12c) hic et in aeterna saecula *CS* 3; qua ratione fixa et sine ulla haesitatione ASSER *Alf.* 103; **1202** cum reverentia et solemniter observari (v. depositio 3b).

6 (correlative *et* .. *et*) both .. and.

'attritus' et 'consultus' et nomina sunt et participia ALDH. *PR* 124; historiam .. tibi .. et prius .. transmisi .. et nunc .. retransmitto BEDE *HE pref.*; *GlC* D 227 (v. discrepatio 2); **875** aet a Deo et angelis ejus *CS* 539; et pater et pastor previgil esto tuis WULF. *Poems* 10; ANSELM I 265 (v. consentire 1a); **c1220** (v. depositio 3b); *Croyl.* 75 (v. 2 dilectio 4a).

7 **a** also, as well; *cf. atque* 1c; **b** (w. *etiam*; *v. et. etiam* 2d); **c** (w. *non solum* .. *sed* or sim.; *v. et. etiam* 2e); **d** (w. *sicut*); **e** (w. *necnon*).

a quadragesimus quartus .. orditur annus .., qui et meae nativitatis est GILDAS *EB* 26; ut episcopus, presbyter, diaconus, vel qui in .. furtu captus est deponatur, non et communione privetur quia .. non judicat Deus bis in id ipsum EGB. *Pen.* 5. 1; **838** ut .. libertas et regula monasterialis vitae .. ab omnibus illis servetur, sed et post dies meos sue libertatis electione .. digni habeantur *CS* 421; religiosa .. femina, nobilis ingenio, nobilis et genere ASSER *Alf.* 2; culmina celsa poli felici calle petisti, / et nobis aperi culmina celsa poli WULF. *Poems* 14; ita permansit et post mortem R. E. *DB* I 2v.; *G. Steph.* I 51 (v. dolose); unde et in egregiis legitur poetarum libris GIR. *TH intr.* p. 3. **b** de semine .. Stuf et Wihtgar, duorum fratrum et etiam comitum ASSER *Alf.* 2; omnis decima ejusdem ville et etiam de terra regis *DB* I 41v.; **1269** maneriorum facta et onera .. tenetur suis propriis sumptibus facere et eciam supportare *Cl* 100; potestatem vendicandi rem et eciam defendendi illam OCKHAM *Pol.* I 305; **s1333** omnes terras .. regni Scocie et eciam forinsecas insulas .. conquestus est *Meaux* II 371. **c** genus .. non solum nobile sed et religiosum BEDE *HE* II 1; **957** (14c) non solum in patriarchis et prophetis verum etiam et in regibus *CS* 995; ille vero ut Salomon pacificus non solum unum templum et plurima in suo regno praecepit renovari BYRHT. *V. Ecgwini* 395. **d** spatio bilustri temporis .. sic ut et nunc GILDAS *EB* 1; **803** praecipio sicut et ego mandatum a domno apostolico Leone papa percepi *CS* 312; [ligamenta] patiuntur sicut et nervi RIC. MED. *Anat.* 219; dicitur potentia inesse materie corporis celestis sicut et elementaris, sed non potentia in substantia proprie KILWARDBY *OS* 260. **e** **853** rex Occidentalium Saxonum nec non et Cantuariorum *CS* 467; necnon et eodem anno Æthelwulfus .. filiam suam Burgredo .. dedit ASSER *Alf.* 9 (cf. ib. 17, 104).

8 **a** (introducing cl. implying consequence). **b** (after vb. of motion, implying purpose). **c** (introducing cl. implying condition) or (?) *f. l.*

a BONIF. *AG* 541 (v. compromissivus); formosus est? expecta paulisper et non erit J. SAL. *Pol.* 633B; MAP *NC* I 22 (v. alapa c); **s1105** hic patrem proprium in vinculis conjecit, quibus et obiit HIGD. VII 14; NETTER *DAF* II 235v. (v. attendentia a); **1454** (v. assuefacere a); ut inquirat que desiderantur et sic historiam .. conscribat FERR. *Kinloss pref.* 3; ne [plebs] Deum ad indignationem provocet et sic in bella seditionesque proruat *Ib.* 6. **b** et i celeriter et adfer de culina pulmentarium ÆLF. BATA 5. 1; **13..** homines ville .. solebant .. ire apud L. et reportare averagium de anguillis *MonA* III 164b. **c** quid mihi vultis dare et [? l. ut] ego eum vobis tradam? *Conc. Scot.* II 40.

9 (in lieu of rel. pron., introducing subordinate cl.).

1283 debet lx opera in gardino .. et valent ij s. v d. *Cust. Battle* 12; **1311** tenet unum curtilagium .. et continet unam acram terre *Ib.* 143.

10 (w. compar. force) as.

tunc et modo pro iiij hidis se defendit *DB* I 19v.

11 (as prep. w. abl.) with.

habet Robertus iiij villanos et v bobus *DB* I 19v.; cum nequeat invalidus et valido, infirmus et sano eque onus sustinere (*Cons. Cnuti*) *GAS* 355 (= *Quad.*, *ib.*: non potest debilis cum strenuo pariter); **c1230** dedi .. xvj[mam] partem piscarii et piscacionis et seinis et retibus *Cart. Cockersand* 213.

et- v. et. aet-.

eta [LL < ἦτα], eta, seventh letter of Greek alphabet. **b** numeral (= 8).

eta, 'e', *H*, viij *Runica Manuscripta* 351; eta NECKAM *Ut.* 117, ita BACON *Maj.* I 75 (v. delta); habent Greci .. unum e breve .. et alterum longum quod vocant eta *Id. Gram. Gk.* 5. **b** *Runica Manuscripta* 351 (v. a supra).

†etactus, *f. l.*

dentibus †etacta [l. contacta] non sit buccella redacta *Doctus dicetur* 26.

etas, etat-, etern- v. aetas, aetat-, aetern-. **etcetera** v. ceterus 2.

etenim [CL], for, and indeed, in fact: **a** (as first word); **b** (as second or third word); **c** (introducing clarification or corroboration of preceding statement).

a ~m reges Romanorum cum orbis imperium obtinuissent .. GILDAS *EB* 5; ~m celeberrimus ille nominis Christi gerulus [sc. S. Paulus] ad exemplum .. agonem protulit ALDH. *VirgP* 3. **b** crevit ~m germine praepollenti GILDAS *EB* 21; **705** quaerere ~m tuae sanctitatis consilium .. WEALDHERE *Ep.* 22; **858** haec sunt ~m marisci quae ad eandem terram .. pertinent *CS* 496; **875** ista aetenim terra praefata his terminibus undique circumcincta est *CS* 539; [palpo] contingens etenim est ad utrumlibet / vel impossibile quod infert quidlibet WALT. WIMB. *Palpo* 64; **1360** confederaciones ~m bone fient semper inter reges (*Tract.*) J. READING 176b (= WALS. *HA* II 293: enim); 'nosti .. talem virum ..?' .. 'nosco ~m' *Latin Stories* 86. **c** rem .. mirabilem .. indicavit... nam ~m post paucos dies .. obitum sancti .. audierunt *V. Cuthb.* I 5; probavit [Gregorius] hoc dogma [Eutycii] orthodoxae fidei .. esse contrarium. catholica ~m fides habet quod corpus nostrum .. subtile .. sit .. sed palpabile BEDE *HE* II 1 p. 76; exercitus in duas se turmas divisit: una ~m turma in .. Franciam perrexit et altera .. Cantiam adiit ASSER *Alf.* 66; ille cujus est verbum aut imago, nec imago nec verbum est. constat igitur quia exprimi non potest quid duo sint summus spiritus et verbum ejus .. . ~m proprium est unius esse ex altero et proprium est alterius alternum esse ex illo ANSELM (*Mon.* 38) I 56; magna in ecclesia Dei columna .. cecidit. vir ~m ille .. cum muliere hac in nocte .. fornicatus est ALEX. CANT. *Mir.* 30 p. 218.

etero- v. hetero-.

etesiae [CL *pl. only* < ἐτησίαι sc. ἄνεμοι], etesian wind.

secunda .. causa [inundationis Nili] sunt ethesie flantes et renitentes ejus cursui GROS. *Hexaem.* XI 12 p. 319.

etesticulare [cf. CL testiculari], to castrate, geld. *V. et. detesticulare.*

to gelde, castrare, emasculare, ~are *CathA*.

etexere [cf. CL detexere], to unweave (fig.), expound.

regulas siquidem perutiles vos docui ~ere per presentes *Dictamen* 335; tenuras diversimodas satis lucide ~ui *Ars notaria* 440; **c1420** tam racionabiles patri vestro ~ui raciones .. ut vestra michi hillariter annuebat *FormOx* 433.

†ethees [Ar. *al-dhahab misr. as edh-dhehef*], (alch.) gold.

hoc aurum quibusdam aurum vel †ethees Romanum solet appellari ROB. ANGL. *Alch.* 519b; †edes est aurum *LC* 239.

ethelia [Ar. *athāliya* < αἰθάλη], (alch.) sublimed vapour.

philosophi decoquere, ~ia imbuere, et terere frequentissime preceperunt DASTIN *Ros.* 14.

ethem- v. etym-. **ether** v. aether. **ethereo-, ethero-** v. hetero-. **ethesia** v. etesia. **ethic-** v. et. hectic-.

ethice [LL; cf. CL ethicōs < ἠθικῶς], ethically, morally.

dictent etice, i.e. moraliter GARL. *Dict.* 134; **s1378** novus pontifex [Urbanus VI] cepit ~e tractare de multis et .. disputare contra cardinalium avariciam WALS. *HA* I 381.

1 ethicus [CL < ἠθικός]

1 ethical, concerned w. moral philosophy.

~a, moralis *GlC* E 316; 'obsecro itaque vos' [*Eph.* iv 1]: ~a admonitio LANFR. *Comment. Paul.* 295; mores .. in ~am consonantiam redigere ADEL. *ED* 26; in ~is disciplinis decenter eruditus GIR. *TH* III 48; virtus activa ~e

subjacet speculationi quoniam ab ea perficiuntur mores J. Blund *An.* 336; casibus ex variis ethica dicta traho Garl. *Tri. Eccl.* 55; talis debet esse sermo poeticus et sermo eticus *Ps.*-Gros. *Gram.* 68.

2 (as sb. m.) moral philosopher. **b** Aristotle. **c** (w. ref. to Classical author); *cf. ethnicus* 2d.

omnes ~i, tam nostri quam ethnici, negligentiam conantur excutere J. Sal. *Ep.* 250 (148); gesta canens ethicus esse volo Garl. *Tri. Eccl.* 42; [dialecticus] nunc est logicus ..; nunc ~us ut hic: utrum summum bonum voluptas; nunc physicus .. Kilwardby *OS* 469. **b** ~us .. in anima tria fieri opinatur: potentiam, passionem, habitum [*Eth. Nic.* II 4] Alf. Angl. *Cor* 16. 10. **c** secutus est hunc ordinem ~us, votorumque seriem in ordine expetendorum eleganter expressit [Horace *Ep.* I 4. 8–11] J. Sal. *Met.* 834D; preclare .. ait ~us .. id unumquemque decet maxime [etc., Cicero *de Off.* I 31. 113] *Id. Pol.* 397A; secundum ~um 'non minor est virtus quam querere, parta tueri' [Ovid *Ars Amat.* II 13] Gerv. Cant. *Imag.* 82; ~orum dicta, hujus incommodi pestem tanto detestantia, in medium deducamus [Cicero, Seneca, Horace, Lucan] Gir. *PI* I 13; tam ex ~is quam theologie paginis notum habuerat matrimoniorum quanta sint onera *Id. Æthelb.* 4; [antonomasia:] ethicus hic culpat, condemnat apostolus Garl. *Hon. Vit.* 158; **s1250** secundum illud ~i: 'judicis auxilium sub iniqua lege rogato' [Cato] M. Par. *Maj.* V 97; **s1459** juxta ~um .. ut ipse asserit in suis Moralibus [etc., Claudian] *Reg. Whet.* I 352.

3 (as sb. usu. n. pl. < τὰ ἠθικά, w. *liber* or ellipt.) Aristotle *Ethica Nicomachea*.

de libro ~orum gratia vestri bene factum est ut mihi videtur Ad. Marsh *Ep.* 25; .. doctor angelorum / librum legit ethicorum / in sullimi cathedra Walt. Wimb. *Virgo* 160; **1329** item lego domui scolarium de Balliolo in Oxon' .. librum Eticorum cum Metaphisicis in uno volumine *DCSal.* (*HMC*) 376; quia bonum commune est melius et divinius quam bonum unius primo ~orum Ockham *Pol.* I 257; ?**a1350** ~a Aristotelis audisse complete *StatOx* 33 (cf. ib.: quod liber ~orum audiatur); **c1439** ~a Aristotelis traducta per Leonardum Arretinum (*Catal. Librorum*) *MunAcOx* 761; **p1440** Burley super libros ~orum (*Catal. Librorum*) *JRL Bull.* XVI 471; annotationum in ~en Aristotelis lib. 10 Ferr. *Kinloss* 46.

4 (f. sg. *ethica, ethice* < ἠθική *sc.* φιλοσοφία) ethics, moral philosophy.

ethica moralis heret sibi [sc. sapientie] collateralis / hec revocat brutos ad legem lege solutos R. Cant. *Malch.* IV 293; ~e regula est quia non omnia sunt semper promissa solvenda J. Sal. *Pol.* 499A; quid iudex, testis, quid femina, vel quid epebus, / quidue senex, facias etica nostra docet A. Meaux *Susanna* 406; animo tuo suam infudit dulcedinem ~e documentum Vinsauf *AV* II 128; exempla quibus vel jocunditas excitetur vel edificetur ~a Map *NC* III 1 f. 34; finis ultima quodammodo totius philosophie est ~a moralis Kilwardby *OS* 409; ~am Socrates primus ad corrigendos componendosque mores instituit W. Burley *Vit. Phil.* 110.

2 ethicus v. hecticus. **ethim-** v. etym-.

ethnicus [LL < ἐθνικός]

1 ethnic, heathen, pagan.

Hilarion .. ~is parentibus .. oriundus Aldh. *VirgP* 29; ethnica sed nullis molliri corda lagonis / cedebant Frith. 1077; **10.** .. ~e, *æthna WW*; ~i reges Danorum .. Angliam invaserunt Ord. Vit. IV 6 p. 201; J. Sal. *Ep.* 250 (148) (v. 1 ethicus 2a); [dies] quam Jovis vocabulo apud gentiles ~a insignivit consuetudo *Lib. Eli.* III 60; **s1328** affirmans .. unum militem Christianum duos canes ~os evincere Fordun *Cont.* XIII 16.

2 (as sb. m.): **a** gentile, non-Jew; **b** (w. ref. to *Matth.* xviii 17); **c** non-Christian; **d** (w. ref. to Classical author); *cf.* 1 *ethicus* 2c.

a Machabeorum .. pignora .. spurcas ~orum culturas .. repudiarunt Aldh. *Met.* 2; vide discipulum ad magistri formam omnibus omnia factum: .. modo cum ~o ~um, modo cum Judeo Judeum H. Bos. *Thom.* III 15; **s1313** hoc .. volunt statuta canonum; et ipsi ~i manifestum nobis reliquerunt exemplum, quando Egiptii .. servituti regie se subjecerunt, pontifices .. liberi remanserunt *V. Ed. II* 193. **b** **c800** si impenitens fuerit, sit vobis sicut ~us et publicanus (*Lit. Papae*) W. Malm. *GR* I 89; regis nuncii vel peregrini .. tractantur durius et sunt ei tanquam ~i et publicani *Itin. Ric.* I 26; fratrem peccantem .. tanquam ~um et publicanum non habendum Ockham *Pol.* I 117; **a1385** quatinus nullum de fratribus predicti loci .. presumatis admittere sed pocius ipsum habeatis tamquam ~um et publicanum *Reg. S. Andr.* 157b. **c** Chrisantus .. torquendus traditur, nisi .. ~orum ritu turificare consentiret Aldh. *VirgP* 35 p. 278; Ord. Vit. X 5 p. 25 (v. eous 2a); missis .. ad Salahadinum nunciis .. cum in redhibitionem .. crucis nulla posset ~us supplicatione deflecti Devizes 36; **s1254** dum [papa] .. vellet .. ossa corporis episcopi Linc' extra ecclesiam proicere et ipsum in tantam infamiam precipitare ut ~us, rebellis et inobediens .. acclamaretur M. Par. *Maj.* V 429; **s1378** invenit tempus nostrum .. homines Christiano nomine insignitos pejores infidelibus et irreverentiores ipsis ~is et paganis Wals. *HA* I 375; milites qui currunt ad ~os id est *into ethynesse Ziz.* 367 (cf. *Concl. Loll. XII* 10: ad paganiam vel sarracenos [ME: *to hethnesse*]); *a payname*, ~us, gentilis, paganus *CathA.* **d** **1187** rixandum iterum si rixa est, ut ait ~us, 'ubi tu pulsas ego vapulo tantum' [Juvenal *Sat.* III 289] *Ep. Cant.* 80; stelle animate secundum ~os angelique in medium venientes induunt corpora Fishacre *Quaest.* 44; si figmenta gentilium, si dicta ~orum in hoc opusculo .. inserantur, Christiane tamen religioni famulantur Higd. I 1 p. 16; talis apud ~os Suetonius domum descripsit Caesariam .. talis Valerius Maximus, .. Tullius, .. Homerus (*Lit. Abbatis*) *Croyl. Cont. A* 108; **s1404** commemorantes illud ~i ita dicentis [etc., Martial XII 6] Wals. *YN* 411.

ethnurus [cf. LL ethnicus + CL nurus], pagan daughter-in-law or (?) *f. l.*

sicut filias †ethnurusque [? l. ethnicas nurusque] alienigenas quondam improbabat Rebecca [cf. *Gen.* xxvi 34–5] Gosc. *V. Mild.* 21.

ethomol- v. etymol-. **ethro-** v. hetero-. **ethym-** v. etym-.

etiam [CL]

1 still, yet.

~m vivente .. fratre suo Asser *Alf.* 42.

2 even; **b** (w. compar.). **c** also, as well. **d** (w. *et*; *v. et. atque* 1b, *et* 7b); **e** (w. *non solum* .. *sed* or sim.; *v. et. etiam* 7c); **f** (introducing end of series or climactic example).

ad Gallias magna comitante satellitum caterva [cf. Virgil *Aen.* II 40], insuper ~m imperatoris insignibus .. Maximum mittit Gildas *EB* 13; ~m antequam baptismi rudimenta susciperet Aldh. *VirgP* 47; gens .. reginam juxta regem sedere non patitur nec ~m reginam appellari .. permittit Asser *Alf.* 13; quantum aut visus aut ~m auditus extenditur Gir. *TH* I 12. **b** post pauca, quod ~m crebrius stilo propheta adjunxit .. Gildas *EB* 49. **c** ista ego .. in scripturis veteribus intuens, convertebar ~m ad novas *Ib.* 1; illud ~m non omittendum reor .. Aldh. *VirgP* 25; **705** quod adhuc infelicius est, ecclesiastici ~m in hanc .. dissensionem .. inplicantur Wealdhere *Ep.* 22; **814** (9c) aetiam nomina testium infra adscribuntur *CS* 343; habet ~m quater xx acras terrae *DB* I 2; **1366** cum omnibus suis pertinenciis .. in hundredo de N. ac essiam in hundredo de A. *Arch. Bridgw.* 151; sic disposuit Deus, quod qui de oculo eruendo ad literam intellexit, de monte movendo ~m miraculose per graciam sue veritatis complevit Knighton I 91. **d** quia in Hibernia scolasticam eruditionem viguisse audivit, ~m et quorundam sanctorum virorum .. conversatione incitatus .. Hiberniam secessit Alcuin *WillP* 4; pecuniam ab illo exigentibus, ~m et non exigentibus .. impendebat Asser *Alf.* 101; super murum clamavit 've urbi ..' et cum addidisset 've ~m et mihi', lapis enormiter missus eum peremit M. Par. *Maj.* I 112. **e** non de firmamento solum temporali, sed de summa ~m caelorum arce Gildas *EB* 8 (cf. ib. 65: non solum laudo, verum ~m .. praefero); non solum audiendis scripturae sanctae verbis .. verum ~m noscendis priorum gestis Bede *HE pref.*; sarcofagum non humo terrae conditum, immo ~m in memoriale quoddam posuit, quod nunc .. conspicimus Felix *Guthl.* 51; **1126** non solum nobis sed aetiam elementis tue more displicent *Ep. Anselm. Bur.* 97. **f** praeter illum solum pauperes aut nullos aut ~m paucissimos habebant adjutores Asser *Alf.* 105; pro aliquorum amore vel timore aut aliorum odio aut ~m pro alicujus pecuniae cupiditate *Ib.* 106.

3 yes. **b** indeed, truly.

responderunt "~m" utrique Bede *HE* III 25 p. 188; dicito "*gae*", quod est lingua Anglorum verbum adfirmandi et consentiendi, id est, ~m *Ib.* V 2; at ille "~m" inquit Felix *Guthl.* 50; "est iste ex tuis sociis?" "~m est" [AS: *gea, he ys*] Ælf. *Coll.* 91; "laetaris quod in fide Christiana moreris?" respondeat "~m" Anselm *Misc.* 353; verbi gratia, diceret Gerbertus, "ero apostolicus?" responderet statua, "~m" W. Malm. *GR* II 172.; dixit uxor viro suo .. "credis tu eos esse filios tuos?" cui respondens, "~m" *Latin Stories* 23. **b** qui .. interrogavit si voluisset tali hospiti ministrare. ille "~m [vv. ll. iam, vero iam]" .. ait [etc.] *V. Cuthb.* I 4; (*Aldhelm*) *ASPR* VI 97 (v. encratia); ~m, *A. forsothe WW.*

etiamnunc [CL; al. div.], even now, still.

c705 quemadmodum te viva voce .. ammonere curavi, ita ~c absentem .. litteris exhortari non piget Aldh. *Ep.* 8 (11).

etiamsi [CL; al. div.], even if, even though: **a** (w. ind.); **b** (w. subj.).

a quod ille, ~si hoc solo dicitur jam non posse peccare, quia nunc hanc habet scientiam ex casu diaboli, tamen illi sit ad gloriam Anselm (*Casus Diab.* 15 *tit.*) I 272. **b** ~si bombicinum .. peplum .. fulgescat Aldh. *VirgP* 9; ~si lingua sileret, vita loqueretur Bede *HE* V 12; certus sum enim, ~si non videam, non illum nisi juste a summe justo damnatum Anselm (*Casus Diab.* 2) I 235; **1423** Amund. I 167 (v. ducalis 1b).

etic- v. ethic-. **etnesceia** v. aesnecia. **etro-** v. hetero-.

etsi [CL; al. div.], even if, although: **a** (w. ind.); **b** (w. subj.); **c** (in parenthesis).

a **a705** etsi te .. non meruimus audire, tuos tamen .. legimus fastos (Cellanus) *Ep. Aldh.* 3 (9); etsi aliis non est apostolus, sed tamen nobis est Bede *HE* II 1; Lanfr. *Corp. & Sang.* 426C (v. devius 2c); nec voluntatem nec conversionem voluntatis puto negari posse aliquid esse. nam etsi non sunt substantiae, non tamen .. Anselm (*Casus Diab.* 8) I 245; qui etsi imminentis pestis considerant periculum, minus tamen .. formidant .. interitum Ord. Vit. VI 9 p. 77. **b** quid pro hoc solo retributionis .. sperares, etsi non talia sequerentur quae secuta sunt Gildas *EB* 33; etsi noluisset veritatis praedicatori credere, tamen .. cum honore remisit eum Alcuin *WillP* 11; etsi difficile sit intelligere quomodo misericordia tua non absit a tua justitia Anselm (*Prosl.* 9) I 108; **1160** J. Sal. *Ep.* 48 (122) (v. cruciare 1b); H. Bos. *Thom.* IV 20 (v. dominicus 2b); Gir. *JS* 3 p. 204 (v. congressio b); Capgr. *Hen.* (*dedic.*) 2 (v. convenientia 2b). **c** quis eorum carissimum discipulum .., etsi non perpetua lepra ut Helisaeus, saltim expulsione multavit? Gildas *EB* 72; quatinus per virum fidelem, etsi fidelis, accresceret devotio mulieris Ord. Vit. VI 9 p. 52; cum aliquid in complexione verborum equivoce dici, etsi non ex additis, contingit Balsh. *AD* 59; mediocris .. competit eis, etsi non scientia, sufficientia Gir. *TH intr.* p. 4.

etymologare [ἐτυμολογεῖν], **~iare, ~izare,** to etymologize, suggest derivation (of); **b** (absol.); **c** (p. ppl. *s. act.*) etymological, concerned w. etymology; *v. et. etymologicus* a.

s1244 papa .. didicit hoc nomen 'mulier' ethimologizare. dicitur enim 'mulier' quasi 'molliens herum' *Flor. Hist.* II 271; Hugutio et Papias dicunt quod 'Parasceue' dicitur 'preparatio cene' et componitur a 'paro' et 'cena'. .. ~izant prius per posterius, et estimant vocabula unius lingue [Grece] esse alterius [Latine] Bacon *CSPhil.* 448; 'Deus' ~izatur quasi 'dans eternam vitam suis' *Ib.*; cum 'proposicio' ethimologatur quasi 'pro alio posicio' Wycl. *Univ.* f. 6 (cf. MS Univ. Prag. IV H 9: ethimoloyzatur); patriam [sc. Angliam], nomen regis [sc. Ælle], et multa alia rethorice ethimologizans [cf. Bede *HE* II 1] Thorne 1757; nomen ~iatum Capgr. *Hen.* (*dedic.*) 2 (v. convenientia 2b). **b** [sonorum] numerus ab Arisotele dicitur oratio, ut equivocetur nomen orationis, secundum quod ~izando dicitur 'oris ratio' Kilwardby *OS* 194; ~izat Augustinus [*Ep.* 147] 'presens' inquit 'dicitur quasi presto sum sensibus' (Kyn.) *Ziz.* 72. **c** **1510** Ysydorus ethimologizatus (*Invent.*) *Cant. Coll. Ox.* I 46.

etymologia [CL < ἐτυμολογία]

1 etymology. **b** (usu. pl.) Isidore *Etymologiarum Libri.*

[Jesus] cujus sacrosancti nominis non tantum aethimologia sed et ipse quem litteris comprehendit numerus .. nostrae salutis myseria redolet Bede *Luke* (ii 21) 338; ethimologia, proprietas, †ethincon [l. ethimon, i.e. etymon] proprium *GlC* E 318–9; templum ei [Veste] et tholum .. ad similitudinem terre †rotunda [l. rotunde] dicit attribui: idque etiam per nominis ~iam .. probare conatur, terram nuncupare asserens Vestam, quod sola quasi vi sua stet Alb. Lond. *DG* 2. 6; ethimologia est sciencia cognoscendi diccionum singularium significaciones et sentenciarum diversitatem secundum varias diccionum conjuncciones *Ps.*-Gros. *Gram.* 67; cum .. 'Deus' sit Grecum non potest habere Latinam ~iam, ut fiat vis in hoc nomine '~ia' Bacon *CSPhil.* 448; *Id. Gram. Gk.* 62 (v. etymum b); de .. nominis ejusdem [Melse] ethimologia *Meaux* I 73 *tit.*; *MGL* I 32 (v. aldermannus 2a). **b** **c1400** libri theologie .. : Ysidorus Ethimologiarum in uno volumine (*Catal. Librorum*) *FormOx* 242; **13.** . liber Ethimologiarum (*Catal. Librorum*) *Chr. Rams.* app. 365; Ysidorus Ethimologiarum in uno volumine .. item Matheus glosatus, ubi est pars Ysodori Ethimologie (*Cart. Reading*) *EHR* III 121, 122; item liber continens Isiderum Ethemolegisarum cum ij tractatibus gramaticalibus Heete *Catal. Coll. Wint.* 69.

2 (?) name.

Ætheldretha vero, cujus ethimologia preclara et simplex sonat *Lib. Eli.* I *prol.* p. 7.

etymologiare v. etymologare.

etymologice, etymologically, by etymology.

'Ricardus' igitur ~e potest dici quasi 'ridens', 'carus', et 'dulcis' R. Bocking *Ric. Cic.* I 9 p. 286; **s1244** didicit enim papa quod 'mulier' ethimologice dicitur, quasi 'moliens herum' *Ann. Lond.* 41; Augustinus [*Ep.* 147] dicit quod 'presens' dicitur ~e quasi 'presto sensui' *Ziz.* app. 475; abbas [R. Wallingford, ob. **1335**] instrumentum astronomie .. 'Albion', quasi totum per unum, ~e vocitabit *G. S. Alb.* II 207.

etymologicus [CL < ἐτυμολογικός], concerned w. etymology, the etymologist (as epithet of Isidore); *v. et. etymologare* c. **b** concerned w. words.

usque huc Isidorus ~us *Eul. Hist.* II 44; Ysodorus Ethimologicus (*Catal. Librorum*) *Chr. Rams. app.* 356. **b** ~us, tropicus, figuratus Osb. Glouc. *Deriv.* 198.

etymologizare v. etymologare.

etymologizatio, etymologization, tracing etymology.

'aldermanni' nominis ethimologizacio *MGL* I 32 *tit.*; **c1430** qui cinis aut fraxinus [? *Thomas Asshe*] appellaris, cujus ethomologisacionem laudabilem tradunt naturales *Cant. Coll. Ox.* III 72.

etymum [CL < ἔτυμον], etymon, primitive meaning or form of word. **b** word.

ac probabile est, veluti e proxima significatione de nomine vetustissimo 'Kynlusche', hoc est 'capita herbarum', regem David hujus loci fundatorem ~um deflexisse aliquantulum et dixisse 'Killusche' .. hoc est 'ecclesia herbarum' FERR. *Kinloss* 13. **b** 'ethymon' est 'verbum', a quo 'ethymologia' sine aspiratione, et est etymologia verus sermo interpretationis alicujus vocabuli BACON *Gram. Gk.* 62.

eu v. eheu.

eu- [εὖ], (in comp.) well. **b** (by misinterp.) naturally.

FRITH. 619 (v. eutyches); MAP *NC* V 4 (v. consonare 1b); BACON *Gram. Gk.* 111 (v. eucharis); *Alph.* 60 (v. euodes). **b** eunuchi naturaliter sunt casti nati, ab *eu* quod est 'naturale', et 'castus -ta -tum', et 'natus', i. qui naturaliter carent testiculis GAD. 37v. 1.

euagetus [εὐάγητος], bright, clear.

humor .. albugineus qui alio nomine dicitur euagaydos BART. ANGL. V 4.

euarguminus v. energumenus.

1 euax [CL]

1 (interj.) hurrah!

680 heu, heu! pro tantis erroribus potius quam ~x, ~x! .. ingeminandum reor ALDH. *Ep.* 4 p. 484; **a690** ~x eugeque! *Ib.* 5 p. 492; primum ve et tristia, post euax et lyre *Poem S. Thom.* 73; ve vertentem in euax, fletum in gaudere *Ib.* 90; sunt .. alii affectus in ipsa [anima] a viribus suis egressi, ut leticia sive contemplacio, spes et amor, ut '~x, heya, ha' et quecumque pulsu passionum anime sine premeditacione emittuntur *Ps.*-GROS. *Gram.* 60.

2 (adj.) welcome.

~x, *wilcume* ÆLF. *Sup.*; avete omnes! .. cuncti ~x [*gl.*: *ealle bliðe*] estis mihi ÆLF. BATA 4. 11 p. 36.

2 euax v. 2 evax.

eubulia [εὐβουλία], good counsel, sound judgement. (*Cf.* Aristotle *Eth. Nic.* VI 9).

item commentator sexto Ethicorum parum ante capitulum de ~ia DUNS *Metaph.* IV 2 p. 158.

euca- v. et. eucha-. **eucatisma** v. encathisma. **eucaton** v. hecaton.

eucharis [LL < εὔχαρις], gracious. **b** (as sb.) gracious man (or as quasi-adv.).

acriter increpatus ab ~i pontifice LANTFR. *Swith.* 1; ~is, *swæs* vel *wynsum* ÆLF. *Sup.*; ~is, gratiosus, gratificus OSB. GLOUC. *Deriv.* 193; vigebat in eo pariter et lingua ~is et dextera liberalis AD. EYNS. *Hug.* V 14 p. 165; NECKAM *Ut.* 107 (v. epicharis); *acharis* ab *a*, quod est 'sine', et *charis*, quod est 'gracia', *eucharis*, ab *eu*, quod est 'bonum' BACON *Gram. Gk.* 111; *gracyows*, eucaris *PP.* **b** astitit eucharis et libamina consecrat aris FRITH. 354.

eucharistia [LL < εὐχαριστία]

1 thanksgiving.

~ias, gratiarum actiones *GlC* E 341.

2 Eucharist: **a** (in Canon of Mass); **b** (element to be consecrated); **c** (Host); **d** (reserved); **e** (distributed to sick); **f** (as sacrament).

a Innocentius statuit osculum ad missam dari in loco ~ie R. NIGER *Chr. II* 128. **b** **1371** pro emendacione ij parium de *irnes* pro eucarista iij s. iiij d. *Fabr. York* 126. **c** post annum et dimedium ~iam sumat GILDAS *Pen.* 1; BEDE *HE* II 5 p. 91 (v. dare 9b); cotidie .. ~iam [AS p. 388: *husel*] accipere non renuant *RegulC* 23; sacerdos communicet, posteaque det ~iam eis (*Jud. Dei*) *GAS* 414; H. BOS. *Thom.* III 37 (v. 1 communio 6a); Silvester .. ~iam in lineo conficiendam instituit R. NIGER *Chr. I* 32; si .. de minutis eukaristie partibus in patena aut corporalibus aliqua acciderit negligencia .., frater cujus culpa hoc contigerit puniatur *Cust. Westm.* 215; tribuens Christus apostolis potestatem ~ie consecrande OCKHAM *Dial.* 846; nam cum adoro hostiam / impendo sibi latriam / et sanguini in poculo. / cum colo eukaristiam / tunc ledo conscientiam (*In Lollardos*) *Pol. Poems* I 247; [sacrista] habebit annuatim de grangia domini unum bussellum boni, mundi, et sicci frumenti pro pane faciendo ad eukaristiam ecclesie predicte contra Pascha (*Wells MSS*) *Arch. Soc. Som* XX (*Sup.*) p. 67; **1415** (v. elevatio 1d). **d** interrogavit si ~iam intus haberent BEDE *HE* IV 22 p. 261; *RegulC* 41 (v. communicatio 4); philatorium [v. l. filitorium], in quo reservatur dignissima eucaristia NECKAM *Ut.* 119; magnum altare nunquam debet esse, quod absit, sine pixide cum eukaristia *Cust. Cant.* 112; **1454** j pixide de cupro .. pro eukaristia conservanda *Ac. Durh.* 241. **e** quid opus est ~ia? neque enim mori adhuc habes BEDE *HE* IV 22 p. 261; infirmis .. devote petentibus post viij dies vel xv ~ia poterit iterato conferri GIR. *GE* I 3; **1229** (v. dare 9b); **1365** capellanus defert eukaristiam per parochiam ad infirmos *Fabr. York* 243; **1545** nulla sacramenta .. ministrentur nisi .. ~ia infirmis *Conc. Scot.* I cclxvi. **f** ORD. VIT. IV 6 p. 211 (v. astructio); **1237** sacramenta principalia .. sunt baptismus, confirmatio, penitentia, eukaristia .. *Conc. Syn.* 246; **1332** sacramentum ~ie personis secularibus .. sepe ministrarunt *Lit. Cant.* I 479; [ecclesia] cujus sacramenta sine signis ministrari non possunt, ut patet de baptismo et ~ia (KYN.) *Ziz.* 64; ad confessionem, quia hoc est sacramentum post eukaristiam [ME: *weofdes sacrament*] et baptismum quod diabolus magis odit *AncrR* 124; **1538** de .. blasphemiis contra sacrosanctum ~ie sacramentum *Form. S. Andr.* II 59.

eucharistialis, eucharistic. **b** (as sb. n.) pyx, vessel for reserved Host.

benedictio ~is vasculi (*Bened. Rob.*) *HBS* XXIV 94 *tit.*; si autem minister altaris accusatus adjutorio amicorum careat, offam judicialem sumat et in ea divinum judicium subeat, nisi eucaristialem probacionem preeligat, et sibi liceat (*Cons. Cnuti*) *GAS* 287 (cf. *Quad.*, *ib.*: nisi super .. corpus Domini permittatur ei se purgare; AS: *buton he on husle geladian mote*). **b** hoc ~e .. quod nos indigni ad mystici corporis tui custodiam consecramus (*Bened. Rob.*) *HBS* XXIV 94; **1493** unum magnum eukaristiale de argento, ponderis clx unciarum (*Invent.*) *Bannatyne Misc.* II 25.

eucharisticus, ~tius, eucharistic.

s1229 prelati .. aliud remedium non habentes calices ~tias et alia sacra .. vasa .. vendiderunt WEND. II 377; panis .. factus ex prophano ~ticus, hoc est .. caro Christi GARDINER *CC* 109.

euchesis v. euexia.

euchymia [LL < εὐχυμία], wholesome juice.

restauratio bone humiditatis non fit nisi ex nutrientibus cibis et precipue euchimiis secundum Plinium BACON V 5; ex euchimiis bene digestis provenientibus ex animalibus et plantis potest restaurari .. humiditas naturalis .. in senibus *Id.* IX 40.

euchymus [LL < εὔχυμος], 'euchymous', well-flavoured, wholesome.

eu quod est 'bonum', .. inde †euthimus *Alph.* 60.

eucrasia [cf. εὐκρασία], good composition, good temperament. *Cf. dyscrasia, eucraticus.*

magnitudo oculorum cum proportione operationum et virtutum multitudinem substantie et bonam ~iam [*gl.*: i.e. bonam temperationem vel temperantiam] ex qua oculi sunt facti ostendit. ex bonitate operationis multam substantiam et eucrasiatam demonstrat [*gl.*: sc. oculorum magnitudo]; cum vitio vero operationum, parvam substantiam non eucrasiatam BACON V 86; *eu* quod .. est 'bonum' ..: inde .. eucrasis et ~ia et eucraticum *Alph.* 60; hoc .. arguit imperfeccionem intellectus, quia nos indigemus tot ycrasiis ad nostram noticiam quod multas veritates non possumus cognoscere WYCL. *Log.* II 211.

eucrasiatus, well-tempered. *V. et eucraticus.*

BACON V 86 (v. eucrasia).

eucrasis v. eucrasia.

eucraticus [cf. εὔκρατος], well-tempered. *V. et. eucrasiatus.*

qualiter [homo] de limo terre †encratico sit factus *Quaest. Salern.* B 3; primi hominis, qui ex limo †encratico fuit creatus *Ib.* N 11; *Alph.* 60 (v. eucrasia).

eucritus [εὔκριτος], (med.) having a favourable crisis. *Cf. dyscritus.*

oportet autem et alia bona signa considerare, ut brevis et ~a judicetur. ut si urina multum intensam albam habeat ypostasim .., brevis et ~a erit egritudo GILB. I 29.

eucta v. euthenia. **eucyclius** v. encyclius.

eudica [dub.], (alch.) dross, scum.

~a (fex vitri) .. bene omnibus corporibus convenit .. . quando ~am querere volueris, in vitreis vasis eam quere ROB. ANGL. *Alch.* 517a; ~a omnium horum [corporum] est secretum, quod sc. alio nomine moszhacumia dicitur, quod .. Latine 'fex vitri' vel 'vitri immunditia' dici potest *Ib.* 518b.

eudolia v. eudulia. **eudolium** v. edulium.

eudoxia [εὐδοξία], good repute, honour.

~ia, claritas *GlC* E 336; ~ia, claritas OSB. GLOUC. *Deriv.* 193.

eudoxus [cf. εὔδοξος *infl. by* ὀρθόδοξος], (?) well-catechized.

archipater gaudet heredem nactus opimum, / cui queat eudoxas moriens committere caulas FRITH. 181.

eudulia [εὖ + δουλεία], good service.

eudolia, bonum servitium *GlC* E 346; ~ia, bonum servitium OSB. GLOUC. *Deriv.* 202; dono non vincitur mors vel edulia / omnes digladiat pari ferocia WALT. WIMB. *Sim.* 182.

Eudymios v. Audynaios. **euechia** v. euexia. **eueria** v. ewera. **euerroima** v. enaeorema.

euexia [εὐεξία], good health.

ab euchesi ad chachesim *Chr. Wallingf.* 59 (v. cachexia); sicut dicit Aristoteles .. 'si euechia est sanitas, egritudo est †cathalepsius' BACON XV 323; laborare causa est ~ie DUNS *Metaph.* V *rub.* p. 189; alimentum .. quo dabatur non solum hilarior corporis euechia [vv. ll. enchia, enethia; *ed.*: energia] sed et diuturnior florens etas R. BURY *Phil.* 16. 212; scripsit [Galienus] .. de inequali distemperancia librum, de †enoxia [v.l. enexia, l. euexia], .. W. BURLEY *Vit. Phil.* 388.

eufamia v. euphemia. **eufonia** v. euphonia. **euforb-** v. euphorb-.

eufortunatus [eu- + CL fortunatus], fortunate.

eu quod est 'bonum' .. : inde .. †infortinatus [v. l. eufortunatus] *Alph.* 60.

eufortunium [eu- + fortunium], good fortune. *Cf. dysfortunium.*

fortuna dividitur in fortunam malam et bonam, sc. in infortunium et ~ium BACON XIII 124; ad bonos mores et ad ~ia in rebus, negociis, officiis, et omnibus *Id. Tert. Sup.* 15; SICCAV. *PN* 199 (v. dysfortunium); bona fortuna est a Deo, qui immediate movet intellectum bene fortunati ad †enfortunia consequenda BRADW. 192A; dicimus enim communiter mirabilis fortuna prospera vel adversa accidit tali viro, volentes dicere quod aliquod †enfortunium vel infortunium ipsi acciderit *Ib.* 271A; *eu* quod est 'bonum' .. : inde .. infortunium [v. l. eufortunium] *Alph.* 60; *happe or good spede*, efortunium *PP.*

eufracticus, eufraticus v. emphracticus. **eufrag-, eufras-** v. euphras-. **eufurb-** v. euphorb-.

euge [CL < εὖγε]

1 good! fine! **b** (as sb.) euge, approval.

a690 ne .. ut .. in squalores trusus praecipitaretur, sed potius — euax ~eque — ingressurus tripudium .. promereatur ALDH. *Ep.* 5; ~e, gaude, bene *GlC* E 327; FRITH. 736 (v. ciere 1e); perpendit .. popularis favoris auram .. undique '~e! ~e!' acclamantem J. FURNESS *Kentig.* 8 p. 175; hinc sunt interjecciones: ~e, hay, atat, heu *Ps.*-GROS. *Gram.* 60. **b** sed nichil esse diu Lachesis permittit, in omni / condicione bonis invidet euge suum A. MEAUX *Susanna* 60.

eugenes [cf. CL eugeneus < εὐγενής], noble.

~es, nobiles *GlC* E 333; ~es, A. *noble, wytty* *WW.*

eugenia [εὐγένεια], nobility.

~ia, nobilitas *GlC* E 343.

euiscus v. hibiscus. **eukaristia** v. eucharistia.

eulogetus [εὐλογητός], blessed.

faber eulogitus respondit episcopo .. LANTFR. *Swith.* 1.

1 eulogia [LL < εὐλογία], **~ium**

1 eulogy, praise. *Cf.* 1 *elogium* 1.

~ium .. Brittaniae .. Nennius .. congregavit NEN. *HB* 143; eulogium tendo divinis, tendoque fisim / hiis qui secretis insenuere suis GARL. *Tri. Eccl.* 100; fuit Willelmus Wykeham .. apud oppidum de Wykeham .. enixus; et sic .. nomen cum loco ~io perpetuo decoravit HEETE *Wykeham* 295.

2 good news. **b** aphorism, 'bon mot'. **c** (biblical) text. **d** (as title of book).

elogium, fama bona *GlC* E 127; elogium, i. fama *GlH* E 213; **s1240** nuntius .. qui ~ium a Terra Sancta transtulit .. nuntiavit .. quod .. Soldanus Damascenus .. proposuit baptismi suscipere sacramentum M. PAR. *Maj.* IV 65; eulogium didici, tauri perient inimici [*gl.*: 'eulogium didici', i. bonum sermonem a Spiritu Sancto, quod 'tauri perient inimici'] (J. BRIDL.) *Pol. Poems* 161, 162. **b** ~ium, responsum aliquod ubi ratio redditur *GlC* E 338; ad .. columpnam .. Fabricii redeo, qui ab hoste Pirro approbatus, hoc est ~io descriptus GREG. *Mir. Rom.* 25; illud nobile Ciceronis ~ium .. ad animum revocantes 'presentes fructus contemnamus, posteritatis glorie serviamus' GIR. *PI* I *pref.*; vulgari dicitur ~io 'quod oculus non videt, cor non desiderat' J. GODARD *Ep.* 239; sapientis ~ium est 'laudet te alienus et non os tuum' J. BURY *Glad. Sal.* 594. **c** elogium, testimonium *GlC* E 113; inanem .. poenitentiam scriptura teste nomino .. qua homines .. dolent. sed quamvis per hanc rem .. ~ii miserabiliter contristentur ASSER *Alf.* 91; Jeremiam prophetam Dominus .. vas electionis .. tali ~io futurum pronuntiat J. FURNESS *Kentig.* 1 p. 162; **s1170** festum faciebat .. de hiis ~iis que 'O sapientia' cum sequentibus nuncupantur M. PAR. *Min.* I 359; quod de Salamone legitur famosum ~ium .. 'magnificatus est rex gloriosus' [etc.; *1 Kings* x 23] J. LOND. *Commend. Ed.* I 13; non sine .. animarum periculo apparent contra divine legis ~ia .. legibus civilibus conantes .. determinare contrarium evangelice veritati PAUL. ANGL. *ASP* 1544. **d** ~ium Johannis Cornubiensis ad Alexandrum Papam tertium J. CORNW. *Eul. tit.*; ~ium contra Dampnatorum errorum (*sic*) (*Catal. Librorum*) *Chr. Rams.* xc; hoc libellum conglobatum ~ium volo nominari *Eul. Hist.* I *proem.* p. 4.

3 blessing. **b** blessed bread, 'Eulogia'.

c720 illum cum caritate suscipias et .. cum tua benedictione et gratia et ~ia dirigere digneris ad .. fratrem .. B. (EANGYTH) *Ep. Bonif.* 14; **10..** ~iae, benedictionis *WW*; ~iae, benedictiones OSB. GLOUC. *Deriv.* 200; quoties pueros .. obvios habebat, eos illico salutatione preveniens ad reciprocam invitabat salutationem, ut .. innocentium ei

benedictio .. cum salutationis ∼io refunderetur Gir. *IK* I 2. **b** alie [oblationes] ad benedicendum in ∼ias, i.e. panem benedictum dandum diebus festis fidelibus illis qui sacramento altaris participare parati non erant Bart. Exon. *Pen.* 116; ut .. daretur .. ∼ia .., id est panis benedictus Beleth *RDO* 48. 55D.

4 gift (also fig.); **b** (w. ref. to *Regula S. Benedicti* 54). **c** grant.

promissum sequentis ∼iae munusculum [sc. librum] non aliter me spopondisse mementote Aldh. *VirgP* 60; elogia, *laac GlC* E 139; **796** magnas mihi ∼ias misisti, dum tuam .. agnovi sanitatem et prosperitatem; quae mihi plus placet quam millena talenta auri et argenti Alcuin *Ep.* 112; Ord. Vit. V 14 p. 420 (v. benedictio 4); tum mater ipsa tum filie crebra dedere Deo .. graciarum ∼ia *Mir. Hen. VI* II 38. **b** qui alicui litteras vel ∼ias seu quelibet munuscula miserit aut acceperit *Cust. Westm.* 265; quod nullatenus liceat monacho nec a parentibus suis neque a quoquam hominum nec sibi invicem literas aut ∼ias vel quelibet munuscula accipere aut dare, sine precepto abbatis *Cust. Cant.* 397; **s1425** inquisivit .. nunquid .. fratres litteras scribunt vel mittunt ∼ias, munerave conferunt Amund. I 207. **c** **940** (14c) caveant haec frangentes claustra infernalia, gaudeantque †Jesu aliginnasio [l. Jesuali ginnasio] haec augentes ∼ia *CS* 750; **942** (13c) fas divini privilegii et ius humani ∼ii iugiter servare *Ch. Burton* 5 (cf. ib. 8 [**949**]: hoc regale ∼ium); **950** (12c) hoc fructuo[s]um ∼ie munusculum [cf. Aldh. *VirgP* 38] in sempiterno graphio .. maneat *CS* 888 (= *MonA* II 321: †eulogige); **961** hoc ∼ium propria manu depinxi *CS* 1066.

5 will, testament. *V. et. elogium* 2.

1309 per .. peticionem .. bonorum decedencium ab intestato que temporalia existere dinoscunter et similiter eorum bonorum que in ∼iis defunctorum post legata nominatim in eis relicta .. distribuenda committuntur (*Lit. Baronum*) *Reg. Heref.* 474; **c1400** decendencium executoribus, quos in suis ultimis deputaverint ∼iis (*Reg. Exon.*) *Conc.* III 250a.

2 eulogia v. holalogium.

eulogiare, ∼izare [εὐλογεῖν, εὐλογίζειν], to eulogize, praise.

∼io, A. *to prayse and alowe WW*; *to prayse*, commendare, canere, .. elogizare *CathA*.

eulogice, eulogically, by commendation, with praise.

sue glorie participem vos faciat qui dicta sua ∼e suis discipulis enucliabat *Dictamen* 369.

eulogige v. 1 eulogia 4c. **eulogitus** v. eulogetus. **eulogium** v. 1 elogium, 1 eulogia. **eulogizare** v. eulogiare. **euluare, euludare, eululare** v. oillare. **eumicizare** v. eunuchizare. **eunodis** v. euodes.

eunuchare [CL], to make a eunuch (of), castrate: **a** (man); **b** (animal). *V. et. eunuchizare* 1.

a rex Willelmus .. plures clericorum ejus fecit evirari et ∼atorum ante se in pelvi afferri membra W. Fitzst. *Thom.* 55; mutilati tales et eunucati, virilibus abscisis Gir. *Spec.* II 32; Sagiensem episcopum enuchaverat Knighton I 143. **b** equus ille .. eunucatus fuerat, hic autem integer est et testiculos habens Gir. *JS* 4 p. 251.

eunuchizare [LL < εὐνουχίζειν]

1 to eunuchize, make a eunuch (of), (man, also fig.). **b** (p. ppl. as sb. m.) gelding. *V. et. eunuchare.*

10.. castraverunt, †eumicizaverit [l. eunucizaverunt] *WW*; 'abscindantur', i.e. ∼entur a malis moribus, ne amplius generent in malum Lanfr. *Comment. Paul.* (*Gal.* v 12) 282; Nicephorus .. volens ∼are filios suos, ne truderent eum in exilium R. Niger *Chr. I* 79; quod per beatam Virginem .. ∼atus et curatus .. fuerit Ad. Eyns. *Hug.* II 2 p. 52. **b** de instrumentis agricolarum: .. spadatus vel ∼atus, *belisnod* Ælf. *Gl.*

2 (intr.) to live as a eunuch, to be chaste.

to lyf chaste, eunuchidare, continere, caste vivere *CathA*.

eunuchus [CL < εὐνοῦχος], eunuch; **b** (w. ref. to *Matth.* xix 12); **c** (w. ref. to *Acts* viii 27–38). **d** official, servant.

semivir, ∼us *Gl. Leid.* 46. 17; quamobrem ipsi soli barbescant, numquam vero aut raro idipsum mulieribus et ∼is contingat Adel. *QN* 20; ∼i per amissionem testiculorum .. versi sunt in femineam naturam *Quaest. Salern.* P 43; ∼us, qui non habet testes, ut spado Bacon *Gram. Gk.* 135; **c1396** sententie vel canones, qui incipiunt 'de enuchis' (*Catal. Librorum*) *Meaux* III lxxxvi. **b** spadones .., qui secundo ∼orum gradui evangelica .. astipulatione deputantur Aldh. *VirgP* 21; de istis ∼is loquitur Dominus in evangelio, qui se castraverunt propter regnum caelorum Ælf. *Ep.* 2. 70; nec ∼os nos ferro facere sed fidei fervore laudabile est Gir. *GE* II 20; Garl. *Syn.* 1585A (v. castrare 2a). **c** **c720** Deus .. per angelum suum .. misit .. Philippum .. ad ∼um (Eangyth) *Ep. Bonif.* 14; venerunt ad locum ubi Philippus baptizavit ∼um Hugeb. *Will.* 4; in curru ∼i Aethiopis J. Sal. *Ep.* 284 (271). **d** ∼us, consul Romanus *Gl. Leid.* 43. 20; dum .. Run in tabernaculo ludens in alea cum suis ∼is [*gl.*: vel apparitoribus] consedisset *VSB* (*Cadoc* 24) 76 (cf. ib.: ∼os [*gl.*: vel assedas]); *a chaumberlayn*, camerarius, .. †eunuphus *CathA*.

euodes [CL < εὐώδης], (med.) sort of salve or ointment.

†eunodis [l. euuodes] interpretatus 'bene olens' et dicitur ab *eu* quod est 'bonum' *Alph.* 60.

euonymus [CL < εὐώνυμος], spindle-tree (*Euonymus europaeus*).

∼us *is called* .. fusago *or* fusaria ..; *it maye be called in Englishe spyndle tree or square tree* Turner *Herb Names* D1.

euouae, (mus.) sequence of vowels from *seculorum amen*, designating liturgical cadence.

help us nu of ure senne potest .. Latine sic exprimi: .. a peccatis nostris nos averte. euouae W. Cant. *Mir. Thom.* I 11; vitam dando volucri quam necarant invidi .. euouae *Offic. Kentig.* xcv; omni sabbato antiphona super 'Benedictus' habet suum euouae, i.e. 'seculorum amen' Maidstone 19.

eupagmasticus v. epacmasticus. **eupatica** v. hepatica.

eupatorium [CL eupatoria < εὐπατόριον], (bot.) agrimony (*Agrimonia eupatorium*) or sim.

pulvis cum succo borraginis aut ∼ii .. coleram nigram educit Gilb. II 100. 2; debent pauca frigida poni in medicina sua .. cum quibusdam calidis, sicut ∼io, ysopo Gad. 4v. 2; herba pulicum est idem quod ∼ium secundum quosdam, ut recitat J. Mesue in medicinis laxativis, capitulo de ∼io *Alph.* 79; *Ib.* 8 (v. ambrosia b); ∼ium, i. salvia agrestis *SB* 20 (cf. ib. 22: gasith, i. ∼ium); ∼ium, A. *ambrosye, or wylde sauge WW*.

euperiston v. euporistus.

eupetalos [CL < εὐπέταλος], (bot.) spurge laurel (*Daphne laureola*).

Turner *Herb.* A4v. (v. daphnoides).

euphemia [LL = *euphemism* < εὐφημία], good repute.

conversacione bona et eufamia fratris Symonis de L., tunc episcopi Eliensis .. papa certificatus J. Reading 190b.

euphemismus [εὐφημισμός], (rhet.) euphemism, substitution of favourable for unfavourable word.

euphesmismos, A. *good chaungynge WW*.

euphonia [LL < εὐφωνία], (gram.) euphony. **b** similar sound, rhyme.

GlC D 379 (v. duo); saepius dictiones semivocalibus quam mutis propter ∼iam, id est sonoritatem, finiuntur Alcuin *Gram.* 855C; quamvis ejus penultima brevis sit, ∼iae causa solet acui, sicut et verba calefacio, calefacis Abbo *QG* 5 (12); ∼ia dulcis sonus vel bonus sonus Osb. Glouc. *Deriv.* 200; syllaba interposita causa ∼ie *Ib.* 439; non enim due acute conveniunt simul nec est ∼ia nec bonus sonus Bacon *Tert.* 239; ∼ia, que est bonitas soni *Ib.* 241. **b** '*hattest þu Urs, have þu Godes kurs*' eleganter in his verbis, sed dure nominum eufonie alludens: [etc.] W. Malm. *GP* III 115.

euphonomaton [cf. εὐφωνία ὀνομάτων], (gram.) euphony.

eufonomaton [v. l. eufonomyaton] est consonantia orationis que consistit in similitudine sive idemptitate replicata tum literarum, tum sillabarum, tum etiam †dictionem [l. dictionum] Gerv. Melkley *AV* 10 (cf. ib. in marg.: eufonomaton quasi bonus sonus in nomine).

euphorbiatus, ∼bius, (med.) made from gum of spurge.

pillule euforbiate: recipe euforb', .. tempera cum succo apii Gilb. II 119. 2 (cf. ib. 115v. 1: pillule tapsie et fetide et †euforbite [l. euforbiate]); **1307** cum pulvere eufurbeo (v. castoreum).

euphorbium, ∼ia [CL < εὐφόρβιον], (bot.) spurge (*Euphorbia*). **b** (med.) gum resin obtained from spurge. **c** infusion made from spurge.

ibique [in Mauritania] crescit herba que dicitur euforbia .., cujus lacteum succum .. extollit in claritate visus Bart. Angl. XV 94; oleum de euforbio est optimum et oleum de croco Gad. 65v. 2. **b** abdellum, euforbium [*gl.*: unguentum], sarcotalla Neckam *Ut.* 110; pro frigore .. fiat inunctio spine cum unguentis .. acutis cum euforbio Gilb. I 39. 2; serapinum, euforbium, oppopenacum, et alie gumme in quibus est caliditas tepida Gad. 65v. 2; euforbium gummi est cujusdam arboris *SB* 20, *Alph.* 60. **d** vomitus .. provocetur cum eufor[bio] Gilb. II 115v. 1.

euphrasia [εὐφρασία = *good cheer*], (bot. & med.) eye-bright (*Euphrasia officinalis*).

pulvis ad quartanam digerens materiam: recipe .. piretri, eufrasie, urtice .. quantum sufficit; ad dulcedinem in cibis utatur Gilb. I 48. 2; thimi, camedreos, sanamunde, eufragie Gad. 103. 2; aloe succotrinum valet pro oculis hominum .. cum aqua fe[niculi] vel eufragie *Ib.* 109. 2; resolutio quoque fit .. per medicinas decoctas in aqua vel vino et superpositas, sicut est ruta, eufrasia, melilotum .. et similia *Ib.* 111. 2; eufragia, eufrasia idem, G. et A. *eufrasye Alph.* 60; hec eufrasia, *a heufrasy WW*.

euporistus [LL < εὐπόριστος], (med.) easily procured, common.

evacuabitur materia cum medicina .. vel purgetur cum theod' euperiston aut alia aliqua competenti medicina Gilb. I 39. 1; *Ib.* I 52v. 2 (v. dyscrasia); †theodoriton emperiston [l. theodoricon euperiston] optimum ad omne vitium capitur et oculorum et cerebri *Ib.* VII 294. 2; tunc trufera magna, vel theodoricon anacardinum, †antheodoricon emperiscon [l. aut theodoricon euperiston] valent specialiter Gad. 79v. 2.

euprepia [εὐπρέπεια], beauty, dignity, majesty.

jam quoque pastoris extremos crede rogatus / ut tua praecluibus gliscens eupraepia sceptris / ardua Romulei servet praecepta vigoris Frith. 1029; nostraque caterva hujus diei ∼ia *Miss. Westm.* I 362; *a bewetye*, ∼ia *CathA*.

eurauster, euriaster v. euroauster.

Euripus [CL < εὔριπος = *Euripus, strait noted for violent current*]

1 violent current (also fig.). **b** quicksand.

c720 quando ventorum violentia et procellarum tempestates .. inormem ∼um inpellunt (Eangyth) *Ep. Bonif.* 14; hic in sentinam ventris recenti crapula ructante exestuantis tanquam ∼o inmergendus abominanter deponitur Pull. *CM* 221; Trevet *Troades* 60 (v. deductio 1b). **b** **10..** aurippus, *cwecesond WW*.

2 (artificial) pool.

∼us vel piscina, *fiscpol* Ælf. *Sup.*

euritides v. uritides.

eurizus [εὔριζος], well-rooted.

obrizon .., i. purum aurum ..; alii exponunt pro purgatissimo auro, quasi ∼on, i. bone radicis aurum *Alph.* 127.

euroafricus [cf. LL euroauster], south-east wind.

∼us, *suðan easten wind* Ælf. *Gl.*

euroauster [LL], south-east (wind). **b** the south-east. **c** (by conf.) north-east or south-west wind.

flante .. vento ∼ro dure, .. undarum culmina in regionem Australium Saxonum .. projecerunt eos Eddi 13; *þe sowthe est wynde*, euriaster, nothus *CathA*. **b** Bede *HE* IV 3 p. 208 (v. exortus 1c); **s1091** discordia ventorum .. ab ∼ro veniens .. plusquam secentas domos effregit W. Malm. *GR* IV 324; hic [sc. Auster] tenet a dextris euraustrum, evolat austro / Affricus a leva Neckam *DS* II 87; invenit locum palustrem .. divertensque se ad ∼um loci .. excidit sibi .. mansiunculam *Chr. Dale* 3. **c** eurus, ∼er, *norðan eastan wind* Ælf. *Gl.*; ∼er, qui medius est inter meridiem et occidentem, tanta violentia flavit quod [etc.] *Meaux* I 181.

euronotus [CL = *south-east wind*], the south-east.

ad euronothum, *eastsuth GlC* A 47; **9..** ad euronothum, *eastsuð WW*; Achoriorum populi Utopiensium insulae ad ∼on oppositi More *Ut.* 85.

Europa [CL]

1 Europa.

∼am .. in specie taurina, i.e. in navi picturam tauri habente, .. asportavit Alb. Lond. *DG* 3. 5; Juppiter ∼e captus amore filie Agenoris regis Sidonie *Natura Deorum* 29.

2 Europe.

per omnes ∼ae provincias Aldh. *VirgP* 25; miracula caelitus acta / finibus in cunctis Europae nota patescunt Wulf. *Swith. pref.* 346; omnis ∼a .. non nescit W. Malm. *GR* III 265; usque ad finem ∼e a parte meridiei, scilicet usque ad montes Pirenos in confinio ∼e et Affrice Stratford *Serm.* 88.

Europaeus [CL], European (person).

qui .. Muselmanni .. dicuntur ab ∼is omnibus Turcae .. nuncupantur Camd. *Br.* 26.

eurus [CL], east or south-east wind. **b** the east or south-east. **c** right-hand. **d** (by conf.) north-east wind.

∼us, nomen venti; flat ab oriente *GlC* E 335; sum Salomone sagacior et velocior euro Tatwine *Aen.* 1 (*Philosophia*) 4; ∼o ab aurora spirante Gir. *EH* I 2; **1423** (v. contradictorius 2a). **b** [Brittanniae] orientalis pars .. a subsolano et ∼o cingitur oceano, ab aquilone .. paludum uligine Abbo *Edm.* 2; **9..** ab ∼o, *eastansuðan WW*; quanto ad ∼i partes magis acceditur Gir. *TH* I 3. **c** ∼us, dexter *Gl. Leid.* 36. 6. **d** Ælf. *Gl.* (v. euroauster c).

Eurynis v. Erinys b.

eusarcia [εὐσαρκία], fullness of flesh, good condition.

†esarbera, i. bona carnositas. . i. *eu* quod est 'bonum';. . inde †eusabera vel †euscarcrea †ad [l. ab] *eu* quod est 'bonum' et *sarcos* quod est 'caro' *Alph.* 60–1.

†euscopus, *f. l.*

s1383 preter captivitatem . . multorum hominum . ., perdidit xx m marcarum †euscoparum [*sic* MS, ? l. episcopalium] ad continuandum werram Wasconie . . . dicta . . pecunia, que collecta fuerat de . . ecclesia Anglicana, fuit regi . . minime fructuosa WALS. *HA app.* 399.

eusebia [LL < εὐσέβεια], piety, reverence.

1237 fines orbis terrarum per tuarum super crucem exaltationem manuum ad ~iam convocasti (*Lit. Archiep. Constant. ad Papam*) M. PAR. *Maj.* III 448; depositum recipientem reddere. pietatem, sc. ~iam, exercere. castitatem amare W. BURLEY *Vit. Phil.* 30.

eusebius [εὐσέβειος], pious.

nos seriem patriam non frivola scripta tenemus, / discipulo eusebii Policarpo dante Johannis FRITH. 256; **1237** nos Graeci nitimur in omnibus observare orthodoxam et ~iam sententiam (*Lit. Archiep. Constant. ad Papam*) M. PAR. *Maj.* III 454; ~ius, i. pius *WW.*

eustomachicus [cf. εὐστόμαχος], (med.) eustomachous, palatable.

componatur [aloe] cum melle . . et sic erit eustomaticum GILB. VI 238. 2; *eu* quod est 'bonum' . . : inde . . eustomacicus *Alph.* 60.

eustrum v. haustrum. **eutheca** v. entheca.

euthenia [εὐθηνία], provisioning, supply, abundance. **b** prosperity.

ex secunde et tertie digestionis †essentia [vv. ll. eucta, euthiata, euthrata; ? l. euthinia] metheora semper confortatur ALF. ANGL. *Cor* 15. 4. **b** *him symle wæs / euthenia oftor on fylste, / æne on eðle ec ðon ðe se is / yfel on gesæd* (*Aldhelm*) *ASPR* VI 97.

euthimus v. euchymus. **euthrogeneus** v. heterogeneus. **eutiches** v. eutyches.

eutopia [εὖ + τόπια], fortunate place (w. play on *utopia*). *Cf. utopia.*

Utopia priscis dicta ob infrequentiam, / nunc civitatis aemula Platonicae, /. . Eutopia merito sum vocanda nomine MORE *Ut. pref.*

eutropia [εὐτροπία , ? *conf. w.* εὐτροφία], good disposition.

sub virtute sunt hujusmodi species, fortitudo, castitas, . . veritas, eutrophoya, que est virtus eligens medium circa ludos, verecundia [etc.] BACON XV 227.

eutyches [εὐτυχής], fortunate (man).

audiit eutiches [*gl.*: vel felix, *eu* Graece, 'bonum' vel 'bene', *tichos*, 'fortuna'] quid rex sibi contrahat FRITH. 619.

euuangelium v. evangelium. **euxhennum** v. exenium.

euzomon [CL < εὔζωμον], (bot.) rocket (*Eruca sativa*).

euzumon TURNER *Herb.* B 1 (v. eruca 1a).

evacio v. evasio 3.

evacuabilis, removable.

cum hoc non sit perfeccio sic nisi secundum quid ponens imperfeccionem ~em WYCL. *Log.* II 86.

evacuare [CL]

1 to empty (container; also fig.); **b** (place). **c** to unload (ship).

cavantur, ~antur, *þyrliaþ GlH* C 576; cave . . ne sic implearis sapore saeculi . . ut ~eris sapore Dei ANSELM (*Ep.* 8) III 110;. . nisi ~averis cor tuum ab omni alio amore *Id.* (*Ep.* 112) III 245; **s681** Aigulfus . . effracto a latere sepulcro, illud ~avit M. PAR. *Maj.* I 303; **s1260** aliorum crumenas immisericorditer ~avit FORDUN *Cont.* X 11. **b** Maximianus Britanniam centum triginta hominum milibus ~avit *Flor. Hist.* I 172 *rub.* (= M. PAR. *Maj.* I 172: vacuavit); **s1386** regnum Anglie gentibus armorum omnino ~atum *Plusc.* IX 40 (= FORDUN *Cont.* XIV 2: vacuatum). **c** **1234** quod mercatores . . [non] possent . . naves suas ~are *Cl* 552; **1264** vina illa in eadem navi duci faciet usque London' . . et . . cum ~ata fuerit reducetur ad partes de Wincheles' *Cl* 392; **1375** quando j batellus sit apud *le Stathe* ad vendendum, j alius batellus vel duo . . erunt apud T. quousque ille primus batellus ~etur *Leet Norw.* 65.

2 (med.) to evacuate, purge: **a** (organ); **b** (matter or humour); **c** (absol.).

a dat medicinam ~antem stomachum ab illo humore GILB. I 16v. 1. **b** dico quod [evacuatio] . . fit in die interpolationis [febris] cum non commiscentur humores boni cum malis: quare non ~antur boni in quantitate multa *Ib.* 17. 1; ~etur . . materia cum medicinis simplicibus seu compositis *Ib.* 17v. 1; de hiis que ~ant et consumunt humorem inducentem accidentia senectutis BACON IX 7; quousque materia peccans fuerit digesta et utiliter ~ata J. MIRFIELD *Brev.* 50; nihil . . sumens alimenti vel poculi, sed neque egestionis quiddam ~ans vel urine *Mir. Hen. VI* IV 127 p. 232. **c** de medicinis ~antibus: . . purgamus . . cum oximelle [etc.] GILB. I 41. 2.

3 to clear (of something). **b** to clean (out). **c** to deprive (w. abl. or *de*).

capsulam . . oculis [puellae caecae] adplicavit, quos statim ~atos tenebris lumen veritatis implevit BEDE *HE* I 18; sicut piger quis . . agrum suum . . tribulis ac spinis obsitum tardius ~at et emundat AILR. *Spec. Car.* II 21. 570B; dum . . agellulum suum . . ab inundatione aquarum pluvialium per rivulos ~aret COGGESH. *Visio* 5. **b** sicut domus scopis mundatur et ~atur AILR. *Serm.* 440C; **1366** injunctum est omnibus tenentibus ville quod ~ent cursum aque apud *le Northgayt Hal. Durh.* 57; **1423** ij ciste, unde j magna, et alia pro mappis ~andis *Ac. Obed. Abingd.* 98. **c** ut caper hirsutus rodit cum dente racemos, / floribus evacuans frondenti palmite vites ALDH. *VirgV* 2846; ecclesia suis pignoribus ~ata ad solum evertitur GOSC. *Transl. Aug.* 39D; crux ea te [demonem] stravit et viribus evacuavit R. CANT. *Malch.* II 459; corda . . quiete . . ~at AD. SCOT *OP* 491C (v. derogatio a); **s1398** ad tertium . . cursum Scotus Anglicum de duobus dentibus ~avit FORDUN *Cont.* XV 6.

4 to expel, drive out (person). **b** to remove, sweep away, get rid (of).

1202 ad ~andum eos [malefactores et latrones] de eis [insulis] *Pat* 15a; **s1312** possunt omnes armatos in civitate extraneos ~are *Ann. Lond.* 216; Octavianus . . infra paucos annos illos [consules] ~avit et regnavit xliiij annos solus *Eul. Hist.* I 313; rex Francie Philippus . . inutiles personas . . a curia sua . . exclusit et de toto regno ~are precepit *Plusc.* VII 1. **b** nil †ovis [l. ovi *or* avis] ~ati inventorem juvat inventio nidi *Collect. Stories* 203; baculus . . S. Cyricii ad glandiculas gibbosasque strumas . . ~andas penitus et delendas speciali quadam virtute prepollet GIR. *IK* I 1 p. 18; **1311** capellarii qui emunt capellas de extraneis habent diem ad deliberandum eos de eisdem . . et [concordatum fuit] quod ~ant falsas capellas citra festum Pasche *MGL* II 103; **c1362** in emendacione unius scope pro aqua ~anda in quarera, ij d. *Ac. Durh.* 566; **1373** injunctum est omnibus tenentibus ville quod ~ent quandam herbam vocatam *gold*, quilibet pro porcione sua *Hal. Durh.* 118; **1374** sustentabit clausur[am] . . pomerii et radices veterum arborum tempore debito ~abit *Ib.* 125; **1378** (v. evacuatio 3b); stirps extirpatur, flos arboris evacuatur GOWER *CT* II 298; **c1400** soluti J. S. . . ~anti pulverem ex quarera lvij s. viij d. *Fabr. York* 20.

5 to evacuate, leave (place); **b** (eccl.).

aiebat rex . . "vel juret mihi . . vel ~et regnum" W. MALM. *GP* I 50; luna meridiem tenente . . oceanus . . australia . . littora . . ~at GIR. *TH* II 3; **s1263** rex universitatem cleri Oxoniam ~are coegit *Flor. Hist.* II 487; redibis ad paginam *NS* usque ille habeat unum jactum, per quem oportebit ipsum ~are punctum *Φ Ludus Angl.* 163. **b** cum, obeuntibus possessoribus suis, ~atas dignitatum sedes hii optarent suis *V. Ed. Conf.* 41v.

6 (w. abstr. obj.) to impair, weaken, cause to disappear. **b** to obviate. **c** (intr.) to disappear.

magicum falsi fantasma Simonis / funditus evacuans taetras detrusit in umbras ALDH. *CE* 4. 1. 26; cum omnes ~atis viribus obstupuissent . . GOSC. *Wulfh.* 14; extirpetur omnis detractio, expellatur murmuratio, . . evanescat inutilium curiositas, . . ~etur indignatio ANSELM (*Ep.* 332) V 268; caloris vi ~ata GIR. *TH* I 6; ne . . quicquam attemptaret contrarium, quo gloriam eorum evacueret G. COLD. *Durh.* 21; **1219** ne . . posset predicte constitutionis vigor ~ari *Ch. Sal.* 95; animorum vim ~antes et enervantes robur corporum AD. MARSH *Ep.* 143; pro . . ~andis abusionibus veterum tyrannorum BRINTON *Serm.* 6; **s1404** in transitu [pape] ad ~andum . . populi pressuram . . jactabantur missilia in vulgus AD. USK 91. **b** ad quorum [bacciliorum] defectus omnes in futurum ~andos eis inveniendis redditus constituit G. COLD. *Durh.* 2. **c** succrescentibus vitiis virtutes in eo [sc. Will. II] penitus ~averunt GERV. CANT. *GR* 65.

7 to set at naught. **b** to bring to naught, frustrate. **c** to annul, nullify (esp. law); **d** (w. ref. to *1 Cor.* xiii 8).

peccatum maximum et negationem contra Deum . . admittere convincitur, divinam ordinationem damnabiliter ~ans AD. MARSH *Ep.* 141; Andromacha ~at minas Ulixis de morte dicens: "o Ulixe, vis cogere Andromacham metu" TREVET *Troades* 43. **b** si quis . . peccatum suum vel furtum detegere voluerit, tua justissima veritas hoc ~are dignetur (*Jud. Dei*) *GAS* 411; de litteris . . perditis et . . legatione . . sic ~ata major [causa contristandi] GIR. *RG* II 21; **s1389** non isto modo ad ~andum visitacionem processum est WALS. *HA* II 191; **1441** justa . . petiturus est que damna nostra ~ent et nobis pergrata existant (*Lit. Regis*) BEKYNTON I 137; furores insurgentium malignantiumque conatus secundum jura regni viriliter ~avit *Croyl. Cont. B* 535. **c** clericus quidam . . prevenerat . . hunc [electum Dubline] suis verbis nitebatur consecrationem illius ~are EADMER *HN* 348; omnia ejus [apostolice sedis pervasoris] facta ~ata W. MALM. *GP* I 23; factio istorum . . non implet sed ~at legem J. SAL. *Pol.* 592A; **1189** neque in posterum privilegia vestra vel cartas concedatis ~ari *Ep. Cant.* 292; **12..** omnes illas consuetudines . . per hanc cartam ~avi *Reg. Malm.* II 20; **s1201** rege Anglorum [Johanne] uxorato, ~ata videbatur illa sponsio quam . . fecerat Lodovico TREVET *Ann.* 168; OCKHAM *Pol.* I 284 (v. caerimonialis 2a); peticionem dux Lancastrie ~avit, dicens non esse equum *Chr. Westm.* 152; ~ato prioris composicionis obligatorio *Meaux* II 224; **1451** (v. annullare 3a); **1530** sciatis nos . . potestatem . . revocasse, ~asse, ac pro nichilo habuisse *Deeds Balliol* 129. **d** in qua videlicet patria [caelesti] sicut prophetia ~abitur . . sic et unda baptismi siccabitur BEDE *Gen.* (viii 11) 102; prophetia et scientia sunt imperfecta, ergo ~abuntur LANFR. *Comment. Paul.* (*1 Cor.* xiii 8) 199; quando prohetie ~abuntur facie ad faciem OCKHAM *Dial.* 749;.

8 to refute, counter. **b** (math.) to cancel. **c** to clear (debt).

800 quibus illius vesaniae litterulis . . respondere curavi, ~ans veracissimis sanctorum patrum sensibus omnes illius adsertiones ALCUIN *Ep.* 200; ut vestras assertiones ~arem W. MALM. *GR* II 202 p. 253; cum opinionem ejus aut fidem adversa probatio nequaquam ~aret J. SAL. *Pol.* 575B; nunc volo quasdam falsitates ~are juxta dicta BACON *Gram. Gk.* 56; demonstrationes geometrice . . ~ant penitus hanc responsionem *Id. Tert.* 128; istam objeccionem . . alii ~are conantur OCKHAM *Dial.* 463; ut penitus ~etur [sc. ista opinio] videndum est primo [etc.] PAUL. ANGL. *ASP* 1549. **b** si radicum medietas cum seipsa multiplicetur, hujus multiplicationis summa, multiplicationem quarte partis cum seipsa ac deinde cum quatuor multiplicate, sufficienter ~et, adequabit, vel delebit ROB. ANGL. *Alg.* 80. **c** **s1255** ut . . ea [maneria] . . donec debita ~arentur, retineret M. PAR. *Abbr.* 346.

9 (log.) to exhaust.

prima contrarietas est illa que ~at totum genus et adequatur illi BACON VIII 35; fieri in facto esse ~at fieri in potencia ut per se terminus DUNS *Metaph.* V 11 p. 284; terminus ~ans potenciam *Ib.*; ordo essencialis per sex ordines dividentes ~atur *Id. Prim. Princ.* 630; harum divisionum ostensio duo adhuc ostendi requirit, sc. quod membra cujuslibet inter se repugnent et quod ~ent racionem divisi *Ib.* 631.

evacuatio [LL]

1 emptying.

cum debilitatio insit corpori, ut quidam asserunt, ex desiccatione et ~one oris stomaci *Quaest. Salern.* B 77; **1399** in ~one dicti toralis calcis per operarios conductos *Fabr. York* 15.

2 (med.) evacuation, purging. **b** *domus evacuationis*, privy.

celebratis ~onibus, fiat bonum condimentum . . debilibus GILB. I 35v. 1; consumptio superflue humiditatis fit cum ~onibus et medicinis consumentibus humiditatem innaturalem BACON IX 5; regimen completum sanitatis . . consistit in his, que sunt cibus, potus, . . quies, ~o [etc.] *Id. NM* 540. **b** H. HUNT. *HA* VI 14 (v. domus 13).

3 expulsion, driving out. **b** removal, sweeping away. **c** drawing off, draining.

quamvis . . ex virtute comprimente facta ~one spirituum sit frigiditas naturaliter gravativa BART. ANGL. IV 2. **b** **1378** per subitam maris intemperiem totaliter cassatus existit, destructus, et evacuatus . . ita quod . . propter destruccionem et ~onem predicti Cobbe sive Conners nulla . . mercandisa venire seu cariari possunt *IMisc* 216/3 m. 2. **c** **s1431** complanata est strata Chirchestret cum . . lapidibus per industriam Willelmi Bakere in ~onem aquarum *Chr. S. Alb.* 63; **c1435** solut' Willelmo T. pro purgacione de *le goters* circa . . B. pro ~one aque infiltratis ibidem tempore pluviali, ij s. *Ac. Durh.* 624; **1472** solut' Johanni W. molendinario . . pro factura *del milnirynes* . . pro ~one aque et reimposicione ejusdem tempore mundacionis molendini de B. *Ib.* 643.

4 evacuation (of place).

c1333 sub pena juris nostri amissionis et tocius domus ~onis *Deeds Balliol* 121.

5 impairment, weakening.

horribilius . . grassari conspiciuntur evangeliorum ~ones, contradictiones legum, ecclesiarum vastationes [etc.] AD. MARSH *Ep.* 246 p. 421; dicta visio et fruicio [sc. divinae essencie], sine aliqua intercisione vel ~one, continuabitur usque ad finale judicium *Meaux* III 39; **s1410** in subversionem ecclesie . . et ~onem tocius religionis regni *Chr. S. Alb.* 56.

6 nullification.

a1104 doctor ille gentium, . . cum totus in legis ~one sudaret (MATHILDA REGINA) *Ep. Anselm.* V 245; est . . libertas ~o servitutis BRACTON 56; post promulgacionem evangelii et ~onem legalium . . temporalium OCKHAM *Pol.* II 657; **1571** pro ~one . . fictorum covinosorum et fraudulentorum feoffamentorum *Entries* 207b.

7 refutation.

propter ~onem unius maximi erroris qui sit in . . philosophia BACON *Tert.* 74; illa ~o est contra sentenciam necessariam de universalibus WYCL. *Ente* 79; pro ~one hujus testimonii non oportet . . glossare dicta istius testis (WYNTERTON) *Ziz.* 219.

evacuativus, (med.) evacuative, purgative; **b** (as sb. n.).

de medicinis ~is GILB. I 17v. 1; si aliquis voluerit dare medicinam ~am, sit hoc cum luna fuerit in signis aquaticis in ascendente ROB. ANGL. (II) 179; flobotomia minorativa et ~a GAD. 5. 1; fluxus ~i qui fit in ano, signa frequentia assellationis pauce *Ib.* 57v. 1. **b** digesta materia .. evacuanda est cum ~is flegmatis et melancholie commixtis GILB. I 43v. 2.

evacuatrix [cf. LL evacuator], dispeller, destroyer (f.).

ablata .. securitate noxia, que mater est et nutrix vitiorum, noverca autem et ~ix virtutum AD. SCOT *Serm.* 358B.

evacuere v. evacuare 6a.

evadare [cf. LL vadare], to ford, wade across.

duos .. ad eos direxit, qui illos ~are fluvium edocerent ORD. VIT. IX 14 p. 585; fluvio .. ~ato *Ib.* 6 p. 495 (v. enatare d).

evadere [CL]

1 to leave (place, fig.). **b** to issue, be emitted.

s1453 si billa dicta transiret, sive ~deret domum illam [sc. inferiorem Parliamenti] absque modificacione ulla, cessarent .. omnes preces *Reg. Whet.* I 93. **b** jam sine voce jacebat, vix tenuis flatus jam ~surus supererat in pectore palpitante supremus P. CORNW. *Rev.* I 205 p. 198.

2 to get away (also fig.); **b** (w. compl.); **c** (from pursuer, custody, or gaol); **d** (dep.). **e** (trans.) to escape (from person).

unam veluti post naufragium, in qua ad vivorum terram ~datis, paenitentiae tabulam .. exquirite GILDAS *EB* 110; reliqui, qui ~serunt, pacem .. pepigerunt ASSER *Alf.* 27; qui †eaudere [l. evadere] potuerunt, venerunt ad concives suos G. MON. V 16; **s1272** qui tandem per fugam ~dere desperans .. Edwardi se obtulit voluntati TREVET *Ann.* 283; **s1350** quidam tamen .. in navibus ~serunt AVESB. f. 121; ~do, A. *to a skapye WW*. **b** Christi suffragio fretus expers periculi sospes ~sit ALDH. *VirgP* 35; ex hujus vitae naufragio nudus ~dens *V. Greg.* p. 76; si vis ~dere liber a me, da mihi vij vaccas *VSH* (*Ciaran of Saigir* 19) I 229; **c1228** navis .. confracta est, omnes tamen homines .. salvi ~serunt (*Attest.*) *Feod. Durh.* 246. **c 1195** quando comes J. fregit gaoliam, ~sit cum aliis prisonibus *CurR RC* 103; **1201** misit ad deliberandum eum et non fuit inventus, set ~sit *SelPlCrown* 2; **1203** cum ~sisset de manibus suis †porrexit [= *SelPlCrown* 45: perrexit] ad villam *CurR* II 180; **1220** cognovit .. quod imprisonatus fuit in carcere .. et quod ~sit de carcere per auxilium vicecomitis *Ib.* VIII 396; **1221** ~sit de gaola et fregit gaolam et fugit *SelPlCrown* 102; **1255** ipse ~sit de prisona *SelPlForest* 12; **1320** de evasione duorum fugitivorum qui ~serunt de custodia predecessoris sui *Lit. Cant.* I 45; **1340** (v. deburgare a); **1440** gaolam .. fregerunt et ab eadem ~serunt *Pat* 448 m. 15. **d** clerici falsi, monachi ~si et quicumque Deum aliquo modo derelinquunt MAP *NC* I 29 f. 22; **1249** quedam dama †evadiata fuit de parco de N. et intravit campum de B. *SelPlForest* 90 (cf. ib.: dama ~sit de parco); **1300** ab eisdem nunciis non minima pericula in mari et itinere .. ~sis (*Lit. Archiep.*) *Ann. Lond.* 106; **1334** cum Simon esset ~sus a manibus eorum ibat querere viridarios *SelPlForest* 69; .. quanto cogor meminisse dolore / temporis illius, quo dolor omnis erat. / nunc tamen evasus quia vivo furore remoto, / cum laudis jubilo cautica solvo deo GOWER *VC* I 2081; **s1142** rege cum magna difficultate ~so BROMPTON 1032. **e** pugnabant contra invicem, qui hostem evaserant, cives BEDE *HE* I 22; non nos incolomis miser evasisse valebis WULF. *Swith.* I 529; **s1350** licet potuisset manus ipsorum cautius ~sisse, noluit .. adversariis tergum dare AVESB. f. 120b.

3 to survive, get by. **b** (med.) to survive, recover.

summa expensarum suarum xxxiij li. per v septimanas eundo redeundo et morando cum xj equis. et non sic ~sisset nisi vectigalia navigio transvexisset, quia hoc anno erat magna caristia bladi *Hist. Roff.* f. 39v.; in communibus in qualibet septimana non minus octo denariis ~dere valeo *Dictamen* 377. **b** in ~suris .. catuli precipue apparent in urina quia tunc malitia morbi expellitur *Quaest. Salern.* B 256; quidam febricitantes .. in fluvium projecti ~dunt *Ib.* Ba 47; M. SCOT *Phys.* 10 (v. determinare 1d); si egrotus manus ad pedes flexerit nullo modo ~det J. MIRFIELD *Brev.* 64.

4 (trans.) to avoid, escape (condition or event); **b** (spiritual). **c** (absol.) to avoid (tax).

sed Deus aeterna defendit ab arce puellam, / ut voti compos flammas evaderet ignis ALDH. *VirgV* 1998; sustentavit innumerabilem multitudinem egenorum qui, periculum famis ~dere cupientes, ad eum .. confugerant WULF. *Æthelwold* 29; si periculum aut naufragium ~seris *Descr. Constant.* 252; pluvias non ~des GIR. *TH* II 8; **s1191** ut mortem ~derent TREVET *Ann.* 127; **1390** (v. constare 3c). **b** ut .. sic mortem ~deret aeternam BEDE *HE* III 23; **957** (12c) sciat se .. tenebrosum Tartarum non ~dere *CS* 994; fac .. ut qui paschalibus remediis innovati similitudinem terreni parentis evassimus [AS: *we wideadon*] *Rit. Durh.* 33; qui pro pecuniis .. praesumunt plures in una die facere missas, aestimo non ~dere condempnationem ÆLF. *Ep.* 3. 76; precor .. ut ~dam .. dolores damnatorum ANSELM (*Or.* 6) III 17; licet poenam illorum qui Deum minime verentur ~dant ALEX. CANT. *Dicta* 10 p. 149; ?**1182** quod .. de transgressione tua canonicam non poteris ~dere disciplinam (*Lit. Papae*) ELMH. *Cant.* 455. **c** nisi commune geldum in villa venerit, unde nullus ~dat *DB* I 30.

5 (log.) to evade (argument). **b** to avoid, escape (conclusion).

fictio illius virtutis .. non ~et hanc objectionem BACON *Maj.* II 435; licet .. hec responsio videatur ~ere argumentum DUNS *Ord.* I 215. **b** dicunt .. impugnatores, quod ipse non ~dit, quin ex verbis suis, que asserit in constitucione [etc.] .. . sequitur quod [etc.] OCKHAM *Pol.* II 532.

6 (w. compl.) to end up, turn out (as).

audio .. te praedicatorem ~sisse perfectissimum et in divinis causas perorandis omnes tibi facile cessisse FREE *Ep.* 54.

evadiare [cf. vadiare], to discharge (debt).

aquiter, aquietare, ~iare, luere pignus, liberare, epignorare *Gl. AN Ox.* f. 153; **13**.. si burgensis queritur de aliquo burgense quod ei debitum debeat et alius cognoverit debitum, precipiet prepositus quod ipse ~iet debitum petenti, et ipse ~iet, et tunc precipiet ut ipse reddat debitum infra octo dies super forisfacturam (*Cust. Preston*) *EHR* XV 498.

evadiari v. evadere 2d.

evagari [CL]

1 (of person, esp. monk or cleric) to stray, wander about; **b** (fig.). **c** (of money) to 'go astray'.

in .. claustris .. cenobite .. clauduntur, ne si per exteriora tanquam Dina [*Gen.* xxxiv] .. impudenter ~antur ORD. VIT. V 14 p. 418; quam cito .. ~atur Dina opprimitur ab Emor filio principis terre R. NIGER *Mil.* I 22; **s1251** fratres .. minores .. non possent ad instantiam monachi qui eos .. suscipit .. quin ~arentur retineri M. PAR. *Maj.* V 264; ordo fratrum subintroductus est in ecclesiam ut suppleat defectus prelatorum et ~ancium clericorum WYCL. *Apost.* 20. **b** seditio plebes commovet .. et per abruta vitiorum letaliter ~ari cogit ORD. VIT. XII 21 p. 380; preceptum .. quo psalmista [*Psalm* xxxi 9] precatur eorum maxillas constringi qui per campos licentie ~antes ad Deum non approximant R. BOCKING *Ric. Cic. prol.*; baculus pastoralis in summitate est allectivus ut desides alliciat ~antes BRINTON *Serm.* 23 p. 95. **c 1441** ne porcio sive dos vicarie predicte ~etur ulterius sub incerto *Reg. Cant.* I 315.

2 (w. inanim. subj.) to spread, extend.

per investigabiles .. vias solus oceanus circumfertur et ~atur GIR. *TH pref.*; quatenus .. non sit in ea [fabricatione cordis] superfluitas ~ans in angulos in quibus lateant nocitiva *Ps.*-RIC. *Anat.* 21.

3 to wander, stray (in thought, speech, or sim.). **b** to digress (in writing).

'in civitate' quippe considemus si intra mentium nostrarum nos claustra constringimus ne loquendo exterius ~emur BEDE *Luke* (xxiv 49) 633; J. SAL. *Pol.* 389B (v. concupiscentia a); dispersis cogitationibus nostris misere .. per innumera ~amur AD. SCOT *QEC* 31 *tit.* 862A; ut .. visus tuus nullatenus ad aliud ~etur J. GODARD *Ep.* 239; sumus cum antiquis patribus una Spiritus Sancti fistula non ~antes per verba a sermonibus Dei extranea WYCL. *Ver.* II 152. **b** non est tempus illud pertractare ne nimis ~emur a proposito KILWARDBY *OS* 169; ne longius a serie propositi videar ~ari *Hist. Arthuri* 88.

evagatio [CL]

1 straying; **b** (of moon).

de .. ~one Dine [*Gen.* xxxiv] R. NIGER *Mil.* I 22 *tit.*; **1219** ~ones monachorum .. inhibeantur et si pro necessitate ecclesie sue .. proficiscantur [etc.] *Doc. Eng. Black Monks* I 17; **1423** (v. dyscrasia a). **b** in .. lasciva lune ~one a latere ad latus zodiaci sese moventis W. DONC. *Aph. Phil.* 3. 37.

2 wandering (of thought or sim.).

oratio .. demonstrans .. partim ~onis imaginarie licentiam BALSH. *Ut.* 45; ne quod lingua quasi orando proferre videtur, efficiente hoc cogitationum instabilium ~one, omni .. fructu spirituali privetur AD. SCOT *QEC* 31. 863C; de accidia nascuntur tristitia, malitia, .. cordis ~o circa prohibita EDMUND *Spec. Relig.* 32; omnes mentis ipsius ~ones transeunt in stabilitatem ROLLE *IA* 255.

evaginare [LL], to unsheathe (dagger or sword); **b** (fig.).

ALDH. *VirgP* 52 (v. capulus 1a); ~ata sub veste sica BEDE *HE* II 9; ~at, *uttihþ GlH* E 373; exerere, i. ~are, proferre, exercere, vel *abredan Ib.* 463; non evagines gladios, cultros alienos, / ni possessorum tibi sit permissa voluntas D. BEC. 1178; non hec [securis] ut gladius ~atur GIR. *TH* III 21; BRACTON 162 (v. compulsivus a); **s1406** dixit .. comes: "Tu es Petrus et super hanc petram [*Matth.* xvi 18] ~abo gladium meum .. " AD. USK 109; **1522** (v. cultellus 1c); **1554** (v. aeruginare c). **b** †**1012** (v. contradictio 2b); os tuum organum Spiritus Sancti esse videbatur, per quod ipsa divinitas sue predicationis ~avit officia *Ep. ad amicum* 2; **s1460** *Reg. Whet.* I 385 (v. evibrare).

evalescere [CL], **evalēre** [LL], to be able.

nec tamen evaluit fugiens evadere mortem ALCUIN *SSEbor* 551; et quis eum [sc. Deum] dignis efferre favoribus ardens / que velit, evaleat? subjacet eger homo L. DURH. *Dial.* III 520.

evallare [CL], to remove or (?) *f. l.*

1296 in stipendiis xxj .. marinariorum operancium per .. ij dies circa malum evallandum [? l. avallandum] de nave et illum trahencium in galeam usque ad schaffaldum *Ac. Galley Newcastle* 181.

evanescere [CL], **evanēre**

1 to lose strength, grow faint.

ab uno te [Deo] aversus in multa ~eo ALCUIN (*Confess. Fid.*) *Dub.* 1029A; divinorum series .. quanto sepius recitatur .. tanto audientis animus auditu expavescit .., magnitudinis consideratione ~escit DOMINIC *V. Ecgwini prol.*; venenosus vigor prorsus ~uit GIR. *TH* I 39; ~escunt WYCL. *Eccl.* 197 (v. evirescere).

2 to shrivel up, wither.

in illo [basilisco] non remanet nisi cutis que omnino desiccata ~escit et arescit *Quaest. Salern.* B 106.

3 to disappear; *v. et. devanescere*; **b** (of phantom or sim.); **c** (of sound); **d** (of abstr.).

aufugit, ~uit *GlC* A 944; ~esco, i. ~eo, *ic fordwine GlH* E 375; fatiscit, i. ~escit, dissolvitur, discedit, *ateorade Ib.* F 108; **1166** ut .. nec metu potestatis aut amore bonorum ~escentium iniquitati consentiat J. SAL. *Ep.* 191 (172); cera liquefacta .. in qua si figure .. protrahuntur, illico ~escunt et confuse fiunt *Quaest. Salern.* N 43; dum [fumus] durat .. facit sordere quousque ~escat TREVET *Troades* 32; *to vanysche away*, †evanare, ~escere, inanescere *CathA*; ~eo, A. *to vanshe a wey WW*; veniet angelus et accipiet librum ..; et claudet librum et †vuanesset [l. evanescet] *Chester Plays* XI 40. **b** arbitrantur .. Chaldearum .. fantasmata .. ~escere ALDH. *VirgP* 35; statim ~uerunt ob oculis meis .. diabolus ac ministri ejus *Descr. Constant.* 248; elegans et fortis cornipes subito deficiens ~uit (*Visio*) ORD. VIT. V 10 p. 384; spiritus blasphemus abscessit et in tenues ~escens auras ulterius non comparuit R. COLD. *Godr.* 220; ad crucis signaculum .. omnes versutie ejus ~escunt ALEX. BATH *Mor.* II 30 p. 151; diabolicas jubet ~escere fraudes H. AVR. *Hugh* 1085. **c** ~uerunt in cogitationibus suis [*Rom.* i 21] ignorantes prophetarum voces BYRHT. *V. Ecgwini* 351; C cum T consillabicatur, sed fere ~escit figuracio C et confunduntur clausiones *Ps.*-GROS. *Gram.* 25. **d** mundi prosperitas .. ut somnium ~escit ALDH. *PR* 142 (*Allocutio ad regem*); luxus, jocus, saltus, libido, luxuria certe ~uerunt ALCH. *Ep.* 299; ~escat inutilium curiositas ANSELM (*Ep.* 332) V 268 (v. evacuare 6a); estas .. debilem pulsum reddit .. propter quod ~escit virtus et debilitatur BART. ANGL. III 24; peccatum Ade .. / procul evanescit LEDREDE *Carm.* 10. 18.

evangelarium, ~iarium, evangelistary, lectionary containing the gospels. *V. et. evangelistarium.*

1245 item ~iarium et epistolarium adeo vetus quod fere nullius est momenti *Invent. S. Paul.* 497; **1401** duas legendas, duo collectoria, unum ~arium, unum epistolarium, sex gradalia *Pat* 363 m. 26; **1518** duo ~iaria quorum unum argenteum .. et aliud cuprum deauratum (*Vis. Thesaurariae*) *Reg. Aberd.* II 173.

evangelicare [cf. LL evangelizare], to announce, proclaim (good news). *V. et. evangelizare* 1.

cui astitit in visione persona ~ans ei nuntia bona. "surge" inquit [etc.] J. WORC. 41.

evangelicus [LL < εὐαγγελικός]

1 evangelical, of the gospel: **a** (w. ref. to book or page). **b** (as sb. m.) lectionary containing the gospels.

a c787 sit manus dextera .. ~is onerata paginis, ut cibis spiritalibus pascatur animus ALCUIN *Ep.* 4; cum liber ~us vel reliquie sanctorum super os obsesse [sc. a diabolo] .. ponerentur, [diabolus] ad inferiorem gutturis partem fugiebat GIR. *IK* I 12 p. 94; pulvinar subtrahitur ~is supponendum lateribus R. BURY *Phil.* 4. 65. **b c1220** unus ~us bene deauratus cum lapidibus viij *Process. Sal.* 169.

2 (w. ref. to specific text): **a** in the gospel; **b** (of person, thing, or story) mentioned in the gospel. **c** (as sb. n.) gospel saying.

a non .. omnes .. virginum catervas .. recipiendas ~us sermo spopondit [*Matth.* xxv 1] ALDH. *VirgP* 16; nota quomodo hoc pulchre priori convenit lectioni .. ~ae [*Matth.* iii 16] *V. Greg.* p. 102; **793** huic ~a auctoritas intonat: 'qui vos audit, me audit' [*Luke* x 16] ALCUIN *Ep.* 23; in quo dinoscimus parabolam ~ae lectionis impletam, quae dicit .. 'Qui .. usque in finem perseveraverit' [etc., *Matth.* x 22] LANTFR. *Swith.* 3; memento ~i precepti quo dicitur 'ego pro te rogavi, Petre' [*Luke* xxii 32] (*Lit. Papae*)

W. MALM. *GP* I 32; sententia illius textus ~i 'Quod factum est in ipso vita erat' [*John* i 3–4] (KYN.) *Ziz.* 83; **1462** cum loquente ewangelista [*Luke* ix] .. satiavit Dominus v milia hominum eo vero respectu ~o vos considerantes [etc.] *Lit. Cant.* III 238. **b 798** ~a vidua [*Mark* xii 42] ALCUIN *Ep.* 145; ut .. ad similitudinem ~ae gallinae [cf. *Matth.* xxiii 37] illos sub alis protectionis suae .. foveat ANSELM (*Ep.* 288) IV 208; servus ille ~us [*Matth.* xxv] qui acceptis in sorte v talentis alia v .. superlucratus est H. BOS. *Thom.* III 3; ille ceci illius ~i [*Mark* x 47] imitator egregius multo magis clamabat AILR. *V. Ed. Conf.* 764C; sal ~um [*Mark* ix 48–9] in omni sacrificio .. offerens ECCLESTON *Adv. Min.* 99; **s1382** J. Wyclif evangelium .. transtulit de Latino in Anglicam linguam non angelicam .. et sic ~a margarita spargitur et a porcis conculcatur [*Matth.* vii 6] KNIGHTON *Cont.* II 152; abbas ipse [A., ob. **1339**] apparatum historie ~e .. circa magnum altare cum decenti pictura preparavit *Meaux* II 312. **c 931** tendentes ad illud ~um, 'date et dabitur vobis' [*Luke* vi 38] *CS* 677; parum intelligens illud ~um 'omne regnum in se ipsum divisum desolabitur' [*Matth.* xii 25] G. MON. XI 9; **s1232** Hubertus .. considerabat illud ~um 'confiteor tibi, Pater celi et terre' [*Matth.* xi 25] M. PAR. *Maj.* III 228; **1235** utinam conveniat mihi illud ~um 'beati eritis cum maledixerint vobis homines' [*Matth.* v 11] GROS. *Ep.* 11.

3 (w. ref. to Christian preaching or doctrine); **b** (tradition or authority); **c** (manner of life).

famis .. ~i cibi culina ipsa vestrae animae viscera excomedens grassatur in vobis GILDAS *EB* 85; videamus .. quid ~a tuba .. sacerdotibus eloquatur *Ib.* 92; **†676** (12c) ~a et apostolica dogmata *CS* 43; Antonius, .. ~i seminis sator ALDH. *VirgP* 28; illas in partes navigare cogitavit et clarissima ~ae praedicationis luce torpentes .. populos .. inlustrare ALCUIN *WillP* I 5; cum tuba nobis personet ~a nisi qui .. certaverit neminem .. coronari T. MON. *Will.* II 2; his evangelica dispergere semina fas est GARL. *Myst. Eccl.* 389; **1301** Salvator Mundi .. postquam durum Mosaice .. ~e gracie suave jugum [*Matth.* xi 30] imposuit (*Lit. Papae*) *MGL* II 161; in .. ~is preceptis OCKHAM *Dial.* 635; **s1413** Lollardi, qui doctrinam ~am et apostolicam atque propheticam depravabant WALS. *YN* 438. **b 680** illud .. a fide catholica discrepat et ab ~a traditione discordat ALDH. *Ep.* 4; BEDE *HE* III 25 p. 186 (v. apostolicus 1a); **c795** cujus devotio a sectis perversi dogmatis fidem catholicam ~a soliditate munire non cessat ALCUIN *Ep.* 41; EADMER *HN* 119 (v. catholicus 2b); que .. synodus [sc. Nicena] habet auctoritatem ~am R. NIGER *Chr. II* 123; quatenus aut sanctio ~a aut canonica traditio non obsistit AD. MARSH *Ep.* 9; **s1297** papa .. in ecclesiis nobilibus plantat contra statuta ~a seculares *Ann. Worc.* 532. **c** sextum ~ae beatitudinis gradum consequi credatur ALDH. *VirgP* 21; quod paupertas ~a .. proprietatem rerum nequaquam excludit OCKHAM *Pol.* III 12; **1506** felicis vite semitam ante oculos depingi ~a frugalitas docet (*Lit. Regis*) *Scot. Grey Friars* II 279.

4 (w. ref. to person or symbol): **a** representing an evangelist, author of gospel. **b** who preaches the gospel. **c** (*doctor evangelicus*) Wycliff. **d** (as sb. m.) evangelist, author of gospel. **e** evangelist, preacher.

a Ezechiel .. propheta, egregius quattuor .. ~orum animalium inspector [*Ezek.* i 4–14] GILDAS *EB* 61. **b** Jacobus, Johannis frater .. protominister martyrque ~us *Ib.* 73; **799** ~o Aquilae [archiepiscopo Salisburgensi] Albinus salutem ALCUIN *Ep.* 185; post antiqua ~i protoparentis Anglorum Augustini solemnia GOSC. *Transl. Aug.* 15A; armis assumptis, quibus apostolus [*Eph.* vi 13] ~um hominem .. armat *G. Steph.* II 79; **1298** totus Christus .. omni die offertur .. per ministros evangelicos *Lit. Cant.* I 25. **c** R. DYMMOK 89 (v. doctor 2c). **d** (K.) iste philosophus non fuit ~us. (A.) non fuit ~us, sed rhetoricus. (K.) cur credimus ei? ALCUIN *Rhet.* 30; nemo rogans ~i sub amore Johannis / munere frustratus a rege recessit inanis *V. Ed. Conf. Metr.* I 412. **e** convertitur princeps ducum in ~um parvulum GOSC. *Aug. Min.* 751D.

5 (?) heavenly.

comminatio ~a mundano statui evidenter convenire videbatur, nam et tonitrus cum .. fulgure premissis adjungebantur M. PAR. *Abbr.* 299.

evangelista [LL < εὐαγγελιστής]

1 announcer of good news, preacher of the gospel; **b** (w. ref. to *2 Tim.* iv 5).

huic .. contubernio prepollebant quatuor ecclesiastici proceres, seu quatuor ~e, Mellitus, Justus, Paulinus, Rufianus GOSC. *Aug. Min.* 752D. **b** opus ~ae est bene vivere et bene dicere; moribus et verbis subjectos instruere LANFR. *Comment. Paul.* [*2 Tim.* iv 5] 367; **1238** ut .. pastor .. non affectet honorem .. sed onus, non divitias sed ~e opus GROS. *Ep.* 60.

2 evangelist, author of gospel.

de .. ~a .. quem Ezechiel [i 10] vultu declarat humano .. ita congruenter adstipulatur .. ALDH. *VirgP* 22; alter ~a ovem perditam ait in montibus, alter vero in deserto *V. Greg.* p. 106; **799** considerandum est, .. quod ille mirabilis ~a ait 'Verbum caro factum est' [*John* i 14] ALCUIN *Ep.* 166; ubi legimus in propheta aut ~a aut apostolo .. Deum unum esse tres personas ..? ANSELM (*Proc. Sp.* 11) I 209; singuli ~e sua volumina ediderunt J. SAL. *Ep.* 143 (209 p. 332); mysticas ~arum formas, nunc senas, nunc quaternas, nunc binas alas habentes GIR. *TH* II 38; AD. EYNS. *Hug.* V 16 p. 194 (v. canonicus 3a); de concordia ewangelistarum (*Catal. Durh.*) *FormOx* 241.

3 (dist. by name): **a** Matthew; **b** Mark; **c** Luke; **d** John.

a quem .. ~a Matheus a Christi genealogia seclusit M. PAR. *Maj.* I 30; **1261** in crastino B. Mathei ~e *Cl* 445; Mattheus ~a primo narrat quod 'diabolus assumpsit eum' [*Matth.* iv 5] OCKHAM *Pol.* I 339. **b** apostolica traditio, quae per beatum Petrum Romae praedicata per Marcum ~am .. confirmata est (*Ep. Ceolfridi*) BEDE *HE* V 21 p. 337; sit beatus Marcus martyr et ~a [AS: *godspellere*] .. adjutor *Rit. Durh.* 52; sanctus Marcus ~a, qui scripsit evangelium *Descr. Constant.* 256; WYCL. *Ver.* I 247 (v. canonicare 1b). **c** evangelium [*Luke* ii] quo virginalem partum .. S. Lucas ~a describit, recitatur AILR. *V. Ed. Conf.* 785B; **1200** a crastino S. Luce ~e *CurR* I 117; bellum in vigilia S. Luce ~e fuit commissum .. ideo dicit auctor 'nam Lucas medicus', i. S. Lucas ~a, qui fuit arte medicus (J. BRIDL.) *Pol. Poems* I 158; **1443** in crastino S. Luce ~e *Lit. Cant.* III 177. **d** beatus ~a Johannes BEDE *HE* III 25 p. 184; **c795** dicit .. Johannes ~a 'si fratrem, quem vides non diligis' [etc., *1 John* iv 20] ALCUIN *Ep.* 79; S. Franciscum, quem quidam .. dixerat sancto Johanni ewangeliste in stigmatum collatione prelatum ECCLESTON *Adv. Min.* 112; **a1447** sunt .. duo altaria .. in honore S. Johannis ~e AMUND. I app. 446.

4 St. John the Divine.

Johannes ~a scripsit Apocalypsim in insula de Patmos (J. BRIDL.) *Pol. Poems* I 129.

evangelistarium, evangelistary, lectionary containing the gospels. *V. et. evangelarium.*

1295 ~ium quo utuntur ad magnum altare est de peroptima litera et novum *Hist. S. Paul.* 327a; librum evangelii .. ad regem .. deportabit ad osculandum, deinde referet ad .. episcopum qui missam celebrat. quo vero ~io a dicto pontifice deosculato .. incipiatur offertorium *Lib. Regal.* 24v.

evangelium [LL < εὐαγγέλιον]

1 evangel, good news, gospel (of Christ); **b** (w. ref. to *Rom.* ii 16). **c** preaching of Christian doctrine, Christianity.

post .. praedicando Christi ~ium orbis paene circuitum GILDAS *EB* 73; ~ium, bona adnuntiatio *GlC Int.* 117; illum [panem] quem et vetus lex elegit ad significandam et ~ium ad exhibendam eandem veritatem ANSELM (*Azym.* 3) II 227; euuangelium domini Jhesu MAP *NC* V 4 f. 62; coruscantis ~ii revelata misteria AD. DORE *Pictor* 142; ~ium dicitur quasi 'bonum nuntium' HALES *Sent.* IV 44. **b** queritur quare dicitur '~ium Pauli' potius quam 'baptismus' *Ib.* **c c634** ut opus ~ii quod cepistis teneatis (*Lit. Papae*) W. MALM. *GP* I 32; a quibus praesulibus .. gratiam ~ii perceperint BEDE *HE pref.*; iterum eum in opus evangeli [v. l. ~ii] remisit ALCUIN *WillP* I 7; **c1240** vos .. estis quidam legis, prophetarum, et ~ii doctores GROS. *Ep.* 90; 'muti dogmate divino' quia non predicant divinam legem seu ~ium (J. BRIDL.) *Pol. Poems* I 158.

2 (pl.; four) gospels; **b** (collect.); **c** (dist. by name); **d** (w. ref. to specific passage); **e** lection from gospel.

iiij ~iorum libros ex ordine didicit BEDE *HE* V 19; **a792** utinam ~ia quattuor, non Aeneades duodecim pectus compleant tuum ALCUIN *Ep.* 13; qui [sc. Graeci] ~ia nobiscum venerantur ANSELM (*Proc. Sp.* 1) II 177; ewangeliorum / scriptores Christi purissima verba perenni / inscripsere libro H. AVR. *Poems* 43. 66; **1329** (v. 1 canon 3). **b** mihi videtur servitium Dei .. primatum tenere, sicut legitur in ~io [AS: *on godspelle*] ÆLF. *Coll.* 99; nomen Jesu venerabatur et verba sancti ~ii devotissime recolebat ECCLESTON *Adv. Min.* 125; **s1382** (v. evangelicus 2b); in ~io Jhesu Christi una et eadem historia per quatuor evangelistas approbatur *Plusc.* VI *prol.* p. 5. **c** in ~ium Marci libros iiij, in ~ium Lucae libros vj BEDE *HE* V 24 p. 358; **793** Augustinus .. in expositione ~ii secundum Johannem .. ait [etc.] ALCUIN *Ep.* 23; S. Kiaranus ~ium Mathei .. cum aliis legebat *VSH* (*Ciaran of Cluain* 17) I 206. **d** iterum in ~io Dominus 'venite ad me omnes' [etc., *Matth.* xi 28] GILDAS *EB* 36; **796** Christus in ~io [*Matth.* ix 14] respondit interrogantibus se quare discipuli illius non jejunarent, dicens [etc.] ALCUIN *Ep.* 109; sicut Dominus in ~io ait 'ubicumque fuerit corpus' [etc. *Luke* xvii 37] ÆLF. *Æthelwold* 2; ex verbis Filii .. / qui fidem recipi .. / duorum judicat vel trium testium [*John* viii 17] / sicut lex edocet et euuangelium WALT. WIMB. *Carm.* 289; in ewangelio [ME: *þe godspel*] de tribus Mariis sic scribitur Marci xvj°, 'ut venientes ungerent Jhesum' *AncrR* 148. **e** THEOD. *Pen.* II 2. 11 (v. cappa 3a); diaconus vero, antequam ad ~ium [AS p. 406: *god spelle*] legendum accedat *RegulC* 34; pronuncietur ~ium et ex eo sermo agatur LANFR. *Const.* 93; **1295** lecta ~ia 'Credo' ibiden incepit *DCCant. Reg. Q* f. 27a.

3 book, lectionary containing gospels; **b** (used in oath-taking).

quattuor ~ia de auro purissimo in membranis depurpuratis .. scribere jussit EDDI 17; **1390** quatuor ewangelia .. in uno volumine *FormOx* 241. **b 855** in iiij ~iorum Christi libris cum suo arrato confixum et sub Dei foenore panum *CS* 490; **1172** super sanctum ~ium unusquisque eorum confirmavit [etc.] *Act. Hen. II* I 582; **c1220** etc. (v. corporaliter 1d); **1304** (v. corporalis 1d); **1474** praestito .. juramento super Dei ewangelia *Lit. Cant.* III 290.

evangelizare [LL < εὐαγγελίζειν]

1 to announce, proclaim (good news or sim.). *V. et. evangelicare.*

angelus .. ~abat pastoribus gaudium magnum [cf. *Luke* ii 10] BEDE *CuthbP* 27; ~at, adnuntiat *GlC* E 322; neomartyris gloriam .. ~atam H. BOS. *Thom.* VI 11 (cf. ib.: ~ata palma).

2 to preach (trans.); **b** (w. acc. & inf.).

qui verbum Dei genti Anglorum ~arent BEDE *HE* V 24 p. 353; sint speciosi pedes ejus ad ~andum verbum tuum [cf. *Rom.* x 15] EGB. *Pont.* 2; qui olim ~ando regnum Dei illuc perveniens OSB. *V. Dunst.* 6; una secum Anglis Christum ~ando GOSC. *Aug. Min.* 757D; Ninia .. qui .. Christi predicationem ~avit W. MALM. *GP* III 118 p. 256; **1235** cum omnibus sitis debitores ~andi verbum salutis GROS. *Ep.* 16. **b** ipse ~at Deum fuisse in Christo mundum reconciliantem sibi [cf. *2 Cor.* v 19] AD. SCOT *Serm.* 407D.

3 (absol.) to preach the gospel: **a** (w. Christ as subj.); **b** (w. preacher as subj.); **c** (pr. ppl. as sb.).

a c790 exemplum Christi .. qui per civitates, .. vicos, villas ~ando iter agebat ALCUIN *Ep.* 28; ait .. Auctor ~andi 'si diligis me, pasce oves meas' [cf. *John* xv 15 etc.] AD. MARSH *Ep.* 100. **b** praebuit palam adsensum ~anti B. Paulino rex BEDE *HE* II 14 p. 113; cum per loca singula discurrendo .. ~andi opus exercuisset ALCUIN *WillP* I 6; ~avit .. qualiter nunquam ante ~avit ADEL. BLANDIN. *Dunst.* 11; Marcus ~andi causa Alexandriam proficiscens J. SAL. *Pol.* 416C; si aliquis ~aret contra apostolicam doctrinam sequitur quod sit anathema OCKHAM *Dial.* 574 (*recte* 575); *CathA* (v. categorare). **c** non ergo stipendium ~antibus est negandum sed non propter hoc evangelizandum GIR. *GE* I 49; si populus fuerit sic obstinatus .. quod non ministret necessaria suo evangelizanti .., tunc necesse est eum ad alium populum declinare WYCL. *Ver.* III 36; [Apostoli] appellantur .. pastores, piscatores, ~antes similiter omnes BEKINSAU 750.

4 (intr.) to read or sing the gospel.

procedente quoque ad ~andum diacono (*Pont. Magd.*) *HBS* XXXIX 160.

evangelizatio [LL], preaching.

a prechynge, catagoria, .. ~o, predicacio, predicamentum *CathA*.

evangelizator [LL], preacher.

1239 episcopi verbi Dei ~ores cum evangelistis celestia sunt animalia GROS. *Ep.* 127; ~or hereticalis doctrine OCKHAM *Dial.* 574 (*recte* 575); baptizatus est a Finano .. assumptisque secum quatuor ~ibus WHITTLESEY *app.* f. 26v. p. 159; **1425** apostolicis .. viris et ~oribus Christi in necessariis usibus nulla tribuere apud Jeronymum seipsum condempnare est *Reg. Cant.* III 137.

evangelus [LL < εὐάγγελος], bringing good news.

invide, corrodis †evangele [l. evangela] scripta Maronis / splendoremque solis diminuisse cupis [cf. Virgil *Ecl.* IV] NECKAM *DS* V 15.

evanidus [CL]

1 becoming feeble.

~us, insipidus *GlH* E 372.

2 transient.

~us, qui cito evanescit OSB. GLOUC. *Deriv.* 193; .. considera cutis florarium / preclarum hodie sed cras inglorium; / quam sit evanidum, quam perfunctorium WALT. WIMB. *Carm.* 338.

evantagium v. avantagium 2d.

evanuare [*backformed from* evanui *perf. of* evanescere], to cause to vanish.

sanctus singulas species illusorias, edito signo crucis, ~avit J. FURNESS *Walth.* 66.

evaporabilis, evaporable, that can be evaporated.

GILB. I 59. 1 (v. consumptibilis); qui [lapides] facile secabiles sunt, humidum unctuosum non facile ~e pro humido continuativo habent *Ps.*-GROS. *Summa* 632.

evaporare [CL]

1 to emit. **b** (fig.) to utter, air (notion).

716 ut .. nihil tam durum foetorem ~ans .. videret quam proprium corpus BONIF. *Ep.* 10; per pororum etiam apertionem ex vi caloris fit spirituum evaporatio, ex quorum presentia corpus levabitur; quibus ~atis per ipsorum absentiam aggravatur BART. ANGL. IV 1; si materia situata est in membro raro, cito ~atur: si spissa, diu durat GILB. I 11. 2. **b** W. MALM. *GP* I 45 (v. decoquere 3c).

2 (intr.) to evaporate, be emitted or dispersed: **a** (of liquid); **b** (of smoke, vapour, or sim.); **c** (med.); **d** (fig.).

a si [pannum humectatum] apropries igni, totam domum obnubilabit aqua inde ~ans S. LANGTON *Gl. Hist. Schol.* 42; quousque humiditas ~et M. SCOT *Lumen* 264 (v. bullire 1a). **b** suavis odoris fragrantia ~ans illius [sancti] infudit se naribus J. FURNESS *Walth.* 134; NECKAM *Ut.* 117 (v. 1 caminus 2b); *Quaest. Salern.* P 83 (v. evaporatio 1a). **c** excoctus .. et purgatus sanguis ~ans unitusque materie temperate .. organum creat spongiosum ALF. ANGL. *Cor* 14. 7; si .. colera menstrua distemperet ea sui levitate .. ascendens et ~ans, cerebrum ad caliditatem disponit *Ib.* 15. 4; sunt quidam qui habent in se corruptos humores et veneno similes unde spiritus ab eis semper per resolutionem ~ans quasi venenum est *Quaest. Salern.* B 56; in .. hominibus amorosis, in quibus spiritus cordis incipiunt ~are UPTON 108. **d** affluunt divitie, influunt delicie, ~at vana gloria, que omnia curam carnis operantur in concupiscentiis R. NIGER *Mil.* III 39.

3 to boil off (trans.).

~a aquam cum lentissimo igne RIPLEY 197; ~etur aqua vel destilletur in lento igne *Ib.* 216.

4 to become hot.

~o, A. *to wexe hote WW.*

evaporatio [CL]

1 evaporation, exhalation; **b** (fig.).

propter multam pororum apertionem et spiritus naturalis ~onem *Quaest. Salern.* B 138; quando exterius [aloe] partes aeree et ignee de facili evaporant cum non habeant quod ~onem prohibeat *Ib.* P 83; per ~onem ipsius [odoris] a corpore odorifero diminuitur ipsum corpus J. BLUND *An.* 201; BART. ANGL. IV 1 (v. evaporare 1a); BACON VIII 203 (v. digestivus c); *Id.* XIV 79 (v. evaporativus a). **b** [Christus dicitur] ignis propter gratie ~onem BART. ANGL. I 21.

2 (med.) treatment inducing evaporation.

fiant ~ones exterius de malva GAD. 119. 2.

evaporativus [LL], evaporative, able or causing to evaporate; **b** (as sb. n.) medicament causing evaporation; *v. et. evaporatorius.*

quoddam est ~um ponens fumum et vaporem materie, ut est jejunium; et quoddam subtiliat et liquefacit GILB. VI 237v. 2; natura saporabilis et saporis est in se terminata, quia non est ~a neque sui multiplicativa .. et ideo non est sapor sui multiplicativus via evaporationis BACON XIV 79. **b** oportet .. apponere ~a; sed quia materie per spiritus qui evolantur per poros debet fieri digestio, cavendum est ut statim apponantur confortativa stiptica GILB. I 23v. 1.

evaporatorius, (as sb. n.) medicament causing evaporation. *V. et. evaporativus* b.

docet facere ~ium siccum, ut quod prehumectatum erat et temperatum sicco evaporetur GILB. IV 192. 1; ~ia et inunctiones et embrocationes GAD. 120v. 1.

evardum v. eswarda 1.

evasio [LL]

1 escape (from danger); **b** (from damnation or sim.).

ministri falsitatis dominum repedarunt iniquitatis, ~onem suam pro magno reputantes HERM. ARCH. 3; **1236** difficilis videtur ~o quin incidam in manus hominum [cf. *Heb.* x 31] GROS. *Ep.* 26; **1263** sicut aviculam que quanto ad ~onem fortius innititur tanto firmius alligatur (*Lit. Imp. Frederici*) W. GUISB. 180; **s1380** cum naufragi post periculorum ~onem monasterium de B. intrassent *Chr. Kirkstall* 123. **b** intercapedo quietis .. nostrae ~onis gratia caelitus donata est BEDE *HE* V 1; stagnum .. ubi anime expiande post purgantis incendii ~onem immergebantur COGGESH. *Visio* 33; **1451** ne majores quam minores magistratus et subditos, ulcionis divine furor .. invadat et invasos sub inevitabilitate ~onis concludat *Reg. Heref.* 9.

2 escape (of king or magnate from captivity).

[Ludovicus] rex [Francorum] de ~one sua letus regreditur Laudunum W. JUM. IV 8; **1234** rex perdonavit ei [sc. Huberto de Burgo] ~onem de castro suo de Divisis *BNB* II 667; **s1302** de restitucione et ~one [prioris] Ricardi de carcere GRAYSTANES 25 *rub.*; **s1413** per omne tempus illud quod fluxit ab ~one ejus [sc. regis] usque ad .. Epiphaniam, discurrebant undique Lollardorum nuncii WALS. *YN* 446; **s1265** de ~one principis Eadwardi et bello de Eveshame FORDUN *Cont.* X 20 *tit.*

3 escape (of criminal from custody) or fine payable by person responsible for escape.

a1188 (v. apprehendio 1c); **1198** Waltero O. dim. m. per plegium pro ~one Thome *CurR RC* I 173; **1221** cepit de eadem thethinga pro ~one c s. *PlCrGlouc* 54; **1242** W. C. .. de prisona evasit, et ideo loquendum de evacione *AssizeR Durh.* 1; **1300** dicti gressemanni, si ~o latronum evenerit, respondebunt de ~one *IPM* 96/32; **s1340** rex .. condonavit omnia catalla felonum .., ~ones incarceratorum, fines et forisfacciones *Eul. Hist.* III 204; **1494** pro carceris ~one et fraccione .. petiit instantissime libertatem *Sanct. Durh.* 55.

4 (fine for) straying (of animal). *V. et evasura.*

1292 quod nullas ~ones nec emendas exhibeant de animalibus predictorum .. infra metas de W. *BBC* (*Warrington*) 383.

5 escape, draining (of water).

1311 G. de S. .. fecit fossatum pro ~one aque molendini sui *Reg. Gasc. A* 305.

6 evasion, excuse; **b** (log.).

multas responsiones et ~ones, que ad quasdam impugnaciones nostras dari poterant, patenter exclusit OCKHAM *Pol.* III 11; **s1304** quem interrogando quo iturus esset .. multas excusaciones et ~ones multiplicavit *Plusc.* IX 6. **b** quia habent quasdam ~ones falsas, ideo alique considerande sunt BACON *Tert.* 124; propter ~onem illius objectionis non debet fingi talis virtus *Id. Maj.* II 435; videtur esse quod .. ex ista ~one videretur destructa omnis via probandi unitatem alicujus conceptus univocam DUNS *Ord.* III 20; aliam ~onem habent sophiste, concedendo quod totum est sue partes; et sic dicunt, copulativam esse universalem et particularem, affirmativam et negativam; et tamen nec est universalis nec affirmativa, sed est ille partes WYCL. *Log.* II 21.

evasor, escaper, fugitive.

fraudulentus ~or dux Andegavie .. filius .. Johannis quondam regis Francie, qui patrem in captivitate .. reliquit J. READING 194b.

evasura, (fine for) straying (of animal). *V. et. evasio* 4.

1236 recepcio .. de ~is averiorum lx, xix s. x d. *KRAc* 131 r. 21.

1 evax v. euax.

2 evax [? cf. CL aevum + -ax], aged lady, dowager (w. ref. to queen mother). *Cf.* 1 *avia.*

955 (13c) Þulfhelm presul, Aldred antistes, Eadgeofu euax [? l. aevax], Eadþig cliton, Eadgar *æþling* et ceteri duces .. consensum prebuerunt *Ch. Burton* 13; **956** (12c) Ædgiva efax genitrix regum *CS* 1346 (= *Lib. Eli.* II 28).

evectio [CL]

1 transporting, conveyance; **b** (w. subj. gen.). **c** unloading (of ship).

que [trabes] magno coempte pro longinquitate itineris ~onis difficultate pretium auxerant W. MALM. *GP* V 216; comitantibus .. se clericis qui sanctum adveherent .. preparant ~oni necessaria AILR. *SS Hex* 15; mercatores possunt percipere pretium laboris sui et ~onis sue T. CHOBHAM *Summa* 301; **1527** pro ~one fimi xxj d. *Cant. Coll. Ox.* II 260. **b** **s1315** [monachi] spretis equorum ~onibus .. in aque medio .. perierunt *Flor. Hist.* III 170 (cf. ib. 173: relictis .. gurgitum evexionibus, ad parliamentum Lincolnie .. accessit). **c** **1393** Thomas dampnum non modicum est perpessus pro eo saltem quod, navis ejus ~one priori frustrata, ad partes suas absque ~one rediit aliquali *Dip. Corr. Ric. II* 144.

2 means of transport, esp. horse. **b** (w. ref. to eccl. procuration) retinue. **c** (pl.) traffic.

quod ubicunque invenietis clericos .. equitantes, vobis liceret eos de suis ~onibus dejicere P. BLOIS *Ep.* 82; indigeo mitti ~ones ut .. versus vos iter arripere valeam AD. MARSH *Ep.* 27; **1263** multis ~onibus indigemus tam pro cariagiis quam negociis aliis *Cl* 306; **s1312** quem [sc. Gaveston] comes simplicem ascendere jussit ~onem et in castellum suum .. secum adduxit *Flor. Hist.* III 152; *G. Hen. V* 12 (v. desidia b). **b** ut .. [quidam episcopi] multas sequelas et ~ones innumeras circumducere possent GIR. *JS* 1 p. 135; **1246** nonnulli archiepiscopi .. personarum et ~onum numero taxato .. non contenti ad vestra monasteria causa procurationis recipiende in anno non semel sed frequenter accedunt (*Lit. Papae*) *Dryburgh* 192; **c1327** de mittendis .. pro adventu vestro ~onibus et familia .. per vestras nos expedit literas premuniri J. MASON *Ep.* 32 p. 216; **1400** deputavimus nocturnam requiem in villa de Kyngeston .., illucque ~ones cum jocalibus, ministros quoque, qui pararent et disponerent pro necessariis, premisimus *Lit. Cant.* III 73; [Alexander III] statuit .. in curia cujuscumque prelati .. certum et paucum numerum fieri ~onum, quia multitudo equorum non necessariorum destruxit sustentacionem FORDUN *Cont.* X 41. **c** **1434** per inhonestata commercia .. denigratur .. cimiterium per bruta animalia .., ventilaciones granorum, aliaque ~onum diversa genera per .. cimiterium .., quod regie strate .. pocius quam cimiterio .. valeat assimilari *Reg. Heref.* 181.

3 'evection', upward movement, exaltation. **b** exalted position.

995 (12c) quos istius aevi fortuna manu tepide ~onis alludit *CD* 692. **b** **c990** talis excellentiae dignitatem, tantaeque ~onis virum B. *Ep.* 386.

evectura [cf. CL evectus], means of transport. *V. et evectio* 2b.

1325 ita quod [decanus .. et canonicus] habeant .. xxiiij equos et in locis singulis per ipsos visitandis in esculentis .. et aliis necessariis pro equis, famulis et ~is suis .. honorifice procurentur *Stat. Linc.* II 127.

evedlonda v. hevedlanda.

evehere [CL]

1 to convey, carry out or away; **b** (person, esp. across water).

~it, portat *GlC* E 344; ~endus *to ferienne GlP* 375; cum .. omnia evecta erant de navibus que erant necessaria itineri *G. Hen. V* 3. **b** GILDAS *EB* 18 (v. 1 curuca); *Ib.* 23 (v. cyula); rex Arturus letaliter vulneratus .. ad sananda vulnera sua in insulam Avallonis evectus .. Constantino .. diadema .. concessit G. MON. XI 2; NETTER *DAF* II 209 (v. cessibilis).

2 to carry or lift up; **b** (to heaven). **c** to exalt. **d** (pass.) to inveigh (against).

798 qui de pulvere evexit Dominus potest de creatura facere quae vult ALCUIN *Ep.* 158; **9..** evectus, *upwegen WW*; candens saxum quadratum offendit, quo paululum evecto, erumpens vapor nardifluus GOSC. *Transl. Aug.* 17C; cum celi .. fragoribus concussa terra tremens ~i sub plantis videretur *Chr. Battle* f. 39v. **b** quis .. ob invidiam melioris hostiae caelestique igni in caelis evectae, ut Abel, occisus? GILDAS *EB* 69; angelicis evectae catervis .. ad caeli sidera scandunt ALDH. *VirgP* 51; qui evectus florentibus / paradisi cespitibus / sociatus sublimibus / angelorum cum milibus / regnat (ÆTHELWALD) *Carm. Aldh.* 2. 89; atque Gregorius hinc evectus ad astra volavit *Kal. Met.* 18; qui sponsam Christi ecclesiam .. strenui naute de salo hujus seculi ad portam vite evexerunt HON. *Spec. Eccl.* 1016B. **c** episcopi ministros .. ambitionis quodam evectos cothurno *Chr. Battle* f. 53. **d** terribilibus minis in hostes .. ~itur ORD. VIT. VII 14 p. 223.

3 (p. ppl. as sb. n.) promontory.

s1176 vario desudans navigio .. ducatum Appulie, Capue principatum, evexa Calabrie .. pertransiit DICETO *YH* I 417.

evellerare [cf. CL vellus], to pluck (wool). *Cf. avellere* a, *evellere* 2b.

1288 Beatrix la Q. et Acilia socia ejus assuete sunt evellere bidentes et ~averunt vellera bidentium J. M. capellani *Leet Norw.* 4; **1324** consuetus tondere et ~are lanam de bidentibus vicinorum *JustIt* 1165 r. 19.

evellere [CL], **~are**

1 to tear up, uproot (plant). **b** to dig up, chip away (stone). **c** to dig out, extract (artifact). **d** to exhume (cadaver).

Orion .. ornos aut ingentia robora de montibus evulsa radicitus traxit *Lib. Monstr.* I 56; **c745** (DAN. WINT.) *Ep. Bonif.* 64 (v. comma 1a); ~et, i. eruet, *alyft*; ~it, i. eradicat, exstirpat, *ut alucþ GlH* E 380–1; OSB. GLOUC. *Deriv.* 199, MAP *NC* I 24, etc. (v. eruncare); tribulos et spinas .. agricola evulsit *V. Gund.* 29; utrum [planta] habeat animam, sive ~atur a ramo vel a radice BACON XI 242; omnes .. herbas qui sub isto curru sunt ~e *VSH* (*Boece* 27) I 95. **b** onagri .. saxa de montibus ~unt *Lib. Monstr.* II 3; de fragmentis que latomi de informi lapide marculis evulserant fideles collegerunt ORD. VIT. XI 27 p. 262; **c1275** in petra ad novam bercariam de Farendone ~anda et carianda xxvj s. vj d. *Ac. Beaulieu* 166. **c** ingens choruscatio .. ferreos de cruce clavos evulsit ORD. VIT. V 3 p. 307; **1349** in factura unius *spatour* pro lectuariis in garderoba prioris de pixidibus ~endis, v d. *Ac. Durh.* 549. **d** si apta videtur [aecclesia] ad consecrandum, inde evulsa [sint cadavera infidelium] et rasis vel lotis lignis ejus, reaedificetur THEOD. *Pen.* II 1. 4.

2 to tear at, pluck out, cut off (part of body). **b** to pluck, pull (hair or wool); *v. et. avellere* a; *cf. evellerare.*

ut .. impleret Christi mandatum dicentis oculum dextrum scandalizantem ~i debere [cf. *Matth.* v 29] GILDAS *EB* 69; **s797** oculos evulserunt *AS Chr.*; citius .. potest in se confidens humana sapientia impingendo cornua sibi ~ere quam innitendo petram hanc evolvere [cf. *Ezek.* xxxiv 21, *Psalm* xliii 6] ANSELM (*Incarn. B*) II 7; si .. homo .. ita peccasset ut dominus ei .. oculos ~ere .. posset .. ALEX. CANT. *Dicta* 1 p. 111; palpebris ejus turpiter evulsis R. COLD. *Cuthb.* 44 (cf. ib.: lumina distorta vibrare); queritur dens apri evulsus ab ore ejus, quare eo vivente radat *Quaest. Salern.* B 162; talis erit quod .. si diem inter nos non tenueris assignatam .. habeam sine condicione omnes carnes tui corporis ~ere cum gladio acuto *Latin Stories* 116. **b** lugentes crines et barbas ~unt ORD. VIT. VII 12 p. 212; **1288** (v. evellerare); **1307** in .. pellibus lanutis ~andis *MinAc* 1079/18 m. 8.

3 to cleave, pull down, tear apart. **b** to root out, get rid of (abstr.).

solo sternerentur .. ima turrium edito cardine evulsarum murorumque celsorum saxa GILDAS *EB* 24; ~it, repulit *GlC* E 334; dum .. [frumentum] conteritur in mortario, aer qui ex concussione calefit, dum ibi iterum pilo ~itur, et exalat, et frigiditas inde succedit *Quaest. Salern.* B 131; **1209** in custo mairemii venientis de foresta .. ad molindinum et carpentario ad ~andum mairemium *Pipe Wint.* 60; **s1265** (v. construere a); **1538** (v. divisivus c). **b** quis memoriam malefacti de corde radicitus, ut Joseph, evulsit? GILDAS *EB* 69; ~endus est error OCKHAM *Pol.* III 280; **1420** pro redintegranda pace ~endisque dissidiis *Ps.*-ELMH. *Hen. V* 91; de mentibus simplicium .. hunc errorem ~ere PAUL. ANGL. *ASP* 1542.

4 (w. personal obj.) to tear away, dislodge (from; partly fig.).

de ergastulo / carnis evulsus (ÆTHELWALD) *Carm. Aldh.* 2. 86; ut . . nihil . . sit quod ab ejus firmitate me valeat ~ere ANSELM (*CurD* 1) II 48; monachus . . vitam claustralem . . fastidit querens . . qualiter ab ea ~atur et transplantetur NIG. *Ep.* 17.

evenire [CL]

1 to come forth or out; **b** (w. abstr. subj.). **c** to go too far, transgress.

si . . soror mea partum edidit masculum, ad me cum partu ~iat *VSH* (*Berach* 4) I 76; **1338** (v. claccum); **1503** pro secularibus sacerdotibus cum ~erint in illo altare missam celebraturis *Invent. Ch. Ch.* 133. **b** ?**a1105** quam intolerabile . . malum inde . . ~turum sit . . cognoscere poteritis ANSELM (*Ep.* 340) V 278; ex hoc . . bonum ~iet *VSH* (*Boece* 29) I 96. **c c1300** si . . contigerit . . aliquos . . contra dictam ordinacionem in aliquo ~ire, et super hoc sint convicti (*Ordinatio*) *MGL* II 94.

2 a (w. dat. or *ad* & acc.) to belong, fall (to). **b** to accrue.

a Fledanburh . . quod sibi ~it ex hereditate uxoris sue DOMINIC *V. Ecgwini* I 9; **1270** terras . . que ad propartem ipsorum . . ~ire debent *Cl* 298. **b c1132** ij s. de Danegeld, i. e. the[n]manetale, quoque anno ~iebant super illas ix carrucatas *Cart. Rievaulx* 142; **c1200** cum omnibus evencionibus que ~ire possunt de . . predicto redditu *AncD* C 4048; **12..** cum omnibus aliis rebus et eschaetis, que mihi . . possent ~ire et accedere *Reg. Malm.* II 90; **12..** coquinarius tenet villam de A. . . et quecunque inde ~irent, sive de placitis sive de ceteris eventionibus coquinarii erunt *Cust. Abingd.* 306.

3 to come about, happen, occur; **b** (w. ref. to date); **c** (w. adverbial pred.); **d** (w. *ut*); **e** (w. inf. or acc. & inf.). **f** (p. ppl. or gdv. *s. act.*).

id si forte casu ~erit . . non prodest GILDAS *EB* 108; cruenta fors ~it ALDH. *VirgP* 38; sicut semper populo qui odium incurrerit Dei ~ire solet ASSER *Alf.* 27; LANFR. *Const.* 168 (v. durus 2a); quod . . anno necdum completo vidimus ~isse GIR. *TH* II 50; **1237** (v. copicia a); BRADW. *CD* 688E (v. certitudinaliter); OCKHAM *Pol.* III 14 (v. contradictio 1a); **1454** (v. discoragium). **b** in vigilia apostolorum Symonis et Jude que ~it sexta feria COGGESH. *Visio* 5. **c** sed secus evenit quam machina straba putabat ALDH. *VirgV* 1005; aliter quam sperabatur ~it ORD. VIT. III 3; adhuc felicius ~it . . filiabus meis quam michi TREVET *Troades* 9. **d** hac morosa tricatione ~it ut pollicita codicelli rescriptio tanto temporis intervallo protelaretur ALDH. *VirgP* 59; si forte ~isset, quod tamen raro ~it, ut ad regis convivium vocaretur BEDE *HE* III 5 p. 136; ex quodam . . libro illi ~it ut recitarem ASSER *Alf.* 88; ~it . . ut aliquis innocentem injuste percutiat ANSELM (*CurD* 7) II 57; *Cust. Westm.* 215 (v. consecratio 1b). **e** ~it per culpam incuriae . . ecclesiam ignibus consumi BEDE *HE* III 17 p. 160; BALSH. *AD* 67 (v. demonstrare 2a). **f s1297** misit filio suo in Angliam potestatem plenam ad parliamentum convocandum . . mandato principi ~to parliamentum edidit *Eul. Hist.* III 167; in . . expellendo omnem ambiguitatem imposterum . . ~iendam *FormA* 71; **1455** omnimoda escapia . . transgressiones [etc.] . . infra . . regnum . . emersa et ~ta (*Lit. Regis*) *Reg. Whet.* I 196.

4 (math.) to result. **b** (of promise or prophecy) to be fulfilled.

quadratum TL, quod ex multiplicatione quinarii cum quinario (in hoc casu) colligitur, nobis ~iet ROB. ANGL. *Alg.* 82. **b** ut . . loquendo . . de . . oboedientia emittas spiritum. sic enim ~iet tibi promissio illa, quae perseverantibus usque in finem promittitur ANSELM (*Ep.* 436) V 384; ita omnia ~erunt sicut S. Yta predixit *VSH* (*Ite* 20) II 123.

5 a (w. compl.) to become; *cf. devenire* 3. **b** (w. *de*) to become of.

a 1130 Rogerus dedit abbati . . xx m. argenti, et ~it homo ejus liges de hoc quod tenet de eo (*Conventio*) *Chr. Rams.* 252. **b 1268** quid de dicto brevi ad curiam domini regis ~erit ignoro *Cl* 9; querit Andromacha quid ~iet de filio abscondito TREVET *Troades* 37.

eventare [LL], (med.) to rid (an organ) of wind. **b** to exhale, discharge (vapour).

aeris ingressu [cor] ~atur fumi expressione ALF. ANGL. *Cor* 11. 16; artarie . . sunt conposite ad hoc, ut per ipsas ~etur cor a suis fumis *Ps.*-RIC. *Anat.* 6. **b** ad fumositatem ~andam GILB. I 17. 1.

eventatio [LL], (med.) ventilation, respiration.

si aer motus habeat liberam exhalationem et ~onem, infrigidatur *Quaest. Salern.* B 176; superveniente estate dissolvitur humor, calore poros aperiente. per ~onem itaque fumositatum ab humore dissolvitur *Ib.* P 92; domus . . retinentes calorem per clausuram fenestrarum et prohibitionem ~onis GILB. I 7. 2; ad sanguinis ~onem et adustionis prohibitionem *Ib.* 18. 2; ex longa mora in corpore cum carentia ~onis . . calefit GAD. 15V. 2; quarto habet basis cordis posicionem versus dextram, ut sic recipiat sanguinem, ~onem, et motum pulsus WYCL. *Mand. Div.* 179.

eventativus [LL], (med.) promoting ventilation or perspiration. *V. et. eventatorius.*

multa sunt calida que licet primo calefaciant, post tamen infrigidant ut sunt omnia ~a et pororum . . aperitiva *Quaest. Salern.* B 281; in colerica vehementis inflammationis [flobotomia] non competit nisi minorativa et ~a GAD. 16V. 1.

eventatorius [LL], (med.) promoting ventilation or perspiration. *V. et. eventativus.*

juscalcus acram habet in se qualitatem et †eventoriam [v. l. ~am] et purgativam *Alph.* 85.

eventilare [CL]

1 to winnow thoroughly (fig.), to consider, discuss.

per multos dies . . omnia capitula plene ~antes EDDI 53; ut . . actus cogitatusque discutiant, ~ent BEDE *Tab.* 498A; [sententiam] quam hucusque studui [? l. distuli] ~are (*Adv. Elipand.* II 13) ALCUIN *Dogm.* 269D; **972** (12c) cum archana cordis indagatione ~ans perhennem gratulationem *CS* 1285; aliquantis controversiis prolatis et ~atis W. MALM. *GP* I 49.

2 to fan away, rid of, dissipate (partly fig.); **b** (person or demon); **c** (abstr.).

~atum cineribus ignem . . frustulis appositis . . incendia aptare contendo ÆLNOTH *Cnut prol.* 3; germina . . etsi . . tenera . . pestilens crebro secularis glorie aura ~aret et niteretur corrumpere H. BOS. *Thom.* II 6; quicquid urget intrinsecus in cogitatione, lingue flabellum exterius in auras ~at J. GODARD *Ep.* 228. **b** quodsi venefici aut magi . . reperiantur, ~entur a patria (*Cons. Cnuti*) *GAS* 311 (= *Quad. ib.*: expellantur a finibus nostris; AS: *fyse hig man georne ut of þysum earde*); virgo . ., manica explicata, omnes [malignantes] pariter ~avit J. FORD *Wulf.* 21. **c** dubietas ~ata est W. MALM. *GP* IV 184; **s1000** predixit . . quod . . dominium . . et honorem sine termino restitutionis ~aret H. HUNT. *HA* VI 1.

eventilatio, arguing, consideration, discussion.

cum . . ad ~onem causarum ventum esset, omnes qui tuendis ecclesie causis . . convenerant . . ita convicti sunt ut . . EADMER *HN* 21.

eventilator, winnower (fig.).

area . . auctoritatis tibi commodate de celis paleas a se statim novit ~oris verbo discutere (*Lit. ad Papam*) NETTER *DAF* I *prol.*

eventio [cf. CL evenire]

1 arrival.

s1213 ~one archiepiscopi cognita . . in obviam adierunt *Eul. Hist.* III 106.

2 casual profit, obvention. *V. et. eventura,* 2 *eventus* 3b.

c1200, 12.. (v. evenire 2b); **1205** omnes ~ones et excaetas que de ipsis et terris eorum accidere potuerunt *RChart* 154b; **1206** ad perpetuam vicariam ecclesie de H. possidendam . . et omnes ~ones altaris reddendo ipsi H. xxx s. *CurR* IV 73; **a1212** neque in aliquo quod ad ecclesiam de M. juste pertineat sive de decimacionibus sive de aliquibus ~onibus injuriam sustinebunt *Reg. S. Aug.* 547.

eventorius v. eventatorius. **eventur** v. 2 eventus 2b.

eventura [cf. CL evenire], casual profit, obvention. *V. et. adventura, eventio* 2, 2 *eventus* 3b.

14.. confirmavi . . Willelmo homagium Margarete . . cum releviis et herietis et escaetis et ~is que . . contingere potuerunt ex illis duabus acris (*Cart. Hosp.*) *MS BL Cotton Nero* E VI f. 196.

1 eventus v. evenire.

2 eventus [CL]

1 coming, arrival. **b** attendance.

~us, incursus *GlC* E 339; quod rex Scotie, audito electi ~u, statim ad sua remeasset GIR. *Galf.* I 3; multa signa . . in mundo visa sunt . . ad insinuandum Magni Regis [sc. Christi] ~um *Eul. Hist.* I 68 (cf. ib.: in signum adventus Magni Regis). **b** nullus intret parliamentum nisi qui sectam et ~um debeat ad parliamentum *Mod. Ten. Parl.* 39 (cf. ib. 5: nisi eorum presentia et ~us . . requiratur).

2 event, incident, occurrence. **b** fate.

hostes . . optatis ~uum successibus . . superati ALDH. *VirgP* 12; *DB* I 252 (v. 3 casus 4c); W. CANT. *Mir. Thom.* III 24 (v. 3 casus 4a); [insula] nuper nata . . cui talis ~us originem dedit GIR. *TH* II 12; rex Offa duos episcopos . . ad investigandam ~ium (*sic*) istorum certitudinem . . destinavit *Id. Æthelb.* 14; ~us futuri BRADW. *CD* 600C (v. antecedentia); 'si fata', id est ~us fortune, 'juvant', id est prosperentur TREVET *Troades* 39. **b** fata, i. fortuna, †eventur [MS: ~us], . . *gewyrda GlH* F 130; **c1078** illorum . . peccatum sive ~um, pro illis orando miti mente dissimulate ANSELM (*Ep.* 63) III 179; diversos et atroces ~us separatim experti sunt ORD. VIT. III 14 p. 152.

3 outcome, result. **b** casual profit, obvention; *v. et. adventura, eventio* 2, *eventura.*

discipulo inter discrimina . . militum ~us rerum praestulanti genetricem . . praecepit tuendam ALDH. *VirgP* 7; ~um discriminis tuto in loco exspectabat BEDE *HE* III 24 p. 178; ut . . rex et ego cum quadam spe boni ~us conveniremus ANSELM (*Ep.* 388) V 332; tu . . quovis in pace quiesce et ~um belli prestolare ORD. VIT. III 14 p. 146; rex Misenorum . . facili ~u plurima bella gessit GREG. *Mir. Rom.* 4; ~us mortalis non debet medico imputari J. MIRFIELD *Flor.* 130; **1410** (v. confluentia d). **b 1214** tenentes sunt atornati, ipsi Rogero de redditu assise, et ipsi Ricardo de aliis ~ibus *CurR* VII 240.

4 (phr.): **a** (w. abl., or *in* & acc. or abl.) in the event, as it happens; **b** (*in omnem* ~*um*) in any case; **c** (w. gen.) in the event of; **d** (w. *si* or rel. pron.).

a 1296 istud vobis scribimus in ~u prout quedam que recepimus pro certo post recessum nostrum a parliamento de S. Edmundo a suffraganeis supradictis prout in adventu vestro ad nos plenius vobis dicemus *DCCant.* (*HMC*) 263; **1312** ut . . habeant facultatem . . seldas vendendi; in aventum predictum volo quod . . *RR K's Lynn* I 78; **1336** ut si in ~um patiamur impulsum, habeamus provisum contra comminancium jacula nobis scutum *Lit. Cant.* II 132; **1340** si quis contra dictum regium curiale preceptum exnunc fecerit, licet sibi male contingat, non miretur in ~um *FormOx* 159. **b 1294** quod duo fratres tantum de tribus predictis nominatis in omnem ~um primo nominarentur domino archiepiscopo ad singula officia predicta *DCCant. Reg.* Q f. 26a. **c 1308** vobis . . nostre absencie in ~u, committimus vices nostras *Lit. Cant.* III 386; **1326** in cujus tractacionis ~um, juxta consilium apostoli, caucius est ambulandum *Ib.* I 203; **a1350** in ~u . . dissensionis arbitrii . . eorumdem majoris partis arbitrio stetur *StatOx* 41; **1419** in ~u vacacionis *Reg. Cant.* I 176; **1427** protestor, me velle . . ~u gravaminis . . appellare (*Appellatio Archiep.*) *Conc.* III 485b; **1520** in ~u non paritionis *Conc. Scot.* I cclxxxv *rub.* **d 1317** quod . . velimus sibi concedere dictam navem . . retinendam in ~u si concordia . . reformata esset *RGasc* IV 1783; **1325** ista . . vobis pronuntio, in ~u si forte . . lingue mendaces . . contraria vobis suggerant *Lit. Cant.* I 150; **1472** in ~u quo . . collector . . nos . . certificet . . quod . . *Reg. Whet.* II 137.

everare v. averare a.

everberare [CL], to beat violently. *V. et. deverberare* 1, *diverberare* 2.

exidere, i. . . excutere, eicere, ~are, admovere *GlH* E 538.

everrae v. everriae.

everrere [CL], to sweep out.

~it, trahit *GlC* E 312; ~it, i. trahit, . . everenda, tollenda *GlH* E 382, 386.

everriae [CL], (pl.) purificatory rites.

everriator, qui facit everras, i. munditias circa mortuos OSB. GLOUC. *Deriv.* 197.

everriator [CL], performer of purificatory rites.

OSB. GLOUC. *Deriv.* 197 (v. everriae).

everroima v. enaeorema.

eversio [CL]

1 overturning, upsetting (fig.); **b** (astr.) or ? *f. l.*

quae . . haeresis sacras litteras male intellexit sed . . sine ulla ~one suo eas statu manere permisit LANFR. *Corp. & Sang.* 420C; **1278** emerserunt . . quedam nova, que ad ~onem jurium, consuetudinum, libertatum, et grave periculum ecclesie Anglicane redundant *Conc. Syn.* 826. **b** dicitur [Thales] de astrologia tractasse necnon et solares ecclipses et ~ones [? l. reversiones] predixit W. BURLEY *Vit. Phil.* 2.

2 destruction.

excidium, ~o *GlC* E 526; excidium, i. ~o, expugnatio, casus, ruina, vel *hereteam GlH* E 528; in Troje ~one . . eam [sc. Palladem] Virgilius arces dicit insedisse ALB. LOND. *DG* 10. 2; hic Waterfordie superbia cecidit . . hinc nobilis urbis cepit ~o GIR. *EH* I 13; urbis [Ninive] ~onem [penitencia] relaxavit UHTRED *Medit.* 203.

eversivus, tending to overthrow.

modo autem ~i scola antichristi, dimissis operibus, contendit circa magnitudinem potestatis WYCL. *Blasph.* 258.

eversor [CL], overthrower, destroyer.

nil obstat quin . . arcem nostrae mentis saevus impugnator et ~or ascendat BEDE *Ezra* 893; †**1066** (12c) (v. constitutor); qui prevaricator vel ~or conscripte legis exstiterit were sue culpa sit (*Leg. Hen.* 34. 8) *GAS* 566; milites nepotis ~ores secum duxit in vinculis MAP *NC* I 30 f. 22v.; juris ~or, assertor injurie *Ib.* V 4 f. 61.

eversus [LL = *refutation*], turning aside, diversion.

13.. de eversu aque Thamisie *MGL* I 476 *rub.*

evertere [CL]

1 to overturn, turn over or back (also fig.); **b** (p. ppl. *eversus*) upside down; **c** (of garment) 'turned'. **d** (w. *in* or *ex*) contrary, backwards.

[Godwini] ~untur oculi, brachia rigescunt AILR. *V. Ed. Conf.* 767A; EADMER *Beat.* 3 (v. divertere 1d); R. COLD. *Cuthb.* 36 (v. evolvere 1b); GIR. *IK* I 12 (v. continere 1b); mulier si acum amiserit . . omnia stramina ~it [ME: *towent uch strea*] quousque invenerit *AncrR* 124; **1423** AMUND. I 178 (v. corrosivus 1b). **b** BACON *Maj.* II 140 (v. confluentia b); **1315** in cruce sancti Petri cum ymagine ~a argentea . . continetur *Invent. Ch. Ch.* 81; ~um, A. *upsodoun WW.* **c 1448** una toga nigra per fullonem ~a *MunAcOx* 579. **d s1385** Deus . ., vento in ~um stante, classim regiam portum predictum exire vetabat THORNE 2181; **s1304** ferris equorum ex ~o confixit [v. l. confixtis] . . ut nullus vestigia equorum . . perciperet *Plusc.* IX 5 (cf. FORDUN *Cont.* XII 6: ferramenta . . retrograde affigi).

2 to upset, overturn, throw down (structure). **b** to overthrow, sack (mil.). **c** to uproot, fell (also fig.).

nefandas simulacrorum effigies . . ad solum diruit, quassavit, ~it ALDH. *VirgP* 36 p. 282; deruta, i. ~a, *ahwerfde GlH* D 236; ~ere †*ahwerfdon* [l. *ahwerfan*], vel *gehwurfan, towurpan Ib.* E 376; GOSC. *Transl. Aug.* 39D (v. evacuare 3c); cum tantam molem [sc. statue] . . non posset ~ere, . . ignem idolo supponi jussit GREG. *Mir. Rom.* 6. **b** ~it, expugnat *GlC* E 340; pleros gladio vindice ferit, aliorum latebras ~it, terras devastat, et domos . . concremat ORD. VIT. IV p. 195; *G. Hen. II* I 219 (v. conventiculum 2b); planctus . . chori de eversa Troja TREVET *Troades* 3. **c** cultor agrestis / pinos evertens altas ALDH. *Aen.* 78. 10; corus . . arbores . . ~ens GIR. *TH* I 6; **c1435** (v. deponere 7a).

3 to overthrow (fig.), frustrate. **b** to divert (from).

hoc vitium [sc. luxuria] . . totius boni ~it statum GILDAS *EB* 21; ut . . adscisceretur quatenus, qui magorum molimina funditus ~eret . . supernorum sacramenta . . cognosceret ALDH. *VirgP* 43; ubi pretium pro dicenda justitia accepit, veritatem vendidit, et quando ipsam ratione sua ~ebat . . veritatem perimebat ALEX. CANT. *Mir.* 46 (II) p. 251; **s1437** Deus qui . . perjuros et pacem turbantes confudit et ~it *Compilatio* 166. **b** sese mutavit in turpem vulpeculam ut vel sic famulum Dei cauda quatienti . . ab intentione Dei sui ~eret B. *V. Dunst.* 16.

4 to turn or convert (something into another form).

sic agnas ~it in lupas MAP *NC* V 3 f. 60v.

evesborda [ME *ēves bord*], eaves-board.

1400 in s[alario] . . serrancium tabulas que vocantur esborde et alias tabulas . . xviij d. *Mem. Ripon* III 131; **1470** in latthis, . . evysbord', meremio *Ac. Obed. Abingd.* 138.

evexus v. evehere.

evibrare [LL < CL = *to set in vibration*], to brandish (also fig.).

s1119 caput regis gladio tota vi ~ato emicantibus scintillis bis percussit M. PAR. *Min.* I 227; in me cum mors evibrat gladium J. HOWD. *Ph.* 920; **s1455** ad ulciscendum . . suum gladium ~are *Reg. Whet.* I 162; **s1460** in signum . . quod Dominus . . evaginaturus ~aturusque esset . . gladium ulcionis *Ib.* 386.

evicerare v. eviscerare.

evictio [CL]

1 (leg.) eviction, acquisition or recovery of land or property by legal process.

post ~onem, si petentem evincere contigerit, regressum inde habere poterit versus evictorem GLANV. XII 24; petens tenetur ad waranciam per . . obligacionem sui antecessoris et quanquam de ~one tenet accio, ipsum ab agendo repellit excepcio *Fleta* 294; **1313** promittentes . . bona fide ipsi Bertrando legitime stipulanti pro se et suis successoribus . . super premissis . . plenam et integram ~onem et garenciam portare in judicio et extra *RGasc* IV 973; **1328** si . . dicta terre particula per legem patrie evicta fuerit et . . alienata . . ego vel heredes . . mei . . infra spacium duorum mensium a tempore dicte ~onis numerandorum tantum de terra nostra . . eisdem . . restituemus *Reg. Newbattle* 153.

2 (leg.) dispossession or (?) *f. l.*; *cf. evectio* 2b.

s1312 nuncii pape . . prelatos et clerum procuracionibus, ~onibus [? l. eveccionibus], et aliis . . gravaminibus vexaverunt AD. MUR. *Chr.* 16.

evictor

1 evictor, dispossessor.

GLANV. XII 24 (v. evictio 1).

2 champion, vindicator.

executor invictus, dubiorum elector velox, et juris et injurie fortis ~or MAP *NC* V 3 f. 60v.; victus voluptatis ~or *Ib.*

evidare v. 1 evitare. **evidens** v. evidere.

evidenter [CL], visibly, perceptibly (to sense). **b** evidently, clearly (to understanding). **c** (rhet.) vividly.

locus . . belli pertranseuntibus ~er patet, ubi . . congeries ossium . . usque hodie jacet ORD. VIT. III 14 p. 144; [dies] lucis sue gratiam ~ius aperire ubique . . cepit AD. EYNS. *Visio pref.* **b** ~er ostendit qualiter se exhibeant suo officio sacerdotes GILDAS *EB* 105; ut ~ius harum rerum ratio claresceret ALDH. *Met.* 8; signa . . his possunt agnoscere satis ~er indiciis *V. Greg.* p. 79; et evitentius ipse per Zachariam dicit . . *Eccl. & Synag.* 100; verbum . . se prolem ejus esse a quo est ~issime probat ANSELM (*Mon.* 55) I 67; si enim licet rapere regnum celorum, ~ius potest quis injuste emere vel vendere regnum celorum WYCL. *Sim.* 15. **c** manifestis exemplorum formulis hoc ~ius reserari rogo ALDH. *Met.* 10 p. 96; per . . Johannem . . magistris et scholaribus responsio vestra et ~er et prudenter et diligenter est recitata AD. MARSH *Ep.* 16.

evidentia [CL]

1 appearance, obviousness.

~ae, *swutulnesse GlN* 27. 25.

2 evidence, proof; **b** (w. subj. or obj. gen.); **c** (*in ~iam*); **d** (*ad majorem ~iam, pro majori ~ia*).

nullam . . ex scriptis Hibernicis ~iam . . inveni GIR. *TH intr.* p. 8; si . . Augustinus vocaret solum scripturam sacram libros scriptos vel literas visibiles, nullam faceret ~iam pro parte sua quia Abraham fuit propheta (KYN.) *Ziz.* 16. **b 1072** contra tantam tantarum auctoritatum ~iam paucissimas contradictiones opposuit LANFR. *Ep.* 3 (4); **1219** ad cujus rei ~iam verba in privilegiis contenta huic scripto inserimus *Ch. Sal.* 89; plus cognoscimus in horrendis rerum ~iis quam ex oraculis vatum . . conjicimus AD. MARSH *Ep.* 8; per ipsius facti ~iam et publicam notitiam ejusdam miraculi *Chr. Evesham* 23; sicut ex principiorum ~ia conclusionis veritas declaratur R. BURY *Phil.* 18. 231; ?**1320** querentes sunt disseisiti absque aliqua ~ia facti hujusmodi manifestanda *MGL* I 448; **c1443** nisi videatur . . accusatum non esse reum . . per certas ~ias fame, sciencie, vite vel private examinacionis que cancellario . . videantur sufficere ad judicandum . . *MunAcOx* 538. **c** in hujus . . rei ~iam sigillum dentibus meis impressi ELMH. *Cant.* 119; **1440** referre dignetur in ~iam premissorum BEKYNTON II 73; **1478** que . . litere patentes . . in ~iam ostense fuerunt *Entries* 25. **d** id tamen hic tantillum ad majorem ~iam addere sufficiat quod . . GIR. *DK* II 2; **1238** ad hujus rei majorem ~iam restituimus . . omnia instrumenta *Reg. Paisley* 25; **c1320** pro majori ~ia sigilla predictorum arbitrorum . . sunt appensa *Reg. Dunferm.* 355.

3 (documentary) evidence.

1332 compertum est per ~ias diversas reddituales quod . . Salamon C. duo habuit tenementa *Reg. S. Aug.* 182; **1381** quod . . diversa . . munimenta, rotuli, ~ie et rentalia . . libertates . . tangencia . . combusta fuerunt (*Cl*) *Foed.* VII 338a; transcriptum ~iarum Edmundi R. armigeri de manerio suo de Borstalle *Cart. Boarstall* 203; quarum alliganciarum tenores et scripta reperies in libro regalium ~iarum et recordorum *G. Hen. V* 2; **1445** Willielmus . . deliberavit Roberto . . ~ias subscriptas. in primis, composicionem . . item testamentum . . item confirmacionem [etc.] *Pri. Cold.* 154; P. VERG. XVII 322 (v. 1 copia 4a).

4 guide.

1258 signum . . quod vocatur Blakeman . . erectum est in portu de Grimmesby ad ~iam piscatorum et mercatorum in eodem portu applicantium *ChartR* 49 m. 5.

evidentialis, documentary.

hujus . . Albini hortatu . . Beda sepe in titulum speculi ~is hujus monasterii memoratus historiam . . composuit ELMH. *Cant.* 294.

evidēre [CL *pr. ppl. only*]

1 (intr.) to be apparent; **b** (impers.).

ex jure divino et racione ~endi colligitur qualiter sit eligendus summus pontifex OCKHAM *Dial.* 953 (*recte* 941); **1407** alia . . statuta specialia . . volenti inquirere ~ebunt ad promptum in . . tabula superius annotata *StatOx* 199. **b** hoc nomen 'ens' est commune ad signandum quamlibet veritatem, sic et hoc nomen 'res'; patet ex modo loquendi scripture quo ad secundam partem que minus ~et ex hoc, quod scriptura vocat tale ens rem WYCL. *Ente Praed.* 76; ex his ~et quanta cautela pastor habet ligare et solvere NETTER *DAF* II 235v. 1; **1513** vicecustos ex mandato . . custodis ut ex ejus litteris ~et, equitavit Londonias ad faciendum compotum cum magistro W. *Reg. Merton* 435.

2 (pr. ppl. as adj.): **a** visible, perceptible (to sense); **b** evident, obvious (to understanding); **c** (*in ~enti*) in the open, in plain view.

a quod . . didicerim ~enti scripto detexam ORD. VIT. VI 10 p. 86; si nigra quelibet nix esse dicitur / . . / in testimonium si palpo trahitur / falsum tam evidens verificabitur WALT. WIMB. *Palpo* 68. **b** ~ens indicium est non esse eum legitimum pastorem GILDAS *EB* 92; ut ~entioribus adhuc astipulationibus . . comprobetur, aliqua annectenda sunt *Ib.* 93; luculentum exemplar et ~ens indicium . . profer ALDH. *PR* 122 (cf. id. *VirgP* 48: satis ~ens documentum); a**957** (12c) (v. ecclesiastes b); veritas . . ~ens et ratio docet . . ANSELM (*Praesc.* 2 3) II 261; Deus . . filiis suis sue benignitatis ~entiora demonstrat indicia DOMINIC *V. Ecgwini prol.*; ad ~entiorem tante diversitatis indaginem GIR. *TH* II 3. **c** in sola Lombardia invente sunt xviij in ~enti [hereticorum secte] R. NIGER *Mil.* III 81; **s1226** cujus rei experimentum in ~enti est WEND. II 303.

evigilare [CL]

1 (intr.) to awake, wake up; **b** (fig.); **c** (w. abstr. subj.); **d** (pr. ppl. as adj.).

mox ~ans sanissimus surrexit BEDE *HE* IV 31; ~at gibber fugiente gravedine somni WULF. *Swith.* I 266; LANFR. *Const.* 89 (v. dormire 1a); ~ans postera die vidit in re juxta quod previderat in visione W. CANT. *Mir. Thom.* VI 166. **b c895** (v. devotatio 1); anima mea, ~a ANSELM (*Or.* 14) III 55; quid . . agendum ut . . ad opera bona ~ent? EADMER *Beat. intr.* p. 274; versiculus [*gl.*: breves sententie biblice] pigras mentes docet ~are GARL. *Myst. Eccl.* 207. **c** si nec corpus nec spiritus infirmarentur . . superbia . . ~aret [ME: *awacnen*] *AncrR* 59. **d** Alfredus . . in servicio Dei ~antissimus *Eul. Hist. Annot.* II 188.

2 to arise from death, be resurrected.

mortuus evigilat disrumpens tartara tetra ALDH. *VirgV* 1413; ne . . nihil . . inveniatis . . in manibus vestris cum ~averitis post finem ANSELM (*Ep.* 54) III 168.

3 to lie awake. **b** to 'burn the midnight oil', study. **c** (trans.) to compose carefully.

pallidus evigilat somni formidine captus ALDH. *VirgV* 618; cogitationes meae . . me nocturnis horis . . ~are fecerunt BYRHT. *V. Ecgwini* 362; prepositus [monasterii] . . adhuc ~ans GOSC. *Wulsin* 17; nocte quadam mulier ~ans GIR. *GE* I 11. **b** patres qui explicandis ~averunt scripturis ANDR. S. VICT. *Comm.* 274. **c** *GlC* E 112 (v. elucubrare 1); elucubratum, i. meditatum, lucidum, ~atum, accensum, purum, *hluttor GlH* E 206.

4 (trans.) to awaken; **b** (fig.).

dum ~aretur a somni gravedine . . LANTFR. *Swith.* 3; in suo lectulo jacet et dormit. . . non audeo excitare eum, quia prohibuit nobis ~are eum ÆLF. BATA 4. 13; Herbertus Cenomannorum comes . . vulgo, sed parum Latine cognominari '~ans canem' pro ingenti probitate promeruit ORD. VIT. IV 12 p. 252; eum ~are non audebat R. COLD. *Cuthb.* 51; **s1312** ipsum Petrum [de Gaverstone] ~avit et ad castrum suum de Warwick secum duxit AD. MUR. *Chr.* 17; **s1327** quadam . . nocte . . Jacobus de D. . . per medium exercitum Anglicanum transivit, . . aliquos occidit, plurimos terribiliter ~avit *G. Ed. III Bridl.* 97. **b** vitis liquor . . / . . rubeus . . / evigilans citius torpentia frigore membra H. AVR. *Poems* 2. 236.

evigilatio [LL], awakening.

s1434 absque ~one compausavit AMUND. II 89 (v. compausare).

evilare v. ejulare a.

evilescere [CL], to become worthless or despicable.

si cura mei apud vos penitus non ~uit (*Lit. Reginae Angliae*) *Ep. Anselmi* V 344.

evillare [cf. CL villa], **a** (intr.) to leave town, be absent; *v. et. devillare*. **b** (trans.) to drive from town, expel.

a s1308 protelato . . assensu regio comites ~arunt, assignato eis die reversionis in quindena Pasche *Ann. Paul.* 262; **1323** dum bercarii querunt tres hurta[r]dos . . in marisco, quia †fuit [? l. sunt *or* fuerunt] ~at' per v dies pro tempestate pluvie *Ac. Wellingb.* 129; **1345** quo die prior ~avit apud Dublin' *Ac. Trin. Dublin* 76. **b c1320** iidem pistores depauperantur et ~antur ad voluntatem populi civitatis *Lond. Ed. I & II* II 160.

evincere [CL]

1 to defeat (enemy). **b** to overcome (obstacle; also fig.); **c** (w. abstr. obj.).

R. COLD. *Godr.* 77 (v. colluctamen). **b** torrens . . uno objectas sibi ~it gurgite moles GILDAS *EB* 17. **c** florentes suae pubertatis annos, evicta juventute, calcavit B. *V. Dunst.* 5; W. MALM. *GR* V 400 (v. domesticus 4b); 'vicimus eos matrum dolos', id est . . percepimus dolos matrum et evicimus eos TREVET *Troades* 42; erit gloriosum tales temptaciones ~ere UHTRED *Medit.* 205.

2 to defeat (in argument). **b** (intr.) to prevail.

[Lanfrancus] profundissimis disputationibus Beringerium Romae . . palam evicit ORD. VIT. IV 6 p. 211. **b** irruit in negata consilia et donec evicerit non est finis instantie MAP *NC* IV 15 f. 56.

3 to evince, prove existence (of); **b** (w. acc. & inf.). **c** to vindicate, prove right (to).

~it ratio gloriam Dei . . bonitati ipsius . . parem PULL. *Sent.* 808B; *Ib.* 692C (v. dissultus); Deus . . permisit eos affligi quousque . . bonis studiis et operibus ~erent salvationem R. NIGER *Mil.* III 85. **b** interseritur . . que . . sequerentur inconvenientia, si dii plures essent, et sic tantum unum Deum esse ~itur PULL. *Sent. prol.* 639C. **c 1167** cum evicerit ecclesie libertatem J. SAL. *Ep.* 252 (220).

4 (leg.) to acquire or recover (land or property) by legal process; **b** (w. pers. obj.); **c** (w. abstr. obj.).

GLANV. XII 24, **1328** (v. evictio 1); GIR. *GE* II 27 (v. delegare 2c); **1238** si evicte fuerint a nobis .. dicte decime, .. illas eisdem solvi faciemus *LTRMem* 12 m. 11(1)*d.*; **1282** manerium non potest ab eo ~i nisi per communem legem *SelCKB* I 107; **12..** (v. canon 5); *Hist. Roff.* 2v. (= *Anglia Sacra* I 357) (v. computus 2c); **1416** si contigerit .. tenementum .. extra eorum possessionem ~i *Deeds Balliol* 125; FORTESCUE *LLA* 53 (v. comparticeps). **b** ipsa [mulier] .. eo [clerico] tanquam suo, puta quem sibi conventionis .. jure jam evicerat licentius utens .. GIR. *GE* II 13 p. 229; res servi domini dicitur esse sui / evicto servo sequitur possessio servum, / et cedunt domino servus et ejus opes GOWER *VC* VII 67. **c** jus .. quod post multas et longas dilationes, per duellum vix ~itur, per beneficium .. [legalis] constitutionis .. acceleracius expeditur GLANV. II 7.

evinculare [cf. LL vinculare], to unchain, release.

Lazare, .. / veni foras prius †est [l. et] post exvinculare *Poem S. Thom.* 85; *deliverer*, ~are *Gl. AN Ox.* f. 154; **1494** episcopus London' dictum dominum Thomam Percy a suis carceribus ~avit *DC Cant. Reg.* S. f. 400b.

evirare [CL], to castrate, unman. **b** (p. ppl. as sb. m.) eunuch.

†ebilantur [l. evirantur], mutilantur *GlC* E 5; Galli Senones obsiderunt Romam, et quoscumque ex illis capiebant Romani ~abant *GlP* 398*n.*; adulter effectus, comprehensus et ~atus est R. COLD. *Godr.* 233; W. FITZST. *Thom.* 55 (v. eunuchare a); vir ~atus hanc tamen ab impiis pietatem consecutus est, quod receptis testibus abscisis vulneribus suis mederetur W. CANT. *Mir. Thom.* VI 13. **b** ~atus, i. .. eunuchus, spado *GlH* E 391; ~atum contempnendo conspuere prevalebunt R. COLD. *Cuthb.* 103.

2 to enfeeble. **b** (p. ppl. as sb. m.) enfeebled man.

haec et hujusmodi innumera ministros antichristi ad ~anda pectora fortium blasphemare non latet BEDE *Sam.* (*1 Sam.* xxii 6–8) 660; nulla temporum mollitie virtutem ~are compulsus W. MALM. *GP* II 74 p. 153; cum nullus eum valeret illecebris ~are R. BURY *Phil.* 15. 193. **b** Mahog, qui in ~atum transfertur, hoc est virili actione mente et virtute privatum BEDE *Sam.* (*1 Sam.* xxvii 3) 695.

evirescere [CL = *to lose strength*; cf. virescere], to grow green, flourish (also fig.).

a vireo, viresco, quod componitur ~esco OSB. GLOUC. *Deriv.* 598; [mundo dediti] virescunt in yeme peregrinacionis, refrigescente caritate multorum, sed in estate diei novissime propter defectum radicacionis in Christo ex ardore solis justicie evanescunt; sed tunc fideles .. cum pastor eorum apparuerit, ~escunt WYCL. *Eccl.* 197; ab hac herba [sc. Ioanne Clemente], †qua [l. quae] et Latinis literis et Graecis coepit ~escere, egregiam .. frugem spero MORE *Ut.* 5.

eviscerare [CL]

1 to eviscerate, disembowel; **b** (person or his innards); **c** (vitals, testicles); **d** (refl., of spider). **e** (fig.) to dig out; **f** (fig.) to 'clean out', rob. **g** (fig.) to exhaust.

~ata, *athed GlC* E 328; ~atis cervis duobus, inter ipsa intestina lanam interseri procuravit GIR. *IK* I 9; ut os lupi vellus eviscerans J. HOWD. *Ph.* 507; exentero .., i. evicero *Alph.* 57. **b** ~andum, *to holdigenne, to befleanne GlP* 338; G. episcopus Dunelmi defunctus est .. parentes ejus .. ~atum et sale conspersum .. eum .. reservaverunt J. HEX. *HR Cont.* 309; **s1252** fuerunt .. non pauci qui optarent ut hi illos excerebrassent, alii reliquos ~antes M. PAR. *Maj.* V 352; **1290** circa exequias Walteri .. viz. pro viceribus de corpore extrahendis et corpore evicerando et reparando et saliando *Chanc. Misc.* 4/5 f. 51v.; **s1305** ~atis intestinis [Willelmi Waleys] ac in ignem crematis *Flor. Hist.* III 124; **s1450** Johannes Cade .. occisus quaternizatus et ~atus HERRISON *Abbr. Chr.* 6. **c** erant qui .. jurarent quod parvo obice impediebantur quin .. nuntios .. vel ~arent vel ementularent *G. S. Alb.* I 186. **d** seipsam ~at aranea, ut materia non desit cassibus contexendis NECKAM *NR* II 113; O. CHERITON *Fab.* 15A (v. aranea 1a). **e** aper .., dente protenso cespitem cujusdam colliculi .. ~are gestiens, .. locum .. ostendit J. FURNESS *Kentig.* 24 p. 202. **f** is febre cotidiana correptus ad medicorum confugit auxilium, inanibus se sumptibus ~ans *Mir. Fridesw.* 51; **s1256** ut .. quos predecessor excoriaverat, successor immisericorditer ~aret M. PAR. *Maj.* V 577; in manus .. latronum incidimus; ~atique de infinitis pecuniis .. vix evadentes *Croyl.* 74. **g** qui seipsos ~ant ob inanem laudis amorem J. SAL. *Pol.* 772B; non dolore tabescas, .. non sollicitudo distrahat, non [te] ~ent cure H. BOS. *Thom.* IV 13 p. 364; clerici .. totos se ~ant ut unicum beneficium capiant O. CHERITON *Fab.* 15A; **1245** ipsos .. gracia optamus prosequi speciali qui hospitalitatis causa se ipsos evicerant *Cart. Osney* III 22.

2 to extract (essential points).

ut rei ipsius ~emus interna BEDE *TR* 46; haec de qualitate temporum et elementorum simul et de aetate hominum sint a nobis ~ata BYRHT. *Man.* 10; quodam compendio ~atis objectarum quaestionum intimis .. terminum his imponere decrevi ABBO *QG* 23 (50).

3 (p. ppl.) 'visceral', drawn from the heart.

1433 pias ipsius matris [sc. universitatis Oxon.] preces lacrimosis ~atas cum suspiriis .. exaudire *EpAcOx* 96.

evisceratio [LL], evisceration, disembowelling; **b** (fig.).

(*Leg. Hen.* 75. 1) *GAS* 591 (v. decomatio); **1264** personis ecclesiasticis captis .. ac male tractatis et demum usque ad ~onem redemptis (*Lit. Episc. Wigorn.*) GERV. CANT. *GR Cont.* 240; **s1427** accusator nequissimus pene traccionis et ~onis [datus est] *Chr. S. Alb.* 19. **b** per .. matrimonium nostre dulcissime regine cessat sediciosa ~o incolarum utriusque regni *Regim. Princ.* 82.

eviscus v. hibiscus.

†evispila, *f. l.*

nonne, si mortuus jacerem †in evispila [v. l. in sandapila, ? l. sine vispillone], intenderes ut .. H. BOS. *Thom.* III 1.

evitabilitas, (phil.) state of being avoidable, contingency.

the contingency of things (~as) (RIC. ARMAGH *Sent. extr.*) *Wycl. & Ox.* 86.

evitabiliter, avoidably.

vel .. nihil fit contingenter, id est ~er, vel primum sic causat immediate quod posset eciam non causare DUNS *Ord.* II 179.

1 evitare [CL]

1 to avoid.

ad ~andas vel repellendas .. gentium .. inruptiones BEDE *HE* I 14; **786** equos .. plerique in vobis comedunt .. quod .. ~ate *Ep. Alcuin.* 3 p. 27; casualia [vitia] .. quia causis exterioribus accidunt, leviori custodia ~ari possunt *Simil. Anselmi* 121; malitiam .. non ~ari GIR. *TH* I 23; luxuria .. est .. lubrica et effrenata mentis prostitucio et ista omni modo †evidanda [l. evitanda] *Spec. Laic.* 49; **13..** (v. correctio 2b); frigus et calorem et sitim et esuriem ~are non valeo CHAUNDLER *Apol.* 23a.

2 to protect, keep (from).

ad ~andum nos .. de periculo, articulos .. brevium .. nobis .. significare velitis *Chr. Rams.* 399.

2 evitare [CL], to kill.

~averit, offocaverit *GlC* E 349; ~atus, perterritus *Ib.* 355; ~atus, i. vita privatus, perterritus, mortuus; ~atur, eviscerat *GlH* E 393–4.

evitatio [CL], avoidance.

cordis contritio .. delicti ~o P. BLOIS *Serm.* 711A; cautio est turpium et adversitatis fortuite ~o W. DONC. *Aph. Phil.* 3. 21; **1236** ad ~onem istius pene in ecclesia integre residere *Stat. Linc.* II 144.

evitenter v. evidenter.

evitus [cf. CL avitus], (?) aged, worn-out. *Cf. envisus.*

1299 vobis mandamus quatinus .. unum bonum equm fortem et non ~um .. mittatis *Cl* 117 m. 14*d.* (cf. ib. m. 6*d.*, 4*d.* [**1300**]; = *Cal.* 379, 403: †enitum; ib. 407: evitum); **1314** tibi precepimus .. quod provideri et emi facias .. carectam cum quatuor equis fortibus, non ~is aut mahemio aliquo debilitatis *RScot* 127a.

evocare [CL]

1 to call forth or out; **b** (w. ref. to death).

~ans presbyterum, rogavit secum venire ad patientem BEDE *HE* III 11 p. 149 (cf. ib. II 12 p. 108: ~atum foras); excitatur, ~atur *GlC* E 452 (cf. ib. 537: exciti, excitari, ~ati). **b** cum quis eorum de saeculo fuisset ~atus BEDE *HE* IV 21 p. 257; MAP *NC* II 27 (v. convicaneus b).

2 to entice.

bellica seditio .. clerum .. a studio religionis .. ~at ORD. VIT. XII 21 p. 380; fortuna blandiens ad dominium de Cobham per conjugium [Johannem de Veteri Castro] ~avit *G. Hen. V* 1.

3 to summon; **b** (w. *placitum* as obj.).

ipse pro .. maturitate consiliorum saepius ad regem solebat ~ari *Hist. Abb. Jarrow* 12; si vicecomes ~at eos ad siremot *DB* I 179; xv archiepiscopi .. apostolico jussu ~ati .. congregati sunt ORD. VIT. XII 21 p. 372; **1165** regem Francorum ~averat ut Purificationis festum ageret secum J. SAL. *Ep.* 161 (144 p. 30); W. FITZST. *Thom. prol.* 12 (v. 2 conventus 2b); RIC. ARMAGH *Def. Cur.* 1397 (v. conservatorius 1b); **1445** (v. diaeta 2d); **1484** (v. comportare 1a). **b** placitum coram vobis in Anglia fecit ~ari *State Tri. Ed. I* 48.

4 to call into existence. **b** (gram.) to supply.

interpretatur Clotho 'evocatio', Lachesis 'sors', Atropos 'sine ordine' .. ~antur primo homines ex non esse in esse sive de matris utero in lucem ALB. LOND. *DG* 6. 23. **b** ad evocacionem oportet quod significatum ~antis sit confusum et persona finita et discreta, et e contrario a parte ~ati BACON XV 2; Oratius [*Ep.* I 16. 18] loquitur ad Quintum .. et est ibi evocatio quia hoc quod dico 'omnis Roma' ~atur ab hoc pronomine 'nos' intellecto, et potest bene ab intellecto ~are *Ib.* 174.

evocatio [CL]

1 calling forth or out; **b** (w. ref. to death).

ecclesia, ~o *GlC Int.* 113; ALB. LOND. *DG* 6. 23 (v. evocare 4a). **b** praescius diei ~onis suae, qua felicitatem .. accepturus erat ut esset semper conjunctus Christo ALCUIN *Hag.* 690C; ante sue ~onis diem longe egritudinis igne decoquitur TURGOT *Marg.* 13; J. LOND. *Commend. Ed. I* 8 (v. corregnatio).

2 calling forth, enticing.

pundbreche fit pluribus modis: emissione, ~one, receptione, excussione (*Leg. Hen.* 40. 2) *GAS* 567.

3 summons.

1259 supplicandum quatenus a predicta ~one et diei assignatione nos habere dignemini excusator (*AncC* II 181) *RL* II 137.

4 manifestation. **b** (gram.) 'evocation', supply.

s870 erat hoc [sc. visio dormientis] quasi quaedam divinae pietatis ~o ut ex Dei munere adepta terra illa mox in Christi floreret titulo *Chr. S. Neoti.* **b** licet major sit discrecio in pronomine tercie persone apcior est persona pronominis ad hoc ut fiat ~o quam persona nominis BACON XV 4; *Ib.* 2, 174 (v. evocare 4b).

evocitare [cf. CL vocitare], to call by name, designate.

[Februarium] evocitant Ebrii Graecique per Tios *Kal. M. A.* I 399 (v. Dios).

evolabilis, that can fly away (fig.).

quam timemus omnem punctulum doloris .. cito medicabilis aut ultro ~is GOSC. *Lib. Confort.* 48.

evolare [CL]

1 to fly away; **b** (fig.); **c** (of speech or sim.). **d** to 'fly', hasten.

[apes] per aethera ~antes .. mortalium visus aufugiunt ALDH. *VirgP* 26; [anates] ~antes in lacu quodam .. se recipiunt GIR. *TH* II 29; **13..** [pavo] ~at et abvolat *Mem. S. Edm.* I app. 366; **s1461** (v. columbella b). **b** **802** ALCUIN *Ep.* 245 (v. educatio 1); Oriensis episcopus infirmatus .. ad superos ~avit ORD. VIT. IX 12 p. 582; crescat et in ramos virtus, fundatur et alta / evolet HANV. VIII 206 p. 366; felices pulli aquilarum illi, qui .. ad corpus Christi ~averunt J. FORD *Serm.* 8. 2. **c** **799** nec ego .. examinare possum quae subito casu ex ore dictantis ~ant ALCUIN *Ep.* 172; poterant hoc verbo, nisi tardius ~asset, plurimi premuniri ne .. DEVIZES 27; fama de sancto ~ans pulsavit aures .. regis J. FURNESS *Kentig.* 30. **d** nisi citissimus ad commilitones tuos ~averis, auxilium prebiturus eis ORD. VIT. IX 15 p. 601.

2 (w. inanim. subj.) to fly or float upwards.

scintille .. †evolebant R. COLD. *Cuthb.* 39 (v. deultra a); faville de rogo ~antes mutate sunt in aves *Natura Deorum* 20; partes [urine] aquose .. subtiliores .. in superficie ~ant *Quaest. Salern.* N 37; *Alph.* 90 (v. allisio a).

3 to escape.

~at, exilit, erumpit *GlH* E 400; qui clausus erat .. / .. / evolat illaesus WULF. *Swith.* II 628; GILB. I 23v. 1 (v. evaporativus b).

evolgare v. evulgare.

evolitare [CL], to fly away frequently (fig.).

de arca, i. e. ecclesia, ~antes .. nusquam ad eam puro corde revolastis GILDAS *EB* 95.

evolutio [CL]

1 unfolding (of tale).

hujus .. historie seriem scribere nunc supersedimus dum ad ejus ~onem vacare donaverit indago certior *V. Ed. Conf.* 49.

2 lapse (of time).

infra mensem post ~onem cujuslibet termini *Melrose* app. 23; post aliquanti temporis ~onem .. Ethelbaldus .. illuc advenit *Croyl.* 2.

evolvere [CL]

1 to roll away (also fig.). **b** to unfold (clothes). **c** to unroll, turn over (scroll, roll, or book; also fig.).

evolutam labilibus / mundi molem rotatibus (ÆTHELWALD) *Carm. Aldh.* 2. 13; citius potest in se confidens humana sapientia .. cornua sibi evellere quam innitendo petram hanc [sc. unum et solum Deum esse] ~vere ANSELM (*Incarn. A* 4) I 283. **b** sacra indumenta explicans et replicans, ~vendo evertens ac palpanter explorans R. COLD. *Cuthb.* 36. **c** schedulam .. ~vunt AILR. *Ed. Conf.* 761B (v. disquirere a); librum coram se oppansum sepius per folia seriatim ~vit R. COLD. *Godr.*

322; **1170** ~vat unusquisque et relegat proprie conscientie librum J. SAL. *Ep.* 296 (300 p. 700); ?**12..** in hoc libello continentur nostrorum transcripta munimentorum ne sit necesse negociorum procuratoribus originalia illorum sepius ~vere *Reg. Plympton* 151.

2 to release, extricate; **b** (refl.). **c** (p. ppl.) unimpeded, free.

'iniquitates meae supergressae caput meum' obvolvunt me . . ~ve me, exonera me . . ANSELM (*Prosl.* 1) I 100. **b** a**1093** vides . . quia . . nescio quomodo me sine peccato possim ~vere ab hac me eligentium intentione *Id.* (*Ep.* 156) IV 19; *Id.* (*Incarn. A* 4) I 285 (v. contemplari b). **c** ut expeditius pateat ad currendum ~utioribus pedibus peragretur J. GODARD *Ep.* 221.

3 to unravel (knot; also fig.), to uncover (something hidden).

ALDH. *PR* 129 (v. enudare 2); Jeronimus . . involuta . . et implicita patenter ~vens et explicans elucidavit ANDR. S. VICT. *Comm.* 273; **1170** ~vere cordis humani latebras J. SAL. *Ep.* 297 (301); **1177** P. BLOIS *Ep.* 66. 198B (v. cuneus 2b); speculatio prima / nec bene nec plene discernit; quando revolvo / rem magis evolvo VINSAUF *PN* 1964; abditas ab antiquo proprietates ~vere GIR. *TH intr.* p. 7.

4 to make known, unfold.

quantae [fuerit] in perversos districtionis non est nostrae facultatis ~vere ABBO *Edm.* 4; nulla camena tuas potis est evolvere laudes WULF. *Poems* 15; quot valet humanis evolvere nemo loquelis *Id. Swith.* I 1376; *demostrer*, . . ~vere *Gl. AN Ox.* f. 154; s**1358** nobilitas hujus solennitatis multa erat nimis, nec est nostre facultatis ejus gloriosa facta ~vere KNIGHTON II 99.

5 (pass., of time) to roll by.

~utis xcviij lustrorum temporum circulis ALDH. *Met.* 2 p. 69; ~utis aliquorum temporum curriculis FELIX *Guthl.* 4; solaris [annus], . . qui trecentis sexaginta quinque diebus ~vitur BYRHT. *Man.* 34; a**1075** paucorum dierum spatio ~uto LANFR. *Ep.* (3); ~utis multis annis HON. *Spec. Eccl.* 864A; s**1306** paucis ~utis diebus post mortem . . Johannis . . Comyn FORDUN *Cont.* XII 9.

evomatio v. evomitio.

evomere [CL]

1 to vomit up, spew out; **b** (fig.). **c** (w. animal or monster as subj.; also fig.) to emit from mouth (partly fig.); **d** to emit, give forth. **e** (absol.) to vomit.

si monachus exundante ventre ~erit sacrificium in die . . deleat culpam GILDAS *Pen.* 7; si per ebrietatem vel voracitatem . . ~erit eucharistiam xl dies peniteat EGB. *Pen.* 11. 7; venenum ~uit citoque sanatus Salvatori suo gratias egit ORD. VIT. VI 10 p. 116; per nares et oris exitum sanguinem nigrum ~entem *Ep. ad amicum* 115; nummos quos . . deglutiverat . . per vomitum reicere coegerunt, quos cum ~uisset, jussit demon eos colligere COGGESH. *Visio* 24; spicam . . e gutture infans ~uit *Mir. Hen. VI* I 3 p. 22. **b** anima tepida et digna ~i [cf. *Apoc.* iii 16] ANSELM (*Medit.* 1) III 77; cum ecclesia . . continere . . plurimos non dubitetur, tandem ~endos, si eorum aliquos . . multos non eveniat PULL. *Sent.* 708A. **c** Arriana perfidia, atrox ceu anguis, transmarina nobis ~ens venena GILDAS *EB* 12; draco qui . . virus . . ~uit ALDH. *VirgP* 12; erat monstrum . . nomine Cacus in antro fluminis Tiberini flammas de pectore ~ens *Lib. Monstr.* I 31; vermiculorum qui sericum ~unt GIR. *TH* I 21; cetus Jonam ~it AD. DORE *Pictor* 163; ungue . . plantam pedis . . infirmi de lardo et istud prohice cani. et si illud comedat et non ~at, vivet infirmus ille J. MIRFIELD *Brev.* 66. **d** de puteo . . sulphureus . . ~ebatur fumus ALEX. CANT. *Mir.* 36 (II) p. 232; constat Hydram locum fuisse ~entem aquas ALB. LOND. *DG* 13. 4; eo moriente tota terra . . mortuos de se ~uit HON. *Spec. Eccl.* 925A; cur terra noxium virus [i. e. ferrum] evomuit? WALT. WIMB. *Carm.* 541; s**1377** (v. effigiare 1a); *Ps.*-ELMH. *Hen. V* 42 (v. diruptivus). **e** fetor . . exibat qui . . tantam . . eis anxietatem generabat, quod quasi penitus crepare debuissent ~ebant ALEX. CANT. *Mir.* 36 (I) p. 232.

2 to give vent to, pour out (usu. emotional thought or speech). **b** to display, reveal, show.

cum . . incestum . . de recessibus falsi pectoris ~uisset ALDH. *VirgP* 32; tu e diverso serpentina lingua mortiferum ~uisti venenum ALCUIN (*Adv. Elipand.*) *Dogm.* 246C; a**1078** ANSELM (*Ep.* 12) III 116 (v. cruditas b); plurima cum lamentis verba ~uit ORD. VIT. IX 9 p. 532; acerba que ruminaverunt ~uerunt *Ib.* XII 21 p. 386; additur . . confessionem secundum esse refugium et quod sicut ore, ita peccatum debet ~i corde PULL. *Sent.* 658A; W. MALM. *GP* I 17 (v. efflator); si totam Tullius spumam evomeret WALT. WIMB. *Palpo* 150; tanta mala . . in confratres suos . . ~uit, ut horrori foret audientibus WALS. *HA* II 158. **b** ~uit, i. ostendit, †degerit [MS: digerit], significat *GlH* E 401.

3 to gush out.

fons iste ita ~uit ut mulierem . . submersit *Eul. Hist.* II 128 (cf. GIR. *TH* II 9).

evomitio [cf. CL vomitio], vomiting up, spewing out.

~o, *spiwinge* ÆLF. *Gl.*; †evomatio, *speowung GlH* E 402.

evulgare [CL], to divulge, publish. *V. et. divulgare.*

1281 nos prefatas composicionem ordinacionem et sentenciam . . approbamus, ratificamus, acceptamus, et evulgamus *Cart. Osney* II 459; **1520** (v. evulgatio).

evulgatio [cf. LL vulgatio], divulging, publication. *V. et. divulgatio.*

1520 simulque videri posses me urgere ad promulgandum opus quasi inde cupias fidem esse factam lectori non te impedisse ~onem operis quod tam impense ambis ut evulgetur *Ep. Erasm.* IV 1061.

evulsio [LL], evulsion, plucking.

cur incisione unguium vel ~one pilorum asellarum minoratur visus? *Quaest. Salern.* C 25.

evysborda v. evesborda.

ewagium [cf. AN *ewage*], 'ewage', toll for passage by water, ferry due. *V. et. aquagium* 2.

1200 nos concessisse . . burgensibus de Dunewichge quod . . quieti sint de theloneo . . de danegeld et de ~io, de wrec et lagan [etc.] *RChart* 51b; **1200** (1230) quod [homines de Beverlaco] sint liberi et quieti . . de wrek et de lagan, de ~io, et de leve (*Ch. Regis*) *CurR* XIII 2651.

ewang- v. evang-. **ewaria** v. eweria.

ewea [AN *ewe*, OF *aigue* < CL aqua], (stretch of) water. *V. et. aqua* 1c.

1155 decimam . . allecium suorum et piscium de eweis suis de Longolio et de Nova Villa et de Puteis *Act. Hen. II* I 102.

ewera, ~um [AN *ewer*], ewer. *V. et. aquarius* 2a.

1268 legamus . . domino Maurianensi episcopo albam nostram novam et eueriam nostram argenteam *Test. Ep. Heref.* 5; **1390** pro . . emendacione unius ~i deaurati fracti *Ac. H. Derby* 6; **1440** deliberaciones . . ciphorum, ollarum, et ~arum de auro vel deauratorum *Pat* 448 m. 33.

eweria, ewery, room or office of ewerer. *Cf. aquarius* 3a.

1400 E. nuper rex Anglie . . pro bono servicio quod G. del S. garcio hwerie hospicii sui sibi impenderat . . *War. Issue* 15. 358 (cf. ib. 17. 268 [**1401**]: garcio ~ie); **1447** sciatis quod . . R. B. servientem ewarie nostre . . accepimus (*Pat*) *Foed.* XI 182a; **1453** vadia pagettorum: . . Thome Paver, pagetto ~ie (*DL Ac. Var.*) *JRL Bull.* XL 411; **1478** dilectus serviens noster Willelmus Burton armiger generosus ewerarie nostre *Pat* 542 m. 20.

ex [CL; *for use w. adv.* v. et. deinde 2b, diu 4, econtra, examodo, exdudum, exhinc, exinde, exintra, exnunc, expost, extunc]

1 out of, from (a place); **b** (in adverbial phr., usu. w. ref. to vantage point).

omnes e finibus depulit GILDAS *EB* 15; e strato festina surgere ALDH. *VirgV* 1278; e . . domu ÆTHELWULF *Abb.* 356 (v. domus 2a); apis . . caris e cellulis consurgens ASSER *Alf.* 76; e refectorio *Cust. Westm.* 138 (v. cursus 7a). **b** videbam e regione quantum . . increverat GILDAS *EB* 1; ex superis prospectans arcibus ultor ALDH. *VirgV* 2599; me delectat sedere ex adverso loco sancto meo in quo orare solebam CUTHB. *Ob. Baedae* clxiv; in viis . . ex utraque parte *DB* I 2; ex adverso A. TEWK. *Thom.* 25, **1321** (v. ascendere 7a); **1178** eum e vestigio sequor P. BLOIS *Ep.* 52. 159B (v. diploma 1b); villam . . e regione monasterii . . sitam *Chr. Abingd.* II 9; pedes e vestigio sequebatur GIR. *GE* II 22 p. 278 (v. cursor 1b); ex omni parte COGGESH. *Visio* 19 (v. exstruere c); **1203** terra . . in corneria piscarie ex opposito fronti ecclesie sancte Marie Magdalene *E. Ch. S. Paul* 79; nemo . . pro quavis re sermonem alicui ex transverso vel a latere dirigere presumat *Cust. Westm.* 190; nec est aliquis jam qui disponat . . stare ex adverso pro ecclesia Dei *Chr. Westm.* 144; a**1400**, **1426** (v. advertere 3c).

2 from the surface of, from off.

melotis, pellis simplex ex uno latere †deperdens [l. dependens] *GlC* M 129; lapsum e ponte AILR. *An.* III 38 f. 56 (v. 1 coxa a); e prora labitur *Id. Ed. Conf.* 749B (v. divaricare 1a).

3 (w. ref. to time) from, after. **b** (w. *quo*, as conj.) after, since.

ex eo tempore nunc cives nunc hostes vincebant GILDAS *EB* 26; ex quo tempore BEDE *HE pref.* p. 7; **838** ex hac die *CS* 421; ex eo usque nunc aecclesia terram perdit *DB* I 252v.; ex illa hora ALEX. CANT. *Mir.* 21 (II) p. 198; sicut ex post facto claruit GIR. *EH* I 45; ex nocte fit dies BACON *Tert.* 197 (v. effective); **1434** ex antiquo (v. antiquus 1b); **1458** ex diu (v. diu 4). **b** ex quo [Brittannia] inhabitata est . . ingrata consurgit GILDAS *EB* 4; a**795** ex quo te sciebam . . semper te amabam ALCUIN *Ep.* 28; gallina ex quo sit scaturizata [v. l. excaturizata, *gl.*: *escaude*] . . cimino condiatur, si elixa fuerit NECKAM *Ut.* 102; hereditatem . . per Clarenses multo tempore perdidimus; sed ex quo perdere debuimus leti sumus GIR. *RG* II 9; ex quo tractavit de errore cleri . . jam intendit tractare de errore virorum religiosorum GOWER *VC* IV *tit.*.

4 (partitively) from among; **b** (math. expr. subtraction or deduction).

peculiari ex omnibus nationibus populo . . dixerat GILDAS *EB* 1; elegerunt ex suo numero virum BEDE *HE* V 11; ex navibus eorum novem naves ceperunt ASSER *Alf.* 6; liberos homines quos habet sub se commend[atos] tenet; et ex eis revocat Robertum *DB* II 311; FL. WORC. I 118 (v. collegium 1a); 'beati qui non viderunt et crediderunt' [*John* xx 29] ex hujusmodi quisquis es, hoc attende T. MON. *Will. prol.* 5; **1187** (v. 1 continentia 3). **b** iiij s. . . ex . . feodis deducendos *StatOx* 456 (v. deducere 3d).

5 (indicating descent): **a** from, by (father); **b** from, out of (mother).

a ex patre fit filius BACON *Tert.* 197 (v. effective). **b** si puellam Dei maculaverit, iij annos paeniteat . ., licet pariat an non pariat filium ex ea THEOD. *Pen.* I 14. 11; liber homo . . plures habens filios ex eadem matre . . legitime procreatos GLANV. VII 1; Henricus . . genuit ex ea Malcolum *G. Walth.* 127; nepos ejus ex sorore W. BURLEY *Vit. Phil.* 252.

6 from (a source); **b** (of payment or acquisition); **c** (of tenure); **d** (of information); **e** (of derivation or translation); **f** (w. ellipsis of sb.).

cum lacrimis . . quae ex Dei caritate profluunt GILDAS *EB* 1 (cf. ib.: potus novus ex rupe [cf. *Exod.* vi 11]); ALDH. *Aen.* 17 (*Perna*) 1 (v. concha 1a); *Id. VirgV* 2800 (v. contundere a); BACON VI 2 (v. computus 1a); miriofillos . . tirsum habet ex una radice mollem *Alph.* 118; relucet claritas spiritalisque majestas ex sanctorum, qui in ea [sc. Anglia] floruerunt, virtutibus et exemplis CAPGR. *Hen.* 200. **b** **749** (12c) ei libenter . . ex eo quod accepi iterum retribuo *CS* 178 p. 255; cum sumptus qui debebatur ex publico non daretur ALCUIN *Rhet.* 14; tota civitas ex omnibus debitis reddebat T. R. E. xv li. [etc.] *DB* II 107; W. MALM. *GR* IV 313 (v. caliga 1a); meremium . . fuit . . ex proprio argento suo emptum *State Tri. Ed. I* 89; ex patrimonio . . vixi GASCOIGNE *Loci* 31. **c** s**1244** ut quilibet baro tenens ex rege in capite haberet . . M. PAR. *Maj.* IV 379. **d** ex scriptis patriae . . non satis claret GILDAS *EB* 4; quod . . illas visiones ex ipsius ore audierit BEDE *HE* III 19 p. 167; cujus patientiae esset ex antedictis ejus gestis ostenditur ALCUIN *WillP* 24; ut possit unusquisque vestrum dicere ex sententia: 'lectulus noster floridus' (*Cant.* i 16) AD. SCOT *QEC* 5. 810C; s**1232** Godefridus . . capellam ingressus precepit ex ore regis ut [Hubertus] exiret de capella WEND. III 36; ex . . locis argumenta elicere GROS. 2; ut ex immediate dictis patet *Mus. Mens.* (*Anon. VI*) 399; elicibiles ex scriptura WYCL. *Blasph.* 46; **1579** (v. desumere a). **e** hic locus ex nitro sortitur Nitria nomen ALDH. *VirgV* 1458; libros . . de Latinitate . . in Saxonicam linguam aliquando sensum ex sensu ponens . . interpretatus est ASSER *Alf.* 77; verbum e verbo transtulit W. MALM. *GP* V 240 (v. construere 3a). **f** ut omnis arrogancia vel inanis gloria, que ex hujusmodi oriri solet, reprimeretur BLAKMAN *Hen. VI* 14.

7 from (source of word or emotion).

egenis eleemosynam esse dandam summis e labiis praedicantes GILDAS *EB* 66; questus e pectore promit ALDH. *VirgV* 1905; [verba] ex ore prodita (ÆTHELWALD) *Carm. Aldh.* 5. 40; profusis ex imo pectore lacrimis BEDE *HE* IV 26 p. 273; s**1239** imperator ex intimo cordis tactus [v. l. tacto] dolore precordiali scripsit M. PAR. *Maj.* III 546; **1360** (v. cor 2a).

8 (indicating change) out of, from being; *cf. de* 2e.

ut . . in agnum ex lupo mutaret GILDAS *EB* 11; WULF. *Æthelwold* 40 (v. efficere 6a); *G. Steph.* II 105 (v. consulatus 4a); distinguit inter illos conversos ex Judeis et inter gentiles OCKHAM *Pol.* II 770.

9 out of, from (physical or mental condition); **b** (w. ref. to death).

subjectos cives . . ex imminenti captivitate liberavit GILDAS *EB* 15; **849** ne . . ex memoria . . labentur (v. 2 condicere 1d). **b** egredi e corpore BEDE *HE* III 17; raptos e mundo *Ib.* IV 15 p. 233; absolutus ex carne CUTHB. *Ob. Baedae* clxiii; ut in admiracionem verteretur . . hominem e vita non ocius emigrasse *Mir. Hen. VI* I 22.

10 (w. ref. to composition or construction) from, of (material); **b** (w. *facere*) to make of, do with; **c** (abstr.); **d** (in qualifying phr., without vb.).

flores / e quis virgineas valeant fabricare coronas ALDH. *VirgV* 139; *Id. VirgP* 3, etc. (v. constare 1c); [Factor] me . . ex nichilo formavit CUTHB. *Ob. Baedae* clxiii; laternam ex lignis et bovinis cornibus . . construere imperavit ASSER *Alf.* 104; **957** (v. creare 2a); est corpus hominis compositum ex quatuor elementis BART. ANGL. IV 1; *Chr. Abingd.* I 7 (v. 1 credere 4b); ex ferro fit cultellus BACON *Tert.* 197 (v. effective). **b** isti homines libere exstiterunt ad Berchingum, set modo ex ipsis potest facere quod sibi placuerit *DB* II 17v.; **1274** de . . catallis Johannis . . nichil sciunt, nec ad quorum manus devenerunt nec quid ex eis factum fuit *CourtR Wakefield* I 13. **c** ALCUIN *Rhet.* 8 (v. constare 1c). **d** *GlC* D 313 (v. discerniculum 1); **1433** lego fratri meo . . unam zonam argenteam ex serico *Reg. Cant.* II 471; **1516** tres pendentes ex blodio sago *Ac. Durh.* 253.

11 (instrumental) with, by means of. **b** by. **c** in, according to.

ut prius ex prosa laudabat littera castos; / sic modo heroica stipulentur carmina laudem ALDH. *VirgV* 19; puer .. decoratus ex .. cesarie *G. Herw.* 320b (v. 2 facies); thecas ex auro .. coopertas *Chr. Abingd.* II 214 (v. eruderare 3). **b** homines ex nomine jurabit (*Leis Will.*) *GAS* 503 (v. appellator a). **c** quae sibi acciderant ex ordine referens ALEX. CANT. *Mir.* 29 p. 217; D. BEC. 1778 (v. concors b); **s1321** predictum casum ex ordine referentes TROKELOWE 107.

12 a by virtue of, in consequence of. **b** (w. *se*) on one's own initiative, in one's own right. **c** (w. *hoc*) accordingly. **d** (*ex eo quod, ex hoc quod, ex quo*) because.

a [Jeremia] propheta ex sua persona loquitur .. et post pauca .. ex persona Dei GILDAS *EB* 48, 49; qualiter ex propria meruissent carne coronas ALDH. *VirgV* 2831; epistulam privilegii ex auctoritate apostolica firmatam BEDE *HE* 16 p. 241; **1082** quidam monachus .. ferrum judicii quod ex antiquo jure in eodem monasterio erat, per ignorantiam et ex quadam simplicitate in alios usus transformavit *Regesta* I p. 122 (v. et. 13b infra); LANFR. *Comment. Paul.* 150 (v. 2 contristare); ex eadem molestia quam in via ceperat lectulo decubuit ALEX. CANT. *Mir.* 21 (II) p. 197; Dominus noster precepit nobis ut ex sua parte 'diceremus vobis quatinus' .. *Ib.* 45 (I) p. 247; ADEL. *Alch.* 21, OCREATUS *Helceph* 133 (v. ducere 8f); H. BOS. *Thom.* III 1 (v. comminatorius 1c); DEVIZES 42v. (v. criticus); GIR. *Symb.* I 31 p. 321 (v. consequi 2a); **1322** in omnibus causis coram cancellario .. ventilatis, sive procedatur ex officio, sive ad instanciam partis *StatOx* 125; **s1342** (v. credentia 3a); OCKHAM *Pol.* I 192, **1505** (v. 3 casus 4b); **1439** BEKYNTON I 51 (v. credentia 3a). **b** si .. principium habet aut ex se vel per se hoc habet aut ex alio vel per aliud .. ANSELM (*Mon.* 18) I 32; ex se ipso ulterius irrotulare fecit quod .. *State Tri. Ed. I* 62; que festivitates ex se habent processionem *Cust. Cant.* 11; **s1314**, etc. ex proprio capite (v. 2 caput 2b); respondens Jesus Pilato dixit 'ex te hoc dicis' [cf. *John* xviii 34: a temetipso] *Eul. Hist.* I 97. **c** revocavit eum ad tutorem; set ipse sibi defuit, et ex hoc dedit ille vadem *DB* II 103; ex hoc nunc nec unum extorquebis inde breviculum MAP *NC* V 6 f. 71. **d** DUNS *Ord.* III 284 (v. dispositio 3a); **1309** dicte .. discordie ex eo quod dicta loca .. certis finibus .. conclusa non fuerant originem habuerunt *RGasc* IV 216; OCKHAM *Pol.* II 602 (v. copulativus b); **1340** bannitus fuit .. pro eo et ex eo quod .. tranquillitatem .. universitatis .. perturbavit *FormOx* 121; **s1398** rex .. propriis manibus, ex quo alii hoc non audebant, ipsum proposuit interemere AD. USK 19; **1484, 1487** (v. declamare 2b); **1514** pro cxviij ulnis pannei linei pro linthiaminibus ex hoc quod antiq' expendebatur in diploidibus pro guerra hoc anno *Ac. Durh.* 160.

13 a in compliance with, in pursuance of. **b** in conformity with. **c** (w. adj. as sb. n., equivalent to adv.) in a (specified) manner; *cf. de* 10e.

a ex quorum consilio hoc factum esse perhibetur ASSER *Alf.* 12; ex discentium consensu BALSH. *AD rec. 2* 126 (v. 1 consensus a); ex condicto juramenti R. NIGER *Chr. I* 86, etc. (v. 2 condicere 1d); **1445** ex parcium .. assensu (v. concorditer c); **1464** ex consideracione auditorum (v. consideratio 3); **1513** in .. stipendiis ex imposicione et assignacione magistri T. C. prioris *Ac. Durh.* 662. **b** navem ex lege tamen populi esse oportet ALCUIN *Rhet.* 15; **1082** (v. 12a supra); ab omnibus peccatis .. eum absolvit et ex more sacre unctionis oleo .. linit *V. Gund.* 41; H. BOS. *Thom.* III 32 (v. 2 edicere 2c); BRACTON 1 (v. consuetudo 2b); *Ib.* 4 (v. consuetudo 2a); **1339** quod mater ex jure non admitteretur ad regnum (*Lit. Regis*) AD. MUR. *Chr.* 94; **1412** quolibet anni quarterio .. missas tres .. ex vi statuti .. celebrabit *StatOx* 220. **c** legebam .. Dominum dixisse 'non veni nisi ad oves perditas domus Israel' et e contrario 'filii .. regni hujus eicientur in tenebras' GILDAS *EB* 1; e diverso ALDH. *Met.* 7, etc. (v. divertere 6b); e contrario BEDE *HE* V 13 p. 313, etc. (v. contrarius 2e); super paganos ex improviso irrumpunt ASSER *Alf.* 54; ex solito reges hic diadema ferunt G. AMIENS *Hast.* 672; e converso ANSELM (*Mon.* 4) I 17, etc. (v. convertere 3c); ex abbundanti (*Leg. Hen.*) *GAS* 563, etc. (v. 2 abundare 4c); **1152** purgationem ab ipso ex superabundanti recepimus (*Lit. Papae*) ELMH. *Cant.* 406; ex accidenti dux ilico subsecutus est GERV. CANT. *GR* 89; **1222** ex conjuncto (v. conjungere 2e); ex facili M. SCOT *Phys.* 83 (v. doctrinalis c); ex necessario, .. ex contingenti GROS. 146 (v. contingere 8a); ex directo GILB. III 173v. 1 (v. dirigere 2b); hoc ex incidenti dictum est BACON II 105; ex consequenti *Ib.* VIII 31 (v. consequi 2d); ex difficili curatur GAD. 81. 1 (v. dislocare 1a); **s1314** ex insperato intrarunt (*Chr. Anon.*) *Illust. Scot.* 2; ex proposito *AncrR* 69 (v. blaese); **s1453** e directo (v. dirigere 2c).

14 to the extent of; **b** (w. adv.).

jussionis ex parte mutationem [fecit] GILDAS *EB* 38; exercitus maxima ex parte equester factus est ASSER *Alf.* 21; ut promptuario memoriae verba ex integro reconderes ABBO *Edm. pref.*; wasta fuit ex parte *DB* I 259; dicant psalterium ex integro LANFR. *Const.* 114; urbem preterea Cantuarie .. isti concessit ex solido W. MALM. *GP* I 48; **s1234** quod .. terram Britannie totam cum castellis et urbibus ex integro resignaret WEND. III 94; nisi .. signum specialiter fecerit presidens, ut ex toto ministret et cum servitoribus postea prandeat *Cust. Westm.* 118. **b** quod .. solvent dicti abbas et conventus .. decimas ex integre sine aliqua subtractione *Cart. Dieul.* 356.

15 by the standard of.

nos ex segnitie sua metientes W. MALM. *GP* IV *prol.*; cum .. monachorum detencio ex quanto gravior seu diuturnior tanto magis discordie esse speretur seminarium *Pri. Cold.* 52.

16 (in new comp., expr.): **a** ('from, of') *v. exannalis.* **b** ('along, across') *v. eportare, evadare.* **c** ('out, away, abroad') *v. effluxus, enavigatio, eradiare, evillare, exaquare, exaspirare, excarriagium, excarriare, ~iatio, excola, ~icus, exhauritorius, exhelus, exspirabilis, ~itas.* **d** (removal, separation, or deprivation) *v. ementulare, ~atio, emoviare, epinguatus, erubiginare, ~atio, etesticulare, evellare, excaedere, excapitare, excolorare, excossiare, excrustare, ~atio, exjudicare, exmonachare, exocreare, expaleare, expedare, explumare, exspinare, exsumptuare, extesticulare, extunicare, 3 exuberare.* **e** (intensification) *v. effaminare, elucrari, ~atio, eluculenter, elusor, emaceratio, emadere, emagnus, emandare, emarcidus, emature, ememorare, emendicatio, emerite, emingere, emordere, emurmurare, emutescere, emutilatio, enector, epatescere, 2 ephoebus, errebellis, erugire, evirescere, evocitare, evomitio, evulgatio, exadmirari, exalacritare, exalienare, exallogeneus, 1 exartare, exasper, exassare, exauctio, exauferre, exbannire, excambire, ~itio, ~itor, excellerarius, excinerare, excogitabilis, excogitate, excomere, excostare, excrebrescere, excrispare, excruciatrix, excultibilis, excurator, excurtare, exebriare, exempticius, exhilarescere, exhilariter, exignire, exnamiare, exoccare, exoccultare, expampinare, exportator, exprodere, exscire, exseminare, exsequax, exsoporare, exsperare, exsumere, exuber, exustulare.* **f** (completion) *v. exprecari.* **g** (privative, 'not') *v. epudoratus, exbracatus, exermis, exjudicaliter, exlegalitas, exsiliquus, exstudiosus, exterror.* **h** ('formerly, no longer') *v. exabbas, exaugustus, exauratus, excancellarius, exconstabularius, exdux, eximperatrix, expontifex, exregina, exromanus, exsacerdos.* **i** (reversal or reciprocity) *v. emutuare, enectere, enormare, esursum, etexere, evadiare, evinculare, exalligare, excanonicare, excardinare, excondicere, exemphracticus, exhominare, 1 exhumare, ~atio, exoppilare, expignerare, expropriare, exsaccare, exsarcinare, extenebrare, extumulare, ~atio, exumectare.*

ex- v. et. es-, exs-, s-.

exa v. 2 axa.

exa- v. et. hexa-.

exabbas [cf. LL abbas], ex-abbot.

juste ~as effectus, officio et loco cessit J. FURNESS *Walth.* 36; **s1213** quum iterum sedisset jam ~as, petii a .. legato ut cogeret eum ad restitutionem quorundam bonorum ecclesie *Chr. Evesham* 250; **s1213** iste abbas [R. Norreys] .. depositus est et ~as factus *MonA* II 27a.

exacerbare [CL]

1 to irritate, distress, enrage; **b** (animal). **c** (intr.) to rail (against).

neminem specialiter sermonum severitas castigando ~avit ALDH. *VirgP* 58; Gundulfus, qui die et nocte lacrimis suis .. me ~at *V. Gund.* 11; **1167** vobis visus est .. legatus in prima salutatione suspicionibus inurendus et gratis ~andus? J. SAL. *Ep.* 220 (227); Anna uxor Tobie virum suum cecitate et inopia laborum verbis ~at AD. DORE *Pictor* 162; ~asti spiritum meum J. FORD *Wulf.* 45. **b** importuna sitis greges animantum graviter ~avit ORD. VIT. XIII 16 p. 39; insidet equo .. factisque discursibus et giris ~at eum MAP *NC* III 2 f. 37v. **c** **c1430** *Reg. Whet.* II 433 (v. atterere 2b).

2 (med.) to exacerbate, aggravate (illness).

dum febris incipit, principium; dum ~atur, augmentum; dum in summa exacerbatione perseverat, statum BACON IX 200.

exacerbatio [LL]

1 irritation, anger, embitterment. **b** harassment.

~o, irritatio, *abolgennes GlH* E 423; **1170** hoc quidem arbitror huic ~oni .. dedisse originem J. SAL. *Ep.* 293 (298 p. 696); **s1171** predicto regi ~o sese nolle infundere acerbiorem *G. Hen. II* 17. **b** **s1301** quia per Scotorum incursionem et Francorum ~onem .. pecunia destituitur *Ann. Ed. I* 454.

2 (med.) exacerbation, aggravation.

BACON IX 200 (v. exacerbare 2); paroximus, i. ~o, inde paroxiticon, i. exacerbativum, ut in Alexandro de frenesi *Alph.* 135.

exacerbativus

1 provocative, exasperating.

querulo itaque et ~o sermone mox enarrant quam precipitanter .. regnum turbaverit H. BOS. *Thom.* V 8.

2 (med.) irritant, exacerbating.

Alph. 135 (v. exacerbatio 2).

exacedron v. hexahedron. **exaconton** v. pyxacanthos.

exactare [*backformed from* exactus *p. ppl. of* exigere], to exact. *V. et. exigere.*

c1148 ne aliquis .. exactiones exigat seu servitia aliqua ex eis ~et [*but ? l.* exartat] *Cart. Sallay* 531.

exacte [CL], exactly, accurately, precisely.

fides verborum tanto ~ius a nobis requiritur quanto clarius .. BALD. CANT. *Sacr. Alt.* 667A.

exactio [CL]

1 question. **b** demand, requisition; **c** (w. obj. gen.). **d** exaction (w. ref. to penalty). **e** calling in (of debt, fig.).

haec est .. perfecta .. humanae naturae oboedientia, cum .. acceptam bonam [Dei] voluntatem sine omni ~one spontanea libertate opere perficit ANSELM (*Medit.* 3) III 88; dum blandis ~onibus omnem vite illius accepisset historiam W. MALM. *Mir. Mariae* 215. **b** ~one principali de Normannia numerosi bellatores acciti sunt ORD. VIT. III 11 p. 124; cum .. exigo et ille quod exigitur denegat, quoniam illum per ~onem irrito, terga vertimus loco ad quem ire debemus ALEX. CANT. *Dicta* 16 p. 173; jejunium summe ~onis est ut in his qui non comedunt nisi radices et herbas BELETH *RDO* 11. 25B; **12..** quidam presbyteri .. ~ones faciunt a laicis corpus Christi tenentes in manibus ac si dicerent 'quid mihi vultis dare et ego eum vobis tradam' *Conc. Scot.* II 40. **c** **796** si melius sit rudibus populis in principio fidei jugum inponere decimarum, ut plena fiat per singulas domus ~o illarum ALCUIN *Ep.* 110; **1178** ut Cantuariensis archiepiscopus te et successores tuos .. absque ~one obedientie .. benedicat (*Lit. Papae*) ELMH. *Cant.* 422; nisi Turstinus .. sine ~one professionis, in Eboracensem reciperetur sedem J. HEX. *HR Cont.* 303; de fidei tamen ~one nichil scit *Feod. Durh.* 286. **d** ipsa .. perversitatis .. satisfactio vel a non satisfaciente poenae ~o .. in eadem universitate suum tenent locum ANSELM (*CurD* I 15) II 73; sic fiat donec veredictum unanimiter proferatur et non per dietam vel prisone ~onem *Fleta* 52. **e** nullam illi [monacho bonam deserenti voluntatem] vim per nos inferentes illum Dei ~oni, cui se debitorem fecit, dimittimus ANSELM (*Ep.* 113) III 248.

2 exaction, toll, tax; **b** (w. *saecularis*).

c733 (15c) totam ~onem navis .. michi .. jure publico in Lundoniensi portu prius competentem *CS* 149; ~o, *geabules monung GlC* E 518; **?a1081** rogo quatinus .. clericos .. quietos ab omni invectione atque ~one .. dimittatis LANFR. *Ep.* 19 (42); **c1148** (v. exactare); **a1172** (v. buttagium); **a1214, 1320** (v. demanda a). **b** **1194** liberi sint .. de omnibus aliis secularibus ~onibus tam per mare quam per terram (*Ch. Regis*) *MGL* II 655; **1213** carucatam terre .. tenendam .. quiete ab operacione et ab omni seculari ~one *Regesta Scot.* II 513; **c1284** reddendo annuatim .. iiij d. pro omni servicio, sectis curie, ~one seculari, et demanda *Deeds Balliol* 2.

3 (leg.) charge, claim.

in causis omnibus .. alii sunt accusatores, alii defensores, alii testes, alii judices .. nullaque simul ~one permixti (*Leg. Hen.* 5. 1) *GAS* 548; si placitum sit furti vel ~onis hujusmodi (*Ib.* 49. 7) *Ib.* 572; **1219** R. petit .. terciam partem ut jus suum, quia terra partibilis est .. consideratum est quod non respondeat .. eo quod terra nuncquam fuit partita ..: et sit in misericordia pro injusta ~one *CurR* VIII xi; **s1232** H., .. cui datus fuerat a rege terminus ille ad respondendum super articulis et ~onibus supradictis, .. non ausus est comparere WEND. III 35.

exactionalis, pertaining to exaction of a due. *V. et. exactorius* a.

nulli vel aliquando vel alicubi necesse sit de causis ~ibus .. inprovise respondere (*Leg. Hen.* 61. 19) *GAS* 582.

exactionare, to plunder.

1432 si vero fortassis in partibus transmarinis aut in mari transeundo aut redeundo captus fuero per inimicos et ~atus *Reg. Cant.* II 493.

exactivus [LL], exactive, exacting; **b** (w. obj. gen.). **c** extortionate.

sunt iiij media citra excommunicacionem ad decimas acquirendum .. non dico ~a, sed secundum caritatem ewangelicam allectiva WYCL. *Civ. Dom.* I 323. **b** ea .. quorum prior justitia legis fuerat ~a, fidei gratia exhibentur voluntaria R. NIGER *Mil.* II 66; ~a responsionis allocutio BALSH. *AD rec. 2* 12; necessitas est ~a refectionis J. GODARD *Ep.* 222; amoris vehemencia ex parte Dei nostre

dileccionis ~a BRINTON *Serm.* 34 p. 174. **c** rex exactivus [v. l. exacturus], vecors, injustus oditur, / fortis diligitur, justus, ratione dativus (*In Franciam*) *Pol. Poems* I 39; vinum contemplacionis .. per statum et potestatem ~am vel secularem extigwitur WYCL. *Ver.* I 68.

exactor [CL]

1 one who expels or drives off.

s1256 fur es .. nocturnus boum ~or M. PAR. *Maj.* V 577.

2 one who exacts, demander (also fig.); **b** (w. obj. gen.). **c** exacter of penalty.

licitum est nobis .. vivere .. de donis quae in munere Deo offeruntur, sed non licet vi extorquere, quia ministri Dei esse debemus, non ~ores ÆLF. *Ep.* 3. 63; ~or, i. .. postulator *GlH* E 424; plebes .. ab iniquis ~oribus atque predonibus patrocinando protexit ORD. VIT. X 16 p. 92; **s1017** [rex Cnut] fecit .. mirabilem censum reddi ... dignum ~orem Dominus justus Anglis imposuit H. HUNT. *HA* VI 15; a pravis ~oribus fiebant iniquitates sub alicujus cause pretextu MAP *NC* IV 2 f. 44; venter noster importunus ~or est J. GODARD *Ep.* 221. **b** **796** esto praedicator pietatis, non decimarum ~or ALCUIN *Ep.* 107; contentus erit ~or juramenti si fidelitatis servande sibi succinctim absolute verba prestentur J. SAL. *Ep.* 192 (202 p. 296); nec laudis ~or nec aure popularis aucupator GIR. *EH* I 4; posuit Deus predicatorem, non ~orem bone vite in aliis GASCOIGNE *Loci* 59. **c** **804** per singula momenta properat dirus ~or quem nullus vitare potest ALCUIN *Ep.* 294; †seminicemque [MS: seminecemque] virum .. / proiceret canibus rabidis exactor edendum WULF. *Swith.* II 450; **1077** non horreant se traditos esse tyranno et ~ori ANSELM (*Ep.* 80) III 203; non huc venimus ut cultores Christi ledamus, sed ut a sevis ~oribus eruamus ORD. VIT. IX 15 p. 608; nullus ~orum in regiam prolem lapidem mittere presumebat *V. Kentig.* 4.

3 collector (of tax), reeve, official.

823 ut omnes agros sint libera (*sic*) .. a pastu regum et principum, ducum et prefectum (*sic*) ~orumque *Ch. Roff.* 18; †**964** (12c) (v. centuriata); ~or regis .. equo insilivit ÆTHELW. III 1; ~or, i. monitor cens[u]um, *scyldlæta GlH* E 424; partim a regiis ~oribus comprehensi .. compedibus astricti sunt OSB. *Mir. Dunst.* 22; Tancredus princeps militie milites et gentiles captivos protinus missis ~oribus collegit ORD. VIT. X 24 p. 153; **s1248** coguntur .. miserabiles negotiatores et truculenter a regiis ~oribus angariantur M. PAR. *Maj.* V 7.

4 executor. *Cf. actor 2, exsecutor.*

a940 (13c) hujus sane cedulae testes et ~ores sunt quorum nomina .. annotantur *CS* 640.

exactorie, in a demanding manner, by compulsion.

'sine consilio .. tuo nihil volui facere, uti ne velut' (ut non) 'ex necessitate' (~ie) 'bonum tuum esset, sed voluntarium' LANFR. *Comment. Paul.* (*Philem.* 14) 374; Christus cum suis apostolis vixit vitam pauperrimam, .. nihil ~ie redonando apostolis sed ex libere collatis simpliciter .. victitanto (*sic*) WYCL. *Compl.* 92; **1423** episcopum ab ipso abbate ~ie, in manifestum prejudicium sue ecclesie vendicatis (*sic*) AMUND. I 73*n*.

exactorius, pertaining to exaction of a due; *v. et. exactionalis.* **b** extortionate.

medietatem decime .. tenebant pacto, ut omnes episcopales consuetudines, et omnes ~ias servitutes persolverent pro illo ORD. VIT. VI 6 p. 34; rotulus ~ius ille est in quo .. annotantur firme regis *Dial. Scac.* I 16 A. **b** Saxoniam .. Angli repedarunt, regis mandata Eadmundo .. detulerunt, et quasi vi ~ia illum in regem petierunt G. FONT. *Inf. S. Edm.* 4 p. 38; **1424** bonum est .. dum res tranquille geritur .. nec aliquid contrarium aut ~ium innovatur previdere qualis sit futurus contencionis exitus AMUND. I 189.

exactrix [LL *as adj.*], exactress, agent.

717 dum ~x invisi Plutonis, mors videlicet .. in limine latrat BONIF. *Ep.* 9.

exacuare v. exacuere.

exacuatio [cf. exacuare, acuatio], sharpening.

1532 Johanni R. pro ~one *le pykks Househ. Bk. Durh.* 88 (cf. ib.: acuacio *le pykks*).

exacuere [CL], **~are**

1 to sharpen; **b** (fig.); **c** (w. ref. to *Ezek.* xxi 9–10).

8.. et .. ~it, *and scerpð WW*; aquila .. fertur .. lapidem .. jam prope, rostrum purgando pariter et ~endo, perforasse GIR. *IK* II 9. **b** exacuere leves inimici frustra ligones / nequiquam ancipites inspicant acrius enses FRITH. 842; contumacie stimulos .. malleolis odii in acies penetrativas ~are non cessavit *Chr. Rams.* 156; philosophie instrumentum quod mentem mira subtilitate ~it J. SAL. *Pol.* 438A; orationum sagitte tunc ~untur J. FORD *Serm.* 15. 3. **c** **1140** gladios in te male juratus miles ~it G. FOLIOT *Ep.* 1; gladius .. ~atus .. et limatus quasi libero suo dimissus arbitrio, vadit 'ad dexteram suam sive ad sinistram' J. FORD *Serm.* 41. 4.

2 to spur (horse). **b** (fig.) to goad, stimulate.

s1298 sonipede calcaribus ~ato (v. congressus c). **b** aliquis .. ad virginis [Etheldride] incorruptionem certius explorandam sotios ~ere temptavit W. MALM. *GP* IV 183; **s1257** improperabant insuper regine quod patrem suum regem Anglie ~erat et vocaverat ut .. hostiliter veniret M. PAR. *Maj.* V 656.

3 to whet (appetite or desire).

questio .. quo federe nodet / oppositos mixtura cibos, quo frixa paratu / exacuant gustus HANV. II 193 p. 264; vota sua in vetitum ~ens NIG. *Ep.* 17; J. HOWD. *Ph.* 990 (v. degustare b).

exacuminare [LL], to sharpen (fig.).

institutionibus apostolicis ~atus, in presbiteros sue diocesis exarsit ORD. VIT. XII 25 p. 406.

exacuriare v. excurare.

exadmirari [cf. CL admirari], to wonder, marvel.

intellectus humanus non quiescit in talibus nisi perveniat ad cognicionem cause; ideo ~ari [*sic*, ? l. ~ati] ceperunt philosophi philosophari MELTON 247.

exadverso v. advertere 3c, ex 1b. **exaenia** v. exenium.

exaequare [CL], to equal, match.

numerus .. 4 cum re multiplicandus erit, et producentur 4 res, substantiam quam divisimus, hoc est 10 sine re ~antes ROB. ANGL. *Alg.* 106; W. CANT. *Mir. Thom.* II 31 (v. 1 coxa 1a); **12..** (v. duodecies).

exaestuare [CL], to blaze out, flare up. **b** to boil up, seethe; **c** (fig.).

calor ~ans GIR. *TH* I 33; ~o, A. *to wexe hote WW*. **b** ~at, fluctuat *GlC* E 459; ~o, A. *to .. byle WW*. **c** PULL. *CM* 221 (v. euripus 1a); caro .. que lasciviendo ~asset GIR. *GE* II 10.

exaestuatio [LL], surging.

ad hoc facinus ~o marina Normannos adjuvit, que ad rivulum quemdam Eduinum morari coegit ORD. VIT. IV 7 p. 216; fortis maris ~o .. abundanter exundans *G. Steph.* I 27.

exaggeranter [LL], in exacerbated or intensified manner.

mox guttur .. cepit intumescere et palatum ipsius cum lingua et faucibus .. ~er per tres dies .. amaricare R. COLD. *Godr.* 234.

exaggerare [CL]

1 to heap up; **b** (fig.). **c** to pile up (accusation, reproach, or threat).

anniversarias avide praedas .. ~abant GILDAS *EB* 17; ~at, i. congregat, accumulat *GlH* E 414; **s1217** M. PAR. *Min.* II 225 (v. cumera b). **b** reges habet Britannia, sed tyrannos, .. immensum montem scelerum ~antes GILDAS *EB* 27; ex corpore sibi anima letitiam vel merorem ~abit PULL. *Sent.* 644D. **c** Sophonias propheta clarus quas minas ~at audite GILDAS *EB* 55; exagerat, †explorat [l. exprobrat] *GlC* E 448; exagerat, †exprobat [MS: exprobrat] *GlH* E 445; execrat, ~at *Ib.* 480; **s1224** comes .. Cestrensis .. tumens et minas ampullosas contra regem et justiciarium ~ans M. PAR. *Min.* II 260.

2 to increase, make greater (partly fig.).

~at, i. .. auget *GlH* E 414; hoc etiam gaudium praeclaro ~atur miraculo GOSC. *Aug. Maj.* 80C; Convallus Eugenii germanus omnibus virtutibus ~atus LESLEY *RGScot.* 147.

3 to emphasise, enlarge on, exaggerate.

quid opus est professionem Nathanaelis protestantis verbis ~are 'rabbi, tu es Filius Dei' [*John* i 49]? ALCUIN (*Adv. Elipand.*) *Dogm.* 91C; **802** scio .. pontificem multas dicturum [v. l. dicendas] esse accusationes contra fratres nostros, et quae gesta sunt ~are *Id. Ep.* 245 p. 394; non dico bonorum virorum virtutes ad exemplum bene vivendi aliis non esse monstrandas, sed eisdem ipsis non esse ~andas ANSELM (*Ep.* 189) IV 75; ~are .. calumnias (*Ib.* 192) *Ib.* 80; hec dicens, virge quam tenebat gravi ad pavimentum illisione, indignitatem rei ~are visus est W. MALM. *GP* I 54; [episcopus] .. enormitatem ~at maleficii AD. EYNS. *Hug.* IV 5 p. 22.

exaggeratim, in heaps.

~im, cumulanter OSB. GLOUC. *Deriv.* 194.

exaggeratio [CL]

1 (rhet.) heaping up (fig.), intensifying (by repetition).

Gl. Leid. 28. 69 (v. emphasis a); 'si linguis hominum loquar et' etiam 'angelorum' (~o) LANFR. *Comment. Paul.* (*1 Cor.* xiii 1) 199; quid sibi velit hec verborum ~o [*Matth.* xxii 37], hec inculcatio tam .. exacta BALD. CANT. *Tract.* 3. 417D.

2 increase.

insoliti vectigalis gravi ~one .. plebes .. oppressit ORD. VIT. VIII 8 p. 312.

3 exaggeration, overstatement.

opus enim, quod tuis exhortationibus et inconsulta, fateor, pollicitatione suscepi, majus est et crebrescentium cotidie malorum innovatione profusum ~onibus, permutationibus, permixturis, ex oppositis, ex adjunctis, verum circumstanciis, contingentium modis (*Quad., dedic.*) *GAS* 529; ~one rerum (ut qui nominant et promittunt grit[h]breche vel hamsocnam ..) (*Leg. Hen.* 22. 1) *Ib.* 561.

exagitare [CL]

1 to stir up. **b** to buffet, toss about.

~at, i. commovet *GlH* E 431; D. BEC. 1031 (v. crustella). **b** ut .. tota nocte inter obstantes undas nunc huc nunc illuc ~ata fuisset [navis] G. MON. XII 4; **s1263** navibus ~atis, grassantibus et conquassatis FORDUN *Cont.* X 16.

2 to sting. **b** to bait, goad (bear or bull). **c** to arouse, excite (person or his emotion).

scorpionis aculeo ~atus occiditur GIR. *TH* I 27. **b** **1349** [*flesh*] taurorum ~atorum *Cal. Pl. Mem. Lond.* I 228; CAIUS *Can.* 7 (v. arctylus). **c** GOSC. *Transl. Aug.* 28 (v. credere 5a); eum quem sepe iracundie furor ~at AILR. *Spir. Amicit.* III 14. 681A; 'moverunt capita sua' [*Psalm* cviii 25] .. ad subsannationem meam, semetipsos invicem ~antes J. FORD *Serm.* 56. 4.

3 to drive from place to place. **b** to persecute, harass.

~ans, persequens, *fesigende GlP* 194; pares in bello victoria sequestravit, et pompa triumphantes, post dejectos et fugaces, ~avit ORD. VIT. XII 18 p. 356; Io objecta, Erinys sub specie oestri [eam] per totum orbem ~avit *Natura Deorum* 23. **b** EADMER *Wilf.* 46 (v. contrarietas 1a); totum regnum injustis exactionibus .. ~avit ORD. VIT. VII 8 p. 191; **s1251** ut .. innotescat quot .. injuriis nos .. Anglos ~at curia Romana M. PAR. *Maj.* V 233; quos etas juvenilior per fumosos libidinum estus .. per temeraria presumptionum precipitia .. vexatos ~at AD. MARSH *Ep.* 59.

4 to harangue, scold. **b** to consider, discuss.

~at, i. .. increpat, fatigat *GlH* E 431; uxor .. castissimum virum quotidianis jurgiis ~abat W. BURLEY *Vit. Phil.* 98. **b** 'si .. tecum exigas', id est ~es et penses apud te quid nobis sit .. faciendum TREVET *Troades* 41.

exagitatio [LL]

1 stirring up, exciting.

ut .. a talis insanie desisteret ~one, nec capud unquam ab motibus inquietis comprimeret R. COLD. *Cuthb.* 112.

2 hunt, chase.

in foresta pulcherrima post longam ferarum ~onem capellam prenobilem ingressus hominem in ea vidi MAP *NC* V 6 f. 66v.

3 harangue, scolding.

quorum [verborum] ~one stimulatus .. fratrem .. percussisset nisi .. G. COLD. *Durh.* 15.

exagium [LL < ἐξάγιον]

1 weighing. *V. et. essaium.*

ALDH. *PR* 140 p. 199 (v. aequamentum).

2 weight, measure.

recipe ceruse ʒ ij, cathimie ~ia duo, tuthie [etc.] .. ana ʒ j GILB. III 134. 2; recipe .. fenug[reci], mirre ana exag' j *Ib.* IV 178v. 2; potest sumi de trociscis eorum a dimidio ~io usque ad unum BACON IX 65; et ʒ j cum dimidio facit solidum, ~ium, et aureum, que tria idem sunt in pondere, licet nomina diversificentur J. MIRFIELD *Brev.* 92; ~ium habet lxxxx grana, que faciunt dragmam et semis .. ~ia 6 vel solidi 6 faciunt unciam unam ... ~ium solido differt in nomine solo *Eng. Weights* 34.

3 balance, scale.

idcirco arsis et thesis aequa sillabarum trutina et aequiperante temporum ~io pariter ponderabuntur ALDH. *PR* 125 p. 174; in .. pedibus aequo divisionis ~io trutinatis *Ib.* 135 p. 189; ~ium, *andmitta GlC* E 416; ~ium, *onmitta GlH* E 413.

exal- v. et. exhal-.

exalacritare [cf. CL alacritas], to cause to hasten, to urge on.

prepara materiam futuro operi .. tuum ~aturus patrem per omnia H. LOS. *Ep.* 57.

exalapare [LL], to beat, strike.

dum .. crebris palmarum contusionibus ~aretur ALDH. *VirgP* 43; ~aretur, *suungen GlC* E 477; ~aretur, flagellatus fuit *GlH* E 425; **9..** ~aretur, *wæs fystslægenu WW*.

exalbatio [cf. CL albatus], clothing in white (mon.). *V. et. dealbatio 5.*

magister eorum maximam circa illos adhibiturus est sollicitudinem, ut .. cum nullo ante ~onem suam signent vel loquantur, nec aliquis cum eis *Cust. Cant.* 271.

exalbidus [CL], off-white, whitish.

satirion .. habet .. florem purpureum vel purpurastrum et ~um *Alph.* 158.

exalere [LL], to feed, nourish.

to growe, adolere, coalere .., ~ere (tercie conjugacionis) *CathA.*

exalienare [cf. CL alienare], to dispossess, disinherit.

exheredet, i. ~at de hereditate, *beyrfeweardige GlH* E 462.

exallage [ἐξαλλαγή], complete change, alteration.

~e, permotatio [i.e. permutatio] *GlC* E 466 (cf. *Gl. Leid.* 28. 29: †exallege).

exalligare [cf. CL alligare], to release, revoke.

1261 nec relaxentur [v. l. exalligantur] sententie .. donec de .. inobedientia .. satisfecerit *Conc.* I 749b (cf. *Conc. Syn.* 676).

exallogeneus [cf. ἀλλογενής], heterogeneous.

sunt et principia heterogenea sive exeleogenea, i.e. alterius nature, quam sint ea quorum ipsa sicut principia NECKAM *NR* II 173.

exallus [ἔξαλλος], of another type, different.

exeleos sive xenos, peregrinum NECKAM *NR* II 173.

exaltabilis, worthy to be exalted.

abbas insuper erit venerabilis, magnificus, et ~is *VSB* (*Iltut* 9) 206; **1420** speramus .. quod Cantuariensem ecclesiam concernentia vestra promocione ~i feliciter reflorescent *Lit. Cant.* III 140.

exaltare [CL]

1 to raise to a higher level; **b** (fig.); **c** (road or bank); **d** (water level).

illi qui ~atum pro signo serpentem aeneum aspiciebant BEDE *Hom.* II 18. 201; cum .. fumum supra muros urbis ~ari conspiceret *Id. HE* III 16; ~atus Mardocheus super equum selle regie non est tactus vana gloria AD. DORE *Pictor* 154; crux exaltatur illic, campana renarrat / ecclesie laudes GARL. *Hon. Vit.* 179; [abbas T., ob. **1236**] ~avit ad majus luminare vestiarii *Chr. Evesham* 271; **1244** iij fenestras ejusdem aule cum operatione cementaria ad modum porticus ~ari faciant *Liberate* 20 m. 14; s**1258** pistores .. non fuerunt positi in pillorio .. sed .. ~ati fuerunt in tumberella *Leg. Ant. Lond.* 41; s**1283** caput [Griffini] supra turrim Londoniensem .. fixum ~averunt *Plusc.* VII 31; edificiorum fabrice .. tali proceritate, que paupertati non convenit, ~ate R. BURY *Phil.* 6. 88. **b** stabat adhuc spiritus procelle et ~ati sunt fluctus ejus AILR. *Ed. Conf.* 743D. **c** **1296** suffodit terricidias de fossato Norwyci ~ando calcetum tente sue *Leet Norw.* 47; **1313** ~avit viam regiam ex opposito messuagii quondam Thome G. cum gravella et sabilone ita quod per illam exaltacionem obstupavit cursum aque de M. *Ib.* 59; **1323** (v. diaeta 3b); **1344** (v. chorda 7b). **d** a**1135** monachi stagnum .. molendini ad nocumentum terre mee vel gardini mei non ~abunt *Cart. Glouc.* I 243; .. quod injuste .. ~avit stagnum molendini sui .. ad nocumentum liberi tenementi GLANV. XIII 36; **1221** J. obstruxit illud *flete* et ~avit stagnum, per quod non possunt trahere buscam *CurR* X 3; prohibetur ne quis faciat in suo per quod nocere possit vicino, ut si stagnum ~averit in suo BRACTON 232.

2 to raise (voice). **b** (mus.) to raise in pitch.

infatigabili clamore .. vocem ~ant GIR. *TH* I 14. **b** psalmi .. dicuntur sub una voce, nullum psalmum ~ando in choro; .. rectores dicant .. totum psalmum 'Venite', nullum versum ~ando *Brev. Sal.* xii.

3 (w. person or institution as obj.): **a** to elevate, exalt (in status); **b** (spiritually). **c** to praise, extol. **d** to make confident or proud, to puff up.

a c**1077** gloria .. Deo, cui vita vestra sic placuit ut eam ad exemplum ~aret ANSELM (*Ep.* 78) III 201; Archgallo .. nobiles .. laborabat deponere, et ignobiles ~are G. MON. III 17; **1341** nos .. in annis adolescentie ad regni solium ~ati (*Lit. Regis*) AVESB. 95; AD. MUR. *Chr.* app. 248 (v. exsultare d); s**1256** episcopatus sui cathedralem .. possessionibus ditavit et prebendis et canonicis ~avit FORDUN *Cont.* X 11. **b** nonnulli edito virginitatis fastigio sublimati et pudicae conversationis arcibus ~ati ALDH. *VirgP* 13; **796** quemcumque voluerit, ~at [sc. Deus] ALCUIN *Ep.* 107; eum miseratio Christi / .. / non tantumque polis sed et exaltavit in arvis WULF. *Swith.* I 482; LANFR. *Comment. Paul.* 177 (v. 1 despicere 2d). **c** adulteria punire, iniquos non ~are O. CANT. *Const.* 2; a**1085** non probo quod .. Clementem tot .. preconiis tam propere ~as LANFR. *Ep.* 59 (52). **d** **796** non te saeculi pompa ~et ALCUIN *Ep.* 114; nisi .. homo prius habuerit voluntatem .. ~andi .. numquam .. extolletur. .. de exaltatione .. avaritia et alia similia *Simil. Anselmi* 36; qui nimis exaltat se confundetur in ymis WALT. ANGL. *Fab.* 42. 31; exaltabuntur in Gallos cornua justi / letificabuntur Angli (cf. *Psalm* lxxiv 11) (J. BRIDL.) *Pol. Poems* I 156.

4 (w. abstr. obj.): **a** to increase. **b** to extol, make much of. **c** to elevate (to higher things). **d** to heighten (anger).

a ut, sicut Deus vestram .. ~at potestatem, ita .. ANSELM (*Ep.* 294) IV 214. **b** vos arroganter verba ~asse GILDAS *EB* 74; horum .. miracula suprafatus auctor [sc. Goscelinus] predicat, signa ~at W. MALM. *GP* I 2; *Fleta* 51 (v. diabolus 1a); comendant et ~ant [ME: *heved up*] elemosinam quam facit *AncrR* 81. **c** usque ad Christum et B. Virginem [philosophi] considerationem suam ~averunt BACON *Tert.* 48. **d** mulieris animum diabolus instigat, regis iram mulier ~at OSB. *V. Dunst.* 27.

5 to increase, raise (price or rent).

post obitum Petri, ~avit archiepiscopus dictam terram ad xvj li. *RDomin* 3; **1319** quod tallagia .. non augmententur seu ~entur nisi de communi consensu majoris et communitatis (*Ch. Regis*) *MGL* I 142; precium rerum .. ~averunt .. a iiij s. usque ad iiij nobilia Anglorum GASCOIGNE *Loci* 104; a**1470** inquiratur .. de hiis qui regratunt grana .. aut alia bona .. ~antes primum precium et .. in cariori foro vendent [v. l. vendentes] quam .. vendi debeant *BBAdm* I 231.

6 (astr., pass.) to be raised to position of greatest 'influence'.

GROS. 43 (v. descensio a); preter istas virtutes planete habent alias virtutes que dicuntur exaltationes; Sol enim ~atur in Ariete, Luna in Tauro, Saturnus in Libra, Jupiter in Cancro, Mars in Capricorno, Venus in Piscibus, Mercurius in Virgine ROB. ANGL. (II) 169; exaltatio Martis 28 gradu. in Aquario nullus ~atur BACON V 22*n*.

7 (alch.): **a** to distill. **b** to raise (to higher 'degree'), refine.

a cum tota calx soluta et ~ata fuerit per alembicum in aquam claram RIPLEY 212. **b** exaltacio parum differt a sublimacione .. si velis tua corpora ~are, illa sublima primo spiritu vite, donec terra sit bene subtiliata per naturalem rectificacionem omnium elementorum *Id. Axiom.* 116.

8 (? intr.) to rise (or, by conf. w. *exhalare*, to emit (odour)).

~avit, *stonc GlC* E 391.

exaltatio [LL]

1 lifting, raising up. **b** erection or heightening (of structure). **c** raising (of water level). **d** (w. ref. to Feast of the Exaltation of the Holy Cross, 14 Sept.).

caelestis .. est ascensio ejus ad vitam sempiternam, terrena vero ~o ejus ad mortem temporalem BEDE *Hom.* II 18. 199 (cf. ib.: ~o .. serpentis aenei); c**1470** pro ~one trium campanarum *Ac. Churchw. Glast.* 282. **b** a**1198** conductum fontis de S. et ~onem molendini et stagni et vivarii *Danelaw* 138; **1242** pro cxj li. xij s. positis in ~one magne turris *KRMem* 20 m. 12*d.*; a**1270** dedi .. canonicis .. [de L.] in emendationem et ~onem .. domus de L. quandam partem bosci mei in S. *Ch. Sal.* 235; **1313** (v. exaltare 1c); **1358** (v. deexaltatio); **1424** pro ~one murorum dicte ecclesie ex utraque parte supra columpnas *Reg. Cant.* II 300. **c** **1181** P. M. r. c. de xl s. pro ~one stagni *Pipe* 44; **1203** de ~one cujusdam stagni in A. [*Norf*] ad nocumentum .. tenementi .. Tebbaldi *CurR* III 49. **d** EGB. *Pont.* 89, etc. (v. crux 3c); iiij dies ante ~onem Sancte Crucis *Descr. Constant.* 247; de Pascha usque ad festum ~onis Sancte Crucis [ME: *from Aster oðet þe Halirode*] *AncrR* 165.

2 raising (of voice).

s**1306** tantus clangor tubarum .. et ~o vocum pre gaudio .. clamancium *Flor. Hist.* III 131.

3 raising (in status), promotion (of person). **b** exalted position, dignity.

796 ut in filii mei karissimi ~one gauderem ALCUIN *Ep.* 114; c**1077** antequam mihi liceret .. litteras exsultationis pro vestra ~one mittere, audivi quod .. ANSELM (*Ep.* 78) III 200; **1165** in promptu erit et Alexandri dejectio et pape nostri Pascalis ~o (*Lit. ad Papam*) *Becket Mat.* V 189. **b** ut de terrena ~one .. ad caeleste regnum .. vos [Hen. I] perducat ANSELM (*Ep.* 402) V 346; **1257** festo .. coronationis nostre .. celebrato .. visum est .. ~oni nostre votive plurimum expedire ut statim .. humiliationi nostrorum rebellium intendamus (*Lit. Regis Romanorum*) *Leg. Ant. Lond.* 28 (cf. *Foed.* I 623b).

4 exaltation, glorification: **a** (of person); **b** (of nation or realm); **c** (of Faith or Church); **d** (spiritual).

a ut .. in mea defensione simul et ~one plurimum exultarem OSB. *Mir. Dunst.* 25; **1339** status vestri [sc. prioris] prosperitatem et ~onem .. affectavimus toto corde *Lit. Cant.* II 215; constituit Petrum summum pontificem .. non propter utilitatem et ~onem vel honorem Petri, sed .. propter utilitatem fidelium OCKHAM *Pol.* I 46; **1439** zelantes .. honorem et ~onem ejusdam [abbatis] (*Lit. ad Papam*) BEKYNTON I 12. **b** **793** aequitas principum populi est ~o ALCUIN *Ep.* 18; c**1261** conservet Dominus personam vestram ad ~onem regni Anglie †pro [l. per] tempora diuturna (*AncC* IV 13) *RL* II 184; **1439** ut .. in .. nacionis Anglicane honoris ~onem et provectum .. nomen cardinalatus .. in se assumeret (*Pat*) BEKYNTON I 43. **c** a**804** Deum .. deprecor ut proficias in ~one aecclesiarum Christi ALCUIN *Ep.* 288; videntes gloriam et ~onem sanctae ecclesiae LANFR. *Comment. Paul.* (*Rom.* x 19) 140; **1337** dilatet imperium et confirmet ad ~onem catholice fidei (*Lit. ad regem*) *Collect. Ox.* I 34; **1481** ad .. honorem .. Domini .. et ecclesie sue .. ~onem *Lit. Cant.* III 307. **d** solemus .. in majorum nostrorum ~one congaudere, ut cum in nataliciis sanctorum festiva exultatione jucundamur ANSELM (*CurD* I 18) II 80; ut mundum relinquendo Christum sequaris et per temporalem humilitatem et paupertatem ~onem et divitias aeternas consequaris *Id.* (*Ep.* 133) III 276.

5 conceit, pride.

~onis genera sunt xv. .. est aliquando ~o in sola opinione, ut si quis opinetur se esse dignum pontificatu nec tamen velit fieri episcopus *Simil. Anselmi* 21.

6 increase, rise (of price or tax).

1362 quod ~o custume predicte ultra dim. m. de sacco ante hec tempora facta eis non cedat in prejudicium *RScot* I 867a; **1382** judicium collistrigii pro ~one mercati (*LBLond.* H f. 157) *MGL* I 606.

7 (astr.) 'exaltation', rise to position of greatest 'influence'.

sunt in signis predictis quedam fortitudines, que planetis attribuuntur; que dicuntur potestates vel dignitates seu testimonia, ut sunt domus, ~o, triplicitas, terminus, facies, aspectus GROS. 42; *Id. Hexaem.* V 9 (v. dinumerabilis); ROB. ANGL. (II) 169, BACON V 22*n.* (v. exaltare 6); dicunt astronomi quod sol ibi habeat suam ~onem, que est major ejus dignitas, vel secunda post majorem BACON *Maj.* I 191; Saturni ~o ELVEDEN *Cal.* 6.

8 (alch.): **a** distillation, evaporation. **b** 'exaltation', raising (to higher 'degree'), refining.

a post hec intendimus .. olei distillationem et aque ~onem BACON *Min.* 314. **b** RIPLEY *Axiom.* 116 (v. exaltare 7b); ~o est sublimatio. est etiam operatio qua res affectionibus mutata ad altiorem substantiae et virtutis dignitatem perducitur, vel est subtiliatio res sensim dissolvendo, in puriorem et majorem virtutis suae gradum transponens, et fit circulatione, aut ablutione *LC*.

exaltator [LL], uplifter, exalter.

sunt .. nomina verbalia in -trix desinentia feminina, sicut masculina in -or terminantur .. ~or, exaltatrix ALDH. *PR* 126; c**923** rex gloriose, sanctae ~or ecclesiae, gentilitatis humiliator pravae (*Lit. Radbodi*) W. MALM. *GP* V 249.

exaltatrix, uplifter, exalter (f.).

ALDH. *PR* 126 (v. exaltator).

examb- v. excamb-.

examen [CL]

1 swarm: **a** (of bees); **b** (of other creatures).

a siquidem, infantulus cum in cunis .. quiesceret .. ~en apium ora .. complevit ALDH. *VirgP* 26 (cf. id. *VirgV* 657: examen apum .. / contexit faciem pueri); ~en, *suearm GlC* E 506; ut .. ~ina favos deserant GIR. *TH* I 6; **1326** dicunt quod prepositus et bedelli consueverunt habere .. de bonis felonii ~ina apium si fuerint *BB St. Davids* 256; propoleos, i. favus sine cera alba et virginia, quam primo faciunt ~ina, i. nove apes *Alph.* 150. **b** vermium ~ina ALDH. *VirgP* 36 (v. ebullire 2).

2 horde, troop (of persons).

collecto ~ine famulorum Christi BEDE *HE* III 22 p. 173; doctor .. Pictorum examina nanctus *Mir. Nin.* 65; FRITH. 1098 (v. barridus); ministrorum ~ina pullulabant H. BOS. *Thom.* II 11; hoc unum virgini dulce solacium / concedat rapidum examen hostium, / ut .. WALT. WIMB. *Carm.* 607; monachorum ~ina FERR. *Kinloss* 6.

3 tongue of balance. **b** assay or specimen for assay; *v. et. examinatio* 1c.

~en, i. †filium [l. filum] in medium qua trutinae †stratera [MS: statera] regitur et lances aequantur, vel lingua lancis dicitur *GlH* E 406; ~en, *wægetunge* ÆLF. *Gl.*; GARL. *Syn.* 1588B (v. bilanx); hoc ~en, lingua bilancis; est examen apum colleccio, lingua bilancis *WW*. **b** facto .. ~ine, defert illud argentarius ad barones .. et .. ponderat illud .. tunc inscribitur idem ~en desuper ducta creta hiis verbis: 'Everwicscira ..' *Dial. Scac.* I 6 H; fusor duos percipit denarios pro ~ine *Ib.* I; **1229** (v. dealbare 2b); **1236** abbas Sancti Eadmundi habet eundem diem ad respondendum de ~ine cunei sui, nisi aliquid velit dicere contra ~en *KRMem* 14 m. 21*d.*; **1280** inter multimodas examinationes ~en per assaium certius reputatur *RBExch* III 992.

4 divine (esp. last) judgement. *V. et. examinatio* 2.

680 supremum vivorum et mortuorum ~en, quando .. retributio aequissimis judicii lancibus trutinabitur ALDH. *Ep.* 4 p. 486; **716** gratias agere non cesso dispensationi superni ~inis una cum .. fratribus qui .. HWÆTBERHT *Ep.*; **858** in die magni aexaminis *CS* 496; in die districti ~inis judici rationem sunt reddituri O. CANT. *Const.* 2;

Deus, .. non me justifico secundum ~en districti judicii tui ANSELM (*Ep.* 156) IV 19; **1146** (v. 2 distringere 3d); AD. MARSH *Ep.* 75 (v. contuitus c).

5 ordeal (esp. of water or iron); *v. et examinatio* 3; **b** (fig.).

WULF. *Swith.* II 320, W. JUM. II 20 (v. chalybs b); festis diebus ferri vel aque judicia (~ina) fieri prohibemus (*Quad.*) *GAS* 297; **a1150** (v. duellum 3c); GIR. *DK* I 14 (v. 1 candere 2c); **s1043** Emma .. scripsit .. se probare Dei judicio ferrique candentis ~ine episcopum fore injuste diffamatum HIGD. VI 23. **b** fiduciam habens quod beata virgo non sineret diu eam manere in hoc ~ine ANSELM BURY *Mir. Virg.* 23.

6 examination, inquisition, questioning; *v. et. examinatio* 4a; **b** (eccl. or acad.); *v. et. examinatio* 4c.

~en, i. .. probatio rectitudinis et justitiae *GlH* E 406; ~inis, inquisitionis *Ib.* 434; GIR. *EH pref.* (v. examinare 5a); **1269** cum W. .. agat coram baronibus .. contra [H.], ubi in inquisicionem respondendo consenciens et inde licet sero penitens et se tractum esse dicens ad ~en vetitum, querelam deposuerit coram vobis *KRMem* 43 m. 15*d.* **b** **s1226** si legatus vellet etiam fidei ~en subire WEND. II 306; **1543** se subjecit arduo et rigoroso et privato ~ini omnium doctorum .. collegii juris civilis *Form. S. Andr.* II 310; **1549** (v. examinare 5c); cur nos e sacris scripturis non convincunt? cur nos ad illarum ~en non revocant? JEWEL *Apol.* A 8.

7 consideration, judgement, weighing up. *V. et. examinatio* 5.

conveniant .. singuli vero ~ine conscientiam suam GILDAS *EB* 92; ALDH. *VirgP* 18 (v. electio 1d); discens examine multo / abdita .. scrutarier antra sophiae FRITH. 173; **a1087** si quae in ipsis culpae invenirentur suspensa interim vindicta ad nostrum ~en servarentur LANFR. *Ep.* 27 (30); si .. aliter vestro [i.e. archiep. Cant.] placuerit ~ini ANSELM (*Ep.* 72) III 193; utrum id recte sit, tuo ~ine velim esse securior ADEL. *QN prol.* p. 2; **c1375** si singula facti intente consideracionis ~ine inspexeritis .. *Pri. Cold.* 51; homines regionis istius apti majus redduntur .. ad discernendum in causis que magni sunt ~inis quam sunt viri qui .. ex ruris familiaritate mentis contrahunt ruditatem FORTESCUE *LLA* 24.

exametus v. hexamitum.

examinabilis [LL], that withstands examination, examinable.

conjunguntur stannum et cuprum cum mercurio, ut appareat hominibus argentum et aliquo modo fabricabile et in igne ~e .. et in examinatione nature *Correct. Alch.* 17.

1 examinare [CL]

1 to weigh, balance. **b** (math.) to distribute (quantity).

librat, ~at trutinatum *GlC* L 188. **b** in hac .. divisione et maximi divisoris continentia est et dividendi ~anda, i.e. comparanda. .. maximum divisorem et dividendum cum eorumdem continentia, i.e. quantitatem esse ~andam, censuimus vocaremus THURKILL *Abac.* 59.

2 to test, try; **b** (fig.). **c** to assay.

~a, i. .. amere *GlH* E 407; ~asti, probasti, *asude Ib.* 433. **b** ut ~ata [ecclesia] adversis, manifestius quam sit fide firma .. clarescat BEDE *Gen.* (xx 16) 184B; placuit .. provisori salutis nostrae .. ejus animam longa .. infirmitate .. ~ari *Id. HE* IV 21 p. 256; **a1104** sicut aurum in fornace probatur, ita mentes electorum suorum igne tribulationis ~at ANSELM (*Ep.* 312) V 239; cum probitatem suam in multis debellationibus ~asset, profectus est Romam G. MON. V 3; quod jubes, faciam; si vis, examina WALT. WIMB. *Carm.* 242. **c** *Dial. Scac.* I 6 F (v. argentarius b).

3 (w. ref. to divine judgement).

rimamini .. pectoris vestri profunda, an .. sacerdotalem gratiam ~andam in Domini revelatione conservetis GILDAS *EB* 106; ne .. ad perpetuam perditionem districtius ~ans tollat BEDE *HE* IV 23 p. 266; *Ib.* V 12 p. 308 (v. castigare 1a); vita ejus discutitur, ~atur, damnatur ALEX. CANT. *Mir.* 46 (I) p. 251.

4 (w. ref. to ordeal).

ferro vel aqua ~andi, si orationem ibi deposuerunt, .. de salute sua tripudiarunt W. MALM. *Glast.* 18; aqua ~antur; evadunt singuli BEN. PET. *Mir. Thom.* IV 79.

5 to examine, question (person, also refl. and fig.); **b** (leg.); **c** (eccl. or acad.).

quicunque .. tali consideratione se studuerit ~are, profecto non residebit in animo suo, quo jure se debeat prae aliis magnificare EADMER *Beat.* 15 p. 290; ut invidi .. judicis .. subdamur examini nos ipsos non ~antes GIR. *EH pref.* p. 222; tu, judex pietas, testes examina / et da sentenciam WALT. WIMB. *Carm.* 288; senes et infantes .. capti ac durissimis tormentis ut ecclesie sue thesauros ostenderent ~ati et examinati sunt *Croyl.* 22. **b** secta Willelmi ~ata est et testatur *BNB* II 583; **1324** Alicia .. in curia .. ~ata .. remitt' et quietumclam' .. jus quod habet .. *CBaron* 138; **1352** cuidam testi ~ato apud Ebor' in causa prioris, xiiij d. *Ac. Durh.* 552. **c** **1238** clericos .. a magistro E. et successoribus suis ~atos absque malitia et cavillatione ad dictas decimas .. admittent, et investient *Ch. Sal.* 247; **c1350** nullus legat nisi .. fuerit ~atus .. et cum ydoneus fuerit licencietur *StatOx* 20 (cf. ib. 201 [**1409**]: secundum magistrorum electorum ad ~andum determinatores estimacionem); cum .. episcopatus propter insufficienciam Roberti de S. electi in literatura, et in Romana curia ~ati propter defectum literature repulsi, per biennium vacavisset BIRCHINGTON *Arch. Cant.* 44; **1549** ut dialecticam artem experiri cupientes priusquam .. admittantur ~entur, et ne ad baccalaureatus seu magisterii lauream recipiantur nisi prius de examinis vigore ad hoc idonei fuerint reperti *Conc. Scot.* II 105; quod nullus infra civitatem Lond' .. super se assumat ad exercendum .. ut medicus .. nisi .. ~etur, approbetur et admittatur per episcopum Lond' *Entries* 463b.

6 to weigh (fig.), consider (proposal, document, or sim.). **b** (p. ppl.) carefully considered, deliberate.

neque abnegavit se .. eandem subiturum esse religionem; si tamen ~ata a prudentibus sanctior .. posset inveniri BEDE *HE* II 9 p. 98; taediosus ~andae in judiciis veritatis arbiter existebat ASSER *Alf.* 105; scripturam ipsam ~andam vestro mitto judicio ANSELM (*Mon., ep. ad Lanfr.*) I 6; **1324** .. et hujusmodi eleccio cancellario universitatis Cantebrig' notificetur, simpliciter approbanda, sed non ~anda *Stat. Mich. Cantab.* 644; **1475** cartam .. ~avimus et diligenter inspeximus, et quia per .. examinacionem .. *Scot. Grey Friars* II 212. **b** antiquorum .. ~atos labores securiori aviditate cupivimus perscrutari R. BURY *Phil.* 9. 145.

2 examinare v. exanimare.

examinarius, of an examiner, judicial.

s1330 simulavit se habere officium ~ium consistorii THORNE 2056.

examinate [LL], **~im,** deliberately, scrupulously.

sacerdos: 'decimas dabis omnium que possides.' .. penitens: 'si ita ~im [v. l. ~e] dande sunt decime, quis salvatur quia de tot milibus quis bene decimat?' ROB. FLAMB. *Pen.* 214.

examinatio [CL]

1 weighing, testing (of metal). **b** (fig.) testing, trial. **c** assay; *v. et. examen* 3b.

veram naturam argenteam non habet in se, sicut apparet in colore et ~one *Correct. Alch.* 17. **b** excipiuntur flammis ignis purgatorii et vel usque ad diem judicii longa hujus ~one a vitiorum sorde mundantur BEDE *Hom.* I 2. 30; putas te tactum virga Dei posse evadere sine ~one terroris? ALEX. CANT. *Mir.* 52 p. 267; multos tuorum hujus rei [i.e. expugnationis nigri militis] ~one vexasti que mei est terminata obsequio *Hist. Meriadoci* 364. **c** **c1248** (v. 1 essaium 1b); **1280** (v. examen 3b); **1361** assaiam de monetis .. cussis tam per ignem .. et pondus quam per ~onem operariorum monetarum *(Pat) Foed.* VI 308.

2 divine (esp. last) judgement. *V. et. examen* 4.

dies ~onis tales vos inveniat quales fons regenerationis purgat EGB. *Pont.* 99; **933** (v. dies 9b); in ~one extremi judicii *Latin Stories* 100; suscitabuntur a sepulcris et cum ipsis unientur anime eorum in ultima ~one ROLLE *IA* 159.

3 (leg.) ordeal. *V. et. examen* 5a. **b** torture.

ab adventu Domini usque ad octabas Epiphanie .. non est tempus leges faciendi, id est .. vel ferri vel aque vel alias legis ~ones tractari (*Leg. Hen.* 62. 1) *GAS* 583; **1167** aliis eruendo oculos, cogendo alios ad duellum, alios ad ~onem ignis vel aque BECKET *Ep.* 287; accusati sunt viri duo et ~oni aque addicti BEN. PET. *Mir. Thom.* IV 78. **b** [Ælfegus] ab eis [sc. paganis] captus et crudeli est ~one occisus EADMER *V. Anselmi* I 30.

4 examination, inquisition, questioning; *v. et. examen* 6a; **b** (leg.); **c** (eccl. or acad.); *v. et. examen* 6b.

quaestio, ~o *GlC* Q 37; BRACTON 80 (v. diligere 5b); **1354** per strictam ~onem dilectorum mercatorum nostrorum .. de ponderibus et custumis lanarum *RScot* 765a. **b** super ~one justiciariorum et narratorum .. facta per episcopum *Stat. Tri. Ed. I* 20; **1295** (v. examinator 3b); **s1376** dominus de Nevyle .. loqui desiit exspectans cum silentio ~onis sue tempus *Chr. Angl.* 80; **c1390** prima ~o testium .. facta in capella beate Marie *SelPlAdm* I 14. **c** **s1093** cum ante ordinandi pontificis ~onem .. Walchelinus .. electionem scriptam legeret EADMER *HN* 49; **1238** in ~one dictorum clericorum *Ch. Sal.* 247; **1268** secundum magistrorum electorum ad ~onem estimacionem *StatOx* 26; papa .. voluit quod .. electus ad Romanam curiam veniret, ~onem personaliter subiturus BIRCHINGTON *Arch. Cant.* 44.

5 consideration, judgement, scrutiny; *v. et. examen* 7; **b** (leg.).

ungebantur reges non per Deum sed qui ceteris crudeliores exstarent et .. ab unctoribus non pro veri ~one trucidabantur GILDAS *EB* 21; si ea .. meliora esse .. habita ~one perspexeris BEDE *HE* II 13 p. 112; cum .. prophetarum dicta considero et ea diligenti ~one perquiro *Eccl. & Synag.* 77; est in hoc volumine ab Elkaurezmo ~o planetarum et temporum secundum medium locum terre dictum Arin ADEL. *Elk. pref.*; sine magna fidelitatis ejus ~one prehabita GIR. *GE* II 32; **s1291** que .. recitata et diligenti ~one ponderata OXNEAD 279; archiepiscopus cum clero .. examinavit .. responsionem, et redacta est ~o in certam formam que sequitur *Ziz.* 326. **b** **1279** subsunt articuli per vos nondum examinati qui magna indigent ~one ad plenam justiciam de eadem loquela faciendam *PQW* 199b; inquisiciones et jurate in placito terre capiende que magne ~onis non sunt capiantur in patria coram uno justiciario et eciam inquisiciones et jurate in placito terre magnam ~onem requirentes coram duobus justiciariis de banco .. capiantur *Reg. Brev. Orig.* 186.

examinator [LL]

1 assayer.

1207 rex .. omnibus monetariis et ~oribus monete .. salutem *Pat* 76a; **1366** cuidam laboranti pro uno ~ore monete adquirendo (*sic*), xl s. *ExchScot* 261.

2 (w. ref. to God) judge.

sicut ~or Deus humane crementi metas indidit nature .. PULL. *Sent.* 693A.

3 (eccl.) judicial examiner; **b** (of specified court).

decanus Suessionensis, .. vir litteratus causarumque ~or incorruptus W. CANT. *Mir. Thom.* VI 34; inter .. episcopos illos iniquarum legum querit ~ores qui fuerunt auctores H. BOS. *Ep.* 20. 1452D; **s1179** Albertus .. Alexandri pape nuntius .. novum genus pene novus ~or culparum indixit DICETO *YH* I 430; **s1251** ~ores dati in causa principali quibusdam subdelegatis vices suas committere curaverunt *Meaux* II 79. **b** **1295** de salario ~orum: ~or pro examinacione cujuslibet testis tantum recipiat [sc. in consistorio de Arcubus] .. quantum recipitur pro scriptura attestacionum *Conc.* II 205a; **1299** R. de H. curie nostre Cantuariensis ~ori generali *Reg. Cant.* 349; **1320** sigillum magistri J. de B. communis ~oris consistorii Norwyc' *AncD* A 2857; **1440** Robertus Alne, ~or generalis curie Eboracensis *Test. Ebor.* II 78.

4 (acad.) examiner.

1469 (v. coeligere 2a); **1477** si inceptores .. ab ~oribus fuerint comperti habiles *StatOx* 170; **1560** hi tres alios tres ~ores singuli singulos et suo collegio artium magistros secum adjungant et ludimagistrum schole Westmonasteriensis *Educ. Ch.* 498.

5 (Chancery official).

1389 omnes predicti clerici de prima et secunda forma, precipue ~ores *Chanc. Orders* 4; CAMD. *Br.* 143 (v. 1 cancellaria 2c).

6 one who examines.

ad magistrum in schola discipulorum ~orem tam districtum H. BOS. *Thom.* III 18 p. 248; licet examinare literas papales .. et tamen ~ores hujusmodi non habent super literas examinatas aliquam potestatem OCKHAM *Dial.* 891 (*recte* 889).

examinatorius [LL]

1 examinatory, probative; **b** (w. *sermo*, acad.).

sic ergo debet credi ecclesie, de quanto caput ecclesie influit in doctorem, cujus speculum ~ium est Scriptura sacra, si in ipsa sit concors sentencia WYCL. *Civ. Dom.* I 417. **b** **1317** sermones ~ii nominati qui per baccallarios .. faciendi sunt antequam magistrentur *FormOx* 20; **1421** quod quilibet frater de ordine mendicancium taliter incepturus ultra sermonem ~ium predicet duos sermones ad clerum in ecclesia S. Marie [Oxon.] inter lecturam sentenciarum et suam incepcionem *Reg. Cant.* III 72; **1462** supplicat pater R. E. .. quatinus viij argumenta, viij responsiones, introitus biblie, lectura libri sentenciarum, sermo ~ius, sermo ad quem tenetur ex novo statuto sufficiant sibi ad effectum quod possit admitti ad incipiendum in sacra theologia *Grey Friars Ox.* 336; **1516** quod predicet sermonem suum ~ium ante gradum *Cant. Coll. Ox.* III 257.

2 (as sb. n.) instrument for examining, means of testing.

sicut in primis ~ium cudens instruxit judicem, sic clientem suum Aristotiles in his ad docentis provehit auctoritatem J. SAL. *Met.* 920B; *Ib.* 916C (v. conflatorium a).

examinatrix [LL], weighing, testing (f.).

examinatrix lanx J. HOWD. *Cant.* 135 p. 28.

examit- v. hexamit-.

examodo [cf. amodo], from now, henceforward.

1321 ideo consideratur quod predictus W. de T. teneat ~o dictam piscariam separalem *CBaron* 133.

examplificare [LL], to enrich.

1149 que ego adhuc propter necessitatem meam in manu mea retineo .. donec me Deus ~et [= *Regesta* 795: exemplificet] quod ego ei reddere possum [= *Regesta*: possim] *Ch. Sal.* 16.

examussim [CL], according to rule, exactly, precisely.

ut id .. per ordinem .. examusim enucleare studeas ALDH. *Met.* 9 p. 85 (cf. id. *VirgP* 22: thesaurum virginitatis examusim inquirentes); examusim, *geornlice*, absolute, certe, vel exquisite *GlC* E 471; libet loci nostri prima rudimenta ~im .. explanare *Chr. Battle* f. 12; subtilitates, quas assequi nequeunt, ~im [*gl.*: i.e. certissime; amussis enim est perpendiculum] comprehendere volunt NECKAM *NR* II 174; quod ideo factum ~im audeo confiteri *Mir. Hen. VI* I 1 p. 16.

exanclare v. exantlare. **exanguis** v. exsanguis.

exangulare [cf. LL angulare], to search out.

to seke, querere, .. ~are, scrutari *CathA.*

exanimare [CL]

1 to deprive of life, kill. **b** (p. ppl.) lifeless, dead (also as sb.).

†examinat, accidit [l. exanimat, occidit] *GlC* E 437; pleri, abjectis armis, acumine saxeo ~ati sunt ORD. VIT. IV p. 175; sceleratam siquis ignorans manducaverit ridendo ~abitur NECKAM *NR* II 62; *Croyl.* 22 (v. 1 examinare 5a). **b** at sicut corpus ~atum cito fetet atque contemnitur, sic exterius genus sine interiori despicitur *Simil. Anselmi* 96; ~atorum cadavera W. MALM. *GR* IV 357.

2 to deprive of courage, dispirit. **b** (p. ppl.) dispirited.

~o, extra animum sum *GlH* E 444; **1170** equum est .. me de vestris .. injuriis compati et .. ~ari defectu J. SAL. *Ep.* 296 (300 p. 700). **b** inermes et ~ati bellum diu rogatum abhorrebant, jamque velut exanimes, inglorii, et inbelles mori preoptabant ORD. VIT. IX 10 p. 549; familiam .. ex Reimundi abscessu ~atam et contristatam GIR. *EH* II 12.

exanimatio [CL], deprivation of soul, death.

corporis mortui viva compositione probante hanc sancti viri ultimam ~onem non exinanitionem fuisse H. BOS. *Thom.* VI 14; s**1243** usque fere ad ~onem jactu lapidis contritus et spiculo vulneratus *Flor. Hist.* II 260; illud diluvium [sc. Noe] est animancium / exanimacio morsque vivencium WALT. WIMB. *Carm.* 176.

exanimis, ~us [CL]

1 deprived of life, dead. **b** inanimate.

unum ex fratribus .. de summo cacumine ligni deorsum cadentem fracto corpore ~em audierunt *V. Cuthb.* IV 10; in capite illum percussit et ~em reddidit ORD. VIT. III 3 p. 44; ~es et mortui reperti sunt GIR. *TH* I 29. **b** vivo, sed exanimis transivi viscera matris HWÆTBERHT *Aen.* 38 (*Pullus*) 4; delicatissimi quondam libri, corrupti .. jam effecti, .. jacebant ~es R. BURY *Phil.* 8. 120.

2 half dead, unconscious.

~us, .. †siminecem [MS: seminecem] *GlH* E 435; dolor .. [eam] tam exsensem pene quam ~em reddidit R. COLD. *Cuthb.* 115; solotenus prostratus jacuit quasi in extasi et ~is *Ghost Stories* 415.

3 deprived of courage, dispirited.

~us, exsanguis *GlH* E 435; ORD. VIT. IX 10 p. 549 (v. exanimare 2b).

exannalis [ex + annalis], 'exannual' (w. ref. to a roll of unrecovered debts).

[**1323** *tutes maneres autres dettes avant ore entrez en roule annal, et que unqore leynz courent en demaunde, sauve arrerages des fermes, soient remues et pleinement escrites en un autre roule, que serra nome 'Roule Exannal', dount le titre soit tiel*: Rotulus de debitis extractis de rotulis annalibus *RB Exch* III 85]; **1333** H. le Scrop xiiij die Octobr. per rotulum ~em in Not[tingham], ad quem diem justic[iarius] non retorn[avit] breve *LTRMem* 105 m. 114*d*.; **14..** rotulus ~is *MS PRO* E. 363/6.

exanthema [CL < ἐξάνθημα], (med.) exanthema, pustule, eruption on skin.

tota cutis cedit a capite, et vocantur [pustule] ex antimata GILB. I 82v. 1; exantimata est quod vitium in capite et alibi *Alph.* 61.

exantlare [LL < ἐξαντλεῖν], to draw out; **b** (fig.). **c** (by misinterp.) to let, allow.

exanthlo [v. l. ~o] (i.e. exaurio, nam rota putei exauritoria 'anthlia' vocatur) ALDH. *PR* 124; *Id. VirgP* 9, *VirgV* 219 (v. antlia a). **b** virgo supra pectus Christi accubitare Johannes / in caena meruit viva exanclando fluenta ALCUIN *Carm.* 71. 1. 17; omnia versifico longum exhantlare relatu FRITH. 767; nec Plato sensibus Minerve calicem / exanclans funditus Cirreque laticem WALT. WIMB. *Sim.* 116; ad hos labores tanta industria ~atos accedebat ROBERTSON *Rolloc* 11. **c** *to latt*, dimittere, †exeuclare [MS: exanclare], pati, permittere, sinere *CathA.*

exaptota v. hexaptota.

exaquare [cf. 1 aquare < CL aquari], to drain, lead water from: **a** (pond); **b** (marsh or crop); **c** (house). *V. et. esseware*, 1 *essewerare.*

a 1231 fraxinos .. combusserunt et vivaria exequiaverunt et pisces ceperunt *BNB* II 492. **b 1293** in blado ~ando *Cant. Cath. Pri.* 183; **1300** pro marisco ~ando *Ib.* 186. **c 1272** in hominibus conductis ad domos curie Cantuarie ~andas et mundandas post quandam magnam tempestatem *MinAc* 1128/1.

exaquia, ~ium

1 drain. **b** drainage channel (for mill). *V. et. essewera* 1.

a**1145** carnis et elixe replet omnia nidor et asse, / halat et †exequium [MS: exaquium] thura nociva novum L. DURH. *Dial.* II 498. **b 1322** in servicio unius carpentarii facientis bayam, ~ias, et alveum subtus rotam parietem aquatic' *MinAc* 1145/21 m. 22; **1323** idem computat xxv s. in ~iis molendini per mundacionem aque asportatis de novo faciendis *MinAc* 1147/11 A 7.

2 ditch, dyke, trench (for draining land). *V. et. essewera* 2.

ad exsequias et guterias faciendas *BNB* II 218; **1227** per commune consilium tocius patrie fecit essequia illa fieri; et talis est consuetudo marisci quod unus homo non potest esse contra communem provisionem patrie de essequiis et guteriis faciendis *CurR* XIII 313.

exararatus v. 1 exartare.

exarare [CL]

1 to plough (land); **b** (fig.). **c** to furrow (face).

pedibus terram ~ans, glebas superiores secuit et terram fodit R. COLD. *Godr.* 100. **b** aratro quippe discipline ~andi sunt qui fuerunt prius heretici et sale sapientie conferendi, ut non fructus malos .. errorum faciunt R. NIGER *Mil.* III 80; virtus exhăret nisi te dolor exăret [*gl.*: pugnat vel laborat] intus H. AVR. *CG* f. 7 19. **c** faciem jam ruga senilis / exarat NECKAM *DS* V 338.

2 to inscribe; **b** (absol.).

a**804** evangelicas habere scriptas ammonitiones in mente magis quam pittaciolis ~atas in collo circumferre ALCUIN *Ep.* 290; **838** ego Ceolnoð .. signum sanctae crucis ~avi *CS* 421; epitaphium .. litteris aureis comiter ~atum est ORD. VIT. VII 9 p. 193; chirographum .. manu Saxonica ~atum ostendi .. archiepiscopo *Croyl.* 95; in sepulcro .. talis erat scriptura litteris Hebraicis, Grecis, et Latinis ~ata *Itin. Mand.* 12. **b 786** stilo diligenti in charta hujus paginae ~averunt, signum sanctae crucis infigentes ALCUIN *Ep.* 3.

3 to express or describe in writing, compose.

798 (12c) Christiana religio sicut primitus .. Gregorio dirigente ~ata est ita credimus *CS* 291; a**804** in dialogis .. Gregorii .. multa [miracula] inveniuntur lucidissima ~ata eloquentia ALCUIN *Ep.* 279; quicquid .. mundi valemus salva ratione excerpere de numeris sacratis, placet in hoc codicello ~are BYRHT. *Man.* 198; si tam decoram materiam incompto et contemptibili dictamine ~are praesumo ANSELM (*CurD* I) II 49; actus apostolorum .. dulci stilo Lucas dinoscitur ~asse J. SAL. *Ep.* 143 (209 p. 332); hec nostre diligentie monumenta, sicut et priora vobis ~ata GIR. *DK pref.* 2; narratione luculenter ~ata COGGESH. *Visio* 3.

exaratio [LL]

1 ploughing; **b** (fig.).

1283 ubi .. erit questio .. de clausura vel impedimento, seu ~one, sacione, seu dirrupcione vie *RGasc* II 206. **b** citra plenam ~onem jugeris, nolite missas ad aratrum revocare manus (cf. *Luke* ix 62) *Reg. Whet.* II 417.

2 written work, writings.

prout seniorum relatione seu scriptorum quorumlibet ~one perpendere potui *Hist. Llanthony* f. 31v.

exarator, scribe, writer.

a**1183** hiis testibus .. Waltero de B. presencium ~ore *Reg. Ant. Linc.* IV 216.

exarcerunt v. exardescere. **exarchimetra** v. exarthrema.

exarchus [LL < ἔξαρχος], **a** exarch, governor of Byzantine province. **b** (eccl.) metropolitan bishop.

a Martinus papa .. per Teodorum exarcum, jussu Constantini nepotis Eraclii .. raptus est ORD. VIT. V 9 p. 346. **b 1274** metropolita Ephesenus, prehonoratus exharchus totius Asie (*Lit. praelat. Graec.*) *Flor. Hist.* III 37.

exardentia, fervour.

1437 ut incultum sermonem nostrum .. minime inspiciant, sed ~iam, fidem, atque caritatem debeant intueri BEKYNTON II 21 (cf. ib. 24: ut ostenderit .. ~iam, desiderium atque amorem ad .. opus).

exardescere [CL], **~ēre** [LL]

1 (intr.): **a** (w. fire or heat as subj., or unspec.) to burn; **b** (fig.). **c** (w. thing as subj.) to catch fire, burn. **d** to become hot.

a in vicina .. casula ~sit incendium (*V. Germani*) BEDE *HE* I 19; **9..** (v. concalescere); a**1103** sicut .. ignem vento agitatum videmus ~descere ita .. ANSELM (*Ep.* 262) IV 177; non potest calor diu ~descere cum .. ei deficiat .. humiditas *Quaest. Salern.* C 30; ~deo, A. *to brenne WW.* **b 1308** ignis in nostris meditacionibus exardessit (*Lit. Papae*) *Reg. Carl.* II 7. **c** candelae .. ~descere citius plus debito .. cogebantur ASSER *Alf.* 104; si dolum volueris igni comparare, / paleas studueris igni tali dare, / que mox ut exarserint, desistunt ardere *Carm. Lew.* 469; quem [sc. Jovem] Semele .. sustinere non potuit; immo suis donis ~sit et exspiravit *Natura Deorum* 32. **d** productus ab igne calibsque / exarsit candens WULF. *Swith.* II 343.

2 (intr., w. personal subj.) to be afire, burn, glow: **a** (w. fever); **b** (w. anger, hatred, or sim.); **c** (w. desire or love). **d** (w. gd.) to burn with desire (for). **e** (mil.) to attack.

a igne infernali in membro percussus, usque in ipsum corpus statim ~sit GIR. *TH* II 52. **b** in emulationem ~dere novoque moveri tumultu Francia coepit W. POIT. I 29; in .. ejus odium canonici .. et quidam laici ~descunt .. ut .. ANSELM (*Ep.* 126) III 267; contra sanctum Dei in iram et odium et scandalum ~sit DOMINIC *V. Ecgwini* I 5; ~dentes in iram MAP *NC* I 14 f. 12; hic pauper .. / hostis est animo, sed frater labiis / animo menciens exardet odiis WALT. WIMB. *Palpo* 63. **c** †**931** (13c) ego .. desiderio regni caelestis ~dens *CS* 670; utinam sic viscera animae meae dulci fervore vestrae dilectionis ~descant ut viscera carnis meae exarescant ANSELM (*Or.* 7) III 24; s**1225** WEND. II 293 (v. convenire 2b). **d** GRIM *Thom.* app. 455 (v. cogitativus b). **e 790** Avari .. ~serunt in Italiam ALCUIN *Ep.* 7; parant vallum rescindere; castellani resistunt. ~dent, audent, aggrediuntur propius et acrius W. POIT. I 33; s**1263** (v. caballicata a).

3 (w. abstr. subj.).

regnante Decio, quando .. tortorum ferocitas contra bellatores Christi ~sit ALDH. *VirgP* 51; quantum prius ardens vehementius ~sit desiderium meum de vobis ANSELM (*Ep.* 120) III 258; ~descens invidia ORD. VIT. III 3 p. 61; *Ib.* VIII 8 p. 312 (v. cupidus a).

4 (trans.) to set afire, burn; **b** (fig.).

HANV. VII 380 (v. exassare); **1255** I. de H. in S. ~sit in altitudine septem pedum unam quercum *SelPlForest* lxxxvi; **1291** villas .. et horrea .. exarcerunt (*sic*) et bona .. asportaverunt *Anglo-Scot. Rel.* 47. **b** si libido carnem [regis] ita ~serit ut in luxuriam .. labatur FORTESCUE *NLN* I 26.

exare v. axare.

exarescere [CL], **exarēre**

1 (intr.) to become very dry, dry out. **b** to wither, waste away, dry up; **c** (fig.).

quia tota tectura pre diuturnitate nimia ~uerat eo citius .. ignis .. excrescebat R. COLD. *Godr.* 157; *Ib.* 70 (v. coctura 1); sic ager in vere floriger ante messem ~uit R. BURY *Phil. prol.* 6. **b** pes ille cum crure statim ~uit GIR. *TH* II 48; ulcus horrendum .. totaliter ~escens .. decrevit in nichilum *Mir. Hen. VI* IV 132. **c** ANSELM (*Or.* 7) III 24 (v. exardescere 2c); exharet H. AVR. *CG* f. 7. 19 (v. exarare 1b); membra tremunt dato judicio, / cor exaret concussum tedio J. HOWD. *Ph.* 547.

2 (trans.) to dry out, wither.

s**1292** ventus validus herbas urendo ~uit *Plusc.* VIII 17.

exaridatio v. exheredatio.

exarmare [CL], to disarm (person). **b** to destroy, dismantle (defences).

~atus, inarmatus *GlH* E 439; qui aliquem ~abit injuste solvat eum secundum suum *halsfang* (*Quad.*) *GAS* 351 (= *Cons. Cnuti, ib.*: dearmaverit; AS: *bewæpnige*); imperavit ut .. Balduinum sociosque suos dum ~ati essent invaderet ORD. VIT. IX 11 p. 565; revertitur cum sociis et sese ~avit G. MON. II 17; cohortibus ~atis urbem Trinovantum venerunt *Ib.* III 7. **b** quantum canelle nostre ex fortalicio .. ~assent de die, ipsi de nocte .. rearmarunt *G. Hen. V* 6.

exarmatio [LL], disarming.

de ~one alicujus (*Inst. Cnuti rub.*) *GAS* 617.

exarsio [cf. arsio, exardescere], burning out. **b** (w. *funiculus*) flame-carrier.

1291 injurias, dampna, et ~ones passi sunt *Anglo-Scot. Rel.* 47. **b** s**1303** misso funiculo exartionis, .. omnia coequans terre funditus dissipavit, ecclesia dumtaxat ab incendio reservata *Flor. Hist.* III 311.

1 exartare [cf. CL artare], to compress, make compact or dense. **b** (fig.) to constrain, enthrall.

†inctus [v. l. incus, *gl.*: *enclume*] .. assit [sc. aurifabro] duritie inexhauste vel †exararate, super quam ferrum positum vel aurum emolliatur NECKAM *Ut.* 118. **b 13..** beneficiati nostre diocesis cupiditatis vic[io] ~ati *Conc. Scot.* II 67.

2 exartare v. exsartare. **exartarius, exartum** v. exsartarius, exsartum.

exarthrema [ἐξάρθρημα], (anat.) dislocation.

†exarchimetra [l. exarthrimata], i. resilicio vel dislocacio ossis *Alph.* 61.

exartio v. exarsio.

exasciare [CL], to hew out (also fig.).

~are, dolare Osb. Glouc. *Deriv.* 202; **1520** nihil tum libri erat facies, nihil edolatum ~iatumve, nihil concinnatum, perfectum nihil in toto opere erat *Ep. Erasmi* IV 1061; s**1527** (v. caelum 4a).

exasper [cf. CL asper], harsh, irritating, provocative.

1288 nec [archiepiscopus] aliqua suffraganeis suis mandata .. immittet ~era, sicut fecit *Reg. Heref.* 185.

exasperare [CL]

1 to roughen, make uneven (surface).

luna .. tumescit et .. equora .. ~ari incipiunt et moveri Gir. *TH* II 3; mors .. / .. / levem .. faciem rugis exasperat Walt. Wimb. *Sim.* 66.

2 (med.) to irritate, make sore.

exulcerat, ~at *GlC* E 436; siccitate ~ando facit homini amittere vocem *Quaest. Salern.* P 75; trachea arteria siccitate ~atur *Ib.* 135; [siccitas] secundarios .. effectus habet multos, sicut est inspissare, ~are Bart. Angl. IV 3.

3 to sharpen (also fig.). **b** to harden.

s**1440** heu! plebs in clerum, laicatus et in monachatum / sic furit ut stimulos exaspret Erinis in ipsos Amund. II 221; ut omnes .. mansiones .. circumdarentur fossatis que palorum ~atorum .. munirentur ordinibus *Ps.*-Elmh. *Hen. V* 59 p. 159. **b** [crystallus] assimilatur Sagittario, quia eo mense .. Decembri aqua in glaciem incipiat ~ari Alb. Lond. *DG* 8. 10.

4 to harshen, make severe; **b** (weather); **c** (rhet.). **d** (intr.) to deal harshly.

†exasperarus [l. ~atus], saevus *GlH* E 440; penitentie .. ad arbitrium sacerdotis ex causis inspectis mitigande sunt et ~ande... mitigabimus eas et forte ~abimus Rob. Flamb. *Pen.* 234. **b** Wallingf. (*EPT*) I 232 (v. 2 dominium 2b). **c** sermo rhetoris primo quidem pulcher videtur, deinde ~atur; ad ultimum vero damnat reum Alb. Lond. *DG* 9. 4. **d** dictum est superius .. modo ~are in prevaricatores legis Wycl. *Ver.* III 70.

5 to exasperate, incense, provoke, goad; **b** (fig.); **c** (pr. ppl. as adj.) exasperating, provocative.

†lactescit [l. lacessit], ~at, provocat, vel frequenter lacerat, detrahit, maledicit *GlC* L 97; patienter toleret divinum judicium .. ne per impatientiam judicem justum ~ans mereatur quod non habet non accipere et quod accepit amittere Anselm (*Ep.* 37) III 147; Turci .. fatigati .., comperientes quod Franci fugiebant, animis ~ati armis hostes insecuti sunt Ord. Vit. X 20 p. 128; **1167** plura congessit quibus animum hominis ~asse potest J. Sal. *Ep.* 222 (223); si te causidicus causis exasperet artis D. Bec. 1536; s**1256** cardinales .. ~arunt .. papam in Bononienses M. Par. *Maj.* V 564. **b** ut .. flamma pinguedine excitata majoris incendii incrementa concipit, sic idem ignis infernalis in morte tiranni quasi ~atus magis furere videbatur Alex. Cant. *Mir.* 35 (I) p. 227. **c** s**1290** Judeorum ~ans multitudo .. jussa est .. ab Anglia secedere *Flor. Hist.* III 70.

exasperascere v. exasperescere.

exasperatio [CL]

1 roughening, irritation.

gustum lingue fervor impedit. ideo ~one preventa suavitas excluditur *Quaest. Salern.* P 3.

2 sharpening.

1473 (v. dilaceratio b); **1533** eisdem, pro ~one *le pykks*, iiij d. *Househ. Bk. Durh.* 178.

3 harshness.

s**1429** apcius inclinabitur ad reddendum vobis quod est vestrum suavitate sermonis quam ~one Amund. I 265.

4 annoyance, exasperation, provocation.

s**1297** rex .. duriciam contra .. ecclesiam exercere disposuit ut ipsam .. ab omni privaret proteccione .. quinpocius videretur ejus infestatoribus ~onum calcaria ministrare *Chr. S. Edm.* 65; **1300** viris .. ecclesiasticis .. exemptis notificatis .. expressius, .. sine .. dictorum exemptorum ~one .. iiij d. .. colligi faciatis *Reg. Carl.* I 44.

exasperescere, (med.) to become rough or irritated.

asperitas .. significat siccitatem materie et lenitas humiditatem, excepta conditione exteriori quum membrum exasperascit per medicinam stipticam vel remollescit per oleum Gilb. VII 310v. 1.

exaspirare [cf. CL aspirare], to breathe out, express.

per os ratio exasspiratur in verba Gros. *Templ.* 2. 5.

exaspr- v. exasper-.

exassare [cf. LL assare], to burn up, torture by burning.

ad Stygias urget properantius undas / quos Flegeton exasset [v. l. exarsit] aquis, Cochitus adustis / elixet lacrimis Hanv. VII 379 p. 354.

exauctio [cf. CL auctio], sale.

a sale, venditatio, ~o; .. *portsale*, ~o Levins *Manip.* 17.8, 24.

exauctorare [CL], **~izare**

1 (mil.) to discharge, dismiss (dishonourably).

~avit, *geheende GlC* E 399; miles ignominiose ~atur quando amor Dei et timor .. ab eo .. elabuntur R. Niger *Mil.* I 34; ille dux Austrie quem rex Anglie apud Accaronem ~averat Devizes 42v.; vagos milites et ~atos Boece 73.

2 (eccl.) to degrade, depose.

archiepiscopus judicio ecclesie fecit eum ~ari et .. cauteriari W. Fitzst. *Thom.* 34; archipresul .. consultus premandavit ut omni privatus beneficio ecclesiastico ~aretur, et in monasterio .. recluderetur H. Bos. *Thom.* III 22; **1222** in degradatione sacerdotis .. hiis verbis usus est: '~amus te' *Conc. Syn.* 105; s**1164** rex Henricus .. decrevit quemlibet clericum, in publico flagitio deprehensum primo ~izari M. Par. *Min.* III 196 (= Diceto *YH* I 313: ut .. episcopus ~aret); ~izamus, exuimus, et degradamus te N. ab ordine sacerdotali *Pont. Sal.* II 332*n*.

3 to deprive of authority. **b** (by conf.) to invest with authority.

~are, extra auctoritatem ponere Osb. Glouc. *Deriv.* 202; **1280** advocatorum officium .. multum ~atur ab illis, qui in ipso infideliter se exercent per quos justitia deperit *Conc. Syn.* 773. **b** ~atus, auctoritate plenus Osb. Glouc. *Deriv.* 193.

exauctorizatio [cf. LL exauctoratio], deprivation of authority.

non nos [sc. episcopos] .. vexationes .. movent, non laborum dispendia frangunt, non damna enormia sollicitant, .. sed frequentes ~ones, sed officii nostri mutilata dignitas, sed fame periclitantis diminutio W. Cant. *V. Thom.* II 30.

exaudibilis [LL], **a** ready to hear. **b** worthy to be heard.

a pie ~is Jesu Christe, exaudi me .. peccatorem Alcuin *Liturg.* 484D; qua in re perpendi potest quam sit ~is pie petitioni qui servorum suorum tam benigne affuit supplicationi Alex. Cant. *Mir.* 23 (I) p. 209. **b** **804** precibus ejus quae ipsi divinae majestati ~es et carae noscuntur Alcuin *Ep.* 306; una .. voce confitentes .. preces Swithuni ~es Lantfr. *Swith.* 25; c**1238** domum Domini decet sanctitudo que orationes orantium in ea fortificat et facit ~es Gros. *Ep.* 57.

exaudire [CL]

1 to hear, listen (to). **b** to understand.

si non revertantur ad Deum ~ita saltim tali admonitione, 'fili, peccasti ..' (*Ecclus.* xxi 1) Gildas *EB* 35; cum legitur evangelium .. stantes curvi reverenter ~iant Gir. *GE* I 7. **b** **1167** hoc .., si fideliter ~iatur nec a nature consortibus vinculum subtrahit caritatis J. Sal. *Ep.* 186 (192).

2 to heed, comply with (prayer or sim.); **b** (w. personal obj.).

Dominus ~ivit preces vestras Bede *HE* IV 14 p. 234; preces populi tui .. Domine, .. ~i *Rit. Durh.* 6; **1231** unde estis religiosi homines et vite perfectionem habitu profitentes omnium preces ~ire tenemini dummodo exauditio puritati fidei vel honestati morum non sit impedimentum Gros. *Ep.* 4; Christe, redemptor omnium / exaudi preces supplicum Ledrede *Carm.* 36. 2. **b** cum .. diutius oraret, nihilo tardius meruit ~iri Bede *HE* IV 10; ~i me, sancte Michael, invocantem te *Nunnam.* 87; Wulf. *Poems* XLVIII 2. 48 (v. dulus); c**1074** ipse .. vos .. clamantes ad se propiciatus ~iat Lanfr. *Ep.* 38 (10); ~i me, domina, sana animam peccatoris servi tui Anselm (*Or.* 5) III 14; ipsum audiens quidem sed non ~iens Gir *PI* III 7; **1437** cum .. sepe requisissent ut ad alterius loci electionem intenderet .. postquam minime ~iti erant .. *RL* II 8.

3 (pass., leg.) to be heard (in court), to be granted a hearing.

si quis verberando fecerit aliquem *blaa* et *blodi*, ipse qui fuerit *blaa* et *blodi*, prius debet ~iri *Leg. IV Burg.* 72; **1235** petierunt judicium .. et non potuerunt ~iri *CurR* XV 1446.

exauditio [LL], hearing, heeding, granting (of prayer); *v. et. exauditus*; **b** (gen., w. *gratia* or sim.).

preces .. Dominus ~one suscipere dignatus est Bede *Mark* (xv 32) 296A; ~onem petitionis dilecti filii *Eccl. & Synag.* 115; ita tua ~o transcendat affectum meae supplicationis Anselm (*Or.* 18) III 72; **1331** ~one dignior est supplicacionis materia quam persona .. supplicantis *Lit. Cant.* I 373. **b** **1242** clerico nostro ~onis aures benivolens prebeatis (*Lit. ad Papam*) *RGasc* I 160; **1254** eisdem in his que digne postulant ad ~onis gratiam nos faciles exhibemus (*Lit. Papae*) *MunAcOx* 26; c**1261** preces nostras .. dignetur excellentia vestra in sinum ~onis admittere (*AncC* V 83) *RL* II 202; **1281** preces hujusmodi ad ~onis effectum .. nullatenus admittentes *Law Merch.* II 34; **1423** ut infra sacrarium vestre ~onis admittere dignemini mee excusacionis preces *Reg. Whet.* II 408.

exauditor [CL], one who hears prayer: **a** God; **b** saint.

a omnium te invocantium .. exauditor Egb. *Pont.* 90; c**790** praesto est ubique pius sanctarum ~or orationum Alcuin *Ep.* 59; gaude .. anima mea. ipse quem tu .. desiderabas ~orem ipse tibi parat intercessorem Anselm (*Or.* 12) III 49; s**1182** Deus autem ~or orationis pauperum votum regis .. non despexit *G. Hen. II* I 285; **1433** omnium mestorum ~or vos .. conservat *Cant. Coll. Ox.* III 94. **b** prope est [Dominus] .. se invocantibus, sed est propior sanctis intervenientibus; quia quo boni praesto sunt interventores, dulciores subsequuntur ~ores Herm. Arch. 49.

exauditus, hearing, heeding (of prayer). *V. et. exauditio* a.

alius .. se .. accusans indignum ~u sanctum magnificavit J. Furness *Walth.* 115; nec ipsorum gemitus ac petitio ab ~u excluduntur divino *NLA* (*Wyro*) II 445.

exauferre [cf. CL auferre], to take away, confiscate, or (?) *f. l.*

s**1239** responderunt quod tociens bona ecclesie exauferat curia Romana quod equanimiter amplius nequiverant tolerare Oxnead 167 (= M. Par. *Maj.* III 567: exhauserat).

exaugēre [CL], to increase greatly.

idem / exauxit studii Parisiensis opes Garl. *Tri. Eccl.* 74; venit ad celestia Paulus / exauctasque Deo reddere gaudet oves *Ib.* 101.

exaugustus [cf. CL augustus], (w. ref. to imperial title) no longer august.

1170 ipse imperator iam ~us patenter expertus est se in augustalem non posse redire dignitatem, nisi pacem cum ecclesia fecerit J. Sal. *Ep.* 293 (298) p. 690.

exaur- v. et. exhaur-.

exauratus [cf. CL auratus], no longer gilded (fig.).

1171 o illustrissima sed nunc ~ata Anglie corona, cujus decoris rose deciderunt (*Lit. monachi ad regem*) *Becket Mat.* VII 450.

exbannire, ~are, ~iare [cf. bannire, ~are], to banish.

s**1212** comes [de Bolonia] .. de regno Francie auctoritate regia ~itur Trevet *Ann.* 184; s**1305** Flandrenses omnes de Anglia ~ivit *Ib.* 406 (= Rish. 228: ~iavit, Wals. *HA* I 108: ~avit); s**1313** ut publicum inimicum terre per communitatem Anglie ex duorum regum assensu tociens ~itum Trokelowe 80; **1423** exceptis duntaxat rebellibus et ~itis nostri communis [Senarum], ad quos presens nostra securitas et salvus conductus .. nullatenus extendatur (*Forma salvi conductus*) Amund. I 141.

exbibere v. ebibere.

exbracatus [cf. CL bracatus], trouserless.

in abundantia virtutis sue adversus inerme hominum genus exbraccatum et pannosum prevalere non possit H. Bos. *Ep.* 20. 1451D.

exbrancare [cf. OF *esbrancher*], to strip of branches, to pollard.

1282 ~ati .. ~ate (v. estronare).

exbrancatura [cf. OF *esbrancheure*], stripping of branches, pollarding. **b** outer branches (of tree).

1198 qui forisfecerit .. per esbrancaturam (v. copatura) (= W. Coventr. II 132: de esbrancathura). **b** **1229** inquirendum utrum bosci deteriorati fuerint de subbosco vel ~a; et deterioratio subbosci et ~e scribatur per se *Pat* 287; **1260** deterioratio subbosci et exbranchiature scribatur per se *Cl* 141; **1270** facta est magna destructio de grosso bosco et de ~a in boscis supradictis *TRBk Forest Proc.* 229 m. 9*d*.; **1330** j carectatam de exbranchiatura querc[uum] *KR Forest Proc.* 2/26.

exbullitio v. ebullitio. **exc-** v. et. esc-.

excaecare [CL]

1 to blind. **b** to 'blind' (w. glare, dust, smoke, or sim.).

a Nabuchodonosor oculi Sedechiae ~ati sunt Bede *Gen.* (x 15–18) 120; s**1180, 1249** (v. ementulare a); contigit sagittam in unum oculum Haraldi vehementer infigi et oculum ~ari Silgrave 79; et tunc ~atur utroque oculo cum Sedichia rege Gascoigne *Loci* 80. **b** fulgur auri oculos intuentium ~abit G. Mon. VII 4; sanguis in .. oculos ejus profluens eorundem ~avit aciem *Ib.* X 3; sicut

.. talpas sol ~at GIR. *TH* I 27; fumus oculos ~at hominis S. LANGTON *Serm.* 2. 5; AD. MARSH *Ep.* 194 (v. exsufflare 1b); cineres que ~ant [ME: *ablent*] insufflantem *AncrR* 76; execat *Ib.* (v. exsufflare 2b); sagittarii nostri ita cum suis sagittis adversarios ~averunt quod infra breve spacium eis compulerunt in fugam *V. Ric. II* 45.

2 (fig.) to blind, confuse; **b** (w. emotion); **c** (w. ref. to *Exod.* xxiii 8 or *Deut.* xvi 19).

799 ipsi, cordibus suis ~ati, ~averunt caput proprium ALCUIN *Ep.* 174; insipiens nimis ~atur ORD. VIT. VIII 24 p. 416; pax est ~ata, discordia propagata *Lib. Mem. Bernewelle* 56; **1296** tortuositas .. animi nostri ferocitatem taliter ~avit (*Lit. Regis Scot.*) FORDUN *Cont.* XI 26; quidam per scienciam sunt exsecati S. GAUNT *Serm.* 208; **1342** (v. devitare a). **b** ~ati furore in monachos fremebant ORD. VIT. XIII 23 p. 61; Venus .. / te magis excecat, luxuriose senex A. MEAUX *Susanna* 43; proprie superbie ~ati pulveribus *Latin Stories* 101; hoc utique non agerent nisi ~arentur perversi amoris igne ROLLE *IA* 149; Gallici, superbia ~ati nociva non previdentes STRECCHE *Hen. V* 150. **c** ~ati ab eo missis ingentis pecunie exeniis ORD. VIT. XI 24 p. 240; expedit tibi muneribus illum ~are W. JUM. IV 5; **s1263** alii muneribus ~ati a fidelitate .. recesserunt RISH. 13; per dona eam ~are non valebat *Latin Stories* 132.

excaecatio [LL], blinding. **b** blindness; **c** (fig.).

Irene .. oculos filiorum Constantini fecit evelli, ne quid mali propter patris ~onem adversus eam machinarent *Eul. Hist.* I 366; ceci videbunt, quia illi qui erunt ceci, per multa tempora forte ante ~onem videbunt (KYN.) *Ziz.* 12. **b** huic viro .. incommodum maximum accidit, viz. oculorum suorum ~io *Mir. J. Bev. A* 318. **c** ut etiam antiquos prophetas de futura suae gentis ~one quae nobis causa illuminationis fuit contristatos .. fuisse cognoscas .. BEDE *Sam.* (*1 Sam.* xvi 1) 603; o .. quam ceca semper ambitionis insatiate ~o! R. COLD. *Cuthb.* 74; **1241** densissimas infernalium ~onum tenebras AD. MARSH *Ep.* 76; de ~one casualis amoris ROLLE *IA* 209 *rub.*

excaedere [cf. CL caedere, 2 excidere, excudere], to cut out or (?) *f. l.*

habeat .. artavum quo surculos exsecet [v. l. excedet, *gl.*: *trenchet*] NECKAM *Ut.* 111.

excaet-, excahet-, excait- v. escaere, escaet-. **excambiatio** v. excambitio.

excambire [cf. LL cambire], **~iare, ~itare**

1 to exchange, give in exchange or compensation. **b** to receive in exchange. *V. et. cambire* 1, *escangiare.*

haec terra est de excambio de T. quam ~iavit (*Beds*) *DB* I 214v.; **1103** terras quas [abbas] Aldwinus dedit aut ~uit de dominio suo *Chr. Rams.* 220 (= *Regesta* 650); **c1115** ut abbas .. habeat illam terram quam .. episcopus ei escambiavit *Chr. Abingd.* II 76 (= *Regesta* 1128); **c1165** donationem .. quam .. Walterus .. domui de W. .. concesserat nobis esscambuit apud Menewde *Reg. Paisley* 3; si [jus suum] donaverit vel vendiderit vel escambierit vel alio modo rite alienaverit GLANV. II 6; **a1200** suum *falde* et *corft* de Guptorp ex campiavit cum eis *DL Cart. Misc.* III 89; **1205** ad recipiendum de eodem abbate terram quam ipse ei escambiaverat *CurR* III 317; **1216** xj acrarum .. quas .. monachi mihi exscambiaverunt *FormA* 255; **1227** si .. contigerit quod ego et fratres mei .. eam [elemosinam] predicte abbacie non possimus garantare, debemus .. ipsam alibi in feodo nostro rationabiliter ~ire *CartINorm* 306; **12..** si ego W. vel heredes mei illam predictam terram Tome et heredibus suis warentizare non possimus, ego vel heredes mei ~itabimus illi et heredibus suis bene ad valenciam illius predicte terre in eadem Stretona *FormA* 18; **12..** quod predictam terram neque vendent neque ~ient .. nec alicui in feodum .. tradent *Cart. Glouc.* II 137; **1507** ~iare (v. cambire 1a); **1583** parcellam possessionum nostrarum cum archiepiscopo Ebor' antehac ~iatam *Pat* 1234 m. 14 (cf. ib. 1235 m. 17: exchambiata). **b** hoc manerium ~iavit Robertus C. de M. pro Pateberie *DB* I 149; rex tenet E.; Reinbaldus tenuit T. R. E.; comes Willelmus ~iavit illud ab eo *DB* I 180v.; **c1170** quia vero partem terre ecclesie que mihi erat neccessaria eis ~iavi et pejorem eis dedi *Kelso* 235; una virgata .. quam W. .. ~iavit pro quadam silva *Chr. Battle* f. 14v.; **1205** quod .. facias habere Willelmo de G. terram .. quam dominus archiepiscopus C. ab eo escambiavit *Cl* 56a.

2 to change, exchange (money). *V. et. cambire* 2.

1203 mandamus vobis quod redditus lx s. Andecavie .. ~iatis ubi et sicut melius poteritis *Pat* 34a; **s1257** volo quod ista moneta currat, denarius pro xx sterlingis, ita quod nullus cogatur ad illum capiendum et qui illum ceperit possit illum escambiare ubi voluerit *Leg. Ant. Lond.* 30.

excambitio, ~iatio, exchange. **b** property given in exchange or compensation. *V. et. cambitio.*

recepit de abbate per ~itionem alterius terrae *DB* I 176; **a1180** (1316) me .. confirmasse .. omnem ~itionem quam R. de B. facit eisdem monachis *CalCh* III 319; **c1200** hec concessio et excambiacio *Cart. S. Neot.* 85v.; **1320** in exambiacione [*of one horse* xviij s. xij d.] *Fabr. Exon.* 126; hec est ~icio facta inter moniales S. Michaelis de Stanford et Galfridum .., sc. quod .. G. excambiavit cum .. monialibus viij acras terre arabilis *FormA* 155. **b c1085** si aliquis dixerit quod .. de meo dono aliquid habeat, mandate mihi magnitudinem terre .. et ego .. aut ei inde escambitionem reddam aut aliud faciam *Regesta* 276; **11..** si .. aliquis .. predictas terras .. auferre poterit providebimus ecclesie de H. .. plenariam ~itionem juxta precium predictarum terrarum *Reg. S. Osm.* I 341; **a1241** ego .. R. et heredes mei .. redditum v s. warantizabimus .., et si necesse fuerit excambiabimus in aliis redditibus nostris magis apparentibus; pro hac venditione .., si necesse fuerit, ~iatione dederunt .. iiij m. *E. Ch. S. Paul.* 114.

excambitor, ~iator, money-changer. *V. et. cambitor.*

s1190 sub Turona ~iatores. postea super portum archiepiscopus Pisanus DICETO *YH* II 80; **1198** (1328) secundum .. cartas .. venditorum vel escambiatorum suorum *CalCh* IV 96; **1199** (1252) sicut .. cyrographa donatorum, venditorum, concessorum, vel ~itorum suorum testantur *CalCh* I 383; **s1235** usuarii asserentes se esse mercatores denariorum et postea specialius se esse mercatores domini pape vel escambiatores M. PAR. *Min.* II 382 (cf. id. *Abbr.* 272: scambiatores); **c1350** de eschambiatore .. qui secundus post monetarium *MonA* III 164a.

excambitrix, ~iatrix, (f.) money-changer.

c1279 H. le T. captus pro eo quod uxor est ~iatrix *Gaol Del.* 35/2 m. 48*d.*

excambium, ~ia

1 exchange (esp. of property for property or for money); *v. et. cambium* 1a, 1 *cangium* a, *decambium, escangium* a. **b** property given in exchange or compensation; *v. et. escangium* b; **c** (fig.). **d** substitute.

pro ~io terrae in qua castellum sedet *DB* I 2; haec supradicta maneria sunt de ~iis Willelmi (*Devon*) *Ib.* 117v.; istas duas praedictas mansiones dedit comes de M. episcopo propter escambium castelli Cornugalliae *Dom. Exon.* 118 (= *DB* I 4v.: pro ~io); **c1110** terras quas dederunt pro escambio terre quam ab eis [monachis] receperunt ad amplificandum cemeterium suum ELMH. *Cant.* 359 (= *Regesta* 1077); **c1160** nos .. concessisse .. unam mansuram in .. escambiam propter quandam aliam mansuram *Danelaw* 252; **c1160** (1235) donationes et ~ias quas H. de P. et O. .. fecerunt in territorio .. ville de Pipewell *CalCh* I 20; **1165** R. de S. xij s. pro eschambio terre sue *Pipe* 77; **c1180** dedi A. filie P. in scambio dim. karucatam terre in K. .. pro dimidia karucata terre in L. *Danelaw* 316; **1186** monachi .. habent culturam illam .. in †escambrium pomerii et curie (*Concordia*) *Reg. Heref.* VI 35; **1197** in ~ium autem predicti manerii de Andeli .. concessimus .. ecclesie Rothomagensi .. omnia molendina que nos habuimus Rothomagi (*Ch. Ric. I*) DICETO *YH* II 155; **11..** sciant .. me dedisse .. in exscambio elemosinarum quas per castellanos amiserunt iiij m. de molendino meo de K. *Cart. Holyrood* 29; **1212** monachi de Lenton tenent j molendinum .. pro l s. que solebant pertinere ad Lindeby pro ~ia de Papelwic *Fees* I 149; **s1264** facto escambio (v. consulatus 4b); **1274** manerium quoddam .. Linc' episcopus in exambium sue jurisdiccionis in proprios usus convertendo accepit *Leg. Ant. Lond.* app. 213; **1320** dedimus unam acram .. in exchambium pro quodam mesuagio *Reg. Heref.* 141; **1411** in solucione pro ~io j olle enee pro potagio famulorum vij s. *Crawley* 307; **1534** ~ium sigillorum: .. summa sigillorum excambiatorum *Househ. Bk. Durh.* 238. **b** scambium *DB* I 84v. (v. cambire 1a); **1130** ut habeant terram quam tenent de abbatia de W. aut escambium ad valens in comitatu *Pipe* 20; **1173** juraverunt quod comes dabit ei legitimum ~ium ad arbitrium abbatis de C. (*Chirog.*) *G. Hen. II* I 41; **1202** concessimus J. de C. .. xxx li. .. annuatim .. percipiendas .. quousque .. racionabile ~ium providerimus pro Curteleis *Pat* 6b; **1203** concordati sunt de terra .. quam .. Gillebertus amisit per defaltam .. Willelmi per sic quod Willelmus dabit ei escambium ad walentiam *CurR* II 234; **1218** de redditu de parvis escambiis ante pontem Torneicium in Rupella *Pat* 166; **1221** Gaufridus de Bere habet essecambium in Lesseby *KRMem* 5 m. 14; **c1225** si .. contigerit quod hanc .. terram .. warrantizare non poterimus eis rationabile eskambium ad valenciam predicte terre plenarie faciemus *Reg. S. Thom. Dublin* 9; **1230** pro hac concessione .. dedimus ascambium et .. confirmamus terram de Kenny .. tenendam sibi .. de nobis .. inperpetuum *Reg. Aberbr.* I 262; **c1280** si ita contigerit ego R. B. predictum warentizare non possum burgagium, faciam sibi unum ecambium ad valorem illius dimidii burgagii *Arch. Bridgw.* 317; **c1440** contulit eciam dictum monasterium de Dunfermlyn .. domino Georgio de Dunbar .. pleno jure et libero ~ium .. certas terras de Aldcambus *Pri. Cold.* 254. **c** Salomon [ait] 'prosperitas stultorum perdet illos' [*Prov.* i 32]. numquam .. hoc nobis Deus ~ium donet GIR. *Symb.* I 31 p. 320. **d** infirmis qui communia comedere non possunt ~ia debet providere [sc. coquinarius] *Obs. Barnwell* 186.

2 exchange (of prisoners).

1310 de ~io Marie, sororis Roberti regis Scotie pro novem hominibus regis Anglie prisonariis apud Scotos *RScot* 86b; **1314** de ~io captivorum *Ib.* 134b; **s1141** interlocutio inter magnates facta est, quod pro rege [Stephano] comes cum suis date [v. l. dati] sint in escambio *Eul. Hist.* III 73.

3 (w. ref. to money): **a** change, exchange; *v. et. cambium* 2a. **b** office or place of exchange; *v. et. cambium* 2c. **c** bill of exchange.

a s1249 ~ium monete factum fuit per totam Angliam *Eul. Hist.* III 138; **s1279** eodem anno fuit ~ium monete .. et annus durissimus propter sterilitatem et escambium simul concurrentia B. COTTON 159; **1331** computat .. pro amissione ~ii de pecunia soluta ad curiam Romanam *ExchScot* 463; **1385** solvit .. xij s. pro naulo et v s. pro scambio monete *CartINorm* 47. **b s1192** rex Ricardus misit puerum suum ad escambium in civitatem G. ut cibos famelicis compararet. ille autem ad escambium veniens cum plures bizantios proferret nimisque .. pompatice se haberet .. WEND. I 220; **1217** liberari faciatis .. justiciario .. cuneum nostrum et ~ium Londonie *Pat* 96; **s1257** dixit .. rex ".. veniat ad ~ium nostrum, et habebit pro quolibet aureo decem et novem denarios et obolum" *Leg. Ant. Lond.* 30; **s1269** statere et pondera eorum [sc. mercatorum extraneorum], quando examinata fuerunt in escambio regis, fuerunt falsa .. inventa *Ib.* 119; **1311** magistro ~ii regis apud Berewicum (v. chaumagium). **c 1526** permutationum litterae quas vulgus ~ium vocat his inclusae ad te mittuntur *Ep. Erasm.* VI 1726.

excamp- v. excamb-.

excancellarius [cf. LL cancellarius], exchancellor.

Guibertus .. ~us, defuncto Ravennate archiepiscopo, .. electus est BOSO *V. Pont.* 360.

excandere v. excandescere.

excandescentia [CL], blazing anger.

W. FITZST. *Thom.* 72 (v. defervere 2c); Parcarum pervicax excandescentia / in omnes simili grassatur furia WALT. WIMB. *Sim.* 182.

excandescere [CL], **~dēre** [LL], to blaze with anger, flare up; **b** (w. abstr. subj.).

~uit, in iracundiam exilivit *GlC* E 502; **1166** ad hec dominus R. aliquantulum adversus hec ~uit J. SAL. *Ep.* 145 (168); sicut preceptor puerilis excessus reprimit nec ~et GIR. *PI* I 6; demones .. ira ~escentes .. miserum .. discerpserunt COGGESH. *Visio* 21; **1291** R. de B. .. exposuit episcopo qualiter magistri universitatis Oxon. in eundem magistrum P. excandeurant pro eo quod portavit commissionem prescriptam (*Reg. Ant. Linc.*) *EHR* XXVI 506; mox furor regis insevit et ~ens in iram KNIGHTON I 327; **s1176** clericus Scotus .. cum .. verba .. probrosa .. audierat ignitum velut ferrum ~ens FORDUN *Cont.* VIII 26. **b** ubi [sc. in communione angelorum] non inflatur superbia .. non ~escit ira BALD. CANT. *Tract* 15. 550A; **1267** [ira] vitium pessimum est et maxime homini innaturale et in periculum ejus ~ens BACON *Maj.* II 298.

excangium v. escangium. **excanirizatus** v. excaturizare.

excanonicare [cf. canonicare], to divest of canonry.

cum esses litteratorie artis .. ignarus, scis quia amici tui epistole, quas depravasti, te fecerunt canonicum: tuque per easdem facile ~ari posses, si significarent summo pontifici .. usurpationis officium quod exerces P. BLOIS *Ep.* 21. 76B.

excap- v. et. escap-.

excapitare [cf. 2 capitare 5], to behead. *V. et. decapitare* a.

cumque tormentis affectus ~andus duceretur, flumen siccatum est per orationem sancti [Albani] H. HUNT. *HA* I 36; **s1016** jussit eum ~ari et caput in stipite .. figi *Ib.* VI 14; **s1377** omnes Picardos .. tanquam proditionis reos ~avit WALS. *HA* I 345.

excardinare [cf. CL cardo], to unhinge (fig.), disorder, perturb.

contenciones que valde cor sacerdotis ~are faciunt MIRK f. 13v.

excari- v. excarri-.

excarnare [LL], to remove flesh from.

[dens] extrahatur cum tenaculis postquam ~averis eum a carne gingivarum GAD. 120. 1.

excarnificare [CL], to torture. **b** to mangle, dismember.

[Piso] comprehensus a militibus Vespasiani redeuntibus a Syria ~atur et unco pertractus in Tiberi necatur R. NIGER *Chr. II* 113. **b** exanimatorum cadavera Turci uncis ferreis in murum trahebant, ludibrio nostrorum ~anda W. MALM. *GR* IV 357.

excarpsum [LL], extract. *V. et. excerpere.*

excarpsum [v. l. excerptio] de canonibus catholicorum patrum vel poeniteniale ad remedium animarum EGB. *Pen. tit.*

excarriagium [cf. carriagium], carrying away. *V. et. excarriatio.*

1446 una cum excariagio rubisi et petrarum post consummacionem operis *DL MinAc* 8235/508 r. 8.

excarriare [cf. 1 carriare], to carry away.

1199 sterkilinia †ecuriare [MS: ecariare] *CurR* I 77.

excarriatio [cf. carriatio], carrying away. *V. et. excarriagium.*

1366 post primam falcacionem et excariacionem feni *AncD* A 11758.

excasus [cf. CL casus], swoon, trance, or (?) *f. l.*

1297 totusque animus meus quasi in excasum [? l. excessum *or* extasim] est deductus *Reg. North.* 131.

excaturizare [cf. LL cauterizare, ? *infl. by* CL scaturire], to scald: **a** (person, also fig.); **b** (animal).

a hospes truncatur dum dormit ab hospite, quosdam / exscaturit fervens hospitis unda feri GARL. *Tri. Eccl.* 129; **1256** (v. ebullire 3); **1259** qui ~atus [MS: excõnizatus] est semel semper aquas fervidas expavescit M. PAR. *Maj.* V 736; **1278** Agnes .. cecidit in quodam plumbo pleno aqua calida ita quod ~ata fuit, ita quod .. obiit *JustIt* 131 r. 1; **1348** est quoddam vas impletum cum granamello calido .. et .. predicta J. in predicto vase cecidit et sic excaterizata fuit *RCoron* 194 m. 13; color .. stomatici [est] quasi †excanirizati [l. excaturizati] vel a sincopi resurgentis GAD. 73. 2; **s1426** Agnes .., ~ata in quodam plumbo, obiit die parasceues *Chr. S. Alb.* 9; exscaturizo, A. *to scaldy WW*; *to scalde*, ~are *CathA*. **b** habeat lixa aquam calidam qua pulli possint ~ari [v. l. possunt encaturizari, *gl.*: *estre eschaudes*] NECKAM *Ut.* 97; *Ib.* 102 (v. ex 3b); **1302** in j plumb' conduct' pro dictis porcis excaturizand' et succid' coquend', xij d. *MinAc* 997/13; **1306** hogetti. inde computat .. mactatos ad larderium in yeme ix, exscaturizatos pro senescallo ad Natale ij, in morina ij, exscaturizatum ad Pascha pro familia j *Ib.* 856/15 m. 2/d./; *pluk bryddys*, excatariso *PP*.

excaturizatio, scalding.

1380 communem domum pro mactacione .. bestiarum et exscaturizatione porcorum *FormOx* 254; **1384** domus in suburbio Oxon' prope collegium de Balliolo pro exscaturizacione porcorum et mactacione bestiarum *IMisc* 231/9.

excavare [CL], to excavate, hollow out; **b** (fig.); **c** (intr. *s. pass.*).

W. CANT. *Mir Thom.* III 41 (v. concavus 2b); speculemur aquam que mollis est, percussione perseverante durum lapidem ~are *Regim. Princ.* 89. **b** spreta apostolica reverencia, ~are nituntur ecclesie fundamenta PECKHAM *Ep.* 432. **c** terre .. ubi prius planities fuerat, altius quinque cubitorum ~averunt ALEX. CANT. *Mir.* 36 (I) p. 231.

excedenter v. 2 excedere 4d.

1 excedere v. excaedere.

2 excedere [CL]

1 (intr.) to go away, withdraw; **b** (fig.); **c** (w. *mente*); **d** (w. ref. to memory). **e** (pass. *s. act.*) to extend (in space).

~o, egredior *GlC* E 430; excessit finibus illis FRITH. 780; GOSC. *Wulfh.* 2 (v. cuniculus 1a). **b** paululum secedit et ~it remotis in partibus quasi verecundis et occultis natura ludit excessibus GIR. *TH pref.* p. 21. **c** si quis Christianus subita temptatione mente sua ~erit vel .. se ipsum occciderit .. THEOD. *Pen.* II 10. 4. **d** **a690** tuum .. discipulatum .. efflagito ut oblitterata nequaquam memoria ~at quod .. ALDH. *Ep.* 5 p. 491; **1266** a memoria vestra non credimus ~isse (*sic*) .. *Cl* 224. **e** planta .. cujus palmites ~untur per unum brachium BACON V 122.

2 (trans.) to leave, quit. **b** to pass from (condition). **c** (w. *hominem*) to die.

nec Romana prius falsi pilotria testes / excedent, justas donec pro crimine poenas / jure luant FRITH. 1190; quid mihi nam prodest, vinclis quod liber apertis / excessi vigiles ..? WULF. *Swith.* II 597 (cf. ib. 930: limen .. excessit). **b** qui ubi infantiles annos .. excessit, puer factus .. ad sanctitatis opera semetipsum cepit informare EADMER *V. Osw.* 1. **c** **s1135** catholicus rex .. Deo se commendavit, sicque .. incipiente nocte hominem excessit ORD. VIT. XIII 19 p. 50.

3 to exceed, go beyond (limit); **b** (w. abstr. obj.). **c** to transcend.

~at, *oferstige GlH* E 673; quandoque invaduntur ipsi limites terrarum et per occupationem ~untur GLANV. IX 13; **s1316** tanta .. aquarum inundancia quod fluvii terminos solitos .. excesserunt GRAYSTANES 36. **b** Erycis .. bellorum instrumenta omnem modum humanum ~entia leguntur *Lib. Monstr.* I 51; vellem aliquanto diffusius scribere, nisi lex epistolae cogeret me brevitatem non ~ere ANSELM (*Ep.* 101) III 233; [siccitas] .. qualitas [est] pessima quando debitam ~it in corporibus proportionem BART. ANGL. IV 3 (cf. 4c infra); res que retinent .. calorem cordis temperatum ne suos ~erit terminos BACON IX 139; singuli per se tropum non ~ant, sc. decimam vocem vel cum semitono undecimam ODINGTON 141. **c** de summa caelorum arce tempora cuncta ~ente GILDAS *EB* 8; virtutes illius amplas / quae modulum et numerum excedunt ALDH. *VirgV* 857; **957** (14c) coelestia regna quae nostrarum mentium sensus ~unt *CS* 988; excessitque modum hoc tam mirabile signum WULF. *Swith.* II 402; immensa bonitas, quae .. omnem intellectum ~is ANSELM (*Prosl.* 9) I 107.

4 to exceed (in number, size, or value); **b** (in time). **c** (absol.) to be in excess; **d** (log.).

Cyclopes .. arborum altitudinem ~ebant *Lib. Monstr.* I 11; adeo ut .. mensura iiij digitorum in sarcofago corpus ~eret BEDE *HE* IV 11; quae est haec enormitas culparum mearum quae ~it multitudinem miserationum vestrarum ANSELM (*Or.* 9) III 32; una sola littera numerum peccatorum [monachi] excessit ORD. VIT. III 3 p. 50; omnis numerus unitatem ~it usque ad decem ROB. ANGL. *Alg.* 66; **a1189** facient .. nobis pro L. et pro W. forinsecum servicium, quod †nos [?l. hos] ~it in denariis, sc. quantum pertinet ad feudum dimidii militis *Ch. Gilb.* 17; Britannia duplo in quantitate Hiberniam ~it GIR. *TH* I 2; R. MARSTON *QD* 77 (v. collimitare b); **c1350** statutum est quod si singula pignora ~ant in aliquo valore partem pecunie mutuo .. accepte *StatOx* 78. **b** data illius brevis .. excessit diem quindene predicte per quinque septimanas et amplius *State Tri. Ed. I* 42. **c** omnes .. versus qui supra dictum sillabarum numerum videntur ~ere ALDH. *Met.* 10 p. 83; BRACTON 93 (v. admensuratio c); [siccitas] pessima est qualitas et mortificativa dum ~it BART. ANGL. IV 3 (cf. 3b supra); **1242** habet de superplus xij s. et x d. blancorum qui non debent ei allocari, quia excesserunt per extensionem maneriorum *Pipe* 61; **1353** summa .. expensarum .. cum excessu compoti anni precedentis .. cclj li. iiij s. iij d. ob. quad. et ~unt lix li. viij s. d. ob. *Sacr. Ely* II 158. **d** primo modo angeli perfectius contemplantur; secundo modo ut ~entia et excessa [cf. Arist. *Metaph.* 1021 a 6–7]; tertio modo plus homines quam angeli HALES *Sent.* III 172 (cf. ib. 173: secundo modo †excedenter [? l. ~entes] et excesse, quia quidam homines majorem habent gratiam quam quidam angeli); primo modo prius [ordo essentialis] dicitur eminens et posterius excessum DUNS *PW* 52; *Id. Prim. Princ.* I 5 (v. eminentia 4).

5 to surpass: **a** (w. acc.); **b** (w. dat.); **c** (pr. ppl.) excessive.

a ~it, i. superat, *geþihþ*, *oferstihþ GlH* E 672; jucundum est intueri in Patre et Filio et utriusque Spiritu, quomodo .. nullus alium ~at ANSELM (*Mon.* 59) I 70; non facile diffiniri poterat quis eorum alterum ~eret G. MON. X 10; **s1399** rex Ricardus in divitiis omnes predecessores suos studuit ~ere *Eul. Hist.* III 384. **b** ditissima femina .. ceteris .. per Angliam comitissis sicut divitiis, ita cultu vestium nitebatur ~ere AILR. *V. Ed. Conf.* 783C. **c** ~entia, i. superhabundantia *GlH* E 674; clericalis ordo quibusdam in locis confusione agebatur, ut .. a vita secularium ~entius nihil haberet OSB. *V. Dunst.* 36; GILB. I 3v. 1 (v. conculcare 2).

6 (intr.) to transgress, go too far.

excesserit, culpaverit *GlC* E 410; **1296** si .. prelatus in aliquo excesserit *Obs. Barnwell* 50; **1344** quamdiu .. corrigibilem in casu quo excesserit seipsum prebuerit *Eng. Clergy* 283; **1514** subditos delinquentes criminosos et ~entes ac de crimine heresis suspectos *Ib.* 198.

3 excelare v. excellare. **excelcissime** v. excelse.

excelebrare [cf. CL celebrare], to celebrate (mass) in an irregular manner.

in aliquibus locis Scotorum quidam fuerant qui contra totius ecclesie consuetudinem missas ~are consueverunt *NLA* (*Marg.*) II 171 (= TURGOT *Marg.* 8: celebrare).

excellare [LL *gl.*], to cohabit with one's wife.

excelare, cum uxore esse *GlC* E 493; tunc excillabit et latronem generabit .. 'excillabit', i. coibit cum uxore sua, quia excillare est manere cum uxore propria, secundum Catholicon (J. BRIDL.) *Pol. Poems* I 159, 160.

excellararius [cf. cellararius], cellarer, 'birler'.

hic exelerarius, *a byrler WW*.

excellenter [CL], excellently, outstandingly. **b** egregiously, infamously.

c710 septimum [diem] .. tam ~er scriptura commendat, 'dies .. septimus erit celebrior' [*Lev.* xxiii 8] (*Ep. Ceolfridi*) BEDE *HE* V 21; **1072** meminisse debet humiliter excellens ~erque humilis beatitudo vestra quia .. LANFR. *Ep.* 3 (4); ~er honorabili et honorabiliter excellenti regine Anglorum Mathilde TURGOT *Marg. prol.*; sapientia astrorum tota .. est in corporibus celestibus ~issime, sed ibi nos latet .. ignobilissime FISHACRE *Sent. Prol.* 82; ~issime transcensis .. voluptatis fede lasciviis AD. MARSH *Ep.* 49; *Ib.* 36 (v. dilatare 2a); cum uni dicitur convenire ~er quod pluribus convenit et dicitur antonomasia *Ps.*-GROS. *Gram.* 74; Plato .. inter omnes discipulos Socratis eum ~issime diligebat *Eul. Hist.* I 424. **b** **s1141** procedit consul [de Albermarle] .. adulter patentissimus et ~er impurus H. HUNT. *HA* VIII 15.

excellentia [CL]

1 excellence, high standard or status; **b** (theol. or spiritual); **c** (gram.). **d** (med.) high degree, excess.

eminentia, i. sublimitas, ~ia, celsitudo, *oferhlifung GlH* E 242; *Ib.* D 481 (v. dignitas 1a); hi pollebant et ~ia preclare generositatis et claritudine religionis ORD. VIT. III 11 p. 121; Ædmundus .. ab ~ia virtutis contraxerat insigne nominis TURGOT *Marg.* 2. **b** cujus ~ia fidei .. claruerit BEDE *HE* III 13; quod illis contullit ~iam [AS: *gicorenscipe*] sempiternam fructibus nostrae devotionis accrescat *Rit. Durh.* 54; Deum propria dignitate et singulari ~ia privare ANSELM (*Incarn. B* 10) II 27; EADMER *Excell. B. M.* 578B (v. dejectio 2a). **c** construccionem .. ad ea que supponuntur vocant ~iam, que .. genitivum querit ut 'virgo virginum, dominus dominorum' *Ps.*-GROS. *Gram.* 65. **d** non .. quod impedit sensus impedit et motus nisi sit in ~ia GILB. II 109. 2; nec motus [impeditur] quamvis destruatur sensus, ut patet in morientibus. prius nam destruitur sensus quam motus, nisi in ~ia .. aut in apopleticis (*sic*) *Ib.*

2 as title: **a** (royal); **b** (papal); **c** (archiepiscopal); **d** (other).

a **601** incolumem ~iam vestram gratia superna custodiat (*Lit. Papae*) BEDE *HE* I 32 p. 70; **799** direxi ~iae vestrae stamen quarundam supputationum de solis .. per signiferum cursu ALCUIN *Ep.* 171; **a1074** quem .. ~ia vestra [sc. Hiberniae regis] ad nos consecrandum transmisit LANFR. *Ep.* 37(9); Deus vestram ~iam et meam parvitatem .. laetificet ANSELM (*Ep.* 347, *ad Reginam Anglorum*) V 286; placuit ~ie vestre, invictissime Anglorum rex GIR. *TH pref.* p. 20; **c1330** reales literas coram regia si placet ~ia recitandas J. MASON *Ep.* 14 p. 203; **1388** (v. dominatio 2). **b** ut .. a vestra ~ia pallium non suscipiat ANSELM (*Ep.* 451, *ad Papam*) V 399; **1204** definitio vero ~ie vestre reservata (*Lit. ad Papam*) *Chr. Evesham* 137. **c** delatis ad nos vestrae ~iae litteris ALCUIN *WillP pref.*; tale aliquid vestrae ~iae [i.e. Lanfranco] narrare valeo OSB. *Mir. Dunst.* 22. **d** **1231** Judeos quos dominus L. de municipio suo expulit .. vestra disposuit ~ia super terram vestram recolligere (*Ad Comitissam Wintoniae*) GROS. *Ep.* 5; **c1365** vestri magistratus ~ie .. innotescat quod .. *FormOx* 365.

1 excellere [CL]

1 (intr.) to excel, be pre-eminent; **b** (gdv. *s. act.*).

BEDE *Sam.* 582 (v. dorcas); hunc inter cunctos aiebant ~uisse ingenio W. POIT. I 11; in divinis .. preditus, sapientia plurimum ~ebat DOMINIC *V. Ecgwini* I 2. **b** ~endus, i. praecellens, supereminens *GlH* E 667; **1340** ~ende sapiencie viro et amico suo predilecto .. salutem *FormOx* 302.

2 (pr. ppl. *excellens*): **a** excellent, pre-eminent; **b** (w. ref. to status); **c** (usu. superl., of royal person, power, or sim.); **d** (theol.).

a sum excellens specie, mirandus in orbe ALDH. *Aen.* 14 (*Pavo*) 1; **a690** tuam .. solertiam .. ~ens fama percrebuit *Id. Ep.* 5 p. 491; vir .. doctissimus atque ~entis ingenii BEDE *HE* IV 21 p. 255; ut illorum [presbyterorum] conversatio .. moribus populi ~entior sit O. CANT. *Const.* 4. **b** **s1196** voluerunt .. ~entiores civium, quos majores et aldermannos dicimus .. seipsos servare indemnes M. PAR. *Maj.* II 418; *Offic. Sal.* 25 (v. classicus 4a); J. READING 179b (v. domina 1b); duo ~enciores presbiteri .. ad sepulchrum accedant *Med. Stage* II 313. **c** **c630** domino ~entissimo atque praecellentissimo filio Aeduino regi Anglorum (*Lit. Papae*) BEDE *HE* II 17 p. 118; **838** ~entissimis regibus nostris Ecgberhto et Æthelwulfo *CS* 421; ad consolationem .. regis .. Ædmundi omnisque populi ~enti imperio ejus subjecti O. CANT. *Const. pref.*; **1254** ~entissimus dominus H. .. rex Anglie (*Pat*) *RGasc* I 349; ipsos regie potestati seu ~enciori de necessitate fore subjectatos WYCL. *Compl.* 91; **1544** ~entissimi, serenissimi, et Christianissimi principis .. Henrici octavi *FormA* 71. **d** ~entioris figura mysterii quo modo tabernaculum .. sanctam designat ecclesiam BEDE *Tab.* 465C; cum Filius Dei haberet ~entiorem nativitatem .. ANSELM (*Incarn. B* 10) II 25; tam ~ens donum [ME: *se he[ch] ȝeove*, i. e. Christum, *Eph.* v] nunquam datum erat tam infimis miseris *AncrR* 152; racio omnium istorum est copiosior, diffusior et omnino ~encior in Cristo quam racio mali est eciam in diabolo WYCL. *Ver.* III 212.

3 (trans.) to excel, outstrip, surpass; **b** (w. dat.).

797 clementia regis omnium hominum .. ~ere decet consuetudines ALCUIN *Ep.* 123; illi qui superioris propositi sunt eos qui inferioris sunt humilitate .. et aliis virtutibus ~ere ANSELM (*Ep.* 189) IV 75; probitate .. omnes Anglie reges precedentes .. ~it ORD. VIT. IV 6 p. 202; Deus bonum quod ~it res omnes debet reddere ALEX. CANT. *Dicta* 10 p. 150; major antiquitas non facit majorem auctoritatem, quia tunc .. scripture prophetarum ~erent epistolas apostolorum (KYN.) *Ziz.* 5. **b** non .. ideo illae duae personae [Trinitatis] ~ent Filio ANSELM (*Incarn. B* 10) II 26.

2 excellere [AN *essiler*, OF *essilier* < LL exīliare], to destroy.

c1300 de .. boscis quod dominus .. possit assartare et ~ere *FormMan* 26.

excelse [CL], pre-eminently, outstandingly.

.. ut apud omnes excelcissime floruerit ROBERTSON *Rolloc* 11.

excelsia [cf. excelsus 3], elevated position, dignity.

antequam in hanc ruinose potestatis ~iam ascendisset erat in eo quedam liberalitatis species adumbrata .. sed honores mutant mores P. BLOIS *Ep.* 18. 68B.

excelsitudo [LL], highness (as title).

1171 nihil nisi sinistrum et vestre ⏜ini [v. l. celsitudini] ignominiosum reportantibus (*Lit. clericorum regis*) G. Hen. II I 22.

excelsus [CL]

1 high, lofty. **b** (w. *in* as adv. phr.) up, on high.

insuper excelsum forti compage sacellum / . . / diruit ad fundum ALDH. *VirgV* 1324; sermo . . velut ⏜i sideris fulgore . . refulsit *Lib. Monstr. prol.*; stella . . ⏜am radiantis flammae quasi columnam praeferens BEDE *HE* IV 12 p. 228; stant excelsa tolis rostrata cacumina turris WULF. *Swith. pref.* 179; in medio . . pulpiti erit preparatus thronus ⏜us W. SAY *Lib. Reg. Cap.* 74. **b** fumum ascendentem in ⏜um Angli . . prospexerant ORD. VIT. XII 18 p. 356.

2 pre-eminent, exalted; **b** (of God). **c** (as sb. m.) Most High, God.

⏜e generositatis lampade renitebat ORD. VIT. III 3 p. 61; [sancti] in morte vitali meritis jam ⏜i GIR. *TH* II 55; hic magnus parvulus, servus fit dominus [cf. *Deut.* xxvii 14] V. *Gund.* 21; ⏜a voce clamare cepit . . OSB. *Mir. Dunst.* 5; ⏜a voce legant, ut . . fratres . . quiescentes per eos excitati surgant *Cust. Westm.* 262. **b** magis in fletum prorumpere cogor quam in ⏜um sermonem G. MON. VI 2.

excennus v. xenodochium. **excentellare** v. estencellare. **excentric-** v. eccentric-.

exceptare [CL], to take or draw out.

⏜at, tractat *GlH* 661.

exceptatio v. acceptatio.

exceptator [cf. CL exceptare], one who takes or draws out.

⏜or, tractator *GlH* E 662.

exceptere [cf. excipere 8, exceptio 4], (leg.) to make objection, to plead.

1463 coram vobis in judicio ponit, ⏜it, et objiciendo objicit contra . . decretum pretensum super eleccione Johannis . . in decanum ecclesie vestre *Reg. Heref.* 80.

exceptio [CL]

1 receiving, reception (of person).

susceptio mali pro bono . ., ⏜o Satanae pro angelo lucis GILDAS *EB* 21; Elsinus [episc. Wint.] . . Cantiam intrusus est. primoque ⏜onis die non abstinuit quin furias . . evomeret W. MALM. *GP* I 17.

2 exception, singling out (of person).

ne personarum arguar ⏜onis GILDAS *EB* 65; in tempore Noe diluvio / fertur mortalium facta perdicio / . . / paucorum admodum erat excepcio WALT. WIMB. *Carm.* 174; **c1530** quod . . sitis caritativi . . et non discordantes convenientesve favoribus, consideracionibus seu personarum ⏜one . . utentes (*Vis. Leic.*) *EHR* IV 309.

3 (log.) exception.

dicendum de hac diccione 'preter' exceptiva, tum quod ⏜o sepe vult cadere super aliquam divisionem et ad eam continuari, tum quia oppositum habet ad ipsam (SHIRWOOD) *GLA* III 21 *n.* 75; 'reliquimus omnia' sc. preter illa sine quibus non potest hec vita transiri: dicunt quod talis ⏜o non potest colligi ex scripturis, sed ejus opposita ex scripturis patenter habetur. ideo talis exceptiva concedi non debet OCKHAM *Pol.* II 428.

4 (leg.) objection, plea; **b** (dist. by form); **c** (w. gen. of description). **d** (? fig.) obstacle, barrier.

1166 ut . . in usus adversariorum non multiplicet ⏜ones J. SAL. *Ep.* 270 (184 p. 220); quod . . per testes ⏜one majores probare parati sumus GIR. *JS* 4 p. 243; **1258** curia dicit quod ista ⏜o nulla est *SelPlMan* 57; **12. .** omnes qui in causa matrimoniali falsas ⏜ones maliciose opponunt *Conc. Scot.* II 27; **1305** non irrotulant . . legitimas ⏜ones *MGL* II 90; si accusatus per modum ⏜onis contra eos nequaquam crimen opponit OCKHAM *Dial.* 597; **1444** lego . . clerico meo . . omnes quaternos meos de practicis curie, viz. libellorum, posicionum, articulorum ⏜onum *Test. Ebor.* II 91; **1456** (v. agreare 1d). **b 1208**, BRACTON 187b (v. dilatorius a); **1271** etc. (v. declinatorius a); **1276, 1289** ⏜oni . . in factum (v. 2 dolus b). **c** GLANV. XIII 11 (v. bastardia); per temporis ⏜onem possum te removere VAC. *Lib. Paup.* 79; RIC. ANGL. *Summa* 38 (v. dilatorius a); **1270** super ⏜one consanguinitatis ex parte prefati J. proposita *SelCCant* 63; **1276, 1289** ⏜oni doli, metus (v. dolus b); **1279** renuncio . . omni juris auxilio . . et maxime ⏜oni non numerate peccunie *Reg. Heref.* 219; **1307** super ⏜one nontenure inde . . allegata *Year Bk.* I *Ed.* II 3; **1541** sentenciam interlocutoriam qua quandam ⏜onem spolii . . repulit *Offic. S. Andr.* 141. **d s1178** Burgundie . . quam Italie vicinantem intelligas ad arcendos hostes ab ea parte cacumina montium, precipitia vallium in modum ⏜onis opponere DICETO *YH* I 427.

5 land exempted from taxation. *Cf. exemptio 2.*

1254 estimatio bonorum . . abbatis et conventus de Waltham in ⏜one sua *Val. Norw.* 520; **1261** W. arrabit omnes ⏜ones predictas aratro suo *DCLinc.* Dij/70/2/62.

6 excerpt, extract. **b** (mus.) part, strain.

CUTHB. *Ob. Baedae* clxii (v. excerptio); ⏜ones de Augustino super Johannem *Text. Roff.* 224v.; ⏜o de penitentia Astulfi qui uxorem suam interfecerat BART. EXON. *Pen.* 50; **12. .** incipiunt ⏜ones de libro Gilde (*MS BL Cotton Nero D viii*) NEN. *HB rub.*; c1396 ⏜ones orthodoxorum patrum de diversis tractatibus (*Catal. Librorum*) *Meaux* III lxxxvi; **1442** in alio libro continentur ⏜ones de Historia Aurea *Ac. Durh.* 471; **14. .** brevis et utilis ⏜o historie veteris et novi testamenti (*Cart. Reading*) *EHR* III 118. **b** *Itin. Ric.* II 13 (v. depressio 2).

exceptive [LL], (gram. & log.) exceptively, by way of exception.

OCKHAM *Summa* II 18 p. 307 (v. diminutive b).

exceptivus [LL]

1 (gram. & log.) exceptive: **a** (of word or phr.) that introduces an exception. **b** (of proposition) containing an exception to the subject. **c** (as sb. f.) exception, exceptive proposition.

a (SHIRWOOD) *GLA* III 21 *n.* 75 (v. exceptio 3); omnes curatos volebat . . intelligere in illa particula ⏜a 'nisi prelati locorum' RIC. ARMAGH *Unusq.* 57; termini ⏜i WYCL. *Log.* I 54 (v. excipere 5e). **b** in proposicionibus exclusivis et ⏜is sed dubitacio, ut sic dicam 'tantum omnis homo currit', non potest converti nisi sic 'ergo tantum quoddam currens est homo', quod falsum est BACON XV 293; circa supposicionem confusam et distributivam immobilem est sciendum quod semper subjectum talem habet supposicionem in proposicione ⏜a . . OCKHAM *Summa* I 74 p. 230; est primo videndum que sunt proposiciones ⏜e *Ib.* II 18 p. 307. **c** si . . ⏜a fuerit negativa, tunc tam subjectum quam predicatum supponit confuse et distributive, sed limitate *Ib.* II 18 p. 308; *Id. Pol.* II 428 (v. exceptio 3); ⏜e sunt universales WYCL. *Log.* I 54 (v. excipere 5e).

2 (leg.) exceptionable.

si reus . . nullam proposuerit materiam contrariam aut ⏜am contra hujusmodi testes . . excusatur ab expensis *Praxis* 68.

exceptor [CL]

1 amanuensis, clerk, scribe.

⏜or, id est, scriptor qui excipiebat omnia in scriptis que proferebantur in judicio ab actore et reo VAC. *Lib. Paup.* 155.

2 'exceptor', objector.

quod in casu objectionis bastardie precise exprimeretur causa, vel pro indefenso haberetur ⏜or *Fleta* 432.

3 excerpter.

claret Prosper . . ⏜or sententiarum S. Augustini R. NIGER *Chr.* II 132.

4 catcher (of person), bailiff.

cachepol, pety serjaunt, angarius, . . ⏜or *PP*.

exceptorius [CL]

1 notarial, scribal.

sic . . Latinorum prolixa depictio a figuris xix transiret in viij que arte ⏜ia volumina maxima in parva spatia contraheret *Ps.-GROS. Gram.* 23.

2 (leg.) exceptional.

1446 quam . . excepcionem predicti . . judices pretensi admiserunt et terminum ad eandem probandam eisdem [partibus] . . assignarunt, que quidem partes in dicta materia ⏜ia nichil probarunt *Pat* 463 m. 23.

3 (as sb. f. or n.) cistern, receptacle for water.

⏜ia, cisterna *GlH* E 664; *synke ffor water or seyvynge*, ⏜ium *PP*.

excera- v. exsecra-. **excerc-** v. exerc-.

excerebrare [LL]

1 to brain, bash (someone's) brains out ; **b** (refl.); **c** (w. inanim. subj.).

nullus quamlibet experti roboris vincula innectere temptaret quin solo ejus [demone afflati] nisu ⏜aretur W. MALM. *GP* V 261; Jacobus . . Hierosolymis lapidatus est . . et pertica fullonis ⏜atus est R. NIGER *Chr.* I 22; **1220** percussit dominum suum . . in fronte . . ita quod ⏜avit eum *CurR* VIII 381*n.*; si vult, accipiat fustem vel baculum / quamvis excerebret me suum servulum / tamen non auferet dulcem caliculum WALT. WIMB. *Carm.* 160; **60**; BLAKMAN *Hen. VI* 17 (v. decollare 1a). **b s1249** ad columpnam ad quam alligatus fuerat caput fortiter allidens seipsum ⏜avit M. PAR. *Maj.* V 69. **c** lapis lapsus de fastigio ecclesie monachum . . ⏜avit DEVIZES 40v.; descendant grandines et malos . . / . . / . . excerebrent saxo tornatili WALT. WIMB. *Carm.* 516; **s1340** lapides a turribus malorum projecti multos ⏜arunt BAKER 117.

2 to remove brain (of corpse).

s1135 corpus . . regis defuncti ita evisceratum et ⏜atum saleque . . respersum est CAPGR. *Hen.* 67.

3 to render brainless (fig.), to stupefy. **b** to outwit.

potus puerorum . . cerebellum / turbat; quam plures sunt potibus excerebrati D. BEC. 2425; ⏜ate miser . . abscede ocius! MAP *NC* IV 16 f. 58v. **b** Sphinx ibi [*Thebes*] portentum stragem facit advenientum. / Oedipus hoc stravit suus hospes et excerebravit R. CANT. *Malch.* IV 351.

excerebrator, one who beats out or removes brains.

a ceruyller, ⏜or CathA.

excernere [CL], to sift out, cleanse.

†excerpno, A. *to clense* WW.

excerpere [CL], to pick out, select (fig.). **b** to excerpt, make extracts from (a book).

tota sancta scriptura, ex qua debes flores ⏜ere EDMUND *Spec. Relig.* 26. **b** a mandatis quae . . ex omni paene sanctarum scripturarum textu . . ⏜tae sunt GILDAS *EB* 106; haec . . ex antiquorum opusculis scriptorum ⏜ere curavi BEDE *AM* 141; his . . testimoniis quae ex multis pauca ⏜si LANFR. *Corp. & Sang.* 435C; quedam ex his ⏜ere et hic interserere non superfluum duxi GIR *IK* II 7; chronicas . . istas vobis de vetustis rotulis . . ⏜simus *Ann. Worc. pref.* 355.

excerpnere v. excernere.

excerptio [CL], excerpt, extract.

in nostram linguam . . convertit . . de libris Isidori episcopi ⏜ones [v. l. exceptiones] quasdam CUTHB. *Ob. Baedae* clxii; has ⏜ones de Prisciano . . vobis puerulis . . ad vestram linguam transferre studui ÆLF. *Gram.* 1.

excertio v. exercitio. **excertus** v. 2 exercitus.

excessio [LL]

1 secession. *Cf. excessus 1a.*

Cartago . . anno ⏜onis sue xcvj recepta est ORD. VIT. V 9 p. 343.

2 excess. *V. et. excessus 4a.*

⏜one caloris et frigoris eliminata ADEL. *QN* 71 (v. distemperantia a).

excessive

1 excessively. **b** (modifying adj.) very, too. **c** more than usual, especially.

Augustinus ⏜e loquitur de illis penis DUNS *Sent.* II 33. 1. 4; **1315** qui hominibus ad pacem et fidem nostram nunc existentibus dampna ⏜e irrogavit . . *RScot* 152b; **1343** quia provisiones facte per sedem apostolicam ⏜ius solito personis alienigenis in corone nostre . . prejudicium . . cedere dignoscuntur (*Cl*) W. GUISB. *Cont.* 410. **b** volo istum facere ⏜e misericordem [ME: *to reuful*] *AncrR* 80. **c** pulsentur insimul due majores campane . . sicut . . ⏜e sonitus fiat *Cust. Westm.* 310.

2 (w. ref. to goods or money): **a** exorbitantly. **b** at an exorbitant price. **c** extravagantly.

a 1349 breve pro sellariis . . et aliis castigandis ne capiant ⏜e (*LB Lond.* F f. 168) *MGL* I 620; **s1377** (v. convicinus c); **s1392** pistores in x quarteriis frumenti vj s. viij d. ⏜e lucrantur *Eul. Hist. Cont.* 368; **1488** W. K. est frunitor et capit lucrum ⏜e *DL CourtR* 126/1875 m. 4d. **b s1340** omnes, etiam non indictati . . ⏜e se redemerunt qui voluerunt carcerem evitare AD. MUR. *Chr.* 118; **1413** (v. extensor); **1419** volo quod . . executores mei vendant dictum tenementum carius quo †poterint, quia ⏜e dedi pro eodem *Wills N. Country* 21. **c 1322** abbas J. . . bona monasterii nostri . . nimis ⏜e consumpsit et dilapidavit (*Chr. Abingd.*) *EHR* XXVI 735.

excessivus

1 excessive, very great; **b** (of natural force); **c** (of number); **d** (of weight).

sanctissimi viri .. vigilias temperabant ~as BACON *Maj.* II 362; caristia bladi fuit nimis ~a per sex annos WHITTLESEY *Cont.* 221; pernecessarium est dilaciones fieri in processibus omnium accionum, dummodo nimium ipse non fuerint ~e FORTESCUE *LLA* 53. **b** nervis hominum .. frigore repentino et ~o hyemis .. repercussis *Croyl.* 16; **s1433** nisi inundaciones ille .. magis solito ~e fuerint et nimis graves (*Indent.*) *Croyl. Cont. B* 517. **c** **s1265** cum scutiferorum et peditum .. numero ~o TREVET *Ann.* 266; **s1346** nostri paucissimi de multitudine hostium ~a crebras victorias reportaverunt AD. MUR. *Chr.* 201; **s1352** convocatis militibus .. numero ~o J. READING 162b. **d** **1388** propter .. pondus ~um ad .. deterioracionem domorum in quibus [pertice] firmantur *MGL* I 453.

2 (of price, tax, or sim.) exorbitant.

propter districtionem nimis transgressivam vel ~am [v. l. concessivam] ultra modum et mensuram debitam BRACTON 217; **s1317** propter .. retenciones armatorum stipendiis insolitis et ~is *G. Ed. II Bridl.* 50; **1343** vos .. per diversas et ~as exacciones et imposiciones decimarum .. multipliciter oprimini onere debitorum *Reg. Heref.* 72; **1381** W. de B. armiger .. captus et ad ~am redempcionem per Scotos positus fuit *RScot* 34a; **1412** (v. carnifex 2); **1425** vendere .. carnes ad precium nimis ~um *Mem. York* I 57.

3 excessive, outrageous.

1324 ne ipsos .. errores seu aliquid aliud ~um permittatis .. predicare (W. MELTON) *Fabr. York* 158n.; **1344** contra dominum C. .. verba nimium ~a protulit *Lit. Cant.* II 280; **s1366** falsata bulla de indulgenciis ~is .. statum illorum [fratres ordinis S. Runcivalle] .. denigravit J. READING 187b; **s1398** rex .. habuit secum in familia cccc ~os viros .. malignissimos et subditos .. impune affligentes AD. USK 23; **s1361** modus criminis interfeccionis ejus nimium ~us fuit *Plusc.* IX 45.

excessorius, excessive, extravagant.

obediencia .. debet .. esse velox et voluntaria, .. simplex non ~ia, hilaris non objurgativa *Spec. Laic.* 58.

excessus [CL]

1 departure, going out (partly fig.); *cf. excessio* 1; **b** (sts. w. *vitae*) death. **c** (w. ref. to *Psalm* xxx 23, *Acts* xi 5, *etc.*) ecstasy.

non autumo, .. omnia apud omnes humanis in ~ibus fore profutura B. *V. Dunst.* 34; ~us, A. .. *passynge oute WW.* **b** **990** (12c) post hujus vitae ~um cuicunque sibi ratum duxerit cleronomo derelinquat *CD* 673; post ~um domini Oswaldi pontificis aecclesiae Eboracensis archiepiscopatum suscaepit WULF. *Æthelwold* 24; fratribus .. meis ~um venerandi patris .. aperui, concitoque gradu ad locum ubi .. corpus .. jacebat .. deveni DOMINIC *V. Ecgwini* I 9; vite vero post excessum non vadat ad tenebras HIL. RONCE. I 157. **c** vidit hominem Dei mire [v. l. miro] stupore in ~u mentis occupatum *V. Cuthb.* IV 10; mentis in excessu transcendit nubila celi *Mir. Nin.* 213; **798** per quoddam mentis ~um .. haec locutus sum ALCUIN *Ep.* 156; ~um mentis patienti apparuit sanctus Dei OSB. *Mir. Dunst.* 18; in mentis raptus ~um biduo fere jacebat exanimis AILR. *Ed. Conf.* 771D; in exstasi neque in ~u mentis omnino non exstitit quia ista pervigil oculo corporeo .. vidit R. COLD. *Cuthb.* 38.

2 digression.

hiis per ~um quemdam necessario anticipatis, ea que cepimus directe narrationis serie prosequamur AD. EYNS. *Hug.* III 12 p. 123; quia ad hec .. quasi per ~um quemdam stilum deflex*imus Ib.* IV 3 p. 11.

3 rising up. **b** (w. *maris*) flood.

~us, A. .. *surmountynge WW.* **b** **s1287** maximum diluvium et ~us maris in omnibus terris maritimis *Feud. Man.* 103 (= *Meaux* II 279 [**s1307**]).

4 excess; *v. et. excessio* 2. **b** excessive number. **c** excessive amount. **d** greatness.

ut et resecet voluntatis ~um et excedendi non amputet potestatem ANSELM (*Casus Diab.* 14) IV 258; non possibilitatis ~um infinitum cognoscibilem reddere proposuimus BALSH. *AD rec.* 2 144; omnis .. malicia est in ~u GILB. III 106. 1; tractatus amorem quem ad libros habuimus ab ~u purgabit R. BURY *Phil. prol.* 12; in re .. qualibet potest esse ~us [ME: *overdon*] *AncrR* 108. **b** **1279** quatenus clamorem .. super intolerabili ~u ferarum vestrarum seu bestiarum sedare velitis (*Ad Comitem Surreye*) PECKHAM *Ep.* 31; **13..** (v. extrahere 6e). **c** ~us [dotis] .., si fuerit per assignacionem alterius quam heredis, per admensuracionem revocabitur per .. statutum *Fleta* 342 (cf. BRACTON 93 s. v. admensuratio c); **1353** (v. 2 excedere 4c). **d** et si Deus se vellet ostendere intellectui nostro .. parvitas potencie nostre intellective et ~us objecti .. hec .. non impediunt BACONTHORPE *Quaest. Sent.* 8B.

5 (moral) excess, sin. **b** (leg.) transgression.

letaniis quibus Dominum pro nostris imploramus ~ibus atque .. peccatis *V. Greg.* p. 110; postulantes multiplicium indulgentiam ~uum [AS p. 401: *misdæde*] dicentes "confiteor" *RegulC* 31; facto jejunio .. de suis ~ibus confessi ALEX. CANT. *Mir.* 36 (I) p. 231; W. NEWB. *HA* I 12 (v. elemosina 1a); GIR. *Symb.* I 3 (v. deferre 10b); quando saccus est inanis / tunc excessus est immanis WALT. WIMB. *Van.* 21. **b** lex .. est .. donum Dei, dogma sapientum, correctio voluntariorum ~uum J. SAL. *Pol.* 515A; si nos ~um non emendaverimus .. predicti iiij barones referant causam illam ad residuos de xxv baronibus *Magna Carta* 60; **1217** ne castra sua .. ei [sc. Waltero de L.] reddere tardetis, occasione ~us per Willelmum de L. nobis illati. ipse enim Walterus manucepit .. quod plene nobis satisfaciet de ~u illo emendando .. pro Willelmo *Pat* 77; **1236** per oblivionem ostensa fuit tallia illa et non per maliciam, et ideo perdonatur ~us *KRMem* 15 m. 18; **1320** de ~ibus vicecomitum vel aliorum ballivorum, .. si aliquem (*sic*) litem foverint *MGL* II 350.

6 insult, outrage.

domine mi rex, quod hic agitur non est ~us aut reverencie vestre contemptus MAP *NC* V 6 f. 70; **s1202** rex Francie fecit summoneri regem Anglie, ut Parisius veniret; .. ei responsurus super quibusdam ~ibus, quos ei imponebat *Ann. S. Edm.* 9; **1345** ut taceres de multis ~ibus per nuncium nostrum .. commissis (*Lit. Papae*) AD. MUR. *Chr.* 178.

7 ? freak.

GIR. *TH pref.* p. 21 (v. 2 excedere 1b).

excetra [CL], water snake (also fig.).

exedra serpens est. si occiditur, surgent de capite ejus plures serpentes nisi citius incenditur *Gl. Leid.* 23. 1; fuit .. hydra .. serpens in Lerna .. cui, uno ceso capite, tria capita excrescebant. unde et ~a a Latinis dicta est ALB. LOND. *DG* 13. 4; si tamen incendat Sinon excetraque sufflet, / non minus inceptum tendo parare stilum GOWER *VC* II prol. 51.

exchaet- v. escaere, escaeta. **exchaire** v. escaere. **exchambium** v. excambium. **exchang-** v. escang-. **exchap-** v. escap-. **exchat-, excheat-, exchet-** v. escaet-. **exchipp-** v. skipp-. **excialis** v. exitialis. **excicialis** v. exercitualis, exitialis. **excicium** v. exitium.

excidamentum [cf. 1 excĭdere 4], escheat. *Cf. escaëta* 1.

1141 concedo .. ut teneat omnia ~a mea que mihi exciderint in comitatu Essexe, reddendo inde firmam rectam quamdiu erunt in dominio meo *Mandeville* 92.

1 excĭdere [CL]

1 (of person) to fall; **b** (fig.); **c** (fig.) to lapse, slip up.

~it occisus, quoniam 'occidit super iracundiam ejus sol' (*Eph.* iv 26) MAP *NC* III 3 f. 40v. **b** **?1165** non est .. dampnum dispendiosius quam siquis a gratia ~at (cf. *Gal.* v 4) J. SAL. *Ep.* 250 (148); omnis homo ~it in primo parente originaliter S. GAUNT *Serm.* 208. **c** [Theodredum] uno ~isse magis errore quam crimine, quod fures .. severitati legum addixerit, patibulis adjudicatos W. MALM. *GP* II 73 p. 144.

2 (of thing) to fall (out or down). **b** (w. abstr. subj.) to fall away, decline.

~it, cecidit vel *gewat GlH* E 529; queritur ante duodecimum annum si dentes ~erint quare renascantur .. *Quaest. Salern.* B 71; **1232** (v. copero 1). **b** sed postquam excidit obediencia / et vindex affuit erubescentia / .. WALT. WIMB. *Carm.* 418.

3 (usu. w. *animo*, *memoria*, or sim.) to slip (away), escape (notice).

~erant †ammo [l. animo], de animo recedebant *GlC* E 446; nihil ~it eorum quae supra ratione investigante comperimus a memoria mea ANSELM (*Casus Diab.* 25) I 273; menti ejus .. penitus ~erat quod Absalon .. turmas .. congesserat ORD. VIT. VII 4 p. 164; ne queso ~at animo quam adipiscemur, angelorum similitudo EADMER *Beat.* 3; non ~at autem quod .. BALSH. *AD rec.* 2 156; ~ente a voluntate ejus omni cura medicinali W. CANT. *Mir. Thom.* III 12.

4 to escheat; *cf. escaëre* a; **b** (pr. ppl. as sb. n. pl.) escheat; *cf. escaëta* 1.

1141 (v. excidamentum); cum in manum regis baronia vel magnum aliquid ~it, .. discreti .. viri diriguntur, qui .. redditus earundem in summam dirigunt *Dial. Scac.* II 27 A; **1227** rex concessit .. comiti Cestrie .. partem honoris Richemund .. cum omnibus escaetis que inde decetero ~ere poterunt *Pat* 124; **1239** (v. escaëta 1); **1243** de aliqua domo competenti que ~erit in manum nostram de dominibus Judeorum .. eidem .. providebimus (cf. *CalPat* 391) *RGasc* I 148. **b** sequitur compotus de ~entibus et occupatis quod nos usitatius dicimus de propresturis et eschaetis *Dial. Scac.* II 10 A (cf. ib. 10 F: tertium genus ~entium).

2 excīdere [CL]

1 to cut away or out (from). **b** to hollow out.

legebam .. oleastri ramum bonae olivae .., si non timuisset .. ~endum (cf. *Rom.* xi 24) GILDAS *EB* 1; BEDE *HE* III 2 p. 129 (v. 1 astula); **8..** ~it, *hio forcearf WW*; sarmentum, rami qui de vineis ~untur *GlC* S 35; excisa glacie GIR. *GE* II 10 (v. congelare 1a); **s1252** ferrum remansit in vulnere; quod .. excisum .. M. PAR. *Maj.* V 319. **b** domus .. rotunda erat excisa in petra BEDE *Hom.* II 10. 153; vagabantur in montaneis vel in excisis prerruptorum cuniculis ORD. VIT. IX 15 p. 600; saxi durities aquis exesa .. tota late concava in modum pene lapidei vasis excisa GIR. *GE* II 10.

2 to carve out, hew; **a** (w. material as obj.); **b** (w. artefact as obj.).

a lapide inpolito, .. non exciso *Gl. Leid.* 23. 5; **1234** tabulamenta petrarum excisarum *Cal. Liberate* VI 2406; lapides .. albos / quos manus artificis omnes excidit in unguem H. AVR. *Hugh* 866. **b** **1259** quinque ymagines regum excisas in franca petra *Ac. Build. Hen. III* 196; AD. EYNS. *Hug.* V 18 (v. diptycha a).

3 to slice.

excisus tenue sit caseus inveteratus D. BEC. 2607.

4 to fell (tree, also fig.). **b** to chop, shape (wood).

ne .. Christi securem sibi ad conburendum se, in crura exciso radicitus convertat [cf. *Matth.* iii 10] *V. Greg.* p. 106; si 'arbor quae non facit fructum bonum' [cf. *Matth.* iii 10] ~itur ut arida ANSELM (*Or.* 10) III 36; **s1254** ligna .. tam silvestria quam fructifera arefacta, solis securibus patuerunt ~enda M. PAR. *Maj.* V 461; arbori excise de cujus trunco nata est TREVET *Troades* 41. **b** **1278** in x[c] iiij[xx] et xij carectatis bosci prosternend', excidend', et cariand' *Ac. Durh.* 488; **1323** in expensis carpentariorum ~encium ligna predicta [i. e. xx ligna quercina empt'] apud Chickissand, j li. *Sacr. Ely* II 33.

5 (w. personal obj.): **a** to cut, strike down. **b** to mutilate.

a GOSC. *Mir. Iv.* lxx (v. effulminare). **b** lumine privatur, miser et caecatur utroque, / naribus excisis, auresque manusque secantur WULF. *Swith.* II 469; excisa soboles Jude repululat / .. / nam Judas reddiit qui jura jugulat WALT. WIMB. *Sim.* 12.

excidium [CL], (mil.) destruction (of place); **b** (of person, institution, or nation); **c** (w. *animae*).

haesit .. tam desperati insulae ~ii .. mentio .. memoriae eorum GILDAS *EB* 26; in ~io Trojae gemini serpentes a Tenedo insula .. natabant *Lib. Monstr.* III 10; ~ium, discidium, .. expugnatio, .. eversio *GlC* E 378, 379, 526; ~ium, i. .. casus, ruina, *hereteam GlH* E 528; sceptri .. apice ante ~ium patriae potitus est bis ter annis *V. Neot. A* 17; Eneas .. ~ium urbis .. diffugiens, Italiam .. adivit G. MON. I 3; Nabuzardan in ~io Jerusalem dimisit in pace pauperes P. BLOIS *Serm.* 693D; M. PAR. *Maj.* III 149 (v. concambium a). **b** T. MON. *Will. prol.* (v. Christianicida); Judei ~io pariter et exterminio, Pylatus exilio penas luit GIR. *IK* I 4; seducens scolares .. ut .. adirent Stanfordiam .., ad .. universitatis [Oxoniensis] †exeodium [l. excidium] *Collect. Ox.* I 16; ~ii ducis Burgundie participes erant *Ps.-*ELMH. *Hen. V* 126. **c** tu .., robuste armis sed animae fortior ~iis GILDAS *EB* 32; **1342** (v. devitare a).

exciere, excire [CL]

1 to cause to move away, rouse, stir. **b** to rouse (from sleep). **c** to stir, incite (to action). **d** (mil.) to muster.

multitudo .. cum conjugibus ac liberis ~ita convenerat BEDE *HE* I 17; ~iti, excitati *GlC* E 537; ~io, .. moveo *GlH* E 535; rumoribus .. viri pugnaces de vicinis regionibus ~iti convenerunt ORD. VIT. III 12 p. 126. **b** Phebo per orbem spargente .., ~itus rex sonum majoris signi audivit in .. basilica *Ib.* VII 16 p. 248; excĭtus exurgit, excĭtus tendit in hostem H. AVR. *CG* 7v. 11 (v. et. 1d infra). **c** erroneus exul ad tantum laborem tyrannum ~ivit ORD. VIT. III 11 p. 124. **d** Uther Pendragon, ~ita armatorum copia, ivit in Kambriam G. MON. VIII 14; regali edicto Normannos et Anglos iterum ~ivit ORD. VIT. IV 12 p. 256; H. AVR. *CG* 7v. 11 (v. 1b supra).

2 to start (animal), to drive (game).

cum die quodam ~ire saltibus feras intenderet GIR. *IK* I 1.

3 to call forth, summon. **b** to evoke, produce.

~iti, .. evocati *GlC* E 537; ~io, .. voco *GlH* E 535; fulgurite, id est fulguratores erant sive qui fulgura per incantationes ~iebant ALB. LOND. *DG* 11. 16. **b** multos fletus ex oculis viduarum .. ~ivit ORD. VIT. VIII 12 p. 336; HANV. IX 306 p. 386 (v. eluctari b).

excillare v. excellare. **excimbium** v. cymbium. **excindere** v. exscindere.

excinerare [cf. cinerare], to burn, reduce to ashes.

ut blasphemus .. tractus et suspensus deinde .. eviscerartus et postremo flammis ~atus est CAPGR. *Hen.* 123.

excipere [CL]

1 to take out, select. **b** to mark or single out. **c** (p. ppl.) select, exceptional.

~iatur, i. [MS: segregatur, *sy fram asceaden*; ed. omits] *GlH* E 532; **9..** excepit, *ut afeng, ut adyde WW*; note .. vel figure, quas abaciste 'caracteres' vocant, omnes sunt xxxvj et diverse. ex his sc. caracteres ix ~iuntur quos proprio

nomine vocamus 'integros' THURKILL *Abac.* f. 55v.; tanquam marinas inter arenas gemmas eligens et ~iens GIR. *TH intr.* p. 8. **b** num centennis tu . . coaevus Mathusalae exceptus paene omni prole servaberis? GILDAS *EB* 30; **1168** sunt . . homines . . quos non etas discernit . ., non titulus professionis . . ~it J. SAL. *Ep.* 251 (246). **c** de cellerario quodam egregio et vere quidem excepte actionis viro GIR. *Spec.* III 17.

2 to excerpt.

dictandi tenorem notariis ~ientibus et antiquariis describentibus ALDH. *VirgP* 59; W. MALM. *GP* I 42 (v. effluere 2b); incipit prologus libri ex universo enucleato jure excepti VAC. *Lib. Paup.* 1; omnia . . de libris . . philosophorum ~iens . . compilavi BART. ANGL. *proem.*; narraciones monstruosas edocet sub diversis auctoribus exceptas *Eul. Hist.* I *proem.* 3.

3 (w. personal obj.): **a** to take (on one's shoulders). **b** to receive, greet, welcome. **c** (refl.) to betake (oneself).

a ~iens . . eum super humeros suos, asportavit . . *Latin Stories* 76. **b** ductus . . ad domum suam lugubriter ~itur ALDH. *VirgP* 50; iterum excoepit, eosque fecit esse in eclesia *V. Greg.* p. 95; ita ut . . gaudenter ab omnibus tamquam Dei famulus ~eretur BEDE *HE* III 26 p. 191; regia classis / caelicolae sotias laeta exceptura phalanges FRITH. 334; latrones . . ipsam cum sarcis exceperunt et . . ad silvam deduxerunt *Latin Stories* 96. **c** s**1141** (v. 2 essentia 6).

4 to take, receive; **b** (punishment); **c** (injury or sim.). **d** to sustain, endure (attack). **e** to take, receive (oath); **f** (abstr. obj.).

debitum . . exactum . . ~ient GILDAS *EB* 1; nuda . . manu timide excipit illam / et portat calibem . . rubentem WULF. *Swith.* II 346; ~iat inde plegium [AS: *fo to þam borge*] (*Quad.*) *GAS* 443; bene pugnaverunt, bene vicerunt et premium victorie hodie exceperunt AILR. *Serm.* 295A; *Chr. Rams.* 33 (v. duodennium); quem [cruorem] exceperunt tam viri quam mulieres et diligenter reposuerunt *Latin Stories* 66. **b** semper . . defleat culpam suam, oboedientiam prae omnibus libentissime ~iat GILDAS *Pen.* 1; quis eorum . . squalores pedoresque carcerum . . excepit? *Id. EB* 72; excipis . . dignas . . poenas FRITH. 95; FOLC. *V. J. Bev.* 11 (v. emaculare); s**1179** juxta jus publicum jure debuerat pro meritis tociens excepisse suspendium DICETO *YH* I 437; c**1380** sub . . penis sibi per vos imponendis et de ipso ~iendis *FormOx* 255. **c** excipiunt ictus . . cruentos FRITH. 391; *Ib.* 701 (v. aerumna); c**1166** ut . . rapinam bonorum . . pro fide . . gaudenter ~iam J. SAL. *Ep.* 194 (188 p. 250). **d** quem Cesar . . pretenso clipeo excepit G. MON. IV 3; homuncio . . / . . / qui quamvis gladium in manu teneat / unum excipere leonem timeat WALT. WIMB. *Carm.* 323. **e** **1415** per . . juramentum de ea exceptum tactis sacrosanctis Dei evangeliis *Reg. Cant.* II 109. **f** omnes Christi tirones . . lucem . . serenam aurae caelestis ~iunt GILDAS *EB* 12; mors unius ex suis multorum in mortibus marchionum Anglis lugubres et Normannis exosas excepit exequias DICETO *YH* I 437; Antipater intolerabile odium populi excepit M. PAR. *Maj.* I 86.

5 to except, exclude; **b** (imper. sg.). **c** to leave out, omit, neglect (duty or obligation). **d** to make exception (of), stipulate; **e** (log., absol.).

~iuntur passiva et deponentia ejusdem modi ALDH. *PR* 128 p. 176; a**1105** qui . . dixit quia 'unusquisque' recipiet 'prout gessit' [cf. *2 Cor.* v 10] . . nullam excepit personam ANSELM (*Ep.* 346) V 284; pannus tertius . . quasi pro ~ienda importuna feditate pulveris superadditus R. COLD. *Cuthb.* 42; [mors] casas conterens sceptra non excipit WALT. WIMB. *Sim.* 97; nec de imperatore seu rege . . [Christus] fecit mencionem specialem, nec regem quemcumque excepit vel exemit OCKHAM *Pol.* III 281; prefatum capitaneum . . convenciones punctuate a suis tam mitibus privilegiis exceperunt *Ps.*-ELMH. *Hen. V* 54. **b** a**1252** conjugatis nulla injungatur penitentia, ~e quando suspecti habentur ad invicem *Conc.* I 689a (= *Conc. Syn.* 455: ex qua suspecti habeantur). **c** volo, ut omnis prepositus habeat gemotum semper ad iiij ebdomadas . . si quis hoc ~iat [AS: *gif hit hwa oferhebbe*], emendet sicut ante dictum est (*Quad.*) *GAS* 145. **d** a**1102** aut . . hanc excommunicationem in Anglia absolvite . . aut eam vos servare velle . . vestris litteris significate; aut si quid discretioni vestrae placet ~ere, eadem certitudine nominatim quid illud sit intimate ANSELM (*Ep.* 280) IV 195. **e** sunt termini exceptivi 'preter quam' et 'nisi' et aliqua que illis equivalent. et differunt in hoc quia duo primi ~iunt indifferenter a distribucione affirmativa vel negativa. et sunt exceptivarum quedam affirmative et quedam negative . . . exceptive sunt universales WYCL. *Log.* I 54.

6 (p. ppl. *exceptus* in abl. absol.): **a** excepted. **b** (w. ref. to time) lacking. **c** not counted.

a Brittannia insula . . milium ducentorum in lato spatium, ~is diversorum prolixioribus promontoriorum tractibus GILDAS *EB* 3; proco fuerat, quo non praestantior alter / regibus exceptis, mundum qui jure gubernant ALDH. *VirgV* 2067; homines ~is paucis quos manu retinuit . . prosiluerunt *V. Cuthb.* II 6; **741** (12c) (v. constructio 1b); et nox in tantum crevit per claustra genarum, / ut nihil exceptis posset sentire tenebris WULF. *Swith.* I 1502; a**1109** ossa S. . . Neoti . . reposui . . in . . scrinio, ~o uno brachio, quod dicitur esse in Cornu Galliae ANSELM (*Ep.* 473) V 421; nullus ~o Corineo aderat G. MON. I 15; **1269** vicecomes accepit securitatem de prosequendo et jussit quod talis caperetur ubicunque inveniretur ~a ecclesia et cimiterio *CBaron* 86; **1335** de quatuor viginti hobelarii in comitatu Wiltshire ~a civitate Sarum et villa de Bath *RScot* 329a. **b** per xvj annorum spatia, ~is xiij ebdomadibus HUGEB. *Wynn.* 13; s**940** Ædestanus . . obiit vj Kal. Nov. xlj anno post mortem Aluredi regis solum modo una nocte ~a *AS Chr.* **c** quattuor milia virorum, ~a secundi sexus caterva ALDH. *Met.* 2 p. 67; ista [regina], ~is sacerdotibus et diaconibus, novem episcopos occidere jussit EDDI 6; nati sunt . . filii et filiae [quinque], . . ~is his qui in infantia . . praeoccupati sunt ASSER *Alf.* 75; intra civitatem et xviij manerii qui in Hereford reddunt firmas suas computantur cccxxxv li. xviij s., ~is placitis de hundredo et de comitatu *DB* I 6; **1221** (v. denarius 8a).

7 (*excepto (hoc) quod* or *quia*) except that; **b** (*excepto* as prep. w. acc.) except; **c** (w. abl. or gen.).

ita ut Sauli . . conparandus videretur, ~o dumtaxat hoc quod divine erat religionis ignarus BEDE *HE* III 23 p. 175; ~o . . hoc quod omnis natura bona dicitur, duo bona et duo his contraria mala usu dicuntur ANSELM (*Casus Diab.* 12) I 255; ~o hoc quia Deus de malis multis modis bona facit *Id.* (*CurD* I 15) II 73; qualis fui hactenus, talis tibi maneo ~o quod quantum religiosior efficeris . . H. LOS. *Ep.* 42; debent facere quantum facit dimidia hida, scilicet sarculando etc., ~o quod non metit nec triturat *Cust. Battle* 29; **1321** (v. denarius 10). **b** qui . . votum voverit in arbore vel in qualibet re ~o aecclesiam, si clerici vel laici excommunicentur EGB. *Pen.* 8. 1. **c** **939** (13c) ~o istis tribus expeditione pontis arcisve constructione *CS* 743; sex millia [sc. anni] . . ~o annis quinque ÆTHELW. III 3; successit in regnum Karulus minor . . et ut dicam proavi sui passim potestatem, exscepto provinciae Liduuicon *Ib.* IV 3; hunc [sc. Alfredum] ut redemptorem suscepere cuncti . . ~o barbarae gentis et his qui sub manu eorum tum captivi tenebantur *Ib.*; ~o vj acris prati DB I 51v.; **1315** omnia rubea ~o una capa de nigris *Invent. Ch. Ch.* 25*n*.

8 (leg.) to plead as exception; **b** (w. *contra*). *Cf. exsumere*.

agendo et probando, defendendo et ~iendo et replicando BRACTON 1b; ~ere poterit, et dicere quod secta non fuit benefacta eo quod statim hutesios non levavit *Fleta* 49; **1275** ad agendum, deffendendum, ~iendum . ., litem contestandum *Reg. Heref.* 12; G. de Nortone . . coram eis [sc. justiciariis] ~iendo proposuit quod ipsi ad dictum placitum tenendum warentum non haberent *MGL* II 172; c**1357** (v. agere 3e). **b** **1249** excepit contra illos quod non debuit illis ad breve respondere *CurR* XIX 946; multipliciter . . ~i poterit contra breve BRACTON 188; s**1237** contra eleccionem excepit rex quod electus erat inimicus regis GRAYSTANES 4; hereticus propter crimen heresis non potest contra ipsum ~ere OCKHAM *Dial.* 597.

9 to take down, note (from dictation). **b** to take in, comprehend. **c** (absol.) to gather (fig.), understand.

exceptis, notatis *GlH* E 665; Parabolas compilaverunt, ante . . a Salomone dictas et . . ab ~ientibus . . vulgatas J. SAL. *Ep.* 143 (209 p. 328); VAC. *Lib. Paup.* 155 (v. exceptor 1). **b** hujus divisionis divisoribus per quorumlibet adjectionem caracterum hic prescripto modo adauctis, qui maximus dicitur est ~iendus THURKILL *Abac.* f. 60v.; in hiis [locutionibus] . . omnes catholici expositores Christum ~iunt, quod si nullus alius homo a Christo ~iendus est et Christus non est aliquis homo, ut vel ipse ~i debeat, nullus homo ~iendus est J. CORNW. *Eul.* 6. **c** c**1390** grandes . . possessiones ex pia largicione fidelium in boriali plaga optinetis, sub ea . . ordinacione, sicut excepimus, usibus vestris ab olim collatas *FormOx* 227 (cf. ib. 228: latorem presencium sine . . debito processu, ut excepimus, . . expulsum).

10 to follow.

cum . . una syllaba brevis remanserit de verbo quae vel in vocalem desinens ~iatur a consonante verbi sequentis vel in consonantem desinens ~iatur a littera vocali BEDE *AM* 90; †excipiatur [MS: excipitur], i. . . sequitur *GlH* E 532.

excipium [cf. CL excipuum], frithed field; intake.

a frithed felde, ~ium *CathA*.

excipula [cf. CL excipulum], receptacle, trap.

1517 formularum, id est, ~arum opifices (*Lit. Budaei*) MORE *Ut.* lxxxi; **1542** septem duodenas ~arum, A. *vij dosen of shrympe leapes* vulgariter vocatarum *willyers HCA Warrant Bk.* 1/47.

excipulum [CL = *receptacle*; cf. LL excipiabulum], hunting-spear.

a sperre for a bayre, ~um, venabulum *CathA*.

excire v. exciere.

1 excisa v. 2 excidere.

2 excisa [Middle Dutch *excijs*; cf. *DuC* s. v. accisia], duty, excise, 'accise'. (*Cf. OED*; *Middelnederlandsch Woordenboek*, ed. E. Verwijs & J. Verdam II iv (1886), *s. v.*)

1490 exsisis . . exsisas (v. datium).

excisio [CL]

1 excision, cutting out.

albus et excisus castos lapis et sapientes / exprimit: albedo pudor est, excisio dogma H. AVR. *Hugh* 923; **1323** in cariagio et ~one petre empte apud Swaffham . . viij s. viiij d. *Sacr. Ely* II 32.

2 cutting up, slashing.

pars utraque . . discessit ab armorum ~one G. CRISPIN *Herl.* 88.

3 destruction.

c**1250** satisfactio consistit in ~one causarum peccati *Conc. Syn.* 454.

excitabilis [LL], excitable, that can be aroused.

qui . . inter adversa et prospera dormire magis patitur, quam acquiescat, ~is est R. NIGER *Mil.* III 33.

excitamentum [LL], stimulus, incitement.

1237 existens . . nostri torporis ~um, titubantis erectio, . . tribulati consolatio GROS. *Ep.* 40; **1485** contra diabolicas fraudes et fantastica ~a contemplative certarunt (*Lit. Archiep. Ardmachensis*) *Anal. Boll.* XXVII 39.

excitare [CL]

1 to arouse, call forth. **b** to awaken (from sleep). **c** to raise (from death).

si ~atus veniat post misam, quicquid cantaverunt replicet ex ordine fratres GILDAS *Pen.* 19; ~atur, evocatur *GlC* E 452; ~a hos pisces . . et orationibus tuis effice ut sint homines, sicut antea fuerunt WULF. *Æthelwold* 39; excĭtat hinc oritur, excītat nascitur inde H. AVR. *CG* 7v. 12. **b** [corcodrilli] sunt rapaces si quos a somno ~ati sibi vicinos perseneserint *Lib. Monstr.* II 25; ÆLF. *Coll.* 103 (v. duriter 1); qui stupuit nimium, quod tempestate soporis / excitat hospes eum WULF. *Swith.* I 273; quam quietius possit infantes ~et LANFR. *Const.* 142; gallus dormientes in profunda nocte cantando ~at ORD. VIT. VI 4 p. 13; "dormisne?" . . "dormiebam, sed ~atus sum" W. CANT. *Mir. Thom.* II 21; ~at gubernator Jonam dormientem in navi, tropologicus intellectus de excitatione Christi dormientis AD. DORE *Pictor* 157; *Cust. Cant.* 106 (v. 1 dependere 1a). **c** excitat horrenda constrictum morte cadaver ALDH. *VirgV* 290; BEDE *Hom.* II 9. 143 (v. desipere a).

2 to excite, stimulate (body or mind). **b** to spur (horse). **c** to stir, cause to move.

qui semen dormiens . . fuderit iij dies jejunet. si [se] ~at ipse, primo xx dies, iterans xl dies THEOD. *Pen.* I 8. 9; novis quibusdam . . lectoris animum ~are GIR. *TH intr.* p. 7. **b** sunt . . calcaria huic militi ad ~andum equum suum pernecessaria *Simil. Anselmi* app. 193. **c** **801** quievit calamus meus quia non fuit qui ~aret eum ALCUIN *Ep.* 214.

3 to encourage, provoke, urge; **b** (w. *ad* or *in*); **c** (w. *ut*); **d** (w. inf.).

quidam . . invidia quadam ~ati . . amaricati sunt ASSER *Alf.* 96. **b** homines . . ad dilectionem . . bonae actionis ~are curabat BEDE *HE* IV 22 p. 261; plura sunt quae videntur liberum arbitrium ad bene operandum ~are ANSELM (*Praesc.* 3. 1) II 264; ad sequendum se ~arunt ORD. VIT. III 3 p. 54; mentem suam in Dei amorem ~at ALEX. CANT. *Dicta* 20 p. 194; si [picture] . . literatos ad amorem ~ent scripturarum AD. DORE *Pictor* 142; octo sunt que nos ~ant ad vigilandum [ME: *ladieð us to waken*] in bono *AncrR* 46 (cf. ib. 115: diabolus non potest aliquem cogere ad peccandum licet ad hoc ~et [ME: *eggi*]). **c** bona voluntas amica monitione ut plus ferveat ~atur ANSELM (*Ep.* 324) V 255; s**1346** ut per hoc ~aret populum regni, ut eo ferventius diligerent regem AD. MUR. *Chr.* 211; **1423** licet sanctos ut orent pro miseris ~are, que quidem excitacio ad sanctos immediate et oracio eciam immediate ad dominum Deum dirigitur *Reg. Cant.* III 163. **d** **1336** ~at nos dilectio spiritalis . . universitatem vestram . . deprecari, ut . . *Lit. Cant.* II 117; a**1350** ne quis eorum absenciam contemptui vel arrogancie ~etur ascribere *StatOx* 57; **1463** veremur ne populus . . ecclesiam . . contemnere ~entur *Conc.* III 586b; Hedda episcopus ~ans Inas regem fundare [ecclesiam] W. WORC. *Itin.* 126.

4 **a** to generate (heat). **b** to ignite (spark), to kindle or stir up (fire; also fig.). **c** to heat (water).

a ut ex magni caloris excitatione et . . veloci confricationis inculcatione calor ~etur et humor dissolvatur *Quaest. Salern.* B 12; propter . . corporis exercitationem que . . pulsum fecit fortem . . quia calor naturalis . . ~atur BART. ANGL. III 24. **b** flante maximo vento, ignis ~atus est *V. Cuthb.* II 7; flamma pinguedine ~ata majoris incendii incrementa concipit ALEX. CANT. *Mir.* 35 (I) p. 227; scintilla . . fomentis ~ata . . erumpit . . in flammam PULL. *Sent.* 721A; quos in reipublicae salutem . . educabamus jam in faces publicaque incendia . . ~ari nostro et omnium malo conspiciemus FERR. *Kinloss* 6. **c** (*Quad.*) *GAS* 386 (v. bullitus).

5 to raise, stir up (element or force).

BEDE *Luke* (v 1) 381 (v. crispare 3b); diabolus . . ~at ventos et tempestates ALEX. CANT. *Dicta* 5 p. 131; clamore ipsius ~abuntur maria G. MON. VII 4; ~abitur Daneum nemus et in humanam vocem erumpens clamabit *Ib.*

6 to erect (structure).

FERR. *Kinloss* 71 (v. corollarium 2); si quis .. imaginem ~et in templis Christianorum JEWEL *Apol.* E 5.

7 (w. abstr. obj.) to bring into existence, cause, arouse. **b** (w. *verba*); **c** (log. & phil.).

ille neglegentiam ~at ALCH. *Ep.* 299; non debet esse contentiosus nec lites ~are ÆLF. *Ep.* 2. 177; unde assumam, nisi de vobis, quod ad ~andam misericordiam vestram obtendam vobis ANSELM (*Or.* 10) III 38; ideo voluit [Deus] in hac sciencia [sc. theologia] .. in cordibus nostris divinam ~are dileccionem; et eciam per modum maxime dileccionis excitativum MIDDLETON *Sent.* I 8; orchis .. dicitur multas vires coeundi ~are *Alph.* 131. **b** s**1253** (v. cubicularius 1b). **c** excitacio †sit [l. fit] semper propter aliquid, quia adminus ~atur substancia ad audiendum vel percipiendum BACON XV 111; si '~are' non sit 'aliquid causare' in potencia intellectiva non aliter se habet in se post excitacionem quam ante, et ita non magis ~atur nunc quam prius DUNS *Ord.* III 253.

excitatio [LL < CL = *liveliness*]

1 arousing, summoning. **b** awakening (from sleep). **c** raising (from death).

ad ~onem viventium de morte animae BEDE *HE* V 12 p. 303; **1459** apparitori pro ~one et vocacione curatorum *Ac. Durh.* 477. **b** AD. DORE *Pictor* 157 (v. excitare 1b); in dormitorio fiat mane ~o cum tintinnabulo *Cust. Westm.* 316. **c** mysterium suae passionis et ~onis a mortuis BEDE *Hom.* II 1. 120.

2 excitation, stimulation (of mind or spirit).

~o mentis ad contemplandum Deum ANSELM (*Prosl.* 1 *tit.*) I 97; pro devocione et ~one animarum universorum Christianorum ad Deum W. WORC. *Itin.* 270.

3 appeal, exhortation, suggestion. **b** incitement.

a**1298** ~o Bathoniensis super liberacione presbiteri *Reg. Cant.* 245; s**1377** J. de Nevill ad ~onem Ricardi de B. terrarii et Johannis de B. feretrarii fecit .. opus marmoreum .. sub feretro S. Cuthberti *Hist. Durh.* 2; c**1380** vestram ~onem in secretis penes .. abbatem impendere sic velitis ut ejus benevolenciam potuero .. optinere *FormOx* 320; rancores cordium, scrupulosas anxiasque mentes inter regem et appellantes si que fuerunt mellifluis ~onibus commissariorum graciose evellerunt FAVENT 19; **1423** (v. excitare 3c); c**1465** ultima ~o .. Johannis Fastolf ad concludendum festinanter cum Johanne P. fuit quod .. intendebat quod executores sui desiderabant vendere colegium *Paston Let.* 61. **b** ad ~onem tandem Sadii suscipit MAP *NC* III 2 f. 36; **1441** [ne] .. caritas .. et .. fraternalis dileccio .. familiarium nostrorum aut aliorum quorumcumque jurgiis aut ~onibus .. violentur BEKYNTON I 139; de intoxicacione .. ignorans .. ad eorum ~onem eundem potum bibebat .. et .. sic intoxicatus obiit *Entries* 51b; quod idem ad excitac[ionem] serviencium suorum .. illas [libras] .. detinuisset .. et ex eorum falsa conspiracione .. *Ib.* 628b.

4 generation (of heat).

Quaest. Salern. B 12 (v. excitare 4a).

5 causing, arousing, stirring up (of abstr.); **b** (log. & phil.).

1305 ad exittacionem devocionis fidelium .. tendere *MonA* III 563a; **14..** sunt .. sicut libri clericis, sic laicis picture .. et figura ad ~onem Dei amoris, et sanctorum suorum cultus pariter et amoris AMUND. I app. 418. **b** omnem .. operationem actualem motio precessit aliqua [vel] ~o, set omnem intentionem et ~onem non semper sequitur operatio actualis BACON VIII 108; *Ib.* XV 111 (v. excitare 7c); [Augustinus] dicit quod 'tertium solius anime est' ergo, secundum eum, illa intencio .. non est illa ~o vel inclinacio, per speciem DUNS *Ord.* IV 104.

excitativus, excitative, arousing, stimulating; *v. et. excitatorius* 1a, *excitatrix*. **b** deserving, worthy.

distinctorum nomina velut signa memorie ~a habere utile erit BALSH. *AD rec.* 2 136; cantus antiphonarum est tanquam .. vox preconia et nostrarum ~a mentium P. BLOIS *Ep.* 243. 558c; sanguis naturalis est purus et calidus .. letificativus, amoris ~us BART. ANGL. IV 7; MIDDLETON *Sent.* I 8 (v. excitare 7a); R. BURY *Phil.* 8. 130 (v. collatio 4b); s**1392** componens .. historiam competentem .. ~am devocionis WALS. *HA* II 207. **b** **1282** in eo tanto laudabilius estimamus .. quanto ex .. rebellione Wallensium .. magis ~a detencionis quam sue liberacionis a carcere procedere viderentur judicia PECKHAM *Ep.* 246.

excitator [LL]

1 rouser (from sleep, fig.).

nos excitator [gl.: *arærend, awreccend*] mentium / jam Christus ad vitam vocat *AS Hymns* 18.

2 stimulator. **b** inciter.

Dunstanus .. artium liberalium .. ~or mirificus W. MALM. *GR* II 149. **b** s**1222** licet .. seditionis ~or .. esset .. dignus .. suspendio *Flor. Hist.* II 176; s**1248** obiit S. de L. archidiaconus Cantuariensis, multimode ~or perturbationis M. PAR. *Abbr.* 305.

excitatorius [cf. LL excitator]

1 excitatory, arousing; *v. et. excitativus, excitatrix*. **b** (as sb. n.) alarm clock.

pocio spumans in libidinem prohibetur et ebrietas .. et .. omnia accessoria vel ~ia ad eandem WYCL. *Ver.* II 194. **b** aliud item minus [horologium] veluti ~ium, quo is utitur ex officio qui .. reliquos fratres excitare consuevit FERR. *Kinloss* 71.

2 (w. *litterae* or sim.) letters exhortatory; **b** (as sb. f.).

s**1235** bulla ~ia ad regem de defendendo (*Chr. S. Aug.*) ELMH. *Cant.* 44; **1313** litteras episcopales ~ias capitulo directas *Stat. Linc.* I 265; **1343** littera ~ia .. missa ad amicum pro beneficio ecclesiastico optinendo *Lit. Cant.* II 268; c**1377** litteras .. ~ias, quod michi c s. pro libris emendis voluerits destinare *FormOx* 384; s**1185** patriarcha cum literis ~iis Lucii pape in Angliam veniens .. auxilium contra Saracenos petiit BROMPTON 1144. **b** **1300** ~ia episcopo Coventrensi pro negocio de Meynel *Reg. Cant.* 699.

excitatrix [LL], excitative, arousing, stimulating. *V. et. excitativus, excitatorius* 1a.

s**1135** hec .. comestio, pessimi humoris illatrix et consimilium [humorum] vehemens ~ix .. fecit perturbationem H. HUNT. *HA* VII 43.

excitialis v. exitialis.

exclamare [CL]

1 to exclaim, cry aloud (absol.); **b** (w. *oratio recta*); **c** (trans.); **d** (w. acc. & inf.).

~avit auditis ejus sermonibus, dicens .. BEDE *HE* II 13 p. 112; exclamat cum praeside turba clientum WULF. *Swith.* II 384; ~avit .. antistes, precipiens ei ne appropinquaret ad se ALEX. CANT. *Mir.* 43 (I) p. 243; quatinus .. ad clementissimum consolatorem me gaudeam ~asse ORD. VIT. III 7 p. 99; ~ans voce altisona .. hostibus metum incussit GIR. *EH* I 13; VINSAUF *CR* 323 (v. exclamatio 1b). **b** Felix .. ~asse fertur "gratias tibi ago, Christe .." ALDH. *VirgP* 27; "miserere misellis," / exclamant "miserere .." WULF. *Swith.* I 1143; celsa voce ~avit "viri Christiana professione insigniti .. " G. MON. IX 4. **c** alleluiam .. sacerdotes ~abant (*V. Germani*) BEDE *HE* I 21; **1265** ~averunt insultum et .. civitatem graviter insultaverunt *IMisc* 12/11. **d** cum ~assem me illum non esse qui querebatur ALEX. CANT. *Mir.* 31 p. 220; uxor .. illum .. mortuum esse .. ~avit *Ib.* 49 p. 259.

2 (w. personal obj.): **a** to call upon. **b** to hail, challenge, raise hue and cry (on). **c** to jeer (at). **d** (w. compl.) to cry out against.

a ~at itaque puer Christum, pavore conterritus OSB. *V. Dunst.* 7. **b** **1251** propter fugam ~atus de dictis H. et R. et secutus est, et captus *SelPlForest* 96; **1255** forestarii non ausi fuerunt ~are dictos malefactores *Ib.* 27; **1270** (v. continuus 2d); **1270** exclammavit (v. cautela 2a). **c** **1207** quidam homo concubuit cum ea sub quodam gardino et pueri ~averunt eam ita quod ipsa reliquit pallium *SelPlCrown* 6; [regina] intercepta est a Londoniensibus et ab eis enormiter blasphemata atque ~ata turpiter WALS. *YN* app. 504. **d** rogo ne statim me aut praesumptorem novitatum aut falsitatis assertorem ~et sed .. ANSELM (*Mon. prol.*) I 8.

3 to proclaim, publish.

~ata et confirmata est hec conventio multorum testimonio *Cart. Carisb.* f. 22v.; Elyas .. irreverenter se intrusit in abbathiam de Selby, se faciens abbatem ~ari *G. S. Alb.* I 120.

4 to 'cry' (wares or service).

reparatores ciphorum ~ant ciphos reparandos cum filo ereo et argenteo GARL. *Dict.* 126.

exclamatio [CL]

1 exclamation, crying aloud; **b** (rhet.).

iratus rex cum ~one dixit "ubi est magnanimitas tua?" ORD. VIT. XIII 10 p. 21; si additur tempus sillabe causa admiracionis vel causa ~onis *Ps.*-GROS. *Gram.* 70; **1519** quoad ~ones puerorum, habent monere patres et matres ut provideant pro eisdem *Fabr. York* 271. **b** *Gl. Leid.* 28. 65 (v. epiphonema); est ~o color quando ex dolore vel indignatione exclamamus ut in hoc patet exemplo: 'o Asie flos, Troja potens ..' VINSAUF *CR* 323.

2 hailing, challenging, hue and cry.

si quis furi obvius factus fuerit et illum sponte abire permiserit sine ~one [AS: *butan hreame*], emendet .. qui ~onem audierit et accurrere neglexerit, solvat .. (*Cons. Cnuti*) *GAS* 331 [cf. (*Quad.*) *ib.*: sine clamore (vociferatione)].

exclamatorie, exclamatorily, with a loud voice.

proponant .. quedam prophonetice, i. e. ~ie GARL. *Dict.* 133; s**1459** quibus, cum aliis invectivis variis, in eos ~ie dictis, timere sibi .. ceperant *Reg. Whet.* I 344.

exclamatrix, exclaimer (f.).

intellexit per Spiritum pia illa ~ix altitudinem sacramenti W. NEWB. *Serm.* 829.

exclamitare [LL], to exclaim, cry aloud (absol.). *V. et. exclamare* 1a.

sicut gaudens in laudem Dei ~at GOSC. *Aug. Maj.* 69C.

exclamm- v. exclam-.

exclarare [CL], to make clear (fig.), demonstrate.

1206 idem G. .. teneat de ballivo nostro quousque ~atum fuerit coram nobis utrum remanere debeat heredi .. G. an heredibus .. W. *Cl* 67a.

exclotura v. esclotura.

excludere [CL]

1 to deny access or entry, shut out.

†hae [l. haec] loci artitudine ~sus praetermitto alibi, Deo aspirante, retexenda GOSC. *Transl. Aug.* 20C; intrabo intra me ipsum, ~dam omnia praeter illum et me ipsum ANSELM (*Or.* 14) III 55; a collocatione pignorum ~si fuerant ORD. VIT. VI 10 p. 108; fumus thuris .. copiose ascendebat; sed teterrimum putorem ~dere non prevalebat *Ib.* VII 16 p. 254; exterius .. domui porta est necessaria ut hostis et indignus ~dantur ab ea R. NIGER *Mil.* III 17; s**1349** WALS. *HA* I 274 (v. deforis 3a).

2 to exclude, cut off, separate (place). **b** to block.

c**1298** foresta .. incipit ad molendinum quod vocatur S. et sic per le Meredyche .. includendo forestam ex parte dextera .. et ~dendo extra forestam ex parte sinistra totum residuum .. *Cart. Boarstall* 574. **b** exclusere duos caesis ex hostibus amnes FRITH. 546 (cf. EDDI 19: duo flumina cadaveribus mortuorum replentes).

3 (p. ppl. *exclusus* as sb. usu. f.): **a** a sluice, lock (usu. w. ref. to mill); *v. et. claudere* 2e, *recludere*; **b** L'Écluse, Sluys (Flanders). **c** dock.

a in eadem j liber homo Edrici, viij acrae et una pars unius ~sae *DB* II 304v.; in ~sa alterius molini habet Robertus Malet partem *Ib.* 382v.; **1111** precipio quod predicti monachi .. perpetualiter .. possideant .. in pascuis, in aquis et molendiis et ~sis *Cart. Colne* 1 v.; c**1115** esclusa (v. excluseta); **1222** ad faciendam ibi ~sam vel gurgitem *Cart. Osney* IV 103; **1232** debet habere anguillas ad ~sam suam cadentes *BNB* II 526; **1276** exclus[e] prioris aperte sunt quando necesse sit transeuntibus *Hund.* I 198; **1293** (v. 2 baia); **1295** in carpenteria pro predictis kaiis .. et pro rota et sklusis reparandis (*Ac. Cliffe*) *DCCant.*; **1300** de forstallo, de sclusa Petri de Molendino *Reg. S. Aug.* 58; **1310** in terra propria dicti domini regis fecit fieri quandam esclausam cujusdam molendini sui *Reg. Gasc. A* I 252; **1331** (v. esclotura); **1344** ~sa .. vocatur Fouremullelok .. que claudit et retinet aquam .. per quatuor pedes in altitudinem plus quam relique ~se superius in predicta aqua de Lye posite retinent *Pub. Works* II 17; **1444** ~sas molendinorum .. a fundo in quo fixe fuerunt extraxerunt et eas in minutas partes cecuerunt *Pat* 458 m. 16d.; **1477** de abbatissa de C. pro redditu unius ~si fixi ad terram domini apud Dunford .. iij d. (*Rent.*) *Mon. Exon.* 125b. **b** **1164** Philippum apud ~sam castrum, a quo tirannis Yprensis tam longa obsidione exclusus est J. SAL. *Ep.* 134 (136 p. 2); s**1202** apud ~sum, quod vulgariter dicitur Le Sleus *Plusc.* VII 1. **c** **1212** quod .. claudi facias bono et forti muro ~sam nostram de Portsmua .. ad galias .. nostras custodiendas *Cl* 117a; **1228** rex J. .. muros fieri fecit prope ~sas illas ad galias suas .. includendas *Cl* 32.

4 to banish, cast out; **b** (w. abstr. obj.). **c** (med.) to expel. **d** to omit, leave out.

~sa multitudine daemonum BEDE *HE* II 4; c**1110** pro filio suo quem a servitio vestro ~sistis ANSELM (*Ep.* 18) III 125; ipsum cum progenie sua de finibus Normannie .. ~de ORD. VIT. VIII 5 p. 293; cherubin .. ~dit Adam et Evam a paradiso AD. DORE *Pictor* 155. **b** quatenus .. vitia .. radicitus .. extirpentur et ~dantur ANSELM (*Ep.* 312) V 239; jejunia metuebat et quantum poterat abhorrens a se procul ~debat ORD. VIT. V 19 p. 445; ejus [voluntatis] .. memoriam a corde vestro ~dite ALEX. CANT. *Mir.* app. p. 269; OCKHAM *Pol.* I 28 (v. despoticus). **c** GILB. II 112. 2 (v. climax 2); lupinus .. cujus ferina cum melle comesta aut cum aceto bibita lumbricos ~dit *Alph.* 106; onomia .. lapidem vesice ~dit *Ib.* 130. **d** nonnulli .. hunc pedem de versu ~dendum censuerunt ALDH. *Met.* 10 p. 82; quem quidam per sinalipham ~dunt *Ib.* p. 89; his .. virginum catervis nequaquam Eustochii et Demetriadis virtutum rumusculus .. a nostris litterarum scedulis .. ~datur *Id. VirgP* 49; BRADW. *CD* 863A (v. exclusive 2).

5 to exclude (person from condition, state, or sim.). **b** (leg.) to exclude, estop.

1237 (v. concludere 2b); s**1297** RISH. 168 (v. denegatio 1). **b** c**1300** ex quo clericus ~detur a purgacione sua per suam confessionem *Year Bk. 30–1 Ed. I* app. 545; **1307** dicunt quod per hoc ~di non debent de isto brevi de forma donacionis que eis competit de jure reversionis secundum formam donacionis *Year Bk. 1 Ed. II* 3.

6 to prevent, preclude, bar; **b** (w. abstr. subj.); **c** (w. acc. & inf.).

p**1082** quod in titulis .. nomini nostro addidi nomen abbatis .. feci ut nominis ~derem aequivocationem ANSELM (*Ep.* 100) III 232; ut omnes excusationes tuas ~dam

Id. (*CurD* 1) II 49. **b** **1093** ut neque justitiam gratia neque gratiam justitia .. ~dat ANSELM (*Ep.* 165) IV 39; qualiter unitatis simplicitas a se ~dat pluralitatem *Id.* (*Proc. Sp.* 1) II 181; ?**1165** cum fraterna [caritas] commendatur non ~ditur .. sororina J. SAL. *Ep.* 250 (148); sicut una operatio aliam a se diversam operationem ~dit, sic cogitatio cogitationem expellit ALEX. CANT. *Dicta* 3 p. 121; AD. MARSH *Ep.* 30 p. 127 (v. dissensio). **c** cum .. veritas .. ~dat plura esse per quae cuncta sint .. ANSELM (*Mon.* 3) I 16.

7 (w. *diem ultimum*) to die. *V. et.* 2 *claudere* 8a.

s**1367** cum uxor .. Henrici de Percy .. diem suum ultimum ~sisset *Meaux* III 163.

8 to open, keep open. Cf. *cludere* 1. **b** (p. ppl. w. *tempus*) open season.

aperi hostium aecclesiae et ~de ante nos, quia intrare modo volumus ÆLF. BATA 4. 11 p. 38. **b** **1270** in tempore ~so predicte tres acre .. sunt communa *IMisc* 16/4.

9 to hatch (chick).

pullos marcidos et rubros et tanquam eadem hora jam ~sos GIR. *TH* II 40; falcones .. qui marinis in rupibus ~duntur *Id. EH* I 29; *to hatch eggs*, ova ~dere LEVINS *Manip.* 38.

exclusa v. excludere 3a.

exclusagium [cf. LL exclusa, *p. ppl. of* excludere], (payment for) sluice. *V. et. excluseta.*

c**1100** dedi in .. elemosinam .. ~ium et stagnum de piscaria et molendino de W. *Reg. Wetherhal* 7; c**1187** terram .. in qua situm est ~ium *Act. Hen. II* II 407; **1189** ex dono Richardi filii L. slusagium unum super terram suam ad molendinum monachorum fullericum *MonA* V 565b; c**1215** concessi .. monachis .. ~ium de Northbroke et terram de F. cum bosco et aquis (*Cart. Buckfast*) *Reg. Exon. 1360–69* III 1573; **1235** (1304) duo molendina .. cum aquis et ~is *Mon. Exon.* 38a; **1606** slusag' (v. ballastagium).

excluseta [cf. LL exclusa, *p. ppl. of* excludere], payment for use of sluice. *V. et. exclusagium.*

c**1115** dederunt quoque esclusetam de molendino de Caravilla, que est super magnam esclusam *Regesta* 79D.

exclusim, decisively, so as to debar further action.

1325 contencio .. finaliter et ~im pausata est in hunc modum *Pat* 399 m. 26.

exclusio [CL]

1 exclusion, keeping out.

1362 custodia walliarum, gutterarum, et fossatorum .. tam pro ~one aque maritime quam pro evacuacione aquarum dulcium *Pat* 262 m. 6d.; c**1410** pro ~one [n]odularum [? l. monedularum] ab ecclesia *Ac. Durh.* 403.

2 prevention, preclusion. **b** leaving out (of consideration), setting aside.

lex donum Dei est .. norma justitie .. ~o et exterminatio vitiorum J. SAL. *Pol.* 777D; o quam gloriosa foret ~o falsitatis perfide et enucliacio veritatis! WYCL. *Apost.* 243. **b** licet dicat apostolos nullum jus proprium .. in illis temporalibus habuisse, sed tantum simplicem facti usum, per ~onem omnis juris proprii collegio apostolorum vel cuilibet apostolo OCKHAM *Pol.* I 367.

3 sluice.

1337 propter infinitos sumptus quos ipsi circa facturam ~onis aque maritime pro salvacione marisci illius facere oporterit (*Pat*) *Cart. Bilsington* 146.

4 hatching.

usque ad plenam pullorum ~onem GIR. *TH* II 28.

exclusive

1 exclusively, not including.

addit unum annum, dicens quod fuerint ab Adam usque ad nativitatem Christi 5199; qui numerus, liceat videatur inclusive intelligi, tamen ~e scribitur in cereo paschali BACON *Tert.* 206; **1259** de dicta comba, prout rectius itur ad pratum Grimoardi T. ~e *RGasc* II 473; cum aliquod mobile ab aliquo gradu ~e ad alium gradum inclusive vel ~e intendet uniformiter motum suum HEYTESBURY *Reg.* 278; legantur .. articuli .. ab illo loco 'porro etc.' .. usque ad illum locum ~e 'licet etc.' (*Abbr. Stat.*) *Mon. Francisc.* II 118; *FormOx* 461 (v. continuare 3a).

2 (log.) by way of exclusion.

ut supponat generaliter omnia esse divisa in tria: futurum, presens, et preteritum, sive factum; et per hoc, quod dicit ~e, solo ipso Deus privatur . . . intendat includere ultimum trium membrorum divisionis premisse, et excludere duo priora BRADW. *CD* 863A.

3 solely.

1421 incepturi in facultate sacre theologie, completa eorum forma in eadem facultate usque ad doctoratum ~e in universitate predicta *Reg. Cant.* III 71.

exclusivus

1 exclusive, that excludes. **b** (w. ref. to rent).

duo precipue sunt exclusiva dolorum NIG. *SS* 1572. **b** **1342** satisfactum est episcopo Abirdonensi de secundis decimis suis de dicto burgo de eodem anno, per assedacionem camerarii ~am *ExchScot* 484.

2 excluded (from reckoning), not including (terminal points).

hoc .. essonium ostendi debet et priori tertio die ~o ante diem datum *Fleta* 387; primum instans temporis et ultimum sunt pro illo instanti, pro quo est idem tempus; termini autem ~i cujuscumque temporis sic finiti non sunt instancia illius temporis, sed alterorum immediatorum WYCL. *Ente Praed.* 207; inter fundacionem vero et dotacionem sex anni in numero ~i probabiliter computantur ELMH. *Cant.* 81.

3 (log.) that excludes all but what is specified.

GROS. *Hexaem.* II 1 (v. discretivus 1a); BACON XV 293 (v. exceptivus 1b); s**1296** archiepiscopus cum coepiscopis suis .. disputantes .. super peticione regia, nec invento modo ~e sentencie .. discesserunt *Flor. Hist.* III 99.

4 (as sb. f.): **a** (gram.) exclusive word. **b** (log.) limiting statement.

a vocabulo 'figuratio' addit ~am 'tantum', quae ~a in Graecis non est GARDINER *CC* 779. **b** imponit appellanti, quod secundum eum Levite habuerunt tantum usum decimarum [sc. sine dominio], cum tamen istam ~am nusquam ponat OCKHAM *Pol.* II 460.

exclusor v. excusor.

1 exclusorius [CL]

1 (leg.) exclusory, that debars.

1282 ad nonum art[iculum] respondet [archiepiscopus] quod .. hoc non denegatur episcopis, immo conceditur eis proponere contrarium, vel mere ~ium *Conc. Syn.* 926; **1295** liceat parti appellate .. factum contrarium et ~ium proponere et probare *Conc.* II 208a; **1342** possit pars appellata factum contrarium seu ~ium proponere *Ib.* 687b; **1507** exceptionem, replicationem, materiam justificatoriam seu ~iam, vel directe contrariam *Ib.* III 650a.

2 (as sb. m.) door- or gate-keeper, janitor. **b** (as sb. n.) sluice-gate.

~ius, janitor OSB. GLOUC. *Deriv.* 202. **b** **1240** facient extrahere ~ia sua de ipsis exclusis quociens opus fuerit in aquarum superhabundacionibus ad deliberacionem aque *Cart. Darley* II 486.

2 exclusorius v. excusorius. **exclusum** v. excludere 3a.

excoctio [LL]

1 cooking, boiling; **b** (of cadaver). **c** concoction.

rectificatur .. aqua per eventationem et excolationem et agitationem .. aut per ~onem et post permittatur residere GILB. VII 362v. 2. **b** s**1190** post multam ~onem ossibus [imperatoris Fretherici] a carne sejunctis, caro .. in .. ecclesia conquiescit, ossa vero .. per mare ducuntur transferenda Jerosolimam *Itin. Ric.* I 24 p. 56. **c** quid .. de piperibus et variis ~onibus loquar? SERLO GRAM. *Mon. Font.* 16.

2 (med.) rise in temperature.

omnis humor albus, vel rubeus .. ut ad viriditatem perveniat, necesse est hoc multis gradibus et generibus ~onis, non remissionis *Quaest. Salern.* N 39.

excoctor [cf. CL coctor], smelter, one who melts metal.

1566 (v. affinator).

excogitabilis, conceivable.

non .. aliquis est alius modus ~is preter predictos et hec est conclusio tertia BACON *Maj.* II 433.

excogitare [CL]

1 to excogitate, think out, devise; **b** (w. inf.); **c** (w. indir. qu.).

c**1072** quicquid tibi opto, i. e. quod optimum ~at mens mea ANSELM (*Ep.* 4) III 104; aliquid .. inventori ~andum sine quo aliquid utroque modo dicatur ut .. BALSH. *AD* 86; precellentius quam vel exprimi vel ~ari possit GIR. *TH* I 13; nec incongrue ~atum est ALB. LOND. *DG* 11. 11. **b** horruit .. quod domus Dei .. quasi speluncam latronum factam agnovit, et mox juxta voluntatem Dei emendare ~avit EDDI 16. **c** ~are coepit qua ratione .. voti sui tenorem .. conservare posset ASSER *Alf.* 103; ~avit unde .. ventorum sufflationem prohibere potuisset *Ib.* 104; parum ~ans quid sibi contingere posset G. MON. X 9; Brutus .. postquam filii sui ordinem susceperunt militarem acriter ~avit [v. l. cogitavit] quomodo illos posset promovere *Eul. Hist.* II 220; s**1067** Willielmus .. multum ~avit .. quomodo .. dominium .. adeptus est, et qualiter Deo satisfacere potuit ~avit *Ib.* III 39.

2 (p. ppl.): **a** thoughtfully contrived, refined. **b** cunning. **c** (w. *malitia*) malice aforethought. **d** (as sb. n. pl.) device, plan.

a ejus [sc. Marie] modica et cotidiana sunt aliorum maxima et ~ata W. MALM. *Mir. Mariae* 171; tormenta exquisita et ~ata .. quantum ad gehenne cruciatus minima reputantur S. LANGTON *Serm.* 2. 10; licet gravitatem tuam, sagacissime pater, scribendi modus ~acior et excelsior deceret CHAUNDLER *Apol.* 11b. **b** ~atum facinus ad multorum lamenta perficere conati sunt ORD. VIT. XII 45 p. 478. **c** **1235** remittitur .. justiciariis misericordia quia potius fuit ibi ignorantia quam ~ata malitia *CurR* XV 1429; **1323** per ~atam maliciam litigancium *StatOx* 127. **d** commenta, ~ata *Gl. Leid.* 35. 100.

3 to think about, bear in mind.

c**793** quid nos homunculi in fine saeculi .. melius ~are poterimus quam ut .. sequamur doctrinam? ALCUIN *Ep.* 23 p. 61; s**1300** regis prudenciam, .. fortitudinem, et graciam, et mortem imminentem ~antes, castellum, corpora, catalla, et omnia que intra erant in regis graciam offerebant *Eul. Hist.* III 171.

excogitate, carefully.

cum .. pars eorum .. progrederetur caute et ~e H. HUNT. *HA* II 14.

excogitatio [CL], excogitation, thinking out, devising.

machinatio, dolor[um] ~o *GlC* M 13; ratiocinatio est diligens et considerata faciendi aliquid aut non faciendi ~o ALCUIN *Rhet.* 17; non vaga et quo ducet casus sed secundum modum quem docebimus diducta inveniendo ~o BALSH. *AD* 83; sermocinalis [scientia] .. de signo est, sc. de signo, cujus ~o facta est propter scientias speculativas et practicas KILWARDBY *OS* 623.

excogitator [CL], contriver, deviser.

tam horrendi sceleris .. nec ~or hic fuerat nec machinatus GIR. *IK* I 4 p. 51*n.*; mirabilis ~or est talium trifarum et astutiarum *Id. Invect.* I 4 p. 96; principalis .. machinator et protractor, ~or et doctor ille magister erat *Id. SD* 96.

excola [cf. CL incola], alien, foreigner.

fistula rurestris cecinit prothemata cannis, / callosas cavi meliger velut excola sannas FRITH. 1391; **1319** volumus .. vestros .. pre ceteris ~is confoveri *Foed.* III 766b.

excolanum v. esculentus 1b.

excolare [LL], to clean by filtering, to filter out; **b** (med.); **c** (w. ref. to *Matth.* xxiii 24); **d** (intr. for pass.) to percolate. **e** (pr. ppl. as sb.) filterer.

~at, siid *GlC* E 461; †exolantes, mandantes [l. excolantes, mundantes] *Ib.* 362; †exolantes, mundantes, a †colendo [l. colando] dicitur *Gl. Leid.* 24. 12; ~at, coquitur *GlH* E 707. **b** trachea et pulmo cordi ministrant aera temperando et ~ando RIC. MED. *Anat.* 221; *Ib.* 224 (v. 1 colon); melancolia .. constringit urinales meatus, ut urina non nisi tenuissima per angustas vias valeat ~ari GILB. VI 238v. 2. **c** ne .. excollantes culicem, camelum .. glutiant AD. MARSH *Ep.* 247 cap. 43 p. 484. **d** fit commotio per totum corpus et ex commotione generantur fumi qui ~ant per poros D. BEC. p. 87*n.* **e** **1228** ut Dominus custodem haberet in vineis, ut manus putantis et suculus non deesset excolantis (*Lit. ad Papam*) *Reg. S. Osm.* II 112.

excolatio [LL], filtering.

GILB. VII 362v. 2 (v. excoctio 1a).

excolere [CL]

1 to cultivate: **a** (land); **b** (fig.); **c** (crop).

a ut cotidiano manuum opere hortum ~endo laboraret WULF. *Æthelwold* 9; si .. agricole terram noluerint ~ere quod (*sic*) aliud poterunt officium explere? *Simil. Anselmi* 128; *Dial. Scac.* I 11 B (v. dominium 3c); cum Fontem Blaadi jussisset ~i cingique muris MAP *NC* V 5 f. 65v.; a**1200** (v. 3 cultus 1a); **1204** concessimus eidem .. lx acras assarti .. et landam de C. excollendam quam habet de dono H. de C. *RChart* 123a; **1221** (v. dimissio 6a). **b** cordis sui agrum pervigili ~ebat sollicitudine DOMINIC *V. Ecgwini* I 2; Ecgwinus tamquam terra exculta de virtutum segete cepit feracius fructum ferre *Ib.* 7. **c** BEDE *Luke* (xx 9) 575 (v. colonus a); c**1327** ut in .. orto dominico novelle plantule excultе proficiant J. MASON *Ep.* 32 p. 215.

2 to care for, give attention to.

tota cura cordis ~endi, non ventris BEDE *HE* III 26 p. 191; non est jam quod capillos hujuscemodi sic excultos, sicque dispositos, comam dicere verearis capiti sponsi decentissime congruentem J. FORD *Serm.* 15. 5.

3 to cultivate, develop, improve.

excoluit plebem doctrina Rotomagensem (*Vers.*) ORD. VIT. V 9 p. 336; a susceptione .. cure ad ~endum incultos transeundum. . . ab incultis vero prius excultis et ab egris sanatis compositis in homine moribus occurrendum est alicubi variis erroribus R. NIGER *Mil.* II 65.

4 to bless, favour, endow. **b** to compensate.

nonne [Deus] per ceteris eos diligit quos a malis exuit, quos virtutibus ~it quos et beatos facit? H. READING (I) *Dial.* 1155B; licet [Hibernenses] ad plenum nature dotibus ~antur GIR. *TH* III 10; Lydia sedes regnorum est

antiqua, quam fluvius Pacto ~it, in divitiis et torrentibus aureis *Eul. Hist.* II 49 (= BART. ANGL. XV 90: fluvius Pacto extulit). **b** gens Northumbrorum .. Eilricum .. abicentes .. regis injurias honoribus et detrimenta muneribus ~uerunt CIREN. II 84 (= FL. WORC. I 135: explеverunt).

5 to worship (as God). **b** to revere (person); **c** (object or place).

induit Hieroboam Samariae stemmata pravus, / qui regum primus excoluit vitulos ALCUIN *Carm.* 69. 122; saecla priora .. / excoluere suos vano terrore tirannos FRITH. 11; ~it, colit, *begæþ GlH* E 708; GARL. *Tri. Eccl.* 131 (v. amorifer). **b** Cuthberti .. quem semper ~uisti et dilexisti R. COLD *Cuthb.* 70; rex .. cepit ab ea diligi .., ~i in tantum et honorari ut .. G. FONT. *Inf. S. Edm.* 4; liquet .. episcopi .. et ceteri magistrum Adam quanta .. honore ~ebant *Chr. Witham* 504. **c** monasterium .. quod .. regina .. multum diligebat, venerabatur, ~ebat BEDE *HE* III 11 p. 148; libros rectae fidei tramitem phylosophantes diligenter ~uit B. *V. Dunst.* 5; reliquias sancti Ebrulfi .. veneratio devotorum ~it ORD. VIT. VI 10 p. 105; J. SAL. *Met* 854B (v. diacrisis).

excoliare v. escuilliare.

excolicus [cf. excola], 'alien', not one's own.

hactenus excolicum quanto sudore sacellum / emerit, exposui FRITH. 1309.

excolorare [cf. CL colorare], to deprive of colour. *Cf. decolorare, discolorare.*

en cuncta obsidens foedarat viscera tabo / excolorata cute erupuerunt pondera lepre *Mir. Nin.* 331.

excoll- v. excol-.

excomere [cf. CL comere], (p. ppl.) refined.

Thomas .. / .. / recubat .. / moribus excomptis et miti pectore charus (*Epitaph*) *Hist. Durh.* 14.

excomesse [LL], to consume, eat up (also fig.).

~edens GILDAS *EB* 85 (v. evangelicus 3a); eviscerat, ~edit *GlC* E 337.

excommunicare [LL]

1 to excommunicate; **b** (dist. by form, as *in genere, in specie, nominatim*); **c** (w. church as obj.). **d** (p. ppl. as sb.) excommunicate; *v. et. excommunicius.*

THEOD. *Pen.* I 12. 1 (v. 1 communicare 5a); S. Gregorius .. eum .. quem edocere .. noluit, ~avit. quam excommunicationis sententiam non facile ferens .. magorum quaesivit adjumenta .. *V. Greg.* p. 97; quod cum episcopus prohibere .. non posset, ~avit [v. l. excommonicavit] eum BEDE *HE* III 22 p. 173; ammonendi sunt episcopi .. neminem nisi juste ~are O. CANT. *Const.* 3; **1081** L. archiepiscopus .. ~amus illos qui consilio vel facto erunt, quod G. separetur a .. usu monachorum *Reg. Malm.* I 327; **c1100** quaerunt quidam .. cur ego regem non ~o; .. mandatum mihi est quia mea excommunicatio .. ab illo .. in derisum converteretur ANSELM (*Ep.* 210) IV 107; H. LOS. *Ep.* 35 p. 71 (v. anathema c); ~ati sunt omnes a domino papa .. qui ecclesias .. spoliare presumunt GIR. *JS* sup. 147; **s1253** M. PAR. *Maj.* V 360 (v. candela 2c); **12..** (v. damnare 3b). **b** **1188** (v. 1 communio 5); **c1214** ~entur in genere solemniter sortiarii, .. incendiarii, usurarii [etc.] *Conc. Syn.* 33; BRAKELOND 147* (v. candela 2c); **s1216** summus pontifex barones Anglie, quos prius ~averat in genere, ad instantiam regis Anglorum .. ~avit nominatim et in specie WEND. II 167; **c1228, 1230** (v. 2a infra); **13..** ne .. quem in vita scivit ~atum a canone vel ab homine .. in genere vel in specie ad ecclesiasticam [sepulturam] admittere presumat *Conc. Scot.* II 69; **1425** causam racionabilem si quam pro se habeant quare .. nominatim et in specie ~ari .. non debeant in forma juris propposituri et allegaturi *Reg. Cant.* II 305. **c** **c800** mirum mihi videtur, qua auctoritate ecclesias Christi ~are voluisti ALCUIN *Ep.* 298. **d** nolo communicare ~atis, nec fieri ~atus ANSELM (*Ep.* 327) V 259; **1166** rex .. a cujus ~ati communione se unquam suspendit? J. SAL. *Ep.* 175 (176); **s1189** GERV. CANT. *Chr.* 458 (v. communicare 4a); **1227** quod postquam litteras .. episcoporum nostrorum Anglie receperimus patentes et testificantes quoscumque ~atos perdurasse per lx dies .. manus regias ad ipsos extendamus *Cl* 166b; **1280, 1488** (v. candela 2c); **1285** sunt plures ~ati hodie in Anglia quam in aliqua terra mundi *Conc. Syn.* 971; **13..** (v. communicare 4b).

2 (w. non-episcopal subj.); **b** (w. ref. to Jew).

GILDAS *Pen.* 12 (v. communicare 4a); nos .. quantum potest rex, ~amus .. quicumque contra hoc †facinus [MS *gl.*: vel actum; v. l. factum] venerit (*Lit. Regis*) DICETO *YH* II 156; **1212** W. offert domino regi j palefridum per sic quod ipse det licenciam ~andi per totum comitatum L. omnes illos qui plagam vel .. roberiam aliquam ipsis fecissent *CurR* VI 210; **1221** monachi et hospitalarii statim ~ant vicecomitem et ballivos suos et ballivos domini regis *PlCrGlouc* 12; **c1228** quidam monachus .. ~avit eos, utrum nominatim vel in genere nescit, et cum .. conquesti fuissent episcopo audivit dici quod monachos idem .. dixit se stulte ~asse et revocavit sententiam (*Attestatio*) *Feod. Durh.* 246; **1230** de consuetudine .. ~andi .. ordinavimus .. quod .. monachi auctoritate nostra [sc. episcopi Dunelm.] .. ter in anno .. accensis candelis et pulsatis campanis sollempniter ~abunt in genere omnes illos, qui in episcopatu .. infringunt jura .. episcopi vel ecclesie D. *Ib.* 214. **b** **1275** dedimus .. consorti nostre A. regine Anglie .. bona .. Cok' Hagini Judei .. que .. ad nos tanquam forisfacta spectant eo quod idem Judeus ~atus est *SelPlJews* 87 (cf. ib. Sadekinus .. Judeus pro culpa sua juxta rectum et consuetudinem Judaismi dudum ~atus fuerit et in ipsa excommunicacione per xl dies .. perseveraverit).

3 to cast out. **b** to exorcize (demon).

qui hoc diabolicum semen [sc. discordiam] seminat, a Deo ~atur *AncrR* 70. **b** GIR. *GE* I 53 (v. accendere 1a).

4 (absol.).

Brand .. ita scripsit et ~avit H. ALBUS 41; rogo autem, immo quantum mihi licet ~o et detestor, ne superbia vel etiam nominetur in vobis P. BLOIS *Serm.* 680D.

excommunicatio [LL]

1 excommunication; **b** (dist. by degree); **c** (of church).

673 susceptor [clerici discurrentis] .. ~oni subjacebit (*Conc. Hertf.*) BEDE *HE* IV 5 p. 216; **799** non pertinax erroris defensio ~onis percutit gladio ALCUIN *Ep.* 166 p. 274; **c1103** qui ante ~onem vel post ~onem .. Sodomitico peccato peccaverunt ANSELM (*Ep.* 257) IV 169; **1196** propter multiplicem contumaciam ~onis sententia innodatus *CurR* I 27; **c1214** sciatis vos ~onis vinculo innodatos *MunAcOx* 3; ut .. si convenit peccato, sustineat sententiam ~onis. est .. hic ~o separatio a communione altaris HALES *Sent.* IV 289; divinus diminuitur cultus per ~ones iniquas et illicita interdicta OCKHAM *I. & P.* 13; **1437** archiepiscopum [Tarentinum] .. sub ~onis, privacionis .. penis .. in domo propria .. detinere .. moliti sunt BEKYNTON II 9. **b** ~o: maxima (hec separat ab omni communione fidelium), major (hec separat a perceptione sacramentorum et ab ingressu ecclesie), minor (hec separat a Deo tantum et non ab ecclesia, et hec pro .. mortali peccato) GROS. *Templ.* 7. 3; **c1240** se sciant majori ~one innodandos *Conc. Syn.* 381; **c1288** quatinus omnes .. tam a jure quam a nobis majoris ~onis sentencia .. innodatos sic excommunicatos esse .. faciatis *FormOx* 359; **c1300** ipsum rectorem esse excommunicatum majori ~one a canone pro violenta manuum injeccione *FormMan* 24; **1432** omnes .. monendo sub pena ~onis majoris .. quam ferimus in hiis scriptis in omnes contravenientes; ne de dicta pecunia quicquid .. auferre .. presumant *StatOx* 252; **1559** quod .. propter suam .. excrescentem contumaciam .. Johannam C. excommunicaverit .. et sic .. Johanna C. majoris excommonicationis sententia .. innodata existit (*Vis. Cant.*) *EHR* XXVIII 669. **c** **1371** pro una litera ~onis ecclesie de Dalton *Ac. Durh.* 179.

2 (of Jew).

1275 (v. excommunicare 2b).

excommunicativus, excommunicative, pertaining to excommunication.

videtur quod ~e exacciones, preter ewangelium adinvente, originantur ex nobis preter alimenta et quibus tegamur propter curiositatem fastus solicitis WYCL. *Civ. Dom.* I 325.

excommunicator [LL], excommunicator, one (usu. bishop) who excommunicates.

12.. idem ~or .. terras .. excommunicati in dyocesi sua sitas ecclesiastico supposuerit interdicto *Conc. Scot.* II 28; talis [sc. injustus] .. ~or videtur plus polluere sanctam ecclesiam quam corporaliter occidens hominem ad altare WYCL. *Eccl.* 153.

excommunicatorialis, (w. *litterae*) letters of excommunication. *V. et. excommunicatorius.*

1541 litteras citatorias .. ~es et ceteras executoriales decernendi, concedendi, et tribuendi *Form S. Andr.* II 126; **1546** per .. litteras ~es aggravatorias .. decernendi *Ib.* 351.

excommunicatorius, excommunicatory. *V. et. excommunicatorialis.*

s680 ~io .. S. Petri gladio .. excidatur H. ALBUS 19; **s1301** bulla ~ia contra detentores decimarum (*Chr. S. Aug.*) ELMH. *Cant.* 58.

excommunicius [cf. LL excommunio], excommunicate person. *V. et excommunicare* 1d.

1188 nos enim predictum Rogerum pro fugitivo et ~io habemus *Ep. Cant.* 270.

excomputare [cf. CL computare], to deduct.

c1400 numquid .. nobiles .. teneantur .. ad solucionem dictorum ccm contribuere seu eadem ccm de bonis .. regis Ricardi idem rex primitus debeat ~are AD. USK 53.

excondicere [cf. CL condicere, OF *escondire*], (refl. leg.) to clear (oneself) by compurgation.

appellatus .. de ecclesie infractione .. ~et (*sic*) seu purget se per xij homines legales *Conc.* I 313b (cf. *GAS* 503: purget se [AN: *s'en escundisse*]).

exconizatus v. excaturizare.

exconstabularius [cf. 2 constabularius], ex-constable.

s1140 Milo ~ius grandi adunato exercitu .. Wincelcumbiam invadit J. WORC. 60.

exconsul [LL], ex-consul.

~ul, *hiredgerefa* ÆLF. *Gl.*

exconsularis [LL], **~ius,** formerly of consular rank.

s1141 Willemus Yprensis, a Flandria oriundus, vir ~is et magne probitatis H. HUNT. *HA* VIII 18; **1452** Consolacionis Liber .. quem .. ediderat Romane urbis quondam patricius ~ius Boecius BEKYNTON I 274.

excoquere [CL]

1 to cook (by baking or boiling). **b** to overcook, burn, dry out. **c** to harden by boiling (leather); *v. et. coquere* 2b. **d** to scald, cauterize (wound). **e** (p. ppl., of eye) inflamed. **f** digested.

potens est Deus absque corporis igne panes vestros ~ere ORD. VIT. VI 9 p. 73; [piscem] in caldarium .. posuit et excoxit R. COLD. *Godr.* 151; ~o, A. *to sethe WW.* **b** cum carnes in aqua illa diu coquerentur nec ~i possent GIR. *TH* II 29; quandoque est .. humiditas aquosa tantum, que dum transducitur ad superiora arboris, tum calore naturali tum exteriori excocta transducitur tota in carnem sine testa .. sicut videmus in ficubus *Quaest. Salern.* B 144; ~o, A. *to .. brenne WW.* **c** ad vitalium .. custodiam multiplois linea varie consuta lorice superponitur .. et subinduitur aut corium excoctum R. NIGER *Mil.* I 19. **d** **1375** ne per sanguinis effusionem scandalizarentur, vulnera ipsius Willelmi cum aqua cocta ~erunt *SelCKB* VI 174. **e** quare .. habes oculos rubeos et excoctos? ANSELM *Misc.* 326. **f** digesti, .. excocti *Gl. Leid.* 2. 51.

2 to smelt, refine (metal). **b** (fig.) to purify. **c** (fig.) to refine away (impurity).

metalla in igne excocta ad ornatum corone sumuntur HON. *GA* 588C. **b** templum Domini .. ingreditur .. gloria resurrectionis ab omni labe mortalitatis excoctus BEDE *Hom.* I 11. 56; sese ut aurum in fornace ab omni scoria vitiorum omnimodis ~ere satagunt ORD. VIT. V 14 p. 418; [Ædeluuoldus] excoctus digne, dum purificatur in igne, / purior extractus, resplenduit illius actus *Lib. Eli.* II 10 (*Vers.*) p. 398. **c** BEDE *HE* IV 9 p. 222 (v. 1 caminus 3c); sicut vas excocta rubigine mundum .. in thesaurum reconditur ORD. VIT. VIII 17 p. 370; ardore devotionis omnem in se peccati rubiginem ~erunt P. BLOIS *Serm.* 693A; discipuli .. preneglectam scoriam [sc. sciencie] ~erunt donec fieret aurum electum R. BURY *Phil.* 10. 158.

3 to temper (iron); **b** (fig.); **c** (w. ref. to illness); **d** (p. ppl.) tried, vexed.

cum faber projicit aquam super ferrum .. unde fortius ferrum ~itur et remollitur *Quaest. Salern.* B 210. **b** **a1077** gloria .. Deo qui .. vos in igne tribulationis collocaret quatinus .. spem vestram usque ad debitum robur ~eret ANSELM (*Ep.* 78) III 201; Malchum tribulatio dura / excoquit R. CANT. *Malch.* I 377; Danais Fortuna caminis / excoxit non seva Friges, majoraque bellis / erudiit perferre viros HANV. I 104 p. 244. **c** abbas .. longa excoctus aegritudine *Hist. Abb. Jarrow* 17; Eadberhtus .. / .. / febribus excoquitur BEDE *CuthbV* 838; diuturni prius cruciatus excocta purgatorio tandem .. curata est *Mir. Fridesw.* 96; **s1257** episcopus Cestrensis diuturna infirmitate .. excoctus cesserat episcopatui M. PAR. *Maj.* V 644. **d** excoctum .. pectus FRITH. 80 (cf. ib. 122: ardent excoctis fibrarum omenta laternis).

excoracio v. excoriatio.

excoriare [LL]

1 to excoriate, flay, strip of skin: **a** (person, also fig.); **b** (part of body); **c** (animal); *cf. excorticare* 3; **d** (w. skin as obj.; *cf. Micah* iii 3); **e** (absol.). **f** to shave off (hair).

a desipio, ~io, febricito ALDH. *PR* 133 p. 186; precipiebat .. vivos ~iari et ~iatos comburi G. MON. III 15; flagellant vere et ~iant animum, et exulcerant tenerum et intentum in Christo affectum G. HOYLAND *Ascet.* 279B; nonne magnum est si te non ~io, si te vivere permitto? O. CHERITON *Fab.* 6; **s1297** quem [sc. H. de Cressingham] Scoti ob odium speciale ~iantes, pellem ejus in particulas diviserunt RISH. 180. **b** ut pars .. brachii ab ipsa manus junctura videretur usque ad os ~iata HERM. ARCH. 48; milites .. capitis mei summitatem, ubi corone mee locus est, ~iaverunt H. BOS. *Thom.* IV 20; captivi .. per cuneos concatenati, pedes exulcerati, humeros ~iati, .. ad manus latomorum .. materiem comportabant DEVIZES 43v.; major digitus dextri pedis qui ~iatus in adventu suo penitus sanatus inventus est *Canon. G. Sempr.* 141v.; **1271** repercussit .. Johannem in dextra parte capitis .. ita quod totum capud suum ~iavit *SelCCoron* 22. **c** **1235** solet furari averia et .. escoriare boves et vaccas *CurR* XV 1146; **1236** quadam jumenta quam escoriavit *JustIt* 775 m. 18*d.*; vulgariter dicitur quod primo oportet cervum capere et postea .. ~iare illum BRACTON 191; **1246** damam ~iatam *SelPlForest* 84 (cf. ib. 109: escoriavit eandem damam); **1320** in j equo ~iando et dicto coreo corriando *Fabr. Exon.* 119; GAD. 71v. 2 (v. excoriatio 1); de duobus canibus

ovium devorationi assuetis .. accidit .. Alriche capi et ~iari *Latin Stories* 108. **d** pelles eorum ab eis ~iaverunt GILDAS *EB* 85; Cambyses .. pellem cujusdam falsi judicis ~iatam fecit involvi circa cathedram judicialem *Eul. Hist.* I 57. **e** qui murdrum aperte fecerit sive combusserit vel decapitaverit vel ~iaverit aliterve diffecerit ne cognosci valeat .. reddatur parentibus interfecti (*Leg. Hen.* 92. 19) *GAS* 609. **f** [gigas] mandaverat Arturo ut barbam suam diligenter ~iaret atque ~iatam sibi dirigeret G. MON. X 3.

2 (med.) to abrade, graze. *Cf. excorticare* 2.

quare quidam legentes fiunt rauci? quia in eis arteria est gracilis, non potest dilatari legendo .. ex nimio conatu facile ~iantur, unde fiunt rauci *Quaest. Salern.* Ba 19; lavetur os .. cum aqua et aceto, ita quod sit duplum de aqua; aliter enim ~iaret linguam GAD. 5v. 1.

3 a to pod, shell. **b** to peel (wood), bark (tree); *cf. escorchiare, excorticare* 1a. **c** to cut (peat); *cf. excorticare* 1c.

a BACON IX 73 (v. amygdala a); subcellario .. ad turbam buscam et novas fabas ~iandas ij. quar. vij. buss. [panis]; .. ij. quar. panis hospitum ad fabas et pisas ~iandas *Ac. Beaulieu* 300, 309. **b** **1309** pro huss[eto] excoriat[o] *CourtR Wakefield* II 222; virgas populeas .. ~iavit *Eul. Hist.* I 36 (= HIGD. II 11 p. 302: decorticans); **1365** de ix arboribus .. per ipsum excorisatis ita quod amplius gessere non possunt *Hal. Durh.* 45. **c** **1246** quod nec prior .. nec Johannes .. possint .. colere vel ~iare .. moram set .. remaneat in communa pastura *Feod. Durh.* 104n.; **1261** de xxij s. iij d. pro licencia ~iandi turbas in mora ibidem *DL CourtR* 128/1919; **1430** soliti sunt brueram eradicare et turbas ~iare ad libitum *Feod. Durh.* 10n.

4 to deprive of property, to 'fleece', 'skin'.

s**1098** H. HUNT. *HA* VII 20 (v. abradere 1b); non tallagiis .. clerum Menevensem ~iet GIR. *JS* sup. 150; GIR. *JS* 1 p. 136, *AncrR* 23 (v. deplumare b); s**1258** A. .. a papa .. missus .. in Angliam ad eam exscoriandam *Flor. Hist.* II 417; **1274** fecit vastum in vivar[iis] et homines ejusdem ville escoriavit *Hund.* I 172; **1275** dedit x li. magis quam alii ballivi dare consueverunt ad ~iandam patriam, et ita fecit *Ib.* 188; **1294** per immoderatas misericordias ~iavit populum *PlRChester* 6 r. 11; tantis .. extorcionibus infestantur viri precipue religiosi, immo pocius ~iantur quod .. WALS. *YN* app. 545.

5 to strip, separate (abstr.).

sicut igitur ~iata fuit malicia ab actu WYCL. *Ente* 242.

excoriatio

1 excoriation, flaying.

excorietur aries juvenis et accipiatur pellis immediate post ~onem GAD. 71v. 2; secundus [labor Herculis] fuit interfectio et ~o leonis in Nemea silva HIGD. II 17; **1322** cum ~one j stalonis et j pultr' *MinAc* 1145/21 m. 35.

2 (med.) abrading, grazing. **b** abrasion, graze.

s**1183** injuriam patris .. vindicat febris, ulciscitur fluxus ventris cum ~one intestinorum R. HOWD. II 279; ~o trachee arterie et lingue et palati GILB. I 74v. 1; carnes tyrie .. educunt [superfluitates] ad cutem et ad exteriora per sudorem vel pediculos vel ~onem BACON IX 65; GAD. 56. 1 (v. diarria 1); *Ib.* 118. 2 (v. cynoglossa a). **b** vulnus .. si fiat in cute vocatur ~o GAD. 122. 1.

3 stripping, removal: **a** (of bark); **b** (of turf); **c** (of text from book by wear).

a **1185** V. C. .. r. c. de dim. m. pro ~one quercuum *Pipe* 114; **1188** villata de C. cum dominiis debet iiij s. ij d. pro ~one quercuum *Ib.* 194; a**1220** (v. cippus 1a); **1370** ad respond' domino de excoracione arborum *Hal. Durh.* 98. **b** **1198** qui foris fecerit in foresta regis .. per foditionem turbarum, sive per esscoriationem more, sive per colpationem de subnemore (*Assisa Forestae*) R. HOWD. IV 65. **c** **1425** libri precum .. quidam ~one, alii tabellarum .. dirupcione .. dehonestantur (*Inq.*) *Reg. Heref.* 67.

4 depriving of property, 'fleecing'.

1269 exactores regii gratiam in ingratitudinem et in novum genus ~onis convertentes iiij denarios .. de singulis marcis ad rectores .. pertinentibus .. extorserunt *Conc. Syn.* 799.

excoriativus, a (med.) abrasive. **b** (alch.) caustic.

a scabies ~a et ulcerativa GAD. 42v. 1. **b** *Ps.*-GROS. *Summa* 643 (v. corrosivus 1c).

excoriator, flayer, skinner. **b** fleecer (fig.), despoiler.

1198 Robertus de Riflei [est] ~or animalium *Pl. K. or J.* 6; Turstan Pigace ~or est bidentium in Beston' *Ib.* 30; **1282** ~oribus boum *KRAc* 4/3; **1285** jus .. habent in .. textoribus, ~oribus, carnificibus [etc.] *RGasc* II 274. **b** spiritualium tonsores ovium, vel potius ~ores GIR. *GE* II 34; homo inprobus et injustus et ~or pauperum hominum BRAKELOND 124; **1238** (v. exossator).

excorisare v. excoriare.

excors [CL], wanting intelligence or discernment, gaumless, gormless.

~s, sine corde *GlC* E 432; **8..** ~s, *modleas WW*; neque adeo ~s sum ut pro vero astruam .. similia J. SAL. *Pol.* 387C; ~s, sine corde OSB. GLOUC. *Deriv.* 202.

excorticare [LL]

1 to excorticate, peel (plant), bark (tree); *v. et. escorchiare; cf. excoriare* 3b. **b** to husk (grain); *cf. excoriare* 3a. **c** to cut (peat); *cf. excoriare* 3c.

de arbore quam fusenum vocant ~atam perticam ei fac ADEL. *CA* 11; **1170** W. L. r. c. de dim. m. pro hominibus qui ~averunt quercus *Pipe* 23; quare Jacob virgas varias et ~atas in aquis ante greges suos ponebat [cf. *Gen.* xxx 37] ut agni varii nascerentur *Quaest. Salern.* P 34; GAD. 6v. 2 (v. 1 costa 2); *CathA* (v. corticare a). **b** J. GODARD *Ep.* 222 (v. amygdalatus); detur .. lac seminum .. ~atorum GILB. I 31v. 1; decoquatur in aqua cum ordeo excortitato J. MIRFIELD *Brev.* 84; triticum ~atum cum lacte bullitum KYMER 19. **c** a**1245** nec .. ~abunt moram in occidente vie de Widemers .. sed integra jacebit *Cart. Newm.* 22.

2 (med.) to abrade, graze, peel off. *Cf. excoriare* 2.

BACON *Maj.* II 16 (v. corticalis a); valet pro lingua ~ata GAD. 7v. 1.

3 to flay, skin (animal). *Cf. excoriare* 1c.

repleatur catus ~atus pinguis et evisceratus, suatur bene et suaviter assetur GILB. VII 318. 2.

excortio, (med.) abrasion, graze, or (?) *f. l.*

alius quidam .. excortione [? l. excoriatione] ventris diutissime gravatus ibi est .. sanatus R. COLD. *Godr.* 424.

excortus v. exserere 2b.

excossiare, to clip off (impurity or bust from wool).

1442 BEKYNTON I 128 (v. claccare).

excostare [cf. 1 costare], to rib (flax).

CathA (v. 1 costare 1b).

excoticus v. exoticus. **excreare, ~atio** v. exscreare, ~atio.

excrebrescere [cf. CL crebrescere], to increase, intensify.

conflictu .. in adventu ejus ~ente *G. Walth.* 109.

1 excrementum [CL; cf. excernere], what is sifted out, esp. excrement, waste matter from body.

~a generaliter sunt omnia superflua per naturam ejecta *LC*; mulierum ~a sunt menstrua *LC*.

2 excrementum [CL; cf. excrescere], increase, encroachment (of natural force). **b** outgrowth. **c** increment, excess, profit.

s**1404** Selandia, Flandria, et Hollandia per undarum ~a innumerabilia sensit dispendia WALS. *YN* 412. **b** ~um, quod supercrescit, sicut ungues OSB. GLOUC. *Deriv.* 193. **c** tanquam .. in superfluis rerum ~is filia fundaretur GIR. *IK* I 3; **1240** de predicta peccunia seu ipsius ~o *StatOx* 75; **1252** summa recepte de frumento cum ~o mcclxxj sum. *DCCant. Reg.* H f. 173b; **1255** mittimus vobis .. lx m., vobis mandantes quod pro eisdem .. nobis habere faciatis vj m. boni auri combusti, et quia intelleximus quod marca hujusmodi non valet ex toto x m. argenti, faciatis nobis habere quantum poteritis de ~o auri pro denariis predictis *Cl* 178; **1288** summa tocius ordei recepti et recipiendi cum ~o mccccxlvj summe iiij busselli et dim. *Cant. Cath. Pri.* 208; [*incres*], excrescencia .., incrementum, ~um *PP*.

excrescentia

1 (med.) outgrowth, excrescence.

polipus est ~ia carnis infra nares GAD. 117v. 1.

2 growth, increase.

BART. ANGL. XIX 121 (v. denarius 1b); procedit continue ~ia ista per additionem unius diei in anno GROS. *Comp.* 224; **1370** si .. eorum redditus augeantur .. juxta ~iam facultatum, numerus [sc. presbyterorum] augeatur *Lit. Cant.* II 499; **1439** (v. desiderare 2c); **1452** exorans ut amicitiam continuare dignemini cum ~ia quam cepistis *Pri. Cold.* 176.

3 profit, surplus; *cf. excrescere* 5b. **b** (w. ref. to increased value of deposit, pledge, or sim.).

1417 lego .. ad ~ias scacarii .. vj li. xiij s. iiij d. (*Test.*) *Reg. Exon.* 417n.; **1423** volumus .. excessum reponi in cista communi ad hunc finem ut cum hiis ~iis exhibeantur hiis cantoribus superpellicia AMUND. I 107; **1479** unacum xiij s. .. de ~ia minutarum custumarum terre de S. *ExchScot* 634; **1485** ita quod .. satisfaciant de frumento .. granatario nostro .. cum ~ia que fuerit de ordio *Reg. Aberbr.* II 222; **1587** canonicatum sive prebendam .. unacum omnibus proficuis, commoditatibus, dividenciis, ~iis [etc.] *Pat* 1300 m. 14. **b** **1336** si quid, venditis pignoribus, ultra sortem excrescat, illud in usus similes cum sorte convertatur, donec venerint qui pignora exposuerint, predictas ~ias recepturi *StatOx* 135; **1340** vj s. de ~iis cujusdam caucionis in .. cista exposite .. pro xx s. vendite *FormOx* 122; **1486** motum est de caucione in cista .. magistri F. .. et visum est ut ~ia, si qua evenerit, servetur collegio *Reg. Merton* 94; **1541** ad ~iam valorum bonorum .. in .. testamentis .. contentorum *Form. S. Andr.* II 132.

excrescere [CL]

1 to grow (intr.); **b** (fig.). **c** (trans., fig.) to overgrow. **d** (p. ppl. *excretus*) mature, full-grown; *cf. crescere* 1e.

in his wastis terris excreverunt silvae *DB* I 186v.; quidam heremita plantavit olera ... una tamen planta olerum non excrevit *Spec. Laic.* 55. **b** papa .. vitiorum frutices que in ecclesia Dei excreverant ligone justitie succidit ALEX. CANT. *Mir.* 28 (II) p. 215; xv rami de arbore dilectionis ~unt HON. *GA* 608C. **c** Ricardus rex Anglie, cujus caput vepres libidinum ~erant (*sic*) BROMPTON 1190. **d** mecum sis .. sospes / .. uberibus pro votis utere glebis, / farris et excreti communis copia vini FRITH. 115.

2 (of natural force) to increase in quantity or strength.

cum tempestas ~it *V. Greg.* p. 76; .. eo citius .. ignis ~ebat R. COLD. *Godr.* 157; quoniam estivus calor jam nimis excreverat BOSO *V. Pont.* 393; ex humiditate lune ~unt aque, unde cum aque ~unt herba illa [sc. nenufar] declinatur *Quaest. Salern.* B 221; s**1253** excrevit aqua Tamisie, ascendens altior quam unquam fecit *Leg. Ant. Lond.* 20; KNIGHTON I 433 (v. celura 1).

3 to increase in number, size, or amount; **b** (w. *ad*).

tertius .. ebdomade modus qui ex septies septem annorum collectione concluditur, quia valde ~endo multiplicatur .. non posse congruere dinoscitur *Eccl. & Synag.* 94; **1167** dampnorum que .. in quadruplum excreverant J. SAL. *Ep.* 222 (223); hinc est qui lunatici dicuntur qui singulis mensibus pro lune augmento cerebro ~ente languescunt GIR. *TH* II 3. **b** ROB. ANGL. *Alg.* 98 (v. duplatio); *G.S. Alb.* II 178 (v. corrediarius); ut semper pensio bienii ad summam ~at xxiij s. *Cart. Carisb.* f. 71v.; Londonie modius tritici .. paulatim usque ad ij s. excrevit *Feud. Man.* 148.

4 to exceed, be in excess: **a** (absol. or w. prep.); **b** (pr. ppl. w. *dies*); **c** (trans.).

a si ultra vij excreverint, eis sublatis, quot remanserint .. BYRHT. *Man.* 54; c**1182** (v. coquina 1b); montes super plana terre sua altitudine excreverunt HON. *Spec. Eccl.* 815B; **1236** ~unt xij d. et iij quad. *Cust. Battle* 133; si plures fuerint oboli quam numerus panum, videndum est quota pars fuerit numerus ~ens de numero panum .. *MGL* I 351. **b** nec major erit annus bisextilis alio anno precedente, die propter diem ~entem, neque hora neque momento secundum quod inferius dicetur plenius de anno et die BRACTON 344b. **c** colossus qui mole vastissima .. cunctos homines excrevit *Lib. Monstr.* I 3; a**1228** ita ut valencia .. servicii detenti .. summam ~eret xv m. *Cart. Eynsham* I 138; si fuerint xx oboli et xxiiij panes .. ~it numerus panum numerum obolorum *MGL* I 350.

5 to accrue; **b** (pr. ppl. n. pl.); *cf. excrescentia* 3.

sic centenarium numerum duplicando et triplicando .. millenarius ~it numerus ROB. ANGL. *Alg.* 66; **1218** ccc .. li. .. cum lucro quod inde excrevit *Pat* 180; **1230** habet de superplus xij s. et xj d. qui non debent vicecomiti allocari quia ~unt per extensionem manerorum (*sic*) *Pipe* 164; **1251** excepta porcione redditus ~entis terre dicti J. *BBC* (*Kilmaclenine*) 313; **1400** una medietas illius quod ~it de amerciamentis assise ultra c s. .. regi solvendos *StatOx* 191; **1469** de arreragiis .. que extendebant ad c li. et ~ebant de grassumis et feodis etc. *ExchScot* 618. **b** **1550** quod super ~entia et resta stallorum .. recipiantur per duos canonicos *Reg. Aberd.* II 121.

6 (w. pers. subj.): **a** to improve. **b** to grow rich. **c** (trans.) to exceed, transgress.

a Willelmus de E. .. per plurimas probitates multipliciter excrevit ORD. VIT. III 9 p. 109; diabolus .. videns fratres in bonis ~ere operibus *Ib.* VI 9 p. 71; nonne super semetipsum excreverat is, qui ait "vivo ego, jam non ego, vivit autem in me Christus?" [*Gal.* ii 20] S. LANGTON *Serm.* 4. 22. **b** si villanus excrevisset [AS: *geþeah*] ut haberet plenarie v hidas terre sue proprie .. erat taini lege dignus (*Quad.*) *GAS* 457. **c** **1356** si tabernarius assisam .. ~eret .. per majorem et ballivos hospicium claudatur *MunAcOx* 183.

7 (w. abstr. subj.) to grow, increase.

601 ut cum Christiana fides in regno vestro excreverit nostra quoque apud vos locutio latior ~at (*Lit. Papae*) BEDE *HE* I 32; quantum in eo crescebat successus temporis, tantum ~ebat .. studium probitatis DOMINIC *V. Ecgwini* I 2; nescientes qualiter tirannidem ejus, que jam super eos nimis excreverat, evaderent ORD. VIT. III 11 p. 119; in me tui dilectio ~it ALEX. CANT. *Dicta* 14 p. 160; s**1190** (v. colligere 4a); magna paupertas que super eum [Christum] semper magis ac magis excrevit [ME: *wox*] *AncrR* 96; **1559** contra Johannam C. .. propter suam multiplicem et ~entem contumaciam judicialiter contractam (*Vis. Cant.*) *EHR* XXVII 669.

8 (trans.) to raise, cause to rise.

[S. Stephanus] deambulabat .. circuiens turrim suam super tabulatum ejusdem turris quam ad illud jam opus excreverat [? sc. Ailsi] quasi circumspiciendo .. opus ecclesie sue P. CORNW. *Rev.* I 6 f. 24.

excretio [LL], growth.

intra illos annos non calciamentum aut vestis illorum [Hebreorum] est attrita nec ulla capillorum vel unguium ~o eis est dominata M. PAR. *Maj.* I 11 (= Orosius I 10).

excrispare [cf. CL crispare], to ripple, curl.

lacus .. aquis crispantibus aura non ventis sed de se ipso sibi ~ans, unde et Genesar dicitur Greco vocabulo BACON *Maj.* I 341.

excruciare [CL], to torture. **b** to torment (mentally). **c** (pr. ppl. as adj.) excruciating, causing pain.

tali femineam sontes molimine spinam / excruciare student membratim quatenus ossa / .. vacuarent cruda medullis ALDH. *VirgV* 1995; **a1081** plerique .. ante baptismum .. diversis ~iati poenis de corpore migraverunt LANFR. *Ep.* 33 (49); **s1135** R... Saresbiriensis episcopus .. captus et ~iatus miserandum sortitus est exterminium H. HUNT. *HA* VIII 1; Jacobus, Simon, et Thadeus enecati, Johannes veneno et exilio ~iatus, Thomas transfossus HON. *GA* 578A; sancti .. ~iati nichil senserunt P. CORNW. *Disp.* 149. **b** ut .. sit .. commissus duro custodi qui ejus animam immisericorditer .. ~iet BYRHT. *V. Ecgwini* 393; dolor acerrimus pectus tenerrimum / angit, excruciat, et torquet WALT. WIMB. *Carm.* 264. **c** non est in calice liquor excrucians, / non acet pristino sapore varians *Ib.* 155.

excruciatio [LL], torture, torment.

quando .. formidatur .. carnis ~o, vel perempcio OCKHAM *Dial.* 544.

excruciatrix [cf. LL excruciator], torturer (f.).

invidia sui ipsius ~ix [v. l. cruciatrix] est, sibi ipsi pestis letifera NECKAM *NR* II 105.

excrustare [cf. CL crustare], to strip, spoil (ornament or cover).

~ato pavimento evulsa crates erigitur, sepulcralis cryptula .. violatur GOSC. *Transl. Aug.* 21C; die uno xij textus, .. viij cruces, viij scrinia argento et auro nudata et ~ata sunt W. MALM. *GP* V 271; thechas reliquiarum sanctarum ~avit R. COLD. *Cuthb.* 29; [Athelwoldus] fecit tres cruces ex auro et argento .. que fracte sunt et ~ate [tempore] regis Stephani *Abbat. Abingd.* 278; utrum feretrum S. Ædmundi saltem in parte ~aretur ad redemptionem regis Ricardi BRAKELOND 148v.; **c1250** imagines .. quarum †una [l. unam] auro et gemmis ~avit *MonA* II 437a.

excrustatio, stripping, spoiling (of ornament or cover).

s1149 appellaverant .. monachi Henricum episcopum .. de ~one magne crucis *Ann. Wint.* 54.

excuba, ~us [cf. LL excubator], guard, watchman; **b** (fig.).

cum quis mentiendi nota inuritur, dici solet quia quovis ~o vigilive mendacior est J. SAL. *Pol.* 462A; super exercitus cura noctes ducebat .. et tanquam ~arum ~a .. nocte tota circumeundo .. errabundus excubare solebat GIR. *EH* II 8; hic ~us, A. *wayte WW*. **b** scelerumque procellas / propulit infracto securus navita clavo / quem precessiva ratio dedit excuba tanto / cum socia virtute viro HANV. V 457.

excubanter, vigilantly.

divine legis sententias exestuans, vitas patrum providissimorum perlegens ~er *NLA* (*J. Bridl.*) II 70.

excubare [CL]

1 (mil., intr.) to mount guard, keep watch; **b** (w. dat.). **c** (trans.) to guard, watch.

rex .. Eadgarus ~abat in portu Sandewic cum classe .. contra externos exercitus GOSC. *Wulfh.* 6; ut pervigiles contra ingeniosos exploratores ~arent ORD. VIT. XII 13 p. 343; GIR. *EH* II 8 (v. excuba a). **b** dux versutias metuebat, et excubitores qui tentoriis ~arent prudenter disposuerat ORD. VIT. IX 6 p. 493. **c** ut .. ij solidi .. solverentur in usus virorum fortium qui perlustrantes et jugiter ~antes maritima impetum hostium reprimerent *Dial. Scac.* I 11 A.

2 to keep vigil. **b** to lurk.

~abat diebus ac noctibus ante tugurium pauperis vulgus BEDE *HE* I 19; ~abant, †vigilibant *GlC* E 555; ~et, evigilet, *bewacige GlP* 57; HERM. ARCH. 38 (v. clericellus a); dum in oratorio sola ~aret ORD. VIT. VIII 21 p. 392; singulis [gruibus] vicissim alternis noctibus ~antibus GIR. *TH* I 14; [mulieres] que ad ostium tabernaculi ~abant P. BLOIS *Serm.* 744C; **a1450** chorus in vigilia nocturna ~et in choro circa funus *Stat. Linc.* II 343. **b** secus viam latrunculi sepe ~ant insidiantes spoliis animarum R. NIGER *Mil.* I 2.

3 (usu. w. dat.) to watch over, to be attentive to.

~at, observat *GlC* E 435; assentiebatur ei [Radulfo, episc. Roff.] Robertus Belesmensis .. patiebaturque hominem libere religioni ~are W. MALM. *GP* I 68; **1169** gratias ago benivolentie vestre que non solum mihi prospicere et meis non desistit utilitatibus ~are G. FOLIOT *Ep.* 205.

excubatio [CL], mounting guard, keeping vigil.

gallina .. procedit .. et ~one pervigil et inexcubatione profusa J. FORD *Serm.* 14. 6.

excubator [LL], guard, watchman. *V. et. excubitor* a.

circa corpus martyris corvi tanquam ~ores assistunt GIR. *TH* II 28.

excubatorius, of a guard or watchman.

ignes ~ios .. accendi fecerunt *Ps.*-ELMH. *Hen. V* 25; vigilum ignes et ~ii sunt accensi LIV. *Hen. V* 6b.

excubiae [CL *pl.*], **~ia**

1 keeping guard, watch. **b** guard duty (feud.).

milites ad ~ias confessorum deputati ALDH. *VirgP* 36; ~ias noctis contra inruptiones hostium BEDE *Ezra* 898; cum .. contingit .. civitatem obsessam tueri, .. in nocte ternis ~iarum ordinibus pernoctando .. cavent BELETH *RDO* 21. 33; felices excubie / .. / angelorum et pastorum / hodie LEDREDE *Carm.* 2. 21. **b** **c1180** liberi .. ab omni pedagio, theloneo, .. passagio, ~iis, exercitu, et equitatu [etc.] *Act. Hen. II* II 355; **1192** sint liberi .. absque venda, telonio, ~iis, exercitu, equitatu (*Ch. Rotomag.*) *Thes. Nov. Anecd.* I 649a; Philippum de B. .. quendam burgensem .. dedisse .. quietum ab omnibus querelis et consuetudinibus preter de ~ia *Cart. Glouc.* II 103.

2 (eccl.) vigil.

proxima nocte .. tribus .. custodibus .. ~ias noctis agentibus *Hist. Abb. Jarrow* 40; nocte .. ordinentur duo fratres .. qui ibidem .. ~ias [AS p. 422: *wæccean*] fideles exerceant *RegulC* 46; discant .. sacras frequenter ~ias celebrare OSB. *V. Dunst.* 40; Christiani .. nocte illa quieverunt nisi quod potius ~iis et orationibus incubuerunt ORD. VIT. IX 16 p. 616; ad sepulcrum regis nocte sequenti accensis cereis ~ias celebravit AILR. *Ed. Conf.* 786D; paraverunt sibi luminaria que manibus in eisdem ~iis [sc. in oratorio] tenerent ALEX. CANT. *Mir.* 23 (II) p. 209; quadam nocte ad matutinales ~ias ipse stans ex una parte chori respexit ad tres novicios suos P. CORNW. *Rev.* II 893.

3 wakefulness, lying awake. **b** watchfulness, vigilance. **c** anxiety, concern; **d** (w. *mentis*).

excubeas patitur juvenis si nocte dieque / sique senex dormit designat morte resolvi J. MIRFIELD *Brev.* 58. **b** excubias timet illa [Fortuna] tuas oculosque manusque: / hos quia non claudis, has quia non aperis SERLO WILT. 17. 5; vestitur sidere celum / .. et orbi / exibet excubias oculis populosior Argus HANV. VIII 356; regina pervigil, cujus ad ipsum semper erant ~ie MAP *NC* III 2 f. 36; illius [cigni] ~ias nullus poterat eludere AD. EYNS. *Hug.* III 7 p. 107. **c 717** aurilegi ambrones .. frustratis adflicti inservire ~iis .. dinoscuntur BONIF. *Ep.* 9; mox et ab humanis sic languidus ille relictus / excubiis supera meruit pietate juvari WULF. *Swith.* I 689; speciali solertia regiis ~iis inherens, propensiore cura quam patri proprio serviens G. FONT. *Inf. S. Edm.* 1. **d** magnanimitas regia .. Gallorum rebellionem a mentis ~iis non expellit *Ps.*-ELMH. *Hen. V* 18 (cf. ib. 48: excidiis a mencium ~iis non expulsis).

4 guard, watchman. **b** guardhouse, sentry-box.

assint .. ~ie [*gl.: waytes*] vigiles, cornibus suis strepitum et clangorem .. facientes NECKAM *Ut.* 106; vigili .. animo .. se undique positis ~iis atrio bene culto providendum est R. NIGER *Mil.* I 21; **1364** in liberacione facta ~iis castri de Dunbretane .. liij s. iiij d. *ExchScot* 169. **b** ~ias, *weardseld GlC* E 527; **9..** ~ias, *weardsetl WW*.

excubialis [LL], of a guard, appropriate to a watchman.

qui excubitali [v. l. excubiali] obsequio concinnator .. credendus erat J. SAL. *Pol.* 461D.

excubitor [LL], guard, watchman; *v. et. excubator*. **b** guardian, supervisor.

~or, vigil, *dægweard* ÆLF. *Sup.*; ~ores, *heafodweardas GlH* E 749; de dangione regios expulit ~ores ORD. VIT. VIII 1 p. 262; *Ib.* IX 6 p. 493 (v. excubare 1b); dum ~ores intentius pernoctant, miserum homunculum a muro demissum .. ceperunt *G. Steph.* I 14; **s1250** cum .. civitati appropinquarent intuebantur eos ~ores .. a turrium .. propugnaculis M. PAR. *Maj.* V 161. **b** Garbald, qui ecclesie civitatis Reginae pastorale ~oris subiit magisterium WILLIB. *Bonif.* 7.

excubitus [CL]

1 guard, watch.

vicissim excubabant noctibus et ubi major ingruebat metus ibi vigilantior preparabatur ~us ORD. VIT. IX 14 p. 59.

2 watch, clock.

1605 unum ~um, A. *a watch HMC Rep.* IX 293a.

excubus v. excuba. **excucio** v. excussio.

excudere [CL]

1 to hammer out, forge (metal); **b** (fig.) **c** to strike (fire).

~unt, fabricant; ~it, malleo quodcumque conponit *GlC* E 385–6; ~it, *ameraþ GlP* 580; arma / fabricat, excudit vincula GARL. *Epith.* I 496. **b** finibus Armonicis excuditur enea pestis [*gl.*: i. bellum; .. nota quod potest dici pestis ~itur] J. CORNW. *Merl.* 67. **c** ignis .. ~itur ex eorum [corporum] impetuosa collisione ADEL. *QN* 65; *Ib.* 66 (v. complodere 1c).

2 to print.

1516 Linacer protinus a Natali quae vertit e Galeno mittet Luteciam ~enda (MORE) *Ep. Erasmi* II 502; **1517** si videtur tuis excusa typis (ERASMUS *Ep.*) MORE *Ut.* lxxviii; **1520** eam statuo esse commodissimam rationem .. qua respondeatur illi epistolae tuae quae nuper Basileae excusa antea apud bibliopolas prostaret quam ad meas manus tota pervenerit *Ep. Erasmi* IV 1061 p. 159; **1552** cujus .. libri exemplaria omnia, ubi excusa fuerint praesentari ipsi .. mandat .. praesens concilium *Conc. Scot.* II 137.

3 to work out (mentally).

cum .. volueris scire defectus lune, illam oppositionem ~e in qua luna caput vel caudam draconis obtineat ADEL. *Elk.* 33; VINSAUF *PN* 1616 (v. cudere 2d).

excudia, ~ium, swinglestock, instrument for beating hemp; *cf. excussorium* a. **b** plough-staff.

instrumenta mulieribus convenientia: .. ~ia [*gl.*: ~ia dicitur ab excutio, et est illud instrumentum cum quo linum †texitur [? l. teritur] .. G. *paissel*; ~ia, G. *soienges*; ~ia, *eclice*] GARL. *Dict.* 134; ~ia, *a swyngylstok*; .. hoc †exculidium, A. *a swyndylstoc*, hoc ~ium, *a swyndilland*; .. hec ~ia, A. *a sungyllestok*, hec †excudiatorium, *a sungyllehand WW*; *a swynglestoke*, ~ia, ~ium *CathA*. **b** *a ploghe-staffe*, scudium, ~ium *Ib.*

excudiare, to swingle, dress (hemp) by beating.

~io, A. *to squyngyl WW*; *to swyngille*, ~iare *CathA*.

excudiatorium, exculidium v. excudia. **exculentus** v. esculentus.

exculpare [LL], to exculpate, free from blame. **b** to free from, get rid of. **c** ? *f.l.*.

ut .. non haec antea reprehendendo judicemus quam ad conscientiam nostram humiliter reversi digito eam discretionis solerter ~emus BEDE *Hom.* I 25. 107. **b** [poenitentia] conficitur .. primum ~ando peccata ALCUIN (*In Heb.*) *Exeg.* 1058B. **c** excipe proficuos, foveas quo te reprehendant, / ut decet †exculpa [? l. ex culpa] letius †arte [? l. arta] feras (*Mors Hen. IV*) *Pol. Poems* II 120.

exculpere v. exsculpere.

excultibilis [cf. cultibilis, LL excultio], cultivable.

1141 concedo .. ut a die illo in antea omnia illa essarta sint amodo ~ia et arrabilia sine forisfacto (*Ch. Imp. Matilde*) *Mandeville* 92; **c1180** (1448) sciatis me dedisse .. illam terram ~em quam habeo apud Norwicum (*Pat*) *MonA* IV 70b.

excultio [LL = *cultivation*], worship.

Dei ~o COLET *Cel. Hier.* 174 (v. effictio).

excurare [LL < CL = *to take care of*], to scour, clean: **a** (ditch); **b** (artefact). *V. et. escurare.*

a **a1294** quod dicta fossata .. ~are debeant *Cart. Chich.* 7; **1504** omnes haias, sepes, et fossata manerio .. pertinentia bene .. ~abit et plantabit *Crawley* 493. **b** **1541** suspiciens an vasculum quoddam vocatum *a trunke* plane †exacuriatur [l. excuriatur] necne *AncIndict* 546 m. 93.

excuratio [cf. excurare, curatio], scouring, cleaning: **a** (of ditch or sewer); *v. et. escuratio* a; **b** (of house).

a **a1294** pro dicta ~one fossatorum *Cart. Chich.* 7; **c1471** Johanni L. pro excuracione volte subterranee et purgacione latrine puerorum (*AuditR Eton*) *Arch. Hist. Camb.* I 414n. **b** **1564** item pro ~one domus fossoris ij d. *Ac. Churchw. Glast.* 383.

excurator [cf. CL curator], guardian. *Cf. escurator.*

1285 quod abbas possit dare tutores et ~ores *RGasc* II 272n. (cf. ib. 272: tutores et curatores).

excurrere [CL]

1 to run (on), rush (out; also fig.). **b** (trans.) to run out from.

celeri festinatione per maris alta ~unt R. COLD. *Cuthb.* 30; equus aliquanto longius conabatur cum milite suo ~ere *Ib.* 128; H. BOS. *Thom.* IV 13 p. 367 (v. effluere 2d); **1204** si canes .. ~unt in .. moras et bruillos *RChart* 122b. **b** velut manus sevas evasurus dormitorium ~ebat W. CANT. *Mir. Thom.* V 8.

2 (of liquid) to pour forth (also fig.). **b** (trans.) to drain.

R. COLD. *Cuthb.* 45 (v. diffluere 1a); ut ~at putredo de vulnere cordis P. BLOIS *Serm.* 602D; **s1376** aquas fecerunt ~ere (v. caput 15a). **b** ADEL. *QN* 55 (v. aquositas).

3 (trans.): **a** to pass, spend (time). **b** to perform (duty), transact (business). **c** to run out of, exhaust (essoin).

a parvissimo spatio serenitatis ad momentum excurso BEDE *HE* II 13; tertia nox aderat mediis excursa tenebris WULF. *Swith.* I 671; excurso denique aliquanti temporis spatio .. natus est .. filius T. MON. *Will.* I 2; elapsa Pentecostis hebdomada et sic mense fere toto post ultimam audientiam excurso GIR. *JS* 3 p. 192; **s1203** pueriIibus autem annis [S. Dominici] innocenter excursis TREVET *Ann.* 172. **b** omnia caritatis officia ~isti GOSC. *Lib. Confort.* 28; his .. omnibus sic excursis, recessit comes Leycestrie AD. MARSH *Ep.* 30 p. 129. **c** excursis omnibus essoniis quibus se essoniare poterit .. GLANV. IV 6.

excursio [CL]

1 (mil.) sortie. *V. et. excursus* 1b.

rex .. opportuna loca contra ~ones hostium communivit ORD. VIT. IV 4 p. 184.

2 passing (of time). *V. et. excursus* 4.

post bis senum annorum ~onem coepit .. filius Dei .. pandere quis esset BYRHT. *V. Ecgwini* 351.

excursus [CL]

1 running, rushing (out; also fig.). **b** (mil.) sortie; *v. et excursio* 1.

allegat praesul, facilis verum ille juventae / excursus trepidat, ne forsan mobilis aetas / praecipitem pravae retrahat per competa sectae FRITH. 238; GOSC. *Wulfh.* 2 (v. conclamare 1f). **b** ~um Christianorum .. expectantes ORD. VIT. IX 14 p. 590; cum enim pro more ad bellorum ferretur †exursus [l. excursus], ab hostibus interfectus .. est W. MALM. *Mir. Mariae* 178.

2 excursion, journey.

est Wiht insula .. nautarum ~ibus frequentata *G. Steph.* I 21.

3 **a** 'play', scope (for movement). **b** winding (of river). **c** spread (of abstr.).

a calculator in medio lateris residet .. ut liberum habeat ministra manus ~um *Dial. Scac.* I 4 M. **b** [flumina] insulam .. longis ~ibus disterminant GIR. *TH intr.* p. 7. **c** scitis .. quam periculosum sit .. adversus innoxium detestabilem suscitare infamiam quam cum abolere volueritis, ipsius ~um non poteris cohibere P. BLOIS *Ep.* 55. 130C.

4 passing (of time). *V. et. excursio* 2.

in hujus seculi transeuntis ~u [AS: *from erninge*] victum nobis spiritalem ne deficiamus inpende *Rit. Durh.* 18; venit post paucorum dierum ~um ad Romam BYRHT. *V. Ecgwini* 358; *Id. V. Osw.* 424 (v. duodenarius 1b); post ~um paucorum dierum .. ordinatus est RIC. HEX. *Hist. Hex.* I 18; **s1186** in facie .. Teobaldi, Thome, Ricardi, Cantuariensium archiepiscoporum, juxta temporis ~um, ordine successoris quatuor presentarat episcopos DICETO *YH* II 42; post sexti mensis a tempore illo ~um AD. EYNS. *Hug.* III 7.

5 discussion. **b** excursus, digression.

in ~u rerum .. aliquantulum perfectionis poteris invenire DICETO *Chr. pref.* 1 p. 3. **b** *Ep. ad amicum* 140 (v. distendere 1e).

6 aberration, bizarre occurrence.

credo quod arta magis presentibus atque futuris / grata forent .. / quam de terrenis excursibus, atque caducis / stemmatibus frustra rimari ORD. VIT. XI (*Vers. prol.*) p. 159; scrutabunda tam cursuum nature quam ~uum inquisitione profeci GIR. *EH intr.* p. 212; nature .. ~us tam stupendos explicare *Id. TH intr.* p. 7.

excurtare [cf. CL curtare], **~iare**, to dock (horse's tail); *v. et. escurtare*. **b** to abbreviate.

jumentum quoddam, .. cui forte obviavit in via, ~avit H. BOS. *Thom.* V 8; **1247** brachium suum fregerunt et caudas equorum suorum ~iaverunt et cappam ipsius canonici assportaverunt *JustIt* 455 m. 7. **b** ne .. quis .. hanc martyris historiam .. aut mutilet aut ~et H. BOS. *Thom.* VII 2.

excusabilis [CL]

1 excusable, pardonable: **a** (of person); **b** (of offence).

a si David sacerdotali cibo pastus ~is est .. quanto magis filius hominis .. evulsarum sabbato spicarum noxa non tenetur BEDE *Luke* (vi 5) 394; examinatus postremo tamen in victoria omnino ~is apparuit EDDI 55; vestra .. reverentia .. ~is apud Deum .. existeret ANSELM (*Ep.* 298) IV 219; nemo eorum qui mortem provocat ~is est; ~iores sunt qui imminentem abhorrent J. SAL. *Pol.* 584A; P. BLOIS *Ep.* 37. 116C (v. accusabilis); **1324** habeat .. discrecio vestra ~es in hac parte racionabiliter excusatos *Lit. Cant.* I 116. **b** juvenilis ~is est levitas GIR. *TH* III 52; talis corrupcio .. vicium .. inexcusabile comprimit, cum impropnetas ~is approbari non poterit per figuras ELMH. *Cant.* 338.

2 providing excuse.

1474 nonnullos esse dubios .. an eorum .. infirmitas vel servicii occupacio sit adeo ~is *Mon. Hib. & Scot.* 475b.

excusabilitas, excusability.

dicunt doctores quod primus parens post statum innocencie non potuit primo venialiter peccavisse, quia tanto dotato virtutibus non affuisset excusacio peccandi, quantumcunque levi peccato de genere; et cum venialitas et ~as a dampnacione, sicut et eorum opposita, corespondent, videtur patere sentencia WYCL. *Civ. Dom.* I 71.

excusabiliter [LL], excusably, with excuse. *V. et. excusatorie* b.

Herodes .. laetabatur occulte quod ea petebatur quae antea facere, si ~er posset, disponebat BEDE *Hom.* II 23. 240; **s1191** nobiles .. declarata inopia sua, redire ad propria ~er proponebant W. NEWB. *HA* IV 23; BACON XV 30 (v. constructibilis); episcopi possunt propter diversas causas absentare se a suis diocesibus et fieri non ibidem residentes ~er et meritorie PECOCK *Abbr.* 617 (= GASCOIGNE *Loci* 27: excusatorie).

excusamen [LL], excusing, pardoning.

1508 in consciencie mee ~en et voluntatis dicti reverendi patris complementum *Cl* 374 m. 24*d*.

excusare [CL]

1 (w. ref. to past or present conduct): **a** to excuse, justify (person); **b** (refl.); **c** (w. abstr. obj.); **d** (w. abstr. subj.); **e** (w. *quin*).

a haec est tua excusatio, quoniam tu eos semper ~as ÆLF. BATA 4. 7; o apostole Dei .. porta me, .. ~a me ANSELM (*Or.* 17) III 70; **1126** si una ovis .. perierit, qua ope suffult[us] apud Deum ~ari poteris? *Ep. Anselm. Bur.* 97; Nichodemus ~at Ihesum apud Judeos AD. DORE *Pictor* 158; metu mortis vel gravium tormentorum potest a pertinacia et pravitate heretica ~ari, sed non a peccato mortali OCKHAM *Dial.* 462. **b** **c1077** non .. vos apud districtum judicem ~are valetis ANSELM (*Ep.* 80) III 203; nec se a rapina ~are poterit quamdiu .. ALEX. CANT. *Dicta* 19 p. 179; in confessione .. debet homo excusare se ipsum et non ~are ALEX. BATH *Mor.* IV 18 p. 156. **c** ~a excessum meum, amor Dei ANSELM (*Or.* 12) III 48; GIR. PI III 13 (v. accusare 1d); dupliciter peccatur ore: uno modo defendendo peccatum suum et ~ando HALES *Sent.* IV 254. **d** Lanfrancum vita ejus multis .. nota .. ab hoc crimine satis ~at ANSELM (*Ep.* 136) III 280; quod .. regia competenter ~at licentia ALB. LOND. *DG* 4. 10; OCKHAM *Dial.* 884 (v. contrafacere 1a). **e** quippe nec locus nec tempus aliquod ~at aliquem quin bene possit vivere ANSELM (*Ep.* 96) III 222; nec amor, nec odium, nec aliquid preter timorem mortis potest quemcunque in hoc casu ~are, quin sit hereticus reputandus OCKHAM *Dial.* 448.

2 to atone (for).

inde thoro meliore redit veteremque repulsam / excusans victor regnat lauroque superbit J. EXON. *BT* I 305.

3 (w. *innocentiam*) to plead innocent.

a1166 si redire tutum fuerit, paratus sum .. regi .. satisfacere ubicumque non potero meam innocentiam ~are J. SAL. *Ep.* 164 (149).

4 (w. ref. to proposed action or task): **a** to excuse (person); **b** (w. *absentia*); **c** (refl.). **d** (absol.) to make excuse. **e** (w. acc. & inf. or *quia*) to plead in excuse (that). **f** (w. *quod*) to deny (rightness of course of action).

a **c795** arcium munimentum, quod omni populo necesse est, ab eo opere nullum excusatum esse *CS* 274; nec aliquis ad ministrandum de cetero ~etur pretextu fragilitatis per sompnium contingentis *Cust. Cant.* 39; **1356** super quo nos habere velit .. vestra sanctitas ~atos (*Lit. Regis ad Papam*) AVESB. 135; **1447** Johanni L. armigero deferenti literam domini regis .. ad ~andum nos penes eundem regem, xx s. *Ac. Durh.* 630. **b** absentia tua, .. nisi necessariis .. causis possit ~ari, in capitis tui periculum redundabit *Dial. Scac.* II 3 A; **1199** †excusa [? l. excusata] tertii conjudicis nostri absentia adjudicavimus .. *Reg. S. Osm.* I 356; **1315** rex vult absenciam suam ad proximum parliamentum suum apud Westmonasterium .. habere excusatam *RScot* 135b. **c** ille, se ~ans et venire non posse contestans, .. misit pro se .. nepotem suum BEDE *HE* III 7; quod .. diu tentare recusavi atque me cum re ipsa comparans multis me rationibus me ~are tentavi ANSELM (*Mon. prol.*) I 7; **1301** si [rex] ~et se quia proceres regni sui .. dicunt se nolle permittere regem jura corone sue .. papam in judicium deducere *Anglo-Scot. Rel.* 93 (v. et. 3e infra). **d** **s1190** in obviam fuit ei [regi Ricardo] Otto .. rogans eum Romam domino pape adventurum. quo tamen ~ante, .. Apuliam introivit *Meaux* I 253. **e** ipse .. se non esse dignum ~ans .. *V. Cuthb.* III 6; ille .. primo abnuens [episcopus fieri], non esse se dignum ~avit, postremo .. noluit .. benedictionem Dei effugere EDDI 11; **1301** (v. 3c supra). **f** quoniam inconveniens existimabam ut frigidus calidum calefacere tentaret, utique volui recusare, sed rursus considerans quia frigido flatu fervens ignis augetur, non omnino quod petebar potui ~are ANSELM (*Ep.* 2) III 99.

excusatio [CL]

1 (w. ref. to past or present conduct) excuse, justification; **b** (w. ref. to *Psalm* cxl 4).

680 fortasse quilibet .. tali se ~onis clipeo defendat .. inquiens .. ALDH. *Ep.* 4 p. 485; ÆLF. BATA 4. 7 (v. excusare 1a); **c1071** ad calumniam vestram quam dicitis rationem ~onis nostrae exposuimus ANSELM (*Ep.* 113) III 248; **1166** ~onem qua diuturnitatem silentii purgare studuistis .. habeo .. acceptam J. SAL. *Ep.* 227 (181). **b** ea que .. tunc confitebatur .. non delicta lugendo sed excusando potius et rationem facti assignando ad excusandas ~ones proponebat GIR. *PI* III 13 (cf. id. *Spec.* III 15).

2 (w. ref. to proposed action or task) excuse, pretext; **b** (w. defining gen.); **c** (w. obj. gen. or *de*).

a1073 precipimus .. quatinus omni ~one summota illuc eatis LANFR. *Ep.* 12 (13); horum [judicum] siquis de *hundret* remanebat die quo sedebat sine ~one manifesta x s. emendabat *DB* I 262v.; **1126** noli .. hac conditione securus promisso tuo ~onem moliri, ut, videlicet .. te volentem jubeat rex longius procedere *Ep. Anselm. Bur.* 97; Godefredus regnum suscipiendum in ~onem duxit, pretextu sancte humilitatis GERV. TILB. II 20 p. 946; **s1323** BLANEFORD 140 (v. comparere 2a). **b** ille [sc. Dunstanus] statim facilis sibi verbi ~onem rejecit, inquiens se non esse hujus pastoralis curae prospectum B. *V. Dunst.* 19; **a1073** ~o incognitae linguae .. nullum apud eos locum invenire praevaluit LANFR. *Ep.* 1. **c** ne quidam causa penuriae saecularis substantiae ~onem negotiandi cum Christo habeant, respondit dominus dicens .. ANSELM *Misc.* 323; **1220** nullam nobis inducit promissio illa obligationem vel vobis ~onem de non faciendo quod .. precepimus *Pat* 226; numquid non potuit nos cum minori gravamine redemisse? .. certe .. sed noluit .. ut auferret nobis omnem ~onem [ME: *bitellunge*] amoris nostri erga eum *AncrR* 154; **1384** quoad allegacionem ejusdem archiepiscopi pro ~one dampnorum *PlRCP* 495 r. 312.

excusative, by way of excuse.

ne .. occupacio claustralis tolleret ~e laborem manualem, .. Augustinus .. injungit ut laborent NETTER *DAF* I 528b.

excusativus, excusative, apologetic.

allocutio ~a ad regem ALDH. *PR* 142 *rub.*; (*Quad. dedic.*) *GAS* 532 (v. concessivus).

excusator [LL]

1 excuser, defender, apologist.

cui .. desunt ~ores, .. ipse solus sibi sufficiat in defensione innocentiae suae EGB. *Dial.* 3; peccata mea .. vos attrahitis accusatores, vos removetis ~ores ANSELM (*Or.* 10) III 34; **1164** ~ores regis et emuli vestri J. SAL. *Ep.* 134 (136 p. 10); qua .. audacia ~ores simoniace heresis putant se verum dicere PAUL. ANGL. *ASP* 1543.

2 bearer of excuse (for failure to appear as summoned).

1166 quod rex Anglie .. ad colloquium accedere non potuerit, sed miserit ~ores .. qui hanc causam absentie ejus volebant astruere J. SAL. *Ep.* 145 (168); .. si citatus super regiis .. negotiis nec veneris nec ~orem miseris *Dial. Scac.* II 3 A; nec adest Haymo sed ~orem mittens se ne illic interesset finxit corporis invalitudine detineri *Chr. Battle* f. 93; *Fleta* 382 (v. essoniator); **s1320** omnes magnates illuc [in parliamentum] venerunt .. excepto comite Lancastrie; tamen misit procuratores et ~ores *Ann. Paul.* 290; **1472** quia capitulo .. interesse nequeo .. abbatem Westmonasteriensem meum .. procuratorem, ~orem, et nuncium specialem .. facio *Reg. Whet.* II 99; **1517** ad comparendum personaliter per se et non per procuratorem seu ~orem *Form. S. Andr.* I 11.

excusatorie, **a** by giving an excuse. **b** excusably, with excuse; *v. et. excusabiliter*.

a **1340** scientes quod si premissa facere neglexeritis aut ~ie tractaveritis per quod periculum in vestri defectu nobis aut regno .. per ejusmodum hostium invasiones eveniat *RScot* I 593a; **1430** [petenti] negatorie, aut dilatorie, seu quomodolibet ~ie, respondere *Reg. Whet.* II app. 454. **b** episcopi possunt .. esse .. non residentes in suis diocesibus ~ie et meritorie GASCOIGNE *Loci* 27 (= PECOCK *Abbr.* 617: excusabiliter).

excusatorius [LL], excusatory. **b** (w. *litterae* or sim.) letters excusatory; **c** (as sb. f. or n.).

c1000 vos .. clementer hanc ~iam suscipientes querimoniam .. insipientiae meae .. promittere dignemini parcere (*Ep. ad Wulstanum*) *Mem. Dunst.* 405; **s1141** post recitata scripta ~ia quibus absentiam suam quidam tutati sunt W. MALM. *HN* 492; omne verbum stultum et vacuum, impudicum, ~ium, detractorium .. ab illis spiritualibus exercitiis .. aliena sunt AD. SCOT *QEC* 17. 829C; **s1224** multiplicatis intercessoribus et intervenientibus quibusdam rationibus ~iis pepercit rex tribus M. PAR. *Min.* II 264; **s1274** decanus Lincolniensis .. pape tradidit cedulam ~iam oppressiones Anglicane ecclesie continentem W. GUISB. 214 (cf. 2 billa 4g); **s1295** dum rex noster ad regem Scottorum literas dirigeret, .. ~ia impotencie et quasi brevis responsio datur *Ib.* 264; cum .. quasdam

causas ~ias nobis in cancellariam .. miseritis quas insufficientes reputamus .. *Reg. Brev. Orig.* 265. **b** legati .. aliorum .. presulum cum ~iis apicibus .. concilio interfuerunt ORD. VIT. IX 3 p. 470; **1226** isti .. [canonici] litteras suas ~ias miserunt, ratihabitionem continentes *Reg. S. Osm.* II 61; **1284** littera ~ia pro priore Spaldingie *Doc. Eng. Black Monks* I 122; **s1264** mittebant literas ad regem barones .. ~ias .. et comminatorias W. GUISB. *Cont.* 314. **c** propter multimoda valetudinum .. discrimina missis ~iis ad ministrum generalem AD. MARSH *Ep.* 183; **1298** regraciatorium .. et ~ium in hiis que secuntur *Reg. Cant.* 297; **1341** ipse [J. archiep. Cant.] dictas ~ias nostras justa et vera .. continentes .. libellos famosos intitulat (*Pat*) BIRCHINGTON *Arch. Cant.* 36.

excusor [CL]

1 smith, metal-worker.

cum castrum illud .. conflandi ferrum locus esset aptissimus et fabris et ferri †exclusoribus [l. excusoribus] maxime repleretur *Chr. Evesham* 26 (= *NLA* I 376).

2 printer.

1573 ipsum Franciscum .. impressorem seu ~orem nostrum .. facimus *Pat* 1116 m. 39.

excusorium v. excussorium.

excusorius, of a metal-worker.

s1186 feretrum .. auro et argento arte †exclusoria [l. excusoria] splendide adornatum *G. S. Alb.* I 205.

excuss- v. et. excus-.

excussio [LL]

1 shaking (of tree). **b** shaking out (fig.).

c1191 concedo .. Willelmo [munitori] .. suum *restingtre* et residuum pomorum meorum post excucionem arborum gardini mei (*Ch. R. Com. Cestr.*) *Rec. Chester City, Earwaken MSS.* **b** Spiritus Sanctus .. habet esse a producentibus ipsum .. per quandam quasi ~onem sive expulsionem aut progressum DUNS *Ord.* II 290.

2 striking, knocking out; **b** (w. obj. gen.); **c** (w. subj. gen.).

ignis ex eo [sc. silice] ~one probatur *Ps.*-GROS. *Summa* 628. **b s1251** os .. comitis usque ad sanguinis effusionem .. et dentium ~onem tundentes M. PAR. *Maj.* V 220; per media capita usque ad ~onem cerebrorum .. fustibus eos percuciebant *NLA* I 474. **c** accesserat .. miraculo vestis siccitas, que, pauculis guttulis madefacta, sola digitorum ~one siccitatem recepit W. MALM. *Mir. Mariae* 151.

3 forcible seizure. **b** (illegal) rescue (of person); *cf. rescussio.*

pundbrech fit pluribus modis, emissione, evocatione, receptione, ~one (*Leg. Hen.* 40. 2) *GAS* 567; **1284** captus pro excucione cujusdam burse .. quam bursam excutit in Guyhald, Lond' *Gaol Del.* 35/2 m. 21d. **b 1240** venerunt ad clamorem et huthesium levatum super malefactores .. quibus A. fuit in auxilio ad ipsorum evasionem et ~onem *CurR* XVI 1368.

4 threshing.

Inst. Sempr. *lxvii (v. excussor a).

5 threshing out (fig.), debate, investigation.

non est homo qui non alicubi careat eo [sc. libero arbitrio] nunc deficiens arbitrii ~one, nunc discusse rei appetitu, aliquando rei appetite obtentu PULL. *Sent.* 720C; **s1254** asserens quod postmodum fieret super eandem taxationem inquisitio cum diligenti et districta ~one M. PAR. *Abbr.* 336; ad partem philsophie moralis ultimam que est de causarum et controversiarum ~one BACON *Tert. Sup.* 76.

excussitus v. 1 excutere.

excussor [LL], beater, thresher. **b** persecutor.

finito autumpno provideatur frater fidelis et ~ores qui eant per grangias ad excutiendum de unoquoque blado .. in ceteris grangiis interim excussione cessante *Inst. Sempr.* *lxvii. **b** ~or, accusator, *wrohtberend GlH* E 744.

excussorium [CL *adj. = for sifting*], implement for threshing or sifting; *cf. excudia* a. **b** (threshing) floor.

~ium, A. *a swyngelstok WW*; **1560** costus pistrini: .. pro duobus ~iis ij s. iiij d. (*Ac. Burs.*) *Ac. Coll. Wint.* **b** ~ium, *flor on huse* ÆLF. *Gl.*; excusorium, pavimentum, *flor GlH* E 740; ad trituratorium sive segetis ~ium, in quo manebat .. servus .. avenam siccans, perrexit *VSB* (*Cadoc* 7) 36.

1 excussus [LL]

1 knocking, striking against.

petulanti ~u ova omnia .. confringunt W. MALM. *GP* II 75 p. 161.

2 ? residue, amount shaken out (on voyage).

1248 ipsi marinelli habebunt ~um navis de eodem blado *CalIMisc* I 16.

2 excussus v. 1 excutere.

1 excutere [CL]

1 to shake. **b** to flap, flutter, ruffle. **c** (w. ref. to *Is.* xxxiii 15) to shake free (from). **d** to shake out (so as to dislodge contents).

torpore gravati / excutiunt sua membra viri WULF. *Swith.* II 646; quasi de alto evigilans sompno, excussit capud AD. EYNS. *Visio* 4. **b** papiliones alis excussis avolant *Simil. Anselmi* 72; coram divitibus tales non excute vestes D. BEC. 2493; [fenix] .. alas frequenter ~it *Quaest. Salern.* N 5. **c s1193** Rothomagensis archiepiscopus .. a munere manus ~iens, clamores equa lance dijudicans DICETO *YH* II 112; munera sibi oblata .. omnino respuens et manus inde prorsus ~iens GIR. *GE* II 27; **1284** clericos seculares, qui ab omni munere didicerint ~ere manus suas PECKHAM *Ep.* II 552. **d** emuncto, purgato, excusso *GlH* E 264; **c1237** plante super illam terram folia et fructus excusse dimittunt GROS. *Ep.* 46; *Babio* 184, J. BLUND *An.* 164 (v. 1 dumus b); **1268** excusserunt pirarium suum totius fructus pretii dimidie marce, et asportaverunt et excusserunt pomeria sua totius fructus precii v s. *Rec. Norw.* I 212; laxativa medela / viscera que laxet excutiatque lutum GARL. *Epith.* III 382; quando judex irritatur / ut offensa remittatur / excute marsupium WALT. WIMB. *Van.* 54 (cf. ib. 19: excussa bursa); neque aliquem pannum in auditu excuttere, sed fieri potest et debet ibidem [sc. in dormitorio] *Cust. Cant.* 188; **s1327** KNIGHTON I 446 (v. deplicare 1c).

2 to elicit.

lacrymas quas compunctio cordis excusserat TURGOT *Marg.* 1; **s1254** [monachorum] oppressiones si quis plenius enarraret lacrimas ~eret compassionis M. PAR. *Maj.* V 468.

3 to shake or knock (out or away from); **b** (w. pers. obj.; also fig.); **c** to shake or rouse (from sleep).

quia .. navem incaute religatam etiam de sinu tuti littoris ~it cum tempestas excrescit *V. Greg.* p. 76; *GlC* E 45, OSB. GLOUC. *Deriv.* 197 (v. edentare a); quid si ipse permittat eandem margaritam ab aliquo invido ~i de manu sua in caenum .. ANSELM (*CurD* I 19) I 85; utrique oculi supra mensam cecidere excussi *V. Kenelmi B* 82rb; vinum †excussitis [l. excussis] doliorum capitibus effuderunt *Dieul.* 144v. **b** [ut] nulla difficultas .. valeat eum a veritate, cui per fidem adhaesit, ~ere ANSELM (*Incarn. A*) I 285; tempestas que ~it hominem de ista navi [i.e. abrenuntiatione mundi] tentatio est AILR. *Serm.* 317B; cum .. mulier caudam levaret, socius meus a cauda excussus in lutum cecidet (*sic*) *Latin Stories* 18. **c** cum, somno excussa, videret ceteras pausantes circa se sorores BEDE *HE* IV 21 p. 257.

4 to shake off, repulse (partly fig.); **b** (w. ref. to *Gen.* xvii 40); **c** (w. abstr. obj.).

nec penetrare sinit stuprorum spicula pectus / sed procul excussit jaculatas fraude sagittas ALDH. *VirgV* 1157; arduus excusso quorum convitia telo / unus pontifici foedo sic ingerit ore FRITH. 789; timeo ne amicos hujusmodi .. facile fortuna ~iat J. SAL. *Ep.* 161 (144 p. 32); non plumam extrahendo, non pulverem, etsi nullus fuerit, ~iendo, sed inter alios palpones tibi scribendo placere constitui GIR. *IK pref.* p. 8; palpo .. / .. / nunc aptat clamidem .. / nunc plumam excutit ymaginariam WALT. WIMB. *Palpo* 72; solaris facies .. / .. / jubar recuperat, umbras excuciens *Id. Carm.* 302; comes Warwic' cum paucis campum tenens curiose viriliterque Scottos cum suis ~iens .. illesus permansit *Compilatio* 176. **b c710** excussum Aegyptiae servitutis jugum (*Ep. Ceolfridi*) BEDE *HE* V 21 p. 341; Christus .. jugum mortis ab homine excussit G. CRISPIN *Serm.* 114; **s1252** M. PAR. *Maj.* V 279 (v. desub a); **s1208** Anglici .. de sub jugo intolerabili talis tiranni cupientes jam ~ere *Flor. Hist.* II 137. **c** ~e cordis mei teporem ANSELM (*Or.* 16) III 67; debet monachus torporem suum ~ere *Id. Misc.* 360; **c1167** excussis curialibus nugis J. SAL. *Ep.* 169 (194); omnes ethici .. negligentiam conantur ~ere *Ib.* 250 (148); H. BOS. *Thom.* III 6 p. 193 (v. expellere 1a); ~iet [ME: *schaken of*] a se sompnum torporis *AncrR* 47.

5 to seize, snatch. **b** to recover. **c** to set free.

qui sanguinis hominum prodigus infesta ~it latrocinia W. MALM. *Mir. Mariae* 191; mors .. / .. puellas speciosas / .. / tenerosas excutit WALT. WIMB. *Van.* 144; **1284** (v. excussio 3a). **b** de omni furtivo pecore .. si a latronum manibus ~iatur [AS: *gyf hit man æt ðeofes handa ahret*] (*Quad.*) *GAS* 391; qui namium excussit, reddat, et overseunessa sit .. ~ere namium est si quis viam tollat et avertat retro namium suum (*Leg. Hen.* 51. 7, 8) *Ib.* 573; **1167** Q. debet v m. pro namis excussis *Pipe* 156. **c** si .. videas eundem virum ita tenentem arietem ut ipse aries sese de manibus ejus ~iat ANSELM (*Lib. Arb.* 7) I 219; qualiter rex Ricardus excussit a Turcis apud Darum mille ducentos Christianos captivos *Itin. Ric.* V 7 *rub.*; Deo .. dispensante .. per regem Ricardum excussi sunt a servitute *Ib.*

6 to thresh. **b** to beat (wool).

in collectione .. frugum .. fratres .. decimas ponant separatim, et cum .. fuerint ~ienda primo .. ~antur decime, et summa .. proveniens annotetur dica. .. deinde cum relique fruges fuerint ~iende .. *Inst. Sempr.* *lxviii; **a1168** debet arare ter in anno et ~ere bladum semel in yeme *Med. E. Anglia* 279; **1218** detinuit eum in prisona sua .. et misit servientes suos ad domum suam .. et excussit bladum suum *Eyre Yorks* 371; debent .. invenire j hominem ad ~iendum segetem abbatis *Reg. S. Aug.* 27; **1251** ~it etiam de frumento et siligine xxiiij garbas *Cart. Rams.* I 310. **b** in virgis et clatis ad lanam ~iendam emptis et cariandis xij d. in xj saccis dim. j petr. lane ad tascam ~iendis xlj s. iij d. ob. *Ac. Beaulieu* 220.

7 to examine, investigate.

~e Virgilium .. et ibi [ethice] invenies condituram J. SAL. *Met.* 854C.

2 †excutere, *f.l.*.

oriundus †excuteras [? l. extiteras] de tam digna stirpe regali FAVENT 15.

exdudum [al. div.], previously, some time ago.

12.. ~um ordinata *Becket to Langton* 193.

exdux [cf. CL dux], ex-duke.

s1107 Henricus ~x, affectans repetere ducatum, occupat oppidum Aquisgrani (SIG. GEMBLOUX) TORIGNI *Chr.* 88.

exebonus v. exhebenus.

exebriare [cf. CL ebriare], to make helplessly drunk, inebriate (fig.).

si [regem] decubuisse cognosceret, .. potatores lectissimos potione pavoris ~iaret Angligenas DEVIZES 41.

execare v. excaecare, 2 exsecare. **execr-** v. exsecr-. **execuscio** v. exsecutio. **execut-** v. exsecut-. **exedere** v. exesse.

1 exedra v. excetra.

2 exedra (exh-) [CL], exedra, recess or bay with seat. **b** ante-room. **c** choir.

~a, sella; .. ~a, locus subselliorum; .. ~a, exterior sedes ubi sedit plebs; edra dicitur interior sedis (*sic*) ubi papa sedit cum communionem dat ad populum *GlC* E 366, 420, 562–3; ~ae, scabelli ad cibos vel subselli *Gl. Leid.* 35. 61; *a treleswyndowe*, cancellus, festra, fenestra cancellata, ~a *CathA*. **b** hinc post modicum in secretiorem transfertur ~am ipsis vestimentorum insigniis .. induendus AD. EYNS. *Hug.* V 20 p. 228. **c** in exhedra monachorum in templo (trito satis nomine chorum vocant) subsellia .. posuit FERR. *Kinloss* 75.

exefegesis v. epexegesis.

exegematicus [LL < ἐξηγηματικός], narrative.

BEDE *AM* 140 (v. enarrativus).

exegesis [LL < ἐξήγησις], exegesis, explanation, exposition.

†extentesion [l. exegeseon], †quaessionum [l. expositio quaestionum] *GlC* E 412 (cf. *Gl. Leid.* 30. 66: †exenteseon, quaestionum); ~in in Divi Augustini regulam conscripsit FERR. *Kinloss* 40.

exeleogeneus v. exallogeneus. **exeleos** v. exallus. **exelerarius** v. excellararius. **exelus** v. exhelus.

exemphracticus [cf. LL emphracticus], (med.) deobstructive.

exemfracticum, i. opilacionem solvens *Alph.* 56; *Ib.* (v. emphracticus).

exemplabilis [LL], that may be formed after an exemplar or from a model.

non enim exemplar et exemplatum referuntur ad invicem, nec idea et ideatum, sed exemplar ad ~e et idea ad ideabile dicuntur ad invicem relative sicut creativum et creabile W. ALNWICK *QD* 104; nemo .. audeat negare ydeas in mente Dei, nisi sciat vere salvare Deum posse proprie et distincte valde intelligere atque racionabiliter formare, exemplare, et producere res extra producibiles ut sunt sic distincte et proprie valde intelligibiles, formabiles, ~es et producibiles racionabiliter, negando proprie proprias et simpliciter necessarias rerum extra producibilium raciones exemplaria, intelligibilitates, et producibilitates WYCL. *Univ.* 5.

exemplar [CL]

1 example, instance. **b** sample, specimen; *v. et. exemplaris* 1b. **c** (gram. & rhet.) illustration, paradigm. *V. et. exemplum* 1.

ne .. praeterita saeculorum ~aria solummodo perscruter ALDH. *Met.* 2 p. 65; **a988** caetera ~aria agiae scripturae (*Ep. ad Archiep.*) *Mem. Dunst.* 372; quadam nocte hujus visionis ~ar post pia precum studia .. conspexit B. *V. Dunst.* 29; quis sacrum esse dubitet quem tot sacrilegiorum ~aria .. predocent GIR. *TH* III 24; per ista pauca ~aria patet fidelibus .. quomodo respondendum est ad .. versucias .. Antichristi WYCL. *Versut.* 103. **b 1341** de quibus vino et frumento ad .. probandum ~ar presencialiter sibi ibidem demonstravit *Plusc.* IX 38. **c** da ~aria verborum ionico minori subdita ALDH. *PR* 131; dicito participiorum ~ar *Ib.* 136; potes verbum transponere in nomen et nomen substantivum in adjectivum .. ut per quedam ~aria apercius pululabant, verbi gracia [etc.] *Dictamen* 339.

2 exemplar, model, pattern; **b** (w. ref. to person). **c** original. *V. et. exemplum* 3.

Romani .. fortia formidoloso populo monita tradunt ~aria instituendorum armorum relinquunt GILDAS *EB* 18; tuum ~ar, quod scriptum est in tabula .. scribe ÆLF. BATA 4. 16 p. 40; quotcunque .. radices simul colligere .. volueris .. juxta hoc ~ar multiplicare poteris ROB. ANGL. *Alg.* 102; factus est liber iste, qui est nobis vivendi positus ~ar GARL. *SM pref.* 87; **1381** in sol. facta uni pictori de Novo Castro pro pictura unius volucris S. Cuthberti pro ~are pro *le rerdos*, xij d. *Ac. Durh.* 591. **b** oportebat vos imitari illum .. qui .. bonitatis et humilitatis .. invictum ~ar est GILDAS *EB* 74; gloriosum illustris Agnae ~ar ALDH. *VirgP* 45; talis erat ~ar patientiae Job BEDE *Hom.* I 17. 265; Calixtus papa .. virtutum ~ar emicuit ORD. VIT. VI 27 p. 421; boni propositi a teneris annis ~ar Sictricius G. FONT. *Inf. S. Edm. prol.*; Maria que mulieribus omnibus esse debet ~ar [ME: *for bisne*] *AncrR* 19; salve, forma pietatis, / exemplar humilitatis *Mir. Hen. VI* I *prol.* p. 2. **c** W. FITZST. *Thom.* 29 (v. echo).

3 (phil. & theol.) archetype, idea. *V. et. exemplum* 5b.

que .. Plato .. in Thimeo demonstrare conatur, mundo opificem et materiam et finem et ~ar et formam assignans BALSH. *AD rec. 2* 164; anima .. quasi reverberata acie contemplationis sue in seipsa reperit quod diffinit, nam et ejus ~ar in ipsa est, exemplum vero in actualibus .. illa itaque ~aria cogitabilia quidem sunt et quasi phantasie et umbre existentium secundum Aristotelem J. SAL. *Met.* 878C; in prima causa res potentialiter sunt solum ... 'unum' .. et 'multa' non sunt differentie entis potentia sed entis actu et ita accidit eis ut ibi sunt esse unum vel multa; sunt tamen ibi per modum ~aris unius HALES *Sent.* I 71; BACON VII 113 (v. exemplare 3a); MIDDLETON *Sent.* I 73 (v. exemplaritas); si loquamur de cognitione veritatis, respondetur quod sicut est duplex ~ar, creatum et increatum, secundum Platonem in Timeo (viz. ~ar .. creatum et noncreatum: '~ar creatum' est species universalis causata a re, '~ar increatum' est idea in mente divina) ita duplex est conformitas ad ~ar et duplex veritas DUNS *Ord.* III 127–8; W. ALNWICK *QD* 104 (v. exemplabilis); sacrilegium .. esset dicere Deum intueri extra se ~ar sui ad extra producti WYCL. *Univ.* 5.

4 copy, transcript. *V. et. exemplum* 6a.

~ar praefatae epistulae hoc est BEDE *HE* I 32; **c747** direxi ~aria epistolarum S. Gregorii quas de scrinio Romanae ecclesiae excepi BONIF. *Ep.* 75; **1072** reliqua .. [privilegia] reliquorum tam autentica quam eorum ~aria in .. combustione .. sunt absumpta LANFR. *Ep.* 3 (4); **a1103** ~ar litterarum quas regi mitto, vobis transmitto ANSELM (*Ep.* 306) IV 228; textus est pro majori parte corruptus horribiliter in ~ari vulgato, hoc est Parisiensi BACON *Min.* 330.

5 recurrence, repetition (of event).

H. CANTOR 7v. (v. exemplum 5).

exemplare [LL]

1 to adduce as example or instance. **b** to show by giving example. *V. et. exemplicare* 1, 2 *exemplificare* 1.

ea que dico .. sunt contra ~ata et consueta et vulgata BACON *Tert.* 25. **b** [Wyclyff] ad ~andum et probandum quod panis qui prefuit in altari ante consecracionem remanet in sacramento post consecracionem posuit multiplex exemplum *Ziz.* 107; certum est quod ipsa [ecclesia triumphans] errare non poterit, ut ~atur inferius WYCL. *Chr. & Antichr.* 654.

2 to adduce as model; **b** (pass., w. *ab*) to be modelled on. **c** (w. ref. to person) to exemplify.

si in exemplaribus scripture nostre regibus sic, quid de tanta qui fuerunt et sunt ~atorum regum multitudine, quorum .. gesta .. in annalibus .. [non] sunt descripta? H. BOS. *LM* 1323B; sacerdocium Romanum factum cum signis et ritibus .. est parve virtutis, nullibi in sacra scriptura ~atum *Concl. Loll. XII* 2. **b** cyclus decemnovenalis, qui ~atus est a lunari BACON VI 123; sicut accidens non est ens nisi quia entis .. sic nec usus creature nisi quia ab usu Domini ~atur WYCL. *Dom. Div.* 33. **c** **s68** Linum et Cletum Petrus ordinavit ad [e]xemplanda exteriora ministeria *AS Chr.*; in .. vita .. quam dominus noster Jhesus in persona propria ~avit UHTRED *Mon. V.* 377; Christus legem evangelicam ad illam regulam ~avit WYCL. *Mand. Div. prol.* 202; Fraunces laboravit / ut posteri sic facerent primus exemplavit (*Contra Relig.* I 179) *Mon. Francisc.* I 597.

3 (phil. & theol.) to form after an (ideal) exemplar; *v. et. 2 exemplificare* 3; **b** (p. ppl. as sb. n.).

de exemplari est loqui dupliciter uno modo per comparationem ad ~antem et sic est unum; alio modo per comparationem ad exemplata et sic sunt plura BACON VII 113; MIDDLETON *Sent.* I 73 (v. exemplaritas); in quantum creatura est ~ata et refertur ad Deum, in quantum est causa exemplaris DUNS *Ord.* III 176; omne exemplatum habet causam ~antem et omne habens causam est causatum W. ALNWICK *QD* 96; 'per' significat circumstanciam cause efficientis vel ~antis ... prius .. est forma exemplaris ~ans creaturam quam forma intrinsice inexistens eidem WYCL. *Form.* 164; *Id. Univ.* 5 (v. exemplabilis). **b** est .. cognitio in universali per distinctionem et simplicitatem illius universalis exemplaris in quo sunt ~ata BACON VII 96; exemplar ~ato conformatur *Ib.* 101; W. ALNWICK *QD* 96 (v. 3a supra); *ib.* 104 (v. exemplabilis); exemplum ~ato non correspondet, sed discordat in multis CONWAY *Def. Mend.* 1420 (*recte* 1320).

4 to copy. **b** (p. ppl. as sb. n.) copy. *V. et.* 2 *exemplificare* 4, *explicare* 2.

799 tu vero ~a illud *Ep. Alcuin.* 183; **1306** eas [sc. litteras] transcripsi, ~avi .. nil addens, nil minuens *Reg. Carl.* I 259; **1435** quia [literas] .. integras invenimus .. easdem .. ~avimus et transumpsimus, ~amus et transumimus per presentes .. *Reg. Heref.* 188; **1465** evidenciam .. per notarium .. transcribi, copiari, et ~ari .. mandavimus *Reg. Aberd.* II 315. **b** **1219** (v. deponere 4a); **1240** eorum [sc. instrumentorum] ~ata .. penes nos retinemus *Reg. Malm.* I 393.

exemplaris [LL < CL = *copy*]

1 exemplary, given as example. **b** (as sb. n.) sample; *v. et. exemplar* 1b, *exemplum* 1b.

facilior est ~is distinctio quam ut opera disciplinali indigeat BALSH. *AD rec. 2* 173; de bono solitudinis per raciones ~es *AncrR proem.* 2. **b** **1433** quoddam ~e de tissuis de auro *Cl* 116 m. 16.

2 exemplary, serving as (moral) example; **b** (of abstr.).

vobis .. presertim exemplum dedit ~is vir iste (*Ep. ad Archiep. Cant.*) H. BOS. *Thom. pref.* p. 156; *Id. LM* 1323B (v. exemplare 2a); constantis fidei datur exemplaris imago / Eligius sanctus GARL. *Tri. Eccl.* 38; ut fidelibus et infidelibus ~iores se preberent OCKHAM *Pol.* II 478; **s1379** factum .. memorabile .. illius .. fortitudinis ~is [v. l. exemplar] .. Hugonis C. WALS. *HA* I 405; **1431** ne .. pompose .. sed cum ea moderacione et honestate, que viros ~es decet, accedatis (*Reg. Exon.*) *Conc.* III 519a; **1573** obitus fratris Johannis .. devoti valde et ~is (*Necrolog.*) *Mon. Francisc.* II 136. **b** ad edificationem populi ad ~em universorum sanctificationem AD. MARSH *Ep.* 100; **1295** [ecclesia Cantuariensis] ut fons luminis honestatis radios ~es cujuscumque decoris emittens *Reg. Cant.* 68; **1319** antiquorum patrum ~is sanxit auctoritas, quod .. *FormOx* 49; spiritualiter pascere oves non contingit nisi tripliciter, sc. salutari doctrina, et vita ~i, et disciplina .. regulari OCKHAM *Dial.* 484.

3 (phil.) archetypal, ideal. **b** (w. *causa* or *forma*) formal cause.

[Deus] non solum vivit per omnia secula ~ia que sunt raciones ~es seculorum temporalium, sed et per omnia secula temporalia (KYN.) *Ziz.* 101. **b** dicunt quod hoc convenit eis ab alio, sc. a Deo, sed non effective secundum genus cause efficientis, sed secundum genus cause ~aris T. SUTTON *Quodl.* 374; res predicamentales, antequam sint in actu, .. reali relacione referuntur ad Deum tamquam ad causam ~arem ab eterno, .. licet non tamquam ad causam efficientem *Ib.*; causa ~aris DUNS *Ord.* III 176; forma ~aris WYCL. *Form.* 164 (v. exemplare 3a).

exemplaritas, exemplarity, archetypal quality.

omnis racio cognoscendi formatur ab ipso [sc. Deo] ut ~ate PECKHAM *QA* 96; racionem enim ~atis omnium eidem [sc. Deo] attribuit [Plato] vel idee in mente intelligencie respectu corporalium compositorum *Ps.*-GROS. *Summa* 354; primo modo procedit creatura a Deo secundum racionem ~atis, quia Deus produxit creaturam secundum exemplar suum, quod habet in mente divina. secundo modo procedit Filius per modum ~atis, quia ipse Filius procedit a Patre per modum exemplandi MIDDLETON *Sent.* I 73.

exemplariter

1 exemplarily, by way of example. *V. et. exemplatim.*

BALSH. *AD rec. 2* 44 (v. commonitive); contingit .. in podagra, ut ~er doceamus, quia quedam est vagativa, quedam quiescens et fixa GILB. VII 310. 1; in proportionibus numerorum tota ratio numeri ~er explicatur BACON *Maj.* I 104; ut ~er loquar *Id. Gram. Gk.* 27; potuit ~er hoc dixisse BRADW. *CD* 720D.

2 by force of (moral) example.

eorum familiari contubernio ~er inflammati W. MALM. *Glast.* 23; **1252** regulares observantias astringimur observare et ad observandum subditos ~er invitare *Doc. Eng. Black Monks* I 49; ut .. sacerdotes Christi .. ~er revocent seculares a candente cupidine *Ziz.* 482; jam episcopi non predicant vocaliter et ~er GASCOIGNE *Loci* 191; mulieris viro subjeccio ydealiter ~erque divino lucebat in verbo FORTESCUE *NLN* II 20.

3 as an archetype, ideally.

dupliciter accipitur exemplare: uno modo ut ~er intelligere, sicut artifex intelligit domum juxta exemplar in anima W. ALNWICK *QD* 104; consummatus est numerus ecclesiasticorum ordinum, qui sunt ~er in mundi sacerdotio in illis choris angelicis, imaginarie in humana hierarchia COLET *Sacr. Eccl.* 48.

exemplarium [CL], copy, transcript.

forte ibi in antiquioribus ~iis 'assumpti hominis' positum fuit ALCUIN (*Adv. Elipand*) *Dogm.* 265A; **798** obsecro .. ut ~ium illius libelli domno dirigatur apostolico *Id. Ep.* 149; **1340** de cruce universitatis cum pertinentibus, de caucionibus et ~iis *FormOx* 118; **a1347** libros et ~ia et summas cistarum et munimenta et cartas *StatOx* 148.

exemplarius, copyist, scribe. *V. et. exemplator* 2.

1246 hiis testibus .. Waltero Aurifabro .. Rogero ~io *Cart. Hosp. S. John* I 89; **c1275** Martino ~io *Ib.* 113 (cf. ib. 39 [**1293**]: sacramentum .. Martini *le Samplarier*); **12..** Willelmo de Aston', exemplar' *AncD* A 9681.

exemplasticus [LL], adhesive.

virtus est illi [sinopide] stiptica et †exfervatica [v. l. exserantica] et †exphastica [v. l. ~a] *Alph.* 121.

exemplatim, exemplarily, by way of example. *V. et. exemplariter* 1.

cui cum tunc eruditorum suorum aliquis in medium ~im proponeret multos ab aula et alios multos a seculo ad pastorale culmen assumptos .. respondit .. H. BOS. *Thom.* III 17.

exemplatio [LL], service as example.

in ista velacione, ubi non est tantummodo similitudo, sed imitacio et ~o passiva, impossibile est idem absolutum referri ad diversa DUNS *Ord.* III 215; quis .. dubitat, quin Christus instar hominum in statu innocencie non transivit per hec temporalia, capiendo eorum usum, nisi de quanto fuit necessarium ad beatitudinem et Christianorum ~onem? WYCL. *Civ. Dom.* III 90; de duodecim tribubus Israel, de quibus .. propter ~onem in moribus .. facit scriptura singulariter mencionem *Id. Ver.* III 247.

exemplativus, exemplary, archetypal.

omnia que sunt .. per bonum et optimum sunt .. et propter ipsum et per ipsum et in ipso omne principium ~um, consummativum, intellectuale BRADW. *CD* 150D (= *Ps.*-Dionysius *Div. Nom.* 5).

exemplator

1 one who shows by example.

quartus liber .. docet auctorem .. fuisse .. in expropriacione temporalium .. ~orem pariter et doctorem AD. EASTON *Def.* 679.

2 copyist, scribe. *V. et. exemplarius.*

1275 Martino ~ore *Cart. Hosp. S. John* I 86; **1291** R. de G., qui se alias coram Martino ~ore, coronatore de Abindon, cognovit esse falsatorem monete *Gaol Del.* 87 r. 1*d.*; **1298** de dono Agathe filie Martini ~oris Oxonie *Cart. Hosp. S. John* I 195.

exemplicare [cf. LL exemplare]

1 to show by example. *V. et. exemplare* 1, 2 *exemplificare* 1.

de ceteris .. caracteribus, de quibus non ~avimus, faciendum est THURKILL *Abac.* f. 56.

2 to copy. *V. et. exemplare* 4a, 2 *exemplificare* 4.

1427 tenorem irrotulamenti .. duximus ~andam *Reg. S. Aug.* 368.

1 exemplificare v. examplificare.

2 exemplificare [cf. LL exemplare]

1 to adduce as example. **b** to show by giving example (also absol.). *V. et. exemplare* 1, *exemplicare* 1.

utimur tribus argumentis pessimis pro omnibus que facimus et dicimus, sc. hoc ~atum est, hoc consuetum est, hoc vulgatum est, ergo faciendum est BACON *Tert.* 71; **1377** non est ~ata potestas a Christo .. excommunicandi subditos (WYCL.) WALS. *HA* I 355 (= *Ziz.* 251: exemplata). **b** in quo [libro] virginitatis gloriam prius predicat et postea non difficilem esse per sanctorum celibatum ~at W. MALM. (*V. Aldh.*) *GP* V 196; quoniam ~andi gratia quedam posteris mandare decrevimus *Chr. Battle* f. 84v.; scio .. quo tendas. non hoc modo michi ~abis CRICKLADE *Spec. Fid.* III 5; refert Tullius .. et ~at de quodam rege qui .. GIR. *PI* I 7; vetera pro novis .. et sophisticum pro non sophistico multipliciter a medicis recipiuntur, sicut ~avi BACON IX 154; volo adhuc ~are de aliis vocabulis *Id. Gram. Gk.* 68; de talibus veritatibus .. ~are nituntur, dicentes quod talis veritas est illa OCKHAM *Dial.* 412; ut de C D ~atum est supra *Ps.*-OCKHAM *Princ. Theol.* 56; magister meus est illius opinionis quod antiquitas scripture maximam auctoritatem facit .. sicut ~at in cartis, in quibus .. (KYN.) *Ziz.* 4; quemadmodum ~avit Sanctus Spiritus per apostolos in Matthia NETTER *DAF* I 258a.

2 to give or serve as (moral) example (also absol.).

W. de E. qui non solum sermone sed in ~ata devotione verbum Dei .. predicaverat ECCLESTON *Adv. Min.* 33; sic .. proficit dolor de quanto pacat personam contra quam delictum fuit commissum, de quanto ~at ad retrahendum

a talibus ex ejus nocumento Wycl. *Act.* 86; si sic proficeret recte predicando, sancte ~ando, .. sobrie inter homines vivendo Gascoigne *Loci* 51.

3 (phil. & theol.) to form after an (ideal) exemplar. *V. et. exemplare* 3a.

omnes veritates create ab ipso ~ate, ipso .. agnito ut ratio exemplaris eorumdem, cognoscuntur, sicut visa luce illa videntur que ad eadem illustrantur Knapwell *Not.* 188*n*.

4 to copy. *V. et. exemplare* 4, *exemplicare* 2.

1284 proferunt cartam Willelmi regis conquestoris quam cartam dominus rex nunc inspexit et ~avit *PQW* 93a; **1335** nos .. tenorem litterarum nostrarum .. per inspeccionem rotulorum duximus exemplificand' *RScot* 358a; **1390** ~atum per Robertum de F. et Thomam de S., clericos *Reg. Heref.* 48; **1416** fecit ~ari in scaccario .. regis .. sub sigillo .. regis inquisicionem *Ib.* 94; **1435** super fide dictorum transumptorum et ~atorum adhibenda et jurium predictorum clausura Amund. II 58; **1542** tenorem decreti predicti duximus ~andum per presentes *Deeds Balliol* 165.

exemplificatio

1 exemplifying, citing an example.

non est vera specificacio, sed magis ~o et explanacio obscuri Bacon XV 169.

2 giving of (moral) example.

virtuose operaciones .. sc. sacramentorum administracio, .. boni ~o, agendorum consiliacio Gascoigne *Loci* 112.

3 copying. **b** (leg.) exemplification, copy.

1354 domino W. de W. pro ~one del Convenit xx s. *Ac. Durh.* 554; **1453** in vadiis .. Roberti T. .. pro ~one actus de Suthampton .. et literis patentibus (*DL Ac. Ver.*) *JRL Bull.* XL 414; **1549** (v. 2 conquestio c). **b** s**1342** ~o recordi et processus decime decimarum manerii de M. (*Chronol.*) Elmh. *Cant.* 64; **1390** prout littere patentes .. avi nostri de ~one cartarum .. testantur *Reg. Heref.* 48; **1494** per .. literas domini H. nuper regis Anglie V .. de ~one diversorum recordorum et brevium in communi banco *Entries* 128; **1583** ~o (*in marg.*) *Pat* 1236 m. 29.

exemplificatorius, (w. *litterae*) letters of exemplification.

1504 auctoritate ejusdem parliamenti .. ac etiam de recordo irrotulari et superinde literas ~ias validas et efficaces *RScot* 564b.

exemplum [CL]

1 (adduced) example, instance. **b** sample; *v. et. exemplaris* 1b. **c** (gram. & rhet.) illustration, paradigm. *V. et. exemplar* 1.

quid immoramur in ~is veteribus? Gildas *EB* 73; [epistulae] quas .. ~i gratia protelaveram Aldh. *Met.* 3; portentuose, monstruose, ~i causa cum sex digitis nati *Gl. Leid.* 1. 95; quod si per ~a consideremus, clarius apparebit Anselm (*Proc. Sp.* 1) II 181; ne hanc artem aliquis error incurrere arbitretur tale damus ~um Rob. Angl. *Alg.* 122; erit horum facilior per ~a cognitio Balsh. *AD* 85. **b** **1344** (*selling grain by samples*) per ~a *Cal. Pl. Mem. Lond.* 160. **c** epitriti promulgentur ~a Aldh. *PR* 137.

2 simile, comparison; **b** (as literary genre) exemplum, anecdote; **c** (log., as mode of argument); **d** demonstration, proof.

portum monasterii petisse ex hujus vitae naufragio nudus evadens .. humilitatis ~o usus gratissimo dixit .. *V. Greg.* p. 76; ne quis balneis ablutus .. per lutosum iter incedat .. per hoc specimen .. temet ipsum intuere et ad correctionem tui hoc ~um converte Ord. Vit. X 23 p. 139. **b** paradigma, narratio per ~a ortans aliquem aut deterrens *Gl. Leid.* 28. 26; ~um hominis cujusdam, de quo in ~is continetur quod .. *Latin Stories* 129. **c** ~um est quando probatur unum particulare per aliud, ut 'in scolis est doctor non sorte sed arte, igitur in navi elegendus est gubernator non sorte sed arte' Bacon XV 303; *Ib.* 289 (v. enthymema). **d** examen, ~um, expositio *GlC* E 490; *Ib.* A 668 (v. apodixis).

3 pattern, model. **b** (moral) example; **c** (w. defining gen.); **d** (w. ref. to deeds contrasted w. words); **e** (w. *in*, pejoratively). *V. et. exemplar* 2.

GlC D 330, 360 (v. documentum 1); alfini .. sunt cornuti ~o episcopi J. Waleys *Schak.* 464. **b** juxta ~a patrum antiquorum .. administrare curavit Bede *HE* IV 3 p. 207; clara .. exempla futuris / prebuit Wulf. *Swith. pref.* 301; c**1077** gloria .. Deo, cui vita vestra sic placuit ut eam ad ~um exaltaret Anselm (*Ep.* 78) III 201; juxta illum qui negligenter vixit, ejus ~o a bono opere non defecit (*Ib.* 231) IV 138; inclusus diu gemuit, ~umque posteris ne similibus inhient dereliquit Ord. Vit. VII 8 p. 192; [Christus] reliquit nobis ~um ut sequamur vestigia ejus M. Rievaulx (*Ep.*) 63. **c** ad ~um rigidae conversationis et ardui formam propositi animos militantium Christo instigantes Aldh. *VirgP* 7; episcopi .. qui debent esse forma et ~um aliis canonicae religionis Anselm (*Ep.* 427) V 374; ~um sanctitatis Ord. Vit. XII 21 p. 388. **d** populum tam ~a quam verba docentes Gildas *EB* 76; plures nam Christo convertit .. turmas / exemplo simul et celebri rumore coruscans Aldh. *VirgV* 2112; c**1077** efficacius bonum ~o quam verbo persuadetur Anselm (*Ep.* 80) III 203; tam verbis quam scriptis et salutaribus ~is subjectos erudiit Ord. Vit. VIII 6 p. 305. **e** parcas larga manus damnans Albania, Scotos / ponit in exemplum dapsilitate sua Garl. *Tri. Eccl.* 33; **1478** quisque paccarius huic ordinacioni contraveniens sic punietur ut aliis sit in ~um et faciet emendam parti gravate *Foed.* XII 81a.

4 mode.

fratres .. me .. precati sunt ut quaedam .. sub quodam eis meditationis ~o describerem Anselm (*Mon. prol.*) I 7.

5 (leg.) precedent. **b** (phil.) archetype, original; *v. et. exemplar* 3.

professione determinata est que non habuit ~um, nec puto habituram exemplar H. Cantor 7v.; nec vult rex Eboracensi ecclesie .. hoc esse in prejudicium nec Cantuariensi in ~um *Ib.* 19v.; quod presens concessio nostra de feodis .. non trahatur in ~o quovis modo *BBAdm* I 375. **b** liquet .. eum in singulorum creatione venerabilis ~i normam secutum, cum cuncta superno ducat ab ~o Alf. Angl. *Cor* 15. 1.

6 copy, transcript; *v. et. exemplar* 4. **b** (phil.) copy of archetype, embodiment of ideal.

c**1168** vobis mittimus ~a cartarum quas vidistis .. quia ipsas originales propter varia pericula circumferre non audent *Reg. Plympton* 162. **b** J. Sal. *Met.* 878c (v. exemplar 3).

exempticius [cf. CL empticius], bought.

~ius, pecuniae emptus *GlH* E 488; Aldredus .. prebendas illas de terra ~ia fecit, set regias consuetudines vel exactiones ab illis emere non potuit, quibus vendere non licebat H. Cantor 8v.

exemptio [CL]

1 taking out, removal.

Stephani regis rebus humanis ~o Gir. *EH* II 31.

2 exemption, immunity; **b** (eccl.); **c** (personal); **d** (mon., esp. from episcopal jurisdiction); **e** (national).

1203 libertates et ~ones secularium exactionum .. [a] Scottorum regibus .. vobis indultas *Reg. Newbattle* 223; **1266** libertates, immunitates, privilegia, et ~ones tam in victualibus vendendis .. quam aliis .. vobis concessa *MunAcOx* 31; **1267** de cartis .. ~onis et libertatis ne ponantur impetrantes in assisis juratis .. provisum est quod .. (*Marlb.* 14) *StRealm* I 23; **1309** quo ad ~onem de terris suis disclamat et bene cognoscit quod .. rex debet habere de terris hominum suorum felonium, annum, et vastum *PQW* 828b; s**1399** propter privilegium ~onis patrie in qua .. facinoroci .. ad illam patriam tanquam nidum facinorum .. receptari solebant Ad. Usk 26. **b** s**1202** causa nostra .. favorabilis est et maxime apud ecclesiam Romanam .. que etiam diligit ~ones *Chr. Evesham* 114; **1321** si ~ones .. processu temporis pariunt dissolutionis materiam *Mon. Hib. & Scot* 216b; cum privilegia et ~o que conceduntur a Deo et a natura magis debeant .. servari quam que indulgentur a papa Ockham *Pol.* I 104; cum omnibus .. terris, ecclesiis, .. immunitatibus, privilegiis, ~onibus, indultis *Conc. Scot.* I cccviii. **c** Hugo .. Rothomagensis archiepiscopus .. personalem optinuit ~onem Diceto *Chr.* 6. **d** S. Dionysii cenobium .. a Parisiensis ecclesie subjectione .. se per ~onem emancipavit Gir. *Spec.* II 16; orta .. inter abbatem .. de M. .. ex parte una et episcopum .. de S. ex altera .. super ~one monasterii questione *Reg. Malm.* I 386; **1245** ecclesia de S. .. a jurisdictione episcopali .. libera et exempta .. ecclesia de F. consimili libertate et ~one *Ch. Sal.* 293; [Sergius I] concessit ~onem monasterii Malmesburie Sancto Adelmo *Eul. Hist.* I 224; s**1312** fuit divulgatum quod .. religiosi exempti ad jus transirent commune; unde solus ordo Cisterciensis papam adiit .. pro ~one sua pristina pacifice obtinenda Wals. *HA* I 127. **e** per rebellionem regni Francie vel ~onem papa non debuit aliqua potestate privari Ockham *Dial.* 888.

exemptor [CL = *extractor*], (eccl.) one who claims exemption.

sicut non mitre .. nec anuli nisi solemnibus diebus ad obsequia divina solum ~oribus hujusmodi dicunt indulti Gir. *Spec.* II 29 p. 92.

exeniare, to present (a gift) to, to bribe. *V. et. xeniare.*

Raimundus miles, a venatu rediens et aucupatu, perdicibus aliisque carnibus ferinis dominam ~at Gerv. Tilb. I 15; quod .. testibus contra ipsum necessariis nuntios continue mitteret et frequenter eos exenniaret *Proc. A. Kyteler* 30; .. qui pecuniam magnam undique mutuans ad magnam summam, inutiliter papam eam ~avit et presentavit *Hist. Roff.* f. 99 (= *Anglia Sacra* I 375).

exeniolum, small gift, token. *V. et. xeniolum.*

p**754** de nostro .. vili vestitu parva exseniola direximus tuo cultui quanquam indigna (Cyneheard) *Ep. Bonif.* 114; s**1179** cum .. ~a quedam in signum dilectionis accepisset a rege Diceto *YH* I 433 (cf. B. Cotton *Hist.* 79: exenniola); [Beda] nonnullis de fratribus familiariorem declarans amicitiam, ~a quedam secretius est largitus M. Par. *Maj.* I 335 (cf. W. Malm. *GR* I 61: xeniola).

exenium [LL < *prosthetic* e + CL xenium < ξένιον], gift, present; **b** (between host and guest); **c** (spec. of food); **d** (dist. by occasion of presentation). **e** customary payment. **f** bribe, extorted payment. **g** benefit. *V. et. xenium.*

601 parva .. ~ia transmisi (*Lit. Papae*) Bede *HE* I 32 p. 69 (cf. *CS* 6 [†**605** (12c)]: quod mihi xenium de domino papa .. directum fuerat); caelestis munificentiae stipendium potius quam humanae liberalitatis ~ium [v. l. xenium; *gl.*: donum, *lac*] Aldh. *VirgP* 38 p. 290; direxit devotio mea .. nonnulla munuscula, id est caucum argenteum intus deauratum pensantem libras tres et semis et due repte. et haec ~ia .. direximus (*Lit. Regis Cantiae*) *Ep. Bonif.* 105 p. 230; non formido minas, exaenia nulla capesso Frith. 1103; **1044** in suo vivere cum prosperitate semper istum ~ium obtineat *CD* 770; premiserat viros .. cum regiis donariis et exenniis que et regem dare et recipere cum honore deceret Gir. *Æthelb.* 5; **1244** dicunt quod semper ad exenna facienda et ad honores debent talliari sicut alii de eadem villa excepto arreragio firme ville *CurR* 131 m. 11; **1275** purpresture .. sine emendacione remanserunt per potestatem majorum civitatis .. pro donis et exhenniis que receperunt *Hund.* I 313; s**1199** Rotomagensibus .. cor suum pro ~io transmisit Wend. I 283; primo aperuerunt [magi] exennium [ME: *þe presenz*] quod portarunt *AncrR* 49; affluxerunt loco xeniorum [MSS: ~iorum, enceniorum] et munerum locoque donorum et jocalium cenulenti quaterni ac decrepiti codices R. Bury *Phil.* 8. 119; **1441** cum eis [sc. apicibus vestris] una vestre gratitudinis ~ia [MS: exennia] Bekynton I 129. **b** ex domini parte portans exennia, non sis / furtivus raptor illorum sive tributor; / cum data sint, tali latori pocula dentur D. Bec. 2497; xenon .. est peregrinum, et inde dicitur xenium, quod est munus presentatum: et non debet dici ~ium sicut multi corrumpunt .. et in antiquis textibus non solum Grecis sed Latinis semper xenium et nunquam ~ium Bacon *Gram. Gk.* 71; tam in conviviis et exenniis quam colloquiis J. Reading f. 168v. **c** exceptis .. victualibus que ipso nomine ~iorum non procurante sibi collata sunt *Dial. Scac.* II 27 A; cibariorum ~ia .. frequenter ferre consueverat Gir. *IK* I 11; **1298** item singula exennia missa monachis ad magnam mensam et non alibi integre deferantur *Reg. Cant.* 817; **1314** in duobus lagenis vini pro exzennio faciendo abbati de Petriburch viij d. *Comp. Worc.* 38; **1302** summa *carkoys* bovium, de exenniis, xij, pretio vj li. *Reg. Whet.* II app. 332; celerarius potest .. qualibet septimana accipere unum exennium de pane et servisia in cellario et mittere in villam suis creditoribus *Cust. Cant.* 125; **1334** in lxviij gallinis pro †euxhennis *Ac. Durh.* 19; **1350** qui ferent caseum et butyrum et omnia exennia ad predictum curiam *Reg. S. Aug.* I 193. **d** miles effectus plurimis ~iis nobiliter honoratus Ord. Vit. III 2 p. 40; s**1189** [in coronatione regis] affuerunt et Judei .. cum ~iorum plurimo apparatu *Ann. Wav.* 246; **1274** expense facte in exennio ad opus regine de Scotia in adventu suo apud Leycestriam *Rec. Leic.* I 147; **1287** pro exhennio providendo contra adventum nunciorum .. regis Francie venientium versus Wind[esor] ad regem Anglie (*AcWardr*) *TRBk* 201 p. 11. **e** **12..** ecclesie dabit corporale exennium et pannum superiorem *Conc. Scot.* II 44; **1301** item debet unum exennium (*sic*) ad Natale Domini, sc. unum panem precii ij d. et ij gallinas precii ij d. *IPM* 101/2 m. 5; **1331** quieti .. de .. vectigalibus et tributis exenniis *PQW* 32. **f** dominibus .. et templis .. depredatis, cum multis ~iis, cum innumeris etiam captivis .. discessere *G. Steph.* I 67. **g** **1044** in suo vivere cum prosperitate semper istum (*sic*) ~ium obtineat *CD* 770.

exennalis v. sexennalis. **exennium** v. exenium. **exens-** v. exsens-. **exentatio** v. exenteratio.

exenterare [CL], to disembowel (person); **b** (bird or beast). **c** to gut (fish). **d** to eviscerate (fig.), reveal.

quodam defuncto ~ato W. Malm. *GR* V 410; s**1135** [corpus regis] in quodam recessu ecclesie majoris exinteratum est ne diuturnitate corruptum nares assidentium .. exacerbaret *Id. HN* 459; s**1199** [Ric. I] corpus ~atum .. humatum est Coggesh. *Chr.* 96; valectus vocatus Hall .. tractus fuit ut proditor, †exerteratus [l. ~atus], ejus internis combustis Otterb. 222. **b** exinteratorum equorum W. Malm. *GP* I 17 p. 26 (v. exta a); suem .. in usum rei familiaris ~avit .. ipsaque intestina .. mensis suis reservavit W. Cant. *Mir. Thom.* VI 61; ejectum pullum rostro corvus rosit, occidit et ~avit Strecche *Hen. V* 148; cervi corpus ~atum ducis partiretur arbitrio Boece 16v. **c** exintera, *anseeat* [*Tob.* vi 5] *GlC* E 411; incipit in Tobia [*Tob.* vi 5]: .. †extentera [l. exentera], initium excoriandi *Gl. Leid.* 20. 6; [pisce] empto .. ex more condiendi ~ato .. clavicula .. in visceribus piscis invenitur Dominic *V. Ecgwini* I 6; piscem incidi et ~ari jubens coram se, .. in eo invenit anulum J. Furness *Kentig.* 36 p. 225; pisces ~ati [*gl.*: *abuellez*] cum salsa coquantur Neckam *Ut.* 102; c**1300** quod pisces non exinterentur in piscariis, set ad mare, super ripam *Doc. Ir.* 233. **d** quia de superficie litterae pauca perstrinximus .. nunc ad exinterandos allegoriae sensus stylum vertamus Bede *Cant.* 1110B; 'facturam meam tibi innotui'. ecce quod diabolus se ipsum ~avit O. Cheriton *Fab.* 167.

exenteratio, ~izatio, disembowelling.

s**1381** Johannem Balle .. traccioni, suspendio, decollacioni, exentracioni .. Robertus adjudicavit WALS. *HA* II 32; s**1397** adjudicatus est traccioni .. exentrizacioni, combustioni interiorum [etc.] *Ib.* 225; *bowelyng*, evisceracio, †exentacio [l. exenteracio] *PP*.

exentesion v. exegesis. **exeodium** v. excidium.

exepiscopus [LL], former bishop.

747 sacrilegi illi et contumaces .. ~i (*Lit. Papae*) *Ep. Bonif.* 77; ut .. intrusorem suum ~um illum ei .. subrogaret GIR. *Invect.* I 11.

exequ- v. et. exsequ-. **exequcio** v. exsecutio. **exequiare** v. exaquare. **exequium** v. exaquia. **exequtio, ~or** v. exsecutio, ~or.

exercere [CL]

1 to train, practise (for improvement); **b** (refl.).

velut .. gimnosofistas .. palestricis disciplinis .. in gimnasio ~eri, qui .. coronam .. difficillimis propriae exercitationis viribus .. nanciscuntur ALDH. *VirgP* 2; relictis dialecticorum disciplinis quibus dudum .. ~ebatur *Ib.* 35; genus illud hominum, .. lingua ~itum, munerum avidum W. MALM. *Mir. Mariae* 188. **b** ~e [AS: *bega þe behwyrf*] temet ipsum in hoc, et esto quod es ÆLF. *Coll.* 100; **1103** in dictamine, et plus in prosa quam in versibus te ~e ANSELM (*Ep.* 290) IV 210; **1409** te ibidem disputando, arguendo et respondendo doctrinaliter ~entes *StatOx* 200.

2 (absol.) to go about one's business; **b** (refl.) to busy oneself. **c** to harass, exhaust.

nolite ~ere quando obscuratur EGB. *Pen.* 8. 3; de Sylvestro II .. legitur, quod diabolo fecit homagium, quem etiam in papatu ~ens consuluit OCKHAM *Dial.* 469. **b** suos .. subditos .. operibus justitiae se ~ere faciebat BEDE *HE* IV 21 p. 254; qui nomen monachi desiderant .. lectione sacra .. se ~entes .. patremfamilias exspectent O. CANT. *Const.* 6; ut .. in sanctis actibus vos ~eatis ANSELM (*Ep.* 420) V 366. **c** exer[ci]tum, sollicitum *GlC* E 382; ~et, i. .. fatigat *GlH* E 449; labore ~itos *abysegode GlP* 38.

3 to use, ply (tool). **b** to exert (force). **c** (w. *vitam*) to lead.

exerere, i. evaginare, proferre, ~ere, vel *abredan GlH* E 463 (cf. ib. 466: exserere, ~ere); W. MALM. *GR* II 126 (v. 1 colus a); ut ubi ~erentur aratra campana planities vix inveniretur GIR. *TH* III 2. **b** sol .. minorem in subjecta vim caloris ~et *Ib.* I 39; leo, si includitur in foveam, impeditus vim suam .. ~ere non potest ALB. LOND. *DG* 6. 11. **c** contra rerum naturam rudis habitator ~uit vitam ALDH. *VirgP* 29; in ~enda vita solitaria BEDE *HE* V 1; Beda .. venustam ~uit vitam BYRHT. *Man. Epil.* 244.

4 to work (land); **b** (saltpan). **c** to exercise (right of way), use (pasture).

[haec terra] si bene ~eretur c s. valeret *DB* I 222; boves [habet] ut terram ~eant *Simil. Anselmi* 128. **b** *DB* I 268 (v. 4 bullio a). **c** a**1246** si quis .. predictam pasturam ~ere voluerit, det pro quolibet equo .. j d. *BBC* (*Saltash*) 73; **1368** injunctum est eisdem quod non exerciant predictam viam de cetero *Hal. Durh.* 72; **1377** injunctum est Thome S. pondero de B. quod arestari faciat omnes homines exercentibus (*sic*) injustas vias infra dominium prioris *Ib.* 138.

5 to lend (money at interest).

J. SAL. *Met.* 831C (v. abaequare); VAC. *Lib. Paup.* 140, 161 (v. faenebris).

6 to rouse (morally). **b** to exercise, tax (mind).

suo populum sermone salubri / instruit, exercet, renovat, meliorat, adornat WULF. *Swith.* I 855; [Deus] creat incommoda quibus ~et et purgat justos ANSELM (*Praesc.* I 7) II 258; diligenter excerce te ipsam [ME: *ruing up sture þe*], .. clama pro succursu *AncrR* 109. **b** ingeniosis ars hec paret nescia mismet: / experientis sensum exercet [*gl.*: exacuit] saepius ipsam, / doctilogorum nam socium dat doctificando OSW. *Vers.* 7; cepit .. in divinarum lectionum studio .. animum .. ~ere TURGOT *Marg.* 3.

7 to execute, perform (action or task); **b** (ritual or dance). **c** to discharge (duty). **d** to commit, perpetrate. **e** to wage (war). **f** to play (part).

dexteram mammam virilem pro ~endis operibus, et ad fetus nutriendos sinistram habet muliebrem *Lib. Monstr.* I 19; hanc oboedientiam mihi furatus es, quam me ignorante ~es ÆLF. *Æthelwold* 10 (= WULF. *Æthelwold* 14); progreditur mulier .. / exercere sibi consueta negotia quaedam WULF. *Swith.* II 101; quanto .. magis tribulationes insurgunt, tanto magis unusquisque .. opus ~eat ANSELM (*Ep.* 382) V 325; boum labores ~eri incipiunt ALB. LOND. *DG* 8. 12; **1269, 1358** (v. actus 3c); **1432** facultatis seu sciencie ordinarium ~ere *StatOx* 240. **b** presbiteratus caeremonias sedulus discere simul et ~ere non omisit *Hist. Abb. Jarrow* 4; cum Spartanae virgines sub hostili metu .. pompam corumque agrestem Dianae de more [non] ~erent .. BONIF. *Met.* 111; **1001** (15c) praevideat rectoris examinatio unde ibidem continue ~eatur ordo psalmodiae *CD* 706; c**1200** concedo etiam eis .. ut divinum officium ~eant *Reg. Dunferm.* 419. **c** officium episcopatus et verbo ~ebat et opere BEDE *HE* IV 13 p. 232; **862** (14c) ne liceat .. alicui hominum nisi ipsius loci .. ministris aliquod officium seculare .. †excercerae aut †excercerae pretendere *CS* 503; **1269** officium vicecomitis .. excercere *Cl* 33; **1279** intendimus .. visitacionis et inquisicionis officium apud vos paternis affectibus excercere *Reg. Ebor.* 20; **1369** vobis mandamus quod predictum episcopum .. officium suum episcopale et spirituale .. excercere permittatis *RScot* 932a; s**1154** officia episcopalia .. ~ere *Plusc.* VI 18. **d** fraudes .. quas non ~uit BYRHT. *V. Ecgwini* 357; malificia malifici ~ent ALB. LOND. *DG* 11. 12. **e** Deus .. ipse .. inimicitias ~et adversus diabolum *Simil. Anselmi* 75; propter guerras quas comes de R. et alii .. adversus dominum Remensem ~ebant J. SAL. *Ep.* 134 (136 p. 6). **f** cum omnes ~eant histrionem, aliquem esse necesse est spectatorem *Id. Pol.* 494A.

8 (w. abstr. obj.): **a** to exercise, show. **b** to indulge.

a sagacissimam animorum industriam .. lectionis instantia ~ere noscuntur ALDH. *VirgP* 3; nobilitatem religionis .. virtute devotionis ~uit BEDE *HE* II 1 p. 74; nisi .. se correxerit .. regularem in eum me ~ere severitatem necesse erit ANSELM (*Ep.* 97) III 225; parsimoniam ~ere nolebat G. CRISPIN *Herl.* 89; [Christus] suis discipulis [? *add* potestatem] ~endi potestatem in alios interdicit OCKHAM *Dial.* 509 (cf. *Matth.* xx 25); **1429** hominem verberando sive aliquam irreverenciam †exiterando [MS: excercendo] (*Pat*) *MonA* V 459a. **b** ALDH. *VirgP* 47 (v. crudelitas a); **716** demones .. rogabant angelos ut .. permitterentur crudelitatis eorum voluntatem in eo ~ere BONIF. *Ep.* 10 p. 14; in sanctum furias exercens immoderatas FRITH. 1282; ~ere crudelitatem TREVET *Troades* 71.

9 to administer (justice).

strictum ne exerceat actus / judicium WULF. *Swith.* I 747; c**1155** P. BLOIS *Ep.* 6. 17A (v. curia 4a); **1167** ut pro .. potentibus eset vigor justicie ~endus J. SAL. *Ep.* 200 (235); **1300** excercere dignemini contra ipsum auxilium brachii secularis *DCCant. Reg.* Q f. 9; **1340** (v. bracchium 2c); Deum super omnia diligentes, justiciam debite ~entes CANTLOW *Orig. Cantab.* 276.

10 to practise (skill, art, or occupation); **b** (law); **c** (w. ref. to trade); **d** (fig.).

ALDH. *PR* 114 p. 156 (v. aucupium); ut libentius artem meam ~eam [AS: *ic begancge*] ÆLF. *Coll.* 93; silvae in quibus .. venationem ~et *DB* I 186v.; magus .. ante lucis ortum .. artem magicam solus in agro ~uit GREG. *Mir. Rom.* 4; ORD. VIT. XI 9 p. 197 (v. apodixis b); hec ipsa, quo omnium studium ~eatur et scientia facilius elucescat, adducemus ROB. ANGL. *Alg.* 102; W. FITZST. *Thom. prol.* 14 (v. agonistica); **1187** in liberatione servientis qui ~et agriculturam xxx s. et v d. *Pipe* 15; **1253** nullus .. ut sutor, pelliparis, fullo .. ~eat officium suum nisi sit in burgo .. (*Ch. Bolton*) *EHR* XVII 293; **1331** cum Johannes K. de Flandria, textor pannorum laneorum, .. infra regnum nostrum Anglie causa mesteri sui inibi ~endi .. accesserit (*Pat*) *Foed.* IV 496a; **1341** ne quis .. turneare, burdeare, justas facere, .. seu alia facta armorum ~ere presumat .. (*Cl*) *Foed.* V 223b; **1363** (v. bolta a); **1380** ne .. mactacionem .. bestiarum .. in domo predicta seu prope collegium .. excerceat *FormOx* 255; **1438** (v. ars 2a); **1446** quod per biennium .. litterarum studium excerceret *Eng. Clergy* 243; **1449** (v. 1 disporta 2). **b** **1415** ut .. legem civilem .. excercerem *FormOx* 432; **1432** (v. curia 8b). **c** c**1185** nisi fuerint aliqui eorum qui mercaturam ~uerint sicut mercatores *Regesta Scot.* 255; sub pacis obtentu et quasi mercature ~ende pretextu .. advenerunt GIR. *TH* III 43; **1242** ut .. per totum regnum nostrum ire possint ad emendum et vendendum et omnimodas mercaturas excercendas (*Ch. Regis Scotiae*) *Reg. Glasg.* 148; **1300** dedi .. libertatem habendi forum .. cum libero usu excercendi merces et mercaturas *FormMan* 6; **1319** nec possumus mercatoribus suas ~entibus mercaturas, ingressum .. denegare (*Chanc. Misc.* 29/8) *Foed.* III 771a; **1401** .. ibidem morari, mercari, mercandisas licitas ~ere .. (*TreatyR*) *Foed.* VIII 192a. **d** dum carnale stirpatur patrimonium spiritale ~etur mercimonium ALDH. *VirgP* 42.

11 to attend. **b** to frequent.

1328 ad scholas grammaticales .. possidendas et excercendas *Reg. Whet.* II app. 306; **1423** volo quod J. et R. .. inveniantur ad scolas .. si voluntarie et libenter velint scolas ~ere et addiscere *Reg. Cant.* II 293; **1464** lego .. Johanni M. ad subsidium sue exhibicionis, dum scholas ~eat Oxonie .. iiij d. (*Test.*) *MunAcOx* 707; **1472** presertim cancellarius [tenetur residere], qui juxta ecclesiam actualiter legere et scholas ibidem ~ere tenetur *Fabr. York* 250. **b** **1286** dicunt quod idem J. ~et tabernas nocte dieque *Gaol Del.* 36/1 m. 36; **1287** mercatores nundinas Hadleiganas ~entes (*CourtR St. Ives*) *Law Merch.* I 19; **1343** nullus .. sacerdotum mercandisas aliquas seu tabernas ~eat (*Stat. Sibthorpe*) *Eng. Clergy* 270; **1448** vicarius .. ~et communes tabernas usque mediam noctem per quod inebriatur (*Court Bk. Linc.*) *Ib.* 230; **1452** comitivas nimis frequentat populares, tabernas ~ens cervisie *Pri. Cold.* 175.

exercicialis v. exercitualis. **exercisium** v. exercitium.

exercitamentum [CL], exercise: **a** (physical); **b** (literary); **c** (acad.).

a decrevit adulescentes .. educarentur .. et cursu exercitarentur assuescerentque ferre arma, ab omni autem ~o quod ad effoeminandos animos attinet abstinerent BOECE 25v. **b** **1520** quin poeta .. fuerit .. exanguis cujus poema .. nullis disserendi ~is formetur? (MORE) *Ep. Erasm.* IV 1106. **c** **1542** juxta .. effectum statuti .. collegii de disceptacionibus et ~is scholasticorum *Deeds Balliol* 323.

exercitare [CL]

1 (trans.) to exercise, train (partly fig.). **b** (p. ppl.) expert, proficient; **c** (w. abstr.). **d** (absol.) to take exercise.

nostrae exercitationis sollicitudine horum exemplis instincta et .. stimulata .. centenas enigmatum propositiones componere nitebatur et velut in .. gimnasio prima ingenioli rudimenta ~ari cupiens .. ALDH. *Met.* 6. **b** ~atae, *ðare getyhtan GlC* E 553; ~atus, *acostnod* ÆLF. *Sup.*; s**1135** rex Henricus .. magna virtutis probitate laudabilis .. in militaribus congressionibus optime ~atus fuit RIC. HEX. *Stand.* 37; in priorum libris ~ati BALSH. *AD* 8; ~atus in prelio et eruditus industrie R. NIGER *Mil.* I 51; animosiores exstiterant et armis ~atiores GIR. *PI* III 12; gradu aut etate provecciores et magis in ordine experti et excercitati *Cust. Westm.* 188; 'rubuit dextram .. rudem', id est non ~atam ad bellum TREVET *Troades* 19. **c** est .. sophisticis abundare mobilioris ingenii et magis exercendi, ceteris altioris et magis ~ati BALSH. *AD* 36; que nunc ambigua sunt .. majori mora et ~atiori indagacione perscrutabor GREG. *Mir. Rom.* 25; maturitatem .. quam purior honestas, quam ~atior industria .. pacificat AD. MARSH *Ep.* 59. **d** solet contingere hec egritudo [sc. frenesis] maxime colicis et tempore estivo et ~antibus multum GILB. II 102. 1; oportet .. quod prelati habeant alios ~andi modos J. MIRFIELD *Flor.* 142.

2 to vex.

~a, miserab[iliter] solicita *GlC* E 361 (cf. ib. 552: ~at, miserabiliter soll[icitat]).

3 to rouse (morally).

per hanc [tribulationem] ~ati ad majora proficitis ANSELM (*Ep.* 332) V 268.

4 (w. abstr. obj.) to practise.

c**1168** tua [caritas] .. perspicua est quod ipsam .. efficaciter ~asti J. SAL. *Ep.* 251 (246).

exercitatio [CL]

1 exercise, practice; **b** (mil.). **c** experience, proficiency.

ALDH. *Met.* 6 (v. exercitare 1a); ~o, i. praeparatio, .. cultus, studium *GlH* E 454; ad ~onem disputandi nobis haec profecisse non negabis ANSELM (*Gram.* 21) I 168; deesse non poterit multimode caritatis exhibitio constantissime ~onis experimento R. COLD. *Osw. pref.* p. 327; dialectica valet ad tria, sc. ad disciplinas philosophicas .. et ad obviationem et ad ~onem KILWARDBY *OS* 506. **b** naumachium, locus navalis ~onis *GlC* N 10; naturale est omnibus se tueri et alium ferire, etiam si armis et ~one non didicerint ALCUIN *Rhet.* 3; naumachium, i. ~o illa que agitur in navi OSB. GLOUC. *Deriv.* 369; in via calcaria et frenum [equo damus], hoc est .. in ~one, cohibitionem, et incitamentum R. NIGER *Mil.* I 14. **c** Gelasius papa .. longa ~one, utpote qui presulum apocrisiarius fere xl annis enituerat, calluit ORD. VIT. XII 1 p. 311.

2 use.

funditores, hoc est qui fundibulorum ~onibus duellum committunt ALDH. *PR* 138; **797** ut sint ibi [sc. in domo Dei] legentes juvenes et .. librorum ~o ALCUIN *Ep.* 128.

3 exertion, effort; **b** (w. *corporalis* or sim.). **c** (spiritual) exercise, meditation (*cf. Psalm* liv 3). *V. et. exercitio* 1.

ALDH. *VirgP* 2 (v. exercere 1a); ~o, i. .. fatigatio, .. industria *GlH* E 554; ecclesiam .. quam bonorum ~o .. decoravit .. incendium .. devastavit ORD. VIT. X 8 p. 43; omnem laborem et ~onem .. fugiunt J. SAL. *Pol.* 595A. **b** non sufficit ad salutem corporalis ~o ubi non fuerit pia virtutum mentis exhibitio ALEX. CANT. *Dicta* 12 p. 155 (cf. *1 Tim.* iv 8); propter laborem et corporis ~onem .. pulsum facit fortem BART. ANGL. III 24; ~o corporis *AncrR* 5. **c** ~o, i. .. meditatio *GlH* E 454.

4 execution (of task), performance (of duty); *v. et. exercitio* 2a, *exercitium* 4. **b** putting into effect (of law).

943 pontis arcisve constructione, et promptissimum itinere (*sic*) expeditionis ~o *CS* 780; necessarie sunt tube, ut earum clangore .. determinetur civilis preliorum ~o R. NIGER *Mil.* III 58; que [mulier libidinosa] libidini tandem aliquando renuntians, otia veneria in operum transfert ~onem ALB. LOND. *DG* 11. 8; affligitur homo perfectus .. assidue .. virtutum ~one W. DAN. *Sent.* 56. **b** legis humane ~o, doctrinacio vel institucio WYCL. *Ver.* II 131.

5 summons. *Cf. citatio* 2.

1297 ~o officiali .. quod .. abbati cedenti faciat providi de porcionibus .. assignatis *Reg. Cant.* 196.

exercitatiuncula, light (physical) exercise.

exercyse the body with labour, corpus ~is versare WHITTINGTON *Vulg.* 43.

exercitativus [LL], as an exercise, affording practice.

est autem ut sophistice incipiatur .. in contentiosa [disputatione] frequenter, in ∼a nonnunquam, in inquisitiva nunquam Balsh. *AD* 36; in viij .. Topicorum determinatur dialectica obviativa et ∼a Kilwardby *OS* 508.

exercitator [CL], practitioner of trade, skill, or art. *V. et. exercitor* 1a.

territi a furcis fures .. artium mechanicarum fiunt ∼ores [v. l. exercitores] W. Fitzst. *Thom.* 10; singulorum officiorum ∼ores .. sunt locis distincti omnes *MGL* II 6 (= W. Fitzst. *Thom. prol.* 10: exercitores); gymnosophiste .. dicuntur ∼ores in sapientia Bacon *Gram. Gk.* 74; hujus facultatis [sc. legis] ∼oribus accidit ut plerumque litibus intendendis indulgeant plus quam paci R. Bury *Phil.* 11. 169.

exercitio [CL]

1 exertion, effort. **b** (spiritual) exercise, meditation. *V. et. exercitamentum, exercitatio* 3, *exercitium* 2.

∼o, i. .. *gymen GlH* E 451. **b** ∼o, i. meditatio *Ib.*

2 execution (of task), performance (of duty); *v. et. exercitatio* 4a, *exercitium* 4. **b** exercising, wielding (of power).

1289 vadia sibi .. pro †excercione .. officii de Judaismo assignata *RGasc* II 293; **15..** dixerunt ipsum .. inhabilem et inexpertem esse in scientia et †exertione ad officia illa .. occupanda, eo quod .. nullum exercitium in eisdem officiis .. habuit *Entries* 443. **b** de ∼one potestatis qua possunt eleemosynas suas subtrahere ab ecclesia delinquente *Ziz.* app. 487.

exercitium [CL]

1 exercise, practice (for improvement). **b** experience, proficiency.

sequuntur nunc harum regularum ∼ii majoris causa questiones xviij Rob. Angl. *Alg.* 144; ea in exemplis ponere studuimus ut .. facile sit ∼ium Balsh. *AD* 8. **b** *Entries* 443 (v. exercitio 2a).

2 exertion, effort, toil. **b** (physical) exercise; **c** (mil.); **d** (log.). **e** (spiritual) exercise, meditation. **f** action, activity. *V. et. exercitamentum, exercitatio* 3; *exercitio* 1.

∼iis, *bigangum GlC* E 387; per ignotas .. pererrans, / divinae gentes sationis tempore passim / dilatans, exercitium non segne gerebat Frith. 563; **1012** (12c) soror .. omnia quae possibilitatis ejus et utilitatis fratris omnibus ∼iis studuit explere *CD* 719; multos .. loris innexos jugis ruralibus ∼iis submittunt Ord. Vit. IX 2 p. 467; bruta .. sunt in assiduo existentia labore et ∼io *Quaest. Salern.* B 300; [Saturnus] in agricultura magnum impendens ∼ium Alb. Lond. *DG* 1. 2; inanitio et repletio, ∼ium atque quies Bart. Angl. IV 4; non consentit .. scholastica ∼ia intermittere Ad. Marsh *Ep.* 26; **c1318** tanto furore incipiunt insanire quod excercicia ruralia, per que victus noster adquiritur, .. fieri non permittunt J. Mason *Ep.* 16 p. 205. **b** bonum est ∼ium corporis Anselm (*Ep.* 446) V 394; oportet ut caveat ab ira, .. et balneis et exertitiis corporis Gilb. IV 194v. 2; patet quod ∼ium corporale sine lassitudine vel tedio affuisset Wycl. *Innoc.* 492; principalis species ∼iorum est deambulans per loca alta et munda J. Mirfield *Flor.* 140. **c** militari ∼io .. certaverunt Ord. Vit. X 8 p. 45; quod .. studio vanitatis hausi de ∼io militari .. converti ad exercitium spirituale R. Niger *Mil.* I *prol.* p. 93; **s1175** [rex] martiis plurimum intentus et detentus ∼iis Anglorum Gir. *EH* II 5. **d** primo, premitto quod oportet omnem theologum concedere. .. secundo, gracia ∼ii dico quod .. Baconthorpe *Quaest. Sent.* 9D. **e** ∼ia, intentiones, meditationes *GlH* E 460; fratres qui voluerint ad suam redeant requiem; qui autem spirituali ∼io [AS p. 411: *onbigencge*] noluerint .. *RegulC* 38; R. Niger *Mil.* I *prol.* p. 93 (v. 2c supra); **1549** ne ullus ecclesiasticus .. immisceat se secularibus negotiis .. lucri causa .. quo a spirituali ∼io, propria cura neglecta, abstrahatur *Conc. Scot.* II 89. **f** [de verbo]: quia .. omnis causa agens circa personam agit in paciens et non simul et sic cum mora, accidit sic significanti in ∼io sive motu temporis adjacencia *Ps.*-Gros. *Gram.* 46.

3 (moral) rousing, stirring up.

religio illa excrevit ut ille de Cistercio forent omnium monachorum ∼ium, studiosorum speculum Higd. VII 10 p. 404; **s1461** misericors .. Dominus qui, peccatis nostris exigentibus, perversorum malitiam .. ad ∼ium nostrum sinit prevalere .. suscitavit nobis propugnatorem *Croyl. Cont. C* 532.

4 execution, carrying out, performance. **b** discharge (of function or duty), performance (of duty). *V. et. exercitatio* 4, *exercitio* 2.

malens scripturam emolumento litterarum carnalis vitae nutrimenta per laboris ∼ium adipisci quam .. Aldh. *PR* 143 p. 203; dum haec ∼ia bonorum operum .. agerentur B. *V. Dunst.* 6; .. ut quietus ad sola piae vitae ∼ia exquirenda sedulo vacet Anselm (*Ep.* 37) III 146; squalorem penitentie converterunt in ∼ium luxurie Ord. Vit. XI 11 p. 208; *Quaest. Salern.* B 8 (v. desiccare 1a); **s1088** Rogerus .. sceleris ∼ium per Estangle .. inchoavit H. Hunt. *HA* VII 1; post amaros gemitus et immensa spiritualium operum ∼ia superne contemplacionis dulcedinem sentire Rolle *IA* 208. **b** **955** (12c) praeter triplum liberum servitium, hoc est arcis pontis expeditionisque ∼ium *CS* 905; Pull. *Sent.* 927C (v. degradatio 1b); in .. ∼io ecclesiasticorum officiorum Gir. *GE* II 25; **1289** rex tradidit .. Bernardo custodiam et ∼ium sigilli regis et contrasigilli quod habet in Agenesio *RGasc* II 305; **1488** concedimus eidem Ricardo pro †excercio [MS: exercicio] et occupatione officiorum xl li. per annum *RScot* 483a; **1549** fideli ∼io tabellionatus [et] officii hujusmodi *Conc. Scot.* II 112 (cf. ib. 121: sequuntur .. ordinationes penes officium procuratorum curiarum consistorialium et †exercitiam [l. ∼ium] in eorum causis deducendis); **1595** decretum .. de ∼iis juristarum et medicorum ordinariis *StatOx* 453; **1597** qui .. de determinationibus suis non curantes ad .. universitatis dedecus .. ∼ia .. omittunt *Ib.* 455.

exercitor [CL]

1 practitioner (of trade); *v. et. exercitator.* **b** cultivator, tiller (of land).

singulorum officiorum ∼ores .. sunt locis distincti omnes W. Fitzst. *Thom. prol.* 10. **b** *GAS* 512 (v. colonus a).

2 (leg.) exercitor, agent. **b** (w. *navis*) master, pilot.

potest .. qui contrahit premeditari et inquirere quis sit, que in ∼ore non potest, et ideo est periculum Vac. *Lib. Paup.* 130; cum .. judicium hoc nomine datur in dominum ∼oris, quo nomine tenetur actio? an de peculio an exercitoria directa an utilis? si voluntate domini, exercitoria. sin autem, de peculio *Ib.*. **b** **1540** magister, ∼or, sive gubernator predicte navis *HCA* 7/81 (cf. ib.: *the sayd shippe mayster or* ∼or).

3 frequenter. *Cf. exercere* 11b.

1397 parochiani dicunt quod .. Robertus R. est communis ∼or tabernarum, prout Johannes B. dicit; alii dicunt quod non (*Vis. Heref.*) *EHR* XLV 95.

exercitorius [CL], (leg.) of an agent.

nota ∼iam actionem ad formam potius quam ad causam pertinere Vac. *Lib. Paup.* 130; *Ib.* (v. exercitor 2).

exercitualis [LL]

1 of an army.

s1186 cesa sunt in hoc †exerciciali [? l. exercituali *or* vv. ll. exciciali, execrabili] bello Christianorum militum ij millia Fordun *GA* 18.

2 (n. pl. as sb.) heriot.

si quis .. ex hac vita migraverit .. propter mortem subitaneam, dominus illius non vendicet sibi .. nisi sua justa ∼ia (*Cons. Cnuti*) *GAS* 357 (= *Inst. Cnuti, ib.*: tantum quod Angli vocant *heregeate*; cf. ib. 359: virronis ∼ia apud Danos; *ib.* 361: omnis .. vidua ∼ia debita infra anni spacium sine forisfacto persolvat).

exercitulus [cf. CL exercitus], small army.

rex recurrit ad pugnam, ad auxiliandum plurimum laborantem ∼um suum *Itin. Ric.* VI 23.

1 exercitus v. exercere.

2 exercitus [CL]

1 exercise, practice.

in cultum Dei .. et in virtutum ∼u Bacon *Maj.* III 71.

2 army, host; **b** (w. ref. to *Is.* i 24 *etc.*); **c** (w. ref. to *Te Deum*); **d** (spiritual); **e** (fig.); **f** (? iron.).

∼us Assyriorum Gildas *EB* 72; serpens .. a Romano ∼u .. repertus describitur *Lib. Monstr.* III 9; venit contra eum cum inmenso ac forti ∼u Bede *HE* I 34; Asser *Alf.* 49 (v. castellum 1a); Ord. Vit. IV 17 p. 290 (v. castrensis 2b); **s1417** rex .. consedit cum ∼u coram .. Caen *Chr. S. Alb.* 111. **b** Adonai, dominus ∼uum vel omnipotens *Gl. Leid.* 21. 17; Ad. Marsh *Ep.* 8 (v. dominus 10a). **c** martyrum et insignis te exercitus undique laudat Wulf. *Swith.* I 994. **d** ut intueri poterit auxiliarium caelestis ∼us .. montem plenum Gildas *EB* 72; supervenit ∼us malignorum spirituum Bede *HE* V 13 p. 312; dux inter magnos duces ∼uum Christi Anselm (*Or.* 15) III 62; cuncto ∼ui Christianorum vita et salus *Pont. Ebor.* 281; sunt in ejus [diaboli] ∼u [ME: *hird*] et ei serviunt in sua curia *AncrR* 75. **e** nunquam .. nidificantium crescit ∼us Gir. *TH* I 12. **f** **1214** Walterus .. misit quendam excercitum ad domum .. Baldrici, bene circa xl homines *CurR* VII 242.

3 (feud.) army, expeditionary force; **b** (w. *Walliae*). **c** (duty of) military service.

soca talis erat quod nichil reddebat sed adjuvabat in ∼u regis in terra et in mari *DB* I 368; de omni forinseco servicio preter unam navem quam cum necesse habuero personaliter ire vel mittere in ∼u propter negotio regni, invenient ad servicium meum (*Ch. Hen. II*) *VCH Essex* I 386; **a1231** (v. 1 creantia 1b); **1243** totum excercitum illud revocatum fuit per .. breve patens *Cl* 56; **1286** (v. 1 constabularia 1a); **1329** vicario de Peblis, pro dampnis que sustinuit per ultimum ∼um, xl s. *ExchScot* 222. **b** **1166** episcopus Bath' debet iiij li. .. de ∼u Walie *Pipe* 98; **1219** (v. 2 broca 1a); **1257** propter quod minus plene fecit regi servicium suum in ultimo excercitu regis Wallie *Cl* 174; **1349** ad sagittand' unam sagittam ad anteriorem ∼um Wall' *CalIPM* IX 359. **c** **a940** (12c) ut maneat ista libertas insolubiliter ab omni seculari servitio .. tribus exceptis, expeditione, pontis arcisque constructione, et ∼u *CS* 737; **c1050** collata fuit villa de K. .. absque omni munere et onere et exactione regis .. et sine refectione pontis et sine ∼u et venatione *E. Ch. Scot.* 5 (cf. ib. 178 [**1147**]: quietas ab omni servitio .. excepto ∼u regis); habet .. molinum ab omni servitio quietum preter ∼um *DB* I 366; **s1100** Willelmus [II] suos ∼ibus frequentissimis et gildis continuis vexabat H. Hunt. *HA* VII 22; **1199** liberi .. ab .. ∼ibus [etc.] *RChart* 2a; ab omni exhercitu et expeditione excepta illa que vocatur nomine belli liberos *Ib.* 8b; **1199**, **1238** (v. caballicata b); **1315** concedimus quod .. burgenses .. ab omni ∼u mutuo et subvencione usque ad decem annos penitus sint immunes *RGasc* IV 1626 p. 473; **1330** ab omni scotto et geldo et .. auxiliis regum .. et hornegeld' et †excertibus et wapentach' et scutag' *PQW* 503b.

exered- v. exhered-. **exerere** v. exserere.

exermis [cf. CL inermis], unarmed.

excutiet pacem, quam dat patientia, nullus; / sit licet exermis, conterit arma tamen J. Sal. *Enth. Pol.* 9; *without wapyn*, ∼is, exermus, inermus, inermis *CathA*.

exert- v. et. exerc-. **exterrare** v. exenterare.

exesse, exedere [CL]

1 to eat up or away, devour; **b** (w. bird, fish, or worm as subj.); **c** (w. fire or iron as subj.); **d** (w. abstr. subj.).

exesus, comestus *GlC* E 534; exesum vel comessum, consumptum, .. esum, .. *þurhetan GlH* E 474; exedi, manduco *Ib.* 475; exedendus, devorandus *Ib.* 487; **9..** exedi, *ic et WW*. **b** vermiculus ligni .. permodicus .. fortissimum ligni robur exedens consumit Bede *Kings* (*2 Kings* viii 2) 721; tradunt iterum quod cujusdam jecur ibi vultur exedat Hon. *Spec. Eccl.* 1057D; cujus corporis pars media .. piscibus devorantibus exesa nunquam comparuit R. Cold. *Godr.* 108; vermis .. lento morsu interiora [impudicatoris] exedens *G. Steph.* II 77; unde et jecur exesum a vulture in penam renasci dicitur Alb. Lond. *DG* 6. 5; adhibita est aquila, ut cor exederet [Promethei] *Ib.* 10. 10; exesa cernimus ligna terredine Walt. Wimb. *Carm.* 405. **c** obstupendum quomodo ignis .. pertransire vel exedere domum non presumpserit R. Cold. *Godr.* 158; [ferrum] lenia renum latera exedendo corruperat *Id. Cuthb.* 94 (cf. ib. 20: ferrei compedis rigor omnem tenere pellicule superficiem exedendo minoraverat). **d** qui ebriosum condemnant virus invidiae quo exeduntur ipsi non videant Bede *Hom.* I 25. 108.

2 to consume, emaciate, waste away.

exese carnes, sanguis exhaustus, ossa suis vacuata medullis Ailr. *Ed. Conf.* 785A; ossa exesa et demolita W. Cant. *Mir. Thom.* II 23; per exesos carnium anfractus *Ib.*; fronde senio exesa R. Cold. *Osw.* 17.

3 to hollow out, cut away.

exesum, .. *aholad GlH* E 474; far per genus mol[l]icionis fit de quolibet grano panifico si solum retundetur exesis capitibus et decorticetur *Alph.* 62.

exeuclare v. exantlare. **exeundare** v. exundare.

exferveficus [cf. LL exfervefacere], (med.) that makes hot.

multa sinopida bona et spissa et gravis colligitur in Cappodocia in spelunca distillans; virtus est illi stiptica et †exfervatica [v. l. exserantica; ? l. exferveficа] et †exphastica [v. l. exemplastica] *Alph.* 121.

exfibulare [LL], to unclasp, untie (also fig.). (*Cf.* Prudentius *Psych.* 633).

GlH E 575 (v. exsolvere 1a); domina lacernam .. effibulabat Osb. Glouc. *Deriv.* 4; effibulare, pallium dissolvere *Ib.* 194; intacta virgo .. / .. modum istum / solvit et effibulat Walt. Wimb. *Virgo* 23; solvit et effibulat fedus matrimonii *Id. Elem.* 324.

exflagrare v. efflagrare.

exforestare [cf. forestare], to remove from forest status. *V. et. deafforestare, deforestare, difforestare, disafforestare.*

c1227 precepimus ut omnia illa tenementa sint ∼ata et ab omni seculari servitio libera (*Ch. Com. Glouc.*) *Cart. Glam.* II 426.

exfrediare v. exfridiare.

exfretare [cf. LL fretare, CL transfretare], to cross (the sea).

∼at, navigat *GlC* E 474.

exfridiare [cf. AS *friðian* = *to keep peace, protect*], to disturb (violently). *V. et. effraiare* a.

si quis ad arma prosiliat et domum exfrediet [v. l. diffrodiet] nec tamen aliquem percutiat, dimidio forisfacto culpa consistat (*Leg. Hen.* 81. 4) *GAS* 598.

exfumigare v. effumigare. **exgartare** v. esgaretare. **exguere** v. exstinguere. **exhabundare** v. 2 abundare 4c.

exhalabilis, exhalable.

videbitur quod .. odor sit exalatio et odorabile exalabile, quia temperat qualitates ipsius cerebri BACON XIV 103.

exhalare [CL]

1 to exhale, breathe out: **a** (breath); **b** (vapour or sim.); **c** (word); **d** (w. *animam* or *spiritum*) to die.

a fetidum exalavit [*gl.: ut apyfhte*, exspiravit] spiraculum ALDH. *VirgP* 32; serpentes .. mortiferos exalabant halitus *Lib. Monstr.* III 7. **b** ~at .. cerebrum calorem qui, si in eo obturaretur, phrenesim .. generaret ADEL. *QN* 20; baratrum patebat exalans sulphureum fumum ALEX. CANT. *Mir.* 35 (II) p. 227; *Quaest. Salern.* W 11 (v. exhalatio 3b). **c** s†**1176** hujusmodi verba cum impetu ~avit FORDUN *Cont.* VIII 26. **d** vermibus scaturiens putidum exalavit spiritum ALDH. *VirgP* 52; sic .. decantans .. ultimum e corpore ~avit spiritum CUTHB. *Ob. Baedae* clxiv; ut .. prius animam exalasse quam finem doloribus excepisse videatur (*Leg. Hen.* 75. 1) *GAS* 591; H. HUNT. *HA* VIII 12 (v. anima 1a); GIR. *GE* II 4 (v. cutis 1a); **1276** (v. decenarius 3a); animam exalans .. migrans e mundo ROLLE *IA* 146; dominus Ricardus C. .. spiritum exalavit et .. apud S. Paulum sepulture datur STRECCHE *Hen. V* 152.

2 to breathe upon.

si sanguis in calice congeletur, tamdiu desuper exaletur donec dissolvatur *Cust. Westm.* 219.

3 to belch or vomit forth (also fig.).

ferrum quod Anglica Avena absorbuerat Romana Tybris ~at! DOMINIC *V. Ecgwini* I 6; s**1248** M. PAR. *Maj.* V 31 (v. crapulare).

4 (intr.) to exhale, issue. **b** to stink.

~at, †anhellam [l. anhelitum] emittit *GlC* E 546; ~et, i. redolet, .. *stemþ GlH* E 405; ad ingressum beati doctoris Botulphi fumus ~at teterrimus FOLC. *V. Bot.* 6; [spiritus] cor distendens, qua ingressus est, erumpit; spiritus vero ~at ALF. ANGL. *Cor* 11. 21; aeris inclusi et per fenestras occultas sensim ~antis .. eruptio GIR. *IK* I 2; fumositates que exterius debent ~are atque evaporare interius retinentur *Quaest. Salern.* B 117; BART. ANGL. IV 1 (v. discoloratīvus); de latrina amoto operculo non exalat nisi fetor ROLLE *IA* 188. **b** †exaltavit [l. exalavit], *stonc GlC* E 391; ~et, i. .. fetet *GlH* E 405; **9..** exalabat, *reac WW*.

exhalatio [CL]

1 breath, gasp. **b** (*sc. ultima*) death; **c** (w. *spiritus*).

crebris in egrotando ~onibus homo .. attenuatur PULL. *Sent.* 691B; morbo .. letali .. usque ad extremam ~onem .. afficiuntur GIR. *TH* II 4. **b** rex omnesque majores natu fere usque ad ~onem perterriti OSB. *V. Dunst.* 36; *sowlyng or deyng*, .. exalacio *PP*. **c** nihil in eo amici ejus preter spiritus ~onem exspectabant W. CANT. *Mir. Thom.* IV 26.

2 exhaled vapour. **b** stench.

799 nebulosa aquarum exalatio ALCUIN *Ep.* 170; exalatio .. est compositum corpus, licet sit aqueum per dominium, habet enim se exalatio ad aquam sicut fumus ad terram BACON XIV 103; *Ib.* (v. exhalabilis). **b** ea que nascuntur de corrupcionibus et purgamentis vel exalacionibus aut cadaverum tabe GROS. *Hexaem.* VII 5; s**1327** per ~onem cadaverum BAKER 107b (= MORE *Chr. Ed. II* 318); jam cernimus ex conclusis exalationes quasdam atras ascendere FORTESCUE *NLN* I 43.

3 exhalation, issuing (of vapour or sim.); **b** (w. ref. to hair).

si non possunt fieri tales exspirationes sine fumali evaporatione et exalatione nichilominus .. cerebrum confortant BACON XIV 104; [ex motu] objecti .. sicut propter velocem motum fluminis non fiunt tante exalationes sicut in aquis marinis PECKHAM *Persp.* III 17. **b** spiritus .. in cerebro generatur qui amissis capillis qui erant cooperimenta capitis et ~ones, [Samson] spiritus exhalavit et sic vires amisit *Quaest. Salern.* W 11.

exhalescere, to issue.

ut tam violenti volutione ~escat aether in flammam ADEL. *QN* 73.

exhantlare v. exantlare. **exharcus** v. exarchus. **exharere** v. exarescere.

exhaurire [CL]

1 to draw off (fluid). **b** to drink up. **c** to take a draught. **d** (fig.) to drink in.

tota aqua ~ritur si arcus fundum pertingat *Quaest. Salern.* Ba 112; W. CANT. *Mir. Thom.* II 77 (v. coctura 3). **b** FRITH. 1357 (v. canistrum 1b); ore desiccato tantum [aque] ~sit quod .. exspiravit GIR. *TH* II 48. **c** **1458** nec .. de illo aureo ~sisti poculo liquoreve nectareo, qui .. *Reg. Whet.* I 314. **d** †exauravit, conprehendit *GlC* E 470; agnoscens illa [sus] illum mireque ejus vocem ~riens venit ad eum BYRHT. *V. Ecgwini* 375; illius primevi exordii et prohemii preloquimina potuimus ~rire R. COLD. *Cuthb.* 2 p. 5.

2 to remove (from container); **b** (fig.). **c** to draw (sword).

ille particulam pulveris, quem de sepulchrali crypta sancti Augustini ~serat, .. remittit GOSC. *Transl. Aug.* 28B; ~riri in corporalibus significat illud non manere in illo unde ~ritur .. DUNS *Ord.* IV 148. **b** **949** sancti viri .. quicquid in semetipsis terrenum sentiunt indesinenter .. operibus sanctis exauriunt *CS* 880. **c** **1577** J. N. .. pugionem ~sit et super insultam predictam .. W. G. .. pugionem eciam ~sit et sic .. simul pugnaverunt *Pat* 1014 m. 18.

3 to empty (of fluid), drain. **b** (p. ppl. *exhaustus*) dried up. **c** to empty (of other contents).

~stas, evacuatas *GlC* E 405; ~stum, i. .. evacuatum *GlH* E 422; in primo propinatu ~sere illud vas medonis ad unius palmulae mensuram B. *V. Dunst.* 10; cor .. cum omnibus corporis sensibus et viribus, sicut ~stis sanguine fieri solet, deficit ANSELM (*Ep.* 39) III 151; c**1218** ille .. plus laudatur qui plures inebriat et calices fecundiores ~rit *Conc. Syn.* 64; nonne oportet ollam multum bullientem ~rire aliquantulum ..? [ME: *nule hit beon ouer leden*] *AncrR* 144. **b** ~stum, i. .. siccatum, .. *aslacod GlH* E 422; quasi immotus pulvis ~sti corporis [S. Withburge] .. imaginem pretenderet integritatis *Lib. Eli.* II 147. **c** tapetia, quae fracta et ~sta sanctorum corporibus monumenta tegebant GOSC. *Transl. Aug.* 26C; pauperum Christi loculos ~rire J. SAL. *Ep.* 217 (196).

4 to exhaust, consume, use up; **b** (refl.); **c** (w. ref. to physical resources); **d** (of abstr.).

ALDH. *VirgV* 1615 (v. 2 crusta 3); †exaureant, consumant *GlC* E 489 (cf. ib. 449: †exanreant, consumant); †exhaureant, consumant; ~stum, i. consumptum *GlH* E 421–2; hauserunt ministri liquorem tota die .. sed nequivit ille liquor ~riri de vase ÆLF. *Æthelwold* 8 (= WULF. *Æthelwold* 12); species .. perutiles ad omnem medicinam, que si ~ste aut imminute sunt .. ne turberis J. SAL. *Ep.* 166 (147); si lignum, ferrum .. ceteraque metalla [igni] imposita fuerint ut caleant, unumquodque .. ardorem excipit nec tamen ab igne calorem ~rit ALEX. CANT. *Dicta* 9 p. 149. **b** se in eleemosinarum largitionibus totum ~riens GIR. *GE* I 9. **c** heremita .. vitam solitariam degens ~sta membrorum vitalia .. quinque caricibus .. sustentasse .. describitur ALDH. *PR* 114; exaustis, defectis *GlC* E 404. **d** exhausta veterum virtute deorum ALDH. *VirgV* 1389; a**803** quid scientiae divitiis locupletius, quae numquam ~riuntur? ALCUIN *Ep.* 262; veritatis ratio tam ampla .. est ut a mortalibus nequeat ~riri ANSELM (*CurD*) II 40.

5 to deprive of (material resources).

s**1080** nimis ~serunt nos carae emptiones leguminum et avenae ANSELM (*Ep.* 89) III 215; ~sta terra hominibus et opibus R. NIGER *Mil.* III 82.

6 to carry through, persist in.

o fraus, o que dolus, quos rex sub ymagine solus / dum scelus exhausit tam longo tempore clausit GOWER *CT* II 24.

exhauritorius [cf. LL hauritorium], that draws out.

exanthlo (id est exaurio, nam rota putei exauritoria anthlia vocatur) ALDH. *PR* 124.

exhaustio [LL], consuming, consumption.

cumque frequentem ~onem nulla suppleret adjectio, ad inopiam etiam diurni panis domus .. defecit W. MALM. *GP* V 272.

exhebenus [CL], sort of precious stone. (*Cf.* Pliny *HN* XXXVII 159).

lapis †exebonus albus est et speciosus †que [v. l. quo] solent aurifices aurum limpidare *Alph.* 91.

exhedra v. 2 exedra.

exhelus [cf. CL anhelus], that exhales an odour, reeking.

labiis serpentis .. / turpiter exelis fetet odore gravi NIG. *Mir. BVM* f. 16vb; vulnus et exeli vulneris atra lues *Ib.*

exhennium v. exenium. **exhercitus** v. 2 exercitus.

exheredare [CL]

1 to disinherit.

s**887** rex Carolus defungitur, quem nepos illius, nomine Ernulfus, sex septimanis antequam decessisset, ~avit *AS Chr.*; dominus suus [Henricus rex], controversiis ortis inter ipsum et filiam .. Mathildem .., ipsam ~avit SILGRAVE 89; in rebus .. immobilibus habent minus dominium quia res illas non possunt vendere .. cum heredes suos de rebus immobilibus ~are non valeant OCKHAM *Pol.* I 308.

2 to deprive (person or institution) of patrimony or rightful possession, to impoverish; **b** (p. ppl. as sb. m., esp. w. ref. to baronial party 1265–6); **c** (fig. or spiritual). *V. et. exhereditare.*

~et, alienat vel abjecit *GlC* E 381; *GlP* 545 (v. exheres); locupletes proscribere exhaeredare [v. l. exhaereditare] ecclesias OSB. *V. Dunst.* 25; a**1094** vestrum peto .. auxilium, quatenus ut fidelis filius matri vestrae contra filium .. volentem eam exhaeredare, subveniatis ANSELM (*Ep.* 170) IV 52; ex rapto vivere nolis / non exheredes aliquos ut sit tuus heres / ex rapto dives D. BEC. 147; **1257** quod faciant habere Warino .. militi ceco et ~ato unam robam *Cl* 163; s**1248** Nicholaus .. juvenes manu valida exhaeredere (*sic*) proponebat *Ann. Cambr.* 86; dominus Simon de Monteforti .. propter inobedienciam suam erga regem ~atus et exlegatus cum filiis suis KNIGHTON I 65; exheredatum set eum jubet esse fugatum GOWER *CT* III 110. **b** mors .. regis eodem die quo Rotomagi defunctus est .. in Calabria quibusdam ~atis nunciata est ORD. VIT. VII 16 p. 249; s**1141** acies ~atorum que preibat percussit aciem regalem H. HUNT. *HA* VIII 18 (= GERV. CANT. *Chr.* 116: exhereditatorum); s**1266** J. de Hexvil et alii ~ati .. ceperunt insulam de Ely *Ann. Cambr.* 102; s**1266** elegerunt .. ut .. providerent et ordinarent tam super tranquillitate regis et regni quam super terris ~atorum sibi reddendis *Ann. Dunstable* 243; **1273** quod .. cartas quas ~ati dudum in insula Eliensi existentes detulerunt a villa .. Cantebrigie .. tempore turbacionis regni .. recipiatis *SelPlJews* 76. **c** certum est quoniam qui Deum ~at vel ecclesias ejus in hac vita .. a regno Dei ~atur in futura vita ANSELM (*Ep.* 270) IV 185; huc usque pacem habuimus de qua nunc nos spoliare et ~are queris *Itin. Mand.* 114.

exheredatio [CL], depriving of patrimony, impoverishment; **b** (spiritual). *V. et. exhereditas, exhereditatio, exhereditio.*

sub duobus regibus .. multa pertulit, labores viz., ~onis damna, exilium, et multa pericula ORD. VIT. VIII 9 p. 320; **1160** si rex Francie habuerit querelam versus eos, que sit ad justitiam corporis vel membrorum sive ~onem .. per consilium regis Anglie deducetur *Act. Hen. II* I 252; **1234** crescere volunt .. per regni perturbationem et aliorum ~onem (*Consilium episcoporum*) WEND. III 76 (= M. PAR. *Maj.* III 270: exhereditionem); **1259** (v. colludium c); **1291** .. quod nullo modo ipsum admitteret ad hujusmodi officium faciendum quod esset ad exeredacionem et prejudicium ecclesie Ram[eseie] et contra libertatem carte nundinarum contentam *Law Merch.* I 42; **1363** episcopus [Cicestr'] .. appropriavit .. medietatem unius diei ultra predictas viij dies [nundinarum] in prejudicium et exaridacionem domini regis *IMisc* 187/8; absque enormi lesione corone Anglie et ~one perpetua ejusdem *G. Hen. V* 2 p. 13; **1464** ~onem et destruccionem .. Johannis que ei per utlagariam .. consecuturam .. evenirent *Paston Let.* 687. **b** quoniam non potuit exhaeredari honore quem nondum habebat .. hanc exhaeredationem praevenire potest reconciliatio et avertere ANSELM (*Praesc.* 3) II 277.

exheredator, disinheritor, dispossessor.

1200 ~or patris ejus et ejusdem Petri *CurR* I 175; s**1218** Saphadinus .. fratrueliumque suorum ~or ac regni Asie usurpator WEND. II 233; **1285** si vicecomes respondeat quod returnum fecit ballivis alterius libertatis .. puniatur vicecomes tanquam ~or domini regis et corone sue (2 *Westm.* 39) *StRealm* I 90; **1321** Hugo pater et Hugo filius Dispensatores tanquam ~ores corone sint perpetuo exheredati (*Act. Parl.*) *G. Ed. II Bridl.* 69.

exheredere v. exheredare.

exhereditare [CL], to disinherit, deprive of patrimony, impoverish; **b** (p. ppl. as sb. m.). *V. et. exheredare 2.*

1012 quod [foedus] qui praesumpsisset infringere ~ari se sciret omnibus habitis *Ch. Roff.* 33; OSB. *V. Dunst.* 25 (v. exheredare 2a); nisi ad eum ~andum vel regnum suum depopulandum Francorum genus .. anhelaret ORD. VIT. IX 14 p. 584; ducis filium .. funditus extorrem ~avit *Ib.* XII 21 p. 376; s**1104** Willelmus .. consul Moretuil causa perfidie ab Anglia ~atus a regi in Normanniam discedens H. HUNT. *HA* VII 235; **1196** Henricus pro defectu Roberti et Isabele debuit esse exhereditari (*sic*) *CurR* I 19; c**1218** testes .. per quorum testimonia .. aliquis .. ~etur .. non absolvantur *Conc. Syn.* 77; s**1265** quod omnes qui apud Lewes vel Evesham .. contra .. regem arma .. detulissent, a terris et possessionibus suis penitus ~arentur *Ann. Lond.* 70; **1360** omnes .. ~ati vel de terris ablati .. restituentur in integrum .. sicut ante guerram (*Tract.*) WALS. *HA* I 293; s**1201** [rex Anglie] a baronibus apud regem Francie, cujus vassalus erat delatus, cum comparere nollet, .. per judicium parium ~atus est FORDUN *Cont.* VIII 63. **b** GERV. CANT. *Chr.* 116 (v. exheredare 2b).

exhereditas, disherison. *V. et. exheredatio, exhereditatio, exhereditio.*

fratres sumus, tuam ~atem non querimus, pronam penatibus larum quandoque reddendus es H. LOS. *Ep.* 29.

exhereditatio [CL v. l.], disherison, loss. *V. et. exheredatio, exhereditas, exhereditio.*

1199 petit considerationem curie utrum pater suus potuit totam terram suam dare in maritagium filie sue ad ~onem suam *CurR* I 87; **1304** burgenses [*of Totnes, Devon*] clamaverunt emendas assise panis fracte quod maxime in prejudicium et ~onem .. Willelmi redundat *Gild Merch.* II 238; **1321** in ipsorum Johannis et Lore dispendium .. et ~onis periculum manifestum (*Breve Regis*) *MGL* II 363; s**1265** ex .. proscripcionibus, ~onibus, et incarceracionibus *Plusc.* VII 27; in comburendo .. xij pomos .. ad ~onem ipsius R. .. *Entries* 689b.

exhereditio, disherison. *V. et. exheredatio, exhereditas, exhereditatio.*

1234 M. PAR. *Maj.* III 270 (v. exheredatio a); **1272** in nostrum et heredum nostrorum ~onem manifestam *Cl* 492; **1292** ad .. dampnum .. Ricardi et †exhereditionis [MS: exheredacionis] periculum manifestum (*IPM*) *Doc. Scot.* I 323.

exheres [CL], disinherited.

c705 ne .. invisi .. aemulorum cunei .. congratulentur, si sobolem opulenti paternae philosophiae censu ~edem .. comperiunt (ÆTHELWALD) *Ep. Aldh.* 2 (7); ~es, exheredatus *bereafod GlP* 545; patet quod multe carte remanent post mortuos ~edes que dicunt hereditatem signatam ipsis mortuis et suis heredibus .. in perpetuum pertinere WYCL. *Ver.* II 134.

exhibere [CL]

1 to exhibit, produce (for inspection). **b** (p. ppl. as sb. n.) exhibit, item presented for inspection. **c** to convey, reveal (information). **d** to produce (effect or result). **e** to fulfil, put into effect.

?**1181** cum .. archiepiscopus .. peteret instrumentorum sibi copiam ~eri .. pars fratrum .. quantum potuit privilegiorum exhibitionem vitavit (*Lit. Papae*) ELMH. *Cant.* 444; **1245** (v. apostolus 2a); **1287** ut dispensaciones .. nobis .. non differant ~ere *Conc. Syn.* 1016; **c1420** dies in quibus querele .. replicaciones rejunccionesque ~entur in filumque ponuntur *Chanc. Orders* 7c; ~eo quasdam indenturas .. et allego hujusmodi exhibita esse subscripta et sigillata respective manibus et sigillis *Praxis* 227 (v. et. 1b infra). **b** **1400** diligenter ponderatis hujusmodi ~itis et ostensis *Cart. Rams.* II 211; **c1540** custos registri et ~itorum in eadem curia [admiralitatis] quorumcunque *Entries* 75b; *Praxis* 227 (v. 1a supra). **c** reperta sunt .. quaedam in veteribus libris vitiose descripta, .. caetera ex relatione veterum, ut ab antiquioribus, sunt eis ~ita FOLC. *V. Bot. pref.* 374; quia jubetis, breviter illud schedula praesens ~eat ANSELM (*Ep.* 61) III 176. **d** carnifex .. catastarum crudelitatem exercuit, lividas palmarum vibices ~uit ALDH. *VirgP* 47; substantia cui si 21 ʒ adjunxeris tota summa simul decem ipsius substantie radices ~eat ROB. ANGL. *Alg.* 74. **e** quod bene proposuit fortior exhibuit (*Vers.*) ANSELM *Misc.* 351; **1448** idem W. diversas condiciones super exhibitione cujusdam sacerdotis .. non ~uit *Ac. Durh.* 236.

2 (w. *praesentiam* or sim.) to appear (in person). **b** (refl.) to present itself, crop up.

1072 si Canturiensis (*sic*) archiepiscopus concilium cogere voluerit .. Eboracensis .. sui praesentiam .. ~eat *Lit. Cant.* III 351 (= *Regesta* 65); **1072** quoadusque concilio seipsum ~uit LANFR. *Ep.* 3 (4); age .. Domine, appare mihi, .. ~e praesentiam tuam ANSELM (*Or.* 2) III 9; A. TEWK. *Add. Thom.* 25 (v. demandare 6b); **1331** die et loco predictis vestram .. studeatis presenciam ~ere *Lit. Cant.* I 361. **b** juxta quod se occasio componendarum rerum ~uit ALDH. *Met.* 6; cum opportunitas se ~et ANSELM (*Ep.* 234) IV 142.

3 to show, display: **a** (w. abstr. obj.); **b** (refl. w. compl.); **c** (w. adv.); **d** (w. inanim. subj.). **e** to present the appearance (of).

a curam .. lectionibus sacris .. ~ebat BEDE *HE* II 19 p. 164; nulla sic gignitur, ut nulla admixta dissimilitudine omnimodam similitudine parentis ~eat ANSELM (*Mon.* 40) I 58; archiepiscopus Lugdunensis gaudet .. se suam mihi munificentiam .. honorifice ~ere, et desiderat me .. secum .. manere *Id.* (*Ep.* 208) IV 103; **1169** de ~ita mansuetudine nascitur .. insolentia J. SAL. *Ep.* 268 (285). **b** exemplum vivendi sese videntibus .. ~ens BEDE *HE* IV 21 p. 255; cum .. fratri nostro .. vos .. beneficos in omnibus ~etis ANSELM (*Ep.* 40) III 151; bone, ne te ultorem ~eas, a quo peto interventorem *Id.* (*Or.* 14) III 56; Edwardus qui se patrem patrie ~uerat TURGOT *Marg.* 2; **1166** me vobis semper fidelem ~ui et devotum J. SAL. *Ep.* 173 (160); **a1184** hoc ei concedimus quamdiu se fidelem nobis †exiguerit [l. exhibuerit] et predictum censum bene reddiderit *Reg. S. Bees* 361; rex se difficilem ~uit TREVET *Troades* 3. **c** quando se male ~ebat filius VAC. *Lib. Paup.* 81; ~ens se curialiter BACON V 142 (v. curialiter 2a). **d** ut [mare] vix .. paucis diebus se navigantibus tranquillum ~eat GIR. *TH* II 1. **e** qui crura natibus adherebant, ~ebat potius quadrupedum quam hominem (*V. Aldh.*) W. MALM. *GP* V 262.

4 a to provide. **b** to offer, present, grant (also absol.). **c** (med.) to administer. **d** to pay. **e** to contribute to. **f** to render (service, honour, or sim.). **g** to take, utter (oath). **h** to dispense (justice), utter (verdict). **i** (w. *fidem*) to give credence.

a **680** nec manibus lomentum .. cum manutergio ~etur ALDH. *Ep.* 4 p. 484; gardianus de manerio .. mattulas .. per domus longitudinem ~ere debet *Cust. Cant.* 195. **b** alimoniae stipendium et stipis edulium ~ens ALDH. *VirgP* 50; Dei servus sui .. cordis thalamum .. redemptori ~uit BYRHT. *V. Ecgwini* 355; bonus annus quando canis corvo exibet [AS: *gyfeð*] *Prov. Durh.* 6; hoc alii ~e quod tibi ~eri optaveris W. DONC. *Aph. Phil.* 10. 5; **1276** pro russeto exibito Thome de B. xlij s. *Rec. Leic.* I 176; quidam diabolo fecit homagium, cochlear argenteum in pignus homagii ~endo *Latin Stories* 37; **1516** ballivus .. possessionem corporalem .. per terram et lapidem denariumque argenti .. ~uit *Scot. Grey Friars* II 12. **c** ~eantur electuaria et syrupi omni mane et vespere et meridie GILB. I 19. 1; opiata .. de tertio in tertium paroxismum potest ~eri *Ib.* 19. 2; diaborraginum .. in causis melancholie ~eatur *Ib.* II 100. 2; mulgeatur et ~eatur statim quia lac citissime corrumpitur J. MIRFIELD *Brev.* 80. **d** **s857** c .. mancusas .. pape precepit ~eri M. PAR. *Maj.* I 387; **s1232** rex .. auxilium pecuniare sibi postulat .. ~eri *Flor. Hist.* II 202; **1275** reddendo .. iiij d. de eadem firma quam exibet pro terra in qua manet *Reg. S. Bees* 296; **1292** (v. emenda 4a). **e** **1341** excusat se prior quod .. non potest expensis ~ere pro incepcione talis in theologia *FormOx* 225. **f** spurcas delubris caeremonias ~entes ALDH. *VirgP* 50; ut nullus honor qui alicui sancto debet ~eri, ~eatur ab illis ANSELM (*Ep.* 236) IV 144; itineranti pervium Meldunum ~uit hospitium W. MALM. *GP* V 262; ministeria que ordini competebant alacriter ~ebat ORD. VIT. III 10 p. 115; **1171** amasii diu ~itum obsequium *Ep. J. Sal.* 305 (307); *Chr. Battle* f. 65 (v. detergere 1b); quod his numinibus ubique gentium veneratio ~eatur ALB. LOND. *DG* 13. 8; **1239** licet .. inviti cogamur ab universis ~itam gratiam revocare .. (*Lit. Imp. Fred.*) M. PAR. *Maj.* III 547; favor abbati ~itus *State Tri. Ed. I* 50. **g** sacramento per legatos ~ito ORD. VIT. IV 5 p. 197. **h** **a1160** meminimus vobis scripsisse ut .. [Waltero] abbati ecclesie de Bello justiciam ~eretis *Doc. Theob.* 12; sin autem contumaces extiterint .. sententia ~enda est R. NIGER *Mil.* III 73; **a1181** ut ipsis .. justicie non differat plenitudinem ~ere (*Lit. Papae*) *Reg. Malm.* I 374; **s1227** rex statuit illis diem .. apud Norhamtonam ut ibi faceret eis plenam rectitudinem ~eri WEND. II 322; **1265** Johanni et aliis jus sibi vendicantibus in maneriis .. plenam et celerem justiciam ~ebimus *Cl* 25; ut .. super predictis recordo et processu justiciam ~eret *State Tri. Ed. I* 46; **1306** intraneo et domestico communis justicia ~eatur *BBC* (*Swansea*) 224. **i** **1410** pater .. mendaciis inimicorum meorum fidem ~uit *FormOx* 427.

5 (w. pers. obj.) to support, maintain; **b** (acad.). **c** to entertain.

1164 ~uit eum dominus Pictavensis .. et primo dedit ei v m., deinde c s. J. SAL. *Ep.* 142 (136 p. 14); MAP *NC* V 5 f. 66v. (v. despicabilis a); **1254** quod .. ipsum in necessariis ~eat donec convalueirt *Cl* 258; **a1350** cum .. servientes in robis et aliis necessariis ab ipso .. ~eantur *StatOx* 68; **1457** hominum sagitariorum .. ~endorum per comitatum *Lit. Cant.* III 227. **b** **1252** faciant habere Johanni de Aula, clerico, quem rex exibet in scolis Oxonie, .. unam robam *Cl* 298; **1287** ut .. pauperes clerici ~erentur in scolis *Conc. Syn.* 1026; a suo avunculo .. ~itus est primo ad scolas grammaticales et postea ad studium Oxonie *Hist. Durh.* 1; **s1402** cujus me pater .. ad scholas ~uit AD. USK 77; **1435** residuum ad ~endum pro termino octo annorum in universitati Oxoniensi pauperes capellanos qui antequam ad exhibicionem .. admittantur sint in artibus baccalarii *Test. Ebor.* II 58. **c** regi .. illum benigne exibendum commendavit *Hist. Abb. Jarrow* 32; hospites .. oleribus et porris .. valde tenuiter ~ere solent GIR. *Spec.* III 13 p. 212; **s1201** Samson abbas exhibuit [regem J.] cum omni sequela sua honorifice *Ann. S. Edm.* 8; **c1237** per totam ebdomadam in mensa sua ministros suos ~ebit *Stat. Linc.* I 294.

6 (w. double acc., by conf. w. *inhibere*) to forbid.

Ancelmus .. tenuit concilium in quo ~uit presbiteros uxores W. WORC. *Itin.* 178.

exhibilis, (phil.) demonstrable.

memoria in quantum hujusmodi recipit speciem ut retentibilem solum, et, ut ita loquar, intellectui ~em; intelligentia vero ut exhibitam et intuibilem; propter quod potentie diverse dici debent KNAPWELL *Not.* 195.

exhibitio [CL]

1 production, bringing into court (of evidence).

si sponsa virum supervixerit dotem et maritationem suam cartarum instrumentis vel testium ~onibus ei traditam perpetualiter habeat (*Leg. Hen.* 70. 22) *GAS* 590; ?**1181** (v. exhibere 1a); **1367** de ~one alienacionis bonorum monasterio de Pasleto *Reg. Paisley* 37 *rub.*; **1391** in exp[ensis] terrar[ii] apud Ebor' pro ~one monumentorum nostrorum coram domino archiepiscopo *Ac. Durh.* 597; **c1585** usque diem ~onis hujus informationis *Entries* 431.

2 (w. *praesentiae* or sim.) appearance.

a1098 ego .. ad sinum .. paternae .. pietatis vestrae per ~onem praesentiae meae confugere disposui ANSELM (*Ep.* 206) IV 99; **1176** tam sollenni .. tante ecclesie vocationi presentie vestre ~one satisfacere maturetis (*Lit. Regis Franciae*) DICETO *YH* I 412; J. WALEYS *Commun.* III 8 f. 23 (v. condescensio).

3 showing, manifestation; **b** (w. *miraculorum* or sim.). **c** (w. gen., of abstr.) display.

in populis suis notificat virtutem, etiam in irrationabilibus invocatione fidelium dans ~onem HERM. ARCH. 53. **b** in ~one miraculorum humani gloriam favoris .. declinare BEDE *Mark* (vii 24) 202A; si nova ipsius miraculorum ~o revocetur R. COLD. *Cuthb.* 64; **1171** post tot signorum ~onem J. SAL. *Ep.* 304 (305 p. 736); ut .. Deus quanti meriti vir .. fuerit demonstraret, jucundus ut erat in vita sua, quasi jocosa miraculorum ~one declaravit ALEX. CANT. *Mir.* 33 p. 225. **c** numquam tanta benignitatis opus est ~one quanta in nova .. de reprobis ad probos mores conversione ANSELM (*Ep.* 67) III 187; Anselmus .. vitam .. in .. virtutum ~onibus exercebat EADMER *V. Anselmi* II 43; **1167** familiaritatis .. jugis et perpetua ad invicem ~o J. SAL. *Ep.* 214 (199); ALEX. CANT. *Dicta* 12 p. 155 (v. exercitatio 3b); ultronea fidelitatis ~one GIR. *TH* III 9; ecclesia .. nulli .. religione caritatisque exibitione gratuita .. habebatur secunda *Chr. Battle* f. 48.

4 performance (of work), rendering (of service); **b** (compared w. words).

per bonorum operum ~onem EGB. *Pont.* 93; timeat .. princeps Dominum et se .. pia ~one operis servum profiteatur J. SAL. *Pol.* 526D; facta est translatio persone absque nova professionis vel obedientie ~one H. BOS. *Ep.* 2. 1423B; **s1311** grata ~one obsequiorum apud dominum suum summi favoris apicem optinuit *V. Ed. II* 168. **b** caesar Henricus scriptis et bonorum operum ~onibus irradiat (*Quad. pref.*) *GAS* 543; hoc fama multiplex adtestatur, hoc operum ~one .. comprobatur ORD. VIT. IV 6 p. 200; **a1170** liberalitas vestra non modo ex relatione amici vestri .. verum ipsa operis ~one fidelius innotescit J. SAL. *Ep.* 135 (141); **1219** attendentes nunc ex ipsius relatione et operis ~one majestatem nostram fallaciter .. esse circumventam *Pat* 392a.

5 giving, granting (w. gen.); **b** dispensing (of justice).

quae vero lingua .. explicabit eleemosynarum ~ones egenis ab eo [i.e. duce Roberto] .. distributas? W. JUM. X 12; **s1152** a domino suo duce Normannorum petierunt .. auxilii ~onem H. HUNT. *HA* VIII 32; **1226** subventionis hujus [sc. quintedecime] ~o *Pat* 103; pro immeritis beneficiorum ~onibus .. regratiari AD. MARSH *Ep.* 78. **b** **1226** ut neuter sibi in juris ~one derogari juste possit conqueri *Pat* 73; **1271** nos .. qui singulis de regno nostro .. in ~onem justicie sumus debitores *Cl* 332; **1340** cum ~one plena justicie (*Lit. Regis*) AVESB. 88b; **1438** quatinus .. in modum effectualem justicie ~onem ministretis BEKYNTON I 254.

6 provision, maintenance, support; **b** (w. gen. of person or institution). **c** (acad.) 'exhibition'. **d** entertainment (of guest). **e** cost, expense.

ipsorum [hospitalarium] illibata crumena largam eis de proprio faciebant ~onem MAP *NC* I 23 f. 16; **1343** clericis ~onem in victualibus tribuat competentem (*Stat. Sibthorpe*) *Eng. Clergy* 269; **1376** fratres, licet infirmi fuerint, nichil percipient de predicta ~one *DCCant.* D.E. 4; tam larga ~one procurati, tam laxa regula sunt contenti *Croyl.* 40. **b** **1214** ad parcamenum et ~onem scriptorum pro libris scribendis (*Cust.*) *Chr. Evesham* 208; **1253** quod .. sitis quieti ab exibucione Simonis de Norwyco *Cl* 457; **s1289** remisimus ei [abbati Persore] ~onem conventus propter combustionem ecclesie illius *Ann. Worc.* 500; de ~one consanguineorum .. sollicitudinem gerere *Spec. Incl.* 1. 2; **1335** in annua ~one hospitalis B. Marie Magdalene vj li. viiij s. iiij d. *Comp. Swith.* 232; **1457** ad invencionem et ~onem .. hominum sagittariorum *Lit. Cant.* III 227. **c** **c1280** quam cito .. plures redditus empti fuerint augeatur numerus et ~o magistrorum *MunAcOx* 782; **1340** aliis .. scolaribus .. infirmantibus .. ~o similis fiat de communi *Deeds Balliol* 291; **1406** in ~one ij scolarium Oxonie studencium xx s. *Comp. Swith.* 288; **1432** lego Willelmo puero meo qui stat apud S. in studio ad exhibucionem suam vj m. argenti si scolas continuare velit *Reg. Cant.* II 492; **1434** pro exhibucione fratrum et puerorum .. collegii in annum tunc futurum; .. pro exhibucione annua *Cant. Coll. Ox.* II 262; **1485** in ~one unius scolaris Oxonie studentis .. x s. *Comp. Swith.* 298. **d** in sumptibus autem ~onis et honore, volunt omnes omnibus .. parificari GIR. *IK* II 5; **1214** expensas factas in ~one domini legati apud S. Albanum per iiij dies *Cl* 210; **12..** quod .. numerus ibidem Deo servientium et hospitum confluentium ~o augeatur juxta facultatum suorum (*sic*) incrementum *Reg. S. Thom. Dublin* 220; **1511** recepi a gardiano maneriorum pro ~one domini cardinalis xxxj li. *Cant. Coll. Ox.* II 271. **e** **1413** omnes monachi quos abbas ad mensam illis festis vocaverit erunt ad ~onem abbatis (*Stat.*) *Croyl. Cont. B* 498.

exhibitor [CL]

1 one who presents legal case.

1437 ut non modo non fuisset admissa .. peticio, verum contra ~orem pocius ut ad carceres traheretur esset acclamatum (*Lit. Papae*) BEKYNTON II 10.

2 (w. *praesentium* or sim.) bearer.

1265 Willelmo .. et Theodosio vestrarum ~oribus litterarum *Cl* 138; **1287** Willelmum et Galfridum presencium ~ores *Reg. Malm.* II app. 400; **1309** Guillelmum de S., clericum ~orem presencium *PQW* 836a; **1418** Thomam de Myrton .. ~orem presencium ad Anglie, Scotie, et nonnullas alias mundi partes *Mon. Hib. & Scot.* 370a.

3 fulfiller (of promise).

s1209 ad opus prefati Othonis [regis Alemannie] magnifici promissoris et parcissimi ~oris M. PAR. *Min.* II 117.

4 supporter, benefactor.

1375 scolaris ~ori *FormOx* 225.

exhibitorius [CL], expressive (of), exhibiting. **b** that gives support or maintenance.

s**1183** hoc etenim vinculo debite subjectionis ~io .. comites Britannie ducibus Normannorum .. tenentur astricti DICETO *YH* II 18. **b 1415** quatinus .. manus vestras ~ias .. michi dignemini expandere .. et me .. cum xx s. recreare *FormOx* 433.

exhibitus, provision (of food or sim.).

[Martha] parat .. [convivium Domino] quoniam spiritus promptus est; sed cum sollicitudine, quoniam caro infirma est: de apparatu sollicitatur, imo et de ~u turbatur PULL. *Sent.* 936D.

exhibutio v. exhibitio. **exhil-** v. et. exil-.

exhilarare [CL]

1 to exhilarate, gladden; **b** (w. inanim. subj. or obj.).

798 repletus sum gaudio .. et totus jocunditate ~atus ALCUIN *Ep.* 143; **8..** †exiraret [l. exilararet], *gegladað WW*; multiplices non numerantur opes, / Altithronum primo quibus exhilaravit ab aevo WULF. *Swith.* I 119; hic nec inferni merore cruciamur nec jucunditate celi ~amur PULL. *Sent.* 702D; **1166** [Domini] cujus muneribus abutentes pestifera dulcedine prosperorum in perniciem totiens ~ati sumus J. SAL. *Ep.* 175 (176); *elecer*, .. gaudere, exhillarare, jubilare *Gl. AN Ox.* f. 154v.; quo audito Jacobus Douglas plurimum exhileratus (*Chr. Anon.*) *Illust. Scot.* 5; s**1306** post diuturna infortunia, multum ~atus FORDUN *Cont.* XII 12 (cf. *Plusc.* IX 8: exhilleratus); *chere thy gestes*, exillera convivas STANBR. *Vulg.* 19. **b** a**1166** me sinceritas vestra .. ~avit J. SAL. *Ep.* 164 (149); [musica] animos tristes non mediocriter ~at GIR. *TH* III 12; ecce dolet cernens sed spes facit exhilarari NIG. *Paul.* f. 50v. 688; facta †relaturum [l. relaturam] bonitas se sperat habere, / exhilarataque per secula nulla perit WALT. ANGL. 18. 28.

2 to enhance or brighten in appearance.

exhilarant frondes silvam VINSAUF *CR* 324 (v. disjungere 3c).

exhilaratio [LL], exhilaration, delight.

non enim [homini erat] laboris afflictio [in paradiso] sed voluntatis ~o ALCUIN *Exeg.* (*Gen.* ii 15) 521D; [Christus dicitur] oleum propter interiorem anime impiguationem et exhillaracionem BART. ANGL. I 21; **1439** permaxima ~one reficitur cor nostrum BEKYNTON I 206.

exhilarescere, to become glad.

ut .. et celi etiam novo gaudio ~erent dum celici cives sue regine .. festive occurrerent HON. *Sig.* 517C.

exhilariter, joyfully.

legite gratulabundi et ~er sanctorum scita et decreta ÆLF. BATA 5. 4.

exhiler- v. exhilar-. **exhill-** v. exhil-.

exhinc [CL]

1 after this, hereafter, then.

multo ~c tempore in ecclesia manens BEDE *HE* II 20; quod utinam ~c etiam nostrarum lectione litterarum fiat! *Ib.* V 14; hactenus incerto mea stamine vita pependit, / .. / exhinc certa sequar, cupiens agnoscere verum ALCUIN *SS Ebor* 175; oceani tumidas exhinc remeavit ad undas FRITH. 1262; pronior existam semperque fidelior exhinc WULF. *Swith.* II 802; **1093** ut ~c abbathia predicta ab omni calumnia secura et libera permaneat *Regesta* p. 132; ~c .. Emmam defuncti regis relictam duxit uxorem AILR. *Ed. Conf.* 744A; ~c [sc. tempore abbatis H., ob. **1349**] ceperunt redditus .. monasterii minui *Meaux* III 37.

2 from this point, hence.

798 plurima ~c dicere potui sed nolui cartulae excedere modum ALCUIN *Ep.* 143; **1289** prout semita transit per medium loci .. et ~c versus Perafita *RGasc* II 440.

3 for this reason, on this account.

quod scriptura sacra non sit ~c falsa WYCL. *Ver.* II 17.

exhominare, to unman.

ut Venus exhominet homines GARL. *Epith.* I 83.

exhonerare v. exonerare.

exhonorare [LL], to dishonour: **a** (person); **b** (God or the Church); **c** (abstr.).

a ANSELM II 68 (v. exhonoratio); ut .. archiepiscopum ~em cui professionem debeo W. MALM. *GP* I 48; non ergo .. ~andi clerici boni propter vitia delinquentium H. LOS. *Ep.* 60; rex .. ne ~aretur, quid .. conducibile esset .. inquisivit J. FURNESS *Kentig.* 37 p. 227. **b** qui tunc consputus est salivis infidelium .. nunc .. vesanis .. fidelium ~atur opprobriis BEDE *Mark* (xiv 65) 281D; **798** defende sponsam Domini Dei tui. cogita de sponsa tua, si quis eam ~are velit ALCUIN *Ep.* 148; hunc honorem debitum qui Deo non reddit .. Deum ~at et hoc est peccare ANSELM *Misc.* 300; s**1141** idem sanctam ecclesiam ~averat W. MALM. *HN* 495; **1166** sponsum ~at Christum quicumque inhonorat ecclesiam sponsam ejus J. SAL. *Ep.* 184 (174). **c** eo .. munere ~anda visa est adolescentia senilis *Id. Pol.* 400B; nulli enim non egrotanti licet jejunium quadragesimale sine penitentia solvere et totam quadragesimam ~are ROB. BRIDL. *Dial.* 114.

exhonoratio [LL], dishonouring.

ita qui honorem alicujus violat non sufficit honorem reddere, si non secundum ~onis factam molestiam aliquid, quod placeat illi quem exhonoravit, restituit ANSELM (*CurD* I 11) II 68.

exhorbitare v. exorbitare. **exhoriri** v. exoriri.

exhorrere, ~escere [CL]

1 to shudder (w. fear), be or become terrified; **b** (w. inf.).

his ita contuitis, exhorruit FRITH. 445. **b** quod tua perfida gens in .. Christo .. tunc implere non exorruit *Eccl. & Synag.* 115; si ipsi debent turpia .. flagitia nostra scire, que etiam ~escimus cogitare? HON. *Eluc.* 1173A; mortis eum .. subigere non ~uit immanitas *Chr. Battle* f. 34.

2 (trans.) to shudder at, fear. **b** (gdv.) horrific.

ALDH. *VirgP* 44 (v. atramentum 1b); commissum, ubi ad cor suum rediit, gravissime ~uit BEDE *HE* IV 23; pater ejus .. ~uit facinus flagitiosissimum ABBO *Edm.* 16; **9..** exorruit, *onscunode WW*; c**1071** si .. quod saepius ore bene promisit diabolica persuasione deceptus ~eat ANSELM (*Ep.* 113) III 248; colligite egentem Christum, ne ~eatis judicem opulentum cum venerit judicare vivos et mortuos H. LOS. *Serm.* 3 p. 90; armate militie robur vehementer ~ens GIR. *EH* II 34; patratum scelus ~escit [virgo] *Pass. Æthelb.* 8. **b** ~endissimam .. addictionem AD. MARSH *Ep.* 247 c. 18 p. 459 (v. 1 addictio).

3 to become horrible or fearsome.

[leprosus] rediens notis .. suis vilescebat eo quod notis fedis ~escebat W. CANT. *Mir. Thom.* VI 55.

exhortamentum [LL], exhortation.

sunt altiora perfectionis praecepta, vel potius ~a BEDE *Mark* (viii 8) 208A; a**804** ~um .. conscribere ut habeeres jugiter inter manus paternae ammonitionis sententias ALCUIN *Ep.* 305; *treatie*, ~um LEVINS *Manip.* 110.

exhortari, ~are [CL]

1 to exhort, encourage; **b** (w. *ut*, *quatinus*, or *ne*); **c** (w. inf.); **d** (absol.).

c**705** te .. litteris ~ari non piget ALDH. *Ep.* 8 (11); **787** optans te non solum in meis [apicibus] proficere, sed etiam tuis me multoties exortari ALCUIN *Ep.* 4; **793** ignorantes instruite, scientes ~ate *Ib.* 17; exhortans omnem divino dogmate plebem WULF. *Swith.* I 1033; fratres semper ad ardua exortans ÆLF. *Æthelwold* 6; a**1097** vos paterna monitione ~or ANSELM (*Ep.* 203) IV 95; s**1333** eosdem ad pugnandum .. exortaverunt *Plusc.* IX 28. **b** sollerter ~ans ne .. aestimarent BEDE *HE* II 19; coeperunt [eum] diligenter ~ari ut .. paenitentiam faceret *Ib.* V 14; **1167** si ~atus est ut evitetis J. SAL. *Ep.* 220 (227); **1201** rogamus et exortamur in Domino quatinus nuntios ejus .. benigne recipere .. velitis *RChart* 100b; **1495** volo quod .. capellanus .. teneatur populum ~are ut dicant unum Pater Noster (*Ch. Regis Scotie*) *Scot. Grey Friars* II 20. **c** ut vestrum .. studium .. mea ~etur commonitio .. ad meliora proficere ANSELM (*Ep.* 185) IV 70. **d** a**1103** ad fratres .. estote vos epistola nostra ad salutandum, ad ~andum, ad confortandum (*Ib.* 307) IV 229; primo regina ~ando planctum modificat dicens .. TREVET *Troades* 13.

2 to advise, recommend (a course of action). *Cf. exhortatus.*

1282 rex .. liberaliter a nobis ~ata concessit PECKHAM *Ep.* I 327.

exhortatio [CL]

1 exhortation, encouragement; **b** (w. subj. gen.); **c** (w. obj. gen.).

non omnibus una eademque exortatio congruit *V. Greg.* p. 109; colimus .. nativitatem Domini .. in qua specialiter angelica ~one docemur vota ei bonae voluntatis offerre BEDE *Hom.* I 6. 339; **799** nescio quae causa .. te ab ~one cessare conpulit ALCUIN *Ep.* 175; licet .. monita piae exortationis .. quempiam docere praesumam O. CANT. *Const. pref.*; ut vos .. excitem amica ~one ANSELM (*Ep.* 270) IV 185; duo .. sunt genera ~onum quibus interior homo exteriorem debet excitare ad opus bonum *Simil. Anselmi* app. p. 100. **b** ego Inae .. exortatione et doctrina C. patris mei .. (*Quad.*) *GAS* 89; fuit .. scribendi occasio .. nobilium principum tam remuneratio quam ~o. honores enim artes nutrire solent GIR. *TH intr.* p. 4; chorus mulierum Trojanarum ad ~onem Hecube plangit infortunia Troje TREVET *Troades* 10. **c** exortatio singulorum et maxime prelatorum ut legitime vivant (*Quad.*) *GAS* 536.

2 sermon.

cum .. ad locum sanctae ~onis suae ventum est, o qualia .. per organum suum Spiritus Sanctus effudit ADEL. BLANDIN. *Dunst.* 11; **1549** (v. contio d).

exhortatiuncula [LL], little exhortation.

hanc ~am meam habuissetis .. nisi .. P. BLOIS *Ep.* 103. 326B.

exhortativus [CL], exhortative.

c**797** illud ~um .. Esaiae prophetae elogium ALCUIN *Ep.* 121.

exhortator [LL], exhorter, encourager.

1410 tanti malificii ~ores *FormOx* 424.

exhortatorie, exhortatively.

'locutus est ad cor' [*2 Chron.* xxxii 6], i. e. ~ie et consolatorie locutus est S. LANGTON *Chron.* 195.

exhortatorius [LL], exhortatory; **b** (w. *sermo*, *verbum*, or sim.); **c** (w. *litterae* or sim., or as sb. f.) letters exhortatory; **d** (papal). **e** (as sb. n. pl.) exhortation.

9.. exortatorium, *trymendlic WW*; ad tale nocumentum exortatoria est consolatio seculi, que invitat hominem ad delectationem ALEX. BATH *Mor.* IV 10 p. 168. **b** dum .. ~io illos sermone reficeret BEDE *CuthbP* 36; verba ~ia [AS p. 367: *mynegyendlice*] ac pacifica pitacio luculentissime caraxata .. destinavit *RegulC* 4; surgens imperavit silentium habuitque ~ium sermonem ad populum AILR. *SS Hex* 2; verbis ~iis, preceptoriis, vel prohibitoriis OCKHAM *Dial.* 538; addidit .. ille qui hec scripsit .. versus .. ~ios *Croyl. Cont. C* 577. **c** BEDE *HE* II 4 (v. epistola 1); **799** saepius desideravi ~ias dilectionis vestrae litteras ALCUIN *Ep.* 175; c**1150** littera exortatoria sancti Thome Cantuar' directa .. episcopis *Doc. Theob.* 238 *tit.*; **1245** clerici .. rogaverunt quatinus .. literam supplicatoriam et ~iam destinare curaremus GROS. *Ep.* 89; **1428** per universum orbem Christianitatis epistolas ~ias transmittere BEKYNTON II 124. **d** ~ias ad fidem litteras a pontifice Bonifatio accepit BEDE *HE* II 10; **991** misi eum illuc cum litteris nostris ~iis (*Lit. Papae*) *Conc. Syn.* 178; misi [apocrisiarium nostrum] .. cum litteris nostris ~iis ut resipiscerent ab hac superstitione (*Lit. Papae*) W. MALM. *GR* II 166; **1324** bulla .. summi pontificis .. ~ia directa .. regi super reformacione pacis *TreatyR* I 246; **1430** asperius post nostras exortatorias quam prius .. in attritum hominem exacerbastis *Reg. Whet.* II 433. **e** s**1259** consimilia .. ~ia .. ad omnes Alemannie magnates .. mandata *Flor. Hist.* II 428; **1435** metrice .. sibi .. talia exortatoria dixit AMUND. II 88.

exhortatus, exhortation. *Cf. exhortari* 2.

1406 ad hoc .. te piis ~ibus invitamus (*Lit. Papae*) *Conc.* III 289a.

1 exhumare [cf. CL humare], to exhume.

s**1290** litere archiepiscopi venerunt ad episcopum jubentes eum corpus H. Poche ~atum fratribus minoribus reddi sepeliendum *Ann. Worc.* 502; **1317** dictum corpus †hesumere [l. exhumare] .. illudque .. ecclesiastice tradiderunt sepulture .. presumpserunt *Mon. Hib. & Scot.* 197b; heretici sepulti in locis sacris sunt ~andi OCKHAM *Pol.* III 270; s**1358** qui ~avit eum et fregit parietem ecclesie et extraxit corpus per foramen et ejecit extra cimiterium KNIGHTON II 104; Henricus Percy, qui .. fuerat sepultus, in crastino .. ~atus est ejusque corpus Salopie reductum *Dieul.* 147; Ricardum regem, apud Langeley sepultum, rex Henricus jussit ~ari STRECCHE *Hen. V* 147.

2 exhumare v. eximere 3b.

exhumatio [cf. CL humatio], exhumation.

1305 super ~one corporis Hugonis le Blak' excommunicati *Reg. Cant.* 488; **1439** pro ~one ossium .. Thome quondam ducis Clarencie *Invent. Ch. Ch.* 152.

exhumator [cf. CL humator], exhumator.

~or cadaveris fraternalis HOLCOT *Wisd.* 39.

exhumectare v. exumectare. **exibere, ~itio** v. exhibere, ~itio. **exibutio** v. exhibitio. **exicc-** v. exsicc-. **exicium** v. exitium. **exigalum** v. oxygala.

exigare [cf. 1 exigere], to summon (to appear in court), to put in exigent (as preliminary to outlawry). *V. et. exigere* 8d.

1353 indictatus .. et per processum ~atus fuit in comitatu *Enf. Stat. Lab.* 242*.

exigentarius [cf. 1 exigere 8], 'exigenter', officer who issues exigent.

1439 officium ~ii comitatuum Lincoln', Norff', Hertf', Essex', Warr', Leyc', Staff', et Salop' *Pat* 445 m. 33.

exigentia

1 exigency, need, necessity; *v. et. exigere* 9b. **b** (gram.) requirement. **c** (math., specification).

1226 familia .. leprosarum .. ad .. ecclesiam veniet .. et secundum ~iam jura sua ibidem recipiet *Ch. Sal.* 173; secundum ~iam ipsius recipientis et quia natura est virtus finita, ideo recipitur modo finito BACON VII 129; ex quibus convincitur ~ia, quod .. perfeccius foret episcopum habere pure alimenta et tegumenta WYCL. *Sim.* 82; venditi sunt ipso [R. abbate, ob. **1335**] dictante .. xxxij libri ..; et .. coquinario x li. .. liberavit. factum infame .. ut .. spirituales epulas quoquo pacto carnalibus ~iis applicarent *G. S. Alb.* II 200. **b** dicendum quod .. hujusmodi concepcio non sit per similes casus propter ~iam preposicionis, quia

preposicio exigit ablativum BACON XV 70; ∼ia casus recti a parte post est gracia copule *Ib.* 99. **c** fiat igitur circulus secundum ∼iam *AF* que dividatur .. in duas partes WALLINGF. (*Quad.* 10) I 42.

2 exigency, requirement (w. *secundum, juxta,* or sim., & gen. of abstr.).

injurias quibus eum citra meritorum suorum ∼iam .. affecisti P. BLOIS *Ep.* 3. 7C; cum posceret hora mensas nec haberet quo reficeretur secundum infirmitatis ∼iam W. CANT. *Mir. Thom.* II 31; restituere .. tenentur custodes hereditatis ipsis heredibus instauratas et debitis aquietas juxta ∼iam temporis custodie et quantitatis hereditatis GLANV. VII 9; secundum ∼iam probitatis et stematis MAP *NC* V 5 f. 66v.; secundum legitimas sacramenti matrimonialis ∼ias AD. MARSH *Ep.* 25; secundum ∼iam cursus nature GROS. *Quaest. Theol.* 200; ut nec fideles dirigantur .. in vita secundum ∼iam fidei nec .. BACON *Tert.* 11; secundum juris ∼iam *Chr. Peterb.* 68; **1281** juxta feodi ∼iam in omnibus respondere paratus existam *Reg. Heref.* 297; **12..** per canonicos fratres .. ipsi domui secundum facultatum suarum ∼iam necessarios *Reg. S. Thom. Dublin* 220; major .. et vicecomites suas liberatas amicis .. honorifice secundum sui gradus ∼iam prebeurunt *MGL* I 29; **1433** juxta ∼iam officii quo fungimur *Deeds Balliol* 302; **1440** in .. universitate .. secundum formam et ∼iam statutorum .. facultatis arcium magister graduatus *FormOx* 464.

3 exaction, demand; **b** (eccl.).

s1187 propter intolerabiles ∼ias quas rex Francie sibi fieri postulavit *G. Hen. II* II 5; **s1190** rex Francie litteris mandaverat regi Tancredo, ut non adquiesceret ∼iis regis Anglie *Itin. Ric.* II 19; **s1253** cum de magna regis ∼ia, qui postulavit sibi peregrinaturo infinitam exhiberi pecuniam, diutius pertractassent, rogatum est .. M. PAR. *Min.* III 136; **1291** quod .. possit .. discutere et terminare nostras calumnias et ∼ias (*Breve Regis*) OXNEAD 282; **1360** rex Anglie filiusque ejus .. renunciabunt .. ∼iis quas fecerunt (*Treug.*) J. READING 176. **b** **1195** (1329) eandem .. ecclesiam [Linc.] .. de predicta ∼ia mantelli de nobis .. carta nostra quietam clamamus *CalCh* IV 147; habeant .. curiam suam .. ita .. ut nulla ∼ia .. in dono, vel in assisa, vel alia consuetudine ab episcopo .. fiat in prebendis eorum *Reg. S. Osm.* I 14; **1300** conceditur .. absque alicujus rei temporalis ∼ia *Dryburgh* 94; liberam .. ab omni servicio et exaccione et consuetudine et absque omni alia ∼ia que exigi vel evenire potest in terra *Reg. Newbattle* 92.

exigere [CL]

1 to drive out.

∼it, i. .. eicit *GlH* E 504; ∼itur, *wæs ut ascofen GlP* 184; exegit, *anydde Ib.* 820.

2 to remove, take off.

∼ebant, *araefndun GlC* E 503; ∼it, i. .. *arœfnaþ GlH* E 504; aliquando manus chirothecis velantur, aliquando exactis chirothecis denudantur HON. *GA* 609B.

3 to thrust out, stretch forward (fig.), or (?) *f. l.*

cum .. reliquie Dacorum nephandum caput exigunt [? l. erigunt] .. contriti sunt sub pedibus ejus [Athelstani] *Plusc.* VI 16.

4 to acquire, achieve. **b** to perform, complete. **c** to perpetrate. **d** (w. *mentionem*) to make mention.

∼e mihi victoriam et perduc me ad coronam ANSELM (*Or.* 15) III 64. **b** ALDH. *VirgV* 1580 (v. concentus a); nec poterant .. mori, nisi exacta illa consecratione ALB. LOND. *DG* 9. 12. **c** post tempus modicum exacto scelere / .. / tirannus moritur WALT. WIMB. *Carm.* 255. **d** Willelmo .., cujus mentionem paulo ante exegimus .. discesso *G. Steph.* II 93.

5 to spend (time). **b** (pass., of period of time) to end, be completed. **c** (absol.) to spend time, live.

cum annos xxx in regno .. exegisset BEDE *HE* IV 11 p. 225; in pelliciis vestibus omnes dies solitariae conversationis suae ∼ebat FELIX *Guthl.* 28. **b** annis .. sedecim exactis *Hist. Abb. Jarrow* 17; non multo .. exacto tempore BEDE *HE* III 9; **1071** exactis .. compluribus annis LANFR. *Ep.* 2; W. MALM. *GP* I 17 (v. efflator); **s1201** Grifinus .. terram .. cepit, sed ante mensem exactum Grifinus .. ibidem obiit *Ann. Cambr.* 62. **c** heremita qui .. in practicae conversationis studio desudans quam Martha .. praefigurat, miro devotionis fervore exegit ad demum .. theoricam .. transegit vitam ALDH. *VirgP* 29.

6 (w. pers. obj. expressed or implied): **a** to ask, demand, exact, compel; **b** (w. double obj.); **c** (w. inf.); **d** (w. acc. & inf.); **e** (w. *ut*); **f** to ask (w. indir. qu.).

a **1179** si quis .. exactus a sua receptione aliquid dederit, ad sanos ordines non accedat; is autem qui eum receperit officii sui privatione mulctetur (*Decr. Papae*) R. HOWD. II 181 (= GERV. CANT. *Chr.* 284: exactus pro); *demonder*, poscere, precari, .. ∼ere, orare *Gl. AN Ox.* f. 154v. **b** **c1075** ut tempus quod aliis .. scripturis sponte vos non piget insumere, vel hoc ad opus quod ∼imini non gravemini addicere ANSELM (*Ep.* 29) III 137; decimas solvere religionis pars est, et eas [decimas] a Deo populus .. ∼itur, at qui eas exigunt irreligiosi sunt J. SAL. *Pol.* 694A; noli diffidere, curam ∼eris non curacionem GIR. *Invect.* V 2; GASCOIGNE *Loci* 59 (v. erogare 5b). **c** cum Filius tuus .. lavari a Johanne undis Jordanicis exigisset EGB. *Pont.* 121; incurvatus pondere criminum alios ∼or erigere ANSELM (*Or.* 17) III 70. **d** **1187** clavem [ecclesie de H.] vobis tradi exegistis (*Lit. Archiep.*) DICETO *YH* II 48; **c1200** omnibus .. de quibus .. ecclesia decimas dari ∼it (*Ch. Regis Scotiae*) *Dryburgh* 37. **e** ab homine Deus ∼ebat ut diabolum vinceret ANSELM (*CurD* II 19) II 131; **1168** Pictavenses .. exegerunt ut eis resarcirentur dampna que rex Anglie .. illis intulerant J. SAL. *Ep.* 246 (279 p. 602); egit, immo exegit ab episcopo Rotomagensi ut confiscata .. predia episcopo redderentur DEVIZES 38v. **f** quid respondebis in illa die cum ∼etur a te .. omne tempus vivendi tibi impensum, qualiter fuerit a te expensum? ANSELM (*Medit.* 1) III 77; ?**1189** debet unus de viris predictis ∼ere ab eo versus quem assisa petitur, si sciat aliquid dicere per quod assisa debeat remanere *MGL* I 330; **1354** Philippus ad .. *morewenspeche* venit .. et exactus quare dispexit majorem suum, verbis suis ipsum parvipendendo *Rec. Leic.* II 93.

7 **a** to require, demand, exact, compel (payment, service, or sim.); **b** (w. abstr. or inanim. subj.; also absol.); **c** (gram. & math.) to require.

a †**693** (14c) siquis .. potius praeditus haec exacta decernit, possideat bona sempiterna *CS* 121; **749** (12c) ut munuscula ab aeclesiis .. minime ∼antur *CS* 178; **858** ut .. vi exactorum operum .. secura .. permaneat *CS* 496; numquid Deus injustus est, ut iterum ∼at quod solutum est? ANSELM (*CurD* I 19) II 86; totum .. quod erit mei juris usque ad ultimum quadrantem ∼am *Simil. Anselmi* 82; scedulam quam vobis perscribendam ∼itis [non] .. pape litteris hoc nobis designatum constat *Chr. Battle* f. 67v.; parvula mihi credita est pecunia quam .. dominus .. ∼et cum usura P. CORNW. *Panth. prol.* 39; **1251** forestarii .. ∼ebant ab eo vadium et plegium *SelPlForest* 94; **1281** que [ovis] si infra unum annum et unum diem ∼atur, obligat se ad restitucionem dicte ovis vel precii *SelPlMan* 31; **1294** (v. de 1c); **1314** (v. erga 6c); **1559** sub poena tantundem pecuniae quantum dotis nomine promissum .. fuerit, solvendi et in alium usum ∼endi, inque pios usus disponendi *Conc. Scot.* II 156. **b** ratio ∼it ut in pleno versu xxiiij tempora sint ALDH. *Met.* 10 p. 82; rex ipse, cum oportunitas exegisset, .. veniebat BEDE *HE* III 26; **793** peccata habitantium hoc exigerunt (*sic*) ALCUIN *Ep.* 20; vestram imprecor benivolam pietatem, nullis licet meis ∼entibus meritis, .. quatenus .. B. *Ep.* 387; ne exientibus (*sic*) vestris peccatis mortem repentinam vitae praesentis incidatis *GAS* 207; **a1089** vita ejus hoc ∼ente ANSELM (*Ep.* 11) III 115; **1215** (v. ericius 4); sicut ad regimen nature ∼untur sensus et virtutes, ita ad perfectionem ejusdem ∼untur .. spiritus quidam BART. ANGL. III 22; cum tempus exigerit (*sic*) lignorum strepitus sit pro cimbalo *Cust. Westm.* 316; **1315** si necessitas exiguat (*sic*) et eis videatur expediens esse *RGasc* IV 1626 p. 475; **1448** prout casus exigerit (*sic*) (*Ch. Regis*) *Reg. Whet.* I 39. **c** natura .. numeri hoc ∼it non .. ROB. ANGL. *Alg.* 98; ex intellectione, cum et id quod designatur et ad id ex eo aliud intelligi usus [sermonis] ∼it BALSH. *AD* 98; tunc est questio communis de omni supposito a parte ante cum verbo cujuscumque sit persone, an construatur ita quod ∼atur; quare si ∼itur, aut ∼itur racione significati aut consignificati BACON XV 8; *Ib.* 70 (v. exigentia 1b).

8 (leg.): **a** (trans.) to claim, demand (right or sim.). **b** (pr. ppl. as sb.) plaintiff. **c** to summon (to appear in court). **d** (w. pers. obj.) to put in exigent (as preliminary to outlawry); *v. et. exigare*. **e** (gdv. f. or n.) proceedings preliminary to outlawry. **f** (*breve exigendi* or sim.) 'exigent', writ of summons.

a sepe .. ex inscitia placitantium cause transeunt in jus aliorum .. tarditate, ut qui in prefectura vel qualibet potestate constitutus, sepe differt ∼ere, dum licet, quod sepe cum labore frustraque prosequitur destitutus (*Leg. Hen.* 22. 1) *GAS* 561; **1217** atornavit .. Robertum .. ad lucrandum vel perdendum de jure quod ipsa ∼it versus Willelmum *Pat* 113; **1228** postquam aliquis fuerit appellatus .. pro morte hominis, non potest ∼ere recognitionem antequam acquietaverit se de appello versus eum facto *MGL* I 92; **1230** si quis autem de terra vel de feudo prioris attachiatus fuerit per ballivos episcopi pro aliqua re pertinente ad curiam prioris, prior vel ballivus suus curiam suam ∼et et habebit sine contradictione, si eam ∼at ad horam et terminum *Feod. Durh.* 215; si .. contigerit aliquem hominem de tenemento prioris de Broke pro aliquo .. crimine attachiari, .. veniet ballivus prioris de Broke et ∼et curiam prioris et .. reus judicetur *Cust. Battle* 136; **1262** (v. curia 8a). **b** **1269** primo de placito terre sic.: .. A. tenens vel ∼ens (seu petens) versus B. de placito terre *CBaron* 81 (cf. ib.: si plures sunt ∼entes ..). **c** **1269** primo ∼antur essoniatores. deinde primo intrantur essonia de sectatoribus curie *CBaron* 80; **1306** commissio facta fuit .. ad calumniandum et ∼endum omnes cives Londoniarum ex quacunque causa attachiati fuerint *MGL* II 180; **1364** dictus Johannes solempniter exactus non venit *Law Merch.* I 112; **1405** predicti J. et A. solempniter exacti sunt et comparuerunt *CourtR Banstead*; **1452** xxiiij juratores impanellati exacti veniunt *Cart. Boarstall* 604; **1468** W. .., licet solempniter exactus, non revenit, set in contemptu curie defaltum fecit (*CourtR Banstead*) *Surrey Arch. Coll.* XXXII 53. **d** **1203** quod vicecomes faciat eum ∼i per comitatum quousque utlagetur *CurR* II 212; **1220** si quos invenerit resistentes illos capiat et habeat coram justiciariis .. et si se subtraxerint et nolint stare recto, faciat illos ∼i et in comitatu utlagari *Ib.* VIII 198; **1221** Willemus et Adam malecreduntur et ideo ∼antur et utlagentur *SelPlCrown* 105; **1226** dicunt quod debet ∼i ad tres hustengos et .. utlagari ad folkesmotum .. et quid .. tempus ∼endi et utlagendi brevissimum est .. *MGL* I 86; **1258** preceptum fuit quod predictus Galfridus ∼eretur de comitatu in comitatum ad utlagandum *JustIt* 1187 r. 15; cum principalis se acquietaverit .. non est necesse quod illi de forcia respondeant, set tunc primo ∼antur cum principales .. fuerint .. utlagati *Fleta* 42; **1364** Johannes et Ricardus exacti fuerunt primo et non comparuerunt. postea secundo, tercio, quarto, et ad istum comitatum exacti fuerunt quinto et non comparuerunt. ideo in judicio utlagantur *SelCCoron* 118. **e** **1275** in itinere justiciariorum predictus Galfridus Payn pro contumatia positus fuit in ∼endis, et per auxilium predicti Rogeri de Colvile de ∼endis amotus fuit propter quod nulla justicia de predicta felonia facta fuit *Hund.* I 448b; principales judicium utlagarie .. prius debent sustinere et .. suspendende sunt ∼ende erga hujusmodi secundarios, eo quod replegiabiles sunt *Fleta* 42; **1313** cum quis ponitur in ∼endo causa felonie, catalla confiscantur, contra est de causa transgressionis *Eyre Kent* 95; **c1320** si quis appellatus defaltam fecerit, ob quam poni debet in ∼endam *Lond. Ed. I & II* II 188 (cf. ib.: .. positus fuit in ∼enda et exactus); **1321** pro eo quod non venit .. postmodum in ∼enda poni, et ea occasione ibidem utlagari *Reg. Exon.* 440; **1439** de .. hominibus fugam facientibus pro ∼enda *Pat* 443 m. 18*d.*; cum .. in ∼endis positi existant in comitatu tuo asserentes ∼endas predictas in ipsos, ipsis .. ignorantibus, processisse nobis supplicaverint .. *Reg. Brev. Orig.* 273; **1585** cum .. in exigend' possitus fuisset in hustengo nostro London' ad utlagandum *Pat* 1303 m. 9. **f** **13..** de brevibus ∼endi et milites faciendi *MGL* I 172; de brevibus de ∼endo *Ib.* 173 (cf. ib. 190: *brief dexigent*); W. clericus Croxton dixit quod fecit novum ∼as in principio termini Michaelis eo quod .. vicecomes non misit breve de exigent W. WORC. *Itin.* 248.

9 (pr. ppl. as adj.) necessary. **b** (as sb. n. pl.) exigencies, necessities; *v. et. exigentia* 1a.

a1184 si contingeret quod siquis eorum depauperetur .. peteret .. necessaria sua in victu et vestitu pro statu suo ∼entia *BBC* (*Tewkesbury*) 70. **b** domus nostra, secundum custuum meorum ∼encia domi, ut in esculentis et poculentis et aliis minutis sumptibus, michi deberet scolatizanti Oxonie allocari *FormOx* 326; **1487** fervidus vestre devotionis affectus .. exigentia digna requirit ut .. vestris beneficiis gratitudinis debito compensemus *Scot. Grey Friars* II 263.

exigitio, exaction.

a1154 prohibeo ne aliquis meorum eis injuriam vel contumeliam vel aliquam novam ∼onem inferre vel exigere presumat (*Cart. Castleacre*) *MS BL Harley* 2110 f. 4v.

exigitivus, requiring, demanding; **b** (w. obj. gen.).

hoc verbum 'debet' .. respicit jus naturale sive evangelicum, et tunc dicitur ∼um S. LANGTON *Quaest.* f. 171v. **b** cuncta laborantum Deus acta remunerat eque; / res est mercedis exigitiva labor H. AVR. *Poems* 6. 86.

exignire [cf. LL ignire], to ignite, set afire (also fig.).

pii laboris desiderio amoreque ∼itus divino Romae .. visitare proposuit limina *V. Neot. A* 6; dea non valet aut deus ullus / exignire faces illas nisi femina sola D. BEC. 1986.

exiguere v. exhibere 3b, exigere 7b.

exiguitas [CL], exiguity, smallness; **b** (as title of humility).

totum quod de Christo creditur .. propter ejus .. humilitatem quasi propter nimiam ∼atem subtile est et incomprehensibile BALD. CANT. *Sacr. Alt.* 748D; pro ingenii mei ∼ate studui demonstrare que .. VAC. *Tract.* 5. **b** istum .. libellum .. quatinus in metricae artis versus transferatis nostra ∼as .. praecatur (*Ep. Wulfrici*) *Mem. Dunst.* 409; si quid .. †exiquitatis [v. l. exiguitatis] mee imperitie imputetur J. FURNESS *Kentig. prol.*; quantum sufficit mea ∼as AD. MARSH *Ep.* 12; ∼ati meae videtur, quod .. OCKHAM *Dial.* 480.

exiguus [CL]

1 exiguous, little, small in size or extent. **b** (as sb. m.) little one.

summa dum exiguis non trano per aethera pennis ALDH. *Aen.* 42 (*Struthio*) 3; exiguo, sulcat qui corpora, verme *Ib.* 100. 66; in hoc ∼uo opere BYRHT. *Man.* 14; exiguo .. poemate WULF. *Swith.* II 514; ∼uum et vile munus quod vobis mittit nostra pauper parvitas ANSELM (*Ep.* 10) III 113; [apri] ∼ui, deformes, et fugitivi GIR. *TH* I 24. **b** ne concedas trudendos hostibus istinc / sed magis exiguos defendens dextera tangat ALDH. *VirgV pref.* 14; servans militiae / castra supernae / praedones cohibit, / daemones arcet, / astans exiguis / causa salutis *Anal. Hymn.* LI 183.

2 small in amount, a little. **b** (pl.) few. **c** (math., of a number) less than the product of its parts. **d** (as sb. n.) little.

exiguae caperent nutrimina crustae ALDH. *VirgV* 2209; alimenta nec ulla / sumeret, excepto facili vegetamine panis / exigui WULF. *Swith.* I 1404. **b** exiguis nec possumus edere verbis / talia signa Dei *Ib.* II 398; quomodo elegit xij apostolos .. praeelegit .. ~uos famulos, fideles, non gnaros BYRHT. *V. Ecgwini* 352. **c** c**798** legimus .. numerorum .. inperfectorum alios esse superfluos, alios ~uos ALCUIN *Ep.* 133. **d** exiguum dixi .. / .. ne lingua pudorem / praesumtrix tulerit FRITH. 482.

3 (of period of time) brief, short.

vix .. exiguo manserunt gaudia lustro FRITH. 1043.

4 (of sound) faint.

levis nubecula patris tonitruum / in aure sibulum mutat exiguum WALT. WIMB. *Carm.* 96.

5 (of person) insignificant, humble. **b** (of abstr.) meagre, slight.

non esse eum legitimum pastorem .. qui haec non tam nostra, qui valde ~ui sumus, quam veteris novique testamenti decreta recusarit GILDAS *EB* 92; **a690** domino .. Ehfredo Aldhelmus ~uus in Domino salutem ALDH. *Ep.* 5; Dionysius ~uus .. alios [annos] .. pari schemate subnexuit BEDE *HE* V 21 p. 341; **722** ego Bonifatius ~uus episcopus BONIF. *Ep.* 16; ~uus, humilis *GlC* E 440; sacerdoti magno Ecgbercto presbiter meritis ~uus Aediluulf .. salutem ÆTHELWULF *Abb. pref.* **b** et famis exigua fugerunt funera stipe ALDH. *CE* 4. 7. 36; exigua tandem virtute resumpta WULF. *Swith.* I 103; feci .. quod potui quamvis omnino ~uum sit quod feci DOMINIC *V. Ecgwini* I 17; **1458** humanitatis exhibite, ~ue quamvis, et exilime (*Lit. Abbatis*) *Reg. Whet.* I 321.

exil- v. et. exhil-, exsil-.

1 exīliare [LL *p. ppl. only*; cf. CL exilis], to weaken, deplete. **b** to ruin, destroy.

~iata, i. consumpta *GlH* E 498. **b** **1205** ita quod boscum illum non vastent, †destruent [l. destruant], vel †exulent [l. exilient] *RChart* 143a.

2 exīliare [LL; cf. CL exilium], to exile, banish; *v. et.* 3 *exulare* 2a. **b** (leg.) to outlaw. **c** to evict.

ducta est Victoria .. in Tribulano territorio .. ut ibidem ~iata famis copia et cibi inopia augeretur ALDH. *VirgP* 52; martir qui multas tribulaciones passus et ~iatus pro nomine Christi erat *Descr. Constant.* 259; aliquanto .. tempore inimicorum accusatione ~iatus W. MALM. *GR* II 199; Flavia .. in insula Pontiana ob fidei testimonium ~iatur *Flor. Hist.* I 130 (= M. PAR. *Maj.* I 115: exulatur); s**1066** ceteri .. recalcitrantes .. trans mare pulsi et ~iati *Croyl.* 70; s**1037** Haraldus .. novercam ~iavit [v. l. exulavit] *Eul. Hist.* III 30; s**1307** Petrum de Gaverstone communi decreto ~iatum .. revocare WALS. *HA* I 115. **b** si quis hominem pro culpa ~iatum tenuerit aut paverit, emendet hoc (*Quad.*) *GAS* 319 (= *Cons. Cnuti*, *ib.*: si quis exlegem servaverit; AS: *friðleasan man* .. *oððe flyman*). **c** **1392** ~iavit duos tenentes nativos .. per magnam durisciam .. et tenementa eorum .. devastavit *IMisc* 252/12/3 (cf. ib.: fecit destruccionem exulando tres tenentes nativos).

exiliatio [cf. 2 exiliare], exile, banishment. *V. et. exulatio.*

s**1321** rex .. post exiliationem ambos [Spensatores], inconsultis magnatibus, ad solum proprium revocavit OTTERB. 110.

exilire v. exsilire.

exīlis [CL]

1 thin, lean, slender. **b** narrow. **c** small.

acus exilis ALDH. *Aen.* 29. 3 (v. 2 acus a); ~em, tenuem; .. ~is, gracilis *GlC* E 365, 367; nullum lupus audax / exillis rapuit lurcon temet faciente GODEMAN 22; si lepus atque canem temptet laniare ferocem, / scorpius exilis tunicatum si crocodrillum *Altercatio* 4; que ~ia sunt arbori debiliter herentia hieme occidunt, que vero grossa firmiter sunt herentia minime cadunt *Quaest. Salern.* Ba 24; potest hoc videri in capillis frigidi cerebri qui ~es apparent *Ib.* P 14. **b** **12**.. declinando parum .. per ~em semitam usque in introitum nemoris *Feod. Durh.* 203*n.* **c** **1264** terras et predia captivorum suo prorsus dominio subjugavit coadjutoribus suis .. ~issimas dividens partes WYKES 153; **1316** minores ville dicti hundredi et ~es *Aids* 388.

2 scanty, meagre, mean.

vix .. iiij canonici erant qui victu ~i .. vitam tolerarent W. MALM. *GP* I 72; **1295** habito imprisonamento, [vagantes] deliberantur etc. quia ~es etc. *Gaol Del.* 39/2 r. 2; contra gulam est ipsius [Christi] ~is piccancia [ME: *poure pitance*] quam habuit in cruce *AncrR* 96; **1410** in cujus inmensi doni .. exilimam recompensam *StatOx* 209; **1459** munus quamquam exillimum [MS: exilimum] apud nos tamen ditissimum (*Concessio Suffragiorum*) *Reg. Whet.* I 327.

3 slight, unsubstantial (also fig.). **b** (of sound), faint, thin.

poeta .. enigmatum propositiones ~i materia sumpta ludibundis apicibus legitur cecinisse ALDH. *Met.* 6; GIR. *TH intr.* p. 6 (v. eloquentia 1); honor mundi .. / .. / est .. / inanis et exilis WALT. WIMB. *Van.* 3; sensus tenui vigens acumine / per linguam funditur exili famine *Id. Palpo* 152; postquam .. ~em facimus introduccionem de sex gradibus ascensivis ad thronum Salomonis .. *Regim. Princ.* 146. **b** L in fine diccionis plenum habet sonum, in principio et secunda cum geminatur ~em ... N .. sonat in medio exiliter *Ps.*-GROS. *Gram.* 29; ypsile, hoc est i tenue, unde Priscianus dicit quod Palemon grammaticus hanc litteram vocavit ~em et Grillius ad Virgilium de accentibus lenem †nominant [l. nominat] BACON *Gram. Gk.* 31.

exilitas [CL]

1 leanness.

exhilitas, *hlænnes GlH* E 525; membrorum ~ate et tenuitate demolitus est W. CANT. *Mir. Thom.* II 43.

2 poor quality, inferiority; **b** (as title of humility).

ut ~atem materie gravior stilus attollat GIR. *TH intr.* p. 6; **1379** condonatur propter ~atem ter[re] *Hal. Durh.* 161. **b** personalem ~atis mee presentiam .. Londini .. exhibere curabo AD. MARSH *Ep.* 3.

3 scarcity, meagreness. **b** poverty (of person or institution).

1302 ex destruccione et ~ate rerum et reddituum temporalium *Reg. Carl.* I 197; ne inopia seu temporalis substancie ~as non paucos a studio scolastico posset revocare .. LEEKE 10; **1406** dictarum capellaniarum debilitate et reddituum ~ate consideratis *Midlothian* 316; per ~atem victus in ecclesiis parochialibus appropriatis .. non sunt .. curati GASCOIGNE *Loci* 20. **b** **1350** ~ati domus sororum de W... pie compatiens (*Cl*) *Mon. Francisc.* II 280; **1416** libri etc. honesta sunt et sufficiencia considerata ~ate et paupertate parochianorum *Fabr. York* 248; **1441** vicario de Dalton propter ~atem vicarie sue, xx s. vj d. ob. *Ac. Durh.* 184; s**1524** non ob malignitatem vel ingratitudinem contra regem, sed propter nimiam paupertatem et ~atem *Reg. Butley* 48.

exiliter [CL]

1 meagrely, meanly.

ea urbs [Cantuaria] est .. nec adeo magna nec ~er parva W. MALM. *GP prol.* p. 3; non tenuiter dilexit nos Deus, non mediocriter, non ~er, sed plenius, sed pinguius BALD. CANT. *Tract.* 13. 535C; disce quomodo Filius Dei penaliter, odibiliter, et ~er se habuit ad hunc mundum WYCL. *Ver.* II 142.

2 lightly.

gens ~er [v. l. leviter] armata et agilitate potius quam robustis viribus confisa GIR. *DK* II 3.

3 unsubstantially, without due consideration. **b** (of sound) faintly.

quid igitur moveret innovare conclusionem .. tam ~er fundatam et scripture contrariam? WYCL. *Ver.* I 276; nec hujus negocii felix execucio modicum seu ~er regio pectori insedebat *Ps.*-ELMH. *Hen. V* 63 p. 175. **b** *Ps.*-GROS. *Gram.* 29 (v. exilis 3b).

4 briefly, concisely.

omnes .. qui vident eas .. sciunt ipsas racionabiliter impugnare ... sed contra rem ipsam .. nullus scit ipsas ~er colorare BRADW. *CD* 136C.

exilium [CL]

1 exile, banishment; **b** (leg.); **c** (fig.). **d** (spiritual, w. ref. to earthly life). **e** (w. *mentis*) insanity.

[monimenta] .. aut ignibus hostium exusta aut civium ~ii classe .. deportata GILDAS *EB* 4; Romam linquens .. virgo / exul in exilium Tribulanae ducitur urbis ALDH. *VirgV* 2386; patriam propter Dominum spontaneo mutavit exilio *Hist. Abb. Jarrow* 21; Uuilfrid post longum ~ium in episcopatum .. receptus BEDE *HE* V 3 p. 285; rex Guillelmus .. proditores .. in ~ium expulit ORD. VIT. IV 7 p. 217; pro te proscribitur et solo patrio / pulsa diutino datur exilio WALT. WIMB. *Carm.* 272; plane scietur quis fuit causa dictorum mortis et exulii *Dieul.* f. 143v. (cf. ib. f. 144: filium in ~io positum .. bannivit). **b** si quis ministrum altaris peremerit, sit ille exlex .. nisi ipse non solum vago ~io plene delictum correxerit, set et cognacioni satis fecerit (*Cons. Cnuti*) *GAS* 341 (= *Inst. Cnuti*, *ib.*: per ~ium; AS: *wræcsið*). **c** non tellure locus mihi, non in parte polorum est: / exilium nullus modo tam crudele veretur ALDH. *Aen.* 3 (*Nubes*) 3; de avibus .. quas hiemali ~io [v. l. consilio] nature rigor relegare solet GIR. *TH* I 20. **d** in hujus vitae ~io ANSELM (*Orig. Pecc.* 27) II 170; da mihi, Domine, in hoc ~io panem doloris *Id.* (*Or.* 16) III 67; in libro .. vite legunt beati spiritus in celo .. in libro vero Scripture legendum nobis est in hoc ~io FISHACRE *Sent. Prol.* 80. **e** custodes in mentis ~ium .. et .. in horrorem resolvi terribiliter coegerunt *Ps.*-ELMH. *Hen. V* 20.

2 (med., w. *linguae*) abscess causing protrusion of tongue.

accidit autem apostema lingue eam nimis magnificans et ab ore exire faciens et vocatur ~ium lingue BART. ANGL. V 21.

3 destruction, ruin, waste; **b** (w. obj. gen., also fig.).

1205 quod permittatis comitissam L. vendere de bosco suo .. sine wasto et sine ~io *Cl* 23a; **1219** attachiati fuerunt ad ostendendum quare fecerunt vastum et ~ium de bosco de H. *CurR* VIII 69; vastum et destructio fere idem sunt ... ~ium vero dici poterit generaliter ubi quid fit ad deformitatem .. capitalis mesuagii, ut si quis domos prostraverit .. item si arbores .. extirpaverint BRACTON 316b-317; **1267** item firmarii tempore firmarum suarum vastum, venditionem, seu ~ium non faciant, in domibus, boscis, hominibus (*Marlb.* 23) *StRealm* I 24; **1302** tenementa et domos eorum in statu debito absque vasto vendicione vel ~io custodiat *BBC* (*Berwick*) 99; **1336** quod ipsos orphanos terras .. et domos eorum in statu debito absque vasto venditione vel ~io custodiat *RScot* 429a. **b** **1199** de placito exilii bosci *CurR RC* II 14; s**1308** homines .. pacifici .. guerram et pacis ~ium valde formidabant *V. Ed. II* 158; bestia pestifera, nuper quam misit Athenas, / destruat ut cives, mota Diana palam / urbis in exilium GOWER *VC* I 455.

4 asylum, sanctuary. *Cf. asylum.*

abbatiis, prioratibus, cantariis, hospitalibus seu aliis ~iis domibus mortificatorum [etc.] *Reg. Brev. Orig.* 180.

exillerare v. exhilarare. **exillis** v. 1 exilis. **exilocataracta** v. xylocerata. **exilon, exilos** v. xylon.

eximere [CL]

1 to take out, extract.

a690 spiculis .. ex faretra exemptis ALDH. *Ep.* 5 p. 493; in quem lacum pars .. arundinis .. si demissa fuerit et postero die exempta .. pars .. exempta invenietur lapidea GIR. *TH* II 7; OCKHAM *Pol.* I 56 (v. coronare 2a); **1393** H. adeo cito exemit gladium et percussit R. B. in collo *PRO Durh.* 3/33 m. 12*d.*

2 to banish, expel.

ipse miserabiles persone non debent ~i de provincia, sed ipse possunt alios ~ere ad audientiam imperatoris VAC. *Lib. Paup.* 77.

3 to set free, rescue. **b** (pass., w. *humanis rebus* or sim.) to die.

argentum .. et aurum non poterit ~ere [*Zeph.* i 18: liberare] eos in die irae GILDAS *EB* 55; si temporis illius aerumnis exemtus ad regni fastigia perveniret BEDE *HE* II 12 p. 107; condecet eniti poenis Acherontis adusti / exemptas justis mentes miscere suadelis FRITH. 290; **a984** Domini gregem .. pastores .. luporum rictibus ~entes .. defendant (ÆTHELWOLD *Ch.*) *Conc. Syn.* 128; [genitrix Dei] per cujus partum de morte aeterna sum exemptus ANSELM (*Or.* 7) III 19; **1164** ut ~atis vos .. a laqueis creditorum J. SAL. *Ep.* 134 (136 p. 14); non potest divitem nummus eximere / a fati nexibus et mesto funere WALT. WIMB. *Sim.* 58. **b** exempto autem homine [AS p. 443: *gefærenum soþlice þam menn*] lavetur corpus *RegulC* 66; rege Athelredo rebus humanis exempto GIR. *Æthelb.* 3; *Dial. Scac.* I 11 C (v. determinatio 1c); **1282** si .. filia nostra rebus humanis .. †exhumatur .. dos ad nos .. revertatur *RGasc* II 159; **1317** [quod] prefatus Johannes .. quingentas libras, prefata Theophania rebus humanis exempta, penes se detineat *Pat* 148 m. 8.

4 to exempt (from obligation or authority); **b** (eccl. or mon.); **c** (p. ppl. *exemptus*, also as sb. m., esp. w. ref. to episcopal jurisdiction).

cives .. magnarum civitatum et villarum exemptarum super nullo placito extra civitates suas vocari debent nisi de .. transgressionibus forinsecis *Fleta* 116; non habere imperatorem pro superiore non ~it aliquem a subjeccione OCKHAM *Pol.* I 139; non video quod papa exemit episcopos ab onere predicandi GASCOIGNE *Loci* 16. **b** c**1167** nunquid ~endus erat a jurisdictione .. episcoporum J. SAL. *Ep.* 198 (213 p. 348); tria [monasteria] superbia .. se prorsus ~ere .. matribus suis .. ecclesiis .. fecit GIR. *Spec.* II 30; **1300** nos .. scholares [universitatis Oxon.] .. ab omni jurisdiccione .. quorumcunque archiepiscoporum .. episcoporum et aliorum ordinariorum judicum .. tenore presencium ~imus (*Lit. Papae*) *MunAcOx* 80; in .. Scriptura sacra, ubi fit mencio de potestate pape collata sibi a Christo, .. [non] ab illa potestate aliquod regnum ~itur OCKHAM *Dial.* 888. **c** **1226** ut .. sciatis qui sint abbates ~i a nobis eos vobis duximus nominandos viz. abbas S. Albani, abbas Westmonasterii, abbas S. Edmundi, abbas S. Augustini Cant. *Conc. Syn.* 158; s**1235** (v. abbas a); **1256** proventus omnium maneriorum religiosorum .., ~is duntaxat exceptis *Val. Norw.* 515; s**1261** contra religiosos et maxime ~os studebunt contendere *Flor. Hist.* II 469; **1320** (v. decanatus 1c); congruit racioni illas tres in capite marginali .. consignare sc. .. 'regem' ut ecclesiam possessionibus dotantem; 'abbatem', sibi commissa conservantem et 'diocesanum', ~os quandoque perturbantem THORNE *prol.* 1758; appetit ipse [frater] scolis nomen sibi ferre magistri, / quem post exemptum regula nulla ligat GOWER *VC* IV 816 (cf. ib. *rub.*: de fratribus .. qui .. quasi ab ordinis sui jugo ~i .. summas in studio scole cathedras affectant); **1452** abbati ~i monaste-

rii *Reg. Whet.* I 67; **1549** de visitatione monasteriorum et inquisitione contra ~os *Conc. Scot.* II 91 *rub.*; ordinarii loca ~a visitent *Ib.* 110.

eximie [CL], excellently, outstandingly.

sunt quidam cupidi qui quadam nobilitate / eximie mensis cenare volunt alienis D. BEC. 1803.

eximietas [LL], excellence. **b** (as honorific title) excellency.

~as, sublimitas *GlC* E 532; ea .. minus eximia .. ut crescant ad ~atem W. NEWB. *Serm.* 895. **b 1231** obtulit quoque se mihi occasio duplex ut ~ati vestre aliquid salubriter commonitorium scriberem GROS. *Ep.* 5.

eximius [CL]

1 excellent, outstanding: **a** (of person); **b** (of thing); **c** (of abstr.). **d** (n. pl. as sb.) finery.

a apparet ergo eum qui vos sacerdotes sciens ex corde dicit non esse ~ium Christianum GILDAS *EB* 108; Joseph, .. castitatis .. executor ac doctor ~ius BEDE *HE* V 21 p. 342; c**803** Cassiodorus, ~ius interpres psalmorum ALCUIN *Ep.* 307 p. 468; in libro Ezechielis, ~ii prophetae BYRHT. *Man.* 202; praesulis eximii FRITH. 402; dominae ~iae .. Frodelinae ANSELM (*Ep.* 45) III 158; s**1100** hoc juraverunt xij ~iores procerum utrimque H. HUNT. *HA* VII 23. **b** virginis eximiam qui scribit commate vitam ALDH. *VirgV* 2188; lux illa campi florentis ~ia in conparatione ejus quae nunc apparuit lucis .. tenuissima videbatur BEDE *HE* V 12 p. 308; opus eximiumque / certatim fabricare student WULF. *Swith.* II 10; scripsit Aenigmata .. et de Laude Virginum .. librum ~ium F. MALM. *V. Aldh.* 71C; **1167** ut vos .. super candelabrum aureum .. tanquam lucernam ~iam collocaret J. SAL. *Ep.* 221 (229); in .. ~ia civitate Exoniensi *Chr. Battle* f. 29; proprium autem epitheton ovibus dabant lectis, porcis ~iis, bobus intactis ALB. LOND. *DG* 6. 32; accedo cominus ad vas eximium / vini desiderans vel stillicidium WALT. WIMB. *Carm.* 173. **c** virum eximiae pietatis et religionis BEDE *HE* III 14 p. 154; **811** ~iae caritatis industria *CS* 332; puer .. / indolis eximiae quidam WULF. *Swith.* II 790; ~ie strenuitatis vestre .. fama GIR. *TH* III 48; domino suo ~iam illius in Christo conversationem .. enarrabant *Chr. Witham* 502. **d** s**1113** Radulphus .. episcopum .. sacris vestibus indutum illudque officium .. infra diocesim suam facere volentem, exutis ~iis cedere coegit CAPGR. *Hen.* 60.

2 great, loud.

valvas / eximium dare quae strepitum volvendo solebant WULF. *Swith.* II 616.

eximperatrix [cf. LL imperatrix], ex-empress.

s**1125** ducens .. filiam suam ~icem .. Anglie heredem GERV. CANT. *Chr.* 93; s**1139** accessunt ~icem, H. regis filiam FL. WORC. *Cont. A* 110; s**1139** ubi autem novit [rex Stephanus] exreginam apud Arundel ~icem .. recepisse graviter ferens, illo movit exercitum J. WORC. 55.

eximursine v. oxymyrsine. **exin** v. exinde.

exinanire [CL]

1 to empty, deplete. **b** (refl., w. ref. to *Phil.* ii 7).

~ire, evacuare *GlC* E 456; de Dublinensi familia, stipendiorum defectu graviter ~ita GIR. *EH* II 17; **1405** villa de Sandwico per diversas pestilencias ac alia jacturas et infortunia .. in tantum ~ita et debilitata existit *Cl* 278 m. 24. **b** tu, si vis esse altare Dei, ~i teipsum BEDE *Tab.* 455; Patrem Christus relinquere visus est, quando semetipsum ~ivit LANFR. *Comment. Paul.* (*Eph.* v 22) 304; P. BLOIS *Serm.* 576B (v. exinanitio 1b).

2 to weaken, wear out. **b** to diminish, worsen.

effeto, i... debilitato, ~ito *GlH* E 95; Deus cujus bonitas non exhauritur, cujus misericordia non ~itur ANSELM (*Or.* 10) III 35; **1166** enervari et ~iri coepit potestas eorum J. SAL. *Ep.* 185 (184 p. 216); **1273** in obsequio felicis recordacionis H. regis Anglie per tempora existens diuturna se ipsum ~ivit *AncC* VII 223; cum adeo [corpus] ex infirmitatis nimia gravitate extenuatum, ymmo ~itum fuerit *Ps.*-ELMH. *Hen. V* 129. **b** rasus .. erat barba et capite .. magis volens aliquantum aspectu ~ire se, et compositos crines amittere, quam adversantes sibi parcere *G. Herw.* 334b; in [torneamentis] milites .. patrimonia sua .. et .. vitas solius vane laudis .. aviditate ~iebant R. NIGER *Mil.* I 36.

3 to bring to naught, destroy.

contradictores imperialium diffinitionum inani poenitentia paene ~iti verecundabuntur ASSER *Alf.* 91; alioquin .. silvesceret vel de se nimium reputaret et sic ~iretur [ME: *swa to nocht iwinden*] *AncrR* 59; **1446** imaginantes .. ipsos vexare opprimere et totaliter destruere et ~ire *Cl* 295 m. 30d.; s**1415** discordia .. mota est inter dominos que ad huc [? *add* non] est ~ita *Plusc.* X 24.

4 to despoil, strip.

nemo tamen judicet tantum virum post ultionem Dei misericordia destitutum, nec bonae voluntatis suae fructu ~itum GOSC. *Transl. Aug.* 33C.

5 to free (from).

944 sit .. praedictum rus liber ab omni fiscali tributo saeculariumque servitutum ~itum *CS* 791 (= *CS* 869 [**948**]).

exinanitio [CL]

1 emptying out. **b** (theol., w. ref. to *Phil.* ii 7).

~one diarrie attenuatus egrotabat ORD. VIT. XIII 18 p. 48; suffocatio .. accidit ex cordis lesione, quando humorum ibi .. existencium fit evacuacio et per consequens spirituum ~o BART. ANGL. III 15. **b** Christus .. exinanivit se ut nos impleret... magna et plusquam magna ~o est P. BLOIS *Serm.* 576B; qui cingi celico nequit cinctorio / cinctus iniciis est in presepio. / o quam mirabilis abbreviacio / vel certe verius exinanicio WALT. WIMB. *Carm.* 109; quidquid dictum est de ~one sua [Christi] et mandacione quod sui debent sequi ipsum in talibus WYCL. *Ver.* I 293; Domini Dei mei .. tanta ~o ut servi naturam susciperet UHTRED *Medit.* 197.

2 weakening. **b** worsening.

GlH E 269 (v. enervatio 1a); intersecta arteria saltuose sanguis egreditur .. sequiturque sincopis ~onem ALF. ANGL. *Cor* 11. 6. **b** in nulla corporis parte ulla poterat extenuatio seu ~o deprehendi... ipsa corporis mortui viva compositione probante hanc sancti viri, exanimationem non ~onem fuisse H. BOS. *Thom.* VI 14; **1312** regnum ipsum ad ~onem devenire instabilem [poterit] (*Lit. Papae*) *Reg. Carl.* II 63.

3 bringing to naught, destruction.

spei alienatio, caritatis ~o [*gl.*: i. revacuatio] J. FURNESS *Kentig.* 18 p. 190.

4 spoliation, impoverishment.

1280 cum .. canonici de Marsey .. per incendii pressure multiplicis et infortunii dispendia ad ultimatam ~onem sui et quasi ad nichilum subito sint redacti *Reg. Ebor.* 70; **1371** compatientes .. dictorum religiosorum paupertati et .. nimie ~oni per depredaciones (*Lit. Episc. Aberd.*) *Mon. Hib. & Scot.* 344b.

exinde, exin [CL]

1 thereafter: **a** from that time; **b** next (in order).

a quis in monte cum Domino locutus et nequaquam concrepantibus tubis ~nde perterritus .. advexit? GILDAS *EB* 69; prima et tertia .. pro eis [defunctis] missa agatur et ~nde post annum .. servatur THEOD. *Pen.* II 5. 2; **686** (13c) terram .. B. Petro ejusque familiae .. tradidi possidendam et quicquid ~nde facere voluerint utpote domini liberi habeant potestatem *CS* 67; exin sacratam perrexit quaerere vitam ALDH. *CE* 3. 8; ~nde autem usque ad tempora praesentia quae .. gesta sint .. cognovimus BEDE *HE pref.* p. 6; ~n coepere plures per dies .. venire Brittaniam *Ib.* III 3; cum aetatis suae xxiiij annum peregisset .. spem .. in Christo tenebat. ~n coepto itinere .. monasterium .. usque pervenit FELIX *Guthl.* 20; aecclesiae suas consuetudines quietas habuerunt regis Edwardi tempore et ~nde .. habeurunt consuetudines suas *DB* I 2; evolutis ~nde paucis diebus T. MON. *Will.* II 4; ~nde vivendi formam accipiat meliorem GIR. *EH* I 35. **b** s**1011** ~n ecclesia Christi spoliata comburitur FL. WORC. I 164 (= M. PAR. *Maj.* I 483: ~nde); **1266** Radulphus .. fecit hostium aperire .. et ~nde perrexerunt ad domum Willelmi M. .. et dictum W. wlneraverunt *SelCCoron* 8; **1319** (v. 2 constabularius 5a).

2 therefrom, thence: **a** (place); **b** (source); **c** (cause); **d** (expr. separation).

a missi a domino suo [Romam] ut ~nde sibi reliquias sanctorum .. adferrent *V. Greg.* p. 94; ut paulatim ablata ~nde terra fossam .. altam reddiderit BEDE *HE* III 9; **957** (14c) Adam .. feliciter collocatus, culpa praevaricationis inventa ~nde pariter expulsus *CS* 995; tertium .. latus .. in sinistram porrectum [Johannis] esse non dubitamus. porro quartum ~nde inceptum .. *Alea Evang.* 174; hinc iterum navigantes devenimus Ortigiam. ~n ad Turrem Faris OSB. BAWDSEY cxlv; unum [brachium maris] Hispaniam interluit atque Britanniam; ac ~nde in boream se convertens Galliam dividit et Britanniam GIR. *TH* I 2; **1298** sic procedendo usque ad S. et sic ~nde usque ad H. et ~nde usque .. *Cart. Boarstall* 576; proximo sequuntur ascendentes cum continuacione veri motus solis, ~nde altitudo meridiana cum gradu ascendentis in meridie ELVEDEN *Cal.* 5. **b 1200** (v. dominium 5d); **1327** pastum .. super .. tabulam .. ponebat ad panes ~nde ad furniendum preparandos *MGL* III 416; **1440** considerans metallum esse derelictum in tempore predecessoris sui, pro tribus campanis ~nde effundendis .. [abbas T., cess. **1399**] emit metallum pro addicione *Meaux* III 240. **c** si aliquis servorum cujusquam rationabilis viri peccavisset, et dum sibi ~nde multe fierent molestie, non reclamaret .. ALEX. CANT. *Dicta* 1 p. 113; ad hoc serpens antiquus homini peccatum suadendo porrexit ut ~nde ad interitum hominis augmentum .. acciperet *Id. Mir.* 50 (I) p. 263; reputans ne .. mala ~nde traheretur consequentia *Chr. Battle* f. 85; **1299** non aliter .. extra .. regni accedere limites voluerunt, nisi per te .. cavaretur eisdem quod .. nullum ~nde .. regni libertatibus posset dispendium imminere *Reg. Cant.* 575. **d** omnes .. qui originali peccato ibidem detinebantur magna potentia ~nde [AS: *of ðon*] liberasti *Rit. Durh.* 101.

3 for that reason. **b** about that matter.

c**1078** si .. didicissem qua infamia diffamaretur caritas vestra .. et ~nde meum consilium .. quaesissetis .. et nullum reddidissem responsum .. ANSELM (*Ep.* 63) III 178; ~nde accepisti me in tuitionem tuam ut nihil noceret animae meae *Id.* (*Medit.* 3) III 90; **1296** ne ~nde quoquo modo turbemini *Reg. Cant.* 128. **b 1266** denarios inde provenientes regi .. habere faciat, ita quod rex diligenciam suam ~nde debeat merito commendare *Cl* 163; **1266** ita .. fideliter vos habeatis in hac parte quod vos ~nde merito commendare debeamus *Cl* 197; **1296** de hoc quoque vobis .. pro parte tetigimus quando simul ~nde ultimo tractabamus *Reg. Cant.* 128.

exint- v. et. exent-.

exintegre [cf. CL integre], completely, entirely.

1203 protestantibus pretaxatam pecuniam ~e [MS: ? ex integro] sine dilatione persolvi faciemus *Pat* 26.

exintra [cf. CL intra], from within, out.

quotiens volebat ad victualia queritanda ~a prodire R. COLD. *Cuthb.* 26.

exiquitas v. exiguitas. **exirare** v. exhilarare.

1 exire [CL]

1 (w. pers. subj.) to exit, go out: **a** (absol.); **b** (w. adv.); **c** (w. prep. or adverbial phr.); **d** (w. gd. or *ut* cl. indicating purpose). **e** (trans.) to go out from. **f** (p. ppl. *s. act.*).

a tunc itaque surgentes exierunt *V. Cuthb.* II 4; **8..** exibit, *utgeð WW*; s**1335** (v. devillare b). **b** in nomine .. Christi .. exi hinc, draco nequissime! ALDH. *VirgP* 52. **c 793** non exeatis post luxurias carnis .. sed in servitio Dei .. permanete ALCUIN *Ep.* 20; pagani insuper juraverunt se citissime de suo regno exituros ASSER *Alf.* 56; ab illis / Gallica rura petens exivit finibus FRITH. 696; mulier .. vidit .. aquilam de ore ipsius exire ÆLF. *Æthelwold* 2; finita .. prece .. unanimiter sequentes eum exierunt ad flumen BYRHT. *V. Ecgwini* 392; **1221** W. et G. .. comederunt .. ad domum Walteri H. et de domo illa exivit ad hoc faciendum et ad domum illam de facto rediit *SelPlCrown* 83; s**1458** (v. culter 2). **d** exeo [AS: *ic ga ut*] diluculo minando boves ÆLF. *Coll.* 90; **1268** cum vellet exire redeundi versus partes suas *JustIt* 618 r. 4; lotis .. pedibus presidentis atque prioris .. exiet continuo servitor aut eciam servitores .. ut aquam mutent *Cust. Cant.* 217. **e** exiens atrium HERM. ARCH. 40 (v. consessus 1a); a**1094** qui .. claustra monasterii libenter exeunt non solum sibi sed et aliis .. noxii sunt ANSELM (*Ep.* 178) IV 62; milites ex Christianis exierunt castra ORD. VIT. IX 15 p. 599; ecclesiam exivit ALEX. CANT. *Mir.* 29 p. 217; non exit grabatum MAP *NC* III 3 f. 40; **1289** cum domum illam exierunt *SelCKB* I 178; exivit [ME: *he wende ut of*] civitatem magnam in Bethaniam *AncrR* 96; WYCL. *Pol.* I 19 (v. cruciare 3c). **f 1235** quando .. J. scivit ipsos exutos (*sic*) de patria .. venit .. et posuit se in terram illam *CurR* XV 1750.

2 (w. inanim. subj.): **a** (absol., esp. of fluid); **b** (w. prep.); **c** (trans.).

a si sanguis exeat *GAS* 611 (v. cravatio); dormiendo .. quare sepius emittat sperma quam urinam cum propinquior sit urina ad exeundum *Quaest. Salern.* B 43; signum est hu[morum] exeuntium GILB. V 211. 2 (v. curabilitas); quod subtile est exit BACON *Min.* 386 (v. electrum 2e); quando mare exiit, id est *ebbyngwater* W. WORC. *Itin.* 262. **b 798** sol .. post dies triginta et decem semis horas exiet de Ariete ALCUIN *Ep.* 148; transigit Euripilum jaculabilis hasta Menalce / occiduas ingressa comas, levumque per orbem / exit et excussum defert in cuspide lumen J. EXON. *BT* VI 229; foratoria per que remi exeunt vel exire possunt NECKAM *Ut.* 115; dicit .. Aristoteles .. quod nichil aliud est visum videre quam quod visus ~eat ad rem visam BART. ANGL. III 17; *SB* 32 (v. ereuxis). **c** corpus naturale .. exibit .. locum BRADW. *CD* 130A (v. coextensio).

3 to come out, begin: **a** (of person) to issue, be born; *cf. egredi* 1e. **b** (of seed) to spring up.

a priusquam [Jeremias] formaretur in utero praescitus et priusquam exiret de vulva sanctificatus GILDAS *EB* 47; puer in septimo mense laborans exire, si non exit longo tempore debilitatur, unde si tunc in octavo mense exierit vivere non potest *Quaest. Salern.* B 27; **1251** nullam poterimus habere vel exigere servitutem sive de aliquibus de eisdem exeuntibus *BBC* (*Higham Ferrers*) 142; obiit .. Johannes sine herede de corpore suo exeunte *State Tri. Ed. I* 17; **1324** etsi .. J.B. et M. uxor ejus obierunt sine herede de corporibus eorum exeunte *CBaron* 136; **1430** (v. carnaliter 2a). **b** exit humo semen et herba viret WALT. ANGL. *Fab.* 25. 6.

4 (of revenue) to issue, accrue.

mille acrae silvae infructuosae de qua exeunt xxiiij s. *DB* I 2; [episcopus] habebat mel et venationem et quicquid exibat *Ib.* 173; c**1090** cuicumque ego postea dederim terras de quibus decime exeunt *Regesta* p. 133; **1212** id quod inde exibit tradatur duobus probis hominibus *MGL* II 86; s**1233** tam male dissipavit bona que exierunt a vicecomitatu quod non permissum est ei ea amplius recipere *Leg. Ant. Lond.* 7; **1324** (v. blanchiatura); **1451** una cum libero redditu v s. exeuncium de iiij bovatis terre *Ac. Durh.* 187; **1533** dedit .. quandam annuitatem sive annualem redditum vj s. viij d. exeuntem de omnibus terris et tenementis suis *Banstead* II 104.

5 a (w. inanim. or abstr. subj.) to originate. **b** (of letter or edict) to issue. **c** (gram.) to derive. **d** (math.) to come out, work out; *cf.* 9a *infra*.

a si ignis civitatem comburebat, de cujus domo exibat .. emendabat per iij oras *DB* I 262v.; a**1078** pati non potest

mens .. ut vel suspicemini ex ore meo exisse quod non amplius vobis libros nostros praestabimus ANSELM (*Ep.* 12) III 116; **a1105** avertat Deus hoc a vobis neque .. permittat tam pravum exemplum ulla opinione exire de vobis (*Ib.* 323) V 252. **b s1196** (v. 2 edicere 2c); **1295** similis littera exivit pro ecclesia de Wrotham *Reg. Cant.* 55; **1315** de brevibus judicialibus habeant [querentes] remedium de placeis unde brevia illa exibunt *RParl* I 322b. **c** figura .. diccionis est in quantum diccio ab alia .. exit aut non exit. namque derivantur dicciones ab aliis et alie non, sed sunt alique principium generacionis sicut et res *Ps.*-GROS. *Gram.* 32; de verbo nomen tamquam de stipite ramus / exit VINSAUF *PN* 1607. **d** manifestum est, si id quod ex aliquo diviso exierit, cum eo in quod ipsum dividitur multiplicaris, quod tum substantia que divisa est adimpleatur ROB. ANGL. *Alg.* 104.

6 to leave, depart (intr.). **b** to retire (from office). **c** (trans., w. abstr. obj.) to pass through, depart from. **d** to diverge. **e** (med. & bot.) to protrude. **f** (trans.) to protrude from.

c792 aurum in fornace .. coquitur ut purius exeat ALCUIN *Ep.* 14; **c798** exorcizatur, id est conjuratur malignus spiritus ut exeat et recedat *Ib.* 134; cum Deus procedit de Deo Patre et Filio nec exit extra Deum: manet Deus, id est Spiritus Sanctus, in Deo de quo procedit ANSELM (*Incarn. B* 15) II 34; **a1077** illa [munera] possunt sine te mare transire sed ista [caritas] non potest de corde tuo exire *Id.* (*Ep.* 68) III 188; permisit .. illum de coenobio ~ire et ad seculum redire ORD. VIT. III 3 p. 44; **1219** quesiti quomodo exivit de seisina illa quam habuit per curiam domini regis .. dicunt quod nesciunt quomodo, nisi tantum quod exivit spontanea voluntate sua de partibus illis *CurR* VIII 16; cum angeli exeunt a celo, .. contra appetitum naturalem exeunt FISHACRE *Quaest.* 46; exeunti a stupha detur tyriaca GILB. IV 206. 1. **b 1254** sciendum quod sumptibus suis, quando exierit, debet intrare blada *DCCant. Reg.* H f. 179; **s970** fuit prior, abbas et episcopus per xxxviiij annos. et anno istius in abbatia exeuntis nono fuit inventio sancti Ivonis *Chr. Rams.* 339. **c** pueritiam jam exivi, senectuti appropinquavi ALEX. CANT. *Dicta* 3 p. 119; tam subtiliter modulos intrant et exeunt GIR. *TH* III 11. **d** ab interiore parte cerebri exeunt duo nervi BART. ANGL. V 6; **1155** usque ad semitam que exit de eadem via et ducit ad S. *Feod. Durh.* 121n. **e 1268** cecidit super gambam suam sinistram .. unde pes suus extra juncturam exiit *Rec. Norw.* I 210; si matrix .. exiverit ad exteriora GAD. 81. 1 (v. dislocare 1a); apium emoroydarum .. habet radicem rotundam sed compressam ad modum vertilis, et ex medio partis inferioris exit unica radix *SB* 11. **f 1271** plagam in capite ultra aurem sinistram longitudinis iiij pollicium quod cerebrum exitum fuit *SelCCoron* 30.

7 to depart this life, to die; **b** (w. *de corpore, vita, saeculo,* or sim.); **c** (w. *in viam patrum*).

c1218 sacramentum extreme unctionis, cum sit sacramentum exeuntium *Conc. Syn.* 90; quintum [sacramentum] exeuntium: unctio extrema HALES *Sent.* IV 40. **b 716** primo gallicinio exiebat de corpore BONIF. *Ep.* 10 p. 15; exeunti de hac vita BEDE *HE* IV 9 p. 222; de saeculo .. exiturus *Ib.* 24 p. 261; cum anima vestra de corpore exiens ante conspectum [Dei] praesentabitur ANSELM (*Ep.* 347) V 285; **s1250** (v. cussinus). **c** in viam patrum exiit exspectans diem Domini in judicio venturo EDDI 15.

8 to escape (intr.); **b** (trans.). **c** to pass (from possession). **d** (of gate) to open, 'give' (onto). **e** (med.) to burst. **f** (of abstr.) to get out, spread abroad.

hic secum mirans cruce se consignat et unde / exeat attonito pectore scire nequit WULF. *Swith. pref.* 56; [anima] temptat exire at aeneo carcere clauditur ANSELM (*Or.* 14) III 58; **1220** idem Johannes fuit in profundo carcere, et .. ibi fregit carcerem ita quod fere potuit exire *CurR* VIII 397; **1220** de custodia Johannis exivit ipsa, eo quod voluit eam facere monialem *Ib.* IX 67. **b** [canis] leporem prendit, fauces lepus exit inhermes WALT. ANGL. *Fab.* 27. 5; **s1340** ipsos turrim exire permisit AD. MUR. *Chr.* 117. **c** [hidae] in acclesia fuerunt ante regem E. sed ignorant quomodo exierunt *DB* I 259. **d 1309** per rectam metodum iri potest per gaulam .. prati, que gaula exit in itinere publico *RGasc* IV 216. **e** cum in junctura †idropisis [l. idropis] exiverit apostema J. MIRFIELD *Brev.* 70. **f** mox proceres inter rumusculus exiit aulae, / scilicet adventasse virum virtute vigetum FRITH. 211; ab ortu solis usque ad occasum exivit sancta opinio ejus ÆTHELW. I 1 p. 5; spiritualem claritatem ejus vultui inesse et inde exire perspexit ALEX. CANT. *Mir.* 50 (I) p. 260.

9 to come (to a result), to issue (in); *cf.* 5d *supra.* **b** (of period of time) to come to an end.

cui ergo hoc miraculum adscribendum est nisi illi cujus jussu ad opus exivit? ÆLF. *Æthelwold* 23; celet bonam voluntatem, ut non nisi cum in opus exit appareat in publico ANSELM (*Ep.* 101) III 234; res omnis que fit in hoc mundo exit in esse per efficiens et materiale principium ex quo producitur per virtutem efficientis BACON *Tert.* 107; *Id.* VIII 149 (v. creabilis b); cum dixit [sc. Deus] "multiplicamini" [*Gen.* i 28], non conferebat potestatem multiplicandi prolem, sed de exeundo in actum potestatis prius collate dedit preceptum OCKHAM *Pol.* II 489. **b 759** exeunte Julio *Ep. Alcuin.* 182 p. 301; **1268, 1292** (v. dies 6c).

10 (trans.) to go beyond, exceed.

nullatenus aliquid creatum potest exire creantis .. immensitatem ANSELM (*Mon.* 14) I 27; si .. exercitium exiverit temperamentum accidit .. pulsus parvus BART. ANGL. III 24; vir .. exit / normam nec causam respicit ille suam GARL. *Epith.* I 253.

11 (inf. as sb.) exit, egress.

1215 omnes mercatores habeant salvum et securum exire de Anglia et venire in Angliam *Magna Carta* 41.

2 exire v. 2 exuere. **exist-** v. exsist-.

existimare [CL]

1 to estimate, value.

1558 dicta rota ~atur ad valenciam vj s. viij d. *AncIndict* 595/1 m. 77.

2 to consider, think, judge; **b** (w. compl.); **c** (w. acc. & inf.); **d** (w. *quia* or *quod*).

conicio, ~o *GlC* C 506; animam procreati hominis non, ut quidam ~ant, .. a patre vel a matre existendi initium sumere WULF. *Æthelwold* 4; *bulewerkis* .. quod in Latina lingua sonat, ut ~o, opus bellicum STRECCHE *Hen. V* 164. **b** contingere solet ut .. qui ~abatur praeteritae conversationis neglegentia posterior .. existat anterior ALDH. *VirgP* 10; se .. infelices ~antes qui nec hoc in juventute didicerant ASSER *Alf.* 106; **a1093** ut .. nihil umquam ~are possis jucundius ANSELM (*Ep.* 232) V 139; **a1103** si quis clericus qui et litteratus et strenuus ~aretur ad ecclesiam nostram .. vellet venire (*Ib.* 307) V 230; non .. inde hoc ~are verum BALSH. *AD* 46; imago Colosei quam quidam statuam Solis ~ant, alii .. GREG. *Mir. Rom.* 6; Arcades soli, ob sterilitatem agrorum commoti non sunt et ideo .. nobiles ~antur ALB. LOND. *DG* 1. 11. **c** nec hoc homines ausos esse ~abat ASSER *Alf.* 97; ~ante abbate illum hoc juvamine ministri peragere ÆLF. *Æthelwold* 10 (= WULF. *Æthelwold* 14); **a1073** ne unde vos mercedem habere apud Deum ~atis inde .. LANFR. *Ep.* 1; ~ando se esse aliquid cum nichil sit, ipse se seducit *V. Gund.* 19; multa cogitamus non esse quae scimus esse, et multa esse quae non esse scimus; non ~ando sed fingendo ita esse ut cogitamus ANSELM (*Resp. Ed.*) I 134. **d** nec silentio praetereundum ~o quod quidam presbiter noster .. opus misericordiae factum recordavit *V. Cuthb.* IV 7; ~ans .. quia quantos .. satelles praeoccuparet ad interitum perducere, tantos .. ABBO *Edm.* 6; **1071** nec ~et .. beatitudo vestra quod .. aut .. injuriis lacessitus aut regalibus angariis .. pergravatus hoc facere velit LANFR. *Ep.* 2; illis vero ~antibus quod alienata mente loqueretur OSB. *Mir. Dunst.* 20.

existimatio [CL]

1 estimating, making judgement.

sicut in illa perfecta felicitate unusquisque plus amabit sine comparatione Deum quam se .., ita plus gaudebit absque ~one de felicitate Dei quam de sua ANSELM (*Prosl.* 25) I 120; inveniunt .. B. Paulum circa animarum ~one nimis sollicitum COGGESH. *Visio* 17.

2 estimate. **b** judgement, opinion.

erat ~o ponderis hujus circiter xv milia librarum ferri GREG. *Mir. Rom.* 9. **b** utinam sic vera esset ~o quam fama hominum temere loquentium quod nesciunt de me vos docuit ANSELM (*Ep.* 85) III 210; ~onem .. eorum .. frustratam vidimus qui .. seculum duraturum putaverunt HARCLAY *Adv.* 70.

existimative, by estimate, as an opinion.

quod hec dicerent ~e, quia potius hoc existimabant quam veraciter scirent R. MELUN *Paul.* 180.

existimator [CL], one who forms opinion, judge.

opinatores, ~ores *GlC* O 217.

exitatio v. excitatio. **exiterare** v. exercere 8a.

exitiabilis [CL], death-dealing, destructive (also fig.).

neque nominatim inclamitans montes ipsos aut colles vel fluvios olim ~es, nunc vero humanis usibus utiles GILDAS *EB* 4; Arriana haeresis .. ~e perfidiae suae virus .. insularum ecclesiis aspersit BEDE *HE* I 8; ~es, i. mortales vel siticulosos *GlH* E 508; propria voluntas .. noxia est omnibus et ~is ANSELM *Misc.* 310; non enim his affectibus excitari vel pulsari valde laudabile existimamus, si boni sunt, nec ~e si mali AILR. *Spec. Car.* III 16. 590D.

exitiabiliter [LL], destructively, fatally.

donec Arriana perfidia .. fratres .. ~er faceret sejungi GILDAS *EB* 12; revera ~er tibi consilium dedit, qui totius Normannici exercitus robur amittere suasit W. JUM. IV 6.

exitialis [CL], death-dealing, destructive.

~em, mortalem *GlH* E 507 (cf. ib. 539: †exciale [l. exitiale], mortiferum); Deus .. constituit .. hunc mundum in quo ~em lacum, id est infernum, constituit HON. *Eluc.* 1113B; dant ibi Sirenes exitiale melos *Brutus* 344; tyrannorum .. finis et exitus ~is ferro plerumque sive veneno maturatur GIR. *PI* I 16; meretur ~e judicium ROB. BRIDL. *Dial.* 27; ab ~i lapidis casu R. BOCKING *Ric. Cic.* I 13; omnes patulis / intendunt auribus sirene modulis; / .. / excicialibus illecti voculis WALT. WIMB. *Palpo* 118; quod .. ab omnibus expectatur, corporis sc. animeque exciciale divorcium *Mir. Hen. VI* III 123.

exitialiter [LL], destructively, perniciously. **b** as if dying, wretchedly.

ut proprium tam ~er virum perdidisse non ei sufficeret AD. EYNS. *Hug.* IV 5; unde ipsemet ~er periclitaretur, committere non precavit *Ib.* V 7. **b** Henricus P. media corporis parte depressus, satis ~er per tres vixit annos *Lib. Eli.* III 138.

exiticius [cf. CL exitus], exiled person.

1421 non dabunt .. auxilium .. Aragonensibus .. ~iisve aut bannitis (*TreatyR*) *Foed.* X 120b.

exitiosus [CL], death-dealing, destructive. **b** dead.

~um, i. periculosum, mortalem *GlH* E 514. **b** devehitur .. ~um funus ad locum usque sepulcri *Mir. Hen. VI* II 40 p. 110.

exitium [CL], disaster, destruction, ruin. **b** outrage, crime. **c** destruction of life, death.

Gabaonitarum .. foedus .. nonnullis intulisse ~ium GILDAS *EB* 1; quos letale virus crudeli mortis ~io .. prostraverat ALDH. *VirgP* 23; cum .. neque inminens oculo ~ium humana manus curare valeret BEDE *HE* IV 30 p. 280; nec .. posset .. Christi ovile .. sine sui ~io custodire B. *V. Dunst.* 19; **1045** (14c) post generale vero istius decursus ~ium *CD* 778; palpo .. / .. / aule primoribus .. / propinat pocula dulcis exicii WALT. WIMB. *Palpo* 76; tremunt exiciis [MS: exciciis] cetus infancium, / cedunt gladiis more bidencium *Planct. Univ. Ox.* 113. **b s1304** deploravit abhominabile ~ium in vicarium Jesu Christi et Petri commissum *Flor. Hist.* III 117. **c** ~ium, mors, periculum *GlC* E 556; ~ium, i. .. †perdictio [l. perditio], *forþsiþ, utsiþ* *GlH* E 506.

exittatio v. excitatio.

exitura [LL], (med.) outflowing, efflux. **b** abscess.

in aliquibus relinquuntur orificia ampla ut non cohibeatur sanguinis ab exitu omnino, unde in palato, naribus, et ano fiunt multotiens sanguinis ~e *Ps.*-RIC. *Anat.* 7; ~a pustule nigre J. MIRFIELD *Brev.* 70. **b** cuidam .. accidit ex comestione ejus [carnis viperarum] ~a in collo magna quam aperuit et exivit caro ejus tota conversa in pediculos BACON V 107; ~a est apostema magnum creticum in quo colligitur materia expulsa GAD. 26. 1; ~a generaliter est omne apostema quod saniem ejicit *LC*.

exitus [CL]

1 coming out, going away (also fig.). **b** (right of) egress, exit. **c** departure, retirement (from office). **d** escape. **e** (w. *mentis*) ecstasy. **f** (phil.) beginning, issuing.

exodus, ~us *GlC Int.* 115; ~us, i. .. egressus, *utgong* *GlH* E 505; peccata, quam faciles aditus, quam difficiles ~us habetis! ANSELM (*Or.* 8) III 28; a die ~us de ventre matris eorum usque in diem sepulture M. RIEVAULX (*Serm.*) 55; **1280** dat' carucariis ad primum ~um carucarum post Natale iiij d. *MinAc* (*Norf*) 935/7; ~us urine GAD. 99. 2 (v. diabetes). **b 1265** clamabant dicti prior et conventus introitum suum et ~um esse ad mariscum de E. cum animalibus suis *Feod. Durh.* 164n.; **1269** cepit ab eo xxij d. pro custodia ij equorum ipsius R., quos detinuit dum [tenuit ipsum] in prisona, et iiij d. ad ~um porte sue *SelPlForest* 50; **12..** libere et quiete .. in moris et pasturis, in introitibus et ~ibus, in omnibus libertatibus et aisiamentis *Feod. Durh.* 23n. **c 1448** per liberacionem factam Alexandro de N. .. ab ultimo scaccario usque ad ~um suum de officio *ExchScot* 317. **d 1221** capti fuerunt pro morte illa, et liberati Gioni de Cancelliis tunc constabulario castri; set de ~u eorum nichil sciunt *PlCrGlouc* 57. **e** Martheque peragunt opus in effectu, / Mariam preferunt mentis in exitu TRYVYTLAM *Laus Ox.* 184. **f** est ~us mirabilis triplex, sc. manifestativus potentie Dei, ut ~us creationis, et .. divine sapientie et talis est ~us miraculorum et .. bonitatis divine, et talis est ~us redemptionis HALES *Sent.* II 160; in primo ~u rerum, qui est per creationem, una est forma .. set in secundo ~u, sc. in esse physico, .. non est una prima forma BACON VIII 42; *Ib.* 48 (v. coexire); consideravi quomodo [res] educitur in esse, an per generacionem de potentia materie, an per ~um ab agente, an per impressionem, sicut sigillum agit in ceram *Id. Tert.* 108.

2 exit, outlet. **b** way out (of difficulty), solution (of problem).

ostia, ~us fluminum in mare *GlC* O 282; latebrae / .. / introitus quarum stat clausus et exitus harum WULF. *Swith. pref.* 129; humorem .. per ~um suum expellit ADEL. *QN* 33 (v. eliquare 1a); GIR. *EH* I 5 (v. aptare 1c); puer .. frangens nervos dum recalcitrat ad ~um, vite idoneus nascitur *Quaest. Salern.* B 27; **c1225** ascendendo per .. fossatum usque ad ~um quem eis dedi et feci versus moram ad communem pasturam meam exercendam (*Reg. Holm Cultram*) *MonA* V 611a; **1375** quod .. non intrent campum nisi ad ~us ville, et quicquid colligerint infra campum differant per eosdem ~us *Hal. Durh.* 126. **b** sicut lignum vetite arboris .. fuit Ade .. introitus ad .. mortem .. ita lignum crucis fuit credituris ~us a peccato ad .. vitam *Eccl. & Synag.* 108; dum vocatis in foveam

vestram .. obdurato omnem ~um obturatis ANSELM (*Or.* 10) III 35; hic duplex est ~us, nam potest dici quod [etc.] .. secundum hoc potest dici [etc.] S. LANGTON *Quaest.* 371.

3 end. **b** (med.) extremity. **c** conclusion (of period of time). **d** (w. *mensis*) latter half of month, in which dates are reckoned back from last day (Fr.).

†exito [l. exitu], *endistaeb GlC* E 394; ~us, i. .. finis, .. terminus *GlH* E 505; *DB* I 2 (v. 1 callis a); **1221** (v. estreciare 1a); **1374** ad ~um ville versus Beurepair est meremium multum de Codesley *Ac. Durh.* 211. **b** tibia incurva tota a principio genuum usque in calcanei exterioris ~um R. COLD. *Cuthb.* 48. **c** tribus .. vita nostra continetur: natura .. fato, cui nonaginta anni, hoc est tres Saturni cursus, ~um creant, .. fortuna ALB. LOND. *DG* 9. 10; **1398** post ~um .. xl dierum erit ad cornu regis (*Stat. Rob. III*) *APScot* 209; cum ad presenciam .. domini accesserit ante ~um anni et diei .. terras suas ad plegium liberari petat *Ib.* 213b. **d** **1315** A.D. m°ccc°xv° .. tercia die ~us mensis Marcii *RGasc* IV 1330.

4 final state (of life). **b** end (of one's life), 'passing away', death.

†**11..** cum omnes medici solius mortis ~um nobis prominere promitterent (*Ch. Archiep. Ebor.*) *Feod. Durh.* lxxvi; felix exitus et sacra passio morsque beata / insignes Petri titulos Paulique coronam / prefert M. RIEVAULX (*Vers.*) 37. **b** filios sacerdotis .. cito ~u periisse GILDAS *EB* 1; in scriptis .. ejus hystoricis de ~u animarum multa narravit miracula *V. Greg.* p. 103; cum .. ~um ejus de hac vita viderent BEDE *HE* IV 21 p. 258; **800** felicior est in bono dies ~us quam nativitatis ALCUIN *Ep.* 198; rennuit ipse tamen, huic ne foret exitus idem FRITH. 199; *RegulC* 65 (v. commendatio 4); anima, cum in ~u .. corporis fuerit, .. manum .. daemonum non timebit ALEX. CANT. *Dicta* 14 p. 163; usque ad ~um vite GIR. *EH* I 40; magnates regni nuper ad parliamentum, modo tamen desolutum per regis exitum, congregati *Ps.*-ELMH. *Hen. V* 8.

5 issue, heir (of person). **b** offspring (of animal).

1285 habuerunt .. potestatem .. exheredandi de tenemento ~um ipsorum contra voluntatem donatorum (*2 Westm.* 1.) *StRealm* I 71; **1293** pater .. Warini fuit servilis condicionis, unde ~us ipsius manet ejusdem condicionis *SelPlMan* 169; **c1340** nullus est ~us inter .. Henricum quondam virum suum et ipsam procreatus *MGL* I 392; **1380** J. et A. obierunt absque ~u et similiter .. R. obiit sine herede *Hal. Durh.* 163; **1389** (v. escaetabilis); Cayin et ~um ejus Dominus involvit undis diluvii FORTESCUE *NLN* I 9. **b** **1251** dedi .. sufficientem .. pasturam .. ad xx vaccas parturientes et unum taurum cum ~u earum ij annorum *ChartR* 44 m. 24; **1395** nullus pisciculus nec ~us piscium vocatus *la frygh'* sive *la shead* .. evadere potest *Pub. Works* I 161.

6 entrails, offal.

~us, intestinis hostiarum *GlC* E 469; **1230** quando custodit porcos .. tempore mactacionis porcorum debet habere ~um unius porci cum dorso *Doc. Bec* 32; **1290** in preparacione ~uum boum recencium et ad eosdem mactandos, iiij d. *Ac. Swinfield* 71; **1298** de .. uno carcosio sine ~u et corio *Pipe* 143 r. 23; **1308** de xxxiiij s. j d. rec' de feodo de *le rangh* et ~ibus animalium et piscium sic venditis per uxorem Roberti *Ac. Durh.* 84; **c1335** in stipendio mulierum .. mundancium intestina et ~us porcorum *Comp. Swith.* 229.

7 issue, produce, revenue, profits; **b** (royal); **c** (eccl.); **d** (man.). **e** (*~um facere*) to inventory, make an account of issue.

DB I 32 (v. applicare 2b); **1167** (v. 2 burgagium b); tradiderunt .. terram .. cum omnibus ~ibus terre *RDomin* 4; **1203** de placito tercie partis ~uum de bosci de S. *CurR* III 14; **1214** etc. (v. escaetor a); castrum de M. tradimus .. Seneroni E. cum omnibus juribus, redditibus, et exsitibus que .. habebamus in dicto castro *RGasc* I sup. p. 39; **1259** (v. approuamentum 1); **1396** cum molendinis, multuris, et eorum sequelis, cum curiis et curiarum ~ibus [etc.] *Reg. Paisley* 91; **1552** proficua, ~us, redditus, et revenciones predictorum mesuagiorum, terrarum, tenementorum *Pat* 850 m. 22. **b** **1225** quod debitum quod debui .. regi .. reddatur .. regi de exutibus custodiarum mearum *Cl* 71a; **1259** rex mittit Johanni P. .. c s. de ~ibus sigilli regis ad operaciones regis de Windes' faciendas *Cl* 442; **1260** denarii provenientes de ~u sigilli nostri Anglie *Cl* 241; **1261** de ~ibus prefati cunei regis *Cl* 352. **c** **1164** cum vacaverit archiepiscopatus, vel episcopatus, vel abbatia, vel prioratus de dominio regis, debet esse in manu ejus et exinde percipiet omnes redditus et ~us sicut dominicos *Const. Clar.* 12; defuncto enim canonico, omnes ~us et obventiones prebende sue totius termini infra quam decedit ei debentur *Offic. Sal.* 10; **1529** xxj li. xviiij s. x d. de proficuis et ~ibus capelle S. Margarete *Ac. Durh.* 162. **d** **1209** ~us grangie: idem reddunt compotum de lxvj quarteriis dimidio de toto ~u frumenti *Pipe Wint.* 51; in alio rotulo particulariter poni debent ~us grangie .. ita quod primo de ~u frumenti, postea siliginis .. consequenter de ~u ordei et avene .. postea debent ordinari multones et oves matrice et agni dictarum ovium, dices de ~u talis anni *FormMan* 12; **1356** de ij s. viij d. de redditu j messuagii .. nihil, quia levatus de ~u *Crawley* 270; **13..** quantum valet [manerium] per annum in omnibus ~ibus juxta verum valorem *Feod. Durh.* 9; **1449** de lxxvj quarteriis .. ordei de toto ~u grangiatoris .. trituratis *Crawley* 481; **1529** lviij li. viiij s. iij d. de prof' et exit' manerii de Elwett, ut patet per compotum prepositi *Ac. Durh.* 162. **e** **1308** in vadio Henrici le D. facientis ~um grangie per ix dies xiij d. ob. *Crawley* 263; **1388** W. L. servus ipsius J. de L. fecit ~um omnium bladorum ipsius J. in M. viz. xix quar. ordei vendidit *IMisc* 332/13.

8 expense, 'outgoing'.

1236 (v. exonerare 5); **1338** summa totius ~us necessarii (*Comp. Wootton*) *Hants Rec. Soc.* (1895) 149.

9 exaction, fine.

†**1204** ut ipsi .. liberi et quieti .. sint ab omnibus ~ibus, exactionibus, redditibus (*Ch. Regis*) *Feod. Durh.* 93; **1331** quod predicti major et civitas [de Bedeford] de ~ibus medio tempore perceptis onerentur [etc.] *PQW* 17b; quo die non venientes ad magnos ~us posuerunt, mittentes postea eidem Ricardo de Wylleby ut ~us suos certo die eis solvisset, alioquin rex novus cum suis ad eum veniret pro ~ibus querendis *Hist. Roff.* 60.

10 outcome, result. **b** (leg., question at) issue. **c** (w. *placiti*) issue of the plea. **d** (w. *patriae*) verdict of jury.

propter secundos bellorum ~us ALDH. *VirgP* 48; quem res ~um haberet solliciti exspectantes BEDE *HE* III 11; quantum gratiarum a rege .. in fine consecutus sit, rei ~us docuit *Chr. Battle* f. 89; spiritus Domini omnia cooperatur in bonum [cf. *Rom.* viii 28], dum et male acta bonos convertit in ~us PULL. *Sent.* 880A; his negotiis ad tam recolendum deductis ~um rex civitatem .. adiit *Ps.*-ELMH. *Hen. V* 126. **b** super veritate ~us sic juncti FORTESCUE *LLA* 26; **1505** hec omnia petit quod inquirantur per patriam .. ideo tam predicte xx li. [salmonum] quam predicte alie x li. .. respectuantur per auditores .. quousque ~us illi triantur *Entries* 16; **1505** relicto ~u predicto per predictos Stephanum Watson [etc.] superius ad patriam junct[o] *KRMem* 284 m. 58d.; **1583** ubi ~us predictus triari non potest *Pat* 1236 m. 35. **c** si coram judice contendentes ad litis perveniant contestacionem, super materia facti, quam legis Anglie periti ~um placiti appellant, ~us hujusmodi veritas per leges civiles, testium deposicione probari debet FORTESCUE *LLA* 20; exponitur eis ~us placiti de cujus veritate jurati illi curiam certificabunt *Ib.* 26. **d** **1433** J. B. et W. .. arrectati pro certis feloniis .. unde indictati de quibus feloniis .. de bono et malo posuerunt se inde in ~um patrie, per quem triati .. convicti fuerunt *Langley* app. 255.

exivi v. 1 exire, 2 exuere.

exjudicialiter [cf. LL judicialiter], extra-judicially. *V. et. extrajudicialiter.*

1515 dicta quorundam .. [*names follow*] .. (licet ~er et nullo eorum mediante juramento) examinatorum *Reg. Heref.* 224.

exjudicare [cf. CL judicare], to deprive by judicial action.

s1321 de aliis qui .. per potestatem regis exheredati et ~ati sunt assensu parium terre minime requisito *G. Ed. II Bridl.* 62.

exkaeta v. escaeta. **exkippare** v. skippare.

exlegalitas [cf. legalitas], illegality, unlawful conduct.

inquiret justicia per .. meliores homines .. de quali vita ipse [emptor] est et si antea audierunt eum calumpniari de ~ate. quodsi testati fuerint eum de legalitate expurget se judicio comitatus quod .. (*Leg. Ed. Conf.*) *GAS* 669.

exlegare, to banish, outlaw.

s1017 consilio perfidi ducis .. Canutus Eaduium .. regis Eadmundi germanum .. ~avit FL. WORC. I 181; **s1009** impetu .. Wulnodi quem rex ~atum ejecerat W. MALM. *GR* II 165; **s1172** Adam de P. .. exivit ab Anglia ~atus *G. Hen. II* I 35; **s1051** rex .. Godwinum et .. v filios ab Anglia ~avit M. PAR. *Maj.* I 521 (= FL. WORC. I 206: exules fore decreverunt); **s1265** qui ~ati principaliter extiterunt, erant Simon et Wido filii .. Simonis de Monte Forti RISH. 38; **s1326** (v. bannire 2b); **s1374** rex .. proposuit predictos monachos ~asse AD. MUR. *Cont. A* 215.

exlex [CL]

1 exempt from law, lawless.

~x, sine lege, dissolutus OSB. GLOUC. *Deriv.* 199; nec mirandum si de gente .. ~ge .. tales .. contra nature legem natura producat GIR. *TH* III 35; **s1235** que leges vel consuetudines longis retroactis temporibus ~ges extiterant et injuriose *Flor. Hist.* II 217; GARL. *Tri. Eccl.* 140 (v. convertere 7a); lex exlex, amor exosus, concordia discors (*Vers.*) M. PAR. *Maj.* V 323; quot et quanti judices †seleges [l. exleges] Pelagianos olim damnatos .. absolvere et reconciliare sollicite machinantur BRADW. *CD pref.*

2 (as sb.) outlaw.

postquam rex W. venit in Angliam, fuit iste Edricus ~x indaciam [l. in Daciam] *DB* II 200; si aliquem dejiciat in mortem sit utlaga (vel ~x) [AS: *utlah*] et prosequatur (*Quad.*) *GAS* 133; (*Cons. Cnuti*) *Ib.* 311 (v. dyscolus a); ibi latrones et ~ges specialem speluncam habebant, inaudita scelera faciebant ORD. VIT. XI 36 p. 288; sublimandus .. non in regem sed ~gem GIR. *TH* III 25; predonum .. sicut et furum ~ges .. quos usitatius uthlagatos dicimus *Dial. Scac.* II 10 L; **1557** complures etiam traditores, rebelles, et ~ges .. expulsi tam extra limites de L. et O. quam de aliis locis *ActPCIr* 39.

exmonachare, to deprive of the status of a monk.

ipsum abstracto religionis habitu, a monasterio turpiter ejectum ~ari procuravit GIR. *Spec.* II 28.

exmonachus [LL], ex-monk.

Adeodatus Romanus ~us .. sedit annis iv ORD. VIT. II 17 p. 435; Erembertus .. cenobita .. ad ~um languentem accurrit *Ib.* VII 13 p. 220; monachi illius, sed moribus ~i, de abbate in abbatem translatio GIR. *Spec.* III 7.

exmursine v. oxymyrsine.

exnamiare [cf. namiare], to distrain: **a** (person); **b** (property).

a **c1158** prohibeo quod [sanctimoniales] non esnamientur pro defectu servicii David de A. .. pro re aliqua que ad me pertineat *Danelaw* 280. **b** **c1111** precipio tibi .. ne amodo terra sua sit esnamiata pro terra tua super x li. forisfacturam meam *Pl. Anglo-Norm.* 110; **1158** prohibeo ne [terra S. Osewyni de Northumberland] sit ~iata propter alterius debitum vel forisfactum nisi propter suum dominicum *CalCh* II 172; **c1160** ne terra .. sine recto clamore exnammetur nec dominica peccunia S. Stephani exnammetur pro alicujus debito *Act. Hen. II* I 273.

exnatus [cf. CL natus], class of servant.

c1250 (v. 1 chevagium 1d).

exnunc [LL; al. div.], from now, henceforth.

1254 ~c decernimus irritum .. si quid super hoc .. fuerit .. attentatum *MunAcOx* I 27; **1271** cessantibus ~c omnibus modis penis et usuris *Cl* 434; **1318** (v. 1 cessio 1c); **1326** illos .. ~c prout ex tunc .. excommunicacionis sentencia .. innodamus *Lit. Cant.* I 202; **1340** (v. 2 eventus 4a); exnunc noli lugere / dic Petro Simoni / tot signa claruere / sciant discipuli LEDREDE *Carm.* 28. 9; **1470** quod .. fide sua media promisit, et ~c firmiter promittit *Pri. Cold.* 217; **1543** (v. extunc a).

exoccare [cf. occare], to break.

occa .. componitur ~o .. et redocco .., ambo pro scindere OSB. GLOUC. *Deriv.* 396.

exoccultare [cf. CL occultare], to conceal, keep hidden, or (?) *f.l.*

Alfredum quem Godwynus .. interfecit exoccultatum [? l. exoculatum] in insula Eliensi *Feud. Man.* 134 (cf. *ASChr.* [s1036]: *Ælfred .. Godwine .. gelette.. man hine blende*).

exoccupare [LL]

1 to seize, occupy completely.

filius .. premisit suos preoccupare pontem .. sed militibus patris concurrentibus ad ~andum pontem, milites filii a ponte repelluntur TORIGNI *Chr.* 87.

2 to prevent, hinder.

to lett, detinere, retinere, tardare, ~are, impedire *CathA.*

3 to free from (activity or occupation).

~atis .. mentibus surrepunt tedia J. SAL. *Pol.* 406A; **s1016** ~ato ab aliis .. negotiis animo *Chr. Rams.* 121; ut exoneratus terrenis et ~atus transitoriis .. ad celestia tendas AD. SCOT *TGC* 823D; audito signo statim .. silebunt, atque, ~atis manibus, si qui tunc scribunt, ecclesiam .. ingredientur *Cust. Westm.* 166; infirmarius .. in claustro tenetur esse .. quando ~atus fuerit *Cust. Cant.* 330.

exoccupatio, hindrance.

a lettynge, detencio, ~o, inpedicio, impedimentum *CathA.*

exocreare [cf. CL ocreatus], to deprive of greaves.

Parca .. / .. / fortes exocreat quos fractis cruribus / ut lutum figuli contundit calcibus WALT. WIMB. *Sim.* 117.

exoculare [CL], **~ari**

1 to put out eyes, blind; *v. et. deoculare, disoculare*; **b** (fig.). **c** (p. ppl. as sb.) blind person.

ut stupet exoculata diei talpa nitorem R. CANT. *Poems* 260; H. HUNT. *HA* VIII 1 (v. deoculare); furtum facit exoculatos, / in cruce suspensos D. BEC. 1785; **c1256** deferebat unam pilam de nive cum qua percussit hominem dicti Ricardi comitis, ita quod eum ~avit *IMisc* 10/7; qui contra sacculum certare nititur / si saccus jubeat, exoculabitur WALT. WIMB. *Sim.* 46; quosdam prelatos statuerunt exoculare *Vers. Hen. V* 161; Johannes .. ~ari et lingua privari mandatur *Extr. Chr. Scot.* 83. **b** rarius .. illum majoris dignitatis ~avit ambitio *Ep. ad amicum* 107. **c** sanctus .. martyr .. ~ato novos oculos reddiderat W. CANT. *Mir. Thom.* VI 10 p. 422.

2 (dep.) to stare at.

sedatur Christiana gens miraculo; parvulique martyrium ~ata, interrogat quomodo evasisset ignem W. MALM. *Mir. Mariae* 201.

exoculatio, blinding.

enormes excessus, super fratrum .. ~onibus GIR. *IK* I 1; cedes atroces et occisiones, ~ones et incarcerationes patientissime pro Christo sufferunt *Id. Spec.* IV 16.

exodium [CL], exode, dramatic postlude.

~ium, cantatio in theatris ludicra et scurilis *GlC* E 487 (cf. ib. 417: †exossum [l. exodium], canticum in teatris).

exodus [LL < ἔξοδος], exodus, going out. **b** Exodus, second book of the Pentateuch.

~us, exitus *GlC Int.* 115; O ante D breviatur ut .. periodus, ~us, synodus BACON *Gram. Gk.* 123. **b** illud .. celeberrimum ~i candelabrum [*Exod.* xxv 31] cujus stipes .. ornabatur ALDH. *Met.* 2 p. 66; unde est illud ~i 'cumque extendisset Moyses manum super mare' [*Exod.* xiv 21] BEDE *Gen.* 98; 'convictus mox morte moriatur' ~i vigesimo primo capitulo RIC. ARMAGH *Def. Cur.* 1398 (*recte* 1298); ad ~um festino et deinde ad reliquos Moisei libros CAPGR. *Gen. pref.* 231.

exolare v. excolare.

exolescere [CL], **exolēre** [LL]

1 to grow up.

~eo, i. .. excresco *GlH* E 698; ~etum *gewexenne GlP* 406; ~etus, excretus OSB. GLOUC. *Deriv.* 195.

2 to deteriorate, waste away. **b** to worsen morally, lose virtue.

~everunt, *gesueðradum GlC* E 395; ~itus, minuatus *Ib.* 443; e[x]olevit, vetustate obscuratus est *Ib.* 538; ~escit, defecit *Ib.* 547; ~iverunt, i. tabuerunt, .. corripuerunt, *geswefredon GlH* E 694; †exolescti [MS: exolescit], i. evanescit, defecit *Ib.* 697. **b** ~itus, superbis *GlC* E 540; ~evit, i. corruptus est vitiis *GlH* E 699.

3 to become destitute, deprived (of).

9.. ~escunt, *aidliaþ WW*; pene dixerim omnes gratia veritatis ~etos, velut eam pariter sacrilega condempnatione proscripserunt (*Quad.*) *GAS* 533.

exolut- v. exsolut-.

exomologesis [LL < ἐξομολόγησις], confession.

~in, confessio *GlC* E 463 (cf. ib. 505: ~in, preces vel confesio); ~is, confessio OSB. GLOUC. *Deriv.* 196; ~i rite peracta FERR. *Kinloss* 82.

exon- v. et. esson-.

exonerare [CL]

1 to unload (freight or ship). **b** to discharge (firearm). **c** (med.) to relieve, evacuate (part of body).

cum naves in portu Hibernico .. ~assent GIR. *TH* I 29; **1253** (v. 3 corallus a); **1303** postquam .. res et mercandise ~ate seu vendite fuerint (*Stat.*) *MGL* II 210; **s1386** (v. 1 artare 1d); **1486** de xx torquibus ferri ~atis in anno precedenti hoc compotum *ExchScot* 411. **b** **1573** tormentum suum .. pulvere tormentali et uno globulo plumbeo oneratum, ~avit *Pat* 1105 m. 34; **1577** videre desiderabat quo modo tormenticulum illud ~are potuit. .. interrogavit pro clave tormenticuli .. et utrum ambo eorum ~ata fuerunt necne *Pat* 1159 m. 11; **1618** plurima tormenta in eam [navem] immiserunt et fulminari et ~ari fecerunt *HCA Libel.* 78/163. **c** intestina tua si casu sint onerata / turbine, quere locum quo possint exonerari D. BEC. 1103; omnia membra simul et semel a superfluis ~antur *Quaest. Salern.* B 16; nervi palpebrarum multa humiditate ~ati *Ib.* 59; cum partes ex superfluitatibus ~ent delectant *Ib.* 314.

2 to relieve (of burden); **b** (iron., of money).

quia abominabilis est sapore, natura cito ~are se laborat *Quaest. Salern.* N 50; accersitis jubet ut seipsum diligenter armis ~ent *Hist. Arthuri* 84; sic se natura ~at ex superfluo sanguine GILB. VII 294. 1. **b** **1177** nuntii vestri a Romana curia redierunt ~ati quidem argento, onerati plumbo P. BLOIS *Ep.* 41; omnes quibus pecunia sua fuit oneri rex officiosissime ~avit DEVIZES f. 27; GERV. CANT. *Chr.* 257 (v. complantare a).

3 to exonerate (person from responsibility or liability); **b** (refl.); **c** (w. abl. or prep. & abl.). **d** (w. inanim. obj.).

iniquitates meae .. obvolvunt me . . . evolve me, ~a me ANSELM (*Prosl.* 1) I 100; **1231** quod .. ad nos exhonerandos cum effectu laboraretis *Cl* 584; **1320** ita quod ipse et coexecutores sui fuissent ~ati *Lit. Cant.* I 44; proice a me culpas meas, ut ego ~atus [ME: *ilichted*] leviter ascendam .. in celum *AncrR* 138; **1415** summa .. pendet quousque dux fuerit informatus quare dictam summam recepit set custumarii inde exhonerantur *ExchScot* 224; **1485** (v. dispunctuare a). **b** me .., tuis provolutus genibus, ~ans affligo B. *V. Dunst.* 1; **1170** unde se possit ~are J. SAL. *Ep.* 299 (303). **c** **c1090** ut .. ab eo debito contigerit eum ~ari ANSELM (*Ep.* 140) III 286; Rogerius .. pastoralis cure sarcina ~ari .. desideravit ORD. VIT. XII 32 p. 433; **1225** quod dominus rex inde a peccato sit exhoneratus *Cl* 27; **1321** animam .. regine de xxviij s. iiij d. .. ~amus per presentes *Lit. Cant.* I 49; **1334** tenuit decem feoda militum de domino rege in capite de quorum servicio ~atus fuit propter custodiam foreste *SelPlForest* 67; **1410** pendent lxxx li. . ., de qua summa .. auditores .. ~averunt custumarios computantes *ExchScot* 113; **s1458** ~ans .. ipsum [sc. custodem gaole] ab officio, subinstituit alterum, qui magis idoneus fuerat *Reg. Whet.* I 290. **d** **c1350** maneria tenuerunt ab omnimodo servicio exhonerata *Reg. S. Aug.* 65; ut a tallagiis ~etur regnum *Eul. Hist. Cont.* 399.

4 to exonerate (trespass), exculpate (fault).

1340 nunquam vaccam dicte Alicie imparcavit ~ando illud ut acciperet donum suum et hoc petit quod inquiratur *CBaron* 106.

5 to relieve of (financial) burden, reimburse.

1236 noluit se de exitibus camerarie onerare, quia secundum assisas scaccarii non habuit warantum per quod se ~are posset *KRMem* 15 m. 16(1)*d.*; **1524** de quibus [receptis] se ~at de arrer' hujus compoti vij li. j d. .. summa .. totius exoneracionis xvij li. xviiij s. j d. *Ac. Durh.* 666.

6 to overstock. *Cf. superonerare.*

1388 R. de M. .. ~avit dictam pasturam cum bidentibus suis continue per quinque annos ultime elapsos per extorcionem et distruccionem tenencium *IMisc* 238/1E.

exoneratio [CL]

1 unloading (of ship). **b** discharging (of firearm). **c** (med.) evacuation.

1196 (c1392) cum .. applicatione, oneratione, et ~one navium, battellorum, et aliorum vasorum (*Ch. Regis*) *MonA* I 240b; **1258** dum tamen ipsi .. ~one navis ferentis victualia illa interfuerint *BBC* (*Grimsby*) 300. **b** **1573** parcum .. circumambulabat querens convenientem .. sagittacionem et ~onem tormenti .. versus .. volucrem *Pat* 1105 m. 34. **c** animus .. desiderium .. excitat .. ad superfluorum ~onem *Quaest. Salern.* B 18.

2 releasing. **b** relief, release.

catholici .. predicant quomodo ecclesia potest .. per ~onem temporalium adjuvari WYCL. *Sim.* 101; **s1339** post .. infantule mortue partus ~onem *Meaux* II 381. **b** **s1260** nunciatus est .. uno eodemque die obitus istorum trium regi, qui magno se consilio et ~one cognoscens destitutum, dolorem .. concepit non modicum *Flor. Hist.* II 451.

3 (w. subj. gen. or poss. pron.) discharge (from responsibility), exoneration (from liability). **b** (w. obj. gen.) discharge (of debt), exoneration (of burden).

1312 quod .. summam nobis ad scaccarium nostrum Berewici ad nostri ~onem faciatis liberare *RScot* I 110; in relevationem nostri monasterii et ~onem .. manerium .. concessit *Croyl.* 65; **s1428** exoneratio fratris Roberti Ownesby ab officiis cellararii et bursarii *Chr. S. Alb.* 30; **1439** litere .. pro plena ~one et acquietacione .. archiepiscopi .. videbuntur necessarie BEKYNTON I 46; **1545** quittantiis .. per vos deliberandis pecuniarium summis .. pro vestra ~one facienda habitis et receptis *Conc. Scot.* I cclx. **b** **1236** precentor .. omnia onera usque ad .. ~onem viij marcarum in solidum sustinebit *Ch. Sal.* 240; **1353** collector quintedecime .. habuit commissionem .. ad .. salaria ponendum in ~onem quintedecime (*AssizeR Sussex*) *EHR* XXI 521; quatinus in ~onem oneris mei et officii .. oculum vigilem volueritis accommodare *Dictamen* 367; **s1425** breve regium in ~onem impositi oneris .. impetravit AMUND. I 198.

4 reimbursement.

1524 (v. exonerare 5).

exoneratorium, (w. *curatorum*), (title of a book).

1528 librum sive codicillum '~ium curatorum' nuncupatum *Conc.* III 712.

exonium v. essonia.

exoperari [LL], to work out, produce.

illa [sc. hierarchia] maxime stabilitatem, scientiam, et amorem ~atur in humana hierarchia COLET *Cel. Hier.* 184.

exoppilare [cf. CL oppilare], (med.) to unblock.

salsa .. ~ant epar et splenem GILB. III 161. 2.

exoptabilis [CL], desirable.

dies Dominica .. triumpho Christi veneranda, nostra quoque resurrectione nobis ~is BEDE *Temp.* 15; **s1088** rex .. populo .. leges promisit ~es H. HUNT. *HA* VII 1.

exoptare [CL], to long for, desire greatly; **b** (w. inf.); **c** (p. ppl. as adj.).

ego Ælfricus .. salutem ~o domno archiepiscopo Sigerico ÆLF. *CH I pref.* 1; PULL. *Sent.* 852B (v. deploratio); **1176** sponso suo .. eam quam sibi salutem ~at (BASILIA *Ep.*) GIR. *EH* II 14; oporteret .. nimirum hoc avide amplecteretur atque ardentissimo ~aret anhelitu ROLLE *IA* 146. **b** quis eorum mori ~ans mundo et vivere Christo .. sensus .. prostravit? GILDAS *EB* 71; progeniemque libens exoptat gignere stirpis ALDH. *VirgV* 128; **c794** hujus te calicis mero inebriare ~o ALCUIN *Ep.* 34; **798** te amare me fateor et a te amari ~o *Id. ad Beatum* 318; qui ~ant indui Christi corporis incorruptionem *Ep. Anselm.* II 234. **c** habebimus impleta illa ~ata promissione Domini BEDE *Tab.* 413; juvenis .. ad tenenda .. regni sceptra ~atissimus *Id. HE* V 19 p. 322.

exorabilis [CL], who can be moved by prayer.

fac illum .. mihi ~em ANSELM (*Or.* 12) III 46; ut supplicanti filio ~is pie condones indulgentiam ORD. VIT. V 10 p. 388; pia semper et ~is gloriosa illa [sc. BVM] D. LOND. *Ep.* 12; ut .. discant se posse faciles in magnis invenire quos in minimis ~es habuere W. CANT. *Mir. Thom.* V 20.

exorare [CL]

1 to entreat, pray (to): **a** (w. dat.); **b** (w. acc.); **c** (w. *quatenus, quod,* or *ut*); **d** (absol.); **e** (w. *quatenus* or *ut*); **f** (supine abl. w. *difficilis* or *facilis*).

a **1341** regi .. ~amus (v. 2 deliberatio 1a); **1361** numerus scolarium .. Deo pro nobis .. ~ancium *Lit. Cant.* II 410. **b** multi .. ad [v. l. *omit* ad] ~andam in adversis divinam clementiam .. sunt .. accensi BEDE *HE* IV 14 p. 236; oro te: ~a eum; peto a te: impetra ab eo ANSELM (*Or.* 17) III 69; ad dominum .. redit, eum ~ans hujusmodi verbis *Simil. Anselmi* 73; Dominum ~aturus GIR. *GE* II 10; **s1300** rex pro pace .. episcopum .. ~abat *G. Durh.* 18. **c** te caelestem sponsum ~ando interpello ut tua .. caritas .. me .. inebriat *Nunnam.* 66; civem .. ~averunt ut se victimam .. faceret GREG. *Mir. Rom.* 5; **1168** ~etur dominus papa ut ecclesie reformet pacem J. SAL. *Ep.* 243 (241 p. 470); **1282** paternitatem .. ~amus quatenus (v. dominabilis 1); **1329** paternitatem vestram .. deprecor et ~o, quod .. *Lit. Cant.* I 287; **1448** vestram reverenciam .. deprecor et ~o quatenus .. supradicta committantur custodie *MunAcOx* 584. **d** sportas .. / quas prius exorans palma benedixerat alma ALDH. *VirgV* 1612; ~ando eam devotissime salutabat *Latin Stories* 97; aut stans aut genua flectens ~avit *Meaux* I 439. **e** **a1200** cum lacrimis et singultibus ~o, ut .. pietas .. concedat *Feod. Durh.* 151*n.*; **1297** dilectos nostros socios .. transmittimus, ~antes quatenus .. quid .. justum visum fuerit distinguatis *Gild. Merch.* I 278. **f** date .. nec sitis ~atu difficiles ANSELM (*Or.* 7) III 25; Petre, ne sis ~atu difficilis (*Ib.* 9) III 31; ut nullus sit in Anglia sanctus Ivone .. ~atu facilior W. MALM. *GP* IV 181.

2 a (w. acc.) to request, pray (for). **b** (w. *pro*) to pray (on behalf of, on account of).

a volumus vos scire .. quid necesse sit .. a Deo precibus ~are ÆLF. *EC* 15; mihi veniam ~are non sufficio ANSELM (*Or.* 18) III 72. **b** quis eorum pro peccatis populi ~ans imo de pectore clamavit? GILDAS *EB* 69; qui novit .. pro persecutoribus ~are [AS: *gebidda*] *Rit. Durh.* 44; **s1234** pro suis fidelibus .. ~are M. PAR. *Maj.* III 290; **1335** pro anima .. Thome .. et aliorum pro quibus ~are tenentur *Eng. Clergy* 258; **1412** pro cleri benefactoribus in publico ~are *StatOx* 220.

3 to marry, wed.

to be wedde, .. ~ari *CathA*.

exoratio [CL], entreaty, prayer.

ferventi ~one ad Deum facta GILDAS *EB* 72; **1372** ista grangia facta .. fuit .. ad ~onem .. ballivi istius loci *MonA* II 298.

exorator [CL], successful suppliant.

sperantes illis [sanctis] exoratoribus ut tu / .. / .. laxes .. debita nobis BEDE *CuthbV* 974; sit apud te pro nobis ~or [Hilarius] qui tunc contra haereticos pro te adstitit assertor EGB. *Pont.* 91.

exorbitantia, error, transgression. *V. et. exorbitare* 1f.

1423 multe ~ie in prioratu de Daventre pullulabant *Doc. Eng. Black Monks* II 153 (= *Conc.* III 426a).

exorbitare [LL]

1 (intr.) to deviate, stray. **b** to err, fail; **c** (morally). **d** (w. *a via* or sim.). **e** (pr. ppl. as adj.) deviant, erroneous, irregular. **f** (as sb. n.) error, transgression; *v. et. exorbitantia.*

~ans, *asuab GlC* E 475; ~antes, i. circuientes, declinantes, *aswifende GlH* E 690. **b** inspiciens clericus .. rescriptum observabat eum, ne ~aret *Dial. Scac.* II 2 C; si seisina sive possessio aliquando ~et ita quod jus merum non sequatur .. BRACTON f. 62b; si .. in aliquo calamus preceps ~averit .. SICCAV. *PN* 131; folia occidunt caduca, flores ~ant et de fructu *FormOx* 448. **c** homo primus, nisi ~asset, penam .. nullam .. meruisset PULL. *Sent.* 746A; H. BOS. *Thom.* III 30, GIR. *PI* III 13 (v. deviare 1b); GIR. *GE* I 34 (v. desperabiliter); **1541** (v. deplorabiliter). **d** ALDH. *VirgP* 38 (v. errabundus); **796** a via veritatis et perpetuae pascuis vitae ~are ALCUIN *Ep.* 94; si ab ejus voluntate .. vos ~asse cognoveritis OSB. *V. Dunst.* 43; H. LOS. *Ep.* 12 (v. effeminate); tua generositas, / a qua non exorbitas, / incepit ab atavis HIL. RONCE. 4. 14; a linea regie stirpis ~averunt W. MALM. *GR* I 43; dum a scientia pietatis ~ant J. SAL. *Pol.* 459D; **s1094** a vestigiis beati Petri videantur Romani pontifices .. ~are M. PAR. *Min.* I 50; **1324** (v.

conservatia b); cunctorum viancium sed non ~ancium via recta RIC. ARMAGH *AP* 19; quod a regulis grammatice nimis patenter ~at (KYN.) *Ziz.* 62. **e** omnes qui a jure communi per ~antes gracias beneficia ecclesiastica sunt adepti PAUL. ANGL. *ASP* 1527; sic ~antes promoventur episcopi inutiles, idiote, scandalosi *Ib.* 1533; **1478** fili ~ans *Reg. Whet.* II 186. **f 1421** cum plura sint ~ia et enormia inter professores ordinis .. nigrorum monachorum in Anglia .. *Doc. Eng. Black Monks* II 110 (= *Conc.* III 413a).

2 (trans.) to stray from.

1323 multos facit sacre religionis semitas exhorbitare *Lit. Cant.* I 111.

exorbitatio [LL]

1 deviation from course.

fit .. longo intervallo mundi circuicionis ~o, quam inflammacionis vastitas sequatur necesse est BRADW. *CD* 102D.

2 error, transgression.

s**1125** rebus que non eque processerant, ne pari ~one amplius procederent, opem pro posse laturus J. WORC. 22; **1242** ne .. nota aliquis vobis possit impingi ab his que tantos decent cives alicujus ex parte aliqua ~onis GROS. *Ep.* 95; s**1422** quanta exhibita fuerat vagandi occasio per tuum recessum flebilem et anormalem ~onem AMUND. I 88; **1452** ut .. Johannem ab hujusmodi ~onibus arcius compescatis *Pri. Cold.* 175.

exorcisma v. exorcismus.

exorcismare [cf. CL exorcizare, LL exorcismus], to exorcize.

1242 in necessitatis articulo puer baptizatus si convalescat ad ecclesiam deferri debet sed non ~ari *Conc. Scot.* II 58.

exorcismus [LL < ἐξορκισμός], **~a**, exorcism, driving out of evil spirit. **b** words or rite of exorcism; **c** (w. ref. to person); **d** (w. ref. to thing).

ALDH. *VirgP* 43 (v. catechizare 1a); [spiritus maligni] simulant se coactos et quasi ~orum virtute extractos fingunt J. SAL. *Pol.* 469A; spiritus extra fertur, ut non incidat semen .. et fit .. ex maleficio et ~ate GILB. VII 285v. 2; per ~um expellitur ab exorcizatis potestas diaboli OCKHAM *Pol.* I 164; *CathA* (v. adjuratio c). **b** BEDE *HE* III 11 (v. dicere 5a); ~um, sermo correptionis *GlC* E 359; exorcista cum ordinatur accipiat de manu episcopi libellum in quo scripti sunt ~i EGB. *Pont.* 13; libros ~orum *Cust. Westm.* 49; *Conc.* III 259 (v. exorcista b). **c** ~o super illum ab archiepiscopo facto OSB. *Mir. Dunst.* 19; jubent .. presbyterum accersiri et super eum pro furore sedando ~um recitari GOSC. *Mir. Iv.* lxxiv; **1281** super sic baptizatos dicantur ~i et catechismi *Conc. Syn.* 897. **d** ~us olei incipit EGB. *Pont.* 122; ~um et benedictionem panis et casei .. isto modo debes facere (*Jud. Dei*) *GAS* 425; pulsatur signum ad ~um salis et aque *Cust. Westm.* 241; ~i .. sive benedicciones .. vini, panis, aque, olei, salis, cere, incensi sive thuris, mense altaris, murorum ecclesie, vestimentorum, mitre, baculi pastoralis, baculorum peregrinorum .. practica sunt necromancie pocius quam sancte theologie R. DYMMOCK 113.

exorcista [LL < ἐξορκιστής], exorcist. **b** holder of third degree in holy orders.

masculina ut proreta, .. ~a ALDH. *PR* 133 p. 185; ~a, adjurans *GlC* E 422; BELETH *RDO* 13. 27 (v. adjurator). **b** ALDH. *Met.* 2 p. 70 (v. acolytus b); [Christus] ~a fuit, quando ejecit septem daemonia de Maria Magdalenae (*sic*) EGB. *Pont.* 10; ÆLF. *Ep.* 2. 118 (v. energumenus b); ~arum est officium ex obsessis corporibus daemonia effugare LANFR. *Cel. Conf.* 629C; c**1400** te W. ~am condemnatum, ab ordine ~e degradamus et deponimus: .. tibi librum exorcismorum auferimus, ac te omni et omnimodo honore ~e privamus *Conc.* III 259; s**1422** cum exorzistis stallum teneas AMUND. I 95; hic ~a, A. *a benet WW.*

exorcizare [CL < ἐξορκίζειν]

1 to exorcize (evil spirit).

e[x]orcizo, adjuro *GlC* E 406; ~o te, maledicte diabole (*Jud. Dei* 14) *GAS* 425.

2 to cleanse of evil spirit: **a** (w. pers. as obj.); **b** (w. thing as obj.).

a c**798** [caticumenus] ~atur, id est conjuratur malignus spiritus, ut exeat et recedat ALCUIN *Ep.* 134; exorcistas habemus qui cathezizandos ~ant BELETH *RDO* 13. 27; OCKHAM *Pol.* I 164 (v. exorcismus a). **b** THEOD. *Pen.* II 9. 2 (v. aqua 2b); ALDH. *VirgP* 32 (v. benedictio 3); ~o te, creatura salis .., ut efficiaris sal ~atum in salutem credentium EGB. *Pont* 34; adjuro te, creatura aquae .., ut fias aqua ~ata, adjurata et obfirmata adversus .. diabolum (*Jud. Dei* 1) *GAS* 405; rebus materialibus in ecclesiis uti nos oportet .. ad usum ecclesiasticum consecratis, exorzisatis, adjuratis et sanctificatis R. DYMMOCK 123.

3 to adjure, beseech.

clamat .. ad Dominum .., exorcisatum habet populum ut maledicat ei terra, provocat ultricem a celo dexteram MAP *NC* IV 6 f. 50; s**1388** obnixius supplicabant, exorcizando regem et proceres parliamenti quod ob amorem Dei .. cessarent a morte justiciariorum FAVENT 20; s**1422** te .. ~antes per Deum vivum, adjurantesque per Ihesum Christum ut taliter tempus deperditum studeas jam iterum redimere AMUND. I 88.

exorcizatio [LL], exorcization, exorcism.

alia [sacramenta] constant in factis, qualia sunt crucis signaculum, exsufflatio ~onis, expansio manuum HALES *Sent.* IV 21; non vident ipsas res mutari propter ipsarum consecracionem vel exorzizacionem R. DYMMOCK 131.

exordiarius [cf. CL exordiri]

1 beginner.

a begynner, ~ius, inceptor *CathA.*

2 precentor.

~ius, elevata in altum voce, dixit "Redemptor mundi conservet vitam vestram" BYRHT. *V. Osw.* 447; ~io cum tribus sociis chorum tenente *Ib.* 464.

exordinare [LL]

1 to disorder, disturb. **b** (intr.) to be disorderly, cause disturbance.

si [tristitia et dolor] invaluerint, ut ~ent et turbent animam, ex ea concussione fit ira J. SAL. *Met.* 922D. **b** si prior aliquam exordinationem in choro viderit, licet ei .. fratrem ~antem reprehendere *Obed. Abingd.* 356.

2 (eccl.) to deprive of orders.

si presbiter hominem occidat, .. ~et [AS: *onhadige*] eum episcopus et tunc ab ecclesia reddatur (*Quad.*) *GAS* 63; si me asseris contra scita canonum ordinatum, libenti animo ~ari concedo EADMER *Wilf.* 17; s**1164** si sacerdos .. flagitium perpetrasset, ~atus ab archiepiscopo, traderetur laicali curie judicandus *Ann. Wint.* 57; s**1202** si ~ati sumus, ecce tribulatio, pena peccati et exordinationis nostre *Chr. Evesham* 114.

exordinatio [LL], (eccl. & mon.) disturbance, breach of rule. (*Cf. Regula S. Benedicti* 65).

~ones, *misfadunga GlH* E 689; **1105** pecunia magna necessaria, labor gravis, ~ones multae ANSELM (*Ep.* 355) V 295; *Obed. Abingd.* 356 (v. exordinare 1b); *Chr. Evesham* 104 (v. chlamys e); *Ib.* 114 (v. exordinare 2); ob suspicionem alicujus ~onis alicubi reperiende .. agatur exploratio *Cust. Cant.* 94; ut tolleretur imposterum ~onis occasio *Meaux* II 22.

exordiri [CL]

1 to begin (speech or written work): **a** (trans.); **b** (w. direct speech); **c** (w. inf.); **d** (absol.).

a hoc modo prophetiam suam ~diens: "revertimini [etc.]" GILDAS *EB* 57; c**1072** unde potissimum ~diar allocutionem meam ANSELM (*Ep.* 4) III 104; de Jove tractatum ~diamur ALB. LOND. *DG* 2. 6. **b** ita ~sus est "patientia autem probationem .." ALDH. *Met.* 4; **798** ita ~si sumus "necessarium est, fratres .." *CS* 291; ad eum ~sus sum "sunt vera an falsa .." BYRHT. *V. Ecgwini* 375. **c** ita loqui ~sus est BEDE *HE* V 19 p. 329. **d** qui bene ~diri volet, prius necesse est ut suae causae genus diligenter agnoscat ALC-UIN *Rhet.* 20; ~diam, incipiam *GlH* E 680; ut veritatem rei enucleare possimus, longius aliquantulum nos ~diri oportet ANSELM (*Casus Diab.* 12) I 252; **1168** unde .. dulcissimi fratres, ~ar? J. SAL. *Ep.* 241 (244 p. 482); taliter ~ditus subintulit "eja, tu, .." R. COLD. *Cuthb.* 18; cujus rei figmentum ut explicemus, paulo altius ~diamur ALB. LOND. *DG* 11. 20; volo alcius ~diri [ME: *biginnen*] et sic ad hoc descendere *AncrR* 135.

2 (p. ppl. *exorsus* as sb. n. pl.) beginning. *V. et. exordium* 3.

sicque interdiu scevo exemplo in ~sis, die diem recrastinante [etc.] *Chr. Battle* f. 13.

exordium [CL]

1 beginning, start: **a** (w. ref. to time); **b** (anat.).

a BEDE *TR* 6 p. 193 (v. annus 1c); incipiunt veris exordia tempore prisco *Kal. M. A.* I 399; ~ia, i. principia *frymþu GlH* E 685; sumamus hoc ~ium. primo omnium veneremur Deum ÆLF. BATA 5. 13. **b** a planta usque ad unguis ~ium, quod inferius patere debuerat, superius prominebat R. COLD. *Cuthb.* 48 p. 99; de vocabulis ad .. membra humani corporis spectantibus: .. hoc ~ium, *a begynnyng WW.*

2 origin, cause, source: **b** (w. *habere* or sim.).

propria voluntas hominis totius est ~ium mali *Simil. Anselmi* 8; querit qualiter bestia intraverit, que causa fuerit, quod ~ium ejus, quisve sit aditus ALEX. CANT. *Dicta* 1 p. 116; ~ium repercussionis *Quaest. Salern.* P 62. **b 680** signum a Nazareis .. sumpsit ~ium ALDH. *Ep.* 4 p. 483; incipit compotus .. incipit, id est .. ~ium accipit BYRHT. *Man.* 2; quis intelligit .. quo modo ad esse veniret, .. unde ~ium subsistendi haberet? PULL. *Sent.* 674D; ex hoc patet unde habuit [sacramentum] ~ium S. LANGTON *Quaest.* 367; causa est sexta circumstancia .. per quem res sumpsit ~ium [ME: *hwer þurch hit bigon*] *AncrR* 122.

3 primal stage, beginnings.

parva mihi primo constant exordia vitae ALDH. *Aen.* 93 (*Scintilla*) 3; Anna .. profetissa .. in divinae nativitatis ~io .. clarescit *Id. VirgP* 13; in ipso ~io nascentis ibi ecclesiae BEDE *HE* II 14; eadem plenius expedienda ab ~io [monasterii] *Chr. Battle* f. 8; eam etiam inter ~ia condite Carthaginis Enee nuptam ALB. LOND. *DG* 9. 13; HIGD. I 4 (v. deviatio c).

4 exordium, preface, prologue (of written work); **b** (rhet.).

Proba .. in ~io Vergiliocentonis .. regulam .. deprompsit ALDH. *PR* 135; a dictis dicenda alio ~io distinguamus ANSELM (*CurD* I 25) II 96; in ~io hujus opusculi EADMER *Beat.* 15 p. 291; cujus doctrine ministerio illius primevi ~ii et prohemii preloquimina potuimus exhaurire R. COLD. *Cuthb.* 2 p. 5. **b** "quid est ~ium?" "oratio animum auditoris idonee comparans ad reliquam dictionem" ALCUIN *Rhet.* 20; et habet [oratio rhetorica] sex partes, sc. proemium sive ~ium .. KILWARDBY *OS* 589; partes epistole .. sunt sex .. sc. salutacio, ~ium .. ~ium, id est proverbium *Dictamen* 338.

exoriri [CL]

1 to arise, appear, come into view (partly fig.). **b** to rise or leap up.

croceum solis jubar ~tum terris infunditur ALDH. *Met.* 3; per culmina / candunt exorta fulmina (ÆTHELWALD) *Carm. Aldh.* 4. 68; **1107** exhortus est sol H. LOS. *Ep.* 12 p. 20; sol .. predicit .. ventos tamen ante ~ientem, cum nubes rubescunt BACON VI 49; **1305** (v. desperare c). **b** erumpens, i. ~iens, *uphleapende GlH* E 339.

2 to come into existence, be born. **b** (of plant) to spring up, sprout. **c** (of fountain) to burst forth.

~tus, natus *GlC* E 388; ~tus, i. natus, ortus, editus, procreatus *GlH* E 677; exorrior, A. *to be born WW.* **b** flores ex .. lignorum ramusculis ~ti ALDH. *VirgP* 9; gratia, quae velut rosa senticosis ~ta surculis .. rubescit *Ib.* 18; dum .. adlatum ultra omne tempus serendi, .. mox copiosa seges ~ta .. refectionem praebebat BEDE *HE* IV 26 p. 272; exorrior, A. *to .. sprynge WW.* **c** ante pedes ejus fons perennis ~tus est BEDE *HE* I 7.

3 (w. abstr. or inanim. subj.) to come about, begin. **b** (of subject in discussion) to crop up.

semper peccatorum reverentia ~itur reverens a terra et qui corrigat inter homines non est GILDAS *EB* 86; cum .. ~tam furentis cunei crudelitatem sedare temptaret ALDH. *VirgP* 38 p. 289; civibus exoritur mox exultatio laetis *Id. VirgV* 553; si aliqua temptatio ~ta foris repente extiterit *V. Cuthb.* II 6; **838** nulla altercatio .. inimicaliter ~ta sit *CS* 421; primo jam ~to mane *V. Neot. A* 16; ~tis quibusdam simultatum causis ORD. VIT. III 3 p. 55; ut [opusculum] .. quod non ex Galfridi Monemutensis fonticulo censeatur ~tum G. MON. I 1; per discordiam inter ipsum et Hugonem .. ~tam GIR. *TH* II 50. **b** cum .. loqueretur .., sermone de Osualdo ~to, diceret quod .. BEDE *HE* III 11.

4 to begin (w. direct speech) or (?) *f. l.*

qui ita ad illos exoritur [? l. exorditur]: "numquid .." *G. Herw.* f. 330b.

exornare [CL]

1 to arrange.

Deus .. ~avit atque adornavit xij menses in binis equinoctiis BYRHT. *Man.* 8.

2 to adorn, decorate (place, partly fig.). **b** to enhance, glorify, honour (abstr. obj.).

quid ~abit civitatem? GILDAS *EB* 54; ~atus, valde ornatus *GlC* E 380; extruit ecclesias donisque exornat opimis ALCUIN *SSEbor* 275; GARL. *Tri. Eccl.* 109 (v. defoedare); mergit in teneris ferrum visceribus, / Judeam martirum exornans floribus WALT. WIMB. *Carm.* 243. **b** tu 'simplicitate cordis' [*Acts* ii 46] interius animam tuam ~a ALCH. *Ep.* 299; c**793** justitia omnes tuos ~et actus ALCUIN *Ep.* 30; de nobilitate et de morum tuorum, quae generis nobilitatem ~at, honestate ANSELM (*Ep.* 133) III 275; delicias dat fastiditior usus / exornatque suos nunc novitas operosa periculum J. EXON. *BT* I 86; prudentia rationem ~at ALB. LOND. *DG* 9. 1.

3 to strip of ornament.

to disaray [v. l. *disray or disgise*], ~are *CathA.*

exornatio [CL]

1 fashioning, adornment.

forme figureque exterioris ~o ADEL. *QN* 76; opus .. quarte diei principium est operum ~onis elementorum mundi R. MELUN *Sent.* I 242.

2 (rhet.) embellishment.

verborum leporem ac ~onem plurium fuisse R. MELUN *Sent.* I 27; in cantilenis rhythmicis et dictamine tam subtiles inveniuntur ut .. tam verborum quam sententiarum proferant ~ones GIR. *DK* I 12; *Ib.* (v. agnominatio); VINSAUF *AV* II 3. 25 (v. denominatio 1b); partem ejus [sc. rhetorice] que dicitur elocutio propter verborum ~onem, ubi requiritur quedam vocum harmonia KILWARDBY *OS* 645; nota quod ~o verborum nichil aliud est nisi flos mellitus idemptitatem et equiparanciam continens sub cujusdam pollencia radiosi coloris *Dictamen* 338.

exorrere v. exhorrere. **exorriri** v. exoriri. **exort-** v. exhort-.

exortus [CL]

1 arising, ascent; **b** (astr.). **c** sunrise (as point of compass), the east.

in cujus ~u [sc. Heliae] aurea quadrupes .. mugitum reboasse describitur ALDH. *VirgP* 20. **b** quare [luna] matutino in ~u nunc erecta nunc supina pareat BEDE *TR* 25 p. 228; solis .. / cujus in exortu cum spicula prima resultant .. WULF. *Swith. pref.* 133; sol aureus suo ~u .. noctis nubila exturbat DOMINIC *V. Ecgwini prol.*; quod si in ~u aut in occasu sit ita ut rubescant nubes BACON VI 49. **c** ab euroaustro, id est ab alto brumalis ~us BEDE *HE* IV 3 p. 208.

2 coming into existence, birth. **b** growth (of plant, fig.). **c** source (of river).

patre .. Hatheguino, matre vero Adelesia genitus, diocesim Rotomagensem .. suo illustravit ~u *V. Gund.* 3. **b** multusque spinarum ~us .. vicario saltem labore .. ab agro vite nostre extirpetur PULL. *Sent.* 907B. **c** sursum in Tamesi et tunc superius in Ligam et tunc in longum usque ad ~um [AS: *æwylm*] ejus (*Quad.*) *GAS* 127.

3 beginning, origin.

ut .. eum in ~u temporum existentem ac .. de Patre natum monstraret BEDE *Hom.* I 8. 39; ecclesie ~um et processum .. repetens ob origine pandam W. MALM. *GR* I 19.

exorz- v. exorc-.

exosculari [CL]

1 to kiss fondly.

dexteram illius humiliter ~antes WULF. *Æthelwold* 40; **1104** pedes ~abor *Ep. Anselm.* V 245; pavimentum ~ans DOMINIC *Mir. Virg.* 146; *to exosculate*, ~ari LEVINS *Manip.* 41.

2 to welcome (fig.).

puer litteris datus .. carius illa ~abatur que .. mentem ad superna dirigerent W. MALM. *GP* I 19 p. 28; auspitia future sanctitatis ~atus in puella *Ib.* II 78 p. 174.

exosculatio [CL], kissing.

sic pedes, sic vulnerum loca assidua ~one demulcet W. S. ALB. *V. Alb. & Amphib.* 9.

exossare [CL], to remove bone from.

edilancinare, .. ~are OSB. GLOUC. *Deriv.* 196.

exossator, one who removes bones.

ne exuentes hominem, induamini imo diabolicam feritatem, hominum facti manibus excoriatores sanguinolentis, ~ores, et tandem comestores GROS. *Ep.* 48 p. 143.

exossum v. exodium.

exosus [CL]

1 hating.

humanum ~us consortium ALDH. *VirgP* 31; illa .. gerulum simulacri ~a .. interimitur *Ib.* 52; [mulier] juxta mortuum ~a vitam ANSELM (*Or.* 16) III 66.

2 hated, hateful, odious: **a** (of person); **b** (of thing or abstr.). **c** (w. *habere*) to hate.

a gens exosa mihi tradebat nomen habendum ALDH. *Aen.* 65 (*Muriceps*) 9; [Saraceni] omnibus ~i et contrarii BEDE *Gen.* (xvi 12) 159B; **966** (13c) temporalis gazae possessio .. incertis heredibus interdum optatis saepe exossis derelinquitur *CS* 1189; abbas, quoniam Angligena erat et Normannis ~us, ab emulis accusatus est ORD. VIT. IV 16 p. 285; principi factus ~us *Dial. Scac.* I 8 E; hinc totum genus mulierum potuit esse ~um et publica exprobratione dignissimum BALD. CANT. *Tract.* 7. 476D; **s1522** comes compluribus Anglicis extitit ~us .. pre nimia judiciis severitate *Reg. Butley* 41. **b** infaustus ille annus et omnibus bonis ~us usque hodie permanet BEDE *HE* III 1 p. 128; misit .. ad revocandum .. abbatem ab ~o .. exilio B. *V. Dunst.* 24; aufertur mensa tunc ~a, convivia vertuntur in lamenta GOSC. *Mir. Iv.* lxii; nihil magis exhorruit quam hominum contubernia que maxime sibi ~a subterfugere omnimodis procuravit R. COLD. *Godr.* 59; *Cust. Westm.* 188 (v. curiositas 1b); modo tuba veritatis / est exosa WALT. WIMB. *Van.* 116; **1418** pluralitas beneficiorum canonibus ~a *Reg. Cant.* IV 195. **c** ~us, odio habetus (*sic*) *GlC* E 541; cognatos .. suos quam aspides ~os habuit R. NIGER *Chr. II* p. 168; quem magis inter ceteros ~um habuerat GIR. *EH* I 4; AD. MUR. *Chr.* 57*n*. (v. despective).

exotericus [CL < ἐξωτερικός], popular, intelligible to general public.

exotherica [studia] J. SAL. *Pol.* 648A (v. acroaticus).

exoterus [ἐξώτερος], outward, external, or (?) *f. l.*

dicunt phisiologi quia lincis aut pantere odorem animalia cetera sequuntur; istos tamen qui musco et speciebus exoteris [? l. exoticis] placant olfactum et provocant velle, si possent, non arbitror in panteram aut lincem transformari J. SAL. *Pol.* 761B.

exothericus v. exotericus.

exoticus [CL], exotic, foreign, imported. **b** strange, unusual. **c** barbarous, unintelligible.

~um, i. odibile, peregrinum *GlH* E 692; nautis .. e Saxonia multam ~am mercem advectantibus W. CANT. *Mir. Thom.* VI 77; vino, speciebus, pannis aureis et holosericis, auro et argento, et lapidibus preciosis, et diversi generis mercibus ~is WALS. *HA* II 146. **b** FRITH. 1392 (v. docmen); non .. rem voveret ~am [sc. virginitatem suam], nisi provideret sibi et aliis incomparabilem inde accumulari gloriam EADMER *Virt.* 582A; in catheractis pugnandi .. usus et modus apud Anglos jam ~i habebantur *Ps.*-ELMH. *Hen. V* 20 p. 45; cum .. famis macies .. perpenderet .. murum ratonumque carnes ~as receptat *Ib.* 68; *uncowth*, .. excoticus *PP*. **c** haec non sunt ~a quae dico verba sed satis cognita BYRHT. *V. Osw.* 443; moderatius .. se agit Aldelmus, nec nisi perraro et necessario [v. l. perrara et necessaria] verba ponit ~a W. MALM. *GP* V 196; ~orum verborum interpretaciones .. jussimus .. annotari R. BURY *Phil.* 12. 176.

expaaltare v. espeltare.

expaleare [cf. CL palea], to remove chaff from, winnow.

s1380 precepit .. ut totum .. fructum celeriter expaliaretur, quod cum factum fuisset .. cc quarteria frumenti purificati in horreo remanserunt *Chr. Kirkstall* 122.

expallescere [CL], **expallēre** [LL], to turn pale.

quem cum in terram .. procumbentem aspicio, non paululum expavescens ~eo *Ep. ad amicum* 83 p. 115; ~uit rex et inhorruit MAP *NC* III 2 f. 36; ave, videns natum / ligno disclavatum / expallescere J. HOWD. *Sal.* 38.

expalmare [LL], to strike with the palm, slap.

scribe palmam veram vincentium / expalmatam palmis cedentium J. HOWD. *Ph.* 553; alapis gravibus ~atos *Mir. J. Bev. C* 329.

expalpare [CL], to obtain by caressing or squeezing.

propter hoc regia fricat ulcuscula, / expalpans pinguia per frictum fercula WALT. WIMB. *Palpo* 91.

expampinare [cf. CL pampinare], to dress, prune shoots from (vine; fig.).

ut hyems algida vites expampinat / et nudat omnia que ver ingraminat WALT. WIMB. *Sim.* 114.

expandere [CL]

1 to spread out (limbs of body, partly fig.). **b** (refl. & pass.) to stretch oneself out. **c** to lay open (fig.).

[corvus] ~sis alis et inclinato capite sedens *V. Cuthb.* III 5; ~sis cruribus *Ib.* I 3 (v. erigere 1b); ~sis manibus Deo gratias agere non cessabat CUTHB. *Ob. Baedae* clxiv; ~dit Athelwoldus alas suas et .. expulsit clericos ÆLF. *Æthelwold* 16 (= WULF. *Æthelwold* 20); manibus in modum crucis ~sis BYRHT. *V. Osw.* 455; ~sis brachiis archiepiscopum divina sacrificia agentem apprehendit OSB. *Mir. Dunst.* 145; laudatas ~dit alas avis junonia *Quaest. Salern.* N 28. **b** Domine, .. ~de te super mortuum istum [cf. *1 Kings* xvii 21] ANSELM (*Or.* 10) III 38; virgo rubet, redolet, expanditur, et duplicatur GARL. *Epith.* IV 309; [rex] pre dolore subito sui impos effectus, corruit ~sus BAKER f. 106. **c** plus miseriam suam coram misericorde pastore ~dendo quam obsecrando exorat ANSELM (*Or.* 9) III 31; ~dam aerumnas meas ante ipsum (*Ib.* 14) III 55; pietatis viscera .. ~dentes .. xx s. .. michi dignemini destinare *FormOx* 422.

2 (of geog. feature) to extend; **b** (phil.). **c** (p. ppl.) extensive.

[Hibernia] a Dublinia usque ad Patricii colles, Connactiumque mare, in latum ~ditur GIR. *TH* I 2; [flumen] duo .. brachia ad oppositas mundi partes ~dit *Ib.* 7. **b** quedam forma substantialis indeterminate materiam ~dens et non terminans KILWARDBY *OS* 183. **c** omnis forma ~sa in subjecto habet continuationem ab eodem; set motus est actus vel forma ~sus in subjecto mobili BACON VIII 145; [in India] ficus est tam ~sa ut .. hominum turme possint discumbere HIGD. I 11; botrix arbor est fructuosa tota ~sa super terram *Alph.* 23; in ~sa diocesi [sc. Lincolniensi] *Reg. Whet.* II 471.

3 to unfold (cloth or net, partly fig.), unfurl (banner). **b** to unroll (rotulet), open (book). **c** (her.) to display. **d** (astr., *annus expansus*) tabulated display of changes of planetary position within a year.

796 retia apostolicae praedicationis .. ~dere jussit ALCUIN *Ep.* 113; LANFR. *Const.* 182 (v. cilicium c); puer sanctus .., veste in gremio collecta et expassa [v. l. expansa], carbones vivos suscepit J. FURNESS *Kentig.* 25 p. 206; reges expandunt vexilla GARL. *Tri. Eccl.* 36; 'diffusis velis', id est ~sis TREVET *Troades* 80; acriter se preparant, vexillum regis contra statuta Anglie ibidem ~dendo FAVENT 11. **b** volumen mortuorum super altare dissolutum palam ~ditur ORD. VIT. III 7 p. 101. **c** aquilae situs triplex, procidens, volans, erectus vel ~sus .. ~sus qui pedibus innitens alas protendit quidpiam foturas .. hodie in armis imperii SPELMAN *Asp.* 127; clypeum vides ex cyano minioque palatim distinctum, tribus argenteis aquilis ~sis *Ib.* 129. **d** in secunda columpna per eundem modum faciemus de annis ~sis Domini usque ad xxx BACON VI 151; tabula annorum ~sorum *Ib.* 152; in ordine annorum ~sorum *Ib.* 153; *entere into thy tables in the first lyne theras is writen* anni collecti et ~si .. . *consider wel that fro j to xx ben* anni ~si *and from xx to iij*m *ben* anni collecti CHAUCER *Astrolabe* II 44.

4 to spill, shed (blood; *cf.* OF *espandre*).

1290 per predictum servientem fuit sanguis in predictam libertatem ~sus *State Tri. Ed. I* 6.

5 to spread (dung).

1224 ~et fimum, sc. j acram pro ij operibus *Ch. & Cust. Caen* (*Felsted*) 91.

6 (p. ppl. as sb. f.) span, measure of length.

latitudo [rotulorum] .. paulo plus una ~sa et semis *Dial. Scac.* I 5 S.

expansio [LL]

1 spreading out.

~o manuum HALES *Sent.* IV 21 (v. exorcizatio); **1424** de ~one et clavacione Christi ad crucem *Mem. York* II 102.

2 extension (phil.)

recipit continuacionem sue extensionis et ~onis BACON VIII 145.

3 expanse.

s1191 buccas .. triplici velorum expassione .. notabiles DICETO *YH* II 93.

4 extent.

~onem .. climatum per sua milliaria .. descripsi BACON *Maj.* I 298.

expapillare [CL *p. ppl. only*], to bare to the breast.

~are, i. denudare OSB. GLOUC. *Deriv.* 190.

expassio v. expansio. **expassus** v. expandere. **expatiari** v. exspatiari.

expavescere, expavēre [CL], (intr.) to become frightened. **b** (trans.) to take fright at (present fact). **c** to dread (fut. prospect). **d** (w. inf.) to fear (to).

tremibundus et pallidus ~it ALDH. *VirgP* 33; ~ere, timuerunt; ~escere, timere *GlH* E 576–7; ~esce memorando, contremisce cogitando ANSELM (*Medit.* 3) III 89; ~escens et ad rei novitatem obstupefactus *V. Gund.* 45; **1207** bestie magis ~ent per latrones quam per barones *Cl* 85b; cepit demon ~escere et fremere *Latin Stories* 99. **b** factum vehementer ~it WULF. *Æthelwold* 5; equum .. umbras ~escentem NECKAM *NR* II 158. **c** horrida mortis discrimina pallidus ~it ALDH. *VirgP* 23; mala futura ~esco, presentia minime reformido PULL. *Sent.* 826C; DICETO *YH* I 388 (v. catarrhus); nec nichilominus vituperaciones ~escens J. MIRFIELD *Flor.* 118. **d** sanguineas manus .. in ipsum inicere non ~isti *Eccl. & Synag.* 107; quod .. summi regis indignationem incurrere ~isset *Chr. Battle* f. 116v.; **1208** manum suam in ecclesiam extendere non ~it (*Lit. Papae*) *Conc.* I 529; **1294** (v. damnabiliter).

expect- v. et. exspect-.

†expecteoli, *f. l.*

s1100 unusquisque cum arcu et sagitta in manu †expecteoli [MSS: exp'oteoli, exp'teoli, ? l. ex parte omni] pro preda capienda KNIGHTON I 111.

expectorare [CL= *to banish from the breast*], to bring forth from the heart.

a pecto .. per compositionem ~o, .. i. exsolvere, unde ~atus OSB. GLOUC. *Deriv.* 435; qui verum animi verbis expectorat / nunquam in domibus potentum anchorat WALT. WIMB. *Palpo* 125.

expedare [cf. CL pedatus], **~ere**, to hamble, law, remove claws or ball from the forefoot of (dog); *v. et. espeltare, expeditare.* **b** (p. ppl. *expedatus*, of man) who has a foot cut off (also as sb. m.).

1166 S. de H. r. c. de j m. pro canibus non ~atis *Pipe* 41; **1200** (1227) episcopus eam [sc. terram liberam] habeat .. de wastis et de rewardis foreste, et de canibus suis †expetendis [l. expedendis] et aliis placitis et querelis et occasionibus foreste que ad nos pertinent *Ch. Sal.* 179; **1208** (1268) libera et quieta .. de canibus suis ~endis *Oak Bk. Southampt.* II 40 (cf. *RChart* 183a [**1208**]: espeltandis). **b** **1168** de catallis Ailrici de Lingefeld ~ati *Pipe* 219; **1177** de xij d. de catallis Siwardi de Niwehalle ~ati *Pipe* 87; de catallis fugitivorum et ~atorum *Ib.* 201.

expedatio, fine for avoidance of hambling (of dog). *V. et. espeltatio, expeditatio* b, *expeditura.*

1252 quod demandam quam facit hominibus de Basingestok de expidacione canum et pannagio porcorum .. in .. foresta, ponat in respectum usque .. *Cl* 44.

expediatio v. expeditatio.

expedibiliter, effectually.

ut possimus ~ius jussa vestra in effectum ducere GIR. *Invect.* II 7.

expedienter, quickly.

s1086 Henricus .. officio clericali est addictus et in eo bene ac ~er profecit M. PAR. *Min.* I 31; **s1193** rex Francorum ~er guerram suam in Normannia continuavit *Flor. Hist.* II 109; **1254** ubi celerius et ~ius fieri poterit, capi faciat ad opus regis .. jocalia *Cl* 320; nunc vado dormire et jam surgam et ~ius [ME: *cwicluker*] faciam tunc quam nunc quod facere modo deberem *AncrR* 100.

expedimentum [LL]

1 solution (of problem).

tribus .. modis, quod ad praesentis impedimenti sufficit ~um, exponi potest ANSELM (*Mon.* 8) I 23; *furtherance,* ~um LEVINS *Manip.* 21; *an expediment,* ~um *Ib.* 67.

2 baggage.

1167 quia miserat eas [sc. literas] cum ~o suo usque Wintoniam BECKET *Ep.* 285.

expediose, quickly.

ut .. liquiditate fleumatis spissitudo sanguinis in temperie conservetur et sic facilius et ~ius ad singula membra nutrimentum sanguinis deportetur BART. ANGL. IV 9.

expedire [CL]

1 to set free; **b** (fig.). **c** to empty. **d** (p. ppl. *expeditus*, of troops) unencumbered, lightly armed (also as sb. m.); **e** (of others, also fig.).

~io, exsolvo *GlC* E 441; ~ior, i. liberor *GlH* E 605; instituit ut .. vinculatos ~iret W. MALM. *GP* I 48; [vacca] suadens socie ut abscissa cauda ab impedimento se solveret et secum ~ita rediret NIG. *Ep.* 18; Chiron sagittis cancrum percussit filiumque ~ivit ALB. LOND. *DG* 15. 4. **b** nec adhuc priorum retibus malorum ~itus priscis recentia auget malis GILDAS *EB* 28; ut .. nos exiguos dignaretur [Deus] ~iri a peccatorum nexibus BYRHT. *V. Ecgwini* 378; peccato .. omnis homo detinetur cujus jugo .. nec quisquam nec unquam se ~it PULL. *Sent.* 755A. **c** sicut .. cito ~iuntur horrea que assidua non fuerint adjectione referta GIR. *EH pref.* p. 223. **d** videbat .. eos [sc. spiritus] fere semper pedites et ~itos et quasi sub forma venatorum *Ib.* II 38; his apparatibus ~itus, miles .. ad prelium accedit R. NIGER. *Mil.* I 1. **e** eum ad regem hujusmodi curarum tumultibus ~itum dirigit ABBO *Edm.* 7; agite gratias Deo quia exonerati estis et ~iti ut .. totis viribus curratis ad Deum ANSELM (*Ep.* 211) IV 108; [mulier] equiti sacculum reddebat, sicque ~ita letior iter agebat ALEX. CANT. *Mir.* 21 (II) p. 197; [vinum] linguam reddit ~itam, liberat a curis, et hominem facit audacem BACON V 92.

2 to prepare; **b** (refl.).

~ierant, *araeddum GlC* E 393; ~itus, i. .. paratus *GlH* E 601. **b** clerici se ad servitium Dei ~iant HON. *GA* 614D.

3 to dispatch, speed (messenger). **b** to expedite, deal w. quickly. **c** to hasten progress (of). **d** (*in expedito*) in hand, in train.

s1281 rex .. ~iens .. nuncios, ad Norwegiensium regem .. remisit FORDUN *Cont.* X 38; **s1281** nunciis .. de consilio prelatorum et procerum ~itis et contentis *Plusc.* VII 31 p. 109. **b** **1220** [Theobaldus] fecit rogari episcopum .. ut ~iret negotium illud *CurR* IX 197; Gerebertus iter ~iens venit ad mare M. PAR. *Maj.* I 477 (= W. MALM. *GR* II 167 p. 195: viam celerans); *Fleta* 164 (v. diaeta 3a); **1380** in expensis domini J. de B. .. usque London .. pro .. negociis ecclesiam tangentibus ~iendis *Ac. Durh.* 589; appropriaciones omnium ecclesiarum .. cognicioni deducere arbitror summopere fore ~iendum THORNE 2090; *G. Hen. V* 14 (v. chronicus 2b). **c** **c1168** si ei subveneritis .. ~ietis famam et vobis et vestris prospicietis in posterum J. SAL. *Ep.* 256 (257); ut plurimum ptisici ~iuntur cum folia cadant ab arboribus J. MIRFIELD *Brev.* 78. **d** non est opus multiloquio, ubi res est in ~ito GIR. *EH* I 15; **1220** dixit ei .. quod totum negotium ejus fuit in ~ito *CurR* IX 197.

4 (p. ppl. *expeditus*): **a** (w. ref. to movement or growth) agile, vigorous (also as sb.); **b** (w. ref. to mental or administrative activity) lively, quick. **c** (of thing) light, readily available or portable.

a generosa progenitus / genetrice, expeditus / statura, [val]de stabilis / statu (ÆTHELWALD) *Carm. Aldh.* 5. 24; Germanus ducem se proelii profitetur, eligit ~itos BEDE *HE* I 20; *GlH* E 113 (v. efficax 1); qui vult habere eum [sc. accipitrem] ~itum in aucupando, faciat ei bonam vesicam gutturis UPTON 191. **b** in per se disserendo ~itiores BALSH. *AD rec. 2* 122 (v. divisio 4); in corpore enim sano ~ita est vivacitas mentis, in egro pigrior ALB. LOND. *DG* 6. 10; vir discretus et circumspectus, jure civili et canonico eleganter ~itus *Flor. Hist.* II 255; bibat et subito fiet facundior, / in verbis prompcior et expedicior WALT. WIMB. *Carm.* 147; *Ps.*-ELMH. *Hen. V* 92 (v. consummatrix); ad .. collegiorum .. fundamen perquisivit .. ~itos virtute et sciencia juvenculos BLAKMAN *Hen. VI* 12. **c** contra inermes .. viros .. ~itiora satis arma sufficiunt GIR. *EH* II 38 p. 396; inquiratur de quercubus et aliis arboribus ~itis in foresta *Fleta* 91.

5 to explain, expound, tell; **b** (refl.); **c** (w. indir. qu.).

strictus hunc pedem commentaturus ~iam ALDH. *PR* 136; causam .. tardae inchoationis ~ire curabo ASSER *Alf.* 87; his ita prefinitis hinc ipsam artem ~ire inchoandum BALSH. *AD* 10; paucis nos ~ientes dicimus quod illud sacramentum non est .. aliqua actio sed quedam qualitas S. LANGTON *Quaest.* 368. **b** **c1230** coitum contra naturam; ut me ~iam, contra naturam est omnis coitus qui non sit inter virum et mulierem *Conc. Syn.* 219. **c** Justina .. quanta .. pertulerit quis mediocri fretus ingenio ~ire se posse gloriatur ALDH. *VirgP* 43; quoniam haec ipsa scienti loquor, his omissis, cur eorum meminerim ~iam ANSELM (*Mon. Ep. ad Lanfrancum*) I 6; GIR. *TH* III 16 (v. enucleatim).

6 to be expedient, suitable, right; *cf.* 8a, 9a *infra.* **b** (med.) to be efficacious. **c** (w. pers. subj.) to have advantage, make profit.

date .. quid ~iat mihi GILDAS *EB* 74; **1073** quid michi ~iat beatitudo vestra .. novit LANFR. *Ep.* 43 (18); Domine, qui das fidei intellectum, da mihi ut quantum scis ~ire intelligam ANSELM (*Prosl.* 2) I 101; **1225** (v. divisim a); **s1242** GROS. *Ep.* 99 (v. conjecturatio 1b); Deus aliqua fecit propter peccata malorum plectenda, et illa ~iunt, quando puniendi sunt mali OCKHAM *Dial.* 878. **b** J. MIRFIELD *Brev.* 50 (v. experimentum 4a). **c** heu mihi! .. bona mea expendidi et in nullo ~ivi *Latin Stories* 115; **1532** dixerunt sibi pro eo quod ipse fuit homo abjuratus, ideo omnes illi pejus expedirent si ipsum ulterius in consortium eorum in naviculam predictam arriperent *CoramR* 1084 *Rex* m. 7.

7 (impers., sts. w. dat.) it is expedient, suitable, right; **b** (w. inf. or acc. & inf.); **c** (w. *ut* or *quod*). **d** (*~ire videre, videri*, or sim.) to seem to be right.

~it, i. utile est, juvat, prodest *GlH* E 630; **c1168** ut .. Christi pauperes prout cuique ~ire cognoverit, consoletur J. SAL. *Ep.* 260 (260). **b** non licet et non ~it oboedire ei THEOD. *Pen.* I 5. 11; **948** (12c) cum .. unicuique mortalium ~iat .. [Deo] gratiarum rependere actiones *CS* 860; LANFR. *Const.* 166 (v. expellere 1a); **1168** interdum ~it .. prenosse temporum motus J. SAL. *Ep.* 244 (272 p. 552); opus est in strepitu bellorum .. ut .. distinguatur .. quando sit instandum et quando cedere ~iat R. NIGER *Mil.* I 39. **c** ~it enim animae suae ut hoc fiat LANFR. *Ep.* 54 (56); ~it ut fiat quod volo *V. Gund.* 45; omnibus .. ~it quod Dominus dormiat juxta majores vel minores S. LANGTON *Ruth* 115; espedit ut nostram pietas divina salutem / provideat GARL. *Epith.* III 493; ~it quod .. recordum et processus .. examinentur *State Tri. Ed. I* 3; ~it ut que sit hec lex nature .. investigemus FORTESCUE *NLN* I 31. **d** **1162** aliis temporibus quibuscunque sibi viderit exspedire (Lit. Abbatis) *Reg. Whet.* II app. 317; **c1165** quatinus michi .. rescribatis quod .. maxime videbitur ~ire J. SAL. *Ep.* 142 (139 p. 20); **1230** sicut ~ire viderit *Feod. Durh.* 213; **1243** [pincerna regis] faciat prout melius viderit ~ire *Cl* 103; **c1250** ut liceat eis firmare stagnum molendini .. ubicumque .. sibi viderit ~iendum *Feod. Durh.* 137n.; **1330** ad consignandum quascunque cartas quas .. viderint ~ire *Reg. Paisley* 32.

8 (pr. ppl. *expediens*) expedient, right, profitable; *cf.* 6a *supra.* **b** (as sb. n. pl.).

de his quae erant itineri meo ~ientia sollicite cogitabam P. BLOIS *Ep.* 65. 191A; bonum .. quod facimus et malum quod facimus proprie ~iens et inexpediens dicitur GROS. 233; **1285** si eisdem ~iens videatur *RGasc* II 272; **1315** fidelium nostrorum consilium et auxilium nobis utilia et ~ientia plurimum reputamus *RScot* 145a; **1407** via cessionis .. compendiosior et .. ~ientior judicata BEKYNTON II 126. **b** **c1168** unctio [Dei] te de omnibus ~ientibus edocebit J. SAL. *Ep.* 259 (258).

9 (phr. *expediens est* or sim.; *cf.* 7 *supra*) it is expedient, suitable, right: **a** (w. inf.); **b** (w. *ut* or *quod*).

a visum fuit ~iens provinciam per custodias dividi ECCLESTON *Adv. Min.* 42; exhortari studentes .. reputamus ~iens R. BURY *Phil.* 17. 216; est tamen ~iens populis .. informari ELMH. *Metr. Hen. V pref.* p. 79; **s1452** an .. restarent aliqua in quibus fuerat ~iens apponere remediacionem *Reg. Whet.* I 25. **b** **1268** cum videretur ~iens et honestum .. ut certa forma provideretur *StatOx* 25; non est ~iens quod tota communitas fidelium .. voto castitatis se astringat OCKHAM *Pol.* I 360; ~iens est et necesse quod vos .. certioremini *Reg. Brev. Orig.* 214.

expeditamentum, hambling, lawing (of dog). *V. et. espeltamentum, expeditatio* a.

1232 sint in perpetuum quieti .. de ~is canum et de omnibus summonitionibus, placitis, querelis .. ad forestarios [et] viridiarios pertinentibus *MonA* VI 932a (cf. *CalCh* 168).

expeditare [cf. expedare], to hamble, law (dog). *V. et. espeltare, expedare.*

1198 quietos ab omnibus oppressionibus et exactionibus, sc. .. canibus ~andis, sartis, vastis [etc.] *CalCh* II 306; **1217** (v. canis 2a, expeditatio b); **s1225** canes, qui solebant ~ari, has libertates se habere sentiebant M. PAR. *Min.* II 273; **1268** (v. expeditatio b); **1276** (v. expeditatio a); [Johannes le Wolfhonte et Thomas] ibunt in foresta .. et habebunt secum unum mastivum non ~atum *DL Forest Proc.* 1/5 r. 14d.; **1343** quod canes non ~entur *Cart. Boarstall* 610; **1406** preceptum est omnibus tenentibus de B. .. quod de cetero canes eorum ~entur *CourtR Banstead.*

expeditatio, hambling, lawing (of dog); *v. et. espeltamentum, expeditamentum.* **b** fine for avoidance of hambling (of dog); *v. et. espeltatio, expedatio, expeditura.*

c1105 volo quod abbas et homines sui sint liberi et quieti de ~one canum *Regesta* 577; *GAS* 559, **1217** (v. canis 2a); **1184** precepit [rex] quod ~o mastivorum fiat ubicunque fere sue pacem habent et habere consueverunt (*Ass. Forestae* 14) *SelCh* 188; **1232** rex .. concessit .. tenentibus infra warrennam regis de Corf' quod ipsi .. sint quieti de ~one canum suorum *Cl* 88; **1276** [Galfridus de Nevill] occasionavit plures villatas adjacentes foreste de Galtres pro non ~one canum ubi canes satis bene fuerunt expeditati *Hund.* I 118a; **1278** quieti .. de canum expediacione *PQW* 276a; **1445** for[isfactura] pro non ~one canum suorum vocat' *dogsilver* secundum usum et consuetudinem foreste *Pat* 459 m. 10. **b** **1217** cujus canis inventus fuerit tunc non expeditatus det pro misericordia iij s. et de cetero nullus bos capiatur pro ~one. talis autem sit expeditatio per assisam communiter quod iij ortilli abscidantur sine pelota de pede anteriori (*Ch. Forestae* 6) *SelCh* 346 (v. et. a supra); **1268** rarissime invenitur ibi aliquis canis non expeditatus, per quod .. nesciunt estimare quantum valere posset predicta ~o per annum *IAQD* 3/13; **1343** denarios .. pro ~one canum suorum exigit *Cart. Boarstall* 610; **1365** omnes denarios de ~one canum et de chiminagio infra dictam forestam [de Shirewood'] *Pat* 273 m. 43.

expedite [CL], **~iter**

1 freely, nimbly.

lapides pugillares .. pre alia gente promptius et ~ius ad manum habent GIR. *TH* III 10; animalia dum surgunt .. graviores et debiliores sui corporis partes prius extollunt .. sicque ~ius eriguntur et celerius *Quaest. Salern.* W 8.

2 quickly.

1253 quod .. ad nos redire valeat ~er *RGasc* I 375 (= *Cl* 198: expeditus).

3 clearly, unambiguously.

sed ut ~ius inquiratur, duo tantum hujusmodi assumenda sunt contraria *Simil. Anselmi* app. p. 95; pretermissa .. ea que in hysteria Anglorum adusque principis Willelmi imperium de predecessoribus satis ~e contexta reperiuntur J. CORNW. *Merl. pref.*; DUNS *Ord.* V 181 (v. expeditio 4b).

expeditio [CL]

1 disencumbrance, preparation (for action).

~o, praeparatio *GlC* E 558, *GlH* E 607; illa denudatio carnis apud Judeos ~oque mentule ad faciliorem coitum COLET *Rom. Enarr.* 225.

2 journey, mission. **b** (mil.) expedition. **c** expeditionary force, army. **d** mil. service. **e** fine for exemption from mil. service.

1467 quatenus [ipsum] in ipsis ~onibus suis moram facere libere permittatis *MunAcOx* 724. **b** Romani, patriae denuntiantes nequaquam se tam laboriosis ~onibus posse frequentius vexari GILDAS *EB* 18; [Claudius] ~onem in Brittaniam movit BEDE *HE* I 3; ~o, *hergiung GlC* E 554; quando rex ibat in ~onem, vel terra vel mari *DB* I 64v.; dicimus aliquem isse in ~onem militum ubi milites liberi et prompti efficiuntur ad bellandum OSB. GLOUC. *Deriv.* 411; omnes eorum [Norwagiensium] ~ones et bella navali certamine fiunt GIR. *TH* II 11. **c** ALDH. *VirgP* 12 (v. duodecies); ~o, *faerd GlC* E 401; **s871** quot millia paganae ~onis occisa perierunt ASSER *Alf.* 42; ~onibus, exercitibus, *fyrdum GlH* E 608; prius itaque republica bene composita ~o est convocanda et ordinanda R. NIGER *Mil.* III 58; **s1299** ipse .. rediit Angliam estivo tempore cum majori ~one reversurus *Chr. S. Edm.* 73. **d** **811** exceptis tribus tantum debitis, i.e. ~onem et arcis munitionem et pontis instructionem adversus paganos *CS* 332; **860** (15c) immunis nisi ~one et pontis factione et arcium munitione *CS* 500; **948** sit .. rus liber ab omni fiscali tributo .. sine expoeditione *CS* 869; **961** sit ab omni regali servitio libera exceptis .. arcis munitione, pontis constructione, et ~one *CS* 1072 (cf. *endorsement* [16c]: hepedicione); siquis in in ~onem summonitus non ibat, totam terram suam erga regem forisfaciebat *DB* I 56v.; *fyrdunga*, i.e. ~onem (*Quad.*) *GAS* 317; *GAS* 444 (v. brigbota); **1213** tenendam .. libere et quiete ab exercitu et ~one *Regesta Scot.* II 513. **e** episcopus reclamabat super .. abbatem .. geldum regis et servitium et ~ones in terra et in mari *Cart. Heming* I 80; *fyrdwite*, i. e. forisfacturam ~onis (*Quad.*) *GAS* 319 (cf. dimissio 2b).

3 drawing up (of document). **b** dispatch, expediting, completion.

1385 in expensis domini Johannis de F. apud Ebor' circa ~onem carte confirmacionis de Farne, xxxiij s. *Ac. Durh.*

526. **b** **1200** quatinus fidem habeatis hiis que G. de C. vobis dicet super ~onem negotiorum meorum *RChart* 58b; **1217** ut [archiepiscopus] agendorum nostrorum .. ~oni per vestrum consilium .. intendat *Pat* 57; **1295** visitacionem .. progressu continuare canonico usque ad finalem ~onem ejusdem *DCCant. Reg.* Q f. 27v.; c**1335** pro ~one tam pii negocii operas vestras petimus impendatis *Collect. Ox.* I 30; **1361** cum ~o dicte fabrice insideat .. nobis cordi .. *Fabr. York* 176; **1414** certificatorium .. de et super ~one permutacionis facte inter dominos J. D. .. et J. G. *Reg. Cant.* I 129; s**1425** ~onem negociorum suorum adepti sunt *Plusc.* XI 3 p. 373; *utterance of sale*, ~o LEVINS *Manip.* 22.

4 liveliness, quickness (of mind).

homo .. per gloriam fit intellectualis et equalis ~onis in intelligendo cum angelis PECKHAM *QA* 118; facilitatio, ~o, et promptitudo ponuntur racione passi ... potest ergo agens expedite et prompte et faciliter agere, propter disposicionem passi DUNS *Ord.* V 181.

5 (?) narrative account, exposition.

1335 nova alia et ~onem parliamenti vobis mittamus in brevi *Lit. Cant.* II 96.

6 advantage. **b** success.

haec est consiliatio, quam Cnutus .. consiliatus est .. Deo ad laudem et sibimet ad regiam dignitatem et ~onem [AS: *to þearfe*] legat quilibet utram malit, sive secularem legem sive divinam ~onem (*Cons. Cnuti*) *GAS* 279; clerici juvenes .. quibus .. concessum et pro ~one populi brevia facere cursoria *Fleta* 78; pro ampliore ~one et honore Dei et ecclesie *Lit. Cant.* I 3; s**1403** [Britones] in magno exercitu ad succursum et ~onem Oweni intrarunt Walliam AD. USK 85. **b** s**1322** plures .. fame et morbo perierunt. propter quod absque ~one aliqua reversus est rex *Meaux* II 345; nosmetipsos ad ejus honorem salvandum indempnem omnibus periculis exponemus, nam ejus ~o nostra est promocio MILEMETE *Nob.* 61; perfectum negociorum finem retinebitis et gloriosam ~onem *Ib.* 73; **1456** grave erit .. pluries flexis genibus petere propria, set frustra semper, et absque ~one ulla *Reg. Whet.* I 221.

expeditionalis [LL], relating to mil. expedition or service. **b** (? as sb.) temporary lodging (for expeditionary force).

739 (11c) rerum regalium ac secularium operum sit inmunis .. nisi tantum ~ium rerum *CS* 1331; **781** (11c) ab ~ibus causis .. libera *CS* 240; c**795** a cunctis operibus .. libera preter ~ibus causis et pontium structionum et arcium munimentum *CS* 274; **933** ut sit .. tutus .. ab .. tributis majoribus et minoribus atque ~ibus taxationibus *CS* 694; **961** (12c) ut communi jugo subiciatur .. i. e. ~ium rerum et arcium munitione pontiumque constructione *CS* 1074. **b** ~es, subitas habitationes *GlH* E 609.

expeditivus [LL], advantageous, profitable (also as sb. n.).

1295 nostre sollicitudinis aciem ad ~a .. undique dirigentes *Reg. Cant.* 26; de triplici fructu .. secundus ~us et meritorius BRINTON *Serm.* 36. 149.

expeditura [cf. expeditare], fine for avoidance of hambling (of dog). *V. et. espeltatio, expedatio, expeditatio* b.

1207 xx s. pro ~a *Pat* 70b.

expedor v. espedor.

expellere [CL]

1 to drive out, expel, send away (person or animal, also fig.). **b** (leg.) to banish, exile, outlaw. **c** (p. ppl. as sb. m.) exiled person, outlaw. **d** to drive off (with stick).

episcopus .. ~ens nos ab eo oravit *V. Cuthb.* IV 5; **957** (14c) Adam .. expulsus in has aerumpnosas orbis plagas *CS* 995; utrum expediat eum vel diutius detineri vel de monasterio ~i LANFR. *Const.* 166; veterem hominem .. concussit, excussit, et expulit ut jam vetustatis nec compareret vestigium H. BOS. *Thom.* III 6 p. 193; sic et adulti jam filii .. a patrum domiciliis .. ~untur GIR. *TH* I 12 p. 35; **1204** (v. dispendere 2b); rigide ~e turpem mastinum [ME: *hat him ut*] et abige eum *AncrR* 109; canes ~ere de ecclesia PAUL. ANGL. *ASP* 1529; BAD. AUR. 207 (v. confragum b). **b** exulat, i. .. alienatur, fugatur, ~itur, *wræclastaþ GlH* E 758; si hominem occiderit, sit exul et cum clamore ~atur ab omnibus qui Dei justitiam volunt (*Inst. Cnuti*) *GAS* 347. **c** **9**.. †extori [? l. exteri *or* extorres], expulsi, *wræccan WW*; si quis fecerit opus expulsi quod Angli vocant *utlages weorc*, videat rex de pace (*Inst. Cnuti*) *GAS* 317 (= *Cons. Cnuti*: exlegis). **d** **1338** expulsit .. Johannem le Harpour in dorso cum puncto baculi ut surgeret de magistro suo et ipsum vulneravit cum puncto .. baculi in dorso *SelCCoron* 44.

2 to throw out (rubbish). **b** to expel (contents or secretions). **c** to banish (pain); **d** (abstr.).

paupercula vidua volens domum suam mundare colligit primo grossiora et ~it [ME: *schuveð hit .. ut*] *AncrR* 119. **b** superfluitates quas natura per singulos menses ~it, unde menstrua nominantur *Quaest. Salern.* B 21; *Ib.* 6 (v. eicere 3c); GILB. VI 268. 1 (v. coadunatio 1a); BACON XI 281 (v. gummi 1a). **c** ille .. ab oculo glaucomiam et algemam expulsit BYRHT. *V. Ecgwini* 364; tactu manuum suarum per signum sancte crucis dolores ~ebat DOMINIC *V. Ecgwini* I 16. **d** expulsa diaboli tyrannide BEDE *HE* IV 14 p. 233; expuleras tenebras omnibus inque locis WULF. *Poems* 11; ut inimici a nobis ~eres [AS: *afirdest*] potestatem *Rit. Durh.* 23; hostilitas ~itur, pax jampridem expulsa revocatur *Chr. Battle* f. 90; inanitatem ~o ALEX. CANT. *Dicta* 3 p. 121; OCKHAM *Pol.* I 164 (v. exorcismus a).

3 to reject, rebut, defeat.

13.. materia allegata in placito per defendentem ad ~endam accionem querentis *MGL* I 177 (cf. ib. 288).

expelt- v. espelt-. **expencio** v. expensio.

expendenter, with great expense, lavishly.

1299 H. de K. .. et W. de B. [et al.] capti .. pro suspicione latrocinii eo quod vagantes nocte .. in warda predicta frequentantes tabernas et lupanar' ibidem ~er et expensas facientes *Gaol Del.* 37/4 m. 3*d*.

expendere [CL]

1 to weigh, measure. **b** (math.) to measure (into parts), divide. **c** to weigh in mind, judge.

~dero, i. .. metiar *GlH* E 614; **9**.. ~datur, *sie awegen oþþe ahangen WW*. **b** si tota summa, i. e. numerus, per septem ~sa, i. e. divisa, fuerit, et nil superfuerit BYRHT. *Man.* 50. **c** ~derunt, i. .. judicaverunt *GlH* E 613.

2 to disburse, spend: **a** (property); **b** (money); **c** (refl., fig.); **d** (absol.).

a ut .. ea, quibus te privas, egenis ~das AD. SCOT *OP* 510A; bona mea ~didi *Latin Stories* 115; **1339** si .. alias res et bona .. ~dideritis *RScot* I 569a; **1340** executores in bonis .. defuncti .. omnia .. fideliter ~didisse *FormOx* 116. **b** dum cernunt amplum sponsas expendere censum ALDH. *VirgV* 2384; pecuniae portionem quam habebat in usum pauperum ~dit WULF. *Æthelwold* 29; ~dam itaque hoc [obolum] in nucleis ALEX. CANT. *Dicta* 3 p. 120; **1189** viij^m brabantinorum .. ~didere DICETO *YH* II 61; **1206** ut .. redditus .. obedientiarum libere et absque omni diminutione ~dantur *Chr. Evesham* 213; **1219** cum [mille marce] .. ~dite fuerint *Pat* 199; **1220** quingente marce, quas ~didit in curia Romana *Ib.* 248; **1227** cum .. T. de G. .. veniret ad nos .. ostendens se multa ~didisse in servicio nostro pro guerra .. sustinenda *Cl* 164b; c**1389** (v. expensor); **1410** pecuniam .. ~didi *FormOx* 419; **1425** custos .. de denariis per eum receptis et ~ditis fidelem reddat computum annuatim *Conc.* III 505b; a**1466** quod .. expendirent (*sic*) residuum (v. extraequitator); exspendidit .. in dimidio anno ij^m li. W. WORC. *Itin.* 72. **c** c**794** Creator ad redemptionis tuae pretium se ipsum ~dit ALCUIN *Ep.* 34. **d** episcopus habet sumptus unde possit ~dere OCKHAM *Pol.* I 302; **1380** quando exspendiderat et in quibus, et ut habeat tallias de expensis *Reg. Rough* 213.

3 (p. ppl. *expensus* as sb. f.): **a** spending, expenditure, outlay (also fig.). **b** funds, money. **c** charge, cost. **d** expenses, money spent.

a nihil nobis deest nisi ~sarum facultas GIR. *RG* III 10 p. 107; **1236** si .. contigerit .. hundredum .. ~sas facere, homines prioris .. secundum portionem suam †debunt [MS: dabunt] cum ceteris hominibus .. hundredi *Cust. Battle* 136; jungitque lacrimas / expensis sanguinis quas facis maximas WALT. WIMB. *Carm.* 617. **b** **1164** quantum ~se permiserint undecumque quesite, quod jusseritis exequar J. SAL. *Ep.* 134 (136 p. 12); cum ~sa sufficiens itineri arripiendo .. in exiguo locatur marsupiola [l. marsupiolo] NECKAM *NR* II 52; oportuit me hostiatim mendicare, sine omni ~sa BRAKELOND f. 134; **1267** etc. (v. apponere 4c). **c** regiis interim exibendum ~sis habui hominem letum MAP *NC* II 3 f. 24v.; a**1294** probi viri duo vel tres de gilda laborabunt cum eo [sc. reo] duas dietas recedendo super ~sas gilde; si vero ultra duas dietas cum ipso laboraverint, reus tunc propriis ~sis suis eos .. adducet *Gild Merch.* I 230; si infirmus dives est, et nichil vult dare adhuc medicus tenetur ipsum curare propriis ~sis J. MIRFIELD *Flor.* 132; **1353** in uno *porpays* empto pro ~sis domini prioris, x s. vj d. *Ac. Durh.* 553; **1450** (v. domicilium 2a); **1460** (v. domicilium 2b); imperator in palacio regis Henrici fuerat London' .. per tres menses in ~sis semper Henrici regis Anglorum STRECCHE *Hen. V* 155; s**1420** (v. caelatura 2a). **d** **1187** in exspensa vj canonicorum .. xij li. et xiiij s. *Pipe* 26; volumus .. ut .. ei saltem medietatem .. restituat ~sarum GIR. *Invect.* III 16; c**1325** (v. duodenus 5); c**1337** nota, infra stilo ~se necessarie, de viij s. solutis pro una piscaria in Sunderland *Ac. Durh.* 534; **1364** ~sa forinseca cum reparacione domorum *Banstead* 343; **1468** pro .. aliis minutis ~sis ad usum .. regis *ExchScot* 590.

4 to consume, use up: **a** (commodity); **b** (foodstuff); *cf. expensare*; **c** (fig.). **d** to waste.

a c**1300** focalia in dicto bosco in domo sua propria ~denda *FormMan* 3; s**1399** cumque utraque pars fere sagittas ~dissent .. *Dieul.* f. 147; **1456** in denariis solutis de cofferis domini pro iij foderis plumbi emptis et ~ditis in opere predicto *Arch. Cant.* LXIII 138; **1514** (v. diplois b). **b** cum tres expendit sportas cum pane refertas ALDH. *VirgV* 1611; **1249** pro vino ~dito in aula xij d. *DCCant.* D.E. 1; **1257** blada .. ~dita (v. dominicus 3c); s**1322** ~ditis .. victualibus TROKELOWE 125. **c** primus quicquid scivit de Anglico ~didit, dicens "nos tres Wallenses." .. secundus Anglicum suum ~didit, dicens, "propter denarium in bursa" *Latin Stories* 128. **d** **1376**, **1445** (v. curriso).

5 (p. ppl. *expensus* as sb. f.) provision, supply (also fig.). **b** spence; *v. et. dispendere* 2b, *spensa*.

~sa, *daeguuini GlC* E 488; ~sa, i. substantia, .. *dægwine GlH* E 610; prescripto legum cohercetur ~sa cenarum J. SAL. *Pol.* 731B; dicit de obsidione, et de defectu victualium et ~sarum (J. BRIDL.) *Pol. Poems* I 159. **b** clericus ~se panis et vini ij s. in die *Domus Reg.* 130; dispensatores ~se *Ib.* 132; **1187** in domo mea [sc. regis Scotiae], sc. in ~sa et coquina *Regesta Scot.* 270; c**1212** per serjantiam custodiendi hostium ~se domini regis *Fees* I 51.

6 to spend, use up (time).

vatis .. / aethereis expendit ovans sub laudibus umbras BEDE *CuthbV* 779; sicque diem totum sacris expendimus ymnis WULF. *Swith.* II 69; postquam expensum est nocturnum spatium WALT. WIMB. *Carm.* 542; dies illos .. non minus diligenter ~dit BLAKMAN *Hen. VI* 15; **1458** concessus est unus dies regentibus, ita quod ~datur infra universitatem *MunAcOx* 740; c**1478** nullus eorum ~dat in anno ultra triginta dies *StatOx* 290.

7 to pay (penalty), suffer (retribution).

~disse, *araefnde GlC* E 373; expe[n]disset, *ðrowode Ib.* 392; ~disset, i. sustinuisset, patiebatur *GlH* E 612.

expendibilis [cf. expendere 4], spendable, for ordinary use. *V. et. expensabilis.*

1325 (v. cuisorius); *spendybylle*, ~is *CathA*.

expendire v. expendere.

expenditio [cf. expendere 4, 5], provision, supply.

x^m anguillarum quae omni anno in villa quae Wellan [*Upwell, Cambs*] dicitur pro ~one redduntur fratribus ad victualia T. ELY *Etheldr. Acta* II 9 p. 525.

expenditor [cf. expendere 5c], dispenser, spender.

1354 dum ipse fuit receptor et ~or bonorum .. ecclesie *Reg. Rough* 285; fiat de collectoribus et ~oribus, ita quod non eligantur .. si domini .. interesse velint *Laws Romney Marsh* 67.

expendium [cf. expendere 2, 3a]

1 expenditure. *V. et. dispendium* 1.

imperator dedit ei maximam pecuniam .. et dixit ei: ".. quantum ~ium miseris in constructione hospicii reddam tibi" *Descr. Constant.* 261; s**532** fecit rex ~ium in lectorium .. tributum de uno anno DICETO *Chr.* I 93.

2 maintenance.

s**1166** [Thomas] in ~iis sufficientiam apud S. Columbam invenit per iiij annos DICETO *YH* I 329.

expensabilis [cf. expensare], spendable, for ordinary use. *V. et. dispensabilis, expendibilis.*

j sextarium de vino claro, et j sextarium de vino ~i *Domus Reg.* 129; **1184** pro vj tonellis vini expensibilis et ij aliis tonellis boni vini *Pipe* 136; s**1194** R. HOWD. III 245 (v. candela 1c); **1206** j dolium vini de vino ~i ad celebrandum missas *Cl* 62b; **1300** j sextarium de vino claro et j sextarium de vino ~i *AcWardr* 201.

expensare [CL = *to pay out*; cf. expendere 4, 5], to consume, use up (foodstuff).

1215 in v doliis vini ~atis .. in hospicio nostro *Cl* 185a.

expensarius [cf. CL expensare, expendere 5b], dispenser, spender. *V. et. dispensarius* 1, *expenditor.*

1213 testibus .. Ricardo filio Michaelis ~io [etc.] *Regesta Scot.* 515.

expensibilis v. expensabilis.

expensio [LL], disbursement, distribution. **b** purchase. **c** expense.

948 pro caducarum ~one substantiarum *CS* 860; possessionum venditionem: earum in pauperes ~onem AD. SCOT *OP* 510A. **b** a**1127** (16c) cappa pro cujus expencione c li. distribuit *Invent. Ch. Ch.* 44. **c** **1508** item in ~onibus in infirmaria tempore infirmitatis *DCCant.* C 11 f. 117v.

expensor [cf. CL expensare, expendere 5c], dispenser, distributor (also fig.). *V. et. expenditor, expensarius.*

s**1135** false monete factores et studiosos ~ores gravi animadversione puniri fecit RIC. HEX. *Stand.* 141; s**1136** pastores, .. spirituales sc. divini verbi ~ores *G. Steph.* I 13; c**1389** hic incipit modus qualiter clericus sive ~or expendet pecuniam domini sui (*MS Dublin, Trinity Coll.* E. 5. 13) *Medium Ævum* VI 207.

expercaria v. espercaria.

experducere [cf. CL perducere], (p. ppl., of metal rod) drawn out to a certain length. *Cf. esperduta.*

c**1300** de j ~to ferro ad Natale Domini ij d. ob. *DCCant. Reg.* J f. 26.

expergefacere [CL], to awaken (person) from sleep, rouse (from inactivity).

~factus [post visionem nocturnam] ALDH. *VirgP* 25; sopor .. quem Dominus .. immisit, non sinens eos ~fieri donec ipse rediens abisset BEDE *Sam.* 692; ad hanc visionis vocem beatus ~factus Dunstanus B. *V. Dunst.* 9; ~facti cives compertis rumoribus valde contristati sunt ORD. VIT. IV 14 p. 267; ad tertium signum †expergestam [MS: expergefacta] surrexit *Canon. G. Sempr.* f. 150; a sompno ~facti *Ps.*-GROS. *Gram.* 52; vir .. sanctus ~factus [ME: *abreid*] vocavit ad se discipulum *AncrR* 87.

expergestus v. expergefacere.

expergiscere, ~i [CL], to awaken (intr.); **b** (fig.); **c** (w. inanim. or abstr. subj.).

quasi de gravi experrectus somno, exsurgens resedit BEDE *HE* V 19 p. 328; expergescens, evigilans *GlC* E 376; experrectus, evigilavit *Ib.* 472; antequam .. possent ~ere *V. Kenelmi B* 81v.; tumultuacione socii experrecti ALEX. CANT. *Mir.* 22 (I) p. 203; ne homo, licet corpore sopitus, excitante doctrina melius ad studium facile videretur per se experrecturus PULL. *Sent.* 765B; cum a tam suavi sompno aculeo inserto de facili non possit ~i vel excitari *Quaest. Salern.* B 161; ego experrectus visionem fixo servavi animo AD. EYNS. *Visio* 9; ~ere, ~or, ~eris, i. *aveiller* vel *esbruscer GlSid* f. 143v.; O David .., jam nunc ~ere et, exorta luce, .. proficiscere *Holy Rood-Tree* 45. **b** s**1298** his rex Anglie expergescens injuriis ad sedandum .. insolenciam .. processit *Chr. S. Edm.* 69. **c** adjuva .. ut accendatur tepor meus, ut ~atur torpor meus ANSELM (*Or.* 7) III 19; terra dormiens non expergescitur WALT. WIMB. *Carm.* 491; ocium et neglegencia sunt sompnus pueri diaboli. sed in tremendo judicio horribiliter ~entur [ME: *schal* .. *abreiden*] cum sono metuendo tubarum *AncrR* 76.

experientia [CL]

1 experiment, proving, testing. *V. et. experimentum* 1a.

~ia, experimentum, probatio, *onfundennes GlH* E 631; ut hujusmodi ~ia exercitatus equivocatorum numerum et equivocationum modos expeditius et plenius dinoscat BALSH. *AD rec. 2* 44; ad caritatis explende tam sufficientiam quam ~iam GIR. *TH* II 40; qui ingrediuntur in religionem ad ~iam T. CHOBHAM *Summa* 158 (cf. ib.: si aliquis fuerit in ~ia potest .. exire et redire ad seculum); ~ia conclusionis .. per ~ias naturales et imperfectas BACON *Tert.* 43 (v. experimentalis); de cognitis per ~iam .. dico quod licet ~ia non habeatur de omnibus singularibus sed de pluribus, .. tamen expertus infallibiliter novit quia ita est et semper et in omnibus DUNS *Ord.* III 141; ista jam apparent falsa ~ia temporum. nam .. ab Adam .. usque ad diluvium sunt ij^m annorum HARCLAY *Adv.* 57.

2 experiencing (of event), situation.

in eadem .. me nunc ~ia video tanquam inter malleum positum et incudem GIR. *Symb.* I 28 p. 301; loquitur expercius reverencia militaris, quam vera ~ia docuit et instruxit *Ps.*-ELMH. *Hen. V* 10 *tit.*.

3 knowledge acquired by experience. *Cf. experimentum* 2b.

cum a proximantibus accolis illius solitudinis ~iam sciscitaretur FELIX *Guthl.* 25; a**1086** ~ia vestra indulgentiam ei praestare valebit LANFR. *Ep.* 22 (24); quantum .. rei auditum superat ~ia, tantum vincit audientis cognitionem experientis scientia ANSELM (*Incarn. A*) I 284; **1165** de sapientia vestra quam litterarum copia tum rerum ~ia J. SAL. *Ep.* 142 (139 p. 20); nemo scit unde sit hoc antidotum, nisi qui didicerit in libro ~ie M. RIEVAULX (*Ep.*) 63; **1438** virum .. magni .. consilii et ~ie in agendis (*Lit. Regis*) BEKYNTON I 2.

experimentalis, experimental, based upon experience.

sciencia ~is, que negligit argumenta .. nisi simul adsit experiencia conclusionis ... et ideo hec docet experiri conclusiones nobiles omnium scienciarum, que in aliis scienciis aut probantur per argumenta aut investigantur per experiencias naturales et imperfectas BACON *Tert.* 43; *Id.* V 11 (v. 1 eclipsis a); **1281** cui et habilitatem ad hoc precipuam ipsius terre ~is cognicio preparavit PECKHAM *Ep.* 159; **1410** de ~i procedit ordine, necnon medicinalis sciencia protestatur, quod singula animalium .. *FormOx* 424.

experimentaliter, experimentally, by experience.

recepto .. antidoto, ~er percepit omnes spiritus interiores paulatim reviviscere *NLA* (*J. Bridl.*) II 76; **1342** ~er .. didicimus *Lit. Cant.* II 261; astronomie miranda diversitas ut ~er visui subderetur R. BURY *Phil.* 16. 211; s**1384** Scoti .. in nemoribus .. delituerunt, nolentes bellum inferre nostratibus, quos ~er cognoverunt illis in locis et illo tempore yemali .. frigore et fame perituros *V. Ric. II* 50; qui .. Dei graciam in seipsis ~er senciunt *Spec. Incl.* 1. 5; **1485** ~er cognoscimus *Reg. Aberbr.* II 242.

experimentare [LL], **~ari**

1 (dep.) to test, try.

omnia de fratribus faciens secundum libitum voluntatis sue .. patientiam fratrum .. ~atus est ECCLESTON *Adv. Min.* 98.

2 to experience.

statur in aliquo 'vero' 'ut in pluribus', cujus extrema experimentum scitum [v. l. †~atum] est frequenter uniri DUNS *Ord.* III 143; nullus .. homo est, qui non vidit somnium quod enunciavit sibi aliquid futurum, et cum homo ~averit hoc multocies, videbit quod hoc non accidit casu BRADW. *CD* 32C.

experimentatio, experimentation, experiment.

philosophia acquiritur .. subtili investigacione, rerum prudenti ~one et sic de aliis que exigunt ad ejus invencionem J. WALEYS *Compend.* I 7 T; isti regule innituntur artifices faciendo multas ~ones, intendendo conquassare ova secundum dyametros longitudinales et sic de multis limitatis a lege nature WYCL. *Ente Praed.* 156.

experimentativus, experimentative, relying upon experiment.

secunda [heresis medicorum] empirica, i. e. ~a, inventa est ab Esculapio, que non indiciorum signis, sed solis constat experimentis W. BURLEY *Vit. Phil.* 184 (cf. Isid. *Etym.* IV 4. 1: experientissima).

experimentator, experimenter. **b** the Experimenter, Rhazes.

ut diversi auctores et ~ores perhibent GROS. 68; ~or .. vult omne combustibile comburere per hoc speculum ad radios solis BACON *Tert.* 45; nec credo quod ~or ex noticia sensuali convincet oppositum WYCL. *Log.* III 68. **b** ~or dicit quod si arthemisia ponatur sub capite pacientis [etc.] J. MIRFIELD *Brev.* 66.

experimentia, experience, situation, or (?) *f. l.*

in simili .. experimentia [? l. experientia *or* experimento] versari dinoscitur propter similes literas nuper ab eodem missas GIR. *Invect.* I 10 p. 114.

experimentum [CL]

1 testing, trial, demonstration; *v. et. experientia* 1. **b** experiment, proof.

fidei Christianae gratia .. cujus ~a permaxima in expugnandis barbaris jam ceperat BEDE *HE* III 3; quod noviter [Deus] probabit ~o *Found. Waltham* 19; fidem Gregorius plane negat habere meritum, si ei humana ratio prebeat ~um GIR. *TH* I 13 p. 43; conclusionem .. hanc Ricardus evidentiori probavi ~o tali, quod movet nos memoriter tenere RIC. MED. *Anat.* 232; scio futura predicere .. que certo ~o cognoscere poteris *Latin Stories* 98. **b** ad propositum etiam facit ~um etiam vulgo notum. humore impleatur urceus .. NECKAM *NR* I 19; hoc .. manifestum est per ~um illud ..: si in vas mittatur quid .. GROS. 74; hoc ~o patet quoniam si ponatur aliquid in profundo vasis mediocris altitudinis .. PECKHAM *Persp.* III 7.

2 experience: **a** (w. ref. to senses); **b** (as means of acquiring knowledge); *cf. experientia* 3.

a quicunque .. de cellis illis discretive egit, idipsum sensuali ~o didicisse auguror ADEL. *QN* 18; quod grando fiat ex grossis guttis candentibus ~o vidimus *Quaest. Salern.* B 163; propositiones .. note apud intellectum per sensus ~um J. BLUND *An.* 137; ex talis sensus et memorie multiplicatione fit ~um KILWARDBY *OS* 9. **b** ~um, *andwisnis GlC* E 375; qui hoc non per fidem, sed per ~um cognoscerent ANSELM (*Praesc.* 9) II 277; *Id. Misc.* 306 (v. doctrina 2b); evidenti jam ~o scientes quod a peccatorum nexibus facillime possent ab illo dissolvi DOMINIC *V. Ecgwini* I 18; quod .. vita hec misera .. sit quamvis .. miseriarum nos doceant ~a AILR. *Serm.* 245C; **1166** que cotidianis rerum ~is luce clarius patent J. SAL. *Ep.* 183 (175 p. 158).

3 knowledge, history, tradition.

Brittanniae insulae ~um juxta traditionem veterum explicare curabo NEN. *HB* 147; si quis scire voluerit quo tempore post diluvium habitata est haec insula, hoc ~um bifarie inveni *Ib.* 149; aliud ~um inveni de isto Bruto ex veteribus libris veterum nostrorum *Ib.* 159.

4 remedy. **b** tried method.

~is uti propono, tum quia breviter expediunt tum quia multi infirmi modernis temporibus valde impacientes sunt. .. intellige quod duplex est ~um, sc. ~um vallatum racione et ~um non vallatum racione. de primo dicitur quod ~um est illud quod a prudentibus racione est inventum .. . ~um autem si non sit vallatum racione tunc timorosum est et fallax J. MIRFIELD *Brev.* 50. **b** realgar vel risalgar est vena terre. inde habemus ~um ad ratos et mures capiendum *Alph.* 156.

5 magical device.

1331, FAVENT 18 (v. character 1b); s**1384** custos castri .. accepit fratrem .. et leves compedes super eum posuit et timens ne forsan ~is uteretur in tuto loco .. ipsum reclusit *Chr. Westm.* 143.

experiolus v. sciurellus.

experiri [CL], **~ire**

1 to measure, test, prove; **b** (*s. pass.*). **c** (absol.) to experiment.

ut in ista gente ~iretur Dominus .. praesentem Israelem GILDAS *EB* 26; totus in preces assurgo et efficaciam earum ~ior J. SAL. *Ep.* 206 (195); dum vires ingenii non ~iuntur igne animi vacui GIR. *TH intr.* p. 5; visne ambulandi vires ~iri? R. BOCKING *Ric. Cic.* II 5; BACON *Tert.* 43 (v. experimentalis); Deus volens ~iri patienciam regis .. tetigit eum in morte unius de amantissimis .. suis *G. Hen. V* 44. **b 13..** (v. 2 constabularius 5b); hoc vero sepius fuerat ~tum [ME: *for that hath ben prouyd oftyn tyme*] *Itin. Mand.* 60. **c** aliquoties, ~iendi gratia, serpentes in ollis eneis delati sunt GIR. *TH* I 29; ~iendi causa *Id. IK* I 5 p. 58.

2 (leg.) to try, put to trial. **b** (intr.) to go to court.

GIR. *IK* I 7 (v. duellum 3f). **b 1163** ipse .. in presentia nostra adversus jamdictum priorem ~iens G. FOLIOT *Ep.* 149.

3 to experience (w. senses); **b** (*s. pass.*).

ALDH. *VirgV* 2425 (v. efflare 1c); ars .. / experientis sensum exercet sepius ipsam OSW. *Vers.* 7; ANSELM I 14 (v. discernere 3a); cum avulsus sum a pedibus vestris tunc primum .. lesionis aculeos ~tus sensi J. SAL. *Ep.* 284 (271); s**1460** consimilia nos ~ire .. verebamur *Croyl. Cont. B* 531. **b** si non possunt virgineo flore pudicitiae, saltem ~tae voluptatis jugi mortificatione ABBO *Edm.* 17.

4 to find by experience, discover; **b** (w. acc. & inf. or *quod*); **c** (w. indir. qu.); **d** (*s. pass.*). **e** to study.

cujus mores et industriam in variis jam rerum eventibus ~tus fuerat H. BOS. *Thom.* II 8; s**1296** quendam .. Robertum .. ad regem Scotie .. demandare, suam [i. e. regis] voluntatem ~turum *Flor. Hist.* III 97. **b** nos .. qui ejus vitam .. cognovimus, hanc illi semper fuisse consuetudinem frequenter ~ti sumus *V. Gund.* 33; **1167** ut eas [preces] apud vos ~iatur alicujus esse momenti J. SAL. *Ep.* 214 (199); **1170** *Ib.* 293 (v. exaugustus); ita .. ~imur in nobis quod possumus appetere majus bonum DUNS *Ord.* II 7. **c** cujus meriti .. sit .. ~tus sum BEDE *HE* V 6; ad ~iendum .. quis eorum majus jus in Galliam haberet G. MON. X 4; de quibus disseritur assignandi dicemus facile fiet ~iri BALSH. *AD* 51; ut ~irentur utrum vox nata esset an disceretur ALB. LOND. *DG* 1. 11; volens ~iri utrum fecerit ex stulticia *Latin Stories* 42; ubi simul ~iemur quis sit dedecoris sine laude dignus in conflictu militari STRECCHE *Hen. V* 165. **d** s**1405** in †grossia ejus urina intoxicacione ~ta AD. USK 100. **e 1549** dialecticam artem ~iri *Conc. Scot.* II 105.

5 (pr. ppl. *experiens* as adj.) enterprising, lively. **b** intelligent.

~iens, i. impiger, navus, celer *GlH* E 629. **b** ~iens, i. .. sciens *Ib.*; cunctis ~ientioris viris scientie R. COLD. *Cuthb.* 42.

6 (p. ppl. *expertus*) expert, knowing, learned; *v. et. expers* 3. **b** (as sb. m.) one who has learned, expert, sage. **c** (*s. pass.*) tested, tried, proved.

aetas tempestatis illius nescia et praesentis tantum serenitatis ~ta GILDAS *EB* 26; ~ta, docta *GlH* E 621; post hec expercior in secularibus / fit cito dicior sua sunt comparibus *Planct. Univ. Ox.* 27. **b** onerosum plurimum, quod illius officii optime norunt ~ti H. BOS. *Thom.* II 8; DUNS *Ord.* III 141 (v. experientia 1); secundum ~tos hujus sciencie TUNST. 247; s**1252** innitatur .. consiliis sapientium et ~torum et timentium Deum FORDUN *Cont.* X 8. **c** ~tus, i. probatus *GlH* E 617; nichil aliud exercebat nisi sanctorum ~tissimorum ritum *V. Neot. A* 2; sirupus in ejectione san[guinis] ~tus, quo nihil est .. melius GILB. IV 194v. 2; *Ib.* I 1. 1 (v. dictio 1d).

experk-, experqu- v. esperc-.

experrectio [cf. CL experrectus *p. ppl. of* expergiscere], awakening.

per ~onem factam a sensu tactus WYCL. *Ente* f. 2.

expers [CL]

1 having no share (of), taking no part (in). **b** deprived (of), devoid (of).

~tia, aliena *GlC* E 473; **956** expeditionis, pontis, et arcis non ~s sit hoc donum, sed ceterarum rerum *CS* 986; ~s, i. .. sine parte *GlH* E 634; **1147** assigno quod Franci .. hostium possessiones .. habeant, omnibus meis et me omnimodo ~tibus (*Ch. Regis Portugalensium*) OSB. BAWDSEY clx; nec jus nature .. divini beneficii ~s FORTESCUE *NLN* I 37. **b** Romani .., patria vini oleique ~te relicta, Italiam petunt GILDAS *EB* 7; signa Judaici velleris imbris caelestis ~tis *Ib.* 70; carcer lanternae luminis expers ALDH. *VirgV* 2318; insula nec vinearum ~s BEDE *HE* I 1 p. 13; at sulcata manens semper sum seminis expers HWÆTBERHT *Aen.* 31 (*Cera*) 2; ~s, i. .. privatus *GlH* E 634; ne ~s et quasi vacuus a mercede .. videretur *V. Gund.* 29.

2 lacking experience or knowledge (of).

antiquitas verae religionis ~s ALDH. *PR* 123; ~s, i. ignarus, .. imperitus, inscius *GlH* E 634; **a1075** novus homo et Anglicae consuetudinis penitus ~s LANFR. *Ep.* 4 (3 p. 40); pecora que sunt rationis ~tia AILR. *Anima* I 12; religionis expertem *Id. Met.* 855A (v. collatio 5a); abbas .. ~s humani consilii, confisus tamen de divino *Chr. Battle* f. 128v.

3 (by conf. w. *expertus*) expert, knowledgeable, learned. *V. et. experiri* 6a.

~s, scius *GlC* E 549; **1280** se gerent sicut iis per aliquos idoneos et ~tes viros a cancellario deputatos dicetur *MunAcOx* 782; secundum ~tes hujus sciencie TUNST. 271.

experte [cf. experiri 6], from experience, wisely.

Dunstanus .. assuetas sibi visiones et hymnos supernorum civium frequentabat, qui hoc etiam fertur ~tissime dixisse quod ubicumque .. pedem vertisses, super aliquem sanctorum calcares GOSC. *Transl. Aug.* 44C.

experv- v. sperv-. **expes** v. exspes.

1 expetere v. espeltare.

2 expetere [CL]

1 to ask, beseech (person).

reges Guent .. ~ivere regem ut dominium et defensionem ab eo .. haberent ASSER *Alf.* 80; **1146** ~isti imperium meum concessionem vie transitusque (*Lit. Imp. ad regem Franc.*) DICETO *YH* I 257 (v. et. 2b infra).

2 to seek (thing). **b** to request (answer or favour), seek after (benefit). **c** to demand (revenge). **d** (absol.) to require.

~endorum, i. exquirendorum, quae ~enda videntur *GlH* E 641; **1027** archiepiscopi .. angari[a]bantur immensitate pecuniarum quae ab eis ~ebatur (*Lit. Regis*) *Conc. Syn.* 510; **1167** ut nichil nobis defuerit probabiliter ~endorum J. SAL. *Ep* 212 (197). **b** nuptiae aliae ~untur non cujuslibet relictae GILDAS *EB* 35; maxima exercitus multitudo undam lavacri salutaris ~it BEDE *HE* I 20; sanctorum .. ~unt colloquia FOLC. *V. Bot.* 2; **1093** auxilium amicorum ~ere ANSELM (*Ep.* 159) IV 26; **1146** (v. 1 supra); unde sit iratus rogat illa vel exanimatus / Malchus; id expetitur, mulieri res aperitur R. CANT. *Malch.* IV 137; nec ab aliquo innocentiam vel beneficium sive prelationem quasi per debitum ~ere ALEX. CANT. *Dicta* 16 p. 170; **1166** remoti principes amicitias ~ebant J. SAL. *Ep.* 145 (168 p. 104). **c** ignis [paganorum] .. justas .. Dei ultiones ~iit BEDE *HE* I 15; **1168** de inimicis optatam ~et ultionem J. SAL. *Ep.* 244 (272 p. 570); pro verbo levi irascimur et vindictam irascendo ~imus P. BLOIS *Serm.* 704C; uxor tua mihi multas inferebat injurias, de ea volebam ~ere ultionem *Latin Stories* 32. **d** **c1165** cum .. res et tempus ~ierint J. SAL. *Ep.* 172 (207); sunt et quedam que, nisi materie cursus ~eret, pudor reticenda persuaderet GIR. *TH* III 25.

3 to seek out, go to (place).

Thetis cur tumidas Zephiro minitante salivas / expetii? FRITH. 125; **1027** [Deus] mihi concessit .. omne sanctuarium .. infra urbem Romam aut extra .. ~ere (*Lit. Regis*) *Conc. Syn.* 509; bis in Jerusalem sepulcrum Domini ~iit ORD. VIT. III 2 p. 6.

4 to seek, contrive (to do something); **b** (w. inf.); **c** (w. *ut*).

quodsi iterum tale facere presumpserit [etc.] .. quodsi majus ~it, oculi ejus eruantur (*Cons. Cnuti* 30. 5) *GAS* 333 (cf. *Inst. Cnuti*: quodsi adhuc majora fecerit; *Quad.*: et si adhuc amplius peccaverit; AS: *ond gif he þonne gyt mare wurc geworht hæbbe*). **b** expetiit revocare virum sat inepte repulsum FRITH. 1000; qui ad plenum nosse ~it, pontificum libros otiosus transcurrat ALB. LOND. *DG* 6. 35. **c** ut regia auctoritate [carta] renovaretur ~iit *Chr. Battle* f. 121.

5 to discover, learn, or (?) *f. l.*

quatenus .. ad expetendum [? l. experiendum] veniret quis eorum majus jus in Galliam haberet *Eul. Hist.* II 342 (= G. MON. X 4: ad experiendum).

expetibilis [CL], desirable.

~is, desiderabilis *GlH* E 649; **c1000** post virtutum omnium ~em ubertatem (*Ep. ad Wulstanum*) *Mem. Dunst.* 404; cum .. omnium ~ium prima sit sapientia J. SAL. *Met.* 857C; **1527** pax bello ~ior *Conc.* III 708b.

expetibilitas, desirability.

que hujus temperantie ~as? quid nostra referet? ADEL. *QN* 72.

exphasticus v. exemplasticus.

expiabilis [LL], expiable. **b** expiatory.

e[x]piabilis, inmundus *GlC* E 464; *clennessabylle*, ~is, purgabilis *CathA*; *expiable*, ~is LEVINS *Manip.* 3. **b** a Domino petere consuevit quatinus anima sua .. in igne ~i et remediabili usque ad districti examinis diem .. purgatoriis suppliciis .. deputaretur GIR. *Spec.* II 24 p. 71.

expiamen [cf. LL expiamentum], expiation.

a clensynge, colacio, .. expiacio, ~en *CathA*.

expiare [CL]

1 to expiate, atone for (sin or offence).

a690 psalmigrafus .. propriae piaculi ~ians flagitium conscientiae .. infit .. ALDH. *Ep.* 5 p. 492; accepto clericali habitu, praeterita piacula ~iare certabat FELIX *Guthl.* 20; utrum [Mauritius] mallet delicta sua in hac vita ~iare an in alia R. NIGER *Chr. II* 141; quousque [injuria] manifeste fuerit ~iata per penam NIG. *Ep.* 19; **1191** (v. distrusus); [Mauritius] suo .. sanguine mundanas maculas et mendas meruit in terris ~iare GIR. *PI* I 20 p. 124.

2 to clear (person or soul) of guilt; **b** (refl.).

qua ratione, si inculpabiles sunt [clerici], possunt ~iari? EGB. *Dial.* 3; Deus .. vos .. ~iet ab omni contagione delicti *Id. Pont.* 81; ut nos .. ~iet a peccatis quibus meremur supplicium ABBO *Edm.* 17; jejunia quae nos ~iando gratiae tuae dignos efficiant et ad remedia perducant aeterna *Rit. Durh.* 23; secundum quod homo [Christus] est sacrificium quo ~iati sumus J. CORNW. *Eul.* 8; anime ~iate COGGESH. *Visio* 30; expiet ut mundum mulier, qui per mulierem / subsidet GARL. *Epith.* I 203. **b** ~iet se inde coram omnibus, petita venia *Cust. Cant. Abbr.* 264.

3 to cleanse, purge (partly fig.).

680 vascula .. et fialas .. cineribus ~ianda purgandaque praecipiunt ALDH. *Ep.* 4 p. 484; illuxit postquam Phebi clarissima lampas / et mundum furvis expiat a tenebris G. AMIENS *Hast.* 568; **11..** hec sacras Iesu lacrimis / .. / mentis tenebras expians *Anal. Hymn.* LI 175.

expiatio [CL]

1 expiation.

749 (12c) pro ~one delictorum suorum *CS* 178; **811** pro ~one piaculorum ejus *CS* 335; **853** pro ~one piaculorum meorum et absolutione criminum meorum *CS* 467; pro nostrorum ~one scelerum R. COLD. *Cuthb.* 42; fit autem ~o holocaustis R. NIGER *Mil.* II 21.

2 cleansing.

ad ~onem Israhelitici populi .. spoponderunt oracula ALDH. *Met.* 2; †**670** (11c) pro ~one animae meae *CS* 723; mensis, in quo animarum ~ones apud antiquos celebrantur, Februarius est appellatus ALB. LOND. *DG* 4. 3; pro ~one lepre AD. DORE *Pictor* 163.

expiator [LL], expiator.

~or est dum fit peccati remissio, propitius dum per remissionem datur reconciliatio PULL. *Sent.* 882D.

expiatorium [cf. LL expiatorius], place of expiation, purgatory.

purgatorium, ~ium, locus ubi purgantur anime OSB. GLOUC. *Deriv.* 473.

expiatrix [CL], expiator (f.). **b** (as adj.) expiatory.

vetusti .. dedecoris ~icem et sexus muliebris nobilitatricem, .. Salvatoris genitricem W. NEWB. *Serm.* 827; hoc proponit pietas, mentis expiatrix GARL. *Epith.* I *Summa* 25. **b** fusus .. pro Christo sanguis .. poscit vicem ~icis aque [baptismatis] W. NEWB. *Serm.* 900.

expidatio v. expedatio.

expignerare [cf. CL pignerare], to redeem (a pledge).

epignorare *Gl. AN Ox.* f. 153 (v. evadiare); *CathA* (v. depignerare).

1 expīlare [CL], to depilate, remove hair from.

equus ille ~atus emarcuit et usque ad interitum suum elanguit, nec operis ullius usui aptus fuit J. FURNESS *Walth.* 76.

2 expīlare [CL]

1 to plunder, rob.

~atam, *apryid, arytrid GlC* E 400; terra .. ita .. Turchis sevientibus ~ata ut vix .. alimoniam ministrare sufficeret W. MALM. *GR* IV 357; omnes bulgias et manticas efferri coram et ~ari imperavit *Id. GP* I 50 p. 95; **1166** novorum aliquid que in ~atis invenitis armariis J. SAL. *Ep.* 199 (185) (cf. Cicero *Pro Cluentio* 64. 181); componitur etiam ~o, -as, i. diripere .. et inde expilator, expilatio OSB. GLOUC. *Deriv.* 418; **1257** bona ecclesiarum diripere, diminuere, vel aliter ~are *Conc. Syn.* 536.

2 (leg.) to deprive (of inheritance).

quisquis patrimonium suum dilapidaverat alienamve hereditatem ~averat *Lib. Eli.* III 52 p. 297; de crimine ~ate hereditatis VAC. *Lib. Paup.* 198.

3 to remove (also fig.).

testule ovi interior tela, que quandoque unguinum preacumine vix pre sui teneritudine de testula confracta ~atur R. COLD. *Godr.* 112; expilat mundus oculos, caro lubrica mentem / glutinat, hanc Sathanae retia multa trahunt GARL. *Tri. Eccl.* 120.

expilatio [CL], plundering, robbing.

OSB. GLOUC. *Deriv.* 418 (v. 2 expilare 1).

expilator [CL]

1 plunderer, robber.

~or divitum, exterminator pauperum W. MALM. *GR* IV 314; OSB. GLOUC. *Deriv.* 418 (v. 2 expilare 1).

2 squanderer of inheritance.

~ores, alienae hereditatis subreptores *GlC* E 486.

expingere [cf. CL pangere, impingere], to prise, force apart.

nec etiam preacutissima extremitate unguium [pannus a cute] in aliquo loco elici, ~i, vel saltem sensu quovis perceptibili diduci prevaluit R. COLD. *Cuthb.* 41.

expir- v. exspir-.

expiscari [CL], to fish for (also fig.), search for.

~abar, capiebam *GlH* E 546; quod cum amiserint summopere requirunt, sed erumnis afflicti ~antes reperire nequeunt ORD. VIT. XII 33 p. 438; ~ari, omnes pisces capere OSB. GLOUC. *Deriv.* 200.

explacitare, (leg.) to gain by pleading, plead for successfully. **b** (refl.) to clear (oneself) by pleading.

a1084 illas terras quas ipse abbas ~avit coram vij schiris .. contra omnes injuste eas quaerentes *Regesta* p. 125; Lanfrancus ~avit illud [manerium de Sunderhersce] contra episcopum Bajocensem *Dom. Cant.* f. 3. **b** alius dies ponatur ei, et tunc ~et se, vel emendet, nisi competens soinus intercedat (*Leg. Hen.* 50. 3) *GAS* 573; **s1051** ut magnates illius castelli blande in curia regis de seditione convenirentur. si se possent ~are, illesi abirent W. MALM. *GR* II 199 p. 242.

explacitatio, (leg.) (successful) pleading.

c1100 haec iij juga non scottabant cum hoc manerio [*Orpington, Kent*] et sunt de ~one quam fecit archiepiscopus contra episcopum Bajocensem *Dom. Cant.* f. 4v.

explanare [CL]

1 to flatten, smooth (also fig.).

~at, ex[a]equat *GlC* E 428; lapidum .. quos caementarius ~are vel quadrare voluerit ANSELM *Misc.* 317; **1430** (v. colonare).

2 to clear (forest or woodland); **b** (fig.).

s1093 nemora ~avit M. PAR. *Min.* I 46; **s1256** ut silvas ~ans omnia devastaret *Id. Maj.* V 589. **b** **s1381** totum illud germen Kentensium et Juttorum statuerunt de terra viventium explanare [? l. explantare] WALS. *HA* II 14.

3 to explain, make intelligible.

quod textus libelli Eugeniae uberius ~at ALDH. *VirgP* 44; ille melius .. lingua Anglorum quam ego per interpretem potest ~are quae sentimus BEDE *HE* III 25 p. 184; opuscula doctor / edidit, explanans obscura volumina sanctae scripturae ALCUIN *SS Ebor* 1306; in ~ando Ysaiam ANDR. S. VICT. *Comm.* 273; **1164** satis ~avi in quantam perniciem ecclesie Romane tendunt hec J. SAL. *Ep.* 134 (136 p. 8); in libello quem .. conscripsimus, dilucida brevitate sunt hec ~ata GIR. *TH* II 3; prout .. potero quamvis balbuciendo aliqua ~abo BART. ANGL. II 8.

4 to unfurl. **b** (her.) to display.

s1388 precedente eos vexillo regis ~ato usque regem .. iter arripuerunt *Chr. Kirkstall* 126. **b** portat [imperator] aquilam fissam et ~atam in campo aureo BAD. AUR. 118.

explanatio [CL]

1 planing, smoothing w. plane.

1514 circa ~one meremii *Ac. Durh.* 253.

2 explanation, exegesis.

de .. pedibus quorum exempla aliquantula ~one .. digessimus ALDH. *PR* 125; in librum .. Tobiae ~onis allegoricae librum j BEDE *HE* V 24 p. 358; hos auctores in hac ~one sumus sequuti ÆLF. *CH I pref.* 1; [Beda] abdita in ~onum libris plus quam lx reseravit ORD. VIT. IV 6 p. 207; quere in festis suis ~onem de processionibus ad vesperas et ad matutinas *Cust. Norw.* 208; ad cujus difficultatis ~onem quidam subtiliter perscrutantes R. MARSTON *QD* 385.

explanatiuncula, brief explanation.

si quid tibi in his ~is gratum dixi BEDE *Kings* 736; proposui .. aliquam ~am super obscura prophetarum scripta cudere ANDR. S. VICT. *Comm.* 272.

explanativus, explanatory.

similiter et metaphysica quodammodo sui ~a est KILWARDBY *OS* 581; ecce quod falsa et viciosa addicio prohibetur, non autem ~a postlacio WYCL. *Civ. Dom.* I 431.

explanator [CL], explainer, exegete.

F., .. in divinis tractatibus ~or profluus ORD. VIT. X 15 p. 85; ceteris prophete ejusdem ~oribus ANDR. S. VICT. *Comm.* 274.

explantare [CL], to extirpate, eradicate, uproot (fig.).

ipsum inimicum eradicare et ~are [AS: *of plantia*] *Rit. Durh.* 121; volo ut .. omnis injusticia .. de finibus nostris sarculetur et ~etur *GAS* 309; ad ~andam heresim Pelagianam GIR. *DK* I 18; canonicis illis a loco suo penitus expulsis et ~atis *Id. Spec.* III 2 p. 144; mundes a sordibus ipsum / carmen et explantes vitium VINSAUF *PN* 1921; regni primatem .. / quem rex explantat, dux ex pietate replantat GOWER *CT* III 255.

explectare [cf. explectum], to exploit, take for esplees.

a**1180** ita quod dicti fratres .. capiant et ~ent quidquid ad usum et edificationem ipsorum .. viderint expedire (*Ch. Grandmont*) *Act. Hen. II* II 121; **1276** sciatis nos dedisse .. Reymundo plateam seu solum .. habendum et tenendum et ~andum *RGasc* II 21b; **1289** quod gentes nostre .. aliqua ~averant et adhuc ~abant per se ipsos et solo nomine nostro, .. in prejudicium ipsius episcopi et contra jus et naturam pariagii jurisdictionis *RGasc* II 364; **1293** si gentes nostre .. aliquid seisiant, capiant, vel ~ent, vel seisire vellent, capere, vel ~are .. (*Lit. Regis Franciae*) *Foed.* I 793; **1310** riperia seu maresium .. consuevit esse locus communis ad ~andum et pascendum ad omnia animalia *Reg. Gasc. A* 45; **1373** G. .. habeat jus et causam tenendi et ~andi predictam domum *Pat* 290 m. 14.

explectatio [cf. explectare], exploitation, taking for esplees.

1422 quod .. personas ecclesiasticas que de solvendo summas .. debitas negligentes fuerint per bonorum suorum ~onem .. compellant *Foed.* X 203b.

explectum, expletia, ~tium [AN *espleit*, OF *esploit* < explicitus *p. ppl. of* explicare], esplees, produce or revenue from land. *V. et. espletum.* **b** right to take esplees.

1193 quatuor virgatas terre .. tenendas .. cum omnibus ~ctis que mihi evenire poterunt *FormA* 130; **1195** jus suum et saisinam patris sui ita quod pater suus cepit inde ~ta ad valenciam v s. *CurR RC* 49; **1218** unde .. fuit saisitus .. capiendo inde ~cia ad valenciam [etc.] *Eyre Yorks* 60; **1219** terram tenuit et cepit inde ~tias *CurR* VIII 37; item nec ~tia capere, quia nondum advenit tempus messium neque vindemiarum. si .. fructus non maturos perceperit vel arbores prostraverit, ista non debent dici ~tia, cum sint potius ad damnum quam ad commodum BRACTON 40; usus quandoque vestimentum prebet et post imaginariam donacionem seisinam declarat, sicut capcio ~ciarum et unde donatarius sic existens .. habet liberum tenementum *Fleta* 291; **1302** episcopus habebit omnia ~cias et proficua quecunque de corona emergencia .. durantibus nundinis *RParl* I 152a; **1330** prior .. fuit seisitus de predicto manerio .. capiendo inde explicia ad valenciam [etc.] *Cart. S. Fridesw.* II 98; **1396** per quod alligatur ~cias de homagiis, redditibus, et arreragiis redituum sufficienter warantizatas *Cart. Glam.* 1388. **b 1279** scripta clericis consilii .. ostensa eisdem dederunt conscienciam, una cum dicto expletto, quod .. abbas, conventus et clericus haberent jus in premissis *AncC* XXIII 115; **1289** licet predecessores nostri eadem ~cta fecissent, ipsius episcopi et ecclesie sue Agennensis optentu, nolentes eisdem ~ctis insistere, .. concedimus quod .. pariagium .. in omnibus observetur, non obstantibus ~ctis nostris predictis *RGasc* II 364–5.

explegitor v. explorator.

explere [CL]

1 to fill out, complete, conclude.

~etis igitur .. masculini sexus exemplis, .. ad .. secundi sexus personas .. contendamus ALDH. *VirgP* 39 p. 291; cessabant verba, lacrimae sermonem ~ebant *V. Gund.* 33 p. 56; secundus ordo [librorum Vet. Test.] continet prophetias, et viij libris ~etur J. SAL. *Ep.* 143 (209 p. 320); vipera mater Adam protendit, suscipit, explet / virus, honus, vulnus GARL. *Epith.* I 413.

2 to fulfil (desire), satisfy (appetite).

ALDH. *VirgV* 2619 (v. amburere b); cum .. ad libidinem ~endam philosophentur J. SAL. *Pol.* 815A; divitiis autem mali abundant, primo ut mala que concupiscunt justo Dei judicio ~ere per pecuniam valeant HON. *Eluc.* 1136D; quomodocumque [concupiscencia] .. ~eatur [ME: *hit eaver is acwenht*] *AncrR* 73.

3 to perform, complete (ritual). **b** to fulfil (duty, obligation, promise, or project). **c** (w. *vices*) to 'fill in for', take place of.

~eta missa THEOD. *Pen.* II 8. 5; ~etis .. hymnis matutinalibus BEDE *HE* V 9 p. 297; omnibus secundum seriem ecclesiasticam ~etis BYRHT. *V. Ecgwini* 380; quibus [orationibus] ~etis [AS p. 418: *þam gefylledum*] per ordinem *RegulC* 44; a**1077** debita servitia sine casula ~everunt LANFR. *Ep.* 13 (14); **1139** ministerium dedicationis ~evi *Act. Ep. Linc.* 33. **b** quis vestrum sponte ~everit id quod sequitur: 'propterea nolite fieri imprudentes' [*Eph.* v 17] GILDAS *EB* 102; **716** ut vos .. seduli munus ~eatis (HWÆTBERHT *Ep.*) *Hist. Abb. Jarrow* 30; opus ~evit mirificum *V. Greg.* p. 109; ~ere votum BEDE *HE* II 12 p. 107; quod aliud poterunt officium ~ere? *Simil. Anselmi* 128; anima .. suum non valet ~ere conatum EDMUND *Spec. Relig.* 127; **1265** ut .. ea que in litteris regis .. plenius exequentur (*sic*) faciant et ~ent *Cl* 103; in opere ~ete promissionis non reperiuntur nisi tria, sc. exigens et promissio et solvens GROS. *Quaest. Theol.* 205. **c** c**1147** ut [supprior] vices prioris sui absentis incunctanter ~eret *Ch. Durh.* 36.

4 a to finish, reach the end of (journey). **b** to spend, complete, pass (period of time).

a namque iteris (*sic*) longos explevit honeste meatus FRITH. 135; presul .. laboriosum iter ~evit ORD. VIT. X 9 p. 55. **b** bilustro .. ~eto GILDAS *EB* 12; omnem in ejus obsequio .. ~evit aetatem BEDE *HE* V 20; nec non expletos post quattuor exitus annos ALCUIN *SS Ebor* 641; **946** (12c) ~eto siquidem dierum tempore suorum *CS* 818; expletum triduum menses dum quinque sequuntur WULF. *Swith.* I 1083; diem totum in ingenti gaudio ~everunt *V. II Off.* 24.

expleta, ~ia v. explectum.

expletio [CL]

1 conclusion.

qui vos ad ~onem hujus fecit pervenire concilii EGB. *Pont.* 98.

2 fulfilment (of desire).

illi .. metuentes .. a pravarum ~onibus voluntatum cohiberi ORD. VIT. XI 36 p. 290; hii spiritus .. veloces ad divine voluntatis ~onem BART. ANGL. II 2; subsequitur libidinis ~o, que per capram designatur ALB. LOND. *DG* 14. 5; per ~onem libidinis [ME: *fule brune cwench*] *AncrR* 73.

3 performance, completion (of ritual). **b** fulfilment.

post ~onem uniuscujusque hore duos psalmos .. peroremus *Comp. Swith.* 183; s**1147** post ~onem misse OSB. BAWDSEY clii. **b** post ~onem signi ab eodem [propheta] praedicti GILDAS *EB* 77.

4 end (of period of time).

quomodo S. Wilfridus, post ~onem octo annorum prime expulsionis sue, episcopatum Haugustaldensem recepit RIC. HEX. *Hist. Hex.* I 11 *tit.*; usque ad alteram diem ~onis hebdomade septime, id est, quinquaginta dies BACON *Maj.* I 201.

expletium v. explectum.

expletivus [LL], (med.) that completes or fulfils (function). **b** (gram. & rhet.) expletive, that completes or clarifies (sense; also as sb.).

quedam [membra] operacionum sunt organa ~a, quedam superfluitatum expurgatoria et receptacula et respirativa RIC. MED. *Anat.* 212. **b** ~ae [conjunctiones] sunt quae vel bonum vel malum explent sensum ALCUIN *Didasc.* 895B; *sume syndon gehatene* ~ae *oððe* completivae *gecwedene, þæt synd gefyllendlice* ÆLF. *Gram.* 261; ~um, vel sc. similitudinem proferam LANFR. *Comment. Paul.* (*1 Cor.* xiv 6) 202.

explettum, expletum v. explectum. **expletus** v. explere.

explicabilis [CL], **a** explicable. **b** compassable.

a quo modo isti defectus habeant in nobis racionem culpe, habet magnam difficultatem et vix ~em R. MARSTON *QD* 161. **b** filii .. Israel paucorum dierum viam commeatu ~em peccatis exigentibus xl annis longis protraxere dispendiis (*Lit. Rogeri prioris Lantoniae*) GIR. *Symb.* I 17.

explicare [CL, *perf.* ~avi, ~ui, *p. ppl.* ~atus, ~itus]

1 to unfold. **b** to unroll (scroll), open (book); *cf.* 6 *infra.* **c** to smooth (wrinkle). **d** to unfurl. *V. et. deplicare* 1.

NECKAM *Ut.* 101 (v. complicare 1a); ~ant pallia altaris .. post missam eadem debeant complicare *Ord. Ebor.* I 71. **b** ~o, i. .. aperio *GlH* E 549. **c** rugas ejus [sc. pellis] ~a G. HOYLAND *Ascet.* 261; numquid non caritas Christi omnem de facie ejus maculam extersit, ~uit rugam? J. FORD *Serm.* 4. 8. **d** M. PAR. *Maj.* V 645, RISH. 26 (v. draco 2d).

2 to extricate, disentangle. **b** (p. ppl. *explicitus*) unencumbered, unhampered.

exemtum, ~itum, exclusum *GlC* E 535; ~uit, i. *utalædde GlH* E 551; quia se a retibus fallacis sapientie ~uerunt AILR. *Serm.* 467A. **b** ~itus, i. expeditus *GlH* E 553; D. BEC. 1543 (v. claudus); quicquid libet, licitum dicit, et a lege / se putat explicitum, quasi major rege *Carm. Lewes* 444.

3 to unfold (fig.), explicate, explain, make clear; **b** (w. indir. qu.). **c** (p. ppl. *explicitus*) explicit.

neque altum ingenium / explicare mortalium / ullus valet (ÆTHELWALD) *Carm. Aldh.* 5. 60; nullius sermone ~ari potest *V. Cuthb.* II 1; in processu epistulae ita suas calamitates ~ant BEDE *HE* I 13; a**795** mentis probamentis vestrae auctoritatis pro nobis ~avit devotionem ALCUIN *Ep.* 41; a**1073** nescio cui aptius calamitates meas ~em quam tibi LANFR. *Ep.* 1; si vera illud ratione ~itum est, qualiter est illa ineffabilis? ANSELM (*Mon.* 65) I 75; ANDR. S. VICT. *Comm.* 273 (v. evolvere 3); quod ut apertius ~eam [v. l. ~em] .. ROB. BRIDL. *Dial.* 33; naturam athomi, si potes, explica WALT. WIMB. *Carm.* 383. **b** quis ~et quomodo sciat [sapientia] .. seipsam? ANSELM (*Mon.* 64) I 75; quid tunc temporis contigerit .. veraciter ~abo ORD. VIT. III 3 p. 52; quot etiam expensarum dispendia sustinuerit nemo est qui facile possit ~are *Chr. Battle* f. 84v. **c 1301** plenam et expressam seu ~itam .. mencionem *Reg. Carl.* I 148; dicentes quod certitudo ~ita [et dubitacio] de eodem se non possunt compati in eodem OCKHAM *Pol.* III 57; est .. catholicus, licet de tali articulo non habeat firmam et ~itam fidem *Id. Dial.* 444; duplex est credulitas, sc. implicita et ~ita WYCL. *Ente* 77.

4 to make explicit, deploy, exercise.

potestas gladii materialis apud ecclesiam est implicita, sed per imperatorem qui eam recipit ~atur OCKHAM *Pol.* I 69.

5 (trans.) to complete, finish.

~o, i. .. finio *GlH* E 549; ~itis devotis orationibus nosmet ipsos sollicite commendavimus dignissimis apostolis BYRHT. *V. Ecgwini* 378; proposueram .. illam prius perficere istudque opus subsequenter ~are nedum uterque labor incumberet G. MON. VII 2; ~ito completorio J. FURNESS *Walth.* 65; ~ata missa, unusquisque .. capam .. bene plicatam .. revestiario ad archam deferat *Cust. Westm.* 60.

6 (intr. 3rd pers. pr. *explicit, expliciunt* < *explicitus* by analogy w. *incipit, incipiunt*) to end; *cf.* 1b *supra*: **a** (w. book or part of book as subj.); **b** (w. title as subj.); **c** (w. subject matter as subj.).

a ~it praefatio, incipiunt capitula BEDE *HE pref.* p. 8; ~iunt capitula, incipit ipse liber *Ib.* I *tit.*; explicit ad domnum specialis epistola patrem WULF. *Swith. pref.* 329; ~it prologus in vitam S. Dunstani OSB. *V. Dunst.* 71; hec [i. e. Liber II] quidem ~iunt H. HUNT. *HA* II *epil.* p. 66; ~iunt capitula librorum anachoritarum *AncrR* 4; ~it titulus secundus ELMH. *Cant.* 126. **b** ~it Vita S. Edwardi regis et confessoris AILR. *Ed. Conf.* 790B; ~iunt Sententie numero centum W. DAN. *Sent.* 100; hic ~iunt Exempla honeste vite GARL. *Hon. Vit. epil.*; ~it Summa magistri Johannis Hauboys HAUBOYS 448. **c** ~it modus et ordo lucerne de principalibus festis *Cust. Westm.* 280; **1269** ~it modus tenendi curias *CBaron* 91; ~it modus omnium cartarum *FormMan* 11; **1391** ~iunt salutaciones secundum usum Oxonie *FormOx* 411; **1470** explicit, expliciunt, qualia scripta ferunt *Reg. Whet.* I 420.

explicatio [CL]

1 unwinding, straightening.

tanquam subita virge circulate ~one GIR. *TH* II 42.

2 explication, explanation.

dictorum ~o BALSH. *AD rec.* 2 43; ad istius igitur difficultatis ~onem humiliter accedentes R. MARSTON *QD* 161; ~o legis nature DUNS *Ord.* I 70.

3 deployment, exercise.

1332 indulgencia .. per quam .. tue jurisdiccionis ~o .. valeat .. impediri *Lit. Cant.* I 515.

explicator [CL], explicator, expositor.

que si non secundum enuntiationem sufficienter distinximus inventori primo set non secundum locutionem convenienter ~ori primo indulgendum est BALSH. *AD rec.* 2 102; ~ores artis *Ib.* 115.

explicatrix [CL *as adj.*], explicator, expositor (f.).

cum artium ista sit inventrix novarum et abstrusissimarum fidelissima ~ix DEE *Monas* 185.

explicia v. explectum. **explicit** v. explicare 6.

explicite [cf. CL explicate, explicitus], explicitly, expressly.

ista dicit specialius et ~e que illa dixit generalius et involute KILWARDBY *OS* 490; secundum quod ponit rem suam circa subjectum in comparacione ad predicatum composicionis implicite; tunc .. est sensus ille 'qui solus est pater est pater': alium secundum quod ponit rem suam circa subjectum in comparacione ad predicatum composicionis ~e; et tunc est sensus 'pater est pater et nullus alius a patre est pater' MIDDLETON *Sent.* I 197a; ~e, sicut definicio exprimit; implicite, sicut definitum exprimit DUNS *Ord.* IV 178; OCKHAM *Pol.* III 46 (v. credere 6a); anime sue salutem implicite vel ~e invenire potest diligens investigator J. MIRFIELD *Flor.* 116; **1451** non propter hoc restituuntur .. nisi hoc eis beneficium ~e impendatur *Mon. Francisc.* II 100.

explicium v. explectum. **expliciunt** v. explicare 6.

explodere [CL]

1 to drive away (by clapping).

virgo .. / ingentem explodit sancta virtute colubrum ALDH. *VirgV* 2404; ~dit, excludit *atynið GlC* E 414; ~datur, i. expellatur, *sy ut aned* vel *awrecen sy GlH* E 723; BALD. CANT. 491C (v. exsibilare).

2 to remove, cast off. **b** (gram.) to elide.

versu / explosis penitus naevis et rusticitate ALDH. *Aen. prol.* 26; ~sa, i. . . evacuata, deleta *GlH* E 721; quod mater audiens et muliebriter stupens de equo quo sedit repente ~sa decidit R. COLD. *Godr.* 344. **b** si prior vocalis ~ditur, erit sinalipha ALDH. *Met.* 9; a poetis per sincopam vocalis U ~ditur *Id. PR* 125; ~sa, elisa *GlC* E 447; ~dita, i. elisa *GlH* E 724.

3 to burst, explode. **b** to destroy, abolish. **c** to show up (pretence), expose (vice), 'explode' (opinion).

ne balena vorax valvas explodat Olimpi ALDH. *VirgV* 2535; ~sa, i. . . fracta *GlH* E 721; cute pluribus subito locis quasi ~sa T. MON. *Will.* VI 14; scis qua vi fulminis ignis exploditur WALT. WIMB. *Carm.* 388. **b** ~si, extincti *GlC* E 363; execrabilia . . lolia . . negligenter respersa fundotenus ~dant B. *V. Dunst.* 1; decreti chirographo . . renuit et vim ejus omnem et auctoritatem ~sit H. BOS. *Thom.* III 29. **c** Dominus . . factiosam farisaicae temptationis calumniam . . ~dit ALDH. *VirgP* 18; **1168** [Stoicorum] opinio ~sa est fidelissima ratione et virtute rectius philosophantium J. SAL. *Ep.* 235 (276 p. 584); sic capellani illius comperta est cupiditas et ~sa GIR. *GE* I 48 p. 128; TURNER *Av.* 16 (v. aurivittis).

4 (p. ppl.) stricken.

cumque jaceret ~sa [mulier a daemone vexata] et jamjamque videretur moritura BEDE *CuthbP* 15; decubuit exanimis et ~sa R. COLD. *Cuthb.* 119 p. 265; *Id. Godr.* 353 (v. epilepsia).

explorare [CL]

1 to explore, reconnoitre (place). **b** to seek out, find (person). **c** to spy on, keep an eye on (person or activity); **d** (absol. & intr.) to explore, spy.

explorat callem quo tendere tanta / turba velit WULF. *Swith.* II 744; locum belli singulis ~at noctibus MAP *NC* IV 15 f. 57v.; circuit [demon] tanquam hostis obsidens, muros clausos ~ans BART. ANGL. II 19; mittit Josue duos ut ~ent urbem Jericho [cf. *Josh.* vi 25] AD. DORE *Pictor* 158. **b** ~at, i. . . petit *GlH* E 717; **1210** sex galiis euntibus . . ad explorand' piratas *Praest.* 179; **1258** ipsos cum omnibus catallis et rebus suis quos ~are poteritis sine dilacione arrestetis *Cl* 318; regem Hymbar undique ~abant. ipso invento irruunt in eum *Eul. Hist.* II 221. **c** **s1016** rex Edmundus in Westsexam proficiscens Cnutonis progressum graviter ~avit M. PAR. *Maj.* I 497; **1258** curialiter et caute ~ari faciat quod magnam pecuniam secum non abducat *Cl* 331; **1266** et in expensis nunciorum ~ancium regem Norwegie per tres vices *ExchScot* 5. **d** ~at, absultat *GlC* E 384; **1340** cuidam exploratori misso usque partes Francie . . ad ~andum ibidem de gestis regis Francie (*AcWardr*) *TRBk* 203 p. 216; **1488** receptor fuit attendans et ~ans super predictum Thomam Lovell (*Ac. T. Lovell*) *Rutland MSS* f. 6.

2 (mon.) to go round as inspector.

tertius et quartus prior, nisi esset ~andi gratia, . . exierunt ac revertebantur *Cust. Westm.* 18 (= *Cust. Cant.* 82); *Obed. Abingd.* 365 (v. exploratio 2).

3 to investigate, inquire into. **b** to discover; **c** (w. acc. & inf.); **d** (w. indir. qu.).

sunt innumerabilia quae, si quis ad ~anda pennis volare posset, . . ficta probaret *Lib. Monstr. prol.*; ut diligentius ~ata scripturae veritas docet (*Ep. Ceolfridi*) BEDE *HE* V 21 p. 335; mentem . . ~are deposco B. *V. Dunst.* 1; **1169** [rex] ~averat vires nostras J. SAL. *Ep.* 286 (286); inquire totum et ~a [ME: *trudde*] tua peccata *AncrR* 132; **1340** cursori domini ducis . . misso usque Erewell' . . ~ando rumores de transitu regis et de inimicis suis *KRAc* 389/6 m. 1. **b** **c798** poteris . . juxta eandem regulam octogenarii ~are diminutionem ALCUIN *Ep.* 133; ~ata conjecturacione hostium . . sopivit illud propositum *G. Hen. V* 6 p. 40. **c** presbyterum quem ~averat porcis abundare GIR. *GE* II 34 p. 330; **s1304** ~atum est in nive vestigia equorum accessisse ad stabulum FORDUN *Cont.* XII 6. **d** quid eum . . vocaret / explorat WULF. *Swith.* I 1169; Aeneas fecit quondam magum mulierem ~are quid haberet in ventre, masculum aut feminam *AS Chr. pref.*; utrum vere amici sint interveniens paupertas ~at AILR. *Spir. Amicit.* III 63. 687; ~antes quando ultimum exalarem spiritum ALEX. CANT. *Mir.* 52 p. 266; **1166** ut . . accedas ad ipsum ~aturus quatenus apud ipsum possis proficere J. SAL. *Ep.* 228 (182); si quis diligenter inquisierit omnes angulos sui cordis nec amplius scit ~are [ME: *rungi mare ut*] si quid lateat *AncrR* 120.

4 to test, prove.

~at, i. . . exprobat *GlH* E 717; **c1168** illos quorum michi fides in Domino fuerat ~ata J. SAL. *Ep.* 251 (246); nunc palis in viscera terre missis soliditas fundamenti ~atur NECKAM *NR* II 172.

exploratio [CL]

1 exploration, reconnoitring, scouting, spying.

xl . . diebus . . fit ~o [cf. *Num.* xiv 33], . . ut qui xl dierum scrutationi non crediderint, xl annis in deserto deputabuntur errori R. NIGER *Mil.* II 43; ipsorum adventus ~one certissima prescius GIR. *EH* II 2; **c1441** conventus fuit coram rege . . super felonia et ~one ac revelacione consilii regis *Pri. Cold.* 249.

2 (mon.) inspection.

prior faciet ~onem et ostia loquutoriorum obserabit . . . prior primo scrutinium ad locutorium hospitum . . ostia obserabit . . . postmodum explorabit ubi noverit esse presentiam hospitum *Obed. Abingd.* 364–5; prior . . potest illud ~onis officium inferiori injungere *Cust. Cant.* 83.

3 inspection, examination.

hec . . non sacrificia erant, sed ad victimarum pertinebant ~onem. si . . non stuperent, apte videbantur ALB. LOND. *DG* 6. 31.

explorator [CL]

1 scout, observer. **b** spy.

c793 resticulum, qui ~ores Jesu Nave de peritura Hierico [cf. *Josh.* ii 15] salvavit ALCUIN *Ep.* 23 p. 61; exploratores silvarum densa peragrant, / predonesque locis investigantur opacis WULF. *Swith.* II 457; ~oribus missis ad lustrandum repromissionis terram *Eccl. & Synag.* 57; duos . . servientes suos fideles constituit speculatores et ~ores . . ne Dani supervenirent H. ALBUS 80; sollicite igitur caveat ~or a falso et provideat ut bene lustret exploranda, quatinus vera referat R. NIGER *Mil.* II 43; GIR. *EH* II 36 (v. dux 1a); significavit duci ~orum assercio quod hostilis exercitus . . in vicina distancia se prepararent ad prelium *Ps.*-ELMH. *Hen. V* 114. **b** sacerdos, qui rerum tam evidens contemplator exstiterat, exitum earum stupidus simul et tacitus ~or observabat OSB. *V. Dunst.* 42; pius . . ~or, aspice per fenestras J. FORD *Serm.* 6. 9; **c1173** diligentem de domesticis nostris ~orem direxi, et audita per eum status melioratione manifesta gavisus sum J. SAL. *Ep.* 322 (310 p. 758); ~ores, i. *espies GlSid* f. 145; **1263** quidam malivoli vestri sanguinem nostrum sitiunt, qui nos †explegitorem [MS: expl.... /orem; ? l. exploratorem] reputant, dicentes quod nichil fit in marchia quod vobis non revelamus (*AncC* III 79) *Foed.* I 755; **1313** postea . . idem R. misit quemdam Johannem Ysoude notorium ~orem suum in felonia facienda de societate sua ut quereret opportunitatem quando idem R. eundem constabularium posset interficere *Eyre Kent* I 98; W. GUISB. 199 (v. exploratrix 1); hic ~or, *a spyer WW*.

2 (mon.) inspector, third or fourth prior charged w. going the rounds.

priori, subpriori, tertio priori, ~ori ob reverentiam ordinis, si scrutinium fecerint, deferendum est signo vel verbo eis *Obed. Abingd.* 361; ~ori incumbit explorationem facere quoties viderit expedire . . et quoties expedit, explorabit ante priores, post priores, in circuitu chori, in loquutorio, in infirmatorio, in refectorio, in promptuario *Ib.* 368; quacunque hora existimaverint ~ores claustri quicquam inordinacionis alicubi reperire *Cust. Westm.* 18 (= *Cust. Cant.* 82); de tercio et quarto priore, sive de ~oribus claustri *Ib.* 25 *rub.* (= *Ib.* 87 *rub.*); habeant ~ores defectuum medietatem pecunie sic amisse *Stat. Wells* 64.

3 inspector, examiner.

1242 ~ori vinorum venientium ad portum de Sandwic' per totum predictum tempus, xxx s. *Pipe* 139.

exploratrix [LL]

1 spy (f.).

1209 Alais de Xanton' ~ici eunti in patriam suam, j m. per regem *Misae* 141; **1213** Aelosie ~ici eunti in patriam suam, de dono j m. per regem *Ib.* 243; **s1265** nunciatum est . . per exploratorem suum Margoth que cum mulier esset in veste tamen virili velud homo gradiebatur. . . accepto nuncio, . . pervenit ad locum quem preordinaverat ~ix ipsa W. GUISB. 199.

2 observer, investigator (f.).

matrona cujus curae aegrotans est creditus, cum usque ad transcensum pinnae indefessa ~ix cuncta prospiceret, coelesti prodigio fidele testimonium perhibuit ADEL. BLANDIN. *Dunst.* 2.

explumare [cf. CL plumare], to strip of feathers, pluck.

ADEL. *CA* 12 (v. aculeus 1a).

expoeditio v. expeditio. **expol-** v. et. exspol-.

expolire [CL]

1 to polish; **b** (fig.). **c** (p. ppl.) smooth, flat. **d** (fig.) worn down.

e[x]politum, ornatum *GlC* E 418; **9**. . ~ietur, *sie areaht WW*; sub ~ita . . materia, ornata, culta *to asworfenum oran GlP* 227; expollio, A. *to pulshe, or furby WW*. **b** **c790** eo magis vestrae indigent [libelli] defensionis quo minus ab auctore proprio ~iti sunt ALCUIN *Ep.* 120; ut . . humanam naturam vetustate ~iens innovaris *Nunnam.* f. 21v.; eloquium . . schematis hujus lima . . ~itum GIR. *DK* I 12. **c** exclusos . . quam . . ~itissima planicies . . indefensos patencius exponebat *Ps.*-ELMH. *Hen. V* 59 p. 151. **d** quid . . facerent Cantuarienses monachi tot tunsionibus et pressuris ~iti GERV. CANT. *Chr.* 404.

2 to improve, finish, perfect.

1173 ad ~ienda suscepte cause merita, que per se patent, mens inops et victa lingua succumbat J. SAL. *Ep.* 311 (313); domus insignitur, / insignis interius foris expolitur, / expolita domine sue custoditur GARL. *Epith.* V *Summa* 30–1.

expompare [LL]

1 to deprive of pomp or splendour.

mors imis supera facit equalia; / elata pompulis expompat omnia WALT. WIMB. *Carm.* 377; expompat Attropos omne pompaticum *Id. Sim.* 138; mors pomposos expompare / mors magnorum incurvare / non veretur vertices *Id. Van.* 140.

2 to flaunt, vaunt.

qui propter popularis aure flatum universa eventilet, et aulico fastu ~et [v. l. exponet] H. BOS. *Thom.* III 2; omni se specie vanitatis ~avit *Ib.* 37 p. 306.

exponere [CL]

1 to put out, bring or carry forth. **b** to set or throw down. **c** to put ashore. **d** to put down, lay out (path).

~sito, . . *geborone GlC* E 390; ut navis, oneribus ~sitis, liberius potuisset . . excurrere R. COLD. *Cuthb.* 75 p. 155; naute . . quam intus habebant scapham ~nunt T. MON. *Will.* VII 17. **b** spolia colliguntur ~sita BEDE *HE* I 20; ~sito, jectato *GlC* E 370; miles . ., aliis progredientibus et suppellectilis varie onera exportantibus, licet equum amiserit, lapidem tamen . . secum sustulit et . . in terra ~suit R. COLD. *Cuthb.* 75 p. 156. **c** exponuntque illam trans aequora, calleque recto / fertur ad Anglorum mulier quasi mortua gentem WULF. *Swith.* II 874. **d** **1565** cum . . ordinatum fuit de ~nendis Anglice *warples* in communibus campis de Wimbledon . . in hac forma . . ordinatum est . . ut jam aut posthac erint ~nenda per homagium hujus curie *CourtR Wimbledon* 128.

2 to set in place. **b** to set out, relate.

a1219 Hug' Gagat' Sibillaque uxor ejus hec timpanna fecerunt ecponi (*Inscr.*) *VCH Bucks* II 116; qui [rex David] concito ad bellum similiter se †exponentes [MSS: exponens] gentes suas in tribus turmis bellicis divisit *Plusc.* IX 40 p. 294. **b** **c700** (11c) post hanc donationis cartulam quam supra ~suimus (*Ch.*) GOSC. *Milb.* 202; sicut superius ~situm est *Hist. Abb. Jarrow* 18.

3 to reveal, expose, disclose.

num adeo . . Dominus . . servis infimis . . se totum ~suit ut . . que sunt . . statim pateant GIR. *TH* I 13; **1167** manifeste ei suspicionis causas ~nere J. SAL. *Ep.* 222 (223 p. 386).

4 to lay open or unprotected; **b** (to the elements); **c** (to physical or moral danger); **d** (w. *in eventum*).

leones . . virum [sc. Danielem] ~situm videbant DOMINIC *V. Ecgwini prol.*; **1168** ~situs tanquam signum ad sagittam J. SAL. *Ep.* 281 (250). **b** ventis . . et mari navis eminus ~nitur T. MON. *Will.* VII 17; GIR. *TH* I 6 (v. defensio 1a); GERV. TILB. II 96 (v. deplumare a); [in exercicio] ~nit se homo bono aeri J. MIRFIELD *Flor.* 140; vento amicabiliter flante, ~suit vela ventis *G. Hen. V* 3 p. 20. **c** innumera cadaverum millia feris avibusque . . ~sita OSB. BAWDSEY clxxxi; **1168** si persecutoribus ecclesie clerum voluisset ~nere J. SAL. *Ep.* 265 (261); ne lupi infernalis de hyatibus rapiendas eas ~nat J. FURNESS *Kentig.* 30 p. 214; ob auram inanis glorie supremis sese periculis ~nunt NECKAM *NR* II 175; proprias . . uxores aliquando prostituunt et ~nunt luxurie [ME: *puttyn hem to foly*] *Itin. Mand.* 76. **d** quod . . se et suos ~neret in eventum *Ps.*-ELMH. *Hen. V* 22.

5 to offer, make available; **b** (w. abstr. obj.). **c** (w. inf.) to dispose (to).

adolescentulus . . cunctis parentum ~sitis rebus . . abegit *V. Neot. A* 1; **1164** et mihi et meis domum et terram comitis pro vestra reverentia ~nentes J. SAL. *Ep.* 134 (136 p. 2); de acervo auri . . quem ~nit ei [Helyseo] Naaman [cf. *2 Kings* v] AD. DORE *Pictor* 155; **1242** quod . . falcones nostros beneplacitis . . fratris nostri, cum voluerit, ~nat (*Pat*) *RGasc* I 71; **1243** rogamus quatinus homines vestros . . ad . . solvendum nobis focagium ~natis nobis *Cl* 60. **b** **1167** licet pro Verbo Dei quod in carne suscepta se . . morti exposuit, ~nere . . animas nostras J. SAL. *Ep.* 225 (225); [musica] nubilos vultus serenat, supercilium ponit, austeritatem reponit, jocunditatem ~nit GIR. *TH* III 12. **c** **1235** omnibus eidem [imperatori] placere sumus ~siti *TreatyR* I 14; **1236** parati et ~siti . . in hiis et aliis inherere consiliis *Ib.* 30.

6 to lay out, put up, expose (for sale); **b** (pledge).

a1104 libros et vestimenta et alia ornamenta ecclesiae . . tu pro voluntate tua ~nis et ea extraneis das ANSELM (*Ep.* 278) IV 192; ludicra sicut anulos, monilia, etc. . . nec semper ~nuntur emptoribus ne deturpentur pluvia et vento *GlSid* f. 144; **1293** equos . . vendicioni ~suimus et de necessitate expendidimus *Reg. Cant.* 1284; **1439** nullus . . vendicioni ~nat seu emat . . aliquam merceriam *Cl* 289 m. 6d.; **1552** nulla venalia durante sacro ~nantur *Conc. Scot.* II 132. **b** **1324** magister J. B. ~suit caucionem pro aula Leonum *Cart. Osney* III 163; **1336** illud [pignus] in usus similes . . convertatur donec venerint qui pignora ~suerunt *StatOx* 135; **1435** omnes cauciones et vadia ~ni vendicioni *MunAcOx* II 511.

7 to lay out, spend. **b** to use (skill). **c** (p. ppl. as sb. n. pl.) expenses.

s1237 rex .. sine thesauro est. .. multa enim ~suit in expensis sororis sue imperatricis *Flor. Hist.* II 220; **s1251** plus quam x^m m. ~suerat OXNEAD *Chr.* 186; **1443** (v. 2 ducatus); **1542** pecuniam que ob necessitatem .. est ~nenda *Deeds Balliol* 323. **b 1383** Dedrico carpentario pro opere et artificio suo ~nendo ad perfectam consummacionem magne machine *ExchScot* 665. **c 1369** pro quibusdam ~sitis ad reparacionem .. castri *ExchScot* 347.

8 to express, put into words. *V. et. extraponere* 2.

profuit iste viro nimium .. / .. / exponens longos animi ferventis agones FRITH. 159; **9**.. edissere, i. ~nere, *asecgan WW*; anxius suspirando ingemescens, altosque cordis anfractus vocibus ~nens R. COLD. *Cuthb.* 75 p. 156; **s1189** Deo et vobis gratias uberes ~no DICETO *YH* II 61.

9 to expound, explain; **b** (w. acc. & inf.); **c** (w. indir. qu.); **d** (absol.) to preach. **e** to identify (as). **f** (pr. ppl.) expounder. **g** (p. ppl. as sb. n.) exposition.

precor hoc lucidius ~ni ALDH. *Met.* 10 p. 84; evangelii verba ~nens *V. Cuthb.* II 6; beatum Job ~nendo *V. Greg.* p. 103; paulo post subjecit ~nens "ex corde exeunt cogitationes malae" [*Matth.* xv 19] BEDE *HE* I 27 p. 57; **793** regula S. Benedicti legatur .. et propria ~natur lingua ALCUIN *Ep.* 19; pacem .. apostolus ~nebat dicens 'ipse est pax nostra' [*Eph.* ii 14] B. *V. Dunst.* 30; hoc est quod ~nere voluimus ROB. ANGL. *Alg.* 88; BACON XV 77, 115 (v. exponibilis); Joseph antiquitus exponens sompnium WALT. WIMB. *Carm.* 253; **1431** primitus textum .. legant: deinde ipsum .. plene et aperte ~nant *StatOx* 236. **b** *Meaux* III 276 (v. dirationare 3). **c** cum ~nerent per ordinem quomodo haec .. didicissent BEDE *HE* IV 21 p. 258; qualiter .. terra .. ex parte fuerit ecclesie .. data .. ex ordine ~suerunt *Chr. Battle* f. 86; **s490** ~suit ei .. quomodo prodiderant eos Saxones M. PAR. *Maj.* I 222. **d 1433** quod in precibus inibi missarum tempore populo ~nendi eis sim nominatim specialiter recommissus *Reg. Cant.* II 486. **e** stacten quidam ~nunt mirram, quidam ammoniacum *SB* 41; G[alen] in epistolis ad Glauconem ~nit lapis pirites, i. milvaris *Alph.* 90. **f** eundem sensum quem habuit revelans habuerunt et ~nentes, quare exponentes verba divine scripture ad primum intellectum ipsorum pervenerunt OCKHAM *Dial.* 836. **g** per illam noticiam predicacionis triplicis .. ut .. loquendum est in ~sito triplici supradicto WYCL. *Conf.* 508.

10 (log.) exponent.

quando ergo [reduplicative proposiciones] sunt causales, tunc dicuntur habere iiij ~nentes, ut ista: 'ex hoc quod tu es homo, tu es animal' dicitur debere sic exponi: 'tu es homo' et 'tu es animal' et 'omnis homo est animal' et 'si aliquid est homo, ipsum est animal' WYCL. *Log.* II 96.

11 ? *f. l.*

1263 quod terram suam excolere, blada et fena colligere, et pacifice intrare possint et de aliis rebus suis exponere [? l. disponere] *Cl* 244; **1453** usurarius est .. excommunicandus, quousque illicitum exinde contractum in statum pristinum juris exposuerit [? l. reposuerit] *Conc.* III 566.

exponibilis [cf. exponere 10], (gram. & log.) exponible.

ipsum inpersonale non exigit actum in quantum sic [prout absolutum] ~e est; si autem exponatur prout transitivum est .. BACON XV 77; necesse est quod habeat aliquid ~e per appositum et aliquid ~e per suppositum. ille .. ablativus qui exponitur per suppositum in subjectum potest indifferenter esse nomen et prenomen *Ib.* 115; *GLA* III 228 (v. consequentia 3); termini ~es sunt omnes dicciones exclusive: ut tantum, solum [etc.] WYCL. *Log.* I 6.

expons- v. spons-.

expontifex [cf. CL pontifex], ex-pope.

ut, nisi servierit, aut ~icem aut exromanum esse necesse sit J. SAL. *Pol.* 814B.

exporrigere [CL], to stretch out.

exertum, i. .. exporrectum *GlH* E 457; exporrecto, protenso *Ib.* 716.

exportare [CL]

1 to carry out or away, snatch (person, animal, or body). **b** to take away (artefact). **c** to remove (abstr.).

noctibus multotiens cognatorum timore meorum a Gaulterio avunculo meo de camera .. furtim ~atus sum ORD. VIT. VII 15 p. 229; **1143** ut .. corpora excommunicatorum in cimiteriis sepulta inde ~entur *Conc. Syn.* 803; malevoli .. salmones furtive ~abant R. COLD. *Godr.* 217; **1327** pastor sollicitus ovem deviantem, luporum morsubus ~ans, reducit ad gregem *Lit. Cant.* I 242; **s98** cadaver populari sandapila per vispiliones ~atum atque ignominiose pollutum est M. PAR. *Maj.* I 117. **b** cum .. naviculam .. nostram ab undis ~aremus BEDE *HE* V 1; inundatio .. pontes omnes .. confractos ~averit R. COLD. *Godr.* 97; *Id. Cuthb.* 75 p. 156 (v. exponere 1b); **1540** (v. contabulare). **c** dolor tamen omnis .. velut ipso episcopo foras eum ~ante, funditus ablatus est BEDE *HE* V 3.

2 to export.

1428 de xj l. xvj s. viij d. de custuma panni lanei empti infra dictum burgum et ~ati de regno *ExchScot* 451.

3 (w. abl.) to clear, empty, rid (of).

laborabant ut non modo sentina sed et irruentibus undis puppim certatim ~arent CIREN. I 376 (= SAMSON *Mir. Edm.* I 11: ut irruentes undas certatim ejicerent).

exportator [cf. LL portator], bearer.

equum meum, tui lapidis ~orem onerarium R. COLD. *Cuthb.* 75 p. 156.

exposcere [CL], to ask for, demand; **b** (w. acc. & inf.). **c** to ask, entreat (a person). **d** (w. abstr. subj.) to need, require.

a1075 cum Lanfrancus scriptam .. professionem .. ~eret LANFR. *Ep.* (3); salutem corporis ~imus aut mentis PULL. *CM* 217; osculum .. dulcissimum ~it ROLLE *IA* 218. **b** ÆLNOTH *Cnut* 32 (v. 1 ducatus 1a); cum .. eum a professione .. absolvi specialiter ~erent *Chr. Battle* f. 117v. **c 706** vos .. subnixa ~o prece nequaquam hujus perturbationis strofa scandalizari ALDH. *Ep.* 9 (12). **d** in .. observatione omnium que ordo ~it *Simil. Anselmi* 79; **1166** ut tempus ~et J. SAL. *Ep.* 168 (167); **1330** si pertinacia eorum hoc ~erit *Lit. Cant.* I 332; **1363** quociens opus fuerit et causa racionabilis hoc ~erit *Ib.* II 439; **1427** quod consuetudo illius loci ~it *Reg. Cant.* II 357.

expositio [CL]

1 bringing out, exposition (of Host).

s1091 nisi feria fuerit ~onis in hebdomeda Pasc', Pentec', et Natalis Domini quando omnes de conventu circulariter percipiunt ad cappam dies suos *Croyl.* 105; **c1400** propter solempnitatem ~onis *Stat. Linc.* I 388.

2 exposure (to danger), risk (to life).

s1229 quod .. cum illo immutabiliter starent usque ad capitum ~ones M. PAR. *Min.* II 306; **s1251** miles strenuus, valens pro ipso contra omnes stare usque capitis ~onem *Id. Maj.* V 214.

3 putting up, exposure (of pledge for sale).

a1380 nullius caucionis .. publice vendicioni exposite .. vendicionem .. ultra tres septimanas, a tempore ~onis .. connumerandas, impedient *StatOx* 184.

4 exposition, exegesis, explanation; **b** (as title of book).

in aliorum catholicorum dictis plenam .. ~onem THEOD. *Pen. epil.*; de aedificatione templi allegoricae ~onis .. libros ij BEDE *HE* V 24 p. 358; **c793** Augustinus in ~one psalmorum ALCUIN *Ep.* 23 p. 63; [lectiones] de ~one psalmi 'Exaudi, Deus' (*Psalm* lxiii) LANFR. *Const.* 105; Jeronimus in ~one catholice fidei J. CORNW. *Eul.* 14; 'nova cudere', id est novas ~ones facere, dumtaxat ad edificationem sit S. LANGTON *Gl. Hist. Schol.* 39; ista ~o — quod opinio in se non videtur dicere — quod illa una racio in se formaliter veritas et bonitas DUNS *Ord.* IV 251. **b 1439** ~o super artem medicine. ~o super aphorismos Hippocratis *MunAcOx* 761; **p1440** ~o super Apocalipsim (*Catal. Librorum*) *JRL Bull.* XVI 469; **1451** ~o aphorismorum in conclusionibus secundum Jacobum Fortunensem *MunAcOx* 614.

expositiuncula [LL], short exposition.

ALCUIN *Ep.* 243 (v. enchiridion a); ~am summariam .. scripture illius 'nova lux Judeis visa est' AD. MARSH *Ep.* 244 p. 408.

expositive, expositively, by way of exposition.

uno modo si ~e teneatur. Bernardus: 'quicquid occurit morbis, quicquid conciliat sanitatem'. ~e tenetur, sic enim occuritur morbus GERV. MELKLEY *AV* 39; comparant .. vitam nostram 'vestigio nubis' .. et sic legitur et tenetur ~e HOLCOT *Wisd.* 62.

expositor [CL]

1 issuer, utterer.

1428 [*a common utterer*] ~or [*of such false money*] *Rec. Norw.* I 303.

2 expositor, exegete, interpreter.

sacrae ~ores scripturae BEDE *TR* 1; ~or, commentator, *dihtere* ÆLF. *Gl.*; **c1080** omnes hujus sententiae ~ores concorditer asseverant LANFR. *Ep.* 33 (49 p. 156); S. LANGTON *Ruth* 106 (v. 2 dispensare 2a); **s1327** falsos suarum litterarum ~ores BAKER f. 107b; **1459** j ~or super metaphisicam *Cant. Coll. Ox.* I 14.

expositorie, expositorily, by way of exposition. **b** (log.) w. expository syllogism.

sic ~e prosequitur Augustinus WYCL. *Ver.* I 171. **b** sequitur enim ~e: ista essencia erit ignis; et ista eadem essencia erit aqua; ergo ignis erit aqua WYCL. *Form.* 182; videtur taliter ~e esse arguendum: hoc ille terminus significat, et hoc est melius Deo, ergo melius Deo iste terminus significat *Id. Trial.* 46; de forma ~e arguendi *Id. Ver.* II 98.

expositorius

1 expository, explanatory. **b** (log. w. *syllogismus*) expository syllogism.

ecce Sybilla, famosissima prophetissa inter gentiles cujus fama nec philosophos latuit, nec poetas, que in libro suo ~io visionis seu somnii .. subjungit de quarto [sc. sole] BRADW. *CD* 34B; sicut patet .. quoad sensum ~ium et alias formas ac opposita predicata WYCL. *Ver.* I 21. **b** de syllogismo ~io affirmativo dico quod in qualibet trium figurarum potest fieri bonus .. 'Socrates est musicus; album est Socrates; igitur album est musicum' (DUNS) *GLA* III 231; ut patet per syllogismum ~ium sic: hoc intelligibile est aurum, hoc idem intelligibile est lapis; igitur lapis est aurum W. ALNWICK *QD* 29; nonne iste sillogismus est ~ius demonstrato predicato? in hac 'homo est animal' hoc predicatum predicatur; hoc predicatum est conceptus; igitur conceptus predicatur? LUTTERELL *Occam* 36; omnia ista probantur per syllogismum ~ium qui perficitur reducendo ipsum in quarto modo prime figure, sicud prius per oppositum conclusionis cum altera premissarum concludendo oppositum alterius premisse *Ps.-*OCKHAM *Princ. Theol.* 64; primo peraloysmo [v. l. peralogismo] quem vocant sylloysmum ~ium WYCL. *Conf.* 506.

2 (as sb. n.) exposition, commentary.

1245 ~ium evangeliorum quorundam in quibusquam festivitatibus, bonum et novum, de grossa littera *Invent. S. Paul.* 497; **p1440** ~ium super eodem [sc. textu philosophie] (*Catal. Librorum*) *JRL Bull.* XVI 479.

expositrix, expositor (f.).

a constirrere, expositor, ~ix, constructor *CathA*.

expost [CL; al. div.], thereafter, afterwards.

eodem anno institutus est cancellarius Anglie. et infra triennium ~t ter adiit regem Francie *Hist. Durh.* 1; ~t regulatus est populus ducatu sacerdotum tribus Levitice WYCL. *Ver.* III 258; proximo sequuntur ascendentes cum continuacione veri motus solis, exinde altitudo meridiana .. et ~t, figure eclipsium depinguntur ELVEDEN *Cal.* 5; **s1385** WALS. *HA* II 121 (v. detentio 2); **a1400** (v. dehonestare 1c); **1470** infra mensem seu sex septimanas immediate ~t sequentes *Pri. Cold.* 218.

expostulare [CL], to demand, ask for; **b** (w. *ut*). **c** (w. abstr. subj.) to require.

Judaei quondam ~abant signum sibi de coelo ALCUIN (*Adv. Felicem* I 20) *Dogm.* 144C; fidelitatem .. offero et .. amicitiam ~o ANSELM (*Ep.* 4) III 105. **b 1102** ut preces nostras dignetur non spernere .. ~o (*Ib.* 280) IV 195; ~o a te, domine Petre, ut non solum scripturas .. contra me inducas P. CORNW. *Disp.* 156. **c 1105** rei necessitas nostram .. precem ad vestram pietatem ~at ANSELM (*Ep.* 340) V 278; **1285** prout seysona ~at *Cust. Suss.* (*Terring*) II 25; **1411** omnes .. campi jacebunt pro warecta prout seisona anni ~averit (*Indent.*) *EHR* XXXVII 410.

expraessi v. exprimere.

exprecari [cf. CL precari], to complete one's prayer.

juxta vestibulum ejusdem ecclesie .. est una latrina summo altari ejusdem ecclesie contigua, nociva valde, in tantum quod tempore estivali vix potest aliquis in choro ~ari propter fetoris abhominacionem ejusdem latrine (*Vis.*) *Fabr. York* 247; propter incursus aquarum et campanilis commocionem, vix audent parochiani .. ad audiendum divina inibi ~ari *Ib.*

expremere v. exprimere.

expressare [cf. expressus *p. ppl. of* exprimere], to mention expressly, to state explicitly. *V. et. exprimere* 5.

1254 ut hec omnia legitime compleant, teneant, et exequantur quemadmodum superius ~antur (*Pat*) *RGasc* I 348; **1317** juxta imposicionem et taxacionem superius ~atas *Reg. Carl.* II 150; **1376** per processum hujusmodi superius ~atum plenius continetur *G.S. Alb.* III 206; **s1379** post ~ata negotia sua WALS. *HA* I 416; **1380** in expensis factis .. ut patet per parcellas in papiro bursarii ~atas iiij li. xvij s. x d. *Ac. Durh.* 589; quamvis non dicatur in symbolo, tamen ~atur in symbolo NETTER *DAF* II 253v. 2; **1438** ex certis tunc nobis ~atis causis BEKYNTON I 201; **1558** prout supra ~atur *Scot. Grey Friars* II 111.

expresse [CL]

1 audibly, distinctly. **b** clearly.

Titus iste interpres apostoli erat, et horum lingua ~ius loquebatur quam apostolus LANFR. *Comment. Paul.* 222A; et quicquid in ore meo est ~e intus ducendo ADEL. *QN* 21. **b** [vacca] pedes ~e cum pilositate et colore cervinos habens GIR. *TH* II 22.

2 explicitly, precisely. *V. et. expressim* 2, *exprimere* 7d.

tanto veriora quanto magis rebus quarum sunt verba similia sunt et eas ~ius signant ANSELM (*Mon.* 10) I 25; non per antifrasim, set ~e GIR. *SD* 6; hoc tamen non ~e dicit Aristoteles KILWARDBY *OS* 508; **1299** ut de suis bladis .. in autumpno jam instanti ~e non deciment, sed .. decimas ipsas a novem partibus non separatas nec ~e distinctas penes se .. retineant *Reg. Cant.* 353; nisi illud ~e [ME: *utterliche*] in confessione dixisset quod in puericia

fecerat *AncrR* 120; verba Innocentii III que contra predicta videntur ~issime militare OCKHAM *Pol.* I 39; *Ib.* 328 (v. contradicere 1d); **1452** dixit exspresse, fatebatur, et recognovit *Reg. Armagh* 228.

expressim [CL]

1 expressly, for express purpose.

nisi forte quod precipitur ~im saluti rei publice inveniatur adversum J. SAL. *Pol.* 605C.

2 explicitly, precisely. *V. et. expresse* 2, *exprimere* 7d.

1168 ~im cavisse publice potestati in id quod salva caritate non potest observari J. SAL. *Ep.* 269 (282); **1285** obligamus et ypotecamus ~im .. omnia bona nostra *RGasc* II 245; H. Bos. *Thom.* V 9 (v. cervicosus); **1317** monasteriorum dignitatibus ac beneficiis subscriptis ~im exceptis *Reg. Carl.* II 158.

expressio [CL]

1 expressing, forcing or sending out. **b** expressed substance.

acinacium, -cii, i. cosse uvarum que post ~onem proiciuntur OSB. GLOUC. *Deriv.* 15; ALF. ANGL. *Cor* 16 (v. eventare a); Verbum sive Filius procedit a Patre per .. excussionem sive expulsionem aut ~onem producti DUNS *Ord.* II 290; Spiritus Sanctus .. habet esse a producentibus ipsum .. per quandam ~onem producti *Ib.*; **c1521** in coquina: .. pelvis eneus cum foraminibus ad ~onem liquorum *Cant. Coll. Ox.* I 64. **b** qui granum frumenti et ~onem botri transformat in corpus suum et sanguinem *Found. Waltham* 11.

2 uttering. **b** utterance.

meditatio .. variis vocum ~onibus demonstratur; ~ones autem hujusmodi non solum ea complectuntur PULL. *Sent.* 682B. **b** certi suarum petitionum articuli, sub ea que fieri poterit ~onis luculentia AD. MARSH *Ep.* 16 p. 100.

3 stating expressly, explicit mention. **b** formula.

1167 si liceret, .. libenter exponerem; sed sine singulorum ~one certum sit hoc pactionibus esse insertum J. SAL. *Ep.* 213 (198); hi suaserunt clam regi ut mox facta obligatione regiarum consuetudinum faceret ~onem H. Bos. *Thom.* III 26; **s1213** petii a domino legato ut cogeret eum ad restitutionem .. bonorum ecclesie .. et expressi que illa erant, et restituit .. secundum ~onem meam clavem sigilli ecclesie et sigillum proprium *Chr. Evesham* 251; **1258** libertates suas, que diu extiterunt in demanda ad scaccarium regis et que propter minorem ~onem adhuc tenentur in suspenso *Cl* 204; vocativus .. bene potest [proferri] sine actuali ~one [persone et numeri] BACON XV 110; post ~onem nominum Apostolorum, sequitur immediate 'hos duodecim misit etc.' OCKHAM *Pol.* II 752; de confessione, que est sola nuda ~o peccatorum CONWAY *Def. Mend.* 1413 (*recte* 1313). **b** **1166** illa ~o, qua sibi et heredibus suis contra omnes mortales caveri vult J. SAL. *Ep.* 214 (177 p. 182); **1330** sub quacumque forma vel ~one verborum (*Lit. Papae*) *Lit. Cant.* I 329.

4 vivid expression, emphasis; **b** (rhet.).

mentis oculus interior .. qualitatem vestium ~one manifestissima contemplatus est AILR. *Ed. Conf.* 768A. **b** in hoc .. verbo tanta ~one probato AD. SCOT *OP* 484B; VINSAUF *AV* II 2. 34 (v. emphasis a).

expressivus

1 that forces or presses out. **b** (as sb.) substance that forces out.

Quaest. Salern. B 170 (v. destillare 1); frigidum humidi ~um, quod et vehementissime coagulat et indurat *Ps.*-GROS. *Summa* 628 (cf. ib.: est calidum humidi extractivum). **b** in omni dolore capitis .. laborandum est cum ~is et alterativis GILB. II 93v. 2.

2 (phil.) that elicits or draws forth.

illud verbum Patris est ~um, non operativum. creaturarum vero est ~um et operativum MIDDLETON *Sent.* I 250.

3 expressive, significant. **b** explicit.

1196 voce caritatis qua nos amplecti videtur ~a, in hec verba prorupit (*Lit. archiep. Rothomag.*) DICETO *YH* II 142; PECKHAM *QR* 26 (v. emphaticus b); potest esse 'sicut' ~um comparacionis BACON VII 54. **b** **1300** nusquam in vobis appareat ~a rebellio ad majores vestros nec aliquod signum murmuris vel animi indignatis *Reg. Cant.* 854.

expresso v. exprimere 7d.

expressor [LL]

1 one who portrays or represents.

pictores vero sunt ymaginum rerum et similitudinum artificio picture ~ores UPTON 97.

2 expresser, one who states.

quod si infirmus .. non posset expresse verba testamenti sui exprimere, et aliquem de amicis constitueret ~orem et executorem, non staret illud testamentum M. PAR. *Min.* III 21 *n.* 2.

exprimere [CL], **~are**

1 to press or squeeze (to extract liquid). **b** to extract (liquid) by squeezing (also fig.). **c** to press, squeeze. **d** to thrust out, expel (also fig.).

racemos .. torcularibus regulariter ~endos ALDH. *VirgP* 30; **s1252** capellanum .. ignorantem vidimus .. acerbas uvas in oculos eorundem [magnatum] ~entem, tanquam expertem penitus rationis M. PAR. *Maj.* V 329. **b** madidus vino de Sodomitana vite expresso GILDAS *EB* 32; quasi ab uberibus ~it butyrum ANSELM *Misc.* 307; quousque [vulnus] aperiatur et putridus humor ~atur EADMER *Beat.* 15 p. 289; ut ab auditoribus eorum ~eretur vinum perfidie AILR. *Serm.* 490C; sic fluunt oculi .. / .. / quasi per oculi venas virginei / expressi fluerent fluctus equorei WALT. WIMB. *Carm.* 620. **c** **8**.. expremit, *ofðrecð WW*; **9**.. exprimatus (v. 2 confricare a); *GlH* E 191 (v. eliquare 1a); ex earundem [cervicarum] lacte coagulato tres caseos expressos et fiscella formatos archiepiscopo presentavit GIR. *IK* II 11 p. 141; [caro decocta] ~atur fortiter inter duos baculos per pannum et cum ista decoccione fiat .. usus gargarismi J. MIRFIELD *Brev.* 84. **d** elisi, i. expressi, percussi, expulsi *GlH* E 195; **a988** ut .. visitaret gentem Cornubiensem ad ~endos [v. l. extirpandos] eorum errores *Conc. Syn.* 169; **1437** si .. Anna post mortem .. Nicholai expressa fuerit de predicto manerio *Cl* 288 m. 20*d*.

2 to impress (seal, sign, or sim.). **b** (absol.) to sign, make mark.

679 manu propria signum sanctae crucis expraessi *CS* 45; **680** utrumque .. signum ~itur in capite clericorum ALDH. *Ep.* 4 p. 483; artifex subtilis expresserat sigillum regium bitumine formaveratque cuprium tam expresse similitudinis ad illum ut nemo differentiam videret MAP *NC* V 6 f. 70v. (v. et. 7a infra). **b** **1254** facta carta apud Burgos, rege ~ante, prima die Nov. .. *RGasc* I sup. 5.

3 to portray, represent. **b** to reproduce, imitate.

per .. aquilam .. praeclarus vir .. ~itur WULF. *Æthelwold* 3; *Found. Waltham* 21 (v. exsanguis d); ars hinc pictoris variavit nube coloris / et foris expressit quod clausum litera gessit *Vers. Worc.* 100; BART. ANGL. V 7 (v. dijudicativus). **b** lupus movet hostia, voce capellam / exprimit, ut pateant hostia clausa sibi WALT. ANGL. *Fab.* 29. 6.

4 to express in words, describe, explain; **b** (refl.); **c** (w. acc. & inf., *quod*, or indir. qu.). **d** (absol.) to speak.

tribus, ut lingua ejus ~itur, cyulis, nostra longis navibus GILDAS *EB* 23; hanc scriptor verax expressit Matheus ALDH. *CE* 4. 10. 15; expraesit, explanavit *GlC* E 507; expraesserunt, *arehton Ib.* 550; **1168** ~o sensum J. SAL. *Ep.* 267 (252); secunda [pars] prodigiosa nature ludentis ~it opera GIR. *TH intr.* p. 7; **1288** per verba mutuum consensum de presenti ~encia *SelCCant* 338; **1357** erumpnas meas ~avi *Lit. Cant.* II 364. **b** ANSELM III 259 (v. expromere 3). **c** quarta pars .. operis ~at qua intentione allegorice diabolum exsuperavit BYRHT. *V. Ecgwini* 351; quam ardenter alii patres gesserant, .. quis roboratus ingenio Homeri potest ~i? [? l. ~ere] *Id. V. Osw.* 434; de catechumenis ~entibus se habere propositum baptizandi OCKHAM *Dial.* 436 (*recte* 438); **s1397** rex expressit quod .. ordinaret remedium AD. USK 17. **d** de vestimentis .. ~it manifeste, nam in constitucione .. dicit in hec verba: 'constat quod vestimenta ..' OCKHAM *Pol.* I 304.

5 to mention expressly, to state explicitly. *V. et. expressare.*

omnia criminalia semel saltem oportet in confessione ~i GIR. *GE* I 37; reddant generaliter compotum, ~endo et integram summam omnium receptorum et specificando usus in quos expendidit quisque dictam pecunie summam *Norw. Cath. Pri.* 109; **1473** de duobus terminis hujus compoti, que particulariter expremuntur in libro *Exch. Scot* 141; **1556** ut .. in quolibet prandio .. ita ut in cena precedenti ~atur per aliquem scholarium textus *StatOx* 372.

6 (math.) to express as number, to represent.

~itur numerus annorum vigeni centies ducenti super et quadraginta duo ÆTHELW. I 1; postea hujus aggregati radicem quadratam accipias, quam scilicet 5 et unius medietas componunt, ex qua medietatem radicum, $2\frac{1}{2}$, subtrahas et manebunt 3, que unam radicem substantie ~unt, quam substantiam novenarius componit numerus ROB. ANGL. *Alg.* 72.

7 (p. ppl. *expressus* as adj.) express, explicit. **b** (as sb. n.) express statement. **c** (phr. *per expressum*) expressly. **d** (abl. as adv.) explicitly, precisely; *v. et. expresse* 2, *expressim* 2.

~ae, i. manifestae, apertae *GlH* E 645; obtulit expressum patribus diploma legendum FRITH. 759; **c1159** votum .. aut ~um aut tacitum J. SAL. *Ep.* 67 (99 p. 154); ~a forma vetule cujusdam apparuit GIR. *TH* II 19 p. 103; MAP *NC* V 6 f. 70 (v. 2a supra); **1219** mandatum nostrum tam ~um contempnendo *Pat* 225; cum sceptris in manibus et coronis in capite ~is signis sanctitatis *G. Hen. V* 15 p. 106; ex scriptura patent plura et ~iora testimonia de pena inferni perpetua quam de pena purgatorii temporali WYCL. *Ver.* II 56. **b** **1339** quod in ~o legali .. corrigitur, multo fortius in tacito prohibetur (*Lit. Regis*) AD. MUR. *Chr.* 93. **c** **1403** denuncietis .. per ~um quod si quis .. mandata .. neglexerit adimplere .. *Conc.* III 277b; **s1453** per hanc nostram invencionem concepimus satis per ~um, quomodo illa grandis summa pecunie .. per quosdam confratres .. subtracta fuerat *Reg. Whet.* I 108; **s1455** ut .. offeret se velle fateri per ~um suum ingressum fuisse .. erroneum *Ib.* 206. **d** **1284** ~o dicunt quod nichil inde scivit *Gaol Del.* 35/2 m. 29; **1289** ordinacionem et voluntatem nos, partes predicte, illico ~o emmologavimus *RGasc* II 295.

exprobare, ~atio v. exprobrare, ~atio.

exprobrare [CL], to reproach; **b** (w. dat. of person); **c** (w. acc. & inf. or *quod*); **d** (absol.).

quid celabunt cives quae .. ~ant .. nationes? GILDAS *EB* 26; **c705** utrum .. infamia sint ~andi qui concessa .. frangunt ALDH. *Ep.* 9 (12) p. 502; liberum arbitrium .. monita contemnit ~are ANSELM (*Praesc.* 3) II 264; avis .. incredulitatem et duritiam cordis ~avit J. FURNESS *Kentig.* 5 p. 170; modo probus exprobratur, / subsannatur sanctitas WALT. WIMB. *Van.* 112. **b** ne ~arent sibi sodales quod timore mortis faceret ea BEDE *HE* V 13 p. 311; inter verbera exprobando ei dicebat "ista .." GOSC. *Mir. Iv.* lxxii; ~abat .. hominibus ea que secretius gesserant GIR. *IK* I 12 p. 94; in theatrali ludibrio coram monstruosis larvis eidem ~antibus sistitur COGGESH. *Visio* 22. **c** Anglorum gentem nimis ~abat absque virtute virium esse *G. Herw.* 321b; cum .. illi frequenter ~aret quod miser et pediculosus esset *Latin Stories* 12. **d** mentitur quandoque, fallaciter loquitur, ~at [ME: *upbreided*], litigat, adulatur *AncrR* 68.

exprobratio [CL], reproach.

exprobatio, i. improperatio, objurgatio, *edwit GlH* E 734; o contemptor humanarum exprobationum DOMINIC *V. Ecgwini* I 6; exprobatione dignissimum BALD. CANT. *Tract.* 7. 476D (v. exosus 2b); G. FONT. *Inf. S. Edm.* 8 (v. genitura 2); AD. MARSH *Ep.* 30 p. 127 (v. despectio 1c); sustinuit .. Dominus ~ones [ME: *upbrud*], derisiones et hujusmodi *AncrR* 32.

exprodere [cf. CL prodere], to give out, publish.

Focas .. grammaticus primo versu sinalipham ~it ALDH. *Met.* 9.

expromere [CL]

1 to bring out.

~it, exerit [i. e. exserit] *GlC* E 514; ructat, ~et *Ib.* R 238.

2 to bring into play, put to use.

c1167 jus est veras ~ere voces J. SAL. *Ep.* 198 (213 p. 346).

3 to disclose, reveal.

haec placidus heros expromserat ore jocundo FRITH. 120; quomodo quaerit se verbis exprimere, sed nulla verba sufficiunt; quanta vult ~ere, sed tempus et carta non capiunt ANSELM (*Ep.* 120) III 259.

expromissio [cf. CL expromittere], promise.

filii .. eorum ducatu justitie adepti sunt beneficium ~onis divine et introierunt terram Chanaan eamque possederunt R. NI-GER *Mil.* III *prol.*

expromissor [CL], vicarious promissor.

c1250 et fidejussor seu ~or absque ulla dilatione .. exigatur *StatCantab* 213; **1254** fidejussores seu ~ores vestri (*Pat*) *RGasc* I 464.

expromittere [CL], to promise, contract.

1165 nollem .. ~ere quod Cantuariensi .. non servirem J. SAL. *Ep.* 141 (150); est enim penitentie subsidium transmigrationi et non obstinationi expromissum R. NIGER *Mil.* III 4.

expropriare [cf. CL propriare], to expropriate, deprive of property.

expropriatio fratrum [Minorum], qua se in professione per votum paupertatis ~iant OCKHAM *Pol.* III 6; **1451** novicii ante professionem sint ~iati omnino *Mon. Francisc.* II 85.

expropriatio, expropriation, renunciation or deprivation of property.

succedunt .. eis [apostolis] .. religiosi in ~one PECKHAM *Kilw.* 135; si eadem sollicitudo quam exigunt temporalia manet post ~onem temporalium que ante inerat, ipsa ~o ad perfeccionem valet nil conferre OCKHAM *Pol.* III 89; *Ib.* 6 (v. expropriare); Christus .. precepit apostolis nichil ferre in via, quod precepit ~onem omnium perpetuam WYCL. *Civ. Dom.* III 133.

exproprietarie, without property.

debemus habere firmum propositum perseverandi ~ie WYCL. *Ver.* I 134; sic debent vivere ~ie vitam pauperem *Ib.* 153; quicunque religiosus assumpserit dignitatem .. abbatis .. possessionate vel ~ie *Id. Sim.* 17.

expropietarius [cf. CL proprietarius], expropriated, propertyless.

'nolite' inquit 'possidere aurum neque argentum neque pecunias in saccis vestris' [*Matth.* x 9]; quod .. oportet intelligere de habicione ~ia vel civili WYCL. *Civ. Dom.* III 196; status vivendi proprietarie in mundi prosperitate est perfeccior atque securior quam vita ~ia in ewangelica paupertate *Id. Ver.* III 161; distinguens inter clericos propria possidentes et clericos ~ios R. MAIDSTONE *PP* f. 160v.; addentes continenciam et paupertatem ~iam ad legem Christi NETTER *DAF* I 471b.

expropietas [cf. CL proprietas], state of being without property.

non repugnat ~atis professori ut sub cura regiminis curam facit dispensacionis NETTER *DAF* I 572b.

expuere v. exspuere.

expugnabilis [CL], open to attack or refutation.

leges .. civiles esse solidas nec ~es suis sentenciis demonstrarunt FORTESCUE *NLN* II 54.

expugnaculum [cf. CL pugnaculum], siege engine.

diffusus est .. exercitus [circa] villam [*Berwick*] in circuitu a parte terrestri, et ceperunt contra eam municiones et ~a properari *V. Ed. II* 242.

expugnare [CL]

1 to attack, fight (trans.); **b** (fig.); **c** (intr.).

ipsi promiserunt ~are inimicos ejus fortiter NEN. *HB* 176; **1168** rex Anglorum eos transmisso exercitu ~abat dum verba concordie tractarentur J. SAL. *Ep.* 244 (272 p. 566); MAP *NC* IV 3 (v. citra 3b); rex .. villam ~avit et in manu forti cepit, et .. exuperata est STRECCHE *Hen. V* 152. **b** nonne .. ad haec [praecepta] ~anda vel potius obruenda .. arma corripitis? GILDAS *EB* 108; pravas expugnans virgo cohortes ALDH. *VirgV* 2485; fidem suam falso testimonio ~antes EGB. *Dial.* 410; cujusdam sanctimonialis virginale ~are ausus est W. MALM. *Mir. Mariae* 190; expugnatores urbium ipsa inexpugnabilis [sc. mors] ~at BALD. CANT. *Tract.* 10. 513B; armatique aeris ira / instrepit et geminis expugnat vela procellis J. EXON. *BT* III 439. **c** s**1301** rex .. in castellum duriter ~ans, cetus interior viriliter resistens, ex utraque parte fit fortis colluctacio *Eul. Hist.* III 171.

2 to defeat in battle, capture. **b** to destroy.

postquam [Alexander] Aornim petram ~avit in India *Lib. Monstr.* II 6; Saxonum gens .. locum manendi quasi pro patria pugnatura, re autem vera hanc ~atura, suscepit BEDE *HE* I 15; ~atis .. Boructuaris a gente Antiquorum Saxonum *Ib.* V 11; nec .. illam civitatem ~are potuerunt, quia cives illi se viriliter defenderunt ASSER *Alf.* 66; Romaneium [*Romney*] accessit, et ~atis his qui intus erant, cladem suorum vindicavit ORD. VIT. III 14 p. 153; qualiter [terra] subacta sit et ~ata GIR. *TH pref.* p. 20; Ilio ~ato occisoque Laomedonte ALB. LOND. *DG* 3. 8. **b** vastat, spoliat, ~at *GlC* U 53.

3 to fight or fend off. **b** to overcome (abstr.). **c** (intr.) to fight back.

cum corpore namque et occurrentem diabolum ~at, ejus tentationibus viriliter resistendo *Simil. Anselmi* app. 193 p. 98; judica, Domine, nocentes me, expugna inpugnantes me *V. Kentig.* 6; s**1295** exercitum fortem adunavit ad Scotorum injuriam ~andam *Flor. Hist.* III app. 286. **b** impugnare namque potest invitam voluntatem, ~are nequit invitam ANSELM (*Lib. Arb.* 6) I 218. **c** ille [diabolus pugnat] invidia, tu amore fraternae dilectionis ~a ALCH. *Ep.* 299.

expugnatio [CL], capture by assault, conquest; **b** (fig.). **c** destruction.

veniens Ulixes ab ~one Trojae *Lib. Monstr.* I 11; de .. ejusdem [gentis] per advenas ~onibus GIR. *TH intr.* p. 8; profectus inde dominus rex in Scociam, apud Berewyk cum toto exercitu primo pervenit, et hanc primam expugnacionem de consilio fore decrevit *V. Ed. II* 242. **b** c**800** melius ex consilio quam aperta ~one ALCUIN *Ep.* 211; OSB. *Mir. Dunst.* 19 (v. diabolicus a). **c** excidium, ~o *GlC* E 379; excidium, i. .. ~o, casus, ruina, vel *hereteam GlH* E 528.

expugnator [CL]

1 assailant.

explorator potius quam ~or advenit GIR. *EH* I 3; BALD. CANT. *Tract.* 10. 513B (v. expugnare 1a); armis enim propriis quasi per se impotens pugnator exutus, alium ~orem .. ad pugnandum armavit *Latin Stories* 85.

2 champion, conqueror.

in adversis propellendum infategabilis ~or GIR. *Invect.* II 10 p. 145; **1265** pacis nostre zelatores et turbatorum ejusdem ~ores *Cl* 125.

expugnatrix [LL], (one) that assails or conquers (f.).

in grandis exercitus ~ice potencia *Ps.*-ELMH. *Hen. V* 81; **1454** avida plantatrix scienciarum et virtutum, et constans ac provida ~ix abusionum et viciorum *Reg. Dunferm.* 442.

expulsare [CL], to expel.

1412 ab aulis ~ati (v. cito 1e).

expulsatio, expulsion. *V. et. expulsio* 1b, 2 *expulsus* 1.

1432 sub pena expulsionis [v. l. ~onis] a convocacione *StatOx* 247; s**1315** post ~onem Johannis de Balliolo *Plusc.* IX 13; ante .. tempus ~onis et disseisine *Entries* 352b.

expulsio [CL]

1 driving out. **b** expulsion (of person); *v. et. expulsatio, 2 expulsus* 1.

sicut amica similitudine fit attractio, ita dissimilitudine inimica sequitur ~o NECKAM *NR* II 98 p. 182; DUNS *Ord.* II 290 (v. expressio 1a). **b** quis .. carissimum discipulum .. ~one multavit? GILDAS *EB* 72; pagani .. post ejus [sc. Burghredi] ~onem totum Merciorum regnum .. subdiderunt ASSER *Alf.* 46; quid petis in ~one nostra [sc. daemonum], cum totus orbis tuis inclarescat meritis? FOLC. *V. Bot.* 7; qui exulem (quem Angli vocant *utlaga*) paverit post ~onem, quod Angli dicunt *fede oþþe fermie* (*Inst. Cnuti*) *GAS* 317; Genesim .. legimus, in qua humani generis ~o a paradiso legitur HON. *GA* 653C; quoniam pecunia aut ~one corrigentur precipue famulorum culpe *Cust. Cant.* 125.

2 (med.) expulsion: **a** (w. ref. to function of heart or lungs); *v. et. 2 expulsus* 2; **b** (w. ref. to elimination from body).

a pulsio .. in ~onem et impulsionem dividitur. expulsum causa movens statim deserit, impulsum vero usque ad finem comitatur ALF. ANGL. *Cor* 11. 22; pulmonem comprimendo aeris ~onem et attractionem impedit *Quaest. Salern.* B 86. **b** prime enim potentie, ut appetitus, retentio, digestio, ~o, anime insunt beneficio ALF. ANGL. *Cor* 8. 2; *Quaest. Salern.* P 65 (v. deportatio 1b); 'colica passio' appellatur angustiosa cibi detencio corrupti, deinde ejus ~o per superiora et inferiora *SB* 17; rascacio est aspera sputi educcio vel ~o *Ib.* 36.

expulsivus

1 expulsive. **b** (med.) eliminative.

[vis] ~a locum habet in rebus corporalibus et immobilibus sicut in terris et tenementis. item locum habet in rebus incorporalibus sicut in iis que in jure consistunt BRACTON 162; nisi .. inclusis obsidionis ~a supervenirent suffragia *Ps.*-ELMH. *Hen. V* 54. **b** in escis carnalibus quedam .. per vim ~am ejiciuntur omnino J. SAL. *Pol.* 659C; W. CANT. *Mir. Thom.* II 65 (v. contentivus a); natura juvante, movetur et ad virgam deportata per collum vesice, et virtute ~a cooperante, emittitur *Quaest. Salern.* B 226; opilatio multis de causis fit .. debilitate ~e [sc. virtutis] aut fortitudine retentive GILB. I 4. 2; [anima vegetativa] quam illustravit gloriosus Deus septem viribus, que sunt vis attractiva, retentiva, digestiva, ~a, nutritiva, generativa, informativa BRADW. *CD* 138D.

2 that repels, keeps out.

forcia edificia lignea, tempestatum hyemalium ~a *Ps.*-ELMH. *Hen. V* 52.

expulsor [CL], expeller.

laudent alii ~orem demonum H. READING (I) *Adjut.* 1351A.

expulsorius [LL], expulsive, that drives out.

hec pro salute veritatis, contra exposicionem ~iam veritatis et perversoriam tantorum doctorum BRADW. *CD* 463B.

1 expulsus v. expellere.

2 expulsus

1 expulsion. *V. et. expulsatio, expulsio* 1b.

1500 de ingressu, ~u, nec disseisina *Entries* 355b.

2 (med.) expulsion, exhaling. *V. et. expulsio* 2a.

cessat quidem tractus ingresso aere, ~us emisso ALF. ANGL. *Cor* 6. 2.

expultrix [CL = *expeller*], (anat.) expulsive.

septum transversum .. interraneis vim ~cem firmat D. EDW. *Anat.* B 3v.

expum- v. exspum-.

expunctio [LL], completion, fulfilment.

suscitatis omnibus .. et reformatis atque recensitis ad utriusque meriti ~onem ALCUIN (*Conf. Fidei*) *Dub.* 1049C.

expungere [CL]

1 to tick off, remove from register. **b** to drive off, expel.

1564 omni tam universitatis libertate quam matriculationis protinus ~antur et deleantur *StatOx* 395. **b** sat erat patria expunxisse beatum FRITH. 682; si me amare vis, cave ne ulterius hac me injuria ~as W. MALM. *GR* III 264; potestas legitima, qua fideles attrahimus et infideles ~imus tamquam baculo pastorali R. NIGER *Mil.* I 16.

2 to complete.

expuncta, expleta *GlC* E 482.

expungn- v. expugn-.

expurgare [CL]

1 to cleanse (of unwanted matter; partly fig.); **b** (w. ref. to *1 Cor.* v 7).

expurgans veterum clemens monumenta malorum ALDH. *VirgV* 2886; ad ~andum triticum ubi exuberantia zizaniorum nimis multiplicata est ORD. VIT. IV 6 p. 205; ecclesiam de heresibus .. ~are OCKHAM *Dial.* 431; *Ib.* 505 (v. disseminare 1c); **1412** decens foret .. quod ecclesia foret ab eorum tradicionibus ~ata *Conc.* III 349b. **b** tota massa ~abitur a veteri fermento, id est tota familia mundabitur ad inveterato furto *Obs. Barnwell* 190.

2 to clear away, get rid of (unwanted matter; fig.); **b** (w. ref. to *1 Cor.* v 7).

discussis penetralibus cordis nostri atque ~atis vitiorum ruderibus BEDE *HE* IV 3 p. 211; a**984** e monasteriis .. vitiorum spurcitias ~ans (ÆTHELWOLD *Ch.*) *Conc. Syn.* 126; **1093** nec nitor me dignum archiepiscopatu probare, sed falsum crimen ~are ANSELM (*Ep.* 156) IV 22; manifesta peccata non sunt occulta correccione purganda, nec sunt sub condicione ~anda OCKHAM *Dial.* 759; **1520** quis rabula, quis scurra, quis mimus, quis latrinarius tam foeda ~asset in quemquam? (E. LEE) *Ep. Erasmi* IV 1061. **b** quomodo ~abitur vetus fermentum, i. e. peccatum? GILDAS *EB* 100.

3 (med.) to purge (also absol.).

[oves pregnantes] debiliores sunt et non possunt a se superfluitates emittere et ~are *Quaest. Salern.* B 69; cassiafistula maturat et ~at GAD. 28v. 1.

4 to clear from blame; **b** (leg.).

Deus .. ipsum ob omni ~ans scelere ORD. VIT. III 9 p. 111. **b** testimonium vitae et sapientiae ejus .. illum ab hoc crimine ~at ANSELM (*Incarn. A*) I 282; ~et se et friborgum suum (*Leg. Ed. Conf.* 20. 3) *GAS* 646; **1337** Adam .. se wlt ~ari secundum ordinacionem domini nostri custodis *ExchScot* 437.

expurgatio [CL], expurgation, purging from sin.

qui electos suos ab omni macula peccatorum expurgaret .. cujus ~onis sacramento congruit apte quod sequitur BEDE *Gen.* (xvii 11) 162B.

expurgatorius, (med.) purgative, excretory. **b** (as sb. n.) drain.

quedam operationum sunt organa expletiva, quedam superfluitatum ~ia RIC. MED. *Anat.* 212. **b** **1220** (*Waltham Abbey*) *MFG.*

exputare [CL], to examine thoroughly.

1322 ceterum predictus Willelmus ~abit cum priore vel cellerario nostre domus in negociis nostris quociescumque requisitus fuerit *Cart. Blyth* 489.

exquiae v. exsequiae. **exquietus** v. exquirere.

exquirenter, inquiringly.

si predictam materiam ~ius indagares OCKHAM *Dial.* 407.

exquirere [CL]

1 to seek out. **b** to search through.

paenitentiae tabulam toto animi nisu ~rite GILDAS *EB* 110; qui auguria .. observant .. in ~rendis aliquam artem maleficiorum THEOD. *Pen.* I 15. 4; consilium et auxilium ~sivimus DOMINIC *V. Ecgwini* I 9; quodsi [canes rabidi] intra septa foreste reperiantur, talis ~ratur herus et emendet (*Ps.-Cnut de Foresta*) *GAS* 626; reges fortes et potentes / rupes altas exquirentes / castra condunt forcia WALT. WIMB. *Van.* 142. **b** manticis omnibus et bulgis in medium prolatis et ~sitis W. MALM. *GR* IV 315.

2 to ask (person). **b** to inquire. **c** to learn by inquiry. **d** to obtain by request.

p**1083** senes .. qualiter in initio apud sanctum ageretur Cuthbertum a me ~siti sedem illius episcopalem in insula Lindisfarnensi fuisse .. responderunt *Ch. Durh.* 3 p. 7. **b** rimanti, ~enti acute *GlC* R 172; ~it, *he axode GlP* 523; ego sollicite de ejus salute ~sieram P. CORNW. *Rev.* I 205 p. 199. **c** **798** his ita ~sitis, una omnium voce ita responsum est (*Clovesho*) *CS* 291; post hanc artem ~rendam atque elevandam vox canora descendit ALB. LOND. *DG* 8. 20; **1326** de magno exercitu in partibus Francie congregato, de quo mihi mandastis, nichil possum ~rere ab illis qui veniunt de partibus predictis *Lit. Cant.* I 173; *Ps.*-ELMH. *Hen. V* 78 (v. ductivus b). **d** ut a suis sibi cibum ~rerent [v. l. exciperent] parentibus *Lib. Monstr.* II 32.

3 to require, demand. **b** (p. ppl. *exquisitus* as sb. n. pl. w. *naturae*) 'nature's need', 'call of nature'.

cum .. in die judicii de ejusdem manibus veluti interfectoris animae ~rantur GILDAS *EB* 110; **1167** ab utroque regum [sc. David & Achab] pauperum et dumtaxat innocentum sanguis ~ritur J. SAL. *Ep.* 200 (235); a te ipsius sanguis ~ritur et tu mortis ejus reus extiteris *Judas Story*

70. **b** per .. privatiorem, ut fertur, cameram, cellis effractis ad ~sita nature perforatis .. evasit GIR. *Spec.* II 29 p. 92; **s1016** dum ad domum secretiorem ad ~sita nature diverteret *Flor. Hist.* I 546 (cf. H. HUNT. *HA* VI 4: in domum evacuationis ad requisita nature).

4 (p. ppl. *exquisitus*): **a** (of food or clothing) exquisite, choice. **b** carefully chosen, discriminating, finished. **c** far-fetched, specious. **d** (of torture) elaborately devised, exquisite.

a fructus .. arborum qui in domum Domini offerebantur purissimi et ~siti esse jubebantur BEDE *Hom.* II 25. 434; **793** melius est animam .. bonis ornare moribus quam corpus .. ~sitis comere vestibus ALCUIN *Ep.* 20; carnes ~sitiores et bajulos exigunt diligentiores GIR. *TH* I 12; **1242** queri facias quindecim lesta optimi et †exquietissimi [l. exquisitissimi] allec' ad os nostrum proprium *Liberate* 19 m. 10; de colore vestis non est multum curandum .. dum tamen non nimis ~site [ME: *bute hit beo unorne*] *AncrR* 170. **b** **c797** ~sitiores eruditionis scolasticae libelli ALCUIN *Ep.* 121; ad ~sitiorem tam subtilium causarum inquisitionem GIR. *TH* II 3; ave, mater, exquisitis / extollenda laudibus WALT. WIMB. *Virgo* 57; nunc referam sine racione ~sita BACON *Gram. Gk.* 69. **c** **1166** omnes blanditie et ~siti colores eo tendunt J. SAL. *Ep.* 231 (175); nec nos .. ullo unquam tempore veniemus in contrarium premissorum .. quoquo modo .. directe vel quovis ~sito colore *Ps.*-ELMH. *Hen. V* 91 p. 266; FORDUN *GA* 170*n.* (v. divortiare b). **d** ~sitis poenarum machinamentis .. artus .. dilacerant ALDH. *VirgP* 33; tormenta ~sita et excogitata in hoc seculo S. LANGTON *Serm.* 2. 10; pudet .. penna ~sitorum ad hec cruciatuum enarrare immania FORTESCUE *LLA* 22 p. 48.

exquirius v. sciurellus.

exquisite [CL]

1 accurately, carefully.

GlC E 471 (v. examussim); in cxx milia passuum satis ~e latitudinem Hibernie diffundi describit GIR. *TH* I 3; **a1265** a laicis .. adultis cum ad confessionem venerint, an sciant hujusmodi ~ius inquiratur *Conc. Syn.* 713 (= *Conc.* II 297b: †exquisitive); [vipera] abluatur cum aqua et sale ablucione ~issime facta BACON V 107; ideo puto quod si questionem specialem super hoc habuisset, aliquid ~e dixisset W. ALNWICK *QD* 161; licet error hic implicite traditus sit ~ius inferius improbandus OCKHAM *Pol.* III 188.

2 beautifully.

tot corpore vitiatos .. in alia non vidimus natione. sicut enim qui bene formantur, ~issime, et nusquam melius GIR. *TH* III 35.

exquisitio [LL]

1 research, investigation.

nec sine certissima ~one rerum gestarum aliquid .. scribere .. praesumpsi BEDE *CuthbP prol.*; numquid que in utroque Testamento tam subtili commendantur ~one numerorum rationes vacare putabimus a mysteriis? AD. MARSH *Ep.* 180 p. 323.

2 (leg.) right of search.

ruricolis quoque ipsis hanc eandem statuo rectitudinem, ut in meis meorumque principum pecoribus et pascuis habeant ~onem [AS: *smeagung*] *GAS* 213.

exquisitive v. exquisite.

exquisitor [LL], seeker, investigator.

c1236 ut sentiunt hujus seculi ~ores prudentie et intelligentie .. GROS. *Ep.* 36 p. 126; veritatis ~or AD. MARSH *Ep.* 12; justorum judiciorum ~or *Eul. Hist. Annot.* II 188 (cf. W. MALM. *GR* II 123: judiciorum .. inquisitor).

exquisitus v. exquirere 4.

exregina [cf. CL regina], ex-queen.

s1139 ~a, regis adventu tremefacta GERV. CANT. *Chr.* 110; novit ~am .. eximperatricem .. recepisse FL. WORC. *Cont. A* 117; J. WORC. 55 (v. eximperatrix).

exromanus [cf. CL Romanus], ex-Roman.

J. SAL. *Pol.* 814B (v. expontifex).

exsaccare [cf. CL saccare], to unsack.

~o, A. *to vnsacke WW.*

exsacerdos [cf. CL sacerdos], ex-priest.

merito illo sacerdotis exutus insigni, quod exturbatus sicut vere exul, sic et quodammodo ~os H. BOS. *Thom.* III 6 p. 196.

exsaginare [cf. CL saginare], (falc.) to rid of superfluous fat. *V. et. essaimare.*

restat .. quatinus eum ~are sciam ADEL. *CA* 14.

exsanguinare [CL *p. ppl. only*], to drain of blood.

deinde ~entur [veruce] cum ungue vel abscindantur circumquaque GAD. 29. 2.

exsanguis [CL], bloodless. **b** weak, feeble (also fig.). **c** pale, white (w. fear). **d** lifeless.

9.. ~es, *orblede WW*; quasi presagium faciunt future dissolutionis membra jam ~ia ac per hoc quodammodo marcentia PULL. *Sent.* 691C; extremitas corporis pallida remanet et exanguis BART. ANGL. IV 7. **b** viribus exangues reparavit FOLC. *Carm.* 21; **1520** exanguis (v. exercitamentum b). **c** diriguere metu et ~es facti desperaverunt ORD. VIT. IX 7 p. 504; **1159** aride lingue color exanguis J. SAL. *Ep.* 60 (110 p. 177); quos timor exangues .. / fecerat NIG. *SS* 1829. **d** cum .. diram .. Stigii Plutonis ingluviem ~ibus miserorum manibus crudeli strage satiaret ALDH. *Met.* 2; **9..** ~e, *orsaule WW*; **s1147** innumera cadaverum millia .. ~ibusque similes vivi OSB. BAWDSEY clxxxi; corpus hominis exangue non consuevit mortuum formam prioris status frequenter exprimere *Found. Waltham* 21.

exsarcinare [cf. LL sarcinare], to unload.

s1191 familia ejus circa ~andas naves erat intenta DEVIZES 35.

exsartare [cf. sartus, *p. ppl. of* sarire], to essart, bring (land) into cultivation. *V. et. essartare* a.

a1224 illam terram quam .. pater suus .. de bosco exartavit *Cart. Sallay* 351; **1289** centum sadones terre .. debet exartisse (*sic*), laborasse et in garegio vertisse [MS: versas esse] ab instanti die Marcii usque ad duos annos proximo .. venturos *RGasc* II 532.

exsartarius [cf. exsartare, OF *essartier*], tenant of assart. *V. et. essartarius.*

c1168 (1256) exartarius pro fossorio iiij d. Andegavenses dabit (*Ch. Alienoris*) *Mémoires de la Société des antiquaires de l'ouest* XIV 180–1.

exsartum [cf. sartus, *p. ppl. of* sarire]

1 essart, area reclaimed from woodland. *V. et. essartum* 1.

de ~is silvae exeunt xvij s. et iiij d. *DB* I 180; **1176** ~a omnium terrarum suarum .. jam facta .. eis in perpetuum quietaclamo (*Ch. Regis*) *MGL* II 660; **c1189** decem acras terre de exarto nemoris *Act. Hen. II* II 421; **1199** unam virgatam terre, xlij acras et ~um totum quod fuit Garmundi, et decem acras juxta idem essartum *RChart* 7a; Alanus in maneria ecclesie .. infra terminos forestarum sita insurgens .. dim. m. .. pro exartis vi exegit *Chr. Battle* f. 88v.; **1224** concessi .. exartum ibi juxta jacens *Cart. Sallay* 351.

2 tax on essart. *V. et. essartum* 2.

1163 habeant quietantiam de exartis et wastis nemorum *Act. Hen. II* I 373; **1205** decimas omnes garbarum .. exceptis exartis (*Compositio*) *FormA* 26.

exsatiare [CL], to satisfy.

studiosa animi intentione circumeunt querentes quos devorent [*1 Pet.* v 8], .. quibus suum demum ~ient famem J. FORD *Serm.* 49. 7.

exsaturare [CL], to satisfy.

cumque jam .. rabiem non tantum ~asset .. ABBO *Edm.* 6; ut cum aliquis ~atus racemis, vinea tamen deambulat, ut quam pulchre in ea racemi dependeant videat *Simil. Anselmi* 16; qui .. propter ~andam libidinem mutuis se fovent amplexibus PULL. *Sent.* 948C.

exsc- v. et. esc-, exc-, sc-. **exscaët-** v. escaët-. **exscamb-** v. excamb-. **exscandescere** v. excandescere. **exscarletum** v. scarletum. **exscatur-** v. excatur-. **exsceptus** v. excipere.

exscindere (exc-) [CL], to destroy.

incendium .. injicere aut urbem excindere W. POIT. I 38; si tuerentur eas moenia Trojana, brevi talis viri manus et consilium excinderint Pergama *Ib.* II 26; **1241** quod .. vos .. interim excindi et prosterni faciatis boscos ubi necesse fuerit ad bonos et latos passus faciendos *Cl* 329.

exscire [cf. CL scire], to learn of.

tertius exscivit In papa nocentius [i. e. papa Innocentius] arma / ecclesie GARL. *Epith.* IV 97; venit .. ad me quidam nigromanticus .. qui famam nostri gressus ~iverat *Eul. Hist.* I 397.

exscitus v. sticus. **exscoriare** v. excoriare.

exscreare (exc-) [CL], to cough up, spit out; **b** (absol.).

excreat, proicit *GlC* E 517; H. ALBUS 93 (v. 1 bacillus 1); excrea quod habes in ore, et expue R. BOCKING *Ric. Cic.* II 6; prohibeatur descensus ejus [catarri] ad profundum; et fiat facilius ad expellendum et excreandum GAD. 51. 2. **b** cum horrendis vocibus incessanter excreavit et expuit .. qui excreaverat dixit se .. fetorem sensisse P. CORNW. *Rev.* II 893.

exscreatio (exc-) [CL], coughing up, spitting out (of phlegm). **b** phlegm, spittle.

quatinus ea que leguntur .. audiantur sine tumultu tam verborum quam sonorum et, si fieri potest, tussis et excreationis ROB. BRIDL. *Dial.* 116; rusticus iste, cum tussi et excreationibus suis, tedium nobis infert O. CHERITON *Fab.* 73B; post missam .. caveat ~ones quantum potest donec comederit et biberit, ne forte aliquid inter dentes remanserit aut in faucibus, quod excreando ejiceretur *Miss. Ebor.* II 224. **b** fleumaticus est .. sputis et excreationibus multis plenus BART. ANGL. IV 9.

exscreatus [LL], phlegm, spittle.

accidencia senectutis .. sunt .. excreatus putridus BACON *Maj.* II 206; ~atus putridus *Id.* IX 18.

exscribere [CL], to transcribe. **b** (p. ppl. as sb. n.) transcript.

itero preces quatinus libros Aristotilis quos habetis michi faciatis ~i J. SAL. *Ep.* 211 (201). **b** **1166** exscriptum earum [sc. litterarum] michi transmisit frater meus *Ib.* 160 (162); ex litteris .. quarum vobis exscriptum mitto *Ib.* 214 (177).

exscrutari [LL], to investigate, search out.

1585 eligerunt Henricum Vincent et Johannem Okes ad signandum, escrutandum et registrandum omnia corria .. ut sint legitima secundum formam statuti *DL CourtR* 119/1838 m. 2*d*.

exsculpere (exc-) [CL]

1 to dig, hollow out. **b** to carve, chisel out (design or inscription). **c** to fashion (literary work). **d** to scrape up (fig.).

in summitate rupis istius est modica quedam concavitas, sanctorum virorum manibus olim ~ta GIR. *TH* II 41; molendinum quod .. in latere cujusdam saxi .. manibus suis ~sit *Ib.* 52. **b** corpora sena tenet .. / tumbaque mirifico praesens fabricata decore / desuper exculpto cohibet cum culmine tecta *Epigr. Milredi* 813; angelus Domini .. per quatuor angulos templi circumvolans digito suo signum crucis ~sit GIR. *GE* I 25 p. 72. **c** qui meditatos in patria et exculptos sermones inferebat Anglis W. MALM. *GP* I 68; ut .. aliquod munimen litterali studio queant exculpere J. CORNW. *Merl. pref.*; vobis .. materiam .. appono: .. lectores appositam ruditatem exculpant, ut eorum industria bona facie prodeat in publicum MAP *NC* II 32 f. 34; quidquid elucubrans exsculpo studio / detur infantibus quorum sum flagio WALT. WIMB. *Palpo* 168. **d** precepit ut ~erem si quid possem et ad transmarina .. accelerarem H. BOS. *Thom.* III 38.

2 to dig out (fig.), discover.

ut .. conscientiam sollerti discretione exculpamus BEDE *Cant.* 1157C; si quis verum diligenter ~at W. MALM. *GR* II 169; licet ex his beatus Gregorius aliquid allegorice significationis ~serit AILR. *An.* III 27; videamus differentiam inter laneam et lineam vestem: exinde aliquid spirituale si possumus ~amus *Id. Serm.* 359A.

exsculptorius [cf. CL exsculpere, sculptor], that digs out (fig.), that discovers.

trutina estimationis .. [novit] .. scintillantia effectuum desideria arte ~ia contueri R. COLD. *Cuthb.* 1 p. 2.

exscur- v. excur-.

1 exsecare v. excaecare.

2 exsecare (exe-) [CL], to cut out or off.

execandas, *to terende GlP* 329; nisi speretur partus posse †exsiccari vivus PULL. *Sent.* 767C; Esculapius, quia a Coronidis utero dicitur ~tus, ipsius fingitur filius ALB. LOND. *DG* 8. 15; habeat .. artavum quo surculos ~et [*gl.*: *trenchet*] NECKAM *Ut.* 111.

execrabilis (exe-) [CL], execrable, accursed, hateful; **b** (w. ref. to papal bull *Execrabilis*).

705 nonne ~is cachinni ridiculo et gannaturae strepitu ab omnibus [digni] ducuntur? ALDH. *Ep.* 9 (12); execrabilia hujus superficiei lolia B. *V. Dunst.* 1; ut aliquis, dum munditiae cordis studere voluerit, immundos et execrabiles cogitatus habeat ALEX. CANT. *Dicta* 14 p. 165; a clero sacro auri tributum execrabile tam exigens quam extorquens GIR. *EH* II 25; crudele nimium / et execrabile puto judicium WALT. WIMB. *Carm.* 589; quia injuriam sui per hujusmodi ~ia juramenta aures mee sustinere non valent FORDUN *Cont.* VIII 27. **b** **s1317** fecit papa unam constitucionem que incipit Execrabilis AD. MUR. *Chr.* 28; **s1345** beneficia .. reservavit, sicut continetur in decretali, que Execrabilis nuncupatur *Ib.* 174; **1419** per constitucionem †Excerabilis [l. Execrabilis] vacet *Pri. Cold.* 91 (cf. ib. 246 [**1422**]: per constitucionem Execrabilis).

exsecrabiliter (exe-) [CL], execrably, damnably; **b** (w. play on *sacramentum*).

innumeras voces jactare execrabiliter in Dominum et in omnes sanctos blasphemias dicere OSB. *Mir. Dunst.* 19 p. 149; ad .. sceleratum ministerium ~er consummandum P. BLOIS *Ep.* 238. 542A; errarent non solum damnabiliter, sed execrabiliter OCKHAM *Dial.* 828; uxores et filios execrabiliter opprimentes WALS. *HA* II 83. **b** **s1138** rex .. Scotorum, quia sacramentum fecerat filie regis Henrici, quasi sub velamento sanctitatis per suos execrabiliter egit; mulieres enim gravidas findebat H. HUNT. *HA* VIII 6; **s1138** exercitum suum promovit in Angliam, et per suos execrabiliter peragebat *Meaux* I 120.

exsecramen (exe-) [LL], execration, cursing. *V. et. exsecratio* a.

a bannynge, detestacio, detestamen, execramen, maledictum, maledictio *CathA*.

exsecrari (exe-) [CL], **~are** [LL]

1 to curse.

execrare, i. maledicere *GlC* E 509; nisi quando perniciosa protervarum opera execrando emendare non poterat HUGEB. *Wynn.* 6; postquam illud execratus fuerit et se ab illo alienare contenderit ALEX. CANT. *Dicta* 1 p. 110; synodus Gangrensis .. in qua statutum est anathema esse qui olera cum carne cocta †exceratur R. NIGER *Chr. II* 124.

2 to profane.

ut inter tot predones execrata potius ecclesia dici possit quam consecrata GIR. *GE* II 27; **c1236** GROS. *Ep.* 32 (v. diabolicus a); **1298** cimiterium .. per .. sanguinis effusionem .. dudum .. ~am *Reg. Cant.* 280.

3 to execrate, hate. **b** (gdv.) execrable, worthy to be cursed, hateful.

illi execrantes monachicam vitam ilico exierunt de aecclesia ÆLF. *Æthelwold* 14; diuturnitatem vita .. summo odio execrabuntur EADMER *Beat.* 15 p. 286; maximum dampnum militum nostrorum incurremus et regem nostrum ad ~andum nos commovebimus G. MON. X 4; dum uti infortunii presagium execrarentur *Chr. Battle* f. 9v. **b** **617** execrandam diabolicae versutiae supplantationem (*Lit. Papae*) BEDE *HE* II 10 p. 103; execrandae formae hippotamos *Lib. Monstr.* II 17; **799** qui salvum fecit servum suum et liberavit a persecutione ~andae infidelitatis ALCUIN *Ep.* 177; **9..** execranda, *þa onscuniendlecan WW*; in presentia ejus .. nihil execrandum facere .. quisquam ausus fuerat TURGOT *Marg.* 4; **1347** cetera innumerabilia detestanda et ~anda mala (*Lit. Papae*) AVESB. f. 111.

exsecratio (exe-) [CL], execration, cursing; *v. et. exsecramen.* **b** curse, evil. **c** execrable deed.

[dii] juramentum per ~onem habent. nam jusjurandum proprie, diis alicunde testibus invocatis, prospera optare, ~o vero adversa deposcere est ALB. LOND. *DG* 6. 3; **1298** de execracione licium agitur *Reg. Cant.* 542. **b** **797** timore mortis aut tormentorum immanitate aut idolatriae execratione ALCUIN *Ep.* 128; quousque pestiferam execrationis suae voluntatem cum adaucta regis inimicitia adimpleret B. *V. Dunst.* 22. **c** ut dicat Egyptios .. execraciones et abhominaciones commisisse BEKINSAU 750.

exsecrator (exe-) [LL]

1 execrator, curser.

a banner, devotator, derogator, detestator, execrator, imprecator, maledicus *CathA*.

2 hater, detester.

hii .. ~ores .. alios .. ad persequendum .. famulum Dei deposcebant B. *V. Dunst.* 13; appetitor honesti, turpitudinis execrator OSB. *V. Dunst.* 8 p. 77.

exsectio [CL], cutting off.

unguibus quod toties dempsit ~o BEDE *Luke* 489.

executio (executio) [CL]

1 performance (of task). **b** carrying into effect (of command, duty, or sim.); **c** (w. obj. gen.); **d** (w. subj. gen.); **e** (w. adverbial phr.). **f** procedure, means of use. **g** (pl.) duties.

ad elimosynas operumque bonorum ~onem BEDE *HE* III 5 p. 136; quedam frigide et humide .. longam et prolixam operis ~onem exigunt *Quaest. Salern.* B 12. **b** quare si qua in disserendo enuntiationes et interrogationes fieri convenit arte docuerimus, quod propositi nunc suscepimus executi erimus, et proposito erit amplior propositi ~o BALSH. *AD* 11 (cf. ib. *rec.* 2 104: propositum enim sic exequi proposuimus ut proposito sit amplior propositi ~o); **1217** cum velitis .. votum peregrinationis vestre instanter ~oni dare *Pat* 54; **c1273**, etc. (v. demandare 1c); **1303** ad execusciones .. procedere (*Lit. Episc. Lond.*) *Chr. Rams.* 381*n.*; **1309** (v. executor 3b); et sic ~o, que est realis operacio agentis, est actualior et principalior quam intencio agentis naturalis, que est talis inclinacio T. SUTTON *Quodl.* 598; **1400** placuit .. quod antiquum statutum .. in ~one ponatur debita *StatOx* 191. **c** cum ex charitate ad moriendum exstitit paratus, ut premio dignior non fieret mortis ~one quam antea moriendi voluntate PULL. *Sent.* 798B; **12..** fiant in hujus ~one statuti *Conc. Scot.* II 39; **1281** quod non fecit exequcionem cujusdam brevis domini regis *PQW* 400a; ~o tamen actuum respicit singularia; sicut lex est de universalibus et ~o legis de singularibus WYCL. *Log.* II 63. **d** primo ponitur regine exhortacio, secundo chori ~o TREVET *Troades* 13; **1452** pro ~one executorum meorum *MunAcOx* 656 (v. et. 4 infra). **e** **1306, 1456** (v. 3a infra); **1321** ~onem de debitis illis levandis .. faciunt *MGL* II 322; **1332** fit ~o per breve de magna districcione returnabile ad diem predictum *LTRMem* 105 m. 7*d*. **f** ~o .. tabule supposite per quam principium mensium arabum inveniatur hec est: signabitur ergo annorum collectorum notula .. ADEL. *Elk.* 4. **g** **1384** ut majori et ballivis civitatis predicte ac aliis ministris domini regis resisterent in regiminibus ejusdem civitatis et ~onibus suis faciendis *IMisc* 234/10.

2 (eccl.) performance, celebration.

Offic. Sal. 72 (v. executor 2).

3 (leg.): **a** executing, carrying out of judgement or sentence; **b** writ to enforce judicial sentence; **c** execution (of sentence of death or person sentenced).

a gladio .. judiciorum ~o irrogatur R. NIGER *Mil.* II 13; **1229** cum aliquis in eadem [curia prioris] judicatus fuerit ad pillorium vel tumberellum, ~o judicii fiat per ballivos prioris *Feod. Durh.* 216; BRACTON 107 (v. delusorius); **1293** quod Simon vos pluries requisierit quod ~onem judicii predicti fieri faceretis *RScot* 20a; **1306** quod .. adjudicentur .. correcciones secundum modum delicti .. et quod in premissis plenaria ~o fiat *BBC* (*Swansea*) 372; **1384** (v. 1 barra 6); **1456** fuit .. adjudicatus pilorie .. et sic ~o super ipsum facta fuit *FormA* 18. **b** **s1206** caute feci ipsam sententiam .. ~oni a capite usque ad finem interseri *Chr. Evesham* 184 (cf. ib. 198: accepta ~one et viatico); **1303** in .. expensis garcionis portantis moniciones et ~ones .. officialibus et decanis *DCWestm.* 72/12335; **1439** in ij brevibus originalibus .. cum diversis mandatis et ~onibus *Ac. Durh.* 73; **1545** monitorium cum ~one parata *Conc. Scot.* I cclvii *rub.*. **c** **s1322** rex .. remisit .. ~onem duarum penarum, quod idem T. comes non traheretur nec suspenderetur, sed quod ~o fieret tantummodo super ipsum quod decapitaretur WALS. *HA* I 165; **1418** Thomas A. ~oni positus fuit *RNorm* 239; **1431** pro ~one certorum insurrectorum contra dominum regem *ActPC* IV 89; **s1489** plurimos exequtioni debite mandavit *Reg. Merton* 122; si, pronuntiata mortis sententia, differri ~onem jubeat princeps MORE *Ut.* 71.

4 execution (of will, usu. w. *testamenti* or sim.).

1227 executores .. comitis Essex' promiserunt domino regi c li. pro habendis catallis que fuerunt ipsius comitis ad ~onem testamenti ipsius comitis faciendam *LTRMem* 9 m. 3(2); **c1230** dabit executoribus meis .. l m. in usus ~onis testamenti mei *Ch. Sal.* 204; si liber homo intestatus .. decesserit, .. ad ecclesiam et ad amicos pertinebit ~o BRACTON 60b; **13..** qualiter ultime voluntates defunctorum .. per .. executores .. debite ~oni mandentur *Conc. Scot.* II 74; **1424** onus ~onis hujus testamenti *Reg. Cant.* II 290; **1452** pro ~one ultime voluntatis mee *MunAcOx* 646.

5 (Gasc.) enforcement of contract under seal.

1304 Johannes G., contrarotulator noster Burdegale, tenens sigillum nostrum ad scaccarium ~onis Burdegale .. te in servientem ~onis sigilli .. ad contractus duxerit preficiendum nos, .. mandamus .. *RGasc* III 443; **1312** (v. executoria 2); **1316** tanquam serjantus et executor ~onum sigilli et contrasigilli [ad contractus] *RGasc* IV 1523.

exsecutionarius (exe-) [cf. exsecutio 2c], executioner. *V. et. exsecutor* 3c.

1686 ad flagellandum per communem ~ium a Newgate ad furcas de Tyburne condemnatus .. fuit *EHR* XXIX 731.

exsecutive (exe-)

1 executively, in execution, in actual fact.

potest .. dominus .. dare mihi dextrarium etsi non habuerit tale, .. sed subserviens non deliberabit michi dextrarium nisi singularem habuerit, ~e michi dando WYCL. *Log.* II 63; 'sacerdos' intelligi potest dupliciter vel nude potestative vel ~e *Id. Ver.* II 241.

2 subsequently.

que autem ~e queruntur, item de uno singillatim non de singulis singula BALSH. *AD rec.* 2 139.

exsecutivus (exe-)

1 executive, able to execute. **b** (w. obj. gen.).

voluntas Dei nullius boni creati est causa nisi mediante potencia ~a, ergo nullius boni est causa immediata MIDDLETON *Sent.* I 401b; si ponatur potencia illa 'operantis extra' esse voluntas illa et non aliqua alia potencia ~a; quod si poneretur aliqua potencia ~a alia a voluntate DUNS *Ord.* VI 308; nec est in eo [sc. Deo] ultra intellectum dictantem et voluntatem consencientem alia virtus ~a ponenda BRADW. *CD* 197B. **b** dixerunt subtiles philosophi quod est dare actum ~um voluntatis divine, distinctum ab illa volicione WYCL. *Log.* III 192; **1408** hoc nostrum antiqui juris ~um statutum *Conc.* III 316a; dic quod istud est preceptum pocius ~um illius, quod primo statutum est, quam auctoritativum LYNDW. 11 c (cf. *Conc. Syn.* 837).

2 subsequent. *V. et. assecutivus.*

ut .. nominatim discernantur duo hec genera .. querendorum, .. quedam initialia, quedam ~a appellavimus BALSH. *AD rec.* 2 163; [liber] qui primo dividitur in partem prooemialem et ~am FISHACRE *Sent. Prol.* 98.

exsecutor (exe-) [CL]

1 performer, doer. **b** one who carries out (task, duty, command, or sim.).

eorum quae agenda docebat erat ~or devotissimus BEDE *HE* V 22; Æ., .. in omni probitate actuum promptissimus ~or DOMINIC *V. Ecgwini* I 9; strenuus in agendis, .. ~or invictus MAP *NC* V 3 f. 60v. **b** non tam delator quam veritatis regulae ~or inveniatur GILDAS *Pen.* 27; ut archiepiscopum Cantuariensem propositi sui ~orem haberet EADMER *Wilf.* 46; **1166** in Moysen et Aaron divine legis ~ores J. SAL. *Ep.* 218 (171); ~or verbi Dei R. NIGER *Mil.* III 74; non auctor sceleris .. sed vel ~or vel executionis non impeditor GIR. *IK* I 4 p. 53.

2 (eccl.) officiant.

~or officii solempni apparatu se induat .. sicut ad executionem misse *Offic. Sal.* 72; **1439** postquam ~or officii inchoaverit missam suam *Stat. Linc.* II 191; quo [psalmo] finito sacerdos ~or officii dicit .. oracionem W. SAY *Lib. Reg. Cap.* 58; **1483** tunc incipiunt †spalmum [l. psalmum] 'Te Deum laudamus' a prelato ~ore officii et finitur a choro et organo *Fabr. York* 211.

3 authorized agent, executor. **b** papal judge delegate appointed to carry out judgement. **c** executioner.

leges sanxit in posterum ut sententie principum super animadversione prolate in diem tricesimum ab ~oribus differrentur H. BOS. *Thom.* IV 13 p. 370; **1343** delegatis, subdelegatis, ~oribus, subexecutoribus (*Lit. Regis*) W. GUISB. *Cont.* 410; ille qui [librum] perdidit vel ejusdem procurator seu etiam ~or R. BURY *Phil.* 19. 244; **1514** vos ~orem per presentes damus .. ut hoc per vos distribuatur *Scot. Grey Friars* II 228. **b** **1200** nullus delegatus vel subdelegatus, ~or, aut etiam observator auctoritate sedis apostolice (*Lit. Papae*) *Reg. Dunferm.* 277; papa .. per judices et ~ores optimos .. filium amoveri et patri ecclesiam denuo conferri .. fecit GIR. *SD* 16; **1255** per magistrum R., negotii crucis ~orem domini pape deputatum *Val. Norw.* 209*n.*; **c1255** domini pape judices delegati sive ~ores *AncC* LV 5; **1309** certis eis juxta morem, quem apostolica sedes servare .. consuevit, ~oribus deputatis, nonnulli .. eisdem ~oribus ipsis temerarie inhibere presumunt, ne commisse ipsis hujusmodi ministerium execucionis exerceant (*Lit. Papae*) *Reg. Cant.* 1032 (cf. *Ann. Lond.* 165); **1435** Ricardus C. .. archdiaconus Roffensis, compulsor, sive ~or, ad infrascripta sub forma in ipsis litteris compulsoriis originalibus quibus presentes annectimus .. annotata .. deputamus (*Lit. R. archidiac.*) AMUND. I 397 (cf. compulsor b); **1449** (v. executorialis a). **c** [Elphegus] inter lapides pro suis ~oribus exorabat ut et in hoc se alterum nobis Stephanum exhiberet [cf. *Acts* vii 60] H. BOS. *Ep.* 1449D.

4 executor of will: **a** (usu. w. *testamenti* or sim.); **b** (w. gen. of testator or poss. pron.). **c** (w. *dativus*).

a testamenti .. ~ores esse debent quos testator ad hoc elegerit et quibus curam ipsam commiserit GLANV. VII 6; **1225** ~oribus testamenti .. archiepiscopi *Pat* 521; **1256** ab exequtoribus testamenti *Cl* 26; ~ores ordinantes de funere facient operum dispersionem et segregacionem HOLCOT *Wisd.* 145; **1340** ~ores testamenti .. Henrici *MGL* I 392; **1352** rex .. uni ~orum testamenti .. Henrici salutem *RScot* I 751a. **b** **1220** quod ~ores Ade decani dederunt (*Vis.*) *Reg. S. Osm.* I 275; **1236, 1336** (v. exequi 5a); **1294** de ~oribus rectoris ecclesie de Overbury *Comp. Worc.* I 23; amplius vobis proderit unus quadrans datus in vita quam totus mundi thesaurus per ~ores vestros post mortem distributus RIC. ARMAGH *Serm.* 39; **1402** pro tractatu habendo cum ~oribus W. Johnson *Ac. Durh.* 300; **1522** nominando ipsum suum ~orem *Scot. Grey Friars* II 78. **c** **1518** (v. dativus 3a); **c1520** (v. datio 2); **1559** de ~oribus testamentorum dativis *Conc. Scot.* II 167; si nullum sit testamentum .. ~ores dativos dent, quorum officium .. a curatore bonis dando in jure civili non multum differt *Jus Feudale* 252.

exsecutoria (exe-)

1 executry, executorship (of will). *Cf. exsecutor* 4.

1559 casu quo agnati .. citati recusaverint onus ~ie acceptare *Conc. Scot.* II 167.

2 (Gasc.) keepership (of seal).

1312 cum .. concesserimus .. officium serjancie, videlicet faciendi in senescalcia Agennes' execuciones sigilli nostri et contrasigilli ad contractus in Agennes' deputatorum .. ac idem officium in custodia sigillorum predictorum et execucione eorumdem consistat et in partibus illis officium ~ie sigillorum predictorum, ut asseritur, vulgariter nuncupetur *RGasc* IV 647; item a magistro Ricardo de B. tenente ad firmam ~iam sigilli et contrasigilli regii quo utitur in Agen' ad contractus *Ib.* app. p. 551.

exsecutorialis (exe-), executorial, authorizing execution of judgement; **b** (w. *litterae*). *V. et. exsecutorius* 2.

1449 [episcopus Norwycensis] advertens quomodo apostolicarum fuerat litterarum .. precipuus executor, protinus .. ~em exercuit potestatem *Reg. Whet.* I 154. **b** **1456** processuum et licterarum ~ium desuper habitorum (*Lit. Papae*) *Mon. Hib. & Scot.* 400b; **1470** juxta vim, formam, et tenorem quarundam literarum ~ium super dicto prioratu de Coldingham in ipsa Romana curia decretarum *Pri. Cold.* 217; **1541** (v. excommunicatorialis).

exsecutorium (exe-), ordinal, service-book. *Cf. exsecutio* 2, *exsecutor* 2.

1446 tria vetera missalia, .. unum vetus portiphorium, unum processionale, unum executor[ium] officii, unum collectuarium *Cl* 296 m. 26*d*.

exsecutorius (exe-) [LL]

1 belonging to an executor. **b** (as sb. m.) executor or (?) *f. l.*

1310 ego .. tam nomine meo proprio quam ego ipsa et dicti Gilbertus et Robertus executores predicti nomine ~io *Deeds Balliol* 168; per R. executorem testamenti .. nomine ~io *Reg. Brev. Orig.* 54. **b 1573** executoriis [? l. executoribus] et assignatis suis *Pat* 1104 m. 25.

2 executory, authorizing execution of judgement; **b** (w. *litterae* or sim.). **c** (as sb. f.) executory letter. *V. et. exsecutorialis.*

1330 execuciones necnon judicialia ~ia eorundem que ad hujusmodi libertates pertinent per ballivos suos faciend' et exercend' *PQW* 642b. **b 1222** de litteris ~iis domini pape de sentencia excommunicacionis *Pat* 380; **s1257** alius .. dominum papam appellavit et ab ipso literas ~ias super mandato papali reportavit *Ann. Dunstable* 205; **s1304** bullas suas ~ias *Plusc.* VIII 29 (= FORDUN *Cont.* XI 35: literas bullatas); **1317** litteras apostolicas tam principales quam ~ias *Reg. Carl.* II 161; **s1378** bullas hujus tanti [negotii] ~ias WALS. *HA* I 356; **1441** cum litera ~ia super archano negocio BEKYNTON I 227. **c** concessit nobis dominus papa ecclesias .. et super eisdem ~ias *G. S. Alb.* I 351 (cf. ib.: ecclesia .. concessa et a domino papa confirmata et super eadem ~ia).

exsecutrix (exe-) [LL]

1 one who performs (action), carries out (task) (f.).

hec eorum [sc. demonum] nuncia nequam et ~ix irarum MAP *NC* II 14 f. 28; ~ix sororum discordias pacificare studeat *Collect. Ox.* I 47; ac si natura inferior esset ~ix in opere eorum que ordinata sunt ab intelligencia movente SICCAV. *PN* 196.

2 executrix (of will): **a** (w. *testamenti* or sim.); **b** (w. gen. of testator).

a 1287 potestatem recipiendi attornatos Johanne de B., ~icis testamenti Thome Brun (*Dedimus Potestatem*) *PRO* C 254/11/117; **1303** testamenti mei .. facio .. uxorem meam ~icem principalem *Deeds Balliol* 167; **1333** Hawys[ia] uxor Johannis de Wykham, ~ix testamenti ejusdem J. supplicavit *LTRMem* 105 m. 24 (*rec.*); I. que fuit uxor H. ~ix testamenti ejusdem H. *Reg. Brev. Orig.* 58; **1520** (v. doaressa); **1549** in denariis .. solutis Elianore comitisse dotisse Rutland', ~ici ultime voluntatis Thome nuper comitis *Rutland MSS Ac. Receiver* 2–3 Ed. VI r. 4. **b 1294** contra Emmam relictam Edmundi P. et ejusdem Edmundi ~icem *SelCCant* 411; **s1302** Dionisia de Monte Caniso, ~ix domini Willelmi de Monte Caniso *Mon. Francisc.* I 503 (= *Grey Friars Lond.* 154).

exseitas [cf. CL ex se], (phil.) 'exseity', quality or condition of existing independently. (*Cf.* Avicenna *Opera philosophica* Venice, 1508, f. 86v.).

[Avicenna] volens docere que sunt extra formalem racionem quidditatis rei, coactus est uti terminis logicalibus, in quibus ponuntur modi perseitatis, ~atis, pro 'ex se', quia per tales proposiciones cognoscitur quid est extra quidditatem rei et quid non W. ALNWICK *QD* 191.

exseminare [cf. CL seminare], to scatter, sow (fig.).

'laudanda est', inquit, 'laudabilis vita eterna ex qua per seipsam vita .. ~atur' BRADW. *CD* 157E (= *Ps.*-Dionysius *Div. Nom.* 6).

exseniolum v. exeniolum.

exsensus (exe-) [CL], **~is** [LL], insensible, without feeling. **b** senseless, foolish.

quum diu ~is et sine voce decubuisset GOSC. *Mir. Iv.* lxiii; morbo crescente, triduo ~us et mutus jacuit W. MALM. *GR* II 193 (= *NLA* I 348: ~is); omnibus membris in corpore toto ~ibus R. COLD. *Cuthb.* 70 p. 143. **b** quedam .. multo tempore adeo pervalide infirmari consueverat ut quicumque illam vidisset insanam et ~em omnino crederet R. COLD. *Godr.* 409; animos .. / saxosos, stupidos, exsenses, inscios WALT. WIMB. *Sim.* 156; *fonde*, .. demens, desipiens, ~is *CathA*.

exsequax (exe-) [cf. CL sequax], follower.

cepit primo adherere Wiclefensibus .., qui sui tenentes doctrinam magistri jam examina multa suorum ~acium Londoniis fecerant *V. Ric. II* 80.

exsequi (exe-) [CL]

1 to follow (also fig.). **b** to imitate.

~etur, i. .. sequitur *GlH* E 468; quod .. concilium .. induci procuraret Benedictum XIII ad viam mutue cessionis celerius ~ende GASCOIGNE *Loci* 164. **b** istum jejunantem, illum ~i nitebatur in pulvere cilicioque quiescentem *V. Neot. A* 2.

2 to strive after. **b** to persist in, continue with (task). **c** (absol.) to persist, continue.

~ens, que sola vere libertas est, nobilitatem *V. Neot. A* 23. **b** solitum sibi opus evangelizandi ~ens BEDE *HE* III 19 p. 163; quod dum multo tempore sedulus ~eretur *Ib.* IV 25 p. 264; videbitis .. qualiter ~emini vocacionem vestram *Spec. Incl.* 3. 1. **c** quocumque in loco Dei omnipotentis famuli Neoti cordetenus ~itur memoria sive consistunt oracula *V. Neot. A* 21.

3 to do, perform. **b** to fulfil (office), execute, carry out (duty, command); **c** to execute, put into effect (judgement); **d** (*s. pass.*).

opera tamen fidei .. diligenter ~i curavit BEDE *HE* III 25 p. 182; juste quod justum est .. ~eris GIR. *GE* II 31 p. 319. **b 1164** ut .. mandatum vestrum ~erer J. SAL. *Ep.* 134 (136 p. 4); **1230** mittimus .. Michaelem de B. .. ad officium suum loco suo ~endum in hiis que ad officium marescalcie .. pertinent *Cl* 410; **1275** que [littera] si forte a casu vobis non venerit, tunc si placet ~amini hic contenta *Reg. Heref.* 19; **1332** ad vestra ~enda negocia in partibus Anglicanis J. MASON *Ep.* 59 p. 201. **c s1080** de his qui de parentela sua uxores tenent .. episcopi canonicam justitiam ~antur (*Statuta*) ORD. VIT. V 5 p. 317; **s1012** cum .. hujus decreti sententia .. absque misericordia ~eretur M. PAR. *Maj.* I 487; **s1387** ut [Robertus] viriliter ~eretur judicia predicti consilii *Chr. Kirkstall* 126; vicecomes .. omnia mandata et judicia curiarum regis in comitatu suo ~enda ~itur FORTESCUE *LLA* 24. **d c1340** quare .. excommunicacionis sentencia ~i contra eum non debeat cum effectu *FormOx* 129; **1400** talia et hujusmodi libertates, jura regalia, consuetudines .. per tales officiarios et ministros gubernentur et ~antur (*Ch. Regis*) *MGL* II 487; **1458** quod extunc dicta recognicio non sit executura, sed perdat suum vigorem (*Lit. Regis*) *Reg. Whet.* I 304; **1545** et presentes debite executas et indorsatas .. reportetis *Conc. Scot.* I cclxix.

4 (eccl.) to perform, celebrate (liturgy).

exequias debita satis veneratione .. per omnia ~ens *V. Gund.* 46; absente episcopo .. [decanus] tenetur ~i officium *Offic. Sal.* 2; cantor .. officium .. cantorie ex moderno usu, licet non rite, ~i solet quousque antiphonam .. reinceperit *Cust. Cant.* 95; **s1490** in quibus exeqiis et missa ipse custos .. officia divina ~atur *Reg. Merton* 141.

5 (w. *testamentum* or sim.) to execute (will); **b** (*s. pass.*).

1236 executoribus dicti Roberti plenam saisinam habere facias de omnibus catallis que fuerint dicti Roberti .. ad ~endum testamentum ipsius Roberti *KRMem* 14 m. 6d.; **1326** ad hanc ultimam voluntatem meam fideliter ~endam hos constituo executores meos *Deeds Balliol* 53; **c1440** ad .. ~endam predictam ultimam voluntatem predicti Roberti Mawteby *Paston Let.* 9. **b 1219** testamentum suum quod plenius executum fuit *CurR* VIII 7; **1414** (v. dispositio 4b); **1424** residuum .. omnium bonorum meorum quod premissis executis superfuerit expendi volo inter pauperes *Reg. Cant.* II 290.

6 to set out, enumerate; **b** to explore (text), to pursue, follow through (course of argument).

1166 licet grandiuscula sit epistola que tamen necessaria sola ~itur J. SAL. *Ep.* 183 (175); Rabanus .. et Cassiodorus .. que ad hunc articulum pertinent latius ~untur *Ib.* 143 (209 p. 324); sane planetarum, quos bonos vel noxios diximus, latius naturas ~itur Plinius ALB. LOND. *DG* 9. 6. **b** est .. que dicta est multiplicium distinctio disserenti plurimum necessaria, ne simpliciter ~endo multiplex conatus frustra adhibeatur BALSH. *AD rec.* 2 168; satis violenter hunc textum ~eris dum nimis judaizare tu niteris ANDR. S. VICT. *Comm.* 136.

7 to attain, arrive at (result).

quinti vero [sc. domicilii] et ceterorum principia simili ratione reperies, hac una differentia .. ut cum in primis iiij duas horas nocturnas retractaveris, cetera per additionem duarum horarum diurnarum de tempore tue regionis ~aris ADEL. *Elk.* 32.

exsequia v. exaquia.

exsequiae (exe-) [CL], **~ia** (n. pl.), exequies, burial rites, funeral. **b** (commemorative) office of the dead. **c** mortal remains.

ALDH. *Met.* 10 p. 88 (v. epigramma 1); **716** cui antea ipse in infirmitate exitus sui ministravi et ~ia prebui BONIF. *Ep.* 10 p. 13 (cf. ib. p. 15: ~ias); miri odoris flagrantia omnium perfuderat nares, ut perspicuae (*sic*) intellegeretur ad ~ia viri sancti angelicum venisse ministerium ALCUIN *WillP* I 25; **9.** .. ~ias, *deaþþenunga* *WW*; *V. Gund.* 46 (v. exsequi 4); ipso tumulationis die dum plebs in ~iis dilecti regis adhuc maderet fletis ORD. VIT. III 11 p. 118; authentice matris nostre tanquam ~ias plangere et funus prosequi lamentabile GIR. *IK* II *pref.*; **1287** pro †exquiis [l. exequiis] funeralibus domini Johannis de Vallibus qui obiit Aquis x die Sept. (*AcWardr*) *TRBk* 201 p. 94; **1315** (v. commendatio 4). **b c1400** ad ~ias dicendas cum missa in crastino *Mon. Francisc.* I 591; **1406** ~ias .. pro .. defuncti anime salute .. celebrare .. teneatur *Lit. Cant.* III 98; **1430** (v. concursorie); **1432** post incepcionem ~iarum vel missarum universitatis *StatOx* 247; solent .. ~ie solennes in capella regis .. in anno quatuor fieri W. SAY. *Lib. Reg. Cap.* 60. **c** translatae sunt .. ~iae regis Glestoniam, ibique .. terrae commendatae OSB. *V. Dunst.* 21; funus juxta Servium proprie est jam ardens cadaver; quod dum portatur, ~ias dicimus; .. crematum, reliquias; conditum jam, sepultum ALB. LOND. *DG* 6. 30.

exsequialis (exe-) [CL], exequial, proper to a funeral. **b** (as sb. n. pl.) funeral.

verbis .. ~ibus *liclicum wordum* *GlP* 936; non ~ibus planctibus, sed triumphalibus cantibus GOSC. *Aug. Maj.* 50B; ~e officium celeberrime egit G. CRISPIN *Herl.* 110; celebratis exsequiis, funeri capam .. injecerunt, vultum tegentes, et missum est ad sacerdotes vicinos ut et ipsi venientes ~e munus impenderent W. CANT. *Mir. Thom.* II 48. **b** post clausos oculos et ~ia adhibita *Ib.* VI 138.

exsequialiter (exe-), with a (commemorative) office of the dead. *Cf. exsequiae* b.

1505 anniversarium deposicionis vestre diem catholicorum more ~er observare *Cl* 370B m. 2.

exsequtio, ~or v. executio, ~or. **exseranticus** v. exferveficus.

exserere (exe-) [CL]

1 to stretch out, put forth.

in sui conditoris injuriam impias ~unt linguas BEDE *Gen.* (xi 8–9) 130; manum quasi ad feriendum minitans ~it *Id. HE* IV 3 p. 211; ~tum, i. .. exporrectum, elevatum .., ~ere, i. .. proferre, .. vel *abredan* *GlH* E 458, 463; H. BOS. *Thom.* III 31 (v. angulatim); et crines Crinius aurosas exerit WALT. WIMB. *Carm.* 307.

2 to expose, lay bare. **b** to draw (weapon, also fig.).

~tum, i. .. extractum, nudatum, expeditum, †*þæs nacodan* [l. nacod], .., *æwæde, benæced* *GlH* E 458; OSB. GLOUC. *Deriv.* 201 (v. exsertare). **b** ~ere, i. evaginare, .. *GlH* E 463; ~ta machaera GOSC. *Aug. Maj.* 89B; si gladium non ~it, aut ~to indignus ferit PULL. *Sent.* 928D; **1169** Petri gladius potenter ~tus est J. SAL. *Ep.* 302 (295); W. CANT. *Mir. Thom.* VI 92 (v. effractor 1c); ~to [v. l. extracto] gladio viam sibi vir animosus viribus aperuit GIR. *EH* II 1; *Id. PI* I 10 p. 34 (v. atrocitas a); hostis civem .. in gladio †excorto [? l. exserto] .. invadere non desistit AD. MARSH *Ep.* 246 p. 482; subito virgam e manica ~uit *Arthur & Gorlagon* 8.

3 to disclose, reveal, demonstrate. **b** (p. ppl. *exsertus*) open, conspicuous.

terroris et comminationis Deus ~ebat indicia DOMINIC *V. Ecgwini prol.*; Gallicos ictus gladio et lancea palam ~emus ORD. VIT. X 24 p. 145; HANV. I 484 (v. epenthesis b); veri sacra fides .. / .. dum culta venis, dum libera frontem / exeris J. EXON. *BT* I 13; simulare ab eorum obsidione recessum, ut attrahantur et occultos errores ~ere et in quibus feriri possunt prudenter elicere R. NIGER *Mil.* III 78. **b** cum bis binis annorum cursibus dira peste vesaniae vastaretur et †exerti [v. l. exerte, sc. ~tae] macilentia arido in corpore vires distaberent [vv. ll.: †distabuerent, †distabuerunt] FELIX *Guthl.* 41; ~tum, i. .., edoctum, .. apertum, .. manifestum *GlH* E 458; gratia quippe seculi hec, velut exterior [v. l. ~tior] carnis pulchritudo, que quidem a Deo, quanquam ipsa sit gratia fallax et vana H. BOS. *Thom.* II 1 p. 164.

4 to stir up, exert; **b** (w. abstr. obj.).

~ere, i. exercere *GlC* E 531; **1169** si vero regem redire contigerit, .. vocem pontifice dignam ~at [episcopus] in spiritu libertatis J. SAL. *Ep.* 292 (289 p. 656); mox totum se ~it et haud segniter strenue se accingit ad opera H. BOS. *Thom.* III 6 p. 193; MAP *NC* IV 4 (v. consolidare 1a); dandis exsertus [*gl.*: ad dandum paratus] bibit hoc de fonte Robertus, / quem sapit ut certus, et in omni jure disertus GARL. *Mor. Scol.* 9. **b a804** refrigerium est quoddam caritatis apicibus ~ere flammas et vice lingue frui litterulis ALCUIN *Ep.* 290; intellectus .. ~it vires suas J. SAL. *Pol.* 437C; sol .. radiorum vim ~ere incipit ALB. LOND. *DG* 8. 11; caritas .. aliquem actum elicit quo majorem .. non posset ~ere R. MARSTON *QD* 320.

5 to untangle, undo.

mox igitur tauri prostratum morte cadaver / suscitat exertis absolvens vincula nodis ALDH. *VirgV* 588; **9.** .. ~tis, *onbundonne* *WW*.

exsertare (exe-) [CL], to exsert, thrust out, expose, lay bare.

~abant, denudabant *GlH* E 458; ~are, denudare OSB. GLOUC. *Deriv.* 195 (cf. ib. 201: expapillare, denudare, expectorare, ~are, exerere).

exsiaimiare v. essaimare.

exsibilare [CL], to exsibilate, hiss off.

~at *hwyslaþ* *GlP* 735; ab omnibus exploditur et ~atur BALD. CANT. *Tract.* 9. 491C.

1 exsiccare v. 2 exsecare.

2 exsiccare (exi-) [CL]

1 (trans.) to exsiccate, dry up (liquids); **b** (watercourse or sim.); **c** (fig.); **d** (intr.).

tradunt quidam quod vis veneni .. omnem defuncti cadaveris humorem ~averat ORD. VIT. III 5 p. 74; autumnus .. adeo cuncta astringit, ut etiam herbe jam marceant, suci arborum ~entur ALB. LOND. *DG* 4. 8; fervore suo omnem sol ~at humorem *Ib.* 8. 1. **b** nimius in Sequana ventus efflavit, et aliquandiu ~avit ORD. VIT.

XII 16 p. 349; in plerisque locis fontes aruerunt, lacus et cisterne ~ate sunt *Ib.* XIII 29 p. 80; s**1136** Deus .. duorum castelli puteorum uberes venas .. ~avit *G. Steph.* I 18; [Hercules] alterum ejus [sc. hydre] alveum, cujus eruptiones immodice agros obruebant, ~avit ALB. LOND. *DG* 13. 4. **c** **797** adducite vobis doctores et magistros sacrae scripturae .. ne fons veritatis in vobis ~etur ALCUIN *Ep.* 129; concede ut, spiritu tuo operante, ~entur ista flumina misera Babilonis GASCOIGNE *Loci* 99. **d** cum jam detinuisset salsus fluvius et litora usque ad recentis aque alveolum ~assent *G. Hen. V* 25 p. 168.

2 to dry out (substance by removing liquid); **b** (med.). **c** (w. pers. subj.) to cause or allow to become dry. **d** to leave (ship) high and dry.

donec absterserat omnem / lux solis limpham, exuviasque exsiccat ab undis ÆTHELWULF *Abb.* 243; pannus in semilunio aqua infusus, naturali glutinosa sui humiditate prorsus sublata, ~atus de facili teritur NECKAM *NR* II 79; ligna in plenilunio corrumpuntur; pori enim eorum et raritates humiditate replentur, quia primo dum calore aeris ~antur in putredinem convertuntur *Quaest. Salern.* N 3; *AncrR* 49 (v. denudatio 2); sol suis radiis segetes ~ans metendas *Deorum Imag.* 23. **b** GILB. III 137v. 2 (v. extenuare 2a); [salia] sunt omnia facile pulverinabilia et calida sicca multum ~antia et constrictiva *Ps.*-GROS. *Summa* 642; myrrha resolvit et aperit et ~at ea [sc. apostemata] absque mordicatione GAD. 30. 1. **c** faeno .. salsuginis .. deciso ~ato et incenso BEDE *Kings* 730; ad pannos ~andos *Domus Reg.* 133 (v. aquarius 3a); vidit .. virum Dei folia .. in manibus terentem et colores madentes ad estus ignis ~antem R. COLD. *Godr.* 596; a**1200** tantum .. more .. dedi eis .. ubi sufficienter possint ~are petas suas *Melrose* 87; **1356** novum meremium .. per tempus estivale poterit ~ari *Fabr. York* 171. **d** s**893** cum ad naves sociorum .. reverti vellent, ~ate sunt ... sed ecce mare ad puppes redeunte .. BROMPTON 813.

3 (fig.) to dry out (corrupting humours).

[laboribus] quibus naturales et velut ingenitas ejus delectationes ~are .. queamus BEDE *Tab.* 456D; ut medullae corporis mei ~entur ANSELM (*Or.* 7) III 24; primates .. urit ambitio, ~at [v. l. excecat] cupiditas, contrahit avaritia et quecumque parit elatio delicie cleri sunt R. NIGER *Mil.* IV 52.

4 (med.) to increase the proportion of 'dryness'.

[accidentalis sterilitas] fiat .. vicio spermatis .. ut si nimium sit calidum, vel nimium siccum, unde nimium consumitur vel ~atur, unde non adherit in vitam. .. in mulo et mula, quarum spermata siccissima sunt et viscosa, .. ex intensa siccitate ~antur et consumuntur *Quaest. Salern.* B 174.

5 (intr.) to wither, become weak.

contabescunt, i. ~ant, *hy aswindaþ*, vel *heo beoþ unbliþe* *GlH* C 1647.

exsiccatio (exi-) [LL]

1 drying. **b** (med.) power to reduce 'humidity' and increase 'dryness'.

desiccentur [trocissi] in umbra .. et oportet ut non cadat super eos radius solis omnino nec ante ~onem nec post ipsam BACON V 107; **1300** (v. 2 decasus 1c); **1313** computat in decasu, mensurando, ~one, perdicione et putrefaccione, in granar' iij quar. vj bus. brasei *KRAc* 375/8 f. 23*d.*; **1460** pannos et vestes .. causa ~onis pendentes in hortis *Reg. Whet.* I 286. **b** caro serpentis, cum in usu habetur, .. prolongat vitam, .. et ~o ejus est fortis sed calefactio ejus non est vehemens BACON IX 66; gumme in quibus est caliditas tepida cum ~one GAD. 65v. 2; *Ib.* 116v. 1 (v. curatio 2a); et si constringatur hanelitus patientis propter ~onem rosarum J. MIRFIELD *Brev.* 82.

2 drain.

1227 quod .. faciat auxilium ad wallias faciendas ... unde .. prior ostendit quod, desicut ipse et alii deberent auxilium facere ad unam ~onem [= *BNB* II 217: †exsucatorem] faciendam .. *CurR* XIII 313.

exsiccativus (exi-), (med.): **a** drying, exsiccative (as sb. n.). **b** reducing proportion of 'humidity'.

a appone ~a sine mordicacione infrigidancia parum cum pauca resolucione GAD. 29v. 1. **b** si est nimia humiditatis, .. dentur cibi ~i et humiditatis consumptivi GILB. 81v. 1.

exsiliquus [cf. CL siliqua, siliquari], (of pulses) shelled.

fabe silique et fabe ~e [*gl.: faves saunz cosses*] NECKAM *Ut.* 96; *schylled pyse*, pise ~e *CathA.*

exsilire (exi-) [CL]

1 to leap, leap out (also fig.). **b** to burst forth (also fig.). **c** to spring forth, appear.

laetis bonorum operum et cogitatuum passibus ~iunt BEDE *Gen.* 168; intravit cum illis in templum, ambulans et ~iens et laudans Dominum [*Acts* iii 8] *Id. HE* V 2; c**798** ut purior ~iat anima de ergastulo carceris sui ALCUIN *Ep.* 161; GERV. CANT. *Chr.* 121 (v. episcopalis 2b); arcum tenens cervam ~ientem sagitta perforavit GIR. *IK* I 1 p. 17; MAP *NC* II 19 (v. consummare 2a); WALS. *HA* II 184 (v. 2 distentio b); in villam jam marcialibus furiis subjiciendam ~iens cum suis sanguinis sitibundis agminibus *Ps.*-ELMH. *Hen. V* 45 p. 110. **b** excanduit, in iracundiam ~ivit *GlC* E 502, *GlH* E 592; *Lib. Eli.* III 60 (v. contingere 1a); flammarum globi de gurgite marino frequentius in terrarum eminentias ~ire cernuntur AD. MARSH *Ep.* 48. **c** [fructus] terris ~ientes appareant ALB. LOND. *DG* 8. 14.

2 (trans.) to leap out from.

corbem ~it HERM. ARCH. 13 (v. corbis a).

exsilium v. exilium. **exsisa** v. 2 excisa.

exsistenter, really, in fact.

cum omnia ista apparenter sint metalla, et non existenter *Correct. Alch.* 10.

exsistentia [LL]

1 a being, living thing. *V. et. ens* 1a, *entitas* 1a, 2 *essentia* 1a.

Deum super omnem ~iam .. credimus esse ALCUIN *Dogm.* 24D; nomine ~ie .. intelligitur quod habeat substantiale esse RIC. S. VICT. *Trin.* IV 16. 940A; ~ie convenit quod habeat substantiale esse HALES *Sent.* III 63.

2 substance, material. *V. et.* 2 *essentia* 2a.

puer natus et spiramen / trinus Deus paris tamen / existentiae *Anal. Hymn.* XLVII 367.

3 existence. *V. et.* 2 *esse* 14c, 2 *essentia* 5.

in rerum quoque ~ia est similiter vera vel falsa significatio ANSELM (*Ver.* 9) I 189; nominamus .. 'aliud' quod .. habet nec conceptionem nec ullam ~iam *Id. Misc.* 336; ut per ~iam ejus in corpore adquirat ipsa anima sibi pure veritatis participationem J. BLUND *An.* 381; est igitur veritas sermonis vel opinionis de futuro presens assertio ~ie rei in futuro cum ~ia rei in futuro GROS. 144; **1231** in eternis et increatis rationibus contuebimur omnium rerum creatarum ~ias *Id. Ep.* 6; potentia divina non habet arctationem et limitationem quantum ad actualem ~iam in pluribus et in infinitis BACON *Maj.* I 145; super existentiam earum [i.e. substantiarum spiritualium] in loco *Id. Tert.* 172; visio est exsistentis ut exsistens est et ut presens est videnti secundum suam ~iam et secundum hoc distinguitur visio ab intellectione abstractiva DUNS *Ord.* II 23; simplex divina apprehensio facit ipsum apprehensum esse presens Deo, sed non secundum ~iam (KYN.) *Ziz.* 40; **1559** de existentia corporis et sanguinis Christi in Eucharistie sacramento *Conc. Scot.* II 164 *tit.*

4 reality (dist. from appearance).

vir .. habens .. plus fraudis quam laudis, plus eminentie quam ~ie GIR. *EH* II 11; quid aliud hoc queso nisi manifestam hypocrisis notam et simulatricis apparentie ubi non subest ~ie veritas *Id. Spec.* III 13 p. 213.

exsistere (exi-) [CL]

1 (absol.) to be, exist; *v. et.* 2 *esse* 1, *exstare* 2a. **b** to be in reality (dist. from appearance). **c** to occur.

quid es, [Deus,] nisi id quod summum omnium solum ~ens per seipsum? ANSELM (*Prosl.* 5) I 104; cum dicimus Deum ~ere de Deo nascendo vel procedendo *Id.* (*Proc. Sp.* 14) II 214; sunt tria, 'sum', 'fio', '~o', a triplici genere compositionis. quedam .. est simplicium que ratione virtutis agendi et patiendi generatur, et dicitur 'esse'; quedam per abjectionem ab aliquo generatur, et dicitur 'fieri'; quedam per compositionem prius entium et dicitur '~ere' *Ps.*-GROS. *Gram.* 62; cum solum illud quod ~it Deus intuetur, multa .. sunt que non ~unt, ut possibilia; omnia tamen preterea et futura ~unt in tempore suo (WYCL.) *Ziz.* 464. **b** utinam .. fuerint .. tam ~entes quam apparentes GIR. *TH* III 27; Haraldus, dictus et ~ens proditor et perjurus .. *Feud. Man.* 138. **c** s**1290** hoc anno pluviarum inundaciones frequenter extiterunt OXNEAD *Chr.* 277.

2 a (w. locative) to be present, located, situated; **b** (w. local adv.); **c** (w. adverbial phr.). **d** (w. local adv.) to be present, appear, attend; **e** (w. adverbial phr.). *V. et.* 2 *esse* 6.

a s**1449** dominus Schalys, London' ~ens *Chr. Hen. VI & Ed. IV* 151. **b** in insulas plurimas dividitur terra illa propter diversa flumina ibi ~encia *Itin. Mand.* 98; exposuit vela ventis in .. navibus, exceptis his que aretro extiterant *G. Hen. V* 3; **1449** omnia alia bona mea residua mobilia, presencia et futura, ubicumque ~encia .. do et lego *Wills Richm.* 6. **c** Orion .. oritur .. cum sole in Tauro ~ente ALB. LOND. *DG* 9. 6; **1237** summitate pertice, ubi signum crucis extiterat, detruncata, que crux etiam, dum videretur fugientibus onerosa, in medio extitit derelicta (*Lit. Frederici Imp.*) M. PAR. *Maj.* III 444 (v. et. 7d infra); **1260** de omnibus terris .. in quibuscunque comitatibus terre ille ~ent *BBC* (*Cinque Ports*) 166; **1283** custos manerii .. inveniet cariagium .. pro antiquis terris in manerio predicto ~entibus *Cust. Battle* 15; **1313** S. de Hoke ~ens super quandam carectam .. cecidit pro mocione unius equi in eadem carecta ~entis *Eyre Kent* I 154–5; **1472** pro *le riddyng* quarrere ~entis juxta molend' de Acley pro recto cursu aque habendo *Ac. Durh.* 644. **d** **1212** cum R... qui foris extitit, audisset matrem suam clamantem, ipse intravit *SelPlCrown* 59; tunc clerico ejusdem Johannis .. ibi ~ente *State Tri. Ed. I* 61. **e** **1217** per consilium fidelium nostrorum nobiscum ~entium *Pat* 21; rege in regno suo non ~ente *Fleta* 28 (*recte* 82); s**1240** ad cujus [ecclesie] dedicacionem exstitit archiepiscopus .. et sex episcopi *Flor. Hist.* II 237*n.*; episcopis et aliis prelatis simul ~entibus in parliamento *Proc. A. Kyteler* 19; s**1313** Thomas .. ~ens in Francia AD. MUR. *Chr.* 19; cum rex extiterat apud portum .. pro disposicione navalis potencie *G. Hen. V* 20.

3 (w. adverbial phr.) to be, become, or remain (in specified condition); *v. et.* 2 *esse* 7, *exstare* 3b. **b** (w. *ultra*) to be in charge of, supervise.

isti homines libere exstiterunt ad Berchingum *DB* II 17v.; in dubio ~ens utrum diutius eos obpugnaret G. MON. I 15; **1275** (v. de 12b); Johannes de R. infra etatem ~ens *State Tri. Ed. I* 24; **1291** dedimus .. domos .. tanquam escaeta .. in manu nostra ~encia *Deeds Balliol* 99; hic quadam die in societate fratrum ~ens *Latin Stories* 113; **1300** (v. de 12c); **1344** (v. de 12e); firma pax teneatur .. inter omnes subditos domini regis ad pacem suam ~entes (*Stat. David II* 31) *RegiamM* II f. 54v.; quilibet sacerdos ~ens in peccato mortali WYCHE *Ep.* 532; **1451** ego .. in mea ultima voluntate ~ens, condo meum testamentum *MunAcOx* 613; in episcopali gradu ~ens antequam fuit archiepiscopus GASCOIGNE *Loci* 231; **1453** in denariis solutis diversis garcionibus .. in singulis officiis suis ~entibus et expectantibus a dicto primo die Octobris .. usque ultimum diem Septembris (*DL Ac. Var.*) *JRL Bull.* XL 410; **1503** quilibet laicus de scholasticorum familia minime ~ens *StatOx* 309; **1575** jamque .. in voluntate ~it predictas litteras patentes .. restituere cancellandas *Pat* 1131 m. 19. **b** **1280** in cibo et potu j hominis ~entis ultra messores per iiij septimanas *Ac. Stratton* 111; **1308** in vadio G. P. existentis ultra trituracionem et facientis exitum grangie per xlv dies *Crawley* 263; **1313** [*plumber & boy*] existent' ultra [*the washing of ashes of lead*] *Fabr. Exon.* 70.

4 (w. adj. as compl.) to be, become, or remain (of specified description); **b** (w. adv.). *V. et.* 2 *esse* 9, *exstare* 3a.

solertissimus extiterat et .. ~ere non desistit BEDE *HE* V 20 p. 332; qui quondam extiterant famosi late per orbem / corpora sena tenet hic marmor *Epigr. Milredi* 813; hoc factum esse autumabant .. diaboli .. invidia qui semper bonis invidus ~at ASSER *Alf.* 74; sub eodem .. momento pauper ex divite, mortuus ex vivo potest ~ere *Simil. Anselmi* 69; ferus cunctis et intolerabilis ~ere *G. Steph.* II 111; **1168** nulli .. exstiti onerosus J. SAL. *Ep.* 273 (283); s**1281** H. Loodiensis episcopus dignitate episcopali eo quod proletarius extiterat .. spoliatus OXNEAD *Chr.* 257; s**1078** (v. exturbatio); **1355** moneta .. que in pondere minor et allaia debilior ~it (*Cl*) *Foed.* V 813a; tuam voluntatem mihi prorsus patere certus ~o *Arthur & Gorlagon* 1; **1553** dictus R., nativus ~ens .. *Crawley* 519. **b** Jesus extitit plus quam propheta [ME: *Jesu Crist was more and grettere than anothir prophete*] *Itin. Mand.* 70.

5 (w. sb. as compl.); **b** (w. sb. or pron. in agreement as compl.); **c** (w. compl. in gen.); **d** (w. inf. as compl.). *V. et.* 2 *esse* 10, *exstare* 3c.

ut ei doctrinae cooperator ~ens diligenter adtenderet BEDE *HE* IV 1; taediosus .. veritatis arbiter ~ebat ASSER *Alf.* 105; **1187** (v. coadjutor); ~ens confessor suus GASCOIGNE *Loci* 2. **b** qui .. miraculi testes extitere GILDAS *EB* 26; a**700** pontificis Offtori ego Ecguuine .. successor in episcopatum ~o *CS* 76; **956** (12c) abbas et omnis congregatio .. testes extitisse memorantur *CS* 931; qui prevaricator vel eversor conscripte legis exstiterit (*Leg. Hen.* 34. 8) *GAS* 566; quia Deus in parte extitit causa .. PULL. *CM* 218; s**679** reges extiterunt Francorum Theodericus et Childericus *Chr. S. Neoti*; respondit se .. caussam uteri ejus intumescentis extitisse L. DURH. *Brig.* 2; cum .. nepos .. ex filio primogenito .. de corpore suo ei heres extiterit GLANV. VII 3; †neutrum [v. l. neuter] .. illorum [sc. regum] de quo agimus ille extitit G. FONT. *Inf. S. Edm.* 3; s**1193** cujus fratrem prius occiderat in curia regis Francie, ipsis ~entibus pueris ad scaccarium ludentibus *Eul. Hist.* I 387; Sigismundo bono tunc ~ente imperatore Romanorum GASCOIGNE *Loci* 163; parochiani ipsi piscatores ~unt FLETE *Westm.* 45; **1467** R. unus valectus regis de corona extiterit (*TRBk*) *JRL Bull.* L 464. **c** **1239** *MonA* V 253a (v. gilbogus); **1300** si quis .. monachorum, cujuscumque condicionis vel status extiterit .. *Vis. Ely* 22; **1315** intencionis nostre non ~it, nec volumus quod .. (*Cl*) *Foed.* III 522a; Jacob xcj annorum ~ens genuit Joseph HIGD. II 11 p. 302; s**1381** quia tenere etatis ~ebat AD. USK 155. **d** emundet se, quod nec velle nec posse nec consilium nec testimonium ejus extiterit (*Leg. Hen.* 87. 2a) *GAS* 601.

6 (w. pr. ppl. as compl.). *Cf.* 4 *supra*, 7 *infra*. *V. et.* 2 *esse* 12b.

c**705** licet adolescens aetate ~as ALDH. *Ep.* 8 (10); **1072** ut .. archiepiscopus .. canonicis dispositionibus oboediens ~at *Lit. Cant.* III 351; vir prudens .. tunc forte presens ~ens GIR. *TH* I 32; de redditibus, .. decimis, elemosinis, et ceteris omnibus, prioribus Dunelm' et monachis per omnia intendentes ~ant *Feod. Durh.* lxx; **1552** in quem inoboediens extiterit *StatOx* 362.

7 (as auxiliary vb. w. p. ppl.): **a** (pres. as pres.); **b** (pres. as perf.); **c** (imperf. as imperf.); **d** (perf. as

perf.); **e** (fut. perf. as fut. perf.). *V. et.* 2 *esse* 13, *exstare* 4.

a **1253** si quis .. gratiam per potentiam .. conetur extorquere .. a societate .. universitatis privatus ~at *StatOx* 49; facientes inquisicionem ac eciam utrum alias beneficiatus ~at *Chr. Peterb.* 82; de errore illorum qui in ecclesia beneficiati ~unt GOWER *VC* III cap. 20 *tit.*; **1583** advantagia, emolumenta, et hereditamenta .. premissis supradictis .. spectantia .. aut cum eisdem .. antehac usualiter dimissa, locata, usitata, occupata seu gavisa ~entia *Pat* 1235 m. 16. **b** **1262** (v. coronare 2b); **1335** quod .. H. et J. diversis aliis negociis prepediti ~ant *RScot* 312b; **1378** (v. evacuatio 3b); **1400** omnia maneria .. que .. nobis forisfacta ~unt (*Pat*) *Foed.* VIII 163a; dicit hoc factum fuisse Philippo ~ente electo *Feod. Durh.* 277; **1688** G. T. per inde .. attinctus seu adjudicatus ~it vel non existit (*Pardon*) *N. & Q.* V (1852) 496. **c** **1375** priorem .. in tantum prosequebantur quod .. abbathia illa de bonis et rebus suis in multo ~ebat pejorata *Pub. Works* I 286. **d** ostenditur eum electum Deo extitisse ÆLF. *Æthelwold* 3 (= WULF. *Æthelwold* 4); extitit derelicta M. PAR. *Maj.* III 444 (v. 2c supra); **c1259** quod per testes .. probatum extitit coram ipso evidenter quod .. *Cl* 19; in justicia extiterunt celi creati et constituti sunt super terram BACON V 123; **1306** villa predicta .. per progenitores nostros situata extitit super portum nostrum predictum *BBC* (*Yarmouth*) 245; extitit ad Romanam curiam appellatum GRAYSTANES 19 p. 67; **s1308** quoniam sine causa exstitit [v. l. fuit] fatigatus AD. MUR. *Chr.* 13; Britannia a Bruto extitit denominata CIREN. I 9; **1453** Margareta .. extitit posita in collistrigio *MunAcOx* 660. **e** si aliqua temptatio exorta foris repente extiterit, .. stabiles estote *V. Cuthb.* II 6.

8 (pr. ppl. as sb. n.) a being, (living) thing. *V. et. ens* 1.

ut .. sit Filius ~ens per Patrem et Pater per Filium, quasi non possit alter ~ens esse nisi per alterum ANSELM (*Mon.* 44) I 60; an aliqua non simul secundum tempus ~entia nunc sint BALSH. *AD rec.* 2 133 p. 87; octava trinitas est secundum quod est in cognitione vel affectu: ~ens pulcrum et delectabile HALES *Sent.* I 52; DUNS *Ord.* II 23 (v. exsistentia 3).

9 (as sb. m.) person present.

a1350 in expensis celerarii et secum ~encium in nundinis de Corbrigge per duos dies, x s. iij d. *Ac. Durh.* 38; **s1460** (v. 2 canon a).

10 (as sb. n.) being, existence: **a** (inf.); **b** (pr. ppl.); **c** (gd.).

a si unquam fabrica mundi sumpserit exordium .. an per se habeat ~ere D. MORLEY 10; ante omne tempus .. nulla creatura habuit ~ere (KYN.) *Ziz.* 40; instruxerunt nos .. doctores quomodo creature habeant triplex esse, sc. esse intelligibile in Deo, esse possibile in causis, et esse ~ere in proprio genere (WYCL.) *Ib.* 464. **b** ANSELM I 20 (v. ens 3). **c** ostenditur .. animam procreati hominis non .. a patre vel a matre ~endi initium sumere WULF. *Æthelwold* 4; quid .. aliud est ejus vel aetas vel ~endi diuturnitas quam ejus aeternitas ANSELM (*Mon.* 21) I 37.

exsitus v. exitus.

exsolanus (exo-) [cf. CL < exsolare; exulanus], one living in exile.

~us, extra solum patrium positus OSB. GLOUC. *Deriv.* 201 (cf. ib. 202: exulaticus, exul, exterminatus, ~us).

exsolare (exo-) [CL < *false etym.* ex + solum + -are], to go into exile, live in exile. (*Cf.* Plautus *Mer.* 593 *etc.*). *Cf. exulare.*

~are, exulari, quasi extra solum proprium ire OSB. GLOUC. *Deriv.* 196.

exsolescere [LL], to become unfamiliar, pass out of currency.

cujus [sc. Swithuni] bonitas jamdudum inchoata nec nostra etate ~escit W. MALM. *GP* II 75 p. 168.

exsolutio (exo-) [CL], **a** outcome, resolution. **b** (med.) 'exolution'. **c** discharge (of debt or sim.).

a patefacere judicii ~onem EDDI 53. **b** lipochomia malefaccio sincopis, ~o vulgariter, idem quod spasmus, i. defectus motus cordis *Alph.* 100. **c** functio, ~o tributorum *GlC* F 401; primo .. negotiandum est de satisfactionis ~one, postea de meritorum acquisitione R. NIGER *Mil.* II 21.

exsolv- v. exsolu-.

exsolvere (exo-) [CL]

1 to unfasten, loose. **b** to set free. **c** to unfold (fig.), explain.

exfibulat, i. ~it, *unspeon, unscrydde GlH* E 575; Cuthbertus ibi sua eum vincula precepit ~ere R. COLD. *Cuthb.* 20 p. 43; extricare, ~ere OSB. GLOUC. *Deriv.* 195. **b** †**663** [? **693** or **708**] (14c) Cerberi .. rictibus reatum ~at proprium *CS* 121; per nimiam caliditatem ~untur spiritus et exhalant *Quaest. Salern.* B 307; *deseriter*, .. decarcerare, ~ere *Gl. AN Ox.* f. 154v. **c** si .. valuissem .. ipse ejus [visionis] interpretationem .. liquefactam ~ere B. *V. Dunst.* 30.

2 to perform, discharge (obligation); **b** (w. ref. to conjugal debt); **c** (eccl., w. ref. to canonical hours or sim.). **d** (w. *gratias* or sim.) to give thanks. **e** (w. *poenam* or sim.) to pay penalty.

obsequium suae servitutis quod domino debuit ~it BEDE *Hom.* II 7. 136. **b** **s34** fuit vir quidam .. et uxor ejus Ciborea, qui dum nocte quadam mutuum sibi debitum ~issent, somniavit mulier quod filium .. peperisset HIGD. IV 6 p. 352. **c** matutinorum hymnos ~ebat Christo voce sonora BYRHT. *V. Ecgwini* 390; **1282** in horis canonicalibus ~endis *Reg. Ebor.* 295; horas canonicas .. cum majori devocione et attencione ~ere si poteris (HILTON) *MS BL Royal* 6 E III f. 122ra. **d** **1002** (12c) (v. 2 cunctari b); debitas Deo gratias ~imus DOMINIC *V. Ecgwini* I 9; grates ~it MAP *NC* III 3 f. 40; **s1147** cives .. laudes et gratias .. ~erunt R. HOWD. I 209; **1340** (v. deprecari 1a). **e** audivit Henricum Scrop .. prodicionis sue penas meritas ~isse WALS. *HA* II 307.

3 to pay (money owed) in discharge of debt.

heinfaram vel forestel .. qui faciebat iiij li. ~ebat *DB* I 262v. (*Cheshire*); *Chr. Abingd.* II 125 (v. geldare 4b); pensiones domorum .. ~antur *StatCantab* 213; **s1350** donec communi ciste universitatis ebdomodalem ~erit bursam suam *StatOx* 152; **1412** (v. contumacia 1b).

exsomnis [CL], unsleeping, wakeful.

hic et hec insompnis et hoc -ne, i. sine somno, et hic et hec ~is et hoc -ne, i. extra somnum OSB. GLOUC. *Deriv.* 549.

exsonium v. essonia.

exsoporare [cf. CL soporare], to send to sleep.

heu quot et quam egregios virtutum viros recumbentes in gremio suo [sc. Dalile] ~avit, decalvavit, excecavit [cf. *Judges* xvi 19] J. FORD *Serm.* 49. 12.

exsorbēre [CL], **~escere,** to swallow, gulp down.

to suppe, clere, haurire, sorbere, con-, ex-, ob-, sorbere, exsorbescere, con-, ex-, sorbillare *CathA.*

exsors [CL], exempt (from), having no share (in).

ab hereditate gratiae .. in aeternum permanebunt ~tes BEDE *Gen.* 190; exanimis jacuit paene et spiraminis exsors ALCUIN *SS Ebor* 618; non eris immunis poenae, non criminis exsors FRITH. 1092; Christiane fidei ~tes H. LOS. *Serm.* 22; peccati ~s permanere PULL. *Sent.* 747C; si .. libertatis spiritualis ~s exstiterit .. W. DONC. *Aph. Phil.* 5. 6.

exsortium, levy (of troops conscripted by drawing lots).

1267 mandamus quatenus .. ad nos cum omni hominum ~io, quod poteritis, personaliter veniatis (*Lit. O. Cardinalis*) *Reg. North.* 8 (= *Reg. Ebor.* 153).

exspatiari (exp-) [CL], **a** to spread out. **b** to wander (from path, also fig.). **c** to expatiate, digress, elaborate (in speech or writing).

a Phrigie tria milia pubis / exiliunt, variis exspatiata modis *Brutus* 220. **b** cor tumet, insanit cervix, pes errat, ocellus / expaciatur GARL. *Epith.* I 242; *Id. Tri. Eccl.* 63 (v. dextrarius a). **c** de eo aliquid ~andum est ALB. LOND. *DG* 11. 9.

exspectabilis (exp-) [LL], outstanding in appearance, excellent. *V. et. spectabilis.*

~es senatores, *þa medumestan ealdres GlH* E 638; [rates] ~i .. ordine flatu secundo Sanduich .. sunt appulsi *Enc. Emmae* II 5; **s1235** R. de S. elegantie singularis, generis ~is, probitatis admirabilis M. PAR. *Maj.* III 334; [Eadfrithus] corpore ~is elegancie et magnitudinis fuit *G. S. Alb.* I 20.

exspectaculum (exp-) [LL = *sight, spectacle*], (by misinterp.) expectation. *V. et. exspectantia, exspectatio.*

~um, expectatio OSB. GLOUC. *Deriv.* 201.

exspectantia (exp-), expectancy, expectation. *V. et. exspectaculum, exspectatio.*

papa non concedit ~iam singulariter super dicta persona, ne expectans conspiret in mortem ejus ex libidine dominandi WYCL. *Civ. Dom.* I 211.

exspectare (exp-) [CL]

1 to look for, expect, await. **b** (gram.) to 'look to', depend on. **c** to refer or apply to, lie in store for. **d** to look upon, consider. **e** (leg.) to admit, allow.

~a me hic parum usque dum rediero *Descr. Constant.* 247; **a1216** mercator foraneus .. in hospitio suo ~et emptorem suum (*Mun. Lond.*) *EHR* XVII 726; fructus est ultimum quod ~atur de arbore DUNS *Ord.* II 47. **b** subtrahitur etiam verbum quando plures clausule unum verbum ~ant ut 'tu labores, tu dolores, tu timores considerras' *Ps.*-GROS. *Gram.* 72. **c** **s1206** (v. decertatio); **1409** coram illo seu illis ad quem seu quos cognitio premissorum ~at et ~are dignocitur *Foed.* VIII 578. **d** **a804** ubi sancti post hujus vitae sudorem aeterna pace fruuntur, qui nostrum de supernis sedibus ~ant agonem ALCUIN *Ep.* 310; **1229** consilium ipsius excommunicati sine periculo animarum non potuimus ~are (*Lit. Patriarchae*) M. PAR. *Maj.* III 182. **e** GLANV. II 7 (v. essonia 1a); **1331** qui est infra etatem et in custodia domini regis et sine quo discussionem libertatum predictarum ~are non potest et pet' quod loquela ista remaneat usque ad etatem etc. *PQW* 44a.

2 to look for, expect (w. longing, hope, fear, *etc.*); **b** (w. ref. to the Lord's coming); **c** (w. ref. to King Arthur). **d** to await. **e** to wait (intr.).

sciens [quia] homini Dei ~anda erat *V. Cuthb.* II 8; **c798** si vulnera corporis carnalis medici manus ~ant, quanto magis vulnera animae spiritalis medici solacia deposcunt ALCUIN *Ep.* 138 p. 217; nichil .. desiderabilius ~abant quam medicum G. MON. VIII 14; populo ~ante quod de eis futurum erat *Ib.* IX 11 p. 449; **1177** ~abamus pacem J. SAL. *Ep.* 472 (183); WYCL. *Civ. Dom.* I 211 (v. exspectantia). **b** ~antes a justo rectore omnium Deo .. severa .. judicia GILDAS *EB* 11; quam .. promissionem .. Domini ~at feliciter *V. Greg.* p. 110; monachi .. Patremfamilias ~ent, ut veniens eos faciat in aeterna requie sine fine permanere O. CANT. *Const.* 6; sancti qui Christi Domini adventum ardenter ~abant *Eccl. & Synag.* 96; qui .. Domini sui misericordiam patienter ~averint .. *Simil. Anselmi* 80. **c** sic Britonum ridenda fides et credulus error / Arturum exspectat exspectabitque perenne J. EXON. *BT* III 473; propter metum Britonum non audens eum [sc. Arturum] dicere mortuum, quem adhuc vere Britones ~ant venturum W. NEWB. *HA proem.* p. 18; quibus si credideris, / exspectare poteris / †Arcturum [l. Arturum] cum Britonibus P. BLOIS *Contra clericos* 1134C. **d** quasi responsum ejus .. cui loquebatur ~ans BEDE *HE* IV 9 p. 223; hujus tuae mihi inauditae assertionis multum a te rationem ~o ANSELM (*Lib. Arb.* 8) I 220; **1164** pro certo accepi .. dominum Remensem ejus [sc. regis] ~are colloquium J. SAL. *Ep.* 134 (136 p. 6). **e** omnes ante januam basilicae discalciati laneisque induti ~ent ÆLF. *EC* 45; lex datur Moysi, ~ante populo in campestribus AD. DORE *Pictor* 157; dum .. illi exterius ~arent ut viderent finem *Latin Stories* 109.

3 to wait, await (a time): **a** (absol.); **b** (w. acc.); **c** (w. *usque, ut,* or sim.). **d** (leg., w. *aetatem*) to await the age (of majority, w. ref. to heir). **e** (w. *mortem*) to outlive (someone).

a si [mulier] in captivitatem per vim ducta est, vir ejus v annos ~et THEOD. *Pen.* II 12. 21; ~a adhuc parum ANSELM (*CurD* 1) II 92; GLANV. I 7 (v. dies 11a). **b** ut horam diei tertiam ad capiendum cibum ~aret .. invitabat *V. Cuthb.* II 2; vesperam ~abant BEDE *Hom.* I 16. 258; cum lacrimis ~emus finem nostrum *V. Gund.* 33 p. 56; *Stat. Tri. Edw. I* 79 (v. gildhalla c); **1441** compotum fidelem reddere et finem ejusdem compoti fideliter expectare [l. expectare] *DL ChancR* 8 m. 7d. **c** **1071** necessitate urgente ~are non potui quoadusque redirent .. legati nostri LANFR. *Ep.* 2; **1164** donec certioretur domi ~at J. SAL. *Ep.* 134 (136 p. 6); **c1165** dissuasit ne sub ea conditione redirem sed ~arem ut ira ejus [sc. regis] aliquantulum deferveret *Ib.* 142 (139 p. 22); **1168** rex .., cum fere usque ad vesperam ~asset, transivit flumen *Ib.* 246 (279 p. 604); ~a usque cras! *AncrR* 125; **s1355** rex .. ~avit ibidem usque dictum diem Martis AVESB. 126v. **d** **1224** Jueta pro se et pro Godefrido etc. dicit quod non debet etatem ~are quia Jordanus pater suus non obiit seisitus ut de feodo *CurR* XI 1995; **1248** R. non potest hoc dedicere. ideo ~et etatem *SelPlMan* 16. **e** **1224** Adam habuit ij filios, Rogerum sc. et Brianum .. set Rogerus non ~avit mortem patris et .. Brianus post mortem Ade intravit hereditatem sui *CurR* XI 2033; **1225** Matillis et Cecilia soror ejus ~erunt mortem Nicholai et ad eas reversa fuit advocacio illa [ecclesie de Eywenthe, *Beds*] *BNB* III 108.

4 to wait, delay, remain. **b** (w. *super*) to wait on, attend.

non debet homo ~are attendendo quid velit consiliari sed celeriter moras rumpere ALEX. CANT. *Dicta* 17 p. 177; **1214** qui B. ~avit ibi per viij dies et R. et G. non venerunt *SelPlCrown* 67; **1253** ~averunt clam insidiantes si aliquis sequeretur *SelPlForest* 79; **1254** fecit R. de P. tunc garcionem suum ibidem ~are ad insidiandum si quis voluit feram illam asportare *Ib.* 112; multi ~ant confiteri [ME: *monimon abit for to schriven him*] usque ad necessitatem extremam *AncrR* 130; **c1370** (v. contus a); **1430** lego Christoforo Pyncus, si ~averit mecum in servicio, xlij s. iiij d. *Test. Ebor.* II 6; plura mala fiunt .. que non fierent si .. domini temporales sua loca debita regerent et in eisdem ~arent GASCOIGNE *Loci* 1. **b** **1419** diversis officiariis ~antibus apud Rouchestre super salve custodiend' divers' †habentes [MS: harnes'] domine regine (*KRAc* 406/30 f. 8b) *JRL Bull.* XXVI 86 (cf. ib.: diversis de Rouchestre vigilantibus †habentes [MS: harnes'] .. regine noctanter).

exspectatio (exp-) [CL]

1 awaiting (person or event), period of waiting in expectation or suspense; **b** (w. obj. gen.).

qui justi Symeonis ~onem [AS: *onbasnung*] inplesti *Rit. Durh.* 4; post diutinam ~onem ORD. VIT. XII 15 p. 348; **1166** si te interim hec angit ~o J. SAL. *Ep.* 165 (164);

gravissima .. medios inter hostes ~o GIR. *IK* II 13. **b** utique torquet me ~o tui longitudine sua ANSELM (*Ep.* 76) III 198; c**1237** de ~one decani in choro. .. vespere .. non inchoabuntur ante adventum decani *Stat. Linc.* I 282 *rub.*; **1270** (v. contrarietas 1b); **1398** graciam provisionis de canonicatu sub ~one prebende in ecclesia cathedrali .. Sar' *Pat* 350 m. 18.

2 expectation (theol.); **b** (w. *gentium*) Christ as the expected one (*cf.* LXX & Vulg. *Gen.* xlix 10: προσδοκία).

quanta sit in spirituali spes et quam delectabilis ~o Christi ANSELM (*Ep.* 168) IV 44; AD. SCOT *TT* 771C (v. desideriosus); '.. et liberavit me de manu Herodis et de ore leonis', i.e. de potestate inimici mei spiritualis et de ~one plebis Judeorum, i.e. de illis malis eternis in que mali spiritus crediderunt me casurum GASCOIGNE *Loci* 81. **b** ~onem illum dicit gentium quia omnes gentes .. servabantur ut per ipsum ad salutem .. vocarentur *Eccl. & Synag.* 76; ille diu promissus, ille singularis ~o gentium G. STANFORD *Cant.* 228; ~o gentium Jesus Christus M. PAR. *Maj.* I 80.

exspectativus (exp-), expectative; (w. *gratia*) reversionary grace (eccl.).

1389 per gracias ~as ecclesie .. fuerunt pregravate *Reg. Heref.* 75; **1462** non obstantibus .. constitucionibus et ordinacionibus apostolicis et quibuscumque aliis graciis expectativis, nominacionibus, .. reservacionibus .. *Mon. Hib. & Scot.* 437b; c**1520** dictus B. .. virtute cujusdam gracie ~e eidem a .. papa .. concesse .. canonicatum et prebendam de A. acceptavit *Form. S. Andr.* I 220.

exspectator (exp-) [LL], **a** one who waits. **b** spectator.

a ne longo suspendio diuturnae ambagis, antequam ad triclinium perveniatur, aeger ~or exanimetur GOSC. *Transl. Aug.* 29C; ille plasmator omnium et gubernator, quanquam longanimis sit ~or, .. gravis est ultor et punitor GIR. *EH* II 31 p. 380. **b** inmensa multitudo .. convenerat, aderat populus expectator [v. l. expectatur] futurus et judex BEDE *HE* I 17 (= Constantius *Vita S. Germani* 14: expectator [vv. ll. expectatur, spectator]).

exspedire v. expedire. **exspen-** v. expen-.

exsperare [cf. CL sperare], to hope.

s**1412** fidelia corda populi .. quorum stabiliri favoribus infallibiliter ~amus *Chr. S. Alb.* 66.

exsperduc- v. esperduc-.

exspernere (exp-) [LL], to despise utterly, reject.

1166 super exspreto mandato suo G. FOLIOT *Ep.* 170 p. 235; consuetudines .. rex jam pridem penitus exsprevisset si non [etc.] *Ib.* p. 242; **1409** expretis peticione et requesta meis *Foed.* VIII 577b.

exspes (exp-) [CL], without hope, hopeless. **b** mad.

s**1136** uxor ejus .. strictissime includebatur, totius ad se refugii supervenientis ~s *G. Steph.* I 9; [juvenis] ~s, quia jam tenebre noctis .. omne humanum sibi precludebant auxilium W. CANT. *Mir. Thom.* III 41; solus, inops, expes, vite peneque relictus GOWER *VC* I 1585. **b** *wode* .. furiosus, interdum ~s indeclinabile, immanis, insanus *CathA.*

exspinare [cf. CL spina], to draw out thorns. *V. et. despinare.*

CathA (v. despinare).

exspirabilis [cf. CL spirabilis], evaporable.

quia ignis in mixto est bene ~e (*sic*) BACON XIV 104.

exspirabilitas, capacity to be exhaled.

aer etiam [omnibus se communicat] per suas [proprietates] scilicet inspirabilitatem, ~atem, transparenciam, et continenciam DOCKING (*Gal.* vi 2) 113.

exspiraculum [cf. CL exspirare, spiraculum], vent, outlet.

fumositas .. non inveniens liberam exhalationem quasi repercutitur. ubi vero liberius invenit ~um, .. *Quaest. Salern.* B 168; quandam fumositatem que quandoque non habens ~um incipit corpus movere et vivificare *Ib.* 262.

exspirare (exp-) [CL]

1 (intr.) to breathe out. **b** (intr., of humours, vapours, or sim.) to vent. **c** (trans.) to exhale, breathe.

RIC. MED. *Anat.* 220 (v. epiglottis). **b** in estate .. velleres [ovium] abraduntur et calore exteriori aperiuntur pori et fumositas superflua ~at *Quaest. Salern.* B 69; ~ans .. corruptio urine [asinorum] *Ib.* C 22; complantatus quidem est spiritus, non quod non exhalet, sed quia nunquam totaliter ~at ALF. ANGL. *Cor* 11. 16; ~ans per poros calor coagulata dissolvit *Ib.* 14. 7. **c** ore naribusque ignem flammasque ~ant *Lib. Monstr.* II 13; J. BLUND *An.* 28 (v. exspiratio a).

2 to breathe out (one's life). **b** (intr.) to breathe one's last, die. **c** to run out, expire (also fig.). **d** (p. ppl. *s. act.*) having expired.

qui .. tam gravi infirmitate detinebatur, ut vitalem videretur ~are spiritum *VSH* (*Berach* 9) I 78; *he is deed* .. ~avit animam. .. efflavit spiritum STANBR. *Vulg.* 21. **b** illa primum .. episcopo poculum letitie dedit qui sibi ~anti calicem mortis auferebat *V. Cuthb.* IV 3; egrotavit tandemque ingravescente morbo .. ~avit ORD. VIT. III 9 p. 107; qui penitus ~asse videbantur .. respirare compellit GIR. *TH* I 27; rex innocens suffocatus ~avit *V. II Off.* 24. **c** quod hujusmodi valeat in brevi ~are mandatum H. BOS. *Ep.* 1435D; ~avit inter eos fere caritas R. NIGER *Mil.* IV 26; s**1217** ~ante treuga (OL. SCHOLASTICUS) M. PAR. *Maj.* III 9; **1309** litem .. propter quam tantam pecuniam effundere oporteret totaliter ~asse *Reg. Cant.* 1053; HARCLAY *Adv.* 74 (v. exspiratio c). **d** **1191** termino ~ato et pactione .. infirmata (*Lit. Regis*) R. HOWD. III 131; **1319** jacuit sub aqua ab hora prima .. diei Lune usque ad horam nonam diei sequentis ~atus .. et .. per Dei gratiam respiravit *Conc.* II 488a; **1577** concesserunt .. terminum annorum .. non ~atum *Entries* 679b.

exspiratio (exp-) [CL], **a** expiration, breathing out. **b** evaporation. **c** expiry.

a motum siquidem cordis ~onemque et respirationem continua esse oportere ALF. ANGL. *Cor* 3. 3; ad constrictionis et dilatationis officium ut ~onem et respirationem cordis operetur *Ib.* 16. 9; quamdiu animal inspirat et exspirat aera, vivit; quamcito deficit inspiratio et ~o aeris moritur J. BLUND *An.* 28; utrum in plantis sit ~o et inspiratio BACON XI 202. **b** [aer] in medio contentus non habens ~onem conculcatus calefit *Quaest. Salern.* P 15; erit aliud genus ~onis que tamen communiter loquendo potest dici evaporatio BACON XIV 104. **c** sub isto centenario v dicit quod pene omne regnum exspirabat .. quod v significat ~onem perfectam HARCLAY *Adv.* 74; **1450** venientes †aut [l. ante] diem ~onis salvi conductus *RScot* II 338b; **1558** a fine et ~one predicti termini annorum *Entries* 254.

exspoliare (exp-) [CL]

1 to despoil, rob; **b** (fig.). **c** to remove (priest).

si quis corpus in terra .. effodere vel ~iare praesumpserit, wargus habeatur (*Leg. Hen.* 83. 5) *GAS* 600; qui viam vadit qua latronibus invenitur, .. invaditur, tunditur, ~iatur ALEX. CANT. *Dicta* 14 p. 161; s**1147** nos .. ad hanc quam possidetis urbem, non vos expugnatum huc neque ~iatum, si vultis, venimus OSB. BAWDSEY clxi; sacrilege beati Cuthberti sanctuaria ~ians R. COLD. *Cuthb.* 28 p. 64; Loth capitur, pastor rapitur, locus expoliatur GOWER *VC* I 1315; audiens unum de famulis suis multis furtive ~iatum bonis BLAKMAN *Hen. VI* 11. **b** dolebas .. te presentia corporee lucis spoliari [MSS: ~ari] EADMER *Wilf.* 35; deridere cave fortunis expoliatum D. BEC. 207; sol naturam destruit et ~iat eos [sc. trocissos] a virtute BACON V 107. **c** **1381** modo guerrino intraverunt ecclesiam de W. et predictum nunc J. prepositum ab eadem ecclesia ibidem ~iaverunt *IMisc* 223/23.

2 to strip (person, of clothing). **b** (other); **c** (fig.). **d** to strip off (covering).

s**694** horrendum est hominibus ~iare Deum vivum et scindere tunicam ejus et hereditatem *AS Chr.*; coram nobis se ~iavit et .. gladio .. se .. cinctum ostendit ANSELM BURY *Mir. Virg.* 20; s**1217** spoliatus [v. l. ~iatus], tenens virgam, petiit et obtinuit absolutionem M. PAR. *Maj.* III 13; **537** Cesar ipsum [sc. Pilatum] illa tunica ~iari fecit (*Mors Pilati*) *Flor. Hist.* I 112; ~iatus et nudus in cruce [ME: *steortnaked he wes to spoilled on þe rode*] *AncrR* 96. **b** serpens per arctum intrat foramen ut se veteri pelle ~iet et novam adquirat CHAUNDLER *Apol.* 31b. **c** ~ia te tuum ab omni forma et imagine corporali EDMUND *Spec. Relig.* 134; ~ia tuum peccatum [ME: *despoille þi sunne*] et fac illud nudum in confessione *AncrR* 123 (cf. ib. 121: ~ia peccatum tuum [ME: *bi clute þu hit naut*], hoc est, non celes aliquam ejus circumstanciam); per affectum boni operis frumenta dominica vitiorum suorum paleis ~ia *NLA* (*Augustine*) I 82; expoliata toga legis nova fit sinagoga *Vers. Worc.* 104. **d** a lichnis cera non dentibus expolietur, / immo manu D. BEC. 2399.

exspoliatio (exp-) [LL],

1 plundering, robbing. **b** removal (of priest).

post templi sacri ~onem OSB. *V. Dunst.* 46; **1208** quandam ~onem in modum exceptionis objecit *Melrose* 101; **1289** bonorum ~o *Conc. Syn.* 1089; est sancta spoliatio [*Ziz.* 367: ~o; ME: *holy robbing*] pauperis populi *Concl. Loll. XII* 10; s**1355** propter vindictam ~onis ecclesie *Plusc.* IX 42; s**1308** omnes quotquot excommunicavit papa Benedictus causa ~onis Bonifacii pape octavi *Ann. Paul.* 266. **b** **1381** W. [et al.] fuerunt consulentes, auxiliantes et manutenentes ad ~onem dicti prepositi ab ecclesia predicta *IMisc* 223/23.

2 (usu. w. ref. to *Coloss.* ii 11, iii 9) putting off, removal.

c**798** ut .. veteris hominis ~o in novae reformationis transeat gloriam ALCUIN *Ep.* 136 p. 208 (cf. id. *Dub.* (*Conf. Fidei*) 1065B: circumcisus est .. in ~one veteris hominis); a**802** [circumcisio] quae in novo homine ~onem carnalium designat voluptatem *Id. Ep.* 243 p. 390 (= *Id. Exeg.* (*In Psalmos*) 572C); si conplexa fuerit luna Jovi, significat dubitacionem et mutacionem ac ~onem a fide HARCLAY *Adv.* 79.

exspresse v. exprese.

exspuere (exp-) [CL], **a** (intr.) to spit (also fig.). **b** (med.) to expectorate. **c** to spew. **d** (fig.) to eject. **e** to reject, despise.

a ~ens, linguam muti ut loqui valeat tangit BEDE *Hom.* II 6. 234; non tamen magis est in semine culpa, quam est in sputo vel sanguine, si quis mala voluntate ~it aut de sanguine suo aliquid emittit ANSELM (*Orig. Pecc.* 6) II 149; OSB. BAWDSEY clxvi (v. extergere a); GIR. *SD* 32 (v. delarvare); si sapis, extra vas expue quando lavas *Doctus dicetur* 28. **b** si patiens tussiat tussi sicca et nil ~at, signum est indigestionis in summo RIC. MED. *Signa* 36; quicumque sanguinem spumosum ~unt, his ex pulmone eductio fit GAD. 52v. 2. **c** hic volo bibere totis conatibus, / donec longissimis exspuem tractibus WALT. WIMB. *Carm.* 165. **d** sicut .. mare non suos habitatores ~it et extraneos hospites eicit R. NIGER *Mil.* III 40; neque Pictagoram infernus expuit WALT. WIMB. *Sim.* 104. **e** se commassant azymis, †expuens [*ed.* ? l. spuentes] fermentum *Poem S. Thom.* 84; [homunculi] ambitiones nostras .. ~ebant GIR. *IK* I 8 p. 76.

exspumare (exp-) [CL], to foam out.

ut odor improbus gustum irritet, gustus ingluviem ingerat, et ingluvies in libidinem ~et R. NIGER *Mil.* III 31; ~at os, ardent oculi *Ib.* 32.

exst- v. et. ext-. **exstamen** v. 2 stagnum.

exstare (ext-) [CL; *perf. forms not dist. from those of* exsistere]

1 to protrude, stand out.

~at, superat, eminet *GlC* E 383; stetit .. carina, puppi duntaxat ~ans et prora .. descensura sub undas W. CANT. *Mir. Thom.* III 46; est archus .. in quo super ~antes longe tabulas lapideas erecte sunt imagines GREG. *Mir. Rom.* 22.

2 (absol.) to be, exist; *v. et.* 2 *esse* 1, *exsistere* 1a. **b** (w. personal subj.) to live. **c** (of document) to be found, (of information) to be recorded. **d** (w. *memoria* as subj.) to endure, survive. **e** (w. abstr. subj.) to be, exist.

~are, adhuc esse *GlC* E 403; ~ant, sunt *Ib.* 567; qui condidit omne quod extat WULF. *Swith. pref.* 406. **b** regulam quae ab omnibus .. sanctis sacerdotibus quibusque temporibus ~antibus .. servata est GILDAS *EB* 75. **c** **1166** cujus retractationis apud nos privilegium ~at J. SAL. *Ep.* 193 (187 p. 238). **d** quorum memoria .. perenniter ~at memoratu dignissima GIR. *TH* II *pref.*; **1285** feria usi sunt a tempore quo non ~at memoria *MunCOx* 211; **1347** cum .. antecessores .. Murielle .. a tempore quo non ~at memoria .. seisiti fuissent *RScot* 697b; **1384** sic .. homines ville .. fecerunt a tempore de quo non ~at memoria *Bury St. E.* 178. **e** malorum mere sunt duo contraria / .. / ab hiis fraus extat et impudencia WALT. WIMB. *Sim.* 31; iste due intellecciones simul ~ant in intellectu BACONTHORPE *Quaest. Sent.* 5b.

3 **a** (w. adj. as compl.) to be (in specified condition or of specified description); *v. et.* 2 *esse* 9, *exsistere* 4a; **b** (w. adverbial phr.); *v. et.* 2 *esse* 7, *exsistere* 3a; **c** (w. sb.); *v. et.* 2 *esse* 10, *exsistere* 5a.

a nullo sc. hoc malo eorum ~ante immuni GILDAS *EB* 98; fato victus pice nigrior exsto ALDH. *Aen.* 44 (*Ignis*) 8; Graecia patres / edidit, ex quo numero celeberrimus extat / Gregorius *Id. VirgV* 711; a**705** mearum litterarum editiunculam .. pandens .. quatenus .. omnibus .. lectorum numerositatibus acceptabilis ~et (ÆTHELWALD) *Ep. Aldh.* II (7); os, oris, longa est, os et ossis sed brevis exstat ALCUIN *Carm.* 118. 13; cunctarumque miser rerum vilissimus extat WULF. *Swith. pref.* 538; **1168** vivis ~antibus argumentis notum est 'fortitudo ejus in lumbis ejus' [*Job* xl 11] J. SAL. *Ep.* 235 (276 p. 586); pecunia .. sine qua rex quilibet ~at desolatus M. PAR. *Maj.* III 380; **1410** dispendia oriuntur, quorum quam loqui ~at honestius insilere *FormOx* 424. **b** Uther in dubio ~ans an verum protulisset Merlinus G. MON. VIII 16. **c** pars major [lapidis] .. in orientali .. ecclesiae loco quadrangulum .. altare .. ~at BEDE *HE* V 16; puellarum juvenumque votum extas publicum HIL. RONCE. 9. 25; **1423** major civitatis London', licet indignus, extiti ut ~o in presenti *Cl* 273 m. 1d.

4 (as auxiliary vb.). *V. et.* 2 *esse* 13, *exsistere* 7.

~ant .. pro quibusdam culpis modi paenitentiae in canonibus inpositi ÆLF. *EC* 35; in exordio venerabilis hujus exigui operis, fundamentum ~at eximium collatum BYRHT. *Man.* 198; **1325** officium thesaurarie .. de quo oneratus sacramentaliter ~at (*DCCant.*) *HMC Rep.* I 271; **1375** que summa .. ~at ipsis custumariis in suo compoto nuper reddito allocata *ExchScot* 503.

exstasis v. 1 ecstasis. **exstensellare** v. estencelare. **exstenta** v. extendere 5e.

exsternare (ext-) [CL], to drive out of one's wits.

~are, alienare OSB. GLOUC. *Deriv.* 201; numquid †esterrateus [*ed.*: externatus] es tu ut dicas *ebolech*, quod est spina, pro *gebolech*, quod dicitur spica? M. RIEVAULX (*Ep.*) 74.

exstimulare [CL], to goad, stir up.

ejus [sc. Bruti] ad exemplum pugnando Britannia major / assumit vires exstimulatque viros GARL. *Tri. Eccl.* 117.

exstinctio (ext-) [CL]

1 putting out (of fire, light, or sim.). **b** (med., of 'heat'). **c** quenching (of heated metal). **d** slaking (of lime or sulphur).

illuminationes et ~ones ALCUIN *Suppos.* 1203B; *Quaest. Salern.* C 6 (v. exstinguere 1d). **b** mors nichil aliud est quam ~o naturalis caloris in corde *Quaest. Salern.* B 84. **c** si esset fluxus ventris, tunc confici debet [potus] cum aqua ~onis ferri GAD. 32v. 2. **d 1476** una cum ~one et *le drawkyng* unius *lymekiln Ac. Durh.* 646.

2 killing. **b** extinction, putting an end to (something). **c** discharge (of debt).

propter Johannis nuper ducis Burgundie detestandam, horrendam, proditoriamque ~onem *Ps.*-ELMH. *Hen. V* 107 p. 292. **b** cordis calefactio, spiritus corruptio, virtutis ~o ALF. ANGL. *Cor* 11. 16. **c** predicta duo scripta aquietancie facta fuerunt .. pro ~one sive solucione predictarum xviij m. *Entries* 180.

exstinctivus (ext-), (med.) tending to reduce 'heat'; **b** (as sb., w. ref. to drug).

queritur quare oleum sit fomentum caloris et aqua ~a *Quaest. Salern.* B 210; somnus infertur superfluus et aliquando caloris naturalis ~us GILB. II 106v. 2. **b** super caput ponatur mucillago psilii et in circuitu ~a GAD. 27v. 2.

exstinctor (ext-) [CL], one who extinguishes (fire). **b** killer, destroyer.

omnia inferioris urbis edificia flamma consumpserat, et ~ores suos vis incendii .. confugisse compulerat R. COLD. *Cuthb.* 39. **b** Nembroth robustus qui venator erat coram Domino, id est .. ~or hominum sicut sunt venatores ferarum, ~ores et non rectores FORTESCUE *NLN* I 7.

exstinctorius (ext-) [LL], **a** (substance) that extinguishes or quenches (fire). **b** causing extinction or death.

a s1218 per liquorem acetosum ac sabulum et cetera ~ia est subventum (OL. SCHOLASTICUS) M. PAR. *Maj.* III 38. **b** ingruente ~ie famis calamitate J. FURNESS *Walth.* 52.

exstinguere (ext-) [CL]

1 to extinguish, put out (fire, lamp, or sim.); **b** (fig.); **c** (astr.) to darken. **d** to quench (heated metal). **e** to slake (lime or sulphur).

non acies flammae .. potuit vel cohiberi vel ~i GILDAS *EB* 5; ad domum quasi inflammatam usque pervenerunt .. ~ere flammam volentes *V. Cuthb.* II 6; flammis .. sopitis atque exstinctis BEDE *HE* II 7; ~untur candelae LANFR. *Const.* 189; lumen quod vi ventorum et inundatione pluviarum extinctum erat, divinitus illuminatum est ORD. VIT. III 13 p. 137; *Quaest. Salern.* C 6 (v. 1d infra); inextinguibile lumen extinguitur WALT. WIMB. *Carm.* 636; **1237** (v. deguttare 1b); **1268** (v. cymbalum 2b). **b** Theodorus .. salutifera exhortatione coeptum tanti periculi funditus ~it incendium BEDE *HE* IV 19; Dominus hanc lucernam extinxit .. set dum corporaliter eam extinxit, spiritualiter eam magis accendit S. LANGTON *Serm.* 4. 38; modicus fuit ignis caritatis .. quem unus flatus extinxit [ME: *þet an puf acwencte*] *AncrR* 38. **c** aspice lunam Februarii .. si †extingurante [MS: extinguitu.. ; ? l. extinguitur ante] vj kl. Martii, et si ante praedictas .. kalendas .. extincta fuerit, fac illam ut sit xxx^ma^ *Kal. M. A.* II 423. **d** ignis .. [fit, qui] descendens ad nubes, que sunt aquose, in eis extinguitur, in qua extinctione sonus magnus efficitur, ut videmus contingere quando fabri ferrum ignitum in aqua ~unt *Quaest. Salern.* C 6 (v. et. 1a supra); videmus .. ferrum candens ~i in aqua *Ib.* N 36; in lacte ubi fuerit ferrum ignitum et extinctum J. MIRFIELD *Brev.* 88. **e 1239** quod .. cariari facias Lond' mille quarter' calcis ad operationes Turris Lond' et .. calcem non facias ~i antequam ibidem veniet *Liberate* 13 m. 15 (*Cal.* p. 379); *Ac. Beaulieu* 37 etc. (v. 2 calx a, b); **1317** in aqua ad †exguend' calce (*sic*) *Rec. Leic.* I 316; sulfur aliud est vivum, aliud extinctum *SB* 41; *Alph.* 180 (v. canellatus); c**1385** pro viij quar. et dim. calcis non extinct' *KRAc* 473/2 m. 8.

2 to kill. **b** (pass. in middle sense) to die.

rex ab infidelibus in bello corporaliter extinctus BEDE *HE* IV 14; quomodo hostis antiquus sanctum virum per casum cujusdam postis ~ere conatus sit WULF. *Æthelwold* 15 *tit.*; inopiae magnitudo plerosque dira clade ~eret *Ib.* 29; adversarios dispersit, quosdam extinxit vel exilio damnavit BYRHT. *HR* 62; mulier, dum mariti sui emulum ~ere putavit, mariti sui unicum fratrem .. occidit ORD. VIT. III 9 p. 106; **1169** lacrime viduarum .. creduntur [comitem Nivernensem] inglorium extinxisse J. SAL. *Ep.* 287 (287); letalem hostem letaliter extinctum GIR. *TH* I 31; nunc ferro, nunc veneno, sese passim et alternatim ~entes *Id. PI* I 17 p. 75. **b** multi profluvio ventris extincti sunt ORD. VIT. III 14 p. 153; **1237** causa castigationis posuit [mater] capud ipsius [puelle] inter tibias suas quamdiu ipsam verberaret, ita quod extincta fuit per infortunium et non per feloniam *CurR* XVI 101.

3 to put an end to (condition or sim.).

omnis culpa funditus ~itur (*Lit. Papae*) BEDE *HE* I 27 p. 54; **798** quatinus haec impia haeresis omnimodis ~atur ALCUIN *Ep.* 148; his .. verbis accensa fides in eo extinxit laetiferum [sc. letiferum] haustum quod bibebat, et maturius surrexit ÆLF. *Æthelwold* 15; ANSELM V 361 (v. cogitare 1a); **1166** rationis aciem ~entes consiliis toxicatis J. SAL. *Ep.* 229 (180); c**1175** ut .. morbus ~eretur et vulnera sanarentur *Ib.* (323); sitim ~unt GIR. *TH* II 7 p. 88; hec comestio esuriem vix ~it M. RIEVAULX (*Ep.*) 63.

4 to render null (right, custom). **b** to cancel (interest).

dicunt eciam molindinarius et filii quod, antequam hoc appellum fuit, appellaverunt ipsi quosdam de nepotibus W. de C. et pro suo appello extinguendo factum est hoc appellum *SelPlCrown* 78; **1285** qualiter extincta sunt feoda domini abbatis que ab ipso petita sunt patebit inferius *Ambrosden* I 432; **1292** jus .. non est estinctum *PQW* 117b; **1312** quia .. dominus habebit reversionem .. mesuagii, terre, et more .. extinguntur (*sic*) de redditu quem solebat reddere per annum xiiij d. *Cust. Battle* 154; eo quod morte crimina ~antur OCKHAM *Pol.* III 217. **b 1253** consideratum est quod extincte sunt usure de dicto debito *SelPlJews* 27.

exstinguibilis (ext-) [LL], extinguishable.

sol .. perlustrat ut .. lucernae jubar minus utile immo ~e reddat BEDE *Sam.* (*1 Sam.* iii 2–3) 519C; ANSELM *Misc.* 302 (v. exstinguibilitas).

exstinguibilitas (ext-), capacity to be extinguished.

splendor quamdiu est in sole est indeficiens et inextinguibilis, sicut et sol ..; appositaque stuppa vel boleto sicco quod vulgo dicitur escha, nascitur splendor extinguibilis, ~atem habens non ex se sed ex sibi conjuncta materie ANSELM *Misc.* 302.

exstirpamentum (ext-), estrepement, stripping, clearance. *V. et. estrepamentum.*

1467 vasta et ~a sive extirpationes terre et tenementorum *Entries* 86.

exstirpare (ext-) [CL]

1 to uproot (vegetation); **b** (fig.). **c** to clear (ground) of vegetation.

in annona depressa peritura olera penitus ~are nituntur B. *V. Dunst. prol.*; c**1127** domos ejus fregit, virgultum ~avit (*Cart. Thorney*) *Eng. Justice* 140; non liceat vidue in dote sua nemora vendere nec virgultum ~are *Cust. Norm.* 5. 6; p**1206** si .. heredes sui nemus quod ibi est ~are voluerint .. *Cart. Boarstall* 26; **1275** (v. exstirpatio 1a); **1278** de bruere extirpand', siccand', et cariand' *Ac. Durh.* 488; **1291** nullum arborem possit succidere vel exterpare *Cart. Wardon* f. 102; **1396** mulieribus ~antibus *le mosse* pro *le Milndam Ac. Durh.* 599. **b** a**804** opus .. est sacerdotis .. ~are de agro dominice possessionis peccatorum spinas ALCUIN *Ep.* 311; B. *V. Dunst.* 2 (v. dumosus b); ANSELM V 239 (v. excludere 4b); sicut .. ille minora in circuitu arbusta prius curat succidere, .. sic et huic vitia minora .. prius sunt ~anda *Simil. Anselmi* 146; presidens vitiorum frutices, que in ecclesia Dei excreverant, ligone justitie succidit et ~avit ALEX. CANT. *Mir.* 28 (II) p. 215. **c** Aldwinus abbas [ob. **1113**] dedit .. quicquid terre Leofwinus monachus ~avit et fructectis mundavit, vel etiam quicquid adhuc ~ari poterit de eadem terra *Cart. Rams.* II 214; c**1205** sex acras terre quas de boscho ~averint *BBC* (*Ayr*) 52; **1304** ad estirpandum multas terras *RGasc* III 4664.

2 to eradicate, eliminate; **b** to consume, use up.

prospera mundi simul et adversa contemnere, terrena a se desideria funditus ~are BEDE *Hom.* II 17. 196; ut .. nec in grege commisso vel ~ent vitia vel inserant virtutes GIR. *TH* III 28 p. 175; volens jocosa quedam insimulatione reprehendere que noverat aspera increpatione nequaquam se posse ~are NIG. *Ep.* 20. **b** hic sic latro est vel raptor, quod male cepit, si ad manum est, reddat; et si illud penitus ~averit, .. in integrum ei cui damnum intulit restituat (*Leg. Ed.* 5. 2) *GAS* 630; judices .. per .. 'terrores' quos populo infligendo ~abunt terram (J. BRIDL.) *Pol. Poems* I 188.

3 to extort.

1470 diversas pecuniarum summas a nobis absque ulla causa racionabili multociens ~ando *Reg. Aberbr.* II 164.

exstirpatio (ext-) [CL]

1 uprooting (of vegetation); **b** (fig.). **c** clearance of ground, estrepement; *cf. estrepamentum.*

ut viderent conculcationem segetum suarum et ~onem vinearum ORD. VIT. VII 14 p. 225; **1205** de placito ~onis arborum et domorum suarum *CurR* III 262; **1275** episcopus Exon' querit de predicto Ricardo quod ipse venit in gardino suo in Egglesheyl [*Cornw*] et extirpavit pomeria et entas et ipsas plantavit in gardino suo. .. Ricardus venit et defendit dictam ~onem *JustIt* 1224 r. 1; **1333** pro qualibet carecta x d. cum ~one ejusdem bruere *LTRMem* 105 m. 194; **1456** pro extrippacione ramalium et arbustorum in gardino manerii de Witton *Ac. Durh.* 241; s**1189** ubi logie invente fuerunt, et combustio facta, et ~o alneti *Croyl. Cont. B* 456. **b 1376** circa ~onem hujus lollii (*Lit. Papae*) *Ziz.* 242. **c 1205** in ~one gardini et bosci et domorum *CurR* III 287; **1262** cumque annus, dies, et catalla felonum et dampnatorum et ~ones terrarum suarum ad nos de jure pertinent *Cl* 142; **1467** (v. exstirpamentum).

2 eradication, extirpation. **b** disturbance. **c** (w. pun on *stirps*) genocide, destruction of lineage.

s**1307** ad ~onem predictorum [sc. Templariorum] *Ann. Ed. I* 494; **1381** fidei extirpatio, / statuum detractio, / virtutum exterminium *Pol. Poems* I 245; **1549** haeresium ~onem *Conc. Scot.* II 82. **b 1276** tenentur .. sicut alii vicini, in ~onibus et maleficiis que fient de nocte vel de die .. respondere *RGasc* II 14. **c** quis .. in ~onem usque ad internicionem de terra repromissionis septem gentium morali intelligentia .. Jesum Nave imitatus est? GILDAS *EB* 70.

exstirpator (ext-) [LL], extirpator, uprooter, destroyer; **b** (w. ref. to heresy).

s**1246** quod dilapidator et ~or substantie ecclesie Cantuariensis extitisset M. PAR. *Abbr.* 297 (cf. id. *Min.* III 4: dilapidator et †suffator); s**1258** malefactorum urbis malleus et ~or *Id. Maj.* V 723; qui deberant viciorum ~ores esse .. facti sunt viciorum promotores J. WALEYS *Schak.* 464. **b** haereticae pravitatis .. devotus ~or ALCUIN (*Adv. Elipand* I 7) *Dogm.* 246C; Theodosius fuit heresium ~or R. NIGER *Chr. II* 129; heresium studioso ~ori .. domino Humfrido CAPGR. *Gen.* 229.

exstocare (ext-) [cf. AS *stoc*], to clear land by 'stocking up' trees, assart. *Cf. stockingum.*

c**1139** dedi eis pratum apud Elmourám quod Rogerus de Tocheham de grava quadam extocaverat *MonA* VI 137a; c**1150** item pratum de Elmora quod Rogerus de Thoch ~averat de grava *Ch. Heref.* 17; **1199** pratum de Elmore quod Rogerus de Tokeham extotavit *RChart* 7a.

exstra v. extra. **exstractio** v. extractio. **exstraneus** v. extraneus. **exstrayus** v. estraia. **exstreciare** v. estreciare. **exstrepere** v. estrepare.

exstringere (extr-) [LL], to restrain, curtail.

1389 volo quod hec omnia infra annum post decessum meum expediantur tempore superius limitato per hanc limitacionem non extricto *Chap. Linc.* MS A 28 f. 43.

exstructio (extr-) [CL = *construction*], building up (fig.), improvement.

quibusdam qui adhuc prefato pontifici .. detrahere non verentur, eo sc. quod nec secularium nec ecclesiasticarum rerum ~onibus ipse, ut dicunt, in sua manu omnia tenens ita studium impenderit, sicut antecessor illius .. fecit, paucis rationem ostendere in mentem venit EADMER *HN* 260.

exstructor [CL], builder, composer.

haec diverse aenigmata torquens / stamine metrorum exstructor conserta retexit TATWINE *Aen. tit.*

exstruere (extr-) [CL], **a** to heap up, make by heaping. **b** to erect, build (building or sim.); **c** (other structure); **d** (w. ref. to living creature).

a extruitur plumis torus ornateque paratur NIG. *Paul.* f. 45v. 50. **b** ut .. juberent templum ~i BEDE *Ezra* 845; vallum .. velut murus ~itur altus supra terram *Id. HE* I 5; ALCUIN *SS Ebor* 275 (v. ecclesia 5a); nec mirificis et corruptibilibus ~cta operibus palatia quesivit *Eccl. & Synag.* 87; ecclesia ipsa ruit quam beatus Ecgwinus ~xerat DOMINIC *V. Ecgwini* I 20; ecclesia .. lapideo tabulatu .. ~cta GIR. *IK* I 3 p. 37. **c** fontem .. miro quondam Romanorum opere ~ctum BEDE *CuthbP* 27 p. 244; sedes .. ex candentibus ferreis circulis et ex omni parte clavatis .. ~cte erant COGGESH. *Visio* 19; diis .. celestibus .. ~ctis focis sacrificabant ALB. LOND. *DG* 6. 31. **d** elephas est animal ossibus ~ctum robustum et firmum BALD. CANT. *Tract.* 16. 568A; indecorum videbatur prudenti Opifici tanto studio machinam estructam non fuisse erectam RIC. MED. *Anat.* 234.

exstudiosus [cf. CL studiosus], unstudious, uninterested.

estne ars [sc. aleatoris] accommoda rationi cujus quanto quisque studentior, tanto erit ~ior? J. SAL. *Pol.* 399A.

exsucare [LL], to draw out juice.

exsucco, A. *to drawe out juse WW.*

exsucator v. exsiccatio.

exsudare (exu-) [CL]

1 to sweat out, exude (liquid). **b** (intr.) to ooze. **c** (fig.) to sweat, toil.

fons exsudat aquas viva de rupe GARL. *Epith.* III 45; virginis hic arbor exsudat balsama *Ib.* IV 127. **b** quoniam .. locus terre ~antem humorem generare non deficit, magna semper inde gutta nascens fons esse non desinit ADEL. *QN* 57. **c** nec ut prelati ad bestias pugnando, resistentes pravitatibus rebellium, sub gravis luctaminis fasce ~ant AD. SCOT *TT* 619A.

2 to dry.

balneat aegrotas [sc. oves], exudat flumine lotas; / tondet oves, fulget lotum pecus R. CANT. *Malch.* II 437; neque enim hora suppetebat ut posset [linteolum vino intinctum] .. ablui et si ablueretur non citius posset ~ari ANSELM BURY *Mir. Virg.* 15.

exsufflare [LL]

1 (trans.) to blow forth. **b** (fig.) to emit (*cf. Ecclus.* xliii 4). **c** (w. *spiritum* or sim.) to give up the ghost, die; **d** (fig.).

dissolvitur humiditas a fumositate calida a vacuitate cordis ad cerebrum ~ata *Quaest. Salern.* N 56; tubatores trahentes interius ventum vane laudis et iterum cum hyatu ~ant [ME: *puffeð hit utward*] *AncrR* 75. **b** utinam sapientia, que desursum est, humane peritie radios igneos ~ans excecet oculos AD. MARSH *Ep.* 194. **c** **s1227** postquam beatam animam ~asset *Flor. Hist.* II 189; 'cum spiritus noster .. cessit in aera' i.e. cum homo ~averit moriendo spiritum TREVET *Troades* 31. **d** ex nimis vehementi ire impetu scientie et consilii ~ato spiritu qui ex eo datur perit modus H. BOS. *Thom* IV 13 p. 372.

2 to breathe upon, blow upon. **b** (intr.) to blow. **c** to extinguish (flame) by blowing, to blow out. **d** to blow away; **e** (fig.) to drive away.

mulieribus solum, et his non oris flatu sed follibus tantum et ventilabris ignem [sc. inextinguibilem S. Brigide] licet ~are GIR. *TH* II 36 (cf. ib. 48: ubicunque ignem invenit .. eum ~avit); [castor] ad ipsum foraminis ingressum in ripa residens, aquam ~at, terram pedibus scalpens immiscet, et ex limpida visuique pervia turbidam reddit et cenulentam *Id. IK* II 3 p. 117 (= *Id. DK* I 5 p. 174); Jacobus .. rector de Kereby sepeliebatur coram capitulo de Bellelande et solebat egredi in noctibus usque Kereby et quadam nocte ~avit oculum concubine sue ibidem; et dicitur quod abbas et conventus fecerunt corpus ejus effodi de tumulo *Ghost Stories* 418. **b** cupidi officium est cineres congregare . . . ~at [ME: *blaweð*] in eis et se ipsum excecat *AncrR* 76. **c** frater .. aspexit favillas candelae jacentes per multas lineas et eas ~ans invenit paginam inlaesam ÆLF. *Æthelwold* 25 (= WULF. *Æthelwold* 36). **d** **s1195** multitudinem paganorum ut paleam ante faciem venti .. ~abit (*Lit. Papae*) DICETO *YH* II 134; **s1305** hoc stridens gelu ~avit pluvialis et tridui Austri flatus *Flor. Hist.* III 128; nemo se jactet .. quia flatu verbi poterit ~ari [ME: *hit mei beo to weaved*] *AncrR* 48; reponere granum in granario et exufflare [ME: *puffen awei*] paleam *Ib.* 101; **s1470** pro ejus vulgariter trita et ~anda citius cenulenta congerie *Croyl. Cont. B* 545. **e** dialectici .. prorsus a spiritualium quaestionum disputatione sunt ~andi ANSELM (*Incarn.*) I 285 (= *Ib.* II 10); **s1386** qui .. jactitabant se cunctos Gallicos ~aturos Anglia [v. l. sufflaturos ex Anglia] WALS. *HA* II 145.

3 (eccl.) to exsufflate, breathe on candidate for baptism in token of driving out evil. **b** to exorcise.

me catechizare ipse curavit, factumque est ut ~ante illo in faciem meam confestim me melius habere sentirem BEDE *HE* V 6 p. 291; **c798** primo paganus caticumenus fit; accedens ad baptismum ut renuntiet maligno spiritu ..; ~atur etiam ut fugato diabolo Christo Deo nostro paretur introitus; exorcizatur .. ALCUIN *Ep.* 134 (cf. ib. 137 p. 214). **b** omnem maligni spiritus potestatem ~avit *NLA* (*Guthlac*) II 6 (cf. FELIX *Guthl.* 41 p. 130: inflans in faciem ejus spiritum salutis, omnem valitudinem maligni spiritus de eo reppulit).

4 a to cast out, reject. **b** to set at nought, cancel out. **c** to extinguish, extirpate.

a qualiter .. provincia Orientalium Saxonum fidem, quam olim ~averit, recuperaverit BEDE *HE pref.* p. 7; abjecta prisca superstitione, ~ata idolatria *Ib.* IV 13 p. 231; non leviter ~ari debet ab eo quod accepit, sed usque in finem perseverare stabilis *Simil. Anselmi* 90; **s616** ~ata Christianitate W. MALM. *GP* I 10; **s1188** mutato vel potius ~ato expeditionis Jerosolymitane proposito W. NEWB. *HA* III 25 p. 276; metus archidiaconi .. ~at .. transactionem GIR. *GE* II 33 p. 325; **1250** excusatio quelibet ~abitur et nullum penitus remedium apparebit GROS. *Ep.* 130 p. 441; **s1164** credebatur ab omnibus rex omnem animi rancorem quam adversus archiepiscopum conceperat exsufflasse [MS: exuflasse] sed non erat ita M. PAR. *Min.* I 330; falsitas regnat, veritas ~atur BACON *Maj.* I 3 (= *Ib.* III 3); hereticos .. Christum ~antes OCKHAM *Dial.* 624. **b** **s1193** fratris in periculo positi fidelitate ~ata, ejus se hostem inverecundissime declaravit W. NEWB. *HA* IV 32; **1228** ne tantis laboribus ~atis et inutiliter sic exhaustis totum dissolveretur negotium (*Lit. Papae*) M. PAR. *Maj.* III 147; **s1242** postquam thesaurum ejus exhauserat et honorem ~averat *Flor. Hist.* II 255; putat .. allegacionem adductam primo capitulo ~ari OCKHAM *Pol.* I 113. **c** **s1233** memoriam omnium gestorum suorum ~avit cum vita multorum M. PAR. *Maj.* III 251; **s1245** exuflata ecclesie libertate qua Christus eam liberavit *Id. Abbr.* 297; rex Willelmus, cum jam pene omnem Anglie nobilitatem ~asset *Flor. Hist.* II 14; nisi .. Cyrillus .. eam [sc. Nestorianam nequitiam] .. in spiritu vehementi penitus ~asset R. BURY *Phil.* 10. 164.

exsufflatio [LL]

1 blowing, breathing out.

miraculum evanescit quod .. aure laudis expositum ~oni patescit J. FURNESS *Walth.* 57; ponit .. Spiritum .. Sanctum produci quasi per expressionem vel ~onem sui DUNS *Ord.* IV 57; cujus consimile imprimeret [cor] in aliis membris per ~onem et transmissionem caloris sui ad ea *Ps.-*RIC. *Anat.* 23.

2 (eccl.) exsufflation, expelling evil by breathing over or upon.

prius .. quam exorcismis et ~onibus clericorum immundus spiritus ab eis pellatur ALCUIN (*Conf. Fid.* III 31) *Dub.* 1076D; HALES *Sent.* IV 21 (v. exorcizatio).

3 rejection, refutation.

ex hiis patet ~o frivolorum sophismatum .. quibus impugnare nituntur crucem penitencie PECKHAM *Paup.* 60.

exsugere [CL], **a** to suck out (liquid); **b** to suck out (also fig.), drain.

a hirudinis in modum ~gentis incumbens languor ossium ~xerat medullas *Mir. J. Bev. C* 330; **s1251** de cujus uberibus .. lac non creditur ~xisse M. PAR. *Maj.* V 241. **b** animus jocundior hostem / nutrit et impinguat, et gaudia suggerit illi / exsugens tua membra dolor VINSAUF *PN* 313; fiat tunc scarificatio .. et ~gatur leviter cum ventosis GAD. 127. 2; mamillam grammatice porreximus ~gendam R. BURY *Phil.* 4. 45.

exsul, exsul- v. exul, exul-.

exsultabilis (exult-) [LL], giving occasion for rejoicing, joyful.

diem susceptionis ad habitum sacrum solenni refectione universis fratribus ~em fecit AD. EYNS. *Hug.* IV 1 p. 154; de tristabili gaudent et rident, de re vero ~i plangunt atque dolent BART. ANGL. IV 11; diem ~em solemniter celebrantes *Lib. Eli.* II 52; **1457** agite dies letitie, et confitemini illi qui .. nobis ~em diem tantopere expectatam videre concessit (*Lit. Papae*) *Ch. Sal.* 375.

exsultanter (exult-) [CL = *with abandon*], rejoicingly.

996 (13c) ego .. ~er munio vel affirmo praesens testis adeo *CD* 1289; omnes Deo gratias ~er reddidere GOSC. *Transl. Aug.* 17A.

exsultare (exult-) [CL], to leap about, behave in unrestrained manner. **b** (pr. ppl., her.) rampant. **c** to exult, rejoice. **d** (trans.) to cause to rejoice, gladden.

elata ~antes fortitudine saxa de montibus evellunt *Lib. Monstr.* II 3. **b** leonum multiplex est in scutis situs, erectus quem rapacem, rapidum, et rabiosum vocant, nos exultantem .. SPELMAN *Asp.* 118. **c** omnes ~ant filii gremio ac si matris ecclesiae confoti GILDAS *EB* 12; horridus exultat crudo certamine Mavors ALDH. *VirgV* 1548; certus de illorum correctione reverentissimus pater ~avit ut videret diem Domini [cf. *John* viii 56] BEDE *HE* V 22 p. 348; quod si tantum de aliis, quos ut se diliget, gaudebit, quantum de Deo, quem supra se diliget, ~abit? *Simil. Anselmi* 71; in gloria ejus mira exsultatione ~abunt EADMER *Beat.* 14; voce letabunda canorus ~at GIR. *TH* III 12 p. 156. **d** sic agendo [sc. premiando bene meritos] dominus ~abit corda subditorum MILEMETE *Nob.* 58; Edwardum exaltavit [v. l. ~avit] firma spes in Domino AD. MUR. *Chr.* app. 248.

exsultatio (exult-) [CL], rejoicing, exultation. **b** (w. obj. gen.) praise.

o quantam ~onem pio omnium patri Deo tua salus servanda praestaret GILDAS *EB* 34; civibus exoritur mox exultatio laetis ALDH. *VirgV* 553; BEDE *Hom.* I 4. 17 (v. demonstrator a); verum haec cordis ~o futurae humiliationis exstitit designatio OSB. *Mir. Dunst.* 19 p. 147; EADMER *Beat.* 14 (v. exsultare c); antequam mihi liceret dulcissime sanctitati vestre litteras ~onis pro vestra exaltatione mittere, audivi quod .. *V. Gund.* 19; cordis jocunditas aut exultacio WALT. WIMB. *Sim.* 174; tota ejus ~o et gaudium erat in Dei laudibus BLAKMAN *Hen. VI* 15. **b** ~ones Dei in guttere ejus sonuerunt [cf. *Psalm* cxlix 6] *Chr. Rams.* 21.

exsumere [cf. CL sumere], (leg.) to raise objection (against). *Cf. excipere* 8.

c1302 *N.* "domine, hic nominantur calumpnie contra plures. vultis quod legam eas publiciter?" *Justiciarius* "non, immo legatis eas prisoni et secrete, quia per os suum debent ~i." et ita factum est. quibus ore suo propositis quia reperiebantur vere calumpnie, illi contra quos proponebantur removebantur ad inquisicionem [*ed.*: ab inquisicione] *Year Bk. 30 & 31 Ed. I* app. 532.

exsumptuare [cf. LL sumptuare], to deprive of wealth.

exsumtuavit, pauperavit *GlC* E 478; ~avit, pauperavit, *geyrmde GlH* E 778.

exsuperare (exu-) [CL]

1 to surmount. **b** (fig.) to overcome, overwhelm. **c** to exceed.

Alpibus ~atis GIR. *GE* I 23. **b** beatus Johannes .. haereticorum perfidiam potenter ~at BEDE *Hom.* I 8. 39; oratio assidua ignita diaboli jacula ~at ALCH. *Ep.* 300; BYRHT. *V. Ecgwini* 351 (v. exprimere 4c); ~at omnem sensum .. illa pulchritudo ANSELM *Misc.* 358; NECKAM *DS* II 491 (v. digestivus a); quandoque ignis exuberat aquam, quandoque e converso *Quaest. Salern.* B 151; aliquando unum [sperma] ~at aliud *Ib.* 175; rex .. villam expugnavit et in manu forti cepit, et in festo .. Mauricii ~ata est STRECCHE *Hen. V* 152. **c** melliferum sucum qui ~at omnem dulcedinem BYRHT. *Man.* 246; ne .. affirmare ausim non tantum laudis tibi tributum esse quin id plane merita ~arunt tua FREE *Ep.* 62.

2 (leg.) to seize (defaulter).

~etur [AS: *gewylde hine man*] et episcopi judicio reservetur (*Quad.*) *GAS* 131; (*Ib.*) *Ib.* 190 (v. consociare a); inveniat .. fidejussores . . . si non possit, ~etur [AS: *gewylde hine man*] quibus modis poterit sic vivus sic mortuus (*Ib.*) *Ib.* 205; inveniat .. plegios . . . si non possit, ~etur [AS: *gewylde man hine*] sicut alterutrum poterit, sive vivus, sive mortuus (*Ib.*) *Ib.* 329.

exsuperatio [CL], (rhet.) exaggeration, hyperbole.

est yperbole superlocutio vel excessio in sententia et colorum nomine ~o nuncupatur GERV. MELKLEY *AV* 86.

exsurgere (exu-) [CL]

1 (w. person as subj.) to stand up, arise (also fig.); **b** (imp.; *cf. Psalm* iii 7 *etc.*); **c** to rise up (in rebellion).

sopitum morte cadaver / exsurrecturum fatali fine quiescit ALDH. *CE* 4. 12. 26; in lectum ambo sternuntur ita ut ne ad sedendum quidem ~ere possent *Hist. Abb. Jarrow* 15; ~ens a somno BEDE *HE* IV 22 p. 260; nos a somno animae ~ere .. amonebat CUTHB. *Ob. Baedae* clxi; Theodorus .. ~ens septimum locum gloriose exornavit BYRHT. *HR* 33; illi, quasi reviviscente spiritu, quam festinantius ~unt R. COLD. *Cuthb.* 30 p. 69; ~ens archiepiscopus eos .. sequebatur W. FITZST. *Thom.* 136; [Anteus] denique tacta terra viridior et validior ~ebat, quia libido quanto ei magis caro consenserit, tanto surgit nocivior ALB. LOND. *DG* 13. 2 (cf. *Deorum Imag.* 22: Anteus erat gigas, filius Terre, cui mater concesserat ut, quotiens terre prostratus occumberet, viribus duplicatis ~eret). **b** **a798** ~e, fili, ~e ALCUIN *Ep.* 131; ~e, Domine, in adjutorium nostrum *Descr. Constant.* 257. **c** **1166** ecclesiam sic deserere, in principem ~ere G. FOLIOT *Ep.* 170 p. 242.

2 to rise. **b** (of plant) to grow.

s870 visum est sibi dormienti .. subito exsurrexisse examen apum *Chr. S. Neoti*; *G. S. Alb.* I 219 (v. domitialis). **b** si herbarum universitas et arborum parva ab origine naturalem ad usque altitudinem ~it PULL. *Sent.* 727A; admissum celo nemus hic exurgit GARL. *Epith.* IV 125.

3 to arise, occur, result; **b** (w. *placitum*); **c** (w. ref. to revenues or charges).

tum sagittae toxicatae facinoris Pilati exsurrexerunt .. adversum Dominum BYRHT. *V. Osw.* 450; dicam quod de medio cornu exortum sit, quia inter prima et ultima exurrexerit [cf. *Dan.* vii 7–8] ANDR. S. VICT. *Comm.* 277; [cum] ardentem in sua carne libidinis fomitem persensisset ~ere GIR. *GE* II 10 p. 215; BACON *NM* 550 (v. citrinitas b). **b** **1108** si amodo ~at placitum de divisione terre (*Lit. Hen. I*) *GAS* 524 (= *Regesta* 892). **c** (*Quad.*) *GAS* 177 (v. ceapgildum); breve regis obtinuit ut quietus esset ab hiis que de terra ipsius pro essartis exigebantur, apposito numero qui de hiis ~ebat *Dial. Scac.* I 11 E; **1378** dicunt quod sunt .. lxxiij s. iiij d. ob. de redditibus assise .. unde xxxv s. ~unt de tenentibus apud R. *IMisc* 23/5 m. 2.

exsuscitare [CL], **a** to rouse from sleep. **b** to stir up, stimulate.

a illa sororem [dormientem] premit, pulsat, et ~at *Mir. Hen. VI* I 9 p. 33. **b** [filios] curis acuunt et ~ant GIR. *TH* I 12; nisi .. precordia sua ad desiderii ejusdem virtutem ~et J. FORD *Serm.* 38. 6; AD. MARSH *Ep.* 92 p. 213 (v. concitare b).

ext- v. et. exst-.

exta [CL], **~um**, entrails, bowels; **b** (used in sacrifice or divination); **c** (as food).

~a, *iesen*; .. ~a, praecordia, *bæcþearm GlC* E 439, 465; ~a, intestina, fibras pectorum, hostiare, *gesen GlH* E 583; eliso cerebro .. procumbebant homines, lorice rumpebantur, ~a fundebantur ORD. VIT. IX 10 p. 560; ut exinteratorum equorum adhuc spirantibus ~is immergeret pedes W. MALM. *GP* I 17 p. 26; ~a, *rede blode, a gibelet WW*; hoc ~um, *a bowyle*; .. A. *a gret paugh*; .. *a trype Ib.* **b** nec Pan, Arcadiae quem gens colit exta litando ALDH. *VirgV* 1383; aruspicium quoque in ~orum inspectione viget. .. ~orum nomine censentur omnia que cutis extremitate teguntur J. SAL. *Pol.* 407D (cf. ib. 461C); quia aruspices aras inspicientes in ~is et fibris sacrificiorum futura considerent ALB. LOND. *DG* 11. 13. **c** fartor, ~orum repletor OSB. GLOUC *Deriv.* 242; despecte vetule que

despectissima / exta, lucanicas, omasum, ozima / popello vendicat et ova pessima, / reginam nobilem lux equat ultima WALT. WIMB. *Sim.* 118.

extabescere [CL], to pine away completely, to die.

~escit, languescens defluit *GlC* E 438; regio non multo post morbo captus ~uit W. MALM. *GP* IV 184.

extaediare [LL], to make weary.

viri deliciis assueti et in hiis enutriti, cum sepe, si non fuissent saturati, murmurarent, ~iati, domum reversi sunt *MonA* IV 608a; **s1290** qui .. ex tumultu curialis strepitus ~iatus .. papatui cessit HIGD. VII 38; Arthurus ~iatus post xxvj annum adventus Cerdici FORDUN *Chr.* III 25*n*.

extalis [LL; cf. CL extaliosus], **~e**, straight gut, rectum.

quem febris torsit anhela / .. / nec non extales multavit poena pudenda ALDH. *CE* 4. 2. 22; *Id. VirgV* 977 (v. egerere b); ~e, *snædilþearm* *GlC* E 419; ~e, *rop*, *snædelþearm* vel *smeruþearm* vel *bacþearm* *GlH* E 583; ~es *snædel*, *bæcþearm* ÆLF. *Gl.*; sextum intestinum ~e sive extensum sive longaon *Ps.*-RIC. *Anat.* 35; *tharme*, intestinum, .. ~is *CathA*.

extare v. exstare. **extas-, extat-** v. ecstas-, ecstat-, ectas-. **extecis** v. 1 ecstasis b.

extemplo [CL], **a** at once, forthwith. **b** suddenly, unexpectedly.

a extimplo .. agnoscentes se inlusos fuisse *V. Cuthb.* II 6; cum dicerent "pax et securitas", ~o .. sunt poena multati BEDE *HE* IV 23 p. 265; ergo ubi trans celsi conscendunt lumina solis / angelici cunei modulantes carmina, caelum / clauditur extimplo ÆTHELWULF *Abb.* 319; orat, et extimplo fit munere laeta superno WULF. *Swith.* II 111; firmitatem illam confestim expugnaverunt et omnes extimplo interfecerunt ORD. VIT. IX 10 p. 544; nemo enim ~o fit optimus ALEX. CANT. *Dicta* 1 p. 114. **b** viderunt viri foris stantes domum illam extimplo quasi ardentem EDDI 1; quae .. vidit per somnium, quasi subito sublatum eum quaesierit .. nullumque ejus uspiam vestigium apparuerit. .. ~o se repperire sub veste sua monile pretiosissimum BEDE *HE* IV 21 p. 256; cum parturiendi tempus immineret .. ~o prodigium divinum .. circumadstantibus .. turbis videbatur FELIX *Guthl.* 4; continuo meritam praesumptor senserat iram, / siquidem extimplo languescens damna oculorum / incidit *Mir. Nin.* 114; regius satelles Rodbertum extimplo recessisse retulit ORD. VIT. XI 3 p. 170.

extemporaliter [LL], **a** extemporaneously, on the moment. **b** unseasonably, out of due season.

a sermonem quamlibet elegantem ~iter facere W. MALM. *GP* IV 139. **b** si se temporaliter vel ~iter reddiderint tempora J. SAL. *Pol.* 417C.

extempus v. extimus. **extencellare** v. estencellare. **extencio** v. extensio.

extendere [CL]

1 to stretch, make taut; **b** to pitch (tent); **c** to extend, spread out. **d** (anat.; pass. in middle sense) to become erect. **e** (p. ppl. *extensum* as sb. n.) straight gut; *cf. extalis*.

1236 ad pannos faciendos, siccandos, ~endos, et alias modis necessariis preparandos (*Pat*) *RL* II 11; GILB. II 89v. 1 (v. extensivus a); GAD. 128v. 2 (v. extrorsum); **1370** cum cultellis extractis et arcubus extensis ad pugnandum *Pat* 281 m. 6; **1378** balistis eorum extensis .. [? l. modo] guerrino *IMisc* 220/7 m. 4. **b** extento [v. l. extenso] desuper papilione BEDE *HE* IV 17 p. 245; Jacob cum filiis in monte Galaad ~it tabernaculum AD. DORE *Pictor* 157; **1233** (v. distendere 2a). **c** distenta, i. extenta, *apened*, *tobræd* *GlH* D 667; festivae mappae super tabulas refectorii sint extensae LANFR. *Const.* 129; partes que infra eandem summam continentur accipe, et eas multiplicando tamdiu per tabulam, i. e. abacum, ~e, donec et ipse, i. e. partes extense, vel equentur vel superent divisores; et tunc divisionem incipe THURKILL *Abac.* 63v.; quia [ferrum] non posset ~i nisi humiditas compararetur ei *Quaest. Salern.* B 162. **d** cum videmus aliquem uti veneriis .. virga movetur, inflatur, et ~itur *Quaest. Salern.* P 8. **e** *Ps.*-RIC. *Anat.* 35 (v. extalis).

2 to reach out (part of body); **b** (w. *bracchium*, fig.) to exert authority; *v. et.* 8a *infra*; **c** (w. *manum* & *ad* or *in*) to lay hands on, take action concerning, interfere with.

extensis manibus Deo gratias agere non est oblitus CUTHB. *Ob. Baedae* clxi; ut neque pedem posset ad ambulandum ~ere LANTFR. *Swith.* 3; ille seminecem [Eadmundum] .. jubet caput extendere ABBO *Edm.* 10; manus ~ere [ME: *putten honden utward*] *AncrR* 34. **b** BYRHT. *V. Osw.* 464, etc. (v. bracchium 2b). **c** manus nisus est ~ere in Deo cernua innocentium colla BYRHT. *HR* 3 p. 7; **a1161** ne quis in bona ecclesie sancte Werburge manum violentam ~at *Doc. Theob.* 69 (= *Cart. Chester* p. 129); **1167** ne scelerosus ille .. in res monachorum .. manum posset ~ere J. SAL. *Ep.* 228 (236 p. 444); **1226** ne ad res sive mercandisas mercatorum partium vestrarum in potestatem et terram nostram venientium manus ~eremus *Pat* 85; **1297** nec ob vestri defectum manus ad id .. gravius ~amus *Reg. Cant.* 173; **1314** inhibemus omnibus nostris officialibus .. ne ad premissa [emolumenta, etc.] modo quolibet manus ~ant *RGasc* IV 1133; licet pro premissis possemus ad vos, exigente justicia, manum ~ere perquam gravem *Ib.* 1182.

3 (pass. in middle sense or refl.) to stretch out (one's body), lie full length; **b** (w. ref. to cross, rack, or sim.). **c** to reach (by stretching).

miser, cur .. sic in trunco jaces extensus? WULF. *Æthelwold* 46 (cf. ÆLF. *Æthelwold* 28); ~itur pro mortuo AD. USK 101 (v. 1 ecstasis b); quidam enim dum cantant ~unt se et hic inde se flectunt ac si febribus essent vexati, quod valde inhonestum est TUNST. 251. **b** ipse [Petrus] postea extensus est in cruce pro fide Christi ÆLF. *Ep.* 2. 187; *Ann. Dunstable* 95, FORTESCUE *LLA* 22 (v. 2 eculeus 2a); ejus preciosum corpus extensum [ME: *isprad*] in cruce *AncrR* 154. **c** **1488** si equitator .. super equum suum sedens .. tenens arcum suum per medium poterit ~ere usque ad summitatem suprem' rame (*sic*) viridis alicujus arboris habentis per majores partes mortuas ramas in cacumine, quod illa arbor vocetur *a ronpyke*, et non aliter (*Sutton Coldfield*) *DL CourtR* 127/1901A m. 1.

4 to extend (in space), have length, area, or volume: **a** (pass. in middle sense); **b** (refl.); **c** (intr.). **d** (w. adverbial acc.).

a monstrum .. cujus corpus per viij jugera ibi porrectum ~itur *Lib. Monstr.* I 47; quae in longitudine et latitudine aequali mensura ~ebatur BYRHT. *V. Ecgwini* 382; cum .. longitudo ab austro in boream extensa jaceat, illa [sc. Britannia] octingenta milia passuum in longum .. habet GIR. *TH* I 2; **a1237** concessi .. dimidiam acram terre .. et xx perticatas terre de longitudine extense a dicta dimidia acra versus Polre *Cart. Bilsington* 86; BACON XIII 145 (v. dimensionaliter); notaret fidelis quomodo concedi debeat quod corpus Christi est extensum in hoc sacramento; quia panis extensus et tamen nec ipsum nec aliqua pars ejus ibi ~itur, sed habet esse spirituale WYCL. *Conf.* 508; (*Id.*) *Ziz.* 115 (v. dimensionaliter). **b** crescentes paulatim ignes usque ad invicem sese ~erunt BEDE *HE* III 19 p. 165; **1230** per medium cujusdam bosci qui se ~it usque ad quandam foreram, que forera se ~it de bosco illo usque ad magnum iter de Irnham *CurR* XIV 167; **1255** (v. abuttare 1a); **1270** tonitrus et fulgur ~it se et percussit dictam Amiciam ita quod .. obiit *RCoron* 1 m. 1d. **1278** Haginus habuit liberum ingressum et exitum per medias domos prefati Cok, quas tenet, per quoddam posternum quod se ~it a prefato capitali mesuagio prefati H. *SelPlJews* 105; opera domini Lincolniensis .. que vidi scripta manu propria .. ~unt se in quantitatem doctoris de Lyra super scripturam sacram GASCOIGNE *Loci* 126. **c** **s1228** ista terra .. ~it ad murum civitatis versus aquilonem *Mon. Francisc.* I app. 496 (= *Grey Friars Lond.* 147); **1236** homines ejusdem ville habent terram suam tam longe ~entem sicut et ipsa *CurR* XV 1922; **1257** regiam viam que ~it versus Chippeam *Reg. Malm.* II 202; **1309** de dimidia acra terre .. ~ente super pratum de Coggemore *Ib.* II lxxix; **1460** (v. diplois a); **1531** (v. braciatio). **d** duodenos pedes ~it R. COLD. *Cuthb.* 92 (v. duodenus 1b).

5 **a** to 'extend', assess (yearly) value of (land, rents, or sim.). **b** (of land, rents, or sim.; pass. in middle sense) to have (yearly) value of; **c** (refl.); **d** (intr.). **e** (p. ppl. *extentus*, ~*a*, as sb., usu. f.) (record of) extent, survey, valuation. **f** annual rent. *Cf. appretiare* 1.

a **1204** mandamus quod ~i faciatis manerium de Uphaven .. ad plus quod poterit ~i secundum quod maneria nostra ~i solent *Cl* 4a; **1218** quod .. terras .. ~i et appreciari faciat . . . et ad diem illum venerunt extensiones et liberate sunt Stephano de S. *BNB* II 5; **1252** secundum quod predicta burgagia et tenementa eis extenta et concessa fuerunt *BBC* (*Weymouth*) 56; **1259** (v. denariata 1d); BRACTON 75–75b (v. extensor); **1268** memorandum quod .. extenta fuit tota baronia domini abbatis S. Edmundi *Val. Norw.* 544; **1268, 1308** (v. extenditor); **1294** ad terras ~endas et assedandas *Doc. Scot.* I 429; mandamus quod .. discrete et rationabiliter ~atis et appreciari faciatis omnes terras [etc.] (*Brev.*) *Fleta* 310; **1313** qui minus sufficienter ~unt terras alicujus in favore ejusdem vel alterius cui custodie terrarum dari vendi vel concedi non debuerunt in decepcione domini regis (*Artic. Coronae*) *Eyre Kent* 39 (*cf. MGL* II 357 [**1320**]); **1325** nichil valet opus ultra reprisam et ideo non ~itur *Banstead* 319; **13..** terre et tenementa defendentis qui moram suam retraxit extra civitatem post quartam defaltam ~entur et liberabuntur querenti *MGL* I 177 (cf. ib. 217: *serrount extenduz et liverez a mesme le pleintif*); **14..** unum messuagium .. per processum coram vobis in banco .. factum ~i .. procuravit *Reg. Brev. Orig.* 149v. **b** **1242** ad valenciam predicte virgate terre .. que stenta est ad x s. per annum *CurR* XVI 2034; **1259** rex de terris et tenementis de quibus Willelmus de Kyme .. fuit seisitus .. et que extensa fuerunt per preceptum regis ad cc iiij^{xx} li. et iiij s. .. assignavit Lucie que fuit uxor ejusdem Willelmi in dotem omnes terras .. ultra Trentam que ~untur ad lxvij li. xj s. v d., et manerium de Imyngham quod ~itur ad xxvj li. xvj s. ij d. *Cl* 455; **1272** warda militum de honore de Cloune, que warda ~itur per annum tempore guerre ad vj li. .. et tempore pacis in nichilo *Ib.* 506; **1305** letam nostram .. que ad ij s. ~itur per annum *BBC* (*Norwich*) 344; **1315** terciam partem manerii .. que ~itur per annum ad viij li. *Year Bk.* 17 *Ed. II* 38; **1336** de terra de Crokeston ad ix li. xiij s. iiij d. extenta per annum . . . de terra de Howeleteston que ad lxvj s. viij d. ~itur per annum (*KRAc*) *Cal. Scot.* III 333. **c** **1332** nos in recompensacionem .. maneriorum de Bistlesham [*Norf*] et parcorum que in valorem lxxviij li. x d. ob. se ~unt, indempnitati juris nostre providere volentes, assignavimus .. manerium de F. *LTRMem* 105 m. 8*d.*; **1366** redd' antiquam firmam que se ~it ad l s. *Hal. Durh.* 54; oblaciones [etc.] .. ~unt se ad sexcenta nobilia, id est m et cc ducatos annuatim W. SAY. *Lib. Reg. Cap.* 63; **1463** accionem .. quam habuit contra Thomam .. virtute cujusdam contractus .. ~entem se ad summam c s. *MunAcOx* 700; **1464** sunt ibidem libere firme ~entes se ad summam xvj s. *Feod. Durh.* 138; **1464** que terre ~unt se in anno ad xl m. *ExchScot* 263; **1559** ubi defuncti pars ad x li. monete Scoticane tantum se ~erit *Conc. Scot.* II 168. **d** **c1377** modio frumenti ad xx d. ~ente *FormOx* 384; **c1450** si hujusmodi bona ~ant ad valorem xxj d. *BBAdm* I 223; **1460** ad valorem ix li. annuatim ~unt vel infra *Paston Let.* 57; **1514** proficuos .. manerii .. ~entes ad summam xxiiij li. x s. *FormA* 413; **1538** (v. deverium b). **e** **1163** summa extensi .. m et cc et liij li. [etc.] *Pipe* 39; **1219** quod xv li. [etc.] qui arestati fuerunt in feria S. Botulfi .. sunt de ~a predicta, et sunt extenti infra ciij li. [etc.] ad quod predicta villa fuit extenta *Cl* 404b; **1230** ad valentiam eorundem exituum per ~am et estimationem factam per sacramentum proborum et legalium hominum *Pat* 404; **1268** est summa ~e totius baronie predicte .. cclvj li. x s. iiij d. *Val. Norw.* 544; **1276** ij s. iiij d. annuatim que excedunt exstentam dicte terre *Reg. Heref.* 90; **1281** per certam arrentacionem, juxta legalem ~am per vos inde faciendam *BBC* (*New Winchelsea*) 1; **1292** per rationabilem extentam fidedignorum (*Indent.*) *Doc. Scot.* I 321; **12..** (v. deinstauratus); **1307** ~a manerii de Bernehorne facta die Mercurii .. anno regni regis Edwardi xxxv^{to} *Cust. Battle* 17; **1325** sic valet redditus plus quam ~a *Banstead* 335; **1332** que quidem extente sunt inter inquis[iciones] et ~as de hoc anno in custodia alter[ius] rememoratoris *LTRMem* 105 m. 8*d.*; **1336** de terra de Ovenland que in ~a nominatur Domland .. non respondet (*KRAc*) *Cal. Scot.* III 330 app.; **1388** coram .. assignatis ad astentam faciendam de manerio predicto *IMisc* 241/6; ~us tenementi quondam Johannis de H. *Reg. Malm.* II lxxvi; **14..** facta ~a terrarum et tenementorum que fuerunt predicti B. *Reg. Brev. Orig.* 170; **1516** quatenus .. per bonum ~um fieri faciatis latori presencium x libratas terre .. ; .. nomen .. dicte terre .. cum metis et divisis .. et modum ~i capelle nostre mittatis *Form. S. Andr.* I 252. **f** **1259** (v. denariata 1d); **1272** manerium de Weston' .. assignatur domino regi in ~a vij li. v s. vj d. [etc.] *Cl* 509; **s1291** solvendo singulis annis ~am illius warde *Chr. Peterb.* 148; **1333** cl li. vij s. j d. quos nobis debet de ~is castri *Reg. Heref.* 53; **1504** in denariis, ~is, wardis [etc.] *Crawley* 493.

6 (w. ref. to number) to add up to: **a** (pass. in middle sense); **b** (refl.); **c** (p. ppl. *extentus* as sb. f.) total, sum.

a qualiter ergo libre in marcas ~antur satis dictum THURKILL *Li.*; que sunt due substantie invicem collecte quibus, si similitudo 10 radicum earum adjuncta fuerit, ad 48 tota ~atur collectio ROB. ANGL. *Alg.* 72. **b** **1317** (v. chargia 1a); **s1340** summa .. navium captarum de Gallicis ad cc .. et bargiarum ad xxx se ~ebat AD. MUR. *Chr.* 109; **s1377** (v. coggo); **1457** se ~unt in toto ad numerum septem millium sagittariorum *Lit. Cant.* III 231; **1460** cujus itineris extractus ~it se ad vj li. *ExchScot* 595; **1460** expense annuales .. secundum fidelem compotum se ~unt .. ad dccc m. *Paston Let.* 610. **c** **s1343** papa Clemens iterum fecit in Anglia provisiones duobus cardinalibus .. ad ~am duorum millium marcarum WALS. *YN* 282.

7 to extend (in time), have duration.

DUNS *Ord.* VII 179 (v. durativus); BRADW. *CD* 839E (v. ampliativus a).

8 to stretch, exert (oneself, one's power or resources), to strive; *v. et.* 2b *supra*. **b** (of abstr.) to reach, extend, apply (also pass. in middle sense); **c** (refl.); **d** (intr.).

801 nullus est talis in hoc saeculo qui non habeat oblivisci quae retro sunt et se ~ere in anteriora ALCUIN *Ep.* 237; ad aeterna .. tota intentione me ~ens LANFR. *Comment. Paul.* (*Phil.* iii 13) 316B; dum .. mentem ad coelestia contemplanda ~eret OSB. *V. Dunst.* 41; [abbas] cum in ecclesiae suae longius protendendae aedificium largum ~eret animum, graviter offendebat eum .. opus impediose productum GOSC. *Transl. Aug.* 34A; *G. Hen. V* 1 (v. conari b). **b** ita ordo precum a summis usque ad finem .. ~itur ANSELM *Misc.* 330; **a1241** per totam terram nostram .. ubicunque posse nostrum ~it *BBC* (*Haverfordwest*) 262; **1423** AMUND. I 141 (v. exbannire). **c** votum vivendi sine proprio non se ~it ad ea quibus necessario eget vita humana OCKHAM *Pol.* III 11; **1386** nec volo quod legacio hec se ~at ad liberos tenentes meos *FormA* 428; **1446** proviso semper quod .. perdonacio nostra aliquo modo valeat, allocetur nec fiat nec aliqualiter se ~at ad Alienoram Cobeham *Cart. Boarstall* 522. **d** **1386** xl s. ad distribuendum inter omnes fratres capellanos .. sicut porcio dicte summe de xl s. possit ~ere per equales porciones *FormA* 428; **1451** volo quod, si bona post debita soluta legataque satisfacta ~ere possunt, quod executores mei inveniant unum presbyterum idoneum celebrantem pro anima mea *MunAcOx* 624; **1457** proviso semper quod .. provisiones .. non ~ant nec in aliquo modo sint prejudiciales preposito et collegio .. Beate Marie *Lit. Cant.* III 229; **1546** de pecuniis .. dominus .. servientibus academie pro stipendiis satisfaciet .. quantum .. summe per ipsum recipiende ~erint et non ultra *StatOx* 341.

9 (log. & phil., pass. in middle sense) to 'extend', possess 'extension' or range of denotation. **b** (p. ppl. *extensus*) extended.

et ideo habitus et actus non ~untur DUNS *Ord.* I 233; quod potencia infinita 'non est in magnitudine finita' extensa per accidens ad extensionem magnitudinis *Ib.* IV 157: quia enim extensione ~itur aliquid, vel si extensio esset per se existens, aliquid esset forma informans extensionem, extensa per accidens, ergo si potencia ista infinita poneretur in magnitudine, quero quid est ista extensio magnitudinis? *Ib.* 158; que figura [sc. alleotheta] secundum Januensem in suo Catholicon, quamvis sit tolerabilis, non est tamen ~enda, quia magis invenitur ex auctoritate quam racione vel usu (KYN.) *Ziz.* 9; oportet, dicit, quod intencio Januensis est talem figuram [sc. alleothetam] que plus habet auctoritatis quam racionis non esse †~endum [l. ~endam] ..; sed grammaticorum concors sentencia dicit quod omnino figura hujusmodi est extensibilis racione. cum igitur talis figura de extensione temporis sit tam crebra in scriptura .. (WYCL.) *Ib.* 462. **b** impugnatores .. dicunt quod licet verba .. ~o modo accepto vocabulo 'possidendi' sensum verum possent habere, accipiendo tamen vocabulum 'possidendi' magis stricte .. verba ista erronea sunt censenda OCKHAM *Pol.* II 440; ea que portabantur in loculis erant communia, quo ad aliquem proprietatem ~o modo accepto nomine 'proprietatis' toti communitati fidelium *Ib.* 711.

extenditor [cf. extendere 5], 'extender', valuer, surveyor. *V. et. extensor, extentator, extentor.*

1268 tres ~ores per partes eligendos ad extendendum per sacramentum suum omnes terras *Cl* 488; **1308** quod maneria predicta .. per certos ~ores ad ibidem constitutos extenderentur *SelCKB* IV 10.

extenebrare [cf. CL tenebrare], to bring to light.

que murmura rerum / occulta extenebrat redditque latentia luci J. EXON. *BT* I 311.

extense [LL], **a** widely, generally. **b** (log.) by way of extension; *cf. extendere* 9.

a cum iste modus loquendi sit tam ~e sparsus in scriptura (WYCL.) *Ziz.* 462. **b** *Ziz.* 115 (v. dimensionaliter).

extensellare v. estencellare.

extensibilis, a (med.) extensible, that can be extended. **b** (log.) capable of extension.

a *Ps.*-RIC. *Anat.* 42 (v. dilatabilis); nec est inconveiens quod epar dissolutum in parvas partes transeat per meseraicas, quia vene ille sunt ~es GAD. 57. 2. **b** appositio non esset continui vel ~is alicui in infinitum BACON VIII 159 (cf. ib.: de appositione continui vel extensionis adinvicem); simplicitas substancie corporee, si per divinam potenciam esset a dimensionibus actualiter separata, .. esset inextensa, ~is tamen MIDDLETON *Sent.* II 112a; sic opponitur duo, ut et ista, 'non-extensibile ad praxim' et '~e ad praxim' DUNS *Ord.* I 222; (WYCL.) *Ziz.* 462 (v. extendere 9).

extensio [CL]

1 stretching, drawing out, making taut. **b** (med.) distention, swelling.

ex malleorum sonitu et chordarum extensione percussa GIR. *TH* III 13 (= Isid. *Etym.* III 16. 1); **s1247** tremula paralitici membra firmavit consolidatione nervorum; contractis artuum ~one subvenit M. PAR. *Maj.* VI 124; spasmus est ~o vel contraccio nervorum et lacertorum *SB* 40. **b** extentio, i. tenacitas ventris, tentigo, †*gebind* [l. *geþind*] *GlH* E 650; satyriasis est immoderata virge erectio; .. fit sine delectatione aliqua quia non est cum appetitu, sed cum dolore et ~one GILB. VII 287v. 1; cum .. habet oculos extensos cum ~one vultus, talis est malitiosus nequam BACON V 168.

2 reaching out (of part of body); **b** holding out.

magis familiaris oblatio quam quae manuum tuarum ~one sacrata est EGB. *Pont.* 112. **b** **716** quem .. videbat angelico quodam umbraculo contra impetum daemoniorum, quasi libri alicujus magni ~one et super positione defensum BONIF. *Ep.* 10 p. 14.

3 stretching out (of body).

~onem membrorum in cruce ostendit *Eccl. & Synag.* 100.

4 extent (in space).

797 propter vastitatem terrarum vestrarum et ~onem regni vestri ALCUIN *Ep.* 127; nulla vel modica caude potest esse ~o, ut in cervo et lepore *Quaest. Salern.* B 73 (cf. ib.: quare complemento caude carent, ut cervi et lepores); si [angelus] locum divisibilem necessario occupabit et omnes ejus partes, hoc non facit propter sui divisibilitatem nec quantitatem nec ~onem BACON *Tert.* 179; de infinitate siquidem secundum duracionem tantummodo, vel secundum ~onem .. nullus videtur velle debere intelligi tale dictum BRADW. *CD* 19E; sic negant quamlibet partem quantitativam corporis esse corpus, cum spiritus indivisibilis quoad molem sit pars quantitativa corporis ecclesie, licet non habeat ~onem WYCL. *Chr. & Antichr.* 661.

5 extent, valuation, survey.

1202 xviij libratas terre in H. ad rationabilem ~onem et ad rationabilem starationem *CurR* II 112; **1204** si valentia illius manerii cum ~one illa excedat l li. *Cl* 4a; **1218** (v. extendere 5a); **1225** excepta ~one quam dominus rex fieri precepit de terra capelle Isolde, .. quam ~onem .. justiciariis Hibernie eidem Thome scire faciet *Pat* 528; **c1266** quod estimari poterint per rationabilem et legitimam ~onem *Deeds Balliol* 327; **1287** quod .. per sacramentum extendat etc. et scire faciat ~onem illam thesaurario et baronibus de scaccario *PQW* 14b; **1553** nullus tenens ibidem custoderit [oves] ultra extincionem in presentibus ordinatis (*CourtR Spelsbury*) *Ditchley Pps.*

6 increase (of number or quantity).

in numero tamen quandam pluralitatis ~onem facimus THURKILL *Li.*; oportet quod alia sit extensio materie ab ~one quantitatis T. SUTTON *Quodl.* 449; antiqui ecclesie doctores, dum agunt de perfeccione religiosorum peculiarium, pocius de ea tractant secundum intensionem gradualem quam secundum ~onem numeralem NETTER *DAF* I 426.

7 extent in time. **b** lengthening of duration.

BACON VIII 231 (v. distantia 1b). **b** (KYN.) *Ziz.* 31 (v. ampliatio d).

8 (log. & phil.) extending (of abstr.). **b** 'extension', range of denotation or application; *cf. intensio.*

intellectus speculativus veritatis per ~onem ejus ad amorem boni fit practicus BACON *Tert.* 10; DUNS *Ord.* IV 157, 158 (v. extendere 9a). **b** quia enim caritas in via extenditur ad omnem hominem, salvandum et dampnandum, caritas autem in patria ad homines salvandos, ideo caritas in via major est quantum ad ~onem, licet minor sit quantum ad intensionem DOCKING 107; dedit Christus apostolis .. principatum ministrativum, qui est .. major quam sit principatus dominativus, licet non sit tantus extencione potestatis OCKHAM *I & P* 15.

extensive, extensively, in extent (of space, number, or time). **b** (log. & phil.) by way of 'extension', w. a wide range of denotation or application.

ille [motus] non ~e nec in infinitum sed orbicolariter et ad primum motionis reciprocabitur locum ADEL. *QN* 61; [estuant] quartanarii plus ~e, quia diutius durat estuatio; .. set calor est major in causone intensive GAD. 15v. 2; sicut addicio denarii ad denarium, non solum facit ~e majorem cumulum sed facit eciam possessorem intensive magis divitem NETTER *DAF* I 426 (*recte* 436). **b** dico quod quantitas virtutis non tantummodo mensuratur quoad numerum objectorum, hoc est quasi ~e secundum similitudinem quantitatis discrete, sed et quantum ad intensionem actus super idem objectum MIDDLETON *Sent.* I 162b; Deus autem supra mensuram magnus et omnifariam .. infinitus .. quodammodo numerose et ~e propter infinitatem omnimodam virtutum et bonitatum quas habet, .. infinitus etiam quodammodo intensive BRADW. *CD* 27A; infinitum .. dicitur ~e et intensive, et hoc dicitur scilicet simpliciter et extra genus et quasi in genere (P. BRIDL.) *Quaest. Ox.* 347; si peculiaris religio perfectorum est ~e perfeccior communi religione vulgi, erit eciam intensive NETTER *DAF* I 426 (*recte* 436).

extensivus [LL < CL = *causing delay*], inducing or capable of extension: **a** (med.); **b** (phil.).

a ~us [dolor] est ex flegmate quod nervum aut musculum .. extendit GILB. II 89v. 1; inflatio que est ex ventositate est tumor ~us et tactui repugnat *Ib.* IV 202v. 1; BACON V 85 (v. deambulativus). **b** ejus [voluntatis] .. proprium est ~am esse in aliud per naturam diversum et operativam per judicium et eleccionem .. atque eciam causati a se conservativam et administrativam esse atque summe perfectivam *Ps.*-GROS. *Summa* 382; 'potest' simpliter pro duobus temporibus dicitur de presenti sc. et futuro quia est verbum ~um seu ampliativum BRADW. *CD* 839E.

extensor [LL = *torturer*], valuer, surveyor. *V. et. extenditor, extentator, extentor.*

1220 de extensione terre .. ~ores ceperunt j molendinum et unum perreinum et j *wasse CurR* VIII 294; **1231** preceptum est vicecomiti quod .. inquirat qui fuerunt ~ores terrarum et tenementorum que fuerunt predicti Willelmi .. ad partitionem faciendam *BNB* II 482; officium ~orum est in rebus hereditariis extendendis et appretiandis, quod imprimis videant quid et quantum sit in dominico in quolibet manerio, sc. quot acre terre arabilis, vel quot virgate, et quantum valeat acra vel virgata per annum. .. et in summa omnia alia que sunt de corpore manerii, et de quibus commodum posset evenire BRACTON 75–75b; cum ~ores .. eligantur ad extensionem et appreciacionem faciendam, tunc fiat breve ~oribus electis quod extensionem illam faciant *Fleta* 311; **1413** bona et catalla .. in favorem .. Johannis C. per ~ores .. nimis alte et excessive extenta et appreciata *Cl* 262 m. 18*d*.

extensus, extenta v. extendere.

extentator [cf. CL extentare], valuer, surveyor. *V. et extenditor, extensor, extentor.*

14.. quousque L. et K. xl li. de terris et catallis ipsorum ~orum per extentam illam levaverint *Reg. Brev. Jud.* 74.

extentera v. exenterare. **extentio** v. extensio.

extentor [cf. extendere 5], valuer, surveyor. *V. et extenditor, extensor, extentator.*

1246 assignet ex parte regis discretos et legales homines qui melius sciant extendere terras et tenementa .. et ea extendi faciat per eosdem quantum valeant per ~ores *Cl* 403; **1270** secundum extentam et particionem quam predicti sex participatores et ~ores electi fecerint *Ib.* 298; petendo pro eo quod .. terra et ten[ementa] nimis alte extenduntur per annum ut permittitur quod .. predictis ~oribus liberentur per extentam per ipsos factam *Entries* 597.

1 extentus v. extendere.

2 extentus [LL = *stretching*], (Sc.) 'extent' (dist. as old or new), valuation, assessment.

1523 viij marcatarum terrarum novi ~us *Offic. S. Andr.* 125; **1555** iiij solidatas terrarum nostrarum antiqui ~us *Melrose* 604; **1596** terras de Rarsay .. extendentes ad viij mercatas antiqui ~us .. reddend' annuatim xxiiij m. et xxx [? l. xiij] s. iiij d. nove augmentacionis *RMSScot* 155.

extenuabilis, that can be lessened or weakened.

[conjugii] sacramentum .. / .. / .. gravibus vix extenuabile causis H. AVR. *Poems* 127. 36.

extenuare [CL]

1 to make thin, lessen; also fig. **b** to weaken. **c** to rarefy. **d** to impoverish. *V. et. attenuare.*

marceat, ~etur, *geþynnige GlP* 53; [luxuria] vires corporis .. enervat .. et totum corpus ~at R. NIGER *Mil.* I 28 p. 112; quidam multum comedunt tamen sunt ~ati, quidam vero parum et sunt pingues *Quaest. Salern.* Ba 87; *Ib.* B 8 (v. desiccare 1a); corpori suo maledicebat, quod nec labor nec abstinentia frangere vel ~are valebant MAP *NC* V 6 f. 68; GILB. II 98. 2 (v. extenuativus); GAD. 45. 1 (v. atrophia); pondera peccati / sic extenuati LEDREDE *Carm.* 17. 11; pulmo bibit humiditatem corporis nutrimentalem. ideo ~atur corpus J. MIRFIELD *Brev.* 74. **b** **1167** ut vos ditet et roboret et adversarios vestros ~et et enervet J. SAL. *Ep.* 200 (235); cocodrillus enim quemlibet solo visu cogit ~ari *Quaest. Salern.* Ba 50; [luxuria] corpus debilitat .., potenciam ~at *Spec. Laic.* 49. **c** humiditates .. aquarum longinquissimo intervallo, dum ad superiora trahuntur ~atas ADEL. *QN* 75. **d** **1332** monasterium ita ~atum esse in substancia J. MASON *Ep.* 59 p. 201; **1437** BEKYNTON I 7 (v. depauperare 1c); **s1450** locupletissimum civem .. usque ad quadrantem novissimum ~abat *Croyl. Cont. B* 526.

2 (med.) to relieve. **b** to belittle, disparage.

apponantur colyria ~antia et exsiccativa GILB. III 137v. 2. **b** **1164** honestatem cause vestre ~antes, excusatores regis et emuli vestri hoc temeritati .. ascribere conabuntur J. SAL. *Ep.* 134 (136 p. 10); nec .. ~amus Coenam Domini aut eam frigidam tantum caeremoniam esse docemus JEWEL *Apol.* B 6.

3 (? by misinterp.) to plead, indict. *Cf. extenuatio* 2.

~ari, judicari vel in[dicari] *GlH* E 655.

extenuatio [CL]

1 thinning, lessening. **b** emaciation. **c** impoverishment. *V. et. attenuatio.*

s1247 tumentem hydropisim corporis ~one curavit M. PAR. *Maj.* VI 124. **b** siccitas naturaliter attenuativa, quia, .. dum dominatur, consumit humiditatem, .. qua consumpta sequitur ~o BART. ANGL. IV 3; *Alph.* 17 (v. atrophia). **c** **1437** BEKYNTON I 11 (v. depauperatio 1b).

2 belittlement, disparagement; **b** (rhet.).

quod quidem in ~onem divini cultus et studii vergeret detrimentum *Dictamen* 348. **b** quot modis fit amplificatio vel ~o causae? duobus: ex impulsione vel ratiocinatione ALCUIN *Rhet.* 17 (cf. ib. 16: defensor ~one ad minuendam causam).

extenuativus, (med.) extenuative, thinning, lessening. *V. et attenuativus, extenuatorius.*

[vomica] pingues extenuat, calide enim et sicce complexionis est et virtutis ~e GILB. II 98. 2; si sanguis .. se ibi coagulaverit oportet ponere ~a et resolutiva *Ib.* III 143v. 1; *Ib.* VI 237v. 2 (v. discontinuativus).

extenuatorius, (med.) extenuative. *V. et extenuativus.*

lothos .. arbor est stiptica et mediocriter ~ia *Alph.* 106; [sulphur] nascitur in moloida et lippata; virtus ei termantica et diaforetica et recorporativa et ~ia *Ib.* 180; *Ib.* 88 (v. crommyon).

extenus v. extimus.

exter [CL], external, foreign; **b** (as sb.) foreigner. *Cf. exterior, externus, extimus, extremus.*

ne .. nomen Romanorum .. ~erarum gentium opprobrio obrosum vilesceret GILDAS *EB* 17 (cf. BEDE *HE* I 12); quiescentibus ad tempus ~eris .. bellis BEDE *HE* I 22 *tit.*; **s1009** defendere Angliam contra ~eras gentes *AS Chr.*; in

~eris exulavit regionibus ORD. VIT. XII 39 p. 462; rex dilexit nobilem pauperem dominam ~ere terre [ME: *of feorrene londe*] *AncrR* 152; **1446** ad aliquas partes ~eras extra regnum nostrum Anglie *Cart. Boarstall* 522. **b** exter, alienus, *fremde*; ~erorum, i. peregrinorum, *utancumenra GlH* E 651, 652; tributarius ~eris, in domesticos predo R. NIGER *Chr. II* 168; non absque enormi domesticorum damno, semper in ~eros ceca largitio GIR. *TH* III 48 p. 192.

exterere [CL = *to wear away*], **a** to elide. **b** to beat on.

a extritae vocalis ALDH. *PR* 141 p. 200 (v. apostropha 2). **b** exterit abiegnas Petri dignissime valvas FRITH. 737.

extergere [LL < CL extergēre], to wipe clean, wipe dry; **b** to wipe away; **c** (fig.).

[lutraeae] pedes ejus .. villo satagebant ~gere BEDE *CuthbP* 10; ~git altare linteo EGB. *Pont.* 39; lavent et ~gant [AS p. 413: *þwean ond drigean*] pedes pauperum *RegulC* 40 (cf. ÆLF. *EC* 9); in ~so et levigato corpore J. SAL. *Pol.* 474A; crucis insuper signum cum magna irrisione ostentare nostris, atque in illam expuentes, feditatis sue posteriora ~gebat ex illa OSB. BAWDSEY clxvi; **1295** (v. abstersorius b); ~gens faciem meam, osculatus est me *NLA* (*Joseph ab Arimathia*) II 80. **b** sanguinem ab oculis ~gens T. MON. *Will.* VI 8; corporis sui sudores ~sit R. COLD. *Godr.* 41 p. 56; extergit manus officiosa cruorem NIG. *Laur.* f. 41rb; de oculis, fronte, vel ore .. sanguinem .. diluerunt et penitus ~serunt AD. EYNS. *Visio* 13A. **c** stercus peccatorum penitentia et confessione ~gamus HON. *Spec. Eccl.* 964D; quia omnis peccatorum tuorum macula hac egritudinis †exturgetur [l. extergetur] pena T. MON. *Will.* V 21 p. 215; spiritum .. abluere ab omni sorde vitiorum, deinde ~gere atque siccare instantia precum ROB. BRIDL. *Dial.* 187; quod veri extergunt tenebras rerumque retrusas / altius effodiunt causas HANV. III 326.

exterior [CL; *compar. of* exter]

1 outer, exterior. **b** (as sb. n. pl.) outer parts. **c** outlying. **d** (w. ref. to plea) outside a certain limit.

melligeris apibus mea prima processit origo, / set pars exterior crescebat cetera silvis ALDH. *Aen.* 32 (*Pugillares*) 2; **1291** (v. 2 gistare); **1304, 1327** (v. 2 baillium b); **s1399** monile, juxta fimbriam .. regis subtus vestem ejus ~iorem .. firmatum *V. Ric. II* 204. **b 9..** ~iora, *þa yttran WW*; cancer fluvialis .. decoquatur .. in aqua .. et abjectis ~ioribus interiora et extremitates fortissime abluantur J. MIRFIELD *Brev.* 82. **c 1221** (v. grangia 1). **d 1190** (v. gilda 3b); **1200** quod nullus eorum placitet extra burgum .. de ullo placito preter placita de tenuris ~ioribus *RChart* 65b; **1381** quod nullus eorum .. placitet extra muros civitatis Wynton' de ullo placito preter placita de tenuris ~ioribus *BB Winchester* f. 3; **1407** quod nullus civis .. placitet extra curiam ejusdem civitatis in ullo placito preter placita de tenueris ~ioribus *Ib.* f. 8b.

2 external, (coming from) outside; **b** (as sb. n. pl.).

lucem ~iorem oculo et videndis contiguam BALSH. *AD rec.* 2 175; *Quaest. Salern.* B 69 (v. exspirare 1b); ab ~iore vicissim vexatione spiritus alacritate respirare GIR. *TH intr.* p. 8; aliter accipitur 'usus' pro actu utendi re aliqua ~iori OCKHAM *Pol.* 300. **b** craneum .. cerebrum defendit ab ~ioribus RIC. MED. *Anat.* 213.

3 outward, visible.

quantum pro industria ~iori regi placens, tantum pro interna suimet neglegentia displicens BEDE *HE* V 13; ORD. VIT. III 5 p. 69 (v. cambuca a); ~ior habitus interiora signabit *Ib.* XII 47 p. 490; cerimonias et observantias ~iores OCKHAM *Pol.* I 29; oportet suavitatem emere cum ~iori amaritudine [ME: *wið bitternesse wið uten*] *AncrR* 148; J. BURY *Glad. Sal.* 589 (v. glossare 2a).

4 worldly, unspiritual; **b** (as sb. n. pl.); **c** (w. ref. to "inner" and "outer" man).

quia pondus ~iorum curarum semper sibi noxium et importabile judicaverat ORD. VIT. XII 32 p. 436; **1234** ut nulli ordinis custodi aliqua obedientia ~ior committatur per quam officium spirituale exequi impediatur (*Vis. Westm.*) *EHR* XXVII 739; non est presumendum, quod careat vicio .. saltem secundum preparacionem cordis, licet constare possit quod careat .. vicio, quantum ad opus ~ius OCKHAM *Dial.* 589. **b** celesti scientia preditum, et in ~iorum pietate spectabilem AD. MARSH *Ep.* 148. **c** sicut ~ioris hominis natura, qui in propatulo formatus visibiliter conspicitur ALDH. *VirgP* 3; **c803** et eat homo ~ior in domum aeternitatis suae [cf. *Eccl.* xii 5] ALCUIN *Ep.* 239; ut .. ad profectum interioris hominis homo vacet ~ior AD. MARSH *Ep.* 28.

exterius [CL], (on the) outside, externally. **b** outwardly.

domum hanc et ~ius obsedit et intus maxima ex parte residens implevit BEDE *HE* V 13 p. 312; pannus .. qui thecam interiorem sancti corporis .. ~ius circumdederat R. COLD. *Cuthb.* 42 p. 89; **c1228** vidit .. monachum qui erat ~ius repulsum *Feod. Durh.* 267; **1250** duas acras terre arabilis .. que jacent ~ius super culturam de Gillebanc *Reg. S. Bees* 321; psalterium .. quod habet ~ius imaginem Christi argenteam ELMH. *Cant.* 98. **b** quod cum ipse presens rogaret ~ius, tu absens persuadebas interius *V. Gund.* 14; in ipsa [sc. simplicitate] est interius et ~ius spiritualiter et profunditas spiritualis finite MIDDLETON *Sent.* II 112a; estne tam grave malum ~ius [ME: *utward*] incaute respicere? *AncrR* 11.

exterminabilis [LL]

1 illimitable, endless.

1457 abnegas Dei Filium, a quo .. ~is vite possessio foret solercius expetenda (*Lit. Papae*) *Reg. Whet.* I 273.

2 deadly.

in exitialem et ~em .. destructionem GIR. *PI* III 28 p. 311; ejus reditum cum exercitu collecto ~em sibi formidaverunt *NLA* (*Edmund*) II 581.

exterminare [CL]

1 to drive beyond boundary, expel, banish. **b** to separate (by change of boundary), detach.

si quis contempserit Nicenae Concilium et fecerit Pascha cum Judaeis .. ~abitur ab omni ecclesia THEOD. *Pen.* I 5. 3 (*cf. ib.* II. 5: ~etur ab aecclesia); praecipiens [corvos] .. de insula discedere ~avit *V. Cuthb.* III 5; ~atus, *ut adryfen* ÆLF. *Sup.* 173; **c1074** consuetudines .. quae a sacris legibus improbantur a regno vestro ~are studete LANFR. *Ep.* 38 (10); ut me .. a finibus meis ~are insistat G. MON. IV 8; [pulvis Hibernie] venenosos abinde vermes procul ~at GIR. *TH* I 30. **b** de villa Winekefeld, versus Wildesoram sita, regis arbitrio, ad forestam illic amplificandam iiij hide tunc ~ate sunt *Chr. Abingd.* II 7.

2 a to exterminate, kill. **b** to raze, destroy. **c** to extirpate, eliminate, reject.

a stragica caede omnes indigenas ~are BEDE *HE* IV 14 p. 237; draco .. eum ~are conabitur G. MON. VII 4; clerus et populus .. timentes ne .. se et sua penitus ~ari contingat *V. Ed. II* 288; quos Thartari poterant invenire in ore gladii ~antes *Meaux* II 70; **s1185** Guillicosum .. latronum in Laudonia principem .. ~avit *Plusc.* VI 32. **b** extirpat, i. ~at, eradicat, *astifecað GlH* E 561; ut totam Normanniam rapinis et incendiis ~arent W. JUM. V 4; GIR. *Spec.* III 16 (v. depauperare 1c); **1305** quod .. Christiani possident .. ~are satagit et .. devorare (*Lit. Cardinalium*) *Reg. Cant.* 676. **c** ~ant hujusmodi mensuras nonnulli clerici imperiti BYRHT. *Man.* 40; **1104** eliminetur negligentia, ~etur invidentia ANSELM (*Ep.* 332) V 268; BART. ANGL. II 19 (v. exterminator 2b); galbanum .. letiferas veneni pernicias ~ans AD. MARSH *Ep.* 147 cap. 12.

3 (intr.) to die.

s1413 sacro igne dicti sancti Fiatri decoctus exterminavit *Plusc.* X 14.

4 to disguise.

s1388 Robertus disfiguraverat seipsum fingens se pauperem .. feceratque sibi barbam prolixam .., et faciem suam ~abat ne agnosceretur KNIGHTON *Cont.* II 293.

exterminatio [LL]

1 banishment, exile.

quam magnam infra sue ~onis terminum benevolentiam sibi comparaverit H. CANTOR 22v.

2 extermination, killing. **b** destruction. **c** extirpation.

gladium ~onis ALEX. CANT. *Mir.* 24 p. 211; ve rubeo draconi, nam ~o ejus festinat G. MON. VII 3; **s1144** indignationem divinam manifestans, ~onem sceleratorum dominantes H. HUNT. *HA* VIII 22; muscam informari in ~onem muscarum J. SAL. *Pol.* 393C; illud genus duelli quod fit propter ~onem finaliter occasione inimiciciarum naturalium precedencium approbare non audeo UPTON 77. **b s1185** quod ~o imperii sui festinabat *G. Hen. II* I 257; cum exitialem Britannie ~onem, et concitati ducis atrocem .. enarrasset expedicionem WALS. *YN* 55. **c** exclusio et ~o vitiorum J. SAL. *Pol.* 777D; **c1174** firmamentum justitie et iniquitatis ~o *Id. Ep.* 313 (316).

exterminator [LL]

1 one who banishes (*cf.* Isid. *Etym.* X 87).

~or, *ut draefere* ÆLF. *Sup.* 172.

2 destroyer; **b** (w. ref. to Satan identified as angel of death; *cf. Apoc.* ix 11). **c** (as adj.) deadly, destructive.

~or, vastator, *westend, ytend GlH* E 653; W. MALM. *GR* IV 314 (v. expilator); **s1143** possessiones abbatie .. ab ~oribus .. occupate sunt *Chr. Rams.* 331; **s1215** rex exinde tyrannus effectus et proprii regni ~or *Flor. Hist.* II 155. **b 1115** fraudulentus ~or .. scandala intolerabilia Cumbrensium ecclesie machinavit *Conc.* I 392a (= *Reg. Glasg.* I 3); [Lucifer] dicitur Appollion [sc. Ἀπολλύων] Grece, i. ~or Latine .. quia bona virtutum .. exterminare desiderat BART. ANGL. II 19; tot linguis .. nomen ~oris exprimitur regis trucis, quot nomen regis salvatoris omnium in ligno crucis ELMH. *Cant.* 214. **c s1247** [annus] Anglie nocivus, Wallie ~or, terre sancte inimicus M. PAR. *Min.* III 31; **c1430** cum .. vinea vindemiatores habeat omnes qui pretergrediuntur viam, ~orem aprum de silva singularemque ferum depascentem in ea [cf. *Psalm* lxxix 14] *Reg. Whet.* II app. 400.

exterminatrix, destroyer (f.).

injustitia caritatis ~rix J. SAL. *Pol.* 778B.

exterminium [LL]

1 banishment, exile; **b** (w. ref. to Jews).

si obtinuerit rex a rege vel dolo vel bello regnum, quantumcumque tyrannus sit, coloni resident, non facit ~ium, patriis licet in finibus aliqua frui letitia, mortemque tyranni .. intra terminos prestolari possunt MAP *NC* I 25 f. 19; **s586** omnes simul in ~ium pellebantur. secesserunt itaque .. in occidentalibus regni partibus M. PAR. *Maj.* I 251; Scotos a Pictis .. trusos in ~ium FORDUN *Chr.* II 50; **1600** decreverunt .. ut ministri .. exules et extorres proscribantur et ab academia perpetuo ~io ejiciantur *StatOx* 456. **b** appropinquante Romano bello et ~io Judaicae gentis BEDE *Mark* (xiii 14–16) 261C; quod in Christi passione palam fuit; ubi et Judas suspendio, Judei excidio pariter et ~io, Pylatus exilio penas luit GIR. *IK* I 4 p. 53; [Cyrus] l millia Judeorum laxatos a captivitate regredi fecit in Judeam, unde magnum factum est [i. e. erat] ~ium Judeorum *Eul. Hist.* I 55.

2 a extermination, killing; **b** destruction, ruin, defeat; **c** extirpation. **d** deterioration, wasting away.

a ut .. pestilentia et ~ium gentis secutum sit BEDE *HE* I 14 *tit.*; diluvio paganorum, ~io populorum, subversione urbium GOSC. *Transl. Aug.* 18A; multi fame vel gladio vel alio quolibet ~io mortui sunt ORD. VIT. IX 7 p. 505; Dominus .. Salahadinum ad obstinate gentis ~ium debacchari permisit *Itin. Ric.* I 1; **1339** gladium nostre ac nostrorum neci et ~io preparatum (*Lit. Regis*) AD. MUR. *Chr.* 95; **s1477** in ~ium Ricardi domini de Beauchamp *Croyl. Cont. C* 561. **b** a pereuntis mundi ~io salvare BEDE *Gen.* (vi 15) 89; conatus est in ~ium adducere totius fines Brittanniae ABBO *Edm.* 5; toto urbis territorio .. cedibus et incendiis ad ~ium fere redacto GIR. *EH* I 11; M. PAR. *Maj.* V 116 (v. effugare 2a); **1318** ut in laqueum cadant quem in universitatis ~ium paraverunt *FormOx* 41; concernentes easdem terras nostras ~io irrecuperabili proximare *Meaux* III 102; **c1435** flores ad exterminum (*sic*) sunt proscripti *FormOx* 449. **c** de ~io religionis idolatrie J. SAL. *Pol.* 473C; **s1226** ~ium heretice pravitatis WEND. II 315; contradictionem veritatis, .. ~ium fidei AD. MARSH *Ep.* 245; **1407** expectamus in Dei virtute pestis hujus ~ium (*Lit. Regis Franciae*) BEKYNTON II 129. **d** nuper enim notavi tue pallentis ~ium faciem J. GODARD *Ep.* 222; passio lumbricorum acutissima est ut interdum ducat patientem in ~ium mentis GILB. V 228v. 2.

3 wreck, ruins.

manebant ~ia civitatum ab hoste derutarum ac desertarum BEDE *HE* I 22.

4 ? *f. l.*

clericorum aggregantur personae paucorum servientium inibi, quorum nomina praelibamus pro veraci testimonio quaeque sine testibus dantes exterminio (*sic*) [? l. ex termino] HERM. ARCH. 1.

exterminum v. exterminium. **externare** v. exsternare. **externeatio** v. extraneatio.

1 externus [CL], foreign, alien; **b** (as sb.) foreigner. **c** adventitious.

augebantur ~ae clades domesticis motibus GILDAS *EB* 19; ~ae peregrinationis participem ALDH. *VirgP* 21; qui subito veniens externis exul ab oris ALCUIN *SS Ebor* 236; internis atque ~is regiae potestatis sollicitudinibus ASSER *Alf.* 25; non in Anglia solum sed in ~is regnis ANSELM (*Ep.* 214) IV 113; ~e dominationis jugo sua colla mancipare ORD. VIT. XIII 26 p. 70. **b** quoniam [Wictberct] ~is prodesse ad fidem non poterat, suis amplius ex virtutum exemplis prodesse curabat BEDE *HE* V 9 p. 298; saepius externis praedantibus undique fines ALCUIN *SS Ebor* 510; consilium ne ab ~is aliquid rancoris inter germanos deprehenderetur occultatum est ORD. VIT. XI 2 p. 162. **c** regnum .. reges dubii vel externi disperdiderunt BEDE *HE* IV 24 p. 268.

2 externus v. hesternus. **exterpare** v. exstirpare 1a.

exterrēre [CL], to frighten; **b** (absol.). **c** to scare off.

describitur quod angues .. Cleopatram ad Nilum fugassent ~itam *Lib. Monstr.* III 23; cujus praesentia cum essem ~itus, dixit mihi ne timerem BEDE *HE* IV 23 p. 264; EADMER *Virt.* 583D (v. deturbare d); W. CANT. *Mir. Thom.* II 41 (v. cratis 1d); NECKAM *NR* II 125 (v. descensus 3a); MAP *NC* III 2 (v. devincere 1a). **b** si mendacitatis rigor ~eat, Salamon eciam illa expavit NETTER *DAF* I 500. **c s1260** eos volebant .. ~ere a tam frequenti .. deinceps adventatione *Flor. Hist.* II 445.

exterritare, to terrify.

febris .. comminans me .. multumque ~ans bis ausa est tangere servum vestrum ANSELM (*Ep.* 139) III 285; sermonum affabilitate credulos decipiens, gnaros autem malitie ~ans W. MALM. *GR* V 398; mare turbulentum navigantes ~at EADMER *HN* 6; Dei virum de loco sui victoriosi certaminis conatus fuerit ~ando propellere R. COLD. *Godr.* 51 p. 64.

exterror, fearless, undismayed.

ab impetu demonum .. ~ores, securos, et invincibiles *Obs. Barnwell* 232.

extersio [cf. CL extergere], wiping off, drying. *V. et. detersio.*

abbas in capitulo leva, prior parte dextra, cum pelvibus et manutergiis in ablutione et ~one ministrabit *Obed. Abingd.* 354.

extersivus [cf. CL extergere], (med.) cleansing, detergent.

danda sunt mundificantia et ~a saniei GILB. V 216v. 1.

extesticulare [cf. CL testiculari], to castrate. *V. et. detesticulare, etesticulare.*

s1096 cecatus et ~atus est W. MALM. *GR* IV 319 (cf. *Eul. Hist.* III 48 [**s1096**]: ~atus est et cecatus).

extestinus [LL *gl.*], alien.

~us, alienigena OSB. GLOUC. *Deriv.* 202.

†exthacius, *s. dub.*; ? domestic servant, envoy, hostage.

1188 Saladinus dixit quandoque in tentorio suo ~io Patricii et Baliani .. quod .. *G. Hen. II* II 52 (cf. DICETO *YH* II 59: †Eustacio).

†extima, offal or (?) *f. l.*

inquisicio facta sub Wauberge de quadam bestia capta in prato unde †extima [? l. exta *or* intestina] inventa fuit (*sic*) *SelPlForest* 74 (cf. ib. 23: quedam bestia capta fuit sub Wauberg' cujus intestina fuerunt inventa in parco).

extimare v. aestimare.

extimescere [CL], **extimēre** [LL]

1 (intr.) to grow fearful, be afraid. **b** (w. inf.) to hesitate.

~uit multum; atque .. suscepit fidem Christi BEDE *HE* II 6 (cf. *ASChr.* [**s616**]: qui videns pontificem sic male tractatum ~uit et, accepta .. Christi fide, ..); hec Eboracheses ut audierunt, ~entes, maturata deditione vim declinaverunt ORD. VIT. IV 4 p. 185. **b** quos aggredi .. Grecorum audacia ~uit BART. ANGL. XV 153.

2 (trans.) to fear, dread.

[Angli] plus eum [sc. Guillelmum ducem] quam regem Noricorum ~entes W. POIT. II 16; princeps apostolorum .. ~uit vocem ancille H. LOS. *Serm.* 9. 268; ille perturbatus tam grave sibi onus [sc. regimen pontificale] ~uit ORD. VIT. IV 6 p. 212; qui arguentem ~uit ancillam H. READING (I) *Haeret.* I 13. 1269D; adolescens adjurationem illam ~escens existimansque obedientem .. meliorem J. FURNESS *Kentig.* 7 p. 174; humanae conditionis fragilitatem ~esco FREE *Ep.* 57.

extimplo v. extemplo.

extimus [CL], outermost, furthest. **b** last, final. **c** last, least. *V. et. extremus.*

†extenus, extremus; .. †extempus, extremus *GlC* E 476, 481; ~e sphere subditarumque stellarum .. cursus ADEL. *QN* 72; egressus ad ~am hostii partem *Ep. ad Amicum* 9; sepem .. ~os horti ejus fines circumdantem R. COLD. *Godr.* 96; quem orbis extimi circumferencia / non ambit, ambiunt ventris centralia WALT. WIMB. *Carm.* 108; **a1350** (v. conformis a). **b** cicli nondecimus cum deficit extimus annus HWÆTBERHT *Aen.* 29 (*De aetate et saltu*) 4; extima vitae / spectanti dum preteritae spiramina reddat FRITH. 866. **c** omnium ~us sacerdotum B. vilisque Saxonum indigena B. *V. Dunst. prol.*

extincctus v. exstinguere. **extincio** v. extensio. **extinct-** v. exstinct-. **extingere, extinguere, extingurante, extinnctus** v. exstinguere. **extinspex, extipex** v. extispex. **extirp-** v. exstirp-. **extisis** v. 1 ecstasis b.

extispex [CL], one who examines entrails, soothsayer.

extipices, *haelsent GlC* E 484; extipices, i. auruspuces, *halseras GlH* E 562; extinspex, -icis, i. augur qui inspicit exta OSB. GLOUC. *Deriv.* 188 (cf. ib. 524).

extocare v. exstocare.

extollenter, with pride.

~er, arroganter OSB. GLOUC. *Deriv.* 202.

extollentia [LL], **a** superiority. **b** extolment, promoting. **c** pride. **d** ambition.

a potest .. ~ia naturalis dominii et inferioritas civilis dominii ex septem accipi WYCL. *Civ. Dom.* III 227. **b** **1452** ad divine laudis ~iam augmentumque *EpAcOx* 309. **c** elatio .. ~iam mentis significat BEDE *Gen.* (x 30) 121; dum ~ia, filia superbiae, .. te pascit .. ANSELM *Misc.* 301; cor illius, ~ie peste minime vexante, famulabatur Domino in cordis timore *Pass. Æthelb.* 1; **1166** quicquid agitis ~ie est aut ire J. SAL. *Ep.* 217 (176); hic arrogancia nostra confunditur, / hic extollencia nostra retunditur WALT. WIMB. *Carm.* 312; ne forte opinio popularis regium animum .. estimaret inflari ~ia singularis fortune ELMH. *Metr. Hen. V prol.* p. 80. **d** **s1395** felicis quidem si non aspirasset ad gradus sublimes, sed propter ~iam infelicitati subacti WALS. *HA* II 219.

extollere [CL], to lift up, raise (also fig.). **b** to promote, advance (person), improve (condition). **c** to extol, praise. **d** to elate with pride. *Cf. attollere.*

825 (14c) post mortem vero Coenulfi .. multae discordiae et innumerabiles dissonantiae ~ebantur *CS* 387; quo [MS: que] enim poterit in te ~i superbia cum audis 'memento homo quia cinis es' ALEX. BATH *Mor.* IV 18 p. 154; cum solis calore [nenufar] juvatur, ~itur ab aqua *Quaest. Salern.* B 221; animalia dum surgunt .. graviores et debiliores sui corporis partes prius ~unt *Ib.* W 8; ~o, A. *to bere up, or to hye WW.* **b** praecepit ne .. id alicui indicaret, ne .. fama ~i foris videretur humana *V. Greg.* p. 102; tibi non nocent jura [? l. jurgia] saeculi nec laudes ~unt te humano favore BYRHT. *V. Ecgwini* 362; **1169** alternat fortuna rerum vices mortaliumque conditionem nunc deicit, nunc ~it J. SAL. *Ep.* 285 (288). **c** laudantes deos suos, id est sensus, ~entes divitias GILDAS *EB* 71; †~at [l. ~it], honorat *GlC* E 426; quandoquidem eos qui hujuscemodi munere donati sunt ~ant catholici patres ABBO *Edm.* 17; **a1078** Augustinus .. excellenti laude eum ~it LANFR. *Ep.* 50 (46); digne laudari meruit et ~i GIR. *IK* I 3 p. 41; *Id. TH intr.* p. 6 (v. eloquentia 1); BART. ANGL. XV 94 (v. euphorbium a); ille tam ~ende nobilitatis Warwici comes eligitur *Ps.*-ELMH. *Hen. V* 88 p. 246. **d** propria itaque voluntas, quia Dei voluntati non subicitur sed supra eam ~itur, ob hoc recte superbia dicitur *Simil. Anselmi* 7; [de generibus exaltationis] .. ~itur homo in opinione simul et voluntate *Ib.* 23.

extolneare [cf. tolneum < AS *toln*], to pay toll.

Flandrenses et Pontejenses et Normannia et Francia monstrabant res suas et ~eabant (*Quad.*) *GAS* 232 (= *EEC* 155); si quis in servum transeat, sicut possessor est, in halimoto vel hundreto vel vicinio coram testibus agatur, eum extol[n]eet, ut nec ille deinceps abneget (*Leg. Hen.* 78. 2) *GAS* 594.

extoppare [cf. AS *topp* = *tuft of hair*], to 'top', poll, shave, scalp.

dictum est de servis: si qui furentur simul ut senior ex eis capiatur et occidatur vel suspendatur, et aliorum singuli verberentur ter et †excorientur [MSS: extopentur, extoppentur, †extorpentur] et truncetur minimus digitus in signum (*Quad.*) *GAS* 191 (cf. ib. 335: decapilletur; (*Inst. Cnuti*) *Ib.*: auferatur .. corium capitis cum capillis, quod Angli dicunt *beheætian*; (*Cons. Cnuti*) *Ib.*: pilletur); (cf. LANTFR. *Swith.* 26: si quispiam cleptes in tota .. invenire- tur patria, .. excruciaretur diutius; et sic demum decoriata pelle capitis cum crinibus, per omnia paene membra mortuus relinqueretur).

extorpare v. extoppare.

extorquēre [CL]

1 to twist out, wrest away. **b** to extract.

ex[t]orti, *aðresti GlC* E 389; ~ti, *aþræste GlH* E 728; **9..** ~sit, *awræste WW*; quod .. Dunstanus tantas sibi turmas diripiendo e manibus ~sisset B. *V. Dunst.* 16; quomodo Ulixes .. filium Hectoris ~sit a matre Andromacha TREVET *Troades* 32. **b** GOSC. *Mir. Aug.* 16 (v. conflare 2a); aurum ex lilio et urtica ~quebitur, et argentum ex ungulis mugientium manabit G. MON. VII 3 p. 387.

2 to obtain by force, extort: **a** (property); **b** (response to request, reaction); **c** (w. *ut* & subj.); **d** (fig.). **e** (w. pers. obj.) to oppress by extortion.

a ÆLF. *Ep.* 3. 63 (v. exactor 2a); [ecclesias] magna .. cum difficultate ~sit et juri monasterii .. de Bello restituit *Chr. Battle* f. 99v.; R. COLD. *Cuthb.* 109 (v. desponsalia); **1250** (v. contributio b); **s1204** confidens de pecunia quam se juravit ab Anglia ~surum *Flor. Hist.* II 129; **1313** qui pro potestate officii alios occasionaverint et per hoc ~serint terras et redditus et alias prestaciones *Eyre Kent* 37; **1354** bona et catalla sua per minas .. ~querunt (*sic*) *Reg. Heref.* 208; **1447** hoc fecit ad ~quendam pecuniam ab ipso (*Court Bk. Linc.*) *Eng. Clergy* 217. **b** foedus callididate licet ~tum GILDAS *EB* 1; opus .. dilectione magis quam scientia ~sum *V. Greg.* p. 106; ut .. ~queat ab eo quod quaerit *Simil. Anselmi* 28; ut dulcem .. cantum ~queant, eas [cicadas] decapitare solent GIR. *TH* I 21; judex in criminibus veritatem ~quet torturis FORTESCUE *NLN* II 50. **c** **1073** ut legeret suarum precum nimietate a vobis ~sit LANFR. *Ep.* 43 (18); AD. MARSH *Ep.* 30 (v. concrepatio). **d** GILDAS *EB* 1 (v. deprehendere 2b); **1093** (v. confixio b); **1166** ut eductas doloris impetu et ~tas verberibus lacrimas redire faciant in sinum oculorum J. SAL. *Ep.* 193 (187 p. 230); casu .. ~quente R. COLD. *Cuthb.* 103 p. 229; ut a 'fio', 'fideo', 'finis' .. etc. magnam partem Latini ~queret *Ps.*-GROS. *Gram.* 33; nunc extorquet cum usura / gemitus quos paritura / nature detinuit (*B. Virg.*) *Holy Rood-Tree* 78. **e** **1276** [ballivi] modo dant xv m., et .. hac de causa ~quent homines *Hund.* I 41b; **c1400** extorsit populum, nam sua cuique rapit [*gl.*: rex iste populum vexabat graviter, pecunias ~quens] (*Mem. Vers.*) *Pol. Poems* I 461.

3 to twist, sprain (joint). **b** to torture (as on the rack).

1302 Oliverus de A. inventus fuit mortuus habens collum ~tum .. . [inimici sui] ipsum ceperunt et collum suum ~serunt *SelCCoron* 61. **b** si justis legibus fur mori debeat, / par dolor animam matris extorqueat WALT. WIMB. *Carm.* 594.

4 (p. ppl. *extortus*) distorted, forced, exaggerated. **b** (*s. act.*) extortionate.

admiror .. hic quorundam magnorum expositionem nimis ~am et intentioni B. Augustini nullatenus dubito contrariam R. MARSTON *QD* 381; in quibus habeurunt fiduciam nec alios adduxerunt nisi ad ~um sensum (TYSS.) *Ziz.* 179. **b** ipsum [sc. papam] falso, violenter et ~a manu primariam ecclesiae potestatem hactenus usurpasse .. affirmare CHAUNCY *Passio* 28v.

5 ? *f. l.*

quare cum ere calido magis extorquetur [? l. excoquetur] quis quam cum ferro vel alio metallo *Quaest. Salern.* N 40 (cf. *nn.* ad loc.: excoctum calore maximo).

extorrēre [CL], to scorch (fig.).

rex [Henricus IV] .. legacionem faciens Henrico suo primogenito, .. ut sibi coronam non appropriaret .. qui mandatum patris parvipendens miserabiliori morte .. igne sacro extostus apud Gallias interiit FORDUN *Cont.* XV 9.

extorris [CL]

1 driven from one's country, exiled. **b** (as sb.) foreigner. **c** (w. play on etym. meaning, *ex* + *terra*) 'Lackland' (epithet of King John).

pro eis qui jam domum reversi fuerant et pro illis qui adhuc ~es patriae durabant BEDE *Ezra* 872; sed rex praefatus non sontem †pelleret [? l. pellerat] arvis / deque suis praedis extorrem trusit inicus *Mir. Nin.* 112; patet .. quid nequam homines, quia regno Dei ~es suo merito fiunt, promereantur EADMER *Beat.* 15 p. 288; ultro in exilium aliqui profugiunt quo ~es vel a potestate Normannorum sint liberi ORD. VIT. IV 3 p. 172; in hoc exilio, quo ~es fere facti sunt a regno GIR. *DK* II 7; **1600** (v. exterminium 1a). **b** ~es, *wræccan GlC* E 515; ~es, i. exules, extranei, *utlendan, wreccean GlH* E 726; gentes Anglorum felices praesule tanto / .. / extorresque supervenientes vosque beati *De libero arbitrio* 181. **c** **s1216** nihil terre, immo nec seipsum possidens [*in marg.*: unde Johannes ~is] M. PAR. *Maj.* II 668; **s1216** nec etiam tantillum terre in pace retinens ut vere Johannis ~is diceretur *Flor. Hist.* II 161 (cf. *Ann. Lond.* 20: ut vere Johannes ~is, id est sine terra, diceretur).

2 deprived of, devoid of, free from.

haec Balaam .. a sorte sanctorum fecit ~em BEDE *Egb.* 17; **c795** cujus luminis quidam ~es Christum .. filium Dei proprium negare non timent ALCUIN *Ep.* 41; omnes vestri familiares amici, qui in hoc loco defuncti fuerint, a gehennalibus erunt ~es suppliciis *VSB* (*Cadoc* 17) 60; peccatorum ~is W. MALM. *GP* I 65; hic .. jam ab omnium penalium locorum cruciatu ~is prestolabatur .. introitum eterne felicitatis COGGESH. *Visio* 31; nervi qui ex nimia strictione sui ~es animalis vivacitatis extiterant *NLA* (*Erkenwald*) I 401.

extorsere [*backformed from* extorsi *perf. of* extorquere], to oppress by extortion. *V. et. extorquere* 2e.

1275 vicecomes tradidit Willelmo de Royinges ballivas ad ~endos homines *Hund.* I 188b.

extorsio, extortio [LL]

1 extortion, exacting by force or sim.; **b** (w. *per*) by way of extortion, illegitimately.

quid .. est subdito intimata principis postulatio, nisi a subdito quasi quedam violenta exactio aut quasi ab invito dura quedam ~sio? H. BOS. *Thom.* III 14 p. 221; **s1245** de multiformi redditum ~sione .. in Anglia M. PAR. *Maj.* IV 441; **1321** absque aliqua ~sione de pecunia ab eis *MunAcOx* 787. **b** **1234** cartas adulterinas et illicitas tum per caliditatem tum per extrosionem (*sic*) impetratas *Reg. Paisley* 164; **1267** scriptum obligatorium de vij m. in quibus eis tenebatur per ~cionem cepit et asportavit *Cl* 353; **1310** adquisivit injuste, vel per ~sionem vel per quemcumque alium modum illicitum *MonA* II 309; **1331** per ~sionem et districcionem vicecomitum .. solverunt pro hidagio eisdem vicecomitibus xl d. per annum *PQW* 324; **1369** per ~cionem levari fecit vj s. viij d. ad usum suum proprium *SelPlForest* xlix.

2 'extortion', exaction; excessive, harsh, or illegal impost.

1213 ne aliquis hec dona et obsequia gratuita exactiones appellare valeat vel ~siones *RChart* I 191b; **c1340** racione alicujus oppressionis, ~sionis, dampni .. *FormOx* 122; **†1032** (14c) duris ~cionibus et diris depredationibus *CD* 748; taxaque cessabit, extortio non fugitabit [*gl.*: quamvis enim taxam ab eis non recipiet, tamen accipiet ~tionem] (J. BRIDL.) *Pol. Poems* I 192; **1421** de et super ~cionibus, pilleriis, roberiis, imposicionibus, appaticiamentis (*RNorm*) *Foed.* X 112a; **1522** nostri tui ordinarii .. damnum non modicum et .. ~siones .. nobis inferri .. fecisti *Form. S. Andr.* I 229.

extorsive [cf. extorquere 2], extortionately. *V. et. extortive.*

1304 auctoritate officii sui et ~e levaverunt de hominibus predictarum villarum predictos denarios de tallagio predicto *SelCExchPl* 219; **1433** terras .. que .. injuste et ~e seisivit et .. in manibus suis extunc tenuit *Langley* app. 261 (cf. ib. 260: episcopus ~e .. compulsit dictos Wil-

lelmum et Johannem contra suam voluntatem per duriciam); ipsum W. P. . . imprisonari fecit et . . ibidem sic in prisona . . quousque finem per ij s. pro deliberacione sua habenda cum prefato C. [ballivo abbatis] fecisset ~e tenuit *Entries* 11b.

extorsor [cf. extorquere 2], extortioner, one who exacts excessive, harsh, or illegal impost (used in formula in *Capitula Itineris*). *V. et. extortor.*

1276 de vic' qui tradiderunt ballivis ~oribus etc. *Hund.* I 41b; de vicecomitibus qui tradiderunt ballivis ~oribus populum gravantibus supra modum . . firmas ut sic suas firmas levarent (*Cap. Itineris*) *Fleta* 29; **1321** de vicecomitibus qui tradiderunt ballivas (*sic*) ~oribus populum gravantibus ultra modum *MGL* II 355.

extorte [cf. extorquere 4a], in a distorted or forced sense.

congrue et convenienter antiquis doctoribus . . utuntur moderni doctores, sequaces Magistri Sententiarum, his vocabulis 'panis et vinum' pro accidentibus panis et vini, et non ~e et contra intentum fidei et ecclesie (WYNTERTON) *Ziz.* 188.

extortio v. extorsio.

extortionaliter [cf. extorsio], extortionately, by way of extortion.

1395 unum equum . . a dicto Johanne . . ~er ceperunt et abduxerunt *Proc. J. P.* 143; **1433** sic ~er compellit dictos tenentes suos de novo prosequi deliberacionem de terris *Langley* app. 257.

extortionativus v. extortivus.

extortiose, extortionately, by way of extortion. *V. et. extortuose.*

1391 decanus . . sub colore officii sui cepit ~e de Johanne Spicer . . vij s. argenti de extorsionibus *Proc. J. P.* 455; tu [vicecomes] spiritu avaricie seductus, machinans . . bona . . predicti A. officii tui colore in usus tuos proprios ~e convertere . . *Entries* 311b.

extortive [cf. extorquere 2], extortionately, by way of extortion. *V. et. extorsive.*

1395 Willelmus Leche . . manucepit . . Thomam . . eum sanare de omnibus infirmitatibus suis et cepit a predicto Thoma et aliis visinis suis ~e xl li. et nihil eis proficuit *Proc. J. P.* 130; **c1448** vicarius ~e adquisivit . . evidencias et munimenta dicte placee (*Court Bk. Linc.*) *Eng. Clergy* 238.

extortivus [cf. extorquere 2], extortionate.

ut delinquentes in dominos exacciones dicuntur ponere se in suis graciis quando subiciunt se extortionative [MS: extor^{tie}, ? l. extortive] potestati eorum (WYCL. *Ente*) *Wycl. & Ox.* 135*n*.

extortor [cf. CL extorquere], extortioner, one who exacts excessive, harsh, or illegal impost. *V. et. extorsor.*

s1252 secundum estimationem novam ad inquisitionem strictissimam ad voluntatem et arbitrium regiorum satellitum et ~orum qui astute nimis in dampnum ecclesie inestimabile . . inhiarent M. PAR. *Maj.* V 325; bonorum ~ores in publicis congressionibus BOECE 75.

extortuose, extortionately, by way of extortion. *V. et. extortiose.*

1275 Reginaldus de M. cepit ~e de Galfrido ad Aquam . . ij s. *Hund.* I 493b.

extortus v. extorquere. **extotare** v. exstocare.

extra [CL]

1 (adv.) outside a place or institution; **b** (w. *ab* or *ad*) from or on the outside.

pagani . . super eos irrumpunt, . . prosternunt intus et ~a ASSER *Alf.* 27; **a1089** clerici et laici tam intus quam ~a LANFR. *Ep.* 31 (59); queritur utrum excommunicatus possit excommunicari. quod non videtur, quia qui est ~a non potest esse magis ~a HALES *Sent.* IV 335; oportet ~a [ME: *ute*] laborare et domi quiescere *AncrR* 139; **1376** xviiij li. iij s. vj d. rec. de diversis obedientiariis infra et ~a, pro *le rerdos Ac. Durh.* 584; duos . . forestarios . . vidit absolvi a monachis ~a ad hostium ecclesie *Feod. Durh.* 275. **b s1333** ut ab ~a adjutorium exspectarent AD. MUR. *Chr.* 67; carpentariis ad ~a laborantibus servus Dei deplanxit BAKER 107b; **1416** etc. (v. ad 2c); **1453** una frocca data domino R. W. communario, in quod morabatur ad ~a per vij annos *Ac. Durh.* 190; **1511** privilegia . . concessa civitati et ecclesie Lismorensi ejusque territorio et maneriis ab ~a *Conc.* III 653; **1534** ferrura equorum ad ~a *Househ. Bk. Durh.* 239.

2 on the outside. **b** protuberantly. **c** outwardly; **d** (w. *ad*).

efficiens quidem et finis [sc. causalitates] veluti ~a existentes tendunt in, forma vero et materia abiciunt ad invicem *Ps.*-GROS. *Gram.* 54; **1295** (v. gladiolatus). **b** quod [oculi] ~a fuerint euntes aut intus nimis existentes J. MIRFIELD *Brev.* 56. **c** quia cecus es intus et extra M. CORNW. *Hen.* 260. **d** sint licet hii versus modice virtutis ad extra, / interior virtus ordine major erit GOWER *VC* II prol. 29; **1452** (v. ad 2c).

3 to the outside, away, abroad.

prohibemus, ne aliquis ~a vendatur (*Quad.*) *GAS* 261; **1230** quod nullus magistratorum nec scolaris trahatur ad ~a *StatOx* 97; **1306** pro Lucya . . maritanda ~a *Crawley* 242; **1499** pro . . *les gutturs* super ecclesiam mundandis et pro nive ~a jactanda ij d. *Ac. Churchw. Glast.* 331.

4 besides, additionally. **b** more.

~a, i. . . praeter *GlH* E 588; DUNS *Ord.* II 351 (v. disgregativus b); visum est regem . . jura . . alienare non posse, ~a, de jure . . tenetur . . jura regni sui . . servare AVESB. 80; **1449** de iiij s. iiij d. de pellibus nudis xxxj multonum . . post tonsionem, ut ~a, precium pellis j d. *Crawley* 478; **1458** liquore . . nectario, qui dudum ad ~a in mensa apponebatur *Reg. Whet.* I 314. **b** ~a, i. . . plus *GlH* E 588.

5 (prep.) outside (a place), beyond (a boundary); **b** (governing abstr. sb.); **c** (w. ellipsis of sb.).

portenta . . diabolica . . liniamentis . . deformibus intra vel ~a deserta moenia GILDAS *EB* 4; ~a fines omnes Brittaniae BEDE *HE* I 1 p. 11; **859** intra villulam et ~a villulam *CS* 497; omnia quae ~a arcem invenit surripuit ASSER *Alf.* 56; **a984** exstra refectorium (ÆTHELWOLD *Ch.*) *Conc. Syn.* 127; stantem ~a balconem LANTFR. *Swith.* 20; WULF. *Swith.* II 166 (v. balco); siquis . . arborem stantem ~a viam intra prostraverit *DB* I 1; erant c et iij homines commanentes intus et ~a murum *Ib.* 179; quecunque res in aqua posita major videtur in aqua quam ~a aquam NECKAM *NR* II 153 p. 234; **1314** cepit . . equum . . quem invenit in campo de B. ~a feodum suum *Eyre Kent* I 70; per viam ~a nemus *Feod. Durh.* 101; *Meaux* III 242 (v. fabrilis 2); **1428** Inverness . . pro expensis regis fiendis ~a montem *ExchScot* 452; **1476** servientibus . . una cum . . asportacione lapidum ~a mare ad dictum molendinum *Ac. Durh.* 646. **b** neque enim leve principis extra / praecipuum fas est subjectos velle meare FRITH. 707. **c** intus civitatem vel ~a *DB* I 2; **a1100** in festo die et ~a *Regesta* 436; **1343** regi, cardinalibus, et Scottis infra aquas et ~a *Ac. Durh.* 170.

6 on the outside of (a body or organ).

SB 34 (v. cacochymia); ~a corpus utuntur foliis et radice, non intra, quod mortifera est [herba] *Alph.* 11.

7 (w. vb. of motion or sim.) out of, away from; **b** (governing vendor) from.

ferreus qui ventrem secabat circulus . . disruptus prosilivit ~a hominis viscera LANTFR. *Swith.* 24; prosiliebat / integer extra hominis quam strinxerat acriter ulnam WULF. *Swith.* II 295; limenque excessit et extra / tecta domus veniens pueris sociatur eisdem *Ib.* 930; COGGESH. *Chr.* 123 (v. glomus 1b); **s1324** de evasione cujusdam ~a turrim Londonearum BLANEFORD 145 *tit.* **b** hoc manerium T. R. E. ~a aecclesiam emptum fuit, eo pacto et conventione ut post tertium haeredem cum omni pecunia manerium aecclesia S. Petri de episcopatu reciperet *DB* I 46v.; **1217** vendidi et quiete clamavi ~a me et heredes meos Ricardo priori . . duodecim denariatas quieti redditus *AncD* A 1845; **a1221** prior et conventus Sancte Trinitatis Lond' quiete clamaverunt Hielie (*sic*) de Cornhill' . . ~a domum suam totum capitale *Ib.* 1851; **1226** habendum dictis priori et conventui ~a me et heredes meos libere quiete *Ib.* 1881; **c1240** habendum et tenendum dicto Johanni Juveni et heredibus suis ~a me et heredes meos *Ib.* 1822.

8 outside, not included in, not reckoned with. **b** not in (condition or state). **c** separated from. **d** extraneous to.

dies quarta decima ~a hunc numerum separatim . . praenotatur BEDE *HE* V 21; **813** (17c) nec alicui foras ~a congregationi *CS* 342; quaedam silva quam isdem Osuuardus posuit ~a manerium *DB* I 2v.; habet . . j hidam quae jacuit in rapo de Leuues; nunc ~a rapum est. non geldat *Ib.* 27v.; R. episcopus posuit eam [sc. hidam] ~a elemosinam S. Pauli injuste *Ib.* 209; **1324** H. filius W. . . est ~a decennam *CBaron* 140. **b** siqui . . sunt clerici ~a sacros ordines constituti qui se continere non possunt (*Lit. Papae*) BEDE *HE* I 27; **1427** de x s. rec' de molendino fullatico . . et non plus, eo quod ~a tenuram pro defectu tenentis *Ac. Durh.* 621; **1439** nil de j piscar', . . quia ~a tenuram *Ib.* 64. **c** paeniteat iiij annos ~a ecclesiam et vj inter auditores et ij adhuc ~a communionem THEOD. *Pen.* I 5. 10; **680** quid . . prosunt bonorum operum emolumenta si ~a catholicam gerantur ecclesiam? ALDH. *Ep.* 4 p. 481; omnes Judeos atque paganos quos ~a Christianismum reperit *Simil. Anselmi* 76. **d** omnia haec [sc. virginitas, castitas, jugalitas] non sunt ~a palatium ALDH. *VirgP* 19.

9 beyond reach, scope, or jurisdiction of. **b** (leg., w. *finem*) (founded) upon a fine, (arising) from an agreement.

ut mens ~a rationis regulam . . nihil faciat (*Lit. Papae*) BEDE *HE* I 27 p. 50; ~a auctoritatem propriam episcopos Galliarum judicare non poteris (*Ib.*) *Ib.* p. 53; in dominica terra regis tenet R. de B. unam domum et unam piscariam . . et est ~a manum regis *DB* I 162; qui fugit, ~a legem habeatur [AS: *si se man utlah*] (*Quad.*) *GAS* 337; **1309** *ne fuist pas receu* quia extra casum statuti *Year Bk. 2 Edw. II* 76; **1334** omnes terre sue quas habuit in foresta sunt ~a regardum racione ballive sue *SelPlForest* 67. **b 1385** quoddam breve de scire facias ~a finem predictum *PlRCP* 496 r. 321.

10 besides, in addition to, other than. **b** more than. **c** except, apart from.

sicera est omnis potio quae ~a vinum inebriare potest . . . ex suco frumentorum et pomorum conficitur *Gl. Leid.* 1. 111; *DB* I 2v. (v. ecclesiola); ~a hos [*solins*] sunt in dominio iiij *solins Ib.*; in Bolehestre . . in dominio est j carucata terrae ~a ij hidas et virg' *Ib.* 211; has iij forisfacturas habebat in dominio rex E. in omni Anglia ~a firmas *Ib.* 252; se non alias inniti aut aliam quesituros ~a cartam probationem asserunt, nil se majus vel minus ~a cartam exigere *Chr. Battle* f. 87. **b** discipulum terrenis ~a solitum ponderibus oneratum GILDAS *EB* 72. **c** ~a abbatem [AS p. 439: *buton þam abbude*] nullus ab hoc debito servitutis excusetur *RegulC* 62; **1493** in diebus piscium . . per totum annum ~a quadragesimam *Ac. Durh.* 652.

11 (w. *se*, *sensum*, or sim.) beside oneself, out of one's mind.

amentes et ~a se facti GIR. *GE* II 54 p. 163; totus ~a se pedetentim longe defertur in nemus MAP *NC* IV 11 f. 52; ut sibi ipse de se discredat et fascinnata mente alias ~a se putet Ollonem *Ib.* 16 f. 58; **1227** de demente et ~a sensum *BNB* III 660; es tu . . ~a te ipsum [ME: *ut of þe seolven*] *AncrR* 106; miles . . immobiliter quasi ~a se positus erectus astabat *Latin Stories* 65; fecit . . miraculum de . . homine ~a sensum W. WORC. *Itin.* 30.

extracapere, ? to withdraw (land) or (?) *f. l.*

c1235 de feudis duorum militum una virgata terre extracapta [? l. extracepta, i.e. extrasaepta] in Cershull' *Fees* 448.

extracludere [cf. LL extraclusus], to exclude.

ex pro extra invenitur poni, ut excludo ~o, exsul extra solum ALCUIN *Orth.* 111.

extracta v. extrahere.

extractio [LL]

1 pulling out, drawing out; **b** (w. ref. to sleeve).

c1410 pro ~one armorum violenta *StatOx* 205. **b 1565** pro extract' unius par' manicarum pro un' tog' . . de velvet' . . cum *lawne Ac. LChamb.* 58 f. 20v. (cf. *Misc. LChamb.* 33 p. 144: *drawinge oute of a paire of sleeves for a Flaunders gown of black velvet . . with lawne*).

2 drawing forth, fetching out (person). **b** taking out (animals from stock); *v. et. extractura.* **c** yelming (of straw).

cum instrumentis horribilibus ipsum vulnerantes graviter et occidentes post extraxionem ejus extra ecclesiam GASCOIGNE *Loci* 159; **1492** postea ipsum J. ab ecclesia . . ceperunt, et usque gaolam . . regis . . duxerunt que est eadem ~o et abductio ipsius J. extra ecclesiam . . in predicto placito . . specificata, absque hoc quod idem T. C. seu . . alii ipsum J. ab ecclesia . . aliter . . extraxerunt vel abduxerunt *Entries* 54b. **b c1230** percipere [debent] . . uxores eorum pro ~one bidentium aliud vellus [*Chisenbury*] *Doc. Bec* 56; **1345** de xl agnis de ~one ante tonsuram venditis *Comp. Swith.* 147. **c 1514** pro ~one straminis, xiiij d. una cum xij d. pro le *cratels Ac. Durh.* 161.

3 drawing off, taking out, removal. **b** drawing (of water). **c** shedding (of blood).

ponatur in furno post ~onem panis GILB. V 221. 1; **1323** in invencione et ~one ij ruscarum, iiij d. *MinAc* 965/5; extractis pecuniis ad curiam Romanam . . domini temporales tenentur de lege consciencie ~onem hujusmodi prohibere (WYCL.) *Ziz.* 261; **1433** sol' diversis operariis laborantibus circa ~onem antiqui meremii et imposicione novi meremii *Ac. Durh.* 622; **1556** nulla [sc. scriptura] . . ex cista communi extrahatur, nisi . . arbitrio congregationis . . et tum schedula in qua de hujusmodi ~one et de nomine ejus cui scriptura extracta traditur mentio fiat, conscribatur, eaque in predicta cista . . conservetur *StatOx* 367. **b 1472** (v. cursus 4a); **1533** pro ~one aque *Househ. Bk. Durh.* 185. **c** pena . . pro sanguinis ~one, x s. *BBAdm* I 231.

4 carrying away, carriage.

1534 *sleydds* pro ~one lapidum ultra aquam de Wiri *Househ. Bk. Durh.* 252.

5 clearing (of land, Gasc.).

1259 pro cultura et ~one dictarum l sadonum *RGasc* II 473.

6 a record (of indictment). **b** compilation of excerpts.

a 1320 exoneratio v m. exactarum in Scaccario per ~onem justiciariorum *MGL* I 685; **c1460** dato Guidoni Rowclif . . in regardo pro ~one indicamenti apud Hoveden, xx s. *Fabr. York* 134. **b 1439** liber de ~one sermonum cum dictis Lincolniensis *MunAcOx* 760; **1501** ~o summaria super libros Ethicorum *Cant. Coll. Ox.* I 26.

7 extraction (as physical or chemical process). **b** refining (of metal). **c** extracted substance, extract, essence.

Bacon IX 156 (v. extrahere 7a); ~o, est digestio e corporea concretione, partes subtiliores et puriores ab affuso aliquo menstruo apprehensas, relictis foecibus dissolvens. vel est segregatio essentiae qua e corpore suo extrahitur *LC* 240. **b** **1323** (v. affinatio 1b). **c** ~ones sunt nobiliores distractionibus *LC* 240.

8 (phil.) eliciting into actuality.

sicut .. totus ignis est factus in actu, sic totus fuit in potencia, et nec est prima ~o ejus quod fuit in potencia objectiva. secunda ~o est secundum quod agens de potencia materie preexistentis .. educit formam Duns *Sent.* II 12. 1. 17.

9 (math.): **a** subtraction. **b** calculation.

a **1308** summa exstraccionis xc li. xvj s. viij d. quad. *Ac. Durh.* 2. **b** tabula ~onis prima ad annos collectos Gros. *Comp.* 239 *rub.*; per radicum ~onem talibus numeris surdis per addicionem multarum ciphrarum ut docet canon ad hoc factus Wallingf. *Quad.* 32; capitulum secundum de multiplicacione, divisione, et radicum ~one Killingworth *Alg.* 714.

extractivus, (med.) drawing off, removing.

sicut opium est ~um caloris innati, ita balsamus et mirra sunt vivificativa ejusdem Gilb. VI 266. 2; calidum humidi ~um et digestivum, inducens coagulationem ad formam lapidis in terrestri *Ps.*-Gros. *Summa* 628.

extractor, extractor, drawer out. **b** miner.

primo tractus sui conamine, dum [piscatores] retia traherent, salmo unus .. apparuit .. in suos ~ores quasi in stupendo deseviens R. Cold. *Cuthb.* 73 p. 150; T. York. *Sap.* II 28 *rub.* (v. datio 1f); **1416** medici, sirurgici, fisici et ~ores dentium *Doc. Bev.* 111. **b** c**1250** Radulfus Bugge de Notingham extraxit minam de predicta minera . . . et similiter Radulfus Bugge de Bathecuelle fuit ~or predicte minere tempore J. de Grey. et J. de Grey cepit chimagium de ~oribus de dictis mineris tempore suo *DL Forest Proc.* 1/3 r. 12.

extractura, taking out (animals from stock). *V. et. estrahura, estraia* 2, *extractio* 2.

c**1300** in extra[ct]ura ad lardarium domini .. ij [sc. vaccas] quia debiles *FormMan* 4; reddit comptum de ij carcosis bovviis (*sic*) retentis de remanente ultimi compoti. et de x de ~a ut supra. et de x multonibus de ~a ut supra *Reg. Rough* 227.

1 extractus [cf. extrahere 6]

1 estreat, extract or copy of record (esp. relating to fines or amercements). *V. et. extrahere* 6d.

1304 ~us totius tallagii predicti liberetis sub sigillis vestris .. ad scaccarium nostrum (*RParl*) *SelCh* 498; omnis justiciarius .. importet ~us justiciarie infra octo dies post xl dies contentos in prefatis ~ibus (*Stat. Rob. III* 27) *RegiamM* II f. 69; ~us: "De re judicata", capitulum "Ad apostolice" Ad. Usk 59; **1460** idem clericus omisit scribere expensas suas in ~u justiciarie *Ib.* VII 5; **1468** prout patet in ~u curie senescallatus ostenso super compotum, x li. *Ib.* 565.

2 fine or amercement. *V. et. extrahere* 6e.

1381 pro secundis decimis sibi debitis de ~u ultimi itineris justiciarii iij li. *ExchScot* I clxxxii; de summa hujus ~us recuperata *Ib.*; **1388** W. B. nuper collector ~us curie *IMisc* 240/17; **1459** pro expensis .. camerarii deputatorum .. eo †quo [l. quod] compotans levavit integrum ~um et nichil solvit pro expensis eorum, et de burgo nullus ~us erat, x li. *ExchScot* 547; **1460** et de xxx li. x s. receptis a ballivis burgi de Edinburgh per ~us unius itineris camerarie . . . *Ib.* 595; **1460** et non onerat se de exitibus unius itineris camerarie .. cujus itineris ~us extendit se ad vj li. *Ib.*

2 extractus v. extrahere.

extradonare, (Scot.) to give, alienate (possession).

1266 (17c) de .. expensis suis factis in ballia predicta usque ad diem quo dictam balliam ~avit *ExchScot* 2; **1523** decernimus dictam Margaretam Somerwell ad judicialiter revocandum et ~andum suam conjunctam infeodacionem ac vitalem reditum *Offic. S. Andr.* 125; **1543** antedictum annuum reditum .. omnino renunciavit, quitclamavit et ~avit imperpetuum, prout per presentes renunciat, quitclamat et ~at *Scot. Grey Friars* II 40; **1575** predictum locum .. in manibus Willelmi .. pure et simpliciter resignavit, ~avit, et dimisit *Ib.* 249.

extraducere, to lead out.

~o, A. *to lede out WW.*

extraëquitator [extra + equitator; cf. ME *outridere*], outrider (mon.).

a**1466** quod abbas, officiarii, et ~ores expendirent (*sic*) residuum in mundanis et riotis *Paston Let.* 61.

extrahere [CL]

1 to pull out, extract. **b** to draw (arms, sword, or sim.). **c** to draw up (ship). **d** to draw out (to full length).

speram facili conamine prensam / extrahit et dicto citius de rupe tenaci Wulf. *Swith.* I 129; si linguam ~at [AS: *gif monnes tunge bið of heafde*] (*Quad.*) *GAS* 81; interposuit clipeum suum in quo mucro .. inhesit ita ut .. ipsum imperator ~ere non potuisset G. Mon. IV 3; **1166** tanquam viscera nostra de claustro pectoris acerbitate ferri extracta J. Sal. *Ep.* 151 (157); **1201** ita quod iij ossa ex capite ejus per .. verberacionem extracta fuerunt *SelPlCrown* 2 (cf. ib. 4: vulneravit eum in capite ita quod xxviij ossa ~untur); **1240** (v. 1 exclusorius 2b); dens ~atur cum tenaculis Gad. 120. 1 (v. excarnare); homines hujus mundi qui omnes de uno sacculo materno ~untur J. Waleys *Schak.* 463; **1290** (v. eviscerare 1b); **1300** extraxit bundas positas inter ipsum et Rogerum de M. *Leet Norw.* 51; **1336** Thomas .. sagitta percussus in femore, illam incaute extraens, venas et nervos rumpens, incontinenti decessit *Illust. Scot.* 59; filipendula .. quando ~itur a terra non debet abluj *SB* 21; **1444** (v. excludere 3a). **b** qui ante archiepiscopum pugnaverit aut arma extraxerit [AS: *wæpne gebregde*] (*Inst. Cnuti*) *GAS* 59; **1166** (v. 1 conserere 2a); **1203** invenit .. Robertum armatum in felonia cum vi sua armata et gladio suo extracto *SelPlCrown* 49; s**1253** (v. alenatius); **1368** de Thoma .. pro cultello suo extracto ad percussendum Johannem *Hal. Durh.* 68; in obviam venit angelus Domini cum gladio extricto [v. l. extracto] *Chester Plays* V 215; **1493** illam sicam quam secundarius Sauder extraxit contra pacem super J. R. *CourtR Ottery St. M.* m. 102d. **c** si navem suam extraxerit [AS: *gyf he his scip upp getogen hæbbe*] .. (*Quad.*) *GAS* 222. **d** filum .. extractum in longum Wycl. *Apost.* 158 (v. globus 1b).

2 to drag out. **b** to stretch out. **c** to draw forth, fetch out (person); **d** (falc.) to draw (hawk) out of mew; **e** to take out (animals from stock). **f** to deliver, rescue.

1201 ipse venit in domum suam et eam per pedes extraxit *CurR* I 293; **1225** non ausi fuerunt ~ere corpus sine visu coronatorum *SelPlCrown* 115; **1258** (v. abjuratio 3); Symonem .. Robertum .. et fratrem Willelmum .. de turri extraxerunt et .. eos decapitaverunt *Chr. Kirkstall* 125; Judei extraxerunt eam et ejecerunt extra civitatem .. et lapidaverunt eam *Holy Rood-Tree* 56; **1371** extraxerunt eam de puteo predicto et duxerunt eam ad domum Margerie Rush *SelCCoron* 46. **b** brachiis [Christi] atque tibiis per cordas in longum et latum extractis *Spec. Incl.* 2. 2. **c** adjurant per Dominum .. donec ipsum [sc. Cuthbertum] .. ~unt latebris atque ad sinodum pertrahunt Bede *CuthbP* 24; ut [hostes] ~antur a suis munitionibus et facilius extra de plano cedantur R. Niger. *Mil.* III 77; Dominus .. parcit debilibus .. et ~it eos [ME: *draȝeð ham ut*] a mundo dulciter et delicate *AncrR* 79. **d** **1204** pro ~endo girfalco regis de muta *Pipe* 120; **1284** eunti apud D. ad ~endum ibidem unum ostorium regis *KRAc* 351/11 m. 4; eidem eunti ad mutas London' ad ~endum unum girfalconem *Ib.* m. 41. **e** c**1300** quot multones mortui fuerunt ante tonsionem, .. et quot extracti fuerunt ad lardarium *FormMan* 41; **1333** mandavimus vobis quod omnes pullanos equicii .. qui ~endi sunt in instanti seisona ~i .. faciatis *Cl* 154 m. 16. **f** ut plurimas de antiqui hostis faucibus ~eret gentes Alcuin *Hag.* 658D; innumerabiles ~ere de inferno Anselm (*Medit.* 3) III 85.

3 to draw off, take out, remove. **b** to draw (wine, blood). **c** to delete, erase.

pistor clibanum calefacit, panes imponit et coctos ~it Ord. Vit. VI 3 p. 11; extracto de loculis suis denario R. Cold. *Cuthb.* 103 p. 231; viator .. nec etiam calciamenta sibi ~i permisit *Id. Godr.* 40; **1200** proprios anulos extraxit de digitis *CurR* I 256; leo iratus erexit palmam et cum unguibus extraxit totum corium de capite lupi *Latin Stories* 54; *Cust. Cant.* 10 (v. denodare 1a); **1477** summa de cista extracta .. pro pecuniis illis ~endis . . . ad me penes quem est hec summa sic extracta *Let. Ch. Ch.* 36; **1556** (v. extractio 3a). **b** Bacon V 92 *gl.* (v. faex 1a); **1281** Ricardus M. extraxit sanguinem de Stephano G. *SelPlMan* 30; **1290** Agnetem verberavit et sanguinem ab ea extraxit *State Tri. Ed. I* 26; **1321** non permiserunt homines potantes in tabernis suis videre dolia nec interesse ubi vina ~untur de doliis (*Eyre*) *Lond. Ed. I & II* II 186. **c** **1429** constat de rasura viz. ubi superius continebatur '*de la fee farm*' etc. ~itur '*fee*' per mandatum domini cancellarii *PS* 690/2036.

4 to carry away.

c**1280** cariabit fenum et †extrahiet [l. ~et] fima *Crawley* 237; **1283** extraxherunt (v. crudwainum); **1285** coadunabit ad fimos quando ~untur *Cust. Suss.* (*Terring*) II 26; **1285** (v. elongare 6a); c**1300** in stipendio W. B. ~entis fimos cum carecta sua *FormMan* 33; c**1330** quatuor mulieribus ~entibus fagot' extra parcum .. viiij d. *Ac. Durh.* 519; **1459** per vendicionem xx petrarum lane receptarum .. a diversis personis ~entibus dicta lanas ad alios burgos et extra privilegia dicti burgi *ExchScot* 510.

5 **a** to clear (land, *Gasc.*). **b** to dig out (ore from mine).

a **1289** quas l sadones terra .. Hodinus debet ~ere, laborare et in garegio vertere *RGasc* II 472. **b** c**1250** (v. extractor b).

6 **a** to excerpt (from a text); **b** to make a copy (of text). **c** (p. ppl. *extractus* as sb. n.) extract, excerpt (from text); **d** (as sb., usu. f.) estreat, extract or copy of record (esp. relating to fines or amercements); *v. et.* 1 *extractus* 1. **e** fine or amercement; *v. et.* 1 *extractus* 2.

a in septimo libro Pantegni Constantini, capitulo iij, de quo hec extraximus Bart. Angl. III 23; s**1331** quedam de antiquis chronicis .. sub compendio sunt extracta Avesb. 79; a**1350** (v. extraordinarie); ex laboribus antiquorum aliqua paucula medullata extraxi *Eul. Hist.* I *proem.* p. 4. **b** **1236** omnia debita que .. episcopus Norwic' regi debuit ~i faciant a rotulis scaccarii et extracta illa liberent executoribus dicti episcopi *KRMem* 15 m. 16 (1); **1289** reficiatis instrumentum [sc. quod reperiri non potest] illud de protocollo seu registro vestro fideliter ~entes *RGasc* II 395; **1323** debitis extractis (v. exannalis); **1517** item evidencie extracte in quodam libro *Ac. Durh.* 293. **c** ~a de antiquis chronicis notanda Avesb. 79 *tit.* (cf. ib. 81b: sufficiunt premissa ~a de antiquis chronicis). **d** **1218** liberari faciatis Willelmo de H. clerico ~as et brevia que penes vos remanserunt *Cl* 382b; **1226** mandatum est vicecomitibus .. quod ~a placitorum .. recipiant *Pat* 87; **1236** (v. 6b supra); s**1254** ~as rotulorum de amerceamentis et omnimodis finibus M. Par. *Min.* III 335; **1260** quod amerciamenta mercatorum Wintonie .. que alias tibi levare precipimus, et quorum ~as tibi transmisimus .. levari facias *Cl* 205; **1290** ~e de predictis finibus facte sunt et liberate in scaccario *State Tri. Ed. I* 40; c**1290** quod omnes justiciarii .. liberent in scaccario ~as suas de finium exitibus et amerciamentis coram eis taxatis *Fleta* 85; s**1276** finem fecerunt per unam marcam; que ponitur in ~is *G. S. Alb.* I 419; **1314** fines et redempciones delinquencium .. capiatis et ~as inde annuatim ad scaccarium nostrum liberetis (*Breve*) *MGL* II 213; **1384** ad liberandum vobis ad scaccarium predictum aliquas ~as finium, exituum, amerciamentorum Thorne 2181. **e** c**1250** ad recipiendum ~as de summonitionibus scaccarii (*AncD* D 134) *EE County Court* 134; **1258** memorandum quod .. liberata fuit Willelmo de Axemuth una ~a auri et alia ~a argenti de finibus factis in cancellaria regis deportande ad scaccarium *Cl* 464; **1282** ~e et districciones que debent fieri pro muro et fossato ville faciendis *Rec. Leic.* I 197; **1284** ~am de Sancto Emiliano pro tercia parte .. vicecomes .. percipere consuevit *RGasc* II 223; **1287** quia dicta cedula .. non est originale sicut recordatum est per eundem Rogerum qui ~as eorundem cc li. postea liberavit ad scaccarium .. (*Pipe*) *EHR* XXII 737; **1313** quod tercia pars leude seu astracte restituatur eidem [vicecomiti] tenenda a rege *MS PRO* E. 175/2/5 m. 5; **1315** tercia pars leude seu ~e S. Emuliani .. restituatur eidem [vicecomiti] tenenda de nobis *RGasc* IV 1327; **13..** infra quas summas non respondent de aliquibus denariis provenientibus de finibus amerciamentis operariorum pro excessu, eo quod justiciarii regis in hoc comitatu nullas extratas dictis collectoribus inde liberaverunt .. (*Lay Subsidy R*) *EHR* XXI 537.

7 to extract (substance) by physical or chemical process. **b** to refine (metal). **c** (p. ppl. as sb. n.) extracted substance, extract, essence.

oportet non solum virtutem venenosam ~i sed alias inutiles; et non solum sic, sed oportet facere resolutiones varias corporum a corporibus, ut in extractione elementorum diversi generis .. et sive illa a quibus ~antur, sint omnino inutilia sive nocivum Bacon IX 156; per vias alkimie ~itur oleum benedictum a lateribus et aqua rosacea a rosis *Ib.*; *Alph.* 2 (v. acinus a); *SB* 9 (v. ahoho); Cutcl. *CL* (v. 2 essentia 2c); Wycl. *Log.* III 77 (v. destillabilis); *LC* 240 (v. extractio 7a). **b** cum .. admisceatur sulphur grossum cum argento vivo grosso, superflue excoquitur et ferrum estrahitur Gros. 6; **1293** (v. affinatio 1b); **1295** (v. glecca); **1323** (v. affinare b). **c** *Ac. Beaulieu* 266 (v. deciduus 2); *LC* 240 (v. 2 essentia 2b).

8 (fig.) to draw out, elicit; **b** (speech); **c** (meaning).

801 nec cum periculo cor leonis ~endum Alcuin *Ep.* 237; aliquid ~ere de nichilo non humani negotii opus fuit R. Cold. *Cuthb.* 22 p. 48; dum [virtus] non applicata est ut ~at ad existenciam actu quod sub possibilitate latet *Ps.*-Gros. *Gram.* 48; generans non facit aliud quam ~ere illud quod est in potentia ad actum Duns *Sent.* II 12. 1. 17. **b** nihil aliud [sc. responsum] poterant ab eo ~ere nisi "xiij libras et iij annos" J. Mirfield *Flor.* 130. **c** si ad rem habentem quidditatem, tunc intellectus natus erit reverti et ~ere quidditatem illam Baconthorpe *Quaest. Sent.* 2b; Elmh. *Cant.* 224 (v. 1 deliberatio c).

9 (math.): **a** to take away, subtract. **b** to work out, calculate.

a *tl* ~amus atque ex eadem area *bg* aream *bt* minuamus Rob. Angl. *Alg.* 82; **1308** ~enda sunt de carnibus, piscibus et allec' furtive asportatis .. xj li. xv s. j d. ob. quad. *Ac. Durh.* 2. **b** cum .. radicem alicujus ~ere voluerimus Adel. *Alch.* 25; verbi gratia volo ~ere radicem de 5625 *Ib.*; de modo ~endo annos et menses Arabum ex annis Christi tam per multiplicationem et divisionem quam per tabulas Gros. *Comp.* 237.

10 to draw out (period of time), prolong, delay. (*Cf.* Virgil *Aen.* X 888).

in consilio privato regni aliquandiu moram traxerat [MS: extraxerat] *G. Hen. V* 2 p. 16.

extrahura v. estrahura. **extrajudiciabiliter** v. extrajudicialiter.

extrajudicialis, extrajudicial.

1316 in secretis ~ibus tractandis per ipsos [majorem et juratos, contrarotulator] non intereit nisi vocatus per eos *RGasc* IV 1539; **1342** in appellacionibus eciam mere ~ibus tuitorie vel directe ad dictam curiam interjectis *Conc.* II 687b; confessio peccatorum .. est ~is, que .. propter impedimentum concurrens ex parte confitentis .. sentenciam virtute clavium ecclesie absolutoriam non attingit .. alia est confessio judicialis, que scilicet omni remoto impedimento attingit sententiam absolucionis predictam CONWAY *Def. Mend.* 1412 (*recte* 1312); **1527** [*J. L. appointed procurators*] ad ipsius nomine et pro eo quandam appellacionem ~em *Form. S. Andr.* I 207.

extrajudicialiter, extrajudicially. *V. et. exjudicialiter.*

1301 per nuncium cum litteris de credencia qui ~er predictas informaciones pape seriatim exponat *Anglo-Scot. Rel.* 93; **1335** nolumus .. de jure suo, si quod habet, in occultis ~er informari *Lit. Cant.* II 81; **1342** quanquam eciam ~er appellans repelli possit a prosecucione appellacionis sue per excommunicacionis objectum *Conc.* II 687a; **1343** (v. amicabiliter); **1347** extrajudiciabiliter et verbaliter duntaxat impetivit coram nobis *Reg. Roff.* 361; **1382** judicaliter vel ~er, publice vel occulte (*Lit. Archiep. Cant.*) *Ziz.* 310; **1494** certos articulos .. eidem episcopo porrigi ~er tamen fecit *DCCant. Reg.* S f. 396b.

extraliberatio, (Sc.) outgoing payment or delivery.

1329 numerus recepte martorum vij^{c} lxviij. de quibus, in ~onibus .. testante rotulo clerici probacionis, lxv *ExchScot* 196.

extramanens, (Sc.) outdweller, burgess whose property lies outside burgh (constr. as pr. ppl.).

1359 pendent eciam in manibus Jacobi de Rossy and Thome Brid, burgensium de Dunde ~encium, iiij li., causa quod non habent possessiones infra burgum predictum, nec extra infra vicecomitatum distringi possunt *ExchScot* 593; **1456** de exitibus unius itineris camerarie .. de ~entibus dictum burgum *Ib.* 158; **1469** [*1460 schorlings*] ~encium burgum *Ib.* 661; **1475** tam de ~entibus regalitatem Sancti Andree quam de infra, cujus custume bine pars est de ~entibus dictam regalitatem et tercia pars de manentibus infra regalitatem *Ib.* 318.

extramarinus, (Sc.) overseas. *V. et. ultramarinus; cf. extramontanus.*

1480 pro sua sustentacione ad scolas in partibus ~is pro medicina studenda *ExchScot* 69 (cf. ib. 155 [**1481**]: in partibus ultramarinis); **1484** pro solucione debitorum suorum in partibus ~is *Ib.* 292; **1530** N. scolaris .. ut ad omnes .. sacros ordines rite promoveri valeat partes ~as visitare .. intendit *Form. S. Andr.* I 366.

extramentum v. stramentum. **extraminor** v. extraneus.

extramissio, (w. ref. to optics) emission, radiation.

GROS. 73 (v. extramittere b); ad hoc in speciali dicunt quidam quod ibi sensus in actu futurus sit non per intussusceptionem, sed per ~onem PECKHAM *QA* 164; imo materialiter et active ac si oculus fixus per ~onem videret partes fluminis succedentes BRADW. *CD* 7D; quemadmodum si poneretur visus punctualis quiescens in centro celi circumvoluti, et videret per ~onem et active non passive, sicut Deus res videt *Ib.* 243D.

extramittere, a to send away, remove (from one's keeping). **b** (w. ref. to optics) to radiate, emit (rays).

a 1115 (v. dominicus 3c); **a1127** investigans si aliqui librorum .. extramissi per aliquem fuerint; quod si fuerint .. ut retromittantur *E. Ch. S. Paul.* 216; vinum abbatis .. nec sine precepto vel licencia abbatis inde aliquid ~at *Cust. Cant.* 52. **b** mathematici .. et physici considerantes ea, que sunt supra naturam, tangentes id, quod est ex parte visus supra naturam et activum, dicunt visum fieri ~endo. hanc partem visus, que fit per extramissionem, exprimit Aristoteles aperte in libro de Animalibus GROS. 73; quod visus fiat intus suscipiendo et non ~endo BACON *Maj.* II 51.

extramontanus, lying beyond the mountains (w. ref. to the Highlands). *V. et. ultramontanus; cf. extramarinus.*

1398 pro expensis domini ducis Albanie .. laborantis in negociis regis et regni ad partes ~as *ExchScot* III 460 (cf. ib. IV 452: Inverness .. pro expensis regis fiendis extra montem).

extraneare [LL]

1 to estrange, treat as a stranger, disown. **b** to alienate, dissociate (person). **c** to alienate (property).

cur sanguinei abinvicem ~eantur? respondeo quod cessavit usus videndi vel offensio intervenit M. SCOT *Phys.* 14; **1291** petit judicium si idem Willelmus filius Willelmi ~eare possit ipsum Henricum, nunc allegando ipsum fuisse bastardum *PlRCP* 89 m. 138; *to make strawnge*, alienare, ~eare *CathA.* **b 1302** Johannes est war[antus] dotis sue per patrem ipsius Johannis assignate, de qua assign[acione] non potest se ~eare *PlRChester* 15 r. 13; diebus festivis vos ab omni negocio mundiali ~eate *Regim. Princ.* 112; **1455** laborarunt cum summo eorum conatu ad elongandum et ~eandum nos a vestra maxime desiderata presencia *Reg. Whet.* I 184. **c** ex quo patet quod nemo potest, servando justiciam, abdicare, alienare, vel ~eare a se vendendo vel aliter commutando dominium naturale; cum enim proprium insit ex natura et non potest ~eari a re cujus est proprium WYCL. *Civ. Dom.* I 126; **c1470** terre .. que per centum annos .. ab ecclesia .. alienate fuerunt et ~eate, redierunt iterum ad naturam suam pristinam *Reg. Whet.* I 433.

2 (phil.) to separate, treat as distinct (from). **b** (intr., sts. pass. in middle sense) to diverge, deviate.

fallacia est accidentis ex identitate aliquorum inter se concludere identitatem respectu tertii respectu cujus ~eatur DUNS *Ord.* II 186; sicut .. inferius ~eatur suo superiori, de quo superiore est primo ille habitus, ita multo magis ~eabitur objectum sue passioni, comparando sive ad habitum sive ad potenciam *Ib.* III 106; nec dicetur racio quare tantum ~eare potest elemosinas ab ordinacione quam Christus instituit WYCL. *Sim.* 56. **b** ista exposicio sive glossa nimis ~eatur a textu BRADW. *CD* 478D; non .. video quod sit .. gratus discipulus qui negat modum suum loquendi et fingit alium gracia ~eandi WYCL. *Ver.* I 55; non .. licet nos equivocare in juramentis ~eando a populo, multo magis non debemus ~eare in sensu a Domino *Ib.* II 39; *Id. Conf.* 508 (v. difficultare b).

3 (p. ppl.) ? made strange, uncharacteristic.

similitudine prodigiali ~eatisque incursibus ipsos comminatorie tentavit in peccatis immergere *NLA* II (*J. Bridl.*) 71.

extraneatio

1 strangeness, extravagance.

pompam seculi testatur sumptuositas et multiplicitas ferculorum, ~o lauti ministerii cibariorum, et paliata exilaracio ad serviendum seculo in excessu et falsitate verborum, sed non sic Christus WYCL. *Civ. Dom.* II 216.

2 (phil.): **a** distinction, differentiation. **b** divergence, deviation. **c** difference, separateness.

a unde numquam esset hic fallacia accidentis 'intelleccione distinguuntur ista, intelleccio est natura, ergo natura distinguuntur', nisi racio intelleccionis extraneaaretur racioni nature, in quantum comparantur ad tercium; ergo illa ~o prevenit 'aliquam distinccionem' racionis ab illa, in quantum comparantur ad tercium, et illa prevenit dictinccionem racionum inter se DUNS *Ord.* IV 260; si homo generaretur ex terra, ipse esset homo equivoce propter ~onem materie WYCL. *Incarn.* 137; talem extereacionem reperies in quolibet tali peraloysmo vocato sylloysmo expositorio *Id. Conf.* 506. **b** non video utilitatem in ~one a logica scripture *Id. Ver.* I 388; impertinencia et ~o glosarum [scripture] quas dant moderni (*Id. Ente*) *Wycl. & Ox.* 164. **c** si papa non sit de numero illorum propter ~onem a sequela in moribus, quid sibi et adverbio illi 'vobiscum'? *Id. Apost.* 201; natura lapsa deficit .. primo propter loci variacionem, .. secundo propter complexionis ~onem *Id. Innoc.* 491.

extranee [LL], strangely.

strawngely, ~e, barbare, peregrine *CathA.*

extraneitas

1 extraneity, estrangement, strangeness.

1284 sit in eis [sc. Wallensibus] cum Anglicis cor unum et anima una ut nulla inter eos ~as nominetur, sed pereat nomen extraneorum per familiare consortium PECKHAM *Ep.* 561 p. 741 (= *Conc.* II 105: †extranietas).

2 (phil.) distinction, differentiation.

hinc sumit raciones ~atis KILWARDBY *OS* 577; propter ~atem medii respectu tercii in quantum comparatur ad primum DUNS *Ord.* VII 91.

extraneus [CL]

1 from outside one's family or household (also as sb.). **b** third-party (also as sb.).

si quis presbiter aut diaconus uxorem ~eam duxerit .. deponatur THEOD. *Pen.* I 9. 4; ille ~is [addictus], hic suis GIR. *TH* III 51; cur quidam conjugales ita se diligunt ardenter cum sint de ~eo sanguine M. SCOT *Phys.* 14; [Deus] non verberat aliquem nisi quem diligit et reputat filium suum, sicut tu nolles verberare puerum ~eum [ME: *fremede*] *AncrR* 62. **b** quia vivente viro vel uxore ~eam copulam querere nulli eorum licet LANFR. *Ep.* 10 (23); si quis vero ~eus eum ad liberandum emeret suis nummis GLANV. V 5; cum quis .. nativum suum a se .. ~eo vendiderit *Ib.*

2 from outside, not local, adventitious; **b** (as sb. m. or f.) outsider, stranger. **c** (mon.) from outside the monastic community (also as sb.).

cepit consuetudines de ~is mercatoribus [*Canterbury*] *DB* I 2; **1221** quidam ~eus eques cum quodam garcione hospitatus fuit in villa *PlCrGlouc* 19; **a1272** nulli mercatori ~io liceat discicionem pannorum facere (*Kilkenny*) *Gild. Merch.* II 134. **b** si quis ~eus in Oxeneford .. vitam finierit, rex habebit quicquid reliquerit [*Oxon*] *DB* I 154v.; **1274** ipsi ~ei sunt quieti alibi de toloneis in foris (*King's Lynn*) *Hund.* I 461; **1366** permisit carectas ~iorum concul- care moram *Hal. Durh.* 61; **1387** super visu corporis cujusdam ~ee submerse .. *RCoron* 189 m. 5; **1605** quidam ~ei non inhabitantes infra burgum *Gild Merch.* (*Devizes*) II 53. **c** fratres eligant sibi abbatem de ipsis si habent; sin autem, de ~eis THEOD. *Pen.* II 6. 1; **a984** reges .. nullam exstraneam personam jus tirannidis super monachos exercentem imponant (ÆTHELWOLD *Ch.*) *Conc. Syn.* 128; **c1060** neque introducatur per violentiam ~ea persona nisi quam concors congregatio preesse elegerit (*Lit. Papae*) AILR. *V. Ed. Conf.* 759C; ab omni ~ea subjectione .. immunis ORD. VIT. III 2 p. 39; **1194** archidiaconi officiales sunt episcopi quorum officium in †extraminoribus [? l. extranioribus] adminstrationibus consistit (*Const. Lichfield*) *Conc.* I 499; **1403** cum amicis, tenentibus, et aliis ~eis *Ac. Durh.* 219 (cf. ib.: confratribus et aliis ~is).

3 foreign. **b** (as sb. m. or f.) foreigner; **c** (as pers. epithet). **d** an exile (also fig.).

donec .. gentem suam ab ~ea invasione liberaret BEDE *HE* IV 24 p. 268; **1360** de v s. vj d. et ob., receptis per custumam l pellium ~eorum, carcatarum in eisdem navibus *ExchScot* 9. **b 1151** nullus ~eus emat merces illarum navium sive aliarum que venerint de ultra mare nisi per manus hominum Rothomagi *Act. Hen. II* I 20; **1221** quidam ~eus de partibus transmarinis *PlCrGlouc* 56; **s1233** turbatio inter regem Anglie et suos quia magis adhesit ~eis quam suis *Feud. Man.* 98; **1292** secundum quod alii ~ei patrie faciunt *BBC* (*Warrington*) 383; cum ~eorum gemitus, ignotorum ululatus, notorum querulosa murmura .. mundum merore replere non desinant *Ps.-*ELMH. *Hen. V* 115. **c** mansura Gileberti ~ei *Chr. Battle* f. 16v.; **1167** Widoni ~eo cx s. *Pipe* 59; **1167** et in liberatione constituta .. Heilewise ~ee xlv s. vij d. ob. *Ib.* 141; **1198** Johanni filio Johannis ~ei *Ib.* 108; **1242** Johannes ~eus *Ib.* 1. **d 799** antichristi discipulus .. ab altario Dei ~eus (ELIPAND) *Ep. Alcuin* 182 p. 301; *GlH* E 726 (v. extorris 1b).

4 strange, peculiar, exotic.

Spiritus loquebatur per os hominis ~ea lingua LANFR. *Comment. Paul.* (*1 Cor.* xiv 13) 202; signum .. naturalis argenti est quod quando percutis cum malleo super incudem facit sonum ~eum, non sicut cuprum nec sicut alia BACON *Min.* 378; **1287** literas vestras .. recepimus familiares plurimum et ~eas, .. ~eas .. quia usque ad hec tempora fuit retroactis inauditum .. PECKHAM *Ep.* 679; pecuniam in vino aut esculentis vel poculentis ~eis .. voluptuose .. consumpsisse *Norw. Cath. Pri.* 112; si pro novis causis questio ventilabatur ~ea R. BURY *Phil.* 8. 134.

5 a foreign, alien (to one's nature or experience). **b** (fig.) exempt from. **c** extraneous, out-of-the-way. **d** deviating from.

a ad id ignorari pertinere dico quod omnibus aut eruditioribus aut cuilibet contra quem disputando insistere dignum dubium esse non est ~eum BALSH. *AD* 20; si Deus .. esset objectum conforme intellectui nostro .. et non .. ~eum BACONTHORPE *Quaest. Sent.* 9B. **b** a dolore mortis ~eus spiritum inter verba vere confessionis efflavit BROMPTON *Chr.* 735. **c 1313** in viis ~eis causa carecte emendend' *Fabr. Exon.* 66. **d** quedam presumpcio, quod eorum assercio esset a veritate ~ea OCKHAM *Dial.* 662.

extranius v. extraneus.

extranominatus, named on the outside (of roll or sim.).

1526 visitacio ordinaria monasterii de Michelney per ~um vicarium in spiritualibus generalem *Vis. Wells* 218.

extranotatus, marked on the outside (of roll or sim.).

visitacio ordinaria prioratus Taunton, xv die mensis Augusti anno salutis ~o *Vis. Wells* 220.

extransverso, extransversum v. transvertere.

extraordinarie [LL], extraordinarily, outrageously. **b** additionally.

1188 equis eorum ablatis ~ie, ignominiose usque ad nos pedites eos redire permisit *Ep. Cant.* 173; **c1430** (v. anomalus b). **b a1350** quod sextus liber Decretalium legatur ordinarie .. et quod certi tituli, extracti secundum disposicionem magistrorum .., ~ie legantur *StatOx* 46; **c1431** a bachilario ~ie legente *Ib.* 235.

extraordinarius [CL], extraordinary; **b** (n. pl. as sb.) 'extraordinaries', irregular payments; **c** (w. *liber* or ellipt.) additional to required reading.

illud ~io opere restituat aut superponat GILDAS *Pen.* 26; **c798** ~iae hujus inquisitor quaestionis ALCUIN *Ep.* 136 p. 207; ~ie sunt penitentie et arbitrarie GIR. *GE* I 46; **c1250** per penam canonicam sive ~iam eis imponendam (*Const. Lond.* 84) *Conc. Syn.* 651; UPTON 33 (v. extravagans 2b). **b s1153** clerus .. muneribus sordidis non gravabitur; ab ~iis vacationem habebit DICETO *YH* I 297. **c a1380** unam collacionem vel unum librum de tribus libris

~iis codicis .. perlegisse *StatOx* 45; **14..** audiantur libri ~ii, in toto vel in parte, ubi facultas mature dispensabit, si fiat defectus .. tempus autem ~iorum committit facultas discrecioni legencium (*Stat. Glasg.*) *EHR* XIV 251*n.*

extrapendere, to hang on the outside.

[**1166** ut mandent vobis per literas suas extra sigillum pendentes quot milites quisquis [v. l. quisque] habeat *RBExch* I 412]; **c1175** hujus conventionis testes sunt et suis eam sigillis ~entibus confirmaverunt J. episcopus Glasg' [etc.] *Dryburgh* 47.

extrapercutere, to knock out (teeth).

1303 quatuor dentes de ore suo extrapercusserunt *JustIt* 945.

extraponere

1 a to put off, lay aside. **b** to exclude (person). **c** to alienate property.

a hec ad bene beateque vivendum potest sola sufficere: adeo ut extraposita universa aut nichil aut minimum perfectionis adiciant J. SAL. *Pol.* 821D. **b** archiepiscopus a gracia, pace, et proteccione regis extrapositus, est a suis possessionibus .. destitutus BIRCHINGTON *Arch. Cant.* 14. **c a1116** si quid inde postea captum est sive in terra sive in hominibus, reddatur eis quia nolo ut inde quicquid ~atur *Regesta* p. 333 (cf. ib.: si quid inde extra positum est, reddatur eis); **c1130** reseiseant in dominio ecclesie sue omnes terras illas que sine concessu meo .. de dominio illo extraposite sunt (*Cart. Tavistock*) *EHR* LXII 356;

2 to express. *V. et. exponere* 8.

suppositum intellegitur quod non debet ~i secundum vocem BACON XV 18.

extraportare, to carry out or away.

1427 lego .. magnum portiphorium meum in thesauraria dicte ecclesie .. quod non inde auferatur vel ~atur *Reg. Cant.* II 349; **1429** de custuma panni lanei empti infra dictum burgum et ~ati de regno per tempus computi *ExchScot* 476.

extrapositio, (phil.) extrusion.

subintracio parcium materie, ut per hoc fiat condensacio et rarefaccio per ~onem illarum DUNS *Metaph.* VII 8 p. 378; quantitas non est nisi ~o parcium seu distancia localis seu situalis parcium faciencium unum totum, ad quam ~onem .. non requiruntur nisi partes ille que distant OCKHAM *Sacr. Alt.* 348.

extrare, to pull out or (?) *f. l.*

1218 inventus fuit submersus in quadam (*sic*) lebete. Robertus .. et Willelmus frater suus extraverunt [? l. extraxerunt] eum *Eyre Yorks* 316.

†extrarium, *f. l.* (by misinterp. of abbr.).

occurrunt beate sorores, precipua regni celestis †extraria [MS: ex^a^ria; l. exemplaria] AD. MARSH *Ep.* 64.

extrarius [CL], out of line.

nec, dum comes improbus instat, / [dens] proximus, urgenti cedens, extrarius errat HANV. I 458.

extrascribere, to copy out.

in martilogio fratrum S. Francisci ecclesie de B. extrascripsi '1419 frater Johannes S. obiit [etc.]' W. WORC. *Itin.* 78.

extrastatum, (as etym. gl. ἔκτασις conf. w. ἐκστασις) ectasis, lengthening of vowel.

Ps.-GROS. *Gram.* 70 (v. ectasis).

extrata v. extrahere 6e.

extratenēre, to keep out, withhold.

1571 ipsum A. firma sua .. inde (termino suo .. nondum finito) ejecit, expulit, et amovit ipsumque A. a possessione inde ~uit et adhuc ~et et alia enormia ei intulit *Entries* 256.

extratensio, (as etym. gl. on *extensio*) outstretching.

extensio .. est ~o partium T. SUTTON *Quodl.* 449.

extratentio, keeping out, withhholding.

1515 consideratum est quod predictum J. [etc.] recuperent versus prefatum W. damna sua .. occasione .. expulsionis, disseisine, et ~onis .. de .. vicesima parte [acre] *Entries* 355.

1 extraura v. estrahura, extractura.

extravagans [extra + CL vagari]

1 itinerant. **b** stray.

1384 confessio facta fratri habenti potestatem a papa seu dioecesano audiendi confessiones aut cuiquam alteri ~anti (CROMPE) *Ziz.* 352. **b 1564** una equa ~ans .. venit infra dominium hic et remansit ibidem (*CourtR Hunmanby*) *Arch. Soc. Yorks J.* X 71.

2 (of payment) supplementary, additional (also as sb.). **b** supplementary, discursive. **c** (as sb. n.) digression.

si talis .. remanserit in areragiis, et oportet super aliquo ~ante respondere, tunc accepta fide debitoris debet mareschallus eidem inhibere *Fleta* 83; **1415** expense ~antes (*Ac. King's Hall*) *Arch. Hist. Camb.* II 671. **b** ut concordantie et notule ~antes suis decenter aptentur locis (H. Bos.) *PL* CXC 1476; alius textus invenitur in titulo de quibusdam aliis extraordinariis capitulis feudorum, que capitula sunt ~antia, nec sunt in corpore decime collacionis UPTON 33. **c** hec enim ~ancia in magnis cronicis repperi, propterea incidentaliter hic inserere utile judicavi *Plusc.* VI 20.

3 (w. *constitutio*, or as sb. f.) papal constitution supplementary to Gratian or the Decretals.

item in extravag' De appellatione Alexandri III [etc.] RIC. ANGL. *Summa* 25 p. 32 (cf. ib. 32 p. 55: ut extra' De fide instrumentorum); ut in ~anti De procuratoribus, cap. prima GIR. *Invect.* V 20; **s1294** nonnullas ~antes constituciones Honorii, Adriani .. et aliorum incorporavit RISH. 146; **s1297** (v. constitutio 4b); ~ante De summa Trinitate (TYSS.) *Ziz.* 171; ~ante De Reliquiis et veneracione sanctorum *Ib.* 172; de privilegio in constitucione ~anti pape Clementis *V. Ric. II* 54; ~antes Johannis XXII glosatum (*Catal.*) *Reg. Aberd.* II 129.

extravagus [cf. CL vagus], vagrant (sb.).

s1428 jam stat ab extravagis locus hic seclusus agrestis (*Vers.*) AMUND. I 261.

extravenditum, (w. *de*) sale outside the bounds.

1185 Robertus de Belmes debet j m. pro ~o de foresta *Pipe* 167 (cf. *SelPlForest* 21 [**1255**]: Norman Sampson vendidit tres quercus in Wauberg' et quod plures alias fecit transgressiones dum fuit forestarius).

extravisio, external vision.

si .. mundus esset unum animal et sol ejus oculus, quo videret per ~onem WYCL. *Ente* 51.

extraxio v. extractio. **extraya** v. estraia.

extremalis [LL], **a** at the extremity (partly fig.). **b** final.

a ex denominacione facta patet quod *GQ* correspondet intensiori gradui ~i, quod est impossibile DUMBLETON *Summa* 321; et hic miror quare theologi admittunt casum ultimum, et tamen dicunt quod Deus non potest auferre punctum a linea nisi addiderit alium, nec continuare duas lineas ad invicem, nisi corrumpendo puncta ~ia et generando terminum communem WYCL. *Log.* III 32; *Id. Ente* 196 (v. curvabilis b); **c1430** inter bifarias anime vires, que, quadam proprietatis congruencia, dicuntur in virtutis latitudine ~es *Reg. Whet.* II app. 469. **b s1460** finale responsum super ultimata ~ique summa solucionis pro reversione ejusdem [sc. manerii] *Reg. Whet.* I 359.

extremaliter, as extremes.

duo circa divicias ~iter collocantur, .. affluencia sc. diviciarum et inopia [cf. *Prov.* xxx 7–8] NETTER *DAF* I 499.

extremare, to place at the end, in last or lowest place.

to make laste, ~are *CathA.*

extremitas [CL]

1 extremity, end: **a** (of body); **b** (of thing); **c** (of line); **d** (of text or proposition).

a [mus et spix] tenui et gracili membrorum ~ate terminantur ALDH. *Met.* 10 p. 95; [semibos vir] habebat totum corpus humanum preter ~ates, que bovine fuerant GIR. *TH* II 21; BACON *Maj.* II 18 (v. glacialis 2b); GAD. 52v. 2 (v. gibbosare); vene fagitide, sc. vene que sunt in carnositate faciei juxta ~ates oris *SB* 20. **b** ORD. VIT. IV 2 p. 168 (v. bubalinus); licet quedam corpora sint in quibus dominatur pars inferioris ~atis, quandoque vero medie, quandoque autem dominantur partes ultime ~atis *Quaest. Salern.* B 121; rudentes .. quorum ~atibus velum malo jungatur [v. l. maritetur] NECKAM *Ut.* 115; **1383** [crux] cum parvis margaritis in quatuor ~atibus .. circulariter affixit *Ac. Durh.* 440; archus .. una ~as satis artificiose requievit in castro *G. Hen. V* 15 p. 108. **c** sicut in ~atibus quadrati majoris *GH* ponuntur ROB. ANGL. *Alg.* 78; GROS. 13 (v. 1 axis 2a). **d** quia longum est, ut sciscitatio et solutio earundem passionum per ordinem enucleetur, saltim ~as pandatur ALDH. *Met.* 10 p. 95; inter majorem ~atem et minorem [syllogismi] interposuerunt mediacionis terminum, ut quamvis bis sumptus ante conclusionem, nihilominus, propter diffidencie spiritum, ingrederetur eciam et eam *Reg. Whet.* II app. 453.

2 utmost, last, or least place. **b** extreme condition.

da nobis ut omnis ~as placeat nobis, quantocumque fuerimus minimi et posteriores omnibus ALCUIN *Liturg.* 503B; fons venenorum ebullit in oriente ... in his .. ~atibus venenosus vigor prorsus evanuit GIR. *TH* I 39. **b s1227** omni ~ate, vilitate, et paupertate pro Christo contenti, non extollantur M. PAR. *Maj.* III 136.

3 (?) setting in place, establishment. *Cf.* 2 *collocatio* 1.

collocatio, i. ~as, *gestaþelung GlH* C 1571.

extremus [CL]

1 situated at the extremity, uttermost. **b** (phil.) opposite (also as sb.). **c** (as sb. n.) extremity.

Britannia insula in ~o ferme orbis limite circium .. versus GILDAS *EB* 3; ~am partem loci illius *V. Cuthb.* III 4; Ceolfridus extremis Anglorum finibus abbas (CEOLFRID) *Epigr. Milredi* 806; fama per ~os mundi cardines divulgata G. MON. IX 11; in occiduis et ~is terrarum finibus GIR. *TH pref.* p. 20. **b** omne medium conficitur ex ~is J. BLUND *An.* 122; duo colores ~i, sc. albus et niger *Quaest. Salern.* B 167; habitudo est immutabilis sic, quia inter ~a non potest esse opposita habitudo, nec non esse ista, positis ~is, sed per destruccionem ~i vel ~orum destruitur DUNS *Ord.* III 151; cum .. ~a non sint in actu rerum nisi et media sint in quibus non est opposicio; media autem inter hec duo ~a sunt HALES *Sent.* I 315. **c** quia per quartam partem in uno ~o et per quartam partem in altero hujus census latus auctum est ROB. ANGL. *Alg.* 130; quod altus homo cum ~is digitorum vix attingeret BRYGG *Itin.* 381.

2 last; **b** (*ad ~um*) finally. **c** least. **d** (as sb. n., log.) final part of categorical proposition.

.. addatur extremis [sc. litteris] prima duabus ALCUIN *Carm.* 63. 4. 5; hic liber extremus scripturae inscribitur almae / divinis totus mysteriis redolens *Ib.* 69. 171; Guillelmus comes Moritoliensis aciem duxit primam, et Rodbertus Belesmensis ~am ORD. VIT. XI 20 p. 230; inpomentum, cibus qui cene ~us inponitur, quod et bellarium dicitur OSB. GLOUC. *Deriv.* 294; horum [regum] ~us ante .. Eadmundum regnavit Offa G. FONT. *Inf. S. Edm.* 1. **b** quod, cum frequenti voce repeteret, nec tamen ei aliquis obtemperaret, ad ~um intulit: "scio quod" [etc.] BEDE *HE* IV 8; pagani fame, frigore, timore, et ad ~um desperatione perterriti ASSER *Alf.* 56; sic ut ad extremum mater cum pignore posset / ire per anfractus securo pectore curvos WULF. *Swith.* II 462. **c c705** Aldhelmus ~us servorum Dei ALDH. *Ep.* 8 (11); **1166** non reges .. elegit, sed ~os hominum Britones Nivicollinos J. SAL. *Ep.* 145 (168); dum suppremus fit extremus / et extremus fit suppremus WALT. WIMB. *Virgo* 99. **d** uno modo vocatur terminus omne illud quod potest esse copula vel ~um proposicionis categorice, subjectum viz. vel predicatum, vel eciam determinacio ~i vel verbi OCKHAM *Summa* 9; multa enim nomina non sunt termini, sc. nomina syncategorematica, quia talia quamvis possint esse ~a proposicionum si sumantur materialiter vel simpliciter, quando tamen sumuntur significative non possunt esse ~a proposicionum *Ib.* 10; proposicio cathegoria de disjuncto ~o *Id. Dial.* 802 (v. disjungere 4e).

3 a (w. ref. to death) last. **b** (w. *unctio*) Extreme Unction. **c** (as sb. n. pl. w. *ad* or *in*) the point of death; **d** (of Last Judgement).

a quis .. crucis affixus pro reverentia Christi patibulo .. ~um halitum fudit? GILDAS *EB* 73; **c790** cani capilli ~um denuntiant properare diem ALCUIN *Ep.* 74; cum in ~o laborasset mortis articulo GIR. *JS* sup. 147; ~a suspiria rapiens *Ps.*-ELMH. *Hen. V* 127 p. 334. **b** unctio ~a quotiens recidivaverit iterari poterit GIR. *GE* I 3; sacramentum ~e unctionis S. LANGTON *Quaest.* 366; exeuncium sacramentum sc. ~a unccio HALES *Sent.* IV 388; **c1250** quintum [sacramentum] est ~a unccio, sc. sacramentum exeuncium, que nos ad Dei preparat vocacionem (*Const. Lond.* 1) *Conc. Syn.* 634; ad officium tandem ~e unccionis deventum est *Mir. Hen. VI* IV 128. **c** percussus .. langore atque ad ~a perductus BEDE *HE* V 14; *RegulC* 65 (v. agere 4e); **1156** cum in ~is agere videremur J. SAL. *Ep.* 22; Petrus languore correptus ad ~a perductus est ALEX. CANT. *Mir.* 46 (I) p. 250; **1220** in ~is agens illud [sc. mesagium] assignavit in subsidium Terre Sancte *CurR* VIII 297; narratur de sancto languente in ~is [ME: *þe lei on his deað uuel*] *AncrR* 120; positus in ~is, sacerdoti ad ultimum quis fuerit confessus est *Meaux* I 153. **d** diem ~um *Chr. Rams.* 107 (v. dies 9b); in ~o examine districte ulcioni subjaceat *NLA* (*Edmund*) II 673; in ~o judicio [ME: *an domesdei*] *AncrR* 14.

4 (with ref. to degree): **a** extreme. **b** (*ad ~um*) utterly, to the limit.

a ~e imperitie genus est hominem ibi totum efflare spiritum ubi .. ORD. VIT. IX 6 p. 496. **b** suis equis .. ad ~um fessis *Ib.* IX 9 p. 541.

extrenneum [OF *estreine* < CL strena], new year's gift.

1376 in ~eo dato Matheo de B., ij s. iiij d. *Ac. Churchw. Bath* 12.

extrepiare v. estrepare. **extreppa** v. estrepum.

extricabilis [LL], extricable, that may be disentangled, solved, escaped. **b** (by misinterp.) inextricable.

1168 doleo quod perversitas quorundam vix ~es ei tetendit insidias J. SAL. *Ep.* 243 (241 p. 462); OSB. GLOUC. *Deriv.* 200 (v. enodabilis). **b** ~e, *unforfeored GlH* E 570; **9..** ~i, *ungebrocenre WW.*

1 extricare v. estreciare.

2 extricare [CL], to loosen, disentangle, unravel; **b** (fig.). **c** to resolve. **d** to prepare, clear.

indumenta .. numquam vetustate ~abantur ALDH. *VirgP* 38 p. 287; **10..** ~abatur, *tolesed wæran WW*; OSB. GLOUC. *Deriv.* 195 (v. exsolvere 1a). **b** **a984** ~ans .. Domini cultura criminum spurcitias, virtutum semine sedulus agricola inserui (ÆTHELWOLD *Ch.*) *Conc. Syn.* 124; monachus iste .. muliebrem tricam firmos ~antem animos et infirmos intricantem .. rapere .. curavit GIR. *Spec.* II 8. **c** ~abatur, terminabatur, resolvebatur; .. ~abuntur, terminentur *GlH* E 569, 571; ~are, solvere vel terminare OSB. GLOUC. *Deriv.* 201. **d** anne illa [anima], cum hospitium suum [sc. corpus] ~aret, cavaret, extenderet, materiam quidem, unde hec faceret, habebat? ADEL. *QN* 43.

extricatio [LL], disentanglement (fig.), solution.

aphorismus est diffinitus: brevitate modesta succinctus. ita ab Oribasio in aphorismorum Ypocratis ~one describitur W. DONC. *Aph. Phil.* 2. 2.

extrictus v. extrahere.

extrinsece, a externally, on the outside. **b** (phil.) extrinsically.

a os aperi et siccum fungum abrade, aut etiam ~e abscide ADEL. *CA* 10. **b** vocamus visum principium sive eciam instrumentum ~e loquendo WYCL. *Quaest. Log.* 245; et patet quod omnia ista ~e denominant corpus Christi (TYSS.) *Ziz.* 169.

extrinsecus [CL *adv.*, LL *adj.*]

1 (adv.) from without. **b** outside.

quaerens ~us quod intrinsecus non habebat, id est in propria regno suo ASSER *Alf.* 76 p. 61; accidit ut [homo] ~us petita arma sibi laboriose adaptet ADEL. *QN* 15; insunt passiones intrinsecus nate, assunt ~us illate NECKAM *NR* II 155 p. 240; **1140** prohibeo et quod nullus super meum forisfactum aliquod namum in predicta terra ullo modo capere presumat pro alterius ~us forisfacto *E. Ch. Scot.* 128. **b** adclinis destinae, quae ~us ecclesiae pro munimine erat adposita BEDE *HE* III 17 p. 160; ~us, i. separatim, *utene GlH* E 567.

2 outwardly.

satis .. perpendo .. ex officio quod mihi ~us exhibetis quam pium circa me intrinsecus affectum habeatis *Chr. Battle* f. 118; *StatOx* 158 (v. difformis).

3 (adj.) external, from the outside. **b** external, on the outside.

nullum .. inveni .. ~i juvaminis adminiculum GIR. *TH intr.* p. 8; **1342** bona .. hospitalis absque remedio et auxilio extrinceco hiis diebus non sufficiunt *Lit. Cant.* II 252. **b** cum concluditur tres angulos trianguli esse equales duobus rectis per angulum ~um qui equipollet duobus intra oppositis KILWARDBY *OS* 497; hostillarii .. ~i incumbit officio omnes regulares .. admittere *Cust. Westm.* 86 (cf. *Cust. Cant.* 141: hostilarii .. incumbit officio in hostilariam ~am omnes regulares .. admittere); dum vento diu persistente contrario ~a pars remigii ad istam intraneam venire non posset *G. Hen. V* 21.

4 outer, outward, visible.

monasteria .. ~is abundanter opibus et non minus locupletavit internis *Hist. Abb. Jarrow* 20; ~a fortune munera GIR. *Symb.* I 9 p. 232; **s1408** satis faciliter in verbis et forma ~a concordarunt *Chr. S. Alb.* 32; hec sciencia non est inventa propter necessaria ~a sed propter necessaria intrinseca (ut videlicet propter ordinem et moderacionem passionum) DUNS *Ord.* I 230; **1440** occupaciones ~as et solicitudines effugere decreveramus (*Lit. Antipapae*) *Cop. Pri. S. Andr.* 194; **1466** per decenciam ~i habitus morum interdum decor intrinsecus designatur *Mem. Ripon* I 169.

5 (from) outside (local community); **b** (w. ref. to feud. service or due); *cf. forinsecus*; **c** (eccl. or mon.). **d** (dist. from *forinsecus*).

1216 bailliam ~am in manum nostrum capientes; mandavimus enim constabulario .. quod .. de terris ~is ipsum volumus bailliam habere *Cl* 273b; **1228** villam de Aulton cum hundredis intrinseco et ~o *Pat* 231; **1263** loquelas que ibidem terminari non poterunt tam de comitatibus ~is quam comitatu predicto *Cl* 236; **1329** burgenses ~i *Gild Merch.* (*Barnstaple*) II 14; **s1388** rex .. ut mercatores ~i possent dividere merces suas et per partes vendere in civitate concessit *Eul. Hist. Cont.* 367; **1455** hostis .. extrincecus *Reg. Whet.* 179. **b** **c1240** liberam et quietam ab omni servicio intrinseco et ~o *Kelso* 247; **1292** tolnetum intrinsecum et ~um *PQW* 121 (v. et. 5b infra). **c** **1105** pars omnium ~arum elemosinarum *MonA* II 81; si quis nostre congregacionis monachus .. super incontinencia convincatur, .. nec administracio ~a sibi ex tunc aliquatenus committatur *Cust. Cant.* 41; **1304** cum ~o senescallo monacho *Ord. Ely* 24. **d** **1311** mercatoribus .. tam †extrincessis quam forincessis *Law Merch.* I 90; **1364** fratres dicti hospitalis de negociis secularibus, tam forinsecis quam ~is, se nimium intromittunt *IMisc* 188/10.

6 (phil.) extrinsic. **b** (of causes) external, efficient.

primo debetur essencie create triplex †mensure [l. mensura]: una intrinseca que est sua propria limitacio in tali genere vel specie; alia ~a in genere tantum, et sic nobilissima essencia illius generis mensura est aliarum essenciarum ejusdem generis; alia ~a et extra genus et sic Deus sub racione qua essencia summe perfecta mensura est cujuslibet essencie create MIDDLETON *Sent.* II 41a; actus quem exercet aliquis circa rem ~am, sicut comededo, bibendo .. et hujusmodi, vocatur usus facti, et additur 'facti' ad distinguendum talem usum ab usu juris OCKHAM *Pol.* I 301; forma .. quedam est intrinseca rei, et quedam ~a WYCL. *Quaest. Log.* 261; de objectis ~is, ut de preteritis et de futuris (KYN.) *Ziz.* 79. **b** sine accione ~a DUNS *Ord.* I 37; si essencia .. esset absoluta, posset perfecte cognosci sine cognicione cause ~e *Ib.* III 186; quantitas .. non potest poni causa intrinseca nec ~a substancie vel qualitatis OCKHAM *Sacr. Alt.* 348; homo non elicit actum de novo nisi moveatur ab objecto ~o [MS: †ex ~o] WYCL. *Ente Praed.* 115.

7 a (as sb. n.) the outside. **b** foreign parts. **c** (as sb. m. or f.) outsider, stranger.

a **1314** nec valet ab ~o aer recencior advenire (*Instr. de Praedicatoribus*) *Flor. Hist.* III 163. **b** **s1344** contra omnes ab ~o venientes AD. MUR. *Chr.* 155. **c** **1320** inquisiciones tam per ~os quam intrinsecos pro hujusmodi malicia abolenda *MunCOx* 36; **1330** ipsi advocant capere de intrinsecis unum tolnetum et de ~is pro eadem re duplum *Gild Merch.* (*Derby*) II 52; quantum ad defectum jurisdiccionis fratrum in ~os suo ordini CONWAY *Def. Mend.* 1417 (*recte* 1317).

extrinsio [dub.], outward movement. *Cf. extensio.*

congregat calor homogenia .. et disgregat eterogenia .. . econtra autem in resolucione gravium que secundum angulum descendunt ad centrum. et propter istam intercepcionem medii, inter levia que secundum dyametrum moventur ab angulo, et †~one [? l. ~onem] medii inter gravia que moventur ad angulum versus centrum, creditur quod hinc inde sunt absoluta raritas et gravitas adquisite, computando cum summo aereo totum medium interceptum WYCL. *Log.* III 68.

extrip- v. estrep-, exstirp-. **extron-** v. et. estron-.

extroniamentum, branch lopped in pollarding. *V. et. estronatura, estronicium.*

Tri. W. Langton 273 (v. extroniare).

extroniare, ~izare [cf. estronare < extruncare], to pollard.

pomeria .. ~iaverunt .. et extroniamenta .. asportaverunt *Tri. W. Langton* 273; **1316** nec aliquas arbores in dictis tenementis prosternet, extirpabit nec ~izabit nisi ad necessariam clausturam tenementorum (*Cart. Chertsey* 1123) *KR Misc. Bk.* 25 f. 345v.

extrorsum [LL], outwards.

coxam accipias et ut .. extendendo volvas juncturam ~um donec ad locum redeat naturalem GAD. 128v. 2.

extrosio v. extorsio. **extrovare** v. estronare. **extruct-** v. exstruct-.

extrudere [CL], to extrude, expel.

†extrudoe [MS: extrudor], depellor *GlH* E 796; febre ~sa .. convaluit GOSC. *Wulsin* 22; antidotum ex serpentibus conficitur quod Tyriacum vocatur. morsus serpentium et mortiferos haustus ~dit, miroque modo venenum veneno exhauritur *Id. Lib. Confort.* 94; sed adversos carnalium passionum atrocissimos hostes, ut eos a cordium receptaculis ~dentes in terra cordis nostri .. templum preparemus AILR. *Serm.* 293C; dum sequens ~dit precedentem ipsa se intrudit BALD. CANT. *Tract.* 10. 517B.

extruncare, to cut short (fig.). *V. et. estronare.*

nisi .. episcopus .. cujusdam magnatis Angligeni ~asset maliciam, omnes fere pedites de Anglia fuissent morte turpissima condempnati *Chr. S. Edm.* 69.

extrusio, extrusion, thrusting out.

utrum ne in auctorem, cujus jussu [anima] intravit, violenta ~o referri debeat? ADEL. *QN* 43; **s1197** cum .. sue olim [sc. cancellarii] ab Anglia ignominiose ~onis homo ingentis animi immemor esse non posset W. NEWB. *HA* V 29.

extrusor, one who sets out wares (for sale), pusher.

si sis mercator .. / .. / et varius rerum variarum venditor, emptor, / perfidus extrusor non sis mercis neque mendax D. BEC. 1759.

extuberare [CL], to wrinkle (eyebrow). **b** to burl (cloth).

extuperat, tumet, †existat [l. exstat] *GlH* E 793; ne Britonibus .. ~arent supercilia GOSC. *Aug. Maj.* 76D. **b** *to burle clothe*, ~are *CathA.*

extuberarius, ~ator, ~atrix, burler.

a burler, ~arius, [extubera]tor, [extubera]trix *CathA.*

extulisse v. efferre. **extum** v. exta.

extumulare [cf. CL tumulare], to disentomb (partly fig.).

ruit ex improviso humus .. de summitate fosse, et eum quidem penitus obruit .. pius pater exaudiens sic obrutum ~are procuravit ut et sibi .. extumulatio communiter ascribi posset W. CANT. *Mir. Thom.* III 2; si .. decessit infidelis .. ~etur GROS. *Templ.* 7. 12; **s1382** nisi prius propriis manibus ~arent et procul ejicerent ab ecclesiastica sepultura WALS. *HA* II 75.

extumulatio, disentombment (partly fig.).

W. CANT. *Mir. Thom.* III 2 (v. extumulare).

extunc [LL; al. div.], **a** thereafter, thenceforward; **b** (in phr. w. *in antea* or *proxime sequens*). **c** then, forthwith.

a fidem .. Cuthberti ~c laude digna predicabant BEDE *CuthbP* 7; **957** (v. constringere 4b); in vigiliis et orationibus ita ~c se armavit assiduitate infatigabili W. DAN. *Ailred* 42; **s1188** quod .. ex tunc manerent omnia in eodem statu TREVET *Ann.* 110; FORTESCUE *LLA* 35 (v. convicinus c); **1543** exnunc prout ~c *Conc. Scot.* I cclvi. **b** **s1238** ut .. ipsi autem ~c in antea ipsi, quasi imperatori et domino, cum debita servirent reverentia M. PAR. *Maj.* III 496; **1317** quod ~c in antea nichil statueretur a cancellario .. nisi [etc.] (R. BURY *Ep.*) *FormOx* 20; **1381** major et cives .. elegerunt .. Simonem de W., Simonem Clapham et Henricum de B. essendi (*sic*) ballivos .. in anno extunc proximo sequenti *Mem. York* I 127; a festo S. Michaelis A.D. 1394, usque idem festum ~c proxime sequens A.D. 1395 per unum annum integrum *Comp. Swith.* 202; **1425** citra festum Pasche proximo ~c sequens *Reg. Cant.* II 304. **c** **c1245** alioquin ipse ~c ex officii sui debito ad institutionem ejusdem in predicta ecclesia faciendam .. procederet GROS. *Ep.* 126; **s1102** (v. concubinarius c); **1290** quandocunque .. rex .. dederit .. lx libratas terre, .. nos ~c .. regi .. reddemus .. custumam et redditum quos habuimus .. in villa et portu de Sandwico *Lit. Cant.* III 383; **1322** posuit ignem in villa de Burtone .. et ~c predictus comes .. exiit (*Lit. Regis*) TROKELOWE 113 (= *Foed.* II 478); **a1400** ~c facta resignacione dicti prioratus *Pri. Cold.* 81; **1425** si predictus Henricus decesserit antequam ad legitimam etatem pervenerit, vult quod ~c predicte lx li. eidem disposite disponantur in cooperturam plumbeam capelle S. Johannis Baptiste *Reg. Cant.* II 326; **1459** a clericis et clero ex tunc presentibus *Conc. Scot.* II 79.

extundere [CL], to beat, strike. **b** to force out, dispel. **c** to extort.

~it, i. elidit, [*ed. omits*: excutit] *GlH* E 791; ut percussione fabri [ferrum] ~atur KYKELY 226. **b** extusit vel extunsit, i. dejecit, extorsit *GlH* E 794. **c** *Ib.* (v. b supra).

extunicare [cf. CL tunicare], to strip. **b** (fig.) to peel away.

in instructione rudium, primum occurrit fortune suis eos ~are panniculosis sarcinis P. BLOIS *Opusc.* 1021D. **b** **c1200** (v. caepa d).

extupare v. stuppare. **extuperare** v. extuberare.

exturbare [CL]

1 to drive out, drive away (also fig.). **b** to displace (by force).

sol aureus suo exortu universa noctis nubila ~at DOMINIC *V. Ecgwini prol.*; scurrilitatem et vaniloquium .. ~are, .. virga correctionis increpare *V. Swith.* 375; quos ego .. pro nefariis ~averam factionibus ORD. VIT. XII 24 p. 401; viam Domino in peccatorum cordibus facinoris ~ando tenebras preparavit R. COLD. *Cuthb.* 17 p. 34; ut hereses et schismata de ecclesia tollant hostesque ecclesie viriliter expugnare et ~are non negligant J. FORD *Serm.* 67. 10. **b** **s1147** nolumus .. vos tam antiquis ~are sedibus OSB. BAWDSEY clxii; equum .. de navis sedibus ~averant et in maris medio proiciendo demerserant R. COLD. *Cuthb.* 75 p. 155; de hac deinde sue paupertatis habitatione eam [sc. avem] ~are volentibus sine rebellione et absque ultione etiam minoribus cedit J. FORD *Serm.* 18. 5.

2 to disturb, upset.

diabolus ut virum sanctum ~et omnia temptamentorum genera percurrit ADEL. BLANDIN. *Dunst.* 6; quos cum suis copiis exercitum regis ~are frequenter dirigebat ORD. VIT. XI 3 p. 173; quia non statim omnia que requiris invenis in eis [sc. sacris scripturis], ~aris H. READING (I) *Mem.* 1299A; in frondibus nidificantes in concussione deinceps ramorum ejus cum ipso simul ~ati sunt J. FORD *Serm.* 36. 4; ~ati naute multumque adversante vento acti J. WALLINGF. *Chr.* 66.

exturbatio, disturbance, interruption.

s1078 Antiochia capitur a paganis, cum adjacente provincia, que extitit Christiana a tempore beati Petri sine ~one *Flor. Hist.* II 10.

exturgere v. extergere.

exuber [cf. CL uber], very abundant.

1302 barones .. regi .. ad gracciarum (*sic*) acciones ~eres assurgentes unanimiter responderunt *Reg. Cant.* 625.

exuberanter, exuberantly, abundantly. *V. et. exubere.*

in Anglia ~ius spe sullimati fuerant ORD. VIT. VI 5 p. 18; hec .. omnia mala post mortem ejus tanto ~ius et vehementius prevaluerunt RIC. HEX. *Stand.* f. 37 p. 139; **1423** concessis .. duobus primis, volumus ut in tercio ~ius crescat vobis concessio (*Lit. Papae*) AMUND. I 158; ut concessa quamvis pascua sibi videantur ~er sufficere *Reg. Whet.* II app. 388; **1541** ut .. pietatis officia illius ~er in omnia vicina loca longe lateque dimanent ad Dei omnipotentis gloriam *MonA* I 106.

exuberantia [CL], copious flowing (of liquid); *v. et. exuberatio*; **b** (fig.). **c** exuberance, abundance.

noctu extitit fluminalis ~ia ÆLF. BATA 5. 6; circumstabant plurimi .. dolores suos lacrymarum ~ia protestantes *Mir. J. Bev. C* 329; onus sibi impositum cum ~ia lacrimarum humiliter suscipiens *Cust. Cant.* 27. **b** exoro, quatinus, de ~ia pectoris .. eam benedicciones graciam dicte dignemini religioni diffundere *Reg. Whet.* II app. 368. **c** ubi ~ia zizaniorum nimis multiplicata est ORD. VIT. IV 6 p. 205; fructuum et piscium cunctarumque rerum ~ia ditissima *Ib.* V 6 p. 324; preter stupendas annuorum provectuum ~ias copiosissimas .. prebitionum profusiones, et multiplicissimas .. contributionum prestationes AD. MARSH *Ep.* 246 p. 430; mecum est testium exuberantia WALT. WIMB. *Carm.* 290; **c1310** domino J... salutum et caritatis ~iam salutifere affluentem *Chr. Rams.* app. 405; **1335** in humilitate spiritus ac mutue dileccionis ~ia *Lit. Cant.* II 101; **1337** quantas possimus grates vobis referimus speciales gerentes in votis expertam gratitudinis vestre constanciam cum .. retribucionis ~ia *RScot* I 516a.

1 exuberare v. exsuperare.

2 exuberare [CL], (of liquids) to flow copiously; **b** (fig.); **c** to be abundant, abound. **d** (pr. ppl. as adj.) flowing, abundant, exuberant. **e** (p. ppl. *s. act.*) supplied with, abounding in.

~at, exundat, superfluit *GlC* E 498; **s1136** cum .. aque largissime ~arint *G. Steph.* I 18; hec .. a rivulo ibi decurrente, et quandoque ad modum torrentis ~ante, Hestild nomine, Hestoldesham, quasi predium Hestild, vocatur RIC. HEX. *Hist. Hex.* I 1; aquas circa castra ~are faciunt ALEX. BATH *Mor.* I 30 p. 145. **b** odor in regione earum tam suavis ~at qui omnia aromatum genera exuperat ANSELM *Misc.* 359. **c** cum .. innumera .. exempla affatim ~ent et ubertim suppeditent ALDH. *VirgP* 22; tanta hodie calculatorum ~at copia (*Ep. Ceolfridi*) BEDE *HE* V 21 p. 341; divine legis prevaricatio nimis ~avit ORD. VIT. VIII 22 p. 394; **1147** (v. egere 2a); eolicis flatibus .. pre aliis terris hec ~at GIR. *TH* I 6 p. 27; ignis ~at ut in alliis quia acuta sunt *Quaest. Salern.* B 151; ~abat dolor vehemens W. CANT. *Mir. Thom.* II 23. **d** famosissimus habetur pro sua ~anti eloquentia COGGESH. *Visio* 23; quod .. gracie invenire debeat ~ancius incrementum (*Lit. Regis*) AD. MUR. *Chr.* 99. **e** vicaria predicta stetit satis pinguis et diversis comoditatibus exuberata *Reg. Rough* 298.

3 exuberare [cf. CL uber = *teat*], to wean.

to spayn, ablactare, elactare, ~are; .. *spaned*, exuberis, ~atus, ablactatus *CathA*.

exuberatio, copious flowing. *V. et. exuberantia* a.

juxta lunares defectus .. residente derivationis ~one GIR. *TH* II 3; ex quorum [humorum] multiplicatione fumositatum fit ~o; ex earum ~one superfluitatum fit collectio *Quaest. Salern.* B 328.

exubere, abundantly. *V. et. exuberanter.*

abundyngly, abundanter, †erupere [*ed.*: exubere] *CathA*.

exuberis [cf. CL uber = *teat*], weaned. **b** (of cow) dry.

~es, i. infantes qui extracti sunt ab ubere, et sububeres qui adhuc sunt sub ubere OSB. GLOUC. *Deriv.* 617; *CathA* (v. 3 exuberare). **b** *dry, as kyne or bestis þat wyl gev no mylke*: ~is, ~e *PP*.

exubiae v. exuviae. **exud-** v. exsud-.

1 exuere v. 1 exire.

2 exuere [CL]

1 to put off (garment or sim.); **b** (fig.). **c** to strip (person of garments); **d** (fig.).

~unt habitum mundi et induunt armaturam Dei FOLC. *V. Bot.* 402; monachus †exivit vestes et cingulo cinxit se et cucurrit S. LANGTON *Exempla* 124; cum cuilibet religioso liceret habitum quemcumque, eciam laycalem, quociescunque et quamdiu libuerit induere atque ~ere WYCL. *Apost.* 4. **b** ut Jhesus exuat / mortalem tunicam WALT. WIMB. *Carm.* 621; nam vultus habitum mutat et exuit *Id. Palpo* 133. **c** propriis ~ta vestibus ALDH. *VirgP* 45; **797** ut pater pius pallio .. non ~atur ALCUIN *Ep.* 128; LANFR. *Const.* 157 (v. cuculla 1a); *GAS* 495 (v. conjuratio 2); dum vestimentis ~eretur ORD. VIT. XII 31 p. 430; quando frater ~tus dorso qui prius recognovit delictum in capitulo venit ante presidentem, et flagellat eum ter cum corrigiis *Conc.* II 356b; armis .. propriis quasi per se impotens pugnator ~tus *Latin Stories* 85; *Croyl.* 22 (v. colobium a); unus locus secretus .. cum igne et aqua calida .. ad nudandum et ~endum ibi infantem ante baptismum W. SAY *Lib. Reg. Cap.* 68. **d** adeo se mundi rebus ~it ut .. veniret ad monasterium BEDE *HE* IV 3 p. 208; tu .. defensor animae meae qui nunquam tegmine ~tus virtutum fuisti *Nunnam.* 71; ~eras, misericors Domine, vetustis pannis originalis peccati et indueras me veste innocentiae ANSELM (*Or.* 8) III 27.

2 to cast off, shed (possessions, attributes, *etc.*). **b** (w. *hominem*) to die. **c** to deprive (of something). **d** to release; **e** (w. ref. to soul set free from body).

ejus filii, sed filii perditionis; ejus homines, sed omnem ~ti humanitatem W. FITZST. *Thom.* 145; sui sexus perversores .. qui .. quod creati sunt et nati ~unt et feminas induunt J. FURNESS *Kentig.* 28 p. 211; formam humanam prorsus ~entes induunt lupinam GIR. *TH* II 19 p. 102; ~ta sua forma induit novam SICCAV. *PN* 158; nomen regis ~it et nomen induit tunc tyranni FORTESCUE *NLN* I 7. **b** ~it hominem rex Ædgarus. quo mortuo .. *Lib. Eli.* II 11 p. 84; Edelredus rex .. non multo post hominem †exivit. rex igitur Chunutus, audita morte regis .. W. JUM. V 9. **c** propter apostasiam regum Anglorum qua se fidei sacramentis ~erant BEDE *HE* III 1 p. 128; velut si aliquis latro aliquem ad se despoliandum incitaret .. aut dicendo ei simplici verbo ut se ~eret *Simil. Anselmi* 122; veniet dies illa qua nitore hoc ~tus horribili appareas cilicio involutus PULL. *CM* 210. **d** exueret mundum ut furva caligine Christus ALDH. *VirgV* 1687; **680** ut crinibus carnis nostrae quasi criminibus ~amur *Id. Ep.* 4 p. 483; **1360** quod ipse ab indignacione aliorum essent ~ti, et erga communitatem .. publice excusati *MunAcOx* 222; **s1298** reges et regnum Scocie a dominio et potestate regis Anglie ~ebantur *Meaux* II 272; **1480** affectans .. ab eodem prioratu ~i et exonerari *Reg. Whet.* II 215; **1504** ut eas [animas] a peccatis omnibus ~as *StatOx* 318. **e** quae et qualia essent quae ~tus corpore videret BEDE *HE* V 12 p. 309 (cf. ib. III 19 p. 164); quomodo .. postquam corpore ~te fuerint .. anime ad astra referantur ALB. LOND. *DG* 6. 17; in conjuncto passiones sunt et non in anima ..; in ~ta autem est apprehensio non corporalis GILB. VI 244v. 2; cum infelix anima a corpore ~ta fuerit ROLLE *IA* 212; dicunt quoque non esse purgatorium post mortem nec evenire animabus ~tis vel penam vel gloriam ante diem judicii *Itin. Mand.* 14.

exuffl-, exufl- v. exsuffl-.

1 exugia, part of body, ? for *axungia*, 'internal fat'.

talias bathma exugiam atque binas idumas (*Lorica*) *Nunnam.* 92 (= *Cerne* 86); ~ia, i. minctura, *micgerne* vel spolia *GlH* E 765; ~ia, *micgern* ÆLF. *Gl.*; **11..** ~ium, *mygern WW Sup.* 471.

2 exugia v. exuviae.

exuitio, a putting off (also fig.). **b** release.

a vestium ~o *Mir. Cuthb. Farne* 4; cum factus fuerit homo divinus per ~onem corupcionis peccati *Ps.*-GROS. *Gram.* 11; conversionem substancie panis cum omni ~one sui in substanciam corporis Christi, sicut fit ~o plenaria a vinculo veteris debiti NETTER *DAF* II 115. 2. **b** NETTER *DAF* II 115. 2 (v. a supra).

exul (exsul) [CL], exile, banished person; **b** (fig.). **c** (leg.) outlaw.

705 (v. eliminare a); ubi suos homines, qui ~es vagabantur, recipere posset BEDE *HE* IV 13 p. 232; **736** sororem .. quae ~em Germanicum [i.e. Bonifatium] spiritali lumine consolata est BONIF. *Ep.* 30; exul qui extra solum suum voluntate peregrinatur *GlC* E 496; exul, i. peregrinus, expulsus a propriis finibus, alienus, *utlenda GlH* E 759; Ecgwinus .. proficiscitur felix exul DOMINIC *V. Ecgwini* I 5; exul abit sine spe reditus patrieque reique; / proscriptus manet in patria sed re spoliatus WALT. WIMB. *App.* 2. 22. **b** totius opis te, amice, video ~em W. MALM. *Mir. Mariae* 179; ave, virgo, mentis dulcor, / in qua reus et exul cor / fundat, figit, anchorat WALT. WIMB. *Virgo* 12. **c** exul, *utlaga* ÆLF. *Sup.*; masura .. quae fuit cujusdam ~is, i. *utlage DB* I 1; latro habeatur exul [AS: *utlah*] (*Inst. Cnuti*) *GAS* 335; sit utlaga, i.e. exul vel exlex (*Quad.*) *Ib.* 192; **1384** (v. cornu 4d).

exulanus, person living in exile. *V. et. exsolanus.*

~us, exul OSB. GLOUC. *Deriv.* 197.

1 exulare v. axelare. **2 exulare** v. 1 exiliare b.

3 exulare (exs-) [CL]

1 (intr.) to live in exile or banishment (also fig.). **b** to go into exile (also fig.). **c** (fig.) to be far from.

filii .. Æedilfridi .. apud Scottos .. ~abant BEDE *HE* III 1 p. 127; Caedwalla .. cum ~aret a patria sua *Ib.* IV 15; errabundo qui sparsim ~averat *V. Neot. A* 13; sentio me ab illa [sc. fide] ~are ANSELM (*Or.* 10) III 36; Fulco .. depositus vij annis ~avit ORD. VIT. X 4 p. 19; **c1164** ab Anglia ~at apud nos et nos domini nostre ~amus cum illo *Ep. J. Sal.* 136 (143); longe proscribitur lex, et jus exulat WALT. WIMB. *Sim.* 12. **b** Aristeus .. terram suam exiens in Ceam insulam ~avit *Natura Deorum* 31; **s1308** fuit .. ordinatum quod .. Petrus de Gavestone .. ~aret de regno Anglie AD. MUR. *Chr.* 12; ~ant igitur inducie et feroces guerre solite redeunt feritates *Ps.*-ELMH. *Hen. V* 59 p. 158. **c** occurrit quod sermo meus a vero non ~at W. MALM. *GR* I 68.

2 (trans.) to exile, banish; *v. et.* 2 *exiliare* a. **b** (pass., w. double obj.) to be banished (the country).

si quis secundum legem ~atus fuerit pro aliquo reatu .. *DB* I 280v.; [Anselmus] ~atus .. Romam venit H. CANTOR 3; **1215** nullus liber homo capiatur .. aut utlagetur aut ~etur .. nisi per legale judicium *Magna Carta* 39; **s1055** rex Eadwardus .. Algarum comitem ab Anglia ~avit M. PAR. *Maj.* I 524 (= FL. WORC. I 212: exlegavit); **1309** rex .. in hiis insulis sicut in Anglia ~avit et exheredavit omnes Normannos in Francia seu Normannia commorantes *PQW* 822a; **s1426** arestatis .. et condampnatis, quibusdam decollatis, .. aliis proscriptis et ~atis *Plusc.* XI 4. **b** **s1290** omnes Judei .. terram Anglie et Aquitanie .. ~antur *Ann. Lond.* 99 (cf. W. NEWB. *HA Cont.* 574: ~ati sunt omnes Judei ab Anglia).

exularis [LL], belonging to exile, of an exiled person.

calamitose et exsularis vite mee residuum .. superimpendere paratus sum H. BOS. *Ep.* 1425A.

exulatio (exs-) [CL], exile, banishment. *V. et. exiliatio.*

hec alias referam cum librum de ~one [MSS: †exultacione] eorum transtulero G. MON. XI 10; ~onis sue tempore per triennium moratus fuerat ORD. VIT. III 9 p. 108; de secunda expulsione Sancti Wilfridi, ~one, et revocatione RIC. HEX. *Hist. Hex.* I 12 *tit.*; **s1321** super injusta ~one domini Hugonis Despenser filii *Ann. Paul.* 300; dominus Thomas de Mortuo Mari fuit preconizatus sub pena .. perpetue ~onis se infra sex menses judicio sisti *V. Ric. II.* 138.

exulator [LL = *one who sends into exile*], outlaw.

~ores hic pompabunt vel unus pro omnibus *Beunans Meriasek* 72; primus ~or: *"me yv outlayer in cois"* [*I am an outlaw in the forest*] *Ib.*

exulatus [CL], exile, banishment.

duas sui ~us causas proponenti BEDE *Sam.* (*1 Sam.* xxvi 21) 694.

exulcerare [CL], to exulcerate, make sore; **b** (fig.). **c** to exasperate, aggravate.

~at, exasperat *GlC* E 436; ~ata sunt brachia ut ossa nudarentur, exesa inguina W. CANT. *Mir. Thom.* III 47; innumeris tormentis corpus illud ~are contendo R. COLD. *Godr.* 155; **s1192** captivi .. pedes ~ati, humeros excoriati, clunes stimulati, terga cesi DEVIZES 43v.; vepribus hirsutis se totum ingerens tantis vulneribus carnem dilacerando ~avit quod tota caro proprio sanguine maderet GIR. *GE* II 10 p. 214; tu scorpionibus Jhesum exulcera WALT. WIMB. *Carm.* 569. **b** cum ad reprimendum quamlibet [v. l. quemlibet] ~ate mentis dolorem congrua cuique medicamenta conficiat J. SAL. *Pol.* 672B; G. HOYLAND *Ascet.* 279B (v. excoriare 1a). **c** quin [sermo] omnium episcoporum regionis aures inquietaret, corda ~aret W. MALM. *GP* I 6 p. 13; **1166** eoque magis cruciat animum in ~ate mentis clausus angustiis J. SAL. *Ep.* 161 (159); **1168** quod .. omnium fidelium mentes ~avit *Ib.* 261 (280 p. 612).

exulium v. exilium. **exult-** v. et. exsult-. **exultatio** v. exsultatio, exulatio.

exulvus, *s. dub.*; ? *cf. exul* or *exsolvere*, or perhaps pers. name such as Æscwulf.

a1233 dedi .. unum burgagium .. libere .. ab omni exaccione seculari et servicio, videlicet, inter exulvum Gonde et Gilbertum fialatorem (*MS BL Add.* 37,769 f. 93v.) *Cart. Cockersand* 641.

exum v. 2 axa.

†exumbratio, *f. l.*

dicunt super sacramentum suum quod J. .. et W. fuerunt jurati in predicta assisa nove disseisine impanellata. et similter [iij alii] fuerunt imbraciatores ejusdem assise ad eam ducendam et procurandam. et ceperunt .. pecuniarum summas et alia dona, viz. pro veredicto suo dicendo predictus D. cepit xx m. [etc.] et predictus W. H. habet .. placeam terre .. in T. quousque levantur inde iij m. pro †exumbracione [l. imbraciacione] assise predicte etc. *Entries* 145b.

exumectare [cf. CL umectare], to dry out.

nolebat [lignum] .. exhumectari G. CRISPIN *Herl.* 88 (v. affectatio).

exundantia [LL], profusion, abundance.

hujus ratio saltus lunaris longa sui facit ~ia crementi lunam aliquoties majorem quam putatur videri BEDE *TR* 43; o si illius inundantiae ~ia inundabit ut diluat malorum meorum abundantiam ANSELM (*Or.* 14) III 57; recolere in memoria amorem et gaudium hujus domine, quibus jugi ~ia in Deum et de Deo jucundabatur tota illius substantia EADMER *Excell. B. M.* 569D; dulcedine .. totos eos inestimabili ~a satiabit *Id. Beat.* 6; nec bonitatis ei plenitudo defuit, quam frequens signorum ~ia commendare non desinit R. COLD. *Cuthb.* 64 p. 126.

exundatio [CL], overflowing.

a796 nec eam .. ∼o fluminum ullatenus impediat ALCUIN *Ep.* 60; flumen quod ∼o pluvialis intransmeabile fecerat J. FURNESS *Walth.* 127.

exundare [CL], **a** (esp. of stream) to rise in flood, overflow (also fig.); **b** (trans.) to spill over, overflow. **c** to overflow (w. liquid). **d** (pr. ppl. as adj.) abundantly flowing.

a ∼avit, *auueol* GlC E 374; imbribus exundans torrens ceu montibus altis / sternit agros segetesque ALCUIN *SSEbor* 525; quia nequaquam adversatur justitiae quod ∼at ex bonitate, quae nulla est sine justitia ANSELM (*Prosl.* 9) I 108; fluvius ∼ans cito collegit lutum ultra modum ALEX. BATH *Mor.* I 13 p. 128; tot interfecit quod cadavera eorum projecta in fluvio .. prohiberunt cursum fluvii, unde relicto canali sanguinolentus ultra ripas ∼avit TREVET *Troades* 16. **b** montanus torrens crebris tempestatum rivulis auctus sonoroque meatu alveos ∼ans GILDAS *EB* 17. **c** ∼ante ventre GILDAS *Pen.* 7 (v. evomere 1a); oculi ejus ut piscine in Esebon de sanctis fontibus ∼abant torrentem suum GOSC. *Lib. Confort.* 31; 1106 velut favum pinguem et ∼antem atque stillantem densas et suaves guttas ANSELM (*Ep.* 434) V 381; flexis genibus et junctis manibus, et ∼antibus oculis, patri suo grates rettulit V. *II Off.* 5; per totum diem fontem olei terra †exeundavit [MS: exundavit] GASCOIGNE *Loci* 144. **d** Bernardus Carnotensis, ∼antissimus modernis temporibus fons litterarum in Gallia J. SAL. *Met.* 854C.

exungia v. axungia.

exunguere, exungere [cf. CL exungui, ungere], to anoint. *V. et. axungiare.*

nec ex magistri hominis eruditione hoc illi, magis autem ex unctione magistra, juxta quod ille pre participibus suis ∼ctus H. BOS. *Thom.* III 14 p. 225; *to vynte,* aromatizare, .. ∼gere *CathA.*

exungulare [LL], to mutilate by pulling out finger-nails.

judex jussit ∼ari eos [sc. SS. Maximum et Venerandum] TORIGNI *Access. Sig.* 17.

exuperare v. exsuperare.

exurere [CL]

1 (of fire) to consume, destroy by burning. **b** (w. ref. to deliberate human action) to burn, destroy by fire. **c** (med.) to burn, cauterize.

ignis .. non quievit accensus, donec cunctam paene ∼ens insulae superficiem rubra .. lingua delamberet GILDAS *EB* 24 (cf. G. MON. XI 8: donec cunctam pene superficiem insule .. exussit); quae mox ignis edax flammis combussit acerbis; / non tamen exussit sanctorum torre lacertos ALDH. *VirgV* 1430; flammarum domitor, qui mundi comprimis ignes, / ne nos exurant, flammas compesce gehennae FOLC. *Carm.* 27; scintillans ignis .. barbas et penes aliosque pilos virorum et mulierum exussit ORD. VIT. V 3 p. 307; ut eis penne estuantibus solis ignibus ∼antur GIR. *TH* I 13 p. 40; phenix novus renascitur de cineribus fenicis exusti AD. DORE *Pictor* 163; tunicam .. super scapulas ejus exustam P. CORNW. *Rev.* II 203; AD. EYNS. *Hug.* IV 14 (v. culina a). **b** evertendi sunt muri obfirmationis eorum et ∼ende domus hereticorum R. NIGER *Mil.* III 79; in eodem volumine .. cujus rei autor apud Athenas exustus est ALB. LOND. *DG* 9. 9; *NLA* II 404 (v. comburere 2a). **c** quare apostema potius frigido ferro quam calido debet incidi ..? [foramen] non potest claudi propter exustam carnem sicut posset si frigido ferro incideretur *Quaest. Salern.* Ba 83.

2 (of fire) to burn away (impurity, also fig.). **b** to purge (something of impurities).

1076 per ustionem rubigo peccatorum ∼itur ANSELM (*Ep.* 53) III 167; triplex est .. animarum purgatio: .. ignis enim, quo omnia ∼untur [cf. Virgil *Aen.* VI 742] de terra est, nam celestis nihil perurit ALB. LOND. *DG* 6. 18; omnis denique iniquorum impietas fornax est ei et lima et malleus ad ∼endum in ea quod impurum est J. FORD *Serm.* 49. 4; sic ignis in terram de celo mittitur, / sic mundi scoria vetus exuritur WALT. WIMB. *Carm.* 43. **b** flamma quedam ∼ens [*Joel* ii 3] que animas nigras et maculosas secundum culparum modum brevius aut diuturnius ∼ebat COGGESH. *Visio* 15.

3 to scorch, parch.

[luna] fructus ∼eret et fontes siccaret ADEL. *QN* 69.

4 to burn (fig.): **a** (w. ref. to fever or sim.); **b** (w. ref. to scandal or sin).

a nos .. febrium languoribus per biennium modo incredibili exusti *Feod. Durh.* lxxvi. **b** ut nos famulos tuos non ∼at flamma vitiorum [AS: *ne giberne leg synna*] *Rit. Durh.* 100; filios .. patrum flagitia ∼unt PULL. *Sent.* 769B; ne libidine ∼atur *Ib.* 948C; 1284 mentes .. illorum .. ∼unt scandala filiorum PECKHAM *Ep.* 516.

1 exurgere v. exsurgere.

2 exurgēre [CL = *to squeeze out*], to urge against, dissuade.

1333 imploramus quatinus .. vestra sinceritas sic †exurgat [l. ∼eat] ipsos ab inceptis .. ut .. *RScot* I 233b.

exursus v. excursus.

exustio [CL], burning. **b** scorching.

mansiones .. wastatae sunt extra metam castelli, .. propter .. ignium ∼onem *DB* I 336v.; componitur etiam uro, exuro, -is, unde exustus, ∼o, unde combustus, combustio OSB. GLOUC. *Deriv.* 608; Hercules .. hydram ∼one interfecit ALB. LOND. *DG* 13. 4. **b** ignis .. calere non ad flagrationis ∼onem cepit R. COLD. *Cuthb.* 47 p. 97 (cf. ib. p. 98: pannus ipse ex ignis ∼one candidior apparuit).

exustor, one who consumes with fire.

s1099 rex Ranulfo placitatori sed perversori, exactori sed ∼ori totius Anglie, dedit episcopatum Dunhelme H. HUNT. *HA* VII 21.

exustulare [cf. CL ustulare], to scorch.

flammas ignium sevire ad miraculum, non autem ∼are ad dispendium, permittit R. COLD. *Cuthb.* 45; ardoris flamma nec etiam exteriores filorum villos ∼avit *Ib.* 66; ignis pannos .. ∼asse non potuit *Ib.*; hec .. gravem .. infirmitatem passa fuit, et .. sepius in capitis regionibus diversis cauteriis ∼ata comparuit *Id. Godr.* 374*.

exutare [*backformed from* exutus *p. ppl. of* 2 exuere], to cast off, release.

hec hamis est lignum bifurcatum quo rete extenditur et ∼atur BACON *Gram. Gk.* 30n.

exutus v. 1 exire, exitus 7b, 2 exuere.

exuviae [CL = *armour stripped from body of defeated enemy in token of victory*]

1 a prize. **b** spoils, plunder.

a qui celer optatam poterit contingere palmam / .. / in numero satrapumque merebitur esse meorum / stemmate regali comptus et exuviis *De libero arbitrio* 82. **b** †exugiae, spolia GlC E 525; c793 ne quid apud te ∼iarum perditae civitatis inveniatur ALCUIN *Ep.* 23 p. 61; ∼iae, i. .. praeda spolie .. vel *reaflac, reaf* GlH E 766; 9. . ∼ias, *deap reaf nelle ic him þæt lif ongenimen WW.*

2 clothing removed from dead body. **b** clothing, garments; **c** (w. ref. to animal skins; also fig.).

exubiae, vestes mortuorum GlC E 524; ∼iae, i. .. vestes mortuorum GlH E 766. **b** quaedam muliercula .. abluebat ∼ias domini sui, quae .. arreptae sunt. senior aut illius, ultramodum iratus eo quod tam negligenter custodiret induvias .. LANTFR. *Swith.* 38. **c** exuvias positura meas, brumalia calcans / frigora HWÆTBERHT *Aen.* 47 (*De scitali serpente*) 5; efferus exuviis populator me spoliavit TATWINE *Aen.* 5 (*De membrano*) 1; ∼iae, i. .. pelles ferarum GlH E 766; ∼iis leonis indutus asellus rudit, non rugit NECKAM *NR* II 180 p. 317.

3 bodily remains, relics.

ossibus hinc lotis portabant lintea munda / solis in aspectu exuvias ÆTHELWULF *Abb.* 234; concurrit ordo monasticus, occurrit et clerus ad beati viri exequias; ruunt catervatim populi .. ad tanti patris ∼ias DOMINIC V. *Ecgwini* I 17; accessit ad lapidem quo gloriosissimi regis ∼ie claudebantur, et stans ante sepulcrum .. AILR. *Ed. Conf.* 780A; W. MALM. *GR* II 160 (v. I emicare 1a).

4 emblem.

habet etiam in acie ∼iam draconis in signum, qui aperto semper ore excipiens ventum comminetur hostibus exterminium imminere R. NIGER *Mil.* II 19.

exvinculare v. evinculare. **exzennio** v. exenium c. **eya** v. I eia. **eylnesca** v. aesnecia. **eyna** v. tina. **eynecia, ∼cya (sb.), ∼cius, ∼scius** v. aesnecia. **∼cius.** **eyrum** v. eirum. **eysiamentum** v. aisiamentum.

Eyza [Ar. 'Īsā], Jesus.

Jesum, quem nos, inquit, Graece Christum nominamus, Arabice autem Eyza *Ps.*-GROS. *Summa* 282.